# The Cubs

# THE CUBS

*The Complete Record
of Chicago Cubs Baseball*

Historical Text by
Art Ahrens and Eddie Gold

Cubs Graphics by
John Warner Davenport

COLLIER BOOKS
MACMILLAN PUBLISHING COMPANY
*New York*

COLLIER MACMILLAN PUBLISHERS
*London*

Macmillan Publishing Company
866 Third Avenue, New York, N.Y. 10022
Collier Macmillan Canada, Inc.

Library of Congress Cataloging-in-Publication Data

Ahrens, Art, 1949–
   The Cubs: the complete record of Chicago Cubs
baseball.

   1. Chicago Cubs (Baseball team)—Statistics.
2. Chicago Cubs (Baseball team)—History. I. Gold,
Eddie, 1932–    . II. Davenport, John Warner,
1931–    . III. Title.
GV875.C6A37   1986   796.357′64′0977311   85-23705
ISBN 0-02-029420-4

Macmillan books are available at special discounts for bulk purchases for
sales promotions, premiums, fund-raising, or educational use. For details,
contact:

Special Sales Director
Macmillan Publishing Company
866 Third Avenue
New York, N.Y. 10022

10 9 8 7 6 5 4 3 2 1

Printed in the United States of America

# Contents

# The All-Time
# Cubs Leaders

This section provides information on individual all-time single season and lifetime Cubs leaders. Included for all the various categories are leaders in batting, base running, fielding, and pitching. All the information is self-explanatory with the possible exception of Home Run Percentage, which is the number of home runs per 100 times at bat.

## LIFETIME LEADERS

*Batting.* The top ten men are shown in batting and base-running categories. For averages, a minimum of 1500 at bats is necessary to qualify, except for pinch-hit batting average where 45 pinch-hit at bats is the minimum necessary to qualify. If required by ties, 11 players are shown. If ties would require more than 11 men to be shown, none of the last tied group is included.

*Pitching.* The top ten pitchers are shown in various categories. For averages, a minimum of 750 innings pitched is necessary to qualify. If required by ties, 11 players are shown. If ties would require more than 11 men to be shown, none of the last tied group is included. For relief pitching categories, the top five are shown.

*Fielding.* The top five in each fielding category are shown for each position. For averages, the minimum for qualification at each position except pitcher is 350 games played. For pitchers, 750 innings pitched are necessary. If required by ties, six players are shown. If ties would require more than six men to be shown, none of the last tied group is shown.

# ALL-TIME SINGLE SEASON LEADERS

*Batting.* The top ten men are shown in batting and base-running categories. For averages, a player must have a total of at least 3.1 plate appearances for every scheduled game to qualify, except for pinch-hit batting average where 30 pinch-hit at bats are the minimum necessary to qualify. If required by ties, 11 players are shown. If ties would require more than 11 men to be shown, none of the last tied group is included.

*Pitching.* The top ten pitchers are shown in various categories. For averages, innings pitched must equal or exceed the number of scheduled games in order for a pitcher to qualify. If required by ties, 11 players are shown. If ties would require more than 11 men to be shown, none of the last tied group is included.

*Fielding.* The top five in each fielding category are shown for each position. For averages, the minimum for qualification at first base, second base, shortstop, third base, and catcher is 100 games played. For outfield, games played must equal or exceed two-thirds of the number of scheduled games. For pitchers, innings pitched must equal or exceed the number of scheduled games. If required by ties, 6 players are shown. If ties would require more than 6 men to be shown, none of the last tied group is shown.

## BATTING AVERAGE

| | |
|---|---|
| 1. Ross Barnes, 1876 | .429 |
| 2. Cap Anson, 1881 | .399 |
| 3. Cap Anson, 1879 | .396 |
| 4. Cap Anson, 1894 | .395 |
| 5. Bill Lange, 1895 | .389 |
| 6. King Kelly, 1886 | .388 |
| 7. Rogers Hornsby, 1929 | .380 |
| 8. Heinie Zimmerman, 1912 | .372 |
| 9. Cap Anson, 1886 | .371 |
| 10. Cal McVey, 1877 | .368 |

## SLUGGING AVERAGE

| | |
|---|---|
| 1. Hack Wilson, 1930 | .723 |
| 2. Rogers Hornsby, 1929 | .679 |
| 3. Gabby Hartnett, 1930 | .630 |
| 4. Hack Wilson, 1929 | .618 |
| 5. Ernie Banks, 1958 | .614 |
| 6. Dave Kingman, 1979 | .613 |
| 7. Billy Williams, 1972 | .606 |
| 8. Ernie Banks, 1959 | .596 |
| 9. Ernie Banks, 1955 | .596 |
| 10. Andy Pafko, 1950 | .591 |

## HITS

| | |
|---|---|
| 1. Rogers Hornsby, 1929 | 229 |
| 2. Kiki Cuyler, 1930 | 228 |
| 3. Billy Herman, 1935 | 227 |
| 4. Woody English, 1930 | 214 |
| 5. Frank Demaree, 1936 | 212 |
| 6. Billy Herman, 1936 | 211 |
| 7. Jigger Statz, 1923 | 209 |
| 8. Hack Wilson, 1930 | 208 |
| 9. Heinie Zimmerman, 1912 | 207 |
| 10. Billy Herman, 1932 | 206 |

## DOUBLES

| | |
|---|---|
| 1. Billy Herman, 1936 | 57 |
| 1. Billy Herman, 1935 | 57 |
| 3. Kiki Cuyler, 1930 | 50 |
| 4. Ned Williamson, 1883 | 49 |
| 4. Riggs Stephenson, 1932 | 49 |
| 6. Rogers Hornsby, 1929 | 47 |
| 7. Riggs Stephenson, 1927 | 46 |
| 8. Ray Grimes, 1922 | 45 |
| 8. Walt Wilmot, 1894 | 45 |

## TRIPLES

| | |
|---|---|
| 1. Vic Saier, 1913 | 21 |
| 1. Wildfire Schulte, 1911 | 21 |
| 3. Bill Dahlen, 1896 | 19 |
| 3. Bill Dahlen, 1892 | 19 |
| 3. Ryne Sandberg, 1984 | 19 |
| 6. Billy Herman, 1939 | 18 |
| 7. Jimmy Ryan, 1897 | 17 |
| 7. Heinie Zimmerman, 1911 | 17 |
| 7. Woody English, 1930 | 17 |
| 7. Kiki Cuyler, 1930 | 17 |

## HOME RUNS

| | |
|---|---|
| 1. Hack Wilson, 1930 | 56 |
| 2. Dave Kingman, 1979 | 48 |
| 3. Ernie Banks, 1958 | 47 |
| 4. Ernie Banks, 1959 | 45 |
| 5. Ernie Banks, 1955 | 44 |
| 6. Ernie Banks, 1957 | 43 |
| 7. Billy Williams, 1970 | 42 |
| 8. Hank Sauer, 1954 | 41 |
| 8. Ernie Banks, 1960 | 41 |
| 10. Hack Wilson, 1929 | 39 |
| 10. Rogers Hornsby, 1929 | 39 |

## RUNS

| | |
|---|---|
| 1. Rogers Hornsby, 1929 | 156 |
| 2. King Kelly, 1886 | 155 |
| 2. Kiki Cuyler, 1930 | 155 |
| 4. Bill Dahlen, 1896 | 153 |
| 5. Woody English, 1930 | 152 |
| 6. George Gore, 1886 | 150 |
| 6. Bill Dahlen, 1894 | 150 |
| 8. Hack Wilson, 1930 | 146 |
| 9. Hugh Duffy, 1889 | 144 |
| 10. Jimmy Ryan, 1889 | 140 |

## RUNS BATTED IN

| | |
|---|---|
| 1. Hack Wilson, 1930 | 190 |
| 2. Hack Wilson, 1929 | 159 |
| 3. Rogers Hornsby, 1929 | 149 |
| 4. Cap Anson, 1886 | 147 |
| 5. Ernie Banks, 1959 | 143 |
| 6. Kiki Cuyler, 1930 | 134 |
| 7. Walt Wilmot, 1894 | 130 |
| 8. Hack Wilson, 1927 | 129 |
| 8. Ernie Banks, 1958 | 129 |
| 8. Billy Williams, 1970 | 129 |

## STOLEN BASES

| | |
|---|---|
| 1. Frank Chance, 1903 | 67 |
| 2. Billy Maloney, 1905 | 59 |
| 3. Frank Chance, 1906 | 57 |
| 4. Ryne Sandberg, 1985 | 54 |
| 5. Johnny Evers, 1906 | 49 |
| 6. Davey Lopes, 1985 | 47 |
| 7. Johnny Evers, 1907 | 46 |
| 8. Sam Mertes, 1899 | 45 |
| 8. Bob Dernier, 1984 | 45 |
| 10. Ivan DeJesus, 1980 | 44 |

## RUNS PER GAME

| | |
|---|---|
| 1. Ross Barnes, 1876 | 1.91 |
| 2. King Kelly, 1886 | 1.31 |
| 3. George Gore, 1886 | 1.27 |
| 4. Bill Dahlen, 1894 | 1.24 |
| 5. Jimmy Ryan, 1894 | 1.23 |
| 6. Bill Dahlen, 1896 | 1.22 |
| 7. George Gore, 1882 | 1.18 |
| 8. George Gore, 1881 | 1.18 |
| 9. King Kelly, 1885 | 1.16 |
| 10. Abner Dalrymple, 1882 | 1.14 |

## RUNS BATTED IN PER GAME

| | |
|---|---|
| 1. Hack Wilson, 1930 | 1.23 |
| 2. Cap Anson, 1894 | 1.19 |
| 3. Cap Anson, 1886 | 1.18 |
| 4. Hack Wilson, 1929 | 1.06 |
| 5. Cap Anson, 1885 | 1.02 |
| 6. Cap Anson, 1882 | 1.01 |
| 7. George Decker, 1894 | 1.01 |
| 8. Walt Wilmot, 1894 | .98 |
| 9. Cap Anson, 1881 | .98 |
| 10. Rogers Hornsby, 1929 | .96 |

## HOME RUN PERCENTAGE

| | |
|---|---|
| 1. Hack Wilson, 1930 | 9.6 |
| 2. Dave Kingman, 1979 | 9.0 |
| 3. Hank Sauer, 1954 | 7.9 |
| 4. Ernie Banks, 1959 | 7.6 |
| 5. Ernie Banks, 1958 | 7.6 |
| 6. Ernie Banks, 1955 | 7.4 |
| 7. Gabby Hartnett, 1930 | 7.3 |
| 8. Ernie Banks, 1957 | 7.2 |
| 9. Andy Pafko, 1950 | 7.0 |
| 10. Ernie Banks, 1960 | 6.9 |

## AT BATS

1. Billy Herman, 1935 ............ 666
2. Don Kessinger, 1969 ............ 664
3. Ken Hubbs, 1962 ............ 661
4. Bill Buckner, 1982 ............ 657
5. Glenn Beckert, 1966 ............ 656
5. Billy Herman, 1932 ............ 656
7. Jigger Statz, 1923 ............ 655
7. Don Kessinger, 1968 ............ 655
9. Billy Williams, 1966 ............ 648
10. Sparky Adams, 1927 ............ 647

## EXTRA BASE HITS

1. Hack Wilson, 1930 ............ 97
2. Rogers Hornsby, 1929 ............ 94
3. Ernie Banks, 1957 ............ 83
4. Ernie Banks, 1955 ............ 82
5. Ernie Banks, 1958 ............ 81
6. Ernie Banks, 1960 ............ 80
6. Billy Williams, 1970 ............ 80
6. Kiki Cuyler, 1930 ............ 80
9. Billy Williams, 1965 ............ 79
10. Billy Williams, 1972 ............ 77

## TOTAL BASES

1. Hack Wilson, 1930 ............ 423
2. Rogers Hornsby, 1929 ............ 409
3. Ernie Banks, 1958 ............ 379
4. Billy Williams, 1970 ............ 373
5. Billy Williams, 1965 ............ 356
6. Hack Wilson, 1929 ............ 355
6. Ernie Banks, 1955 ............ 355
8. Ernie Banks, 1959 ............ 351
8. Kiki Cuyler, 1930 ............ 351
10. Billy Williams, 1972 ............ 348

## BASES ON BALLS

1. Jimmy Sheckard, 1911 ............ 147
2. Jimmy Sheckard, 1912 ............ 122
3. Richie Ashburn, 1960 ............ 116
4. Cap Anson, 1890 ............ 113
5. Johnny Evers, 1910 ............ 108
6. Hack Wilson, 1930 ............ 105
7. Gary Matthews, 1984 ............ 103
8. George Gore, 1886 ............ 102
9. Woody English, 1930 ............ 100
10. Stan Hack, 1941 ............ 99
10. Stan Hack, 1945 ............ 99

## STRIKEOUTS

1. Byron Browne, 1966 ............ 143
2. Adolfo Phillips, 1966 ............ 135
3. Dave Kingman, 1979 ............ 131
4. Ken Hubbs, 1962 ............ 129
5. Billy Cowan, 1964 ............ 128
6. Rick Monday, 1976 ............ 125
7. Rick Monday, 1973 ............ 124
8. Lou Brock, 1963 ............ 122
9. Roy Smalley, 1950 ............ 114
10. Randy Hundley, 1966 ............ 113

## HIGHEST STRIKEOUT AVERAGE

1. Billy Cowan, 1964 ............ .258
2. Dave Kingman, 1979 ............ .246
3. Larry Corcoran, 1883 ............ .236
4. Rick Monday, 1972 ............ .235
5. Rick Monday, 1976 ............ .234
6. Rick Monday, 1973 ............ .224
7. Lou Brock, 1963 ............ .223
8. Jerry Martin, 1980 ............ .217
9. Randy Hundley, 1966 ............ .215
10. Ron Cey, 1984 ............ .214

## BB AVERAGE

1. Jimmy Sheckard, 1911 ............ .214
2. Johnny Evers, 1910 ............ .200
3. Jimmy Sheckard, 1912 ............ .189
4. George Gore, 1886 ............ .187
5. Cap Anson, 1890 ............ .183
6. Richie Ashburn, 1960 ............ .175
7. Gary Matthews, 1984 ............ .173
8. Bob O'Farrell, 1922 ............ .168
9. Frank Chance, 1905 ............ .166
10. Ned Williamson, 1886 ............ .157

## PINCH HITS

1. Thad Bosley, 1985 ............ 20
2. Merritt Ranew, 1963 ............ 17
2. Jim Bolger, 1957 ............ 17
2. Bob Will, 1962 ............ 17
5. Frankie Baumholtz, 1955 ............ 15
5. Babe Twombly, 1921 ............ 15
5. Jesus Figueroa, 1980 ............ 15
8. Chick Tolson, 1926 ............ 14
8. Champ Summers, 1975 ............ 14
10. Larry Biittner, 1979 ............ 13

## PINCH HIT AT BATS

1. Bob Will, 1962 ............ 67
2. Thad Bosley, 1985 ............ 60
3. Richie Hebner, 1985 ............ 59
4. Bob Molinaro, 1982 ............ 53
4. Chuck Tanner, 1958 ............ 53
4. Jesus Figueroa, 1980 ............ 53
7. Bob Will, 1961 ............ 52
7. Larry Biittner, 1980 ............ 52
9. Jim Bolger, 1958 ............ 51
10. Jim McKnight, 1962 ............ 49
10. Chris Ward, 1974 ............ 49

## PINCH HIT BATTING AVERAGE

1. Merritt Ranew, 1963 ............ .415
2. Frankie Baumholtz, 1955 ............ .405
3. Babe Twombly, 1921 ............ .395
4. Mike Vail, 1978 ............ .367
5. Scot Thompson, 1979 ............ .364
5. Phil Cavarretta, 1951 ............ .364
7. Jim Bolger, 1957 ............ .354
8. Chick Tolson, 1926 ............ .350

### GAMES

1. Ted Abernathy, 1965 ........ 84
1. Dick Tidrow, 1980 ........ 84
3. Bill Campbell, 1983 ........ 82
4. Bill Hutchison, 1892 ........ 75
4. Willie Hernandez, 1982 ........ 75
6. Bill Caudill, 1980 ........ 72
6. Lee Smith, 1982 ........ 72
8. Bill Hutchison, 1890 ........ 71
8. Lindy McDaniel, 1965 ........ 71
8. Phil Regan, 1969 ........ 71
8. Donnie Moore, 1978 ........ 71

### WINS

1. John Clarkson, 1885 ........ 53
2. Al Spalding, 1876 ........ 47
3. Larry Corcoran, 1880 ........ 43
3. Bill Hutchison, 1891 ........ 43
5. Bill Hutchison, 1890 ........ 42
6. John Clarkson, 1887 ........ 38
7. Bill Hutchison, 1892 ........ 37
8. John Clarkson, 1886 ........ 35
8. Larry Corcoran, 1884 ........ 35
10. Larry Corcoran, 1883 ........ 34

### LOSSES

1. Bill Hutchison, 1892 ........ 34
2. Terry Larkin, 1878 ........ 26
3. Bill Hutchison, 1890 ........ 25
4. Bill Hutchison, 1893 ........ 23
4. George Bradley, 1877 ........ 23
4. Terry Larkin, 1879 ........ 23
4. Larry Corcoran, 1884 ........ 23
8. Dick Ellsworth, 1966 ........ 22
8. Bill Bonham, 1974 ........ 22

### COMPLETE GAMES

1. John Clarkson, 1885 ........ 68
2. Bill Hutchison, 1892 ........ 67
3. Bill Hutchison, 1890 ........ 65
4. Terry Larkin, 1879 ........ 57
4. Larry Corcoran, 1884 ........ 57
4. Larry Corcoran, 1880 ........ 57
7. Terry Larkin, 1878 ........ 56
7. Bill Hutchison, 1891 ........ 56
7. John Clarkson, 1887 ........ 56
10. Al Spalding, 1876 ........ 53

### WINNING PERCENTAGE

1. Fred Goldsmith, 1880 ........ .875
2. Hank Borowy, 1945 ........ .846
3. King Cole, 1910 ........ .833
3. Jim McCormick, 1885 ........ .833
5. Ed Reulbach, 1906 ........ .826
6. Three Finger Brown, 1906 ........ .813
7. Ed Reulbach, 1907 ........ .810
8. Jocko Flynn, 1886 ........ .800
8. Bert Humphries, 1913 ........ .800
8. Orval Overall, 1906 ........ .800
8. Jack Taylor, 1906 ........ .800

### EARNED RUN AVERAGE

1. Three Finger Brown, 1906 ........ 1.04
2. Jack Pfiester, 1907 ........ 1.15
3. Carl Lundgren, 1907 ........ 1.17
4. Three Finger Brown, 1909 ........ 1.31
5. Jack Taylor, 1902 ........ 1.33
6. Three Finger Brown, 1907 ........ 1.39
7. Ed Reulbach, 1905 ........ 1.42
7. Orval Overall, 1909 ........ 1.42
9. Three Finger Brown, 1908 ........ 1.47
10. Jack Pfiester, 1906 ........ 1.56

### INNINGS PITCHED

1. Bill Hutchison, 1892 ........ 627
2. John Clarkson, 1885 ........ 623
3. Bill Hutchison, 1890 ........ 603
4. Bill Hutchison, 1891 ........ 561
5. Larry Corcoran, 1880 ........ 536
6. Al Spalding, 1876 ........ 529
7. John Clarkson, 1887 ........ 523
8. Larry Corcoran, 1884 ........ 517
9. Terry Larkin, 1879 ........ 513
10. Terry Larkin, 1878 ........ 506

### STRIKEOUTS

1. John Clarkson, 1886 ........ 340
2. John Clarkson, 1885 ........ 318
3. Bill Hutchison, 1892 ........ 316
4. Bill Hutchison, 1890 ........ 289
5. Ferguson Jenkins, 1970 ........ 274
6. Ferguson Jenkins, 1969 ........ 273
7. Larry Corcoran, 1884 ........ 272
8. Larry Corcoran, 1880 ........ 268
9. Ferguson Jenkins, 1971 ........ 263
10. Bill Hutchison, 1891 ........ 261

### BASES ON BALLS

1. Bill Hutchison, 1890 ........ 199
2. Bill Hutchison, 1892 ........ 187
3. Sam Jones, 1955 ........ 185
4. Willie McGill, 1893 ........ 181
5. Bill Hutchison, 1891 ........ 178
6. Bill Hutchison, 1893 ........ 156
7. Bill Hutchison, 1894 ........ 140
7. Larry Cheney, 1914 ........ 140
9. Danny Friend, 1896 ........ 139
10. Adonis Terry, 1895 ........ 131

## HITS PER 9 INNINGS

1. Ed Reulbach, 1906 .......... 5.33
2. Carl Lundgren, 1907 .......... 5.65
3. Three Finger Brown, 1908 .. ... 6.17
4. Ed Reulbach, 1905 .......... 6.41
5. Three Finger Brown, 1906 .. 6.43
6. Orval Overall, 1909 .......... 6.44
7. Jack Pfiester, 1906 .......... 6.44
8. Three Finger Brown, 1909 .. 6.46
9. Sam Jones, 1955 .......... 6.52
10. King Cole, 1910 .......... 6.53

## STRIKEOUTS PER 9 INNINGS

1. Dick Selma, 1969 .......... 8.59
2. Sam Jones, 1956 .......... 8.40
3. Ferguson Jenkins, 1969 ...... 7.90
4. Ferguson Jenkins, 1970 .. 7.88
5. John Clarkson, 1884 .......... 7.78
6. Ferguson Jenkins, 1968 .. ... 7.60
7. Sam Jones, 1955 .......... 7.37
8. Ferguson Jenkins, 1967 .. 7.34
9. Ferguson Jenkins, 1966 .. 7.32
10. Ferguson Jenkins, 1971 ...... 7.28

## BASES ON BALLS PER 9 INNINGS

1. Al Spalding, 1876 .......... .44
2. Terry Larkin, 1879 .......... .53
3. Terry Larkin, 1878 .......... .55
4. Fred Goldsmith, 1880 .......... .77
5. Fred Goldsmith, 1882 .......... .84
6. Grover Alexander, 1923 ...... .89
7. George Bradley, 1877 .......... .89
8. Fred Goldsmith, 1883 .......... .92
9. Dennis Eckersley, 1985 ...... 1.01
10. Ferguson Jenkins, 1971 ...... 1.02

## SHUTOUTS

1. Three Finger Brown, 1906 ...... 10
1. John Clarkson, 1885 .......... 10
3. Grover Alexander, 1919 ...... 9
3. Three Finger Brown, 1908 .. 9
3. Orval Overall, 1909 .......... 9
3. Bill Lee, 1938 .......... 9

## RELIEF GAMES

1. Ted Abernathy, 1965 .......... 84
1. Dick Tidrow, 1980 .......... 84
3. Bill Campbell, 1983 .......... 82
4. Willie Hernandez, 1982 .......... 75
5. Lindy McDaniel, 1965 .......... 71
5. Phil Regan, 1969 .......... 71

## RELIEF WINS

1. Lindy McDaniel, 1963 .......... 13
2. Phil Regan, 1969 .......... 12
3. Dick Tidrow, 1979 .......... 11

## SAVES

1. Bruce Sutter, 1979 .......... 37
2. Lee Smith, 1985 .......... 33
2. Lee Smith, 1984 .......... 33
4. Ted Abernathy, 1965 .......... 31
4. Bruce Sutter, 1977 .......... 31

## RELIEF WINS PLUS SAVES

1. Bruce Sutter, 1979 .......... 43
2. Lee Smith, 1984 .......... 42
3. Lee Smith, 1985 .......... 40
4. Bruce Sutter, 1977 .......... 38

## RELIEF WINNING PERCENTAGE

1. Emil Kush, 1946 .......... 1.000
1. Charlie Root, 1937 .......... 1.000
3. Willie Hernandez, 1978 .......... .800
4. Dick Tidrow, 1982 .......... .727
5. Dick Tidrow, 1979 .......... .688

| PUTOUTS | ASSISTS | FIELDING AVERAGE |
|---|---|---|

**1B**

| PUTOUTS | | ASSISTS | | FIELDING AVERAGE | |
|---|---|---|---|---|---|
| 1. Ernie Banks, 1965 | 1682 | 1. Bill Buckner, 1983 | 161 | 1. Ernie Banks, 1969 | .997 |
| 2. Vic Saier, 1916 | 1622 | 2. Bill Buckner, 1982 | 159 | 2. Eddie Waitkus, 1946 | .996 |
| 3. Ernie Banks, 1964 | 1565 | 3. Ernie Banks, 1964 | 132 | 3. Charlie Grimm, 1933 | .996 |
| 4. Bill Buckner, 1982 | 1547 | 4. Bill Buckner, 1979 | 124 | 4. Ernie Banks, 1968 | .996 |
| 5. Ray Grimes, 1921 | 1544 | 5. Charlie Grimm, 1932 | 123 | 5. Ripper Collins, 1938 | .996 |

**2B**

| PUTOUTS | | ASSISTS | | FIELDING AVERAGE | |
|---|---|---|---|---|---|
| 1. Billy Herman, 1933 | 466 | 1. Ryne Sandberg, 1983 | 571 | 1. Ryne Sandberg, 1984 | .993 |
| 2. Billy Herman, 1936 | 457 | 2. Sparky Adams, 1925 | 551 | 2. Glenn Beckert, 1971 | .986 |
| 3. Fred Pfeffer, 1889 | 452 | 3. Ryne Sandberg, 1984 | 550 | 3. Ryne Sandberg, 1985 | .986 |
| 4. Gene Baker, 1955 | 432 | 4. Rogers Hornsby, 1929 | 547 | 4. Ryne Sandberg, 1983 | .986 |
| 5. Fred Pfeffer, 1891 | 429 | 5. Billy Herman, 1932 | 527 | 5. Ken Hubbs, 1962 | .983 |
| | | 5. Manny Trillo, 1976 | 527 | | |

**3B**

| PUTOUTS | | ASSISTS | | FIELDING AVERAGE | |
|---|---|---|---|---|---|
| 1. Tom Burns, 1889 | 225 | 1. Ron Santo, 1967 | 393 | 1. Ken Reitz, 1981 | .977 |
| 2. Randy Jackson, 1951 | 198 | 2. Ron Santo, 1966 | 391 | 2. Stan Hack, 1945 | .975 |
| 3. Stan Hack, 1945 | 195 | 3. Ron Santo, 1968 | 378 | 3. Woody English, 1933 | .973 |
| 4. Tom Burns, 1888 | 194 | 4. Ron Santo, 1963 | 374 | 4. Charlie Deal, 1921 | .973 |
| 5. Tom Burns, 1890 | 188 | 5. Ron Santo, 1965 | 373 | 5. Charlie Deal, 1920 | .973 |

**SS**

| PUTOUTS | | ASSISTS | | FIELDING AVERAGE | |
|---|---|---|---|---|---|
| 1. Bill Dahlen, 1898 | 369 | 1. Ivan DeJesus, 1977 | 595 | 1. Ernie Banks, 1959 | .985 |
| 2. Joe Tinker, 1912 | 354 | 2. Don Kessinger, 1968 | 573 | 2. Larry Bowa, 1983 | .984 |
| 3. Bill Jurges, 1935 | 348 | 3. Joe Tinker, 1908 | 570 | 3. Ernie Banks, 1960 | .977 |
| 4. Joe Tinker, 1905 | 345 | 4. Ivan DeJesus, 1978 | 558 | 4. Don Kessinger, 1969 | .976 |
| 5. Jimmy Cooney, 1926 | 344 | 5. Don Kessinger, 1969 | 542 | 5. Bill Jurges, 1937 | .975 |

**OF**

| PUTOUTS | | ASSISTS | | FIELDING AVERAGE | |
|---|---|---|---|---|---|
| 1. Jigger Statz, 1923 | 438 | 1. Orator Shaffer, 1879 | 50 | 1. Rick Monday, 1972 | .996 |
| 2. Hack Wilson, 1927 | 400 | 2. King Kelly, 1883 | 38 | 2. Andy Pafko, 1945 | .995 |
| 3. Augie Galan, 1936 | 381 | 3. Jimmy Ryan, 1889 | 36 | 3. Wildfire Schulte, 1908 | .994 |
| 4. Hack Wilson, 1929 | 380 | 4. Jimmy Ryan, 1888 | 34 | 4. Lee Walls, 1958 | .992 |
| 5. Kiki Cuyler, 1930 | 377 | 5. Jimmy Ryan, 1887 | 33 | 5. Bob Will, 1960 | .992 |

**C**

| PUTOUTS | | ASSISTS | | FIELDING AVERAGE | |
|---|---|---|---|---|---|
| 1. Randy Hundley, 1969 | 978 | 1. Johnny Kling, 1903 | 189 | 1. Gabby Hartnett, 1937 | .996 |
| 2. Randy Hundley, 1968 | 885 | 2. Johnny Kling, 1902 | 158 | 2. Randy Hundley, 1967 | .996 |
| 3. Randy Hundley, 1966 | 871 | 3. Johnny Kling, 1908 | 149 | 3. Gabby Hartnett, 1934 | .996 |
| 4. Randy Hundley, 1967 | 865 | 3. Jimmy Archer, 1912 | 149 | 4. Randy Hundley, 1972 | .995 |
| 5. Jody Davis, 1984 | 811 | 5. Tom Daly, 1887 | 148 | 5. Randy Hundley, 1968 | .995 |

**P**

| PUTOUTS | | ASSISTS | |
|---|---|---|---|
| 1. Larry Corcoran, 1884 | 47 | 1. John Clarkson, 1885 | 174 |
| 2. Al Spalding, 1876 | 45 | 2. Bill Hutchison, 1892 | 156 |
| 3. Bill Hutchison, 1890 | 44 | 3. Larry Corcoran, 1884 | 132 |
| 4. Jake Weimer, 1904 | 37 | 4. Bill Hutchison, 1890 | 128 |
| 4. Larry Corcoran, 1883 | 37 | 5. John Clarkson, 1887 | 125 |

| TOTAL CHANCES | TOTAL CHANCES PER GAME | DOUBLE PLAYS |
|---|---|---|

**1B**

| | | |
|---|---|---|
| 1. Ernie Banks, 1965 ........ 1790 | 1. Cap Anson, 1879 ........ 12.6 | 1. Charlie Grimm, 1928 ........ 147 |
| 2. Vic Saier, 1916 ........ 1723 | 2. Joe Start, 1878 ........ 12.5 | 2. Ernie Banks, 1965 ........ 143 |
| 3. Bill Buckner, 1982 ........ 1718 | 3. Cap Anson, 1885 ........ 12.0 | 3. Charlie Grimm, 1926 ........ 139 |
| 4. Ernie Banks, 1964 ........ 1707 | 4. Bill Everett, 1899 ........ 12.0 | 4. Dee Fondy, 1955 ........ 135 |
| 5. Bill Everett, 1899 ........ 1633 | 5. Fred Merkle, 1919 ........ 11.9 | 5. Ernie Banks, 1962 ........ 134 |

**2B**

| | | |
|---|---|---|
| 1. Billy Herman, 1933 ........ 1023 | 1. Fred Pfeffer, 1884 ........ 8.1 | 1. Freddie Maguire, 1928 ........ 126 |
| 2. Fred Pfeffer, 1889 ........ 991 | 2. Joe Quest, 1879 ........ 7.7 | 1. Ryne Sandberg, 1983 ........ 126 |
| 3. Fred Pfeffer, 1891 ........ 980 | 3. Fred Pfeffer, 1883 ........ 7.5 | 3. Billy Herman, 1933 ........ 114 |
| 4. Billy Herman, 1936 ........ 973 | 4. Fred Pfeffer, 1889 ........ 7.4 | 3. Gene Baker, 1955 ........ 114 |
| 5. Billy Herman, 1935 ........ 971 | 5. Fred Pfeffer, 1885 ........ 7.4 | 5. Billy Herman, 1938 ........ 111 |

**3B**

| | | |
|---|---|---|
| 1. Ron Santo, 1967 ........ 606 | 1. Cap Anson, 1876 ........ 5.0 | 1. Ron Santo, 1961 ........ 41 |
| 2. Tom Burns, 1889 ........ 598 | 2. Bill Bradley, 1900 ........ 4.9 | 2. Ron Santo, 1970 ........ 36 |
| 3. Ron Santo, 1966 ........ 566 | 3. Frank Hankinson, 1878 ........ 4.6 | 2. Ron Santo, 1966 ........ 36 |
| 4. Ron Santo, 1965 ........ 552 | 4. Ned Williamson, 1883 ........ 4.6 | |
| 5. Randy Jackson, 1951 ........ 545 | 5. Ned Williamson, 1879 ........ 4.5 | |

**SS**

| | | |
|---|---|---|
| 1. Bill Dahlen, 1898 ........ 956 | 1. Bill Dahlen, 1895 ........ 6.9 | 1. Roy Smalley, 1950 ........ 115 |
| 2. Joe Tinker, 1905 ........ 928 | 2. Bill Dahlen, 1893 ........ 6.8 | 2. Don Kessinger, 1973 ........ 109 |
| 3. Roy Smalley, 1950 ........ 924 | 3. Bill Dahlen, 1898 ........ 6.7 | 3. Jimmy Cooney, 1926 ........ 107 |
| 4. Joe Tinker, 1908 ........ 923 | 4. Bill Dahlen, 1896 ........ 6.7 | 3. Woody English, 1929 ........ 107 |
| 5. Bill Dahlen, 1895 ........ 894 | 5. Johnny Peters, 1877 ........ 6.4 | 5. Ernie Banks, 1954 ........ 105 |

**OF**

| | | |
|---|---|---|
| 1. Jigger Statz, 1923 ........ 476 | 1. Jigger Statz, 1924 ........ 3.1 | 1. Jimmy Sheckard, 1911 ........ 12 |
| 2. Hack Wilson, 1927 ........ 427 | 2. Jigger Statz, 1923 ........ 3.1 | 2. Bill Lange, 1899 ........ 11 |
| 3. Jigger Statz, 1924 ........ 411 | 3. Jigger Statz, 1922 ........ 3.1 | 2. Danny Green, 1899 ........ 11 |
| 4. Hack Wilson, 1929 ........ 406 | 4. Peanuts Lowrey, 1943 ........ 3.0 | 4. Bill Lange, 1894 ........ 10 |
| 5. Kiki Cuyler, 1930 ........ 406 | 5. Andy Pafko, 1944 ........ 3.0 | 4. Wilbur Good, 1914 ........ 10 |

**C**

| | | |
|---|---|---|
| 1. Randy Hundley, 1969 ........ 1065 | 1. Tom Daly, 1887 ........ 8.4 | 1. Bob O'Farrell, 1922 ........ 22 |
| 2. Randy Hundley, 1968 ........ 971 | 2. Silver Flint, 1880 ........ 8.1 | 2. Gabby Hartnett, 1927 ........ 21 |
| 3. Randy Hundley, 1966 ........ 970 | 3. Bill Harbidge, 1878 ........ 7.4 | 3. Gabby Hartnett, 1933 ........ 17 |
| 4. Randy Hundley, 1967 ........ 928 | 4. Silver Flint, 1885 ........ 7.2 | 3. Randy Hundley, 1969 ........ 17 |
| 5. Jody Davis, 1984 ........ 915 | 5. Silver Flint, 1884 ........ 7.2 | |

**P**

| | | |
|---|---|---|
| 1. John Clarkson, 1885 ........ 220 | 1. Guy Bush, 1933 ........ 6.5 | 1. Guy Bush, 1932 ........ 10 |
| 2. Larry Corcoran, 1884 ........ 203 | 2. John Clarkson, 1884 ........ 3.9 | 2. Claude Passeau, 1942 ........ 9 |
| 3. Bill Hutchison, 1892 ........ 190 | 3. Jock Menefee, 1903 ........ 3.9 | 2. Rick Reuschel, 1979 ........ 9 |
| 4. Bill Hutchison, 1890 ........ 186 | 4. Nixey Callahan, 1900 ........ 3.7 | 4. Johnny Schmitz, 1949 ........ 8 |
| 5. John Clarkson, 1887 ........ 166 | 5. Nixey Callahan, 1899 ........ 3.6 | 4. Jack Taylor, 1899 ........ 8 |
| | | 4. John Clarkson, 1885 ........ 8 |

| PUTOUTS PER GAME | | ASSISTS PER GAME | |
|---|---|---|---|
| **1B** | | | |
| 1. Cap Anson, 1879 | 12.2 | 1. Bill Buckner, 1983 | 1.1 |
| 2. Joe Start, 1878 | 11.8 | 2. Bill Buckner, 1982 | 1.0 |
| 3. Fred Merkle, 1919 | 11.3 | 3. Bill Buckner, 1979 | .9 |
| 4. Cap Anson, 1885 | 11.2 | 4. Dee Fondy, 1954 | .9 |
| 5. Vic Saier, 1916 | 11.0 | 5. Frank Chance, 1904 | .9 |
| **2B** | | | |
| 1. Fred Pfeffer, 1884 | 3.5 | 1. Joe Quest, 1879 | 4.0 |
| 2. Fred Pfeffer, 1889 | 3.4 | 2. Sparky Adams, 1925 | 3.8 |
| 3. Fred Pfeffer, 1883 | 3.3 | 3. Freddie Maguire, 1928 | 3.8 |
| 4. Fred Pfeffer, 1887 | 3.2 | 4. Fred Pfeffer, 1884 | 3.8 |
| 5. Joe Quest, 1879 | 3.2 | 5. Footsie Blair, 1930 | 3.7 |
| **3B** | | | |
| 1. Cap Anson, 1876 | 2.0 | 1. Ned Williamson, 1879 | 2.8 |
| 2. Cap Anson, 1877 | 1.9 | 2. Bill Bradley, 1900 | 2.7 |
| 3. Tom Burns, 1889 | 1.7 | 3. Ned Williamson, 1883 | 2.6 |
| 4. Frank Hankinson, 1878 | 1.6 | 4. Ron Santo, 1966 | 2.6 |
| 5. Tom Burns, 1887 | 1.6 | 5. Ned Williamson, 1881 | 2.6 |
| **SS** | | | |
| 1. Bill Dahlen, 1893 | 2.6 | 1. Bill Dahlen, 1895 | 4.1 |
| 2. Bill Dahlen, 1898 | 2.6 | 2. Bob Ferguson, 1878 | 4.0 |
| 3. Joe Tinker, 1912 | 2.5 | 3. Ivan DeJesus, 1977 | 3.9 |
| 4. Bill Dahlen, 1896 | 2.5 | 4. Bill Jurges, 1932 | 3.8 |
| 5. Jimmy Cooney, 1926 | 2.4 | 5. Jimmy Cooney, 1891 | 3.7 |
| **OF** | | | |
| 1. Jigger Statz, 1924 | 2.8 | 1. Orator Shaffer, 1879 | .7 |
| 2. Jigger Statz, 1923 | 2.8 | 2. King Kelly, 1880 | .5 |
| 3. Jigger Statz, 1922 | 2.8 | 2. John Cassidy, 1878 | .5 |
| 4. Peanuts Lowrey, 1943 | 2.8 | 4. King Kelly, 1883 | .5 |
| 5. Hack Wilson, 1927 | 2.7 | 5. King Kelly, 1881 | .4 |
| **C** | | | |
| 1. Randy Hundley, 1969 | 6.5 | 1. Tom Daly, 1887 | 2.3 |
| 2. Cal Neeman, 1957 | 6.0 | 2. Silver Flint, 1880 | 1.7 |
| 3. Randy Hundley, 1966 | 5.8 | 3. Duke Farrell, 1889 | 1.6 |
| 4. Silver Flint, 1880 | 5.8 | 4. Silver Flint, 1884 | 1.5 |
| 5. George Mitterwald, 1977 | 5.7 | 5. Silver Flint, 1885 | 1.5 |
| **P** | | | |
| 1. Guy Bush, 1933 | 1.3 | 1. Guy Bush, 1933 | 5.1 |
| 2. Rube Waddell, 1901 | 1.1 | 2. Jack Taylor, 1902 | 2.9 |
| 3. Jake Weimer, 1904 | 1.0 | 3. Nixey Callahan, 1900 | 2.9 |
| 4. Nixey Callahan, 1898 | .9 | 4. Clark Griffith, 1899 | 2.9 |
| 5. George Van Haltren, 1888 | .8 | 5. Grover Alexander, 1919 | 2.8 |
| 5. Jim McCormick, 1885 | .8 | | |

## GAMES

| | | |
|---|---|---|
| 1. Ernie Banks | | 2528 |
| 2. Cap Anson | | 2276 |
| 3. Billy Williams | | 2213 |
| 4. Ron Santo | | 2126 |
| 5. Phil Cavarretta | | 1953 |
| 6. Stan Hack | | 1938 |
| 7. Gabby Hartnett | | 1926 |
| 8. Jimmy Ryan | | 1660 |
| 9. Don Kessinger | | 1648 |
| 10. Wildfire Schulte | | 1564 |

## DOUBLES

| | | |
|---|---|---|
| 1. Cap Anson | | 532 |
| 2. Ernie Banks | | 407 |
| 3. Billy Williams | | 402 |
| 4. Gabby Hartnett | | 391 |
| 5. Stan Hack | | 363 |
| 6. Jimmy Ryan | | 362 |
| 7. Ron Santo | | 353 |
| 8. Billy Herman | | 346 |
| 9. Phil Cavarretta | | 341 |
| 10. Charlie Grimm | | 270 |

## BATTING AVERAGE

| | | |
|---|---|---|
| 1. Riggs Stephenson | | .336 |
| 2. Cap Anson | | .334 |
| 3. Bill Lange | | .330 |
| 4. Kiki Cuyler | | .325 |
| 5. Bill Everett | | .323 |
| 6. Hack Wilson | | .322 |
| 7. King Kelly | | .316 |
| 8. George Gore | | .315 |
| 9. Jimmy Ryan | | .310 |
| 10. Frank Demaree | | .309 |

## AT BATS

| | | |
|---|---|---|
| 1. Ernie Banks | | 9421 |
| 2. Cap Anson | | 9108 |
| 3. Billy Williams | | 8479 |
| 4. Ron Santo | | 7768 |
| 5. Stan Hack | | 7278 |
| 6. Jimmy Ryan | | 6770 |
| 7. Phil Cavarretta | | 6592 |
| 8. Don Kessinger | | 6355 |
| 9. Gabby Hartnett | | 6282 |
| 10. Wildfire Schulte | | 5835 |

## TRIPLES

| | | |
|---|---|---|
| 1. Jimmy Ryan | | 142 |
| 2. Cap Anson | | 124 |
| 3. Wildfire Schulte | | 117 |
| 4. Bill Dahlen | | 106 |
| 5. Phil Cavarretta | | 99 |
| 6. Joe Tinker | | 93 |
| 7. Ernie Banks | | 9C |
| 8. Billy Williams | | 87 |
| 9. Stan Hack | | 81 |

## SLUGGING AVERAGE

| | | |
|---|---|---|
| 1. Hack Wilson | | .590 |
| 2. Hank Sauer | | .512 |
| 3. Billy Williams | | .503 |
| 4. Ernie Banks | | .500 |
| 5. Gabby Hartnett | | .490 |
| 6. Leon Durham | | .487 |
| 7. Kiki Cuyler | | .485 |
| 8. Ron Santo | | .472 |
| 9. Bill Nicholson | | .471 |
| 10. Riggs Stephenson | | .469 |

## HITS

| | | |
|---|---|---|
| 1. Cap Anson | | 3041 |
| 2. Ernie Banks | | 2583 |
| 3. Billy Williams | | 2510 |
| 4. Stan Hack | | 2193 |
| 5. Ron Santo | | 2171 |
| 6. Jimmy Ryan | | 2102 |
| 7. Phil Cavarretta | | 1927 |
| 8. Gabby Hartnett | | 1867 |
| 9. Billy Herman | | 1710 |
| 10. Don Kessinger | | 1619 |

## HOME RUNS

| | | |
|---|---|---|
| 1. Ernie Banks | | 512 |
| 2. Billy Williams | | 392 |
| 3. Ron Santo | | 337 |
| 4. Gabby Hartnett | | 231 |
| 5. Bill Nicholson | | 205 |
| 6. Hank Sauer | | 198 |
| 7. Hack Wilson | | 190 |
| 8. Andy Pafko | | 126 |
| 9. Rick Monday | | 106 |

## HOME RUN PERCENTAGE

| | | |
|---|---|---|
| 1. Hank Sauer | | 6.3 |
| 2. Hack Wilson | | 6.0 |
| 3. Ernie Banks | | 5.4 |
| 4. Jim Hickman | | 4.9 |
| 5. Billy Williams | | 4.6 |
| 6. Ron Cey | | 4.5 |
| 7. Ron Santo | | 4.3 |
| 8. Bill Nicholson | | 4.2 |
| 9. Rick Monday | | 4.2 |
| 10. Walt Moryn | | 4.0 |

## EXTRA BASE HITS

| | | |
|---|---|---|
| 1. Ernie Banks | | 1009 |
| 2. Billy Williams | | 881 |
| 3. Ron Santo | | 756 |
| 4. Cap Anson | | 752 |
| 5. Gabby Hartnett | | 686 |
| 6. Jimmy Ryan | | 603 |
| 7. Phil Cavarretta | | 532 |
| 8. Bill Nicholson | | 503 |
| 9. Stan Hack | | 501 |
| 10. Wildfire Schulte | | 463 |

## TOTAL BASES

| | | |
|---|---|---|
| 1. Ernie Banks | | 4706 |
| 2. Billy Williams | | 4262 |
| 3. Cap Anson | | 4109 |
| 4. Ron Santo | | 3667 |
| 5. Gabby Hartnett | | 3079 |
| 6. Jimmy Ryan | | 3045 |
| 7. Stan Hack | | 2889 |
| 8. Phil Cavarretta | | 2742 |
| 9. Wildfire Schulte | | 2354 |
| 10. Billy Herman | | 2305 |

## STOLEN BASES

| | | |
|---|---|---|
| 1. Frank Chance | | 404 |
| 2. Joe Tinker | | 304 |
| 3. Johnny Evers | | 291 |
| 4. Wildfire Schulte | | 214 |
| 5. Jimmy Slagle | | 198 |
| 6. Stan Hack | | 165 |
| 7. Jimmy Sheckard | | 163 |
| 8. Kiki Cuyler | | 161 |
| 9. Solly Hofman | | 158 |
| 10. Ryne Sandberg | | 155 |

## RUNS

| | | |
|---|---|---|
| 1. | Cap Anson | 1719 |
| 2. | Jimmy Ryan | 1410 |
| 3. | Billy Williams | 1306 |
| 4. | Ernie Banks | 1305 |
| 5. | Stan Hack | 1239 |
| 6. | Ron Santo | 1109 |
| 7. | Phil Cavarretta | 968 |
| 8. | Bill Dahlen | 918 |
| 9. | Billy Herman | 875 |
| 10. | Gabby Hartnett | 847 |

## RUNS BATTED IN PER GAME

| | | |
|---|---|---|
| 1. | Hack Wilson | .90 |
| 2. | Cap Anson | .75 |
| 3. | Bill Lange | .71 |
| 4. | Walt Wilmot | .68 |
| 5. | Hank Sauer | .68 |
| 6. | Ernie Banks | .65 |
| 7. | Kiki Cuyler | .63 |
| 8. | Bill Nicholson | .62 |
| 9. | George Decker | .62 |
| 10. | Billy Williams | .61 |

## STRIKEOUTS

| | | |
|---|---|---|
| 1. | Ron Santo | 1271 |
| 2. | Ernie Banks | 1236 |
| 3. | Billy Williams | 934 |
| 4. | Gabby Hartnett | 683 |
| 5. | Bill Nicholson | 676 |
| 6. | Don Kessinger | 629 |
| 7. | Phil Cavarretta | 585 |
| 8. | Rick Monday | 540 |
| 9. | Randy Hundley | 519 |
| 10. | Ned Williamson | 482 |

## RUNS BATTED IN

| | | |
|---|---|---|
| 1. | Cap Anson | 1715 |
| 2. | Ernie Banks | 1636 |
| 3. | Billy Williams | 1353 |
| 4. | Ron Santo | 1290 |
| 5. | Gabby Hartnett | 1153 |
| 6. | Jimmy Ryan | 914 |
| 7. | Phil Cavarretta | 896 |
| 8. | Bill Nicholson | 833 |
| 9. | Hack Wilson | 768 |
| 10. | Wildfire Schulte | 743 |

## BASES ON BALLS

| | | |
|---|---|---|
| 1. | Stan Hack | 1092 |
| 2. | Ron Santo | 1071 |
| 3. | Cap Anson | 952 |
| 4. | Billy Williams | 911 |
| 5. | Phil Cavarretta | 794 |
| 6. | Ernie Banks | 763 |
| 7. | Bill Nicholson | 696 |
| 8. | Gabby Hartnett | 691 |
| 9. | Jimmy Ryan | 683 |
| 10. | Jimmy Sheckard | 629 |

## HIGHEST STRIKEOUTS PER AT BAT

| | | |
|---|---|---|
| 1. | Rick Monday | .212 |
| 2. | Roy Smalley | .203 |
| 3. | Andre Rodgers | .198 |
| 4. | Jim Hickman | .190 |
| 5. | Ron Cey | .189 |
| 6. | Jody Davis | .187 |
| 7. | George Altman | .185 |
| 8. | Leon Durham | .179 |
| 9. | Barry McCormick | .179 |
| 10. | Silver Flint | .172 |

## RUNS PER GAME

| | | |
|---|---|---|
| 1. | George Gore | 1.07 |
| 2. | King Kelly | 1.07 |
| 3. | Abner Dalrymple | .94 |
| 4. | Bill Dahlen | .93 |
| 5. | Bill Lange | .85 |
| 6. | Jimmy Ryan | .85 |
| 7. | Walt Wilmot | .80 |
| 8. | Bill Everett | .78 |
| 9. | Hack Wilson | .77 |
| 10. | Cap Anson | .76 |

## BB AVERAGE

| | | |
|---|---|---|
| 1. | Jimmy Sheckard | .151 |
| 2. | Dom Dallessandro | .136 |
| 3. | Jim Hickman | .132 |
| 4. | Rick Monday | .131 |
| 5. | Stan Hack | .130 |
| 6. | Hack Wilson | .128 |
| 7. | Bill Nicholson | .125 |
| 8. | Ron Santo | .121 |
| 9. | Jimmy Slagle | .118 |
| 10. | Bob O'Farrell | .117 |

## LOWEST STRIKEOUTS PER AT BAT

| | | |
|---|---|---|
| 1. | Charlie Deal | .031 |
| 2. | Charlie Hollocher | .032 |
| 3. | Cap Anson | .034 |
| 4. | Eddie Waitkus | .034 |
| 5. | Sparky Adams | .038 |
| 6. | Johnny Evers | .040 |
| 7. | Bill Buckner | .042 |
| 8. | Bill Lange | .046 |
| 9. | Walt Wilmot | .046 |
| 10. | Charlie Grimm | .047 |

## PINCH HITS

| | | |
|---|---|---|
| 1. | Larry Biittner | 46 |
| 1. | Phil Cavarretta | 46 |
| 1. | Bob Will | 46 |
| 4. | Dom Dallessandro | 45 |
| 5. | Scot Thompson | 39 |
| 6. | Mike Vail | 31 |
| 7. | Thad Bosley | 30 |
| 7. | George Altman | 30 |
| 9. | Jerry Morales | 29 |
| 9. | Gabby Hartnett | 29 |

## PH BATTING AVERAGE

| | | |
|---|---|---|
| 1. | Frankie Baumholtz | .308 |
| 2. | Riggs Stephenson | .304 |
| 3. | Thad Bosley | .297 |
| 4. | Jim Bolger | .280 |
| 5. | Champ Summers | .280 |
| 6. | Willie Smith | .274 |
| 7. | Pete LaCock | .273 |
| 7. | Scot Thompson | .273 |
| 9. | Dom Dallessandro | .271 |
| 10. | Larry Biittner | .271 |

## GAMES

1. Charlie Root .......... 605
2. Don Elston .......... 449
3. Guy Bush .......... 428
4. Ferguson Jenkins .......... 401
5. Bill Hutchison .......... 367
6. Bill Lee .......... 364
7. Rick Reuschel .......... 358
8. Three Finger Brown .......... 346
9. Bob Rush .......... 339
10. Lee Smith .......... 330

## COMPLETE GAMES

1. Bill Hutchison .......... 317
2. Larry Corcoran .......... 253
3. Clark Griffith .......... 240
4. Three Finger Brown .......... 206
5. Jack Taylor .......... 188
6. John Clarkson .......... 186
7. Hippo Vaughn .......... 177
7. Charlie Root .......... 177
9. Fred Goldsmith .......... 163
10. Grover Alexander .......... 159

## INNINGS PITCHED

1. Charlie Root .......... 3138
2. Bill Hutchison .......... 3026
3. Ferguson Jenkins .......... 2673
4. Larry Corcoran .......... 2338
5. Three Finger Brown .......... 2329
6. Rick Reuschel .......... 2291
7. Bill Lee .......... 2271
8. Hippo Vaughn .......... 2216
9. Guy Bush .......... 2201
10. Clark Griffith .......... 2189

## WINS

1. Charlie Root .......... 201
2. Three Finger Brown .......... 188
3. Bill Hutchison .......... 181
4. Larry Corcoran .......... 175
5. Ferguson Jenkins .......... 167
6. Clark Griffith .......... 152
6. Guy Bush .......... 152
8. Hippo Vaughn .......... 151
9. Bill Lee .......... 139
10. John Clarkson .......... 136
10. Ed Reulbach .......... 136

## WINNING PERCENTAGE

1. John Clarkson .......... .705
2. Three Finger Brown .......... .689
3. Ed Reulbach .......... .680
4. Larry Corcoran .......... .670
5. Orval Overall .......... .662
6. Jack Pfiester .......... .636
7. Fred Goldsmith .......... .633
8. Jake Weimer .......... .628
9. Carl Lundgren .......... .621
10. Clark Griffith .......... .620

## STRIKEOUTS

1. Ferguson Jenkins .......... 2038
2. Charlie Root .......... 1432
3. Rick Reuschel .......... 1367
4. Bill Hutchison .......... 1226
5. Hippo Vaughn .......... 1138
6. Larry Corcoran .......... 1086
7. Bob Rush .......... 1076
8. Three Finger Brown .......... 1043
9. John Clarkson .......... 997
10. Ken Holtzman .......... 988

## LOSSES

1. Charlie Root .......... 156
2. Bill Hutchison .......... 154
3. Bob Rush .......... 140
4. Ferguson Jenkins .......... 132
5. Rick Reuschel .......... 127
6. Bill Lee .......... 123
7. Dick Ellsworth .......... 110
8. Hippo Vaughn .......... 104
9. Guy Bush .......... 101
10. Claude Passeau .......... 94

## EARNED RUN AVERAGE

1. Three Finger Brown .......... 1.80
2. Jack Pfiester .......... 1.86
3. Orval Overall .......... 1.92
4. Jake Weimer .......... 2.15
5. Ed Reulbach .......... 2.24
6. Larry Corcoran .......... 2.26
7. Hippo Vaughn .......... 2.33
8. Terry Larkin .......... 2.34
9. John Clarkson .......... 2.39
10. Carl Lundgren .......... 2.42

## BASES ON BALLS

1. Bill Hutchison .......... 1106
2. Charlie Root .......... 871
3. Guy Bush .......... 734
4. Bob Rush .......... 725
5. Bill Lee .......... 704
6. Sheriff Blake .......... 661
7. Ed Reulbach .......... 650
8. Rick Reuschel .......... 640
9. Hippo Vaughn .......... 621
10. Ferguson Jenkins .......... 600

## HITS PER 9 INNINGS

1. Orval Overall ............................ 6.86
2. Ed Reulbach ............................ 7.04
3. Jack Pfiester ............................ 7.20
4. Three Finger Brown ............... 7.26
5. Jake Weimer ........................... 7.32
6. Larry Cheney .......................... 7.63
7. Carl Lundgren ......................... 7.69
8. John Clarkson ......................... 7.92
9. Hippo Vaughn ......................... 8.00
10. Larry Corcoran ........................ 8.02

## SHUTOUTS

1. Three Finger Brown ............... 50
2. Hippo Vaughn ......................... 35
3. Ed Reulbach ............................ 31
4. Ferguson Jenkins .................... 29
5. Orval Overall ........................... 28
6. Bill Lee .................................... 25
7. Grover Alexander .................... 24
8. Claude Passeau ...................... 23
8. Larry Corcoran ........................ 23

## SAVES

1. Bruce Sutter ............................ 133
2. Lee Smith ................................ 113
3. Don Elston ............................... 63
4. Phil Regan ............................... 60
5. Charlie Root ............................. 40

## STRIKEOUTS PER 9 INNINGS

1. Ferguson Jenkins .................... 6.86
2. Bill Bonham ............................. 6.33
3. Don Elston ............................... 6.18
4. Ken Holtzman ......................... 6.14
5. Mike Krukow ........................... 5.85
6. Orval Overall ........................... 5.78
7. Rick Reuschel ......................... 5.37
8. Bob Anderson ......................... 5.35
9. John Clarkson ......................... 5.18
10. Bill Hands ............................... 5.18

## RELIEF GAMES

1. Don Elston ............................... 434
2. Lee Smith ................................ 324
3. Willie Hernandez .................... 312
4. Bruce Sutter ............................ 300
5. Charlie Root ............................. 266

## WINS PLUS SAVES

1. Bruce Sutter ............................ 165
2. Lee Smith ................................ 140
3. Don Elston ............................... 109
4. Phil Regan ............................... 91
5. Charlie Root ............................. 82

## BASES ON BALLS PER 9 INNINGS

1. Terry Larkin ............................. .54
2. Fred Goldsmith ....................... 1.00
3. Grover Alexander .................... 1.28
4. John Clarkson ......................... 1.56
5. Three Finger Brown ............... 1.72
6. Larry Corcoran ........................ 1.78
7. Jack Taylor .............................. 1.84
8. Larry Jackson ......................... 1.86
9. Milt Pappas ............................. 1.97
10. Ferguson Jenkins .................... 2.02

## RELIEF WINS

1. Don Elston ............................... 46
2. Charlie Root ............................. 42
3. Guy Bush ................................. 34
4. Bruce Sutter ............................ 32
5. Phil Regan ............................... 31

## RELIEF WINNING PERCENTAGE

1. Percy Jones ............................. .762
2. Guy Bush ................................. .739
3. Emil Kush ................................ .704
4. Charlie Root ............................. .636
4. Three Finger Brown ............... .636

| GAMES | CHANCES PER GAME | FIELDING AVERAGE |
|---|---|---|

**1B**

| | | |
|---|---|---|
| 1. Cap Anson — 2058 | 1. Fred Merkle — 11.4 | 1. Ernie Banks — .994 |
| 2. Charlie Grimm — 1321 | 2. Ray Grimes — 10.8 | 2. Eddie Waitkus — .993 |
| 3. Ernie Banks — 1259 | 3. Cap Anson — 10.8 | 3. Charlie Grimm — .992 |
| 4. Phil Cavarretta — 1207 | 4. Frank Chance — 10.7 | 4. Bill Buckner — .992 |
| 5. Frank Chance — 989 | 5. Vic Saier — 10.7 | 5. Phil Cavarretta — .990 |

**2B**

| | | |
|---|---|---|
| 1. Johnny Evers — 1368 | 1. Fred Pfeffer — 7.1 | 1. Ryne Sandberg — .989 |
| 2. Billy Herman — 1340 | 2. Billy Herman — 6.3 | 2. Sparky Adams — .976 |
| 3. Glenn Beckert — 1206 | 3. Sparky Adams — 6.2 | 3. Manny Trillo — .974 |
| 4. Fred Pfeffer — 1073 | 4. Gene Baker — 5.8 | 4. Glenn Beckert — .974 |
| 5. Manny Trillo — 607 | 5. Manny Trillo — 5.7 | |

**3B**

| | | |
|---|---|---|
| 1. Ron Santo — 2102 | 1. Ned Williamson — 4.3 | 1. Woody English — .964 |
| 2. Stan Hack — 1836 | 2. Tom Burns — 4.1 | 2. Charlie Deal — .964 |
| 3. Harry Steinfeldt — 730 | 3. Heinie Zimmerman — 3.5 | 3. Stan Hack — .957 |
| 4. Tom Burns — 696 | 4. Charlie Deal — 3.3 | 4. Ron Cey — .955 |
| 5. Randy Jackson — 687 | 5. Randy Jackson — 3.2 | 5. Ron Santo — .954 |

**SS**

| | | |
|---|---|---|
| 1. Don Kessinger — 1618 | 1. Bill Dahlen — 6.8 | 1. Larry Bowa — .976 |
| 2. Joe Tinker — 1500 | 2. Joe Tinker — 5.9 | 2. Ernie Banks — .969 |
| 3. Ernie Banks — 1125 | 3. Charlie Hollocher — 5.8 | 3. Don Kessinger — .964 |
| 4. Bill Jurges — 960 | 4. Bill Jurges — 5.5 | 4. Ivan DeJesus — .963 |
| 5. Charlie Hollocher — 751 | 5. Woody English — 5.5 | 5. Bill Jurges — .963 |

**OF**

| | | |
|---|---|---|
| 1. Billy Williams — 2087 | 1. Jigger Statz — 3.1 | 1. Andy Pafko — .986 |
| 2. Jimmy Ryan — 1591 | 2. Bill Lange — 2.8 | 2. Rick Monday — .983 |
| 3. Wildfire Schulte — 1540 | 3. Andy Pafko — 2.7 | 3. Jerry Morales — .982 |
| 4. Bill Nicholson — 1292 | 4. Hack Wilson — 2.6 | 4. Peanuts Lowrey — .982 |
| 5. Jimmy Sheckard — 999 | 5. Walt Wilmot — 2.5 | 5. Dom Dallessandro — .981 |

**C**

| | | |
|---|---|---|
| 1. Gabby Hartnett — 1756 | 1. Silver Flint — 6.8 | 1. Randy Hundley — .992 |
| 2. Johnny Kling — 960 | 2. Johnny Kling — 6.2 | 2. Dick Bertell — .984 |
| 3. Randy Hundley — 939 | 3. Randy Hundley — 6.2 | 3. Jody Davis — .984 |
| 4. Jimmy Archer — 681 | 4. Jimmy Archer — 6.1 | 4. Gabby Hartnett — .984 |
| 5. Silver Flint — 668 | 5. Jody Davis — 5.7 | 5. Clyde McCullough — .983 |

**P**

| | | |
|---|---|---|
| 1. Charlie Root — 605 | 1. Frank Corridon — 4.4 | |
| 2. Don Elston — 449 | 2. Rube Waddell — 3.4 | |
| 3. Guy Bush — 401 | 3. Nixey Callahan — 3.3 | |
| 4. Ferguson Jenkins — 401 | 4. Frank Hankinson — 3.3 | |
| 5. Bill Hutchison — 367 | 5. Matt Kilroy — 3.0 | |
| | 5. Roscoe Coughlin — 3.0 | |

| PUTOUTS | PUTOUTS PER GAME | ASSISTS |
|---|---|---|

**1B**

| PUTOUTS | PUTOUTS PER GAME | ASSISTS |
|---|---|---|
| 1. Cap Anson — 20761 | 1. Fred Merkle — 10.7 | 1. Cap Anson — 955 |
| 2. Charlie Grimm — 12668 | 2. Ray Grimes — 10.3 | 2. Charlie Grimm — 815 |
| 3. Ernie Banks — 12005 | 3. Cap Anson — 10.1 | 3. Ernie Banks — 809 |
| 4. Phil Cavarretta — 11111 | 4. Vic Saier — 10.0 | 4. Phil Cavarretta — 779 |
| 5. Frank Chance — 9798 | 5. Frank Chance — 9.9 | 5. Bill Buckner — 744 |

**2B**

| PUTOUTS | PUTOUTS PER GAME | ASSISTS |
|---|---|---|
| 1. Billy Herman — 3658 | 1. Fred Pfeffer — 3.1 | 1. Billy Herman — 4453 |
| 2. Fred Pfeffer — 3322 | 2. Billy Herman — 2.7 | 2. Johnny Evers — 4130 |
| 3. Johnny Evers — 3072 | 3. Gene Baker — 2.7 | 3. Fred Pfeffer — 3633 |
| 4. Glenn Beckert — 2640 | 4. Sparky Adams — 2.4 | 4. Glenn Beckert — 3632 |
| 5. Manny Trillo — 1383 | 5. Don Johnson — 2.4 | 5. Manny Trillo — 2008 |

**3B**

| PUTOUTS | PUTOUTS PER GAME | ASSISTS |
|---|---|---|
| 1. Stan Hack — 1944 | 1. Tom Burns — 1.5 | 1. Ron Santo — 4532 |
| 2. Ron Santo — 1930 | 2. Ned Williamson — 1.2 | 2. Stan Hack — 3494 |
| 3. Tom Burns — 1033 | 3. Heinie Zimmerman — 1.2 | 3. Ned Williamson — 1500 |
| 4. Harry Steinfeldt — 807 | 4. Doc Casey — 1.2 | 4. Tom Burns — 1484 |
| 5. Ned Williamson — 737 | 5. Charlie Deal — 1.2 | 5. Randy Jackson — 1388 |

**SS**

| PUTOUTS | PUTOUTS PER GAME | ASSISTS |
|---|---|---|
| 1. Joe Tinker — 3248 | 1. Bill Dahlen — 2.5 | 1. Don Kessinger — 5346 |
| 2. Don Kessinger — 2642 | 2. Joe Tinker — 2.2 | 2. Joe Tinker — 5083 |
| 3. Ernie Banks — 2087 | 3. Charlie Hollocher — 2.1 | 3. Ernie Banks — 3441 |
| 4. Bill Jurges — 1995 | 4. Woody English — 2.1 | 4. Bill Jurges — 3098 |
| 5. Bill Dahlen — 1796 | 5. Bill Jurges — 2.1 | 5. Bill Dahlen — 2622 |

**OF**

| PUTOUTS | PUTOUTS PER GAME | ASSISTS |
|---|---|---|
| 1. Billy Williams — 3562 | 1. Jigger Statz — 2.9 | 1. Jimmy Ryan — 327 |
| 2. Jimmy Ryan — 2873 | 2. Andy Pafko — 2.5 | 2. King Kelly — 206 |
| 3. Bill Nicholson — 2627 | 3. Bill Lange — 2.4 | 3. Wildfire Schulte — 181 |
|  | 4. Hack Wilson — 2.4 | 4. George Gore — 160 |
|  | 5. Peanuts Lowrey — 2.3 | 5. Billy Williams — 143 |

**C**

| PUTOUTS | PUTOUTS PER GAME | ASSISTS |
|---|---|---|
| 1. Gabby Hartnett — 7154 | 1. Randy Hundley — 5.7 | 1. Johnny Kling — 1244 |
| 2. Randy Hundley — 5346 | 2. Steve Swisher — 5.0 | 2. Gabby Hartnett — 1239 |
| 3. Johnny Kling — 4585 | 3. Jody Davis — 5.0 | 3. Silver Flint — 950 |
| 4. Silver Flint — 3215 | 4. Silver Flint — 4.8 | 4. Jimmy Archer — 903 |
| 5. Jimmy Archer — 3131 | 5. Johnny Kling — 4.8 | 5. Bob O'Farrell — 584 |

**P**

| PUTOUTS | PUTOUTS PER GAME | ASSISTS |
|---|---|---|
| 1. Rick Reuschel — 227 | 1. Rube Waddell — 1.1 | 1. Bill Hutchison — 645 |
| 2. Ferguson Jenkins — 187 | 2. Chuck Rainey — .7 | 2. Three Finger Brown — 600 |
| 3. Larry Corcoran — 175 | 3. Al Spalding — .7 | 3. Hippo Vaughn — 571 |
| 4. Three Finger Brown — 149 | 4. Jake Weimer — .7 | 4. Ed Reulbach — 568 |
| 5. Bob Rush — 148 | 5. Walt Woods — .7 | 5. Clark Griffith — 544 |

| ASSISTS PER GAME | | DOUBLE PLAYS | | CHANCES | |
|---|---|---|---|---|---|
| **1B** | | | | | |
| 1. Bill Buckner | .9 | 1. Cap Anson | 1189 | 1. Cap Anson | 22299 |
| 2. Eddie Waitkus | .8 | 2. Charlie Grimm | 1147 | 2. Charlie Grimm | 13586 |
| 3. Dee Fondy | .7 | 3. Ernie Banks | 1005 | 3. Ernie Banks | 12894 |
| 4. Phil Cavarretta | .6 | 4. Phil Cavarretta | 981 | 4. Phil Cavarretta | 12011 |
| 5. Ernie Banks | .6 | 5. Bill Buckner | 663 | 5. Frank Chance | 10543 |
| **2B** | | | | | |
| 1. Sparky Adams | 3.6 | 1. Billy Herman | 918 | 1. Billy Herman | 8396 |
| 2. Ryne Sandberg | 3.5 | 2. Glenn Beckert | 742 | 2. Fred Pfeffer | 7591 |
| 3. Fred Pfeffer | 3.4 | 3. Fred Pfeffer | 614 | 3. Johnny Evers | 7568 |
| 4. Billy Herman | 3.3 | 4. Johnny Evers | 525 | 4. Glenn Beckert | 6441 |
| 5. Manny Trillo | 3.3 | 5. Manny Trillo | 386 | 5. Manny Trillo | 3481 |
| **3B** | | | | | |
| 1. Ned Williamson | 2.5 | 1. Ron Santo | 389 | 1. Ron Santo | 6777 |
| 2. Ron Santo | 2.2 | 2. Stan Hack | 255 | 2. Stan Hack | 5684 |
| 3. Tom Burns | 2.1 | 3. Randy Jackson | 121 | 3. Tom Burns | 2835 |
| 4. Steve Ontiveros | 2.1 | 4. Tom Burns | 118 | 4. Ned Williamson | 2571 |
| 5. Charlie Deal | 2.1 | 5. Charlie Deal | 108 | 5. Harry Steinfeldt | 2304 |
| **SS** | | | | | |
| 1. Bill Dahlen | 3.7 | 1. Don Kessinger | 982 | 1. Joe Tinker | 8905 |
| 2. Ivan DeJesus | 3.4 | 2. Ernie Banks | 724 | 2. Don Kessinger | 8284 |
| 3. Charlie Hollocher | 3.4 | 3. Bill Jurges | 598 | 3. Ernie Banks | 5702 |
| 4. Joe Tinker | 3.4 | 4. Joe Tinker | 585 | 4. Bill Jurges | 5288 |
| 5. Don Kessinger | 3.3 | 5. Ivan DeJesus | 467 | 5. Bill Dahlen | 4861 |
| **OF** | | | | | |
| 1. King Kelly | .5 | 1. Jimmy Ryan | 65 | 1. Billy Williams | 3806 |
| 2. George Gore | .2 | 2. Bill Lange | 39 | 2. Jimmy Ryan | 3514 |
| 3. Jimmy Ryan | .2 | 3. Jimmy Slagle | 38 | 3. Bill Nicholson | 2798 |
| 4. Bill Lange | .2 | 3. Wildfire Schulte | 38 | 4. Wildfire Schulte | 2629 |
| 5. Jigger Statz | .2 | 5. Cliff Heathcote | 30 | | |
| | | 5. Jimmy Sheckard | 30 | | |
| **C** | | | | | |
| 1. Silver Flint | 1.4 | 1. Gabby Hartnett | 172 | 1. Gabby Hartnett | 8531 |
| 2. Jimmy Archer | 1.3 | 2. Johnny Kling | 97 | 2. Johnny Kling | 5990 |
| 3. Johnny Kling | 1.3 | 3. Jimmy Archer | 69 | 3. Randy Hundley | 5840 |
| 4. Malachi Kittredge | 1.0 | 4. Bob O'Farrell | 63 | 4. Silver Flint | 4562 |
| 5. Bob O'Farrell | 1.0 | 5. Randy Hundley | 59 | 5. Jimmy Archer | 4154 |
| **P** | | | | | |
| 1. Frank Corridon | 3.5 | 1. Guy Bush | 42 | 1. Bill Hutchison | 855 |
| 2. Frank Hankinson | 2.5 | 2. Claude Passeau | 32 | 2. Three Finger Brown | 770 |
| 3. Pop Williams | 2.5 | 2. Rick Reuschel | 32 | 3. Clark Griffith | 728 |
| 4. Nixey Callahan | 2.5 | 4. Bill Lee | 30 | 4. Larry Corcoran | 722 |
| 5. Ned Garvin | 2.4 | 5. Ed Reulbach | 28 | 5. Bill Lee | 705 |

# The Cubs and Their Players
# Year-by-Year

This section is a chronological listing of every Chicago Cubs season through 1985. All format information and abbreviations are explained below.

## ROSTER INFORMATION

| | | | |
|---|---|---|---|
| POS | Fielding Position | R | Runs |
| B | Bats B(oth), L(eft), or | RBI | Runs Batted In |
| | R(ight) | BB | Bases on Balls |
| G | Games | SO | Strikeouts |
| AB | At Bats | SB | Stolen Bases |
| H | Hits | | |
| 2B | Doubles | *Pinch-Hit* | |
| 3B | Triples | AB | Pinch-Hit At Bats |
| HR | Home Runs | H | Pinch Hits |
| HR% | Home Run Percentage | | |
| | (the number of home | BA | Batting Average |
| | runs per 100 times at | SA | Slugging Average |
| | bat) | | |

*Regulars.* The men who appear first on the team roster are considered the regulars for that team at the positions indicated. There are several factors for determining regulars of which "most games played at a position" and "most fielding chances at a position," are the two prime considerations.

*Substitutes.* Appearing directly beneath the regulars are the substitutes for the team. Substitutes are listed by position: first infielders, then outfielders, then catchers. Within these areas, substitutes are listed in order of most at bats, and can be someone who played most of the team's games as a regular, but not at one position. The rules for determining the listed positions of substitutes are as follows:

*One Position Substitutes.* If a man played at least 70% of his games in the field at one position, then he is listed only at that position, except for outfielders, where all three outfield positions are included under one category.

*Two Position Substitutes.* If a man did not play at least 70% of his games in the field at one position, but did play more than 90% of his total games at two positions, then he is shown with a combination fielding position. For example, if a player has an "S2" shown in his position column, it would mean that he played at least 90% of his games at shortstop and second base. These combinations are always indicated by the first letter or number of the position. The position listed first is where the most games were played.

*Utility Players.* If a player has a "UT" shown in his position column, it means that he did not meet the above 70% or 90% requirement and is listed as a utility player.

*Individual League Leaders.* (Applies to batting, fielding, and pitching.) Statistics that appear in bold-faced print indicate the player led or tied for the league lead in the particular statistical category.

*Traded League Leaders.* (Applies to batting, fielding, and pitching.) An asterisk (*) next to a particular figure indicates that the player led the league that year in the particular statistical category, but since he played for more than one team, the figure does not necessarily represent his league-leading total or average.

## TEAM AND LEAGUE INFORMATION

| | | | | |
|---|---|---|---|---|
| W | Wins | | *Fielding* | |
| L | Losses | | E | Errors |
| PCT | Winning Percentage | | DP | Double Plays |
| GB | Games Behind the League Leader | | FA | Fielding Average |
| R | Runs Scored | | | |
| OR | Opponents' Runs (Runs Scored Against) | | *Pitching* | |
| | | | CG | Complete Games |
| *Batting* | | | BB | Bases on Balls |
| | | | SO | Strikeouts |
| 2B | Doubles | | ShO | Shutouts |
| 3B | Triples | | SV | Saves |
| HR | Home Runs | | ERA | Earned Run Average |
| BA | Batting Average | | | |
| SA | Slugging Average | | | |
| SB | Stolen Bases | | | |

*Team League Leaders.* Statistics that appear in bold-faced print indicate the team led or tied for the league lead in the particular statistical category. When teams are tied for league lead, the figures for all teams who tied are shown in boldface.

## INDIVIDUAL FIELDING INFORMATION

| | | | | |
|---|---|---|---|---|
| T | Throws L(eft) or R(ight) | | E | Errors |
| | (blank if not available) | | DP | Double Plays |
| G | Games | | TC/G | Total Chances per |
| PO | Putouts | | | Game |
| A | Assists | | FA | Fielding Average |

Each man's fielding record is shown for each position he played during the year. Fielding information for pitchers is not included.

## INDIVIDUAL PITCHING INFORMATION

| | | | | |
|---|---|---|---|---|
| T | Throws R(ight) or L(eft) | | BB | Bases on Balls Allowed |
| W | Wins | | SO | Strikeouts |
| L | Losses | | R | Runs Allowed |
| PCT | Winning Percentage | | ER | Earned Runs Allowed |
| ERA | Earned Run Average | | ShO | Shutouts |
| SV | Saves | | H/9 | Hits Allowed Per 9 |
| G | Games Pitched | | | Innings Pitched |
| GS | Games Started | | BB/9 | Bases on Balls Allowed |
| CG | Complete Games | | | Per 9 Innings Pitched |
| IP | Innings Pitched | | SO/9 | Strikeouts Per 9 |
| H | Hits Allowed | | | Innings Pitched |

The abbreviations for the teams appear as listed below.

| | | | | |
|---|---|---|---|---|
| ATL | Atlanta | | LOU | Louisville |
| BAL | Baltimore | | MIL | Milwaukee |
| BKN | Brooklyn | | MON | Montreal |
| BOS | Boston | | NY | New York |
| BUF | Buffalo | | PHI | Philadelphia |
| CHI | Chicago | | PIT | Pittsburgh |
| CIN | Cincinnati | | PRO | Providence |
| CLE | Cleveland | | SD | San Diego |
| DET | Detroit | | SF | San Francisco |
| HAR | Hartford | | STL | St. Louis |
| HOU | Houston | | SYR | Syracuse |
| IND | Indianapolis | | TRO | Troy |
| KC | Kansas City | | WAS | Washington |
| LA | Los Angeles | | WOR | Worcester |

| MANAGER | W | L | PCT |
|---|---|---|---|
| Al Spalding | 52 | 14 | .788 |

| POS | Player | B | G | AB | H | 2B | 3B | HR | HR % | R | RBI | BB | SO | SB | Pinch Hit AB | Pinch Hit H | BA | SA |
|---|---|---|---|---|---|---|---|---|---|---|---|---|---|---|---|---|---|---|
| **REGULARS** | | | | | | | | | | | | | | | | | | |
| 1B | Cal McVey | R | 63 | 308 | 107 | 15 | 0 | 1 | 0.3 | 62 | 53 | 2 | 4 | | 0 | 0 | .347 | .406 |
| 2B | Ross Barnes | R | 66 | 322 | **138** | 21 | 14 | 1 | 0.3 | **126** | 59 | **20** | 8 | | 0 | 0 | **.429** | **.590** |
| SS | Johnny Peters | R | 66 | 316 | 111 | 14 | 2 | 1 | 0.3 | 70 | 47 | 3 | 2 | | 0 | 0 | .351 | .418 |
| 3B | Cap Anson | R | 66 | 309 | 110 | 13 | 7 | 1 | 0.3 | 63 | 59 | 12 | 8 | | 0 | 0 | .356 | .453 |
| RF | Bob Addy | L | 32 | 142 | 40 | 4 | 1 | 0 | 0.0 | 36 | 16 | 5 | 0 | | 0 | 0 | .282 | .324 |
| CF | Paul Hines | R | 64 | 305 | 101 | 21 | 3 | 2 | 0.7 | 62 | 59 | 1 | 3 | | 0 | 0 | .331 | .439 |
| LF | John Glenn | R | 66 | 276 | 84 | 9 | 2 | 0 | 0.0 | 55 | 32 | 12 | 6 | | 0 | 0 | .304 | .351 |
| C | Deacon White | L | 66 | 303 | 104 | 18 | 1 | 1 | 0.3 | 66 | **60** | 7 | 3 | | 0 | 0 | .343 | .419 |
| **SUBSTITUTES** | | | | | | | | | | | | | | | | | | |
| OF | Oscar Bielaski | R | 32 | 139 | 29 | 3 | 0 | 0 | 0.0 | 24 | 10 | 2 | 3 | | 0 | 0 | .209 | .230 |
| OF | Fred Andrus | R | 8 | 36 | 11 | 3 | 0 | 0 | 0.0 | 6 | 2 | 0 | 5 | | 0 | 0 | .306 | .389 |
| **PITCHERS** | | | | | | | | | | | | | | | | | | |
| P | Al Spalding | R | 66 | 292 | 91 | 14 | 2 | 0 | 0.0 | 54 | 44 | 6 | 3 | | 0 | 0 | .312 | .373 |
| | TEAM TOTAL | | | 2748 | 926 | 135 | 32 | 7 | 0.3 | 62 | 441 | 70 | 45 | 0 | 0 | 0 | .337 | .417 |

## INDIVIDUAL  FIELDING

| POS | Player | T | G | PO | A | E | DP | TC/G | FA | POS | Player | T | G | PO | A | E | DP | TC/G | FA |
|---|---|---|---|---|---|---|---|---|---|---|---|---|---|---|---|---|---|---|---|
| 1B | C. McVey | R | 55 | 485 | 10 | 21 | 21 | 9.4 | .959 | OF | P. Hines | R | 64 | 159 | 8 | 14 | 4 | 2.8 | **.923** |
| | J. Glenn | R | 15 | 112 | 0 | 8 | 4 | 8.0 | .933 | | J. Glenn | R | 56 | 128 | 5 | 18 | 1 | 2.7 | .881 |
| | D. White | R | 3 | 15 | 0 | 3 | 0 | 6.0 | .833 | | B. Addy | L | 32 | 46 | 6 | 13 | 0 | 2.0 | .800 |
| | A. Spalding | R | 3 | 6 | 0 | 0 | 0 | 2.0 | 1.000 | | O. Bielaski | R | 32 | 41 | 4 | 14 | 1 | 1.8 | .763 |
| | | | | | | | | | | | C. McVey | R | 1 | 0 | 0 | 0 | 0 | 0.0 | .000 |
| 2B | R. Barnes | R | 66 | 167 | 199 | 36 | 22 | 6.1 | **.910** | | A. Spalding | R | 10 | 7 | 2 | 3 | 0 | 1.2 | .750 |
| | P. Hines | R | 1 | 0 | 0 | 0 | 0 | 0.0 | .000 | | D. White | R | 3 | 8 | 0 | 2 | 0 | 3.3 | .800 |
| SS | J. Peters | R | 66 | 95 | 193 | 21 | **16** | 4.7 | **.932** | | F. Andrus | R | 8 | 5 | 0 | 2 | 0 | 0.9 | .714 |
| 3B | C. Anson | R | 66 | **135** | 147 | 50 | **8** | 5.0 | .849 | C | D. White | R | 63 | 295 | 50 | 64 | 3 | 6.5 | .844 |
| | D. White | R | 1 | 0 | 0 | 0 | 0 | 0.0 | .000 | | C. McVey | R | 6 | 23 | 1 | 2 | 0 | 4.3 | .923 |
| | C. McVey | R | 1 | 2 | 0 | 0 | 0 | 2.0 | 1.000 | | C. Anson | R | 2 | 2 | 0 | 0 | 0 | 1.0 | 1.000 |

In 1876 Ulysses S. Grant was president, Custer met his end at Little Big Horn, the United States had 38 states, and the Chicago Cubs were the White Stockings, for the simple reason that they wore white hose.

Largely through the efforts of White Stockings' owner William Hulbert, the National League was formed as an outgrowth of the earlier National Association. Appropriately, the White Stockings won the first pennant, thanks to such stars as Albert Spalding, Adrian Anson, Deacon White, Ross Barnes, and Cal McVey, all of whom had been signed away from eastern teams. Barnes, whose specialty was the "fair-foul" hit, walked off with nearly all the batting honors, leading the league in average, hits, runs, doubles, and triples. At that time, any ball hit in fair territory remained in play even if it rolled foul while going down the baseline; even the partisan Chicago press regarded some of Barnes' safeties as questionable.

Spalding, with his canny underhand delivery, was the league's winningest pitcher. On his "rest" days he played first base while McVey took over in the pitcher's box.

The team's high point came from July 20 through 27, when it scored 88 runs in four consecutive games to set a record that still stands. However, the record is a bit dubious when one considers that in those days fielders caught barehanded.

When the Stockings clinched the pennant on September 26 with a 7–6 win over Hartford, the *Chicago Tribune* proudly announced that "they won and now, despite every combination, every abuse, every unfairness, they have played themselves fairly to the front, and so cleanly that nothing can throw off the grip they have on the flag."

It was a great way for the club to begin its history. But with a start like that, what do you do for an encore?

## TEAM  STATISTICS

| | W | L | PCT | GB | R | OR | Batting 2B | 3B | HR | BA | SA | SB | Fielding E | DP | FA | CG | B | Pitching SO | ShO | SV | ERA |
|---|---|---|---|---|---|---|---|---|---|---|---|---|---|---|---|---|---|---|---|---|---|
| HI | 52 | 14 | .788 | | 624 | 257 | 131 | 32 | 7 | .337 | .416 | 0 | 282 | 33 | .899 | 58 | 29 | 51 | 8 | 4 | 1.76 |
| TL | 45 | 19 | .703 | 6 | 386 | 229 | 73 | 27 | 2 | .259 | .313 | 0 | 268 | 33 | .902 | 63 | 39 | 103 | 16 | 0 | 1.22 |
| AR | 47 | 21 | .691 | 6 | 429 | 261 | 96 | 22 | 2 | .267 | .322 | 0 | 337 | 27 | .888 | 69 | 27 | 114 | 11 | 0 | 1.67 |
| OS | 39 | 31 | .557 | 15 | 471 | 450 | 96 | 24 | 9 | .266 | .328 | 0 | 442 | 42 | .860 | 49 | 104 | 77 | 3 | 7 | 2.51 |
| OU | 30 | 36 | .455 | 22 | 280 | 344 | 68 | 14 | 6 | .249 | .294 | 0 | 397 | 44 | .875 | 67 | 38 | 125 | 5 | 0 | 1.69 |
| Y | 21 | 35 | .375 | 26 | 260 | 412 | 39 | 15 | 2 | .227 | .261 | 0 | 473 | 18 | .825 | 56 | 24 | 37 | 2 | 0 | 2.94 |
| HI | 14 | 45 | .237 | 34.5 | 378 | 534 | 79 | 35 | 7 | .271 | .342 | 0 | 456 | 32 | .839 | 53 | 41 | 22 | 1 | 2 | 3.22 |
| IN | 9 | 56 | .138 | 42.5 | 238 | 579 | 51 | 12 | 4 | .234 | .271 | 0 | 469 | 45 | .841 | 57 | 34 | 60 | 0 | 0 | 3.62 |
| EAGUE TOTAL | | | | | 3066 | 3066 | 633 | 181 | 39 | .265 | .321 | 0 | 3124 | 274 | .866 | 472 | 336 | 589 | 46 | 13 | 2.31 |

## INDIVIDUAL  PITCHING

| TCHER | T | W | L | PCT | ERA | SV | G | GS | CG | IP | H | BB | SO | R | ER | ShO | H/9 | BB/9 | SO/9 |
|---|---|---|---|---|---|---|---|---|---|---|---|---|---|---|---|---|---|---|---|
| Spalding | R | 47 | 13 | .783 | 1.75 | 0 | 61 | 60 | 53 | 528.2 | 542 | 26 | 39 | 226 | 103 | 8 | 9.23 | 0.44 | 0.66 |
| al McVey | R | 5 | 1 | .833 | 1.52 | 2 | 11 | 6 | 5 | 59.1 | 57 | 2 | 9 | 22 | 10 | 0 | 8.65 | 0.30 | 1.37 |
| eacon White | R | 0 | 0 | – | 0.00 | 1 | 1 | 0 | 0 | 2 | 1 | 0 | 3 | 0 | 0 | 0 | 4.50 | 0.00 | 13.50 |
| oss Barnes | R | 0 | 0 | – | 20.25 | 0 | 1 | 0 | 0 | 1.1 | 7 | 0 | 0 | 8 | 3 | 0 | 47.25 | 0.00 | 0.00 |
| ohnny Peters | R | 0 | 0 | – | 0.00 | 1 | 1 | 0 | 0 | 1 | 1 | 1 | 0 | 1 | 0 | 0 | 9.00 | 9.00 | 0.00 |
| EAM TOTAL | | 52 | 14 | .788 | 1.76 | 4 | 75 | 66 | 58 | 592.1 | 608 | 29 | 51 | 257 | 116 | 8 | 9.24 | 0.44 | 0.77 |

| MANAGER | W | L | PCT |
|---|---|---|---|
| Al Spalding | 26 | 33 | .441 |

| POS | Player | B | G | AB | H | 2B | 3B | HR | HR % | R | RBI | BB | SO | SB | Pinch Hit AB | Pinch Hit H | BA | SA |
|---|---|---|---|---|---|---|---|---|---|---|---|---|---|---|---|---|---|---|
| **REGULARS** | | | | | | | | | | | | | | | | | | |
| 1B | Al Spalding | R | 60 | 254 | 65 | 7 | 6 | 0 | 0.0 | 29 | 35 | 3 | 16 | | 0 | 0 | .256 | .331 |
| 2B | Ross Barnes | R | 22 | 92 | 25 | 1 | 0 | 0 | 0.0 | 16 | 5 | 7 | 4 | | 0 | 0 | .272 | .283 |
| SS | Johnny Peters | R | 60 | 265 | 84 | 10 | 3 | 0 | 0.0 | 45 | 41 | 1 | 7 | | 0 | 0 | .317 | .377 |
| 3B | Cap Anson | R | 59 | 255 | 86 | 19 | 1 | 0 | 0.0 | 52 | 32 | 9 | 3 | | 0 | 0 | .337 | .420 |
| RF | Paul Hines | R | 60 | 261 | 73 | 11 | 7 | 0 | 0.0 | 44 | 23 | 1 | 8 | | 0 | 0 | .280 | .375 |
| CF | Dave Eggler | R | 33 | 136 | 36 | 3 | 0 | 0 | 0.0 | 20 | 20 | 1 | 5 | | 0 | 0 | .265 | .287 |
| LF | John Glenn | R | 50 | 202 | 46 | 6 | 1 | 0 | 0.0 | 31 | 20 | 8 | 16 | | 0 | 0 | .228 | .267 |
| C | Cal McVey | R | 60 | 266 | 98 | 9 | 7 | 0 | 0.0 | 58 | 36 | 8 | 11 | | 0 | 0 | .368 | .455 |
| **SUBSTITUTES** | | | | | | | | | | | | | | | | | | |
| P3 | George Bradley | R | 55 | 214 | 52 | 7 | 3 | 0 | 0.0 | 31 | 12 | 6 | 19 | | 0 | 0 | .243 | .304 |
| 2O | Harry Smith | R | 24 | 94 | 19 | 1 | 0 | 0 | 0.0 | 7 | 3 | 4 | 6 | | 0 | 0 | .202 | .213 |
| 3B | Cherokee Fisher | R | 1 | 4 | 0 | 0 | 0 | 0 | 0.0 | 0 | 0 | 0 | 2 | | 0 | 0 | .000 | .000 |
| OF | Jimmy Hallinan | L | 19 | 89 | 25 | 4 | 1 | 0 | 0.0 | 17 | 11 | 4 | 2 | | 0 | 0 | .281 | .348 |
| OF | Charlie Eden | R | 15 | 55 | 12 | 0 | 1 | 0 | 0.0 | 9 | 5 | 3 | 6 | | 0 | 0 | .218 | .255 |
| OF | Charlie Waitt | | 10 | 41 | 4 | 0 | 0 | 0 | 0.0 | 2 | 2 | 0 | 3 | | 0 | 0 | .098 | .098 |
| OF | Joe Quinn | | 4 | 14 | 1 | 0 | 0 | 0 | 0.0 | 1 | 0 | 1 | 0 | | 0 | 0 | .071 | .071 |
| OF | Charley Jones | R | 2 | 8 | 3 | 1 | 0 | 0 | 0.0 | 1 | 2 | 1 | 0 | | 0 | 0 | .375 | .500 |
| OP | Dave Rowe | R | 2 | 7 | 2 | 0 | 0 | 0 | 0.0 | 0 | 0 | 0 | 3 | | 0 | 0 | .286 | .286 |
| **PITCHERS** | | | | | | | | | | | | | | | | | | |
| P | Laurie Reis | L | 4 | 16 | 2 | 0 | 0 | 0 | 0.0 | 3 | 1 | 0 | 0 | | 0 | 0 | .125 | .125 |
| | TEAM TOTAL | | | 2273 | 633 | 79 | 30 | 0 | 0.0 | 36 | 248 | 57 | 111 | 0 | 0 | 0 | .278 | .340 |

## INDIVIDUAL FIELDING

| POS | Player | T | G | PO | A | E | DP | TC/G | FA | POS | Player | T | G | PO | A | E | DP | TC/G | FA |
|---|---|---|---|---|---|---|---|---|---|---|---|---|---|---|---|---|---|---|---|
| 1B | A. Spalding | R | 45 | 472 | 21 | 21 | 23 | 11.4 | .959 | OF | P. Hines | R | 49 | 75 | 4 | 19 | 1 | 2.0 | .806 |
| | J. Glenn | R | 14 | 160 | 4 | 13 | 9 | 12.6 | .927 | | D. Eggler | R | 33 | 60 | 8 | 11 | 3 | 2.4 | .861 |
| | C. McVey | R | 1 | 17 | 0 | 1 | 0 | 18.0 | .944 | | J. Glenn | R | 36 | 66 | 7 | 4 | 1 | 2.1 | .948 |
| | G. Bradley | R | 3 | 12 | 0 | 0 | 0 | 4.0 | 1.000 | | J. Hallinan | L | 19 | 27 | 1 | 7 | 1 | 1.8 | .800 |
| 2B | R. Barnes | R | 22 | 49 | 70 | 23 | 5 | 6.5 | .838 | | C. Eden | R | 15 | 17 | 2 | 9 | 1 | 1.9 | .679 |
| | A. Spalding | R | 13 | 37 | 50 | 8 | 6 | 7.3 | .916 | | G. Bradley | R | 1 | 0 | 0 | 0 | 0 | 0.0 | .000 |
| | P. Hines | R | 11 | 27 | 36 | 17 | 4 | 7.3 | .788 | | C. Waitt | | 10 | 20 | 3 | 6 | 1 | 2.9 | .793 |
| | H. Smith | R | 14 | 32 | 32 | 11 | 2 | 5.4 | .853 | | H. Smith | R | 10 | 15 | 0 | 7 | 0 | 2.2 | .682 |
| | C. McVey | R | 1 | 1 | 4 | 0 | 1 | 5.0 | 1.000 | | J. Quinn | | 4 | 7 | 1 | 4 | 0 | 3.0 | .667 |
| SS | J. Peters | R | 60 | 124 | 215 | 45 | 23 | 6.4 | .883 | | C. Jones | R | 2 | 5* | 1 | 0* | 0 | 3.0* | 1.000 |
| 3B | C. Anson | R | 40 | 74 | 77 | 20 | 9 | 4.3 | .883 | | D. Rowe | R | 2 | 2 | 0 | 1 | 0 | 1.5 | .667 |
| | C. McVey | R | 17 | 18 | 23 | 8 | 0 | 2.9 | .837 | C | C. McVey | R | 40 | 137 | 34 | 28 | 3 | 5.0 | .859 |
| | G. Bradley | R | 16 | 11 | 18 | 13 | 1 | 2.6 | .690 | | C. Anson | R | 31 | 103 | 41 | 22 | 5 | 5.4 | .867 |
| | A. Spalding | R | 2 | 0 | 5 | 3 | 0 | 4.0 | .625 | | | | | | | | | | |
| | C. Fisher | R | 1 | 0 | 2 | 1 | 0 | 3.0 | .667 | | | | | | | | | | |

After winning the first pennant, the White Stockings of 1877 became the first great collapse in major-league history. In a league that had been reduced to six teams (New York and Philadelphia were expelled for refusing to make western trips), Chicago plummeted to fifth place.

There were several reasons for the demise. The "fair-foul" hit was outlawed, which caused Ross Barnes's batting average to drop 157 points. Spalding, who developed arm trouble, moved to first base while George Bradley did most of the pitching, with indifferent success. Since the reserve clause was still a few years away, Deacon White signed with Boston, leaving a gap in the catcher's box. Hitting slackened off also, as only Anson, McVey, and Peters maintained their 1876 pace.

### TEAM STATISTICS

|  | W | L | PCT | GB | R | OR | Batting 2B | 3B | HR | BA | SA | SB | Fielding E | DP | FA | CG | B | Pitching SO | ShO | SV | ERA |
|---|---|---|---|---|---|---|---|---|---|---|---|---|---|---|---|---|---|---|---|---|---|
| OS | 42 | 18 | .700 |  | 419 | 263 | 91 | 37 | 4 | .296 | .370 | 0 | 290 | 36 | .889 | 61 | 38 | 177 | 7 | 0 | 2.15 |
| OU | 35 | 25 | .583 | 7 | 339 | 288 | 75 | 36 | 9 | .280 | .354 | 0 | 267 | 37 | .904 | 61 | 41 | 141 | 4 | 0 | 2.25 |
| AR | 31 | 27 | .534 | 10 | 341 | 311 | 63 | 31 | 4 | .270 | .328 | 0 | 313 | 32 | .885 | 59 | 56 | 99 | 4 | 0 | 2.32 |
| TL | 28 | 32 | .467 | 14 | 284 | 318 | 51 | 36 | 1 | .244 | .302 | 0 | 281 | 29 | .892 | 52 | 92 | 132 | 1 | 0 | 2.66 |
| HI | 26 | 33 | .441 | 15.5 | 366 | 375 | 79 | 30 | 0 | .278 | .340 | 0 | 313 | 43 | .883 | 45 | 58 | 92 | 3 | 3 | 3.37 |
| IN | 15 | 42 | .263 | 25.5 | 291 | 485 | 72 | 34 | 6 | .255 | .329 | 0 | 394 | 33 | .852 | 48 | 61 | 85 | 1 | 1 | 4.19 |
| LEAGUE TOTAL |  |  |  |  | 2040 | 2040 | 431 | 204 | 24 | .271 | .338 | 0 | 1858 | 210 | .884 | 326 | 346 | 726 | 20 | 4 | 2.81 |

### INDIVIDUAL PITCHING

| PITCHER | T | W | L | PCT | ERA | SV | G | GS | CG | IP | H | BB | SO | R | ER | ShO | H/9 | BB/9 | SO/9 |
|---|---|---|---|---|---|---|---|---|---|---|---|---|---|---|---|---|---|---|---|
| George Bradley | R | 18 | 23 | .439 | 3.31 | 0 | 50 | 44 | 35 | 394 | 452 | 39 | 59 | 267 | 145 | 2 | 10.32 | 0.89 | 1.35 |
| al McVey | R | 4 | 8 | .333 | 4.50 | 2 | 17 | 10 | 6 | 92 | 129 | 11 | 20 | 86 | 46 | 0 | 12.62 | 1.08 | 1.96 |
| aurie Reis | R | 3 | 1 | .750 | 0.75 | 4 | 4 | 4 | 4 | 36 | 29 | 6 | 11 | 8 | 3 | 1 | 7.25 | 1.50 | 2.75 |
| Spalding | R | 1 | 0 | 1.000 | 3.27 | 1 | 4 | 1 | 0 | 11 | 17 | 0 | 2 | 12 | 4 | 0 | 13.91 | 0.00 | 1.64 |
| ave Rowe | R | 0 | 1 | .000 | 18.00 | 4 | 1 | 1 | 0 | 1 | 3 | 2 | 0 | 2 | 2 | 0 | 27.00 | 18.00 | 0.00 |
| EAM TOTAL |  | 26 | 33 | .441 | 3.37 | 3 | 76 | 60 | 45 | 534 | 630 | 58 | 92 | 375 | 200 | 3 | 10.62 | 0.98 | 1.55 |

| MANAGER | W | L | PCT |
|---------|----|----|------|
| Bob Ferguson | 30 | 30 | .500 |

| POS | Player | B | G | AB | H | 2B | 3B | HR | HR % | R | RBI | BB | SO | SB | Pinch Hit AB | Pinch Hit H | BA | SA |
|------|--------|---|---|-----|-----|----|----|----|------|----|-----|----|----|----|----|----|------|------|
| **REGULARS** | | | | | | | | | | | | | | | | | | |
| 1B | Joe Start | L | 61 | 285 | 100 | 12 | 5 | 1 | 0.4 | 58 | 27 | 2 | 3 | | 0 | 0 | .351 | .439 |
| 2B | Bill McClellan | L | 48 | 205 | 46 | 6 | 1 | 0 | 0.0 | 26 | 29 | 2 | 13 | | 0 | 0 | .224 | .263 |
| SS | Bob Ferguson | B | 61 | 259 | 91 | 10 | 2 | 0 | 0.0 | 44 | 39 | 10 | 12 | | 0 | 0 | .351 | .405 |
| 3B | Frank Hankinson | R | 58 | 240 | 64 | 8 | 3 | 1 | 0.4 | 38 | 27 | 5 | 36 | | 0 | 0 | .267 | .338 |
| RF | John Cassidy | R | 60 | 256 | 68 | 7 | 1 | 0 | 0.0 | 33 | 29 | 9 | 11 | | 0 | 0 | .266 | .301 |
| CF | Jack Remsen | R | 56 | 224 | 52 | 11 | 1 | 1 | 0.4 | 32 | 19 | 17 | 33 | | 0 | 0 | .232 | .304 |
| LF | Cap Anson | R | 60 | 261 | 89 | 12 | 2 | 0 | 0.0 | 55 | 40 | 13 | 1 | | 0 | 0 | .341 | .402 |
| C | Bill Harbidge | L | 54 | 240 | 71 | 12 | 0 | 0 | 0.0 | 32 | 37 | 6 | 13 | | 0 | 0 | .296 | .346 |
| **SUBSTITUTES** | | | | | | | | | | | | | | | | | | |
| 2B | Al Spalding | R | 1 | 4 | 2 | 0 | 0 | 0 | 0.0 | 0 | 0 | 0 | 0 | | 0 | 0 | .500 | .500 |
| O2 | Jimmy Hallinan | L | 16 | 67 | 19 | 3 | 0 | 0 | 0.0 | 14 | 2 | 5 | 6 | | 0 | 0 | .284 | .328 |
| OF | Bill Sullivan | | 2 | 6 | 1 | 0 | 0 | 0 | 0.0 | 1 | 0 | 0 | 0 | | 0 | 0 | .167 | .167 |
| C | Phil Powers | R | 8 | 31 | 5 | 1 | 1 | 0 | 0.0 | 2 | 2 | 1 | 5 | | 0 | 0 | .161 | .258 |
| C | Bill Traffley | R | 2 | 9 | 1 | 0 | 0 | 0 | 0.0 | 1 | 1 | 0 | 1 | | 0 | 0 | .111 | .111 |
| **PITCHERS** | | | | | | | | | | | | | | | | | | |
| P | Terry Larkin | R | 58 | 226 | 65 | 9 | 4 | 0 | 0.0 | 33 | 32 | 17 | 17 | | 0 | 0 | .288 | .363 |
| P | Laurie Reis | L | 5 | 20 | 3 | 0 | 0 | 0 | 0.0 | 2 | 0 | 1 | 6 | | 0 | 0 | .150 | .150 |
| | TEAM TOTAL | | | 2333 | 677 | 91 | 20 | 3 | 0.1 | 37 | 284 | 88 | 157 | 0 | 0 | 0 | .290 | .350 |

## INDIVIDUAL FIELDING

| POS | Player | T | G | PO | A | E | DP | TC/G | FA |
|------|--------|---|----|-----|-----|----|----|------|------|
| 1B | J. Start | L | 61 | 719 | 13 | 33 | 28 | 12.5 | .957 |
| 2B | McClellan | L | 42 | 87 | 139 | 35 | 15 | 6.2 | .866 |
| | C. Anson | R | 9 | 21 | 26 | 7 | 4 | 6.0 | .870 |
| | J. Hallinan | L | 5 | 12 | 12 | 8 | 1 | 6.4 | .750 |
| | B. Ferguson | R | 4 | 13 | 10 | 4 | 0 | 6.8 | .852 |
| | A. Spalding | R | 1 | 3 | 0 | 4 | 0 | 7.0 | .429 |
| SS | B. Ferguson | R | 57 | 71 | 226 | 40 | 17 | 5.9 | .881 |
| | McClellan | L | 5 | 2 | 20 | 5 | 0 | 5.4 | .815 |
| 3B | F. Hankinson | R | 57 | 94 | 138 | 33 | 9 | 4.6 | .875 |
| | T. Larkin | R | 1 | 1 | 4 | 3 | 0 | 8.0 | .625 |
| | C. Anson | R | 3 | 0 | 5 | 3 | 0 | 2.7 | .625 |

| POS | Player | T | G | PO | A | E | DP | TC/G | FA |
|------|--------|---|----|-----|-----|----|----|------|------|
| OF | J. Cassidy | L | 60 | 89 | 30 | 28 | 6 | 2.5 | .810 |
| | J. Remsen | R | 56 | 103 | 14 | 7 | 5 | 2.2 | .944 |
| | C. Anson | R | 48 | 60 | 6 | 14 | 0 | 1.7 | .825 |
| | McClellan | L | 1 | 0 | 0 | 0 | 0 | 0.0 | .000 |
| | J. Hallinan | L | 11 | 14 | 2 | 4 | 0 | 1.8 | .800 |
| | B. Harbidge | L | 8 | 8 | 1 | 1 | 0 | 1.3 | .900 |
| | T. Larkin | R | 1 | 0 | 1 | 0 | 0 | 1.0 | 1.000 |
| | L. Reis | L | 1 | 1 | 0 | 0 | 0 | 1.0 | 1.000 |
| | B. Sullivan | | 2 | 1 | 0 | 0 | 0 | 0.5 | 1.000 |
| C | B. Harbidge | L | 50 | 257 | 66 | 45 | 1 | 7.4 | .878 |
| | P. Powers | R | 8 | 47 | 19 | 5 | 0 | 8.9 | .930 |
| | C. Anson | R | 3 | 13 | 5 | 1 | 3 | 6.3 | .947 |
| | B. Ferguson | R | 1 | 7 | 2 | 2 | 0 | 11.0 | .818 |
| | B. Traffley | R | 2 | 7 | 3 | 0 | 0 | 5.0 | 1.000 |
| | J. Cassidy | L | 1 | 2 | 1 | 0 | 0 | 3.0 | 1.000 |

Having previously played at Twenty-third and State streets on Chicago's South Side, the White Stockings relocated to Lakefront Park at Michigan Avenue and Randolph Street, which would be their address through 1884. In the home opener on May 14, Indianapolis beat the White Stockings, 5–3.

By now only Anson remained from the 1876 lineup, and he had been moved to left field. The new manager, shortstop Bob Ferguson, brought the team back up to .500 with a fourth place finish, but, according to Anson, was a mediocre manager unable to establish discipline. Ferguson was tough with his bat, however, finishing with a .351 average, as did first baseman Joe Start, whose 100 hits topped the league. Anson followed with a .341 mark, but beyond that it was an undistinguished roster with little punch. Terry Larkin did nearly all of the pitching, winning all but one of the team's 30 victories.

## TEAM STATISTICS

| | W | L | PCT | GB | R | OR | Batting 2B | 3B | HR | BA | SA | SB | Fielding E | DP | FA | CG | B | Pitching SO | ShO | SV | ERA |
|---|---|---|---|---|---|---|---|---|---|---|---|---|---|---|---|---|---|---|---|---|---|
| OS | 41 | 19 | .683 | | 298 | 241 | 75 | 25 | 2 | .241 | .300 | 0 | 228 | 48 | .914 | 58 | 38 | 184 | 9 | 0 | 2.32 |
| IN | 37 | 23 | .617 | 4 | 333 | 281 | 67 | 22 | 5 | .276 | .331 | 0 | 269 | 37 | .900 | 61 | 63 | 220 | 6 | 0 | 1.84 |
| RO | 33 | 27 | .550 | 8 | 353 | 337 | 107 | 30 | 8 | .263 | .346 | 0 | 311 | 42 | .892 | 59 | 86 | 173 | 6 | 0 | 2.38 |
| HI | 30 | 30 | .500 | 11 | 371 | 331 | 91 | 20 | 3 | .290 | .350 | 0 | 304 | 37 | .891 | 61 | 35 | 175 | 1 | 0 | 2.37 |
| ND | 24 | 36 | .400 | 17 | 293 | 328 | 76 | 15 | 3 | .236 | .286 | 0 | 290 | 37 | .898 | 59 | 87 | 182 | 2 | 1 | 2.32 |
| IL | 15 | 45 | .250 | 26 | 256 | 386 | 65 | 20 | 2 | .250 | .300 | 0 | 376 | 32 | .866 | 54 | 55 | 147 | 1 | 0 | 2.60 |
| LEAGUE TOTAL | | | | | 1904 | 1904 | 481 | 132 | 23 | .259 | .319 | 0 | 1778 | 233 | .893 | 352 | 364 | 1081 | 25 | 1 | 2.30 |

## INDIVIDUAL PITCHING

| PITCHER | T | W | L | PCT | ERA | SV | G | GS | CG | IP | H | BB | SO | R | ER | ShO | H/9 | BB/9 | SO/9 |
|---|---|---|---|---|---|---|---|---|---|---|---|---|---|---|---|---|---|---|---|
| Terry Larkin | R | 29 | 26 | .527 | 2.24 | 0 | 56 | 56 | 56 | 506 | 511 | 31 | 163 | 288 | 126 | 1 | 9.09 | 0.55 | 2.90 |
| Laurie Reis | R | 1 | 3 | .250 | 3.25 | 4 | 4 | 4 | 4 | 36 | 55 | 4 | 8 | 34 | 13 | 0 | 13.75 | 1.00 | 2.00 |
| Frank Hankinson | R | 0 | 1 | .000 | 6.00 | 4 | 1 | 1 | 1 | 9 | 11 | 0 | 4 | 9 | 6 | 0 | 11.00 | 0.00 | 4.00 |
| TEAM TOTAL | | 30 | 30 | .500 | 2.37 | 0 | 61 | 61 | 61 | 551 | 577 | 35 | 175 | 331 | 145 | 1 | 9.42 | 0.57 | 2.86 |

| MANAGER | W | L | PCT |
|---|---|---|---|
| Cap Anson | 46 | 33 | .582 |

| POS | Player | B | G | AB | H | 2B | 3B | HR | HR % | R | RBI | BB | SO | SB | Pinch Hit AB | Pinch Hit H | BA | SA |
|---|---|---|---|---|---|---|---|---|---|---|---|---|---|---|---|---|---|---|
| **REGULARS** | | | | | | | | | | | | | | | | | | |
| 1B | Cap Anson | R | 51 | 227 | 90 | 20 | 1 | 0 | 0.0 | 40 | 34 | 2 | 2 | | 0 | 0 | .396 | .493 |
| 2B | Joe Quest | R | 83 | 334 | 69 | 16 | 1 | 0 | 0.0 | 38 | 22 | 9 | 33 | | 0 | 0 | .207 | .260 |
| SS | Johnny Peters | R | 83 | 379 | 93 | 13 | 2 | 1 | 0.3 | 45 | 31 | 1 | 19 | | 0 | 0 | .245 | .298 |
| 3B | Ned Williamson | R | 80 | 320 | 94 | 20 | 13 | 1 | 0.3 | 66 | 36 | 24 | 31 | | 0 | 0 | .294 | .447 |
| RF | Orator Shaffer | L | 73 | 316 | 96 | 13 | 0 | 0 | 0.0 | 53 | 35 | 6 | 28 | | 0 | 0 | .304 | .345 |
| CF | George Gore | L | 63 | 266 | 70 | 17 | 4 | 0 | 0.0 | 43 | 32 | 8 | 30 | | 0 | 0 | .263 | .357 |
| LF | Abner Dalrymple | L | 71 | 333 | 97 | 25 | 1 | 0 | 0.0 | 47 | 23 | 4 | 29 | | 0 | 0 | .291 | .372 |
| C | Silver Flint | R | 79 | 324 | 92 | 22 | 6 | 1 | 0.3 | 46 | 41 | 6 | 44 | | 0 | 0 | .284 | .398 |
| **SUBSTITUTES** | | | | | | | | | | | | | | | | | | |
| 1B | Lew Brown | R | 6 | 21 | 6 | 1 | 0 | 0 | 0.0 | 2 | 1 | 1 | 4 | | 0 | 0 | .286 | .333 |
| 3B | Stedronsky | | 4 | 12 | 1 | 0 | 0 | 0 | 0.0 | 0 | 0 | 0 | 3 | | 0 | 0 | .083 | .083 |
| 3B | Herm Doscher | | 3 | 11 | 2 | 0 | 0 | 0 | 0.0 | 1 | 1 | 0 | 3 | | 0 | 0 | .182 | .182 |
| UT | Frank Hankinson | R | 44 | 171 | 31 | 4 | 0 | 0 | 0.0 | 14 | 8 | 2 | 14 | | 0 | 0 | .181 | .205 |
| O1 | Jack Remsen | R | 42 | 152 | 33 | 4 | 2 | 0 | 0.0 | 14 | 8 | 2 | 23 | | 0 | 0 | .217 | .270 |
| OF | Bill Harbidge | L | 4 | 18 | 2 | 0 | 0 | 0 | 0.0 | 2 | 1 | 0 | 5 | | 0 | 0 | .111 | .111 |
| C | Tom Dolan | R | 1 | 4 | 0 | 0 | 0 | 0 | 0.0 | 0 | 0 | 0 | 2 | | 0 | 0 | .000 | .000 |
| **PITCHERS** | | | | | | | | | | | | | | | | | | |
| P | Terry Larkin | R | 60 | 228 | 50 | 12 | 2 | 0 | 0.0 | 26 | 18 | 8 | 24 | | 0 | 0 | .219 | .289 |
| | TEAM TOTAL | | | 3116 | 826 | 167 | 32 | 3 | 0.1 | 43 | 291 | 73 | 294 | 0 | 0 | 0 | .265 | .342 |

## INDIVIDUAL FIELDING

| POS | Player | T | G | PO | A | E | DP | TC/G | FA | POS | Player | T | G | PO | A | E | DP | TC/G | FA |
|---|---|---|---|---|---|---|---|---|---|---|---|---|---|---|---|---|---|---|---|
| 1B | C. Anson | R | 51 | 620 | 8 | 16 | 26 | 12.6 | .975 | OF | O. Shaffer | R | 72 | 99 | 50 | 37 | 3 | 2.6 | .801 |
| | J. Remsen | R | 11 | 135 | 5 | 13 | 2 | 13.9 | .915 | | A. Dalrymple | R | 71 | 103 | 4 | 40 | 1 | 2.1 | .728 |
| | G. Gore | R | 9 | 108 | 2 | 5 | 3 | 12.8 | .957 | | G. Gore | R | 54 | 93 | 9 | 15 | 0 | 2.2 | .872 |
| | Williamson | R | 6 | 77 | 1 | 3 | 2 | 13.5 | .963 | | J. Remsen | R | 31 | 52 | 4 | 9 | 1 | 2.1 | .862 |
| | L. Brown | R | 6 | 72 | 2 | 2 | 5 | 12.7 | .974 | | F. Hankinson | R | 14 | 21 | 3 | 2 | 0 | 1.9 | .923 |
| 2B | J. Quest | R | 83 | 263 | 331 | 48 | 30 | 7.7 | .925 | | B. Harbidge | L | 4 | 3 | 1 | 3 | 0 | 1.8 | .571 |
| | | | | | | | | | | | S. Flint | R | 1 | 2 | 0 | 0 | 0 | 2.0 | 1.000 |
| SS | J. Peters | R | 83 | 94 | 271 | 71 | 14 | 5.3 | .837 | | T. Larkin | R | 3 | 0 | 1 | 1 | 0 | 0.7 | .500 |
| 3B | Williamson | R | 70 | 84 | 193 | 41 | 13 | 4.5 | .871 | C | S. Flint | R | 78 | 341 | 109 | 42 | 6 | 6.3 | .915 |
| | F. Hankinson | R | 5 | 5 | 17 | 6 | 0 | 5.6 | .786 | | Williamson | R | 4 | 22 | 5 | 5 | 0 | 8.0 | .844 |
| | Stedronsky | | 4 | 4 | 11 | 4 | 1 | 4.8 | .789 | | T. Dolan | R | 1 | 6 | 2 | 0 | 0 | 8.0 | 1.000 |
| | H. Doscher | | 3 | 2 | 5 | 3 | 0 | 3.3 | .700 | | | | | | | | | | |
| | O. Shaffer | R | 1 | 0 | 1 | 1 | 0 | 2.0 | .500 | | | | | | | | | | |

The Milwaukee and Indianapolis clubs had disbanded during the off-season, and the White Stockings were quick to grab the cream of their crop. From Milwaukee came outfielder Abner Dalrymple, while catcher Silver Flint and third baseman Ned Williamson were plucked from the Indianapolis squad. More importantly, Anson was named manager and became known as "Cap," short for "Captain."

On May 1, 1879, Anson made his managerial debut a memorable one, collecting two singles and driving in a run in a 4–3 victory over Syracuse. The rejuvenated White Stockings led the league until early August, when Anson was sidelined by a kidney infection. Around the same time, Terry Larkin was struck on the head by a line drive, which not only ruined his pitching career but drove him to insanity and, eventually, suicide.

Chicago sank rapidly thereafter, winding up in fourth place, but with hopes for a bright future.

### TEAM STATISTICS

| | W | L | PCT | GB | R | OR | 2B | 3B | HR | BA | SA | SB | E | DP | FA | CG | B | SO | ShO | SV | ERA |
|---|---|---|---|---|---|---|---|---|---|---|---|---|---|---|---|---|---|---|---|---|---|
| | | | | | | | Batting | | | | | | Fielding | | | | | Pitching | | | |
| O | 59 | 25 | .702 | | 612 | 355 | 142 | 55 | 12 | .296 | .381 | 0 | 382 | 41 | .902 | 73 | 62 | 329 | 2 | 2 | 2.18 |
| S | 54 | 30 | .643 | 5 | 562 | 348 | 138 | 51 | 20 | .274 | .368 | 0 | 319 | 58 | .913 | 79 | 46 | 230 | 12 | 1 | 2.19 |
| F | 46 | 32 | .590 | 10 | 394 | 365 | 105 | 54 | 2 | .252 | .328 | 0 | 331 | 62 | .906 | 78 | 47 | 198 | 8 | 0 | 2.34 |
| I | 46 | 33 | .582 | 10.5 | 437 | 411 | 167 | 32 | 3 | .259 | .336 | 0 | 381 | 52 | .900 | 82 | 57 | 211 | 5 | 0 | 2.46 |
| N | 43 | 37 | .538 | 14 | 485 | 464 | 127 | 53 | 8 | .264 | .347 | 0 | 454 | 48 | .877 | 79 | 81 | 246 | 4 | 0 | 2.29 |
| E | 27 | 55 | .329 | 31 | 322 | 461 | 116 | 29 | 4 | .223 | .285 | 0 | 406 | 42 | .889 | 79 | 116 | 287 | 3 | 0 | 2.65 |
| R | 22 | 48 | .314 | 30 | 276 | 462 | 61 | 19 | 5 | .227 | .270 | 0 | 398 | 37 | .872 | 64 | 52 | 132 | 5 | 0 | 3.19 |
| O | 19 | 56 | .253 | 35.5 | 321 | 543 | 102 | 24 | 4 | .237 | .294 | 0 | 460 | 44 | .875 | 75 | 47 | 210 | 3 | 0 | 2.80 |
| LEAGUE TOTAL | | | | | 3409 | 3409 | 958 | 317 | 58 | .255 | .329 | 0 | 3131 | 384 | .892 | 609 | 508 | 1843 | 42 | 3 | 2.50 |

### INDIVIDUAL PITCHING

| PITCHER | T | W | L | PCT | ERA | SV | G | GS | CG | IP | H | BB | SO | R | ER | ShO | H/9 | BB/9 | SO/9 |
|---|---|---|---|---|---|---|---|---|---|---|---|---|---|---|---|---|---|---|---|
| Terry Larkin | R | 31 | 23 | .574 | 2.44 | 0 | 58 | 58 | 57 | 513.1 | 514 | 30 | 142 | 278 | 139 | 3 | 9.01 | 0.53 | 2.49 |
| Frank Hankinson | R | 15 | 10 | .600 | 2.50 | 0 | 26 | 25 | 25 | 230.2 | 248 | 27 | 69 | 133 | 64 | 2 | 9.68 | 1.05 | 2.69 |
| TEAM TOTAL | | 46 | 33 | .582 | 2.46 | 0 | 84 | 83 | 82 | 744 | 762 | 57 | 211 | 411 | 203 | 5 | 9.22 | 0.69 | 2.55 |

| MANAGER | W | L | PCT |
|---|---|---|---|
| Cap Anson | 67 | 17 | .798 |

| POS | Player | B | G | AB | H | 2B | 3B | HR | HR % | R | RBI | BB | SO | SB | Pinch Hit AB | Pinch Hit H | BA | SA |
|---|---|---|---|---|---|---|---|---|---|---|---|---|---|---|---|---|---|---|
| **REGULARS** | | | | | | | | | | | | | | | | | | |
| 1B | Cap Anson | R | 86 | 356 | 120 | 24 | 1 | 1 | 0.3 | 54 | 74 | 14 | 12 | | 0 | 0 | .337 | .419 |
| 2B | Joe Quest | R | 82 | 300 | 71 | 12 | 1 | 0 | 0.0 | 37 | 27 | 8 | 16 | | 0 | 0 | .237 | .283 |
| SS | Tom Burns | L | 85 | 333 | 103 | 17 | 3 | 0 | 0.0 | 47 | 43 | 12 | 23 | | 0 | 0 | .309 | .378 |
| 3B | Ned Williamson | R | 75 | 311 | 78 | 20 | 2 | 0 | 0.0 | 65 | 31 | 15 | 26 | | 0 | 0 | .251 | .328 |
| RF | King Kelly | R | 84 | 344 | 100 | 17 | 9 | 1 | 0.3 | 72 | 60 | 12 | 22 | | 0 | 0 | .291 | .401 |
| CF | George Gore | L | 77 | 322 | 116 | 23 | 2 | 2 | 0.6 | 70 | 47 | 21 | 10 | | 0 | 0 | .360 | .463 |
| LF | Abner Dalrymple | L | 86 | 382 | 126 | 25 | 12 | 0 | 0.0 | 91 | 36 | 3 | 18 | | 0 | 0 | .330 | .458 |
| C | Silver Flint | R | 74 | 284 | 46 | 10 | 4 | 0 | 0.0 | 30 | 17 | 5 | 32 | | 0 | 0 | .162 | .225 |
| **SUBSTITUTES** | | | | | | | | | | | | | | | | | | |
| UT | Larry Corcoran | | 72 | 286 | 66 | 11 | 1 | 0 | 0.0 | 41 | 25 | 10 | 33 | | 0 | 0 | .231 | .276 |
| PO | Fred Goldsmith | R | 35 | 142 | 37 | 4 | 2 | 0 | 0.0 | 24 | 15 | 2 | 15 | | 0 | 0 | .261 | .317 |
| O2 | Tommy Beals | R | 13 | 46 | 7 | 0 | 0 | 0 | 0.0 | 4 | 3 | 1 | 6 | | 0 | 0 | .152 | .152 |
| OP | Tom Poorman | L | 7 | 25 | 5 | 1 | 2 | 0 | 0.0 | 3 | 0 | 0 | 2 | | 0 | 0 | .200 | .400 |
| **PITCHERS** | | | | | | | | | | | | | | | | | | |
| P | Charlie Guth | | 1 | 4 | 1 | 0 | 0 | 0 | 0.0 | 0 | 0 | 1 | 2 | | 0 | 0 | .250 | .250 |
| | TEAM TOTAL | | | 3135 | 876 | 164 | 39 | 4 | 0.1 | 53 | 378 | 104 | 217 | 0 | 0 | 0 | .279 | .360 |

## INDIVIDUAL FIELDING

| POS | Player | T | G | PO | A | E | DP | TC/G | FA |
|---|---|---|---|---|---|---|---|---|---|
| 1B | C. Anson | R | 81 | 833 | 15 | 20 | 28 | 10.7 | **.977** |
| | G. Gore | R | 7 | 56 | 0 | 2 | 2 | 8.3 | .966 |
| | F. Goldsmith | R | 4 | 34 | 0 | 3 | 0 | 9.3 | .919 |
| 2B | J. Quest | R | 80 | 223 | 270 | 58 | 26 | 6.9 | .895 |
| | C. Anson | R | 1 | 0 | 0 | 0 | 0 | 0.0 | .000 |
| | Williamson | R | 3 | 7 | 11 | 1 | 2 | 6.3 | .947 |
| | T. Beals | | 3 | 7 | 2 | 4 | 1 | 4.3 | .692 |
| | K. Kelly | R | 1 | 0 | 1 | 0 | 0 | 1.0 | 1.000 |
| SS | T. Burns | R | 79 | 62 | 186 | 39 | 9 | 3.6 | .864 |
| | K. Kelly | R | 1 | 0 | 0 | 0 | 0 | 0.0 | .000 |
| | L. Corcoran | R | 8 | 4 | 21 | 5 | 1 | 3.8 | .833 |
| | J. Quest | R | 2 | 2 | 8 | 1 | 0 | 5.5 | .909 |
| | C. Anson | R | 1 | 2 | 1 | 1 | 0 | 4.0 | .750 |
| 3B | Williamson | R | 63 | 83 | 143 | 27 | 5 | 4.0 | **.893** |
| | K. Kelly | R | 14 | 22 | 20 | 7 | 0 | 3.5 | .857 |
| | C. Anson | R | 9 | 14 | 14 | 4 | 1 | 3.6 | .875 |
| | T. Burns | R | 9 | 8 | 14 | 5 | 0 | 3.0 | .815 |
| | J. Quest | R | 1 | 1 | 0 | 1 | 0 | 2.0 | .500 |

| POS | Player | T | G | PO | A | E | DP | TC/G | FA |
|---|---|---|---|---|---|---|---|---|---|
| OF | A. Dalrymple | R | 86 | 157 | 19 | 29 | 4 | 2.4 | .859 |
| | G. Gore | R | 74 | 124 | 18 | 21 | 4 | 2.2 | .871 |
| | K. Kelly | R | 64 | 49 | 32 | 23 | 1 | 1.6 | .779 |
| | F. Goldsmith | R | 10 | 10 | 4 | 6 | 0 | 2.0 | .700 |
| | S. Flint | R | 13 | 6 | 2 | 2 | 1 | 0.8 | .800 |
| | T. Poorman | R | 7 | 6 | 1 | 2 | 0 | 1.3 | .778 |
| | T. Beals | | 10 | 7 | 1 | 1 | 0 | 0.9 | .889 |
| | L. Corcoran | R | 8 | 4 | 3 | 1 | 1 | 1.0 | .875 |
| C | S. Flint | R | 67 | 388 | 117 | 37 | 4 | 8.1 | **.932** |
| | K. Kelly | R | 17 | 40 | 15 | 12 | 2 | 3.9 | .821 |
| | Williamson | R | 11 | 57 | 22 | 6 | 2 | 7.7 | .929 |
| | T. Burns | R | 2 | 3 | 2 | 2 | 0 | 3.5 | .714 |

The reserve clause was instituted during the off-season, enabling ownership to retain a player indefinitely. Meanwhile, new faces among the White Stockings of 1880 were rookie shortstop Tommy Burns, catcher-outfielder Mike "King" Kelly, and pitchers Larry Corcoran and Fred Goldsmith. Goldsmith is often credited with inventing the curveball.

One of Anson's managerial strategies was to use two pitchers instead of just one. Rookie Corcoran won 43 games, including the first Cub no-hitter, a 6–0 victory over Boston on August 19.

A 21-game winning streak from June 2 through July 8 propelled the White Stockings so far in front that for all practical purposes the race was already over, even though the pennant was not clinched until September 15, with a 5–2 win over the Reds. The club's won-lost percentage of .798 remains the highest in National League annals, although it is questionable whether they could have maintained that torrid a pace over a longer schedule. George Gore won the batting title with .360, and Goldsmith's winning percentage of .875 is still tops in Cub history.

## TEAM STATISTICS

|  | W | L | PCT | GB | R | OR | 2B | Batting 3B | HR | BA | SA | SB | Fielding E | DP | FA | CG | B | Pitching SO | ShO | SV | ERA |
|---|---|---|---|---|---|---|---|---|---|---|---|---|---|---|---|---|---|---|---|---|---|
| CHI | 67 | 17 | .798 |  | 538 | 317 | 164 | 39 | 4 | .279 | .360 | 0 | 329 | 41 | .911 | 80 | 129 | 367 | 9 | 3 | 1.93 |
| PRO | 52 | 32 | .619 | 15 | 419 | 299 | 114 | 34 | 8 | .248 | .313 | 0 | 357 | 53 | .910 | 75 | 51 | 286 | 12 | 2 | 1.64 |
| CLE | 47 | 37 | .560 | 20 | 387 | 337 | 130 | 52 | 7 | .242 | .327 | 0 | 330 | 52 | .910 | 83 | 98 | 289 | 7 | 1 | 1.90 |
| TRO | 41 | 42 | .494 | 25.5 | 392 | 438 | 114 | 37 | 5 | .251 | .319 | 0 | 366 | 58 | .900 | 81 | 113 | 173 | 4 | 0 | 2.74 |
| WOR | 40 | 43 | .482 | 26.5 | 412 | 370 | 129 | 52 | 8 | .231 | .316 | 0 | 355 | 49 | .905 | 68 | 97 | 297 | 7 | 5 | 2.27 |
| BOS | 40 | 44 | .476 | 27 | 416 | 456 | 134 | 41 | 20 | .253 | .343 | 0 | 367 | 54 | .901 | 70 | 86 | 187 | 3 | 0 | 3.08 |
| BUF | 24 | 58 | .293 | 42 | 331 | 502 | 104 | 37 | 3 | .226 | .289 | 0 | 408 | 55 | .890 | 72 | 78 | 186 | 6 | 1 | 3.09 |
| CIN | 21 | 59 | .263 | 44 | 296 | 472 | 91 | 36 | 7 | .224 | .288 | 0 | 437 | 49 | .877 | 79 | 88 | 208 | 3 | 0 | 2.44 |
| LEAGUE TOTAL |  |  |  |  | 3191 | 3191 | 980 | 328 | 62 | .245 | .320 | 0 | 2949 | 411 | .901 | 608 | 740 | 1993 | 51 | 12 | 2.37 |

## INDIVIDUAL PITCHING

| PITCHER | T | W | L | PCT | ERA | SV | G | GS | CG | IP | H | BB | SO | R | ER | ShO | H/9 | BB/9 | SO/9 |
|---|---|---|---|---|---|---|---|---|---|---|---|---|---|---|---|---|---|---|---|
| Larry Corcoran | R | 43 | 14 | .754 | 1.95 | 2 | 63 | 60 | 57 | 536.1 | 404 | 99 | 268 | 216 | 116 | 5 | 6.78 | 1.66 | 4.50 |
| Fred Goldsmith | R | 21 | 3 | .875 | 1.75 | 1 | 26 | 24 | 22 | 210.1 | 189 | 18 | 90 | 82 | 41 | 4 | 8.09 | 0.77 | 3.85 |
| Tom Poorman | R | 2 | 0 | 1.000 | 2.40 | 0 | 2 | 1 | 0 | 15 | 12 | 8 | 0 | 5 | 4 | 0 | 7.20 | 4.80 | 0.00 |
| Charlie Guth |  | 1 | 0 | 1.000 | 5.00 | 0 | 1 | 1 | 1 | 9 | 12 | 1 | 7 | 8 | 5 | 0 | 12.00 | 1.00 | 7.00 |
| King Kelly | R | 0 | 0 | — | 0.00 | 0 | 1 | 0 | 0 | 3 | 3 | 1 | 1 | 2 | 0 | 0 | 9.00 | 3.00 | 3.00 |
| Tom Burns | R | 0 | 0 | — | 0.00 | 0 | 1 | 0 | 0 | 1.1 | 2 | 2 | 1 | 4 | 0 | 0 | 13.50 | 13.50 | 6.75 |
| TEAM TOTAL |  | 67 | 17 | .798 | 1.93 | 3 | 94 | 86 | 80 | 775 | 622 | 129 | 367 | 317 | 166 | 9 | 7.22 | 1.50 | 4.26 |

| MANAGER | W | L | PCT |
|---|---|---|---|
| Cap Anson | 56 | 28 | .667 |

| POS | Player | B | G | AB | H | 2B | 3B | HR | HR % | R | RBI | BB | SO | SB | Pinch Hit AB | H | BA | SA |
|---|---|---|---|---|---|---|---|---|---|---|---|---|---|---|---|---|---|---|
| **REGULARS** | | | | | | | | | | | | | | | | | | |
| 1B | Cap Anson | R | 84 | 343 | **137** | 21 | 7 | 1 | 0.3 | 67 | **82** | 26 | 4 | | 0 | 0 | **.399** | .510 |
| 2B | Joe Quest | R | 78 | 293 | 72 | 6 | 0 | 1 | 0.3 | 35 | 26 | 2 | 29 | | 0 | 0 | .246 | .276 |
| SS | Tom Burns | L | 84 | 342 | 95 | 20 | 3 | 4 | 1.2 | 41 | 42 | 14 | 22 | | 0 | 0 | .278 | .389 |
| 3B | Ned Williamson | R | 82 | 343 | 92 | 12 | 6 | 1 | 0.3 | 56 | 48 | 19 | 19 | | 0 | 0 | .268 | .347 |
| RF | King Kelly | R | 82 | 353 | 114 | **27** | 3 | 2 | 0.6 | 84 | 55 | 16 | 14 | | 0 | 0 | .323 | .433 |
| CF | George Gore | L | 73 | 309 | 92 | 18 | 9 | 1 | 0.3 | **86** | 44 | 27 | 23 | | 0 | 0 | .298 | .424 |
| LF | Abner Dalrymple | L | 82 | 362 | 117 | 22 | 4 | 1 | 0.3 | 72 | 37 | 15 | 22 | | 0 | 0 | .323 | .414 |
| C | Silver Flint | R | 80 | 306 | 95 | 18 | 0 | 1 | 0.3 | 46 | 34 | 6 | 39 | | 0 | 0 | .310 | .379 |
| **SUBSTITUTES** | | | | | | | | | | | | | | | | | | |
| 23 | Andy Piercy | | 2 | 8 | 2 | 0 | 0 | 0 | 0.0 | 1 | 0 | 0 | 1 | | 0 | 0 | .250 | .250 |
| OF | Hugh Nicol | R | 26 | 108 | 22 | 2 | 0 | 0 | 0.0 | 13 | 7 | 4 | 12 | | 0 | 0 | .204 | .222 |
| **PITCHERS** | | | | | | | | | | | | | | | | | | |
| P | Larry Corcoran | | 47 | 189 | 42 | 8 | 0 | 0 | 0.0 | 25 | 9 | 5 | 22 | | 0 | 0 | .222 | .265 |
| P | Fred Goldsmith | R | 42 | 158 | 38 | 3 | 4 | 0 | 0.0 | 24 | 16 | 6 | 17 | | 0 | 0 | .241 | .310 |
| | TEAM TOTAL | | | 3114 | 918 | 157 | 36 | 12 | 0.4 | 55 | 400 | 140 | 224 | 0 | 0 | 0 | .295 | .380 |

## INDIVIDUAL FIELDING

| POS | Player | T | G | PO | A | E | DP | TC/G | FA |
|---|---|---|---|---|---|---|---|---|---|
| 1B | C. Anson | R | 84 | **892** | **43** | 24 | 48 | 11.4 | **.975** |
| | G. Gore | R | 1 | 8 | 1 | 0 | 1 | 9.0 | 1.000 |
| | S. Flint | R | 1 | 4 | 0 | 0 | 0 | 4.0 | 1.000 |
| 2B | J. Quest | R | 77 | 238 | 249 | 37 | 28 | 6.8 | .929 |
| | Williamson | R | 4 | 11 | 17 | 4 | 2 | 8.0 | .875 |
| | T. Burns | R | 3 | 10 | 13 | 1 | 1 | 8.0 | .958 |
| | A. Piercy | R | 1 | 3 | 3 | 2 | 0 | 8.0 | .750 |
| SS | T. Burns | R | 80 | 100 | 249 | **52** | 20 | 5.0 | .870 |
| | C. Anson | R | 1 | 0 | 0 | 0 | 0 | 0.0 | .000 |
| | Williamson | R | 2 | 6 | 7 | 1 | 1 | 7.0 | .929 |
| | L. Corcoran | R | 2 | 2 | 7 | 0 | 0 | 4.5 | 1.000 |
| | J. Quest | R | 1 | 4 | 3 | 0 | 0 | 7.0 | 1.000 |
| | H. Nicol | R | 1 | 1 | 1 | 1 | 0 | 3.0 | .667 |
| 3B | Williamson | R | 76 | 117 | **194** | 31 | 10 | 4.5 | **.909** |
| | K. Kelly | R | 8 | 8 | 12 | 1 | 0 | 2.6 | .952 |
| | T. Burns | R | 3 | 6 | 1 | 3 | 1 | 3.3 | .700 |
| | A. Piercy | R | 1 | 3 | 0 | 1 | 0 | 4.0 | .750 |
| | G. Gore | R | 1 | 0 | 0 | 1 | 0 | 1.0 | .000 |

| POS | Player | T | G | PO | A | E | DP | TC/G | FA |
|---|---|---|---|---|---|---|---|---|---|
| OF | G. Gore | R | 72 | 146 | 21 | 24 | 3 | 2.7 | .874 |
| | A. Dalrymple | R | 82 | 143 | 14 | **31** | 1 | 2.3 | .835 |
| | K. Kelly | R | 72 | 85 | 31 | 22 | 2 | 1.9 | .841 |
| | H. Nicol | R | 26 | 44 | 11 | 4 | 1 | 2.3 | .932 |
| | L. Corcoran | R | 1 | 0 | 0 | 0 | 0 | 0.0 | .000 |
| | F. Goldsmith | R | 3 | 3 | 2 | 3 | 0 | 2.7 | .625 |
| | S. Flint | R | 8 | 3 | 0 | 0 | 0 | 0.4 | 1.000 |
| C | S. Flint | R | 80 | 319 | 92 | 27 | 6 | 5.5 | .938 |
| | Williamson | R | 1 | 0 | 0 | 0 | 0 | 0.0 | .000 |
| | K. Kelly | R | 11 | 28 | 9 | 10 | 1 | 4.3 | .787 |
| | C. Anson | R | 2 | 2 | 0 | 0 | 0 | 1.0 | 1.000 |

Playing with the same lineup as the year before, the White Stockings made it back-to-back pennants with another championship in 1881, beating out second-place Providence by 9 games. With a .399 average, Anson led the league in batting, hits, and RBI, while Corcoran topped the league with 31 victories. Both Kelly and Dalrymple hit .323. Burns fell victim to the "sophomore jinx" as his batting average dropped to .278.

There were no no-hitters, but Goldsmith came close with a 17–0 one-hit victory over Detroit on August 11. Gore set a major league record by stealing seven bases in one game, during a 12–8 victory over Providence. On his way to scoring five runs, he stole second base five times and third twice. The final game of the season was played in a driving rainstorm at Troy, N.Y., before a paid attendance of 12, the smallest crowd in major league history. Incidentally, Chicago won, 10–8.

### TEAM  STATISTICS

| | W | L | PCT | GB | R | OR | Batting | | | | | | SB | Fielding | | | Pitching | | | | | |
|---|---|---|---|---|---|---|---|---|---|---|---|---|---|---|---|---|---|---|---|---|---|---|
| | | | | | | | 2B | 3B | HR | BA | SA | | E | DP | FA | CG | B | SO | ShO | SV | ERA |
| CHI | 56 | 28 | .667 | | 550 | 379 | 157 | 36 | 12 | .295 | .380 | 0 | 309 | 54 | .916 | 81 | 122 | 228 | 9 | 0 | 2.43 |
| PRO | 47 | 37 | .560 | 9 | 447 | 426 | 144 | 37 | 11 | .253 | .335 | 0 | 390 | 66 | .896 | 76 | 138 | 264 | 7 | 0 | 2.40 |
| BUF | 45 | 38 | .542 | 10.5 | 440 | 447 | 157 | 50 | 12 | .264 | .361 | 0 | 408 | 48 | .891 | 72 | 89 | 185 | 5 | 0 | 2.84 |
| DET | 41 | 43 | .488 | 15 | 439 | 429 | 131 | 53 | 17 | .260 | .357 | 0 | 338 | 80 | .905 | 83 | 137 | 265 | 10 | 0 | 2.65 |
| TRO | 39 | 45 | .464 | 17 | 399 | 429 | 124 | 31 | 5 | .248 | .314 | 0 | 311 | 70 | .917 | 85 | 159 | 207 | 7 | 0 | 2.97 |
| BOS | 38 | 45 | .458 | 17.5 | 349 | 410 | 121 | 27 | 5 | .251 | .317 | 0 | 325 | 54 | .909 | 72 | 143 | 199 | 6 | 3 | 2.71 |
| CLE | 36 | 48 | .429 | 20 | 392 | 414 | 120 | 39 | 7 | .255 | .326 | 0 | 348 | 68 | .904 | 82 | 126 | 240 | 2 | 0 | 2.68 |
| WOR | 32 | 50 | .390 | 23 | 410 | 492 | 114 | 31 | 7 | .253 | .316 | 0 | 353 | 50 | .903 | 80 | 120 | 196 | 5 | 0 | 3.54 |
| LEAGUE TOTAL | | | | | 3426 | 3426 | 1068 | 304 | 76 | .260 | .338 | 0 | 2782 | 490 | .905 | 631 | 1034 | 1784 | 51 | 3 | 2.77 |

### INDIVIDUAL  PITCHING

| PITCHER | T | W | L | PCT | ERA | SV | G | GS | CG | IP | H | BB | SO | R | ER | ShO | H/9 | BB/9 | SO/9 |
|---|---|---|---|---|---|---|---|---|---|---|---|---|---|---|---|---|---|---|---|
| Larry Corcoran | R | 31 | 14 | .689 | 2.31 | 0 | 45 | 44 | 43 | 396.2 | 380 | 78 | 150 | 204 | 102 | 4 | 8.62 | 1.77 | 3.40 |
| Fred Goldsmith | R | 24 | 13 | .649 | 2.59 | 0 | 39 | 39 | 37 | 330 | 328 | 44 | 76 | 166 | 95 | 5 | 8.95 | 1.20 | 2.07 |
| Ned Williamson | R | 1 | 1 | .500 | 2.00 | 0 | 3 | 1 | 1 | 18 | 14 | 0 | 2 | 9 | 4 | 0 | 7.00 | 0.00 | 1.00 |
| TEAM TOTAL | | 56 | 28 | .667 | 2.43 | 0 | 87 | 84 | 81 | 744.2 | 722 | 122 | 228 | 379 | 201 | 9 | 8.73 | 1.47 | 2.76 |

| MANAGER | W | L | PCT |
|---|---|---|---|
| Cap Anson | 55 | 29 | .655 |

| POS | Player | B | G | AB | H | 2B | 3B | HR | HR% | R | RBI | BB | SO | SB | Pinch Hit AB | Pinch Hit H | BA | SA |
|---|---|---|---|---|---|---|---|---|---|---|---|---|---|---|---|---|---|---|
| **REGULARS** | | | | | | | | | | | | | | | | | | |
| 1B | Cap Anson | R | 82 | 348 | 126 | 29 | 8 | 1 | 0.3 | 69 | 83 | 20 | 7 | | 0 | 0 | .362 | .500 |
| 2B | Tom Burns | L | 84 | 355 | 88 | 23 | 6 | 0 | 0.0 | 55 | 48 | 15 | 28 | | 0 | 0 | .248 | .346 |
| SS | King Kelly | R | 84 | 377 | 115 | 37 | 4 | 1 | 0.3 | 81 | 55 | 10 | 27 | | 0 | 0 | .305 | .432 |
| 3B | Ned Williamson | R | 83 | 348 | 98 | 27 | 4 | 3 | 0.9 | 66 | 60 | 27 | 21 | | 0 | 0 | .282 | .408 |
| RF | Hugh Nicol | R | 47 | 186 | 37 | 9 | 1 | 1 | 0.5 | 19 | 16 | 7 | 29 | | 0 | 0 | .199 | .274 |
| CF | George Gore | L | 84 | 367 | 117 | 15 | 7 | 3 | 0.8 | 99 | 51 | 29 | 19 | | 0 | 0 | .319 | .422 |
| LF | Abner Dalrymple | L | 84 | 397 | 117 | 25 | 11 | 1 | 0.3 | 96 | 36 | 14 | 18 | | 0 | 0 | .295 | .421 |
| C | Silver Flint | R | 81 | 331 | 83 | 18 | 8 | 4 | 1.2 | 48 | 44 | 2 | 50 | | 0 | 0 | .251 | .390 |
| **SUBSTITUTES** | | | | | | | | | | | | | | | | | | |
| 2B | Joe Quest | R | 42 | 159 | 32 | 5 | 2 | 0 | 0.0 | 24 | 15 | 8 | 16 | | 0 | 0 | .201 | .258 |
| 1B | Milt Scott | | 1 | 5 | 2 | 0 | 0 | 0 | 0.0 | 1 | 0 | 0 | 0 | | 0 | 0 | .400 | .400 |
| **PITCHERS** | | | | | | | | | | | | | | | | | | |
| P | Fred Goldsmith | R | 45 | 183 | 42 | 11 | 1 | 0 | 0.0 | 23 | 19 | 4 | 29 | | 0 | 0 | .230 | .301 |
| P | Larry Corcoran | | 40 | 169 | 35 | 10 | 2 | 1 | 0.6 | 23 | 24 | 6 | 18 | | 0 | 0 | .207 | .308 |
| | TEAM TOTAL | | | 3225 | 892 | 209 | 54 | 15 | 0.5 | 60 | 451 | 142 | 262 | 0 | 0 | 0 | .277 | .389 |

## INDIVIDUAL FIELDING

| POS | Player | T | G | PO | A | E | DP | TC/G | FA |
|---|---|---|---|---|---|---|---|---|---|
| 1B | C. Anson | R | 82 | 810 | 27 | 45 | 42 | 10.8 | .949 |
| | F. Goldsmith | R | 1 | 7 | 0 | 1 | 0 | 8.0 | .875 |
| | K. Kelly | R | 1 | 3 | 2 | 2 | 0 | 7.0 | .714 |
| | M. Scott | | 1 | 3 | 0 | 0 | 0 | 3.0 | 1.000 |
| 2B | T. Burns | R | 43 | 129 | 127 | 25 | 21 | 6.5 | .911 |
| | J. Quest | R | 41 | 113 | 127 | 33 | 18 | 6.7 | .879 |
| SS | T. Burns | R | 41 | 60 | 131 | 40 | 9 | 5.6 | .827 |
| | K. Kelly | R | 42 | 66 | 117 | 43 | 9 | 5.4 | .810 |
| | H. Nicol | R | 8 | 3 | 8 | 4 | 1 | 1.9 | .733 |
| | J. Quest | R | 1 | 0 | 1 | 2 | 0 | 3.0 | .333 |
| 3B | Williamson | R | 83 | 108 | 210 | 43 | 16 | 4.3 | .881 |
| | L. Corcoran | R | 1 | 0 | 0 | 0 | 0 | 0.0 | .000 |
| | K. Kelly | R | 3 | 1 | 6 | 1 | 0 | 2.7 | .875 |

| POS | Player | T | G | PO | A | E | DP | TC/G | FA |
|---|---|---|---|---|---|---|---|---|---|
| OF | A. Dalrymple | R | 84 | 185 | 8 | 27 | 4 | 2.6 | .877 |
| | G. Gore | R | 84 | 153 | 23 | 33 | 5 | 2.5 | .842 |
| | H. Nicol | R | 47 | 59 | 27 | 11 | 1 | 2.1 | .887 |
| | K. Kelly | R | 38 | 50 | 21 | 9 | 3 | 2.1 | .888 |
| | S. Flint | R | 10 | 6 | 0 | 1 | 0 | 0.7 | .857 |
| C | S. Flint | R | 81 | 440 | 91 | 37 | 3 | 7.0 | .935 |
| | K. Kelly | R | 12 | 13 | 3 | 4 | 0 | 1.7 | .800 |
| | C. Anson | R | 1 | 3 | 0 | 1 | 0 | 4.0 | .750 |

In 1882 the White Stockings became the first team to win three straight pennants. This time, however, it was close, as second place Providence finished only 3 games behind. The pennant was not clinched until September 29, with an 11–5 romp over Buffalo.

Predictably, Anson was the batting star with a .362 mark, with plenty of support from Kelly, Gore, and Dalrymple. On July 24 the White Stockings became white hot in a 35–4 massacre of Cleveland. Seven players—Dalrymple, Kelly, Gore, Williamson, Burns, Flint, and Hugh Nichol—collected four hits to set a major-league record. Corcoran, on his way to another great year in the pitcher's box, hit the first grand slam homer in Cub history on June 20 in a 13–3 shelling of Worcester, adding two singles and a double for good measure. Three months later to the day, he posted his second of three career no-hitters with a 5–0 win over Worcester. Finally, on September 30, 16-year-old Milton Scott became the youngest player in Cub history, taking Anson's place at first base and going two-for-five as the White Stockings beat Buffalo, 6–5.

## TEAM  STATISTICS

|      | W | L | PCT | GB | R | OR | 2B | Batting 3B | HR | BA | SA | SB | Fielding E | DP | FA | CG | B | Pitching SO | ShO | SV | ERA |
|------|---|---|-----|----|---|----|----|----|----|----|----|----|----|----|----|----|----|----|-----|----|-----|
| CHI | 55 | 29 | .655 |   | 604 | 353 | 209 | 54 | 15 | .277 | .389 | 0 | 376 | 54 | .898 | 83 | 102 | 279 | 7 | 0 | 2.22 |
| PRO | 52 | 32 | .619 | 3 | 463 | 356 | 121 | 54 | 10 | .250 | .333 | 0 | 371 | 67 | .901 | 80 | 87 | 273 | 9 | 1 | 2.27 |
| BOS | 45 | 39 | .536 | 10 | 472 | 414 | 114 | 50 | 15 | .264 | .347 | 0 | 314 | 37 | .910 | 81 | 77 | 352 | 4 | 0 | 2.80 |
| BUF | 45 | 39 | .536 | 10 | 500 | 461 | 146 | 47 | 18 | .274 | .368 | 0 | 315 | 42 | .910 | 79 | 114 | 287 | 3 | 0 | 3.25 |
| CLE | 42 | 40 | .512 | 12 | 402 | 411 | 139 | 40 | 20 | .238 | .331 | 0 | 358 | 71 | .905 | 81 | 132 | 232 | 4 | 0 | 2.75 |
| DET | 42 | 41 | .506 | 12.5 | 407 | 488 | 117 | 44 | 20 | .230 | .315 | 0 | 396 | 44 | .893 | 82 | 129 | 354 | 7 | 0 | 2.98 |
| TRO | 35 | 48 | .422 | 19.5 | 430 | 522 | 116 | 59 | 12 | .244 | .333 | 0 | 432 | 70 | .887 | 81 | 168 | 189 | 6 | 0 | 3.08 |
| WOR | 18 | 66 | .214 | 37 | 379 | 652 | 109 | 57 | 16 | .231 | .322 | 0 | 468 | 66 | .877 | 75 | 151 | 195 | 0 | 0 | 3.75 |
| LEAGUE TOTAL |  |  |  |  | 3657 | 3657 | 1071 | 405 | 126 | .251 | .343 | 0 | 3030 | 451 | .897 | 642 | 960 | 2161 | 40 | 1 | 2.89 |

## INDIVIDUAL  PITCHING

| PITCHER | T | W | L | PCT | ERA | SV | G | GS | CG | IP | H | BB | SO | R | ER | ShO | H/9 | BB/9 | SO/9 |
|---------|---|---|---|-----|-----|----|---|----|----|----|----|----|----|----|----|-----|-----|------|------|
| Fred Goldsmith | R | 28 | 16 | .636 | 2.42 | 0 | 44 | 44 | 44 | 405 | 377 | 38 | 109 | 194 | 109 | 4 | 8.38 | 0.84 | 2.42 |
| Larry Corcoran | R | 27 | 13 | .675 | 1.95 | 0 | 40 | 40 | 39 | 355.2 | 281 | 63 | 170 | 151 | 77 | 3 | 7.11 | 1.59 | 4.30 |
| Ned Williamson | R | 0 | 0 | — | 6.00 | 0 | 1 | 0 | 0 | 3 | 9 | 1 | 0 | 8 | 2 | 0 | 27.00 | 3.00 | 0.00 |
| TEAM TOTAL |   | 55 | 29 | .655 | 2.22 | 0 | 85 | 84 | 83 | 763.2 | 667 | 102 | 279 | 353 | 188 | 7 | 7.86 | 1.20 | 3.29 |

| MANAGER | W | L | PCT |
|---|---|---|---|
| Cap Anson | 59 | 39 | .602 |

| POS | Player | B | G | AB | H | 2B | 3B | HR | HR % | R | RBI | BB | SO | SB | Pinch Hit AB | Pinch Hit H | BA | SA |
|---|---|---|---|---|---|---|---|---|---|---|---|---|---|---|---|---|---|---|
| **REGULARS** | | | | | | | | | | | | | | | | | | |
| 1B | Cap Anson | R | 98 | 413 | 127 | 36 | 5 | 0 | 0.0 | 70 | | 18 | 9 | | 0 | 0 | .308 | .419 |
| 2B | Fred Pfeffer | R | 96 | 371 | 87 | 22 | 7 | 1 | 0.3 | 41 | | 8 | 50 | | 0 | 0 | .235 | .340 |
| SS | Tom Burns | L | 97 | 405 | 119 | 37 | 7 | 2 | 0.5 | 69 | | 13 | 31 | | 0 | 0 | .294 | .435 |
| 3B | Ned Williamson | R | 98 | 402 | 111 | 49 | 5 | 2 | 0.5 | 83 | | 22 | 48 | | 0 | 0 | .276 | .438 |
| RF | King Kelly | R | 98 | 428 | 109 | 28 | 10 | 3 | 0.7 | 92 | | 16 | 35 | | 0 | 0 | .255 | .388 |
| CF | George Gore | L | 92 | 392 | 131 | 30 | 9 | 2 | 0.5 | 105 | | 27 | 13 | | 0 | 0 | .334 | .472 |
| LF | Abner Dalrymple | L | 80 | 363 | 108 | 24 | 4 | 2 | 0.6 | 78 | | 11 | 29 | | 0 | 0 | .298 | .402 |
| C | Silver Flint | R | 85 | 332 | 88 | 23 | 4 | 0 | 0.0 | 57 | | 3 | 69 | | 0 | 0 | .265 | .358 |
| **SUBSTITUTES** | | | | | | | | | | | | | | | | | | |
| PO | Larry Corcoran | | 68 | 263 | 55 | 12 | 7 | 0 | 0.0 | 40 | | 6 | 62 | | 0 | 0 | .209 | .308 |
| PO | Fred Goldsmith | R | 60 | 235 | 52 | 12 | 3 | 1 | 0.4 | 38 | | 4 | 35 | | 0 | 0 | .221 | .311 |
| OF | Billy Sunday | L | 14 | 54 | 13 | 4 | 0 | 0 | 0.0 | 6 | | 1 | 18 | | 0 | 0 | .241 | .315 |
| | TEAM TOTAL | | | 3658 | 1000 | 277 | 61 | 13 | 0.4 | 67 | 0 | 129 | 399 | 0 | 0 | 0 | .273 | .393 |

## INDIVIDUAL FIELDING

| POS | Player | T | G | PO | A | E | DP | TC/G | FA |
|---|---|---|---|---|---|---|---|---|---|
| 1B | C. Anson | R | 98 | 1031 | 41 | 40 | 59 | 11.3 | .964 |
| | F. Goldsmith | R | 2 | 4 | 0 | 0 | 0 | 2.0 | 1.000 |
| | F. Pfeffer | R | 1 | 2 | 0 | 0 | 1 | 2.0 | 1.000 |
| 2B | F. Pfeffer | R | 79 | 264 | 264 | 67 | 49 | 7.5 | .887 |
| | T. Burns | R | 19 | 59 | 57 | 28 | 5 | 7.6 | .806 |
| | K. Kelly | R | 3 | 6 | 11 | 8 | 0 | 8.3 | .680 |
| | L. Corcoran | R | 1 | 1 | 1 | 0 | 1 | 2.0 | 1.000 |
| SS | T. Burns | R | 79 | 121 | 260 | 56 | 25 | 5.5 | .872 |
| | F. Pfeffer | R | 18 | 15 | 63 | 19 | 6 | 5.4 | .804 |
| | L. Corcoran | R | 3 | 5 | 5 | 3 | 0 | 4.3 | .769 |
| 3B | Williamson | R | 97 | 111 | 252 | 87 | 20 | 4.6 | .807 |
| | K. Kelly | R | 2 | 3 | 4 | 2 | 0 | 4.5 | .778 |
| | F. Pfeffer | R | 1 | 0 | 1 | 0 | 0 | 1.0 | 1.000 |

| POS | Player | T | G | PO | A | E | DP | TC/G | FA |
|---|---|---|---|---|---|---|---|---|---|
| OF | G. Gore | R | 92 | 195 | 27 | 34 | 4 | 2.8 | .867 |
| | A. Dalrymple | R | 80 | 149 | 12 | 34 | 3 | 2.4 | .826 |
| | K. Kelly | R | 82 | 101 | 38 | 32 | 5 | 2.1 | .813 |
| | F. Goldsmith | R | 16 | 28 | 3 | 7 | 0 | 2.4 | .816 |
| | S. Flint | R | 23 | 10 | 2 | 4 | 0 | 0.7 | .750 |
| | T. Burns | R | 1 | 0 | 0 | 0 | 0 | 0.0 | .000 |
| | L. Corcoran | R | 13 | 13 | 0 | 5 | 0 | 1.4 | .722 |
| | B. Sunday | R | 14 | 10 | 1 | 6 | 0 | 1.2 | .647 |
| | C. Anson | R | 1 | 1 | 0 | 0 | 0 | 1.0 | 1.000 |
| C | S. Flint | R | 83 | 301 | 104 | 57 | 4 | 5.6 | .877 |
| | K. Kelly | R | 38 | 73 | 37 | 21 | 2 | 3.4 | .840 |
| | Williamson | R | 3 | 4 | 5 | 1 | 0 | 3.3 | .900 |
| | C. Anson | R | 1 | 2 | 0 | 2 | 0 | 4.0 | .500 |

Although the White Stockings made a noble effort to make it four pennants in a row, they had to be content with the runner-up slot to Boston. Joe Quest had been replaced at second base by Fred Pfeffer, who cemented the famed "stonewall infield." Covering as much ground as a modern tarpaulin, Pfeffer became one of the greatest glovemen of his era—without the aid of a glove. Another newcomer was part-time outfielder Billy Sunday, who went on to world renown as an evangelist. As a player, Billy was a competent fielder and base runner, but did not have a prayer as a batter. Consequently, his big-league stay was brief.

These were the only changes in the roster as the White Stockings continued to make entries in the record books. On July 3 they slugged 14 doubles, including four each by Anson and Dalrymple, in a 31–7 drubbing of Buffalo. An even more spectacular outing came September 6, as Chicago scored a record 18 times in the bottom of the seventh inning to rock Detroit, 26–6. Tommy Burns was especially remarkable with two doubles and a home run in that inning.

## TEAM STATISTICS

|  | W | L | PCT | GB | R | OR | 2B | Batting 3B | HR | BA | SA | SB | Fielding E | DP | FA | CG | B | Pitching SO | ShO | SV | ERA |
|---|---|---|---|---|---|---|---|---|---|---|---|---|---|---|---|---|---|---|---|---|---|
| BOS | 63 | 35 | .643 |  | 669 | 456 | 209 | 86 | 34 | .276 | .408 | 0 | 409 | 58 | .901 | 89 | 90 | 538 | 5 | 3 | 2.55 |
| CHI | 59 | 39 | .602 | 4 | 679 | 540 | 277 | 61 | 13 | .273 | .393 | 0 | 543 | 76 | .879 | 91 | 123 | 299 | 5 | 1 | 2.78 |
| PRO | 58 | 40 | .592 | 5 | 636 | 436 | 189 | 59 | 21 | .272 | .372 | 0 | 419 | 75 | .903 | 88 | 111 | 376 | 4 | 1 | 2.37 |
| CLE | 55 | 42 | .567 | 7.5 | 476 | 443 | 184 | 38 | 8 | .246 | .329 | 0 | 389 | 69 | .909 | 92 | 217 | 402 | 5 | 2 | 2.22 |
| BUF | 52 | 45 | .536 | 10.5 | 614 | 576 | 184 | 59 | 8 | .284 | .371 | 0 | 445 | 52 | .896 | 90 | 101 | 362 | 5 | 2 | 3.32 |
| NY | 46 | 50 | .479 | 16 | 530 | 577 | 138 | 69 | 25 | .255 | .355 | 0 | 468 | 52 | .889 | 87 | 170 | 323 | 5 | 0 | 2.94 |
| DET | 40 | 58 | .408 | 23 | 524 | 650 | 164 | 48 | 13 | .250 | .330 | 0 | 470 | 77 | .893 | 89 | 184 | 324 | 4 | 2 | 3.56 |
| PHI | 17 | 81 | .173 | 46 | 437 | 887 | 181 | 47 | 4 | .240 | .320 | 0 | 639 | 62 | .858 | 91 | 125 | 253 | 3 | 0 | 5.33 |
| LEAGUE TOTAL |  |  |  |  | 4565 | 4565 | 1526 | 467 | 126 | .262 | .360 | 0 | 3782 | 521 | .891 | 717 | 1121 | 2877 | 36 | 11 | 3.13 |

## INDIVIDUAL PITCHING

| PITCHER | T | W | L | PCT | ERA | SV | G | GS | CG | IP | H | BB | SO | R | ER | ShO | H/9 | BB/9 | SO/9 |
|---|---|---|---|---|---|---|---|---|---|---|---|---|---|---|---|---|---|---|---|
| Larry Corcoran | R | 34 | 20 | .630 | 2.49 | 0 | 56 | 53 | 51 | 473.2 | 483 | 82 | 216 | 281 | 131 | 3 | 9.18 | 1.56 | 4.10 |
| Fred Goldsmith | R | 25 | 19 | .568 | 3.15 | 0 | 46 | 45 | 40 | 383.1 | 456 | 39 | 82 | 256 | 134 | 2 | 10.71 | 0.92 | 1.93 |
| Cap Anson | R | 0 | 0 | – | 0.00 | 1 | 2 | 0 | 0 | 3 | 1 | 1 | 0 | 1 | 0 | 0 | 3.00 | 3.00 | 0.00 |
| King Kelly | R | 0 | 0 | – | 0.00 | 0 | 1 | 0 | 0 | 1 | 1 | 0 | 0 | 0 | 0 | 0 | 9.00 | 0.00 | 0.00 |
| Ned Williamson | R | 0 | 0 | – | 9.00 | 0 | 1 | 0 | 0 | 1 | 1 | 1 | 1 | 2 | 1 | 0 | 9.00 | 9.00 | 9.00 |
| TEAM TOTAL |  | 59 | 39 | .602 | 2.78 | 1 | 106 | 98 | 91 | 862 | 942 | 123 | 299 | 540 | 266 | 5 | 9.84 | 1.28 | 3.12 |

| MANAGER | W | L | PCT |
|---|---|---|---|
| Cap Anson | 62 | 50 | .554 |

| POS | Player | B | G | AB | H | 2B | 3B | HR | HR % | R | RBI | BB | SO | SB | Pinch Hit AB | Pinch Hit H | BA | SA |
|---|---|---|---|---|---|---|---|---|---|---|---|---|---|---|---|---|---|---|
| **REGULARS** | | | | | | | | | | | | | | | | | | |
| 1B | Cap Anson | R | 112 | 475 | 159 | 30 | 3 | 21 | 4.4 | 108 | | 29 | 13 | | 0 | 0 | .335 | .543 |
| 2B | Fred Pfeffer | R | 112 | 467 | 135 | 10 | 10 | 25 | 5.4 | 105 | | 25 | 47 | | 0 | 0 | .289 | .514 |
| SS | Tom Burns | L | 83 | 343 | 84 | 14 | 2 | 7 | 2.0 | 54 | | 13 | 50 | | 0 | 0 | .245 | .359 |
| 3B | Ned Williamson | R | 107 | 417 | 116 | 18 | 8 | 27 | 6.5 | 84 | | 42 | 56 | | 0 | 0 | .278 | .554 |
| RF | King Kelly | R | 108 | 452 | 160 | 28 | 5 | 13 | 2.9 | 120 | | 46 | 24 | | 0 | 0 | **.354** | .524 |
| CF | George Gore | L | 103 | 422 | 134 | 18 | 4 | 5 | 1.2 | 104 | | 61 | 26 | | 0 | 0 | .318 | .415 |
| LF | Abner Dalrymple | L | 111 | 521 | 161 | 18 | 9 | 22 | 4.2 | 111 | | 14 | 39 | | 0 | 0 | .309 | .505 |
| C | Silver Flint | R | 73 | 279 | 57 | 5 | 2 | 9 | 3.2 | 35 | | 7 | 57 | | 0 | 0 | .204 | .333 |
| **SUBSTITUTES** | | | | | | | | | | | | | | | | | | |
| SS | Walt Kinzie | | 19 | 82 | 13 | 3 | 0 | 2 | 2.4 | 4 | | 0 | 13 | | 0 | 0 | .159 | .268 |
| P1 | Thomas Lynch | L | 1 | 4 | 0 | 0 | 0 | 0 | 0.0 | 0 | 0 | 0 | 2 | | 0 | 0 | .000 | .000 |
| OF | Billy Sunday | L | 43 | 176 | 39 | 4 | 1 | 4 | 2.3 | 25 | | 4 | 36 | | 0 | 0 | .222 | .324 |
| UT | John Clarkson | R | 21 | 84 | 22 | 6 | 2 | 3 | 3.6 | 16 | | 2 | 16 | | 0 | 0 | .262 | .488 |
| UT | Joe Brown | | 15 | 61 | 13 | 1 | 0 | 0 | 0.0 | 6 | | 0 | 15 | | 0 | 0 | .213 | .230 |
| C | Sy Sutcliffe | L | 4 | 15 | 3 | 1 | 0 | 0 | 0.0 | 4 | | 2 | 4 | | 0 | 0 | .200 | .267 |
| **PITCHERS** | | | | | | | | | | | | | | | | | | |
| P | Larry Corcoran | | 64 | 251 | 61 | 3 | 4 | 1 | 0.4 | 43 | | 10 | 33 | | 0 | 0 | .243 | .299 |
| P | Fred Goldsmith | R | 22 | 81 | 11 | 2 | 0 | 2 | 2.5 | 11 | | 7 | 26 | | 0 | 0 | .136 | .235 |
| P | Tom Lee | | 6 | 24 | 3 | 1 | 0 | 0 | 0.0 | 0 | | 0 | 6 | | 0 | 0 | .125 | .167 |
| P | George Crosby | | 3 | 13 | 4 | 0 | 0 | 1 | 7.7 | 1 | | 0 | 1 | | 0 | 0 | .308 | .538 |
| P | John Hibbard | | 2 | 7 | 0 | 0 | 0 | 0 | 0.0 | 0 | | 0 | 4 | | 0 | 0 | .000 | .000 |
| P | Fred Andrus | R | 1 | 5 | 1 | 0 | 0 | 0 | 0.0 | 3 | | 1 | 0 | | 0 | 0 | .200 | .200 |
| P | Mike Corcoran | | 1 | 3 | 0 | 0 | 0 | 0 | 0.0 | 0 | | 0 | 1 | | 0 | 0 | .000 | .000 |
| | TEAM TOTAL | | | 4182 | 1176 | 162 | 50 | 142 | 3.4 | 83 | 0 | 264 | 469 | 0 | 0 | 0 | .281 | .446 |

## INDIVIDUAL FIELDING

| POS | Player | T | G | PO | A | E | DP | TC/G | FA |
|---|---|---|---|---|---|---|---|---|---|
| 1B | C. Anson | R | 112 | **1211** | 40 | 58 | 86 | 11.7 | .956 |
| | K. Kelly | R | 2 | 8 | 2 | 2 | 1 | 6.0 | .833 |
| | J. Clarkson | R | 1 | 3 | 0 | 3 | 0 | 6.0 | .500 |
| | T. Lynch | | 1 | 5 | 0 | 0 | 0 | 5.0 | 1.000 |
| | J. Brown | | 1 | 3 | 0 | 0 | 0 | 3.0 | 1.000 |
| 2B | F. Pfeffer | R | 112 | **395** | **422** | 88 | 85 | 8.1 | .903 |
| SS | T. Burns | R | 80 | 99 | 254 | 68 | 21 | 5.3 | .838 |
| | W. Kinzie | | 17 | 18 | 46 | 13 | 4 | 4.5 | .831 |
| | K. Kelly | R | 12 | 7 | 37 | 18 | 3 | 5.2 | .710 |
| | L. Corcoran | R | 2 | 2 | 10 | 1 | 0 | 6.5 | .923 |
| | T. Lee | | 1 | 1 | 5 | 0 | 0 | 6.0 | 1.000 |
| | C. Anson | R | 1 | 1 | 3 | 1 | 0 | 5.0 | .800 |
| 3B | Williamson | R | 99 | 121 | **250** | 60 | 25 | 4.4 | .861 |
| | K. Kelly | R | 10 | 12 | 16 | 8 | 2 | 3.6 | .778 |
| | W. Kinzie | | 2 | 4 | 5 | 1 | 0 | 5.0 | .900 |
| | T. Burns | R | 3 | 3 | 5 | 1 | 0 | 3.0 | .889 |
| | J. Clarkson | R | 2 | 0 | 2 | 2 | 0 | 2.0 | .500 |

| POS | Player | T | G | PO | A | E | DP | TC/G | FA |
|---|---|---|---|---|---|---|---|---|---|
| OF | G. Gore | R | 103 | 185 | 25 | 32 | 5 | 2.3 | .868 |
| | A. Dalrymple | R | 111 | 176 | 18 | 26 | 5 | 2.0 | .882 |
| | K. Kelly | R | 63 | 69 | 31 | 26 | 1 | 2.0 | .794 |
| | B. Sunday | R | 43 | 45 | 8 | 27 | 1 | 1.9 | .663 |
| | J. Clarkson | R | 8 | 5 | 5 | 4 | 1 | 1.8 | .714 |
| | J. Brown | | 9 | 5 | 1 | 2 | 0 | 0.9 | .750 |
| | F. Goldsmith | R | 2 | 1 | 1 | 0 | 0 | 1.0 | 1.000 |
| | L. Corcoran | R | 4 | 2 | 0 | 0 | 0 | 0.5 | 1.000 |
| C | S. Flint | R | 73 | 354 | 110 | 61 | 9 | 7.2 | .884 |
| | K. Kelly | R | 28 | 105 | 55 | 32 | 3 | 6.9 | .833 |
| | Williamson | R | 10 | 34 | 20 | 7 | 1 | 6.1 | .885 |
| | S. Sutcliffe | | 4 | 34 | 6 | 1 | 1 | 10.3 | .976 |
| | C. Anson | R | 3 | 4 | 4 | 3 | 0 | 3.7 | .727 |
| | J. Brown | | 1 | 3 | 1 | 0 | 0 | 4.0 | 1.000 |

Prior to 1884 any ball hit over the short right field fence at Lakefront Park was a ground-rule double, but then the rule was changed to give the batter a home run. As a result, the White Stockings hit 142 "home runs," which remained the record until surpassed by the 1927 Yankees.

Ned Williamson led the league with 27 (which stood until Babe Ruth hit 29 in 1919), while Pfeffer had 25, Dalrymple 22, and Anson 21. On May 30 Williamson became the first major leaguer to belt three homers in one game. On August 5 and 6 Anson became the first to collect five in two games, setting a record that has been matched by several players but not exceeded.

In spite of their ersatz power, the White Stockings were not a factor in the pennant race. Due largely to the decline of Goldsmith's pitching, the team spent most of the campaign in the second division. However, a surge in August and September enabled them to catch a tie for fourth place. An encouraging sign was the arrival of pitcher John Clarkson, who won 10 of 13 decisions in September, and eventually made it to the Hall of Fame. Larry Corcoran pitched his third no-hit game with a 6–0 shellacking of Providence on June 27.

## TEAM STATISTICS

| | W | L | PCT | GB | R | OR | Batting 2B | 3B | HR | BA | SA | SB | Fielding E | DP | FA | CG | B | Pitching SO | ShO | SV | ERA |
|---|---|---|---|---|---|---|---|---|---|---|---|---|---|---|---|---|---|---|---|---|---|
| PRO | 84 | 28 | .750 | | 665 | 388 | 153 | 43 | 21 | .241 | .315 | 0 | 398 | 50 | .918 | 107 | 172 | 639 | 16 | 2 | 1.59 |
| BOS | 73 | 38 | .658 | 10.5 | 684 | 468 | 179 | 60 | 36 | .254 | .351 | 0 | 384 | 46 | .922 | 109 | 135 | 742 | 14 | 2 | 2.47 |
| BUF | 64 | 47 | .577 | 19.5 | 700 | 626 | 163 | 69 | 39 | .262 | .361 | 0 | 462 | 71 | .905 | 108 | 189 | 534 | 14 | 1 | 2.95 |
| CHI | 62 | 50 | .554 | 22 | 834 | 647 | 162 | 50 | 142 | .281 | .446 | 0 | 595 | 107 | .886 | 106 | 231 | 472 | 9 | 0 | 3.03 |
| NY | 62 | 50 | .554 | 22 | 693 | 623 | 148 | 67 | 24 | .255 | .341 | 0 | 514 | 69 | .895 | 111 | 326 | 567 | 4 | 0 | 3.12 |
| PHI | 39 | 73 | .348 | 45 | 549 | 824 | 149 | 39 | 14 | .234 | .301 | 0 | 536 | 67 | .888 | 106 | 254 | 411 | 3 | 1 | 3.93 |
| CLE | 35 | 77 | .313 | 49 | 458 | 716 | 147 | 49 | 16 | .237 | .312 | 0 | 512 | 75 | .897 | 107 | 269 | 482 | 7 | 0 | 3.43 |
| DET | 28 | 84 | .250 | 56 | 445 | 736 | 114 | 47 | 31 | .208 | .284 | 0 | 549 | 60 | .886 | 109 | 245 | 488 | 3 | 0 | 3.38 |
| LEAGUE TOTAL | | | | | 5028 | 5028 | 1215 | 424 | 323 | .247 | .340 | 0 | 3950 | 545 | .900 | 863 | 1821 | 4335 | 70 | 6 | 2.98 |

## INDIVIDUAL PITCHING

| PITCHER | T | W | L | PCT | ERA | SV | G | GS | CG | IP | H | BB | SO | R | ER | ShO | H/9 | BB/9 | SO/9 |
|---|---|---|---|---|---|---|---|---|---|---|---|---|---|---|---|---|---|---|---|
| Larry Corcoran | R | 35 | 23 | .603 | 2.40 | 0 | 60 | 59 | 57 | 516.2 | 473 | 116 | 272 | 286 | 138 | 7 | 8.24 | 2.02 | 4.74 |
| Fred Goldsmith | R | 9 | 11 | .450 | 4.26 | 0 | 21 | 21 | 20 | 188 | 245 | 29 | 34 | 141 | 89 | 1 | 11.73 | 1.39 | 1.63 |
| John Clarkson | R | 10 | 3 | .769 | 2.14 | 0 | 14 | 13 | 12 | 118 | 94 | 25 | 102 | 64 | 28 | 0 | 7.17 | 1.91 | 7.78 |
| Joe Brown | | 4 | 2 | .667 | 4.68 | 0 | 7 | 6 | 5 | 50 | 56 | 7 | 27 | 36 | 26 | 0 | 10.08 | 1.26 | 4.86 |
| Tom Lee | | 1 | 4 | .200 | 3.77 | 0 | 5 | 5 | 5 | 45.1 | 55 | 15 | 14 | 43 | 19 | 0 | 10.92 | 2.98 | 2.78 |
| George Crosby | | 1 | 2 | .333 | 3.54 | 0 | 3 | 3 | 3 | 28 | 27 | 12 | 11 | 21 | 11 | 0 | 8.68 | 3.86 | 3.54 |
| John Hibbard | | 1 | 1 | .500 | 2.65 | 0 | 2 | 2 | 2 | 17 | 18 | 9 | 4 | 10 | 5 | 1 | 9.53 | 4.76 | 2.12 |
| Fred Andrus | R | 1 | 0 | 1.000 | 2.00 | 0 | 1 | 1 | 1 | 9 | 11 | 2 | 2 | 3 | 2 | 0 | 11.00 | 2.00 | 2.00 |
| Mike Corcoran | | 0 | 1 | .000 | 4.00 | 0 | 1 | 1 | 1 | 9 | 16 | 7 | 2 | 14 | 4 | 0 | 16.00 | 7.00 | 2.00 |
| Thomas Lynch | | 0 | 0 | – | 2.57 | 0 | 1 | 1 | 0 | 7 | 7 | 3 | 2 | 4 | 2 | 0 | 9.00 | 3.86 | 2.57 |
| King Kelly | R | 0 | 1 | .000 | 8.44 | 0 | 2 | 0 | 0 | 5.1 | 12 | 2 | 1 | 11 | 5 | 0 | 20.25 | 3.38 | 1.69 |
| Ned Williamson | R | 0 | 0 | – | 18.00 | 0 | 2 | 0 | 0 | 2 | 8 | 2 | 0 | 8 | 4 | 0 | 36.00 | 9.00 | 0.00 |
| Cap Anson | R | 0 | 1 | .000 | 18.00 | 0 | 1 | 0 | 0 | 1 | 3 | 1 | 1 | 4 | 2 | 0 | 27.00 | 9.00 | 9.00 |
| Fred Pfeffer | R | 0 | 0 | – | 9.00 | 0 | 1 | 0 | 0 | 1 | 3 | 1 | 0 | 2 | 1 | 0 | 27.00 | 9.00 | 0.00 |
| TEAM TOTAL | | 62 | 49 | .559 | 3.03 | 0 | 121 | 112 | 106 | 997.1 | 1028 | 231 | 472 | 647 | 336 | 9 | 9.28 | 2.08 | 4.26 |

| MANAGER | W | L | PCT |
|---|---|---|---|
| Cap Anson | 87 | 25 | .777 |

| POS | Player | B | G | AB | H | 2B | 3B | HR | HR % | R | RBI | BB | SO | SB | Pinch Hit AB | Pinch Hit H | BA | SA |
|---|---|---|---|---|---|---|---|---|---|---|---|---|---|---|---|---|---|---|
| **REGULARS** | | | | | | | | | | | | | | | | | | |
| 1B | Cap Anson | R | 112 | 464 | 144 | **35** | 7 | 7 | 1.5 | 100 | 114 | 34 | 13 | | 0 | 0 | .310 | .461 |
| 2B | Fred Pfeffer | R | 112 | 469 | 113 | 12 | 6 | 6 | 1.3 | 90 | 71 | 26 | 47 | | 0 | 0 | .241 | .330 |
| SS | Tom Burns | L | 111 | 445 | 121 | 23 | 9 | 7 | 1.6 | 82 | 70 | 16 | 48 | | 0 | 0 | .272 | .411 |
| 3B | Ned Williamson | R | 113 | 407 | 97 | 16 | 5 | 3 | 0.7 | 87 | 64 | **75** | 60 | | 0 | 0 | .238 | .324 |
| RF | King Kelly | R | 107 | 438 | 126 | 24 | 7 | 9 | 2.1 | **124** | 74 | 46 | 24 | | 0 | 0 | .288 | .436 |
| CF | George Gore | L | 109 | 441 | 138 | 21 | 13 | 5 | 1.1 | 115 | 51 | 68 | 25 | | 0 | 0 | .313 | .454 |
| LF | Abner Dalrymple | L | 113 | **492** | 135 | 27 | 12 | **11** | **2.2** | 109 | 58 | 46 | 42 | | 0 | 0 | .274 | .445 |
| C | Silver Flint | R | 68 | 249 | 52 | 8 | 2 | 1 | 0.4 | 27 | 19 | 2 | 52 | | 0 | 0 | .209 | .269 |
| **SUBSTITUTES** | | | | | | | | | | | | | | | | | | |
| SO | Jimmy Ryan | R | 3 | 13 | 6 | 1 | 0 | 0 | 0.0 | 2 | 2 | 1 | 1 | | 0 | 0 | .462 | .538 |
| OF | Billy Sunday | L | 46 | 172 | 44 | 3 | 3 | 2 | 1.2 | 36 | 20 | 12 | 33 | | 0 | 0 | .256 | .343 |
| PO | Wash Williams | | 1 | 4 | 1 | 0 | 0 | 0 | 0.0 | 0 | 0 | 0 | 0 | | 0 | 0 | .250 | .250 |
| OF | Bill Krieg | R | 1 | 3 | 0 | 0 | 0 | 0 | 0.0 | 0 | 0 | 0 | 2 | | 0 | 0 | .000 | .000 |
| C | Sy Sutcliffe | L | 11 | 43 | 8 | 1 | 1 | 0 | 0.0 | 5 | 4 | 2 | 5 | | 0 | 0 | .186 | .256 |
| CO | Jim McCauley | | 3 | 6 | 1 | 0 | 0 | 0 | 0.0 | 1 | 0 | 2 | 3 | | 0 | 0 | .167 | .167 |
| C | Ed Gastfield | | 1 | 3 | 0 | 0 | 0 | 0 | 0.0 | 0 | 0 | 0 | 1 | | 0 | 0 | .000 | .000 |
| **PITCHERS** | | | | | | | | | | | | | | | | | | |
| P | John Clarkson | R | 72 | 283 | 61 | 11 | 5 | 4 | 1.4 | 34 | 31 | 3 | 44 | | 0 | 0 | .216 | .332 |
| P | Jim McCormick | R | 25 | 103 | 23 | 1 | 4 | 0 | 0.0 | 13 | 16 | 1 | 18 | | 0 | 0 | .223 | .311 |
| P | Ted Kennedy | L | 9 | 36 | 3 | 0 | 0 | 0 | 0.0 | 3 | 0 | 0 | 10 | | 0 | 0 | .083 | .083 |
| P | Larry Corcoran | | 7 | 22 | 6 | 1 | 0 | 0 | 0.0 | 6 | 4 | 6 | 1 | | 0 | 0 | .273 | .318 |
| TEAM TOTAL | | | | 4093 | 1079 | 184 | 74 | 55 | 1.3 | 83 | 598 | 340 | 429 | 0 | 0 | 0 | .264 | .385 |

## INDIVIDUAL FIELDING

| POS | Player | T | G | PO | A | E | DP | TC/G | FA |
|---|---|---|---|---|---|---|---|---|---|
| 1B | C. Anson | R | 112 | **1253** | 39 | **57** | 62 | **12.0** | .958 |
| | K. Kelly | R | 2 | 9 | 1 | 3 | 0 | 6.5 | .769 |
| 2B | F. Pfeffer | R | 109 | **325** | **391** | 86 | 66 | **7.4** | .893 |
| | T. Burns | R | 1 | 0 | 0 | 0 | 0 | 0.0 | .000 |
| | K. Kelly | R | 6 | 7 | 15 | 3 | 1 | 4.2 | .880 |
| SS | T. Burns | R | 111 | 151 | 370 | **96** | 35 | 5.6 | .844 |
| | J. Ryan | L | 2 | 3 | 11 | 5 | 0 | 9.5 | .737 |
| | L. Corcoran | R | 1 | 0 | 1 | 0 | 0 | 1.0 | 1.000 |
| 3B | Williamson | R | 113 | 113 | **258** | 45 | **18** | 3.7 | **.892** |
| | K. Kelly | R | 2 | 2 | 3 | 3 | 0 | 4.0 | .625 |
| | J. Clarkson | R | 1 | 0 | 1 | 0 | 0 | 1.0 | 1.000 |
| | T. Kennedy | | 1 | 0 | 1 | 0 | 0 | 1.0 | 1.000 |

| POS | Player | T | G | PO | A | E | DP | TC/G | FA |
|---|---|---|---|---|---|---|---|---|---|
| OF | G. Gore | R | 109 | 204 | 17 | 29 | 2 | 2.3 | .884 |
| | A. Dalrymple | R | 113 | 180 | 16 | 27 | 2 | 2.0 | .879 |
| | K. Kelly | R | 69 | 95 | **29** | 19 | 2 | 2.1 | .867 |
| | B. Sunday | R | 46 | 46 | 6 | 11 | 2 | 1.4 | .825 |
| | S. Flint | R | 1 | 0 | 0 | 0 | 0 | 0.0 | .000 |
| | J. McCauley | | 2 | 0 | 0 | 0 | 0 | 0.0 | .000 |
| | B. Krieg | R | 1 | 6 | 2 | 2 | 0 | 10.0 | .800 |
| | J. Ryan | L | 1 | 3 | 0 | 2 | 0 | 5.0 | .600 |
| | F. Pfeffer | R | 1 | 2 | 0 | 0 | 0 | 2.0 | 1.000 |
| | S. Sutcliffe | | 1 | 1 | 1 | 0 | 0 | 2.0 | 1.000 |
| | W. Williams | | 1 | 1 | 0 | 1 | 0 | 2.0 | .500 |
| | McCormick | R | 1 | 1 | 0 | 0 | 0 | 1.0 | 1.000 |
| | J. Clarkson | R | 3 | 1 | 0 | 0 | 0 | 0.3 | 1.000 |
| C | S. Flint | R | 68 | **356** | 100 | 36 | 2 | 7.2 | **.927** |
| | K. Kelly | R | 37 | 146 | 64 | 30 | 2 | 6.5 | .875 |
| | S. Sutcliffe | | 11 | 46 | 11 | 11 | 0 | 6.2 | .838 |
| | E. Gastfield | | 1 | 10 | 1 | 0 | 1 | 11.0 | 1.000 |
| | J. McCauley | | 2 | 7 | 1 | 2 | 0 | 5.0 | .800 |
| | Williamson | R | 1 | 6 | 1 | 0 | 0 | 7.0 | 1.000 |
| | C. Anson | R | 1 | 2 | 0 | 0 | 0 | 2.0 | 1.000 |

The 1885 race was a two-way struggle between the White Stockings and the New York Giants, creating an intense rivalry that would peak during the Frank Chance era. Although Chicago enjoyed an early 18-game winning streak, they could never venture far ahead, as the Giants usually matched them win for win.

The team had vacated its lakeside location for West Side Park at Congress and Loomis streets, which would be their home until 1893. Without the short right-field fence, home run production dipped to 53, which was still good enough to lead the league.

Corcoran departed in May because of a lame arm, and John Clarkson began pitching on an everyday basis, gathering an amazing 53 wins. Later in the year, however, the White Stockings signed Jim McCormick, who relieved some of John's burden by winning 20 himself.

The big bats continued to be Anson, Kelly, Gore, and, Dalrymple but it was light-hitting Fred Pfeffer who rose to the occasion when it counted the most. His seventh-inning homer in the final game of the playoffs gave the White Stockings the edge they needed to squeeze by the Giants, 2–1, to clinch the pennant.

Shortly after the flag was captured, Chicago brought up young outfielder Jimmy Ryan, who quickly became a superstar. In the postseason competition, their opponents were the American Association St. Louis Browns, not to be confused with the latter-day Browns of the AL. The series was a cross between a World Series and a barnstorming tour, as games were played in Chicago, St. Louis, Pittsburgh, and Cincinnati. After an eventful seven games that included violence on and off the field and frequent disputes over the umpiring, a special committee declared the series over with the teams tied at three wins and a tie apiece.

## TEAM STATISTICS

| | W | L | PCT | GB | R | OR | 2B | Batting 3B | HR | BA | SA | SB | Fielding E | DP | FA | CG | B | Pitching SO | ShO | SV | ERA |
|---|---|---|---|---|---|---|---|---|---|---|---|---|---|---|---|---|---|---|---|---|---|
| CHI | 87 | 25 | .777 | | 834 | 470 | 184 | 74 | 55 | .264 | .385 | 0 | 496 | 80 | .903 | 108 | 202 | 458 | 14 | 4 | 2.23 |
| NY | 85 | 27 | .759 | 2 | 691 | 370 | 150 | 82 | 16 | .269 | .359 | 0 | 331 | 85 | .929 | 109 | 266 | 519 | 15 | 1 | 1.72 |
| PHI | 56 | 54 | .509 | 30 | 513 | 511 | 156 | 35 | 20 | .229 | .302 | 0 | 447 | 66 | .905 | 108 | 218 | 378 | 9 | 0 | 2.39 |
| PRO | 53 | 57 | .482 | 33 | 442 | 531 | 114 | 30 | 6 | .220 | .272 | 0 | 459 | 70 | .903 | 108 | 235 | 371 | 8 | 0 | 2.71 |
| BOS | 46 | 66 | .411 | 41 | 528 | 589 | 144 | 53 | 22 | .232 | .312 | 0 | 478 | 79 | .901 | 111 | 188 | 480 | 10 | 0 | 3.03 |
| DET | 41 | 67 | .380 | 44 | 514 | 582 | 149 | 65 | 26 | .243 | .338 | 0 | 463 | 61 | .901 | 105 | 224 | 475 | 6 | 1 | 2.88 |
| BUF | 38 | 74 | .339 | 49 | 495 | 761 | 149 | 50 | 23 | .251 | .333 | 0 | 464 | 65 | .901 | 107 | 234 | 320 | 3 | 1 | 4.30 |
| STL | 36 | 72 | .333 | 49 | 390 | 593 | 121 | 21 | 8 | .221 | .270 | 0 | 398 | 67 | .916 | 107 | 278 | 337 | 4 | 0 | 3.37 |
| LEAGUE TOTAL | | | | | 4407 | 4407 | 1167 | 410 | 176 | .241 | .322 | 0 | 3536 | 573 | .908 | 863 | 1845 | 3338 | 69 | 7 | 2.82 |

## INDIVIDUAL PITCHING

| PITCHER | T | W | L | PCT | ERA | SV | G | GS | CG | IP | H | BB | SO | R | ER | ShO | H/9 | BB/9 | SO/9 |
|---|---|---|---|---|---|---|---|---|---|---|---|---|---|---|---|---|---|---|---|
| John Clarkson | R | 53 | 16 | .768 | 1.85 | 0 | 70 | 70 | 68 | 623 | 497 | 97 | 318 | 255 | 128 | 10 | 7.18 | 1.40 | 4.59 |
| Jim McCormick | R | 20 | 4 | .833 | 2.43 | 0 | 24 | 24 | 24 | 215 | 187 | 40 | 88 | 103 | 58 | 3 | 7.83 | 1.67 | 3.68 |
| Ted Kennedy | | 7 | 2 | .778 | 3.43 | 0 | 9 | 9 | 8 | 78.2 | 91 | 28 | 36 | 54 | 30 | 0 | 10.41 | 3.20 | 4.12 |
| Larry Corcoran | R | 5 | 2 | .714 | 3.64 | 0 | 7 | 7 | 6 | 59.1 | 63 | 24 | 10 | 38 | 24 | 1 | 9.56 | 3.64 | 1.52 |
| Fred Pfeffer | R | 2 | 1 | .667 | 2.56 | 2 | 5 | 2 | 2 | 31.2 | 26 | 8 | 13 | 15 | 9 | 0 | 7.39 | 2.27 | 3.69 |
| Ned Williamson | R | 0 | 0 | — | 0.00 | 2 | 2 | 0 | 0 | 6 | 2 | 0 | 3 | 0 | 0 | 0 | 3.00 | 0.00 | 4.50 |
| Wash Williams | | 0 | 0 | — | 13.50 | 0 | 1 | 1 | 0 | 2 | 2 | 5 | 0 | 5 | 3 | 0 | 9.00 | 22.50 | 0.00 |
| TEAM TOTAL | | 87 | 25 | .777 | 2.23 | 4 | 118 | 113 | 108 | 1015.2 | 868 | 202 | 468 | 470 | 252 | 14 | 7.69 | 1.79 | 4.15 |

| MANAGER | W | L | PCT |
|---|---|---|---|
| Cap Anson | 90 | 34 | .726 |

| POS | Player | B | G | AB | H | 2B | 3B | HR | HR % | R | RBI | BB | SO | SB | Pinch Hit AB | Pinch Hit H | BA | SA |
|---|---|---|---|---|---|---|---|---|---|---|---|---|---|---|---|---|---|---|
| **REGULARS** | | | | | | | | | | | | | | | | | | |
| 1B | Cap Anson | R | 125 | 504 | 187 | 35 | 11 | 10 | 2.0 | 117 | 147 | 55 | 19 | 29 | 0 | 0 | .371 | .544 |
| 2B | Fred Pfeffer | R | 118 | 474 | 125 | 17 | 8 | 7 | 1.5 | 88 | 95 | 36 | 46 | | 0 | 0 | .264 | .378 |
| SS | Ned Williamson | R | 121 | 430 | 93 | 17 | 8 | 6 | 1.4 | 69 | 58 | 80 | 71 | | 0 | 0 | .216 | .335 |
| 3B | Tom Burns | L | 112 | 445 | 123 | 18 | 10 | 3 | 0.7 | 64 | 65 | 14 | 40 | | 0 | 0 | .276 | .382 |
| RF | Jimmy Ryan | R | 84 | 327 | 100 | 17 | 6 | 4 | 1.2 | 58 | 53 | 12 | 28 | | 0 | 0 | .306 | .431 |
| CF | George Gore | L | 118 | 444 | 135 | 20 | 12 | 6 | 1.4 | 150 | 63 | 102 | 30 | | 0 | 0 | .304 | .444 |
| LF | Abner Dalrymple | L | 82 | 331 | 77 | 7 | 12 | 3 | 0.9 | 62 | 26 | 33 | 44 | | 0 | 0 | .233 | .353 |
| C | Silver Flint | R | 54 | 173 | 35 | 6 | 2 | 1 | 0.6 | 30 | 13 | 12 | 36 | | 0 | 0 | .202 | .277 |
| **SUBSTITUTES** | | | | | | | | | | | | | | | | | | |
| UT | King Kelly | R | 118 | 451 | 175 | 32 | 11 | 4 | 0.9 | 155 | 79 | 83 | 33 | | 0 | 0 | **.388** | .534 |
| PO | Jocko Flynn | | 57 | 205 | 41 | 6 | 2 | 4 | 2.0 | 40 | 19 | 18 | 45 | | 0 | 0 | .200 | .307 |
| OF | Billy Sunday | L | 28 | 103 | 25 | 2 | 2 | 0 | 0.0 | 16 | 6 | 7 | 26 | | 0 | 0 | .243 | .301 |
| C | George Moolic | R | 16 | 56 | 8 | 3 | 0 | 0 | 0.0 | 9 | 2 | 2 | 17 | | 0 | 0 | .143 | .196 |
| C | Lew Hardie | | 16 | 51 | 9 | 0 | 0 | 0 | 0.0 | 4 | 3 | 4 | 10 | | 0 | 0 | .176 | .176 |
| **PITCHERS** | | | | | | | | | | | | | | | | | | |
| P | John Clarkson | R | 55 | 210 | 49 | 9 | 1 | 3 | 1.4 | 21 | 23 | 0 | 38 | | 0 | 0 | .233 | .329 |
| P | Jim McCormick | R | 42 | 174 | 41 | 9 | 2 | 2 | 1.1 | 17 | 21 | 2 | 30 | | 0 | 0 | .236 | .345 |
| | TEAM TOTAL | | | 4378 | 1223 | 198 | 87 | 53 | 1.2 | 90 | 673 | 460 | 513 | 29 | 0 | 0 | .279 | .401 |

## INDIVIDUAL FIELDING

| POS | Player | T | G | PO | A | E | DP | TC/G | FA |
|---|---|---|---|---|---|---|---|---|---|
| 1B | C. Anson | R | 125 | 1188 | 66 | 48 | 69 | 10.4 | .963 |
| | K. Kelly | R | 9 | 41 | 4 | 2 | 0 | 5.2 | .957 |
| | S. Flint | R | 3 | 13 | 1 | 0 | 1 | 4.7 | 1.000 |
| | F. Pfeffer | R | 1 | 1 | 0 | 0 | 0 | 1.0 | 1.000 |
| 2B | F. Pfeffer | R | 118 | 343 | 340 | 73 | 66 | 6.4 | .903 |
| | K. Kelly | R | 6 | 14 | 12 | 5 | 4 | 5.2 | .839 |
| | J. Ryan | L | 5 | 9 | 9 | 0 | 1 | 3.6 | 1.000 |
| SS | Williamson | R | 121 | 161 | 355 | 78 | 36 | 4.9 | .869 |
| | J. Ryan | L | 6 | 4 | 14 | 3 | 0 | 3.5 | .857 |
| | K. Kelly | R | 5 | 3 | 1 | 1 | 1 | 1.0 | .800 |
| 3B | T. Burns | R | 112 | 149 | 247 | 49 | 12 | 4.0 | .890 |
| | L. Hardie | | 1 | 0 | 0 | 0 | 0 | 0.0 | .000 |
| | J. Ryan | L | 6 | 9 | 7 | 3 | 0 | 3.2 | .842 |
| | K. Kelly | R | 8 | 8 | 6 | 3 | 2 | 2.1 | .824 |

| POS | Player | T | G | PO | A | E | DP | TC/G | FA |
|---|---|---|---|---|---|---|---|---|---|
| OF | G. Gore | R | 118 | 184 | 20 | 29 | 4 | 2.0 | .876 |
| | A. Dalrymple | R | 82 | 126 | 15 | 7 | 1 | 1.8 | **.953** |
| | J. Ryan | L | 70 | 93 | 18 | 23 | 3 | 1.9 | .828 |
| | K. Kelly | R | 56 | 62 | 24 | 20 | 1 | 1.9 | .811 |
| | B. Sunday | R | 28 | 50 | 3 | 5 | 0 | 2.1 | .914 |
| | J. Flynn | | 28 | 15 | 2 | 2 | 1 | 0.7 | .895 |
| | G. Moolic | R | 2 | 0 | 0 | 0 | 0 | 0.0 | .000 |
| | L. Hardie | | 2 | 3 | 1 | 0 | 1 | 2.0 | 1.000 |
| | McCormick | R | 4 | 1 | 1 | 0 | 0 | 0.5 | 1.000 |
| | J. Clarkson | R | 5 | 1 | 0 | 0 | 0 | 0.2 | 1.000 |
| C | S. Flint | R | 54 | 300 | 93 | 47 | 2 | 8.1 | .893 |
| | K. Kelly | R | 53 | 259 | 94 | 28 | 3 | 7.2 | .927 |
| | G. Moolic | R | 15 | 96 | 25 | 7 | 3 | 8.5 | .945 |
| | L. Hardie | | 13 | 65 | 15 | 3 | 0 | 6.4 | .964 |
| | C. Anson | R | 12 | 32 | 18 | 5 | 1 | 4.6 | .909 |
| | Williamson | R | 4 | 1 | 1 | 1 | 0 | 0.8 | .667 |

With the playing schedule extended to an unprecedented 124 games, the White Stockings expanded their pitching staff to a three-man operation. Rookie John Flynn was brought in to share McCormick's and Clarkson's duties. He responded with a 24–6 record for an .800 winning percentage, best in the league. In the meantime, McCormick enjoyed a 16-game winning streak while Clarkson continued to be the workhorse with 36 wins.

In his first season as a regular, Jimmy Ryan proved himself an asset to the team with a .306 average and a deadly throwing arm. Since Dalrymple was fading, Ryan could not have come along at a better time. Kelly, between nighttime drinking bouts, peaked at .388 to lead the league, while Anson followed with .371. On May 28 the White Stockings enjoyed the most lopsided shutout win in the team's history, rampaging Washington, 20–0. Once again, it was a tight pennant race. The White Stockings didn't clinch the flag until October 9 (with a 12–3 win at Boston), while runner-up Detroit finished only 2 1/2 games out. The White Stockings again met the St. Louis Browns in the championship series. St. Louis won in six games, allegedly because some of the Chicago players did not take it seriously and clowned around rather than concentrating.

## TEAM STATISTICS

| | W | L | PCT | GB | R | OR | 2B | Batting 3B | HR | BA | SA | SB | Fielding E | DP | FA | CG | B | Pitching SO | ShO | SV | ERA |
|---|---|---|---|---|---|---|---|---|---|---|---|---|---|---|---|---|---|---|---|---|---|
| CHI | 90 | 34 | .726 | | 900 | 555 | 198 | 87 | 53 | .279 | .401 | 0 | 475 | 82 | .912 | 116 | 262 | 647 | 7 | 3 | 2.54 |
| DET | 87 | 36 | .707 | 2.5 | 829 | 538 | 176 | 80 | 54 | .280 | .391 | 0 | 373 | 82 | .928 | 122 | 270 | 592 | 8 | 0 | 2.85 |
| NY | 75 | 44 | .630 | 12.5 | 692 | 558 | 175 | 67 | 22 | .269 | .356 | 0 | 359 | 70 | .927 | 119 | 278 | 582 | 3 | 1 | 2.85 |
| PHI | 71 | 43 | .623 | 14 | 621 | 498 | 145 | 66 | 26 | .240 | .327 | 0 | 393 | 46 | .921 | 110 | 264 | 540 | 9 | 2 | 2.45 |
| BOS | 56 | 61 | .479 | 30.5 | 657 | 661 | 151 | 59 | 24 | .260 | .341 | 0 | 457 | 63 | .906 | 116 | 298 | 511 | 3 | 0 | 3.24 |
| STL | 43 | 79 | .352 | 46 | 547 | 712 | 183 | 46 | 30 | .236 | .321 | 0 | 452 | 92 | .914 | 118 | 392 | 501 | 6 | 0 | 3.41 |
| KC | 30 | 91 | .248 | 58.5 | 494 | 872 | 177 | 48 | 19 | .228 | .306 | 0 | 482 | 79 | .910 | 117 | 246 | 442 | 4 | 0 | 4.85 |
| WAS | 28 | 92 | .233 | 60 | 445 | 791 | 135 | 51 | 23 | .210 | .285 | 0 | 458 | 69 | .910 | 116 | 379 | 500 | 4 | 0 | 4.30 |
| LEAGUE TOTAL | | | | | 5185 | 5185 | 1340 | 504 | 251 | .251 | .342 | 0 | 3449 | 583 | .916 | 934 | 2389 | 4315 | 44 | 6 | 3.31 |

## INDIVIDUAL PITCHING

| PITCHER | T | W | L | PCT | ERA | SV | G | GS | CG | IP | H | BB | SO | R | ER | ShO | H/9 | BB/9 | SO/9 |
|---|---|---|---|---|---|---|---|---|---|---|---|---|---|---|---|---|---|---|---|
| John Clarkson | R | 35 | 17 | .673 | 2.41 | 0 | 55 | 55 | 50 | 466.2 | 419 | 86 | 340 | 246 | 125 | 3 | 8.08 | 1.66 | 6.56 |
| Jim McCormick | R | 31 | 11 | .738 | 2.82 | 0 | 42 | 42 | 38 | 347.2 | 341 | 100 | 172 | 165 | 109 | 2 | 8.83 | 2.59 | 4.45 |
| Jocko Flynn | | 24 | 6 | .800 | 2.24 | 1 | 32 | 29 | 28 | 257 | 207 | 63 | 146 | 127 | 64 | 2 | 7.25 | 2.21 | 5.11 |
| Jimmy Ryan | L | 0 | 0 | – | 4.63 | 1 | 5 | 0 | 0 | 23.1 | 19 | 13 | 15 | 15 | 12 | 0 | 7.33 | 5.01 | 5.79 |
| Ned Williamson | R | 0 | 0 | – | 0.00 | 1 | 2 | 0 | 0 | 3 | 2 | 0 | 1 | 2 | 0 | 0 | 6.00 | 0.00 | 3.00 |
| TEAM TOTAL | | 90 | 34 | .726 | 2.54 | 3 | 136 | 126 | 116 | 1097.2 | 988 | 262 | 674 | 555 | 310 | 7 | 8.10 | 2.15 | 5.53 |

| MANAGER | W | L | PCT |
|---|---|---|---|
| Cap Anson | 71 | 50 | .587 |

| POS | Player | B | G | AB | H | 2B | 3B | HR | HR % | R | RBI | BB | SO | SB | Pinch Hit AB | Pinch Hit H | BA | SA |
|---|---|---|---|---|---|---|---|---|---|---|---|---|---|---|---|---|---|---|
| **REGULARS** | | | | | | | | | | | | | | | | | | |
| 1B | Cap Anson | R | 122 | 472 | 164 | 33 | 13 | 7 | 1.5 | 107 | 102 | 60 | 18 | 27 | 0 | 0 | .347 | .517 |
| 2B | Fred Pfeffer | R | 123 | 479 | 133 | 21 | 6 | 16 | 3.3 | 95 | 89 | 34 | 20 | 57 | 0 | 0 | .278 | .447 |
| SS | Ned Williamson | R | 127 | 439 | 117 | 20 | 14 | 9 | 2.1 | 77 | 78 | 73 | 57 | 45 | 0 | 0 | .267 | .437 |
| 3B | Tom Burns | L | 115 | 424 | 112 | 20 | 10 | 3 | 0.7 | 57 | 60 | 34 | 32 | 32 | 0 | 0 | .264 | .380 |
| RF | Billy Sunday | L | 50 | 199 | 58 | 6 | 6 | 3 | 1.5 | 41 | 32 | 21 | 20 | 34 | 0 | 0 | .291 | .427 |
| CF | Jimmy Ryan | R | 126 | 508 | 145 | 23 | 10 | 11 | 2.2 | 117 | 74 | 53 | 19 | 50 | 0 | 0 | .285 | .435 |
| LF | Marty Sullivan | R | 115 | 472 | 134 | 13 | 16 | 7 | 1.5 | 98 | 77 | 36 | 53 | 35 | 0 | 0 | .284 | .424 |
| C | Tom Daly | B | 74 | 256 | 53 | 10 | 4 | 2 | 0.8 | 45 | 17 | 22 | 25 | 29 | 0 | 0 | .207 | .301 |
| **SUBSTITUTES** | | | | | | | | | | | | | | | | | | |
| 3B | Patsy Tebeau | R | 20 | 68 | 11 | 3 | 0 | 0 | 0.0 | 8 | 10 | 4 | 4 | 8 | 0 | 0 | .162 | .206 |
| UT | Emil Geis | R | 3 | 12 | 1 | 0 | 0 | 0 | 0.0 | 0 | 0 | 0 | 7 | 0 | 0 | 0 | .083 | .083 |
| OP | George Van Haltren | L | 45 | 172 | 35 | 4 | 0 | 3 | 1.7 | 30 | 17 | 15 | 15 | 12 | 0 | 0 | .203 | .279 |
| OF | Bob Pettit | L | 32 | 138 | 36 | 3 | 3 | 2 | 1.4 | 29 | 12 | 8 | 15 | 16 | 0 | 0 | .261 | .370 |
| PO | Charlie Sprague | L | 3 | 13 | 2 | 0 | 0 | 0 | 0.0 | 0 | 0 | 0 | 2 | 0 | 0 | 0 | .154 | .154 |
| OF | Jocko Flynn | | 1 | 0 | 0 | 0 | 0 | 0 | – | 0 | 0 | 0 | 0 | 0 | 0 | 0 | – | – |
| C | Silver Flint | R | 49 | 187 | 50 | 8 | 6 | 3 | 1.6 | 22 | 21 | 4 | 28 | 7 | 0 | 0 | .267 | .422 |
| CO | Dell Darling | R | 38 | 141 | 45 | 7 | 4 | 3 | 2.1 | 28 | 20 | 22 | 18 | 19 | 0 | 0 | .319 | .489 |
| **PITCHERS** | | | | | | | | | | | | | | | | | | |
| P | John Clarkson | R | 63 | 215 | 52 | 5 | 5 | 6 | 2.8 | 40 | 25 | 11 | 25 | 6 | 0 | 0 | .242 | .395 |
| P | Mark Baldwin | R | 41 | 139 | 26 | 1 | 1 | 4 | 2.9 | 18 | 17 | 10 | 42 | 4 | 0 | 0 | .187 | .295 |
| P | Shadow Pyle | | 4 | 16 | 3 | 1 | 0 | 1 | 6.3 | 1 | 4 | 0 | 0 | 1 | 0 | 0 | .188 | .438 |
| | TEAM TOTAL | | | 4350 | 1177 | 178 | 98 | 80 | 1.8 | 81 | 655 | 407 | 400 | 382 | 0 | 0 | .271 | .412 |

## INDIVIDUAL  FIELDING

| POS | Player | T | G | PO | A | E | DP | TC/G | FA |
|---|---|---|---|---|---|---|---|---|---|
| 1B | C. Anson | R | 122 | 1232 | 70 | 36 | 75 | 11.0 | .973 |
| | S. Flint | R | 2 | 25 | 1 | 1 | 1 | 13.5 | .963 |
| | T. Daly | R | 2 | 20 | 0 | 0 | 3 | 10.0 | 1.000 |
| | E. Geis | | 1 | 11 | 0 | 0 | 0 | 11.0 | 1.000 |
| | M. Baldwin | R | 1 | 3 | 0 | 0 | 1 | 3.0 | 1.000 |
| 2B | F. Pfeffer | R | 123 | 393 | 402 | 72 | 68 | 7.0 | .917 |
| | T. Daly | R | 2 | 5 | 9 | 1 | 1 | 7.5 | .933 |
| | J. Ryan | L | 3 | 4 | 4 | 3 | 1 | 3.7 | .727 |
| | E. Geis | | 1 | 2 | 2 | 3 | 0 | 7.0 | .571 |
| SS | Williamson | R | 127 | 133 | 361 | 61 | 31 | 4.4 | .890 |
| | T. Daly | R | 2 | 2 | 2 | 1 | 0 | 2.5 | .800 |
| 3B | T. Burns | R | 107 | 168 | 246 | 61 | 23 | 4.4 | .872 |
| | P. Tebeau | R | 20 | 19 | 34 | 9 | 4 | 3.1 | .855 |

| POS | Player | T | G | PO | A | E | DP | TC/G | FA |
|---|---|---|---|---|---|---|---|---|---|
| OF | M. Sullivan | R | 115 | 189 | 10 | 36 | 0 | 2.0 | .847 |
| | J. Ryan | L | 122 | 164 | 33 | 33 | 7 | 1.9 | .857 |
| | B. Sunday | R | 50 | 78 | 4 | 25 | 2 | 2.1 | .766 |
| | B. Pettit | | 32 | 34 | 8 | 5 | 0 | 1.5 | .894 |
| | Van Haltren | L | 27 | 37 | 1 | 3 | 1 | 1.5 | .927 |
| | D. Darling | R | 20 | 18 | 4 | 6 | 1 | 1.4 | .786 |
| | C. Sprague | L | 1 | 0 | 0 | 0 | 0 | 0.0 | .000 |
| | T. Burns | R | 8 | 16 | 2 | 0 | 2 | 2.3 | 1.000 |
| | T. Daly | R | 8 | 9 | 2 | 2 | 1 | 1.6 | .846 |
| | J. Clarkson | R | 5 | 5 | 0 | 1 | 0 | 1.2 | .833 |
| | M. Baldwin | R | 5 | 3 | 0 | 2 | 0 | 1.0 | .600 |
| | J. Flynn | | 1 | 0 | 0 | 1 | 0 | 1.0 | .000 |
| | S. Pyle | | 1 | 0 | 0 | 1 | 0 | 1.0 | .000 |
| | F. Pfeffer | R | 2 | 1 | 0 | 0 | 0 | 0.5 | 1.000 |
| C | T. Daly | R | 64 | 354 | 148 | 35 | 12 | 8.4 | .935 |
| | S. Flint | R | 47 | 255 | 73 | 33 | 3 | 7.7 | .909 |
| | D. Darling | R | 20 | 114 | 41 | 17 | 2 | 8.6 | .901 |
| | C. Anson | R | 1 | 1 | 0 | 1 | 0 | 2.0 | .500 |
| | B. Pettit | | 1 | 1 | 0 | 1 | 0 | 2.0 | .500 |

Spalding had blamed the 1886 championship series loss on the nighttime carousing of Kelly, Gore, and McCormick, and sold all of them. Kelly's price, an unprecedented $10,000, created front- page headlines. The slumping Dalrymple was also dealt away. John Flynn, the pitching sensation of the year before, developed arm trouble and appeared in but one game.

The established stars were replaced by a cast of youngsters, or "Colts," as the press called them. Among them were pitcher Mark Baldwin, pitcher-outfielder George Van Haltren, catcher Dell Darling, and outfielder Marty Sullivan. In spite of an obviously weakened lineup, the White Stockings took an early lead and held it into August. Then the heat took its toll, and Chicago fell apart, finishing third. In 1887—and in that year alone—walks were counted as base hits, the result being ridiculously inflated batting averages. Anson batted .421 to lead the league; Williamson, 371; Ryan, .355; Sullivan, .334; Pfeffer, .325, and Burns, .317. When the averages were scaled down to their proper size years later, Anson proved the only .300 hitter with .347, which fell to second in the league behind Sam Thompson's .372.

### TEAM STATISTICS

| | W | L | PCT | GB | R | OR | Batting 2B | 3B | HR | BA | SA | SB | Fielding E | DP | FA | CG | B | Pitching SO | ShO | SV | ERA |
|---|---|---|---|---|---|---|---|---|---|---|---|---|---|---|---|---|---|---|---|---|---|
| DET | 79 | 45 | .637 | | 969 | 714 | 213 | 126 | 59 | .299 | .436 | 267 | 394 | 92 | .925 | 122 | 344 | 337 | 3 | 1 | 3.95 |
| PHI | 75 | 48 | .610 | 3.5 | 901 | 702 | 213 | 89 | 47 | .274 | .389 | 355 | 471 | 76 | .912 | 119 | 305 | 435 | 7 | 1 | 3.47 |
| CHI | 71 | 50 | .587 | 6.5 | 813 | 716 | 178 | 98 | 80 | .271 | .412 | 382 | 472 | 99 | .914 | 117 | 338 | 510 | 4 | 3 | 3.46 |
| NY | 68 | 55 | .553 | 10.5 | 816 | 723 | 167 | 93 | 48 | .279 | .389 | 415 | 431 | 83 | .921 | 123 | 373 | 412 | 5 | 1 | 3.57 |
| BOS | 61 | 60 | .504 | 16.5 | 831 | 792 | 185 | 94 | 54 | .277 | .395 | 373 | 522 | 94 | .905 | 123 | 396 | 254 | 4 | 1 | 4.41 |
| PIT | 55 | 69 | .444 | 24 | 621 | 750 | 183 | 78 | 20 | .258 | .349 | 221 | 425 | 70 | .921 | 123 | 246 | 248 | 3 | 0 | 4.12 |
| WAS | 46 | 76 | .377 | 32 | 601 | 818 | 149 | 63 | 47 | .242 | .336 | 334 | 483 | 77 | .910 | 124 | 299 | 396 | 4 | 0 | 4.19 |
| IND | 37 | 89 | .294 | 43 | 628 | 965 | 162 | 70 | 33 | .247 | .339 | 334 | 479 | 105 | .912 | 119 | 431 | 245 | 4 | 1 | 5.25 |
| LEAGUE TOTAL | | | | | 6180 | 6180 | 1450 | 711 | 388 | .269 | .381 | 2681 | 3677 | 696 | .915 | 970 | 2732 | 2837 | 34 | 8 | 4.05 |

### INDIVIDUAL PITCHING

| PITCHER | T | W | L | PCT | ERA | SV | G | GS | CG | IP | H | BB | SO | R | ER | ShO | H/9 | BB/9 | SO/9 |
|---|---|---|---|---|---|---|---|---|---|---|---|---|---|---|---|---|---|---|---|
| John Clarkson | R | 38 | 21 | .644 | 3.08 | 0 | 60 | 59 | 56 | 523 | 513 | 92 | 237 | 283 | 179 | 2 | 8.83 | 1.58 | 4.08 |
| Mark Baldwin | R | 18 | 17 | .514 | 3.40 | 1 | 40 | 39 | 35 | 334 | 329 | 122 | 164 | 218 | 126 | 1 | 8.87 | 3.29 | 4.42 |
| George Van Haltren | L | 11 | 7 | .611 | 3.86 | 1 | 20 | 18 | 18 | 161 | 177 | 66 | 76 | 113 | 69 | 1 | 9.89 | 3.69 | 4.25 |
| Jimmy Ryan | L | 2 | 1 | .667 | 4.20 | 0 | 8 | 3 | 2 | 45 | 53 | 17 | 14 | 36 | 21 | 0 | 10.60 | 3.40 | 2.80 |
| Shadow Pyle | | 1 | 3 | .250 | 4.73 | 0 | 4 | 4 | 3 | 26.2 | 32 | 21 | 5 | 27 | 14 | 0 | 10.80 | 7.09 | 1.69 |
| Charlie Sprague | L | 1 | 0 | 1.000 | 4.91 | 0 | 3 | 3 | 2 | 22 | 24 | 13 | 9 | 16 | 12 | 0 | 9.82 | 5.32 | 3.68 |
| Emil Geis | | 0 | 1 | .000 | 8.00 | 0 | 1 | 1 | 1 | 9 | 17 | 3 | 4 | 17 | 8 | 0 | 17.00 | 3.00 | 4.00 |
| Marty Sullivan | R | 0 | 0 | – | 7.71 | 0 | 1 | 0 | 0 | 2.1 | 6 | 1 | 1 | 2 | 2 | 0 | 23.14 | 3.86 | 3.86 |
| Ned Williamson | R | 0 | 0 | – | 9.00 | 0 | 1 | 0 | 0 | 2 | 2 | 1 | 0 | 2 | 2 | 0 | 9.00 | 4.50 | 0.00 |
| Bob Pettit | | 0 | 0 | – | 0.00 | 1 | 1 | 0 | 0 | 1 | 3 | 2 | 0 | 8 | 0 | 0 | 27.00 | 18.00 | 0.00 |
| TEAM TOTAL | | 71 | 50 | .587 | 3.46 | 3 | 139 | 127 | 117 | 1126 | 1156 | 338 | 510 | 716 | 433 | 4 | 9.24 | 2.70 | 4.08 |

| MANAGER | W | L | PCT |
|---|---|---|---|
| Cap Anson | 77 | 58 | .570 |

| POS | Player | B | G | AB | H | 2B | 3B | HR | HR % | R | RBI | BB | SO | SB | Pinch Hit AB | Pinch Hit H | BA | SA |
|---|---|---|---|---|---|---|---|---|---|---|---|---|---|---|---|---|---|---|
| **REGULARS** | | | | | | | | | | | | | | | | | | |
| 1B | Cap Anson | R | 134 | 515 | 177 | 20 | 12 | 12 | 2.3 | 101 | 84 | 47 | 24 | 28 | 0 | 0 | .344 | .499 |
| 2B | Fred Pfeffer | R | 135 | 517 | 129 | 22 | 10 | 8 | 1.5 | 90 | 57 | 32 | 38 | 64 | 0 | 0 | .250 | .377 |
| SS | Ned Williamson | R | 132 | 452 | 113 | 9 | 14 | 8 | 1.8 | 75 | 73 | 65 | 71 | 25 | 0 | 0 | .250 | .385 |
| 3B | Tom Burns | L | 134 | 483 | 115 | 12 | 6 | 3 | 0.6 | 60 | 70 | 26 | 49 | 34 | 0 | 0 | .238 | .306 |
| RF | Hugh Duffy | R | 71 | 298 | 84 | 10 | 4 | 7 | 2.3 | 60 | 41 | 9 | 32 | 13 | 0 | 0 | .282 | .413 |
| CF | Jimmy Ryan | R | 129 | 549 | 182 | 33 | 10 | 16 | 2.9 | 115 | 64 | 35 | 50 | 60 | 0 | 0 | .332 | .515 |
| LF | Marty Sullivan | R | 75 | 314 | 74 | 12 | 6 | 7 | 2.2 | 40 | 39 | 15 | 32 | 9 | 0 | 0 | .236 | .379 |
| C | Tom Daly | B | 65 | 219 | 42 | 2 | 6 | 0 | 0.0 | 34 | 29 | 10 | 26 | 10 | 0 | 0 | .192 | .256 |
| **SUBSTITUTES** | | | | | | | | | | | | | | | | | | |
| OP | George Van Haltren | L | 81 | 318 | 90 | 9 | 14 | 4 | 1.3 | 46 | 34 | 22 | 34 | 21 | 0 | 0 | .283 | .437 |
| OF | Bob Pettit | L | 43 | 169 | 43 | 1 | 4 | 4 | 2.4 | 23 | 23 | 7 | 9 | 7 | 0 | 0 | .254 | .379 |
| PO | George Borchers | | 10 | 33 | 2 | 2 | 0 | 0 | 0.0 | 3 | 2 | 1 | 13 | 1 | 0 | 0 | .061 | .121 |
| PO | Ad Gumbert | R | 7 | 24 | 8 | 0 | 1 | 0 | 0.0 | 3 | 2 | 0 | 2 | 0 | 0 | 0 | .333 | .417 |
| PO | Charlie Brynan | R | 3 | 11 | 2 | 0 | 1 | 0 | 0.0 | 1 | 1 | 0 | 3 | 0 | 0 | 0 | .182 | .364 |
| PO | Dad Clarke | B | 2 | 7 | 2 | 0 | 1 | 1 | 14.3 | 4 | 2 | 1 | 2 | 0 | 0 | 0 | .286 | 1.000 |
| PO | Willard Mains | | 2 | 7 | 1 | 0 | 0 | 0 | 0.0 | 1 | 0 | 1 | 3 | 0 | 0 | 0 | .143 | .143 |
| CO | Duke Farrell | B | 64 | 241 | 56 | 6 | 3 | 3 | 1.2 | 34 | 19 | 4 | 41 | 8 | 0 | 0 | .232 | .320 |
| C | Silver Flint | R | 22 | 77 | 14 | 3 | 0 | 0 | 0.0 | 6 | 3 | 1 | 21 | 1 | 0 | 0 | .182 | .221 |
| C | Dell Darling | R | 20 | 75 | 16 | 3 | 1 | 2 | 2.7 | 12 | 7 | 3 | 12 | 0 | 0 | 0 | .213 | .360 |
| **PITCHERS** | | | | | | | | | | | | | | | | | | |
| P | Gus Krock | | 39 | 134 | 22 | 0 | 0 | 1 | 0.7 | 9 | 11 | 5 | 34 | 1 | 0 | 0 | .164 | .187 |
| P | Mark Baldwin | R | 30 | 106 | 16 | 1 | 2 | 1 | 0.9 | 11 | 5 | 5 | 47 | 4 | 0 | 0 | .151 | .226 |
| P | John Tener | R | 12 | 46 | 9 | 1 | 0 | 0 | 0.0 | 4 | 1 | 1 | 15 | 1 | 0 | 0 | .196 | .217 |
| P | Frank Dwyer | R | 5 | 21 | 4 | 1 | 0 | 0 | 0.0 | 2 | 2 | 0 | 5 | 0 | 0 | 0 | .190 | .238 |
| | TEAM TOTAL | | | 4616 | 1201 | 147 | 95 | 77 | 1.7 | 73 | 569 | 290 | 563 | 287 | 0 | 0 | .260 | .383 |

## INDIVIDUAL FIELDING

| POS | Player | T | G | PO | A | E | DP | TC/G | FA |
|---|---|---|---|---|---|---|---|---|---|
| 1B | C. Anson | R | 134 | 1314 | 65 | 20 | 85 | 10.4 | .986 |
| | D. Farrell | R | 1 | 10 | 0 | 0 | 0 | 10.0 | 1.000 |
| 2B | F. Pfeffer | R | 135 | 421 | 457 | 65 | 78 | 7.0 | .931 |
| SS | Williamson | R | 132 | 120 | 375 | 65 | 48 | 4.2 | .884 |
| | H. Duffy | R | 3 | 1 | 9 | 3 | 0 | 4.3 | .769 |
| 3B | T. Burns | R | 134 | 194 | 273 | 49 | 16 | 3.9 | .905 |
| | H. Duffy | R | 1 | 3 | 2 | 2 | 0 | 7.0 | .714 |
| OF | J. Ryan | L | 128 | 217 | 34 | 35 | 5 | 2.2 | .878 |
| | M. Sullivan | R | 75 | 114 | 13 | 10 | 7 | 1.8 | .927 |
| | H. Duffy | R | 67 | 103 | 19 | 12 | 5 | 2.0 | .910 |
| | Van Haltren | L | 57 | 73 | 9 | 12 | 0 | 1.6 | .872 |
| | D. Farrell | R | 31 | 50 | 3 | 7 | 1 | 1.9 | .883 |
| | B. Pettit | | 43 | 46 | 8 | 4 | 3 | 1.3 | .931 |
| | C. Brynan | R | 1 | 0 | 0 | 0 | 0 | 0.0 | .000 |
| | D. Clarke | R | 1 | 0 | 0 | 0 | 0 | 0.0 | .000 |
| | J. Tener | R | 1 | 0 | 0 | 0 | 0 | 0.0 | .000 |
| | T. Daly | R | 4 | 11 | 0 | 1 | 0 | 3.0 | .917 |
| | G. Borchers | | 3 | 5 | 0 | 3 | 0 | 2.7 | .625 |
| | M. Baldwin | R | 3 | 2 | 2 | 1 | 0 | 1.7 | .800 |
| | A. Gumbert | R | 2 | 3 | 0 | 0 | 0 | 1.5 | 1.000 |
| | W. Mains | R | 1 | 0 | 0 | 1 | 0 | 1.0 | .000 |
| C | T. Daly | R | 62 | 400 | 107 | 33 | 10 | 8.7 | .939 |
| | D. Farrell | R | 33 | 171 | 50 | 32 | 3 | 7.7 | .874 |
| | D. Darling | R | 20 | 139 | 26 | 12 | 5 | 8.9 | .932 |
| | S. Flint | R | 22 | 96 | 42 | 11 | 7 | 6.8 | .926 |

Albert Spalding had dollar signs in his eyes when—against Anson's advice—he sold John Clarkson to Boston for $10,000. Clarkson and Mike Kelly subsequently became known as "the $20,000 battery." Billy Sunday also departed to Pittsburgh.

Rookie Gus Krock, the first left-handed pitcher in Cub history, won 25 games. Another rookie hurler, John Tener, later became governor of Pennsylvania. Outfielder Hugh Duffy, also a rookie, batted .282 in 71 games. He would go on to bat a record .438 for Boston in 1894.

Although the commanding presence of Clarkson was sorely missed, the White Stockings still played exciting ball, pulling home second to the Giants. Anson led the league in batting with .344 while Ryan, now approaching his prime, hit .332 with a league-leading 16 homers. On July 28, Ryan became the first Cub to hit for the cycle, collecting a single, a double, a triple, and a home run in the same game. Anson added two homers as the White Stockings outslugged Detroit 21–17. Following the close of the season, the White Stockings and a team of "All-Americans" embarked on baseball's first world tour, bringing the national game to a host of foreign capitals.

### TEAM STATISTICS

| | W | L | PCT | GB | R | OR | 2B | 3B | HR | BA | SA | SB | E | DP | FA | CG | B | SO | ShO | SV | ERA |
|---|---|---|---|---|---|---|---|---|---|---|---|---|---|---|---|---|---|---|---|---|---|
| NY | 84 | 47 | .641 | | 659 | 479 | 130 | 76 | 55 | .242 | .336 | 314 | 432 | 76 | .924 | **136** | 308 | **724** | 19 | 1 | **1.96** |
| CHI | 77 | 58 | .570 | 9 | **734** | 659 | 147 | **95** | **77** | .260 | **.383** | 287 | 417 | **112** | .927 | 123 | 308 | 588 | 13 | 1 | 2.96 |
| PHI | 69 | 61 | .531 | 14.5 | 535 | 509 | 151 | 46 | 16 | .225 | .290 | 246 | 424 | 70 | .923 | 125 | 196 | 519 | 9 | **3** | 2.38 |
| BOS | 70 | 64 | .522 | 15.5 | 669 | 619 | 167 | 89 | 56 | .245 | .351 | 293 | 494 | 91 | .917 | 134 | 269 | 484 | 7 | 0 | 2.61 |
| DET | 68 | 63 | .519 | 16 | 721 | 629 | 177 | 71 | 52 | **.263** | .361 | 193 | 463 | 83 | .919 | 130 | **183** | 522 | 9 | 1 | 2.74 |
| PIT | 66 | 68 | .493 | 19.5 | 534 | 580 | 150 | 49 | 14 | .227 | .289 | 287 | **416** | 88 | **.927** | 135 | 223 | 367 | 13 | 0 | 2.67 |
| IND | 50 | 85 | .370 | 36 | 603 | 731 | **180** | 33 | 33 | .238 | .313 | **350** | 449 | 84 | .921 | 132 | 308 | 388 | 6 | 0 | 3.81 |
| WAS | 48 | 86 | .358 | 37.5 | 482 | 731 | 98 | 49 | 31 | .208 | .271 | 331 | 494 | 69 | .912 | 133 | 298 | 406 | 6 | 0 | 3.54 |
| LEAGUE TOTAL | | | | | 4937 | 4937 | 1200 | 508 | 334 | .239 | .325 | 2301 | 3589 | 673 | .921 | 1048 | 2093 | 3998 | 82 | 6 | 2.83 |

*Batting: 2B, 3B, HR, BA, SA, SB. Fielding: E, DP, FA. Pitching: CG, B, SO, ShO, SV, ERA.*

### INDIVIDUAL PITCHING

| PITCHER | T | W | L | PCT | ERA | SV | G | GS | CG | IP | H | BB | SO | R | ER | ShO | H/9 | BB/9 | SO/9 |
|---|---|---|---|---|---|---|---|---|---|---|---|---|---|---|---|---|---|---|---|
| Gus Krock | L | 24 | 14 | .632 | 2.44 | 0 | 39 | 39 | 39 | 339.2 | 295 | 45 | 161 | 143 | 92 | 4 | 7.82 | 1.19 | 4.27 |
| Mark Baldwin | R | 13 | 15 | .464 | 2.76 | 0 | 30 | 30 | 27 | 251 | 241 | 99 | 157 | 136 | 77 | 2 | 8.64 | 3.55 | 5.63 |
| George Van Haltren | L | 13 | 13 | .500 | 3.52 | 1 | 30 | 24 | 24 | 245.2 | 263 | 60 | 139 | 148 | 96 | 4 | 9.64 | 2.20 | 5.09 |
| John Tener | R | 7 | 5 | .583 | 2.74 | 0 | 12 | 12 | 11 | 102 | 90 | 25 | 39 | 59 | 31 | 1 | 7.94 | 2.21 | 3.44 |
| George Borchers | | 4 | 4 | .500 | 3.49 | 4 | 10 | 10 | 7 | 67 | 67 | 29 | 26 | 45 | 26 | 1 | 9.00 | 3.90 | 3.49 |
| Ad Gumbert | R | 3 | 3 | .500 | 3.14 | 4 | 6 | 6 | 5 | 48.2 | 44 | 10 | 16 | 24 | 17 | 0 | 8.14 | 1.85 | 2.96 |
| Frank Dwyer | R | 4 | 1 | .800 | 1.07 | 4 | 5 | 5 | 5 | 42 | 32 | 9 | 17 | 20 | 5 | 1 | 6.86 | 1.93 | 3.64 |
| Jimmy Ryan | L | 4 | 0 | 1.000 | 3.05 | 0 | 8 | 2 | 1 | 38.1 | 47 | 12 | 11 | 30 | 13 | 0 | 11.03 | 2.82 | 2.58 |
| Charlie Brynan | R | 2 | 1 | .667 | 6.48 | 4 | 3 | 3 | 2 | 25 | 29 | 7 | 11 | 25 | 18 | 0 | 10.44 | 2.52 | 3.96 |
| Dad Clarke | R | 1 | 0 | 1.000 | 5.06 | 4 | 2 | 2 | 1 | 16 | 23 | 6 | 6 | 17 | 9 | 0 | 12.94 | 3.38 | 3.38 |
| Willard Mains | R | 1 | 1 | .500 | 4.91 | 4 | 2 | 2 | 1 | 11 | 8 | 6 | 5 | 12 | 6 | 0 | 6.55 | 4.91 | 4.09 |
| TEAM TOTAL | | 76 | 57 | .571 | 2.96 | 1 | 147 | 135 | 123 | 1186.1 | 1139 | 308 | 588 | 659 | 390 | 13 | 8.64 | 2.34 | 4.46 |

| MANAGER | W | L | PCT |
|---|---|---|---|
| Cap Anson | 67 | 65 | .508 |

| POS | Player | B | G | AB | H | 2B | 3B | HR | HR % | R | RBI | BB | SO | SB | Pinch Hit AB | Pinch Hit H | BA | SA |
|---|---|---|---|---|---|---|---|---|---|---|---|---|---|---|---|---|---|---|
| **REGULARS** | | | | | | | | | | | | | | | | | | |
| 1B | Cap Anson | R | 134 | 518 | 177 | 32 | 7 | 7 | 1.4 | 100 | 117 | 86 | 19 | 27 | 0 | 0 | .342 | .471 |
| 2B | Fred Pfeffer | R | 134 | 531 | 121 | 15 | 7 | 7 | 1.3 | 85 | 77 | 53 | 51 | 45 | 0 | 0 | .228 | .322 |
| SS | Ned Williamson | R | 47 | 173 | 41 | 3 | 1 | 1 | 0.6 | 16 | 30 | 23 | 22 | 2 | 0 | 0 | .237 | .283 |
| 3B | Tom Burns | L | 136 | 525 | 127 | 27 | 6 | 4 | 0.8 | 64 | 66 | 32 | 57 | 18 | 0 | 0 | .242 | .339 |
| RF | Hugh Duffy | R | 136 | 584 | 182 | 21 | 7 | 12 | 2.1 | 144 | 89 | 46 | 30 | 52 | 0 | 0 | .312 | .433 |
| CF | Jimmy Ryan | R | 135 | 576 | 187 | 31 | 14 | 17 | 3.0 | 140 | 72 | 70 | 62 | 45 | 0 | 0 | .325 | .516 |
| LF | George Van Haltren | L | 134 | 543 | 168 | 20 | 10 | 9 | 1.7 | 126 | 81 | 82 | 41 | 28 | 0 | 0 | .309 | .433 |
| C | Duke Farrell | B | 101 | 407 | 101 | 19 | 7 | 11 | 2.7 | 66 | 75 | 41 | 21 | 13 | 0 | 0 | .248 | .410 |
| **SUBSTITUTES** | | | | | | | | | | | | | | | | | | |
| SS | Charlie Bastian | R | 46 | 155 | 21 | 0 | 0 | 0 | 0.0 | 19 | 10 | 25 | 46 | 1 | 0 | 0 | .135 | .135 |
| PO | Ad Gumbert | R | 41 | 153 | 44 | 3 | 2 | 7 | 4.6 | 30 | 29 | 11 | 36 | 2 | 0 | 0 | .288 | .471 |
| C | Dell Darling | R | 36 | 120 | 23 | 1 | 1 | 0 | 0.0 | 14 | 7 | 25 | 22 | 5 | 0 | 0 | .192 | .217 |
| C | Silver Flint | R | 15 | 56 | 13 | 1 | 0 | 1 | 1.8 | 6 | 9 | 3 | 18 | 1 | 0 | 0 | .232 | .304 |
| C | Pete Sommers | R | 12 | 45 | 10 | 5 | 0 | 0 | 0.0 | 5 | 8 | 2 | 8 | 0 | 0 | 0 | .222 | .333 |
| **PITCHERS** | | | | | | | | | | | | | | | | | | |
| P | John Tener | R | 42 | 150 | 41 | 4 | 2 | 1 | 0.7 | 18 | 19 | 7 | 22 | 1 | 0 | 0 | .273 | .347 |
| P | Frank Dwyer | R | 36 | 135 | 27 | 1 | 1 | 1 | 0.7 | 14 | 6 | 4 | 8 | 0 | 0 | 0 | .200 | .244 |
| P | Bill Hutchison | R | 37 | 133 | 21 | 1 | 1 | 1 | 0.8 | 14 | 7 | 7 | 40 | 2 | 0 | 0 | .158 | .203 |
| P | Gus Krock | | 7 | 24 | 4 | 0 | 0 | 0 | 0.0 | 4 | 2 | 0 | 6 | 0 | 0 | 0 | .167 | .167 |
| P | Egyptian Healy | R | 5 | 20 | 2 | 0 | 0 | 0 | 0.0 | 2 | 1 | 0 | 6 | 0 | 0 | 0 | .100 | .100 |
| P | Bill Bishop | | 2 | 1 | 0 | 0 | 0 | 0 | 0.0 | 0 | 0 | 1 | 1 | 0 | 0 | 0 | .000 | .000 |
| TEAM TOTAL | | | | 4849 | 1310 | 184 | 66 | 79 | 1.6 | 86 | 705 | 518 | 516 | 243 | 0 | 0 | .270 | .384 |

## INDIVIDUAL FIELDING

| POS | Player | T | G | PO | A | E | DP | TC/G | FA | POS | Player | T | G | PO | A | E | DP | TC/G | FA |
|---|---|---|---|---|---|---|---|---|---|---|---|---|---|---|---|---|---|---|---|
| 1B | C. Anson | R | 134 | 1409 | 79 | 27 | 73 | 11.3 | .982 | OF | J. Ryan | L | 106 | 252 | 36 | 23 | 9 | 2.9 | .926 |
| | J. Tener | R | 2 | 23 | 2 | 0 | 0 | 12.5 | 1.000 | | Van Haltren | L | 130 | 222 | 25 | 28 | 3 | 2.1 | .898 |
| 2B | F. Pfeffer | R | 134 | 452 | 483 | 56 | 69 | 7.4 | .943 | | H. Duffy | R | 126 | 184 | 19 | 24 | 2 | 1.8 | .894 |
| | C. Bastian | R | 1 | 4 | 10 | 0 | 1 | 14.0 | 1.000 | | D. Farrell | R | 25 | 54 | 4 | 7 | 0 | 2.6 | .892 |
| | Van Haltren | L | 1 | 4 | 1 | 0 | 0 | 5.0 | 1.000 | | B. Hutchison | R | 1 | 0 | 0 | 0 | 0 | 0.0 | .000 |
| | | | | | | | | | | | P. Sommers | | 1 | 0 | 0 | 0 | 0 | 0.0 | .000 |
| SS | C. Bastian | R | 45 | 63 | 153 | 19 | 9 | 5.2 | .919 | | A. Gumbert | R | 13 | 31 | 0 | 9 | 0 | 3.1 | .775 |
| | Williamson | R | 47 | 48 | 130 | 33 | 7 | 4.5 | .844 | | J. Tener | R | 6 | 3 | 2 | 3 | 0 | 1.3 | .625 |
| | J. Ryan | L | 29 | 34 | 97 | 34 | 10 | 5.7 | .794 | | F. Dwyer | R | 3 | 5 | 1 | 0 | 0 | 2.0 | 1.000 |
| | H. Duffy | R | 10 | 3 | 27 | 8 | 2 | 3.8 | .789 | C | D. Farrell | R | 76 | 344 | 119 | 46 | 3 | 6.7 | .910 |
| | Van Haltren | L | 3 | 4 | 9 | 4 | 2 | 5.7 | .765 | | D. Darling | R | 36 | 172 | 45 | 9 | 2 | 6.3 | .960 |
| | F. Dwyer | R | 2 | 7 | 5 | 2 | 3 | 7.0 | .857 | | S. Flint | R | 15 | 65 | 19 | 9 | 0 | 6.2 | .903 |
| 3B | T. Burns | R | 136 | 225 | 301 | 72 | 30 | 4.4 | .880 | | P. Sommers | | 11 | 45 | 11 | 11 | 1 | 6.1 | .836 |

Having just returned from baseball's first world tour, the White Stockings were already half worn out when the season opened. Williamson had suffered a broken kneecap during the trip, and was never the same afterward. It was the beginning of the end of the "stonewall infield."

Gus Krock, their pitching sensation of the previous year, developed arm trouble and was dealt away early in the season. Meanwhile, the White Stockings floundered, playing sub-.500 ball most of the season. Only a late surge enabled them to reach third place with a winning record—and just barely at that.

Nevertheless, there were many bright spots. Bill Hutchison, a rookie pitcher, won 16 games. Anson and Ryan continued to pound the ball, the latter connecting for 17 home runs. His six leadoff homers were a record until broken by Bobby Bonds in 1973. George Van Haltren, moved from the pitcher's box to left field, responded with a .309 average, while rightfielder Hugh Duffy hit .305 in his first full season. An outfield of Ryan, Duffy, and Van Haltren could have become one of the Cubs' greatest, but it was not destined to last. A players' revolt was brewing, and all hell would soon break loose.

## TEAM STATISTICS

|  | W | L | PCT | GB | R | OR | 2B | 3B | Batting HR | BA | SA | SB | E | Fielding DP | FA | CG | B | Pitching SO | ShO | SV | ERA |
|---|---|---|---|---|---|---|---|---|---|---|---|---|---|---|---|---|---|---|---|---|---|
| NY | 83 | 43 | .659 |  | 935 | 708 | 207 | 77 | 53 | .282 | .394 | 292 | 437 | 90 | .920 | 118 | 523 | 542 | 6 | 3 | 3.47 |
| BOS | 83 | 45 | .648 | 1 | 826 | 626 | 196 | 53 | 43 | .270 | .363 | 331 | 413 | 105 | .926 | 121 | 413 | 497 | 10 | 4 | 3.36 |
| CHI | 67 | 65 | .508 | 19 | 867 | 814 | 184 | 66 | 79 | .263 | .377 | 243 | 463 | 91 | .923 | 123 | 408 | 434 | 6 | 2 | 3.73 |
| PHI | 63 | 64 | .496 | 20.5 | 742 | 748 | 215 | 52 | 44 | .266 | .362 | 269 | 466 | 92 | .915 | 106 | 428 | 443 | 4 | 2 | 4.00 |
| PIT | 61 | 71 | .462 | 25 | 726 | 801 | 209 | 65 | 42 | .253 | .351 | 231 | 385 | 94 | .931 | 125 | 374 | 345 | 5 | 1 | 4.51 |
| CLE | 61 | 72 | .459 | 25.5 | 656 | 720 | 131 | 59 | 25 | .250 | .319 | 237 | 365 | 108 | .936 | 132 | 519 | 435 | 6 | 1 | 3.66 |
| IND | 59 | 75 | .440 | 28 | 819 | 894 | 228 | 35 | 62 | .278 | .377 | 252 | 420 | 102 | .926 | 109 | 420 | 408 | 3 | 2 | 4.85 |
| WAS | 41 | 83 | .331 | 41 | 632 | 892 | 151 | 57 | 25 | .251 | .329 | 232 | 519 | 91 | .904 | 113 | 527 | 388 | 1 | 0 | 4.68 |
| LEAGUE TOTAL |  |  |  |  | 6203 | 6203 | 1521 | 464 | 373 | .264 | .359 | 2087 | 3468 | 773 | .923 | 947 | 3612 | 3492 | 41 | 15 | 4.02 |

## INDIVIDUAL PITCHING

| PITCHER | T | W | L | PCT | ERA | SV | G | GS | CG | IP | H | BB | SO | R | ER | ShO | H/9 | BB/9 | SO/9 |
|---|---|---|---|---|---|---|---|---|---|---|---|---|---|---|---|---|---|---|---|
| Bill Hutchison | R | 16 | 17 | .485 | 3.54 | 0 | 37 | 36 | 33 | 318 | 306 | 117 | 136 | 206 | 125 | 3 | 8.66 | 3.31 | 3.85 |
| John Tener | R | 15 | 15 | .500 | 3.64 | 0 | 35 | 30 | 28 | 287 | 302 | 105 | 105 | 192 | 116 | 1 | 9.47 | 3.29 | 3.29 |
| Frank Dwyer | R | 16 | 13 | .552 | 3.59 | 0 | 32 | 30 | 27 | 276 | 307 | 72 | 63 | 177 | 110 | 0 | 10.01 | 2.35 | 2.05 |
| Ad Gumbert | R | 16 | 13 | .552 | 3.62 | 0 | 31 | 28 | 25 | 246.1 | 258 | 76 | 91 | 148 | 99 | 2 | 9.43 | 2.78 | 3.32 |
| Gus Krock | L | 3 | 3 | .500 | 4.90 | 4 | 7 | 7 | 5 | 60.2 | 86 | 14 | 16 | 43 | 33 | 0 | 12.76 | 2.08 | 2.37 |
| Egyptian Healy | R | 1 | 4 | .200 | 4.50 | 4 | 5 | 5 | 5 | 46 | 48 | 18 | 22 | 35 | 23 | 0 | 9.39 | 3.52 | 4.30 |
| Bill Bishop |  | 0 | 0 | — | 18.00 | 2 | 2 | 0 | 0 | 3 | 6 | 6 | 1 | 13 | 6 | 0 | 18.00 | 18.00 | 3.00 |
| TEAM TOTAL |  | 67 | 65 | .508 | 3.73 | 2 | 149 | 136 | 123 | 1237 | 1313 | 408 | 434 | 814 | 512 | 6 | 9.55 | 2.97 | 3.16 |

| MANAGER | W | L | PCT |
|---|---|---|---|
| Cap Anson | 84 | 53 | .613 |

| POS | Player | B | G | AB | H | 2B | 3B | HR | HR % | R | RBI | BB | SO | SB | Pinch Hit AB | Pinch Hit H | BA | SA |
|---|---|---|---|---|---|---|---|---|---|---|---|---|---|---|---|---|---|---|
| **REGULARS** | | | | | | | | | | | | | | | | | | |
| 1B | Cap Anson | R | 139 | 504 | 157 | 14 | 5 | 7 | 1.4 | 95 | 107 | **113** | 23 | 29 | 0 | 0 | .312 | .401 |
| 2B | Bob Glenalvin | | 66 | 250 | 67 | 10 | 3 | 4 | 1.6 | 43 | 26 | 19 | 31 | 30 | 0 | 0 | .268 | .380 |
| SS | Jimmy Cooney | R | 135 | 574 | 156 | 19 | 10 | 4 | 0.7 | 114 | 52 | 73 | 23 | 45 | 0 | 0 | .272 | .361 |
| 3B | Tom Burns | L | 139 | 538 | 149 | 16 | 6 | 6 | 1.1 | 86 | 86 | 57 | 45 | 44 | 0 | 0 | .277 | .362 |
| RF | Jim Andrews | | 53 | 202 | 38 | 4 | 2 | 3 | 1.5 | 32 | 17 | 23 | 41 | 11 | 0 | 0 | .188 | .272 |
| CF | Walt Wilmot | B | 139 | 571 | 159 | 15 | 12 | 14 | 2.5 | 114 | 99 | 64 | 44 | 76 | 0 | 0 | .278 | .420 |
| LF | Cliff Carroll | B | 136 | **582** | 166 | 16 | 6 | 7 | 1.2 | 134 | 65 | 53 | 34 | 34 | 0 | 0 | .285 | .369 |
| C | Malachi Kittredge | R | 96 | 333 | 67 | 8 | 3 | 3 | 0.9 | 46 | 35 | 39 | 53 | 7 | 0 | 0 | .201 | .270 |
| **SUBSTITUTES** | | | | | | | | | | | | | | | | | | |
| 2B | Pete O'Brien | | 27 | 106 | 30 | 7 | 0 | 3 | 2.8 | 15 | 16 | 5 | 10 | 4 | 0 | 0 | .283 | .434 |
| 2B | Ed Hutchinson | L | 4 | 17 | 1 | 1 | 0 | 0 | 0.0 | 0 | 0 | 0 | 0 | 0 | 0 | 0 | .059 | .118 |
| 2B | Pat Wright | B | 1 | 2 | 0 | 0 | 0 | 0 | 0.0 | 0 | 0 | 1 | 0 | 0 | 0 | 0 | .000 | .000 |
| O2 | Howard Earl | | 92 | 384 | 95 | 10 | 3 | 6 | 1.6 | 57 | 57 | 18 | 47 | 17 | 0 | 0 | .247 | .336 |
| OF | Elmer Foster | R | 27 | 105 | 26 | 4 | 2 | 5 | 4.8 | 20 | 23 | 9 | 21 | 18 | 0 | 0 | .248 | .467 |
| OF | Pop Lytle | R | 1 | 4 | 0 | 0 | 0 | 0 | 0.0 | 1 | 0 | 0 | 1 | 0 | 0 | 0 | .000 | .000 |
| C | Tom Nagle | R | 38 | 144 | 39 | 5 | 1 | 1 | 0.7 | 21 | 11 | 7 | 24 | 4 | 0 | 0 | .271 | .340 |
| CO | Jake Stenzel | R | 11 | 41 | 11 | 1 | 0 | 0 | 0.0 | 3 | 3 | 1 | 0 | 0 | 0 | 0 | .268 | .293 |
| C | Chuck Lauer | | 2 | 8 | 2 | 1 | 0 | 0 | 0.0 | 1 | 2 | 0 | 0 | 0 | 0 | 0 | .250 | .375 |
| C | Marty Honan | | 1 | 3 | 0 | 0 | 0 | 0 | 0.0 | 0 | 1 | 0 | 2 | 0 | 0 | 0 | .000 | .000 |
| **PITCHERS** | | | | | | | | | | | | | | | | | | |
| P | Bill Hutchison | R | 71 | 261 | 53 | 7 | 2 | 2 | 0.8 | 28 | 27 | 13 | 63 | 6 | 0 | 0 | .203 | .268 |
| P | Pat Luby | | 36 | 116 | 31 | 5 | 3 | 3 | 2.6 | 27 | 17 | 9 | 6 | 3 | 0 | 0 | .267 | .440 |
| P | Ed Stein | | 20 | 59 | 9 | 1 | 0 | 0 | 0.0 | 4 | 7 | 7 | 20 | 1 | 0 | 0 | .153 | .169 |
| P | Mike Sullivan | L | 12 | 40 | 5 | 1 | 0 | 0 | 0.0 | 1 | 7 | 2 | 12 | 0 | 0 | 0 | .125 | .150 |
| P | Roscoe Coughlin | | 11 | 39 | 10 | 1 | 1 | 0 | 0.0 | 5 | 1 | 2 | 12 | 0 | 0 | 0 | .256 | .333 |
| P | Bob Gibson | R | 1 | 4 | 0 | 0 | 0 | 0 | 0.0 | 0 | 0 | 1 | 0 | 0 | 0 | 0 | .000 | .000 |
| P | Fred Demarris | | 1 | 2 | 0 | 0 | 0 | 0 | 0.0 | 0 | 0 | 0 | 1 | 0 | 0 | 0 | .000 | .000 |
| P | Ed Eiteljorg | R | 1 | 1 | 0 | 0 | 0 | 0 | 0.0 | 0 | 0 | 0 | 1 | 0 | 0 | 0 | .000 | .000 |
| P | Ossie France | L | 1 | 1 | 0 | 0 | 0 | 0 | 0.0 | 0 | 0 | 0 | 0 | 0 | 0 | 0 | .000 | .000 |
| TEAM TOTAL | | | | 4891 | 1271 | 146 | 59 | 68 | 1.4 | 84 | 653 | 516 | 514 | 329 | 0 | 0 | .260 | .356 |

## INDIVIDUAL FIELDING

| POS | Player | T | G | PO | A | E | DP | TC/G | FA |
|---|---|---|---|---|---|---|---|---|---|
| 1B | C. Anson | R | 135 | 1345 | **49** | 31 | 61 | 10.6 | .978 |
| | H. Earl | | 3 | 31 | 2 | 2 | 1 | 11.7 | .943 |
| | P. Luby | R | 2 | 19 | 2 | 1 | 0 | 11.0 | .955 |
| 2B | B. Glenalvin | R | 66 | 128 | 194 | 25 | 20 | 5.3 | .928 |
| | H. Earl | | 39 | 84 | 137 | 31 | 10 | 6.5 | .877 |
| | P. O'Brien | | 27 | 65 | 80 | 11 | 11 | 5.8 | .929 |
| | Hutchinson | | 4 | 6 | 12 | 0 | 1 | 4.5 | 1.000 |
| | C. Anson | R | 2 | 7 | 5 | 1 | 0 | 6.5 | .923 |
| | P. Wright | R | 1 | 1 | 3 | 0 | 0 | 4.0 | 1.000 |
| SS | J. Cooney | R | 135 | 237 | 452 | 47 | 50 | 5.5 | **.936** |
| | H. Earl | | 4 | 3 | 11 | 2 | 0 | 4.0 | .875 |
| 3B | T. Burns | R | 139 | 188 | 290 | 54 | 25 | 3.8 | .898 |

| POS | Player | T | G | PO | A | E | DP | TC/G | FA |
|---|---|---|---|---|---|---|---|---|---|
| OF | W. Wilmot | L | 139 | **320** | 26 | 23 | 4 | 2.7 | .938 |
| | C. Carroll | R | 136 | 265 | 28 | 20 | 7 | 2.3 | .936 |
| | J. Andrews | | 53 | 80 | 10 | 10 | 1 | 1.9 | .900 |
| | H. Earl | | 49 | 60 | 8 | 11 | 1 | 1.6 | .861 |
| | E. Foster | L | 27 | 69 | 2 | 1 | 0 | 2.7 | .986 |
| | T. Nagle | R | 6 | 6 | 0 | 1 | 0 | 1.2 | .857 |
| | J. Stenzel | R | 6 | 6 | 0 | 1 | 0 | 1.2 | .857 |
| | P. Lytle | R | 1 | 3 | 1 | 0 | 0 | 4.0 | 1.000 |
| C | M. Kittredge | R | 96 | 458 | 113 | 34 | 9 | 6.3 | .944 |
| | T. Nagle | R | 33 | 161 | 25 | 12 | 0 | 6.0 | .939 |
| | J. Stenzel | R | 6 | 25 | 6 | 1 | 0 | 5.3 | .969 |
| | C. Lauer | R | 2 | 12 | 3 | 3 | 0 | 9.0 | .833 |
| | C. Anson | R | 3 | 9 | 2 | 0 | 0 | 3.7 | 1.000 |
| | M. Honan | | 1 | 6 | 0 | 1 | 0 | 7.0 | .857 |
| | J. Cooney | R | 1 | 1 | 0 | 0 | 0 | 1.0 | 1.000 |

In 1886 the first ballplayers' union, the Brotherhood of Professional Baseball Players, was formed, demanding an end to the reserve clause and the salary limitation. When the NL balked at these demands, the Brotherhood bolted in 1890 to form its own circuit, the Players' League. Since Fred Pfeffer was one of the leaders in the movement, he took nearly the entire team with him. Only Anson, Burns, and Bill Hutchison remained loyal to the NL.

Quickly recruiting a team of youngsters, the White Stockings now became known as the Colts on a full-time basis. Considering all the unknown quantities he had to work with, Anson did a creditable job in piloting the team to a second place finish. Some of the recruits were competent players, including outfielder Walt Wilmot, a good hitter, and shortstop Jimmy Cooney, a slick glove man whose son later played short for the Cubs also. Rookie pitcher Pat Luby set a club record by winning 17 consecutive games. Hutchison emerged as the staff workhorse with 42 wins in 603 innings, including a complete-game doubleheader victory at Brooklyn on Memorial Day.

### TEAM STATISTICS

| | W | L | PCT | GB | R | OR | Batting | | | BA | SA | SB | Fielding | | FA | CG | B | Pitching | | | ERA |
|---|---|---|---|---|---|---|---|---|---|---|---|---|---|---|---|---|---|---|---|---|---|
| | | | | | | | 2B | 3B | HR | | | | E | DP | | | | SO | ShO | SV | |
| BKN | 86 | 43 | .667 | | 884 | 620 | 184 | 75 | 43 | .264 | .369 | 349 | 320 | 92 | .940 | 115 | 401 | 403 | 6 | 2 | 3.05 |
| CHI | 84 | 53 | .613 | 6 | 847 | 692 | 146 | 59 | 68 | .260 | .356 | 329 | 344 | 89 | .940 | 126 | 481 | 504 | 6 | 3 | 3.24 |
| PHI | 78 | 54 | .591 | 9.5 | 823 | 707 | 220 | 78 | 23 | .269 | .364 | 334 | 398 | 122 | .929 | 122 | 486 | 507 | 8 | 2 | 3.32 |
| CIN | 77 | 55 | .583 | 10.5 | 753 | 633 | 150 | 120 | 28 | .259 | .361 | 312 | 382 | 106 | .932 | 124 | 407 | 488 | 9 | 1 | 3.05 |
| BOS | 76 | 57 | .571 | 12 | 763 | 593 | 175 | 62 | 31 | .258 | .341 | 285 | 359 | 77 | .934 | 132 | 354 | 506 | 13 | 1 | 2.93 |
| NY | 63 | 68 | .481 | 24 | 713 | 698 | 208 | 89 | 25 | .259 | .354 | 289 | 449 | 104 | .921 | 115 | 607 | 612 | 6 | 1 | 3.06 |
| CLE | 44 | 88 | .333 | 43.5 | 630 | 832 | 132 | 59 | 21 | .232 | .299 | 152 | 405 | 108 | .929 | 129 | 462 | 306 | 2 | 0 | 4.13 |
| PIT | 23 | 113 | .169 | 66.5 | 597 | 1235 | 160 | 43 | 20 | .230 | .294 | 208 | 607 | 94 | .896 | 119 | 573 | 381 | 3 | 0 | 5.97 |
| LEAGUE TOTAL | | | | | 6010 | 6010 | 1375 | 585 | 259 | .254 | .342 | 2258 | 3264 | 792 | .927 | 982 | 3771 | 3707 | 53 | 10 | 3.60 |

### INDIVIDUAL PITCHING

| PITCHER | T | W | L | PCT | ERA | SV | G | GS | CG | IP | H | BB | SO | R | ER | ShO | H/9 | BB/9 | SO/9 |
|---|---|---|---|---|---|---|---|---|---|---|---|---|---|---|---|---|---|---|---|
| Bill Hutchison | R | 42 | 25 | .627 | 2.70 | 2 | 71 | 66 | 65 | 603 | 505 | 199 | 289 | 315 | 181 | 5 | 7.54 | 2.97 | 4.31 |
| Pat Luby | R | 20 | 9 | .690 | 3.19 | 1 | 34 | 31 | 26 | 267.2 | 226 | 95 | 85 | 129 | 95 | 0 | 7.60 | 3.19 | 2.86 |
| Ed Stein | R | 12 | 6 | .667 | 3.81 | 0 | 20 | 18 | 14 | 160.2 | 147 | 83 | 65 | 100 | 68 | 1 | 8.23 | 4.65 | 3.64 |
| Mike Sullivan | | 5 | 6 | .455 | 4.59 | 0 | 12 | 12 | 10 | 96 | 108 | 58 | 33 | 77 | 49 | 0 | 10.13 | 5.44 | 3.09 |
| Roscoe Coughlin | R | 4 | 4 | .500 | 4.26 | 0 | 11 | 10 | 10 | 95 | 102 | 40 | 29 | 60 | 45 | 0 | 9.66 | 3.79 | 2.75 |
| Bob Gibson | R | 1 | 0 | 1.000 | 0.00 | 0 | 1 | 1 | 1 | 9 | 6 | 2 | 1 | 1 | 0 | 0 | 6.00 | 2.00 | 1.00 |
| Fred Demarris | R | 0 | 0 | – | 0.00 | 0 | 1 | 0 | 0 | 2 | 1 | 1 | 1 | 0 | 0 | 0 | 4.50 | 4.50 | 4.50 |
| Ed Eiteljorg | R | 0 | 1 | .000 | 22.50 | 0 | 1 | 1 | 0 | 2 | 5 | 1 | 1 | 7 | 5 | 0 | 22.50 | 4.50 | 4.50 |
| Ossie France | | 0 | 0 | – | 13.50 | 0 | 1 | 0 | 0 | 2 | 3 | 2 | 0 | 3 | 3 | 0 | 13.50 | 9.00 | 0.00 |
| TEAM TOTAL | | 84 | 51 | .622 | 3.24 | 3 | 152 | 139 | 126 | 1237.1 | 1103 | 481 | 504 | 692 | 446 | 6 | 8.02 | 3.50 | 3.67 |

| MANAGER | W | L | PCT |
|---|---|---|---|
| Cap Anson | 82 | 53 | .607 |

| POS | Player | B | G | AB | H | 2B | 3B | HR | HR % | R | RBI | BB | SO | SB | Pinch Hit AB | Pinch Hit H | BA | SA |
|---|---|---|---|---|---|---|---|---|---|---|---|---|---|---|---|---|---|---|
| **REGULARS** | | | | | | | | | | | | | | | | | | |
| 1B | Cap Anson | R | 136 | 540 | 157 | 24 | 8 | 8 | 1.5 | 81 | 120 | 75 | 29 | 17 | 0 | 0 | .291 | .409 |
| 2B | Fred Pfeffer | R | 137 | 498 | 123 | 12 | 9 | 7 | 1.4 | 93 | 77 | 79 | 60 | 40 | 0 | 0 | .247 | .349 |
| SS | Jimmy Cooney | R | 118 | 465 | 114 | 15 | 3 | 0 | 0.0 | 84 | 42 | 48 | 17 | 21 | 0 | 0 | .245 | .290 |
| 3B | Bill Dahlen | R | 135 | 551 | 145 | 20 | 13 | 9 | 1.6 | 116 | 76 | 67 | 60 | 29 | 0 | 0 | .263 | .396 |
| RF | Cliff Carroll | B | 130 | 515 | 132 | 20 | 8 | 7 | 1.4 | 87 | 80 | 50 | 42 | 31 | 0 | 0 | .256 | .367 |
| CF | Jimmy Ryan | R | 118 | 505 | 145 | 22 | 15 | 9 | 1.8 | 110 | 66 | 53 | 38 | 27 | 0 | 0 | .287 | .444 |
| LF | Walt Wilmot | B | 121 | 498 | 139 | 14 | 10 | 11 | 2.2 | 102 | 71 | 55 | 21 | 42 | 0 | 0 | .279 | .414 |
| C | Malachi Kittredge | R | 79 | 296 | 62 | 8 | 5 | 2 | 0.7 | 26 | 27 | 17 | 28 | 4 | 0 | 0 | .209 | .291 |
| **SUBSTITUTES** | | | | | | | | | | | | | | | | | | |
| 3B | Tom Burns | L | 59 | 243 | 55 | 8 | 1 | 1 | 0.4 | 36 | 17 | 21 | 21 | 18 | 0 | 0 | .226 | .280 |
| OF | Elmer Foster | R | 4 | 16 | 3 | 0 | 0 | 1 | 6.3 | 3 | 1 | 1 | 2 | 1 | 0 | 0 | .188 | .375 |
| C | Pop Schriver | R | 27 | 90 | 30 | 1 | 4 | 1 | 1.1 | 15 | 21 | 10 | 9 | 1 | 0 | 0 | .333 | .467 |
| C | Bill Bowman | | 15 | 45 | 4 | 1 | 0 | 0 | 0.0 | 2 | 5 | 5 | 9 | 0 | 0 | 0 | .089 | .111 |
| C | Bill Merritt | R | 11 | 42 | 9 | 1 | 0 | 0 | 0.0 | 4 | 4 | 2 | 2 | 0 | 0 | 0 | .214 | .238 |
| C | Tom Nagle | R | 8 | 25 | 3 | 0 | 0 | 0 | 0.0 | 3 | 1 | 1 | 3 | 0 | 0 | 0 | .120 | .120 |
| C | Marty Honan | | 5 | 12 | 2 | 0 | 0 | 1 | 8.3 | 1 | 3 | 1 | 3 | 0 | 0 | 0 | .167 | .417 |
| **PITCHERS** | | | | | | | | | | | | | | | | | | |
| P | Bill Hutchison | R | 67 | 243 | 45 | 4 | 2 | 2 | 0.8 | 27 | 25 | 17 | 62 | 5 | 0 | 0 | .185 | .243 |
| P | Ad Gumbert | R | 34 | 105 | 32 | 7 | 4 | 0 | 0.0 | 18 | 16 | 13 | 14 | 4 | 0 | 0 | .305 | .448 |
| P | Pat Luby | | 32 | 98 | 24 | 2 | 4 | 2 | 2.0 | 19 | 24 | 8 | 16 | 3 | 0 | 0 | .245 | .408 |
| P | Ed Stein | | 14 | 43 | 7 | 1 | 0 | 0 | 0.0 | 4 | 4 | 3 | 10 | 0 | 0 | 0 | .163 | .186 |
| P | Tom Vickery | | 14 | 39 | 7 | 1 | 0 | 0 | 0.0 | 3 | 1 | 0 | 10 | 3 | 0 | 0 | .179 | .205 |
| P | George Nicol | | 3 | 6 | 2 | 0 | 0 | 0 | 0.0 | 0 | 3 | 0 | 1 | 0 | 0 | 0 | .333 | .667 |
| TEAM TOTAL | | | | 4875 | 1240 | 161 | 87 | 61 | 1.3 | 83 | 684 | 526 | 457 | 246 | 0 | 0 | .254 | .361 |

### INDIVIDUAL FIELDING

| POS | Player | T | G | PO | A | E | DP | TC/G | FA | POS | Player | T | G | PO | A | E | DP | TC/G | FA |
|---|---|---|---|---|---|---|---|---|---|---|---|---|---|---|---|---|---|---|---|
| 1B | C. Anson | R | 136 | 1407 | 79 | 29 | 86 | 11.1 | .981 | OF | J. Ryan | L | 117 | 231 | 25 | 27 | 3 | 2.4 | .905 |
| | P. Schriver | R | 2 | 0 | 0 | 0 | 0 | 0.0 | .000 | | W. Wilmot | L | 121 | 223 | 15 | 20 | 0 | 2.1 | .922 |
| | B. Merritt | R | 1 | 10 | 0 | 1 | 1 | 11.0 | .909 | | C. Carroll | R | 130 | 168 | 15 | 17 | 5 | 1.5 | .915 |
| | P. Luby | R | 1 | 5 | 0 | 0 | 0 | 5.0 | 1.000 | | B. Dahlen | R | 37 | 69 | 7 | 6 | 4 | 2.2 | .927 |
| | A. Gumbert | R | 1 | 1 | 1 | 0 | 1 | 2.0 | 1.000 | | A. Gumbert | R | 1 | 0 | 0 | 0 | 0 | 0.0 | .000 |
| 2B | F. Pfeffer | R | 137 | 429 | 474 | 77 | 78 | 7.2 | .921 | | B. Hutchison | R | 1 | 0 | 0 | 0 | 0 | 0.0 | .000 |
| | | | | | | | | | | | T. Nagle | R | 1 | 0 | 0 | 0 | 0 | 0.0 | .000 |
| SS | J. Cooney | R | 118 | 145 | 433 | 52 | 39 | 5.3 | .917 | | E. Foster | L | 4 | 6 | 1 | 1 | 0 | 2.0 | .875 |
| | B. Dahlen | R | 15 | 28 | 46 | 16 | 4 | 6.0 | .822 | | T. Burns | R | 2 | 7 | 0 | 0 | 0 | 3.5 | 1.000 |
| | T. Burns | R | 4 | 7 | 11 | 4 | 1 | 5.5 | .818 | | P. Luby | R | 2 | 1 | 0 | 1 | 0 | 1.0 | .500 |
| | J. Ryan | L | 2 | 4 | 4 | 1 | 0 | 4.5 | .889 | C | M. Kittredge | R | 79 | 384 | 87 | 30 | 5 | 6.3 | .940 |
| | T. Vickery | | 1 | 1 | 2 | 1 | 1 | 4.0 | .750 | | P. Schriver | R | 27 | 135 | 27 | 6 | 3 | 6.2 | .964 |
| 3B | B. Dahlen | R | 84 | 120 | 211 | 42 | 13 | 4.4 | .887 | | B. Bowman | | 15 | 41 | 13 | 5 | 1 | 3.9 | .915 |
| | T. Burns | R | 53 | 92 | 107 | 24 | 11 | 4.2 | .892 | | B. Merritt | R | 11 | 31 | 11 | 2 | 1 | 4.0 | .955 |
| | | | | | | | | | | | T. Nagle | R | 7 | 25 | 4 | 3 | 1 | 4.6 | .906 |
| | | | | | | | | | | | M. Honan | | 5 | 18 | 8 | 1 | 0 | 5.4 | .963 |
| | | | | | | | | | | | C. Anson | R | 2 | 2 | 1 | 0 | 0 | 1.5 | 1.000 |

Following the collapse of the Players' League, Ryan, Pfeffer, and pitcher Ad Gumbert were returned to the Colts. The others, however, were not, the losses of Duffy and Van Haltren being especially aggravating. The loss was partially offset by freshman infielder Bill Dahlen, who displayed skill with both bat and glove. Hutchison, more than ever the workhorse of the staff, won 43 games.

The Colts were at the top of the totem pole most of the year and at one point enjoyed an 8-game lead, thanks largely to an 11-game winning streak in late August. But the Boston Beaneaters came on strong during the final month to pass Chicago, winning the pennant by 3 1/2 games. Included in the Boston surge were four straight wins over the Giants during the last week of the season under suspicious circumstances. Anson charged that the Giants had thrown the games so that an eastern team could win the pennant, and the league conducted an investigation. Although nothing was proven, many a sportswriter regarded the Boston pennant as tainted. For Anson, it was a bitter pill to swallow, as this would be the last time his team was in solid contention.

Even so, the season was not without its humorous aspects. Now a 40-year-old, Anson was hitting under .300 (although not by much) for the first time in his career, and writers began hinting he should retire. So, on September 4, he played an entire game wearing false whiskers in mockery of his detractors.

## TEAM STATISTICS

| | W | L | PCT | GB | R | OR | Batting | | | | | SB | Fielding | | | CG | B | Pitching | | | |
|---|---|---|---|---|---|---|---|---|---|---|---|---|---|---|---|---|---|---|---|---|---|
| | | | | | | | 2B | 3B | HR | BA | SA | | E | DP | FA | | | SO | ShO | SV | ERA |
| )S | 87 | 51 | .630 | | 847 | 658 | 181 | 82 | 51 | .255 | .356 | 289 | 358 | 96 | .938 | 126 | 364 | 525 | 9 | 6 | 2.76 |
| HI | 82 | 53 | .607 | 3.5 | 832 | 730 | 159 | 87 | 61 | .253 | .359 | 238 | 397 | 119 | .932 | 114 | 475 | 477 | 6 | 3 | 3.47 |
| Y | 71 | 61 | .538 | 13 | 754 | 711 | 189 | 72 | 48 | .263 | .362 | 224 | 384 | 104 | .933 | 117 | 593 | 651 | 11 | 3 | 2.99 |
| HI | 68 | 69 | .496 | 18.5 | 756 | 773 | 180 | 51 | 21 | .252 | .322 | 232 | 443 | 108 | .925 | 105 | 505 | 343 | 3 | 5 | 3.73 |
| E | 65 | 74 | .468 | 22.5 | 835 | 888 | 183 | 87 | 23 | .255 | .339 | 242 | 485 | 86 | .920 | 118 | 476 | 400 | 1 | 3 | 3.50 |
| N | 61 | 76 | .445 | 25.5 | 765 | 820 | 200 | 69 | 23 | .260 | .345 | 337 | 432 | 73 | .924 | 121 | 459 | 407 | 8 | 3 | 3.86 |
| N | 56 | 81 | .409 | 30.5 | 646 | 790 | 148 | 90 | 40 | .242 | .335 | 244 | 409 | 101 | .931 | 125 | 465 | 393 | 6 | 1 | 3.55 |
| T | 55 | 80 | .407 | 30.5 | 679 | 744 | 148 | 71 | 28 | .239 | .317 | 205 | 475 | 76 | .917 | 122 | 465 | 446 | 7 | 2 | 2.89 |
| AGUE TOTAL | | | | | 6114 | 6114 | 1388 | 609 | | 295 | .252 | .342 | 2011 | 3383 | 763 | .928 | 948 | 3802 | 3642 | 51 | 26 | 3.34 |

## INDIVIDUAL PITCHING

| TCHER | T | W | L | PCT | ERA | SV | G | GS | CG | IP | H | BB | SO | R | ER | ShO | H/9 | BB/9 | SO/9 |
|---|---|---|---|---|---|---|---|---|---|---|---|---|---|---|---|---|---|---|---|
| l Hutchison | R | 43 | 19 | .694 | 2.81 | 1 | 66 | 58 | 56 | 561 | 508 | 178 | 261 | 283 | 175 | 4 | 8.15 | 2.86 | 4.19 |
| l Gumbert | R | 17 | 11 | .607 | 3.58 | 0 | 32 | 31 | 24 | 256.1 | 282 | 90 | 73 | 149 | 102 | 1 | 9.90 | 3.16 | 2.56 |
| t Luby | R | 8 | 11 | .421 | 4.76 | 1 | 30 | 24 | 18 | 206 | 221 | 94 | 52 | 148 | 109 | 0 | 9.66 | 4.11 | 2.27 |
| Stein | R | 7 | 6 | .538 | 3.74 | 0 | 14 | 10 | 9 | 101 | 99 | 57 | 38 | 68 | 42 | 1 | 8.82 | 5.08 | 3.39 |
| m Vickery | | 5 | 5 | .500 | 4.07 | 0 | 14 | 12 | 7 | 79.2 | 72 | 44 | 39 | 55 | 36 | 0 | 8.13 | 4.97 | 4.41 |
| eorge Nicol | L | 0 | 1 | .000 | 4.91 | 0 | 3 | 2 | 0 | 11 | 14 | 10 | 12 | 20 | 6 | 0 | 11.45 | 8.18 | 9.82 |
| nmy Ryan | L | 0 | 0 | — | 1.59 | 1 | 2 | 0 | 0 | 5.2 | 11 | 2 | 2 | 7 | 1 | 0 | 17.47 | 3.18 | 3.18 |
| AM TOTAL | | 80 | 53 | .602 | 3.47 | 3 | 161 | 137 | 114 | 1220.2 | 1207 | 475 | 477 | 730 | 471 | 6 | 8.90 | 3.50 | 3.52 |

| MANAGER | W | L | PCT |
|---|---|---|---|
| Cap Anson | 70 | 76 | .479 |

| POS | Player | B | G | AB | H | 2B | 3B | HR | HR % | R | RBI | BB | SO | SB | Pinch Hit AB | Pinch Hit H | BA | SA |
|---|---|---|---|---|---|---|---|---|---|---|---|---|---|---|---|---|---|---|
| **REGULARS** | | | | | | | | | | | | | | | | | | |
| 1B | Cap Anson | R | 146 | 559 | 152 | 25 | 9 | 1 | 0.2 | 62 | 74 | 67 | 30 | 13 | 0 | 0 | .272 | .354 |
| 2B | Jimmy Canavan | R | 118 | 439 | 73 | 10 | 11 | 0 | 0.0 | 48 | 32 | 48 | 48 | 33 | 0 | 0 | .166 | .239 |
| SS | Bill Dahlen | R | 143 | 587 | 173 | 23 | 19 | 5 | 0.9 | 116 | 58 | 45 | 56 | 60 | 0 | 0 | .295 | .424 |
| 3B | Jiggs Parrott | | 78 | 335 | 72 | 9 | 5 | 2 | 0.6 | 40 | 22 | 8 | 30 | 7 | 0 | 0 | .215 | .290 |
| RF | Sam Dungan | R | 113 | 433 | 123 | 19 | 7 | 0 | 0.0 | 46 | 53 | 35 | 19 | 15 | 0 | 0 | .284 | .360 |
| CF | Jimmy Ryan | R | 128 | 505 | 148 | 21 | 11 | 10 | 2.0 | 105 | 65 | 61 | 41 | 27 | 0 | 0 | .293 | .438 |
| LF | Walt Wilmot | B | 92 | 380 | 82 | 7 | 7 | 2 | 0.5 | 47 | 35 | 40 | 20 | 31 | 0 | 0 | .216 | .287 |
| C | Pop Schriver | R | 92 | 326 | 73 | 10 | 6 | 1 | 0.3 | 40 | 34 | 27 | 25 | 4 | 0 | 0 | .224 | .301 |
| **SUBSTITUTES** | | | | | | | | | | | | | | | | | | |
| SS | Jimmy Cooney | R | 65 | 238 | 41 | 1 | 0 | 0 | 0.0 | 18 | 20 | 23 | 5 | 10 | 0 | 0 | .172 | .176 |
| 2B | Jim Connor | | 9 | 34 | 2 | 0 | 0 | 0 | 0.0 | 0 | 0 | 1 | 7 | 0 | 0 | 0 | .059 | .059 |
| 2B | Fred Roat | | 8 | 31 | 6 | 0 | 1 | 0 | 0.0 | 4 | 2 | 2 | 3 | 2 | 0 | 0 | .194 | .258 |
| O2 | George Decker | | 78 | 291 | 66 | 6 | 7 | 1 | 0.3 | 32 | 28 | 20 | 49 | 9 | 0 | 0 | .227 | .306 |
| PO | Pat Luby | | 45 | 163 | 31 | 3 | 2 | 2 | 1.2 | 14 | 20 | 12 | 27 | 3 | 0 | 0 | .190 | .270 |
| OF | Charlie Newman | R | 16 | 61 | 10 | 0 | 0 | 0 | 0.0 | 4 | 2 | 1 | 6 | 2 | 0 | 0 | .164 | .164 |
| C | Malachi Kittredge | R | 69 | 229 | 41 | 5 | 0 | 0 | 0.0 | 19 | 10 | 11 | 27 | 2 | 0 | 0 | .179 | .201 |
| **PITCHERS** | | | | | | | | | | | | | | | | | | |
| P | Bill Hutchison | R | 77 | 263 | 57 | 10 | 5 | 1 | 0.4 | 23 | 22 | 10 | 60 | 8 | 0 | 0 | .217 | .304 |
| P | Ad Gumbert | R | 52 | 178 | 42 | 1 | 2 | 1 | 0.6 | 18 | 8 | 14 | 24 | 5 | 0 | 0 | .236 | .281 |
| P | Harry DeMiller | | 4 | 10 | 3 | 0 | 0 | 0 | 0.0 | 2 | 5 | 2 | 1 | 2 | 0 | 0 | .300 | .300 |
| P | George Meakim | R | 1 | 5 | 2 | 0 | 0 | 0 | 0.0 | 1 | 2 | 0 | 0 | 0 | 0 | 0 | .400 | .400 |
| P | John Hollison | R | 1 | 3 | 0 | 0 | 0 | 0 | 0.0 | 0 | 0 | 0 | 3 | 0 | 0 | 0 | .000 | .000 |
| P | Frank Griffith | L | 1 | 1 | 0 | 0 | 0 | 0 | 0.0 | 0 | 0 | 0 | 1 | 0 | 0 | 0 | .000 | .000 |
| | TEAM TOTAL | | | 5071 | 1197 | 150 | 92 | 26 | 0.5 | 63 | 492 | 427 | 482 | 233 | 0 | 0 | .236 | .317 |

## INDIVIDUAL FIELDING

| POS | Player | T | G | PO | A | E | DP | TC/G | FA | POS | Player | T | G | PO | A | E | DP | TC/G | FA |
|---|---|---|---|---|---|---|---|---|---|---|---|---|---|---|---|---|---|---|---|
| 1B | C. Anson | R | 146 | 1491 | 67 | 44 | 62 | 11.0 | .973 | OF | J. Ryan | L | 120 | 241 | 26 | 23 | 5 | 2.4 | .921 |
| 2B | J. Canavan | R | 112 | 282 | 349 | 53 | 40 | 6.1 | .923 | | W. Wilmot | L | 92 | 197 | 8 | 22 | 0 | 2.5 | .903 |
| | G. Decker | | 16 | 22 | 37 | 10 | 3 | 4.3 | .855 | | S. Dungan | | 113 | 183 | 8 | 20 | 2 | 1.9 | .905 |
| | F. Roat | R | 8 | 11 | 24 | 4 | 1 | 4.9 | .897 | | G. Decker | | 62 | 73 | 12 | 12 | 3 | 1.6 | .876 |
| | J. Connor | | 9 | 14 | 19 | 3 | 0 | 4.0 | .917 | | P. Luby | R | 16 | 17 | 1 | 2 | 0 | 1.3 | .900 |
| | B. Dahlen | R | 1 | 3 | 2 | 1 | 0 | 6.0 | .833 | | C. Newman | R | 16 | 18 | 1 | 1 | 1 | 1.3 | .950 |
| SS | B. Dahlen | R | 72 | 178 | 232 | 41 | 29 | 6.3 | .909 | | P. Schriver | R | 10 | 12 | 1 | 1 | 0 | 1.4 | .929 |
| | J. Cooney | R | 65 | 101 | 211 | 30 | 15 | 5.3 | .912 | | A. Gumbert | R | 7 | 10 | 0 | 2 | 0 | 1.7 | .833 |
| | J. Ryan | L | 9 | 17 | 24 | 7 | 2 | 5.3 | .854 | | J. Canavan | R | 4 | 6 | 1 | 0 | 0 | 1.8 | 1.000 |
| | J. Canavan | R | 2 | 6 | 5 | 1 | 1 | 6.0 | .917 | | B. Hutchison | R | 2 | 4 | 0 | 1 | 0 | 2.5 | .800 |
| 3B | B. Dahlen | R | 68 | 113 | 189 | 19 | 14 | 4.7 | .941 | | B. Dahlen | R | 2 | 3 | 0 | 0 | 0 | 1.5 | 1.000 |
| | J. Parrott | | 78 | 115 | 164 | 34 | 7 | 4.0 | .891 | C | P. Schriver | R | 82 | 367 | 102 | 36 | 5 | 6.2 | .929 |
| | | | | | | | | | | | M. Kittredge | R | 69 | 359 | 87 | 26 | 5 | 6.8 | .945 |

The American Association folded after the 1891 campaign, with the result that four of its clubs were absorbed into the National League, bloating it to 12 teams. There were significant developments in Chicago also. Gradually withdrawing from team operations, Spalding appointed James Hart as president, much to Anson's consternation. Hart called Anson out of date in his methods, while Anson countered by charging Hart with being a cheapskate and undermining his authority over the players. Regardless of who was right, the conflict caused much dissension in the ranks.

The NL experimented that year with a split-season concept in which the winner of the first half would play the winner of the second half for the pennant. This was of no consequence to the Colts, who were not in the race during either portion. For the first time an Anson team slipped below the .500 mark as Chicago dropped to seventh place with a 70–76 record. Fred Pfeffer had been sold to Louisville, and his loss left a gaping hole at second base that was not adequately filled for a decade. Anson, Ryan, and Dahlen were the brunt of an otherwise anemic attack. For the third straight year, Hutchison led the league in wins but was beginning to show signs of overwork.

| First Half | W | L | PCT | GB | | Second Half | W | L | PCT | GB |
|---|---|---|---|---|---|---|---|---|---|---|
| BOS* | 52 | 22 | .702 | | | CLE | 53 | 23 | .697 | |
| BKN | 51 | 26 | .662 | 2.5 | | BOS | 50 | 26 | .658 | 3 |
| PHI | 46 | 30 | .605 | 7 | | BKN | 44 | 33 | .571 | 9.5 |
| CIN | 44 | 31 | .587 | 8.5 | | PIT | 43 | 34 | .558 | 10.5 |
| CLE | 40 | 33 | .548 | 11.5 | | PHI | 41 | 36 | .532 | 12.5 |
| PIT | 37 | 39 | .487 | 16 | | NY | 40 | 37 | .519 | 13.5 |
| WAS | 35 | 41 | .461 | 18 | | CHI | 39 | 37 | .513 | 14 |
| CHI | 31 | 39 | .443 | 21 | | CIN | 38 | 37 | .507 | 14.5 |
| STL | 31 | 42 | .425 | 22.5 | | LOU | 33 | 42 | .440 | 19.5 |
| NY | 31 | 43 | .419 | 23 | | BAL | 26 | 46 | .361 | 25 |
| LOU | 30 | 47 | .390 | 25.5 | | STL | 25 | 52 | .325 | 28.5 |
| BAL | 20 | 55 | .267 | 34.5 | | WAS | 23 | 52 | .307 | 29.5 |

*Defeated Cleveland in playoff 5 games to 0 (1 tie).

## TEAM STATISTICS

| | W | L | PCT | GB | R | OR | Batting | | | | | | Fielding | | | Pitching | | | | | |
|---|---|---|---|---|---|---|---|---|---|---|---|---|---|---|---|---|---|---|---|---|---|
| | | | | | | | 2B | 3B | HR | BA | SA | SB | E | DP | FA | CG | B | SO | ShO | SV | ERA |
| BOS | 102 | 48 | .680 | | 862 | 649 | 203 | 51 | 34 | .250 | .327 | 338 | 454 | 128 | .929 | 143 | 460 | 509 | 15 | 1 | 2.86 |
| CLE | 93 | 56 | .624 | 8.5 | 855 | 613 | 196 | 96 | 26 | .254 | .340 | 225 | 407 | 95 | .935 | 140 | 413 | 472 | 11 | 2 | 2.41 |
| BKN | 95 | 59 | .617 | 9 | 935 | 733 | 183 | 105 | 30 | .262 | .350 | 409 | 398 | 98 | .940 | 132 | 600 | 597 | 12 | 5 | 3.25 |
| PHI | 87 | 66 | .569 | 16.5 | 860 | 690 | 225 | 95 | 50 | .262 | .367 | 216 | 393 | 128 | .939 | 131 | 492 | 502 | 10 | 5 | 2.93 |
| CIN | 82 | 68 | .547 | 20 | 766 | 731 | 155 | 75 | 44 | .241 | .322 | 270 | 402 | 140 | .939 | 131 | 535 | 437 | 8 | 2 | 3.17 |
| PIT | 80 | 73 | .523 | 23.5 | 802 | 796 | 143 | 108 | 38 | .236 | .322 | 222 | 483 | 113 | .927 | 130 | 537 | 455 | 3 | 1 | 3.10 |
| CHI | 70 | 76 | .479 | 30 | 635 | 735 | 149 | 92 | 26 | .235 | .316 | 233 | 424 | 85 | .932 | 133 | 424 | 518 | 6 | 1 | 3.16 |
| NY | 71 | 80 | .470 | 31.5 | 811 | 826 | 173 | 85 | 38 | .251 | .337 | 301 | 565 | 97 | .912 | 139 | 635 | 641 | 5 | 1 | 3.29 |
| LOU | 63 | 89 | .414 | 40 | 649 | 804 | 133 | 61 | 18 | .226 | .284 | 275 | 471 | 133 | .928 | 137 | 447 | 430 | 9 | 0 | 3.34 |
| WAS | 58 | 93 | .384 | 44.5 | 731 | 869 | 148 | 78 | 38 | .239 | .320 | 276 | 547 | 122 | .916 | 129 | 556 | 479 | 5 | 3 | 3.46 |
| STL | 56 | 94 | .373 | 46 | 703 | 922 | 138 | 53 | 45 | .226 | .298 | 209 | 452 | 100 | .929 | 139 | 543 | 478 | 4 | 1 | 4.20 |
| BAL | 46 | 101 | .313 | 54.5 | 779 | 1020 | 160 | 111 | 30 | .254 | .343 | 227 | 584 | 100 | .910 | 131 | 536 | 437 | 2 | 1 | 4.28 |
| LEAGUE TOTAL | | | | | 9388 | 9388 | 2006 | 1010 | 417 | .245 | .327 | 3201 | 5580 | 1339 | .928 | 1625 | 6178 | 5955 | 90 | 23 | 3.28 |

## INDIVIDUAL PITCHING

| PITCHER | T | W | L | PCT | ERA | SV | G | GS | CG | IP | H | BB | SO | R | ER | ShO | H/9 | BB/9 | SO/9 |
|---|---|---|---|---|---|---|---|---|---|---|---|---|---|---|---|---|---|---|---|
| Bill Hutchison | R | 37 | 34 | .521 | 2.74 | 0 | 75 | 71 | 67 | 627 | 572 | 187 | 316 | 323 | 191 | 5 | 8.21 | 2.68 | 4.54 |
| Ad Gumbert | R | 22 | 19 | .537 | 3.41 | 0 | 46 | 45 | 39 | 382.2 | 399 | 107 | 118 | 220 | 145 | 0 | 9.38 | 2.52 | 2.78 |
| Pat Luby | R | 10 | 17 | .370 | 3.13 | 1 | 31 | 26 | 24 | 247.1 | 247 | 106 | 64 | 150 | 86 | 1 | 8.99 | 3.86 | 2.33 |
| Harry DeMiller | | 1 | 1 | .500 | 6.38 | 0 | 4 | 2 | 2 | 24 | 29 | 16 | 15 | 22 | 17 | 0 | 10.88 | 6.00 | 5.63 |
| George Meakim | R | 0 | 1 | .000 | 11.00 | 0 | 1 | 1 | 1 | 9 | 18 | 2 | 0 | 14 | 11 | 0 | 18.00 | 2.00 | 0.00 |
| Frank Griffith | L | 0 | 1 | .000 | 11.25 | 0 | 1 | 1 | 0 | 4 | 3 | 6 | 3 | 5 | 5 | 0 | 6.75 | 13.50 | 6.75 |
| John Hollison | L | 0 | 0 | – | 2.25 | 0 | 1 | 0 | 0 | 4 | 1 | 0 | 2 | 1 | 1 | 0 | 2.25 | 0.00 | 4.50 |
| TEAM TOTAL | | 70 | 73 | .490 | 3.16 | 1 | 159 | 146 | 133 | 1298 | 1269 | 424 | 518 | 735 | 456 | 6 | 8.80 | 2.94 | 3.59 |

| MANAGER | W | L | PCT |
|---|---|---|---|
| Cap Anson | 56 | 71 | .441 |

| POS | Player | B | G | AB | H | 2B | 3B | HR | HR % | R | RBI | BB | SO | SB | Pinch Hit AB | Pinch Hit H | BA | SA |
|---|---|---|---|---|---|---|---|---|---|---|---|---|---|---|---|---|---|---|
| **REGULARS** | | | | | | | | | | | | | | | | | | |
| 1B | Cap Anson | R | 103 | 398 | 125 | 24 | 2 | 0 | 0.0 | 70 | 91 | 68 | 12 | 13 | 1 | 1 | .314 | .384 |
| 2B | Bill Lange | R | 117 | 469 | 132 | 8 | 7 | 8 | 1.7 | 92 | 88 | 52 | 20 | 47 | 0 | 0 | .281 | .380 |
| SS | Bill Dahlen | R | 116 | 485 | 146 | 28 | 15 | 5 | 1.0 | 113 | 64 | 58 | 30 | 31 | 0 | 0 | .301 | .452 |
| 3B | Jiggs Parrott | | 110 | 455 | 111 | 10 | 9 | 1 | 0.2 | 54 | 65 | 13 | 25 | 25 | 0 | 0 | .244 | .312 |
| RF | Sam Dungan | R | 107 | 465 | 138 | 23 | 7 | 2 | 0.4 | 86 | 64 | 29 | 8 | 11 | 0 | 0 | .297 | .389 |
| CF | Jimmy Ryan | R | 83 | 341 | 102 | 21 | 7 | 3 | 0.9 | 82 | 30 | 59 | 25 | 8 | 0 | 0 | .299 | .428 |
| LF | Walt Wilmot | B | 94 | 392 | 118 | 14 | 14 | 3 | 0.8 | 69 | 61 | 40 | 8 | 39 | 1 | 0 | .301 | .431 |
| C | Malachi Kittredge | R | 70 | 255 | 59 | 9 | 5 | 2 | 0.8 | 32 | 30 | 17 | 15 | 3 | 0 | 0 | .231 | .329 |
| **SUBSTITUTES** | | | | | | | | | | | | | | | | | | |
| UT | Llewellan Camp | L | 38 | 156 | 41 | 7 | 7 | 2 | 1.3 | 37 | 17 | 19 | 19 | 30 | 0 | 0 | .263 | .436 |
| SS | Charlie Irwin | R | 21 | 82 | 25 | 6 | 2 | 0 | 0.0 | 14 | 13 | 10 | 1 | 4 | 0 | 0 | .305 | .427 |
| 2B | Bob Glenalvin | | 16 | 61 | 21 | 3 | 1 | 0 | 0.0 | 11 | 12 | 7 | 3 | 7 | 0 | 0 | .344 | .426 |
| UT | Tom Parrott | R | 7 | 27 | 7 | 1 | 0 | 0 | 0.0 | 4 | 3 | 1 | 2 | 0 | 0 | 0 | .259 | .296 |
| 2B | Bad Bill Eagan | | 6 | 19 | 5 | 0 | 0 | 0 | 0.0 | 3 | 2 | 5 | 5 | 4 | 0 | 0 | .263 | .263 |
| 2B | John O'Brien | L | 4 | 14 | 5 | 0 | 1 | 0 | 0.0 | 3 | 1 | 2 | 2 | 0 | 0 | 0 | .357 | .500 |
| UT | George Decker | | 81 | 328 | 89 | 9 | 8 | 2 | 0.6 | 57 | 48 | 24 | 22 | 22 | 0 | 0 | .271 | .366 |
| OF | Henry Lynch | | 4 | 14 | 3 | 2 | 0 | 0 | 0.0 | 0 | 2 | 1 | 1 | 0 | 0 | 0 | .214 | .357 |
| OF | Bob Caruthers | L | 1 | 3 | 0 | 0 | 0 | 0 | 0.0 | 0 | 0 | 1 | 0 | 0 | 0 | 0 | .000 | .000 |
| C | Pop Schriver | R | 64 | 229 | 65 | 8 | 3 | 4 | 1.7 | 49 | 34 | 14 | 9 | 4 | . 3 | 0 | .284 | .397 |
| **PITCHERS** | | | | | | | | | | | | | | | | | | |
| P | Bill Hutchison | R | 46 | 162 | 41 | 7 | 3 | 0 | 0.0 | 14 | 25 | 7 | 20 | 2 | 0 | 0 | .253 | .333 |
| P | Willie McGill | | 40 | 124 | 29 | 4 | 0 | 0 | 0.0 | 18 | 13 | 20 | 13 | 5 | 1 | 0 | .234 | .266 |
| P | Hal Mauck | | 23 | 61 | 9 | 0 | 0 | 0 | 0.0 | 2 | 4 | 3 | 9 | 0 | 0 | 0 | .148 | .148 |
| P | Fritz Clausen | R | 10 | 33 | 4 | 0 | 0 | 0 | 0.0 | 2 | 0 | 2 | 1 | 0 | 0 | 0 | .121 | .121 |
| P | Bert Abbey | R | 7 | 26 | 6 | 1 | 0 | 0 | 0.0 | 2 | 2 | 2 | 3 | 0 | 0 | 0 | .231 | .269 |
| P | Gus McGinnis | | 13 | 25 | 6 | 0 | 0 | 0 | 0.0 | 8 | 7 | 9 | 2 | 0 | 0 | 0 | .240 | .240 |
| P | Frank Donnelly | | 7 | 18 | 8 | 1 | 2 | 0 | 0.0 | 4 | 3 | 2 | 2 | 0 | 0 | 0 | .444 | .722 |
| P | Clark Griffith | R | 4 | 11 | 2 | 0 | 0 | 0 | 0.0 | 1 | 2 | 0 | 1 | 0 | 0 | 0 | .182 | .182 |
| P | Sam Shaw | R | 2 | 7 | 2 | 0 | 0 | 0 | 0.0 | 1 | 1 | 0 | 2 | 0 | 0 | 0 | .286 | .286 |
| P | Jim Hughey | | 2 | 2 | 0 | 0 | 0 | 0 | 0.0 | 1 | 0 | 1 | 1 | 0 | 0 | 0 | .000 | .000 |
| P | Doc Parker | R | 1 | 1 | 0 | 0 | 0 | 0 | 0.0 | 0 | 0 | 0 | 0 | 0 | 0 | 0 | .000 | .000 |
| P | Gus Yost | | 1 | 1 | 0 | 0 | 0 | 0 | 0.0 | 0 | 0 | 0 | 0 | 0 | 0 | 0 | .000 | .000 |
| P | Abe Johnson | | 1 | 0 | 0 | 0 | 0 | 0 | — | 0 | 0 | 0 | 0 | 0 | 0 | 0 | — | — |
| | TEAM TOTAL | | | 4664 | 1299 | 186 | 93 | 32 | 0.7 | 82 | 682 | 466 | 261 | 255 | 6 | 1 | .279 | .379 |

## INDIVIDUAL FIELDING

| POS | Player | T | G | PO | A | E | DP | TC/G | FA |
|---|---|---|---|---|---|---|---|---|---|
| 1B | C. Anson | R | 101 | 997 | 44 | 20 | 59 | 10.5 | .981 |
| | G. Decker | | 27 | 245 | 10 | 5 | 18 | 9.6 | .981 |
| 2B | B. Lange | R | 57 | 151 | 181 | 42 | 21 | 6.6 | .888 |
| | G. Decker | | 20 | 32 | 55 | 17 | 5 | 5.2 | .837 |
| | B. Glenalvin | R | 16 | 35 | 42 | 6 | 4 | 5.2 | .928 |
| | B. Dahlen | R | 10 | 27 | 24 | 4 | 1 | 5.5 | .927 |
| | L. Camp | R | 9 | 16 | 31 | 3 | 5 | 5.6 | .940 |
| | J. Parrott | | 7 | 13 | 23 | 2 | 2 | 5.4 | .947 |
| | B. Eagan | | 6 | 12 | 19 | 3 | 4 | 5.7 | .912 |
| | J. O'Brien | R | 4 | 10 | 8 | 2 | 1 | 5.0 | .900 |
| | T. Parrott | R | 1 | 1 | 4 | 0 | 0 | 5.0 | 1.000 |
| SS | B. Dahlen | R | 88 | 229 | 306 | 65 | 33 | **6.8** | .892 |
| | C. Irwin | R | 21 | 55 | 66 | 12 | 10 | 6.3 | .910 |
| | J. Ryan | L | 10 | 20 | 23 | 7 | 2 | 5.0 | .860 |
| | B. Lange | R | 7 | 18 | 25 | 6 | 2 | 7.0 | .878 |
| | L. Camp | R | 3 | 2 | 8 | 2 | 0 | 4.0 | .833 |
| | G. Decker | | 2 | 1 | 4 | 2 | 0 | 3.5 | .714 |
| 3B | J. Parrott | | 99 | 145 | 251 | 42 | 21 | 4.4 | .904 |
| | L. Camp | R | 16 | 23 | 27 | 9 | 2 | 3.7 | .847 |
| | B. Lange | R | 8 | 14 | 25 | 4 | 3 | 5.4 | .907 |
| | B. Dahlen | R | 3 | 3 | 5 | 1 | 0 | 3.0 | .889 |
| | T. Parrott | R | 2 | 2 | 2 | 0 | 0 | 2.0 | 1.000 |

| POS | Player | T | G | PO | A | E | DP | TC/G | FA |
|---|---|---|---|---|---|---|---|---|---|
| OF | W. Wilmot | L | 93 | 198 | 16 | 31 | 1 | 2.6 | .873 |
| | S. Dungan | | 107 | 175 | 20 | 17 | 3 | 2.0 | .920 |
| | J. Ryan | L | 73 | 162 | 16 | 18 | 2 | 2.7 | .908 |
| | B. Lange | R | 40 | 97 | 7 | 5 | 1 | 2.7 | .954 |
| | G. Decker | | 33 | 55 | 10 | 9 | 2 | 2.2 | .878 |
| | B. Dahlen | R | 17 | 27 | 2 | 2 | 1 | 1.8 | .935 |
| | L. Camp | R | 11 | 14 | 0 | 4 | 0 | 1.6 | .778 |
| | P. Schriver | R | 5 | 9 | 1 | 1 | 0 | 2.2 | .909 |
| | H. Lynch | | 4 | 5 | 0 | 1 | 0 | 1.5 | .833 |
| | J. Parrott | | 4 | 5 | 0 | 1 | 0 | 1.5 | .833 |
| | B. Hutchison | R | 2 | 2 | 0 | 2 | 0 | 2.0 | .500 |
| | B. Caruthers | R | 1 | 1 | 0 | 0 | 0 | 1.0 | 1.000 |
| | G. McGinnis | | 1 | 1 | 0 | 0 | 0 | 1.0 | 1.000 |
| C | M. Kittredge | R | 70 | 260 | 81 | 22 | 4 | 5.2 | .939 |
| | P. Schriver | R | 56 | 215 | 62 | 22 | 8 | 5.3 | .926 |
| | B. Lange | R | 7 | 23 | 12 | 3 | 1 | 5.4 | .921 |

By now the Colts had moved into the fabled West Side Ground at Taylor Street and Wolcott Avenue, which would be their home for the next 22 years. They played their first game at the new location on May 14; it was the first Sunday game in Chicago.

This was also the year when the pitching distance was extended to 60 feet, 6 inches. Predictably, the immediate effect was devastating on pitchers. The Colts team batting average jumped from .235 to .279 while the staff ERA soared from 3.16 to 4.81. Many pitchers were unable to make the adjustment, including Colt ace Bill Hutchison, who never enjoyed another winning season.

Weak in both pitching and defense, Anson's men sank to ninth place, their poorest showing yet. The only bright spots among newcomers were rookie outfielder Bill Lange and Clark Griffith, a young pitcher.

## TEAM  STATISTICS

| | W | L | PCT | GB | R | OR | Batting 2B | 3B | HR | BA | SA | SB | Fielding E | DP | FA | CG | B | Pitching SO | ShO | SV | ERA |
|---|---|---|---|---|---|---|---|---|---|---|---|---|---|---|---|---|---|---|---|---|---|
| BOS | 86 | 43 | .667 | | 1008 | 795 | 178 | 50 | 64 | .290 | .391 | 243 | 353 | 118 | .936 | 115 | 402 | 253 | 2 | 2 | 4.43 |
| PIT | 81 | 48 | .628 | 5 | 970 | 766 | 176 | 127 | 37 | .299 | .411 | 210 | 347 | 112 | .938 | 104 | 504 | 280 | 8 | 1 | 4.08 |
| CLE | 73 | 55 | .570 | 12.5 | 976 | 839 | 222 | 98 | 31 | .300 | .408 | 252 | 395 | 92 | .929 | 110 | 356 | 242 | 2 | 2 | 4.20 |
| PHI | 72 | 57 | .558 | 14 | 1011 | 841 | 246 | 90 | 79 | .301 | .430 | 202 | 318 | 121 | .944 | 107 | 521 | 283 | 4 | 2 | 4.68 |
| NY | 68 | 64 | .515 | 19.5 | 941 | 845 | 182 | 101 | 62 | .293 | .410 | 299 | 432 | 95 | .927 | 111 | 581 | 395 | 6 | 4 | 4.29 |
| BKN | 65 | 63 | .508 | 20.5 | 775 | 845 | 173 | 83 | 44 | .266 | .370 | 213 | 385 | 88 | .930 | 109 | 547 | 297 | 3 | 3 | 4.55 |
| CIN | 65 | 63 | .508 | 20.5 | 759 | 814 | 161 | 65 | 28 | .259 | .340 | 238 | 321 | 138 | .943 | 97 | 549 | 258 | 4 | 5 | 4.59 |
| BAL | 60 | 70 | .462 | 26.5 | 820 | 893 | 164 | 86 | 27 | .275 | .365 | 233 | 384 | 95 | .929 | 104 | 534 | 275 | 1 | 2 | 4.97 |
| CHI | 56 | 71 | .441 | 29 | 829 | 874 | 186 | 93 | 32 | .279 | .379 | 255 | 421 | 92 | .922 | 101 | 553 | 273 | 4 | 5 | 4.81 |
| STL | 57 | 75 | .432 | 30.5 | 745 | 829 | 152 | 98 | 10 | .264 | .341 | 250 | 398 | 110 | .930 | 114 | 542 | 301 | 3 | 4 | 4.06 |
| LOU | 50 | 75 | .400 | 34 | 759 | 942 | 178 | 73 | 18 | .260 | .342 | 203 | 330 | 111 | .937 | 114 | 479 | 190 | 4 | 1 | 5.90 |
| WAS | 40 | 89 | .310 | 46 | 722 | 1032 | 180 | 83 | 24 | .266 | .354 | 154 | 497 | 96 | .912 | 110 | 574 | 292 | 2 | 0 | 5.56 |
| LEAGUE TOTAL | | | | | 10315 | 10315 | 2198 | 1047 | 456 | .280 | .379 | 2752 | 4581 | 1268 | .931 | 1296 | 6142 | 3339 | 43 | 31 | 4.66 |

## INDIVIDUAL  PITCHING

| PITCHER | T | W | L | PCT | ERA | SV | G | GS | CG | IP | H | BB | SO | R | ER | ShO | H/9 | BB/9 | SO/9 |
|---|---|---|---|---|---|---|---|---|---|---|---|---|---|---|---|---|---|---|---|
| Bill Hutchison | R | 16 | 23 | .410 | 4.75 | 0 | 44 | 40 | 38 | 348.1 | 420 | 156 | 80 | 266 | 184 | 2 | 10.85 | 4.03 | 2.07 |
| Willie McGill | L | 17 | 18 | .486 | 4.61 | 0 | 39 | 34 | 26 | 302.2 | 311 | 181 | 91 | 206 | 155 | 1 | 9.25 | 5.38 | 2.71 |
| Hal Mauck | | 8 | 10 | .444 | 4.41 | 0 | 23 | 18 | 12 | 143 | 168 | 60 | 23 | 112 | 70 | 1 | 10.57 | 3.78 | 1.45 |
| Fritz Clausen | L | 6 | 2 | .750 | 3.08 | 1 | 10 | 9 | 8 | 76 | 71 | 39 | 31 | 46 | 26 | 0 | 8.41 | 4.62 | 3.67 |
| Gus McGinnis | | 2 | 5 | .286 | 5.35 | 0 | 13 | 5 | 3 | 67.1 | 85 | 31 | 13 | 67 | 40 | 0 | 11.36 | 4.14 | 1.74 |
| Bert Abbey | R | 2 | 4 | .333 | 5.46 | 0 | 7 | 7 | 5 | 56 | 74 | 20 | 6 | 52 | 34 | 0 | 11.89 | 3.21 | 0.96 |
| Frank Donnelly | | 3 | 1 | .750 | 5.36 | 2 | 7 | 5 | 3 | 42 | 51 | 17 | 6 | 42 | 25 | 0 | 10.93 | 3.64 | 1.29 |
| Tom Parrott | R | 0 | 3 | .000 | 6.67 | 0 | 4 | 3 | 2 | 27 | 35 | 17 | 7 | 30 | 20 | 0 | 11.67 | 5.67 | 2.33 |
| Clark Griffith | R | 1 | 1 | .500 | 5.03 | 0 | 4 | 2 | 2 | 19.2 | 24 | 5 | 9 | 14 | 11 | 0 | 10.98 | 2.29 | 4.12 |
| Sam Shaw | R | 1 | 0 | 1.000 | 5.63 | 0 | 2 | 2 | 1 | 16 | 12 | 13 | 1 | 12 | 10 | 0 | 6.75 | 7.31 | 0.56 |
| Jim Hughey | R | 0 | 1 | .000 | 11.00 | 0 | 2 | 2 | 1 | 9 | 14 | 3 | 4 | 16 | 11 | 0 | 14.00 | 3.00 | 4.00 |
| Jimmy Ryan | L | 0 | 0 | — | 0.00 | 0 | 1 | 0 | 0 | 4.2 | 3 | 0 | 1 | 0 | 0 | 0 | 5.79 | 0.00 | 1.93 |
| Gus Yost | | 0 | 1 | .000 | 13.50 | 0 | 1 | 1 | 0 | 2.2 | 3 | 8 | 1 | 4 | 4 | 0 | 10.13 | 27.00 | 3.38 |
| Doc Parker | R | 0 | 0 | — | 13.50 | 1 | 1 | 0 | 0 | 2 | 5 | 1 | 0 | 3 | 3 | 0 | 22.50 | 4.50 | 0.00 |
| Abe Johnson | | 0 | 0 | — | 36.00 | 1 | 1 | 0 | 0 | 1 | 2 | 2 | 0 | 4 | 4 | 0 | 18.00 | 18.00 | 0.00 |
| TEAM TOTAL | | 56 | 69 | .448 | 4.81 | 5 | 159 | 128 | 101 | 1117.1 | 1278 | 553 | 273 | 874 | 597 | 4 | 10.29 | 4.45 | 2.20 |

| MANAGER | W | L | PCT |
|---|---|---|---|
| Cap Anson | 57 | 75 | .432 |

| POS | Player | B | G | AB | H | 2B | 3B | HR | HR % | R | RBI | BB | SO | SB | Pinch Hit AB | Pinch Hit H | BA | SA |
|---|---|---|---|---|---|---|---|---|---|---|---|---|---|---|---|---|---|---|
| **REGULARS** | | | | | | | | | | | | | | | | | | |
| 1B | Cap Anson | R | 83 | 347 | 137 | 28 | 4 | 5 | 1.4 | 82 | 99 | 40 | 15 | 17 | 0 | 0 | .395 | .542 |
| 2B | Jiggs Parrott | | 127 | 532 | 139 | 17 | 9 | 3 | 0.6 | 83 | 64 | 16 | 35 | 30 | 0 | 0 | .261 | .344 |
| SS | Bill Dahlen | R | 121 | 508 | 184 | 32 | 14 | 15 | 3.0 | 150 | 107 | 76 | 33 | 42 | 0 | 0 | .362 | .569 |
| 3B | Charlie Irwin | R | 128 | 498 | 144 | 24 | 9 | 8 | 1.6 | 84 | 95 | 63 | 23 | 35 | 0 | 0 | .289 | .422 |
| RF | Jimmy Ryan | R | 108 | 481 | 173 | 37 | 7 | 3 | 0.6 | 133 | 62 | 50 | 23 | 11 | 0 | 0 | .360 | .484 |
| CF | Bill Lange | R | 111 | 442 | 145 | 16 | 9 | 6 | 1.4 | 84 | 90 | 56 | 18 | 65 | 0 | 0 | .328 | .446 |
| LF | Walt Wilmot | B | 133 | 597 | 197 | 45 | 12 | 5 | 0.8 | 134 | 130 | 35 | 23 | 74 | 0 | 0 | .330 | .471 |
| C | Pop Schriver | R | 96 | 349 | 96 | 12 | 3 | 3 | 0.9 | 55 | 47 | 29 | 21 | 9 | 1 | 0 | .275 | .352 |
| **SUBSTITUTES** | | | | | | | | | | | | | | | | | | |
| UT | George Decker | | 91 | 384 | 120 | 17 | 6 | 8 | 2.1 | 74 | 92 | 24 | 17 | 23 | 4 | 1 | .313 | .451 |
| 2B | Llewellan Camp | L | 8 | 33 | 6 | 2 | 0 | 0 | 0.0 | 1 | 1 | 1 | 6 | 0 | 0 | 0 | .182 | .242 |
| S2 | John Houseman | | 4 | 15 | 6 | 3 | 1 | 0 | 0.0 | 5 | 4 | 5 | 3 | 2 | 0 | 0 | .400 | .733 |
| PO | Scott Stratton | L | 23 | 96 | 36 | 5 | 4 | 3 | 3.1 | 29 | 23 | 6 | 1 | 3 | 1 | 0 | .375 | .604 |
| PO | Adonis Terry | R | 30 | 95 | 33 | 4 | 2 | 0 | 0.0 | 19 | 17 | 11 | 12 | 3 | 0 | 0 | .347 | .432 |
| OF | Sam Dungan | R | 10 | 39 | 9 | 2 | 0 | 0 | 0.0 | 5 | 3 | 7 | 1 | 1 | 0 | 0 | .231 | .282 |
| C | Malachi Kittredge | R | 51 | 168 | 53 | 8 | 2 | 0 | 0.0 | 36 | 23 | 26 | 20 | 2 | 0 | 0 | .315 | .387 |
| **PITCHERS** | | | | | | | | | | | | | | | | | | |
| P | Clark Griffith | R | 46 | 142 | 33 | 5 | 4 | 0 | 0.0 | 27 | 15 | 23 | 9 | 6 | 2 | 1 | .232 | .324 |
| P | Bill Hutchison | R | 39 | 136 | 42 | 3 | 0 | 6 | 4.4 | 30 | 16 | 11 | 17 | 2 | 0 | 0 | .309 | .463 |
| P | Willie McGill | | 27 | 82 | 20 | 5 | 0 | 0 | 0.0 | 10 | 3 | 15 | 12 | 1 | 0 | 0 | .244 | .305 |
| P | Bert Abbey | R | 11 | 39 | 5 | 0 | 0 | 0 | 0.0 | 3 | 4 | 2 | 7 | 1 | 0 | 0 | .128 | .128 |
| P | Kid Camp | | 3 | 11 | 0 | 0 | 0 | 0 | 0.0 | 0 | 0 | 0 | 1 | 0 | 0 | 0 | .000 | .000 |
| P | Fritz Clausen | R | 1 | 1 | 0 | 0 | 0 | 0 | 0.0 | 0 | 0 | 0 | 1 | 0 | 0 | 0 | .000 | .000 |
| | TEAM TOTAL | | | 4995 | 1578 | 265 | 86 | 65 | 1.3 | 104 | 895 | 496 | 298 | 327 | 8 | 2 | .316 | .442 |

## INDIVIDUAL FIELDING

| POS | Player | T | G | PO | A | E | DP | TC/G | FA |
|---|---|---|---|---|---|---|---|---|---|
| 1B | C. Anson | R | 82 | 739 | 47 | 8 | 52 | 9.7 | **.990** |
| | G. Decker | | 48 | 429 | 15 | 12 | 29 | 9.5 | .974 |
| | P. Schriver | R | 2 | 14 | 4 | 1 | 1 | 9.5 | .947 |
| | S. Stratton | R | 2 | 17 | 0 | 1 | 2 | 9.0 | .944 |
| | A. Terry | R | 2 | 5 | 0 | 0 | 1 | 2.5 | 1.000 |
| 2B | J. Parrott | | 123 | 285 | 379 | 49 | 56 | 5.8 | .931 |
| | L. Camp | | 8 | 26 | 18 | 9 | 4 | 6.6 | .830 |
| | G. Decker | | 2 | 4 | 7 | 0 | 0 | 5.5 | 1.000 |
| | J. Houseman | | 1 | 1 | 4 | 1 | 2 | 6.0 | .833 |
| | C. Anson | R | 1 | 4 | 1 | 0 | 0 | 5.0 | 1.000 |
| SS | B. Dahlen | R | 66 | 186 | 253 | 50 | 43 | 7.4 | .898 |
| | C. Irwin | R | 61 | 118 | 218 | 43 | 20 | 6.2 | .887 |
| | J. Houseman | | 3 | 7 | 12 | 1 | 2 | 6.7 | .950 |
| | B. Lange | R | 2 | 1 | 3 | 4 | 0 | 4.0 | .500 |
| | G. Decker | | 1 | 3 | 1 | 1 | 2 | 5.0 | .800 |
| | P. Schriver | R | 3 | 2 | 2 | 1 | 0 | 1.7 | .800 |
| | C. Griffith | R | 1 | 0 | 0 | 3 | 0 | 3.0 | .000 |
| 3B | C. Irwin | R | 67 | 89 | 123 | 46 | 15 | 3.9 | .822 |
| | B. Dahlen | R | 55 | 96 | 129 | 25 | 10 | 4.5 | .900 |
| | G. Decker | | 7 | 7 | 7 | 7 | 1 | 3.0 | .667 |
| | P. Schriver | R | 3 | 4 | 9 | 2 | 0 | 5.0 | .867 |
| | B. Lange | R | 1 | 2 | 1 | 3 | 0 | 6.0 | .500 |
| | J. Parrott | | 1 | 2 | 1 | 0 | 0 | 3.0 | 1.000 |
| OF | B. Lange | R | 109 | 267 | 25 | 29 | 10 | 2.9 | .910 |
| | W. Wilmot | L | 133 | 264 | 16 | 41 | 5 | 2.4 | .872 |
| | J. Ryan | L | 108 | 221 | 22 | 24 | 3 | 2.5 | .910 |
| | G. Decker | | 29 | 54 | 9 | 12 | 0 | 2.6 | .840 |
| | S. Dungan | | 10 | 15 | 2 | 0 | 1 | 1.7 | 1.000 |
| | C. Griffith | R | 7 | 7 | 1 | 3 | 0 | 1.6 | .727 |
| | S. Stratton | R | 5 | 9 | 0 | 0 | 0 | 1.8 | 1.000 |
| | A. Terry | R | 7 | 7 | 1 | 1 | 0 | 1.3 | .889 |
| | B. Hutchison | R | 4 | 1 | 0 | 0 | 0 | 0.3 | 1.000 |
| C | P. Schriver | R | 88 | 290 | 91 | 32 | 12 | 4.7 | .923 |
| | M. Kittredge | R | 51 | 209 | 36 | 20 | 4 | 5.2 | .925 |

As pitchers continued to reel from the effects of the extended pitching distance, batting averages soared to heavenly heights in 1894. The Colts hit .314 for a club record (excluding 1876, when only 66 games were played) while scoring 1,041 runs for another team high. On the other side of the coin, the pitching staff gave up 1,066 runs on a 5.68 ERA, also Cub records. To add to the futility, they did not record a shutout victory the entire season, the only time this has happened in Cub annals. Clark Griffith, who led the pack with 21 wins, also had the lowest ERA, a not very stingy 4.92.

Although Anson had the highest average, the real batting hero was Bill Dahlen, who put together back-to-back hitting streaks of 42 games (June 20 through August 6, a Cub record) and 28 games (August 8 through September 9). Batting .362 for the year with 15 homers and 107 RBI, Dahlen hit .397 in his 42-game streak (he was hitting only .257 when it began), and .415 in his 28-game run. His first streak marked the only prolonged successful period the Colts enjoyed, as they won 25 of the 42 contests.

## TEAM STATISTICS

| | W | L | PCT | GB | R | OR | Batting 2B | 3B | HR | BA | SA | SB | Fielding E | DP | FA | CG | B | Pitching SO | ShO | SV | ERA |
|---|---|---|---|---|---|---|---|---|---|---|---|---|---|---|---|---|---|---|---|---|---|
| AL | 89 | 39 | .695 | | 1171 | 820 | 271 | 150 | 33 | .343 | .483 | 324 | 293 | 105 | .944 | 97 | 472 | 275 | 1 | 11 | 5.00 |
| Y | 88 | 44 | .667 | 3 | 940 | 789 | 197 | 96 | 44 | .301 | .409 | 319 | 443 | 101 | .924 | 111 | 539 | 395 | 5 | 5 | 3.83 |
| OS | 83 | 49 | .629 | 8 | 1222 | 1002 | 272 | 93 | 103 | .331 | .484 | 241 | 415 | 120 | .925 | 108 | 411 | 262 | 3 | 1 | 5.41 |
| HI | 71 | 57 | .555 | 18 | 1143 | 966 | 252 | 131 | 40 | .349 | .476 | 273 | 338 | 111 | .935 | 102 | 469 | 262 | 3 | 4 | 5.63 |
| KN | 70 | 61 | .534 | 20.5 | 1021 | 1007 | 228 | 130 | 42 | .313 | .440 | 282 | 390 | 85 | .928 | 105 | 555 | 285 | 3 | 5 | 5.51 |
| LE | 68 | 61 | .527 | 21.5 | 932 | 896 | 241 | 90 | 37 | .303 | .414 | 220 | 344 | 107 | .935 | 107 | 435 | 254 | 6 | 1 | 4.97 |
| IT | 65 | 65 | .500 | 25 | 955 | 972 | 222 | 123 | 49 | .312 | .443 | 256 | 354 | 106 | .936 | 106 | 457 | 304 | 2 | 0 | 5.60 |
| HI | 57 | 75 | .432 | 34 | 1041 | 1066 | 265 | 86 | 65 | .314 | .441 | 327 | 452 | 113 | .918 | 117 | 557 | 281 | 0 | 0 | 5.68 |
| TL | 56 | 76 | .424 | 35 | 771 | 954 | 171 | 113 | 54 | .286 | .408 | 190 | 426 | 109 | .923 | 114 | 500 | 319 | 2 | 0 | 5.29 |
| IN | 55 | 75 | .423 | 35 | 910 | 1085 | 224 | 68 | 60 | .294 | .410 | 215 | 423 | 119 | .925 | 110 | 491 | 219 | 4 | 3 | 5.99 |
| VAS | 45 | 87 | .341 | 46 | 882 | 1122 | 218 | 118 | 59 | .287 | .425 | 249 | 499 | 81 | .908 | 102 | 446 | 190 | 1 | 4 | 5.51 |
| OU | 36 | 94 | .277 | 54 | 692 | 1001 | 173 | 88 | 42 | .269 | .375 | 217 | 428 | 130 | .920 | 113 | 475 | 258 | 2 | 1 | 5.45 |
| LEAGUE TOTAL | | | | | 11680 | 11680 | 2734 | 1286 | 628 | .309 | .435 | 3113 | 4805 | 1287 | .927 | 1292 | 5807 | 3304 | 32 | 35 | 5.32 |

## INDIVIDUAL PITCHING

| PITCHER | T | W | L | PCT | ERA | SV | G | GS | CG | IP | H | BB | SO | R | ER | ShO | H/9 | BB/9 | SO/9 |
|---|---|---|---|---|---|---|---|---|---|---|---|---|---|---|---|---|---|---|---|
| ill Hutchison | R | 14 | 15 | .483 | 6.06 | 0 | 36 | 34 | 28 | 277.2 | 373 | 140 | 59 | 257 | 187 | 0 | 12.09 | 4.54 | 1.91 |
| lark Griffith | R | 21 | 11 | .656 | 4.92 | 0 | 36 | 30 | 28 | 261.1 | 328 | 85 | 71 | 193 | 143 | 0 | 11.30 | 2.93 | 2.45 |
| illie McGill | L | 7 | 19 | .269 | 5.84 | 0 | 27 | 23 | 22 | 208 | 272 | 117 | 58 | 195 | 135 | 0 | 11.77 | 5.06 | 2.51 |
| donis Terry | R | 5 | 11 | .313 | 5.84 | 0 | 23 | 21 | 16 | 163.1 | 232 | 123 | 39 | 191 | 106 | 0 | 12.78 | 6.78 | 2.15 |
| cott Stratton | R | 8 | 5 | .615 | 6.03 | 0 | 15 | 12 | 11 | 119.1 | 198 | 40 | 23 | 127 | 80 | 0 | 14.93 | 3.02 | 1.73 |
| ert Abbey | R | 2 | 7 | .222 | 5.18 | 0 | 11 | 11 | 10 | 92 | 119 | 37 | 24 | 74 | 53 | 0 | 11.64 | 3.62 | 2.35 |
| id Camp | | 0 | 1 | .000 | 6.55 | 0 | 3 | 2 | 2 | 22 | 34 | 12 | 6 | 24 | 16 | 0 | 13.91 | 4.91 | 2.45 |
| ritz Clausen | L | 0 | 1 | .000 | 10.38 | 0 | 1 | 1 | 0 | 4.1 | 5 | 3 | 1 | 5 | 5 | 0 | 10.38 | 6.23 | 2.08 |
| EAM TOTAL | | 57 | 70 | .449 | 5.68 | 0 | 152 | 134 | 117 | 1148 | 1561 | 557 | 281 | 1066 | 725 | 0 | 12.24 | 4.37 | 2.20 |

| MANAGER | W | L | PCT |
|---|---|---|---|
| Cap Anson | 72 | 58 | .554 |

| POS | Player | B | G | AB | H | 2B | 3B | HR | HR % | R | RBI | BB | SO | SB | Pinch Hit AB | Pinch Hit H | BA | SA |
|---|---|---|---|---|---|---|---|---|---|---|---|---|---|---|---|---|---|---|
| **REGULARS** | | | | | | | | | | | | | | | | | | |
| 1B | Cap Anson | R | 122 | 474 | 159 | 23 | 6 | 2 | 0.4 | 87 | 91 | 55 | 23 | 12 | 0 | 0 | .335 | .422 |
| 2B | Ace Stewart | R | 97 | 365 | 88 | 8 | 10 | 8 | 2.2 | 52 | 76 | 39 | 40 | 14 | 0 | 0 | .241 | .384 |
| SS | Bill Dahlen | R | 129 | 509 | 139 | 19 | 10 | 7 | 1.4 | 107 | 62 | 61 | 51 | 38 | 0 | 0 | .273 | .391 |
| 3B | Bill Everett | L | 133 | 550 | 197 | 16 | 10 | 3 | 0.5 | 129 | 88 | 33 | 42 | 47 | 0 | 0 | .358 | .440 |
| RF | Jimmy Ryan | R | 108 | 443 | 143 | 22 | 8 | 6 | 1.4 | 83 | 49 | 48 | 22 | 18 | 0 | 0 | .323 | .449 |
| CF | Bill Lange | R | 123 | 478 | 186 | 27 | 16 | 10 | 2.1 | 120 | 98 | 55 | 24 | 67 | 0 | 0 | .389 | .575 |
| LF | Walt Wilmot | B | 108 | 466 | 132 | 16 | 6 | 8 | 1.7 | 86 | 72 | 30 | 19 | 28 | 0 | 0 | .283 | .395 |
| C | Tim Donahue | L | 63 | 219 | 59 | 9 | 1 | 2 | 0.9 | 29 | 36 | 20 | 25 | 5 | 0 | 0 | .269 | .347 |
| **SUBSTITUTES** | | | | | | | | | | | | | | | | | | |
| 2B | Harry Truby | | 33 | 119 | 40 | 3 | 0 | 0 | 0.0 | 17 | 16 | 10 | 7 | 7 | 0 | 0 | .336 | .361 |
| SS | Charlie Irwin | R | 3 | 10 | 2 | 0 | 0 | 0 | 0.0 | 4 | 0 | 2 | 1 | 0 | 0 | 0 | .200 | .200 |
| O1 | George Decker | | 73 | 297 | 82 | 9 | 7 | 2 | 0.7 | 51 | 41 | 17 | 22 | 11 | 0 | 0 | .276 | .374 |
| PO | Scott Stratton | L | 10 | 24 | 7 | 1 | 1 | 0 | 0.0 | 3 | 2 | 4 | 2 | 1 | 1 | 0 | .292 | .417 |
| UT | Jiggs Parrott | | 3 | 4 | 1 | 0 | 0 | 0 | 0.0 | 0 | 0 | 0 | 0 | 0 | 0 | 0 | .250 | .250 |
| C | Malachi Kittredge | R | 60 | 212 | 48 | 6 | 3 | 3 | 1.4 | 30 | 29 | 16 | 9 | 6 | 0 | 0 | .226 | .325 |
| C | Bill Moran | | 15 | 55 | 9 | 2 | 1 | 1 | 1.8 | 8 | 9 | 3 | 2 | 2 | 0 | 0 | .164 | .291 |
| **PITCHERS** | | | | | | | | | | | | | | | | | | |
| P | Clark Griffith | R | 43 | 144 | 46 | 3 | 0 | 1 | 0.7 | 20 | 27 | 16 | 9 | 2 | 0 | 0 | .319 | .361 |
| P | Adonis Terry | R | 40 | 137 | 30 | 3 | 2 | 1 | 0.7 | 18 | 10 | 2 | 17 | 1 | 0 | 0 | .219 | .292 |
| P | Bill Hutchison | R | 38 | 126 | 25 | 3 | 3 | 0 | 0.0 | 12 | 11 | 5 | 23 | 1 | 0 | 0 | .198 | .270 |
| P | Doc Parker | R | 7 | 22 | 7 | 0 | 1 | 0 | 0.0 | 3 | 2 | 1 | 1 | 0 | 0 | 0 | .318 | .409 |
| P | Walter Thornton | | 8 | 22 | 7 | 1 | 0 | 1 | 4.5 | 4 | 7 | 3 | 1 | 0 | 0 | 0 | .318 | .500 |
| P | Danny Friend | | 5 | 17 | 4 | 0 | 0 | 0 | 0.0 | 4 | 1 | 1 | 1 | 0 | 0 | 0 | .235 | .235 |
| P | Monte McFarland | | 2 | 7 | 1 | 0 | 0 | 0 | 0.0 | 0 | 0 | 0 | 3 | 0 | 0 | 0 | .143 | .143 |
| P | Bert Abbey | R | 1 | 3 | 1 | 0 | 0 | 0 | 0.0 | 0 | 0 | 0 | 0 | 0 | 0 | 0 | .333 | .333 |
| P | John Dolan | | 2 | 3 | 0 | 0 | 0 | 0 | 0.0 | 0 | 0 | 1 | 0 | 0 | 0 | 0 | .000 | .000 |
| TEAM TOTAL | | | | 4706 | 1413 | 171 | 85 | 55 | 1.2 | 86 | 727 | 422 | 344 | 260 | 1 | 0 | .300 | .408 |

## INDIVIDUAL  FIELDING

| POS | Player | T | G | PO | A | E | DP | TC/G | FA |
|---|---|---|---|---|---|---|---|---|---|
| 1B | C. Anson | R | 122 | 1176 | 60 | 19 | 82 | 10.3 | .985 |
| | J. Parrott | | 1 | 0 | 0 | 0 | 0 | 0.0 | .000 |
| | G. Decker | | 11 | 110 | 3 | 0 | 10 | 10.3 | 1.000 |
| | W. Thornton | L | 1 | 3 | 0 | 0 | 0 | 3.0 | 1.000 |
| 2B | A. Stewart | R | 97 | 252 | 281 | 52 | 53 | 6.0 | .911 |
| | H. Truby | R | 33 | 98 | 93 | 10 | 21 | 6.1 | .950 |
| | G. Decker | | 1 | 0 | 0 | 0 | 0 | 0.0 | .000 |
| | B. Everett | R | 3 | 4 | 9 | 1 | 0 | 4.7 | .929 |
| SS | B. Dahlen | R | 129 | 281 | 527 | 86 | 70 | 6.9 | .904 |
| | C. Irwin | R | 3 | 3 | 6 | 1 | 1 | 3.3 | .900 |
| | G. Decker | | 1 | 2 | 2 | 0 | 0 | 4.0 | 1.000 |
| | A. Terry | R | 1 | 1 | 2 | 1 | 0 | 4.0 | .750 |
| | J. Parrott | | 1 | 2 | 1 | 0 | 0 | 3.0 | 1.000 |
| 3B | B. Everett | R | 130 | 174 | 263 | 75 | 12 | 3.9 | .854 |
| | G. Decker | | 3 | 2 | 8 | 2 | 0 | 4.0 | .833 |

| POS | Player | T | G | PO | A | E | DP | TC/G | FA |
|---|---|---|---|---|---|---|---|---|---|
| OF | B. Lange | R | 123 | 298 | 28 | 27 | 6 | 2.9 | .924 |
| | W. Wilmot | L | 108 | 226 | 19 | 23 | 5 | 2.5 | .914 |
| | J. Ryan | L | 108 | 161 | 18 | 12 | 6 | 1.8 | .937 |
| | G. Decker | | 57 | 98 | 3 | 10 | 0 | 1.9 | .910 |
| | J. Parrott | | 1 | 0 | 0 | 0 | 0 | 0.0 | .000 |
| | S. Stratton | R | 4 | 5 | 0 | 2 | 0 | 1.8 | .714 |
| | A. Terry | R | 1 | 3 | 0 | 1 | 0 | 4.0 | .750 |
| | B. Dahlen | R | 1 | 1 | 0 | 0 | 0 | 1.0 | 1.000 |
| | C. Griffith | R | 1 | 1 | 0 | 0 | 0 | 1.0 | 1.000 |
| C | T. Donahue | R | 63 | 234 | 45 | 26 | 8 | 4.8 | .915 |
| | M. Kittredge | R | 59 | 197 | 48 | 6 | 4 | 4.3 | .976 |
| | B. Moran | | 15 | 49 | 18 | 14 | 0 | 5.4 | .827 |

Shortly before the 1895 campaign began, Anson, again being urged to retire, answered, "I will play first base this year or die in the attempt." That he was far from dead was proven by his .335 average and 91 RBI. Furthermore, his Colts kicked themselves up to fourth place, thanks to a strong finish.

Bill Lange enjoyed his greatest year with a sizzling .389 mark while rookie third baseman Bill Everett batted .358, still the all-time high for a Cub freshman. Griffith grew into a more unbeatable pitcher every day while Bill "Adonis" Terry, a Brooklyn castoff, won 21 games to prove he was no washup.

Sunday ball had now been played in Chicago for two years without objection, but a pressure group called the Sunday Observance League succeeded in having the entire team arrested in the third inning on June 23 for "aiding and abetting the forming of a noisy crowd on a Sunday." Club president James Hart posted bail, and the Colts finished the game, whipping Cleveland, 13–4.

If anything, such incidents only brought more fans to the park as 382,299 patrons clicked through the turnstiles during the season. During the July 4 afternoon game, a then-record 22,913—the first baseball crowd in Chicago over 20,000—paid their way in to see the Colts beat the Reds, 9–5, after winning the morning contest, 8–7. Baseball was getting to be big business.

## TEAM STATISTICS

| | W | L | PCT | GB | R | OR | 2B | 3B | HR | BA | SA | SB | E | DP | FA | CG | B | SO | ShO | SV | ERA |
|---|---|---|---|---|---|---|---|---|---|---|---|---|---|---|---|---|---|---|---|---|---|
| | | | | | | | **Batting** | | | | | | **Fielding** | | | | | **Pitching** | | | |
| AL | 87 | 43 | .669 | | 1009 | 646 | 235 | 89 | 25 | .324 | .427 | 310 | **288** | 108 | **.946** | 104 | 430 | 244 | 10 | 4 | **3.80** |
| LE | 84 | 46 | .646 | 3 | 917 | 720 | 194 | 67 | 29 | .305 | .395 | 187 | 348 | 77 | .936 | 108 | **346** | 326 | 6 | 3 | 3.90 |
| HI | 78 | 53 | .595 | 9.5 | **1068** | 957 | **272** | 73 | **61** | **.330** | **.450** | 276 | 369 | 93 | .933 | 106 | 485 | 330 | 2 | 7 | 5.47 |
| HI | 72 | 58 | .554 | 15 | 866 | 854 | 171 | 85 | 55 | .298 | .405 | 260 | 401 | **113** | .928 | **119** | 432 | 297 | 3 | 1 | 4.67 |
| KN | 71 | 60 | .542 | 16.5 | 867 | 834 | 189 | 77 | 39 | .282 | .379 | 183 | 325 | 96 | .941 | 103 | 395 | 216 | 5 | 6 | 4.94 |
| OS | 71 | 60 | .542 | 16.5 | 907 | 826 | 197 | 57 | 54 | .290 | .391 | 199 | 364 | 104 | .934 | 115 | 363 | 370 | 4 | 4 | 4.27 |
| T | 71 | 61 | .538 | 17 | 811 | 787 | 190 | 89 | 26 | .290 | .386 | 257 | 392 | 95 | .930 | 106 | 500 | 382 | 4 | 6 | 4.05 |
| N | 66 | 64 | .508 | 21 | 903 | 854 | 235 | **107** | 33 | .298 | .415 | **326** | 377 | 112 | .931 | 97 | 362 | 245 | 2 | 6 | 4.81 |
| Y | 66 | 65 | .504 | 21.5 | 852 | 834 | 191 | 90 | 32 | .288 | .389 | 292 | 438 | 106 | .922 | 115 | **409** | 258 | 6 | 1 | 4.51 |
| AS | 43 | 85 | .336 | 43 | 837 | 1048 | 207 | 101 | 55 | .287 | .412 | 237 | 447 | 96 | .917 | 99 | 465 | 258 | 0 | 5 | 5.28 |
| TL | 39 | 92 | .298 | 48.5 | 747 | 1032 | 155 | 89 | 36 | .281 | .373 | 205 | 380 | 94 | .930 | 105 | 439 | 280 | 1 | 1 | 5.76 |
| OU | 35 | 96 | .267 | 52.5 | 698 | 1090 | 171 | 73 | 34 | .279 | .368 | 156 | 477 | 104 | .913 | 104 | 469 | 245 | 3 | 1 | 5.90 |
| AGUE TOTAL | | | | | 10482 | 10482 | 2407 | 997 | 479 | .296 | .399 | 2888 | 4606 | 1198 | .930 | 1281 | 5101 | 3602 | 46 | 45 | 4.78 |

## INDIVIDUAL  PITCHING

| TCHER | T | W | L | PCT | ERA | SV | G | GS | CG | IP | H | BB | SO | R | ER | ShO | H/9 | BB/9 | SO/9 |
|---|---|---|---|---|---|---|---|---|---|---|---|---|---|---|---|---|---|---|---|
| ark Griffith | R | 25 | 13 | .658 | 3.93 | 0 | 42 | 41 | 39 | 353 | 434 | 91 | 79 | 228 | 154 | 0 | 11.07 | 2.32 | 2.01 |
| donis Terry | R | 21 | 14 | .600 | 4.80 | 0 | 38 | 34 | 31 | 311.1 | 346 | 131 | 88 | 228 | 166 | 0 | 10.00 | 3.79 | 2.54 |
| ll Hutchison | R | 13 | 21 | .382 | 4.73 | 0 | 38 | 35 | 30 | 291 | 371 | 129 | 85 | 218 | 153 | 2 | 11.47 | 3.99 | 2.63 |
| oc Parker | R | 4 | 2 | .667 | 3.68 | 0 | 7 | 6 | 5 | 51.1 | 65 | 9 | 9 | 30 | 21 | 1 | 11.40 | 1.58 | 1.58 |
| anny Friend | L | 2 | 2 | .500 | 5.27 | 0 | 5 | 5 | 5 | 41 | 50 | 14 | 10 | 27 | 24 | 0 | 10.98 | 3.07 | 2.20 |
| alter Thornton | L | 2 | 0 | 1.000 | 6.08 | 1 | 7 | 2 | 2 | 40 | 58 | 31 | 13 | 50 | 27 | 0 | 13.05 | 6.98 | 2.93 |
| cott Stratton | R | 2 | 3 | .400 | 9.60 | 0 | 5 | 5 | 3 | 30 | 51 | 14 | 4 | 42 | 32 | 0 | 15.30 | 4.20 | 1.20 |
| onte McFarland | | 2 | 0 | 1.000 | 5.14 | 0 | 2 | 2 | 2 | 14 | 21 | 5 | 5 | 11 | 8 | 0 | 13.50 | 3.21 | 3.21 |
| ohn Dolan | R | 0 | 1 | .000 | 6.55 | 0 | 2 | 2 | 1 | 11 | 16 | 6 | 1 | 12 | 8 | 0 | 13.09 | 4.91 | 0.82 |
| ert Abbey | R | 0 | 1 | .000 | 4.50 | 0 | 1 | 1 | 1 | 8 | 10 | 2 | 3 | 8 | 4 | 0 | 11.25 | 2.25 | 3.38 |
| EAM TOTAL | | 71 | 57 | .555 | 4.67 | 1 | 147 | 133 | 119 | 1150.2 | 1422 | 432 | 297 | 854 | 597 | 3 | 11.12 | 3.38 | 2.32 |

| MANAGER | W | L | PCT |
|---|---|---|---|
| Cap Anson | 71 | 57 | .555 |

| POS | Player | B | G | AB | H | 2B | 3B | HR | HR % | R | RBI | BB | SO | SB | Pinch Hit AB | Pinch Hit H | BA | SA |
|---|---|---|---|---|---|---|---|---|---|---|---|---|---|---|---|---|---|---|
| **REGULARS** | | | | | | | | | | | | | | | | | | |
| 1B | Cap Anson | R | 108 | 402 | 133 | 18 | 2 | 2 | 0.5 | 72 | 90 | 49 | 10 | 24 | 1 | 0 | .331 | .400 |
| 2B | Fred Pfeffer | R | 94 | 360 | 88 | 16 | 7 | 2 | 0.6 | 45 | 52 | 23 | 20 | 22 | 0 | 0 | .244 | .344 |
| SS | Bill Dahlen | R | 125 | 476 | 172 | 30 | 19 | 9 | 1.9 | 153 | 74 | 64 | 36 | 51 | 0 | 0 | .361 | .561 |
| 3B | Bill Everett | L | 132 | 575 | 184 | 16 | 13 | 2 | 0.3 | 130 | 46 | 41 | 43 | 46 | 0 | 0 | .320 | .403 |
| RF | Jimmy Ryan | R | 128 | 490 | 153 | 24 | 10 | 3 | 0.6 | 83 | 86 | 46 | 16 | 29 | 0 | 0 | .312 | .420 |
| CF | Bill Lange | R | 122 | 469 | 153 | 21 | 16 | 4 | 0.9 | 114 | 92 | 65 | 24 | 84 | 0 | 0 | .326 | .465 |
| LF | George Decker | | 107 | 421 | 118 | 23 | 11 | 5 | 1.2 | 68 | 61 | 23 | 14 | 20 | 0 | 0 | .280 | .423 |
| C | Malachi Kittredge | R | 65 | 215 | 48 | 4 | 1 | 1 | 0.5 | 17 | 19 | 14 | 14 | 6 | 0 | 0 | .223 | .265 |
| **SUBSTITUTES** | | | | | | | | | | | | | | | | | | |
| 3S | Barry McCormick | | 45 | 168 | 37 | 3 | 1 | 1 | 0.6 | 22 | 23 | 14 | 30 | 9 | 0 | 0 | .220 | .268 |
| 2B | Harry Truby | | 29 | 109 | 28 | 2 | 2 | 2 | 1.8 | 13 | 31 | 6 | 5 | 4 | 0 | 0 | .257 | .367 |
| 2B | Josh Reilly | | 9 | 42 | 9 | 1 | 0 | 0 | 0.0 | 6 | 2 | 1 | 1 | 2 | 0 | 0 | .214 | .238 |
| OF | George Flynn | | 29 | 106 | 27 | 1 | 2 | 0 | 0.0 | 15 | 4 | 11 | 9 | 12 | 0 | 0 | .255 | .302 |
| OF | Algie McBride | L | 9 | 29 | 7 | 1 | 1 | 1 | 3.4 | 2 | 7 | 7 | 3 | 0 | 0 | 0 | .241 | .448 |
| PO | Walter Thornton | | 9 | 22 | 8 | 0 | 1 | 0 | 0.0 | 6 | 1 | 5 | 2 | 2 | 1 | 0 | .364 | .455 |
| C | Tim Donahue | L | 57 | 188 | 41 | 10 | 1 | 0 | 0.0 | 27 | 20 | 11 | 15 | 11 | 0 | 0 | .218 | .282 |
| C | Con Daily | L | 9 | 27 | 2 | 0 | 0 | 0 | 0.0 | 1 | 1 | 1 | 2 | 1 | 0 | 0 | .074 | .074 |
| **PITCHERS** | | | | | | | | | | | | | | | | | | |
| P | Clark Griffith | R | 38 | 135 | 36 | 5 | 2 | 1 | 0.7 | 22 | 16 | 9 | 7 | 3 | 2 | 0 | .267 | .356 |
| P | Danny Friend | | 37 | 126 | 30 | 3 | 3 | 1 | 0.8 | 12 | 10 | 3 | 5 | 2 | 0 | 0 | .238 | .333 |
| P | Adonis Terry | R | 30 | 99 | 26 | 4 | 2 | 0 | 0.0 | 14 | 15 | 8 | 12 | 4 | 0 | 0 | .263 | .343 |
| P | Buttons Briggs | R | 26 | 78 | 10 | 0 | 2 | 0 | 0.0 | 5 | 6 | 7 | 14 | 0 | 0 | 0 | .128 | .179 |
| P | Doc Parker | R | 10 | 36 | 10 | 0 | 1 | 0 | 0.0 | 4 | 4 | 1 | 5 | 0 | 0 | 0 | .278 | .333 |
| P | Monte McFarland | | 4 | 12 | 0 | 0 | 0 | 0 | 0.0 | 0 | 0 | 0 | 3 | 0 | 0 | 0 | .000 | .000 |
| | TEAM TOTAL | | | 4585 | 1320 | 182 | 97 | 34 | 0.7 | 83 | 660 | 409 | 290 | 332 | 4 | 0 | .288 | .392 |

## INDIVIDUAL  FIELDING

| POS | Player | T | G | PO | A | E | DP | TC/G | FA | POS | Player | T | G | PO | A | E | DP | TC/G | FA |
|---|---|---|---|---|---|---|---|---|---|---|---|---|---|---|---|---|---|---|---|
| 1B | C. Anson | R | 98 | 880 | 54 | 16 | 67 | 9.7 | .983 | OF | B. Lange | R | 121 | 313 | 18 | 24 | 3 | 2.9 | .932 |
| | G. Decker | | 36 | 351 | 19 | 6 | 25 | 10.4 | .984 | | J. Ryan | L | 128 | 207 | 21 | 22 | 4 | 2.0 | .912 |
| 2B | F. Pfeffer | R | 94 | 227 | 307 | 30 | 43 | 6.0 | .947 | | G. Decker | | 71 | 131 | 10 | 11 | 0 | 2.1 | .928 |
| | H. Truby | R | 28 | 76 | 82 | 11 | 17 | 6.0 | .935 | | G. Flynn | | 29 | 66 | 6 | 10 | 3 | 2.8 | .878 |
| | J. Reilly | | 8 | 20 | 28 | 8 | 1 | 7.0 | .857 | | B. Everett | R | 35 | 65 | 4 | 9 | 0 | 2.2 | .885 |
| | McCormick | R | 3 | 8 | 3 | 2 | 3 | 4.3 | .846 | | A. McBride | L | 9 | 21 | 1 | 2 | 0 | 2.7 | .917 |
| SS | B. Dahlen | R | 125 | 310 | 456 | 71 | 66 | 6.7 | .915 | | W. Thornton | | 3 | 7 | 0 | 2 | 0 | 3.0 | .778 |
| | McCormick | R | 6 | 8 | 23 | 8 | 4 | 6.5 | .795 | | D. Friend | L | 1 | 2 | 0 | 0 | 0 | 2.0 | 1.000 |
| | J. Reilly | | 1 | 1 | 4 | 3 | 0 | 8.0 | .625 | | McCormick | R | 1 | 1 | 0 | 0 | 0 | 1.0 | 1.000 |
| 3B | B. Everett | R | 97 | 148 | 180 | 44 | 10 | 3.8 | .882 | | D. Parker | R | 1 | 1 | 0 | 0 | 0 | 1.0 | 1.000 |
| | McCormick | R | 35 | 34 | 72 | 21 | 5 | 3.6 | .835 | C | M. Kittredge | R | 64 | 251 | 56 | 12 | 12 | 5.0 | .962 |
| | | | | | | | | | | | T. Donahue | R | 57 | 235 | 60 | 20 | 7 | 5.5 | .937 |
| | | | | | | | | | | | C. Anson | R | 10 | 21 | 8 | 4 | 0 | 3.3 | .879 |
| | | | | | | | | | | | C. Daily | | 9 | 24 | 7 | 1 | 0 | 3.6 | .969 |
| | | | | | | | | | | | B. Lange | R | 1 | 1 | 0 | 0 | 0 | 1.0 | 1.000 |

Although the Colts slipped to fifth place in 1896, their record was virtually identical to that of the year before, and optimism remained high. Although pitchers were growing accustomed to the new pitching distance, batting remained the team's primary asset. Lange, Ryan, Anson, Dahlen, and Everett all checked in at a .300-plus clip. Fred Pfeffer was back at second base after a five-year absence, but he had slowed down considerably, so the middle of the infield was still a sore spot.

Hutchison had retired, and Terry was starting to show his age, but two rookie hurlers, Danny Friend and Herb "Buttons" Briggs, showed promise by winning 18 and 12 games. History was made July 13 when Ed Delahanty of the Phillies smashed four home runs—all of them inside the park—and a single, driving in seven runs at West Side Grounds. In spite of this prolific attack, the Colts won, 9–8. And for trivia buffs: Crackerjack advertisements appeared on the team programs for the first time.

## TEAM STATISTICS

| | W | L | PCT | GB | R | OR | 2B | Batting 3B | HR | BA | SA | SB | Fielding E | DP | FA | CG | B | Pitching SO | ShO | SV | ERA |
|---|---|---|---|---|---|---|---|---|---|---|---|---|---|---|---|---|---|---|---|---|---|
| BAL | 90 | 39 | .698 | | 995 | 662 | 207 | 100 | 23 | .328 | .429 | 441 | 296 | 114 | .945 | 115 | 339 | 302 | 9 | 1 | 3.67 |
| CLE | 80 | 48 | .625 | 9.5 | 840 | 650 | 207 | 72 | 28 | .301 | .391 | 175 | 288 | 117 | .949 | 113 | 280 | 336 | 9 | 5 | 3.46 |
| CIN | 77 | 50 | .606 | 12 | 783 | 620 | 205 | 73 | 19 | .294 | .388 | 350 | 252 | 107 | .951 | 105 | 310 | 219 | 12 | 4 | 3.67 |
| BOS | 74 | 57 | .565 | 17 | 860 | 761 | 175 | 74 | 36 | .300 | .392 | 241 | 368 | 94 | .934 | 110 | 397 | 277 | 6 | 3 | 3.78 |
| CHI | 71 | 57 | .555 | 18.5 | 815 | 799 | 182 | 97 | 34 | .286 | .390 | 332 | 366 | 115 | .934 | 118 | 467 | 353 | 2 | 1 | 4.41 |
| PIT | 66 | 63 | .512 | 24 | 787 | 741 | 169 | 94 | 27 | .292 | .385 | 217 | 317 | 103 | .941 | 108 | 439 | 362 | 8 | 1 | 4.30 |
| NY | 64 | 67 | .489 | 27 | 829 | 821 | 159 | 87 | 40 | .297 | .394 | 274 | 365 | 90 | .933 | 104 | 403 | 312 | 1 | 2 | 4.54 |
| PHI | 62 | 68 | .477 | 28.5 | 890 | 891 | 234 | 84 | 49 | .295 | .413 | 191 | 313 | 112 | .941 | 107 | 387 | 243 | 3 | 2 | 5.20 |
| BKN | 58 | 73 | .443 | 33 | 692 | 764 | 174 | 87 | 28 | .284 | .379 | 198 | 297 | 104 | .945 | 97 | 400 | 259 | 3 | 1 | 4.25 |
| WAS | 58 | 73 | .443 | 33 | 818 | 920 | 179 | 79 | 45 | .286 | .388 | 258 | 398 | 99 | .927 | 106 | 435 | 292 | 2 | 3 | 4.61 |
| STL | 40 | 90 | .308 | 50.5 | 593 | 929 | 134 | 78 | 37 | .257 | .346 | 185 | 345 | 73 | .936 | 115 | 456 | 279 | 1 | 1 | 5.33 |
| LOU | 38 | 93 | .290 | 53 | 653 | 997 | 142 | 80 | 37 | .261 | .351 | 195 | 475 | 110 | .916 | 108 | 541 | 288 | 1 | 4 | 5.12 |
| LEAGUE TOTAL | | | | | 9555 | 9555 | 2167 | 1005 | 403 | .290 | .387 | 3057 | 4080 | 1238 | .938 | 1306 | 4854 | 3522 | 57 | 28 | 4.36 |

## INDIVIDUAL PITCHING

| PITCHER | T | W | L | PCT | ERA | SV | G | GS | CG | IP | H | BB | SO | R | ER | ShO | H/9 | BB/9 | SO/9 |
|---|---|---|---|---|---|---|---|---|---|---|---|---|---|---|---|---|---|---|---|
| Clark Griffith | R | 22 | 13 | .629 | 3.54 | 0 | 36 | 35 | 35 | 317.2 | 370 | 70 | 81 | 189 | 125 | 0 | 10.48 | 1.98 | 2.29 |
| Danny Friend | L | 18 | 14 | .563 | 4.74 | 0 | 36 | 33 | 28 | 290.2 | 298 | 139 | 86 | 196 | 153 | 1 | 9.23 | 4.30 | 2.66 |
| Adonis Terry | R | 15 | 13 | .536 | 4.28 | 0 | 30 | 28 | 25 | 235.1 | 268 | 88 | 74 | 161 | 112 | 1 | 10.25 | 3.37 | 2.83 |
| Buttons Briggs | R | 12 | 8 | .600 | 4.31 | 1 | 26 | 21 | 19 | 194 | 202 | 108 | 84 | 129 | 93 | 0 | 9.37 | 5.01 | 3.90 |
| Doc Parker | R | 1 | 5 | .167 | 6.16 | 0 | 9 | 7 | 7 | 73 | 100 | 27 | 15 | 71 | 50 | 0 | 12.33 | 3.33 | 1.85 |
| Monte McFarland | | 0 | 4 | .000 | 7.20 | 0 | 4 | 3 | 2 | 25 | 32 | 21 | 3 | 25 | 20 | 0 | 11.52 | 7.56 | 1.08 |
| Walter Thornton | L | 2 | 1 | .667 | 5.70 | 0 | 5 | 5 | 2 | 23.2 | 30 | 13 | 10 | 26 | 15 | 0 | 11.41 | 4.94 | 3.80 |
| Malachi Kittredge | R | 0 | 0 | – | 5.40 | 0 | 1 | 0 | 0 | 1.2 | 2 | 1 | 0 | 2 | 1 | 0 | 10.80 | 5.40 | 0.00 |
| TEAM TOTAL | | 70 | 58 | .547 | 4.41 | 1 | 147 | 132 | 118 | 1161 | 1302 | 467 | 353 | 799 | 569 | 2 | 10.09 | 3.62 | 2.74 |

| MANAGER | W | L | PCT |
|---|---|---|---|
| Cap Anson | 59 | 73 | .447 |

| POS | Player | B | G | AB | H | 2B | 3B | HR | HR % | R | RBI | BB | SO | SB | Pinch Hit AB | Pinch Hit H | BA | SA |
|---|---|---|---|---|---|---|---|---|---|---|---|---|---|---|---|---|---|---|
| **REGULARS** | | | | | | | | | | | | | | | | | | |
| 1B | Cap Anson | R | 114 | 424 | 128 | 17 | 3 | 3 | 0.7 | 67 | 75 | 60 | | 11 | 0 | 0 | .302 | .377 |
| 2B | Jim Connor | | 77 | 285 | 83 | 10 | 5 | 3 | 1.1 | 40 | 38 | 24 | | 10 | 2 | 1 | .291 | .393 |
| SS | Bill Dahlen | R | 75 | 277 | 82 | 18 | 8 | 6 | 2.2 | 67 | 40 | 43 | | 15 | 0 | 0 | .296 | .484 |
| 3B | Bill Everett | L | 92 | 379 | 119 | 14 | 7 | 5 | 1.3 | 63 | 39 | 36 | | 26 | 1 | 0 | .314 | .427 |
| RF | Jimmy Ryan | R | 136 | 520 | 160 | 33 | 17 | 5 | 1.0 | 103 | 85 | 50 | | 27 | 0 | 0 | .308 | .465 |
| CF | Bill Lange | R | 118 | 479 | 163 | 24 | 14 | 5 | 1.0 | 119 | 83 | 48 | | 73 | 0 | 0 | .340 | .480 |
| LF | George Decker | | 111 | 428 | 124 | 12 | 7 | 5 | 1.2 | 72 | 63 | 24 | | 11 | 1 | 0 | .290 | .386 |
| C | Malachi Kittredge | R | 79 | 262 | 53 | 5 | 5 | 1 | 0.4 | 25 | 30 | 22 | | 9 | 0 | 0 | .202 | .271 |
| **SUBSTITUTES** | | | | | | | | | | | | | | | | | | |
| 3S | Barry McCormick | | 101 | 419 | 112 | 8 | 10 | 2 | 0.5 | 87 | 55 | 33 | | 44 | 0 | 0 | .267 | .348 |
| UT | Nixey Callahan | R | 94 | 360 | 105 | 18 | 6 | 3 | 0.8 | 60 | 47 | 10 | | 12 | 2 | 0 | .292 | .400 |
| 2B | Fred Pfeffer | R | 32 | 114 | 26 | 0 | 1 | 0 | 0.0 | 10 | 11 | 12 | | 5 | 0 | 0 | .228 | .246 |
| OP | Walter Thornton | | 75 | 265 | 85 | 9 | 6 | 0 | 0.0 | 39 | 55 | 30 | | 13 | 1 | 0 | .321 | .400 |
| OF | Tom Hernon | | 4 | 16 | 1 | 0 | 0 | 0 | 0.0 | 2 | 2 | 0 | | 1 | 0 | 0 | .063 | .063 |
| C | Tim Donahue | L | 58 | 188 | 45 | 7 | 3 | 0 | 0.0 | 28 | 21 | 9 | | 3 | 1 | 1 | .239 | .309 |
| **PITCHERS** | | | | | | | | | | | | | | | | | | |
| P | Clark Griffith | R | 46 | 162 | 38 | 8 | 4 | 0 | 0.0 | 27 | 21 | 18 | | 2 | 0 | 0 | .235 | .333 |
| P | Danny Friend | | 25 | 88 | 25 | 5 | 0 | 0 | 0.0 | 12 | 9 | 5 | | 1 | 0 | 0 | .284 | .341 |
| P | Buttons Briggs | R | 22 | 81 | 13 | 0 | 1 | 0 | 0.0 | 5 | 5 | 3 | | 1 | 0 | 0 | .160 | .185 |
| P | Roger Denzer | L | 12 | 39 | 6 | 1 | 0 | 0 | 0.0 | 4 | 1 | 1 | | 0 | 0 | 0 | .154 | .179 |
| P | Jim Korwan | | 5 | 12 | 0 | 0 | 0 | 0 | 0.0 | 0 | 0 | 1 | | 0 | 0 | 0 | .000 | .000 |
| P | Adonis Terry | R | 1 | 3 | 0 | 0 | 0 | 0 | 0.0 | 1 | 0 | 0 | | 0 | 0 | 0 | .000 | .000 |
| P | Dave Wright | R | 1 | 3 | 1 | 0 | 0 | 0 | 0.0 | 1 | 1 | 1 | | 0 | 0 | 0 | .333 | .333 |
| | TEAM TOTAL | | | 4804 | 1369 | 189 | 97 | 38 | 0.8 | 83 | 681 | 430 | 0 | 264 | 8 | 2 | .285 | .388 |

## INDIVIDUAL FIELDING

| POS | Player | T | G | PO | A | E | DP | TC/G | FA |
|---|---|---|---|---|---|---|---|---|---|
| 1B | C. Anson | R | 103 | 933 | 62 | 25 | 67 | 9.9 | .975 |
| | G. Decker | | 38 | 394 | 23 | 5 | 22 | 11.1 | .988 |
| | C. Griffith | R | 1 | 0 | 0 | 0 | 0 | 0.0 | .000 |
| | T. Donahue | R | 1 | 3 | 0 | 1 | 0 | 4.0 | .750 |
| 2B | J. Connor | | 76 | 176 | 293 | 32 | 40 | 6.6 | .936 |
| | F. Pfeffer | R | 32 | 73 | 93 | 22 | 12 | 5.9 | .883 |
| | N. Callahan | R | 30 | 65 | 92 | 14 | 10 | 5.7 | .918 |
| | G. Decker | | 1 | 1 | 0 | 1 | 0 | 2.0 | .500 |
| | McCormick | | 1 | 0 | 1 | 0 | 0 | 1.0 | 1.000 |
| SS | B. Dahlen | R | 75 | 215 | 291 | 38 | 48 | 7.3 | .930 |
| | McCormick | R | 46 | 109 | 153 | 28 | 16 | 6.3 | .903 |
| | N. Callahan | R | 18 | 26 | 53 | 14 | 9 | 5.2 | .849 |
| | C. Griffith | R | 2 | 5 | 8 | 1 | 1 | 7.0 | .929 |
| | T. Donahue | R | 2 | 1 | 4 | 1 | 0 | 3.0 | .833 |
| 3B | B. Everett | R | 83 | 119 | 147 | 42 | 9 | 3.7 | .864 |
| | McCormick | R | 56 | 62 | 115 | 31 | 10 | 3.7 | .851 |
| | C. Griffith | R | 1 | 3 | 3 | 3 | 0 | 9.0 | .667 |
| | N. Callahan | R | 2 | 2 | 3 | 1 | 1 | 3.0 | .833 |

| POS | Player | T | G | PO | A | E | DP | TC/G | FA |
|---|---|---|---|---|---|---|---|---|---|
| OF | B. Lange | R | 118 | 264 | 17 | 16 | 4 | 2.5 | .946 |
| | J. Ryan | L | 136 | 211 | 28 | 14 | 7 | 1.9 | .945 |
| | G. Decker | | 75 | 112 | 12 | 10 | 1 | 1.8 | .925 |
| | W. Thornton | L | 59 | 74 | 8 | 23 | 0 | 1.8 | .781 |
| | N. Callahan | R | 21 | 40 | 8 | 6 | 1 | 2.6 | .889 |
| | B. Everett | R | 8 | 18 | 0 | 1 | 0 | 2.4 | .947 |
| | T. Hernon | | 4 | 10 | 0 | 0 | 0 | 2.5 | 1.000 |
| | C. Griffith | R | 2 | 0 | 0 | 2 | 0 | 1.0 | .000 |
| | D. Friend | L | 1 | 1 | 0 | 0 | 0 | 1.0 | 1.000 |
| C | M. Kittredge | R | 79 | 324 | 75 | 20 | 6 | 5.3 | .952 |
| | T. Donahue | R | 55 | 218 | 64 | 15 | 2 | 5.4 | .949 |
| | C. Anson | R | 11 | 36 | 13 | 2 | 2 | 4.6 | .961 |

Following strong showings the previous two years, Anson felt the Colts could go all the way in 1897, but such was not the case. Injuries to Dahlen and Everett hurt the team severely, and Friend and Briggs were largely ineffective on the mound. Also, they still did not have a reliable catcher or second baseman. Spending much of the season in 10th or 11th place, they finally rallied late to finish ninth.

In spite of this, it was a historic season. Anson, who had announced that it would be his last year as a player, was given his own "Day," May 4, to start a Cub tradition that has continued ever since. At age 46, he became the oldest player to hit .300 in a full season, batting .302. On July 18 he collected the 3,000th hit of his career (first to do so) in a 6–3 win over Baltimore. On June 29, the Colts went wild in a 36–7 carnage over Louisville, establishing a major-league record for most runs scored in a game by one team. Barry McCormick gathered six hits while pitcher Nixey Callahan went five-for-seven. Finally, on August 13, Clark Griffith, who considered it bad luck to pitch a shutout, hurled the first of his career, a 2–0 win over the Reds.

## TEAM STATISTICS

| | W | L | PCT | GB | R | OR | 2B | 3B | HR | BA | SA | SB | E | DP | FA | CG | B | SO | ShO | SV | ERA |
|---|---|---|---|---|---|---|---|---|---|---|---|---|---|---|---|---|---|---|---|---|---|
| | | | | | | | Batting | | | | | | Fielding | | | Pitching | | | | |
| BOS | 93 | 39 | .705 | | 1025 | 665 | 230 | 83 | 45 | .319 | .426 | 233 | 272 | 80 | .951 | 115 | 393 | 329 | 8 | 7 | 3.65 |
| BAL | 90 | 40 | .692 | 2 | 964 | 674 | 243 | 66 | 20 | .325 | .414 | 401 | 277 | 110 | .951 | 118 | 382 | 361 | 3 | 0 | 3.55 |
| NY | 83 | 48 | .634 | 9.5 | 895 | 695 | 188 | 84 | 31 | .299 | .392 | 328 | 397 | 109 | .930 | 118 | 486 | 456 | 8 | 3 | 3.47 |
| CIN | 76 | 56 | .576 | 17 | 763 | 705 | 219 | 69 | 22 | .290 | .383 | 194 | 273 | 100 | .948 | 100 | 329 | 270 | 4 | 2 | 4.09 |
| CLE | 69 | 62 | .527 | 23.5 | 773 | 680 | 192 | 88 | 16 | .298 | .389 | 181 | 261 | 74 | .950 | 111 | 289 | 277 | 6 | 0 | 3.95 |
| BKN | 61 | 71 | .462 | 32 | 802 | 845 | 202 | 72 | 22 | .279 | .365 | 187 | 364 | 99 | .936 | 114 | 410 | 256 | 4 | 2 | 4.60 |
| WAS | 61 | 71 | .462 | 32 | 781 | 793 | 194 | 77 | 36 | .297 | .395 | 208 | 369 | 103 | .933 | 103 | 400 | 348 | 7 | 5 | 4.01 |
| PIT | 60 | 71 | .458 | 32.5 | 676 | 835 | 140 | 108 | 25 | .276 | .370 | 170 | 346 | 70 | .936 | 112 | 318 | 342 | 2 | 2 | 4.67 |
| CHI | 59 | 73 | .447 | 34 | 832 | 894 | 189 | 97 | 38 | .282 | .386 | 264 | 296 | 72 | .944 | 115 | 364 | 253 | 4 | 2 | 4.60 |
| PHI | 55 | 77 | .417 | 38 | 752 | 792 | 213 | 83 | 40 | .293 | .398 | 163 | 395 | 85 | .929 | 114 | 459 | 267 | 2 | 0 | 4.42 |
| LOU | 52 | 78 | .400 | 40 | 669 | 859 | 160 | 70 | 40 | .265 | .358 | 195 | 375 | 84 | .933 | 109 | 453 | 207 | 1 | 1 | 6.21 |
| STL | 29 | 102 | .221 | 63.5 | 588 | 1083 | 149 | 67 | 31 | .275 | .356 | 172 | | | | | | | | | |
| LEAGUE TOTAL | | | | | 9520 | 9520 | 2319 | 964 | 366 | .292 | .386 | 2696 | 4018 | 1098 | .939 | 1360 | 4716 | 3727 | 51 | 25 | 4.31 |

## INDIVIDUAL PITCHING

| PITCHER | T | W | L | PCT | ERA | SV | G | GS | CG | IP | H | BB | SO | R | ER | ShO | H/9 | BB/9 | SO/9 |
|---|---|---|---|---|---|---|---|---|---|---|---|---|---|---|---|---|---|---|---|
| Clark Griffith | R | 21 | 19 | .525 | 3.72 | 1 | 41 | 38 | 38 | 343.2 | 410 | 86 | 102 | 231 | 142 | 1 | 10.74 | 2.25 | 2.67 |
| Danny Friend | L | 12 | 11 | .522 | 4.52 | 0 | 24 | 24 | 23 | 203 | 244 | 86 | 58 | 144 | 102 | 0 | 10.82 | 3.81 | 2.57 |
| Nixey Callahan | R | 12 | 9 | .571 | 4.03 | 0 | 23 | 22 | 21 | 189.2 | 221 | 55 | 52 | 111 | 85 | 1 | 10.49 | 2.61 | 2.47 |
| Buttons Briggs | R | 4 | 17 | .190 | 5.26 | 0 | 22 | 22 | 21 | 186.2 | 246 | 85 | 60 | 166 | 109 | 0 | 11.86 | 4.10 | 2.89 |
| Walter Thornton | L | 6 | 7 | .462 | 4.70 | 0 | 16 | 16 | 15 | 130.1 | 164 | 51 | 55 | 91 | 68 | 0 | 11.32 | 3.52 | 3.80 |
| Roger Denzer | R | 2 | 8 | .200 | 5.13 | 0 | 12 | 10 | 8 | 94.2 | 125 | 34 | 17 | 91 | 54 | 0 | 11.88 | 3.23 | 1.62 |
| Jim Korwan | | 1 | 2 | .333 | 5.82 | 0 | 5 | 4 | 3 | 34 | 47 | 28 | 12 | 36 | 22 | 0 | 12.44 | 7.41 | 3.18 |
| Adonis Terry | R | 0 | 1 | .000 | 10.13 | 0 | 1 | 1 | 1 | 8 | 11 | 6 | 1 | 10 | 9 | 0 | 12.38 | 6.75 | 1.13 |
| Dave Wright | R | 1 | 0 | 1.000 | 15.43 | 0 | 1 | 1 | 1 | 7 | 17 | 2 | 4 | 14 | 12 | 0 | 21.86 | 2.57 | 5.14 |
| TEAM TOTAL | | 59 | 74 | .444 | 4.53 | 1 | 145 | 138 | 131 | 1197 | 1485 | 433 | 361 | 894 | 603 | 2 | 11.17 | 3.26 | 2.71 |

| MANAGER | W | L | PCT |
|---|---|---|---|
| Tom Burns | 85 | 65 | .567 |

| POS | Player | B | G | AB | H | 2B | 3B | HR | HR % | R | RBI | BB | SO | SB | Pinch Hit AB | Pinch Hit H | BA | SA |
|---|---|---|---|---|---|---|---|---|---|---|---|---|---|---|---|---|---|---|
| **REGULARS** | | | | | | | | | | | | | | | | | | |
| 1B | Bill Everett | L | 149 | 596 | 190 | 15 | 6 | 0 | 0.0 | 102 | 69 | 53 | | 28 | 0 | 0 | .319 | .364 |
| 2B | Jim Connor | | 138 | 505 | 114 | 9 | 9 | 0 | 0.0 | 51 | 67 | 42 | | 11 | 0 | 0 | .226 | .279 |
| SS | Bill Dahlen | R | 142 | 524 | 152 | 35 | 8 | 1 | 0.2 | 96 | 79 | 58 | | 27 | 0 | 0 | .290 | .393 |
| 3B | Barry McCormick | | 137 | 530 | 131 | 15 | 9 | 2 | 0.4 | 76 | 78 | 47 | | 15 | 0 | 0 | .247 | .321 |
| RF | Sam Mertes | R | 83 | 269 | 80 | 4 | 8 | 1 | 0.4 | 45 | 47 | 34 | | 27 | 5 | 0 | .297 | .383 |
| CF | Bill Lange | R | 113 | 442 | 141 | 16 | 10 | 6 | 1.4 | 79 | 69 | 36 | | 22 | 0 | 0 | .319 | .441 |
| LF | Jimmy Ryan | R | 144 | 572 | 185 | 32 | 13 | 4 | 0.7 | 122 | 79 | 73 | | 29 | 0 | 0 | .323 | .446 |
| C | Tim Donahue | L | 122 | 396 | 87 | 12 | 3 | 0 | 0.0 | 52 | 39 | 49 | | 17 | 0 | 0 | .220 | .265 |
| **SUBSTITUTES** | | | | | | | | | | | | | | | | | | |
| 3B | Harry Wolverton | L | 13 | 49 | 16 | 1 | 0 | 0 | 0.0 | 4 | 2 | 1 | | 1 | 0 | 0 | .327 | .347 |
| 2B | Frank Martin | | 1 | 4 | 0 | 0 | 0 | 0 | 0.0 | 0 | 0 | 0 | | 0 | 0 | 0 | .000 | .000 |
| OP | Walter Thornton | | 62 | 210 | 62 | 5 | 2 | 0 | 0.0 | 34 | 14 | 22 | | 8 | 2 | 0 | .295 | .338 |
| OF | Danny Green | L | 47 | 188 | 59 | 4 | 3 | 4 | 2.1 | 26 | 27 | 7 | | 12 | 0 | 0 | .314 | .431 |
| PO | Nixey Callahan | R | 43 | 164 | 43 | 7 | 5 | 0 | 0.0 | 27 | 22 | 4 | | 3 | 0 | 0 | .262 | .366 |
| UT | Frank Isbell | L | 45 | 159 | 37 | 4 | 0 | 0 | 0.0 | 17 | 8 | 3 | | 3 | 0 | 0 | .233 | .258 |
| UT | Walt Woods | | 48 | 154 | 27 | 1 | 0 | 0 | 0.0 | 16 | 8 | 4 | | 3 | 0 | 0 | .175 | .182 |
| PO | Matt Kilroy | L | 26 | 96 | 22 | 4 | 1 | 0 | 0.0 | 20 | 10 | 13 | | 0 | 1 | 0 | .229 | .292 |
| PO | Henry Clarke | R | 2 | 4 | 1 | 0 | 0 | 0 | 0.0 | 0 | 0 | 1 | | 0 | 0 | 0 | .250 | .250 |
| CO | Frank Chance | R | 53 | 147 | 42 | 4 | 3 | 1 | 0.7 | 32 | 14 | 7 | | 7 | 2 | 1 | .286 | .374 |
| C | Art Nichols | R | 14 | 42 | 12 | 1 | 0 | 0 | 0.0 | 7 | 6 | 4 | | 6 | 0 | 0 | .286 | .310 |
| **PITCHERS** | | | | | | | | | | | | | | | | | | |
| P | Clark Griffith | R | 38 | 122 | 20 | 2 | 3 | 0 | 0.0 | 15 | 15 | 13 | | 1 | 0 | 0 | .164 | .230 |
| P | Jack Taylor | R | 5 | 15 | 3 | 2 | 0 | 0 | 0.0 | 4 | 2 | 3 | | 0 | 0 | 0 | .200 | .333 |
| P | Buttons Briggs | R | 4 | 14 | 6 | 1 | 0 | 0 | 0.0 | 2 | 1 | 0 | | 0 | 0 | 0 | .429 | .500 |
| P | Bill Phyle | | 4 | 9 | 1 | 0 | 0 | 0 | 0.0 | 1 | 0 | 2 | | 0 | 0 | 0 | .111 | .111 |
| P | Danny Friend | | 2 | 7 | 2 | 1 | 0 | 0 | 0.0 | 0 | 0 | 0 | | 0 | 0 | 0 | .286 | .429 |
| P | John Katoll | R | 2 | 4 | 0 | 0 | 0 | 0 | 0.0 | 0 | 0 | 0 | | 0 | 0 | 0 | .000 | .000 |
| | TEAM TOTAL | | | 5222 | 1433 | 175 | 83 | 19 | 0.4 | 82 | 656 | 476 | 0 | 220 | 10 | 1 | .274 | .351 |

## INDIVIDUAL FIELDING

| POS | Player | T | G | PO | A | E | DP | TC/G | FA | | POS | Player | T | G | PO | A | E | DP | TC/G | FA |
|---|---|---|---|---|---|---|---|---|---|---|---|---|---|---|---|---|---|---|---|---|
| 1B | B. Everett | R | 149 | 1519 | 70 | 42 | 123 | 10.9 | .974 | | OF | J. Ryan | L | 144 | 267 | 20 | 27 | 2 | 2.2 | .914 |
| | F. Chance | R | 3 | 18 | 0 | 2 | 0 | 6.7 | .900 | | | B. Lange | R | 111 | 269 | 19 | 9 | 4 | 2.7 | .970 |
| | B. Lange | R | 2 | 17 | 0 | 0 | 1 | 8.5 | 1.000 | | | S. Mertes | R | 60 | 97 | 13 | 15 | 6 | 2.1 | .880 |
| | N. Callahan | R | 1 | 1 | 0 | 0 | 0 | 1.0 | 1.000 | | | D. Green | | 47 | 87 | 10 | 3 | 5 | 2.1 | .970 |
| | S. Mertes | R | 2 | 1 | 0 | 0 | 0 | 0.5 | 1.000 | | | W. Thornton | L | 34 | 66 | 5 | 10 | 2 | 2.4 | .877 |
| 2B | J. Connor | | 138 | 330 | 437 | 44 | 75 | 5.9 | .946 | | | F. Isbell | R | 28 | 40 | 3 | 2 | 0 | 1.6 | .956 |
| | S. Mertes | | 4 | 11 | 17 | 5 | 6 | 8.3 | .848 | | | F. Chance | R | 17 | 23 | 5 | 7 | 1 | 2.1 | .800 |
| | W. Woods | R | 6 | 4 | 16 | 2 | 1 | 3.7 | .909 | | | H. Clarke | R | 1 | 0 | 0 | 0 | 0 | 0.0 | .000 |
| | F. Isbell | R | 3 | 2 | 8 | 5 | 0 | 5.0 | .667 | | | M. Kilroy | L | 12 | 14 | 2 | 1 | 1 | 1.4 | .941 |
| | F. Martin | | 1 | 5 | 2 | 0 | 0 | 7.0 | 1.000 | | | N. Callahan | R | 9 | 10 | 2 | 3 | 0 | 1.7 | .800 |
| | McCormick | R | 1 | 2 | 3 | 1 | 0 | 6.0 | .833 | | | W. Woods | R | 11 | 8 | 2 | 0 | 0 | 0.9 | 1.000 |
| | N. Callahan | R | 1 | 1 | 0 | 1 | 0 | 2.0 | .500 | | C | T. Donahue | R | 122 | 450 | 107 | 22 | 16 | 4.7 | .962 |
| SS | B. Dahlen | R | 142 | 369 | 511 | 76 | 77 | 6.7 | .921 | | | F. Chance | R | 33 | 62 | 14 | 4 | 3 | 2.4 | .950 |
| | S. Mertes | R | 14 | 19 | 23 | 7 | 4 | 3.5 | .857 | | | A. Nichols | R | 14 | 47 | 13 | 2 | 1 | 4.4 | .968 |
| | W. Woods | R | 3 | 7 | 8 | 5 | 1 | 6.7 | .750 | | | | | | | | | | | |
| | F. Isbell | R | 2 | 3 | 6 | 3 | 2 | 6.0 | .750 | | | | | | | | | | | |
| | N. Callahan | R | 1 | 3 | 2 | 2 | 0 | 7.0 | .714 | | | | | | | | | | | |
| | McCormick | R | 1 | 1 | 1 | 2 | 0 | 4.0 | .500 | | | | | | | | | | | |
| 3B | McCormick | R | 136 | 152 | 322 | 60 | 31 | 3.9 | .888 | | | | | | | | | | | |
| | H. Wolverton | R | 13 | 21 | 35 | 10 | 1 | 5.1 | .848 | | | | | | | | | | | |
| | F. Isbell | R | 3 | 2 | 7 | 3 | 1 | 4.0 | .750 | | | | | | | | | | | |
| | W. Woods | R | 3 | 4 | 5 | 3 | 0 | 4.0 | .750 | | | | | | | | | | | |

February 1, 1898 marked the end of an era when Cap Anson was given his pink slip and replaced by former infielder Tommy Burns. Without Anson, the Colts became the Orphans, a nickname that stuck for the next three years.

They finished a strong fourth in Burns's first season, thanks mainly to their pitching. The staff ERA of 2.83 was best in the league. Griffith enjoyed his greatest year with a 26–10 mark and a 1.88 ERA. Nixey Callahan posted 20 wins. Walt Thornton, whose career was otherwise undistinguished, hurled a 2–0 no-hitter against Brooklyn on August 21.

Rookie outfielder Danny Green displayed skill both at bat and on the basepaths, as did Sam Mertes, another newcomer. Jack Taylor, a freshman pitcher, had a spectacular late-season debut, hurling five complete games and winning all of them. Everett was moved to first base in place of the retired Anson. He was just as poor a fielder at first as at third, but continued to hit well.

Although the fans resented the firing of Anson, it did not prevent them from coming to the park in record numbers. For the first time in Chicago baseball, home attendance climbed over the 400,000 mark.

## TEAM STATISTICS

| | W | L | PCT | GB | R | OR | 2B | Batting 3B | HR | BA | SA | SB | Fielding E | DP | FA | CG | B | Pitching SO | ShO | SV | ERA |
|---|---|---|---|---|---|---|---|---|---|---|---|---|---|---|---|---|---|---|---|---|---|
| BOS | 102 | 47 | .685 | | 872 | 614 | 190 | 55 | **53** | .290 | **.377** | 172 | 310 | 102 | .950 | 127 | 470 | 432 | 9 | **7** | 2.98 |
| BAL | 96 | 53 | .644 | 6 | **933** | 623 | 154 | 77 | 12 | **.302** | .368 | **250** | 326 | 105 | .947 | 138 | 400 | 422 | 12 | 0 | 2.90 |
| CIN | 92 | 60 | .605 | 11.5 | 831 | 740 | 207 | **101** | 19 | .271 | .359 | 165 | 325 | 128 | .950 | 131 | 449 | 294 | 10 | 2 | 3.50 |
| CHI | 85 | 65 | .567 | 17.5 | 828 | 679 | 175 | 83 | 19 | .274 | .350 | 220 | 412 | **149** | .936 | 137 | 364 | 323 | **13** | 0 | **2.83** |
| CLE | 81 | 68 | .544 | 21 | 730 | 683 | 162 | 56 | 18 | .263 | .325 | 93 | **301** | 95 | **.952** | **142** | **309** | 339 | 9 | 0 | 3.20 |
| PHI | 78 | 71 | .523 | 24 | 823 | 784 | **238** | 81 | 33 | .280 | .377 | 182 | 379 | 102 | .937 | 129 | 399 | 325 | 10 | 0 | 3.72 |
| NY | 77 | 73 | .513 | 25.5 | 837 | 800 | 190 | 86 | 33 | .266 | .352 | 214 | 447 | 113 | .932 | 141 | 587 | **558** | 9 | 1 | 3.44 |
| PIT | 72 | 76 | .486 | 29.5 | 634 | 694 | 140 | 88 | 14 | .258 | .328 | 107 | 340 | 105 | .946 | 131 | 346 | 330 | 10 | 3 | 3.41 |
| LOU | 70 | 81 | .464 | 33 | 728 | 833 | 150 | 71 | 32 | .267 | .342 | 235 | 382 | 114 | .939 | 137 | 470 | 271 | 4 | 0 | 4.24 |
| BKN | 54 | 91 | .372 | 46 | 638 | 811 | 156 | 66 | 17 | .256 | .322 | 130 | 334 | 125 | .947 | 134 | 476 | 294 | 1 | 0 | 4.01 |
| WAS | 51 | 101 | .336 | 52.5 | 704 | 939 | 177 | 81 | 35 | .271 | .355 | 197 | 443 | 119 | .929 | 129 | 450 | 371 | 0 | 1 | 4.52 |
| STL | 39 | 111 | .260 | 63.5 | 571 | 929 | 149 | 55 | 13 | .247 | .305 | 104 | 388 | 97 | .939 | 133 | 372 | 288 | 0 | 2 | 4.53 |
| LEAGUE TOTAL | | | | | 9129 | 9129 | 2088 | 900 | 298 | .271 | .347 | 2069 | 4387 | 1354 | .942 | 1609 | 5092 | 4247 | 87 | 16 | 3.60 |

## INDIVIDUAL PITCHING

| PITCHER | T | W | L | PCT | ERA | SV | G | GS | CG | IP | H | BB | SO | R | ER | ShO | H/9 | BB/9 | SO/9 |
|---|---|---|---|---|---|---|---|---|---|---|---|---|---|---|---|---|---|---|---|
| Clark Griffith | R | 26 | 10 | .722 | **1.88** | 0 | 38 | 38 | 36 | 325.2 | 305 | 64 | 97 | 105 | 68 | 4 | 8.43 | 1.77 | 2.68 |
| Nixey Callahan | R | 20 | 10 | .667 | 2.46 | 0 | 31 | 31 | 30 | 274.1 | 267 | 71 | 73 | 137 | 75 | 2 | 8.76 | 2.33 | 2.39 |
| Walter Thornton | L | 13 | 10 | .565 | 3.34 | 0 | 28 | 25 | 21 | 215.1 | 226 | 56 | 56 | 116 | 80 | 2 | 9.45 | 2.34 | 2.34 |
| Walt Woods | R | 9 | 13 | .409 | 3.14 | 0 | 27 | 22 | 18 | 215 | 224 | 59 | 26 | 128 | 75 | 3 | 9.38 | 2.47 | 1.09 |
| Matt Kilroy | L | 6 | 7 | .462 | 4.31 | 0 | 13 | 11 | 10 | 100.1 | 119 | 30 | 18 | 67 | 48 | 0 | 10.67 | 2.69 | 1.61 |
| Frank Isbell | R | 4 | 7 | .364 | 3.56 | 0 | 13 | 9 | 7 | 81 | 86 | 42 | 16 | 54 | 32 | 0 | 9.56 | 4.67 | 1.78 |
| Jack Taylor | R | 5 | 0 | 1.000 | 2.20 | 0 | 5 | 5 | 5 | 41 | 32 | 10 | 11 | 12 | 10 | 0 | 7.02 | 2.20 | 2.41 |
| Buttons Briggs | R | 1 | 3 | .250 | 5.70 | 0 | 4 | 4 | 3 | 30 | 38 | 10 | 14 | 22 | 19 | 0 | 11.40 | 3.00 | 4.20 |
| Bill Phyle | R | 2 | 1 | .667 | 0.78 | 0 | 3 | 3 | 3 | 23 | 24 | 6 | 4 | 15 | 2 | 2 | 9.39 | 2.35 | 1.57 |
| Danny Friend | L | 0 | 2 | .000 | 5.29 | 0 | 2 | 2 | 2 | 17 | 20 | 10 | 4 | 15 | 10 | 0 | 10.59 | 5.29 | 2.12 |
| John Katoll | R | 0 | 1 | .000 | 0.82 | 0 | 2 | 1 | 1 | 11 | 8 | 1 | 3 | 4 | 1 | 0 | 6.55 | 0.82 | 2.45 |
| Henry Clarke | R | 1 | 0 | 1.000 | 2.00 | 0 | 1 | 1 | 1 | 9 | 8 | 5 | 1 | 4 | 2 | 0 | 8.00 | 5.00 | 1.00 |
| TEAM TOTAL | | 87 | 64 | .576 | 2.83 | 0 | 167 | 152 | 137 | 1342.2 | 1357 | 364 | 323 | 679 | 422 | 13 | 9.10 | 2.44 | 2.17 |

| MANAGER | W | L | PCT |
|---|---|---|---|
| Tom Burns | 75 | 73 | .507 |

| POS | Player | B | G | AB | H | 2B | 3B | HR | HR % | R | RBI | BB | SO | SB | Pinch Hit AB | Pinch Hit H | BA | SA |
|---|---|---|---|---|---|---|---|---|---|---|---|---|---|---|---|---|---|---|
| **REGULARS** | | | | | | | | | | | | | | | | | | |
| 1B | Bill Everett | L | 136 | 536 | 166 | 17 | 5 | 1 | 0.2 | 87 | 74 | 31 | | 30 | 0 | 0 | .310 | .366 |
| 2B | Barry McCormick | | 102 | 376 | 97 | 15 | 2 | 2 | 0.5 | 48 | 52 | 25 | | 14 | 0 | 0 | .258 | .324 |
| SS | Gene DeMontreville | R | 82 | 310 | 87 | 6 | 3 | 0 | 0.0 | 43 | 40 | 17 | | 26 | 0 | 0 | .281 | .319 |
| 3B | Harry Wolverton | L | 99 | 389 | 111 | 14 | 11 | 1 | 0.3 | 50 | 49 | 30 | | 14 | 0 | 0 | .285 | .386 |
| RF | Danny Green | L | 117 | 475 | 140 | 12 | 11 | 6 | 1.3 | 90 | 56 | 35 | | 18 | 2 | 0 | .295 | .404 |
| CF | Bill Lange | R | 107 | 416 | 135 | 21 | 7 | 1 | 0.2 | 81 | 58 | 38 | | 41 | 0 | 0 | .325 | .416 |
| LF | Jimmy Ryan | R | 125 | 525 | 158 | 20 | 10 | 3 | 0.6 | 91 | 68 | 43 | | 9 | 0 | 0 | .301 | .394 |
| C | Tim Donahue | L | 92 | 278 | 69 | 9 | 3 | 0 | 0.0 | 39 | 29 | 34 | | 10 | 0 | 0 | .248 | .302 |
| **SUBSTITUTES** | | | | | | | | | | | | | | | | | | |
| 23 | Jim Connor | | 69 | 234 | 48 | 7 | 1 | 0 | 0.0 | 26 | 24 | 18 | | 6 | 0 | 0 | .205 | .244 |
| SS | George Magoon | R | 59 | 189 | 43 | 5 | 1 | 0 | 0.0 | 24 | 21 | 24 | | 5 | 0 | 0 | .228 | .265 |
| 3B | Bill Bradley | R | 35 | 129 | 40 | 6 | 1 | 2 | 1.6 | 26 | 18 | 12 | | 4 | 0 | 0 | .310 | .419 |
| 2B | Doc Curley | R | 10 | 37 | 4 | 0 | 1 | 0 | 0.0 | 7 | 2 | 3 | | 0 | 0 | 0 | .108 | .162 |
| OF | Sam Mertes | R | 117 | 426 | 127 | 13 | 16 | 9 | 2.1 | 83 | 81 | 33 | | 45 | 5 | 1 | .298 | .467 |
| PO | Nixey Callahan | R | 47 | 150 | 39 | 4 | 3 | 0 | 0.0 | 21 | 18 | 8 | | 9 | 1 | 0 | .260 | .327 |
| OF | Frank Quinn | | 12 | 34 | 6 | 0 | 1 | 0 | 0.0 | 6 | 1 | 6 | | 1 | 1 | 0 | .176 | .235 |
| PO | Dick Cogan | R | 8 | 25 | 5 | 1 | 2 | 0 | 0.0 | 4 | 4 | 2 | | 0 | 0 | 0 | .200 | .400 |
| C | Frank Chance | R | 64 | 192 | 55 | 6 | 2 | 1 | 0.5 | 37 | 22 | 15 | | 10 | 3 | 0 | .286 | .354 |
| C | Art Nichols | R | 17 | 47 | 12 | 2 | 0 | 1 | 2.1 | 5 | 11 | 0 | | 3 | 2 | 0 | .255 | .362 |
| **PITCHERS** | | | | | | | | | | | | | | | | | | |
| P | Jack Taylor | R | 42 | 139 | 37 | 9 | 2 | 0 | 0.0 | 25 | 17 | 16 | | 0 | 1 | 1 | .266 | .360 |
| P | Clark Griffith | R | 39 | 120 | 31 | 5 | 0 | 0 | 0.0 | 15 | 14 | 14 | | 2 | 0 | 0 | .258 | .300 |
| P | Ned Garvin | | 24 | 71 | 11 | 0 | 0 | 0 | 0.0 | 1 | 1 | 1 | | 0 | 0 | 0 | .155 | .155 |
| P | Bill Phyle | | 10 | 34 | 6 | 0 | 0 | 0 | 0.0 | 2 | 1 | 0 | | 0 | 0 | 0 | .176 | .176 |
| P | John Katoll | R | 2 | 7 | 0 | 0 | 0 | 0 | 0.0 | 0 | 0 | 0 | | 0 | 0 | 0 | .000 | .000 |
| P | John Malarkey | | 1 | 5 | 1 | 1 | 0 | 0 | 0.0 | 0 | 0 | 0 | | 0 | 0 | 0 | .200 | .400 |
| P | Skel Roach | R | 1 | 4 | 0 | 0 | 0 | 0 | 0.0 | 0 | 0 | 0 | | 0 | 0 | 0 | .000 | .000 |
| | TEAM TOTAL | | | 5148 | 1428 | 173 | 82 | 27 | 0.5 | 81 | 661 | 406 | 0 | 247 | 15 | 2 | .277 | .359 |

## INDIVIDUAL FIELDING

| POS | Player | T | G | PO | A | E | DP | TC/G | FA |
|---|---|---|---|---|---|---|---|---|---|
| 1B | B. Everett | R | 136 | **1491** | 95 | **47** | 103 | 12.0 | .971 |
| | B. Lange | R | 14 | 149 | 4 | 5 | 9 | 11.3 | .968 |
| | S. Mertes | R | 3 | 24 | 4 | 2 | 4 | 10.0 | .933 |
| | F. Chance | R | 1 | 2 | 0 | 0 | 0 | 2.0 | 1.000 |
| | T. Donahue | R | 1 | 1 | 0 | 0 | 0 | 1.0 | 1.000 |
| 2B | McCormick | R | 99 | 200 | 344 | 34 | 47 | 5.8 | .941 |
| | J. Connor | | 44 | 82 | 147 | 14 | 20 | 5.5 | .942 |
| | D. Curley | R | 10 | 12 | 27 | 4 | 2 | 4.3 | .907 |
| | N. Callahan | R | 1 | 3 | 4 | 0 | 1 | 7.0 | 1.000 |
| | F. Quinn | | 1 | 0 | 1 | 0 | 0 | 1.0 | 1.000 |
| SS | DeMontreville | R | 82 | 192 | 306 | 54 | 38 | 6.7 | .902 |
| | G. Magoon | R | 59 | 138 | 216 | 41 | 34 | 6.7 | .896 |
| | B. Bradley | R | 5 | 15 | 14 | 8 | 1 | 7.4 | .784 |
| | McCormick | R | 3 | 5 | 7 | 3 | 2 | 5.0 | .800 |
| | N. Callahan | R | 2 | 4 | 4 | 2 | 1 | 5.0 | .800 |
| | S. Mertes | R | 1 | 2 | 3 | 1 | 1 | 6.0 | .833 |
| | C. Griffith | R | 1 | 1 | 1 | 2 | 0 | 4.0 | .500 |
| | H. Wolverton | R | 1 | 1 | 1 | 1 | 0 | 3.0 | .667 |
| 3B | H. Wolverton | R | 98 | 123 | 227 | 57 | 12 | 4.2 | .860 |
| | B. Bradley | R | 30 | 46 | 68 | 15 | 7 | 4.3 | .884 |
| | J. Connor | | 25 | 19 | 64 | 12 | 5 | 3.8 | .874 |

| POS | Player | T | G | PO | A | E | DP | TC/G | FA |
|---|---|---|---|---|---|---|---|---|---|
| OF | J. Ryan | L | 125 | 266 | 18 | 13 | 6 | 2.4 | .956 |
| | B. Lange | R | 94 | 224 | 22 | 6 | 11 | 2.7 | .976 |
| | S. Mertes | R | 108 | 197 | 20 | 18 | 4 | 2.2 | .923 |
| | D. Green | | 115 | 175 | 22 | 11 | 11 | 1.8 | .947 |
| | N. Callahan | R | 9 | 15 | 0 | 0 | 0 | 1.7 | 1.000 |
| | F. Quinn | | 10 | 10 | 0 | 1 | 0 | 1.1 | .909 |
| | D. Cogan | R | 3 | 3 | 0 | 0 | 0 | 1.0 | 1.000 |
| C | T. Donahue | R | 91 | 304 | 100 | 21 | 13 | 4.7 | .951 |
| | F. Chance | R | 57 | 166 | 64 | 12 | 6 | 4.2 | .950 |
| | A. Nichols | R | 15 | 44 | 10 | 4 | 3 | 3.9 | .931 |

Following the Orphans' strong showing in 1898, the new season began with great expectations. Off to a fast start, the team was consistently at or near the lead during the early part of the year, and fan enthusiasm was never higher. On April 30, a crowd of 27,489—the largest in baseball history at that point—paid its way into West Side Grounds to see a 4–0 victory over the Cardinals.

However, by mid-July the Cubs had settled firmly in the second division, finally ending in eighth place. Bill Dahlen had been traded over the winter, and his loss weakened an infield front line that was already lackluster. Callahan and Griffith each topped 20 wins (Griffith for the sixth straight year) but Taylor did not live up to expectations, nor did Ned Garvin.

Batting and base-stealing remained strong as Ryan, Lange, Green, Mertes, and Everett all had productive seasons. However, at the end of the season Lange retired at the peak of his career. His departure had a devastating effect on the team's already numerous problems. Finally, Burns was fired as manager.

### TEAM STATISTICS

| | W | L | PCT | GB | R | OR | 2B | 3B | Batting HR | BA | SA | SB | E | Fielding DP | FA | CG | B | Pitching SO | ShO | SV | ERA |
|---|---|---|---|---|---|---|---|---|---|---|---|---|---|---|---|---|---|---|---|---|---|
| BKN | 101 | 47 | .682 | | 892 | 658 | 178 | 97 | 26 | .291 | .382 | 271 | 314 | 125 | .948 | 121 | 463 | 331 | 9 | 9 | **3.25** |
| BOS | 95 | 57 | .625 | 8 | 858 | **645** | 178 | 89 | 40 | .287 | .377 | 185 | **303** | 124 | **.952** | 138 | 432 | 385 | 13 | 4 | 3.26 |
| PHI | 94 | 58 | .618 | 9 | **916** | 743 | **241** | 84 | 30 | **.301** | **.395** | 212 | 379 | 110 | .940 | 129 | 370 | 281 | **15** | 2 | 3.47 |
| BAL | 86 | 62 | .581 | 15 | 827 | 691 | 204 | 71 | 17 | .297 | .376 | **364** | 308 | 96 | .949 | 133 | 349 | 294 | 9 | 4 | 3.31 |
| STL | 84 | 67 | .556 | 18.5 | 819 | 739 | 172 | 89 | 46 | .285 | .377 | 210 | 397 | 117 | .939 | 134 | **321** | 331 | 7 | 1 | 3.36 |
| CIN | 83 | 67 | .553 | 19 | 856 | 770 | 194 | 105 | 13 | .275 | .360 | 228 | 339 | 111 | .947 | 130 | 370 | 360 | 8 | 5 | 3.70 |
| PIT | 76 | 73 | .510 | 25.5 | 834 | 765 | 196 | **121** | 27 | .289 | .384 | 179 | 361 | 98 | .945 | 117 | 437 | 334 | 9 | 4 | 3.60 |
| CHI | 75 | 73 | .507 | 26 | 812 | 763 | 173 | 82 | 27 | .277 | .359 | 247 | 428 | **145** | .935 | **147** | 330 | 313 | 8 | 1 | 3.37 |
| LOU | 75 | 77 | .493 | 28 | 827 | 775 | 192 | 68 | 40 | .280 | .364 | 233 | 394 | 102 | .939 | 134 | 323 | 287 | 5 | 2 | 3.45 |
| NY | 60 | 90 | .400 | 42 | 734 | 863 | 161 | 65 | 23 | .281 | .352 | 234 | 433 | 140 | .932 | 138 | 628 | **397** | 4 | 0 | 4.29 |
| WAS | 54 | 98 | .355 | 49 | 743 | 983 | 162 | 87 | **47** | .272 | .363 | 176 | 403 | 99 | .935 | 131 | 422 | 328 | 3 | 0 | 4.93 |
| CLE | 20 | 134 | .130 | 84 | 529 | 1252 | 142 | 50 | 12 | .253 | .305 | 127 | 388 | 121 | .937 | 138 | 527 | 215 | 0 | 0 | 6.37 |
| LEAGUE TOTAL | | | | | 9647 | 9647 | 2193 | 1008 | 348 | .282 | .366 | 2666 | 4447 | 1388 | .942 | 1590 | 4972 | 3856 | 90 | 32 | 3.85 |

### INDIVIDUAL PITCHING

| PITCHER | T | W | L | PCT | ERA | SV | G | GS | CG | IP | H | BB | SO | R | ER | ShO | H/9 | BB/9 | SO/9 |
|---|---|---|---|---|---|---|---|---|---|---|---|---|---|---|---|---|---|---|---|
| Jack Taylor | R | 18 | 21 | .462 | 3.76 | 0 | 41 | 39 | 39 | 354.2 | 380 | 84 | 67 | 223 | 148 | 1 | 9.64 | 2.13 | 1.70 |
| Clark Griffith | R | 22 | 13 | .629 | 2.79 | 0 | 38 | 38 | 35 | 319.2 | 329 | 65 | 73 | 163 | 99 | 0 | 9.26 | 1.83 | 2.06 |
| Nixey Callahan | R | 21 | 12 | .636 | 3.06 | 0 | 35 | 34 | 33 | 294.1 | 327 | 76 | 77 | 155 | 100 | 3 | 10.00 | 2.32 | 2.35 |
| Ned Garvin | R | 9 | 13 | .409 | 2.85 | 0 | 24 | 23 | 22 | 199 | 202 | 42 | 69 | 101 | 63 | 4 | 9.14 | 1.90 | 3.12 |
| Bill Phyle | R | 1 | 8 | .111 | 4.20 | 1 | 10 | 9 | 9 | 83.2 | 92 | 29 | 10 | 58 | 39 | 0 | 9.90 | 3.12 | 1.08 |
| Dick Cogan | R | 2 | 3 | .400 | 4.30 | 0 | 5 | 5 | 5 | 44 | 54 | 24 | 9 | 32 | 21 | 0 | 11.05 | 4.91 | 1.84 |
| John Katoll | R | 1 | 1 | .500 | 6.00 | 0 | 2 | 2 | 2 | 18 | 17 | 4 | 1 | 15 | 12 | 0 | 8.50 | 2.00 | 0.50 |
| John Malarkey | R | 0 | 1 | .000 | 13.00 | 0 | 1 | 1 | 1 | 9 | 19 | 5 | 7 | 13 | 13 | 0 | 19.00 | 5.00 | 7.00 |
| Skel Roach | R | 1 | 0 | 1.000 | 3.00 | 0 | 1 | 1 | 1 | 9 | 13 | 1 | 0 | 3 | 3 | 0 | 13.00 | 1.00 | 0.00 |
| TEAM TOTAL | | 75 | 72 | .510 | 3.37 | 1 | 157 | 152 | 147 | 1331.1 | 1433 | 330 | 313 | 763 | 498 | 8 | 9.69 | 2.23 | 2.12 |

| MANAGER | W | L | PCT |
|---|---|---|---|
| Tom Loftus | 65 | 75 | .464 |

| POS | Player | B | G | AB | H | 2B | 3B | HR | HR % | R | RBI | BB | SO | SB | Pinch Hit AB | Pinch Hit H | BA | SA |
|---|---|---|---|---|---|---|---|---|---|---|---|---|---|---|---|---|---|---|
| **REGULARS** | | | | | | | | | | | | | | | | | | |
| 1B | John Ganzel | R | 78 | 284 | 78 | 14 | 4 | 4 | 1.4 | 29 | 32 | 10 | | 5 | 0 | 0 | .275 | .394 |
| 2B | Cupid Childs | L | 138 | 538 | 131 | 14 | 5 | 0 | 0.0 | 70 | 44 | 57 | | 15 | 0 | 0 | .243 | .288 |
| SS | Barry McCormick | | 110 | 379 | 83 | 13 | 5 | 3 | 0.8 | 35 | 48 | 38 | | 8 | 0 | 0 | .219 | .303 |
| 3B | Bill Bradley | R | 122 | 444 | 125 | 21 | 8 | 5 | 1.1 | 63 | 49 | 27 | | 14 | 1 | 1 | .282 | .399 |
| RF | Jimmy Ryan | R | 105 | 415 | 115 | 25 | 4 | 5 | 1.2 | 66 | 59 | 29 | | 19 | 0 | 0 | .277 | .393 |
| CF | Danny Green | L | 103 | 389 | 116 | 21 | 5 | 5 | 1.3 | 63 | 49 | 17 | | 28 | 2 | 1 | .298 | .416 |
| LF | Jack McCarthy | L | 124 | 503 | 148 | 16 | 7 | 0 | 0.0 | 68 | 48 | 24 | | 22 | 1 | 0 | .294 | .354 |
| C | Tim Donahue | L | 67 | 216 | 51 | 10 | 1 | 0 | 0.0 | 21 | 17 | 19 | | 8 | 0 | 0 | .236 | .292 |
| **SUBSTITUTES** | | | | | | | | | | | | | | | | | | |
| SS | Billy Clingman | B | 47 | 159 | 33 | 6 | 0 | 0 | 0.0 | 15 | 11 | 17 | | 6 | 0 | 0 | .208 | .245 |
| 3S | Sammy Strang | B | 27 | 102 | 29 | 3 | 0 | 0 | 0.0 | 15 | 9 | 8 | | 1 | 0 | 0 | .284 | .314 |
| 1B | Bill Everett | L | 23 | 91 | 24 | 4 | 0 | 0 | 0.0 | 10 | 17 | 3 | | 2 | 0 | 0 | .264 | .308 |
| 3B | Harry Wolverton | L | 3 | 11 | 2 | 0 | 0 | 0 | 0.0 | 2 | 0 | 2 | | 1 | 0 | 0 | .182 | .182 |
| O1 | Sam Mertes | R | 127 | 481 | 142 | 25 | 4 | 7 | 1.5 | 72 | 60 | 42 | | 38 | 0 | 0 | .295 | .407 |
| OF | Cozy Dolan | L | 13 | 48 | 13 | 1 | 0 | 0 | 0.0 | 5 | 2 | 2 | | 2 | 0 | 0 | .271 | .292 |
| OF | Sam Dungan | R | 6 | 15 | 4 | 0 | 0 | 0 | 0.0 | 1 | 1 | 1 | | 0 | 3 | 1 | .267 | .267 |
| C | Frank Chance | R | 56 | 151 | 46 | 8 | 4 | 0 | 0.0 | 26 | 13 | 15 | | 8 | 4 | 1 | .305 | .411 |
| CO | Charlie Dexter | | 40 | 125 | 25 | 5 | 0 | 2 | 1.6 | 7 | 20 | 1 | | 2 | 4 | 1 | .200 | .288 |
| C | Johnny Kling | R | 15 | 51 | 15 | 3 | 1 | 0 | 0.0 | 8 | 7 | 2 | | 0 | 0 | 0 | .294 | .392 |
| C | Art Nichols | R | 8 | 25 | 5 | 0 | 0 | 0 | 0.0 | 1 | 0 | 3 | | 1 | 1 | 0 | .200 | .200 |
| C | Roger Bresnahan | R | 2 | 2 | 0 | 0 | 0 | 0 | 0.0 | 0 | 0 | 0 | | 0 | 0 | 0 | .000 | .000 |
| **PITCHERS** | | | | | | | | | | | | | | | | | | |
| P | Nixey Callahan | R | 32 | 115 | 27 | 3 | 2 | 0 | 0.0 | 16 | 9 | 6 | | 5 | 0 | 0 | .235 | .296 |
| P | Clark Griffith | R | 30 | 95 | 24 | 4 | 1 | 1 | 1.1 | 16 | 7 | 8 | | 2 | 0 | 0 | .253 | .347 |
| P | Ned Garvin | | 30 | 91 | 14 | 1 | 0 | 0 | 0.0 | 12 | 4 | 3 | | 0 | 0 | 0 | .154 | .165 |
| P | Jack Taylor | R | 28 | 81 | 19 | 3 | 1 | 1 | 1.2 | 7 | 6 | 3 | | 1 | 0 | 0 | .235 | .333 |
| P | Jock Menefee | R | 17 | 46 | 5 | 0 | 0 | 0 | 0.0 | 5 | 4 | 2 | | 0 | 1 | 0 | .109 | .109 |
| P | Bert Cunningham | R | 8 | 27 | 4 | 1 | 0 | 0 | 0.0 | 5 | 1 | 1 | | 1 | 0 | 0 | .148 | .185 |
| P | Frank Killen | L | 6 | 20 | 3 | 0 | 0 | 0 | 0.0 | 5 | 0 | 2 | | 0 | 0 | 0 | .150 | .150 |
| P | Long Tom Hughes | R | 3 | 6 | 0 | 0 | 0 | 0 | 0.0 | 0 | 0 | 2 | | 0 | 0 | 0 | .000 | .000 |
| P | Mal Eason | | 1 | 3 | 0 | 0 | 0 | 0 | 0.0 | 0 | 0 | 0 | | 0 | 0 | 0 | .000 | .000 |
| P | Ervin Harvey | L | 2 | 3 | 0 | 0 | 0 | 0 | 0.0 | 0 | 0 | 0 | | 0 | 1 | 0 | .000 | .000 |
| TEAM TOTAL | | | | 4916 | 1281 | 201 | 52 | 33 | 0.7 | 63 | 519 | 343 | 0 | 189 | 18 | 5 | .261 | .343 |

## INDIVIDUAL FIELDING

| POS | Player | T | G | PO | A | E | DP | TC/G | FA |
|---|---|---|---|---|---|---|---|---|---|
| 1B | J. Ganzel | R | 78 | 817 | 34 | 17 | 40 | 11.1 | .980 |
| | S. Mertes | R | 33 | 340 | 17 | 10 | 16 | 11.1 | .973 |
| | B. Everett | R | 23 | 264 | 10 | 6 | 14 | 12.2 | .979 |
| | B. Bradley | R | 15 | 128 | 13 | 2 | 10 | 9.5 | .986 |
| | F. Chance | R | 1 | 5 | 1 | 1 | 0 | 7.0 | .857 |
| 2B | C. Childs | R | 137 | 323 | 431 | 52 | 57 | 5.9 | .935 |
| | McCormick | R | 5 | 8 | 14 | 3 | 1 | 5.0 | .880 |
| | S. Strang | R | 2 | 2 | 5 | 1 | 0 | 4.0 | .875 |
| | T. Donahue | R | 1 | 2 | 1 | 1 | 0 | 4.0 | .750 |
| | C. Dexter | R | 1 | 0 | 1 | 0 | 0 | 1.0 | 1.000 |
| SS | McCormick | R | 84 | 161 | 307 | 48 | 32 | 6.1 | .907 |
| | B. Clingman | R | 47 | 81 | 150 | 34 | 19 | 5.6 | .872 |
| | S. Strang | R | 9 | 12 | 26 | 9 | 2 | 5.2 | .809 |
| | S. Mertes | R | 7 | 12 | 19 | 2 | 2 | 4.7 | .939 |
| 3B | B. Bradley | R | 106 | 164 | 291 | 61 | 11 | 4.9 | .882 |
| | McCormick | R | 21 | 29 | 57 | 13 | 1 | 4.7 | .869 |
| | S. Strang | R | 16 | 16 | 31 | 6 | 3 | 3.3 | .887 |
| | H. Wolverton | R | 3 | 2 | 5 | 1 | 0 | 2.7 | .875 |

| POS | Player | T | G | PO | A | E | DP | TC/G | FA |
|---|---|---|---|---|---|---|---|---|---|
| OF | J. McCarthy | L | 123 | 233 | 20 | 15 | 4 | 2.2 | .944 |
| | D. Green | | 101 | 218 | 10 | 15 | 2 | 2.4 | .938 |
| | S. Mertes | R | 88 | 180 | 13 | 16 | 4 | 2.4 | .923 |
| | J. Ryan | L | 105 | 177 | 12 | 18 | 3 | 2.0 | .913 |
| | C. Dexter | R | 13 | 31 | 3 | 0 | 2 | 2.6 | 1.000 |
| | C. Dolan | L | 13 | 18 | 1 | 4 | 0 | 1.8 | .826 |
| | S. Dungan | | 3 | 4 | 0 | 1 | 0 | 1.7 | .800 |
| C | T. Donahue | R | 66 | 232 | 63 | 23 | 6 | 4.8 | .928 |
| | F. Chance | R | 51 | 155 | 65 | 16 | 2 | 4.6 | .932 |
| | C. Dexter | R | 22 | 67 | 33 | 6 | 2 | 4.8 | .943 |
| | J. Kling | R | 15 | 49 | 15 | 7 | 2 | 4.7 | .901 |
| | R. Bresnahan | R | 1 | 0 | 0 | 0 | 0 | 0.0 | .000 |
| | A. Nichols | R | 7 | 21 | 9 | 2 | 0 | 4.6 | .938 |

In the final year of the 19th century Tom Loftus was appointed the Orphans' new manager. Things looked fairly promising at the start, as the team played winning ball well into July. But eventually the leaky defense betrayed Chicago again, as it sank into a tie for fifth place with the Cardinals.

Clark Griffith renounced his old superstition about shutouts to lead the league with four, but otherwise it was a subpar year by his standards, as it was for Callahan. On May 17, Bill Everett was traded to Kansas City of the American League (still a minor circuit at that time) for first baseman John Ganzel. It was also the last year for veteran Jimmy Ryan, who was released in October; he was their last link to the great teams of the 1880s. Another changing of the guard came late in the year when Johnny Kling came up from the Western League team based in St. Louis, Missouri. Kling replaced Tim Donahue as the regular catcher. He was to be their first dependable receiver in more than a decade.

## TEAM STATISTICS

| | W | L | PCT | GB | R | OR | Batting 2B | 3B | HR | BA | SA | SB | Fielding E | DP | FA | CG | B | Pitching SO | ShO | SV | ERA |
|---|---|---|---|---|---|---|---|---|---|---|---|---|---|---|---|---|---|---|---|---|---|
| KN | 82 | 54 | .603 | | **816** | 722 | 199 | 81 | 26 | **.293** | **.383** | **274** | 303 | 102 | .948 | 104 | 405 | 300 | 8 | **4** | 3.89 |
| T | 79 | 60 | .568 | 4.5 | 733 | **612** | 185 | **100** | 25 | .272 | .368 | 174 | 322 | 106 | .945 | 114 | **295** | **415** | 11 | 1 | **3.06** |
| HI | 75 | 63 | .543 | 8 | 810 | 791 | 187 | 82 | 29 | .290 | .378 | 205 | 330 | **125** | .945 | 116 | 402 | 284 | 7 | 3 | 4.12 |
| OS | 66 | 72 | .478 | 17 | 778 | 739 | 163 | 68 | **48** | .283 | .373 | 182 | **273** | 86 | **.953** | 116 | 463 | 340 | 8 | 2 | 3.72 |
| HI | 65 | 75 | .464 | 19 | 635 | 751 | **202** | 51 | 33 | .260 | .342 | 189 | 418 | 98 | .933 | **137** | 324 | 357 | 9 | 1 | 3.23 |
| TL | 65 | 75 | .464 | 19 | 743 | 747 | 141 | 81 | 36 | .291 | .375 | 243 | 331 | 73 | .943 | 117 | 299 | 325 | **12** | 0 | 3.75 |
| N | 62 | 77 | .446 | 21.5 | 702 | 745 | 178 | 83 | 33 | .266 | .354 | 183 | 341 | 120 | .945 | 118 | 404 | 399 | 9 | 1 | 3.83 |
| Y | 60 | 78 | .435 | 23 | 713 | 823 | 177 | 61 | 23 | .279 | .357 | 236 | 439 | 124 | .928 | 114 | 442 | 277 | 4 | 0 | 3.96 |
| AGUE TOTAL | | | | | 5930 | 5930 | 1432 | 607 | 253 | .279 | .366 | 1686 | 2757 | 834 | .942 | 936 | 3034 | 2697 | 68 | 12 | 3.69 |

## INDIVIDUAL PITCHING

| TCHER | T | W | L | PCT | ERA | SV | G | GS | CG | IP | H | BB | SO | R | ER | ShO | H/9 | BB/9 | SO/9 |
|---|---|---|---|---|---|---|---|---|---|---|---|---|---|---|---|---|---|---|---|
| ixey Callahan | R | 13 | 16 | .448 | 3.82 | 0 | 32 | 32 | 32 | 285.1 | 347 | 74 | 77 | 195 | 121 | 2 | 10.95 | 2.33 | 2.43 |
| ark Griffith | R | 14 | 13 | .519 | 3.05 | 0 | 30 | 30 | 27 | 248 | 245 | 51 | 61 | 126 | 84 | 4 | 8.89 | 1.85 | 2.21 |
| ed Garvin | R | 10 | 18 | .357 | 2.41 | 0 | 30 | 28 | 25 | 246.1 | 225 | 63 | 107 | 126 | 66 | 1 | 8.22 | 2.30 | 3.91 |
| ck Taylor | R | 10 | 17 | .370 | 2.55 | 1 | 28 | 26 | 25 | 222.1 | 226 | 58 | 57 | 130 | 63 | 2 | 9.15 | 2.35 | 2.31 |
| ck Menefee | R | 9 | 4 | .692 | 3.85 | 0 | 16 | 13 | 11 | 117 | 140 | 35 | 30 | 74 | 50 | 0 | 10.77 | 2.69 | 2.31 |
| ert Cunningham | R | 4 | 3 | .571 | 4.36 | 0 | 8 | 7 | 7 | 64 | 84 | 21 | 7 | 53 | 31 | 0 | 11.81 | 2.95 | 0.98 |
| ank Killen | L | 3 | 3 | .500 | 4.67 | 0 | 6 | 6 | 6 | 54 | 65 | 11 | 4 | 31 | 28 | 0 | 10.83 | 1.83 | 0.67 |
| ong Tom Hughes | R | 1 | 1 | .500 | 5.14 | 0 | 3 | 3 | 3 | 21 | 31 | 7 | 12 | 31 | 12 | 0 | 13.29 | 3.00 | 5.14 |
| al Eason | R | 1 | 0 | 1.000 | 1.00 | 0 | 1 | 1 | 1 | 9 | 9 | 3 | 2 | 2 | 1 | 0 | 9.00 | 3.00 | 2.00 |
| vin Harvey | L | 0 | 0 | — | 0.00 | 0 | 1 | 0 | 0 | 4 | 3 | 1 | 0 | 0 | 0 | 0 | 6.75 | 2.25 | 0.00 |
| EAM TOTAL | | 65 | 75 | .464 | 3.23 | 1 | 155 | 146 | 137 | 1271 | 1375 | 324 | 357 | 751 | 456 | 9 | 9.74 | 2.29 | 2.53 |

| MANAGER | W | L | PCT |
|---|---|---|---|
| Tom Loftus | 53 | 86 | .381 |

| POS | Player | B | G | AB | H | 2B | 3B | HR | HR % | R | RBI | BB | SO | SB | Pinch Hit AB | Pinch Hit H | BA | SA |
|---|---|---|---|---|---|---|---|---|---|---|---|---|---|---|---|---|---|---|
| **REGULARS** | | | | | | | | | | | | | | | | | | |
| 1B | Jack Doyle | R | 75 | 285 | 66 | 9 | 2 | 0 | 0.0 | 21 | 39 | 7 | | 8 | 0 | 0 | .232 | .277 |
| 2B | Cupid Childs | L | 63 | 237 | 61 | 9 | 0 | 0 | 0.0 | 24 | 21 | 29 | | 3 | 0 | 0 | .257 | .295 |
| SS | Barry McCormick | | 115 | 427 | 100 | 15 | 6 | 1 | 0.2 | 45 | 32 | 31 | | 12 | 0 | 0 | .234 | .304 |
| 3B | Fred Raymer | | 120 | 463 | 108 | 14 | 2 | 0 | 0.0 | 41 | 43 | 11 | | 18 | 1 | 1 | .233 | .272 |
| RF | Frank Chance | R | 69 | 241 | 67 | 12 | 4 | 0 | 0.0 | 38 | 36 | 29 | | 30 | 2 | 1 | .278 | .361 |
| CF | Danny Green | L | 133 | 537 | 168 | 16 | 12 | 6 | 1.1 | 82 | 60 | 40 | | 31 | 0 | 0 | .313 | .421 |
| LF | Topsy Hartsel | L | 140 | 558 | 187 | 25 | 16 | 7 | 1.3 | 111 | 54 | 74 | | 41 | 0 | 0 | .335 | .475 |
| C | Johnny Kling | R | 74 | 253 | 70 | 6 | 3 | 0 | 0.0 | 26 | 21 | 9 | | 7 | 4 | 1 | .277 | .324 |
| **SUBSTITUTES** | | | | | | | | | | | | | | | | | | |
| UT | Charlie Dexter | | 116 | 460 | 123 | 9 | 5 | 1 | 0.2 | 46 | 66 | 16 | | 22 | 2 | 0 | .267 | .315 |
| 2B | Pete Childs | | 61 | 213 | 48 | 5 | 1 | 0 | 0.0 | 23 | 14 | 27 | | 4 | 0 | 0 | .225 | .258 |
| 3B | Jim Delahanty | R | 17 | 63 | 12 | 2 | 0 | 0 | 0.0 | 4 | 4 | 3 | | 5 | 0 | 0 | .190 | .222 |
| 3B | Mike Hickey | R | 10 | 37 | 6 | 0 | 0 | 0 | 0.0 | 4 | 3 | 2 | | 1 | 0 | 0 | .162 | .162 |
| 3B | Larry Hoffman | R | 6 | 22 | 7 | 1 | 0 | 0 | 0.0 | 2 | 6 | 0 | | 1 | 0 | 0 | .318 | .364 |
| 23 | Germany Schaefer | R | 2 | 5 | 3 | 1 | 0 | 0 | 0.0 | 0 | 0 | 2 | | 0 | 0 | 0 | .600 | .800 |
| OF | Cozy Dolan | L | 43 | 171 | 45 | 1 | 2 | 0 | 0.0 | 29 | 16 | 7 | | 3 | 2 | 0 | .263 | .292 |
| OP | Jock Menefee | R | 48 | 152 | 39 | 5 | 3 | 0 | 0.0 | 19 | 13 | 8 | | 4 | 1 | 0 | .257 | .329 |
| OF | Bill Gannon | | 15 | 61 | 9 | 0 | 0 | 0 | 0.0 | 2 | 0 | 1 | | 5 | 0 | 0 | .148 | .148 |
| OF | Harry Croft | | 3 | 12 | 4 | 0 | 0 | 0 | 0.0 | 1 | 4 | 0 | | 0 | 0 | 0 | .333 | .333 |
| C | Mike Kahoe | R | 67 | 237 | 53 | 12 | 2 | 1 | 0.4 | 21 | 21 | 8 | | 5 | 0 | 0 | .224 | .304 |
| **PITCHERS** | | | | | | | | | | | | | | | | | | |
| P | Long Tom Hughes | R | 38 | 118 | 14 | 1 | 0 | 0 | 0.0 | 7 | 5 | 2 | | 0 | 0 | 0 | .119 | .127 |
| P | Jack Taylor | R | 35 | 106 | 23 | 6 | 0 | 0 | 0.0 | 12 | 2 | 4 | | 0 | 2 | 0 | .217 | .274 |
| P | Rube Waddell | R | 30 | 98 | 25 | 3 | 3 | 2 | 2.0 | 16 | 14 | 2 | | 2 | 0 | 0 | .255 | .408 |
| P | Mal Eason | | 27 | 87 | 12 | 1 | 0 | 0 | 0.0 | 4 | 6 | 1 | | 1 | 0 | 0 | .138 | .149 |
| P | Bert Cunningham | R | 1 | 1 | 0 | 0 | 0 | 0 | 0.0 | 0 | 0 | 1 | | 0 | 0 | 0 | .000 | .000 |
| P | Charlie Ferguson | | 1 | 1 | 0 | 0 | 0 | 0 | 0.0 | 0 | 0 | 0 | | 0 | 0 | 0 | .000 | .000 |
| | TEAM TOTAL | | | 4845 | 1250 | 153 | 61 | 18 | 0.4 | 57 | 480 | 314 | 0 | 203 | 14 | 3 | .258 | .326 |

## INDIVIDUAL FIELDING

| POS | Player | T | G | PO | A | E | DP | TC/G | FA |
|---|---|---|---|---|---|---|---|---|---|
| 1B | J. Doyle | R | 75 | 698 | 60 | 21 | 32 | 10.4 | .973 |
| | C. Dexter | R | 54 | 499 | 39 | 10 | 28 | 10.1 | .982 |
| | F. Raymer | R | 5 | 54 | 4 | 1 | 1 | 11.8 | .983 |
| | M. Kahoe | R | 6 | 37 | 4 | 5 | 2 | 7.7 | .891 |
| | F. Chance | R | 6 | 27 | 3 | 4 | 1 | 5.7 | .882 |
| | J. Menefee | R | 2 | 15 | 0 | 4 | 1 | 9.5 | .789 |
| | J. Kling | R | 1 | 6 | 0 | 1 | 0 | 7.0 | .857 |
| | R. Waddell | L | 1 | 6 | 0 | 0 | 1 | 6.0 | 1.000 |
| 2B | C. Childs | R | 62 | 146 | 192 | 22 | 34 | 5.8 | .939 |
| | P. Childs | R | 61 | 128 | 198 | 14 | 19 | 5.6 | .959 |
| | J. Delahanty | R | 1 | 0 | 0 | 0 | 0 | 0.0 | .000 |
| | C. Dexter | R | 13 | 34 | 33 | 4 | 3 | 5.5 | .944 |
| | F. Raymer | R | 3 | 6 | 12 | 1 | 0 | 6.3 | .947 |
| | G. Schaefer | R | 1 | 3 | 2 | 0 | 1 | 5.0 | 1.000 |
| | L. Hoffman | R | 1 | 1 | 1 | 0 | 0 | 2.0 | 1.000 |
| | J. Menefee | R | 1 | 0 | 1 | 0 | 0 | 1.0 | 1.000 |
| SS | McCormick | R | 112 | 202 | 405 | 59 | 47 | 5.9 | .911 |
| | F. Raymer | R | 29 | 47 | 76 | 10 | 9 | 4.6 | .925 |
| 3B | F. Raymer | R | 82 | 79 | 143 | 30 | 5 | 3.1 | .881 |
| | C. Dexter | R | 25 | 39 | 48 | 11 | 0 | 3.9 | .888 |
| | J. Delahanty | R | 17 | 21 | 29 | 7 | 2 | 3.4 | .877 |
| | M. Hickey | R | 10 | 8 | 18 | 9 | 2 | 3.5 | .743 |
| | L. Hoffman | R | 5 | 5 | 7 | 3 | 0 | 3.0 | .800 |
| | McCormick | R | 3 | 4 | 6 | 1 | 0 | 3.7 | .909 |
| | G. Schaefer | R | 1 | 3 | 2 | 0 | 0 | 5.0 | 1.000 |
| OF | D. Green | | 133 | 312 | 17 | 24 | 7 | 2.7 | .932 |
| | T. Hartsel | L | 140 | 273 | 16 | 15 | 3 | 2.2 | .951 |
| | C. Dolan | L | 41 | 63 | 9 | 10 | 3 | 2.0 | .878 |
| | F. Chance | R | 50 | 61 | 7 | 5 | 0 | 1.5 | .932 |
| | J. Menefee | R | 24 | 39 | 3 | 4 | 1 | 1.9 | .913 |
| | C. Dexter | R | 21 | 38 | 0 | 2 | 0 | 1.9 | .950 |
| | B. Gannon | | 15 | 16 | 2 | 0 | 1 | 1.2 | 1.000 |
| | L. Hughes | R | 1 | 0 | 0 | 0 | 0 | 0.0 | .000 |
| | H. Croft | | 3 | 5 | 3 | 0 | 0 | 2.7 | 1.000 |
| | J. Kling | R | 1 | 3 | 0 | 0 | 0 | 3.0 | 1.000 |
| C | M. Kahoe | R | 63 | 368 | 74 | 12 | 8 | 7.2 | .974 |
| | J. Kling | R | 69 | 319 | 75 | 20 | 7 | 6.0 | .952 |
| | F. Chance | R | 13 | 55 | 20 | 1 | 2 | 5.8 | .987 |
| | C. Dexter | R | 3 | 8 | 5 | 0 | 1 | 4.3 | 1.000 |

In 1901 the youthful American League declared itself a major league, "raiding" players from NL clubs with lucrative contracts. The Chicago Cubs were among the hardest hit by the raids, as seven players from the 1900 roster jumped to the new league. To make matters worse, three stars—Griffith, Callahan, and Mertes—were on the South Side playing for Charles Comiskey's White Sox.

Their ranks decimated, the Orphans were renamed the Remnants, an appropriate label for the raggedy collection of has-beens and greenhorns who represented the club. Hovering at or near the cellar all year, they finished a poor sixth, escaping the basement by only one game. The only redeeming features were the hitting of Danny Green and Topsy Tully Hartsel, and the pitching of Rube Waddell. By the following season, all three were in the AL.

### TEAM STATISTICS

| | W | L | PCT | GB | R | OR | 2B | 3B | Batting HR | BA | SA | SB | E | Fielding DP | FA | CG | B | Pitching SO | ShO | SV | ERA |
|---|---|---|---|---|---|---|---|---|---|---|---|---|---|---|---|---|---|---|---|---|---|
| PIT | 90 | 49 | .647 | | 776 | 534 | 185 | 92 | 28 | .286 | .378 | 203 | 287 | 97 | .950 | 119 | 244 | 505 | 15 | 4 | 2.58 |
| PHI | 83 | 57 | .593 | 7.5 | 668 | 543 | 194 | 58 | 24 | .267 | .347 | 199 | 262 | 65 | .954 | 125 | 259 | 480 | 16 | 0 | 2.87 |
| BKN | 79 | 57 | .581 | 9.5 | 744 | 600 | 206 | 97 | 32 | .288 | .390 | 178 | 281 | 99 | .950 | 111 | 435 | 583 | 7 | 3 | 3.14 |
| STL | 76 | 64 | .543 | 14.5 | 792 | 689 | 187 | 97 | 39 | .285 | .383 | 190 | 305 | 89 | .949 | 118 | 332 | 445 | 5 | 5 | 3.68 |
| BOS | 69 | 69 | .500 | 20.5 | 531 | 556 | 135 | 36 | 28 | .250 | .312 | 157 | 282 | 89 | .952 | 128 | 349 | 558 | 11 | 0 | 2.90 |
| CHI | 53 | 86 | .381 | 37 | 578 | 699 | 153 | 61 | 18 | .258 | .326 | 203 | 336 | 87 | .943 | 131 | 324 | 586 | 2 | 0 | 3.33 |
| NY | 52 | 85 | .380 | 37 | 544 | 755 | 166 | 47 | 19 | .255 | .321 | 133 | 348 | 81 | .941 | 118 | 377 | 542 | 11 | 1 | 3.87 |
| CIN | 52 | 87 | .374 | 38 | 561 | 818 | 179 | 70 | 38 | .251 | .339 | 137 | 355 | 102 | .940 | 126 | 365 | 542 | 4 | 0 | 4.17 |
| LEAGUE TOTAL | | | | | 5194 | 5194 | 1405 | 558 | 226 | .268 | .350 | 1400 | 2456 | 728 | .947 | 976 | 2685 | 4241 | 71 | 13 | 3.32 |

### INDIVIDUAL PITCHING

| PITCHER | T | W | L | PCT | ERA | SV | G | GS | CG | IP | H | BB | SO | R | ER | ShO | H/9 | BB/9 | SO/9 |
|---|---|---|---|---|---|---|---|---|---|---|---|---|---|---|---|---|---|---|---|
| Long Tom Hughes | R | 11 | 21 | .344 | 3.24 | 0 | 37 | 35 | 32 | 308.1 | 309 | 115 | 225 | 166 | 111 | 1 | 9.02 | 3.36 | 6.57 |
| Jack Taylor | R | 13 | 19 | .406 | 3.36 | 0 | 33 | 31 | 30 | 275.2 | 341 | 44 | 68 | 165 | 103 | 0 | 11.13 | 1.44 | 2.22 |
| Rube Waddell | L | 13 | 15 | .464 | 2.81 | 0 | 29 | 28 | 26 | 243.2 | 239 | 66 | 168 | 123 | 76 | 0 | 8.83 | 2.44 | 6.21 |
| Mal Eason | R | 8 | 17 | .320 | 3.59 | 0 | 27 | 25 | 23 | 220.2 | 246 | 60 | 68 | 136 | 88 | 1 | 10.03 | 2.45 | 2.77 |
| Jock Menefee | R | 8 | 13 | .381 | 3.80 | 0 | 21 | 20 | 19 | 182.1 | 201 | 34 | 55 | 102 | 77 | 0 | 9.92 | 1.68 | 2.71 |
| Bert Cunningham | R | 0 | 1 | .000 | 5.00 | 0 | 1 | 1 | 1 | 9 | 11 | 3 | 2 | 6 | 5 | 0 | 11.00 | 3.00 | 2.00 |
| Charlie Ferguson | R | 0 | 0 | — | 0.00 | 0 | 1 | 0 | 0 | 2 | 1 | 2 | 0 | 0 | 0 | 0 | 4.50 | 9.00 | 0.00 |
| TEAM TOTAL | | 53 | 86 | .381 | 3.33 | 0 | 149 | 140 | 131 | 1241.2 | 1348 | 324 | 586 | 698 | 460 | 2 | 9.77 | 2.35 | 4.25 |

| MANAGER | W | L | PCT |
|---|---|---|---|
| Frank Selee | 68 | 69 | .496 |

| POS | Player | B | G | AB | H | 2B | 3B | HR | HR % | R | RBI | BB | SO | SB | Pinch Hit AB | Pinch Hit H | BA | SA |
|---|---|---|---|---|---|---|---|---|---|---|---|---|---|---|---|---|---|---|
| **REGULARS** | | | | | | | | | | | | | | | | | | |
| 1B | Frank Chance | R | 75 | 236 | 67 | 9 | 4 | 1 | 0.4 | 40 | 31 | 35 | | 28 | 4 | 1 | .284 | .369 |
| 2B | Bobby Lowe | R | 121 | 472 | 116 | 13 | 3 | 0 | 0.0 | 41 | 31 | 11 | | 16 | 0 | 0 | .246 | .286 |
| SS | Joe Tinker | R | 133 | 501 | 137 | 19 | 5 | 2 | 0.4 | 54 | 54 | 26 | | 27 | 0 | 0 | .273 | .343 |
| 3B | Germany Schaefer | R | 81 | 291 | 57 | 2 | 3 | 0 | 0.0 | 32 | 14 | 19 | | 12 | 0 | 0 | .196 | .223 |
| RF | Davy Jones | L | 64 | 243 | 74 | 12 | 3 | 0 | 0.0 | 41 | 14 | 38 | | 12 | 0 | 0 | .305 | .379 |
| CF | John Dobbs | L | 59 | 235 | 71 | 8 | 2 | 0 | 0.0 | 31 | 35 | 18 | | 3 | 0 | 0 | .302 | .353 |
| LF | Jimmy Slagle | L | 115 | 454 | 143 | 11 | 4 | 0 | 0.0 | 64 | 34 | 53 | | 40 | 2 | 1 | .315 | .357 |
| C | Johnny Kling | R | 114 | 434 | 124 | 19 | 3 | 0 | 0.0 | 50 | 57 | 29 | | 23 | 1 | 0 | .286 | .343 |
| **SUBSTITUTES** | | | | | | | | | | | | | | | | | | |
| UT | Charlie Dexter | | 69 | 266 | 60 | 12 | 0 | 2 | 0.8 | 30 | 26 | 19 | | 13 | 0 | 0 | .226 | .293 |
| UT | Jack Taylor | R | 55 | 186 | 44 | 6 | 1 | 0 | 0.0 | 18 | 17 | 8 | | 6 | 1 | 0 | .237 | .280 |
| 1B | Hal O'Hagan | | 31 | 108 | 21 | 1 | 3 | 0 | 0.0 | 10 | 10 | 11 | | 8 | 0 | 0 | .194 | .259 |
| 2S | Johnny Evers | L | 26 | 89 | 20 | 0 | 0 | 0 | 0.0 | 7 | 2 | 3 | | 1 | 0 | 0 | .225 | .225 |
| 1B | Fred Clark | | 12 | 43 | 8 | 1 | 0 | 0 | 0.0 | 1 | 2 | 4 | | 1 | 0 | 0 | .186 | .209 |
| P3 | Deacon Morrissey | | 7 | 22 | 2 | 0 | 0 | 0 | 0.0 | 1 | 0 | 3 | | 0 | 0 | 0 | .091 | .091 |
| SS | Mike Jacobs | | 5 | 19 | 4 | 0 | 0 | 0 | 0.0 | 1 | 2 | 0 | | 0 | 0 | 0 | .211 | .211 |
| 23 | Sammy Strang | B | 3 | 11 | 4 | 0 | 0 | 0 | 0.0 | 1 | 0 | 1 | | 1 | 0 | 0 | .364 | .364 |
| SS | Ed Glenn | | 2 | 7 | 0 | 0 | 0 | 0 | 0.0 | 0 | 0 | 1 | | 0 | 0 | 0 | .000 | .000 |
| UT | Jock Menefee | R | 65 | 216 | 50 | 4 | 1 | 0 | 0.0 | 24 | 15 | 15 | | 4 | 0 | 0 | .231 | .259 |
| OF | Dakin Miller | L | 51 | 187 | 46 | 4 | 1 | 0 | 0.0 | 17 | 13 | 7 | | 10 | 0 | 0 | .246 | .278 |
| OF | Bunk Congalton | L | 45 | 179 | 40 | 3 | 0 | 1 | 0.6 | 14 | 24 | 7 | | 3 | 0 | 0 | .223 | .257 |
| O1 | Art Williams | | 47 | 160 | 37 | 3 | 0 | 0 | 0.0 | 17 | 14 | 15 | | 9 | 4 | 0 | .231 | .250 |
| OF | Jim Murray | R | 12 | 47 | 8 | 0 | 0 | 0 | 0.0 | 3 | 1 | 2 | | 0 | 0 | 0 | .170 | .170 |
| UT | Larry Schlafly | R | 10 | 31 | 10 | 0 | 3 | 0 | 0.0 | 5 | 5 | 6 | | 2 | 0 | 0 | .323 | .516 |
| OF | Mike Lynch | | 7 | 28 | 4 | 0 | 0 | 0 | 0.0 | 4 | 0 | 2 | | 0 | 0 | 0 | .143 | .143 |
| OF | Jack Hendricks | L | 2 | 7 | 4 | 0 | 1 | 0 | 0.0 | 0 | 0 | 0 | | 0 | 0 | 0 | .571 | .857 |
| OF | Chick Pedroes | | 2 | 6 | 0 | 0 | 0 | 0 | 0.0 | 0 | 0 | 0 | | 0 | 0 | 0 | .000 | .000 |
| OF | Snapper Kennedy | B | 1 | 5 | 0 | 0 | 0 | 0 | 0.0 | 0 | 0 | 0 | | 0 | 0 | 0 | .000 | .000 |
| OF | R. E. Hildebrand | | 1 | 4 | 0 | 0 | 0 | 0 | 0.0 | 1 | 0 | 1 | | 0 | 0 | 0 | .000 | .000 |
| OF | Ed Hughes | | 1 | 3 | 0 | 0 | 0 | 0 | 0.0 | 0 | 0 | 0 | | 0 | 0 | 0 | .000 | .000 |
| UT | Mike Kahoe | R | 7 | 18 | 4 | 1 | 0 | 0 | 0.0 | 0 | 2 | 0 | | 0 | 0 | 0 | .222 | .278 |
| C | Pete Lamer | | 2 | 9 | 2 | 0 | 0 | 0 | 0.0 | 2 | 0 | 0 | | 0 | 0 | 0 | .222 | .222 |
| **PITCHERS** | | | | | | | | | | | | | | | | | | |
| P | Pop Williams | R | 38 | 116 | 23 | 1 | 2 | 0 | 0.0 | 14 | 13 | 11 | | 0 | 1 | 0 | .198 | .241 |
| P | Carl Lundgren | R | 20 | 66 | 7 | 1 | 0 | 0 | 0.0 | 2 | 5 | 2 | | 2 | 0 | 0 | .106 | .121 |
| P | Bob Rhoads | R | 16 | 45 | 10 | 0 | 0 | 0 | 0.0 | 0 | 2 | 2 | | 1 | 0 | 0 | .222 | .222 |
| P | Jim St. Vrain | | 12 | 31 | 3 | 0 | 0 | 0 | 0.0 | 2 | 0 | 2 | | 0 | 0 | 0 | .097 | .097 |
| P | Alex Hardy | | 4 | 14 | 3 | 1 | 0 | 0 | 0.0 | 3 | 4 | 1 | | 0 | 0 | 0 | .214 | .286 |
| P | Jim Gardner | | 3 | 10 | 2 | 0 | 0 | 0 | 0.0 | 0 | 2 | 1 | | 0 | 0 | 0 | .200 | .200 |
| P | Mal Eason | | 2 | 5 | 1 | 0 | 0 | 0 | 0.0 | 0 | 0 | 1 | | 0 | 0 | 0 | .200 | .200 |
| P | Fred Glade | R | 1 | 3 | 1 | 0 | 1 | 0 | 0.0 | 0 | 0 | 0 | | 0 | 0 | 0 | .333 | 1.000 |
| TEAM TOTAL | | | | 4807 | 1207 | 131 | 40 | 6 | 0.1 | 53 | 423 | 353 | 0 | 222 | 13 | 2 | .251 | .299 |

## INDIVIDUAL FIELDING

| POS | Player | T | G | PO | A | E | DP | TC/G | FA |
|---|---|---|---|---|---|---|---|---|---|
| 1B | F. Chance | R | 38 | 391 | 20 | 13 | 21 | 11.2 | .969 |
| | H. O'Hagan | | 31 | 311 | 24 | 6 | 19 | 11.0 | .982 |
| | C. Dexter | R | 22 | 223 | 10 | 6 | 15 | 10.9 | .975 |
| | A. Williams | R | 19 | 194 | 14 | 8 | 10 | 11.4 | .963 |
| | J. Menefee | R | 18 | 177 | 7 | 6 | 4 | 10.6 | .968 |
| | F. Clark | L | 12 | 115 | 6 | 8 | 9 | 10.8 | .938 |
| | G. Schaefer | R | 3 | 35 | 1 | 1 | 2 | 12.3 | .973 |
| | J. Taylor | R | 2 | 16 | 1 | 0 | 2 | 8.5 | 1.000 |
| 2B | B. Lowe | R | 117 | 326 | 406 | 33 | 59 | 6.5 | .957 |
| | J. Evers | R | 18 | 38 | 58 | 1 | 5 | 5.4 | .990 |
| | J. Taylor | R | 1 | 0 | 0 | 0 | 0 | 0.0 | .000 |
| | L. Schlafly | R | 4 | 7 | 9 | 3 | 0 | 4.8 | .842 |
| | J. Menefee | R | 1 | 1 | 2 | 1 | 0 | 4.0 | .750 |
| | S. Strang | R | 2 | 2 | 1 | 0 | 2 | 1.5 | 1.000 |
| SS | J. Tinker | R | 124 | 243 | 453 | 72 | 47 | 6.2 | .906 |
| | J. Evers | R | 8 | 10 | 29 | 4 | 1 | 5.4 | .907 |
| | M. Jacobs | | 5 | 9 | 13 | 3 | 1 | 5.0 | .880 |
| | C. Lundgren | R | 2 | 1 | 6 | 3 | 1 | 5.0 | .700 |
| | E. Glenn | | 2 | 0 | 6 | 0 | 0 | 3.0 | 1.000 |
| | J. Kling | R | 1 | 1 | 2 | 2 | 1 | 5.0 | .600 |
| | G. Schaefer | R | 1 | 1 | 2 | 2 | 0 | 5.0 | .600 |
| | M. Kahoe | R | 1 | 0 | 1 | 0 | 0 | 1.0 | 1.000 |
| 3B | G. Schaefer | R | 75 | 103 | 152 | 40 | 11 | 3.9 | .864 |
| | C. Dexter | R | 39 | 62 | 60 | 21 | 5 | 3.7 | .853 |
| | J. Taylor | R | 12 | 12 | 25 | 4 | 0 | 3.4 | .902 |
| | J. Tinker | R | 8 | 10 | 15 | 2 | 1 | 3.4 | .926 |
| | L. Schlafly | R | 2 | 3 | 6 | 0 | 1 | 4.5 | 1.000 |
| | B. Lowe | R | 2 | 3 | 4 | 0 | 0 | 3.5 | 1.000 |
| | S. Strang | R | 2 | 3 | 3 | 1 | 0 | 3.5 | .857 |
| | D. Morrissey | | 2 | 2 | 1 | 2 | 0 | 2.5 | .600 |
| | M. Kahoe | R | 2 | 0 | 2 | 1 | 1 | 1.5 | .667 |
| | J. Menefee | R | 2 | 1 | 1 | 1 | 0 | 1.5 | .667 |

| POS | Player | T | G | PO | A | E | DP | TC/G | FA |
|---|---|---|---|---|---|---|---|---|---|
| OF | J. Slagle | R | 113 | 262 | 15 | 10 | 5 | 2.5 | .965 |
| | D. Jones | R | 64 | 146 | 3 | 7 | 1 | 2.4 | .955 |
| | J. Dobbs | R | 59 | 122 | 8 | 3 | 5 | 2.3 | .977 |
| | D. Miller | R | 51 | 97 | 9 | 5 | 0 | 2.2 | .955 |
| | B. Congalton | L | 45 | 71 | 6 | 1 | 1 | 1.7 | .987 |
| | J. Menefee | R | 23 | 38 | 2 | 2 | 1 | 1.8 | .952 |
| | A. Williams | R | 24 | 32 | 1 | 3 | 0 | 1.5 | .917 |
| | E. Hughes | | 1 | 0 | 0 | 0 | 0 | 0.0 | .000 |
| | C. Dexter | R | 10 | 18 | 1 | 0 | 0 | 1.9 | 1.000 |
| | J. Murray | L | 12 | 17 | 1 | 0 | 0 | 1.5 | 1.000 |
| | M. Lynch | R | 7 | 12 | 1 | 1 | 0 | 2.0 | .929 |
| | P. Williams | R | 6 | 8 | 0 | 1 | 0 | 1.5 | .889 |
| | J. Hendricks | L | 2 | 6 | 0 | 0 | 0 | 3.0 | 1.000 |
| | S. Kennedy | R | 1 | 5 | 0 | 0 | 0 | 5.0 | 1.000 |
| | G. Schaefer | R | 2 | 4 | 1 | 0 | 1 | 2.5 | 1.000 |
| | F. Chance | R | 4 | 4 | 0 | 0 | 0 | 1.0 | 1.000 |
| | L. Schlafly | R | 5 | 4 | 0 | 0 | 0 | 0.8 | 1.000 |
| | C. Pedroes | | 2 | 2 | 0 | 0 | 0 | 1.0 | 1.000 |
| | J. Taylor | R | 3 | 1 | 1 | 0 | 0 | 0.7 | 1.000 |
| | Hildebrand | | 1 | 1 | 0 | 0 | 0 | 1.0 | 1.000 |
| C | J. Kling | R | 112 | 471 | 158 | 17 | 16 | 5.8 | .974 |
| | F. Chance | R | 29 | 113 | 27 | 4 | 2 | 5.0 | .972 |
| | M. Kahoe | R | 4 | 17 | 4 | 3 | 0 | 6.0 | .875 |
| | P. Lamer | R | 2 | 9 | 3 | 2 | 1 | 7.0 | .857 |

This season was a turning point in the team's course. Frank Selee, the new manager, emphasized youth in his rebuilding program; hence a new nickname—Cubs. The term was coined by the *Chicago Daily News* on March 27, but it took a while to catch on, as Colts remained in popular usage for several years.

Jimmy Slagle was the new centerfielder, Joe Tinker nailed down the shortstop slot immediately, and Carl Lundgren, a University of Illinois graduate, became a vital addition to the pitching corps. Johnny Kling came into his own both as a hitter and defensive catcher, while Jack Taylor was brilliant on the mound. With seven shutouts to his credit, he won 22 games, including a 19-inning, 3–2 duel with the Pirates on June 22. Although Chicago finished only fifth, there were 15 more victories to count over the previous season.

Late in the season, the youthful Johnny Evers was given a trial at second base while Selee converted Frank Chance from a catcher to a first baseman. On September 15, the first Tinker-to-Evers-to-Chance double play was recorded in a 6–3 victory over the Reds at West Side Grounds. A new era was dawning.

### TEAM STATISTICS

| | W | L | PCT | GB | R | OR | Batting 2B | 3B | HR | BA | SA | SB | Fielding E | DP | FA | CG | B | Pitching SO | ShO | SV | ERA |
|---|---|---|---|---|---|---|---|---|---|---|---|---|---|---|---|---|---|---|---|---|---|
| PIT | 103 | 36 | .741 | | 775 | 440 | 199 | 94 | 19 | .287 | .377 | 222 | 247 | 87 | .958 | 131 | 250 | 564 | 21 | 3 | 2.30 |
| BKN | 75 | 63 | .543 | 27.5 | 564 | 519 | 147 | 50 | 19 | .257 | .320 | 145 | 275 | 79 | .952 | 131 | 363 | 536 | 15 | 1 | 2.69 |
| BOS | 73 | 64 | .533 | 29 | 572 | 516 | 142 | 39 | 14 | .250 | .305 | 189 | 240 | 90 | .959 | 124 | 372 | 523 | 14 | 4 | 2.61 |
| CIN | 70 | 70 | .500 | 33.5 | 633 | 566 | 188 | 77 | 18 | .282 | .363 | 131 | 322 | 118 | .945 | 130 | 352 | 430 | 9 | 1 | 2.67 |
| CHI | 68 | 69 | .496 | 34 | 530 | 501 | 131 | 40 | 6 | .251 | .299 | 222 | 327 | 111 | .946 | 132 | 279 | 437 | 18 | 2 | 2.21 |
| STL | 56 | 78 | .418 | 44.5 | 517 | 695 | 116 | 37 | 10 | .258 | .304 | 158 | 336 | 107 | .944 | 112 | 338 | 400 | 7 | 2 | 3.47 |
| PHI | 56 | 81 | .409 | 46 | 484 | 649 | 113 | 42 | 5 | .247 | .293 | 108 | 305 | 81 | .946 | 118 | 334 | 504 | 8 | 2 | 3.50 |
| NY | 48 | 88 | .353 | 53.5 | 401 | 590 | 149 | 34 | 8 | .238 | .291 | 187 | 330 | 104 | .943 | 118 | 332 | 501 | 11 | 1 | 2.82 |
| LEAGUE TOTAL | | | | | 4476 | 4476 | 1185 | 413 | 99 | .259 | .320 | 1362 | 2382 | 777 | .949 | 996 | 2620 | 3895 | 103 | 16 | 2.78 |

### INDIVIDUAL PITCHING

| PITCHER | T | W | L | PCT | ERA | SV | G | GS | CG | IP | H | BB | SO | R | ER | ShO | H/9 | BB/9 | SO/9 |
|---|---|---|---|---|---|---|---|---|---|---|---|---|---|---|---|---|---|---|---|
| Jack Taylor | R | 22 | 11 | .667 | 1.33 | 1 | 36 | 33 | 33 | 324.2 | 271 | 43 | 83 | 86 | 48 | 8 | 7.51 | 1.19 | 2.30 |
| Pop Williams | R | 12 | 16 | .429 | 2.51 | 0 | 31 | 31 | 26 | 254.1 | 259 | 63 | 94 | 108 | 71 | 1 | 9.17 | 2.23 | 3.33 |
| Jock Menefee | R | 12 | 10 | .545 | 2.42 | 0 | 22 | 21 | 20 | 197.1 | 202 | 26 | 60 | 81 | 53 | 5 | 9.21 | 1.19 | 2.74 |
| Carl Lundgren | R | 9 | 9 | .500 | 1.97 | 0 | 18 | 18 | 17 | 160 | 158 | 45 | 68 | 59 | 35 | 1 | 8.89 | 2.53 | 3.83 |
| Bob Rhoads | R | 4 | 8 | .333 | 3.20 | 1 | 16 | 12 | 12 | 118 | 131 | 42 | 43 | 66 | 42 | 1 | 9.99 | 3.20 | 3.28 |
| Jim St. Vrain | L | 4 | 6 | .400 | 2.08 | 0 | 12 | 11 | 10 | 95 | 88 | 25 | 51 | 36 | 22 | 1 | 8.34 | 2.37 | 4.83 |
| Deacon Morrissey | | 1 | 3 | .250 | 2.25 | 0 | 5 | 5 | 5 | 40 | 40 | 8 | 13 | 16 | 10 | 0 | 9.00 | 1.80 | 2.93 |
| Alex Hardy | L | 2 | 2 | .500 | 3.60 | 0 | 4 | 4 | 4 | 35 | 29 | 12 | 12 | 19 | 14 | 1 | 7.46 | 3.09 | 3.09 |
| Jim Gardner | R | 1 | 2 | .333 | 2.88 | 0 | 3 | 3 | 2 | 25 | 23 | 10 | 6 | 12 | 8 | 0 | 8.28 | 3.60 | 2.16 |
| Mal Eason | R | 1 | 1 | .500 | 1.00 | 0 | 2 | 2 | 2 | 18 | 21 | 2 | 4 | 7 | 2 | 0 | 10.50 | 1.00 | 2.00 |
| Fred Glade | R | 0 | 1 | .000 | 9.00 | 0 | 1 | 1 | 1 | 8 | 13 | 3 | 3 | 11 | 8 | 0 | 14.63 | 3.38 | 3.38 |
| TEAM TOTAL | | 68 | 69 | .496 | 2.21 | 2 | 150 | 141 | 132 | 1275.1 | 1235 | 279 | 437 | 501 | 313 | 18 | 8.72 | 1.97 | 3.08 |

| MANAGER | W | L | PCT |
|---|---|---|---|
| Frank Selee | 82 | 56 | .594 |

| POS | Player | B | G | AB | H | 2B | 3B | HR | HR % | R | RBI | BB | SO | SB | Pinch Hit AB | Pinch Hit H | BA | SA |
|---|---|---|---|---|---|---|---|---|---|---|---|---|---|---|---|---|---|---|
| **REGULARS** | | | | | | | | | | | | | | | | | | |
| 1B | Frank Chance | R | 125 | 441 | 144 | 24 | 10 | 2 | 0.5 | 83 | 81 | 78 | | 67 | 2 | 1 | .327 | .440 |
| 2B | Johnny Evers | L | 124 | 464 | 136 | 27 | 7 | 0 | 0.0 | 70 | 52 | 19 | | 25 | 0 | 0 | .293 | .381 |
| SS | Joe Tinker | R | 124 | 460 | 134 | 21 | 7 | 2 | 0.4 | 67 | 70 | 37 | | 27 | 0 | 0 | .291 | .380 |
| 3B | Doc Casey | L | 112 | 435 | 126 | 8 | 3 | 1 | 0.2 | 56 | 40 | 19 | | 11 | 0 | 0 | .290 | .329 |
| RF | Dick Harley | L | 104 | 386 | 89 | 9 | 1 | 0 | 0.0 | 72 | 33 | 45 | | 27 | 2 | 2 | .231 | .259 |
| CF | Davy Jones | L | 130 | 497 | 140 | 18 | 3 | 1 | 0.2 | 64 | 62 | 53 | | 15 | 0 | 0 | .282 | .336 |
| LF | Jimmy Slagle | L | 139 | 543 | 162 | 20 | 6 | 0 | 0.0 | 104 | 44 | 81 | | 33 | 0 | 0 | .298 | .357 |
| C | Johnny Kling | R | 132 | 491 | 146 | 29 | 13 | 3 | 0.6 | 67 | 68 | 22 | | 23 | 0 | 0 | .297 | .428 |
| **SUBSTITUTES** | | | | | | | | | | | | | | | | | | |
| UT | Otto Williams | R | 38 | 130 | 29 | 5 | 0 | 0 | 0.0 | 14 | 13 | 4 | | 8 | 0 | 0 | .223 | .262 |
| 21 | Bobby Lowe | R | 32 | 105 | 28 | 5 | 3 | 0 | 0.0 | 14 | 15 | 4 | | 5 | 1 | 1 | .267 | .371 |
| 1B | Bill Hanlon | | 8 | 21 | 2 | 0 | 0 | 0 | 0.0 | 4 | 2 | 6 | | 1 | 0 | 0 | .095 | .095 |
| 3B | George Moriarty | R | 1 | 5 | 0 | 0 | 0 | 0 | 0.0 | 1 | 0 | 0 | | 0 | 0 | 0 | .000 | .000 |
| OF | Jack McCarthy | L | 24 | 101 | 28 | 5 | 0 | 0 | 0.0 | 11 | 14 | 4 | | 8 | 0 | 0 | .277 | .327 |
| OF | John Dobbs | L | 16 | 61 | 14 | 1 | 1 | 0 | 0.0 | 8 | 4 | 7 | | 0 | 0 | 0 | .230 | .279 |
| UT | Jim Cook | | 8 | 26 | 4 | 1 | 0 | 0 | 0.0 | 3 | 2 | 2 | | 1 | 0 | 0 | .154 | .192 |
| UT | Tommy Raub | R | 36 | 84 | 19 | 3 | 2 | 0 | 0.0 | 6 | 7 | 5 | | 3 | 8 | 3 | .226 | .310 |
| C | Larry McLean | R | 1 | 4 | 0 | 0 | 0 | 0 | 0.0 | 0 | 1 | 1 | | 0 | 0 | 0 | .000 | .000 |
| **PITCHERS** | | | | | | | | | | | | | | | | | | |
| P | Jack Taylor | R | 40 | 126 | 28 | 3 | 4 | 0 | 0.0 | 13 | 17 | 6 | | 3 | 0 | 0 | .222 | .310 |
| P | Jake Weimer | L | 35 | 107 | 21 | 4 | 0 | 0 | 0.0 | 10 | 6 | 9 | | 0 | 0 | 0 | .196 | .234 |
| P | Bob Wicker | R | 32 | 98 | 24 | 5 | 2 | 0 | 0.0 | 18 | 8 | 4 | | 1 | 0 | 0 | .245 | .337 |
| P | Jock Menefee | R | 22 | 64 | 13 | 3 | 0 | 0 | 0.0 | 3 | 2 | 3 | | 0 | 0 | 0 | .203 | .250 |
| P | Carl Lundgren | R | 27 | 61 | 7 | 0 | 0 | 0 | 0.0 | 6 | 3 | 11 | | 1 | 0 | 0 | .115 | .115 |
| P | Clarence Currie | R | 6 | 12 | 5 | 0 | 0 | 0 | 0.0 | 1 | 3 | 1 | | 0 | 0 | 0 | .417 | .417 |
| P | Alex Hardy | | 3 | 6 | 1 | 0 | 0 | 0 | 0.0 | 0 | 1 | 1 | | 0 | 0 | 0 | .167 | .167 |
| P | Peaches Graham | R | 1 | 2 | 0 | 0 | 0 | 0 | 0.0 | 0 | 0 | 0 | | 0 | 0 | 0 | .000 | .000 |
| P | Pop Williams | R | 2 | 2 | 0 | 0 | 0 | 0 | 0.0 | 0 | 0 | 0 | | 0 | 1 | 0 | .000 | .000 |
| P | John Doscher | R | 1 | 0 | 0 | 0 | 0 | 0 | 0.0 | 0 | 0 | 0 | | 0 | 0 | 0 | .000 | .000 |
| TEAM TOTAL | | | | 4733 | 1300 | 191 | 62 | 9 | 0.2 | 69 | 548 | 422 | 0 | 259 | 14 | 7 | .275 | .347 |

## INDIVIDUAL FIELDING

| POS | Player | T | G | PO | A | E | DP | TC/G | FA | POS | Player | T | G | PO | A | E | DP | TC/G | FA |
|---|---|---|---|---|---|---|---|---|---|---|---|---|---|---|---|---|---|---|---|
| 1B | F. Chance | R | 121 | 1204 | 68 | 36 | 49 | 10.8 | .972 | OF | J. Slagle | R | 139 | 292 | 16 | 21 | 8 | 2.4 | .936 |
| | B. Hanlon | | 8 | 92 | 4 | 2 | 2 | 12.3 | .980 | | D. Jones | R | 130 | 249 | 14 | 8 | 3 | 2.1 | .970 |
| | B. Lowe | R | 6 | 52 | 4 | 2 | 5 | 9.7 | .966 | | D. Harley | R | 103 | 162 | 18 | 15 | 2 | 1.9 | .923 |
| | T. Raub | R | 6 | 41 | 4 | 8 | 3 | 8.8 | .849 | | J. Dobbs | R | 16 | 37 | 1 | 0 | 0 | 2.4 | 1.000 |
| | O. Williams | R | 3 | 20 | 0 | 0 | 1 | 6.7 | 1.000 | | J. McCarthy | L | 24 | 33 | 3 | 2 | 1 | 1.6 | .947 |
| | J. Menefee | R | 2 | 18 | 0 | 0 | 0 | 9.0 | 1.000 | | J. Cook | R | 5 | 11 | 0 | 0 | 0 | 2.2 | 1.000 |
| | J. Cook | R | 1 | 5 | 0 | 0 | 0 | 5.0 | 1.000 | | T. Raub | R | 5 | 7 | 0 | 0 | 0 | 1.4 | 1.000 |
| 2B | J. Evers | R | 110 | 245 | 306 | 37 | 39 | 5.3 | .937 | C | J. Kling | R | 132 | 565 | 189 | 24 | 13 | 5.9 | .969 |
| | B. Lowe | R | 22 | 37 | 72 | 6 | 8 | 5.2 | .948 | | T. Raub | R | 12 | 38 | 7 | 5 | 0 | 4.2 | .900 |
| | O. Williams | R | 7 | 12 | 24 | 4 | 0 | 5.7 | .900 | | L. McLean | R | 1 | 7 | 1 | 1 | 0 | 9.0 | .889 |
| | J. Cook | R | 2 | 1 | 3 | 2 | 0 | 3.0 | .667 | | F. Chance | R | 2 | 8 | 0 | 1 | 0 | 4.5 | .889 |
| | J. Taylor | R | 1 | 0 | 0 | 1 | 0 | 1.0 | .000 | | | | | | | | | | |
| SS | J. Tinker | R | 107 | 229 | 362 | 61 | 37 | 6.1 | .906 | | | | | | | | | | |
| | O. Williams | R | 26 | 60 | 88 | 10 | 9 | 6.1 | .937 | | | | | | | | | | |
| | J. Evers | R | 11 | 21 | 26 | 12 | 1 | 5.4 | .797 | | | | | | | | | | |
| 3B | D. Casey | R | 112 | 143 | 190 | 31 | 5 | 3.3 | .915 | | | | | | | | | | |
| | J. Tinker | R | 17 | 17 | 38 | 6 | 0 | 3.6 | .902 | | | | | | | | | | |
| | T. Raub | R | 4 | 4 | 9 | 2 | 0 | 3.8 | .867 | | | | | | | | | | |
| | B. Lowe | R | 1 | 2 | 4 | 3 | 0 | 9.0 | .667 | | | | | | | | | | |
| | J. Evers | R | 2 | 2 | 4 | 2 | 0 | 4.0 | .750 | | | | | | | | | | |
| | G. Moriarty | R | 1 | 3 | 1 | 0 | 0 | 4.0 | 1.000 | | | | | | | | | | |
| | O. Williams | R | 1 | 2 | 0 | 1 | 0 | 3.0 | .667 | | | | | | | | | | |
| | J. Taylor | R | 1 | 2 | 0 | 0 | 0 | 2.0 | 1.000 | | | | | | | | | | |

The Tinker-Evers-Chance trio was now getting into full swing, to give the Colts their best infield front line since the heydey of the "stonewall infield." With a .327 average and 67 stolen bases, Chance had finally found himself. Furthermore, the team soared to third place, its highest finish since 1891. Their pitching was becoming increasingly dominant as the 1903 edition boasted 20-game winners Taylor (21–14) and rookie Tornado Jake Weimer (20–8), with Bob Wicker right behind at 19–0.

The NL and AL had finally declared a truce, so that in October the first modern World Series was played, with the Boston Puritans (Red Sox) defeating the Pirates, five games to three. In Chicago, Selee's men met Charlie Comiskey's White Sox in the first City Series, which ended up being called after each side had won seven games. Jack Taylor, after winning the opener 11–0, lost his next three starts by sound margins, raising rumors that he had thrown them. Although the charges were never substantiated, Taylor was subsequently traded to the Cardinals for pitcher Mordecai "Three Finger" Brown.

### TEAM STATISTICS

| | W | L | PCT | GB | R | OR | 2B | 3B | HR | BA | SA | SB | E | DP | FA | CG | B | SO | ShO | SV | ERA |
|---|---|---|---|---|---|---|---|---|---|---|---|---|---|---|---|---|---|---|---|---|---|
| PIT | 91 | 49 | .650 | | 793 | 613 | 208 | 110 | 34 | .287 | .393 | 172 | 295 | 100 | .951 | 117 | 384 | 454 | 16 | 5 | 2.91 |
| NY | 84 | 55 | .604 | 6.5 | 729 | 567 | 181 | 49 | 20 | .272 | .344 | 264 | 287 | 87 | .951 | 115 | 371 | 628 | 8 | 8 | 2.95 |
| CHI | 82 | 56 | .594 | 8 | 695 | 599 | 191 | 62 | 9 | .275 | .347 | 259 | 338 | 78 | .942 | 117 | 354 | 451 | 6 | 6 | 2.77 |
| CIN | 74 | 65 | .532 | 16.5 | 765 | 656 | 228 | 92 | 28 | .288 | .390 | 144 | 312 | 84 | .946 | 126 | 480 | 480 | 11 | 1 | 3.07 |
| BKN | 70 | 66 | .515 | 19 | 667 | 682 | 177 | 56 | 15 | .265 | .339 | 273 | 284 | 98 | .951 | 118 | 377 | 438 | 11 | 4 | 3.44 |
| BOS | 58 | 80 | .420 | 32 | 578 | 699 | 176 | 47 | 25 | .245 | .318 | 159 | 361 | 89 | .937 | 125 | 460 | 516 | 5 | 0 | 3.34 |
| PHI | 49 | 86 | .363 | 39.5 | 617 | 738 | 186 | 62 | 12 | .268 | .341 | 120 | 300 | 76 | .947 | 126 | 425 | 381 | 5 | 2 | 3.97 |
| STL | 43 | 94 | .314 | 46.5 | 505 | 795 | 138 | 65 | 8 | .251 | .313 | 171 | 354 | 111 | .940 | 111 | 430 | 419 | 4 | 2 | 3.76 |
| LEAGUE TOTAL | | | | | 5349 | 5349 | 1485 | 543 | 151 | .269 | .349 | 1562 | 2531 | 723 | .946 | 955 | 3179 | 3767 | 66 | 28 | 3.27 |

### INDIVIDUAL  PITCHING

| PITCHER | T | W | L | PCT | ERA | SV | G | GS | CG | IP | H | BB | SO | R | ER | ShO | H/9 | BB/9 | SO/9 |
|---|---|---|---|---|---|---|---|---|---|---|---|---|---|---|---|---|---|---|---|
| Jack Taylor | R | 21 | 14 | .600 | 2.45 | 1 | 37 | 33 | 33 | 312.1 | 277 | 57 | 83 | 137 | 85 | 1 | 7.98 | 1.64 | 2.39 |
| Jake Weimer | L | 21 | 9 | .700 | 2.30 | 0 | 35 | 33 | 27 | 282 | 241 | 104 | 128 | 111 | 72 | 3 | 7.69 | 3.32 | 4.09 |
| Bob Wicker | R | 19 | 10 | .655 | 3.02 | 1 | 32 | 27 | 24 | 247 | 236 | 74 | 110 | 114 | 83 | 1 | 8.60 | 2.70 | 4.01 |
| Carl Lundgren | R | 10 | 9 | .526 | 2.94 | 3 | 27 | 20 | 16 | 193 | 191 | 60 | 67 | 98 | 63 | 0 | 8.91 | 2.80 | 3.12 |
| Jock Menefee | R | 8 | 8 | .500 | 3.00 | 0 | 20 | 17 | 13 | 147 | 157 | 38 | 39 | 85 | 49 | 1 | 9.61 | 2.33 | 2.39 |
| Clarence Currie | R | 1 | 2 | .333 | 2.97 | 1 | 6 | 3 | 2 | 33.1 | 35 | 9 | 9 | 10 | 9 | 0 | 9.45 | 2.43 | 2.43 |
| Alex Hardy | L | 2 | 1 | .667 | 6.39 | 0 | 3 | 3 | 1 | 12.2 | 21 | 7 | 4 | 10 | 9 | 0 | 14.92 | 4.97 | 2.84 |
| Peaches Graham | R | 0 | 1 | .000 | 5.40 | 0 | 1 | 1 | 0 | 5 | 9 | 3 | 4 | 6 | 3 | 0 | 16.20 | 5.40 | 7.20 |
| Pop Williams | R | 0 | 1 | .000 | 5.40 | 0 | 1 | 1 | 1 | 5 | 9 | 0 | 2 | 3 | 3 | 0 | 16.20 | 0.00 | 3.60 |
| John Doscher | R | 0 | 1 | .000 | 12.00 | 0 | 1 | 1 | 0 | 3 | 6 | 2 | 5 | 5 | 4 | 0 | 18.00 | 6.00 | 15.00 |
| TEAM TOTAL | | 82 | 56 | .594 | 2.77 | 6 | 163 | 139 | 117 | 1240.1 | 1182 | 354 | 451 | 594 | 382 | 6 | 8.58 | 2.57 | 3.27 |

| MANAGER | W | L | PCT |
|---|---|---|---|
| Frank Selee | 93 | 60 | .608 |

| POS | Player | B | G | AB | H | 2B | 3B | HR | HR % | R | RBI | BB | SO | SB | Pinch Hit AB | Pinch Hit H | BA | SA |
|---|---|---|---|---|---|---|---|---|---|---|---|---|---|---|---|---|---|---|
| **REGULARS** | | | | | | | | | | | | | | | | | | |
| 1B | Frank Chance | R | 124 | 451 | 140 | 16 | 10 | 6 | 1.3 | 89 | 49 | 36 | | 42 | 0 | 0 | .310 | .430 |
| 2B | Johnny Evers | L | 152 | 532 | 141 | 14 | 7 | 0 | 0.0 | 49 | 47 | 28 | | 26 | 0 | 0 | .265 | .318 |
| SS | Joe Tinker | R | 141 | 488 | 108 | 12 | 13 | 3 | 0.6 | 55 | 41 | 29 | | 41 | 0 | 0 | .221 | .318 |
| 3B | Doc Casey | L | 136 | 548 | 147 | 20 | 4 | 1 | 0.2 | 71 | 43 | 18 | | 21 | 0 | 0 | .268 | .325 |
| RF | Davy Jones | L | 98 | 336 | 82 | 11 | 5 | 3 | 0.9 | 44 | 39 | 41 | | 14 | 0 | 0 | .244 | .333 |
| CF | Jack McCarthy | L | 115 | 432 | 114 | 14 | 2 | 0 | 0.0 | 36 | 51 | 23 | | 14 | 0 | 0 | .264 | .306 |
| LF | Jimmy Slagle | L | 120 | 481 | 125 | 12 | 10 | 1 | 0.2 | 73 | 31 | 41 | | 28 | 0 | 0 | .260 | .318 |
| C | Johnny Kling | R | 123 | 452 | 110 | 18 | 0 | 2 | 0.4 | 41 | 46 | 16 | | 7 | 2 | 0 | .243 | .296 |
| **SUBSTITUTES** | | | | | | | | | | | | | | | | | | |
| UT | Frank Corridon | R | 19 | 58 | 13 | 1 | 0 | 0 | 0.0 | 3 | 1 | 1 | | 0 | 0 | 0 | .224 | .241 |
| UT | Shad Barry | R | 73 | 263 | 69 | 7 | 2 | 1 | 0.4 | 29 | 26 | 17 | | 12 | 1 | 0 | .262 | .316 |
| UT | Otto Williams | R | 57 | 185 | 37 | 4 | 1 | 0 | 0.0 | 21 | 8 | 13 | | 9 | 2 | 1 | .200 | .232 |
| PO | Bob Wicker | R | 50 | 155 | 34 | 1 | 0 | 0 | 0.0 | 17 | 9 | 4 | | 4 | 0 | 0 | .219 | .226 |
| OF | Harry McChesney | R | 22 | 88 | 23 | 6 | 2 | 0 | 0.0 | 9 | 11 | 4 | | 2 | 0 | 0 | .261 | .375 |
| OF | Wildfire Schulte | L | 20 | 84 | 24 | 4 | 3 | 2 | 2.4 | 16 | 13 | 2 | | 1 | 0 | 0 | .286 | .476 |
| UT | Broadway Aleck Smith | | 10 | 29 | 6 | 1 | 0 | 0 | 0.0 | 0 | 2 | 3 | | 1 | 2 | 0 | .207 | .241 |
| OF | Solly Hofman | R | 7 | 26 | 7 | 0 | 0 | 1 | 3.8 | 7 | 4 | 1 | | 2 | 0 | 0 | .269 | .385 |
| O3 | George Moriarty | R | 4 | 13 | 0 | 0 | 0 | 0 | 0.0 | 0 | 0 | 1 | | 0 | 0 | 0 | .000 | .000 |
| OF | Ike Van Zandt | L | 3 | 11 | 0 | 0 | 0 | 0 | 0.0 | 0 | 0 | 0 | | 0 | 0 | 0 | .000 | .000 |
| OF | Bill Carney | B | 2 | 7 | 0 | 0 | 0 | 0 | 0.0 | 0 | 0 | 0 | | 0 | 0 | 0 | .000 | .000 |
| OF | Dutch Rudolph | L | 2 | 3 | 1 | 0 | 0 | 0 | 0.0 | 0 | 0 | 1 | | 0 | 0 | 0 | .333 | .333 |
| C | Jack O'Neill | R | 51 | 168 | 36 | 5 | 0 | 1 | 0.6 | 8 | 19 | 6 | | 1 | 2 | 0 | .214 | .262 |
| C | Fred Holmes | R | 1 | 3 | 1 | 1 | 0 | 0 | 0.0 | 1 | 0 | 0 | | 0 | 0 | 0 | .333 | .667 |
| C | Tom Stanton | B | 1 | 3 | 0 | 0 | 0 | 0 | 0.0 | 0 | 0 | 0 | | 0 | 0 | 0 | .000 | .000 |
| **PITCHERS** | | | | | | | | | | | | | | | | | | |
| P | Jake Weimer | L | 37 | 115 | 21 | 3 | 0 | 0 | 0.0 | 5 | 11 | 1 | | 1 | 0 | 0 | .183 | .209 |
| P | Buttons Briggs | R | 34 | 94 | 16 | 1 | 0 | 1 | 1.1 | 6 | 4 | 5 | | 0 | 0 | 0 | .170 | .213 |
| P | Carl Lundgren | R | 31 | 90 | 20 | 3 | 2 | 0 | 0.0 | 7 | 8 | 5 | | 1 | 0 | 0 | .222 | .300 |
| P | Three Finger Brown | B | 31 | 89 | 19 | 3 | 1 | 0 | 0.0 | 8 | 8 | 2 | | 0 | 2 | 1 | .213 | .270 |
| P | Ed Groth | | 3 | 6 | 0 | 0 | 0 | 0 | 0.0 | 0 | 0 | 0 | | 0 | 0 | 0 | .000 | .000 |
| TEAM TOTAL | | | | 5210 | 1294 | 157 | 62 | 22 | 0.4 | 59 | 470 | 298 | 0 | 227 | 11 | 2 | .248 | .315 |

## INDIVIDUAL FIELDING

| POS | Player | T | G | PO | A | E | DP | TC/G | FA |
|---|---|---|---|---|---|---|---|---|---|
| 1B | F. Chance | R | 123 | 1205 | 106 | 13 | 48 | 10.8 | .990 |
| | S. Barry | R | 18 | 181 | 8 | 5 | 11 | 10.8 | .974 |
| | O. Williams | R | 11 | 98 | 5 | 2 | 2 | 9.5 | .981 |
| | J. Kling | R | 6 | 51 | 0 | 2 | 2 | 8.8 | .962 |
| | F. Corridon | R | 5 | 22 | 1 | 1 | 2 | 4.8 | .958 |
| 2B | J. Evers | R | 152 | 381 | 518 | 54 | 53 | 6.3 | .943 |
| | T. Brown | R | 1 | 0 | 0 | 0 | 0 | 0.0 | .000 |
| | O. Williams | R | 6 | 10 | 18 | 0 | 0 | 4.7 | 1.000 |
| | S. Barry | R | 2 | 3 | 2 | 0 | 1 | 2.5 | 1.000 |
| SS | J. Tinker | R | 140 | 327 | 465 | 64 | 54 | 6.1 | .925 |
| | S. Barry | R | 8 | 13 | 30 | 8 | 4 | 6.4 | .843 |
| | O. Williams | R | 10 | 16 | 29 | 2 | 0 | 4.7 | .957 |
| | S. Hofman | R | 1 | 1 | 2 | 1 | 0 | 4.0 | .750 |
| 3B | D. Casey | R | 134 | 157 | 241 | 39 | 11 | 3.3 | .911 |
| | S. Barry | R | 16 | 21 | 30 | 3 | 0 | 3.4 | .944 |
| | O. Williams | R | 6 | 4 | 12 | 4 | 0 | 3.3 | .800 |
| | G. Moriarty | R | 2 | 4 | 3 | 2 | 0 | 4.5 | .778 |
| | B. Smith | R | 1 | 0 | 2 | 0 | 0 | 2.0 | 1.000 |

| POS | Player | T | G | PO | A | E | DP | TC/G | FA |
|---|---|---|---|---|---|---|---|---|---|
| OF | J. McCarthy | L | 115 | 213 | 8 | 9 | 0 | 2.0 | .961 |
| | J. Slagle | R | 120 | 194 | 15 | 18 | 7 | 1.9 | .921 |
| | D. Jones | R | 97 | 128 | 8 | 10 | 0 | 1.5 | .932 |
| | S. Barry | R | 30 | 52 | 3 | 5 | 0 | 2.0 | .917 |
| | W. Schulte | R | 20 | 34 | 3 | 2 | 0 | 2.0 | .949 |
| | O. Williams | R | 21 | 33 | 3 | 1 | 1 | 1.8 | .973 |
| | B. Wicker | R | 20 | 30 | 1 | 2 | 0 | 1.7 | .939 |
| | McChesney | R | 22 | 27 | 2 | 1 | 1 | 1.4 | .967 |
| | T. Brown | R | 1 | 0 | 0 | 0 | 0 | 0.0 | .000 |
| | J. Kling | R | 10 | 10 | 0 | 1 | 0 | 1.1 | .909 |
| | S. Hofman | R | 6 | 7 | 2 | 0 | 1 | 1.5 | 1.000 |
| | B. Smith | R | 6 | 7 | 0 | 2 | 0 | 1.5 | .778 |
| | G. Moriarty | R | 2 | 4 | 0 | 1 | 0 | 2.5 | .800 |
| | J. Tinker | R | 1 | 4 | 0 | 0 | 0 | 4.0 | 1.000 |
| | I. Van Zandt | | 3 | 3 | 0 | 0 | 0 | 1.0 | 1.000 |
| | F. Corridon | R | 2 | 1 | 0 | 1 | 0 | 1.0 | .500 |
| | B. Carney | R | 2 | 0 | 1 | 0 | 0 | 0.5 | 1.000 |
| | D. Rudolph | L | 2 | 1 | 0 | 0 | 0 | 0.5 | 1.000 |
| C | J. Kling | R | 104 | 499 | 135 | 17 | 6 | 6.3 | .974 |
| | J. O'Neill | R | 49 | 256 | 62 | 6 | 5 | 6.6 | .981 |
| | F. Chance | R | 1 | 8 | 1 | 0 | 0 | 9.0 | 1.000 |
| | D. Casey | R | 2 | 6 | 3 | 0 | 0 | 4.5 | 1.000 |
| | F. Holmes | R | 1 | 4 | 1 | 0 | 0 | 5.0 | 1.000 |
| | T. Stanton | R | 1 | 4 | 1 | 0 | 0 | 5.0 | 1.000 |
| | B. Smith | R | 1 | 1 | 1 | 0 | 1 | 2.0 | 1.000 |

The arrival of Mordecai "Three Finger" Brown bolstered a pitching staff that was already one of the strongest in baseball. Brown had lost his right index finger in a childhood accident, but the alleged handicap gave him a natural sinkerball. Weimer and Wicker continued to be tough to beat while Lundgren began pitching up to his potential with 17 wins.

As John McGraw's Giants and Selee's Colts battled for supremacy in May and June, the rivalry intensified. On June 11, Giant ace Joe McGinnity was going for his 13th straight win against Bob Wicker before 35,000 at the Polo Grounds. Wicker held the Giants hitless for nine innings, allowed one single in the tenth, then held them hitless again before winning 1–0 in the 12th on Johnny Evers's single. Even the New York fans were impressed, and a crowd carried Wicker off the diamond to the clubhouse on their shoulders.

The Giants surged well ahead thereafter, and Chicago had to be satisfied with a second-place finish, 13 games behind in spite of a 93–60 record. The end of the year saw the debut of outfielder Frank "Wildfire" Schulte, who soon became a star.

## TEAM STATISTICS

| | W | L | PCT | GB | R | OR | Batting 2B | 3B | HR | BA | SA | SB | Fielding E | DP | FA | CG | B | Pitching SO | ShO | SV | ERA |
|---|---|---|---|---|---|---|---|---|---|---|---|---|---|---|---|---|---|---|---|---|---|
| NY | 106 | 47 | .693 | | 744 | 476 | 202 | 65 | 31 | .262 | .344 | 283 | 294 | 93 | .956 | 127 | 349 | 707 | 21 | 14 | 2.17 |
| CHI | 93 | 60 | .608 | 13 | 599 | 517 | 157 | 62 | 22 | .248 | .315 | 227 | 298 | 89 | .954 | 139 | 402 | 618 | 18 | 5 | 2.30 |
| CIN | 88 | 65 | .575 | 18 | 695 | 547 | 189 | 92 | 21 | .255 | .338 | 179 | 301 | 81 | .954 | 142 | 343 | 502 | 12 | 2 | 2.35 |
| PIT | 87 | 66 | .569 | 19 | 675 | 592 | 164 | 102 | 15 | .258 | .338 | 178 | 291 | 93 | .955 | 133 | 379 | 455 | 15 | 1 | 2.89 |
| STL | 75 | 79 | .487 | 31.5 | 602 | 595 | 175 | 66 | 24 | .253 | .327 | 199 | 307 | 83 | .952 | 146 | 319 | 529 | 7 | 2 | 2.64 |
| BKN | 56 | 97 | .366 | 50 | 497 | 614 | 159 | 53 | 15 | .232 | .295 | 205 | 343 | 87 | .945 | 135 | 414 | 453 | 12 | 2 | 2.70 |
| BOS | 55 | 98 | .359 | 51 | 491 | 749 | 153 | 50 | 24 | .237 | .300 | 143 | 348 | 91 | .946 | 136 | 500 | 544 | 14 | 0 | 3.43 |
| PHI | 52 | 100 | .342 | 53.5 | 571 | 784 | 170 | 54 | 23 | .248 | .316 | 159 | 403 | 93 | .937 | 131 | 425 | 469 | 10 | 2 | 3.39 |
| LEAGUE TOTAL | | | | | 4874 | 4874 | 1369 | 544 | 175 | .249 | .322 | 1573 | 2585 | 710 | .950 | 1089 | 3131 | 4277 | 109 | 28 | 2.73 |

## INDIVIDUAL PITCHING

| PITCHER | T | W | L | PCT | ERA | SV | G | GS | CG | IP | H | BB | SO | R | ER | ShO | H/9 | BB/9 | SO/9 |
|---|---|---|---|---|---|---|---|---|---|---|---|---|---|---|---|---|---|---|---|
| Jake Weimer | L | 20 | 14 | .588 | 1.91 | 0 | 37 | 37 | 31 | 307 | 229 | 97 | 177 | 96 | 65 | 5 | 6.71 | 2.84 | 5.19 |
| Buttons Briggs | R | 19 | 11 | .633 | 2.05 | 2 | 34 | 30 | 28 | 277 | 252 | 77 | 112 | 102 | 63 | 3 | 8.19 | 2.50 | 3.64 |
| Carl Lundgren | R | 17 | 10 | .630 | 2.60 | 1 | 31 | 27 | 25 | 242 | 203 | 77 | 106 | 97 | 70 | 2 | 7.55 | 2.86 | 3.94 |
| Bob Wicker | R | 17 | 8 | .680 | 2.67 | 0 | 30 | 27 | 23 | 229 | 201 | 58 | 99 | 92 | 68 | 4 | 7.90 | 2.28 | 3.89 |
| Three Finger Brown | R | 15 | 10 | .600 | 1.86 | 1 | 26 | 23 | 21 | 212.1 | 155 | 50 | 81 | 74 | 44 | 4 | 6.57 | 2.12 | 3.43 |
| Frank Corridon | R | 5 | 5 | .500 | 3.05 | 0 | 12 | 10 | 9 | 100.1 | 88 | 37 | 34 | 43 | 34 | 0 | 7.89 | 3.32 | 3.05 |
| Ed Groth | | 0 | 2 | .000 | 5.63 | 1 | 3 | 2 | 2 | 16 | 22 | 6 | 9 | 13 | 10 | 0 | 12.38 | 3.38 | 5.06 |
| TEAM TOTAL | | 93 | 60 | .608 | 2.30 | 5 | 173 | 156 | 139 | 1383.2 | 1150 | 402 | 618 | 517 | 354 | 18 | 7.48 | 2.61 | 4.02 |

| MANAGER | W | L | PCT |
|---|---|---|---|
| Frank Selee | 52 | 38 | .578 |
| Frank Chance | 40 | 23 | .635 |

| POS | Player | B | G | AB | H | 2B | 3B | HR | HR % | R | RBI | BB | SO | SB | Pinch Hit AB | Pinch Hit H | BA | SA |
|---|---|---|---|---|---|---|---|---|---|---|---|---|---|---|---|---|---|---|
| **REGULARS** | | | | | | | | | | | | | | | | | | |
| 1B | Frank Chance | R | 118 | 392 | 124 | 16 | 12 | 2 | 0.5 | 92 | 70 | 78 | | 38 | 3 | 0 | .316 | .434 |
| 2B | Johnny Evers | L | 99 | 340 | 94 | 11 | 2 | 1 | 0.3 | 44 | 37 | 27 | | 19 | 0 | 0 | .276 | .329 |
| SS | Joe Tinker | R | 149 | 547 | 135 | 18 | 8 | 2 | 0.4 | 70 | 66 | 34 | | 31 | 0 | 0 | .247 | .320 |
| 3B | Doc Casey | L | 144 | 526 | 122 | 21 | 10 | 1 | 0.2 | 66 | 56 | 41 | | 22 | 2 | 0 | .232 | .316 |
| RF | Billy Maloney | L | 145 | 558 | 145 | 17 | 14 | 2 | 0.4 | 78 | 56 | 43 | | 59 | 0 | 0 | .260 | .351 |
| CF | Jimmy Slagle | L | 155 | 568 | 153 | 19 | 4 | 0 | 0.0 | 96 | 37 | 97 | | 27 | 0 | 0 | .269 | .317 |
| LF | Wildfire Schulte | L | 123 | 493 | 135 | 15 | 14 | 1 | 0.2 | 67 | 47 | 32 | | 16 | 0 | 0 | .274 | .367 |
| C | Johnny Kling | R | 111 | 380 | 83 | 8 | 6 | 1 | 0.3 | 26 | 52 | 28 | | 13 | 1 | 0 | .218 | .279 |
| **SUBSTITUTES** | | | | | | | | | | | | | | | | | | |
| UT | Solly Hofman | R | 86 | 287 | 68 | 14 | 4 | 1 | 0.3 | 43 | 38 | 20 | | 15 | 1 | 1 | .237 | .324 |
| 1B | Shad Barry | R | 27 | 104 | 22 | 2 | 0 | 0 | 0.0 | 10 | 10 | 5 | | 5 | 1 | 0 | .212 | .231 |
| 3B | Hans Lobert | R | 14 | 46 | 9 | 2 | 0 | 0 | 0.0 | 7 | 1 | 3 | | 4 | 0 | 0 | .196 | .239 |
| OF | Jack McCarthy | L | 59 | 170 | 47 | 4 | 3 | 0 | 0.0 | 16 | 14 | 10 | | 8 | 15 | 6 | .276 | .335 |
| C | Jack O'Neill | R | 53 | 172 | 34 | 4 | 2 | 0 | 0.0 | 16 | 12 | 8 | | 6 | 3 | 0 | .198 | .244 |
| **PITCHERS** | | | | | | | | | | | | | | | | | | |
| P | Ed Reulbach | R | 35 | 110 | 14 | 0 | 0 | 0 | 0.0 | 6 | 7 | 1 | | 0 | 1 | 0 | .127 | .127 |
| P | Three Finger Brown | B | 31 | 93 | 13 | 1 | 1 | 1 | 1.1 | 6 | 3 | 4 | | 1 | 0 | 0 | .140 | .204 |
| P | Jake Weimer | L | 33 | 92 | 19 | 1 | 1 | 0 | 0.0 | 8 | 6 | 4 | | 0 | 0 | 0 | .207 | .239 |
| P | Bob Wicker | R | 25 | 72 | 10 | 0 | 0 | 0 | 0.0 | 5 | 3 | 4 | | 1 | 0 | 0 | .139 | .139 |
| P | Carl Lundgren | R | 24 | 61 | 11 | 1 | 1 | 0 | 0.0 | 6 | 3 | 5 | | 0 | 1 | 0 | .180 | .230 |
| P | Buttons Briggs | R | 20 | 57 | 3 | 0 | 0 | 0 | 0.0 | 1 | 1 | 4 | | 0 | 0 | 0 | .053 | .053 |
| P | Big Jeff Pfeffer | R | 15 | 40 | 8 | 3 | 0 | 0 | 0.0 | 4 | 3 | 0 | | 2 | 0 | 0 | .200 | .275 |
| | TEAM TOTAL | | | 5108 | 1249 | 157 | 82 | 12 | 0.2 | 66 | 522 | 448 | 0 | 267 | 28 | 7 | .245 | .314 |

## INDIVIDUAL FIELDING

| POS | Player | T | G | PO | A | E | DP | TC/G | FA | POS | Player | T | G | PO | A | E | DP | TC/G | FA |
|---|---|---|---|---|---|---|---|---|---|---|---|---|---|---|---|---|---|---|---|
| 1B | F. Chance | R | 115 | 1165 | 75 | 13 | 54 | 10.9 | .990 | OF | J. Slagle | R | 155 | 306 | 27 | 13 | 6 | 2.2 | .962 |
| | S. Barry | R | 26 | 257 | 18 | 5 | 10 | 10.8 | .982 | | B. Maloney | R | 145 | 251 | 18 | 13 | 4 | 1.9 | .954 |
| | S. Hofman | R | 9 | 86 | 6 | 3 | 2 | 10.6 | .968 | | W. Schulte | R | 123 | 189 | 14 | 4 | 0 | 1.7 | .981 |
| | J. McCarthy | L | 6 | 44 | 3 | 3 | 5 | 8.3 | .940 | | J. McCarthy | L | 37 | 63 | 9 | 1 | 4 | 2.0 | .986 |
| | J. Kling | R | 1 | 7 | 1 | 0 | 0 | 8.0 | 1.000 | | H. Lobert | R | 1 | 0 | 0 | 0 | 0 | 0.0 | .000 |
| 2B | J. Evers | R | 99 | 249 | 290 | 36 | 38 | 5.8 | .937 | | S. Hofman | R | 3 | 4 | 1 | 0 | 0 | 1.7 | 1.000 |
| | S. Hofman | R | 59 | 138 | 178 | 15 | 13 | 5.6 | .955 | | B. Wicker | R | 3 | 5 | 0 | 0 | 0 | 1.7 | 1.000 |
| SS | J. Tinker | R | 149 | 345 | 527 | 56 | 67 | 6.2 | .940 | | J. Kling | R | 4 | 4 | 0 | 0 | 0 | 1.0 | 1.000 |
| | S. Hofman | R | 9 | 17 | 19 | 3 | 3 | 4.3 | .923 | C | J. Kling | R | 106 | 538 | 136 | 24 | 12 | 6.6 | .966 |
| | D. Casey | R | 1 | 2 | 2 | 0 | 0 | 4.0 | 1.000 | | J. O'Neill | R | 50 | 276 | 63 | 9 | 8 | 7.0 | .974 |
| 3B | D. Casey | R | 142 | 160 | 252 | 22 | 7 | 3.1 | .949 | | | | | | | | | | |
| | H. Lobert | R | 13 | 20 | 25 | 4 | 2 | 3.8 | .918 | | | | | | | | | | |
| | S. Hofman | R | 3 | 3 | 8 | 2 | 0 | 4.3 | .846 | | | | | | | | | | |

The Cubs dropped to third place in 1905, posting an almost identical record to that of the year before. Ed Reulbach, a rookie pitcher, became an immediate mainstay with 18 victories and a sparkling 1.42 ERA. On June 24, he went the distance to beat former Cub Jack Taylor of the Cardinals, 2–1, in 18 innings. Exactly two months later, he again went the route to defeat Tully Sparks of the Phillies, 2–1, in 20 innings. Wildfire Schulte, in his first complete season, batted .274 while outfielder Bill Maloney, who was a Cub for that season only, led the league in stolen bases with 59.

His body ravaged with tuberculosis, manager Frank Selee resigned August 1 in favor of his hand-picked successor, Frank Chance. Chance, who soon became known as the "Peerless Leader," went on to a Cub managerial record of 778–396 (a .649 percentage, highest in Cub history), four pennants, and two world championships—after his team blew a 5–0 lead and lost to the lowly Phillies, 7–6, in his debut as manager. Chance also preferred the nickname Cubs (Selee had been partial to the established title of Colts), and his preference spurred increased usage of the new name. Tinker and Evers, previously on good terms, engaged in a fistfight during an exhibition game at Washington, Ind., and didn't speak to each other for the rest of their careers, although they performed brilliantly on the field.

## TEAM STATISTICS

| | W | L | PCT | GB | R | OR | 2B | 3B | Batting HR | BA | SA | SB | E | Fielding DP | FA | CG | B | Pitching SO | ShO | SV | ERA |
|---|---|---|---|---|---|---|---|---|---|---|---|---|---|---|---|---|---|---|---|---|---|
| NY | 105 | 48 | .686 | | 778 | 505 | 191 | 88 | 39 | .273 | .368 | 291 | 258 | 93 | .960 | 118 | 364 | 760 | 18 | 14 | 2.39 |
| PIT | 96 | 57 | .627 | 9 | 692 | 570 | 190 | 91 | 22 | .266 | .350 | 202 | 255 | 112 | .961 | 113 | 389 | 512 | 12 | 4 | 2.86 |
| CHI | 92 | 61 | .601 | 13 | 667 | 442 | 157 | 82 | 12 | .245 | .314 | 267 | 248 | 99 | .962 | 133 | 385 | 627 | 23 | 2 | 2.04 |
| PHI | 83 | 69 | .546 | 21.5 | 708 | 602 | 187 | 82 | 16 | .260 | .336 | 180 | 275 | 99 | .957 | 119 | 411 | 516 | 12 | 5 | 2.81 |
| CIN | 79 | 74 | .516 | 26 | 735 | 698 | 160 | 101 | 27 | .269 | .354 | 181 | 310 | 122 | .953 | 119 | 439 | 547 | 10 | 1 | 3.01 |
| STL | 58 | 96 | .377 | 47.5 | 535 | 734 | 140 | 85 | 20 | .248 | .321 | 162 | 274 | 83 | .957 | 135 | 367 | 411 | 10 | 2 | 3.59 |
| BOS | 51 | 103 | .331 | 54.5 | 468 | 731 | 148 | 52 | 17 | .234 | .293 | 132 | 325 | 89 | .951 | 139 | 433 | 533 | 14 | 0 | 3.52 |
| BKN | 48 | 104 | .316 | 56.5 | 506 | 807 | 154 | 60 | 29 | .246 | .317 | 186 | 411 | 101 | .936 | 125 | 476 | 556 | 7 | 3 | 3.76 |
| LEAGUE TOTAL | | | | | 5089 | 5089 | 1327 | 641 | 182 | .255 | .332 | 1601 | 2356 | 798 | .954 | 1001 | 3264 | 4462 | 106 | 31 | 2.99 |

## INDIVIDUAL PITCHING

| PITCHER | T | W | L | PCT | ERA | SV | G | GS | CG | IP | H | BB | SO | R | ER | ShO | H/9 | BB/9 | SO/9 |
|---|---|---|---|---|---|---|---|---|---|---|---|---|---|---|---|---|---|---|---|
| Ed Reulbach | R | 18 | 13 | .581 | 1.42 | 1 | 34 | 29 | 28 | 292 | 208 | 73 | 152 | 71 | 46 | 5 | 6.41 | 2.25 | 4.68 |
| Jake Weimer | L | 18 | 12 | .600 | 2.27 | 1 | 33 | 30 | 26 | 250 | 212 | 80 | 107 | 84 | 63 | 2 | 7.63 | 2.88 | 3.85 |
| Three Finger Brown | R | 18 | 12 | .600 | 2.17 | 0 | 30 | 24 | 24 | 249 | 219 | 47 | 89 | 89 | 60 | 4 | 7.92 | 1.59 | 3.22 |
| Bob Wicker | R | 13 | 7 | .650 | 2.02 | 0 | 22 | 22 | 17 | 178 | 139 | 47 | 86 | 46 | 40 | 4 | 7.03 | 2.38 | 4.35 |
| Carl Lundgren | R | 13 | 4 | .765 | 2.24 | 0 | 23 | 19 | 16 | 169 | 132 | 53 | 69 | 58 | 42 | 3 | 7.03 | 2.82 | 3.67 |
| Buttons Briggs | R | 8 | 8 | .500 | 2.14 | 0 | 20 | 20 | 13 | 168 | 141 | 52 | 68 | 58 | 40 | 5 | 7.55 | 2.79 | 3.64 |
| Big Jeff Pfeffer | R | 4 | 5 | .444 | 2.50 | 0 | 15 | 11 | 9 | 101 | 84 | 36 | 56 | 36 | 28 | 0 | 7.49 | 3.21 | 4.99 |
| TEAM TOTAL | | 92 | 61 | .601 | 2.04 | 2 | 177 | 155 | 133 | 1407 | 1135 | 385 | 627 | 442 | 319 | 23 | 7.26 | 2.46 | 4.01 |

| MANAGER | W | L | PCT |
|---|---|---|---|
| Frank Chance | 116 | 36 | .763 |

| POS | Player | B | G | AB | H | 2B | 3B | HR | HR % | R | RBI | BB | SO | SB | Pinch Hit AB | Pinch Hit H | BA | SA |
|---|---|---|---|---|---|---|---|---|---|---|---|---|---|---|---|---|---|---|
| **REGULARS** | | | | | | | | | | | | | | | | | | |
| 1B | Frank Chance | R | 136 | 474 | 151 | 24 | 10 | 3 | 0.6 | 103 | 71 | 70 | | 57 | 0 | 0 | .319 | .430 |
| 2B | Johnny Evers | L | 154 | 533 | 136 | 17 | 6 | 1 | 0.2 | 65 | 51 | 36 | | 49 | 0 | 0 | .255 | .315 |
| SS | Joe Tinker | R | 148 | 523 | 122 | 18 | 4 | 1 | 0.2 | 75 | 64 | 43 | | 30 | 0 | 0 | .233 | .289 |
| 3B | Harry Steinfeldt | R | 151 | 539 | 176 | 27 | 10 | 3 | 0.6 | 81 | 83 | 47 | | 29 | 0 | 0 | .327 | .430 |
| RF | Wildfire Schulte | L | 146 | 563 | 158 | 18 | 13 | 7 | 1.2 | 77 | 60 | 31 | | 25 | 0 | 0 | .281 | .396 |
| CF | Jimmy Slagle | L | 127 | 498 | 119 | 8 | 6 | 0 | 0.0 | 71 | 33 | 63 | | 25 | 0 | 0 | .239 | .279 |
| LF | Jimmy Sheckard | L | 149 | 549 | 144 | 27 | 10 | 1 | 0.2 | 90 | 45 | 67 | | 30 | 0 | 0 | .262 | .353 |
| C | Johnny Kling | R | 107 | 343 | 107 | 15 | 8 | 2 | 0.6 | 45 | 46 | 23 | | 14 | 7 | 2 | .312 | .420 |
| **SUBSTITUTES** | | | | | | | | | | | | | | | | | | |
| 1B | Pete Noonan | R | 5 | 3 | 1 | 0 | 0 | 0 | 0.0 | 0 | 0 | 0 | | 0 | 3 | 1 | .333 | .333 |
| UT | Solly Hofman | R | 64 | 195 | 50 | 2 | 3 | 2 | 1.0 | 30 | 20 | 20 | | 13 | 3 | 0 | .256 | .328 |
| OF | Doc Gessler | L | 34 | 83 | 21 | 3 | 0 | 0 | 0.0 | 8 | 10 | 12 | | 4 | 11 | 2 | .253 | .289 |
| C | Pat Moran | | 70 | 226 | 57 | 13 | 1 | 0 | 0.0 | 22 | 35 | 7 | | 6 | 9 | 0 | .252 | .319 |
| C | Tom Walsh | R | 2 | 1 | 0 | 0 | 0 | 0 | 0.0 | 0 | 0 | 0 | | 0 | 0 | 0 | .000 | .000 |
| PH | Bull Smith | R | 1 | 1 | 0 | 0 | 0 | 0 | 0.0 | 0 | 0 | 0 | | 0 | 1 | 0 | .000 | .000 |
| **PITCHERS** | | | | | | | | | | | | | | | | | | |
| P | Three Finger Brown | B | 36 | 98 | 20 | 1 | 0 | 0 | 0.0 | 11 | 4 | 6 | | 0 | 0 | 0 | .204 | .214 |
| P | Jack Pfiester | R | 31 | 84 | 4 | 0 | 0 | 0 | 0.0 | 5 | 1 | 3 | | 0 | 0 | 0 | .048 | .048 |
| P | Ed Reulbach | R | 34 | 83 | 13 | 0 | 0 | 0 | 0.0 | 4 | 4 | 2 | | 0 | 0 | 0 | .157 | .157 |
| P | Carl Lundgren | R | 28 | 67 | 12 | 0 | 0 | 0 | 0.0 | 4 | 2 | 9 | | 0 | 0 | 0 | .179 | .224 |
| P | Orval Overall | B | 18 | 53 | 9 | 1 | 0 | 0 | 0.0 | 6 | 3 | 2 | | 1 | 0 | 0 | .170 | .189 |
| P | Jack Taylor | R | 17 | 53 | 11 | 3 | 0 | 0 | 0.0 | 5 | 3 | 4 | | 0 | 0 | 0 | .208 | .264 |
| P | Fred Beebe | R | 14 | 29 | 3 | 1 | 0 | 0 | 0.0 | 1 | 3 | 1 | | 0 | 0 | 0 | .103 | .138 |
| P | Bob Wicker | R | 10 | 20 | 2 | 0 | 0 | 0 | 0.0 | 1 | 1 | 2 | | 0 | 0 | 0 | .100 | .100 |
| P | Jack Harper | R | 1 | 0 | 0 | 0 | 0 | 0 | — | 0 | 0 | 0 | | 0 | 0 | 0 | — | — |
| TEAM TOTAL | | | | 5018 | 1316 | 181 | 71 | 20 | 0.4 | 70 | 539 | 448 | 0 | 283 | 34 | 5 | .262 | .339 |

## INDIVIDUAL FIELDING

| POS | Player | T | G | PO | A | E | DP | TC/G | FA | POS | Player | T | G | PO | A | E | DP | TC/G | FA |
|---|---|---|---|---|---|---|---|---|---|---|---|---|---|---|---|---|---|---|---|
| 1B | F. Chance | R | 136 | 1376 | 82 | 16 | 71 | 10.8 | .989 | OF | J. Slagle | R | 127 | 276 | 9 | 7 | 5 | 2.3 | .976 |
| | S. Hofman | R | 21 | 186 | 9 | 2 | 10 | 9.4 | .990 | | J. Sheckard | R | 149 | 264 | 13 | 4 | 1 | 1.9 | .986 |
| | D. Gessler | R | 1 | 4 | 0 | 0 | 0 | 4.0 | 1.000 | | W. Schulte | R | 146 | 218 | 18 | 6 | 7 | 1.7 | .975 |
| | P. Noonan | R | 1 | 1 | 0 | 0 | 1 | 1.0 | 1.000 | | S. Hofman | R | 23 | 38 | 2 | 1 | 1 | 1.8 | .976 |
| 2B | J. Evers | R | 153 | 344 | 441 | 44 | 51 | 5.4 | .947 | | D. Gessler | R | 21 | 27 | 4 | 0 | 0 | 1.5 | 1.000 |
| | S. Hofman | R | 4 | 4 | 2 | 0 | 0 | 1.5 | 1.000 | | E. Reulbach | R | 1 | 1 | 1 | 0 | 0 | 2.0 | 1.000 |
| | C. Lundgren | R | 1 | 3 | 2 | 0 | 0 | 5.0 | 1.000 | | J. Kling | R | 3 | 0 | 1 | 0 | 0 | 0.3 | 1.000 |
| | Steinfeldt | | 1 | 0 | 1 | 0 | 0 | 1.0 | 1.000 | C | J. Kling | R | 96 | 520 | 126 | 12 | 7 | 6.9 | .982 |
| SS | J. Tinker | R | 147 | 288 | 472 | 45 | 55 | 5.5 | .944 | | P. Moran | R | 61 | 335 | 78 | 9 | 6 | 6.9 | .979 |
| | S. Hofman | R | 9 | 20 | 32 | 3 | 7 | 6.1 | .945 | | T. Walsh | R | 2 | 1 | 1 | 0 | 0 | 1.0 | 1.000 |
| 3B | Steinfeldt | R | 150 | 160 | 253 | 20 | 13 | 2.9 | .954 | | | | | | | | | | |
| | J. Evers | R | 1 | 0 | 0 | 0 | 0 | 0.0 | .000 | | | | | | | | | | |
| | S. Hofman | R | 4 | 5 | 7 | 1 | 0 | 3.3 | .923 | | | | | | | | | | |
| | J. Tinker | R | 1 | 1 | 2 | 1 | 0 | 4.0 | .750 | | | | | | | | | | |

In 1906 Chicago was baseball and baseball was Chicago. The very outset found the Cubs a much stronger club. Outfielder Jimmy Sheckard and third baseman Harry Steinfeldt had been picked up in trades while pitcher Jack Pfiester was signed from Omaha. In midseason they were joined by pitcher Orval Overall and a recycled Jack Taylor, both obtained in trades.

The result was a nearly invincible machine that dominated the NL like no other Cub team before or since. Winning a record 116 games, they left their closest rivals, the Giants, 20 games behind. John McGraw's worst humiliation came on June 7, when the Cubs pulverized New York, 19–0, knocking Christy Mathewson out during an 11 run first inning. In August alone the Cubs posted a 26–3 record, and the pennant was clinched with two weeks to play. They stole 283 bases for a modern Cubs team record.

Meanwhile, the White Sox had won the AL pennant to create the first crosstown World Series, and Chicago's only one so far. Although the Cubs were 3–1 favorites with the oddsmakers, the Sox won the series in six games, for the first upset in World Series play.

### TEAM STATISTICS

|    | W | L | PCT | GB | R | OR | 2B | 3B | Batting HR | BA | SA | SB | E | Fielding DP | FA | CG | B | Pitching SO | ShO | SV | ERA |
|----|---|---|-----|----|---|----|----|----|----|----|----|----|---|----|----|----|---|----|-----|----|-----|
| HI | 116 | 36 | .763 |  | 705 | 381 | 181 | 71 | 20 | .262 | .339 | 283 | 194 | 100 | .969 | 125 | 446 | 702 | 31 | 9 | 1.76 |
| Y  | 96 | 56 | .632 | 20 | 625 | 510 | 162 | 53 | 15 | .255 | .321 | 288 | 233 | 84 | .963 | 105 | 394 | 639 | 19 | 16 | 2.49 |
| IT | 93 | 60 | .608 | 23.5 | 623 | 470 | 164 | 67 | 12 | .261 | .327 | 162 | 228 | 109 | .964 | 116 | 309 | 532 | 27 | 2 | 2.21 |
| HI | 71 | 82 | .464 | 45.5 | 528 | 564 | 197 | 47 | 12 | .241 | .307 | 180 | 271 | 83 | .956 | 108 | 436 | 500 | 21 | 5 | 2.58 |
| KN | 66 | 86 | .434 | 50 | 496 | 625 | 141 | 68 | 25 | .236 | .308 | 175 | 283 | 73 | .955 | 119 | 453 | 476 | 22 | 9 | 3.13 |
| IN | 64 | 87 | .424 | 51.5 | 533 | 582 | 140 | 71 | 16 | .238 | .304 | 170 | 262 | 97 | .959 | 126 | 470 | 567 | 11 | 5 | 2.69 |
| TL | 52 | 98 | .347 | 63 | 470 | 607 | 137 | 69 | 10 | .235 | .296 | 110 | 272 | 92 | .957 | 118 | 479 | 559 | 4 | 2 | 3.04 |
| OS | 49 | 102 | .325 | 66.5 | 408 | 649 | 136 | 43 | 16 | .226 | .281 | 93 | 337 | 102 | .947 | 137 | 436 | 562 | 10 | 0 | 3.17 |
| EAGUE TOTAL |  |  |  |  | 4388 | 4388 | 1258 | 489 | 126 | .244 | .310 | 1461 | 2080 | 740 | .959 | 954 | 3423 | 4537 | 145 | 48 | 2.63 |

### INDIVIDUAL PITCHING

| ITCHER | T | W | L | PCT | ERA | SV | G | GS | CG | IP | H | BB | SO | R | ER | ShO | H/9 | BB/9 | SO/9 |
|--------|---|---|---|-----|-----|----|---|----|----|----|---|----|----|---|----|-----|-----|------|------|
| hree Finger Brown | R | 26 | 6 | .813 | 1.04 | 3 | 36 | 32 | 27 | 277.1 | 198 | 61 | 144 | 56 | 32 | 10 | 6.43 | 1.98 | 4.67 |
| ack Pfiester | L | 20 | 8 | .714 | 1.56 | 0 | 31 | 29 | 20 | 241.2 | 173 | 63 | 153 | 63 | 42 | 4 | 6.44 | 2.35 | 5.70 |
| d Reulbach | R | 19 | 4 | .826 | 1.65 | 2 | 33 | 24 | 20 | 218 | 129 | 92 | 94 | 51 | 40 | 6 | 5.33 | 3.80 | 3.88 |
| arl Lundgren | R | 17 | 6 | .739 | 2.21 | 2 | 27 | 24 | 21 | 207.2 | 160 | 89 | 103 | 63 | 51 | 5 | 6.93 | 3.86 | 4.46 |
| ack Taylor | R | 12 | 3 | .800 | 1.83 | 0 | 17 | 16 | 15 | 147.1 | 116 | 39 | 34 | 42 | 30 | 2 | 7.09 | 2.38 | 2.08 |
| rval Overall | R | 12 | 3 | .800 | 1.88 | 1 | 18 | 14 | 13 | 144 | 116 | 51 | 94 | 43 | 30 | 2 | 7.25 | 3.19 | 5.88 |
| ob Wicker | R | 3 | 5 | .375 | 2.99 | 0 | 10 | 8 | 5 | 72.1 | 70 | 19 | 25 | 36 | 24 | 0 | 8.71 | 2.36 | 3.11 |
| red Beebe | R | 7 | 1 | .875 | 2.70 | 1 | 14 | 6 | 4 | 70 | 56 | 32 | 55* | 27 | 21 | 0 | 7.20 | 4.11 | 7.07 |
| ack Harper | R | 0 | 0 | – | 0.00 | 0 | 1 | 1 | 0 | 1 | 0 | 0 | 0 | 0 | 0 | 0 | 0.00 | 0.00 | 0.00 |
| EAM TOTAL |  | 116 | 36 | .763 | 1.76 | 9 | 187 | 154 | 125 | 1379.1 | 1018 | 446 | 702 | 381 | 270 | 29 | 6.64 | 2.91 | 4.58 |

| MANAGER | W | L | PCT |
|---|---|---|---|
| Frank Chance | 107 | 45 | .704 |

| POS | Player | B | G | AB | H | 2B | 3B | HR | HR % | R | RBI | BB | SO | SB | Pinch Hit AB | Pinch Hit H | BA | SA |
|---|---|---|---|---|---|---|---|---|---|---|---|---|---|---|---|---|---|---|
| **REGULARS** | | | | | | | | | | | | | | | | | | |
| 1B | Frank Chance | R | 111 | 382 | 112 | 19 | 2 | 1 | 0.3 | 58 | 49 | 51 | | 35 | 2 | 1 | .293 | .361 |
| 2B | Johnny Evers | L | 151 | 508 | 127 | 18 | 4 | 2 | 0.4 | 66 | 51 | 38 | | 46 | 0 | 0 | .250 | .313 |
| SS | Joe Tinker | R | 117 | 402 | 89 | 11 | 3 | 1 | 0.2 | 36 | 36 | 25 | | 20 | 3 | 0 | .221 | .271 |
| 3B | Harry Steinfeldt | R | 152 | 542 | 144 | 25 | 5 | 1 | 0.2 | 52 | 70 | 37 | | 19 | 1 | 0 | .266 | .336 |
| RF | Wildfire Schulte | L | 97 | 342 | 98 | 14 | 7 | 2 | 0.6 | 44 | 32 | 22 | | 7 | 5 | 1 | .287 | .386 |
| CF | Jimmy Slagle | L | 136 | 489 | 126 | 6 | 6 | 0 | 0.0 | 71 | 32 | 76 | | 28 | 0 | 0 | .258 | .294 |
| LF | Jimmy Sheckard | L | 142 | 484 | 129 | 23 | 1 | 1 | 0.2 | 76 | 36 | 76 | | 31 | 1 | 0 | .267 | .324 |
| C | Johnny Kling | R | 104 | 334 | 95 | 15 | 8 | 1 | 0.3 | 44 | 43 | 27 | | 9 | 3 | 0 | .284 | .386 |
| **SUBSTITUTES** | | | | | | | | | | | | | | | | | | |
| 1B | Del Howard | L | 51 | 148 | 34 | 2 | 2 | 0 | 0.0 | 10 | 13 | 6 | | 3 | 9 | 2 | .230 | .270 |
| SS | Bill Sweeney | R | 3 | 10 | 1 | 0 | 0 | 0 | 0.0 | 1 | 1 | 1 | | 1 | 0 | 0 | .100 | .100 |
| UT | Heinie Zimmerman | R | 5 | 9 | 2 | 1 | 0 | 0 | 0.0 | 0 | 1 | 0 | | 0 | 0 | 0 | .222 | .333 |
| UT | Solly Hofman | R | 134 | 470 | 126 | 11 | 3 | 1 | 0.2 | 67 | 36 | 41 | | 29 | 0 | 0 | .268 | .311 |
| OF | Newt Randall | R | 22 | 78 | 16 | 4 | 2 | 0 | 0.0 | 6 | 4 | 8 | | 2 | 1 | 0 | .205 | .308 |
| PO | Kid Durbin | L | 11 | 18 | 6 | 0 | 0 | 0 | 0.0 | 2 | 0 | 1 | | 0 | 1 | 0 | .333 | .333 |
| C | Pat Moran | | 65 | 198 | 45 | 5 | 1 | 1 | 0.5 | 8 | 19 | 10 | | 5 | 6 | 2 | .227 | .278 |
| C1 | Mike Kahoe | R | 5 | 10 | 4 | 0 | 0 | 0 | 0.0 | 0 | 1 | 0 | | 0 | 1 | 1 | .400 | .400 |
| C | Jack Hardy | R | 1 | 4 | 1 | 0 | 0 | 0 | 0.0 | 0 | 0 | 0 | | 0 | 0 | 0 | .250 | .250 |
| **PITCHERS** | | | | | | | | | | | | | | | | | | |
| P | Orval Overall | B | 36 | 94 | 20 | 4 | 2 | 0 | 0.0 | 6 | 9 | 3 | | 0 | 0 | 0 | .213 | .298 |
| P | Three Finger Brown | B | 36 | 85 | 13 | 0 | 2 | 1 | 1.2 | 6 | 7 | 1 | | 0 | 0 | 0 | .153 | .235 |
| P | Carl Lundgren | R | 28 | 66 | 7 | 0 | 0 | 0 | 0.0 | 4 | 3 | 4 | | 0 | 0 | 0 | .106 | .106 |
| P | Jack Pfiester | R | 30 | 64 | 6 | 1 | 0 | 0 | 0.0 | 4 | 1 | 5 | | 0 | 0 | 0 | .094 | .109 |
| P | Ed Reulbach | R | 27 | 63 | 11 | 1 | 0 | 1 | 1.6 | 4 | 3 | 1 | | 0 | 0 | 0 | .175 | .238 |
| P | Jack Taylor | R | 18 | 47 | 9 | 2 | 0 | 0 | 0.0 | 2 | 1 | 0 | | 0 | 0 | 0 | .191 | .234 |
| P | Chick Fraser | R | 22 | 45 | 3 | 0 | 0 | 0 | 0.0 | 4 | 2 | 2 | | 0 | 0 | 0 | .067 | .067 |
| TEAM TOTAL | | | | 4892 | 1224 | 162 | 48 | 13 | 0.3 | 57 | 450 | 435 | 0 | 235 | 33 | 7 | .250 | .311 |

## INDIVIDUAL  FIELDING

| POS | Player | T | G | PO | A | E | DP | TC/G | FA |
|---|---|---|---|---|---|---|---|---|---|
| 1B | F. Chance | R | 109 | 1129 | 80 | 10 | 64 | 11.2 | **.992** |
| | D. Howard | R | 33 | 301 | 16 | 9 | 17 | 9.9 | .972 |
| | S. Hofman | R | 18 | 204 | 4 | 2 | 7 | 11.7 | .990 |
| | J. Kling | R | 2 | 10 | 2 | 0 | 1 | 6.0 | 1.000 |
| | M. Kahoe | R | 1 | 4 | 0 | 0 | 0 | 4.0 | 1.000 |
| 2B | J. Evers | R | 151 | 346 | **500** | 32 | 58 | 5.8 | .964 |
| | S. Hofman | R | 3 | 10 | 8 | 1 | 4 | 6.3 | .947 |
| | H. Zimmerman | R | 4 | 7 | 8 | 4 | 2 | 4.8 | .789 |
| SS | J. Tinker | R | 113 | 215 | 390 | 39 | 45 | 5.7 | .939 |
| | S. Hofman | R | 42 | 81 | 116 | 17 | 21 | 5.1 | .921 |
| | B. Sweeney | R | 3 | 2 | 6 | 6 | 0 | 4.7 | .571 |
| | H. Zimmerman | R | 1 | 1 | 0 | 0 | 0 | 1.0 | 1.000 |
| 3B | Steinfeldt | R | 151 | 161 | 307 | 16 | 18 | 3.2 | **.967** |
| | S. Hofman | R | 4 | 4 | 2 | 1 | 0 | 1.8 | .857 |

| POS | Player | T | G | PO | A | E | DP | TC/G | FA |
|---|---|---|---|---|---|---|---|---|---|
| OF | J. Slagle | R | 135 | 239 | 15 | 10 | 5 | 2.0 | .962 |
| | J. Sheckard | R | 142 | 223 | 13 | 6 | 2 | 1.7 | .975 |
| | S. Hofman | R | 68 | 134 | 14 | 10 | 4 | 2.3 | .937 |
| | W. Schulte | R | 91 | 130 | 11 | 4 | 1 | 1.6 | .972 |
| | N. Randall | R | 21 | 44 | 3 | 5 | 1 | 2.5 | .904 |
| | D. Howard | R | 8 | 11 | 0 | 1 | 0 | 1.5 | .917 |
| | K. Durbin | L | 5 | 3 | 2 | 0 | 0 | 1.0 | 1.000 |
| | H. Zimmerman | R | 1 | 2 | 0 | 0 | 0 | 2.0 | 1.000 |
| | T. Brown | R | 1 | 1 | 0 | 0 | 0 | 1.0 | 1.000 |
| C | J. Kling | R | 98 | 499 | 109 | 8 | 11 | 6.3 | **.987** |
| | P. Moran | R | 59 | 258 | 72 | 9 | 9 | 5.7 | .973 |
| | J. Hardy | R | 1 | 9 | 1 | 1 | 0 | 11.0 | .909 |
| | M. Kahoe | R | 3 | 5 | 1 | 0 | 0 | 2.0 | 1.000 |

The 1907 season brought another one-team pennant race, namely the Cubs. Although they could not pile up as many victories as the year before, their 107–45 mark was still good for a 17-game edge over the second-place Pirates. The Cub lead was not seriously challenged all year. And all this without a .300 hitter on the team, as Chance was the leader with a modest .293. Even injuries to Tinker and Schulte could not stop them.

Pitching was better than ever as the staff hurled 30 shutouts with a collective ERA of 1.73, still the all-time low. Individual figures were equally incredible—Pfiester, 1.15; Lundgren, 1.17; Brown, 1.39; Reulbach, 1.69; Overall, 1.70. Taylor, whose ERA had ballooned to an unspeakable 3.29, was released in September.

This time the Cubs met the Detroit Tigers of Ty Cobb, Hughie Jennings, Sam Crawford and company in the World Series. Following a 3–3, 12-inning tie in Game One, the Cubs skinned the Tigers in four straight. Cub pitching held Cobb, who had won the first of his 12 batting crowns with a .350 average, to a mere .200, while the Cubs stole a record 18 bases, including six by Slagle.

## TEAM STATISTICS

| | W | L | PCT | GB | R | OR | 2B | 3B | HR | BA | SA | SB | E | DP | FA | CG | B | SO | ShO | SV | ERA |
|---|---|---|---|---|---|---|---|---|---|---|---|---|---|---|---|---|---|---|---|---|---|
| HI | 107 | 45 | .704 | | 572 | 370 | **162** | 48 | 13 | .250 | .311 | 235 | 211 | 110 | **.967** | 114 | 402 | 584 | **30** | 7 | **1.73** |
| IT | 91 | 63 | .591 | 17 | **634** | 510 | 133 | 78 | 19 | .254 | **.324** | 264 | 256 | 75 | .959 | 111 | **368** | 497 | 24 | 4 | 2.30 |
| HI | 83 | 64 | .565 | 21.5 | 512 | 476 | **162** | 65 | 12 | .236 | .305 | 154 | 256 | 104 | .957 | 110 | 422 | 499 | 21 | 3 | 2.43 |
| Y | 82 | 71 | .536 | 25.5 | 574 | 510 | 160 | 48 | **23** | .251 | .317 | 205 | 232 | 75 | .963 | 109 | 369 | **655** | 20 | **11** | 2.45 |
| KN | 65 | 83 | .439 | 40 | 446 | 522 | 142 | 63 | 18 | .232 | .298 | 121 | 262 | 94 | .959 | 125 | 463 | 479 | 20 | 1 | 2.38 |
| IN | 66 | 87 | .431 | 41.5 | 526 | 519 | 126 | **90** | 15 | .247 | .318 | 158 | 227 | 118 | .963 | 118 | 444 | 481 | 10 | 2 | 2.41 |
| OS | 58 | 90 | .392 | 47 | 502 | 652 | 142 | 61 | 22 | .243 | .309 | 120 | 249 | **128** | .961 | 121 | 458 | 426 | 9 | 2 | 3.33 |
| TL | 52 | 101 | .340 | 55.5 | 419 | 606 | 121 | 51 | 19 | .232 | .288 | 125 | 349 | 105 | .947 | **126** | 499 | 589 | 20 | 2 | 2.70 |
| EAGUE TOTAL | | | | | 4185 | 4165 | 1148 | 504 | 141 | .243 | .309 | 1382 | 2042 | 809 | .959 | 934 | 3425 | 4210 | 154 | 32 | 2.46 |

## INDIVIDUAL PITCHING

| PITCHER | T | W | L | PCT | ERA | SV | G | GS | CG | IP | H | BB | SO | R | ER | ShO | H/9 | BB/9 | SO/9 |
|---|---|---|---|---|---|---|---|---|---|---|---|---|---|---|---|---|---|---|---|
| rval Overall | R | 23 | 8 | .742 | 1.70 | 3 | 35 | 29 | 26 | 265.1 | 199 | 69 | 139 | 62 | 50 | **8** | 6.75 | 2.34 | 4.71 |
| hree Finger Brown | R | 20 | 6 | .769 | 1.39 | 3 | 34 | 27 | 20 | 233 | 180 | 40 | 107 | 51 | 36 | 6 | 6.95 | 1.55 | 4.13 |
| arl Lundgren | R | 18 | 7 | .720 | 1.17 | 0 | 28 | 25 | 21 | 207 | 130 | 92 | 84 | 42 | 27 | 7 | **5.65** | 4.00 | 3.65 |
| ack Pfiester | L | 15 | 9 | .625 | **1.15** | 0 | 30 | 22 | 13 | 195 | 143 | 48 | 90 | 61 | 25 | 3 | 6.60 | 2.22 | 4.15 |
| d Reulbach | R | 17 | 4 | **.810** | 1.69 | 0 | 27 | 22 | 16 | 192 | 147 | 64 | 96 | 48 | 36 | 4 | 6.89 | 3.00 | 4.50 |
| hick Fraser | R | 8 | 5 | .615 | 2.28 | 0 | 22 | 15 | 9 | 138.1 | 112 | 46 | 41 | 51 | 35 | 2 | 7.29 | 2.99 | 2.67 |
| ack Taylor | R | 6 | 5 | .545 | 3.29 | 0 | 18 | 13 | 8 | 123 | 127 | 33 | 22 | 62 | 45 | 0 | 9.29 | 2.41 | 1.61 |
| d Durbin | L | 0 | 1 | .000 | 5.40 | 1 | 5 | 1 | 1 | 16.2 | 14 | 10 | 5 | 13 | 10 | 0 | 7.56 | 5.40 | 2.70 |
| EAM TOTAL | | 107 | 45 | .704 | 1.73 | 7 | 199 | 154 | 114 | 1370.1 | 1052 | 402 | 584 | 390 | 264 | 30 | 6.91 | 2.64 | 3.84 |

| MANAGER | W | L | PCT |
|---|---|---|---|
| Frank Chance | 99 | 55 | .643 |

| POS | Player | B | G | AB | H | 2B | 3B | HR | HR % | R | RBI | BB | SO | SB | Pinch Hit AB | Pinch Hit H | BA | SA |
|---|---|---|---|---|---|---|---|---|---|---|---|---|---|---|---|---|---|---|
| **REGULARS** | | | | | | | | | | | | | | | | | | |
| 1B | Frank Chance | R | 129 | 452 | 123 | 27 | 4 | 2 | 0.4 | 65 | 55 | 37 | | 27 | 4 | 2 | .272 | .363 |
| 2B | Johnny Evers | L | 126 | 416 | 125 | 19 | 6 | 0 | 0.0 | 83 | 37 | 66 | | 36 | 2 | 1 | .300 | .375 |
| SS | Joe Tinker | R | 157 | 548 | 146 | 23 | 14 | 6 | 1.1 | 67 | 68 | 32 | | 30 | 0 | 0 | .266 | .392 |
| 3B | Harry Steinfeldt | R | 150 | 539 | 130 | 20 | 6 | 1 | 0.2 | 63 | 62 | 36 | | 12 | 1 | 0 | .241 | .306 |
| RF | Wildfire Schulte | L | 102 | 386 | 91 | 20 | 2 | 1 | 0.3 | 42 | 43 | 29 | | 15 | 0 | 0 | .236 | .306 |
| CF | Jimmy Slagle | L | 104 | 352 | 78 | 4 | 1 | 0 | 0.0 | 38 | 26 | 43 | | 17 | 2 | 0 | .222 | .239 |
| LF | Jimmy Sheckard | L | 115 | 403 | 93 | 18 | 3 | 2 | 0.5 | 54 | 22 | 62 | | 18 | 0 | 0 | .231 | .305 |
| C | Johnny Kling | R | 126 | 424 | 117 | 23 | 5 | 4 | 0.9 | 51 | 59 | 21 | | 16 | 2 | 0 | .276 | .382 |
| **SUBSTITUTES** | | | | | | | | | | | | | | | | | | |
| 2O | Heinie Zimmerman | R | 46 | 113 | 33 | 4 | 1 | 0 | 0.0 | 17 | 9 | 1 | | 2 | 15 | 2 | .292 | .345 |
| UT | Solly Hofman | R | 120 | 411 | 100 | 15 | 5 | 2 | 0.5 | 55 | 42 | 33 | | 15 | 4 | 2 | .243 | .319 |
| OF | Del Howard | L | 96 | 315 | 88 | 7 | 3 | 1 | 0.3 | 42 | 26 | 23 | | 11 | 6 | 2 | .279 | .330 |
| OF | Jack Hayden | R | 11 | 45 | 9 | 2 | 0 | 0 | 0.0 | 3 | 2 | 1 | | 1 | 0 | 0 | .200 | .244 |
| OF | Kid Durbin | L | 14 | 28 | 7 | 1 | 0 | 0 | 0.0 | 3 | 0 | 2 | | 0 | 2 | 0 | .250 | .286 |
| C | Pat Moran | | 50 | 150 | 39 | 5 | 1 | 0 | 0.0 | 12 | 12 | 13 | | 6 | 4 | 0 | .260 | .307 |
| CO | Doc Marshall | R | 12 | 20 | 6 | 0 | 1 | 0 | 0.0 | 4 | 3 | 0 | | 0 | 2 | 1 | .300 | .400 |
| PH | Vin Campbell | L | 1 | 1 | 0 | 0 | 0 | 0 | 0.0 | 0 | 0 | 0 | | 0 | 1 | 0 | .000 | .000 |
| **PITCHERS** | | | | | | | | | | | | | | | | | | |
| P | Three Finger Brown | B | 46 | 121 | 25 | 0 | 0 | 0 | 0.0 | 5 | 4 | 2 | | 2 | 1 | 0 | .207 | .207 |
| P | Ed Reulbach | R | 46 | 99 | 23 | 6 | 2 | 0 | 0.0 | 10 | 9 | 6 | | 1 | 0 | 0 | .232 | .333 |
| P | Jack Pfiester | R | 33 | 79 | 8 | 1 | 0 | 0 | 0.0 | 2 | 2 | 3 | | 1 | 0 | 0 | .101 | .114 |
| P | Orval Overall | B | 38 | 70 | 9 | 1 | 1 | 0 | 0.0 | 3 | 9 | 5 | | 1 | 1 | 0 | .129 | .171 |
| P | Chick Fraser | R | 26 | 50 | 6 | 1 | 0 | 0 | 0.0 | 3 | 1 | 2 | | 1 | 0 | 0 | .120 | .140 |
| P | Carl Lundgren | R | 23 | 47 | 7 | 0 | 0 | 0 | 0.0 | 2 | 1 | 0 | | 0 | 0 | 0 | .149 | .149 |
| P | Andy Coakley | L | 4 | 6 | 0 | 0 | 0 | 0 | 0.0 | 0 | 0 | 0 | | 0 | 0 | 0 | .000 | .000 |
| P | Rube Kroh | L | 2 | 4 | 0 | 0 | 0 | 0 | 0.0 | 0 | 0 | 1 | | 0 | 0 | 0 | .000 | .000 |
| P | Bill Mack | L | 2 | 3 | 2 | 0 | 1 | 0 | 0.0 | 1 | 0 | 0 | | 0 | 0 | 0 | .667 | 1.333 |
| P | Carl Spongburg | R | 1 | 3 | 2 | 0 | 0 | 0 | 0.0 | 0 | 0 | 0 | | 0 | 0 | 0 | .667 | .667 |
| TEAM TOTAL | | | | 5085 | 1267 | 197 | 56 | 19 | 0.4 | 62 | 492 | 418 | 0 | 212 | 47 | 10 | .249 | .321 |

## INDIVIDUAL  FIELDING

| POS | Player | T | G | PO | A | E | DP | TC/G | FA | POS | Player | T | G | PO | A | E | DP | TC/G | FA |
|---|---|---|---|---|---|---|---|---|---|---|---|---|---|---|---|---|---|---|---|
| 1B | F. Chance | R | 126 | 1291 | 86 | 15 | 56 | 11.0 | .989 | OF | J. Sheckard | R | 115 | 201 | 13 | 10 | 3 | 1.9 | .955 |
| | S. Hofman | R | 37 | 357 | 20 | 11 | 10 | 10.5 | .972 | | J. Slagle | R | 101 | 199 | 6 | 5 | 2 | 2.1 | .976 |
| | D. Howard | R | 5 | 26 | 2 | 1 | 0 | 5.8 | .966 | | W. Schulte | R | 102 | 148 | 11 | 1 | 3 | 1.6 | .994 |
| | J. Kling | R | 2 | 5 | 0 | 0 | 0 | 2.5 | 1.000 | | D. Howard | R | 81 | 129 | 10 | 5 | 1 | 1.8 | .965 |
| 2B | J. Evers | R | 123 | 237 | 361 | 25 | 39 | 5.1 | .960 | | S. Hofman | R | 50 | 118 | 9 | 6 | 1 | 2.7 | .955 |
| | S. Hofman | R | 22 | 41 | 55 | 6 | 5 | 4.6 | .941 | | J. Hayden | L | 11 | 19 | 0 | 0 | 0 | 1.7 | 1.000 |
| | H. Zimmerman | R | 20 | 41 | 43 | 7 | 2 | 4.6 | .923 | | D. Marshall | R | 3 | 13 | 2 | 1 | 0 | 5.3 | .938 |
| SS | J. Tinker | R | 157 | 314 | 570 | 39 | 48 | 5.9 | .958 | | K. Durbin | L | 11 | 15 | 0 | 0 | 0 | 1.4 | 1.000 |
| | H. Zimmerman | R | 1 | 1 | 2 | 1 | 0 | 4.0 | .750 | | J. Kling | R | 6 | 6 | 4 | 1 | 1 | 1.8 | .909 |
| 3B | Steinfeldt | R | 150 | 166 | 275 | 28 | 15 | 3.1 | .940 | | H. Zimmerman | R | 8 | 5 | 0 | 0 | 0 | 0.6 | 1.000 |
| | S. Hofman | R | 9 | 16 | 13 | 0 | 0 | 3.2 | 1.000 | C | J. Kling | R | 117 | 596 | 149 | 16 | 11 | 6.5 | .979 |
| | H. Zimmerman | R | 1 | 1 | 3 | 1 | 0 | 5.0 | .800 | | P. Moran | R | 45 | 242 | 56 | 10 | 5 | 6.8 | .968 |
| | | | | | | | | | | | D. Marshall | R | 4 | 9 | 2 | 0 | 1 | 2.8 | 1.000 |

Unlike the two previous seasons, in which the Cubs ran away with the pennant, the 1908 race was a three-way battle to the finish between the Cubs, the Giants, and the Pirates. The Chicago–New York enmity reached its zenith.

On the race's road to its exciting finish, Brown and Reulbach posted their greatest seasons, with records of 29–9 and 24–7. Brown's victory total is still the most by a Cub since the institution of the 60-foot pitching distance. In addition, both pitchers enjoyed streaks of four consecutive shutouts, which remained a league record until broken by Don Drysdale 60 years later. Included in Reulbach's quartet was a shutout doubleheader victory over Brooklyn September 26 by scores of 5–0 and 3–0, the only such occurrence in major-league history.

On September 23, Moose McCormick of the Giants crossed home plate in the bottom of the ninth in what appeared to be the winning run for a 2–1 victory. But Johnny Evers got ahold of a ball and stepped on second base to force Fred Merkle, the runner on first who had failed to touch second but had instead headed for the clubhouse. Umpire Hank O'Day ruled Merkle out, and the game was declared a tie because the fans had already swarmed onto the field, and it was impossible to resume play. In the replay on October 8, the Cubs beat Christy Mathewson, 4–2, to capture the pennant. In the World Series, they were again challenged by the Tigers, who this time eked out one victory. The Cubs went on to become the first team to win two consecutive series.

## TEAM STATISTICS

| | W | L | PCT | GB | R | OR | Batting 2B | 3B | HR | BA | SA | SB | Fielding E | DP | FA | Pitching CG | B | SO | ShO | SV | ERA |
|---|---|---|---|---|---|---|---|---|---|---|---|---|---|---|---|---|---|---|---|---|---|
| CHI | 99 | 55 | .643 | | 624 | 461 | 197 | 56 | 19 | .249 | .321 | 212 | 206 | 76 | .969 | 108 | 437 | 668 | 28 | 10 | 2.14 |
| NY | 98 | 56 | .636 | 1 | 652 | 456 | 182 | 43 | 20 | .267 | .333 | 181 | 250 | 79 | .962 | 95 | 288 | 656 | 25 | 15 | 2.14 |
| PIT | 98 | 56 | .636 | 1 | 585 | 469 | 162 | 98 | 25 | .247 | .332 | 186 | 226 | 74 | .964 | 100 | 406 | 468 | 24 | 8 | 2.12 |
| PHI | 83 | 71 | .539 | 16 | 504 | 445 | 194 | 68 | 11 | .244 | .316 | 200 | 238 | 75 | .963 | 116 | 379 | 476 | 22 | 6 | 2.10 |
| CIN | 73 | 81 | .474 | 26 | 489 | 544 | 129 | 77 | 14 | .227 | .294 | 196 | 255 | 72 | .959 | 110 | 415 | 433 | 17 | 7 | 2.37 |
| BOS | 63 | 91 | .409 | 36 | 537 | 622 | 137 | 43 | 17 | .239 | .293 | 134 | 252 | 90 | .962 | 92 | 423 | 416 | 14 | 1 | 2.79 |
| BKN | 53 | 101 | .344 | 46 | 377 | 516 | 110 | 60 | 28 | .213 | .277 | 113 | 247 | 66 | .961 | 118 | 444 | 535 | 20 | 3 | 2.47 |
| STL | 49 | 105 | .318 | 50 | 371 | 626 | 134 | 57 | 17 | .223 | .283 | 150 | 348 | 68 | .946 | 97 | 430 | 528 | 13 | 4 | 2.64 |
| LEAGUE TOTAL | | | | | 4139 | 4139 | 1245 | 502 | 151 | .239 | .306 | 1372 | 2022 | 600 | .961 | 836 | 3222 | 4180 | 163 | 54 | 2.35 |

## INDIVIDUAL PITCHING

| PITCHER | T | W | L | PCT | ERA | SV | G | GS | CG | IP | H | BB | SO | R | ER | ShO | H/9 | BB/9 | SO/9 |
|---|---|---|---|---|---|---|---|---|---|---|---|---|---|---|---|---|---|---|---|
| Three Finger Brown | R | 29 | 9 | .763 | 1.47 | 5 | 44 | 31 | 27 | 312.1 | 214 | 49 | 123 | 64 | 51 | 9 | 6.17 | 1.41 | 3.54 |
| Ed Reulbach | R | 24 | 7 | .774 | 2.03 | 1 | 46 | 35 | 25 | 297.2 | 227 | 106 | 133 | 81 | 67 | 7 | 6.86 | 3.20 | 4.02 |
| Jack Pfiester | L | 12 | 10 | .545 | 2.00 | 0 | 33 | 29 | 18 | 252 | 204 | 70 | 117 | 87 | 56 | 3 | 7.29 | 2.50 | 4.18 |
| Orval Overall | R | 15 | 11 | .577 | 1.92 | 2 | 37 | 27 | 16 | 225 | 165 | 78 | 167 | 74 | 48 | 4 | 6.60 | 3.12 | 6.68 |
| Chick Fraser | R | 11 | 9 | .550 | 2.27 | 2 | 26 | 17 | 11 | 162.2 | 141 | 61 | 66 | 71 | 41 | 2 | 7.80 | 3.38 | 3.65 |
| Carl Lundgren | R | 6 | 9 | .400 | 4.22 | 0 | 23 | 15 | 9 | 138.2 | 149 | 56 | 38 | 72 | 65 | 1 | 9.67 | 3.63 | 2.47 |
| Andy Coakley | R | 2 | 0 | 1.000 | 0.89 | 0 | 4 | 3 | 2 | 20.1 | 14 | 6 | 7 | 4 | 2 | 1 | 6.20 | 2.66 | 3.10 |
| Rube Kroh | L | 0 | 0 | – | 1.50 | 0 | 2 | 1 | 0 | 12 | 9 | 4 | 11 | 3 | 2 | 0 | 6.75 | 3.00 | 8.25 |
| Carl Spongburg | R | 0 | 0 | – | 9.00 | 0 | 1 | 0 | 0 | 7 | 9 | 6 | 4 | 7 | 7 | 0 | 11.57 | 7.71 | 5.14 |
| Bill Mack | L | 0 | 0 | – | 2.84 | 0 | 2 | 0 | 0 | 6.1 | 5 | 1 | 2 | 3 | 2 | 0 | 7.11 | 1.42 | 2.84 |
| TEAM TOTAL | | 99 | 55 | .643 | 2.14 | 10 | 218 | 158 | 108 | 1434 | 1137 | 437 | 668 | 466 | 341 | 27 | 7.14 | 2.74 | 4.19 |

| MANAGER | W | L | PCT |
|---|---|---|---|
| Frank Chance | 104 | 49 | .680 |

| POS | Player | B | G | AB | H | 2B | 3B | HR | HR % | R | RBI | BB | SO | SB | Pinch Hit AB | Pinch Hit H | BA | SA |
|---|---|---|---|---|---|---|---|---|---|---|---|---|---|---|---|---|---|---|
| **REGULARS** | | | | | | | | | | | | | | | | | | |
| 1B | Frank Chance | R | 93 | 324 | 88 | 16 | 4 | 0 | 0.0 | 53 | 46 | 30 | | 29 | 0 | 0 | .272 | .346 |
| 2B | Johnny Evers | L | 127 | 463 | 122 | 19 | 6 | 1 | 0.2 | 88 | 24 | 73 | | 28 | 0 | 0 | .263 | .337 |
| SS | Joe Tinker | R | 143 | 516 | 132 | 26 | 11 | 4 | 0.8 | 56 | 57 | 17 | | 23 | 0 | 0 | .256 | .372 |
| 3B | Harry Steinfeldt | R | 151 | 528 | 133 | 27 | 6 | 2 | 0.4 | 73 | 59 | 57 | | 22 | 0 | 0 | .252 | .337 |
| RF | Wildfire Schulte | L | 140 | 538 | 142 | 16 | 11 | 4 | 0.7 | 57 | 60 | 24 | | 23 | 0 | 0 | .264 | .357 |
| CF | Solly Hofman | R | 153 | 527 | 150 | 21 | 4 | 2 | 0.4 | 60 | 58 | 53 | | 20 | 0 | 0 | .285 | .351 |
| LF | Jimmy Sheckard | L | 148 | 525 | 134 | 29 | 5 | 1 | 0.2 | 81 | 43 | 72 | | 15 | 0 | 0 | .255 | .335 |
| C | Jimmy Archer | R | 80 | 261 | 60 | 9 | 2 | 1 | 0.4 | 31 | 30 | 12 | | 5 | 0 | 0 | .230 | .291 |
| **SUBSTITUTES** | | | | | | | | | | | | | | | | | | |
| 1B | Del Howard | L | 69 | 203 | 40 | 4 | 2 | 1 | 0.5 | 25 | 24 | 18 | | 6 | 8 | 0 | .197 | .251 |
| UT | Heinie Zimmerman | R | 65 | 183 | 50 | 9 | 2 | 0 | 0.0 | 23 | 21 | 3 | | 7 | 18 | 6 | .273 | .344 |
| 1B | Fred Luderus | L | 11 | 37 | 11 | 1 | 1 | 1 | 2.7 | 8 | 9 | 3 | | 0 | 0 | 0 | .297 | .459 |
| OF | Joe Stanley | B | 22 | 52 | 7 | 1 | 0 | 0 | 0.0 | 4 | 2 | 6 | | 0 | 6 | 0 | .135 | .154 |
| UT | John Kane | R | 20 | 45 | 4 | 1 | 0 | 0 | 0.0 | 6 | 5 | 2 | | 1 | 2 | 0 | .089 | .111 |
| OF | George Browne | L | 12 | 39 | 8 | 0 | 1 | 0 | 0.0 | 7 | 1 | 5 | | 3 | 0 | 0 | .205 | .256 |
| OF | Bill Davidson | R | 2 | 7 | 1 | 0 | 0 | 0 | 0.0 | 2 | 0 | 1 | | 1 | 0 | 0 | .143 | .143 |
| C | Pat Moran | | 77 | 246 | 54 | 11 | 1 | 1 | 0.4 | 18 | 23 | 16 | | 2 | 2 | 1 | .220 | .285 |
| C | Tom Needham | R | 13 | 28 | 4 | 0 | 0 | 0 | 0.0 | 3 | 0 | 0 | | 0 | 6 | 2 | .143 | .143 |
| **PITCHERS** | | | | | | | | | | | | | | | | | | |
| P | Three Finger Brown | B | 50 | 125 | 22 | 3 | 1 | 0 | 0.0 | 13 | 9 | 5 | | 0 | 0 | 0 | .176 | .216 |
| P | Orval Overall | B | 38 | 96 | 22 | 6 | 1 | 2 | 2.1 | 7 | 11 | 7 | | 0 | 0 | 0 | .229 | .375 |
| P | Ed Reulbach | R | 35 | 86 | 12 | 2 | 1 | 0 | 0.0 | 3 | 7 | 5 | | 0 | 0 | 0 | .140 | .186 |
| P | Jack Pfiester | R | 29 | 65 | 11 | 1 | 0 | 0 | 0.0 | 5 | 4 | 5 | | 1 | 0 | 0 | .169 | .185 |
| P | Rube Kroh | L | 17 | 40 | 6 | 0 | 0 | 0 | 0.0 | 4 | 0 | 4 | | 1 | 0 | 0 | .150 | .150 |
| P | Irv Higginbotham | R | 19 | 26 | 6 | 0 | 0 | 0 | 0.0 | 1 | 0 | 0 | | 0 | 0 | 0 | .231 | .231 |
| P | Rip Hagerman | R | 13 | 23 | 3 | 1 | 0 | 0 | 0.0 | 2 | 1 | 1 | | 0 | 0 | 0 | .130 | .174 |
| P | King Cole | R | 1 | 4 | 3 | 0 | 1 | 0 | 0.0 | 1 | 0 | 0 | | 0 | 0 | 0 | .750 | 1.250 |
| P | Rudy Schwenck | | 3 | 4 | 1 | 0 | 0 | 0 | 0.0 | 0 | 0 | 1 | | 0 | 0 | 0 | .250 | .250 |
| P | Ray Brown | | 1 | 3 | 0 | 0 | 0 | 0 | 0.0 | 0 | 1 | 0 | | 0 | 0 | 0 | .000 | .000 |
| P | Carl Lundgren | R | 2 | 2 | 1 | 0 | 0 | 0 | 0.0 | 1 | 1 | 0 | | 0 | 0 | 0 | .500 | .500 |
| P | Pat Ragan | R | 2 | 2 | 0 | 0 | 0 | 0 | 0.0 | 0 | 0 | 0 | | 0 | 0 | 0 | .000 | .000 |
| P | Chick Fraser | R | 1 | 1 | 0 | 0 | 0 | 0 | 0.0 | 0 | 0 | 0 | | 0 | 0 | 0 | .000 | .000 |
| P | Andy Coakley | L | 0 | 0 | 0 | 0 | 0 | 0 | | 0 | 0 | 0 | | 0 | 0 | 0 | – | – |
| | TEAM TOTAL | | - | 4999 | 1227 | 203 | 60 | 20 | 0.4 | 63 | 496 | 420 | 0 | 187 | 42 | 9 | .245 | .322 |

## INDIVIDUAL  FIELDING

| POS | Player | T | G | PO | A | E | DP | TC/G | FA | POS | Player | T | G | PO | A | E | DP | TC/G | FA |
|---|---|---|---|---|---|---|---|---|---|---|---|---|---|---|---|---|---|---|---|
| 1B | F. Chance | R | 92 | 901 | 40 | 6 | 43 | 10.3 | .994 | OF | S. Hofman | R | 153 | 347 | 16 | 13 | 5 | 2.5 | .965 |
| | D. Howard | R | 57 | 593 | 32 | 13 | 29 | 11.2 | .980 | | J. Sheckard | R | 148 | 277 | 18 | 10 | 5 | 2.1 | .967 |
| | F. Luderus | R | 11 | 110 | 4 | 6 | 4 | 10.9 | .950 | | W. Schulte | R | 140 | 169 | 14 | 6 | 1 | 1.4 | .968 |
| 2B | J. Evers | R | 126 | 262 | 354 | 38 | 29 | 5.2 | .942 | | J. Stanley | R | 16 | 17 | 1 | 1 | 0 | 1.2 | .947 |
| | H. Zimmerman | R | 27 | 38 | 23 | 2 | 7 | 2.3 | .968 | | G. Browne | R | 12 | 16 | 1 | 1 | 0 | 1.5 | .944 |
| | J. Kane | R | 2 | 7 | 9 | 0 | 1 | 8.0 | 1.000 | | J. Kane | R | 8 | 9 | 2 | 1 | 0 | 1.5 | .917 |
| SS | J. Tinker | R | 143 | 320 | 470 | 50 | 49 | 5.9 | **.940** | | B. Davidson | R | 2 | 3 | 0 | 0 | 0 | 1.5 | 1.000 |
| | H. Zimmerman | R | 12 | 28 | 32 | 10 | 4 | 5.8 | .857 | C | J. Archer | R | 80 | 408 | 97 | 21 | 7 | 6.6 | .960 |
| | J. Kane | R | 3 | 7 | 9 | 0 | 1 | 5.3 | 1.000 | | P. Moran | R | 74 | 181 | 97 | 8 | 3 | 3.9 | .972 |
| 3B | Steinfeldt | R | 151 | 183 | 299 | 31 | 16 | 3.4 | .940 | | T. Needham | R | 7 | 43 | 5 | 1 | 0 | 7.0 | .980 |
| | H. Zimmerman | R | 16 | 34 | 38 | 7 | 1 | 4.9 | .911 | | | | | | | | | | |
| | J. Kane | R | 3 | 3 | 4 | 2 | 1 | 3.0 | .778 | | | | | | | | | | |

Following the 1908 season Johnny Kling retired because he won the pocket billiard championship. In his absence, the catching was done by Pat Moran and Dublin-born Jimmy Archer, and the Cubs finished second. Although Johnny returned in 1910, the ownership never forgave his "desertion," blaming that for the Cubs' failure to repeat.

The real reason was that the Pirates simply outdid them, winning 110 games to the Cubs' 104, which normally would be more than enough. Against Boston alone, the Cubs had an incredible 21–1 record. Their pitching was as strong as ever, as the staff hurled a league-record 32 shutouts. Lundgren was gone, but the other "big four" of Brown, Reulbach, Overall, and Pfiester easily handled the load, with Reulbach winning 14 in a row. Jimmy Slagle had retired and was replaced in center field by utility man Solly Hofman, who batted .285 to pace the club. But after three straight pennants and two world championships, second fiddle was not much fun.

### TEAM  STATISTICS

| | W | L | PCT | GB | R | OR | 2B | 3B | HR | BA | SA | SB | E | DP | FA | CG | B | SO | ShO | SV | ERA |
|---|---|---|---|---|---|---|---|---|---|---|---|---|---|---|---|---|---|---|---|---|---|
| | | | | | | | | Batting | | | | | | Fielding | | | | Pitching | | | |
| T | 110 | 42 | .724 | | 699 | 447 | 218 | 92 | 25 | .260 | .353 | 185 | 227 | 100 | .964 | 94 | 320 | 490 | 20 | 9 | 2.07 |
| HI | 104 | 49 | .680 | 6.5 | 635 | 390 | 203 | 60 | 20 | .245 | .322 | 187 | 244 | 95 | .961 | 111 | 364 | 680 | 32 | 9 | 1.75 |
| Y | 92 | 61 | .601 | 18.5 | 623 | 546 | 173 | 68 | 26 | .255 | .329 | 230 | 307 | 99 | .954 | 105 | 397 | 735 | 16 | 12 | 2.27 |
| IN | 77 | 76 | .503 | 33.5 | 606 | 599 | 159 | 72 | 22 | .250 | .323 | 280 | 308 | 120 | .952 | 91 | 510 | 477 | 10 | 9 | 2.52 |
| HI | 74 | 79 | .484 | 36.5 | 516 | 518 | 185 | 53 | 12 | .244 | .309 | 185 | 241 | 97 | .961 | 89 | 470 | 610 | 17 | 6 | 2.44 |
| KN | 55 | 98 | .359 | 55.5 | 444 | 627 | 176 | 59 | 16 | .229 | .296 | 141 | 282 | 86 | .954 | 126 | 528 | 594 | 18 | 2 | 3.10 |
| TL | 54 | 98 | .355 | 56 | 583 | 731 | 148 | 56 | 15 | .243 | .303 | 161 | 322 | 90 | .950 | 84 | 483 | 435 | 4 | 2 | 3.41 |
| OS | 45 | 108 | .294 | 65.5 | 435 | 683 | 124 | 43 | 15 | .223 | .274 | 135 | 340 | 101 | .947 | 98 | 543 | 414 | 12 | 6 | 3.20 |
| AGUE TOTAL | | | | | 4541 | 4541 | 1386 | 503 | 151 | .244 | .314 | 1504 | 2271 | 788 | .955 | 798 | 3615 | 4435 | 129 | 55 | 2.59 |

### INDIVIDUAL  PITCHING

| TCHER | T | W | L | PCT | ERA | SV | G | GS | CG | IP | H | BB | SO | R | ER | ShO | H/9 | BB/9 | SO/9 |
|---|---|---|---|---|---|---|---|---|---|---|---|---|---|---|---|---|---|---|---|
| hree Finger Brown | R | 27 | 9 | .750 | 1.31 | 7 | 50 | 34 | 32 | 342.2 | 246 | 53 | 172 | 78 | 50 | 8 | 6.46 | 1.39 | 4.52 |
| rval Overall | R | 20 | 11 | .645 | 1.42 | 2 | 38 | 32 | 23 | 285 | 204 | 80 | 205 | 66 | 45 | 9 | 6.44 | 2.53 | 6.47 |
| d Reulbach | R | 19 | 10 | .655 | 1.78 | 0 | 35 | 32 | 23 | 262.2 | 194 | 82 | 105 | 69 | 52 | 6 | 6.65 | 2.81 | 3.60 |
| ack Pfiester | L | 17 | 6 | .739 | 2.43 | 0 | 29 | 25 | 13 | 196.2 | 179 | 49 | 73 | 67 | 53 | 5 | 8.19 | 2.24 | 3.34 |
| ube Kroh | L | 9 | 4 | .692 | 1.65 | 0 | 17 | 13 | 10 | 120.1 | 97 | 30 | 51 | 26 | 22 | 2 | 7.25 | 2.24 | 3.81 |
| p Hagerman | R | 4 | 4 | .500 | 1.82 | 0 | 13 | 7 | 4 | 79 | 64 | 28 | 32 | 29 | 16 | 1 | 7.29 | 3.19 | 3.65 |
| v Higginbotham | R | 5 | 2 | .714 | 2.19 | 0 | 19 | 6 | 4 | 78 | 64 | 20 | 32 | 32 | 19 | 0 | 7.38 | 2.31 | 3.69 |
| ay Brown | | 1 | 0 | 1.000 | 2.00 | 0 | 1 | 1 | 1 | 9 | 5 | 4 | 2 | 3 | 2 | 0 | 5.00 | 4.00 | 2.00 |
| ng Cole | R | 1 | 0 | 1.000 | 0.00 | 0 | 1 | 1 | 1 | 9 | 6 | 3 | 1 | 0 | 0 | 1 | 6.00 | 3.00 | 1.00 |
| arl Lundgren | R | 0 | 1 | .000 | 4.15 | 0 | 2 | 1 | 0 | 4.1 | 6 | 4 | 0 | 2 | 2 | 0 | 12.46 | 8.31 | 0.00 |
| dy Schwenck | | 1 | 1 | .500 | 13.50 | 0 | 3 | 2 | 0 | 4 | 16 | 3 | 3 | 7 | 6 | 0 | 36.00 | 6.75 | 6.75 |
| at Ragan | R | 0 | 0 | – | 2.45 | 0 | 2 | 0 | 0 | 3.2 | 4 | 1 | 2 | 2 | 1 | 0 | 9.82 | 2.45 | 4.91 |
| hick Fraser | R | 0 | 0 | – | 0.00 | 0 | 1 | 0 | 0 | 3 | 2 | 4 | 1 | 1 | 0 | 0 | 6.00 | 12.00 | 3.00 |
| ndy Coakley | R | 0 | 1 | .000 | 18.00 | 0 | 1 | 1 | 0 | 2 | 7 | 3 | 1 | 7 | 4 | 0 | 31.50 | 13.50 | 4.50 |
| EAM TOTAL | | 104 | 49 | .680 | 1.75 | 9 | 212 | 155 | 111 | 1399.1 | 1094 | 364 | 680 | 389 | 272 | 32 | 7.04 | 2.34 | 4.37 |

| MANAGER | W | L | PCT |
|---|---|---|---|
| Frank Chance | 104 | 50 | .675 |

| POS | Player | B | G | AB | H | 2B | 3B | HR | HR % | R | RBI | BB | SO | SB | Pinch Hit AB | Pinch Hit H | BA | SA |
|---|---|---|---|---|---|---|---|---|---|---|---|---|---|---|---|---|---|---|
| **REGULARS** | | | | | | | | | | | | | | | | | | |
| 1B | Frank Chance | R | 88 | 295 | 88 | 12 | 8 | 0 | 0.0 | 54 | 36 | 37 | 15 | 16 | 1 | 0 | .298 | .393 |
| 2B | Johnny Evers | L | 125 | 433 | 114 | 11 | 7 | 0 | 0.0 | 87 | 28 | 108 | 18 | 28 | 0 | 0 | .263 | .321 |
| SS | Joe Tinker | R | 133 | 473 | 136 | 25 | 9 | 3 | 0.6 | 48 | 69 | 24 | 35 | 20 | 2 | 0 | .288 | .397 |
| 3B | Harry Steinfeldt | R | 129 | 448 | 113 | 21 | 1 | 2 | 0.4 | 70 | 58 | 36 | 29 | 10 | 1 | 0 | .252 | .317 |
| RF | Wildfire Schulte | L | 151 | 559 | 168 | 29 | 15 | 10 | 1.8 | 93 | 68 | 39 | 57 | 22 | 1 | 0 | .301 | .460 |
| CF | Solly Hofman | R | 136 | 477 | 155 | 24 | 16 | 3 | 0.6 | 83 | 86 | 65 | 34 | 29 | 0 | 0 | .325 | .461 |
| LF | Jimmy Sheckard | L | 144 | 507 | 130 | 27 | 6 | 5 | 1.0 | 82 | 51 | 83 | 53 | 22 | 1 | 1 | .256 | .363 |
| C | Johnny Kling | R | 91 | 297 | 80 | 17 | 2 | 2 | 0.7 | 31 | 32 | 37 | 27 | 3 | 4 | 0 | .269 | .360 |
| **SUBSTITUTES** | | | | | | | | | | | | | | | | | | |
| UT | Heinie Zimmerman | R | 99 | 335 | 95 | 16 | 6 | 3 | 0.9 | 35 | 38 | 20 | 36 | 7 | 12 | 3 | .284 | .394 |
| 1B | Fred Luderus | L | 24 | 54 | 11 | 1 | 1 | 0 | 0.0 | 5 | 3 | 4 | 3 | 0 | 6 | 2 | .204 | .259 |
| OF | Ginger Beaumont | L | 56 | 172 | 46 | 5 | 1 | 2 | 1.2 | 30 | 22 | 28 | 14 | 4 | 13 | 3 | .267 | .343 |
| UT | John Kane | R | 32 | 62 | 15 | 0 | 0 | 1 | 1.6 | 11 | 12 | 9 | 10 | 2 | 0 | 0 | .242 | .290 |
| C1 | Jimmy Archer | R | 98 | 313 | 81 | 17 | 6 | 2 | 0.6 | 36 | 41 | 14 | 49 | 6 | 8 | 3 | .259 | .371 |
| C | Tom Needham | R | 31 | 76 | 14 | 3 | 1 | 0 | 0.0 | 9 | 10 | 10 | 10 | 1 | 3 | 0 | .184 | .250 |
| PH | Doc Miller | L | 1 | 1 | 0 | 0 | 0 | 0 | 0.0 | 0 | 0 | 0 | 0 | 0 | 1 | 0 | .000 | .000 |
| **PITCHERS** | | | | | | | | | | | | | | | | | | |
| P | Three Finger Brown | B | 46 | 103 | 18 | 1 | 2 | 0 | 0.0 | 9 | 6 | 6 | 17 | 1 | 0 | 0 | .175 | .223 |
| P | King Cole | R | 34 | 91 | 21 | 2 | 1 | 0 | 0.0 | 7 | 9 | 3 | 25 | 1 | 1 | 0 | .231 | .275 |
| P | Harry McIntyre | R | 30 | 66 | 17 | 2 | 0 | 1 | 1.5 | 3 | 8 | 4 | 13 | 0 | 2 | 0 | .258 | .333 |
| P | Ed Reulbach | R | 24 | 56 | 6 | 0 | 0 | 0 | 0.0 | 4 | 2 | 3 | 20 | 1 | 0 | 0 | .107 | .107 |
| P | Orval Overall | B | 25 | 41 | 5 | 1 | 0 | 0 | 0.0 | 4 | 1 | 5 | 6 | 0 | 0 | 0 | .122 | .146 |
| P | Lew Richie | R | 30 | 40 | 9 | 4 | 1 | 0 | 0.0 | 6 | 1 | 3 | 8 | 0 | 0 | 0 | .225 | .375 |
| P | Jack Pfiester | R | 14 | 33 | 3 | 0 | 0 | 0 | 0.0 | 1 | 2 | 2 | 12 | 0 | 0 | 0 | .091 | .091 |
| P | Big Jeff Pfeffer | R | 14 | 17 | 3 | 1 | 1 | 0 | 0.0 | 1 | 2 | 1 | 1 | 0 | 0 | 0 | .176 | .353 |
| P | Orlie Weaver | R | 7 | 13 | 2 | 0 | 0 | 0 | 0.0 | 1 | 0 | 0 | 2 | 0 | 0 | 0 | .154 | .154 |
| P | Rube Kroh | L | 6 | 12 | 3 | 0 | 0 | 0 | 0.0 | 1 | 1 | 0 | 5 | 0 | 0 | 0 | .250 | .250 |
| P | Bill Foxen | L | 2 | 2 | 0 | 0 | 0 | 0 | 0.0 | 0 | 0 | 1 | 1 | 0 | 0 | 0 | .000 | .000 |
| P | Alex Carson | | 2 | 1 | 0 | 0 | 0 | 0 | 0.0 | 0 | 0 | 1 | 1 | 0 | 0 | 0 | .000 | .000 |
| TEAM TOTAL | | | | 4977 | 1333 | 219 | 84 | 34 | 0.7 | 71 | 586 | 542 | 501 | 173 | 56 | 12 | .268 | .366 |

## INDIVIDUAL FIELDING

| POS | Player | T | G | PO | A | E | DP | TC/G | FA |
|---|---|---|---|---|---|---|---|---|---|
| 1B | F. Chance | R | 87 | 773 | 38 | 3 | 48 | 9.4 | .996 |
| | J. Archer | R | 40 | 381 | 17 | 10 | 25 | 10.2 | .975 |
| | S. Hofman | R | 24 | 212 | 8 | 5 | 10 | 9.4 | .978 |
| | F. Luderus | R | 17 | 151 | 7 | 4 | 7 | 9.5 | .975 |
| | O. Overall | R | 1 | 0 | 0 | 0 | 0 | 0.0 | .000 |
| | H. Zimmerman | R | 1 | 3 | 0 | 0 | 0 | 3.0 | 1.000 |
| | T. Needham | R | 1 | 2 | 0 | 0 | 0 | 2.0 | 1.000 |
| 2B | J. Evers | R | 125 | 282 | 347 | 33 | 55 | 5.3 | .950 |
| | H. Zimmerman | R | 33 | 73 | 73 | 8 | 15 | 4.7 | .948 |
| | J. Kane | R | 6 | 4 | 4 | 1 | 1 | 1.5 | .889 |
| SS | J. Tinker | R | 131 | 277 | 411 | 42 | 54 | 5.6 | .942 |
| | H. Zimmerman | R | 26 | 46 | 69 | 24 | 9 | 5.3 | .827 |
| | J. Kane | R | 2 | 2 | 3 | 0 | 0 | 2.5 | 1.000 |
| 3B | Steinfeldt | R | 128 | 137 | 246 | 22 | 16 | 3.2 | .946 |
| | H. Zimmerman | R | 22 | 37 | 38 | 1 | 4 | 3.5 | .987 |
| | J. Kane | R | 4 | 4 | 7 | 2 | 0 | 3.3 | .846 |
| | S. Hofman | R | 1 | 0 | 1 | 0 | 0 | 1.0 | 1.000 |

| POS | Player | T | G | PO | A | E | DP | TC/G | FA |
|---|---|---|---|---|---|---|---|---|---|
| OF | J. Sheckard | R | 143 | 308 | 21 | 8 | 3 | 2.4 | .976 |
| | S. Hofman | R | 110 | 249 | 19 | 7 | 4 | 2.5 | .975 |
| | W. Schulte | R | 150 | 221 | 18 | 8 | 5 | 1.6 | .968 |
| | G. Beaumont | R | 56 | 107 | 5 | 5 | 0 | 2.1 | .957 |
| | J. Kane | R | 18 | 21 | 0 | 0 | 0 | 1.2 | 1.000 |
| | O. Overall | R | 1 | 0 | 0 | 0 | 0 | 0.0 | .000 |
| | H. Zimmerman | R | 4 | 5 | 1 | 0 | 0 | 1.5 | 1.000 |
| | B. Pfeffer | R | 1 | 1 | 0 | 0 | 0 | 1.0 | 1.000 |
| C | J. Kling | R | 86 | 407 | 118 | 11 | 10 | 6.2 | .979 |
| | J. Archer | R | 49 | 239 | 80 | 10 | 6 | 6.7 | .970 |
| | T. Needham | R | 27 | 131 | 31 | 3 | 0 | 6.1 | .982 |

Following a one-year hiatus, the Cubs won their fourth pennant in five years with 104 victories and a 13-game lead over the hated Giants. Kling had returned to the team, but his best days were obviously behind him as he shared the catching chores with Jimmy Archer. Brown won 25 games but it was rookie Len "King" Cole who stole the show with a 20–4 mark, including a 4–0 no-hitter over the Cardinals on July 31 that was called after the seventh inning because both teams had to catch a train.

It looked as if the Cubs were putting their hitting shoes back on, too. Their league-leading 34 home runs were the most by a Cub team since 1897, while the team batting average was the club's highest in seven years. Solly Hofman batted a solid .325, while Schulte led the league in homers with 10. Utility infielder Heinie Zimmerman began appearing on a semiregular basis and grew more proficient at the plate every day. On the negative side, Evers suffered a broken leg late in the season and could not play in the World Series. On June 28, Tinker became the only Cub to steal home twice in one game during an 11–1 romp over the Reds, while the pennant clincher, an 8–4 victory at Cincinnati, featured a triple play.

The Cubs entered the World Series as favorites, but a younger and faster Philadelphia Athletic squad made mincemeat out of them in five games. It was the first sign that Chance's machine was starting to grow old.

## TEAM STATISTICS

| | W | L | PCT | GB | R | OR | 2B | Batting 3B | HR | BA | SA | SB | E | Fielding DP | FA | CG | B | Pitching SO | ShO | SV | ERA |
|---|---|---|---|---|---|---|---|---|---|---|---|---|---|---|---|---|---|---|---|---|---|
| CHI | 104 | 50 | .675 | | 712 | 499 | 219 | 84 | 34 | .268 | .366 | 173 | 230 | 110 | .963 | 99 | 474 | 609 | 27 | 11 | 2.51 |
| NY | 91 | 63 | .591 | 13 | 715 | 567 | 204 | 83 | 31 | .275 | .366 | 282 | 291 | 117 | .955 | 96 | 397 | 717 | 9 | 8 | 2.68 |
| PIT | 86 | 67 | .562 | 17.5 | 655 | 576 | 214 | 83 | 33 | .266 | .360 | 148 | 245 | 102 | .961 | 73 | 392 | 479 | 13 | 11 | 2.83 |
| PHI | 78 | 75 | .510 | 25.5 | 674 | 639 | 223 | 71 | 22 | .255 | .338 | 199 | 258 | 132 | .960 | 84 | 547 | 657 | 16 | 7 | 3.05 |
| CIN | 75 | 79 | .487 | 29 | 620 | 684 | 150 | 79 | 23 | .259 | .333 | 310 | 291 | 103 | .955 | 86 | 528 | 497 | 16 | 9 | 3.08 |
| BKN | 64 | 90 | .416 | 40 | 497 | 623 | 166 | 73 | 25 | .229 | .305 | 151 | 235 | 125 | .964 | 103 | 545 | 555 | 15 | 4 | 3.07 |
| STL | 63 | 90 | .412 | 40.5 | 639 | 718 | 167 | 70 | 15 | .248 | .319 | 179 | 261 | 109 | .959 | 83 | 541 | 466 | 3 | 12 | 3.78 |
| BOS | 53 | 100 | .346 | 50.5 | 495 | 701 | 173 | 49 | 31 | .246 | .317 | 152 | 305 | 137 | .954 | 74 | 599 | 531 | 12 | 7 | 3.22 |
| LEAGUE TOTAL | | | | | 5007 | 5007 | 1516 | 592 | 214 | .256 | .338 | 1594 | 2116 | 935 | .959 | 698 | 4023 | 4511 | 111 | 69 | 3.02 |

## INDIVIDUAL PITCHING

| PITCHER | T | W | L | PCT | ERA | SV | G | GS | CG | IP | H | BB | SO | R | ER | ShO | H/9 | BB/9 | SO/9 |
|---|---|---|---|---|---|---|---|---|---|---|---|---|---|---|---|---|---|---|---|
| Three Finger Brown | R | 25 | 13 | .658 | 1.86 | 7 | 46 | 31 | 27 | 295.1 | 256 | 64 | 143 | 95 | 61 | 7 | 7.80 | 1.95 | 4.36 |
| King Cole | R | 20 | 4 | .833 | 1.80 | 0 | 33 | 29 | 21 | 239.2 | 174 | 130 | 114 | 64 | 48 | 4 | 6.53 | 4.88 | 4.28 |
| Harry McIntyre | R | 13 | 9 | .591 | 3.07 | 0 | 28 | 19 | 10 | 176 | 152 | 50 | 65 | 70 | 60 | 2 | 7.77 | 2.56 | 3.32 |
| Ed Reulbach | R | 12 | 8 | .600 | 3.12 | 0 | 24 | 23 | 13 | 173.1 | 161 | 49 | 55 | 76 | 60 | 1 | 8.36 | 2.54 | 2.86 |
| Orval Overall | R | 12 | 6 | .667 | 2.68 | 1 | 23 | 21 | 11 | 144.2 | 106 | 54 | 92 | 44 | 43 | 4 | 6.59 | 3.36 | 5.72 |
| Lew Richie | R | 11 | 4 | .733 | 2.70 | 0 | 30 | 11 | 8 | 130 | 117 | 51 | 53 | 45 | 39 | 3 | 8.10 | 3.53 | 3.67 |
| Jack Pfiester | L | 6 | 3 | .667 | 1.79 | 0 | 14 | 13 | 5 | 100.1 | 82 | 26 | 34 | 28 | 20 | 2 | 7.36 | 2.33 | 3.05 |
| Big Jeff Pfeffer | R | 1 | 0 | 1.000 | 3.27 | 0 | 13 | 1 | 1 | 41.1 | 43 | 16 | 11 | 31 | 15 | 0 | 9.36 | 3.48 | 2.40 |
| Rube Kroh | L | 3 | 1 | .750 | 4.46 | 0 | 6 | 4 | 1 | 34.1 | 33 | 15 | 16 | 19 | 17 | 0 | 8.65 | 3.93 | 4.19 |
| Orlie Weaver | R | 1 | 2 | .333 | 3.66 | 0 | 7 | 2 | 2 | 32 | 34 | 15 | 22 | 17 | 13 | 0 | 9.56 | 4.22 | 6.19 |
| Alex Carson | R | 0 | 0 | – | 4.05 | 0 | 2 | 0 | 0 | 6.2 | 6 | 1 | 2 | 5 | 3 | 0 | 8.10 | 1.35 | 2.70 |
| Bill Foxen | L | 0 | 0 | – | 9.00 | 0 | 2 | 0 | 0 | 5 | 7 | 3 | 2 | 5 | 5 | 0 | 12.60 | 5.40 | 3.60 |
| TEAM TOTAL | | 104 | 50 | .675 | 2.51 | 11 | 228 | 154 | 99 | 1378.2 | 1171 | 474 | 609 | 499 | 384 | 23 | 7.64 | 3.09 | 3.98 |

| MANAGER | W | L | PCT |
|---|---|---|---|
| Frank Chance | 92 | 62 | .597 |

| POS | Player | B | G | AB | H | 2B | 3B | HR | HR % | R | RBI | BB | SO | SB | Pinch Hit AB | Pinch Hit H | BA | SA |
|---|---|---|---|---|---|---|---|---|---|---|---|---|---|---|---|---|---|---|
| **REGULARS** | | | | | | | | | | | | | | | | | | |
| 1B | Vic Saier | L | 86 | 259 | 67 | 15 | 1 | 1 | 0.4 | 42 | 37 | 25 | 37 | 11 | 12 | 4 | .259 | .336 |
| 2B | Heinie Zimmerman | R | 143 | 535 | 164 | 22 | 17 | 9 | 1.7 | 80 | 85 | 25 | 50 | 23 | 4 | 1 | .307 | .462 |
| SS | Joe Tinker | R | 144 | 536 | 149 | 24 | 12 | 4 | 0.7 | 61 | 69 | 39 | 31 | 30 | 0 | 0 | .278 | .390 |
| 3B | Jim Doyle | R | 130 | 472 | 133 | 23 | 12 | 5 | 1.1 | 69 | 62 | 40 | 54 | 19 | 3 | 1 | .282 | .413 |
| RF | Wildfire Schulte | L | 154 | 577 | 173 | 30 | 21 | 21 | 3.6 | 105 | 121 | 76 | 68 | 23 | 0 | 0 | .300 | .534 |
| CF | Solly Hofman | R | 143 | 512 | 129 | 17 | 2 | 2 | 0.4 | 66 | 70 | 66 | 40 | 30 | 0 | 0 | .252 | .305 |
| LF | Jimmy Sheckard | L | 156 | 539 | 149 | 26 | 11 | 4 | 0.7 | 121 | 50 | 147 | 58 | 32 | 0 | 0 | .276 | .388 |
| C | Jimmy Archer | R | 116 | 387 | 98 | 18 | 5 | 4 | 1.0 | 41 | 41 | 18 | 43 | 5 | 3 | 0 | .253 | .357 |
| **SUBSTITUTES** | | | | | | | | | | | | | | | | | | |
| 23 | Johnny Evers | L | 46 | 155 | 35 | 4 | 3 | 0 | 0.0 | 29 | 7 | 34 | 10 | 6 | 2 | 0 | .226 | .290 |
| 2S | Dave Shean | R | 54 | 145 | 28 | 4 | 0 | 0 | 0.0 | 17 | 15 | 8 | 15 | 4 | 9 | 1 | .193 | .221 |
| 1B | Frank Chance | R | 31 | 88 | 21 | 6 | 3 | 1 | 1.1 | 23 | 17 | 25 | 13 | 9 | 1 | 0 | .239 | .409 |
| 1B | Kitty Bransfield | R | 3 | 10 | 4 | 2 | 0 | 0 | 0.0 | 0 | 0 | 2 | 2 | 0 | 0 | 0 | .400 | .600 |
| OF | Wilbur Good | L | 58 | 145 | 39 | 5 | 4 | 2 | 1.4 | 27 | 21 | 11 | 17 | 10 | 12 | 1 | .269 | .400 |
| OF | Al Kaiser | R | 27 | 84 | 21 | 0 | 5 | 0 | 0.0 | 16 | 7 | 7 | 12 | 6 | 4 | 1 | .250 | .369 |
| OF | Bill Collins | R | 7 | 5 | 1 | 1 | 0 | 0 | 0.0 | 2 | 0 | 1 | 3 | 0 | 1 | 1 | .200 | .400 |
| C | Johnny Kling | R | 27 | 80 | 14 | 3 | 2 | 1 | 1.3 | 8 | 5 | 8 | 14 | 1 | 2 | 0 | .175 | .300 |
| C | Peaches Graham | R | 36 | 71 | 17 | 3 | 0 | 0 | 0.0 | 6 | 8 | 11 | 8 | 2 | 8 | 2 | .239 | .282 |
| C | Tom Needham | R | 27 | 62 | 12 | 2 | 0 | 0 | 0.0 | 4 | 5 | 9 | 14 | 2 | 3 | 0 | .194 | .226 |
| **PITCHERS** | | | | | | | | | | | | | | | | | | |
| P | Three Finger Brown | B | 53 | 91 | 23 | 4 | 1 | 0 | 0.0 | 8 | 6 | 6 | 12 | 0 | 0 | 0 | .253 | .319 |
| P | Lew Richie | R | 36 | 91 | 14 | 0 | 1 | 0 | 0.0 | 7 | 4 | 3 | 23 | 0 | 0 | 0 | .154 | .176 |
| P | King Cole | R | 32 | 79 | 12 | 1 | 1 | 0 | 0.0 | 7 | 0 | 1 | 23 | 1 | 0 | 0 | .152 | .190 |
| P | Ed Reulbach | R | 33 | 67 | 6 | 3 | 0 | 0 | 0.0 | 6 | 3 | 13 | 32 | 0 | 0 | 0 | .090 | .134 |
| P | Harry McIntyre | R | 26 | 53 | 14 | 4 | 0 | 0 | 0.0 | 9 | 2 | 5 | 10 | 0 | 1 | 1 | .264 | .340 |
| P | Fred Toney | R | 18 | 18 | 2 | 0 | 0 | 0 | 0.0 | 1 | 0 | 0 | 5 | 0 | 0 | 0 | .111 | .111 |
| P | Orlie Weaver | R | 6 | 17 | 1 | 0 | 0 | 0 | 0.0 | 0 | 0 | 1 | 7 | 0 | 0 | 0 | .059 | .059 |
| P | Charlie Smith | R | 7 | 13 | 1 | 0 | 0 | 0 | 0.0 | 0 | 1 | 0 | 2 | 0 | 0 | 0 | .077 | .077 |
| P | Jack Pfiester | R | 6 | 11 | 2 | 0 | 0 | 0 | 0.0 | 0 | 2 | 1 | 5 | 0 | 0 | 0 | .182 | .182 |
| P | Reggie Richter | R | 22 | 10 | 1 | 0 | 0 | 0 | 0.0 | 1 | 1 | 0 | 7 | 0 | 0 | 0 | .100 | .100 |
| P | Cy Slapnicka | B | 3 | 9 | 2 | 0 | 0 | 0 | 0.0 | 0 | 1 | 0 | 0 | 0 | 0 | 0 | .222 | .222 |
| P | Larry Cheney | R | 3 | 4 | 1 | 0 | 0 | 0 | 0.0 | 0 | 0 | 1 | 0 | 0 | 0 | 0 | .250 | .250 |
| P | Bill Foxen | L | 3 | 4 | 1 | 1 | 0 | 0 | 0.0 | 0 | 0 | 1 | 0 | 0 | 0 | 0 | .250 | .500 |
| P | Cliff Curtis | R | 4 | 2 | 1 | 0 | 0 | 0 | 0.0 | 1 | 0 | 0 | 0 | 0 | 0 | 0 | .500 | .500 |
| P | Jack Rowan | R | 1 | 1 | 0 | 0 | 0 | 0 | 0.0 | 0 | 0 | 0 | 0 | 0 | 0 | 0 | .000 | .000 |
| P | Hank Griffin | R | 1 | 0 | 0 | 0 | 0 | 0 | — | 0 | 0 | 0 | 0 | 0 | 0 | 0 | — | — |
| P | Ernie Ovitz | R | 1 | 0 | 0 | 0 | 0 | 0 | — | 0 | 0 | 1 | 0 | 0 | 0 | 0 | — | — |
| TEAM TOTAL | | | | 5132 | 1335 | 218 | 101 | 54 | 1.1 | 75 | 640 | 585 | 617 | 214 | 65 | 13 | .260 | .374 |

## INDIVIDUAL  FIELDING

| POS | Player | T | G | PO | A | E | DP | TC/G | FA | POS | Player | T | G | PO | A | E | DP | TC/G | FA |
|---|---|---|---|---|---|---|---|---|---|---|---|---|---|---|---|---|---|---|---|
| 1B | V. Saier | R | 73 | 715 | 33 | 15 | 44 | 10.5 | .980 | OF | J. Sheckard | R | 156 | 332 | 32 | 14 | 12 | 2.4 | .963 |
| | S. Hofman | R | 36 | 353 | 17 | 6 | 17 | 10.4 | .984 | | W. Schulte | R | 154 | 246 | 19 | 8 | 8 | 1.8 | .971 |
| | F. Chance | R | 29 | 289 | 11 | 3 | 12 | 10.4 | .990 | | S. Hofman | R | 107 | 230 | 11 | 8 | 5 | 2.3 | .968 |
| | H. Zimmerman | R | 11 | 107 | 10 | 1 | 8 | 10.7 | .992 | | W. Good | L | 40 | 74 | 3 | 6 | 1 | 2.1 | .928 |
| | J. Archer | R | 10 | 84 | 4 | 1 | 6 | 8.9 | .989 | | A. Kaiser | R | 23 | 35 | 3 | 4 | 0 | 1.8 | .905 |
| | Bransfield | R | 3 | 27 | 1 | 0 | 6 | 9.3 | 1.000 | | B. Collins | R | 4 | 1 | 0 | 0 | 0 | 0.3 | 1.000 |
| 2B | H. Zimmerman | R | 108 | 256 | 304 | 32 | 42 | 5.5 | .946 | C | J. Archer | R | 102 | 476 | 124 | 14 | 11 | 6.0 | .977 |
| | J. Evers | R | 33 | 66 | 90 | 4 | 17 | 4.8 | .975 | | J. Kling | R | 25 | 122 | 34* | 5* | 2 | 6.4 | .969 |
| | D. Shean | R | 23 | 43 | 64 | 6 | 5 | 4.9 | .947 | | T. Needham | R | 23 | 94 | 32 | 2 | 2 | 5.6 | .984 |
| | J. Archer | R | 1 | 0 | 0 | 0 | 0 | 0.0 | .000 | | P. Graham | R | 28 | 78 | 25 | 3 | 3 | 3.8 | .972 |
| SS | J. Tinker | R | 143 | 333 | 486 | 55 | 56 | 6.1 | .937 | | | | | | | | | | |
| | D. Shean | R | 19 | 37 | 42 | 6 | 12 | 4.5 | .929 | | | | | | | | | | |
| 3B | J. Doyle | R | 127 | 134 | 278 | 35 | 25 | 3.5 | .922 | | | | | | | | | | |
| | H. Zimmerman | R | 20 | 25 | 34 | 9 | 2 | 3.4 | .868 | | | | | | | | | | |
| | J. Evers | R | 11 | 13 | 15 | 3 | 2 | 2.8 | .903 | | | | | | | | | | |
| | D. Shean | R | 1 | 1 | 1 | 0 | 0 | 2.0 | 1.000 | | | | | | | | | | |

By 1911, the Cubs were clearly an aging team, as they finished a respectable but distant second. Vic Saier was supplanting Chance at first base, while Evers missed most of the season because of a nervous breakdown. Overall retired, and Kling was dealt to the Braves.

On the positive side, Heinie Zimmerman began to reach his prime, leading the club in batting, while Schulte clubbed 21 homers and was awarded a Chalmers automobile for his efforts. On June 11, Zimmerman set a Cub record by driving in nine runs in a 20–2 scalping of the Braves.

Jimmy Archer was now the first-string catcher, gaining renown for his deadly throwing arm. Jim Doyle replaced Harry Steinfeldt at third but died the following winter of appendicitis.

Joe Tinker, one of the few batters to hit well against Christy Mathewson, enjoyed his greatest outing off Matty on August 7, collecting two singles, a double, and a triple, scoring three times and stealing home in an 8–6 victory over the Giants.

Pitching was still strong as Brown won 20 or more games for the sixth straight year, while King Cole followed his spectacular rookie year with a follow-up that was nearly as good. Nevertheless, the younger and speedier Giants ran away with the pennant.

## TEAM  STATISTICS

| | W | L | PCT | GB | R | OR | 2B | Batting 3B | HR | BA | SA | SB | Fielding E | DP | FA | CG | B | Pitching SO | ShO | SV | ERA |
|---|---|---|---|---|---|---|---|---|---|---|---|---|---|---|---|---|---|---|---|---|---|
| Y | 99 | 54 | .647 | | 756 | **542** | 225 | 105 | 41 | **.279** | **.391** | **347** | 255 | 86 | .959 | **95** | **369** | **771** | 19 | 11 | **2.69** |
| HI | 92 | 62 | .597 | 7.5 | **757** | 607 | 218 | 101 | 54 | .260 | .374 | 214 | 260 | 114 | .960 | 85 | 525 | 582 | 12 | **16** | 2.90 |
| T | 85 | 69 | .552 | 14.5 | 744 | 557 | 206 | **106** | 48 | .262 | .371 | 160 | 232 | **131** | .963 | 91 | 375 | 605 | 14 | 10 | 2.84 |
| HI | 79 | 73 | .520 | 19.5 | 658 | 669 | 214 | 56 | **60** | .259 | .359 | 153 | **231** | 113 | **.963** | 90 | 598 | 697 | **20** | 9 | 3.30 |
| TL | 75 | 74 | .503 | 22 | 671 | 745 | 199 | 85 | 27 | .252 | .340 | 175 | 261 | 106 | .960 | 88 | 701 | 561 | 6 | 9 | 3.68 |
| IN | 70 | 83 | .458 | 29 | 682 | 706 | 180 | 105 | 21 | .261 | .346 | 290 | 295 | 108 | .955 | 77 | 476 | 557 | 4 | 10 | 3.26 |
| KN | 64 | 86 | .427 | 33.5 | 539 | 659 | 151 | 71 | 28 | .237 | .311 | 184 | 243 | 112 | .962 | 81 | 566 | 533 | 14 | 10 | 3.39 |
| OS | 44 | 107 | .291 | 54 | 699 | 1021 | **249** | 54 | 37 | .267 | .355 | 169 | 347 | 110 | .947 | 73 | 672 | 486 | 5 | 6 | 5.08 |
| EAGUE TOTAL | | | | | 5506 | 5506 | 1642 | 683 | 316 | .260 | .356 | 1692 | 2124 | 880 | .958 | 680 | 4282 | 4792 | 94 | 81 | 3.39 |

## INDIVIDUAL  PITCHING

| ITCHER | T | W | L | PCT | ERA | SV | G | GS | CG | IP | H | BB | SO | R | ER | ShO | H/9 | BB/9 | SO/9 |
|---|---|---|---|---|---|---|---|---|---|---|---|---|---|---|---|---|---|---|---|
| hree Finger Brown | R | 21 | 11 | .656 | 2.80 | 13 | **53** | 27 | 21 | 270 | 267 | 55 | 129 | 110 | 84 | 0 | 8.90 | 1.83 | 4.30 |
| ew Richie | R | 15 | 11 | .577 | 2.31 | 1 | 36 | 28 | 18 | 253 | 213 | 103 | 78 | 88 | 65 | 4 | 7.58 | 3.66 | 2.77 |
| d Reulbach | R | 16 | 9 | .640 | 2.96 | 0 | 33 | 29 | 15 | 221.2 | 191 | 103 | 79 | 97 | 73 | 2 | 7.75 | 4.18 | 3.21 |
| ing Cole | R | 18 | 7 | .720 | 3.13 | 0 | 32 | 27 | 13 | 221.1 | 188 | 99 | 101 | 87 | 77 | 2 | 7.64 | 4.03 | 4.11 |
| arry McIntyre | R | 11 | 7 | .611 | 4.11 | 0 | 25 | 17 | 9 | 149 | 147 | 33 | 56 | 81 | 68 | 1 | 8.88 | 1.99 | 3.38 |
| red Toney | R | 1 | 1 | .500 | 2.42 | 0 | 18 | 4 | 1 | 67 | 55 | 35 | 27 | 36 | 18 | 0 | 7.39 | 4.70 | 3.63 |
| eggie Richter | R | 1 | 3 | .250 | 3.13 | 2 | 22 | 5 | 0 | 54.2 | 62 | 20 | 34 | 30 | 19 | 0 | 10.21 | 3.29 | 5.60 |
| rlie Weaver | R | 3 | 2 | .600 | 2.06 | 0 | 6 | 4 | 1 | 43.2 | 29 | 17 | 20 | 12 | 10 | 1 | 5.98 | 3.50 | 4.12 |
| harlie Smith | R | 3 | 2 | .600 | 1.42 | 0 | 7 | 5 | 3 | 38 | 31 | 7 | 11 | 11 | 6 | 1 | 7.34 | 1.66 | 2.61 |
| ack Pfiester | L | 0 | 4 | .000 | 4.01 | 0 | 6 | 5 | 3 | 33.2 | 34 | 18 | 15 | 25 | 15 | 0 | 9.09 | 4.81 | 4.01 |
| y Slapnicka | R | 0 | 2 | .000 | 3.38 | 0 | 3 | 2 | 1 | 24 | 21 | 7 | 10 | 12 | 9 | 0 | 7.88 | 2.63 | 3.75 |
| ll Foxen | L | 1 | 1 | .500 | 2.08 | 0 | 3 | 1 | 0 | 13 | 12 | 12 | 6 | 6 | 3 | 0 | 8.31 | 8.31 | 4.15 |
| arry Cheney | R | 1 | 0 | 1.000 | 0.00 | 0 | 3 | 1 | 0 | 10 | 8 | 3 | 11 | 0 | 0 | 0 | 7.20 | 2.70 | 9.90 |
| liff Curtis | R | 1 | 2 | .333 | 3.86 | 0 | 4 | 1 | 0 | 7 | 7 | 5 | 4 | 4 | 3 | 0 | 9.00 | 6.43 | 5.14 |
| rnie Ovitz | R | 0 | 0 | – | 4.50 | 0 | 1 | 0 | 0 | 2 | 3 | 3 | 0 | 2 | 1 | 0 | 13.50 | 13.50 | 0.00 |
| ack Rowan | R | 0 | 0 | – | 4.50 | 0 | 1 | 0 | 0 | 2 | 1 | 2 | 0 | 4 | 1 | 0 | 4.50 | 9.00 | 0.00 |
| ank Griffin | R | 0 | 0 | – | 18.00 | 0 | 1 | 1 | 0 | 1 | 1 | 3 | 1 | 2 | 2 | 0 | 9.00 | 27.00 | 9.00 |
| EAM TOTAL | | 92 | 62 | .597 | 2.90 | 16 | 254 | 157 | 85 | 1411 | 1270 | 525 | 582 | 607 | 454 | 11 | 8.10 | 3.35 | 3.71 |

| MANAGER | W | L | PCT |
|---|---|---|---|
| Frank Chance | 91 | 59 | .607 |

| POS | Player | B | G | AB | H | 2B | 3B | HR | HR % | R | RBI | BB | SO | SB | Pinch Hit AB | Pinch Hit H | BA | SA |
|---|---|---|---|---|---|---|---|---|---|---|---|---|---|---|---|---|---|---|
| **REGULARS** | | | | | | | | | | | | | | | | | | |
| 1B | Vic Saier | L | 122 | 451 | 130 | 25 | 14 | 2 | 0.4 | 74 | 61 | 34 | 65 | 11 | 1 | 0 | .288 | .419 |
| 2B | Johnny Evers | L | 143 | 478 | 163 | 23 | 11 | 1 | 0.2 | 73 | 63 | 74 | 18 | 16 | 0 | 0 | .341 | .441 |
| SS | Joe Tinker | R | 142 | 550 | 155 | 24 | 7 | 0 | 0.0 | 80 | 75 | 38 | 21 | 25 | 0 | 0 | .282 | .351 |
| 3B | Heinie Zimmerman | R | 145 | 557 | **207** | 41 | 14 | **14** | 2.5 | 95 | **103** | 38 | 60 | 23 | 2 | 0 | **.372** | **.571** |
| RF | Wildfire Schulte | L | 139 | 553 | 146 | 27 | 11 | 13 | 2.4 | 90 | 70 | 53 | 70 | 17 | 0 | 0 | .264 | .423 |
| CF | Tommy Leach | R | 82 | 265 | 64 | 10 | 3 | 2 | 0.8 | 50 | 32 | 55 | 20 | 14 | 1 | 1 | .242 | .325 |
| LF | Jimmy Sheckard | L | 146 | 523 | 128 | 22 | 10 | 3 | 0.6 | 85 | 47 | **122** | 81 | 15 | 0 | 0 | .245 | .342 |
| C | Jimmy Archer | R | 120 | 385 | 109 | 20 | 2 | 5 | 1.3 | 35 | 58 | 22 | 36 | 7 | 1 | 0 | .283 | .384 |
| **SUBSTITUTES** | | | | | | | | | | | | | | | | | | |
| UT | Red Downs | R | 43 | 95 | 25 | 4 | 3 | 1 | 1.1 | 9 | 14 | 9 | 17 | 5 | 11 | 2 | .263 | .400 |
| 3B | Ed Lennox | R | 27 | 81 | 19 | 4 | 1 | 1 | 1.2 | 13 | 16 | 12 | 10 | 1 | 2 | 1 | .235 | .346 |
| UT | Tom Downey | R | 13 | 22 | 4 | 0 | 2 | 0 | 0.0 | 4 | 4 | 1 | 5 | 0 | 3 | 0 | .182 | .364 |
| UT | Charley Moore | R | 5 | 9 | 2 | 0 | 1 | 0 | 0.0 | 2 | 2 | 0 | 1 | 0 | 0 | 0 | .222 | .444 |
| 1B | Frank Chance | R | 2 | 5 | 1 | 0 | 0 | 0 | 0.0 | 2 | 0 | 3 | 0 | 1 | 0 | 0 | .200 | .200 |
| OF | Ward Miller | L | 86 | 241 | 74 | 11 | 4 | 0 | 0.0 | 45 | 22 | 26 | 18 | 11 | 15 | 6 | .307 | .386 |
| O1 | Solly Hofman | R | 36 | 125 | 34 | 11 | 0 | 0 | 0.0 | 28 | 18 | 22 | 13 | 5 | 0 | 0 | .272 | .360 |
| OF | Cy Williams | L | 28 | 62 | 15 | 1 | 1 | 0 | 0.0 | 3 | 1 | 6 | 14 | 2 | 5 | 0 | .242 | .290 |
| OF | Wilbur Good | L | 39 | 35 | 5 | 0 | 0 | 0 | 0.0 | 7 | 1 | 3 | 7 | 3 | 21 | 3 | .143 | .143 |
| C | Tom Needham | R | 33 | 90 | 16 | 5 | 0 | 0 | 0.0 | 12 | 10 | 7 | 13 | 3 | 1 | 0 | .178 | .233 |
| C | Dick Cotter | R | 26 | 54 | 15 | 0 | 2 | 0 | 0.0 | 6 | 10 | 6 | 13 | 1 | 1 | 0 | .278 | .352 |
| C | Harry Chapman | R | 1 | 4 | 1 | 0 | 1 | 0 | 0.0 | 1 | 1 | 0 | 0 | 1 | 0 | 0 | .250 | .750 |
| C | Mike Hechinger | R | 2 | 3 | 0 | 0 | 0 | 0 | 0.0 | 0 | 0 | 2 | 0 | 0 | 0 | 0 | .000 | .000 |
| C | George Yantz | R | 1 | 1 | 1 | 0 | 0 | 0 | 0.0 | 0 | 0 | 0 | 0 | 0 | 0 | 0 | 1.000 | 1.000 |
| **PITCHERS** | | | | | | | | | | | | | | | | | | |
| P | Larry Cheney | R | 42 | 106 | 24 | 5 | 2 | 1 | 0.9 | 13 | 12 | 6 | 25 | 0 | 0 | 0 | .226 | .340 |
| P | Jimmy Lavender | R | 42 | 87 | 13 | 3 | 0 | 0 | 0.0 | 6 | 5 | 5 | 34 | 0 | 0 | 0 | .149 | .184 |
| P | Lew Richie | R | 39 | 76 | 10 | 1 | 0 | 0 | 0.0 | 7 | 4 | 5 | 19 | 2 | 0 | 0 | .132 | .145 |
| P | Ed Reulbach | R | 39 | 55 | 6 | 2 | 0 | 0 | 0.0 | 3 | 4 | 4 | 23 | 0 | 0 | 0 | .109 | .145 |
| P | Charlie Smith | R | 21 | 35 | 9 | 1 | 0 | 0 | 0.0 | 4 | 2 | 1 | 4 | 0 | 1 | 0 | .257 | .286 |
| P | Three Finger Brown | B | 16 | 31 | 9 | 1 | 0 | 0 | 0.0 | 3 | 5 | 2 | 6 | 1 | 1 | 1 | .290 | .323 |
| P | Lefty Leifield | L | 13 | 26 | 3 | 1 | 1 | 0 | 0.0 | 3 | 1 | 1 | 12 | 0 | 0 | 0 | .115 | .231 |
| P | Harry McIntyre | R | 8 | 10 | 3 | 0 | 1 | 0 | 0.0 | 1 | 5 | 1 | 1 | 0 | 4 | 3 | .300 | .500 |
| P | Jim Maroney | L | 10 | 6 | 3 | 0 | 0 | 0 | 0.0 | 1 | 1 | 0 | 1 | 0 | 0 | 0 | .500 | .667 |
| P | George Pearce | L | 3 | 6 | 1 | 1 | 0 | 0 | 0.0 | 1 | 0 | 0 | 2 | 0 | 0 | 0 | .167 | .333 |
| P | King Cole | R | 8 | 5 | 2 | 1 | 0 | 0 | 0.0 | 0 | 1 | 0 | 2 | 0 | 0 | 0 | .400 | .600 |
| P | Fred Toney | R | 9 | 5 | 0 | 0 | 0 | 0 | 0.0 | 0 | 0 | 1 | 0 | 0 | 0 | 0 | .000 | .000 |
| P | Grover Lowdermilk | R | 2 | 4 | 0 | 0 | 0 | 0 | 0.0 | 0 | 0 | 0 | 1 | 0 | 0 | 0 | .000 | .000 |
| P | Len Madden | L | 6 | 4 | 1 | 0 | 0 | 0 | 0.0 | 0 | 0 | 0 | 3 | 0 | 0 | 0 | .250 | .250 |
| P | Joe Vernon | R | 1 | 2 | 0 | 0 | 0 | 0 | 0.0 | 0 | 0 | 0 | 0 | 0 | 0 | 0 | .000 | .000 |
| P | Ensign Cottrell | L | 1 | 1 | 0 | 0 | 0 | 0 | 0.0 | 0 | 0 | 0 | 0 | 0 | 0 | 0 | .000 | .000 |
| P | Bill Powell | R | 1 | 0 | 0 | 0 | 0 | 0 | — | 0 | 0 | 0 | 0 | 0 | 0 | 0 | — | — |
| P | Rudy Sommers | L | 1 | 0 | 0 | 0 | 0 | 0 | — | 0 | 1 | 1 | 0 | 0 | 0 | 0 | — | — |
| TEAM TOTAL | | | | 5048 | 1398 | 245 | 91 | 43 | 0.9 | 75 | 649 | 560 | 615 | 164 | 70 | 17 | .277 | .387 |

## INDIVIDUAL FIELDING

| POS | Player | T | G | PO | A | E | DP | TC/G | FA | POS | Player | T | G | PO | A | E | DP | TC/G | FA |
|---|---|---|---|---|---|---|---|---|---|---|---|---|---|---|---|---|---|---|---|
| 1B | V. Saier | R | 120 | 1165 | 52 | 10 | 67 | 10.2 | .992 | OF | J. Sheckard | R | 146 | 332 | **26** | 14 | 4 | 2.5 | .962 |
| | H. Zimmerman | R | 22 | 212 | 11 | 4 | 15 | 10.3 | .982 | | W. Schulte | R | 139 | 219 | 19 | 12 | 6 | 1.8 | .952 |
| | S. Hofman | R | 9 | 77 | 2 | 2 | 7 | 9.0 | .975 | | T. Leach | R | 73 | 181 | 11 | 5 | 4 | 2.7* | .975* |
| | F. Chance | R | 2 | 22 | 0 | 0 | 1 | 11.0 | 1.000 | | W. Miller | R | 64 | 109 | 6 | 7 | 2 | 1.9 | .943 |
| 2B | J. Evers | R | 143 | 319 | 439 | 32 | 71 | 5.5 | .959 | | S. Hofman | L | 27 | 67 | 7 | 1 | 4 | 2.8 | .987 |
| | R. Downs | R | 16 | 19 | 31 | 5 | 6 | 3.4 | .909 | | C. Williams | L | 22 | 36 | 3 | 0 | 0 | 1.8 | 1.000 |
| | T. Downey | R | 1 | 0 | 3 | 0 | 0 | 3.0 | 1.000 | | W. Good | L | 10 | 7 | 1 | 0 | 0 | 0.8 | 1.000 |
| | C. Moore | R | 1 | 0 | 3 | 0 | 0 | 3.0 | 1.000 | C | J. Archer | R | 118 | 504 | **149** | **23** | 15 | 5.7 | .966 |
| SS | J. Tinker | R | 142 | **354** | 470 | 50 | 73 | **6.2** | .943 | | T. Needham | R | 32 | 116 | 39 | 1 | 3 | 4.9 | .994 |
| | R. Downs | R | 9 | 13 | 28 | 3 | 3 | 4.9 | .932 | | D. Cotter | R | 24 | 64 | 19 | 4 | 0 | 3.6 | .954 |
| | T. Downey | R | 5 | 8 | 11 | 5 | 0 | 4.8 | .792 | | G. Yantz | R | 1 | 0 | 0 | 0 | 0 | 0.0 | .000 |
| | C. Moore | R | 2 | 2 | 2 | 1 | 0 | 2.5 | .800 | | H. Chapman | R | 1 | 7 | 3 | 0 | 0 | 10.0 | 1.000 |
| 3B | H. Zimmerman | R | 121 | 142 | 242 | **35** | 16 | 3.5 | .916 | | M. Hechinger | R | 2 | 7 | 2 | 0 | 0 | 4.5 | 1.000 |
| | E. Lennox | R | 24 | 25 | 32 | 4 | 1 | 2.5 | .934 | | | | | | | | | | |
| | R. Downs | R | 5 | 3 | 15 | 2 | 1 | 4.0 | .900 | | | | | | | | | | |
| | T. Leach | R | 4 | 9 | 7 | 1 | 0 | 4.3 | .941 | | | | | | | | | | |
| | T. Downey | R | 3 | 3 | 4 | 1 | 0 | 2.7 | .875 | | | | | | | | | | |
| | C. Moore | R | 1 | 1 | 1 | 0 | 0 | 2.0 | 1.000 | | | | | | | | | | |

The Cub empire continued its gradual decline in 1912, as the team slipped to third place. It was the season dominated by Heinie Zimmerman. En route to becoming the first Cub to amass 200 hits in a season, Heinie led the league in batting, home runs, RBI, hits, doubles, slugging, and total bases; he also enjoyed a 23-game hitting streak. Third base had been made his new home, but he was no Steinfeldt as a glove man.

Evers shook off his nerve problems to hit a career high .341, while Archer peaked at .283. With Brown and Reulbach on the way out, the pitching slack was taken up by rookie spitballers Larry Cheney and Jimmy Lavender, both of whom showed promise. Cheney's 26 wins remain the most by a Cub freshman since the institution of the 60-foot pitching distance, while Lavender halted Giant Rube Marquard's winning streak at 19.

In contract difficulties with owner Charles Murphy, Frank Chance was fired September 28. When Joe Tinker was traded to the Reds over the winter, only Johnny Evers remained of the trio.

## TEAM STATISTICS

|  | W | L | PCT | GB | R | OR | Batting 2B | 3B | HR | BA | SA | SB | Fielding E | DP | FA | CG | B | Pitching SO | ShO | SV | ERA |
|---|---|---|---|---|---|---|---|---|---|---|---|---|---|---|---|---|---|---|---|---|---|
| NY | 103 | 48 | .682 |  | 823 | 571 | 231 | 89 | 47 | .286 | .395 | 319 | 280 | 123 | .956 | 93 | 338 | 652 | 8 | 13 | 2.58 |
| PIT | 93 | 58 | .616 | 10 | 751 | 565 | 222 | 129 | 39 | .284 | .398 | 177 | 169 | 125 | .972 | 94 | 497 | 664 | 18 | 6 | 2.85 |
| CHI | 91 | 59 | .607 | 11.5 | 756 | 668 | 245 | 91 | 43 | .277 | .387 | 164 | 249 | 125 | .960 | 80 | 493 | 554 | 14 | 8 | 3.42 |
| CIN | 75 | 78 | .490 | 29 | 656 | 722 | 183 | 89 | 21 | .256 | .339 | 248 | 247 | 102 | .960 | 86 | 452 | 561 | 12 | 10 | 3.42 |
| PHI | 73 | 79 | .480 | 30.5 | 670 | 688 | 244 | 68 | 43 | .267 | .367 | 159 | 231 | 98 | .963 | 82 | 515 | 616 | 10 | 8 | 3.25 |
| STL | 63 | 90 | .412 | 41 | 659 | 830 | 190 | 77 | 27 | .268 | .352 | 193 | 274 | 113 | .957 | 62 | 560 | 487 | 6 | 11 | 3.85 |
| BKN | 58 | 95 | .379 | 46 | 651 | 754 | 220 | 73 | 32 | .268 | .358 | 179 | 255 | 96 | .959 | 71 | 510 | 553 | 10 | 7 | 3.64 |
| BOS | 52 | 101 | .340 | 52 | 693 | 861 | 227 | 68 | 35 | .273 | .360 | 137 | 295 | 129 | .954 | 92 | 521 | 542 | 5 | 3 | 4.17 |
| LEAGUE TOTAL |  |  |  |  | 5659 | 5659 | 1762 | 684 | 287 | .272 | .369 | 1576 | 2000 | 911 | .960 | 660 | 3886 | 4629 | 83 | 66 | 3.40 |

## INDIVIDUAL PITCHING

| PITCHER | T | W | L | PCT | ERA | SV | G | GS | CG | IP | H | BB | SO | R | ER | ShO | H/9 | BB/9 | SO/9 |
|---|---|---|---|---|---|---|---|---|---|---|---|---|---|---|---|---|---|---|---|
| Larry Cheney | R | 26 | 10 | .722 | 2.85 | 0 | 42 | 37 | 28 | 303.1 | 262 | 111 | 140 | 122 | 96 | 4 | 7.77 | 3.29 | 4.15 |
| Jimmy Lavender | R | 16 | 13 | .552 | 3.04 | 3 | 42 | 31 | 15 | 251.2 | 240 | 89 | 109 | 116 | 85 | 3 | 8.58 | 3.18 | 3.90 |
| Lew Richie | R | 16 | 8 | .667 | 2.95 | 0 | 39 | 27 | 15 | 238 | 222 | 74 | 69 | 102 | 78 | 4 | 8.39 | 2.80 | 2.61 |
| Ed Reulbach | R | 10 | 6 | .625 | 3.78 | 3 | 39 | 19 | 8 | 169 | 161 | 60 | 75 | 86 | 71 | 0 | 8.57 | 3.20 | 3.99 |
| Charlie Smith | R | 7 | 4 | .636 | 4.21 | 1 | 21 | 5 | 1 | 94 | 92 | 31 | 47 | 56 | 44 | 0 | 8.81 | 2.97 | 4.50 |
| Three Finger Brown | R | 5 | 6 | .455 | 2.64 | 0 | 15 | 8 | 5 | 88.2 | 92 | 20 | 34 | 35 | 26 | 2 | 9.34 | 2.03 | 3.45 |
| Lefty Leifield | L | 7 | 2 | .778 | 2.42 | 0 | 13 | 9 | 4 | 70.2 | 68 | 21 | 23 | 26 | 19 | 1 | 8.66 | 2.67 | 2.93 |
| Fred Toney | R | 1 | 2 | .333 | 5.25 | 0 | 9 | 2 | 0 | 24 | 21 | 11 | 9 | 19 | 14 | 0 | 7.88 | 4.13 | 3.38 |
| Jim Maroney | L | 1 | 1 | .500 | 4.56 | 1 | 10 | 3 | 1 | 23.2 | 25 | 17 | 5 | 13 | 12 | 0 | 9.51 | 6.46 | 1.90 |
| Harry McIntyre | R | 1 | 2 | .333 | 3.80 | 0 | 4 | 3 | 2 | 23.2 | 22 | 6 | 8 | 11 | 10 | 0 | 8.37 | 2.28 | 3.04 |
| King Cole | R | 1 | 2 | .333 | 10.89 | 0 | 8 | 3 | 0 | 19 | 36 | 8 | 9 | 26 | 23 | 0 | 17.05 | 3.79 | 4.26 |
| George Pearce | L | 0 | 0 | — | 5.52 | 0 | 3 | 2 | 0 | 14.2 | 15 | 12 | 9 | 13 | 9 | 0 | 9.20 | 7.36 | 5.52 |
| Grover Lowdermilk | R | 0 | 1 | .000 | 9.69 | 0 | 2 | 1 | 1 | 13 | 17 | 14 | 8 | 18 | 14 | 0 | 11.77 | 9.69 | 5.54 |
| Len Madden | L | 0 | 1 | .000 | 2.92 | 0 | 6 | 2 | 0 | 12.1 | 16 | 9 | 5 | 10 | 4 | 0 | 11.68 | 6.57 | 3.65 |
| Ensign Cottrell | L | 0 | 0 | — | 9.00 | 0 | 1 | 0 | 0 | 4 | 8 | 1 | 1 | 4 | 4 | 0 | 18.00 | 2.25 | 2.25 |
| Joe Vernon | R | 0 | 0 | — | 11.25 | 0 | 1 | 0 | 0 | 4 | 4 | 6 | 1 | 6 | 5 | 0 | 9.00 | 13.50 | 2.25 |
| Rudy Sommers | L | 0 | 1 | .000 | 3.00 | 0 | 1 | 0 | 0 | 3 | 4 | 2 | 2 | 1 | 1 | 0 | 12.00 | 6.00 | 6.00 |
| Bill Powell | R | 0 | 0 | — | 9.00 | 0 | 1 | 0 | 0 | 2 | 2 | 1 | 0 | 2 | 2 | 0 | 9.00 | 4.50 | 0.00 |
| TEAM TOTAL |  | 91 | 59 | .607 | 3.42 | 8 | 257 | 152 | 80 | 1358.2 | 1307 | 493 | 554 | 666 | 517 | 14 | 8.66 | 3.27 | 3.67 |

| MANAGER | W | L | PCT |
|---|---|---|---|
| Johnny Evers | 88 | 65 | .575 |

| POS | Player | B | G | AB | H | 2B | 3B | HR | HR % | R | RBI | BB | SO | SB | Pinch Hit AB | Pinch Hit H | BA | SA |
|---|---|---|---|---|---|---|---|---|---|---|---|---|---|---|---|---|---|---|
| **REGULARS** | | | | | | | | | | | | | | | | | | |
| 1B | Vic Saier | L | 148 | 518 | 149 | 14 | 21 | 14 | 2.7 | 93 | 92 | 62 | 62 | 26 | 1 | 0 | .288 | .477 |
| 2B | Johnny Evers | L | 135 | 444 | 126 | 20 | 5 | 3 | 0.7 | 81 | 49 | 50 | 14 | 11 | 0 | 0 | .284 | .372 |
| SS | Al Bridwell | L | 135 | 405 | 97 | 6 | 6 | 1 | 0.2 | 35 | 37 | 74 | 28 | 12 | 0 | 0 | .240 | .291 |
| 3B | Heinie Zimmerman | R | 127 | 447 | 140 | 28 | 12 | 9 | 2.0 | 69 | 95 | 41 | 40 | 18 | 1 | 0 | .313 | .490 |
| RF | Wildfire Schulte | L | 132 | 495 | 138 | 28 | 6 | 9 | 1.8 | 85 | 72 | 39 | 68 | 21 | 2 | 1 | .279 | .414 |
| CF | Tommy Leach | R | 130 | 454 | 131 | 23 | 10 | 6 | 1.3 | 99 | 32 | 77 | 44 | 21 | 7 | 3 | .289 | .423 |
| LF | Mike Mitchell | R | 81 | 278 | 72 | 11 | 6 | 4 | 1.4 | 37 | 35 | 32 | 33 | 15 | 0 | 0 | .259 | .385 |
| C | Jimmy Archer | R | 110 | 367 | 98 | 14 | 7 | 2 | 0.5 | 38 | 44 | 19 | 27 | 4 | 3 | 1 | .267 | .360 |
| **SUBSTITUTES** | | | | | | | | | | | | | | | | | | |
| 23 | Art Phelan | R | 90 | 259 | 65 | 11 | 6 | 2 | 0.8 | 41 | 35 | 29 | 25 | 8 | 7 | 3 | .251 | .363 |
| SS | Red Corriden | R | 45 | 97 | 17 | 3 | 0 | 2 | 2.1 | 13 | 9 | 9 | 14 | 4 | 4 | 1 | .175 | .268 |
| 1B | Fritz Mollwitz | R | 2 | 7 | 3 | 0 | 0 | 0 | 0.0 | 1 | 0 | 0 | 0 | 0 | 0 | 0 | .429 | .429 |
| SS | Chick Keating | R | 2 | 5 | 1 | 1 | 0 | 0 | 0.0 | 1 | 0 | 0 | 1 | 0 | 0 | 0 | .200 | .400 |
| OF | Ward Miller | L | 80 | 203 | 48 | 5 | 7 | 1 | 0.5 | 23 | 16 | 34 | 33 | 13 | 13 | 8 | .236 | .345 |
| OF | Cy Williams | L | 49 | 156 | 35 | 3 | 3 | 4 | 2.6 | 17 | 32 | 5 | 26 | 5 | 5 | 2 | .224 | .359 |
| OF | Otis Clymer | B | 30 | 105 | 24 | 5 | 1 | 0 | 0.0 | 16 | 7 | 14 | 18 | 9 | 3 | 0 | .229 | .295 |
| OF | Wilbur Good | L | 49 | 91 | 23 | 3 | 2 | 1 | 1.1 | 11 | 12 | 11 | 16 | 5 | 16 | 4 | .253 | .363 |
| OF | Tuffy Stewart | L | 9 | 8 | 1 | 1 | 0 | 0 | 0.0 | 1 | 2 | 2 | 5 | 1 | 5 | 0 | .125 | .250 |
| OF | Milo Allison | L | 2 | 6 | 2 | 0 | 0 | 0 | 0.0 | 1 | 0 | 0 | 1 | 0 | 1 | 0 | .333 | .333 |
| C | Roger Bresnahan | R | 68 | 161 | 37 | 5 | 2 | 1 | 0.6 | 20 | 21 | 21 | 11 | 7 | 9 | 4 | .230 | .304 |
| C | Tom Needham | R | 20 | 42 | 10 | 4 | 1 | 0 | 0.0 | 5 | 11 | 4 | 8 | 0 | 4 | 0 | .238 | .381 |
| C | Bubbles Hargrave | R | 3 | 3 | 1 | 0 | 0 | 0 | 0.0 | 0 | 1 | 0 | 0 | 0 | 1 | 0 | .333 | .333 |
| PH | Mike Hechinger | R | 2 | 2 | 0 | 0 | 0 | 0 | 0.0 | 0 | 0 | 0 | 0 | 0 | 2 | 0 | .000 | .000 |
| PH | Pete Knisely | R | 2 | 2 | 0 | 0 | 0 | 0 | 0.0 | 0 | 0 | 0 | 1 | 0 | 2 | 0 | .000 | .000 |
| PH | Ed McDonald | R | 1 | 0 | 0 | 0 | 0 | 0 | | 0 | 0 | 0 | 0 | 0 | 0 | 0 | — | — |
| **PITCHERS** | | | | | | | | | | | | | | | | | | |
| P | Larry Cheney | R | 56 | 104 | 20 | 3 | 0 | 0 | 0.0 | 6 | 7 | 10 | 34 | 0 | 1 | 0 | .192 | .221 |
| P | Jimmy Lavender | R | 40 | 68 | 8 | 1 | 0 | 0 | 0.0 | 2 | 1 | 0 | 30 | 0 | 0 | 0 | .118 | .132 |
| P | Bert Humphries | R | 28 | 62 | 12 | 1 | 0 | 0 | 0.0 | 8 | 3 | 6 | 17 | 0 | 0 | 0 | .194 | .210 |
| P | George Pearce | L | 25 | 55 | 4 | 1 | 0 | 0 | 0.0 | 5 | 1 | 4 | 24 | 0 | 0 | 0 | .073 | .091 |
| P | Charlie Smith | R | 20 | 45 | 4 | 0 | 0 | 0 | 0.0 | 1 | 0 | 2 | 17 | 0 | 0 | 0 | .089 | .089 |
| P | Orval Overall | B | 11 | 24 | 6 | 2 | 0 | 0 | 0.0 | 1 | 2 | 2 | 3 | 0 | 0 | 0 | .250 | .333 |
| P | Hippo Vaughn | B | 7 | 21 | 4 | 0 | 0 | 0 | 0.0 | 3 | 1 | 0 | 7 | 0 | 0 | 0 | .190 | .190 |
| P | Lew Richie | R | 16 | 17 | 2 | 1 | 0 | 0 | 0.0 | 2 | 0 | 2 | 4 | 0 | 0 | 0 | .118 | .176 |
| P | Eddie Stack | R | 11 | 16 | 1 | 0 | 0 | 0 | 0.0 | 0 | 2 | 0 | 6 | 0 | 0 | 0 | .063 | .063 |
| P | Ed Reulbach | R | 9 | 12 | 3 | 0 | 0 | 0 | 0.0 | 1 | 0 | 0 | 5 | 0 | 0 | 0 | .250 | .250 |
| P | Fred Toney | R | 7 | 12 | 3 | 0 | 1 | 0 | 0.0 | 0 | 2 | 1 | 1 | 0 | 0 | 0 | .250 | .417 |
| P | Earl Moore | R | 7 | 8 | 1 | 0 | 0 | 0 | 0.0 | 2 | 0 | 1 | 5 | 0 | 0 | 0 | .125 | .125 |
| P | Lefty Leifield | L | 7 | 7 | 0 | 0 | 0 | 0 | 0.0 | 1 | 0 | 0 | 3 | 0 | 0 | 0 | .000 | .000 |
| P | Doc Watson | R | 1 | 2 | 0 | 0 | 0 | 0 | 0.0 | 1 | 0 | 1 | 1 | 0 | 0 | 0 | .000 | .000 |
| P | Zip Zabel | R | 1 | 2 | 0 | 0 | 0 | 0 | 0.0 | 0 | 0 | 0 | 0 | 0 | 0 | 0 | .000 | .000 |
| TEAM TOTAL | | | | 5010 | 1286 | 194 | 96 | 59 | 1.2 | 72 | 621 | 553 | 633 | 181 | 86 | 27 | .257 | .369 |

## INDIVIDUAL FIELDING

| POS | Player | T | G | PO | A | E | DP | TC/G | FA | POS | Player | T | G | PO | A | E | DP | TC/G | FA |
|---|---|---|---|---|---|---|---|---|---|---|---|---|---|---|---|---|---|---|---|
| 1B | V. Saier | R | 148 | 1469 | 71 | 26 | 79 | 10.6 | .983 | OF | T. Leach | R | 119 | 270 | 15 | 3 | 5 | 2.4 | .990 |
| | J. Archer | R | 8 | 58 | 5 | 2 | 4 | 8.1 | .969 | | M. Mitchell | R | 81 | 176 | 14 | 12* | 0 | 2.5 | .941 |
| | F. Mollwitz | R | 2 | 19 | 0 | 0 | 0 | 9.5 | 1.000 | | W. Schulte | R | 129 | 180 | 13 | 9 | 2 | 1.6 | .955 |
| | T. Needham | R | 1 | 2 | 0 | 0 | 0 | 2.0 | 1.000 | | W. Miller | R | 63 | 136 | 9 | 3 | 5 | 2.3 | .980 |
| 2B | J. Evers | R | 135 | 303 | 426 | 30 | 70 | 5.6 | .960 | | C. Williams | L | 44 | 77 | 4 | 2 | 0 | 1.9 | .976 |
| | A. Phelan | R | 46 | 56 | 79 | 10 | 9 | 3.2 | .931 | | O. Clymer | R | 26 | 54 | 2 | 4 | 0 | 2.3 | .933 |
| | R. Corriden | R | 2 | 4 | 3 | 1 | 0 | 4.0 | .875 | | W. Good | L | 26 | 37 | 1 | 1 | 0 | 1.5 | .974 |
| SS | A. Bridwell | R | 135 | 282 | 399 | 37 | 46 | 5.3 | .948 | | M. Allison | R | 1 | 3 | 0 | 0 | 0 | 3.0 | 1.000 |
| | R. Corriden | R | 36 | 46 | 80 | 13 | 12 | 3.9 | .906 | | T. Stewart | L | 1 | 2 | 0 | 0 | 0 | 2.0 | 1.000 |
| | C. Keating | R | 2 | 6 | 1 | 0 | 0 | 3.5 | 1.000 | C | J. Archer | R | 103 | 454 | 138 | 19 | 6 | 5.9 | .969 |
| | A. Phelan | R | 1 | 0 | 1 | 0 | 0 | 1.0 | 1.000 | | R. Bresnahan | R | 58 | 194 | 67 | 10 | 2 | 4.7 | .963 |
| 3B | H. Zimmerman | R | 125 | 139 | 232 | 36 | 18 | 3.3 | .912 | | T. Needham | R | 14 | 51 | 24 | 3 | 4 | 5.6 | .962 |
| | A. Phelan | R | 38 | 46 | 68 | 9 | 3 | 3.2 | .927 | | B. Hargrave | R | 2 | 3 | 1 | 0 | 0 | 2.0 | 1.000 |
| | T. Leach | R | 2 | 6 | 2 | 3 | 0 | 5.5 | .727 | | | | | | | | | | |
| | R. Corriden | R | 1 | 1 | 0 | 0 | 0 | 1.0 | 1.000 | | | | | | | | | | |

In 1913 Johnny Evers was appointed Cub manager in a move that turned out to be unsettling for all concerned. The moody Evers was just as difficult to get along with as his nickname "The Crab" implied. Joe Tinker asked to be traded and was. Al Bridwell, the new shortstop, almost came to blows with Evers on the diamond during an argument. Heinie Zimmerman was fined for "backtalk," and on another occasion, Tommy Leach came in from center field and threatened to rearrange Johnny's face. All the dissension considered, it was surprising that the Cubs finished as high as they did.

Zimmerman, although not nearly as hot as he had been in 1912, still led the club with a .313 average and 95 RBI. He also set a major-league record by getting ejected from three games in a five-day period in mid-June. Vic Saier tied a Cub record with 21 triples, while Cheney was still the big winner with 21 wins. Two new additions to the staff, Bert Humphries and George Pearce, won 16 and 13 games. At the end of the season, Evers found himself both out of a job and traded to Boston.

## TEAM  STATISTICS

| | W | L | PCT | GB | R | OR | 2B | 3B | HR | BA | SA | SB | E | DP | FA | CG | B | SO | ShO | SV | ERA |
|---|---|---|---|---|---|---|---|---|---|---|---|---|---|---|---|---|---|---|---|---|---|
| | | | | | | | **Batting** | | | | | | **Fielding** | | | **Pitching** | | | | | |
| NY | 101 | 51 | .664 | | 684 | 515 | 226 | 70 | 31 | **.273** | .361 | **296** | 254 | 107 | .961 | 82 | **315** | 651 | 12 | **16** | **2.43** |
| PHI | 88 | 63 | .583 | 12.5 | 693 | 636 | **257** | 78 | **73** | .265 | **.382** | 156 | **214** | 112 | **.968** | 77 | 512 | **667** | **20** | 11 | 3.15 |
| CHI | 88 | 65 | .575 | 13.5 | **720** | 625 | 194 | **96** | 59 | .257 | .369 | 181 | 259 | 106 | .959 | 89 | 478 | 556 | 12 | 14 | 3.13 |
| PIT | 78 | 71 | .523 | 21.5 | 673 | 585 | 210 | 86 | 35 | .263 | .356 | 181 | 226 | 94 | .964 | 74 | 434 | 590 | 9 | 7 | 2.90 |
| BOS | 69 | 82 | .457 | 31.5 | 641 | 690 | 191 | 60 | 32 | .256 | .335 | 177 | 273 | 82 | .957 | **105** | 419 | 597 | 12 | 3 | 3.19 |
| BKN | 65 | 84 | .436 | 34.5 | 595 | 613 | 193 | 86 | 39 | .270 | .363 | 188 | 243 | **125** | .961 | 70 | 439 | 548 | 9 | 6 | 3.13 |
| CIN | 64 | 89 | .418 | 37.5 | 607 | 717 | 170 | **96** | 27 | .261 | .347 | 226 | 251 | 104 | .961 | 71 | 456 | 522 | 10 | 10 | 3.46 |
| STL | 51 | 99 | .340 | 49 | 523 | 755 | 152 | 72 | 14 | .247 | .315 | 171 | 219 | 113 | .965 | 73 | 476 | 464 | 6 | 10 | 4.24 |
| LEAGUE TOTAL | | | | | 5136 | 5136 | 1593 | 644 | 310 | .262 | .354 | 1576 | 1939 | 843 | .962 | 641 | 3529 | 4595 | 90 | 77 | 3.20 |

## INDIVIDUAL  PITCHING

| PITCHER | T | W | L | PCT | ERA | SV | G | GS | CG | IP | H | BB | SO | R | ER | ShO | H/9 | BB/9 | SO/9 |
|---|---|---|---|---|---|---|---|---|---|---|---|---|---|---|---|---|---|---|---|
| Larry Cheney | R | 21 | 14 | .600 | 2.57 | **11** | **54** | 36 | 25 | 305 | 271 | 98 | 136 | 117 | 87 | 2 | 8.00 | 2.89 | 4.01 |
| Jimmy Lavender | R | 10 | 14 | .417 | 3.66 | 2 | 40 | 20 | 10 | 204 | 206 | 98 | 91 | 111 | 83 | 0 | 9.09 | 4.32 | 4.01 |
| Bert Humphries | R | 16 | 4 | **.800** | 2.69 | 0 | 28 | 20 | 13 | 181 | 169 | 24 | 61 | 80 | 54 | 2 | 8.40 | 1.19 | 3.03 |
| George Pearce | L | 13 | 5 | .722 | 2.31 | 0 | 25 | 21 | 14 | 163.1 | 137 | 59 | 73 | 60 | 42 | 3 | 7.55 | 3.25 | 4.02 |
| Charlie Smith | R | 7 | 9 | .438 | 2.55 | 0 | 20 | 17 | 8 | 137.2 | 138 | 34 | 47 | 53 | 39 | 1 | 9.02 | 2.22 | 3.07 |
| Orval Overall | R | 4 | 5 | .444 | 3.31 | 0 | 11 | 9 | 6 | 68 | 73 | 26 | 30 | 33 | 25 | 1 | 9.66 | 3.44 | 3.97 |
| Lew Richie | R | 2 | 4 | .333 | 5.82 | 0 | 16 | 6 | 1 | 65 | 77 | 30 | 15 | 53 | 42 | 0 | 10.66 | 4.15 | 2.08 |
| Hippo Vaughn | L | 5 | 1 | .833 | 1.45 | 0 | 7 | 6 | 5 | 56 | 37 | 27 | 36 | 13 | 9 | 2 | 5.95 | 4.34 | 5.79 |
| Eddie Stack | R | 4 | 2 | .667 | 4.24 | 1 | 11 | 7 | 3 | 51 | 56 | 15 | 28 | 29 | 24 | 1 | 9.88 | 2.65 | 4.94 |
| Fred Toney | R | 2 | 2 | .500 | 6.00 | 0 | 7 | 5 | 2 | 39 | 52 | 22 | 12 | 29 | 26 | 0 | 12.00 | 5.08 | 2.77 |
| Ed Reulbach | R | 1 | 3 | .250 | 4.42 | 0 | 9 | 2 | 1 | 38.2 | 41 | 21 | 10 | 27 | 19 | 0 | 9.54 | 4.89 | 2.33 |
| Earl Moore | R | 1 | 1 | .500 | 4.45 | 0 | 7 | 2 | 0 | 28.1 | 34 | 12 | 12 | 19 | 14 | 0 | 10.80 | 3.81 | 3.81 |
| Lefty Leifield | L | 0 | 1 | .000 | 5.48 | 0 | 6 | 1 | 0 | 21.1 | 28 | 5 | 4 | 14 | 13 | 0 | 11.81 | 2.11 | 1.69 |
| Doc Watson | L | 1 | 0 | 1.000 | 1.00 | 0 | 1 | 1 | 1 | 9 | 8 | 6 | 1 | 2 | 1 | 0 | 8.00 | 6.00 | 1.00 |
| Zip Zabel | R | 1 | 0 | 1.000 | 0.00 | 0 | 1 | 1 | 0 | 5 | 3 | 1 | 0 | 0 | 0 | 0 | 5.40 | 1.80 | 0.00 |
| TEAM TOTAL | | 88 | 65 | .575 | 3.13 | 14 | 243 | 154 | 89 | 1372.1 | 1330 | 478 | 556 | 640 | 478 | 12 | 8.72 | 3.13 | 3.65 |

| MANAGER | W | L | PCT |
|---|---|---|---|
| Hank O'Day | 78 | 76 | .506 |

| POS | Player | B | G | AB | H | 2B | 3B | HR | HR % | R | RBI | BB | SO | SB | Pinch Hit AB | H | BA | SA |
|---|---|---|---|---|---|---|---|---|---|---|---|---|---|---|---|---|---|---|
| **REGULARS** | | | | | | | | | | | | | | | | | | |
| 1B | Vic Saier | L | 153 | 537 | 129 | 24 | 8 | 18 | 3.4 | 87 | 72 | 94 | 61 | 19 | 0 | 0 | .240 | .415 |
| 2B | Bill Sweeney | R | 134 | 463 | 101 | 14 | 5 | 1 | 0.2 | 45 | 38 | 53 | 15 | 18 | 0 | 0 | .218 | .276 |
| SS | Red Corriden | R | 107 | 318 | 73 | 9 | 5 | 3 | 0.9 | 42 | 29 | 35 | 33 | 13 | 6 | 2 | .230 | .318 |
| 3B | Heinie Zimmerman | R | 146 | 564 | 167 | 36 | 12 | 4 | 0.7 | 75 | 87 | 20 | 46 | 17 | 1 | 1 | .296 | .424 |
| RF | Wilbur Good | L | 154 | 580 | 158 | 24 | 7 | 2 | 0.3 | 70 | 43 | 53 | 74 | 31 | 0 | 0 | .272 | .348 |
| CF | Tommy Leach | R | 153 | 577 | 152 | 24 | 9 | 7 | 1.2 | 80 | 46 | 79 | 50 | 16 | 1 | 0 | .263 | .373 |
| LF | Wildfire Schulte | L | 137 | 465 | 112 | 22 | 7 | 5 | 1.1 | 54 | 61 | 39 | 55 | 16 | 3 | 1 | .241 | .351 |
| C | Roger Bresnahan | R | 86 | 248 | 69 | 10 | 4 | 0 | 0.0 | 42 | 24 | 49 | 20 | 14 | 4 | 1 | .278 | .351 |
| **SUBSTITUTES** | | | | | | | | | | | | | | | | | | |
| SS | Claud Derrick | R | 28 | 96 | 21 | 3 | 1 | 0 | 0.0 | 5 | 13 | 5 | 13 | 2 | 0 | 0 | .219 | .271 |
| SS | Bob Fisher | R | 15 | 50 | 15 | 2 | 2 | 0 | 0.0 | 5 | 5 | 3 | 4 | 2 | 0 | 0 | .300 | .420 |
| UT | Art Phelan | R | 25 | 46 | 13 | 2 | 1 | 0 | 0.0 | 5 | 3 | 4 | 3 | 0 | 13 | 6 | .283 | .370 |
| 3B | Art Bues | R | 14 | 45 | 10 | 1 | 1 | 0 | 0.0 | 3 | 4 | 5 | 6 | 1 | 2 | 0 | .222 | .289 |
| SS | Chick Keating | R | 20 | 30 | 3 | 0 | 1 | 0 | 0.0 | 3 | 0 | 6 | 9 | 0 | 0 | 0 | .100 | .167 |
| 1B | Fritz Mollwitz | R | 13 | 20 | 3 | 0 | 0 | 0 | 0.0 | 0 | 1 | 0 | 3 | 1 | 6 | 0 | .150 | .150 |
| 3B | Herman Bronkie | R | 1 | 1 | 1 | 1 | 0 | 0 | 0.0 | 1 | 1 | 0 | 0 | 0 | 0 | 0 | 1.000 | 2.000 |
| OF | Jimmy Johnston | R | 50 | 101 | 23 | 3 | 2 | 1 | 1.0 | 9 | 8 | 4 | 9 | 3 | 11 | 2 | .228 | .327 |
| OF | Cy Williams | L | 55 | 94 | 19 | 2 | 2 | 0 | 0.0 | 12 | 5 | 13 | 13 | 2 | 22 | 4 | .202 | .266 |
| OF | Pete Knisely | R | 37 | 69 | 9 | 0 | 1 | 0 | 0.0 | 5 | 5 | 5 | 6 | 0 | 19 | 4 | .130 | .159 |
| OF | Johnny Bates | L | 9 | 8 | 1 | 0 | 0 | 0 | 0.0 | 2 | 1 | 1 | 1 | 0 | 4 | 0 | .125 | .125 |
| C | Jimmy Archer | R | 79 | 248 | 64 | 9 | 2 | 0 | 0.0 | 17 | 19 | 9 | 9 | 1 | 3 | 1 | .258 | .310 |
| C | Bubbles Hargrave | R | 23 | 36 | 8 | 2 | 0 | 0 | 0.0 | 3 | 2 | 0 | 4 | 2 | 7 | 1 | .222 | .278 |
| C | Tom Needham | R | 9 | 17 | 2 | 1 | 0 | 0 | 0.0 | 3 | 3 | 1 | 4 | 1 | 2 | 0 | .118 | .176 |
| C | Earl Tyree | R | 1 | 4 | 0 | 0 | 0 | 0 | 0.0 | 1 | 0 | 0 | 0 | 0 | 0 | 0 | .000 | .000 |
| PH | Milo Allison | L | 1 | 1 | 1 | 0 | 0 | 0 | 0.0 | 0 | 0 | 0 | 0 | 0 | 1 | 1 | 1.000 | 1.000 |
| PH | Tuffy Stewart | L | 2 | 1 | 0 | 0 | 0 | 0 | 0.0 | 0 | 0 | 0 | 0 | 0 | 1 | 0 | .000 | .000 |
| **PITCHERS** | | | | | | | | | | | | | | | | | | |
| P | Larry Cheney | R | 50 | 100 | 18 | 2 | 2 | 0 | 0.0 | 8 | 10 | 8 | 35 | 1 | 0 | 0 | .180 | .240 |
| P | Hippo Vaughn | B | 42 | 97 | 14 | 3 | 1 | 1 | 1.0 | 10 | 3 | 5 | 33 | 2 | 0 | 0 | .144 | .227 |
| P | Jimmy Lavender | R | 37 | 63 | 11 | 3 | 1 | 0 | 0.0 | 8 | 5 | 6 | 25 | 2 | 0 | 0 | .175 | .254 |
| P | Bert Humphries | R | 35 | 55 | 13 | 0 | 0 | 0 | 0.0 | 4 | 6 | 3 | 10 | 0 | 1 | 0 | .236 | .236 |
| P | George Pearce | L | 30 | 45 | 4 | 1 | 0 | 0 | 0.0 | 2 | 3 | 0 | 19 | 0 | 0 | 0 | .089 | .111 |
| P | Zip Zabel | R | 29 | 38 | 7 | 0 | 0 | 0 | 0.0 | 2 | 4 | 0 | 5 | 0 | 0 | 0 | .184 | .184 |
| P | Casey Hageman | R | 16 | 15 | 7 | 1 | 0 | 0 | 0.0 | 2 | 1 | 0 | 5 | 0 | 0 | 0 | .467 | .533 |
| P | Charlie Smith | R | 16 | 11 | 1 | 0 | 0 | 0 | 0.0 | 0 | 0 | 0 | 4 | 0 | 0 | 0 | .091 | .091 |
| P | Eddie Stack | R | 7 | 4 | 0 | 0 | 0 | 0 | 0.0 | 0 | 0 | 1 | 2 | 0 | 0 | 0 | .000 | .000 |
| P | George McConnell | R | 1 | 2 | 0 | 0 | 0 | 0 | 0.0 | 0 | 0 | 0 | 1 | 0 | 0 | 0 | .000 | .000 |
| P | Elmer Koestner | R | 5 | 1 | 0 | 0 | 0 | 0 | 0.0 | 0 | 0 | 0 | 0 | 0 | 0 | 0 | .000 | .000 |
| | TEAM TOTAL | | | 5050 | 1229 | 199 | 74 | 42 | 0.8 | 60 | 502 | 501 | 577 | 164 | 107 | 24 | .243 | .337 |

## INDIVIDUAL FIELDING

| POS | Player | T | G | PO | A | E | DP | TC/G | FA | | POS | Player | T | G | PO | A | E | DP | TC/G | FA |
|---|---|---|---|---|---|---|---|---|---|---|---|---|---|---|---|---|---|---|---|---|
| 1B | V. Saier | R | 153 | 1521 | 59 | 22 | 62 | 10.5 | .986 | | OF | T. Leach | R | 137 | 321 | 16 | 11 | 5 | 2.5 | .968 |
| | F. Mollwitz | R | 4 | 24 | 1 | 1 | 1 | 6.5 | .962 | | | W. Good | L | 154 | 242 | 25 | 20 | 10 | 1.9 | .930 |
| 2B | B. Sweeney | R | 134 | 301 | 426 | 35 | 40 | 5.7 | .954 | | | W. Schulte | R | 134 | 217 | 9 | 11 | 2 | 1.8 | .954 |
| | R. Corriden | R | 3 | 0 | 0 | 0 | 0 | 0.0 | .000 | | | J. Johnston | R | 28 | 58 | 7 | 5 | 3 | 2.5 | .929 |
| | H. Zimmerman | R | 12 | 25 | 36 | 5 | 3 | 5.5 | .924 | | | C. Williams | L | 27 | 46 | 2 | 3 | 0 | 1.9 | .941 |
| | R. Bresnahan | R | 14 | 11 | 18 | 1 | 0 | 2.1 | .967 | | | P. Knisely | R | 16 | 36 | 3 | 1 | 2 | 2.5 | .975 |
| | J. Johnston | R | 4 | 11 | 9 | 3 | 0 | 5.8 | .870 | | | F. Mollwitz | R | 1 | 0 | 0 | 0 | 0 | 0.0 | .000 |
| | A. Phelan | R | 3 | 1 | 2 | 0 | 0 | 1.0 | 1.000 | | | J. Bates | L | 3 | 5 | 0 | 0 | 0 | 1.7 | 1.000 |
| SS | R. Corriden | R | 96 | 174 | 212 | 46 | 29 | 4.5 | .894 | | | R. Bresnahan | R | 1 | 1 | 0 | 0 | 0 | 1.0 | 1.000 |
| | C. Derrick | R | 28 | 65 | 88 | 18 | 9 | 6.1 | .895 | | C | R. Bresnahan | R | 85 | 365 | 113 | 11 | 6 | 5.8 | .978 |
| | H. Zimmerman | R | 15 | 30 | 37 | 10 | 3 | 5.1 | .870 | | | J. Archer | R | 76 | 367 | 105 | 13 | 8 | 6.4 | .973 |
| | B. Fisher | R | 15 | 20 | 46 | 4 | 3 | 4.7 | .943 | | | B. Hargrave | R | 16 | 34 | 6 | 3 | 0 | 2.7 | .930 |
| | C. Keating | R | 16 | 15 | 24 | 2 | 2 | 2.6 | .951 | | | T. Needham | R | 7 | 22 | 11 | 2 | 0 | 5.0 | .943 |
| | A. Phelan | R | 2 | 6 | 5 | 1 | 1 | 6.0 | .917 | | | E. Tyree | R | 1 | 2 | 1 | 0 | 0 | 3.0 | 1.000 |
| 3B | H. Zimmerman | R | 119 | 141 | 197 | 39 | 13 | 3.2 | .897 | | | | | | | | | | | |
| | T. Leach | R | 16 | 25 | 26 | 7 | 0 | 3.6 | .879 | | | | | | | | | | | |
| | A. Bues | R | 12 | 14 | 16 | 1 | 0 | 2.6 | .968 | | | | | | | | | | | |
| | A. Phelan | R | 7 | 5 | 14 | 2 | 0 | 3.0 | .905 | | | | | | | | | | | |
| | R. Corriden | R | 8 | 5 | 11 | 2 | 1 | 2.3 | .889 | | | | | | | | | | | |
| | H. Bronkie | R | 1 | 0 | 0 | 1 | 0 | 1.0 | .000 | | | | | | | | | | | |

The off-season firing of Johnny Evers left the Cub infield north of first base leakier than a sieve. Impenetrable only a few years earlier, the defense committed 310 errors.

Hippo Vaughn, on his way to becoming the Cubs' greatest southpaw, was a 21-game winner while Cheney won 20. Beyond those two, however, the staff was inconsistent at best. The slumping of such key players as Zimmerman, Schulte, and Archer did not help matters.

In spite of their glaring weaknesses, the Cubs had a good first half, standing in second place with a 48–37 record on July 21. But once the "dog days" of August set in, the team's slipshod infield and lack of pitching depth brought about the inevitable decline. By season's end they were lucky to finish fourth, barely over .500. With Cub managers now going in and out on a revolving-door basis, Hank O'Day, who had replaced Evers, was himself given the pink slip.

## TEAM STATISTICS

| | W | L | PCT | GB | R | OR | 2B | 3B | HR | BA | SA | SB | E | DP | FA | CG | B | SO | ShO | SV | ERA |
|---|---|---|---|---|---|---|---|---|---|---|---|---|---|---|---|---|---|---|---|---|---|
| | | | | | | | Batting | | | | | | Fielding | | | Pitching | | | | | |
| BOS | 94 | 59 | .614 | | 657 | 548 | 213 | 60 | 35 | .251 | .335 | 139 | 246 | 143 | .963 | 104 | 477 | 606 | 19 | 5 | 2.74 |
| NY | 84 | 70 | .545 | 10.5 | 672 | 576 | 222 | 59 | 30 | .265 | .348 | 239 | 254 | 119 | .961 | 88 | 367 | 563 | 20 | 9 | 2.94 |
| STL | 81 | 72 | .529 | 13 | 558 | 540 | 203 | 65 | 33 | .248 | .333 | 204 | 239 | 109 | .964 | 83 | 422 | 531 | 16 | 11 | 2.38 |
| CHI | 78 | 76 | .506 | 16.5 | 605 | 638 | 199 | 74 | 42 | .243 | .337 | 164 | 310 | 87 | .951 | 70 | 528 | 651 | 14 | 9 | 2.71 |
| BKN | 75 | 79 | .487 | 19.5 | 622 | 618 | 172 | 90 | 31 | .269 | .355 | 173 | 248 | 112 | .961 | 80 | 466 | 605 | 11 | 10 | 2.82 |
| PHI | 74 | 80 | .481 | 20.5 | 651 | 687 | 211 | 52 | 62 | .263 | .361 | 145 | 324 | 81 | .950 | 85 | 452 | 650 | 14 | 6 | 3.06 |
| PIT | 69 | 85 | .448 | 25.5 | 503 | 540 | 148 | 79 | 18 | .233 | .303 | 147 | 223 | 96 | .966 | 86 | 392 | 488 | 10 | 9 | 2.70 |
| CIN | 60 | 94 | .390 | 34.5 | 530 | 651 | 142 | 64 | 16 | .236 | .299 | 224 | 314 | 113 | .952 | 74 | 489 | 607 | 15 | 14 | 2.94 |
| LEAGUE TOTAL | | | | | 4798 | 4798 | 1510 | 543 | 267 | .251 | .334 | 1435 | 2158 | 860 | .958 | 670 | 3593 | 4701 | 119 | 73 | 2.78 |

## INDIVIDUAL PITCHING

| PITCHER | T | W | L | PCT | ERA | SV | G | GS | CG | IP | H | BB | SO | R | ER | ShO | H/9 | BB/9 | SO/9 |
|---|---|---|---|---|---|---|---|---|---|---|---|---|---|---|---|---|---|---|---|
| Larry Cheney | R | 20 | 18 | .526 | 2.54 | 5 | 50 | 40 | 21 | 311.1 | 239 | 140 | 157 | 136 | 88 | 6 | 6.91 | 4.05 | 4.54 |
| Hippo Vaughn | L | 21 | 13 | .618 | 2.05 | 1 | 42 | 35 | 23 | 293.2 | 236 | 109 | 165 | 119 | 67 | 4 | 7.23 | 3.34 | 5.06 |
| Jimmy Lavender | R | 11 | 11 | .500 | 3.07 | 0 | 37 | 28 | 11 | 214.1 | 191 | 87 | 87 | 106 | 73 | 2 | 8.02 | 3.65 | 3.65 |
| Bert Humphries | R | 10 | 11 | .476 | 2.68 | 0 | 34 | 22 | 8 | 171 | 162 | 65 | 78 | 82 | 55 | 0 | 7.79 | 4.15 | 4.98 |
| George Pearce | L | 8 | 12 | .400 | 3.51 | 1 | 30 | 16 | 4 | 141 | 122 | 65 | 78 | 45 | 31 | 0 | 7.31 | 3.16 | 3.52 |
| Zip Zabel | R | 4 | 4 | .500 | 2.18 | 1 | 29 | 7 | 2 | 128 | 104 | 45 | 50 | 45 | 31 | 0 | 7.31 | 3.16 | 3.52 |
| Charlie Smith | R | 2 | 4 | .333 | 3.86 | 0 | 16 | 5 | 1 | 53.2 | 49 | 15 | 17 | 27 | 23 | 0 | 8.22 | 2.52 | 2.85 |
| Casey Hageman | R | 2 | 1 | .667 | 3.47 | 1 | 16 | 1 | 0 | 46.2 | 44 | 12 | 17 | 26 | 18 | 0 | 8.49 | 2.31 | 3.28 |
| Eddie Stack | R | 0 | 1 | .000 | 4.96 | 0 | 7 | 1 | 0 | 16.1 | 13 | 11 | 9 | 11 | 9 | 0 | 7.16 | 6.06 | 4.96 |
| George McConnell | R | 0 | 1 | .000 | 1.29 | 0 | 1 | 1 | 0 | 7 | 3 | 3 | 3 | 1 | 1 | 0 | 3.86 | 3.86 | 3.86 |
| Elmer Koestner | R | 0 | 0 | – | 2.84 | 0 | 4 | 0 | 0 | 6.1 | 6 | 4 | 6 | 5 | 2 | 0 | 8.53 | 5.68 | 8.53 |
| TEAM TOTAL | | 78 | 76 | .506 | 2.71 | 9 | 266 | 156 | 70 | 1389.1 | 1169 | 528 | 651 | 638 | 418 | 14 | 7.57 | 3.42 | 4.22 |

| | | W | L | PCT |
|---|---|---|---|---|
| **MANAGER** | | | | |
| Roger Bresnahan | | 73 | 80 | .477 |

| POS | Player | B | G | AB | H | 2B | 3B | HR | HR % | R | RBI | BB | SO | SB | Pinch Hit AB | Pinch Hit H | BA | SA |
|---|---|---|---|---|---|---|---|---|---|---|---|---|---|---|---|---|---|---|
| **REGULARS** | | | | | | | | | | | | | | | | | | |
| 1B | Vic Saier | L | 144 | 497 | 131 | 35 | 11 | 11 | 2.2 | 74 | 64 | 64 | 62 | 29 | 4 | 1 | .264 | .445 |
| 2B | Heinie Zimmerman | R | 139 | 520 | 138 | 28 | 11 | 3 | 0.6 | 65 | 62 | 21 | 33 | 19 | 1 | 1 | .265 | .379 |
| SS | Bob Fisher | R | 147 | 568 | 163 | 22 | 5 | 5 | 0.9 | 70 | 53 | 30 | 51 | 9 | 2 | 0 | .287 | .370 |
| 3B | Art Phelan | R | 133 | 448 | 98 | 16 | 7 | 3 | 0.7 | 41 | 35 | 55 | 42 | 12 | 0 | 0 | .219 | .306 |
| RF | Wilbur Good | L | 128 | 498 | 126 | 18 | 9 | 2 | 0.4 | 66 | 27 | 34 | 65 | 19 | 2 | 1 | .253 | .337 |
| CF | Cy Williams | L | 151 | 518 | 133 | 22 | 6 | 13 | 2.5 | 59 | 64 | 26 | 49 | 15 | 1 | 1 | .257 | .398 |
| LF | Wildfire Schulte | L | 151 | 550 | 137 | 20 | 6 | 12 | 2.2 | 66 | 69 | 49 | 68 | 19 | 3 | 1 | .249 | .373 |
| C | Jimmy Archer | R | 97 | 309 | 75 | 11 | 5 | 1 | 0.3 | 21 | 27 | 11 | 38 | 5 | 5 | 2 | .243 | .320 |
| **SUBSTITUTES** | | | | | | | | | | | | | | | | | | |
| 12 | Polly McLarry | L | 68 | 127 | 25 | 3 | 0 | 1 | 0.8 | 16 | 12 | 14 | 20 | 2 | 21 | 2 | .197 | .244 |
| 23 | Alex McCarthy | R | 23 | 72 | 19 | 3 | 0 | 1 | 1.4 | 4 | 6 | 5 | 7 | 2 | 0 | 0 | .264 | .347 |
| SS | Eddie Mulligan | R | 11 | 22 | 8 | 1 | 0 | 0 | 0.0 | 5 | 2 | 5 | 1 | 2 | 0 | 0 | .364 | .409 |
| SS | Chick Keating | R | 4 | 8 | 0 | 0 | 0 | 0 | 0.0 | 1 | 0 | 0 | 3 | 1 | 1 | 0 | .000 | .000 |
| 2B | Joe Schultz | R | 7 | 8 | 2 | 0 | 0 | 0 | 0.0 | 1 | 3 | 0 | 2 | 0 | 4 | 1 | .250 | .250 |
| OF | Red Murray | R | 51 | 144 | 43 | 6 | 1 | 0 | 0.0 | 20 | 11 | 8 | 8 | 6 | 9 | 5 | .299 | .354 |
| O2 | Pete Knisely | R | 64 | 134 | 33 | 9 | 0 | 0 | 0.0 | 12 | 17 | 15 | 18 | 1 | 17 | 4 | .246 | .313 |
| OF | John Fluhrer | R | 6 | 6 | 2 | 0 | 0 | 0 | 0.0 | 0 | 0 | 1 | 0 | 1 | 3 | 0 | .333 | .333 |
| O3 | Red Corriden | R | 6 | 3 | 0 | 0 | 0 | 0 | 0.0 | 1 | 0 | 2 | 1 | 0 | 2 | 0 | .000 | .000 |
| C | Roger Bresnahan | R | 77 | 221 | 45 | 8 | 1 | 1 | 0.5 | 19 | 19 | 29 | 23 | 19 | 6 | 0 | .204 | .262 |
| C | Bubbles Hargrave | R | 15 | 19 | 3 | 0 | 1 | 0 | 0.0 | 2 | 2 | 1 | 5 | 0 | 6 | 1 | .158 | .263 |
| C | Jack Wallace | R | 2 | 7 | 2 | 0 | 0 | 0 | 0.0 | 0 | 0 | 0 | 2 | 0 | 0 | 0 | .286 | .286 |
| C | Bob O'Farrell | R | 2 | 3 | 1 | 0 | 0 | 0 | 0.0 | 0 | 0 | 0 | 0 | 0 | 0 | 0 | .333 | .333 |
| **PITCHERS** | | | | | | | | | | | | | | | | | | |
| P | Hippo Vaughn | B | 43 | 86 | 14 | 3 | 0 | 0 | 0.0 | 8 | 9 | 7 | 27 | 3 | 0 | 0 | .163 | .198 |
| P | Jimmy Lavender | R | 46 | 67 | 9 | 3 | 0 | 0 | 0.0 | 1 | 0 | 1 | 31 | 0 | 0 | 0 | .134 | .179 |
| P | George Pearce | L | 36 | 56 | 11 | 2 | 1 | 0 | 0.0 | 4 | 2 | 3 | 16 | 0 | 0 | 0 | .196 | .268 |
| P | Zip Zabel | R | 37 | 54 | 4 | 0 | 0 | 0 | 0.0 | 2 | 0 | 0 | 7 | 2 | 0 | 0 | .074 | .074 |
| P | Bert Humphries | R | 31 | 46 | 8 | 0 | 1 | 0 | 0.0 | 3 | 1 | 2 | 11 | 0 | 0 | 0 | .174 | .217 |
| P | Larry Cheney | R | 25 | 40 | 6 | 0 | 0 | 0 | 0.0 | 2 | 2 | 3 | 13 | 0 | 0 | 0 | .150 | .150 |
| P | Pete Standridge | R | 30 | 40 | 9 | 2 | 1 | 0 | 0.0 | 5 | 4 | 4 | 16 | 0 | 0 | 0 | .225 | .325 |
| P | Karl Adams | R | 26 | 30 | 0 | 0 | 0 | 0 | 0.0 | 0 | 0 | 0 | 16 | 0 | 0 | 0 | .000 | .000 |
| P | Phil Douglas | R | 4 | 8 | 0 | 0 | 0 | 0 | 0.0 | 0 | 0 | 0 | 3 | 0 | 0 | 0 | .000 | .000 |
| P | Brad Hogg | L | 2 | 3 | 0 | 0 | 0 | 0 | 0.0 | 0 | 0 | 0 | 0 | 0 | 0 | 0 | .000 | .000 |
| P | Ed Schorr | R | 2 | 2 | 1 | 0 | 0 | 0 | 0.0 | 1 | 0 | 0 | 1 | 0 | 0 | 0 | .500 | .500 |
| P | Bob Wright | R | 2 | 0 | 0 | 0 | 0 | 0 | – | 0 | 0 | 0 | 0 | 0 | 0 | 0 | – | – |
| | TEAM TOTAL | | | 5114 | 1246 | 212 | 66 | 53 | 1.0 | 57 | 492 | 393 | 639 | 166 | 87 | 20 | .244 | .342 |

## INDIVIDUAL FIELDING

| POS | Player | T | G | PO | A | E | DP | TC/G | FA |
|---|---|---|---|---|---|---|---|---|---|
| 1B | V. Saier | R | 139 | 1348 | 65 | 21 | 71 | 10.3 | .985 |
| | P. McLarry | R | 25 | 167 | 7 | 4 | 5 | 7.1 | .978 |
| 2B | H. Zimmerman | R | 100 | 211 | 267 | 29 | 30 | 5.1 | .943 |
| | A. Phelan | R | 24 | 61 | 64 | 6 | 5 | 5.5 | .954 |
| | P. McLarry | R | 20 | 41 | 48 | 4 | 3 | 4.7 | .957 |
| | A. McCarthy | R | 12 | 34 | 35 | 2 | 8 | 5.9 | .972 |
| | P. Knisely | R | 9 | 15 | 13 | 5 | 2 | 3.7 | .848 |
| | J. Schultz | R | 2 | 3 | 3 | 1 | 0 | 3.5 | .857 |
| | R. Murray | R | 1 | 0 | 4 | 0 | 0 | 4.0 | 1.000 |
| SS | B. Fisher | R | 147 | 277 | 434 | 51 | 35 | 5.2 | .933 |
| | A. McCarthy | R | 1 | 0 | 0 | 0 | 0 | 0.0 | .000 |
| | E. Mulligan | R | 10 | 23 | 26 | 5 | 9 | 5.4 | .907 |
| | C. Keating | R | 2 | 4 | 5 | 3 | 0 | 6.0 | .750 |
| | H. Zimmerman | R | 4 | 2 | 6 | 0 | 2 | 2.0 | 1.000 |
| 3B | A. Phelan | R | 110 | 136 | 203 | 22 | 14 | 3.3 | .939 |
| | H. Zimmerman | R | 36 | 39 | 71 | 11 | 3 | 3.4 | .909 |
| | E. Mulligan | R | 1 | 0 | 0 | 0 | 0 | 0.0 | .000 |
| | A. McCarthy | R | 12 | 13 | 33 | 0 | 3 | 3.8 | 1.000 |
| | R. Corriden | R | 1 | 1 | 1 | 1 | 0 | 3.0 | .667 |

| POS | Player | T | G | PO | A | E | DP | TC/G | FA |
|---|---|---|---|---|---|---|---|---|---|
| OF | C. Williams | L | 151 | 347 | 14 | 12 | 2 | 2.5 | .968 |
| | W. Schulte | R | 147 | 280 | 24 | 12 | 3 | 2.1 | .962 |
| | W. Good | L | 125 | 192 | 13 | 14 | 4 | 1.8 | .936 |
| | R. Murray | R | 39 | 82 | 4 | 3 | 1 | 2.3 | .966 |
| | P. Knisely | R | 34 | 44 | 3 | 3 | 2 | 1.5 | .940 |
| | R. Corriden | R | 1 | 0 | 0 | 0 | 0 | 0.0 | .000 |
| | J. Fluhrer | R | 2 | 1 | 0 | 1 | 0 | 1.0 | .500 |
| C | J. Archer | R | 88 | 447 | 126 | 13 | 11 | 6.7 | .978 |
| | R. Bresnahan | R | 68 | 345 | 95 | 8 | 9 | 6.6 | .982 |
| | B. Hargrave | R | 9 | 13 | 7 | 0 | 0 | 2.2 | 1.000 |
| | J. Wallace | R | 2 | 13 | 6 | 0 | 0 | 9.5 | 1.000 |
| | B. O'Farrell | R | 2 | 1 | 1 | 1 | 0 | 1.5 | .667 |

In the Cubs' last year in their West Side location, catcher Roger Bresnahan became the third in a succession of one-year managers. Although the team again pulled in fourth, it was their first below-.500 finish in 13 years. Furthermore, they were only 3 1/2 games out of the cellar, as the bottom five teams were squeezed close together. Cub pitching was even less effective than it had been in 1914, as batters began catching on to Cheney's wet deliveries. Attendance was low as fans abandoned the Cubs for the pennant-winning Chicago Whales of the Federal League and the second-place White Sox.

It was a dull season and an unexciting team. Even so, there were three events of historical significance. Zip Zabel, an otherwise obscure pitcher, set a major league record by hurling 18 1/3 innings in relief, beating Brooklyn, 4–3, in 19 innings on June 17. On August 18, Cub outfielder Wilbur Good became the only Cub to steal second, third, and home plate in the same inning, during a 9–0 shellacking of the Dodgers. Finally, on August 31, Jimmy Lavender no-hit the hated Giants, 2–0.

### TEAM STATISTICS

|  | W | L | PCT | GB | R | OR | Batting 2B | 3B | HR | BA | SA | SB | Fielding E | DP | FA | CG | B | Pitching SO | ShO | SV | ERA |
|---|---|---|---|---|---|---|---|---|---|---|---|---|---|---|---|---|---|---|---|---|---|
| PHI | 90 | 62 | .592 |  | 589 | 463 | 202 | 39 | **58** | .247 | .340 | 121 | 216 | 99 | .966 | **98** | 342 | 652 | **20** | 8 | **2.17** |
| BOS | 83 | 69 | .546 | 7 | 582 | 545 | **231** | 57 | 17 | .240 | .319 | 121 | **213** | 115 | **.966** | 95 | 366 | 630 | 15 | 9 | 2.57 |
| BKN | 80 | 72 | .526 | 10 | 536 | 560 | 165 | 75 | 14 | .248 | .317 | 131 | 238 | 96 | .963 | 87 | 473 | 499 | 16 | 7 | 2.66 |
| CHI | 73 | 80 | .477 | 17.5 | 570 | 620 | 212 | 66 | 53 | .244 | **.342** | 166 | 268 | 94 | .958 | 71 | 480 | **657** | 18 | 6 | 3.11 |
| PIT | 73 | 81 | .474 | 18 | 557 | 520 | 197 | 91 | 24 | .246 | .334 | **182** | 214 | 100 | .966 | 91 | 384 | 544 | 18 | 10 | 2.60 |
| STL | 72 | 81 | .471 | 18.5 | **590** | 601 | 159 | **92** | 20 | **.254** | .333 | 162 | 235 | 109 | .964 | 79 | 402 | 538 | 13 | 9 | 2.89 |
| CIN | 71 | 83 | .461 | 20 | 516 | 585 | 194 | 84 | 15 | .253 | .331 | 156 | 222 | **148** | .966 | 80 | 497 | 572 | 19 | **12** | 2.84 |
| NY | 69 | 83 | .454 | 21 | 582 | 628 | 195 | 68 | 24 | .251 | .329 | 155 | 256 | 119 | .960 | 78 | **325** | 637 | 15 | 8 | 3.11 |
| LEAGUE TOTAL |  |  |  |  | 4522 | 4522 | 1555 | 572 | 225 | .248 | .331 | 1194 | 1862 | 880 | .964 | 679 | 3269 | 4729 | 134 | 69 | 2.75 |

### INDIVIDUAL PITCHING

| PITCHER | T | W | L | PCT | ERA | SV | G | GS | CG | IP | H | BB | SO | R | ER | ShO | H/9 | BB/9 | SO/9 |
|---|---|---|---|---|---|---|---|---|---|---|---|---|---|---|---|---|---|---|---|
| Hippo Vaughn | L | 20 | 12 | .625 | 2.87 | 1 | 41 | 34 | 18 | 269.2 | 240 | 77 | 148 | 105 | 86 | 4 | 8.01 | 2.57 | 4.94 |
| Jimmy Lavender | R | 10 | 16 | .385 | 2.58 | 3 | 41 | 24 | 13 | 220 | 178 | 67 | 117 | 77 | 63 | 1 | 7.28 | 2.74 | 4.79 |
| George Pearce | L | 13 | 9 | .591 | 3.32 | 0 | 36 | 20 | 8 | 176 | 158 | 77 | 96 | 83 | 65 | 2 | 8.08 | 3.94 | 4.91 |
| Bert Humphries | R | 8 | 13 | .381 | 2.31 | 2 | 31 | 22 | 10 | 171.2 | 183 | 23 | 45 | 69 | 44 | 4 | 9.59 | 1.21 | 2.36 |
| Zip Zabel | R | 7 | 10 | .412 | 3.20 | 0 | 36 | 17 | 8 | 163 | 124 | 84 | 60 | 81 | 58 | 2 | 6.85 | 4.64 | 3.31 |
| Larry Cheney | R | 8 | 9 | .471 | 3.56 | 0 | 25 | 18 | 6 | 131.1 | 120 | 55 | 68 | 69 | 52 | 2 | 8.22 | 3.77 | 4.66 |
| Pete Standridge | R | 4 | 1 | .800 | 3.61 | 0 | 29 | 3 | 2 | 112.1 | 120 | 36 | 42 | 56 | 45 | 0 | 9.61 | 2.88 | 3.36 |
| Karl Adams | R | 1 | 9 | .100 | 4.71 | 0 | 26 | 12 | 3 | 107 | 105 | 43 | 57 | 62 | 56 | 0 | 8.83 | 3.62 | 4.79 |
| Phil Douglas | R | 1 | 1 | .500 | 2.16 | 0 | 4 | 4 | 2 | 25 | 17 | 7 | 18 | 9 | 6 | 1 | 6.12 | 2.52 | 6.48 |
| Brad Hogg | R | 1 | 0 | 1.000 | 2.08 | 0 | 2 | 2 | 1 | 13 | 12 | 6 | 0 | 3 | 3 | 1 | 8.31 | 4.15 | 0.00 |
| Ed Schorr | R | 0 | 0 | – | 7.50 | 0 | 2 | 0 | 0 | 6 | 9 | 5 | 3 | 5 | 5 | 0 | 13.50 | 7.50 | 4.50 |
| Bob Wright | R | 0 | 0 | – | 2.25 | 0 | 2 | 0 | 0 | 4 | 6 | 3 | 0 | 3 | 3 | 1 | 13.50 | 0.00 | 6.75 |
| TEAM TOTAL |  | 73 | 80 | .477 | 3.11 | 6 | 275 | 156 | 71 | 1399 | 1272 | 480 | 657 | 622 | 484 | 18 | 8.18 | 3.09 | 4.23 |

| MANAGER | W | L | PCT |
|---|---|---|---|
| Joe Tinker | 67 | 86 | .438 |

| POS | Player | B | G | AB | H | 2B | 3B | HR | HR % | R | RBI | BB | SO | SB | Pinch Hit AB | Pinch Hit H | BA | SA |
|---|---|---|---|---|---|---|---|---|---|---|---|---|---|---|---|---|---|---|
| **REGULARS** | | | | | | | | | | | | | | | | | | |
| 1B | Vic Saier | L | 147 | 498 | 126 | 25 | 3 | 7 | 1.4 | 60 | 50 | 79 | 68 | 20 | 0 | 0 | .253 | .357 |
| 2B | Otto Knabe | R | 57 | 145 | 40 | 8 | 0 | 0 | 0.0 | 17 | 7 | 9 | 18 | 3 | 5 | 2 | .276 | .331 |
| SS | Chuck Wortman | R | 69 | 234 | 47 | 4 | 2 | 0 | 0.9 | 17 | 16 | 18 | 22 | 4 | 0 | 0 | .201 | .261 |
| 3B | Heinie Zimmerman | R | 107 | 398 | 116 | 25 | 5 | 6 | 1.5 | 54 | 64* | 16 | 33 | 15 | 4 | 1 | .291 | .425 |
| RF | Max Flack | L | 141 | 465 | 120 | 14 | 3 | 3 | 0.6 | 65 | 20 | 42 | 43 | 24 | 3 | 0 | .258 | .320 |
| CF | Cy Williams | L | 118 | 405 | 113 | 19 | 9 | 12 | 3.0 | 55 | 66 | 51 | 64 | 6 | 2 | 0 | .279 | .459 |
| LF | Les Mann | R | 127 | 415 | 113 | 13 | 9 | 2 | 0.5 | 46 | 29 | 19 | 31 | 11 | 9 | 1 | .272 | .361 |
| C | Jimmy Archer | R | 77 | 205 | 45 | 6 | 2 | 1 | 0.5 | 11 | 30 | 12 | 24 | 3 | 16 | 2 | .220 | .283 |
| **SUBSTITUTES** | | | | | | | | | | | | | | | | | | |
| UT | Rollie Zeider | R | 98 | 345 | 81 | 11 | 2 | 1 | 0.3 | 29 | 22 | 26 | 26 | 9 | 1 | 0 | .235 | .287 |
| SS | Eddie Mulligan | R | 58 | 189 | 29 | 3 | 4 | 0 | 0.0 | 13 | 9 | 8 | 30 | 1 | 0 | 0 | .153 | .212 |
| 2B | Steve Yerkes | R | 44 | 137 | 36 | 6 | 2 | 1 | 0.7 | 12 | 10 | 9 | 7 | 1 | 3 | 1 | .263 | .358 |
| 2B | Alex McCarthy | R | 37 | 107 | 26 | 2 | 3 | 0 | 0.0 | 10 | 6 | 11 | 7 | 1 | 0 | 0 | .243 | .318 |
| 1O | Fritz Mollwitz | R | 33 | 71 | 19 | 2 | 0 | 0 | 0.0 | 1 | 11 | 7 | 6 | 4 | 9 | 2 | .268 | .296 |
| SS | Mickey Doolan | R | 28 | 70 | 15 | 2 | 1 | 0 | 0.0 | 4 | 5 | 8 | 7 | 0 | 3 | 0 | .214 | .271 |
| 3B | Charlie Pechous | R | 22 | 69 | 10 | 1 | 1 | 0 | 0.0 | 5 | 4 | 3 | 21 | 1 | 0 | 0 | .145 | .188 |
| 2B | Larry Doyle | L | 9 | 38 | 15 | 5 | 1 | 1 | 2.6 | 6 | 7 | 1 | 1 | 0 | 0 | 0 | .395 | .658 |
| S3 | Joe Tinker | R | 7 | 10 | 1 | 0 | 0 | 0 | 0.0 | 0 | 1 | 1 | 1 | 0 | 1 | 0 | .100 | .100 |
| 3B | Charlie Deal | R | 2 | 8 | 2 | 1 | 0 | 0 | 0.0 | 2 | 3 | 0 | 0 | 0 | 0 | 0 | .250 | .375 |
| SS | Marty Shay | R | 2 | 7 | 2 | 0 | 0 | 0 | 0.0 | 0 | 0 | 0 | 1 | 0 | 0 | 0 | .286 | .286 |
| 3B | Herb Hunter | L | 2 | 4 | 0 | 0 | 0 | 0 | 0.0 | 0 | 0 | 0 | 0 | 0 | 1 | 0 | .000 | .000 |
| OF | Wildfire Schulte | L | 72 | 230 | 68 | 11 | 1 | 5 | 2.2 | 31 | 27 | 20 | 35 | 9 | 5 | 0 | .296 | .417 |
| OF | Joe Kelly | R | 54 | 169 | 43 | 7 | 1 | 2 | 1.2 | 18 | 15 | 9 | 16 | 10 | 8 | 1 | .254 | .343 |
| OF | Dutch Zwilling | L | 35 | 53 | 6 | 1 | 0 | 1 | 1.9 | 4 | 8 | 4 | 6 | 0 | 23 | 4 | .113 | .189 |
| OF | Earl Smith | L | 14 | 27 | 7 | 1 | 1 | 0 | 0.0 | 2 | 4 | 2 | 5 | 1 | 7 | 1 | .259 | .370 |
| OF | Solly Hofman | R | 5 | 16 | 5 | 2 | 1 | 0 | 0.0 | 2 | 2 | 2 | 2 | 0 | 1 | 0 | .313 | .563 |
| OF | Merwin Jacobson | L | 4 | 13 | 3 | 0 | 0 | 0 | 0.0 | 2 | 0 | 1 | 4 | 2 | 0 | 0 | .231 | .231 |
| C | Bill Fischer | L | 65 | 179 | 35 | 9 | 2 | 1 | 0.6 | 15 | 14 | 11 | 8 | 2 | 6 | 0 | .196 | .285 |
| C | Art Wilson | R | 36 | 114 | 22 | 3 | 1 | 0 | 0.0 | 5 | 5 | 6 | 14 | 1 | 2 | 1 | .193 | .237 |
| C | Rowdy Elliott | R | 23 | 55 | 14 | 3 | 0 | 0 | 0.0 | 5 | 3 | 3 | 5 | 1 | 4 | 0 | .255 | .309 |
| C | Nick Allen | R | 5 | 16 | 1 | 0 | 0 | 0 | 0.0 | 1 | 1 | 0 | 3 | 0 | 1 | 0 | .063 | .063 |
| C | Clem Clemens | R | 10 | 15 | 0 | 0 | 0 | 0 | 0.0 | 0 | 0 | 1 | 6 | 0 | 1 | 0 | .000 | .000 |
| C | John O'Connor | | 1 | 0 | 0 | 0 | 0 | 0 | – | 0 | 0 | 0 | 0 | 0 | 0 | 0 | – | – |
| C | Bob O'Farrell | | 1 | 0 | 0 | 0 | 0 | 0 | – | 0 | 0 | 0 | 0 | 0 | 0 | 0 | – | – |
| PH | Eddie Sicking | B | 1 | 1 | 0 | 0 | 0 | 0 | 0.0 | 0 | 0 | 0 | 0 | 0 | 1 | 0 | .000 | .000 |
| **PITCHERS** | | | | | | | | | | | | | | | | | | |
| P | Hippo Vaughn | B | 44 | 104 | 14 | 1 | 1 | 0 | 0.0 | 4 | 7 | 3 | 46 | 0 | 0 | 0 | .135 | .163 |
| P | Claude Hendrix | R | 45 | 80 | 16 | 3 | 0 | 1 | 1.3 | 4 | 5 | 6 | 24 | 0 | 7 | 1 | .200 | .275 |
| P | George McConnell | R | 48 | 57 | 9 | 0 | 0 | 0 | 0.0 | 2 | 0 | 2 | 4 | 0 | 0 | 0 | .158 | .158 |
| P | Gene Packard | L | 44 | 54 | 7 | 3 | 0 | 0 | 0.0 | 9 | 1 | 4 | 13 | 0 | 0 | 0 | .130 | .185 |
| P | Jimmy Lavender | R | 36 | 53 | 8 | 1 | 0 | 0 | 0.0 | 1 | 0 | 2 | 21 | 0 | 0 | 0 | .151 | .170 |
| P | Mike Prendergast | R | 35 | 46 | 7 | 0 | 0 | 0 | 0.0 | 1 | 1 | 1 | 17 | 0 | 0 | 0 | .152 | .152 |
| P | Tom Seaton | L | 35 | 38 | 7 | 1 | 1 | 0 | 0.0 | 4 | 2 | 1 | 15 | 2 | 0 | 0 | .184 | .263 |
| P | Three Finger Brown | B | 12 | 16 | 4 | 0 | 0 | 0 | 0.0 | 2 | 0 | 1 | 4 | 0 | 0 | 0 | .250 | .250 |
| P | Paul Carter | L | 8 | 12 | 2 | 0 | 0 | 0 | 0.0 | 1 | 0 | 0 | 2 | 0 | 0 | 0 | .167 | .167 |
| P | Scott Perry | L | 4 | 11 | 3 | 1 | 0 | 0 | 0.0 | 0 | 1 | 0 | 2 | 0 | 0 | 0 | .273 | .364 |
| P | George Pearce | L | 4 | 0 | 0 | 0 | 0 | 0 | – | 0 | 0 | 0 | 0 | 0 | 0 | 0 | – | – |
| | TEAM TOTAL | | | 5179 | 1237 | 194 | 56 | 46 | 0.9 | 52 | 456 | 399 | 662 | 133 | 123 | 17 | .239 | .325 |

## INDIVIDUAL   FIELDING

| POS | Player | T | G | PO | A | E | DP | TC/G | FA |
|---|---|---|---|---|---|---|---|---|---|
| 1B | V. Saier | R | 147 | 1622 | 74 | 27 | 78 | 11.7 | .984 |
| | F. Mollwitz | R | 19 | 116 | 7 | 3 | 6 | 6.6 | .976 |
| | R. Zeider | R | 2 | 6 | 0 | 0 | 0 | 3.0 | 1.000 |
| 2B | O. Knabe | R | 42 | 72 | 128 | 13 | 17 | 5.1 | .939 |
| | S. Yerkes | R | 41 | 79 | 114 | 17 | 14 | 5.1 | .919 |
| | A. McCarthy | R | 34 | 54 | 95 | 11 | 9 | 4.7 | .931 |
| | R. Zeider | R | 33 | 59 | 81 | 6 | 7 | 4.4 | .959 |
| | H. Zimmerman | R | 14 | 22 | 46 | 5 | 6 | 5.2 | .932 |
| | L. Doyle | R | 9 | 19 | 35 | 1 | 10 | 6.1 | .982 |
| SS | E. Mulligan | R | 58 | 116 | 200 | 40 | 27 | 6.1 | .888 |
| | C. Wortman | R | 69 | 124 | 191 | 32 | 24 | 5.0 | .908 |
| | M. Doolan | R | 24 | 46 | 77 | 11 | 8 | 5.6 | .918 |
| | R. Zeider | R | 5 | 9 | 9 | 2 | 2 | 4.0 | .900 |
| | H. Zimmerman | R | 4 | 6 | 8 | 1 | 1 | 3.8 | .933 |
| | M. Shay | R | 2 | 6 | 5 | 1 | 2 | 6.0 | .917 |
| | J. Tinker | R | 4 | 3 | 7 | 1 | 0 | 2.8 | .909 |
| | A. McCarthy | R | 3 | 2 | 2 | 1 | 0 | 1.7 | .800 |
| | O. Knabe | R | 1 | 0 | 1 | 0 | 0 | 1.0 | 1.000 |
| 3B | H. Zimmerman | R | 75 | 88 | 198 | 21 | 11 | 4.1* | .932 |
| | R. Zeider | R | 55 | 59 | 108 | 13 | 10 | 3.3 | .928 |
| | C. Pechous | R | 22 | 22 | 56 | 5 | 2 | 3.8 | .940 |
| | J. Archer | R | 1 | 0 | 0 | 0 | 0 | 0.0 | .000 |
| | O. Knabe | R | 1 | 0 | 0 | 0 | 0 | 0.0 | .000 |
| | C. Deal | R | 2 | 2 | 8 | 0 | 1 | 5.0 | 1.000 |
| | H. Hunter | R | 1 | 1 | 2 | 1 | 0 | 4.0 | .750 |
| | J. Tinker | R | 2 | 1 | 2 | 0 | 0 | 1.5 | 1.000 |

| POS | Player | T | G | PO | A | E | DP | TC/G | FA |
|---|---|---|---|---|---|---|---|---|---|
| OF | C. Williams | L | 116 | 260 | 7 | 3 | 0 | 2.3 | .989 |
| | M. Flack | L | 136 | 193 | 22 | 2 | 4 | 1.6 | .991 |
| | L. Mann | R | 115 | 200 | 9 | 6 | 1 | 1.9 | .972 |
| | W. Schulte | R | 65 | 108 | 8 | 6 | 0 | 1.9 | .951 |
| | J. Kelly | R | 46 | 98 | 4 | 5 | 0 | 2.3 | .953 |
| | D. Zwilling | L | 10 | 11 | 0 | 0 | 0 | 1.1 | 1.000 |
| | F. Mollwitz | R | 6 | 8 | 0 | 1 | 0 | 1.5 | .889 |
| | S. Hofman | R | 4 | 7 | 1 | 0 | 0 | 2.0 | 1.000 |
| | M. Jacobson | L | 4 | 8 | 0 | 0 | 0 | 2.0 | 1.000 |
| | R. Zeider | R | 7 | 7 | 1 | 0 | 0 | 1.1 | 1.000 |
| | E. Smith | R | 7 | 4 | 0 | 1 | 0 | 0.7 | .800 |
| | G. Packard | L | 3 | 3 | 0 | 1 | 0 | 1.3 | .750 |
| | O. Knabe | R | 1 | 2 | 0 | 0 | 0 | 2.0 | 1.000 |
| C | B. Fischer | R | 56 | 246 | 73 | 9 | 3 | 5.9 | .973 |
| | J. Archer | R | 65 | 236 | 84 | 7 | 5 | 5.0 | .979 |
| | A. Wilson | R | 34 | 140 | 43 | 9 | 2 | 5.6 | .953 |
| | R. Elliott | R | 18 | 77 | 17 | 3 | 1 | 5.4 | .969 |
| | J. O'Connor | R | 1 | 0 | 0 | 0 | 0 | 0.0 | .000 |
| | B. O'Farrell | R | 1 | 0 | 0 | 0 | 0 | 0.0 | .000 |
| | C. Clemens | R | 9 | 26 | 6 | 2 | 0 | 3.8 | .941 |
| | N. Allen | R | 4 | 19 | 4 | 1 | 1 | 6.0 | .958 |

In 1916, Joe Tinker was named Cub manager, chewing–gum magnate William Wrigley purchased an interest in the club, and the Cubs moved to their present location at Clark and Addison streets on the North Side. The new stadium, then called Weeghman Park, had been built two years earlier to house the Chicago Whales of the Federal League. After the FL folded, the Whale ownership bought the Cubs and vacated West Side Grounds.

The Cubs' first game at the new site was an 11-inning nail-biter on April 20, in which the Cubs edged the Reds, 7–6, on Vic Saier's game-winning single. Unfortunately, it was not an omen of things to come, as the Cubs ended up a poor fifth with their worst record in 15 years. Other than an occasional Cy Williams home run and the pitching of Vaughn, there was not much to cheer about. Two old standbys, Schulte and Zimmerman, were dealt away in midseason. Three Finger Brown returned to the team but was over the hill and retired after the season. When Tinker was fired in the off-season to be replaced by Fred Mitchell, the last link to the 1906-10 glory years was gone.

## TEAM STATISTICS

| | W | L | PCT | GB | R | OR | 2B | 3B | HR | BA | SA | SB | E | DP | FA | CG | B | SO | ShO | SV | ERA |
|---|---|---|---|---|---|---|---|---|---|---|---|---|---|---|---|---|---|---|---|---|---|
| | | | | | | | Batting | | | | | | Fielding | | | Pitching | | | | | |
| BKN | 94 | 60 | .610 | | 585 | 471 | 195 | 80 | 28 | **.261** | **.345** | 187 | 224 | 90 | .965 | 96 | 372 | 634 | 22 | 9 | **2.12** |
| PHI | 91 | 62 | .595 | 2.5 | 581 | 489 | **223** | 53 | 42 | .250 | .341 | 149 | 234 | 119 | .963 | **97** | **295** | 601 | **26** | 9 | 2.36 |
| BOS | 89 | 63 | .586 | 4 | 542 | **453** | 166 | 73 | 22 | .233 | .307 | 141 | **212** | 124 | **.967** | **97** | 325 | **644** | 21 | 11 | 2.19 |
| NY | 86 | 66 | .566 | 7 | **597** | 504 | 188 | 74 | 42 | .253 | .343 | **206** | 217 | 108 | .966 | 88 | 310 | 638 | 22 | 11 | 2.60 |
| CHI | 67 | 86 | .438 | 26.5 | 520 | 541 | 194 | 56 | **46** | .239 | .325 | 133 | 286 | 104 | .957 | 72 | 365 | 616 | 17 | 13 | 2.65 |
| PIT | 65 | 89 | .422 | 29 | 484 | 586 | 147 | **91** | 20 | .240 | .316 | 173 | 260 | 97 | .959 | 88 | 443 | 596 | 10 | 7 | 2.76 |
| CIN | 60 | 93 | .392 | 33.5 | 505 | 617 | 187 | 88 | 14 | .254 | .331 | 157 | 228 | **126** | .965 | 86 | 458 | 569 | 7 | 6 | 3.10 |
| STL | 60 | 93 | .392 | 33.5 | 476 | 629 | 155 | 74 | 25 | .243 | .318 | 182 | 278 | 124 | .957 | 58 | 445 | 529 | 11 | **14** | 3.14 |
| LEAGUE TOTAL | | | | | 4290 | 4290 | 1455 | 589 | 239 | .247 | .328 | 1328 | 1939 | 892 | .963 | 682 | 3013 | 4827 | 136 | 80 | 2.61 |

## INDIVIDUAL PITCHING

| PITCHER | T | W | L | PCT | ERA | SV | G | GS | CG | IP | H | BB | SO | R | ER | ShO | H/9 | BB/9 | SO/9 |
|---|---|---|---|---|---|---|---|---|---|---|---|---|---|---|---|---|---|---|---|
| Hippo Vaughn | L | 17 | 14 | .548 | 2.20 | 1 | 44 | 35 | 21 | 294 | 269 | 67 | 144 | 94 | 72 | 4 | 8.23 | 2.05 | 4.41 |
| Claude Hendrix | R | 8 | 16 | .333 | 2.68 | 2 | 36 | 24 | 15 | 218 | 193 | 67 | 117 | 81 | 65 | 3 | 7.97 | 2.77 | 4.83 |
| Jimmy Lavender | R | 10 | 14 | .417 | 2.82 | 2 | 36 | 25 | 9 | 188 | 163 | 62 | 91 | 76 | 59 | 4 | 7.80 | 2.97 | 4.36 |
| George McConnell | R | 4 | 12 | .250 | 2.57 | 0 | 28 | 20 | 8 | 171.1 | 137 | 35 | 82 | 66 | 49 | 1 | 7.20 | 1.84 | 4.31 |
| Gene Packard | L | 10 | 6 | .625 | 2.78 | 5 | 37 | 15 | 5 | 155.1 | 154 | 38 | 36 | 60 | 48 | 2 | 8.92 | 2.20 | 2.09 |
| Mike Prendergast | R | 6 | 11 | .353 | 2.31 | 2 | 35 | 10 | 4 | 152 | 127 | 23 | 56 | 53 | 39 | 2 | 7.52 | 1.36 | 3.32 |
| Tom Seaton | R | 6 | 6 | .500 | 3.27 | 1 | 31 | 14 | 4 | 121 | 108 | 43 | 45 | 54 | 44 | 0 | 8.03 | 3.20 | 3.35 |
| Three Finger Brown | R | 2 | 3 | .400 | 3.91 | 0 | 12 | 4 | 2 | 48.1 | 52 | 9 | 21 | 27 | 21 | 0 | 9.68 | 1.68 | 3.91 |
| Paul Carter | R | 2 | 2 | .500 | 2.75 | 0 | 8 | 5 | 2 | 36 | 26 | 17 | 14 | 16 | 11 | 0 | 6.50 | 4.25 | 3.50 |
| Scott Perry | R | 2 | 1 | .667 | 2.54 | 0 | 4 | 3 | 2 | 28.1 | 30 | 3 | 10 | 9 | 8 | 1 | 9.53 | 0.95 | 3.18 |
| George Pearce | L | 0 | 0 | – | 2.08 | 0 | 4 | 1 | 0 | 4.1 | 6 | 1 | 0 | 5 | 1 | 0 | 12.46 | 2.08 | 0.00 |
| TEAM TOTAL | | 67 | 85 | .441 | 2.65 | 13 | 275 | 156 | 72 | 1416.2 | 1265 | 365 | 616 | 541 | 417 | 17 | 8.04 | 2.32 | 3.91 |

| MANAGER | W | L | PCT |
|---|---|---|---|
| Fred Mitchell | 74 | 80 | .481 |

| POS | Player | B | G | AB | H | 2B | 3B | HR | HR % | R | RBI | BB | SO | SB | Pinch Hit AB | Pinch Hit H | BA | SA |
|---|---|---|---|---|---|---|---|---|---|---|---|---|---|---|---|---|---|---|
| **REGULARS** | | | | | | | | | | | | | | | | | | |
| 1B | Fred Merkle | R | 146 | 549 | 146 | 30 | 9 | 3 | 0.5 | 65 | 57 | 42 | 60 | 13 | 1 | 0 | .266 | .370 |
| 2B | Larry Doyle | L | 135 | 476 | 121 | 19 | 5 | 6 | 1.3 | 48 | 61 | 48 | 28 | 5 | 7 | 3 | .254 | .353 |
| SS | Chuck Wortman | R | 75 | 190 | 33 | 4 | 1 | 0 | 0.0 | 24 | 9 | 18 | 23 | 6 | 0 | 0 | .174 | .205 |
| 3B | Charlie Deal | R | 135 | 449 | 114 | 11 | 3 | 0 | 0.0 | 46 | 47 | 19 | 18 | 10 | 5 | 1 | .254 | .292 |
| RF | Max Flack | L | 131 | 447 | 111 | 18 | 7 | 0 | 0.0 | 65 | 21 | 51 | 34 | 17 | 10 | 3 | .248 | .320 |
| CF | Cy Williams | L | 138 | 468 | 113 | 22 | 4 | 5 | 1.1 | 53 | 42 | 38 | 78 | 8 | 1 | 1 | .241 | .338 |
| LF | Les Mann | R | 117 | 444 | 121 | 19 | 10 | 1 | 0.2 | 63 | 44 | 27 | 46 | 14 | 1 | 0 | .273 | .367 |
| C | Art Wilson | R | 81 | 211 | 45 | 9 | 2 | 2 | 0.9 | 17 | 25 | 32 | 36 | 6 | 4 | 2 | .213 | .303 |
| **SUBSTITUTES** | | | | | | | | | | | | | | | | | | |
| UT | Rollie Zeider | R | 108 | 354 | 86 | 14 | 2 | 0 | 0.0 | 36 | 27 | 28 | 30 | 17 | 15 | 2 | .243 | .294 |
| SS | Pete Kilduff | R | 56 | 202 | 56 | 9 | 5 | 0 | 0.0 | 23 | 15 | 12 | 19 | 11 | 0 | 0 | .277 | .371 |
| P1 | Dutch Ruether | L | 31 | 44 | 12 | 1 | 3 | 0 | 0.0 | 3 | 11 | 8 | 11 | 0 | 13 | 4 | .273 | .432 |
| 3S | Charlie Pechous | R | 13 | 41 | 10 | 0 | 0 | 0 | 0.0 | 2 | 1 | 2 | 9 | 1 | 0 | 0 | .244 | .244 |
| 23 | Paddy Driscoll | R | 13 | 28 | 3 | 1 | 0 | 0 | 0.0 | 2 | 3 | 2 | 6 | 2 | 0 | 0 | .107 | .143 |
| 1B | Vic Saier | L | 6 | 21 | 5 | 1 | 0 | 0 | 0.0 | 5 | 2 | 2 | 1 | 0 | 0 | 0 | .238 | .286 |
| 1B | Roy Leslie | R | 7 | 19 | 4 | 0 | 0 | 0 | 0.0 | 1 | 1 | 1 | 5 | 1 | 1 | 0 | .211 | .211 |
| 23 | Herb Hunter | L | 3 | 3 | 0 | 0 | 0 | 0 | 0.0 | 0 | 0 | 0 | 0 | 0 | 1 | 0 | .000 | .000 |
| OF | Harry Wolter | L | 117 | 353 | 88 | 15 | 7 | 0 | 0.0 | 44 | 28 | 38 | 40 | 7 | 16 | 7 | .249 | .331 |
| OF | Morrie Schick | R | 14 | 34 | 5 | 0 | 0 | 0 | 0.0 | 3 | 3 | 3 | 10 | 0 | 0 | 0 | .147 | .147 |
| OF | Turner Barber | L | 7 | 28 | 6 | 1 | 0 | 0 | 0.0 | 2 | 2 | 2 | 8 | 1 | 0 | 0 | .214 | .250 |
| OF | Bill Marriott | L | 2 | 6 | 0 | 0 | 0 | 0 | 0.0 | 0 | 0 | 0 | 1 | 0 | 0 | 0 | .000 | .000 |
| OS | Harry Wolfe | R | 9 | 5 | 2 | 0 | 0 | 0 | 0.0 | 1 | 1 | 1 | 1 | 0 | 2 | 0 | .400 | .400 |
| C | Rowdy Elliott | R | 85 | 223 | 56 | 8 | 5 | 0 | 0.0 | 18 | 28 | 11 | 11 | 4 | 12 | 2 | .251 | .332 |
| C | Pickles Dillhoefer | R | 42 | 95 | 12 | 1 | 1 | 0 | 0.0 | 3 | 8 | 2 | 9 | 1 | 4 | 0 | .126 | .158 |
| C | Bob O'Farrell | R | 3 | 8 | 3 | 2 | 0 | 0 | 0.0 | 1 | 1 | 1 | 0 | 1 | 0 | 0 | .375 | .625 |
| PH | Jimmy Archer | R | 2 | 2 | 0 | 0 | 0 | 0 | 0.0 | 0 | 0 | 0 | 1 | 0 | 2 | 0 | .000 | .000 |
| PH | Earl Blackburn | R | 2 | 2 | 0 | 0 | 0 | 0 | 0.0 | 0 | 0 | 0 | 0 | 0 | 2 | 0 | .000 | .000 |
| **PITCHERS** | | | | | | | | | | | | | | | | | | |
| P | Hippo Vaughn | B | 41 | 100 | 16 | 2 | 1 | 0 | 0.0 | 7 | 6 | 9 | 33 | 1 | 0 | 0 | .160 | .200 |
| P | Phil Douglas | R | 51 | 89 | 11 | 0 | 1 | 0 | 0.0 | 3 | 3 | 3 | 18 | 0 | 0 | 0 | .124 | .146 |
| P | Claude Hendrix | R | 48 | 86 | 22 | 3 | 1 | 0 | 0.0 | 7 | 7 | 5 | 20 | 1 | 5 | 1 | .256 | .314 |
| P | Al Demaree | L | 24 | 41 | 5 | 0 | 0 | 0 | 0.0 | 0 | 1 | 4 | 17 | 0 | 0 | 0 | .122 | .122 |
| P | Paul Carter | L | 23 | 33 | 6 | 1 | 0 | 0 | 0.0 | 3 | 0 | 2 | 10 | 0 | 0 | 0 | .182 | .212 |
| P | Vic Aldridge | R | 30 | 29 | 4 | 0 | 0 | 0 | 0.0 | 3 | 1 | 0 | 9 | 0 | 0 | 0 | .138 | .138 |
| P | Mike Prendergast | R | 35 | 28 | 7 | 2 | 0 | 0 | 0.0 | 1 | 0 | 1 | 4 | 0 | 0 | 0 | .250 | .321 |
| P | Tom Seaton | L | 16 | 21 | 5 | 1 | 0 | 0 | 0.0 | 2 | 1 | 3 | 7 | 0 | 0 | 0 | .238 | .286 |
| P | Harry Weaver | R | 4 | 5 | 1 | 0 | 0 | 0 | 0.0 | 0 | 0 | 0 | 2 | 0 | 0 | 0 | .200 | .200 |
| P | Roy Walker | R | 2 | 1 | 0 | 0 | 0 | 0 | 0.0 | 0 | 0 | 0 | 0 | 0 | 0 | 0 | .000 | .000 |
| P | Gene Packard | L | 2 | 0 | 0 | 0 | 0 | 0 | — | 0 | 0 | 0 | 0 | 0 | 0 | 0 | — | — |
| | TEAM TOTAL | | | 5135 | 1229 | 194 | 67 | 17 | 0.3 | 55 | 458 | 415 | 599 | 127 | 104 | 26 | .239 | .313 |

## INDIVIDUAL FIELDING

| POS | Player | T | G | PO | A | E | DP | TC/G | FA | POS | Player | T | G | PO | A | E | DP | TC/G | FA |
|---|---|---|---|---|---|---|---|---|---|---|---|---|---|---|---|---|---|---|---|
| 1B | F. Merkle | R | 140 | 1415 | 66 | 26 | 84 | 10.8 | .983 | OF | C. Williams | L | 136 | 340 | 23 | 15 | 4 | 2.8 | .960 |
| | R. Leslie | R | 6 | 59 | 3 | 2 | 3 | 10.7 | .969 | | L. Mann | R | 116 | 203 | 20 | 11 | 2 | 2.0 | .953 |
| | V. Saier | R | 6 | 56 | 7 | 0 | 3 | 10.5 | 1.000 | | M. Flack | L | 117 | 199 | 14 | 12 | 3 | 1.9 | .947 |
| | D. Ruether | L | 5 | 41 | 2 | 0 | 2 | 8.6 | 1.000 | | H. Wolter | L | 97 | 131 | 14 | 9 | 5 | 1.6 | .942 |
| | H. Wolter | L | 1 | 3 | 0 | 0 | 0 | 3.0 | 1.000 | | C. Hendrix | R | 2 | 0 | 0 | 0 | 0 | 0.0 | .000 |
| | R. Zeider | R | 1 | 2 | 0 | 0 | 0 | 2.0 | 1.000 | | M. Schick | R | 12 | 21 | 3 | 1 | 0 | 2.1 | .960 |
| 2B | L. Doyle | R | 128 | 300 | 348 | 33 | 54 | 5.3 | .952 | | F. Merkle | R | 6 | 15 | 2 | 0 | 1 | 2.8 | 1.000 |
| | R. Zeider | R | 24 | 51 | 76 | 3 | 13 | 5.4 | .977 | | T. Barber | R | 7 | 13 | 2 | 0 | 0 | 2.1 | 1.000 |
| | P. Driscoll | R | 8 | 12 | 18 | 4 | 4 | 4.3 | .882 | | B. Marriott | R | 1 | 2 | 0 | 1 | 0 | 3.0 | .667 |
| | P. Kilduff | R | 5 | 11 | 17 | 0 | 2 | 5.6 | 1.000 | | R. Zeider | R | 1 | 1 | 0 | 0 | 0 | 1.0 | 1.000 |
| | H. Hunter | R | 1 | 2 | 0 | 0 | 0 | 2.0 | 1.000 | | H. Wolfe | R | 2 | 1 | 0 | 0 | 0 | 0.5 | 1.000 |
| | C. Wortman | R | 1 | 0 | 2 | 0 | 0 | 2.0 | 1.000 | C | A. Wilson | R | 75 | 361 | 92 | 15 | 5 | 6.2 | .968 |
| SS | C. Wortman | R | 65 | 85 | 162 | 22 | 26 | 4.1 | .918 | | R. Elliott | R | 73 | 307 | 93 | 13 | 9 | 5.7 | .969 |
| | P. Kilduff | R | 51 | 91 | 128 | 19 | 19 | 4.7 | .920 | | Dillhoefer | R | 37 | 146 | 49 | 3 | 2 | 5.4 | .985 |
| | R. Zeider | R | 48 | 77 | 95 | 19 | 16 | 4.0 | .901 | | B. O'Farrell | R | 3 | 9 | 1 | 0 | 1 | 3.3 | 1.000 |
| | C. Pechous | R | 5 | 7 | 15 | 4 | 2 | 5.2 | .846 | | | | | | | | | | |
| | H. Wolfe | R | 1 | 2 | 1 | 0 | 0 | 3.0 | 1.000 | | | | | | | | | | |
| | P. Driscoll | R | 1 | 0 | 2 | 0 | 0 | 2.0 | 1.000 | | | | | | | | | | |
| 3B | C. Deal | R | 130 | 151 | 254 | 18 | 31 | 3.3 | .957 | | | | | | | | | | |
| | R. Zeider | R | 26 | 20 | 55 | 6 | 6 | 3.1 | .926 | | | | | | | | | | |
| | C. Wortman | R | 1 | 0 | 0 | 0 | 0 | 0.0 | .000 | | | | | | | | | | |
| | C. Pechous | R | 7 | 12 | 8 | 0 | 0 | 2.9 | 1.000 | | | | | | | | | | |
| | P. Driscoll | R | 2 | 3 | 4 | 3 | 0 | 5.0 | .700 | | | | | | | | | | |
| | H. Hunter | R | 1 | 1 | 2 | 1 | 0 | 4.0 | .750 | | | | | | | | | | |

On May 2, 1917, Hippo Vaughn of the Cubs and Fred Toney of the Reds locked horns in the greatest pitching duel in history—a double no-hitter for nine innings. Finally, Cincinnati eked out two hits in the 10th to win, 1–0. There were no more than 2,500 at Wrigley Field on that cold day, but according to Vaughn, at least 10 times that number later claimed to have been there. Vaughn, who took the loss lightheartedly, went on to win 23 games, a career high.

Otherwise, it was a bland, ho-hum season with another fifth place finish. Phil Douglas, the number two pitching ace, was an alcoholic spitballer who had great potential but was betrayed both by his own weaknesses and lack of hitting. The Cub offense, such as it was, was led by Les Mann at .273. On an ironic note, the new first baseman was Fred Merkle, whose "boner" nine years earlier had enabled the Cubs to win the pennant. He had been picked up hastily from Brooklyn after Vic Saier suffered a broken leg, and remained the regular first baseman for the next four years.

## TEAM  STATISTICS

| | W | L | PCT | GB | R | OR | Batting 2B | 3B | HR | BA | SA | SB | Fielding E | DP | FA | CG | B | Pitching SO | ShO | SV | ERA |
|---|---|---|---|---|---|---|---|---|---|---|---|---|---|---|---|---|---|---|---|---|---|
| NY | 98 | 56 | .636 | | 635 | 457 | 170 | 71 | **39** | .261 | .343 | **162** | **208** | 122 | **.968** | 92 | **327** | 551 | 18 | **14** | **2.27** |
| PHI | 87 | 65 | .572 | 10 | 578 | 500 | **225** | 60 | 38 | .248 | .339 | 109 | 212 | 112 | .967 | 103 | **327** | 617 | **22** | 4 | 2.46 |
| STL | 82 | 70 | .539 | 15 | 531 | 567 | 159 | 93 | 26 | .250 | .333 | 159 | 221 | **153** | .967 | 66 | 421 | 502 | 16 | 10 | 3.03 |
| CIN | 78 | 76 | .506 | 20 | 601 | 611 | 196 | **100** | 26 | **.264** | **.354** | 153 | 247 | 120 | .962 | 95 | 404 | 492 | 12 | 6 | 2.66 |
| CHI | 74 | 80 | .481 | 24 | 552 | 567 | 194 | 67 | 17 | .239 | .313 | 127 | 267 | 121 | .959 | 79 | 374 | **654** | 15 | 9 | 2.62 |
| BOS | 72 | 81 | .471 | 25.5 | 536 | 552 | 169 | 75 | 22 | .246 | .320 | 155 | 224 | 122 | .966 | **105** | 371 | 593 | 21 | 3 | 2.77 |
| BKN | 70 | 81 | .464 | 26.5 | 511 | 559 | 159 | 78 | 25 | .247 | .322 | 130 | 245 | 102 | .962 | 99 | 405 | 582 | 7 | 9 | 2.78 |
| PIT | 51 | 103 | .331 | 47 | 464 | 595 | 160 | 61 | 9 | .238 | .298 | 150 | 251 | 119 | .961 | 84 | 432 | 509 | 17 | 6 | 3.01 |
| LEAGUE TOTAL | | | | | 4408 | 4408 | 1432 | 605 | 202 | .249 | .328 | 1145 | 1875 | 971 | .964 | 723 | 3061 | 4500 | 128 | 61 | 2.70 |

## INDIVIDUAL  PITCHING

| PITCHER | T | W | L | PCT | ERA | SV | G | GS | CG | IP | H | BB | SO | R | ER | ShO | H/9 | BB/9 | SO/9 |
|---|---|---|---|---|---|---|---|---|---|---|---|---|---|---|---|---|---|---|---|
| Hippo Vaughn | L | 23 | 13 | .639 | 2.01 | 0 | 41 | 39 | 27 | 295.2 | 255 | 91 | 195 | 97 | 66 | 5 | 7.76 | 2.77 | **5.94** |
| Phil Douglas | R | 14 | 20 | .412 | 2.55 | 1 | **51** | 37 | 20 | 293.1 | 269 | 50 | 151 | 123 | 83 | 5 | 8.25 | 1.53 | 4.63 |
| Claude Hendrix | R | 10 | 12 | .455 | 2.60 | 1 | 40 | 21 | 13 | 215 | 202 | 72 | 81 | 94 | 62 | 1 | 8.46 | 3.01 | 3.39 |
| Al Demaree | R | 5 | 9 | .357 | 2.55 | 1 | 24 | 18 | 6 | 141.1 | 125 | 37 | 43 | 53 | 40 | 1 | 7.96 | 2.36 | 2.74 |
| Paul Carter | R | 5 | 8 | .385 | 3.26 | 2 | 23 | 13 | 6 | 113.1 | 115 | 19 | 34 | 47 | 41 | 0 | 9.13 | 1.51 | 2.70 |
| Vic Aldridge | R | 6 | 6 | .500 | 3.12 | 2 | 30 | 6 | 1 | 106.2 | 100 | 37 | 44 | 52 | 37 | 1 | 8.44 | 3.12 | 3.71 |
| Mike Prendergast | R | 3 | 6 | .333 | 3.35 | 1 | 35 | 8 | 1 | 99.1 | 112 | 21 | 43 | 42 | 37 | 0 | 10.15 | 1.90 | 3.90 |
| Tom Seaton | R | 5 | 4 | .556 | 2.53 | 1 | 16 | 9 | 3 | 74.2 | 60 | 23 | 27 | 30 | 21 | 1 | 7.23 | 2.77 | 3.25 |
| Dutch Ruether | L | 2 | 0 | 1.000 | 2.48 | 0 | 10 | 4 | 1 | 36.1 | 37 | 12 | 23 | 12 | 10 | 0 | 9.17 | 2.97 | 5.70 |
| Harry Weaver | R | 1 | 1 | .500 | 2.75 | 0 | 4 | 2 | 1 | 19.2 | 17 | 7 | 8 | 10 | 6 | 0 | 7.78 | 3.20 | 3.66 |
| Roy Walker | R | 0 | 1 | .000 | 3.86 | 0 | 2 | 1 | 0 | 7 | 8 | 5 | 4 | 5 | 3 | 0 | 10.29 | 6.43 | 5.14 |
| Gene Packard | L | 0 | 0 | – | 10.80 | 0 | 2 | 0 | 0 | 1.2 | 3 | 0 | 1 | 2 | 2 | 0 | 16.20 | 0.00 | 5.40 |
| TEAM TOTAL | | 74 | 80 | .481 | 2.62 | 9 | 278 | 158 | 79 | 1404 | 1303 | 374 | 654 | 567 | 408 | 14 | 8.35 | 2.40 | 4.19 |

| MANAGER | | W | L | PCT |
|---|---|---|---|---|
| Fred Mitchell | | 84 | 45 | .651 |

| POS | Player | B | G | AB | H | 2B | 3B | HR | HR % | R | RBI | BB | SO | SB | Pinch Hit AB | Pinch Hit H | BA | SA |
|---|---|---|---|---|---|---|---|---|---|---|---|---|---|---|---|---|---|---|
| **REGULARS** | | | | | | | | | | | | | | | | | | |
| 1B | Fred Merkle | R | 129 | 482 | 143 | 25 | 5 | 3 | 0.6 | 55 | 65 | 35 | 36 | 21 | 0 | 0 | .297 | .388 |
| 2B | Rollie Zeider | R | 82 | 251 | 56 | 3 | 2 | 0 | 0.0 | 31 | 26 | 23 | 20 | 16 | 7 | 1 | .223 | .251 |
| SS | Charlie Hollocher | L | 131 | 509 | 161 | 23 | 6 | 2 | 0.4 | 72 | 38 | 47 | 30 | 26 | 0 | 0 | .316 | .397 |
| 3B | Charlie Deal | R | 119 | 414 | 99 | 9 | 3 | 2 | 0.5 | 43 | 34 | 21 | 13 | 11 | 1 | 0 | .239 | .290 |
| RF | Max Flack | L | 123 | 478 | 123 | 17 | 10 | 4 | 0.8 | 74 | 41 | 56 | 19 | 17 | 0 | 0 | .257 | .360 |
| CF | Dode Paskert | R | 127 | 461 | 132 | 24 | 3 | 3 | 0.7 | 69 | 59 | 53 | 49 | 20 | 0 | 0 | .286 | .371 |
| LF | Les Mann | R | 129 | 489 | 141 | 27 | 7 | 2 | 0.4 | 69 | 55 | 38 | 45 | 21 | 0 | 0 | .288 | .384 |
| C | Bill Killefer | R | 104 | 331 | 77 | 10 | 3 | 0 | 0.0 | 30 | 22 | 17 | 10 | 5 | 0 | 0 | .233 | .281 |
| **SUBSTITUTES** | | | | | | | | | | | | | | | | | | |
| 2B | Pete Kilduff | R | 30 | 93 | 19 | 2 | 2 | 0 | 0.0 | 7 | 13 | 7 | 7 | 1 | 0 | 0 | .204 | .269 |
| 23 | Charlie Pick | L | 29 | 89 | 29 | 4 | 1 | 0 | 0.0 | 13 | 12 | 14 | 4 | 7 | 0 | 0 | .326 | .393 |
| 2O | Bill McCabe | B | 29 | 45 | 8 | 0 | 1 | 0 | 0.0 | 9 | 5 | 4 | 7 | 2 | 6 | 1 | .178 | .222 |
| 2S | Chuck Wortman | R | 17 | 17 | 2 | 0 | 0 | 1 | 5.9 | 4 | 3 | 1 | 2 | 3 | 0 | 0 | .118 | .294 |
| OF | Turner Barber | L | 55 | 123 | 29 | 3 | 2 | 0 | 0.0 | 11 | 10 | 9 | 16 | 3 | 20 | 4 | .236 | .293 |
| C | Bob O'Farrell | R | 52 | 113 | 32 | 7 | 3 | 1 | 0.9 | 9 | 14 | 10 | 15 | 0 | 7 | 2 | .283 | .425 |
| C | Rowdy Elliott | R | 5 | 10 | 0 | 0 | 0 | 0 | 0.0 | 0 | 0 | 2 | 1 | 0 | 0 | 0 | .000 | .000 |
| C | Tom Daly | R | 1 | 1 | 0 | 0 | 0 | 0 | 0.0 | 0 | 0 | 0 | 0 | 0 | 0 | 0 | .000 | .000 |
| C | Tommy Clarke | R | 1 | 0 | 0 | 0 | 0 | 0 | – | 0 | 0 | 0 | 0 | 0 | 0 | 0 | – | – |
| PH | Fred Lear | R | 2 | 1 | 0 | 0 | 0 | 0 | 0.0 | 0 | 0 | 1 | 0 | 0 | 1 | 0 | .000 | .000 |
| **PITCHERS** | | | | | | | | | | | | | | | | | | |
| P | Lefty Tyler | L | 38 | 100 | 21 | 1 | 0 | 0 | 0.0 | 9 | 8 | 9 | 15 | 0 | 2 | 0 | .210 | .220 |
| P | Hippo Vaughn | B | 35 | 96 | 23 | 3 | 2 | 0 | 0.0 | 13 | 8 | 6 | 21 | 4 | 0 | 0 | .240 | .313 |
| P | Claude Hendrix | R | 35 | 91 | 24 | 3 | 3 | 3 | 3.3 | 14 | 17 | 4 | 11 | 1 | 3 | 1 | .264 | .462 |
| P | Phil Douglas | R | 25 | 55 | 14 | 1 | 0 | 0 | 0.0 | 2 | 5 | 0 | 5 | 0 | 0 | 0 | .255 | .273 |
| P | Paul Carter | L | 21 | 25 | 6 | 0 | 0 | 0 | 0.0 | 2 | 2 | 0 | 3 | 0 | 0 | 0 | .240 | .240 |
| P | Speed Martin | R | 9 | 16 | 3 | 1 | 0 | 0 | 0.0 | 0 | 0 | 0 | 2 | 0 | 0 | 0 | .188 | .250 |
| P | Roy Walker | R | 13 | 11 | 0 | 0 | 0 | 0 | 0.0 | 0 | 0 | 1 | 5 | 0 | 0 | 0 | .000 | .000 |
| P | Grover Alexander | R | 3 | 10 | 1 | 0 | 0 | 0 | 0.0 | 1 | 0 | 0 | 2 | 0 | 0 | 0 | .100 | .100 |
| P | Harry Weaver | R | 8 | 8 | 2 | 1 | 0 | 0 | 0.0 | 0 | 0 | 0 | 3 | 1 | 0 | 0 | .250 | .250 |
| P | Vic Aldridge | R | 3 | 3 | 1 | 1 | 0 | 0 | 0.0 | 1 | 1 | 0 | 0 | 0 | 0 | 0 | .333 | .667 |
| P | Buddy Napier | R | 1 | 3 | 1 | 0 | 0 | 0 | 0.0 | 0 | 0 | 0 | 2 | 0 | 0 | 0 | .333 | .333 |
| TEAM TOTAL | | | | 4325 | 1147 | 164 | 53 | 21 | 0.5 | 53 | 438 | 358 | 343 | 159 | 47 | 9 | .265 | .342 |

## INDIVIDUAL FIELDING

| POS | Player | T | G | PO | A | E | DP | TC/G | FA |
|---|---|---|---|---|---|---|---|---|---|
| 1B | F. Merkle | R | 129 | 1388 | 82 | 15 | 69 | 11.5 | .990 |
| | T. Barber | R | 4 | 37 | 3 | 1 | 3 | 10.3 | .976 |
| | R. Zeider | R | 1 | 4 | 1 | 0 | 0 | 5.0 | 1.000 |
| 2B | R. Zeider | R | 79 | 142 | 207 | 16 | 22 | 4.6 | .956 |
| | P. Kilduff | R | 30 | 72 | 72 | 10 | 18 | 5.1 | .935 |
| | C. Pick | R | 20 | 42 | 66 | 4 | 0 | 5.6 | .964 |
| | B. McCabe | R | 13 | 21 | 41 | 4 | 1 | 5.1 | .939 |
| | C. Wortman | R | 8 | 8 | 11 | 3 | 1 | 2.8 | .864 |
| SS | C. Hollocher | R | 131 | 278 | 418 | 53 | 39 | 5.7 | .929 |
| | C. Wortman | R | 4 | 5 | 2 | 0 | 1 | 1.8 | 1.000 |
| 3B | C. Deal | R | 118 | 144 | 247 | 24 | 21 | 3.5 | .942 |
| | D. Paskert | R | 6 | 6 | 14 | 3 | 2 | 3.8 | .870 |
| | C. Pick | R | 8 | 3 | 11 | 3 | 6 | 2.1 | .824 |
| | R. Zeider | R | 1 | 1 | 1 | 0 | 0 | 2.0 | 1.000 |

| POS | Player | T | G | PO | A | E | DP | TC/G | FA |
|---|---|---|---|---|---|---|---|---|---|
| OF | D. Paskert | R | 121 | 283 | 12 | 6 | 1 | 2.5 | .980 |
| | L. Mann | R | 129 | 229 | 15 | 10 | 3 | 2.0 | .961 |
| | M. Flack | L | 121 | 199 | 20 | 5 | 5 | 1.9 | .978 |
| | T. Barber | R | 27 | 45 | 2 | 3 | 0 | 1.9 | .940 |
| | B. McCabe | R | 4 | 2 | 1 | 0 | 0 | 0.8 | 1.000 |
| C | B. Killefer | R | 104 | 487 | 110 | 11 | 12 | 5.8 | .982 |
| | B. O'Farrell | R | 45 | 115 | 36 | 4 | 3 | 3.4 | .974 |
| | T. Clarke | R | 1 | 0 | 0 | 0 | 0 | 0.0 | .000 |
| | R. Elliott | R | 5 | 15 | 5 | 1 | 0 | 4.2 | .952 |
| | T. Daly | R | 1 | 2 | 0 | 1 | 0 | 3.0 | .667 |

The Cubs were expected to be greatly strengthened by the acquisition of pitcher Grover Alexander and his batterymate, Bill Killefer, only to see Alex drafted into the army. Instead, the big three of Vaughn, Lefty Tyler, and Claude Hendrix proved nearly unbeatable in leading the Cubs to an easy pennant in William Wrigley's first year as primary stockholder. Provost Marshal General Crowder's "work or fight" order resulted in the baseball season being curtailed after Labor Day. Since there was not time enough for anyone else to put on a stretch drive, the Cubs glided to the pennant.

The sparkplug of the team was rookie shortstop Charlie Hollocher, an intense hustler who batted .316 to pace the club, collected 161 hits to lead the league, and stole 26 bases. In the earliest (by the calendar) World Series ever played, the Cubs met the Red Sox. It was a brilliantly pitched series on both sides, with Boston coming out ahead in six games, even though the Cubs outscored them, 10–9. Babe Ruth, who would later haunt the Cubs in a Yankee jersey, won two games for the Red Sox, while the Chicago contests were played in Comiskey Park because of its larger seating capacity. This was the only time in history that the Cubs played home games at the White Sox location.

## TEAM STATISTICS

| | W | L | PCT | GB | R | OR | 2B | 3B | Batting HR | BA | SA | SB | Fielding E | DP | FA | CG | B | Pitching SO | ShO | SV | ERA |
|---|---|---|---|---|---|---|---|---|---|---|---|---|---|---|---|---|---|---|---|---|---|
| CHI | 84 | 45 | .651 | | 538 | 393 | 164 | 53 | 21 | .265 | .342 | 159 | 188 | 91 | .966 | 92 | 296 | 472 | 25 | 6 | 2.18 |
| NY | 71 | 53 | .573 | 10.5 | 480 | 415 | 150 | 53 | 13 | .260 | .330 | 130 | 152 | 78 | .970 | 74 | 228 | 330 | 18 | 11 | 2.64 |
| CIN | 68 | 60 | .531 | 15.5 | 530 | 496 | 165 | 84 | 15 | .278 | .366 | 128 | 192 | 127 | .964 | 84 | 381 | 321 | 14 | 6 | 3.00 |
| PIT | 65 | 60 | .520 | 17 | 466 | 412 | 107 | 72 | 15 | .248 | .321 | 200 | 179 | 108 | .966 | 85 | 320 | 395 | 17 | 2 | 2.48 |
| BKN | 57 | 69 | .452 | 25.5 | 360 | 463 | 121 | 62 | 10 | .250 | .315 | 113 | 193 | 74 | .963 | 85 | 299 | 312 | 10 | 6 | 2.81 |
| PHI | 55 | 68 | .447 | 26 | 430 | 507 | 158 | 28 | 25 | .244 | .313 | 97 | 211 | 91 | .961 | 78 | 369 | 340 | 13 | 0 | 3.15 |
| BOS | 53 | 71 | .427 | 28.5 | 424 | 469 | 107 | 59 | 13 | .244 | .307 | 83 | 184 | 89 | .965 | 96 | 277 | 361 | 3 | 5 | 2.90 |
| STL | 51 | 78 | .395 | 33 | 454 | 527 | 147 | 64 | 27 | .244 | .325 | 119 | 220 | 116 | .962 | 72 | 352 | 361 | 3 | 5 | 2.96 |
| LEAGUE TOTAL | | | | | 3682 | 3682 | 1119 | 475 | 139 | .254 | .328 | 1029 | 1519 | 774 | .965 | 666 | 2522 | 2898 | 112 | 43 | 2.76 |

## INDIVIDUAL PITCHING

| PITCHER | T | W | L | PCT | ERA | SV | G | GS | CG | IP | H | BB | SO | R | ER | ShO | H/9 | BB/9 | SO/9 |
|---|---|---|---|---|---|---|---|---|---|---|---|---|---|---|---|---|---|---|---|
| Hippo Vaughn | L | 22 | 10 | .688 | 1.74 | 0 | 35 | 33 | 27 | 290.1 | 216 | 76 | 148 | 75 | 56 | 8 | 6.70 | 2.36 | 4.59 |
| Lefty Tyler | L | 19 | 9 | .679 | 2.00 | 1 | 33 | 30 | 22 | 269.1 | 218 | 67 | 102 | 72 | 60 | 8 | 7.28 | 2.24 | 3.41 |
| Claude Hendrix | R | 19 | 7 | .731 | 2.78 | 0 | 32 | 27 | 21 | 233 | 229 | 54 | 86 | 87 | 72 | 3 | 8.85 | 2.09 | 3.32 |
| Phil Douglas | R | 9 | 9 | .500 | 2.13 | 2 | 25 | 19 | 11 | 156.2 | 145 | 31 | 51 | 57 | 37 | 2 | 8.33 | 1.78 | 2.93 |
| Paul Carter | R | 4 | 1 | .800 | 2.71 | 1 | 21 | 4 | 1 | 73 | 78 | 19 | 13 | 29 | 22 | 4 | 9.62 | 2.34 | 1.60 |
| Speed Martin | R | 6 | 2 | .750 | 1.84 | 0 | 9 | 5 | 4 | 53.2 | 47 | 14 | 20 | 27 | 13 | 0 | 10.38 | 3.12 | 4.15 |
| Roy Walker | R | 1 | 3 | .250 | 2.70 | 1 | 13 | 7 | 2 | 43.1 | 50 | 15 | 16 | 19 | 11 | 1 | 7.88 | 2.35 | 2.68 |
| Harry Weaver | R | 2 | 2 | .500 | 2.20 | 1 | 8 | 3 | 1 | 32.2 | 27 | 7 | 9 | 13 | 8 | 1 | 7.44 | 1.93 | 2.48 |
| Grover Alexander | R | 2 | 1 | .667 | 1.73 | 0 | 3 | 3 | 3 | 26 | 19 | 3 | 15 | 7 | 5 | 0 | 6.58 | 1.04 | 5.19 |
| Vic Aldridge | R | 0 | 1 | .000 | 1.46 | 0 | 3 | 0 | 0 | 12.1 | 11 | 6 | 10 | 3 | 2 | 0 | 8.03 | 4.38 | 7.30 |
| Buddy Napier | R | 0 | 0 | – | 5.40 | 0 | 1 | 0 | 0 | 6.2 | 10 | 4 | 2 | 4 | 4 | 0 | 13.50 | 5.40 | 2.70 |
| TEAM TOTAL | | 84 | 45 | .651 | 2.18 | 6 | 183 | 131 | 92 | 1197 | 1050 | 296 | 472 | 393 | 290 | 23 | 7.89 | 2.23 | 3.55 |

| MANAGER | W | L | PCT |
|---|---|---|---|
| Fred Mitchell | 75 | 65 | .536 |

| POS | Player | B | G | AB | H | 2B | 3B | HR | HR % | R | RBI | BB | SO | SB | Pinch Hit AB | Pinch Hit H | BA | SA |
|---|---|---|---|---|---|---|---|---|---|---|---|---|---|---|---|---|---|---|
| **REGULARS** | | | | | | | | | | | | | | | | | | |
| 1B | Fred Merkle | R | 133 | 498 | 133 | 20 | 6 | 3 | 0.6 | 52 | 62 | 33 | 35 | 20 | 0 | 0 | .267 | .349 |
| 2B | Charlie Pick | L | 75 | 269 | 65 | 8 | 6 | 0 | 0.0 | 27 | 18 | 14 | 12 | 17 | 0 | 0 | .242 | .316 |
| SS | Charlie Hollocher | L | 115 | 430 | 116 | 14 | 5 | 3 | 0.7 | 51 | 26 | 44 | 19 | 16 | 0 | 0 | .270 | .347 |
| 3B | Charlie Deal | R | 116 | 405 | 117 | 23 | 5 | 2 | 0.5 | 37 | 52 | 12 | 12 | 11 | 0 | 0 | .289 | .385 |
| RF | Max Flack | L | 116 | 469 | 138 | 20 | 4 | 6 | 1.3 | 71 | 35 | 34 | 18 | 18 | 0 | 0 | .294 | .392 |
| CF | Dode Paskert | R | 87 | 270 | 53 | 11 | 3 | 2 | 0.7 | 21 | 29 | 28 | 33 | 7 | 8 | 1 | .196 | .281 |
| LF | Les Mann | R | 80 | 299 | 68 | 8 | 8 | 1 | 0.3 | 31 | 22 | 11 | 29 | 12 | 1 | 0 | .227 | .318 |
| C | Bill Killefer | R | 103 | 315 | 90 | 10 | 2 | 0 | 0.0 | 17 | 22 | 15 | 8 | 5 | 3 | 0 | .286 | .330 |
| **SUBSTITUTES** | | | | | | | | | | | | | | | | | | |
| 2B | Buck Herzog | R | 52 | 193 | 53 | 4 | 4 | 0 | 0.0 | 15 | 17 | 10 | 7 | 12 | 0 | 0 | .275 | .337 |
| UT | Pete Kilduff | R | 31 | 88 | 24 | 4 | 2 | 0 | 0.0 | 5 | 8 | 10 | 5 | 1 | 1 | 1 | .273 | .364 |
| UT | Fred Lear | R | 40 | 76 | 17 | 3 | 1 | 1 | 1.3 | 8 | 11 | 8 | 11 | 2 | 14 | 2 | .224 | .329 |
| UT | Lee Magee | B | 79 | 267 | 78 | 12 | 4 | 1 | 0.4 | 36 | 17 | 18 | 16 | 14 | 7 | 2 | .292 | .378 |
| OF | Turner Barber | L | 76 | 230 | 72 | 9 | 4 | 0 | 0.0 | 26 | 21 | 14 | 17 | 7 | 6 | 1 | .313 | .387 |
| OF | Dave Robertson | L | 27 | 96 | 20 | 2 | 0 | 1 | 1.0 | 8 | 10 | 1 | 10 | 3 | 2 | 0 | .208 | .260 |
| OS | Bill McCabe | B | 33 | 84 | 13 | 3 | 1 | 0 | 0.0 | 8 | 5 | 9 | 15 | 3 | 3 | 0 | .155 | .214 |
| OF | Barney Friberg | R | 8 | 20 | 4 | 1 | 0 | 0 | 0.0 | 1 | 0 | 1 | 2 | 0 | 1 | 0 | .200 | .250 |
| OF | Hal Reilly | | 1 | 3 | 0 | 0 | 0 | 0 | 0.0 | 0 | 0 | 0 | 1 | 0 | 0 | 0 | .000 | .000 |
| C | Bob O'Farrell | R | 49 | 125 | 27 | 4 | 2 | 0 | 0.0 | 11 | 9 | 7 | 10 | 2 | 9 | 1 | .216 | .280 |
| C | Tom Daly | R | 25 | 50 | 11 | 0 | 1 | 0 | 0.0 | 4 | 1 | 2 | 5 | 0 | 6 | 0 | .220 | .260 |
| **PITCHERS** | | | | | | | | | | | | | | | | | | |
| P | Hippo Vaughn | B | 38 | 98 | 17 | 4 | 0 | 0 | 0.0 | 5 | 2 | 8 | 27 | 0 | 0 | 0 | .173 | .214 |
| P | Claude Hendrix | R | 36 | 78 | 15 | 1 | 0 | 1 | 1.3 | 6 | 6 | 2 | 19 | 0 | 3 | 1 | .192 | .244 |
| P | Grover Alexander | R | 30 | 70 | 12 | 1 | 0 | 0 | 0.0 | 6 | 4 | 10 | 18 | 0 | 0 | 0 | .171 | .186 |
| P | Phil Douglas | R | 25 | 51 | 8 | 2 | 0 | 0 | 0.0 | 3 | 3 | 1 | 10 | 0 | 0 | 0 | .157 | .196 |
| P | Speed Martin | R | 35 | 44 | 8 | 1 | 0 | 0 | 0.0 | 3 | 2 | 1 | 15 | 0 | 0 | 0 | .182 | .205 |
| P | Paul Carter | L | 29 | 26 | 7 | 0 | 0 | 0 | 0.0 | 2 | 2 | 0 | 4 | 0 | 0 | 0 | .269 | .269 |
| P | Sweetbreads Bailey | R | 21 | 18 | 7 | 1 | 0 | 0 | 0.0 | 1 | 1 | 3 | 3 | 0 | 0 | 0 | .389 | .444 |
| P | Lefty Tyler | L | 6 | 7 | 1 | 0 | 0 | 0 | 0.0 | 0 | 1 | 3 | 2 | 0 | 0 | 0 | .143 | .143 |
| P | Joel Newkirk | R | 1 | 1 | 0 | 0 | 0 | 0 | 0.0 | 0 | 0 | 0 | 1 | 0 | 0 | 0 | .000 | .000 |
| P | Harry Weaver | R | 2 | 1 | 0 | 0 | 0 | 0 | 0.0 | 0 | 0 | 0 | 0 | 0 | 0 | 0 | .000 | .000 |
| TEAM TOTAL | | | | 4581 | 1174 | 166 | 58 | 21 | 0.5 | 45 | 387 | 298 | 359 | 150 | 64 | 9 | .256 | .332 |

## INDIVIDUAL FIELDING

| POS | Player | T | G | PO | A | E | DP | TC/G | FA |
|---|---|---|---|---|---|---|---|---|---|
| 1B | F. Merkle | R | 132 | **1494** | 56 | **23** | 66 | 11.9 | .985 |
| | F. Lear | R | 9 | 100 | 2 | 1 | 4 | 11.4 | .990 |
| 2B | C. Pick | R | 71 | 135 | 253 | 22* | 31 | 5.8 | .946 |
| | B. Herzog | R | 52 | 81 | 151 | 3 | 14 | 4.5 | .987 |
| | F. Lear | R | 9 | 18 | 20 | 2 | 1 | 4.4 | .950 |
| | L. Magee | R | 7 | 13 | 19 | 2 | 0 | 4.9 | .941 |
| | P. Kilduff | R | 8 | 8 | 20 | 1 | 3 | 3.6 | .966 |
| SS | C. Hollocher | R | 115 | 219 | 418 | 40 | 49 | 5.9 | .941 |
| | L. Magee | R | 13 | 26 | 46 | 6 | 4 | 6.0 | .923 |
| | P. Kilduff | R | 7 | 16 | 15 | 6 | 2 | 5.3 | .838 |
| | B. McCabe | R | 4 | 7 | 7 | 2 | 2 | 4.0 | .875 |
| | F. Lear | R | 3 | 3 | 5 | 2 | 1 | 3.3 | .800 |
| 3B | C. Deal | R | 116 | 157 | 233 | 11 | 14 | 3.5 | **.973** |
| | P. Kilduff | R | 14 | 11 | 26 | 1 | 2 | 2.7 | .974 |
| | L. Magee | R | 10 | 11 | 16 | 3 | 0 | 3.0 | .900 |
| | C. Pick | R | 3 | 2 | 6 | 1 | 0 | 3.0 | .889 |
| | B. McCabe | R | 1 | 0 | 1 | 0 | 0 | 1.0 | 1.000 |

| POS | Player | T | G | PO | A | E | DP | TC/G | FA |
|---|---|---|---|---|---|---|---|---|---|
| OF | M. Flack | L | 116 | 194 | 18 | 3 | 1 | 1.9 | .986 |
| | L. Mann | R | 78 | 155 | 10 | 3 | 2 | 2.2 | .982 |
| | D. Paskert | R | 80 | 146 | 12 | 5 | 1 | 2.0 | .969 |
| | T. Barber | R | 68 | 123 | 7 | 7 | 1 | 2.0 | .949 |
| | L. Magee | R | 44 | 80 | 7 | 2 | 1 | 2.0 | .978 |
| | D. Robertson | L | 25 | 53 | 2 | 4 | 0 | 2.4 | .932 |
| | B. McCabe | R | 19 | 36 | 2 | 2 | 1 | 2.1 | .950 |
| | H. Reilly | | 1 | 0 | 0 | 0 | 0 | 0.0 | .000 |
| | B. Friberg | R | 7 | 13 | 0 | 0 | 0 | 1.9 | 1.000 |
| C | B. Killefer | R | 100 | **478** | 124 | 8 | 7 | **6.1** | **.987** |
| | B. O'Farrell | R | 38 | 119 | 48 | 6 | 5 | 4.6 | .965 |
| | T. Daly | R | 18 | 55 | 10 | 3 | 2 | 3.8 | .956 |

Following their splendid showing in the final year of the "war to end all wars," the Cubs of 1919 were a disappointing third, one of the main reasons being that Hollocher fell victim to the proverbial "sophomore jinx."

Grover Alexander, back from the army, won 16 games with 9 shutouts to tie the club record. One of them was the shortest nine-inning game in Cub history as he blanked the Braves 3–0 in 58 minutes on September 21. Vaughn won 21 games, but Tyler and Hendrix were not up to previous form. In addition to this, the Cubs finally soured on Phil Douglas's drinking sprees, trading him to the Giants on July 23 for outfielder Dave Robertson. On August 9, Vaughn became the last Cub pitcher to steal home plate during a 3–1 victory over the Giants. Hitting tapered off also as outfielder Max Flack and third baseman Charlie Deal were the only regulars over .275. The real headlines that year went to the White Sox, whose suspicious play in the World Series lead to an investigation and the subsequent "Black Sox" scandal.

### TEAM STATISTICS

| | W | L | PCT | GB | R | OR | 2B | 3B | Batting HR | BA | SA | SB | Fielding E | DP | FA | CG | B | Pitching SO | ShO | SV | ERA |
|---|---|---|---|---|---|---|---|---|---|---|---|---|---|---|---|---|---|---|---|---|---|
| CIN | 96 | 44 | .686 | | 577 | 401 | 135 | 83 | 20 | .263 | .342 | 143 | 152 | 98 | .974 | 89 | 298 | 407 | 23 | 9 | 2.23 |
| NY | 87 | 53 | .621 | 9 | 605 | 470 | 204 | 64 | 40 | .269 | .366 | 157 | 216 | 96 | .964 | 72 | 305 | 340 | 11 | 13 | 2.70 |
| CHI | 75 | 65 | .536 | 21 | 454 | 407 | 166 | 58 | 21 | .256 | .332 | 150 | 186 | 87 | .969 | 80 | 294 | 495 | 21 | 5 | 2.21 |
| PIT | 71 | 68 | .511 | 24.5 | 472 | 466 | 130 | 82 | 17 | .249 | .325 | 196 | 166 | 89 | .970 | 92 | 263 | 391 | 16 | 4 | 2.88 |
| BKN | 69 | 71 | .493 | 27 | 525 | 513 | 167 | 66 | 25 | .263 | .340 | 112 | 218 | 84 | .972 | 98 | 292 | 476 | 12 | 1 | 2.73 |
| BOS | 57 | 82 | .410 | 38.5 | 465 | 563 | 142 | 62 | 24 | .253 | .324 | 145 | 204 | 111 | .966 | 79 | 337 | 374 | 5 | 9 | 3.17 |
| STL | 54 | 83 | .394 | 40.5 | 463 | 552 | 163 | 52 | 18 | .256 | .326 | 148 | 217 | 112 | .963 | 55 | 415 | 414 | 6 | 8 | 3.23 |
| PHI | 47 | 90 | .343 | 47.5 | 510 | 699 | 208 | 50 | 42 | .251 | .342 | 114 | 219 | 112 | .963 | 93 | 408 | 397 | 6 | 2 | 4.17 |
| LEAGUE TOTAL | | | | | 4071 | 4071 | 1315 | 517 | 207 | .258 | .337 | 1165 | 1578 | 789 | .968 | 658 | 2612 | 3294 | 100 | 51 | 2.91 |

### INDIVIDUAL PITCHING

| PITCHER | T | W | L | PCT | ERA | SV | G | GS | CG | IP | H | BB | SO | R | ER | ShO | H/9 | BB/9 | SO/9 |
|---|---|---|---|---|---|---|---|---|---|---|---|---|---|---|---|---|---|---|---|
| Hippo Vaughn | L | 21 | 14 | .600 | 1.79 | 1 | 38 | 37 | 25 | 306.2 | 264 | 62 | 141 | 83 | 61 | 4 | 7.75 | 1.82 | 4.14 |
| Grover Alexander | R | 16 | 11 | .593 | 1.72 | 1 | 30 | 27 | 20 | 235 | 180 | 38 | 121 | 51 | 45 | 9 | 6.89 | 1.46 | 4.63 |
| Claude Hendrix | R | 10 | 14 | .417 | 2.62 | 0 | 33 | 25 | 15 | 206.1 | 208 | 42 | 69 | 79 | 60 | 2 | 9.07 | 1.83 | 3.01 |
| Speed Martin | R | 8 | 8 | .500 | 2.47 | 2 | 35 | 14 | 7 | 163.2 | 158 | 52 | 54 | 58 | 45 | 2 | 8.69 | 2.86 | 2.97 |
| Phil Douglas | R | 10 | 6 | .625 | 2.00 | 0 | 25 | 19 | 8 | 161.2 | 133 | 34 | 63 | 52 | 36 | 4 | 7.40 | 1.89 | 3.51 |
| Paul Carter | R | 5 | 4 | .556 | 2.65 | 1 | 28 | 7 | 2 | 85 | 81 | 28 | 17 | 36 | 25 | 0 | 8.58 | 2.96 | 1.80 |
| Sweetbreads Bailey | R | 3 | 5 | .375 | 3.15 | 0 | 21 | 5 | 0 | 71.1 | 75 | 20 | 19 | 30 | 25 | 0 | 9.46 | 2.52 | 2.40 |
| Lefty Tyler | L | 2 | 2 | .500 | 2.10 | 0 | 6 | 5 | 3 | 30 | 20 | 13 | 9 | 8 | 7 | 0 | 6.00 | 3.90 | 2.70 |
| Harry Weaver | R | 0 | 1 | .000 | 10.80 | 0 | 2 | 1 | 0 | 3.1 | 6 | 2 | 1 | 7 | 4 | 0 | 16.20 | 5.40 | 2.70 |
| Joel Newkirk | R | 0 | 0 | – | 13.50 | 0 | 1 | 0 | 0 | 2 | 2 | 3 | 1 | 3 | 3 | 0 | 9.00 | 13.50 | 4.50 |
| TEAM TOTAL | | 75 | 65 | .536 | 2.21 | 5 | 219 | 140 | 80 | 1265 | 1127 | 294 | 495 | 407 | 311 | 21 | 8.02 | 2.09 | 3.52 |

| MANAGER | W | L | PCT |
|---|---|---|---|
| Fred Mitchell | 75 | 79 | .487 |

| POS | Player | B | G | AB | H | 2B | 3B | HR | HR % | R | RBI | BB | SO | SB | Pinch Hit AB | Pinch Hit H | BA | SA |
|---|---|---|---|---|---|---|---|---|---|---|---|---|---|---|---|---|---|---|
| **REGULARS** | | | | | | | | | | | | | | | | | | |
| 1B | Fred Merkle | R | 92 | 330 | 94 | 20 | 4 | 3 | 0.9 | 33 | 38 | 24 | 32 | 3 | 6 | 0 | .285 | .397 |
| 2B | Zeb Terry | R | 133 | 496 | 139 | 26 | 9 | 0 | 0.0 | 56 | 52 | 44 | 22 | 12 | 0 | 0 | .280 | .369 |
| SS | Charlie Hollocher | L | 80 | 301 | 96 | 17 | 2 | 0 | 0.0 | 53 | 22 | 41 | 15 | 20 | 0 | 0 | .319 | .389 |
| 3B | Charlie Deal | R | 129 | 450 | 108 | 10 | 5 | 3 | 0.7 | 48 | 39 | 20 | 14 | 5 | 1 | 1 | .240 | .304 |
| RF | Max Flack | L | 135 | 520 | 157 | 30 | 6 | 4 | 0.8 | 85 | 49 | 52 | 15 | 13 | 2 | 0 | .302 | .406 |
| CF | Dode Paskert | R | 139 | 487 | 136 | 22 | 10 | 5 | 1.0 | 57 | 57 | 64 | 58 | 16 | 1 | 0 | .279 | .396 |
| LF | Dave Robertson | L | 134 | 500 | 150 | 29 | 11 | 10 | 2.0 | 68 | 75 | 40 | 44 | 17 | 0 | 0 | .300 | .462 |
| C | Bob O'Farrell | R | 94 | 270 | 67 | 11 | 4 | 3 | 1.1 | 29 | 19 | 34 | 23 | 1 | 8 | 0 | .248 | .352 |
| **SUBSTITUTES** | | | | | | | | | | | | | | | | | | |
| 1O | Turner Barber | L | 94 | 340 | 90 | 10 | 5 | 0 | 0.0 | 27 | 50 | 9 | 26 | 5 | 5 | 2 | .265 | .324 |
| 23 | Buck Herzog | R | 91 | 305 | 59 | 9 | 2 | 0 | 0.0 | 39 | 19 | 20 | 21 | 8 | 2 | 0 | .193 | .236 |
| 2B | Bill Marriott | L | 14 | 43 | 12 | 4 | 2 | 0 | 0.0 | 7 | 5 | 6 | 5 | 1 | 0 | 0 | .279 | .465 |
| S2 | Hal Leathers | L | 9 | 23 | 7 | 1 | 0 | 1 | 4.3 | 3 | 1 | 1 | 1 | 1 | 1 | 0 | .304 | .478 |
| 3B | Sumpter Clarke | R | 1 | 3 | 1 | 0 | 0 | 0 | 0.0 | 0 | 0 | 0 | 1 | 0 | 0 | 0 | .333 | .333 |
| OF | Babe Twombly | L | 78 | 183 | 43 | 1 | 1 | 2 | 1.1 | 25 | 14 | 17 | 20 | 5 | 22 | 4 | .235 | .284 |
| O2 | Barney Friberg | R | 50 | 114 | 24 | 5 | 1 | 0 | 0.0 | 11 | 7 | 6 | 20 | 2 | 2 | 0 | .211 | .272 |
| C | Bill Killefer | R | 62 | 191 | 42 | 7 | 1 | 0 | 0.0 | 16 | 16 | 8 | 5 | 2 | 1 | 0 | .220 | .267 |
| C | Tom Daly | R | 44 | 90 | 28 | 6 | 0 | 0 | 0.0 | 12 | 13 | 2 | 6 | 1 | 14 | 4 | .311 | .378 |
| PH | Bill McCabe | B | 3 | 2 | 1 | 0 | 0 | 0 | 0.0 | 1 | 0 | 0 | 0 | 0 | 2 | 1 | .500 | .500 |
| **PITCHERS** | | | | | | | | | | | | | | | | | | |
| P | Grover Alexander | R | 46 | 118 | 27 | 4 | 1 | 1 | 0.8 | 9 | 14 | 11 | 26 | 0 | 0 | 0 | .229 | .305 |
| P | Hippo Vaughn | B | 40 | 102 | 22 | 3 | 1 | 1 | 1.0 | 14 | 12 | 12 | 23 | 0 | 0 | 0 | .216 | .294 |
| P | Claude Hendrix | R | 34 | 83 | 15 | 3 | 0 | 0 | 0.0 | 10 | 6 | 3 | 11 | 2 | 7 | 1 | .181 | .217 |
| P | Lefty Tyler | L | 29 | 65 | 17 | 3 | 1 | 0 | 0.0 | 6 | 6 | 9 | 7 | 0 | 2 | 2 | .262 | .338 |
| P | Speed Martin | R | 35 | 44 | 7 | 1 | 0 | 1 | 2.3 | 5 | 4 | 3 | 10 | 1 | 0 | 0 | .159 | .250 |
| P | Paul Carter | L | 31 | 35 | 6 | 1 | 1 | 0 | 0.0 | 3 | 4 | 1 | 5 | 0 | 0 | 0 | .171 | .257 |
| P | Sweetbreads Bailey | R | 21 | 7 | 1 | 0 | 0 | 0 | 0.0 | 0 | 0 | 0 | 4 | 0 | 0 | 0 | .143 | .143 |
| P | Virgil Cheeves | R | 5 | 4 | 0 | 0 | 0 | 0 | 0.0 | 0 | 0 | 1 | 2 | 0 | 0 | 0 | .000 | .000 |
| P | Chippy Gaw | R | 6 | 4 | 1 | 0 | 0 | 0 | 0.0 | 1 | 0 | 0 | 1 | 0 | 0 | 0 | .250 | .250 |
| P | Joel Newkirk | R | 2 | 3 | 0 | 0 | 0 | 0 | 0.0 | 1 | 0 | 0 | 0 | 0 | 0 | 0 | .000 | .000 |
| P | Percy Jones | R | 4 | 2 | 0 | 0 | 0 | 0 | 0.0 | 0 | 0 | 0 | 2 | 0 | 0 | 0 | .000 | .000 |
| P | Joe Jaeger | R | 2 | 1 | 0 | 0 | 0 | 0 | 0.0 | 0 | 0 | 0 | 1 | 0 | 0 | 0 | .000 | .000 |
| P | Ted Turner | R | 1 | 1 | 0 | 0 | 0 | 0 | 0.0 | 0 | 0 | 0 | 1 | 0 | 0 | 0 | .000 | .000 |
| TEAM TOTAL | | | | 5117 | 1350 | 223 | 67 | 34 | 0.7 | 61 | 536 | 428 | 421 | 115 | 76 | 15 | .264 | .354 |

## INDIVIDUAL FIELDING

| POS | Player | T | G | PO | A | E | DP | TC/G | FA | POS | Player | T | G | PO | A | E | DP | TC/G | FA |
|---|---|---|---|---|---|---|---|---|---|---|---|---|---|---|---|---|---|---|---|
| 1B | F. Merkle | R | 85 | 906 | 54 | 15 | 52 | 11.5 | .985 | OF | D. Paskert | R | 137 | 306 | 23 | 15 | 3 | 2.5 | .956 |
| | T. Barber | R | 69 | 739 | 30 | 9 | 40 | 11.3 | .988 | | D. Robertson | L | 134 | 230 | 10 | 8 | 1 | 1.9 | .968 |
| | B. Herzog | R | 1 | 1 | 0 | 0 | 0 | 1.0 | 1.000 | | M. Flack | L | 132 | 216 | 16 | 8 | 2 | 1.8 | .967 |
| 2B | Z. Terry | R | 63 | 138 | 222 | 9 | 30 | 5.9 | .976 | | B. Twombly | R | 45 | 91 | 6 | 3 | 0 | 2.2 | .970 |
| | B. Herzog | R | 59 | 128 | 175 | 20 | 25 | 5.5 | .938 | | B. Friberg | R | 24 | 28 | 2 | 1 | 0 | 1.3 | .968 |
| | B. Friberg | R | 24 | 57 | 74 | 5 | 9 | 5.7 | .963 | | T. Barber | R | 17 | 27 | 1 | 1 | 0 | 1.7 | .966 |
| | B. Marriott | R | 14 | 26 | 40 | 8 | 2 | 5.3 | .892 | | F. Merkle | R | 1 | 0 | 0 | 0 | 0 | 0.0 | .000 |
| | H. Leathers | R | 3 | 0 | 3 | 0 | 0 | 1.0 | 1.000 | C | B. O'Farrell | R | 86 | 317 | 100 | 19 | 6 | 5.1 | .956 |
| | T. Barber | R | 2 | 1 | 1 | 0 | 0 | 1.0 | 1.000 | | B. Killefer | R | 61 | 304 | 80 | 9 | 6 | 6.4 | .977 |
| | B. Twombly | R | 2 | 0 | 1 | 0 | 0 | 0.5 | 1.000 | | T. Daly | R | 29 | 88 | 18 | 2 | 0 | 3.7 | .981 |
| SS | C. Hollocher | R | 80 | 196 | 280 | 23 | 34 | 6.2 | .954 | | | | | | | | | | |
| | Z. Terry | R | 70 | 153 | 249 | 16 | 32 | 6.0 | .962 | | | | | | | | | | |
| | H. Leathers | R | 6 | 15 | 18 | 7 | 0 | 6.7 | .825 | | | | | | | | | | |
| 3B | C. Deal | R | 128 | 129 | 268 | 11 | 22 | 3.2 | **.973** | | | | | | | | | | |
| | B. Herzog | R | 28 | 25 | 66 | 9 | 7 | 3.6 | .910 | | | | | | | | | | |
| | S. Clarke | R | 1 | 0 | 1 | 0 | 0 | 1.0 | 1.000 | | | | | | | | | | |

The descent continued as the Cubs dropped to fifth place, in the year Weeghman Field was rechristened Cubs Park. There have been many seasons dominated by one player, and in 1920 it was Grover Alexander's turn. Pitching 363 innings for a 20th-century Cub high, "Old Pete" went the distance 33 times en route to a 27–14 mark. He had an 11-game winning streak, won his own game with a 10th-inning homer to beat the Reds, 3–2, on May 31, and outlasted Jesse Haines of the Cardinals in a 17–inning duel 3–2 on October 1. Alex led the league in wins, ERA (1.91), strikeouts (173), complete games (33), innings pitched (363.1), and strikeouts per nine innings (4.29). He was second in winning percentage with .659, and in shutouts with 7, saves (5), and games pitched (46).

Hippo Vaughn's effectiveness was beginning to wane, but he was still good for 19 wins. Hendrix was benched late in the season for allegedly betting against his own teammates, and was not invited back the following spring, for obvious reasons. Hollocher missed much of the season with a stomach problem, but performed well when he was healthy.

## TEAM STATISTICS

| | W | L | PCT | GB | R | OR | Batting 2B | 3B | HR | BA | SA | SB | Fielding E | DP | FA | CG | B | Pitching SO | ShO | SV | ERA |
|---|---|---|---|---|---|---|---|---|---|---|---|---|---|---|---|---|---|---|---|---|---|
| BKN | 93 | 61 | .604 | | 660 | 528 | 205 | 99 | 28 | .277 | .367 | 70 | 226 | 118 | .966 | 89 | 327 | 553 | 17 | 10 | 2.62 |
| NY | 86 | 68 | .558 | 7 | 682 | 543 | 210 | 76 | 46 | .269 | .363 | 131 | 210 | 137 | .969 | 86 | 297 | 380 | 18 | 9 | 2.80 |
| CIN | 82 | 71 | .536 | 10.5 | 639 | 569 | 169 | 76 | 18 | .277 | .349 | 158 | 200 | 125 | .968 | 90 | 393 | 435 | 12 | 9 | 2.84 |
| PIT | 79 | 75 | .513 | 14 | 530 | 552 | 162 | 90 | 16 | .257 | .332 | 181 | 186 | 119 | .971 | 92 | 280 | 444 | 17 | 10 | 2.89 |
| CHI | 75 | 79 | .487 | 18 | 619 | 635 | 223 | 67 | 34 | .264 | .354 | 115 | 225 | 112 | .965 | 95 | 382 | 508 | 13 | 9 | 3.27 |
| STL | 75 | 79 | .487 | 18 | 675 | 682 | 238 | 96 | 32 | .289 | .385 | 126 | 256 | 136 | .961 | 72 | 479 | 529 | 9 | 12 | 3.43 |
| BOS | 62 | 90 | .408 | 30 | 523 | 670 | 168 | 86 | 23 | .260 | .339 | 88 | 239 | 125 | .964 | 93 | 415 | 368 | 13 | 6 | 3.54 |
| PHI | 62 | 91 | .405 | 30.5 | 565 | 714 | 229 | 54 | 64 | .263 | .364 | 100 | 232 | 135 | .964 | 77 | 444 | 419 | 8 | 11 | 3.63 |
| LEAGUE TOTAL | | | | | 4893 | 4893 | 1604 | 644 | 261 | .270 | .357 | 969 | 1774 | 1007 | .966 | 694 | 3017 | 3636 | 107 | 76 | 3.13 |

## INDIVIDUAL PITCHING

| PITCHER | T | W | L | PCT | ERA | SV | G | GS | CG | IP | H | BB | SO | R | ER | ShO | H/9 | BB/9 | SO/9 |
|---|---|---|---|---|---|---|---|---|---|---|---|---|---|---|---|---|---|---|---|
| Grover Alexander | R | 27 | 14 | .659 | 1.91 | 5 | 46 | 40 | 33 | 363.1 | 335 | 69 | 173 | 96 | 77 | 7 | 8.30 | 1.71 | 4.29 |
| Hippo Vaughn | L | 19 | 16 | .543 | 2.54 | 0 | 40 | 38 | 24 | 301 | 301 | 81 | 131 | 113 | 85 | 4 | 9.00 | 2.42 | 3.92 |
| Claude Hendrix | R | 9 | 12 | .429 | 3.58 | 0 | 27 | 23 | 12 | 203.2 | 216 | 54 | 72 | 101 | 81 | 0 | 9.55 | 2.39 | 3.18 |
| Lefty Tyler | L | 11 | 12 | .478 | 3.31 | 0 | 27 | 27 | 18 | 193 | 193 | 57 | 57 | 83 | 71 | 2 | 9.00 | 2.66 | 2.66 |
| Speed Martin | R | 4 | 15 | .211 | 4.83 | 2 | 35 | 13 | 6 | 136 | 165 | 50 | 44 | 96 | 73 | 0 | 10.92 | 3.31 | 2.91 |
| Paul Carter | R | 3 | 6 | .333 | 4.67 | 2 | 31 | 8 | 2 | 106 | 131 | 36 | 14 | 68 | 55 | 0 | 11.12 | 3.06 | 1.19 |
| Sweetbreads Bailey | R | 1 | 2 | .333 | 7.12 | 0 | 21 | 1 | 0 | 36.2 | 38 | 11 | 8 | 38 | 29 | 0 | 9.33 | 2.70 | 1.96 |
| Virgil Cheeves | R | 0 | 0 | – | 3.50 | 0 | 5 | 2 | 0 | 18 | 16 | 7 | 3 | 7 | 7 | 0 | 8.00 | 3.50 | 1.50 |
| Chippy Gaw | R | 1 | 1 | .500 | 4.85 | 0 | 6 | 1 | 0 | 13 | 16 | 3 | 4 | 9 | 7 | 0 | 11.08 | 2.08 | 2.77 |
| Percy Jones | L | 0 | 0 | – | 11.57 | 0 | 4 | 0 | 0 | 7 | 15 | 3 | 0 | 10 | 9 | 0 | 19.29 | 3.86 | 0.00 |
| Joel Newkirk | R | 0 | 1 | .000 | 5.40 | 0 | 2 | 1 | 0 | 6.2 | 8 | 6 | 2 | 6 | 4 | 0 | 10.80 | 8.10 | 2.70 |
| Joe Jaeger | R | 0 | 0 | – | 12.00 | 0 | 2 | 0 | 0 | 3 | 6 | 4 | 0 | 6 | 4 | 0 | 18.00 | 12.00 | 0.00 |
| Ted Turner | R | 0 | 0 | – | 13.50 | 0 | 1 | 0 | 0 | 1.1 | 2 | 1 | 0 | 2 | 2 | 0 | 13.50 | 6.75 | 0.00 |
| TEAM TOTAL | | 75 | 79 | .487 | 3.27 | 9 | 247 | 154 | 95 | 1388.2 | 1442 | 382 | 508 | 635 | 504 | 13 | 9.35 | 2.48 | 3.29 |

| MANAGER | W | L | PCT |
|---|---|---|---|
| Johnny Evers | 42 | 56 | .429 |
| Bill Killefer | 22 | 33 | .400 |

| POS | Player | B | G | AB | H | 2B | 3B | HR | HR % | R | RBI | BB | SO | SB | Pinch Hit AB | Pinch Hit H | BA | SA |
|---|---|---|---|---|---|---|---|---|---|---|---|---|---|---|---|---|---|---|
| **REGULARS** | | | | | | | | | | | | | | | | | | |
| 1B | Ray Grimes | R | 147 | 530 | 170 | 38 | 6 | 6 | 1.1 | 91 | 79 | 70 | 55 | 5 | 0 | 0 | .321 | .449 |
| 2B | Zeb Terry | R | 123 | 488 | 134 | 18 | 1 | 2 | 0.4 | 59 | 45 | 27 | 19 | 1 | 1 | 0 | .275 | .328 |
| SS | Charlie Hollocher | L | 140 | 558 | 161 | 28 | 8 | 3 | 0.5 | 71 | 37 | 43 | 13 | 5 | 3 | 1 | .289 | .384 |
| 3B | Charlie Deal | R | 115 | 422 | 122 | 19 | 8 | 3 | 0.7 | 52 | 66 | 13 | 9 | 3 | 2 | 0 | .289 | .393 |
| RF | Max Flack | L | 133 | 572 | 172 | 31 | 4 | 6 | 1.0 | 80 | 37 | 32 | 15 | 17 | 3 | 1 | .301 | .400 |
| CF | George Maisel | R | 111 | 393 | 122 | 7 | 2 | 0 | 0.0 | 54 | 43 | 11 | 13 | 17 | 1 | 1 | .310 | .338 |
| LF | Turner Barber | L | 127 | 452 | 142 | 14 | 4 | 1 | 0.2 | 73 | 54 | 41 | 24 | 5 | 2 | 1 | .314 | .369 |
| C | Bob O'Farrell | R | 96 | 260 | 65 | 12 | 7 | 4 | 1.5 | 32 | 32 | 18 | 14 | 2 | 6 | 1 | .250 | .396 |
| **SUBSTITUTES** | | | | | | | | | | | | | | | | | | |
| UT | John Kelleher | R | 95 | 301 | 93 | 11 | 7 | 4 | 1.3 | 31 | 47 | 16 | 16 | 2 | 9 | 5 | .309 | .432 |
| UT | Bill Marriott | L | 30 | 38 | 12 | 1 | 1 | 0 | 0.0 | 3 | 7 | 4 | 1 | 0 | 20 | 4 | .316 | .395 |
| 3B | Hooks Warner | L | 14 | 38 | 8 | 1 | 0 | 0 | 0.0 | 4 | 3 | 2 | 1 | 1 | 3 | 0 | .211 | .237 |
| SS | Carter Elliott | L | 12 | 28 | 7 | 2 | 0 | 0 | 0.0 | 5 | 0 | 5 | 3 | 0 | 0 | 0 | .250 | .321 |
| 2B | Joe Klugman | R | 6 | 21 | 6 | 0 | 0 | 0 | 0.0 | 3 | 2 | 1 | 2 | 0 | 1 | 1 | .286 | .286 |
| OF | John Sullivan | R | 76 | 240 | 79 | 14 | 4 | 4 | 1.7 | 28 | 41 | 19 | 26 | 3 | 9 | 3 | .329 | .471 |
| OF | Babe Twombly | L | 87 | 175 | 66 | 8 | 1 | 1 | 0.6 | 22 | 18 | 11 | 10 | 4 | 38 | 15 | .377 | .451 |
| OF | Dave Robertson | L | 22 | 36 | 8 | 3 | 0 | 0 | 0.0 | 7 | 14 | 1 | 3 | 0 | 13 | 4 | .222 | .306 |
| OF | Red Thomas | R | 8 | 30 | 8 | 3 | 0 | 1 | 3.3 | 5 | 5 | 4 | 5 | 0 | 0 | 0 | .267 | .467 |
| C | Tom Daly | R | 51 | 143 | 34 | 7 | 1 | 0 | 0.0 | 12 | 22 | 8 | 8 | 1 | 4 | 1 | .238 | .301 |
| C | Bill Killefer | R | 45 | 133 | 43 | 1 | 0 | 0 | 0.0 | 11 | 16 | 4 | 4 | 3 | 3 | 1 | .323 | .331 |
| C | Kettle Wirtz | R | 7 | 11 | 2 | 0 | 0 | 0 | 0.0 | 0 | 1 | 0 | 3 | 0 | 2 | 2 | .182 | .182 |
| **PITCHERS** | | | | | | | | | | | | | | | | | | |
| P | Grover Alexander | R | 31 | 95 | 29 | 3 | 1 | 1 | 1.1 | 8 | 14 | 2 | 13 | 0 | 0 | 0 | .305 | .389 |
| P | Speed Martin | R | 37 | 73 | 17 | 4 | 1 | 0 | 0.0 | 2 | 6 | 1 | 16 | 1 | 0 | 0 | .233 | .315 |
| P | Buck Freeman | B | 38 | 53 | 11 | 1 | 0 | 0 | 0.0 | 3 | 2 | 3 | 27 | 0 | 0 | 0 | .208 | .226 |
| P | Virgil Cheeves | R | 37 | 48 | 8 | 1 | 0 | 0 | 0.0 | 3 | 0 | 1 | 13 | 0 | 0 | 0 | .167 | .188 |
| P | Hippo Vaughn | B | 17 | 41 | 10 | 2 | 0 | 1 | 2.4 | 2 | 5 | 2 | 12 | 0 | 0 | 0 | .244 | .366 |
| P | Lefty York | L | 40 | 39 | 5 | 1 | 0 | 0 | 0.0 | 2 | 5 | 1 | 12 | 0 | 0 | 0 | .128 | .154 |
| P | Elmer Ponder | R | 16 | 33 | 4 | 1 | 0 | 0 | 0.0 | 0 | 2 | 0 | 9 | 0 | 0 | 0 | .121 | .152 |
| P | Percy Jones | R | 32 | 27 | 6 | 0 | 0 | 0 | 0.0 | 1 | 3 | 1 | 14 | 0 | 0 | 0 | .222 | .222 |
| P | Lefty Tyler | L | 19 | 26 | 6 | 2 | 0 | 0 | 0.0 | 4 | 2 | 1 | 5 | 0 | 7 | 2 | .231 | .308 |
| P | Tony Kaufmann | R | 2 | 5 | 2 | 1 | 0 | 0 | 0.0 | 0 | 0 | 0 | 1 | 0 | 0 | 0 | .400 | .600 |
| P | Vic Keen | R | 5 | 5 | 0 | 0 | 0 | 0 | 0.0 | 0 | 0 | 1 | 3 | 0 | 0 | 0 | .000 | .000 |
| P | Ollie Hanson | R | 2 | 3 | 0 | 0 | 0 | 0 | 0.0 | 0 | 0 | 0 | 2 | 0 | 0 | 0 | .000 | .000 |
| P | George Stueland | B | 2 | 3 | 1 | 0 | 0 | 0 | 0.0 | 0 | 1 | 0 | 2 | 0 | 0 | 0 | .333 | .333 |
| P | Oscar Fuhr | R | 1 | 1 | 0 | 0 | 0 | 0 | 0.0 | 0 | 0 | 0 | 1 | 0 | 0 | 0 | .000 | .000 |
| P | Sweetbreads Bailey | R | 3 | 0 | 0 | 0 | 0 | 0 | | 0 | 0 | 0 | 0 | 0 | 0 | 0 | | |
| TEAM TOTAL | | | | 5321 | 1553 | 234 | 56 | 37 | 0.7 | 66 | 609 | 343 | 374 | 70 | 127 | 43 | .292 | .378 |

## INDIVIDUAL FIELDING

| POS | Player | T | G | PO | A | E | DP | TC/G | FA |
|---|---|---|---|---|---|---|---|---|---|
| 1B | R. Grimes | R | 147 | 1544 | 68 | 12 | 93 | 11.0 | .993 |
| | J. Kelleher | R | 11 | 76 | 3 | 0 | 9 | 7.2 | 1.000 |
| 2B | Z. Terry | R | 123 | 272 | 413 | 20 | 57 | 5.7 | .972 |
| | J. Kelleher | R | 27 | 61 | 83 | 7 | 8 | 5.6 | .954 |
| | J. Klugman | R | 5 | 15 | 16 | 1 | 1 | 6.4 | .969 |
| | B. Marriott | R | 6 | 9 | 10 | 4 | 1 | 3.8 | .826 |
| SS | C. Hollocher | R | 137 | 282 | 491 | 30 | 72 | 5.9 | .963 |
| | J. Kelleher | R | 11 | 22 | 33 | 2 | 7 | 5.2 | .965 |
| | C. Elliott | R | 10 | 24 | 30 | 2 | 4 | 5.6 | .964 |
| | B. Marriott | R | 1 | 1 | 1 | 0 | 0 | 2.0 | 1.000 |
| 3B | C. Deal | R | 113 | 122 | 239 | 10 | 19 | 3.3 | .973 |
| | J. Kelleher | R | 37 | 33 | 75 | 6 | 7 | 3.1 | .947 |
| | H. Warner | R | 10 | 4 | 18 | 1 | 1 | 2.3 | .957 |
| | B. Marriott | R | 1 | 1 | 1 | 1 | 1 | 3.0 | .667 |

| POS | Player | T | G | PO | A | E | DP | TC/G | FA |
|---|---|---|---|---|---|---|---|---|---|
| OF | G. Maisel | R | 108 | 259 | 12 | 6 | 2 | 2.6 | .978 |
| | M. Flack | L | 130 | 244 | 19 | 3 | 2 | 2.0 | .989 |
| | T. Barber | R | 123 | 234 | 23 | 8 | 4 | 2.2 | .970 |
| | J. Sullivan | R | 65 | 122 | 3 | 5 | 0 | 2.0 | .962 |
| | B. Twombly | R | 45 | 81 | 11 | 3 | 0 | 2.1 | .968 |
| | J. Kelleher | R | 1 | 0 | 0 | 0 | 0 | 0.0 | .000 |
| | R. Thomas | R | 8 | 24 | 1 | 1 | 0 | 3.3 | .962 |
| | D. Robertson | L | 7 | 9 | 0 | 0 | 0 | 1.3 | 1.000 |
| | B. Marriott | R | 1 | 0 | 1 | 0 | 0 | 1.0 | 1.000 |
| C | B. O'Farrell | R | 90 | 269 | 87 | 12 | 8 | 4.1 | .967 |
| | T. Daly | R | 47 | 171 | 48 | 6 | 10 | 4.8 | .973 |
| | B. Killefer | R | 42 | 147 | 43 | 7 | 6 | 4.7 | .964 |
| | K. Wirtz | R | 5 | 13 | 3 | 0 | 1 | 3.2 | 1.000 |

By 1921 William Wrigley was the sole owner, and the Cubs did their spring training on the family-owned Catalina Island for the first time. This would be their preseason headquarters until 1952, when they relocated to Mesa, Arizona.

Johnny Evers had been recycled as manager in what was a long and trying season. As had been the case in 1913, the fiery-tempered Evers could not communicate effectively with his underlings. Hippo Vaughn who made no bones about his dislike for Evers, quit the team in a fit of anger, never to return, after pitching his last game July 9. Barely a month later, Evers was gone, too, having been fired in favor of Bill Killefer. At the time of Evers's firing, the Cubs were 42–56 and in seventh place, but it was too late to halt the losing trend. The team sank to 35 games below .500, remaining in seventh. The pitching was terrible, as only Alexander could boast a winning record and an ERA under 4.00. Other than that, the only players Cub fans could write home about were Flack, Hollocher, and rookie first baseman Ray Grimes, who batted a solid .321.

### TEAM  STATISTICS

|     | W | L | PCT | GB | R | OR | 2B | Batting 3B | HR | BA | SA | SB | Fielding E | DP | FA | CG | B | Pitching SO | ShO | SV | ERA |
|-----|---|---|-----|----|---|----|----|----|----|----|----|----|----|----|----|----|----|----|----|----|----|
| NY  | 94 | 59 | .614 |     | 840 | 637 | 237 | 93 | 75 | .298 | .421 | 137 | 187 | 155 | .971 | 71 | 295 | 357 | 9 | 18 | 3.55 |
| PIT | 90 | 63 | .588 | 4 | 692 | 595 | 231 | 104 | 37 | .285 | .387 | 134 | 172 | 129 | .973 | 88 | 322 | 500 | 10 | 10 | 3.17 |
| STL | 87 | 66 | .569 | 7 | 809 | 681 | 260 | 88 | 83 | .308 | .437 | 94 | 219 | 130 | .965 | 71 | 399 | 464 | 10 | 16 | 3.62 |
| BOS | 79 | 74 | .516 | 15 | 721 | 697 | 209 | 100 | 61 | .290 | .400 | 94 | 199 | 122 | .969 | 74 | 420 | 382 | 11 | 12 | 3.90 |
| BKN | 77 | 75 | .507 | 16.5 | 667 | 681 | 209 | 85 | 59 | .280 | .386 | 91 | 232 | 142 | .964 | 82 | 361 | 471 | 8 | 12 | 3.70 |
| CIN | 70 | 83 | .458 | 24 | 618 | 649 | 221 | 94 | 20 | .278 | .370 | 117 | 193 | 139 | .969 | 83 | 305 | 408 | 7 | 9 | 3.46 |
| CHI | 64 | 89 | .418 | 30 | 668 | 773 | 234 | 56 | 37 | .292 | .378 | 70 | 166 | 129 | .974 | 73 | 409 | 441 | 7 | 7 | 4.39 |
| PHI | 51 | 103 | .331 | 43.5 | 617 | 919 | 238 | 50 | 88 | .284 | .397 | 66 | 295 | 127 | .955 | 82 | 371 | 333 | 5 | 8 | 4.48 |
| LEAGUE TOTAL |  |  |  |  | 5632 | 5632 | 1839 | 670 | 460 | .289 | .397 | 803 | 1663 | 1073 | .967 | 624 | 2882 | 3356 | 67 | 92 | 3.78 |

### INDIVIDUAL  PITCHING

| PITCHER | T | W | L | PCT | ERA | SV | G | GS | CG | IP | H | BB | SO | R | ER | ShO | H/9 | BB/9 | SO/9 |
|---------|---|---|---|-----|-----|----|----|----|----|----|----|----|----|----|----|----|----|----|----|
| Grover Alexander | R | 15 | 13 | .536 | 3.39 | 1 | 31 | 29 | 21 | 252 | 286 | 33 | 77 | 110 | 95 | 3 | 10.21 | 1.18 | 2.75 |
| Speed Martin | R | 11 | 15 | .423 | 4.35 | 1 | 37 | 28 | 13 | 217.1 | 245 | 68 | 86 | 115 | 105 | 1 | 10.15 | 2.82 | 3.56 |
| Buck Freeman | R | 9 | 10 | .474 | 4.11 | 3 | 38 | 20 | 6 | 177.1 | 189 | 70 | 42 | 96 | 81 | 0 | 9.59 | 3.55 | 2.13 |
| Virgil Cheeves | R | 11 | 12 | .478 | 4.64 | 0 | 37 | 22 | 9 | 163 | 192 | 47 | 39 | 97 | 84 | 1 | 10.60 | 2.60 | 2.15 |
| Lefty York | L | 5 | 9 | .357 | 4.73 | 1 | 40 | 10 | 4 | 139 | 170 | 63 | 57 | 82 | 73 | 1 | 11.01 | 4.08 | 3.69 |
| Hippo Vaughn | L | 3 | 11 | .214 | 6.01 | 0 | 17 | 14 | 7 | 109.1 | 153 | 31 | 30 | 90 | 73 | 0 | 12.59 | 2.55 | 2.47 |
| Percy Jones | L | 3 | 5 | .375 | 4.56 | 0 | 32 | 5 | 1 | 98.2 | 116 | 39 | 46 | 57 | 50 | 0 | 10.58 | 3.56 | 4.20 |
| Elmer Ponder | R | 3 | 6 | .333 | 4.74 | 0 | 16 | 11 | 5 | 89.1 | 117 | 17 | 31 | 58 | 47 | 0 | 11.79 | 1.71 | 3.12 |
| Lefty Tyler | L | 3 | 2 | .600 | 3.24 | 0 | 10 | 6 | 4 | 50 | 59 | 14 | 8 | 22 | 18 | 0 | 10.62 | 2.52 | 1.44 |
| Vic Keen | R | 0 | 3 | .000 | 4.68 | 0 | 5 | 4 | 1 | 25 | 29 | 9 | 9 | 17 | 13 | 0 | 10.44 | 3.24 | 3.24 |
| Tony Kaufmann | R | 1 | 0 | 1.000 | 4.15 | 1 | 2 | 1 | 1 | 13 | 12 | 3 | 6 | 6 | 6 | 0 | 8.31 | 2.08 | 4.15 |
| George Stueland | R | 0 | 1 | .000 | 5.73 | 0 | 2 | 1 | 0 | 11 | 11 | 7 | 4 | 7 | 7 | 0 | 9.00 | 5.73 | 3.27 |
| Ollie Hanson | R | 0 | 2 | .000 | 7.00 | 0 | 2 | 2 | 1 | 9 | 9 | 6 | 2 | 7 | 7 | 0 | 10.80 | 3.60 | 3.60 |
| Sweetbreads Bailey | R | 0 | 0 | – | 3.60 | 0 | 3 | 0 | 0 | 5 | 6 | 2 | 2 | 2 | 2 | 0 | 10.80 | 3.60 | 3.60 |
| Oscar Fuhr | L | 0 | 0 | – | 9.00 | 0 | 1 | 0 | 0 | 4 | 11 | 0 | 2 | 9 | 4 | 0 | 24.75 | 0.00 | 4.50 |
| TEAM TOTAL |  | 64 | 89 | .418 | 4.39 | 7 | 273 | 153 | 73 | 1363 | 1605 | 409 | 441 | 775 | 665 | 6 | 10.60 | 2.70 | 2.91 |

| MANAGER | W | L | PCT |
|---|---|---|---|
| Bill Killefer | 80 | 74 | .519 |

| POS | Player | B | G | AB | H | 2B | 3B | HR | HR % | R | RBI | BB | SO | SB | Pinch Hit AB | Pinch Hit H | BA | SA |
|---|---|---|---|---|---|---|---|---|---|---|---|---|---|---|---|---|---|---|
| **REGULARS** | | | | | | | | | | | | | | | | | | |
| 1B | Ray Grimes | R | 138 | 509 | 180 | 45 | 12 | 14 | 2.8 | 99 | 99 | 75 | 33 | 7 | 0 | 0 | .354 | .572 |
| 2B | Zeb Terry | R | 131 | 496 | 142 | 24 | 2 | 0 | 0.0 | 56 | 67 | 34 | 16 | 2 | 0 | 0 | .286 | .343 |
| SS | Charlie Hollocher | L | 152 | 592 | 201 | 37 | 8 | 3 | 0.5 | 90 | 69 | 58 | 5 | 19 | 0 | 0 | .340 | .444 |
| 3B | Marty Krug | R | 127 | 450 | 124 | 23 | 4 | 4 | 0.9 | 67 | 60 | 43 | 43 | 7 | 0 | 0 | .276 | .371 |
| RF | Barney Friberg | R | 97 | 296 | 92 | 8 | 2 | 0 | 0.0 | 51 | 29 | 37 | 37 | 8 | 12 | 2 | .311 | .351 |
| CF | Jigger Statz | B | 110 | 462 | 137 | 19 | 5 | 1 | 0.2 | 77 | 34 | 41 | 31 | 16 | 0 | 0 | .297 | .366 |
| LF | Hack Miller | R | 122 | 466 | 164 | 28 | 5 | 12 | 2.6 | 61 | 78 | 26 | 39 | 3 | 6 | 2 | .352 | .511 |
| C | Bob O'Farrell | R | 128 | 392 | 127 | 18 | 8 | 4 | 1.0 | 68 | 60 | 79 | 34 | 5 | 2 | 1 | .324 | .441 |
| **SUBSTITUTES** | | | | | | | | | | | | | | | | | | |
| 3B | John Kelleher | R | 63 | 193 | 50 | 7 | 1 | 0 | 0.0 | 23 | 20 | 15 | 14 | 5 | 6 | 0 | .259 | .306 |
| 2B | Sparky Adams | R | 11 | 44 | 11 | 0 | 1 | 0 | 0.0 | 5 | 3 | 4 | 3 | 1 | 0 | 0 | .250 | .295 |
| 3B | George Grantham | L | 7 | 23 | 4 | 1 | 1 | 0 | 0.0 | 3 | 3 | 1 | 3 | 2 | 1 | 0 | .174 | .304 |
| 1B | Walt Golvin | L | 2 | 2 | 0 | 0 | 0 | 0 | 0.0 | 0 | 1 | 0 | 0 | 0 | 0 | 0 | .000 | .000 |
| 2B | Joe Klugman | R | 2 | 2 | 0 | 0 | 0 | 0 | 0.0 | 0 | 0 | 0 | 0 | 0 | 0 | 0 | .000 | .000 |
| OF | Cliff Heathcote | L | 76 | 243 | 68 | 8 | 7 | 1 | 0.4 | 37 | 34 | 18 | 15 | 5 | 12 | 3 | .280 | .383 |
| O1 | Turner Barber | L | 84 | 226 | 70 | 7 | 4 | 0 | 0.0 | 35 | 29 | 30 | 9 | 7 | 19 | 2 | .310 | .376 |
| OF | Marty Callaghan | L | 74 | 175 | 45 | 7 | 4 | 0 | 0.0 | 31 | 20 | 17 | 17 | 2 | 17 | 3 | .257 | .343 |
| OF | George Maisel | R | 38 | 84 | 16 | 1 | 1 | 0 | 0.0 | 9 | 6 | 8 | 2 | 1 | 5 | 1 | .190 | .226 |
| OF | Max Flack | L | 17 | 54 | 12 | 1 | 0 | 0 | 0.0 | 7 | 6 | 2 | 4 | 2 | 1 | 0 | .222 | .241 |
| OF | Howie Fitzgerald | L | 10 | 24 | 8 | 1 | 0 | 0 | 0.0 | 3 | 4 | 3 | 2 | 1 | 3 | 2 | .333 | .375 |
| C | Gabby Hartnett | R | 31 | 72 | 14 | 1 | 1 | 0 | 0.0 | 4 | 4 | 6 | 8 | 1 | 4 | 1 | .194 | .236 |
| C | Kettle Wirtz | R | 31 | 58 | 10 | 2 | 0 | 1 | 1.7 | 7 | 6 | 12 | 15 | 0 | 3 | 0 | .172 | .259 |
| PH | Butch Weis | L | 2 | 2 | 1 | 0 | 0 | 0 | 0.0 | 2 | 0 | 0 | 0 | 0 | 2 | 1 | .500 | .500 |
| PH | Harvey Cotter | L | 1 | 1 | 1 | 1 | 0 | 0 | 0.0 | 0 | 0 | 0 | 0 | 0 | 1 | 1 | 1.000 | 2.000 |
| **PITCHERS** | | | | | | | | | | | | | | | | | | |
| P | Vic Aldridge | R | 36 | 100 | 26 | 1 | 3 | 0 | 0.0 | 8 | 13 | 1 | 6 | 1 | 0 | 0 | .260 | .330 |
| P | Grover Alexander | R | 33 | 85 | 15 | 1 | 0 | 0 | 0.0 | 4 | 11 | 6 | 16 | 0 | 0 | 0 | .176 | .188 |
| P | Tiny Osborne | L | 41 | 67 | 9 | 2 | 0 | 0 | 0.0 | 6 | 4 | 0 | 17 | 1 | 0 | 0 | .134 | .164 |
| P | Virgil Cheeves | R | 39 | 62 | 13 | 1 | 1 | 1 | 1.6 | 6 | 3 | 2 | 16 | 0 | 0 | 0 | .210 | .306 |
| P | Percy Jones | R | 44 | 47 | 4 | 0 | 0 | 0 | 0.0 | 2 | 3 | 2 | 18 | 0 | 0 | 0 | .085 | .085 |
| P | Tony Kaufmann | R | 38 | 45 | 9 | 2 | 1 | 1 | 2.2 | 4 | 4 | 2 | 14 | 0 | 1 | 1 | .200 | .356 |
| P | George Stueland | B | 35 | 31 | 4 | 0 | 0 | 0 | 0.0 | 2 | 2 | 1 | 17 | 0 | 0 | 0 | .129 | .129 |
| P | Vic Keen | R | 7 | 12 | 4 | 0 | 0 | 0 | 0.0 | 1 | 0 | 0 | 5 | 0 | 0 | 0 | .333 | .333 |
| P | Buck Freeman | R | 11 | 8 | 1 | 1 | 0 | 0 | 0.0 | 1 | 0 | 0 | 2 | 0 | 0 | 0 | .125 | .250 |
| P | Fred Fussell | L | 3 | 6 | 0 | 0 | 0 | 0 | 0.0 | 1 | 0 | 1 | 4 | 0 | 0 | 0 | .000 | .000 |
| P | Ed Morris | R | 5 | 4 | 1 | 0 | 0 | 0 | 0.0 | 0 | 1 | 0 | 2 | 0 | 0 | 0 | .250 | .250 |
| P | Uel Eubanks | R | 2 | 1 | 1 | 1 | 0 | 0 | 0.0 | 1 | 0 | 0 | 0 | 0 | 1 | 1 | 1.000 | 2.000 |
| P | Speed Martin | R | 1 | 1 | 0 | 0 | 0 | 0 | 0.0 | 0 | 0 | 1 | 1 | 0 | 0 | 0 | .000 | .000 |
| TEAM TOTAL | | | | 5335 | 1564 | 248 | 71 | 42 | 0.8 | 77 | 667 | 525 | 447 | 97 | 95 | 20 | .293 | .390 |

## INDIVIDUAL FIELDING

| POS | Player | T | G | PO | A | E | DP | TC/G | FA |
|---|---|---|---|---|---|---|---|---|---|
| 1B | R. Grimes | R | 138 | 1378 | 68 | 19 | 106 | 10.6 | .987 |
| | T. Barber | R | 16 | 164 | 4 | 0 | 10 | 10.5 | 1.000 |
| | J. Kelleher | R | 4 | 41 | 4 | 0 | 3 | 11.3 | 1.000 |
| | B. Friberg | R | 6 | 44 | 1 | 0 | 4 | 7.5 | 1.000 |
| | W. Golvin | L | 2 | 4 | 0 | 0 | 0 | 2.0 | 1.000 |
| 2B | Z. Terry | R | 125 | 298 | 442 | 28 | 75 | 6.1 | .964 |
| | M. Krug | R | 23 | 44 | 66 | 11 | 10 | 5.3 | .909 |
| | S. Adams | R | 11 | 18 | 35 | 5 | 5 | 5.3 | .914 |
| | B. Friberg | R | 3 | 2 | 4 | 0 | 2 | 2.0 | 1.000 |
| | J. Klugman | R | 2 | 2 | 3 | 0 | 1 | 2.5 | 1.000 |
| SS | C. Hollocher | R | 152 | 332 | 502 | 30 | 89 | 5.7 | **.965** |
| | J. Kelleher | R | 7 | 9 | 15 | 2 | 1 | 3.7 | .923 |
| | Z. Terry | R | 4 | 10 | 10 | 1 | 2 | 5.3 | .952 |
| | M. Krug | R | 1 | 1 | 5 | 0 | 1 | 6.0 | 1.000 |
| 3B | M. Krug | R | 104 | 129 | 184 | 21 | 19 | 3.2 | .937 |
| | J. Kelleher | R | 46 | 44 | 93 | 10 | 9 | 3.2 | .932 |
| | Z. Terry | R | 3 | 2 | 9 | 0 | 0 | 3.7 | 1.000 |
| | G. Grantham | R | 5 | 5 | 4 | 0 | 1 | 1.8 | 1.000 |
| | B. Friberg | R | 5 | 3 | 3 | 0 | 0 | 1.2 | 1.000 |

| POS | Player | T | G | PO | A | E | DP | TC/G | FA |
|---|---|---|---|---|---|---|---|---|---|
| OF | J. Statz | R | 110 | 309 | 16 | 14 | 4 | 3.1 | .959 |
| | H. Miller | R | 116 | 219 | 15 | 10 | 3 | 2.1 | .959 |
| | B. Friberg | R | 74 | 126 | 13 | 4 | 5 | 1.9 | .972 |
| | C. Heathcote | L | 60 | 131 | 5 | 2 | 1 | 2.3 | .986 |
| | M. Callaghan | L | 53 | 85 | 2 | 5 | 0 | 1.7 | .946 |
| | T. Barber | R | 47 | 78 | 4 | 4 | 2 | 1.8 | .953 |
| | G. Maisel | R | 38 | 50 | 2 | 0 | 0 | 1.4 | 1.000 |
| | M. Flack | L | 17 | 28 | 0 | 2 | 0 | 1.8 | .933 |
| | Fitzgerald | L | 10 | 9 | 0 | 2 | 0 | 1.1 | .818 |
| C | B. O'Farrell | R | 125 | **446** | **143** | 14 | **22** | 4.8 | .977 |
| | G. Hartnett | R | 27 | 79 | 29 | 2 | 0 | 4.1 | .982 |
| | K. Wirtz | R | 27 | 55 | 6 | 2 | 1 | 2.3 | .968 |

Following their horrendous finish the previous year, the Cubs of 1922 were a pleasant surprise, pulling home a respectable fifth, six games over .500.

Heavy hitting was the main factor, as their .293 team batting average was the club's highest in 27 years. Grimes and Hollocher enjoyed the best years of their careers, while Bob O'Farrell, now the first-string catcher, and utility man Barney Friberg also began to carry hot bats.

A newcomer to the squad was Lawrence "Hack" Miller, the colorful leftfielder. The son of German immigrants, Miller had grown up in a slum neighborhood on Chicago's near North Side, which made him a natural hero. The beer-loving Miller would twist iron bars, uproot trees, and pound nails with his bare fists. His .352 average is still the 20th-century high for a Cub rookie. Two other rookies, Gabby Hartnett and Sparky Adams, were inconspicuous at this point.

The record books were rewritten August 25, when the Cubs outslugged the Phillies 26–23 in the highest scoring game of all time. At one time the Cubs led, 25–6, and Philadelphia left the bases full in the top of the ninth. Batting heroes were Miller, with two homers and six RBI, and Cliff Heathcote, who garnered five hits.

The pitching, however, remained shaky. Alexander and Vic Aldridge were a good one-two punch, but beyond that it was a weak staff. This ultimately prevented the Cubs from finishing higher.

## TEAM  STATISTICS

|  | W | L | PCT | GB | R | OR | Batting 2B | 3B | HR | BA | SA | SB | Fielding E | DP | FA | CG | B | Pitching SO | ShO | SV | ERA |
|---|---|---|---|---|---|---|---|---|---|---|---|---|---|---|---|---|---|---|---|---|---|
| NY | 93 | 61 | .604 |  | 852 | 658 | 253 | 90 | 80 | .305 | .428 | 116 | 194 | 145 | .970 | 73 | 393 | 388 | 7 | 15 | 3.45 |
| CIN | 86 | 68 | .558 | 7 | 766 | 677 | 226 | 99 | 45 | .296 | .401 | 130 | 205 | 147 | .968 | 88 | 326 | 357 | 8 | 3 | 3.53 |
| PIT | 85 | 69 | .552 | 8 | 865 | 736 | 239 | 110 | 52 | .308 | .419 | 145 | 187 | 126 | .970 | 88 | 358 | 490 | 15 | 7 | 3.98 |
| STL | 85 | 69 | .552 | 8 | 863 | 819 | 280 | 88 | 107 | .301 | .444 | 73 | 239 | 122 | .961 | 60 | 447 | 465 | 8 | 12 | 4.44 |
| CHI | 80 | 74 | .519 | 13 | 771 | 808 | 248 | 71 | 42 | .293 | .390 | 97 | 204 | 154 | .968 | 74 | 475 | 402 | 8 | 12 | 4.34 |
| BKN | 76 | 78 | .494 | 17 | 743 | 754 | 235 | 76 | 56 | .290 | .392 | 79 | 208 | 139 | .967 | 82 | 490 | 499 | 12 | 8 | 4.05 |
| PHI | 57 | 96 | .373 | 35.5 | 738 | 920 | 268 | 55 | 116 | .282 | .415 | 48 | 225 | 152 | .965 | 73 | 460 | 394 | 6 | 5 | 4.64 |
| BOS | 53 | 100 | .346 | 39.5 | 596 | 822 | 162 | 73 | 32 | .263 | .341 | 67 | 215 | 121 | .965 | 62 | 489 | 360 | 7 | 6 | 4.37 |
| LEAGUE TOTAL |  |  |  |  | 6194 | 6194 | 1911 | 662 | 530 | .292 | .404 | 755 | 1677 | 1106 | .967 | 600 | 3438 | 3355 | 71 | 68 | 4.10 |

## INDIVIDUAL  PITCHING

| PITCHER | T | W | L | PCT | ERA | SV | G | GS | CG | IP | H | BB | SO | R | ER | ShO | H/9 | BB/9 | SO/9 |
|---|---|---|---|---|---|---|---|---|---|---|---|---|---|---|---|---|---|---|---|
| Vic Aldridge | R | 16 | 15 | .516 | 3.52 | 0 | 36 | 34 | 20 | 258.1 | 287 | 56 | 66 | 129 | 101 | 2 | 10.00 | 1.95 | 2.30 |
| Grover Alexander | R | 16 | 13 | .552 | 3.63 | 1 | 33 | 31 | 20 | 245.2 | 283 | 34 | 48 | 111 | 99 | 1 | 10.37 | 1.25 | 1.76 |
| Tiny Osborne | R | 9 | 5 | .643 | 4.50 | 3 | 41 | 14 | 7 | 184 | 183 | 95 | 81 | 113 | 92 | 1 | 8.95 | 4.65 | 3.96 |
| Virgil Cheeves | R | 12 | 11 | .522 | 4.09 | 2 | 39 | 23 | 9 | 182.2 | 195 | 76 | 40 | 99 | 83 | 1 | 9.61 | 3.74 | 1.97 |
| Percy Jones | L | 8 | 9 | .471 | 4.72 | 1 | 44 | 26 | 7 | 164 | 197 | 69 | 46 | 104 | 86 | 2 | 10.81 | 3.79 | 2.52 |
| Tony Kaufmann | R | 7 | 13 | .350 | 4.06 | 3 | 37 | 9 | 4 | 153 | 161 | 57 | 45 | 81 | 69 | 1 | 9.47 | 3.35 | 2.65 |
| George Stueland | R | 9 | 4 | .692 | 5.92 | 0 | 34 | 12 | 4 | 111 | 129 | 48 | 43 | 81 | 73 | 0 | 10.46 | 3.89 | 3.49 |
| Vic Keen | R | 1 | 2 | .333 | 3.89 | 1 | 7 | 3 | 2 | 34.2 | 36 | 10 | 11 | 20 | 15 | 0 | 9.35 | 2.60 | 2.86 |
| Buck Freeman | R | 0 | 1 | .000 | 8.77 | 1 | 11 | 1 | 0 | 25.2 | 47 | 10 | 10 | 28 | 25 | 0 | 16.48 | 3.51 | 3.51 |
| Fred Fussell | L | 1 | 1 | .500 | 4.74 | 0 | 3 | 2 | 1 | 19 | 24 | 8 | 4 | 11 | 10 | 0 | 11.37 | 3.79 | 1.89 |
| Ed Morris | R | 0 | 0 | – | 8.25 | 0 | 5 | 0 | 0 | 12 | 22 | 6 | 5 | 17 | 11 | 0 | 16.50 | 4.50 | 3.75 |
| Speed Martin | R | 1 | 0 | 1.000 | 7.50 | 0 | 1 | 1 | 0 | 6 | 10 | 2 | 2 | 5 | 5 | 0 | 15.00 | 3.00 | 3.00 |
| Jel Eubanks | R | 0 | 0 | – | 27.00 | 0 | 2 | 0 | 0 | 1.2 | 5 | 4 | 1 | 9 | 5 | 0 | 27.00 | 21.60 | 5.40 |
| TEAM TOTAL |  | 80 | 74 | .519 | 4.34 | 12 | 293 | 156 | 74 | 1397.2 | 1579 | 475 | 402 | 808 | 674 | 8 | 10.17 | 3.06 | 2.59 |

| MANAGER | W | L | PCT |
|---|---|---|---|
| Bill Killefer | 83 | 71 | .539 |

| POS | Player | B | G | AB | H | 2B | 3B | HR | HR % | R | RBI | BB | SO | SB | Pinch Hit AB | Pinch Hit H | BA | SA |
|---|---|---|---|---|---|---|---|---|---|---|---|---|---|---|---|---|---|---|
| **REGULARS** | | | | | | | | | | | | | | | | | | |
| 1B | Ray Grimes | R | 64 | 216 | 71 | 7 | 2 | 2 | 0.9 | 32 | 36 | 24 | 17 | 5 | 2 | 0 | .329 | .407 |
| 2B | George Grantham | L | 152 | 570 | 160 | 36 | 8 | 8 | 1.4 | 81 | 70 | 71 | 92 | 43 | 2 | 0 | .281 | .414 |
| SS | Sparky Adams | R | 95 | 311 | 90 | 12 | 0 | 4 | 1.3 | 40 | 35 | 26 | 10 | 20 | 10 | 4 | .289 | .367 |
| 3B | Barney Friberg | R | 146 | 547 | 174 | 27 | 11 | 12 | 2.2 | 91 | 88 | 45 | 49 | 13 | 0 | 0 | .318 | .473 |
| RF | Cliff Heathcote | L | 117 | 393 | 98 | 14 | 3 | 1 | 0.3 | 48 | 27 | 25 | 22 | 32 | 2 | 0 | .249 | .308 |
| CF | Jigger Statz | R | 154 | 655 | 209 | 33 | 8 | 10 | 1.5 | 110 | 70 | 56 | 42 | 29 | 0 | 0 | .319 | .440 |
| LF | Hack Miller | R | 135 | 485 | 146 | 24 | 2 | 20 | 4.1 | 74 | 88 | 27 | 39 | 6 | 4 | 4 | .301 | .482 |
| C | Bob O'Farrell | R | 131 | 452 | 144 | 25 | 4 | 12 | 2.7 | 73 | 84 | 67 | 38 | 10 | 6 | 3 | .319 | .471 |
| **SUBSTITUTES** | | | | | | | | | | | | | | | | | | |
| SS | Charlie Hollocher | L | 66 | 260 | 89 | 14 | 2 | 1 | 0.4 | 46 | 28 | 26 | 5 | 9 | 1 | 0 | .342 | .423 |
| UT | John Kelleher | R | 66 | 193 | 59 | 10 | 0 | 6 | 3.1 | 27 | 21 | 14 | 9 | 2 | 15 | 6 | .306 | .451 |
| 1B | Allen Elliott | L | 53 | 168 | 42 | 8 | 2 | 2 | 1.2 | 21 | 29 | 2 | 12 | 3 | 0 | 0 | .250 | .357 |
| SS | Pete Turgeon | R | 3 | 6 | 1 | 0 | 0 | 0 | 0.0 | 1 | 0 | 0 | 0 | 0 | 0 | 0 | .167 | .167 |
| OF | Marty Callaghan | L | 61 | 129 | 29 | 1 | 3 | 0 | 0.0 | 18 | 14 | 8 | 18 | 2 | 16 | 3 | .225 | .279 |
| OF | Otto Vogel | R | 41 | 81 | 17 | 0 | 1 | 1 | 1.2 | 10 | 6 | 7 | 11 | 2 | 6 | 1 | .210 | .272 |
| OF | Denver Grigsby | L | 24 | 72 | 21 | 5 | 2 | 0 | 0.0 | 8 | 5 | 7 | 5 | 1 | 1 | 1 | .292 | .417 |
| OF | Butch Weis | L | 22 | 26 | 6 | 1 | 0 | 0 | 0.0 | 2 | 2 | 5 | 8 | 0 | 13 | 3 | .231 | .269 |
| OF | Tony Murray | R | 2 | 4 | 1 | 0 | 0 | 0 | 0.0 | 0 | 0 | 0 | 0 | 0 | 0 | 0 | .250 | .250 |
| C1 | Gabby Hartnett | R | 85 | 231 | 62 | 12 | 2 | 8 | 3.5 | 28 | 39 | 25 | 22 | 4 | 15 | 2 | .268 | .442 |
| C | Kettle Wirtz | R | 5 | 5 | 1 | 0 | 0 | 0 | 0.0 | 2 | 1 | 2 | 0 | 0 | 0 | 0 | .200 | .200 |
| PH | Bob Barrett | R | 3 | 3 | 1 | 0 | 0 | 0 | 0.0 | 0 | 0 | 0 | 0 | 0 | 3 | 1 | .333 | .333 |
| **PITCHERS** | | | | | | | | | | | | | | | | | | |
| P | Grover Alexander | R | 39 | 111 | 24 | 3 | 1 | 1 | 0.9 | 10 | 10 | 1 | 11 | 0 | 0 | 0 | .216 | .288 |
| P | Tony Kaufmann | R | 33 | 74 | 16 | 2 | 0 | 2 | 2.7 | 10 | 10 | 7 | 17 | 0 | 0 | 0 | .216 | .324 |
| P | Vic Aldridge | R | 30 | 71 | 19 | 3 | 0 | 0 | 0.0 | 5 | 4 | 6 | 6 | 0 | 0 | 0 | .268 | .310 |
| P | Tiny Osborne | L | 37 | 60 | 12 | 2 | 0 | 0 | 0.0 | 3 | 3 | 0 | 19 | 0 | 0 | 0 | .200 | .233 |
| P | Vic Keen | R | 35 | 53 | 8 | 2 | 0 | 0 | 0.0 | 9 | 2 | 1 | 16 | 0 | 0 | 0 | .151 | .189 |
| P | Nick Dumovich | L | 28 | 29 | 7 | 0 | 1 | 0 | 0.0 | 4 | 0 | 2 | 3 | 0 | 0 | 0 | .241 | .310 |
| P | Virgil Cheeves | R | 19 | 23 | 4 | 1 | 0 | 0 | 0.0 | 1 | 1 | 0 | 6 | 0 | 0 | 0 | .174 | .217 |
| P | Fred Fussell | L | 28 | 20 | 4 | 1 | 0 | 0 | 0.0 | 2 | 0 | 1 | 7 | 0 | 0 | 0 | .200 | .250 |
| P | Rip Wheeler | R | 3 | 9 | 1 | 0 | 0 | 0 | 0.0 | 0 | 2 | 0 | 0 | 0 | 0 | 0 | .111 | .111 |
| P | Phil Collins | R | 1 | 2 | 0 | 0 | 0 | 0 | 0.0 | 0 | 0 | 0 | 1 | 0 | 0 | 0 | .000 | .000 |
| P | Guy Bush | R | 1 | 1 | 0 | 0 | 0 | 0 | – | 0 | 0 | 0 | 0 | 0 | 0 | 0 | – | – |
| P | Ed Stauffer | R | 1 | 0 | 0 | 0 | 0 | 0 | – | 0 | 0 | 0 | 0 | 0 | 0 | 0 | – | – |
| P | George Stueland | B | 6 | 0 | 0 | 0 | 0 | 0 | – | 0 | 0 | 0 | 0 | 0 | 0 | 0 | – | – |
| TEAM TOTAL | | | | 5259 | 1516 | 243 | 52 | 90 | 1.7 | 75 | 675 | 455 | 485 | 181 | 96 | 28 | .288 | .406 |

### INDIVIDUAL FIELDING

| POS | Player | T | G | PO | A | E | DP | TC/G | FA | POS | Player | T | G | PO | A | E | DP | TC/G | FA |
|---|---|---|---|---|---|---|---|---|---|---|---|---|---|---|---|---|---|---|---|
| 1B | R. Grimes | R | 62 | 629 | 30 | 6 | 46 | 10.7 | .991 | OF | J. Statz | R | 154 | 438 | 26 | 12 | 7 | 3.1 | .975 |
| | A. Elliott | R | 52 | 450 | 19 | 4 | 36 | 9.1 | .992 | | H. Miller | R | 129 | 256 | 17 | 6 | 4 | 2.2 | .978 |
| | G. Hartnett | R | 31 | 270 | 15 | 4 | 23 | 9.3 | .986 | | C. Heathcote | L | 112 | 231 | 14 | 5 | 1 | 2.2 | .980 |
| | J. Kelleher | R | 22 | 183 | 9 | 5 | 11 | 9.0 | .975 | | M. Callaghan | L | 38 | 60 | 3 | 2 | 0 | 1.7 | .969 |
| 2B | G. Grantham | R | 150 | 374 | 518 | 55 | 90 | 6.3 | .942 | | D. Grigsby | R | 22 | 41 | 1 | 0 | 0 | 1.9 | 1.000 |
| | J. Kelleher | R | 6 | 9 | 17 | 3 | 2 | 4.8 | .897 | | O. Vogel | R | 24 | 36 | 3 | 3 | 0 | 1.8 | .929 |
| | | | | | | | | | | | B. Weis | L | 6 | 9 | 0 | 0 | 0 | 1.5 | 1.000 |
| SS | S. Adams | R | 79 | 153 | 248 | 28 | 45 | 5.4 | .935 | | S. Adams | R | 1 | 3 | 1 | 0 | 0 | 4.0 | 1.000 |
| | C. Hollocher | R | 65 | 124 | 212 | 13 | 35 | 5.4 | .963 | | T. Murray | R | 2 | 2 | 0 | 0 | 0 | 1.0 | 1.000 |
| | J. Kelleher | R | 14 | 30 | 47 | 8 | 7 | 6.1 | .906 | | | | | | | | | | |
| | P. Turgeon | R | 2 | 4 | 3 | 1 | 2 | 4.0 | .875 | C | B. O'Farrell | R | 124 | 418 | 118 | 13 | 11 | 4.4 | .976 |
| 3B | B. Friberg | R | 146 | 168 | 294 | 22 | 33 | 3.3 | .955 | | G. Hartnett | R | 39 | 143 | 24 | 1 | 2 | 4.3 | .994 |
| | J. Kelleher | R | 11 | 6 | 11 | 6 | 1 | 2.1 | .739 | | K. Wirtz | R | 3 | 10 | 0 | 0 | 0 | 3.3 | 1.000 |
| | O. Vogel | R | 1 | 1 | 1 | 0 | 1 | 2.0 | 1.000 | | | | | | | | | | |

The 1923 season was marred by ailments to two star players, Grimes and Hollocher. Grimes suffered a slipped disc, and Hollocher was beset with stomach problems. For both, it was the beginning of the end of their careers. In spite of these setbacks, the Cubs climbed up to fourth place and home attendance crossed the 700,000 mark for the first time.

The Cubs powered a new team high (excluding the phony 1884 record) of 90 home runs, led by Miller's 20. The team was also fast, leading the league with 181 steals, the most by a Cub team in the lively ball era. Friberg, O'Farrell, and Jigger Statz contributed solid seasons while Alexander appeared to be mellowing with age, winning 22 games. During one stretch he went 51 consecutive innings without issuing a base on balls, a Cub record. Guy Bush made his Cub debut while Gabby Hartnett and Sparky Adams began to appear on a semiregular basis.

## TEAM STATISTICS

|  | W | L | PCT | GB | R | OR | Batting 2B | 3B | HR | BA | SA | SB | Fielding E | DP | FA | CG | B | Pitching SO | ShO | SV | ERA |
|---|---|---|---|---|---|---|---|---|---|---|---|---|---|---|---|---|---|---|---|---|---|
| Y | 95 | 58 | .621 |  | 854 | 679 | 248 | 76 | 85 | .295 | .415 | 106 | 176 | 141 | .972 | 62 | 424 | 453 | 10 | 18 | 3.90 |
| IN | 91 | 63 | .591 | 4.5 | 708 | 629 | 237 | 95 | 45 | .285 | .392 | 96 | 202 | 144 | .969 | 88 | 359 | 450 | 11 | 9 | 3.21 |
| T | 87 | 67 | .565 | 8.5 | 786 | 696 | 224 | 111 | 49 | .295 | .404 | 154 | 179 | 157 | .971 | 92 | 402 | 414 | 5 | 9 | 3.87 |
| HI | 83 | 71 | .539 | 12.5 | 756 | 704 | 243 | 52 | 90 | .288 | .406 | 181 | 208 | 144 | .967 | 80 | 435 | 408 | 8 | 11 | 3.82 |
| L | 79 | 74 | .516 | 16 | 746 | 732 | 274 | 76 | 63 | .286 | .398 | 89 | 232 | 141 | .963 | 77 | 456 | 398 | 9 | 7 | 3.87 |
| KN | 76 | 78 | .494 | 19.5 | 753 | 741 | 214 | 81 | 62 | .285 | .387 | 71 | 293 | 137 | .955 | 94 | 477 | 549 | 8 | 5 | 3.73 |
| OS | 54 | 100 | .351 | 41.5 | 636 | 798 | 213 | 58 | 32 | .273 | .353 | 57 | 230 | 157 | .964 | 55 | 394 | 351 | 13 | 7 | 4.22 |
| HI | 50 | 104 | .325 | 45.5 | 748 | 1008 | 259 | 39 | 112 | .278 | .401 | 70 | 217 | 172 | .966 | 68 | 549 | 385 | 3 | 8 | 5.30 |
| AGUE TOTAL |  |  |  |  | 5987 | 5987 | 1912 | 588 | 538 | .286 | .395 | 824 | 1737 | 1193 | .966 | 616 | 3496 | 3408 | 67 | 74 | 3.99 |

## INDIVIDUAL PITCHING

| ITCHER | T | W | L | PCT | ERA | SV | G | GS | CG | IP | H | BB | SO | R | ER | ShO | H/9 | BB/9 | SO/9 |
|---|---|---|---|---|---|---|---|---|---|---|---|---|---|---|---|---|---|---|---|
| rover Alexander | R | 22 | 12 | .647 | 3.19 | 2 | 39 | 36 | 26 | 305 | 308 | 30 | 72 | 128 | 108 | 3 | 9.09 | 0.89 | 2.12 |
| c Aldridge | R | 16 | 9 | .640 | 3.48 | 0 | 30 | 30 | 15 | 217 | 209 | 67 | 64 | 101 | 84 | 2 | 8.67 | 2.78 | 2.65 |
| ony Kaufmann | R | 14 | 10 | .583 | 3.10 | 3 | 33 | 24 | 18 | 206.1 | 209 | 67 | 72 | 97 | 71 | 2 | 9.12 | 2.92 | 3.14 |
| ny Osborne | R | 8 | 15 | .348 | 4.56 | 1 | 37 | 25 | 8 | 179.2 | 174 | 89 | 69 | 117 | 91 | 1 | 8.72 | 4.46 | 3.46 |
| c Keen | R | 12 | 8 | .600 | 3.00 | 1 | 35 | 17 | 10 | 177 | 169 | 57 | 46 | 70 | 59 | 0 | 8.59 | 2.90 | 2.34 |
| ick Dumovich | L | 3 | 5 | .375 | 4.60 | 1 | 28 | 8 | 1 | 94 | 118 | 45 | 23 | 60 | 48 | 0 | 11.30 | 4.31 | 2.20 |
| ed Fussell | L | 3 | 5 | .375 | 5.54 | 3 | 28 | 2 | 1 | 76.1 | 90 | 31 | 38 | 51 | 47 | 0 | 10.61 | 3.66 | 4.48 |
| rgil Cheeves | R | 3 | 4 | .429 | 6.18 | 0 | 19 | 8 | 0 | 71.1 | 89 | 37 | 13 | 54 | 49 | 0 | 11.23 | 4.67 | 1.64 |
| p Wheeler | R | 1 | 2 | .333 | 4.88 | 0 | 3 | 3 | 1 | 24 | 28 | 5 | 5 | 14 | 13 | 0 | 10.50 | 1.88 | 1.88 |
| eorge Stueland | R | 0 | 1 | .000 | 5.63 | 0 | 6 | 0 | 0 | 8 | 11 | 5 | 2 | 7 | 5 | 0 | 12.38 | 5.63 | 2.25 |
| hil Collins | R | 1 | 0 | 1.000 | 3.60 | 0 | 1 | 1 | 0 | 5 | 8 | 1 | 2 | 2 | 2 | 0 | 14.40 | 1.80 | 3.60 |
| d Stauffer | R | 0 | 0 | – | 13.50 | 0 | 1 | 0 | 0 | 2 | 5 | 1 | 0 | 3 | 3 | 0 | 22.50 | 4.50 | 0.00 |
| uy Bush | R | 0 | 0 | – | 0.00 | 0 | 1 | 0 | 0 | 1 | 1 | 0 | 2 | 0 | 0 | 0 | 9.00 | 0.00 | 18.00 |
| EAM TOTAL |  | 83 | 71 | .539 | 3.82 | 11 | 261 | 154 | 80 | 1366.2 | 1419 | 435 | 408 | 704 | 580 | 8 | 9.34 | 2.86 | 2.69 |

| MANAGER | W | L | PCT |
|---|---|---|---|
| Bill Killefer | 81 | 72 | .529 |

| POS | Player | B | G | AB | H | 2B | 3B | HR | HR % | R | RBI | BB | SO | SB | Pinch Hit AB | Pinch Hit H | BA | SA |
|---|---|---|---|---|---|---|---|---|---|---|---|---|---|---|---|---|---|---|
| **REGULARS** | | | | | | | | | | | | | | | | | | |
| 1B | Harvey Cotter | L | 98 | 310 | 81 | 16 | 4 | 4 | 1.3 | 39 | 33 | 36 | 31 | 3 | 7 | 2 | .261 | .377 |
| 2B | George Grantham | L | 127 | 469 | 148 | 19 | 6 | 12 | 2.6 | 85 | 60 | 55 | 63 | 21 | 2 | 0 | .316 | .458 |
| SS | Sparky Adams | R | 117 | 418 | 117 | 11 | 5 | 1 | 0.2 | 66 | 27 | 40 | 20 | 15 | 7 | 2 | .280 | .337 |
| 3B | Barney Friberg | R | 142 | 495 | 138 | 19 | 3 | 5 | 1.0 | 67 | 82 | 66 | 53 | 19 | 0 | 0 | .279 | .360 |
| RF | Cliff Heathcote | L | 113 | 392 | 121 | 19 | 7 | 0 | 0.0 | 66 | 30 | 28 | 28 | 26 | 1 | 0 | .309 | .393 |
| CF | Jigger Statz | R | 135 | 549 | 152 | 22 | 5 | 3 | 0.5 | 69 | 49 | 37 | 50 | 13 | 2 | 1 | .277 | .352 |
| LF | Denver Grigsby | L | 124 | 411 | 123 | 18 | 2 | 3 | 0.7 | 58 | 48 | 31 | 47 | 10 | 2 | 0 | .299 | .375 |
| C | Gabby Hartnett | R | 111 | 354 | 106 | 17 | 7 | 16 | 4.5 | 56 | 67 | 39 | 37 | 10 | 4 | 0 | .299 | .523 |
| **SUBSTITUTES** | | | | | | | | | | | | | | | | | | |
| SS | Charlie Hollocher | L | 76 | 286 | 70 | 12 | 4 | 2 | 0.7 | 28 | 21 | 18 | 7 | 4 | 5 | 1 | .245 | .336 |
| 1B | Ray Grimes | R | 51 | 177 | 53 | 6 | 5 | 5 | 2.8 | 33 | 34 | 28 | 15 | 4 | 1 | 0 | .299 | .475 |
| UT | Bob Barrett | R | 54 | 133 | 32 | 2 | 3 | 5 | 3.8 | 12 | 21 | 7 | 29 | 1 | 10 | 2 | .241 | .414 |
| 1B | Ted Kearns | R | 4 | 16 | 4 | 0 | 1 | 0 | 0.0 | 0 | 1 | 1 | 1 | 0 | 0 | 0 | .250 | .375 |
| 1B | Allen Elliott | L | 10 | 14 | 2 | 0 | 0 | 0 | 0.0 | 0 | 0 | 0 | 1 | 0 | 0 | 0 | .143 | .143 |
| SS | Ralph Michaels | R | 8 | 11 | 4 | 0 | 0 | 0 | 0.0 | 0 | 2 | 0 | 1 | 0 | 3 | 1 | .364 | .364 |
| OF | Otto Vogel | R | 70 | 172 | 46 | 11 | 2 | 1 | 0.6 | 28 | 24 | 10 | 26 | 4 | 9 | 2 | .267 | .372 |
| OF | Butch Weis | L | 39 | 133 | 37 | 8 | 1 | 0 | 0.0 | 19 | 23 | 15 | 14 | 4 | 1 | 1 | .278 | .353 |
| OF | Hack Miller | R | 53 | 131 | 44 | 8 | 1 | 4 | 3.1 | 17 | 25 | 8 | 11 | 1 | 20 | 7 | .336 | .504 |
| OF | Howie Fitzgerald | L | 7 | 19 | 3 | 0 | 0 | 0 | 0.0 | 1 | 2 | 0 | 2 | 0 | 2 | 0 | .158 | .158 |
| C | Bob O'Farrell | R | 71 | 183 | 44 | 6 | 2 | 3 | 1.6 | 25 | 28 | 30 | 13 | 2 | 10 | 3 | .240 | .344 |
| C | John Churry | R | 6 | 7 | 1 | 1 | 0 | 0 | 0.0 | 0 | 0 | 2 | 0 | 0 | 2 | 0 | .143 | .286 |
| **PITCHERS** | | | | | | | | | | | | | | | | | | |
| P | Vic Aldridge | R | 32 | 85 | 15 | 3 | 0 | 0 | 0.0 | 6 | 11 | 2 | 7 | 0 | 0 | 0 | .176 | .212 |
| P | Vic Keen | R | 40 | 77 | 12 | 1 | 0 | 0 | 0.0 | 2 | 8 | 4 | 23 | 0 | 0 | 0 | .156 | .169 |
| P | Tony Kaufmann | R | 35 | 76 | 24 | 5 | 0 | 1 | 1.3 | 6 | 14 | 3 | 10 | 0 | 0 | 0 | .316 | .421 |
| P | Grover Alexander | R | 21 | 65 | 15 | 2 | 0 | 1 | 1.5 | 3 | 10 | 2 | 8 | 0 | 0 | 0 | .231 | .308 |
| P | Elmer Jacobs | R | 38 | 54 | 6 | 0 | 0 | 0 | 0.0 | 3 | 5 | 3 | 13 | 0 | 0 | 0 | .111 | .111 |
| P | Rip Wheeler | R | 29 | 32 | 7 | 0 | 0 | 0 | 0.0 | 3 | 2 | 0 | 3 | 0 | 0 | 0 | .219 | .219 |
| P | Sheriff Blake | L | 29 | 31 | 9 | 0 | 1 | 0 | 0.0 | 5 | 3 | 1 | 1 | 0 | 0 | 0 | .290 | .355 |
| P | Guy Bush | R | 16 | 26 | 4 | 1 | 0 | 0 | 0.0 | 1 | 4 | 1 | 5 | 0 | 0 | 0 | .154 | .192 |
| P | George Milstead | L | 13 | 6 | 1 | 0 | 0 | 0 | 0.0 | 0 | 0 | 2 | 2 | 0 | 0 | 0 | .167 | .167 |
| P | Herb Brett | R | 1 | 2 | 0 | 0 | 0 | 0 | 0.0 | 0 | 0 | 0 | 0 | 0 | 0 | 0 | .000 | .000 |
| P | Tiny Osborne | L | 2 | 0 | 0 | 0 | 0 | 0 | – | 0 | 0 | 0 | 0 | 0 | 0 | 0 | – | – |
| P | Ray Pierce | L | 6 | 0 | 0 | 0 | 0 | 0 | – | 0 | 0 | 0 | 0 | 0 | 0 | 0 | – | – |
| TEAM TOTAL | | | | 5134 | 1419 | 207 | 59 | 66 | 1.3 | 69 | 634 | 469 | 521 | 137 | 88 | 22 | .276 | .378 |

## INDIVIDUAL FIELDING

| POS | Player | T | G | PO | A | E | DP | TC/G | FA | POS | Player | T | G | PO | A | E | DP | TC/G | FA |
|---|---|---|---|---|---|---|---|---|---|---|---|---|---|---|---|---|---|---|---|
| 1B | H. Cotter | L | 90 | 873 | 59 | 10 | 72 | 10.5 | .989 | OF | J. Statz | R | 131 | 373 | 22 | 16 | 5 | 3.1 | .961 |
| | R. Grimes | R | 50 | 530 | 12 | 10 | 40 | 11.0 | .982 | | D. Grigsby | R | 121 | 244 | 16 | 7 | 4 | 2.2 | .974 |
| | B. Barrett | R | 10 | 69 | 5 | 4 | 8 | 7.8 | .949 | | C. Heathcote | L | 111 | 228 | 7 | 5 | 3 | 2.2 | .979 |
| | A. Elliott | R | 10 | 46 | 1 | 0 | 3 | 4.7 | 1.000 | | O. Vogel | R | 53 | 101 | 7 | 5 | 2 | 2.1 | .956 |
| | T. Kearns | R | 4 | 29 | 2 | 0 | 3 | 7.8 | 1.000 | | B. Weis | L | 36 | 81 | 8 | 2 | 2 | 2.5 | .978 |
| 2B | G. Grantham | R | 118 | 273 | 426 | 44 | 78 | 6.3 | .941 | | H. Miller | R | 32 | 54 | 1 | 3 | 0 | 1.8 | .948 |
| | S. Adams | R | 19 | 55 | 66 | 3 | 17 | 6.5 | .976 | | Fitzgerald | L | 5 | 4 | 0 | 0 | 0 | 0.8 | 1.000 |
| | B. Barrett | R | 25 | 48 | 67 | 7 | 11 | 4.9 | .943 | C | G. Hartnett | R | 105 | 369 | 97 | 18 | 12 | 4.6 | .963 |
| | J. Statz | R | 1 | 4 | 4 | 3 | 0 | 11.0 | .727 | | B. O'Farrell | R | 57 | 204 | 40 | 4 | 5 | 4.4 | .984 |
| SS | S. Adams | R | 88 | 169 | 277 | 28 | 62 | 5.4 | .941 | | J. Churry | R | 3 | 7 | 1 | 0 | 0 | 2.7 | 1.000 |
| | C. Hollocher | R | 71 | 156 | 248 | 13 | 42 | 5.9 | .969 | | | | | | | | | | |
| | R. Michaels | R | 4 | 6 | 7 | 1 | 1 | 3.5 | .929 | | | | | | | | | | |
| 3B | B. Friberg | R | 142 | 163 | 268 | 21 | 21 | 3.2 | .954 | | | | | | | | | | |
| | G. Grantham | R | 6 | 4 | 16 | 4 | 0 | 4.0 | .833 | | | | | | | | | | |
| | B. Barrett | R | 8 | 6 | 8 | 2 | 1 | 2.0 | .875 | | | | | | | | | | |
| | O. Vogel | R | 2 | 0 | 3 | 0 | 0 | 1.5 | 1.000 | | | | | | | | | | |

This season saw the Cubs slide back into fifth place, although they again had a winning record. Gabby Hartnett became the first-string catcher when Bob O'Farrell fractured his skull. Grover Alexander took a liking to Hartnett's style, so the now-expendable O'Farrell was traded to the Cardinals the following year. Sparky Adams supplanted Hollocher as the regular shortstop, and Alexander captured his 300th career victory with a 7–3 win over the Giants September 20.

Led by speedsters George Grantham and Cliff Heathcote, the Cubs were reckless on the basepaths, stealing 137 bases but getting caught a record 149 times. Grantham had a good season at the plate, batting .316, but was an erratic second baseman. Hack Miller sat on the bench most of the year, being relegated to pinch-hitting roles, while Statz and Friberg were not up to previous form. The 1924 City Series, which the White Sox won in six games, was the first Chicago baseball event to be broadcast over radio.

## TEAM STATISTICS

| | W | L | PCT | GB | R | OR | 2B | Batting 3B | HR | BA | SA | SB | Fielding E | DP | FA | CG | B | Pitching SO | ShO | SV | ERA |
|---|---|---|---|---|---|---|---|---|---|---|---|---|---|---|---|---|---|---|---|---|---|
| Y | 93 | 60 | .608 | | 857 | 641 | 269 | 81 | 95 | .300 | .432 | 82 | 186 | 160 | .971 | 71 | 392 | 406 | 4 | 21 | 3.62 |
| KN | 92 | 62 | .597 | 1.5 | 717 | 675 | 227 | 54 | 72 | .287 | .391 | 34 | 196 | 121 | .968 | 98 | 403 | 640 | 10 | 5 | 3.64 |
| T | 90 | 63 | .588 | 3 | 724 | 588 | 222 | 122 | 43 | .287 | .399 | 181 | 183 | 161 | .971 | 85 | 323 | 364 | 15 | 5 | 3.27 |
| IN | 83 | 70 | .542 | 10 | 649 | 579 | 236 | 111 | 36 | .290 | .397 | 103 | 217 | 142 | .966 | 77 | 293 | 451 | 14 | 9 | 3.12 |
| HI | 81 | 72 | .529 | 12 | 698 | 699 | 207 | 59 | 66 | .276 | .378 | 137 | 218 | 153 | .966 | 85 | 438 | 416 | 4 | 6 | 3.83 |
| TL | 65 | 89 | .422 | 28.5 | 740 | 750 | 270 | 87 | 67 | .290 | .411 | 86 | 191 | 162 | .969 | 79 | 486 | 393 | 7 | 6 | 4.15 |
| HI | 55 | 96 | .364 | 37 | 676 | 849 | 256 | 56 | 94 | .275 | .397 | 57 | 175 | 168 | .972 | 59 | 469 | 349 | 7 | 10 | 4.87 |
| OS | 53 | 100 | .346 | 40 | 520 | 800 | 194 | 52 | 25 | .256 | .327 | 74 | 168 | 154 | .973 | 66 | 402 | 364 | 10 | 4 | 4.46 |
| EAGUE TOTAL | | | | | 5581 | 5581 | 1881 | 622 | 498 | .283 | .392 | 754 | 1534 | 1221 | .970 | 620 | 3206 | 3383 | 71 | 66 | 3.87 |

## INDIVIDUAL PITCHING

| ITCHER | T | W | L | PCT | ERA | SV | G | GS | CG | IP | H | BB | SO | R | ER | ShO | H/9 | BB/9 | SO/9 |
|---|---|---|---|---|---|---|---|---|---|---|---|---|---|---|---|---|---|---|---|
| c Aldridge | R | 15 | 12 | .556 | 3.50 | 0 | 32 | 32 | 20 | 244.1 | 261 | 80 | 74 | 110 | 95 | 0 | 9.61 | 2.95 | 2.73 |
| c Keen | R | 15 | 14 | .517 | 3.80 | 3 | 40 | 28 | 15 | 234.2 | 242 | 80 | 75 | 112 | 99 | 0 | 9.28 | 3.07 | 2.88 |
| ony Kaufmann | R | 16 | 11 | .593 | 4.02 | 0 | 34 | 26 | 16 | 208.1 | 218 | 66 | 79 | 104 | 93 | 3 | 9.42 | 2.85 | 3.41 |
| mer Jacobs | R | 11 | 12 | .478 | 3.74 | 1 | 38 | 22 | 13 | 190.1 | 181 | 72 | 50 | 93 | 79 | 1 | 8.56 | 3.40 | 2.36 |
| rover Alexander | R | 12 | 5 | .706 | 3.03 | 0 | 21 | 20 | 12 | 169.1 | 183 | 25 | 33 | 82 | 57 | 0 | 9.73 | 1.33 | 1.75 |
| heriff Blake | R | 6 | 6 | .500 | 4.57 | 1 | 29 | 11 | 4 | 106.1 | 123 | 44 | 42 | 58 | 54 | 0 | 10.41 | 3.72 | 3.55 |
| p Wheeler | R | 3 | 6 | .333 | 3.91 | 0 | 29 | 4 | 0 | 101.1 | 103 | 21 | 16 | 53 | 44 | 0 | 9.15 | 1.87 | 1.42 |
| uy Bush | R | 2 | 5 | .286 | 4.02 | 0 | 16 | 8 | 4 | 80.2 | 91 | 24 | 36 | 51 | 36 | 0 | 10.15 | 2.68 | 4.02 |
| eorge Milstead | L | 1 | 1 | .500 | 6.07 | 0 | 13 | 2 | 1 | 29.2 | 41 | 13 | 6 | 25 | 20 | 0 | 12.44 | 3.94 | 1.82 |
| ay Pierce | L | 0 | 0 | – | 7.36 | 0 | 6 | 0 | 0 | 7.1 | 7 | 4 | 2 | 6 | 6 | 0 | 8.59 | 4.91 | 2.45 |
| erb Brett | R | 0 | 0 | – | 5.06 | 0 | 1 | 1 | 0 | 5.1 | 6 | 7 | 1 | 4 | 3 | 0 | 10.13 | 11.81 | 1.69 |
| ny Osborne | R | 0 | 0 | – | 3.00 | 1 | 2 | 0 | 0 | 3 | 3 | 2 | 2 | 1 | 1 | 0 | 9.00 | 6.00 | 6.00 |
| EAM TOTAL | | 81 | 72 | .529 | 3.83 | 6 | 261 | 154 | 85 | 1380.2 | 1459 | 438 | 416 | 699 | 587 | 4 | 9.51 | 2.86 | 2.71 |

| MANAGER | W | L | PCT |
|---|---|---|---|
| Bill Killefer | 33 | 42 | .440 |
| Rabbit Maranville | 23 | 30 | .434 |
| George Gibson | 12 | 14 | .462 |

| POS | Player | B | G | AB | H | 2B | 3B | HR | HR % | R | RBI | BB | SO | SB | Pinch Hit AB | Pinch Hit H | BA | SA |
|---|---|---|---|---|---|---|---|---|---|---|---|---|---|---|---|---|---|---|
| **REGULARS** | | | | | | | | | | | | | | | | | | |
| 1B | Charlie Grimm | L | 141 | 519 | 159 | 29 | 5 | 10 | 1.9 | 73 | 76 | 38 | 25 | 4 | 2 | 0 | .306 | .439 |
| 2B | Sparky Adams | R | 149 | 627 | 180 | 29 | 8 | 2 | 0.3 | 95 | 48 | 44 | 15 | 26 | 0 | 0 | .287 | .368 |
| SS | Rabbit Maranville | R | 75 | 266 | 62 | 10 | 3 | 0 | 0.0 | 37 | 23 | 29 | 20 | 6 | 1 | 0 | .233 | .293 |
| 3B | Howard Freigau | R | 117 | 476 | 146 | 22 | 10 | 8 | 1.7 | 77 | 71 | 30 | 31 | 10 | 0 | 0 | .307 | .445 |
| RF | Cliff Heathcote | L | 109 | 380 | 100 | 14 | 5 | 5 | 1.3 | 57 | 39 | 39 | 26 | 15 | 10 | 1 | .263 | .366 |
| CF | Mandy Brooks | R | 90 | 349 | 98 | 25 | 7 | 13 | 3.7 | 55 | 72 | 19 | 28 | 10 | 1 | 0 | .281 | .504 |
| LF | Art Jahn | R | 58 | 226 | 68 | 10 | 8 | 0 | 0.0 | 30 | 37 | 11 | 20 | 2 | 0 | 0 | .301 | .416 |
| C | Gabby Hartnett | R | 117 | 398 | 115 | 28 | 3 | 24 | 6.0 | 61 | 67 | 36 | 77 | 1 | 6 | 2 | .289 | .555 |
| **SUBSTITUTES** | | | | | | | | | | | | | | | | | | |
| S3 | Pinky Pittenger | R | 59 | 173 | 54 | 7 | 2 | 0 | 0.0 | 21 | 15 | 12 | 7 | 5 | 6 | 1 | .312 | .376 |
| UT | Barney Friberg | R | 44 | 152 | 39 | 5 | 3 | 1 | 0.7 | 12 | 16 | 14 | 22 | 0 | 2 | 0 | .257 | .349 |
| SS | Ike McAuley | R | 37 | 125 | 35 | 7 | 2 | 0 | 0.0 | 10 | 11 | 11 | 12 | 1 | 0 | 0 | .280 | .368 |
| 3B | Ralph Michaels | R | 22 | 50 | 14 | 1 | 0 | 0 | 0.0 | 10 | 6 | 6 | 9 | 1 | 3 | 0 | .280 | .300 |
| 32 | Bob Barrett | R | 14 | 32 | 10 | 1 | 0 | 0 | 0.0 | 1 | 7 | 1 | 4 | 1 | 4 | 2 | .313 | .344 |
| 2B | Gale Staley | L | 7 | 26 | 11 | 2 | 0 | 0 | 0.0 | 2 | 3 | 2 | 1 | 0 | 0 | 0 | .423 | .500 |
| 1B | Ted Kearns | R | 3 | 2 | 1 | 0 | 0 | 0 | 0.0 | 0 | 0 | 0 | 0 | 0 | 0 | 0 | .500 | .500 |
| OF | Tommy Griffith | L | 76 | 235 | 67 | 12 | 1 | 7 | 3.0 | 38 | 27 | 21 | 11 | 2 | 13 | 3 | .285 | .434 |
| OF | Butch Weis | L | 67 | 180 | 48 | 5 | 3 | 2 | 1.1 | 16 | 25 | 23 | 22 | 2 | 20 | 3 | .267 | .361 |
| OF | Jigger Statz | R | 38 | 148 | 38 | 6 | 3 | 2 | 1.4 | 21 | 14 | 11 | 16 | 4 | 1 | 0 | .257 | .378 |
| OF | Denver Grigsby | L | 51 | 137 | 35 | 5 | 0 | 0 | 0.0 | 20 | 20 | 19 | 12 | 1 | 8 | 0 | .255 | .292 |
| OF | Hack Miller | R | 24 | 86 | 24 | 3 | 2 | 2 | 2.3 | 10 | 9 | 2 | 9 | 0 | 3 | 2 | .279 | .430 |
| OF | Alex Metzler | L | 9 | 38 | 7 | 2 | 0 | 0 | 0.0 | 2 | 2 | 3 | 7 | 0 | 0 | 0 | .184 | .237 |
| OF | Joe Munson | L | 9 | 35 | 13 | 3 | 1 | 0 | 0.0 | 5 | 3 | 3 | 1 | 1 | 0 | 0 | .371 | .514 |
| OF | Chink Taylor | R | 8 | 6 | 0 | 0 | 0 | 0 | 0.0 | 2 | 0 | 0 | 0 | 0 | 2 | 0 | .000 | .000 |
| C | Mike Gonzalez | R | 70 | 197 | 52 | 13 | 1 | 3 | 1.5 | 26 | 18 | 13 | 15 | 2 | 9 | 2 | .264 | .386 |
| C | Bob O'Farrell | R | 17 | 22 | 4 | 0 | 1 | 0 | 0.0 | 2 | 3 | 2 | 5 | 0 | 12 | 4 | .182 | .273 |
| C | John Churry | R | 3 | 6 | 3 | 0 | 0 | 0 | 0.0 | 1 | 1 | 0 | 0 | 0 | 0 | 0 | .500 | .500 |
| PH | Mel Kerr | L | 1 | 0 | 0 | 0 | 0 | 0 | — | 1 | 0 | 0 | 0 | 0 | 0 | 0 | — | — |
| **PITCHERS** | | | | | | | | | | | | | | | | | | |
| P | Wilbur Cooper | R | 32 | 82 | 17 | 2 | 1 | 2 | 2.4 | 12 | 10 | 1 | 4 | 0 | 0 | 0 | .207 | .329 |
| P | Grover Alexander | R | 32 | 79 | 19 | 4 | 1 | 2 | 2.5 | 7 | 12 | 1 | 5 | 0 | 0 | 0 | .241 | .392 |
| P | Sheriff Blake | R | 36 | 79 | 12 | 1 | 0 | 0 | 0.0 | 4 | 7 | 2 | 21 | 0 | 0 | 0 | .152 | .165 |
| P | Tony Kaufmann. | R | 31 | 78 | 15 | 7 | 0 | 2 | 2.6 | 8 | 13 | 2 | 17 | 0 | 0 | 0 | .192 | .359 |
| P | Guy Bush | R | 42 | 57 | 11 | 0 | 0 | 0 | 0.0 | 3 | 2 | 2 | 5 | 0 | 0 | 0 | .193 | .193 |
| P | Percy Jones | R | 28 | 39 | 6 | 0 | 0 | 0 | 0.0 | 2 | 2 | 0 | 9 | 0 | 0 | 0 | .154 | .154 |
| P | Vic Keen | R | 30 | 25 | 6 | 1 | 0 | 0 | 0.0 | 2 | 1 | 0 | 8 | 0 | 0 | 0 | .240 | .280 |
| P | Elmer Jacobs | R | 18 | 13 | 3 | 0 | 0 | 0 | 0.0 | 0 | 0 | 0 | 0 | 0 | 0 | 0 | .231 | .231 |
| P | George Milstead | L | 5 | 7 | 0 | 0 | 0 | 0 | 0.0 | 0 | 0 | 0 | 4 | 0 | 0 | 0 | .000 | .000 |
| P | Herb Brett | R | 10 | 1 | 0 | 0 | 0 | 0 | 0.0 | 0 | 0 | 0 | 1 | 0 | 0 | 0 | .000 | .000 |
| P | Jumbo Brown | R | 2 | 1 | 0 | 0 | 0 | 0 | 0.0 | 0 | 0 | 0 | 0 | 0 | 0 | 0 | .000 | .000 |
| P | George Stueland | R | 2 | 1 | 1 | 0 | 0 | 0 | 0.0 | 0 | 0 | 0 | 0 | 0 | 0 | 0 | 1.000 | 1.000 |
| P | Bob Osborn | R | 1 | 0 | 0 | 0 | 0 | 0 | — | 0 | 0 | 0 | 0 | 0 | 0 | 0 | — | — |
| | TEAM TOTAL | | | 5353 | 1473 | 254 | 70 | 85 | 1.6 | 72 | 660 | 397 | 470 | 94 | 103 | 20 | .275 | .396 |

## INDIVIDUAL FIELDING

| POS | Player | T | G | PO | A | E | DP | TC/G | FA |
|---|---|---|---|---|---|---|---|---|---|
| 1B | C. Grimm | L | 139 | 1317 | 73 | 15 | 125 | 10.1 | .989 |
| | M. Gonzalez | R | 9 | 91 | 6 | 0 | 6 | 10.8 | 1.000 |
| | B. Friberg | R | 6 | 46 | 3 | 0 | 3 | 8.2 | 1.000 |
| | H. Freigau | R | 7 | 47 | 1 | 1 | 3 | 7.0 | .980 |
| | R. Michaels | R | 1 | 11 | 0 | 0 | 1 | 11.0 | 1.000 |
| | T. Kearns | R | 3 | 3 | 0 | 0 | 1 | 1.0 | 1.000 |
| 2B | S. Adams | R | 144 | 354 | 551 | 16 | 90 | 6.4 | .983 |
| | G. Staley | R | 7 | 19 | 28 | 1 | 7 | 6.9 | .979 |
| | B. Barrett | R | 4 | 7 | 7 | 0 | 1 | 3.5 | 1.000 |
| | R. Michaels | R | 1 | 1 | 0 | 0 | 0 | 1.0 | 1.000 |
| SS | Maranville | R | 74 | 162 | 261 | 20 | 51 | 6.0 | .955 |
| | I. McAuley | R | 37 | 94 | 93 | 10 | 21 | 5.3 | .949 |
| | P. Pittenger | R | 24 | 48 | 77 | 8 | 10 | 5.5 | .940 |
| | H. Freigau | R | 17 | 31 | 56 | 8 | 14 | 5.6 | .916 |
| | S. Adams | R | 5 | 13 | 22 | 0 | 5 | 7.0 | 1.000 |
| | R. Michaels | R | 1 | 1 | 0 | 0 | 0 | 1.0 | 1.000 |
| | B. Friberg | R | 2 | 0 | 0 | 1 | 0 | 0.5 | .000 |
| 3B | H. Freigau | R | 96 | 98 | 185 | 27 | 20 | 3.2 | .913 |
| | P. Pittenger | R | 24 | 23 | 50 | 3 | 3 | 3.2 | .961 |
| | B. Friberg | R | 26 | 24 | 40 | 8 | 2 | 2.8 | .889 |
| | R. Michaels | R | 15 | 13 | 26 | 1 | 3 | 2.7 | .975 |
| | B. Barrett | R | 6 | 6 | 2 | 0 | 2 | 1.3 | 1.000 |

| POS | Player | T | G | PO | A | E | DP | TC/G | FA |
|---|---|---|---|---|---|---|---|---|---|
| OF | C. Heathcote | L | 99 | 241 | 21 | 8 | 8 | 2.7 | .970 |
| | M. Brooks | R | 89 | 249 | 9 | 6 | 2 | 3.0 | .977 |
| | A. Jahn | R | 58 | 124 | 5 | 2 | 3 | 2.3 | .985 |
| | T. Griffith | R | 60 | 109 | 9 | 8 | 1 | 2.1 | .937 |
| | J. Statz | R | 37 | 112 | 3 | 7 | 0 | 3.3 | .943 |
| | D. Grigsby | R | 39 | 81 | 4 | 3 | 2 | 2.3 | .966 |
| | B. Weis | L | 46 | 78 | 3 | 3 | 0 | 1.8 | .964 |
| | H. Miller | R | 21 | 35 | 1 | 5 | 0 | 2.0 | .878 |
| | A. Metzler | R | 9 | 24 | 3 | 0 | 0 | 3.0 | 1.000 |
| | B. Friberg | R | 12 | 18 | 1 | 0 | 0 | 1.6 | 1.000 |
| | J. Munson | R | 9 | 17 | 1 | 0 | 1 | 2.0 | 1.000 |
| | C. Taylor | R | 2 | 2 | 0 | 0 | 0 | 1.0 | 1.000 |
| C | G. Hartnett | R | 110 | 409 | 114 | 23 | 15 | 5.0 | .958 |
| | M. Gonzalez | R | 50 | 155 | 31 | 2 | 7 | 3.8 | .989 |
| | B. O'Farrell | R | 3 | 6 | 0 | 0 | 0 | 2.0 | 1.000 |
| | J. Churry | R | 3 | 1 | 3 | 0 | 0 | 1.3 | 1.000 |

The most significant event of this season was the arrival of first baseman Charlie Grimm, who batted .306 and went on to become one of the greatest figures in Cub history, both as player and manager. Opening day, April 14, was the first regular-season Cub game broadcast on radio, as Alexander the Great scuttled the Pirates, 8–2, before 38,000 at Cubs Park.

Otherwise, it was a tumultuous season as the Cubs fell to last place for the first time ever. Three captains tried to steer the ship—Killefer, shortstop Rabbit Maranville, and finally George Gibson. The hard-drinking, fun-loving Maranville distinguished his brief managerial career by beating up a cab driver in Brooklyn, dumping water out of a hotel window onto the head of traveling secretary John O. Seys, and running through a Pullman car anointing the passengers from a spittoon. After the last incident, club president Bill Veeck, Sr., decided he was not the man for the job, which the Rabbit really never wanted anyway. Fortunately, better days were ahead.

## TEAM STATISTICS

| | W | L | PCT | GB | R | OR | Batting 2B | 3B | HR | BA | SA | SB | Fielding E | DP | FA | CG | B | Pitching SO | ShO | SV | ERA |
|---|---|---|---|---|---|---|---|---|---|---|---|---|---|---|---|---|---|---|---|---|---|
| T | 95 | 58 | .621 | | 912 | 715 | 316 | 105 | 77 | .307 | .448 | 159 | 224 | 171 | .964 | 77 | 387 | 386 | 2 | 13 | 3.87 |
| Y | 86 | 66 | .566 | 8.5 | 736 | 702 | 239 | 61 | 114 | .283 | .415 | 79 | 199 | 129 | .968 | 80 | 408 | 446 | 6 | 8 | 3.94 |
| 'N | 80 | 73 | .523 | 15 | 690 | 643 | 221 | 90 | 44 | .285 | .387 | 108 | 203 | 161 | .968 | 92 | 324 | 437 | 11 | 12 | 3.38 |
| 'L | 77 | 76 | .503 | 18 | 828 | 764 | 292 | 80 | 109 | .299 | .445 | 70 | 204 | 156 | .966 | 82 | 470 | 428 | 8 | 7 | 4.36 |
| OS | 70 | 83 | .458 | 25 | 708 | 802 | 260 | 70 | 41 | .292 | .390 | 77 | 221 | 145 | .964 | 77 | 458 | 351 | 5 | 4 | 4.39 |
| KN | 68 | 85 | .444 | 27 | 786 | 866 | 250 | 80 | 64 | .296 | .406 | 37 | 210 | 130 | .966 | 82 | 477 | 518 | 4 | 4 | 4.77 |
| HI | 68 | 85 | .444 | 27 | 812 | 930 | 288 | 58 | 100 | .295 | .425 | 48 | 211 | 147 | .966 | 69 | 444 | 371 | 8 | 9 | 5.02 |
| HI | 68 | 86 | .442 | 27.5 | 723 | 773 | 254 | 70 | 85 | .275 | .396 | 94 | 198 | 161 | .969 | 75 | 485 | 435 | 5 | 10 | 4.41 |
| LEAGUE TOTAL | | | | | 6195 | 6195 | 2120 | 614 | 634 | .292 | .414 | 672 | 1670 | 1200 | .966 | 634 | 3453 | 3372 | 49 | 67 | 4.27 |

## INDIVIDUAL PITCHING

| PITCHER | T | W | L | PCT | ERA | SV | G | GS | CG | IP | H | BB | SO | R | ER | ShO | H/9 | BB/9 | SO/9 |
|---|---|---|---|---|---|---|---|---|---|---|---|---|---|---|---|---|---|---|---|
| Grover Alexander | R | 15 | 11 | .577 | 3.39 | 0 | 32 | 30 | 20 | 236 | 270 | 29 | 63 | 106 | 89 | 1 | 10.30 | 1.11 | 2.40 |
| Sheriff Blake | R | 10 | 18 | .357 | 4.86 | 2 | 36 | 31 | 14 | 231.1 | 260 | 114 | 93 | 144 | 125 | 0 | 10.12 | 4.44 | 3.62 |
| Wilbur Cooper | L | 12 | 14 | .462 | 4.28 | 0 | 32 | 26 | 13 | 212.1 | 249 | 61 | 41 | 115 | 101 | 0 | 10.55 | 2.59 | 1.74 |
| Tony Kaufmann | R | 13 | 13 | .500 | 4.50 | 2 | 31 | 23 | 14 | 196 | 221 | 77 | 49 | 107 | 98 | 2 | 10.15 | 3.54 | 2.25 |
| Guy Bush | R | 6 | 13 | .316 | 4.30 | 4 | 42 | 15 | 5 | 182 | 213 | 52 | 76 | 102 | 87 | 0 | 10.53 | 2.57 | 3.76 |
| Percy Jones | L | 6 | 6 | .500 | 4.65 | 0 | 28 | 13 | 6 | 124 | 123 | 71 | 60 | 74 | 64 | 1 | 8.93 | 5.15 | 4.35 |
| Vic Keen | R | 2 | 6 | .250 | 6.26 | 1 | 30 | 8 | 1 | 83.1 | 125 | 41 | 19 | 61 | 58 | 0 | 13.50 | 4.43 | 2.05 |
| Elmer Jacobs | R | 2 | 3 | .400 | 5.17 | 1 | 18 | 4 | 1 | 55.2 | 63 | 22 | 19 | 37 | 32 | 1 | 10.19 | 3.56 | 3.07 |
| George Milstead | L | 1 | 1 | .500 | 3.00 | 0 | 5 | 3 | 1 | 21 | 26 | 8 | 7 | 12 | 7 | 0 | 11.14 | 3.43 | 3.00 |
| Herb Brett | R | 1 | 1 | .500 | 3.63 | 0 | 10 | 1 | 0 | 17.1 | 12 | 3 | 6 | 7 | 7 | 0 | 6.23 | 1.56 | 3.12 |
| Jumbo Brown | R | 0 | 0 | – | 3.00 | 0 | 2 | 0 | 0 | 6 | 5 | 4 | 0 | 5 | 2 | 0 | 7.50 | 6.00 | 0.00 |
| George Stueland | R | 0 | 0 | – | 3.00 | 0 | 2 | 0 | 0 | 3 | 2 | 3 | 2 | 1 | 1 | 0 | 6.00 | 9.00 | 6.00 |
| Bob Osborn | R | 0 | 0 | – | 0.00 | 0 | 1 | 0 | 0 | 2 | 6 | 0 | 0 | 2 | 0 | 0 | 27.00 | 0.00 | 0.00 |
| Barney Friberg | R | 0 | 0 | – | 0.00 | 0 | 0 | 0 | 0 | 0 | 0 | 0 | 0 | 0 | 0 | 0 | – | – | – |
| TEAM TOTAL | | 68 | 86 | .442 | 4.41 | 10 | 269 | 154 | 75 | 1370 | 1575 | 485 | 435 | 773 | 671 | 5 | 10.35 | 3.19 | 2.86 |

| MANAGER | W | L | PCT |
|---|---|---|---|
| Joe McCarthy | 82 | 72 | .532 |

| POS | Player | B | G | AB | H | 2B | 3B | HR | HR % | R | RBI | BB | SO | SB | Pinch Hit AB | Pinch Hit H | BA | SA |
|---|---|---|---|---|---|---|---|---|---|---|---|---|---|---|---|---|---|---|
| **REGULARS** | | | | | | | | | | | | | | | | | | |
| 1B | Charlie Grimm | L | 147 | 524 | 145 | 30 | 6 | 8 | 1.5 | 58 | 82 | 49 | 25 | 3 | 0 | 0 | .277 | .403 |
| 2B | Sparky Adams | R | 154 | 624 | 193 | 35 | 3 | 0 | 0.0 | 95 | 39 | 52 | 27 | 27 | 2 | 0 | .309 | .375 |
| SS | Jimmy Cooney | R | 141 | 513 | 129 | 18 | 5 | 1 | 0.2 | 52 | 47 | 23 | 10 | 11 | 0 | 0 | .251 | .312 |
| 3B | Howard Freigau | R | 140 | 508 | 137 | 27 | 7 | 3 | 0.6 | 51 | 51 | 43 | 42 | 6 | 4 | 2 | .270 | .368 |
| RF | Cliff Heathcote | L | 139 | 510 | 141 | 33 | 3 | 10 | 2.0 | 98 | 53 | 58 | 30 | 18 | 3 | 1 | .276 | .412 |
| CF | Hack Wilson | R | 142 | 529 | 170 | 36 | 8 | 21 | 4.0 | 97 | 109 | 69 | 61 | 10 | 2 | 1 | .321 | .539 |
| LF | Riggs Stephenson | R | 82 | 281 | 95 | 18 | 3 | 3 | 1.1 | 40 | 44 | 31 | 16 | 2 | 6 | 2 | .338 | .456 |
| C | Gabby Hartnett | R | 93 | 284 | 78 | 25 | 3 | 8 | 2.8 | 35 | 41 | 32 | 37 | 0 | 3 | 1 | .275 | .468 |
| **SUBSTITUTES** | | | | | | | | | | | | | | | | | | |
| 2B | Clyde Beck | R | 30 | 81 | 16 | 0 | 0 | 1 | 1.2 | 10 | 4 | 7 | 15 | 0 | 0 | 0 | .198 | .235 |
| 1B | Chick Tolson | R | 57 | 80 | 25 | 6 | 1 | 1 | 1.3 | 4 | 8 | 5 | 8 | 0 | 40 | 14 | .313 | .450 |
| SS | Red Shannon | B | 19 | 51 | 17 | 5 | 0 | 0 | 0.0 | 9 | 4 | 6 | 3 | 0 | 5 | 2 | .333 | .431 |
| UT | Hank Schreiber | R | 10 | 18 | 1 | 1 | 0 | 0 | 0.0 | 2 | 0 | 0 | 1 | 0 | 0 | 0 | .056 | .111 |
| 3B | Joe Graves | L | 2 | 5 | 0 | 0 | 0 | 0 | 0.0 | 0 | 0 | 0 | 1 | 0 | 0 | 0 | .000 | .000 |
| OF | Pete Scott | R | 77 | 189 | 54 | 13 | 1 | 3 | 1.6 | 34 | 34 | 22 | 31 | 3 | 4 | 1 | .286 | .413 |
| OF | Joe Kelly | L | 65 | 176 | 59 | 15 | 3 | 0 | 0.0 | 16 | 32 | 7 | 11 | 0 | 24 | 9 | .335 | .455 |
| OF | Joe Munson | L | 33 | 101 | 26 | 2 | 2 | 3 | 3.0 | 17 | 15 | 8 | 4 | 0 | 4 | 1 | .257 | .406 |
| OF | Mandy Brooks | R | 26 | 48 | 9 | 1 | 0 | 1 | 2.1 | 7 | 6 | 5 | 5 | 0 | 6 | 1 | .188 | .271 |
| C | Mike Gonzalez | R | 80 | 253 | 63 | 13 | 3 | 1 | 0.4 | 24 | 23 | 13 | 17 | 3 | 2 | 0 | .249 | .336 |
| C | John Churry | R | 2 | 4 | 0 | 0 | 0 | 0 | 0.0 | 0 | 0 | 1 | 2 | 0 | 1 | 0 | .000 | .000 |
| PH | Ralph Michaels | R | 2 | 0 | 0 | 0 | 0 | 0 | – | 1 | 0 | 0 | 0 | 0 | 0 | 0 | – | – |
| **PITCHERS** | | | | | | | | | | | | | | | | | | |
| P | Charlie Root | R | 42 | 91 | 13 | 1 | 0 | 1 | 1.1 | 8 | 7 | 2 | 25 | 0 | 0 | 0 | .143 | .187 |
| P | Sheriff Blake | R | 39 | 65 | 14 | 0 | 0 | 0 | 0.0 | 2 | 4 | 2 | 9 | 0 | 0 | 0 | .215 | .215 |
| P | Tony Kaufmann | R | 30 | 60 | 15 | 2 | 0 | 1 | 1.7 | 9 | 7 | 2 | 10 | 1 | 0 | 0 | .250 | .333 |
| P | Percy Jones | R | 30 | 50 | 13 | 4 | 0 | 0 | 0.0 | 4 | 6 | 5 | 15 | 0 | 0 | 0 | .260 | .340 |
| P | Guy Bush | R | 35 | 48 | 8 | 0 | 0 | 0 | 0.0 | 1 | 2 | 1 | 7 | 0 | 0 | 0 | .167 | .167 |
| P | Bob Osborn | R | 31 | 41 | 6 | 1 | 0 | 0 | 0.0 | 1 | 4 | 0 | 16 | 0 | 0 | 0 | .146 | .171 |
| P | Bill Piercy | R | 19 | 35 | 9 | 3 | 0 | 0 | 0.0 | 2 | 3 | 2 | 0 | 0 | 0 | 0 | .257 | .343 |
| P | George Milstead | L | 18 | 19 | 1 | 0 | 0 | 0 | 0.0 | 1 | 0 | 0 | 14 | 0 | 0 | 0 | .053 | .053 |
| P | Wilbur Cooper | R | 8 | 18 | 7 | 0 | 1 | 0 | 0.0 | 2 | 2 | 2 | 0 | 1 | 0 | 0 | .389 | .500 |
| P | Grover Alexander | R | 7 | 15 | 7 | 2 | 0 | 0 | 0.0 | 1 | 3 | 0 | 1 | 0 | 0 | 0 | .467 | .600 |
| P | Walter Huntzinger | R | 11 | 7 | 1 | 0 | 0 | 0 | 0.0 | 1 | 0 | 0 | 2 | 0 | 0 | 0 | .143 | .143 |
| P | Johnny Welch | L | 3 | 1 | 1 | 0 | 0 | 0 | 0.0 | 0 | 0 | 0 | 0 | 0 | 0 | 0 | 1.000 | 1.000 |
| TEAM TOTAL | | | | 5229 | 1453 | 291 | 49 | 66 | 1.3 | 68 | 630 | 445 | 447 | 85 | 106 | 35 | .278 | .390 |

## INDIVIDUAL FIELDING

| POS | Player | T | G | PO | A | E | DP | TC/G | FA |
|---|---|---|---|---|---|---|---|---|---|
| 1B | C. Grimm | L | 147 | 1416 | 68 | 18 | 139 | 10.2 | .988 |
| | C. Tolson | R | 13 | 104 | 7 | 1 | 11 | 8.6 | .991 |
| 2B | S. Adams | R | 136 | 324 | 485 | 29 | 93 | 6.2 | .965 |
| | C. Beck | R | 27 | 68 | 80 | 1 | 19 | 5.5 | .993 |
| | H. Schreiber | R | 1 | 2 | 1 | 0 | 0 | 3.0 | 1.000 |
| SS | J. Cooney | R | 141 | 344 | 492 | 24 | 107 | 6.1 | .972 |
| | R. Shannon | R | 13 | 25 | 42 | 3 | 6 | 5.4 | .957 |
| | S. Adams | R | 2 | 2 | 3 | 0 | 0 | 2.5 | 1.000 |
| | H. Schreiber | R | 3 | 1 | 4 | 0 | 0 | 1.7 | 1.000 |
| | H. Freigau | R | 2 | 1 | 2 | 0 | 0 | 1.5 | 1.000 |
| 3B | H. Freigau | R | 135 | 133 | 242 | 13 | 22 | 2.9 | .966 |
| | S. Adams | R | 19 | 12 | 35 | 2 | 4 | 2.6 | .959 |
| | H. Schreiber | R | 3 | 4 | 6 | 0 | 0 | 3.3 | 1.000 |
| | P. Scott | R | 1 | 2 | 2 | 1 | 1 | 5.0 | .800 |
| | J. Graves | R | 2 | 0 | 1 | 3 | 1 | 2.0 | .250 |

| POS | Player | T | G | PO | A | E | DP | TC/G | FA |
|---|---|---|---|---|---|---|---|---|---|
| OF | H. Wilson | R | 140 | 348 | 11 | 10 | 5 | 2.6 | .973 |
| | C. Heathcote | L | 133 | 306 | 22 | 5 | 8 | 2.5 | .985 |
| | Stephenson | R | 74 | 126 | 7 | 7 | 0 | 1.9 | .950 |
| | P. Scott | R | 59 | 114 | 7 | 4 | 2 | 2.1 | .968 |
| | J. Kelly | L | 39 | 58 | 3 | 3 | 0 | 1.6 | .953 |
| | J. Munson | R | 28 | 51 | 2 | 6 | 1 | 2.1 | .898 |
| | M. Brooks | R | 18 | 23 | 2 | 0 | 2 | 1.4 | 1.000 |
| | H. Freigau | R | 1 | 2 | 0 | 0 | 0 | 2.0 | 1.000 |
| C | G. Hartnett | R | 88 | 307 | 86 | 9 | 6 | 4.6 | .978 |
| | M. Gonzalez | R | 78 | 306 | 53 | 4 | 5 | 4.7 | .989 |
| | J. Churry | R | 1 | 5 | 0 | 0 | 0 | 5.0 | 1.000 |

The 1920s began to roar in earnest in 1926, a pivotal year for the Cubs. The main reason was the appointment of Joe McCarthy as manager. He embarked at once on a rebuilding and disciplinary program. Ace Grover Alexander, whose habits came into conflict with McCarthy, was dealt to the Cardinals on waivers.

New players on the roster included leftfielder Riggs Stephenson, pitcher Charlie Root, and centerfielder Hack Wilson, the hard-drinking home run slugger who best symbolized Cub baseball in the 1920s. Under McCarthy's tutelage, Guy Bush began pitching like a major leaguer, while Grimm and Hartnett started to reach their stride. Sparky Adams had rounded into the best leadoff man in the majors. With the tightened-up infield defense and improvements both at the plate and on the mound, McCarthy's Cubs made a dramatic turnaround, pulling home a solid fourth, only seven games out of first.

### TEAM  STATISTICS

|     | W | L | PCT | GB | R | OR | 2B | 3B | HR | BA | SA | SB | E | DP | FA | CG | B | SO | ShO | SV | ERA |
|-----|---|---|-----|----|---|----|----|----|----|----|----|----|---|----|----|----|---|----|----|----|-----|
| TL | 89 | 65 | .578 |  | 817 | 678 | 259 | 82 | 90 | .286 | .415 | 83 | 198 | 141 | .969 | 90 | 397 | 365 | 10 | 6 | 3.67 |
| IN | 87 | 67 | .565 | 2 | 747 | 651 | 242 | 120 | 35 | .290 | .400 | 51 | 183 | 160 | .972 | 88 | 324 | 424 | 14 | 8 | 3.42 |
| T | 84 | 69 | .549 | 4.5 | 769 | 689 | 243 | 106 | 44 | .285 | .396 | 91 | 220 | 161 | .965 | 83 | 455 | 387 | 12 | 18 | 3.67 |
| HI | 82 | 72 | .532 | 7 | 682 | 602 | 291 | 49 | 66 | .278 | .390 | 85 | 162 | 174 | .974 | 77 | 486 | 508 | 13 | 14 | 3.26 |
| Y | 74 | 77 | .490 | 13.5 | 663 | 668 | 214 | 58 | 73 | .278 | .384 | 94 | 186 | 150 | .970 | 61 | 427 | 419 | 4 | 15 | 3.77 |
| KN | 71 | 82 | .464 | 17.5 | 623 | 705 | 246 | 62 | 40 | .263 | .358 | 76 | 229 | 95 | .963 | 83 | 472 | 517 | 5 | 9 | 3.82 |
| OS | 66 | 86 | .434 | 22 | 624 | 719 | 209 | 62 | 16 | .277 | .350 | 81 | 208 | 150 | .967 | 60 | 455 | 408 | 9 | 9 | 4.03 |
| HI | 58 | 93 | .384 | 29.5 | 687 | 900 | 244 | 50 | 75 | .281 | .390 | 47 | 224 | 153 | .964 | 68 | 454 | 331 | 5 | 5 | 5.19 |
| EAGUE TOTAL |  |  |  |  | 5612 | 5612 | 1948 | 589 | 439 | .280 | .386 | 608 | 1610 | 1184 | .968 | 610 | 3470 | 3359 | 72 | 84 | 3.84 |

### INDIVIDUAL  PITCHING

| ITCHER | T | W | L | PCT | ERA | SV | G | GS | CG | IP | H | BB | SO | R | ER | ShO | H/9 | BB/9 | SO/9 |
|--------|---|---|---|-----|-----|----|----|----|----|----|---|----|----|---|----|----|-----|------|------|
| harlie Root | R | 18 | 17 | .514 | 2.82 | 2 | 42 | 32 | 21 | 271.1 | 267 | 62 | 127 | 104 | 85 | 2 | 8.86 | 2.06 | 4.21 |
| heriff Blake | R | 11 | 12 | .478 | 3.60 | 1 | 39 | 27 | 11 | 197.2 | 204 | 92 | 95 | 91 | 79 | 4 | 9.29 | 4.19 | 4.33 |
| ony Kaufmann | R | 9 | 7 | .563 | 3.02 | 2 | 26 | 21 | 14 | 169.2 | 169 | 44 | 52 | 71 | 57 | 1 | 8.96 | 2.33 | 2.76 |
| ercy Jones | L | 12 | 7 | .632 | 3.09 | 2 | 30 | 20 | 10 | 160.1 | 151 | 90 | 80 | 64 | 55 | 2 | 8.48 | 5.05 | 4.49 |
| uy Bush | R | 13 | 9 | .591 | 2.86 | 2 | 35 | 16 | 7 | 157.1 | 149 | 42 | 32 | 58 | 50 | 2 | 8.52 | 2.40 | 1.83 |
| ob Osborn | R | 6 | 5 | .545 | 3.63 | 1 | 31 | 15 | 6 | 136.1 | 157 | 58 | 43 | 64 | 55 | 0 | 10.36 | 3.83 | 2.84 |
| ll Piercy | R | 6 | 5 | .545 | 4.48 | 0 | 19 | 5 | 1 | 90.1 | 96 | 37 | 31 | 52 | 45 | 0 | 9.56 | 3.69 | 3.09 |
| eorge Milstead | L | 1 | 5 | .167 | 3.58 | 2 | 18 | 4 | 0 | 55.1 | 63 | 24 | 14 | 30 | 22 | 0 | 10.25 | 3.90 | 2.28 |
| ilbur Cooper | L | 2 | 1 | .667 | 4.42 | 0 | 8 | 8 | 3 | 55 | 65 | 21 | 18 | 32 | 27 | 2 | 10.64 | 3.44 | 2.95 |
| rover Alexander | R | 3 | 3 | .500 | 3.46 | 0 | 7 | 7 | 4 | 52 | 55 | 7 | 12 | 26 | 20 | 0 | 9.52 | 1.21 | 2.08 |
| alter Huntzinger | R | 1 | 1 | .500 | 0.94 | 2 | 11 | 0 | 0 | 28.2 | 26 | 8 | 4 | 8 | 3 | 0 | 8.16 | 2.51 | 1.26 |
| ohnny Welch | R | 0 | 0 | – | 2.08 | 0 | 3 | 0 | 0 | 4.1 | 5 | 1 | 0 | 2 | 1 | 0 | 10.38 | 2.08 | 0.00 |
| EAM TOTAL |  | 82 | 72 | .532 | 3.26 | 14 | 269 | 155 | 77 | 1378.1 | 1407 | 486 | 508 | 602 | 499 | 13 | 9.19 | 3.17 | 3.32 |

| MANAGER | W | L | PCT |
|---|---|---|---|
| Joe McCarthy | 85 | 68 | .556 |

| POS | Player | B | G | AB | H | 2B | 3B | HR | HR% | R | RBI | BB | SO | SB | Pinch Hit AB | Pinch Hit H | BA | SA |
|---|---|---|---|---|---|---|---|---|---|---|---|---|---|---|---|---|---|---|
| **REGULARS** | | | | | | | | | | | | | | | | | | |
| 1B | Charlie Grimm | L | 147 | 543 | 169 | 29 | 6 | 2 | 0.4 | 68 | 74 | 45 | 21 | 3 | 0 | 0 | .311 | .398 |
| 2B | Clyde Beck | R | 117 | 391 | 101 | 20 | 5 | 2 | 0.5 | 44 | 44 | 43 | 37 | 0 | 0 | 0 | .258 | .350 |
| SS | Woody English | R | 87 | 334 | 97 | 14 | 4 | 1 | 0.3 | 46 | 28 | 16 | 26 | 1 | 0 | 0 | .290 | .365 |
| 3B | Sparky Adams | R | 146 | 647 | 189 | 17 | 7 | 0 | 0.0 | 100 | 49 | 42 | 26 | 26 | 0 | 0 | .292 | .340 |
| RF | Earl Webb | L | 102 | 332 | 100 | 18 | 4 | 14 | 4.2 | 58 | 52 | 48 | 31 | 3 | 15 | 3 | .301 | .506 |
| CF | Hack Wilson | R | 146 | 551 | 175 | 30 | 12 | 30 | 5.4 | 119 | 129 | 71 | 70 | 13 | 0 | 0 | .318 | .579 |
| LF | Riggs Stephenson | R | 152 | 579 | 199 | 46 | 9 | 7 | 1.2 | 101 | 82 | 65 | 28 | 8 | 0 | 0 | .344 | .491 |
| C | Gabby Hartnett | R | 127 | 449 | 132 | 32 | 5 | 10 | 2.2 | 56 | 80 | 44 | 42 | 2 | 2 | 1 | .294 | .454 |
| **SUBSTITUTES** | | | | | | | | | | | | | | | | | | |
| 3B | Eddie Pick | B | 54 | 181 | 31 | 5 | 2 | 2 | 1.1 | 23 | 15 | 20 | 26 | 0 | 0 | 0 | .171 | .254 |
| SS | Jimmy Cooney | R | 33 | 132 | 32 | 2 | 0 | 0 | 0.0 | 16 | 6 | 8 | 7 | 1 | 0 | 0 | .242 | .258 |
| 3B | Howard Freigau | R | 30 | 86 | 20 | 5 | 0 | 0 | 0.0 | 12 | 10 | 9 | 10 | 0 | 0 | 0 | .233 | .291 |
| 1B | Chick Tolson | R | 39 | 54 | 16 | 4 | 0 | 2 | 3.7 | 6 | 17 | 4 | 9 | 0 | 27 | 7 | .296 | .481 |
| 3B | Elmer Yoter | R | 13 | 27 | 6 | 1 | 1 | 0 | 0.0 | 2 | 5 | 4 | 4 | 0 | 1 | 0 | .222 | .333 |
| 3B | Harry Wilke | R | 3 | 9 | 0 | 0 | 0 | 0 | 0.0 | 0 | 0 | 0 | 1 | 0 | 0 | 0 | .000 | .000 |
| OF | Cliff Heathcote | L | 83 | 228 | 67 | 12 | 4 | 2 | 0.9 | 28 | 25 | 20 | 16 | 6 | 17 | 0 | .294 | .408 |
| OF | Pete Scott | R | 71 | 156 | 49 | 18 | 1 | 0 | 0.0 | 28 | 21 | 19 | 18 | 1 | 31 | 7 | .314 | .442 |
| C | Mike Gonzalez | R | 39 | 108 | 26 | 4 | 1 | 1 | 0.9 | 15 | 15 | 10 | 8 | 1 | 3 | 1 | .241 | .324 |
| C | John Churry | R | 1 | 1 | 1 | 0 | 0 | 0 | 0.0 | 0 | 0 | 0 | 0 | 0 | 0 | 0 | 1.000 | 1.000 |
| PH | Fred Haney | R | 4 | 3 | 0 | 0 | 0 | 0 | 0.0 | 0 | 0 | 0 | 0 | 0 | 3 | 0 | .000 | .000 |
| PH | Tommy Sewell | L | 1 | 1 | 0 | 0 | 0 | 0 | 0.0 | 0 | 0 | 0 | 0 | 0 | 1 | 0 | .000 | .000 |
| **PITCHERS** | | | | | | | | | | | | | | | | | | |
| P | Charlie Root | R | 48 | 122 | 27 | 6 | 1 | 0 | 0.0 | 15 | 8 | 4 | 35 | 0 | 0 | 0 | .221 | .287 |
| P | Sheriff Blake | R | 32 | 83 | 16 | 0 | 0 | 0 | 0.0 | 2 | 3 | 1 | 10 | 0 | 0 | 0 | .193 | .193 |
| P | Hal Carlson | R | 27 | 67 | 11 | 0 | 0 | 0 | 0.0 | 1 | 9 | 0 | 7 | 0 | 0 | 0 | .164 | .164 |
| P | Guy Bush | R | 36 | 65 | 8 | 1 | 0 | 0 | 0.0 | 2 | 1 | 1 | 10 | 0 | 0 | 0 | .123 | .138 |
| P | Jim Brillheart | R | 32 | 44 | 1 | 0 | 0 | 0 | 0.0 | 1 | 1 | 2 | 19 | 0 | 0 | 0 | .023 | .023 |
| P | Percy Jones | R | 30 | 40 | 14 | 1 | 0 | 0 | 0.0 | 3 | 4 | 0 | 11 | 0 | 0 | 0 | .350 | .375 |
| P | Bob Osborn | R | 24 | 39 | 8 | 0 | 1 | 0 | 0.0 | 1 | 4 | 0 | 14 | 0 | 0 | 0 | .205 | .256 |
| P | Tony Kaufmann | R | 9 | 16 | 5 | 0 | 0 | 1 | 6.3 | 2 | 6 | 4 | 4 | 0 | 0 | 0 | .313 | .500 |
| P | Art Nehf | L | 8 | 7 | 3 | 1 | 0 | 0 | 0.0 | 0 | 3 | 1 | 0 | 0 | 0 | 0 | .429 | .571 |
| P | Lefty Weinert | L | 5 | 5 | 1 | 0 | 0 | 0 | 0.0 | 1 | 0 | 1 | 1 | 0 | 0 | 0 | .200 | .200 |
| P | Luther Roy | R | 11 | 3 | 1 | 0 | 0 | 0 | 0.0 | 0 | 1 | 0 | 0 | 0 | 0 | 0 | .333 | .333 |
| P | Wayland Dean | L | 2 | 0 | 0 | 0 | 0 | 0 | – | 0 | 0 | 0 | 0 | 0 | 0 | 0 | – | – |
| P | Henry Grampp | R | 0 | 0 | 0 | 0 | 0 | 0 | – | 0 | 0 | 0 | 0 | 0 | 0 | 0 | – | – |
| P | Johnny Welch | L | 1 | 0 | 0 | 0 | 0 | 0 | – | 0 | 0 | 0 | 0 | 0 | 0 | 0 | – | – |
| TEAM TOTAL | | | | 5303 | 1505 | 266 | 63 | 74 | 1.4 | 75 | 692 | 481 | 492 | 65 | 100 | 19 | .284 | .400 |

## INDIVIDUAL FIELDING

| POS | Player | T | G | PO | A | E | DP | TC/G | FA |
|---|---|---|---|---|---|---|---|---|---|
| 1B | C. Grimm | L | 147 | 1437 | 99 | 15 | 117 | 10.6 | .990 |
| | C. Tolson | R | 8 | 74 | 5 | 0 | 3 | 9.9 | 1.000 |
| 2B | C. Beck | R | 99 | 238 | 358 | 19 | 62 | 6.2 | .969 |
| | S. Adams | R | 60 | 149 | 194 | 2 | 34 | 5.8 | .994 |
| | E. Pick | R | 1 | 1 | 2 | 0 | 0 | 3.0 | 1.000 |
| SS | W. English | R | 84 | 177 | 281 | 29 | 47 | 5.8 | .940 |
| | S. Adams | R | 40 | 82 | 142 | 10 | 23 | 5.9 | .957 |
| | J. Cooney | R | 33 | 75 | 102 | 5 | 13 | 5.5 | .973* |
| | C. Beck | R | 1 | 2 | 1 | 0 | 0 | 3.0 | 1.000 |
| 3B | S. Adams | R | 53 | 45 | 107 | 6 | 12 | 3.0 | .962 |
| | E. Pick | R | 49 | 60 | 71 | 13 | 9 | 2.9 | .910 |
| | H. Freigau | R | 30 | 22 | 46 | 9 | 3 | 2.6 | .883 |
| | C. Beck | R | 17 | 27 | 43 | 5 | 5 | 4.4 | .933 |
| | Stephenson | R | 6 | 12 | 7 | 2 | 2 | 3.5 | .905 |
| | E. Yoter | R | 11 | 4 | 14 | 1 | 0 | 1.7 | .947 |
| | H. Wilke | R | 3 | 2 | 5 | 0 | 0 | 2.3 | 1.000 |
| | W. English | R | 1 | 2 | 4 | 0 | 0 | 6.0 | 1.000 |

| POS | Player | T | G | PO | A | E | DP | TC/G | FA |
|---|---|---|---|---|---|---|---|---|---|
| OF | H. Wilson | R | 146 | 400 | 13 | 14 | 3 | 2.9 | .967 |
| | Stephenson | R | 146 | 297 | 18 | 8 | 5 | 2.2 | .975 |
| | E. Webb | R | 86 | 171 | 14 | 8 | 5 | 2.2 | .959 |
| | C. Heathcote | L | 57 | 136 | 13 | 2 | 7 | 2.6 | .987 |
| | P. Scott | R | 36 | 70 | 3 | 1 | 1 | 2.1 | .986 |
| | E. Pick | R | 1 | 0 | 0 | 0 | 0 | 0.0 | .000 |
| C | G. Hartnett | R | 125 | 479 | 99 | 16 | 21 | 4.8 | .973 |
| | M. Gonzalez | R | 36 | 136 | 29 | 1 | 6 | 4.6 | .994 |
| | J. Churry | R | 1 | 2 | 0 | 0 | 0 | 2.0 | 1.000 |

Three of the most memorable dates in Cub history occurred in May 1927. On May 14, Guy Bush went the distance as the Cubs beat the Braves, 7–2, in 18 innings. Three days later, they edged the same club, 4–3, in 22 innings, for the longest game—in innings—in Cub annals. In the first game of a Memorial Day doubleheader, Cub shortstop Jimmy Cooney became the last NL player to complete an unassisted triple play, in a 7–6 victory at Pittsburgh. Eight days later he was traded to the Phillies for pitcher Hal Carlson. Cooney's replacement, Woody English, quickly achieved stardom.

The Cubs zoomed into contention with a 12-game winning streak in June, and were at the top for several weeks. However, a September collapse (sound familiar?) dropped them to fourth place.

In his first complete season, Riggs Stephenson paced the club with a .344 mark while Hack Wilson became the first Cub to hit 30 home runs, and Charlie Root became the last Chicago pitcher—Cubs or White Sox—to win 25 games, with a 26–15 log. In a Wrigley Field that had just been double-decked, the Cubs were the first NL team to draw an attendance of more than one million, as 1,163,347 patrons paid their way in.

### TEAM STATISTICS

|     | W | L | PCT | GB | R | OR | 2B | 3B | HR | BA | SA | SB | E | DP | FA | CG | B | SO | ShO | SV | ERA |
|-----|---|---|-----|----|---|----|----|----|----|----|----|----|---|----|----|----|---|----|-----|----|-----|
| IT | 94 | 60 | .610 | | 817 | 659 | 258 | 78 | 54 | .305 | .412 | 65 | 187 | 130 | .969 | 90 | 418 | 435 | 10 | 10 | 3.66 |
| TL | 92 | 61 | .601 | 1.5 | 754 | 665 | 264 | 79 | 84 | .278 | .408 | 110 | 213 | 170 | .966 | 89 | 363 | 394 | 14 | 11 | 3.57 |
| Y | 92 | 62 | .597 | 2 | 817 | 720 | 251 | 62 | 109 | .297 | .427 | 73 | 195 | 160 | .969 | 65 | 453 | 442 | 7 | 16 | 3.97 |
| HI | 85 | 68 | .556 | 8.5 | 750 | 661 | 266 | 63 | 74 | .284 | .400 | 65 | 181 | 152 | .971 | 75 | 514 | 465 | 11 | 5 | 3.65 |
| IN | 75 | 78 | .490 | 18.5 | 643 | 653 | 222 | 77 | 29 | .278 | .367 | 62 | 165 | 160 | .973 | 87 | 316 | 407 | 12 | 12 | 3.54 |
| KN | 65 | 88 | .425 | 28.5 | 541 | 619 | 195 | 74 | 39 | .253 | .342 | 106 | 229 | 117 | .963 | 74 | 418 | 574 | 7 | 10 | 3.36 |
| OS | 60 | 94 | .390 | 34 | 651 | 771 | 216 | 61 | 37 | .279 | .363 | 100 | 231 | 130 | .963 | 52 | 468 | 402 | 3 | 11 | 4.22 |
| HI | 51 | 103 | .331 | 43 | 678 | 903 | 216 | 46 | 57 | .280 | .370 | 68 | 169 | 152 | .972 | 81 | 462 | 377 | 5 | 6 | 5.35 |
| LEAGUE TOTAL | | | | | 5651 | 5651 | 1888 | 540 | | 483 | .282 | .386 | 649 | 1570 | 1171 | .969 | 613 | 3412 | 3496 | 69 | 81 | 3.91 |

### INDIVIDUAL PITCHING

| PITCHER | T | W | L | PCT | ERA | SV | G | GS | CG | IP | H | BB | SO | R | ER | ShO | H/9 | BB/9 | SO/9 |
|---------|---|---|---|-----|-----|----|---|----|----|----|---|----|----|---|----|-----|-----|------|------|
| Charlie Root | R | 26 | 15 | .634 | 3.76 | 2 | 48 | 36 | 21 | 309 | 296 | 117 | 145 | 148 | 129 | 4 | 8.62 | 3.41 | 4.22 |
| Sheriff Blake | R | 13 | 14 | .481 | 3.29 | 0 | 32 | 27 | 13 | 224.1 | 238 | 82 | 64 | 101 | 82 | 2 | 9.55 | 3.29 | 2.57 |
| Guy Bush | R | 10 | 10 | .500 | 3.03 | 2 | 36 | 22 | 9 | 193.1 | 177 | 79 | 62 | 76 | 65 | 1 | 8.24 | 3.68 | 2.89 |
| Hal Carlson | R | 12 | 8 | .600 | 3.17 | 0 | 27 | 22 | 15 | 184.1 | 201 | 27 | 27 | 73 | 65 | 2 | 9.81 | 1.32 | 1.32 |
| Jim Brillheart | L | 4 | 2 | .667 | 4.13 | 0 | 32 | 12 | 4 | 128.2 | 140 | 38 | 36 | 67 | 59 | 0 | 9.79 | 2.66 | 2.52 |
| Percy Jones | L | 7 | 8 | .467 | 4.07 | 0 | 30 | 11 | 5 | 112.2 | 123 | 72 | 37 | 67 | 51 | 1 | 9.83 | 5.75 | 2.96 |
| Bob Osborn | R | 5 | 5 | .500 | 4.18 | 0 | 24 | 12 | 2 | 107.2 | 125 | 48 | 45 | 54 | 50 | 0 | 10.45 | 4.01 | 3.76 |
| Tony Kaufmann | R | 3 | 3 | .500 | 6.41 | 0 | 9 | 6 | 3 | 53.1 | 75 | 19 | 21 | 44 | 38 | 0 | 12.66 | 3.21 | 3.54 |
| Art Nehf | L | 1 | 1 | .500 | 1.37 | 1 | 8 | 2 | 2 | 26.1 | 25 | 9 | 12 | 5 | 4 | 1 | 8.54 | 3.08 | 4.10 |
| Luther Roy | R | 3 | 1 | .750 | 2.29 | 0 | 11 | 0 | 0 | 19.2 | 14 | 11 | 5 | 9 | 5 | 0 | 6.41 | 5.03 | 2.29 |
| Lefty Weinert | L | 1 | 1 | .500 | 4.58 | 0 | 5 | 3 | 1 | 19.2 | 21 | 6 | 5 | 13 | 10 | 0 | 9.61 | 2.75 | 2.29 |
| Henry Grampp | R | 0 | 0 | – | 9.00 | 0 | 2 | 0 | 0 | 3 | 4 | 1 | 3 | 3 | 3 | 0 | 12.00 | 3.00 | 9.00 |
| Wayland Dean | R | 0 | 0 | – | 0.00 | 0 | 2 | 0 | 0 | 2 | 0 | 2 | 2 | 0 | 0 | 0 | 0.00 | 9.00 | 9.00 |
| Johnny Welch | R | 0 | 0 | – | 9.00 | 0 | 1 | 0 | 0 | 1 | 0 | 3 | 1 | 1 | 1 | 0 | 0.00 | 27.00 | 9.00 |
| TEAM TOTAL | | 85 | 68 | .556 | 3.65 | 5 | 267 | 153 | 75 | 1385 | 1439 | 514 | 465 | 661 | 562 | 11 | 9.35 | 3.34 | 3.02 |

| MANAGER | W | L | PCT |
|---|---|---|---|
| Joe McCarthy | 91 | 63 | .591 |

| POS | Player | B | G | AB | H | 2B | 3B | HR | HR % | R | RBI | BB | SO | SB | Pinch Hit AB | Pinch Hit H | BA | SA |
|---|---|---|---|---|---|---|---|---|---|---|---|---|---|---|---|---|---|---|
| **REGULARS** | | | | | | | | | | | | | | | | | | |
| 1B | Charlie Grimm | L | 147 | 547 | 161 | 25 | 5 | 5 | 0.9 | 67 | 62 | 39 | 20 | 7 | 0 | 0 | .294 | .386 |
| 2B | Freddie Maguire | R | 140 | 574 | 160 | 24 | 7 | 1 | 0.2 | 67 | 41 | 25 | 38 | 6 | 2 | 1 | .279 | .350 |
| SS | Woody English | R | 116 | 475 | 142 | 22 | 4 | 2 | 0.4 | 68 | 34 | 30 | 28 | 4 | 0 | 0 | .299 | .375 |
| 3B | Clyde Beck | R | 131 | 483 | 124 | 18 | 4 | 3 | 0.6 | 72 | 52 | 58 | 58 | 3 | 1 | 1 | .257 | .329 |
| RF | Kiki Cuyler | R | 133 | 499 | 142 | 25 | 9 | 17 | 3.4 | 92 | 79 | 51 | 61 | 37 | 5 | 0 | .285 | .473 |
| CF | Hack Wilson | R | 145 | 520 | 163 | 32 | 9 | 31 | 6.0 | 89 | 120 | 77 | 94 | 4 | 2 | 0 | .313 | .588 |
| LF | Riggs Stephenson | R | 137 | 512 | 166 | 36 | 9 | 8 | 1.6 | 75 | 90 | 68 | 29 | 8 | 2 | 1 | .324 | .477 |
| C | Gabby Hartnett | R | 120 | 388 | 117 | 26 | 9 | 14 | 3.6 | 61 | 57 | 65 | 32 | 3 | 2 | 0 | .302 | .523 |
| **SUBSTITUTES** | | | | | | | | | | | | | | | | | | |
| 3B | Johnny Butler | R | 62 | 174 | 47 | 7 | 0 | 0 | 0.0 | 17 | 16 | 19 | 7 | 2 | 1 | 0 | .270 | .310 |
| 23 | Norm McMillan | R | 49 | 123 | 27 | 2 | 2 | 1 | 0.8 | 11 | 12 | 13 | 19 | 0 | 9 | 1 | .220 | .293 |
| 1B | Joe Kelly | L | 32 | 52 | 11 | 1 | 0 | 1 | 1.9 | 3 | 7 | 1 | 3 | 0 | 21 | 3 | .212 | .288 |
| 3B | Elmer Yoter | R | 1 | 0 | 0 | 0 | 0 | 0 | – | 0 | 0 | 0 | 0 | 0 | 0 | 0 | – | – |
| OF | Earl Webb | L | 62 | 140 | 35 | 7 | 3 | 3 | 2.1 | 22 | 23 | 14 | 17 | 0 | 24 | 8 | .250 | .407 |
| OF | Cliff Heathcote | L | 67 | 137 | 39 | 8 | 0 | 3 | 2.2 | 26 | 18 | 17 | 12 | 6 | 21 | 5 | .285 | .409 |
| C | Mike Gonzalez | R | 49 | 158 | 43 | 9 | 2 | 1 | 0.6 | 12 | 21 | 12 | 7 | 2 | 4 | 0 | .272 | .373 |
| PH | Johnny Moore | L | 4 | 4 | 0 | 0 | 0 | 0 | 0.0 | 0 | 0 | 0 | 0 | 0 | 4 | 0 | .000 | .000 |
| PH | Ray Jacobs | R | 2 | 2 | 0 | 0 | 0 | 0 | 0.0 | 0 | 0 | 0 | 1 | 0 | 2 | 0 | .000 | .000 |
| **PITCHERS** | | | | | | | | | | | | | | | | | | |
| P | Pat Malone | L | 42 | 95 | 18 | 3 | 0 | 1 | 1.1 | 8 | 11 | 4 | 21 | 0 | 0 | 0 | .189 | .253 |
| P | Sheriff Blake | L | 35 | 88 | 19 | 1 | 0 | 0 | 0.0 | 10 | 5 | 1 | 13 | 0 | 0 | 0 | .216 | .227 |
| P | Guy Bush | R | 42 | 73 | 6 | 0 | 0 | 0 | 0.0 | 3 | 2 | 2 | 18 | 0 | 0 | 0 | .082 | .082 |
| P | Charlie Root | R | 40 | 73 | 13 | 5 | 0 | 0 | 0.0 | 5 | 5 | 2 | 18 | 0 | 0 | 0 | .178 | .247 |
| P | Art Nehf | L | 31 | 58 | 11 | 0 | 1 | 1 | 1.7 | 4 | 3 | 7 | 8 | 0 | 0 | 0 | .190 | .276 |
| P | Percy Jones | R | 39 | 56 | 11 | 0 | 0 | 0 | 0.0 | 1 | 5 | 2 | 11 | 1 | 0 | 0 | .196 | .196 |
| P | Hal Carlson | R | 20 | 19 | 5 | 0 | 0 | 0 | 0.0 | 1 | 1 | 0 | 2 | 0 | 0 | 0 | .263 | .263 |
| P | Ed Holley | R | 13 | 5 | 0 | 0 | 0 | 0 | 0.0 | 0 | 1 | 1 | 0 | 0 | 0 | 0 | .000 | .000 |
| P | Ben Tincup | L | 2 | 3 | 0 | 0 | 0 | 0 | 0.0 | 0 | 0 | 0 | 0 | 0 | 0 | 0 | .000 | .000 |
| P | Lefty Weinert | L | 10 | 2 | 0 | 0 | 0 | 0 | 0.0 | 0 | 0 | 0 | 0 | 0 | 0 | 0 | .000 | .000 |
| P | Johnny Welch | L | 3 | 0 | 0 | 0 | 0 | 0 | – | 0 | 0 | 0 | 0 | 0 | 0 | 0 | – | – |
| | TEAM TOTAL | | | 5260 | 1460 | 251 | 64 | 92 | 1.7 | 71 | 665 | 508 | 517 | 83 | 100 | 20 | .278 | .402 |

## INDIVIDUAL FIELDING

| POS | Player | T | G | PO | A | E | DP | TC/G | FA |
|---|---|---|---|---|---|---|---|---|---|
| 1B | C. Grimm | L | 147 | 1458 | 70 | 10 | 147 | 10.5 | **.993** |
| | J. Kelly | L | 10 | 105 | 6 | 3 | 8 | 11.4 | .974 |
| 2B | F. Maguire | R | 138 | **410** | **524** | 23 | **126** | 6.9 | .976 |
| | N. McMillan | R | 19 | 32 | 53 | 2 | 12 | 4.6 | .977 |
| | C. Beck | R | 1 | 5 | 4 | 0 | 1 | 9.0 | 1.000 |
| SS | W. English | R | 114 | 245 | 382 | 36 | 85 | 5.8 | .946 |
| | C. Beck | R | 47 | 88 | 139 | 8 | 28 | 5.0 | .966 |
| | J. Butler | R | 2 | 2 | 4 | 1 | 1 | 3.5 | .857 |
| 3B | C. Beck | R | 87 | 74 | 156 | 10 | 24 | 2.8 | .958 |
| | J. Butler | R | 59 | 51 | 120 | 9 | 9 | 3.1 | .950 |
| | N. McMillan | R | 18 | 12 | 31 | 3 | 1 | 2.6 | .935 |
| | E. Yoter | R | 1 | 0 | 0 | 0 | 0 | 0.0 | .000 |
| | W. English | R | 2 | 0 | 0 | 0 | 0 | 0.0 | .000 |

| POS | Player | T | G | PO | A | E | DP | TC/G | FA |
|---|---|---|---|---|---|---|---|---|---|
| OF | H. Wilson | R | 143 | 321 | 11 | 14 | 2 | 2.4 | .960 |
| | Stephenson | R | 135 | 268 | 10 | 5 | 1 | 2.1 | .982 |
| | K. Cuyler | R | 127 | 257 | 18 | 5 | 3 | 2.2 | .982 |
| | C. Heathcote | L | 39 | 67 | 5 | 2 | 0 | 1.9 | .973 |
| | E. Webb | R | 31 | 65 | 4 | 1 | 0 | 2.3 | .986 |
| C | G. Hartnett | R | 118 | 455 | **103** | 6 | 14 | **4.8** | **.989** |
| | M. Gonzalez | R | 45 | 198 | 35 | 4 | 8 | 5.3 | .983 |

In 1928 the Cubs were solidified even more by the addition of outfielder Kiki Cuyler and pitcher Pat Malone. Although the Cubs had to part with Sparky Adams in order to get Cuyler from Pittsburgh, he proved to be worth more than the price. Together with Wilson and Stephenson, Cuyler helped form what was undoubtedly the greatest outfield in Cub history. He also became the first Cub to lead the league in stolen bases in 22 years. Malone, after losing his first seven decisions, settled down into an 18-game winner.

A 13-game winning streak in May gave the Cubs the momentum to stay in contention the entire year. In a tight battle with the Cardinals and the Giants, the Cubs finished a threatening third, only four games behind pennant-winning St. Louis. Woody English, in his first full season, hit .299 while Gabby Hartnett crossed the .300 level for the first time. Guy Bush had his best season yet, and Art Nehf was a pleasant surprise, but Charlie Root, after his banner season, slipped to 14–18. A year more typical of Root might have made the difference.

## TEAM STATISTICS

| | W | L | PCT | GB | R | OR | 2B | 3B | HR | BA | SA | SB | E | DP | FA | CG | B | SO | ShO | SV | ERA |
|---|---|---|---|---|---|---|---|---|---|---|---|---|---|---|---|---|---|---|---|---|---|
| | | | | | | | Batting | | | | | | Fielding | | | | | Pitching | | | |
| TL | 95 | 59 | .617 | | 807 | 636 | 292 | 70 | 113 | .281 | .425 | 82 | 160 | 134 | .974 | 83 | 399 | 422 | 4 | 21 | 3.38 |
| Y | 93 | 61 | .604 | 2 | 807 | 653 | 276 | 59 | 118 | .293 | .430 | 62 | 178 | 175 | .972 | 79 | 405 | 399 | 7 | 16 | 3.67 |
| HI | 91 | 63 | .591 | 4 | 714 | 615 | 251 | 64 | 92 | .278 | .402 | 83 | 156 | 176 | .975 | 75 | 508 | 531 | 12 | 14 | 3.40 |
| T | 85 | 67 | .559 | 9 | 837 | 704 | 246 | 100 | 52 | .309 | .421 | 64 | 201 | 123 | .967 | 82 | 446 | 385 | 8 | 11 | 3.95 |
| N | 78 | 74 | .513 | 16 | 648 | 686 | 229 | 67 | 32 | .280 | .368 | 83 | 162 | 194 | .974 | 68 | 410 | 355 | 11 | 11 | 3.94 |
| KN | 77 | 76 | .503 | 17.5 | 665 | 640 | 229 | 70 | 66 | .266 | .374 | 81 | 217 | 113 | .965 | 75 | 468 | 551 | 16 | 15 | 3.25 |
| OS | 50 | 103 | .327 | 44.5 | 631 | 878 | 241 | 41 | 52 | .275 | .367 | 60 | 193 | 141 | .969 | 54 | 524 | 343 | 1 | 6 | 4.83 |
| HI | 43 | 109 | .283 | 51 | 660 | 957 | 257 | 47 | 85 | .267 | .382 | 53 | 181 | 171 | .971 | 42 | 671 | 403 | 4 | 11 | 5.52 |
| AGUE TOTAL | | | | | 5769 | 5769 | 2021 | 518 | 610 | .281 | .397 | 568 | 1448 | 1227 | .971 | 558 | 3831 | 3389 | 63 | 105 | 3.98 |

## INDIVIDUAL  PITCHING

| TCHER | T | W | L | PCT | ERA | SV | G | GS | CG | IP | H | BB | SO | R | ER | ShO | H/9 | BB/9 | SO/9 |
|---|---|---|---|---|---|---|---|---|---|---|---|---|---|---|---|---|---|---|---|
| at Malone | R | 18 | 13 | .581 | 2.84 | 2 | 42 | 25 | 16 | 250.2 | 218 | 99 | 155 | 99 | 79 | 2 | 7.83 | 3.55 | 5.57 |
| heriff Blake | R | 17 | 11 | .607 | 2.47 | 1 | 34 | 29 | 16 | 240.2 | 209 | 101 | 78 | 80 | 66 | 4 | 7.82 | 3.78 | 2.92 |
| harlie Root | R | 14 | 18 | .438 | 3.57 | 2 | 40 | 30 | 13 | 237 | 214 | 73 | 122 | 109 | 94 | 1 | 8.13 | 2.77 | 4.63 |
| uy Bush | R | 15 | 6 | .714 | 3.83 | 2 | 42 | 24 | 9 | 204.1 | 229 | 86 | 61 | 104 | 87 | 2 | 10.09 | 3.79 | 2.69 |
| rt Nehf | L | 13 | 7 | .650 | 2.65 | 0 | 31 | 21 | 10 | 176.2 | 190 | 52 | 40 | 62 | 52 | 2 | 9.68 | 2.65 | 2.04 |
| ercy Jones | L | 10 | 6 | .625 | 4.03 | 3 | 39 | 18 | 9 | 154 | 164 | 56 | 41 | 80 | 69 | 1 | 9.58 | 3.27 | 2.40 |
| al Carlson | R | 3 | 2 | .600 | 5.91 | 4 | 20 | 5 | 2 | 56.1 | 74 | 15 | 11 | 42 | 37 | 0 | 11.82 | 2.40 | 1.76 |
| d Holley | R | 0 | 0 | – | 3.77 | 0 | 13 | 1 | 0 | 31 | 31 | 16 | 10 | 15 | 13 | 0 | 9.00 | 4.65 | 2.90 |
| efty Weinert | L | 1 | 0 | 1.000 | 5.29 | 0 | 10 | 1 | 0 | 17 | 24 | 9 | 8 | 10 | 10 | 0 | 12.71 | 4.76 | 4.24 |
| en Tincup | R | 0 | 0 | – | 7.00 | 0 | 2 | 0 | 0 | 9 | 14 | 1 | 3 | 7 | 7 | 0 | 14.00 | 1.00 | 3.00 |
| ohnny Welch | R | 0 | 0 | – | 15.75 | 0 | 3 | 0 | 0 | 4 | 13 | 0 | 2 | 7 | 7 | 0 | 29.25 | 0.00 | 4.50 |
| EAM TOTAL | | 91 | 63 | .591 | 3.40 | 14 | 276 | 154 | 75 | 1380.2 | 1380 | 508 | 531 | 615 | 521 | 12 | 9.00 | 3.31 | 3.46 |

| MANAGER | W | L | PCT |
|---|---|---|---|
| Joe McCarthy | 98 | 54 | .645 |

| POS | Player | B | G | AB | H | 2B | 3B | HR | HR % | R | RBI | BB | SO | SB | Pinch Hit AB | Pinch Hit H | BA | SA |
|---|---|---|---|---|---|---|---|---|---|---|---|---|---|---|---|---|---|---|
| **REGULARS** | | | | | | | | | | | | | | | | | | |
| 1B | Charlie Grimm | L | 120 | 463 | 138 | 28 | 3 | 10 | 2.2 | 66 | 91 | 42 | 25 | 3 | 0 | 0 | .298 | .436 |
| 2B | Rogers Hornsby | R | 156 | 602 | 229 | 47 | 8 | 39 | 6.5 | 156 | 149 | 87 | 65 | 2 | 0 | 0 | .380 | .679 |
| SS | Woody English | R | 144 | 608 | 168 | 29 | 3 | 1 | 0.2 | 131 | 52 | 68 | 50 | 13 | 0 | 0 | .276 | .339 |
| 3B | Norm McMillan | R | 124 | 495 | 134 | 35 | 5 | 5 | 1.0 | 77 | 55 | 36 | 43 | 13 | 3 | 2 | .271 | .392 |
| RF | Kiki Cuyler | R | 139 | 509 | 183 | 29 | 7 | 15 | 2.9 | 111 | 102 | 66 | 56 | 43 | 9 | 4 | .360 | .532 |
| CF | Hack Wilson | R | 150 | 574 | 198 | 30 | 5 | 39 | 6.8 | 135 | 159 | 78 | 83 | 3 | 0 | 0 | .345 | .618 |
| LF | Riggs Stephenson | R | 136 | 495 | 179 | 36 | 6 | 17 | 3.4 | 91 | 110 | 67 | 21 | 10 | 5 | 3 | .362 | .562 |
| C | Zack Taylor | R | 64 | 215 | 59 | 16 | 3 | 1 | 0.5 | 29 | 31 | 19 | 18 | 0 | 0 | 0 | .274 | .391 |
| **SUBSTITUTES** | | | | | | | | | | | | | | | | | | |
| 3S | Clyde Beck | R | 54 | 190 | 40 | 7 | 0 | 0 | 0.0 | 28 | 9 | 19 | 24 | 3 | 5 | 1 | .211 | .247 |
| 1B | Chick Tolson | R | 32 | 109 | 28 | 5 | 0 | 1 | 0.9 | 13 | 19 | 9 | 16 | 0 | 0 | 0 | .257 | .330 |
| UT | Footsie Blair | L | 26 | 72 | 23 | 5 | 0 | 1 | 1.4 | 10 | 8 | 3 | 4 | 1 | 3 | 2 | .319 | .431 |
| OF | Cliff Heathcote | L | 82 | 224 | 70 | 17 | 0 | 2 | 0.9 | 45 | 31 | 25 | 17 | 9 | 22 | 7 | .313 | .415 |
| OF | Johnny Moore | L | 37 | 63 | 18 | 1 | 0 | 2 | 3.2 | 13 | 8 | 4 | 6 | 0 | 15 | 5 | .286 | .397 |
| OF | Danny Taylor | R | 2 | 3 | 0 | 0 | 0 | 0 | 0.0 | 0 | 0 | 1 | 1 | 0 | 1 | 0 | .000 | .000 |
| C | Mike Gonzalez | R | 60 | 167 | 40 | 3 | 0 | 0 | 0.0 | 15 | 18 | 18 | 14 | 1 | 0 | 0 | .240 | .257 |
| C | Earl Grace | L | 27 | 80 | 20 | 1 | 0 | 2 | 2.5 | 7 | 17 | 9 | 7 | 0 | 0 | 0 | .250 | .338 |
| C | Johnny Schulte | L | 31 | 69 | 18 | 3 | 0 | 0 | 0.0 | 6 | 9 | 7 | 11 | 0 | 1 | 1 | .261 | .304 |
| C | Gabby Hartnett | R | 25 | 22 | 6 | 2 | 1 | 1 | 4.5 | 2 | 9 | 5 | 5 | 1 | 20 | 6 | .273 | .591 |
| C | Tom Angley | L | 5 | 16 | 4 | 1 | 0 | 0 | 0.0 | 1 | 6 | 2 | 2 | 0 | 0 | 0 | .250 | .313 |
| **PITCHERS** | | | | | | | | | | | | | | | | | | |
| P | Pat Malone | L | 40 | 105 | 22 | 3 | 0 | 2 | 1.9 | 8 | 11 | 4 | 23 | 0 | 0 | 0 | .210 | .295 |
| P | Charlie Root | R | 43 | 96 | 15 | 3 | 4 | 1 | 1.0 | 8 | 15 | 4 | 28 | 0 | 0 | 0 | .156 | .302 |
| P | Guy Bush | R | 50 | 91 | 15 | 0 | 0 | 0 | 0.0 | 5 | 3 | 3 | 19 | 1 | 0 | 0 | .165 | .165 |
| P | Sheriff Blake | L | 38 | 81 | 14 | 2 | 0 | 0 | 0.0 | 11 | 4 | 4 | 10 | 0 | 0 | 0 | .173 | .198 |
| P | Art Nehf | L | 32 | 45 | 13 | 3 | 0 | 0 | 0.0 | 3 | 5 | 5 | 3 | 0 | 0 | 0 | .289 | .356 |
| P | Hal Carlson | R | 31 | 39 | 9 | 2 | 0 | 0 | 0.0 | 4 | 8 | 2 | 7 | 0 | 0 | 0 | .231 | .282 |
| P | Mike Cvengros | L | 33 | 15 | 6 | 1 | 0 | 0 | 0.0 | 5 | 1 | 2 | 1 | 0 | 0 | 0 | .400 | .467 |
| P | Claude Jonnard | R | 12 | 10 | 2 | 1 | 1 | 0 | 0.0 | 1 | 2 | 0 | 5 | 0 | 0 | 0 | .200 | .500 |
| P | Trader Horne | R | 11 | 5 | 2 | 0 | 0 | 0 | 0.0 | 1 | 0 | 0 | 1 | 0 | 0 | 0 | .400 | .400 |
| P | Bob Osborn | R | 3 | 4 | 1 | 0 | 0 | 0 | 0.0 | 0 | 0 | 0 | 1 | 0 | 0 | 0 | .250 | .250 |
| P | Ken Penner | L | 5 | 4 | 1 | 0 | 0 | 0 | 0.0 | 0 | 1 | 0 | 1 | 0 | 0 | 0 | .250 | .250 |
| P | Henry Grampp | R | 1 | 0 | 0 | 0 | 0 | 0 | – | 0 | 0 | 0 | 0 | 0 | 0 | 0 | – | – |
| TEAM TOTAL | | | | 5471 | 1655 | 310 | 46 | 139 | 2.5 | 98 | 933 | 589 | 567 | 103 | 84 | 31 | .303 | .452 |

## INDIVIDUAL FIELDING

| POS | Player | T | G | PO | A | E | DP | TC/G | FA | POS | Player | T | G | PO | A | E | DP | TC/G | FA |
|---|---|---|---|---|---|---|---|---|---|---|---|---|---|---|---|---|---|---|---|
| 1B | C. Grimm | L | 120 | 1228 | 74 | 10 | 114 | 10.9 | .992 | OF | H. Wilson | R | 150 | 380 | 14 | 12 | 4 | 2.7 | .970 |
| | C. Tolson | R | 32 | 289 | 16 | 7 | 21 | 9.8 | .978 | | K. Cuyler | R | 129 | 288 | 15 | 8 | 6 | 2.4 | .974 |
| | F. Blair | R | 7 | 64 | 3 | 0 | 3 | 9.6 | 1.000 | | Stephenson | R | 130 | 245 | 9 | 4 | 4 | 2.0 | .984 |
| 2B | R. Hornsby | R | 156 | 286 | 547 | 23 | 106 | 5.5 | .973 | | C. Heathcote | L | 52 | 131 | 4 | 2 | 2 | 2.6 | .985 |
| | F. Blair | R | 2 | 6 | 6 | 0 | 3 | 6.0 | 1.000 | | J. Moore | R | 15 | 32 | 1 | 1 | 0 | 2.3 | .971 |
| SS | W. English | R | 144 | 332 | 497 | 39 | 107 | 6.0 | .955 | | D. Taylor | R | 1 | 1 | 0 | 0 | 0 | 1.0 | 1.000 |
| | C. Beck | R | 14 | 24 | 48 | 4 | 15 | 5.4 | .947 | C | Z. Taylor | R | 64 | 247 | 36 | 6 | 4 | 4.5* | .979 |
| 3B | N. McMillan | R | 120 | 131 | 226 | 21 | 21 | 3.2 | .944 | | M. Gonzalez | R | 60 | 212 | 34 | 2 | 7 | 4.1 | .992 |
| | C. Beck | R | 33 | 18 | 70 | 2 | 5 | 2.7 | .978 | | E. Grace | R | 27 | 106 | 18 | 0 | 1 | 4.6 | 1.000 |
| | F. Blair | R | 8 | 12 | 14 | 3 | 0 | 3.6 | .897 | | J. Schulte | R | 30 | 74 | 16 | 2 | 3 | 3.1 | .978 |
| | | | | | | | | | | | T. Angley | R | 5 | 23 | 7 | 1 | 0 | 6.2 | .968 |
| | | | | | | | | | | | G. Hartnett | R | 1 | 4 | 0 | 0 | 0 | 4.0 | 1.000 |

If the Cubs were only one player short of a pennant in 1928, that problem was solved in November when William Wrigley gave the Braves $200,000 plus five players for second baseman Rogers Hornsby, possibly the greatest hitter in National League history. The addition of the Rajah proved to be the final piece in the jigsaw puzzle, as the lineup of Hornsby, Wilson, Cuyler, Stephenson, Grimm, and English gave the Cubs their most fearsome "murderers' row" ever. The 1929 Cubs batted .303 as a team, scored 982 runs, and socked 140 homers. Three times they scored 16 runs against the Phillies while on another occasion they slapped out 10 successive hits in one inning during a contest against the Braves. The Cub attack would have been even more formidable if Gabby Hartnett had not been relegated to the role of pinch-hitter because of a sore arm.

In spite of all their power, the Cubs took their time in building up steam. However, once they took possession of the lead with a 9–5 victory over the Cardinals June 28, they never relinquished it, finishing 10 1/2 games ahead of the runner-up Pirates. Hornsby put in one of the most lavish performances in Cub history, batting .380 with 229 hits, 156 runs, 47 doubles, 39 homers, and 149 RBI. With Hartnett on the bench, Zack Taylor and Mike Gonzales split the catching chores and filled in adequately. In the World Series, the Cubs met the Athletics, who had a murderers' row of their own in Jimmie Foxx, Al Simmons, Mickey Cochrane, Mule Haas, and Jimmy Dykes. Although the teams appeared to be about even, the A's took the series in five games, sparked by their memorable comeback from an 8–0 deficit with a 10-run seventh in game four.

## TEAM STATISTICS

| | W | L | PCT | GB | R | OR | Batting 2B | 3B | HR | BA | SA | SB | Fielding E | DP | FA | Pitching CG | B | SO | ShO | SV | ERA |
|---|---|---|---|---|---|---|---|---|---|---|---|---|---|---|---|---|---|---|---|---|---|
| CHI | 98 | 54 | .645 | | 982 | 758 | 310 | 45 | 140 | .303 | .452 | 103 | 154 | 169 | .975 | 79 | 537 | 548 | 14 | 21 | 4.16 |
| PIT | 88 | 65 | .575 | 10.5 | 904 | 780 | 285 | 116 | 60 | .303 | .430 | 94 | 181 | 136 | .970 | 79 | 439 | 409 | 5 | 13 | 4.36 |
| NY | 84 | 67 | .556 | 13.5 | 897 | 709 | 251 | 47 | 136 | .296 | .436 | 85 | 158 | 163 | .975 | 68 | 387 | 431 | 9 | 13 | **3.97** |
| STL | 78 | 74 | .513 | 20 | 831 | 806 | 310 | 84 | 100 | .293 | .438 | 72 | 174 | 149 | .971 | 83 | 474 | 453 | 6 | 8 | 4.66 |
| PHI | 71 | 82 | .464 | 27.5 | 897 | 1032 | 305 | 51 | 153 | .309 | .467 | 59 | 191 | 153 | .969 | 45 | 616 | 369 | 5 | 24 | 6.13 |
| BKN | 70 | 83 | .458 | 28.5 | 755 | 888 | 282 | 69 | 99 | .291 | .427 | 80 | 192 | 113 | .968 | 59 | 549 | 549 | 7 | 16 | 4.92 |
| CIN | 66 | 88 | .429 | 33 | 686 | 760 | 258 | 79 | 34 | .281 | .379 | 134 | 162 | 148 | .974 | 75 | 413 | 347 | 5 | 8 | 4.41 |
| BOS | 56 | 98 | .364 | 43 | 657 | 876 | 252 | 78 | 32 | .280 | .375 | 65 | 204 | 146 | .967 | 78 | 530 | 366 | 4 | 12 | 5.12 |
| LEAGUE TOTAL | | | | | 6609 | 6609 | 2253 | 569 | 754 | .294 | .426 | 692 | 1416 | 1177 | .971 | 566 | 3945 | 3472 | 55 | 115 | 4.71 |

## INDIVIDUAL PITCHING

| PITCHER | T | W | L | PCT | ERA | SV | G | GS | CG | IP | H | BB | SO | R | ER | ShO | H/9 | BB/9 | SO/9 |
|---|---|---|---|---|---|---|---|---|---|---|---|---|---|---|---|---|---|---|---|
| Charlie Root | R | 19 | 6 | **.760** | 3.47 | 5 | 43 | 31 | 19 | 272 | 286 | 83 | 124 | 120 | 105 | 4 | 9.46 | 2.75 | 4.10 |
| Guy Bush | R | 18 | 7 | .720 | 3.66 | **8** | **50** | 29 | 18 | 270.2 | 277 | 107 | 82 | 135 | 110 | 2 | 9.21 | 3.56 | 2.73 |
| Pat Malone | R | **22** | 10 | .688 | 3.57 | 2 | 40 | 30 | 19 | 267 | 283 | 102 | **166** | 120 | 106 | **5** | 9.54 | 3.44 | **5.60** |
| Sheriff Blake | R | 14 | 13 | .519 | 4.29 | 1 | 35 | 30 | 13 | 218.1 | 244 | 103 | 70 | 122 | 104 | 1 | 10.06 | 4.25 | 2.89 |
| Art Nehf | L | 8 | 5 | .615 | 5.59 | 1 | 32 | 15 | 4 | 120.2 | 148 | 39 | 27 | 85 | 75 | 0 | 11.04 | 2.91 | 2.01 |
| Hal Carlson | R | 11 | 5 | .688 | 5.16 | 2 | 31 | 14 | 6 | 111.2 | 131 | 31 | 35 | 71 | 64 | 2 | 10.56 | 2.50 | 2.82 |
| Mike Cvengros | L | 5 | 4 | .556 | 4.64 | 2 | 32 | 2 | 0 | 64 | 82 | 29 | 23 | 39 | 33 | 0 | 11.53 | 4.08 | 3.23 |
| Claude Jonnard | R | 0 | 1 | .000 | 7.48 | 0 | 12 | 2 | 0 | 27.2 | 41 | 11 | 11 | 27 | 23 | 0 | 13.34 | 3.58 | 3.58 |
| Trader Horne | R | 1 | 1 | .500 | 5.09 | 0 | 11 | 1 | 0 | 23 | 24 | 21 | 6 | 20 | 13 | 0 | 9.39 | 8.22 | 2.35 |
| Ken Penner | R | 0 | 1 | .000 | 2.84 | 0 | 5 | 0 | 0 | 12.2 | 14 | 6 | 3 | 11 | 4 | 0 | 9.95 | 4.26 | 2.13 |
| Bob Osborn | R | 0 | 0 | – | 3.00 | 0 | 3 | 1 | 0 | 9 | 8 | 2 | 1 | 3 | 3 | 0 | 8.00 | 2.00 | 1.00 |
| Henry Grampp | R | 0 | 1 | .000 | 27.00 | 0 | 1 | 1 | 0 | 2 | 4 | 3 | 0 | 6 | 6 | 0 | 18.00 | 13.50 | 0.00 |
| TEAM TOTAL | | 98 | 54 | .645 | 4.16 | 21 | 295 | 156 | 79 | 1398.2 | 1542 | 537 | 548 | 759 | 646 | 14 | 9.92 | 3.46 | 3.53 |

| MANAGER | W | L | PCT |
|---|---|---|---|
| Joe McCarthy | 86 | 64 | .573 |
| Rogers Hornsby | 4 | 0 | 1.000 |

| POS | Player | B | G | AB | H | 2B | 3B | HR | HR % | R | RBI | BB | SO | SB | Pinch Hit AB | Pinch Hit H | BA | SA |
|---|---|---|---|---|---|---|---|---|---|---|---|---|---|---|---|---|---|---|
| **REGULARS** | | | | | | | | | | | | | | | | | | |
| 1B | Charlie Grimm | L | 114 | 429 | 124 | 27 | 2 | 6 | 1.4 | 58 | 66 | 41 | 26 | 1 | 1 | 0 | .289 | .403 |
| 2B | Footsie Blair | L | 134 | 578 | 158 | 24 | 12 | 6 | 1.0 | 97 | 59 | 20 | 58 | 9 | 6 | 1 | .273 | .388 |
| SS | Woody English | R | 156 | 638 | 214 | 36 | 17 | 14 | 2.2 | 152 | 59 | 100 | 72 | 3 | 0 | 0 | .335 | .511 |
| 3B | Clyde Beck | R | 83 | 244 | 52 | 7 | 0 | 6 | 2.5 | 32 | 34 | 36 | 32 | 2 | 0 | 0 | .213 | .316 |
| RF | Kiki Cuyler | R | 156 | 642 | 228 | 50 | 17 | 13 | 2.0 | 155 | 134 | 72 | 49 | 37 | 0 | 0 | .355 | .547 |
| CF | Hack Wilson | R | 155 | 585 | 208 | 35 | 6 | 56 | 9.6 | 146 | 190 | 105 | 84 | 3 | 0 | 0 | .356 | **.723** |
| LF | Riggs Stephenson | R | 109 | 341 | 125 | 21 | 1 | 5 | 1.5 | 56 | 68 | 32 | 20 | 2 | 27 | 11 | .367 | .478 |
| C | Gabby Hartnett | R | 141 | 508 | 172 | 31 | 3 | 37 | 7.3 | 84 | 122 | 55 | 62 | 0 | 3 | 2 | .339 | .630 |
| **SUBSTITUTES** | | | | | | | | | | | | | | | | | | |
| 3B | Les Bell | R | 74 | 248 | 69 | 15 | 4 | 5 | 2.0 | 35 | 47 | 24 | 27 | 1 | 2 | 0 | .278 | .431 |
| 1B | George Kelly | R | 39 | 166 | 55 | 6 | 1 | 3 | 1.8 | 22 | 19 | 7 | 16 | 0 | 0 | 0 | .331 | .434 |
| SS | Doc Farrell | R | 46 | 113 | 33 | 6 | 0 | 1 | 0.9 | 21 | 16 | 9 | 5 | 0 | 1 | 0 | .292 | .372 |
| 2B | Rogers Hornsby | R | 42 | 104 | 32 | 5 | 1 | 2 | 1.9 | 15 | 18 | 12 | 12 | 0 | 15 | 2 | .308 | .433 |
| 1B | Chick Tolson | R | 13 | 20 | 6 | 1 | 0 | 0 | 0.0 | 0 | 1 | 6 | 5 | 1 | 7 | 2 | .300 | .350 |
| OF | Danny Taylor | R | 74 | 219 | 62 | 14 | 3 | 2 | 0.9 | 43 | 37 | 27 | 34 | 6 | 14 | 7 | .283 | .402 |
| OF | Cliff Heathcote | L | 70 | 150 | 39 | 10 | 1 | 9 | 6.0 | 30 | 18 | 18 | 15 | 4 | 31 | 5 | .260 | .520 |
| C | Zack Taylor | R | 32 | 95 | 22 | 2 | 1 | 1 | 1.1 | 12 | 11 | 2 | 12 | 0 | 2 | 0 | .232 | .305 |
| **PITCHERS** | | | | | | | | | | | | | | | | | | |
| P | Pat Malone | L | 45 | 105 | 26 | 0 | 0 | 4 | 3.8 | 12 | 10 | 7 | 19 | 0 | 0 | 0 | .248 | .362 |
| P | Charlie Root | R | 37 | 80 | 21 | 8 | 0 | 1 | 1.3 | 4 | 6 | 4 | 21 | 1 | 0 | 0 | .263 | .400 |
| P | Guy Bush | R | 46 | 78 | 22 | 0 | 1 | 0 | 0.0 | 7 | 7 | 6 | 19 | 0 | 0 | 0 | .282 | .308 |
| P | Sheriff Blake | L | 36 | 66 | 15 | 0 | 0 | 0 | 0.0 | 5 | 2 | 2 | 14 | 0 | 0 | 0 | .227 | .227 |
| P | Bud Teachout | R | 42 | 63 | 17 | 4 | 1 | 0 | 0.0 | 8 | 5 | 2 | 11 | 0 | 0 | 0 | .270 | .365 |
| P | Bob Osborn | R | 35 | 42 | 4 | 0 | 0 | 0 | 0.0 | 0 | 3 | 0 | 6 | 0 | 0 | 0 | .095 | .095 |
| P | Hal Carlson | R | 8 | 20 | 5 | 0 | 0 | 0 | 0.0 | 1 | 3 | 1 | 5 | 0 | 0 | 0 | .250 | .250 |
| P | Lynn Nelson | L | 37 | 18 | 4 | 1 | 1 | 0 | 0.0 | 0 | 2 | 0 | 1 | 0 | 0 | 0 | .222 | .389 |
| P | Jesse Petty | R | 9 | 13 | 3 | 1 | 0 | 0 | 0.0 | 1 | 1 | 0 | 6 | 0 | 0 | 0 | .231 | .308 |
| P | Mal Moss | R | 12 | 11 | 3 | 0 | 0 | 0 | 0.0 | 0 | 2 | 0 | 3 | 0 | 0 | 0 | .273 | .273 |
| P | Al Shealy | R | 24 | 5 | 3 | 1 | 0 | 0 | 0.0 | 2 | 0 | 0 | 1 | 0 | 0 | 0 | .600 | .800 |
| P | Bill McAfee | R | 2 | 0 | 0 | 0 | 0 | 0 | – | 0 | 0 | 0 | 0 | 0 | 0 | 0 | – | – |
| P | Lon Warneke | R | 1 | 0 | 0 | 0 | 0 | 0 | – | 0 | 0 | 0 | 0 | 0 | 0 | 0 | – | – |
| TEAM TOTAL | | | | 5581 | 1722 | 305 | 72 | 171 | 3.1 | 99 | 940 | 588 | 635 | 70 | 109 | 30 | .309 | .481 |

## INDIVIDUAL FIELDING

| POS | Player | T | G | PO | A | E | DP | TC/G | FA | | POS | Player | T | G | PO | A | E | DP | TC/G | FA |
|---|---|---|---|---|---|---|---|---|---|---|---|---|---|---|---|---|---|---|---|---|
| 1B | C. Grimm | L | 113 | 1040 | 68 | 6 | 103 | 9.9 | **.995** | | OF | K. Cuyler | R | 156 | 377 | 21 | 8 | 7 | 2.6 | .980 |
| | G. Kelly | R | 39 | 414 | 32 | 1 | 31 | 11.5 | .998 | | | H. Wilson | R | 155 | 357 | 9 | 19 | 2 | 2.5 | .951 |
| | C. Tolson | R | 5 | 43 | 4 | 1 | 6 | 9.6 | .979 | | | Stephenson | R | 80 | 132 | 5 | 6 | 1 | 1.8 | .958 |
| | L. Bell | R | 2 | 18 | 3 | 0 | 1 | 10.5 | 1.000 | | | D. Taylor | R | 52 | 97 | 3 | 3 | 0 | 2.0 | .971 |
| 2B | F. Blair | R | 115 | 257 | 429 | 30 | 83 | 6.2 | .958 | | | C. Heathcote | L | 35 | 66 | 4 | 1 | 0 | 2.0 | .986 |
| | R. Hornsby | R | 25 | 44 | 76 | 11 | 16 | 5.2 | .916 | | C | G. Hartnett | R | 136 | **646** | 68 | 8 | 11 | 5.3 | **.989** |
| | C. Beck | R | 24 | 52 | 68 | 7 | 17 | 5.3 | .945 | | | Z. Taylor | R | 28 | 92 | 18 | 0 | 1 | 3.9 | 1.000 |
| | D. Farrell | R | 1 | 2 | 0 | 0 | 0 | 2.0 | 1.000 | | | | | | | | | | | |
| SS | W. English | R | 78 | 173 | 251 | 16 | 57 | 5.6 | .964 | | | | | | | | | | | |
| | C. Beck | R | 57 | 97 | 165 | 13 | 36 | 4.8 | .953 | | | | | | | | | | | |
| | D. Farrell | R | 38 | 67 | 110 | 12 | 20 | 5.0 | .937 | | | | | | | | | | | |
| 3B | W. English | R | 83 | 83 | 135 | 6 | 19 | 2.7 | .973 | | | | | | | | | | | |
| | L. Bell | R | 70 | 63 | 102 | 9 | 14 | 2.5 | .948 | | | | | | | | | | | |
| | F. Blair | R | 13 | 9 | 27 | 4 | 2 | 3.1 | .900 | | | | | | | | | | | |
| | C. Beck | R | 2 | 0 | 3 | 0 | 1 | 1.5 | 1.000 | | | | | | | | | | | |

Riggs Stephenson said it best about Hack Wilson's walloping season. When asked why he himself drove in only 68 runs, Stephenson replied: "I batted behind Wilson, and he didn't leave any runners on base for me to drive in." Wilson, a roly-poly slugger with a miniblacksmith build, had the type of year that legends are built around. He drove in an all-time insurmountable record of 190 runs. And that's not all. He hit an NL-record 56 homers and batted .356. Stephenson led the club with a .367 average, and Kiki Cuyler, the third member of the powerhouse outfield, batted .355. Catcher Gabby Hartnett rebounded from arm miseries and had 37 homers, 122 RBI, and batted .339. Shortstop Woody English reached base a club record 321 times and hit .335. Yet, with all those staggering statistics, the Cubs won only 90 games and finished second, two games behind the Cardinals. Why? The obvious reason was second baseman Roger Hornsby's early-season ankle injury that limited his play to 42 games. A sad note was the death of pitcher Hal Carlson of a stomach hemorrhage on May 28. Pat Malone repeated as a 20-game winner, but Charlie Root dropped to 16 victories and Guy Bush to 15. But the biggest jolt came in the final week when manager Joe McCarthy resigned. Hornsby took the reins for the final four games.

## TEAM STATISTICS

| | W | L | PCT | GB | R | OR | 2B | 3B | Batting HR | BA | SA | SB | E | Fielding DP | FA | CG | B | Pitching SO | ShO | SV | ERA |
|---|---|---|---|---|---|---|---|---|---|---|---|---|---|---|---|---|---|---|---|---|---|
| STL | 92 | 62 | .597 | | 1004 | 784 | 373 | 89 | 104 | .314 | .471 | 72 | 183 | 176 | .970 | 63 | 477 | 641 | 5 | 21 | 4.40 |
| CHI | 90 | 64 | .584 | 2 | 998 | 870 | 305 | 72 | 171 | .309 | .481 | 70 | 170 | 167 | .973 | 67 | 528 | 601 | 6 | 12 | 4.80 |
| NY | 87 | 67 | .565 | 5 | 959 | 814 | 264 | 83 | 143 | .319 | .473 | 59 | 164 | 164 | .974 | 64 | 439 | 522 | 6 | 19 | 4.59 |
| BKN | 86 | 68 | .558 | 6 | 871 | 738 | 303 | 73 | 122 | .304 | .454 | 53 | 174 | 167 | .972 | 74 | 394 | 526 | 13 | 15 | 4.03 |
| PIT | 80 | 74 | .519 | 12 | 891 | 928 | 285 | 119 | 86 | .303 | .449 | 76 | 216 | 164 | .965 | 80 | 438 | 393 | 7 | 13 | 5.24 |
| BOS | 70 | 84 | .455 | 22 | 693 | 835 | 246 | 78 | 66 | .281 | .393 | 69 | 178 | 167 | .971 | 71 | 475 | 424 | 6 | 11 | 4.91 |
| CIN | 59 | 95 | .383 | 33 | 665 | 857 | 265 | 67 | 74 | .281 | .400 | 48 | 161 | 164 | .973 | 61 | 394 | 361 | 6 | 11 | 5.08 |
| PHI | 52 | 102 | .338 | 40 | 944 | 1199 | 345 | 44 | 126 | .315 | .458 | 34 | 239 | 169 | .962 | 54 | 543 | 384 | 3 | 7 | 6.71 |
| LEAGUE TOTAL | | | | | 7025 | 7025 | 2386 | 625 | 892 | .303 | .448 | 481 | 1485 | 1338 | .970 | 534 | 3688 | 3852 | 52 | 109 | 4.97 |

## INDIVIDUAL PITCHING

| PITCHER | T | W | L | PCT | ERA | SV | G | GS | CG | IP | H | BB | SO | R | ER | ShO | H/9 | BB/9 | SO/9 |
|---|---|---|---|---|---|---|---|---|---|---|---|---|---|---|---|---|---|---|---|
| Pat Malone | R | 20 | 9 | .690 | 3.94 | 4 | 45 | 35 | 22 | 271.2 | 290 | 96 | 142 | 145 | 119 | 2 | 9.61 | 3.18 | 4.70 |
| Guy Bush | R | 15 | 10 | .600 | 6.20 | 3 | 46 | 25 | 11 | 225 | 291 | 86 | 75 | 174 | 164 | 0 | 11.64 | 3.44 | 3.00 |
| Charlie Root | R | 16 | 14 | .533 | 4.33 | 3 | 37 | 30 | 15 | 220.1 | 247 | 63 | 124 | 122 | 106 | 4 | 10.09 | 2.57 | 5.07 |
| Sheriff Blake | R | 10 | 14 | .417 | 4.82 | 0 | 34 | 24 | 7 | 186.2 | 213 | 99 | 80 | 127 | 100 | 0 | 10.27 | 4.77 | 3.86 |
| Bud Teachout | L | 11 | 4 | .733 | 4.06 | 0 | 40 | 16 | 6 | 153 | 178 | 48 | 59 | 80 | 69 | 0 | 10.47 | 2.82 | 3.47 |
| Bob Osborn | R | 10 | 6 | .625 | 4.97 | 1 | 35 | 13 | 3 | 126.2 | 147 | 53 | 42 | 74 | 70 | 0 | 10.44 | 3.77 | 2.98 |
| Lynn Nelson | R | 3 | 2 | .600 | 5.09 | 0 | 37 | 3 | 0 | 81.1 | 97 | 28 | 29 | 52 | 46 | 0 | 10.73 | 3.10 | 3.21 |
| Hal Carlson | R | 4 | 2 | .667 | 5.05 | 0 | 8 | 6 | 3 | 51.2 | 68 | 14 | 14 | 31 | 29 | 0 | 11.85 | 2.44 | 2.44 |
| Jesse Petty | L | 1 | 3 | .250 | 2.97 | 0 | 9 | 3 | 0 | 39.1 | 51 | 6 | 18 | 18 | 13 | 0 | 11.67 | 1.37 | 4.12 |
| Al Shealy | R | 0 | 0 | – | 8.00 | 0 | 24 | 0 | 0 | 27 | 37 | 14 | 14 | 24 | 24 | 0 | 12.33 | 4.67 | 4.67 |
| Mal Moss | L | 0 | 0 | – | 6.27 | 1 | 12 | 1 | 0 | 18.2 | 18 | 14 | 4 | 13 | 13 | 0 | 8.68 | 6.75 | 1.93 |
| Lon Warneke | R | 0 | 0 | – | 33.75 | 0 | 1 | 0 | 0 | 1.1 | 2 | 5 | 0 | 5 | 5 | 0 | 13.50 | 33.75 | 0.00 |
| Bill McAfee | R | 0 | 0 | – | 0.00 | 0 | 2 | 0 | 0 | 1 | 3 | 2 | 0 | 5 | 0 | 0 | 27.00 | 18.00 | 0.00 |
| TEAM TOTAL | | 90 | 64 | .584 | 4.80 | 12 | 330 | 156 | 67 | 1403.2 | 1642 | 528 | 601 | 870 | 749 | 6 | 10.53 | 3.39 | 3.85 |

| MANAGER | W | L | PCT |
|---|---|---|---|
| Rogers Hornsby | 84 | 70 | .545 |

| POS | Player | B | G | AB | H | 2B | 3B | HR | HR % | R | RBI | BB | SO | SB | Pinch Hit AB | Pinch Hit H | BA | SA |
|---|---|---|---|---|---|---|---|---|---|---|---|---|---|---|---|---|---|---|
| **REGULARS** | | | | | | | | | | | | | | | | | | |
| 1B | Charlie Grimm | L | 146 | 531 | 176 | 33 | 11 | 4 | 0.8 | 65 | 66 | 53 | 29 | 1 | 1 | 0 | .331 | .458 |
| 2B | Rogers Hornsby | R | 100 | 357 | 118 | 37 | 1 | 16 | 4.5 | 64 | 90 | 56 | 23 | 1 | 4 | 2 | .331 | .574 |
| SS | Woody English | R | 156 | 634 | 202 | 38 | 8 | 2 | 0.3 | 117 | 53 | 68 | 80 | 12 | 0 | 0 | .319 | .413 |
| 3B | Les Bell | R | 75 | 252 | 71 | 17 | 1 | 4 | 1.6 | 30 | 32 | 19 | 22 | 0 | 5 | 1 | .282 | .405 |
| RF | Kiki Cuyler | R | 154 | 613 | 202 | 37 | 12 | 9 | 1.5 | 110 | 88 | 72 | 54 | 13 | 1 | 0 | .330 | .473 |
| CF | Hack Wilson | R | 112 | 395 | 103 | 22 | 4 | 13 | 3.3 | 66 | 61 | 63 | 69 | 1 | 8 | 2 | .261 | .435 |
| LF | Riggs Stephenson | R | 80 | 263 | 84 | 14 | 4 | 1 | 0.4 | 34 | 52 | 37 | 14 | 1 | 14 | 2 | .319 | .414 |
| C | Gabby Hartnett | R | 116 | 380 | 107 | 32 | 1 | 8 | 2.1 | 53 | 70 | 52 | 48 | 3 | 10 | 0 | .282 | .434 |
| **SUBSTITUTES** | | | | | | | | | | | | | | | | | | |
| 32 | Bill Jurges | R | 88 | 293 | 59 | 15 | 5 | 0 | 0.0 | 34 | 23 | 25 | 41 | 2 | 1 | 0 | .201 | .287 |
| 21 | Footsie Blair | L | 86 | 240 | 62 | 19 | 5 | 2 | 0.8 | 31 | 29 | 14 | 26 | 1 | 16 | 2 | .258 | .404 |
| 2B | Billy Herman | R | 25 | 98 | 32 | 7 | 0 | 0 | 0.0 | 14 | 16 | 13 | 6 | 2 | 0 | 0 | .327 | .398 |
| SS | Jimmy Adair | R | 18 | 76 | 21 | 3 | 1 | 0 | 0.0 | 9 | 3 | 1 | 8 | 1 | 0 | 0 | .276 | .342 |
| OF | Danny Taylor | R | 88 | 270 | 81 | 13 | 6 | 5 | 1.9 | 48 | 41 | 31 | 46 | 4 | 18 | 6 | .300 | .448 |
| OF | Vince Barton | L | 66 | 239 | 57 | 10 | 1 | 13 | 5.4 | 45 | 50 | 21 | 40 | 1 | 4 | 1 | .238 | .452 |
| OF | Johnny Moore | L | 39 | 104 | 25 | 3 | 1 | 2 | 1.9 | 19 | 16 | 7 | 5 | 1 | 15 | 3 | .240 | .346 |
| OF | Mike Kreevich | R | 5 | 12 | 2 | 0 | 0 | 0 | 0.0 | 0 | 0 | 0 | 6 | 1 | 1 | 0 | .167 | .167 |
| C | Rollie Hemsley | R | 66 | 204 | 63 | 17 | 4 | 3 | 1.5 | 28 | 31 | 17 | 30 | 4 | 9 | 3 | .309 | .475 |
| C | Earl Grace | L | 7 | 9 | 1 | 0 | 0 | 0 | 0.0 | 2 | 1 | 4 | 1 | 0 | 4 | 0 | .111 | .111 |
| C | Zack Taylor | R | 8 | 4 | 1 | 0 | 0 | 0 | 0.0 | 0 | 0 | 2 | 1 | 0 | 1 | 0 | .250 | .250 |
| **PITCHERS** | | | | | | | | | | | | | | | | | | |
| P | Charlie Root | R | 39 | 90 | 20 | 8 | 0 | 0 | 0.0 | 7 | 8 | 4 | 31 | 0 | 0 | 0 | .222 | .311 |
| P | Bob Smith | R | 36 | 87 | 19 | 2 | 0 | 0 | 0.0 | 7 | 4 | 5 | 2 | 0 | 0 | 0 | .218 | .241 |
| P | Pat Malone | L | 36 | 79 | 17 | 2 | 0 | 1 | 1.3 | 12 | 4 | 3 | 16 | 0 | 0 | 0 | .215 | .278 |
| P | Guy Bush | R | 39 | 57 | 7 | 1 | 0 | 0 | 0.0 | 6 | 9 | 5 | 11 | 0 | 0 | 0 | .123 | .140 |
| P | Jakie May | R | 31 | 22 | 5 | 2 | 0 | 0 | 0.0 | 3 | 2 | 1 | 6 | 0 | 0 | 0 | .227 | .318 |
| P | Les Sweetland | B | 29 | 56 | 15 | 4 | 2 | 0 | 0.0 | 8 | 9 | 4 | 11 | 0 | 3 | 2 | .268 | .411 |
| P | Bud Teachout | R | 37 | 21 | 5 | 0 | 0 | 0 | 0.0 | 4 | 0 | 0 | 3 | 0 | 0 | 0 | .238 | .238 |
| P | Lon Warneke | R | 20 | 19 | 5 | 2 | 0 | 0 | 0.0 | 3 | 2 | 0 | 5 | 0 | 0 | 0 | .263 | .368 |
| P | Ed Baecht | R | 22 | 18 | 5 | 0 | 0 | 0 | 0.0 | 3 | 2 | 0 | 3 | 0 | 0 | 0 | .278 | .278 |
| P | Sheriff Blake | L | 16 | 16 | 8 | 0 | 0 | 0 | 0.0 | 4 | 1 | 0 | 2 | 0 | 0 | 0 | .500 | .500 |
| P | Johnny Welch | L | 8 | 12 | 5 | 2 | 0 | 0 | 0.0 | 2 | 2 | 0 | 2 | 0 | 0 | 0 | .417 | .583 |
| TEAM TOTAL | | | | 5451 | 1578 | 340 | 67 | 83 | 1.5 | 82 | 765 | 577 | 641 | 49 | 115 | 24 | .289 | .422 |

## INDIVIDUAL FIELDING

| POS | Player | T | G | PO | A | E | DP | TC/G | FA | POS | Player | T | G | PO | A | E | DP | TC/G | FA |
|---|---|---|---|---|---|---|---|---|---|---|---|---|---|---|---|---|---|---|---|
| 1B | C. Grimm | L | 144 | 1357 | 79 | 10 | 107 | 10.0 | **.993** | OF | K. Cuyler | R | 153 | 347 | 11 | 11 | 4 | 2.4 | .970 |
| | F. Blair | R | 23 | 142 | 5 | 2 | 10 | 6.5 | .987 | | H. Wilson | R | 103 | 210 | 9 | 5 | 1 | 2.2 | .978 |
| | | | | | | | | | | | D. Taylor | R | 67 | 170 | 3 | 2 | 0 | 2.6 | .989 |
| 2B | R. Hornsby | R | 69 | 107 | 205 | 16 | 24 | 4.8 | .951 | | V. Barton | R | 61 | 133 | 2 | 5 | 0 | 2.3 | .964 |
| | F. Blair | R | 44 | 103 | 115 | 10 | 18 | 5.2 | .956 | | Stephenson | R | 80 | 134 | 1 | 2 | 1 | 1.7 | .985 |
| | B. Herman | R | 25 | 76 | 79 | 10 | 17 | 6.6 | .939 | | J. Moore | R | 22 | 51 | 3 | 2 | 0 | 2.5 | .964 |
| | B. Jurges | R | 33 | 66 | 83 | 5 | 21 | 4.7 | .968 | | M. Kreevich | R | 4 | 5 | 1 | 0 | 0 | 1.5 | 1.000 |
| | | | | | | | | | | | B. Teachout | L | 3 | 5 | 0 | 0 | 0 | 1.7 | 1.000 |
| SS | W. English | R | 138 | **322** | 441 | 28 | 75 | 5.7 | .965 | | | | | | | | | | |
| | J. Adair | R | 18 | 37 | 55 | 5 | 9 | 5.4 | .948 | C | G. Hartnett | R | 105 | 444 | 68 | 10 | **16** | 5.0 | .981 |
| | B. Jurges | R | 3 | 5 | 4 | 0 | 0 | 3.0 | 1.000 | | R. Hemsley | R | 66 | 236 | 40 | 7 | 5 | 4.3 | .975 |
| | | | | | | | | | | | E. Grace | R | 2 | 9 | 1 | 0 | 0 | 5.0 | 1.000 |
| 3B | L. Bell | R | 70 | 66 | 118 | 11 | 18 | 2.8 | .944 | | Z. Taylor | R | 5 | 5 | 2 | 0 | 0 | 1.4 | 1.000 |
| | B. Jurges | R | 54 | 42 | 115 | 6 | 11 | 3.0 | .963 | | | | | | | | | | |
| | R. Hornsby | R | 26 | 21 | 50 | 6 | 6 | 3.0 | .922 | | | | | | | | | | |
| | W. English | R | 18 | 18 | 41 | 1 | 3 | 3.3 | .983 | | | | | | | | | | |
| | F. Blair | R | 1 | 0 | 0 | 1 | 0 | 1.0 | .000 | | | | | | | | | | |

Hack Wilson's batting figures dropped faster than the declining stock market. His final tally of 13 homers, 61 RBI, and a .261 average went from bullish to unbearable. There were many factors that prevented Wilson from Hacking it. The National League took the juice out of the ball in 1931, but Wilson remained juiced from too many nights on the town. He missed the guidance of former manager Joe McCarthy. Before the season ended, Wilson was suspended, and by December he was gone. The Cubs acquired pitcher Burleigh Grimes from the Cardinals for Wilson and Bud Teachout. Baseball also abolished the sacrifice fly, which sent averages tumbling.

Although they led the league in runs scored with 828, the Cubs were never a factor, finishing third with an 84–70 record, 17 games behind the Cardinals. Manager Rogers Hornsby led the team with 16 homers and 90 RBI and tied Charlie Grimm for batting leadership at .331; Kiki Cuyler was a notch behind at .330. The pitching, while not spectacular, was well balanced with Charlie Root winning 17, Pat Malone and Guy Bush 16, and newcomer Bob Smith, obtained from the Phillies for Sheriff Blake, 15. Best of the rookies was second baseman Billy Herman, who was Hornsby's heir apparent. Herman batted .327 as a late-season addition.

## TEAM   STATISTICS

| | W | L | PCT | GB | R | OR | 2B | Batting 3B | HR | BA | SA | SB | E | Fielding DP | FA | CG | B | Pitching SO | ShO | SV | ERA |
|---|---|---|---|---|---|---|---|---|---|---|---|---|---|---|---|---|---|---|---|---|---|
| STL | 101 | 53 | .656 | | 815 | 614 | 353 | 74 | 60 | .286 | .411 | 114 | 160 | 169 | .974 | 80 | 449 | 626 | 17 | 20 | 3.45 |
| NY | 87 | 65 | .572 | 13 | 768 | 599 | 251 | 64 | 101 | .289 | .416 | 83 | 159 | 126 | .974 | 90 | 421 | 571 | 17 | 12 | 3.30 |
| CHI | 84 | 70 | .545 | 17 | 828 | 710 | 340 | 67 | 83 | .289 | .422 | 49 | 169 | 141 | .973 | 80 | 524 | 541 | 8 | 8 | 3.97 |
| BKN | 79 | 73 | .520 | 21 | 681 | 673 | 240 | 77 | 71 | .276 | .390 | 45 | 187 | 154 | .969 | 64 | 351 | 546 | 9 | 18 | 3.84 |
| PIT | 75 | 79 | .487 | 26 | 636 | 691 | 243 | 70 | 41 | .266 | .360 | 59 | 194 | 167 | .968 | 89 | 442 | 345 | 9 | 5 | 3.66 |
| PHI | 66 | 88 | .429 | 35 | 684 | 828 | 299 | 52 | 81 | .279 | .400 | 42 | 210 | 149 | .966 | 60 | 511 | 499 | 4 | 16 | 4.58 |
| BOS | 64 | 90 | .416 | 37 | 533 | 680 | 221 | 59 | 34 | .258 | .341 | 46 | 170 | 141 | .973 | 78 | 406 | 419 | 12 | 9 | 3.90 |
| CIN | 58 | 96 | .377 | 43 | 592 | 742 | 241 | 70 | 21 | .269 | .352 | 24 | 165 | 194 | .973 | 70 | 399 | 317 | 4 | 6 | 4.22 |
| LEAGUE TOTAL | | | | | 5537 | 5537 | 2188 | 533 | 492 | .277 | .387 | 462 | 1414 | 1241 | .971 | 611 | 3503 | 3864 | 80 | 94 | 3.86 |

## INDIVIDUAL   PITCHING

| PITCHER | T | W | L | PCT | ERA | SV | G | GS | CG | IP | H | BB | SO | R | ER | ShO | H/9 | BB/9 | SO/9 |
|---|---|---|---|---|---|---|---|---|---|---|---|---|---|---|---|---|---|---|---|
| Charlie Root | R | 17 | 14 | .548 | 3.48 | 2 | 39 | 31 | 19 | 251 | 240 | 71 | 131 | 109 | 97 | 3 | 8.61 | 2.55 | 4.70 |
| Bob Smith | R | 15 | 12 | .556 | 3.22 | 2 | 36 | 29 | 18 | 240.1 | 239 | 62 | 63 | 101 | 86 | 2 | 8.95 | 2.32 | 2.36 |
| Pat Malone | R | 16 | 9 | .640 | 3.90 | 0 | 36 | 30 | 12 | 228.1 | 229 | 88 | 112 | 115 | 99 | 2 | 9.03 | 3.47 | 4.41 |
| Guy Bush | R | 16 | 8 | .667 | 4.49 | 2 | 39 | 24 | 14 | 180.1 | 190 | 66 | 54 | 104 | 90 | 1 | 9.48 | 3.29 | 2.70 |
| Les Sweetland | L | 8 | 7 | .533 | 5.04 | 0 | 26 | 14 | 9 | 130.1 | 156 | 61 | 32 | 89 | 73 | 0 | 10.77 | 4.21 | 2.21 |
| Jakie May | L | 5 | 5 | .500 | 3.87 | 2 | 31 | 4 | 1 | 79 | 81 | 43 | 38 | 35 | 34 | 0 | 9.23 | 4.90 | 4.33 |
| Ed Baecht | R | 2 | 4 | .333 | 3.76 | 2 | 22 | 6 | 2 | 67 | 64 | 32 | 34 | 34 | 28 | 0 | 8.60 | 4.30 | 4.57 |
| Lon Warneke | R | 2 | 4 | .333 | 3.22 | 0 | 20 | 7 | 3 | 64.1 | 67 | 37 | 27 | 33 | 23 | 0 | 9.37 | 5.18 | 3.78 |
| Bud Teachout | L | 1 | 2 | .333 | 5.72 | 0 | 27 | 3 | 1 | 61.1 | 79 | 28 | 14 | 40 | 39 | 0 | 11.59 | 4.11 | 2.05 |
| Sheriff Blake | R | 0 | 4 | .000 | 5.22 | 0 | 16 | 5 | 0 | 50 | 64 | 26 | 29 | 34 | 29 | 0 | 11.52 | 4.68 | 5.22 |
| Johnny Welch | R | 2 | 1 | .667 | 3.74 | 0 | 8 | 3 | 1 | 33.2 | 39 | 10 | 7 | 16 | 14 | 0 | 10.43 | 2.67 | 1.87 |
| TEAM TOTAL | | 84 | 70 | .545 | 3.97 | 8 | 300 | 156 | 80 | 1385.2 | 1448 | 524 | 541 | 710 | 612 | 8 | 9.40 | 3.40 | 3.51 |

| MANAGER | W | L | PCT |
|---|---|---|---|
| Rogers Hornsby | 53 | 44 | .546 |
| Charlie Grimm | 37 | 20 | .649 |

| POS | Player | B | G | AB | H | 2B | 3B | HR | HR % | R | RBI | BB | SO | SB | Pinch Hit AB | H | BA | SA |
|---|---|---|---|---|---|---|---|---|---|---|---|---|---|---|---|---|---|---|
| **REGULARS** | | | | | | | | | | | | | | | | | | |
| 1B | Charlie Grimm | L | 149 | 570 | 175 | 42 | 2 | 7 | 1.2 | 66 | 80 | 35 | 22 | 2 | 0 | 0 | .307 | .425 |
| 2B | Billy Herman | R | 154 | 656 | 206 | 42 | 7 | 1 | 0.2 | 102 | 51 | 40 | 33 | 14 | 0 | 0 | .314 | .404 |
| SS | Bill Jurges | R | 115 | 396 | 100 | 24 | 4 | 2 | 0.5 | 40 | 52 | 19 | 26 | 1 | 1 | 0 | .253 | .348 |
| 3B | Woody English | R | 127 | 522 | 142 | 23 | 7 | 3 | 0.6 | 70 | 47 | 55 | 73 | 5 | 1 | 0 | .272 | .360 |
| RF | Kiki Cuyler | R | 110 | 446 | 130 | 19 | 9 | 10 | 2.2 | 58 | 77 | 29 | 43 | 9 | 1 | 0 | .291 | .442 |
| CF | Johnny Moore | L | 119 | 443 | 135 | 24 | 5 | 13 | 2.9 | 59 | 64 | 22 | 38 | 4 | 10 | 4 | .305 | .470 |
| LF | Riggs Stephenson | R | 147 | 583 | 189 | 49 | 4 | 4 | 0.7 | 86 | 85 | 54 | 27 | 3 | 0 | 0 | .324 | .443 |
| C | Gabby Hartnett | R | 121 | 406 | 110 | 25 | 3 | 12 | 3.0 | 52 | 52 | 51 | 59 | 0 | 2 | 1 | .271 | .436 |
| **SUBSTITUTES** | | | | | | | | | | | | | | | | | | |
| 3B | Stan Hack | L | 72 | 178 | 42 | 5 | 6 | 2 | 1.1 | 32 | 19 | 17 | 16 | 5 | 14 | 2 | .236 | .365 |
| SS | Mark Koenig | B | 33 | 102 | 36 | 5 | 1 | 3 | 2.9 | 15 | 11 | 3 | 5 | 0 | 2 | 0 | .353 | .510 |
| 1B | Harry Taylor | L | 10 | 8 | 1 | 0 | 0 | 0 | 0.0 | 1 | 0 | 1 | 1 | 0 | 7 | 1 | .125 | .125 |
| OF | Lance Richbourg | L | 44 | 148 | 38 | 2 | 2 | 1 | 0.7 | 22 | 21 | 8 | 4 | 0 | 10 | 3 | .257 | .318 |
| OF | Vince Barton | L | 36 | 134 | 30 | 2 | 3 | 3 | 2.2 | 19 | 15 | 8 | 22 | 0 | 2 | 0 | .224 | .351 |
| O1 | Marv Gudat | L | 60 | 94 | 24 | 4 | 1 | 1 | 1.1 | 15 | 15 | 16 | 10 | 0 | 30 | 10 | .255 | .351 |
| O3 | Rogers Hornsby | R | 19 | 58 | 13 | 2 | 0 | 1 | 1.7 | 10 | 7 | 10 | 4 | 0 | 3 | 1 | .224 | .310 |
| OF | Frank Demaree | R | 23 | 56 | 14 | 3 | 0 | 0 | 0.0 | 4 | 6 | 2 | 7 | 0 | 5 | 1 | .250 | .304 |
| OF | Danny Taylor | R | 6 | 22 | 5 | 2 | 0 | 0 | 0.0 | 3 | 3 | 3 | 1 | 1 | 0 | 0 | .227 | .318 |
| C | Rollie Hemsley | R | 60 | 151 | 36 | 10 | 3 | 4 | 2.6 | 27 | 20 | 10 | 16 | 2 | 8 | 3 | .238 | .424 |
| C | Zack Taylor | R | 21 | 30 | 6 | 1 | 0 | 0 | 0.0 | 2 | 3 | 1 | 4 | 0 | 7 | 1 | .200 | .233 |
| **PITCHERS** | | | | | | | | | | | | | | | | | | |
| P | Lon Warneke | R | 35 | 99 | 19 | 1 | 1 | 0 | 0.0 | 8 | 9 | 3 | 20 | 0 | 0 | 0 | .192 | .222 |
| P | Guy Bush | R | 40 | 84 | 15 | 2 | 1 | 0 | 0.0 | 6 | 1 | 4 | 12 | 0 | 0 | 0 | .179 | .226 |
| P | Pat Malone | L | 37 | 78 | 14 | 2 | 0 | 1 | 1.3 | 7 | 7 | 3 | 17 | 0 | 0 | 0 | .179 | .244 |
| P | Charlie Root | R | 39 | 76 | 13 | 1 | 0 | 1 | 1.3 | 4 | 10 | 0 | 29 | 0 | 0 | 0 | .171 | .224 |
| P | Burleigh Grimes | R | 30 | 44 | 11 | 1 | 0 | 0 | 0.0 | 4 | 5 | 0 | 9 | 1 | 0 | 0 | .250 | .273 |
| P | Bob Smith | R | 36 | 42 | 10 | 4 | 1 | 0 | 0.0 | 5 | 4 | 0 | 2 | 1 | 0 | 0 | .238 | .381 |
| P | Bud Tinning | B | 24 | 23 | 2 | 1 | 0 | 0 | 0.0 | 3 | 1 | 3 | 12 | 0 | 0 | 0 | .087 | .130 |
| P | Jakie May | R | 35 | 8 | 1 | 0 | 0 | 0 | 0.0 | 0 | 0 | 1 | 1 | 0 | 0 | 0 | .125 | .125 |
| P | Carroll Yerkes | R | 2 | 3 | 1 | 0 | 0 | 0 | 0.0 | 0 | 0 | 0 | 0 | 0 | 0 | 0 | .333 | .333 |
| P | LeRoy Herrmann | R | 7 | 2 | 1 | 0 | 0 | 0 | 0.0 | 0 | 0 | 0 | 1 | 0 | 0 | 0 | .500 | .500 |
| P | Ed Baecht | R | 1 | 0 | 0 | 0 | 0 | 0 | – | 0 | 0 | 0 | 0 | 0 | 0 | 0 | – | – |
| P | Bobo Newsom | R | 1 | 0 | 0 | 0 | 0 | 0 | – | 0 | 0 | 0 | 0 | 0 | 0 | 0 | – | – |
| TEAM TOTAL | | | | 5462 | 1519 | 296 | 60 | 69 | 1.3 | 72 | 665 | 398 | 514 | 48 | 103 | 27 | .278 | .392 |

## INDIVIDUAL FIELDING

| POS | Player | T | G | PO | A | E | DP | TC/G | FA |
|---|---|---|---|---|---|---|---|---|---|
| 1B | C. Grimm | L | 149 | 1429 | 123 | 11 | 127 | 10.5 | .993 |
| | M. Gudat | L | 8 | 63 | 4 | 1 | 4 | 8.5 | .985 |
| | G. Hartnett | R | 1 | 14 | 0 | 0 | 2 | 14.0 | 1.000 |
| | H. Taylor | L | 1 | 5 | 0 | 0 | 0 | 5.0 | 1.000 |
| 2B | B. Herman | R | 154 | 401 | 527 | 38 | 102 | 6.3 | .961 |
| | B. Smith | R | 2 | 1 | 10 | 0 | 1 | 5.5 | 1.000 |
| SS | B. Jurges | R | 103 | 223 | 394 | 23 | 69 | 6.2 | .964 |
| | M. Koenig | R | 33 | 58 | 106 | 12 | 21 | 5.3 | .932 |
| | W. English | R | 38 | 66 | 102 | 8 | 17 | 4.6 | .955 |
| 3B | W. English | R | 93 | 96 | 173 | 12 | 13 | 3.0 | .957 |
| | S. Hack | R | 51 | 36 | 90 | 12 | 5 | 2.7 | .913 |
| | R. Hornsby | R | 6 | 1 | 10 | 4 | 0 | 2.5 | .733 |
| | B. Jurges | R | 5 | 4 | 7 | 0 | 1 | 2.2 | 1.000 |

| POS | Player | T | G | PO | A | E | DP | TC/G | FA |
|---|---|---|---|---|---|---|---|---|---|
| OF | Stephenson | R | 147 | 298 | 7 | 5 | 2 | 2.1 | .984 |
| | J. Moore | R | 109 | 272 | 12 | 5 | 2 | 2.7 | .983 |
| | K. Cuyler | R | 109 | 239 | 7 | 8 | 1 | 2.3 | .969 |
| | L. Richbourg | R | 33 | 70 | 2 | 1 | 1 | 2.2 | .986 |
| | V. Barton | R | 34 | 64 | 3 | 0 | 1 | 2.0 | 1.000 |
| | F. Demaree | R | 17 | 31 | 2 | 0 | 1 | 1.9 | 1.000 |
| | D. Taylor | R | 6 | 18 | 0 | 2 | 0 | 3.3 | .900 |
| | R. Hornsby | R | 10 | 16 | 0 | 0 | 0 | 1.6 | 1.000 |
| | M. Gudat | L | 14 | 14 | 0 | 1 | 0 | 1.1 | .933 |
| | R. Hemsley | R | 1 | 1 | 1 | 0 | 0 | 2.0 | 1.000 |
| C | G. Hartnett | R | 117 | 484 | 75 | 10 | 8 | 4.9 | .982 |
| | R. Hemsley | R | 47 | 173 | 17 | 5 | 3 | 4.1 | .974 |
| | Z. Taylor | R | 14 | 39 | 4 | 0 | 0 | 3.1 | 1.000 |

The year began on a sad note with the death of owner William Wrigley at age 70 on January 26. From the time he gained control of the Cubs, Wrigley had played a dominant role in rebuilding the ballclub. He fraternized with the players, and manager Rogers Hornsby was among his favorites. With Wrigley gone, club president William Veeck, who was often at odds with Hornsby, dismissed him as manager on August 2.

Hornsby departed with the team in third place at 53–44. The Cubs rallied under Charlie Grimm to beat out the Pirates by four games with a 90–64 record. Lacking a true power hitter—their leader was little-known outfielder Johnny Moore with 13 homers—the Cubs relied on tight defense and pitching. Their biggest asset was Lon Warneke, who in his first full season led the league in wins with 22 and ERA at 2.37. Shortstop Mark Koenig helped key the pennant drive. Rescued from the minors, the former Yankee batted a solid .353 in 33 games. But the Cubs voted him only half a share of the World Series loot. That misguided lack of generosity was not lost on the Yankees, their Series rival. Led by Babe Ruth, the Yankees rode the Cubs unmercifully and swept the Series in four games. In the third game, Ruth silenced the Cub catcalls by pointing to the Wrigley Field bleachers and depositing the ball there for his famed called shot, one of the game's most enduring legends.

## TEAM STATISTICS

| | W | L | PCT | GB | R | OR | 2B | Batting 3B | HR | BA | SA | SB | Fielding E | DP | FA | CG | B | Pitching SO | ShO | SV | ERA |
|---|---|---|---|---|---|---|---|---|---|---|---|---|---|---|---|---|---|---|---|---|---|
| CHI | 90 | 64 | .584 | | 720 | 633 | 296 | 60 | 69 | .278 | .392 | 48 | 173 | 146 | .973 | 79 | 409 | 527 | 9 | 7 | **3.44** |
| PIT | 86 | 68 | .558 | 4 | 701 | 711 | 274 | 90 | 47 | .285 | .394 | 71 | 185 | 124 | .969 | 72 | 338 | 377 | 12 | 12 | 3.75 |
| BKN | 81 | 73 | .526 | 9 | 752 | 747 | 296 | 59 | 109 | .283 | .419 | 61 | 183 | 169 | .971 | 61 | 403 | 499 | 7 | 16 | 4.28 |
| PHI | 78 | 76 | .506 | 12 | 844 | 796 | 330 | 67 | 122 | .292 | .442 | 71 | 194 | 133 | .968 | 59 | 450 | 459 | 4 | 17 | 4.47 |
| BOS | 77 | 77 | .500 | 13 | 649 | 655 | 262 | 53 | 63 | .265 | .366 | 36 | 152 | 145 | .976 | 72 | 420 | 440 | 8 | 8 | 3.53 |
| NY | 72 | 82 | .468 | 18 | 755 | 706 | 263 | 54 | 116 | .276 | .406 | 31 | 191 | 143 | .969 | 57 | 387 | 506 | 3 | 16 | 3.83 |
| STL | 72 | 82 | .468 | 18 | 684 | 717 | 307 | 51 | 76 | .269 | .385 | 92 | 175 | 155 | .971 | 70 | 455 | 681 | 13 | 9 | 3.97 |
| CIN | 60 | 94 | .390 | 30 | 575 | 715 | 265 | 68 | 47 | .263 | .362 | 35 | 178 | 129 | .971 | 83 | 276 | 359 | 6 | 6 | 3.79 |
| LEAGUE TOTAL | | | | | 5680 | 5680 | 2293 | 502 | 649 | .276 | .396 | 445 | 1431 | 1144 | .971 | 553 | 3138 | 3848 | 62 | 91 | 3.88 |

## INDIVIDUAL PITCHING

| PITCHER | T | W | L | PCT | ERA | SV | G | GS | CG | IP | H | BB | SO | R | ER | ShO | H/9 | BB/9 | SO/9 |
|---|---|---|---|---|---|---|---|---|---|---|---|---|---|---|---|---|---|---|---|
| Lon Warneke | R | 22 | 6 | .786 | 2.37 | 0 | 35 | 32 | 25 | 277 | 247 | 64 | 106 | 84 | 73 | 4 | 8.03 | 2.08 | 3.44 |
| Guy Bush | R | 19 | 11 | .633 | 3.21 | 0 | 40 | 30 | 15 | 238.2 | 262 | 70 | 73 | 106 | 85 | 1 | 9.88 | 2.64 | 2.75 |
| Pat Malone | R | 15 | 17 | .469 | 3.38 | 0 | 37 | 33 | 17 | 237 | 222 | 78 | 120 | 111 | 89 | 2 | 8.43 | 2.96 | 4.56 |
| Charlie Root | R | 15 | 10 | .600 | 3.58 | 3 | 39 | 23 | 11 | 216.1 | 211 | 55 | 96 | 99 | 86 | 0 | 8.78 | 2.29 | 3.99 |
| Burleigh Grimes | R | 6 | 11 | .353 | 4.78 | 1 | 30 | 18 | 5 | 141.1 | 174 | 50 | 36 | 89 | 75 | 1 | 11.08 | 3.18 | 2.29 |
| Bob Smith | R | 4 | 3 | .571 | 4.61 | 2 | 34 | 11 | 4 | 119 | 148 | 36 | 35 | 64 | 61 | 1 | 11.19 | 2.72 | 2.65 |
| Bud Tinning | R | 5 | 3 | .625 | 2.80 | 0 | 24 | 7 | 2 | 93.1 | 93 | 24 | 30 | 34 | 29 | 0 | 8.97 | 2.31 | 2.89 |
| Jakie May | L | 2 | 2 | .500 | 4.36 | 1 | 35 | 0 | 0 | 53.2 | 61 | 19 | 20 | 34 | 26 | 0 | 10.23 | 3.19 | 3.35 |
| LeRoy Herrmann | R | 2 | 1 | .667 | 6.39 | 0 | 7 | 0 | 0 | 12.2 | 18 | 9 | 5 | 9 | 9 | 0 | 12.79 | 6.39 | 3.55 |
| Carroll Yerkes | L | 0 | 0 | — | 3.00 | 0 | 2 | 0 | 0 | 9 | 5 | 3 | 4 | 3 | 3 | 0 | 5.00 | 3.00 | 4.00 |
| Ed Baecht | R | 0 | 0 | — | 0.00 | 0 | 1 | 0 | 0 | 1 | 1 | 1 | 0 | 0 | 0 | 0 | 9.00 | 9.00 | 0.00 |
| Marv Gudat | L | 0 | 0 | — | 0.00 | 0 | 1 | 0 | 0 | 1 | 1 | 0 | 2 | 0 | 0 | 0 | 9.00 | 0.00 | 18.00 |
| Bobo Newsom | R | 0 | 0 | — | 0.00 | 0 | 1 | 0 | 0 | 1 | 1 | 0 | 0 | 0 | 0 | 0 | 9.00 | 0.00 | 0.00 |
| TEAM TOTAL | | 90 | 64 | .584 | 3.44 | 7 | 286 | 154 | 79 | 1401 | 1444 | 409 | 527 | 633 | 536 | 9 | 9.28 | 2.63 | 3.39 |

| MANAGER | W | L | PCT |
|---|---|---|---|
| Charlie Grimm | 86 | 68 | .558 |

| POS | Player | B | G | AB | H | 2B | 3B | HR | HR % | R | RBI | BB | SO | SB | Pinch Hit AB | Pinch Hit H | BA | SA |
|---|---|---|---|---|---|---|---|---|---|---|---|---|---|---|---|---|---|---|
| **REGULARS** | | | | | | | | | | | | | | | | | | |
| 1B | Charlie Grimm | L | 107 | 384 | 95 | 15 | 2 | 3 | 0.8 | 38 | 37 | 23 | 15 | 1 | 2 | 0 | .247 | .320 |
| 2B | Billy Herman | R | 153 | 619 | 173 | 35 | 2 | 0 | 0.0 | 82 | 44 | 45 | 34 | 5 | 0 | 0 | .279 | .342 |
| SS | Bill Jurges | R | 143 | 487 | 131 | 17 | 6 | 5 | 1.0 | 49 | 50 | 26 | 39 | 3 | 0 | 0 | .269 | .359 |
| 3B | Woody English | R | 105 | 398 | 104 | 19 | 2 | 3 | 0.8 | 54 | 41 | 53 | 44 | 5 | 0 | 0 | .261 | .342 |
| RF | Babe Herman | L | 137 | 508 | 147 | 36 | 12 | 16 | 3.1 | 77 | 93 | 50 | 57 | 6 | 5 | 4 | .289 | .502 |
| CF | Frank Demaree | R | 134 | 515 | 140 | 24 | 6 | 6 | 1.2 | 68 | 51 | 22 | 42 | 4 | 0 | 0 | .272 | .377 |
| LF | Riggs Stephenson | R | 97 | 346 | 114 | 17 | 4 | 4 | 1.2 | 45 | 51 | 34 | 16 | 5 | 3 | 0 | .329 | .436 |
| C | Gabby Hartnett | R | 140 | 490 | 135 | 21 | 4 | 16 | 3.3 | 55 | 88 | 37 | 51 | 1 | 0 | 0 | .276 | .433 |
| **SUBSTITUTES** | | | | | | | | | | | | | | | | | | |
| 3S | Mark Koenig | B | 80 | 218 | 62 | 12 | 1 | 3 | 1.4 | 32 | 25 | 15 | 9 | 5 | 15 | 4 | .284 | .390 |
| 1B | Harvey Hendrick | L | 69 | 189 | 55 | 13 | 3 | 4 | 2.1 | 30 | 23 | 13 | 17 | 4 | 19 | 6 | .291 | .455 |
| 3B | Stan Hack | L | 20 | 60 | 21 | 3 | 1 | 1 | 1.7 | 10 | 2 | 8 | 3 | 4 | 0 | 0 | .350 | .483 |
| 1B | Dolf Camilli | L | 16 | 58 | 13 | 2 | 1 | 2 | 3.4 | 8 | 7 | 4 | 11 | 3 | 0 | 0 | .224 | .397 |
| OF | Kiki Cuyler | R | 70 | 262 | 83 | 13 | 3 | 5 | 1.9 | 37 | 35 | 21 | 29 | 4 | 1 | 0 | .317 | .447 |
| OF | Jim Mosolf | L | 31 | 82 | 22 | 5 | 1 | 1 | 1.2 | 13 | 9 | 5 | 8 | 0 | 8 | 3 | .268 | .390 |
| OF | Taylor Douthit | R | 27 | 71 | 16 | 5 | 0 | 0 | 0.0 | 8 | 5 | 11 | 7 | 2 | 1 | 0 | .225 | .296 |
| C | Gilly Campbell | L | 46 | 89 | 25 | 3 | 1 | 1 | 1.1 | 11 | 10 | 7 | 4 | 0 | 23 | 6 | .281 | .371 |
| C | Zack Taylor | R | 16 | 11 | 0 | 0 | 0 | 0 | 0.0 | 0 | 0 | 0 | 1 | 0 | 4 | 0 | .000 | .000 |
| C | Babe Phelps | L | 3 | 7 | 2 | 0 | 0 | 0 | 0.0 | 0 | 2 | 0 | 1 | 0 | 1 | 0 | .286 | .286 |
| **PITCHERS** | | | | | | | | | | | | | | | | | | |
| P | Lon Warneke | R | 39 | 100 | 30 | 6 | 1 | 2 | 2.0 | 9 | 13 | 3 | 13 | 0 | 0 | 0 | .300 | .440 |
| P | Guy Bush | R | 41 | 88 | 11 | 4 | 0 | 0 | 0.0 | 4 | 3 | 8 | 16 | 0 | 0 | 0 | .125 | .170 |
| P | Charlie Root | R | 35 | 85 | 8 | 3 | 0 | 0 | 0.0 | 1 | 0 | 4 | 22 | 0 | 0 | 0 | .094 | .129 |
| P | Bud Tinning | B | 32 | 67 | 14 | 2 | 0 | 0 | 0.0 | 3 | 10 | 1 | 17 | 0 | 0 | 0 | .209 | .239 |
| P | Pat Malone | L | 31 | 63 | 10 | 0 | 0 | 0 | 0.0 | 5 | 4 | 0 | 9 | 0 | 0 | 0 | .159 | .159 |
| P | Lynn Nelson | L | 29 | 21 | 5 | 1 | 1 | 0 | 0.0 | 5 | 1 | 1 | 3 | 0 | 0 | 0 | .238 | .381 |
| P | Burleigh Grimes | R | 17 | 20 | 3 | 0 | 0 | 0 | 0.0 | 1 | 4 | 1 | 4 | 0 | 0 | 0 | .150 | .150 |
| P | Roy Henshaw | R | 21 | 10 | 2 | 0 | 0 | 0 | 0.0 | 1 | 0 | 1 | 2 | 0 | 0 | 0 | .200 | .200 |
| P | LeRoy Herrmann | R | 9 | 6 | 1 | 0 | 0 | 0 | 0.0 | 0 | 0 | 0 | 0 | 0 | 0 | 0 | .167 | .167 |
| P | Beryl Richmond | R | 4 | 1 | 0 | 0 | 0 | 0 | 0.0 | 0 | 0 | 0 | 0 | 0 | 0 | 0 | .000 | .000 |
| P | Carroll Yerkes | R | 1 | 0 | 0 | 0 | 0 | 0 | – | 0 | 0 | 0 | 0 | 0 | 0 | 0 | – | – |
| TEAM TOTAL | | | | 5255 | 1422 | 256 | 51 | 72 | 1.4 | 64 | 608 | 392 | 475 | 52 | 82 | 23 | .271 | .380 |

## INDIVIDUAL FIELDING

| POS | Player | T | G | PO | A | E | DP | TC/G | FA |
|---|---|---|---|---|---|---|---|---|---|
| 1B | C. Grimm | L | 104 | 979 | 84 | 4 | 94 | 10.3 | **.996** |
| | H. Hendrick | R | 38 | 328 | 23 | 6 | 31 | 9.4 | .983 |
| | D. Camilli | L | 16 | 163 | 14 | 1 | 21 | 11.1 | .994 |
| 2B | B. Herman | R | 153 | 466 | 512 | 45 | 114 | 6.7 | .956 |
| | M. Koenig | R | 2 | 7 | 2 | 0 | 1 | 4.5 | 1.000 |
| SS | B. Jurges | R | 143 | 298 | 476 | 34 | 95 | 5.7 | .958 |
| | M. Koenig | R | 26 | 33 | 58 | 5 | 15 | 3.7 | .948 |
| | W. English | R | 1 | 0 | 1 | 0 | 0 | 1.0 | 1.000 |
| 3B | W. English | R | 103 | 80 | 173 | 7 | 9 | 2.5 | **.973** |
| | M. Koenig | R | 37 | 32 | 74 | 9 | 9 | 3.1 | .922 |
| | S. Hack | R | 17 | 19 | 40 | 1 | 8 | 3.5 | .983 |
| | H. Hendrick | R | 1 | 0 | 1 | 0 | 0 | 1.0 | 1.000 |

| POS | Player | T | G | PO | A | E | DP | TC/G | FA |
|---|---|---|---|---|---|---|---|---|---|
| OF | F. Demaree | R | 133 | 321 | 12 | 12 | 1 | 2.6 | .965 |
| | B. Herman | L | 131 | 252 | 12 | 12 | 1 | 2.1 | .957 |
| | Stephenson | R | 91 | 187 | 5 | 3 | 2 | 2.1 | .985 |
| | K. Cuyler | R | 69 | 130 | 2 | 3 | 0 | 2.0 | .978 |
| | J. Mosolf | R | 22 | 51 | 2 | 2 | 0 | 2.5 | .964 |
| | T. Douthit | R | 18 | 37 | 3 | 3 | 0 | 2.4 | .930 |
| | H. Hendrick | R | 8 | 16 | 1 | 2 | 8 | 2.4 | .895 |
| C | G. Hartnett | R | 140 | 550 | 77 | 7 | 17 | 4.5 | .989 |
| | G. Campbell | R | 20 | 66 | 9 | 4 | 1 | 4.0 | .949 |
| | B. Phelps | R | 2 | 6 | 2 | 0 | 1 | 4.0 | 1.000 |
| | Z. Taylor | R | 12 | 8 | 0 | 0 | 0 | 0.7 | 1.000 |

The Cubs' quest for a second pennant in a row may have been shattered during spring training, when Kiki Cuyler broke an ankle sliding home. Cuyler didn't return until midsummer and played only 70 games. Another jolt was the poor play of Babe Herman; after angling for the slugging outfielder for four years, the Cubs finally landed the Babe, giving the Reds four players and cash. Herman batted only .289, and his power contribution was 16 homers and 93 RBI. The Babe did have one big day, hitting three homers and driving in eight runs in a 10–1 triumph on July 1.

The inability to win consistently on the road led to the Cubs' third-place finish. They were 50–27 at home, but fell to 36–41 when they packed their bags. Despite all those setbacks they finished only six games behind the Giants with an 86–68 record. Riggs Stephenson led the batting parade at .329, while Gabby Hartnett tied Babe Herman with 16 homers. Guy Bush had his only 20-win season after receiving 16 four-leaf clovers from fans. Lon Warneke, 18–13, was the most effective pitcher with a 2.00 earned-run average and 26 complete games. Another factor was the 163 double plays turned in by the Billys—Herman and Jurges—around the keystone.

## TEAM   STATISTICS

| | W | L | PCT | GB | R | OR | 2B | 3B | Batting HR | BA | SA | SB | E | Fielding DP | FA | CG | B | Pitching SO | ShO | SV | ERA |
|---|---|---|---|---|---|---|---|---|---|---|---|---|---|---|---|---|---|---|---|---|---|
| NY | 91 | 61 | .599 | | 636 | 515 | 204 | 41 | **82** | .263 | .361 | 31 | 178 | 156 | .973 | 75 | 400 | 555 | **22** | 15 | **2.71** |
| PIT | 87 | 67 | .565 | 5 | 667 | 619 | 249 | **84** | 39 | **.285** | **.383** | 34 | 166 | 133 | .972 | 70 | 313 | 401 | 16 | 12 | 3.27 |
| CHI | 86 | 68 | .558 | 6 | 646 | 536 | **256** | 51 | 72 | .271 | .380 | 52 | 168 | **163** | .973 | **95** | 413 | 488 | 16 | 9 | 2.93 |
| BOS | 83 | 71 | .539 | 9 | 552 | 531 | 217 | 56 | 54 | .252 | .345 | 25 | **138** | 148 | **.978** | 85 | 355 | 383 | 14 | **16** | 2.96 |
| STL | 82 | 71 | .536 | 9.5 | **687** | 609 | **256** | 61 | 57 | .276 | .378 | **99** | 162 | 119 | .973 | 73 | 452 | **635** | 10 | **16** | 3.37 |
| BKN | 65 | 88 | .425 | 26.5 | 617 | 695 | 224 | 51 | 62 | .263 | .359 | 82 | 177 | 120 | .971 | 71 | 374 | 415 | 9 | 10 | 3.73 |
| PHI | 60 | 92 | .395 | 31 | 607 | 760 | 240 | 41 | 60 | .274 | .369 | 55 | 183 | 156 | .970 | 52 | 410 | 341 | 10 | 13 | 4.34 |
| CIN | 58 | 94 | .382 | 33 | 496 | 643 | 208 | 37 | 34 | .246 | .320 | 30 | 177 | 139 | .971 | 74 | **257** | 310 | 13 | 8 | 3.42 |
| LEAGUE TOTAL | | | | | 4908 | 4908 | 1854 | 422 | 460 | .266 | .362 | 408 | 1349 | 1134 | .973 | 595 | 2974 | 3528 | 110 | 99 | 3.34 |

## INDIVIDUAL   PITCHING

| PITCHER | T | W | L | PCT | ERA | SV | G | GS | CG | IP | H | BB | SO | R | ER | ShO | H/9 | BB/9 | SO/9 |
|---|---|---|---|---|---|---|---|---|---|---|---|---|---|---|---|---|---|---|---|
| Lon Warneke | R | 18 | 13 | .581 | 2.00 | 1 | 36 | 34 | **26** | 287.1 | 262 | 75 | 133 | 83 | 64 | 4 | 8.21 | 2.35 | 4.17 |
| Guy Bush | R | 20 | 12 | .625 | 2.75 | 2 | 41 | 32 | 20 | 258.2 | 261 | 68 | 84 | 98 | 79 | 4 | 9.08 | 2.37 | 2.92 |
| Charlie Root | R | 15 | 10 | .600 | 2.60 | 0 | 35 | 30 | 20 | 242.1 | 232 | 61 | 86 | 85 | 70 | 2 | 8.62 | 2.27 | 3.19 |
| Pat Malone | R | 10 | 14 | .417 | 3.91 | 0 | 31 | 26 | 13 | 186.1 | 186 | 59 | 72 | 91 | 81 | 2 | 8.98 | 2.85 | 3.48 |
| Bud Tinning | R | 13 | 6 | .684 | 3.18 | 1 | 32 | 21 | 10 | 175.1 | 169 | 60 | 59 | 73 | 62 | 3 | 8.67 | 3.08 | 3.03 |
| Lynn Nelson | R | 5 | 5 | .500 | 3.21 | 1 | 24 | 3 | 3 | 75.2 | 65 | 30 | 20 | 34 | 27 | 0 | 7.73 | 3.57 | 2.38 |
| Burleigh Grimes | R | 3 | 6 | .333 | 3.49 | 3 | 17 | 7 | 3 | 69.2 | 71 | 29 | 12 | 29 | 27 | 1 | 9.17 | 3.75 | 1.55 |
| Roy Henshaw | L | 2 | 1 | .667 | 4.19 | 0 | 21 | 0 | 0 | 38.2 | 32 | 20 | 16 | 22 | 18 | 0 | 7.45 | 4.66 | 3.72 |
| LeRoy Herrmann | R | 0 | 1 | .000 | 5.57 | 1 | 9 | 1 | 0 | 21 | 26 | 8 | 4 | 19 | 13 | 0 | 11.14 | 3.43 | 1.71 |
| Beryl Richmond | L | 0 | 0 | – | 1.93 | 0 | 4 | 0 | 0 | 4.2 | 10 | 2 | 2 | 1 | 1 | 0 | 19.29 | 3.86 | 3.86 |
| Carroll Yerkes | L | 0 | 0 | – | 4.50 | 0 | 1 | 0 | 0 | 2 | 2 | 1 | 0 | 1 | 1 | 0 | 9.00 | 4.50 | 0.00 |
| TEAM TOTAL | | 86 | 68 | .558 | 2.93 | 9 | 251 | 154 | 95 | 1361.2 | 1316 | 413 | 488 | 536 | 443 | 16 | 8.70 | 2.73 | 3.23 |

| MANAGER | W | L | PCT |
|---|---|---|---|
| Charlie Grimm | 86 | 65 | .570 |

| POS | Player | B | G | AB | H | 2B | 3B | HR | HR % | R | RBI | BB | SO | SB | Pinch Hit AB | Pinch Hit H | BA | SA |
|---|---|---|---|---|---|---|---|---|---|---|---|---|---|---|---|---|---|---|
| **REGULARS** | | | | | | | | | | | | | | | | | | |
| 1B | Charlie Grimm | L | 75 | 267 | 79 | 8 | 1 | 5 | 1.9 | 24 | 47 | 16 | 12 | 1 | 1 | 0 | .296 | .390 |
| 2B | Billy Herman | R | 113 | 456 | 138 | 21 | 6 | 3 | 0.7 | 79 | 42 | 34 | 31 | 6 | 1 | 0 | .303 | .395 |
| SS | Bill Jurges | R | 100 | 358 | 88 | 15 | 2 | 8 | 2.2 | 43 | 33 | 19 | 34 | 1 | 2 | 1 | .246 | .366 |
| 3B | Stan Hack | L | 111 | 402 | 116 | 16 | 6 | 1 | 0.2 | 54 | 21 | 45 | 42 | 11 | 2 | 0 | .289 | .366 |
| RF | Babe Herman | L | 125 | 467 | 142 | 34 | 5 | 14 | 3.0 | 65 | 84 | 35 | 71 | 1 | 6 | 2 | .304 | .488 |
| CF | Kiki Cuyler | R | 142 | 559 | 189 | 42 | 8 | 6 | 1.1 | 80 | 69 | 31 | 62 | 15 | 0 | 0 | .338 | .474 |
| LF | Chuck Klein | L | 115 | 435 | 131 | 27 | 2 | 20 | 4.6 | 78 | 80 | 47 | 38 | 3 | 5 | 2 | .301 | .510 |
| C | Gabby Hartnett | R | 130 | 438 | 131 | 21 | 1 | 22 | 5.0 | 58 | 90 | 37 | 46 | 0 | 1 | 0 | .299 | .502 |
| **SUBSTITUTES** | | | | | | | | | | | | | | | | | | |
| S3 | Woody English | R | 109 | 421 | 117 | 26 | 5 | 3 | 0.7 | 65 | 31 | 48 | 65 | 6 | 0 | 0 | .278 | .385 |
| 2B | Augie Galan | B | 66 | 192 | 50 | 6 | 2 | 5 | 2.6 | 31 | 22 | 16 | 15 | 4 | 12 | 5 | .260 | .391 |
| 1B | Don Hurst | L | 51 | 151 | 30 | 5 | 0 | 3 | 2.0 | 13 | 12 | 8 | 18 | 0 | 3 | 1 | .199 | .291 |
| 1B | Dolf Camilli | L | 32 | 120 | 33 | 8 | 0 | 4 | 3.3 | 17 | 19 | 5 | 25* | 1 | 0 | 0 | .275 | .442 |
| 1B | Phil Cavarretta | L | 7 | 21 | 8 | 0 | 1 | 1 | 4.8 | 5 | 6 | 2 | 3 | 1 | 2 | 0 | .381 | .619 |
| OF | Tuck Stainback | R | 104 | 359 | 110 | 14 | 3 | 2 | 0.6 | 47 | 46 | 8 | 42 | 7 | 8 | 3 | .306 | .379 |
| OF | Riggs Stephenson | R | 38 | 74 | 16 | 0 | 0 | 0 | 0.0 | 5 | 7 | 7 | 5 | 0 | 22 | 5 | .216 | .216 |
| C | Babe Phelps | L | 44 | 70 | 20 | 5 | 2 | 2 | 2.9 | 7 | 12 | 1 | 8 | 0 | 26 | 9 | .286 | .500 |
| C | Bob O'Farrell | R | 22 | 67 | 15 | 3 | 0 | 0 | 0.0 | 3 | 5 | 3 | 11 | 0 | 0 | 0 | .224 | .269 |
| C | Bennie Tate | L | 11 | 24 | 3 | 0 | 0 | 0 | 0.0 | 1 | 0 | 1 | 3 | 0 | 3 | 0 | .125 | .125 |
| **PITCHERS** | | | | | | | | | | | | | | | | | | |
| P | Lon Warneke | R | 52 | 113 | 22 | 3 | 0 | 0 | 0.0 | 12 | 8 | 3 | 9 | 0 | 1 | 0 | .195 | .221 |
| P | Bill Lee | R | 40 | 76 | 10 | 3 | 0 | 0 | 0.0 | 6 | 7 | 4 | 11 | 0 | 0 | 0 | .132 | .171 |
| P | Guy Bush | R | 41 | 70 | 16 | 1 | 0 | 0 | 0.0 | 4 | 10 | 2 | 13 | 2 | 0 | 0 | .229 | .243 |
| P | Pat Malone | L | 34 | 64 | 11 | 0 | 0 | 0 | 0.0 | 2 | 6 | 2 | 20 | 0 | 0 | 0 | .172 | .172 |
| P | Jim Weaver | R | 27 | 52 | 3 | 0 | 0 | 0 | 0.0 | 1 | 0 | 1 | 26 | 0 | 0 | 0 | .058 | .058 |
| P | Charlie Root | R | 34 | 40 | 7 | 3 | 0 | 2 | 5.0 | 3 | 4 | 0 | 13 | 0 | 0 | 0 | .175 | .400 |
| P | Bud Tinning | R | 39 | 39 | 7 | 2 | 0 | 0 | 0.0 | 2 | 3 | 0 | 4 | 0 | 0 | 0 | .179 | .231 |
| P | Roy Joiner | L | 20 | 10 | 2 | 0 | 0 | 0 | 0.0 | 0 | 0 | 0 | 2 | 0 | 0 | 0 | .200 | .200 |
| P | Dick Ward | R | 3 | 1 | 0 | 0 | 0 | 0 | 0.0 | 0 | 0 | 0 | 0 | 0 | 0 | 0 | .000 | .000 |
| P | Charlie Wiedemeyer | L | 4 | 1 | 0 | 0 | 0 | 0 | 0.0 | 0 | 0 | 0 | 1 | 0 | 0 | 0 | .000 | .000 |
| P | Lynn Nelson | L | 2 | 0 | 0 | 0 | 0 | 0 | – | 0 | 0 | 0 | 0 | 0 | 0 | 0 | – | – |
| | TEAM TOTAL | | | 5347 | 1494 | 263 | 44 | 101 | 1.9 | 70 | 664 | 375 | 630 | 59 | 95 | 28 | .279 | .402 |

## INDIVIDUAL FIELDING

| POS | Player | T | G | PO | A | E | DP | TC/G | FA | POS | Player | T | G | PO | A | E | DP | TC/G | FA |
|---|---|---|---|---|---|---|---|---|---|---|---|---|---|---|---|---|---|---|---|
| 1B | C. Grimm | L | 74 | 683 | 43 | 4 | 39 | 9.9 | .995 | OF | K. Cuyler | R | 142 | 319 | 15 | 10 | 1 | 2.4 | .971 |
| | D. Hurst | L | 47 | 413 | 18 | 6 | 39 | 9.3 | .986 | | C. Klein | R | 110 | 222 | 6 | 9 | 2 | 2.2 | .962 |
| | D. Camilli | L | 32 | 294 | 24 | 4* | 27 | 10.1 | .988 | | B. Herman | L | 113 | 192 | 7 | 6 | 2 | 1.8 | .971 |
| | B. Herman | L | 7 | 59 | 3 | 1 | 5 | 9.0 | .984 | | T. Stainback | R | 96 | 185 | 4 | 9 | 1 | 2.1 | .955 |
| | Cavarretta | L | 5 | 53 | 5 | 0 | 6 | 11.6 | 1.000 | | Stephenson | R | 15 | 26 | 3 | 0 | 1 | 1.9 | 1.000 |
| 2B | B. Herman | R | 111 | 278 | 385 | 17 | 64 | 6.1 | .975 | C | G. Hartnett | R | 129 | 605 | 86 | 3 | 11 | 5.4 | .996 |
| | A. Galan | R | 43 | 90 | 106 | 8 | 16 | 4.7 | .961 | | B. O'Farrell | R | 22 | 93 | 10 | 0 | 2 | 4.7 | 1.000 |
| | W. English | R | 7 | 73 | 134 | 6 | 4 | 30.4 | .972 | | B. Phelps | R | 18 | 44 | 7 | 1 | 0 | 2.9 | .981 |
| SS | B. Jurges | R | 98 | 205 | 334 | 19 | 63 | 5.7 | .966 | | B. Tate | R | 8 | 12 | 3 | 0 | 0 | 1.9 | 1.000 |
| | W. English | R | 56 | 61 | 109 | 5 | 22 | 3.1 | .971 | | | | | | | | | | |
| | A. Galan | R | 1 | 1 | 1 | 0 | 0 | 2.0 | 1.000 | | | | | | | | | | |
| 3B | S. Hack | R | 109 | 102 | 198 | 16 | 10 | 2.9 | .949 | | | | | | | | | | |
| | W. English | R | 46 | 11 | 17 | 3 | 5 | 0.7 | .903 | | | | | | | | | | |
| | A. Galan | R | 3 | 1 | 8 | 0 | 2 | 3.0 | 1.000 | | | | | | | | | | |
| | T. Stainback | R | 1 | 1 | 1 | 0 | 0 | 2.0 | 1.000 | | | | | | | | | | |

The Cubs thought their long search for a slugger to replace Hack Wilson had ended when they obtained Phillies outfielder Chuck Klein for $65,000 plus Mark Koenig, Harvey Hendrick, and Ted Kleinhans. Klein, however, played most of the season with a charley horse, and missed rattling the tin fences of the Baker Bowl. His figures fell to 20 homers, 80 RBI, and a .301 average. As a result, the Cubs remained in third place with an 86–65 mark, eight games behind the Cardinals' Gashouse Gang. Lon Warneke, who pitched back-to-back one-hitters at the outset of the season, had a 22–10 record, but couldn't offset the demise of Charlie Root, who was 4–7. Two newcomers, pitcher Bill Lee, 13–14, and third baseman Stan Hack, who batted .289, showed promise of being Cub mainstays for the next decade. Outfielder Kiki Cuyler had his last hurrah by leading the Cubs with a .338 average, and tied the Phillies' Ethan Allen in doubles with 42. Catcher Gabby Hartnett led the Cubs in homers with 22 and RBI with 90. The Cubs also pulled one of their worst trades, sending promising first baseman Dolph Camilli to the Phillies for veteran Don Hurst, who batted .199 for the Cubs.

## TEAM  STATISTICS

| | W | L | PCT | GB | R | OR | 2B | Batting 3B | HR | BA | SA | SB | E | Fielding DP | FA | CG | B | Pitching SO | ShO | SV | ERA |
|---|---|---|---|---|---|---|---|---|---|---|---|---|---|---|---|---|---|---|---|---|---|
| STL | 95 | 58 | .621 | | 799 | 656 | 294 | 75 | 104 | .288 | .425 | 69 | 166 | 141 | .972 | 78 | 411 | 689 | 15 | 16 | 3.69 |
| NY | 93 | 60 | .608 | 2 | 760 | 583 | 240 | 41 | 126 | .275 | .405 | 19 | 179 | 141 | .972 | 66 | 351 | 499 | 12 | 30 | 3.19 |
| CHI | 86 | 65 | .570 | 8 | 705 | 639 | 263 | 44 | 101 | .279 | .402 | 59 | 137 | 135 | .977 | 73 | 417 | 633 | 11 | 9 | 3.76 |
| BOS | 78 | 73 | .517 | 16 | 683 | 714 | 233 | 44 | 83 | .272 | .378 | 30 | 169 | 120 | .972 | 62 | 405 | 462 | 11 | 20 | 4.11 |
| PIT | 74 | 76 | .493 | 19.5 | 735 | 713 | 281 | 77 | 52 | .287 | .398 | 44 | 145 | 118 | .975 | 61 | 354 | 487 | 8 | 8 | 4.20 |
| BKN | 71 | 81 | .467 | 23.5 | 748 | 795 | 284 | 52 | 79 | .281 | .396 | 55 | 180 | 141 | .970 | 66 | 476 | 520 | 6 | 12 | 4.48 |
| PHI | 56 | 93 | .376 | 37 | 675 | 794 | 286 | 35 | 56 | .284 | .384 | 52 | 197 | 140 | .966 | 52 | 437 | 416 | 8 | 15 | 4.76 |
| CIN | 52 | 99 | .344 | 42 | 590 | 801 | 227 | 65 | 55 | .266 | .364 | 34 | 181 | 136 | .970 | 51 | 389 | 438 | 3 | 19 | 4.37 |
| LEAGUE TOTAL | | | | | 5695 | 5695 | 2108 | 433 | 656 | .279 | .394 | 362 | 1354 | 1072 | .972 | 509 | 3240 | 4144 | 74 | 129 | 4.06 |

## INDIVIDUAL  PITCHING

| PITCHER | T | W | L | PCT | ERA | SV | G | GS | CG | IP | H | BB | SO | R | ER | ShO | H/9 | BB/9 | SO/9 |
|---|---|---|---|---|---|---|---|---|---|---|---|---|---|---|---|---|---|---|---|
| Lon Warneke | R | 22 | 10 | .688 | 3.21 | 3 | 43 | 35 | 23 | 291.1 | 273 | 66 | 143 | 116 | 104 | 3 | 8.43 | 2.04 | 4.42 |
| Bill Lee | R | 13 | 14 | .481 | 3.40 | 1 | 35 | 29 | 16 | 214.1 | 218 | 74 | 104 | 91 | 81 | 4 | 9.15 | 3.11 | 4.37 |
| Guy Bush | R | 18 | 10 | .643 | 3.83 | 2 | 40 | 27 | 15 | 209.1 | 213 | 54 | 75 | 96 | 89 | 1 | 9.16 | 2.32 | 3.22 |
| Pat Malone | R | 14 | 7 | .667 | 3.53 | 0 | 34 | 21 | 8 | 191 | 200 | 55 | 111 | 85 | 75 | 1 | 9.42 | 2.59 | 5.23 |
| Jim Weaver | R | 11 | 9 | .550 | 3.91 | 0 | 27 | 20 | 8 | 159 | 163 | 54 | 98 | 77 | 69 | 1 | 9.23 | 3.06 | 5.55 |
| Bud Tinning | R | 4 | 6 | .400 | 3.34 | 3 | 39 | 7 | 1 | 129.1 | 134 | 46 | 44 | 59 | 48 | 1 | 9.32 | 3.20 | 3.06 |
| Charlie Root | R | 4 | 7 | .364 | 4.28 | 0 | 34 | 9 | 2 | 117.2 | 141 | 53 | 46 | 62 | 56 | 0 | 10.78 | 4.05 | 3.52 |
| Roy Joiner | L | 0 | 1 | .000 | 8.21 | 0 | 20 | 2 | 0 | 34 | 61 | 8 | 9 | 33 | 31 | 0 | 16.15 | 2.12 | 2.38 |
| Charlie Wiedemeyer | L | 0 | 0 | – | 9.72 | 0 | 4 | 1 | 0 | 8.1 | 16 | 4 | 2 | 10 | 9 | 0 | 17.28 | 4.32 | 2.16 |
| Dick Ward | R | 0 | 0 | – | 3.18 | 0 | 3 | 0 | 0 | 5.2 | 9 | 2 | 1 | 6 | 2 | 0 | 14.29 | 3.18 | 1.59 |
| Lynn Nelson | R | 0 | 1 | .000 | 36.00 | 0 | 2 | 1 | 0 | 1 | 4 | 1 | 0 | 4 | 4 | 0 | 36.00 | 9.00 | 0.00 |
| TEAM TOTAL | | 86 | 65 | .570 | 3.76 | 9 | 281 | 152 | 73 | 1361 | 1432 | 417 | 633 | 639 | 568 | 11 | 9.47 | 2.76 | 4.19 |

| MANAGER | W | L | PCT |
|---|---|---|---|
| Charlie Grimm | 100 | 54 | .649 |

| POS | Player | B | G | AB | H | 2B | 3B | HR | HR % | R | RBI | BB | SO | SB | Pinch Hit AB | Pinch Hit H | BA | SA |
|---|---|---|---|---|---|---|---|---|---|---|---|---|---|---|---|---|---|---|
| **REGULARS** | | | | | | | | | | | | | | | | | | |
| 1B | Phil Cavarretta | L | 146 | 589 | 162 | 28 | 12 | 8 | 1.4 | 85 | 82 | 39 | 61 | 4 | 1 | 0 | .275 | .404 |
| 2B | Billy Herman | R | 154 | 666 | 227 | 57 | 6 | 7 | 1.1 | 113 | 83 | 42 | 29 | 6 | 0 | 0 | .341 | .476 |
| SS | Bill Jurges | R | 146 | 519 | 125 | 33 | 1 | 1 | 0.2 | 69 | 59 | 42 | 39 | 3 | 0 | 0 | .241 | .314 |
| 3B | Stan Hack | L | 124 | 427 | 133 | 23 | 9 | 4 | 0.9 | 75 | 64 | 65 | 17 | 14 | 5 | 2 | .311 | .436 |
| RF | Chuck Klein | L | 119 | 434 | 127 | 14 | 4 | 21 | 4.8 | 71 | 73 | 41 | 42 | 4 | 6 | 1 | .293 | .488 |
| CF | Frank Demaree | R | 107 | 385 | 125 | 19 | 4 | 2 | 0.5 | 60 | 66 | 26 | 23 | 6 | 8 | 2 | .325 | .410 |
| LF | Augie Galan | B | 154 | 646 | 203 | 41 | 11 | 12 | 1.9 | 133 | 79 | 87 | 53 | 22 | 0 | 0 | .314 | .467 |
| C | Gabby Hartnett | R | 116 | 413 | 142 | 32 | 6 | 13 | 3.1 | 67 | 91 | 41 | 46 | 1 | 6 | 1 | .344 | .545 |
| **SUBSTITUTES** | | | | | | | | | | | | | | | | | | |
| 3S | Woody English | R | 34 | 84 | 17 | 2 | 0 | 2 | 2.4 | 11 | 8 | 20 | 4 | 1 | 4 | 2 | .202 | .298 |
| 1B | Charlie Grimm | L | 2 | 8 | 0 | 0 | 0 | 0 | 0.0 | 0 | 0 | 0 | 1 | 0 | 0 | 0 | .000 | .000 |
| O3 | Freddie Lindstrom | R | 90 | 342 | 94 | 22 | 4 | 3 | 0.9 | 49 | 62 | 10 | 13 | 1 | 6 | 1 | .275 | .389 |
| OF | Kiki Cuyler | R | 45 | 157 | 42 | 5 | 1 | 4 | 2.5 | 22 | 18 | 10 | 16 | 3 | 3 | 2 | .268 | .389 |
| OF | Tuck Stainback | R | 47 | 94 | 24 | 4 | 0 | 3 | 3.2 | 16 | 11 | 0 | 13 | 1 | 10 | 3 | .255 | .394 |
| C | Ken O'Dea | L | 76 | 202 | 52 | 13 | 2 | 6 | 3.0 | 30 | 38 | 26 | 18 | 0 | 9 | 1 | .257 | .431 |
| C | Walter Stephenson | R | 16 | 26 | 10 | 1 | 1 | 0 | 0.0 | 2 | 2 | 1 | 5 | 0 | 9 | 2 | .385 | .500 |
| PH | Johnny Gill | L | 3 | 3 | 1 | 1 | 0 | 0 | 0.0 | 2 | 1 | 0 | 1 | 0 | 3 | 1 | .333 | .667 |
| **PITCHERS** | | | | | | | | | | | | | | | | | | |
| P | Bill Lee | R | 39 | 102 | 24 | 3 | 0 | 0 | 0.0 | 8 | 11 | 2 | 15 | 0 | 0 | 0 | .235 | .265 |
| P | Lon Warneke | R | 44 | 91 | 20 | 1 | 0 | 0 | 0.0 | 9 | 15 | 3 | 9 | 0 | 0 | 0 | .220 | .231 |
| P | Larry French | R | 42 | 85 | 12 | 1 | 0 | 0 | 0.0 | 4 | 5 | 1 | 14 | 0 | 0 | 0 | .141 | .153 |
| P | Charlie Root | R | 38 | 69 | 14 | 2 | 1 | 1 | 1.4 | 8 | 7 | 3 | 22 | 0 | 0 | 0 | .203 | .304 |
| P | Tex Carleton | B | 31 | 62 | 8 | 0 | 0 | 0 | 0.0 | 4 | 2 | 2 | 12 | 0 | 0 | 0 | .129 | .129 |
| P | Roy Henshaw | R | 31 | 51 | 13 | 1 | 0 | 0 | 0.0 | 5 | 2 | 1 | 11 | 0 | 0 | 0 | .255 | .275 |
| P | Fabian Kowalik | B | 20 | 15 | 3 | 0 | 0 | 0 | 0.0 | 1 | 1 | 0 | 2 | 0 | 0 | 0 | .200 | .200 |
| P | Clay Bryant | R | 12 | 6 | 2 | 0 | 0 | 1 | 16.7 | 2 | 2 | 2 | 2 | 0 | 0 | 0 | .333 | .833 |
| P | Hugh Casey | R | 13 | 6 | 1 | 0 | 0 | 0 | 0.0 | 1 | 0 | 0 | 3 | 0 | 0 | 0 | .167 | .167 |
| P | Clyde Shoun | L | 5 | 3 | 0 | 0 | 0 | 0 | 0.0 | 0 | 0 | 0 | 0 | 0 | 0 | 0 | .000 | .000 |
| P | Roy Joiner | L | 2 | 1 | 0 | 0 | 0 | 0 | 0.0 | 0 | 0 | 0 | 0 | 0 | 0 | 0 | .000 | .000 |
| | TEAM TOTAL | | | 5486 | 1581 | 303 | 62 | 88 | 1.6 | 84 | 782 | 464 | 471 | 66 | 70 | 18 | .288 | .414 |

## INDIVIDUAL  FIELDING

| POS | Player | T | G | PO | A | E | DP | TC/G | FA |
|---|---|---|---|---|---|---|---|---|---|
| 1B | Cavarretta | L | 145 | 1347 | 98 | 20 | 129 | 10.1 | .986 |
| | S. Hack | R | 7 | 66 | 7 | 1 | 5 | 10.6 | .986 |
| | C. Grimm | L | 2 | 27 | 1 | 0 | 4 | 14.0 | 1.000 |
| 2B | B. Herman | R | 154 | 416 | 520 | 35 | 109 | 6.3 | .964 |
| SS | B. Jurges | R | 146 | 348 | 484 | 31 | 99 | 5.9 | .964 |
| | W. English | R | 12 | 21 | 29 | 1 | 4 | 4.3 | .980 |
| 3B | S. Hack | R | 111 | 87 | 237 | 20 | 21 | 3.1 | .942 |
| | F. Lindstrom | R | 33 | 31 | 35 | 4 | 7 | 2.1 | .943 |
| | W. English | R | 16 | 8 | 25 | 5 | 2 | 2.4 | .868 |

| POS | Player | T | G | PO | A | E | DP | TC/G | FA |
|---|---|---|---|---|---|---|---|---|---|
| OF | A. Galan | R | 154 | 351 | 12 | 8 | 4 | 2.4 | .978 |
| | C. Klein | R | 111 | 215 | 11 | 10 | 7 | 2.1 | .958 |
| | F. Demaree | R | 98 | 204 | 13 | 6 | 3 | 2.3 | .973 |
| | F. Lindstrom | R | 50 | 136 | 5 | 3 | 0 | 2.9 | .979 |
| | K. Cuyler | R | 42 | 98 | 5 | 2 | 1 | 2.5 | .981 |
| | T. Stainback | R | 28 | 40 | 1 | 3 | 0 | 1.6 | .932 |
| C | G. Hartnett | R | 110 | 477 | 77 | 9 | 11 | 5.1 | .984 |
| | K. O'Dea | R | 63 | 213 | 27 | 9 | 3 | 4.0 | .964 |
| | Stephenson | R | 6 | 17 | 6 | 0 | 1 | 3.8 | 1.000 |

Superstitious manager Charlie Grimm nailed 21 tacks into his shoes as the Cubs hammered out 21 straight victories to win the pennant. In third place behind the Cardinals and Giants on September 4, the Cubs were unbeatable down the stretch until the final game of the season. But by then they had clinched the pennant with a 100–54 record, four games ahead of the Cardinals. Pitchers Larry French and Bill Lee won five games each during the streak, while Lon Warneke and Charlie Root won four apiece, Roy Henshaw won two, and Tex Carleton one. Warneke and Lee were 20-game winners.

Two long homestands keyed the Cubs' spree. In addition to a 19–1 September record at Wrigley Field, they were 20–5 before the home folks in July. And the Cubs didn't do it on pitching alone. A well-balanced attack that featured five .300 hitters gave the Cubs a league-leading .288 average. Catcher Gabby Hartnett led the club with .344 and 91 RBI and won the Most Valuable Player Award; second baseman Billy Herman had 227 hits and 57 doubles and hit .341; leftfielder Augie Galan, who didn't ground into a double play all season, scored 133 runs, stole 22 bases, and hit .314; Frank Demaree batted .325; and Stan Hack hit .311. Slugger Chuck Klein continued to disappoint with a .293 average, but led with 21 homers. Grimm entrusted first base to teenager Phil Cavarretta, and the youngster responded with 82 RBI and a .275 average. But in the World Series only Warneke stood out for the Cubbies, posting both of the Chicago victories as Detroit won in six games.

## TEAM STATISTICS

| | W | L | PCT | GB | R | OR | Batting 2B | 3B | HR | BA | SA | SB | Fielding E | DP | FA | CG | B | Pitching SO | ShO | SV | ERA |
|---|---|---|---|---|---|---|---|---|---|---|---|---|---|---|---|---|---|---|---|---|---|
| CHI | 100 | 54 | .649 | | 847 | 597 | 303 | 62 | 88 | **.288** | .414 | 66 | 186 | **163** | .970 | **81** | 400 | 589 | 12 | 14 | **3.26** |
| STL | 96 | 58 | .623 | 4 | 829 | 625 | 286 | 59 | 86 | .284 | .405 | 71 | **164** | 133 | **.972** | 73 | 382 | **594** | 9 | 18 | 3.54 |
| NY | 91 | 62 | .595 | 8.5 | 770 | 675 | 248 | 56 | **123** | .286 | **.416** | 32 | 174 | 129 | .972 | 76 | 411 | 524 | 10 | 11 | 3.78 |
| PIT | 86 | 67 | .562 | 13.5 | 743 | 647 | 255 | **90** | 66 | .285 | .402 | 30 | 190 | 94 | .968 | 76 | **312** | 549 | **15** | 11 | 3.42 |
| BKN | 70 | 83 | .458 | 29.5 | 711 | 767 | 235 | 62 | 59 | .277 | .376 | 60 | 188 | 146 | .969 | 62 | 436 | 480 | 11 | **20** | 4.22 |
| CIN | 68 | 85 | .444 | 31.5 | 646 | 772 | 244 | 68 | 73 | .265 | .378 | **72** | 204 | 139 | .966 | 59 | 438 | 500 | 9 | 12 | 4.30 |
| PHI | 64 | 89 | .418 | 35.5 | 685 | 871 | 249 | 32 | 92 | .269 | .378 | 52 | 228 | 145 | .963 | 53 | 505 | 475 | 8 | 15 | 4.76 |
| BOS | 38 | 115 | .248 | 61.5 | 575 | 852 | 233 | 33 | 75 | .263 | .362 | 20 | 197 | 101 | .967 | 54 | 404 | 355 | 6 | 5 | 4.93 |
| LEAGUE TOTAL | | | | | 5806 | 5806 | 2053 | 462 | 662 | .277 | .391 | 403 | 1531 | 1050 | .968 | 534 | 3288 | 4066 | 80 | 106 | 4.02 |

## INDIVIDUAL PITCHING

| PITCHER | T | W | L | PCT | ERA | SV | G | GS | CG | IP | H | BB | SO | R | ER | ShO | H/9 | BB/9 | SO/9 |
|---|---|---|---|---|---|---|---|---|---|---|---|---|---|---|---|---|---|---|---|
| Lon Warneke | R | 20 | 13 | .606 | 3.06 | 4 | 42 | 30 | 20 | 261.2 | 257 | 50 | 120 | 102 | 89 | 1 | 8.84 | 1.72 | 4.13 |
| Bill Lee | R | 20 | 6 | **.769** | 2.96 | 1 | 39 | 32 | 18 | 252 | 241 | 84 | 100 | 106 | 83 | 3 | 8.61 | 3.00 | 3.57 |
| Larry French | L | 17 | 10 | .630 | 2.96 | 2 | 42 | 30 | 16 | 246.1 | 279 | 44 | 90 | 94 | 81 | 4 | 10.19 | 1.61 | 3.29 |
| Charlie Root | R | 15 | 8 | .652 | 3.08 | 2 | 38 | 18 | 11 | 201.1 | 193 | 47 | 94 | 85 | 69 | 1 | 8.63 | 2.10 | 4.20 |
| Tex Carleton | R | 11 | 8 | .579 | 3.89 | 1 | 31 | 22 | 8 | 171 | 169 | 60 | 84 | 82 | 74 | 0 | 8.89 | 3.16 | 4.42 |
| Roy Henshaw | L | 13 | 5 | .722 | 3.28 | 1 | 31 | 18 | 7 | 142.2 | 135 | 68 | 53 | 60 | 52 | 3 | 8.52 | 4.29 | 3.34 |
| Fabian Kowalik | R | 2 | 2 | .500 | 3.86 | 0 | 13 | 0 | 0 | 55 | 60 | 19 | 20 | 31 | 27 | 0 | 9.82 | 3.11 | 3.27 |
| Hugh Casey | R | 0 | 0 | — | 3.86 | 0 | 13 | 0 | 0 | 25.2 | 29 | 14 | 10 | 13 | 11 | 0 | 10.17 | 4.91 | 3.51 |
| Clay Bryant | R | 1 | 2 | .333 | 5.16 | 2 | 9 | 1 | 0 | 22.2 | 34 | 7 | 13 | 15 | 13 | 0 | 13.50 | 2.78 | 5.16 |
| Clyde Shoun | L | 1 | 0 | 1.000 | 2.84 | 0 | 5 | 1 | 0 | 12.2 | 14 | 5 | 5 | 4 | 4 | 0 | 9.95 | 3.55 | 3.55 |
| Roy Joiner | L | 0 | 0 | — | 5.40 | 0 | 2 | 0 | 0 | 3.1 | 6 | 2 | 0 | 4 | 2 | 0 | 16.20 | 5.40 | 0.00 |
| TEAM TOTAL | | 100 | 54 | .649 | 3.26 | 14 | 272 | 154 | 81 | 1394.1 | 1417 | 400 | 589 | 596 | 505 | 12 | 9.15 | 2.58 | 3.80 |

| MANAGER | W | L | PCT |
|---|---|---|---|
| Charlie Grimm | 87 | 67 | .565 |

| POS | Player | B | G | AB | H | 2B | 3B | HR | HR % | R | RBI | BB | SO | SB | Pinch Hit AB | Pinch Hit H | BA | SA |
|---|---|---|---|---|---|---|---|---|---|---|---|---|---|---|---|---|---|---|
| **REGULARS** | | | | | | | | | | | | | | | | | | |
| 1B | Phil Cavarretta | L | 124 | 458 | 125 | 18 | 1 | 9 | 2.0 | 55 | 56 | 17 | 36 | 8 | 8 | 4 | .273 | .376 |
| 2B | Billy Herman | R | 153 | 632 | 211 | 57 | 7 | 5 | 0.8 | 101 | 93 | 59 | 30 | 5 | 0 | 0 | .334 | .470 |
| SS | Bill Jurges | R | 118 | 429 | 120 | 25 | 1 | 1 | 0.2 | 51 | 42 | 23 | 25 | 4 | 0 | 0 | .280 | .350 |
| 3B | Stan Hack | L | 149 | 561 | 167 | 27 | 4 | 6 | 1.1 | 102 | 78 | 89 | 39 | 17 | 0 | 0 | .298 | .392 |
| RF | Frank Demaree | R | 154 | 605 | 212 | 34 | 3 | 16 | 2.6 | 93 | 96 | 49 | 30 | 4 | 0 | 0 | .350 | .496 |
| CF | Augie Galan | B | 145 | 575 | 152 | 26 | 4 | 8 | 1.4 | 74 | 81 | 67 | 50 | 16 | 2 | 0 | .264 | .365 |
| LF | Ethan Allen | R | 91 | 373 | 110 | 18 | 6 | 3 | 0.8 | 47 | 39 | 13 | 30 | 12 | 0 | 0 | .295 | .399 |
| C | Gabby Hartnett | R | 121 | 424 | 130 | 25 | 6 | 7 | 1.7 | 49 | 64 | 30 | 36 | 0 | 7 | 0 | .307 | .443 |
| **SUBSTITUTES** | | | | | | | | | | | | | | | | | | |
| S3 | Woody English | R | 64 | 182 | 45 | 9 | 0 | 0 | 0.0 | 33 | 20 | 40 | 28 | 1 | 5 | 0 | .247 | .297 |
| 1B | Charlie Grimm | L | 39 | 132 | 33 | 4 | 0 | 1 | 0.8 | 13 | 16 | 5 | 8 | 0 | 4 | 1 | .250 | .303 |
| S3 | Gene Lillard | R | 19 | 34 | 7 | 1 | 0 | 0 | 0.0 | 6 | 2 | 3 | 8 | 0 | 10 * | 3 | .206 | .235 |
| OF | Johnny Gill | L | 71 | 174 | 44 | 8 | 0 | 7 | 4.0 | 20 | 28 | 13 | 19 | 0 | 25 | 6 | .253 | .420 |
| OF | Chuck Klein | L | 29 | 109 | 32 | 5 | 0 | 5 | 4.6 | 19 | 18 | 16 | 14 | 0 | 0 | 0 | .294 | .477 |
| OF | Tuck Stainback | R | 44 | 75 | 13 | 3 | 0 | 1 | 1.3 | 13 | 5 | 6 | 14 | 1 | 9 | 1 | .173 | .253 |
| C | Ken O'Dea | L | 80 | 189 | 58 | 10 | 3 | 2 | 1.1 | 36 | 38 | 38 | 18 | 0 | 22 | 7 | .307 | .423 |
| C | Walter Stephenson | R | 6 | 12 | 1 | 0 | 0 | 0 | 0.0 | 0 | 1 | 0 | 5 | 0 | 2 | 0 | .083 | .083 |
| **PITCHERS** | | | | | | | | | | | | | | | | | | |
| P | Bill Lee | R | 43 | 87 | 12 | 0 | 1 | 1 | 1.1 | 5 | 3 | 2 | 14 | 0 | 0 | 0 | .138 | .195 |
| P | Larry French | R | 43 | 85 | 18 | 2 | 0 | 0 | 0.0 | 5 | 5 | 4 | 12 | 0 | 0 | 0 | .212 | .235 |
| P | Lon Warneke | R | 40 | 84 | 17 | 1 | 0 | 1 | 1.2 | 9 | 5 | 2 | 9 | 0 | 0 | 0 | .202 | .250 |
| P | Tex Carleton | B | 35 | 60 | 14 | 1 | 0 | 3 | 5.0 | 9 | 11 | 10 | 13 | 0 | 0 | 0 | .233 | .383 |
| P | Curt Davis | R | 24 | 53 | 8 | 1 | 0 | 0 | 0.0 | 6 | 3 | 2 | 13 | 0 | 0 | 0 | .151 | .170 |
| P | Roy Henshaw | R | 39 | 44 | 6 | 1 | 0 | 0 | 0.0 | 3 | 1 | 1 | 7 | 0 | 0 | 0 | .136 | .159 |
| P | Charlie Root | R | 33 | 15 | 5 | 0 | 0 | 0 | 0.0 | 1 | 0 | 2 | 4 | 0 | 0 | 0 | .333 | .333 |
| P | Clay Bryant | R | 32 | 12 | 5 | 0 | 0 | 0 | 0.0 | 4 | 2 | 0 | 0 | 0 | 0 | 0 | .417 | .417 |
| P | Fabian Kowalik | R | 6 | 5 | 0 | 0 | 0 | 0 | 0.0 | 1 | 0 | 0 | 0 | 0 | 0 | 0 | .000 | .000 |
| P | Clyde Shoun | L | 4 | 0 | 0 | 0 | 0 | 0 | – | 0 | 0 | 0 | 0 | 0 | 0 | 0 | – | – |
| TEAM TOTAL | | | | 5409 | 1545 | 275 | 36 | 76 | 1.4 | 75 | 707 | 491 | 462 | 68 | 94 | 22 | .286 | .392 |

## INDIVIDUAL FIELDING

| POS | Player | T | G | PO | A | E | DP | TC/G | FA |
|---|---|---|---|---|---|---|---|---|---|
| 1B | Cavarretta | L | 115 | 980 | 71 | 14 | 93 | 9.3 | .987 |
| | C. Grimm | L | 35 | 297 | 33 | 0 | 31 | 9.4 | 1.000 |
| | S. Hack | R | 11 | 104 | 8 | 0 | 15 | 10.2 | 1.000 |
| 2B | B. Herman | R | 153 | **457** | 492 | 24 | 110 | 6.4 | **.975** |
| | W. English | R | 1 | 3 | 4 | 0 | 0 | 7.0 | 1.000 |
| SS | B. Jurges | R | 116 | 249 | 379 | 26 | 80 | 5.6 | .960 |
| | W. English | R | 42 | 75 | 127 | 5 | 27 | 4.9 | .976 |
| | G. Lillard | R | 4 | 9 | 9 | 1 | 2 | 4.8 | .947 |
| 3B | S. Hack | R | 140 | 121 | 202 | 17 | 13 | 2.4 | .950 |
| | W. English | R | 17 | 14 | 21 | 0 | 3 | 2.1 | 1.000 |
| | G. Lillard | R | 3 | 2 | 4 | 1 | 0 | 2.3 | .857 |

| POS | Player | T | G | PO | A | E | DP | TC/G | FA |
|---|---|---|---|---|---|---|---|---|---|
| OF | A. Galan | R | 145 | 381 | 9 | 5 | 3 | 2.7 | .987 |
| | F. Demaree | R | 154 | 285 | 16 | 10 | 1 | 2.0 | .968 |
| | E. Allen | R | 89 | 191 | 2 | 4 | 2 | 2.2 | .980 |
| | J. Gill | R | 41 | 72 | 3 | 5 | 1 | 2.0 | .938 |
| | C. Klein | R | 29 | 63 | 3 | 6* | 0 | 2.5 | .917 |
| | T. Stainback | R | 26 | 38 | 1 | 0 | 0 | 1.5 | 1.000 |
| C | G. Hartnett | R | 114 | 504 | 75 | 5 | 8 | **5.1** | **.991** |
| | K. O'Dea | R | 55 | 211 | 27 | 5 | 1 | 4.4 | .979 |
| | Stephenson | R | 4 | 10 | 1 | 0 | 0 | 2.8 | 1.000 |

Wrigley Field was indeed the friendly confines for the Cubs, who lost only one home game during the month of June. Charlie Grimm's team surged into first place with 15 straight victories, which included 11 at home. Overall the Cubs were 50–27 at their Addison and Clark address and 37–40 on the road. But the Giants prevailed by five games over the Cubs and Cardinals, who tied for second with 87–67 marks. While the Cubs and Cardinals were trading punches in September, the Giants were beating their three weak eastern rivals: Boston, Brooklyn, and Philly. The three teams finished sixth through eighth and combined for 270 losses.

Outfielder Frank Demaree was the Cubs' leading batter at .350 and nosed teammate Billy Herman in hits, 212–211. Herman, who hit .334, had 57 doubles for the second year in a row. Catcher Gabby Hartnett was the Cubs' third .300 hitter at .307. Right-hander Bill Lee and southpaw Larry French shared pitching honors with 18 victories each. Lon Warneke, who had arm trouble at the outset of the season, bounced back with 16 wins. The Cubs finally gave up on slugger Chuck Klein and shipped him to Philly for outfielder Ethan Allen and pitcher Curt Davis. Outfielder Augie Galan became the first Cub to homer in an All-Star Game when the NL topped the AL for the first time, 4–3, on July 7 at Boston.

## TEAM STATISTICS

| | W | L | PCT | GB | R | OR | 2B | 3B | Batting HR | BA | SA | SB | Fielding E | DP | FA | CG | B | Pitching SO | ShO | SV | ERA |
|---|---|---|---|---|---|---|---|---|---|---|---|---|---|---|---|---|---|---|---|---|---|
| NY | 92 | 62 | .597 | | 742 | 621 | 237 | 48 | 97 | .281 | .395 | 31 | 168 | 164 | .974 | 58 | 401 | 500 | 12 | 22 | **3.46** |
| CHI | 87 | 67 | .565 | 5 | 755 | **603** | 275 | 36 | 76 | .286 | .392 | 68 | **146** | 156 | **.976** | 77 | 434 | 597 | **18** | 10 | 3.53 |
| STL | 87 | 67 | .565 | 5 | 795 | 794 | **332** | 60 | 88 | .281 | **.410** | **69** | 156 | 134 | .974 | 65 | 477 | 561 | 5 | **24** | 4.48 |
| PIT | 84 | 70 | .545 | 8 | **804** | 718 | 283 | **80** | 60 | **.286** | .397 | 37 | 199 | 113 | .967 | 67 | **379** | 559 | 5 | 12 | 3.89 |
| CIN | 74 | 80 | .481 | 18 | 722 | 760 | 224 | 73 | 82 | .274 | .388 | 68 | 191 | 150 | .969 | 50 | 418 | 459 | 6 | 23 | 4.22 |
| BOS | 71 | 83 | .461 | 21 | 631 | 715 | 207 | 44 | 68 | .265 | .356 | 23 | 189 | **175** | .971 | 60 | 451 | 421 | 7 | 13 | 3.94 |
| BKN | 67 | 87 | .435 | 25 | 662 | 752 | 263 | 43 | 68 | .272 | .353 | 55 | 208 | 107 | .966 | 59 | 528 | **654** | 7 | 18 | 3.98 |
| PHI | 54 | 100 | .351 | 38 | 726 | 874 | 250 | 46 | **103** | .281 | **.401** | 50 | 252 | 144 | .959 | 51 | 515 | 454 | 7 | 14 | 4.64 |
| LEAGUE TOTAL | | | | | 5837 | 5837 | 2071 | 430 | 607 | .278 | .386 | 401 | 1509 | 1143 | .969 | 487 | 3603 | 4205 | 67 | 136 | 4.02 |

## INDIVIDUAL PITCHING

| PITCHER | T | W | L | PCT | ERA | SV | G | GS | CG | IP | H | BB | SO | R | ER | ShO | H/9 | BB/9 | SO/9 |
|---|---|---|---|---|---|---|---|---|---|---|---|---|---|---|---|---|---|---|---|
| Bill Lee | R | 18 | 11 | .621 | 3.31 | 1 | 43 | 33 | 20 | 258.2 | 238 | 93 | 102 | 103 | 95 | 4 | 8.28 | 3.24 | 3.55 |
| Larry French | L | 18 | 9 | .667 | 3.39 | 3 | 43 | 28 | 16 | 252.1 | 262 | 54 | 104 | 103 | 95 | 4 | 9.34 | 1.93 | 3.71 |
| Lon Warneke | R | 16 | 13 | .552 | 3.44 | 1 | 40 | 29 | 13 | 240.2 | 246 | 76 | 113 | 108 | 92 | 4 | 9.20 | 2.84 | 4.23 |
| Tex Carleton | R | 14 | 10 | .583 | 3.65 | 1 | 35 | 26 | 12 | 197.1 | 204 | 67 | 88 | 85 | 80 | 4 | 9.30 | 3.06 | 4.01 |
| Curt Davis | R | 11 | 9 | .550 | 3.00 | 1 | 24 | 20 | 10 | 153 | 146 | 31 | 52 | 60 | 51 | 0 | 8.59 | 1.82 | 3.06 |
| Roy Henshaw | L | 6 | 5 | .545 | 3.97 | 1 | 39 | 14 | 6 | 129.1 | 152 | 56 | 69 | 67 | 57 | 2 | 10.58 | 3.90 | 4.80 |
| Charlie Root | R | 3 | 6 | .333 | 4.15 | 1 | 33 | 4 | 0 | 73.2 | 81 | 20 | 32 | 34 | 34 | 0 | 9.90 | 2.44 | 3.91 |
| Clay Bryant | R | 1 | 2 | .333 | 3.30 | 0 | 26 | 0 | 0 | 57.1 | 57 | 24 | 35 | 25 | 21 | 0 | 8.95 | 3.77 | 5.49 |
| Fabian Kowalik | R | 0 | 2 | .000 | 6.75 | 1 | 6 | 0 | 0 | 16 | 24 | 7 | 1 | 12 | 12 | 0 | 13.50 | 3.94 | 0.56 |
| Clyde Shoun | L | 0 | 0 | – | 12.46 | 0 | 4 | 0 | 0 | 4.1 | 3 | 6 | 1 | 6 | 6 | 0 | 6.23 | 12.46 | 2.08 |
| TEAM TOTAL | | 87 | 67 | .565 | 3.53 | 10 | 293 | 154 | 77 | 1382.2 | 1413 | 434 | 597 | 603 | 543 | 18 | 9.20 | 2.82 | 3.89 |

| MANAGER | W | L | PCT |
|---|---|---|---|
| Charlie Grimm | 93 | 61 | .604 |

| POS | Player | B | G | AB | H | 2B | 3B | HR | HR % | R | RBI | BB | SO | SB | Pinch Hit AB | Pinch Hit H | BA | SA |
|---|---|---|---|---|---|---|---|---|---|---|---|---|---|---|---|---|---|---|
| **REGULARS** | | | | | | | | | | | | | | | | | | |
| 1B | Ripper Collins | B | 115 | 456 | 125 | 16 | 5 | 16 | 3.5 | 77 | 71 | 32 | 46 | 2 | 4 | 0 | .274 | .436 |
| 2B | Billy Herman | R | 138 | 564 | 189 | 35 | 11 | 8 | 1.4 | 106 | 65 | 56 | 22 | 2 | 1 | 0 | .335 | .479 |
| SS | Bill Jurges | R | 129 | 450 | 134 | 18 | 10 | 1 | 0.2 | 53 | 65 | 42 | 41 | 2 | 0 | 0 | .298 | .389 |
| 3B | Stan Hack | L | 154 | 582 | 173 | 27 | 6 | 2 | 0.3 | 106 | 63 | 83 | 42 | 16 | 1 | 0 | .297 | .375 |
| RF | Frank Demaree | R | 154 | 615 | 199 | 36 | 6 | 17 | 2.8 | 104 | 115 | 57 | 31 | 6 | 0 | 0 | .324 | .485 |
| CF | Joe Marty | R | 88 | 290 | 84 | 17 | 2 | 5 | 1.7 | 41 | 44 | 28 | 30 | 3 | 3 | 2 | .290 | .414 |
| LF | Augie Galan | B | 147 | 611 | 154 | 24 | 10 | 18 | 2.9 | 104 | 78 | 79 | 48 | 23 | 0 | 0 | .252 | .412 |
| C | Gabby Hartnett | R | 110 | 356 | 126 | 21 | 6 | 12 | 3.4 | 47 | 82 | 43 | 19 | 0 | 8 | 2 | .354 | .548 |
| **SUBSTITUTES** | | | | | | | | | | | | | | | | | | |
| UT | Lonny Frey | B | 78 | 198 | 55 | 9 | 3 | 1 | 0.5 | 33 | 22 | 33 | 15 | 6 | 14 | 2 | .278 | .369 |
| O1 | Phil Cavarretta | L | 106 | 329 | 94 | 18 | 7 | 5 | 1.5 | 43 | 56 | 32 | 35 | 7 | 11 | 4 | .286 | .429 |
| OF | Tuck Stainback | R | 72 | 160 | 37 | 7 | 1 | 0 | 0.0 | 18 | 14 | 7 | 16 | 3 | 10 | 2 | .231 | .288 |
| OF | Carl Reynolds | R | 7 | 11 | 3 | 1 | 0 | 0 | 0.0 | 0 | 1 | 2 | 2 | 0 | 4 | 1 | .273 | .364 |
| C | Ken O'Dea | L | 83 | 219 | 66 | 7 | 5 | 4 | 1.8 | 31 | 32 | 24 | 26 | 1 | 13 | 3 | .301 | .434 |
| C | John Bottarini | R | 26 | 40 | 11 | 3 | 0 | 1 | 2.5 | 3 | 7 | 5 | 10 | 0 | 7 | 2 | .275 | .425 |
| PH | Bob Garbark | R | 1 | 1 | 0 | 0 | 0 | 0 | 0.0 | 0 | 0 | 0 | 0 | 0 | 1 | 0 | .000 | .000 |
| PH | Dutch Meyer | R | 1 | 0 | 0 | 0 | 0 | 0 | – | 0 | 0 | 0 | 0 | 0 | 0 | 0 | – | – |
| **PITCHERS** | | | | | | | | | | | | | | | | | | |
| P | Bill Lee | R | 42 | 87 | 15 | 2 | 0 | 1 | 1.1 | 4 | 4 | 3 | 23 | 0 | 0 | 0 | .172 | .230 |
| P | Tex Carleton | B | 34 | 71 | 12 | 3 | 1 | 0 | 0.0 | 4 | 9 | 6 | 22 | 0 | 0 | 0 | .169 | .239 |
| P | Larry French | R | 42 | 71 | 9 | 1 | 0 | 0 | 0.0 | 1 | 0 | 0 | 12 | 0 | 0 | 0 | .127 | .141 |
| P | Charlie Root | R | 43 | 67 | 12 | 2 | 0 | 1 | 1.5 | 7 | 9 | 1 | 19 | 0 | 0 | 0 | .179 | .254 |
| P | Roy Parmelee | R | 37 | 52 | 9 | 0 | 0 | 2 | 3.8 | 7 | 8 | 1 | 19 | 0 | 0 | 0 | .173 | .288 |
| P | Clay Bryant | R | 47 | 45 | 14 | 2 | 1 | 1 | 2.2 | 13 | 7 | 2 | 4 | 0 | 2 | 1 | .311 | .467 |
| P | Curt Davis | R | 28 | 40 | 12 | 2 | 0 | 1 | 2.5 | 6 | 9 | 2 | 3 | 0 | 0 | 0 | .300 | .425 |
| P | Clyde Shoun | L | 37 | 29 | 4 | 2 | 0 | 0 | 0.0 | 3 | 1 | 0 | 5 | 0 | 0 | 0 | .138 | .207 |
| P | Kirby Higbe | R | 1 | 3 | 0 | 0 | 0 | 0 | 0.0 | 0 | 0 | 0 | 1 | 0 | 0 | 0 | .000 | .000 |
| P | Newt Kimball | R | 2 | 1 | 0 | 0 | 0 | 0 | 0.0 | 0 | 0 | 0 | 0 | 0 | 0 | 0 | .000 | .000 |
| P | Bob Logan | R | 4 | 1 | 0 | 0 | 0 | 0 | 0.0 | 0 | 0 | 0 | 0 | 0 | 0 | 0 | .000 | .000 |
| | TEAM TOTAL | | | 5349 | 1537 | 253 | 74 | 96 | 1.8 | 81 | 762 | 538 | 496 | 71 | 79 | 19 | .287 | .416 |

## INDIVIDUAL FIELDING

| POS | Player | T | G | PO | A | E | DP | TC/G | FA |
|---|---|---|---|---|---|---|---|---|---|
| 1B | R. Collins | L | 111 | 1068 | 80 | 11 | 94 | 10.4 | .991 |
| | Cavarretta | L | 43 | 355 | 33 | 7 | 27 | 9.2 | .982 |
| | S. Hack | R | 4 | 21 | 4 | 1 | 5 | 6.5 | .962 |
| 2B | B. Herman | R | 137 | 384 | 468 | 41 | 97 | 6.5 | .954 |
| | L. Frey | R | 13 | 24 | 32 | 1 | 5 | 4.4 | .982 |
| | A. Galan | R | 8 | 10 | 33 | 2 | 4 | 5.6 | .956 |
| SS | B. Jurges | R | 128 | 258 | 370 | 16 | 74 | 5.0 | .975 |
| | L. Frey | R | 30 | 53 | 67 | 8 | 11 | 4.3 | .938 |
| | A. Galan | R | 2 | 0 | 2 | 0 | 0 | 1.0 | 1.000 |
| 3B | S. Hack | R | 150 | 151 | 247 | 13 | 25 | 2.7 | .968 |
| | L. Frey | R | 9 | 6 | 2 | 1 | 2 | 1.0 | .889 |

| POS | Player | T | G | PO | A | E | DP | TC/G | FA |
|---|---|---|---|---|---|---|---|---|---|
| OF | A. Galan | R | 140 | 328 | 9 | 7 | 3 | 2.5 | .980 |
| | F. Demaree | R | 154 | 283 | 17 | 6 | 6 | 2.0 | .980 |
| | J. Marty | R | 84 | 196 | 4 | 5 | 0 | 2.4 | .976 |
| | Cavarretta | L | 53 | 99 | 7 | 3 | 1 | 2.1 | .972 |
| | T. Stainback | R | 49 | 99 | 4 | 2 | 1 | 2.1 | .981 |
| | J. Bottarini | R | 1 | 0 | 0 | 0 | 0 | 0.0 | 0.000 |
| | L. Frey | R | 5 | 7 | 0 | 0 | 0 | 1.4 | 1.000 |
| | C. Reynolds | R | 2 | 4 | 0 | 1 | 0 | 2.5 | .800 |
| C | G. Hartnett | R | 101 | 436 | 65 | 2 | 7 | 5.0 | .996 |
| | K. O'Dea | R | 64 | 234 | 29 | 4 | 4 | 4.2 | .985 |
| | J. Bottarini | R | 18 | 44 | 9 | 0 | 0 | 2.9 | 1.000 |

The Cubs traded away their pennant seven months before the season began. On October 8, 1936, they gift-wrapped pitcher Lon Warneke to the Cardinals for pitcher Roy Parmelee and first baseman Ripper Collins. Warneke won 18 games for the Cardinals. Parmelee won only seven, while Collins broke a leg in the stretch drive. The Cubs finished only two games behind the pennant-winning Giants. They could have used Warneke's strong right arm and his 18 victories. So much for hindsight.

The Cubs started slowly, but bolted into first place on June 15 and virtually held it every day until overtaken by the Giants in September. Catcher Gabby Hartnett caught fire with a 26-game hitting streak, batting .433 from June 29 through August 25, and temporarily took over the club when manager Charlie Grimm became ill. Hartnett finished with a solid .354 average. Billy Herman was next at .335, followed by Frank Demaree's .324. That trio helped the Cubs lead the league in batting at .287. Augie Galan led the club with a modest 18 homers, while Demaree topped it in RBI with 115. The Cubs were also in front of the league in fielding with a .975 average. Although Tex Carleton and Larry French won 16 each, the Cubs rated only sixth in pitching. Warneke would have been the difference.

## TEAM STATISTICS

| | W | L | PCT | GB | R | OR | Batting | | | | | | | Fielding | | | Pitching | | | | |
| --- | --- | --- | --- | --- | --- | --- | --- | --- | --- | --- | --- | --- | --- | --- | --- | --- | --- | --- | --- | --- | --- |
| | | | | | | | 2B | 3B | HR | BA | SA | SB | E | DP | FA | CG | B | SO | ShO | SV | ERA |
| NY | 95 | 57 | .625 | | 732 | 602 | 251 | 41 | 111 | .278 | .403 | 45 | 159 | 143 | .974 | 67 | 404 | **653** | 11 | 17 | 3.43 |
| CHI | 93 | 61 | .604 | 3 | **811** | 682 | 253 | 74 | 96 | **.287** | **.416** | 71 | 151 | 141 | **.975** | 73 | 502 | 596 | 11 | 13 | 3.97 |
| PIT | 86 | 68 | .558 | 10 | 704 | 646 | 223 | **86** | 47 | .285 | .384 | 32 | 181 | 135 | .970 | 67 | 428 | 643 | 12 | 17 | 3.56 |
| STL | 81 | 73 | .526 | 15 | 789 | 733 | **264** | 67 | 94 | .282 | .406 | **78** | 164 | 127 | .973 | 81 | 448 | 573 | 10 | 4 | 3.95 |
| BOS | 79 | 73 | .520 | 16 | 579 | 556 | 200 | 41 | 63 | .247 | .339 | 45 | 157 | 128 | .975 | **85** | **372** | 387 | **16** | 10 | **3.22** |
| BKN | 62 | 91 | .405 | 33.5 | 616 | 772 | 258 | 53 | 37 | .265 | .354 | 69 | 217 | 127 | .964 | 63 | 476 | 592 | 5 | 8 | 4.13 |
| PHI | 61 | 92 | .399 | 34.5 | 724 | 869 | 258 | 37 | 103 | .273 | .391 | 66 | 184 | **157** | .970 | 59 | 501 | 529 | 6 | 15 | 5.06 |
| CIN | 56 | 98 | .364 | 40 | 612 | 707 | 215 | 59 | 73 | .254 | .360 | 53 | 208 | 139 | .966 | 64 | 533 | 581 | 10 | **18** | 3.94 |
| LEAGUE TOTAL | | | | | 5567 | 5567 | 1922 | 458 | 624 | .272 | .382 | 459 | 1421 | 1097 | .971 | 559 | 3664 | 4554 | 81 | 102 | 3.91 |

## INDIVIDUAL PITCHING

| PITCHER | T | W | L | PCT | ERA | SV | G | GS | CG | IP | H | BB | SO | R | ER | ShO | H/9 | BB/9 | SO/9 |
| --- | --- | --- | --- | --- | --- | --- | --- | --- | --- | --- | --- | --- | --- | --- | --- | --- | --- | --- | --- |
| Bill Lee | R | 14 | 15 | .483 | 3.54 | 3 | 42 | 33 | 17 | 272.1 | 289 | 73 | 108 | 122 | 107 | 2 | 9.55 | 2.41 | 3.57 |
| Tex Carleton | R | 16 | 8 | .667 | 3.15 | 0 | 32 | 27 | 18 | 208.1 | 183 | 94 | 105 | 80 | 73 | 4 | 7.91 | 4.06 | 4.54 |
| Larry French | L | 16 | 10 | .615 | 3.98 | 0 | 42 | 28 | 11 | 208 | 229 | 65 | 100 | 106 | 92 | 4 | 9.91 | 2.81 | 4.33 |
| Charlie Root | R | 13 | 5 | .722 | 3.38 | 5 | 43 | 15 | 5 | 178.2 | 173 | 32 | 74 | 71 | 67 | 0 | 8.71 | 1.61 | 3.73 |
| Roy Parmelee | R | 7 | 8 | .467 | 5.13 | 0 | 33 | 18 | 8 | 145.2 | 165 | 79 | 55 | 93 | 83 | 0 | 10.19 | 4.88 | 3.40 |
| Clay Bryant | R | 9 | 3 | .750 | 4.26 | 3 | 38 | 10 | 4 | 135.1 | 117 | 78 | 75 | 69 | 64 | 1 | 7.78 | 5.19 | 4.99 |
| Curt Davis | R | 10 | 5 | .667 | 4.08 | 1 | 28 | 14 | 8 | 123.2 | 138 | 30 | 32 | 64 | 56 | 0 | 10.04 | 2.18 | 2.33 |
| Clyde Shoun | L | 7 | 7 | .500 | 5.61 | 0 | 37 | 9 | 2 | 93 | 118 | 45 | 43 | 65 | 58 | 0 | 11.42 | 4.35 | 4.16 |
| Bob Logan | L | 0 | 0 | – | 1.42 | 1 | 4 | 0 | 0 | 6.1 | 6 | 4 | 2 | 1 | 1 | 0 | 8.53 | 5.68 | 2.84 |
| Kirby Higbe | R | 1 | 0 | 1.000 | 5.40 | 0 | 1 | 0 | 0 | 5 | 4 | 1 | 2 | 3 | 3 | 0 | 7.20 | 1.80 | 3.60 |
| Newt Kimball | R | 0 | 0 | – | 10.80 | 0 | 2 | 0 | 0 | 5 | 12 | 1 | 0 | 8 | 6 | 0 | 21.60 | 1.80 | 0.00 |
| TEAM TOTAL | | 93 | 61 | .604 | 3.97 | 13 | 302 | 154 | 73 | 1381.1 | 1434 | 502 | 596 | 682 | 610 | 11 | 9.34 | 3.27 | 3.88 |

| MANAGER | W | L | PCT |
|---|---|---|---|
| Charlie Grimm | 45 | 36 | .556 |
| Gabby Hartnett | 44 | 27 | .620 |

| POS | Player | B | G | AB | H | 2B | 3B | HR | HR % | R | RBI | BB | SO | SB | Pinch Hit AB | Pinch Hit H | BA | SA |
|---|---|---|---|---|---|---|---|---|---|---|---|---|---|---|---|---|---|---|
| **REGULARS** | | | | | | | | | | | | | | | | | | |
| 1B | Ripper Collins | B | 143 | 490 | 131 | 22 | 8 | 13 | 2.7 | 78 | 61 | 54 | 48 | 1 | 7 | 0 | .267 | .424 |
| 2B | Billy Herman | R | 152 | 624 | 173 | 34 | 7 | 1 | 0.2 | 86 | 56 | 59 | 31 | 3 | 1 | 0 | .277 | .359 |
| SS | Bill Jurges | R | 137 | 465 | 114 | 18 | 3 | 1 | 0.2 | 53 | 47 | 58 | 53 | 3 | 0 | 0 | .245 | .303 |
| 3B | Stan Hack | L | 152 | 609 | 195 | 34 | 11 | 4 | 0.7 | 109 | 67 | 94 | 39 | 16 | 0 | 0 | .320 | .432 |
| RF | Frank Demaree | R | 129 | 476 | 130 | 15 | 7 | 8 | 1.7 | 63 | 62 | 45 | 34 | 1 | 4 | 1 | .273 | .384 |
| CF | Carl Reynolds | R | 125 | 497 | 150 | 28 | 10 | 3 | 0.6 | 59 | 67 | 22 | 32 | 9 | 0 | 0 | .302 | .416 |
| LF | Augie Galan | B | 110 | 395 | 113 | 16 | 9 | 6 | 1.5 | 52 | 69 | 49 | 17 | 8 | 6 | 0 | .286 | .418 |
| C | Gabby Hartnett | R | 88 | 299 | 82 | 19 | 1 | 10 | 3.3 | 40 | 59 | 48 | 17 | 1 | 4 | 2 | .274 | .445 |
| **SUBSTITUTES** | | | | | | | | | | | | | | | | | | |
| UT | Tony Lazzeri | R | 54 | 120 | 32 | 5 | 0 | 5 | 4.2 | 21 | 23 | 22 | 30 | 0 | 14 | 2 | .267 | .433 |
| SS | Steve Mesner | R | 2 | 4 | 1 | 0 | 0 | 0 | 0.0 | 2 | 0 | 1 | 1 | 0 | 1 | 0 | .250 | .250 |
| SS | Bobby Mattick | R | 1 | 1 | 1 | 0 | 0 | 0 | 0.0 | 0 | 1 | 0 | 0 | 0 | 0 | 0 | 1.000 | 1.000 |
| O1 | Phil Cavarretta | L | 92 | 268 | 64 | 11 | 4 | 1 | 0.4 | 29 | 28 | 14 | 27 | 4 | 13 | 1 | .239 | .321 |
| OF | Joe Marty | R | 76 | 235 | 57 | 8 | 3 | 7 | 3.0 | 32 | 35 | 18 | 26 | 0 | 7 | 0 | .243 | .391 |
| OF | Coaker Triplett | R | 12 | 36 | 9 | 2 | 1 | 0 | 0.0 | 4 | 2 | 0 | 1 | 0 | 3 | 0 | .250 | .361 |
| OF | Jim Asbell | R | 17 | 33 | 6 | 2 | 0 | 0 | 0.0 | 6 | 3 | 3 | 9 | 0 | 6 | 3 | .182 | .242 |
| C | Ken O'Dea | L | 86 | 247 | 65 | 12 | 1 | 3 | 1.2 | 22 | 33 | 12 | 18 | 1 | 13 | 2 | .263 | .356 |
| C | Bob Garbark | R | 23 | 54 | 14 | 0 | 0 | 0 | 0.0 | 2 | 5 | 1 | 0 | 0 | 1 | 0 | .259 | .259 |
| **PITCHERS** | | | | | | | | | | | | | | | | | | |
| P | Clay Bryant | R | 50 | 106 | 24 | 2 | 1 | 3 | 2.8 | 16 | 15 | 2 | 10 | 0 | 1 | 0 | .226 | .349 |
| P | Bill Lee | R | 44 | 101 | 20 | 3 | 1 | 0 | 0.0 | 10 | 13 | 4 | 20 | 1 | 0 | 0 | .198 | .248 |
| P | Tex Carleton | B | 33 | 65 | 15 | 4 | 1 | 0 | 0.0 | 9 | 7 | 3 | 10 | 1 | 0 | 0 | .231 | .323 |
| P | Larry French | R | 43 | 62 | 13 | 3 | 1 | 0 | 0.0 | 7 | 7 | 5 | 9 | 0 | 0 | 0 | .210 | .290 |
| P | Charlie Root | R | 44 | 48 | 8 | 1 | 0 | 0 | 0.0 | 2 | 3 | 4 | 16 | 0 | 0 | 0 | .167 | .188 |
| P | Jack Russell | R | 42 | 32 | 7 | 1 | 1 | 0 | 0.0 | 4 | 3 | 2 | 15 | 0 | 0 | 0 | .219 | .313 |
| P | Dizzy Dean | R | 13 | 26 | 5 | 1 | 0 | 0 | 0.0 | 3 | 1 | 0 | 2 | 0 | 0 | 0 | .192 | .231 |
| P | Vance Page | R | 13 | 26 | 4 | 0 | 0 | 0 | 0.0 | 2 | 1 | 0 | 7 | 0 | 0 | 0 | .154 | .154 |
| P | Al Epperly | L | 9 | 8 | 2 | 1 | 0 | 0 | 0.0 | 2 | 5 | 2 | 3 | 0 | 0 | 0 | .250 | .375 |
| P | Kirby Higbe | R | 2 | 3 | 0 | 0 | 0 | 0 | 0.0 | 0 | 0 | 0 | 1 | 0 | 0 | 0 | .000 | .000 |
| P | Bob Logan | R | 14 | 3 | 0 | 0 | 0 | 0 | 0.0 | 0 | 0 | 0 | 0 | 0 | 0 | 0 | .000 | .000 |
| P | Newt Kimball | R | 1 | 0 | 0 | 0 | 0 | 0 | 0.0 | 0 | 0 | 0 | 0 | 0 | 0 | 0 | – | – |
| TEAM TOTAL | | | | 5333 | 1435 | 242 | 70 | 65 | 1.2 | 71 | 673 | 522 | 476 | 49 | 81 | 11 | .269 | .377 |

## INDIVIDUAL FIELDING

| POS | Player | T | G | PO | A | E | DP | TC/G | FA | POS | Player | T | G | PO | A | E | DP | TC/G | FA |
|---|---|---|---|---|---|---|---|---|---|---|---|---|---|---|---|---|---|---|---|
| 1B | R. Collins | L | 135 | 1264 | 111 | 6 | 118 | 10.2 | **.996** | OF | C. Reynolds | R | 125 | 328 | 10 | 6 | 4 | 2.8 | .983 |
| | Cavarretta | L | 28 | 206 | 16 | 1 | 14 | 8.0 | .996 | | A. Galan | R | 103 | 211 | 10 | 3 | 3 | 2.2 | .987 |
| | B. Garbark | R | 1 | 2 | 0 | 0 | 0 | 2.0 | 1.000 | | F. Demaree | R | 125 | 199 | 12 | 6 | 1 | 1.7 | .972 |
| 2B | B. Herman | R | 151 | **404** | 517 | 18 | 111 | 6.2 | **.981** | | J. Marty | R | 68 | 143 | 6 | 2 | 1 | 2.2 | .987 |
| | T. Lazzeri | R | 4 | 8 | 17 | 0 | 1 | 6.3 | 1.000 | | Cavarretta | L | 52 | 71 | 5 | 3 | 0 | 1.5 | .962 |
| SS | B. Jurges | R | 136 | 277 | 417 | 34 | 82 | 5.4 | .953 | | J. Asbell | R | 17 | 14 | 1 | 0 | 1 | 0.9 | 1.000 |
| | T. Lazzeri | R | 25 | 33 | 54 | 5 | 11 | 3.7 | .946 | | C. Triplett | R | 9 | 15 | 1 | 0 | 0 | 1.8 | 1.000 |
| | B. Mattick | R | 1 | 0 | 0 | 0 | 0 | 0.0 | .000 | | T. Lazzeri | R | 1 | 2 | 0 | 0 | 0 | 2.0 | 1.000 |
| | S. Mesner | R | 1 | 0 | 2 | 1 | 0 | 3.0 | .667 | C | G. Hartnett | R | 83 | 358 | 40 | 2 | 8 | 4.8 | .995 |
| 3B | S. Hack | R | 152 | **178** | 300 | 23 | **26** | 3.3 | .954 | | K. O'Dea | R | 71 | 294 | 32 | 10 | 3 | 4.7 | .970 |
| | T. Lazzeri | R | 7 | 6 | 4 | 2 | 0 | 1.7 | .833 | | B. Garbark | R | 20 | 64 | 7 | 0 | 0 | 3.6 | 1.000 |

It had to be the greatest moment in Cub history. The date was September 28. The time was 5:37 P.M. Darkness had set in at Wrigley Field. It was the ninth inning, and the score was tied, 5–5. Player-manager Gabby Hartnett connected off the Pirates' Mace Brown for his famed "Homer in the Gloamin." That blow put the Cubs ahead of the Pirates, and Chicago went on to clinch the pennant three days later with a 10–3 romp over the Cardinals. The season began with much fanfare as the Cubs purchased sore-armed Dizzy Dean from the Cardinals for three players and $185,000. Dean, used infrequently, was 7–1, but was a drawing card. The Cubs began slowly and were in fourth place with a 45–36 mark on July 20 when Charlie Grimm was replaced by Hartnett as manager. The Pirates, meanwhile, took first in July and held it throughout the stretch. They even built an auxiliary press box to handle the World Series crowd. But the Cubs rallied with a 44–27 mark under Hartnett and left the Pirates in the dark, winning the pennant by two games with an 89–63 record. Bill Lee, who pitched four consecutive shutouts in September for a seasonal total of 9, also led the league in victories with 22 and had a 2.66 ERA. He was ably assisted by Clay Bryant, who led in strikeouts with 135 and had 19 victories. Stan Hack was the top offensive weapon, batting .320 with 109 runs scored and 195 hits. Rip Collins was high in homers with only 13. In the World Series, the Yankees showed the Cubbies real power with a one-sided four-game sweep.

## TEAM STATISTICS

|   | W | L | PCT | GB | R | OR | Batting 2B | 3B | HR | BA | SA | SB | Fielding E | DP | FA | Pitching CG | B | SO | ShO | SV | ERA |
|---|---|---|---|---|---|---|---|---|---|---|---|---|---|---|---|---|---|---|---|---|---|
| HI | 89 | 63 | .586 |  | 713 | 598 | 242 | 70 | 65 | .269 | .377 | 49 | 135 | 151 | .978 | 67 | 454 | 583 | 16 | 18 | 3.37 |
| IT | 86 | 64 | .573 | 2 | 707 | 630 | 265 | 66 | 65 | .279 | .388 | 47 | 163 | 168 | .974 | 57 | 432 | 557 | 8 | 15 | 3.46 |
| Y | 83 | 67 | .553 | 5 | 705 | 637 | 210 | 36 | 125 | .271 | .396 | 31 | 168 | 147 | .973 | 59 | 389 | 497 | 8 | 18 | 3.62 |
| IN | 82 | 68 | .547 | 6 | 723 | 634 | 251 | 57 | 110 | .277 | .406 | 19 | 172 | 133 | .971 | 72 | 463 | 542 | 11 | 16 | 3.62 |
| OS | 77 | 75 | .507 | 12 | 561 | 618 | 199 | 39 | 54 | .250 | .333 | 49 | 173 | 136 | .972 | 83 | 465 | 413 | 15 | 12 | 3.40 |
| TL | 71 | 80 | .470 | 17.5 | 725 | 721 | 288 | 74 | 91 | .279 | .407 | 55 | 199 | 145 | .967 | 58 | 474 | 534 | 10 | 16 | 3.84 |
| KN | 69 | 80 | .463 | 18.5 | 704 | 710 | 225 | 79 | 61 | .257 | .367 | 66 | 157 | 148 | .973 | 56 | 446 | 469 | 12 | 14 | 4.07 |
| HI | 45 | 105 | .300 | 43 | 550 | 840 | 233 | 29 | 40 | .254 | .333 | 38 | 201 | 135 | .966 | 68 | 582 | 492 | 3 | 6 | 4.93 |
| AGUE TOTAL |  |  |  |  | 5388 | 5388 | 1913 | 450 | 611 | .267 | .376 | 354 | 1368 | 1163 | .972 | 520 | 3705 | 4087 | 83 | 115 | 3.78 |

## INDIVIDUAL PITCHING

| TCHER | T | W | L | PCT | ERA | SV | G | GS | CG | IP | H | BB | SO | R | ER | ShO | H/9 | BB/9 | SO/9 |
|---|---|---|---|---|---|---|---|---|---|---|---|---|---|---|---|---|---|---|---|
| ll Lee | R | 22 | 9 | .710 | 2.66 | 2 | 44 | 37 | 19 | 291 | 281 | 74 | 121 | 95 | 86 | 9 | 8.69 | 2.29 | 3.74 |
| ay Bryant | R | 19 | 11 | .633 | 3.10 | 2 | 44 | 30 | 17 | 270.1 | 235 | 125 | 135 | 105 | 93 | 3 | 7.82 | 4.16 | 4.49 |
| arry French | L | 10 | 19 | .345 | 3.80 | 0 | 43 | 27 | 10 | 201.1 | 210 | 62 | 83 | 95 | 85 | 3 | 9.39 | 2.77 | 3.71 |
| ex Carleton | R | 10 | 9 | .526 | 5.42 | 0 | 33 | 24 | 9 | 167.2 | 213 | 74 | 80 | 118 | 101 | 0 | 11.43 | 3.97 | 4.29 |
| harlie Root | R | 8 | 7 | .533 | 2.86 | 8 | 44 | 11 | 5 | 160.2 | 163 | 30 | 70 | 62 | 51 | 0 | 9.13 | 1.68 | 3.92 |
| ack Russell | R | 6 | 1 | .857 | 3.34 | 3 | 42 | 0 | 0 | 102.1 | 100 | 30 | 29 | 43 | 38 | 0 | 8.79 | 2.64 | 2.55 |
| zzy Dean | R | 7 | 1 | .875 | 1.81 | 0 | 13 | 10 | 3 | 74.2 | 63 | 8 | 22 | 20 | 15 | 1 | 7.59 | 0.96 | 2.65 |
| ance Page | R | 5 | 4 | .556 | 3.84 | 1 | 13 | 9 | 3 | 68 | 90 | 13 | 18 | 33 | 29 | 0 | 11.91 | 1.72 | 2.38 |
| Epperly | R | 2 | 0 | 1.000 | 3.67 | 0 | 9 | 4 | 1 | 27 | 28 | 15 | 10 | 11 | 11 | 0 | 9.33 | 5.00 | 3.33 |
| bb Logan | L | 0 | 2 | .000 | 2.78 | 2 | 14 | 0 | 0 | 22.2 | 18 | 17 | 10 | 9 | 7 | 0 | 7.15 | 6.75 | 3.97 |
| rby Higbe | R | 0 | 0 | — | 5.40 | 0 | 2 | 2 | 0 | 10 | 10 | 6 | 4 | 6 | 6 | 0 | 9.00 | 5.40 | 3.60 |
| ewt Kimball | R | 0 | 0 | — | 9.00 | 0 | 1 | 0 | 0 | 1 | 3 | 0 | 1 | 1 | 1 | 0 | 27.00 | 0.00 | 9.00 |
| EAM TOTAL |  | 89 | 63 | .586 | 3.37 | 18 | 302 | 154 | 67 | 1396.2 | 1414 | 454 | 583 | 598 | 523 | 16 | 9.11 | 2.93 | 3.76 |

| MANAGER | W | L | PCT |
|---|---|---|---|
| Gabby Hartnett | 84 | 70 | .545 |

| POS | Player | B | G | AB | H | 2B | 3B | HR | HR % | R | RBI | BB | SO | SB | Pinch Hit AB | Pinch Hit H | BA | SA |
|---|---|---|---|---|---|---|---|---|---|---|---|---|---|---|---|---|---|---|
| **REGULARS** | | | | | | | | | | | | | | | | | | |
| 1B | Rip Russell | R | 143 | 542 | 148 | 24 | 5 | 9 | 1.7 | 55 | 79 | 36 | 56 | 2 | 0 | 0 | .273 | .386 |
| 2B | Billy Herman | R | 156 | 623 | 191 | 34 | 18 | 7 | 1.1 | 111 | 70 | 66 | 31 | 9 | 0 | 0 | .307 | .453 |
| SS | Dick Bartell | R | 105 | 336 | 80 | 24 | 2 | 3 | 0.9 | 37 | 34 | 42 | 25 | 6 | 3 | 1 | .238 | .348 |
| 3B | Stan Hack | L | 156 | 641 | 191 | 28 | 6 | 8 | 1.2 | 112 | 56 | 65 | 35 | 17 | 0 | 0 | .298 | .398 |
| RF | Jim Gleeson | B | 111 | 332 | 74 | 19 | 6 | 4 | 1.2 | 43 | 45 | 39 | 46 | 7 | 17 | 4 | .223 | .352 |
| CF | Hank Leiber | R | 112 | 365 | 113 | 16 | 1 | 24 | 6.6 | 65 | 88 | 59 | 42 | 1 | 8 | 1 | .310 | .556 |
| LF | Augie Galan | B | 148 | 549 | 167 | 36 | 8 | 6 | 1.1 | 104 | 71 | 75 | 26 | 8 | 3 | 0 | .304 | .432 |
| C | Gabby Hartnett | R | 97 | 306 | 85 | 18 | 2 | 12 | 3.9 | 36 | 59 | 37 | 32 | 0 | 8 | 3 | .278 | .467 |
| **SUBSTITUTES** | | | | | | | | | | | | | | | | | | |
| SS | Bobby Mattick | R | 51 | 178 | 51 | 12 | 1 | 0 | 0.0 | 16 | 23 | 6 | 19 | 1 | 1 | 0 | .287 | .365 |
| 1B | Phil Cavarretta | L | 22 | 55 | 15 | 3 | 1 | 0 | 0.0 | 4 | 0 | 4 | 3 | 2 | 7 | 3 | .273 | .364 |
| SS | Steve Mesner | R | 17 | 43 | 12 | 4 | 0 | 0 | 0.0 | 7 | 6 | 3 | 4 | 0 | 3 | 0 | .279 | .372 |
| OF | Carl Reynolds | R | 88 | 281 | 69 | 10 | 6 | 4 | 1.4 | 33 | 44 | 16 | 38 | 5 | 14 | 3 | .246 | .367 |
| OF | Bill Nicholson | L | 58 | 220 | 65 | 12 | 5 | 5 | 2.3 | 37 | 38 | 20 | 29 | 0 | 0 | 0 | .295 | .464 |
| OF | Joe Marty | R | 23 | 76 | 10 | 1 | 0 | 2 | 2.6 | 6 | 10 | 4 | 13 | 2 | 2 | 0 | .132 | .224 |
| C | Gus Mancuso | R | 80 | 251 | 58 | 10 | 0 | 2 | 0.8 | 17 | 17 | 24 | 19 | 0 | 3 | 0 | .231 | .295 |
| C | Bob Garbark | R | 24 | 21 | 3 | 0 | 0 | 0 | 0.0 | 1 | 0 | 0 | 3 | 0 | 2 | 0 | .143 | .143 |
| **PITCHERS** | | | | | | | | | | | | | | | | | | |
| P | Bill Lee | R | 37 | 103 | 13 | 0 | 0 | 1 | 1.0 | 3 | 3 | 4 | 16 | 0 | 0 | 0 | .126 | .155 |
| P | Claude Passeau | R | 35 | 77 | 12 | 2 | 0 | 1 | 1.3 | 6 | 6 | 2 | 27 | 0 | 0 | 0 | .156 | .221 |
| P | Larry French | R | 36 | 73 | 14 | 2 | 0 | 1 | 1.4 | 6 | 7 | 4 | 26 | 0 | 0 | 0 | .192 | .260 |
| P | Charlie Root | R | 35 | 57 | 10 | 2 | 1 | 2 | 3.5 | 4 | 6 | 2 | 21 | 0 | 0 | 0 | .175 | .351 |
| P | Vance Page | R | 27 | 47 | 12 | 3 | 0 | 0 | 0.0 | 2 | 6 | 3 | 11 | 0 | 0 | 0 | .255 | .319 |
| P | Dizzy Dean | R | 19 | 34 | 5 | 1 | 0 | 0 | 0.0 | 4 | 1 | 1 | 7 | 1 | 0 | 0 | .147 | .176 |
| P | Earl Whitehill | L | 24 | 29 | 3 | 0 | 0 | 0 | 0.0 | 1 | 0 | 2 | 7 | 0 | 0 | 0 | .103 | .103 |
| P | Jack Russell | R | 43 | 17 | 0 | 0 | 0 | 0 | 0.0 | 1 | 0 | 0 | 8 | 0 | 0 | 0 | .000 | .000 |
| P | Clay Bryant | R | 28 | 14 | 3 | 1 | 0 | 0 | 0.0 | 9 | 1 | 1 | 1 | 0 | 1 | 0 | .214 | .286 |
| P | Gene Lillard | R | 23 | 10 | 1 | 0 | 0 | 0 | 0.0 | 3 | 0 | 6 | 3 | 0 | 0 | 0 | .100 | .100 |
| P | Kirby Higbe | R | 9 | 7 | 2 | 1 | 0 | 0 | 0.0 | 0 | 1 | 0 | 3 | 0 | 0 | 0 | .286 | .429 |
| P | Ray Harrell | R | 4 | 5 | 0 | 0 | 0 | 0 | 0.0 | 0 | 0 | 2 | 1 | 0 | 0 | 0 | .000 | .000 |
| P | Vern Olsen | R | 4 | 0 | 0 | 0 | 0 | 0 | 0.0 | 1 | 0 | 2 | 1 | 0 | 0 | 0 | .000 | .000 |
| TEAM TOTAL | | | | 5293 | 1407 | 263 | 62 | 91 | 1.7 | 72 | 671 | 523 | 553 | 61 | 72 | 15 | .266 | .391 |

## INDIVIDUAL FIELDING

| POS | Player | T | G | PO | A | E | DP | TC/G | FA | POS | Player | T | G | PO | A | E | DP | TC/G | FA |
|---|---|---|---|---|---|---|---|---|---|---|---|---|---|---|---|---|---|---|---|
| 1B | R. Russell | R | 143 | 1383 | 83 | 18 | 109 | 10.4 | .988 | OF | A. Galan | R | 145 | 290 | 6 | 9 | 0 | 2.1 | .970 |
| | Cavarretta | L | 13 | 106 | 6 | 1 | 10 | 8.7 | .991 | | H. Leiber | R | 98 | 249 | 5 | 6 | 0 | 2.7 | .977 |
| 2B | B. Herman | R | 156 | 377 | 485 | 29 | 95 | 5.7 | .967 | | J. Gleeson | R | 91 | 175 | 5 | 8 | 1 | 2.1 | .957 |
| | S. Mesner | R | 1 | 3 | 4 | 0 | 1 | 7.0 | 1.000 | | C. Reynolds | R | 72 | 168 | 5 | 5 | 1 | 2.5 | .972 |
| SS | D. Bartell | R | 101 | 241 | 307 | 33 | 62 | 5.8 | .943 | | B. Nicholson | R | 58 | 123 | 5 | 6 | 0 | 2.3 | .955 |
| | B. Mattick | R | 48 | 102 | 179 | 22 | 28 | 6.3 | .927 | | J. Marty | R | 21 | 24 | 4 | 2 | 0 | 1.4 | .933 |
| | S. Mesner | R | 12 | 12 | 39 | 4 | 7 | 4.6 | .927 | | Cavarretta | L | 1 | 0 | 0 | 0 | 0 | 0.0 | .000 |
| 3B | S. Hack | R | 156 | 177 | 278 | 21 | 15 | 3.1 | .956 | | C. Bryant | R | 1 | 3 | 0 | 0 | 0 | 3.0 | 1.000 |
| | D. Bartell | R | 1 | 0 | 0 | 0 | 0 | 0.0 | .000 | C | G. Hartnett | R | 86 | 336 | 47 | 3 | 3 | 4.5 | .992 |
| | S. Mesner | R | 1 | 1 | 0 | 0 | 0 | 1.0 | 1.000 | | G. Mancuso | R | 76 | 333 | 36 | 7 | 6 | 4.9 | .981 |
| | | | | | | | | | | | B. Garbark | R | 21 | 22 | 3 | 0 | 0 | 1.2 | 1.000 |

The Cubs went from contenders to pretenders with the loss of smooth-fielding shortstop Billy Jurges in a six-player trade. Shipped to the Giants along with Jurges were outfielder Frank Demaree and catcher Ken O'Dea. In return the Cubs received shortstop Dick Bartell, outfielder Hank Leiber, and catcher Gus Mancuso.

For seven seasons Jurges and second baseman Billy Herman had formed the majors' best double-play combination. Bartell became a target of boobirds with his erratic play. Leiber, however, did supply much-needed power, leading the club with 24 homers and 88 runs batted in. The acquisition of pitcher Claude Passeau from the Phillies helped offset the loss of sore-armed Clay Bryant, who won only two games. Passeau was a 13-game winner and tied the Reds' Bucky Walters for the strikeout lead with 137. In addition to Bryant, first baseman Phil Cavarretta suffered a broken leg and was limited to 22 games.

Late in the season, the Cubs unveiled a new slugger named Bill Nicholson, who was to become a fan favorite throughout the 1940s. With all their injuries, the Cubs did manage to finish fourth with an 84–70 record, 13 1/2 games out.

### TEAM STATISTICS

| | W | L | PCT | GB | R | OR | 2B | Batting 3B | HR | BA | SA | SB | Fielding E | DP | FA | CG | B | Pitching SO | ShO | SV | ERA |
|---|---|---|---|---|---|---|---|---|---|---|---|---|---|---|---|---|---|---|---|---|---|
| IN | 97 | 57 | .630 | | 767 | 595 | 269 | 60 | 98 | .278 | .405 | 46 | 162 | 170 | .974 | 86 | 499 | **637** | 13 | 9 | **3.27** |
| TL | 92 | 61 | .601 | 4.5 | **779** | 633 | **332** | 62 | 98 | **.294** | **.432** | 44 | 177 | 140 | .971 | 45 | 498 | 603 | **18** | **32** | 3.59 |
| KN | 84 | 69 | .549 | 12.5 | 708 | 645 | 265 | 57 | 78 | .265 | .380 | 59 | 176 | 157 | .972 | 69 | **399** | 528 | 9 | 13 | 3.64 |
| HI | 84 | 70 | .545 | 13 | 724 | 678 | 263 | 62 | 91 | .266 | .391 | **61** | 186 | 126 | .970 | 72 | 430 | 584 | 8 | 13 | 3.80 |
| Y | 77 | 74 | .510 | 18.5 | 703 | 685 | 211 | 38 | **116** | .272 | .396 | 26 | **153** | 152 | **.975** | 55 | 478 | 505 | 6 | 20 | 4.07 |
| T | 68 | 85 | .444 | 28.5 | 666 | 721 | 261 | 60 | 63 | .276 | .384 | 44 | 168 | 153 | .972 | 53 | 423 | 524 | 10 | 15 | 4.15 |
| OS | 63 | 88 | .417 | 32.5 | 572 | 659 | 199 | 39 | 56 | .264 | .348 | 41 | 181 | **178** | .971 | 68 | 513 | 430 | 11 | 15 | 3.71 |
| HI | 45 | 106 | .298 | 50.5 | 553 | 856 | 232 | 40 | 49 | .261 | .351 | 47 | 171 | 133 | .970 | 67 | 579 | 447 | 3 | 12 | 5.17 |
| AGUE TOTAL | | | | | 5472 | 5472 | 2032 | 418 | 649 | .272 | .386 | 368 | 1374 | 1209 | .972 | 515 | 3819 | 4258 | 78 | 129 | 3.92 |

### INDIVIDUAL PITCHING

| ITCHER | T | W | L | PCT | ERA | SV | G | GS | CG | IP | H | BB | SO | R | ER | ShO | H/9 | BB/9 | SO/9 |
|---|---|---|---|---|---|---|---|---|---|---|---|---|---|---|---|---|---|---|---|
| ll Lee | R | 19 | 15 | .559 | 3.44 | 0 | 37 | **36** | 20 | 282.1 | 295 | 85 | 105 | 125 | 108 | 1 | 9.40 | 2.71 | 3.35 |
| aude Passeau | R | 13 | 9 | .591 | 3.05 | 3 | 34 | 27 | 13 | 221 | 215 | 48 | 108* | 86 | 75 | 1 | 8.76 | 1.95 | 4.40 |
| arry French | L | 15 | 8 | .652 | 3.29 | 1 | 36 | 21 | 10 | 194 | 205 | 50 | 98 | 80 | 71 | 2 | 9.51 | 2.32 | **4.55** |
| harlie Root | R | 8 | 8 | .500 | 4.03 | 4 | 35 | 16 | 8 | 167.1 | 189 | 34 | 65 | 83 | 75 | 0 | 10.17 | 1.83 | 3.50 |
| ance Page | R | 7 | 7 | .500 | 3.88 | 1 | 27 | 17 | 8 | 139.1 | 169 | 37 | 43 | 77 | 60 | 1 | 10.92 | 2.39 | 2.78 |
| zzy Dean | R | 6 | 4 | .600 | 3.36 | 0 | 19 | 13 | 7 | 96.1 | 98 | 17 | 27 | 40 | 36 | 2 | 9.16 | 1.59 | 2.52 |
| arl Whitehill | L | 4 | 7 | .364 | 5.14 | 1 | 24 | 11 | 2 | 89.1 | 102 | 50 | 42 | 59 | 51 | 1 | 10.28 | 5.04 | 4.23 |
| ack Russell | R | 4 | 3 | .571 | 3.67 | 3 | 39 | 0 | 0 | 68.2 | 78 | 24 | 32 | 32 | 28 | 0 | 10.22 | 3.15 | 4.19 |
| ene Lillard | R | 3 | 5 | .375 | 6.55 | 0 | 20 | 7 | 2 | 55 | 68 | 36 | 31 | 48 | 40 | 0 | 11.13 | 5.89 | 5.07 |
| ay Bryant | R | 2 | 1 | .667 | 5.74 | 0 | 4 | 4 | 2 | 31.1 | 42 | 14 | 9 | 23 | 20 | 0 | 12.06 | 4.02 | 2.59 |
| rby Higbe | R | 2 | 1 | .667 | 3.18 | 0 | 9 | 2 | 0 | 22.2 | 12 | 22* | 16 | 9 | 8 | 0 | 4.76 | 8.74 | 6.35 |
| ay Harrell | R | 0 | 2 | .000 | 8.31 | 0 | 4 | 2 | 0 | 17.1 | 26 | 6 | 5 | 16 | 16 | 0 | 13.50 | 3.12 | 2.60 |
| ern Olsen | L | 1 | 0 | 1.000 | 0.00 | 0 | 4 | 0 | 0 | 7.2 | 2 | 7 | 3 | 0 | 0 | 0 | 2.35 | 8.22 | 3.52 |
| oe Marty | R | 0 | 0 | — | 0.00 | 0 | 0 | 0 | 0 | 0 | 0 | 0 | 0 | 0 | 0 | 0 | — | — | — |
| EAM TOTAL | | 84 | 70 | .545 | 3.80 | 13 | 292 | 156 | 72 | 1392.1 | 1501 | 430 | 584 | 678 | 588 | 8 | 9.70 | 2.78 | 3.77 |

| MANAGER | W | L | PCT |
|---|---|---|---|
| Gabby Hartnett | 75 | 79 | .487 |

| POS | Player | B | G | AB | H | 2B | 3B | HR | HR % | R | RBI | BB | SO | SB | Pinch Hit AB | Pinch Hit H | BA | SA |
|---|---|---|---|---|---|---|---|---|---|---|---|---|---|---|---|---|---|---|
| **REGULARS** | | | | | | | | | | | | | | | | | | |
| 1B | Phil Cavarretta | L | 65 | 193 | 54 | 11 | 4 | 2 | 1.0 | 34 | 22 | 31 | 18 | 3 | 10 | 0 | .280 | .409 |
| 2B | Billy Herman | R | 135 | 558 | 163 | 24 | 4 | 5 | 0.9 | 77 | 57 | 47 | 30 | 1 | 0 | 0 | .292 | .376 |
| SS | Bobby Mattick | R | 128 | 441 | 96 | 15 | 0 | 0 | 0.0 | 30 | 33 | 19 | 33 | 5 | 1 | 0 | .218 | .252 |
| 3B | Stan Hack | L | 149 | 603 | **191** | 38 | 6 | 8 | 1.3 | 101 | 40 | 75 | 24 | 21 | 0 | 0 | .317 | .439 |
| RF | Bill Nicholson | L | 135 | 491 | 146 | 27 | 7 | 25 | 5.1 | 78 | 98 | 50 | 67 | 2 | 9 | 2 | .297 | .534 |
| CF | Hank Leiber | R | 117 | 440 | 133 | 24 | 2 | 17 | 3.9 | 68 | 86 | 45 | 68 | 1 | 3 | 0 | .302 | .482 |
| LF | Jim Gleeson | B | 129 | 485 | 152 | 39 | 11 | 5 | 1.0 | 76 | 61 | 54 | 52 | 4 | 5 | 1 | .313 | .470 |
| C | Al Todd | R | 104 | 381 | 97 | 13 | 2 | 6 | 1.6 | 31 | 42 | 11 | 29 | 1 | 0 | 0 | .255 | .346 |
| **SUBSTITUTES** | | | | | | | | | | | | | | | | | | |
| 1B | Rip Russell | R | 68 | 215 | 53 | 7 | 2 | 5 | 2.3 | 15 | 33 | 8 | 23 | 1 | 15 | 5 | .247 | .367 |
| 1B | Zeke Bonura | R | 49 | 182 | 48 | 14 | 0 | 4 | 2.2 | 20 | 20 | 10 | 4 | 1 | 5 | 1 | .264 | .407 |
| S2 | Rabbit Warstler | R | 45 | 159 | 36 | 4 | 1 | 1 | 0.6 | 19 | 18 | 8 | 19 | 1 | 0 | 0 | .226 | .283 |
| UT | Billy Rogell | B | 33 | 59 | 8 | 0 | 0 | 1 | 1.7 | 7 | 3 | 2 | 8 | 1 | 6 | 1 | .136 | .186 |
| SS | Bobby Sturgeon | R | 7 | 21 | 4 | 1 | 0 | 0 | 0.0 | 1 | 2 | 0 | 1 | 0 | 0 | 0 | .190 | .238 |
| OF | Dom Dallessandro | L | 107 | 287 | 77 | 19 | 6 | 1 | 0.3 | 33 | 36 | 34 | 13 | 4 | 29 | 10 | .268 | .387 |
| OF | Augie Galan | B | 68 | 209 | 48 | 14 | 2 | 3 | 1.4 | 33 | 22 | 37 | 23 | 9 | 9 | 2 | .230 | .359 |
| C | Bob Collins | R | 47 | 120 | 25 | 3 | 0 | 1 | 0.8 | 11 | 14 | 14 | 18 | 4 | 4 | 1 | .208 | .258 |
| C | Gabby Hartnett | R | 37 | 64 | 17 | 3 | 0 | 1 | 1.6 | 3 | 12 | 8 | 7 | 0 | 13 | 5 | .266 | .359 |
| C | Clyde McCullough | R | 9 | 26 | 4 | 1 | 0 | 0 | 0.0 | 4 | 1 | 5 | 5 | 0 | 2 | 0 | .154 | .192 |
| **PITCHERS** | | | | | | | | | | | | | | | | | | |
| P | Claude Passeau | R | 46 | 98 | 20 | 5 | 1 | 1 | 1.0 | 12 | 6 | 9 | 33 | 2 | 0 | 0 | .204 | .306 |
| P | Larry French | B | 40 | 85 | 14 | 3 | 0 | 0 | 0.0 | 5 | 9 | 7 | 20 | 0 | 0 | 0 | .165 | .200 |
| P | Bill Lee | R | 37 | 76 | 10 | 2 | 0 | 0 | 0.0 | 4 | 3 | 2 | 20 | 0 | 0 | 0 | .132 | .158 |
| P | Vern Olsen | R | 35 | 57 | 15 | 3 | 0 | 0 | 0.0 | 4 | 5 | 2 | 9 | 2 | 1 | 0 | .263 | .316 |
| P | Jake Mooty | R | 24 | 38 | 10 | 0 | 0 | 0 | 0.0 | 2 | 2 | 1 | 6 | 0 | 0 | 0 | .263 | .263 |
| P | Charlie Root | R | 36 | 31 | 4 | 0 | 0 | 0 | 0.0 | 4 | 1 | 2 | 10 | 0 | 0 | 0 | .129 | .129 |
| P | Ken Raffensberger | R | 43 | 30 | 5 | 0 | 0 | 0 | 0.0 | 2 | 0 | 0 | 18 | 0 | 0 | 0 | .167 | .167 |
| P | Dizzy Dean | R | 10 | 18 | 4 | 0 | 0 | 0 | 0.0 | 2 | 0 | 0 | 2 | 0 | 0 | 0 | .222 | .222 |
| P | Vance Page | R | 31 | 13 | 4 | 2 | 0 | 0 | 0.0 | 1 | 0 | 1 | 2 | 0 | 0 | 0 | .308 | .462 |
| P | Clay Bryant | R | 16 | 9 | 3 | 0 | 0 | 0 | 0.0 | 4 | 1 | 0 | 4 | 0 | 0 | 0 | .333 | .333 |
| P | Julio Bonetti | R | 1 | 0 | 0 | 0 | 0 | 0 | — | 0 | 0 | 0 | 0 | 0 | 0 | 0 | — | — |
| | TEAM TOTAL | | | 5389 | 1441 | 272 | 48 | 86 | 1.6 | 68 | 627 | 482 | 566 | 63 | 112 | 28 | .267 | .384 |

## INDIVIDUAL FIELDING

| POS | Player | T | G | PO | A | E | DP | TC/G | FA | | POS | Player | T | G | PO | A | E | DP | TC/G | FA |
|---|---|---|---|---|---|---|---|---|---|---|---|---|---|---|---|---|---|---|---|---|
| 1B | Cavarretta | L | 52 | 524 | 30 | 5 | 57 | 10.8 | .991 | | OF | J. Gleeson | R | 123 | 273 | 14 | 5 | 3 | 2.4 | .983 |
| | R. Russell | R | 51 | 518 | 18 | 10 | 22 | 10.7 | .982 | | | B. Nicholson | R | 123 | 235 | 10 | 13 | 2 | 2.1 | .950 |
| | Z. Bonura | R | 44 | 408 | 40 | 4 | 34 | 10.3 | .991 | | | H. Leiber | R | 103 | 187 | 8 | 3 | 0 | 1.9 | .985 |
| | H. Leiber | R | 12 | 115 | 11 | 2 | 10 | 10.7 | .984 | | | Dallessandro | L | 74 | 156 | 1 | 5 | 0 | 2.2 | .969 |
| | S. Hack | R | 1 | 7 | 2 | 0 | 0 | 9.0 | 1.000 | | | A. Galan | R | 54 | 114 | 6 | 2 | 2 | 2.3 | .984 |
| | G. Hartnett | R | 1 | 1 | 1 | 0 | 0 | 2.0 | 1.000 | | C | A. Todd | R | 104 | 418 | 59 | 8 | 11 | 4.7 | .984 |
| 2B | B. Herman | R | 135 | **366** | 448 | 22 | 94 | **6.2** | .974 | | | B. Collins | R | 42 | 133 | 23 | 8 | 3 | 3.9 | .951 |
| | R. Warstler | R | 17 | 41 | 51 | 5 | 7 | 5.7 | .948 | | | G. Hartnett | R | 22 | 69 | 9 | 4 | 2 | 3.7 | .951 |
| | A. Galan | R | 2 | 5 | 5 | 2 | 0 | 6.0 | .833 | | | McCullough | R | 7 | 44 | 4 | 0 | 1 | 6.9 | 1.000 |
| | B. Rogell | R | 3 | 4 | 3 | 0 | 0 | 2.3 | 1.000 | | | | | | | | | | | |
| SS | B. Mattick | R | 126 | 233 | 431 | 38 | 76 | 5.6 | .946 | | | | | | | | | | | |
| | R. Warstler | R | 28 | 49 | 90 | 9 | 13 | 5.3 | .939 | | | | | | | | | | | |
| | B. Sturgeon | R | 7 | 19 | 20 | 7 | 5 | 6.6 | .848 | | | | | | | | | | | |
| | B. Rogell | R | 14 | 7 | 11 | 2 | 2 | 1.4 | .900 | | | | | | | | | | | |
| 3B | S. Hack | R | 148 | **175** | **302** | 23 | **27** | 3.4 | .954 | | | | | | | | | | | |
| | B. Mattick | R | 1 | 0 | 0 | 0 | 0 | 0.0 | .000 | | | | | | | | | | | |
| | B. Rogell | R | 9 | 8 | 10 | 4 | 0 | 2.4 | .818 | | | | | | | | | | | |
| | R. Russell | R | 3 | 1 | 4 | 0 | 0 | 1.7 | 1.000 | | | | | | | | | | | |

So much for tradition. After 14 straight first-division finishes, the Cubs faltered to fifth. After 19 seasons as a Cub catching and hitting hero, manager Gabby Hartnett was given the heave-ho. Hartnett, limiting his playing time to only 22 games, had the Cubs in contention until an August collapse. Ailments and injuries took their toll, sending Phil Cavarretta, Rip Russell, Hank Leiber, and Augie Galan to the sidelines. Clay Bryant and Dizzy Dean had sore arms and were of little use. Dean, 3–3, was waived to Tulsa in the hope that warmer weather would restore his effectiveness. The biggest disappointment was Bill Lee, who tumbled to 9–17. Claude Passeau was the new ace of the staff with a 20–13 record, a 2.50 ERA, 20 complete games, and only 8 homers allowed in 281 innings. A rarity, at least for the Cubs, was three left-handed starters compiling 34 victories. Larry French had 14 and rookies Vern Olsen and Ken Raffensberger had 13 and 7. In addition, the Cubs boasted a trio of .300 hitters. Stan Hack led with .317, newcomer Jimmy Gleeson batted .313 with 39 doubles, and Leiber hit .302. Bill Nicholson, in his first full season, led with 25 homers and 98 RBI and had a .534 slugging average.

### TEAM STATISTICS

| | W | L | PCT | GB | R | OR | Batting 2B | 3B | HR | BA | SA | SB | Fielding E | DP | FA | Pitching CG | B | SO | ShO | SV | ERA |
|---|---|---|---|---|---|---|---|---|---|---|---|---|---|---|---|---|---|---|---|---|---|
| IN | 100 | 53 | .654 | | 707 | 528 | 264 | 38 | 89 | .266 | .379 | 72 | 117 | 158 | .981 | 91 | 445 | 557 | 10 | 11 | 3.05 |
| KN | 88 | 65 | .575 | 12 | 697 | 621 | 256 | 70 | 93 | .260 | .383 | 56 | 183 | 110 | .970 | 65 | 393 | 634 | 17 | 14 | 3.50 |
| TL | 84 | 69 | .549 | 16 | 747 | 699 | 266 | 61 | 119 | .275 | .411 | 97 | 174 | 134 | .971 | 71 | 488 | 550 | 10 | 14 | 3.83 |
| T | 78 | 76 | .506 | 22.5 | 809 | 783 | 276 | 68 | 76 | .276 | .394 | 69 | 217 | 160 | .966 | 49 | 492 | 491 | 8 | 24 | 4.36 |
| HI | 75 | 79 | .487 | 25.5 | 681 | 636 | 272 | 48 | 86 | .267 | .384 | 63 | 199 | 143 | .968 | 69 | 430 | 564 | 12 | 14 | 3.54 |
| Y | 72 | 80 | .474 | 27.5 | 663 | 659 | 201 | 46 | 91 | .267 | .374 | 45 | 139 | 132 | .977 | 57 | 473 | 606 | 11 | 18 | 3.79 |
| OS | 65 | 87 | .428 | 34.5 | 623 | 745 | 219 | 50 | 59 | .256 | .349 | 48 | 184 | 169 | .970 | 76 | 573 | 435 | 9 | 12 | 4.36 |
| HI | 50 | 103 | .327 | 50 | 494 | 750 | 180 | 35 | 75 | .238 | .331 | 25 | 181 | 136 | .970 | 66 | 475 | 485 | 5 | 8 | 4.40 |
| AGUE TOTAL | | | | | 5421 | 5421 | 1934 | 416 | 688 | .264 | .376 | 475 | 1394 | 1142 | .972 | 544 | 3769 | 4322 | 82 | 115 | 3.85 |

### INDIVIDUAL PITCHING

| ITCHER | T | W | L | PCT | ERA | SV | G | GS | CG | IP | H | BB | SO | R | ER | ShO | H/9 | BB/9 | SO/9 |
|---|---|---|---|---|---|---|---|---|---|---|---|---|---|---|---|---|---|---|---|
| aude Passeau | R | 20 | 13 | .606 | 2.50 | 5 | 46 | 31 | 20 | 280.2 | 259 | 59 | 124 | 97 | 78 | 4 | 8.31 | 1.89 | 3.98 |
| arry French | L | 14 | 14 | .500 | 3.29 | 2 | 40 | 33 | 18 | 246 | 240 | 64 | 107 | 93 | 90 | 3 | 8.78 | 2.34 | 3.91 |
| ll Lee | R | 9 | 17 | .346 | 5.03 | 0 | 37 | 30 | 9 | 211.1 | 246 | 70 | 70 | 129 | 118 | 1 | 10.48 | 2.98 | 2.98 |
| ern Olsen | L | 13 | 9 | .591 | 2.97 | 0 | 34 | 20 | 9 | 172.2 | 172 | 62 | 71 | 64 | 57 | 4 | 8.97 | 3.23 | 3.70 |
| en Raffensberger | L | 7 | 9 | .438 | 3.38 | 3 | 43 | 10 | 3 | 114.2 | 120 | 29 | 55 | 54 | 43 | 0 | 9.42 | 2.28 | 4.32 |
| ake Mooty | R | 6 | 6 | .500 | 2.92 | 1 | 20 | 12 | 6 | 114 | 101 | 49 | 42 | 45 | 37 | 0 | 7.97 | 3.87 | 3.32 |
| harlie Root | R | 2 | 4 | .333 | 3.82 | 1 | 36 | 8 | 1 | 113 | 118 | 33 | 50 | 61 | 48 | 0 | 9.40 | 2.63 | 3.98 |
| ance Page | R | 1 | 3 | .250 | 4.42 | 2 | 30 | 1 | 0 | 59 | 65 | 26 | 22 | 38 | 29 | 0 | 9.92 | 3.97 | 3.36 |
| zzy Dean | R | 3 | 3 | .500 | 5.17 | 0 | 10 | 9 | 3 | 54 | 68 | 20 | 18 | 35 | 31 | 0 | 11.33 | 3.33 | 3.00 |
| ay Bryant | R | 0 | 1 | .000 | 4.78 | 0 | 8 | 0 | 0 | 26.1 | 26 | 14 | 5 | 17 | 14 | 0 | 8.89 | 4.78 | 1.71 |
| lio Bonetti | R | 0 | 0 | — | 20.25 | 0 | 1 | 0 | 0 | 1.1 | 3 | 4 | 0 | 3 | 3 | 0 | 20.25 | 27.00 | 0.00 |
| EAM TOTAL | | 75 | 79 | .487 | 3.54 | 14 | 305 | 154 | 69 | 1393 | 1418 | 430 | 564 | 636 | 548 | 12 | 9.16 | 2.78 | 3.64 |

| MANAGER | W | L | PCT |
|---|---|---|---|
| Jimmie Wilson | 70 | 84 | .455 |

| POS | Player | B | G | AB | H | 2B | 3B | HR | HR % | R | RBI | BB | SO | SB | Pinch Hit AB | Pinch Hit H | BA | SA |
|---|---|---|---|---|---|---|---|---|---|---|---|---|---|---|---|---|---|---|
| **REGULARS** | | | | | | | | | | | | | | | | | | |
| 1B | Babe Dahlgren | R | 99 | 359 | 101 | 20 | 1 | 16 | 4.5 | 50 | 59 | 43 | 39 | 2 | 1 | 0 | .281 | .476 |
| 2B | Lou Stringer | R | 145 | 512 | 126 | 31 | 4 | 5 | 1.0 | 59 | 53 | 59 | 86 | 3 | 0 | 0 | .246 | .352 |
| SS | Bobby Sturgeon | R | 129 | 433 | 106 | 15 | 3 | 0 | 0.0 | 45 | 25 | 9 | 30 | 5 | 0 | 0 | .245 | .293 |
| 3B | Stan Hack | L | 151 | 586 | 186 | 33 | 5 | 7 | 1.2 | 111 | 45 | 99 | 40 | 10 | 0 | 0 | .317 | .427 |
| RF | Bill Nicholson | L | 147 | 532 | 135 | 26 | 1 | 26 | 4.9 | 74 | 98 | 82 | 91 | 1 | 4 | 0 | .254 | .453 |
| CF | Phil Cavarretta | L | 107 | 346 | 99 | 18 | 4 | 6 | 1.7 | 46 | 40 | 53 | 28 | 2 | 5 | 2 | .286 | .413 |
| LF | Dom Dallessandro | L | 140 | 486 | 132 | 36 | 2 | 6 | 1.2 | 73 | 85 | 68 | 37 | 3 | 7 | 1 | .272 | .391 |
| C | Clyde McCullough | R | 125 | 418 | 95 | 9 | 2 | 9 | 2.2 | 41 | 53 | 34 | 67 | 5 | 5 | 1 | .227 | .323 |
| **SUBSTITUTES** | | | | | | | | | | | | | | | | | | |
| UT | Johnny Hudson | R | 50 | 99 | 20 | 4 | 0 | 0 | 0.0 | 8 | 6 | 3 | 15 | 3 | 11 | 0 | .202 | .242 |
| SS | Billy Myers | R | 24 | 63 | 14 | 1 | 0 | 1 | 1.6 | 10 | 4 | 7 | 25 | 1 | 0 | 0 | .222 | .286 |
| 2B | Billy Herman | R | 11 | 36 | 7 | 0 | 1 | 0 | 0.0 | 4 | 0 | 9 | 5 | 0 | 0 | 0 | .194 | .250 |
| 1B | Eddie Waitkus | L | 12 | 28 | 5 | 0 | 0 | 0 | 0.0 | 1 | 0 | 0 | 3 | 0 | 3 | 1 | .179 | .179 |
| SS | Lennie Merullo | R | 7 | 17 | 6 | 1 | 0 | 0 | 0.0 | 3 | 1 | 2 | 0 | 1 | 0 | 0 | .353 | .412 |
| 1B | Rip Russell | R | 6 | 17 | 5 | 1 | 0 | 0 | 0.0 | 1 | 1 | 1 | 5 | 0 | 0 | 0 | .294 | .353 |
| OF | Lou Novikoff | R | 62 | 203 | 49 | 8 | 0 | 5 | 2.5 | 22 | 24 | 11 | 15 | 0 | 8 | 3 | .241 | .355 |
| O1 | Hank Leiber | R | 53 | 162 | 35 | 5 | 0 | 7 | 4.3 | 20 | 25 | 16 | 25 | 0 | 9 | 0 | .216 | .377 |
| OF | Augie Galan | B | 65 | 120 | 25 | 3 | 0 | 1 | 0.8 | 18 | 13 | 22 | 10 | 0 | 28 | 4 | .208 | .258 |
| OF | Charlie Gilbert | L | 39 | 86 | 24 | 2 | 1 | 0 | 0.0 | 11 | 12 | 11 | 6 | 1 | 14 | 2 | .279 | .326 |
| OF | Barney Olsen | R | 24 | 73 | 21 | 6 | 1 | 1 | 1.4 | 13 | 4 | 4 | 11 | 0 | 1 | 1 | .288 | .438 |
| OF | Frank Jelincich | R | 4 | 8 | 1 | 0 | 0 | 0 | 0.0 | 0 | 2 | 1 | 2 | 0 | 2 | 0 | .125 | .125 |
| C | Bob Scheffing | R | 51 | 132 | 32 | 8 | 0 | 1 | 0.8 | 9 | 20 | 5 | 19 | 2 | 17 | 3 | .242 | .326 |
| C | Greek George | R | 35 | 64 | 10 | 2 | 0 | 0 | 0.0 | 4 | 6 | 2 | 10 | 0 | 17 | 0 | .156 | .188 |
| PH | Al Todd | R | 6 | 6 | 1 | 0 | 0 | 0 | 0.0 | 1 | 0 | 0 | 1 | 0 | 6 | 1 | .167 | .167 |
| **PITCHERS** | | | | | | | | | | | | | | | | | | |
| P | Claude Passeau | R | 34 | 86 | 19 | 2 | 0 | 3 | 3.5 | 6 | 12 | 2 | 22 | 0 | 0 | 0 | .221 | .349 |
| P | Vern Olsen | R | 37 | 63 | 15 | 2 | 0 | 1 | 1.6 | 7 | 5 | 2 | 10 | 0 | 0 | 0 | .238 | .317 |
| P | Bill Lee | R | 28 | 59 | 11 | 0 | 0 | 2 | 3.4 | 8 | 5 | 1 | 9 | 0 | 0 | 0 | .186 | .288 |
| P | Jake Mooty | R | 33 | 50 | 10 | 1 | 0 | 0 | 0.0 | 5 | 1 | 2 | 7 | 0 | 0 | 0 | .200 | .220 |
| P | Larry French | B | 26 | 47 | 9 | 0 | 0 | 0 | 0.0 | 5 | 3 | 4 | 15 | 0 | 0 | 0 | .191 | .191 |
| P | Paul Erickson | R | 32 | 46 | 7 | 4 | 0 | 1 | 2.2 | 5 | 2 | 0 | 12 | 0 | 0 | 0 | .152 | .304 |
| P | Charlie Root | R | 19 | 33 | 5 | 1 | 0 | 1 | 3.0 | 4 | 4 | 5 | 10 | 0 | 0 | 0 | .152 | .273 |
| P | Vallie Eaves | R | 12 | 20 | 2 | 0 | 0 | 0 | 0.0 | 0 | 0 | 0 | 2 | 0 | 0 | 0 | .100 | .100 |
| P | Tot Pressnell | R | 29 | 15 | 3 | 0 | 0 | 0 | 0.0 | 1 | 0 | 1 | 1 | 0 | 0 | 0 | .200 | .200 |
| P | Vance Page | R | 25 | 7 | 2 | 0 | 0 | 0 | 0.0 | 0 | 0 | 1 | 1 | 0 | 0 | 0 | .286 | .286 |
| P | Johnny Schmitz | R | 6 | 7 | 4 | 0 | 0 | 0 | 0.0 | 1 | 2 | 0 | 0 | 0 | 1 | 0 | .571 | .571 |
| P | Ken Raffensberger | R | 10 | 5 | 0 | 0 | 0 | 0 | 0.0 | 0 | 0 | 0 | 2 | 0 | 0 | 0 | .000 | .000 |
| P | Russ Meers | L | 1 | 2 | 0 | 0 | 0 | 0 | 0.0 | 0 | 0 | 0 | 1 | 0 | 0 | 0 | .000 | .000 |
| P | Wimpy Quinn | R | 3 | 2 | 1 | 0 | 0 | 0 | 0.0 | 0 | 0 | 0 | 0 | 0 | 0 | 0 | .500 | .500 |
| P | Emil Kush | R | 2 | 1 | 0 | 0 | 0 | 0 | 0.0 | 0 | 0 | 0 | 0 | 0 | 0 | 0 | .000 | .000 |
| P | Walt Lanfranconi | R | 2 | 1 | 0 | 0 | 0 | 0 | 0.0 | 0 | 0 | 0 | 1 | 0 | 0 | 0 | .000 | .000 |
| P | Dizzy Dean | R | 1 | 0 | 0 | 0 | 0 | 0 | — | 0 | 0 | 0 | 0 | 0 | 0 | 0 | — | — |
| P | Hank Gornicki | R | 1 | 0 | 0 | 0 | 0 | 0 | — | 0 | 0 | 0 | 0 | 0 | 0 | 0 | — | — |
| TEAM TOTAL | | | | 5230 | 1323 | 239 | 25 | 99 | 1.9 | 66 | 610 | 559 | 668 | 39 | 139 | 19 | .253 | .365 |

## INDIVIDUAL FIELDING

| POS | Player | T | G | PO | A | E | DP | TC/G | FA |
|---|---|---|---|---|---|---|---|---|---|
| 1B | B. Dahlgren | R | 98 | 957 | 38 | 9 | 84 | 10.2 | .991 |
| | Cavarretta | L | 33 | 335 | 12 | 4 | 18 | 10.6 | .989 |
| | H. Leiber | R | 15 | 140 | 7 | 3 | 13 | 10.0 | .980 |
| | E. Waitkus | L | 9 | 71 | 3 | 4 | 8 | 8.7 | .949 |
| | R. Russell | R | 5 | 36 | 3 | 1 | 4 | 8.0 | .975 |
| | S. Hack | R | 1 | 1 | 0 | 0 | 0 | 1.0 | 1.000 |
| 2B | L. Stringer | R | 137 | 356 | 455 | 34 | 84 | 6.2 | .960 |
| | B. Sturgeon | R | 1 | 0 | 0 | 0 | 0 | 0.0 | .000 |
| | B. Herman | R | 11 | 33 | 20 | 6 | 5 | 5.4 | .898 |
| | J. Hudson | R | 13 | 15 | 23 | 3 | 3 | 3.2 | .927 |
| | B. Myers | R | 1 | 4 | 6 | 0 | 1 | 10.0 | 1.000 |
| SS | B. Sturgeon | R | 126 | 215 | 366 | 27 | 68 | 4.8 | .956 |
| | B. Myers | R | 19 | 33 | 60 | 6 | 12 | 5.2 | .939 |
| | J. Hudson | R | 17 | 22 | 27 | 5 | 6 | 3.2 | .907 |
| | L. Merullo | R | 7 | 12 | 18 | 1 | 5 | 4.4 | .968 |
| | L. Stringer | R | 7 | 3 | 7 | 4 | 1 | 2.0 | .714 |
| 3B | S. Hack | R | 150 | 138 | 295 | 21 | 22 | 3.0 | .954 |
| | B. Sturgeon | R | 1 | 0 | 0 | 0 | 0 | 0.0 | .000 |
| | J. Hudson | R | 10 | 4 | 18 | 1 | 0 | 2.3 | .957 |

| POS | Player | T | G | PO | A | E | DP | TC/G | FA |
|---|---|---|---|---|---|---|---|---|---|
| OF | B. Nicholson | R | 143 | 293 | 10 | 9 | 2 | 2.2 | .971 |
| | Dallessandro | L | 131 | 292 | 4 | 4 | 0 | 2.3 | .987 |
| | Cavarretta | L | 66 | 128 | 3 | 1 | 2 | 2.0 | .992 |
| | L. Novikoff | R | 54 | 92 | 3 | 0 | 0 | 1.8 | 1.000 |
| | B. Olsen | R | 23 | 51 | 3 | 3 | 1 | 2.5 | .947 |
| | H. Leiber | R | 29 | 52 | 1 | 2 | 0 | 1.9 | .964 |
| | C. Gilbert | L | 22 | 51 | 0 | 0 | 0 | 2.3 | 1.000 |
| | A. Galan | R | 31 | 45 | 2 | 2 | 0 | 1.6 | .959 |
| | F. Jelincich | R | 2 | 1 | 0 | 0 | 0 | 0.5 | 1.000 |
| C | McCullough | R | 119 | 481 | 64 | 10 | 6 | 4.7 | .982 |
| | B. Scheffing | R | 34 | 126 | 17 | 5 | 1 | 4.4 | .966 |
| | G. George | R | 18 | 63 | 9 | 2 | 2 | 4.1 | .973 |

   The Cubs had a long tradition of player-managers: from Anson to Chance to Hornsby to Grimm to Hartnett. And after Gabby was fired, Cub fans expected second baseman Billy Herman to take command. Owner P. K. Wrigley pulled a surprise by naming Reds' coach Jimmie Wilson as manager. Wilson's first move was obvious—getting rid of Herman. The Cubs gift-wrapped Herman to the Dodgers for outfielder Charlie Gilbert, infielder Johnny Hudson, and $40,000. Herman, one of eight former Cubs in Brooklyn flannels, helped the Dodgers win the pennant. The Cubs, under Wilson, were never in contention. They wound up sixth, with a 70–84 mark, their lowest finish and worst record since 1925. Stan Hack, one of the few survivors from the glory years, scored 111 runs, led the league in hits with 186, and topped the Cub hitters with a .317 average. Bill Nicholson supplied the power with 26 homers and 98 RBI, but there was no other offensive punch. The lone dependable pitcher was Claude Passeau, who had 20 complete games despite his 14–14 record. Rifle-armed catcher Clyde McCullough with 9 homers and 53 RBI was the best of a much-ballyhooed but poor-producing rookie crop. Pitcher Russell Meers was the first Cub to join the armed forces; he entered the navy.

### TEAM STATISTICS

| | W | L | PCT | GB | R | OR | 2B | 3B | HR | BA | SA | SB | E | DP | FA | CG | B | SO | ShO | SV | ERA |
|---|---|---|---|---|---|---|---|---|---|---|---|---|---|---|---|---|---|---|---|---|---|
| | | | | | | | | Batting | | | | | | Fielding | | | | Pitching | | | |
| KN | 100 | 54 | .649 | | 800 | 581 | 286 | 69 | 101 | .272 | .405 | 36 | 162 | 125 | .974 | 66 | 495 | 603 | 17 | 22 | 3.14 |
| L | 97 | 56 | .634 | 2.5 | 734 | 589 | 254 | 56 | 70 | .272 | .377 | 47 | 172 | 146 | .973 | 64 | 502 | 659 | 15 | 20 | 3.19 |
| N | 88 | 66 | .571 | 12 | 616 | 564 | 213 | 33 | 64 | .247 | .337 | 68 | 152 | 147 | .975 | 89 | 510 | 627 | 19 | 10 | 3.17 |
| F | 81 | 73 | .526 | 19 | 690 | 643 | 233 | 65 | 56 | .268 | .368 | 59 | 196 | 130 | .968 | 71 | 492 | 410 | 8 | 12 | 3.48 |
| Y | 74 | 79 | .484 | 25.5 | 667 | 706 | 248 | 35 | 95 | .260 | .371 | 36 | 160 | 144 | .974 | 55 | 539 | 566 | 12 | 18 | 3.94 |
| HI | 70 | 84 | .455 | 30 | 666 | 670 | 239 | 25 | 99 | .253 | .365 | 39 | 180 | 139 | .970 | 74 | 449 | 548 | 8 | 9 | 3.72 |
| )S | 62 | 92 | .403 | 38 | 592 | 720 | 231 | 38 | 48 | .251 | .334 | 61 | 191 | 174 | .969 | 62 | 554 | 446 | 10 | 9 | 3.95 |
| HI | 43 | 111 | .279 | 57 | 501 | 793 | 188 | 38 | 64 | .244 | .331 | 65 | 187 | 147 | .969 | 35 | 606 | 552 | 4 | 9 | 4.50 |
| AGUE TOTAL | | | | | 5266 | 5266 | 1892 | 359 | 597 | .258 | .361 | 411 | 1400 | 1152 | .972 | 516 | 4147 | 4411 | 93 | 109 | 3.63 |

### INDIVIDUAL PITCHING

| TCHER | T | W | L | PCT | ERA | SV | G | GS | CG | IP | H | BB | SO | R | ER | ShO | H/9 | BB/9 | SO/9 |
|---|---|---|---|---|---|---|---|---|---|---|---|---|---|---|---|---|---|---|---|
| aude Passeau | R | 14 | 14 | .500 | 3.35 | 0 | 34 | 30 | 20 | 231 | 262 | 52 | 80 | 99 | 86 | 3 | 10.21 | 2.03 | 3.12 |
| rn Olsen | L | 10 | 8 | .556 | 3.15 | 1 | 37 | 23 | 10 | 185.2 | 202 | 59 | 73 | 84 | 65 | 2 | 9.79 | 2.86 | 3.54 |
| l Lee | R | 8 | 14 | .364 | 3.76 | 1 | 28 | 22 | 12 | 167.1 | 179 | 43 | 62 | 87 | 70 | 0 | 9.63 | 2.31 | 3.33 |
| ke Mooty | R | 8 | 9 | .471 | 3.35 | 4 | 33 | 14 | 7 | 153.1 | 143 | 56 | 45 | 69 | 57 | 1 | 8.39 | 3.29 | 2.64 |
| ul Erickson | R | 5 | 7 | .417 | 3.70 | 1 | 32 | 15 | 7 | 141 | 126 | 64 | 85 | 70 | 58 | 1 | 8.04 | 4.09 | 5.43 |
| rry French | L | 5 | 14 | .263 | 4.63 | 0 | 26 | 18 | 6 | 138 | 161 | 43 | 60 | 88 | 71 | 1 | 10.50 | 2.80 | 3.91 |
| arlie Root | R | 8 | 7 | .533 | 5.40 | 0 | 19 | 15 | 6 | 106.2 | 133 | 37 | 46 | 68 | 64 | 0 | 11.22 | 3.12 | 3.88 |
| t Pressnell | R | 5 | 3 | .625 | 3.09 | 1 | 29 | 1 | 0 | 70 | 69 | 23 | 27 | 26 | 24 | 0 | 8.87 | 2.96 | 3.47 |
| llie Eaves | R | 3 | 3 | .500 | 3.53 | 0 | 12 | 7 | 4 | 58.2 | 56 | 21 | 24 | 27 | 23 | 0 | 8.59 | 3.22 | 3.68 |
| nce Page | R | 2 | 2 | .500 | 4.28 | 1 | 25 | 3 | 1 | 48.1 | 48 | 30 | 17 | 24 | 23 | 0 | 8.94 | 5.59 | 3.17 |
| hnny Schmitz | L | 2 | 0 | 1.000 | 1.31 | 0 | 5 | 3 | 1 | 20.2 | 12 | 9 | 11 | 5 | 3 | 0 | 5.23 | 3.92 | 4.79 |
| n Raffensberger | L | 0 | 1 | .000 | 4.50 | 0 | 10 | 1 | 0 | 18 | 17 | 7 | 5 | 9 | 9 | 0 | 8.50 | 3.50 | 2.50 |
| ss Meers | L | 0 | 1 | .000 | 1.13 | 0 | 1 | 1 | 0 | 8 | 5 | 0 | 5 | 2 | 1 | 0 | 5.63 | 0.00 | 5.63 |
| alt Lanfranconi | R | 0 | 1 | .000 | 3.00 | 0 | 2 | 1 | 0 | 6 | 7 | 2 | 1 | 3 | 2 | 0 | 10.50 | 3.00 | 1.50 |
| mpy Quinn | R | 0 | 0 | — | 7.20 | 0 | 3 | 0 | 0 | 5 | 3 | 3 | 2 | 4 | 4 | 0 | 5.40 | 5.40 | 3.60 |
| hil Kush | R | 0 | 0 | — | 2.25 | 0 | 2 | 0 | 0 | 4 | 2 | 0 | 2 | 1 | 1 | 0 | 4.50 | 0.00 | 4.50 |
| nk Gornicki | R | 0 | 0 | — | 4.50 | 0 | 1 | 0 | 0 | 2 | 3 | 0 | 2 | 1 | 1 | 0 | 13.50 | 0.00 | 9.00 |
| zzy Dean | R | 0 | 0 | — | 18.00 | 0 | 1 | 1 | 0 | 1 | 3 | 0 | 1 | 3 | 2 | 0 | 27.00 | 0.00 | 9.00 |
| AM TOTAL | | 70 | 84 | .455 | 3.72 | 9 | 300 | 155 | 74 | 1364.2 | 1431 | 449 | 548 | 670 | 564 | 8 | 9.44 | 2.96 | 3.61 |

| MANAGER | W | L | PCT |
|---|---|---|---|
| Jimmie Wilson | 68 | 86 | .442 |

| POS | Player | B | G | AB | H | 2B | 3B | HR | HR % | R | RBI | BB | SO | SB | Pinch Hit AB | Pinch Hit H | BA | SA |
|---|---|---|---|---|---|---|---|---|---|---|---|---|---|---|---|---|---|---|
| **REGULARS** | | | | | | | | | | | | | | | | | | |
| 1B | Phil Cavarretta | L | 136 | 482 | 130 | 28 | 4 | 3 | 0.6 | 59 | 54 | 71 | 42 | 7 | 6 | 0 | .270 | .363 |
| 2B | Lou Stringer | R | 121 | 406 | 96 | 10 | 5 | 9 | 2.2 | 45 | 41 | 31 | 55 | 3 | 7 | 3 | .236 | .352 |
| SS | Lennie Merullo | R | 143 | 515 | 132 | 23 | 3 | 2 | 0.4 | 53 | 37 | 35 | 45 | 14 | 0 | 0 | .256 | .324 |
| 3B | Stan Hack | L | 140 | 553 | 166 | 36 | 3 | 6 | 1.1 | 91 | 39 | 94 | 40 | 9 | 0 | 0 | .300 | .409 |
| RF | Bill Nicholson | L | 152 | 588 | 173 | 22 | 11 | 21 | 3.6 | 83 | 78 | 76 | 80 | 8 | 1 | 0 | .294 | .476 |
| CF | Dom Dallessandro | L | 96 | 264 | 69 | 12 | 4 | 4 | 1.5 | 30 | 43 | 36 | 18 | 4 | 26 | 9 | .261 | .383 |
| LF | Lou Novikoff | R | 128 | 483 | 145 | 25 | 5 | 7 | 1.4 | 48 | 64 | 24 | 28 | 3 | 8 | 2 | .300 | .416 |
| C | Clyde McCullough | R | 109 | 337 | 95 | 22 | 1 | 5 | 1.5 | 39 | 31 | 25 | 47 | 7 | 8 | 2 | .282 | .398 |
| **SUBSTITUTES** | | | | | | | | | | | | | | | | | | |
| UT | Rip Russell | R | 102 | 302 | 73 | 9 | 0 | 8 | 2.6 | 32 | 41 | 17 | 21 | 0 | 31 | 5 | .242 | .351 |
| 1B | Jimmie Foxx | R | 70 | 205 | 42 | 8 | 0 | 3 | 1.5 | 25 | 19 | 22 | 55 | 1 | 16 | 3 | .205 | .288 |
| 2S | Bobby Sturgeon | R | 63 | 162 | 40 | 7 | 1 | 0 | 0.0 | 8 | 7 | 4 | 13 | 2 | 2 | 0 | .247 | .302 |
| 1B | Babe Dahlgren | R | 17 | 56 | 12 | 1 | 0 | 0 | 0.0 | 4 | 6 | 4 | 2 | 0 | 1 | 0 | .214 | .232 |
| 3B | Cy Block | R | 9 | 33 | 12 | 1 | 1 | 0 | 0.0 | 6 | 4 | 3 | 3 | 2 | 0 | 0 | .364 | .455 |
| OF | Charlie Gilbert | L | 74 | 179 | 33 | 6 | 3 | 0 | 0.0 | 18 | 7 | 25 | 24 | 1 | 23 | 2 | .184 | .251 |
| OF | Peanuts Lowrey | R | 27 | 58 | 11 | 0 | 0 | 1 | 1.7 | 4 | 4 | 4 | 4 | 0 | 3 | 0 | .190 | .241 |
| OF | Marv Rickert | L | 8 | 26 | 7 | 0 | 0 | 0 | 0.0 | 5 | 1 | 1 | 5 | 0 | 1 | 0 | .269 | .269 |
| OF | Whitey Platt | R | 4 | 16 | 1 | 0 | 0 | 0 | 0.0 | 1 | 2 | 0 | 3 | 0 | 0 | 0 | .063 | .063 |
| C | Chico Hernandez | R | 47 | 118 | 27 | 5 | 0 | 0 | 0.0 | 6 | 7 | 11 | 13 | 0 | 3 | 1 | .229 | .271 |
| C | Bob Scheffing | R | 44 | 102 | 20 | 3 | 0 | 2 | 2.0 | 7 | 12 | 7 | 11 | 2 | 12 | 1 | .196 | .284 |
| C | Paul Gillespie | L | 5 | 16 | 4 | 0 | 0 | 2 | 12.5 | 3 | 4 | 1 | 2 | 0 | 1 | 0 | .250 | .625 |
| C | Marv Felderman | R | 3 | 6 | 1 | 0 | 0 | 0 | 0.0 | 0 | 0 | 1 | 4 | 0 | 0 | 0 | .167 | .167 |
| **PITCHERS** | | | | | | | | | | | | | | | | | | |
| P | Claude Passeau | R | 35 | 105 | 19 | 1 | 0 | 2 | 1.9 | 7 | 10 | 0 | 26 | 0 | 0 | 0 | .181 | .248 |
| P | Bill Lee | R | 32 | 69 | 11 | 2 | 0 | 0 | 0.0 | 2 | 7 | 7 | 13 | 0 | 0 | 0 | .159 | .188 |
| P | Hi Bithorn | R | 38 | 57 | 7 | 1 | 0 | 0 | 0.0 | 3 | 1 | 5 | 9 | 0 | 0 | 0 | .123 | .140 |
| P | Vern Olsen | R | 32 | 48 | 9 | 1 | 0 | 0 | 0.0 | 4 | 4 | 5 | 2 | 0 | 0 | 0 | .188 | .208 |
| P | Bill Fleming | R | 33 | 39 | 2 | 0 | 0 | 0 | 0.0 | 2 | 0 | 0 | 13 | 0 | 0 | 0 | .051 | .051 |
| P | Lon Warneke | R | 12 | 32 | 6 | 0 | 0 | 0 | 0.0 | 1 | 1 | 0 | 5 | 0 | 0 | 0 | .188 | .188 |
| P | Jake Mooty | R | 19 | 28 | 6 | 0 | 0 | 0 | 0.0 | 3 | 2 | 0 | 0 | 0 | 0 | 0 | .214 | .214 |
| P | Johnny Schmitz | R | 23 | 26 | 4 | 0 | 0 | 0 | 0.0 | 1 | 0 | 0 | 5 | 0 | 0 | 0 | .154 | .154 |
| P | Paul Erickson | R | 18 | 21 | 3 | 0 | 0 | 0 | 0.0 | 0 | 1 | 0 | 11 | 0 | 0 | 0 | .143 | .143 |
| P | Hank Wyse | R | 4 | 8 | 1 | 0 | 0 | 0 | 0.0 | 1 | 1 | 1 | 2 | 0 | 0 | 0 | .125 | .125 |
| P | Dick Errickson | L | 21 | 5 | 0 | 0 | 0 | 0 | 0.0 | 0 | 0 | 0 | 0 | 0 | 0 | 0 | .000 | .000 |
| P | Ed Hanyzewski | R | 6 | 5 | 1 | 0 | 0 | 0 | 0.0 | 0 | 2 | 0 | 2 | 0 | 0 | 0 | .200 | .200 |
| P | Tot Pressnell | R | 27 | 3 | 2 | 1 | 0 | 0 | 0.0 | 0 | 3 | 1 | 1 | 0 | 0 | 0 | .667 | 1.000 |
| P | Emil Kush | R | 1 | 1 | 0 | 0 | 0 | 0 | – | 0 | 0 | 0 | 0 | 0 | 0 | 0 | .000 | .000 |
| P | Joe Berry | R | 2 | 0 | 0 | 0 | 0 | 0 | – | 0 | 0 | 0 | 0 | 0 | 0 | 0 | – | – |
| P | Bob Bowman | R | 1 | 0 | 0 | 0 | 0 | 0 | – | 0 | 0 | 0 | 0 | 0 | 0 | 0 | – | – |
| P | Vallie Eaves | R | 0 | 0 | 0 | 0 | 0 | 0 | – | 0 | 0 | 0 | 0 | 0 | 0 | 0 | – | – |
| P | Jesse Flores | R | 4 | 0 | 0 | 0 | 0 | 0 | – | 0 | 0 | 0 | 0 | 0 | 0 | 0 | – | – |
| | TEAM TOTAL | | | 5354 | 1360 | 224 | 41 | 75 | 1.4 | 59 | 533 | 511 | 606 | 63 | 149 | 28 | .254 | .353 |

## INDIVIDUAL FIELDING

| POS | Player | T | G | PO | A | E | DP | TC/G | FA |
|---|---|---|---|---|---|---|---|---|---|
| 1B | Cavarretta | L | 61 | 567 | 44 | 5 | 48 | 10.1 | .992 |
| | J. Foxx | R | 52 | 489 | 24 | 9 | 32 | 10.0 | .983 |
| | R. Russell | R | 35 | 328 | 13 | 9 | 30 | 10.0 | .974 |
| | B. Dahlgren | R | 14 | 136 | 10 | 2 | 7 | 10.6 | .986 |
| 2B | L. Stringer | R | 113 | 268 | 343 | 29 | 59 | 5.7 | .955 |
| | B. Sturgeon | R | 32 | 69 | 99 | 2 | 18 | 5.3 | .988 |
| | R. Russell | R | 24 | 51 | 69 | 4 | 10 | 5.2 | .968 |
| | C. Block | R | 1 | 2 | 3 | 0 | 1 | 5.0 | 1.000 |
| SS | L. Merullo | R | 143 | 299 | 438 | 42 | 80 | 5.4 | .946 |
| | B. Sturgeon | R | 29 | 43 | 64 | 2 | 15 | 3.8 | .982 |
| 3B | S. Hack | R | 139 | 154 | 261 | 15 | 21 | 3.1 | .965 |
| | L. Stringer | R | 1 | 0 | 0 | 0 | 0 | 0.0 | .000 |
| | C. Block | R | 8 | 10 | 12 | 2 | 1 | 3.0 | .917 |
| | R. Russell | R | 10 | 6 | 8 | 1 | 0 | 1.5 | .933 |
| | B. Sturgeon | R | 2 | 1 | 0 | 0 | 0 | 0.5 | 1.000 |

| POS | Player | T | G | PO | A | E | DP | TC/G | FA |
|---|---|---|---|---|---|---|---|---|---|
| OF | B. Nicholson | R | 151 | 327 | 18 | 5 | 2 | 2.3 | .986 |
| | L. Novikoff | R | 120 | 232 | 11 | 9 | 2 | 2.1 | .964 |
| | Cavarretta | L | 70 | 177 | 5 | 2 | 1 | 2.6 | .989 |
| | Dallessandro | L | 66 | 134 | 6 | 2 | 1 | 2.2 | .986 |
| | C. Gilbert | L | 47 | 99 | 6 | 2 | 2 | 2.3 | .981 |
| | P. Lowrey | R | 19 | 43 | 2 | 1 | 1 | 2.4 | .978 |
| | M. Rickert | R | 6 | 18 | 1 | 0 | 0 | 3.2 | 1.000 |
| | W. Platt | R | 4 | 7 | 1 | 0 | 0 | 2.0 | 1.000 |
| | R. Russell | R | 3 | 7 | 0 | 0 | 0 | 2.3 | 1.000 |
| C | McCullough | R | 97 | 386 | 61 | 9 | 10 | 4.7 | .980 |
| | C. Hernandez | R | 43 | 140 | 17 | 4 | 0 | 3.7 | .975 |
| | B. Scheffing | R | 32 | 122 | 16 | 2 | 6 | 4.4 | .986 |
| | P. Gillespie | R | 4 | 13 | 2 | 0 | 0 | 3.8 | 1.000 |
| | M. Felderman | R | 2 | 8 | 2 | 0 | 0 | 5.0 | 1.000 |
| | J. Foxx | R | 1 | 2 | 0 | 0 | 0 | 2.0 | 1.000 |

President Roosevelt gave baseball the green light, but the Cubs were in no rush to go anywhere. They remained a dull sixth, finishing 38 games behind the front-running Cardinals. After bouncing around the bushes with bulging batting averages, Lou "The Mad Russian" Novikoff finally became a regular and tied steady Stan Hack for team leadership at .300. Bill Nicholson was the lone power source with 21 homers and 78 runs batted in and had a .294 average. Claude Passeau just missed a 20-win season with a 19–14 record as team stopper. In addition, Passeau pitched 24 complete games. Best of the rookies was pitcher Hi Bithorn, who showed promise despite a 9–14 record. Two old faces, added via the waiver route, made minimal contributions. Lon Warneke was reacquired from the Cardinals and was 5–7, while slugging star Jimmie Foxx provided little power with 3 homers, 19 RBI, and a .205 average. The Cubs were hit by the draft board, as Uncle Sam reached out and grabbed Johnny Schmitz, Eddie Waitkus, Bob Scheffing, Cy Block, Lou Stringer, and Bobby Sturgeon off the roster. But the Braves and Phillies were in even worse shape, with the Philadelphia club trailing the Cards home by 62 1/2 games.

## TEAM STATISTICS

| | W | L | PCT | GB | R | OR | 2B | Batting 3B | HR | BA | SA | SB | Fielding E | DP | FA | CG | B | Pitching SO | ShO | SV | ERA |
|---|---|---|---|---|---|---|---|---|---|---|---|---|---|---|---|---|---|---|---|---|---|
| TL | 106 | 48 | .688 | | 755 | 482 | 282 | 69 | 60 | .268 | .379 | 71 | 169 | 137 | .972 | 70 | 473 | 651 | 18 | 15 | 2.55 |
| KN | 104 | 50 | .675 | 2 | 742 | 510 | 263 | 34 | 62 | .265 | .362 | 79 | 138 | 150 | .977 | 67 | 493 | 612 | 16 | 24 | 2.84 |
| Y | 85 | 67 | .559 | 20 | 675 | 600 | 162 | 35 | 109 | .254 | .361 | 39 | 138 | 128 | .977 | 70 | 493 | 497 | 12 | 13 | 3.31 |
| IN | 76 | 76 | .500 | 29 | 527 | 545 | 198 | 39 | 66 | .231 | .321 | 42 | 177 | 158 | .971 | 80 | 526 | 616 | 12 | 8 | 2.82 |
| IT | 66 | 81 | .449 | 36.5 | 585 | 631 | 173 | 49 | 54 | .245 | .330 | 41 | 184 | 129 | .969 | 64 | 435 | 426 | 13 | 11 | 3.58 |
| HI | 68 | 86 | .442 | 38 | 591 | 665 | 224 | 41 | 75 | .254 | .353 | 61 | 170 | 169 | .973 | 71 | 525 | 507 | 10 | 14 | 3.60 |
| OS | 59 | 89 | .399 | 44 | 515 | 645 | 210 | 19 | 68 | .240 | .329 | 49 | 142 | 138 | .976 | 68 | 518 | 414 | 9 | 8 | 3.76 |
| HI | 42 | 109 | .278 | 62.5 | 394 | 706 | 168 | 37 | 44 | .232 | .306 | 37 | 194 | 147 | .968 | 51 | 605 | 472 | 2 | 6 | 4.12 |
| EAGUE TOTAL | | | | | 4784 | 4784 | 1680 | 323 | 538 | .249 | .343 | 419 | 1312 | 1156 | .973 | 541 | 4068 | 4195 | 92 | 99 | 3.31 |

## INDIVIDUAL PITCHING

| ITCHER | T | W | L | PCT | ERA | SV | G | GS | CG | IP | H | BB | SO | R | ER | ShO | H/9 | BB/9 | SO/9 |
|---|---|---|---|---|---|---|---|---|---|---|---|---|---|---|---|---|---|---|---|
| laude Passeau | R | 19 | 14 | .576 | 2.68 | 0 | 35 | 34 | 24 | 278.1 | 284 | 74 | 89 | 116 | 83 | 3 | 9.18 | 2.39 | 2.88 |
| ll Lee | R | 13 | 13 | .500 | 3.85 | 0 | 32 | 30 | 18 | 219.2 | 221 | 67 | 75 | 99 | 94 | 1 | 9.05 | 2.75 | 3.07 |
| Bithorn | R | 9 | 14 | .391 | 3.68 | 2 | 38 | 16 | 9 | 171.1 | 191 | 81 | 65 | 93 | 70 | 0 | 10.03 | 4.25 | 3.41 |
| ern Olsen | L | 6 | 9 | .400 | 4.49 | 1 | 32 | 17 | 4 | 140.1 | 161 | 55 | 46 | 75 | 70 | 1 | 10.33 | 3.53 | 2.95 |
| ll Fleming | R | 5 | 6 | .455 | 3.01 | 2 | 33 | 14 | 4 | 134.1 | 117 | 63 | 59 | 51 | 45 | 2 | 7.84 | 4.22 | 3.95 |
| on Warneke | R | 5 | 7 | .417 | 2.27 | 2 | 15 | 12 | 8 | 99 | 97 | 21 | 28 | 33 | 25 | 1 | 8.82 | 1.91* | 2.55 |
| ohnny Schmitz | L | 3 | 7 | .300 | 3.43 | 2 | 23 | 10 | 1 | 86.2 | 70 | 45 | 51 | 41 | 33 | 0 | 7.27 | 4.67 | 5.30 |
| ake Mooty | R | 2 | 5 | .286 | 4.70 | 1 | 19 | 10 | 1 | 84.1 | 89 | 44 | 28 | 48 | 44 | 0 | 9.50 | 4.70 | 2.99 |
| aul Erickson | R | 1 | 6 | .143 | 5.43 | 0 | 18 | 7 | 1 | 63 | 70 | 41 | 26 | 40 | 38 | 0 | 10.00 | 5.86 | 3.71 |
| ot Pressnell | R | 1 | 1 | .500 | 5.49 | 4 | 27 | 0 | 0 | 39.1 | 40 | 5 | 9 | 28 | 24 | 0 | 9.15 | 1.14 | 2.06 |
| ank Wyse | R | 2 | 1 | .667 | 1.93 | 0 | 4 | 4 | 1 | 28 | 33 | 6 | 8 | 10 | 6 | 1 | 10.61 | 1.93 | 2.57 |
| ick Errickson | R | 1 | 1 | .500 | 4.13 | 0 | 13 | 0 | 0 | 24 | 39 | 8 | 9 | 12 | 11 | 0 | 14.63 | 3.00 | 3.38 |
| d Hanyzewski | R | 1 | 1 | .500 | 3.79 | 0 | 6 | 1 | 0 | 19 | 17 | 8 | 6 | 9 | 8 | 0 | 8.05 | 3.79 | 2.84 |
| esse Flores | R | 0 | 1 | .000 | 3.38 | 0 | 4 | 0 | 0 | 5.1 | 5 | 2 | 6 | 5 | 2 | 0 | 8.44 | 3.38 | 10.13 |
| allie Eaves | R | 0 | 0 | – | 9.00 | 0 | 2 | 0 | 0 | 3 | 4 | 2 | 0 | 3 | 3 | 0 | 12.00 | 6.00 | 0.00 |
| oe Berry | R | 0 | 0 | – | 18.00 | 0 | 2 | 0 | 0 | 2 | 7 | 2 | 1 | 4 | 4 | 0 | 31.50 | 9.00 | 4.50 |
| mil Kush | R | 0 | 0 | – | 0.00 | 0 | 1 | 0 | 0 | 2 | 1 | 1 | 1 | 0 | 0 | 0 | 4.50 | 4.50 | 4.50 |
| ob Bowman | R | 0 | 0 | – | 0.00 | 0 | 1 | 0 | 0 | 1 | 1 | 0 | 0 | 0 | 0 | 0 | 9.00 | 0.00 | 0.00 |
| EAM TOTAL | | 68 | 86 | .442 | 3.60 | 14 | 305 | 155 | 71 | 1400.2 | 1447 | 525 | 507 | 667 | 560 | 9 | 9.30 | 3.37 | 3.26 |

| MANAGER | W | L | PCT |
|---|---|---|---|
| Jimmie Wilson | 74 | 79 | .484 |

| POS | Player | B | G | AB | H | 2B | 3B | HR | HR % | R | RBI | BB | SO | SB | Pinch Hit AB | Pinch Hit H | BA | SA |
|---|---|---|---|---|---|---|---|---|---|---|---|---|---|---|---|---|---|---|
| **REGULARS** | | | | | | | | | | | | | | | | | | |
| 1B | Phil Cavarretta | L | 143 | 530 | 154 | 27 | 9 | 8 | 1.5 | 93 | 73 | 75 | 42 | 3 | 2 | 0 | .291 | .421 |
| 2B | Eddie Stanky | R | 142 | 510 | 125 | 15 | 1 | 0 | 0.0 | 92 | 47 | 92 | 42 | 4 | 0 | 0 | .245 | .278 |
| SS | Lennie Merullo | R | 129 | 453 | 115 | 18 | 3 | 1 | 0.2 | 37 | 25 | 26 | 42 | 7 | 0 | 0 | .254 | .313 |
| 3B | Stan Hack | L | 144 | 533 | 154 | 24 | 4 | 3 | 0.6 | 78 | 35 | 82 | 27 | 5 | 7 | 0 | .289 | .366 |
| RF | Bill Nicholson | L | 154 | 608 | 188 | 30 | 9 | **29** | **4.8** | 95 | **128** | 71 | 78 | 4 | 0 | 0 | .309 | .531 |
| CF | Peanuts Lowrey | R | 130 | 480 | 140 | 25 | 12 | 1 | 0.2 | 59 | 63 | 35 | 24 | 13 | 4 | 1 | .292 | .400 |
| LF | Ival Goodman | L | 80 | 225 | 72 | 10 | 5 | 3 | 1.3 | 31 | 45 | 24 | 20 | 4 | 17 | 5 | .320 | .449 |
| C | Clyde McCullough | R | 87 | 266 | 63 | 5 | 2 | 2 | 0.8 | 20 | 23 | 24 | 33 | 6 | 4 | 0 | .237 | .293 |
| **SUBSTITUTES** | | | | | | | | | | | | | | | | | | |
| 23 | Stu Martin | L | 64 | 118 | 26 | 4 | 0 | 0 | 0.0 | 13 | 5 | 15 | 10 | 1 | 25 | 5 | .220 | .254 |
| 1B | Heinz Becker | B | 24 | 69 | 10 | 0 | 0 | 0 | 0.0 | 5 | 2 | 9 | 6 | 0 | 3 | 0 | .145 | .145 |
| SS | Bill Schuster | R | 13 | 51 | 15 | 2 | 1 | 0 | 0.0 | 3 | 0 | 3 | 2 | 0 | 0 | 0 | .294 | .373 |
| 2B | Don Johnson | R | 10 | 42 | 8 | 2 | 0 | 0 | 0.0 | 5 | 1 | 2 | 4 | 0 | 0 | 0 | .190 | .238 |
| 3B | Pete Elko | R | 9 | 30 | 4 | 0 | 0 | 0 | 0.0 | 1 | 0 | 4 | 5 | 0 | 0 | 0 | .133 | .133 |
| OF | Lou Novikoff | R | 78 | 233 | 65 | 7 | 3 | 0 | 0.0 | 22 | 28 | 18 | 15 | 0 | 15 | 6 | .279 | .335 |
| OF | Dom Dallessandro | L | 87 | 176 | 39 | 8 | 3 | 1 | 0.6 | 13 | 31 | 40 | 14 | 1 | 32 | 8 | .222 | .318 |
| OF | Andy Pafko | R | 13 | 58 | 22 | 3 | 0 | 0 | 0.0 | 7 | 10 | 2 | 5 | 1 | 0 | 0 | .379 | .431 |
| OF | Ed Sauer | R | 14 | 55 | 15 | 3 | 0 | 0 | 0.0 | 3 | 9 | 3 | 6 | 1 | 0 | 0 | .273 | .327 |
| OF | Whitey Platt | R | 20 | 41 | 7 | 3 | 0 | 0 | 0.0 | 2 | 2 | 1 | 7 | 0 | 4 | 1 | .171 | .244 |
| O3 | John Ostrowski | R | 10 | 29 | 6 | 0 | 1 | 0 | 0.0 | 2 | 3 | 3 | 8 | 0 | 0 | 0 | .207 | .276 |
| OF | Charlie Gilbert | L | 8 | 20 | 3 | 0 | 0 | 0 | 0.0 | 1 | 0 | 3 | 3 | 1 | 2 | 0 | .150 | .150 |
| C | Chico Hernandez | R | 43 | 126 | 34 | 4 | 0 | 0 | 0.0 | 10 | 9 | 9 | 9 | 0 | 2 | 0 | .270 | .302 |
| C | Mickey Livingston | R | 36 | 111 | 29 | 5 | 1 | 4 | 3.6 | 11 | 16 | 12 | 8 | 1 | 2 | 0 | .261 | .432 |
| C | Al Todd | R | 21 | 45 | 6 | 0 | 0 | 0 | 0.0 | 1 | 1 | 1 | 5 | 0 | 4 | 1 | .133 | .133 |
| C | Billy Holm | R | 7 | 15 | 1 | 0 | 0 | 0 | 0.0 | 0 | 0 | 2 | 4 | 0 | 0 | 0 | .067 | .067 |
| C | Mickey Krietner | R | 3 | 8 | 3 | 0 | 0 | 0 | 0.0 | 0 | 2 | 1 | 2 | 0 | 0 | 0 | .375 | .375 |
| **PITCHERS** | | | | | | | | | | | | | | | | | | |
| P | Claude Passeau | R | 35 | 96 | 19 | 4 | 2 | 0 | 0.0 | 5 | 5 | 0 | 30 | 0 | 0 | 0 | .198 | .281 |
| P | Hi Bithorn | R | 39 | 92 | 16 | 3 | 0 | 0 | 0.0 | 7 | 8 | 4 | 10 | 0 | 0 | 0 | .174 | .207 |
| P | Paul Derringer | R | 32 | 58 | 13 | 3 | 0 | 0 | 0.0 | 4 | 2 | 0 | 6 | 0 | 0 | 0 | .224 | .276 |
| P | Hank Wyse | R | 40 | 50 | 4 | 1 | 0 | 0 | 0.0 | 3 | 1 | 2 | 16 | 0 | 0 | 0 | .080 | .100 |
| P | Ed Hanyzewski | R | 33 | 41 | 2 | 0 | 0 | 0 | 0.0 | 0 | 0 | 0 | 15 | 0 | 0 | 0 | .049 | .049 |
| P | Bill Lee | R | 13 | 26 | 7 | 0 | 0 | 0 | 0.0 | 3 | 1 | 2 | 4 | 0 | 0 | 0 | .269 | .269 |
| P | Lon Warneke | R | 21 | 26 | 5 | 1 | 0 | 0 | 0.0 | 2 | 0 | 5 | 6 | 1 | 0 | 0 | .192 | .231 |
| P | Paul Erickson | R | 15 | 15 | 3 | 0 | 0 | 0 | 0.0 | 0 | 3 | 1 | 6 | 0 | 0 | 0 | .200 | .200 |
| P | Ray Prim | R | 29 | 12 | 2 | 0 | 0 | 0 | 0.0 | 2 | 1 | 1 | 2 | 0 | 0 | 0 | .167 | .167 |
| P | Dick Barrett | R | 15 | 9 | 1 | 0 | 0 | 0 | 0.0 | 1 | 0 | 0 | 2 | 0 | 0 | 0 | .111 | .111 |
| P | Bill Fleming | R | 11 | 8 | 0 | 0 | 0 | 0 | 0.0 | 0 | 0 | 0 | 2 | 0 | 0 | 0 | .000 | .000 |
| P | Walter Signer | R | 4 | 8 | 2 | 0 | 0 | 0 | 0.0 | 0 | 0 | 1 | 2 | 0 | 0 | 0 | .250 | .250 |
| P | Dale Alderson | R | 4 | 3 | 0 | 0 | 0 | 0 | 0.0 | 0 | 0 | 0 | 1 | 0 | 0 | 0 | .000 | .000 |
| P | John Burrows | R | 23 | 3 | 2 | 0 | 0 | 0 | 0.0 | 0 | 0 | 1 | 0 | 0 | 0 | 0 | .667 | .667 |
| P | Jake Mooty | R | 2 | 0 | 0 | 0 | 0 | 0 | – | 0 | 0 | 0 | 0 | 0 | 0 | 0 | | |
| | TEAM TOTAL | | | 5279 | 1380 | 207 | 56 | 52 | 1.0 | 63 | 579 | 574 | 523 | 53 | 123 | 27 | .261 | .351 |

## INDIVIDUAL FIELDING

| POS | Player | T | G | PO | A | E | DP | TC/G | FA |
|---|---|---|---|---|---|---|---|---|---|
| 1B | Cavarretta | L | 134 | 1290 | 67 | **18** | 103 | 10.3 | .987 |
| | H. Becker | R | 18 | 161 | 15 | 3 | 9 | 9.9 | .983 |
| | Livingston | R | 4 | 36 | 4 | 0 | 6 | 10.0 | 1.000 |
| | S. Martin | R | 2 | 23 | 1 | 0 | 1 | 12.0 | 1.000 |
| 2B | E. Stanky | R | 131 | 362 | 416 | 27 | 78 | 6.1 | .966 |
| | S. Martin | R | 22 | 37 | 63 | 2 | 10 | 4.6 | .980 |
| | L. Merullo | R | 1 | 0 | 0 | 0 | 0 | 0.0 | .000 |
| | D. Johnson | R | 10 | 32 | 35 | 3 | 8 | 7.0 | .957 |
| | P. Lowrey | R | 3 | 6 | 10 | 1 | 3 | 5.7 | .941 |
| SS | L. Merullo | R | 125 | 218 | 396 | 39 | 68 | 5.2 | .940 |
| | P. Lowrey | R | 16 | 20 | 39 | 3 | 4 | 3.9 | .952 |
| | B. Schuster | R | 13 | 34 | 52 | 2 | 14 | 6.8 | .977 |
| | E. Stanky | R | 12 | 16 | 20 | 2 | 7 | 3.2 | .947 |
| 3B | S. Hack | R | 136 | 149 | 264 | 17 | 11 | 3.2 | .960 |
| | P. Elko | R | 9 | 8 | 15 | 4 | 1 | 3.0 | .852 |
| | J. Ostrowski | R | 4 | 3 | 5 | 2 | 1 | 2.5 | .800 |
| | S. Martin | R | 8 | 4 | 5 | 0 | 1 | 1.1 | 1.000 |
| | E. Stanky | R | 2 | 1 | 5 | 2 | 0 | 4.0 | .750 |
| | E. Sauer | R | 1 | 3 | 0 | 1 | 0 | 4.0 | .750 |
| | L. Merullo | R | 2 | 4 | 0 | 0 | 0 | 2.0 | 1.000 |

| POS | Player | T | G | PO | A | E | DP | TC/G | FA |
|---|---|---|---|---|---|---|---|---|---|
| OF | B. Nicholson | R | 154 | 340 | 16 | 8 | 2 | 2.4 | .978 |
| | P. Lowrey | R | 113 | 315 | 13 | 6 | 4 | 3.0 | .982 |
| | I. Goodman | R | 61 | 120 | 2 | 4 | 1 | 2.1 | .968 |
| | L. Novikoff | R | 61 | 96 | 2 | 2 | 1 | 1.6 | .980 |
| | Dallessandro | L | 45 | 87 | 2 | 3 | 0 | 2.0 | .967 |
| | E. Sauer | R | 13 | 37 | 1 | 0 | 0 | 2.9 | 1.000 |
| | A. Pafko | R | 13 | 25 | 0 | 0 | 0 | 1.9 | 1.000 |
| | W. Platt | R | 14 | 20 | 0 | 1 | 0 | 1.5 | .952 |
| | Cavarretta | L | 7 | 15 | 0 | 0 | 0 | 2.1 | 1.000 |
| | C. Gilbert | R | 6 | 9 | 1 | 0 | 0 | 1.7 | 1.000 |
| | J. Ostrowski | R | 5 | 8 | 0 | 0 | 0 | 1.6 | 1.000 |
| C | McCullough | R | 81 | 271 | 25 | 7 | 2 | 3.7 | .977 |
| | C. Hernandez | R | 41 | 132 | 21 | 3 | 1 | 3.8 | .981 |
| | Livingston | R | 31 | 114 | 13 | 0 | 0 | 4.1 | 1.000* |
| | A. Todd | R | 17 | 62 | 7 | 1 | 2 | 4.1 | .986 |
| | B. Holm | R | 7 | 21 | 4 | 0 | 0 | 3.6 | 1.000 |
| | M. Krietner | R | 3 | 8 | 1 | 0 | 0 | 3.0 | 1.000 |

Baseball was decimated by the draft, leaving a thin layer of playing talent. The Cubs, like the others, carried on. Because of wartime travel restrictions, the Cubs had to abandon the warm climes of Catalina Island for wintry French Lick, Indiana. That could've been one of the reasons for their cold start. Other factors were Lou Novikoff's salary holdout, Bill Nicholson's frozen bat, and a nine-game losing streak in May. Novikoff returned but was of little use. Nicholson finally hit his first homer on May 30 and went on to lead the league with 29. He also led with 128 RBI and batted .309 to help the Cubs climb to fifth place and a 74–79 record. Another factor in the Cubs rise was pitcher Hi Bithorn, who had 7 shutouts and 19 complete games among his 18 victories. Claude Passeau contributed 15 wins. The Cubs unveiled some rookies with big-league futures. They were second baseman Eddie Stanky, who batted only .245 but drew 92 walks, and outfielder Peanuts Lowrey, who hit .292 and led the Cubs with 12 triples. Near the conclusion of the season, they brought up strong-armed centerfielder Andy Pafko, who batted .379 in 13 games. Catcher Clyde McCullough marched off to war in midseason, while Lowrey and Bithorn were gone at the end of it.

## TEAM STATISTICS

| | W | L | PCT | GB | R | OR | Batting | | | | | | | Fielding | | | CG | B | Pitching | | | |
|---|---|---|---|---|---|---|---|---|---|---|---|---|---|---|---|---|---|---|---|---|---|---|
| | | | | | | | 2B | 3B | HR | BA | SA | SB | | E | DP | FA | | | SO | ShO | SV | ERA |
| 'L | 105 | 49 | .682 | | 679 | 475 | 259 | 72 | 70 | .279 | .391 | 40 | | 151 | 183 | .976 | 94 | 477 | 639 | 21 | 15 | 2.57 |
| N | 87 | 67 | .565 | 18 | 608 | 543 | 229 | 47 | 43 | .256 | .340 | 49 | | 125 | 193 | .980 | 78 | 581 | 498 | 18 | 17 | 3.13 |
| KN | 81 | 72 | .529 | 23.5 | 716 | 674 | 263 | 35 | 39 | .272 | .357 | 58 | | 168 | 137 | .972 | 50 | 585 | 588 | 12 | 22 | 3.88 |
| T | 80 | 74 | .519 | 25 | 669 | 605 | 240 | 73 | 42 | .262 | .357 | 64 | | 170 | 159 | .973 | 74 | 421 | 396 | 11 | 12 | 3.06 |
| HI | 74 | 79 | .484 | 30.5 | 632 | 600 | 207 | 56 | 52 | .261 | .351 | 53 | | 168 | 138 | .973 | 67 | 394 | 394 | 12 | 14 | 3.24 |
| DS | 68 | 85 | .444 | 36.5 | 465 | 612 | 202 | 36 | 39 | .233 | .309 | 56 | | 176 | 139 | .972 | 87 | 440 | 409 | 13 | 4 | 3.25 |
| HI | 64 | 90 | .416 | 41 | 571 | 676 | 186 | 36 | 66 | .249 | .335 | 29 | | 189 | 143 | .969 | 66 | 456 | 431 | 11 | 14 | 3.79 |
| V | 55 | 98 | .359 | 49.5 | 558 | 713 | 153 | 33 | 81 | .247 | .335 | 35 | | 166 | 140 | .973 | 35 | 626 | 588 | 6 | 19 | 4.08 |
| AGUE TOTAL | | | | | 4898 | 4898 | 1739 | 388 | 432 | .258 | .347 | 384 | | 1313 | 1232 | .974 | 551 | 3980 | 4062 | 104 | 117 | 3.37 |

## INDIVIDUAL PITCHING

| TCHER | T | W | L | PCT | ERA | SV | G | GS | CG | IP | H | BB | SO | R | ER | ShO | H/9 | BB/9 | SO/9 |
|---|---|---|---|---|---|---|---|---|---|---|---|---|---|---|---|---|---|---|---|
| aude Passeau | R | 15 | 12 | .556 | 2.91 | 1 | 35 | 31 | 18 | 257 | 245 | 66 | 93 | 96 | 83 | 2 | 8.58 | 2.31 | 3.26 |
| Bithorn | R | 18 | 12 | .600 | 2.60 | 2 | 39 | 30 | 19 | 249.2 | 226 | 65 | 86 | 79 | 72 | 7 | 8.15 | 2.34 | 3.10 |
| aul Derringer | R | 10 | 14 | .417 | 3.57 | 3 | 32 | 22 | 10 | 174 | 184 | 39 | 75 | 90 | 69 | 2 | 9.52 | 2.02 | 3.88 |
| ank Wyse | R | 9 | 7 | .563 | 2.94 | 5 | 38 | 15 | 8 | 156 | 160 | 34 | 45 | 57 | 51 | 2 | 9.23 | 1.96 | 2.60 |
| d Hanyzewski | R | 8 | 7 | .533 | 2.56 | 0 | 33 | 16 | 3 | 130 | 120 | 45 | 55 | 54 | 37 | 0 | 8.31 | 3.12 | 3.81 |
| n Warneke | R | 4 | 5 | .444 | 3.16 | 0 | 21 | 10 | 4 | 88.1 | 82 | 18 | 30 | 40 | 31 | 0 | 8.35 | 1.83 | 3.06 |
| ll Lee | R | 3 | 7 | .300 | 3.56 | 0 | 13 | 12 | 4 | 78.1 | 83 | 27 | 18 | 37 | 31 | 0 | 9.54 | 3.10 | 2.07 |
| ay Prim | L | 4 | 3 | .571 | 2.55 | 1 | 29 | 5 | 0 | 60 | 67 | 14 | 27 | 24 | 17 | 0 | 10.05 | 2.10 | 4.05 |
| ck Barrett | R | 0 | 4 | .000 | 4.80 | 0 | 15 | 4 | 0 | 45 | 52 | 28 | 20 | 28 | 24 | 0 | 10.40 | 5.60 | 4.00 |
| aul Erickson | R | 1 | 3 | .250 | 6.12 | 0 | 15 | 4 | 0 | 42.2 | 47 | 22 | 24 | 32 | 29 | 0 | 9.91 | 4.64 | 5.06 |
| hn Burrows | L | 0 | 2 | .000 | 3.86 | 2 | 23 | 1 | 0 | 32.2 | 25 | 16 | 18 | 17 | 14 | 0 | 6.89 | 4.41 | 4.96 |
| ll Fleming | R | 0 | 1 | .000 | 6.40 | 0 | 11 | 0 | 0 | 32.1 | 40 | 12 | 12 | 24 | 23 | 0 | 11.13 | 3.34 | 3.34 |
| alter Signer | R | 2 | 1 | .667 | 2.88 | 0 | 4 | 2 | 1 | 25 | 24 | 4 | 5 | 8 | 8 | 0 | 8.64 | 1.44 | 1.80 |
| ale Alderson | R | 0 | 1 | .000 | 6.43 | 0 | 4 | 2 | 0 | 14 | 21 | 3 | 4 | 12 | 10 | 0 | 13.50 | 1.93 | 2.57 |
| ke Mooty | R | 0 | 0 | — | 0.00 | 0 | 2 | 0 | 0 | 1 | 2 | 1 | 1 | 0 | 0 | 0 | 18.00 | 9.00 | 9.00 |
| AM TOTAL | | 74 | 79 | .484 | 3.24 | 14 | 314 | 154 | 67 | 1386 | 1378 | 394 | 513 | 598 | 499 | 13 | 8.95 | 2.56 | 3.33 |

| MANAGER | W | L | PCT |
|---|---|---|---|
| Jimmie Wilson | 1 | 9 | .100 |
| Roy Johnson | 0 | 1 | .000 |
| Charlie Grimm | 74 | 69 | .517 |

| POS | Player | B | G | AB | H | 2B | 3B | HR | HR % | R | RBI | BB | SO | SB | Pinch Hit AB | Pinch Hit H | BA | SA |
|---|---|---|---|---|---|---|---|---|---|---|---|---|---|---|---|---|---|---|
| **REGULARS** | | | | | | | | | | | | | | | | | | |
| 1B | Phil Cavarretta | L | 152 | 614 | **197** | 35 | 15 | 5 | 0.8 | 106 | 82 | 67 | 42 | 4 | 0 | 0 | .321 | .451 |
| 2B | Don Johnson | R | 154 | 608 | 169 | 37 | 1 | 2 | 0.3 | 50 | 71 | 28 | 48 | 8 | 0 | 0 | .278 | .352 |
| SS | Lennie Merullo | R | 66 | 193 | 41 | 8 | 1 | 1 | 0.5 | 20 | 16 | 16 | 18 | 3 | 6 | 1 | .212 | .280 |
| 3B | Stan Hack | L | 98 | 383 | 108 | 16 | 1 | 3 | 0.8 | 65 | 32 | 53 | 21 | 5 | 4 | 1 | .282 | .352 |
| RF | Bill Nicholson | L | 156 | 582 | 167 | 35 | 8 | **33** | 5.7 | **116** | **122** | 93 | 71 | 3 | 0 | 0 | .287 | .545 |
| CF | Andy Pafko | R | 128 | 469 | 126 | 16 | 2 | 6 | 1.3 | 47 | 62 | 28 | 23 | 2 | 5 | 1 | .269 | .350 |
| LF | Dom Dallessandro | L | 117 | 381 | 116 | 19 | 4 | 8 | 2.1 | 53 | 74 | 61 | 29 | 1 | 11 | 3 | .304 | .438 |
| C | Dewey Williams | R | 79 | 262 | 63 | 7 | 2 | 0 | 0.0 | 23 | 27 | 23 | 18 | 2 | 1 | 0 | .240 | .282 |
| **SUBSTITUTES** | | | | | | | | | | | | | | | | | | |
| 3S | Roy Hughes | R | 126 | 478 | 137 | 16 | 6 | 1 | 0.2 | 86 | 28 | 35 | 30 | 16 | 7 | 4 | .287 | .351 |
| 2S | Bill Schuster | R | 60 | 154 | 34 | 7 | 1 | 1 | 0.6 | 14 | 14 | 12 | 16 | 4 | 11 | 3 | .221 | .299 |
| S3 | Tony York | R | 28 | 85 | 20 | 1 | 0 | 0 | 0.0 | 4 | 7 | 4 | 11 | 0 | 0 | 0 | .235 | .247 |
| SS | Charlie Brewster | R | 10 | 44 | 11 | 2 | 0 | 0 | 0.0 | 4 | 2 | 5 | 7 | 0 | 0 | 0 | .250 | .295 |
| UT | Eddie Stanky | R | 13 | 25 | 6 | 0 | 1 | 0 | 0.0 | 4 | 0 | 2 | 2 | 1 | 4 | 0 | .240 | .320 |
| 3B | Pete Elko | R | 7 | 22 | 5 | 1 | 0 | 0 | 0.0 | 2 | 0 | 0 | 1 | 0 | 1 | 1 | .227 | .273 |
| 3C | Jimmie Foxx | R | 15 | 20 | 1 | 1 | 0 | 0 | 0.0 | 0 | 2 | 2 | 5 | 0 | 11 | 0 | .050 | .100 |
| OF | Ival Goodman | L | 62 | 141 | 37 | 8 | 1 | 1 | 0.7 | 24 | 16 | 23 | 15 | 0 | 23 | 6 | .262 | .355 |
| OF | Lou Novikoff | R | 71 | 139 | 39 | 4 | 2 | 3 | 2.2 | 15 | 19 | 10 | 11 | 1 | 39 | 12 | .281 | .403 |
| OF | Frank Secory | R | 22 | 56 | 18 | 1 | 0 | 4 | 7.1 | 10 | 17 | 6 | 8 | 1 | 4 | 0 | .321 | .554 |
| OF | Ed Sauer | R | 23 | 50 | 11 | 4 | 0 | 0 | 0.0 | 3 | 5 | 2 | 6 | 0 | 9 | 2 | .220 | .300 |
| OF | John Ostrowski | R | 8 | 13 | 2 | 1 | 0 | 0 | 0.0 | 2 | 2 | 1 | 4 | 0 | 5 | 2 | .154 | .231 |
| C | Billy Holm | R | 54 | 132 | 18 | 2 | 0 | 0 | 0.0 | 10 | 6 | 16 | 19 | 1 | 3 | 0 | .136 | .152 |
| C | Mickey Krietner | R | 39 | 85 | 13 | 2 | 0 | 0 | 0.0 | 3 | 1 | 8 | 16 | 0 | 0 | 0 | .153 | .176 |
| C | Roy Easterwood | R | 17 | 33 | 7 | 2 | 0 | 1 | 3.0 | 1 | 2 | 1 | 11 | 0 | 5 | 1 | .212 | .364 |
| C | Paul Gillespie | L | 9 | 26 | 7 | 1 | 0 | 1 | 3.8 | 2 | 2 | 3 | 3 | 0 | 2 | 0 | .269 | .423 |
| C | Joe Stephenson | R | 4 | 8 | 1 | 0 | 0 | 0 | 0.0 | 0 | 1 | 1 | 3 | 1 | 1 | 0 | .125 | .125 |
| PH | Ben Mann | R | 1 | 0 | 0 | 0 | 0 | 0 | – | 1 | 0 | 0 | 0 | 0 | 0 | 0 | – | – |
| **PITCHERS** | | | | | | | | | | | | | | | | | | |
| P | Hank Wyse | R | 41 | 90 | 16 | 3 | 0 | 0 | 0.0 | 11 | 8 | 2 | 12 | 0 | 0 | 0 | .178 | .211 |
| P | Claude Passeau | R | 34 | 80 | 13 | 3 | 0 | 0 | 0.0 | 6 | 3 | 4 | 17 | 0 | 0 | 0 | .163 | .200 |
| P | Paul Derringer | R | 42 | 57 | 9 | 1 | 0 | 0 | 0.0 | 2 | 4 | 1 | 9 | 0 | 0 | 0 | .158 | .175 |
| P | Bill Fleming | R | 40 | 53 | 9 | 2 | 0 | 0 | 0.0 | 4 | 6 | 1 | 4 | 0 | 0 | 0 | .170 | .208 |
| P | Bob Chipman | L | 26 | 48 | 5 | 0 | 0 | 0 | 0.0 | 1 | 0 | 3 | 11 | 0 | 0 | 0 | .104 | .104 |
| P | Hy Vandenberg | R | 35 | 38 | 9 | 0 | 0 | 0 | 0.0 | 3 | 5 | 1 | 2 | 0 | 0 | 0 | .237 | .237 |
| P | Paul Erickson | R | 33 | 36 | 2 | 0 | 1 | 1 | 2.8 | 2 | 1 | 3 | 15 | 0 | 0 | 0 | .056 | .194 |
| P | Red Lynn | R | 22 | 29 | 6 | 1 | 0 | 0 | 0.0 | 4 | 2 | 1 | 4 | 0 | 0 | 0 | .207 | .241 |
| P | Ed Hanyzewski | R | 14 | 17 | 1 | 0 | 0 | 0 | 0.0 | 2 | 1 | 3 | 5 | 0 | 0 | 0 | .059 | .059 |
| P | Dale Alderson | R | 12 | 4 | 0 | 0 | 0 | 0 | 0.0 | 0 | 0 | 0 | 1 | 0 | 0 | 0 | .000 | .000 |
| P | Charlie Gassaway | L | 2 | 4 | 1 | 0 | 0 | 0 | 0.0 | 0 | 0 | 1 | 1 | 0 | 0 | 0 | .250 | .250 |
| P | John Miklos | L | 2 | 2 | 0 | 0 | 0 | 0 | 0.0 | 0 | 0 | 0 | 1 | 0 | 0 | 0 | .000 | .000 |
| P | Mack Stewart | R | 8 | 1 | 0 | 0 | 0 | 0 | 0.0 | 0 | 0 | 0 | 1 | 0 | 0 | 0 | .000 | .000 |
| P | John Burrows | R | 3 | 0 | 0 | 0 | 0 | 0 | – | 0 | 0 | 0 | 0 | 0 | 0 | 0 | – | – |
| | TEAM TOTAL | | | 5462 | 1425 | 236 | 46 | 71 | 1.3 | 70 | 639 | 520 | 521 | 53 | 152 | 37 | .261 | .360 |

## INDIVIDUAL FIELDING

| POS | Player | T | G | PO | A | E | DP | TC/G | FA |
|---|---|---|---|---|---|---|---|---|---|
| 1B | Cavarretta | L | 139 | 1337 | 77 | 11 | 121 | 10.3 | .992 |
| | S. Hack | R | 18 | 130 | 10 | 2 | 16 | 7.9 | .986 |
| | L. Merullo | R | 1 | 1 | 0 | 0 | 0 | 1.0 | 1.000 |
| 2B | D. Johnson | R | 154 | **385** | 462 | 47 | 85 | 5.8 | .947 |
| | B. Schuster | R | 66 | 14 | 9 | 0 | 3 | 0.3 | 1.000 |
| | E. Stanky | R | 3 | 4 | 3 | 1 | 3 | 2.7 | .875 |
| SS | L. Merullo | R | 56 | 115 | 167 | 19 | 26 | 5.4 | .937 |
| | R. Hughes | R | 52 | 133 | 157 | 8 | 36 | 5.7 | .973 |
| | B. Schuster | R | 38 | 57 | 100 | 9 | 18 | 4.4 | .946 |
| | T. York | R | 15 | 26 | 52 | 5 | 5 | 5.5 | .940 |
| | C. Brewster | R | 10 | 27 | 29 | 6 | 9 | 6.2 | .903 |
| | E. Stanky | R | 3 | 1 | 1 | 0 | 0 | 0.7 | 1.000 |
| 3B | S. Hack | R | 75 | 96 | 164 | 17 | 7 | 3.7 | .939 |
| | R. Hughes | R | 66 | 87 | 146 | 12 | 18 | 3.7 | .951 |
| | T. York | R | 12 | 13 | 29 | 0 | 2 | 3.5 | 1.000 |
| | E. Stanky | R | 3 | 3 | 11 | 2 | 1 | 5.3 | .875 |
| | P. Elko | R | 6 | 6 | 8 | 0 | 1 | 2.3 | 1.000 |
| | J. Foxx | R | 2 | 2 | 6 | 0 | 0 | 4.0 | 1.000 |

| POS | Player | T | G | PO | A | E | DP | TC/G | FA |
|---|---|---|---|---|---|---|---|---|---|
| OF | A. Pafko | R | 123 | 333 | **24** | 6 | 4 | 3.0 | .983 |
| | B. Nicholson | R | 156 | 305 | 18 | 7 | 4 | 2.1 | .979 |
| | Dallessandro | L | 106 | 212 | 9 | 4 | 2 | 2.1 | .982 |
| | I. Goodman | R | 35 | 65 | 0 | 0 | 0 | 1.9 | 1.000 |
| | F. Secory | R | 17 | 44 | 0 | 0 | 0 | 2.6 | 1.000 |
| | L. Novikoff | R | 29 | 39 | 1 | 1 | 0 | 1.4 | .976 |
| | Cavarretta | L | 13 | 26 | 1 | 2 | 0 | 2.2 | .931 |
| | E. Sauer | R | 12 | 23 | 1 | 1 | 0 | 2.1 | .960 |
| | J. Ostrowski | R | 2 | 1 | 0 | 1 | 0 | 1.0 | .500 |
| C | D. Williams | R | 77 | 317 | 50 | 7 | 7 | 4.9 | .981 |
| | B. Holm | R | 50 | 166 | 18 | 4 | 2 | 3.8 | .979 |
| | M. Krietner | R | 39 | 104 | 13 | 1 | 3 | 3.0 | .992 |
| | Easterwood | R | 12 | 29 | 4 | 0 | 1 | 2.8 | 1.000 |
| | P. Gillespie | R | 7 | 22 | 6 | 3 | 0 | 4.4 | .903 |
| | Stephenson | R | 3 | 13 | 2 | 0 | 0 | 5.0 | 1.000 |
| | J. Foxx | R | 1 | 7 | 0 | 0 | 0 | 7.0 | 1.000 |

After winning their opener the Cubs experienced the worst losing streak in team history, dropping 13 straight. Jimmie Wilson resigned as manager after the streak hit nine. Coach Roy Johnson took charge for one game before Charlie Grimm was summoned for his second stint at the helm. The losing streak ended on May 11 when Grimm gave pitcher Eddie Hanyzewski a four-leaf clover. Hanyzewski placed it under his cap and beat Philadelphia, 5–3. Grimm then coaxed third baseman Stan Hack out of retirement, and the club showed steady improvement, eventually escaping the cellar on July 6. In the All-Star Game, Phil Cavarretta set a record by reaching base five straight times on a triple, single, and three walks. Bill Nicholson tied a record by hitting four consecutive homers on July 22–23. He hit 33 homers and drove in 122 runs, thus becoming the first NL player to lead in those departments in successive seasons. An 11-game winning streak in late July and early August helped propel the Cubs into fourth place, where they finished with a 75–79 mark. Cavarretta batted .321, and Dom Dallessandro was next at .304. Hank Wyse led the pitchers with 16 victories, and Claude Passeau had 15. Shortstop Marty Marion of the pennant-winning Cardinals nosed out Nicholson by one vote (190–189) for the MVP Award.

## TEAM STATISTICS

| | W | L | PCT | GB | R | OR | 2B | 3B | Batting HR | BA | SA | SB | E | Fielding DP | FA | CG | B | Pitching SO | ShO | SV | ERA |
|---|---|---|---|---|---|---|---|---|---|---|---|---|---|---|---|---|---|---|---|---|---|
| TL | 105 | 49 | .682 | | 772 | 490 | 274 | 59 | 100 | .275 | .402 | 37 | 112 | 162 | .982 | 89 | 468 | 637 | 26 | 12 | 2.67 |
| IT | 90 | 63 | .588 | 14.5 | 744 | 662 | 248 | 80 | 70 | .265 | .379 | 87 | 191 | 122 | .970 | 77 | 435 | 452 | 10 | 19 | 3.44 |
| IN | 89 | 65 | .578 | 16 | 573 | 537 | 229 | 31 | 51 | .254 | .338 | 51 | 137 | 153 | .978 | 93 | 384 | 359 | 17 | 12 | 2.97 |
| HI | 75 | 79 | .487 | 30 | 702 | 669 | 236 | 46 | 71 | .261 | .360 | 53 | 186 | 151 | .970 | 70 | 452 | 535 | 11 | 13 | 3.59 |
| IY | 67 | 87 | .435 | 38 | 682 | 773 | 191 | 47 | 93 | .263 | .370 | 38 | 179 | 128 | .971 | 47 | 587 | 499 | 4 | 21 | 4.29 |
| OS | 65 | 89 | .422 | 40 | 593 | 674 | 250 | 39 | 79 | .246 | .353 | 37 | 182 | 160 | .971 | 70 | 527 | 454 | 13 | 12 | 3.67 |
| KN | 63 | 91 | .409 | 42 | 690 | 832 | 255 | 51 | 56 | .269 | .366 | 43 | 197 | 112 | .966 | 50 | 660 | 487 | 4 | 13 | 4.68 |
| HI | 61 | 92 | .399 | 43.5 | 539 | 658 | 199 | 42 | 55 | .251 | .336 | 32 | 177 | 138 | .972 | 66 | 459 | 496 | 11 | 6 | 3.64 |
| EAGUE TOTAL | | | | | 5295 | 5295 | 1882 | 395 | 575 | .261 | .363 | 378 | 1361 | 1126 | .972 | 562 | 3972 | 3919 | 96 | 108 | 3.61 |

## INDIVIDUAL PITCHING

| ITCHER | T | W | L | PCT | ERA | SV | G | GS | CG | IP | H | BB | SO | R | ER | ShO | H/9 | BB/9 | SO/9 |
|---|---|---|---|---|---|---|---|---|---|---|---|---|---|---|---|---|---|---|---|
| lank Wyse | R | 16 | 15 | .516 | 3.15 | 1 | 41 | 34 | 14 | 257.1 | 277 | 57 | 86 | 113 | 90 | 3 | 9.69 | 1.99 | 3.01 |
| laude Passeau | R | 15 | 9 | .625 | 2.89 | 3 | 34 | 27 | 18 | 227 | 234 | 50 | 89 | 80 | 73 | 2 | 9.28 | 1.98 | 3.53 |
| aul Derringer | R | 7 | 13 | .350 | 4.15 | 2 | 42 | 16 | 7 | 180 | 205 | 39 | 69 | 96 | 83 | 0 | 10.25 | 1.95 | 3.45 |
| ill Fleming | R | 9 | 10 | .474 | 3.13 | 0 | 39 | 18 | 9 | 158.1 | 163 | 62 | 42 | 74 | 55 | 1 | 9.27 | 3.52 | 2.39 |
| ob Chipman | L | 9 | 9 | .500 | 3.49 | 2 | 26 | 21 | 8 | 129 | 147 | 40 | 41 | 62 | 50 | 1 | 10.26 | 2.79 | 2.86 |
| ly Vandenberg | R | 7 | 4 | .636 | 3.63 | 2 | 35 | 9 | 2 | 126.1 | 123 | 51 | 54 | 67 | 51 | 0 | 8.76 | 3.63 | 3.85 |
| aul Erickson | R | 5 | 9 | .357 | 3.55 | 1 | 33 | 15 | 5 | 124.1 | 113 | 67 | 82 | 59 | 49 | 3 | 8.18 | 4.85 | 5.94 |
| ed Lynn | R | 5 | 4 | .556 | 4.06 | 1 | 22 | 7 | 4 | 84.1 | 80 | 37 | 35 | 41 | 38 | 1 | 8.54 | 3.95 | 3.74 |
| d Hanyzewski | R | 2 | 5 | .286 | 4.47 | 0 | 14 | 7 | 3 | 58.1 | 61 | 20 | 19 | 33 | 29 | 0 | 9.41 | 3.09 | 2.93 |
| ale Alderson | R | 0 | 0 | – | 6.65 | 0 | 12 | 1 | 0 | 21.2 | 31 | 9 | 7 | 18 | 16 | 0 | 12.88 | 3.74 | 2.91 |
| lack Stewart | R | 0 | 0 | – | 1.46 | 0 | 8 | 0 | 0 | 12.1 | 11 | 4 | 3 | 2 | 2 | 0 | 8.03 | 2.92 | 2.19 |
| harlie Gassaway | L | 0 | 1 | .000 | 7.71 | 0 | 2 | 2 | 0 | 11.2 | 20 | 10 | 7 | 11 | 10 | 0 | 15.43 | 7.71 | 5.40 |
| ohn Miklos | L | 0 | 0 | – | 7.71 | 0 | 2 | 0 | 0 | 7 | 9 | 3 | 0 | 6 | 6 | 0 | 11.57 | 3.86 | 0.00 |
| ohn Burrows | L | 0 | 0 | – | 18.00 | 0 | 3 | 0 | 0 | 3 | 7 | 3 | 1 | 7 | 6 | 0 | 21.00 | 9.00 | 3.00 |
| EAM TOTAL | | 75 | 79 | .487 | 3.59 | 13 | 313 | 157 | 70 | 1400.2 | 1481 | 452 | 535 | 669 | 558 | 11 | 9.52 | 2.90 | 3.44 |

| MANAGER | W | L | PCT |
|---|---|---|---|
| Charlie Grimm | 98 | 56 | .636 |

| POS | Player | B | G | AB | H | 2B | 3B | HR | HR % | R | RBI | BB | SO | SB | Pinch Hit AB | Pinch Hit H | BA | SA |
|---|---|---|---|---|---|---|---|---|---|---|---|---|---|---|---|---|---|---|
| **REGULARS** | | | | | | | | | | | | | | | | | | |
| 1B | Phil Cavarretta | L | 132 | 498 | 177 | 34 | 10 | 6 | 1.2 | 94 | 97 | 81 | 34 | 5 | 0 | 0 | **.355** | .500 |
| 2B | Don Johnson | R | 138 | 557 | 168 | 23 | 2 | 2 | 0.4 | 94 | 58 | 32 | 34 | 9 | 0 | 0 | .302 | .361 |
| SS | Lennie Merullo | R | 121 | 394 | 94 | 18 | 0 | 2 | 0.5 | 40 | 37 | 31 | 30 | 7 | 0 | 0 | .239 | .299 |
| 3B | Stan Hack | L | 150 | 597 | 193 | 29 | 7 | 2 | 0.3 | 110 | 43 | 99 | 30 | 12 | 0 | 0 | .323 | .405 |
| RF | Bill Nicholson | L | 151 | 559 | 136 | 28 | 4 | 13 | 2.3 | 82 | 88 | 92 | 73 | 4 | 0 | 0 | .243 | .377 |
| CF | Andy Pafko | R | 144 | 534 | 159 | 24 | 12 | 12 | 2.2 | 64 | 110 | 45 | 36 | 5 | 4 | 1 | .298 | .455 |
| LF | Peanuts Lowrey | R | 143 | 523 | 148 | 22 | 7 | 7 | 1.3 | 72 | 89 | 48 | 27 | 11 | 5 | 1 | .283 | .392 |
| C | Mickey Livingston | R | 71 | 224 | 57 | 4 | 2 | 2 | 0.9 | 19 | 23 | 19 | 6 | 2 | 2 | 0 | .254 | .317 |
| **SUBSTITUTES** | | | | | | | | | | | | | | | | | | |
| UT | Roy Hughes | R | 69 | 222 | 58 | 8 | 1 | 0 | 0.0 | 34 | 8 | 16 | 18 | 6 | 5 | 1 | .261 | .306 |
| 1B | Heinz Becker | B | 67 | 133 | 38 | 8 | 2 | 2 | 1.5 | 25 | 27 | 17 | 16 | 0 | 36 | 5 | .286 | .421 |
| SS | Bill Schuster | R | 45 | 47 | 9 | 2 | 1 | 0 | 0.0 | 8 | 2 | 7 | 4 | 2 | 2 | 0 | .191 | .277 |
| 1B | Reggie Otero | L | 14 | 23 | 9 | 0 | 0 | 0 | 0.0 | 1 | 5 | 2 | 2 | 0 | 6 | 0 | .391 | .391 |
| 3B | John Ostrowski | R | 7 | 10 | 3 | 2 | 0 | 0 | 0.0 | 4 | 1 | 0 | 0 | 0 | 2 | 0 | .300 | .500 |
| 23 | Cy Block | R | 2 | 7 | 1 | 0 | 0 | 0 | 0.0 | 1 | 1 | 0 | 0 | 0 | 0 | 0 | .143 | .143 |
| OF | Ed Sauer | R | 49 | 93 | 24 | 4 | 1 | 2 | 2.2 | 8 | 11 | 8 | 23 | 2 | 15 | 3 | .258 | .387 |
| OF | Frank Secory | R | 35 | 57 | 9 | 1 | 0 | 0 | 0.0 | 4 | 6 | 2 | 7 | 0 | 21 | 2 | .158 | .175 |
| OF | Lloyd Christopher | R | 1 | 0 | 0 | 0 | 0 | 0 | – | 0 | 0 | 0 | 0 | 0 | 0 | 0 | – | – |
| C | Paul Gillespie | L | 75 | 163 | 47 | 6 | 0 | 3 | 1.8 | 12 | 25 | 18 | 9 | 2 | 24 | 7 | .288 | .380 |
| C | Dewey Williams | R | 59 | 100 | 28 | 2 | 2 | 2 | 2.0 | 16 | 5 | 13 | 13 | 0 | 4 | 1 | .280 | .400 |
| C | Len Rice | R | 32 | 99 | 23 | 3 | 0 | 0 | 0.0 | 10 | 7 | 5 | 8 | 2 | 2 | 0 | .232 | .263 |
| PH | Johnny Moore | L | 7 | 6 | 1 | 0 | 0 | 0 | 0.0 | 0 | 2 | 1 | 1 | 0 | 6 | 1 | .167 | .167 |
| **PITCHERS** | | | | | | | | | | | | | | | | | | |
| P | Hank Wyse | R | 38 | 101 | 17 | 2 | 0 | 0 | 0.0 | 6 | 7 | 0 | 16 | 0 | 0 | 0 | .168 | .188 |
| P | Claude Passeau | R | 34 | 91 | 17 | 2 | 0 | 2 | 2.2 | 10 | 9 | 2 | 22 | 0 | 0 | 0 | .187 | .275 |
| P | Paul Derringer | R | 35 | 75 | 15 | 3 | 0 | 0 | 0.0 | 3 | 8 | 0 | 12 | 0 | 0 | 0 | .200 | .240 |
| P | Ray Prim | R | 38 | 51 | 13 | 0 | 0 | 0 | 0.0 | 4 | 1 | 5 | 9 | 0 | 0 | 0 | .255 | .255 |
| P | Hank Borowy | R | 15 | 41 | 7 | 1 | 0 | 0 | 0.0 | 5 | 0 | 4 | 11 | 0 | 0 | 0 | .171 | .195 |
| P | Paul Erickson | R | 28 | 32 | 5 | 2 | 0 | 0 | 0.0 | 2 | 0 | 3 | 8 | 0 | 0 | 0 | .156 | .219 |
| P | Hy Vandenberg | R | 30 | 32 | 4 | 0 | 1 | 0 | 0.0 | 4 | 2 | 1 | 4 | 0 | 0 | 0 | .125 | .188 |
| P | Bob Chipman | L | 25 | 17 | 3 | 1 | 0 | 0 | 0.0 | 1 | 2 | 2 | 4 | 0 | 0 | 0 | .176 | .235 |
| P | Jorge Comellas | R | 7 | 3 | 0 | 0 | 0 | 0 | 0.0 | 0 | 0 | 0 | 2 | 0 | 0 | 0 | .000 | .000 |
| P | Mack Stewart | R | 16 | 3 | 1 | 0 | 0 | 0 | 0.0 | 0 | 0 | 0 | 1 | 0 | 0 | 0 | .333 | .333 |
| P | Ray Starr | R | 9 | 2 | 1 | 0 | 0 | 0 | 0.0 | 1 | 0 | 0 | 0 | 0 | 0 | 0 | .500 | .500 |
| P | Lon Warneke | R | 9 | 2 | 0 | 0 | 0 | 0 | 0.0 | 1 | 0 | 1 | 0 | 0 | 0 | 0 | .000 | .000 |
| P | Ed Hanyzewski | R | 2 | 1 | 0 | 0 | 0 | 0 | 0.0 | 0 | 0 | 1 | 1 | 0 | 0 | 0 | .000 | .000 |
| P | Walter Signer | R | 6 | 1 | 0 | 0 | 0 | 0 | 0.0 | 0 | 0 | 1 | 0 | 0 | 0 | 0 | .000 | .000 |
| P | George Hennessey | R | 2 | 0 | 0 | 0 | 0 | 0 | – | 0 | 0 | 0 | 0 | 0 | 0 | 0 | – | – |
| | TEAM TOTAL | | | 5298 | 1465 | 229 | 52 | 57 | 1.1 | 73 | 674 | 555 | 462 | 69 | 134 | 22 | .277 | .372 |

## INDIVIDUAL FIELDING

| POS | Player | T | G | PO | A | E | DP | TC/G | FA |
|---|---|---|---|---|---|---|---|---|---|
| 1B | Cavarretta | L | 120 | 1149 | 77 | 9 | 83 | 10.3 | .993 |
| | H. Becker | R | 28 | 222 | 12 | 0 | 21 | 8.4 | 1.000 |
| | R. Otero | R | 8 | 54 | 4 | 2 | 4 | 7.5 | .967 |
| | S. Hack | R | 5 | 38 | 2 | 1 | 2 | 8.2 | .976 |
| | R. Hughes | R | 2 | 4 | 0 | 0 | 0 | 2.0 | 1.000 |
| | Livingston | R | 1 | 1 | 0 | 0 | 0 | 1.0 | 1.000 |
| 2B | D. Johnson | R | 138 | 309 | 440 | 19 | 74 | 5.6 | .975 |
| | R. Hughes | R | 21 | 47 | 48 | 1 | 6 | 4.6 | .990 |
| | C. Block | R | 1 | 2 | 5 | 0 | 0 | 7.0 | 1.000 |
| | B. Schuster | R | 3 | 0 | 3 | 0 | 0 | 1.0 | 1.000 |
| SS | L. Merullo | R | 118 | 209 | 336 | 30 | 49 | 4.9 | .948 |
| | R. Hughes | R | 36 | 61 | 100 | 12 | 21 | 4.8 | .931 |
| | B. Schuster | R | 22 | 38 | 37 | 4 | 8 | 3.6 | .949 |
| | P. Lowrey | R | 2 | 1 | 2 | 1 | 0 | 2.0 | .750 |
| 3B | S. Hack | R | 146 | 195 | 312 | 13 | 27 | 3.6 | .975 |
| | B. Schuster | R | 1 | 0 | 0 | 0 | 0 | 0.0 | .000 |
| | R. Hughes | R | 9 | 8 | 9 | 0 | 1 | 1.9 | 1.000 |
| | J. Ostrowski | R | 4 | 1 | 2 | 1 | 0 | 1.0 | .750 |
| | C. Block | R | 1 | 1 | 2 | 0 | 0 | 3.0 | 1.000 |

| POS | Player | T | G | PO | A | E | DP | TC/G | FA |
|---|---|---|---|---|---|---|---|---|---|
| OF | A. Pafko | R | 140 | 371 | 11 | 2 | 0 | 2.7 | **.995** |
| | B. Nicholson | R | 151 | 300 | 12 | 3 | 4 | 2.1 | .990 |
| | P. Lowrey | R | 138 | 280 | 17 | 4 | 1 | 2.2 | .987 |
| | E. Sauer | R | 26 | 44 | 1 | 0 | 1 | 1.7 | 1.000 |
| | Christopher | R | 1 | 0 | 0 | 0 | 0 | 0.0 | .000 |
| | Cavarretta | L | 11 | 23 | 1 | 0 | 0 | 2.2 | 1.000 |
| | F. Secory | R | 12 | 20 | 0 | 0 | 0 | 1.7 | 1.000 |
| | P. Gillespie | R | 1 | 1 | 0 | 0 | 0 | 1.0 | 1.000 |
| C | Livingston | R | 68 | 263 | 27 | 3 | 2 | 4.3 | .990 |
| | P. Gillespie | R | 45 | 161 | 20 | 2 | 1 | 4.1 | .989 |
| | D. Williams | R | 54 | 114 | 20 | 3 | 1 | 2.5 | .978 |
| | L. Rice | R | 29 | 115 | 8 | 3 | 1 | 4.3 | .976 |

It took a war for the Cubs to win their last league pennant. Perhaps the biggest boost came when the navy found Cardinals' star Stan Musial in shipshape condition. Even without Stan the Man, St. Louis beat the Cubs 16 times in 22 tries, but still finished three games behind Jolly Cholly Grimm's crew. How did the Cubs manage to wave the flag? Well, if they couldn't deck the Cards, they found a patsy in Cincy, mopping up the Reds 21 of 22 times. In addition, the Cubbies set an all-time record by sweeping 20 doubleheaders. In home games, the Cubs were 49–26, and they felt equally at home on the road with a 49–30 record, for an 98–56 overall log. The Cubs surfaced to first to stay on July 8. Their biggest boost came on July 27 when they purchased pitcher Hank Borowy from the Yankees for $97,000 in a weird waiver deal. But Borowy, the ace of the Yanks with a 10–5 mark, was sensational down the stretch, winning 11 and losing only 2 for the Cubs. Borowy was not a one-man gang. Hank Wyse surprised with a 22–10 mark, while dependable Claude Passeau was 17–9. Phil Cavarretta enjoyed his greatest season, winning the batting title with a .355 average and capturing the MVP honors. Veteran Stan Hack batted .323, and Don Johnson hit .302. Slugger Bill Nicholson had an offseason with 13 homers, while youngster Andy Pafko drove in 110 runs. The Cubs regained catcher Mickey Livingston and leftfielder Peanuts Lowrey from the military service and both played regular roles, Lowrey driving in 89 runs. The Cubs clinched the pennant on September 29 against the Pirates, but lost the World Series in seven games to the Tigers, despite Passeau's one-hitter in Game Three.

### TEAM STATISTICS

| | W | L | PCT | GB | R | OR | 2B | 3B | Batting HR | BA | SA | SB | E | Fielding DP | FA | CG | B | Pitching SO | ShO | SV | ERA |
|---|---|---|---|---|---|---|---|---|---|---|---|---|---|---|---|---|---|---|---|---|---|
| CHI | 98 | 56 | .636 | | 735 | 532 | 229 | 52 | 57 | .277 | .372 | 69 | 121 | 124 | .980 | 86 | 385 | 541 | 15 | 14 | 2.98 |
| STL | 95 | 59 | .617 | 3 | 756 | 583 | 256 | 44 | 64 | .273 | .371 | 55 | 137 | 150 | .977 | 77 | 497 | 510 | 18 | 9 | 3.24 |
| BKN | 87 | 67 | .565 | 11 | 795 | 724 | 257 | 71 | 57 | .271 | .376 | 75 | 230 | 144 | .962 | 61 | 586 | 557 | 7 | 18 | 3.70 |
| PIT | 82 | 72 | .532 | 16 | 753 | 686 | 259 | 56 | 72 | .267 | .377 | 81 | 178 | 141 | .971 | 73 | 455 | 518 | 8 | 16 | 3.76 |
| NY | 78 | 74 | .513 | 19 | 668 | 700 | 175 | 35 | 114 | .269 | .379 | 38 | 166 | 112 | .973 | 53 | 529 | 530 | 13 | 21 | 4.06 |
| BOS | 67 | 85 | .441 | 30 | 721 | 728 | 229 | 25 | 101 | .267 | .374 | 82 | 193 | 160 | .969 | 57 | 557 | 404 | 7 | 13 | 4.04 |
| CIN | 61 | 93 | .396 | 37 | 536 | 694 | 221 | 26 | 56 | .249 | .333 | 71 | 146 | 138 | .976 | 77 | 534 | 372 | 11 | 6 | 4.00 |
| PHI | 46 | 108 | .299 | 52 | 548 | 865 | 197 | 27 | 56 | .246 | .326 | 54 | 234 | 150 | .962 | 31 | 608 | 433 | 4 | 26 | 4.64 |
| LEAGUE TOTAL | | | | | 5512 | 5512 | 1823 | 336 | 577 | .265 | .364 | 525 | 1405 | 1119 | .971 | 515 | 4151 | 3865 | 83 | 123 | 3.80 |

### INDIVIDUAL PITCHING

| PITCHER | T | W | L | PCT | ERA | SV | G | GS | CG | IP | H | BB | SO | R | ER | ShO | H/9 | BB/9 | SO/9 |
|---|---|---|---|---|---|---|---|---|---|---|---|---|---|---|---|---|---|---|---|
| Hank Wyse | R | 22 | 10 | .688 | 2.68 | 0 | 38 | 34 | 23 | 278.1 | 272 | 55 | 77 | 95 | 83 | 2 | 8.80 | 1.78 | 2.49 |
| Claude Passeau | R | 17 | 9 | .654 | 2.46 | 1 | 34 | 27 | 19 | 227 | 205 | 59 | 98 | 70 | 62 | 5 | 8.13 | 2.34 | 3.89 |
| Paul Derringer | R | 16 | 11 | .593 | 3.45 | 4 | 35 | 30 | 15 | 213.2 | 223 | 51 | 86 | 99 | 82 | 1 | 9.39 | 2.15 | 3.62 |
| Ray Prim | L | 13 | 8 | .619 | 2.40 | 2 | 34 | 19 | 9 | 165.1 | 142 | 23 | 88 | 58 | 44 | 2 | 7.73 | 1.25 | 4.79 |
| Hank Borowy | R | 11 | 2 | .846 | 2.13 | 1 | 15 | 14 | 11 | 122.1 | 105 | 47 | 47 | 33 | 29 | 1 | 7.72 | 3.46 | 3.46 |
| Paul Erickson | R | 7 | 4 | .636 | 3.32 | 3 | 28 | 9 | 3 | 108.1 | 94 | 48 | 53 | 41 | 40 | 0 | 7.81 | 3.99 | 4.40 |
| Hy Vandenberg | R | 6 | 3 | .667 | 3.49 | 2 | 30 | 7 | 3 | 95.1 | 91 | 33 | 35 | 44 | 37 | 1 | 8.59 | 3.12 | 3.30 |
| Bob Chipman | L | 4 | 5 | .444 | 3.50 | 0 | 25 | 10 | 3 | 72 | 63 | 34 | 29 | 37 | 28 | 1 | 7.88 | 4.25 | 3.63 |
| Mack Stewart | R | 0 | 1 | .000 | 4.76 | 0 | 16 | 1 | 0 | 28.1 | 37 | 14 | 9 | 16 | 15 | 0 | 11.75 | 4.45 | 2.86 |
| Lon Warneke | R | 1 | 1 | .500 | 3.86 | 0 | 9 | 1 | 0 | 14 | 16 | 1 | 6 | 9 | 6 | 0 | 10.29 | 0.64 | 3.86 |
| Ray Starr | R | 1 | 0 | 1.000 | 7.43 | 0 | 9 | 1 | 0 | 13.1 | 17 | 7 | 5 | 11 | 11 | 0 | 11.48 | 4.73 | 3.38 |
| Jorge Comellas | R | 0 | 2 | .000 | 4.50 | 0 | 7 | 1 | 0 | 12 | 11 | 6 | 6 | 7 | 6 | 0 | 8.25 | 4.50 | 4.50 |
| Walter Signer | R | 0 | 0 | – | 3.38 | 1 | 6 | 0 | 0 | 8 | 11 | 5 | 0 | 6 | 3 | 0 | 12.38 | 5.63 | 0.00 |
| Ed Hanyzewski | R | 0 | 0 | – | 5.79 | 0 | 2 | 1 | 0 | 4.2 | 7 | 1 | 2 | 4 | 3 | 0 | 13.50 | 1.93 | 0.00 |
| George Hennessey | R | 0 | 0 | – | 7.36 | 0 | 2 | 0 | 0 | 3.2 | 7 | 1 | 2 | 3 | 3 | 0 | 17.18 | 2.45 | 4.91 |
| TEAM TOTAL | | 98 | 56 | .636 | 2.98 | 14 | 290 | 155 | 86 | 1366.1 | 1301 | 385 | 541 | 533 | 452 | 13 | 8.57 | 2.54 | 3.56 |

| MANAGER | W | L | PCT |
|---|---|---|---|
| Charlie Grimm | 82 | 71 | .536 |

| POS | Player | B | G | AB | H | 2B | 3B | HR | HR % | R | RBI | BB | SO | SB | Pinch Hit AB | Pinch Hit H | BA | SA |
|---|---|---|---|---|---|---|---|---|---|---|---|---|---|---|---|---|---|---|
| **REGULARS** | | | | | | | | | | | | | | | | | | |
| 1B | Eddie Waitkus | L | 113 | 441 | 134 | 24 | 5 | 4 | 0.9 | 50 | 55 | 23 | 14 | 3 | 5 | 2 | .304 | .408 |
| 2B | Don Johnson | R | 83 | 314 | 76 | 10 | 1 | 1 | 0.3 | 37 | 19 | 26 | 39 | 6 | 0 | 0 | .242 | .290 |
| SS | Bill Jurges | R | 82 | 221 | 49 | 9 | 2 | 0 | 0.0 | 26 | 17 | 43 | 28 | 3 | 0 | 0 | .222 | .281 |
| 3B | Stan Hack | L | 92 | 323 | 92 | 13 | 4 | 0 | 0.0 | 55 | 26 | 83 | 32 | 3 | 2 | 0 | .285 | .350 |
| RF | Phil Cavarretta | L | 139 | 510 | 150 | 28 | 10 | 8 | 1.6 | 89 | 78 | 88 | 54 | 2 | 2 | 0 | .294 | .435 |
| CF | Peanuts Lowrey | R | 144 | 540 | 139 | 24 | 5 | 4 | 0.7 | 75 | 54 | 56 | 22 | 10 | 0 | 0 | .257 | .343 |
| LF | Marv Rickert | L | 111 | 392 | 103 | 18 | 3 | 7 | 1.8 | 44 | 47 | 28 | 54 | 3 | 6 | 0 | .263 | .378 |
| C | Clyde McCullough | R | 95 | 307 | 88 | 18 | 5 | 4 | 1.3 | 38 | 34 | 22 | 39 | 2 | 5 | 0 | .287 | .417 |
| **SUBSTITUTES** | | | | | | | | | | | | | | | | | | |
| S2 | Bobby Sturgeon | R | 100 | 294 | 87 | 12 | 2 | 1 | 0.3 | 26 | 21 | 10 | 18 | 0 | 7 | 3 | .296 | .361 |
| 2B | Lou Stringer | R | 80 | 209 | 51 | 3 | 1 | 3 | 1.4 | 26 | 19 | 26 | 34 | 0 | 5 | 0 | .244 | .311 |
| 3B | John Ostrowski | R | 64 | 160 | 34 | 4 | 2 | 3 | 1.9 | 20 | 12 | 20 | 31 | 1 | 10 | 0 | .213 | .319 |
| SS | Lennie Merullo | R | 65 | 126 | 19 | 8 | 0 | 0 | 0.0 | 14 | 7 | 11 | 13 | 2 | 1 | 0 | .151 | .214 |
| 3B | Cy Block | R | 6 | 13 | 3 | 0 | 0 | 0 | 0.0 | 2 | 0 | 4 | 0 | 1 | 1 | 0 | .231 | .231 |
| 3B | Hank Schenz | R | 6 | 11 | 2 | 0 | 0 | 0 | 0.0 | 0 | 1 | 0 | 0 | 1 | 0 | 0 | .182 | .182 |
| S2 | Al Glossop | B | 4 | 10 | 0 | 0 | 0 | 0 | 0.0 | 2 | 0 | 1 | 3 | 0 | 0 | 0 | .000 | .000 |
| OF | Bill Nicholson | L | 105 | 296 | 65 | 13 | 2 | 8 | 2.7 | 36 | 41 | 44 | 44 | 1 | 18 | 6 | .220 | .358 |
| OF | Andy Pafko | R | 65 | 234 | 66 | 6 | 4 | 3 | 1.3 | 18 | 39 | 27 | 15 | 4 | 1 | 0 | .282 | .380 |
| OF | Dom Dallessandro | L | 65 | 89 | 20 | 2 | 2 | 1 | 1.1 | 4 | 9 | 23 | 12 | 1 | 29 | 6 | .225 | .326 |
| OF | Frank Secory | R | 33 | 43 | 10 | 3 | 0 | 3 | 7.0 | 6 | 12 | 6 | 6 | 0 | 22 | 4 | .233 | .512 |
| OF | Charlie Gilbert | L | 15 | 13 | 1 | 0 | 0 | 0 | 0.0 | 2 | 1 | 1 | 4 | 0 | 12 | 0 | .077 | .077 |
| OF | Clarence Maddern | R | 3 | 3 | 0 | 0 | 0 | 0 | 0.0 | 0 | 0 | 0 | 0 | 0 | 1 | 0 | .000 | .000 |
| C | Mickey Livingston | R | 66 | 176 | 45 | 14 | 0 | 2 | 1.1 | 14 | 20 | 20 | 19 | 0 | 8 | 1 | .256 | .369 |
| C | Bob Scheffing | R | 63 | 115 | 32 | 4 | 1 | 0 | 0.0 | 8 | 18 | 12 | 18 | 0 | 19 | 7 | .278 | .330 |
| C | Dewey Williams | R | 4 | 5 | 1 | 0 | 0 | 0 | 0.0 | 0 | 0 | 0 | 2 | 0 | 2 | 1 | .200 | .200 |
| C | Ted Pawelek | L | 4 | 4 | 1 | 1 | 0 | 0 | 0.0 | 0 | 0 | 0 | 0 | 0 | 3 | 1 | .250 | .500 |
| PH | Heinz Becker | B | 9 | 7 | 2 | 0 | 0 | 0 | 0.0 | 0 | 1 | 1 | 1 | 0 | 7 | 2 | .286 | .286 |
| PH | Rabbit Garriott | B | 6 | 5 | 0 | 0 | 0 | 0 | 0.0 | 1 | 0 | 0 | 2 | 0 | 5 | 0 | .000 | .000 |
| **PITCHERS** | | | | | | | | | | | | | | | | | | |
| P | Hank Wyse | R | 40 | 74 | 18 | 1 | 0 | 0 | 0.0 | 4 | 7 | 0 | 10 | 1 | 0 | 0 | .243 | .257 |
| P | Hank Borowy | R | 33 | 72 | 13 | 4 | 1 | 0 | 0.0 | 9 | 8 | 1 | 18 | 0 | 0 | 0 | .181 | .264 |
| P | Johnny Schmitz | R | 42 | 70 | 9 | 0 | 0 | 1 | 1.4 | 3 | 3 | 4 | 13 | 0 | 0 | 0 | .129 | .171 |
| P | Claude Passeau | R | 21 | 49 | 10 | 1 | 0 | 3 | 6.1 | 7 | 7 | 0 | 7 | 0 | 0 | 0 | .204 | .408 |
| P | Paul Erickson | R | 32 | 40 | 2 | 1 | 0 | 0 | 0.0 | 1 | 0 | 0 | 16 | 0 | 0 | 0 | .050 | .075 |
| P | Emil Kush | R | 40 | 38 | 8 | 1 | 0 | 0 | 0.0 | 3 | 1 | 0 | 5 | 0 | 0 | 0 | .211 | .237 |
| P | Bob Chipman | L | 34 | 33 | 2 | 0 | 0 | 0 | 0.0 | 1 | 3 | 1 | 17 | 0 | 0 | 0 | .061 | .061 |
| P | Hi Bithorn | R | 26 | 28 | 5 | 0 | 0 | 0 | 0.0 | 4 | 2 | 1 | 2 | 0 | 0 | 0 | .179 | .179 |
| P | Russ Bauers | L | 15 | 10 | 3 | 1 | 0 | 0 | 0.0 | 1 | 2 | 2 | 1 | 0 | 0 | 0 | .300 | .400 |
| P | Doyle Lade | B | 3 | 5 | 1 | 0 | 0 | 0 | 0.0 | 0 | 0 | 0 | 0 | 0 | 0 | 0 | .200 | .200 |
| P | Russ Meyer | B | 4 | 5 | 1 | 0 | 0 | 0 | 0.0 | 0 | 0 | 1 | 0 | 0 | 0 | 0 | .200 | .200 |
| P | Ray Prim | R | 14 | 5 | 1 | 0 | 0 | 0 | 0.0 | 0 | 1 | 1 | 2 | 0 | 0 | 0 | .200 | .200 |
| P | Bill Fleming | R | 14 | 3 | 0 | 0 | 0 | 0 | 0.0 | 0 | 0 | 0 | 0 | 0 | 0 | 0 | .000 | .000 |
| P | Hal Manders | R | 2 | 2 | 0 | 0 | 0 | 0 | 0.0 | 0 | 0 | 0 | 1 | 0 | 0 | 0 | .000 | .000 |
| P | Red Adams | R | 8 | 1 | 0 | 0 | 0 | 0 | 0.0 | 0 | 0 | 0 | 0 | 0 | 0 | 0 | .000 | .000 |
| P | Ed Hanyzewski | R | 3 | 1 | 0 | 0 | 0 | 0 | 0.0 | 0 | 0 | 0 | 0 | 0 | 0 | 0 | .000 | .000 |
| P | Russ Meers | L | 7 | 1 | 1 | 0 | 0 | 0 | 0.0 | 0 | 1 | 0 | 0 | 0 | 0 | 0 | 1.000 | 1.000 |
| P | Vern Olsen | R | 5 | 0 | 0 | 0 | 0 | 0 | – | 0 | 0 | 0 | 0 | 0 | 0 | 0 | – | – |
| P | Emmett O'Neill | R | 1 | 0 | 0 | 0 | 0 | 0 | – | 0 | 0 | 0 | 0 | 0 | 0 | 0 | – | – |
| TEAM TOTAL | | | | 5298 | 1344 | 223 | 50 | 56 | 1.1 | 62 | 566 | 586 | 599 | 43 | 171 | 33 | .254 | .346 |

## INDIVIDUAL FIELDING

| POS | Player | T | G | PO | A | E | DP | TC/G | FA | POS | Player | T | G | PO | A | E | DP | TC/G | FA |
|---|---|---|---|---|---|---|---|---|---|---|---|---|---|---|---|---|---|---|---|
| 1B | E. Waitkus | L | 106 | 992 | 81 | 4 | 76 | 10.2 | .996 | OF | P. Lowrey | R | 126 | 308 | 15 | 7 | 3 | 2.6 | .979 |
| | Cavarretta | L | 51 | 450 | 40 | 4 | 26 | 9.7 | .992 | | M. Rickert | R | 104 | 200 | 5 | 6 | 1 | 2.0 | .972 |
| 2B | D. Johnson | R | 83 | 192 | 228 | 8 | 34 | 5.2 | .981 | | Cavarretta | L | 86 | 196 | 7 | 7 | 2 | 2.4 | .967 |
| | L. Stringer | R | 62 | 135 | 150 | 13 | 17 | 4.8 | .956 | | B. Nicholson | R | 80 | 179 | 4 | 5 | 1 | 2.4 | .973 |
| | B. Sturgeon | R | 21 | 51 | 51 | 3 | 13 | 5.0 | .971 | | A. Pafko | R | 64 | 165 | 13 | 4 | 4 | 2.8 | .978 |
| | B. Jurges | R | 2 | 0 | 0 | 0 | 0 | 0.0 | .000 | | Dallessandro | L | 20 | 33 | 0 | 1 | 0 | 1.7 | .971 |
| | A. Glossop | R | 2 | 4 | 2 | 0 | 0 | 3.0 | 1.000 | | F. Secory | R | 9 | 10 | 0 | 2 | 0 | 1.3 | .833 |
| | J. Ostrowski | R | 1 | 2 | 2 | 0 | 0 | 4.0 | 1.000 | | C. Maddern | R | 2 | 4 | 0 | 0 | 0 | 2.0 | 1.000 |
| SS | B. Jurges | R | 73 | 119 | 204 | 8 | 26 | 4.5 | .976 | | C. Gilbert | L | 2 | 1 | 1 | 0 | 0 | 1.0 | 1.000 |
| | B. Sturgeon | R | 72 | 109 | 158 | 19 | 31 | 4.0 | .934 | C | McCullough | R | 89 | 390 | 40 | 4 | 4 | 4.9 | .991 |
| | L. Merullo | R | 44 | 78 | 131 | 12 | 23 | 5.0 | .946 | | Livingston | R | 56 | 239 | 25 | 5 | 3 | 4.8 | .981 |
| | A. Glossop | R | 2 | 5 | 5 | 1 | 0 | 5.5 | .909 | | B. Scheffing | R | 43 | 97 | 10 | 0 | 3 | 2.5 | 1.000 |
| | L. Stringer | R | 1 | 0 | 2 | 0 | 0 | 2.0 | 1.000 | | T. Pawelek | R | 1 | 0 | 0 | 0 | 0 | 0.0 | .000 |
| 3B | S. Hack | R | 90 | 102 | 168 | 9 | 6 | 3.1 | .968 | | D. Williams | R | 2 | 3 | 1 | 0 | 0 | 2.0 | 1.000 |
| | J. Ostrowski | R | 50 | 33 | 80 | 8 | 5 | 2.4 | .934 | | | | | | | | | | |
| | P. Lowrey | R | 20 | 22 | 34 | 5 | 2 | 3.1 | .918 | | | | | | | | | | |
| | L. Stringer | R | 1 | 0 | 0 | 0 | 0 | 0.0 | .000 | | | | | | | | | | |
| | B. Jurges | R | 7 | 8 | 8 | 0 | 0 | 2.3 | 1.000 | | | | | | | | | | |
| | C. Block | R | 4 | 4 | 7 | 0 | 3 | 2.8 | 1.000 | | | | | | | | | | |
| | H. Schenz | R | 5 | 2 | 4 | 0 | 1 | 1.2 | 1.000 | | | | | | | | | | |

As far as the Cubs are concerned, hardly anything of significance happened in baseball following World War II. There were no banner seasons for waving pennants. While the other teams welcomed war heroes home, the Cubs elected to stand pat with their pennant-winning lineup. Only three returning veterans—Clyde McCullough, Johnny Schmitz, and Eddie Waitkus—played regular roles. Schmitz, a lanky lefty, was 11–11, but led the league in strikeouts with 135, had a 2.61 earned-run average, and knocked St. Louis into a playoff for first with Brooklyn by defeating the Cardinals on the final day of the season. Waitkus, a fancy-fielding first baseman, shoved veteran Phil Cavarretta into the outfield and led the team with a .304 average. Cavarretta shared the homer lead with slugger Bill Nicholson, each hitting eight; it was the lowest total for a Cub leader in 25 years. The biggest disappointment was pitcher Hank Borowy, who developed blisters on his flinging fingers and fell to a 12–10 record. Promising centerfielder Andy Pafko was sidelined most of the season with ankle and elbow injuries. Despite this and other assorted injuries, the Cubs managed to finish third, 14 1/2 games out.

## TEAM STATISTICS

| | W | L | PCT | GB | R | OR | Batting 2B | 3B | HR | BA | SA | SB | Fielding E | DP | FA | CG | B | Pitching SO | ShO | SV | ERA |
|---|---|---|---|---|---|---|---|---|---|---|---|---|---|---|---|---|---|---|---|---|---|
| STL | 98 | 58 | .628 | | 712 | 545 | 265 | 56 | 81 | .265 | .381 | 58 | 124 | 167 | .980 | 75 | 493 | 607 | 18 | 15 | 3.01 |
| BKN | 96 | 60 | .615 | 2 | 701 | 570 | 233 | 66 | 55 | .260 | .361 | 100 | 174 | 154 | .972 | 52 | 671 | 647 | 14 | 28 | 3.05 |
| CHI | 82 | 71 | .536 | 14.5 | 626 | 581 | 223 | 50 | 56 | .254 | .346 | 43 | 146 | 119 | .976 | 59 | 527 | 609 | 14 | 11 | 3.24 |
| BOS | 81 | 72 | .529 | 15.5 | 630 | 592 | 238 | 48 | 44 | .264 | .353 | 60 | 169 | 129 | .972 | 74 | 478 | 531 | 10 | 12 | 3.37 |
| PHI | 69 | 85 | .448 | 28 | 560 | 705 | 209 | 40 | 80 | .258 | .359 | 41 | 148 | 144 | .975 | 55 | 542 | 490 | 11 | 23 | 3.99 |
| CIN | 67 | 87 | .435 | 30 | 523 | 570 | 206 | 33 | 65 | .239 | .327 | 82 | 155 | 192 | .975 | 69 | 467 | 506 | 16 | 11 | 3.07 |
| PIT | 63 | 91 | .409 | 34 | 552 | 668 | 202 | 52 | 60 | .250 | .344 | 48 | 184 | 127 | .970 | 61 | 541 | 458 | 10 | 6 | 3.72 |
| NY | 61 | 93 | .396 | 36 | 612 | 685 | 176 | 37 | 121 | .255 | .374 | 46 | 159 | 121 | .973 | 48 | 660 | 581 | 8 | 13 | 3.92 |
| LEAGUE TOTAL | | | | | 4916 | 4916 | 1752 | 382 | 562 | .256 | .355 | 478 | 1259 | 1153 | .974 | 493 | 4379 | 4429 | 101 | 119 | 3.42 |

## INDIVIDUAL PITCHING

| PITCHER | T | W | L | PCT | ERA | SV | G | GS | CG | IP | H | BB | SO | R | ER | ShO | H/9 | BB/9 | SO/9 |
|---|---|---|---|---|---|---|---|---|---|---|---|---|---|---|---|---|---|---|---|
| Johnny Schmitz | L | 11 | 11 | .500 | 2.61 | 2 | 41 | 31 | 14 | 224.1 | 184 | 94 | 135 | 77 | 65 | 3 | 7.38 | 3.77 | 5.42 |
| Hank Wyse | R | 14 | 12 | .538 | 2.68 | 1 | 40 | 27 | 12 | 201.1 | 206 | 52 | 52 | 73 | 60 | 2 | 9.21 | 2.32 | 2.32 |
| Hank Borowy | R | 12 | 10 | .545 | 3.76 | 0 | 32 | 28 | 8 | 201 | 220 | 61 | 95 | 96 | 84 | 1 | 9.85 | 2.73 | 4.25 |
| Paul Erickson | R | 9 | 7 | .563 | 2.43 | 0 | 32 | 14 | 5 | 137 | 119 | 65 | 70 | 46 | 37 | 1 | 7.82 | 4.27 | 4.60 |
| Emil Kush | R | 9 | 2 | .818 | 3.05 | 2 | 40 | 6 | 1 | 129.2 | 120 | 43 | 50 | 47 | 44 | 1 | 8.33 | 2.98 | 3.47 |
| Claude Passeau | R | 9 | 8 | .529 | 3.13 | 0 | 21 | 21 | 10 | 129.1 | 118 | 42 | 47 | 53 | 45 | 2 | 8.21 | 2.92 | 3.27 |
| Bob Chipman | L | 6 | 5 | .545 | 3.13 | 2 | 34 | 10 | 5 | 109.1 | 103 | 54 | 42 | 44 | 38 | 3 | 8.48 | 4.45 | 3.46 |
| Hi Bithorn | R | 6 | 5 | .545 | 3.84 | 1 | 26 | 7 | 2 | 86.2 | 97 | 25 | 34 | 42 | 37 | 1 | 10.07 | 2.60 | 3.53 |
| Russ Bauers | R | 2 | 1 | .667 | 3.53 | 1 | 15 | 2 | 2 | 43.1 | 45 | 19 | 22 | 17 | 17 | 0 | 9.35 | 3.95 | 4.57 |
| Bill Fleming | R | 0 | 1 | .000 | 6.14 | 0 | 14 | 1 | 0 | 29.1 | 37 | 12 | 10 | 23 | 20 | 0 | 11.35 | 3.68 | 3.07 |
| Ray Prim | L | 2 | 3 | .400 | 5.79 | 1 | 14 | 2 | 0 | 23.1 | 28 | 10 | 10 | 17 | 15 | 0 | 10.80 | 3.86 | 3.86 |
| Russ Meyer | R | 0 | 0 | – | 3.18 | 1 | 4 | 1 | 0 | 17 | 21 | 10 | 10 | 7 | 6 | 0 | 11.12 | 5.29 | 5.29 |
| Doyle Lade | R | 0 | 2 | .000 | 4.11 | 0 | 3 | 2 | 0 | 15.1 | 15 | 3 | 8 | 8 | 7 | 0 | 8.80 | 1.76 | 4.70 |
| Red Adams | R | 0 | 1 | .000 | 8.25 | 0 | 8 | 0 | 0 | 12 | 18 | 7 | 8 | 12 | 11 | 0 | 13.50 | 5.25 | 6.00 |
| Russ Meers | L | 1 | 2 | .333 | 3.18 | 0 | 7 | 2 | 0 | 11.1 | 10 | 10 | 2 | 6 | 4 | 0 | 7.94 | 7.94 | 1.59 |
| Vern Olsen | L | 0 | 0 | – | 2.79 | 0 | 5 | 0 | 0 | 9.2 | 10 | 9 | 8 | 3 | 3 | 0 | 9.31 | 8.38 | 7.45 |
| Ed Hanyzewski | R | 1 | 0 | 1.000 | 4.50 | 0 | 3 | 0 | 0 | 6 | 8 | 5 | 1 | 3 | 3 | 0 | 12.00 | 7.50 | 1.50 |
| Hal Manders | R | 0 | 1 | .000 | 9.00 | 0 | 2 | 1 | 0 | 6 | 11 | 3 | 4 | 6 | 6 | 0 | 16.50 | 4.50 | 6.00 |
| Emmett O'Neill | R | 0 | 0 | | 0.00 | 0 | 1 | 0 | 0 | 1 | 0 | 3 | 1 | 0 | 0 | 0 | 0.00 | 27.00 | 9.00 |
| TEAM TOTAL | | 82 | 71 | .536 | 3.24 | 11 | 342 | 155 | 59 | 1393 | 1370 | 527 | 609 | 580 | 502 | 14 | 8.85 | 3.40 | 3.93 |

| MANAGER | W | L | PCT |
|---|---|---|---|
| Charlie Grimm | 69 | 85 | .448 |

| POS | Player | B | G | AB | H | 2B | 3B | HR | HR % | R | RBI | BB | SO | SB | Pinch Hit AB | H | BA | SA |
|---|---|---|---|---|---|---|---|---|---|---|---|---|---|---|---|---|---|---|
| **REGULARS** | | | | | | | | | | | | | | | | | | |
| 1B | Eddie Waitkus | L | 130 | 514 | 150 | 28 | 6 | 2 | 0.4 | 60 | 35 | 32 | 17 | 3 | 2 | 0 | .292 | .381 |
| 2B | Don Johnson | R | 120 | 402 | 104 | 17 | 2 | 3 | 0.7 | 33 | 26 | 24 | 45 | 2 | 5 | 1 | .259 | .333 |
| SS | Lennie Merullo | R | 108 | 373 | 90 | 16 | 1 | 0 | 0.0 | 24 | 29 | 15 | 26 | 4 | 0 | 0 | .241 | .290 |
| 3B | Peanuts Lowrey | R | 115 | 448 | 126 | 17 | 5 | 5 | 1.1 | 56 | 37 | 38 | 26 | 2 | 1 | 0 | .281 | .375 |
| RF | Bill Nicholson | L | 148 | 487 | 119 | 28 | 1 | 26 | 5.3 | 69 | 75 | 87 | 83 | 1 | 7 | 0 | .244 | .466 |
| CF | Andy Pafko | R | 129 | 513 | 155 | 25 | 7 | 13 | 2.5 | 68 | 66 | 31 | 39 | 4 | 2 | 0 | .302 | .454 |
| LF | Phil Cavarretta | L | 127 | 459 | 144 | 22 | 5 | 2 | 0.4 | 56 | 63 | 56 | 35 | 2 | 3 | 2 | .314 | .397 |
| C | Bob Scheffing | R | 110 | 363 | 96 | 11 | 5 | 5 | 1.4 | 33 | 50 | 25 | 25 | 2 | 13 | 5 | .264 | .364 |
| **SUBSTITUTES** | | | | | | | | | | | | | | | | | | |
| 3B | Stan Hack | L | 76 | 240 | 65 | 11 | 2 | 0 | 0.0 | 28 | 12 | 41 | 19 | 0 | 10 | 2 | .271 | .333 |
| S2 | Bobby Sturgeon | R | 87 | 232 | 59 | 10 | 5 | 0 | 0.0 | 16 | 21 | 7 | 12 | 0 | 10 | 3 | .254 | .341 |
| 2B | Ray Mack | R | 21 | 78 | 17 | 6 | 0 | 2 | 2.6 | 9 | 12 | 5 | 15 | 0 | 0 | 0 | .218 | .372 |
| 2B | Lonny Frey | L | 24 | 43 | 9 | 0 | 0 | 0 | 0.0 | 4 | 3 | 4 | 6 | 0 | 11 | 3 | .209 | .209 |
| SS | Bill Jurges | R | 14 | 40 | 8 | 2 | 0 | 1 | 2.5 | 5 | 2 | 9 | 9 | 0 | 0 | 0 | .200 | .325 |
| SS | Sal Madrid | R | 8 | 24 | 3 | 1 | 0 | 0 | 0.0 | 0 | 1 | 1 | 6 | 0 | 0 | 0 | .125 | .167 |
| 3B | Hank Schenz | R | 7 | 14 | 1 | 0 | 0 | 0 | 0.0 | 2 | 0 | 2 | 1 | 0 | 0 | 0 | .071 | .071 |
| OF | Cliff Aberson | R | 47 | 140 | 39 | 6 | 3 | 4 | 2.9 | 24 | 20 | 20 | 32 | 0 | 6 | 2 | .279 | .450 |
| OF | Marv Rickert | L | 71 | 137 | 20 | 0 | 0 | 2 | 1.5 | 7 | 15 | 15 | 17 | 0 | 27 | 6 | .146 | .190 |
| OF | Dom Dallessandro | L | 66 | 115 | 33 | 7 | 1 | 1 | 0.9 | 18 | 14 | 21 | 11 | 0 | 32 | 8 | .287 | .391 |
| C | Clyde McCullough | R | 86 | 234 | 59 | 12 | 4 | 3 | 1.3 | 25 | 30 | 20 | 20 | 1 | 17 | 3 | .252 | .376 |
| C | Mickey Livingston | R | 19 | 33 | 7 | 2 | 0 | 0 | 0.0 | 2 | 3 | 1 | 5 | 0 | 11 | 5 | .212 | .273 |
| C | Dewey Williams | R | 3 | 2 | 0 | 0 | 0 | 0 | 0.0 | 0 | 0 | 0 | 1 | 0 | 2 | 0 | .000 | .000 |
| **PITCHERS** | | | | | | | | | | | | | | | | | | |
| P | Johnny Schmitz | R | 38 | 68 | 9 | 0 | 0 | 0 | 0.0 | 3 | 3 | 4 | 30 | 0 | 0 | 0 | .132 | .132 |
| P | Paul Erickson | R | 40 | 60 | 15 | 2 | 0 | 1 | 1.7 | 2 | 3 | 0 | 19 | 0 | 0 | 0 | .250 | .333 |
| P | Doyle Lade | B | 35 | 60 | 13 | 2 | 0 | 0 | 0.0 | 3 | 4 | 5 | 18 | 1 | 1 | 0 | .217 | .250 |
| P | Hank Borowy | R | 41 | 56 | 7 | 3 | 0 | 0 | 0.0 | 5 | 6 | 2 | 14 | 0 | 0 | 0 | .125 | .179 |
| P | Hank Wyse | R | 37 | 45 | 5 | 0 | 1 | 0 | 0.0 | 3 | 4 | 1 | 10 | 0 | 0 | 0 | .111 | .156 |
| P | Bob Chipman | L | 33 | 44 | 4 | 0 | 0 | 0 | 0.0 | 4 | 0 | 1 | 16 | 0 | 0 | 0 | .091 | .091 |
| P | Emil Kush | R | 47 | 20 | 5 | 2 | 0 | 0 | 0.0 | 2 | 1 | 0 | 1 | 0 | 0 | 0 | .250 | .350 |
| P | Russ Meers | L | 35 | 14 | 2 | 0 | 0 | 0 | 0.0 | 1 | 0 | 1 | 6 | 0 | 0 | 0 | .143 | .143 |
| P | Claude Passeau | R | 19 | 14 | 0 | 0 | 0 | 0 | 0.0 | 0 | 0 | 0 | 7 | 0 | 0 | 0 | .000 | .000 |
| P | Russ Meyer | B | 23 | 12 | 3 | 0 | 0 | 0 | 0.0 | 2 | 1 | 0 | 1 | 0 | 0 | 0 | .250 | .250 |
| P | Ralph Hamner | R | 3 | 8 | 1 | 0 | 0 | 0 | 0.0 | 0 | 0 | 0 | 3 | 0 | 0 | 0 | .125 | .125 |
| P | Ox Miller | R | 4 | 7 | 3 | 1 | 0 | 1 | 14.3 | 3 | 4 | 0 | 2 | 0 | 0 | 0 | .429 | 1.000 |
| P | Bill Lee | R | 14 | 3 | 1 | 0 | 0 | 0 | 0.0 | 0 | 0 | 0 | 0 | 0 | 0 | 0 | .333 | .333 |
| P | Freddy Schmidt | R | 1 | 2 | 0 | 0 | 0 | 0 | 0.0 | 0 | 0 | 0 | 1 | 0 | 0 | 0 | .000 | .000 |
| P | Bob Carpenter | R | 4 | 1 | 1 | 0 | 0 | 0 | 0.0 | 0 | 0 | 0 | 0 | 0 | 0 | 0 | 1.000 | 1.000 |
| TEAM TOTAL | | | | 5305 | 1373 | 231 | 48 | 71 | 1.3 | 56 | 540 | 469 | 578 | 22 | 160 | 40 | .259 | .361 |

## INDIVIDUAL  FIELDING

| POS | Player | T | G | PO | A | E | DP | TC/G | FA |
|---|---|---|---|---|---|---|---|---|---|
| 1B | E. Waitkus | L | 126 | 1161 | 101 | 8 | 109 | 10.1 | .994 |
| | Cavarretta | L | 24 | 217 | 13 | 3 | 23 | 9.7 | .987 |
| | M. Rickert | R | 7 | 71 | 6 | 0 | 8 | 11.0 | 1.000 |
| 2B | D. Johnson | R | 108 | 255 | 291 | 17 | 65 | 5.2 | .970 |
| | R. Mack | R | 21 | 58 | 78 | 5 | 15 | 6.7 | .965 |
| | B. Sturgeon | R | 30 | 60 | 72 | 1 | 18 | 4.4 | .992 |
| | L. Frey | R | 24 | 17 | 20 | 0 | 4 | 1.5 | 1.000 |
| | P. Lowrey | R | 6 | 5 | 4 | 0 | 0 | 1.5 | 1.000 |
| SS | L. Merullo | R | 108 | 219 | 322 | 29 | 77 | 5.3 | .949 |
| | B. Sturgeon | R | 45 | 75 | 120 | 5 | 24 | 4.4 | .975 |
| | B. Jurges | R | 14 | 13 | 36 | 4 | 10 | 3.8 | .925 |
| | S. Madrid | R | 8 | 16 | 27 | 2 | 5 | 5.6 | .956 |
| 3B | P. Lowrey | R | 91 | 83 | 194 | 16 | 21 | 3.2 | .945 |
| | S. Hack | R | 66 | 64 | 136 | 8 | 11 | 3.2 | .962 |
| | D. Johnson | R | 6 | 5 | 11 | 0 | 4 | 2.7 | 1.000 |
| | H. Schenz | R | 5 | 2 | 9 | 1 | 0 | 2.4 | .917 |
| | B. Sturgeon | R | 5 | 2 | 10 | 0 | 1 | 2.4 | 1.000 |

| POS | Player | T | G | PO | A | E | DP | TC/G | FA |
|---|---|---|---|---|---|---|---|---|---|
| OF | A. Pafko | R | 127 | 327 | 9 | 5 | 3 | 2.7 | .985 |
| | B. Nicholson | R | 140 | 281 | 7 | 3 | 1 | 2.1 | .990 |
| | Cavarretta | L | 100 | 203 | 11 | 5 | 3 | 2.2 | .977 |
| | C. Aberson | R | 40 | 62 | 7 | 6 | 1 | 1.9 | .920 |
| | M. Rickert | R | 30 | 52 | 2 | 1 | 0 | 1.8 | .982 |
| | P. Lowrey | R | 25 | 50 | 2 | 1 | 0 | 2.1 | .981 |
| | Dallessandro | L | 28 | 50 | 1 | 0 | 1 | 1.8 | 1.000 |
| C | B. Scheffing | R | 97 | 379 | 52 | 7 | 4 | 4.5 | .984 |
| | McCullough | R | 64 | 280 | 35 | 5 | 3 | 5.0 | .984 |
| | D. Williams | R | 1 | 0 | 0 | 0 | 0 | 0.0 | .000 |
| | Livingston | R | 7 | 27 | 1 | 0 | 0 | 4.0 | 1.000 |

The Cubs walked the stepladder, wrong by wrong, in 1947. Starting from first place in May and going into June with a 21–16 record, they skidded to sixth in July and stayed there, finishing at 69–85. At the conclusion of the season they made a thorough house-cleaning. The season marked the last hurrah for such notables as Stan Hack, Billy Jurges, Bill Lee, Claude Passeau, and Hank Wyse. But it was a comeback season for Bill Nicholson, who led the team with 26 homers and 75 runs batted in. Among his homers was a prodigious shot that almost hit the scoreboard, sailing onto Sheffield Avenue and striking the hood of a southbound auto. Phil Cavarretta led the hitters at .314, followed by Andy Pafko's .302. Lefty Johnny Schmitz was the top winner with 13 triumphs, but was also a tough-luck loser, leading the league with 18 setbacks. Emil Kush continued his fine work in the bullpen with an 8–3 record, developing into the Cubs' first genuine relief pitcher. The Cubbies did set one team record when 47,801 fans (46,572 paid) shoehorned their way into Wrigley Field on May 18 to see the Dodgers' Jackie Robinson make his Chicago debut.

## TEAM STATISTICS

| | W | L | PCT | GB | R | OR | Batting 2B | 3B | HR | BA | SA | SB | Fielding E | DP | FA | Pitching CG | B | SO | ShO | SV | ERA |
|---|---|---|---|---|---|---|---|---|---|---|---|---|---|---|---|---|---|---|---|---|---|
| BKN | 94 | 60 | .610 | | 774 | 668 | 241 | 50 | 83 | .272 | .384 | **88** | 129 | 164 | .978 | 47 | 626 | 592 | **14** | **34** | 3.82 |
| STL | 89 | 65 | .578 | 5 | 780 | 634 | 235 | **65** | 115 | .270 | .401 | 28 | **128** | **169** | **.979** | **74** | 495 | 642 | 13 | 20 | **3.53** |
| BOS | 86 | 68 | .558 | 8 | 701 | 622 | **265** | 42 | 85 | **.275** | .390 | 58 | 153 | 124 | .974 | 58 | 453 | 486 | **14** | 13 | 3.62 |
| NY | 81 | 73 | .526 | 13 | **830** | 761 | 220 | 48 | **221** | .271 | **.454** | 29 | 155 | 136 | .974 | 54 | 590 | 633 | 13 | 13 | 4.41 |
| CIN | 73 | 81 | .474 | 21 | 681 | 755 | 242 | 43 | 95 | .259 | .375 | 46 | 138 | 134 | .977 | 46 | 589 | 571 | 8 | 15 | 4.10 |
| CHI | 69 | 85 | .448 | 25 | 567 | 722 | 231 | 48 | 71 | .259 | .361 | 22 | 150 | 159 | .975 | 46 | 618 | 514 | 8 | 14 | 3.96 |
| PHI | 62 | 92 | .403 | 32 | 589 | 687 | 210 | 52 | 60 | .258 | .352 | 60 | 152 | 140 | .974 | 70 | 501 | 501 | 9 | 13 | 4.68 |
| PIT | 62 | 92 | .403 | 32 | 744 | 817 | 216 | 44 | 156 | .261 | .406 | 30 | 149 | 131 | .975 | 44 | 592 | 501 | 9 | 13 | 4.68 |
| LEAGUE TOTAL | | | | | 5666 | 5666 | 1860 | 392 | 886 | .265 | .390 | 361 | 1154 | 1157 | .976 | 458 | 4464 | 4492 | 85 | 136 | 4.07 |

## INDIVIDUAL PITCHING

| PITCHER | T | W | L | PCT | ERA | SV | G | GS | CG | IP | H | BB | SO | R | ER | ShO | H/9 | BB/9 | SO/9 |
|---|---|---|---|---|---|---|---|---|---|---|---|---|---|---|---|---|---|---|---|
| Johnny Schmitz | L | 13 | **18** | .419 | 3.22 | 4 | 38 | 28 | 10 | 207 | 209 | 80 | 97 | 91 | 74 | 3 | 9.09 | 3.48 | 4.22 |
| Doyle Lade | R | 11 | 10 | .524 | 3.94 | 0 | 34 | 25 | 7 | 187.1 | 202 | 79 | 62 | 105 | 82 | 1 | 9.70 | 3.80 | 2.98 |
| Hank Borowy | R | 8 | 12 | .400 | 4.38 | 2 | 40 | 25 | 7 | 183 | 190 | 63 | 75 | 99 | 89 | 1 | 9.34 | 3.10 | 3.69 |
| Paul Erickson | R | 7 | 12 | .368 | 4.34 | 1 | 40 | 20 | 6 | 174 | 179 | 93 | 82 | 90 | 84 | 0 | 9.26 | 4.81 | 4.24 |
| Hank Wyse | R | 6 | 9 | .400 | 4.31 | 1 | 37 | 19 | 5 | 142 | 158 | 64 | 53 | 84 | 68 | 1 | 10.01 | 4.06 | 3.36 |
| Bob Chipman | L | 7 | 6 | .538 | 3.68 | 0 | 32 | 17 | 5 | 134.2 | 135 | 66 | 51 | 58 | 55 | 1 | 9.02 | 4.41 | 3.41 |
| Emil Kush | R | 8 | 3 | .727 | 3.36 | 5 | 47 | 1 | 1 | 91 | 80 | 53 | 44 | 38 | 34 | 0 | 7.91 | 5.24 | 4.35 |
| Russ Meers | L | 2 | 0 | 1.000 | 4.48 | 0 | 35 | 1 | 0 | 64.1 | 61 | 38 | 28 | 34 | 32 | 1 | 8.53 | 5.32 | 3.92 |
| Claude Passeau | R | 2 | 6 | .250 | 6.25 | 2 | 19 | 6 | 1 | 63.1 | 97 | 24 | 26 | 54 | 44 | 1 | 13.78 | 3.41 | 3.69 |
| Russ Meyer | R | 3 | 2 | .600 | 3.40 | 0 | 23 | 2 | 1 | 45 | 43 | 14 | 22 | 17 | 17 | 0 | 8.60 | 2.80 | 4.40 |
| Ralph Hamner | R | 1 | 2 | .333 | 2.52 | 0 | 3 | 3 | 2 | 25 | 24 | 16 | 14 | 10 | 7 | 0 | 8.64 | 5.76 | 5.04 |
| Bill Lee | R | 0 | 2 | .000 | 4.50 | 0 | 14 | 2 | 0 | 24 | 26 | 14 | 9 | 16 | 12 | 0 | 9.75 | 5.25 | 3.38 |
| Ox Miller | R | 1 | 2 | .333 | 10.13 | 0 | 4 | 4 | 1 | 16 | 31 | 5 | 7 | 18 | 18 | 0 | 17.44 | 2.81 | 3.94 |
| Bob Carpenter | R | 0 | 1 | .000 | 4.91 | 0 | 4 | 1 | 0 | 7.1 | 10 | 4 | 1 | 5 | 4 | 0 | 12.27 | 4.91 | 1.23 |
| Freddy Schmidt | R | 0 | 0 | — | 9.00 | 0 | 1 | 1 | 0 | 3 | 4 | 5 | 0 | 3 | 3 | 0 | 12.00 | 15.00 | 0.00 |
| TEAM TOTAL | | 69 | 85 | .448 | 4.10 | 15 | 371 | 155 | 46 | 1367 | 1449 | 618 | 571 | 722 | 623 | 8 | 9.54 | 4.07 | 3.76 |

| MANAGER | W | L | PCT |
|---|---|---|---|
| Charlie Grimm | 64 | 90 | .416 |

| POS | Player | B | G | AB | H | 2B | 3B | HR | HR % | R | RBI | BB | SO | SB | Pinch Hit AB | Pinch Hit H | BA | SA |
|---|---|---|---|---|---|---|---|---|---|---|---|---|---|---|---|---|---|---|
| **REGULARS** | | | | | | | | | | | | | | | | | | |
| 1B | Eddie Waitkus | L | 139 | 562 | 166 | 27 | 10 | 7 | 1.2 | 87 | 44 | 43 | 19 | 11 | 2 | 0 | .295 | .416 |
| 2B | Hank Schenz | R | 96 | 337 | 88 | 17 | 1 | 1 | 0.3 | 43 | 14 | 18 | 15 | 3 | 10 | 1 | .261 | .326 |
| SS | Roy Smalley | R | 124 | 361 | 78 | 11 | 4 | 4 | 1.1 | 25 | 36 | 23 | 76 | 0 | 0 | 0 | .216 | .302 |
| 3B | Andy Pafko | R | 142 | 548 | 171 | 30 | 2 | 26 | 4.7 | 82 | 101 | 50 | 50 | 3 | 2 | 1 | .312 | .516 |
| RF | Bill Nicholson | L | 143 | 494 | 129 | 24 | 5 | 19 | 3.8 | 68 | 67 | 81 | 60 | 2 | 4 | 3 | .261 | .445 |
| CF | Hal Jeffcoat | R | 134 | 473 | 132 | 16 | 4 | 4 | 0.8 | 53 | 42 | 24 | 68 | 8 | 14 | 6 | .279 | .355 |
| LF | Peanuts Lowrey | R | 129 | 435 | 128 | 12 | 3 | 2 | 0.5 | 47 | 54 | 34 | 31 | 2 | 13 | 3 | .294 | .349 |
| C | Bob Scheffing | R | 102 | 293 | 88 | 18 | 2 | 5 | 1.7 | 23 | 45 | 22 | 27 | 0 | 23 | 6 | .300 | .427 |
| **SUBSTITUTES** | | | | | | | | | | | | | | | | | | |
| 1O | Phil Cavarretta | L | 111 | 334 | 93 | 16 | 5 | 3 | 0.9 | 41 | 40 | 35 | 29 | 4 | 23 | 3 | .278 | .383 |
| 2B | Emil Verban | R | 56 | 248 | 73 | 15 | 1 | 1 | 0.4 | 37 | 16 | 4 | 7 | 4 | 0 | 0 | .294 | .375 |
| 2S | Gene Mauch | R | 53 | 138 | 28 | 3 | 2 | 1 | 0.7 | 18 | 7 | 26 | 10 | 1 | 7 | 0 | .203 | .275 |
| SS | Dick Culler | R | 48 | 89 | 15 | 2 | 0 | 0 | 0.0 | 4 | 5 | 13 | 3 | 0 | 1 | 0 | .169 | .191 |
| SS | Jeff Cross | R | 16 | 20 | 2 | 0 | 0 | 0 | 0.0 | 1 | 0 | 0 | 4 | 0 | 4 | 0 | .100 | .100 |
| 23 | Don Johnson | R | 6 | 12 | 3 | 0 | 0 | 0 | 0.0 | 0 | 0 | 0 | 1 | 0 | 2 | 0 | .250 | .250 |
| 2B | Dummy Lynch | R | 7 | 7 | 2 | 0 | 0 | 1 | 14.3 | 3 | 1 | 1 | 1 | 0 | 4 | 1 | .286 | .714 |
| OF | Clarence Maddern | R | 80 | 214 | 54 | 12 | 1 | 4 | 1.9 | 16 | 27 | 10 | 25 | 0 | 23 | 5 | .252 | .374 |
| OF | Cliff Aberson | R | 12 | 32 | 6 | 1 | 0 | 1 | 3.1 | 1 | 6 | 5 | 10 | 0 | 3 | 1 | .188 | .313 |
| OF | Carmen Mauro | L | 3 | 5 | 1 | 0 | 0 | 1 | 20.0 | 2 | 1 | 2 | 0 | 0 | 0 | 0 | .200 | .800 |
| C | Clyde McCullough | R | 69 | 172 | 36 | 4 | 2 | 1 | 0.6 | 10 | 7 | 15 | 25 | 0 | 15 | 2 | .209 | .273 |
| C | Rube Walker | L | 79 | 171 | 47 | 8 | 0 | 5 | 2.9 | 17 | 26 | 24 | 17 | 0 | 32 | 7 | .275 | .409 |
| PH | Carl Sawatski | L | 2 | 2 | 0 | 0 | 0 | 0 | 0.0 | 0 | 0 | 0 | 0 | 0 | 2 | 0 | .000 | .000 |
| **PITCHERS** | | | | | | | | | | | | | | | | | | |
| P | Johnny Schmitz | R | 34 | 84 | 11 | 1 | 1 | 0 | 0.0 | 3 | 4 | 3 | 19 | 0 | 0 | 0 | .131 | .167 |
| P | Russ Meyer | B | 29 | 56 | 6 | 0 | 1 | 0 | 0.0 | 1 | 3 | 0 | 19 | 0 | 0 | 0 | .107 | .143 |
| P | Dutch McCall | L | 30 | 53 | 9 | 2 | 0 | 0 | 0.0 | 3 | 6 | 4 | 8 | 0 | 0 | 0 | .170 | .208 |
| P | Bob Rush | R | 38 | 39 | 5 | 1 | 0 | 0 | 0.0 | 1 | 0 | 0 | 9 | 0 | 0 | 0 | .128 | .154 |
| P | Hank Borowy | R | 39 | 36 | 8 | 3 | 0 | 0 | 0.0 | 4 | 0 | 2 | 8 | 0 | 0 | 0 | .222 | .306 |
| P | Ralph Hamner | R | 27 | 33 | 6 | 1 | 0 | 1 | 3.0 | 1 | 5 | 0 | 12 | 0 | 0 | 0 | .182 | .303 |
| P | Doyle Lade | R | 19 | 32 | 5 | 0 | 0 | 0 | 0.0 | 3 | 2 | 1 | 10 | 0 | 0 | 0 | .156 | .156 |
| P | Cliff Chambers | L | 29 | 30 | 4 | 1 | 0 | 0 | 0.0 | 0 | 0 | 3 | 3 | 0 | 0 | 0 | .133 | .167 |
| P | Bob Chipman | L | 34 | 16 | 4 | 0 | 0 | 0 | 0.0 | 2 | 2 | 2 | 4 | 0 | 0 | 0 | .250 | .250 |
| P | Emil Kush | R | 34 | 13 | 2 | 0 | 0 | 0 | 0.0 | 1 | 0 | 2 | 3 | 0 | 0 | 0 | .154 | .154 |
| P | Jess Dobernic | R | 54 | 10 | 2 | 0 | 0 | 0 | 0.0 | 0 | 0 | 0 | 0 | 0 | 0 | 0 | .200 | .200 |
| P | Ben Wade | R | 2 | 2 | 0 | 0 | 0 | 0 | 0.0 | 0 | 0 | 0 | 1 | 0 | 0 | 0 | .000 | .000 |
| P | Paul Erickson | R | 3 | 1 | 0 | 0 | 0 | 0 | 0.0 | 0 | 0 | 0 | 0 | 0 | 0 | 0 | .000 | .000 |
| P | Don Carlsen | R | 1 | 0 | 0 | 0 | 0 | 0 | – | 0 | 0 | 0 | 0 | 0 | 0 | 0 | – | – |
| P | Warren Hacker | R | 3 | 0 | 0 | 0 | 0 | 0 | – | 0 | 0 | 0 | 0 | 0 | 0 | 0 | – | – |
| P | Tony Jacobs | B | 1 | 0 | 0 | 0 | 0 | 0 | – | 0 | 0 | 0 | 0 | 0 | 0 | 0 | – | – |
| TEAM TOTAL | | | | 5352 | 1402 | 225 | 44 | 87 | 1.6 | 59 | 564 | 444 | 574 | 39 | 184 | 39 | .262 | .369 |

## INDIVIDUAL FIELDING

| POS | Player | T | G | PO | A | E | DP | TC/G | FA | POS | Player | T | G | PO | A | E | DP | TC/G | FA |
|---|---|---|---|---|---|---|---|---|---|---|---|---|---|---|---|---|---|---|---|
| 1B | E. Waitkus | L | 116 | 1064 | 92 | 9 | 77 | 10.0 | .992 | OF | H. Jeffcoat | R | 119 | 307 | 12 | 8 | 3 | 2.7 | .976 |
| | Cavarretta | L | 41 | 374 | 28 | 1 | 46 | 9.8 | .998 | | B. Nicholson | R | 136 | 244 | 7 | 5 | 1 | 1.9 | .980 |
| 2B | H. Schenz | R | 78 | 184 | 190 | 10 | 45 | 4.9 | .974 | | P. Lowrey | R | 103 | 225 | 9 | 4 | 2 | 2.3 | .983 |
| | E. Verban | R | 56 | 134 | 164 | 11 | 47 | 5.5 | .964 | | C. Maddern | R | 55 | 98 | 6 | 2 | 0 | 1.9 | .981 |
| | G. Mauch | R | 26 | 56 | 55 | 9 | 18 | 4.6 | .925 | | Cavarretta | L | 40 | 72 | 4 | 2 | 0 | 2.0 | .974 |
| | J. Cross | R | 1 | 0 | 0 | 0 | 0 | 0.0 | .000 | | E. Waitkus | L | 20 | 43 | 0 | 1 | 0 | 2.2 | .977 |
| | P. Lowrey | R | 2 | 4 | 5 | 0 | 1 | 4.5 | 1.000 | | C. Aberson | R | 8 | 12 | 1 | 2 | 1 | 1.9 | .867 |
| | D. Culler | R | 2 | 3 | 1 | 0 | 0 | 2.0 | 1.000 | | C. Mauro | R | 2 | 7 | 0 | 0 | 0 | 3.5 | 1.000 |
| | D. Johnson | R | 2 | 2 | 1 | 0 | 1 | 1.5 | 1.000 | | | | | | | | | | |
| | D. Lynch | R | 1 | 0 | 2 | 0 | 0 | 2.0 | 1.000 | C | B. Scheffing | R | 78 | 332 | 36 | 4 | 5 | 4.8 | .989 |
| SS | R. Smalley | R | 124 | 189 | 351 | 34 | 70 | 4.6 | .941 | | McCullough | R | 51 | 225 | 25 | 7 | 5 | 5.0 | .973 |
| | D. Culler | R | 43 | 65 | 114 | 6 | 18 | 4.3 | .968 | | R. Walker | R | 44 | 178 | 22 | 4 | 3 | 4.6 | .980 |
| | G. Mauch | R | 19 | 21 | 43 | 2 | 6 | 3.5 | .970 | | | | | | | | | | |
| | P. Lowrey | R | 1 | 0 | 0 | 0 | 0 | 0.0 | .000 | | | | | | | | | | |
| | J. Cross | R | 9 | 3 | 8 | 3 | 0 | 1.6 | .786 | | | | | | | | | | |
| 3B | A. Pafko | R | 139 | 125 | 314 | 29 | 29 | 3.4 | .938 | | | | | | | | | | |
| | P. Lowrey | R | 9 | 9 | 15 | 1 | 2 | 2.8 | .960 | | | | | | | | | | |
| | H. Schenz | R | 5 | 3 | 6 | 0 | 0 | 1.8 | 1.000 | | | | | | | | | | |
| | D. Johnson | R | 2 | 1 | 2 | 2 | 1 | 2.5 | .600 | | | | | | | | | | |

Call it a coincidence, but the Cubs remained the lone holdout for daytime baseball and dropped into last place for the first time in 25 years. Charlie Grimm's crew found a snug spot in the cellar in April and stayed there. The club went all out with its so-called youth movement. The results were a failure. Rookie pitcher Dutch McCall lost a team record 13 in a row. Rookie Roy Smalley batted a robust .216 and led all shortstops with 34 errors. Only two rookies made strides: Hal Jeffcoat actually shoved Andy Pafko out of center field, batted .279, and displayed a rifle arm, while high-kicking Bob Rush looked like a comer despite a 5–11 record.

The Cubs concluded the campaign with a 64–90 record. Pafko made a successful switch to third base and was the main offensive threat with 26 homers, 101 RBI, and a .312 average. Bill Nicholson maintained some of his luster with 19 homers and 67 RBI. Schmitz was a virtual one-man staff with an 18–13 record, 18 complete games, and a 2.64 ERA. In addition, he gained notoriety as a Dodger killer, beating Dem Bums six times. While the Braves won the pennant with "Spahn and Sain and pray for rain," the Cubs finished last with "Kush and Rush and two days of slush."

## TEAM STATISTICS

| | W | L | PCT | GB | R | OR | Batting | | | | | | SB | Fielding | | | CG | B | Pitching | | | |
|---|---|---|---|---|---|---|---|---|---|---|---|---|---|---|---|---|---|---|---|---|---|---|
| | | | | | | | 2B | 3B | HR | BA | SA | | | E | DP | FA | | | SO | ShO | SV | ERA |
| OS | 91 | 62 | .595 | | 739 | 584 | 272 | 49 | 95 | .275 | .399 | 43 | 143 | 132 | .976 | 70 | 430 | 579 | 10 | 17 | 3.38 |
| TL | 85 | 69 | .552 | 6.5 | 742 | 646 | 238 | 58 | 105 | .263 | .389 | 24 | 119 | 138 | .980 | 60 | 476 | 635 | 13 | 18 | 3.91 |
| KN | 84 | 70 | .545 | 7.5 | 744 | 667 | 256 | 54 | 91 | .261 | .381 | 114 | 161 | 151 | .973 | 52 | 633 | 670 | 9 | 22 | 3.75 |
| IT | 83 | 71 | .539 | 8.5 | 706 | 699 | 191 | 54 | 108 | .263 | .380 | 68 | 137 | 150 | .977 | 65 | 564 | 519 | 5 | 19 | 4.15 |
| IY | 78 | 76 | .506 | 13.5 | 780 | 704 | 210 | 49 | 164 | .256 | .408 | 51 | 156 | 134 | .974 | 54 | 551 | 527 | 15 | 21 | 3.93 |
| HI | 66 | 88 | .429 | 25.5 | 591 | 729 | 227 | 39 | 91 | .259 | .368 | 68 | 210 | 126 | .964 | 61 | 561 | 552 | 6 | 15 | 4.08 |
| IN | 64 | 89 | .418 | 27 | 588 | 752 | 221 | 37 | 104 | .247 | .365 | 42 | 158 | 135 | .973 | 40 | 572 | 599 | 9 | 20 | 4.47 |
| HI | 64 | 90 | .416 | 27.5 | 597 | 706 | 225 | 44 | 87 | .262 | .369 | 39 | 172 | 152 | .972 | 51 | 609 | 636 | 7 | 10 | 4.00 |
| EAGUE TOTAL | | | | | 5487 | 5487 | 1840 | 384 | 845 | .261 | .383 | 449 | 1256 | 1118 | .974 | 453 | 4396 | 4717 | 74 | 142 | 3.95 |

## INDIVIDUAL PITCHING

| PITCHER | T | W | L | PCT | ERA | SV | G | GS | CG | IP | H | BB | SO | R | ER | ShO | H/9 | BB/9 | SO/9 |
|---|---|---|---|---|---|---|---|---|---|---|---|---|---|---|---|---|---|---|---|
| ohnny Schmitz | L | 18 | 13 | .581 | 2.64 | 1 | 34 | 30 | 18 | 242 | 186 | 97 | 100 | 92 | 71 | 2 | 6.92 | 3.61 | 3.72 |
| uss Meyer | R | 10 | 10 | .500 | 3.66 | 0 | 29 | 26 | 8 | 164.2 | 157 | 77 | 89 | 75 | 67 | 3 | 8.58 | 4.21 | 4.86 |
| utch McCall | L | 4 | 13 | .235 | 4.82 | 0 | 30 | 20 | 5 | 151.1 | 158 | 85 | 89 | 93 | 81 | 0 | 9.40 | 5.06 | 5.29 |
| ob Rush | R | 5 | 11 | .313 | 3.92 | 0 | 36 | 16 | 4 | 133.1 | 153 | 37 | 72 | 70 | 58 | 0 | 10.33 | 2.50 | 4.86 |
| ank Borowy | R | 5 | 10 | .333 | 4.89 | 1 | 39 | 17 | 2 | 127 | 156 | 49 | 50 | 80 | 69 | 1 | 11.06 | 3.47 | 3.54 |
| alph Hamner | R | 5 | 9 | .357 | 4.69 | 0 | 27 | 17 | 5 | 111.1 | 110 | 69 | 53 | 63 | 58 | 0 | 8.89 | 5.58 | 4.28 |
| liff Chambers | L | 2 | 9 | .182 | 4.43 | 0 | 29 | 12 | 3 | 103.2 | 100 | 48 | 51 | 57 | 51 | 1 | 8.68 | 4.17 | 4.43 |
| oyle Lade | R | 5 | 6 | .455 | 4.02 | 0 | 19 | 12 | 6 | 87.1 | 99 | 31 | 29 | 44 | 39 | 0 | 10.20 | 3.19 | 2.99 |
| ess Dobernic | R | 7 | 2 | .778 | 3.15 | 1 | 54 | 0 | 0 | 85.2 | 67 | 40 | 48 | 33 | 30 | 0 | 7.04 | 4.20 | 5.04 |
| mil Kush | R | 1 | 4 | .200 | 4.38 | 3 | 34 | 1 | 0 | 72 | 70 | 37 | 31 | 39 | 35 | 0 | 8.75 | 4.63 | 3.88 |
| ob Chipman | L | 2 | 1 | .667 | 3.58 | 4 | 34 | 3 | 0 | 60.1 | 73 | 24 | 16 | 34 | 24 | 0 | 10.89 | 3.58 | 2.39 |
| aul Erickson | R | 0 | 0 | – | 6.35 | 0 | 3 | 0 | 0 | 5.2 | 7 | 6 | 4 | 5 | 4 | 0 | 11.12 | 9.53 | 6.35 |
| en Wade | R | 0 | 1 | .000 | 7.20 | 0 | 2 | 0 | 0 | 5 | 4 | 4 | 1 | 4 | 4 | 0 | 7.20 | 7.20 | 1.80 |
| Varren Hacker | R | 0 | 1 | .000 | 21.00 | 0 | 3 | 1 | 0 | 3 | 7 | 3 | 0 | 7 | 7 | 0 | 21.00 | 9.00 | 0.00 |
| ony Jacobs | R | 0 | 0 | | 4.50 | 0 | 1 | 0 | 0 | 2 | 3 | 0 | 2 | 1 | 1 | 0 | 13.50 | 0.00 | 9.00 |
| on Carlsen | R | 0 | 0 | – | 36.00 | 0 | 1 | 0 | 0 | 1 | 5 | 2 | 1 | 4 | 4 | 0 | 45.00 | 18.00 | 9.00 |
| EAM TOTAL | | 64 | 90 | .416 | 4.00 | 10 | 375 | 155 | 51 | 1355.1 | 1355 | 609 | 636 | 701 | 603 | 7 | 9.00 | 4.04 | 4.22 |

| MANAGER | W | L | PCT |
|---|---|---|---|
| Charlie Grimm | 19 | 31 | .380 |
| Frankie Frisch | 42 | 62 | .404 |

| POS | Player | B | G | AB | H | 2B | 3B | HR | HR % | R | RBI | BB | SO | SB | Pinch Hit AB | Pinch Hit H | BA | SA |
|---|---|---|---|---|---|---|---|---|---|---|---|---|---|---|---|---|---|---|
| **REGULARS** | | | | | | | | | | | | | | | | | | |
| 1B | Herm Reich | R | 108 | 386 | 108 | 18 | 2 | 3 | 0.8 | 43 | 34 | 13 | 32 | 4 | 8 | 1 | .280 | .360 |
| 2B | Emil Verban | R | 98 | 343 | 99 | 11 | 1 | 0 | 0.0 | 38 | 22 | 8 | 2 | 3 | 7 | 1 | .289 | .327 |
| SS | Roy Smalley | R | 135 | 477 | 117 | 21 | 10 | 8 | 1.7 | 57 | 35 | 36 | 77 | 2 | 3 | 1 | .245 | .382 |
| 3B | Frankie Gustine | R | 76 | 261 | 59 | 13 | 4 | 4 | 1.5 | 29 | 27 | 18 | 22 | 3 | 5 | 0 | .226 | .352 |
| RF | Hal Jeffcoat | R | 108 | 363 | 89 | 18 | 6 | 2 | 0.6 | 43 | 26 | 20 | 48 | 12 | 5 | 2 | .245 | .344 |
| CF | Andy Pafko | R | 144 | 519 | 146 | 29 | 2 | 18 | 3.5 | 79 | 69 | 63 | 33 | 4 | 1 | 1 | .281 | .449 |
| LF | Hank Sauer | R | 96 | 357 | 104 | 17 | 1 | 27 | 7.6 | 59 | 83 | 37 | 47 | 0 | 0 | 0 | .291 | .571 |
| C | Mickey Owen | R | 62 | 198 | 54 | 9 | 3 | 2 | 1.0 | 15 | 18 | 12 | 13 | 1 | 3 | 1 | .273 | .379 |
| **SUBSTITUTES** | | | | | | | | | | | | | | | | | | |
| 1O | Phil Cavarretta | L | 105 | 360 | 106 | 22 | 4 | 8 | 2.2 | 46 | 49 | 45 | 31 | 2 | 9 | 2 | .294 | .444 |
| 3S | Bob Ramazzotti | R | 65 | 190 | 34 | 3 | 1 | 0 | 0.0 | 14 | 6 | 5 | 33 | 9 | 9 | 2 | .179 | .205 |
| UT | Gene Mauch | R | 72 | 150 | 37 | 6 | 2 | 1 | 0.7 | 15 | 7 | 21 | 15 | 3 | 13 | 4 | .247 | .333 |
| 2B | Wayne Terwilliger | R | 36 | 112 | 25 | 2 | 1 | 2 | 1.8 | 11 | 10 | 16 | 22 | 0 | 1 | 0 | .223 | .313 |
| 3B | Bill Serena | R | 12 | 37 | 8 | 3 | 0 | 1 | 2.7 | 3 | 7 | 7 | 9 | 0 | 1 | 0 | .216 | .378 |
| 3B | Hank Schenz | R | 7 | 14 | 6 | 0 | 0 | 0 | 0.0 | 2 | 1 | 1 | 0 | 2 | 0 | 0 | .429 | .429 |
| 1B | Clarence Maddern | R | 10 | 9 | 3 | 0 | 0 | 1 | 11.1 | 1 | 2 | 2 | 0 | 0 | 7 | 1 | .333 | .667 |
| OF | Hank Edwards | L | 58 | 176 | 51 | 8 | 4 | 7 | 4.0 | 25 | 21 | 19 | 22 | 0 | 6 | 1 | .290 | .500 |
| OF | Frankie Baumholtz | L | 58 | 164 | 37 | 4 | 2 | 1 | 0.6 | 15 | 15 | 9 | 21 | 2 | 15 | 5 | .226 | .293 |
| OF | Harry Walker | L | 42 | 159 | 42 | 6 | 3 | 1 | 0.6 | 20 | 14 | 11 | 6 | 2 | 3 | 0 | .264 | .358 |
| OF | Peanuts Lowrey | R | 38 | 111 | 30 | 5 | 0 | 2 | 1.8 | 18 | 10 | 9 | 8 | 3 | 5 | 3 | .270 | .369 |
| OF | Cliff Aberson | R | 4 | 7 | 0 | 0 | 0 | 0 | 0.0 | 0 | 0 | 0 | 0 | 2 | 3 | 0 | .000 | .000 |
| C | Rube Walker | L | 56 | 172 | 42 | 4 | 1 | 3 | 1.7 | 11 | 22 | 9 | 18 | 0 | 12 | 3 | .244 | .331 |
| C | Bob Scheffing | R | 55 | 149 | 40 | 6 | 1 | 3 | 2.0 | 12 | 19 | 9 | 9 | 0 | 14 | 3 | .268 | .383 |
| C | Rube Novotney | R | 22 | 67 | 18 | 2 | 1 | 0 | 0.0 | 4 | 6 | 3 | 11 | 0 | 2 | 1 | .269 | .328 |
| C | Smoky Burgess | L | 46 | 56 | 15 | 0 | 0 | 1 | 1.8 | 4 | 12 | 4 | 4 | 0 | 37 | 12 | .268 | .321 |
| PH | Jim Kirby | R | 3 | 2 | 1 | 0 | 0 | 0 | 0.0 | 0 | 0 | 0 | 0 | 0 | 2 | 1 | .500 | .500 |
| **PITCHERS** | | | | | | | | | | | | | | | | | | |
| P | Johnny Schmitz | R | 36 | 70 | 10 | 2 | 1 | 0 | 0.0 | 4 | 4 | 4 | 10 | 0 | 0 | 0 | .143 | .200 |
| P | Bob Rush | R | 35 | 63 | 2 | 0 | 0 | 0 | 0.0 | 4 | 2 | 1 | 19 | 0 | 0 | 0 | .032 | .032 |
| P | Dutch Leonard | R | 33 | 59 | 12 | 1 | 0 | 0 | 0.0 | 4 | 5 | 2 | 15 | 0 | 0 | 0 | .203 | .220 |
| P | Warren Hacker | R | 32 | 38 | 7 | 0 | 0 | 0 | 0.0 | 1 | 1 | 0 | 2 | 0 | 0 | 0 | .184 | .184 |
| P | Monk Dubiel | R | 33 | 35 | 10 | 0 | 2 | 0 | 0.0 | 2 | 3 | 2 | 7 | 0 | 0 | 0 | .286 | .400 |
| P | Doyle Lade | R | 36 | 32 | 7 | 0 | 0 | 0 | 0.0 | 4 | 4 | 5 | 7 | 1 | 0 | 0 | .219 | .219 |
| P | Bob Chipman | L | 38 | 24 | 3 | 0 | 0 | 0 | 0.0 | 2 | 0 | 3 | 5 | 0 | 0 | 0 | .125 | .125 |
| P | Dewey Adkins | R | 30 | 20 | 4 | 1 | 0 | 1 | 5.0 | 1 | 2 | 0 | 10 | 0 | 0 | 0 | .200 | .400 |
| P | Bob Muncrief | R | 34 | 14 | 4 | 0 | 1 | 0 | 0.0 | 1 | 1 | 1 | 6 | 0 | 0 | 0 | .286 | .429 |
| P | Emil Kush | R | 26 | 9 | 3 | 1 | 0 | 0 | 0.0 | 2 | 1 | 1 | 3 | 0 | 0 | 0 | .333 | .444 |
| P | Cal McLish | R | 9 | 9 | 3 | 0 | 0 | 1 | 11.1 | 1 | 4 | 0 | 3 | 0 | 0 | 0 | .333 | .667 |
| P | Ralph Hamner | R | 6 | 2 | 0 | 0 | 0 | 0 | 0.0 | 0 | 0 | 0 | 1 | 0 | 0 | 0 | .000 | .000 |
| P | Mort Cooper | R | 1 | 0 | 0 | 0 | 0 | 0 | – | 0 | 0 | 0 | 0 | 0 | 0 | 0 | – | – |
| P | Jess Dobernic | R | 4 | 0 | 0 | 0 | 0 | 0 | – | 0 | 0 | 0 | 0 | 0 | 0 | 0 | – | – |
| P | Dwain Sloat | R | 5 | 0 | 0 | 0 | 0 | 0 | – | 0 | 0 | 0 | 0 | 0 | 0 | 0 | – | – |
| TEAM TOTAL | | | | 5214 | 1336 | 212 | 53 | 97 | 1.9 | 59 | 539 | 396 | 573 | 53 | 171 | 45 | .256 | .373 |

## INDIVIDUAL FIELDING

| POS | Player | T | G | PO | A | E | DP | TC/G | FA |
|---|---|---|---|---|---|---|---|---|---|
| 1B | H. Reich | L | 85 | 759 | 83 | 9 | 57 | 10.0 | .989 |
| | Cavarretta | L | 70 | 673 | 63 | 5 | 58 | 10.6 | .993 |
| | C. Maddern | R | 1 | 2 | 1 | 0 | 0 | 3.0 | 1.000 |
| 2B | E. Verban | R | 88 | 218 | 249 | 17 | 60 | 5.5 | .965 |
| | Terwilliger | R | 34 | 77 | 103 | 4 | 11 | 5.4 | .978 |
| | G. Mauch | R | 25 | 58 | 74 | 4 | 17 | 5.4 | .971 |
| | F. Gustine | R | 16 | 52 | 47 | 4 | 15 | 6.4 | .961 |
| | Ramazzotti | R | 4 | 11 | 15 | 3 | 5 | 7.3 | .897 |
| SS | R. Smalley | R | 132 | 265 | 438 | 39 | 91 | 5.6 | .947 |
| | G. Mauch | R | 19 | 35 | 42 | 5 | 9 | 4.3 | .939 |
| | Ramazzotti | R | 12 | 20 | 35 | 0 | 7 | 4.6 | 1.000 |
| 3B | F. Gustine | R | 55 | 52 | 110 | 12 | 13 | 3.2 | .931 |
| | A. Pafko | R | 49 | 40 | 101 | 10 | 10 | 3.1 | .934 |
| | Ramazzotti | R | 36 | 28 | 77 | 3 | 8 | 3.0 | .972 |
| | B. Serena | R | 11 | 9 | 15 | 2 | 0 | 2.4 | .923 |
| | G. Mauch | R | 7 | 5 | 9 | 0 | 1 | 2.0 | 1.000 |
| | H. Schenz | R | 5 | 1 | 9 | 0 | 3 | 2.0 | 1.000 |
| | P. Lowrey | R | 1 | 1 | 1 | 1 | 0 | 3.0 | .667 |
| OF | H. Jeffcoat | R | 101 | 250 | 12 | 10 | 2 | 2.7 | .963 |
| | A. Pafko | R | 98 | 217 | 8 | 3 | 2 | 2.3 | .987 |
| | H. Sauer | R | 96 | 199 | 10* | 4 | 2 | 2.2 | .981 |
| | H. Edwards | L | 51 | 80 | 4 | 1 | 2 | 1.7 | .988 |
| | H. Walker | R | 39 | 69 | 3 | 4 | 0 | 1.9 | .947 |
| | F. Baumholtz | L | 43 | 67 | 3 | 1 | 3 | 1.7 | .986 |
| | P. Lowrey | R | 31 | 56 | 1 | 2 | 0 | 1.9 | .966 |
| | Cavarretta | L | 25 | 39 | 4 | 0 | 1 | 1.7 | 1.000 |
| | H. Reich | L | 16 | 27 | 4 | 1 | 1 | 2.0 | .969 |
| | C. Aberson | R | 1 | 2 | 0 | 0 | 0 | 2.0 | 1.000 |
| C | M. Owen | R | 59 | 219 | 35 | 8 | 5 | 4.4 | .969 |
| | R. Walker | R | 43 | 166 | 23 | 7 | 2 | 4.6 | .964 |
| | B. Scheffing | R | 40 | 152 | 18 | 4 | 3 | 4.4 | .977 |
| | R. Novotney | R | 20 | 82 | 9 | 4 | 3 | 4.8 | .958 |
| | S. Burgess | R | 8 | 21 | 6 | 0 | 2 | 3.4 | 1.000 |

Andy Pafko's "inside-the-glove" homer catch was typical of what kind of season the Cubs were to experience. The Cubs were leading 3–2 with two out and Cardinal runner Eddie Kazak on first in the ninth inning at Wrigley Field on April 30. Pinch-hitter Rocky Nelson hit a fly ball to left center, and Pafko made a sensational, diving, one-handed stab to end the game. Or so he thought. But umpire Al Barlick claimed Pafko trapped the ball. While Pafko ran in holding the ball aloft in triumph, the Cardinals runners raced around the bases with the winning runs of a 4–3 St. Louis victory.

From then on, the Cubs were trapped in the cellar. Charlie Grimm gave way to Frankie Frisch as manager early in the season with the same losing results. One bright note was the acquisition of outfielders Hank Sauer and Frankie Baumholtz from the Reds for Harry Walker and Peanuts Lowrey. Sauer hit 27 of his 31 homers in a Cubs uniform, drove in 83 runs, batted .291, and combined with Pafko for a solid one-two punch in an otherwise drab lineup. Johnny Schmitz was the big winner with 11 hard-earned victories. A leaky defense committed a league-leading 186 errors, led by erratic Roy Smalley's 39 at shortstop. All this resulted in 111 consecutive days in eighth place and a 61–93 log.

### TEAM STATISTICS

| | W | L | PCT | GB | R | OR | Batting 2B | 3B | HR | BA | SA | SB | Fielding E | DP | FA | CG | B | Pitching SO | ShO | SV | ERA |
|---|---|---|---|---|---|---|---|---|---|---|---|---|---|---|---|---|---|---|---|---|---|
| BKN | 97 | 57 | .630 | | 879 | 651 | 236 | 47 | 152 | .274 | .419 | 117 | 122 | 162 | .980 | 62 | 582 | 743 | 15 | 17 | 3.80 |
| STL | 96 | 58 | .623 | 1 | 766 | 616 | 281 | 54 | 102 | .277 | .404 | 17 | 146 | 149 | .976 | 64 | 506 | 606 | 13 | 19 | 3.45 |
| PHI | 81 | 73 | .526 | 16 | 662 | 668 | 232 | 55 | 122 | .254 | .388 | 27 | 156 | 141 | .974 | 58 | 502 | 495 | 12 | 15 | 3.89 |
| BOS | 75 | 79 | .487 | 22 | 706 | 719 | 246 | 33 | 103 | .258 | .374 | 28 | 148 | 144 | .976 | 68 | 520 | 591 | 12 | 11 | 3.99 |
| NY | 73 | 81 | .474 | 24 | 736 | 693 | 203 | 52 | 147 | .261 | .401 | 43 | 161 | 134 | .973 | 68 | 544 | 516 | 10 | 9 | 3.82 |
| PIT | 71 | 83 | .461 | 26 | 681 | 760 | 191 | 41 | 126 | .259 | .384 | 48 | 132 | 173 | .978 | 53 | 535 | 556 | 9 | 15 | 4.57 |
| CIN | 62 | 92 | .403 | 35 | 627 | 770 | 264 | 35 | 86 | .260 | .368 | 31 | 138 | 150 | .977 | 55 | 640 | 538 | 10 | 6 | 4.33 |
| CHI | 61 | 93 | .396 | 36 | 593 | 773 | 212 | 53 | 97 | .256 | .373 | 53 | 186 | 160 | .970 | 44 | 564 | 532 | 8 | 17 | 4.50 |
| LEAGUE TOTAL | | | | | 5650 | 5650 | 1865 | 370 | 935 | .262 | .389 | 364 | 1189 | 1213 | .975 | 472 | 4393 | 4577 | 89 | 109 | 4.04 |

### INDIVIDUAL PITCHING

| PITCHER | T | W | L | PCT | ERA | SV | G | GS | CG | IP | H | BB | SO | R | ER | ShO | H/9 | BB/9 | SO/9 |
|---|---|---|---|---|---|---|---|---|---|---|---|---|---|---|---|---|---|---|---|
| Johnny Schmitz | L | 11 | 13 | .458 | 4.35 | 3 | 36 | 31 | 9 | 207 | 227 | 92 | 75 | 117 | 100 | 3 | 9.87 | 4.00 | 3.26 |
| Bob Rush | R | 10 | 18 | .357 | 4.07 | 4 | 35 | 27 | 9 | 201 | 197 | 79 | 80 | 104 | 91 | 1 | 8.82 | 3.54 | 3.58 |
| Dutch Leonard | R | 7 | 16 | .304 | 4.15 | 0 | 33 | 28 | 10 | 180 | 198 | 43 | 83 | 94 | 83 | 1 | 9.90 | 2.15 | 4.15 |
| Monk Dubiel | R | 6 | 9 | .400 | 4.14 | 4 | 32 | 20 | 3 | 147.2 | 142 | 54 | 52 | 75 | 68 | 1 | 8.65 | 3.29 | 3.17 |
| Doyle Lade | R | 4 | 5 | .444 | 5.00 | 1 | 36 | 13 | 5 | 129.2 | 141 | 58 | 43 | 73 | 72 | 1 | 10.10 | 3.80 | 2.98 |
| Warren Hacker | R | 5 | 8 | .385 | 4.23 | 0 | 30 | 12 | 3 | 125.2 | 141 | 53 | 40 | 68 | 59 | 0 | 10.10 | 3.80 | 2.86 |
| Bob Chipman | L | 7 | 8 | .467 | 3.97 | 1 | 38 | 11 | 3 | 113.1 | 110 | 63 | 46 | 65 | 50 | 1 | 8.74 | 5.00 | 3.65 |
| Dewey Adkins | R | 2 | 4 | .333 | 5.68 | 0 | 30 | 5 | 1 | 82.1 | 98 | 39 | 43 | 58 | 52 | 0 | 10.71 | 4.26 | 4.70 |
| Bob Muncrief | R | 5 | 6 | .455 | 4.56 | 2 | 34 | 3 | 1 | 75 | 80 | 31 | 36 | 42 | 38 | 0 | 9.60 | 3.72 | 4.32 |
| Emil Kush | R | 3 | 3 | .500 | 3.78 | 2 | 26 | 0 | 0 | 47.2 | 51 | 24 | 22 | 21 | 20 | 0 | 9.63 | 4.53 | 4.15 |
| Cal McLish | R | 1 | 1 | .500 | 5.87 | 0 | 8 | 2 | 0 | 23 | 31 | 12 | 6 | 21 | 15 | 0 | 12.13 | 4.70 | 2.35 |
| Ralph Hamner | R | 0 | 2 | .000 | 8.76 | 0 | 6 | 1 | 0 | 12.1 | 22 | 8 | 3 | 13 | 12 | 0 | 16.05 | 5.84 | 2.19 |
| Dwain Sloat | L | 0 | 0 | — | 7.00 | 0 | 5 | 1 | 0 | 9 | 14 | 3 | 3 | 7 | 7 | 0 | 14.00 | 3.00 | 3.00 |
| Jess Dobernic | R | 0 | 0 | — | 20.25 | 0 | 4 | 0 | 0 | 4 | 9 | 4 | 0 | 9 | 9 | 0 | 20.25 | 9.00 | 0.00 |
| Mort Cooper | R | 0 | 0 | — | 0.00 | 0 | 1 | 0 | 0 | 2 | 1 | 1 | 0 | 3 | 3 | 0 | ∞ | ∞ | — |
| TEAM TOTAL | | 61 | 93 | .396 | 4.50 | 17 | 354 | 154 | 44 | 1357.2 | 1463 | 564 | 532 | 770 | 679 | 8 | 9.70 | 3.74 | 3.53 |

| MANAGER | W | L | PCT |
|---|---|---|---|
| Frankie Frisch | 64 | 89 | .418 |

| POS | Player | B | G | AB | H | 2B | 3B | HR | HR % | R | RBI | BB | SO | SB | Pinch Hit AB | Pinch Hit H | BA | SA |
|---|---|---|---|---|---|---|---|---|---|---|---|---|---|---|---|---|---|---|
| **REGULARS** | | | | | | | | | | | | | | | | | | |
| 1B | Preston Ward | L | 80 | 285 | 72 | 11 | 2 | 6 | 2.1 | 31 | 33 | 27 | 42 | 3 | 14 | 1 | .253 | .368 |
| 2B | Wayne Terwilliger | R | 133 | 480 | 116 | 22 | 3 | 10 | 2.1 | 63 | 32 | 43 | 63 | 13 | 4 | 1 | .242 | .363 |
| SS | Roy Smalley | R | 154 | 557 | 128 | 21 | 9 | 21 | 3.8 | 58 | 85 | 49 | 114 | 2 | 0 | 0 | .230 | .413 |
| 3B | Bill Serena | R | 127 | 435 | 104 | 20 | 4 | 17 | 3.9 | 56 | 61 | 65 | 75 | 1 | 2 | 1 | .239 | .421 |
| RF | Bob Borkowski | R | 85 | 256 | 70 | 7 | 4 | 4 | 1.6 | 27 | 29 | 16 | 30 | 1 | 14 | 2 | .273 | .379 |
| CF | Andy Pafko | R | 146 | 514 | 156 | 24 | 8 | 36 | 7.0 | 95 | 92 | 69 | 32 | 4 | 2 | 0 | .304 | .591 |
| LF | Hank Sauer | R | 145 | 540 | 148 | 32 | 2 | 32 | 5.9 | 85 | 103 | 60 | 67 | 1 | 3 | 2 | .274 | .519 |
| C | Mickey Owen | R | 86 | 259 | 63 | 11 | 0 | 2 | 0.8 | 22 | 21 | 13 | 16 | 2 | 1 | 0 | .243 | .309 |
| **SUBSTITUTES** | | | | | | | | | | | | | | | | | | |
| 1B | Phil Cavarretta | L | 82 | 256 | 70 | 11 | 1 | 10 | 3.9 | 49 | 31 | 40 | 31 | 1 | 9 | 2 | .273 | .441 |
| 23 | Bob Ramazzotti | R | 61 | 145 | 38 | 3 | 3 | 1 | 0.7 | 19 | 6 | 4 | 16 | 3 | 6 | 2 | .262 | .345 |
| 3B | Randy Jackson | R | 34 | 111 | 25 | 4 | 3 | 3 | 2.7 | 13 | 6 | 7 | 25 | 4 | 7 | 0 | .225 | .396 |
| UT | Emil Verban | R | 45 | 37 | 4 | 1 | 0 | 0 | 0.0 | 7 | 1 | 3 | 5 | 0 | 13 | 1 | .108 | .135 |
| OF | Carmen Mauro | L | 62 | 185 | 42 | 4 | 3 | 1 | 0.5 | 19 | 10 | 13 | 31 | 3 | 9 | 1 | .227 | .297 |
| OF | Hal Jeffcoat | R | 66 | 179 | 42 | 13 | 1 | 2 | 1.1 | 21 | 18 | 6 | 23 | 7 | 8 | 1 | .235 | .352 |
| OF | Ron Northey | L | 53 | 114 | 32 | 9 | 0 | 4 | 3.5 | 11 | 20 | 10 | 9 | 0 | 25 | 5 | .281 | .465 |
| OF | Hank Edwards | L | 41 | 110 | 40 | 11 | 1 | 2 | 1.8 | 13 | 21 | 10 | 13 | 0 | 10 | 0 | .364 | .536 |
| C | Rube Walker | L | 74 | 213 | 49 | 7 | 1 | 6 | 2.8 | 19 | 16 | 18 | 34 | 0 | 14 | 1 | .230 | .357 |
| C | Carl Sawatski | L | 38 | 103 | 18 | 1 | 0 | 1 | 1.0 | 4 | 7 | 11 | 19 | 0 | 7 | 0 | .175 | .214 |
| C | Bob Scheffing | R | 12 | 16 | 3 | 1 | 0 | 0 | 0.0 | 0 | 1 | 0 | 2 | 0 | 9 | 3 | .188 | .250 |
| C | Harry Chiti | R | 3 | 6 | 2 | 0 | 0 | 0 | 0.0 | 0 | 0 | 0 | 0 | 0 | 2 | 0 | .333 | .333 |
| **PITCHERS** | | | | | | | | | | | | | | | | | | |
| P | Bob Rush | R | 40 | 90 | 15 | 2 | 0 | 1 | 1.1 | 6 | 5 | 3 | 36 | 1 | 1 | 0 | .167 | .222 |
| P | Johnny Schmitz | R | 39 | 67 | 8 | 2 | 0 | 0 | 0.0 | 3 | 5 | 1 | 19 | 0 | 0 | 0 | .119 | .149 |
| P | Paul Minner | L | 43 | 65 | 14 | 0 | 1 | 1 | 1.5 | 6 | 7 | 4 | 16 | 0 | 3 | 0 | .215 | .292 |
| P | Monk Dubiel | R | 39 | 45 | 9 | 2 | 0 | 0 | 0.0 | 4 | 0 | 2 | 16 | 0 | 0 | 0 | .200 | .244 |
| P | Frank Hiller | R | 38 | 44 | 5 | 0 | 0 | 0 | 0.0 | 2 | 1 | 1 | 7 | 0 | 0 | 0 | .114 | .114 |
| P | Doyle Lade | R | 34 | 35 | 10 | 2 | 0 | 0 | 0.0 | 5 | 1 | 3 | 4 | 0 | 0 | 0 | .286 | .343 |
| P | Johnny Klippstein | R | 35 | 33 | 11 | 3 | 0 | 1 | 3.0 | 4 | 3 | 0 | 5 | 0 | 2 | 1 | .333 | .515 |
| P | Dutch Leonard | R | 35 | 16 | 1 | 0 | 0 | 0 | 0.0 | 0 | 0 | 1 | 5 | 0 | 0 | 0 | .063 | .063 |
| P | Johnny Vander Meer | R | 35 | 16 | 2 | 0 | 1 | 0 | 0.0 | 1 | 0 | 1 | 9 | 0 | 0 | 0 | .125 | .250 |
| P | Bill Voiselle | R | 19 | 13 | 1 | 0 | 0 | 0 | 0.0 | 0 | 0 | 0 | 3 | 0 | 0 | 0 | .077 | .077 |
| P | Warren Hacker | R | 5 | 5 | 0 | 0 | 0 | 0 | 0.0 | 0 | 0 | 0 | 0 | 0 | 0 | 0 | .000 | .000 |
| P | Andy Varga | R | 1 | 0 | 0 | 0 | 0 | 0 | — | 0 | 0 | 0 | 0 | 0 | 0 | 0 | | |
| | TEAM TOTAL | | | 5230 | 1298 | 224 | 47 | 161 | 3.1 | 64 | 615 | 479 | 767 | 46 | 165 | 24 | .248 | .401 |

## INDIVIDUAL FIELDING

| POS | Player | T | G | PO | A | E | DP | TC/G | FA |
|---|---|---|---|---|---|---|---|---|---|
| 1B | P. Ward | R | 76 | 734 | 73 | 4 | 78 | 10.7 | .995 |
| | Cavarretta | L | 67 | 606 | 47 | 9 | 55 | 9.9 | .986 |
| | H. Sauer | R | 18 | 145 | 17 | 4 | 11 | 9.2 | .976 |
| | Terwilliger | R | 1 | 0 | 0 | 0 | 0 | 0.0 | .000 |
| | B. Borkowski | R | 1 | 5 | 1 | 0 | 0 | 6.0 | 1.000 |
| 2B | Terwilliger | R | 126 | 314 | 380 | 24 | 80 | 5.7 | .967 |
| | Ramazzotti | R | 31 | 65 | 81 | 6 | 17 | 4.9 | .961 |
| | E. Verban | R | 8 | 11 | 17 | 1 | 6 | 3.6 | .966 |
| SS | R. Smalley | R | 154 | 332 | 541 | 51 | 115 | 6.0 | .945 |
| | Ramazzotti | R | 3 | 3 | 3 | 0 | 0 | 2.0 | 1.000 |
| | E. Verban | R | 3 | 2 | 1 | 0 | 0 | 1.0 | 1.000 |
| 3B | B. Serena | R | 125 | 122 | 274 | 23 | 24 | 3.4 | .945 |
| | R. Jackson | R | 27 | 26 | 56 | 8 | 3 | 3.3 | .911 |
| | Terwilliger | R | 1 | 0 | 0 | 0 | 0 | 0.0 | .000 |
| | Ramazzotti | R | 10 | 5 | 8 | 3 | 2 | 1.6 | .813 |
| | E. Verban | R | 1 | 0 | 0 | 1 | 0 | 1.0 | .000 |
| OF | A. Pafko | R | 144 | 342 | 12 | 8 | 1 | 2.5 | .978 |
| | H. Sauer | R | 125 | 236 | 12 | 9 | 1 | 2.1 | .965 |
| | B. Borkowski | R | 65 | 150 | 3 | 4 | 1 | 2.4 | .975 |
| | C. Mauro | R | 49 | 86 | 2 | 5 | 0 | 1.9 | .946 |
| | H. Jeffcoat | R | 53 | 83 | 6 | 3 | 0 | 1.7 | .967 |
| | R. Northey | R | 27 | 38 | 3 | 1 | 2 | 1.6 | .976 |
| | H. Edwards | L | 29 | 38 | 2 | 1 | 0 | 1.4 | .976 |
| | Terwilliger | R | 1 | 0 | 0 | 0 | 0 | 0.0 | .000 |
| | E. Verban | R | 1 | 0 | 0 | 0 | 0 | 0.0 | .000 |
| | Cavarretta | L | 3 | 3 | 0 | 0 | 0 | 1.0 | 1.000 |
| C | M. Owen | R | 86 | 318 | 39 | 8 | 1 | 4.2 | .978 |
| | R. Walker | R | 62 | 240 | 34 | 7 | 6 | 4.5 | .975 |
| | C. Sawatski | R | 32 | 100 | 19 | 2 | 6 | 3.8 | .983 |
| | B. Scheffing | R | 3 | 11 | 0 | 1 | 1 | 4.0 | .917 |
| | H. Chiti | R | 1 | 1 | 1 | 0 | 0 | 2.0 | 1.000 |

The Roy Smalley era—or was it error?—reached its peak. The lanky shortstop led the Cubs boot camp with 51 bobbles. His erratic mishaps inspired the poets of the pressbox with takeoffs or variations on the Tinker to Evers to Chance ballad of a brighter era. Some went from bad to verse with such lines as "Terwilliger to Smalley to the Dugout." The final tally had the Cubs finishing last in fielding with a league-leading 201 errors.

Although Smalley enjoyed his greatest season at the plate with 21 homers and 85 RBI, he was no match for the Cubs' slugging duo of Pafko, who had 36 homers and 92 RBI, and Sauer, 32 and 103. In addition, Pafko batted .304, but the Cubs ranked last in the league in hitting with a .248 average. And the pitching? Schmitz slipped to 10–16, while Bob Rush was a 20-game loser. Yankee castoff Frank Hiller was a mild surprise with a 12–5 record. Manager Frankie Frisch had the club in contention with a 31–30 record on July 1, but from that date on, the Cubs were 33–69 and wound up seventh, topping only the hapless Pirates.

## TEAM STATISTICS

| | W | L | PCT | GB | R | OR | Batting 2B | 3B | HR | BA | SA | SB | Fielding E | DP | FA | CG | B | Pitching SO | ShO | SV | ERA |
|---|---|---|---|---|---|---|---|---|---|---|---|---|---|---|---|---|---|---|---|---|---|
| PHI | 91 | 63 | .591 | | 722 | 624 | 225 | 55 | 125 | .265 | .396 | 33 | 151 | 155 | .975 | 57 | 530 | 620 | 13 | 27 | 3.50 |
| BKN | 89 | 65 | .578 | 2 | 847 | 724 | 247 | 46 | 194 | .272 | .444 | 77 | 127 | 183 | .979 | 62 | 591 | 772 | 10 | 21 | 4.28 |
| NY | 86 | 68 | .558 | 5 | 735 | 643 | 204 | 50 | 133 | .258 | .392 | 42 | 137 | 181 | .977 | 70 | 536 | 596 | 19 | 15 | 3.71 |
| BOS | 83 | 71 | .539 | 8 | 785 | 736 | 246 | 36 | 148 | .263 | .405 | 71 | 182 | 146 | .970 | 88 | 554 | 615 | 7 | 10 | 4.14 |
| STL | 78 | 75 | .510 | 12.5 | 693 | 670 | 255 | 50 | 102 | .259 | .386 | 23 | 130 | 172 | .978 | 57 | 535 | 603 | 10 | 14 | 3.97 |
| CIN | 66 | 87 | .431 | 24.5 | 654 | 734 | 257 | 27 | 99 | .260 | .376 | 37 | 140 | 132 | .976 | 67 | 582 | 686 | 7 | 13 | 4.32 |
| CHI | 64 | 89 | .418 | 26.5 | 643 | 772 | 224 | 47 | 161 | .248 | .401 | 46 | 201 | 169 | .968 | 55 | 593 | 559 | 9 | 19 | 4.28 |
| PIT | 57 | 96 | .373 | 33.5 | 681 | 857 | 227 | 59 | 138 | .264 | .406 | 43 | 136 | 165 | .977 | 42 | 616 | 556 | 6 | 16 | 4.96 |
| LEAGUE TOTAL | | | | | 5760 | 5760 | 1885 | 370 | 1100 | .261 | .401 | 372 | 1204 | 1303 | .975 | 498 | 4537 | 5007 | 81 | 135 | 4.14 |

## INDIVIDUAL PITCHING

| PITCHER | T | W | L | PCT | ERA | SV | G | GS | CG | IP | H | BB | SO | R | ER | ShO | H/9 | BB/9 | SO/9 |
|---|---|---|---|---|---|---|---|---|---|---|---|---|---|---|---|---|---|---|---|
| Bob Rush | R | 13 | 20 | .394 | 3.71 | 1 | 39 | 34 | 19 | 254.2 | 261 | 93 | 93 | 124 | 105 | 1 | 9.22 | 3.29 | 3.29 |
| Johnny Schmitz | L | 10 | 16 | .385 | 4.99 | 0 | 39 | 27 | 8 | 193 | 217 | 91 | 75 | 122 | 107 | 3 | 10.12 | 4.24 | 3.50 |
| Paul Minner | L | 8 | 13 | .381 | 4.11 | 4 | 39 | 24 | 9 | 190.1 | 217 | 72 | 99 | 105 | 87 | 1 | 10.26 | 3.40 | 4.68 |
| Frank Hiller | R | 12 | 5 | .706 | 3.53 | 1 | 38 | 17 | 9 | 153 | 153 | 32 | 55 | 68 | 60 | 2 | 9.00 | 1.88 | 3.24 |
| Monk Dubiel | R | 6 | 10 | .375 | 4.16 | 2 | 39 | 12 | 4 | 142.2 | 152 | 67 | 51 | 79 | 66 | 2 | 9.59 | 4.23 | 3.22 |
| Doyle Lade | R | 5 | 6 | .455 | 4.74 | 2 | 34 | 12 | 2 | 117.2 | 126 | 50 | 36 | 68 | 62 | 0 | 9.64 | 3.82 | 2.75 |
| Johnny Klippstein | R | 2 | 9 | .182 | 5.25 | 1 | 33 | 11 | 3 | 104.2 | 112 | 64 | 51 | 69 | 61 | 0 | 9.63 | 5.50 | 4.39 |
| Dutch Leonard | R | 5 | 1 | .833 | 3.77 | 6 | 35 | 1 | 0 | 74 | 70 | 27 | 28 | 41 | 31 | 0 | 8.51 | 3.28 | 3.41 |
| Johnny Vander Meer | L | 3 | 4 | .429 | 3.79 | 1 | 32 | 6 | 0 | 73.2 | 60 | 59 | 41 | 46 | 31 | 0 | 7.33 | 7.21 | 5.01 |
| Bill Voiselle | R | 0 | 4 | .000 | 5.79 | 0 | 19 | 7 | 0 | 51.1 | 64 | 29 | 25 | 39 | 33 | 0 | 11.22 | 5.08 | 4.38 |
| Warren Hacker | R | 0 | 1 | .000 | 5.28 | 1 | 5 | 3 | 1 | 15.1 | 20 | 8 | 5 | 11 | 9 | 0 | 11.74 | 4.70 | 2.93 |
| Andy Varga | L | 0 | 0 | — | 0.00 | 0 | 1 | 0 | 0 | 1 | 0 | 1 | 0 | 0 | 0 | 0 | 0.00 | 9.00 | 0.00 |
| TEAM TOTAL | | 64 | 89 | .418 | 4.28 | 19 | 353 | 154 | 55 | 1371.1 | 1452 | 593 | 559 | 772 | 652 | 9 | 9.53 | 3.89 | 3.67 |

| MANAGER | W | L | PCT |
|---|---|---|---|
| Frankie Frisch | 35 | 45 | .438 |
| Phil Cavarretta | 27 | 47 | .365 |

| POS | Player | B | G | AB | H | 2B | 3B | HR | HR % | R | RBI | BB | SO | SB | Pinch Hit AB | Pinch Hit H | BA | SA |
|---|---|---|---|---|---|---|---|---|---|---|---|---|---|---|---|---|---|---|
| **REGULARS** | | | | | | | | | | | | | | | | | | |
| 1B | Chuck Connors | L | 66 | 201 | 48 | 5 | 1 | 2 | 1.0 | 16 | 18 | 12 | 25 | 4 | 10 | 1 | .239 | .303 |
| 2B | Eddie Miksis | R | 102 | 421 | 112 | 13 | 3 | 4 | 1.0 | 48 | 35 | 33 | 36 | 11 | 0 | 0 | .266 | .340 |
| SS | Roy Smalley | R | 79 | 238 | 55 | 7 | 4 | 8 | 3.4 | 24 | 31 | 25 | 53 | 0 | 4 | 2 | .231 | .395 |
| 3B | Randy Jackson | R | 145 | 557 | 153 | 24 | 6 | 16 | 2.9 | 78 | 76 | 47 | 44 | 14 | 2 | 1 | .275 | .425 |
| RF | Hal Jeffcoat | R | 113 | 278 | 76 | 20 | 2 | 4 | 1.4 | 44 | 27 | 16 | 23 | 8 | 9 | 3 | .273 | .403 |
| CF | Frankie Baumholtz | L | 146 | 560 | 159 | 28 | 10 | 2 | 0.4 | 62 | 50 | 49 | 36 | 5 | 4 | 2 | .284 | .380 |
| LF | Hank Sauer | R | 141 | 525 | 138 | 19 | 4 | 30 | 5.7 | 77 | 89 | 45 | 77 | 2 | 8 | 1 | .263 | .486 |
| C | Smoky Burgess | L | 94 | 219 | 55 | 4 | 2 | 2 | 0.9 | 21 | 20 | 21 | 12 | 2 | 30 | 5 | .251 | .315 |
| **SUBSTITUTES** | | | | | | | | | | | | | | | | | | |
| 1B | Phil Cavarretta | L | 89 | 206 | 64 | 7 | 1 | 6 | 2.9 | 24 | 28 | 27 | 28 | 0 | 33 | 12 | .311 | .442 |
| 2B | Wayne Terwilliger | R | 50 | 192 | 41 | 6 | 0 | 0 | 0.0 | 26 | 10 | 29 | 21 | 3 | 0 | 0 | .214 | .245 |
| 1B | Dee Fondy | L | 49 | 170 | 46 | 7 | 2 | 3 | 1.8 | 23 | 20 | 11 | 20 | 5 | 5 | 1 | .271 | .388 |
| SS | Jack Cusick | R | 65 | 164 | 29 | 3 | 2 | 2 | 1.2 | 16 | 16 | 17 | 29 | 2 | 3 | 1 | .177 | .256 |
| SS | Bob Ramazzotti | R | 73 | 158 | 39 | 5 | 2 | 1 | 0.6 | 13 | 15 | 10 | 23 | 0 | 9 | 2 | .247 | .323 |
| 3B | Bill Serena | R | 13 | 39 | 13 | 3 | 1 | 1 | 2.6 | 8 | 4 | 11 | 4 | 0 | 0 | 0 | .333 | .538 |
| 1B | Fred Richards | L | 10 | 27 | 8 | 2 | 0 | 0 | 0.0 | 1 | 4 | 2 | 3 | 0 | 1 | 0 | .296 | .370 |
| OF | Gene Hermanski | L | 75 | 231 | 65 | 12 | 1 | 3 | 1.3 | 28 | 20 | 35 | 30 | 3 | 11 | 5 | .281 | .381 |
| OF | Andy Pafko | R | 49 | 178 | 47 | 5 | 3 | 12 | 6.7 | 26 | 35 | 17 | 10 | 1 | 0 | 0 | .264 | .528 |
| OF | Bob Borkowski | R | 58 | 89 | 14 | 1 | 0 | 0 | 0.0 | 9 | 10 | 3 | 16 | 0 | 23 | 3 | .157 | .169 |
| OF | Carmen Mauro | L | 13 | 29 | 5 | 1 | 0 | 0 | 0.0 | 3 | 3 | 2 | 6 | 0 | 6 | 1 | .172 | .207 |
| C1 | Bruce Edwards | R | 51 | 141 | 33 | 9 | 2 | 3 | 2.1 | 19 | 17 | 16 | 14 | 1 | 13 | 5 | .234 | .390 |
| C | Mickey Owen | R | 58 | 125 | 23 | 6 | 0 | 0 | 0.0 | 10 | 15 | 19 | 13 | 1 | 1 | 0 | .184 | .232 |
| C | Rube Walker | L | 37 | 107 | 25 | 4 | 0 | 2 | 1.9 | 9 | 5 | 12 | 13 | 0 | 5 | 1 | .234 | .327 |
| C | Harry Chiti | R | 9 | 31 | 11 | 2 | 0 | 0 | 0.0 | 1 | 5 | 2 | 2 | 0 | 1 | 0 | .355 | .419 |
| **PITCHERS** | | | | | | | | | | | | | | | | | | |
| P | Paul Minner | L | 36 | 71 | 18 | 4 | 0 | 1 | 1.4 | 8 | 6 | 5 | 10 | 0 | 2 | 0 | .254 | .352 |
| P | Bob Rush | R | 37 | 68 | 13 | 2 | 0 | 0 | 0.0 | 5 | 2 | 1 | 20 | 0 | 0 | 0 | .191 | .221 |
| P | Frank Hiller | R | 24 | 48 | 6 | 0 | 0 | 0 | 0.0 | 4 | 2 | 1 | 9 | 1 | 0 | 0 | .125 | .125 |
| P | Cal McLish | R | 31 | 42 | 5 | 0 | 1 | 0 | 0.0 | 2 | 1 | 3 | 20 | 0 | 0 | 0 | .119 | .167 |
| P | Turk Lown | R | 31 | 39 | 8 | 1 | 0 | 0 | 0.0 | 4 | 1 | 4 | 5 | 0 | 0 | 0 | .205 | .231 |
| P | Johnny Klippstein | R | 35 | 37 | 4 | 0 | 0 | 1 | 2.7 | 1 | 4 | 0 | 12 | 0 | 0 | 0 | .108 | .189 |
| P | Bob Kelly | R | 35 | 31 | 5 | 0 | 0 | 0 | 0.0 | 1 | 0 | 1 | 8 | 0 | 0 | 0 | .161 | .161 |
| P | Bob Schultz | R | 17 | 29 | 4 | 0 | 0 | 0 | 0.0 | 2 | 1 | 0 | 11 | 0 | 0 | 0 | .138 | .138 |
| P | Dutch Leonard | R | 41 | 21 | 0 | 0 | 0 | 0 | 0.0 | 1 | 1 | 0 | 5 | 0 | 0 | 0 | .000 | .000 |
| P | Joe Hatten | R | 23 | 17 | 4 | 0 | 0 | 0 | 0.0 | 0 | 1 | 0 | 4 | 0 | 0 | 0 | .235 | .235 |
| P | Monk Dubiel | R | 22 | 12 | 0 | 0 | 0 | 0 | 0.0 | 0 | 0 | 1 | 4 | 0 | 0 | 0 | .000 | .000 |
| P | Johnny Schmitz | R | 8 | 6 | 1 | 0 | 0 | 0 | 0.0 | 0 | 0 | 0 | 1 | 0 | 0 | 0 | .167 | .167 |
| P | Warren Hacker | R | 2 | 0 | 0 | 0 | 0 | 0 | – | 0 | 0 | 0 | 0 | 0 | 0 | 0 | – | – |
| P | Andy Varga | R | 2 | 0 | 0 | 0 | 0 | 0 | – | 0 | 0 | 0 | 0 | 0 | 0 | 0 | – | – |
| TEAM TOTAL | | | | 5307 | 1327 | 200 | 47 | 103 | 1.9 | 61 | 572 | 477 | 647 | 63 | 180 | 46 | .250 | .364 |

## INDIVIDUAL FIELDING

| POS | Player | T | G | PO | A | E | DP | TC/G | FA | POS | Player | T | G | PO | A | E | DP | TC/G | FA |
|---|---|---|---|---|---|---|---|---|---|---|---|---|---|---|---|---|---|---|---|
| 1B | C. Connors | L | 57 | 452 | 33 | 8 | 41 | 8.6 | .984 | OF | F. Baumholtz | L | 140 | 307 | 6 | 8 | 2 | 2.3 | .975 |
| | Cavarretta | L | 53 | 444 | 42 | 3 | 51 | 9.2 | .994 | | H. Sauer | R | 132 | 286 | 19 | 6 | 2 | 2.4 | .981 |
| | D. Fondy | L | 44 | 387 | 27 | 10 | 40 | 9.6 | .976 | | H. Jeffcoat | R | 87 | 166 | 11 | 2 | 5 | 2.1 | .989 |
| | B. Edwards | R | 9 | 69 | 8 | 4 | 5 | 9.0 | .951 | | G. Hermanski | R | 75 | 134 | 9 | 5 | 1 | 2.0 | .966 |
| | F. Richards | L | 9 | 62 | 8 | 0 | 3 | 7.8 | 1.000 | | A. Pafko | R | 48 | 119 | 6 | 1 | 3 | 2.6 | .992 |
| 2B | E. Miksis | R | 102 | 279 | 317 | 19 | 71 | 6.0* | .969 | | B. Borkowski | R | 25 | 41 | 1 | 3 | 0 | 1.8 | .933 |
| | Terwilliger | R | 49 | 136 | 142 | 9 | 37 | 5.9 | .969 | | C. Mauro | R | 6 | 17 | 1 | 2 | 0 | 3.3 | .900 |
| | Ramazzotti | R | 6 | 10 | 15 | 0 | 3 | 4.2 | 1.000 | C | S. Burgess | R | 64 | 210 | 35 | 5 | 6 | 3.9 | .980 |
| SS | R. Smalley | R | 74 | 117 | 190 | 15 | 42 | 4.4 | .953 | | M. Owen | R | 57 | 188 | 28 | 7 | 6 | 3.9 | .969 |
| | J. Cusick | R | 56 | 78 | 147 | 11 | 25 | 4.2 | .953 | | B. Edwards | R | 28 | 113 | 14 | 5 | 4 | 4.7 | .962 |
| | Ramazzotti | R | 51 | 73 | 137 | 11 | 32 | 4.3 | .950 | | R. Walker | R | 31 | 111 | 15 | 4 | 2 | 4.2 | .969 |
| 3B | R. Jackson | R | 143 | 198 | 323 | 24 | 32 | 3.8 | .956 | | H. Chiti | R | 8 | 34 | 8 | 4 | 1 | 5.8 | .913 |
| | Ramazzotti | R | 1 | 0 | 0 | 0 | 0 | 0.0 | .000 | | | | | | | | | | |
| | B. Serena | R | 12 | 15 | 17 | 2 | 1 | 2.8 | .941 | | | | | | | | | | |

One day doesn't make a season. But Cub manager Phil Cavarretta will always savor July 29, 1951, at Wrigley Field. The Cubs had dropped five in a row and were scoreless for 31 innings. Cavy broke the drought with a two-run triple to help beat the Phillies, 5–4, in the first game of the doubleheader. And with the score tied 4–4 and the bases loaded in the seventh inning of the second game, Cavarretta hit a pinch grand-slam off Robin Roberts for a sweet sweep.

The rest of the season? Forget it. The Cubs had won 21 of 41 to climb as high as second at the outset. Then they lost 9 of 11 and panicked by trading popular centerfielder Andy Pafko to the Dodgers in an eight-player deal. One of the new Cubbies was infielder Eddie Miksis. Cub GM Wid Matthews further angered the faithful by uttering his ridiculous "Miksis will fix us" remark. The following week manager Frankie Frisch was fired, departing with a 35–45 record. He was replaced by Cavaretta, whose hustle and spirited play couldn't lift the team from the cellar, where they resided at 62–92. Hank Sauer carried the heavy lumber with 30 homers and 89 RBI, and Frankie Baumholtz topped the hitters at .284. Bob Rush was the big winner at 11–12, but 41-year-old knuckleballing reliever Dutch Leonard was the most dependable, logging a 10–6 mark with a 2.64 ERA. The top rookie was Handsome Ransom Jackson, who hit 16 homers and drove in 76 runs. Another rookie was elongated first baseman Chuck Connors, who hit only .239 but later carved out a career in movies and TV.

## TEAM STATISTICS

| | W | L | PCT | GB | R | OR | 2B | 3B | HR | BA | SA | SB | E | DP | FA | CG | B | SO | ShO | SV | ERA |
|---|---|---|---|---|---|---|---|---|---|---|---|---|---|---|---|---|---|---|---|---|---|
| NY | 98 | 59 | .624 | | 781 | 641 | 201 | 53 | 179 | .260 | .418 | 55 | 171 | 175 | .972 | 64 | **482** | 625 | 9 | 18 | **3.48** |
| BKN | 97 | 60 | .618 | 1 | **855** | 672 | **249** | 37 | **184** | **.275** | **.434** | **89** | 129 | **192** | .979 | 64 | 549 | **693** | 10 | 13 | 3.88 |
| STL | 81 | 73 | .526 | 15.5 | 683 | 671 | 230 | **57** | 95 | .264 | .382 | 30 | **125** | 187 | **.980** | 58 | 568 | 546 | 9 | **23** | 3.95 |
| BOS | 76 | 78 | .494 | 20.5 | 723 | 662 | 234 | 37 | 130 | .262 | .394 | 78 | 145 | 157 | .976 | **73** | 595 | 604 | 10 | 12 | 3.75 |
| PHI | 73 | 81 | .474 | 23.5 | 648 | 644 | 199 | 47 | 108 | .260 | .375 | 64 | 138 | 146 | .977 | 57 | 496 | 570 | **19** | 15 | 3.81 |
| CIN | 68 | 86 | .442 | 28.5 | 559 | 667 | 215 | 33 | 88 | .248 | .351 | 44 | 140 | 141 | .977 | 55 | 490 | 584 | 14 | **23** | 3.70 |
| PIT | 64 | 90 | .416 | 32.5 | 689 | 845 | 218 | 56 | 137 | .258 | .397 | 26 | 170 | 178 | .972 | 40 | 627 | 582 | 9 | 22 | 4.78 |
| CHI | 62 | 92 | .403 | 34.5 | 614 | 750 | 200 | 47 | 103 | .250 | .364 | 63 | 181 | 161 | .971 | 48 | 572 | 544 | 10 | 10 | 4.34 |
| LEAGUE TOTAL | | | | | 5552 | 5552 | 1746 | 367 | 1024 | .260 | .390 | 449 | 1199 | 1337 | .975 | 459 | 4379 | 4748 | 90 | 136 | 3.96 |

## INDIVIDUAL PITCHING

| PITCHER | T | W | L | PCT | ERA | SV | G | GS | CG | IP | H | BB | SO | R | ER | ShO | H/9 | BB/9 | SO/9 |
|---|---|---|---|---|---|---|---|---|---|---|---|---|---|---|---|---|---|---|---|
| Bob Rush | R | 11 | 12 | .478 | 3.83 | 2 | 37 | 29 | 12 | 211.1 | 219 | 68 | 129 | 108 | 90 | 2 | 9.33 | 2.90 | 5.49 |
| Paul Minner | L | 6 | **17** | .261 | 3.79 | 1 | 33 | 28 | 14 | 201.2 | 219 | 64 | 68 | 97 | 85 | 3 | 9.77 | 2.86 | 3.03 |
| Cal McLish | R | 4 | 10 | .286 | 4.45 | 0 | 30 | 17 | 5 | 145.2 | 159 | 52 | 46 | 76 | 72 | 1 | 9.82 | 3.21 | 2.84 |
| Frank Hiller | R | 6 | 12 | .333 | 4.84 | 1 | 24 | 21 | 6 | 141.1 | 147 | 31 | 50 | 83 | 76 | 2 | 9.36 | 1.97 | 3.18 |
| Turk Lown | R | 4 | 9 | .308 | 5.46 | 0 | 31 | 18 | 3 | 127 | 80 | 90 | 39 | 80 | 77 | 1 | 5.67 | 6.38 | 2.76 |
| Bob Kelly | R | 7 | 4 | .636 | 4.66 | 0 | 35 | 11 | 4 | 123.2 | 130 | 55 | 48 | 70 | 64 | 0 | 9.46 | 4.00 | 3.49 |
| Johnny Klippstein | R | 6 | 6 | .500 | 4.29 | 2 | 35 | 11 | 1 | 123.2 | 121 | 53 | 56 | 71 | 59 | 1 | 8.81 | 3.86 | 4.08 |
| Dutch Leonard | R | 10 | 6 | .625 | 2.64 | 3 | 41 | 1 | 0 | 81.2 | 69 | 28 | 30 | 30 | 24 | 0 | 7.60 | 3.09 | 3.31 |
| Bob Schultz | L | 3 | 6 | .333 | 5.24 | 0 | 17 | 10 | 2 | 77.1 | 75 | 51 | 27 | 51 | 45 | 0 | 8.73 | 5.94 | 3.14 |
| Joe Hatten | L | 2 | 6 | .250 | 5.14 | 0 | 23 | 6 | 1 | 75.1 | 82 | 37 | 23 | 48 | 43 | 0 | 9.80 | 4.42 | 2.75 |
| Monk Dubiel | R | 2 | 2 | .500 | 2.30 | 1 | 22 | 0 | 0 | 54.2 | 46 | 22 | 19 | 17 | 14 | 0 | 7.57 | 3.62 | 3.13 |
| Johnny Schmitz | L | 1 | 2 | .333 | 8.00 | 0 | 8 | 3 | 0 | 18 | 22 | 15 | 6 | 16 | 16 | 0 | 11.00 | 7.50 | 3.00 |
| Andy Varga | L | 0 | 0 | — | 3.00 | 0 | 2 | 0 | 0 | 3 | 2 | 6 | 1 | 1 | 1 | 0 | 6.00 | 18.00 | 3.00 |
| Warren Hacker | R | 0 | 0 | — | 13.50 | 0 | 2 | 0 | 0 | 1.1 | 3 | 0 | 2 | 2 | 2 | 0 | 20.25 | 0.00 | 13.50 |
| TEAM TOTAL | | 62 | 92 | .403 | 4.34 | 10 | 340 | 155 | 48 | 1385.2 | 1374 | 572 | 544 | 750 | 668 | 10 | 8.92 | 3.72 | 3.53 |

| MANAGER | W | L | PCT |
|---|---|---|---|
| Phil Cavarretta | 77 | 77 | .500 |

| POS | Player | B | G | AB | H | 2B | 3B | HR | HR % | R | RBI | BB | SO | SB | Pinch Hit AB | Pinch Hit H | BA | SA |
|---|---|---|---|---|---|---|---|---|---|---|---|---|---|---|---|---|---|---|
| **REGULARS** | | | | | | | | | | | | | | | | | | |
| 1B | Dee Fondy | L | 145 | 554 | 166 | 21 | 9 | 10 | 1.8 | 69 | 67 | 28 | 60 | 13 | 2 | 0 | .300 | .424 |
| 2B | Eddie Miksis | R | 93 | 383 | 89 | 20 | 1 | 2 | 0.5 | 44 | 19 | 20 | 32 | 4 | 1 | 0 | .232 | .305 |
| SS | Roy Smalley | R | 87 | 261 | 58 | 14 | 1 | 5 | 1.9 | 36 | 30 | 29 | 58 | 0 | 5 | 1 | .222 | .341 |
| 3B | Randy Jackson | R | 116 | 379 | 88 | 8 | 5 | 9 | 2.4 | 44 | 34 | 27 | 42 | 6 | 10 | 2 | .232 | .351 |
| RF | Frankie Baumholtz | L | 103 | 409 | 133 | 17 | 4 | 4 | 1.0 | 59 | 35 | 27 | 27 | 5 | 2 | 0 | .325 | .416 |
| CF | Hal Jeffcoat | R | 102 | 297 | 65 | 17 | 2 | 4 | 1.3 | 29 | 30 | 15 | 40 | 7 | 1 | 0 | .219 | .330 |
| LF | Hank Sauer | R | 151 | 567 | 153 | 31 | 3 | 37 | 6.5 | 89 | 121 | 77 | 92 | 1 | 0 | 0 | .270 | .531 |
| C | Toby Atwell | L | 107 | 362 | 105 | 16 | 3 | 2 | 0.6 | 36 | 31 | 40 | 22 | 2 | 5 | 0 | .290 | .367 |
| **SUBSTITUTES** | | | | | | | | | | | | | | | | | | |
| 32 | Bill Serena | R | 122 | 390 | 107 | 21 | 5 | 15 | 3.8 | 49 | 61 | 39 | 83 | 1 | 14 | 4 | .274 | .469 |
| S2 | Tommy Brown | R | 61 | 200 | 64 | 11 | 0 | 3 | 1.5 | 24 | 24 | 12 | 24 | 1 | 5 | 1 | .320 | .420 |
| 2B | Bob Ramazzotti | R | 50 | 183 | 52 | 5 | 3 | 1 | 0.5 | 26 | 12 | 14 | 14 | 3 | 0 | 0 | .284 | .361 |
| 1B | Phil Cavarretta | L | 41 | 63 | 15 | 1 | 1 | 1 | 1.6 | 7 | 8 | 9 | 3 | 0 | 26 | 5 | .238 | .333 |
| SS | Leon Brinkopf | R | 9 | 22 | 4 | 0 | 0 | 0 | 0.0 | 1 | 2 | 4 | 5 | 0 | 2 | 1 | .182 | .182 |
| S2 | Bud Hardin | R | 3 | 7 | 1 | 0 | 0 | 0 | 0.0 | 1 | 0 | 0 | 0 | 0 | 1 | 0 | .143 | .143 |
| OF | Bob Addis | L | 93 | 292 | 86 | 13 | 2 | 1 | 0.3 | 38 | 20 | 23 | 30 | 4 | 15 | 4 | .295 | .363 |
| OF | Gene Hermanski | L | 99 | 275 | 70 | 6 | 0 | 4 | 1.5 | 28 | 34 | 29 | 32 | 2 | 21 | 10 | .255 | .320 |
| C | Harry Chiti | R | 32 | 113 | 31 | 5 | 0 | 5 | 4.4 | 14 | 13 | 5 | 8 | 0 | 0 | 0 | .274 | .451 |
| C | Bruce Edwards | R | 50 | 94 | 23 | 2 | 2 | 1 | 1.1 | 7 | 12 | 8 | 12 | 0 | 24 | 7 | .245 | .340 |
| C | Johnny Pramesa | R | 22 | 46 | 13 | 1 | 0 | 1 | 2.2 | 1 | 5 | 4 | 4 | 0 | 5 | 2 | .283 | .370 |
| PH | Ron Northey | L | 1 | 1 | 0 | 0 | 0 | 0 | 0.0 | 0 | 0 | 0 | 0 | 0 | 1 | 0 | .000 | .000 |
| PH | Bob Usher | R | 1 | 0 | 0 | 0 | 0 | 0 | – | 0 | 0 | 1 | 0 | 0 | 0 | 0 | – | – |
| **PITCHERS** | | | | | | | | | | | | | | | | | | |
| P | Bob Rush | R | 34 | 96 | 28 | 5 | 1 | 0 | 0.0 | 5 | 15 | 1 | 35 | 0 | 0 | 0 | .292 | .365 |
| P | Paul Minner | L | 29 | 64 | 15 | 5 | 1 | 1 | 1.6 | 8 | 5 | 5 | 19 | 0 | 0 | 0 | .234 | .391 |
| P | Johnny Klippstein | R | 41 | 63 | 11 | 1 | 1 | 1 | 1.6 | 3 | 9 | 1 | 24 | 0 | 0 | 0 | .175 | .270 |
| P | Warren Hacker | R | 34 | 58 | 7 | 0 | 0 | 0 | 0.0 | 1 | 4 | 1 | 11 | 1 | 0 | 0 | .121 | .121 |
| P | Turk Lown | R | 33 | 50 | 7 | 1 | 1 | 0 | 0.0 | 3 | 2 | 2 | 11 | 0 | 0 | 0 | .140 | .200 |
| P | Bob Kelly | R | 31 | 37 | 8 | 0 | 0 | 0 | 0.0 | 2 | 1 | 0 | 7 | 0 | 0 | 0 | .216 | .216 |
| P | Willie Ramsdell | R | 19 | 18 | 1 | 1 | 0 | 0 | 0.0 | 0 | 0 | 1 | 7 | 0 | 0 | 0 | .056 | .111 |
| P | Bob Schultz | R | 29 | 18 | 4 | 1 | 0 | 0 | 0.0 | 2 | 1 | 0 | 3 | 0 | 0 | 0 | .222 | .278 |
| P | Joe Hatten | R | 17 | 15 | 1 | 0 | 0 | 0 | 0.0 | 2 | 0 | 0 | 5 | 0 | 0 | 0 | .067 | .067 |
| P | Dutch Leonard | R | 45 | 10 | 2 | 0 | 0 | 0 | 0.0 | 0 | 0 | 0 | 1 | 0 | 0 | 0 | .200 | .200 |
| P | Dick Manville | R | 11 | 2 | 1 | 0 | 0 | 0 | 0.0 | 0 | 0 | 0 | 1 | 0 | 0 | 0 | .500 | .500 |
| P | Vern Fear | B | 4 | 1 | 0 | 0 | 0 | 0 | 0.0 | 0 | 0 | 0 | 0 | 0 | 0 | 0 | .000 | .000 |
| P | Monk Dubiel | R | 1 | 0 | 0 | 0 | 0 | 0 | – | 0 | 0 | 0 | 0 | 0 | 0 | 0 | – | – |
| P | Cal Howe | L | 1 | 0 | 0 | 0 | 0 | 0 | – | 0 | 0 | 0 | 0 | 0 | 0 | 0 | – | – |
| TEAM TOTAL | | | | 5330 | 1408 | 223 | 45 | 107 | 2.0 | 62 | 595 | 422 | 712 | 50 | 140 | 37 | .264 | .383 |

## INDIVIDUAL FIELDING

| POS | Player | T | G | PO | A | E | DP | TC/G | FA | POS | Player | T | G | PO | A | E | DP | TC/G | FA |
|---|---|---|---|---|---|---|---|---|---|---|---|---|---|---|---|---|---|---|---|
| 1B | D. Fondy | L | 143 | 1257 | 103 | 14 | 92 | 9.6 | .990 | OF | H. Sauer | R | 151 | 327 | 17 | 6 | 3 | 2.3 | .983 |
| | Cavarretta | L | 13 | 98 | 10 | 1 | 13 | 8.4 | .991 | | F. Baumholtz | L | 101 | 248 | 10 | 7 | 3 | 2.6 | .974 |
| | T. Brown | R | 5 | 37 | 1 | 1 | 3 | 7.8 | .974 | | H. Jeffcoat | R | 95 | 218 | 16 | 1 | 2 | 2.5 | .996 |
| 2B | E. Miksis | R | 54 | 126 | 140 | 14 | 22 | 5.2 | .950 | | B. Addis | R | 76 | 160 | 8 | 2 | 2 | 2.2 | .988 |
| | B. Serena | R | 49 | 128 | 134 | 3 | 25 | 5.4 | .989 | | G. Hermanski | R | 76 | 146 | 7 | 3 | 3 | 2.1 | .981 |
| | Ramazzotti | R | 50 | 90 | 143 | 5 | 28 | 4.8 | .979 | | R. Jackson | R | 1 | 2 | 0 | 0 | 0 | 2.0 | 1.000 |
| | B. Edwards | R | 1 | 0 | 0 | 0 | 0 | 0.0 | .000 | | | | | | | | | | |
| | T. Brown | R | 10 | 27 | 23 | 2 | 4 | 5.2 | .962 | C | T. Atwell | R | 101 | 451 | 50 | 12 | 6 | 5.1 | .977 |
| | B. Hardin | R | 1 | 4 | 1 | 0 | 0 | 5.0 | 1.000 | | H. Chiti | R | 32 | 170 | 13 | 3 | 6 | 5.8 | .984 |
| SS | R. Smalley | R | 82 | 139 | 200 | 17 | 33 | 4.3 | .952 | | B. Edwards | R | 22 | 82 | 8 | 1 | 2 | 4.1 | .989 |
| | E. Miksis | R | 40 | 81 | 114 | 4 | 21 | 5.0 | .980 | | J. Pramesa | R | 17 | 62 | 6 | 3 | 3 | 4.2 | .958 |
| | T. Brown | R | 39 | 58 | 85 | 14 | 17 | 4.0 | .911 | | | | | | | | | | |
| | L. Brinkopf | R | 6 | 4 | 17 | 1 | 1 | 3.7 | .955 | | | | | | | | | | |
| | B. Hardin | R | 2 | 2 | 3 | 0 | 1 | 2.5 | 1.000 | | | | | | | | | | |
| 3B | R. Jackson | R | 104 | 91 | 203 | 13 | 13 | 3.0 | .958 | | | | | | | | | | |
| | B. Serena | R | 58 | 70 | 100 | 5 | 5 | 3.0 | .971 | | | | | | | | | | |

Left field resembled Tobacco Road following the many Hank Sauer clouts at Wrigley Field. Bleacher fans would toss packets of tobacco after Hank hammered a homer. It was quite a year for Sauer, who led the league with 121 runs batted in and tied the Pirates' Ralph Kiner for homer leadership at 37. Sauer and his 40-ounce wagon tongue he called a bat carried the Cubs on his broad back throughout the season. The result was a surprise fifth-place finish after most experts relegated Phil Cavarretta's club to the cellar. The Cubs held third place with a 38–30 record, but a nine-game losing streak in mid-June dropped them back. With Sauer supplying the punch, the Cubs rallied for a respectable 77–77 record. Hank's reward was being named Most Valuable Player of the Year. In addition, he was the batting hero of the rain-shortened All-Star Game. With the NL trailing, 2–1, in the fourth inning, Sauer hit a two-run homer off Bob Lemon for a 3–2 triumph.

The Cubs were far from a one-man gang. Outfield teammate Frankie Baumholtz batted .325, second only to the Cardinals' Stan Musial. The pitching parade was led by Bob Rush, who rose to 17–13 and was credited with the All-Star Game victory. The most pleasant surprise was Warren Hacker, who didn't draw his first start until June 7. Hacker was 15–9 record and had a 2.58 ERA. And he walked only 31 batters in 185 innings.

## TEAM STATISTICS

| | W | L | PCT | GB | R | OR | 2B | 3B | HR | BA | SA | SB | E | DP | FA | CG | B | SO | ShO | SV | ERA |
|---|---|---|---|---|---|---|---|---|---|---|---|---|---|---|---|---|---|---|---|---|---|
| | | | | | | | | Batting | | | | | | Fielding | | | | Pitching | | | |
| BKN | 96 | 57 | .627 | | 775 | 603 | 199 | 32 | 153 | .262 | .399 | 90 | 106 | 169 | .982 | 45 | 544 | 773 | 11 | 24 | 3.53 |
| NY | 92 | 62 | .597 | 4.5 | 722 | 639 | 186 | 56 | 151 | .256 | .399 | 30 | 158 | 175 | .974 | 49 | 538 | 655 | 11 | 31 | 3.59 |
| STL | 88 | 66 | .571 | 8.5 | 677 | 630 | 247 | 54 | 97 | .267 | .391 | 33 | 141 | 159 | .977 | 49 | 501 | 712 | 11 | 27 | 3.66 |
| PHI | 87 | 67 | .565 | 9.5 | 657 | 552 | 237 | 45 | 93 | .260 | .376 | 60 | 150 | 145 | .975 | 80 | 373 | 609 | 16 | 16 | 3.07 |
| CHI | 77 | 77 | .500 | 19.5 | 628 | 631 | 223 | 45 | 107 | .264 | .383 | 50 | 146 | 123 | .976 | 59 | 534 | 661 | 15 | 15 | 3.58 |
| CIN | 69 | 85 | .448 | 27.5 | 615 | 659 | 212 | 45 | 104 | .249 | .366 | 32 | 107 | 145 | .982 | 56 | 517 | 579 | 11 | 12 | 4.01 |
| BOS | 64 | 89 | .418 | 32 | 569 | 651 | 187 | 31 | 110 | .233 | .343 | 58 | 154 | 143 | .975 | 63 | 525 | 687 | 11 | 13 | 3.78 |
| PIT | 42 | 112 | .273 | 54.5 | 515 | 793 | 181 | 30 | 92 | .231 | .331 | 43 | 182 | 167 | .970 | 43 | 615 | 564 | 4 | 8 | 4.65 |
| LEAGUE TOTAL | | | | | 5158 | 5158 | 1672 | 338 | 907 | .253 | .374 | 396 | 1144 | 1226 | .976 | 444 | 4147 | 5240 | 90 | 146 | 3.73 |

## INDIVIDUAL PITCHING

| PITCHER | T | W | L | PCT | ERA | SV | G | GS | CG | IP | H | BB | SO | R | ER | ShO | H/9 | BB/9 | SO/9 |
|---|---|---|---|---|---|---|---|---|---|---|---|---|---|---|---|---|---|---|---|
| Bob Rush | R | 17 | 13 | .567 | 2.70 | 0 | 34 | 32 | 17 | 250.1 | 205 | 81 | 157 | 99 | 75 | 4 | 7.37 | 2.91 | 5.64 |
| Johnny Klippstein | R | 9 | 14 | .391 | 4.44 | 3 | 41 | 25 | 7 | 202.2 | 208 | 89 | 110 | 110 | 100 | 2 | 9.24 | 3.95 | 4.88 |
| Warren Hacker | R | 15 | 9 | .625 | 2.58 | 1 | 33 | 20 | 12 | 185 | 144 | 31 | 84 | 56 | 53 | 5 | 7.01 | 1.51 | 4.09 |
| Paul Minner | L | 14 | 9 | .609 | 3.74 | 0 | 28 | 27 | 12 | 180.2 | 180 | 54 | 61 | 84 | 75 | 2 | 8.97 | 2.69 | 3.04 |
| Turk Lown | R | 4 | 11 | .267 | 4.37 | 0 | 33 | 19 | 5 | 156.2 | 154 | 93 | 73 | 87 | 76 | 0 | 8.85 | 5.34 | 4.19 |
| Bob Kelly | R | 4 | 9 | .308 | 3.59 | 0 | 31 | 15 | 3 | 125.1 | 114 | 46 | 50 | 62 | 50 | 2 | 8.19 | 3.30 | 3.59 |
| Bob Schultz | L | 6 | 3 | .667 | 4.01 | 0 | 29 | 5 | 1 | 74 | 63 | 51 | 31 | 34 | 33 | 0 | 7.66 | 6.20 | 3.77 |
| Willie Ramsdell | R | 2 | 3 | .400 | 2.42 | 0 | 19 | 4 | 0 | 67 | 41 | 24 | 30 | 22 | 18 | 0 | 5.51 | 3.22 | 4.03 |
| Dutch Leonard | R | 2 | 2 | .500 | 2.16 | 11 | 45 | 0 | 0 | 66.2 | 56 | 24 | 37 | 18 | 16 | 0 | 7.56 | 3.24 | 5.00 |
| Joe Hatten | L | 4 | 4 | .500 | 6.08 | 0 | 13 | 8 | 2 | 50.1 | 65 | 25 | 15 | 35 | 34 | 0 | 11.62 | 4.47 | 2.68 |
| Dick Manville | R | 0 | 0 | — | 7.94 | 0 | 11 | 0 | 0 | 17 | 25 | 12 | 6 | 17 | 15 | 0 | 13.24 | 6.35 | 3.18 |
| Vern Fear | R | 0 | 0 | — | 7.88 | 0 | 4 | 0 | 0 | 8 | 9 | 3 | 4 | 7 | 7 | 0 | 10.13 | 3.38 | 4.50 |
| Cal Howe | L | 0 | 0 | — | 0.00 | 0 | 1 | 0 | 0 | 2 | 0 | 1 | 2 | 0 | 0 | 0 | 0.00 | 4.50 | 9.00 |
| Monk Dubiel | R | 0 | 0 | — | 0.00 | 0 | 1 | 0 | 0 | .2 | 1 | 0 | 1 | 0 | 0 | 0 | 13.50 | 0.00 | 13.50 |
| TEAM TOTAL | | 77 | 77 | .500 | 3.58 | 15 | 323 | 155 | 59 | 1386.1 | 1265 | 534 | 661 | 631 | 552 | 15 | 8.21 | 3.47 | 4.29 |

| MANAGER | W | L | PCT |
|---|---|---|---|
| Phil Cavarretta | 65 | 89 | .422 |

| POS | Player | B | G | AB | H | 2B | 3B | HR | HR % | R | RBI | BB | SO | SB | Pinch Hit AB | Pinch Hit H | BA | SA |
|---|---|---|---|---|---|---|---|---|---|---|---|---|---|---|---|---|---|---|
| **REGULARS** | | | | | | | | | | | | | | | | | | |
| 1B | Dee Fondy | L | 150 | 595 | 184 | 24 | 11 | 18 | 3.0 | 79 | 78 | 44 | 106 | 10 | 1 | 0 | .309 | .477 |
| 2B | Eddie Miksis | R | 142 | 577 | 145 | 17 | 6 | 8 | 1.4 | 61 | 39 | 33 | 59 | 13 | 0 | 0 | .251 | .343 |
| SS | Roy Smalley | R | 82 | 253 | 63 | 9 | 0 | 6 | 2.4 | 20 | 25 | 28 | 57 | 0 | 5 | 1 | .249 | .356 |
| 3B | Randy Jackson | R | 139 | 498 | 142 | 22 | 8 | 19 | 3.8 | 61 | 66 | 42 | 61 | 8 | 7 | 0 | .285 | .476 |
| RF | Hank Sauer | R | 108 | 395 | 104 | 16 | 5 | 19 | 4.8 | 61 | 60 | 50 | 56 | 0 | 5 | 1 | .263 | .473 |
| CF | Frankie Baumholtz | L | 133 | 520 | 159 | 36 | 7 | 3 | 0.6 | 75 | 25 | 42 | 36 | 3 | 3 | 0 | .306 | .419 |
| LF | Ralph Kiner | R | 117 | 414 | 117 | 14 | 2 | 28 | 6.8 | 73 | 87 | 75 | 67 | 1 | 1 | 0 | .283 | .529 |
| C | Clyde McCullough | R | 77 | 229 | 59 | 3 | 2 | 6 | 2.6 | 21 | 23 | 15 | 23 | 0 | 4 | 1 | .258 | .367 |
| **SUBSTITUTES** | | | | | | | | | | | | | | | | | | |
| 23 | Bill Serena | R | 93 | 275 | 69 | 10 | 5 | 10 | 3.6 | 30 | 52 | 41 | 46 | 0 | 13 | 4 | .251 | .433 |
| SS | Tommy Brown | R | 65 | 138 | 27 | 7 | 1 | 2 | 1.4 | 19 | 13 | 13 | 17 | 1 | 30 | 5 | .196 | .304 |
| 2B | Bob Ramazzotti | R | 26 | 39 | 6 | 2 | 0 | 0 | 0.0 | 3 | 4 | 3 | 4 | 0 | 3 | 0 | .154 | .205 |
| SS | Ernie Banks | R | 10 | 35 | 11 | 1 | 1 | 2 | 5.7 | 3 | 6 | 4 | 5 | 0 | 0 | 0 | .314 | .571 |
| 2B | Gene Baker | R | 7 | 22 | 5 | 1 | 0 | 0 | 0.0 | 1 | 0 | 1 | 4 | 1 | 1 | 0 | .227 | .273 |
| OF | Hal Jeffcoat | R | 106 | 183 | 43 | 3 | 1 | 4 | 2.2 | 22 | 22 | 21 | 26 | 5 | 2 | 0 | .235 | .328 |
| OF | Catfish Metkovich | L | 61 | 124 | 29 | 9 | 0 | 2 | 1.6 | 19 | 12 | 16 | 10 | 2 | 18 | 5 | .234 | .355 |
| O1 | Preston Ward | L | 33 | 100 | 23 | 5 | 0 | 4 | 4.0 | 10 | 12 | 18 | 21 | 3 | 3 | 1 | .230 | .400 |
| OF | Gene Hermanski | L | 18 | 40 | 6 | 1 | 0 | 0 | 0.0 | 1 | 1 | 4 | 7 | 1 | 5 | 0 | .150 | .175 |
| OF | Dale Talbot | R | 8 | 30 | 10 | 0 | 1 | 0 | 0.0 | 5 | 0 | 0 | 4 | 1 | 0 | 0 | .333 | .400 |
| OF | Bob Addis | L | 10 | 12 | 2 | 1 | 0 | 0 | 0.0 | 2 | 1 | 2 | 0 | 0 | 5 | 1 | .167 | .250 |
| OF | Paul Schramka | L | 2 | 0 | 0 | 0 | 0 | 0 | — | 0 | 0 | 0 | 0 | 0 | 0 | 0 | — | — |
| C | Joe Garagiola | L | 74 | 228 | 62 | 9 | 4 | 1 | 0.4 | 21 | 21 | 21 | 23 | 0 | 7 | 2 | .272 | .360 |
| C | Toby Atwell | L | 24 | 74 | 17 | 2 | 0 | 1 | 1.4 | 10 | 8 | 13 | 7 | 0 | 1 | 0 | .230 | .297 |
| C | Carl Sawatski | L | 43 | 59 | 13 | 3 | 0 | 1 | 1.7 | 5 | 5 | 7 | 7 | 0 | 29 | 6 | .220 | .322 |
| PH | Phil Cavarretta | L | 27 | 21 | 6 | 3 | 0 | 0 | 0.0 | 3 | 3 | 6 | 3 | 0 | 21 | 6 | .286 | .429 |
| **PITCHERS** | | | | | | | | | | | | | | | | | | |
| P | Warren Hacker | R | 42 | 78 | 17 | 1 | 1 | 0 | 0.0 | 8 | 4 | 1 | 8 | 0 | 0 | 0 | .218 | .256 |
| P | Paul Minner | L | 31 | 68 | 15 | 1 | 1 | 1 | 1.5 | 5 | 6 | 3 | 16 | 0 | 0 | 0 | .221 | .309 |
| P | Johnny Klippstein | R | 48 | 58 | 9 | 2 | 0 | 1 | 1.7 | 5 | 4 | 1 | 20 | 0 | 0 | 0 | .155 | .241 |
| P | Bob Rush | R | 29 | 54 | 6 | 0 | 1 | 0 | 0.0 | 2 | 5 | 3 | 23 | 0 | 0 | 0 | .111 | .148 |
| P | Turk Lown | R | 49 | 48 | 6 | 1 | 0 | 0 | 0.0 | 3 | 2 | 2 | 8 | 0 | 0 | 0 | .125 | .146 |
| P | Bubba Church | R | 27 | 33 | 7 | 0 | 0 | 1 | 3.0 | 1 | 1 | 1 | 6 | 0 | 0 | 0 | .212 | .303 |
| P | Howie Pollet | L | 25 | 31 | 4 | 0 | 0 | 0 | 0.0 | 2 | 0 | 3 | 6 | 0 | 0 | 0 | .129 | .129 |
| P | Dutch Leonard | R | 45 | 10 | 3 | 1 | 0 | 0 | 0.0 | 0 | 2 | 0 | 1 | 0 | 0 | 0 | .300 | .400 |
| P | Jim Willis | L | 13 | 9 | 0 | 0 | 0 | 0 | 0.0 | 1 | 1 | 1 | 3 | 0 | 0 | 0 | .000 | .000 |
| P | Duke Simpson | R | 30 | 8 | 2 | 0 | 0 | 0 | 0.0 | 1 | 0 | 0 | 1 | 0 | 0 | 0 | .250 | .250 |
| P | Sheldon Jones | R | 22 | 7 | 0 | 0 | 0 | 0 | 0.0 | 0 | 0 | 0 | 2 | 0 | 0 | 0 | .000 | .000 |
| P | Bob Schultz | R | 7 | 3 | 0 | 0 | 0 | 0 | 0.0 | 0 | 0 | 0 | 1 | 0 | 0 | 0 | .000 | .000 |
| P | Fred Baczewski | L | 9 | 2 | 1 | 0 | 0 | 0 | 0.0 | 0 | 0 | 0 | 1 | 0 | 0 | 0 | .500 | .500 |
| P | Don Elston | R | 2 | 1 | 0 | 0 | 0 | 0 | — | 0 | 0 | 0 | 0 | 0 | 0 | 0 | .000 | .000 |
| P | Bob Kelly | R | 14 | 1 | 0 | 0 | 0 | 0 | 0.0 | 0 | 0 | 0 | 1 | 0 | 0 | 0 | .000 | .000 |
| P | Bill Moisan | L | 3 | 0 | 0 | 0 | 0 | 0 | — | 0 | 0 | 0 | 0 | 0 | 0 | 0 | — | — |
| | TEAM TOTAL | | | 5272 | 1372 | 204 | 57 | 137 | 2.6 | 63 | 588 | 514 | 746 | 49 | 164 | 33 | .260 | .399 |

### INDIVIDUAL FIELDING

| POS | Player | T | G | PO | A | E | DP | TC/G | FA |
|---|---|---|---|---|---|---|---|---|---|
| 1B | D. Fondy | L | 149 | 1274 | 115 | 18 | 105 | 9.4 | .987 |
| | P. Ward | R | 7 | 49 | 1 | 0 | 9 | 7.1 | 1.000 |
| | C. Metkovich | L | 7 | 37 | 1 | 2 | 2 | 5.7 | .950 |
| 2B | E. Miksis | R | 92 | 210 | 262 | 23 | 65 | 5.4 | .954 |
| | B. Serena | R | 49 | 106 | 120 | 4 | 24 | 4.7 | .983 |
| | Ramazzotti | R | 18 | 28 | 23 | 5 | 6 | 3.1 | .911 |
| | G. Baker | R | 6 | 11 | 11 | 2 | 3 | 4.0 | .917 |
| SS | R. Smalley | R | 77 | 153 | 191 | 25 | 39 | 4.8 | .932 |
| | E. Miksis | R | 53 | 105 | 144 | 12 | 31 | 4.9 | .954 |
| | T. Brown | R | 25 | 44 | 68 | 12 | 13 | 5.0 | .903 |
| | E. Banks | R | 10 | 19 | 33 | 1 | 9 | 5.3 | .981 |
| 3B | R. Jackson | R | 133 | 141 | 265 | 22 | 24 | 3.2 | .949 |
| | B. Serena | R | 28 | 29 | 40 | 3 | 7 | 2.6 | .958 |

| POS | Player | T | G | PO | A | E | DP | TC/G | FA |
|---|---|---|---|---|---|---|---|---|---|
| OF | F. Baumholtz | L | 130 | 290 | 6 | 6 | 0 | 2.3 | .980 |
| | H. Sauer | R | 105 | 221 | 5 | 7 | 1 | 2.2 | .970 |
| | R. Kiner | R | 116 | 211 | 6 | 8 | 2 | 1.9 | .964 |
| | H. Jeffcoat | R | 100 | 175 | 6 | 5 | 0 | 1.9 | .973 |
| | C. Metkovich | L | 38 | 67 | 1 | 0 | 0 | 1.8 | 1.000 |
| | P. Ward | R | 27 | 49 | 0 | 2 | 0 | 1.9 | .961 |
| | P. Schramka | L | 1 | 0 | 0 | 0 | 0 | 0.0 | .000 |
| | D. Talbot | R | 7 | 20 | 3 | 0 | 1 | 3.3 | 1.000 |
| | G. Hermanski | R | 13 | 18 | 0 | 0 | 0 | 1.4 | 1.000 |
| | B. Addis | R | 3 | 7 | 1 | 0 | 1 | 2.7 | 1.000 |
| | T. Brown | R | 6 | 4 | 2 | 1 | 0 | 1.2 | .857 |
| C | J. Garagiola | R | 68 | 296 | 34 | 4 | 2 | 4.9 | .988 |
| | McCullough | R | 73 | 273 | 31 | 4 | 7 | 4.2 | .987 |
| | T. Atwell | R | 24 | 108 | 17 | 8* | 0 | 5.5 | .940 |
| | C. Sawatski | R | 15 | 45 | 5 | 3 | 0 | 3.5 | .943 |

The Cubs finally recruited black talent, coming up with a double-play combination of shortstop Ernie Banks and second baseman Gene Baker. Both reported to the team in September. Baker, 28, was a seasoned veteran in the minor leagues, while Banks, 22, was purchased from the Kansas City Monarchs for $10,000, perhaps the biggest bargain in Cub history. Banks, destined to become Mr. Cub, hit .314 with 2 homers and 6 RBI as the Cubs won 10 in a row.

But he couldn't prevent them from finishing seventh. A nightmarish start in which the team won only 14 of its first 50 games was too much to overcome. Phil Cavarretta's team lost 12 of 14 games in one stretch and dropped 15 of 18 in another. Injuries to Hank Sauer contributed to their poor showing. Sauer fractured a finger during spring training, fractured another digit in June, and suffered a third finger fracture in July as his homer production dropped to 19. Slugger Ralph Kiner was acquired from the Pirates in a 10-player swap on June 4. Kiner led the teams in homers with 28 after hitting 7 for Pittsburgh. Luckily for the Cubs, the Pirates won only 50 and finished 15 games behind Chicago.

### TEAM STATISTICS

| | W | L | PCT | GB | R | OR | 2B | 3B | Batting HR | BA | SA | SB | Fielding E | DP | FA | CG | B | Pitching SO | ShO | SV | ERA |
|---|---|---|---|---|---|---|---|---|---|---|---|---|---|---|---|---|---|---|---|---|---|
| BKN | 105 | 49 | .682 | | 955 | 689 | 274 | 59 | 208 | .285 | .474 | 90 | 118 | 161 | .980 | 51 | 509 | 819 | 11 | 29 | 4.10 |
| MIL | 92 | 62 | .597 | 13 | 738 | 589 | 227 | 52 | 156 | .266 | .415 | 46 | 143 | 169 | .976 | 72 | 539 | 738 | 14 | 15 | 3.30 |
| PHI | 83 | 71 | .539 | 22 | 716 | 666 | 228 | 62 | 115 | .265 | .396 | 42 | 147 | 161 | .975 | 76 | 410 | 637 | 13 | 15 | 3.80 |
| STL | 83 | 71 | .539 | 22 | 768 | 713 | 281 | 56 | 140 | .273 | .424 | 18 | 138 | 161 | .977 | 51 | 533 | 732 | 11 | 36 | 4.23 |
| NY | 70 | 84 | .455 | 35 | 768 | 747 | 195 | 45 | 176 | .271 | .422 | 31 | 151 | 151 | .975 | 46 | 610 | 647 | 10 | 20 | 4.25 |
| CIN | 68 | 86 | .442 | 37 | 714 | 788 | 190 | 34 | 166 | .261 | .403 | 25 | 129 | 176 | .978 | 47 | 488 | 506 | 7 | 15 | 4.64 |
| CHI | 65 | 89 | .422 | 40 | 633 | 835 | 204 | 57 | 137 | .260 | .399 | 49 | 193 | 141 | .967 | 38 | 554 | 623 | 3 | 22 | 4.79 |
| PIT | 50 | 104 | .325 | 55 | 622 | 887 | 178 | 49 | 99 | .247 | .356 | 41 | 163 | 139 | .973 | 49 | 577 | 607 | 4 | 10 | 5.22 |
| LEAGUE TOTAL | | | | | 5914 | 5914 | 1777 | 414 | 1197 | .266 | .411 | 342 | 1182 | 1259 | .975 | 430 | 4220 | 5309 | 73 | 162 | 4.29 |

### INDIVIDUAL PITCHING

| PITCHER | T | W | L | PCT | ERA | SV | G | GS | CG | IP | H | BB | SO | R | ER | ShO | H/9 | BB/9 | SO/9 |
|---|---|---|---|---|---|---|---|---|---|---|---|---|---|---|---|---|---|---|---|
| Warren Hacker | R | 12 | 19 | .387 | 4.38 | 2 | 39 | 32 | 9 | 221.2 | 225 | 54 | 106 | 123 | 108 | 0 | 9.14 | 2.19 | 4.30 |
| Paul Minner | L | 12 | 15 | .444 | 4.21 | 1 | 31 | 27 | 9 | 201 | 227 | 40 | 64 | 109 | 94 | 2 | 10.16 | 1.79 | 2.87 |
| Johnny Klippstein | R | 10 | 11 | .476 | 4.83 | 6 | 48 | 20 | 5 | 167.2 | 169 | 107 | 113 | 115 | 90 | 0 | 9.07 | 5.74 | 6.07 |
| Bob Rush | R | 9 | 14 | .391 | 4.54 | 0 | 29 | 28 | 8 | 166.2 | 177 | 66 | 84 | 97 | 84 | 1 | 9.56 | 3.56 | 4.54 |
| Turk Lown | R | 8 | 7 | .533 | 5.16 | 3 | 49 | 12 | 2 | 148.1 | 166 | 84 | 76 | 93 | 85 | 0 | 10.07 | 5.10 | 4.61 |
| Howie Pollet | L | 5 | 6 | .455 | 4.12 | 1 | 25 | 16 | 2 | 111.1 | 120 | 44 | 45 | 62 | 51 | 0 | 9.70 | 3.56 | 3.64 |
| Bubba Church | R | 4 | 5 | .444 | 5.00 | 1 | 27 | 11 | 1 | 104.1 | 115 | 49 | 47 | 67 | 58 | 0 | 9.92 | 4.23 | 4.05 |
| Dutch Leonard | R | 2 | 3 | .400 | 4.60 | 8 | 45 | 0 | 0 | 62.2 | 72 | 24 | 27 | 34 | 32 | 0 | 10.34 | 3.45 | 3.88 |
| Duke Simpson | R | 2 | 2 | .333 | 8.00 | 0 | 30 | 1 | 0 | 45 | 60 | 25 | 21 | 47 | 40 | 0 | 12.00 | 5.00 | 4.20 |
| Jim Willis | R | 2 | 1 | .667 | 3.12 | 0 | 13 | 3 | 2 | 43.1 | 37 | 17 | 15 | 15 | 15 | 0 | 7.68 | 3.53 | 3.12 |
| Sheldon Jones | R | 0 | 2 | .000 | 5.40 | 0 | 22 | 2 | 0 | 38.1 | 47 | 16 | 9 | 24 | 23 | 0 | 11.03 | 3.76 | 2.11 |
| Bob Kelly | R | 0 | 1 | .000 | 9.53 | 0 | 14 | 0 | 0 | 17 | 27 | 9 | 6 | 19 | 18 | 0 | 14.29 | 4.76 | 3.18 |
| Bob Schultz | L | 0 | 2 | .000 | 5.40 | 0 | 7 | 2 | 0 | 11.2 | 13 | 11 | 4 | 10 | 7 | 0 | 10.03 | 8.49 | 3.09 |
| Fred Baczewski | L | 0 | 0 | — | 6.30 | 0 | 9 | 0 | 0 | 10 | 20 | 6 | 3 | 9 | 7 | 0 | 18.00 | 5.40 | 2.70 |
| Don Elston | R | 0 | 1 | .000 | 14.40 | 0 | 2 | 1 | 0 | 5 | 11 | 0 | 2 | 8 | 8 | 0 | 19.80 | 0.00 | 3.60 |
| Bill Moisan | R | 0 | 0 | — | 5.40 | 0 | 3 | 0 | 0 | 5 | 5 | 2 | 1 | 3 | 3 | 0 | 9.00 | 3.60 | 1.80 |
| TEAM TOTAL | | 65 | 89 | .422 | 4.79 | 22 | 393 | 155 | 38 | 1359 | 1491 | 554 | 623 | 835 | 723 | 3 | 9.87 | 3.67 | 4.13 |

| MANAGER | W | L | PCT |
|---|---|---|---|
| Stan Hack | 64 | 90 | .416 |

| POS | Player | B | G | AB | H | 2B | 3B | HR | HR % | R | RBI | BB | SO | SB | Pinch Hit AB | Pinch Hit H | BA | SA |
|---|---|---|---|---|---|---|---|---|---|---|---|---|---|---|---|---|---|---|
| **REGULARS** | | | | | | | | | | | | | | | | | | |
| 1B | Dee Fondy | L | 141 | 568 | 162 | 30 | 4 | 9 | 1.6 | 77 | 49 | 35 | 84 | 20 | 2 | 1 | .285 | .400 |
| 2B | Gene Baker | R | 135 | 541 | 149 | 32 | 5 | 13 | 2.4 | 68 | 61 | 47 | 55 | 4 | 0 | 0 | .275 | .425 |
| SS | Ernie Banks | R | 154 | 593 | 163 | 19 | 7 | 19 | 3.2 | 70 | 79 | 40 | 50 | 6 | 0 | 0 | .275 | .427 |
| 3B | Randy Jackson | R | 126 | 484 | 132 | 17 | 6 | 19 | 3.9 | 77 | 67 | 44 | 55 | 2 | 2 | 0 | .273 | .450 |
| RF | Hank Sauer | R | 142 | 520 | 150 | 18 | 1 | 41 | 7.9 | 98 | 103 | 70 | 68 | 2 | 1 | 0 | .288 | .563 |
| CF | Dale Talbot | R | 114 | 403 | 97 | 15 | 4 | 1 | 0.2 | 45 | 19 | 16 | 25 | 3 | 1 | 0 | .241 | .305 |
| LF | Ralph Kiner | L | 147 | 557 | 159 | 36 | 5 | 22 | 3.9 | 88 | 73 | 76 | 90 | 2 | 0 | 0 | .285 | .487 |
| C | Joe Garagiola | L | 63 | 153 | 43 | 5 | 0 | 5 | 3.3 | 16 | 21 | 28 | 12 | 0 | 9 | 2 | .281 | .412 |
| **SUBSTITUTES** | | | | | | | | | | | | | | | | | | |
| 2B | Eddie Miksis | R | 38 | 99 | 20 | 3 | 0 | 2 | 2.0 | 9 | 3 | 3 | 9 | 1 | 10 | 0 | .202 | .293 |
| 1B | Steve Bilko | R | 47 | 92 | 22 | 8 | 1 | 4 | 4.3 | 11 | 12 | 11 | 24 | 0 | 23 | 6 | .239 | .478 |
| 3B | Vern Morgan | L | 24 | 64 | 15 | 2 | 0 | 0 | 0.0 | 3 | 2 | 1 | 10 | 0 | 7 | 1 | .234 | .266 |
| 3B | Bill Serena | R | 41 | 63 | 10 | 0 | 1 | 4 | 6.3 | 8 | 13 | 14 | 18 | 0 | 22 | 4 | .159 | .381 |
| SS | Chris Kitsos | B | 1 | 0 | 0 | 0 | 0 | 0 | — | 0 | 0 | 0 | 0 | 0 | 0 | 0 | — | — |
| OF | Frankie Baumholtz | L | 90 | 303 | 90 | 12 | 6 | 4 | 1.3 | 38 | 28 | 20 | 15 | 1 | 17 | 2 | .297 | .416 |
| OF | Hal Rice | R | 51 | 72 | 11 | 0 | 0 | 0 | 0.0 | 5 | 5 | 8 | 15 | 0 | 24 | 2 | .153 | .153 |
| OF | Luis Marquez | R | 17 | 12 | 1 | 0 | 0 | 0 | 0.0 | 2 | 0 | 2 | 4 | 3 | 0 | 0 | .083 | .083 |
| OF | Don Robertson | L | 14 | 6 | 0 | 0 | 0 | 0 | 0.0 | 2 | 0 | 0 | 2 | 0 | 4 | 0 | .000 | .000 |
| C | Walker Cooper | R | 57 | 158 | 49 | 10 | 2 | 7 | 4.4 | 21 | 32 | 21 | 23 | 0 | 11 | 2 | .310 | .532 |
| C | El Tappe | R | 46 | 119 | 22 | 3 | 0 | 0 | 0.0 | 5 | 4 | 10 | 9 | 0 | 0 | 0 | .185 | .210 |
| C | Clyde McCullough | R | 31 | 81 | 21 | 7 | 0 | 3 | 3.7 | 9 | 17 | 5 | 5 | 0 | 2 | 0 | .259 | .457 |
| C | Jim Fanning | R | 11 | 38 | 7 | 0 | 0 | 0 | 0.0 | 2 | 1 | 1 | 7 | 0 | 0 | 0 | .184 | .184 |
| PH | Bruce Edwards | R | 4 | 3 | 0 | 0 | 0 | 0 | 0.0 | 1 | 1 | 2 | 2 | 0 | 3 | 0 | .000 | .000 |
| **PITCHERS** | | | | | | | | | | | | | | | | | | |
| P | Bob Rush | R | 33 | 83 | 23 | 4 | 1 | 2 | 2.4 | 6 | 9 | 3 | 23 | 0 | 0 | 0 | .277 | .422 |
| P | Paul Minner | L | 33 | 76 | 13 | 3 | 0 | 2 | 2.6 | 7 | 14 | 8 | 19 | 0 | 1 | 0 | .171 | .289 |
| P | Warren Hacker | R | 43 | 55 | 13 | 0 | 1 | 0 | 0.0 | 4 | 6 | 1 | 8 | 0 | 0 | 0 | .236 | .273 |
| P | Howie Pollet | L | 20 | 47 | 13 | 2 | 0 | 0 | 0.0 | 6 | 4 | 1 | 6 | 0 | 0 | 0 | .277 | .319 |
| P | Johnny Klippstein | R | 36 | 45 | 6 | 1 | 0 | 0 | 0.0 | 2 | 3 | 0 | 14 | 0 | 0 | 0 | .133 | .156 |
| P | Jim Davis | B | 46 | 32 | 2 | 0 | 0 | 0 | 0.0 | 3 | 0 | 7 | 22 | 0 | 0 | 0 | .063 | .063 |
| P | Hal Jeffcoat | R | 56 | 31 | 8 | 2 | 1 | 1 | 3.2 | 13 | 6 | 1 | 7 | 2 | 0 | 0 | .258 | .484 |
| P | Dave Cole | R | 19 | 28 | 6 | 0 | 0 | 1 | 3.6 | 1 | 4 | 2 | 4 | 0 | 0 | 0 | .214 | .321 |
| P | Jim Brosnan | R | 18 | 8 | 1 | 0 | 0 | 0 | 0.0 | 1 | 2 | 0 | 1 | 0 | 0 | 0 | .125 | .125 |
| P | Bill Tremel | R | 33 | 8 | 2 | 0 | 0 | 0 | 0.0 | 0 | 2 | 1 | 2 | 0 | 0 | 0 | .250 | .250 |
| P | Bubba Church | R | 8 | 5 | 0 | 0 | 0 | 0 | 0.0 | 0 | 0 | 0 | 0 | 0 | 0 | 0 | .000 | .000 |
| P | Jim Willis | L | 14 | 5 | 0 | 0 | 0 | 0 | 0.0 | 0 | 0 | 0 | 3 | 0 | 0 | 0 | .000 | .000 |
| P | Bob Zick | L | 10 | 4 | 1 | 0 | 0 | 0 | 0.0 | 2 | 0 | 0 | 1 | 0 | 0 | 0 | .250 | .250 |
| P | Al Lary | R | 2 | 2 | 1 | 0 | 0 | 0 | 0.0 | 0 | 0 | 0 | 1 | 0 | 0 | 0 | .500 | .500 |
| P | John Pyecha | R | 1 | 1 | 0 | 0 | 0 | 0 | 0.0 | 0 | 0 | 0 | 0 | 0 | 0 | 0 | .000 | .000 |
| P | Turk Lown | R | 16 | 0 | 0 | 0 | 0 | 0 | — | 0 | 0 | 0 | 0 | 0 | 0 | 0 | — | — |
| TEAM TOTAL | | | | 5359 | 1412 | 229 | 45 | 159 | 3.0 | 70 | 640 | 478 | 693 | 46 | 139 | 20 | .263 | .412 |

## INDIVIDUAL FIELDING

| POS | Player | T | G | PO | A | E | DP | TC/G | FA | POS | Player | T | G | PO | A | E | DP | TC/G | FA |
|---|---|---|---|---|---|---|---|---|---|---|---|---|---|---|---|---|---|---|---|
| 1B | D. Fondy | L | 138 | 1228 | 119 | 9 | 129 | 9.8 | .993 | OF | R. Kiner | R | 147 | 298 | 6 | 9 | 1 | 2.1 | .971 |
| | S. Bilko | R | 22 | 182 | 28 | 0 | 17 | 9.5 | 1.000 | | H. Sauer | R | 141 | 282 | 8 | 11 | 2 | 2.1 | .963 |
| 2B | G. Baker | R | 134 | 355 | 385 | 25 | 102 | 5.7 | .967 | | D. Talbot | R | 110 | 245 | 10 | 4 | 1 | 2.4 | .985 |
| | E. Miksis | R | 21 | 62 | 61 | 5 | 16 | 6.1 | .961 | | F. Baumholtz | L | 71 | 168 | 2 | 2 | 0 | 2.4 | .988 |
| | B. Serena | R | 2 | 2 | 1 | 0 | 0 | 1.5 | 1.000 | | H. Rice | R | 24 | 24 | 2 | 3 | 0 | 1.2 | .897 |
| SS | E. Banks | R | 154 | 312 | 475 | 34 | 105 | 5.3 | .959 | | E. Miksis | R | 1 | 0 | 0 | 0 | 0 | 0.0 | .000 |
| | C. Kitsos | R | 1 | 0 | 2 | 0 | 0 | 2.0 | 1.000 | | L. Marquez | R | 14 | 16 | 0 | 0 | 0 | 1.1 | 1.000 |
| 3B | R. Jackson | R | 124 | 118 | 266 | 18 | 21 | 3.2 | .955 | | H. Jeffcoat | R | 3 | 1 | 0 | 0 | 0 | 0.3 | 1.000 |
| | V. Morgan | R | 15 | 8 | 26 | 4 | 1 | 2.5 | .895 | | D. Robertson | L | 6 | 1 | 0 | 0 | 0 | 0.2 | 1.000 |
| | B. Serena | R | 12 | 3 | 25 | 2 | 0 | 2.5 | .933 | | | | | | | | | | |
| | McCullough | R | 3 | 2 | 4 | 0 | 3 | 2.0 | 1.000 | C | W. Cooper | R | 48 | 190 | 31 | 5 | 4 | 4.7 | .978 |
| | E. Miksis | R | 2 | 2 | 2 | 0 | 0 | 2.0 | 1.000 | | J. Garagiola | R | 55 | 191 | 23 | 4 | 0 | 4.0 | .982 |
| | | | | | | | | | | | E. Tappe | R | 46 | 185 | 22 | 3 | 2 | 4.0 | .986 |
| | | | | | | | | | | | McCullough | R | 26 | 103 | 3 | 2 | 1 | 4.2 | .981 |
| | | | | | | | | | | | J. Fanning | R | 11 | 40 | 6 | 0 | 0 | 4.2 | 1.000 |

Phil Cavarretta became the first manager to be fired during spring training. After posting a 5–15 record, Cavy huddled with owner P. K. Wrigley for a team appraisal. He told Wrigley the Cubs were doomed to another second-division finish. Wrigley called it a "defeatist attitude" and fired Cavarretta on March 29, replacing him with Stan Hack. Rookie pitcher Bob Zick then introduced himself to Hack and said, "Hi, I'm Zick." Hack replied, "I'm not feeling too well myself." He had good reason. The Cubbies clubbed the Cardinals, 23–13, on April 17 in a league-record 3 hours and 43 minutes. And in May, they posted a 16–16 log. Then followed perhaps the worst month in Cub history, a 4–21 June swoon that included 11 losses in a row. Cavarretta had been right. The Cubs dropped to seventh and stayed there for a 64–90 record. Only the Pirates, who were 53–101, kept the Cubs from a complete disaster.

On the bright side was the rookie double-play combo of Ernie Banks and Gene Baker. Both batted .275. Ernie had 19 homers and 79 RBI, while Baker had 13 homers and 61 RBI. Later in the season, the Cubs acquired Steve Bilko and the fans took up the chant "Bingo to Bango to Bilko." Rightfielder Hank Sauer, now dubbed the "Mayor of Wrigley Field," satisfied his constituents by slugging 41 homers and driving in 103 runs. But a team can't win without solid pitching. Bob Rush was the big winner with only 13 victories.

## TEAM STATISTICS

| | W | L | PCT | GB | R | OR | 2B | Batting 3B | HR | BA | SA | SB | E | Fielding DP | FA | CG | B | Pitching SO | ShO | SV | ERA |
|---|---|---|---|---|---|---|---|---|---|---|---|---|---|---|---|---|---|---|---|---|---|
| NY | 97 | 57 | .630 | | 732 | 550 | 194 | 42 | 186 | .264 | .424 | 30 | 154 | 172 | .975 | 45 | 613 | 692 | 19 | 33 | 3.09 |
| BKN | 92 | 62 | .597 | 5 | 778 | 740 | 246 | 56 | 186 | .270 | .444 | 46 | 129 | 138 | .978 | 39 | 533 | 762 | 8 | 36 | 4.31 |
| MIL | 89 | 65 | .578 | 8 | 670 | 556 | 217 | 41 | 139 | .265 | .401 | 54 | 116 | 171 | .981 | 63 | 553 | 698 | 13 | 21 | 3.19 |
| PHI | 75 | 79 | .487 | 22 | 659 | 614 | 243 | 58 | 102 | .267 | .395 | 30 | 145 | 133 | .975 | 78 | 450 | 570 | 14 | 12 | 3.59 |
| CIN | 74 | 80 | .481 | 23 | 729 | 763 | 221 | 46 | 147 | .262 | .406 | 47 | 137 | 194 | .977 | 34 | 547 | 537 | 8 | 27 | 4.50 |
| STL | 72 | 82 | .468 | 25 | 799 | 790 | 285 | 58 | 119 | .281 | .421 | 63 | 146 | 178 | .976 | 40 | 535 | 680 | 11 | 18 | 4.50 |
| CHI | 64 | 90 | .416 | 33 | 700 | 766 | 229 | 45 | 159 | .263 | .412 | 46 | 154 | 164 | .974 | 41 | 619 | 622 | 6 | 19 | 4.51 |
| PIT | 53 | 101 | .344 | 44 | 557 | 845 | 181 | 57 | 76 | .248 | .350 | 21 | 173 | 136 | .971 | 37 | 564 | 525 | 4 | 15 | 4.92 |
| LEAGUE TOTAL | | | | | 5624 | 5624 | 1816 | 403 | 1114 | .265 | .407 | 337 | 1154 | 1286 | .976 | 377 | 4414 | 5086 | 83 | 181 | 4.07 |

## INDIVIDUAL PITCHING

| PITCHER | T | W | L | PCT | ERA | SV | G | GS | CG | IP | H | BB | SO | R | ER | ShO | H/9 | BB/9 | SO/9 |
|---|---|---|---|---|---|---|---|---|---|---|---|---|---|---|---|---|---|---|---|
| Bob Rush | R | 13 | 15 | .464 | 3.77 | 0 | 33 | 32 | 11 | 236.1 | 213 | 103 | 124 | 102 | 99 | 0 | 8.11 | 3.92 | 4.72 |
| Paul Minner | L | 11 | 11 | .500 | 3.96 | 1 | 32 | 29 | 12 | 218 | 236 | 50 | 79 | 107 | 96 | 0 | 9.74 | 2.06 | 3.26 |
| Warren Hacker | R | 6 | 13 | .316 | 4.25 | 2 | 39 | 18 | 4 | 158.2 | 157 | 37 | 80 | 89 | 75 | 1 | 8.91 | 2.10 | 4.54 |
| Johnny Klippstein | R | 4 | 11 | .267 | 5.29 | 1 | 36 | 21 | 4 | 148 | 155 | 96 | 69 | 104 | 87 | 0 | 9.43 | 5.84 | 4.20 |
| Howie Pollet | L | 8 | 10 | .444 | 3.58 | 0 | 20 | 20 | 4 | 128.1 | 131 | 54 | 58 | 60 | 51 | 2 | 9.19 | 3.79 | 4.07 |
| Jim Davis | L | 11 | 7 | .611 | 3.52 | 4 | 46 | 12 | 2 | 127.2 | 114 | 51 | 58 | 57 | 50 | 0 | 8.04 | 3.60 | 4.09 |
| Hal Jeffcoat | R | 5 | 6 | .455 | 5.19 | 7 | 43 | 3 | 1 | 104 | 110 | 58 | 35 | 63 | 60 | 0 | 9.52 | 5.02 | 3.03 |
| Dave Cole | R | 3 | 8 | .273 | 5.36 | 0 | 18 | 14 | 2 | 84 | 74 | 62 | 37 | 56 | 50 | 1 | 7.93 | 6.64 | 3.96 |
| Bill Tremel | R | 1 | 2 | .333 | 4.21 | 4 | 33 | 0 | 0 | 51.1 | 45 | 28 | 21 | 27 | 24 | 0 | 7.89 | 4.91 | 3.68 |
| Jim Brosnan | R | 1 | 0 | 1.000 | 9.45 | 0 | 18 | 0 | 0 | 33.1 | 44 | 18 | 17 | 35 | 35 | 0 | 11.88 | 4.86 | 4.59 |
| Jim Willis | R | 0 | 1 | .000 | 3.91 | 0 | 14 | 1 | 0 | 23 | 22 | 18 | 5 | 10 | 10 | 0 | 8.61 | 7.04 | 1.96 |
| Turk Lown | R | 0 | 2 | .000 | 6.14 | 0 | 15 | 0 | 0 | 22 | 23 | 15 | 16 | 18 | 15 | 0 | 9.41 | 6.14 | 6.55 |
| Bob Zick | R | 0 | 0 | — | 8.27 | 0 | 8 | 0 | 0 | 16.1 | 23 | 7 | 9 | 15 | 15 | 0 | 12.67 | 3.86 | 4.96 |
| Bubba Church | R | 1 | 3 | .250 | 9.82 | 0 | 7 | 3 | 1 | 14.2 | 21 | 13 | 8 | 18 | 16 | 0 | 12.89 | 7.98 | 4.91 |
| Al Lary | R | 0 | 0 | — | 3.00 | 0 | 1 | 1 | 0 | 6 | 3 | 7 | 4 | 2 | 2 | 0 | 4.50 | 10.50 | 6.00 |
| John Pyecha | R | 0 | 1 | .000 | 10.13 | 0 | 1 | 0 | 0 | 2.2 | 4 | 2 | 2 | 3 | 3 | 0 | 13.50 | 6.75 | 6.75 |
| TEAM TOTAL | | 64 | 90 | .416 | 4.51 | 19 | 364 | 154 | 41 | 1374.1 | 1375 | 619 | 622 | 766 | 688 | 4 | 9.00 | 4.05 | 4.07 |

| MANAGER | W | L | PCT |
|---|---|---|---|
| Stan Hack | 72 | 81 | .471 |

| POS | Player | B | G | AB | H | 2B | 3B | HR | HR % | R | RBI | BB | SO | SB | Pinch Hit AB | Pinch Hit H | BA | SA |
|---|---|---|---|---|---|---|---|---|---|---|---|---|---|---|---|---|---|---|
| **REGULARS** | | | | | | | | | | | | | | | | | | |
| 1B | Dee Fondy | L | 150 | 574 | 152 | 23 | 8 | 17 | 3.0 | 69 | 65 | 35 | 87 | 8 | 0 | 0 | .265 | .422 |
| 2B | Gene Baker | R | 154 | 609 | 163 | 29 | 7 | 11 | 1.8 | 82 | 52 | 49 | 57 | 9 | 0 | 0 | .268 | .392 |
| SS | Ernie Banks | R | 154 | 596 | 176 | 29 | 9 | 44 | 7.4 | 98 | 117 | 45 | 72 | 9 | 0 | 0 | .295 | .596 |
| 3B | Randy Jackson | R | 138 | 499 | 132 | 13 | 7 | 21 | 4.2 | 73 | 70 | 58 | 58 | 0 | 3 | 1 | .265 | .445 |
| RF | Jim King | L | 113 | 301 | 77 | 12 | 3 | 11 | 3.7 | 43 | 45 | 24 | 39 | 2 | 18 | 4 | .256 | .425 |
| CF | Eddie Miksis | R | 131 | 481 | 113 | 14 | 2 | 9 | 1.9 | 52 | 41 | 32 | 55 | 3 | 2 | 0 | .235 | .328 |
| LF | Hank Sauer | R | 79 | 261 | 55 | 8 | 1 | 12 | 4.6 | 29 | 28 | 26 | 47 | 0 | 10 | 0 | .211 | .387 |
| C | Harry Chiti | R | 113 | 338 | 78 | 6 | 1 | 11 | 3.3 | 24 | 41 | 25 | 68 | 0 | 1 | 0 | .231 | .352 |
| **SUBSTITUTES** | | | | | | | | | | | | | | | | | | |
| 3S | Owen Friend | R | 6 | 10 | 1 | 0 | 0 | 0 | 0.0 | 0 | 0 | 0 | 3 | 0 | 3 | 0 | .100 | .100 |
| 3B | Vern Morgan | R | 7 | 7 | 1 | 0 | 0 | 0 | 0.0 | 1 | 1 | 3 | 4 | 0 | 3 | 0 | .143 | .143 |
| OF | Frankie Baumholtz | L | 105 | 280 | 81 | 12 | 5 | 1 | 0.4 | 23 | 27 | 16 | 24 | 0 | 37 | 15 | .289 | .379 |
| OF | Bob Speake | L | 95 | 261 | 57 | 9 | 5 | 12 | 4.6 | 36 | 43 | 28 | 71 | 3 | 24 | 5 | .218 | .429 |
| OF | Jim Bolger | R | 64 | 160 | 33 | 5 | 4 | 0 | 0.0 | 19 | 7 | 9 | 17 | 2 | 1 | 1 | .206 | .288 |
| OF | Lloyd Merriman | L | 72 | 145 | 31 | 6 | 1 | 1 | 0.7 | 15 | 8 | 21 | 21 | 1 | 19 | 4 | .214 | .290 |
| OF | Ted Tappe | L | 23 | 50 | 13 | 2 | 0 | 4 | 8.0 | 12 | 10 | 11 | 11 | 0 | 8 | 2 | .260 | .540 |
| OF | Gale Wade | L | 9 | 33 | 6 | 1 | 0 | 1 | 3.0 | 5 | 1 | 4 | 3 | 0 | 0 | 0 | .182 | .303 |
| C | Walker Cooper | R | 54 | 111 | 31 | 8 | 1 | 7 | 6.3 | 11 | 15 | 6 | 19 | 0 | 28 | 6 | .279 | .559 |
| C | Clyde McCullough | R | 44 | 81 | 16 | 0 | 0 | 0 | 0.0 | 7 | 10 | 8 | 15 | 0 | 7 | 3 | .198 | .198 |
| C | Jim Fanning | R | 5 | 10 | 0 | 0 | 0 | 0 | 0.0 | 0 | 0 | 1 | 2 | 0 | 0 | 0 | .000 | .000 |
| C | El Tappe | R | 2 | 0 | 0 | 0 | 0 | 0 | — | 0 | 0 | 0 | 0 | 0 | 0 | 0 | — | — |
| PH | Al Lary | R | 4 | 0 | 0 | 0 | 0 | 0 | — | 1 | 0 | 0 | 0 | 0 | 0 | 0 | — | — |
| **PITCHERS** | | | | | | | | | | | | | | | | | | |
| P | Bob Rush | R | 33 | 82 | 9 | 2 | 0 | 1 | 1.2 | 6 | 5 | 6 | 40 | 0 | 0 | 0 | .110 | .171 |
| P | Sam Jones | R | 36 | 77 | 14 | 1 | 0 | 0 | 0.0 | 2 | 5 | 3 | 27 | 0 | 0 | 0 | .182 | .195 |
| P | Warren Hacker | R | 35 | 72 | 18 | 3 | 1 | 0 | 0.0 | 6 | 3 | 0 | 9 | 0 | 0 | 0 | .250 | .319 |
| P | Paul Minner | L | 22 | 56 | 13 | 2 | 0 | 0 | 0.0 | 5 | 1 | 5 | 7 | 0 | 0 | 0 | .232 | .268 |
| P | Jim Davis | B | 42 | 37 | 1 | 0 | 0 | 0 | 0.0 | 1 | 1 | 3 | 21 | 0 | 0 | 0 | .027 | .027 |
| P | Hal Jeffcoat | R | 52 | 23 | 4 | 0 | 0 | 1 | 4.3 | 3 | 1 | 2 | 9 | 0 | 0 | 0 | .174 | .304 |
| P | Howie Pollet | L | 24 | 15 | 6 | 2 | 0 | 0 | 0.0 | 0 | 0 | 2 | 5 | 0 | 0 | 0 | .400 | .533 |
| P | Harry Perkowski | L | 26 | 13 | 2 | 0 | 0 | 0 | 0.0 | 2 | 0 | 1 | 2 | 0 | 1 | 0 | .154 | .154 |
| P | Dave Hillman | R | 26 | 10 | 1 | 0 | 0 | 0 | 0.0 | 1 | 0 | 3 | 5 | 0 | 0 | 0 | .100 | .100 |
| P | John Andre | L | 22 | 9 | 1 | 0 | 0 | 0 | 0.0 | 0 | 0 | 0 | 4 | 0 | 0 | 0 | .111 | .111 |
| P | Bill Tremel | R | 23 | 7 | 2 | 0 | 0 | 0 | 0.0 | 0 | 0 | 1 | 2 | 0 | 0 | 0 | .286 | .286 |
| P | Hy Cohen | R | 7 | 3 | 0 | 0 | 0 | 0 | 0.0 | 0 | 0 | 1 | 1 | 0 | 0 | 0 | .000 | .000 |
| P | Don Kaiser | R | 11 | 2 | 0 | 0 | 0 | 0 | 0.0 | 0 | 0 | 0 | 1 | 0 | 0 | 0 | .000 | .000 |
| P | Bubba Church | R | 3 | 1 | 0 | 0 | 0 | 0 | 0.0 | 0 | 0 | 0 | 0 | 0 | 0 | 0 | .000 | .000 |
| P | Vincente Amor | R | 4 | 0 | 0 | 0 | 0 | 0 | — | 0 | 0 | 0 | 0 | 0 | 0 | 0 | — | — |
| P | Bob Thorpe | R | 2 | 0 | 0 | 0 | 0 | 0 | — | 0 | 0 | 0 | 0 | 0 | 0 | 0 | — | — |
| TEAM TOTAL | | | | 5214 | 1287 | 187 | 55 | 164 | 3.1 | 62 | 597 | 428 | 806 | 37 | 165 | 41 | .247 | .398 |

## INDIVIDUAL FIELDING

| POS | Player | T | G | PO | A | E | DP | TC/G | FA |
|---|---|---|---|---|---|---|---|---|---|
| 1B | D. Fondy | L | 147 | 1304 | 107 | 13 | 135 | 9.7 | .991 |
| | B. Speake | L | 8 | 69 | 7 | 2 | 7 | 9.8 | .974 |
| 2B | G. Baker | R | 154 | 432 | 444 | 30 | 114 | 5.9 | .967 |
| SS | E. Banks | R | 154 | 290 | 482 | 22 | 102 | 5.2 | .972 |
| | O. Friend | R | 1 | 1 | 0 | 0 | 0 | 1.0 | 1.000 |
| 3B | R. Jackson | R | 134 | 125 | 247 | 20 | 26 | 2.9 | .949 |
| | E. Miksis | R | 18 | 23 | 46 | 3 | 5 | 4.0 | .958 |
| | V. Morgan | R | 2 | 2 | 2 | 2 | 0 | 3.0 | .667 |
| | O. Friend | R | 2 | 2 | 2 | 0 | 0 | 2.0 | 1.000 |

| POS | Player | T | G | PO | A | E | DP | TC/G | FA |
|---|---|---|---|---|---|---|---|---|---|
| OF | E. Miksis | R | 111 | 267 | 6 | 3 | 1 | 2.5 | .989 |
| | J. King | R | 93 | 184 | 10 | 2 | 2 | 2.1 | .990 |
| | F. Baumholtz | L | 63 | 131 | 3 | 1 | 1 | 2.1 | .993 |
| | J. Bolger | R | 51 | 125 | 1 | 6 | 0 | 2.6 | .955 |
| | H. Sauer | R | 68 | 122 | 4 | 2 | 1 | 1.9 | .984 |
| | B. Speake | L | 55 | 90 | 4 | 4 | 1 | 1.8 | .959 |
| | L. Merriman | L | 49 | 82 | 2 | 2 | 2 | 1.8 | .977 |
| | T. Tappe | R | 15 | 18 | 1 | 0 | 0 | 1.3 | 1.000 |
| | G. Wade | R | 9 | 12 | 1 | 2 | 0 | 1.7 | .867 |
| C | H. Chiti | R | 113 | 495 | 69 | 9 | 10 | 5.1 | .984 |
| | McCullough | R | 37 | 160 | 12 | 2 | 0 | 4.7 | .989 |
| | W. Cooper | R | 31 | 88 | 11 | 4 | 1 | 3.3 | .961 |
| | J. Fanning | R | 5 | 30 | 2 | 0 | 0 | 6.4 | 1.000 |
| | E. Tappe | R | 2 | 3 | 1 | 0 | 0 | 2.0 | 1.000 |

A rookie named Bob Speake enjoyed a merry month of May and made the Cubs the surprise team of the league. Speake replaced the ailing Hank Sauer in the outfield and hit 10 homers that month as the Cubs won 20 and lost 9 and surged to second behind the Dodgers. Going into June Speake was batting .304 and had driven in 31 runs on only 91 at bats. His clutch hits provided 10 of the 20 victories. But Speake's hot bat cooled off in June, and he finished the season with only 12 homers and a .218 average.

Another May sensation was pitcher Sad Sam Jones, who was obtained in a winter trade with the Indians for Ralph Kiner. Jones pitched a memorable no-hitter, beating the Pirates, 4–0, on May 12 at Wrigley Field. The tense moment came in the ninth inning when he walked three batters and then struck out Dick Groat, Roberto Clemente, and Frank Thomas. But wildness was Jones's downfall. Although he led the NL in strikeouts with 198, Jones walked a Cub record 185 and lost 20 games. His 14 wins were high for the Cub staff.

Manager Stan Hack had the team in third place with a 45–40 record at the All-Star break, but then they dropped 12 of 13 and collapsed into sixth place with a 72–81 log. Ernie Banks was the season-long standout, setting a record of five grand-slam homers in one season. In addition, his 44 homers were the most ever hit by a shortstop. Banks also led the team in RBI with 117 and batted .295.

### TEAM STATISTICS

| | W | L | PCT | GB | R | OR | 2B | 3B | HR | BA | SA | SB | E | DP | FA | CG | B | SO | ShO | SV | ERA |
|---|---|---|---|---|---|---|---|---|---|---|---|---|---|---|---|---|---|---|---|---|---|
| | | | | | | | Batting | | | | | | Fielding | | | Pitching | | | | | |
| KN | 98 | 55 | .641 | | 857 | 650 | 230 | 44 | 201 | .271 | .448 | 79 | 133 | 156 | .978 | 46 | 483 | 773 | 11 | 37 | 3.68 |
| IIL | 85 | 69 | .552 | 13.5 | 743 | 668 | 219 | 55 | 182 | .261 | .427 | 42 | 152 | 155 | .975 | 61 | 591 | 654 | 5 | 12 | 3.85 |
| Y | 80 | 74 | .519 | 18.5 | 702 | 673 | 173 | 34 | 169 | .260 | .402 | 38 | 142 | 165 | .976 | 52 | 560 | 721 | 6 | 14 | 3.77 |
| HI | 77 | 77 | .500 | 21.5 | 675 | 666 | 214 | 50 | 132 | .255 | .395 | 44 | 110 | 117 | .981 | 58 | 477 | 657 | 11 | 21 | 3.93 |
| IN | 75 | 79 | .487 | 23.5 | 761 | 684 | 216 | 28 | 181 | .270 | .425 | 51 | 139 | 169 | .977 | 38 | 443 | 576 | 12 | 22 | 3.95 |
| HI | 72 | 81 | .471 | 26 | 626 | 713 | 187 | 55 | 164 | .247 | .398 | 37 | 147 | 147 | .975 | 47 | 601 | 686 | 10 | 23 | 4.17 |
| TL | 68 | 86 | .442 | 30.5 | 654 | 757 | 228 | 36 | 143 | .261 | .400 | 64 | 146 | 152 | .975 | 42 | 549 | 730 | 10 | 15 | 4.56 |
| IT | 60 | 94 | .390 | 38.5 | 560 | 767 | 210 | 60 | 91 | .244 | .361 | 22 | 166 | 175 | .972 | 41 | 536 | 622 | 5 | 16 | 4.39 |
| EAGUE TOTAL | | | | | 5578 | 5578 | 1677 | 362 | 1263 | .259 | .407 | 377 | 1135 | 1236 | .976 | 385 | 4240 | 5419 | 70 | 160 | 4.04 |

### INDIVIDUAL PITCHING

| ITCHER | T | W | L | PCT | ERA | SV | G | GS | CG | IP | H | BB | SO | R | ER | ShO | H/9 | BB/9 | SO/9 |
|---|---|---|---|---|---|---|---|---|---|---|---|---|---|---|---|---|---|---|---|
| am Jones | R | 14 | 20 | .412 | 4.10 | 0 | 36 | 34 | 12 | 241.2 | 175 | 185 | 198 | 118 | 110 | 4 | 6.52 | 6.89 | 7.37 |
| ob Rush | R | 13 | 11 | .542 | 3.50 | 0 | 33 | 33 | 14 | 234 | 204 | 73 | 130 | 95 | 91 | 3 | 7.85 | 2.81 | 5.00 |
| arren Hacker | R | 11 | 15 | .423 | 4.27 | 3 | 35 | 30 | 13 | 213 | 202 | 43 | 80 | 112 | 101 | 0 | 8.54 | 1.82 | 3.38 |
| aul Minner | L | 9 | 9 | .500 | 3.48 | 0 | 22 | 22 | 7 | 157.2 | 173 | 47 | 53 | 67 | 61 | 1 | 9.88 | 2.68 | 3.03 |
| m Davis | L | 7 | 11 | .389 | 4.44 | 3 | 42 | 16 | 0 | 133.2 | 122 | 58 | 62 | 79 | 66 | 0 | 8.21 | 3.91 | 4.17 |
| al Jeffcoat | R | 8 | 6 | .571 | 2.95 | 6 | 50 | 1 | 0 | 100.2 | 107 | 53 | 32 | 46 | 33 | 0 | 9.57 | 4.74 | 2.86 |
| owie Pollet | L | 4 | 3 | .571 | 5.61 | 5 | 24 | 7 | 1 | 61 | 62 | 27 | 27 | 41 | 38 | 1 | 9.15 | 3.98 | 3.98 |
| ave Hillman | R | 0 | 0 | – | 5.31 | 0 | 25 | 3 | 0 | 57.2 | 63 | 25 | 23 | 36 | 34 | 0 | 9.83 | 3.90 | 3.59 |
| arry Perkowski | L | 3 | 4 | .429 | 5.29 | 2 | 25 | 4 | 0 | 47.2 | 53 | 25 | 28 | 32 | 28 | 0 | 10.01 | 4.72 | 5.29 |
| ohn Andre | R | 0 | 1 | .000 | 5.80 | 1 | 22 | 3 | 0 | 45 | 45 | 28 | 19 | 34 | 29 | 0 | 9.00 | 5.60 | 3.80 |
| Il Tremel | R | 3 | 0 | 1.000 | 3.72 | 2 | 23 | 0 | 0 | 38.2 | 33 | 18 | 13 | 18 | 16 | 0 | 7.68 | 4.19 | 3.03 |
| on Kaiser | R | 0 | 0 | – | 5.40 | 0 | 11 | 0 | 0 | 18.1 | 20 | 5 | 11 | 11 | 11 | 0 | 9.82 | 2.45 | 5.40 |
| y Cohen | R | 0 | 0 | – | 7.94 | 0 | 7 | 1 | 0 | 17 | 28 | 10 | 4 | 17 | 15 | 0 | 14.82 | 5.29 | 2.12 |
| incente Amor | R | 0 | 1 | .000 | 4.50 | 0 | 4 | 0 | 0 | 6 | 11 | 3 | 3 | 3 | 3 | 0 | 16.50 | 4.50 | 4.50 |
| ubba Church | R | 0 | 0 | – | 5.40 | 1 | 2 | 0 | 0 | 3.1 | 4 | 1 | 3 | 2 | 2 | 0 | 10.80 | 2.70 | 8.10 |
| ob Thorpe | R | 0 | 0 | – | 3.00 | 0 | 2 | 0 | 0 | 3 | 4 | 1 | 0 | 0 | 2 | 0 | 12.00 | 0.00 | 0.00 |
| EAM TOTAL | | 72 | 81 | .471 | 4.17 | 23 | 363 | 154 | 47 | 1378.1 | 1306 | 601 | 686 | 713 | 639 | 9 | 8.53 | 3.92 | 4.48 |

| MANAGER | W | L | PCT |
|---|---|---|---|
| Stan Hack | 60 | 94 | .390 |

| POS | Player | B | G | AB | H | 2B | 3B | HR | HR % | R | RBI | BB | SO | SB | Pinch Hit AB | Pinch Hit H | BA | SA |
|---|---|---|---|---|---|---|---|---|---|---|---|---|---|---|---|---|---|---|
| **REGULARS** | | | | | | | | | | | | | | | | | | |
| 1B | Dee Fondy | L | 137 | 543 | 146 | 22 | 9 | 9 | 1.7 | 52 | 46 | 20 | 74 | 9 | 4 | 1 | .269 | .392 |
| 2B | Gene Baker | R | 140 | 546 | 141 | 23 | 3 | 12 | 2.2 | 65 | 57 | 39 | 54 | 4 | 0 | 0 | .258 | .377 |
| SS | Ernie Banks | R | 139 | 538 | 160 | 25 | 8 | 28 | 5.2 | 82 | 85 | 52 | 62 | 6 | 0 | 0 | .297 | .530 |
| 3B | Don Hoak | R | 121 | 424 | 91 | 18 | 4 | 5 | 1.2 | 51 | 37 | 41 | 46 | 8 | 5 | 1 | .215 | .311 |
| RF | Walt Moryn | L | 147 | 529 | 151 | 27 | 3 | 23 | 4.3 | 69 | 67 | 50 | 67 | 4 | 6 | 0 | .285 | .478 |
| CF | Pete Whisenant | R | 103 | 314 | 75 | 16 | 3 | 11 | 3.5 | 37 | 46 | 24 | 53 | 8 | 8 | 2 | .239 | .414 |
| LF | Monte Irvin | R | 111 | 339 | 92 | 13 | 3 | 15 | 4.4 | 44 | 50 | 41 | 41 | 1 | 18 | 7 | .271 | .460 |
| C | Hobie Landrith | L | 111 | 312 | 69 | 10 | 3 | 4 | 1.3 | 22 | 32 | 39 | 38 | 0 | 15 | 4 | .221 | .311 |
| **SUBSTITUTES** | | | | | | | | | | | | | | | | | | |
| UT | Eddie Miksis | R | 114 | 356 | 85 | 10 | 3 | 9 | 2.5 | 54 | 27 | 32 | 40 | 4 | 13 | 6 | .239 | .360 |
| 1B | Frank Kellert | R | 71 | 129 | 24 | 3 | 1 | 4 | 3.1 | 10 | 17 | 12 | 22 | 0 | 41 | 10 | .186 | .318 |
| SS | Jerry Kindall | R | 32 | 55 | 9 | 1 | 1 | 0 | 0.0 | 7 | 0 | 6 | 17 | 1 | 0 | 0 | .164 | .218 |
| 3B | Ed Winceniak | R | 15 | 17 | 2 | 0 | 0 | 0 | 0.0 | 1 | 0 | 1 | 3 | 0 | 7 | 0 | .118 | .118 |
| OF | Jim King | L | 118 | 317 | 79 | 13 | 2 | 15 | 4.7 | 32 | 54 | 30 | 40 | 1 | 34 | 6 | .249 | .445 |
| OF | Solly Drake | B | 65 | 215 | 55 | 9 | 1 | 2 | 0.9 | 29 | 15 | 23 | 35 | 9 | 8 | 3 | .256 | .335 |
| OF | Gale Wade | L | 10 | 12 | 0 | 0 | 0 | 0 | 0.0 | 0 | 0 | 1 | 0 | 0 | 3 | 0 | .000 | .000 |
| C | Harry Chiti | R | 72 | 203 | 43 | 6 | 4 | 4 | 2.0 | 17 | 18 | 19 | 35 | 0 | 5 | 2 | .212 | .340 |
| C | Clyde McCullough | R | 14 | 19 | 4 | 1 | 0 | 0 | 0.0 | 0 | 1 | 0 | 5 | 0 | 7 | 1 | .211 | .263 |
| C | Jim Fanning | R | 1 | 4 | 1 | 0 | 0 | 0 | 0.0 | 0 | 0 | 0 | 0 | 0 | 0 | 0 | .250 | .250 |
| C | El Tappe | R | 3 | 1 | 0 | 0 | 0 | 0 | 0.0 | 0 | 0 | 1 | 0 | 0 | 0 | 0 | .000 | .000 |
| PH | Owen Friend | R | 2 | 2 | 0 | 0 | 0 | 0 | 0.0 | 0 | 0 | 0 | 2 | 0 | 2 | 0 | .000 | .000 |
| PH | Richie Myers | R | 4 | 1 | 0 | 0 | 0 | 0 | 0.0 | 1 | 0 | 0 | 0 | 0 | 1 | 0 | .000 | .000 |
| **PITCHERS** | | | | | | | | | | | | | | | | | | |
| P | Bob Rush | R | 38 | 82 | 8 | 1 | 0 | 0 | 0.0 | 6 | 2 | 6 | 37 | 0 | 0 | 0 | .098 | .110 |
| P | Sam Jones | R | 33 | 57 | 10 | 0 | 0 | 0 | 0.0 | 3 | 1 | 4 | 19 | 0 | 0 | 0 | .175 | .175 |
| P | Warren Hacker | R | 34 | 54 | 8 | 0 | 0 | 0 | 0.0 | 2 | 4 | 0 | 6 | 0 | 0 | 0 | .148 | .148 |
| P | Don Kaiser | R | 27 | 47 | 2 | 0 | 0 | 0 | 0.0 | 1 | 1 | 0 | 30 | 0 | 0 | 0 | .043 | .043 |
| P | Jim Davis | B | 46 | 28 | 5 | 0 | 0 | 0 | 0.0 | 3 | 0 | 1 | 10 | 0 | 0 | 0 | .179 | .179 |
| P | Turk Lown | R | 61 | 23 | 5 | 0 | 1 | 1 | 4.3 | 2 | 2 | 2 | 11 | 0 | 0 | 0 | .217 | .435 |
| P | Jim Brosnan | R | 30 | 22 | 4 | 1 | 0 | 0 | 0.0 | 2 | 0 | 0 | 6 | 0 | 0 | 0 | .182 | .227 |
| P | Vito Valentinetti | R | 42 | 20 | 2 | 0 | 0 | 0 | 0.0 | 0 | 0 | 1 | 10 | 0 | 0 | 0 | .100 | .100 |
| P | Moe Drabowsky | R | 9 | 16 | 4 | 0 | 0 | 0 | 0.0 | 1 | 0 | 0 | 3 | 0 | 0 | 0 | .250 | .250 |
| P | Russ Meyer | B | 20 | 12 | 1 | 0 | 0 | 0 | 0.0 | 0 | 0 | 1 | 3 | 0 | 0 | 0 | .083 | .083 |
| P | Paul Minner | L | 10 | 12 | 3 | 2 | 1 | 0 | 0.0 | 2 | 0 | 0 | 6 | 0 | 0 | 0 | .250 | .583 |
| P | Jim Hughes | R | 25 | 7 | 2 | 1 | 0 | 0 | 0.0 | 2 | 1 | 0 | 0 | 0 | 0 | 0 | .286 | .429 |
| P | Dave Hillman | R | 2 | 4 | 0 | 0 | 0 | 0 | 0.0 | 0 | 0 | 0 | 1 | 0 | 0 | 0 | .000 | .000 |
| P | Johnny Briggs | R | 3 | 0 | 0 | 0 | 0 | 0 | – | 0 | 0 | 0 | 0 | 0 | 0 | 0 | – | – |
| P | George Piktuzis | R | 2 | 0 | 0 | 0 | 0 | 0 | – | 0 | 0 | 0 | 0 | 0 | 0 | 0 | – | – |
| P | Bill Tremel | R | 1 | 0 | 0 | 0 | 0 | 0 | – | 0 | 0 | 0 | 0 | 0 | 0 | 0 | – | – |
| TEAM TOTAL | | | | 5260 | 1281 | 202 | 50 | 142 | 2.7 | 59 | 563 | 446 | 776 | 55 | 177 | 43 | .244 | .382 |

## INDIVIDUAL FIELDING

| POS | Player | T | G | PO | A | E | DP | TC/G | FA | POS | Player | T | G | PO | A | E | DP | TC/G | FA |
|---|---|---|---|---|---|---|---|---|---|---|---|---|---|---|---|---|---|---|---|
| 1B | D. Fondy | L | 133 | 1048 | 94 | 17 | 101 | 8.7 | .985 | OF | W. Moryn | R | 141 | 268 | 18 | 5 | 2 | 2.1 | .983 |
| | F. Kellert | R | 27 | 209 | 24 | 2 | 22 | 8.7 | .991 | | P. Whisenant | R | 93 | 242 | 6 | 2 | 0 | 2.7 | .992 |
| 2B | G. Baker | R | 140 | 362 | 426 | 25 | 99 | 5.8 | .969 | | M. Irvin | R | 96 | 215 | 6 | 2 | 0 | 2.3 | .991 |
| | E. Miksis | R | 19 | 30 | 52 | 2 | 9 | 4.4 | .976 | | J. King | R | 82 | 187 | 10 | 2 | 2 | 2.4 | .990 |
| | E. Winceniak | R | 1 | 1 | 0 | 0 | 0 | 1.0 | 1.000 | | S. Drake | R | 53 | 142 | 3 | 1 | 1 | 2.8 | .993 |
| SS | E. Banks | R | 139 | 279 | 357 | 25 | 92 | 4.8 | .962 | | E. Miksis | R | 33 | 54 | 1 | 1 | 0 | 1.7 | .982 |
| | J. Kindall | R | 18 | 33 | 53 | 4 | 12 | 5.0 | .956 | | G. Wade | R | 3 | 7 | 0 | 1 | 0 | 2.7 | .875 |
| | E. Miksis | R | 2 | 1 | 2 | 0 | 0 | 1.5 | 1.000 | C | H. Landrith | R | 99 | 483 | 55 | 14 | 9 | 5.6 | .975 |
| 3B | D. Hoak | R | 110 | 122 | 158 | 15 | 16 | 2.7 | .949 | | H. Chiti | R | 67 | 327 | 35 | 7 | 2 | 5.5 | .981 |
| | E. Miksis | R | 48 | 59 | 96 | 4 | 5 | 3.3 | .975 | | McCullough | R | 7 | 24 | 3 | 0 | 0 | 3.9 | 1.000 |
| | E. Winceniak | R | 4 | 5 | 3 | 1 | 0 | 2.3 | .889 | | J. Fanning | R | 1 | 5 | 3 | 2 | 1 | 10.0 | .800 |
| | | | | | | | | | | | E. Tappe | R | 3 | 4 | 0 | 0 | 0 | 1.3 | 1.000 |

Talk about dull seasons. This was it. The Cubs dropped a dozen doubleheaders. They were shut out 15 times. Their road record was a dismal 21–56. They were never higher than sixth after the first 10 days of the season. Manager Stan Hack had the dubious distinction of directing the drab doormats to the dungeon, finishing with a 60–94 record. It all began on a Sauer note. During spring training the Cubs traded fan favorite Hank Sauer to the Cardinals for Pete Whisenant. Everyone screamed, "What is a Whisenant?" With Sauer gone, Cub supporters sought a new hero. It was an easy choice. Sinewy shortstop Ernie Banks stepped forward with 28 homers and 85 RBI and batted a team-high .297. Banks was ably supported by Moose Moryn, who had 23 homers and batted .285. Through all the losses, pitcher Bob Rush somehow managed a 13–10 record. Third baseman Don Hoak had a typical day on May 2. He struck out six times against the Giants. General manager Wid Matthews, in the seventh year of his five-year plan to bring home a winner, was given the ax along with Hack at the end of the season.

## TEAM STATISTICS

| | W | L | PCT | GB | R | OR | Batting 2B | 3B | HR | BA | SA | SB | Fielding E | DP | FA | CG | B | Pitching SO | ShO | SV | ERA |
|---|---|---|---|---|---|---|---|---|---|---|---|---|---|---|---|---|---|---|---|---|---|
| BKN | 93 | 61 | .604 | | 720 | 601 | 212 | 36 | 179 | .258 | .419 | 65 | 111 | 149 | .981 | 46 | 441 | 772 | 12 | 30 | 3.57 |
| MIL | 92 | 62 | .597 | 1 | 709 | 569 | 212 | 54 | 177 | .259 | .423 | 29 | 130 | 159 | .979 | 64 | 467 | 639 | 12 | 27 | 3.11 |
| CIN | 91 | 63 | .591 | 2 | 775 | 658 | 201 | 32 | 221 | .266 | .441 | 45 | 113 | 147 | .981 | 47 | 458 | 653 | 4 | 29 | 3.85 |
| STL | 76 | 78 | .494 | 17 | 678 | 698 | 234 | 49 | 124 | .268 | .399 | 41 | 134 | 172 | .978 | 41 | 546 | 709 | 12 | 30 | 3.97 |
| PHI | 71 | 83 | .461 | 22 | 668 | 738 | 207 | 49 | 121 | .252 | .381 | 45 | 144 | 140 | .975 | 57 | 437 | 750 | 4 | 15 | 4.20 |
| NY | 67 | 87 | .435 | 26 | 540 | 650 | 192 | 45 | 145 | .244 | .382 | 67 | 144 | 143 | .976 | 31 | 551 | 765 | 9 | 28 | 3.78 |
| PIT | 66 | 88 | .429 | 27 | 588 | 653 | 199 | 57 | 110 | .257 | .380 | 24 | 162 | 140 | .973 | 37 | 469 | 662 | 8 | 24 | 3.74 |
| CHI | 60 | 94 | .390 | 33 | 597 | 708 | 202 | 50 | 142 | .244 | .382 | 55 | 144 | 141 | .976 | 37 | 613 | 744 | 6 | 17 | 3.96 |
| LEAGUE TOTAL | | | | | 5275 | 5275 | 1659 | 372 | 1219 | .256 | .401 | 371 | 1082 | 1191 | .977 | 360 | 3982 | 5694 | 67 | 200 | 3.77 |

## INDIVIDUAL PITCHING

| PITCHER | T | W | L | PCT | ERA | SV | G | GS | CG | IP | H | BB | SO | R | ER | ShO | H/9 | BB/9 | SO/9 |
|---|---|---|---|---|---|---|---|---|---|---|---|---|---|---|---|---|---|---|---|
| Bob Rush | R | 13 | 10 | .565 | 3.19 | 0 | 32 | 32 | 13 | 239.2 | 210 | 59 | 104 | 101 | 85 | 1 | 7.89 | 2.22 | 3.91 |
| Sam Jones | R | 9 | 14 | .391 | 3.91 | 0 | 33 | 28 | 8 | 188.2 | 155 | 115 | 176 | 93 | 82 | 2 | 7.39 | 5.49 | 8.40 |
| Warren Hacker | R | 3 | 13 | .188 | 4.66 | 0 | 34 | 24 | 4 | 168 | 190 | 44 | 65 | 103 | 87 | 0 | 10.18 | 2.36 | 3.48 |
| Don Kaiser | R | 4 | 9 | .308 | 3.59 | 0 | 27 | 22 | 5 | 150.1 | 144 | 52 | 74 | 69 | 60 | 1 | 8.62 | 3.11 | 4.43 |
| Jim Davis | L | 5 | 7 | .417 | 3.66 | 2 | 46 | 11 | 2 | 120.1 | 116 | 59 | 66 | 56 | 49 | 1 | 8.68 | 4.41 | 4.94 |
| Turk Lown | R | 9 | 8 | .529 | 3.58 | 13 | 61 | 0 | 0 | 110.2 | 95 | 78 | 74 | 49 | 44 | 0 | 7.73 | 6.34 | 6.02 |
| Vito Valentinetti | R | 6 | 4 | .600 | 3.78 | 1 | 42 | 2 | 0 | 95.1 | 84 | 36 | 26 | 47 | 40 | 0 | 7.93 | 3.40 | 2.45 |
| Jim Brosnan | R | 5 | 9 | .357 | 3.79 | 1 | 30 | 10 | 1 | 95 | 95 | 45 | 51 | 44 | 40 | 1 | 9.00 | 4.26 | 4.83 |
| Russ Meyer | R | 1 | 6 | .143 | 6.32 | 0 | 20 | 9 | 0 | 57 | 71 | 26 | 28 | 41 | 40 | 0 | 11.21 | 4.11 | 4.42 |
| Moe Drabowsky | R | 2 | 4 | .333 | 2.47 | 0 | 9 | 7 | 3 | 51 | 37 | 39 | 36 | 19 | 14 | 0 | 6.53 | 6.88 | 6.35 |
| Paul Minner | L | 2 | 5 | .286 | 6.89 | 0 | 10 | 9 | 1 | 47 | 60 | 19 | 14 | 38 | 36 | 0 | 11.49 | 3.64 | 2.68 |
| Jim Hughes | R | 1 | 3 | .250 | 5.16 | 0 | 25 | 1 | 0 | 45.1 | 43 | 30 | 20 | 35 | 26 | 0 | 8.54 | 5.96 | 3.97 |
| Dave Hillman | R | 0 | 2 | .000 | 2.19 | 0 | 2 | 2 | 0 | 12.1 | 11 | 5 | 6 | 7 | 3 | 0 | 8.03 | 3.65 | 4.38 |
| Johnny Briggs | R | 0 | 0 | — | 1.69 | 0 | 3 | 0 | 0 | 5.1 | 5 | 4 | 1 | 1 | 1 | 0 | 8.44 | 6.75 | 1.69 |
| George Piktuzis | L | 0 | 0 | — | 7.20 | 0 | 2 | 0 | 0 | 5 | 6 | 2 | 3 | 4 | 4 | 0 | 10.80 | 3.60 | 5.40 |
| Bill Tremel | R | 0 | 0 | — | 13.50 | 0 | 1 | 0 | 0 | .2 | 3 | 0 | 0 | 1 | 1 | 0 | 40.50 | 0.00 | 0.00 |
| TEAM TOTAL | | 60 | 94 | .390 | 3.96 | 17 | 377 | 157 | 37 | 1391.2 | 1325 | 613 | 744 | 708 | 612 | 6 | 8.57 | 3.96 | 4.81 |

| MANAGER | W | L | PCT |
|---|---|---|---|
| Bob Scheffing | 62 | 92 | .403 |

| POS | Player | B | G | AB | H | 2B | 3B | HR | HR % | R | RBI | BB | SO | SB | Pinch Hit AB | Pinch Hit H | BA | SA |
|---|---|---|---|---|---|---|---|---|---|---|---|---|---|---|---|---|---|---|
| **REGULARS** |
| 1B | Dale Long | L | 123 | 397 | 121 | 19 | 0 | 21 | 5.3 | 55 | 62 | 52 | 63 | 1 | 17 | 5 | .305 | .511 |
| 2B | Bobby Morgan | R | 125 | 425 | 88 | 20 | 2 | 5 | 1.2 | 43 | 27 | 52 | 87 | 5 | 0 | 0 | .207 | .299 |
| 3B | Ernie Banks | R | 156 | 594 | 169 | 34 | 6 | 43 | 7.2 | 113 | 102 | 70 | 85 | 8 | 0 | 0 | .285 | .579 |
| RF | Walt Moryn | L | 149 | 568 | 164 | 33 | 0 | 19 | 3.3 | 76 | 88 | 50 | 90 | 0 | 4 | 1 | .289 | .447 |
| CF | Chuck Tanner | L | 95 | 318 | 91 | 16 | 2 | 7 | 2.2 | 42 | 42 | 23 | 20 | 0 | 12 | 3 | .286 | .415 |
| LF | Lee Walls | R | 117 | 366 | 88 | 10 | 5 | 6 | 1.6 | 42 | 33 | 27 | 67 | 5 | 20 | 8 | .240 | .344 |
| C | Cal Neeman | R | 122 | 415 | 107 | 17 | 1 | 10 | 2.4 | 37 | 39 | 22 | 87 | 0 | 4 | 0 | .258 | .376 |
| **SUBSTITUTES** |
| 3B | Bobby Adams | R | 60 | 187 | 47 | 10 | 2 | 1 | 0.5 | 21 | 10 | 17 | 28 | 0 | 8 | 1 | .251 | .342 |
| UT | Jerry Kindall | R | 72 | 181 | 29 | 3 | 0 | 6 | 3.3 | 18 | 12 | 8 | 48 | 1 | 10 | 2 | .160 | .276 |
| SS | Jack Littrell | R | 61 | 153 | 29 | 4 | 2 | 1 | 0.7 | 8 | 13 | 9 | 43 | 0 | 2 | 1 | .190 | .261 |
| 2B | Casey Wise | B | 43 | 106 | 19 | 3 | 1 | 0 | 0.0 | 12 | 7 | 11 | 14 | 0 | 4 | 0 | .179 | .226 |
| 1B | Dee Fondy | L | 11 | 51 | 16 | 3 | 1 | 0 | 0.0 | 3 | 2 | 0 | 9 | 1 | 0 | 0 | .314 | .412 |
| UT | Ed Winceniak | R | 17 | 50 | 12 | 3 | 0 | 1 | 2.0 | 5 | 8 | 2 | 9 | 0 | 5 | 1 | .240 | .360 |
| 3B | Gene Baker | R | 12 | 44 | 11 | 3 | 1 | 1 | 2.3 | 4 | 10 | 6 | 3 | 0 | 0 | 0 | .250 | .432 |
| 3B | John Goryl | R | 9 | 38 | 8 | 2 | 0 | 0 | 0.0 | 7 | 1 | 5 | 9 | 0 | 0 | 0 | .211 | .263 |
| 1B | Ed Mickelson | R | 6 | 12 | 0 | 0 | 0 | 0 | 0.0 | 0 | 1 | 0 | 4 | 0 | 4 | 0 | .000 | .000 |
| O1 | Bob Speake | L | 129 | 418 | 97 | 14 | 5 | 16 | 3.8 | 65 | 50 | 38 | 68 | 5 | 23 | 9 | .232 | .404 |
| OF | Jim Bolger | R | 112 | 273 | 75 | 4 | 1 | 5 | 1.8 | 28 | 29 | 10 | 36 | 0 | 48 | 17 | .275 | .352 |
| OF | Bob Will | L | 70 | 112 | 25 | 3 | 0 | 1 | 0.9 | 13 | 10 | 5 | 21 | 1 | 36 | 8 | .223 | .277 |
| OF | Bobby Del Greco | R | 20 | 40 | 8 | 2 | 0 | 0 | 0.0 | 2 | 3 | 10 | 17 | 1 | 6 | 1 | .200 | .250 |
| OF | Frank Ernaga | R | 20 | 35 | 11 | 3 | 2 | 2 | 5.7 | 9 | 7 | 9 | 14 | 0 | 7 | 1 | .314 | .686 |
| OF | Eddie Haas | L | 14 | 24 | 5 | 1 | 0 | 0 | 0.0 | 1 | 4 | 1 | 5 | 0 | 8 | 2 | .208 | .250 |
| OF | Bob Lennon | L | 9 | 21 | 3 | 1 | 0 | 1 | 4.8 | 2 | 3 | 1 | 9 | 0 | 5 | 0 | .143 | .333 |
| C | Jim Fanning | R | 47 | 89 | 16 | 2 | 0 | 0 | 0.0 | 3 | 4 | 4 | 17 | 0 | 12 | 1 | .180 | .202 |
| C | Charlie Silvera | R | 26 | 53 | 11 | 3 | 0 | 0 | 0.0 | 1 | 2 | 4 | 5 | 0 | 0 | 0 | .208 | .264 |
| C | Gordon Massa | L | 6 | 15 | 7 | 1 | 0 | 0 | 0.0 | 2 | 3 | 4 | 3 | 0 | 0 | 0 | .467 | .533 |
| PH | Jim Woods | R | 2 | 0 | 0 | 0 | 0 | 0 | — | 1 | 0 | 0 | 0 | 0 | 0 | 0 | — | — |
| **PITCHERS** |
| P | Moe Drabowsky | R | 36 | 82 | 15 | 2 | 0 | 1 | 1.2 | 3 | 10 | 6 | 32 | 0 | 0 | 0 | .183 | .244 |
| P | Dick Drott | R | 38 | 80 | 8 | 0 | 0 | 0 | 0.0 | 3 | 0 | 2 | 25 | 0 | 0 | 0 | .100 | .100 |
| P | Bob Rush | R | 31 | 69 | 14 | 3 | 0 | 0 | 0.0 | 3 | 3 | 3 | 26 | 0 | 0 | 0 | .203 | .246 |
| P | Don Elston | R | 39 | 37 | 4 | 0 | 0 | 0 | 0.0 | 0 | 2 | 0 | 7 | 0 | 0 | 0 | .108 | .108 |
| P | Dave Hillman | R | 36 | 24 | 0 | 0 | 0 | 0 | 0.0 | 1 | 0 | 3 | 16 | 0 | 0 | 0 | .000 | .000 |
| P | Jim Brosnan | R | 41 | 20 | 5 | 4 | 0 | 0 | 0.0 | 2 | 0 | 1 | 4 | 0 | 0 | 0 | .250 | .450 |
| P | Don Kaiser | R | 20 | 19 | 2 | 0 | 0 | 0 | 0.0 | 1 | 1 | 1 | 7 | 0 | 0 | 0 | .105 | .105 |
| P | Tom Poholsky | R | 28 | 19 | 2 | 0 | 0 | 0 | 0.0 | 1 | 1 | 2 | 3 | 0 | 0 | 0 | .105 | .105 |
| P | Dick Littlefield | L | 48 | 11 | 2 | 0 | 0 | 0 | 0.0 | 0 | 0 | 1 | 3 | 0 | 0 | 0 | .182 | .182 |
| P | Turk Lown | R | 67 | 10 | 2 | 0 | 0 | 0 | 0.0 | 0 | 1 | 1 | 1 | 0 | 0 | 0 | .200 | .200 |
| P | Bob Anderson | R | 8 | 4 | 0 | 0 | 0 | 0 | 0.0 | 0 | 0 | 0 | 3 | 0 | 0 | 0 | .000 | .000 |
| P | Elmer Singleton | B | 6 | 3 | 0 | 0 | 0 | 0 | 0.0 | 0 | 0 | 0 | 1 | 0 | 0 | 0 | .000 | .000 |
| P | Glen Hobbie | R | 2 | 2 | 0 | 0 | 0 | 0 | 0.0 | 1 | 0 | 0 | 0 | 0 | 0 | 0 | .000 | .000 |
| P | Ed Mayer | L | 3 | 2 | 1 | 0 | 0 | 0 | 0.0 | 0 | 0 | 0 | 0 | 0 | 0 | 0 | .500 | .500 |
| P | Vito Valentinetti | R | 9 | 2 | 0 | 0 | 0 | 0 | 0.0 | 0 | 0 | 1 | 0 | 0 | 0 | 0 | .000 | .000 |
| P | Johnny Briggs | R | 3 | 0 | 0 | 0 | 0 | 0 | — | 0 | 0 | 0 | 0 | 0 | 0 | 0 | — | — |
| P | Jackie Collum | L | 9 | 0 | 0 | 0 | 0 | 0 | — | 0 | 0 | 0 | 0 | 0 | 0 | 0 | — | — |
| | TEAM TOTAL | | | 5369 | 1312 | 223 | 31 | 147 | 2.7 | 62 | 590 | 461 | 989 | 28 | 235 | 61 | .244 | .380 |

## INDIVIDUAL FIELDING

| POS | Player | T | G | PO | A | E | DP | TC/G | FA |
|---|---|---|---|---|---|---|---|---|---|
| 1B | D. Long | L | 104 | 908 | 72 | 5 | 81 | 9.5 | .995 |
| | B. Speake | L | 39 | 337 | 36 | 3 | 21 | 9.6 | .992 |
| | D. Fondy | L | 11 | 103 | 6 | 1 | 10 | 10.0 | .991 |
| | E. Mickelson | R | 2 | 21 | 3 | 0 | 3 | 12.0 | 1.000 |
| 2B | B. Morgan | R | 116 | 220 | 343 | 14 | 58 | 5.0 | .976 |
| | C. Wise | R | 31 | 62 | 80 | 9 | 18 | 4.9 | .940 |
| | J. Kindall | R | 28 | 52 | 63 | 10 | 7 | 4.5 | .920 |
| | E. Winceniak | R | 3 | 8 | 3 | 2 | 0 | 4.3 | .846 |
| | J. Littrell | R | 6 | 6 | 6 | 0 | 0 | 2.0 | 1.000 |
| | B. Adams | R | 1 | 1 | 0 | 0 | 0 | 1.0 | 1.000 |
| SS | E. Banks | R | 100 | 168 | 261 | 11 | 59 | 4.4 | .975 |
| | J. Littrell | R | 47 | 77 | 124 | 12 | 23 | 4.5 | .944 |
| | J. Kindall | R | 9 | 8 | 16 | 4 | 2 | 3.1 | .857 |
| | E. Winceniak | R | 5 | 8 | 8 | 0 | 2 | 3.2 | 1.000 |
| | C. Wise | R | 5 | 7 | 4 | 1 | 3 | 2.4 | .917 |
| 3B | E. Banks | R | 58 | 73 | 87 | 3 | 12 | 2.8 | .982 |
| | B. Adams | R | 47 | 43 | 68 | 6 | 5 | 2.5 | .949 |
| | J. Kindall | R | 19 | 13 | 30 | 1 | 1 | 2.3 | .977 |
| | B. Morgan | R | 12 | 15 | 18 | 1 | 1 | 2.8 | .971 |
| | G. Baker | R | 12 | 11 | 15 | 4 | 1 | 2.5 | .867 |
| | J. Goryl | R | 9 | 6 | 14 | 1 | 4 | 2.3 | .952 |
| | E. Winceniak | R | 4 | 4 | 9 | 0 | 3 | 3.3 | 1.000 |
| | J. Bolger | R | 3 | 2 | 3 | 2 | 0 | 2.3 | .714 |
| | J. Littrell | R | 5 | 1 | 1 | 0 | 0 | 0.4 | 1.000 |
| | L. Walls | R | 1 | 1 | 0 | 0 | 0 | 1.0 | 1.000 |
| OF | W. Moryn | R | 147 | 276 | 13 | 12 | 3 | 2.0 | .960 |
| | L. Walls | R | 94 | 174 | 6 | 3 | 0 | 1.9 | .984 |
| | C. Tanner | L | 82 | 156 | 5 | 2 | 2 | 2.0 | .988 |
| | J. Bolger | R | 63 | 152 | 4 | 2 | 1 | 2.5 | .987 |
| | B. Speake | L | 60 | 143 | 5 | 4 | 0 | 2.5 | .974 |
| | B. Will | L | 30 | 51 | 1 | 2 | 0 | 1.8 | .963 |
| | B. Del Greco | R | 16 | 27 | 2 | 1 | 0 | 1.9 | .967 |
| | F. Ernaga | R | 10 | 19 | 0 | 1 | 0 | 2.0 | .950 |
| | E. Haas | R | 4 | 4 | 0 | 0 | 0 | 1.0 | 1.000 |
| | B. Lennon | L | 4 | 4 | 0 | 0 | 0 | 1.0 | 1.000 |
| C | C. Neeman | R | 118 | 703 | 56 | 8 | 13 | 6.5 | .990 |
| | J. Fanning | R | 35 | 138 | 14 | 3 | 4 | 4.4 | .981 |
| | C. Silvera | R | 26 | 97 | 11 | 2 | 2 | 4.2 | .982 |
| | G. Massa | R | 6 | 21 | 0 | 0 | 0 | 3.5 | 1.000 |

Bob Scheffing was the new manager, John Holland took over the general manager's duties, and the Cubs showed vast improvement by tying for the cellar. They played hide-and-seek with the Pirates before sharing the spoils with 62–92 records. Holland pulled a couple of bad trades, sending Sad Sam Jones to the Cardinals for Tom Poholsky. Jones won a dozen while Poholsky was 1–7 with the Cubbies. In addition, Holland broke up the Banks-Baker DP combo by trading Gene Baker and Dee Fondy to the Pirates for Lee Walls and Dale Long. It helped homer production, but created confusion around the keystone. Shortstop Ernie Banks worked with six second basemen, such immortals as Bobby Adams, Jerry Kindall, Jack Littrell, Bobby Morgan, Ed Winceniak, and Casey Wise. Banks finished second to the Braves' Hank Aaron in homers, 44 to 43 and drove in 102 runs.

The Cubs uncovered a couple of young pitchers, Dick Drott and Moe Drabowsky. Drott won 15 games and struck out 170 batters, including 15 Braves in one game. Drabowsky won 13, also fanned 170, and pitched a one-hitter. There were a few weird events to make the year memorable. Cub pitchers Drabowsky, Jackie Collum, and Jim Brosnan walked a record nine Reds in the fifth inning of a 9–5 loss on April 24. Brosnan was relieved on the mound without throwing a pitch against the Giants on June 21. After replacing Drott, Brosnan tossed a warmup pitch, caught his jersey in his zipper, and pulled an Achilles tendon.

### TEAM STATISTICS

| | W | L | PCT | GB | R | OR | 2B | 3B | HR | BA | SA | SB | E | DP | FA | CG | B | SO | ShO | SV | ERA |
|---|---|---|---|---|---|---|---|---|---|---|---|---|---|---|---|---|---|---|---|---|---|
| | | | | | | | | Batting | | | | | | Fielding | | | | | Pitching | | |
| L | 95 | 59 | .617 | | 772 | 613 | 221 | 62 | 199 | .269 | .442 | 35 | 120 | 173 | .981 | 60 | 570 | 693 | 9 | 24 | 3.47 |
| L | 87 | 67 | .565 | 8 | 737 | 666 | 235 | 43 | 132 | .274 | .405 | 58 | 131 | 168 | .979 | 46 | 506 | 778 | 11 | 29 | 3.78 |
| KN | 84 | 70 | .545 | 11 | 690 | 591 | 188 | 38 | 147 | .253 | .387 | 60 | 127 | 136 | .979 | 44 | 456 | 891 | 18 | 29 | 3.35 |
| N | 80 | 74 | .519 | 15 | 747 | 781 | 251 | 33 | 187 | .269 | .432 | 51 | 107 | 139 | .982 | 40 | 429 | 707 | 5 | 29 | 4.62 |
| HI | 77 | 77 | .500 | 18 | 623 | 656 | 213 | 44 | 117 | .250 | .375 | 57 | 136 | 117 | .976 | 54 | 412 | 858 | 9 | 23 | 3.80 |
| | 69 | 85 | .448 | 26 | 643 | 701 | 171 | 54 | 157 | .252 | .393 | 64 | 161 | 180 | .974 | 35 | 471 | 701 | 9 | 20 | 4.01 |
| HI | 62 | 92 | .403 | 33 | 628 | 722 | 223 | 31 | 147 | .244 | .380 | 28 | 149 | 140 | .975 | 30 | 601 | 859 | 5 | 26 | 4.13 |
| | 62 | 92 | .403 | 33 | 586 | 696 | 231 | 60 | 92 | .268 | .384 | 46 | 170 | 143 | .972 | 47 | 421 | 663 | 9 | 15 | 3.88 |
| AGUE TOTAL | | | | | 5426 | 5426 | 1733 | 365 | 1178 | .260 | .400 | 399 | 1101 | 1196 | .977 | 356 | 3866 | 6150 | 75 | 195 | 3.88 |

### INDIVIDUAL PITCHING

| TCHER | T | W | L | PCT | ERA | SV | G | GS | CG | IP | H | BB | SO | R | ER | ShO | H/9 | BB/9 | SO/9 |
|---|---|---|---|---|---|---|---|---|---|---|---|---|---|---|---|---|---|---|---|
| oe Drabowsky | R | 13 | 15 | .464 | 3.53 | 0 | 36 | 33 | 12 | 239.2 | 214 | 94 | 170 | 103 | 94 | 2 | 8.04 | 3.53 | 6.38 |
| ck Drott | R | 15 | 11 | .577 | 3.58 | 0 | 38 | 32 | 7 | 229 | 200 | 129 | 170 | 107 | 91 | 3 | 7.86 | 5.07 | 6.68 |
| b Rush | R | 6 | 16 | .273 | 4.38 | 0 | 31 | 29 | 5 | 205.1 | 211 | 66 | 103 | 111 | 100 | 0 | 9.25 | 2.89 | 4.51 |
| n Elston | R | 6 | 7 | .462 | 3.56 | 8 | 39 | 14 | 2 | 144 | 139 | 55 | 102 | 61 | 57 | 0 | 8.69 | 3.44 | 6.38 |
| ve Hillman | R | 6 | 11 | .353 | 4.35 | 1 | 32 | 14 | 1 | 103.1 | 115 | 37 | 53 | 52 | 50 | 0 | 10.02 | 3.22 | 4.62 |
| n Brosnan | R | 5 | 5 | .500 | 3.38 | 0 | 41 | 5 | 1 | 98.2 | 79 | 46 | 73 | 38 | 37 | 0 | 7.21 | 4.20 | 6.66 |
| rk Lown | R | 5 | 7 | .417 | 3.77 | 12 | 67 | 0 | 0 | 93 | 74 | 51 | 51 | 45 | 39 | 0 | 7.16 | 4.94 | 4.94 |
| m Poholsky | R | 1 | 7 | .125 | 4.93 | 0 | 28 | 11 | 1 | 84 | 117 | 22 | 28 | 55 | 46 | 0 | 12.54 | 2.36 | 3.00 |
| n Kaiser | R | 2 | 6 | .250 | 5.00 | 0 | 20 | 13 | 1 | 72 | 91 | 28 | 23 | 48 | 40 | 0 | 11.38 | 3.50 | 2.88 |
| ck Littlefield | L | 2 | 3 | .400 | 5.35 | 4 | 48 | 2 | 0 | 65.2 | 76 | 37 | 51 | 46 | 39 | 0 | 10.42 | 5.07 | 6.99 |
| b Anderson | R | 0 | 1 | .000 | 7.71 | 0 | 8 | 0 | 0 | 16.1 | 20 | 8 | 7 | 16 | 14 | 0 | 11.02 | 4.41 | 3.86 |
| ner Singleton | R | 0 | 1 | .000 | 6.75 | 0 | 5 | 2 | 0 | 13.1 | 20 | 2 | 6 | 11 | 10 | 0 | 13.50 | 1.35 | 4.05 |
| to Valentinetti | R | 0 | 0 | — | 2.25 | 0 | 9 | 0 | 0 | 12 | 12 | 7 | 8 | 5 | 3 | 0 | 9.00 | 5.25 | 6.00 |
| ckie Collum | L | 1 | 1 | .500 | 6.75 | 1 | 9 | 0 | 0 | 10.2 | 8 | 9 | 7 | 8 | 8 | 0 | 6.75 | 7.59 | 5.91 |
| l Mayer | L | 0 | 0 | — | 5.87 | 0 | 3 | 1 | 0 | 7.2 | 8 | 2 | 3 | 5 | 5 | 0 | 9.39 | 2.35 | 3.52 |
| hnny Briggs | R | 0 | 1 | .000 | 12.46 | 0 | 3 | 0 | 0 | 4.1 | 7 | 3 | 1 | 6 | 6 | 0 | 14.54 | 6.23 | 2.08 |
| en Hobbie | R | 0 | 0 | — | 10.38 | 0 | 2 | 0 | 0 | 4.1 | 6 | 5 | 3 | 5 | 5 | 0 | 12.46 | 10.38 | 6.23 |
| AM TOTAL | | 62 | 92 | .403 | 4.13 | 26 | 419 | 156 | 30 | 1403.1 | 1397 | 601 | 859 | 722 | 644 | 5 | 8.96 | 3.85 | 5.51 |

| MANAGER | W | L | PCT |
|---|---|---|---|
| Bob Scheffing | 72 | 82 | .468 |

| POS | Player | B | G | AB | H | 2B | 3B | HR | HR % | R | RBI | BB | SO | SB | Pinch Hit AB | Pinch Hit H | BA | SA |
|---|---|---|---|---|---|---|---|---|---|---|---|---|---|---|---|---|---|---|
| **REGULARS** | | | | | | | | | | | | | | | | | | |
| 1B | Dale Long | L | 142 | 480 | 130 | 26 | 4 | 20 | 4.2 | 68 | 75 | 66 | 64 | 2 | 5 | 2 | .271 | .467 |
| 2B | Tony Taylor | R | 140 | 497 | 117 | 15 | 3 | 6 | 1.2 | 63 | 27 | 40 | 93 | 21 | 0 | 0 | .235 | .314 |
| SS | Ernie Banks | R | 154 | 617 | 193 | 23 | 11 | 47 | 7.6 | 119 | 129 | 52 | 87 | 4 | 0 | 0 | .313 | .614 |
| 3B | Alvin Dark | R | 114 | 464 | 137 | 16 | 4 | 3 | 0.6 | 54 | 43 | 29 | 23 | 1 | 3 | 1 | .295 | .366 |
| RF | Lee Walls | R | 136 | 513 | 156 | 19 | 3 | 24 | 4.7 | 80 | 72 | 47 | 62 | 4 | 4 | 2 | .304 | .493 |
| CF | Bobby Thomson | R | 152 | 547 | 155 | 27 | 5 | 21 | 3.8 | 67 | 82 | 56 | 82 | 0 | 1 | 1 | .283 | .466 |
| LF | Walt Moryn | L | 143 | 512 | 135 | 26 | 7 | 26 | 5.1 | 77 | 77 | 62 | 83 | 1 | 6 | 4 | .264 | .494 |
| C | Sammy Taylor | L | 96 | 301 | 78 | 12 | 2 | 6 | 2.0 | 30 | 36 | 27 | 46 | 2 | 12 | 4 | .259 | .372 |
| **SUBSTITUTES** | | | | | | | | | | | | | | | | | | |
| 32 | John Goryl | R | 83 | 219 | 53 | 9 | 3 | 4 | 1.8 | 27 | 14 | 27 | 34 | 0 | 10 | 3 | .242 | .365 |
| UT | Bobby Adams | R | 62 | 96 | 27 | 4 | 4 | 0 | 0.0 | 14 | 4 | 6 | 15 | 2 | 35 | 9 | .281 | .406 |
| 1O | Jim Marshall | L | 26 | 81 | 22 | 2 | 0 | 5 | 6.2 | 12 | 11 | 12 | 13 | 1 | 1 | 0 | .272 | .481 |
| 1B | Paul Smith | L | 18 | 20 | 3 | 0 | 0 | 0 | 0.0 | 1 | 1 | 3 | 4 | 0 | 10 | 2 | .150 | .150 |
| 2B | Jerry Kindall | R | 3 | 6 | 1 | 1 | 0 | 0 | 0.0 | 0 | 0 | 0 | 3 | 0 | 0 | 0 | .167 | .333 |
| OF | Jim Bolger | R | 84 | 120 | 27 | 4 | 1 | 1 | 0.8 | 15 | 11 | 9 | 20 | 0 | 51 | 10 | .225 | .300 |
| OF | Chuck Tanner | L | 73 | 103 | 27 | 6 | 0 | 4 | 3.9 | 10 | 17 | 9 | 10 | 1 | 53 | 12 | .262 | .437 |
| OF | Lou Jackson | L | 24 | 35 | 6 | 2 | 1 | 1 | 2.9 | 5 | 6 | 1 | 9 | 0 | 11 | 1 | .171 | .371 |
| OF | Charlie King | R | 8 | 8 | 2 | 0 | 0 | 0 | 0.0 | 1 | 1 | 3 | 1 | 0 | 1 | 0 | .250 | .250 |
| OF | Bob Will | L | 6 | 4 | 1 | 0 | 0 | 0 | 0.0 | 1 | 0 | 2 | 0 | 0 | 4 | 1 | .250 | .250 |
| C | Cal Neeman | R | 76 | 201 | 52 | 7 | 0 | 12 | 6.0 | 30 | 29 | 21 | 41 | 0 | 8 | 0 | .259 | .473 |
| C | El Tappe | R | 17 | 28 | 6 | 0 | 0 | 0 | 0.0 | 2 | 4 | 3 | 1 | 0 | 1 | 0 | .214 | .214 |
| C | Moe Thacker | R | 11 | 24 | 6 | 1 | 0 | 2 | 8.3 | 4 | 3 | 1 | 7 | 0 | 2 | 1 | .250 | .542 |
| PH | Frank Ernaga | R | 9 | 8 | 1 | 0 | 0 | 0 | 0.0 | 0 | 0 | 0 | 2 | 0 | 8 | 1 | .125 | .125 |
| PH | Dick Johnson | L | 8 | 5 | 0 | 0 | 0 | 0 | 0.0 | 1 | 0 | 0 | 1 | 0 | 5 | 0 | .000 | .000 |
| PH | Bill Gabler | L | 3 | 3 | 0 | 0 | 0 | 0 | 0.0 | 0 | 0 | 0 | 0 | 0 | 3 | 0 | .000 | .000 |
| PH | Gordon Massa | L | 2 | 2 | 0 | 0 | 0 | 0 | 0.0 | 0 | 0 | 0 | 2 | 0 | 2 | 0 | .000 | .000 |
| PH | Bobby Morgan | R | 1 | 1 | 0 | 0 | 0 | 0 | 0.0 | 0 | 0 | 0 | 1 | 0 | 1 | 0 | .000 | .000 |
| **PITCHERS** | | | | | | | | | | | | | | | | | | |
| P | Dick Drott | R | 39 | 55 | 15 | 0 | 0 | 0 | 0.0 | 6 | 6 | 3 | 18 | 0 | 0 | 0 | .273 | .273 |
| P | Taylor Phillips | L | 39 | 54 | 3 | 0 | 0 | 0 | 0.0 | 2 | 2 | 3 | 24 | 0 | 0 | 0 | .056 | .056 |
| P | Glen Hobbie | R | 55 | 48 | 7 | 0 | 0 | 0 | 0.0 | 3 | 1 | 1 | 26 | 0 | 0 | 0 | .146 | .146 |
| P | Moe Drabowsky | R | 22 | 45 | 7 | 1 | 0 | 0 | 0.0 | 3 | 3 | 0 | 11 | 0 | 0 | 0 | .156 | .178 |
| P | Dave Hillman | R | 32 | 41 | 6 | 2 | 0 | 0 | 0.0 | 4 | 3 | 0 | 20 | 0 | 0 | 0 | .146 | .195 |
| P | Johnny Briggs | R | 20 | 35 | 9 | 1 | 1 | 0 | 0.0 | 3 | 6 | 0 | 14 | 0 | 0 | 0 | .257 | .343 |
| P | Marcelino Solis | L | 15 | 20 | 5 | 1 | 0 | 0 | 0.0 | 1 | 0 | 1 | 3 | 0 | 0 | 0 | .250 | .300 |
| P | Jim Brosnan | R | 8 | 19 | 2 | 1 | 0 | 0 | 0.0 | 0 | 1 | 0 | 6 | 0 | 0 | 0 | .105 | .158 |
| P | Bob Anderson | R | 17 | 17 | 2 | 0 | 0 | 0 | 0.0 | 1 | 0 | 0 | 8 | 0 | 0 | 0 | .118 | .118 |
| P | Bill Henry | L | 44 | 17 | 4 | 1 | 0 | 0 | 0.0 | 2 | 1 | 2 | 6 | 0 | 0 | 0 | .235 | .294 |
| P | Don Elston | R | 69 | 14 | 5 | 0 | 0 | 0 | 0.0 | 1 | 0 | 0 | 2 | 0 | 0 | 0 | .357 | .357 |
| P | John Buzhardt | R | 6 | 8 | 1 | 0 | 0 | 0 | 0.0 | 0 | 0 | 0 | 5 | 0 | 0 | 0 | .125 | .125 |
| P | Gene Fodge | R | 16 | 7 | 0 | 0 | 0 | 0 | 0.0 | 1 | 0 | 1 | 1 | 0 | 0 | 0 | .000 | .000 |
| P | Ed Mayer | L | 19 | 5 | 1 | 0 | 0 | 0 | 0.0 | 1 | 1 | 0 | 1 | 0 | 0 | 0 | .200 | .200 |
| P | Dolan Nichols | R | 24 | 5 | 0 | 0 | 0 | 0 | 0.0 | 0 | 0 | 0 | 3 | 0 | 0 | 0 | .000 | .000 |
| P | Dick Ellsworth | L | 1 | 1 | 0 | 0 | 0 | 0 | 0.0 | 0 | 0 | 0 | 1 | 0 | 0 | 0 | .000 | .000 |
| P | Hersh Freeman | R | 9 | 1 | 0 | 0 | 0 | 0 | 0.0 | 0 | 0 | 0 | 0 | 0 | 0 | 0 | .000 | .000 |
| P | Freddy Rodriguez | R | 7 | 1 | 0 | 0 | 0 | 0 | 0.0 | 0 | 0 | 0 | 1 | 0 | 0 | 0 | .000 | .000 |
| P | Elmer Singleton | B | 2 | 1 | 0 | 0 | 0 | 0 | 0.0 | 0 | 0 | 0 | 1 | 0 | 0 | 0 | .000 | .000 |
| P | Turk Lown | R | 4 | 0 | 0 | 0 | 0 | 0 | – | 0 | 0 | 0 | 0 | 0 | 0 | 0 | – | – |
| TEAM TOTAL | | | | 5289 | 1402 | 207 | 49 | 182 | 3.4 | 70 | 666 | 487 | 853 | 39 | 237 | 54 | .265 | .426 |

## INDIVIDUAL FIELDING

| POS | Player | T | G | PO | A | E | DP | TC/G | FA |
|---|---|---|---|---|---|---|---|---|---|
| 1B | D. Long | L | 137 | 1173 | 84 | 10 | 130 | 9.2 | .992 |
| | J. Marshall | L | 15 | 114 | 7 | 1 | 11 | 8.1 | .992 |
| | B. Adams | R | 11 | 44 | 5 | 2 | 1 | 4.6 | .961 |
| | P. Smith | L | 4 | 14 | 2 | 1 | 0 | 4.3 | .941 |
| 2B | T. Taylor | R | 137 | 311 | 374 | 23 | 103 | 5.2 | .968 |
| | J. Goryl | R | 35 | 45 | 65 | 6 | 13 | 3.3 | .948 |
| | B. Adams | R | 7 | 15 | 13 | 1 | 5 | 4.1 | .966 |
| | J. Kindall | R | 3 | 6 | 5 | 0 | 2 | 3.7 | 1.000 |
| SS | E. Banks | R | 154 | 292 | 468 | 32 | 100 | 5.1 | .960 |
| 3B | A. Dark | R | 111 | 107 | 225 | 18 | 24 | 3.2 | .949 |
| | J. Goryl | R | 44 | 46 | 88 | 10 | 13 | 3.3 | .931 |
| | T. Taylor | R | 1 | 0 | 0 | 0 | 0 | 0.0 | .000 |
| | B. Adams | R | 9 | 4 | 6 | 0 | 0 | 1.1 | 1.000 |
| | B. Thomson | R | 4 | 5 | 3 | 1 | 1 | 2.3 | .889 |

| POS | Player | T | G | PO | A | E | DP | TC/G | FA |
|---|---|---|---|---|---|---|---|---|---|
| OF | B. Thomson | R | 148 | 353 | 13 | 4 | 3 | 2.5 | .989 |
| | W. Moryn | R | 141 | 265 | 4 | 6 | 1 | 2.0 | .978 |
| | L. Walls | R | 132 | 241 | 10 | 2 | 1 | 1.9 | .992 |
| | J. Bolger | R | 37 | 46 | 1 | 3 | 0 | 1.4 | .940 |
| | C. Tanner | L | 15 | 21 | 0 | 1 | 0 | 1.5 | .955 |
| | B. Will | L | 1 | 0 | 0 | 0 | 0 | 0.0 | .000 |
| | L. Jackson | R | 12 | 9 | 0 | 0 | 0 | 0.8 | 1.000 |
| | C. King | R | 7 | 6 | 0 | 0 | 0 | 0.8 | 1.000 |
| | J. Marshall | L | 11 | 5 | 1 | 0 | 0 | 0.5 | 1.000 |
| C | S. Taylor | R | 87 | 460 | 23 | 6 | 4 | 5.6 | .988 |
| | C. Neeman | R | 71 | 340 | 25 | 3 | 6 | 5.2 | .992 |
| | E. Tappe | R | 16 | 46 | 4 | 2 | 0 | 3.3 | .962 |
| | M. Thacker | R | 9 | 34 | 6 | 2 | 1 | 4.7 | .952 |
| | D. Long | L | 2 | 0 | 1 | 0 | 0 | 0.5 | 1.000 |

Ernie Banks became the first member of a team with a losing record to win the Most Valuable Player Award as the Cubs tied the Cardinals for fifth place, both with 72–82 records. Banks was the bell cow of a bullish batting attack that featured five Cubs with 20 or more home runs. The Cubs smashed a team-record 182 homers, Banks leading the league with 47, an all-time record for a major-league shortstop. In addition, Moose Moryn hit 26; Lee Walls, 24; Bobby Thomson, 21; and Dale Long, 20. Besides homers, Banks led the league with 129 runs batted in, 379 total bases, and a .614 slugging average, and was second to the Giants' Willie Mays in runs scored, 121–119. Banks hit .313 to lead the club, and Walls chipped in with a .304 average. The Cubs' downfall was a leaky defense and lack of experienced pitching. Rookie Glen Hobbie was the lone pitcher to win at least 10 games, finishing with a 10–6 mark. The Cubs led the NL at the outset with a 13–7 ledger and were still only 4 1/2 games out on July 4. But a 12–20 August slump dropped them into the cellar. They rallied in September for their highest finish since 1952.

## TEAM STATISTICS

| | W | L | PCT | GB | R | OR | 2B | 3B | HR | BA | SA | SB | E | DP | FA | CG | B | SO | ShO | SV | ERA |
|---|---|---|---|---|---|---|---|---|---|---|---|---|---|---|---|---|---|---|---|---|---|
| IL | 92 | 62 | .597 | | 675 | 541 | 221 | 21 | 167 | .266 | .412 | 26 | 120 | 152 | .980 | 72 | 426 | 773 | 16 | 17 | 3.21 |
| T | 84 | 70 | .545 | 8 | 662 | 607 | 229 | 68 | 134 | .264 | .410 | 30 | 133 | 173 | .978 | 43 | 470 | 679 | 10 | 41 | 3.56 |
| F | 80 | 74 | .519 | 12 | 727 | 698 | 250 | 42 | 170 | .263 | .422 | 64 | 152 | 156 | .975 | 38 | 512 | 775 | 7 | 25 | 3.98 |
| IN | 76 | 78 | .494 | 16 | 695 | 621 | 242 | 40 | 123 | .258 | .389 | 61 | 100 | 148 | .983 | 50 | 419 | 705 | 7 | 20 | 3.73 |
| HI | 72 | 82 | .468 | 20 | 709 | 725 | 207 | 49 | 182 | .265 | .426 | 39 | 150 | 161 | .975 | 27 | 619 | 805 | 5 | 24 | 4.22 |
| TL | 72 | 82 | .468 | 20 | 619 | 704 | 216 | 39 | 111 | .261 | .380 | 44 | 153 | 163 | .974 | 45 | 567 | 822 | 6 | 25 | 4.12 |
| A | 71 | 83 | .461 | 21 | 668 | 761 | 166 | 50 | 172 | .251 | .402 | 73 | 146 | 198 | .975 | 30 | 606 | 855 | 7 | 31 | 4.47 |
| HI | 69 | 85 | .448 | 23 | 664 | 762 | 238 | 56 | 124 | .266 | .400 | 51 | 129 | 136 | .978 | 51 | 446 | 778 | 6 | 15 | 4.32 |
| EAGUE TOTAL | | | | | 5419 | 5419 | 1769 | 365 | 1183 | .262 | .405 | 388 | 1083 | 1287 | .977 | 356 | 4065 | 6192 | 64 | 198 | 3.95 |

## INDIVIDUAL PITCHING

| PITCHER | T | W | L | PCT | ERA | SV | G | GS | CG | IP | H | BB | SO | R | ER | ShO | H/9 | BB/9 | SO/9 |
|---|---|---|---|---|---|---|---|---|---|---|---|---|---|---|---|---|---|---|---|
| aylor Phillips | L | 7 | 10 | .412 | 4.76 | 1 | 39 | 27 | 5 | 170.1 | 178 | 79 | 102 | 102 | 90 | 1 | 9.41 | 4.17 | 5.39 |
| len Hobbie | R | 10 | 6 | .625 | 3.74 | 2 | 55 | 16 | 2 | 168.1 | 163 | 93 | 91 | 80 | 70 | 1 | 8.71 | 4.97 | 4.87 |
| ick Drott | R | 7 | 11 | .389 | 5.43 | 0 | 39 | 31 | 4 | 167.1 | 156 | 99 | 127 | 118 | 101 | 0 | 8.39 | 5.32 | 6.83 |
| oe Drabowsky | R | 9 | 11 | .450 | 4.51 | 0 | 22 | 20 | 4 | 125.2 | 118 | 73 | 77 | 73 | 63 | 1 | 8.45 | 5.23 | 5.51 |
| ave Hillman | R | 4 | 8 | .333 | 3.15 | 1 | 31 | 16 | 3 | 125.2 | 132 | 31 | 65 | 57 | 44 | 0 | 9.45 | 2.22 | 4.66 |
| on Elston | R | 9 | 8 | .529 | 2.88 | 10 | 69 | 0 | 0 | 97 | 75 | 39 | 84 | 35 | 31 | 0 | 6.96 | 3.62 | 7.79 |
| ohnny Briggs | R | 5 | 5 | .500 | 4.52 | 0 | 20 | 17 | 3 | 95.2 | 99 | 45 | 46 | 52 | 48 | 1 | 9.31 | 4.23 | 4.33 |
| ll Henry | L | 5 | 4 | .556 | 2.88 | 6 | 44 | 0 | 0 | 81.1 | 63 | 17 | 58 | 27 | 26 | 0 | 6.97 | 1.88 | 6.42 |
| ob Anderson | R | 3 | 3 | .500 | 3.97 | 0 | 17 | 8 | 2 | 65.2 | 61 | 29 | 51 | 29 | 29 | 0 | 8.36 | 3.97 | 6.99 |
| Marcelino Solis | L | 3 | 3 | .500 | 6.06 | 0 | 15 | 4 | 0 | 52 | 74 | 20 | 15 | 41 | 35 | 0 | 12.81 | 3.46 | 2.60 |
| m Brosnan | R | 3 | 4 | .429 | 3.14 | 0 | 8 | 8 | 2 | 51.2 | 41 | 29 | 24 | 20 | 18 | 0 | 7.14 | 5.05 | 4.18 |
| olan Nichols | R | 0 | 4 | .000 | 5.01 | 1 | 24 | 0 | 0 | 41.1 | 46 | 16 | 9 | 27 | 23 | 0 | 10.02 | 3.48 | 1.96 |
| ene Fodge | R | 1 | 1 | .500 | 4.76 | 0 | 16 | 4 | 1 | 39.2 | 47 | 11 | 15 | 22 | 21 | 0 | 10.66 | 2.50 | 3.40 |
| ohn Buzhardt | R | 3 | 0 | 1.000 | 1.85 | 0 | 6 | 2 | 1 | 24.1 | 16 | 7 | 9 | 5 | 5 | 0 | 5.92 | 2.59 | 3.33 |
| d Mayer | L | 2 | 2 | .500 | 3.80 | 1 | 19 | 0 | 0 | 23.2 | 15 | 16 | 14 | 12 | 10 | 0 | 5.70 | 6.08 | 5.32 |
| ersh Freeman | R | 0 | 1 | .000 | 8.31 | 0 | 9 | 0 | 0 | 13 | 23 | 3 | 7 | 13 | 12 | 0 | 15.92 | 2.08 | 4.85 |
| eddy Rodriguez | R | 0 | 0 | – | 7.36 | 2 | 7 | 0 | 0 | 7.1 | 8 | 5 | 5 | 6 | 6 | 0 | 9.82 | 6.14 | 6.14 |
| mer Singleton | R | 1 | 0 | 1.000 | 0.00 | 0 | 2 | 0 | 0 | 4.2 | 1 | 1 | 2 | 0 | 0 | 0 | 1.93 | 1.93 | 3.86 |
| urk Lown | R | 0 | 0 | – | 4.50 | 0 | 4 | 0 | 0 | 4 | 2 | 3 | 4 | 2 | 2 | 0 | 4.50 | 6.75 | 9.00 |
| ick Ellsworth | L | 0 | 1 | .000 | 15.43 | 0 | 1 | 1 | 0 | 2.1 | 4 | 3 | 0 | 4 | 4 | 0 | 15.43 | 11.57 | 0.00 |
| EAM TOTAL | | 72 | 82 | .468 | 4.22 | 24 | 447 | 154 | 27 | 1361 | 1322 | 619 | 805 | 725 | 638 | 4 | 8.74 | 4.09 | 5.32 |

| MANAGER | W | L | PCT |
|---|---|---|---|
| Bob Scheffing | 74 | 80 | .481 |

| POS | Player | B | G | AB | H | 2B | 3B | HR | HR % | R | RBI | BB | SO | SB | Pinch Hit AB | Pinch Hit H | BA | SA |
|---|---|---|---|---|---|---|---|---|---|---|---|---|---|---|---|---|---|---|
| **REGULARS** | | | | | | | | | | | | | | | | | | |
| 1B | Dale Long | L | 110 | 296 | 70 | 10 | 3 | 14 | 4.7 | 34 | 37 | 31 | 53 | 0 | 27 | 6 | .236 | .432 |
| 2B | Tony Taylor | R | 150 | 624 | 175 | 30 | 8 | 8 | 1.3 | 96 | 38 | 45 | 86 | 23 | 0 | 0 | .280 | .393 |
| SS | Ernie Banks | R | 155 | 589 | 179 | 25 | 6 | 45 | 7.6 | 97 | 143 | 64 | 72 | 2 | 1 | 0 | .304 | .596 |
| 3B | Alvin Dark | R | 136 | 477 | 126 | 22 | 9 | 6 | 1.3 | 60 | 45 | 55 | 50 | 1 | 1 | 0 | .264 | .386 |
| RF | Lee Walls | R | 120 | 354 | 91 | 18 | 3 | 8 | 2.3 | 43 | 33 | 42 | 73 | 0 | 4 | 0 | .257 | .393 |
| CF | George Altman | L | 135 | 420 | 103 | 14 | 4 | 12 | 2.9 | 54 | 47 | 34 | 80 | 1 | 15 | 4 | .245 | .383 |
| LF | Bobby Thomson | R | 122 | 374 | 97 | 15 | 2 | 11 | 2.9 | 55 | 52 | 35 | 50 | 1 | 9 | 4 | .259 | .398 |
| C | Sammy Taylor | L | 110 | 353 | 95 | 13 | 2 | 13 | 3.7 | 41 | 43 | 35 | 47 | 1 | 9 | 1 | .269 | .428 |
| **SUBSTITUTES** | | | | | | | | | | | | | | | | | | |
| 1B | Jim Marshall | L | 108 | 294 | 74 | 10 | 1 | 11 | 3.7 | 39 | 40 | 33 | 39 | 0 | 33 | 8 | .252 | .405 |
| 1O | Art Schult | R | 42 | 118 | 32 | 7 | 0 | 2 | 1.7 | 17 | 14 | 7 | 14 | 0 | 9 | 2 | .271 | .381 |
| 3B | Randy Jackson | R | 41 | 74 | 18 | 5 | 1 | 1 | 1.4 | 7 | 10 | 11 | 10 | 0 | 15 | 1 | .243 | .378 |
| 23 | John Goryl | R | 25 | 48 | 9 | 3 | 1 | 1 | 2.1 | 1 | 6 | 5 | 3 | 1 | 8 | 1 | .188 | .354 |
| 1B | Bobby Adams | R | 3 | 2 | 0 | 0 | 0 | 0 | 0.0 | 0 | 0 | 0 | 1 | 0 | 2 | 0 | .000 | .000 |
| 3B | Don Eaddy | R | 15 | 1 | 0 | 0 | 0 | 0 | 0.0 | 3 | 0 | 0 | 1 | 0 | 0 | 0 | .000 | .000 |
| OF | Walt Moryn | L | 117 | 381 | 89 | 14 | 1 | 14 | 3.7 | 41 | 48 | 44 | 66 | 0 | 13 | 5 | .234 | .386 |
| OF | Irv Noren | L | 65 | 156 | 50 | 6 | 2 | 4 | 2.6 | 27 | 19 | 13 | 24 | 2 | 24 | 12 | .321 | .462 |
| OF | Billy Williams | L | 18 | 33 | 5 | 0 | 1 | 0 | 0.0 | 0 | 2 | 1 | 7 | 0 | 6 | 0 | .152 | .212 |
| OF | Charlie King | R | 7 | 3 | 0 | 0 | 0 | 0 | 0.0 | 3 | 0 | 0 | 1 | 0 | 0 | 0 | .000 | .000 |
| UT | Earl Averill | R | 74 | 186 | 44 | 10 | 0 | 10 | 5.4 | 22 | 34 | 15 | 39 | 0 | 25 | 10 | .237 | .452 |
| C | Cal Neeman | R | 44 | 105 | 17 | 2 | 0 | 3 | 2.9 | 7 | 9 | 11 | 23 | 0 | 5 | 0 | .162 | .267 |
| PH | Lou Jackson | L | 6 | 4 | 1 | 0 | 0 | 0 | 0.0 | 2 | 1 | 0 | 2 | 0 | 4 | 1 | .250 | .250 |
| **PITCHERS** | | | | | | | | | | | | | | | | | | |
| P | Bob Anderson | R | 37 | 80 | 6 | 1 | 0 | 0 | 0.0 | 6 | 3 | 3 | 34 | 0 | 0 | 0 | .075 | .088 |
| P | Glen Hobbie | R | 46 | 79 | 9 | 0 | 0 | 0 | 0.0 | 3 | 2 | 2 | 30 | 0 | 0 | 0 | .114 | .127 |
| P | Dave Hillman | R | 42 | 60 | 9 | 0 | 0 | 0 | 0.0 | 0 | 3 | 6 | 32 | 0 | 0 | 0 | .150 | .150 |
| P | Moe Drabowsky | R | 31 | 45 | 5 | 1 | 0 | 0 | 0.0 | 2 | 2 | 2 | 20 | 0 | 0 | 0 | .111 | .133 |
| P | Art Ceccarelli | R | 18 | 33 | 3 | 0 | 0 | 0 | 0.0 | 2 | 0 | 3 | 16 | 0 | 0 | 0 | .091 | .091 |
| P | Bill Henry | L | 65 | 31 | 6 | 0 | 0 | 0 | 0.0 | 4 | 2 | 0 | 12 | 0 | 0 | 0 | .194 | .194 |
| P | John Buzhardt | R | 31 | 29 | 2 | 1 | 0 | 0 | 0.0 | 4 | 0 | 1 | 15 | 0 | 0 | 0 | .069 | .103 |
| P | Don Elston | R | 65 | 19 | 4 | 0 | 0 | 0 | 0.0 | 2 | 1 | 0 | 2 | 0 | 0 | 0 | .211 | .211 |
| P | Dick Drott | R | 8 | 8 | 1 | 0 | 0 | 0 | 0.0 | 0 | 0 | 0 | 2 | 0 | 0 | 0 | .125 | .125 |
| P | Elmer Singleton | R | 21 | 6 | 0 | 0 | 0 | 0 | 0.0 | 0 | 0 | 0 | 4 | 0 | 0 | 0 | .000 | .000 |
| P | Ben Johnson | R | 4 | 4 | 0 | 0 | 0 | 0 | 0.0 | 0 | 1 | 0 | 1 | 0 | 0 | 0 | .000 | .000 |
| P | Taylor Phillips | L | 7 | 4 | 0 | 0 | 0 | 0 | 0.0 | 0 | 0 | 0 | 1 | 0 | 0 | 0 | .000 | .000 |
| P | Joe Schaffernoth | R | 5 | 3 | 0 | 0 | 0 | 0 | 0.0 | 0 | 0 | 0 | 1 | 0 | 0 | 0 | .000 | .000 |
| P | Seth Morehead | L | 11 | 2 | 1 | 1 | 0 | 0 | 0.0 | 0 | 0 | 0 | 0 | 0 | 0 | 0 | .500 | 1.000 |
| P | Bob Porterfield | R | 4 | 1 | 0 | 0 | 0 | 0 | 0.0 | 1 | 0 | 0 | 0 | 0 | 0 | 0 | .000 | .000 |
| P | Ed Donnelly | R | 9 | 0 | 0 | 0 | 0 | 0 | – | 0 | 0 | 0 | 0 | 0 | 0 | 0 | – | – |
| P | Morrie Martin | L | 3 | 0 | 0 | 0 | 0 | 0 | – | 0 | 0 | 0 | 0 | 0 | 0 | 0 | – | – |
| P | Riverboat Smith | B | 1 | 0 | 0 | 0 | 0 | 0 | – | 0 | 0 | 0 | 0 | 0 | 0 | 0 | – | – |
| TEAM TOTAL | | | | 5296 | 1321 | 209 | 44 | 163 | 3.1 | 67 | 635 | 498 | 911 | 32 | 210 | 55 | .249 | .398 |

## INDIVIDUAL FIELDING

| POS | Player | T | G | PO | A | E | DP | TC/G | FA | POS | Player | T | G | PO | A | E | DP | TC/G | FA |
|---|---|---|---|---|---|---|---|---|---|---|---|---|---|---|---|---|---|---|---|
| 1B | D. Long | L | 85 | 731 | 49 | 12 | 63 | 9.3 | .985 | OF | G. Altman | R | 121 | 278 | 7 | 3 | 2 | 2.4 | .990 |
| | J. Marshall | L | 72 | 558 | 51 | 2 | 52 | 8.5 | .997 | | B. Thomson | R | 116 | 223 | 9 | 3 | 4 | 2.0 | .987 |
| | A. Schult | R | 23 | 126 | 6 | 2 | 15 | 5.8 | .985 | | L. Walls | R | 119 | 203 | 1 | 7 | 0 | 1.8 | .967 |
| | A. Dark | R | 4 | 26 | 4 | 1 | 1 | 7.8 | .968 | | W. Moryn | R | 104 | 175 | 9 | 2 | 1 | 1.8 | .989 |
| | B. Adams | R | 1 | 2 | 0 | 1 | 0 | 3.0 | .667 | | I. Noren | L | 40 | 81 | 4 | 0 | 1 | 2.1 | 1.000 |
| | I. Noren | L | 1 | 3 | 0 | 0 | 0 | 3.0 | 1.000 | | A. Schult | R | 15 | 26 | 0 | 0 | 0 | 1.7 | 1.000 |
| | | | | | | | | | | | R. Jackson | R | 1 | 0 | 0 | 0 | 0 | 0.0 | .000 |
| 2B | T. Taylor | R | 149 | 352 | 456 | 25 | 105 | 5.6 | .970 | | B. Williams | R | 10 | 18 | 0 | 0 | 0 | 1.8 | 1.000 |
| | J. Goryl | R | 11 | 11 | 25 | 1 | 1 | 3.4 | .973 | | J. Marshall | L | 8 | 7 | 1 | 0 | 0 | 1.0 | 1.000 |
| | E. Averill | R | 2 | 3 | 6 | 0 | 1 | 4.5 | 1.000 | | E. Averill | R | 5 | 5 | 0 | 1 | 0 | 1.2 | .833 |
| SS | E. Banks | R | 154 | 271 | 519 | 12 | 95 | 5.2 | .985 | | C. King | R | 1 | 2 | 0 | 0 | 0 | 2.0 | 1.000 |
| | T. Taylor | R | 2 | 3 | 0 | 0 | 0 | 1.5 | 1.000 | C | S. Taylor | R | 109 | 497 | 37 | 10 | 1 | 5.0 | .982 |
| | A. Dark | R | 1 | 1 | 1 | 0 | 0 | 2.0 | 1.000 | | E. Averill | R | 32 | 173 | 11 | 7 | 1 | 6.0 | .963 |
| 3B | A. Dark | R | 131 | 111 | 255 | 20 | 20 | 2.9 | .948 | | C. Neeman | R | 38 | 158 | 9 | 1 | 1 | 4.4 | .994 |
| | R. Jackson | R | 22 | 20 | 28 | 3 | 2 | 2.3 | .941 | | | | | | | | | | |
| | E. Averill | R | 13 | 16 | 32 | 5 | 2 | 4.1 | .906 | | | | | | | | | | |
| | J. Goryl | R | 4 | 0 | 6 | 0 | 1 | 1.5 | 1.000 | | | | | | | | | | |
| | D. Eaddy | R | 1 | 0 | 1 | 1 | 0 | 2.0 | .500 | | | | | | | | | | |

Bob Scheffing had just directed the Cubs to their best record (74–80) since 1952 when he was summoned to owner P. K. Wrigley's office. Scheffing was all smiles and expected a pay hike. Wrigley, apparently unaccustomed to a lofty fifth-place finish, glared at Scheffing and said: "You're fired." So much for even keel. The Cubs were 8–7 in April; 15–16 in May; 13–13 in June; 14–14 in July; 12–16 in August; and 12–13 in September. They were also a one-man wrecking crew. A chap named Ernie Banks drove home 143 runs, most for a Cub since Hack Wilson in 1930. He also had 45 homers and batted .304. Afield, he set two records (both since broken) for a shortstop: fewest errors (12) and highest average (.985). Banks was justly rewarded by winning the Most Valuable Player Award for the second season in a row. But Glen Hobbie was the lone dependable pitcher, with a 16–13 record.

One of the most bizarre plays in Cub history occurred in the fourth inning on June 30 at Wrigley Field when two balls were in play at the same time. It would have taken an Einstein to untangle the mess, but can you picture Stan Musial of the Cardinals sliding into second base while shortstop Banks applied the tag and second baseman Tony Taylor leaped for a wild heave that sailed into centerfield? Was Musial safe or out? Plate umpire Vic Delmore, who was the main culprit involved on that play, was fired at the end of the season.

### TEAM STATISTICS

| | W | L | PCT | GB | R | OR | 2B | 3B | HR | BA | SA | SB | E | DP | FA | CG | B | SO | ShO | SV | ERA |
|---|---|---|---|---|---|---|---|---|---|---|---|---|---|---|---|---|---|---|---|---|---|
| A | 88 | 68 | .564 | | 705 | 670 | 196 | 46 | 148 | .257 | .396 | 84 | 114 | 154 | .981 | 43 | 614 | 1077 | 14 | 26 | 3.79 |
| IL | 86 | 70 | .551 | 2 | 724 | 623 | 216 | 36 | 177 | .265 | .417 | 41 | 127 | 138 | .979 | 69 | 429 | 775 | 18 | 18 | 3.51 |
| F | 83 | 71 | .539 | 4 | 705 | 613 | 239 | 35 | 167 | .261 | .414 | 81 | 152 | 118 | .974 | 52 | 500 | 873 | 12 | 23 | 3.47 |
| IT | 78 | 76 | .506 | 9 | 651 | 680 | 230 | 42 | 112 | .263 | .384 | 32 | 154 | 165 | .975 | 48 | 418 | 730 | 7 | 17 | 3.90 |
| HI | 74 | 80 | .481 | 13 | 673 | 688 | 209 | 44 | 163 | .249 | .398 | 32 | 140 | 142 | .977 | 30 | 519 | 765 | 11 | 25 | 4.01 |
| IN | 74 | 80 | .481 | 13 | 764 | 738 | 258 | 34 | 161 | .274 | .427 | 65 | 126 | 157 | .978 | 44 | 456 | 690 | 7 | 26 | 4.31 |
| TL | 71 | 83 | .461 | 16 | 641 | 725 | 244 | 49 | 118 | .269 | .400 | 65 | 146 | 158 | .975 | 36 | 564 | 846 | 8 | 25 | 4.34 |
| HI | 64 | 90 | .416 | 23 | 599 | 725 | 196 | 38 | 113 | .242 | .362 | 39 | 154 | 132 | .973 | 54 | 474 | 769 | 8 | 15 | 4.27 |
| LEAGUE TOTAL | | | | | 5462 | 5462 | 1788 | 324 | 1159 | .260 | .400 | 439 | 1113 | 1164 | .977 | 376 | 3974 | 6525 | 85 | 175 | 3.95 |

### INDIVIDUAL PITCHING

| PITCHER | T | W | L | PCT | ERA | SV | G | GS | CG | IP | H | BB | SO | R | ER | ShO | H/9 | BB/9 | SO/9 |
|---|---|---|---|---|---|---|---|---|---|---|---|---|---|---|---|---|---|---|---|
| Bob Anderson | R | 12 | 13 | .480 | 4.13 | 0 | 37 | 36 | 7 | 235.1 | 245 | 77 | 113 | 117 | 108 | 1 | 9.37 | 2.94 | 4.32 |
| Glen Hobbie | R | 16 | 13 | .552 | 3.69 | 0 | 46 | 33 | 10 | 234 | 204 | 106 | 138 | 105 | 96 | 3 | 7.85 | 4.08 | 5.31 |
| Dave Hillman | R | 8 | 11 | .421 | 3.53 | 0 | 39 | 24 | 4 | 191 | 178 | 43 | 88 | 84 | 75 | 1 | 8.39 | 2.03 | 4.15 |
| Moe Drabowsky | R | 5 | 10 | .333 | 4.13 | 0 | 31 | 23 | 3 | 141.2 | 138 | 75 | 70 | 78 | 65 | 1 | 8.77 | 4.76 | 4.45 |
| Bill Henry | L | 9 | 8 | .529 | 2.68 | 12 | 65 | 0 | 0 | 134.1 | 111 | 26 | 115 | 42 | 40 | 0 | 7.44 | 1.74 | 7.70 |
| Art Ceccarelli | L | 5 | 5 | .500 | 4.76 | 0 | 18 | 15 | 4 | 102 | 95 | 37 | 56 | 58 | 54 | 2 | 8.38 | 3.26 | 4.94 |
| John Buzhardt | R | 4 | 5 | .444 | 4.97 | 0 | 31 | 10 | 1 | 101.1 | 107 | 29 | 33 | 64 | 56 | 1 | 9.50 | 2.58 | 2.93 |
| Don Elston | R | 10 | 8 | .556 | 3.32 | 13 | 65 | 0 | 0 | 97.2 | 77 | 46 | 82 | 40 | 36 | 0 | 7.10 | 4.24 | 7.56 |
| Elmer Singleton | R | 2 | 1 | .667 | 2.72 | 0 | 21 | 1 | 0 | 43 | 40 | 12 | 25 | 15 | 13 | 0 | 8.37 | 2.51 | 5.23 |
| Dick Drott | R | 1 | 2 | .333 | 5.93 | 0 | 8 | 6 | 1 | 27.1 | 25 | 26 | 15 | 19 | 18 | 1 | 8.23 | 8.56 | 4.94 |
| Seth Morehead | L | 0 | 1 | .000 | 4.82 | 0 | 11 | 2 | 0 | 18.2 | 25 | 8 | 9 | 13 | 10 | 0 | 12.05 | 3.86 | 4.34 |
| Ken Johnson | R | 0 | 0 | — | 2.16 | 0 | 4 | 2 | 0 | 16.2 | 17 | 4 | 6 | 5 | 4 | 0 | 9.18 | 2.16 | 3.24 |
| Taylor Phillips | L | 0 | 2 | .000 | 7.56 | 0 | 7 | 2 | 0 | 16.2 | 22 | 11 | 5 | 14 | 14 | 0 | 11.88 | 5.94 | 2.70 |
| Ed Donnelly | R | 1 | 1 | .500 | 3.14 | 0 | 9 | 0 | 0 | 14.1 | 18 | 9 | 6 | 7 | 5 | 0 | 11.30 | 5.65 | 3.77 |
| Joe Schaffernoth | R | 1 | 0 | 1.000 | 8.22 | 0 | 5 | 1 | 0 | 7.2 | 11 | 4 | 3 | 7 | 7 | 0 | 12.91 | 4.70 | 3.52 |
| Bob Porterfield | R | 0 | 0 | — | 11.37 | 0 | 4 | 0 | 0 | 6.1 | 14 | 3 | 0 | 9 | 8 | 0 | 19.89 | 4.26 | 0.00 |
| Morrie Martin | L | 0 | 0 | — | 19.29 | 0 | 3 | 0 | 0 | 2.1 | 5 | 1 | 1 | 5 | 5 | 0 | 19.29 | 3.86 | 3.86 |
| Riverboat Smith | L | 0 | 0 | — | 81.00 | 0 | 1 | 0 | 0 | .2 | 5 | 2 | 0 | 6 | 6 | 0 | 67.50 | 27.00 | 0.00 |
| TEAM TOTAL | | 74 | 80 | .481 | 4.01 | 25 | 405 | 155 | 30 | 1391 | 1337 | 519 | 765 | 688 | 620 | 10 | 8.65 | 3.36 | 4.95 |

| MANAGER | W | L | PCT |
|---|---|---|---|
| Charlie Grimm | 6 | 11 | .353 |
| Lou Boudreau | 54 | 83 | .394 |

| POS | Player | B | G | AB | H | 2B | 3B | HR | HR % | R | RBI | BB | SO | SB | Pinch Hit AB | Pinch Hit H | BA | SA |
|---|---|---|---|---|---|---|---|---|---|---|---|---|---|---|---|---|---|---|
| **REGULARS** | | | | | | | | | | | | | | | | | | |
| 1B | Ed Bouchee | L | 98 | 299 | 71 | 11 | 1 | 5 | 1.7 | 33 | 44 | 45 | 51 | 2 | 16 | 1 | .237 | .331 |
| 2B | Jerry Kindall | B | 89 | 246 | 59 | 16 | 2 | 2 | 0.8 | 17 | 23 | 5 | 52 | 4 | 3 | 0 | .240 | .346 |
| SS | Ernie Banks | R | 156 | 597 | 162 | 32 | 7 | 41 | 6.9 | 94 | 117 | 71 | 69 | 1 | 0 | 0 | .271 | .554 |
| 3B | Ron Santo | R | 95 | 347 | 87 | 24 | 2 | 9 | 2.6 | 44 | 44 | 31 | 44 | 0 | 1 | 0 | .251 | .409 |
| RF | Bob Will | L | 138 | 475 | 121 | 20 | 9 | 6 | 1.3 | 58 | 53 | 47 | 54 | 1 | 20 | 5 | .255 | .373 |
| CF | Richie Ashburn | L | 151 | 547 | 159 | 16 | 5 | 0 | 0.0 | 99 | 40 | 116 | 50 | 16 | 6 | 1 | .291 | .338 |
| LF | George Altman | L | 119 | 334 | 89 | 16 | 4 | 13 | 3.9 | 50 | 51 | 32 | 67 | 4 | 20 | 8 | .266 | .455 |
| C | Moe Thacker | R | 54 | 90 | 14 | 1 | 0 | 0 | 0.0 | 5 | 6 | 14 | 20 | 1 | 4 | 1 | .156 | .167 |
| **SUBSTITUTES** | | | | | | | | | | | | | | | | | | |
| UT | Frank Thomas | R | 135 | 479 | 114 | 12 | 1 | 21 | 4.4 | 54 | 64 | 28 | 74 | 1 | 11 | 4 | .238 | .399 |
| 23 | Don Zimmer | R | 132 | 368 | 95 | 16 | 7 | 6 | 1.6 | 37 | 35 | 27 | 56 | 8 | 13 | 3 | .258 | .389 |
| 1O | Dick Gernert | R | 52 | 96 | 24 | 3 | 0 | 0 | 0.0 | 8 | 11 | 10 | 19 | 1 | 27 | 7 | .250 | .281 |
| 2B | Tony Taylor | R | 19 | 76 | 20 | 3 | 3 | 1 | 1.3 | 14 | 9 | 8 | 12 | 2 | 0 | 0 | .263 | .421 |
| 2B | Grady Hatton | L | 28 | 38 | 13 | 0 | 0 | 0 | 0.0 | 3 | 7 | 2 | 5 | 0 | 16 | 3 | .342 | .342 |
| 32 | Sammy Drake | B | 15 | 15 | 1 | 0 | 0 | 0 | 0.0 | 5 | 0 | 1 | 4 | 0 | 4 | 1 | .067 | .067 |
| OF | Walt Moryn | L | 38 | 109 | 32 | 4 | 0 | 2 | 1.8 | 12 | 11 | 13 | 19 | 2 | 8 | 2 | .294 | .385 |
| OF | Al Heist | R | 41 | 102 | 28 | 5 | 3 | 1 | 1.0 | 11 | 6 | 10 | 12 | 3 | 10 | 2 | .275 | .412 |
| OF | Danny Murphy | L | 31 | 75 | 9 | 2 | 0 | 1 | 1.3 | 7 | 6 | 4 | 13 | 0 | 7 | 0 | .120 | .187 |
| OF | Lou Johnson | R | 34 | 68 | 14 | 2 | 1 | 0 | 0.0 | 6 | 1 | 5 | 19 | 3 | 6 | 0 | .206 | .265 |
| OF | Billy Williams | L | 12 | 47 | 13 | 0 | 2 | 2 | 4.3 | 4 | 7 | 5 | 12 | 0 | 0 | 0 | .277 | .489 |
| OF | Art Schult | R | 12 | 15 | 2 | 1 | 0 | 0 | 0.0 | 1 | 1 | 1 | 3 | 0 | 7 | 1 | .133 | .200 |
| O1 | Irv Noren | L | 12 | 11 | 1 | 0 | 0 | 0 | 0.0 | 0 | 1 | 3 | 4 | 0 | 7 | 0 | .091 | .091 |
| OF | Nelson Mathews | R | 3 | 8 | 2 | 0 | 0 | 0 | 0.0 | 1 | 0 | 0 | 2 | 0 | 1 | 1 | .250 | .250 |
| O2 | Jim McKnight | R | 3 | 6 | 2 | 0 | 0 | 0 | 0.0 | 0 | 1 | 0 | 1 | 0 | 1 | 0 | .333 | .333 |
| C | Sammy Taylor | L | 74 | 150 | 31 | 9 | 0 | 3 | 2.0 | 14 | 17 | 6 | 18 | 0 | 36 | 6 | .207 | .327 |
| C | El Tappe | R | 51 | 103 | 24 | 7 | 0 | 0 | 0.0 | 11 | 3 | 11 | 12 | 0 | 2 | 0 | .233 | .301 |
| C | Earl Averill | R | 52 | 102 | 24 | 4 | 0 | 1 | 1.0 | 14 | 13 | 11 | 16 | 1 | 25 | 5 | .235 | .304 |
| C | Del Rice | R | 18 | 52 | 12 | 3 | 0 | 0 | 0.0 | 2 | 4 | 2 | 7 | 0 | 0 | 0 | .231 | .288 |
| C | Jim Hegan | R | 24 | 43 | 9 | 2 | 1 | 1 | 2.3 | 4 | 5 | 1 | 10 | 0 | 2 | 0 | .209 | .372 |
| C | Dick Bertell | R | 5 | 15 | 2 | 0 | 0 | 0 | 0.0 | 0 | 0 | 3 | 1 | 0 | 0 | 0 | .133 | .133 |
| C | Cal Neeman | R | 9 | 13 | 2 | 1 | 0 | 0 | 0.0 | 0 | 0 | 0 | 5 | 0 | 0 | 0 | .154 | .231 |
| **PITCHERS** | | | | | | | | | | | | | | | | | | |
| P | Glen Hobbie | R | 46 | 86 | 13 | 1 | 0 | 1 | 1.2 | 6 | 6 | 6 | 31 | 0 | 0 | 0 | .151 | .198 |
| P | Bob Anderson | R | 39 | 71 | 12 | 0 | 0 | 0 | 0.0 | 4 | 1 | 4 | 26 | 0 | 0 | 0 | .169 | .169 |
| P | Don Cardwell | R | 33 | 69 | 14 | 1 | 0 | 3 | 4.3 | 9 | 6 | 0 | 30 | 1 | 2 | 1 | .203 | .348 |
| P | Dick Ellsworth | L | 31 | 48 | 2 | 0 | 0 | 0 | 0.0 | 3 | 1 | 6 | 30 | 0 | 0 | 0 | .042 | .042 |
| P | Seth Morehead | L | 45 | 29 | 4 | 1 | 0 | 0 | 0.0 | 1 | 2 | 1 | 13 | 0 | 0 | 0 | .138 | .172 |
| P | Don Elston | R | 60 | 24 | 3 | 0 | 0 | 0 | 0.0 | 0 | 0 | 0 | 10 | 0 | 0 | 0 | .125 | .125 |
| P | Mark Freeman | R | 30 | 20 | 3 | 0 | 0 | 0 | 0.0 | 2 | 1 | 1 | 9 | 0 | 0 | 0 | .150 | .150 |
| P | Dick Drott | R | 23 | 10 | 1 | 0 | 0 | 0 | 0.0 | 0 | 0 | 0 | 6 | 0 | 0 | 0 | .100 | .100 |
| P | Joe Schaffernoth | R | 33 | 7 | 2 | 0 | 0 | 0 | 0.0 | 0 | 1 | 0 | 2 | 0 | 0 | 0 | .286 | .286 |
| P | Jim Brewer | L | 6 | 6 | 1 | 0 | 0 | 0 | 0.0 | 0 | 0 | 1 | 2 | 0 | 1 | 0 | .167 | .167 |
| P | Moe Drabowsky | R | 33 | 6 | 0 | 0 | 0 | 0 | 0.0 | 0 | 0 | 0 | 3 | 0 | 0 | 0 | .000 | .000 |
| P | Dick Burwell | R | 3 | 3 | 1 | 0 | 0 | 0 | 0.0 | 1 | 0 | 0 | 1 | 0 | 0 | 0 | .333 | .333 |
| P | Ben Johnson | R | 17 | 2 | 0 | 0 | 0 | 0 | 0.0 | 0 | 0 | 0 | 2 | 0 | 0 | 0 | .000 | .000 |
| P | Mel Wright | R | 9 | 2 | 0 | 0 | 0 | 0 | 0.0 | 0 | 0 | 0 | 1 | 0 | 0 | 0 | .000 | .000 |
| P | John Goetz | R | 4 | 1 | 0 | 0 | 0 | 0 | 0.0 | 0 | 0 | 0 | 1 | 0 | 0 | 0 | .000 | .000 |
| P | Al Schroll | R | 2 | 1 | 1 | 0 | 0 | 0 | 0.0 | 0 | 0 | 0 | 0 | 0 | 0 | 0 | 1.000 | 1.000 |
| P | Art Ceccarelli | R | 7 | 0 | 0 | 0 | 0 | 0 | — | 0 | 0 | 0 | 0 | 0 | 0 | 0 | — | — |
| | TEAM TOTAL | | | 5311 | 1293 | 213 | 48 | 119 | 2.2 | 63 | 600 | 531 | 897 | 51 | 256 | 52 | .243 | .369 |

## INDIVIDUAL FIELDING

| POS | Player | T | G | PO | A | E | DP | TC/G | FA |
|---|---|---|---|---|---|---|---|---|---|
| 1B | E. Bouchee | L | 80 | 709 | 56 | 7 | 56 | 9.7 | .991 |
| | F. Thomas | R | 50 | 426 | 34 | 8 | 36 | 9.4 | .983 |
| | G. Altman | R | 21 | 164 | 14 | 1 | 15 | 8.5 | .994 |
| | D. Gernert | R | 18 | 132 | 16 | 2 | 13 | 8.3 | .987 |
| | I. Noren | L | 1 | 5 | 0 | 1 | 1 | 6.0 | .833 |
| | A. Schult | R | 1 | 1 | 0 | 0 | 0 | 1.0 | 1.000 |
| 2B | D. Zimmer | R | 75 | 170 | 215 | 8 | 25 | 5.2 | .980 |
| | J. Kindall | R | 82 | 147 | 218 | 13 | 44 | 4.6 | .966 |
| | T. Taylor | R | 19 | 36 | 50 | 2 | 20 | 4.6 | .977 |
| | G. Hatton | R | 8 | 11 | 16 | 2 | 2 | 3.6 | .931 |
| | J. McKnight | R | 1 | 0 | 2 | 1 | 1 | 3.0 | .667 |
| | S. Drake | R | 2 | 2 | 1 | 0 | 0 | 1.5 | 1.000 |
| SS | E. Banks | R | 156 | 283 | 488 | 18 | 94 | 5.1 | .977 |
| | D. Zimmer | R | 5 | 3 | 8 | 0 | 1 | 2.2 | 1.000 |
| | J. Kindall | R | 2 | 0 | 4 | 0 | 1 | 2.0 | 1.000 |
| 3B | R. Santo | R | 94 | 78 | 144 | 13 | 6 | 2.5 | .945 |
| | D. Zimmer | R | 45 | 38 | 51 | 8 | 5 | 2.2 | .918 |
| | F. Thomas | R | 33 | 25 | 55 | 6 | 4 | 2.6 | .930 |
| | E. Averill | R | 1 | 0 | 0 | 0 | 0 | 0.0 | .000 |
| | S. Drake | R | 6 | 1 | 2 | 0 | 0 | 0.5 | 1.000 |

| POS | Player | T | G | PO | A | E | DP | TC/G | FA |
|---|---|---|---|---|---|---|---|---|---|
| OF | R. Ashburn | R | 146 | 317 | 11 | 8 | 2 | 2.3 | .976 |
| | B. Will | L | 121 | 224 | 10 | 2 | 2 | 2.0 | .992 |
| | G. Altman | R | 79 | 144 | 2 | 1 | 0 | 1.9 | .993 |
| | F. Thomas | R | 49 | 77 | 3 | 3 | 0 | 1.7 | .964 |
| | A. Heist | R | 33 | 65 | 2 | 1 | 0 | 2.1 | .985 |
| | W. Moryn | R | 30 | 52 | 2 | 2 | 1 | 1.9 | .964 |
| | L. Johnson | R | 25 | 43 | 4 | 0 | 0 | 1.9 | 1.000 |
| | D. Murphy | R | 21 | 40 | 1 | 1 | 1 | 2.0 | .976 |
| | J. McKnight | R | 1 | 0 | 0 | 0 | 0 | 0.0 | .000 |
| | D. Zimmer | R | 2 | 0 | 0 | 0 | 0 | 0.0 | .000 |
| | B. Williams | L | 12 | 25 | 0 | 1 | 0 | 2.2 | .962 |
| | D. Gernert | R | 5 | 10 | 1 | 0 | 0 | 2.2 | 1.000 |
| | N. Mathews | R | 2 | 5 | 0 | 0 | 0 | 2.5 | 1.000 |
| | A. Schult | R | 4 | 3 | 0 | 0 | 0 | 0.8 | 1.000 |
| | E. Averill | R | 1 | 1 | 0 | 0 | 0 | 1.0 | 1.000 |
| | I. Noren | L | 1 | 1 | 0 | 0 | 0 | 1.0 | 1.000 |
| C | E. Tappe | R | 49 | 215 | 27 | 2 | 4 | 5.0 | .992 |
| | M. Thacker | R | 50 | 170 | 23 | 4 | 2 | 3.9 | .980 |
| | S. Taylor | R | 43 | 152 | 24 | 4 | 2 | 4.2 | .978 |
| | E. Averill | R | 34 | 130 | 8 | 3 | 1 | 4.1 | .979 |
| | D. Rice | R | 18 | 85 | 7 | 3 | 0 | 5.3 | .968 |
| | J. Hegan | R | 22 | 76 | 9 | 2 | 2 | 4.0 | .977 |
| | C. Neeman | R | 9 | 34 | 4 | 0 | 0 | 4.2 | 1.000 |
| | D. Bertell | R | 5 | 18 | 6 | 0 | 0 | 4.8 | 1.000 |

Another strange managerial maneuver was made by owner P. K. Wrigley at the outset of the season. Charlie Grimm, beginning his third stint at the Cub helm, lasted only 17 games. With the Cubs in the cellar, Wrigley summoned Lou Boudreau from the radio booth and handed the mike to Jolly Cholly. A 6–11 start was too much for Boudreau to overcome. The Cubs didn't make their bold move until August 1, when they streaked past the Phillies into seventh place. They were 54–83 under Boudreau. When Boudreau asked for a three-year contract, Wrigley refused, and Boudreau went back to broadcasting the Cub losses.

The drab season had one bright spot, a no-hitter by Don Cardwell in his Cub debut on May 15. Cardwell was obtained from the Phillies in a six-player swap two days earlier. It took a brilliant play by Moose Moryn with two out in the ninth inning to ensure Cardwell's classic effort. Joe Cunningham of the Cardinals hit a vicious low liner to left field. The lumbering Moose charged in and made a shoetop catch to end the game. To show their gratitude the Cubs shipped Moryn to the Cardinals one month later.

As usual, Ernie Banks was the Cubs' big gun, leading the league in homers with 41 and driving home 117 runs. Glen Hobbie led in victories with 16, but he topped the NL in losses with 20. Best of the newcomers was third baseman Ron Santo, who was plucked from the minors in June and contributed 9 homers and 44 RBI.

## TEAM STATISTICS

| | W | L | PCT | GB | R | OR | 2B | Batting 3B | HR | BA | SA | SB | E | Fielding DP | FA | CG | B | Pitching SO | ShO | SV | ERA |
|---|---|---|---|---|---|---|---|---|---|---|---|---|---|---|---|---|---|---|---|---|---|
| PIT | 95 | 59 | .617 | | 734 | 593 | 236 | 56 | 120 | .276 | .407 | 34 | 128 | 163 | .979 | 47 | 386 | 811 | 11 | 33 | 3.49 |
| MIL | 88 | 66 | .571 | 7 | 724 | 658 | 198 | 48 | 170 | .265 | .417 | 69 | 141 | 137 | .976 | 55 | 518 | 807 | 13 | 28 | 3.76 |
| STL | 86 | 68 | .558 | 9 | 639 | 616 | 213 | 48 | 138 | .254 | .393 | 48 | 141 | 152 | .976 | 37 | 511 | 906 | 11 | 30 | 3.64 |
| LA | 82 | 72 | .532 | 13 | 662 | 593 | 216 | 38 | 126 | .255 | .383 | 95 | 125 | 142 | .979 | 46 | 564 | 1122 | 13 | 20 | 3.40 |
| SF | 79 | 75 | .513 | 16 | 671 | 631 | 220 | 62 | 130 | .255 | .393 | 86 | 166 | 117 | .972 | 55 | 512 | 897 | 16 | 26 | 3.44 |
| CIN | 67 | 87 | .435 | 28 | 640 | 692 | 230 | 40 | 119 | .243 | .388 | 73 | 143 | 133 | .979 | 36 | 565 | 740 | 8 | 35 | 4.00 |
| CHI | 60 | 94 | .390 | 35 | 634 | 776 | 213 | 48 | 119 | .243 | .369 | 51 | 155 | 133 | .977 | 36 | 565 | 805 | 6 | 25 | 4.35 |
| PHI | 59 | 95 | .383 | 36 | 546 | 691 | 196 | 44 | 99 | .239 | .351 | 45 | 155 | 129 | .974 | 45 | 439 | 736 | 6 | 16 | 4.01 |
| LEAGUE TOTAL | | | | | 5250 | 5250 | 1722 | 384 | 1042 | .255 | .388 | 501 | 1124 | 1128 | .977 | 354 | 3937 | 6824 | 84 | 213 | 3.76 |

## INDIVIDUAL PITCHING

| PITCHER | T | W | L | PCT | ERA | SV | G | GS | CG | IP | H | BB | SO | R | ER | ShO | H/9 | BB/9 | SO/9 |
|---|---|---|---|---|---|---|---|---|---|---|---|---|---|---|---|---|---|---|---|
| Glen Hobbie | R | 16 | 20 | .444 | 3.97 | 1 | 46 | 36 | 16 | 258.2 | 253 | 101 | 134 | 130 | 114 | 4 | 8.80 | 3.51 | 4.66 |
| Bob Anderson | R | 9 | 11 | .450 | 4.11 | 1 | 38 | 30 | 5 | 203.2 | 201 | 68 | 115 | 105 | 93 | 0 | 8.88 | 3.00 | 5.08 |
| Don Cardwell | R | 8 | 14 | .364 | 4.37 | 0 | 31 | 26 | 6 | 177 | 166 | 68 | 129 | 101 | 86 | 1 | 8.44 | 3.46 | 6.56 |
| Dick Ellsworth | L | 7 | 13 | .350 | 3.72 | 0 | 31 | 27 | 6 | 176.2 | 170 | 72 | 94 | 83 | 73 | 0 | 8.66 | 3.67 | 4.79 |
| Don Elston | R | 8 | 9 | .471 | 3.40 | 11 | 60 | 0 | 0 | 127 | 109 | 55 | 85 | 57 | 48 | 0 | 7.72 | 3.90 | 6.02 |
| Seth Morehead | L | 2 | 9 | .182 | 3.94 | 4 | 45 | 7 | 2 | 123.1 | 123 | 46 | 64 | 61 | 54 | 0 | 8.98 | 3.36 | 4.67 |
| Mark Freeman | R | 3 | 3 | .500 | 5.63 | 1 | 30 | 8 | 1 | 76.2 | 70 | 33 | 50 | 51 | 48 | 0 | 8.22 | 3.87 | 5.87 |
| Dick Drott | R | 0 | 6 | .000 | 7.16 | 0 | 23 | 9 | 0 | 55.1 | 63 | 42 | 32 | 49 | 44 | 0 | 10.25 | 6.83 | 5.20 |
| Joe Schaffernoth | R | 2 | 3 | .400 | 2.78 | 3 | 33 | 0 | 0 | 55 | 46 | 17 | 33 | 21 | 17 | 0 | 7.53 | 2.78 | 5.40 |
| Moe Drabowsky | R | 3 | 1 | .750 | 6.44 | 1 | 32 | 7 | 0 | 50.1 | 71 | 23 | 26 | 44 | 36 | 0 | 12.70 | 4.11 | 4.65 |
| Ben Johnson | R | 2 | 1 | .667 | 4.91 | 1 | 17 | 0 | 0 | 29.1 | 39 | 11 | 9 | 21 | 16 | 0 | 11.97 | 3.38 | 2.76 |
| Jim Brewer | L | 0 | 3 | .000 | 5.82 | 0 | 5 | 4 | 0 | 21.2 | 25 | 6 | 7 | 14 | 14 | 0 | 10.38 | 2.49 | 2.91 |
| Mel Wright | R | 0 | 1 | .000 | 4.96 | 2 | 9 | 0 | 0 | 16.1 | 17 | 3 | 8 | 9 | 9 | 0 | 9.37 | 1.65 | 4.41 |
| Art Ceccarelli | L | 0 | 0 | – | 5.54 | 0 | 7 | 1 | 0 | 13 | 16 | 4 | 10 | 12 | 8 | 0 | 11.08 | 2.77 | 6.92 |
| Dick Burwell | R | 0 | 0 | – | 5.59 | 0 | 3 | 1 | 0 | 9.2 | 11 | 7 | 1 | 6 | 6 | 0 | 10.24 | 6.52 | 0.93 |
| John Goetz | R | 0 | 0 | – | 12.79 | 0 | 4 | 0 | 0 | 6.1 | 10 | 4 | 6 | 9 | 9 | 0 | 14.21 | 5.68 | 8.53 |
| Al Schroll | R | 0 | 0 | – | 10.13 | 0 | 2 | 0 | 0 | 2.2 | 3 | 5 | 2 | 3 | 3 | 0 | 10.13 | 16.88 | 6.75 |
| TEAM TOTAL | | 60 | 94 | .390 | 4.35 | 25 | 416 | 156 | 36 | 1402.2 | 1393 | 565 | 805 | 776 | 678 | 5 | 8.94 | 3.63 | 5.17 |

## MANAGER

| MANAGER | W | L | PCT |
|---|---|---|---|
| Vedie Himsl | 10 | 21 | .323 |
| Harry Craft | 7 | 9 | .438 |
| El Tappe | 42 | 53 | .442 |
| Lou Klein | 5 | 7 | .417 |

| POS | Player | B | G | AB | H | 2B | 3B | HR | HR % | R | RBI | BB | SO | SB | Pinch Hit AB | Pinch Hit H | BA | SA |
|---|---|---|---|---|---|---|---|---|---|---|---|---|---|---|---|---|---|---|
| **REGULARS** | | | | | | | | | | | | | | | | | | |
| 1B | Ed Bouchee | L | 112 | 319 | 79 | 12 | 3 | 12 | 3.8 | 49 | 38 | 58 | 77 | 1 | 12 | 1 | .248 | .417 |
| 2B | Don Zimmer | R | 128 | 477 | 120 | 25 | 4 | 13 | 2.7 | 57 | 40 | 25 | 70 | 5 | 8 | 1 | .252 | .403 |
| SS | Ernie Banks | R | 138 | 511 | 142 | 22 | 4 | 29 | 5.7 | 75 | 80 | 54 | 75 | 1 | 4 | 1 | .278 | .507 |
| 3B | Ron Santo | R | 154 | 578 | 164 | 32 | 6 | 23 | 4.0 | 84 | 83 | 73 | 77 | 2 | 1 | 1 | .284 | .479 |
| RF | George Altman | L | 138 | 518 | 157 | 28 | 12 | 27 | 5.2 | 77 | 96 | 40 | 92 | 6 | 6 | 0 | .303 | .560 |
| CF | Al Heist | R | 109 | 321 | 82 | 14 | 3 | 7 | 2.2 | 48 | 37 | 39 | 51 | 3 | 8 | 1 | .255 | .383 |
| LF | Billy Williams | L | 146 | 529 | 147 | 20 | 7 | 25 | 4.7 | 75 | 86 | 45 | 70 | 6 | 13 | 6 | .278 | .484 |
| C | Dick Bertell | R | 92 | 267 | 73 | 7 | 1 | 2 | 0.7 | 20 | 33 | 15 | 33 | 0 | 6 | 2 | .273 | .330 |
| **SUBSTITUTES** | | | | | | | | | | | | | | | | | | |
| 2S | Jerry Kindall | R | 96 | 310 | 75 | 22 | 3 | 9 | 2.9 | 37 | 44 | 18 | 89 | 2 | 7 | 1 | .242 | .419 |
| 1S | Andre Rodgers | R | 73 | 214 | 57 | 17 | 0 | 6 | 2.8 | 27 | 23 | 25 | 54 | 1 | 7 | 1 | .266 | .430 |
| 12 | Mel Roach | R | 23 | 39 | 5 | 2 | 0 | 0 | 0.0 | 1 | 1 | 3 | 9 | 1 | 11 | 2 | .128 | .179 |
| 2B | Ken Hubbs | R | 10 | 28 | 5 | 1 | 1 | 1 | 3.6 | 4 | 2 | 0 | 8 | 0 | 2 | 0 | .179 | .393 |
| 1B | Moe Morhardt | L | 7 | 18 | 5 | 0 | 0 | 0 | 0.0 | 3 | 1 | 3 | 5 | 0 | 0 | 0 | .278 | .278 |
| OF | Richie Ashburn | L | 109 | 307 | 79 | 7 | 4 | 0 | 0.0 | 49 | 19 | 55 | 27 | 7 | 34 | 10 | .257 | .306 |
| OF | Bob Will | L | 86 | 113 | 29 | 9 | 0 | 0 | 0.0 | 9 | 8 | 15 | 19 | 0 | 52 | 11 | .257 | .336 |
| O1 | Frank Thomas | R | 15 | 50 | 13 | 2 | 0 | 2 | 4.0 | 7 | 6 | 2 | 8 | 0 | 2 | 0 | .260 | .420 |
| OF | Danny Murphy | L | 4 | 13 | 5 | 0 | 0 | 2 | 15.4 | 3 | 3 | 1 | 5 | 0 | 0 | 0 | .385 | .846 |
| OF | Lou Brock | L | 4 | 11 | 1 | 0 | 0 | 0 | 0.0 | 1 | 0 | 1 | 3 | 0 | 0 | 0 | .091 | .091 |
| OF | Jim McAnany | R | 11 | 10 | 3 | 1 | 0 | 0 | 0.0 | 1 | 0 | 1 | 3 | 0 | 10 | 3 | .300 | .400 |
| OF | Nelson Mathews | R | 3 | 9 | 1 | 0 | 0 | 0 | 0.0 | 0 | 0 | 0 | 2 | 0 | 1 | 0 | .111 | .111 |
| OF | Sammy Drake | B | 13 | 5 | 0 | 0 | 0 | 0 | 0.0 | 1 | 0 | 1 | 1 | 0 | 2 | 0 | .000 | .000 |
| C | Sammy Taylor | L | 89 | 235 | 56 | 8 | 2 | 8 | 3.4 | 26 | 23 | 23 | 39 | 0 | 14 | 0 | .238 | .391 |
| C | Moe Thacker | R | 25 | 35 | 6 | 0 | 0 | 0 | 0.0 | 3 | 2 | 11 | 11 | 0 | 0 | 0 | .171 | .171 |
| C | Cuno Barragan | R | 10 | 28 | 6 | 0 | 0 | 1 | 3.6 | 3 | 2 | 2 | 7 | 0 | 0 | 0 | .214 | .321 |
| PH | George Freese | R | 9 | 7 | 2 | 0 | 0 | 0 | 0.0 | 0 | 1 | 1 | 4 | 0 | 7 | 2 | .286 | .286 |
| **PITCHERS** | | | | | | | | | | | | | | | | | | |
| P | Don Cardwell | R | 40 | 95 | 10 | 3 | 0 | 3 | 3.2 | 6 | 6 | 6 | 55 | 0 | 0 | 0 | .105 | .232 |
| P | Glen Hobbie | R | 36 | 66 | 11 | 3 | 0 | 2 | 3.0 | 5 | 6 | 5 | 30 | 0 | 0 | 0 | .167 | .303 |
| P | Jack Curtis | L | 31 | 60 | 10 | 2 | 0 | 2 | 3.3 | 8 | 4 | 10 | 23 | 0 | 0 | 0 | .167 | .300 |
| P | Dick Ellsworth | L | 37 | 56 | 2 | 1 | 0 | 0 | 0.0 | 1 | 0 | 3 | 29 | 0 | 0 | 0 | .036 | .054 |
| P | Bob Anderson | R | 57 | 42 | 6 | 0 | 0 | 2 | 4.8 | 5 | 5 | 1 | 22 | 0 | 0 | 0 | .143 | .286 |
| P | Jim Brewer | L | 36 | 22 | 4 | 0 | 0 | 0 | 0.0 | 1 | 0 | 2 | 10 | 0 | 0 | 0 | .182 | .182 |
| P | Dick Drott | R | 35 | 22 | 6 | 0 | 1 | 0 | 0.0 | 1 | 1 | 1 | 7 | 0 | 1 | 0 | .273 | .364 |
| P | Don Elston | R | 58 | 11 | 2 | 0 | 0 | 0 | 0.0 | 1 | 0 | 0 | 4 | 0 | 0 | 0 | .182 | .182 |
| P | Barney Schultz | R | 41 | 10 | 1 | 0 | 0 | 0 | 0.0 | 0 | 0 | 0 | 5 | 0 | 0 | 0 | .100 | .100 |
| P | Joe Schaffernoth | R | 21 | 5 | 0 | 0 | 0 | 0 | 0.0 | 1 | 0 | 1 | 1 | 0 | 0 | 0 | .000 | .000 |
| P | Mel Wright | R | 11 | 2 | 0 | 0 | 0 | 0 | 0.0 | 0 | 0 | 0 | 1 | 0 | 0 | 0 | .000 | .000 |
| P | Dick Burwell | R | 2 | 1 | 0 | 0 | 0 | 0 | 0.0 | 0 | 0 | 0 | 0 | 0 | 0 | 0 | .000 | .000 |
| | TEAM TOTAL | | | 5344 | 1364 | 238 | 51 | 176 | 3.3 | 68 | 650 | 539 | 1027 | 35 | 208 | 43 | .255 | .418 |

### INDIVIDUAL FIELDING

| POS | Player | T | G | PO | A | E | DP | TC/G | FA | POS | Player | T | G | PO | A | E | DP | TC/G | FA |
|---|---|---|---|---|---|---|---|---|---|---|---|---|---|---|---|---|---|---|---|
| 1B | E. Bouchee | L | 107 | 852 | 76 | 16 | 97 | 8.8 | .983 | OF | G. Altman | R | 130 | 258 | 11 | 6 | 2 | 2.1 | .978 |
| | A. Rodgers | R | 42 | 369 | 26 | 7 | 34 | 9.6 | .983 | | B. Williams | R | 135 | 220 | 9 | 11 | 3 | 1.8 | .954 |
| | M. Morhardt | L | 7 | 72 | 3 | 3 | 9 | 11.1 | .962 | | A. Heist | R | 99 | 211 | 9 | 5 | 0 | 2.3 | .978 |
| | E. Banks | R | 7 | 68 | 6 | 1 | 8 | 10.7 | .987 | | R. Ashburn | R | 76 | 131 | 4 | 3 | 0 | 1.8 | .978 |
| | M. Roach | R | 7 | 50 | 3 | 1 | 8 | 7.7 | .981 | | E. Banks | R | 23 | 32 | 6 | 1 | 0 | 1.7 | .974 |
| | F. Thomas | R | 6 | 41 | 2 | 0 | 2 | 7.2 | 1.000 | | B. Will | L | 30 | 33 | 0 | 0 | 0 | 1.1 | 1.000 |
| | G. Altman | R | 3 | 20 | 1 | 0 | 3 | 7.0 | 1.000 | | J. McAnany | R | 1 | 0 | 0 | 0 | 0 | 0.0 | .000 |
| | B. Will | L | 1 | 3 | 0 | 1 | 1 | 4.0 | .750 | | D. Zimmer | R | 1 | 0 | 0 | 0 | 0 | 0.0 | .000 |
| 2B | D. Zimmer | R | 116 | 282 | 323 | 17 | 99 | 5.4 | .973 | | F. Thomas | R | 10 | 9 | 2 | 0 | 0 | 1.1 | 1.000 |
| | J. Kindall | R | 50 | 124 | 122 | 13 | 34 | 5.2 | .950 | | L. Brock | L | 3 | 6 | 0 | 2 | 0 | 2.7 | .750 |
| | K. Hubbs | R | 8 | 13 | 15 | 0 | 2 | 3.5 | 1.000 | | D. Murphy | R | 4 | 5 | 1 | 0 | 0 | 1.5 | 1.000 |
| | M. Roach | R | 7 | 3 | 5 | 1 | 0 | 1.3 | .889 | | N. Mathews | R | 2 | 5 | 0 | 0 | 0 | 2.5 | 1.000 |
| | A. Rodgers | R | 1 | 1 | 0 | 0 | 0 | 1.0 | 1.000 | | A. Rodgers | R | 2 | 3 | 0 | 0 | 0 | 1.5 | 1.000 |
| SS | E. Banks | R | 104 | 173 | 358 | 19 | 68 | 5.3 | .965 | | S. Drake | R | 1 | 1 | 0 | 0 | 0 | 1.0 | 1.000 |
| | J. Kindall | R | 47 | 82 | 111 | 13 | 27 | 4.4 | .937 | C | D. Bertell | R | 90 | 396 | 49 | 8 | 10 | 5.0 | .982 |
| | A. Rodgers | R | 24 | 35 | 57 | 2 | 10 | 3.9 | .979 | | S. Taylor | R | 75 | 319 | 25 | 4 | 5 | 4.6 | .989 |
| 3B | R. Santo | R | 153 | 157 | 307 | 31 | 41 | 3.2 | .937 | | M. Thacker | R | 25 | 67 | 5 | 2 | 0 | 3.0 | .973 |
| | D. Zimmer | R | 5 | 2 | 9 | 3 | 1 | 2.8 | .786 | | C. Barragan | R | 10 | 35 | 4 | 0 | 1 | 3.9 | 1.000 |

Owner P. K. Wrigley dropped a bombshell that turned out to be a dud. If the Cubs could finish seventh with a manager, then they could finish seventh without one. His noble experiment was the so-called College of Coaches. Such big names as Vedie Himsl, Harry Craft, and Elvin Tappe took turns as head coach without any success. All finished with below-.500 results. Luckily, the Phillies went into a tailspin, losing a record 23 games in a row to finish in the cellar and save seventh heaven for the Cubbies with a 64–90 mark. It was also an offseason for shortstop Ernie Banks, who suffered a knee injury, and was bothered with an impairment of depth perception in his left eye. The injuries ended Banks' 717-game playing streak and dropped his average to .278. Ernie did lead the team in homers with 29, while outfielder George Altman batted .303 and had 96 RBI. Outfielder Billy Williams won Rookie of the Year honors after hitting 25 homers, driving in 86, and batting .278. Ron Santo had a solid sophomore season with 23 homers, 83 RBI, and a .284 average. Don Cardwell topped the pitchers with a 15–14 record.

## TEAM  STATISTICS

| | W | L | PCT | GB | R | OR | 2B | 3B | HR | BA | SA | SB | E | DP | FA | CG | B | SO | ShO | SV | ERA |
|---|---|---|---|---|---|---|---|---|---|---|---|---|---|---|---|---|---|---|---|---|---|
| IN | 93 | 61 | .604 | | 710 | 653 | 247 | 35 | 158 | .270 | .421 | 70 | 134 | 124 | .977 | 46 | 500 | 829 | 12 | 40 | 3.78 |
| A | 89 | 65 | .578 | 4 | 735 | 697 | 193 | 40 | 157 | .262 | .405 | 86 | 144 | 162 | .975 | 40 | 544 | 1105 | 10 | 35 | 4.04 |
| F | 85 | 69 | .552 | 8 | 773 | 655 | 219 | 32 | 183 | .264 | .423 | 79 | 133 | 126 | .977 | 39 | 502 | 924 | 9 | 30 | 3.77 |
| IIL | 83 | 71 | .539 | 10 | 712 | 656 | 199 | 34 | 188 | .258 | .415 | 70 | 111 | 152 | .982 | 57 | 493 | 652 | 8 | 16 | 3.89 |
| TL | 80 | 74 | .519 | 13 | 703 | 668 | 236 | 51 | 103 | .271 | .393 | 46 | 166 | 165 | .972 | 49 | 570 | 823 | 10 | 24 | 3.74 |
| IT | 75 | 79 | .487 | 18 | 694 | 675 | 232 | 57 | 128 | .273 | .410 | 26 | 150 | 187 | .975 | 34 | 400 | 759 | 9 | 29 | 3.92 |
| HI | 64 | 90 | .416 | 29 | 689 | 800 | 238 | 51 | 176 | .255 | .418 | 35 | 183 | 175 | .970 | 34 | 465 | 755 | 6 | 25 | 4.48 |
| HI | 47 | 107 | .305 | 46 | 584 | 796 | 185 | 50 | 103 | .243 | .357 | 56 | 146 | 179 | .976 | 29 | 521 | 775 | 9 | 13 | 4.61 |
| EAGUE TOTAL | | | | | 5600 | 5600 | 1749 | 350 | 1196 | .262 | .405 | 468 | 1167 | 1270 | .976 | 328 | 3995 | 6622 | 73 | 212 | 4.03 |

## INDIVIDUAL  PITCHING

| ITCHER | T | W | L | PCT | ERA | SV | G | GS | CG | IP | H | BB | SO | R | ER | ShO | H/9 | BB/9 | SO/9 |
|---|---|---|---|---|---|---|---|---|---|---|---|---|---|---|---|---|---|---|---|
| on Cardwell | R | 15 | 14 | .517 | 3.82 | 0 | 39 | 38 | 13 | 259.1 | 243 | 88 | 156 | 121 | 110 | 3 | 8.43 | 3.05 | 5.41 |
| len Hobbie | R | 7 | 13 | .350 | 4.26 | 2 | 36 | 29 | 7 | 198.2 | 207 | 54 | 103 | 113 | 94 | 2 | 9.38 | 2.45 | 4.67 |
| ick Ellsworth | L | 10 | 11 | .476 | 3.86 | 0 | 37 | 31 | 7 | 186.2 | 213 | 48 | 91 | 90 | 80 | 1 | 10.27 | 2.31 | 4.39 |
| ack Curtis | L | 10 | 13 | .435 | 4.89 | 0 | 31 | 27 | 6 | 180.1 | 220 | 51 | 57 | 117 | 98 | 0 | 10.98 | 2.55 | 2.84 |
| ob Anderson | R | 7 | 10 | .412 | 4.26 | .8 | 57 | 12 | 1 | 152 | 162 | 56 | 96 | 85 | 72 | 0 | 9.59 | 3.32 | 5.68 |
| ick Drott | R | 1 | 4 | .200 | 4.22 | 0 | 35 | 8 | 0 | 98 | 75 | 51 | 48 | 54 | 46 | 0 | 6.89 | 4.68 | 4.41 |
| on Elston | R | 6 | 7 | .462 | 5.59 | 8 | 58 | 0 | 0 | 93.1 | 108 | 45 | 59 | 64 | 58 | 0 | 10.41 | 4.34 | 5.69 |
| im Brewer | L | 1 | 7 | .125 | 5.82 | 0 | 36 | 11 | 0 | 86.2 | 116 | 21 | 57 | 65 | 56 | 0 | 12.05 | 2.18 | 5.92 |
| arney Schultz | R | 7 | 6 | .538 | 2.70 | 7 | 41 | 0 | 0 | 66.2 | 57 | 25 | 59 | 32 | 20 | 0 | 7.70 | 3.38 | 7.97 |
| oe Schaffernoth | R | 0 | 4 | .000 | 6.34 | 0 | 21 | 0 | 0 | 38.1 | 43 | 18 | 23 | 29 | 27 | 0 | 10.10 | 4.23 | 5.40 |
| Mel Wright | R | 0 | 1 | .000 | 10.71 | 0 | 11 | 0 | 0 | 21 | 42 | 4 | 6 | 26 | 25 | 0 | 18.00 | 1.71 | 2.57 |
| ick Burwell | R | 0 | 0 | – | 9.00 | 0 | 2 | 0 | 0 | 4 | 6 | 4 | 0 | 4 | 4 | 0 | 13.50 | 9.00 | 0.00 |
| EAM TOTAL | | 64 | 90 | .416 | 4.48 | 25 | 404 | 156 | 34 | 1385 | 1492 | 465 | 755 | 800 | 690 | 6 | 9.70 | 3.02 | 4.91 |

| MANAGER | W | L | PCT |
|---|---|---|---|
| El Tappe | 4 | 16 | .200 |
| Lou Klein | 12 | 18 | .400 |
| Charlie Metro | 43 | 69 | .384 |

| POS | Player | B | G | AB | H | 2B | 3B | HR | HR % | R | RBI | BB | SO | SB | Pinch Hit AB | Pinch Hit H | BA | SA |
|---|---|---|---|---|---|---|---|---|---|---|---|---|---|---|---|---|---|---|
| **REGULARS** | | | | | | | | | | | | | | | | | | |
| 1B | Ernie Banks | R | 154 | 610 | 164 | 20 | 6 | 37 | 6.1 | 87 | 104 | 30 | 71 | 5 | 4 | 2 | .269 | .503 |
| 2B | Ken Hubbs | R | 160 | 661 | 172 | 24 | 9 | 5 | 0.8 | 90 | 49 | 35 | 129 | 3 | 1 | 0 | .260 | .346 |
| SS | Andre Rodgers | R | 138 | 461 | 128 | 20 | 8 | 5 | 1.1 | 40 | 44 | 44 | 93 | 5 | 6 | 0 | .278 | .388 |
| 3B | Ron Santo | R | 162 | 604 | 137 | 20 | 4 | 17 | 2.8 | 44 | 83 | 65 | 94 | 4 | 2 | 0 | .227 | .358 |
| RF | George Altman | L | 147 | 534 | 170 | 27 | 5 | 22 | 4.1 | 74 | 74 | 62 | 89 | 19 | 6 | 1 | .318 | .511 |
| CF | Lou Brock | L | 123 | 434 | 114 | 24 | 7 | 9 | 2.1 | 73 | 35 | 35 | 96 | 16 | 15 | 2 | .263 | .412 |
| LF | Billy Williams | L | 159 | 618 | 184 | 22 | 8 | 22 | 3.6 | 94 | 91 | 70 | 72 | 9 | 0 | 0 | .298 | .466 |
| C | Dick Bertell | R | 77 | 215 | 65 | 6 | 2 | 2 | 0.9 | 19 | 18 | 13 | 30 | 0 | 5 | 1 | .302 | .377 |
| **SUBSTITUTES** | | | | | | | | | | | | | | | | | | |
| UT | Jim McKnight | R | 60 | 85 | 19 | 0 | 1 | 0 | 0.0 | 6 | 5 | 2 | 13 | 0 | 49 | 11 | .224 | .247 |
| S2 | Alex Grammas | R | 23 | 60 | 14 | 3 | 0 | 0 | 0.0 | 3 | 3 | 2 | 7 | 1 | 3 | 0 | .233 | .283 |
| SS | Elder White | R | 23 | 53 | 8 | 2 | 0 | 0 | 0.0 | 4 | 1 | 8 | 11 | 3 | 6 | 1 | .151 | .189 |
| SS | Daryl Robertson | R | 9 | 19 | 2 | 0 | 0 | 0 | 0.0 | 0 | 2 | 2 | 10 | 0 | 2 | 0 | .105 | .105 |
| OF | Don Landrum | L | 83 | 238 | 67 | 5 | 2 | 1 | 0.4 | 29 | 15 | 30 | 31 | 9 | 17 | 2 | .282 | .332 |
| OF | Bob Will | L | 87 | 92 | 22 | 3 | 0 | 2 | 2.2 | 6 | 15 | 13 | 22 | 0 | 67 | 17 | .239 | .337 |
| OF | Nelson Mathews | R | 15 | 49 | 15 | 2 | 0 | 2 | 4.1 | 5 | 13 | 5 | 4 | 3 | 1 | 0 | .306 | .469 |
| OF | Danny Murphy | L | 14 | 35 | 7 | 3 | 1 | 0 | 0.0 | 5 | 3 | 2 | 9 | 0 | 6 | 0 | .200 | .343 |
| OF | Bobby Gene Smith | R | 13 | 29 | 5 | 0 | 0 | 1 | 3.4 | 3 | 2 | 2 | 6 | 0 | 6 | 1 | .172 | .276 |
| OF | Billy Ott | B | 12 | 28 | 4 | 0 | 0 | 1 | 3.6 | 3 | 2 | 2 | 10 | 0 | 5 | 1 | .143 | .250 |
| C | Cuno Barragan | R | 58 | 134 | 27 | 6 | 1 | 0 | 0.0 | 11 | 12 | 21 | 28 | 0 | 7 | 0 | .201 | .261 |
| C | Moe Thacker | R | 65 | 107 | 20 | 5 | 0 | 0 | 0.0 | 8 | 9 | 14 | 40 | 0 | 1 | 0 | .187 | .234 |
| C | El Tappe | R | 26 | 53 | 11 | 0 | 0 | 0 | 0.0 | 3 | 6 | 4 | 3 | 0 | 0 | 0 | .208 | .208 |
| C | Sammy Taylor | L | 7 | 15 | 2 | 1 | 0 | 0 | 0.0 | 0 | 1 | 3 | 3 | 0 | 0 | 0 | .133 | .200 |
| PH | Moe Morhardt | L | 18 | 16 | 2 | 0 | 0 | 0 | 0.0 | 1 | 2 | 2 | 8 | 0 | 16 | 2 | .125 | .125 |
| PH | Jim McAnany | R | 7 | 6 | 0 | 0 | 0 | 0 | 0.0 | 0 | 0 | 1 | 2 | 0 | 6 | 0 | .000 | .000 |
| **PITCHERS** | | | | | | | | | | | | | | | | | | |
| P | Bob Buhl | R | 34 | 69 | 0 | 0 | 0 | 0 | 0.0 | 2 | 1 | 6 | 35 | 1 | 0 | 0 | .000 | .000 |
| P | Cal Koonce | R | 35 | 64 | 6 | 1 | 0 | 0 | 0.0 | 7 | 2 | 1 | 25 | 0 | 0 | 0 | .094 | .109 |
| P | Dick Ellsworth | L | 37 | 62 | 7 | 1 | 0 | 0 | 0.0 | 5 | 2 | 14 | 28 | 0 | 0 | 0 | .113 | .129 |
| P | Don Cardwell | R | 41 | 61 | 9 | 0 | 1 | 0 | 0.0 | 2 | 3 | 4 | 27 | 0 | 0 | 0 | .148 | .180 |
| P | Glen Hobbie | R | 42 | 49 | 6 | 0 | 0 | 0 | 0.0 | 4 | 0 | 3 | 24 | 0 | 0 | 0 | .122 | .122 |
| P | Bob Anderson | R | 57 | 23 | 3 | 0 | 1 | 0 | 0.0 | 1 | 1 | 2 | 10 | 0 | 0 | 0 | .130 | .217 |
| P | Paul Toth | R | 6 | 11 | 2 | 0 | 0 | 0 | 0.0 | 1 | 1 | 1 | 1 | 0 | 0 | 0 | .182 | .182 |
| P | Don Elston | R | 57 | 8 | 0 | 0 | 0 | 0 | 0.0 | 0 | 0 | 0 | 3 | 0 | 0 | 0 | .000 | .000 |
| P | Jug Gerard | R | 39 | 8 | 3 | 0 | 0 | 0 | 0.0 | 0 | 0 | 1 | 2 | 0 | 0 | 0 | .375 | .375 |
| P | Al Lary | R | 23 | 6 | 1 | 0 | 0 | 0 | 0.0 | 1 | 0 | 2 | 1 | 0 | 0 | 0 | .167 | .167 |
| P | Tony Balsamo | R | 18 | 5 | 1 | 1 | 0 | 0 | 0.0 | 1 | 0 | 0 | 3 | 0 | 0 | 0 | .200 | .400 |
| P | Barney Schultz | R | 51 | 5 | 0 | 0 | 0 | 0 | 0.0 | 0 | 1 | 1 | 2 | 0 | 0 | 0 | .000 | .000 |
| P | Jack Curtis | L | 4 | 4 | 1 | 0 | 0 | 0 | 0.0 | 0 | 0 | 1 | 2 | 0 | 0 | 0 | .250 | .250 |
| P | Freddie Burdette | R | 8 | 1 | 0 | 0 | 0 | 0 | 0.0 | 0 | 0 | 0 | 0 | 0 | 0 | 0 | .000 | .000 |
| P | George Gerberman | R | 1 | 1 | 0 | 0 | 0 | 0 | 0.0 | 0 | 0 | 1 | 0 | 0 | 0 | 0 | .000 | .000 |
| P | Morrie Steevens | L | 12 | 0 | 0 | 0 | 0 | 0 | 0.0 | 0 | 0 | 0 | 0 | 0 | 0 | 0 | .000 | .000 |
| P | Jim Brewer | L | 6 | 0 | 0 | 0 | 0 | 0 | – | 0 | 0 | 0 | 0 | 0 | 0 | 0 | – | – |
| P | Don Prince | R | 1 | 0 | 0 | 0 | 0 | 0 | – | 0 | 0 | 0 | 0 | 0 | 0 | 0 | – | – |
| P | Jack Warner | R | 7 | 0 | 0 | 0 | 0 | 0 | – | 0 | 0 | 0 | 0 | 0 | 0 | 0 | – | – |
| TEAM TOTAL | | | | 5534 | 1398 | 196 | 56 | 126 | 2.3 | 63 | 600 | 504 | 1044 | 78 | 231 | 41 | .253 | .377 |

## INDIVIDUAL FIELDING

| POS | Player | T | G | PO | A | E | DP | TC/G | FA | | POS | Player | T | G | PO | A | E | DP | TC/G | FA |
|---|---|---|---|---|---|---|---|---|---|---|---|---|---|---|---|---|---|---|---|---|
| 1B | E. Banks | R | 149 | **1458** | 106 | 11 | 134 | 10.6 | .993 | | OF | B. Williams | R | 159 | 273 | 18 | 10 | 4 | 1.9 | .967 |
| | G. Altman | R | 16 | 121 | 8 | 0 | 13 | 8.1 | 1.000 | | | L. Brock | L | 106 | 243 | 7 | 9 | 2 | 2.4 | .965 |
| | A. Rodgers | R | 1 | 11 | 1 | 0 | 1 | 12.0 | 1.000 | | | G. Altman | R | 129 | 234 | 8 | 7 | 3 | 1.9 | .972 |
| 2B | K. Hubbs | R | 159 | 363 | 489 | 15 | 103 | 5.5 | .983 | | | D. Landrum | R | 59 | 122 | 3 | 4 | 3 | 2.2 | .969 |
| | A. Grammas | R | 3 | 3 | 7 | 0 | 1 | 3.3 | 1.000 | | | N. Mathews | R | 14 | 25 | 0 | 1 | 0 | 1.9 | .962 |
| | J. McKnight | R | 2 | 4 | 5 | 0 | 2 | 4.5 | 1.000 | | | B. Will | L | 9 | 14 | 0 | 0 | 0 | 1.6 | 1.000 |
| | E. White | R | 1 | 0 | 3 | 0 | 0 | 3.0 | 1.000 | | | B. Ott | R | 7 | 9 | 1 | 0 | 0 | 1.4 | 1.000 |
| SS | A. Rodgers | R | 133 | 239 | 433 | 28 | 91 | 5.3 | .960 | | | B. Smith | R | 7 | 9 | 1 | 0 | 0 | 1.4 | 1.000 |
| | E. White | R | 15 | 25 | 44 | 1 | 6 | 4.7 | .986 | | | J. McKnight | R | 5 | 6 | 1 | 1 | 1 | 1.6 | .875 |
| | A. Grammas | R | 13 | 20 | 42 | 0 | 11 | 4.8 | 1.000 | | | D. Murphy | R | 9 | 5 | 0 | 0 | 0 | 0.6 | 1.000 |
| | D. Robertson | R | 6 | 6 | 14 | 0 | 1 | 3.3 | 1.000 | | C | D. Bertell | R | 76 | 306 | 36 | 5 | 0 | 4.6 | .986 |
| | R. Santo | R | 8 | 6 | 11 | 1 | 2 | 2.3 | .944 | | | M. Thacker | R | 65 | 219 | 34 | 1 | 8 | 3.9 | .996 |
| 3B | R. Santo | R | 157 | 161 | 332 | 23 | 33 | 3.3 | .955 | | | C. Barragan | R | 55 | 207 | 27 | 7 | 2 | 4.4 | .971 |
| | A. Grammas | R | 1 | 0 | 0 | 0 | 0 | 0.0 | .000 | | | E. Tappe | R | 26 | 101 | 13 | 0 | 4 | 4.4 | 1.000 |
| | J. McKnight | R | 9 | 7 | 14 | 1 | 2 | 2.4 | .955 | | | S. Taylor | R | 6 | 23 | 1 | 0 | 0 | 4.0 | 1.000 |
| | E. Banks | R | 3 | 4 | 1 | 0 | 1 | 1.7 | 1.000 | | | | | | | | | | | |
| | D. Robertson | R | 1 | 2 | 0 | 0 | 0 | 2.0 | 1.000 | | | | | | | | | | | |

Thank God for the Mets. The spanking new New York franchise was spanked for 120 losses against only 40 victories. But they had an excuse. Their first-season roster included 10 former Cubs. The Cubs, meanwhile, compiled their worst record, hitting the century mark in losses for the first time in team history dating back to 1876. In finishing ninth with 59 wins and 103 losses, the Cubs also tied an all-time record of 16 straight seasons in the second division.

Elvin Tappe was tapped as first head coach and led the Cubs to a futile 4–16 mark in April. Lou Klein was next at 12–18, and Charlie Metro, minus Goldwyn and Mayer, was 43–69. The club was never higher than ninth all season and drew 609,802 fans, the lowest in the majors. As usual, Ernie Banks supplied the punch with 37 homers and 104 RBI, while George Altman batted .318. Two newcomers pumped some life into the lethargic lineup. Ken Hubbs set a record by playing 78 successive games without an error at second base and was named Rookie of the Year. And Lou Brock became the first left-handed batter to homer into the center-field bleachers at the Polo Grounds. He also showed fleetness of foot with 16 stolen bases. The pitching-poor Cubs had their usual 20-game loser. This time it was Dick Ellsworth's turn with a 9–20 record. At the conclusion, the Cubs were 42 1/2 games behind the Giants.

## TEAM STATISTICS

| | W | L | PCT | GB | R | OR | 2B | Batting 3B | HR | BA | SA | SB | Fielding E | DP | FA | CG | B | Pitching SO | ShO | SV | ERA |
|---|---|---|---|---|---|---|---|---|---|---|---|---|---|---|---|---|---|---|---|---|---|
| SF | 103 | 62 | .624 | | 878 | 690 | 235 | 32 | 204 | .278 | .441 | 73 | 142 | 153 | .977 | 62 | 503 | 886 | 10 | 39 | 3.79 |
| LA | 102 | 63 | .618 | 1 | 842 | 697 | 192 | 65 | 140 | .268 | .400 | 198 | 193 | 144 | .970 | 44 | 588 | 1104 | 8 | 46 | 3.62 |
| CIN | 98 | 64 | .605 | 3.5 | 802 | 685 | 252 | 40 | 167 | .270 | .417 | 66 | 145 | 144 | .977 | 51 | 567 | 964 | 13 | 35 | 3.75 |
| PIT | 93 | 68 | .578 | 8 | 706 | 626 | 240 | 65 | 108 | .268 | .394 | 50 | 152 | 177 | .976 | 40 | 466 | 897 | 13 | 41 | 3.37 |
| MIL | 86 | 76 | .531 | 15.5 | 730 | 665 | 204 | 38 | 181 | .252 | .403 | 57 | 124 | 154 | .980 | 59 | 407 | 802 | 10 | 24 | 3.68 |
| STL | 84 | 78 | .519 | 17.5 | 774 | 664 | 221 | 31 | 137 | .271 | .394 | 86 | 132 | 170 | .979 | 53 | 517 | 914 | 17 | 25 | 3.55 |
| PHI | 81 | 80 | .503 | 20 | 705 | 759 | 199 | 39 | 142 | .260 | .390 | 79 | 138 | 167 | .977 | 43 | 471 | 1047 | 9 | 19 | 3.83 |
| HOU | 64 | 96 | .400 | 36.5 | 592 | 717 | 170 | 47 | 105 | .246 | .351 | 42 | 173 | 149 | .973 | 34 | 471 | 863 | 7 | 24 | 4.28 |
| CHI | 59 | 103 | .364 | 42.5 | 632 | 827 | 196 | 56 | 126 | .253 | .377 | 78 | 146 | 171 | .977 | 29 | 601 | 783 | 4 | 26 | 4.54 |
| NY | 40 | 120 | .250 | 60.5 | 617 | 948 | 166 | 40 | 139 | .240 | .361 | 59 | 210 | 167 | .967 | 43 | 571 | 772 | 4 | 10 | 5.04 |
| LEAGUE TOTAL | | | | | 7278 | 7278 | 2075 | 453 | 1449 | .261 | .393 | 788 | 1555 | 1596 | .975 | 458 | 5265 | 9032 | 95 | 289 | 3.94 |

## INDIVIDUAL PITCHING

| PITCHER | T | W | L | PCT | ERA | SV | G | GS | CG | IP | H | BB | SO | R | ER | ShO | H/9 | BB/9 | SO/9 |
|---|---|---|---|---|---|---|---|---|---|---|---|---|---|---|---|---|---|---|---|
| Bob Buhl | R | 12 | 13 | .480 | 3.69 | 0 | 34 | 30 | 8 | 212 | 204 | 94 | 109 | 108 | 87 | 1 | 8.66 | 3.99 | 4.63 |
| Dick Ellsworth | L | 9 | 20 | .310 | 5.09 | 1 | 37 | 33 | 6 | 208.2 | 241 | 77 | 113 | 131 | 118 | 0 | 10.39 | 3.32 | 4.87 |
| Don Cardwell | R | 7 | 16 | .304 | 4.92 | 4 | 41 | 29 | 6 | 195.2 | 205 | 60 | 104 | 116 | 107 | 1 | 9.43 | 2.76 | 4.78 |
| Cal Koonce | R | 10 | 10 | .500 | 3.97 | 0 | 35 | 30 | 3 | 190.2 | 200 | 86 | 84 | 93 | 84 | 1 | 9.44 | 4.06 | 3.97 |
| Glen Hobbie | R | 5 | 14 | .263 | 5.22 | 0 | 42 | 23 | 5 | 162 | 198 | 62 | 87 | 112 | 94 | 0 | 11.00 | 3.44 | 4.83 |
| Bob Anderson | R | 2 | 7 | .222 | 5.02 | 4 | 57 | 4 | 0 | 107.2 | 111 | 60 | 82 | 70 | 60 | 0 | 9.28 | 5.02 | 6.85 |
| Barney Schultz | R | 5 | 5 | .500 | 3.82 | 5 | 51 | 0 | 0 | 77.2 | 66 | 23 | 58 | 36 | 33 | 0 | 7.65 | 2.67 | 6.72 |
| Don Elston | R | 4 | 8 | .333 | 2.44 | 8 | 57 | 0 | 0 | 66.1 | 57 | 32 | 37 | 25 | 18 | 0 | 7.73 | 4.34 | 5.02 |
| Jug Gerard | R | 2 | 3 | .400 | 4.91 | 3 | 39 | 0 | 0 | 58.2 | 67 | 28 | 30 | 40 | 32 | 0 | 10.28 | 4.30 | 4.60 |
| Al Lary | R | 0 | 1 | .000 | 7.15 | 0 | 15 | 3 | 0 | 34 | 42 | 15 | 18 | 27 | 27 | 0 | 11.12 | 3.97 | 4.76 |
| Paul Toth | R | 3 | 1 | .750 | 4.24 | 0 | 6 | 4 | 1 | 34 | 29 | 10 | 11 | 17 | 16 | 0 | 7.68 | 2.65 | 2.91 |
| Tony Balsamo | R | 0 | 1 | .000 | 6.44 | 0 | 18 | 0 | 0 | 29.1 | 34 | 20 | 27 | 22 | 21 | 0 | 10.43 | 6.14 | 8.28 |
| Jack Curtis | L | 0 | 2 | .000 | 3.50 | 0 | 4 | 3 | 0 | 18 | 18 | 6 | 8 | 8 | 7 | 0 | 9.00 | 3.00 | 4.00 |
| Morrie Steevens | L | 0 | 1 | .000 | 2.40 | 0 | 12 | 1 | 0 | 15 | 10 | 11 | 5 | 4 | 4 | 0 | 6.00 | 6.60 | 3.00 |
| Freddie Burdette | R | 0 | 0 | — | 3.72 | 1 | 8 | 0 | 0 | 9.2 | 5 | 8 | 5 | 4 | 4 | 0 | 4.66 | 7.45 | 4.66 |
| Jack Warner | R | 0 | 0 | — | 7.71 | 0 | 7 | 0 | 0 | 7 | 9 | 0 | 3 | 7 | 6 | 0 | 11.57 | 0.00 | 3.86 |
| Jim Brewer | L | 0 | 1 | .000 | 9.53 | 0 | 6 | 1 | 0 | 5.2 | 10 | 3 | 1 | 6 | 6 | 0 | 15.88 | 4.76 | 1.59 |
| George Gerberman | R | 0 | 0 | — | 1.69 | 0 | 1 | 1 | 0 | 5.1 | 3 | 5 | 1 | 1 | 1 | 0 | 5.06 | 8.44 | 1.69 |
| Don Prince | R | 0 | 0 | — | 0.00 | 0 | 1 | 0 | 0 | 1 | 0 | 1 | 0 | 0 | 0 | 0 | 0.00 | 9.00 | 0.00 |
| TEAM TOTAL | | 59 | 103 | .364 | 4.54 | 26 | 471 | 162 | 29 | 1438.1 | 1509 | 601 | 783 | 827 | 725 | 3 | 9.44 | 3.76 | 4.90 |

| MANAGER | W | L | PCT |
|---|---|---|---|
| Bob Kennedy | 82 | 80 | .506 |

| POS | Player | B | G | AB | H | 2B | 3B | HR | HR % | R | RBI | BB | SO | SB | Pinch Hit AB | Pinch Hit H | BA | SA |
|---|---|---|---|---|---|---|---|---|---|---|---|---|---|---|---|---|---|---|
| **REGULARS** | | | | | | | | | | | | | | | | | | |
| 1B | Ernie Banks | R | 130 | 432 | 98 | 20 | 1 | 18 | 4.2 | 41 | 64 | 39 | 73 | 0 | 5 | 1 | .227 | .403 |
| 2B | Ken Hubbs | R | 154 | 566 | 133 | 19 | 3 | 8 | 1.4 | 54 | 47 | 39 | 93 | 8 | 2 | 1 | .235 | .322 |
| SS | Andre Rodgers | R | 150 | 516 | 118 | 17 | 4 | 5 | 1.0 | 51 | 33 | 65 | 90 | 5 | 0 | 0 | .229 | .306 |
| 3B | Ron Santo | R | 162 | 630 | 187 | 29 | 6 | 25 | 4.0 | 79 | 99 | 42 | 92 | 6 | 0 | 0 | .297 | .481 |
| RF | Lou Brock | L | 148 | 547 | 141 | 19 | 11 | 9 | 1.6 | 79 | 37 | 31 | 122 | 24 | 10 | 2 | .258 | .382 |
| CF | Ellis Burton | B | 93 | 322 | 74 | 16 | 1 | 12 | 3.7 | 45 | 41 | 36 | 59 | 6 | 3 | 0 | .230 | .398 |
| LF | Billy Williams | L | 161 | 612 | 175 | 36 | 9 | 25 | 4.1 | 87 | 95 | 68 | 78 | 7 | 1 | 0 | .286 | .497 |
| C | Dick Bertell | R | 100 | 322 | 75 | 7 | 2 | 2 | 0.6 | 15 | 14 | 24 | 41 | 0 | 1 | 0 | .233 | .286 |
| **SUBSTITUTES** | | | | | | | | | | | | | | | | | | |
| 1O | Steve Boros | R | 41 | 90 | 19 | 5 | 1 | 3 | 3.3 | 9 | 7 | 12 | 19 | 0 | 17 | 2 | .211 | .389 |
| 1B | John Boccabella | R | 24 | 74 | 14 | 4 | 1 | 1 | 1.4 | 7 | 5 | 6 | 21 | 0 | 1 | 0 | .189 | .311 |
| 21 | Leo Burke | R | 27 | 49 | 9 | 0 | 0 | 2 | 4.1 | 4 | 7 | 4 | 13 | 0 | 12 | 4 | .184 | .306 |
| SS | Jimmy Stewart | B | 13 | 37 | 11 | 2 | 0 | 0 | 0.0 | 1 | 1 | 1 | 7 | 1 | 5 | 1 | .297 | .351 |
| 21 | Ken Aspromonte | R | 20 | 34 | 5 | 3 | 0 | 0 | 0.0 | 2 | 4 | 4 | 4 | 0 | 8 | 0 | .147 | .235 |
| SS | Alex Grammas | R | 16 | 27 | 5 | 0 | 0 | 0 | 0.0 | 1 | 0 | 0 | 3 | 0 | 3 | 0 | .185 | .185 |
| 1B | Bob Will | L | 23 | 23 | 4 | 0 | 0 | 0 | 0.0 | 0 | 1 | 1 | 3 | 0 | 20 | 4 | .174 | .174 |
| OF | Don Landrum | L | 84 | 227 | 55 | 4 | 1 | 1 | 0.4 | 27 | 10 | 13 | 42 | 6 | 24 | 3 | .242 | .282 |
| OF | Nelson Mathews | R | 61 | 155 | 24 | 3 | 2 | 4 | 2.6 | 12 | 10 | 16 | 48 | 3 | 8 | 0 | .155 | .277 |
| OF | Billy Cowan | R | 14 | 36 | 9 | 1 | 1 | 1 | 2.8 | 1 | 2 | 0 | 11 | 0 | 4 | 1 | .250 | .417 |
| C | Merritt Ranew | L | 78 | 154 | 52 | 8 | 1 | 3 | 1.9 | 18 | 15 | 9 | 32 | 1 | 41 | 17 | .338 | .461 |
| C | Jimmie Schaffer | R | 57 | 142 | 34 | 7 | 0 | 7 | 4.9 | 17 | 19 | 11 | 35 | 0 | 1 | 0 | .239 | .437 |
| C | Cuno Barragan | R | 1 | 1 | 0 | 0 | 0 | 0 | 0.0 | 0 | 0 | 0 | 1 | 0 | 0 | 0 | .000 | .000 |
| **PITCHERS** | | | | | | | | | | | | | | | | | | |
| P | Dick Ellsworth | L | 37 | 94 | 9 | 0 | 0 | 0 | 0.0 | 8 | 5 | 8 | 38 | 0 | 0 | 0 | .096 | .096 |
| P | Larry Jackson | R | 37 | 87 | 17 | 5 | 0 | 0 | 0.0 | 5 | 6 | 2 | 24 | 0 | 0 | 0 | .195 | .253 |
| P | Bob Buhl | R | 37 | 74 | 8 | 0 | 0 | 0 | 0.0 | 2 | 5 | 0 | 28 | 1 | 0 | 0 | .108 | .108 |
| P | Glen Hobbie | R | 36 | 50 | 4 | 0 | 0 | 0 | 0.0 | 2 | 0 | 2 | 27 | 0 | 0 | 0 | .080 | .080 |
| P | Paul Toth | R | 27 | 39 | 1 | 0 | 0 | 0 | 0.0 | 0 | 0 | 2 | 19 | 0 | 0 | 0 | .026 | .026 |
| P | Lindy McDaniel | R | 57 | 22 | 2 | 0 | 0 | 1 | 4.5 | 1 | 2 | 0 | 8 | 0 | 0 | 0 | .091 | .227 |
| P | Cal Koonce | R | 21 | 19 | 2 | 0 | 0 | 0 | 0.0 | 1 | 0 | 1 | 8 | 0 | 0 | 0 | .105 | .105 |
| P | Jim Brewer | L | 29 | 6 | 0 | 0 | 0 | 0 | 0.0 | 0 | 1 | 3 | 4 | 0 | 0 | 0 | .000 | .000 |
| P | Don Elston | R | 51 | 4 | 0 | 0 | 0 | 0 | 0.0 | 1 | 0 | 0 | 1 | 0 | 0 | 0 | .000 | .000 |
| P | Barney Schultz | R | 15 | 4 | 0 | 0 | 0 | 0 | 0.0 | 0 | 0 | 0 | 1 | 0 | 0 | 0 | .000 | .000 |
| P | Jack Warner | R | 8 | 4 | 1 | 0 | 0 | 0 | 0.0 | 0 | 0 | 0 | 1 | 0 | 0 | 0 | .250 | .250 |
| P | Tom Baker | L | 10 | 3 | 0 | 0 | 0 | 0 | 0.0 | 0 | 0 | 0 | 2 | 0 | 0 | 0 | .000 | .000 |
| P | Dick LeMay | L | 9 | 2 | 0 | 0 | 0 | 0 | 0.0 | 0 | 0 | 0 | 1 | 0 | 0 | 0 | .000 | .000 |
| P | Freddie Burdette | R | 4 | 0 | 0 | 0 | 0 | 0 | – | 0 | 0 | 0 | 0 | 0 | 0 | 0 | – | – |
| P | Phil Mudrock | R | 1 | 0 | 0 | 0 | 0 | 0 | – | 0 | 0 | 0 | 0 | 0 | 0 | 0 | – | – |
| | TEAM TOTAL | | | 5404 | 1286 | 205 | 44 | 127 | 2.4 | 57 | 530 | 439 | 1049 | 68 | 166 | 36 | .238 | .363 |

## INDIVIDUAL FIELDING

| POS | Player | T | G | PO | A | E | DP | TC/G | FA | POS | Player | T | G | PO | A | E | DP | TC/G | FA |
|---|---|---|---|---|---|---|---|---|---|---|---|---|---|---|---|---|---|---|---|
| 1B | E. Banks | R | 125 | 1178 | 78 | 9 | 97 | 10.1 | .993 | OF | B. Williams | R | 160 | 298 | 13 | 4 | 2 | 2.0 | .987 |
| | Boccabella | R | 24 | 234 | 12 | 1 | 29 | 10.3 | .996 | | L. Brock | L | 140 | 269 | 17 | 8 | 7 | 2.1 | .973 |
| | S. Boros | R | 14 | 111 | 7 | 3 | 7 | 8.6 | .975 | | E. Burton | R | 90 | 151 | 6 | 4 | 1 | 1.8 | .975 |
| | M. Ranew | R | 7 | 75 | 7 | 0 | 10 | 11.7 | 1.000 | | D. Landrum | R | 57 | 100 | 3 | 3 | 0 | 1.9 | .972 |
| | L. Burke | R | 4 | 31 | 2 | 1 | 1 | 8.5 | .971 | | N. Mathews | R | 46 | 91 | 1 | 2 | 1 | 2.0 | .979 |
| | B. Will | L | 1 | 10 | 0 | 0 | 1 | 10.0 | 1.000 | | S. Boros | R | 11 | 15 | 0 | 1 | 0 | 1.5 | .938 |
| | Aspromonte | R | 2 | 5 | 1 | 0 | 0 | 3.0 | 1.000 | | B. Cowan | R | 10 | 10 | 1 | 1 | 0 | 1.2 | .917 |
| 2B | K. Hubbs | R | 152 | 338 | 493 | 22 | 96 | 5.6 | .974 | C | D. Bertell | R | 99 | 549 | 84 | 8 | 15 | 6.5 | .988 |
| | L. Burke | R | 10 | 22 | 27 | 4 | 6 | 5.3 | .925 | | J. Schaffer | R | 54 | 231 | 23 | 1 | 3 | 4.7 | .996 |
| | Aspromonte | R | 7 | 14 | 25 | 2 | 4 | 5.9 | .951 | | M. Ranew | R | 37 | 138 | 12 | 3 | 4 | 4.1 | .980 |
| | J. Stewart | R | 1 | 2 | 4 | 0 | 1 | 6.0 | 1.000 | | C. Barragan | R | 1 | 1 | 0 | 0 | 0 | 1.0 | 1.000 |
| SS | A. Rodgers | R | 150 | 271 | 454 | 35 | 100 | 5.1 | .954 | | | | | | | | | | |
| | J. Stewart | R | 9 | 11 | 25 | 1 | 7 | 4.1 | .973 | | | | | | | | | | |
| | A. Grammas | R | 13 | 8 | 13 | 1 | 1 | 1.7 | .955 | | | | | | | | | | |
| 3B | R. Santo | R | 162 | 136 | 374 | 26 | 25 | 3.3 | .951 | | | | | | | | | | |

Imagine a Cub pitching staff with a 3.08 earned-run average. Bob Kennedy, who was designated head coach, actually served all season as "manager" and set up a regular pitching rotation and bullpen, and the team finished with an 82–80 record, best in 17 years. Wrigley added more nonsense to his College of Coaches by hiring an Air Force colonel named Robert V. Whitlow as athletic director. The Cubs finally got the better of an off-season trade, acquiring pitchers Larry Jackson and Lindy McDaniel for slugger George Altman. McDaniel was 13–7 and led the league in saves with 22. Jackson, a heady veteran, had 14 victories. But the standout was lefty Dick Ellsworth, who reversed a 9–20 season with a sparkling 22–10 record, had 19 complete games and was second to the Dodgers' Sandy Koufax with a 2.11 ERA.

Kennedy had the Cubs as high as second as late as July 19. But an August slumber in which they lost 11 of 15 dropped them to seventh. Ernie Banks had his worst season, batting only .229, but contributed 18 homers and 64 RBI. It was later disclosed he was suffering from subclinical mumps. Ron Santo and Billy Williams were the big guns; Santo batted .295 and had 25 homers with 99 RBI, and Williams hit .286 to go with 25 homers and 95 RBI. McDaniel, meanwhile, was the hero of a June 6 dream game against the Giants. He entered the contest with one out and bases loaded in the 12th inning, picked Willie Mays off second base and struck out Ed Bailey. McDaniel then slugged a game-winning homer in the bottom of the 12th inning for a 3–2 victory.

## TEAM STATISTICS

| | W | L | PCT | GB | R | OR | 2B | 3B | Batting HR | BA | SA | SB | E | Fielding DP | FA | CG | B | Pitching SO | ShO | SV | ERA |
|---|---|---|---|---|---|---|---|---|---|---|---|---|---|---|---|---|---|---|---|---|---|
| LA | 99 | 63 | .611 | | 640 | 550 | 178 | 34 | 110 | .251 | .357 | 124 | 159 | 129 | .975 | 51 | 402 | 1095 | 24 | 29 | 2.85 |
| STL | 93 | 69 | .574 | 6 | 747 | 628 | 231 | 66 | 128 | .271 | .403 | 77 | 147 | 136 | .976 | 49 | 463 | 978 | 17 | 32 | 3.32 |
| SF | 88 | 74 | .543 | 11 | 725 | 641 | 206 | 35 | 197 | .258 | .414 | 55 | 156 | 113 | .975 | 46 | 464 | 954 | 9 | 30 | 3.35 |
| PHI | 87 | 75 | .537 | 12 | 642 | 578 | 228 | 54 | 126 | .252 | .381 | 56 | 142 | 147 | .978 | 45 | 553 | 1052 | 12 | 31 | 3.09 |
| CIN | 86 | 76 | .531 | 13 | 648 | 594 | 225 | 44 | 122 | .246 | .371 | 92 | 135 | 127 | .978 | 55 | 425 | 1048 | 22 | 36 | 3.29 |
| MIL | 84 | 78 | .519 | 15 | 677 | 603 | 204 | 39 | 139 | .244 | .370 | 75 | 129 | 161 | .980 | 56 | 489 | 924 | 18 | 25 | 3.26 |
| CHI | 82 | 80 | .506 | 17 | 570 | 578 | 205 | 44 | 127 | .238 | .363 | 68 | 155 | 172 | .976 | 45 | 457 | 900 | 16 | 33 | 3.08 |
| PIT | 74 | 88 | .457 | 25 | 567 | 595 | 181 | 49 | 108 | .250 | .359 | 57 | 182 | 195 | .972 | 34 | 457 | 900 | 16 | 33 | 3.10 |
| HOU | 66 | 96 | .407 | 33 | 464 | 640 | 170 | 39 | 62 | .220 | .301 | 39 | 162 | 100 | .974 | 36 | 378 | 937 | 16 | 20 | 3.44 |
| NY | 51 | 111 | .315 | 48 | 501 | 774 | 156 | 35 | 96 | .219 | .315 | 41 | 210 | 151 | .967 | 42 | 529 | 806 | 5 | 12 | 4.12 |
| LEAGUE TOTAL | | | | | 6181 | 6181 | 1984 | 439 | 1215 | .245 | .364 | 684 | 1577 | 1431 | .975 | 459 | 4560 | 9545 | 154 | 276 | 3.29 |

## INDIVIDUAL PITCHING

| PITCHER | T | W | L | PCT | ERA | SV | G | GS | CG | IP | H | BB | SO | R | ER | ShO | H/9 | BB/9 | SO/9 |
|---|---|---|---|---|---|---|---|---|---|---|---|---|---|---|---|---|---|---|---|
| Dick Ellsworth | L | 22 | 10 | .688 | 2.11 | 0 | 37 | 37 | 19 | 290.2 | 223 | 75 | 185 | 75 | 68 | 4 | 6.90 | 2.32 | 5.73 |
| Larry Jackson | R | 14 | 18 | .438 | 2.55 | 0 | 37 | 37 | 13 | 275 | 256 | 54 | 153 | 102 | 78 | 4 | 8.38 | 1.77 | 5.01 |
| Bob Buhl | R | 11 | 14 | .440 | 3.38 | 0 | 37 | 34 | 6 | 226 | 219 | 62 | 108 | 96 | 85 | 0 | 8.72 | 2.47 | 4.30 |
| Glen Hobbie | R | 7 | 10 | .412 | 3.92 | 0 | 36 | 24 | 4 | 165.1 | 172 | 49 | 94 | 80 | 72 | 1 | 9.36 | 2.67 | 5.12 |
| Paul Toth | R | 5 | 9 | .357 | 3.10 | 0 | 27 | 14 | 3 | 130.2 | 115 | 35 | 66 | 50 | 45 | 2 | 7.92 | 2.41 | 4.55 |
| Lindy McDaniel | R | 13 | 7 | .650 | 2.86 | 22 | 57 | 0 | 0 | 88 | 82 | 27 | 75 | 32 | 28 | 0 | 8.39 | 2.76 | 7.67 |
| Cal Koonce | R | 2 | 6 | .250 | 4.58 | 0 | 21 | 13 | 0 | 72.2 | 75 | 32 | 44 | 43 | 37 | 0 | 9.29 | 3.96 | 5.45 |
| Don Elston | R | 4 | 1 | .800 | 2.83 | 4 | 51 | 0 | 0 | 70 | 57 | 21 | 41 | 26 | 22 | 0 | 7.33 | 2.70 | 5.27 |
| Jim Brewer | L | 3 | 2 | .600 | 4.89 | 0 | 29 | 1 | 0 | 49.2 | 59 | 15 | 35 | 32 | 27 | 0 | 10.69 | 2.72 | 6.34 |
| Barney Schultz | R | 1 | 0 | 1.000 | 3.62 | 2 | 15 | 0 | 0 | 27.1 | 25 | 9 | 18 | 11 | 11 | 0 | 8.23 | 2.96 | 5.93 |
| Jack Warner | R | 0 | 1 | .000 | 2.78 | 0 | 8 | 0 | 0 | 22.2 | 21 | 8 | 7 | 7 | 7 | 0 | 8.34 | 3.18 | 2.78 |
| Tom Baker | L | 0 | 1 | .000 | 3.00 | 0 | 10 | 1 | 0 | 18 | 20 | 7 | 14 | 12 | 6 | 0 | 10.00 | 3.50 | 7.00 |
| Dick LeMay | L | 0 | 1 | .000 | 5.28 | 0 | 9 | 1 | 0 | 15.1 | 26 | 4 | 10 | 9 | 9 | 0 | 15.26 | 2.35 | 5.87 |
| Freddie Burdette | R | 0 | 0 | – | 3.86 | 0 | 4 | 0 | 0 | 4.2 | 5 | 2 | 1 | 2 | 2 | 0 | 9.64 | 3.86 | 1.93 |
| Phil Mudrock | R | 0 | 0 | – | 9.00 | 0 | 1 | 0 | 0 | 1 | 2 | 0 | 0 | 1 | 1 | 0 | 18.00 | 0.00 | 0.00 |
| TEAM TOTAL | | 82 | 80 | .506 | 3.08 | 28 | 379 | 162 | 45 | 1457 | 1357 | 400 | 851 | 578 | 498 | 11 | 8.38 | 2.47 | 5.26 |

| MANAGER | W | L | PCT |
|---|---|---|---|
| Bob Kennedy | 76 | 86 | .469 |

| POS | Player | B | G | AB | H | 2B | 3B | HR | HR % | R | RBI | BB | SO | SB | Pinch Hit AB | Pinch Hit H | BA | SA |
|---|---|---|---|---|---|---|---|---|---|---|---|---|---|---|---|---|---|---|
| **REGULARS** | | | | | | | | | | | | | | | | | | |
| 1B | Ernie Banks | R | 157 | 591 | 156 | 29 | 6 | 23 | 3.9 | 67 | 95 | 36 | 84 | 1 | 0 | 0 | .264 | .450 |
| 2B | Joey Amalfitano | R | 100 | 324 | 78 | 19 | 6 | 4 | 1.2 | 51 | 27 | 40 | 42 | 2 | 10 | 3 | .241 | .373 |
| SS | Andre Rodgers | R | 129 | 448 | 107 | 17 | 3 | 12 | 2.7 | 50 | 46 | 53 | 88 | 5 | 3 | 0 | .239 | .371 |
| 3B | Ron Santo | R | 161 | 592 | 185 | 33 | 13 | 30 | 5.1 | 94 | 114 | 86 | 96 | 3 | 0 | 0 | .313 | .564 |
| RF | Len Gabrielson | L | 89 | 272 | 67 | 11 | 2 | 5 | 1.8 | 22 | 23 | 19 | 37 | 9 | 14 | 5 | .246 | .357 |
| CF | Billy Cowan | R | 139 | 497 | 120 | 16 | 4 | 19 | 3.8 | 52 | 50 | 18 | 128 | 12 | 4 | 2 | .241 | .404 |
| LF | Billy Williams | L | 162 | 645 | 201 | 39 | 2 | 33 | 5.1 | 100 | 98 | 59 | 84 | 10 | 1 | 0 | .312 | .532 |
| C | Dick Bertell | R | 112 | 353 | 84 | 11 | 3 | 4 | 1.1 | 29 | 35 | 33 | 67 | 2 | 3 | 0 | .238 | .320 |
| **SUBSTITUTES** | | | | | | | | | | | | | | | | | | |
| 2S | Jimmy Stewart | B | 132 | 415 | 105 | 17 | 0 | 3 | 0.7 | 59 | 33 | 49 | 61 | 10 | 31 | 9 | .253 | .316 |
| 2B | Ron Campbell | R | 26 | 92 | 25 | 6 | 1 | 1 | 1.1 | 7 | 10 | 1 | 21 | 0 | 0 | 0 | .272 | .391 |
| 1O | John Boccabella | R | 9 | 23 | 9 | 2 | 1 | 0 | 0.0 | 4 | 6 | 0 | 3 | 0 | 3 | 1 | .391 | .565 |
| SS | Don Kessinger | R | 4 | 12 | 2 | 0 | 0 | 0 | 0.0 | 1 | 0 | 0 | 1 | 0 | 2 | 0 | .167 | .167 |
| OF | Lou Brock | L | 52 | 215 | 54 | 9 | 2 | 2 | 0.9 | 30 | 14 | 13 | 40 | 10 | 0 | 0 | .251 | .340 |
| OF | Doug Clemens | L | 54 | 140 | 39 | 10 | 2 | 2 | 1.4 | 23 | 12 | 18 | 22 | 0 | 11 | 1 | .279 | .421 |
| OF | Ellis Burton | B | 42 | 105 | 20 | 3 | 2 | 2 | 1.9 | 12 | 7 | 17 | 22 | 4 | 12 | 2 | .190 | .314 |
| UT | Leo Burke | R | 59 | 103 | 27 | 3 | 1 | 1 | 1.0 | 11 | 14 | 7 | 31 | 0 | 34 | 10 | .262 | .340 |
| OF | Billy Ott | B | 20 | 39 | 7 | 3 | 0 | 0 | 0.0 | 4 | 1 | 3 | 10 | 0 | 10 | 2 | .179 | .256 |
| OF | Don Landrum | L | 11 | 11 | 0 | 0 | 0 | 0 | 0.0 | 2 | 0 | 1 | 2 | 0 | 8 | 0 | .000 | .000 |
| C | Jimmie Schaffer | R | 54 | 122 | 25 | 6 | 1 | 2 | 1.6 | 9 | 9 | 17 | 17 | 2 | 9 | 3 | .205 | .320 |
| C | Vic Roznovsky | L | 35 | 76 | 15 | 1 | 0 | 0 | 0.0 | 2 | 2 | 5 | 18 | 0 | 16 | 1 | .197 | .211 |
| C | Merritt Ranew | L | 16 | 33 | 3 | 0 | 0 | 0 | 0.0 | 0 | 1 | 2 | 6 | 0 | 5 | 1 | .091 | .091 |
| PH | Paul Popovich | R | 1 | 1 | 1 | 0 | 0 | 0 | 0.0 | 0 | 0 | 0 | 0 | 0 | 1 | 1 | 1.000 | 1.000 |
| **PITCHERS** | | | | | | | | | | | | | | | | | | |
| P | Larry Jackson | R | 40 | 114 | 20 | 3 | 0 | 0 | 0.0 | 2 | 6 | 1 | 26 | 0 | 0 | 0 | .175 | .202 |
| P | Dick Ellsworth | L | 37 | 87 | 4 | 0 | 0 | 0 | 0.0 | 4 | 1 | 4 | 43 | 0 | 0 | 0 | .046 | .046 |
| P | Bob Buhl | R | 36 | 73 | 7 | 0 | 0 | 0 | 0.0 | 3 | 1 | 6 | 31 | 0 | 0 | 0 | .096 | .096 |
| P | Lew Burdette | R | 28 | 43 | 12 | 0 | 0 | 2 | 4.7 | 6 | 4 | 3 | 12 | 0 | 0 | 0 | .279 | .465 |
| P | Ernie Broglio | R | 18 | 35 | 10 | 1 | 0 | 0 | 0.0 | 2 | 0 | 1 | 7 | 0 | 0 | 0 | .286 | .314 |
| P | Lindy McDaniel | R | 63 | 16 | 2 | 0 | 0 | 0 | 0.0 | 0 | 0 | 0 | 9 | 0 | 0 | 0 | .125 | .125 |
| P | Lee Gregory | L | 19 | 13 | 1 | 0 | 0 | 0 | 0.0 | 0 | 0 | 3 | 6 | 0 | 9 | 0 | .077 | .077 |
| P | Sterling Slaughter | R | 20 | 12 | 1 | 0 | 0 | 0 | 0.0 | 1 | 0 | 1 | 8 | 0 | 0 | 0 | .083 | .083 |
| P | Fred Norman | L | 8 | 11 | 1 | 0 | 0 | 0 | 0.0 | 1 | 0 | 0 | 5 | 0 | 0 | 0 | .091 | .091 |
| P | Cal Koonce | R | 6 | 10 | 0 | 0 | 0 | 0 | 0.0 | 0 | 0 | 0 | 4 | 0 | 0 | 0 | .000 | .000 |
| P | Don Elston | R | 48 | 6 | 1 | 0 | 0 | 0 | 0.0 | 0 | 1 | 0 | 1 | 0 | 0 | 0 | .167 | .167 |
| P | Glen Hobbie | R | 8 | 5 | 0 | 0 | 0 | 0 | 0.0 | 0 | 0 | 2 | 2 | 0 | 0 | 0 | .000 | .000 |
| P | Wayne Schurr | R | 26 | 5 | 0 | 0 | 0 | 0 | 0.0 | 0 | 0 | 1 | 5 | 0 | 0 | 0 | .000 | .000 |
| P | Paul Toth | R | 4 | 3 | 1 | 0 | 0 | 0 | 0.0 | 0 | 0 | 0 | 2 | 0 | 0 | 0 | .333 | .333 |
| P | Freddie Burdette | R | 18 | 1 | 1 | 0 | 0 | 0 | 0.0 | 0 | 0 | 0 | 0 | 0 | 0 | 0 | 1.000 | 1.000 |
| P | John Flavin | L | 5 | 1 | 0 | 0 | 0 | 0 | 0.0 | 0 | 0 | 0 | 0 | 0 | 0 | 0 | .000 | .000 |
| P | Paul Jaeckel | R | 4 | 1 | 0 | 0 | 0 | 0 | 0.0 | 0 | 0 | 0 | 0 | 0 | 0 | 0 | .000 | .000 |
| P | Dick Scott | R | 3 | 0 | 0 | 0 | 0 | 0 | – | 0 | 0 | 0 | 0 | 0 | 0 | 0 | – | – |
| P | Bobby Shantz | R | 20 | 0 | 0 | 0 | 0 | 0 | – | 0 | 0 | 0 | 0 | 0 | 0 | 0 | – | – |
| P | Jack Spring | R | 7 | 0 | 0 | 0 | 0 | 0 | – | 0 | 0 | 0 | 0 | 0 | 0 | 0 | – | – |
| P | Jack Warner | R | 7 | 0 | 0 | 0 | 0 | 0 | – | 0 | 0 | 0 | 0 | 0 | 0 | 0 | – | – |
| TEAM TOTAL | | | | 5545 | 1391 | 239 | 50 | 145 | 2.6 | 64 | 609 | 499 | 1041 | 70 | 186 | 41 | .251 | .390 |

## INDIVIDUAL FIELDING

| POS | Player | T | G | PO | A | E | DP | TC/G | FA | POS | Player | T | G | PO | A | E | DP | TC/G | FA |
|---|---|---|---|---|---|---|---|---|---|---|---|---|---|---|---|---|---|---|---|
| 1B | E. Banks | R | 157 | **1565** | 132 | 10 | 122 | 10.9 | .994 | OF | B. Cowan | R | 134 | 297 | 2 | 10 | 0 | 2.3 | .968 |
| | Amalfitano | R | 1 | 0 | 0 | 0 | 0 | 0.0 | .000 | | B. Williams | R | 162 | 233 | 14 | 13 | 0 | 1.6 | .950 |
| | Gabrielson | R | 8 | 63 | 5 | 0 | 7 | 8.5 | 1.000 | | Gabrielson | R | 68 | 116 | 5 | 2 | 0 | 1.8 | .984 |
| | Boccabella | R | 5 | 41 | 3 | 0 | 3 | 8.8 | 1.000 | | L. Brock | L | 52 | 86 | 8 | 4* | 1 | 1.9 | .959 |
| | L. Burke | R | 2 | 13 | 1 | 0 | 1 | 7.0 | 1.000 | | D. Clemens | R | 40 | 67 | 5 | 6 | 1 | 2.0 | .923 |
| 2B | Amalfitano | R | 86 | 201 | 254 | 17 | 47 | 5.5 | .964 | | E. Burton | R | 29 | 51 | 0 | 1 | 0 | 1.8 | .981 |
| | J. Stewart | R | 61 | 130 | 180 | 6 | 40 | 5.2 | .981 | | L. Burke | R | 18 | 25 | 1 | 0 | 1 | 1.4 | 1.000 |
| | R. Campbell | R | 26 | 64 | 95 | 10 | 15 | 6.5 | .941 | | Boccabella | R | 2 | 0 | 0 | 0 | 0 | 0.0 | .000 |
| | L. Burke | R | 5 | 5 | 4 | 2 | 0 | 2.2 | .818 | | B. Ott | R | 10 | 12 | 0 | 0 | 0 | 1.2 | 1.000 |
| SS | A. Rodgers | R | 126 | 232 | 428 | 24 | 68 | 5.4 | .965 | | J. Stewart | R | 4 | 3 | 0 | 1 | 0 | 1.0 | .750 |
| | J. Stewart | R | 45 | 84 | 127 | 6 | 24 | 4.8 | .972 | | D. Landrum | R | 1 | 1 | 1 | 0 | 0 | 2.0 | 1.000 |
| | Amalfitano | R | 1 | 0 | 0 | 0 | 0 | 0.0 | .000 | C | D. Bertell | R | 110 | 531 | 52 | 11 | 3 | 5.4 | .981 |
| | D. Kessinger | R | 4 | 3 | 7 | 0 | 1 | 2.5 | 1.000 | | J. Schaffer | R | 43 | 143 | 19 | 5 | 1 | 3.9 | .970 |
| 3B | R. Santo | R | 161 | 156 | 367 | 20 | 31 | 3.4 | .963 | | V. Roznovsky | R | 26 | 67 | 14 | 2 | 2 | 3.2 | .976 |
| | L. Burke | R | 4 | 2 | 5 | 0 | 0 | 1.8 | 1.000 | | M. Ranew | R | 9 | 42 | 8 | 0 | 0 | 5.6 | 1.000 |
| | J. Stewart | R | 1 | 0 | 1 | 0 | 0 | 1.0 | 1.000 | | L. Burke | R | 1 | 1 | 0 | 0 | 0 | 1.0 | 1.000 |

The year started on a tragic note when promising second baseman Ken Hubbs was killed in a plane crash near Provo, Utah, on February 15. Hubbs, who had recently obtained his pilot's license, was en route to his home in Colton, California, when his Cessna encountered a snowstorm. The Cubs then committed perhaps the worst blunder in their history on June 15, sending Lou Brock, a fleet, young outfielder to the Cardinals for Ernie Broglio, a shopworn, sore-armed pitcher. Actually, it was a six-player deal, but Brock and Broglio were the principal players. Brock stole 43 bases, batted .315, and helped St. Louis win the World Series. Broglio, meanwhile, was 4–7 in Cub flannels. The Cubs did boast the league's winningest pitcher in Larry Jackson, who had a 24–11 record, including nine victories in a row. In addition, the trio of Billy Williams (33), Ron Santo (30), and Ernie Banks (23) combined for 86 homers. Santo also hit .313, drove in 114 runs, and ranked second to the Giants' Willie Mays in slugging at .564. Disappointments were southpaw Dick Ellsworth, who slipped from 22–10 to 14–18 and reliever Lindy McDaniel, who was of little late-inning value with a 1–7 mark. Head coach Bob Kennedy, who was replaced by Lou Klein, late in the season, had the Cubs as high as fifth place in June, but the team suffered its traditional cold spell during the heat of summer, losing 36 games in July and August and falling into eighth place.

## TEAM STATISTICS

| | W | L | PCT | GB | R | OR | 2B | 3B | HR | BA | SA | SB | E | DP | FA | CG | B | SO | ShO | SV | ERA |
|---|---|---|---|---|---|---|---|---|---|---|---|---|---|---|---|---|---|---|---|---|---|
| | | | | | | | | Batting | | | | | | Fielding | | | | Pitching | | | |
| STL | 93 | 69 | .574 | | 715 | 652 | 240 | 53 | 109 | .272 | .392 | 73 | 172 | 147 | .973 | 47 | 410 | 877 | 10 | 38 | 3.43 |
| CIN | 92 | 70 | .568 | 1 | 660 | **566** | 220 | 38 | 130 | .249 | .372 | 90 | **130** | 137 | **.979** | 54 | 436 | **1122** | 14 | 35 | 3.07 |
| PHI | 92 | 70 | .568 | 1 | 693 | 632 | 241 | 51 | 130 | .258 | .391 | 30 | 157 | 150 | .975 | 37 | 440 | 1009 | 17 | **41** | 3.36 |
| SF | 90 | 72 | .556 | 3 | 656 | 587 | 185 | 38 | **165** | .246 | .382 | 64 | 159 | 136 | .975 | 48 | 480 | 1023 | 17 | 30 | 3.19 |
| MIL | 88 | 74 | .543 | 5 | **803** | 744 | **274** | 32 | 159 | **.272** | **.418** | 53 | 143 | 139 | .977 | 45 | 452 | 906 | 14 | 39 | 4.12 |
| LA | 80 | 82 | .494 | 13 | 614 | 572 | 180 | 39 | 79 | .250 | .340 | **141** | 170 | 126 | .973 | 47 | 458 | 1062 | **19** | 27 | **2.95** |
| PIT | 80 | 82 | .494 | 13 | 663 | 636 | 225 | **54** | 121 | .264 | .389 | 39 | 177 | **179** | .972 | 42 | 476 | 951 | 14 | 29 | 3.52 |
| CHI | 76 | 86 | .469 | 17 | 649 | 724 | 239 | 50 | 145 | .251 | .390 | 70 | 162 | 147 | .975 | **58** | 423 | 737 | 11 | 19 | 4.08 |
| HOU | 66 | 96 | .407 | 27 | 495 | 628 | 162 | 41 | 70 | .229 | .315 | 40 | 149 | 124 | .976 | 30 | **353** | 852 | 9 | 31 | 3.41 |
| NY | 53 | 109 | .327 | 40 | 569 | 776 | 195 | 31 | 103 | .246 | .348 | 36 | 167 | 154 | .974 | 40 | 466 | 717 | 10 | 15 | 4.25 |
| LEAGUE TOTAL | | | | | 6517 | 6517 | 2161 | 427 | 1211 | .254 | .374 | 636 | 1586 | 1439 | .975 | 448 | 4394 | 9256 | 135 | 304 | 3.54 |

## INDIVIDUAL   PITCHING

| PITCHER | T | W | L | PCT | ERA | SV | G | GS | CG | IP | H | BB | SO | R | ER | ShO | H/9 | BB/9 | SO/9 |
|---|---|---|---|---|---|---|---|---|---|---|---|---|---|---|---|---|---|---|---|
| Larry Jackson | R | 24 | 11 | .686 | 3.14 | 0 | 40 | 38 | 19 | 297.2 | 265 | 58 | 148 | 114 | 104 | 3 | 8.01 | 1.75 | 4.47 |
| Dick Ellsworth | L | 14 | 18 | .438 | 3.75 | 0 | 37 | 36 | 16 | 256.2 | 267 | 71 | 148 | 129 | 107 | 1 | 9.36 | 2.49 | 5.19 |
| Bob Buhl | R | 15 | 14 | .517 | 3.83 | 0 | 36 | 35 | 11 | 227.2 | 208 | 68 | 107 | 103 | 97 | 3 | 8.22 | 2.69 | 4.23 |
| Lew Burdette | R | 9 | 9 | .500 | 4.88 | 0 | 28 | 17 | 8 | 131 | 152 | 19 | 40 | 74 | 71 | 2 | 10.44 | 1.31 | 2.75 |
| Ernie Broglio | R | 4 | 7 | .364 | 4.04 | 1 | 18 | 16 | 3 | 100.1 | 111 | 30 | 46 | 51 | 45 | 0 | 9.96 | 2.69 | 4.13 |
| Lindy McDaniel | R | 1 | 7 | .125 | 3.88 | 15 | 63 | 0 | 0 | 95 | 104 | 23 | 71 | 43 | 41 | 0 | 9.85 | 2.18 | 6.73 |
| Don Elston | R | 2 | 5 | .286 | 5.30 | 1 | 48 | 0 | 0 | 54.1 | 68 | 34 | 26 | 38 | 32 | 0 | 11.26 | 5.63 | 4.31 |
| Sterling Slaughter | R | 2 | 4 | .333 | 5.75 | 0 | 20 | 6 | 1 | 51.2 | 64 | 32 | 32 | 35 | 33 | 0 | 11.15 | 5.57 | 5.57 |
| Wayne Schurr | R | 0 | 0 | – | 3.72 | 0 | 26 | 0 | 0 | 48.1 | 57 | 11 | 29 | 22 | 20 | 0 | 10.61 | 2.05 | 5.40 |
| Fred Norman | L | 0 | 4 | .000 | 6.54 | 0 | 8 | 5 | 0 | 31.2 | 34 | 21 | 20 | 25 | 23 | 0 | 9.66 | 5.97 | 5.68 |
| Cal Koonce | R | 3 | 0 | 1.000 | 2.03 | 0 | 6 | 2 | 0 | 31 | 30 | 7 | 17 | 8 | 7 | 0 | 8.71 | 2.03 | 4.94 |
| Glen Hobbie | R | 0 | 3 | .000 | 7.90 | 0 | 8 | 4 | 0 | 27.1 | 39 | 10 | 14 | 29 | 24 | 0 | 12.84 | 3.29 | 4.61 |
| Freddie Burdette | R | 1 | 0 | 1.000 | 3.15 | 0 | 18 | 0 | 0 | 20 | 17 | 10 | 4 | 7 | 7 | 0 | 7.65 | 4.50 | 1.80 |
| Lee Gregory | L | 0 | 0 | – | 3.50 | 0 | 11 | 0 | 0 | 18 | 23 | 5 | 8 | 8 | 7 | 0 | 11.50 | 2.50 | 4.00 |
| Bobby Shantz | L | 0 | 1 | .000 | 5.56 | 1 | 20 | 0 | 0 | 11.1 | 15 | 6 | 12 | 7 | 7 | 0 | 11.91 | 4.76 | 9.53 |
| Paul Toth | R | 0 | 2 | .000 | 8.44 | 0 | 4 | 2 | 0 | 10.2 | 15 | 5 | 0 | 10 | 10 | 0 | 12.66 | 4.22 | 0.00 |
| Jack Warner | R | 0 | 0 | – | 2.89 | 0 | 7 | 0 | 0 | 9.1 | 12 | 4 | 6 | 3 | 3 | 0 | 11.57 | 3.86 | 5.79 |
| Paul Jaeckel | R | 1 | 0 | 1.000 | 0.00 | 0 | 4 | 0 | 0 | 8 | 4 | 3 | 2 | 0 | 0 | 0 | 4.50 | 3.38 | 2.25 |
| Jack Spring | L | 0 | 0 | – | 6.00 | 0 | 7 | 0 | 0 | 6 | 4 | 2 | 1 | 5 | 4 | 0 | 6.00 | 3.00 | 1.50 |
| John Flavin | L | 0 | 1 | .000 | 13.50 | 0 | 5 | 1 | 0 | 4.2 | 11 | 3 | 5 | 7 | 7 | 0 | 21.21 | 5.79 | 9.64 |
| Dick Scott | L | 0 | 0 | – | 12.46 | 0 | 3 | 0 | 0 | 4.1 | 10 | 1 | 1 | 6 | 6 | 0 | 20.77 | 2.08 | 2.08 |
| TEAM TOTAL | | 76 | 86 | .469 | 4.08 | 19 | 417 | 162 | 58 | 1445 | 1510 | 423 | 737 | 724 | 655 | 9 | 9.40 | 2.63 | 4.59 |

| MANAGER | W | L | PCT |
|---|---|---|---|
| Bob Kennedy | 24 | 32 | .429 |
| Lou Klein | 48 | 58 | .453 |

| POS | Player | B | G | AB | H | 2B | 3B | HR | HR % | R | RBI | BB | SO | SB | Pinch Hit AB | Pinch Hit H | BA | SA |
|---|---|---|---|---|---|---|---|---|---|---|---|---|---|---|---|---|---|---|
| **REGULARS** | | | | | | | | | | | | | | | | | | |
| 1B | Ernie Banks | R | 163 | 612 | 162 | 25 | 3 | 28 | 4.6 | 79 | 106 | 55 | 64 | 3 | 2 | 1 | .265 | .453 |
| 2B | Glenn Beckert | R | 154 | 614 | 147 | 21 | 3 | 3 | 0.5 | 73 | 30 | 28 | 52 | 6 | 2 | 2 | .239 | .298 |
| SS | Don Kessinger | R | 106 | 309 | 62 | 4 | 3 | 0 | 0.0 | 19 | 14 | 20 | 44 | 1 | 0 | 0 | .201 | .233 |
| 3B | Ron Santo | R | 164 | 608 | 173 | 30 | 4 | 33 | 5.4 | 88 | 101 | 88 | 109 | 3 | 0 | 0 | .285 | .510 |
| RF | Billy Williams | L | 164 | 645 | 203 | 39 | 6 | 34 | 5.3 | 115 | 108 | 65 | 76 | 10 | 0 | 0 | .315 | .552 |
| CF | Don Landrum | L | 131 | 425 | 96 | 20 | 4 | 6 | 1.4 | 60 | 34 | 36 | 84 | 14 | 15 | 2 | .226 | .334 |
| LF | Doug Clemens | L | 128 | 340 | 75 | 11 | 0 | 4 | 1.2 | 36 | 26 | 38 | 53 | 5 | 25 | 6 | .221 | .288 |
| C | Vic Roznovsky | L | 71 | 172 | 38 | 4 | 1 | 3 | 1.7 | 9 | 15 | 16 | 30 | 1 | 11 | 4 | .221 | .308 |
| **SUBSTITUTES** | | | | | | | | | | | | | | | | | | |
| SS | Roberto Pena | R | 51 | 170 | 37 | 5 | 1 | 2 | 1.2 | 17 | 12 | 16 | 19 | 1 | 1 | 0 | .218 | .294 |
| 2B | Joey Amalfitano | R | 67 | 96 | 26 | 4 | 0 | 0 | 0.0 | 13 | 8 | 12 | 14 | 2 | 37 | 8 | .271 | .313 |
| 1O | John Boccabella | R | 6 | 12 | 4 | 0 | 0 | 2 | 16.7 | 2 | 4 | 1 | 2 | 0 | 2 | 1 | .333 | .833 |
| OS | Jimmy Stewart | B | 116 | 282 | 63 | 9 | 4 | 0 | 0.0 | 26 | 19 | 30 | 53 | 13 | 41 | 6 | .223 | .284 |
| OF | George Altman | L | 90 | 196 | 46 | 7 | 1 | 4 | 2.0 | 24 | 23 | 19 | 36 | 3 | 43 | 6 | .235 | .342 |
| OF | Harvey Kuenn | R | 54 | 120 | 26 | 5 | 0 | 0 | 0.0 | 11 | 6 | 22 | 13 | 1 | 22 | 5 | .217 | .258 |
| OF | Len Gabrielson | L | 28 | 48 | 12 | 0 | 0 | 3 | 6.3 | 4 | 5 | 7 | 16 | 0 | 13 | 2 | .250 | .438 |
| OF | Ellis Burton | B | 17 | 40 | 7 | 1 | 0 | 0 | 0.0 | 6 | 4 | 1 | 10 | 1 | 8 | 2 | .175 | .200 |
| OF | Don Young | R | 11 | 35 | 2 | 0 | 0 | 1 | 2.9 | 1 | 2 | 0 | 11 | 0 | 3 | 1 | .057 | .143 |
| OF | Byron Browne | R | 4 | 6 | 0 | 0 | 0 | 0 | 0.0 | 0 | 0 | 0 | 2 | 0 | 1 | 0 | .000 | .000 |
| C | Chris Krug | R | 60 | 169 | 34 | 5 | 0 | 5 | 3.0 | 16 | 24 | 13 | 52 | 0 | 3 | 0 | .201 | .320 |
| C | Ed Bailey | L | 66 | 150 | 38 | 6 | 0 | 5 | 3.3 | 13 | 23 | 34 | 28 | 0 | 14 | 1 | .253 | .393 |
| C | Dick Bertell | R | 34 | 84 | 18 | 2 | 0 | 0 | 0.0 | 6 | 7 | 11 | 10 | 0 | 0 | 0 | .214 | .238 |
| CO | Leo Burke | R | 12 | 10 | 2 | 0 | 0 | 0 | 0.0 | 0 | 0 | 0 | 4 | 0 | 9 | 1 | .200 | .200 |
| PH | Harry Bright | R | 27 | 25 | 7 | 1 | 0 | 0 | 0.0 | 1 | 4 | 0 | 8 | 0 | 25 | 7 | .280 | .320 |
| PH | Ron Campbell | R | 2 | 2 | 0 | 0 | 0 | 0 | 0.0 | 0 | 0 | 0 | 0 | 0 | 2 | 0 | .000 | .000 |
| PH | Chuck Hartenstein | R | 1 | 0 | 0 | 0 | 0 | 0 | — | 0 | 0 | 0 | 0 | 0 | 0 | 0 | — | — |
| **PITCHERS** | | | | | | | | | | | | | | | | | | |
| P | Larry Jackson | R | 49 | 86 | 11 | 0 | 2 | 1 | 1.2 | 6 | 5 | 5 | 29 | 0 | 1 | 0 | .128 | .209 |
| P | Dick Ellsworth | L | 36 | 73 | 7 | 0 | 1 | 0 | 0.0 | 1 | 2 | 4 | 30 | 0 | 0 | 0 | .096 | .123 |
| P | Bob Buhl | R | 32 | 67 | 4 | 0 | 0 | 0 | 0.0 | 3 | 2 | 3 | 36 | 0 | 0 | 0 | .060 | .060 |
| P | Cal Koonce | R | 38 | 49 | 5 | 1 | 0 | 0 | 0.0 | 2 | 1 | 5 | 21 | 0 | 0 | 0 | .102 | .122 |
| P | Bill Faul | R | 17 | 30 | 3 | 1 | 0 | 0 | 0.0 | 2 | 2 | 1 | 14 | 0 | 0 | 0 | .100 | .133 |
| P | Ted Abernathy | R | 84 | 18 | 3 | 0 | 0 | 0 | 0.0 | 1 | 2 | 0 | 7 | 0 | 0 | 0 | .167 | .167 |
| P | Bob Hendley | R | 18 | 14 | 0 | 0 | 0 | 0 | 0.0 | 0 | 1 | 0 | 10 | 0 | 0 | 0 | .000 | .000 |
| P | Billy Hoeft | L | 29 | 11 | 3 | 0 | 0 | 0 | 0.0 | 1 | 0 | 0 | 3 | 0 | 0 | 0 | .273 | .273 |
| P | Lindy McDaniel | R | 71 | 8 | 0 | 0 | 0 | 0 | 0.0 | 0 | 0 | 1 | 4 | 0 | 0 | 0 | .000 | .000 |
| P | Lew Burdette | R | 8 | 6 | 2 | 1 | 0 | 0 | 0.0 | 0 | 0 | 0 | 1 | 1 | 0 | 0 | .333 | .500 |
| P | Ernie Broglio | R | 26 | 4 | 0 | 0 | 0 | 0 | 0.0 | 0 | 0 | 1 | 2 | 0 | 0 | 0 | .000 | .000 |
| P | Bob Humphreys | R | 41 | 3 | 0 | 0 | 0 | 0 | 0.0 | 0 | 0 | 0 | 0 | 0 | 0 | 0 | .000 | .000 |
| P | Jack Warner | R | 11 | 1 | 0 | 0 | 0 | 0 | 0.0 | 0 | 0 | 0 | 1 | 0 | 0 | 0 | .000 | .000 |
| P | Frank Baumann | L | 4 | 0 | 0 | 0 | 0 | 0 | — | 0 | 0 | 0 | 0 | 0 | 0 | 0 | — | — |
| P | Ken Holtzman | R | 3 | 0 | 0 | 0 | 0 | 0 | — | 0 | 0 | 0 | 0 | 0 | 0 | 0 | — | — |
| TEAM TOTAL | | | | 5540 | 1316 | 202 | 33 | 134 | 2.4 | 63 | 590 | 532 | 948 | 65 | 280 | 55 | .238 | .358 |

## INDIVIDUAL FIELDING

| POS | Player | T | G | PO | A | E | DP | TC/G | FA | POS | Player | T | G | PO | A | E | DP | TC/G | FA |
|---|---|---|---|---|---|---|---|---|---|---|---|---|---|---|---|---|---|---|---|
| 1B | E. Banks | R | 162 | **1682** | 93 | 15 | 143 | **11.0** | .992 | OF | B. Williams | R | 164 | 296 | 10 | 10 | 2 | 1.9 | .968 |
| | G. Altman | R | 2 | 12 | 0 | 0 | 1 | 6.0 | 1.000 | | D. Landrum | R | 115 | 241 | 3 | 3 | 0 | 2.1 | .988 |
| | Boccabella | R | 2 | 11 | 1 | 0 | 0 | 6.0 | 1.000 | | D. Clemens | R | 105 | 145 | 7 | 3 | 0 | 1.5 | .981 |
| | H. Kuenn | R | 1 | 4 | 0 | 2 | 0 | 6.0 | .667 | | J. Stewart | R | 55 | 80 | 4 | 4 | 0 | 1.6 | .955 |
| | E. Bailey | R | 3 | 4 | 0 | 0 | 1 | 1.3 | 1.000 | | G. Altman | R | 45 | 66 | 0 | 4 | 0 | 1.6 | .943 |
| | Gabrielson | R | 1 | 1 | 0 | 0 | 0 | 1.0 | 1.000 | | H. Kuenn | R | 35 | 36 | 3 | 1 | 1 | 1.1 | .975 |
| | | | | | | | | | | | L. Burke | R | 1 | 0 | 0 | 0 | 0 | 0.0 | .000 |
| 2B | G. Beckert | R | 153 | 326 | **494** | 23 | 101 | 5.5 | .973 | | E. Burton | R | 12 | 19 | 1 | 0 | 0 | 1.7 | 1.000 |
| | Amalfitano | R | 24 | 28 | 65 | 1 | 9 | 3.9 | .989 | | D. Young | R | 11 | 14 | 0 | 1 | 0 | 1.4 | .933 |
| | | | | | | | | | | | Gabrielson | R | 14 | 14 | 0 | 0 | 0 | 1.0 | 1.000 |
| SS | D. Kessinger | R | 105 | 176 | 338 | **28** | 69 | 5.2 | .948 | | B. Browne | R | 4 | 2 | 0 | 1 | 0 | 0.8 | .667 |
| | R. Pena | R | 50 | 74 | 151 | 17 | 29 | 4.8 | .930 | | Boccabella | R | 1 | 1 | 0 | 1 | 0 | 2.0 | .500 |
| | J. Stewart | R | 48 | 37 | 54 | 4 | 11 | 2.0 | .958 | C | C. Krug | R | 58 | 273 | 27 | 6 | 5 | 5.3 | .980 |
| | Amalfitano | R | 4 | 3 | 2 | 1 | 0 | 1.5 | .833 | | V. Roznovsky | R | 63 | 270 | 30 | 5 | 6 | 4.8 | .984 |
| 3B | R. Santo | R | 164 | **155** | **373** | 24 | 27 | **3.4** | .957 | | E. Bailey | R | 54 | 237 | 23 | 5 | 3 | 4.9 | .981 |
| | | | | | | | | | | | D. Bertell | R | 34 | 128 | 29 | 3 | 2 | 4.7 | .981 |
| | | | | | | | | | | | L. Burke | R | 2 | 2 | 0 | 0 | 0 | 1.0 | 1.000 |

The Cubs were a hollow triple threat. In Billy Williams (108), Ernie Banks (106), and Ron Santo (101), they were the only team with three 100-RBI players. They also tied a record with three triple plays, all three games with hypnotist Bill Faul on the mound. But the Cubs tripped through the season, winning only nine games after August and finishing eighth with a 72–90 record. Head coach Bob Kennedy was kicked upstairs as a vice-president when the team was 24–32. Lou Klein mopped up with a 48–58 mark. Biggest loser among the pitchers was Larry Jackson, who had 21 losses to go with 14 wins. Dick Ellsworth, who at one stage was 12–6, dropped 9 of his last 11 to wind up at 14–15. The best acquisition was submarine reliever Ted Abernathy, who was kept busy with 84 appearances and 31 saves. A new double-play combo of Glenn Beckert and Don Kessinger was uncovered and loomed as a future fixture. Lost among all the losses was a solid Williams season. The sweet-swinging leftfielder scored 115 runs, had 203 hits, 39 doubles, 34 homers, 356 total bases, a .552 slugging average, and batted .315. Incidentally, Ernie Broglio, the chap dropped into the Cubs' lap for speedy Lou Brock, contributed one victory.

## TEAM STATISTICS

|  | W | L | PCT | GB | R | OR | 2B | 3B | Batting HR | BA | SA | SB | E | Fielding DP | FA | CG | B | Pitching SO | ShO | SV | ERA |
|---|---|---|---|---|---|---|---|---|---|---|---|---|---|---|---|---|---|---|---|---|---|
| LA | 97 | 65 | .599 |  | 608 | 521 | 193 | 32 | 78 | .245 | .335 | 172 | 134 | 135 | .979 | 58 | 425 | 1079 | 23 | 34 | 2.81 |
| SF | 95 | 67 | .586 | 2 | 682 | 593 | 169 | 43 | 159 | .252 | .385 | 47 | 148 | 124 | .976 | 42 | 408 | 1060 | 17 | 42 | 3.20 |
| PIT | 90 | 72 | .556 | 7 | 675 | 580 | 217 | 57 | 111 | .265 | .382 | 51 | 152 | 189 | .977 | 49 | 469 | 882 | 17 | 27 | 3.01 |
| CIN | 89 | 73 | .549 | 8 | 825 | 704 | 268 | 61 | 183 | .273 | .439 | 82 | 117 | 142 | .981 | 43 | 587 | 1113 | 9 | 34 | 3.88 |
| MIL | 86 | 76 | .531 | 11 | 708 | 633 | 243 | 28 | 196 | .256 | .416 | 64 | 140 | 145 | .978 | 43 | 541 | 966 | 4 | 38 | 3.52 |
| PHI | 85 | 76 | .528 | 11.5 | 654 | 667 | 205 | 53 | 144 | .250 | .384 | 46 | 157 | 153 | .975 | 50 | 466 | 1071 | 18 | 21 | 3.53 |
| STL | 80 | 81 | .497 | 16.5 | 707 | 674 | 234 | 46 | 109 | .254 | .371 | 100 | 130 | 152 | .979 | 40 | 467 | 916 | 11 | 35 | 3.77 |
| CHI | 72 | 90 | .444 | 25 | 635 | 723 | 202 | 33 | 134 | .238 | .358 | 65 | 171 | 166 | .974 | 33 | 481 | 855 | 9 | 35 | 3.78 |
| HOU | 65 | 97 | .401 | 32 | 569 | 711 | 188 | 42 | 97 | .237 | .340 | 90 | 166 | 130 | .974 | 29 | 388 | 931 | 7 | 26 | 3.84 |
| NY | 50 | 112 | .309 | 47 | 495 | 752 | 203 | 27 | 107 | .221 | .327 | 28 | 171 | 153 | .974 | 29 | 498 | 776 | 11 | 14 | 4.06 |
| LEAGUE TOTAL |  |  |  |  | 6558 | 6558 | 2122 | 422 | 1318 | .249 | .374 | 745 | 1486 | 1489 | .977 | 416 | 4730 | 9649 | 126 | 306 | 3.54 |

## INDIVIDUAL  PITCHING

| PITCHER | T | W | L | PCT | ERA | SV | G | GS | CG | IP | H | BB | SO | R | ER | ShO | H/9 | BB/9 | SO/9 |
|---|---|---|---|---|---|---|---|---|---|---|---|---|---|---|---|---|---|---|---|
| Larry Jackson | R | 14 | 21 | .400 | 3.85 | 0 | 39 | 39 | 12 | 257.1 | 268 | 57 | 131 | 126 | 110 | 4 | 9.37 | 1.99 | 4.58 |
| Dick Ellsworth | L | 14 | 15 | .483 | 3.81 | 1 | 36 | 34 | 8 | 222.1 | 227 | 57 | 130 | 108 | 94 | 0 | 9.19 | 2.31 | 5.26 |
| Bob Buhl | R | 13 | 11 | .542 | 4.39 | 0 | 32 | 31 | 2 | 184.1 | 207 | 57 | 92 | 100 | 90 | 0 | 10.11 | 2.78 | 4.49 |
| Cal Koonce | R | 7 | 9 | .438 | 3.69 | 0 | 38 | 23 | 3 | 173 | 181 | 52 | 88 | 83 | 71 | 1 | 9.42 | 2.71 | 4.58 |
| Ted Abernathy | R | 4 | 6 | .400 | 2.57 | 31 | 84 | 0 | 0 | 136.1 | 113 | 56 | 104 | 49 | 39 | 0 | 7.46 | 3.70 | 6.87 |
| Lindy McDaniel | R | 5 | 6 | .455 | 2.59 | 2 | 71 | 0 | 0 | 128.2 | 115 | 47 | 92 | 45 | 37 | 0 | 8.04 | 3.29 | 6.44 |
| Bill Faul | R | 6 | 6 | .500 | 3.54 | 0 | 17 | 16 | 5 | 96.2 | 83 | 18 | 59 | 43 | 38 | 3 | 7.73 | 1.68 | 5.49 |
| Bob Humphreys | R | 2 | 0 | 1.000 | 3.15 | 0 | 41 | 0 | 0 | 65.2 | 59 | 27 | 38 | 25 | 23 | 0 | 8.09 | 3.70 | 5.21 |
| Bob Hendley | L | 4 | 4 | .500 | 4.35 | 0 | 18 | 10 | 2 | 62 | 59 | 25 | 38 | 39 | 30 | 0 | 8.56 | 3.63 | 5.52 |
| Billy Hoeft | L | 2 | 2 | .500 | 2.81 | 1 | 29 | 2 | 1 | 51.1 | 41 | 20 | 44 | 21 | 16 | 0 | 7.19 | 3.51 | 7.71 |
| Ernie Broglio | R | 1 | 6 | .143 | 6.93 | 0 | 26 | 6 | 0 | 50.2 | 63 | 46 | 22 | 44 | 39 | 0 | 11.19 | 8.17 | 3.91 |
| Lew Burdette | R | 0 | 2 | .000 | 5.31 | 0 | 7 | 3 | 0 | 20.1 | 26 | 4 | 5 | 17 | 12 | 0 | 11.51 | 1.77 | 2.21 |
| Jack Warner | R | 0 | 1 | .000 | 8.62 | 0 | 11 | 0 | 0 | 15.2 | 22 | 9 | 7 | 16 | 15 | 0 | 12.64 | 5.17 | 4.02 |
| Ken Holtzman | L | 0 | 0 | — | 2.25 | 0 | 3 | 0 | 0 | 4 | 2 | 3 | 3 | 4 | 1 | 0 | 4.50 | 6.75 | 6.75 |
| Frank Baumann | L | 0 | 1 | .000 | 7.36 | 0 | 4 | 0 | 0 | 3.2 | 4 | 3 | 2 | 3 | 3 | 0 | 9.82 | 7.36 | 4.91 |
| TEAM TOTAL |  | 72 | 90 | .444 | 3.78 | 35 | 456 | 164 | 33 | 1472 | 1470 | 481 | 855 | 723 | 618 | 8 | 8.99 | 2.94 | 5.23 |

| MANAGER | W | L | PCT |
|---|---|---|---|
| Leo Durocher | 59 | 103 | .364 |

| POS | Player | B | G | AB | H | 2B | 3B | HR | HR % | R | RBI | BB | SO | SB | Pinch Hit AB | Pinch Hit H | BA | SA |
|---|---|---|---|---|---|---|---|---|---|---|---|---|---|---|---|---|---|---|
| **REGULARS** | | | | | | | | | | | | | | | | | | |
| 1B | Ernie Banks | R | 141 | 511 | 139 | 23 | 7 | 15 | 2.9 | 52 | 75 | 29 | 59 | 0 | 8 | 1 | .272 | .432 |
| 2B | Glenn Beckert | R | 153 | 656 | 188 | 23 | 7 | 1 | 0.2 | 73 | 59 | 26 | 36 | 10 | 1 | 0 | .287 | .348 |
| SS | Don Kessinger | B | 150 | 533 | 146 | 8 | 2 | 1 | 0.2 | 50 | 43 | 26 | 46 | 13 | 0 | 0 | .274 | .302 |
| 3B | Ron Santo | R | 155 | 561 | 175 | 21 | 8 | 30 | 5.3 | 93 | 94 | 95 | 78 | 4 | 0 | 0 | .312 | .538 |
| RF | Billy Williams | L | 162 | 648 | 179 | 23 | 5 | 29 | 4.5 | 100 | 91 | 69 | 61 | 6 | 0 | 0 | .276 | .461 |
| CF | Adolfo Phillips | R | 116 | 416 | 109 | 29 | 1 | 16 | 3.8 | 68 | 36 | 43 | 135 | 32 | 4 | 1 | .262 | .452 |
| LF | Byron Browne | R | 120 | 419 | 102 | 15 | 7 | 16 | 3.8 | 46 | 51 | 40 | 143 | 3 | 5 | 0 | .243 | .427 |
| C | Randy Hundley | R | 149 | 526 | 124 | 22 | 3 | 19 | 3.6 | 50 | 63 | 35 | 113 | 1 | 0 | 0 | .236 | .397 |
| **SUBSTITUTES** | | | | | | | | | | | | | | | | | | |
| 1O | Lee Thomas | L | 75 | 149 | 36 | 4 | 0 | 1 | 0.7 | 15 | 9 | 14 | 15 | 0 | 31 | 8 | .242 | .289 |
| S3 | Ron Campbell | R | 24 | 60 | 13 | 1 | 0 | 0 | 0.0 | 4 | 4 | 6 | 5 | 1 | 5 | 1 | .217 | .233 |
| UT | Joey Amalfitano | R | 41 | 38 | 6 | 2 | 0 | 0 | 0.0 | 8 | 3 | 4 | 10 | 0 | 9 | 2 | .158 | .211 |
| 1B | John Herrnstein | L | 9 | 17 | 3 | 0 | 0 | 0 | 0.0 | 3 | 0 | 3 | 8 | 0 | 5 | 0 | .176 | .176 |
| SS | Roberto Pena | R | 6 | 17 | 3 | 2 | 0 | 0 | 0.0 | 0 | 1 | 0 | 4 | 0 | 2 | 0 | .176 | .294 |
| 2B | Paul Popovich | R | 2 | 6 | 0 | 0 | 0 | 0 | 0.0 | 0 | 0 | 0 | 2 | 0 | 0 | 0 | .000 | .000 |
| O1 | John Boccabella | R | 75 | 206 | 47 | 9 | 0 | 6 | 2.9 | 22 | 25 | 14 | 39 | 0 | 16 | 2 | .228 | .359 |
| OF | George Altman | L | 88 | 185 | 41 | 6 | 0 | 5 | 2.7 | 19 | 17 | 14 | 37 | 2 | 44 | 9 | .222 | .335 |
| UT | Jimmy Stewart | B | 57 | 90 | 16 | 4 | 1 | 0 | 0.0 | 4 | 4 | 7 | 12 | 1 | 31 | 6 | .178 | .244 |
| OF | Bob Raudman | L | 8 | 29 | 7 | 2 | 0 | 0 | 0.0 | 1 | 2 | 1 | 4 | 0 | 0 | 0 | .241 | .310 |
| OF | Marty Keough | L | 33 | 26 | 6 | 1 | 0 | 0 | 0.0 | 3 | 5 | 5 | 9 | 1 | 21 | 5 | .231 | .269 |
| OF | Carl Warwick | R | 16 | 22 | 5 | 0 | 0 | 0 | 0.0 | 3 | 0 | 5 | 6 | 0 | 7 | 2 | .227 | .227 |
| OF | Ty Cline | L | 7 | 17 | 6 | 0 | 0 | 0 | 0.0 | 3 | 2 | 0 | 2 | 1 | 4 | 0 | .353 | .353 |
| OF | Wes Covington | L | 9 | 11 | 1 | 0 | 0 | 0 | 0.0 | 0 | 0 | 1 | 2 | 0 | 7 | 0 | .091 | .091 |
| OF | Harvey Kuenn | R | 3 | 3 | 1 | 0 | 0 | 0 | 0.0 | 0 | 0 | 0 | 1 | 0 | 3 | 1 | .333 | .333 |
| C | Chris Krug | R | 11 | 28 | 6 | 1 | 0 | 0 | 0.0 | 1 | 1 | 1 | 8 | 0 | 1 | 0 | .214 | .250 |
| C | Don Bryant | R | 13 | 26 | 8 | 2 | 0 | 0 | 0.0 | 2 | 4 | 1 | 4 | 1 | 3 | 0 | .308 | .385 |
| PH | Frank Thomas | R | 5 | 5 | 0 | 0 | 0 | 0 | 0.0 | 0 | 0 | 0 | 1 | 0 | 5 | 0 | .000 | .000 |
| **PITCHERS** | | | | | | | | | | | | | | | | | | |
| P | Dick Ellsworth | L | 38 | 90 | 14 | 0 | 1 | 0 | 0.0 | 7 | 5 | 4 | 36 | 0 | 0 | 0 | .156 | .178 |
| P | Ken Holtzman | R | 34 | 73 | 9 | 1 | 0 | 0 | 0.0 | 2 | 2 | 1 | 25 | 0 | 0 | 0 | .123 | .137 |
| P | Ferguson Jenkins | R | 60 | 51 | 7 | 0 | 1 | 1 | 2.0 | 6 | 2 | 3 | 25 | 0 | 0 | 0 | .137 | .235 |
| P | Bill Hands | R | 41 | 49 | 2 | 1 | 0 | 0 | 0.0 | 2 | 1 | 3 | 23 | 0 | 0 | 0 | .041 | .061 |
| P | Cal Koonce | R | 45 | 23 | 3 | 1 | 0 | 0 | 0.0 | 2 | 1 | 3 | 9 | 0 | 0 | 0 | .130 | .174 |
| P | Ernie Broglio | R | 15 | 19 | 7 | 1 | 0 | 0 | 0.0 | 2 | 0 | 2 | 7 | 0 | 0 | 0 | .368 | .421 |
| P | Bob Hendley | R | 43 | 18 | 3 | 1 | 0 | 0 | 0.0 | 2 | 2 | 2 | 8 | 0 | 0 | 0 | .167 | .222 |
| P | Curt Simmons | L | 19 | 18 | 2 | 0 | 0 | 0 | 0.0 | 0 | 0 | 2 | 8 | 0 | 0 | 0 | .111 | .111 |
| P | Bill Faul | R | 17 | 13 | 0 | 0 | 0 | 0 | 0.0 | 0 | 1 | 0 | 5 | 0 | 0 | 0 | .000 | .000 |
| P | Robin Roberts | B | 11 | 10 | 2 | 0 | 0 | 0 | 0.0 | 1 | 0 | 2 | 4 | 0 | 0 | 0 | .200 | .200 |
| P | Ted Abernathy | R | 20 | 4 | 0 | 0 | 0 | 0 | 0.0 | 0 | 0 | 0 | 0 | 0 | 0 | 0 | .000 | .000 |
| P | Billy Hoeft | L | 36 | 4 | 1 | 0 | 0 | 0 | 0.0 | 0 | 0 | 0 | 1 | 0 | 0 | 0 | .250 | .250 |
| P | Rich Nye | L | 3 | 4 | 1 | 0 | 0 | 0 | 0.0 | 0 | 0 | 0 | 0 | 0 | 0 | 0 | .250 | .250 |
| P | Chuck Estrada | R | 9 | 3 | 0 | 0 | 0 | 0 | 0.0 | 0 | 0 | 0 | 0 | 0 | 0 | 0 | .000 | .000 |
| P | Larry Jackson | R | 3 | 3 | 0 | 0 | 0 | 0 | 0.0 | 0 | 0 | 0 | 2 | 0 | 0 | 0 | .000 | .000 |
| P | Dave Dowling | R | 1 | 2 | 0 | 0 | 0 | 0 | 0.0 | 0 | 0 | 0 | 2 | 0 | 0 | 0 | .000 | .000 |
| P | Bob Buhl | B | 1 | 1 | 0 | 0 | 0 | 0 | 0.0 | 0 | 0 | 0 | 0 | 0 | 0 | 0 | .000 | .000 |
| P | Len Church | B | 4 | 1 | 0 | 0 | 0 | 0 | 0.0 | 0 | 0 | 0 | 0 | 0 | 0 | 0 | .000 | .000 |
| P | Arnie Earley | L | 13 | 1 | 0 | 0 | 0 | 0 | 0.0 | 0 | 0 | 0 | 1 | 0 | 0 | 0 | .000 | .000 |
| P | Bill Connors | R | 11 | 0 | 0 | 0 | 0 | 0 | – | 0 | 0 | 1 | 0 | 0 | 0 | 0 | – | – |
| P | Chuck Hartenstein | R | 5 | 0 | 0 | 0 | 0 | 0 | – | 0 | 0 | 0 | 0 | 0 | 0 | 0 | – | – |
| P | Don Lee | R | 16 | 0 | 0 | 0 | 0 | 0 | – | 0 | 0 | 0 | 0 | 0 | 0 | 0 | – | – |
| P | Fred Norman | L | 2 | 0 | 0 | 0 | 0 | 0 | – | 0 | 0 | 0 | 0 | 0 | 0 | 0 | – | – |
| TEAM TOTAL | | | | 5592 | 1418 | 203 | 43 | 140 | 2.5 | 64 | 603 | 457 | 998 | 76 | 212 | 38 | .254 | .380 |

### INDIVIDUAL FIELDING

| POS | Player | T | G | PO | A | E | DP | TC/G | FA | | POS | Player | T | G | PO | A | E | DP | TC/G | FA |
|---|---|---|---|---|---|---|---|---|---|---|---|---|---|---|---|---|---|---|---|---|
| 1B | E. Banks | R | 130 | 1178 | 81 | 10 | 88 | 9.8 | .992 | | OF | B. Williams | R | 162 | 319 | 9 | 8 | 3 | 2.1 | .976 |
| | Boccabella | R | 30 | 182 | 15 | 0 | 12 | 6.6 | 1.000 | | | A. Phillips | R | 111 | 258 | 14 | 6 | 2 | 2.5 | .978 |
| | L. Thomas | L | 20 | 121 | 8 | 1 | 13 | 6.5 | .992 | | | B. Browne | R | 114 | 200 | 3 | 7 | 0 | 1.8 | .967 |
| | Herrnstein | L | 4 | 39 | 0 | 1 | 3 | 10.0 | .975 | | | Boccabella | R | 33 | 48 | 3 | 1 | 1 | 1.6 | .981 |
| | G. Altman | R | 4 | 27 | 2 | 0 | 1 | 7.3 | 1.000 | | | G. Altman | R | 42 | 42 | 4 | 2 | 0 | 1.1 | .958 |
| 2B | G. Beckert | R | 152 | 373 | 402 | 24 | 89 | 5.3 | .970 | | | J. Stewart | R | 15 | 31 | 1 | 0 | 0 | 2.1 | 1.000 |
| | Amalfitano | R | 12 | 23 | 19 | 1 | 5 | 3.6 | .977 | | | L. Thomas | L | 17 | 23 | 1 | 0 | 0 | 1.4 | 1.000 |
| | P. Popovich | R | 2 | 5 | 3 | 1 | 1 | 4.5 | .889 | | | Herrnstein | L | 1 | 0 | 0 | 0 | 0 | 0.0 | .000 |
| | J. Stewart | R | 4 | 5 | 2 | 0 | 0 | 1.8 | 1.000 | | | H. Kuenn | R | 1 | 0 | 0 | 0 | 0 | 0.0 | .000 |
| SS | D. Kessinger | R | 148 | 202 | 474 | 35 | 68 | 4.8 | .951 | | | B. Raudman | L | 8 | 8 | 2 | 1 | 0 | 1.4 | .909 |
| | Amalfitano | R | 2 | 0 | 0 | 0 | 0 | 0.0 | .000 | | | C. Warwick | L | 10 | 8 | 1 | 0 | 0 | 0.9 | 1.000 |
| | J. Stewart | R | 2 | 0 | 0 | 0 | 0 | 0.0 | .000 | | | T. Cline | L | 5 | 7 | 0 | 0 | 0 | 1.4 | 1.000 |
| | R. Campbell | R | 11 | 9 | 40 | 1 | 6 | 4.5 | .980 | | | W. Covington | R | 1 | 2 | 0 | 0 | 0 | 2.0 | 1.000 |
| | R. Santo | R | 8 | 7 | 17 | 1 | 5 | 3.1 | .960 | | | M. Keough | L | 5 | 2 | 0 | 0 | 0 | 0.4 | 1.000 |
| | R. Pena | R | 5 | 10 | 12 | 1 | 2 | 4.6 | .957 | | C | R. Hundley | R | 149 | 871 | 85 | 14 | 8 | 6.5 | .986 |
| | G. Beckert | R | 1 | 0 | 1 | 0 | 0 | 1.0 | 1.000 | | | C. Krug | R | 10 | 55 | 5 | 0 | 2 | 6.0 | 1.000 |
| 3B | R. Santo | R | 152 | 150 | 391 | 25 | 36 | 3.7 | .956 | | | D. Bryant | R | 10 | 42 | 3 | 1 | 2 | 4.6 | .978 |
| | J. Stewart | R | 2 | 0 | 0 | 0 | 0 | 0.0 | .000 | | | Boccabella | R | 5 | 25 | 2 | 0 | 0 | 5.4 | 1.000 |
| | Amalfitano | R | 3 | 0 | 0 | 0 | 0 | 0.0 | .000 | | | | | | | | | | | |
| | R. Campbell | R | 7 | 8 | 13 | 1 | 3 | 3.1 | .955 | | | | | | | | | | | |
| | E. Banks | R | 8 | 5 | 11 | 3 | 0 | 2.4 | .842 | | | | | | | | | | | |

"This ain't no eighth-place ballclub," bellowed manager Leo Durocher. He was right. The Cubs finished 10th. In the process they tied their all-time losing record of 59–103. At least they had a manager. The five semesters of the College of Coaches flunked out. Durocher returned to managing after a 10-year hiatus and engineered trades with the Giants and Phillies, bringing in, for fading veterans, such fresh faces at catcher Randy Hundley, centerfielder Adolfo Phillips, and pitchers Fergie Jenkins and Bill Hands. The Cubs lost eight of their first nine and plunged into the cellar, where they remained.

Actually, the team wasn't that bad, if one discounts pitching. The infield of Ernie Banks, Glenn Beckert, Don Kessinger, and Ron Santo was top grade. Santo had a 28-game hitting streak and led the team with 30 homers, 94 RBI, and a .312 average. Beckert had a 21-game hitting string and batted .287. Kessinger, normally a righty, turned switch-hitter and checked in at .274. Hundley proved the best Cub catcher since Gabby Hartnett. He had 19 homers and was an iron man behind the plate, playing in 149 games. But the hitters couldn't overcome a pitching staff with a fat 4.33 ERA. Dick Ellsworth continued to disappoint with his 22 defeats against 8 victories. The top winner was rookie Ken Holtzman with 11 wins, including a two-hit, 2–1 victory in a head-on duel with the Dodgers' Sandy Koufax. There was hope for the future. The Cubs played 27–30 ball in August and September, and they unloaded sore-armed Ernie Broglio, the last remnant of the ill-fated Lou Brock trade.

## TEAM STATISTICS

| | W | L | PCT | GB | R | OR | 2B | 3B | HR | BA | SA | SB | E | DP | FA | CG | B | SO | ShO | SV | ERA |
|---|---|---|---|---|---|---|---|---|---|---|---|---|---|---|---|---|---|---|---|---|---|
| | | | | | | | | | **Batting** | | | | | **Fielding** | | | | **Pitching** | | | |
| LA | 95 | 67 | .586 | | 606 | 490 | 201 | 27 | 108 | .256 | .362 | 94 | 133 | 128 | .979 | 52 | 356 | 1084 | 20 | 35 | **2.62** |
| SF | 93 | 68 | .578 | 1.5 | 675 | 626 | 195 | 31 | 181 | .248 | .392 | 29 | 168 | 131 | .974 | 52 | 359 | 973 | 14 | 27 | 3.24 |
| PIT | 92 | 70 | .568 | 3 | 759 | 641 | **238** | **66** | 158 | **.279** | **.428** | 64 | 141 | **215** | .978 | 35 | 463 | 898 | 12 | **43** | 3.52 |
| PHI | 87 | 75 | .537 | 8 | 696 | 640 | 224 | 49 | 117 | .258 | .378 | 56 | **113** | 147 | **.982** | 52 | 412 | 928 | 15 | 23 | 3.57 |
| ATL | 85 | 77 | .525 | 10 | **782** | 683 | 220 | 32 | **207** | .263 | .424 | 59 | 154 | 139 | .976 | 37 | 448 | 892 | 19 | 32 | 3.11 |
| STL | 83 | 79 | .512 | 12 | 571 | 577 | 196 | 61 | 108 | .251 | .368 | **144** | 145 | 166 | .977 | 47 | 490 | 1043 | 10 | 35 | 4.08 |
| CIN | 76 | 84 | .475 | 18 | 692 | 702 | 232 | 33 | 149 | .260 | .395 | 70 | 122 | 133 | .980 | 28 | 490 | 929 | 13 | 26 | 3.76 |
| HOU | 72 | 90 | .444 | 23 | 612 | 695 | 203 | 35 | 112 | .255 | .365 | 90 | 174 | 126 | .972 | 34 | 391 | 929 | 13 | 26 | 4.17 |
| NY | 66 | 95 | .410 | 28.5 | 587 | 761 | 187 | 35 | 98 | .239 | .342 | 55 | 159 | 171 | .975 | 37 | 521 | 773 | 9 | 22 | 4.17 |
| CHI | 59 | 103 | .364 | 36 | 644 | 809 | 203 | 43 | 140 | .254 | .384 | 76 | 166 | 132 | .974 | 28 | 479 | 908 | 6 | 24 | **4.33** |
| LEAGUE TOTAL | | | | | 6624 | 6624 | 2099 | 412 | 1378 | .256 | .384 | 737 | 1475 | 1488 | .977 | 402 | 4404 | 9312 | 128 | 303 | 3.61 |

## INDIVIDUAL PITCHING

| PITCHER | T | W | L | PCT | ERA | SV | G | GS | CG | IP | H | BB | SO | R | ER | ShO | H/9 | BB/9 | SO/9 |
|---|---|---|---|---|---|---|---|---|---|---|---|---|---|---|---|---|---|---|---|
| Dick Ellsworth | L | 8 | 22 | .267 | 3.98 | 0 | 38 | 37 | 9 | 269.1 | 321 | 51 | 144 | **150** | 119 | 0 | 10.73 | 1.70 | 4.81 |
| Ken Holtzman | L | 11 | 16 | .407 | 3.79 | 0 | 34 | 33 | 9 | 220.2 | 194 | 68 | 171 | 104 | 93 | 0 | 7.91 | 2.77 | 6.97 |
| Ferguson Jenkins | R | 6 | 8 | .429 | 3.31 | 5 | 60 | 12 | 2 | 182 | 147 | 51 | 148 | 75 | 67 | 1 | 7.27 | 2.52 | 7.32 |
| Bill Hands | R | 8 | 13 | .381 | 4.58 | 2 | 41 | 26 | 0 | 159 | 168 | 59 | 93 | 91 | 81 | 0 | 9.51 | 3.34 | 5.26 |
| Cal Koonce | R | 5 | 5 | .500 | 3.81 | 2 | 45 | 5 | 0 | 108.2 | 113 | 35 | 65 | 57 | 46 | 0 | 9.36 | 2.90 | 5.38 |
| Bob Hendley | L | 4 | 5 | .444 | 3.91 | 7 | 43 | 6 | 0 | 89.2 | 98 | 39 | 65 | 46 | 39 | 0 | 9.84 | 3.91 | 6.52 |
| Curt Simmons | L | 4 | 7 | .364 | 4.07 | 0 | 19 | 10 | 3 | 77.1 | 79 | 21 | 24 | 39 | 35 | 1 | 9.19 | 2.44 | 2.79 |
| Ernie Broglio | R | 2 | 6 | .250 | 6.35 | 1 | 15 | 11 | 2 | 62.1 | 70 | 38 | 34 | 46 | 44 | 0 | 10.11 | 5.49 | 4.91 |
| Bill Faul | R | 1 | 4 | .200 | 5.08 | 0 | 17 | 6 | 1 | 51.1 | 47 | 18 | 32 | 31 | 29 | 0 | 8.24 | 3.16 | 5.61 |
| Robin Roberts | R | 2 | 3 | .400 | 6.14 | 0 | 11 | 9 | 1 | 48.1 | 62 | 11 | 28 | 35 | 33 | 0 | 11.54 | 2.05 | 5.21 |
| Billy Hoeft | L | 1 | 2 | .333 | 4.61 | 3 | 36 | 0 | 0 | 41 | 43 | 14 | 30 | 28 | 21 | 0 | 9.44 | 3.07 | 6.59 |
| Ted Abernathy | R | 1 | 3 | .250 | 6.18 | 4 | 20 | 0 | 0 | 27.2 | 26 | 17 | 18 | 19 | 19 | 0 | 8.46 | 5.53 | 5.86 |
| Don Lee | R | 2 | 1 | .667 | 7.11 | 0 | 16 | 0 | 0 | 19 | 28 | 12 | 7 | 19 | 15 | 0 | 13.26 | 5.68 | 3.32 |
| Arnie Earley | L | 2 | 1 | .667 | 3.57 | 0 | 13 | 0 | 0 | 17.2 | 14 | 9 | 12 | 11 | 7 | 0 | 7.13 | 4.58 | 6.11 |
| Rich Nye | L | 0 | 2 | .000 | 2.12 | 0 | 3 | 2 | 0 | 17 | 16 | 7 | 9 | 4 | 4 | 0 | 8.47 | 3.71 | 4.76 |
| Bill Connors | R | 0 | 1 | .000 | 7.31 | 0 | 11 | 0 | 0 | 16 | 20 | 7 | 3 | 13 | 13 | 0 | 11.25 | 3.94 | 1.69 |
| Chuck Estrada | R | 1 | 1 | .500 | 7.30 | 0 | 9 | 1 | 0 | 12.1 | 16 | 5 | 3 | 12 | 10 | 0 | 11.68 | 3.65 | 2.19 |
| Chuck Hartenstein | R | 0 | 0 | – | 1.93 | 0 | 5 | 0 | 0 | 9.1 | 8 | 3 | 4 | 2 | 2 | 0 | 7.71 | 2.89 | 3.86 |
| Dave Dowling | L | 1 | 0 | 1.000 | 2.00 | 0 | 1 | 1 | 1 | 9 | 10 | 0 | 3 | 2 | 2 | 0 | 10.00 | 0.00 | 3.00 |
| Larry Jackson | R | 0 | 2 | .000 | 13.50 | 0 | 3 | 2 | 0 | 8 | 14 | 4 | 5 | 13 | 12 | 0* | 15.75 | 4.50 | 5.63 |
| Len Church | R | 0 | 1 | .000 | 7.50 | 0 | 4 | 0 | 0 | 6 | 10 | 7 | 3 | 6 | 5 | 0 | 11.25 | 10.50 | 4.50 |
| Fred Norman | L | 0 | 0 | – | 4.50 | 0 | 2 | 0 | 0 | 4 | 5 | 2 | 6 | 2 | 2 | 0 | 11.25 | 4.50 | 13.50 |
| Bob Buhl | R | 0 | 0 | – | 15.43 | 0 | 1 | 1 | 0 | 2.1 | 4 | 1 | 1 | 4 | 4 | 0 | 15.43 | 3.86 | 3.86 |
| TEAM TOTAL | | 59 | 103 | .364 | 4.33 | 24 | 447 | 162 | 28 | 1458 | 1513 | 479 | 908 | 809 | 702 | 2 | 9.34 | 2.96 | 5.60 |

| MANAGER | W | L | PCT |
|---|---|---|---|
| Leo Durocher | 87 | 74 | .540 |

| POS | Player | B | G | AB | H | 2B | 3B | HR | HR % | R | RBI | BB | SO | SB | Pinch Hit AB | Pinch Hit H | BA | SA |
|---|---|---|---|---|---|---|---|---|---|---|---|---|---|---|---|---|---|---|
| **REGULARS** | | | | | | | | | | | | | | | | | | |
| 1B | Ernie Banks | R | 151 | 573 | 158 | 26 | 4 | 23 | 4.0 | 68 | 95 | 27 | 93 | 2 | 5 | 1 | .276 | .455 |
| 2B | Glenn Beckert | R | 146 | 597 | 167 | 32 | 3 | 5 | 0.8 | 91 | 40 | 30 | 25 | 10 | 1 | 0 | .280 | .369 |
| SS | Don Kessinger | B | 145 | 580 | 134 | 10 | 7 | 0 | 0.0 | 61 | 42 | 33 | 80 | 6 | 0 | 0 | .231 | .272 |
| 3B | Ron Santo | R | 161 | 586 | 176 | 23 | 4 | 31 | 5.3 | 107 | 98 | 96 | 103 | 1 | 0 | 0 | .300 | .512 |
| RF | Ted Savage | R | 96 | 225 | 49 | 10 | 1 | 5 | 2.2 | 40 | 33 | 40 | 54 | 7 | 9 | 3 | .218 | .338 |
| CF | Adolfo Phillips | R | 144 | 448 | 120 | 20 | 7 | 17 | 3.8 | 66 | 70 | 80 | 93 | 24 | 2 | 0 | .268 | .458 |
| LF | Billy Williams | L | 162 | 634 | 176 | 21 | 12 | 28 | 4.4 | 92 | 84 | 68 | 67 | 6 | 0 | 0 | .278 | .481 |
| C | Randy Hundley | R | 152 | 539 | 144 | 25 | 3 | 14 | 2.6 | 68 | 60 | 44 | 75 | 2 | 2 | 0 | .267 | .403 |
| **SUBSTITUTES** | | | | | | | | | | | | | | | | | | |
| S2 | Paul Popovich | R | 49 | 159 | 34 | 4 | 0 | 0 | 0.0 | 18 | 2 | 9 | 12 | 0 | 5 | 0 | .214 | .239 |
| 2O | Norm Gigon | R | 34 | 70 | 12 | 3 | 1 | 1 | 1.4 | 8 | 6 | 4 | 14 | 0 | 15 | 2 | .171 | .286 |
| OF | Lee Thomas | L | 77 | 191 | 42 | 4 | 1 | 2 | 1.0 | 16 | 23 | 15 | 22 | 1 | 22 | 4 | .220 | .283 |
| O1 | Clarence Jones | L | 53 | 135 | 34 | 7 | 0 | 2 | 1.5 | 13 | 16 | 14 | 33 | 0 | 9 | 3 | .252 | .348 |
| OF | Al Spangler | L | 62 | 130 | 33 | 7 | 0 | 0 | 0.0 | 18 | 13 | 23 | 17 | 2 | 23 | 4 | .254 | .308 |
| O1 | John Boccabella | R | 25 | 35 | 6 | 1 | 1 | 0 | 0.0 | 0 | 8 | 3 | 7 | 0 | 11 | 2 | .171 | .257 |
| OF | Bob Raudman | L | 8 | 26 | 4 | 0 | 0 | 0 | 0.0 | 0 | 1 | 1 | 4 | 0 | 0 | 0 | .154 | .154 |
| OF | Byron Browne | R | 10 | 19 | 3 | 2 | 0 | 0 | 0.0 | 3 | 2 | 4 | 5 | 1 | 2 | 0 | .158 | .263 |
| OF | George Altman | L | 15 | 18 | 2 | 2 | 0 | 0 | 0.0 | 1 | 1 | 2 | 8 | 0 | 9 | 2 | .111 | .222 |
| OF | Joe Campbell | R | 1 | 3 | 0 | 0 | 0 | 0 | 0.0 | 0 | 0 | 0 | 3 | 0 | 0 | 0 | .000 | .000 |
| C | Johnny Stephenson | L | 18 | 49 | 11 | 3 | 1 | 0 | 0.0 | 3 | 5 | 1 | 6 | 0 | 3 | 1 | .224 | .327 |
| C | Dick Bertell | R | 2 | 6 | 1 | 0 | 1 | 0 | 0.0 | 1 | 0 | 0 | 1 | 0 | 0 | 0 | .167 | .500 |
| PH | Jimmy Stewart | B | 6 | 6 | 1 | 0 | 0 | 0 | 0.0 | 1 | 1 | 0 | 0 | 0 | 6 | 1 | .167 | .167 |
| PH | Joey Amalfitano | R | 4 | 1 | 0 | 0 | 0 | 0 | 0.0 | 0 | 0 | 0 | 1 | 0 | 1 | 0 | .000 | .000 |
| **PITCHERS** | | | | | | | | | | | | | | | | | | |
| P | Ferguson Jenkins | R | 39 | 93 | 14 | 3 | 1 | 0 | 0.0 | 5 | 10 | 6 | 35 | 0 | 0 | 0 | .151 | .204 |
| P | Rich Nye | L | 35 | 75 | 16 | 4 | 0 | 0 | 0.0 | 5 | 4 | 2 | 29 | 0 | 0 | 0 | .213 | .267 |
| P | Ray Culp | R | 30 | 51 | 5 | 0 | 2 | 0 | 0.0 | 4 | 5 | 0 | 29 | 0 | 0 | 0 | .098 | .176 |
| P | Joe Niekro | R | 36 | 46 | 9 | 2 | 0 | 0 | 0.0 | 5 | 11 | 1 | 13 | 1 | 0 | 0 | .196 | .239 |
| P | Bill Hands | R | 49 | 38 | 4 | 0 | 0 | 0 | 0.0 | 0 | 3 | 3 | 26 | 0 | 0 | 0 | .105 | .105 |
| P | Ken Holtzman | R | 12 | 35 | 7 | 1 | 0 | 0 | 0.0 | 4 | 2 | 0 | 11 | 0 | 0 | 0 | .200 | .229 |
| P | Curt Simmons | L | 17 | 28 | 4 | 0 | 0 | 0 | 0.0 | 1 | 3 | 0 | 7 | 0 | 0 | 0 | .143 | .143 |
| P | Chuck Hartenstein | R | 45 | 16 | 1 | 0 | 0 | 0 | 0.0 | 0 | 1 | 0 | 9 | 0 | 0 | 0 | .063 | .063 |
| P | Bill Stoneman | R | 28 | 13 | 0 | 0 | 0 | 0 | 0.0 | 0 | 0 | 1 | 11 | 0 | 0 | 0 | .000 | .000 |
| P | Cal Koonce | R | 34 | 7 | 0 | 0 | 0 | 0 | 0.0 | 0 | 0 | 0 | 3 | 0 | 0 | 0 | .000 | .000 |
| P | Rob Gardner | R | 18 | 6 | 0 | 0 | 0 | 0 | 0.0 | 1 | 0 | 1 | 4 | 0 | 0 | 0 | .000 | .000 |
| P | Bob Hendley | R | 7 | 6 | 0 | 0 | 0 | 0 | 0.0 | 0 | 0 | 1 | 4 | 0 | 0 | 0 | .000 | .000 |
| P | Jim Ellis | R | 8 | 5 | 1 | 0 | 0 | 0 | 0.0 | 0 | 0 | 0 | 5 | 0 | 0 | 0 | .200 | .400 |
| P | Dick Radatz | R | 20 | 4 | 1 | 1 | 0 | 0 | 0.0 | 0 | 1 | 0 | 3 | 0 | 0 | 0 | .250 | .250 |
| P | Bob Shaw | R | 9 | 4 | 1 | 0 | 0 | 0 | 0.0 | 0 | 0 | 1 | 2 | 0 | 0 | 0 | .250 | .250 |
| P | John Upham | L | 8 | 3 | 2 | 0 | 0 | 0 | 0.0 | 1 | 0 | 0 | 0 | 0 | 3 | 2 | .667 | .667 |
| P | Dick Calmus | R | 1 | 2 | 1 | 0 | 0 | 0 | 0.0 | 1 | 2 | 0 | 1 | 0 | 0 | 0 | .500 | .500 |
| P | Rick James | R | 3 | 1 | 0 | 0 | 0 | 0 | 0.0 | 0 | 0 | 0 | 1 | 0 | 0 | 0 | .000 | .000 |
| P | Don Larsen | R | 3 | 0 | 0 | 0 | 0 | 0 | – | 0 | 0 | 0 | 0 | 0 | 0 | 0 | – | – |
| P | Pete Mikkelsen | R | 7 | 0 | 0 | 0 | 0 | 0 | – | 0 | 0 | 0 | 0 | 0 | 0 | 0 | – | – |
| P | Fred Norman | L | 1 | 0 | 0 | 0 | 0 | 0 | – | 0 | 0 | 0 | 0 | 0 | 0 | 0 | – | – |
| | TEAM TOTAL | | | 5463 | 1373 | 211 | 49 | 128 | 2.3 | 70 | 642 | 509 | 912 | 63 | 128 | 25 | .251 | .378 |

## INDIVIDUAL FIELDING

| POS | Player | T | G | PO | A | E | DP | TC/G | FA | POS | Player | T | G | PO | A | E | DP | TC/G | FA |
|---|---|---|---|---|---|---|---|---|---|---|---|---|---|---|---|---|---|---|---|
| 1B | E. Banks | R | 147 | 1383 | 91 | 10 | 111 | 10.1 | .993 | OF | A. Phillips | R | 141 | 340 | 13 | 7 | 0 | 2.6 | .981 |
| | C. Jones | L | 13 | 88 | 5 | 2 | 7 | 7.3 | .979 | | B. Williams | R | 162 | 271 | 3 | 3 | 1 | 1.7 | .989 |
| | L. Thomas | L | 10 | 71 | 5 | 0 | 9 | 7.6 | 1.000 | | T. Savage | R | 86 | 133 | 5 | 3 | 1 | 1.6 | .979 |
| | Boccabella | R | 3 | 22 | 1 | 0 | 3 | 7.7 | 1.000 | | A. Spangler | L | 41 | 71 | 0 | 1 | 0 | 1.8 | .986 |
| | G. Altman | R | 1 | 2 | 0 | 0 | 1 | 2.0 | 1.000 | | L. Thomas | L | 43 | 60 | 2 | 2 | 0 | 1.5 | .969 |
| 2B | G. Beckert | R | 144 | 327 | 422 | 25 | 89 | 5.4 | .968 | | C. Jones | L | 31 | 45 | 0 | 1 | 0 | 1.5 | .978 |
| | P. Popovich | R | 17 | 26 | 39 | 1 | 11 | 3.9 | .985 | | J. Campbell | R | 1 | 0 | 0 | 0 | 0 | 0.0 | .000 |
| | N. Gigon | R | 12 | 20 | 34 | 1 | 6 | 4.6 | .982 | | B. Raudman | L | 8 | 13 | 1 | 2 | 1 | 2.0 | .875 |
| SS | D. Kessinger | R | 143 | 215 | 457 | 19 | 77 | 4.8 | .973 | | B. Browne | R | 8 | 12 | 0 | 0 | 0 | 1.5 | 1.000 |
| | P. Popovich | R | 31 | 40 | 77 | 4 | 12 | 3.9 | .967 | | Boccabella | R | 9 | 11 | 0 | 0 | 0 | 1.2 | 1.000 |
| 3B | R. Santo | R | 161 | 187 | 393 | 26 | 33 | 3.8 | .957 | | G. Altman | R | 4 | 2 | 0 | 0 | 0 | 0.5 | 1.000 |
| | P. Popovich | R | 2 | 0 | 0 | 0 | 0 | 0.0 | .000 | | N. Gigon | R | 4 | 1 | 0 | 0 | 0 | 0.3 | 1.000 |
| | T. Savage | R | 1 | 0 | 2 | 0 | 1 | 2.0 | 1.000 | C | R. Hundley | R | 152 | 865 | 59 | 4 | 7 | 6.1 | .996 |
| | N. Gigon | R | 1 | 0 | 2 | 0 | 0 | 2.0 | 1.000 | | Stephenson | R | 13 | 67 | 8 | 0 | 0 | 5.8 | 1.000 |
| | | | | | | | | | | | D. Bertell | R | 2 | 12 | 1 | 0 | 0 | 6.5 | 1.000 |
| | | | | | | | | | | | Boccabella | R | 1 | 2 | 0 | 0 | 0 | 2.0 | 1.000 |

There was no June swoon for Leo Durocher's Cubs. The team was 20–10 for the merry month that included almost back-to-back seven-game winning streaks and 14 of 15 victories. As a result, the Cubs were the surprise team of baseball, jumping from 10th to third in a single season. With virtually the same personnel, the Cubs cut their errors from 166 to 121, going from eighth to first in fielding. The pitching staff earned run average improved from 4.33 to 3.48. The end result was 28 more victories for an 87–74 record.

It was apparent that Durocher was putting the puzzle together. Fergie Jenkins emerged as the ace of the staff with a 20–13 record, setting the new all-time Cub strikeout record with 236. Lefty Ken Holtzman, who spent most of the season in the army, had enough weekend passes to muster a 9–0 mark. The Banks-Santo-Williams slugging trio continued to be the punch producers, helping the Cubs lead the league in runs scored with 702. Santo led the Cubs with 31 homers, 98 RBI, and .300 average. Banks had 23 homers and 95 RBI, while Williams had 28 homers and 84 RBI. Don Kessinger and Glenn Beckert developed into the Cubs' best double-play combo since the heyday of Jurges and Herman. And Randy Hundley was easily the club's best catcher since Gabby Hartnett. He set a major league record by making just four errors while catching more than 150 games.

## TEAM  STATISTICS

| | W | L | PCT | GB | R | OR | 2B | 3B | HR | BA | SA | SB | E | DP | FA | CG | B | SO | ShO | SV | ERA |
|---|---|---|---|---|---|---|---|---|---|---|---|---|---|---|---|---|---|---|---|---|---|
| | | | | | | | **Batting** | | | | | | **Fielding** | | | | | **Pitching** | | | |
| STL | 101 | 60 | .627 | | 695 | 557 | 225 | 40 | 115 | .263 | .379 | **102** | 140 | 127 | .978 | 44 | 431 | 956 | 17 | **45** | 3.05 |
| SF | 91 | 71 | .562 | 10.5 | 652 | **551** | 201 | 39 | 140 | .245 | .372 | 22 | 134 | 149 | .979 | **64** | 453 | 990 | 17 | 25 | **2.92** |
| CHI | 87 | 74 | .540 | 14 | **702** | 624 | 211 | 49 | 128 | .251 | .378 | 63 | **121** | 143 | **.981** | 47 | 463 | 888 | 7 | 28 | 3.48 |
| CIN | 87 | 75 | .537 | 14.5 | 604 | 563 | 251 | 54 | 109 | .248 | .372 | 92 | **121** | 124 | .980 | 34 | 498 | **1065** | **18** | 39 | 3.05 |
| PHI | 82 | 80 | .506 | 19.5 | 612 | 581 | 221 | 47 | 103 | .242 | .357 | 79 | 137 | 174 | .978 | 46 | 403 | 967 | 17 | 23 | 3.10 |
| PIT | 81 | 81 | .500 | 20.5 | 679 | 693 | 193 | **62** | 91 | **.277** | **.380** | 79 | 141 | **186** | .978 | 35 | 561 | 820 | 5 | 35 | 3.74 |
| ATL | 77 | 85 | .475 | 24.5 | 631 | 640 | 191 | 29 | **158** | .240 | .372 | 55 | 138 | 148 | .978 | 35 | 449 | 862 | 5 | 32 | 3.47 |
| LA | 73 | 89 | .451 | 28.5 | 519 | 595 | 203 | 38 | 82 | .236 | .332 | 56 | 160 | 144 | .975 | 41 | **393** | 967 | 17 | 24 | 3.21 |
| HOU | 69 | 93 | .426 | 32.5 | 626 | 742 | **259** | 46 | 93 | .249 | .364 | 88 | 159 | 120 | .974 | 35 | 485 | 1060 | 8 | 21 | 4.03 |
| NY | 61 | 101 | .377 | 40.5 | 498 | 672 | 178 | 23 | 83 | .238 | .325 | 58 | 157 | 147 | .975 | 36 | 536 | 893 | 10 | 19 | 3.73 |
| LEAGUE TOTAL | | | | | 6218 | 6218 | 2133 | 427 | 1102 | .249 | .363 | 694 | 1408 | 1462 | .978 | 417 | 4672 | 9468 | 121 | 291 | 3.38 |

## INDIVIDUAL  PITCHING

| PITCHER | T | W | L | PCT | ERA | SV | G | GS | CG | IP | H | BB | SO | R | ER | ShO | H/9 | BB/9 | SO/9 |
|---|---|---|---|---|---|---|---|---|---|---|---|---|---|---|---|---|---|---|---|
| Ferguson Jenkins | R | 20 | 13 | .606 | 2.80 | 0 | 38 | 38 | 20 | 289.1 | 230 | 83 | 236 | 101 | 90 | 3 | 7.15 | 2.58 | 7.34 |
| Rich Nye | L | 13 | 10 | .565 | 3.20 | 0 | 35 | 30 | 7 | 205 | 179 | 52 | 119 | 82 | 73 | 0 | 7.86 | 2.28 | 5.22 |
| Joe Niekro | R | 10 | 7 | .588 | 3.34 | 0 | 36 | 22 | 7 | 169.2 | 171 | 32 | 77 | 68 | 63 | 2 | 9.07 | 1.70 | 4.08 |
| Ray Culp | R | 8 | 11 | .421 | 3.89 | 0 | 30 | 22 | 4 | 152.2 | 138 | 59 | 111 | 69 | 66 | 1 | 8.14 | 3.48 | 6.54 |
| Bill Hands | R | 7 | 8 | .467 | 2.46 | 6 | 49 | 11 | 3 | 150 | 134 | 48 | 84 | 46 | 41 | 1 | 8.04 | 2.88 | 5.04 |
| Ken Holtzman | L | 9 | 0 | 1.000 | 2.53 | 0 | 12 | 12 | 3 | 92.2 | 76 | 44 | 62 | 31 | 26 | 0 | 7.38 | 4.27 | 6.02 |
| Curt Simmons | L | 3 | 7 | .300 | 4.94 | 0 | 17 | 14 | 3 | 82 | 100 | 23 | 31 | 54 | 45 | 0 | 10.98 | 2.52 | 3.40 |
| Chuck Hartenstein | R | 9 | 5 | .643 | 3.08 | 10 | 45 | 0 | 0 | 73 | 74 | 17 | 20 | 27 | 25 | 0 | 9.12 | 2.10 | 2.47 |
| Bill Stoneman | R | 2 | 4 | .333 | 3.29 | 2 | 28 | 2 | 0 | 63 | 51 | 22 | 52 | 24 | 23 | 0 | 7.29 | 3.14 | 7.43 |
| Cal Koonce | R | 2 | 2 | .500 | 4.59 | 2 | 34 | 0 | 0 | 51 | 52 | 21 | 28 | 27 | 26 | 0 | 9.18 | 3.71 | 4.94 |
| Rob Gardner | L | 0 | 2 | .000 | 3.98 | 0 | 18 | 5 | 0 | 31.2 | 33 | 6 | 16 | 14 | 14 | 0 | 9.38 | 1.71 | 4.55 |
| Dick Radatz | R | 1 | 0 | 1.000 | 6.56 | 5 | 20 | 0 | 0 | 23.1 | 12 | 24 | 18 | 21 | 17 | 0 | 4.63 | 9.26 | 6.94 |
| Bob Shaw | R | 0 | 2 | .000 | 6.04 | 0 | 9 | 3 | 0 | 22.1 | 33 | 9 | 7 | 16 | 15 | 0 | 13.30 | 3.63 | 2.82 |
| Jim Ellis | L | 1 | 1 | .500 | 3.24 | 0 | 8 | 1 | 0 | 16.2 | 20 | 9 | 8 | 7 | 6 | 0 | 10.80 | 4.86 | 4.32 |
| Bob Hendley | L | 2 | 0 | 1.000 | 6.57 | 1 | 7 | 0 | 0 | 12.1 | 17 | 3 | 10 | 10 | 9 | 0 | 12.41 | 2.19 | 7.30 |
| Pete Mikkelsen | R | 0 | 0 | — | 6.43 | 0 | 7 | 0 | 0 | 7 | 9 | 5 | 0 | 6 | 5 | 0 | 11.57 | 6.43 | 0.00 |
| Rick James | R | 0 | 1 | .000 | 13.50 | 0 | 3 | 1 | 0 | 4.2 | 9 | 2 | 2 | 8 | 7 | 0 | 17.36 | 3.86 | 3.86 |
| Dick Calmus | R | 0 | 0 | — | 8.31 | 0 | 1 | 1 | 0 | 4.1 | 5 | 0 | 1 | 4 | 4 | 0 | 10.38 | 0.00 | 2.08 |
| Don Larsen | R | 0 | 0 | — | 9.00 | 0 | 3 | 0 | 0 | 4 | 5 | 2 | 1 | 4 | 4 | 0 | 11.25 | 4.50 | 2.25 |
| John Upham | L | 0 | 1 | .000 | 33.75 | 0 | 5 | 0 | 0 | 1.1 | 4 | 2 | 2 | 5 | 5 | 0 | 27.00 | 13.50 | 13.50 |
| Fred Norman | L | 0 | 0 | — | 0.00 | 0 | 1 | 0 | 0 | 1 | 0 | 0 | 3 | 0 | 0 | 0 | 0.00 | 0.00 | 27.00 |
| TEAM TOTAL | | 87 | 74 | .540 | 3.48 | 28 | 406 | 162 | 47 | 1457 | 1352 | 463 | 888 | 624 | 564 | 7 | 8.35 | 2.86 | 5.49 |

| MANAGER | W | L | PCT |
|---|---|---|---|
| Leo Durocher | 84 | 78 | .519 |

| POS | Player | B | G | AB | H | 2B | 3B | HR | HR % | R | RBI. | BB | SO | SB | Pinch Hit AB | Pinch Hit H | BA | SA |
|---|---|---|---|---|---|---|---|---|---|---|---|---|---|---|---|---|---|---|
| **REGULARS** | | | | | | | | | | | | | | | | | | |
| 1B | Ernie Banks | R | 150 | 552 | 136 | 27 | 0 | 32 | 5.8 | 71 | 83 | 27 | 67 | 2 | 4 | 1 | .246 | .469 |
| 2B | Glenn Beckert | R | 155 | 643 | 189 | 28 | 4 | 4 | 0.6 | 98 | 37 | 31 | 20 | 8 | 0 | 0 | .294 | .369 |
| SS | Don Kessinger | B | 160 | 655 | 157 | 14 | 7 | 1 | 0.2 | 63 | 32 | 38 | 86 | 9 | 1 | 0 | .240 | .287 |
| 3B | Ron Santo | R | 162 | 577 | 142 | 17 | 3 | 26 | 4.5 | 86 | 98 | 96 | 106 | 3 | 0 | 0 | .246 | .421 |
| RF | Jim Hickman | R | 75 | 188 | 42 | 6 | 3 | 5 | 2.7 | 22 | 23 | 18 | 38 | 1 | 12 | 2 | .223 | .367 |
| CF | Adolfo Phillips | R | 143 | 439 | 106 | 20 | 5 | 13 | 3.0 | 49 | 33 | 47 | 90 | 9 | 2 | 0 | .241 | .399 |
| LF | Billy Williams | L | 163 | 642 | 185 | 30 | 8 | 30 | 4.7 | 91 | 98 | 48 | 53 | 4 | 0 | 0 | .288 | .500 |
| C | Randy Hundley | R | 160 | 553 | 125 | 18 | 4 | 7 | 1.3 | 41 | 65 | 39 | 69 | 1 | 0 | 0 | .226 | .311 |
| **SUBSTITUTES** | | | | | | | | | | | | | | | | | | |
| 1B | Dick Nen | L | 81 | 94 | 17 | 1 | 1 | 2 | 2.1 | 8 | 16 | 6 | 17 | 0 | 28 | 4 | .181 | .277 |
| UT | Lee Elia | R | 15 | 17 | 3 | 0 | 0 | 0 | 0.0 | 1 | 3 | 0 | 6 | 0 | 10 | 2 | .176 | .176 |
| UT | Gene Oliver | R | 8 | 11 | 4 | 0 | 0 | 0 | 0.0 | 1 | 1 | 3 | 2 | 0 | 2 | 1 | .364 | .364 |
| 1B | Clarence Jones | L | 5 | 2 | 0 | 0 | 0 | 0 | 0.0 | 0 | 0 | 2 | 1 | 0 | 2 | 0 | .000 | .000 |
| S2 | Vic LaRose | R | 4 | 2 | 0 | 0 | 0 | 0 | 0.0 | 0 | 0 | 0 | 1 | 0 | 0 | 0 | .000 | .000 |
| OF | Lou Johnson | R | 62 | 205 | 50 | 14 | 3 | 1 | 0.5 | 14 | 14 | 6 | 23 | 3 | 4 | 1 | .244 | .356 |
| OF | Al Spangler | L | 88 | 177 | 48 | 9 | 3 | 2 | 1.1 | 21 | 18 | 20 | 24 | 0 | 41 | 10 | .271 | .390 |
| OF | Willie Smith | L | 55 | 142 | 39 | 8 | 2 | 5 | 3.5 | 13 | 25 | 12 | 33 | 0 | 15 | 5 | .275 | .465 |
| UT | Jose Arcia | R | 59 | 84 | 16 | 4 | 0 | 1 | 1.2 | 15 | 8 | 3 | 24 | 1 | 5 | 1 | .190 | .274 |
| OF | Jimmy McMath | L | 6 | 14 | 2 | 0 | 0 | 0 | 0.0 | 0 | 2 | 0 | 6 | 0 | 3 | 0 | .143 | .143 |
| PO | John Upham | L | 13 | 10 | 2 | 0 | 0 | 0 | 0.0 | 0 | 0 | 0 | 3 | 0 | 6 | 1 | .200 | .200 |
| OF | Ted Savage | R | 3 | 8 | 2 | 0 | 0 | 0 | 0.0 | 0 | 0 | 0 | 1 | 0 | 3 | 1 | .250 | .250 |
| C | John Boccabella | R | 7 | 14 | 1 | 0 | 0 | 0 | 0.0 | 0 | 1 | 2 | 2 | 0 | 2 | 0 | .071 | .071 |
| C | Randy Bobb | R | 7 | 8 | 1 | 0 | 0 | 0 | 0.0 | 0 | 0 | 1 | 2 | 0 | 1 | 0 | .125 | .125 |
| C | Bill Plummer | R | 2 | 2 | 0 | 0 | 0 | 0 | 0.0 | 0 | 0 | 0 | 1 | 0 | 1 | 0 | .000 | .000 |
| C | John Felske | R | 4 | 2 | 0 | 0 | 0 | 0 | 0.0 | 0 | 0 | 0 | 1 | 0 | 1 | 0 | .000 | .000 |
| PH | Johnny Stephenson | L | 2 | 2 | 0 | 0 | 0 | 0 | 0.0 | 0 | 0 | 0 | 0 | 0 | 2 | 0 | .000 | .000 |
| **PITCHERS** | | | | | | | | | | | | | | | | | | |
| P | Ferguson Jenkins | R | 40 | 100 | 16 | 4 | 0 | 1 | 1.0 | 4 | 10 | 6 | 41 | 0 | 0 | 0 | .160 | .230 |
| P | Bill Hands | R | 38 | 82 | 5 | 0 | 0 | 0 | 0.0 | 2 | 0 | 3 | 50 | 0 | 0 | 0 | .061 | .061 |
| P | Ken Holtzman | R | 35 | 80 | 10 | 1 | 0 | 0 | 0.0 | 4 | 5 | 1 | 26 | 0 | 0 | 0 | .125 | .138 |
| P | Joe Niekro | R | 34 | 60 | 6 | 0 | 0 | 0 | 0.0 | 2 | 0 | 4 | 23 | 0 | 0 | 0 | .100 | .100 |
| P | Rich Nye | L | 27 | 44 | 8 | 0 | 0 | 0 | 0.0 | 0 | 2 | 0 | 18 | 0 | 0 | 0 | .182 | .182 |
| P | Phil Regan | R | 68 | 20 | 3 | 1 | 0 | 0 | 0.0 | 3 | 1 | 0 | 8 | 0 | 0 | 0 | .150 | .200 |
| P | Gary Ross | R | 13 | 11 | 1 | 0 | 0 | 0 | 0.0 | 1 | 1 | 0 | 4 | 0 | 0 | 0 | .091 | .091 |
| P | Jack Lamabe | R | 42 | 5 | 1 | 0 | 0 | 0 | 0.0 | 0 | 0 | 1 | 3 | 1 | 0 | 0 | .200 | .200 |
| P | Bill Stoneman | R | 18 | 4 | 0 | 0 | 0 | 0 | 0.0 | 0 | 0 | 0 | 3 | 0 | 0 | 0 | .000 | .000 |
| P | Darcy Fast | L | 8 | 3 | 0 | 0 | 0 | 0 | 0.0 | 0 | 0 | 0 | 1 | 0 | 0 | 0 | .000 | .000 |
| P | Chuck Hartenstein | R | 28 | 2 | 0 | 0 | 0 | 0 | 0.0 | 0 | 0 | 0 | 0 | 0 | 0 | 0 | .000 | .000 |
| P | Archie Reynolds | R | 7 | 2 | 1 | 1 | 0 | 0 | 0.0 | 0 | 0 | 0 | 1 | 0 | 0 | 0 | .500 | 1.000 |
| P | Pete Mikkelsen | R | 3 | 1 | 1 | 0 | 0 | 0 | 0.0 | 0 | 0 | 0 | 0 | 0 | 0 | 0 | 1.000 | 1.000 |
| P | Bobby Tiefenauer | R | 9 | 1 | 0 | 0 | 0 | 0 | 0.0 | 0 | 0 | 0 | 0 | 0 | 0 | 0 | .000 | .000 |
| P | Ramon Hernandez | B | 8 | 0 | 0 | 0 | 0 | 0 | – | 0 | 0 | 0 | 0 | 0 | 0 | 0 | – | – |
| P | Frank Reberger | R | 3 | 0 | 0 | 0 | 0 | 0 | 0.0 | 0 | 0 | 1 | 0 | 0 | 0 | 0 | – | – |
| P | Jophery Brown | L | 1 | 0 | 0 | 0 | 0 | 0 | – | 0 | 0 | 0 | 0 | 0 | 0 | 0 | – | – |
| TEAM TOTAL | | | | 5458 | 1319 | 203 | 43 | 130 | 2.4 | 61 | 576 | 415 | 854 | 41 | 144 | 29 | .242 | .366 |

## INDIVIDUAL FIELDING

| POS | Player | T | G | PO | A | E | DP | TC/G | FA |
|---|---|---|---|---|---|---|---|---|---|
| 1B | E. Banks | R | 147 | 1379 | 88 | 6 | 118 | 10.0 | .996 |
| | D. Nen | L | 52 | 219 | 11 | 3 | 12 | 4.5 | .987 |
| | W. Smith | L | 4 | 16 | 1 | 0 | 0 | 4.3 | 1.000 |
| | G. Oliver | R | 2 | 14 | 0 | 0 | 0 | 7.0 | 1.000 |
| | C. Jones | L | 1 | 2 | 0 | 0 | 0 | 2.0 | 1.000 |
| 2B | G. Beckert | R | 155 | 356 | 461 | 19 | 107 | 5.4 | .977 |
| | J. Arcia | R | 10 | 22 | 19 | 0 | 2 | 4.1 | 1.000 |
| | V. LaRose | R | 2 | 1 | 1 | 0 | 1 | 1.0 | 1.000 |
| | L. Elia | R | 1 | 1 | 0 | 0 | 0 | 1.0 | 1.000 |
| SS | D. Kessinger | R | 159 | 263 | 573 | 33 | 97 | 5.5 | .962 |
| | J. Arcia | R | 7 | 8 | 15 | 2 | 1 | 3.6 | .920 |
| | V. LaRose | R | 2 | 0 | 4 | 1 | 0 | 2.5 | .800 |
| | L. Elia | R | 2 | 1 | 1 | 0 | 0 | 1.0 | 1.000 |
| 3B | R. Santo | R | 162 | 130 | 378 | 15 | 33 | 3.2 | .971 |
| | J. Arcia | R | 1 | 0 | 0 | 0 | 0 | 0.0 | .000 |
| | L. Elia | R | 1 | 1 | 1 | 0 | 0 | 2.0 | 1.000 |

| POS | Player | T | G | PO | A | E | DP | TC/G | FA |
|---|---|---|---|---|---|---|---|---|---|
| OF | A. Phillips | R | 141 | 311 | 11 | 7 | 3 | 2.3 | .979 |
| | B. Williams | R | 163 | 261 | 4 | 9 | 0 | 1.7 | .967 |
| | J. Hickman | R | 66 | 115 | 4 | 3 | 0 | 1.8 | .975 |
| | L. Johnson | R | 57 | 97 | 0 | 3 | 0 | 1.8 | .970 |
| | A. Spangler | L | 48 | 71 | 2 | 2 | 1 | 1.6 | .973 |
| | W. Smith | L | 38 | 42 | 1 | 0 | 0 | 1.1 | 1.000 |
| | J. Arcia | R | 17 | 19 | 0 | 0 | 0 | 1.1 | 1.000 |
| | Boccabella | R | 1 | 0 | 0 | 0 | 0 | 0.0 | .000 |
| | J. Upham | L | 2 | 0 | 0 | 0 | 0 | 0.0 | .000 |
| | J. McMath | L | 3 | 6 | 0 | 0 | 0 | 2.0 | 1.000 |
| | T. Savage | R | 2 | 3 | 0 | 0 | 0 | 1.5 | 1.000 |
| | G. Oliver | R | 1 | 1 | 0 | 0 | 0 | 1.0 | 1.000 |
| C | R. Hundley | R | 160 | 885 | 81 | 5 | 11 | 6.1 | .995 |
| | Boccabella | R | 4 | 27 | 0 | 0 | 0 | 6.8 | 1.000 |
| | R. Bobb | R | 7 | 14 | 2 | 0 | 0 | 2.3 | 1.000 |
| | G. Oliver | R | 1 | 10 | 1 | 0 | 0 | 11.0 | 1.000 |
| | J. Felske | R | 3 | 5 | 0 | 1 | 0 | 2.0 | .833 |
| | B. Plummer | R | 1 | 2 | 0 | 0 | 0 | 2.0 | 1.000 |

The Cubs took manager Leo Durocher on a roller-coaster ride, and he survived to lead them into third place with an 84–78 record. It was a season of streaks—good and bad. The Cubbies struggled to reach the .500 mark in May. Then they hit perhaps their worst scoring drought in club history, going 48 consecutive innings without a run and dropping 12 of 13 games in June. But July was another story. They won 29 of 39 and streaked from ninth to third. Second baseman Glenn Beckert enjoyed a 27-game hitting streak during that span with a solid .362 average. Fergie Jenkins was perhaps the toughest-luck 20-game winner ever. He lost five 1–0 games and still wound up with a 20–15 mark. Fergie was an iron man on the mound, pitching 308 innings, starting 40 games, completing 20, and fanning 260 to go with his sparkling 2.63 ERA. The Cubs were low in errors with 119 and high in homers with 130. Ernie Banks led the homer production with 32, Billy Williams had 30, and Ron Santo 26. Williams and Santo shared RBI honors with 98 each, and Beckert topped the batting parade at .294. For a change, the Cubs swindled the Dodgers in a trade on April 23, getting reliever Phil Regan and Jim Hickman for Ted Savage and Jim Ellis. Regan led the NL with 25 saves and gained 10 victories, and even survived a strip search by ump Chris Pelakoudas on August 18. Pelakoudas was looking for a foreign substance that helped doctor the ball. No evidence was found, and league president Warren Giles later ordered the umpire to apologize to Regan. After all, no team managed by Durocher would try anything illegal.

### TEAM STATISTICS

| | W | L | PCT | GB | R | OR | Batting 2B | 3B | HR | BA | SA | SB | Fielding E | DP | FA | CG | B | Pitching SO | ShO | SV | ERA |
|---|---|---|---|---|---|---|---|---|---|---|---|---|---|---|---|---|---|---|---|---|---|
| STL | 97 | 65 | .599 | | 583 | 472 | 227 | 48 | 73 | .249 | .346 | 110 | 140 | 135 | .978 | 63 | 375 | 971 | 30 | 32 | 2.49 |
| SF | 88 | 74 | .543 | 9 | 599 | 529 | 162 | 33 | 108 | .239 | .341 | 50 | 162 | 125 | .975 | 77 | 344 | 942 | 20 | 16 | 2.71 |
| CHI | 84 | 78 | .519 | 13 | 612 | 611 | 203 | 43 | 130 | .242 | .366 | 41 | 119 | 149 | .981 | 46 | 392 | 894 | 12 | 32 | 3.41 |
| CIN | 83 | 79 | .512 | 14 | 690 | 673 | 281 | 36 | 106 | .273 | .389 | 59 | 144 | 144 | .978 | 24 | 573 | 963 | 16 | 38 | 3.56 |
| ATL | 81 | 81 | .500 | 16 | 514 | 549 | 179 | 31 | 80 | .252 | .343 | 83 | 125 | 139 | .980 | 44 | 362 | 871 | 16 | 29 | 2.92 |
| PIT | 80 | 82 | .494 | 17 | 583 | 532 | 180 | 44 | 80 | .252 | .343 | 130 | 139 | 162 | .979 | 42 | 485 | 897 | 19 | 30 | 2.74 |
| LA | 76 | 86 | .469 | 21 | 470 | 509 | 202 | 36 | 67 | .230 | .319 | 57 | 144 | 144 | .977 | 38 | 414 | 994 | 23 | 31 | 2.69 |
| PHI | 76 | 86 | .469 | 21 | 543 | 615 | 178 | 30 | 100 | .233 | .333 | 58 | 127 | 163 | .980 | 42 | 421 | 935 | 12 | 27 | 3.36 |
| NY | 73 | 89 | .451 | 24 | 473 | 499 | 178 | 30 | 81 | .228 | .315 | 72 | 133 | 142 | .979 | 45 | 430 | 1014 | 25 | 32 | 2.72 |
| HOU | 72 | 90 | .444 | 25 | 510 | 588 | 205 | 28 | 66 | .231 | .317 | 44 | 156 | 129 | .975 | 50 | 479 | 1021 | 12 | 23 | 3.26 |
| LEAGUE TOTAL | | | | | 5577 | 5577 | 1995 | 359 | 891 | .243 | .341 | 704 | 1389 | 1432 | .978 | 471 | 4275 | 9502 | 185 | 290 | 2.99 |

### INDIVIDUAL PITCHING

| PITCHER | T | W | L | PCT | ERA | SV | G | GS | CG | IP | H | BB | SO | R | ER | ShO | H/9 | BB/9 | SO/9 |
|---|---|---|---|---|---|---|---|---|---|---|---|---|---|---|---|---|---|---|---|
| Ferguson Jenkins | R | 20 | 15 | .571 | 2.63 | 0 | 40 | 40 | 20 | 308 | 255 | 65 | 260 | 96 | 90 | 3 | 7.45 | 1.90 | 7.60 |
| Bill Hands | R | 16 | 10 | .615 | 2.89 | 0 | 38 | 34 | 11 | 258.2 | 221 | 36 | 148 | 91 | 83 | 4 | 7.69 | 1.25 | 5.15 |
| Ken Holtzman | L | 11 | 14 | .440 | 3.35 | 1 | 34 | 32 | 6 | 215 | 201 | 76 | 151 | 89 | 80 | 3 | 8.41 | 3.18 | 6.32 |
| Joe Niekro | R | 14 | 10 | .583 | 4.31 | 2 | 34 | 29 | 2 | 177.1 | 204 | 59 | 65 | 93 | 85 | 1 | 10.35 | 2.99 | 3.30 |
| Rich Nye | L | 7 | 12 | .368 | 3.80 | 1 | 27 | 20 | 6 | 132.2 | 145 | 34 | 74 | 65 | 56 | 1 | 9.84 | 2.31 | 5.02 |
| Phil Regan | R | 10 | 5 | .667 | 2.20 | 25* | 68 | 0 | 0 | 127 | 109 | 24 | 60 | 36 | 31 | 0 | 7.72 | 1.70 | 4.25 |
| Jack Lamabe | R | 3 | 2 | .600 | 4.30 | 1 | 42 | 0 | 0 | 60.2 | 68 | 24 | 30 | 33 | 29 | 0 | 10.09 | 3.56 | 4.45 |
| Gary Ross | R | 1 | 1 | .500 | 4.17 | 0 | 13 | 5 | 1 | 41 | 44 | 25 | 31 | 22 | 19 | 0 | 9.66 | 5.49 | 6.80 |
| Chuck Hartenstein | R | 2 | 4 | .333 | 4.54 | 1 | 28 | 0 | 0 | 35.2 | 41 | 11 | 17 | 19 | 18 | 0 | 10.35 | 2.78 | 4.29 |
| Bill Stoneman | R | 0 | 1 | .000 | 5.52 | 0 | 18 | 0 | 0 | 29.1 | 35 | 14 | 18 | 19 | 18 | 0 | 10.74 | 4.30 | 5.52 |
| Bobby Tiefenauer | R | 0 | 1 | .000 | 6.08 | 1 | 9 | 0 | 0 | 13.1 | 20 | 2 | 9 | 12 | 9 | 0 | 13.50 | 1.35 | 6.08 |
| Archie Reynolds | R | 0 | 1 | .000 | 6.75 | 0 | 7 | 1 | 0 | 13.1 | 14 | 7 | 6 | 10 | 10 | 0 | 9.45 | 4.73 | 4.05 |
| Darcy Fast | L | 0 | 1 | .000 | 5.40 | 0 | 8 | 1 | 0 | 10 | 8 | 8 | 10 | 6 | 6 | 0 | 7.20 | 7.20 | 9.00 |
| Ramon Hernandez | L | 0 | 0 | — | 9.00 | 0 | 8 | 0 | 0 | 9 | 14 | 0 | 3 | 11 | 9 | 0 | 14.00 | 0.00 | 3.00 |
| John Upham | L | 0 | 0 | — | 0.00 | 0 | 2 | 0 | 0 | 7 | 2 | 3 | 2 | 0 | 0 | 0 | 2.57 | 3.86 | 2.57 |
| Frank Reberger | R | 0 | 1 | .000 | 4.50 | 0 | 3 | 1 | 0 | 6 | 9 | 2 | 3 | 4 | 3 | 0 | 13.50 | 3.00 | 4.50 |
| Pete Mikkelsen | R | 0 | 0 | — | 7.71 | 0 | 3 | 0 | 0 | 4.2 | 7 | 1 | 5 | 4 | 4 | 0 | 13.50 | 1.93 | 9.64 |
| Willie Smith | L | 0 | 0 | — | 0.00 | 0 | 1 | 0 | 0 | 2.2 | 0 | 0 | 2 | 0 | 0 | 0 | 0.00 | 0.00 | 6.75 |
| Jophery Brown | R | 0 | 0 | — | 4.50 | 0 | 1 | 0 | 0 | 2 | 2 | 1 | 0 | 1 | 1 | 0 | 9.00 | 4.50 | 0.00 |
| TEAM TOTAL | | 84 | 78 | .519 | 3.41 | 32 | 384 | 163 | 46 | 1453.1 | 1399 | 392 | 894 | 611 | 551 | 12 | 8.66 | 2.43 | 5.54 |

| MANAGER | W | L | PCT |
|---|---|---|---|
| Leo Durocher | 92 | 70 | .568 |

| POS | Player | B | G | AB | H | 2B | 3B | HR | HR % | R | RBI | BB | SO | SB | Pinch Hit AB | Pinch Hit H | BA | SA |
|---|---|---|---|---|---|---|---|---|---|---|---|---|---|---|---|---|---|---|
| **REGULARS** |
| 1B | Ernie Banks | R | 155 | 565 | 143 | 19 | 2 | 23 | 4.1 | 60 | 106 | 42 | 101 | 0 | 2 | 2 | .253 | .416 |
| 2B | Glenn Beckert | R | 131 | 543 | 158 | 22 | 1 | 1 | 0.2 | 69 | 37 | 24 | 24 | 6 | 1 | 0 | .291 | .341 |
| SS | Don Kessinger | B | 158 | 664 | 181 | 38 | 6 | 4 | 0.6 | 109 | 53 | 61 | 70 | 11 | 1 | 0 | .273 | .366 |
| 3B | Ron Santo | R | 160 | 575 | 166 | 18 | 4 | 29 | 5.0 | 97 | 123 | 96 | 97 | 1 | 1 | 0 | .289 | .485 |
| RF | Jim Hickman | R | 134 | 338 | 80 | 11 | 2 | 21 | 6.2 | 38 | 54 | 47 | 74 | 2 | 18 | 5 | .237 | .467 |
| CF | Don Young | R | 101 | 272 | 65 | 12 | 3 | 6 | 2.2 | 36 | 27 | 38 | 74 | 1 | 0 | 0 | .239 | .371 |
| LF | Billy Williams | L | 163 | 642 | 188 | 33 | 10 | 21 | 3.3 | 103 | 95 | 59 | 70 | 3 | 2 | 0 | .293 | .474 |
| C | Randy Hundley | R | 151 | 522 | 133 | 15 | 1 | 18 | 3.4 | 67 | 64 | 61 | 90 | 2 | 1 | 0 | .255 | .391 |
| **SUBSTITUTES** |
| UT | Paul Popovich | R | 60 | 154 | 48 | 6 | 0 | 1 | 0.6 | 26 | 14 | 18 | 14 | 0 | 22 | 7 | .312 | .370 |
| 2B | Nate Oliver | R | 44 | 44 | 7 | 3 | 0 | 1 | 2.3 | 15 | 4 | 1 | 10 | 0 | 3 | 0 | .159 | .295 |
| 1B | Rick Bladt | R | 10 | 13 | 2 | 0 | 0 | 0 | 0.0 | 1 | 1 | 0 | 5 | 0 | 1 | 0 | .154 | .154 |
| OF | Al Spangler | L | 82 | 213 | 45 | 8 | 1 | 4 | 1.9 | 23 | 23 | 21 | 16 | 0 | 26 | 1 | .211 | .315 |
| O1 | Willie Smith | L | 103 | 195 | 48 | 9 | 1 | 9 | 4.6 | 21 | 25 | 25 | 49 | 1 | 40 | 12 | .246 | .441 |
| OF | Jim Qualls | B | 43 | 120 | 30 | 5 | 3 | 0 | 0.0 | 12 | 9 | 2 | 14 | 2 | 4 | 2 | .250 | .342 |
| OF | Oscar Gamble | L | 24 | 71 | 16 | 1 | 1 | 1 | 1.4 | 6 | 5 | 10 | 12 | 0 | 0 | 0 | .225 | .310 |
| OF | Adolfo Phillips | R | 28 | 49 | 11 | 3 | 1 | 0 | 0.0 | 5 | 1 | 16 | 15 | 1 | 1 | 0 | .224 | .327 |
| OF | Jimmie Hall | L | 11 | 24 | 5 | 1 | 0 | 0 | 0.0 | 1 | 1 | 1 | 5 | 0 | 1 | 1 | .208 | .250 |
| CO | Ken Rudolph | R | 27 | 34 | 7 | 1 | 0 | 1 | 2.9 | 7 | 6 | 6 | 11 | 0 | 10 | 3 | .206 | .324 |
| C | Bill Heath | L | 27 | 32 | 5 | 0 | 1 | 0 | 0.0 | 1 | 1 | 12 | 4 | 0 | 12 | 2 | .156 | .219 |
| C | Gene Oliver | R | 23 | 27 | 6 | 3 | 0 | 0 | 0.0 | 0 | 0 | 1 | 9 | 0 | 14 | 4 | .222 | .333 |
| CO | John Hairston | R | 3 | 4 | 1 | 0 | 0 | 0 | 0.0 | 0 | 0 | 0 | 2 | 0 | 1 | 1 | .250 | .250 |
| C | Randy Bobb | R | 3 | 2 | 0 | 0 | 0 | 0 | 0.0 | 0 | 0 | 0 | 1 | 0 | 0 | 0 | .000 | .000 |
| PH | Manny Jimenez | L | 6 | 6 | 1 | 0 | 0 | 0 | 0.0 | 0 | 0 | 0 | 2 | 0 | 6 | 1 | .167 | .167 |
| PH | Charley Smith | R | 2 | 2 | 0 | 0 | 0 | 0 | 0.0 | 0 | 0 | 0 | 0 | 0 | 2 | 0 | .000 | .000 |
| **PITCHERS** |
| P | Ferguson Jenkins | R | 43 | 108 | 15 | 2 | 1 | 1 | 0.9 | 6 | 9 | 6 | 42 | 0 | 0 | 0 | .139 | .204 |
| P | Ken Holtzman | R | 39 | 100 | 15 | 1 | 1 | 1 | 1.0 | 5 | 7 | 2 | 32 | 0 | 0 | 0 | .150 | .210 |
| P | Bill Hands | R | 41 | 98 | 9 | 0 | 0 | 0 | 0.0 | 5 | 3 | 4 | 45 | 0 | 0 | 0 | .092 | .092 |
| P | Dick Selma | R | 36 | 52 | 8 | 1 | 1 | 0 | 0.0 | 3 | 0 | 1 | 17 | 0 | 0 | 0 | .154 | .212 |
| P | Rich Nye | L | 36 | 16 | 1 | 0 | 0 | 0 | 0.0 | 1 | 0 | 0 | 7 | 0 | 0 | 0 | .063 | .063 |
| P | Phil Regan | R | 71 | 15 | 1 | 0 | 0 | 0 | 0.0 | 0 | 0 | 2 | 2 | 0 | 0 | 0 | .067 | .133 |
| P | Ted Abernathy | R | 56 | 8 | 2 | 1 | 0 | 0 | 0.0 | 1 | 1 | 0 | 2 | 0 | 0 | 0 | .250 | .375 |
| P | Hank Aguirre | R | 41 | 5 | 2 | 0 | 0 | 0 | 0.0 | 2 | 0 | 0 | 1 | 0 | 0 | 0 | .400 | .400 |
| P | Joe Niekro | R | 4 | 5 | 1 | 1 | 0 | 0 | 0.0 | 0 | 2 | 0 | 1 | 0 | 0 | 0 | .200 | .400 |
| P | Ken Johnson | R | 9 | 4 | 0 | 0 | 0 | 0 | 0.0 | 0 | 0 | 0 | 4 | 0 | 0 | 0 | .000 | .000 |
| P | Jim Colborn | R | 6 | 3 | 0 | 0 | 0 | 0 | 0.0 | 0 | 0 | 0 | 2 | 0 | 0 | 0 | .000 | .000 |
| P | Joe Decker | R | 4 | 2 | 0 | 0 | 0 | 0 | 0.0 | 0 | 0 | 0 | 1 | 0 | 0 | 0 | .000 | .000 |
| P | Don Nottebart | R | 16 | 1 | 0 | 0 | 0 | 0 | 0.0 | 0 | 0 | 0 | 1 | 0 | 0 | 0 | .000 | .000 |
| P | Archie Reynolds | R | 2 | 1 | 0 | 0 | 0 | 0 | 0.0 | 0 | 0 | 2 | 1 | 0 | 0 | 0 | .000 | .000 |
| P | Dave Lemonds | L | 2 | 1 | 0 | 0 | 0 | 0 | 0.0 | 0 | 0 | 0 | 1 | 0 | 0 | 0 | .000 | .000 |
| P | Gary Ross | R | 2 | 0 | 0 | 0 | 0 | 0 | – | 0 | 0 | 0 | 0 | 0 | 0 | 0 | – | – |
| P | Alec Distaso | R | 2 | 0 | 0 | 0 | 0 | 0 | – | 0 | 0 | 0 | 0 | 0 | 0 | 0 | – | – |
| | TEAM TOTAL | | | 5530 | 1400 | 215 | 40 | 142 | 2.6 | 72 | 671 | 559 | 928 | 30 | 169 | 41 | .253 | .384 |

## INDIVIDUAL FIELDING

| POS | Player | T | G | PO | A | E | DP | TC/G | FA |
|---|---|---|---|---|---|---|---|---|---|
| 1B | E. Banks | R | 153 | **1419** | 87 | 4 | 116 | 9.9 | **.997** |
| | W. Smith | L | 24 | 159 | 9 | 1 | 14 | 7.0 | .994 |
| | R. Bladt | R | 7 | 12 | 1 | 0 | 0 | 1.9 | 1.000 |
| 2B | G. Beckert | R | 129 | 262 | 401 | **24** | 71 | 5.3 | .965 |
| | P. Popovich | R | 25 | 50 | 64 | 3 | 13 | 4.7 | .974 |
| | N. Oliver | R | 13 | 22 | 31 | 0 | 9 | 4.1 | 1.000 |
| | J. Qualls | R | 4 | 7 | 4 | 0 | 2 | 2.8 | 1.000 |
| SS | D. Kessinger | R | 157 | **266** | 542 | 20 | **101** | 5.3 | **.976** |
| | P. Popovich | R | 7 | 13 | 23 | 0 | 7 | 5.1 | 1.000 |
| 3B | R. Santo | R | 160 | **144** | 334 | 27 | 23 | 3.2 | .947 |
| | P. Popovich | R | 6 | 2 | 9 | 1 | 1 | 2.0 | .917 |

| POS | Player | T | G | PO | A | E | DP | TC/G | FA |
|---|---|---|---|---|---|---|---|---|---|
| OF | B. Williams | R | 159 | 250 | 15 | 12 | 2 | 1.7 | .957 |
| | D. Young | R | 100 | 191 | 4 | 5 | 0 | 2.0 | .975 |
| | J. Hickman | R | 125 | 153 | 6 | 3 | 0 | 1.3 | .981 |
| | A. Spangler | L | 58 | 75 | 1 | 4 | 0 | 1.4 | .950 |
| | J. Qualls | R | 35 | 55 | 1 | 0 | 0 | 1.6 | 1.000 |
| | O. Gamble | R | 24 | 41 | 1 | 4 | 0 | 1.9 | .913 |
| | A. Phillips | R | 25 | 43 | 0 | 2 | 0 | 1.8 | .956 |
| | W. Smith | L | 33 | 26 | 0 | 2 | 0 | 0.8 | .929 |
| | J. Hairston | R | 1 | 0 | 0 | 0 | 0 | 0.0 | .000 |
| | J. Hall | R | 5 | 5 | 0 | 0 | 0 | 1.0 | 1.000 |
| | K. Rudolph | R | 3 | 2 | 0 | 0 | 0 | 0.7 | 1.000 |
| | P. Popovich | R | 1 | 1 | 0 | 0 | 0 | 1.0 | 1.000 |
| C | R. Hundley | R | 151 | 978 | **79** | 8 | **17** | 7.1 | .992 |
| | B. Heath | R | 9 | 44 | 3 | 1 | 1 | 5.3 | .979 |
| | K. Rudolph | R | 11 | 39 | 3 | 1 | 0 | 3.9 | .977 |
| | G. Oliver | R | 6 | 28 | 2 | 0 | 1 | 5.0 | 1.000 |
| | J. Hairston | R | 1 | 3 | 1 | 0 | 0 | 4.0 | 1.000 |
| | R. Bobb | R | 2 | 4 | 0 | 0 | 0 | 2.0 | 1.000 |

The stereo blared "Hey, hey, holy mackeral, no doubt about it. The Cubs are on their way." For 155 glorious days, from the opener to September 10, the Cubs held first place. Willie Smith walloped a game-winning homer in the 11th inning of the opener to start the Wrigley Field faithful throbbing with enthusiasm unmatched in Cub history. An all-time record 1,674,993 jammed the old ballyard. Dick Selma led the yellow-hatted Bleacher Bums in raucous cheers. Ron Santo clicked his heels after each triumph. Ken Holtzman pitched a no-hitter on August 19, beating the Braves, 3–0, before a packed house. The Cubs swept through April at 16–7. In May they were 16–9. In June they remained steady with a 17–11 mark, followed by 15–14 in July and 18–11 in August. Then came September mourn. The Cubs collapsed to 9–17 in that most vital month. Meanwhile, the Mets won 38 of 49 to march from 8 1/2 back on August 13 to their final 8-game margin. The Cubbies limped home second with a 92–70 record, their best since 1945, but not good enough.

What happened? There were some early indications of incohesiveness when manager Leo Durocher and captain Santo tore into outfielder Don Young for failing to catch two late-inning fly balls in a 4–3 loss to the Mets in July. Then the pitchers allowed Al Weis of the Mets his only two homers of the season in back-to-back defeats at Wrigley a week later. In addition, there was the defection of Durocher, going AWOL in midsummer to Camp Objiwa. Many observers said the team was involved in too many outside activities. Others say Leo should have rested his regulars during the sweltering dog days of summer. Or perhaps the Mets were better. On paper the Cubs looked superior; they had more power, with Santo hitting 29 homers, Ernie Banks 23, Billy Williams and Jim Hickman 21, and Randy Hundley 18. Fergie Jenkins was a 21-game winner, Bill Hands won 20 and Holtzman 17. Glenn Beckert and Don Kessinger were a perfect DP duo. "Hey, hey. Holy mackeral. The Cubs are. . . ."

## TEAM STATISTICS

| | W | L | PCT | GB | R | OR | 2B | 3B | HR | BA | SA | SB | E | DP | FA | CG | B | SO | ShO | SV | ERA |
|---|---|---|---|---|---|---|---|---|---|---|---|---|---|---|---|---|---|---|---|---|---|
| **EAST** | | | | | | | | | | | | | | | | | | | | | |
| NY | 100 | 62 | .617 | | 632 | 541 | 184 | 41 | 109 | .242 | .351 | 66 | 122 | 146 | .980 | 51 | 517 | 1012 | **28** | 35 | 2.99 |
| CHI | 92 | 70 | .568 | 8 | 720 | 611 | 215 | 40 | 142 | .253 | .384 | 30 | 136 | 149 | .979 | 58 | 475 | 1017 | 22 | 27 | 3.34 |
| PIT | 88 | 74 | .543 | 12 | 725 | 652 | 220 | **52** | 119 | **.277** | .398 | 74 | 155 | 169 | .975 | 39 | 553 | 1124 | 9 | 33 | 3.61 |
| STL | 87 | 75 | .537 | 13 | 595 | 540 | **228** | 44 | 90 | .253 | .359 | 87 | 138 | 144 | .978 | 63 | 511 | 1004 | 12 | 26 | **2.94** |
| PHI | 63 | 99 | .389 | 37 | 645 | 745 | 227 | 35 | 137 | .241 | .372 | 73 | 136 | 157 | .978 | 47 | 570 | 921 | 14 | 21 | 4.17 |
| MON | 52 | 110 | .321 | 48 | 582 | 791 | 202 | 33 | 125 | .240 | .359 | 52 | 184 | **179** | .971 | 26 | 702 | 973 | 8 | 21 | 4.33 |
| **WEST** | | | | | | | | | | | | | | | | | | | | | |
| ATL | 93 | 69 | .574 | | 691 | 631 | 195 | 22 | 141 | .258 | .380 | 59 | **115** | 114 | **.981** | 38 | 438 | 893 | 7 | 42 | 3.53 |
| SF | 90 | 72 | .556 | 3 | 713 | 636 | 187 | 28 | 136 | .242 | .361 | 71 | 169 | 155 | .974 | **71** | 461 | 906 | 15 | 17 | 3.25 |
| CIN | 89 | 73 | .549 | 4 | **798** | 768 | 224 | 42 | **171** | .277 | **.422** | 79 | 168 | 158 | .973 | 23 | 611 | 818 | 11 | **44** | 4.13 |
| LA | 85 | 77 | .525 | 8 | 645 | 561 | 185 | **52** | 97 | .254 | .359 | 80 | 126 | 130 | .980 | 47 | **420** | 975 | 20 | 31 | 3.09 |
| HOU | 81 | 81 | .500 | 12 | 676 | 668 | 208 | 40 | 104 | .240 | .352 | **101** | 153 | 136 | .975 | 52 | 547 | **1221** | 11 | 34 | 3.60 |
| SD | 52 | 110 | .321 | 41 | 468 | 746 | 180 | 42 | 99 | .225 | .329 | 45 | 156 | 140 | .975 | 16 | 592 | 764 | 9 | 25 | 4.24 |
| LEAGUE TOTAL | | | | | 7890 | 7890 | 2455 | 471 | 1470 | .250 | .369 | 817 | 1758 | 1777 | .977 | 531 | 6397 | 11628 | 166 | 356 | 3.60 |

## INDIVIDUAL PITCHING

| PITCHER | T | W | L | PCT | ERA | SV | G | GS | CG | IP | H | BB | SO | R | ER | ShO | H/9 | BB/9 | SO/9 |
|---|---|---|---|---|---|---|---|---|---|---|---|---|---|---|---|---|---|---|---|
| Ferguson Jenkins | R | 21 | 15 | .583 | 3.21 | 1 | 43 | **42** | 23 | 311 | 284 | 71 | **273** | 122 | 111 | 7 | 8.22 | 2.05 | 7.90 |
| Bill Hands | R | 20 | 14 | .588 | 2.49 | 0 | 41 | 41 | 18 | 300 | 268 | 73 | 181 | 102 | 83 | 3 | 8.04 | 2.19 | 5.43 |
| Ken Holtzman | L | 17 | 13 | .567 | 3.59 | 0 | 39 | 39 | 12 | 261 | 248 | 93 | 176 | 117 | 104 | 6 | 8.55 | 3.21 | 6.07 |
| Dick Selma | R | 10 | 8 | .556 | 3.63 | 1 | 36 | 25 | 4 | 168.2 | 137 | 72 | 161 | 74 | 68 | 2 | 7.31 | 3.84 | 8.59 |
| Phil Regan | R | 12 | 6 | .667 | 3.70 | 17 | 71 | 0 | 0 | 112 | 120 | 35 | 56 | 49 | 46 | 0 | 9.64 | 2.81 | 4.50 |
| Ted Abernathy | R | 4 | 3 | .571 | 3.18 | 3 | 56 | 0 | 0 | 85 | 75 | 42 | 55 | 38 | 30 | 0 | 7.94 | 4.45 | 5.82 |
| Rich Nye | L | 3 | 5 | .375 | 5.09 | 3 | 34 | 5 | 1 | 69 | 72 | 21 | 39 | 43 | 39 | 0 | 9.39 | 2.74 | 5.09 |
| Hank Aguirre | L | 1 | 0 | 1.000 | 2.60 | 1 | 41 | 0 | 0 | 45 | 45 | 12 | 19 | 13 | 13 | 0 | 9.00 | 2.40 | 3.80 |
| Joe Niekro | R | 0 | 1 | .000 | 3.72 | 0 | 4 | 3 | 0 | 19.1 | 24 | 6 | 7 | 9 | 8 | 0 | 11.17 | 2.79 | 3.26 |
| Ken Johnson | R | 1 | 2 | .333 | 2.84 | 1 | 9 | 1 | 0 | 19 | 17 | 13 | 18 | 8 | 6 | 0 | 8.05 | 6.16 | 8.53 |
| Don Nottebart | R | 1 | 1 | .500 | 7.00 | 0 | 16 | 0 | 0 | 18 | 28 | 7 | 8 | 14 | 14 | 0 | 14.00 | 3.50 | 4.00 |
| Jim Colborn | R | 1 | 0 | 1.000 | 3.00 | 0 | 6 | 2 | 0 | 15 | 15 | 9 | 4 | 6 | 5 | 0 | 9.00 | 5.40 | 2.40 |
| Joe Decker | R | 1 | 0 | 1.000 | 3.00 | 0 | 4 | 1 | 0 | 12 | 10 | 6 | 13 | 4 | 4 | 0 | 7.50 | 4.50 | 9.75 |
| Archie Reynolds | R | 0 | 1 | .000 | 2.57 | 0 | 2 | 2 | 0 | 7 | 11 | 7 | 4 | 5 | 2 | 0 | 14.14 | 9.00 | 5.14 |
| Alec Distaso | R | 0 | 0 | — | 3.60 | 0 | 2 | 0 | 0 | 5 | 6 | 1 | 1 | 2 | 2 | 0 | 10.80 | 1.80 | 1.80 |
| Dave Lemonds | L | 0 | 1 | .000 | 3.60 | 0 | 2 | 1 | 0 | 5 | 5 | 5 | 0 | 2 | 2 | 0 | 9.00 | 9.00 | 0.00 |
| Gary Ross | R | 0 | 0 | — | 13.50 | 0 | 2 | 1 | 0 | 2 | 3 | 2 | 2 | 3 | 3 | 0 | 4.50 | 9.00 | 9.00 |
| TEAM TOTAL | | 92 | 70 | .568 | 3.34 | 27 | 408 | 163 | 58 | 1454 | 1366 | 475 | 1017 | 611 | 540 | 18 | 8.46 | 2.94 | 6.30 |

| MANAGER | W | L | PCT |
|---|---|---|---|
| Leo Durocher | 84 | 78 | .519 |

| POS | Player | B | G | AB | H | 2B | 3B | HR | HR % | R | RBI | BB | SO | SB | Pinch Hit AB | Pinch Hit H | BA | SA |
|---|---|---|---|---|---|---|---|---|---|---|---|---|---|---|---|---|---|---|
| **REGULARS** | | | | | | | | | | | | | | | | | | |
| 1B | Jim Hickman | R | 149 | 514 | 162 | 33 | 4 | 32 | 6.2 | 102 | 115 | 93 | 99 | 0 | 2 | 0 | .315 | .582 |
| 2B | Glenn Beckert | R | 143 | 591 | 170 | 15 | 6 | 3 | 0.5 | 99 | 36 | 32 | 22 | 4 | 3 | 0 | .288 | .349 |
| SS | Don Kessinger | B | 154 | 631 | 168 | 21 | 14 | 1 | 0.2 | 100 | 39 | 66 | 59 | 12 | 2 | 0 | .266 | .349 |
| 3B | Ron Santo | R | 154 | 555 | 148 | 30 | 4 | 26 | 4.7 | 83 | 114 | 92 | 108 | 2 | 2 | 1 | .267 | .476 |
| RF | Johnny Callison | L | 147 | 477 | 126 | 23 | 2 | 19 | 4.0 | 65 | 68 | 60 | 63 | 7 | 3 | 1 | .264 | .440 |
| CF | Cleo James | R | 100 | 176 | 37 | 7 | 2 | 3 | 1.7 | 33 | 14 | 17 | 24 | 5 | 6 | 0 | .210 | .324 |
| LF | Billy Williams | L | 161 | 636 | **205** | 34 | 4 | 42 | 6.6 | 137 | 129 | 72 | 65 | 7 | 0 | 0 | .322 | .586 |
| C | Randy Hundley | R | 73 | 250 | 61 | 5 | 0 | 7 | 2.8 | 13 | 36 | 16 | 52 | 0 | 0 | 0 | .244 | .348 |
| **SUBSTITUTES** | | | | | | | | | | | | | | | | | | |
| 1B | Ernie Banks | R | 72 | 222 | 56 | 6 | 2 | 12 | 5.4 | 25 | 44 | 20 | 33 | 0 | 9 | 2 | .252 | .459 |
| UT | Paul Popovich | R | 78 | 186 | 47 | 5 | 1 | 4 | 2.2 | 22 | 20 | 18 | 18 | 0 | 26 | 2 | .253 | .355 |
| 1B | Willie Smith | L | 87 | 167 | 36 | 9 | 1 | 5 | 3.0 | 15 | 24 | 11 | 32 | 2 | 40 | 9 | .216 | .371 |
| 2B | Phil Gagliano | R | 26 | 40 | 6 | 0 | 0 | 0 | 0.0 | 5 | 5 | 5 | 5 | 0 | 8 | 1 | .150 | .150 |
| SS | Roger Metzger | B | 1 | 2 | 0 | 0 | 0 | 0 | 0.0 | 0 | 0 | 0 | 0 | 0 | 0 | 0 | .000 | .000 |
| OF | Joe Pepitone | L | 56 | 213 | 57 | 9 | 2 | 12 | 5.6 | 38 | 44 | 15 | 15 | 0 | 0 | 0 | .268 | .498 |
| OF | Tommy Davis | R | 11 | 42 | 11 | 2 | 0 | 2 | 4.8 | 4 | 8 | 1 | 1 | 0 | 1 | 1 | .262 | .452 |
| OF | Jimmie Hall | L | 28 | 32 | 3 | 1 | 0 | 0 | 0.0 | 2 | 1 | 4 | 12 | 0 | 1 | 0 | .094 | .125 |
| OF | Al Spangler | L | 21 | 14 | 2 | 1 | 0 | 1 | 7.1 | 2 | 1 | 3 | 3 | 0 | 19 | 2 | .143 | .429 |
| OF | Boots Day | L | 11 | 8 | 2 | 0 | 0 | 0 | 0.0 | 2 | 0 | 0 | 3 | 0 | 11 | 2 | .250 | .250 |
| OF | Brock Davis | L | 6 | 3 | 0 | 0 | 0 | 0 | 0.0 | 0 | 0 | 0 | 1 | 0 | 3 | 0 | .000 | .000 |
| O3 | Terry Hughes | R | 2 | 3 | 1 | 0 | 0 | 0 | 0.0 | 0 | 0 | 0 | 0 | 0 | 1 | 1 | .333 | .333 |
| C | Jack Hiatt | R | 66 | 178 | 43 | 12 | 1 | 2 | 1.1 | 19 | 22 | 31 | 48 | 0 | 2 | 0 | .242 | .354 |
| C | J. C. Martin | L | 40 | 77 | 12 | 1 | 0 | 1 | 1.3 | 11 | 4 | 20 | 11 | 0 | 3 | 0 | .156 | .208 |
| C | Ken Rudolph | R | 20 | 40 | 4 | 1 | 0 | 0 | 0.0 | 1 | 2 | 1 | 12 | 0 | 3 | 0 | .100 | .125 |
| PH | Adrian Garrett | L | 3 | 3 | 0 | 0 | 0 | 0 | 0.0 | 0 | 0 | 0 | 3 | 0 | 3 | 0 | .000 | .000 |
| PH | Roe Skidmore | R | 1 | 1 | 1 | 0 | 0 | 0 | 0.0 | 0 | 0 | 0 | 0 | 0 | 1 | 1 | 1.000 | 1.000 |
| **PITCHERS** | | | | | | | | | | | | | | | | | | |
| P | Ferguson Jenkins | R | 40 | 113 | 14 | 2 | 0 | 3 | 2.7 | 4 | 11 | 1 | 36 | 0 | 0 | 0 | .124 | .221 |
| P | Ken Holtzman | R | 40 | 105 | 21 | 5 | 0 | 0 | 0.0 | 6 | 6 | 5 | 22 | 0 | 1 | 0 | .200 | .248 |
| P | Bill Hands | R | 39 | 75 | 10 | 2 | 0 | 0 | 0.0 | 6 | 6 | 15 | 33 | 0 | 0 | 0 | .133 | .160 |
| P | Milt Pappas | R | 21 | 50 | 12 | 2 | 1 | 2 | 4.0 | 7 | 5 | 2 | 17 | 0 | 0 | 0 | .240 | .440 |
| P | Joe Decker | R | 24 | 34 | 6 | 1 | 0 | 1 | 2.9 | 3 | 3 | 2 | 16 | 0 | 0 | 0 | .176 | .294 |
| P | Jim Colborn | R | 34 | 15 | 1 | 0 | 0 | 0 | 0.0 | 0 | 1 | 0 | 11 | 0 | 0 | 0 | .067 | .067 |
| P | Larry Gura | L | 20 | 10 | 0 | 0 | 0 | 0 | 0.0 | 0 | 0 | 0 | 5 | 0 | 0 | 0 | .000 | .000 |
| P | Phil Regan | R | 54 | 9 | 0 | 0 | 0 | 0 | 0.0 | 1 | 0 | 1 | 7 | 0 | 0 | 0 | .000 | .000 |
| P | Roberto Rodriguez | R | 26 | 8 | 1 | 0 | 0 | 1 | 12.5 | 1 | 1 | 1 | 1 | 0 | 0 | 0 | .125 | .500 |
| P | Jim Dunegan | R | 10 | 4 | 1 | 1 | 0 | 0 | 0.0 | 0 | 2 | 0 | 2 | 0 | 0 | 0 | .250 | .500 |
| P | Juan Pizarro | L | 12 | 3 | 0 | 0 | 0 | 0 | 0.0 | 0 | 0 | 1 | 3 | 0 | 0 | 0 | .000 | .000 |
| P | Hank Aguirre | R | 17 | 2 | 0 | 0 | 0 | 0 | 0.0 | 0 | 0 | 0 | 0 | 0 | 0 | 0 | .000 | .000 |
| P | Archie Reynolds | R | 7 | 2 | 0 | 0 | 0 | 0 | 0.0 | 0 | 0 | 1 | 0 | 0 | 0 | 0 | .000 | .000 |
| P | Ted Abernathy | R | 11 | 0 | 0 | 0 | 0 | 0 | – | 0 | 0 | 0 | 0 | 0 | 0 | 0 | – | – |
| P | Steve Barber | L | 5 | 0 | 0 | 0 | 0 | 0 | – | 0 | 0 | 0 | 0 | 0 | 0 | 0 | – | – |
| P | Jim Cosman | R | 1 | 0 | 0 | 0 | 0 | 0 | – | 0 | 0 | 0 | 0 | 0 | 0 | 0 | – | – |
| P | Bob Miller | R | 7 | 0 | 0 | 0 | 0 | 0 | – | 0 | 0 | 0 | 0 | 0 | 0 | 0 | – | – |
| P | Hoyt Wilhelm | R | 3 | 0 | 0 | 0 | 0 | 0 | – | 0 | 0 | 0 | 0 | 0 | 0 | 0 | – | – |
| TEAM TOTAL | | | | 5491 | 1424 | 228 | 44 | 179 | 3.3 | 80 | 761 | 607 | 844 | 39 | 149 | 24 | .259 | .415 |

## INDIVIDUAL FIELDING

| POS | Player | T | G | PO | A | E | DP | TC/G | FA | POS | Player | T | G | PO | A | E | DP | TC/G | FA |
|---|---|---|---|---|---|---|---|---|---|---|---|---|---|---|---|---|---|---|---|
| 1B | J. Hickman | R | 74 | 563 | 60 | 6 | 46 | 8.5 | .990 | OF | B. Williams | R | 160 | 259 | 13 | 3 | 1 | 1.7 | .989 |
| | E. Banks | R | 62 | 528 | 35 | 4 | 53 | 9.1 | .993 | | J. Callison | R | 144 | 244 | 8 | 7 | 3 | 1.8 | .973 |
| | W. Smith | L | 43 | 318 | 11 | 2 | 32 | 7.7 | .994 | | J. Hickman | R | 79 | 143 | 7 | 4 | 1 | 1.9 | .974 |
| | J. Pepitone | L | 13 | 27 | 2 | 0 | 0 | 2.2 | 1.000 | | J. Pepitone | L | 56 | 121 | 1 | 1 | 0 | 2.2 | .992 |
| | P. Gagliano | R | 1 | 11 | 0 | 0 | 0 | 11.0 | 1.000 | | C. James | R | 90 | 115 | 5 | 0 | 1 | 1.3 | 1.000 |
| | J. Hiatt | R | 2 | 7 | 1 | 0 | 0 | 4.0 | 1.000 | | B. Davis | L | 1 | 0 | 0 | 0 | 0 | 0.0 | .000 |
| | J. Martin | R | 3 | 1 | 1 | 2 | 0 | 1.3 | .500 | | W. Smith | L | 1 | 1 | 0 | 0 | 0 | 1.0 | 1.000 |
| 2B | G. Beckert | R | 138 | 302 | 412 | **22** | 88 | 5.3 | .970 | | T. Hughes | R | 1 | 0 | 0 | 0 | 0 | 0.0 | .000 |
| | P. Popovich | R | 22 | 42 | 58 | 1 | 18 | 4.6 | .990 | | T. Davis | R | 10 | 15 | 0 | 1 | 0 | 1.6 | .938 |
| | P. Gagliano | R | 16 | 14 | 25 | 0 | 2 | 2.4 | 1.000 | | J. Hall | R | 8 | 10 | 0 | 0 | 0 | 1.3 | 1.000 |
| SS | D. Kessinger | R | 154 | 257 | **501** | 22 | 86 | 5.1 | .972 | | B. Day | L | 7 | 6 | 1 | 1 | 0 | 1.1 | .875 |
| | P. Popovich | R | 17 | 24 | 27 | 2 | 7 | 3.1 | .962 | | A. Spangler | L | 6 | 5 | 0 | 0 | 0 | 0.8 | 1.000 |
| | R. Metzger | R | 1 | 1 | 4 | 1 | 1 | 6.0 | .833 | | G. Beckert | R | 1 | 1 | 0 | 0 | 0 | 1.0 | 1.000 |
| 3B | R. Santo | R | 152 | 143 | 320 | 27 | 36 | 3.2 | .945 | | R. Santo | R | 1 | 1 | 0 | 0 | 0 | 1.0 | 1.000 |
| | P. Popovich | R | 16 | 9 | 12 | 1 | 1 | 1.4 | .955 | C | R. Hundley | R | 73 | 455 | 26 | 5 | 2 | 6.7 | .990 |
| | T. Hughes | R | 1 | 0 | 0 | 0 | 0 | 0.0 | .000 | | J. Hiatt | R | 63 | 380 | 22 | 4 | 1 | 6.4 | .990 |
| | P. Gagliano | R | 1 | 0 | 0 | 1 | 0 | 1.0 | .000 | | J. Martin | R | 36 | 163 | 15 | 3 | 2 | 5.0 | .983 |
| | | | | | | | | | | | K. Rudolph | R | 16 | 67 | 6 | 0 | 1 | 4.6 | 1.000 |

There were milestones, but first place might as well have been a millstone around the Cub club's neck. On April 30, Billy Williams became the first National Leaguer to play 1,000 consecutive games. He extended his streak to 1,117 games before benching himself on September 3. And on May 12, Ernie Banks connected for his 500th homer off the Braves' Pat Jarvis in a 4–3 victory. The Cubs again displayed good early foot, leading the division for 64 days through mid-June. Another fall fadeout placed them five behind the Pirates at the wire with an 84–78 record. Williams was the siege gun as the Cubs hit 179 homers, second best in club history. Williams accounted for 42 homers, drove in 129 runs, had 205 hits, a .586 slugging average, 373 total bases, and batted .322. He was ably supported by Jim Hickman's 32 homers and 115 RBI and Ron Santo's 26 homers and 114 RBI. The starting pitchers were also solid with Fergie Jenkins's 22 victories, 274 strikeouts, and 24 complete games. Bill Hands added 18 victories, and Ken Holtzman 17. Their downfall was a soft bullpen. Manager Leo Durocher was reluctant to take out his starters as the Cubs led the majors with 59 complete games. They were way down the list with only 25 saves.

## TEAM STATISTICS

| | W | L | PCT | GB | R | OR | 2B | Batting 3B | HR | BA | SA | SB | E | Fielding DP | FA | CG | B | Pitching SO | ShO | SV | ERA |
|---|---|---|---|---|---|---|---|---|---|---|---|---|---|---|---|---|---|---|---|---|---|
| **EAST** | | | | | | | | | | | | | | | | | | | | | |
| PIT | 89 | 73 | .549 | | 729 | 664 | 235 | **70** | 130 | .270 | .406 | 66 | 137 | **195** | .979 | 36 | 625 | 990 | 13 | 43 | 3.70 |
| CHI | 84 | 78 | .519 | 5 | 806 | 679 | 228 | 44 | 179 | .259 | .415 | 39 | 137 | 146 | .978 | **59** | **475** | 1000 | 9 | 25 | 3.76 |
| NY | 83 | 79 | .512 | 6 | 695 | **630** | 211 | 42 | 120 | .249 | .370 | 118 | 124 | 136 | .979 | 47 | 575 | **1064** | 10 | 32 | **3.46** |
| STL | 76 | 86 | .469 | 13 | 744 | 747 | 218 | 51 | 113 | .263 | .379 | 117 | 150 | 159 | .977 | 51 | 632 | 960 | 11 | 20 | 4.05 |
| PHI | 73 | 88 | .453 | 15.5 | 594 | 730 | 224 | 58 | 101 | .238 | .356 | 72 | **114** | 134 | **.981** | 24 | 538 | 1047 | 8 | 36 | 4.17 |
| MON | 73 | 89 | .451 | 16 | 687 | 807 | 211 | 35 | 136 | .237 | .365 | 65 | 141 | 193 | .977 | 29 | 716 | 914 | 10 | 32 | 4.50 |
| **WEST** | | | | | | | | | | | | | | | | | | | | | |
| CIN | 102 | 60 | .630 | | 775 | 681 | 253 | 45 | **191** | .270 | **.436** | 115 | 151 | 173 | .976 | 32 | 592 | 843 | 15 | **60** | 3.71 |
| LA | 87 | 74 | .540 | 14.5 | 749 | 684 | 233 | 67 | 87 | .270 | .382 | **138** | 135 | 135 | .978 | 37 | 496 | 880 | **17** | 42 | 3.82 |
| SF | 86 | 76 | .531 | 16 | **831** | 826 | **257** | 35 | 165 | .262 | .409 | 83 | 170 | 153 | .973 | 50 | 604 | 931 | 7 | 30 | 4.50 |
| HOU | 79 | 83 | .488 | 23 | 744 | 763 | 250 | 47 | 129 | .259 | .391 | 114 | 140 | 144 | .978 | 36 | 577 | 942 | 6 | 35 | 4.23 |
| ATL | 76 | 86 | .469 | 26 | 736 | 772 | 215 | 24 | 160 | .270 | .404 | 58 | 141 | 118 | .977 | 45 | 478 | 960 | 9 | 24 | 4.35 |
| SD | 63 | 99 | .389 | 39 | 681 | 788 | 208 | 36 | 172 | .246 | .391 | 60 | 158 | 159 | .975 | 24 | 611 | 886 | 9 | 32 | 4.38 |
| LEAGUE TOTAL | | | | | 8771 | 8771 | 2743 | 554 | 1683 | .258 | .392 | 1045 | 1698 | 1845 | .977 | 470 | 6919 | 11417 | 124 | 411 | 4.05 |

## INDIVIDUAL PITCHING

| PITCHER | T | W | L | PCT | ERA | SV | G | GS | CG | IP | H | BB | SO | R | ER | ShO | H/9 | BB/9 | SO/9 |
|---|---|---|---|---|---|---|---|---|---|---|---|---|---|---|---|---|---|---|---|
| Ferguson Jenkins | R | 22 | 16 | .579 | 3.39 | 0 | 40 | 39 | **24** | 313 | 265 | 60 | 274 | 128 | **118** | 3 | 7.62 | **1.73** | 7.88 |
| Ken Holtzman | L | 17 | 11 | .607 | 3.38 | 0 | 39 | 38 | 15 | 288 | 271 | 94 | 202 | 125 | 108 | 1 | 8.47 | 2.94 | 6.31 |
| Bill Hands | R | 18 | 15 | .545 | 3.70 | 1 | 39 | 38 | 12 | 265 | 278 | 76 | 170 | 121 | 109 | 2 | 9.44 | 2.58 | 5.77 |
| Milt Pappas | R | 10 | 8 | .556 | 2.68 | 0 | 21 | 20 | 6 | 144.2 | 135 | 36 | 80 | 53 | 43 | 2 | 8.40 | 2.24 | 4.98 |
| Joe Decker | R | 2 | 7 | .222 | 4.62 | 0 | 24 | 17 | 1 | 109 | 108 | 56 | 79 | 64 | 56 | 0 | 8.92 | 4.62 | 6.52 |
| Phil Regan | R | 5 | 9 | .357 | 4.74 | 12 | 54 | 0 | 0 | 76 | 81 | 32 | 31 | 43 | 40 | 0 | 9.59 | 3.79 | 3.67 |
| Jim Colborn | R | 3 | 1 | .750 | 3.58 | 0 | 34 | 5 | 0 | 73 | 88 | 23 | 50 | 37 | 29 | 0 | 10.85 | 2.84 | 6.16 |
| Roberto Rodriguez | R | 3 | 2 | .600 | 5.82 | 2 | 26 | 0 | 0 | 43.1 | 50 | 15 | 46 | 33 | 28 | 0 | 10.38 | 3.12 | 9.55 |
| Larry Gura | L | 1 | 3 | .250 | 3.79 | 1 | 20 | 3 | 1 | 38 | 35 | 23 | 21 | 18 | 16 | 0 | 8.29 | 5.45 | 4.97 |
| Juan Pizarro | L | 0 | 0 | – | 4.50 | 1 | 12 | 0 | 0 | 16 | 16 | 9 | 14 | 9 | 8 | 0 | 9.00 | 5.06 | 7.88 |
| Archie Reynolds | R | 0 | 2 | .000 | 6.60 | 0 | 7 | 1 | 0 | 15 | 17 | 9 | 9 | 11 | 11 | 0 | 10.20 | 5.40 | 5.40 |
| Hank Aguirre | L | 3 | 0 | 1.000 | 4.50 | 1 | 17 | 0 | 0 | 14 | 13 | 9 | 11 | 10 | 7 | 0 | 8.36 | 5.79 | 7.07 |
| Jim Dunegan | R | 0 | 2 | .000 | 4.85 | 0 | 7 | 0 | 0 | 13 | 13 | 12 | 3 | 7 | 7 | 0 | 9.00 | 8.31 | 2.08 |
| Ted Abernathy | R | 0 | 0 | – | 2.00 | 1 | 11 | 0 | 0 | 9 | 9 | 5 | 2 | 2 | 2 | 0 | 9.00 | 5.00 | 2.00 |
| Bob Miller | R | 0 | 0 | – | 5.00 | 2 | 7 | 1 | 0 | 9 | 6 | 6 | 4 | 5 | 5 | 0 | 6.00 | 6.00 | 4.00 |
| Steve Barber | L | 0 | 1 | .000 | 9.53 | 0 | 5 | 0 | 0 | 5.2 | 10 | 6 | 3 | 6 | 6 | 0 | 15.88 | 9.53 | 4.76 |
| Hoyt Wilhelm | R | 0 | 1 | .000 | 9.82 | 0 | 3 | 0 | 0 | 3.2 | 4 | 3 | 1 | 4 | 4 | 0 | 9.82 | 7.36 | 2.45 |
| Jim Cosman | R | 0 | 0 | – | 27.00 | 0 | 1 | 0 | 0 | 1 | 3 | 1 | 0 | 3 | 3 | 0 | 27.00 | 9.00 | 0.00 |
| TEAM TOTAL | | 84 | 78 | .519 | 3.76 | 25 | 367 | 162 | 59 | 1436.1 | 1402 | 475 | 1000 | 679 | 600 | 8 | 8.78 | 2.98 | 6.27 |

| MANAGER | W | L | PCT |
|---|---|---|---|
| Leo Durocher | 83 | 79 | .512 |

| POS | Player | B | G | AB | H | 2B | 3B | HR | HR % | R | RBI | BB | SO | SB | Pinch Hit AB | Pinch Hit H | BA | SA |
|---|---|---|---|---|---|---|---|---|---|---|---|---|---|---|---|---|---|---|
| **REGULARS** | | | | | | | | | | | | | | | | | | |
| 1B | Joe Pepitone | L | 115 | 427 | 131 | 19 | 4 | 16 | 3.7 | 50 | 61 | 24 | 41 | 1 | 2 | 1 | .307 | .482 |
| 2B | Glenn Beckert | R | 131 | 530 | 181 | 18 | 5 | 2 | 0.4 | 80 | 42 | 24 | 24 | 3 | 2 | 1 | .342 | .406 |
| SS | Don Kessinger | B | 155 | 617 | 159 | 18 | 6 | 2 | 0.3 | 77 | 38 | 52 | 54 | 15 | 2 | 0 | .258 | .316 |
| 3B | Ron Santo | R | 154 | 555 | 148 | 22 | 1 | 21 | 3.8 | 77 | 88 | 79 | 95 | 4 | 1 | 0 | .267 | .423 |
| RF | Johnny Callison | L | 103 | 290 | 61 | 12 | 1 | 8 | 2.8 | 27 | 38 | 36 | 55 | 2 | 14 | 1 | .210 | .341 |
| CF | Brock Davis | L | 106 | 301 | 77 | 7 | 5 | 0 | 0.0 | 22 | 28 | 35 | 34 | 0 | 10 | 1 | .256 | .312 |
| LF | Billy Williams | L | 157 | 594 | 179 | 27 | 5 | 28 | 4.7 | 86 | 93 | 77 | 44 | 7 | 5 | 1 | .301 | .505 |
| C | Chris Cannizzaro | R | 71 | 197 | 42 | 8 | 1 | 5 | 2.5 | 18 | 23 | 28 | 24 | 0 | 0 | 0 | .213 | .340 |
| **SUBSTITUTES** | | | | | | | | | | | | | | | | | | |
| 23 | Paul Popovich | R | 89 | 226 | 49 | 7 | 1 | 4 | 1.8 | 24 | 28 | 14 | 17 | 0 | 30 | 2 | .217 | .310 |
| 1B | Ernie Banks | R | 39 | 83 | 16 | 2 | 0 | 3 | 3.6 | 4 | 6 | 6 | 14 | 0 | 18 | 2 | .193 | .325 |
| SS | Hector Torres | R | 31 | 58 | 13 | 3 | 0 | 0 | 0.0 | 4 | 2 | 4 | 10 | 0 | 4 | 1 | .224 | .276 |
| 1B | Pat Bourque | L | 14 | 37 | 7 | 0 | 1 | 1 | 2.7 | 3 | 3 | 3 | 9 | 0 | 3 | 1 | .189 | .324 |
| 1B | Hal Breeden | R | 23 | 36 | 5 | 1 | 0 | 1 | 2.8 | 1 | 2 | 2 | 7 | 0 | 14 | 0 | .139 | .250 |
| 1B | Ramon Webster | L | 16 | 16 | 5 | 2 | 0 | 0 | 0.0 | 1 | 0 | 1 | 3 | 0 | 14 | 3 | .313 | .438 |
| 3B | Garry Jestadt | R | 3 | 3 | 0 | 0 | 0 | 0 | 0.0 | 0 | 0 | 0 | 0 | 0 | 2 | 0 | .000 | .000 |
| O1 | Jim Hickman | R | 117 | 383 | 98 | 13 | 2 | 19 | 5.0 | 50 | 60 | 50 | 61 | 0 | 12 | 2 | .256 | .449 |
| OF | Cleo James | R | 54 | 150 | 43 | 7 | 0 | 2 | 1.3 | 25 | 13 | 10 | 16 | 6 | 3 | 1 | .287 | .373 |
| OF | Jose Ortiz | R | 36 | 88 | 26 | 7 | 1 | 0 | 0.0 | 10 | 3 | 4 | 10 | 2 | 1 | 0 | .295 | .398 |
| UT | Carmen Fanzone | R | 12 | 43 | 8 | 2 | 0 | 2 | 4.7 | 5 | 5 | 2 | 7 | 0 | 2 | 1 | .186 | .372 |
| OF | Gene Hiser | L | 17 | 29 | 6 | 0 | 0 | 0 | 0.0 | 4 | 1 | 4 | 8 | 1 | 5 | 1 | .207 | .207 |
| OF | Billy North | B | 8 | 16 | 6 | 0 | 0 | 0 | 0.0 | 3 | 0 | 4 | 6 | 1 | 0 | 0 | .375 | .375 |
| C | J. C. Martin | L | 47 | 125 | 33 | 5 | 0 | 2 | 1.6 | 13 | 17 | 12 | 16 | 1 | 5 | 0 | .264 | .352 |
| C | Ken Rudolph | R | 25 | 76 | 15 | 3 | 0 | 0 | 0.0 | 5 | 7 | 6 | 20 | 0 | 1 | 0 | .197 | .237 |
| C | Danny Breeden | R | 25 | 65 | 10 | 1 | 0 | 0 | 0.0 | 3 | 4 | 9 | 18 | 0 | 0 | 0 | .154 | .169 |
| C | Frank Fernandez | R | 17 | 41 | 7 | 1 | 0 | 4 | 9.8 | 11 | 4 | 17 | 15 | 0 | 2 | 0 | .171 | .488 |
| C | Randy Hundley | R | 9 | 21 | 7 | 1 | 0 | 0 | 0.0 | 1 | 2 | 0 | 2 | 0 | 1 | 0 | .333 | .381 |
| PH | Al Spangler | L | 5 | 5 | 2 | 0 | 0 | 0 | 0.0 | 0 | 0 | 0 | 1 | 0 | 5 | 2 | .400 | .400 |
| **PITCHERS** | | | | | | | | | | | | | | | | | | |
| P | Ferguson Jenkins | R | 39 | 115 | 28 | 7 | 1 | 6 | 5.2 | 13 | 20 | 7 | 40 | 0 | 0 | 0 | .243 | .478 |
| P | Milt Pappas | R | 35 | 91 | 14 | 2 | 0 | 0 | 0.0 | 6 | 2 | 4 | 30 | 1 | 0 | 0 | .154 | .176 |
| P | Bill Hands | R | 36 | 72 | 6 | 3 | 0 | 0 | 0.0 | 3 | 6 | 6 | 42 | 0 | 0 | 0 | .083 | .125 |
| P | Ken Holtzman | R | 30 | 69 | 9 | 2 | 0 | 1 | 1.4 | 4 | 5 | 3 | 15 | 0 | 0 | 0 | .130 | .203 |
| P | Juan Pizarro | L | 16 | 34 | 6 | 1 | 0 | 1 | 2.9 | 3 | 2 | 2 | 11 | 0 | 0 | 0 | .176 | .294 |
| P | Bill Bonham | R | 33 | 12 | 2 | 0 | 0 | 0 | 0.0 | 2 | 0 | 0 | 4 | 0 | 0 | 0 | .167 | .167 |
| P | Phil Regan | R | 48 | 8 | 0 | 0 | 0 | 0 | 0.0 | 0 | 0 | 0 | 3 | 0 | 0 | 0 | .000 | .000 |
| P | Joe Decker | R | 22 | 8 | 2 | 1 | 0 | 0 | 0.0 | 1 | 0 | 1 | 5 | 0 | 0 | 0 | .250 | .375 |
| P | Burt Hooton | R | 3 | 7 | 0 | 0 | 0 | 0 | 0.0 | 0 | 0 | 1 | 6 | 0 | 0 | 0 | .000 | .000 |
| P | Ray Newman | L | 30 | 6 | 0 | 0 | 0 | 0 | 0.0 | 0 | 0 | 1 | 3 | 0 | 0 | 0 | .000 | .000 |
| P | Earl Stephenson | L | 16 | 2 | 0 | 0 | 0 | 0 | 0.0 | 0 | 0 | 0 | 2 | 0 | 0 | 0 | .000 | .000 |
| P | Bob Miller | R | 2 | 1 | 0 | 0 | 0 | 0 | 0.0 | 0 | 0 | 0 | 0 | 0 | 0 | 0 | .000 | .000 |
| P | Larry Gura | L | 6 | 1 | 0 | 0 | 0 | 0 | 0.0 | 0 | 0 | 0 | 0 | 0 | 0 | 0 | .000 | .000 |
| P | Ron Tompkins | R | 35 | 0 | 0 | 0 | 0 | 0 | – | 0 | 0 | 0 | 0 | 0 | 0 | 0 | – | – |
| P | Jim Colborn | R | 14 | 0 | 0 | 0 | 0 | 0 | – | 0 | 0 | 0 | 0 | 0 | 0 | 0 | – | – |
| TEAM TOTAL | | | | 5438 | 1401 | 202 | 34 | 128 | 2.4 | 63 | 603 | 527 | 772 | 44 | 157 | 21 | .258 | .378 |

## INDIVIDUAL FIELDING

| POS | Player | T | G | PO | A | E | DP | TC/G | FA | POS | Player | T | G | PO | A | E | DP | TC/G | FA |
|---|---|---|---|---|---|---|---|---|---|---|---|---|---|---|---|---|---|---|---|
| 1B | J. Pepitone | L | 95 | 872 | 64 | 9 | 75 | 9.9 | .990 | OF | B. Williams | R | 154 | 284 | 8 | 7 | 3 | 1.9 | .977 |
| | J. Hickman | R | 44 | 364 | 31 | 1 | 28 | 9.0 | .997 | | B. Davis | L | 93 | 213 | 5 | 4 | 1 | 2.4 | .982 |
| | E. Banks | R | 20 | 167 | 12 | 0 | 15 | 9.0 | 1.000 | | J. Callison | R | 89 | 158 | 3 | 3 | 0 | 1.8 | .982 |
| | P. Bourque | L | 11 | 75 | 13 | 4 | 6 | 8.4 | .957 | | J. Hickman | R | 69 | 106 | 3 | 2 | 0 | 1.6 | .982 |
| | H. Breeden | L | 8 | 48 | 7 | 1 | 2 | 7.0 | .982 | | C. James | R | 48 | 89 | 4 | 2 | 2 | 2.0 | .979 |
| | C. Fanzone | R | 2 | 11 | 1 | 0 | 2 | 6.0 | 1.000 | | J. Ortiz | R | 20 | 53 | 1 | 0 | 1 | 2.7 | 1.000 |
| | R. Webster | L | 1 | 2 | 1 | 0 | 1 | 3.0 | 1.000 | | J. Pepitone | L | 23 | 32 | 0 | 1 | 0 | 1.4 | .970 |
| | | | | | | | | | | | J. Martin | R | 1 | 0 | 0 | 0 | 0 | 0.0 | .000 |
| 2B | G. Beckert | R | 129 | 275 | 382 | 9 | 76 | 5.2 | .986 | | G. Hiser | L | 9 | 19 | 0 | 0 | 0 | 2.1 | 1.000 |
| | P. Popovich | R | 40 | 74 | 119 | 3 | 26 | 4.9 | *.985 | | R. Santo | R | 6 | 10 | 1 | 1 | 0 | 2.0 | .917 |
| | H. Torres | R | 4 | 1 | 5 | 1 | 1 | 1.8 | .857 | | C. Fanzone | R | 6 | 9 | 0 | 0 | 0 | 1.5 | 1.000 |
| | | | | | | | | | | | B. North | R | 6 | 4 | 0 | 0 | 0 | 0.7 | 1.000 |
| SS | D. Kessinger | R | 154 | 263 | 512 | 27 | 97 | 5.2 | .966 | | | | | | | | | | |
| | H. Torres | R | 18 | 11 | 40 | 2 | 6 | 2.9 | .962 | C | Cannizzaro | R | 70 | 311 | 26 | 6 | 2 | 4.9 | .983 |
| | P. Popovich | R | 1 | 0 | 0 | 0 | 0 | 0.0 | .000 | | J. Martin | R | 43 | 218 | 21 | 1 | 2 | 5.6 | .996 |
| | | | | | | | | | | | K. Rudolph | R | 25 | 153 | 16 | 0 | 1 | 6.8 | 1.000 |
| 3B | R. Santo | R | 149 | 118 | 274 | 17 | 29 | 2.7 | .958 | | D. Breeden | R | 25 | 150 | 7 | 4 | 0 | 6.4 | .975 |
| | P. Popovich | R | 16 | 4 | 27 | 1 | 1 | 2.0 | .969 | | F. Fernandez | R | 16 | 91 | 6 | 2 | 0 | 6.2 | .980 |
| | G. Jestadt | R | 1 | 0 | 0 | 0 | 0 | 0.0 | .000 | | R. Hundley | R | 8 | 43 | 3 | 1 | 0 | 5.9 | .979 |
| | C. Fanzone | R | 3 | 2 | 8 | 2 | 0 | 4.0 | .833 | | | | | | | | | | |
| | C. James | R | 2 | 1 | 1 | 0 | 0 | 1.0 | 1.000 | | | | | | | | | | |

This was the summer of discontent between manager Leo Durocher and his veteran players. Although it was smoldering throughout much of the season, it reached its peak following an August 23 meeting in which the players aired their grievances. That prompted owner P. K. Wrigley to take out a full-page ad in all the newspapers, defending his manager and telling the "Dump Durocher Clique" to give up. The ad didn't help. The Cubs lost 9 of their next 11 and dropped out of sight. With all their squandering of talent, the Cubs shared third with the Mets at 83–79, 14 games behind the Pirates.

Perhaps the Cubs' downfall was Durocher's lack of confidence in his bullpen, which picked up only 13 saves, lowest in the majors. His starters had to go the route 75 times, high in the majors. Fergie Jenkins wasted a superb season, leading the NL with 24 victories, 30 complete games, and 325 innings pitched and was second to the Mets' Tom Seaver with 263 strikeouts. In addition, Fergie flogged six homers. Ken Holtzman hurled his second no-hitter, beating the Reds 1–0 on June 3, but was 9–15 for the season. Second baseman Glenn Beckert led the hit parade with a lofty .342. Billy Williams, who batted .301, was high with 28 homers and 93 RBI.

## TEAM STATISTICS

| | W | L | PCT | GB | R | OR | 2B | Batting 3B | HR | BA | SA | SB | E | Fielding DP | FA | CG | B | Pitching SO | ShO | SV | ERA |
|---|---|---|---|---|---|---|---|---|---|---|---|---|---|---|---|---|---|---|---|---|---|
| **EAST** | | | | | | | | | | | | | | | | | | | | | |
| PIT | 97 | 65 | .599 | | 788 | 599 | 223 | 61 | 154 | .274 | .416 | 65 | 133 | 164 | .979 | 43 | 470 | 813 | 15 | 48 | 3.31 |
| STL | 90 | 72 | .556 | 7 | 739 | 699 | 225 | 54 | 95 | .275 | .385 | 124 | 142 | 155 | .978 | 56 | 576 | 911 | 14 | 22 | 3.87 |
| CHI | 83 | 79 | .512 | 14 | 637 | 648 | 202 | 34 | 128 | .258 | .378 | 44 | 126 | 150 | .980 | 75 | 411 | 900 | 17 | 13 | 3.61 |
| NY | 83 | 79 | .512 | 14 | 588 | 550 | 203 | 29 | 98 | .249 | .351 | 89 | 114 | 135 | .981 | 42 | 529 | 1157 | 13 | 22 | 3.00 |
| MON | 71 | 90 | .441 | 25.5 | 622 | 729 | 197 | 29 | 88 | .246 | .343 | 51 | 150 | 164 | .976 | 49 | 658 | 829 | 8 | 25 | 4.12 |
| PHI | 67 | 95 | .414 | 30 | 558 | 688 | 209 | 35 | 123 | .233 | .350 | 63 | 122 | 158 | .981 | 31 | 525 | 838 | 10 | 25 | 3.71 |
| **WEST** | | | | | | | | | | | | | | | | | | | | | |
| SF | 90 | 72 | .556 | | 706 | 644 | 224 | 36 | 140 | .247 | .378 | 101 | 179 | 153 | .972 | 45 | 471 | 831 | 14 | 30 | 3.33 |
| LA | 89 | 73 | .549 | 1 | 663 | 587 | 213 | 38 | 95 | .266 | .370 | 76 | 131 | 159 | .979 | 48 | 399 | 853 | 18 | 33 | 3.23 |
| ATL | 82 | 80 | .506 | 8 | 643 | 699 | 192 | 30 | 153 | .257 | .385 | 57 | 146 | 180 | .977 | 40 | 485 | 823 | 11 | 31 | 3.75 |
| CIN | 79 | 83 | .488 | 11 | 586 | 581 | 203 | 28 | 138 | .241 | .366 | 59 | 103 | 174 | .984 | 27 | 501 | 750 | 11 | 38 | 3.35 |
| HOU | 79 | 83 | .488 | 11 | 585 | 567 | 230 | 52 | 71 | .240 | .340 | 101 | 106 | 152 | .983 | 43 | 475 | 914 | 10 | 25 | 3.13 |
| SD | 61 | 100 | .379 | 28.5 | 486 | 610 | 184 | 31 | 96 | .233 | .332 | 70 | 161 | 144 | .974 | 47 | 559 | 923 | 10 | 17 | 3.23 |
| LEAGUE TOTAL | | | | | 7601 | 7601 | 2505 | 457 | 1379 | .252 | .366 | 900 | 1613 | 1888 | .979 | 546 | 6059 | 10542 | 151 | 329 | 3.47 |

## INDIVIDUAL   PITCHING

| PITCHER | T | W | L | PCT | ERA | SV | G | GS | CG | IP | H | BB | SO | R | ER | ShO | H/9 | BB/9 | SO/9 |
|---|---|---|---|---|---|---|---|---|---|---|---|---|---|---|---|---|---|---|---|
| Ferguson Jenkins | R | 24 | 13 | .649 | 2.77 | 0 | 39 | 39 | 30 | 325 | 304 | 37 | 263 | 114 | 100 | 3 | 8.42 | 1.02 | 7.28 |
| Milt Pappas | R | 17 | 14 | .548 | 3.52 | 0 | 35 | 35 | 14 | 261 | 279 | 62 | 99 | 109 | 102 | 5 | 9.62 | 2.14 | 3.41 |
| Bill Hands | R | 12 | 18 | .400 | 3.42 | 0 | 36 | 35 | 14 | 242 | 248 | 50 | 128 | 112 | 92 | 1 | 9.22 | 1.86 | 4.76 |
| Ken Holtzman | L | 9 | 15 | .375 | 4.48 | 0 | 30 | 29 | 9 | 195 | 213 | 64 | 143 | 108 | 97 | 3 | 9.83 | 2.95 | 6.60 |
| Juan Pizarro | L | 7 | 6 | .538 | 3.48 | 0 | 16 | 14 | 6 | 101 | 78 | 40 | 67 | 43 | 39 | 3 | 6.95 | 3.56 | 5.97 |
| Phil Regan | R | 5 | 5 | .500 | 3.95 | 6 | 48 | 1 | 0 | 73 | 84 | 33 | 28 | 37 | 32 | 0 | 10.36 | 4.07 | 3.45 |
| Bill Bonham | R | 2 | 1 | .667 | 4.65 | 0 | 33 | 2 | 0 | 60 | 63 | 36 | 41 | 38 | 31 | 0 | 9.45 | 5.40 | 6.15 |
| Joe Decker | R | 3 | 2 | .600 | 4.70 | 0 | 21 | 4 | 0 | 46 | 62 | 25 | 37 | 24 | 24 | 0 | 12.13 | 4.89 | 7.24 |
| Ron Tompkins | R | 0 | 2 | .000 | 4.05 | 3 | 35 | 0 | 0 | 40 | 31 | 21 | 20 | 18 | 18 | 0 | 6.98 | 4.73 | 4.50 |
| Ray Newman | L | 1 | 2 | .333 | 3.55 | 2 | 30 | 0 | 0 | 38 | 30 | 17 | 35 | 15 | 15 | 0 | 7.11 | 4.03 | 8.29 |
| Burt Hooton | R | 2 | 0 | 1.000 | 2.14 | 0 | 3 | 3 | 2 | 21 | 8 | 10 | 22 | 5 | 5 | 1 | 3.43 | 4.29 | 9.43 |
| Earl Stephenson | L | 1 | 0 | 1.000 | 4.50 | 1 | 16 | 0 | 0 | 20 | 24 | 11 | 11 | 10 | 10 | 0 | 10.80 | 4.95 | 4.95 |
| Jim Colborn | R | 0 | 1 | .000 | 7.20 | 0 | 14 | 0 | 0 | 10 | 18 | 3 | 2 | 8 | 8 | 0 | 16.20 | 2.70 | 1.80 |
| Bob Miller | R | 0 | 0 | — | 5.14 | 0 | 2 | 0 | 0 | 7 | 10 | 1 | 2 | 4 | 4 | 0 | 12.86 | 1.29 | 2.57 |
| Larry Gura | L | 0 | 0 | — | 6.00 | 1 | 6 | 0 | 0 | 3 | 6 | 1 | 2 | 3 | 2 | 0 | 18.00 | 3.00 | 6.00 |
| TEAM TOTAL | | 83 | 79 | .512 | 3.61 | 13 | 364 | 162 | 75 | 1442 | 1458 | 411 | 900 | 648 | 579 | 16 | 9.10 | 2.57 | 5.62 |

| MANAGER | W | L | PCT |
|---|---|---|---|
| Leo Durocher | 46 | 44 | .511 |
| Whitey Lockman | 39 | 26 | .600 |

| POS | Player | B | G | AB | H | 2B | 3B | HR | HR % | R | RBI | BB | SO | SB | Pinch Hit AB | Pinch Hit H | BA | SA |
|---|---|---|---|---|---|---|---|---|---|---|---|---|---|---|---|---|---|---|
| **REGULARS** | | | | | | | | | | | | | | | | | | |
| 1B | Jim Hickman | R | 115 | 368 | 100 | 15 | 2 | 17 | 4.6 | 65 | 64 | 52 | 64 | 3 | 13 | 3 | .272 | .462 |
| 2B | Glenn Beckert | R | 120 | 474 | 128 | 22 | 2 | 3 | 0.6 | 51 | 43 | 23 | 17 | 2 | 2 | 1 | .270 | .344 |
| SS | Don Kessinger | B | 149 | 577 | 158 | 20 | 6 | 1 | 0.2 | 77 | 39 | 67 | 44 | 8 | 3 | 0 | .274 | .334 |
| 3B | Ron Santo | R | 133 | 464 | 140 | 25 | 5 | 17 | 3.7 | 68 | 74 | 69 | 75 | 1 | 1 | 1 | .302 | .487 |
| RF | Jose Cardenal | R | 143 | 533 | 155 | 24 | 6 | 17 | 3.2 | 96 | 70 | 55 | 58 | 25 | 5 | 2 | .291 | .454 |
| CF | Rick Monday | L | 138 | 434 | 108 | 22 | 5 | 11 | 2.5 | 68 | 42 | 78 | 102 | 12 | 3 | 0 | .249 | .399 |
| LF | Billy Williams | L | 150 | 574 | 191 | 34 | 6 | 37 | 6.4 | 95 | 122 | 62 | 59 | 3 | 2 | 1 | **.333** | **.606** |
| C | Randy Hundley | R | 114 | 357 | 78 | 12 | 0 | 5 | 1.4 | 23 | 30 | 22 | 62 | 1 | 2 | 1 | .218 | .294 |
| **SUBSTITUTES** | | | | | | | | | | | | | | | | | | |
| UT | Carmen Fanzone | R | 86 | 222 | 50 | 11 | 0 | 8 | 3.6 | 26 | 42 | 35 | 45 | 2 | 15 | 4 | .225 | .383 |
| 1B | Joe Pepitone | L | 66 | 214 | 56 | 5 | 0 | 8 | 3.7 | 23 | 21 | 13 | 22 | 1 | 5 | 1 | .262 | .397 |
| 2B | Paul Popovich | R | 58 | 129 | 25 | 3 | 2 | 1 | 0.8 | 8 | 11 | 12 | 8 | 0 | 12 | 2 | .194 | .271 |
| 1B | Pat Bourque | L | 11 | 27 | 7 | 1 | 0 | 0 | 0.0 | 3 | 5 | 2 | 2 | 0 | 4 | 0 | .259 | .296 |
| 1O | Tommy Davis | R | 15 | 26 | 7 | 1 | 0 | 0 | 0.0 | 3 | 6 | 2 | 3 | 0 | 9 | 1 | .269 | .308 |
| 1B | Art Shamsky | L | 15 | 16 | 2 | 0 | 0 | 0 | 0.0 | 1 | 1 | 3 | 3 | 0 | 8 | 2 | .125 | .125 |
| SS | Dave Rosello | R | 5 | 12 | 3 | 0 | 0 | 1 | 8.3 | 2 | 3 | 3 | 2 | 0 | 0 | 0 | .250 | .500 |
| 2B | Allan Montreuil | R | 5 | 11 | 1 | 0 | 0 | 0 | 0.0 | 0 | 0 | 1 | 4 | 0 | 0 | 0 | .091 | .091 |
| OF | Billy North | B | 66 | 127 | 23 | 2 | 3 | 0 | 0.0 | 22 | 4 | 13 | 33 | 6 | 13 | 3 | .181 | .244 |
| OF | Gene Hiser | L | 32 | 46 | 9 | 0 | 0 | 0 | 0.0 | 2 | 4 | 6 | 8 | 1 | 11 | 1 | .196 | .196 |
| OF | Jim Tyrone | R | 13 | 8 | 0 | 0 | 0 | 0 | 0.0 | 1 | 0 | 0 | 3 | 1 | 3 | 0 | .000 | .000 |
| OF | Pete LaCock | L | 5 | 6 | 3 | 0 | 0 | 0 | 0.0 | 3 | 4 | 0 | 1 | 1 | 1 | 1 | .500 | .500 |
| C | Ken Rudolph | R | 42 | 106 | 25 | 1 | 1 | 2 | 1.9 | 10 | 9 | 6 | 14 | 1 | 1 | 0 | .236 | .321 |
| C | J. C. Martin | L | 25 | 50 | 12 | 3 | 0 | 0 | 0.0 | 3 | 7 | 5 | 9 | 1 | 9 | 2 | .240 | .300 |
| C | Ellie Hendricks | L | 17 | 43 | 5 | 1 | 0 | 2 | 4.7 | 7 | 6 | 13 | 8 | 0 | 0 | 0 | .116 | .279 |
| C | Frank Fernandez | R | 3 | 3 | 0 | 0 | 0 | 0 | 0.0 | 0 | 0 | 0 | 2 | 0 | 2 | 0 | .000 | .000 |
| PH | Frank Coggins | B | 6 | 1 | 0 | 0 | 0 | 0 | 0.0 | 0 | 1 | 1 | 0 | 0 | 1 | 0 | .000 | .000 |
| PH | Chris Ward | L | 1 | 1 | 0 | 0 | 0 | 0 | 0.0 | 0 | 0 | 0 | 0 | 0 | 1 | 0 | .000 | .000 |
| **PITCHERS** | | | | | | | | | | | | | | | | | | |
| P | Ferguson Jenkins | R | 36 | 109 | 20 | 1 | 1 | 1 | 0.9 | 8 | 8 | 5 | 34 | 0 | 0 | 0 | .183 | .239 |
| P | Burt Hooton | R | 33 | 72 | 9 | 1 | 0 | 1 | 1.4 | 4 | 6 | 4 | 37 | 0 | 0 | 0 | .125 | .181 |
| P | Milt Pappas | R | 29 | 68 | 13 | 1 | 0 | 1 | 1.5 | 5 | 8 | 2 | 33 | 0 | 0 | 0 | .191 | .250 |
| P | Bill Hands | R | 32 | 57 | 1 | 0 | 0 | 0 | 0.0 | 1 | 0 | 5 | 30 | 0 | 0 | 0 | .018 | .018 |
| P | Rick Reuschel | R | 21 | 44 | 6 | 1 | 0 | 0 | 0.0 | 3 | 3 | 2 | 15 | 0 | 0 | 0 | .136 | .159 |
| P | Juan Pizarro | L | 16 | 21 | 3 | 0 | 0 | 0 | 0.0 | 2 | 0 | 1 | 3 | 0 | 0 | 0 | .143 | .143 |
| P | Tom Phoebus | R | 37 | 15 | 2 | 0 | 0 | 0 | 0.0 | 0 | 0 | 0 | 6 | 0 | 0 | 0 | .133 | .133 |
| P | Bill Bonham | R | 19 | 14 | 4 | 0 | 0 | 0 | 0.0 | 3 | 1 | 2 | 3 | 0 | 0 | 0 | .286 | .286 |
| P | Dan McGinn | L | 43 | 8 | 2 | 0 | 1 | 0 | 0.0 | 0 | 1 | 0 | 1 | 0 | 0 | 0 | .250 | .500 |
| P | Jack Aker | R | 48 | 6 | 0 | 0 | 0 | 0 | 0.0 | 0 | 0 | 1 | 3 | 0 | 0 | 0 | .000 | .000 |
| P | Joe Decker | R | 5 | 2 | 0 | 0 | 0 | 0 | 0.0 | 1 | 0 | 0 | 0 | 0 | 0 | 0 | .000 | .000 |
| P | Steve Hamilton | L | 22 | 1 | 0 | 0 | 0 | 0 | 0.0 | 0 | 0 | 0 | 1 | 0 | 0 | 0 | .000 | .000 |
| P | Larry Gura | L | 7 | 1 | 0 | 0 | 0 | 0 | 0.0 | 0 | 0 | 0 | 1 | 0 | 0 | 0 | .000 | .000 |
| P | Phil Regan | R | 5 | 0 | 0 | 0 | 0 | 0 | – | 0 | 0 | 0 | 0 | 0 | 0 | 0 | – | – |
| P | Clint Compton | L | 1 | 0 | 0 | 0 | 0 | 0 | – | 0 | 0 | 0 | 0 | 0 | 0 | 0 | – | – |
| | TEAM TOTAL | | | 5247 | 1346 | 206 | 40 | 133 | 2.5 | 68 | 634 | 565 | 815 | 69 | 126 | 26 | .257 | .387 |

## INDIVIDUAL  FIELDING

| POS | Player | T | G | PO | A | E | DP | TC/G | FA | POS | Player | T | G | PO | A | E | DP | TC/G | FA |
|---|---|---|---|---|---|---|---|---|---|---|---|---|---|---|---|---|---|---|---|
| 1B | J. Hickman | R | 77 | 670 | 70 | 6 | 61 | 9.7 | .992 | OF | R. Monday | L | 134 | 268 | 6 | 1 | 2 | 2.1 | **.996** |
| | J. Pepitone | L | 66 | 552 | 31 | 2 | 51 | 8.9 | .997 | | B. Williams | R | 144 | 233 | 9 | 4 | 0 | 1.7 | .984 |
| | C. Fanzone | R | 21 | 187 | 5 | 1 | 12 | 9.2 | .995 | | J. Cardenal | R | 137 | 223 | 11 | 7 | 1 | 1.8 | .971 |
| | P. Bourque | L | 7 | 57 | 6 | 0 | 8 | 9.0 | 1.000 | | B. North | R | 48 | 61 | 3 | 3 | 1 | 1.4 | .955 |
| | B. Williams | R | 5 | 42 | 4 | 0 | 5 | 9.2 | 1.000 | | J. Hickman | R | 27 | 38 | 0 | 0 | 0 | 1.4 | 1.000 |
| | A. Shamsky | L | 4 | 30 | 1 | 0 | 1 | 7.8 | 1.000 | | G. Hiser | L | 15 | 21 | 2 | 0 | 1 | 1.5 | 1.000 |
| | T. Davis | R | 3 | 27 | 1 | 0 | 0 | 9.3 | 1.000 | | J. Tyrone | R | 4 | 6 | 1 | 0 | 0 | 1.8 | 1.000 |
| 2B | G. Beckert | R | 118 | 256 | 396 | 16 | 71 | 5.7 | .976 | | T. Davis | R | 2 | 4 | 0 | 1 | 0 | 2.5 | .800 |
| | P. Popovich | R | 36 | 59 | 98 | 3 | 22 | 4.4 | .981 | | P. LaCock | L | 3 | 2 | 0 | 0 | 0 | 0.7 | 1.000 |
| | C. Fanzone | R | 13 | 26 | 43 | 0 | 2 | 5.3 | 1.000 | | R. Santo | R | 1 | 1 | 0 | 0 | 0 | 1.0 | 1.000 |
| | R. Santo | R | 3 | 9 | 8 | 1 | 4 | 6.0 | .944 | | C. Fanzone | R | 1 | 1 | 0 | 0 | 0 | 1.0 | 1.000 |
| | A. Montreuil | R | 5 | 8 | 8 | 0 | 1 | 3.2 | 1.000 | | | | | | | | | | |
| SS | D. Kessinger | R | 146 | 259 | 504 | 28 | 90 | 5.4 | .965 | C | R. Hundley | R | 113 | 569 | 53 | 3 | 7 | 5.5 | **.995** |
| | C. Fanzone | R | 1 | 0 | 0 | 0 | 0 | 0.0 | .000 | | K. Rudolph | R | 41 | 178 | 23 | 7 | 2 | 5.1 | .966 |
| | P. Popovich | R | 8 | 18 | 29 | 1 | 8 | 6.0 | .979 | | E. Hendricks | R | 16 | 83 | 7 | 2 | 0 | 5.8 | .978 |
| | D. Rosello | R | 5 | 11 | 11 | 4 | 4 | 5.2 | .846 | | J. Martin | R | 17 | 60 | 4 | 2 | 1 | 3.9 | .970 |
| | R. Santo | R | 1 | 1 | 0 | 0 | 0 | 1.0 | 1.000 | | F. Fernandez | R | 1 | 1 | 0 | 0 | 0 | 1.0 | 1.000 |
| 3B | R. Santo | R | 129 | 108 | 274 | 21 | 19 | 3.1 | .948 | | | | | | | | | | |
| | C. Fanzone | R | 36 | 29 | 67 | 8 | 7 | 2.9 | .923 | | | | | | | | | | |
| | P. Popovich | R | 1 | 0 | 0 | 0 | 0 | 0.0 | .000 | | | | | | | | | | |

No-hitters by Burt Hooton and Milt Pappas. A batting title for Billy Williams. Another 20-win season for Fergie Jenkins. But the big news was the departure of Leo Durocher as manager. Was he fired, or did he resign? It didn't matter. Friction between Durocher and his players came to an end on July 24 when he was replaced by Whitey Lockman. The Cubs started slowly under Durocher, losing 9 of 11, including 8 in a row. They were barely above .500 with a 46–44 mark when Leo stepped aside. The Cubs rallied under Lockman with a 39–26 record, but finished 11 games out. The Cubs were never a factor and finished second to the Pirates with an 85–70 record. Williams led the NL in batting (.333), slugging (.606), and total bases (348) and hit 37 homers with 122 RBI in his finest season. Jenkins tied Cub immortals Clark Griffith and Mordecai Brown with his sixth 20-win season in a row, finishing at 20–12. Fergie, however, was overshadowed by Pappas, who reached the 200-victory plateau, won 11 in a row for a 17–7 mark, and came within one pitch of a perfect game on September 2 at Wrigley Field when umpire Bruce Froemming called a marginal pitch ball four on Padres' pinch-hitter Larry Stahl. Rookie Hooton, making his fourth career start and first of the season on April 16, no-hit the Phillies, 4–0, at frigid Wrigley Field. Hooton (11–14) joined another newcomer in the pitching rotation, the hefty Rick Reuschel, who showed promise with a 10–8 record.

## TEAM  STATISTICS

| | W | L | PCT | GB | R | OR | Batting 2B | 3B | HR | BA | SA | SB | Fielding E | DP | FA | CG | B | Pitching SO | ShO | SV | ERA |
|---|---|---|---|---|---|---|---|---|---|---|---|---|---|---|---|---|---|---|---|---|---|
| **EAST** | | | | | | | | | | | | | | | | | | | | | |
| PIT | 96 | 59 | .619 | | 691 | 512 | 251 | 47 | 110 | .274 | .397 | 49 | 136 | 171 | .978 | 39 | 433 | 838 | 15 | 48 | 2.81 |
| CHI | 85 | 70 | .548 | 11 | 685 | 567 | 206 | 40 | 133 | .257 | .387 | 69 | 132 | 148 | .979 | 54 | 421 | 824 | 19 | 32 | 3.22 |
| NY | 83 | 73 | .532 | 13.5 | 528 | 578 | 175 | 31 | 105 | .225 | .332 | 41 | 116 | 122 | .980 | 32 | 486 | 1059 | 12 | 41 | 3.27 |
| STL | 75 | 81 | .481 | 21.5 | 568 | 600 | 214 | 42 | 70 | .260 | .355 | 104 | 141 | 146 | .977 | 64 | 531 | 912 | 13 | 13 | 3.42 |
| MON | 70 | 86 | .449 | 26.5 | 513 | 609 | 156 | 22 | 91 | .234 | .325 | 68 | 134 | 141 | .978 | 39 | 579 | 888 | 11 | 23 | 3.60 |
| PHI | 59 | 97 | .378 | 37.5 | 503 | 635 | 200 | 36 | 98 | .236 | .344 | 42 | 116 | 142 | .981 | 43 | 536 | 927 | 13 | 15 | 3.67 |
| **WEST** | | | | | | | | | | | | | | | | | | | | | |
| CIN | 95 | 59 | .617 | | 707 | 557 | 214 | 44 | 124 | .251 | .380 | 140 | 110 | 143 | .982 | 25 | 435 | 806 | 15 | 60 | 3.21 |
| HOU | 84 | 69 | .549 | 10.5 | 708 | 636 | 233 | 38 | 134 | .258 | .393 | 111 | 116 | 151 | .980 | 38 | 498 | 971 | 14 | 31 | 3.77 |
| LA | 85 | 70 | .548 | 10.5 | 584 | 527 | 178 | 39 | 98 | .256 | .360 | 82 | 162 | 145 | .974 | 50 | 429 | 856 | 23 | 29 | 2.78 |
| ATL | 70 | 84 | .455 | 25 | 628 | 730 | 186 | 17 | 144 | .258 | .382 | 47 | 156 | 130 | .974 | 40 | 512 | 732 | 4 | 27 | 4.27 |
| SF | 69 | 86 | .445 | 26.5 | 662 | 649 | 211 | 36 | 150 | .244 | .384 | 123 | 156 | 121 | .974 | 44 | 507 | 771 | 8 | 23 | 3.70 |
| SD | 58 | 95 | .379 | 36.5 | 488 | 665 | 168 | 38 | 102 | .227 | .332 | 78 | 144 | 146 | .976 | 39 | 618 | 960 | 17 | 19 | 3.78 |
| LEAGUE TOTAL | | | | | 7265 | 7265 | 2392 | 430 | 1359 | .248 | .365 | 954 | 1619 | 1706 | .978 | 507 | 5985 | 10544 | 164 | 361 | 3.46 |

## INDIVIDUAL  PITCHING

| PITCHER | T | W | L | PCT | ERA | SV | G | GS | CG | IP | H | BB | SO | R | ER | ShO | H/9 | BB/9 | SO/9 |
|---|---|---|---|---|---|---|---|---|---|---|---|---|---|---|---|---|---|---|---|
| Ferguson Jenkins | R | 20 | 12 | .625 | 3.21 | 0 | 36 | 36 | 23 | 289 | 253 | 62 | 184 | 111 | 103 | 5 | 7.88 | 1.93 | 5.73 |
| Burt Hooton | R | 11 | 14 | .440 | 2.80 | 0 | 33 | 31 | 9 | 218.1 | 201 | 81 | 132 | 78 | 68 | 3 | 8.29 | 3.34 | 5.44 |
| Milt Pappas | R | 17 | 7 | .708 | 2.77 | 0 | 29 | 28 | 10 | 195 | 187 | 29 | 80 | 72 | 60 | 3 | 8.63 | 1.34 | 3.69 |
| Bill Hands | R | 11 | 8 | .579 | 2.99 | 0 | 32 | 28 | 6 | 189.1 | 168 | 47 | 96 | 73 | 63 | 3 | 7.99 | 2.23 | 4.56 |
| Rick Reuschel | R | 10 | 8 | .556 | 2.93 | 0 | 21 | 18 | 5 | 129 | 127 | 29 | 87 | 46 | 42 | 4 | 8.86 | 2.02 | 6.07 |
| Tom Phoebus | R | 3 | 3 | .500 | 3.78 | 6 | 37 | 1 | 0 | 83.1 | 76 | 45 | 59 | 40 | 35 | 0 | 8.21 | 4.86 | 6.37 |
| Jack Aker | R | 6 | 6 | .500 | 2.96 | 17 | 48 | 0 | 0 | 67 | 65 | 23 | 36 | 31 | 22 | 0 | 8.73 | 3.09 | 4.84 |
| Dan McGinn | L | 0 | 5 | .000 | 5.86 | 4 | 42 | 2 | 0 | 63 | 78 | 29 | 42 | 46 | 41 | 0 | 11.14 | 4.14 | 6.00 |
| Juan Pizarro | L | 4 | 5 | .444 | 3.97 | 1 | 16 | 7 | 1 | 59 | 66 | 32 | 24 | 28 | 26 | 0 | 10.07 | 4.88 | 3.66 |
| Bill Bonham | R | 1 | 1 | .500 | 3.10 | 4 | 19 | 4 | 0 | 58 | 56 | 25 | 49 | 22 | 20 | 0 | 8.69 | 3.88 | 7.60 |
| Steve Hamilton | L | 1 | 0 | 1.000 | 4.76 | 0 | 22 | 0 | 0 | 17 | 24 | 8 | 13 | 9 | 9 | 0 | 12.71 | 4.24 | 6.88 |
| Joe Decker | R | 1 | 0 | 1.000 | 2.08 | 0 | 5 | 1 | 0 | 13 | 9 | 4 | 7 | 3 | 3 | 0 | 6.23 | 2.77 | 4.85 |
| Larry Gura | L | 0 | 0 | – | 3.75 | 0 | 7 | 0 | 0 | 12 | 11 | 3 | 13 | 5 | 5 | 0 | 8.25 | 2.25 | 9.75 |
| Phil Regan | R | 0 | 1 | .000 | 2.25 | 0 | 5 | 0 | 0 | 4 | 6 | 2 | 2 | 1 | 1 | 0 | 13.50 | 4.50 | 4.50 |
| Clint Compton | L | 0 | 0 | – | 9.00 | 0 | 1 | 0 | 0 | 2 | 2 | 2 | 0 | 2 | 2 | 0 | 9.00 | 9.00 | 0.00 |
| TEAM TOTAL | | 85 | 70 | .548 | 3.22 | 32 | 353 | 156 | 54 | 1399 | 1329 | 421 | 824 | 567 | 500 | 18 | 8.55 | 2.71 | 5.30 |

| MANAGER | W | L | PCT |
|---|---|---|---|
| Whitey Lockman | 77 | 84 | .478 |

| POS | Player | B | G | AB | H | 2B | 3B | HR | HR % | R | RBI | BB | SO | SB | Pinch Hit AB | Pinch Hit H | BA | SA |
|---|---|---|---|---|---|---|---|---|---|---|---|---|---|---|---|---|---|---|
| **REGULARS** | | | | | | | | | | | | | | | | | | |
| 1B | Jim Hickman | R | 92 | 201 | 49 | 1 | 2 | 3 | 1.5 | 27 | 20 | 42 | 42 | 1 | 34 | 6 | .244 | .313 |
| 2B | Glenn Beckert | R | 114 | 372 | 95 | 13 | 0 | 0 | 0.0 | 38 | 29 | 30 | 15 | 0 | 25 | 6 | .255 | .290 |
| SS | Don Kessinger | B | 160 | 577 | 151 | 23 | 3 | 0 | 0.0 | 52 | 43 | 57 | 44 | 6 | 2 | 0 | .262 | .310 |
| 3B | Ron Santo | R | 149 | 536 | 143 | 29 | 2 | 20 | 3.7 | 65 | 77 | 63 | 97 | 1 | 2 | 0 | .267 | .440 |
| RF | Jose Cardenal | R | 145 | 522 | 158 | 33 | 2 | 11 | 2.1 | 80 | 68 | 58 | 62 | 19 | 2 | 1 | .303 | .437 |
| CF | Rick Monday | L | 149 | 554 | 148 | 24 | 5 | 26 | 4.7 | 93 | 56 | 92 | 124 | 5 | 3 | 1 | .267 | .469 |
| LF | Billy Williams | L | 156 | 576 | 166 | 22 | 2 | 20 | 3.5 | 72 | 86 | 76 | 72 | 4 | 3 | 1 | .288 | .438 |
| C | Randy Hundley | R | 124 | 368 | 83 | 11 | 1 | 10 | 2.7 | 35 | 43 | 30 | 51 | 5 | 3 | 1 | .226 | .342 |
| **SUBSTITUTES** | | | | | | | | | | | | | | | | | | |
| 2B | Paul Popovich | R | 99 | 280 | 66 | 6 | 3 | 2 | 0.7 | 24 | 24 | 18 | 27 | 3 | 9 | 1 | .236 | .300 |
| UT | Carmen Fanzone | R | 64 | 150 | 41 | 7 | 0 | 6 | 4.0 | 22 | 22 | 20 | 38 | 1 | 15 | 5 | .273 | .440 |
| 1B | Pat Bourque | L | 57 | 139 | 29 | 6 | 0 | 7 | 5.0 | 11 | 20 | 16 | 21 | 1 | 17 | 4 | .209 | .403 |
| 1B | Joe Pepitone | L | 31 | 112 | 30 | 3 | 0 | 3 | 2.7 | 16 | 18 | 8 | 6 | 3 | 3 | 1 | .268 | .375 |
| 1B | Gonzalo Marquez | L | 19 | 58 | 13 | 2 | 0 | 1 | 1.7 | 5 | 4 | 3 | 4 | 0 | 2 | 1 | .224 | .310 |
| 2B | Dave Rosello | R | 16 | 38 | 10 | 2 | 0 | 0 | 0.0 | 4 | 2 | 2 | 4 | 2 | 1 | 0 | .263 | .316 |
| 1B | Andre Thornton | R | 17 | 35 | 7 | 3 | 0 | 0 | 0.0 | 3 | 2 | 7 | 9 | 0 | 9 | 3 | .200 | .286 |
| OF | Gene Hiser | L | 100 | 109 | 19 | 3 | 0 | 1 | 0.9 | 15 | 6 | 11 | 17 | 4 | 37 | 6 | .174 | .229 |
| OF | Rico Carty | R | 22 | 70 | 15 | 0 | 0 | 1 | 1.4 | 4 | 8 | 6 | 10 | 0 | 2 | 0 | .214 | .257 |
| OC | Adrian Garrett | L | 36 | 54 | 12 | 0 | 0 | 3 | 5.6 | 7 | 8 | 4 | 18 | 1 | 21 | 6 | .222 | .389 |
| OF | Cleo James | R | 44 | 45 | 5 | 0 | 0 | 0 | 0.0 | 9 | 0 | 1 | 6 | 5 | 10 | 1 | .111 | .111 |
| OF | Pete LaCock | L | 11 | 16 | 4 | 1 | 0 | 0 | 0.0 | 1 | 3 | 1 | 2 | 0 | 7 | 3 | .250 | .313 |
| OF | Matt Alexander | B | 12 | 5 | 1 | 0 | 0 | 0 | 0.0 | 4 | 1 | 1 | 1 | 2 | 1 | 0 | .200 | .200 |
| C | Ken Rudolph | R | 64 | 170 | 35 | 8 | 1 | 2 | 1.2 | 12 | 17 | 7 | 25 | 1 | 0 | 0 | .206 | .300 |
| C | Tom Lundstedt | R | 4 | 5 | 0 | 0 | 0 | 0 | 0.0 | 0 | 0 | 0 | 1 | 0 | 0 | 0 | .000 | .000 |
| PH | Tony LaRussa | R | 1 | 0 | 0 | 0 | 0 | 0 | — | 1 | 0 | 0 | 0 | 0 | 0 | 0 | — | — |
| **PITCHERS** | | | | | | | | | | | | | | | | | | |
| P | Ferguson Jenkins | R | 38 | 84 | 10 | 4 | 0 | 0 | 0.0 | 2 | 4 | 6 | 40 | 0 | 0 | 0 | .119 | .167 |
| P | Rick Reuschel | R | 36 | 73 | 9 | 1 | 0 | 0 | 0.0 | 3 | 2 | 1 | 27 | 0 | 0 | 0 | .123 | .137 |
| P | Burt Hooton | R | 42 | 70 | 9 | 0 | 0 | 0 | 0.0 | 4 | 3 | 10 | 24 | 0 | 0 | 0 | .129 | .129 |
| P | Milt Pappas | R | 30 | 48 | 3 | 0 | 0 | 1 | 2.1 | 2 | 2 | 2 | 28 | 0 | 0 | 0 | .063 | .125 |
| P | Bill Bonham | R | 44 | 43 | 4 | 0 | 0 | 0 | 0.0 | 1 | 1 | 0 | 17 | 0 | 0 | 0 | .093 | .093 |
| P | Bob Locker | R | 63 | 15 | 1 | 0 | 0 | 0 | 0.0 | 0 | 0 | 0 | 9 | 1 | 0 | 0 | .067 | .067 |
| P | Larry Gura | L | 22 | 15 | 3 | 0 | 0 | 0 | 0.0 | 1 | 1 | 1 | 5 | 0 | 0 | 0 | .200 | .200 |
| P | Jack Aker | R | 47 | 7 | 0 | 0 | 0 | 0 | 0.0 | 0 | 0 | 0 | 3 | 0 | 0 | 0 | .000 | .000 |
| P | Ray Burris | R | 31 | 7 | 1 | 0 | 0 | 0 | 0.0 | 0 | 0 | 1 | 3 | 0 | 0 | 0 | .143 | .143 |
| P | Mike Paul | L | 11 | 4 | 0 | 0 | 0 | 0 | 0.0 | 0 | 0 | 0 | 3 | 0 | 0 | 0 | .000 | .000 |
| P | Dave LaRoche | L | 45 | 4 | 2 | 0 | 0 | 0 | 0.0 | 1 | 0 | 1 | 0 | 0 | 0 | 0 | .500 | .500 |
| P | Juan Pizarro | L | 2 | 1 | 0 | 0 | 0 | 0 | 0.0 | 0 | 0 | 0 | 0 | 0 | 0 | 0 | .000 | .000 |
| TEAM TOTAL | | | | 5363 | 1322 | 201 | 21 | 117 | 2.2 | 61 | 570 | 575 | 855 | 65 | 208 | 47 | .247 | .357 |

## INDIVIDUAL FIELDING

| POS | Player | T | G | PO | A | E | DP | TC/G | FA | POS | Player | T | G | PO | A | E | DP | TC/G | FA |
|---|---|---|---|---|---|---|---|---|---|---|---|---|---|---|---|---|---|---|---|
| 1B | J. Hickman | R | 51 | 398 | 31 | 5 | 37 | 8.5 | .988 | OF | R. Monday | L | 148 | 317 | 9 | 9 | 2 | 2.3 | .973 |
| | P. Bourque | L | 38 | 327 | 35 | 5 | 32 | 9.7 | .986 | | B. Williams | R | 138 | 253 | 14 | 4 | 1 | 2.0 | .985 |
| | J. Pepitone | L | 28 | 240 | 19 | 4 | 28 | 9.4 | .985 | | J. Cardenal | R | 142 | 234 | 13 | 5 | 2 | 1.8 | .980 |
| | B. Williams | R | 19 | 167 | 20 | 2 | 14 | 9.9 | .989 | | G. Hiser | L | 64 | 48 | 0 | 1 | 0 | 0.8 | .980 |
| | C. Fanzone | R | 24 | 164 | 11 | 4 | 13 | 7.5 | .978 | | R. Carty | R | 19 | 36 | 0 | 2 | 0 | 2.0 | .947 |
| | G. Marquez | L | 18 | 154 | 15 | 1 | 14 | 9.4 | .994 | | C. James | R | 22 | 23 | 1 | 1 | 0 | 1.1 | .960 |
| | A. Thornton | R | 9 | 81 | 10 | 1 | 3 | 10.2 | .989 | | J. Hickman | R | 13 | 13 | 0 | 0 | 0 | 1.0 | 1.000 |
| 2B | G. Beckert | R | 88 | 163 | 262 | 7 | 50 | 4.9 | .984 | | C. Fanzone | R | 6 | 12 | 0 | 0 | 0 | 2.0 | 1.000 |
| | P. Popovich | R | 84 | 171 | 247 | 8 | 53 | 5.1 | .981 | | A. Garrett | R | 7 | 9 | 0 | 0 | 0 | 1.3 | 1.000 |
| | D. Rosello | R | 13 | 27 | 26 | 2 | 5 | 4.2 | .964 | | P. LaCock | L | 5 | 5 | 1 | 0 | 0 | 1.2 | 1.000 |
| SS | D. Kessinger | R | 158 | 274 | 526 | 30 | 109 | 5.3 | .964 | | M. Alexander | R | 3 | 2 | 0 | 0 | 0 | 0.7 | 1.000 |
| | P. Popovich | R | 9 | 8 | 14 | 0 | 5 | 2.4 | 1.000 | C | R. Hundley | R | 122 | 648 | 59 | 5 | 7 | 5.8 | .993 |
| | D. Rosello | R | 1 | 3 | 3 | 1 | 2 | 7.0 | .857 | | K. Rudolph | R | 64 | 259 | 28 | 9 | 4 | 4.6 | .970 |
| 3B | R. Santo | R | 146 | 107 | 271 | 20 | 17 | 2.7 | .950 | | A. Garrett | R | 6 | 26 | 6 | 2 | 0 | 5.7 | .941 |
| | C. Fanzone | R | 25 | 17 | 30 | 4 | 0 | 2.0 | .922 | | T. Lundstedt | R | 4 | 10 | 1 | 0 | 0 | 2.8 | 1.000 |
| | P. Popovich | R | 1 | 0 | 1 | 0 | 0 | 1.0 | 1.000 | | | | | | | | | | |

They wouldn't fold this time. Cub manager Whitey Lockman was pulling all the right strings. Ron Santo was batting .369. Glenn Beckert had a 26-game hitting streak. Rick Monday had 20 homers by midseason. At the end of April the Cubs were 12–8. At the end of May they were 30–19. At the end of June they were 47–32. It wouldn't happen again.

Oh, yeah. Then came the dog days of summer. They hit the skids with an 8–19 record in July that included 11 losses in a row. They were nearly as bad in August at 9–18. But mediocrity prevailed in the NL East, and the division leadership was up for grabs in September. The Cubs found themselves only 3 1/2 games out going into the final week. But Lockman's losers wound up fourth with a 77–84 log, five games behind the first-place Mets. Santo finished with a .267 average. Beckert closed at .255. Monday hit only six more homers to finish with 26. Santo and Billy Williams were next with 20 each. Jose Cardenal was the only consistent hitter at .303. After six straight 20-win seasons, Fergie Jenkins was down to 14–16. Rick Reuschel was 14–15, and Burt Hooton 14–17. The team that Leo Durocher built grew old together. A major shakeup was in order for next spring.

### TEAM STATISTICS

| | W | L | PCT | GB | R | OR | 2B | 3B | HR | BA | SA | SB | E | DP | FA | CG | B | SO | ShO | SV | ERA |
|---|---|---|---|---|---|---|---|---|---|---|---|---|---|---|---|---|---|---|---|---|---|
| **AST** | | | | | | | | | | | | | | | | | | | | | |
| Y | 82 | 79 | .509 | | 608 | 588 | 198 | 24 | 85 | .246 | .338 | 27 | 126 | 140 | .980 | 47 | 490 | **1027** | 15 | 40 | 3.27 |
| TL | 81 | 81 | .500 | 1.5 | 643 | 603 | 240 | 35 | 75 | .259 | .357 | 100 | 159 | 149 | .975 | 42 | 486 | 867 | 14 | 36 | 3.25 |
| T | 80 | 82 | .494 | 2.5 | 704 | 693 | **257** | 44 | 154 | .261 | .405 | 23 | 151 | 156 | .976 | 26 | 564 | 839 | 11 | **44** | 3.74 |
| ON | 79 | 83 | .488 | 3.5 | 668 | 702 | 190 | 23 | 125 | .251 | .364 | 77 | 163 | 156 | .974 | 26 | 681 | 866 | 6 | 38 | 3.73 |
| HI | 77 | 84 | .478 | 5 | 614 | 655 | 201 | 21 | 117 | .247 | .357 | 65 | 157 | 155 | .975 | 27 | **438** | 885 | 13 | 40 | 3.66 |
| HI | 71 | 91 | .438 | 11.5 | 642 | 717 | 218 | 29 | 134 | .249 | .371 | 51 | 134 | **179** | .979 | **49** | 632 | 919 | 11 | 22 | 4.00 |
| **EST** | | | | | | | | | | | | | | | | | | | | | |
| N | 99 | 63 | .611 | | 741 | 621 | 232 | 34 | 137 | .254 | .383 | **148** | **115** | 162 | **.982** | 39 | 518 | 801 | **17** | 43 | 3.43 |
| A | 95 | 66 | .590 | 3.5 | 675 | 565 | 219 | 29 | 110 | .263 | .371 | 109 | 125 | 166 | .981 | 45 | 461 | 961 | 15 | 38 | **3.00** |
| F | 88 | 74 | .543 | 11 | 739 | 702 | 212 | **52** | 161 | .262 | .407 | 112 | 163 | 138 | .974 | 33 | 485 | 787 | 8 | **44** | 3.79 |
| OU | 82 | 80 | .506 | 17 | 681 | 672 | 216 | 35 | 134 | .251 | .376 | 92 | 116 | 140 | .981 | 45 | 575 | 907 | 14 | 26 | 3.78 |
| TL | 76 | 85 | .472 | 22.5 | **799** | 774 | 219 | 34 | **206** | **.266** | **.427** | 84 | 166 | 142 | .974 | 34 | 575 | 803 | 9 | 35 | 4.25 |
| D | 60 | 102 | .370 | 39 | 548 | 770 | 198 | 26 | 112 | .244 | .351 | 88 | 170 | 152 | .973 | 34 | 548 | 845 | 10 | 23 | 4.16 |
| AGUE TOTAL | | | | | 8062 | 8062 | 2600 | 386 | 1550 | .254 | .376 | 976 | 1745 | 1835 | .977 | 447 | 6453 | 10507 | 143 | 429 | 3.67 |

### INDIVIDUAL PITCHING

| TCHER | T | W | L | PCT | ERA | SV | G | GS | CG | IP | H | BB | SO | R | ER | ShO | H/9 | BB/9 | SO/9 |
|---|---|---|---|---|---|---|---|---|---|---|---|---|---|---|---|---|---|---|---|
| rguson Jenkins | R | 14 | 16 | .467 | 3.89 | 0 | 38 | 38 | 7 | 271 | 267 | 57 | 170 | 133 | 117 | 2 | 8.87 | 1.89 | 5.65 |
| urt Hooton | R | 14 | 17 | .452 | 3.68 | 0 | 42 | 34 | 9 | 240 | 248 | 73 | 134 | 107 | 98 | 2 | 9.30 | 2.74 | 5.03 |
| ck Reuschel | R | 14 | 15 | .483 | 3.00 | 0 | 36 | 36 | 7 | 237 | 244 | 62 | 168 | 95 | 79 | 3 | 9.27 | 2.35 | 6.38 |
| ilt Pappas | R | 7 | 12 | .368 | 4.28 | 0 | 30 | 29 | 1 | 162 | 192 | 40 | 48 | 82 | 77 | 1 | 10.67 | 2.22 | 2.67 |
| ll Bonham | R | 7 | 5 | .583 | 3.02 | 6 | 44 | 15 | 3 | 152 | 126 | 64 | 121 | 55 | 51 | 0 | 7.46 | 3.79 | 7.16 |
| ob Locker | R | 10 | 6 | .625 | 2.55 | 18 | 63 | 0 | 0 | 106 | 96 | 42 | 76 | 40 | 30 | 0 | 8.15 | 3.57 | 6.45 |
| arry Gura | L | 2 | 4 | .333 | 4.85 | 0 | 21 | 7 | 0 | 65 | 79 | 11 | 43 | 39 | 35 | 0 | 10.94 | 1.52 | 5.95 |
| ay Burris | R | 1 | 1 | .500 | 2.91 | 0 | 31 | 1 | 0 | 65 | 65 | 27 | 57 | 22 | 21 | 0 | 9.00 | 3.74 | 7.89 |
| ck Aker | R | 4 | 5 | .444 | 4.08 | 12 | 47 | 0 | 0 | 64 | 76 | 23 | 25 | 33 | 29 | 0 | 10.69 | 3.23 | 3.52 |
| ave LaRoche | L | 4 | 1 | .800 | 5.83 | 4 | 45 | 0 | 0 | 54 | 55 | 29 | 34 | 37 | 35 | 0 | 9.17 | 4.83 | 5.67 |
| ike Paul | L | 0 | 1 | .000 | 3.50 | 0 | 11 | 1 | 0 | 18 | 17 | 9 | 6 | 7 | 7 | 0 | 8.50 | 4.50 | 3.00 |
| an Pizarro | L | 0 | 1 | .000 | 11.25 | 0 | 2 | 0 | 0 | 4 | 6 | 1 | 3 | 5 | 5 | 0 | 13.50 | 2.25 | 6.75 |
| AM TOTAL | | 77 | 84 | .478 | 3.66 | 40 | 410 | 161 | 27 | 1438 | 1471 | 438 | 885 | 655 | 584 | 8 | 9.21 | 2.74 | 5.54 |

| MANAGER | W | L | PCT |
|---|---|---|---|
| Whitey Lockman | 41 | 52 | .441 |
| Jim Marshall | 25 | 44 | .362 |

| POS | Player | B | G | AB | H | 2B | 3B | HR | HR % | R | RBI | BB | SO | SB | Pinch Hit AB | Pinch Hit H | BA | SA |
|---|---|---|---|---|---|---|---|---|---|---|---|---|---|---|---|---|---|---|
| **REGULARS** | | | | | | | | | | | | | | | | | | |
| 1B | Andre Thornton | R | 107 | 303 | 79 | 16 | 4 | 10 | 3.3 | 41 | 46 | 48 | 50 | 2 | 19 | 6 | .261 | .439 |
| 2B | Vic Harris | B | 62 | 200 | 39 | 6 | 3 | 0 | 0.0 | 18 | 11 | 29 | 26 | 9 | 4 | 0 | .195 | .255 |
| SS | Don Kessinger | B | 153 | 599 | 155 | 20 | 7 | 1 | 0.2 | 83 | 42 | 62 | 54 | 7 | 3 | 0 | .259 | .321 |
| 3B | Bill Madlock | R | 128 | 453 | 142 | 21 | 5 | 9 | 2.0 | 65 | 54 | 42 | 39 | 11 | 8 | 4 | .313 | .442 |
| RF | Jose Cardenal | R | 143 | 542 | 159 | 35 | 3 | 13 | 2.4 | 75 | 72 | 56 | 67 | 23 | 8 | 2 | .293 | .441 |
| CF | Rick Monday | L | 142 | 538 | 158 | 19 | 7 | 20 | 3.7 | 84 | 58 | 70 | 94 | 7 | 4 | 0 | .294 | .467 |
| LF | Jerry Morales | R | 151 | 534 | 146 | 21 | 7 | 15 | 2.8 | 70 | 82 | 46 | 63 | 2 | 8 | 2 | .273 | .423 |
| C | Steve Swisher | R | 90 | 280 | 60 | 5 | 0 | 5 | 1.8 | 21 | 27 | 37 | 63 | 0 | 0 | 0 | .214 | .286 |
| **SUBSTITUTES** | | | | | | | | | | | | | | | | | | |
| 1O | Billy Williams | L | 117 | 404 | 113 | 22 | 0 | 16 | 4.0 | 55 | 68 | 67 | 44 | 4 | 10 | 2 | .280 | .453 |
| UT | Carmen Fanzone | R | 65 | 158 | 30 | 6 | 0 | 4 | 2.5 | 13 | 22 | 15 | 27 | 0 | 15 | 4 | .190 | .304 |
| 2B | Dave Rosello | R | 62 | 148 | 30 | 7 | 0 | 0 | 0.0 | 9 | 10 | 10 | 28 | 1 | 2 | 1 | .203 | .250 |
| UT | Billy Grabarkewitz | R | 53 | 125 | 31 | 3 | 2 | 1 | 0.8 | 21 | 12 | 21 | 28 | 1 | 0 | 0 | .248 | .328 |
| 2B | Rob Sperring | R | 42 | 107 | 22 | 3 | 0 | 1 | 0.9 | 9 | 5 | 9 | 28 | 1 | 1 | 0 | .206 | .262 |
| 23 | Ron Dunn | R | 23 | 68 | 20 | 7 | 0 | 2 | 2.9 | 6 | 15 | 12 | 8 | 0 | 1 | 0 | .294 | .485 |
| 3O | Matt Alexander | B | 45 | 54 | 11 | 2 | 1 | 0 | 0.0 | 15 | 0 | 12 | 12 | 8 | 11 | 3 | .204 | .278 |
| 1B | Gonzalo Marquez | L | 11 | 11 | 0 | 0 | 0 | 0 | 0.0 | 1 | 0 | 1 | 2 | 0 | 10 | 0 | .000 | .000 |
| O1 | Chris Ward | L | 92 | 137 | 28 | 4 | 0 | 1 | 0.7 | 8 | 15 | 18 | 13 | 0 | 49 | 9 | .204 | .255 |
| O1 | Pete LaCock | L | 35 | 110 | 20 | 4 | 1 | 1 | 0.9 | 9 | 8 | 12 | 16 | 0 | 4 | 1 | .182 | .264 |
| OF | Jim Tyrone | R | 57 | 81 | 15 | 0 | 1 | 3 | 3.7 | 19 | 3 | 6 | 8 | 1 | 28 | 7 | .185 | .321 |
| OF | Gene Hiser | L | 12 | 17 | 4 | 1 | 0 | 0 | 0.0 | 2 | 1 | 0 | 3 | 0 | 5 | 1 | .235 | .294 |
| C | George Mitterwald | R | 78 | 215 | 54 | 7 | 0 | 7 | 3.3 | 17 | 28 | 18 | 42 | 1 | 11 | 3 | .251 | .381 |
| C | Rick Stelmaszek | L | 25 | 44 | 10 | 2 | 0 | 1 | 2.3 | 2 | 7 | 10 | 6 | 0 | 10 | 2 | .227 | .341 |
| C | Tom Lundstedt | R | 22 | 32 | 3 | 0 | 0 | 0 | 0.0 | 1 | 0 | 5 | 7 | 0 | 0 | 0 | .094 | .094 |
| UT | Adrian Garrett | L | 10 | 8 | 0 | 0 | 0 | 0 | 0.0 | 0 | 0 | 1 | 1 | 0 | 6 | 0 | .000 | .000 |
| **PITCHERS** | | | | | | | | | | | | | | | | | | |
| P | Rick Reuschel | R | 41 | 86 | 19 | 4 | 1 | 0 | 0.0 | 4 | 2 | 0 | 27 | 0 | 0 | 0 | .221 | .291 |
| P | Bill Bonham | R | 48 | 84 | 12 | 2 | 0 | 0 | 0.0 | 8 | 4 | 2 | 25 | 0 | 0 | 0 | .143 | .167 |
| P | Steve Stone | R | 42 | 58 | 7 | 0 | 0 | 0 | 0.0 | 2 | 2 | 2 | 20 | 0 | 0 | 0 | .121 | .121 |
| P | Burt Hooton | R | 48 | 50 | 3 | 1 | 0 | 0 | 0.0 | 1 | 1 | 2 | 22 | 0 | 0 | 0 | .060 | .080 |
| P | Ken Frailing | L | 58 | 31 | 8 | 0 | 0 | 0 | 0.0 | 4 | 6 | 1 | 10 | 0 | 0 | 0 | .258 | .258 |
| P | Dave LaRoche | L | 50 | 27 | 9 | 2 | 0 | 0 | 0.0 | 4 | 2 | 1 | 4 | 0 | 0 | 0 | .333 | .407 |
| P | Tom Dettore | L | 16 | 20 | 5 | 1 | 0 | 0 | 0.0 | 1 | 5 | 3 | 4 | 0 | 0 | 0 | .250 | .300 |
| P | Jim Todd | L | 43 | 16 | 1 | 0 | 0 | 0 | 0.0 | 0 | 1 | 0 | 7 | 0 | 0 | 0 | .063 | .063 |
| P | Ray Burris | R | 41 | 13 | 1 | 0 | 0 | 0 | 0.0 | 0 | 0 | 2 | 4 | 0 | 0 | 0 | .077 | .077 |
| P | Oscar Zamora | R | 56 | 11 | 2 | 0 | 0 | 0 | 0.0 | 0 | 1 | 0 | 1 | 0 | 0 | 0 | .182 | .182 |
| P | Horacio Pina | R | 34 | 5 | 1 | 0 | 0 | 0 | 0.0 | 0 | 0 | 0 | 0 | 0 | 0 | 0 | .200 | .200 |
| P | Jim Kremmel | L | 23 | 3 | 0 | 0 | 0 | 0 | 0.0 | 1 | 0 | 1 | 3 | 0 | 0 | 0 | .000 | .000 |
| P | Herb Hutson | R | 20 | 2 | 0 | 0 | 0 | 0 | 0.0 | 0 | 0 | 0 | 1 | 0 | 0 | 0 | .000 | .000 |
| P | Mike Paul | L | 2 | 0 | 0 | 0 | 0 | 0 | | 0 | 0 | 0 | 0 | 0 | 0 | 0 | — | — |
| TEAM TOTAL | | | | 5574 | 1397 | 221 | 42 | 110 | 2.0 | 66 | 610 | 621 | 857 | 78 | 217 | 47 | .251 | .365 |

## INDIVIDUAL FIELDING

| POS | Player | T | G | PO | A | E | DP | TC/G | FA |
|---|---|---|---|---|---|---|---|---|---|
| 1B | A. Thornton | R | 90 | 760 | 70 | 7 | 61 | 9.3 | .992 |
| | B. Williams | R | 65 | 566 | 49 | 9 | 48 | 9.6 | .986 |
| | P. LaCock | L | 11 | 98 | 10 | 1 | 5 | 9.9 | .991 |
| | C. Ward | L | 6 | 53 | 5 | 0 | 4 | 9.7 | 1.000 |
| | C. Fanzone | R | 7 | 50 | 7 | 0 | 4 | 8.1 | 1.000 |
| | G. Marquez | L | 1 | 2 | 0 | 0 | 0 | 2.0 | 1.000 |
| | A. Garrett | R | 1 | 1 | 0 | 0 | 0 | 1.0 | 1.000 |
| 2B | V. Harris | R | 56 | 122 | 144 | 16 | 20 | 5.0 | .943 |
| | D. Rosello | R | 49 | 77 | 95 | 5 | 32 | 3.6 | .972 |
| | Grabarkewitz | R | 45 | 67 | 100 | 8 | 8 | 3.9 | .954 |
| | R. Sperring | R | 35 | 55 | 85 | 7 | 16 | 4.2 | .952 |
| | R. Dunn | R | 21 | 28 | 38 | 6 | 6 | 3.4 | .917 |
| | C. Fanzone | R | 10 | 10 | 16 | 4 | 2 | 3.0 | .867 |
| | M. Alexander | R | 2 | 0 | 1 | 0 | 0 | 0.5 | 1.000 |
| SS | D. Kessinger | R | 150 | 259 | 476 | 32 | 87 | 5.1 | .958 |
| | D. Rosello | R | 12 | 20 | 19 | 3 | 5 | 3.5 | .929 |
| | R. Sperring | R | 8 | 9 | 16 | 3 | 0 | 3.5 | .893 |
| | Grabarkewitz | R | 7 | 6 | 18 | 0 | 2 | 3.4 | 1.000 |
| 3B | B. Madlock | R | 121 | 84 | 229 | 18 | 14 | 2.7 | .946 |
| | C. Fanzone | R | 35 | 26 | 59 | 11 | 8 | 2.7 | .885 |
| | M. Alexander | R | 19 | 12 | 23 | 3 | 3 | 2.0 | .921 |
| | A. Thornton | R | 1 | 0 | 0 | 0 | 0 | 0.0 | .000 |
| | R. Dunn | R | 6 | 3 | 8 | 1 | 0 | 2.0 | .917 |
| | Grabarkewitz | R | 6 | 2 | 4 | 0 | 0 | 1.0 | 1.000 |
| | J. Tyrone | R | 1 | 2 | 1 | 0 | 0 | 3.0 | 1.000 |

| POS | Player | T | G | PO | A | E | DP | TC/G | FA |
|---|---|---|---|---|---|---|---|---|---|
| OF | R. Monday | L | 139 | 302 | 10 | 5 | 5 | 2.3 | .984 |
| | J. Cardenal | R | 136 | 262 | 15 | 10 | 4 | 2.1 | .965 |
| | J. Morales | R | 143 | 266 | 5 | 7 | 2 | 1.9 | .975 |
| | B. Williams | R | 43 | 69 | 4 | 2 | 2 | 1.7 | .973 |
| | C. Ward | R | 22 | 41 | 1 | 1 | 0 | 2.0 | .977 |
| | P. LaCock | L | 22 | 36 | 2 | 1 | 0 | 1.8 | .974 |
| | J. Tyrone | R | 32 | 24 | 1 | 1 | 0 | 0.8 | .962 |
| | G. Hiser | L | 8 | 8 | 0 | 0 | 0 | 1.0 | 1.000 |
| | A. Garrett | R | 1 | 0 | 1 | 0 | 0 | 1.0 | 1.000 |
| | C. Fanzone | R | 1 | 1 | 0 | 0 | 0 | 1.0 | 1.000 |
| | M. Alexander | R | 4 | 1 | 0 | 0 | 0 | 0.3 | 1.000 |
| C | S. Swisher | R | 90 | 493 | 50 | 7 | 8 | 6.1 | .987 |
| | Mitterwald | R | 68 | 335 | 40 | 10 | 4 | 5.7 | .974 |
| | T. Lundstedt | R | 22 | 70 | 4 | 1 | 0 | 3.4 | .987 |
| | Stelmaszek | R | 16 | 55 | 2 | 1 | 1 | 3.6 | .983 |
| | A. Garrett | R | 3 | 2 | 0 | 0 | 0 | 0.7 | 1.000 |

They broke up that old Durocher gang. Such veterans as Fergie Jenkins, Randy Hundley, Ron Santo, Glenn Beckert, Milt Pappas, Jim Hickman, and Paul Popovich departed before the season. Even sweet-singing Billy Williams became an irregular regular and was traded to the A's at the end of the year, leaving shortstop Don Kessinger as the lone holdover. The result of the rebuilding was a wreck. Attendance dropped by 300,000, and the Cubs, never in contention, lounged in the cellar the last 66 days of the season. Manager Whitey Lockman was replaced by Jim Marshall in midsummer with little change. The team was lacking in all aspects of play, finishing last in fielding, next to last in pitching, and fourth from the bottom in batting. Yet, there were some bright spots in the new lineup. Third baseman Bill Madlock displayed a nice short batting stroke, leading the team with a .313 average. The outfield trio of Jose Cardenal, Rick Monday, and Jerry Morales was big league, combining for 48 homers. Monday led in homers with 20 and Morales in RBI with 82. Rick Reuschel emerged as the pitching leader with a modest 13–12 record. Bill Bonham showed promise with 191 strikeouts and 11 victories, but tied for the league lead in losses with 22. In one department, the Cubs were consistent. They played below .500 ball every month from April through October.

## TEAM STATISTICS

| | W | L | PCT | GB | R | OR | 2B | Batting 3B | HR | BA | SA | SB | E | Fielding DP | FA | CG | B | Pitching SO | ShO | SV | ERA |
|---|---|---|---|---|---|---|---|---|---|---|---|---|---|---|---|---|---|---|---|---|---|
| **EAST** | | | | | | | | | | | | | | | | | | | | | |
| PIT | 88 | 74 | .543 | | 751 | 657 | 238 | 46 | 114 | .274 | .391 | 55 | 162 | 154 | .975 | 51 | 543 | 721 | 9 | 17 | 3.49 |
| STL | 86 | 75 | .534 | 1.5 | 677 | 643 | 216 | 46 | 83 | .265 | .365 | 172 | 147 | 192 | .977 | 37 | 616 | 794 | 13 | 20 | 3.48 |
| PHI | 80 | 82 | .494 | 8 | 676 | 701 | 233 | 50 | 95 | .261 | .373 | 115 | 148 | 168 | .976 | 46 | 682 | 892 | 4 | 19 | 3.92 |
| MON | 79 | 82 | .491 | 8.5 | 662 | 657 | 201 | 29 | 86 | .254 | .350 | 124 | 153 | 157 | .976 | 35 | 544 | 822 | 8 | 27 | 3.60 |
| NY | 71 | 91 | .438 | 17 | 572 | 646 | 183 | 22 | 96 | .235 | .329 | 43 | 158 | 150 | .975 | 46 | 504 | 908 | 15 | 14 | 3.42 |
| CHI | 66 | 96 | .407 | 22 | 669 | 826 | 221 | 42 | 110 | .251 | .365 | 78 | 199 | 141 | .969 | 23 | 576 | 895 | 6 | 26 | 4.28 |
| **WEST** | | | | | | | | | | | | | | | | | | | | | |
| LA | 102 | 60 | .630 | | 798 | 561 | 231 | 34 | 139 | .272 | .401 | 149 | 157 | 122 | .975 | 33 | 464 | 943 | 19 | 23 | 2.97 |
| CIN | 98 | 64 | .605 | 4 | 776 | 631 | 271 | 35 | 135 | .260 | .394 | 146 | 134 | 151 | .979 | 34 | 536 | 875 | 11 | 27 | 3.42 |
| ATL | 88 | 74 | .543 | 14 | 661 | 563 | 202 | 37 | 120 | .249 | .363 | 72 | 132 | 161 | .979 | 46 | 488 | 772 | 21 | 22 | 3.05 |
| HOU | 81 | 81 | .500 | 21 | 653 | 632 | 222 | 41 | 110 | .263 | .378 | 108 | 113 | 161 | .982 | 36 | 601 | 738 | 18 | 18 | 3.48 |
| SF | 72 | 90 | .444 | 30 | 634 | 723 | 228 | 38 | 93 | .252 | .358 | 107 | 175 | 153 | .972 | 27 | 559 | 756 | 11 | 25 | 3.80 |
| SD | 60 | 102 | .370 | 42 | 541 | 830 | 196 | 27 | 99 | .229 | .330 | 85 | 170 | 126 | .973 | 25 | 715 | 855 | 7 | 19 | 4.61 |
| **LEAGUE TOTAL** | | | | | 8070 | 8070 | 2642 | 447 | 1280 | .255 | .367 | 1254 | 1848 | 1836 | .976 | 439 | 6828 | 9971 | 142 | 257 | 3.62 |

## INDIVIDUAL PITCHING

| PITCHER | T | W | L | PCT | ERA | SV | G | GS | CG | IP | H | BB | SO | R | ER | ShO | H/9 | BB/9 | SO/9 |
|---|---|---|---|---|---|---|---|---|---|---|---|---|---|---|---|---|---|---|---|
| Bill Bonham | R | 11 | 22 | .333 | 3.85 | 1 | 44 | 36 | 10 | 243 | 246 | 109 | 191 | 133 | 104 | 2 | 9.11 | 4.04 | 7.07 |
| Rick Reuschel | R | 13 | 12 | .520 | 4.29 | 0 | 41 | 38 | 8 | 241 | 262 | 83 | 160 | 130 | 115 | 2 | 9.78 | 3.10 | 5.98 |
| Burt Hooton | R | 7 | 11 | .389 | 4.81 | 1 | 48 | 21 | 3 | 176 | 214 | 51 | 94 | 112 | 94 | 1 | 10.94 | 2.61 | 4.81 |
| Steve Stone | R | 8 | 6 | .571 | 4.13 | 0 | 38 | 23 | 1 | 170 | 185 | 64 | 90 | 92 | 78 | 0 | 9.79 | 3.39 | 4.76 |
| Ken Frailing | L | 6 | 9 | .400 | 3.89 | 1 | 55 | 16 | 1 | 125 | 150 | 43 | 71 | 65 | 54 | 0 | 10.80 | 3.10 | 5.11 |
| Dave LaRoche | L | 5 | 6 | .455 | 4.79 | 5 | 49 | 4 | 0 | 92 | 103 | 47 | 49 | 54 | 49 | 0 | 10.08 | 4.60 | 4.79 |
| Jim Todd | R | 4 | 2 | .667 | 3.89 | 3 | 43 | 6 | 0 | 88 | 82 | 41 | 42 | 45 | 38 | 0 | 8.39 | 4.19 | 4.30 |
| Oscar Zamora | R | 3 | 9 | .250 | 3.11 | 10 | 56 | 0 | 0 | 84 | 82 | 19 | 38 | 33 | 29 | 0 | 8.79 | 2.04 | 4.07 |
| Ray Burris | R | 3 | 5 | .375 | 6.60 | 1 | 40 | 5 | 0 | 75 | 91 | 26 | 40 | 61 | 55 | 0 | 10.92 | 3.12 | 4.80 |
| Tom Dettore | R | 3 | 5 | .375 | 4.15 | 0 | 16 | 9 | 0 | 65 | 64 | 31 | 43 | 39 | 30 | 0 | 8.86 | 4.29 | 5.95 |
| Horacio Pina | R | 3 | 4 | .429 | 4.02 | 4 | 34 | 0 | 0 | 47 | 49 | 28 | 32 | 22 | 21 | 0 | 9.38 | 5.36 | 6.13 |
| Jim Kremmel | L | 0 | 2 | .000 | 5.23 | 0 | 23 | 2 | 0 | 31 | 37 | 18 | 22 | 21 | 18 | 0 | 10.74 | 5.23 | 6.39 |
| Herb Hutson | R | 0 | 2 | .000 | 3.41 | 0 | 20 | 2 | 0 | 29 | 24 | 15 | 22 | 15 | 11 | 0 | 7.45 | 4.66 | 6.83 |
| Mike Paul | L | 0 | 1 | .000 | 36.00 | 0 | 2 | 0 | 0 | 1 | 4 | 1 | 1 | 4 | 4 | 0 | 36.00 | 9.00 | 9.00 |
| **TEAM TOTAL** | | 66 | 96 | .407 | 4.29 | 26 | 509 | 162 | 23 | 1467 | 1593 | 576 | 895 | 826 | 700 | 5 | 9.77 | 3.53 | 5.49 |

| MANAGER | W | L | PCT |
|---|---|---|---|
| Jim Marshall | 75 | 87 | .463 |

| POS | Player | B | G | AB | H | 2B | 3B | HR | HR % | R | RBI | BB | SO | SB | Pinch Hit AB | Pinch Hit H | BA | SA |
|---|---|---|---|---|---|---|---|---|---|---|---|---|---|---|---|---|---|---|
| **REGULARS** | | | | | | | | | | | | | | | | | | |
| 1B | Andre Thornton | R | 120 | 372 | 109 | 21 | 4 | 18 | 4.8 | 70 | 60 | 88 | 63 | 3 | 9 | 1 | .293 | .516 |
| 2B | Manny Trillo | R | 154 | 545 | 135 | 12 | 2 | 7 | 1.3 | 55 | 70 | 45 | 78 | 1 | 1 | 0 | .248 | .316 |
| SS | Don Kessinger | B | 154 | 601 | 146 | 26 | 10 | 0 | 0.0 | 77 | 46 | 68 | 47 | 4 | 2 | 0 | .243 | .319 |
| 3B | Bill Madlock | R | 130 | 514 | 182 | 29 | 7 | 7 | 1.4 | 77 | 64 | 42 | 34 | 9 | 0 | 0 | .354 | .479 |
| RF | Jose Cardenal | R | 154 | 574 | 182 | 21 | 9 | 9 | 1.6 | 85 | 68 | 77 | 50 | 34 | 5 | 1 | .317 | .423 |
| CF | Rick Monday | L | 136 | 491 | 131 | 29 | 4 | 17 | 3.5 | 89 | 60 | 83 | 95 | 8 | 4 | 1 | .267 | .446 |
| LF | Jerry Morales | R | 153 | 578 | 156 | 21 | 0 | 12 | 2.1 | 62 | 91 | 50 | 65 | 3 | 2 | 2 | .270 | .369 |
| C | Steve Swisher | R | 93 | 254 | 54 | 16 | 2 | 1 | 0.4 | 20 | 22 | 30 | 57 | 1 | 0 | 0 | .213 | .303 |
| **SUBSTITUTES** | | | | | | | | | | | | | | | | | | |
| 1O | Pete LaCock | L | 106 | 249 | 57 | 8 | 1 | 6 | 2.4 | 30 | 30 | 37 | 27 | 0 | 26 | 9 | .229 | .341 |
| UT | Rob Sperring | R | 65 | 144 | 30 | 4 | 1 | 1 | 0.7 | 25 | 9 | 16 | 31 | 0 | 1 | 0 | .208 | .271 |
| SS | Dave Rosello | R | 19 | 58 | 15 | 2 | 0 | 1 | 1.7 | 7 | 8 | 9 | 8 | 0 | 0 | 0 | .259 | .345 |
| 3O | Ron Dunn | R | 32 | 44 | 7 | 3 | 0 | 1 | 2.3 | 2 | 6 | 6 | 17 | 0 | 17 | 3 | .159 | .295 |
| 1B | Adrian Garrett | L | 16 | 21 | 2 | 0 | 0 | 1 | 4.8 | 1 | 6 | 1 | 8 | 0 | 8 | 0 | .095 | .238 |
| OF | Champ Summers | L | 76 | 91 | 21 | 5 | 1 | 1 | 1.1 | 14 | 16 | 10 | 13 | 0 | 46 | 14 | .231 | .341 |
| OF | Gene Hiser | L | 45 | 62 | 15 | 3 | 0 | 0 | 0.0 | 11 | 6 | 11 | 7 | 0 | 24 | 8 | .242 | .290 |
| OF | Joe Wallis | L | 16 | 56 | 16 | 2 | 2 | 1 | 1.8 | 9 | 4 | 5 | 14 | 2 | 3 | 1 | .286 | .446 |
| UT | Vic Harris | B | 51 | 56 | 10 | 0 | 0 | 0 | 0.0 | 6 | 5 | 6 | 7 | 0 | 24 | 4 | .179 | .179 |
| OF | Jim Tyrone | R | 11 | 22 | 5 | 0 | 1 | 0 | 0.0 | 0 | 3 | 1 | 4 | 1 | 5 | 1 | .227 | .318 |
| C | George Mitterwald | R | 84 | 200 | 44 | 4 | 3 | 5 | 2.5 | 19 | 26 | 19 | 42 | 0 | 15 | 3 | .220 | .345 |
| C | Tim Hosley | R | 62 | 141 | 36 | 7 | 0 | 6 | 4.3 | 22 | 20 | 27 | 25 | 1 | 10 | ·2 | .255 | .433 |
| **PITCHERS** | | | | | | | | | | | | | | | | | | |
| P | Bill Bonham | R | 40 | 82 | 15 | 1 | 1 | 0 | 0.0 | 8 | 6 | 1 | 19 | 0 | 0 | 0 | .183 | .220 |
| P | Ray Burris | R | 38 | 82 | 15 | 2 | 0 | 0 | 0.0 | 10 | 4 | 7 | 24 | 0 | 0 | 0 | .183 | .207 |
| P | Rick Reuschel | R | 38 | 77 | 16 | 2 | 0 | 1 | 1.3 | 3 | 7 | 3 | 11 | 0 | 0 | 0 | .208 | .273 |
| P | Steve Stone | R | 34 | 72 | 8 | 2 | 0 | 0 | 0.0 | 3 | 3 | 3 | 29 | 0 | 0 | 0 | .111 | .139 |
| P | Tom Dettore | L | 36 | 24 | 6 | 0 | 0 | 0 | 0.0 | 2 | 2 | 1 | 7 | 0 | 0 | 0 | .250 | .250 |
| P | Darold Knowles | L | 58 | 15 | 1 | 0 | 0 | 0 | 0.0 | 0 | 1 | 1 | 8 | 0 | 0 | 0 | .067 | .067 |
| P | Geoff Zahn | L | 16 | 15 | 2 | 0 | 0 | 0 | 0.0 | 1 | 1 | 0 | 3 | 0 | 0 | 0 | .133 | .133 |
| P | Ken Frailing | L | 41 | 7 | 1 | 0 | 0 | 0 | 0.0 | 2 | 0 | 1 | 1 | 0 | 0 | 0 | .143 | .143 |
| P | Oscar Zamora | R | 52 | 6 | 1 | 0 | 0 | 0 | 0.0 | 0 | 0 | 0 | 0 | 0 | 0 | 0 | .167 | .167 |
| P | Willie Prall | L | 3 | 4 | 0 | 0 | 0 | 0 | 0.0 | 0 | 1 | 1 | 0 | 0 | 0 | 0 | .000 | .000 |
| P | Paul Reuschel | R | 28 | 4 | 0 | 0 | 0 | 0 | 0.0 | 0 | 0 | 1 | 2 | 0 | 0 | 0 | .000 | .000 |
| P | Donnie Moore | L | 4 | 3 | 0 | 0 | 0 | 0 | 0.0 | 0 | 0 | 0 | 3 | 0 | 0 | 0 | .000 | .000 |
| P | Burt Hooton | R | 3 | 3 | 0 | 0 | 0 | 0 | 0.0 | 0 | 0 | 0 | 0 | 0 | 0 | 0 | .000 | .000 |
| P | Milt Wilcox | R | 25 | 3 | 1 | 0 | 0 | 0 | 0.0 | 0 | 0 | 0 | 0 | 0 | 0 | 0 | .333 | .333 |
| P | Bob Locker | R | 22 | 0 | 0 | 0 | 0 | 0 | – | 0 | 0 | 0 | 0 | 0 | 0 | 0 | – | – |
| P | Eddie Watt | R | 6 | 0 | 0 | 0 | 0 | 0 | – | 0 | 0 | 0 | 0 | 0 | 0 | 0 | – | – |
| P | Buddy Schultz | R | 6 | 0 | 0 | 0 | 0 | 0 | – | 0 | 0 | 0 | 0 | 0 | 0 | 0 | – | – |
| P | Ken Crosby | R | 9 | 0 | 0 | 0 | 0 | 0 | – | 1 | 0 | 1 | 0 | 0 | 0 | 0 | – | – |
| P | Eddie Solomon | R | 6 | 0 | 0 | 0 | 0 | 0 | – | 0 | 0 | 0 | 0 | 0 | 0 | 0 | – | – |
| TEAM TOTAL | | | | 5470 | 1419 | 229 | 41 | 95 | 1.7 | 71 | 645 | 650 | 802 | 67 | 202 | 50 | .259 | .368 |

## INDIVIDUAL FIELDING

| POS | Player | T | G | PO | A | E | DP | TC/G | FA | POS | Player | T | G | PO | A | E | DP | TC/G | FA |
|---|---|---|---|---|---|---|---|---|---|---|---|---|---|---|---|---|---|---|---|
| 1B | A. Thornton | R | 113 | 982 | 77 | 13 | 88 | 9.5 | .988 | OF | J. Cardenal | R | 151 | 313 | 14 | 8 | 3 | 2.2 | .976 |
| | P. LaCock | L | 53 | 453 | 43 | 6 | 39 | 9.5 | .988 | | R. Monday | L | 131 | 315 | 6 | 9 | 0 | 2.5 | .973 |
| | Mitterwald | R | 10 | 68 | 6 | 1 | 6 | 7.5 | .987 | | J. Morales | R | 151 | 273 | 11 | 6 | 1 | 1.9 | .979 |
| | A. Garrett | R | 4 | 22 | 4 | 0 | 6 | 6.5 | 1.000 | | J. Wallis | R | 15 | 31 | 1 | 0 | 0 | 2.1 | 1.000 |
| | G. Hiser | L | 1 | 3 | 0 | 0 | 1 | 3.0 | 1.000 | | P. LaCock | L | 26 | 26 | 2 | 0 | 0 | 1.1 | 1.000 |
| 2B | M. Trillo | R | 153 | 350 | 509 | 29 | 103 | 5.8 | .967 | | G. Hiser | L | 18 | 25 | 0 | 0 | 0 | 1.4 | 1.000 |
| | R. Sperring | R | 17 | 22 | 32 | 1 | 4 | 3.2 | .982 | | C. Summers | R | 18 | 16 | 0 | 2 | 0 | 1.0 | .889 |
| | V. Harris | R | 5 | 6 | 8 | 1 | 2 | 3.0 | .933 | | R. Dunn | R | 2 | 0 | 0 | 0 | 0 | 0.0 | .000 |
| | R. Dunn | R | 1 | 0 | 1 | 0 | 0 | 1.0 | 1.000 | | R. Sperring | R | 8 | 11 | 0 | 1 | 0 | 1.5 | .917 |
| SS | D. Kessinger | R | 140 | 205 | 436 | 22 | 100 | 4.7 | .967 | | V. Harris | R | 11 | 9 | 0 | 1 | 0 | 0.9 | .900 |
| | D. Rosello | R | 19 | 27 | 53 | 4 | 7 | 4.4 | .952 | | J. Tyrone | R | 8 | 7 | 1 | 0 | 0 | 1.0 | 1.000 |
| | R. Sperring | R | 16 | 27 | 40 | 7 | 12 | 4.6 | .905 | C | S. Swisher | R | 93 | 426 | 36 | 10 | 5 | 5.1 | .979 |
| | M. Trillo | R | 1 | 0 | 0 | 0 | 0 | 0.0 | .000 | | Mitterwald | R | 59 | 247 | 32 | 7 | 4 | 4.8 | .976 |
| 3B | B. Madlock | R | 128 | 79 | 250 | 20 | 14 | 2.7 | .943 | | T. Hosley | R | 53 | 254 | 16 | 9 | 3 | 5.3 | .968 |
| | R. Sperring | R | 22 | 10 | 43 | 3 | 2 | 2.5 | .946 | | | | | | | | | | |
| | D. Kessinger | R | 13 | 5 | 28 | 2 | 3 | 2.7 | .943 | | | | | | | | | | |
| | R. Dunn | R | 11 | 6 | 16 | 1 | 0 | 2.1 | .957 | | | | | | | | | | |
| | V. Harris | R | 7 | 0 | 6 | 0 | 0 | 0.9 | 1.000 | | | | | | | | | | |
| | A. Thornton | R | 2 | 2 | 0 | 0 | 0 | 1.0 | 1.000 | | | | | | | | | | |

After losing their opener the Cubs won seven in a row and held first place until Mother's Day. After that, it was oh, brother. They remained weak and wound up sharing the cellar with the Expos at 75–87. Amid the gloom, manager Jim Marshall saw some positive signs. His crew did win eight more games than the previous season, and he boasted a batting champion in third baseman Bill Madlock, who stroked a nifty .354. Madlock also was the hitting hero of the 6–3 NL victory in the All-Star Game. It was his two-run single in the ninth inning that provided the winning margin. Jose Cardenal contributed a .317 average and stole 34 bases, most for a Cub since the heyday of Kiki Cuyler. Jerry Morales was the leading run producer, driving in 91 runs, while Andre Thornton edged Rick Monday in homers, 18–17. Another pleasant surprise was fancy-fielding second baseman Manny Trillo, obtained in the Billy Williams trade. Trillo hit in the clutch with 70 RBI.

But the pitching was the worst in both leagues—a fat 4.57 earned-run average. Even Ray Burris and his 15–10 record was suspect with a 4.12 ERA. Only the Reuschel brothers, Rick and Paul, were under 4.00, but Rick had a horrendous 11–17 record. The Reuschels made pitching history by combining on a 7–0 victory against the Dodgers on August 21 for the first all-brother shutout. The Cubs' biggest tormentors were the world champion Reds, who topped them 11 of 12 times.

## TEAM STATISTICS

| | W | L | PCT | GB | R | OR | 2B | 3B | HR | BA | SA | SB | E | DP | FA | CG | B | SO | ShO | SV | ERA |
|---|---|---|---|---|---|---|---|---|---|---|---|---|---|---|---|---|---|---|---|---|---|
| **EAST** | | | | | | | | | | | | | | | | | | | | | |
| PIT | 92 | 69 | .571 | | 712 | 565 | 255 | 47 | **138** | .263 | **.402** | 49 | 151 | 147 | .976 | 43 | 551 | 768 | 14 | 31 | 3.02 |
| PHI | 86 | 76 | .531 | 6.5 | 735 | 694 | **283** | 42 | 125 | .269 | .402 | 126 | 152 | 156 | .976 | 33 | 546 | 897 | 11 | 30 | 3.82 |
| NY | 82 | 80 | .506 | 10.5 | 646 | 625 | 217 | 34 | 101 | .256 | .361 | 32 | 151 | 144 | .976 | 40 | 580 | **989** | 14 | 31 | 3.39 |
| STL | 82 | 80 | .506 | 10.5 | 662 | 689 | 239 | 46 | 81 | **.273** | .375 | 116 | 171 | 140 | .973 | 33 | 571 | 824 | 13 | 36 | 3.58 |
| CHI | 75 | 87 | .463 | 17.5 | 712 | 827 | 229 | 41 | 95 | .259 | .368 | 67 | 179 | 152 | .972 | 27 | 551 | 850 | 8 | 33 | 4.57 |
| MON | 75 | 87 | .463 | 17.5 | 601 | 690 | 216 | 31 | 98 | .244 | .348 | 108 | 180 | **179** | .973 | 30 | 665 | 831 | 12 | 25 | 3.73 |
| **WEST** | | | | | | | | | | | | | | | | | | | | | |
| CIN | 108 | 54 | .667 | | **840** | 586 | 278 | 37 | 124 | .271 | .401 | **168** | **102** | 173 | **.984** | 22 | 487 | 663 | 8 | **50** | 3.37 |
| LA | 88 | 74 | .543 | 20 | 648 | **534** | 217 | 31 | 118 | .248 | .365 | 138 | 127 | 106 | .979 | **51** | **448** | 894 | **18** | 21 | **2.92** |
| SF | 80 | 81 | .497 | 27.5 | 659 | 671 | 235 | 45 | 84 | .259 | .365 | 99 | 146 | 164 | .976 | 37 | 612 | 856 | 9 | 24 | 3.74 |
| SD | 71 | 91 | .438 | 37 | 552 | 683 | 215 | 22 | 78 | .244 | .335 | 85 | 188 | 163 | .971 | 40 | 521 | 713 | 12 | 20 | 3.51 |
| ATL | 67 | 94 | .416 | 40.5 | 583 | 739 | 179 | 28 | 107 | .244 | .346 | 55 | 175 | 147 | .972 | 32 | 519 | 669 | 4 | 25 | 3.93 |
| HOU | 64 | 97 | .398 | 43.5 | 664 | 711 | 218 | **54** | 84 | .254 | .359 | 133 | 137 | 166 | .979 | 39 | 679 | 839 | 6 | 25 | 4.05 |
| LEAGUE TOTAL | | | | | 8014 | 8014 | 2781 | 458 | 1233 | .257 | .369 | 1176 | 1859 | 1837 | .976 | 427 | 6730 | 9793 | 129 | 351 | 3.63 |

## INDIVIDUAL  PITCHING

| PITCHER | T | W | L | PCT | ERA | SV | G | GS | CG | IP | H | BB | SO | R | ER | ShO | H/9 | BB/9 | SO/9 |
|---|---|---|---|---|---|---|---|---|---|---|---|---|---|---|---|---|---|---|---|
| Ray Burris | R | 15 | 10 | .600 | 4.12 | 0 | 36 | 35 | 8 | 238 | 259 | 73 | 108 | 121 | 109 | 2 | 9.79 | 2.76 | 4.08 |
| Rick Reuschel | R | 11 | 17 | .393 | 3.73 | 1 | 38 | 37 | 6 | 234 | 244 | 67 | 155 | 116 | 97 | 0 | 9.38 | 2.58 | 5.96 |
| Bill Bonham | R | 13 | 15 | .464 | 4.72 | 0 | 38 | 36 | 7 | 229 | 254 | 109 | 165 | 133 | 120 | 2 | 9.98 | 4.28 | 6.48 |
| Steve Stone | R | 12 | 8 | .600 | 3.95 | 0 | 33 | 32 | 6 | 214 | 198 | 80 | 139 | 103 | 94 | 1 | 8.33 | 3.36 | 5.85 |
| Darold Knowles | L | 6 | 9 | .400 | 5.83 | 15 | 58 | 0 | 0 | 88 | 107 | 36 | 63 | 61 | 57 | 0 | 10.94 | 3.68 | 6.44 |
| Tom Dettore | R | 5 | 4 | .556 | 5.40 | 0 | 36 | 5 | 0 | 85 | 88 | 31 | 46 | 57 | 51 | 0 | 9.32 | 3.28 | 4.87 |
| Oscar Zamora | R | 5 | 2 | .714 | 5.07 | 10 | 52 | 0 | 0 | 71 | 84 | 15 | 28 | 42 | 40 | 0 | 10.65 | 1.90 | 3.55 |
| Geoff Zahn | L | 2 | 7 | .222 | 4.45 | 1 | 16 | 10 | 0 | 62.2 | 67 | 26 | 21 | 37 | 31 | 0 | 9.62 | 3.73 | 3.02 |
| Ken Frailing | L | 2 | 5 | .286 | 5.43 | 1 | 41 | 0 | 0 | 53 | 61 | 26 | 39 | 37 | 32 | 0 | 10.36 | 4.42 | 6.62 |
| Milt Wilcox | R | 0 | 1 | .000 | 5.68 | 0 | 25 | 0 | 0 | 38 | 50 | 17 | 21 | 27 | 24 | 0 | 11.84 | 4.03 | 4.97 |
| Paul Reuschel | R | 1 | 3 | .250 | 3.50 | 5 | 28 | 0 | 0 | 36 | 44 | 13 | 12 | 15 | 14 | 0 | 11.00 | 3.25 | 3.00 |
| Bob Locker | R | 0 | 1 | .000 | 4.91 | 0 | 22 | 0 | 0 | 33 | 38 | 16 | 14 | 21 | 18 | 0 | 10.36 | 4.36 | 3.82 |
| Willie Prall | L | 0 | 2 | .000 | 8.40 | 0 | 3 | 3 | 0 | 15 | 21 | 8 | 7 | 15 | 14 | 0 | 12.60 | 4.80 | 4.20 |
| Burt Hooton | R | 0 | 2 | .000 | 8.18 | 0 | 3 | 3 | 0 | 11 | 18 | 4 | 5 | 12 | 10 | 0 | 14.73 | 3.27 | 4.09 |
| Donnie Moore | R | 0 | 0 | — | 4.00 | 0 | 4 | 1 | 0 | 9 | 12 | 4 | 8 | 4 | 4 | 0 | 12.00 | 4.00 | 8.00 |
| Ken Crosby | R | 1 | 0 | 1.000 | 3.38 | 0 | 9 | 0 | 0 | 8 | 10 | 7 | 6 | 3 | 3 | 0 | 11.25 | 7.88 | 6.75 |
| Eddie Solomon | R | 0 | 0 | — | 1.29 | 0 | 6 | 0 | 0 | 7 | 7 | 6 | 3 | 1 | 1 | 0 | 9.00 | 7.71 | 3.86 |
| Eddie Watt | R | 0 | 1 | .000 | 13.50 | 0 | 6 | 0 | 0 | 6 | 14 | 8 | 6 | 11 | 9 | 0 | 21.00 | 12.00 | 9.00 |
| Buddy Schultz | L | 2 | 0 | 1.000 | 6.00 | 0 | 6 | 0 | 0 | 6 | 11 | 5 | 4 | 6 | 4 | 0 | 16.50 | 7.50 | 6.00 |
| TEAM TOTAL | | 75 | 87 | .463 | 4.56 | 33 | 460 | 162 | 27 | 1443.2 | 1587 | 551 | 850 | 827 | 732 | 5 | 9.89 | 3.44 | 5.30 |

| MANAGER | W | L | PCT |
|---|---|---|---|
| Jim Marshall | 75 | 87 | .463 |

| POS | Player | B | G | AB | H | 2B | 3B | HR | HR % | R | RBI | BB | SO | SB | Pinch Hit AB | Pinch Hit H | BA | SA |
|---|---|---|---|---|---|---|---|---|---|---|---|---|---|---|---|---|---|---|
| **REGULARS** | | | | | | | | | | | | | | | | | | |
| 1B | Pete LaCock | L | 106 | 244 | 54 | 9 | 2 | 8 | 3.3 | 34 | 28 | 42 | 37 | 1 | 39 | 7 | .221 | .373 |
| 2B | Manny Trillo | R | 158 | 582 | 139 | 24 | 3 | 4 | 0.7 | 42 | 59 | 53 | 70 | 17 | 1 | 0 | .239 | .311 |
| SS | Mick Kelleher | R | 124 | 337 | 77 | 12 | 1 | 0 | 0.0 | 28 | 22 | 15 | 32 | 0 | 3 | 1 | .228 | .270 |
| 3B | Bill Madlock | R | 142 | 514 | 174 | 36 | 1 | 15 | 2.9 | 68 | 84 | 56 | 27 | 15 | 5 | 1 | .339 | .500 |
| RF | Jerry Morales | R | 140 | 537 | 147 | 17 | 0 | 16 | 3.0 | 66 | 67 | 41 | 49 | 3 | 5 | 1 | .274 | .395 |
| CF | Rick Monday | L | 137 | 534 | 145 | 20 | 5 | 32 | 6.0 | 107 | 77 | 60 | 125 | 5 | 4 | 1 | .272 | .507 |
| LF | Jose Cardenal | R | 136 | 521 | 156 | 25 | 2 | 8 | 1.5 | 64 | 47 | 32 | 39 | 23 | 8 | 1 | .299 | .401 |
| C | Steve Swisher | R | 109 | 377 | 89 | 13 | 3 | 5 | 1.3 | 25 | 42 | 20 | 82 | 2 | 4 | 1 | .236 | .326 |
| **SUBSTITUTES** | | | | | | | | | | | | | | | | | | |
| SS | Dave Rosello | R | 91 | 227 | 55 | 5 | 1 | 1 | 0.4 | 27 | 11 | 41 | 33 | 1 | 1 | 0 | .242 | .286 |
| 1O | Larry Biittner | L | 78 | 192 | 47 | 13 | 1 | 0 | 0.0 | 21 | 17 | 10 | 6 | 0 | 28 | 6 | .245 | .323 |
| UT | Rob Sperring | R | 43 | 93 | 24 | 3 | 0 | 0 | 0.0 | 8 | 7 | 9 | 25 | 0 | 1 | 0 | .258 | .290 |
| 1B | Andre Thornton | R | 27 | 85 | 17 | 6 | 0 | 2 | 2.4 | 8 | 14 | 20 | 14 | 2 | 4 | 1 | .200 | .341 |
| 1B | Jerry Tabb | L | 11 | 24 | 7 | 0 | 0 | 0 | 0.0 | 2 | 0 | 3 | 2 | 0 | 6 | 1 | .292 | .292 |
| OF | Joe Wallis | L | 121 | 338 | 86 | 11 | 5 | 5 | 1.5 | 51 | 21 | 33 | 62 | 3 | 26 | 4 | .254 | .361 |
| O1 | Champ Summers | L | 83 | 126 | 26 | 2 | 0 | 3 | 2.4 | 11 | 13 | 13 | 31 | 1 | 47 | 12 | .206 | .294 |
| UT | Wayne Tyrone | R | 30 | 57 | 13 | 1 | 0 | 1 | 1.8 | 3 | 8 | 3 | 21 | 0 | 14 | 4 | .228 | .298 |
| UT | Mike Adams | R | 25 | 29 | 4 | 2 | 0 | 0 | 0.0 | 1 | 2 | 8 | 7 | 0 | 16 | 1 | .138 | .207 |
| C1 | George Mitterwald | R | 101 | 303 | 65 | 7 | 0 | 5 | 1.7 | 19 | 28 | 16 | 63 | 1 | 16 | 1 | .215 | .287 |
| C | Randy Hundley | R | 13 | 18 | 3 | 2 | 0 | 0 | 0.0 | 3 | 1 | 1 | 4 | 0 | 4 | 0 | .167 | .278 |
| C1 | Ed Putman | R | 5 | 7 | 3 | 0 | 0 | 0 | 0.0 | 0 | 0 | 0 | 0 | 0 | 2 | 1 | .429 | .429 |
| **PITCHERS** | | | | | | | | | | | | | | | | | | |
| P | Rick Reuschel | R | 38 | 83 | 19 | 4 | 0 | 0 | 0.0 | 9 | 6 | 6 | 16 | 0 | 0 | 0 | .229 | .277 |
| P | Ray Burris | R | 39 | 81 | 9 | 0 | 0 | 0 | 0.0 | 4 | 1 | 1 | 28 | 0 | 0 | 0 | .111 | .111 |
| P | Bill Bonham | R | 32 | 65 | 13 | 4 | 0 | 0 | 0.0 | 6 | 2 | 2 | 15 | 0 | 0 | 0 | .200 | .262 |
| P | Steve Renko | R | 29 | 53 | 5 | 0 | 0 | 0 | 0.0 | 3 | 1 | 0 | 16 | 0 | 0 | 0 | .094 | .094 |
| P | Steve Stone | R | 17 | 21 | 3 | 0 | 0 | 0 | 0.0 | 1 | 0 | 0 | 9 | 0 | 0 | 0 | .143 | .143 |
| P | Joe Coleman | R | 39 | 13 | 2 | 0 | 0 | 0 | 0.0 | 0 | 0 | 0 | 4 | 0 | 0 | 0 | .154 | .154 |
| P | Paul Reuschel | R | 50 | 13 | 2 | 0 | 0 | 0 | 0.0 | 0 | 1 | 1 | 4 | 0 | 0 | 0 | .154 | .154 |
| P | Oscar Zamora | R | 40 | 9 | 0 | 0 | 0 | 0 | 0.0 | 0 | 0 | 0 | 3 | 0 | 0 | 0 | .000 | .000 |
| P | Bruce Sutter | R | 52 | 8 | 0 | 0 | 0 | 0 | 0.0 | 0 | 0 | 1 | 6 | 0 | 0 | 0 | .000 | .000 |
| P | Darold Knowles | L | 58 | 7 | 1 | 0 | 0 | 0 | 0.0 | 0 | 0 | 3 | 0 | 0 | 0 | 0 | .143 | .143 |
| P | Mike Garman | R | 47 | 7 | 0 | 0 | 0 | 0 | 0.0 | 0 | 0 | 0 | 4 | 0 | 0 | 0 | .000 | .000 |
| P | Buddy Schultz | R | 29 | 4 | 0 | 0 | 0 | 0 | 0.0 | 0 | 0 | 0 | 0 | 0 | 0 | 0 | .000 | .000 |
| P | Ken Frailing | L | 6 | 3 | 0 | 0 | 0 | 0 | 0.0 | 0 | 0 | 0 | 0 | 0 | 0 | 0 | .000 | .000 |
| P | Geoff Zahn | L | 3 | 3 | 0 | 0 | 0 | 0 | 0.0 | 0 | 0 | 0 | 0 | 0 | 0 | 0 | .000 | .000 |
| P | Ken Crosby | R | 7 | 2 | 1 | 0 | 0 | 0 | 0.0 | 0 | 0 | 0 | 0 | 0 | 0 | 0 | .500 | .500 |
| P | Mike Krukow | R | 2 | 1 | 0 | 0 | 0 | 0 | 0.0 | 0 | 0 | 0 | 0 | 0 | 0 | 0 | .000 | .000 |
| P | Ramon Hernandez | B | 2 | 0 | 0 | 0 | 0 | 0 | – | 0 | 0 | 0 | 0 | 0 | 0 | 0 | – | – |
| P | Tom Dettore | L | 4 | 0 | 0 | 0 | 0 | 0 | – | 0 | 0 | 0 | 0 | 0 | 0 | 0 | – | – |
| | TEAM TOTAL | | | 5518 | 1386 | 216 | 24 | 105 | 1.9 | 61 | 559 | 490 | 834 | 74 | 234 | 44 | .251 | .356 |

## INDIVIDUAL FIELDING

| POS | Player | T | G | PO | A | E | DP | TC/G | FA | | POS | Player | T | G | PO | A | E | DP | TC/G | FA |
|---|---|---|---|---|---|---|---|---|---|---|---|---|---|---|---|---|---|---|---|---|
| 1B | P. LaCock | L | 54 | 435 | 30 | 12 | 47 | 8.8 | .975 | | OF | J. Morales | R | 136 | 273 | 12 | 5 | 6 | 2.1 | .983 |
| | R. Monday | L | 32 | 309 | 22 | 3 | 17 | 10.4 | .991 | | | R. Monday | L | 103 | 278 | 4 | 2 | 0 | 2.8 | .993 |
| | L. Biittner | L | 33 | 232 | 33 | 4 | 20 | 8.2 | .985 | | | J. Cardenal | R | 128 | 246 | 10 | 5 | 1 | 2.0 | .981 |
| | A. Thornton | R | 25 | 202 | 19 | 3 | 17 | 9.0 | .987 | | | J. Wallis | R | 90 | 193 | 11 | 5 | 3 | 2.3 | .976 |
| | Mitterwald | R | 25 | 192 | 10 | 1 | 11 | 8.1 | .995 | | | L. Biittner | L | 24 | 34 | 1 | 0 | 0 | 1.5 | 1.000 |
| | C. Summers | R | 10 | 69 | 4 | 0 | 10 | 7.3 | 1.000 | | | C. Summers | R | 26 | 26 | 1 | 1 | 0 | 1.1 | .964 |
| | J. Tabb | R | 6 | 52 | 2 | 0 | 4 | 9.0 | 1.000 | | | P. LaCock | L | 19 | 19 | 3 | 1 | 0 | 1.2 | .957 |
| | W. Tyrone | R | 5 | 30 | 3 | 0 | 6 | 6.6 | 1.000 | | | R. Sperring | R | 3 | 8 | 0 | 0 | 0 | 2.7 | 1.000 |
| | E. Putman | R | 1 | 12 | 0 | 0 | 0 | 12.0 | 1.000 | | | W. Tyrone | R | 7 | 4 | 0 | 0 | 0 | 0.6 | 1.000 |
| 2B | M. Trillo | R | 156 | 349 | **527** | 17 | 103 | 5.7 | .981 | | | M. Adams | R | 4 | 3 | 0 | 0 | 0 | 0.8 | 1.000 |
| | M. Kelleher | R | 5 | 8 | 14 | 1 | 4 | 4.6 | .957 | | C | S. Swisher | R | 107 | 574 | 49 | 11 | 6 | 5.9 | .983 |
| | R. Sperring | R | 4 | 7 | 6 | 0 | 0 | 3.3 | 1.000 | | | Mitterwald | R | 64 | 320 | 40 | 7 | 2 | 5.7 | .981 |
| | M. Adams | R | 1 | 1 | 1 | 0 | 0 | 2.0 | 1.000 | | | C. Summers | R | 1 | 0 | 0 | 0 | 0 | 0.0 | .000 |
| | D. Rosello | R | 1 | 1 | 0 | 0 | 0 | 1.0 | 1.000 | | | R. Hundley | R | 9 | 22 | 2 | 2 | 0 | 2.9 | .923 |
| SS | M. Kelleher | R | 101 | 147 | 289 | 9 | 52 | 4.4 | .980 | | | E. Putman | R | 3 | 4 | 0 | 0 | 0 | 1.3 | 1.000 |
| | D. Rosello | R | 86 | 128 | 217 | 12 | 45 | 4.2 | .966 | | | | | | | | | | | |
| | R. Sperring | R | 15 | 11 | 23 | 0 | 4 | 2.3 | 1.000 | | | | | | | | | | | |
| | M. Trillo | R | 1 | 1 | 0 | 0 | 0 | 1.0 | 1.000 | | | | | | | | | | | |
| 3B | B. Madlock | R | 136 | 107 | 234 | 14 | 21 | 2.6 | .961 | | | | | | | | | | | |
| | M. Kelleher | R | 22 | 12 | 21 | 2 | 1 | 1.6 | .943 | | | | | | | | | | | |
| | R. Sperring | R | 20 | 10 | 11 | 1 | 1 | 1.1 | .955 | | | | | | | | | | | |
| | W. Tyrone | R | 5 | 5 | 7 | 0 | 0 | 2.4 | 1.000 | | | | | | | | | | | |
| | M. Adams | R | 3 | 0 | 1 | 0 | 0 | 0.3 | 1.000 | | | | | | | | | | | |

For once, the Cubs saved the best for last. Third baseman Bill Madlock went four-for-four on the final day of the season to wrest the batting championship from the Reds' Ken Griffey. Madlock finished with a .339 average to retain his batting title. At the outset of the season owner P. K. Wrigley sprang his usual surprise by naming concessions salesman Salty Saltwell as general manager. But the Cubs were constantly assaulted by the opposition. Their worst skid came in June when they dropped 13 of 15, including 9 in a row, and were called "a bunch of clowns" by Wrigley.

The pitching was atrocious until a young bullpen artist named Bruce Sutter was summoned from the bushes. Sutter, displaying a so-called split-fingered fastball, went on to win six and save 10 games. From July 20 on, the Cubs were 39–34 to finish fourth in the division with a 75–87 record. Topping the turnabout was pitcher Ray Burris, who had a 4–11 log on the 4th of July. After that, he was hotter than a firecracker, winning 11, dropping 2, with 9 complete games and 4 shutouts. He was the big gun of August with a 6–1 mark. Although hitting in the leadoff spot, outfielder Rick Monday supplied the power with 32 homers, while Madlock led in RBI with 84. Outfielder Jose Cardenal, who went six-for-six on May 2, just missed the .300 mark, winding up at .299. At the conclusion of the season, baseball held its historic reentry draft. A total of 24 players, who played out their options, were available in the open market. The Cubs selected zilch.

## TEAM STATISTICS

| | W | L | PCT | GB | R | OR | Batting 2B | 3B | HR | BA | SA | SB | Fielding E | DP | FA | CG | B | Pitching SO | ShO | SV | ERA |
|---|---|---|---|---|---|---|---|---|---|---|---|---|---|---|---|---|---|---|---|---|---|
| **AST** | | | | | | | | | | | | | | | | | | | | | |
| HI | 101 | 61 | .623 | | 770 | 557 | 259 | 45 | 110 | .272 | .395 | 127 | 115 | 148 | .981 | 34 | **397** | 918 | 9 | 44 | 3.10 |
| IT | 92 | 70 | .568 | 9 | 708 | 630 | 249 | 56 | 110 | .267 | .391 | 130 | 163 | 142 | .975 | 45 | 460 | 762 | 12 | 35 | 3.37 |
| IY | 86 | 76 | .531 | 15 | 615 | 538 | 198 | 34 | 102 | .246 | .352 | 66 | 131 | 116 | .979 | 53 | 419 | **1025** | 18 | 25 | **2.94** |
| HI | 75 | 87 | .463 | 26 | 611 | 728 | 216 | 24 | 105 | .251 | .356 | 74 | 140 | 145 | .978 | 27 | 490 | 850 | 12 | 33 | 3.93 |
| TL | 72 | 90 | .444 | 29 | 629 | 671 | 243 | 57 | 63 | .260 | .359 | 123 | 174 | 163 | .973 | 35 | 581 | 731 | 15 | 26 | 3.61 |
| MON | 55 | 107 | .340 | 46 | 531 | 734 | 224 | 32 | 94 | .235 | .340 | 86 | 155 | 179 | .976 | 26 | 659 | 783 | 10 | 21 | 3.99 |
| **VEST** | | | | | | | | | | | | | | | | | | | | | |
| IN | 102 | 60 | .630 | | **857** | 633 | **271** | **63** | 141 | **.280** | **.424** | 210 | 102 | 157 | **.984** | 33 | 491 | 790 | 12 | **45** | 3.51 |
| A | 92 | 70 | .568 | 10 | 608 | 543 | 200 | 34 | 91 | .251 | .349 | 144 | 128 | 154 | .980 | 47 | 479 | 747 | 17 | 28 | 3.02 |
| OU | 80 | 82 | .494 | 22 | 625 | 657 | 195 | 50 | 66 | .256 | .347 | 150 | 140 | 155 | .978 | 42 | 662 | 780 | 17 | 29 | 3.55 |
| F | 74 | 88 | .457 | 28 | 595 | 686 | 211 | 37 | 85 | .246 | .345 | 88 | 186 | 153 | .971 | 27 | 518 | 746 | **18** | 31 | 3.53 |
| D | 73 | 89 | .451 | 29 | 570 | 662 | 216 | 37 | 64 | .247 | .337 | 92 | 141 | 148 | .978 | 47 | 543 | 652 | 11 | 18 | 3.65 |
| TL | 70 | 92 | .432 | 32 | 620 | 700 | 170 | 30 | 82 | .245 | .334 | 74 | 167 | 151 | .973 | 33 | 564 | 818 | 13 | 27 | 3.87 |
| EAGUE TOTAL | | | | | 7739 | 7739 | 2652 | 499 | 1113 | .255 | .361 | 1364 | 1742 | 1811 | .977 | 449 | 6263 | 9602 | 164 | 362 | 3.50 |

## INDIVIDUAL PITCHING

| PITCHER | T | W | L | PCT | ERA | SV | G | GS | CG | IP | H | BB | SO | R | ER | ShO | H/9 | BB/9 | SO/9 |
|---|---|---|---|---|---|---|---|---|---|---|---|---|---|---|---|---|---|---|---|
| Rick Reuschel | R | 14 | 12 | .538 | 3.46 | 1 | 38 | 37 | 9 | 260 | 260 | 64 | 146 | **117** | 100 | 2 | 9.00 | 2.22 | 5.05 |
| Ray Burris | R | 15 | 13 | .536 | 3.11 | 0 | 37 | 36 | 10 | 249 | 251 | 70 | 112 | 102 | 86 | 4 | 9.07 | 2.53 | 4.05 |
| Bill Bonham | R | 9 | 13 | .409 | 4.27 | 0 | 32 | 31 | 3 | 196 | 215 | 96 | 110 | 102 | 93 | 0 | 9.87 | 4.41 | 5.05 |
| Steve Renko | R | 8 | 11 | .421 | 3.86 | 0 | 28 | 27 | 4 | 163.1 | 164 | 43 | 112 | 79 | 70 | 0 | 9.04 | 2.37 | 6.17 |
| Paul Reuschel | R | 4 | 2 | .667 | 4.55 | 3 | 50 | 2 | 0 | 87 | 94 | 33 | 55 | 46 | 44 | 0 | 9.72 | 3.41 | 5.69 |
| Bruce Sutter | R | 6 | 3 | .667 | 2.71 | 10 | 52 | 0 | 0 | 83 | 63 | 26 | 73 | 27 | 25 | 0 | 6.83 | 2.82 | 7.92 |
| Joe Coleman | R | 2 | 8 | .200 | 4.10 | 4 | 39 | 4 | 0 | 79 | 72 | 35 | 66 | 43 | 36 | 0 | 8.20 | 3.99 | 7.52 |
| Mike Garman | R | 2 | 4 | .333 | 4.97 | 1 | 47 | 2 | 0 | 76 | 79 | 35 | 37 | 48 | 42 | 0 | 9.36 | 4.14 | 4.38 |
| Steve Stone | R | 3 | 6 | .333 | 4.08 | 0 | 17 | 15 | 1 | 75 | 70 | 21 | 33 | 36 | 34 | 1 | 8.40 | 2.52 | 3.96 |
| Darold Knowles | L | 5 | 7 | .417 | 2.88 | 9 | 58 | 0 | 0 | 72 | 61 | 22 | 39 | 30 | 23 | 0 | 7.63 | 2.75 | 4.88 |
| Oscar Zamora | R | 5 | 3 | .625 | 5.24 | 3 | 40 | 2 | 0 | 55 | 70 | 17 | 27 | 34 | 32 | 0 | 11.45 | 2.78 | 4.42 |
| Buddy Schultz | L | 1 | 1 | .500 | 6.00 | 2 | 29 | 0 | 0 | 24 | 37 | 9 | 15 | 19 | 16 | 0 | 13.88 | 3.38 | 5.63 |
| Ken Frailing | L | 1 | 2 | .333 | 2.37 | 0 | 6 | 3 | 0 | 19 | 20 | 5 | 10 | 7 | 5 | 0 | 9.47 | 2.37 | 4.74 |
| Ken Crosby | R | 0 | 0 | — | 12.00 | 0 | 7 | 1 | 0 | 12 | 20 | 8 | 5 | 16 | 16 | 0 | 15.00 | 6.00 | 3.75 |
| Geoff Zahn | L | 0 | 1 | .000 | 11.25 | 0 | 3 | 2 | 0 | 8 | 16 | 2 | 4 | 10 | 10 | 0 | 18.00 | 2.25 | 4.50 |
| Tom Dettore | R | 0 | 1 | .000 | 10.29 | 0 | 4 | 0 | 0 | 7 | 11 | 2 | 4 | 8 | 8 | 0 | 14.14 | 2.57 | 5.14 |
| Mike Krukow | R | 0 | 0 | — | 9.00 | 0 | 2 | 0 | 0 | 4 | 6 | 2 | 1 | 4 | 4 | 0 | 13.50 | 4.50 | 2.25 |
| Ramon Hernandez | L | 0 | 0 | — | 0.00 | 0 | 2 | 0 | 0 | 1.2 | 2 | 0 | 1 | 0 | 0 | 0 | 10.80 | 0.00 | 5.40 |
| TEAM TOTAL | | 75 | 87 | .463 | 3.94 | 33 | 491 | 162 | 27 | 1471 | 1511 | 490 | 850 | 728 | 644 | 7 | 9.24 | 3.00 | 5.20 |

| MANAGER | W | L | PCT |
|---|---|---|---|
| Herman Franks | 81 | 81 | .500 |

| POS | Player | B | G | AB | H | 2B | 3B | HR | HR % | R | RBI | BB | SO | SB | Pinch Hit AB | Pinch Hit H | BA | SA |
|---|---|---|---|---|---|---|---|---|---|---|---|---|---|---|---|---|---|---|
| **REGULARS** | | | | | | | | | | | | | | | | | | |
| 1B | Bill Buckner | L | 122 | 426 | 121 | 27 | 0 | 11 | 2.6 | 40 | 60 | 21 | 23 | 7 | 22 | 7 | .284 | .425 |
| 2B | Manny Trillo | R | 152 | 504 | 141 | 18 | 5 | 7 | 1.4 | 51 | 57 | 44 | 58 | 3 | 5 | 0 | .280 | .377 |
| SS | Ivan DeJesus | R | 155 | 624 | 166 | 31 | 7 | 3 | 0.5 | 91 | 40 | 56 | 90 | 24 | 0 | 0 | .266 | .353 |
| 3B | Steve Ontiveros | B | 156 | 546 | 163 | 32 | 3 | 10 | 1.8 | 54 | 68 | 81 | 69 | 3 | 3 | 1 | .299 | .423 |
| RF | Bobby Murcer | L | 154 | 554 | 147 | 18 | 3 | 27 | 4.9 | 90 | 89 | 80 | 77 | 16 | 5 | 2 | .265 | .455 |
| CF | Jerry Morales | R | 136 | 490 | 142 | 34 | 5 | 11 | 2.2 | 56 | 69 | 43 | 75 | 0 | 11 | 3 | .290 | .447 |
| LF | Greg Gross | L | 115 | 239 | 77 | 10 | 4 | 5 | 2.1 | 43 | 32 | 33 | 19 | 0 | 39 | 10 | .322 | .460 |
| C | George Mitterwald | R | 110 | 349 | 83 | 22 | 0 | 9 | 2.6 | 26 | 40 | 28 | 69 | 3 | 2 | 0 | .238 | .378 |
| **SUBSTITUTES** | | | | | | | | | | | | | | | | | | |
| 1O | Larry Biittner | L | 138 | 493 | 147 | 28 | 1 | 12 | 2.4 | 74 | 62 | 35 | 36 | 2 | 15 | 5 | .298 | .432 |
| 2S | Mick Kelleher | R | 63 | 122 | 28 | 5 | 2 | 0 | 0.0 | 14 | 11 | 9 | 12 | 0 | 0 | 0 | .230 | .303 |
| 3S | Dave Rosello | R | 56 | 82 | 18 | 2 | 1 | 1 | 1.2 | 18 | 9 | 12 | 12 | 0 | 22 | 7 | .220 | .305 |
| 2B | Mike Sember | R | 3 | 4 | 1 | 0 | 0 | 0 | 0.0 | 0 | 0 | 0 | 2 | 0 | 2 | 0 | .250 | .250 |
| OF | Gene Clines | R | 101 | 239 | 70 | 12 | 2 | 3 | 1.3 | 27 | 41 | 25 | 25 | 1 | 39 | 10 | .293 | .397 |
| OF | Jose Cardenal | R | 100 | 226 | 54 | 12 | 1 | 3 | 1.3 | 33 | 18 | 28 | 30 | 5 | 31 | 10 | .239 | .341 |
| OF | Joe Wallis | L | 56 | 80 | 20 | 3 | 0 | 2 | 2.5 | 14 | 8 | 16 | 25 | 0 | 16 | 2 | .250 | .363 |
| OF | Bobby Darwin | R | 11 | 12 | 2 | 1 | 0 | 0 | 0.0 | 2 | 0 | 0 | 5 | 0 | 8 | 2 | .167 | .250 |
| OF | Mike Adams | R | 2 | 2 | 0 | 0 | 0 | 0 | 0.0 | 0 | 0 | 0 | 1 | 0 | 1 | 0 | .000 | .000 |
| C | Steve Swisher | R | 74 | 205 | 39 | 7 | 0 | 5 | 2.4 | 21 | 15 | 9 | 47 | 0 | 4 | 1 | .190 | .298 |
| C | Mike Gordon | B | 8 | 23 | 1 | 0 | 0 | 0 | 0.0 | 0 | 2 | 2 | 8 | 0 | 0 | 0 | .043 | .043 |
| C | Randy Hundley | R | 2 | 4 | 0 | 0 | 0 | 0 | 0.0 | 0 | 0 | 0 | 1 | 0 | 0 | 0 | .000 | .000 |
| **PITCHERS** | | | | | | | | | | | | | | | | | | |
| P | Rick Reuschel | R | 41 | 87 | 18 | 3 | 1 | 1 | 1.1 | 9 | 8 | 1 | 18 | 0 | 0 | 0 | .207 | .299 |
| P | Ray Burris | R | 40 | 69 | 12 | 2 | 1 | 1 | 1.4 | 4 | 8 | 4 | 22 | 0 | 1 | 0 | .174 | .275 |
| P | Bill Bonham | R | 35 | 65 | 15 | 3 | 0 | 0 | 0.0 | 3 | 3 | 1 | 14 | 0 | 0 | 0 | .231 | .277 |
| P | Mike Krukow | R | 34 | 55 | 11 | 1 | 0 | 0 | 0.0 | 4 | 2 | 1 | 14 | 0 | 0 | 0 | .200 | .218 |
| P | Bruce Sutter | R | 62 | 20 | 3 | 0 | 0 | 0 | 0.0 | 4 | 0 | 2 | 10 | 0 | 0 | 0 | .150 | .150 |
| P | Dave Roberts | L | 17 | 17 | 1 | 0 | 0 | 0 | 0.0 | 0 | 1 | 0 | 5 | 0 | 0 | 0 | .059 | .059 |
| P | Willie Hernandez | L | 67 | 16 | 1 | 0 | 0 | 0 | 0.0 | 0 | 0 | 0 | 9 | 0 | 0 | 0 | .063 | .063 |
| P | Steve Renko | R | 13 | 12 | 2 | 0 | 0 | 0 | 0.0 | 0 | 0 | 2 | 7 | 0 | 0 | 0 | .167 | .167 |
| P | Paul Reuschel | R | 69 | 11 | 0 | 0 | 0 | 0 | 0.0 | 0 | 0 | 0 | 3 | 0 | 0 | 0 | .000 | .000 |
| P | Donnie Moore | L | 27 | 10 | 3 | 0 | 1 | 0 | 0.0 | 0 | 1 | 1 | 5 | 0 | 0 | 0 | .300 | .500 |
| P | Dennis Lamp | R | 11 | 8 | 3 | 0 | 0 | 0 | 0.0 | 0 | 2 | 0 | 2 | 0 | 0 | 0 | .375 | .375 |
| P | Pete Broberg | R | 22 | 6 | 0 | 0 | 0 | 0 | 0.0 | 0 | 0 | 0 | 2 | 0 | 0 | 0 | .000 | .000 |
| P | Dave Giusti | R | 20 | 2 | 0 | 0 | 0 | 0 | 0.0 | 0 | 0 | 0 | 1 | 0 | 0 | 0 | .000 | .000 |
| P | Ramon Hernandez | B | 6 | 1 | 0 | 0 | 0 | 0 | 0.0 | 0 | 0 | 0 | 0 | 0 | 0 | 0 | .000 | .000 |
| P | Jim Todd | L | 20 | 1 | 0 | 0 | 0 | 0 | 0.0 | 0 | 0 | 0 | 0 | 0 | 0 | 0 | .000 | .000 |
| | TEAM TOTAL | | | 5604 | 1489 | 271 | 37 | 111 | 2.0 | 69 | 649 | 534 | 796 | 64 | 226 | 60 | .266 | .387 |

## INDIVIDUAL FIELDING

| POS | Player | T | G | PO | A | E | DP | TC/G | FA |
|---|---|---|---|---|---|---|---|---|---|
| 1B | B. Buckner | L | 99 | 966 | 58 | 10 | 75 | 10.4 | .990 |
| | L. Biittner | L | 80 | 713 | 64 | 10 | 50 | 9.8 | .987 |
| | Mitterwald | R | 1 | 2 | 0 | 0 | 0 | 2.0 | 1.000 |
| 2B | M. Trillo | R | 149 | 330 | 467 | 25 | 81 | 5.5 | .970 |
| | M. Kelleher | R | 40 | 65 | 99 | 4 | 16 | 4.2 | .976 |
| | M. Sember | R | 1 | 2 | 2 | 0 | 1 | 4.0 | 1.000 |
| | D. Rosello | R | 3 | 2 | 1 | 0 | 0 | 1.0 | 1.000 |
| | J. Cardenal | R | 1 | 0 | 0 | 1 | 0 | 1.0 | .000 |
| | B. Murcer | R | 1 | 1 | 0 | 0 | 0 | 1.0 | 1.000 |
| SS | I. DeJesus | R | 154 | 234 | 595 | 33 | 94 | 5.6 | .962 |
| | B. Murcer | R | 1 | 0 | 0 | 0 | 0 | 0.0 | .000 |
| | M. Kelleher | R | 14 | 13 | 27 | 0 | 5 | 2.9 | 1.000 |
| | D. Rosello | R | 10 | 2 | 15 | 4 | 0 | 2.1 | .810 |
| 3B | S. Ontiveros | R | 155 | 100 | 324 | 20 | 24 | 2.9 | .955 |
| | D. Rosello | R | 21 | 4 | 26 | 2 | 2 | 1.5 | .938 |
| | J. Cardenal | R | 1 | 0 | 0 | 0 | 0 | 0.0 | .000 |
| | M. Kelleher | R | 1 | 0 | 0 | 0 | 0 | 0.0 | .000 |

| POS | Player | T | G | PO | A | E | DP | TC/G | FA |
|---|---|---|---|---|---|---|---|---|---|
| OF | J. Morales | R | 128 | 247 | 8 | 4 | 3 | 2.0 | .985 |
| | B. Murcer | R | 150 | 237 | 11 | 5 | 5 | 1.7 | .980 |
| | G. Gross | L | 71 | 109 | 3 | 1 | 0 | 1.6 | .991 |
| | J. Cardenal | R | 62 | 85 | 1 | 1 | 0 | 1.4 | .989 |
| | L. Biittner | L | 52 | 79 | 1 | 1 | 1 | 1.6 | .988 |
| | G. Clines | R | 63 | 68 | 3 | 1 | 0 | 1.1 | .986 |
| | J. Wallis | R | 35 | 36 | 2 | 1 | 0 | 1.1 | .974 |
| | B. Darwin | R | 1 | 0 | 0 | 0 | 0 | 0.0 | .000 |
| | M. Adams | R | 2 | 0 | 0 | 0 | 0 | 0.0 | .000 |
| C | Mitterwald | R | 109 | 621 | 78 | 8 | 13 | 6.5 | .989 |
| | S. Swisher | R | 72 | 327 | 38 | 9 | 3 | 5.2 | .976 |
| | M. Gordon | R | 8 | 31 | 1 | 1 | 1 | 4.1 | .970 |
| | R. Hundley | R | 2 | 10 | 0 | 0 | 0 | 5.0 | 1.000 |

   Never in Cubs' history had a team depended on one player as they did now. Bruce Sutter, the right-handed reliever with the split-fingered fastball, was the head, the arm, and the heart that pumped late-inning victories. At one stage the Cubs were 25 games over .500 and enjoyed an 8 1/2 game lead in the NL East. For 69 days they held onto first place. Then came the collapse, which was less publicized, but greater than the 1969 fadeout. Sutter developed a swelling under his right shoulder blade. It developed into a knot, and the Cubs became have-nots. With Sutter on the sidelines, manager Herman Franks saw his club disintegrate. From August 25 on, the Cubs won 12 and lost 24 and wound up fourth with an 81–81 record. Sutter somehow managed to win seven and save 31 games. Pitcher Rick Reuschel, who at one stage was 15–3, won only one game the final month and finished with a 20–10 record. Second baseman Manny Trillo, a surprise batting leader at .362 in midsummer, plummeted to .280. The batting leaders were third baseman Steve Ontiveros at .299 and outfielder Bobby Murcer with 27 homers. Both were acquired from the Giants for 1976 batting champ Bill Madlock. Newly acquired first baseman Bill Buckner missed 40 games but managed to hit .284 on a gimpy ankle.

## TEAM  STATISTICS

| | W | L | PCT | GB | R | OR | 2B | 3B | HR | BA | SA | SB | E | DP | FA | CG | B | SO | ShO | SV | ERA |
|---|---|---|---|---|---|---|---|---|---|---|---|---|---|---|---|---|---|---|---|---|---|
| | | | | | | | | Batting | | | | | | Fielding | | | | | Pitching | | |
| AST | | | | | | | | | | | | | | | | | | | | | |
| HI | 101 | 61 | .623 | | 847 | 668 | 266 | 56 | 186 | **.279** | **.448** | 135 | 120 | 168 | .981 | 31 | 482 | 856 | 4 | **47** | 3.71 |
| IT | 96 | 66 | .593 | 5 | 734 | 665 | 278 | 57 | 133 | .274 | .413 | **260** | 145 | 137 | .977 | 25 | 485 | 890 | **15** | 39 | 3.61 |
| TL | 83 | 79 | .512 | 18 | 737 | 688 | 252 | 56 | 96 | .270 | .388 | 134 | 139 | **174** | .978 | 26 | 532 | 768 | 10 | 31 | 3.81 |
| HI | 81 | 81 | .500 | 20 | 692 | 739 | 271 | 37 | 111 | .266 | .387 | 64 | 153 | 147 | .977 | 16 | 489 | **942** | 10 | 44 | 4.01 |
| ION | 75 | 87 | .463 | 26 | 665 | 736 | **294** | 54 | 138 | .260 | .402 | 88 | 129 | 128 | .980 | 31 | 579 | 856 | 11 | 33 | 4.01 |
| Y | 64 | 98 | .395 | 37 | 587 | 663 | 227 | 30 | 88 | .244 | .346 | 98 | 134 | 132 | .978 | 27 | 490 | 911 | 12 | 28 | 3.77 |
| VEST | | | | | | | | | | | | | | | | | | | | | |
| A | 98 | 64 | .605 | | 769 | **582** | 223 | 28 | **191** | .266 | .418 | 114 | 124 | 160 | .981 | 34 | **438** | 930 | 13 | 39 | **3.22** |
| IN | 88 | 74 | .543 | 10 | 802 | 725 | 269 | 42 | 181 | .274 | .436 | 170 | **95** | 154 | **.984** | 33 | 544 | 868 | 12 | 32 | 4.22 |
| IOU | 81 | 81 | .500 | 17 | 680 | 650 | 263 | **60** | 114 | .254 | .385 | 187 | 142 | 136 | .978 | **37** | 545 | 871 | 11 | 28 | 3.54 |
| F | 75 | 87 | .463 | 23 | 673 | 711 | 227 | 41 | 134 | .253 | .383 | 90 | 179 | 136 | .972 | 27 | 529 | 854 | 10 | 33 | 3.75 |
| D | 69 | 93 | .426 | 29 | 692 | 834 | 245 | 49 | 120 | .249 | .375 | 133 | 189 | 142 | .971 | 6 | 673 | 827 | 5 | 44 | 4.43 |
| TL | 61 | 101 | .377 | 37 | 678 | 895 | 218 | 20 | 139 | .254 | .376 | 82 | 175 | 127 | .972 | 28 | 701 | 915 | 5 | 31 | 4.85 |
| EAGUE TOTAL | | | | | 8556 | 8556 | 3033 | 526 | 1631 | .262 | .396 | 1555 | 1724 | 1741 | .977 | 321 | 6487 | 10488 | 118 | 429 | 3.91 |

## INDIVIDUAL  PITCHING

| ITCHER | T | W | L | PCT | ERA | SV | G | GS | CG | IP | H | BB | SO | R | ER | ShO | H/9 | BB/9 | SO/9 |
|---|---|---|---|---|---|---|---|---|---|---|---|---|---|---|---|---|---|---|---|
| ick Reuschel | R | 20 | 10 | .667 | 2.79 | 1 | 39 | 37 | 8 | 252 | 233 | 74 | 166 | 84 | 78 | 4 | 8.32 | 2.64 | 5.93 |
| ay Burris | R | 14 | 16 | .467 | 4.72 | 0 | 39 | 39 | 5 | 221 | 270 | 67 | 105 | 132 | 116 | 1 | 11.00 | 2.73 | 4.28 |
| ill Bonham | R | 10 | 13 | .435 | 4.35 | 0 | 34 | 34 | 1 | 215 | 207 | 82 | 134 | 111 | 104 | 0 | 8.67 | 3.43 | 5.61 |
| like Krukow | R | 8 | 14 | .364 | 4.40 | 0 | 34 | 33 | 1 | 172 | 195 | 61 | 106 | 96 | 84 | 1 | 10.20 | 3.19 | 5.55 |
| Villie Hernandez | L | 8 | 7 | .533 | 3.03 | 4 | 67 | 1 | 0 | 110 | 94 | 28 | 78 | 42 | 37 | 0 | 7.69 | 2.29 | 6.38 |
| aul Reuschel | R | 5 | 6 | .455 | 4.37 | 4 | 69 | 0 | 0 | 107 | 105 | 40 | 62 | 58 | 52 | 0 | 8.83 | 3.36 | 5.21 |
| ruce Sutter | R | 7 | 3 | .700 | 1.35 | 31 | 62 | 0 | 0 | 107 | 69 | 23 | 129 | 21 | 16 | 0 | 5.80 | 1.93 | 10.85 |
| ave Roberts | L | 1 | 1 | .500 | 3.23 | 1 | 17 | 6 | 1 | 53 | 55 | 12 | 23 | 22 | 19 | 0 | 9.34 | 2.04 | 3.91 |
| onnie Moore | R | 4 | 2 | .667 | 4.04 | 0 | 27 | 1 | 0 | 49 | 51 | 18 | 34 | 27 | 22 | 0 | 9.37 | 3.31 | 6.24 |
| ete Renko | R | 2 | 2 | .500 | 4.59 | 1 | 13 | 8 | 0 | 51 | 51 | 21 | 34 | 32 | 26 | 0 | 9.00 | 3.71 | 6.00 |
| ete Broberg | R | 1 | 2 | .333 | 4.75 | 0 | 22 | 0 | 0 | 36 | 34 | 18 | 20 | 22 | 19 | 0 | 8.50 | 4.50 | 5.00 |
| m Todd | R | 1 | 1 | .500 | 9.00 | 0 | 20 | 0 | 0 | 31 | 47 | 19 | 17 | 37 | 31 | 0 | 13.65 | 5.52 | 4.94 |
| ennis Lamp | R | 0 | 2 | .000 | 6.30 | 0 | 11 | 3 | 0 | 30 | 43 | 8 | 12 | 21 | 21 | 0 | 12.90 | 2.40 | 3.60 |
| ave Giusti | R | 0 | 2 | .000 | 6.12 | 1 | 20 | 0 | 0 | 25 | 30 | 14 | 15 | 19 | 17 | 0 | 10.80 | 5.04 | 5.40 |
| amon Hernandez | L | 0 | 0 | – | 7.88 | 0 | 6 | 0 | 0 | 8 | 11 | 3 | 4 | 9 | 7 | 0 | 12.38 | 3.38 | 4.50 |
| arry Biittner | L | 0 | 0 | – | 54.00 | 0 | 1 | 0 | 0 | 1 | 5 | 1 | 3 | 6 | 6 | 0 | 45.00 | 9.00 | 27.00 |
| EAM TOTAL | | 81 | 81 | .500 | 4.02 | 44 | 481 | 162 | 16 | 1468 | 1500 | 489· | 942 | 739 | 655 | 6 | 9.20 | 3.00 | 5.78 |

| MANAGER | W | L | PCT |
|---|---|---|---|
| Herman Franks | 79 | 83 | .488 |

| POS | Player | B | G | AB | H | 2B | 3B | HR | HR % | R | RBI | BB | SO | SB | Pinch Hit AB | Pinch Hit H | BA | SA |
|---|---|---|---|---|---|---|---|---|---|---|---|---|---|---|---|---|---|---|
| **REGULARS** | | | | | | | | | | | | | | | | | | |
| 1B | Bill Buckner | L | 117 | 446 | 144 | 26 | 1 | 5 | 1.1 | 47 | 74 | 18 | 17 | 7 | 12 | 2 | .323 | .419 |
| 2B | Manny Trillo | R | 152 | 552 | 144 | 17 | 5 | 4 | 0.7 | 53 | 55 | 50 | 67 | 0 | 2 | 2 | .261 | .332 |
| SS | Ivan DeJesus | R | 160 | 619 | 172 | 24 | 7 | 3 | 0.5 | 104 | 35 | 74 | 78 | 41 | 0 | 0 | .278 | .354 |
| 3B | Steve Ontiveros | B | 82 | 276 | 67 | 14 | 4 | 1 | 0.4 | 34 | 22 | 34 | 33 | 0 | 4 | 2 | .243 | .333 |
| RF | Bobby Murcer | L | 146 | 499 | 140 | 22 | 6 | 9 | 1.8 | 66 | 64 | 80 | 57 | 14 | 10 | 4 | .281 | .403 |
| CF | Greg Gross | L | 124 | 347 | 92 | 12 | 7 | 1 | 0.3 | 34 | 39 | 33 | 19 | 3 | 20 | 5 | .265 | .349 |
| LF | Dave Kingman | R | 119 | 395 | 105 | 17 | 4 | 28 | 7.1 | 65 | 79 | 39 | 111 | 3 | 8 | 1 | .266 | .542 |
| C | Dave Rader | L | 116 | 305 | 62 | 13 | 3 | 3 | 1.0 | 29 | 36 | 34 | 26 | 1 | 13 | 4 | .203 | .295 |
| **SUBSTITUTES** | | | | | | | | | | | | | | | | | | |
| 1O | Larry Biittner | L | 120 | 343 | 88 | 15 | 1 | 4 | 1.2 | 32 | 50 | 23 | 37 | 0 | 33 | 11 | .257 | .341 |
| UT | Rodney Scott | R | 78 | 227 | 64 | 5 | 1 | 0 | 0.0 | 41 | 15 | 43 | 41 | 27 | 3 | 0 | .282 | .313 |
| UT | Mick Kelleher | R | 68 | 95 | 24 | 1 | 0 | 0 | 0.0 | 8 | 6 | 7 | 11 | 4 | 3 | 1 | .253 | .263 |
| 3B | Davy Johnson | R | 24 | 49 | 15 | 1 | 1 | 2 | 4.1 | 5 | 6 | 5 | 9 | 0 | 11 | 4 | .306 | .490 |
| 23 | Rudi Meoli | L | 47 | 29 | 3 | 0 | 1 | 0 | 0.0 | 10 | 2 | 6 | 4 | 1 | 19 | 2 | .103 | .172 |
| UT | Ed Putman | R | 17 | 25 | 5 | 0 | 0 | 0 | 0.0 | 2 | 3 | 4 | 6 | 0 | 5 | 2 | .200 | .200 |
| 3B | Mike Sember | R | 9 | 3 | 1 | 0 | 0 | 0 | 0.0 | 2 | 0 | 1 | 1 | 0 | 2 | 1 | .333 | .333 |
| OF | Gene Clines | R | 109 | 229 | 59 | 10 | 2 | 0 | 0.0 | 31 | 17 | 21 | 28 | 4 | 43 | 10 | .258 | .319 |
| OF | Mike Vail | R | 74 | 180 | 60 | 6 | 2 | 4 | 2.2 | 15 | 33 | 3 | 24 | 0 | 30 | 11 | .333 | .456 |
| OF | Jerry White | B | 59 | 136 | 37 | 6 | 0 | 1 | 0.7 | 22 | 10 | 23 | 16 | 4 | 4 | 2 | .272 | .338 |
| O3 | Hector Cruz | R | 30 | 76 | 18 | 5 | 0 | 2 | 2.6 | 8 | 9 | 3 | 6 | 0 | 10 | 2 | .237 | .382 |
| OF | Joe Wallis | L | 28 | 55 | 17 | 2 | 1 | 1 | 1.8 | 7 | 6 | 5 | 13 | 0 | 4 | 2 | .309 | .436 |
| O1 | Scot Thompson | L | 19 | 36 | 15 | 3 | 0 | 0 | 0.0 | 7 | 2 | 2 | 4 | 0 | 12 | 6 | .417 | .500 |
| C | Larry Cox | R | 59 | 121 | 34 | 5 | 0 | 2 | 1.7 | 10 | 18 | 12 | 16 | 0 | 0 | 0 | .281 | .372 |
| C | Tim Blackwell | B | 49 | 103 | 23 | 3 | 0 | 0 | 0.0 | 8 | 7 | 23 | 17 | 0 | 0 | 0 | .223 | .252 |
| C | Mike Gordon | B | 4 | 5 | 1 | 0 | 0 | 0 | 0.0 | 0 | 0 | 3 | 2 | 0 | 0 | 0 | .200 | .200 |
| **PITCHERS** | | | | | | | | | | | | | | | | | | |
| P | Dennis Lamp | R | 37 | 73 | 15 | 2 | 0 | 0 | 0.0 | 1 | 3 | 0 | 17 | 0 | 0 | 0 | .205 | .233 |
| P | Rick Reuschel | R | 35 | 73 | 10 | 2 | 0 | 0 | 0.0 | 5 | 4 | 4 | 23 | 1 | 0 | 0 | .137 | .164 |
| P | Ray Burris | R | 41 | 61 | 7 | 1 | 2 | 0 | 0.0 | 3 | 2 | 2 | 13 | 0 | 0 | 0 | .115 | .197 |
| P | Dave Roberts | L | 37 | 52 | 17 | 3 | 0 | 2 | 3.8 | 4 | 7 | 2 | 7 | 0 | 2 | 1 | .327 | .500 |
| P | Mike Krukow | R | 27 | 45 | 11 | 5 | 0 | 0 | 0.0 | 4 | 3 | 2 | 13 | 0 | 0 | 0 | .244 | .356 |
| P | Woodie Fryman | R | 13 | 16 | 1 | 1 | 0 | 0 | 0.0 | 0 | 1 | 0 | 5 | 0 | 0 | 0 | .063 | .125 |
| P | Donnie Moore | L | 71 | 15 | 4 | 1 | 0 | 0 | 0.0 | 2 | 4 | 2 | 6 | 0 | 0 | 0 | .267 | .333 |
| P | Bruce Sutter | R | 64 | 13 | 1 | 0 | 0 | 0 | 0.0 | 1 | 0 | 2 | 8 | 0 | 0 | 0 | .077 | .077 |
| P | Lynn McGlothen | L | 49 | 13 | 3 | 1 | 0 | 0 | 0.0 | 1 | 0 | 1 | 1 | 0 | 0 | 0 | .231 | .308 |
| P | Ken Holtzman | R | 23 | 10 | 2 | 1 | 0 | 0 | 0.0 | 2 | 0 | 1 | 5 | 0 | 0 | 0 | .200 | .300 |
| P | Paul Reuschel | R | 16 | 4 | 0 | 0 | 0 | 0 | 0.0 | 0 | 0 | 0 | 1 | 0 | 0 | 0 | .000 | .000 |
| P | Dave Geisel | L | 18 | 3 | 0 | 0 | 0 | 0 | 0.0 | 0 | 0 | 0 | 2 | 0 | 0 | 0 | .000 | .000 |
| P | Willie Hernandez | L | 55 | 1 | 0 | 0 | 0 | 0 | 0.0 | 1 | 0 | 0 | 0 | 0 | 0 | 0 | .000 | .000 |
| P | Manny Seoane | R | 7 | 0 | 0 | 0 | 0 | 0 | – | 0 | 0 | 0 | 0 | 0 | 0 | 0 | – | – |
| TEAM TOTAL | | | | 5530 | 1461 | 224 | 48 | 72 | 1.3 | 66 | 612 | 562 | 744 | 110 | 250 | 75 | .264 | .361 |

## INDIVIDUAL FIELDING

| POS | Player | T | G | PO | A | E | DP | TC/G | FA | | POS | Player | T | G | PO | A | E | DP | TC/G | FA |
|---|---|---|---|---|---|---|---|---|---|---|---|---|---|---|---|---|---|---|---|---|
| 1B | B. Buckner | L | 105 | 1075 | 83 | 6 | 85 | 11.1 | .995 | | OF | B. Murcer | R | 138 | 225 | 8 | 5 | 0 | 1.7 | .979 |
| | L. Biittner | L | 62 | 554 | 52 | 8 | 53 | 9.9 | .987 | | | G. Gross | L | 111 | 182 | 6 | 4 | 1 | 1.7 | .979 |
| | D. Kingman | R | 6 | 56 | 2 | 2 | 4 | 10.0 | .967 | | | D. Kingman | R | 100 | 170 | 8 | 4 | 2 | 1.8 | .978 |
| | E. Putman | R | 3 | 9 | 0 | 1 | 0 | 3.3 | .900 | | | J. White | R | 54 | 102 | 4 | 2 | 1 | 2.0 | .981 |
| | S. Thompson | L | 2 | 8 | 1 | 0 | 1 | 4.5 | 1.000 | | | G. Clines | R | 66 | 84 | 6 | 2 | 0 | 1.4 | .978 |
| | S. Ontiveros | R | 1 | 7 | 0 | 0 | 0 | 7.0 | 1.000 | | | M. Vail | R | 45 | 50 | 1 | 1 | 0 | 1.2 | .981 |
| 2B | M. Trillo | R | 149 | 354 | 505 | 19 | 99 | 5.9 | .978 | | | L. Biittner | L | 29 | 47 | 1 | 1 | 0 | 1.7 | .980 |
| | M. Kelleher | R | 17 | 33 | 48 | 0 | 6 | 4.8 | 1.000 | | | J. Wallis | R | 25 | 36 | 1 | 0 | 0 | 1.5 | 1.000 |
| | R. Scott | R | 6 | 16 | 10 | 1 | 1 | 4.5 | .963 | | | H. Cruz | R | 14 | 30 | 0 | 0 | 0 | 2.1 | 1.000 |
| | R. Meoli | R | 6 | 4 | 5 | 1 | 0 | 1.7 | .900 | | | R. Scott | R | 10 | 14 | 1 | 1 | 0 | 1.6 | .938 |
| SS | I. DeJesus | R | 160 | 232 | 558 | 27 | 96 | 5.1 | .967 | | | S. Thompson | L | 5 | 6 | 0 | 0 | 0 | 1.2 | 1.000 |
| | M. Kelleher | R | 10 | 8 | 11 | 0 | 1 | 1.9 | 1.000 | | C | D. Rader | R | 114 | 412 | 51 | 11 | 7 | 4.2 | .977 |
| | R. Scott | R | 6 | 4 | 7 | 1 | 1 | 2.0 | .917 | | | T. Blackwell | R | 49 | 213 | 20 | 3 | 3 | 4.8 | .987 |
| | M. Sember | R | 1 | 1 | 1 | 0 | 1 | 2.0 | 1.000 | | | L. Cox | R | 58 | 178 | 26 | 7 | 3 | 3.6 | .967 |
| 3B | S. Ontiveros | R | 77 | 57 | 194 | 9 | 16 | 3.4 | .965 | | | E. Putman | R | 2 | 0 | 0 | 0 | 0 | 0.0 | .000 |
| | R. Scott | R | 60 | 43 | 101 | 11 | 15 | 2.6 | .929 | | | M. Gordon | R | 4 | 14 | 0 | 0 | 0 | 3.5 | 1.000 |
| | M. Kelleher | R | 37 | 11 | 41 | 0 | 3 | 1.4 | 1.000 | | | | | | | | | | | |
| | M. Vail | R | 1 | 0 | 0 | 0 | 0 | 0.0 | .000 | | | | | | | | | | | |
| | D. Johnson | R | 12 | 4 | 22 | 5 | 1 | 2.6 | .839 | | | | | | | | | | | |
| | E. Putman | R | 8 | 6 | 13 | 1 | 1 | 2.5 | .950 | | | | | | | | | | | |
| | H. Cruz | R | 7 | 2 | 14 | 0 | 0 | 2.3 | 1.000 | | | | | | | | | | | |
| | R. Meoli | R | 5 | 2 | 9 | 0 | 0 | 2.2 | 1.000 | | | | | | | | | | | |
| | M. Sember | R | 7 | 0 | 2 | 1 | 0 | 0.4 | .667 | | | | | | | | | | | |

In a most unusual season, the Cubs shed their conservative image and finished in the rare atmosphere of third place. Most of the players grew beards and became the "Grubby Cubbies." They also signed their first reentry free agent, Dave Kingman, a slugger unwanted by other clubs. Kingman was the heart of a homer-hungry team, hitting 28 of the Cubs' total of 72, the second lowest in the big leagues. Despite their lack of heavy firepower, the Cubs led the NL in hitting with a .264 average. Manager Herman Franks had the Cubs on top for 30 days before bowing out with a 79–83 record. There was no long losing streak. Their failure was their futility against the division-winning Phillies, dropping 14 of 18 games.

Kingman led in RBI with 79, while Bill Buckner was the top hitter with a .323 mark, and struck out only 17 times in 446 trips. Bobby Murcer was the offensive bust, his homer production dropping from 27 to 9. Ivan DeJesus, who teamed spectacularly with Manny Trillo as a double play duo, gave the usually slew-footed Cubs some speed afoot with 41 stolen bases. Rodney Scott added 27 steals as the Cubs wound up with 110 thefts, their most since 1924. Bruce Sutter had an off season in the bullpen with "only" 27 saves, while Rick Reuschel slid to 14–15. Rookie pitchers included Mike Krukow, 9–3, and Dennis Lamp, 7–15. The Cubs were blanked six times Lamp pitched, including three 1–0 losses.

### TEAM STATISTICS

| | W | L | PCT | GB | R | OR | 2B | 3B | HR | BA | SA | SB | E | DP | FA | CG | B | SO | ShO | SV | ERA |
|---|---|---|---|---|---|---|---|---|---|---|---|---|---|---|---|---|---|---|---|---|---|
| **EAST** | | | | | | | | | | | | | | | | | | | | | |
| PHI | 90 | 72 | .556 | | 708 | 586 | 248 | 32 | 133 | .258 | .388 | 152 | **104** | 155 | **.983** | 38 | 393 | 813 | 9 | 29 | 3.33 |
| PIT | 88 | 73 | .547 | 1.5 | 684 | 637 | 239 | 54 | 115 | .257 | .385 | **213** | 167 | 133 | .973 | 30 | 499 | 880 | 13 | 44 | 3.41 |
| CHI | 79 | 83 | .488 | 11 | 664 | 724 | 224 | 48 | 72 | **.264** | .361 | 110 | 144 | 154 | .978 | 24 | 539 | 768 | 7 | 38 | 4.05 |
| MON | 76 | 86 | .469 | 14 | 633 | 611 | 269 | 31 | 121 | .254 | .379 | 80 | 134 | 150 | .979 | 42 | 572 | 740 | 13 | 32 | 3.42 |
| STL | 69 | 93 | .426 | 21 | 600 | 657 | 263 | 44 | 79 | .249 | .358 | 97 | 136 | 155 | .978 | 32 | 600 | 859 | 13 | 22 | 3.58 |
| NY | 66 | 96 | .407 | 24 | 607 | 690 | 227 | 47 | 86 | .245 | .352 | 100 | 132 | 159 | .979 | 21 | 531 | 775 | 7 | 26 | 3.87 |
| **WEST** | | | | | | | | | | | | | | | | | | | | | |
| LA | 95 | 67 | .586 | | **727** | 573 | 251 | 27 | **149** | .264 | **.402** | 137 | 140 | 138 | .978 | 46 | 440 | 800 | 16 | 38 | **3.12** |
| CIN | 92 | 69 | .571 | 2.5 | 710 | 688 | **270** | 32 | 136 | .256 | .393 | 137 | 134 | 120 | .978 | 16 | 567 | 908 | 10 | 46 | 3.81 |
| SF | 89 | 73 | .549 | 6 | 613 | 594 | 240 | 41 | 117 | .248 | .374 | 87 | 146 | 118 | .977 | 42 | 453 | 840 | 17 | 29 | 3.30 |
| SD | 84 | 78 | .519 | 11 | 591 | 598 | 208 | 42 | 75 | .252 | .348 | 152 | 160 | 171 | .975 | 21 | 483 | 744 | 10 | **55** | 3.28 |
| HOU | 74 | 88 | .457 | 21 | 605 | 634 | 231 | 45 | 70 | .258 | .355 | 178 | 133 | 109 | .978 | **48** | 578 | **930** | 17 | 23 | 3.63 |
| ATL | 69 | 93 | .426 | 26 | 600 | 750 | 191 | 39 | 123 | .244 | .363 | 90 | 153 | 126 | .975 | 29 | 624 | 848 | 12 | 32 | 4.08 |
| LEAGUE TOTAL | | | | | 7742 | 7742 | 2861 | 482 | 1276 | .254 | .372 | 1533 | 1683 | 1688 | .978 | 389 | 6279 | 9905 | 144 | 414 | 3.58 |

### INDIVIDUAL PITCHING

| PITCHER | T | W | L | PCT | ERA | SV | G | GS | CG | IP | H | BB | SO | R | ER | ShO | H/9 | BB/9 | SO/9 |
|---|---|---|---|---|---|---|---|---|---|---|---|---|---|---|---|---|---|---|---|
| Rick Reuschel | R | 14 | 15 | .483 | 3.41 | 0 | 35 | 35 | 9 | 243 | 235 | 54 | 115 | 98 | 92 | 1 | 8.70 | 2.00 | 4.26 |
| Dennis Lamp | R | 7 | 15 | .318 | 3.29 | 0 | 37 | 36 | 6 | 224 | 221 | 56 | 73 | 96 | 82 | 3 | 8.88 | 2.25 | 2.93 |
| Ray Burris | R | 7 | 13 | .350 | 4.75 | 1 | 40 | 32 | 4 | 199 | 210 | 79 | 94 | 112 | 105 | 1 | 9.50 | 3.57 | 4.25 |
| Dave Roberts | L | 6 | 8 | .429 | 5.26 | 1 | 35 | 20 | 2 | 142 | 159 | 56 | 54 | 87 | 83 | 1 | 10.08 | 3.55 | 3.42 |
| Mike Krukow | R | 9 | 3 | .750 | 3.91 | 0 | 27 | 20 | 3 | 138 | 125 | 53 | 81 | 62 | 60 | 1 | 8.15 | 3.46 | 5.28 |
| Donnie Moore | R | 9 | 7 | .563 | 4.11 | 4 | 71 | 1 | 0 | 103 | 117 | 31 | 50 | 55 | 47 | 0 | 10.22 | 2.71 | 4.37 |
| Bruce Sutter | R | 8 | 10 | .444 | 3.18 | 27 | 64 | 0 | 0 | 99 | 82 | 34 | 106 | 44 | 35 | 0 | 7.45 | 3.09 | 9.64 |
| Lynn McGlothen | R | 5 | 3 | .625 | 3.04 | 0 | 49 | 1 | 0 | 80 | 77 | 39 | 60 | 33 | 27 | 0 | 8.66 | 4.39 | 6.75 |
| Willie Hernandez | L | 8 | 2 | .800 | 3.75 | 3 | 54 | 0 | 0 | 60 | 57 | 35 | 38 | 26 | 25 | 0 | 8.55 | 5.25 | 5.70 |
| Woodie Fryman | L | 2 | 4 | .333 | 5.17 | 0 | 13 | 9 | 0 | 55.2 | 64 | 37 | 28 | 37 | 32 | 0 | 10.35 | 5.98 | 4.53 |
| Ken Holtzman | L | 0 | 3 | .000 | 6.11 | 2 | 23 | 6 | 0 | 53 | 61 | 35 | 36 | 40 | 36 | 0 | 10.36 | 5.94 | 6.11 |
| Paul Reuschel | R | 2 | 0 | 1.000 | 5.14 | 0 | 16 | 0 | 0 | 28 | 29 | 13 | 13 | 16 | 16 | 0 | 9.32 | 4.18 | 4.18 |
| Dave Geisel | L | 1 | 0 | 1.000 | 4.30 | 0 | 18 | 1 | 0 | 23 | 27 | 11 | 15 | 12 | 11 | 0 | 10.57 | 4.30 | 5.87 |
| Manny Seoane | R | 1 | 0 | 1.000 | 5.63 | 0 | 7 | 1 | 0 | 8 | 11 | 6 | 5 | 6 | 5 | 0 | 12.38 | 6.75 | 5.63 |
| TEAM TOTAL | | 79 | 83 | .488 | 4.06 | 38 | 489 | 162 | 24 | 1455.2 | 1475 | 539 | 768 | 724 | 656 | 7 | 9.12 | 3.33 | 4.75 |

| MANAGER | W | L | PCT |
|---|---|---|---|
| Herman Franks | 78 | 77 | .503 |
| Joey Amalfitano | 2 | 5 | .286 |

| POS | Player | B | G | AB | H | 2B | 3B | HR | HR % | R | RBI | BB | SO | SB | Pinch Hit AB | Pinch Hit H | BA | SA |
|---|---|---|---|---|---|---|---|---|---|---|---|---|---|---|---|---|---|---|
| **REGULARS** | | | | | | | | | | | | | | | | | | |
| 1B | Bill Buckner | L | 149 | 591 | 168 | 34 | 7 | 14 | 2.4 | 72 | 66 | 30 | 28 | 9 | 8 | 3 | .284 | .437 |
| 2B | Ted Sizemore | R | 98 | 330 | 82 | 17 | 0 | 2 | 0.6 | 36 | 24 | 32 | 25 | 3 | 2 | 0 | .248 | .318 |
| SS | Ivan DeJesus | R | 160 | 636 | 180 | 26 | 10 | 5 | 0.8 | 92 | 52 | 59 | 82 | 24 | 0 | 0 | .283 | .379 |
| 3B | Steve Ontiveros | B | 152 | 519 | 148 | 28 | 2 | 4 | 0.8 | 58 | 57 | 58 | 68 | 0 | 9 | 3 | .285 | .370 |
| RF | Scot Thompson | L | 128 | 346 | 100 | 13 | 5 | 2 | 0.6 | 36 | 29 | 17 | 37 | 4 | 33 | 12 | .289 | .373 |
| CF | Jerry Martin | R | 150 | 534 | 145 | 34 | 3 | 19 | 3.6 | 74 | 73 | 38 | 85 | 2 | 8 | 1 | .272 | .453 |
| LF | Dave Kingman | R | 145 | 532 | 153 | 19 | 5 | **48** | **9.0** | 97 | 115 | 45 | **131** | 4 | 5 | 3 | .288 | **.613** |
| C | Barry Foote | R | 132 | 429 | 109 | 26 | 0 | 16 | 3.7 | 47 | 56 | 34 | 49 | 5 | 5 | 0 | .254 | .427 |
| **SUBSTITUTES** | | | | | | | | | | | | | | | | | | |
| 2B | Steve Dillard | R | 89 | 166 | 47 | 6 | 1 | 5 | 3.0 | 31 | 24 | 17 | 24 | 1 | 17 | 6 | .283 | .422 |
| UT | Mick Kelleher | R | 73 | 142 | 36 | 4 | 1 | 0 | 0.0 | 14 | 10 | 7 | 9 | 2 | 0 | 0 | .254 | .296 |
| 23 | Steve Macko | L | 19 | 40 | 9 | 1 | 0 | 0 | 0.0 | 2 | 3 | 4 | 8 | 0 | 5 | 0 | .225 | .250 |
| 23 | Steve Davis | R | 3 | 4 | 0 | 0 | 0 | 0 | 0.0 | 0 | 1 | 0 | 0 | 0 | 0 | 0 | .000 | .000 |
| 3B | Kurt Seibert | B | 7 | 2 | 0 | 0 | 0 | 0 | 0.0 | 2 | 0 | 0 | 1 | 0 | 1 | 0 | .000 | .000 |
| O1 | Larry Biittner | L | 111 | 272 | 79 | 13 | 3 | 3 | 1.1 | 35 | 50 | 21 | 23 | 1 | 42 | 13 | .290 | .393 |
| OF | Bobby Murcer | L | 58 | 190 | 49 | 4 | 1 | 7 | 3.7 | 22 | 22 | 36 | 20 | 2 | 3 | 1 | .258 | .400 |
| OF | Mike Vail | R | 87 | 179 | 60 | 8 | 2 | 7 | 3.9 | 28 | 35 | 14 | 27 | 0 | 44 | 12 | .335 | .520 |
| OF | Ken Henderson | B | 62 | 81 | 19 | 2 | 0 | 2 | 2.5 | 11 | 8 | 15 | 16 | 0 | 44 | 8 | .235 | .333 |
| OF | Miguel Dilone | B | 43 | 36 | 11 | 0 | 0 | 0 | 0.0 | 14 | 1 | 2 | 5 | 15 | 0 | 0 | .306 | .306 |
| OF | Sam Mejias | R | 31 | 11 | 2 | 0 | 0 | 0 | 0.0 | 4 | 0 | 2 | 5 | 0 | 6 | 1 | .182 | .182 |
| C | Tim Blackwell | B | 63 | 122 | 20 | 3 | 1 | 0 | 0.0 | 8 | 12 | 32 | 25 | 0 | 1 | 0 | .164 | .205 |
| C | Bruce Kimm | R | 9 | 11 | 1 | 0 | 0 | 0 | 0.0 | 0 | 0 | 0 | 0 | 0 | 0 | 0 | .091 | .091 |
| **PITCHERS** | | | | | | | | | | | | | | | | | | |
| P | Rick Reuschel | R | 38 | 79 | 13 | 2 | 1 | 0 | 0.0 | 8 | 6 | 7 | 26 | 0 | 0 | 0 | .165 | .215 |
| P | Lynn McGlothen | L | 42 | 71 | 16 | 3 | 0 | 0 | 0.0 | 6 | 3 | 1 | 10 | 0 | 0 | 0 | .225 | .268 |
| P | Dennis Lamp | R | 38 | 58 | 9 | 1 | 0 | 0 | 0.0 | 2 | 1 | 2 | 9 | 0 | 0 | 0 | .155 | .172 |
| P | Mike Krukow | R | 28 | 51 | 16 | 2 | 0 | 1 | 2.0 | 4 | 8 | 0 | 8 | 0 | 0 | 0 | .314 | .412 |
| P | Ken Holtzman | R | 24 | 43 | 10 | 3 | 0 | 0 | 0.0 | 2 | 1 | 2 | 9 | 0 | 0 | 0 | .233 | .302 |
| P | Bill Caudill | R | 29 | 17 | 1 | 0 | 0 | 0 | 0.0 | 0 | 0 | 0 | 10 | 0 | 0 | 0 | .059 | .059 |
| P | Donnie Moore | L | 39 | 13 | 2 | 0 | 1 | 0 | 0.0 | 0 | 1 | 0 | 5 | 0 | 0 | 0 | .154 | .308 |
| P | Bruce Sutter | R | 62 | 12 | 3 | 0 | 0 | 0 | 0.0 | 0 | 3 | 1 | 5 | 1 | 0 | 0 | .250 | .250 |
| P | Dick Tidrow | R | 63 | 10 | 2 | 0 | 0 | 0 | 0.0 | 0 | 1 | 1 | 2 | 0 | 0 | 0 | .200 | .200 |
| P | Willie Hernandez | L | 52 | 8 | 2 | 1 | 0 | 0 | 0.0 | 0 | 1 | 0 | 5 | 0 | 0 | 0 | .250 | .375 |
| P | George Riley | L | 4 | 2 | 0 | 0 | 0 | 0 | 0.0 | 0 | 0 | 0 | 2 | 0 | 0 | 0 | .000 | .000 |
| P | Dave Geisel | L | 7 | 1 | 0 | 0 | 0 | 0 | 0.0 | 0 | 0 | 0 | 1 | 0 | 0 | 0 | .000 | .000 |
| P | Ray Burris | R | 14 | 1 | 0 | 0 | 0 | 0 | 0.0 | 1 | 0 | 1 | 0 | 0 | 0 | 0 | .000 | .000 |
| P | Doug Capilla | L | 13 | 0 | 0 | 0 | 0 | 0 | — | 0 | 0 | 0 | 0 | 0 | 0 | 0 | — | — |
| TEAM TOTAL | | | | 5539 | 1492 | 250 | 43 | 135 | 2.4 | 70 | 663 | 478 | 760 | 73 | 233 | 63 | .269 | .403 |

## INDIVIDUAL FIELDING

| POS | Player | T | G | PO | A | E | DP | TC/G | FA |
|---|---|---|---|---|---|---|---|---|---|
| 1B | B. Buckner | L | 140 | 1258 | 124 | 7 | 118 | 9.9 | .995 |
| | L. Biittner | L | 32 | 236 | 20 | 2 | 24 | 8.1 | .992 |
| | S. Ontiveros | R | 1 | 7 | 1 | 0 | 1 | 8.0 | 1.000 |
| 2B | T. Sizemore | R | 96 | 230 | 312 | 15 | 68 | 5.8 | .973 |
| | S. Dillard | R | 60 | 111 | 132 | 3 | 31 | 4.1 | .988 |
| | M. Kelleher | R | 29 | 52 | 84 | 3 | 16 | 4.8 | .978 |
| | S. Macko | R | 10 | 18 | 21 | 0 | 4 | 3.9 | 1.000 |
| | S. Davis | R | 2 | 0 | 1 | 0 | 0 | 0.5 | 1.000 |
| SS | I. DeJesus | R | 160 | 235 | 507 | 32 | 97 | 4.8 | .959 |
| | M. Kelleher | R | 14 | 9 | 24 | 1 | 4 | 2.4 | .971 |
| 3B | S. Ontiveros | R | 142 | 98 | 268 | 23 | 27 | 2.7 | .941 |
| | M. Kelleher | R | 32 | 17 | 40 | 2 | 4 | 1.8 | .966 |
| | S. Macko | R | 4 | 3 | 12 | 0 | 0 | 3.8 | 1.000 |
| | S. Dillard | R | 9 | 3 | 6 | 1 | 1 | 1.1 | .900 |
| | S. Davis | R | 1 | 0 | 2 | 0 | 0 | 2.0 | 1.000 |
| | K. Seibert | R | 1 | 2 | 0 | 0 | 0 | 2.0 | 1.000 |
| | M. Vail | R | 2 | 0 | 1 | 0 | 0 | 0.5 | 1.000 |

| POS | Player | T | G | PO | A | E | DP | TC/G | FA |
|---|---|---|---|---|---|---|---|---|---|
| OF | J. Martin | R | 144 | 297 | 11 | 6 | 4 | 2.2 | .981 |
| | D. Kingman | R | 139 | 240 | 11 | 12 | 3 | 1.9 | .954 |
| | S. Thompson | L | 100 | 161 | 7 | 5 | 3 | 1.7 | .971 |
| | B. Murcer | R | 54 | 110 | 4 | 0 | 0 | 2.1 | 1.000 |
| | M. Vail | R | 39 | 51 | 3 | 2 | 0 | 1.4 | .964 |
| | L. Biittner | L | 44 | 46 | 3 | 4 | 0 | 1.2 | .925 |
| | M. Dilone | R | 22 | 27 | 0 | 0 | 0 | 1.2 | 1.000 |
| | K. Henderson | R | 23 | 19 | 0 | 1 | 0 | 0.9 | .950 |
| | S. Mejias | R | 23 | 7 | 0 | 1 | 0 | 0.3 | .875 |
| C | B. Foote | R | 129 | 713 | 63 | 17 | 9 | 6.1 | .979 |
| | T. Blackwell | R | 63 | 245 | 28 | 7 | 3 | 4.4 | .975 |
| | B. Kimm | R | 9 | 30 | 1 | 1 | 0 | 3.6 | .969 |

It was an eerie scene when Dave Kingman would step to the plate at Wrigley Field. Vendors would stop hawking their ale. There was a hushed silence of anticipation. All eyes were focused on the lanky slugger. It was as if life stood still. He was awesome. Sometimes he connected. Sometimes he didn't. But he provided excitement with his 48 homers as 1,648,587 fans spun through the turnstiles to see him swing. Kingman's .613 slugging average topped the league. And, surprisingly, he even batted .288. A typical Cub-Kingman contest occurred on May 17. The Cubs, sparked by the Kong's three homers, came from a 17–6 deficit only to lose, 23–22, when the Phillies' Mike Schmidt homered off relief ace Bruce Sutter in the 10th inning. But Sutter kept the Cubs afloat with his NL record-tying 37 saves.

Somehow Kingman and Sutter couldn't keep the Cubs from another late-season swoon. A 9–22 September collapse sent them spinning into fifth place with an 80–82 record, after boasting a 67–54 mark in mid-August. Manager Herman Franks called some of his players "crazy" and "whiners." The downfall reportedly came during a trip to Montreal. Cub management treated the players to a posh restaurant, but set a two-bottle wine limit per table. That's when the diners turned to whiners. Coach Joey Amalfitano finished the season at the Cub helm.

## TEAM STATISTICS

| | W | L | PCT | GB | R | OR | 2B | 3B | HR | BA | SA | SB | E | DP | FA | CG | B | SO | ShO | SV | ERA |
|---|---|---|---|---|---|---|---|---|---|---|---|---|---|---|---|---|---|---|---|---|---|
| **EAST** | | | | | | | | | | | | | | | | | | | | | |
| PIT | 98 | 64 | .605 | | **775** | 643 | 264 | 52 | 148 | .272 | **.416** | 180 | 134 | 163 | .979 | 24 | 504 | 904 | 7 | **52** | 3.41 |
| MON | 95 | 65 | .594 | 2 | 701 | 581 | 273 | 42 | 143 | .264 | .408 | 121 | 131 | 123 | .979 | 33 | **450** | 813 | 18 | 39 | **3.14** |
| STL | 86 | 76 | .531 | 12 | 731 | 693 | **279** | **63** | 100 | **.278** | .401 | 116 | 132 | 166 | .980 | 38 | 501 | 788 | 10 | 25 | 3.72 |
| PHI | 84 | 78 | .519 | 14 | 683 | 718 | 250 | 53 | 119 | .266 | .396 | 128 | **106** | 148 | **.983** | 33 | 477 | 787 | 14 | 29 | 4.16 |
| CHI | 80 | 82 | .494 | 18 | 706 | 707 | 250 | 43 | 135 | .269 | .403 | 73 | 159 | 163 | .975 | 20 | 521 | **933** | 11 | 44 | 3.88 |
| NY | 63 | 99 | .389 | 35 | 593 | 706 | 255 | 41 | 74 | .250 | .350 | 135 | 140 | **168** | .978 | 16 | 607 | 819 | 10 | 36 | 3.84 |
| **WEST** | | | | | | | | | | | | | | | | | | | | | |
| CIN | 90 | 71 | .559 | | 731 | 644 | 266 | 31 | 132 | .264 | .396 | 99 | 124 | 152 | .980 | 27 | 485 | 773 | 10 | 40 | 3.58 |
| HOU | 89 | 73 | .549 | 1.5 | 583 | 582 | 224 | 52 | 49 | .256 | .344 | **190** | 138 | 146 | .978 | 55 | 504 | 854 | **19** | 34 | 3.19 |
| LA | 79 | 83 | .488 | 11.5 | 739 | 717 | 220 | 24 | **183** | .263 | .412 | 106 | 118 | 123 | .981 | 30 | 555 | 811 | 6 | 34 | 3.83 |
| SF | 71 | 91 | .438 | 19.5 | 672 | 751 | 192 | 36 | 125 | .246 | .365 | 140 | 163 | 138 | .974 | 25 | 577 | 880 | 6 | 34 | 4.16 |
| SD | 68 | 93 | .422 | 22 | 603 | 681 | 193 | 53 | 93 | .242 | .348 | 100 | 141 | 154 | .978 | 29 | 513 | 779 | 7 | 25 | 3.69 |
| ATL | 66 | 94 | .413 | 23.5 | 669 | 763 | 220 | 28 | 126 | .256 | .377 | 98 | 183 | 139 | .970 | 32 | 494 | 779 | 3 | 34 | 4.18 |
| LEAGUE TOTAL | | | | | 8186 | 8186 | 2886 | 518 | 1427 | .261 | .385 | 1486 | 1669 | 1783 | .978 | 362 | 6188 | 9920 | 121 | 423 | 3.73 |

## INDIVIDUAL PITCHING

| PITCHER | T | W | L | PCT | ERA | SV | G | GS | CG | IP | H | BB | SO | R | ER | ShO | H/9 | BB/9 | SO/9 |
|---|---|---|---|---|---|---|---|---|---|---|---|---|---|---|---|---|---|---|---|
| Rick Reuschel | R | 18 | 12 | .600 | 3.62 | 0 | 36 | 36 | 5 | 239 | 251 | 75 | 125 | 104 | 96 | 1 | 9.45 | 2.82 | 4.71 |
| Lynn McGlothen | R | 13 | 14 | .481 | 4.12 | 2 | 42 | 29 | 6 | 212 | 236 | 55 | 147 | 103 | 97 | 1 | 10.02 | 2.33 | 6.24 |
| Dennis Lamp | R | 11 | 10 | .524 | 3.51 | 0 | 38 | 32 | 6 | 200 | 223 | 46 | 86 | 96 | 78 | 1 | 10.04 | 2.07 | 3.87 |
| Mike Krukow | R | 9 | 9 | .500 | 4.20 | 0 | 28 | 28 | 0 | 165 | 172 | 81 | 119 | 84 | 77 | 0 | 9.38 | 4.42 | 6.49 |
| Ken Holtzman | L | 6 | 9 | .400 | 4.58 | 0 | 23 | 20 | 3 | 118 | 133 | 53 | 44 | 70 | 60 | 2 | 10.14 | 4.04 | 3.36 |
| Dick Tidrow | R | 11 | 5 | .688 | 2.71 | 4 | 63 | 0 | 0 | 103 | 86 | 42 | 68 | 35 | 31 | 0 | 7.51 | 3.67 | 5.94 |
| Bruce Sutter | R | 6 | 6 | .500 | 2.23 | 37 | 62 | 0 | 0 | 101 | 67 | 32 | 110 | 29 | 25 | 0 | 5.97 | 2.85 | 9.80 |
| Bill Caudill | R | 1 | 7 | .125 | 4.80 | 0 | 29 | 12 | 0 | 90 | 89 | 41 | 104 | 57 | 48 | 0 | 8.90 | 4.10 | 10.40 |
| Willie Hernandez | L | 4 | 4 | .500 | 5.01 | 0 | 51 | 2 | 0 | 79 | 85 | 39 | 53 | 50 | 44 | 0 | 9.68 | 4.44 | 6.04 |
| Donnie Moore | R | 1 | 4 | .200 | 5.18 | 1 | 39 | 1 | 0 | 73 | 95 | 25 | 43 | 46 | 42 | 0 | 11.71 | 3.08 | 5.30 |
| Ray Burris | R | 0 | 0 | — | 6.23 | 0 | 14 | 0 | 0 | 21.2 | 23 | 15 | 14 | 17 | 15 | 0 | 9.55 | 6.23 | 5.82 |
| Doug Capilla | L | 0 | 1 | .000 | 2.60 | 0 | 13 | 1 | 0 | 17.1 | 14 | 7 | 10 | 6 | 5 | 0 | 7.27 | 3.63 | 5.19 |
| Dave Geisel | L | 0 | 0 | — | 0.60 | 0 | 7 | 0 | 0 | 15 | 10 | 4 | 5 | 1 | 1 | 0 | 6.00 | 2.40 | 3.00 |
| George Riley | L | 0 | 1 | .000 | 5.54 | 0 | 4 | 1 | 0 | 13 | 16 | 6 | 5 | 9 | 8 | 0 | 11.08 | 4.15 | 3.46 |
| TEAM TOTAL | | 80 | 82 | .494 | 3.90 | 44 | 449 | 162 | 20 | 1447 | 1500 | 521 | 933 | 707 | 627 | 5 | 9.33 | 3.24 | 5.80 |

| MANAGER | W | L | PCT |
|---|---|---|---|
| Preston Gomez | 38 | 52 | .422 |
| Joey Amalfitano | 26 | 46 | .361 |

| POS | Player | B | G | AB | H | 2B | 3B | HR | HR % | R | RBI | BB | SO | SB | Pinch Hit AB | Pinch Hit H | BA | SA |
|---|---|---|---|---|---|---|---|---|---|---|---|---|---|---|---|---|---|---|
| **REGULARS** | | | | | | | | | | | | | | | | | | |
| 1B | Bill Buckner | L | 145 | 578 | 187 | 41 | 3 | 10 | 1.7 | 69 | 68 | 30 | 18 | 1 | 6 | 0 | .324 | .457 |
| 2B | Mike Tyson | R | 123 | 341 | 81 | 19 | 3 | 3 | 0.9 | 34 | 23 | 15 | 61 | 1 | 6 | 2 | .238 | .337 |
| SS | Ivan DeJesus | R | 157 | 618 | 160 | 26 | 3 | 3 | 0.5 | 78 | 33 | 60 | 81 | 44 | 0 | 0 | .259 | .325 |
| 3B | Lenny Randle | R | 130 | 489 | 135 | 19 | 6 | 5 | 1.0 | 67 | 39 | 50 | 55 | 19 | 8 | 4 | .276 | .370 |
| RF | Scot Thompson | L | 102 | 226 | 48 | 10 | 1 | 2 | 0.9 | 26 | 13 | 28 | 31 | 6 | 21 | 6 | .212 | .292 |
| CF | Jerry Martin | R | 141 | 494 | 112 | 22 | 2 | 23 | 4.7 | 57 | 73 | 38 | 107 | 8 | 11 | 2 | .227 | .419 |
| LF | Dave Kingman | R | 81 | 255 | 71 | 8 | 0 | 18 | 7.1 | 31 | 57 | 21 | 44 | 2 | 16 | 6 | .278 | .522 |
| C | Tim Blackwell | B | 103 | 320 | 87 | 16 | 4 | 5 | 1.6 | 24 | 30 | 41 | 62 | 0 | 0 | 0 | .272 | .394 |
| **SUBSTITUTES** | | | | | | | | | | | | | | | | | | |
| 1O | Larry Biittner | L | 127 | 273 | 68 | 12 | 2 | 1 | 0.4 | 21 | 34 | 18 | 33 | 1 | 52 | 11 | .249 | .319 |
| 32 | Steve Dillard | R | 100 | 244 | 55 | 8 | 1 | 4 | 1.6 | 31 | 27 | 20 | 54 | 2 | 13 | 3 | .225 | .316 |
| 1B | Cliff Johnson | R | 68 | 196 | 46 | 8 | 0 | 10 | 5.1 | 28 | 34 | 29 | 35 | 0 | 17 | 2 | .235 | .429 |
| UT | Mick Kelleher | R | 105 | 96 | 14 | 1 | 1 | 0 | 0.0 | 12 | 4 | 9 | 17 | 1 | 3 | 1 | .146 | .177 |
| 3B | Steve Ontiveros | B | 31 | 77 | 16 | 3 | 0 | 1 | 1.3 | 7 | 3 | 14 | 17 | 0 | 6 | 0 | .208 | .286 |
| UT | Steve Macko | L | 6 | 20 | 6 | 2 | 0 | 0 | 0.0 | 2 | 2 | 0 | 3 | 0 | 0 | 0 | .300 | .400 |
| OF | Mike Vail | R | 114 | 312 | 93 | 17 | 2 | 6 | 1.9 | 30 | 47 | 14 | 77 | 2 | 45 | 8 | .298 | .423 |
| OF | Jesus Figueroa | L | 115 | 198 | 50 | 5 | 0 | 1 | 0.5 | 20 | 11 | 14 | 16 | 2 | 53 | 15 | .253 | .293 |
| OF | Jim Tracy | L | 42 | 122 | 31 | 3 | 3 | 3 | 2.5 | 12 | 9 | 13 | 37 | 2 | 12 | 2 | .254 | .402 |
| OF | Carlos Lezcano | R | 42 | 88 | 18 | 4 | 1 | 3 | 3.4 | 15 | 12 | 11 | 29 | 1 | 2 | 0 | .205 | .375 |
| OF | Ken Henderson | B | 44 | 82 | 16 | 3 | 0 | 2 | 2.4 | 7 | 9 | 17 | 19 | 0 | 19 | 3 | .195 | .305 |
| C | Barry Foote | R | 63 | 202 | 48 | 13 | 1 | 6 | 3.0 | 16 | 28 | 13 | 18 | 1 | 9 | 2 | .238 | .401 |
| C | Mike O'Berry | R | 19 | 48 | 10 | 1 | 0 | 0 | 0.0 | 7 | 5 | 5 | 13 | 0 | 0 | 0 | .208 | .229 |
| C | Bill Hayes | R | 4 | 9 | 2 | 1 | 0 | 0 | 0.0 | 0 | 0 | 0 | 3 | 0 | 1 | 0 | .222 | .333 |
| **PITCHERS** | | | | | | | | | | | | | | | | | | |
| P | Rick Reuschel | R | 44 | 82 | 13 | 3 | 1 | 0 | 0.0 | 4 | 5 | 1 | 23 | 0 | 0 | 0 | .159 | .220 |
| P | Mike Krukow | R | 34 | 65 | 16 | 0 | 0 | 1 | 1.5 | 5 | 6 | 2 | 12 | 0 | 0 | 0 | .246 | .292 |
| P | Dennis Lamp | R | 41 | 61 | 6 | 0 | 0 | 0 | 0.0 | 3 | 1 | 4 | 9 | 0 | 0 | 0 | .098 | .098 |
| P | Lynn McGlothen | L | 41 | 51 | 10 | 4 | 0 | 0 | 0.0 | 6 | 1 | 4 | 8 | 0 | 1 | 0 | .196 | .275 |
| P | Doug Capilla | L | 40 | 21 | 4 | 0 | 1 | 0 | 0.0 | 1 | 1 | 0 | 9 | 0 | 0 | 0 | .190 | .286 |
| P | Willie Hernandez | L | 53 | 19 | 4 | 1 | 0 | 0 | 0.0 | 0 | 1 | 0 | 7 | 0 | 0 | 0 | .211 | .263 |
| P | Bruce Sutter | R | 60 | 9 | 1 | 0 | 0 | 0 | 0.0 | 0 | 1 | 0 | 6 | 0 | 0 | 0 | .111 | .111 |
| P | Bill Caudill | R | 72 | 9 | 2 | 1 | 0 | 0 | 0.0 | 0 | 1 | 0 | 2 | 0 | 0 | 0 | .222 | .333 |
| P | Randy Martz | L | 6 | 9 | 1 | 0 | 0 | 0 | 0.0 | 0 | 0 | 0 | 5 | 0 | 0 | 0 | .111 | .111 |
| P | Dick Tidrow | R | 84 | 4 | 0 | 0 | 0 | 0 | 0.0 | 1 | 0 | 0 | 1 | 0 | 0 | 0 | .000 | .000 |
| P | George Riley | L | 22 | 1 | 0 | 0 | 0 | 0 | 0.0 | 0 | 0 | 0 | 0 | 0 | 0 | 0 | .000 | .000 |
| P | Lee Smith | R | 18 | 0 | 0 | 0 | 0 | 0 | — | 0 | 0 | 0 | 0 | 0 | 0 | 0 | — | — |
| | TEAM TOTAL | | | 5619 | 1411 | 251 | 35 | 107 | 1.9 | 61 | 578 | 471 | 912 | 93 | 301 | 67 | .251 | .365 |

## INDIVIDUAL FIELDING

| POS | Player | T | G | PO | A | E | DP | TC/G | FA |
|---|---|---|---|---|---|---|---|---|---|
| 1B | B. Buckner | L | 94 | 826 | 73 | 6 | 67 | 9.6 | .993 |
| | C. Johnson | R | 46 | 468 | 16 | 4 | 34 | 10.6 | .992 |
| | L. Biittner | L | 41 | 250 | 19 | 1 | 14 | 6.6 | .996 |
| | S. Thompson | L | 12 | 49 | 2 | 0 | 6 | 4.3 | 1.000 |
| | D. Kingman | R | 2 | 16 | 2 | 1 | 0 | 9.5 | .947 |
| | J. Tracy | R | 1 | 6 | 0 | 0 | 1 | 6.0 | 1.000 |
| 2B | M. Tyson | R | 117 | 222 | 329 | 18 | 69 | 4.9 | .968 |
| | M. Kelleher | R | 57 | 62 | 87 | 4 | 17 | 2.7 | .974 |
| | S. Dillard | R | 38 | 64 | 85 | 3 | 13 | 4.0 | .980 |
| | L. Randle | R | 17 | 40 | 48 | 2 | 5 | 5.3 | .978 |
| | S. Macko | R | 1 | 2 | 1 | 0 | 0 | 3.0 | 1.000 |
| SS | I. DeJesus | R | 156 | 229 | 529 | 24 | 99 | 5.0 | .969 |
| | M. Kelleher | R | 17 | 12 | 33 | 0 | 4 | 2.6 | 1.000 |
| | S. Macko | R | 3 | 7 | 13 | 0 | 4 | 6.7 | 1.000 |
| | S. Dillard | R | 2 | 3 | 2 | 0 | 0 | 2.5 | 1.000 |
| 3B | L. Randle | R | 111 | 76 | 225 | 23 | 7 | 2.9 | .929 |
| | S. Dillard | R | 51 | 25 | 84 | 11 | 6 | 2.4 | .908 |
| | S. Ontiveros | R | 24 | 13 | 39 | 4 | 1 | 2.3 | .929 |
| | M. Kelleher | R | 31 | 8 | 9 | 3 | 2 | 0.6 | .850 |
| | S. Macko | R | 2 | 2 | 0 | 0 | 0 | 1.0 | 1.000 |

| POS | Player | T | G | PO | A | E | DP | TC/G | FA |
|---|---|---|---|---|---|---|---|---|---|
| OF | J. Martin | R | 129 | 262 | 8 | 6 | 0 | 2.1 | .978 |
| | M. Vail | R | 77 | 126 | 5 | 5 | 1 | 1.8 | .963 |
| | D. Kingman | R | 61 | 103 | 8 | 7 | 0 | 1.9 | .941 |
| | S. Thompson | L | 66 | 100 | 4 | 4 | 2 | 1.6 | .963 |
| | B. Buckner | L | 50 | 90 | 5 | 2 | 2 | 1.9 | .979 |
| | J. Figueroa | L | 57 | 89 | 6 | 2 | 2 | 1.7 | .979 |
| | C. Lezcano | R | 39 | 70 | 3 | 4 | 0 | 2.0 | .948 |
| | L. Biittner | L | 38 | 55 | 4 | 1 | 2 | 1.6 | .983 |
| | J. Tracy | R | 31 | 38 | 0 | 2 | 0 | 1.3 | .950 |
| | K. Henderson | R | 22 | 31 | 3 | 2 | 1 | 1.6 | .944 |
| | C. Johnson | R | 3 | 2 | 0 | 1 | 0 | 1.0 | .667 |
| | L. Randle | R | 6 | 3 | 0 | 0 | 0 | 0.5 | 1.000 |
| C | T. Blackwell | R | 103 | 572 | 93 | 12 | 16 | 6.6 | .982 |
| | B. Foote | R | 55 | 317 | 36 | 3 | 5 | 6.5 | .992 |
| | M. O'Berry | R | 19 | 94 | 16 | 2 | 2 | 5.9 | .982 |
| | B. Hayes | R | 3 | 9 | 2 | 0 | 0 | 3.7 | 1.000 |
| | C. Johnson | R | 1 | 1 | 0 | 0 | 0 | 1.0 | 1.000 |

The newspapers conducted a fan poll to select a new Cub manager. The big vote-getter was Whitey Herzog. The Cubs hired Preston Gomez, who received no mention in the balloting. Gomez declared during spring training he wanted a running ballclub. His first move was to get rid of Miguel Dilone. Dilone went to the Indians and stole 61 bases. Gomez made a speedy exit on July 25. When he was fired, the team was in shambles with a 38–52 record. Joey Amalfitano, the team's perennial replacement, was 26–46 the rest of the way as the Cubs finished in the cellar with a 64–98 record. Most of the blame was put on sore-shouldered Dave Kingman, who was in and out of the lineup, poured a water bucket on a sports writer, put out a horrid ghost-written column for one of the papers, and even failed to show up at Wrigley Field for "Dave Kingman T-Shirt Day." His power production dwindled to 18 homers and 57 RBI. In addition, the Cubs were last in fielding with 174 errors.

Somehow, there were some bright spots. Bill Buckner, who constantly ripped the organization for a poor attitude, won the batting title with a .324 average. Ivan DeJesus was steady at shortstop and stole 44 bases. The bullpen, led by Bruce Sutter and his 28 saves, was perhaps the best in team history. Sutter, who won an arbitration salary of $700,000, was ably backed by Dick Tidrow, Bill Caudill, Willie Hernandez, and newcomer Lee Smith. The starters, however, all had losing records.

## TEAM STATISTICS

| | W | L | PCT | GB | R | OR | 2B | 3B | HR | BA | SA | SB | E | DP | FA | CG | B | SO | ShO | SV | ERA |
|---|---|---|---|---|---|---|---|---|---|---|---|---|---|---|---|---|---|---|---|---|---|
| **EAST** | | | | | | | | | | | | | | | | | | | | | |
| PHI | 91 | 71 | .562 | | 728 | 639 | 272 | 54 | 117 | .270 | .400 | 140 | 136 | 136 | .979 | 25 | 530 | 889 | 8 | 40 | 3.43 |
| MON | 90 | 72 | .556 | 1 | 694 | 629 | 250 | 61 | 114 | .257 | .388 | 237 | 144 | 126 | .977 | 33 | 460 | 823 | 15 | 36 | 3.48 |
| PIT | 83 | 79 | .512 | 8 | 666 | 646 | 249 | 38 | 116 | .266 | .388 | 209 | 137 | 154 | .978 | 25 | 451 | 832 | 8 | 43 | 3.58 |
| STL | 74 | 88 | .457 | 17 | 738 | 710 | 300 | 49 | 101 | .275 | .400 | 117 | 122 | 174 | .981 | 34 | 495 | 664 | 9 | 27 | 3.93 |
| NY | 67 | 95 | .414 | 24 | 611 | 702 | 218 | 41 | 61 | .257 | .345 | 158 | 154 | 132 | .975 | 17 | 510 | 886 | 9 | 33 | 3.85 |
| CHI | 64 | 98 | .395 | 27 | 614 | 728 | 251 | 35 | 107 | .251 | .365 | 93 | 174 | 149 | .974 | 13 | 589 | 923 | 6 | 35 | 3.89 |
| **WEST** | | | | | | | | | | | | | | | | | | | | | |
| HOU | 93 | 70 | .571 | | 637 | 589 | 231 | 67 | 75 | .261 | .367 | 194 | 140 | 145 | .978 | 31 | 466 | 929 | 18 | 41 | 3.10 |
| LA | 92 | 71 | .564 | 1 | 663 | 591 | 209 | 24 | 148 | .263 | .388 | 123 | 123 | 149 | .981 | 24 | 480 | 835 | 19 | 42 | 3.24 |
| CIN | 89 | 73 | .549 | 3.5 | 707 | 670 | 256 | 45 | 113 | .262 | .386 | 156 | 106 | 144 | .983 | 30 | 506 | 833 | 12 | 37 | 3.85 |
| ATL | 81 | 80 | .503 | 11 | 630 | 660 | 226 | 22 | 144 | .250 | .380 | 73 | 162 | 156 | .975 | 29 | 454 | 696 | 9 | 37 | 3.77 |
| SF | 75 | 86 | .466 | 17 | 573 | 634 | 199 | 44 | 80 | .244 | .342 | 100 | 159 | 124 | .975 | 27 | 492 | 811 | 10 | 35 | 3.46 |
| SD | 73 | 89 | .451 | 19.5 | 591 | 654 | 195 | 43 | 67 | .255 | .342 | 239 | 132 | 157 | .980 | 19 | 536 | 728 | 9 | 39 | 3.65 |
| LEAGUE TOTAL | | | | | 7852 | 7852 | 2856 | 523 | 1243 | .259 | .374 | 1839 | 1689 | 1746 | .978 | 307 | 5969 | 9849 | 132 | 445 | 3.60 |

## INDIVIDUAL PITCHING

| PITCHER | T | W | L | PCT | ERA | SV | G | GS | CG | IP | H | BB | SO | R | ER | ShO | H/9 | BB/9 | SO/9 |
|---|---|---|---|---|---|---|---|---|---|---|---|---|---|---|---|---|---|---|---|
| Rick Reuschel | R | 11 | 13 | .458 | 3.40 | 4 | 38 | 38 | 6 | 257 | 281 | 76 | 140 | 111 | 97 | 0 | 9.84 | 2.66 | 4.90 |
| Mike Krukow | R | 10 | 15 | .400 | 4.39 | 0 | 34 | 34 | 3 | 205 | 200 | 80 | 130 | 117 | 100 | 0 | 8.78 | 3.51 | 5.71 |
| Dennis Lamp | R | 10 | 14 | .417 | 5.19 | 0 | 41 | 37 | 2 | 203 | 259 | 82 | 83 | 123 | 117 | 1 | 11.48 | 3.64 | 3.68 |
| Lynn McGlothen | R | 12 | 14 | .462 | 4.80 | 0 | 39 | 27 | 2 | 182 | 211 | 64 | 119 | 105 | 97 | 2 | 10.43 | 3.16 | 5.88 |
| Bill Caudill | R | 4 | 6 | .400 | 2.18 | 1 | 72 | 2 | 0 | 128 | 100 | 59 | 112 | 37 | 31 | 0 | 7.03 | 4.15 | 7.88 |
| Dick Tidrow | R | 6 | 5 | .545 | 2.79 | 6 | 84 | 0 | 0 | 116 | 97 | 53 | 97 | 44 | 36 | 0 | 7.53 | 4.11 | 7.53 |
| Willie Hernandez | L | 1 | 9 | .100 | 4.42 | 0 | 53 | 7 | 0 | 108 | 115 | 45 | 75 | 58 | 53 | 0 | 9.58 | 3.75 | 6.25 |
| Bruce Sutter | R | 5 | 8 | .385 | 2.65 | 28 | 60 | 0 | 0 | 102 | 90 | 34 | 76 | 46 | 41 | 0 | 7.94 | 3.00 | 6.71 |
| Doug Capilla | L | 2 | 8 | .200 | 4.10 | 0 | 39 | 11 | 0 | 90 | 82 | 51 | 51 | 46 | 41 | 0 | 8.20 | 5.10 | 5.10 |
| George Riley | L | 0 | 4 | .000 | 5.75 | 0 | 22 | 0 | 0 | 36 | 41 | 20 | 18 | 29 | 23 | 0 | 10.25 | 5.00 | 4.50 |
| Randy Martz | R | 1 | 2 | .333 | 2.10 | 0 | 6 | 6 | 0 | 30 | 28 | 11 | 5 | 14 | 7 | 0 | 8.40 | 3.30 | 1.50 |
| Lee Smith | R | 2 | 0 | 1.000 | 2.86 | 0 | 18 | 0 | 0 | 22 | 21 | 14 | 17 | 9 | 7 | 0 | 8.59 | 5.73 | 6.95 |
| TEAM TOTAL | | 64 | 98 | .395 | 3.89 | 35 | 506 | 162 | 13 | 1479 | 1525 | 589 | 923 | 728 | 639 | 3 | 9.28 | 3.58 | 5.62 |

| MANAGER | W | L | PCT |
|---|---|---|---|
| Joey Amalfitano | 15 | 37 | .288 |
| Joey Amalfitano | 23 | 28 | .451 |

| POS | Player | B | G | AB | H | 2B | 3B | HR | HR % | R | RBI | BB | SO | SB | Pinch Hit AB | Pinch Hit H | BA | SA |
|---|---|---|---|---|---|---|---|---|---|---|---|---|---|---|---|---|---|---|
| **REGULARS** | | | | | | | | | | | | | | | | | | |
| 1B | Bill Buckner | L | 106 | 421 | 131 | 35 | 3 | 10 | 2.4 | 45 | 75 | 26 | 16 | 5 | 2 | 1 | .311 | .480 |
| 2B | Pat Tabler | R | 35 | 101 | 19 | 3 | 1 | 1 | 1.0 | 11 | 5 | 13 | 26 | 0 | 0 | 0 | .188 | .267 |
| SS | Ivan DeJesus | R | 106 | 403 | 78 | 8 | 4 | 0 | 0.0 | 49 | 13 | 46 | 61 | 21 | 0 | 0 | .194 | .233 |
| 3B | Ken Reitz | R | 82 | 260 | 56 | 9 | 1 | 2 | 0.8 | 10 | 28 | 15 | 56 | 0 | 1 | 0 | .215 | .281 |
| RF | Leon Durham | L | 87 | 328 | 95 | 14 | 6 | 10 | 3.0 | 42 | 35 | 27 | 53 | 25 | 3 | 1 | .290 | .460 |
| CF | Steve Henderson | R | 82 | 287 | 84 | 9 | 5 | 5 | 1.7 | 32 | 35 | 42 | 61 | 5 | 4 | 0 | .293 | .411 |
| LF | Jerry Morales | R | 84 | 245 | 70 | 6 | 2 | 1 | 0.4 | 27 | 25 | 22 | 29 | 1 | 12 | 3 | .286 | .339 |
| C | Jody Davis | R | 56 | 180 | 46 | 5 | 1 | 4 | 2.2 | 14 | 21 | 21 | 28 | 0 | 0 | 0 | .256 | .361 |
| **SUBSTITUTES** | | | | | | | | | | | | | | | | | | |
| 23 | Steve Dillard | R | 53 | 119 | 26 | 7 | 1 | 2 | 1.7 | 18 | 11 | 8 | 20 | 0 | 11 | 3 | .218 | .345 |
| 3O | Hector Cruz | R | 53 | 109 | 25 | 5 | 0 | 7 | 6.4 | 15 | 15 | 17 | 24 | 2 | 17 | 3 | .229 | .468 |
| 2B | Mike Tyson | R | 50 | 92 | 17 | 2 | 0 | 2 | 2.2 | 6 | 8 | 7 | 15 | 1 | 13 | 4 | .185 | .272 |
| 2B | Joe Strain | R | 25 | 74 | 14 | 1 | 0 | 0 | 0.0 | 7 | 1 | 5 | 7 | 0 | 3 | 2 | .189 | .203 |
| UT | Ty Waller | R | 30 | 71 | 19 | 2 | 1 | 3 | 4.2 | 10 | 13 | 4 | 18 | 2 | 1 | 1 | .268 | .451 |
| 2S | Scott Fletcher | R | 19 | 46 | 10 | 4 | 0 | 0 | 0.0 | 6 | 1 | 2 | 4 | 0 | 0 | 0 | .217 | .304 |
| OF | Bobby Bonds | R | 45 | 163 | 35 | 7 | 1 | 6 | 3.7 | 26 | 19 | 24 | 44 | 5 | 0 | 0 | .215 | .380 |
| OF | Scot Thompson | L | 57 | 115 | 19 | 5 | 0 | 0 | 0.0 | 8 | 8 | 7 | 8 | 2 | 22 | 2 | .165 | .209 |
| OF | Jim Tracy | L | 45 | 63 | 15 | 2 | 1 | 0 | 0.0 | 6 | 5 | 12 | 14 | 1 | 29 | 5 | .238 | .302 |
| OF | Mike Lum | L | 41 | 58 | 14 | 1 | 0 | 2 | 3.4 | 5 | 7 | 5 | 5 | 0 | 24 | 7 | .241 | .362 |
| OF | Carlos Lezcano | R | 7 | 14 | 1 | 0 | 0 | 0 | 0.0 | 1 | 2 | 0 | 4 | 0 | 2 | 0 | .071 | .071 |
| OF | Mel Hall | L | 10 | 11 | 1 | 0 | 0 | 1 | 9.1 | 1 | 2 | 1 | 4 | 0 | 7 | 1 | .091 | .364 |
| C | Tim Blackwell | B | 58 | 158 | 37 | 10 | 2 | 1 | 0.6 | 21 | 11 | 23 | 23 | 2 | 2 | 0 | .234 | .342 |
| C | Barry Foote | R | 9 | 22 | 0 | 0 | 0 | 0 | 0.0 | 0 | 1 | 3 | 7 | 0 | 3 | 0 | .000 | .000 |
| C | Bill Hayes | R | 1 | 0 | 0 | 0 | 0 | 0 | — | 0 | 0 | 0 | 0 | 0 | 0 | 0 | — | — |
| **PITCHERS** | | | | | | | | | | | | | | | | | | |
| P | Mike Krukow | R | 25 | 50 | 9 | 2 | 0 | 0 | 0.0 | 5 | 3 | 0 | 13 | 0 | 0 | 0 | .180 | .220 |
| P | Randy Martz | L | 34 | 28 | 6 | 0 | 0 | 0 | 0.0 | 0 | 2 | 3 | 13 | 0 | 0 | 0 | .214 | .214 |
| P | Rick Reuschel | R | 16 | 25 | 2 | 0 | 0 | 0 | 0.0 | 1 | 1 | 1 | 7 | 0 | 0 | 0 | .080 | .080 |
| P | Doug Bird | R | 12 | 20 | 2 | 0 | 0 | 0 | 0.0 | 0 | 0 | 1 | 11 | 0 | 0 | 0 | .100 | .100 |
| P | Ken Kravec | L | 25 | 15 | 0 | 0 | 0 | 0 | 0.0 | 1 | 0 | 2 | 8 | 0 | 0 | 0 | .000 | .000 |
| P | Bill Caudill | R | 30 | 14 | 2 | 0 | 0 | 0 | 0.0 | 0 | 1 | 2 | 6 | 0 | 0 | 0 | .143 | .143 |
| P | Mike Griffin | R | 16 | 13 | 2 | 0 | 0 | 0 | 0.0 | 0 | 0 | 0 | 8 | 0 | 0 | 0 | .154 | .154 |
| P | Lynn McGlothen | L | 20 | 12 | 1 | 1 | 0 | 0 | 0.0 | 1 | 0 | 0 | 3 | 0 | 0 | 0 | .083 | .167 |
| P | Lee Smith | R | 40 | 9 | 0 | 0 | 0 | 0 | 0.0 | 0 | 0 | 0 | 7 | 0 | 0 | 0 | .000 | .000 |
| P | Dick Tidrow | R | 51 | 5 | 0 | 0 | 0 | 0 | 0.0 | 0 | 0 | 0 | 0 | 0 | 0 | 0 | .000 | .000 |
| P | Doug Capilla | L | 42 | 3 | 0 | 0 | 0 | 0 | 0.0 | 0 | 0 | 0 | 1 | 0 | 0 | 0 | .000 | .000 |
| P | Dave Geisel | L | 11 | 3 | 0 | 0 | 0 | 0 | 0.0 | 0 | 0 | 1 | 2 | 0 | 0 | 0 | .000 | .000 |
| P | Rawley Eastwick | R | 30 | 2 | 0 | 0 | 0 | 0 | 0.0 | 0 | 0 | 0 | 2 | 0 | 0 | 0 | .000 | .000 |
| P | Jay Howell | R | 10 | 2 | 0 | 0 | 0 | 0 | 0.0 | 2 | 0 | 1 | 0 | 0 | 0 | 0 | .000 | .000 |
| P | Willie Hernandez | L | 13 | 0 | 0 | 0 | 0 | 0 | — | 0 | 0 | 0 | 0 | 0 | 0 | 0 | — | — |
| TEAM TOTAL | | | | 3541 | 836 | 138 | 29 | 57 | 1.6 | 37 | 348 | 341 | 610 | 72 | 156 | 33 | .236 | .340 |

## INDIVIDUAL FIELDING

| POS | Player | T | G | PO | A | E | DP | TC/G | FA |
|---|---|---|---|---|---|---|---|---|---|
| 1B | B. Buckner | L | 105 | 996 | 81 | 17 | 92 | 10.4 | .984 |
| | L. Durham | L | 3 | 16 | 0 | 0 | 1 | 5.3 | 1.000 |
| | S. Thompson | L | 3 | 7 | 0 | 1 | 0 | 2.7 | .875 |
| | M. Lum | L | 1 | 1 | 1 | 0 | 0 | 1.0 | 1.000 |
| 2B | P. Tabler | R | 35 | 70 | 93 | 3 | 17 | 4.7 | .982 |
| | S. Dillard | R | 32 | 54 | 96 | 4 | 21 | 4.8 | .974 |
| | M. Tyson | R | 36 | 50 | 76 | 8 | 14 | 3.7 | .940 |
| | J. Strain | R | 20 | 38 | 81 | 3 | 10 | 6.1 | .975 |
| | S. Fletcher | R | 13 | 31 | 39 | 2 | 10 | 5.5 | .972 |
| | T. Waller | R | 3 | 5 | 2 | 0 | 0 | 2.3 | 1.000 |
| SS | I. DeJesus | R | 106 | 221 | 343 | 24 | 81 | 5.5 | .959 |
| | M. Tyson | R | 1 | 0 | 0 | 0 | 0 | 0.0 | .000 |
| | S. Fletcher | R | 4 | 2 | 4 | 1 | 0 | 1.8 | .857 |
| | S. Dillard | R | 2 | 2 | 0 | 0 | 1 | 1.0 | 1.000 |
| 3B | K. Reitz | R | 81 | 57 | 157 | 5 | 11 | 2.7 | .977 |
| | T. Waller | R | 22 | 11 | 33 | 1 | 2 | 2.0 | .978 |
| | H. Cruz | R | 18 | 12 | 25 | 3 | 0 | 2.2 | .925 |
| | S. Dillard | R | 7 | 3 | 0 | 2 | 0 | 0.7 | .600 |
| | S. Fletcher | R | 1 | 1 | 1 | 0 | 0 | 2.0 | 1.000 |

| POS | Player | T | G | PO | A | E | DP | TC/G | FA |
|---|---|---|---|---|---|---|---|---|---|
| OF | L. Durham | L | 83 | 159 | 4 | 5 | 1 | 2.0 | .970 |
| | S. Henderson | R | 77 | 152 | 4 | 8 | 2 | 2.1 | .951 |
| | J. Morales | R | 72 | 142 | 2 | 2 | 1 | 2.0 | .986 |
| | B. Bonds | R | 45 | 108 | 2 | 2 | 0 | 2.5 | .982 |
| | S. Thompson | L | 30 | 49 | 1 | 1 | 0 | 1.7 | .980 |
| | H. Cruz | R | 16 | 21 | 1 | 0 | 0 | 1.4 | 1.000 |
| | M. Hall | L | 3 | 0 | 0 | 0 | 0 | 0.0 | .000 |
| | J. Tracy | R | 11 | 16 | 0 | 0 | 0 | 1.5 | 1.000 |
| | M. Lum | L | 14 | 12 | 0 | 1 | 0 | 0.9 | .923 |
| | C. Lezcano | R | 5 | 7 | 0 | 0 | 0 | 1.4 | 1.000 |
| | T. Waller | R | 3 | 2 | 0 | 0 | 0 | 0.7 | 1.000 |
| C | J. Davis | R | 56 | 274 | 44 | 9 | 4 | 5.8 | .972 |
| | T. Blackwell | R | 56 | 268 | 28 | 2 | 1 | 5.3 | .993 |
| | B. Hayes | R | 1 | 0 | 0 | 0 | 0 | 0.0 | .000 |
| | B. Foote | R | 8 | 30 | 3 | 0 | 2 | 4.1 | 1.000 |

For the Cubs, the 50-day players' strike couldn't have come at a better time. They had the worst record in the majors, a 15–37 mark, when the players walked out on June 12. The Cubs lost their credibility by trading ace reliever Bruce Sutter to the Cardinals over the winter. They lost their power with the trade of Dave Kingman to the Mets in spring training, and they lost their ace Rick Reuschel in a June deal with the Yankees. General manager Bob Kennedy was fired and replaced by former manager Herman Franks. Then followed the blockbuster news: On June 16, William Wrigley sold the Cubs to the Chicago Tribune Co. for an estimated $20.5 million, ending the family's 65-year association with the team.

Somehow, the Cubs benefitted from the long layoff and the new ownership, rallying to a 23–28 second half record. They were last in team batting at .236, but had one .300 hitter in Bill Buckner, whose 75 RBIs ranked third in the league. And the Cubs salvaged something from the Sutter deal with Leon Durham's .290 average and 25 steals.

| | First Half | | | | | Second Half | | | |
|---|---|---|---|---|---|---|---|---|---|
| | W | L | PCT | GB | | W | L | PCT | GB |
| **EAST** | | | | | **EAST** | | | | |
| PHI | 34 | 21 | .618 | | MON* | 30 | 23 | .566 | |
| STL | 30 | 20 | .600 | 1.5 | STL | 29 | 23 | .558 | .5 |
| MON | 30 | 25 | .545 | 4 | PHI | 25 | 27 | .481 | 4.5 |
| PIT | 25 | 23 | .521 | 5.5 | NY | 24 | 28 | .462 | 5.5 |
| NY | 17 | 34 | .333 | 15 | CHI | 23 | 28 | .451 | 6 |
| CHI | 15 | 37 | .288 | 17.5 | PIT | 21 | 33 | .389 | 9.5 |

*Defeated Philadelphia in playoff 3 games to 2.

| | First Half | | | | | Second Half | | | |
|---|---|---|---|---|---|---|---|---|---|
| **WEST** | | | | | **WEST** | | | | |
| LA* | 36 | 21 | .632 | | HOU | 33 | 20 | .623 | |
| CIN | 35 | 21 | .625 | .5 | CIN | 31 | 21 | .596 | 1.5 |
| HOU | 28 | 29 | .491 | 8 | SF | 29 | 23 | .558 | 3.5 |
| ATL | 25 | 29 | .463 | 9.5 | LA | 27 | 26 | .509 | 6 |
| SF | 27 | 32 | .458 | 10 | ATL | 25 | 27 | .481 | 7.5 |
| SD | 23 | 33 | .411 | 12.5 | SD | 18 | 36 | .333 | 15.5 |

*Defeated Houston in playoff 3 games to 2.

## TEAM STATISTICS

| | W | L | PCT | GB | R | OR | Batting | | | | | | Fielding | | | Pitching | | | | |
|---|---|---|---|---|---|---|---|---|---|---|---|---|---|---|---|---|---|---|---|---|
| | | | | | | | 2B | 3B | HR | BA | SA | SB | E | DP | FA | CG | B | SO | ShO | SV | ERA |
| **EAST** | | | | | | | | | | | | | | | | | | | | | |
| STL | 59 | 43 | .578 | | 464 | 417 | 158 | 45 | 50 | .265 | .377 | 88 | 82 | 108 | **.981** | 11 | 290 | 388 | 5 | **33** | 3.63 |
| MON | 60 | 48 | .556 | 2 | 443 | 394 | 146 | 28 | 81 | .246 | .370 | **138** | 81 | 88 | .980 | 20 | **268** | 520 | 12 | 23 | 3.30 |
| PHI | 59 | 48 | .551 | 2.5 | **491** | 472 | 165 | 25 | 69 | **.273** | **.389** | 103 | 86 | 90 | .980 | 19 | 347 | 580 | 5 | 23 | 4.05 |
| PIT | 46 | 56 | .451 | 13 | 407 | 425 | 176 | 30 | 55 | .257 | .369 | 122 | 86 | 106 | .979 | 11 | 346 | 492 | 5 | 29 | 3.56 |
| NY | 41 | 62 | .398 | 18.5 | 348 | 432 | 136 | 35 | 57 | .248 | .356 | 103 | 130 | 89 | .968 | 7 | 336 | 490 | 3 | 24 | 3.55 |
| CHI | 38 | 65 | .369 | 21.5 | 370 | 483 | 138 | 29 | 57 | .236 | .340 | 72 | 113 | 103 | .974 | 6 | 388 | 532 | 2 | 20 | 4.01 |
| **WEST** | | | | | | | | | | | | | | | | | | | | | |
| CIN | 66 | 42 | .611 | | 464 | 440 | **190** | 24 | 64 | .267 | .385 | 58 | **80** | 99 | .981 | 25 | 393 | 593 | 14 | 20 | 3.73 |
| LA | 63 | 47 | .573 | 4 | 450 | 356 | 133 | 20 | **82** | .262 | .374 | 73 | 87 | 101 | .980 | **26** | 302 | 603 | 19 | 24 | 3.01 |
| HOU | 61 | 49 | .555 | 6 | 394 | **331** | 160 | 35 | 45 | .257 | .356 | 81 | 87 | 81 | .980 | 23 | 300 | **610** | 19 | 25 | **2.66** |
| SF | 56 | 55 | .505 | 11.5 | 427 | 414 | 161 | 26 | 63 | .250 | .357 | 89 | 102 | 102 | .977 | 8 | 393 | 561 | 9 | **33** | 3.28 |
| ATL | 50 | 56 | .472 | 15 | 395 | 416 | 148 | 22 | 64 | .243 | .349 | 98 | 102 | 93 | .976 | 11 | 330 | 471 | 4 | 24 | 3.45 |
| SD | 41 | 69 | .373 | 26 | 382 | 455 | 170 | 35 | 32 | .256 | .346 | 83 | 102 | **117** | **.977** | 9 | 414 | 492 | 6 | 23 | 3.72 |
| LEAGUE TOTAL | | | | | 5035 | 5035 | 1881 | 354 | 719 | .255 | .364 | 1108 | 1138 | 1177 | .978 | 176 | 4107 | 6332 | 103 | 301 | 3.49 |

### INDIVIDUAL  PITCHING

| PITCHER | T | W | L | PCT | ERA | SV | G | GS | CG | IP | H | BB | SO | R | ER | ShO | H/9 | BB/9 | SO/9 |
|---|---|---|---|---|---|---|---|---|---|---|---|---|---|---|---|---|---|---|---|
| Mike Krukow | R | 9 | 9 | .500 | 3.69 | 0 | 25 | **25** | 2 | 144 | 146 | 55 | 101 | 68 | 59 | 1 | 9.13 | 3.44 | 6.31 |
| Randy Martz | R | 5 | 7 | .417 | 3.67 | 6 | 33 | 14 | 1 | 108 | 103 | 49 | 32 | 49 | 44 | 0 | 8.58 | 4.08 | 2.67 |
| Rick Reuschel | R | 4 | 7 | .364 | 3.45 | 0 | 13 | 13 | 1 | 86 | 87 | 23 | 53 | 40 | 33 | 0 | 9.10 | 2.41 | 5.55 |
| Ken Kravec | L | 1 | 6 | .143 | 5.08 | 0 | 24 | 12 | 0 | 78 | 80 | 39 | 50 | 48 | 44 | 0 | 8.76 | 3.60 | 5.77 |
| Dick Tidrow | R | 3 | 10 | .231 | 5.04 | 9 | 51 | 0 | 0 | 75 | 73 | 30 | 39 | 45 | 42 | 1 | 8.64 | 1.92 | 4.08 |
| Doug Bird | R | 4 | 5 | .444 | 3.60 | 0 | 12 | 12 | 2 | 75 | 72 | 16 | 34 | 34 | 30 | 1 | 8.64 | 1.92 | 4.08 |
| Bill Caudill | R | 1 | 5 | .167 | 5.83 | 0 | 30 | 10 | 0 | 71 | 87 | 31 | 45 | 50 | 46 | 0 | 11.03 | 3.93 | 5.70 |
| Lee Smith | R | 3 | 6 | .333 | 3.49 | 1 | 40 | 1 | 0 | 67 | 57 | 31 | 50 | 31 | 26 | 0 | 7.66 | 4.16 | 6.72 |
| Lynn McGlothen | R | 1 | 4 | .200 | 4.75 | 0 | 20 | 6 | 0 | 55 | 71 | 28 | 26 | 32 | 29 | 0 | 11.62 | 4.58 | 4.25 |
| Mike Griffin | R | 2 | 5 | .286 | 4.50 | 1 | 16 | 9 | 0 | 52 | 64 | 9 | 20 | 27 | 26 | 0 | 11.08 | 1.56 | 3.46 |
| Doug Capilla | L | 1 | 0 | 1.000 | 3.18 | 0 | 42 | 0 | 0 | 51 | 52 | 34 | 28 | 20 | 18 | 0 | 9.18 | 6.00 | 4.94 |
| Rawley Eastwick | R | 0 | 1 | .000 | 2.30 | 1 | 30 | 0 | 0 | 43 | 43 | 15 | 24 | 16 | 11 | 0 | 9.00 | 3.14 | 5.02 |
| Jay Howell | R | 2 | 0 | 1.000 | 4.91 | 0 | 10 | 2 | 0 | 22 | 23 | 10 | 10 | 13 | 12 | 0 | 9.41 | 4.09 | 4.09 |
| Dave Geisel | L | 2 | 0 | 1.000 | 0.56 | 0 | 11 | 2 | 0 | 16 | 11 | 10 | 7 | 3 | 1 | 0 | 6.19 | 5.63 | 3.94 |
| Willie Hernandez | L | 0 | 0 | | 3.86 | 2 | 12 | 0 | 0 | 14 | 14 | 8 | 13 | 7 | 6 | 0 | 9.00 | 5.14 | 8.36 |
| TEAM TOTAL | | 38 | 65 | .369 | 4.02 | 20 | 369 | 106 | 6 | 957 | 983 | 388 | 532 | 483 | 427 | 2 | 9.24 | 3.65 | 5.00 |

| MANAGER | W | L | PCT |
|---|---|---|---|
| Lee Elia | 73 | 89 | .451 |

| POS | Player | B | G | AB | H | 2B | 3B | HR | HR % | R | RBI | BB | SO | SB | Pinch Hit AB | Pinch Hit H | BA | SA |
|---|---|---|---|---|---|---|---|---|---|---|---|---|---|---|---|---|---|---|
| **REGULARS** | | | | | | | | | | | | | | | | | | |
| 1B | Bill Buckner | L | 161 | 657 | 201 | 34 | 5 | 15 | 2.3 | 93 | 105 | 36 | 26 | 15 | 0 | 0 | .306 | .441 |
| 2B | Bump Wills | B | 128 | 419 | 114 | 18 | 4 | 6 | 1.4 | 64 | 38 | 46 | 76 | 35 | 21 | 6 | .272 | .377 |
| SS | Larry Bowa | B | 142 | 499 | 123 | 15 | 7 | 0 | 0.0 | 50 | 29 | 39 | 38 | 8 | 2 | 1 | .246 | .305 |
| 3B | Ryne Sandberg | R | 156 | 635 | 172 | 33 | 5 | 7 | 1.1 | 103 | 54 | 36 | 90 | 32 | 1 | 0 | .271 | .372 |
| RF | Jay Johnstone | L | 98 | 269 | 67 | 13 | 1 | 10 | 3.7 | 39 | 43 | 40 | 41 | 0 | 13 | 2 | .249 | .416 |
| CF | Leon Durham | L | 148 | 539 | 168 | 33 | 7 | 22 | 4.1 | 84 | 90 | 66 | 77 | 28 | 5 | 2 | .312 | .521 |
| LF | Keith Moreland | R | 138 | 476 | 124 | 17 | 2 | 15 | 3.2 | 50 | 68 | 44 | 71 | 0 | 6 | 1 | .261 | .399 |
| C | Jody Davis | R | 130 | 418 | 109 | 20 | 2 | 12 | 2.9 | 41 | 52 | 36 | 92 | 0 | 1 | 0 | .261 | .404 |
| **SUBSTITUTES** | | | | | | | | | | | | | | | | | | |
| 2S | Junior Kennedy | R | 105 | 242 | 53 | 3 | 1 | 2 | 0.8 | 22 | 25 | 21 | 34 | 1 | 4 | 0 | .219 | .264 |
| 3B | Pat Tabler | R | 25 | 85 | 20 | 4 | 2 | 1 | 1.2 | 9 | 7 | 6 | 20 | 0 | 0 | 0 | .235 | .365 |
| SS | Scott Fletcher | R | 11 | 24 | 4 | 0 | 0 | 0 | 0.0 | 4 | 1 | 4 | 5 | 1 | 0 | 0 | .167 | .167 |
| OF | Steve Henderson | R | 92 | 257 | 60 | 12 | 4 | 2 | 0.8 | 23 | 29 | 22 | 64 | 6 | 25 | 6 | .233 | .335 |
| OF | Gary Woods | R | 117 | 245 | 66 | 15 | 1 | 4 | 1.6 | 28 | 30 | 21 | 48 | 3 | 22 | 4 | .269 | .388 |
| OF | Jerry Morales | R | 65 | 116 | 33 | 2 | 2 | 4 | 3.4 | 14 | 30 | 9 | 7 | 1 | 30 | 10 | .284 | .440 |
| OF | Mel Hall | L | 24 | 80 | 21 | 3 | 2 | 0 | 0.0 | 6 | 4 | 5 | 17 | 0 | 1 | 0 | .263 | .350 |
| OF | Scot Thompson | L | 49 | 74 | 27 | 5 | 1 | 0 | 0.0 | 11 | 7 | 5 | 4 | 0 | 27 | 7 | .365 | .459 |
| OF | Bob Molinaro | L | 65 | 66 | 13 | 1 | 0 | 1 | 1.5 | 6 | 12 | 6 | 5 | 1 | 53* | 10 | .197 | .258 |
| O1 | Dan Briggs | L | 48 | 48 | 6 | 0 | 0 | 0 | 0.0 | 1 | 1 | 0 | 9 | 0 | 37 | 4 | .125 | .125 |
| OF | Ty Waller | R | 17 | 21 | 5 | 0 | 0 | 0 | 0.0 | 4 | 1 | 2 | 5 | 0 | 6 | 2 | .238 | .238 |
| OF | Hector Cruz | R | 17 | 19 | 4 | 1 | 0 | 0 | 0.0 | 1 | 0 | 2 | 4 | 0 | 15 | 3 | .211 | .263 |
| C | Butch Benton | R | 4 | 7 | 1 | 0 | 0 | 0 | 0.0 | 0 | 1 | 0 | 1 | 0 | 0 | 0 | .143 | .143 |
| C | Larry Cox | R | 2 | 4 | 0 | 0 | 0 | 0 | 0.0 | 1 | 0 | 2 | 1 | 0 | 0 | 0 | .000 | .000 |
| **PITCHERS** | | | | | | | | | | | | | | | | | | |
| P | Ferguson Jenkins | R | 34 | 67 | 10 | 2 | 0 | 0 | 0.0 | 2 | 6 | 0 | 23 | 0 | 0 | 0 | .149 | .179 |
| P | Dickie Noles | R | 31 | 56 | 6 | 3 | 0 | 0 | 0.0 | 5 | 2 | 1 | 35 | 0 | 0 | 0 | .107 | .161 |
| P | Doug Bird | R | 35 | 56 | 8 | 1 | 0 | 0 | 0.0 | 0 | 3 | 0 | 20 | 0 | 0 | 0 | .143 | .161 |
| P | Randy Martz | L | 28 | 42 | 6 | 2 | 0 | 0 | 0.0 | 6 | 6 | 6 | 17 | 0 | 0 | 0 | .143 | .190 |
| P | Allen Ripley | R | 28 | 38 | 5 | 0 | 0 | 0 | 0.0 | 3 | 1 | 0 | 10 | 0 | 0 | 0 | .132 | .132 |
| P | Lee Smith | R | 72 | 16 | 1 | 0 | 0 | 1 | 6.3 | 2 | 1 | 1 | 9 | 0 | 0 | 0 | .063 | .250 |
| P | Mike Proly | R | 44 | 14 | 4 | 1 | 0 | 0 | 0.0 | 0 | 1 | 0 | 1 | 0 | 0 | 0 | .286 | .357 |
| P | Tom Filer | R | 8 | 12 | 1 | 1 | 0 | 0 | 0.0 | 1 | 0 | 0 | 7 | 0 | 0 | 0 | .083 | .167 |
| P | Dan Larson | R | 12 | 11 | 3 | 0 | 0 | 0 | 0.0 | 2 | 0 | 0 | 2 | 0 | 0 | 0 | .273 | .273 |
| P | Bill Campbell | R | 62 | 7 | 1 | 0 | 0 | 0 | 0.0 | 0 | 0 | 0 | 3 | 0 | 0 | 0 | .143 | .143 |
| P | Dick Tidrow | R | 65 | 6 | 0 | 0 | 0 | 0 | 0.0 | 0 | 0 | 0 | 3 | 0 | 0 | 0 | .000 | .000 |
| P | Ken Kravec | L | 13 | 3 | 0 | 0 | 0 | 0 | 0.0 | 0 | 0 | 1 | 1 | 0 | 0 | 0 | .000 | .000 |
| P | Willie Hernandez | L | 75 | 3 | 0 | 0 | 0 | 0 | 0.0 | 1 | 0 | 1 | 3 | 1 | 0 | 0 | .000 | .000 |
| P | Randy Stein | R | 6 | 0 | 0 | 0 | 0 | 0 | – | 0 | 0 | 0 | 0 | 0 | 0 | 0 | – | – |
| P | Herman Segelke | R | 3 | 0 | 0 | 0 | 0 | 0 | – | 0 | 0 | 0 | 0 | 0 | 0 | 0 | – | – |
| TEAM TOTAL | | | | 5531 | 1436 | 239 | 46 | 102 | 1.8 | 67 | 647 | 460 | 869 | 132 | 269 | 58 | .260 | .375 |

## INDIVIDUAL  FIELDING

| POS | Player | T | G | PO | A | E | DP | TC/G | FA |
|---|---|---|---|---|---|---|---|---|---|
| 1B | B. Buckner | L | 161 | 1547 | 159 | 12 | 89 | 10.7 | .993 |
| | L. Durham | L | 1 | 10 | 1 | 0 | 0 | 11.0 | 1.000 |
| | D. Briggs | L | 4 | 9 | 0 | 0 | 1 | 2.3 | 1.000 |
| | S. Thompson | L | 4 | 3 | 1 | 0 | 0 | 1.0 | 1.000 |
| 2B | B. Wills | R | 103 | 199 | 297 | 19 | 45 | 5.0 | .963 |
| | J. Kennedy | R | 71 | 109 | 160 | 6 | 25 | 3.9 | .978 |
| | R. Sandberg | R | 24 | 57 | 95 | 1 | 9 | 6.4 | .993 |
| SS | L. Bowa | R | 140 | 210 | 396 | 17 | 64 | 4.5 | .973 |
| | J. Kennedy | R | 28 | 28 | 60 | 6 | 10 | 3.4 | .936 |
| | S. Fletcher | R | 11 | 11 | 23 | 0 | 3 | 3.1 | 1.000 |
| 3B | R. Sandberg | R | 133 | 79 | 278 | 11 | 19 | 2.8 | .970 |
| | P. Tabler | R | 25 | 23 | 33 | 3 | 3 | 2.4 | .949 |
| | J. Kennedy | R | 7 | 1 | 8 | 0 | 0 | 1.3 | 1.000 |
| | K. Moreland | R | 2 | 4 | 2 | 0 | 0 | 3.0 | 1.000 |
| | T. Waller | R | 1 | 1 | 1 | 1 | 0 | 3.0 | .667 |

| POS | Player | T | G | PO | A | E | DP | TC/G | FA |
|---|---|---|---|---|---|---|---|---|---|
| OF | L. Durham | L | 143 | 301 | 11 | 12 | 1 | 2.3 | .963 |
| | K. Moreland | R | 86 | 169 | 9 | 2 | 0 | 2.1 | .975 |
| | G. Woods | R | 103 | 161 | 6 | 0 | 1 | 1.6 | 1.000 |
| | J. Johnstone | R | 86 | 154 | 8 | 3 | 0 | 1.9 | .982 |
| | S. Henderson | R | 70 | 126 | 5 | 6 | 0 | 2.0 | .956 |
| | J. Morales | R | 41 | 72 | 5 | 0 | 1 | 1.9 | 1.000 |
| | M. Hall | L | 22 | 42 | 4 | 3 | 1 | 2.2 | .939 |
| | S. Thompson | L | 23 | 36 | 2 | 0 | 1 | 1.7 | 1.000 |
| | T. Waller | R | 7 | 9 | 0 | 0 | 0 | 1.3 | 1.000 |
| | D. Briggs | L | 10 | 5 | 2 | 1 | 0 | 0.8 | .875 |
| | B. Molinaro | R | 4 | 2 | 0 | 0 | 0 | 0.5 | 1.000 |
| | H. Cruz | R | 4 | 1 | 0 | 0 | 0 | 0.3 | 1.000 |
| C | J. Davis | R | 129 | 598 | 89 | 11 | 11 | 5.4 | .984 |
| | K. Moreland | R | 44 | 211 | 27 | 6 | 2 | 5.5 | .975 |
| | B. Benton | R | 4 | 20 | 1 | 0 | 0 | 5.3 | 1.000 |
| | L. Cox | R | 2 | 9 | 2 | 0 | 1 | 5.5 | 1.000 |

At times it was tough to distinguish whether this club was the Cubs or the Phillies. The Tribune Co. hired Phillies' manager Dallas Green as executive vice-president, and he brought along his coaching sidekick Lee Elia as manager. Green then set out to bring a lethargic team into the 20th century. He lost on many counts. Wrigleyville residents resisted his attempts to install lights. The old scoreboard remained intact, except for an electronic message board on the bottom.

Meanwhile, there were many new faces in the playing ranks, mostly recycled Phillies. At the outset, they resembled the same old Cubs. Elia suffered through a team record-tying 13-game losing streak and another of nine games. He got into a dugout shoving match with first baseman Bill Buckner. The outlook was grim. Suddenly, the club caught fire with an 18–10 July that led to a strong finish and hope for the future. However, they finished with a 73–89 record and beat out only the Mets in the NL East. Two holdovers from the old era, Buckner and Leon Durham, supplied the punch. Buckner had 201 hits, drove in 105 runs, and batted .306. Durham was high in homers with 22, stole 28 bases, and batted .312. Best of the newcomers was infielder Ryne Sandberg, acquired from the Phillies, who despite a 1-for-31 beginning, finished at .271, stole 32 bases, and set a team rookie record by scoring 103 runs. Free agent Fergie Jenkins was resurrected for a 14–15 record and a 3.15 ERA to top an undistinguished pitching staff.

### TEAM STATISTICS

| | W | L | PCT | GB | R | OR | Batting 2B | 3B | HR | BA | SA | SB | Fielding E | DP | FA | CG | B | Pitching SO | ShO | SV | ERA |
|---|---|---|---|---|---|---|---|---|---|---|---|---|---|---|---|---|---|---|---|---|---|
| **EAST** | | | | | | | | | | | | | | | | | | | | | |
| STL | 92 | 70 | .568 | | 685 | 609 | 239 | 52 | 67 | .264 | .364 | 200 | 124 | 169 | .981 | 25 | 502 | 689 | 10 | 47 | 3.37 |
| PHI | 89 | 73 | .549 | 3 | 664 | 654 | 245 | 25 | 112 | .260 | .376 | 128 | 121 | 138 | .981 | 38 | 472 | 1002 | 13 | 33 | 3.61 |
| MON | 86 | 76 | .531 | 6 | 697 | 616 | 270 | 38 | 133 | .262 | .396 | 156 | 122 | 117 | .980 | 34 | 448 | 936 | 10 | 43 | 3.31 |
| PIT | 84 | 78 | .519 | 8 | 724 | 696 | 272 | 40 | 134 | .273 | .408 | 161 | 145 | 133 | .977 | 19 | 521 | 933 | 7 | 39 | 3.81 |
| CHI | 73 | 89 | .451 | 19 | 676 | 709 | 239 | 46 | 102 | .260 | .375 | 132 | 132 | 110 | .979 | 9 | 452 | 764 | 7 | 43 | 3.92 |
| NY | 65 | 97 | .401 | 27 | 609 | 723 | 227 | 26 | 97 | .247 | .350 | 137 | 175 | 134 | .972 | 15 | 582 | 759 | 5 | 37 | 3.88 |
| **WEST** | | | | | | | | | | | | | | | | | | | | | |
| ATL | 89 | 73 | .549 | | 739 | 702 | 215 | 22 | 146 | .256 | .383 | 151 | 137 | 186 | .979 | 15 | 502 | 813 | 11 | 51 | 3.82 |
| LA | 88 | 74 | .543 | 1 | 691 | 612 | 222 | 32 | 138 | .264 | .388 | 151 | 139 | 131 | .979 | 37 | 468 | 932 | 16 | 28 | 3.26 |
| SF | 87 | 75 | .537 | 2 | 673 | 687 | 213 | 30 | 133 | .253 | .376 | 130 | 173 | 125 | .973 | 18 | 466 | 810 | 4 | 45 | 3.64 |
| SD | 81 | 81 | .500 | 8 | 675 | 658 | 217 | 52 | 81 | .257 | .376 | 165 | 152 | 142 | .976 | 20 | 502 | 765 | 11 | 41 | 3.52 |
| HOU | 77 | 85 | .475 | 12 | 569 | 620 | 236 | 48 | 74 | .247 | .349 | 140 | 136 | 154 | .978 | 37 | 479 | 899 | 16 | 31 | 3.41 |
| CIN | 61 | 101 | .377 | 28 | 545 | 661 | 228 | 34 | 82 | .251 | .350 | 131 | 128 | 158 | .980 | 22 | 570 | 998 | 7 | 31 | 3.66 |
| LEAGUE TOTAL | | | | | 7947 | 7947 | 2823 | 445 | 1299 | .258 | .373 | 1782 | 1684 | 1697 | .978 | 289 | 5964 | 10300 | 117 | 469 | 3.60 |

### INDIVIDUAL PITCHING

| PITCHER | T | W | L | PCT | ERA | SV | G | GS | CG | IP | H | BB | SO | R | ER | ShO | H/9 | BB/9 | SO/9 |
|---|---|---|---|---|---|---|---|---|---|---|---|---|---|---|---|---|---|---|---|
| Ferguson Jenkins | R | 14 | 15 | .483 | 3.15 | 0 | 34 | 34 | 4 | 217.1 | 221 | 68 | 134 | 92 | 76 | 1 | 9.15 | 2.82 | 5.55 |
| Doug Bird | R | 9 | 14 | .391 | 5.14 | 0 | 35 | 33 | 2 | 191 | 230 | 30 | 71 | 119 | 109 | 1 | 10.84 | 1.41 | 3.35 |
| Dickie Noles | R | 10 | 13 | .435 | 4.42 | 0 | 31 | 30 | 2 | 171 | 180 | 61 | 85 | 99 | 84 | 2 | 9.47 | 3.21 | 4.47 |
| Randy Martz | R | 11 | 10 | .524 | 4.21 | 1 | 28 | 24 | 1 | 147.2 | 157 | 36 | 40 | 80 | 69 | 0 | 9.57 | 2.19 | 2.44 |
| Allen Ripley | R | 5 | 7 | .417 | 4.26 | 0 | 28 | 19 | 0 | 122.2 | 130 | 38 | 57 | 61 | 58 | 0 | 9.54 | 2.79 | 4.18 |
| Lee Smith | R | 2 | 5 | .286 | 2.69 | 17 | 72 | 5 | 0 | 117 | 105 | 37 | 99 | 38 | 35 | 0 | 8.08 | 2.85 | 7.62 |
| Dick Tidrow | R | 8 | 3 | .727 | 3.39 | 6 | 65 | 0 | 0 | 103.2 | 106 | 29 | 62 | 45 | 39 | 0 | 9.20 | 2.52 | 5.38 |
| Bill Campbell | R | 3 | 6 | .333 | 3.69 | 0 | 62 | 0 | 0 | 100 | 89 | 40 | 71 | 44 | 41 | 0 | 8.01 | 3.60 | 6.39 |
| Mike Proly | R | 5 | 3 | .625 | 2.30 | 1 | 44 | 1 | 0 | 82 | 77 | 22 | 24 | 22 | 21 | 0 | 8.45 | 2.41 | 2.63 |
| Willie Hernandez | L | 4 | 6 | .400 | 3.00 | 10 | 75 | 0 | 0 | 75 | 74 | 24 | 54 | 26 | 25 | 0 | 8.88 | 2.88 | 6.48 |
| Tom Filer | R | 1 | 2 | .333 | 5.53 | 0 | 8 | 8 | 0 | 40.2 | 50 | 18 | 15 | 25 | 25 | 0 | 11.07 | 3.98 | 3.32 |
| Dan Larson | R | 0 | 4 | .000 | 5.67 | 0 | 12 | 6 | 0 | 39.2 | 51 | 18 | 22 | 30 | 25 | 0 | 11.57 | 4.08 | 4.99 |
| Ken Kravec | L | 1 | 1 | .500 | 6.12 | 0 | 13 | 2 | 0 | 25 | 27 | 18 | 20 | 20 | 17 | 0 | 9.72 | 6.48 | 7.20 |
| Randy Stein | R | 0 | 0 | – | 3.48 | 0 | 6 | 0 | 0 | 10.1 | 7 | 7 | 6 | 4 | 4 | 0 | 6.10 | 6.10 | 5.23 |
| Herman Segelke | R | 0 | 0 | – | 8.31 | 0 | 3 | 0 | 0 | 4.1 | 6 | 4 | 4 | 4 | 4 | 0 | 12.46 | 12.46 | 8.31 |
| TEAM TOTAL | | 73 | 89 | .451 | 3.93 | 43 | 516 | 162 | 9 | 1447.1 | 1510 | 452 | 764 | 709 | 632 | 4 | 9.39 | 2.81 | 4.75 |

| MANAGER | W | L | PCT |
|---|---|---|---|
| Lee Elia | 54 | 69 | .439 |
| Charlie Fox | 17 | 22 | .436 |

| POS | Player | B | G | AB | H | 2B | 3B | HR | HR % | R | RBI | BB | SO | SB | Pinch Hit AB | Pinch Hit H | BA | SA |
|---|---|---|---|---|---|---|---|---|---|---|---|---|---|---|---|---|---|---|
| **REGULARS** | | | | | | | | | | | | | | | | | | |
| 1B | Bill Buckner | L | 153 | 626 | 175 | 38 | 6 | 16 | 2.6 | 79 | 66 | 25 | 30 | 12 | 2 | 1 | .280 | .436 |
| 2B | Ryne Sandberg | R | 158 | 633 | 165 | 25 | 4 | 8 | 1.3 | 94 | 48 | 51 | 79 | 37 | 4 | 2 | .261 | .351 |
| SS | Larry Bowa | B | 147 | 499 | 133 | 20 | 5 | 2 | 0.4 | 73 | 43 | 35 | 30 | 7 | 4 | 1 | .267 | .339 |
| 3B | Ron Cey | R | 159 | 581 | 160 | 33 | 1 | 24 | 4.1 | 73 | 90 | 62 | 85 | 0 | 1 | 0 | .275 | .460 |
| RF | Keith Moreland | R | 154 | 533 | 161 | 30 | 3 | 16 | 3.0 | 76 | 70 | 68 | 73 | 0 | 2 | 0 | .302 | .460 |
| CF | Mel Hall | L | 112 | 410 | 116 | 23 | 5 | 17 | 4.1 | 60 | 56 | 42 | 101 | 6 | 2 | 1 | .283 | .488 |
| LF | Leon Durham | L | 100 | 337 | 87 | 18 | 8 | 12 | 3.6 | 58 | 55 | 66 | 83 | 12 | 1 | 0 | .258 | .466 |
| C | Jody Davis | R | 151 | 510 | 138 | 31 | 2 | 24 | 4.7 | 56 | 84 | 33 | 93 | 0 | 2 | 0 | .271 | .480 |
| **SUBSTITUTES** | | | | | | | | | | | | | | | | | | |
| 1B | Carmelo Martinez | R | 29 | 89 | 23 | 3 | 0 | 6 | 6.7 | 8 | 16 | 4 | 19 | 0 | 4 | 1 | .258 | .494 |
| S3 | Tom Veryzer | R | 59 | 88 | 18 | 3 | 0 | 1 | 1.1 | 5 | 3 | 3 | 13 | 0 | 11 | 3 | .205 | .273 |
| 2B | Dan Rohn | L | 23 | 31 | 12 | 3 | 2 | 0 | 0.0 | 3 | 6 | 2 | 2 | 1 | 17 | 6 | .387 | .613 |
| 23 | Junior Kennedy | R | 17 | 22 | 3 | 0 | 0 | 0 | 0.0 | 3 | 3 | 1 | 6 | 0 | 2 | 0 | .136 | .136 |
| SS | Dave Owen | B | 16 | 22 | 2 | 0 | 1 | 0 | 0.0 | 1 | 2 | 2 | 7 | 1 | 0 | 0 | .091 | .182 |
| 3B | Fritz Connally | R | 8 | 10 | 1 | 0 | 0 | 0 | 0.0 | 0 | 0 | 0 | 5 | 0 | 7 | 1 | .100 | .100 |
| OF | Gary Woods | R | 93 | 190 | 46 | 9 | 0 | 4 | 2.1 | 25 | 22 | 15 | 27 | 5 | 31 | 6 | .242 | .353 |
| OF | Jay Johnstone | L | 86 | 140 | 36 | 7 | 0 | 6 | 4.3 | 16 | 22 | 20 | 24 | 1 | 38 | 6 | .257 | .436 |
| OF | Scot Thompson | L | 53 | 88 | 17 | 3 | 1 | 0 | 0.0 | 4 | 10 | 3 | 14 | 0 | 28 | 6 | .193 | .250 |
| OF | Jerry Morales | R | 63 | 87 | 17 | 9 | 0 | 0 | 0.0 | 11 | 11 | 7 | 19 | 0 | 41 | 8 | .195 | .299 |
| OF | Thad Bosley | L | 43 | 72 | 21 | 4 | 1 | 2 | 2.8 | 12 | 12 | 10 | 12 | 1 | 18 | 4 | .292 | .458 |
| OF | Joe Carter | R | 23 | 51 | 9 | 1 | 1 | 0 | 0.0 | 6 | 1 | 0 | 21 | 1 | 5 | 1 | .176 | .235 |
| OF | Wayne Nordhagen | R | 21 | 35 | 5 | 1 | 0 | 1 | 2.9 | 1 | 4 | 0 | 5 | 0 | 15 | 2 | .143 | .257 |
| OF | Tom Grant | L | 16 | 20 | 3 | 1 | 0 | 0 | 0.0 | 2 | 2 | 3 | 4 | 0 | 5 | 0 | .150 | .200 |
| C | Steve Lake | R | 38 | 85 | 22 | 4 | 1 | 1 | 1.2 | 9 | 7 | 2 | 6 | 0 | 5 | 0 | .259 | .365 |
| C | Mike Diaz | R | 6 | 7 | 2 | 1 | 0 | 0 | 0.0 | 2 | 1 | 0 | 0 | 0 | 3 | 1 | .286 | .429 |
| **PITCHERS** | | | | | | | | | | | | | | | | | | |
| P | Steve Trout | L | 34 | 62 | 12 | 0 | 0 | 0 | 0.0 | 6 | 1 | 2 | 20 | 0 | 0 | 0 | .194 | .194 |
| P | Chuck Rainey | R | 34 | 56 | 9 | 0 | 0 | 0 | 0.0 | 4 | 0 | 6 | 20 | 0 | 0 | 0 | .161 | .161 |
| P | Ferguson Jenkins | R | 33 | 53 | 13 | 2 | 1 | 0 | 0.0 | 3 | 5 | 1 | 8 | 0 | 0 | 0 | .245 | .321 |
| P | Dick Ruthven | R | 25 | 53 | 12 | 1 | 0 | 0 | 0.0 | 5 | 3 | 2 | 13 | 0 | 0 | 0 | .226 | .245 |
| P | Dickie Noles | R | 24 | 38 | 9 | 1 | 0 | 0 | 0.0 | 1 | 5 | 1 | 17 | 0 | 0 | 0 | .237 | .237 |
| P | Craig Lefferts | L | 56 | 18 | 2 | 0 | 0 | 0 | 0.0 | 1 | 0 | 1 | 9 | 0 | 0 | 0 | .111 | .111 |
| P | Mike Proly | R | 60 | 11 | 1 | 0 | 0 | 0 | 0.0 | 1 | 0 | 1 | 3 | 0 | 0 | 0 | .091 | .091 |
| P | Paul Moskau | R | 8 | 11 | 2 | 1 | 0 | 0 | 0.0 | 0 | 0 | 0 | 3 | 0 | 0 | 0 | .182 | .273 |
| P | Bill Campbell | R | 82 | 10 | 1 | 0 | 0 | 0 | 0.0 | 0 | 1 | 0 | 3 | 0 | 0 | 0 | .100 | .100 |
| P | Lee Smith | R | 66 | 9 | 1 | 0 | 0 | 0 | 0.0 | 0 | 0 | 1 | 5 | 0 | 0 | 0 | .111 | .111 |
| P | Rick Reuschel | R | 4 | 7 | 1 | 0 | 0 | 0 | 0.0 | 1 | 0 | 0 | 2 | 0 | 0 | 0 | .143 | .143 |
| P | Reggie Patterson | R | 5 | 6 | 0 | 0 | 0 | 0 | 0.0 | 1 | 0 | 0 | 2 | 0 | 0 | 0 | .000 | .000 |
| P | Warren Brusstar | R | 59 | 4 | 0 | 0 | 0 | 0 | 0.0 | 0 | 0 | 0 | 3 | 0 | 0 | 0 | .000 | .000 |
| P | Rich Bordi | R | 11 | 4 | 0 | 0 | 0 | 0 | 0.0 | 0 | 0 | 0 | 3 | 0 | 0 | 0 | .000 | .000 |
| P | Willie Hernandez | L | 11 | 2 | 1 | 0 | 0 | 0 | 0.0 | 0 | 0 | 0 | 0 | 0 | 0 | 0 | .500 | .500 |
| P | Don Schulze | R | 4 | 1 | 0 | 0 | 0 | 0 | 0.0 | 0 | 0 | 1 | 1 | 0 | 0 | 0 | .000 | .000 |
| P | Alan Hargesheimer | R | 5 | 0 | 0 | 0 | 0 | 0 | — | 0 | 0 | 0 | 0 | 0 | 0 | 0 | — | — |
| P | Bill Johnson | R | 10 | 0 | 0 | 0 | 0 | 0 | — | 0 | 0 | 0 | 0 | 0 | 0 | 0 | — | — |
| | TEAM TOTAL | | | 5511 | 1436 | 272 | 42 | 140 | 2.5 | 70 | 649 | 470 | 867 | 84 | 248 | 50 | .261 | .401 |

## INDIVIDUAL  FIELDING

| POS | Player | T | G | PO | A | E | DP | TC/G | FA |
|---|---|---|---|---|---|---|---|---|---|
| 1B | B. Buckner | L | 144 | 1366 | 161 | 13 | 132 | 10.7 | .992 |
| | C. Martinez | R | 26 | 231 | 15 | 2 | 18 | 9.5 | .992 |
| | S. Thompson | L | 1 | 0 | 0 | 0 | 0 | 0.0 | .000 |
| | L. Durham | L | 6 | 35 | 2 | 0 | 2 | 6.2 | 1.000 |
| 2B | R. Sandberg | R | 157 | 330 | 571 | 13 | 126 | 5.8 | .986 |
| | G. Woods | R | 1 | 0 | 0 | 0 | 0 | 0.0 | .000 |
| | J. Kennedy | R | 7 | 11 | 17 | 0 | 3 | 4.0 | 1.000 |
| | D. Rohn | R | 6 | 12 | 12 | 2 | 2 | 4.3 | .923 |
| SS | L. Bowa | R | 145 | 230 | 464 | 11 | 102 | 4.9 | .984 |
| | T. Veryzer | R | 28 | 23 | 66 | 2 | 16 | 3.3 | .978 |
| | R. Sandberg | R | 1 | 0 | 0 | 0 | 0 | 0.0 | .000 |
| | D. Rohn | R | 1 | 0 | 0 | 0 | 0 | 0.0 | .000 |
| | D. Owen | R | 14 | 10 | 28 | 0 | 5 | 2.7 | 1.000 |
| | J. Kennedy | R | 1 | 1 | 0 | 0 | 0 | 1.0 | 1.000 |
| 3B | R. Cey | R | 157 | 90 | 270 | 17 | 12 | 2.4 | .955 |
| | T. Veryzer | R | 17 | 4 | 7 | 0 | 1 | 0.6 | 1.000 |
| | J. Kennedy | R | 4 | 0 | 0 | 0 | 0 | 0.0 | .000 |
| | F. Connally | R | 3 | 1 | 3 | 0 | 0 | 1.3 | 1.000 |
| | C. Martinez | R | 1 | 1 | 2 | 0 | 0 | 3.0 | 1.000 |
| | D. Owen | R | 3 | 0 | 1 | 0 | 0 | 0.3 | 1.000 |

| POS | Player | T | G | PO | A | E | DP | TC/G | FA |
|---|---|---|---|---|---|---|---|---|---|
| OF | M. Hall | L | 112 | 239 | 8 | 3 | 2 | 2.2 | .988 |
| | K. Moreland | R | 151 | 236 | 7 | 6 | 1 | 1.6 | .976 |
| | L. Durham | L | 95 | 168 | 2 | 6 | 0 | 1.9 | .966 |
| | G. Woods | R | 73 | 97 | 4 | 3 | 0 | 1.4 | .971 |
| | J. Johnstone | R | 44 | 55 | 3 | 4 | 1 | 1.4 | .935 |
| | J. Morales | R | 29 | 29 | 1 | 0 | 0 | 1.0 | 1.000 |
| | S. Thompson | L | 29 | 29 | 0 | 0 | 0 | 1.0 | 1.000 |
| | T. Bosley | L | 20 | 27 | 1 | 0 | 1 | 1.4 | 1.000 |
| | J. Carter | R | 16 | 26 | 0 | 0 | 0 | 1.6 | 1.000 |
| | B. Buckner | L | 15 | 25 | 0 | 0 | 0 | 1.7 | 1.000 |
| | W. Nordhagen | R | 7 | 7 | 0 | 0 | 0 | 1.0 | 1.000 |
| | T. Grant | R | 10 | 6 | 1 | 0 | 0 | 0.7 | 1.000 |
| | C. Martinez | R | 1 | 1 | 0 | 0 | 0 | 1.0 | 1.000 |
| C | J. Davis | R | 150 | 730 | 75 | 13 | 7 | 5.5 | .984 |
| | S. Lake | R | 32 | 115 | 22 | 0 | 3 | 4.3 | 1.000 |
| | K. Moreland | R | 3 | 8 | 0 | 0 | 0 | 2.7 | 1.000 |
| | M. Diaz | R | 3 | 5 | 0 | 0 | 0 | 1.7 | 1.000 |

While the crosstown White Sox were "winning ugly," the Cubs were whining ugly. Manager Lee Elia was seething after the Cubs got off to a 0–6 start. Several weeks later he went into a tirade, exploding expletives. His target was, of all things, Cub fans. Elia addressed them as unemployed unmentionables. On August 22, Elia joined the ranks of the unemployed. The team rallied following Elia's blistering speech, getting to within one game of the .500 mark in mid-June, but fell back into their losing pattern. The Cubs were consistent in all respects with a losing record in doubleheaders, one-run games, extra-inning games, road games, artificial turf, and night games. They finished with a 71–91 record, 54–69 under Elia and 17–22 under Charlie Fox, his replacement, beating out only the Mets for fifth place. Lack of starting pitchers led to the Cub demise. Chuck Rainey, obtained from the Red Sox for Doug Bird in GM Dallas Green's best trade, was the top winner with 14, including a near-miss no-hitter against the Reds as John Milner singled with two out in the ninth. Lee Smith was the lone bona fide reliever, leading the NL in saves with 29, but he also had some bad moments, as attested by his 4–10 record. The entire staff had only nine complete games, worst in the majors. Somehow the defense set a team record with only 115 errors. Keith Moreland led all batters with a .302 average, while Ron Cey was tops in RBI with 90 and tied Jody Davis in homers with 24. Bowlegged centerfielder Mel Hall was best of the rookies, batting .283 with 17 homers. Some of Green's authority was stripped when the Cubs named football executive Jim Finks as team president near the conclusion of the season.

### TEAM STATISTICS

| | W | L | PCT | GB | R | OR | 2B | 3B | HR | BA | SA | SB | E | DP | FA | CG | B | SO | ShO | SV | ERA |
|---|---|---|---|---|---|---|---|---|---|---|---|---|---|---|---|---|---|---|---|---|---|
| EAST |
| PHI | 90 | 72 | .556 | | 696 | 635 | 209 | 45 | 125 | .249 | .373 | 143 | 152 | 117 | .976 | 20 | **464** | **1092** | 10 | 41 | 3.34 |
| PIT | 84 | 78 | .519 | 6 | 659 | 648 | 238 | 29 | 121 | .264 | .383 | 124 | 115 | 165 | .982 | 25 | 563 | 1061 | 14 | 41 | 3.55 |
| MON | 82 | 80 | .506 | 8 | 677 | 646 | **297** | 41 | 102 | .264 | .386 | 138 | 116 | 130 | .981 | **38** | 479 | 899 | **15** | 34 | 3.58 |
| STL | 79 | 83 | .488 | 11 | 679 | 710 | 262 | **63** | 83 | .270 | .384 | **207** | 152 | 173 | .976 | 22 | 525 | 709 | 10 | 27 | 3.79 |
| CHI | 71 | 91 | .438 | 19 | 701 | 719 | 272 | 42 | 140 | .261 | .401 | 84 | 115 | 164 | **.982** | 9 | 498 | 807 | 10 | 42 | 4.07 |
| NY | 68 | 94 | .420 | 22 | 575 | 680 | 172 | 26 | 112 | .241 | .344 | 141 | 151 | 171 | .976 | 18 | 615 | 717 | 7 | 33 | 3.68 |
| WEST |
| LA | 91 | 71 | .562 | | 654 | **609** | 197 | 34 | **146** | .250 | .379 | 166 | 168 | 132 | .974 | 27 | 495 | 1000 | 12 | 40 | **3.10** |
| ATL | 88 | 74 | .543 | 3 | **746** | 640 | 218 | 45 | 130 | **.272** | **.400** | 146 | 137 | **176** | .978 | 18 | 540 | 895 | 4 | **48** | 3.67 |
| HOU | 85 | 77 | .525 | 6 | 643 | 646 | 239 | 60 | 97 | .257 | .375 | 164 | 147 | 165 | .977 | 22 | 570 | 904 | 14 | **48** | 3.45 |
| SD | 81 | 81 | .500 | 10 | 653 | 653 | 207 | 34 | 93 | .250 | .351 | 179 | 129 | 135 | .979 | 23 | 528 | 850 | 5 | 44 | 3.62 |
| SF | 79 | 83 | .488 | 12 | 687 | 697 | 206 | 30 | 142 | .247 | .375 | 140 | 171 | 109 | .973 | 20 | 520 | 881 | 9 | 47 | 3.70 |
| CIN | 74 | 88 | .457 | 17 | 623 | 710 | 236 | 35 | 107 | .239 | .356 | 154 | **114** | 121 | .981 | 34 | 627 | 934 | 5 | 29 | 3.98 |
| LEAGUE TOTAL | | | | | 7993 | 7993 | 2753 | 484 | 1398 | .255 | .376 | 1786 | 1667 | 1758 | .978 | 276 | 6424 | 10749 | 115 | 474 | 3.63 |

### INDIVIDUAL PITCHING

| PITCHER | T | W | L | PCT | ERA | SV | G | GS | CG | IP | H | BB | SO | R | ER | ShO | H/9 | BB/9 | SO/9 |
|---|---|---|---|---|---|---|---|---|---|---|---|---|---|---|---|---|---|---|---|
| Chuck Rainey | R | 14 | 13 | .519 | 4.48 | 0 | 34 | 34 | 1 | 191 | 219 | 74 | 84 | 109 | 95 | 1 | 10.32 | 3.49 | 3.96 |
| Steve Trout | L | 10 | 14 | .417 | 4.65 | 0 | 34 | 32 | 1 | 180 | 217 | 59 | 80 | 105 | 93 | 0 | 10.85 | 2.95 | 4.00 |
| Ferguson Jenkins | R | 6 | 9 | .400 | 4.30 | 0 | 33 | 29 | 1 | 167.1 | 176 | 46 | 96 | 89 | 80 | 1 | 9.47 | 2.47 | 5.16 |
| Dick Ruthven | R | 12 | 9 | .571 | 4.10 | 0 | 25 | 25 | 5 | 149.1 | 156 | 28 | 73 | 78 | 68 | 2 | 9.40 | 1.69 | 4.40 |
| Bill Campbell | R | 6 | 8 | .429 | 4.49 | 8 | 82 | 0 | 0 | 122.1 | 128 | 49 | 97 | 65 | 61 | 0 | 9.42 | 3.60 | 7.14 |
| Dickie Noles | R | 5 | 10 | .333 | 4.72 | 0 | 24 | 18 | 1 | 116.1 | 133 | 37 | 59 | 69 | 61 | 1 | 10.29 | 2.86 | 4.56 |
| Lee Smith | R | 4 | 10 | .286 | 1.65 | 29 | 66 | 0 | 0 | 103.1 | 70 | 41 | 91 | 23 | 19 | 0 | 6.10 | 3.57 | 7.93 |
| Craig Lefferts | L | 3 | 4 | .429 | 3.13 | 1 | 56 | 5 | 0 | 89 | 80 | 29 | 60 | 35 | 31 | 0 | 8.09 | 2.93 | 6.07 |
| Mike Proly | R | 1 | 5 | .167 | 3.58 | 1 | 60 | 0 | 0 | 83 | 79 | 38 | 31 | 35 | 33 | 0 | 8.57 | 4.12 | 3.36 |
| Warren Brusstar | R | 3 | 1 | .750 | 2.35 | 1 | 59 | 0 | 0 | 80.1 | 67 | 37 | 46 | 21 | 21 | 0 | 7.51 | 4.15 | 5.15 |
| Paul Moskau | R | 3 | 2 | .600 | 6.75 | 0 | 8 | 8 | 0 | 32 | 44 | 14 | 16 | 25 | 24 | 0 | 12.38 | 3.94 | 4.50 |
| Rich Bordi | R | 0 | 2 | .000 | 4.97 | 1 | 11 | 1 | 0 | 25.1 | 34 | 12 | 20 | 15 | 14 | 0 | 12.08 | 4.26 | 7.11 |
| Rick Reuschel | R | 1 | 1 | .500 | 3.92 | 0 | 4 | 4 | 0 | 20.2 | 18 | 10 | 9 | 9 | 9 | 0 | 7.84 | 4.35 | 3.92 |
| Willie Hernandez | L | 1 | 0 | 1.000 | 3.20 | 1 | 11 | 1 | 0 | 19.2 | 16 | 6 | 18 | 8 | 7 | 0 | 7.32 | 2.75 | 8.24 |
| Reggie Patterson | R | 1 | 2 | .333 | 4.82 | 0 | 5 | 2 | 0 | 18.2 | 17 | 6 | 10 | 12 | 10 | 0 | 8.20 | 2.89 | 4.82 |
| Don Schulze | R | 0 | 1 | .000 | 7.07 | 0 | 4 | 3 | 0 | 14 | 19 | 7 | 8 | 11 | 11 | 0 | 12.21 | 4.50 | 5.14 |
| Bill Johnson | R | 1 | 0 | 1.000 | 4.38 | 0 | 10 | 0 | 0 | 12.1 | 17 | 3 | 4 | 6 | 6 | 0 | 12.41 | 2.19 | 2.92 |
| Alan Hargesheimer | R | 0 | 0 | — | 9.00 | 0 | 5 | 0 | 0 | 4 | 6 | 2 | 5 | 4 | 4 | 0 | 13.50 | 4.50 | 11.25 |
| TEAM TOTAL | | 71 | 91 | .438 | 4.08 | 42 | 531 | 162 | 9 | 1428.2 | 1496 | 498 | 807 | 719 | 647 | 5 | 9.42 | 3.14 | 5.08 |

# Chicago 1984     Won 96  Lost 65  Pct. .596  1st

| MANAGER | W | L | PCT |
|---|---|---|---|
| Jim Frey | 96 | 65 | .596 |

| POS | Player | B | G | AB | H | 2B | 3B | HR | HR % | R | RBI | BB | SO | SB | Pinch Hit AB | Pinch Hit H | BA | SA |
|---|---|---|---|---|---|---|---|---|---|---|---|---|---|---|---|---|---|---|
| **REGULARS** | | | | | | | | | | | | | | | | | | |
| 1B | Leon Durham | L | 137 | 473 | 132 | 30 | 4 | 23 | 4.9 | 86 | 96 | 69 | 86 | 16 | 8 | 2 | .279 | .505 |
| 2B | Ryne Sandberg | R | 156 | 636 | 200 | 36 | 19 | 19 | 3.0 | 114 | 84 | 52 | 101 | 32 | 0 | 0 | .314 | .520 |
| SS | Larry Bowa | B | 133 | 391 | 87 | 14 | 2 | 0 | 0.0 | 33 | 17 | 28 | 24 | 10 | 2 | 1 | .223 | .269 |
| 3B | Ron Cey | R | 146 | 505 | 121 | 27 | 0 | 25 | 5.0 | 71 | 97 | 61 | 108 | 3 | 2 | 1 | .240 | .442 |
| RF | Keith Moreland | R | 140 | 495 | 138 | 17 | 3 | 16 | 3.2 | 59 | 80 | 34 | 71 | 1 | 15 | 2 | .279 | .422 |
| CF | Bob Dernier | R | 143 | 536 | 149 | 26 | 5 | 3 | 0.6 | 94 | 32 | 63 | 60 | 45 | 2 | 0 | .278 | .362 |
| LF | Gary Matthews | R | 147 | 491 | 143 | 21 | 2 | 14 | 2.9 | 101 | 82 | 103 | 97 | 17 | 3 | 0 | .291 | .428 |
| C | Jody Davis | R | 150 | 523 | 134 | 24 | 2 | 19 | 3.6 | 55 | 94 | 47 | 99 | 5 | 4 | 1 | .256 | .419 |
| **SUBSTITUTES** | | | | | | | | | | | | | | | | | | |
| S3 | Dave Owen | B | 47 | 93 | 18 | 2 | 2 | 1 | 1.1 | 8 | 10 | 8 | 15 | 1 | 3 | 2 | .194 | .290 |
| UT | Richie Hebner | L | 44 | 81 | 27 | 3 | 0 | 2 | 2.5 | 12 | 8 | 10 | 15 | 1 | 26 | 8 | .333 | .444 |
| SS | Tom Veryzer | R | 44 | 74 | 14 | 1 | 0 | 0 | 0.0 | 5 | 4 | 3 | 11 | 0 | 0 | 0 | .189 | .203 |
| 1O | Bill Buckner | L | 21 | 43 | 9 | 0 | 0 | 0 | 0.0 | 3 | 2 | 1 | 1 | 0 | 12 | 3 | .209 | .209 |
| UT | Dan Rohn | L | 25 | 31 | 4 | 0 | 0 | 1 | 3.2 | 1 | 3 | 1 | 6 | 0 | 13 | 2 | .129 | .226 |
| OF | Mel Hall | L | 48 | 150 | 42 | 11 | 3 | 4 | 2.7 | 25 | 22 | 12 | 23 | 2 | 4 | 0 | .280 | .473 |
| OF | Henry Cotto | R | 105 | 146 | 40 | 5 | 0 | 0 | 0.0 | 24 | 8 | 10 | 23 | 9 | 13 | 3 | .274 | .308 |
| OF | Gary Woods | R | 87 | 98 | 23 | 4 | 1 | 3 | 3.1 | 13 | 10 | 15 | 21 | 2 | 31 | 7 | .235 | .388 |
| OF | Thad Bosley | L | 55 | 98 | 29 | 2 | 2 | 2 | 2.0 | 17 | 14 | 13 | 22 | 5 | 23 | 6 | .296 | .418 |
| OF | Jay Johnstone | L | 52 | 73 | 21 | 2 | 2 | 0 | 0.0 | 8 | 3 | 7 | 18 | 0 | 39 | 10 | .288 | .370 |
| OF | Billy Hatcher | R | 8 | 9 | 1 | 0 | 0 | 0 | 0.0 | 1 | 0 | 1 | 0 | 2 | 3 | 0 | .111 | .111 |
| C | Steve Lake | R | 25 | 54 | 12 | 4 | 0 | 2 | 3.7 | 4 | 7 | 0 | 7 | 0 | 1 | 0 | .222 | .407 |
| C1 | Ron Hassey | L | 19 | 33 | 11 | 0 | 0 | 2 | 6.1 | 5 | 5 | 4 | 6 | 0 | 8 | 2 | .333 | .515 |
| PH | Davey Lopes | R | 16 | 17 | 4 | 1 | 0 | 0 | 0.0 | 5 | 0 | 6 | 5 | 3 | 5 | 1 | .235 | .294 |
| **PITCHERS** | | | | | | | | | | | | | | | | | | |
| P | Steve Trout | L | 32 | 61 | 8 | 0 | 0 | 0 | 0.0 | 4 | 3 | 4 | 21 | 0 | 0 | 0 | .131 | .131 |
| P | Rick Sutcliffe | L | 20 | 56 | 14 | 3 | 0 | 0 | 0.0 | 3 | 6 | 2 | 18 | 0 | 0 | 0 | .250 | .304 |
| P | Dennis Eckersley | R | 24 | 55 | 6 | 0 | 0 | 0 | 0.0 | 1 | 1 | 1 | 25 | 0 | 0 | 0 | .109 | .109 |
| P | Dick Ruthven | R | 25 | 44 | 7 | 3 | 0 | 0 | 0.0 | 2 | 2 | 1 | 18 | 0 | 1 | 0 | .159 | .227 |
| P | Scott Sanderson | R | 24 | 42 | 5 | 0 | 0 | 0 | 0.0 | 3 | 5 | 3 | 18 | 0 | 0 | 0 | .119 | .119 |
| P | Chuck Rainey | R | 17 | 31 | 3 | 0 | 0 | 0 | 0.0 | 2 | 3 | 2 | 12 | 0 | 0 | 0 | .097 | .097 |
| P | Rick Reuschel | R | 20 | 29 | 7 | 3 | 0 | 0 | 0.0 | 2 | 3 | 2 | 8 | 0 | 1 | 0 | .241 | .345 |
| P | Rich Bordi | R | 31 | 19 | 1 | 0 | 0 | 0 | 0.0 | 0 | 0 | 1 | 7 | 0 | 0 | 0 | .053 | .053 |
| P | Lee Smith | R | 69 | 13 | 1 | 0 | 0 | 0 | 0.0 | 0 | 1 | 0 | 8 | 0 | 0 | 0 | .077 | .077 |
| P | Tim Stoddard | R | 58 | 11 | 1 | 0 | 0 | 0 | 0.0 | 0 | 0 | 0 | 5 | 0 | 0 | 0 | .091 | .091 |
| P | Dickie Noles | R | 21 | 10 | 0 | 0 | 0 | 0 | 0.0 | 0 | 0 | 1 | 6 | 0 | 0 | 0 | .000 | .000 |
| P | George Frazier | R | 37 | 7 | 2 | 0 | 0 | 0 | 0.0 | 0 | 0 | 0 | 1 | 0 | 0 | 0 | .286 | .286 |
| P | Warren Brusstar | R | 41 | 5 | 1 | 0 | 0 | 0 | 0.0 | 1 | 1 | 2 | 1 | 0 | 0 | 0 | .200 | .200 |
| P | Reggie Patterson | R | 3 | 2 | 0 | 0 | 0 | 0 | 0.0 | 0 | 0 | 0 | 0 | 0 | 0 | 0 | .000 | .000 |
| P | Porfirio Altamirano | R | 5 | 2 | 0 | 0 | 0 | 0 | 0.0 | 0 | 0 | 0 | 0 | 0 | 0 | 0 | .000 | .000 |
| P | Bill Johnson | R | 4 | 0 | 0 | 0 | 0 | 0 | – | 0 | 0 | 0 | 0 | 0 | 0 | 0 | – | – |
| P | Don Schulze | R | 1 | 0 | 0 | 0 | 0 | 0 | 0.0 | 0 | 0 | 0 | 0 | 0 | 0 | 0 | – | – |
| P | Ron Meridith | L | 3 | 0 | 0 | 0 | 0 | 0 | – | 0 | 0 | 0 | 0 | 0 | 0 | 0 | – | – |
| TEAM TOTAL | | | | 5437 | 1415 | 239 | 47 | 136 | 2.5 | 76 | 703 | 567 | 967 | 154 | 219 | 51 | .260 | .397 |

## INDIVIDUAL FIELDING

| POS | Player | T | G | PO | A | E | DP | TC/G | FA |
|---|---|---|---|---|---|---|---|---|---|
| 1B | L. Durham | L | 130 | 1162 | 96 | 7 | 96 | 9.7 | .994 |
| | K. Moreland | R | 29 | 230 | 20 | 6 | 18 | 8.8 | .977 |
| | B. Buckner | L | 7 | 66 | 5 | 0 | 5 | 10.1 | 1.000 |
| | R. Hebner | R | 3 | 35 | 2 | 0 | 4 | 12.3 | 1.000 |
| | R. Hassey | R | 4 | 23 | 1 | 1 | 2 | 6.3 | .960 |
| 2B | R. Sandberg | R | 156 | 314 | 550 | 6 | 102 | 5.6 | .993 |
| | T. Veryzer | R | 4 | 7 | 15 | 1 | 3 | 5.8 | .957 |
| | D. Owen | R | 4 | 1 | 3 | 3 | 0 | 1.8 | .571 |
| | D. Rohn | R | 5 | 3 | 4 | 0 | 1 | 1.4 | 1.000 |
| | D. Lopes | R | 2 | 0 | 2 | 0 | 0 | 1.0 | 1.000 |
| | G. Woods | R | 3 | 1 | 1 | 0 | 0 | 0.7 | 1.000 |
| SS | L. Bowa | R | 132 | 217 | 378 | 16 | 64 | 4.6 | .974 |
| | D. Owen | R | 35 | 37 | 86 | 4 | 19 | 3.6 | .969 |
| | T. Veryzer | R | 36 | 37 | 48 | 3 | 10 | 2.4 | .966 |
| | D. Rohn | R | 5 | 1 | 3 | 0 | 0 | 1.0 | 1.000 |
| 3B | R. Cey | R | 144 | 97 | 230 | 11 | 22 | 2.3 | .967 |
| | R. Hebner | R | 14 | 2 | 24 | 1 | 2 | 1.9 | .963 |
| | D. Rohn | R | 7 | 1 | 8 | 0 | 1 | 1.3 | 1.000 |
| | K. Moreland | R | 8 | 5 | 4 | 0 | 1 | 1.1 | 1.000 |
| | D. Owen | R | 6 | 2 | 2 | 0 | 0 | 0.7 | 1.000 |
| | T. Veryzer | R | 5 | 0 | 0 | 1 | 0 | 0.2 | .000 |

| POS | Player | T | G | PO | A | E | DP | TC/G | FA |
|---|---|---|---|---|---|---|---|---|---|
| OF | B. Dernier | R | 140 | 355 | 5 | 5 | 1 | 2.6 | .986 |
| | G. Matthews | R | 145 | 224 | 7 | 11 | 0 | 1.7 | .955 |
| | K. Moreland | R | 103 | 154 | 6 | 4 | 0 | 1.6 | .976 |
| | H. Cotto | R | 88 | 117 | 3 | 2 | 1 | 1.4 | .984 |
| | M. Hall | L | 46 | 69 | 5 | 3 | 2 | 1.7 | .961 |
| | G. Woods | R | 62 | 53 | 2 | 0 | 1 | 0.9 | 1.000 |
| | T. Bosley | L | 33 | 39 | 2 | 1 | 0 | 1.3 | .976 |
| | J. Johnstone | R | 15 | 12 | 0 | 0 | 0 | 0.8 | 1.000 |
| | B. Buckner | L | 2 | 5 | 1 | 0 | 0 | 3.0 | 1.000 |
| | D. Lopes | R | 9 | 6 | 0 | 0 | 0 | 0.7 | 1.000 |
| | B. Hatcher | R | 4 | 2 | 1 | 0 | 0 | 0.8 | 1.000 |
| | R. Hebner | R | 3 | 2 | 0 | 0 | 0 | 0.7 | 1.000 |
| C | J. Davis | R | 146 | 811 | 89 | 15 | 9 | 6.3 | .984 |
| | S. Lake | R | 24 | 72 | 13 | 4 | 0 | 3.7 | .955 |
| | R. Hassey | R | 6 | 30 | 1 | 0 | 0 | 5.2 | 1.000 |
| | K. Moreland | R | 3 | 4 | 0 | 0 | 0 | 1.3 | 1.000 |

"Hey, hey, whaddya say. The Cubs are going to win today!" Everything was on the upbeat until they were beat up by the Padres in the playoffs. The 1984 edition of the Cubs came within four innings of winning the pennant. Four lousy innings.

The Cubs enjoyed a super summer before their pratfall. During spring training, they dropped 11 in a row and were 3–20. Then GM Dallas Green swindled the Phillies out of Gary Matthews and Bob Dernier, gaining two-thirds of an outfield.

Next came the pitching. On May 25 Green dealt popular Bill Buckner to the Red Sox for pitcher Dennis Eckersley. With starters Dick Ruthven and Scott Sanderson sidelined in mid-June, Green made his master stroke. He obtained pitcher Rick Sutcliffe in a seven-player deal with the Indians. Sutcliffe outdid Hank Borowy, who had led the Cubs to the 1945 pennant with an 11–2 record. The 6-foot-7-inch red-bearded mountain became the team stopper, winning 14 in a row for an astounding 16–1 record.

Perhaps the turning point of the season came on June 23 at Wrigley Field. A young second baseman named Ryne Sandberg emerged from obscurity by hitting game-tying homers in the 9th and 10th innings. The Cubs beat the Cardinals, 12–11, in 11 and were rolling. Their main obstacle was the equally surprising Mets, who held onto first place, but the Cubs bolted past the New Yorkers by winning 11 of their 14 late-season encounters. The Cubs eventually clinched the NL East title on September 24, beating the Pirates, 4–1, in Pittsburgh with Sutcliffe (who else?) on the mound. The Cubs finished with a 96–65 record, 6 1/2 games ahead of the Mets and finally erased the stigma of the 1969 Cubs. Sandberg took MVP honors, and Sutcliffe won the Cy Young Award.

After 13–0 and 4–2 playoff triumphs, it was on to San Diego for the clincher. Just one more victory. That's when they reverted back to Cubby lore as lovable losers.

### TEAM  STATISTICS

| | W | L | PCT | GB | R | OR | 2B | 3B | HR | BA | SA | SB | E | DP | FA | CG | B | SO | ShO | SV | ERA |
|---|---|---|---|---|---|---|---|---|---|---|---|---|---|---|---|---|---|---|---|---|---|
| | | | | | | | | Batting | | | | | | Fielding | | | | Pitching | | | |
| **EAST** | | | | | | | | | | | | | | | | | | | | | |
| CHI | 96 | 65 | .596 | | 762 | 658 | 239 | 47 | 136 | .260 | .397 | 154 | 121 | 137 | .981 | 19 | 442 | 879 | 8 | 50 | 3.75 |
| NY | 90 | 72 | .556 | 6.5 | 652 | 676 | 235 | 25 | 107 | .257 | .369 | 149 | 129 | 154 | .979 | 12 | 573 | 1028 | 15 | 50 | 3.60 |
| STL | 84 | 78 | .519 | 12.5 | 652 | 645 | 225 | 44 | 75 | .252 | .351 | 220 | 118 | 184 | .982 | 19 | 494 | 808 | 12 | 51 | 3.58 |
| PHI | 81 | 81 | .500 | 15.5 | 720 | 690 | 248 | 51 | 147 | .266 | .407 | 186 | 161 | 112 | .975 | 11 | 448 | 904 | 6 | 35 | 3.62 |
| MON | 78 | 83 | .484 | 18 | 593 | 585 | 242 | 36 | 96 | .251 | .362 | 131 | 132 | 147 | .978 | 19 | 461 | 861 | 10 | 48 | 3.31 |
| PIT | 75 | 87 | .463 | 21.5 | 615 | 567 | 237 | 33 | 98 | .255 | .363 | 96 | 128 | 142 | .980 | 27 | 502 | 995 | 13 | 34 | 3.11 |
| **WEST** | | | | | | | | | | | | | | | | | | | | | |
| SD | 92 | 70 | .568 | | 686 | 634 | 207 | 42 | 109 | .259 | .371 | 152 | 138 | 144 | .978 | 13 | 563 | 812 | 17 | 44 | 3.48 |
| ATL | 80 | 82 | .494 | 12 | 632 | 655 | 234 | 27 | 111 | .247 | .361 | 140 | 139 | 153 | .978 | 17 | 525 | 859 | 7 | 49 | 3.57 |
| HOU | 80 | 82 | .494 | 12 | 693 | 630 | 222 | 67 | 79 | .264 | .371 | 105 | 133 | 160 | .979 | 24 | 502 | 950 | 13 | 29 | 3.32 |
| LA | 79 | 83 | .488 | 13 | 580 | 600 | 213 | 23 | 102 | .244 | .348 | 109 | 163 | 146 | .975 | 39 | 499 | 1033 | 16 | 27 | 3.17 |
| CIN | 70 | 92 | .432 | 22 | 627 | 747 | 238 | 30 | 106 | .244 | .356 | 160 | 139 | 116 | .977 | 25 | 578 | 854 | 7 | 38 | 4.16 |
| SF | 66 | 96 | .407 | 26 | 682 | 807 | 229 | 26 | 112 | .265 | .375 | 126 | 173 | 134 | .973 | 9 | 549 | 995 | 7 | 38 | 4.39 |
| LEAGUE TOTAL | | | | | 7894 | 7894 | 2769 | 451 | 1278 | .255 | .369 | 1728 | 1674 | 1729 | .978 | 234 | 6149 | 10929 | 130 | 480 | 3.59 |

### INDIVIDUAL  PITCHING

| PITCHER | T | W | L | PCT | ERA | SV | G | GS | CG | IP | H | BB | SO | R | ER | ShO | H/9 | BB/9 | SO/9 |
|---|---|---|---|---|---|---|---|---|---|---|---|---|---|---|---|---|---|---|---|
| Steve Trout | L | 13 | 7 | .650 | 3.41 | 0 | 32 | 31 | 6 | 190 | 205 | 59 | 81 | 80 | 72 | 2 | 9.71 | 2.79 | 3.84 |
| Dennis Eckersley | R | 10 | 8 | .556 | 3.03 | 0 | 24 | 24 | 2 | 160.1 | 152 | 36 | 81 | 59 | 54 | 0 | 8.53 | 2.02 | 4.55 |
| Rick Sutcliffe | R | 16 | 1 | .941 | 2.69 | 0 | 20 | 20 | 7 | 150.1 | 123 | 39 | 155 | 53 | 45 | 3 | 7.36 | 2.33 | 9.28 |
| Scott Sanderson | R | 8 | 5 | .615 | 3.14 | 0 | 24 | 24 | 3 | 140.2 | 140 | 24 | 76 | 54 | 49 | 0 | 8.96 | 1.54 | 4.86 |
| Dick Ruthven | R | 6 | 10 | .375 | 5.04 | 0 | 23 | 22 | 0 | 126.2 | 154 | 41 | 55 | 75 | 71 | 0 | 10.94 | 2.91 | 3.91 |
| Lee Smith | R | 9 | 7 | .563 | 3.65 | 33 | 69 | 0 | 0 | 101 | 98 | 35 | 86 | 42 | 41 | 0 | 8.73 | 3.12 | 7.66 |
| Rick Reuschel | R | 5 | 5 | .500 | 5.17 | 0 | 19 | 14 | 1 | 92.1 | 123 | 23 | 43 | 57 | 53 | 0 | 11.99 | 2.24 | 4.19 |
| Tim Stoddard | R | 10 | 6 | .625 | 3.82 | 7 | 58 | 0 | 0 | 92 | 77 | 57 | 87 | 41 | 39 | 0 | 7.53 | 5.58 | 8.51 |
| Chuck Rainey | R | 5 | 7 | .417 | 4.28 | 0 | 17 | 16 | 0 | 88.1 | 102 | 38 | 45 | 55 | 42 | 0 | 10.39 | 3.87 | 4.58 |
| Rich Bordi | R | 5 | 2 | .714 | 3.46 | 4 | 31 | 7 | 0 | 83.1 | 78 | 20 | 41 | 37 | 32 | 0 | 8.42 | 2.16 | 4.43 |
| Warren Brusstar | R | 1 | 1 | .500 | 3.11 | 3 | 41 | 0 | 0 | 63.2 | 57 | 21 | 36 | 23 | 22 | 0 | 8.06 | 2.97 | 5.09 |
| George Frazier | R | 6 | 3 | .667 | 4.10 | 3 | 37 | 0 | 0 | 63.2 | 53 | 26 | 58 | 30 | 29 | 0 | 7.49 | 3.68 | 8.20 |
| Dickie Noles | R | 2 | 2 | .500 | 5.15 | 0 | 21 | 1 | 0 | 50.2 | 60 | 16 | 14 | 29 | 29 | 0 | 10.66 | 2.84 | 2.49 |
| Porfirio Altamirano | R | 0 | 0 | – | 4.76 | 0 | 5 | 0 | 0 | 11.1 | 8 | 1 | 7 | 6 | 6 | 0 | 6.35 | 0.79 | 5.56 |
| Reggie Patterson | R | 0 | 1 | .000 | 10.50 | 0 | 3 | 1 | 0 | 6 | 10 | 2 | 5 | 7 | 7 | 0 | 15.00 | 3.00 | 7.50 |
| Bill Johnson | R | 0 | 0 | – | 1.69 | 0 | 4 | 0 | 0 | 5.1 | 4 | 1 | 3 | 1 | 1 | 0 | 6.75 | 1.69 | 5.06 |
| Ron Meridith | L | 0 | 0 | – | 3.38 | 0 | 3 | 0 | 0 | 5.1 | 6 | 2 | 4 | 5 | 2 | 0 | 10.13 | 3.38 | 6.75 |
| Don Schulze | R | 0 | 0 | – | 12.00 | 0 | 1 | 1 | 0 | 3 | 8 | 1 | 2 | 4 | 4 | 0 | 24.00 | 3.00 | 6.00 |
| TEAM TOTAL | | 96 | 65 | .596 | 3.75 | 50 | 432 | 161 | 19 | 1434 | 1458 | 442 | 879 | 658 | 598 | 5 | 9.15 | 2.77 | 5.52 |

| MANAGER | W | L | PCT |
|---|---|---|---|
| Jim Frey | 77 | 84 | .478 |

| POS | Player | B | G | AB | H | 2B | 3B | HR | HR % | R | RBI | BB | SO | SB | Pinch Hit AB | Pinch Hit H | BA | SA |
|---|---|---|---|---|---|---|---|---|---|---|---|---|---|---|---|---|---|---|
| **REGULARS** | | | | | | | | | | | | | | | | | | |
| 1B | Leon Durham | L | 153 | 542 | 153 | 32 | 2 | 21 | 3.9 | 58 | 75 | 64 | 99 | 7 | 2 | 0 | .282 | .465 |
| 2B | Ryne Sandberg | R | 153 | 609 | 186 | 31 | 6 | 26 | 4.3 | 113 | 83 | 57 | 97 | 54 | 1 | 0 | .305 | .504 |
| SS | Shawon Dunston | R | 74 | 250 | 65 | 12 | 4 | 4 | 1.6 | 40 | 18 | 19 | 42 | 11 | 0 | 0 | .260 | .388 |
| 3B | Ron Cey | R | 145 | 500 | 116 | 18 | 2 | 22 | 4.4 | 64 | 63 | 58 | 106 | 1 | 7 | 2 | .232 | .408 |
| RF | Keith Moreland | R | 161 | 587 | 180 | 30 | 3 | 14 | 2.4 | 74 | 106 | 68 | 58 | 12 | 2 | 1 | .307 | .440 |
| CF | Bob Dernier | R | 121 | 469 | 119 | 20 | 3 | 1 | 0.2 | 63 | 21 | 40 | 44 | 31 | 4 | 0 | .254 | .316 |
| LF | Gary Matthews | R | 97 | 298 | 70 | 12 | 0 | 13 | 4.4 | 45 | 40 | 59 | 64 | 2 | 11 | 2 | .235 | .406 |
| C | Jody Davis | R | 142 | 482 | 112 | 30 | 0 | 17 | 3.5 | 47 | 58 | 48 | 83 | 1 | 11 | 2 | .232 | .400 |
| **SUBSTITUTES** | | | | | | | | | | | | | | | | | | |
| UT | Chris Speier | R | 106 | 218 | 53 | 11 | 0 | 4 | 1.8 | 16 | 24 | 17 | 34 | 1 | 12 | 5 | .243 | .349 |
| SS | Larry Bowa | B | 72 | 195 | 48 | 6 | 4 | 0 | 0.0 | 13 | 13 | 11 | 20 | 5 | 2 | 0 | .246 | .318 |
| 13 | Richie Hebner | L | 83 | 120 | 26 | 2 | 0 | 3 | 2.5 | 10 | 22 | 7 | 15 | 0 | 59 | 12 | .217 | .308 |
| UT | Dave Owen | B | 22 | 19 | 7 | 0 | 0 | 0 | 0.0 | 6 | 4 | 1 | 5 | 1 | 3 | 0 | .368 | .368 |
| OF | Davey Lopes | R | 99 | 275 | 78 | 11 | 0 | 11 | 4.0 | 52 | 44 | 46 | 37 | 47 | 22 | 4 | .284 | .444 |
| OF | Thad Bosley | L | 108 | 180 | 59 | 6 | 3 | 7 | 3.9 | 25 | 27 | 20 | 29 | 5 | 60 | 20 | .328 | .511 |
| OF | Billy Hatcher | R | 53 | 163 | 40 | 12 | 1 | 2 | 1.2 | 24 | 10 | 8 | 12 | 2 | 9 | 1 | .245 | .368 |
| OF | Gary Woods | R | 81 | 82 | 20 | 3 | 0 | 0 | 0.0 | 11 | 4 | 14 | 18 | 0 | 27 | 7 | .244 | .280 |
| OF | Brian Dayett | R | 22 | 26 | 6 | 0 | 1 | 1 | 3.8 | 1 | 4 | 0 | 6 | 0 | 14 | 4 | .231 | .346 |
| O2 | Chico Walker | B | 21 | 12 | 1 | 0 | 0 | 0 | 0.0 | 3 | 0 | 0 | 5 | 1 | 8 | 1 | .083 | .083 |
| OF | Darrin Jackson | R | 5 | 11 | 1 | 0 | 0 | 0 | 0.0 | 0 | 0 | 0 | 3 | 0 | 1 | 0 | .091 | .091 |
| C | Steve Lake | R | 58 | 119 | 18 | 2 | 0 | 1 | 0.8 | 5 | 11 | 3 | 21 | 1 | 4 | 1 | .151 | .193 |
| **PITCHERS** | | | | | | | | | | | | | | | | | | |
| P | Dennis Eckersley | R | 26 | 56 | 7 | 0 | 0 | 1 | 1.8 | 1 | 1 | 7 | 25 | 0 | 0 | 0 | .125 | .179 |
| P | Steve Trout | L | 24 | 46 | 5 | 1 | 0 | 0 | 0.0 | 2 | 2 | 2 | 13 | 0 | 0 | 0 | .109 | .130 |
| P | Rick Sutcliffe | L | 20 | 43 | 10 | 0 | 0 | 1 | 2.3 | 4 | 3 | 2 | 10 | 0 | 0 | 0 | .233 | .302 |
| P | Ray Fontenot | L | 38 | 41 | 2 | 0 | 0 | 0 | 0.0 | 2 | 0 | 0 | 18 | 0 | 0 | 0 | .049 | .049 |
| P | Scott Sanderson | R | 19 | 31 | 2 | 0 | 0 | 0 | 0.0 | 1 | 1 | 1 | 17 | 0 | 0 | 0 | .065 | .065 |
| P | Dick Ruthven | R | 20 | 24 | 5 | 0 | 0 | 0 | 0.0 | 1 | 1 | 0 | 7 | 0 | 0 | 0 | .208 | .208 |
| P | Steve Engel | R | 11 | 16 | 3 | 0 | 0 | 1 | 6.3 | 1 | 4 | 3 | 7 | 0 | 0 | 0 | .188 | .375 |
| P | Derek Botelho | R | 11 | 14 | 2 | 0 | 0 | 0 | 0.0 | 2 | 0 | 1 | 5 | 0 | 0 | 0 | .143 | .143 |
| P | Reggie Patterson | R | 8 | 10 | 1 | 0 | 0 | 0 | 0.0 | 1 | 0 | 1 | 4 | 0 | 0 | 0 | .100 | .100 |
| P | Johnny Abrego | R | 6 | 9 | 0 | 0 | 0 | 0 | 0.0 | 0 | 1 | 0 | 2 | 0 | 0 | 0 | .000 | .000 |
| P | Jay Baller | R | 20 | 8 | 0 | 0 | 0 | 0 | 0.0 | 0 | 0 | 0 | 6 | 0 | 0 | 0 | .000 | .000 |
| P | Warren Brusstar | R | 51 | 7 | 1 | 0 | 0 | 0 | 0.0 | 0 | 0 | 1 | 5 | 0 | 0 | 0 | .143 | .143 |
| P | Larry Gura | L | 5 | 6 | 0 | 0 | 0 | 0 | 0.0 | 0 | 0 | 0 | 4 | 0 | 0 | 0 | .000 | .000 |
| P | Lary Sorensen | R | 45 | 6 | 0 | 0 | 0 | 0 | 0.0 | 1 | 0 | 1 | 4 | 0 | 0 | 0 | .000 | .000 |
| P | George Frazier | R | 51 | 6 | 0 | 0 | 0 | 0 | 0.0 | 0 | 0 | 0 | 4 | 0 | 0 | 0 | .000 | .000 |
| P | Lee Smith | R | 65 | 6 | 0 | 0 | 0 | 0 | 0.0 | 0 | 0 | 1 | 5 | 0 | 0 | 0 | .000 | .000 |
| P | Ron Meridith | L | 32 | 4 | 1 | 0 | 0 | 0 | 0.0 | 0 | 0 | 1 | 1 | 0 | 0 | 0 | .250 | .250 |
| P | Dave Gumpert | R | 9 | 1 | 0 | 0 | 0 | 0 | 0.0 | 0 | 0 | 0 | 1 | 0 | 0 | 0 | .000 | .000 |
| P | Jon Perlman | L | 6 | 1 | 0 | 0 | 0 | 0 | 0.0 | 0 | 0 | 0 | 1 | 0 | 0 | 0 | .000 | .000 |
| P | Dave Beard | L | 9 | 0 | 0 | 0 | 0 | 0 | 0.0 | 0 | 0 | 0 | 0 | 0 | 0 | 0 | — | — |
| TEAM TOTAL | | | | 5492 | 1397 | 239 | 28 | 150 | 2.7 | 68 | 640 | 562 | 937 | 182 | 259 | 62 | .254 | .390 |

## INDIVIDUAL FIELDING

| POS | Player | T | G | PO | A | E | DP | TC/G | FA |
|---|---|---|---|---|---|---|---|---|---|
| 1B | L. Durham | L | 151 | 1421 | 107 | 7 | 121 | 10.2 | .995 |
| | R. Hebner | R | 12 | 108 | 6 | 1 | 15 | 9.6 | .991 |
| | K. Moreland | R | 12 | 70 | 6 | 3 | 4 | 6.6 | .962 |
| 2B | R. Sandberg | R | 153 | 353 | 500 | 12 | 99 | 5.7 | .986 |
| | C. Speier | R | 13 | 21 | 28 | 2 | 9 | 3.9 | .961 |
| | D. Lopes | R | 1 | 1 | 2 | 0 | 1 | 3.0 | 1.000 |
| | D. Owen | R | 4 | 1 | 1 | 0 | 0 | 0.5 | 1.000 |
| | C. Walker | R | 2 | 1 | 0 | 0 | 0 | 0.5 | 1.000 |
| SS | S. Dunston | R | 73 | 144 | 248 | 17 | 39 | 5.6 | .958 |
| | L. Bowa | R | 66 | 91 | 197 | 9 | 34 | 4.5 | .970 |
| | C. Speier | R | 58 | 61 | 125 | 7 | 33 | 3.3 | .964 |
| | D. Owen | R | 7 | 3 | 8 | 1 | 2 | 1.7 | .917 |
| | R. Sandberg | R | 1 | 0 | 1 | 0 | 0 | 1.0 | 1.000 |
| 3B | R. Cey | R | 140 | 75 | 273 | 21 | 21 | 2.6 | .943 |
| | C. Speier | R | 31 | 5 | 24 | 2 | 1 | 1.0 | .935 |
| | K. Moreland | R | 11 | 8 | 13 | 4 | 1 | 2.3 | .840 |
| | R. Hebner | R | 7 | 2 | 18 | 3 | 0 | 3.3 | .870 |
| | D. Owen | R | 7 | 2 | 5 | 1 | 0 | 1.1 | .875 |
| | D. Lopes | R | 4 | 1 | 2 | 0 | 0 | 0.8 | 1.000 |
| OF | B. Dernier | R | 116 | 310 | 4 | 9 | 1 | 2.8 | .972 |
| | K. Moreland | R | 148 | 233 | 10 | 6 | 2 | 1.7 | .976 |
| | G. Matthews | R | 85 | 119 | 7 | 3 | 2 | 1.5 | .977 |
| | D. Lopes | R | 79 | 113 | 2 | 1 | 0 | 1.5 | .991 |
| | T. Bosley | L | 55 | 84 | 0 | 1 | 0 | 1.5 | .988 |
| | B. Hatcher | R | 44 | 77 | 2 | 1 | 0 | 1.8 | .988 |
| | G. Woods | R | 56 | 42 | 1 | 0 | 0 | 0.8 | 1.000 |
| | R. Hebner | R | 1 | 0 | 0 | 0 | 0 | 0.0 | .000 |
| | B. Dayett | R | 10 | 8 | 0 | 0 | 0 | 0.8 | 1.000 |
| | D. Jackson | R | 4 | 7 | 0 | 0 | 0 | 1.8 | 1.000 |
| | C. Walker | R | 6 | 3 | 0 | 0 | 0 | 0.5 | 1.000 |
| C | J. Davis | R | 138 | 694 | 84 | 8 | 7 | 5.7 | .990 |
| | S. Lake | R | 55 | 182 | 25 | 1 | 1 | 3.8 | .995 |
| | K. Moreland | R | 2 | 2 | 0 | 0 | 0 | 1.0 | 1.000 |

It was the most teeth-gnashing season in Cub history. They opened as defending NL East champions and, despite little timely hitting and much horrendous middle-inning relief, were in first place through April and May.

The slide began May 19 when Rick Sutcliffe, 1984's Cy Young Award winner with a 16–1 record, ran out a grounder, pulled up with a partial tear of his left hamstring, and was placed on the disabled list. The Cubs then lost Bob Dernier to an ankle injury and Gary Matthews to a torn-up knee. Sutcliffe came back too soon, hurt his arm, and was sidelined through most of the season. He finished with an 8–8 record. Soon the entire starting rotation was decimated. Joining Sutcliffe on the DL were Steve Trout (sore elbow), Dennis Eckersley (sore shoulder), Scott Sanderson (sore back and torn knee ligaments), and Dick Ruthven (broken toe).

On June 12, the Cubs started a club record-tying 13-game losing streak, dropping them from first to fourth. GM Dallas Green had to reach into the barren farm system for pitching help, with disastrous results. The Cubs slipped to fifth, but regained fourth when the Phillies went into a late-season tailspin.

There were a few bright spots. Ryne Sandberg batted .305, and his 26 homers were the most for a Cubs second baseman since Rogers Hornsby's 39 in 1929. He also stole 54 bases, the most by a Cub since Frank Chance stole 57 in 1905. Moreland led the club with a .307 average and had a career-high 106 RBI. Rookie shortstop Shawon Dunston provided hope for the future by rebounding from a shaky start. After being handed the starting job in the spring, he batted .194 and made foolish errors in the field before being optioned to Iowa. He returned in mid-August after the Cubs unloaded veteran shortstop Larry Bowa, and fielded brilliantly while bringing his average up to .260.

## TEAM STATISTICS

| | W | L | PCT | GB | R | OR | 2B | 3B | HR | BA | SA | SB | E | DP | FA | CG | B | SO | ShO | SV | ERA |
|---|---|---|---|---|---|---|---|---|---|---|---|---|---|---|---|---|---|---|---|---|---|
| EAST | | | | | | | | | | | | | | | | | | | | | |
| STL | 101 | 61 | .623 | | 747 | 572 | 245 | 59 | 87 | .264 | .379 | 314 | 108 | 166 | .983 | 37 | 453 | 798 | 20 | 44 | 3.10 |
| NY | 98 | 64 | .605 | 3 | 695 | 568 | 239 | 35 | 134 | .257 | .385 | 117 | 115 | 138 | .982 | 32 | 515 | 1039 | 19 | 37 | 3.11 |
| MON | 84 | 77 | .522 | 16.5 | 633 | 636 | 242 | 49 | 118 | .247 | .375 | 169 | 121 | 152 | .981 | 13 | 509 | 870 | 13 | 54 | 3.55 |
| CHI | 77 | 84 | .478 | 23.5 | 686 | 729 | 239 | 28 | 150 | .254 | .390 | 182 | 134 | 150 | .979 | 20 | 519 | 820 | 8 | 42 | 4.16 |
| PHI | 75 | 87 | .463 | 26 | 667 | 673 | 238 | 47 | 141 | .245 | .383 | 122 | 139 | 142 | .978 | 24 | 596 | 899 | 9 | 30 | 3.68 |
| PIT | 57 | 104 | .354 | 43.5 | 568 | 708 | 252 | 28 | 80 | .247 | .347 | 110 | 133 | 127 | .979 | 15 | 584 | 962 | 6 | 29 | 3.97 |
| WEST | | | | | | | | | | | | | | | | | | | | | |
| LA | 95 | 67 | .586 | | 682 | 579 | 226 | 28 | 129 | .261 | .382 | 136 | 166 | 131 | .974 | 37 | 462 | 979 | 21 | 36 | 2.96 |
| CIN | 89 | 72 | .553 | 5.5 | 677 | 666 | 249 | 34 | 114 | .255 | .376 | 159 | 122 | 142 | .980 | 24 | 535 | 910 | 11 | 45 | 3.71 |
| HOU | 83 | 79 | .512 | 12 | 706 | 691 | 261 | 42 | 121 | .261 | .388 | 96 | 152 | 159 | .976 | 17 | 543 | 909 | 9 | 42 | 3.66 |
| SD | 83 | 79 | .512 | 12 | 650 | 622 | 241 | 28 | 109 | .255 | .368 | 60 | 124 | 158 | .980 | 26 | 443 | 727 | 19 | 44 | 3.41 |
| ATL | 66 | 96 | .407 | 29 | 632 | 781 | 213 | 28 | 126 | .246 | .363 | 72 | 159 | 197 | .976 | 9 | 642 | 776 | 9 | 29 | 4.19 |
| SF | 62 | 100 | .383 | 33 | 556 | 674 | 217 | 31 | 115 | .233 | .348 | 99 | 148 | 134 | .976 | 13 | 572 | 985 | 5 | 24 | 3.61 |
| LEAGUE TOTAL | | | | | 7899 | 7899 | 2862 | 437 | 1424 | .252 | .374 | 1636 | 1621 | 1796 | .979 | 267 | 6373 | 10674 | 149 | 456 | 3.59 |

## INDIVIDUAL PITCHING

| PITCHER | T | W | L | PCT | ERA | SV | G | GS | CG | IP | H | BB | SO | R | ER | ShO | H/9 | BB/9 | SO/9 |
|---|---|---|---|---|---|---|---|---|---|---|---|---|---|---|---|---|---|---|---|
| Dennis Eckersley | R | 11 | 7 | .611 | 3.08 | 0 | 25 | 25 | 6 | 169.1 | 145 | 19 | 117 | 61 | 58 | 2 | 7.71 | 1.01 | 6.22 |
| Ray Fontenot | L | 6 | 10 | .375 | 4.36 | 0 | 38 | 23 | 0 | 154.2 | 177 | 45 | 70 | 86 | 75 | 0 | 10.30 | 2.62 | 4.07 |
| Steve Trout | L | 9 | 7 | .563 | 3.39 | 0 | 24 | 24 | 3 | 140.2 | 142 | 63 | 44 | 57 | 53 | 1 | 9.09 | 4.03 | 2.82 |
| Rick Sutcliffe | R | 8 | 8 | .500 | 3.18 | 0 | 20 | 20 | 6 | 130 | 119 | 44 | 102 | 51 | 46 | 3 | 8.24 | 3.05 | 7.06 |
| Scott Sanderson | R | 5 | 6 | .455 | 3.12 | 0 | 19 | 19 | 2 | 121 | 100 | 27 | 80 | 49 | 42 | 0 | 7.44 | 2.01 | 5.95 |
| Lee Smith | R | 7 | 4 | .636 | 3.04 | 33 | 65 | 0 | 0 | 97.2 | 87 | 32 | 112 | 35 | 33 | 0 | 8.02 | 2.95 | 10.32 |
| Dick Ruthven | R | 4 | 7 | .364 | 4.53 | 0 | 20 | 15 | 0 | 87.1 | 103 | 37 | 26 | 49 | 44 | 0 | 10.61 | 3.81 | 2.68 |
| Lary Sorensen | R | 3 | 7 | .300 | 4.26 | 0 | 45 | 3 | 0 | 82.1 | 86 | 24 | 34 | 44 | 39 | 0 | 9.40 | 2.62 | 3.72 |
| George Frazier | R | 7 | 8 | .467 | 6.39 | 2 | 51 | 0 | 0 | 76 | 88 | 52 | 46 | 57 | 54 | 0 | 10.42 | 6.16 | 5.45 |
| Warren Brusstar | R | 4 | 3 | .571 | 6.05 | 4 | 51 | 0 | 0 | 74.1 | 87 | 36 | 34 | 55 | 50 | 0 | 10.53 | 4.36 | 4.12 |
| Jay Baller | R | 2 | 3 | .400 | 3.46 | 1 | 20 | 4 | 0 | 52 | 52 | 17 | 31 | 21 | 20 | 0 | 9.00 | 2.94 | 5.37 |
| Steve Engel | L | 1 | 5 | .167 | 5.57 | 1 | 11 | 8 | 1 | 51.2 | 61 | 26 | 29 | 36 | 32 | 0 | 10.63 | 4.53 | 5.05 |
| Ron Meridith | L | 3 | 2 | .600 | 4.47 | 1 | 32 | 0 | 0 | 46.1 | 53 | 24 | 23 | 24 | 23 | 0 | 10.29 | 4.66 | 4.47 |
| Derek Botelho | R | 1 | 3 | .250 | 5.32 | 0 | 11 | 7 | 1 | 44 | 52 | 23 | 23 | 27 | 26 | 0 | 10.64 | 4.70 | 4.70 |
| Reggie Patterson | R | 3 | 0 | 1.000 | 3.00 | 0 | 8 | 5 | 1 | 39 | 36 | 10 | 17 | 13 | 13 | 0 | 8.31 | 2.31 | 3.92 |
| Johnny Abrego | R | 1 | 1 | .500 | 6.38 | 4 | 6 | 5 | 0 | 24 | 32 | 12 | 13 | 18 | 17 | 0 | 12.00 | 4.50 | 4.88 |
| Larry Gura | L | 0 | 3 | .000 | 8.41 | 4 | 5 | 4 | 0 | 20.1 | 34 | 6 | 7 | 19 | 19 | 0 | 15.05 | 2.66 | 3.10 |
| Dave Beard | R | 0 | 0 | – | 6.39 | 0 | 9 | 0 | 0 | 12.2 | 16 | 7 | 4 | 9 | 9 | 0 | 11.37 | 4.97 | 2.84 |
| Dave Gumpert | R | 1 | 0 | 1.000 | 3.48 | 0 | 9 | 0 | 0 | 10.1 | 12 | 7 | 4 | 7 | 4 | 0 | 10.45 | 6.10 | 3.48 |
| Jon Perlman | R | 1 | 0 | 1.000 | 11.42 | 0 | 6 | 0 | 0 | 8.2 | 10 | 8 | 4 | 11 | 11 | 0 | 10.38 | 8.31 | 4.15 |
| TEAM TOTAL | | 77 | 84 | .478 | 4.17 | 42 | 475 | 162 | 20 | 1442.1 | 1492 | 519 | 820 | 729 | 668 | 6 | 9.31 | 3.24 | 5.12 |

# Cubs Graphics

Graphs are not everyone's cup of tea. That's a shame, because a clear, well-drawn graph can present an enormous amount of information in an instant. And baseball is the perfect subject for a graphic treatment that can make quick sense of the wealth of statistics and measures generated by that most measured of all sports.

The graphs that follow paint a clear portrait of more than eighty years of accumulated results, and communicate them at a glance. Take a look at the graph below, which charts the Cubs' finishes and won-lost percentage for every season from 1901 through 1985. The Cubs rose smartly from near the bottom of the league to the top in the century's first decade, stayed there awhile, and then bobbed up and down until the '30s. They stayed as close to the top in the '30s as they did to the cellar in the years to come. Leo Durocher's clubs of the 1960s stand out as a recent high point—at least until the '80s, when the club rose smartly from the bottom of the division to the top.

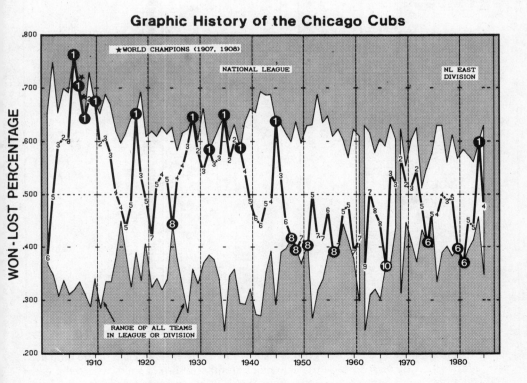

### Graphic History of the Chicago Cubs

The white space indicates the range of won-lost percentages for all teams in the league or division for the given season; the numbers represent the Cubs' finish for the year. In case of ties, the higher finish is listed.

WON-LOST PERCENTAGE

EQUALS POSITION IN FINAL STANDINGS EXCEPT IN 1981

(t = TIE)

TEAM EARNED RUN AVERAGE

ABBREVIATIONS: B = BRAVES   D = DODGERS   E = EXPOS   F = PHILLIES   G = GIANTS   H = ASTROS   M = METS   O = PADRES   P = PIRATES   R = REDS

Decade panels: 1901-1910, 1911-1920, 1921-1930, 1931-1940, 1941-1950, 1951-1960, 1961-1970, 1971-1980

Part graph, part table, these "grables" show the Cubs' rank in each of the indicated categories year by year since 1901. The black numbered boxes show where the Cubs finished; the white lettered boxes show the finish of every other team in the league.

The first two panels here show how vital pitching has been to the Cubs. Surprisingly, until the '84 season, the Cubs had never won a title without finishing first or second in earned run average. The pattern of the Cubs' finishes mirrors that of their ERA ranking—not the most comforting thought when looking at their rankings of the 1980s.

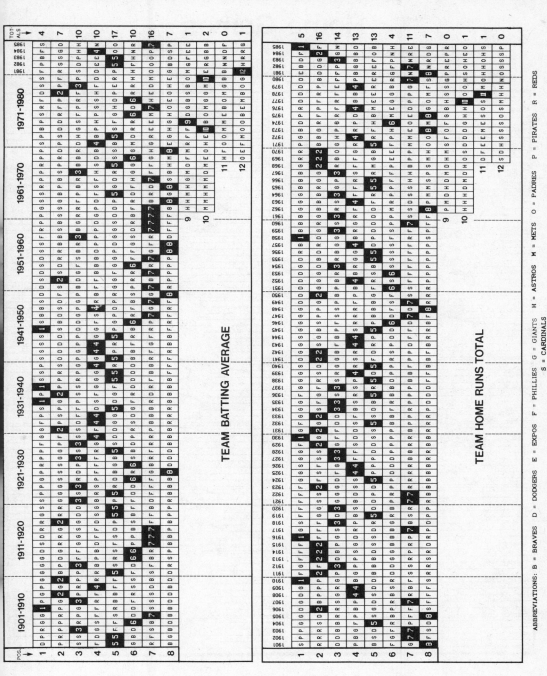

**TEAM BATTING AVERAGE**

**TEAM HOME RUNS TOTAL**

ABBREVIATIONS: B = BRAVES  D = DODGERS  E = EXPOS  F = PHILLIES  G = GIANTS  H = ASTROS  M = METS  O = PADRES  P = PIRATES  R = REDS
S = CARDINALS

These two grables look at the team's performance in the traditional offensive categories, batting average and home runs. The Cubs have always been among the leaders in homers, with only a few brief periods like the late 1940s or early '70s in which the club sank to the lower half of the league. But even when they were hitting homers, they weren't hitting much else; their rankings in average are surprisingly low, even in their glory years. And the home run grable bears no resemblance at all to the won-lost record grable, suggesting that the ability to hit home runs is overrated as a factor in what it takes to win at Wrigley Field.

# Home Games

## Defense

CHI H

← RUNS ALLOWED PER GAME    RUNS SCORED PER GAME →

## Offense

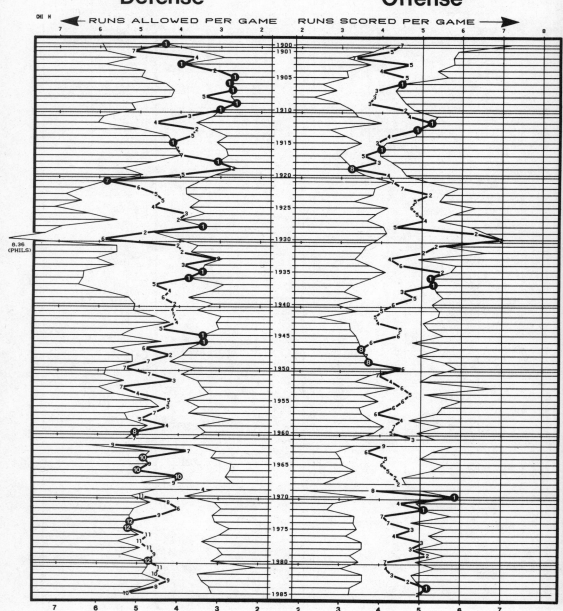

Just how great is the influence of Wrigley? The best way to look at this is to compare the Cubs' performance at home and on the road. The graphs on these two pages show where the Cubs have ranked, year by year, in runs scored and allowed per game at home and on the road. The Home Games graphs, particularly for the last fifteen years, show the Cubs at or near the top of the league in runs scored at home, and clinging to the bottom in runs allowed.

# Road Games

## Defense

## Offense

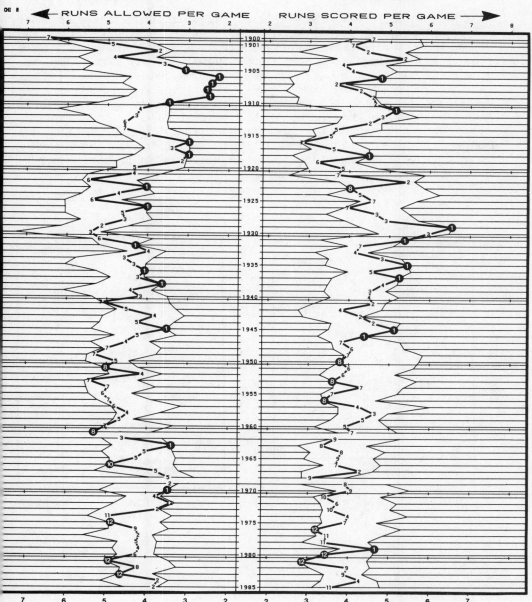

The Road Games graphs, however, give a more balanced view of the team. The pitching, outside the friendly confines, was terrific in the late '60s, middle-of-the-pack in the mid-'70s, and quite good for the last two seasons—second in both '84 and '85. The offense, though, looks like an illusion of the home field; they've ranked in the top half of the league in runs scored on the road only four times in the last twenty years. And last year they fell to 11th, indicating that the reasons for their drop from the division title had less to do with the injuries to the pitching staff than to Dernier and Matthews.

# THE PENNANT RACES

Graphs provide an excellent way of showing the patterns and results of a pennant race. John Davenport's method is to chart each team's progress above or below the .500 mark. Each win moves a team up one step; each loss takes them down one. It takes a two-game difference in record over or under .500 to make a one-game difference in the standings; a team with a 10-1 record, nine games over .500, is one game ahead of a team at 9-2, seven games over .500.

The graphs below show, as examples, two great Cubs pennant wins of the '30s. In 1935, in Dutch Reagan's favorite race, the Cubs were two games behind the Cardinals on September 2, then won 21 straight to clinch the pennant. In 1938, the Cubs came from much farther back to overtake a fading Pirates club. The race was interrupted by the great hurricane of '38, and was clinched on the next-to-last day of the season by Gabby Hartnett's homer in the gloamin'.

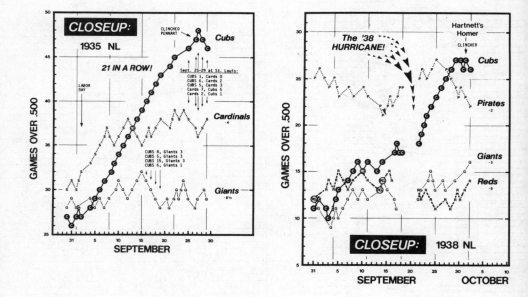

The graphs on the following pages track the Cubs' standing from start to finish for every season since 1901. The black space shows the range of all the clubs in the league (or division since 1969). The numbers in the white circles show where the Cubs stood on the date indicated at the bottom of the graph.

*248*

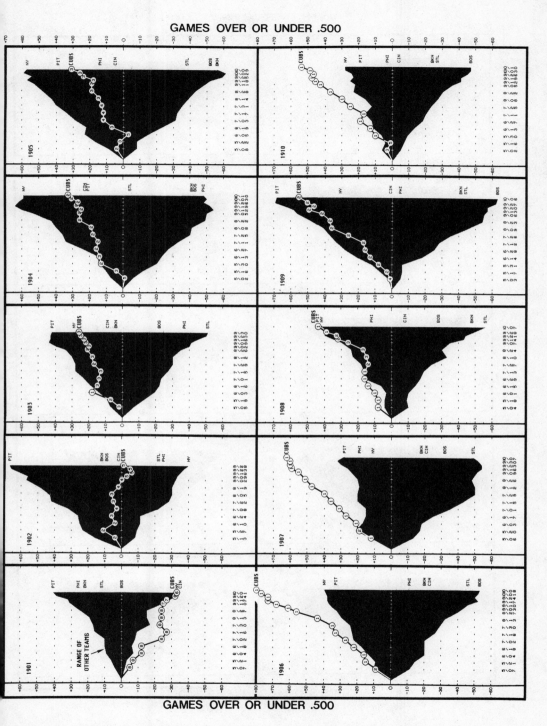

Four pennants and a second in five years: the first decade of the century was as good as it could be for Cubs fans. The Pirates won 96 games in 1906, and still finished 20 games back.

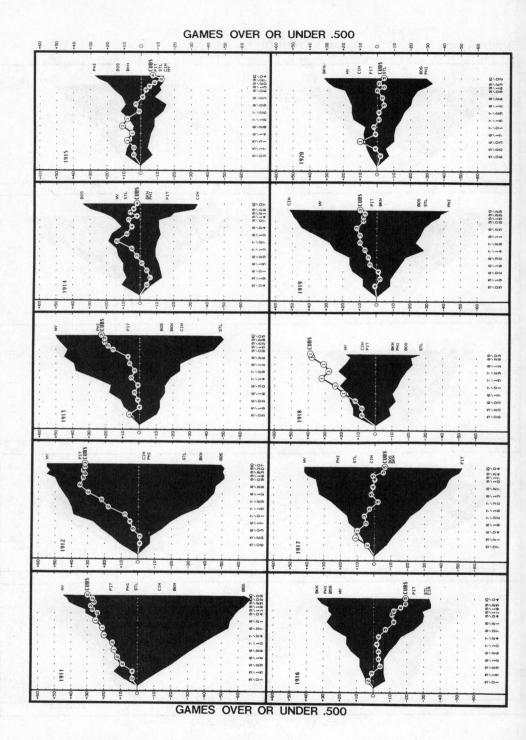

GAMES OVER OR UNDER .500

After making a run at the pennant in 1911, the Cubs faded back into the pack, with the exception of the title in 1918 in a season shortened because of World War I.

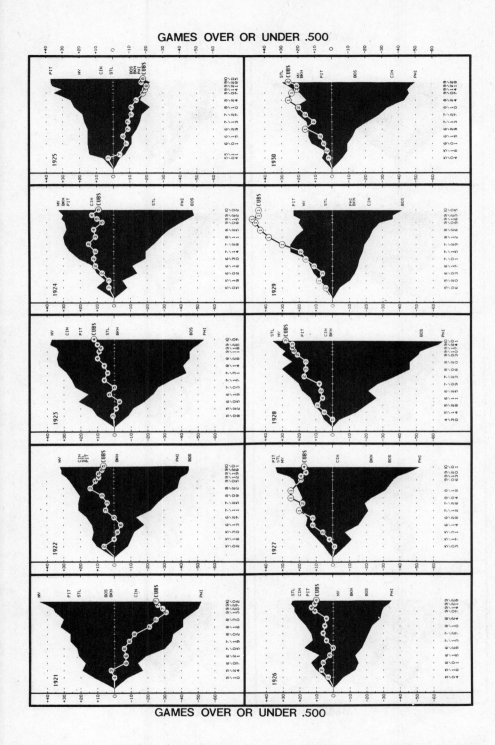

Like a diver pushing off the bottom of the pool, the Cubs fell to the cellar in 1925, and bounced right back, thanks to bats like Wilson's and arms like Root's.

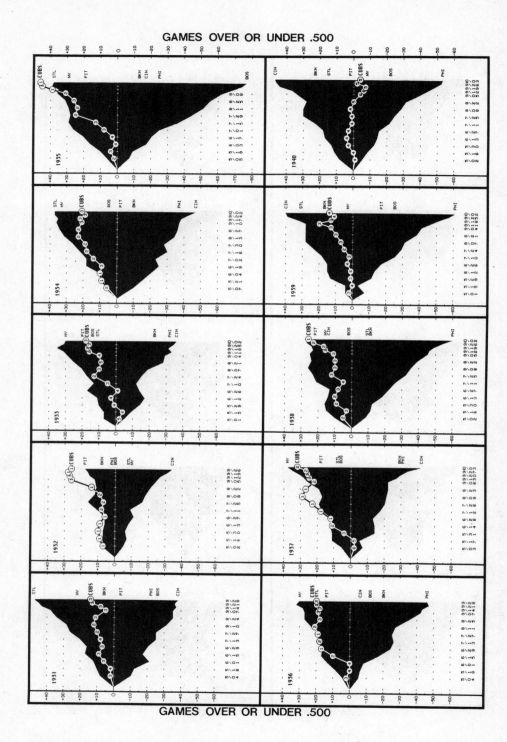

If the Oughties were the golden era, the Thirties were at least sterling silver: three firsts, two seconds, and three thirds, with not a September swoon in the bunch.

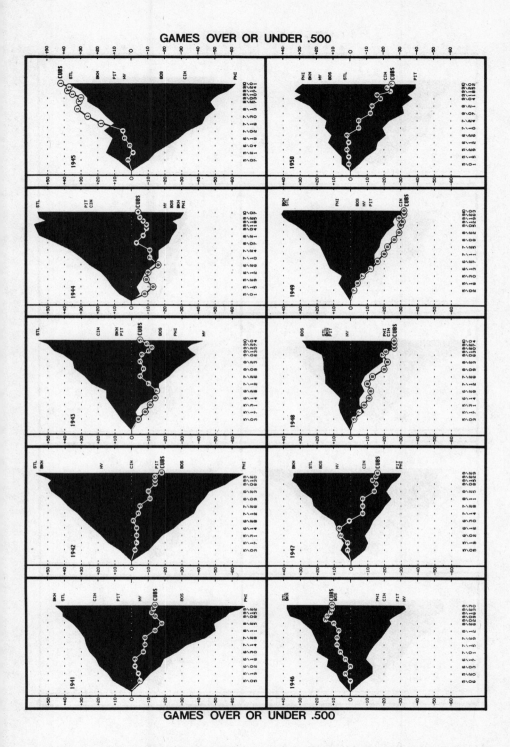

GAMES OVER OR UNDER .500

The surprise pennant of '45 stands out in stark contrast to a dismal decade, as the Cubs fell farther and farther behind the contending Cardinals and Dodgers.

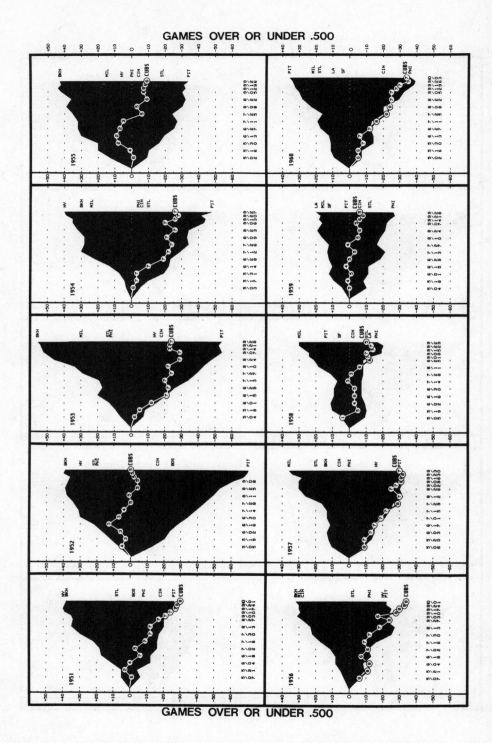

Don't try to tell us the '50s were the best decade of baseball ever: only one year as lofty as .500, and only two in which the Cubs were within ten games of first at midseason.

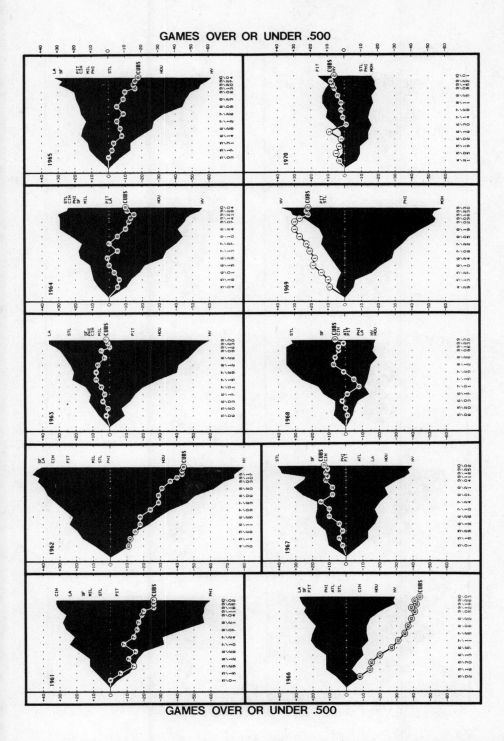

Leo sure was right about the '66 Cubs: they weren't even close to being an eighth-place ballclub. Feel free to skip the 1969 graph altogether.

255

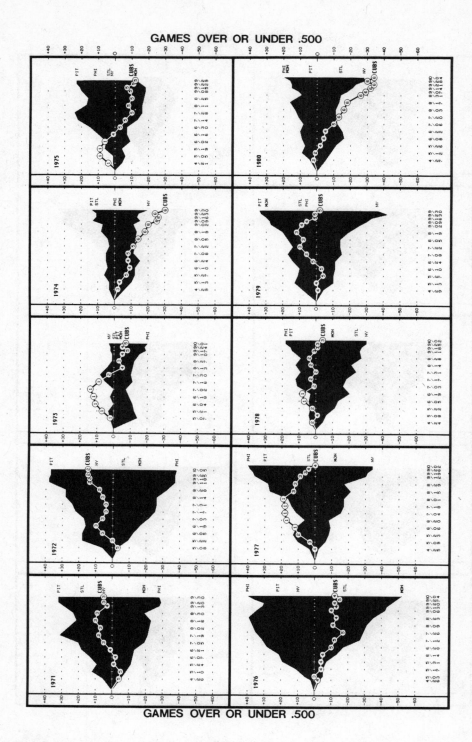

There were only a few brief periods of glory in the '70s, as every year seemed to take a downward turn, an impression visually confirmed by these graphic pictures of the pennant races.

256

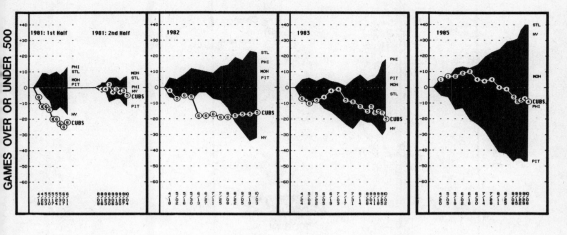

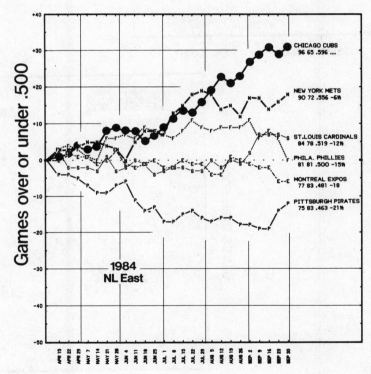

Revenge was sweet, as the September swoon never came in 1984; the Cubs just kept climbing, and the Mets fell by the wayside. And the hopes for the future can be seen in the club's proximity to first in '85 before all the injuries caught up with them.

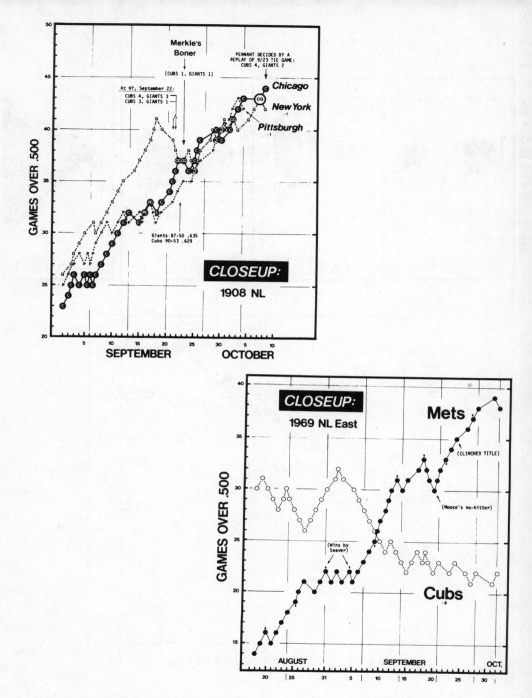

Two more closeups: the greatest pennant race in National League history, and one of the most lamented. The Cubs, Giants, and Pirates fought all season in 1908, with no team opening up any room over the other two. The season ultimately came down to a replay of the tie game resulting from Merkle's Boner; the Cubs beat the New Yorkers 4-2. The other race is all too familiar; the Mets overtook the Cubs when their ten-game winning streak coincided with a Cubs eight-game loss skein.

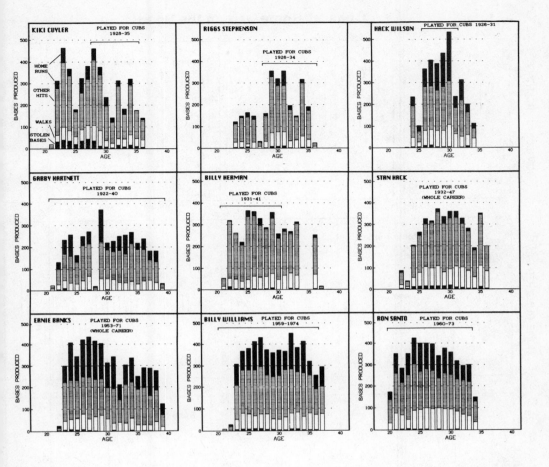

How do you compare the offensive statistics of great ballplayers? One useful way is to treat every component—hits, homers, walks, steals—as Bases Produced, and stack them all up side by side. These graphs make a strong case for the latter trio, Banks, Williams, and Santo, as the most productive threesome in Cubs history. Wilson hit higher highs but burned out too fast; Hartnett only had one year that would look at home with their records. And boosters of the late Riggs Stephenson for the Hall of Fame have a heavy burden of proof on their shoulders; Stan Hack's 80-90 walks a season made him consistently more valuable.

# Cubs at Home and on the Road

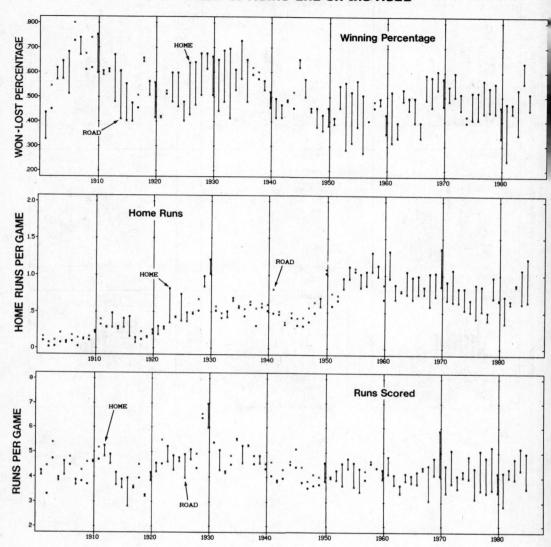

A last look at Wrigley effects. In each panel, home totals are indicated with a small black square, and road totals with an x. Lines connect the home total with the road total whenever the home total is higher. The effects of Wrigley on the Cubs' offense have grown more and more pronounced; in recent years, they have been scoring over a run a game more at home than on the road, and hitting better than a homer every two games more at home. In '84 and '85, though, the winning percentage disparity was very small, perhaps reflecting the organization's realization that to win a pennant, the Cubs will have to be able to win consistently on the road as well as at home.

# Player Register

The Player Register is an alphabetical listing of every man who has played in the major leagues and played or managed for the Chicago Cubs from 1876 through today, except those players who were primarily pitchers. However, pitchers who pinch-hit and played in other positions for a total of 25 games or more are listed in this Player Register. Included are facts about the players and their year-by-year batting records and their lifetime totals of League Championship Series and World Series.

Much of this information has never been compiled, especially for the period 1876 through 1919. For certain other years some statistics are still missing or incomplete. Research in this area is still in progress, and the years that lack complete information are indicated. In fact, all information and abbreviations that may appear unfamiliar are explained in the sample format presented below. John Doe, the player used in the sample, is fictitious and serves only to illustrate the information.

| | G | AB | H | 2B | 3B | HR | HR % | R | RBI | BB | SO | SB | BA | SA | Pinch Hit AB | Pinch Hit H | G by POS |
|---|---|---|---|---|---|---|---|---|---|---|---|---|---|---|---|---|---|

**John Doe**

DOE, JOHN LEE (Slim)
Played as John Cherry part of 1900.
Born John Lee Doughnut.   Brother of Bill Doe.
B. Jan. 1,1850, New York, N. Y.   D. July 1, 1955, New York, N. Y.
Manager 1908-15.
Hall of Fame 1946.

BR TR 6'2"   165 lbs.
BB 1884 BL 1906

| Year | Team | Lg | G | AB | H | 2B | 3B | HR | HR % | R | RBI | BB | SO | SB | BA | SA | PH AB | PH H | G by POS |
|---|---|---|---|---|---|---|---|---|---|---|---|---|---|---|---|---|---|---|---|
| 1884 | STL | U | 125 | 435 | 121 | 18 | 1 | 3 | 0.7 | 44 | | 37 | 42 | 7 | .278 | .345 | 9 | 2 | SS-99, P-26 |
| 1885 | LOU | AA | 155 | 547 | 138 | 22 | 3 | 3 | 0.6 | 50 | 58 | 42 | 48 | 8 | .252 | .320 | 8 | 4 | SS-115, P-40 |
| 1886 | CLE | N | 147 | 485 | 134 | 38 | 5 | 0 | 0.0 | 66 | 54 | 48 | 50 | 8 | .276 | .375 | 7 | 1 | SS-107, P-40 |
| 1887 | BOS | N | 129 | 418 | 117 | 15 | 3 | 1 | 0.2 | 38 | 52 | 32 | 37 | 1 | .280 | .337 | 1 | 0 | SS-102, P-27 |
| 1888 | NY | N | 144 | 506 | 135 | 26 | 2 | 6 | 1.2 | 50 | 63 | 43 | 50 | 1 | .267 | .362 | 10 | 8 | SS-105, P-39 |
| 1889 | 3 teams | | DET | N | (10G – .300) | | | PIT | N | (32G – .241) | | | PHI | N | (41G – .364) | | | |
| " | total | | 83 | 237 | 75 | 31 | 16 | 7 | 3.0 | 90 | 42 | 25 | 35 | 3 | .316 | .671 | 6 | 3 | SS-61, P-22 |
| 1890 | NY | P | 123 | 430 | 119 | 27 | 5 | 1 | 0.2 | 63 | 59 | 39 | 39 | 2 | .277 | .370 | 12 | 10 | SS-85, P-38 |
| 1900 | CHI | A | 146 | 498 | 116 | 29 | 4 | 3 | 0.6 | 51 | 46 | 59 | 53 | 1 | .233 | .325 | 13 | 8 | SS-111, P-35 |
| 1901 | NY | N | 149 | 540 | 147 | 19 | 6 | 4 | 0.7 | 57 | 74 | 49 | 58 | 3 | .272 | .352 | 23 | 15 | SS-114, P-35 |
| 1906 | CHI | N | 144 | 567 | 143 | 26 | 4 | 4 | 0.7 | 70 | 43 | 37 | 54 | 1 | .252 | .333 | 7 | 1 | SS-113, P-31 |
| 1907 | | | 134 | 515 | 140 | 31 | 2 | 5 | 1.0 | 61 | 70 | 37 | 42 | 0 | .272 | .369 | 13 | 8 | SS-97, P-37 |
| 1908 | | | 106 | 372 | 92 | 10 | 2 | 4 | 1.1 | 36 | 40 | 4 | 55 | 1 | .247 | .317 | 1 | 0 | SS-105, P-1 |
| 1914 | CHI | F | 6 | 6 | 0 | 0 | 0 | 0 | 0.0 | 0 | 0 | 0 | 1 | 0 | .000 | .000 | 0 | 0 | P-6 |
| 1915 | NY | A | 1 | 0 | 0 | 0 | 0 | 0 | – | 0 | 0 | 0 | 0 | 0 | – | – | 0 | 0 | SS-1 |
| 14 yrs. | | | 1592 | 5556 | 1927 | 292 4th | 53 | 41 | 0.7 | 676 | 601 | 452 | 564 | 36 | .266 | .360 | 110 | 60 | SS-1215, P-377 |
| 3 yrs. | | | 384 | 1454 | 375 | 67 | 8 | 13 | 0.9 | 167 | 153 | 78 | 151 | 2 | .258 | .342 6th | 21 | 9 | SS-315, P-96 |

**LEAGUE CHAMPIONSHIP SERIES**

| Year | Team | Lg | G | AB | H | 2B | 3B | HR | HR % | R | RBI | BB | SO | SB | BA | SA | PH AB | PH H | G by POS |
|---|---|---|---|---|---|---|---|---|---|---|---|---|---|---|---|---|---|---|---|
| 1901 | NY | N | 3 | 14 | 5 | 2 | 0 | 3 | 21.4 | 3 | 7 | 0 | 1 | 0 | .357 | 1.143 | 0 | 0 | OF-3 |

**WORLD SERIES**

| Year | Team | Lg | G | AB | H | 2B | 3B | HR | HR % | R | RBI | BB | SO | SB | BA | SA | PH AB | PH H | G by POS |
|---|---|---|---|---|---|---|---|---|---|---|---|---|---|---|---|---|---|---|---|
| 1901 | NY | N | 7 | 28 | 9 | 1 | 0 | 6 | 21.4 | 12 | 14 | 3 | 4 | 0 | .321 | 1.000 | 0 | 0 | SS-5, P-2 |
| 1906 | STL | N | 5 | 10 | 5 | 1 | 0 | 1 | 10.0 | 3 | 2 | 0 | 2 | 0 | .500 | .900 | 2 | 0 | P-4, SS-1 |
| 2 yrs. | | | 12 | 38 | 14 | 2 | 0 | 7 | 18.4 | 15 | 16 5th | 3 | 6 | 0 | .368 | .974 9th | 2 | 0 | SS-6, P-6 |

# PLAYER INFORMATION

| | |
|---|---|
| John Doe | This shortened version of the player's full name is the name most familiar to the fans. All players in this section are alphabetically arranged by the last name part of this name. |
| DOE, JOHN LEE | Player's full name. The arrangement is last name first, then first and middle name(s). |
| (Slim) | Player's nickname. Any name or names appearing in parentheses indicates a nickname. |

| | |
|---|---|
| The player's main batting and throwing style. Doe, for instance, batted and threw righthanded. The information listed directly below the main batting information indicates that at various times in a player's career he changed his batting style. The "BB" for Doe in 1884 means he was a switch hitter that year, and the "BL" means he batted lefthanded in 1906. For the years that are not shown it can be assumed that Doe batted right, as his main batting information indicates. | BR TR<br>BB 1884<br>BL 1906 |
| Player's height. | 6'2" |
| Player's average playing weight. | 165 lbs |
| The player at one time in his major league career played under another name and can be found only in box scores or newspaper stories under that name. | Played as John Cherry part of 1900 |
| The name the player was given at birth. (For the most part, the player never used this name while playing in the major leagues, but, if he did, it would be listed as "played as," which is explained above under the heading "Played as John Cherry part of 1900.") | Born John Lee Doughnut |
| The player's brother. (Relatives indicated here are fathers, sons, brothers, grandfathers, and grandsons who played or managed in the major leagues and the National Association.) | Brother of Bill Doe |

Date and place of birth.

B. Jan. 1, 1850, New York, N.Y.

Date and place of death. (For those players who are listed simply as "deceased," it means that, although no certification of death or other information is presently available, it is reasonably certain they are dead.)

D. July 1, 1955, New York, N.Y.

Doe also served as a major league manager. All men who were managers for the Cubs can be found in the Manager Register, where their complete managerial record is shown.

Manager
1908–15

Doe was elected to the Baseball Hall of Fame in 1946.

Hall of Fame
1946

## COLUMN HEADINGS INFORMATION

| G | AB | H | 2B | 3B | HR | HR % | R | RBI | BB | SO | SB | BA | SA | Pinch Hit AB H | G by POS |
|---|----|----|----|----|----|------|---|-----|----|----|----|----|----|----------------|----------|
| | | | | | | | | | | | | | | | |

| | |
|---|---|
| G | Games |
| AB | At Bats |
| H | Hits |
| 2B | Doubles |
| 3B | Triples |
| HR | Home Runs |
| HR % | Home Run Percentage (the number of home runs per 100 times at bat) |
| R | Runs Scored |
| RBI | Runs Batted In |
| BB | Bases on Balls |
| SO | Strikeouts |
| SB | Stolen Bases |
| BA | Batting Average |
| SA | Slugging Average |

*Pinch Hit*

| | |
|---|---|
| AB | Pinch Hit At Bats |
| H | Pinch Hits |
| G by POS | Games by Position. (All fielding positions a man played within the given year are shown. The position where the most games were played is listed first. Any man who pitched, as Doe did, is listed also in the alphabetically arranged Pitcher Register, where his complete pitching record can be found.) If no fielding positions are shown in a particular year, it means the player only pinch-hit, pinch-ran, or was a "designated hitter." |

# TEAM AND LEAGUE INFORMATION

Doe's record has been exaggerated so that his playing career spans all the years of the six different major leagues. Directly alongside the year and team information is the symbol for the league:

N  National League (1876 to date)
A  American League (1901 to date)
F  Federal League (1914–15)
AA  American Association (1882–91)
P  Players' League (1890)
U  Union Association (1884)

STL—The abbreviation of the city in which the team played. Doe, for example, played for St. Louis in 1884. All teams in this section are listed by an abbreviation of the city in which the team played. The abbreviations follow:

| | | | |
|---|---|---|---|
| ALT | Altoona | NWK | Newark |
| ATL | Atlanta | NY | New York |
| BAL | Baltimore | OAK | Oakland |
| BOS | Boston | PHI | Philadelphia |
| BKN | Brooklyn | PIT | Pittsburgh |
| BUF | Buffalo | PRO | Providence |
| CAL | California | RIC | Richmond |
| CHI | Chicago | ROC | Rochester |
| CIN | Cincinnati | SD | San Diego |
| CLE | Cleveland | SEA | Seattle |
| COL | Columbus | SF | San Francisco |
| DET | Detroit | STL | St. Louis |
| HAR | Hartford | STP | St. Paul |
| HOU | Houston | SYR | Syracuse |
| IND | Indianapolis | TEX | Texas |
| KC | Kansas City | TOL | Toledo |
| LA | Los Angeles | TOR | Toronto |
| LOU | Louisville | TRO | Troy |
| MIL | Milwaukee | WAS | Washington |
| MIN | Minnesota | WIL | Wilmington |
| MON | Montreal | WOR | Worcester |

Three franchises in the history of major league baseball changed their location during the season. These teams are designated by the first letter of the two cities they represented. They are:

B-B   Brooklyn-Baltimore (American Association, 1890)
C-M   Cincinnati-Milwaukee (American Association, 1891)
C-P   Chicago-Pittsburgh (Union Association, 1884)

Blank space appearing beneath a team and league indicates that the team and league are the same. Doe, for example, played for Chicago in the National League from 1906 through 1908.

*3 Teams Total*. Indicates a player played for more than one team in the same year. Doe played for three teams in 1889. The number of games he played and his batting average for each team are also shown. Directly beneath this line, following the word "total," is Doe's combined record for all three teams for 1889.

*Total Playing Years*. This information, which appears as the first item on the player's lifetime total line, indicates the total number of years in which he played at least one game. Doe, for example, played in at least one game for fourteen years.

*Cubs Playing Years*. This information, which appears as the first item on the player's Cubs career total line, indicates the total number of years in which he played at least one game for the Cubs.

## STATISTICAL INFORMATION

*League Leaders*. Statistics that appear in bold-faced print indicate the player led his league that year in a particular statistical category. Doe, for example, led the National League in doubles in 1889. When there is a tie for league lead, the figures for all the men who tied are shown in boldface.

*All-Time Single Season Leaders*. Indicated by the small number that appears next to the statistic. Doe, for example, is shown with a small number "1" next to his doubles total in 1889. This means he is first on the all-time major league list for hitting the most doubles in a single season. All players who tied for first are also shown by the same number.

*Lifetime Leaders*. Indicated by the figure that appears beneath the line showing the player's lifetime totals. Doe has a "4th" shown below his lifetime triples total. This means that, lifetime, Doe ranks fourth among major league players for hitting the most triples. Once again, only the top ten are indicated, and players who are tied receive the same number.

*Unavailable Information*. Any time a blank space is shown in a particular statistical column, such as in Doe's 1884 RBI total, it indicates the information was unavailable or incomplete.

*Meaningless Averages.* Indicated by use of a dash (—). In the case of Doe, a dash is shown for his 1915 batting average. This means that, although he played one game, he had no official at bats. A batting average of .000 would mean he had at least one at bat with no hits.

*Cubs Career Totals.* The statistical line appearing below Doe's major league career totals indicates his totals for his career with the Chicago Cubs. In Doe's case, the totals are for the years 1906—1908.

*Cubs Lifetime Leaders.* Indicated by the figure that appears beneath his Cubs career total. Doe has a "6th" shown below his Cubs career pinch hit at bats total. This means that he ranks sixth among Cubs in that category, counting only his years with the club.

*World Series Lifetime Leaders.* Indicated by the figure that appears beneath the player's lifetime World Series totals. Doe as a "5th" shown below his lifetime home run total. This means that, lifetime, Doe ranks fifth among major league players for hitting the most home runs in total World Series play. Players who tied for a position in the top ten are shown by the same number, so that, if two men tied for fourth and fifth place, the appropriate information for both men would be followed by the small number "4," and the next man would be considered sixth in the ranking. Cubs career totals are not provided for post-season play; the indicated totals are for Doe's entire career.

| | G | AB | H | 2B | 3B | HR | HR % | R | RBI | BB | SO | SB | BA | SA | Pinch Hit AB | Pinch Hit H | G by POS |
|---|---|---|---|---|---|---|---|---|---|---|---|---|---|---|---|---|---|

## Cliff Aberson

**ABERSON, CLIFFORD ALEXANDER**  BR  TR  6'  200 lbs.
B. Aug. 28, 1921, Chicago, Ill.  D. June 23, 1973, Vallejo, Calif.

| | G | AB | H | 2B | 3B | HR | HR % | R | RBI | BB | SO | SB | BA | SA | AB | H | G by POS |
|---|---|---|---|---|---|---|---|---|---|---|---|---|---|---|---|---|---|
| 1947 CHI N | 47 | 140 | 39 | 6 | 3 | 4 | 2.9 | 24 | 20 | 20 | 32 | 0 | .279 | .450 | 6 | 2 | OF-40 |
| 1948 | 12 | 32 | 6 | 1 | 0 | 1 | 3.1 | 1 | 6 | 5 | 10 | 0 | .188 | .313 | 3 | 1 | OF-8 |
| 1949 | 4 | 7 | 0 | 0 | 0 | 0 | 0.0 | 0 | 0 | 0 | 2 | 0 | .000 | .000 | 3 | 0 | OF-1 |
| 3 yrs. | 63 | 179 | 45 | 7 | 3 | 5 | 2.8 | 25 | 26 | 25 | 44 | 0 | .251 | .408 | 12 | 3 | OF-49 |
| 3 yrs. | 63 | 179 | 45 | 7 | 3 | 5 | 2.8 | 25 | 26 | 25 | 44 | 0 | .251 | .408 | 12 | 3 | OF-49 |

## Jimmy Adair

**ADAIR, JAMES AUBREY (Choppy)**  BR  TR  5'10½" 154 lbs.
B. Jan. 25, 1907, Waxahachie, Tex.  D. Dec. 9, 1982, Dallas, Tex.

| | G | AB | H | 2B | 3B | HR | HR % | R | RBI | BB | SO | SB | BA | SA | AB | H | G by POS |
|---|---|---|---|---|---|---|---|---|---|---|---|---|---|---|---|---|---|
| 1931 CHI N | 18 | 76 | 21 | 3 | 1 | 0 | 0.0 | 9 | 3 | 1 | 8 | 1 | .276 | .342 | 0 | 0 | SS-18 |

## Bobby Adams

**ADAMS, ROBERT HENRY**  BR  TR  5'10½" 160 lbs.
Brother of Dick Adams.  Father of Mike Adams.
B. Dec. 14, 1921, Tuolumne, Calif.

| | G | AB | H | 2B | 3B | HR | HR % | R | RBI | BB | SO | SB | BA | SA | AB | H | G by POS |
|---|---|---|---|---|---|---|---|---|---|---|---|---|---|---|---|---|---|
| 1946 CIN N | 94 | 311 | 76 | 13 | 3 | 4 | 1.3 | 35 | 24 | 18 | 32 | 16 | .244 | .344 | 13 | 4 | 2B-74, OF-2, 3B-1 |
| 1947 | 81 | 217 | 59 | 11 | 2 | 4 | 1.8 | 39 | 20 | 25 | 23 | 9 | .272 | .396 | 1 | 1 | 2B-69 |
| 1948 | 87 | 262 | 78 | 20 | 3 | 1 | 0.4 | 33 | 21 | 25 | 23 | 6 | .298 | .408 | 14 | 5 | 2B-64, 3B-7 |
| 1949 | 107 | 277 | 70 | 16 | 2 | 0 | 0.0 | 32 | 25 | 26 | 36 | 4 | .253 | .325 | 23 | 6 | 2B-63, 3B-14 |
| 1950 | 115 | 348 | 98 | 21 | 8 | 3 | 0.9 | 57 | 25 | 43 | 29 | 7 | .282 | .414 | 9 | 1 | 2B-53, 3B-42 |
| 1951 | 125 | 403 | 107 | 12 | 5 | 5 | 1.2 | 57 | 24 | 43 | 40 | 4 | .266 | .357 | 30 | 10 | 3B-60, 2B-42, OF-1 |
| 1952 | 154 | 637 | 180 | 25 | 4 | 6 | 0.9 | 85 | 48 | 49 | 67 | 11 | .283 | .363 | 0 | 0 | 3B-154 |
| 1953 | 150 | 607 | 167 | 14 | 6 | 8 | 1.3 | 99 | 49 | 58 | 67 | 3 | .275 | .357 | 0 | 0 | 3B-150 |
| 1954 | 110 | 390 | 105 | 25 | 6 | 3 | 0.8 | 69 | 23 | 55 | 46 | 2 | .269 | .387 | 11 | 4 | 3B-93, 2B-2 |
| 1955 2 teams | | CIN | N (64G – | .273) | | CHI | A (28G – | .095) | | | | | | | | | |
| " total | 92 | 171 | 43 | 11 | 3 | 2 | 1.2 | 31 | 23 | 24 | 25 | 2 | .251 | .386 | 20 | 5 | 3B-51, 2B-6 |
| 1956 BAL A | 41 | 111 | 25 | 6 | 1 | 0 | 0.0 | 19 | 7 | 25 | 15 | 1 | .225 | .297 | 0 | 0 | 3B-24, 2B-18 |
| 1957 CHI N | 60 | 187 | 47 | 10 | 2 | 1 | 0.5 | 21 | 10 | 17 | 28 | 0 | .251 | .342 | 8 | 1 | 3B-47, 2B-1 |
| 1958 | 62 | 96 | 27 | 4 | 4 | 0 | 0.0 | 14 | 4 | 6 | 15 | 2 | .281 | .406 | 35 | 9 | 1B-11, 3B-9, 2B-7 |
| 1959 | 3 | 2 | 0 | 0 | 0 | 0 | 0.0 | 0 | 0 | 0 | 1 | 0 | .000 | .000 | 2 | 0 | 1B-1 |
| 14 yrs. | 1281 | 4019 | 1082 | 188 | 49 | 37 | 0.9 | 591 | 303 | 414 | 447 | 67 | .269 | .368 | 166 | 46 | 3B-652, 2B-399, 1B-12, OF-3 |
| 3 yrs. | 125 | 285 | 74 | 14 | 6 | 1 | 0.4 | 35 | 14 | 23 | 44 | 2 | .260 | .361 | 45 | 10 | 3B-56, 1B-12, 2B-8 |

## Mike Adams

**ADAMS, ROBERT MICHAEL**  BR  TR  5'9"  180 lbs.
Son of Bobby Adams.
B. July 22, 1948, Cincinnati, Ohio

| | G | AB | H | 2B | 3B | HR | HR % | R | RBI | BB | SO | SB | BA | SA | AB | H | G by POS |
|---|---|---|---|---|---|---|---|---|---|---|---|---|---|---|---|---|---|
| 1972 MIN A | 3 | 6 | 2 | 0 | 0 | 0 | 0.0 | 0 | 0 | 0 | 1 | 0 | .333 | .333 | 1 | 1 | OF-1 |
| 1973 | 55 | 66 | 14 | 2 | 0 | 3 | 4.5 | 21 | 6 | 17 | 18 | 2 | .212 | .379 | 1 | 0 | OF-24, DH-2 |
| 1976 CHI N | 25 | 29 | 4 | 2 | 0 | 0 | 0.0 | 1 | 2 | 8 | 7 | 0 | .138 | .207 | 16 | 1 | OF-4, 3B-3, 2B-1 |
| 1977 | 2 | 2 | 0 | 0 | 0 | 0 | 0.0 | 0 | 0 | 0 | 1 | 0 | .000 | .000 | 1 | 0 | OF-2 |
| 1978 OAK A | 15 | 15 | 3 | 1 | 0 | 0 | 0.0 | 5 | 1 | 7 | 2 | 0 | .200 | .267 | 5 | 0 | 2B-6, DH-3, 3B-3 |
| 5 yrs. | 100 | 118 | 23 | 5 | 0 | 3 | 2.5 | 27 | 9 | 32 | 29 | 2 | .195 | .314 | 24 | 1 | OF-31, 2B-7, 3B-6, DH-5 |
| 2 yrs. | 27 | 31 | 4 | 2 | 0 | 0 | 0.0 | 1 | 2 | 8 | 8 | 0 | .129 | .194 | 17 | 1 | OF-6, 3B-3, 2B-1 |

## Sparky Adams

**ADAMS, EARL JOHN**  BR  TR  5'5½" 151 lbs.
B. Aug. 26, 1894, Newtown, Pa.

| | G | AB | H | 2B | 3B | HR | HR % | R | RBI | BB | SO | SB | BA | SA | AB | H | G by POS |
|---|---|---|---|---|---|---|---|---|---|---|---|---|---|---|---|---|---|
| 1922 CHI N | 11 | 44 | 11 | 0 | 1 | 0 | 0.0 | 5 | 3 | 4 | 3 | 1 | .250 | .295 | 0 | 0 | 2B-11 |
| 1923 | 95 | 311 | 90 | 12 | 0 | 4 | 1.3 | 40 | 35 | 26 | 10 | 20 | .289 | .367 | 10 | 4 | SS-79, OF-1 |
| 1924 | 117 | 418 | 117 | 11 | 5 | 1 | 0.2 | 66 | 27 | 40 | 20 | 15 | .280 | .337 | 7 | 2 | SS-88, 2B-19 |
| 1925 | 149 | 627 | 180 | 29 | 8 | 2 | 0.3 | 95 | 48 | 44 | 15 | 26 | .287 | .368 | 0 | 0 | 2B-144, SS-5 |
| 1926 | 154 | 624 | 193 | 35 | 3 | 0 | 0.0 | 95 | 39 | 52 | 27 | 27 | .309 | .375 | 2 | 0 | 2B-136, 3B-19, SS-2 |
| 1927 | 146 | 647 | 189 | 17 | 7 | 0 | 0.0 | 100 | 49 | 42 | 26 | 26 | .292 | .340 | 0 | 0 | 2B-60, 3B-53, SS-40 |
| 1928 PIT N | 135 | 539 | 149 | 14 | 6 | 0 | 0.0 | 91 | 38 | 64 | 18 | 8 | .276 | .325 | 1 | 0 | 2B-107, SS-27, OF-1 |
| 1929 | 74 | 196 | 51 | 8 | 1 | 0 | 0.0 | 37 | 11 | 15 | 5 | 3 | .260 | .311 | 4 | 2 | SS-30, 2B-20, 3B-15, OF-2 |
| 1930 STL N | 137 | 570 | 179 | 36 | 9 | 0 | 0.0 | 98 | 55 | 45 | 27 | 7 | .314 | .409 | 2 | 1 | 3B-104, 2B-25, SS-7 |
| 1931 | 143 | 608 | 178 | 46 | 5 | 1 | 0.2 | 97 | 40 | 42 | 24 | 16 | .293 | .390 | 1 | 0 | 3B-138, SS-6 |
| 1932 | 31 | 127 | 35 | 3 | 1 | 0 | 0.0 | 22 | 13 | 14 | 5 | 0 | .276 | .315 | 0 | 0 | 3B-30 |
| 1933 2 teams | | STL | N (8G – | .167) | | CIN | N (137G – | .262) | | | | | | | | | |
| " total | 145 | 568 | 146 | 22 | 1 | 1 | 0.2 | 60 | 22 | 45 | 33 | 3 | .257 | .305 | 0 | 0 | 3B-135, SS-13 |
| 1934 CIN N | 87 | 278 | 70 | 16 | 1 | 0 | 0.0 | 38 | 14 | 20 | 10 | 2 | .252 | .317 | 12 | 4 | 3B-38, 2B-29 |
| 13 yrs. | 1424 | 5557 | 1588 | 249 | 48 | 9 | 0.2 | 844 | 394 | 453 | 223 | 154 | .286 | .353 | 39 | 13 | 2B-551, 3B-532, SS-297, OF-4 |
| 6 yrs. | 672 | 2671 | 780 | 104 | 24 | 7 | 0.3 | 401 | 201 | 208 | 101 | 115 | .292 | .357 | 19 | 6 | 2B-370, SS-214, 3B-72, OF-1 |

| WORLD SERIES | | | | | | | | | | | | | | | | | |
|---|---|---|---|---|---|---|---|---|---|---|---|---|---|---|---|---|---|
| 1930 STL N | 6 | 21 | 3 | 0 | 0 | 0 | 0.0 | 0 | 1 | 0 | 4 | 0 | .143 | .143 | 0 | 0 | 3B-6 |
| 1931 | 2 | 4 | 1 | 0 | 0 | 0 | 0.0 | 0 | 0 | 0 | 1 | 0 | .250 | .250 | 0 | 0 | 3B-2 |
| 2 yrs. | 8 | 25 | 4 | 0 | 0 | 0 | 0.0 | 0 | 1 | 0 | 5 | 0 | .160 | .160 | 0 | 0 | 3B-8 |

## Bob Addis

**ADDIS, ROBERT GORDON**  BL  TR  6'  175 lbs.
B. Nov. 6, 1925, Mineral, Ohio

| | G | AB | H | 2B | 3B | HR | HR % | R | RBI | BB | SO | SB | BA | SA | AB | H | G by POS |
|---|---|---|---|---|---|---|---|---|---|---|---|---|---|---|---|---|---|
| 1950 BOS N | 16 | 28 | 7 | 1 | 0 | 0 | 0.0 | 7 | 2 | 3 | 5 | 1 | .250 | .286 | 10 | 1 | OF-7 |
| 1951 | 85 | 199 | 55 | 7 | 0 | 1 | 0.5 | 23 | 24 | 9 | 10 | 3 | .276 | .327 | 36 | 12 | OF-46 |
| 1952 CHI N | 93 | 292 | 86 | 13 | 2 | 1 | 0.3 | 38 | 20 | 23 | 30 | 4 | .295 | .363 | 15 | 4 | OF-76 |
| 1953 2 teams | | CHI | N (10G – | .167) | | PIT | N (4G – | .000) | | | | | | | | | |
| " total | 14 | 15 | 2 | 1 | 0 | 0 | 0.0 | 2 | 1 | 2 | 2 | 0 | .133 | .200 | 8 | 1 | OF-3 |
| 4 yrs. | 208 | 534 | 150 | 22 | 2 | 2 | 0.4 | 70 | 47 | 37 | 47 | 8 | .281 | .341 | 69 | 18 | OF-132 |
| 2 yrs. | 103 | 304 | 88 | 14 | 2 | 1 | 0.3 | 40 | 21 | 25 | 30 | 4 | .289 | .359 | 20 | 5 | OF-79 |

| | G | AB | H | 2B | 3B | HR | HR % | R | RBI | BB | SO | SB | BA | SA | Pinch Hit AB | Pinch Hit H | G by POS |
|---|---|---|---|---|---|---|---|---|---|---|---|---|---|---|---|---|---|

## Bob Addy

**ADDY, ROBERT EDWARD (The Magnet)**
B. 1838, Rochester, N. Y.    D. Apr. 10, 1910, Pocatello, Ida.
Manager 1877.

BL  TL  5'8"    160 lbs.

| | G | AB | H | 2B | 3B | HR | HR % | R | RBI | BB | SO | SB | BA | SA | AB | H | G by POS |
|---|---|---|---|---|---|---|---|---|---|---|---|---|---|---|---|---|---|
| 1876 CHI N | 32 | 142 | 40 | 4 | 1 | 0 | 0.0 | 36 | 16 | 5 | | 0 | .282 | .324 | 0 | 0 | OF-32 |
| 1877 CIN N | 57 | 245 | 68 | 2 | 3 | 0 | 0.0 | 27 | 31 | 6 | 5 | | .278 | .310 | 0 | 0 | OF-57 |
| 2 yrs. | 89 | 387 | 108 | 6 | 4 | 0 | 0.0 | 63 | 47 | 11 | 5 | | .279 | .315 | 0 | 0 | OF-89 |
| 1 yr. | 32 | 142 | 40 | 4 | 1 | 0 | 0.0 | 36 | 16 | 5 | | 0 | .282 | .324 | 0 | 0 | OF-32 |

## Matt Alexander

**ALEXANDER, MATTHEW**
B. Jan. 30, 1947, Shreveport, La.

BB  TR  5'11"    168 lbs.

| | G | AB | H | 2B | 3B | HR | HR % | R | RBI | BB | SO | SB | BA | SA | AB | H | G by POS |
|---|---|---|---|---|---|---|---|---|---|---|---|---|---|---|---|---|---|
| 1973 CHI N | 12 | 5 | 1 | 0 | 0 | 0 | 0.0 | 4 | 1 | 1 | 2 | | .200 | .200 | 1 | | OF-3 |
| 1974 | 45 | 54 | 11 | 2 | 1 | 0 | 0.0 | 15 | 0 | 12 | 12 | 8 | .204 | .278 | 11 | 3 | 3B-19, OF-4, 2B-2 |
| 1975 OAK A | 63 | 10 | 1 | 0 | 0 | 0 | 0.0 | 16 | 0 | 1 | 1 | 17 | .100 | .100 | 2 | 0 | DH-17, OF-11, 2B-3, 3B-2 |
| 1976 | 61 | 30 | 1 | 0 | 0 | 0 | 0.0 | 16 | 0 | 0 | 5 | 20 | .033 | .033 | 1 | 0 | OF-23, DH-19 |
| 1977 | 90 | 42 | 10 | 1 | 0 | 0 | 0.0 | 24 | 2 | 4 | 6 | 26 | .238 | .262 | 0 | 0 | OF-31, DH-12, SS-12, 2B-4, 3B-1 |
| 1978 PIT N | 7 | 0 | 0 | 0 | 0 | 0 | – | 2 | 0 | 0 | 0 | 4 | – | – | 0 | 0 | |
| 1979 | 44 | 13 | 7 | 0 | 1 | 0 | 0.0 | 16 | 1 | 0 | 0 | 13 | .538 | .692 | 1 | 0 | OF-11, SS-1 |
| 1980 | 37 | 3 | 1 | 1 | 0 | 0 | 0.0 | 13 | 0 | 0 | 0 | 10 | .333 | .667 | 0 | 0 | OF-4, 2B-1 |
| 1981 | 15 | 11 | 4 | 0 | 0 | 0 | 0.0 | 5 | 0 | 0 | 1 | 3 | .364 | .364 | 4 | 0 | OF-6 |
| 9 yrs. | 374 | 168 | 36 | 4 | 2 | 0 | 0.0 | 111 | 4 | 18 | 26 | 103 | .214 | .262 | 20 | 3 | OF-93, DH-48, 3B-22, SS-13, 2B-10 |
| 2 yrs. | 57 | 59 | 12 | 2 | 1 | 0 | 0.0 | 19 | 1 | 13 | 13 | 10 | .203 | .271 | 12 | 3 | 3B-19, OF-7, 2B-2 |

LEAGUE CHAMPIONSHIP SERIES

| | G | AB | H | 2B | 3B | HR | HR % | R | RBI | BB | SO | SB | BA | SA | AB | H | G by POS |
|---|---|---|---|---|---|---|---|---|---|---|---|---|---|---|---|---|---|
| 1979 PIT N | 1 | 0 | 0 | 0 | 0 | 0 | – | 1 | 0 | 0 | 0 | 0 | – | – | 0 | 0 | |

WORLD SERIES

| | G | AB | H | 2B | 3B | HR | HR % | R | RBI | BB | SO | SB | BA | SA | AB | H | G by POS |
|---|---|---|---|---|---|---|---|---|---|---|---|---|---|---|---|---|---|
| 1979 PIT N | 1 | 0 | 0 | 0 | 0 | 0 | – | 0 | 0 | 0 | 0 | 0 | – | – | 0 | 0 | OF-1 |

## Ethan Allen

**ALLEN, ETHAN NATHAN**
B. Jan. 1, 1904, Cincinnati, Ohio

BR  TR  6'1"    180 lbs.

| | G | AB | H | 2B | 3B | HR | HR % | R | RBI | BB | SO | SB | BA | SA | AB | H | G by POS |
|---|---|---|---|---|---|---|---|---|---|---|---|---|---|---|---|---|---|
| 1926 CIN N | 18 | 13 | 4 | 1 | 0 | 0 | 0.0 | 3 | 0 | 1 | 0 | 3 | .308 | .385 | 2 | 0 | OF-9 |
| 1927 | 111 | 359 | 106 | 26 | 4 | 2 | 0.6 | 54 | 20 | 14 | 23 | 12 | .295 | .407 | 2 | 1 | OF-98 |
| 1928 | 129 | 485 | 148 | 30 | 7 | 1 | 0.2 | 55 | 62 | 27 | 29 | 6 | .305 | .402 | 2 | 0 | OF-129 |
| 1929 | 143 | 538 | 157 | 27 | 11 | 6 | 1.1 | 69 | 64 | 20 | 21 | 21 | .292 | .416 | 2 | 0 | OF-137 |
| 1930 2 teams | | CIN | N (21G – | .217) | NY | N | (76G – | .307) | | | | | | | | | |
| " total | 97 | 284 | 83 | 10 | 2 | 10 | 3.5 | 58 | 38 | 17 | 25 | 6 | .292 | .447 | 18 | 5 | OF-77 |
| 1931 NY N | 94 | 298 | 98 | 18 | 2 | 5 | 1.7 | 58 | 43 | 15 | 15 | 6 | .329 | .453 | 14 | 8 | OF-77 |
| 1932 | 54 | 103 | 18 | 6 | 2 | 1 | 1.0 | 13 | 7 | 1 | 12 | 0 | .175 | .301 | 14 | 2 | OF-24 |
| 1933 STL N | 91 | 261 | 63 | 7 | 3 | 0 | 0.0 | 25 | 36 | 13 | 22 | 3 | .241 | .291 | 21 | 3 | OF-67 |
| 1934 PHI N | 145 | 581 | 192 | 42 | 4 | 10 | 1.7 | 87 | 85 | 33 | 47 | 6 | .330 | .468 | 0 | 0 | OF-145 |
| 1935 | 156 | 645 | 198 | 46 | 1 | 8 | 1.2 | 90 | 63 | 43 | 54 | 5 | .307 | .419 | 0 | 0 | OF-156 |
| 1936 2 teams | | PHI | N (30G – | .296) | CHI | N | (91G – | .295) | | | | | | | | | |
| " total | 121 | 498 | 147 | 21 | 7 | 4 | 0.8 | 68 | 48 | 17 | 38 | 16 | .295 | .390 | 0 | 0 | OF-119 |
| 1937 STL A | 103 | 320 | 101 | 18 | 1 | 0 | 0.0 | 39 | 31 | 21 | 17 | 3 | .316 | .378 | 23 | 8 | OF-78 |
| 1938 | 19 | 33 | 10 | 3 | 1 | 0 | 0.0 | 4 | 4 | 2 | 4 | 0 | .303 | .455 | 12 | 3 | OF-7 |
| 13 yrs. | 1281 | 4418 | 1325 | 255 | 45 | 47 | 1.1 | 623 | 501 | 223 | 310 | 84 | .300 | .410 | 116 | 29 | OF-1123 |
| 1 yr. | 91 | 373 | 110 | 18 | 6 | 3 | 0.8 | 47 | 39 | 13 | 30 | 12 | .295 | .399 | 0 | 0 | OF-89 |

## Nick Allen

**ALLEN, ARTEMUS WARD**
B. Sept. 14, 1888, Udall, Kans.    D. Oct. 16, 1939, Hines, Ill.

BR  TR  6'    180 lbs.

| | G | AB | H | 2B | 3B | HR | HR % | R | RBI | BB | SO | SB | BA | SA | AB | H | G by POS |
|---|---|---|---|---|---|---|---|---|---|---|---|---|---|---|---|---|---|
| 1914 BUF F | 32 | 63 | 15 | 1 | 0 | 0 | 0.0 | 3 | 4 | 3 | | 4 | .238 | .254 | 5 | 2 | C-26 |
| 1915 | 84 | 215 | 44 | 7 | 1 | 0 | 0.0 | 14 | 17 | 18 | | 4 | .205 | .247 | 4 | 1 | C-80 |
| 1916 CHI N | 5 | 16 | 1 | 0 | 0 | 0 | 0.0 | 1 | 1 | 0 | 3 | 0 | .063 | .063 | 1 | 0 | C-4 |
| 1918 CIN N | 37 | 96 | 25 | 2 | 2 | 0 | 0.0 | 6 | 5 | 4 | 7 | 0 | .260 | .323 | 4 | 3 | C-31 |
| 1919 | 15 | 25 | 8 | 0 | 1 | 0 | 0.0 | 7 | 5 | 2 | 6 | 0 | .320 | .400 | 2 | 0 | C-12 |
| 1920 | 43 | 85 | 23 | 3 | 1 | 0 | 0.0 | 10 | 4 | 6 | 11 | 0 | .271 | .329 | 6 | 2 | C-36 |
| 6 yrs. | 216 | 500 | 116 | 13 | 5 | 0 | 0.0 | 41 | 36 | 33 | 27 | 8 | .232 | .278 | 22 | 8 | C-189 |
| 1 yr. | 5 | 16 | 1 | 0 | 0 | 0 | 0.0 | 1 | 1 | 0 | 3 | 0 | .063 | .063 | 1 | 0 | C-4 |

## Milo Allison

**ALLISON, MILO HENRY (Pete)**
B. Oct. 16, 1890, Elk Rapids, Mich.    D. June 18, 1957, Kenosha, Wis.

BL  TR  6'    163 lbs.

| | G | AB | H | 2B | 3B | HR | HR % | R | RBI | BB | SO | SB | BA | SA | AB | H | G by POS |
|---|---|---|---|---|---|---|---|---|---|---|---|---|---|---|---|---|---|
| 1913 CHI N | 2 | 6 | 2 | 0 | 0 | 0 | 0.0 | 1 | 0 | 0 | 1 | 1 | .333 | .333 | 0 | 0 | OF-1 |
| 1914 | 1 | 1 | 1 | 0 | 0 | 0 | 0.0 | 0 | 0 | 0 | 0 | 0 | 1.000 | 1.000 | 1 | 1 | |
| 1916 CLE A | 14 | 18 | 5 | 0 | 0 | 0 | 0.0 | 10 | 0 | 6 | 1 | 0 | .278 | .278 | 1 | 0 | OF-5 |
| 1917 | 32 | 35 | 5 | 0 | 0 | 0 | 0.0 | 4 | 0 | 9 | 7 | 3 | .143 | .143 | 14 | 0 | OF-11 |
| 4 yrs. | 49 | 60 | 13 | 0 | 0 | 0 | 0.0 | 15 | 0 | 15 | 9 | 4 | .217 | .217 | 16 | 1 | OF-17 |
| 2 yrs. | 3 | 7 | 3 | 0 | 0 | 0 | 0.0 | 1 | 0 | 0 | 1 | 1 | .429 | .429 | 1 | 1 | OF-1 |

## George Altman

**ALTMAN, GEORGE LEE**
B. Mar. 20, 1933, Goldsboro, N. C.

BL  TR  6'4"    200 lbs.

| | G | AB | H | 2B | 3B | HR | HR % | R | RBI | BB | SO | SB | BA | SA | AB | H | G by POS |
|---|---|---|---|---|---|---|---|---|---|---|---|---|---|---|---|---|---|
| 1959 CHI N | 135 | 420 | 103 | 14 | 4 | 12 | 2.9 | 54 | 47 | 34 | 80 | 1 | .245 | .383 | 15 | 4 | OF-121 |
| 1960 | 119 | 334 | 89 | 16 | 4 | 13 | 3.9 | 50 | 51 | 32 | 67 | 4 | .266 | .455 | 20 | 8 | OF-79, 1B-21 |
| 1961 | 138 | 518 | 157 | 28 | 12 | 27 | 5.2 | 77 | 96 | 40 | 92 | 6 | .303 | .560 | 6 | 0 | OF-130, 1B-3 |
| 1962 | 147 | 534 | 170 | 27 | 5 | 22 | 4.1 | 74 | 74 | 62 | 89 | 19 | .318 | .511 | 6 | 1 | OF-129, 1B-16 |
| 1963 STL N | 135 | 464 | 127 | 18 | 7 | 9 | 1.9 | 62 | 47 | 47 | 93 | 13 | .274 | .401 | 12 | 3 | OF-124 |
| 1964 NY N | 124 | 422 | 97 | 14 | 1 | 9 | 2.1 | 48 | 47 | 18 | 70 | 4 | .230 | .332 | 18 | 6 | OF-109 |
| 1965 CHI N | 90 | 196 | 46 | 7 | 1 | 4 | 2.0 | 24 | 23 | 19 | 36 | 3 | .235 | .342 | 43 | 6 | OF-45, 1B-2 |
| 1966 | 88 | 185 | 41 | 6 | 0 | 5 | 2.7 | 19 | 17 | 14 | 37 | 2 | .222 | .335 | 44 | 9 | OF-42, 1B-4 |
| 1967 | 15 | 18 | 2 | 2 | 0 | 0 | 0.0 | 1 | 1 | 2 | 8 | 0 | .111 | .222 | 9 | 1 | OF-4, 1B-1 |
| 9 yrs. | 991 | 3091 | 832 | 132 | 34 | 101 | 3.3 | 409 | 403 | 268 | 572 | 52 | .269 | .432 | 173 | 39 | OF-783, 1B-47 |
| 7 yrs. | 732 | 2205 | 608 | 100 | 26 | 83 | 3.8 | 299 | 309 | 203 | 409 | 35 | .276 | .458 | 143 | 30 | OF-550, 1B-47 |
| | | | | | | | | | | | | | | | 5th | 7th | |

| | G | AB | H | 2B | 3B | HR | HR % | R | RBI | BB | SO | SB | BA | SA | Pinch Hit AB | Pinch Hit H | G by POS |
|---|---|---|---|---|---|---|---|---|---|---|---|---|---|---|---|---|---|

## Joey Amalfitano

**AMALFITANO, JOHN JOSEPH**      BR TR 5'11"   175 lbs.
B. Jan. 23, 1934, San Pedro, Calif.
Manager 1979-81.

| | G | AB | H | 2B | 3B | HR | HR % | R | RBI | BB | SO | SB | BA | SA | AB | H | G by POS |
|---|---|---|---|---|---|---|---|---|---|---|---|---|---|---|---|---|---|
| 1954 NY N | 9 | 5 | 0 | 0 | 0 | 0 | 0.0 | 2 | 0 | 0 | 4 | 0 | .000 | .000 | 0 | 0 | 3B-4, 2B-1 |
| 1955 | 36 | 22 | 5 | 1 | 1 | 0 | 0.0 | 8 | 1 | 2 | 2 | 0 | .227 | .364 | 4 | 0 | SS-5, 3B-2 |
| 1960 SF N | 106 | 328 | 91 | 15 | 3 | 1 | 0.3 | 47 | 27 | 26 | 31 | 2 | .277 | .351 | 13 | 5 | 3B-63, 2B-33, SS-3, OF-1 |
| 1961 | 109 | 384 | 98 | 11 | 4 | 2 | 0.5 | 64 | 23 | 44 | 59 | 7 | .255 | .320 | 12 | 4 | 2B-95, 3B-6 |
| 1962 HOU N | 117 | 380 | 90 | 12 | 5 | 1 | 0.3 | 44 | 27 | 45 | 43 | 4 | .237 | .303 | 2 | 1 | 2B-110, 3B-5 |
| 1963 SF N | 54 | 137 | 24 | 3 | 0 | 1 | 0.7 | 11 | 7 | 12 | 18 | 2 | .175 | .219 | 18 | 1 | 2B-37, 3B-7 |
| 1964 CHI N | 100 | 324 | 78 | 19 | 6 | 4 | 1.2 | 51 | 27 | 40 | 42 | 2 | .241 | .373 | 10 | 3 | 2B-86, SS-1, 1B-1 |
| 1965 | 67 | 96 | 26 | 4 | 0 | 0 | 0.0 | 13 | 8 | 12 | 14 | 2 | .271 | .313 | 37 | 8 | 2B-24, SS-4 |
| 1966 | 41 | 38 | 6 | 2 | 0 | 0 | 0.0 | 8 | 3 | 4 | 10 | 0 | .158 | .211 | 9 | 2 | 2B-12, 3B-3, SS-2 |
| 1967 | 4 | 1 | 0 | 0 | 0 | 0 | 0.0 | 0 | 0 | 0 | 1 | 0 | .000 | .000 | 0 | 0 | |
| 10 yrs. | 643 | 1715 | 418 | 67 | 19 | 9 | 0.5 | 248 | 123 | 185 | 224 | 19 | .244 | .321 | 106 | 24 | 2B-398, 3B-90, SS-15, OF-1, 1B-1 |
| 4 yrs. | 212 | 459 | 110 | 25 | 6 | 4 | 0.9 | 72 | 38 | 56 | 67 | 4 | .240 | .346 | 57 | 13 | 2B-122, SS-7, 3B-3, 1B-1 |

## Jim Andrews

**ANDREWS, JAMES PRATT**
B. June 5, 1865, Shelburne Falls, Mass.   D. Dec. 27, 1907, Chicago, Ill.

| | G | AB | H | 2B | 3B | HR | HR % | R | RBI | BB | SO | SB | BA | SA | AB | H | G by POS |
|---|---|---|---|---|---|---|---|---|---|---|---|---|---|---|---|---|---|
| 1890 CHI N | 53 | 202 | 38 | 4 | 2 | 3 | 1.5 | 32 | 17 | 23 | 41 | 11 | .188 | .272 | 0 | 0 | OF-53 |

## Fred Andrus

**ANDRUS, FREDERICK HOTHAM**      BR TR 6'2"   185 lbs.
B. Aug. 23, 1850, Washington, Mich.   D. Nov. 10, 1937, Detroit, Mich.

| | G | AB | H | 2B | 3B | HR | HR % | R | RBI | BB | SO | SB | BA | SA | AB | H | G by POS |
|---|---|---|---|---|---|---|---|---|---|---|---|---|---|---|---|---|---|
| 1876 CHI N | 8 | 36 | 11 | 3 | 0 | 0 | 0.0 | 6 | 2 | 0 | 5 | | .306 | .389 | 0 | 0 | OF-8 |
| 1884 | 1 | 5 | 1 | 0 | 0 | 0 | 0.0 | 3 | | 1 | 0 | | .200 | .200 | 0 | 0 | P-1 |
| 2 yrs. | 9 | 41 | 12 | 3 | 0 | 0 | 0.0 | 9 | 2 | 1 | 5 | | .293 | .366 | 0 | 0 | OF-8, P-1 |
| 2 yrs. | 9 | 41 | 12 | 3 | 0 | 0 | 0.0 | 9 | 2 | 1 | 5 | | .293 | .366 | 0 | 0 | OF-8, P-1 |

## Tom Angley

**ANGLEY, THOMAS SAMUEL**      BL TR 5'8"   190 lbs.
B. Oct. 2, 1904, Baltimore, Md.   D. Oct. 26, 1952, Wichita, Kans.

| | G | AB | H | 2B | 3B | HR | HR % | R | RBI | BB | SO | SB | BA | SA | AB | H | G by POS |
|---|---|---|---|---|---|---|---|---|---|---|---|---|---|---|---|---|---|
| 1929 CHI N | 5 | 16 | 4 | 1 | 0 | 0 | 0.0 | 1 | 6 | 2 | 2 | 0 | .250 | .313 | 0 | 0 | C-5 |

## Cap Anson

**ANSON, ADRIAN CONSTANTINE (Pop)**      BR TR 6'2"   202 lbs.
B. Apr. 17, 1852, Marshalltown, Iowa   D. Apr. 14, 1922, Chicago, Ill.
Manager 1879-98.
Hall of Fame 1939.

| | G | AB | H | 2B | 3B | HR | HR % | R | RBI | BB | SO | SB | BA | SA | AB | H | G by POS |
|---|---|---|---|---|---|---|---|---|---|---|---|---|---|---|---|---|---|
| 1876 CHI N | 66 | 309 | 110 | 13 | 7 | 1 | 0.3 | 63 | 59 | 12 | 8 | | .356 | .453 | 0 | 0 | 3B-66, C-2 |
| 1877 | 59 | 255 | 86 | 19 | 1 | 0 | 0.0 | 52 | 32 | 9 | 3 | | .337 | .420 | 0 | 0 | 3B-40, C-31 |
| 1878 | 60 | 261 | 89 | 12 | 0 | 0 | 0.0 | 55 | 40 | 13 | 1 | | .341 | .402 | 0 | 0 | OF-48, 2B-9, 3B-3, C-3 |
| 1879 | 51 | 227 | 90 | 20 | 1 | 0 | 0.0 | 40 | 34 | 2 | 2 | | .396 | .493 | 0 | 0 | 1B-51 |
| 1880 | 86 | 356 | 120 | 24 | 1 | 1 | 0.3 | 54 | 74 | 14 | 12 | | .337 | .419 | 0 | 0 | 1B-81, 3B-9, SS-1, 2B-1 |
| 1881 | 84 | 343 | 137 | 21 | 7 | 1 | 0.3 | 67 | 82 | 26 | 4 | | .399 | .510 | 0 | 0 | 1B-84, C-2, SS-1 |
| 1882 | 82 | 348 | 126 | 29 | 8 | 1 | 0.3 | 69 | 83 | 20 | 7 | | .362 | .500 | 0 | 0 | 1B-82, C-1 |
| 1883 | 98 | 413 | 127 | 36 | 5 | 0 | 0.0 | 70 | | 18 | 9 | | .308 | .419 | 0 | 0 | 1B-98, P-2, OF-1, C-1 |
| 1884 | 112 | 475 | 159 | 30 | 3 | 21 | 4.4 | 108 | | 29 | 13 | | .335 | .543 | 0 | 0 | 1B-112, C-3, SS-1, P-1 |
| 1885 | 112 | 464 | 144 | 35 | 7 | 7 | 1.5 | 100 | 114 | 34 | 13 | | .310 | .461 | 0 | 0 | 1B-112, C-1 |
| 1886 | 125 | 504 | 187 | 35 | 11 | 10 | 2.0 | 117 | 147 | 55 | 19 | 29 | .371 | .544 | 0 | 0 | 1B-125, C-12 |
| 1887 | 122 | 472 | 164 | 33 | 13 | 7 | 1.5 | 107 | 102 | 60 | 18 | 27 | .347 | .517 | 0 | 0 | 1B-122, C-1 |
| 1888 | 134 | 515 | 177 | 20 | 12 | 12 | 2.3 | 101 | 84 | 47 | 24 | 28 | .344 | .499 | 0 | 0 | 1B-134 |
| 1889 | 134 | 518 | 177 | 32 | 7 | 7 | 1.4 | 100 | 117 | 86 | 19 | 27 | .342 | .471 | 0 | 0 | 1B-134 |
| 1890 | 139 | 504 | 157 | 14 | 5 | 7 | 1.4 | 95 | 107 | 113 | 23 | 29 | .312 | .401 | 0 | 0 | 1B-135, C-3, 2B-2 |
| 1891 | 136 | 540 | 157 | 24 | 8 | 8 | 1.5 | 81 | 120 | 75 | 29 | 17 | .291 | .409 | 0 | 0 | 1B-136, C-2 |
| 1892 | 146 | 559 | 152 | 25 | 9 | 1 | 0.2 | 62 | 74 | 67 | 30 | 13 | .272 | .354 | 0 | 0 | 1B-146 |
| 1893 | 103 | 398 | 125 | 24 | 2 | 0 | 0.0 | 70 | 91 | 68 | 12 | 13 | .314 | .384 | 1 | 1 | 1B-101 |
| 1894 | 83 | 347 | 137 | 28 | 4 | 5 | 1.4 | 82 | 99 | 40 | 15 | 17 | .395 | .542 | 0 | 0 | 1B-82, 2B-1 |
| 1895 | 122 | 474 | 159 | 23 | 6 | 2 | 0.4 | 87 | 91 | 55 | 23 | 12 | .335 | .422 | 0 | 0 | 1B-122 |
| 1896 | 108 | 402 | 133 | 18 | 2 | 2 | 0.5 | 72 | 90 | 49 | 10 | 24 | .331 | .400 | 1 | 0 | 1B-98, C-10 |
| 1897 | 114 | 424 | 128 | 17 | 3 | 3 | 0.7 | 67 | 75 | 60 | | 11 | .302 | .377 | 0 | 0 | 1B-103, C-11 |
| 22 yrs. | 2276 | 9108 | 3041 | 532 | 124 | 96 | 1.1 | 1719 | 1715 | 952 | 294 | 247 | .334 | .451 | 2 | 1 | 1B-2058, 3B-118, C-83, OF-49, 2B-13, SS-3, P-3 |
| 22 yrs. | 2276 | 9108 | 3041 | 532 | 124 | 96 | 1.1 | 1719 | 1715 | 952 | 294 | 247 | .334 | .451 | 2 | 1 | 1B-2058, 3B-118, C-83, OF-49, 2B-13, SS-3, P-3 |
| | **2nd** | **2nd** | **1st** | **1st** | **2nd** | | | **1st** | **1st** | **3rd** | | **2nd** | | | | | |

## Jimmy Archer

**ARCHER, JAMES PETER**      BR TR 5'10"   168 lbs.
B. May 13, 1883, Dublin, Ireland   D. Mar. 29, 1958, Milwaukee, Wis.

| | G | AB | H | 2B | 3B | HR | HR % | R | RBI | BB | SO | SB | BA | SA | AB | H | G by POS |
|---|---|---|---|---|---|---|---|---|---|---|---|---|---|---|---|---|---|
| 1904 PIT N | 7 | 20 | 3 | 0 | 0 | 0 | 0.0 | 1 | 1 | 0 | | 0 | .150 | .150 | 0 | 0 | C-7, OF-1 |
| 1907 DET A | 18 | 42 | 5 | 0 | 0 | 0 | 0.0 | 6 | 0 | 4 | | 0 | .119 | .119 | 0 | 0 | C-17, 2B-1 |
| 1909 CHI N | 80 | 261 | 60 | 9 | 2 | 1 | 0.4 | 31 | 30 | 12 | | 5 | .230 | .291 | 0 | 0 | C-80 |
| 1910 | 98 | 313 | 81 | 17 | 6 | 2 | 0.6 | 36 | 41 | 14 | 49 | 6 | .259 | .371 | 8 | 3 | C-49, 1B-40 |
| 1911 | 116 | 387 | 98 | 18 | 5 | 4 | 1.0 | 41 | 41 | 18 | 43 | 5 | .253 | .357 | 3 | 0 | C-102, 1B-10, 2B-1 |
| 1912 | 120 | 385 | 109 | 20 | 2 | 5 | 1.3 | 35 | 58 | 22 | 36 | 7 | .283 | .384 | 1 | 0 | C-118 |
| 1913 | 110 | 367 | 98 | 14 | 7 | 2 | 0.5 | 38 | 44 | 19 | 27 | 4 | .267 | .360 | 3 | 1 | C-103, 1B-8 |
| 1914 | 79 | 248 | 64 | 9 | 2 | 0 | 0.0 | 17 | 19 | 9 | 9 | 1 | .258 | .310 | 3 | 1 | C-76 |
| 1915 | 97 | 309 | 75 | 11 | 5 | 1 | 0.3 | 21 | 27 | 11 | 38 | 5 | .243 | .320 | 5 | 2 | C-88 |
| 1916 | 77 | 205 | 45 | 6 | 2 | 1 | 0.5 | 11 | 30 | 12 | 24 | 3 | .220 | .283 | 16 | 2 | C-65, 3B-1 |
| 1917 | 2 | 2 | 0 | 0 | 0 | 0 | 0.0 | 0 | 0 | 0 | 1 | 0 | .000 | .000 | 2 | 0 | |
| 1918 3 teams | PIT N (24G – .155) | | BKN N (9G – .273) | | | CIN N (9G – .269) | | | | | | | | | | | |
| " total | 42 | 106 | 22 | 2 | 2 | 0 | 0.0 | 10 | 5 | 3 | 14 | 0 | .208 | .283 | 5 | 1 | C-35, 1B-2 |
| 12 yrs. | 846 | 2645 | 660 | 106 | 34 | 16 | 0.6 | 247 | 296 | 124 | 241 | 36 | .250 | .333 | 46 | 10 | C-740, 1B-60, 2B-2, OF-1, 3B-1 |
| 9 yrs. | 779 | 2477 | 630 | 104 | 31 | 16 | 0.6 | 230 | 290 | 117 | 227 | 36 | .254 | .341 | 41 | 9 | C-681, 1B-58, 3B-1, 2B-1 |

| | G | AB | H | 2B | 3B | HR | HR % | R | RBI | BB | SO | SB | BA | SA | Pinch Hit AB | Pinch Hit H | G by POS |
|---|---|---|---|---|---|---|---|---|---|---|---|---|---|---|---|---|---|

## Jimmy Archer continued

WORLD SERIES

| | G | AB | H | 2B | 3B | HR | HR % | R | RBI | BB | SO | SB | BA | SA | AB | H | G by POS |
|---|---|---|---|---|---|---|---|---|---|---|---|---|---|---|---|---|---|
| 1907 DET A | 1 | 3 | 0 | 0 | 0 | 0 | 0.0 | 0 | 0 | 0 | 1 | 0 | .000 | .000 | 0 | 0 | C-1 |
| 1910 CHI N | 3 | 11 | 2 | 1 | 0 | 0 | 0.0 | 1 | 0 | 0 | 4 | 0 | .182 | .273 | 0 | 0 | 1B-1 |
| 2 yrs. | 4 | 14 | 2 | 1 | 0 | 0 | 0.0 | 1 | 0 | 0 | 5 | 0 | .143 | .214 | 0 | 0 | 1B-1, C-1 |

## Jose Arcia

ARCIA, JOSE RAIMUNDO ORTA (Flaco)    BR TR 6'3"    170 lbs.
B. Aug. 22, 1943, Havana, Cuba

| | G | AB | H | 2B | 3B | HR | HR % | R | RBI | BB | SO | SB | BA | SA | AB | H | G by POS |
|---|---|---|---|---|---|---|---|---|---|---|---|---|---|---|---|---|---|
| 1968 CHI N | 59 | 84 | 16 | 4 | 0 | 1 | 1.2 | 15 | 8 | 3 | 24 | 0 | .190 | .274 | 5 | 1 | OF-17, 2B-10, SS-7, 3B-1 |
| 1969 SD N | 120 | 302 | 65 | 11 | 3 | 0 | 0.0 | 35 | 10 | 14 | 47 | 14 | .215 | .272 | 0 | 0 | 2B-68, SS-37, 3B-8, OF-4, 1B-1 |
| 1970 | 114 | 229 | 51 | 9 | 3 | 0 | 0.0 | 28 | 17 | 12 | 36 | 3 | .223 | .288 | 1 | 0 | SS-67, 2B-20, 3B-9, OF-7 |
| 3 yrs. | 293 | 615 | 132 | 24 | 6 | 1 | 0.2 | 78 | 35 | 29 | 107 | 17 | .215 | .278 | 6 | 1 | SS-111, 2B-98, OF-28, 3B-18, 1B-1 |
| 1 yr. | 59 | 84 | 16 | 4 | 0 | 1 | 1.2 | 15 | 8 | 3 | 24 | 0 | .190 | .274 | 5 | 1 | OF-17, 2B-10, SS-7, 3B-1 |

## Jim Asbell

ASBELL, JAMES MARION    BR TR 6'    210 lbs.
B. June 22, 1914, Dallas, Tex.    D. July 6, 1967, San Mateo, Calif.

| | G | AB | H | 2B | 3B | HR | HR % | R | RBI | BB | SO | SB | BA | SA | AB | H | G by POS |
|---|---|---|---|---|---|---|---|---|---|---|---|---|---|---|---|---|---|
| 1938 CHI N | 17 | 33 | 6 | 2 | 0 | 0 | 0.0 | 6 | 3 | 3 | 9 | 0 | .182 | .242 | 6 | 3 | OF-17 |

## Richie Ashburn

ASHBURN, DON RICHARD (Whitey)    BL TR 5'10"    170 lbs.
B. Mar. 19, 1927, Tilden, Neb.

| | G | AB | H | 2B | 3B | HR | HR % | R | RBI | BB | SO | SB | BA | SA | AB | H | G by POS |
|---|---|---|---|---|---|---|---|---|---|---|---|---|---|---|---|---|---|
| 1948 PHI N | 117 | 463 | 154 | 17 | 4 | 2 | 0.4 | 78 | 40 | 60 | 22 | 32 | .333 | .400 | 1 | 0 | OF-116 |
| 1949 | 154 | 662 | 188 | 18 | 11 | 1 | 0.2 | 84 | 37 | 58 | 38 | 9 | .284 | .349 | 0 | 0 | OF-154 |
| 1950 | 151 | 594 | 180 | 25 | 14 | 2 | 0.3 | 84 | 41 | 63 | 32 | 14 | .303 | .402 | 2 | 0 | OF-147 |
| 1951 | 154 | 643 | 221 | 31 | 5 | 4 | 0.6 | 92 | 63 | 50 | 37 | 29 | .344 | .426 | 0 | 0 | OF-154 |
| 1952 | 154 | 613 | 173 | 31 | 6 | 1 | 0.2 | 93 | 42 | 75 | 30 | 16 | .282 | .357 | 1 | 1 | OF-154 |
| 1953 | 156 | 622 | 205 | 25 | 9 | 2 | 0.3 | 110 | 57 | 61 | 35 | 14 | .330 | .408 | 0 | 0 | OF-156 |
| 1954 | 153 | 559 | 175 | 16 | 8 | 1 | 0.2 | 111 | 41 | 125 | 46 | 11 | .313 | .376 | 0 | 0 | OF-153 |
| 1955 | 140 | 533 | 180 | 32 | 9 | 3 | 0.6 | 91 | 42 | 105 | 36 | 12 | .338 | .448 | 1 | 1 | OF-140 |
| 1956 | 154 | 628 | 190 | 26 | 8 | 3 | 0.5 | 94 | 50 | 79 | 45 | 10 | .303 | .384 | 0 | 0 | OF-154 |
| 1957 | 156 | 626 | 186 | 26 | 8 | 0 | 0.0 | 93 | 33 | 94 | 44 | 13 | .297 | .364 | 0 | 0 | OF-156 |
| 1958 | 152 | 615 | 215 | 24 | 13 | 2 | 0.3 | 98 | 33 | 97 | 48 | 30 | .350 | .441 | 0 | 0 | OF-152 |
| 1959 | 153 | 564 | 150 | 16 | 2 | 1 | 0.2 | 86 | 20 | 79 | 42 | 9 | .266 | .307 | 4 | 1 | OF-149 |
| 1960 CHI N | 151 | 547 | 159 | 16 | 5 | 0 | 0.0 | 99 | 40 | 116 | 50 | 16 | .291 | .338 | 6 | 1 | OF-146 |
| 1961 | 109 | 307 | 79 | 7 | 4 | 0 | 0.0 | 49 | 19 | 55 | 27 | 7 | .257 | .306 | 34 | 10 | OF-76 |
| 1962 NY N | 135 | 389 | 119 | 7 | 3 | 7 | 1.8 | 60 | 28 | 81 | 39 | 12 | .306 | .393 | 31 | 13 | OF-97, 2B-2 |
| 15 yrs. | 2189 | 8365 | 2574 | 317 | 109 | 29 | 0.3 | 1322 | 586 | 1198 | 571 | 234 | .308 | .382 | 80 | 27 | OF-2104, 2B-2 |
| 2 yrs. | 260 | 854 | 238 | 23 | 9 | 0 | 0.0 | 148 | 59 | 171 | 77 | 23 | .279 | .327 | 40 | 11 | OF-222 |

WORLD SERIES

| | G | AB | H | 2B | 3B | HR | HR % | R | RBI | BB | SO | SB | BA | SA | AB | H | G by POS |
|---|---|---|---|---|---|---|---|---|---|---|---|---|---|---|---|---|---|
| 1950 PHI N | 4 | 17 | 3 | 1 | 0 | 0 | 0.0 | 0 | 1 | 0 | 4 | 0 | .176 | .235 | 0 | 0 | OF-4 |

## Ken Aspromonte

ASPROMONTE, KENNETH JOSEPH    BR TR 6'    180 lbs.
Brother of Bob Aspromonte.
B. Sept. 22, 1931, Brooklyn, N. Y.
Manager 1972-74.

| | G | AB | H | 2B | 3B | HR | HR % | R | RBI | BB | SO | SB | BA | SA | AB | H | G by POS |
|---|---|---|---|---|---|---|---|---|---|---|---|---|---|---|---|---|---|
| 1957 BOS A | 24 | 78 | 21 | 5 | 0 | 0 | 0.0 | 9 | 4 | 17 | 10 | 0 | .269 | .333 | 0 | 0 | 2B-24 |
| 1958 2 teams | | BOS | A (6G – | .125) | | | WAS | A (92G – | .225) | | | | | | | | |
| " total | 98 | 269 | 59 | 9 | 1 | 5 | 1.9 | 15 | 27 | 28 | 29 | 1 | .219 | .316 | 9 | 2 | 2B-78, 3B-11, SS-1 |
| 1959 WAS A | 70 | 225 | 55 | 12 | 0 | 2 | 0.9 | 31 | 14 | 26 | 39 | 2 | .244 | .324 | 5 | 0 | 2B-52, SS-12, OF-1, 1B-1 |
| 1960 2 teams | | WAS | A (4G – | .000) | | | CLE | A (117G – | .290) | | | | | | | | |
| " total | 121 | 462 | 133 | 20 | 1 | 10 | 2.2 | 65 | 48 | 53 | 34 | 4 | .288 | .400 | 6 | 0 | 2B-80, 3B-36 |
| 1961 2 teams | | LA | A (66G – | .223) | | | CLE | A (22G – | .229) | | | | | | | | |
| " total | 88 | 308 | 69 | 16 | 1 | 2 | 0.6 | 34 | 19 | 39 | 24 | 0 | .224 | .302 | 3 | 1 | 2B-83 |
| 1962 2 teams | | CLE | A (20G – | .143) | | | MIL | N (34G – | .291) | | | | | | | | |
| " total | 54 | 107 | 27 | 4 | 0 | 0 | 0.0 | 15 | 8 | 12 | 10 | 0 | .252 | .290 | 21 | 5 | 2B-18, 3B-9 |
| 1963 CHI N | 20 | 34 | 5 | 3 | 0 | 0 | 0.0 | 2 | 4 | 4 | 4 | 0 | .147 | .235 | 8 | 0 | 2B-7, 1B-2 |
| 7 yrs. | 475 | 1483 | 369 | 69 | 3 | 19 | 1.3 | 171 | 124 | 179 | 150 | 7 | .249 | .338 | 52 | 8 | 2B-342, 3B-56, SS-13, 1B-3, OF-1 |
| 1 yr. | 20 | 34 | 5 | 3 | 0 | 0 | 0.0 | 2 | 4 | 4 | 4 | 0 | .147 | .235 | 8 | 0 | 2B-7, 1B-2 |

## Toby Atwell

ATWELL, MAURICE DAILEY    BL TR 5'9½"    185 lbs.
B. Mar. 8, 1924, Leesburg, Va.

| | G | AB | H | 2B | 3B | HR | HR % | R | RBI | BB | SO | SB | BA | SA | AB | H | G by POS |
|---|---|---|---|---|---|---|---|---|---|---|---|---|---|---|---|---|---|
| 1952 CHI N | 107 | 362 | 105 | 16 | 3 | 2 | 0.6 | 36 | 31 | 40 | 22 | 2 | .290 | .367 | 5 | 0 | C-101 |
| 1953 2 teams | | CHI | N (24G – | .230) | | | PIT | N (53G – | .245) | | | | | | | | |
| " total | 77 | 213 | 51 | 8 | 1 | 1 | 0.5 | 21 | 25 | 33 | 19 | 0 | .239 | .291 | 11 | 2 | C-68 |
| 1954 PIT N | 96 | 287 | 83 | 8 | 4 | 3 | 1.0 | 36 | 26 | 43 | 21 | 2 | .289 | .376 | 8 | 4 | C-88 |
| 1955 | 71 | 207 | 44 | 8 | 0 | 1 | 0.5 | 21 | 18 | 40 | 16 | 0 | .213 | .266 | 6 | 2 | C-67 |
| 1956 2 teams | | PIT | N (12G – | .111) | | | MIL | N (15G – | .167) | | | | | | | | |
| " total | 27 | 48 | 7 | 1 | 0 | 2 | 4.2 | 2 | 10 | 5 | 6 | 0 | .146 | .292 | 7 | 0 | C-19 |
| 5 yrs. | 378 | 1117 | 290 | 41 | 7 | 9 | 0.8 | 116 | 110 | 161 | 84 | 4 | .260 | .333 | 37 | 6 | C-343 |
| 2 yrs. | 131 | 436 | 122 | 18 | 3 | 3 | 0.7 | 46 | 39 | 53 | 29 | 2 | .280 | .356 | 6 | 0 | C-125 |

## Earl Averill

AVERILL, EARL DOUGLAS    BR TR 5'10"    185 lbs.
Son of Earl Averill.
B. Sept. 9, 1931, Cleveland, Ohio

| | G | AB | H | 2B | 3B | HR | HR % | R | RBI | BB | SO | SB | BA | SA | AB | H | G by POS |
|---|---|---|---|---|---|---|---|---|---|---|---|---|---|---|---|---|---|
| 1956 CLE A | 42 | 93 | 22 | 6 | 0 | 3 | 3.2 | 12 | 14 | 14 | 25 | 0 | .237 | .398 | 8 | 2 | C-34 |
| 1958 | 17 | 55 | 10 | 1 | 0 | 2 | 3.6 | 2 | 7 | 4 | 7 | 1 | .182 | .309 | 0 | 0 | 3B-17 |
| 1959 CHI N | 74 | 186 | 44 | 10 | 0 | 10 | 5.4 | 22 | 34 | 15 | 39 | 0 | .237 | .452 | 25 | 10 | C-32, 3B-13, OF-5, 2B-2 |

| | G | AB | H | 2B | 3B | HR | HR % | R | RBI | BB | SO | SB | BA | SA | Pinch Hit AB | Pinch Hit H | G by POS |
|---|---|---|---|---|---|---|---|---|---|---|---|---|---|---|---|---|---|

## Earl Averill continued

| | | G | AB | H | 2B | 3B | HR | HR % | R | RBI | BB | SO | SB | BA | SA | AB | H | G by POS |
|---|---|---|---|---|---|---|---|---|---|---|---|---|---|---|---|---|---|---|
| 1960 | **2 teams** | | **CHI** | **N** | (52G – | .235) | | **CHI** | **A** | (10G – | .214) | | | | | | | |
| " | total | 62 | 116 | 27 | 4 | 0 | 1 | 0.9 | 16 | 15 | 15 | 18 | 1 | .233 | .293 | 30 | 6 | C-39, OF-1, 3B-1 |
| 1961 | LA A | 115 | 323 | 86 | 9 | 0 | 21 | 6.5 | 56 | 59 | 62 | 70 | 1 | .266 | .489 | 21 | 7 | C-88, OF-9, 2B-1 |
| 1962 | | 92 | 187 | 41 | 9 | 0 | 4 | 2.1 | 21 | 22 | 43 | 47 | 0 | .219 | .332 | 34 | 7 | OF-49, C-6 |
| 1963 | PHI N | 47 | 71 | 19 | 2 | 0 | 3 | 4.2 | 8 | 8 | 9 | 14 | 0 | .268 | .423 | 24 | 4 | C-20, OF-8, 3B-1, 1B-1 |
| 7 yrs. | | 449 | 1031 | 249 | 41 | 0 | 44 | 4.3 | 137 | 159 | 162 | 220 | 3 | .242 | .409 | 142 | 36 | C-219, OF-72, 3B-32, 2B-3, 1B-1 |
| 2 yrs. | | 126 | 288 | 68 | 14 | 0 | 11 | 3.8 | 36 | 47 | 26 | 55 | 1 | .236 | .399 | 50 | 15 | C-66, 3B-14, OF-6, 2B-2 |

## Ed Bailey

**BAILEY, LONAS EDGAR**
Brother of Jim Bailey.
B. Apr. 15, 1931, Strawberry Plains, Tenn.                                BL  TR  6'2"    205 lbs.

| | | G | AB | H | 2B | 3B | HR | HR % | R | RBI | BB | SO | SB | BA | SA | AB | H | G by POS |
|---|---|---|---|---|---|---|---|---|---|---|---|---|---|---|---|---|---|---|
| 1953 | CIN N | 2 | 8 | 3 | 1 | 0 | 0 | 0.0 | 1 | 1 | 1 | 3 | 0 | .375 | .500 | 0 | 0 | C-2 |
| 1954 | | 73 | 183 | 36 | 2 | 3 | 9 | 4.9 | 21 | 20 | 35 | 34 | 1 | .197 | .388 | 12 | 0 | C-61 |
| 1955 | | 21 | 39 | 8 | 1 | 1 | 1 | 2.6 | 3 | 4 | 4 | 10 | 0 | .205 | .359 | 9 | 3 | C-11 |
| 1956 | | 118 | 383 | 115 | 8 | 2 | 28 | 7.3 | 59 | 75 | 52 | 50 | 2 | .300 | .551 | 13 | 8 | C-106 |
| 1957 | | 122 | 391 | 102 | 15 | 2 | 20 | 5.1 | 54 | 48 | 73 | 69 | 5 | .261 | .463 | 6 | 2 | C-115 |
| 1958 | | 112 | 360 | 90 | 23 | 1 | 11 | 3.1 | 39 | 59 | 47 | 61 | 2 | .250 | .411 | 11 | 1 | C-99 |
| 1959 | | 121 | 379 | 100 | 13 | 0 | 12 | 3.2 | 43 | 40 | 62 | 53 | 2 | .264 | .393 | 8 | 2 | C-117 |
| 1960 | | 133 | 441 | 115 | 19 | 3 | 13 | 2.9 | 52 | 67 | 59 | 70 | 1 | .261 | .406 | 9 | 2 | C-129 |
| 1961 | **2 teams** | 119 | **CIN** | **N** | (12G – | .302) | | **SF** | **N** | (107G – | .238) | | | | | | | |
| " | total | 119 | 383 | 94 | 13 | 1 | 13 | 3.4 | 43 | 53 | 45 | 46 | 1 | .245 | .386 | 9 | 5 | C-115, OF-1 |
| 1962 | SF N | 96 | 254 | 59 | 9 | 1 | 17 | 6.7 | 32 | 45 | 42 | 42 | 1 | .232 | .476 | 18 | 6 | C-75 |
| 1963 | | 105 | 308 | 81 | 8 | 0 | 21 | 6.8 | 41 | 68 | 50 | 64 | 0 | .263 | .494 | 16 | 3 | C-88 |
| 1964 | MIL N | 95 | 271 | 71 | 10 | 1 | 5 | 1.8 | 30 | 34 | 34 | 39 | 2 | .262 | .362 | 14 | 3 | C-80 |
| 1965 | **2 teams** | 90 | **SF** | **N** | (24G – | .107) | | **CHI** | **N** | (66G – | .253) | | | | | | | |
| " | total | 90 | 178 | 41 | 6 | 0 | 5 | 2.8 | 14 | 26 | 40 | 35 | 0 | .230 | .348 | 22 | 2 | C-66, 1B-5 |
| 1966 | CAL N | 5 | 3 | 0 | 0 | 0 | 0 | 0.0 | 0 | 0 | 1 | 1 | 0 | .000 | .000 | 3 | 0 | |
| 14 yrs. | | 1212 | 3581 | 915 | 128 | 15 | 155 | 4.3 | 432 | 540 | 545 | 577 | 17 | .256 | .429 | 150 | 37 | C-1064, 1B-5, OF-1 |
| 1 yr. | | 66 | 150 | 38 | 6 | 0 | 5 | 3.3 | 13 | 23 | 34 | 28 | 0 | .253 | .393 | 14 | 1 | C-54, 1B-3 |

**WORLD SERIES**

| | | G | AB | H | 2B | 3B | HR | HR % | R | RBI | BB | SO | SB | BA | SA | AB | H | G by POS |
|---|---|---|---|---|---|---|---|---|---|---|---|---|---|---|---|---|---|---|
| 1962 | SF N | 6 | 14 | 1 | 0 | 0 | 1 | 7.1 | 1 | 2 | 0 | 3 | 0 | .071 | .286 | 2 | 0 | C-3 |

## Gene Baker

**BAKER, EUGENE WALTER**
B. June 15, 1925, Davenport, Iowa                                          BR  TR  6'1"    170 lbs.

| | | G | AB | H | 2B | 3B | HR | HR % | R | RBI | BB | SO | SB | BA | SA | AB | H | G by POS |
|---|---|---|---|---|---|---|---|---|---|---|---|---|---|---|---|---|---|---|
| 1953 | CHI N | 7 | 22 | 5 | 1 | 0 | 0 | 0.0 | 1 | 0 | 1 | 4 | 1 | .227 | .273 | 1 | 0 | 2B-6 |
| 1954 | | 135 | 541 | 149 | 32 | 5 | 13 | 2.4 | 68 | 61 | 47 | 55 | 4 | .275 | .425 | 0 | 0 | 2B-134 |
| 1955 | | 154 | 609 | 163 | 29 | 7 | 11 | 1.8 | 82 | 52 | 49 | 57 | 9 | .268 | .392 | 0 | 0 | 2B-154 |
| 1956 | | 140 | 546 | 141 | 23 | 3 | 12 | 2.2 | 65 | 57 | 39 | 54 | 4 | .258 | .377 | 0 | 0 | 2B-140 |
| 1957 | **2 teams** | | **CHI** | **N** | (12G – | .250) | | **PIT** | **N** | (111G – | .266) | | | | | | | |
| " | total | 123 | 409 | 108 | 22 | 5 | 3 | 0.7 | 40 | 46 | 35 | 32 | 3 | .264 | .364 | 16 | 3 | 3B-72, SS-28, 2B-13 |
| 1958 | PIT N | 29 | 56 | 14 | 2 | 1 | 0 | 0.0 | 3 | 7 | 8 | 6 | 0 | .250 | .321 | 14 | 6 | 3B-11, 2B-3 |
| 1960 | | 33 | 37 | 9 | 0 | 0 | 0 | 0.0 | 5 | 4 | 2 | 9 | 0 | .243 | .243 | 18 | 4 | 3B-7, 2B-1 |
| 1961 | | 9 | 10 | 1 | 0 | 0 | 0 | 0.0 | 1 | 0 | 3 | 2 | 0 | .100 | .100 | 3 | 0 | 3B-3 |
| 8 yrs. | | 630 | 2230 | 590 | 109 | 21 | 39 | 1.7 | 265 | 227 | 184 | 219 | 21 | .265 | .385 | 52 | 13 | 2B-451, 3B-93, SS-28 |
| 5 yrs. | | 448 | 1762 | 469 | 88 | 16 | 37 | 2.1 | 220 | 180 | 142 | 173 | 18 | .266 | .397 | 1 | 0 | 2B-434, 3B-12 |

**WORLD SERIES**

| | | G | AB | H | 2B | 3B | HR | HR % | R | RBI | BB | SO | SB | BA | SA | AB | H | G by POS |
|---|---|---|---|---|---|---|---|---|---|---|---|---|---|---|---|---|---|---|
| 1960 | PIT N | 3 | 3 | 0 | 0 | 0 | 0 | 0.0 | 0 | 0 | 0 | 1 | 0 | .000 | .000 | 3 | 0 | |

## Ernie Banks

**BANKS, ERNEST**
B. Jan. 31, 1931, Dallas, Tex.
Hall of Fame 1977.                                                          BR  TR  6'1"    180 lbs.

| | | G | AB | H | 2B | 3B | HR | HR % | R | RBI | BB | SO | SB | BA | SA | AB | H | G by POS |
|---|---|---|---|---|---|---|---|---|---|---|---|---|---|---|---|---|---|---|
| 1953 | CHI N | 10 | 35 | 11 | 1 | 1 | 2 | 5.7 | 3 | 6 | 4 | 5 | 0 | .314 | .571 | 0 | 0 | SS-10 |
| 1954 | | 154 | 593 | 163 | 19 | 7 | 19 | 3.2 | 70 | 79 | 40 | 50 | 6 | .275 | .427 | 0 | 0 | SS-154 |
| 1955 | | 154 | 596 | 176 | 29 | 9 | 44 | 7.4 | 98 | 117 | 45 | 72 | 9 | .295 | .596 | 0 | 0 | SS-154 |
| 1956 | | 139 | 538 | 160 | 25 | 8 | 28 | 5.2 | 82 | 85 | 52 | 62 | 6 | .297 | .530 | 0 | 0 | SS-139 |
| 1957 | | 156 | 594 | 169 | 34 | 6 | 43 | 7.2 | 113 | 102 | 70 | 85 | 8 | .285 | .579 | 0 | 0 | SS-100, 3B-58 |
| 1958 | | 154 | **617** | 193 | 23 | 11 | **47** | **7.6** | 119 | **129** | 52 | 87 | 4 | .313 | **.614** | 0 | 0 | SS-154 |
| 1959 | | 155 | 589 | 179 | 25 | 6 | 45 | 7.6 | 97 | 143 | 64 | 72 | 2 | .304 | .596 | 1 | 0 | SS-154 |
| 1960 | | 156 | 597 | 162 | 32 | 7 | 41 | 6.9 | 94 | 117 | 71 | 69 | 1 | .271 | .554 | 0 | 0 | SS-156 |
| 1961 | | 138 | 511 | 142 | 22 | 4 | 29 | 5.7 | 75 | 80 | 54 | 75 | 1 | .278 | .507 | 4 | 1 | SS-104, OF-23, 1B-7 |
| 1962 | | 154 | 610 | 164 | 20 | 6 | 37 | 6.1 | 87 | 104 | 30 | 71 | 5 | .269 | .503 | 4 | 2 | 1B-149, 3B-3 |
| 1963 | | 130 | 432 | 98 | 20 | 1 | 18 | 4.2 | 41 | 64 | 39 | 73 | 0 | .227 | .403 | 5 | 1 | 1B-125 |
| 1964 | | 157 | 591 | 156 | 29 | 6 | 23 | 3.9 | 67 | 95 | 36 | 84 | 1 | .264 | .450 | 0 | 0 | 1B-157 |
| 1965 | | 163 | 612 | 162 | 25 | 3 | 28 | 4.6 | 79 | 106 | 55 | 64 | 3 | .265 | .453 | 2 | 1 | 1B-162 |
| 1966 | | 141 | 511 | 139 | 23 | 7 | 15 | 2.9 | 52 | 75 | 29 | 59 | 0 | .272 | .432 | 8 | 1 | 1B-139, 3B-8 |
| 1967 | | 151 | 573 | 158 | 26 | 4 | 23 | 4.0 | 68 | 95 | 27 | 93 | 2 | .276 | .455 | 5 | 1 | 1B-147 |
| 1968 | | 150 | 552 | 136 | 27 | 0 | 32 | 5.8 | 71 | 83 | 27 | 67 | 2 | .246 | .469 | 4 | 1 | 1B-147 |
| 1969 | | 155 | 565 | 143 | 19 | 2 | 23 | 4.1 | 60 | 106 | 42 | 101 | 0 | .253 | .416 | 2 | 2 | 1B-153 |
| 1970 | | 72 | 222 | 56 | 6 | 2 | 12 | 5.4 | 25 | 44 | 20 | 33 | 0 | .252 | .459 | 9 | 2 | 1B-62 |
| 1971 | | 39 | 83 | 16 | 2 | 0 | 3 | 3.6 | 4 | 6 | 6 | 14 | 0 | .193 | .325 | 18 | 2 | 1B-20 |
| 19 yrs. | | 2528 | 9421 | 2583 | 407 | 90 | 512 | 5.4 | 1305 | 1636 | 763 | 1236 | 50 | .274 | .500 | 62 | 14 | 1B-1259, SS-1125, 3B-69, OF-23 |
| 19 yrs. | | 2528 | 9421 | 2583 | 407 | 90 | 512 | 5.4 | 1305 | 1636 | 763 | 1236 | 50 | .274 | .500 | 62 | 14 | 1B-1259, SS-1125, 3B-69, OF-23 |
| | | **1st** | **1st** | **1st** | **2nd** | **7th** | **1st** | | **3rd** | **2nd** | **6th** | **2nd** | | | **4th** | | | |

## Turner Barber

**BARBER, TYRUS TURNER**
B. July 9, 1893, Lavinia, Tenn.   D. Oct. 20, 1968, Milan, Tenn.            BL  TR  5'11"   170 lbs.

| | | G | AB | H | 2B | 3B | HR | HR % | R | RBI | BB | SO | SB | BA | SA | AB | H | G by POS |
|---|---|---|---|---|---|---|---|---|---|---|---|---|---|---|---|---|---|---|
| 1915 | WAS A | 20 | 53 | 16 | 1 | 1 | 0 | 0.0 | 9 | 6 | 6 | 7 | 0 | .302 | .358 | 1 | 0 | OF-19 |
| 1916 | | 15 | 33 | 7 | 0 | 1 | 1 | 3.0 | 3 | 5 | 2 | 3 | 0 | .212 | .364 | 3 | 1 | OF-9 |
| 1917 | CHI N | 7 | 28 | 6 | 1 | 0 | 0 | 0.0 | 2 | 2 | 2 | 8 | 1 | .214 | .250 | 0 | 0 | OF-7 |
| 1918 | | 55 | 123 | 29 | 3 | 2 | 0 | 0.0 | 11 | 10 | 9 | 16 | 3 | .236 | .293 | 20 | 4 | OF-27, 1B-4 |

| | G | AB | H | 2B | 3B | HR | HR % | R | RBI | BB | SO | SB | BA | SA | Pinch Hit AB | Pinch Hit H | G by POS |
|---|---|---|---|---|---|---|---|---|---|---|---|---|---|---|---|---|---|

## Turner Barber continued

| | G | AB | H | 2B | 3B | HR | HR% | R | RBI | BB | SO | SB | BA | SA | PH AB | PH H | G by POS |
|---|---|---|---|---|---|---|---|---|---|---|---|---|---|---|---|---|---|
| 1919 | 76 | 230 | 72 | 9 | 4 | 0 | 0.0 | 26 | 21 | 14 | 17 | 7 | .313 | .387 | 6 | 1 | OF-68 |
| 1920 | 94 | 340 | 90 | 10 | 5 | 0 | 0.0 | 27 | 50 | 9 | 26 | 5 | .265 | .324 | 5 | 2 | 1B-69, OF-17, 2B-2 |
| 1921 | 127 | 452 | 142 | 14 | 4 | 1 | 0.2 | 73 | 54 | 41 | 24 | 5 | .314 | .369 | 2 | 1 | OF-123 |
| 1922 | 84 | 226 | 70 | 7 | 4 | 0 | 0.0 | 35 | 29 | 30 | 9 | 7 | .310 | .376 | 19 | 2 | OF-47, 1B-16 |
| 1923 BKN N | 13 | 46 | 10 | 2 | 0 | 0 | 0.0 | 3 | 8 | 2 | 2 | 0 | .217 | .261 | 1 | 1 | OF-12 |
| 9 yrs. | 491 | 1531 | 442 | 47 | 21 | 2 | 0.1 | 189 | 185 | 115 | 112 | 28 | .289 | .351 | 57 | 12 | OF-329, 1B-89, 2B-2 |
| 6 yrs. | 443 | 1399 | 409 | 44 | 19 | 1 | 0.1 | 174 | 166 | 105 | 100 | 28 | .292 | .353 | 52 | 10 | OF-289, 1B-89, 2B-2 |

WORLD SERIES

| | G | AB | H | 2B | 3B | HR | HR% | R | RBI | BB | SO | SB | BA | SA | PH AB | PH H | G by POS |
|---|---|---|---|---|---|---|---|---|---|---|---|---|---|---|---|---|---|
| 1918 CHI N | 3 | 2 | 0 | 0 | 0 | 0 | 0.0 | 0 | 0 | | 0 | 0 | .000 | .000 | 2 | 0 | |

## Ross Barnes

**BARNES, ROSCOE CHARLES**
B. May 8, 1850, New Jersey    D. Feb. 5, 1915, Chicago, Ill.    BR TR 5'8½" 145 lbs.

| | G | AB | H | 2B | 3B | HR | HR% | R | RBI | BB | SO | SB | BA | SA | PH AB | PH H | G by POS |
|---|---|---|---|---|---|---|---|---|---|---|---|---|---|---|---|---|---|
| 1876 CHI N | 66 | 322 | 138 | 21 | 14 | 1 | 0.3 | 126 | 59 | 20 | | 8 | .429 | .590 | 0 | 0 | 2B-66, P-1 |
| 1877 | 22 | 92 | 25 | 1 | 0 | 0 | 0.0 | 16 | 5 | 7 | | 4 | .272 | .283 | 0 | 0 | 2B-22 |
| 1879 CIN N | 77 | 323 | 86 | 9 | 2 | 1 | 0.3 | 55 | 30 | 16 | | 25 | .266 | .316 | 0 | 0 | SS-61, 2B-16 |
| 1881 BOS N | 69 | 295 | 80 | 14 | 1 | 0 | 0.0 | 42 | 17 | 16 | | 16 | .271 | .325 | 0 | 0 | SS-63, 2B-7 |
| 4 yrs. | 234 | 1032 | 329 | 45 | 17 | 2 | 0.2 | 239 | 111 | 59 | | 53 | .319 | .401 | 0 | 0 | SS-124, 2B-111, P-1 |
| 2 yrs. | 88 | 414 | 163 | 22 | 14 | 1 | 0.2 | 142 | 64 | 27 | | 12 | .394 | .522 | 0 | 0 | 2B-88, P-1 |

## Cuno Barragan

**BARRAGAN, FACUNDO ANTHONY**
B. June 20, 1932, Sacramento, Calif.    BR TR 5'11" 180 lbs.

| | G | AB | H | 2B | 3B | HR | HR% | R | RBI | BB | SO | SB | BA | SA | PH AB | PH H | G by POS |
|---|---|---|---|---|---|---|---|---|---|---|---|---|---|---|---|---|---|
| 1961 CHI N | 10 | 28 | 6 | 0 | 0 | 1 | 3.6 | 3 | 2 | 2 | 7 | 0 | .214 | .321 | 0 | 0 | C-10 |
| 1962 | 58 | 134 | 27 | 6 | 1 | 0 | 0.0 | 11 | 12 | 21 | 28 | 0 | .201 | .261 | 7 | 0 | C-55 |
| 1963 | 1 | 1 | 0 | 0 | 0 | 0 | 0.0 | 0 | 0 | 0 | 1 | 0 | .000 | .000 | 0 | 0 | C-1 |
| 3 yrs. | 69 | 163 | 33 | 6 | 1 | 1 | 0.6 | 14 | 14 | 23 | 36 | 0 | .202 | .270 | 7 | 0 | C-66 |
| 3 yrs. | 69 | 163 | 33 | 6 | 1 | 1 | 0.6 | 14 | 14 | 23 | 36 | 0 | .202 | .270 | 7 | 0 | C-66 |

## Bob Barrett

**BARRETT, ROBERT SCHLEY (Jumbo)**
B. Jan. 27, 1899, Atlanta, Ga.    D. Jan. 18, 1982, Atlanta, Ga.    BR TR 5'11" 175 lbs.

| | G | AB | H | 2B | 3B | HR | HR% | R | RBI | BB | SO | SB | BA | SA | PH AB | PH H | G by POS |
|---|---|---|---|---|---|---|---|---|---|---|---|---|---|---|---|---|---|
| 1923 CHI N | 3 | 3 | 1 | 0 | 0 | 0 | 0.0 | 0 | 0 | 0 | 0 | 0 | .333 | .333 | 3 | 1 | |
| 1924 | 54 | 133 | 32 | 2 | 3 | 5 | 3.8 | 12 | 21 | 7 | 29 | 1 | .241 | .414 | 10 | 2 | 2B-25, 1B-10, 3B-8 |
| 1925 2 teams | CHI N (14G – .313) | | | BKN N (1G – .000) | | | | | | | | | | | | | |
| " total | 15 | 33 | 10 | 1 | 0 | 0 | 0.0 | 1 | 8 | 1 | 4 | 1 | .303 | .333 | 5 | 2 | 3B-6, 2B-4 |
| 1927 BKN N | 99 | 355 | 92 | 10 | 2 | 5 | 1.4 | 29 | 38 | 14 | 22 | 1 | .259 | .341 | 3 | 0 | 3B-96 |
| 1929 BOS A | 68 | 126 | 34 | 10 | 0 | 0 | 0.0 | 15 | 19 | 10 | 6 | 3 | .270 | .349 | 23 | 7 | 3B-34, 1B-4, 2B-2, OF-1 |
| 5 yrs. | 239 | 650 | 169 | 23 | 5 | 10 | 1.5 | 57 | 86 | 32 | 61 | 6 | .260 | .357 | 44 | 12 | 3B-144, 2B-31, 1B-14, OF-1 |
| 3 yrs. | 71 | 168 | 43 | 3 | 3 | 5 | 3.0 | 13 | 28 | 8 | 33 | 2 | .256 | .399 | 17 | 5 | 2B-29, 3B-14, 1B-10 |

## Shad Barry

**BARRY, JOHN C.**
B. Sept. 23, 1878, Newburgh, N.Y.    D. Nov. 27, 1936, Los Angeles, Calif.    BR TR

| | G | AB | H | 2B | 3B | HR | HR% | R | RBI | BB | SO | SB | BA | SA | PH AB | PH H | G by POS |
|---|---|---|---|---|---|---|---|---|---|---|---|---|---|---|---|---|---|
| 1899 WAS N | 78 | 247 | 71 | 7 | 5 | 1 | 0.4 | 31 | 33 | 12 | | 11 | .287 | .368 | 3 | 0 | OF-23, 1B-22, SS-13, 3B-13, 2B-7 |
| 1900 BOS N | 81 | 254 | 66 | 10 | 7 | 1 | 0.4 | 40 | 37 | 13 | | 9 | .260 | .366 | 14 | 3 | OF-24, SS-18, 2B-16, 1B-10, 3B-1 |
| 1901 2 teams | BOS N (11G – .175) | | | PHI N (67G – .246) | | | | | | | | | | | | | |
| " total | 78 | 292 | 69 | 12 | 0 | 1 | 0.3 | 38 | 28 | 17 | | 14 | .236 | .288 | 4 | 0 | 2B-35, OF-24, 3B-16, SS-1 |
| 1902 PHI N | 138 | 543 | 156 | 20 | 6 | 3 | 0.6 | 65 | 57 | 44 | | 14 | .287 | .363 | 0 | 0 | OF-137, 1B-1 |
| 1903 | 138 | 550 | 152 | 24 | 5 | 1 | 0.2 | 75 | 60 | 30 | | 26 | .276 | .344 | 0 | 0 | OF-107, 1B-30, 3B-1 |
| 1904 2 teams | PHI N (35G – .205) | | | CHI N (73G – .262) | | | | | | | | | | | | | |
| " total | 108 | 385 | 94 | 9 | 2 | 1 | 0.3 | 44 | 29 | 28 | | 14 | .244 | .286 | 3 | 0 | OF-62, 1B-18, 3B-17, SS-8, 2B-2 |
| 1905 2 teams | CHI N (27G – .212) | | | CIN N (125G – .324) | | | | | | | | | | | | | |
| " total | 152 | 598 | 182 | 13 | 12 | 1 | 0.2 | 100 | 66 | 38 | | 21 | .304 | .371 | 1 | 0 | 1B-149, OF-2 |
| 1906 2 teams | CIN N (73G – .287) | | | STL N (62G – .249) | | | | | | | | | | | | | |
| " total | 135 | 516 | 139 | 19 | 6 | 1 | 0.2 | 64 | 45 | 41 | | 17 | .269 | .335 | 0 | 0 | OF-65, 1B-64, 3B-6 |
| 1907 STL N | 80 | 292 | 72 | 14 | 2 | 0 | 0.0 | 35 | 19 | 28 | | 4 | .247 | .277 | 0 | 0 | OF-81 |
| 1908 2 teams | STL N (74G – .228) | | | NY N (37G – .149) | | | | | | | | | | | | | |
| " total | 111 | 335 | 71 | 9 | 2 | 0 | 0.0 | 29 | 16 | 28 | | 10 | .212 | .251 | 7 | 1 | OF-100, SS-2 |
| 10 yrs. | 1099 | 4012 | 1072 | 128 | 47 | 10 | 0.2 | 516 | 390 | 279 | | 140 | .267 | .330 | 32 | 4 | OF-625, 1B-294, 2B-60, 3B-54, SS-42 |
| 2 yrs. | 100 | 367 | 91 | 9 | 3 | 1 | 0.3 | 39 | 36 | 22 | | 17 | .248 | .292 | 2 | 0 | 1B-44, OF-30, 3B-16, SS-8, 2B-2 |

## Dick Bartell

**BARTELL, RICHARD WILLIAM (Rowdy Richard)**
B. Nov. 22, 1907, Chicago, Ill.    BR TR 5'9" 160 lbs.

| | G | AB | H | 2B | 3B | HR | HR% | R | RBI | BB | SO | SB | BA | SA | PH AB | PH H | G by POS |
|---|---|---|---|---|---|---|---|---|---|---|---|---|---|---|---|---|---|
| 1927 PIT N | 1 | 2 | 0 | 0 | 0 | 0 | 0.0 | 0 | 0 | 0 | 0 | 0 | .000 | .000 | 0 | 0 | SS-1 |
| 1928 | 72 | 233 | 71 | 8 | 4 | 1 | 0.4 | 27 | 36 | 21 | 18 | 4 | .305 | .386 | 2 | 0 | 2B-39, SS-27, 3B-1 |
| 1929 | 143 | 610 | 184 | 40 | 13 | 2 | 0.3 | 101 | 57 | 40 | 29 | 11 | .302 | .420 | 0 | 0 | SS-97, 2B-70 |
| 1930 | 129 | 475 | 152 | 32 | 13 | 4 | 0.8 | 69 | 75 | 39 | 34 | 8 | .320 | .467 | 3 | 0 | SS-126 |
| 1931 PHI N | 135 | 554 | 160 | 43 | 7 | 0 | 0.0 | 88 | 34 | 27 | 38 | 6 | .289 | .392 | 0 | 0 | SS-133, 2B-3 |
| 1932 | 154 | 614 | 189 | 48 | 7 | 1 | 0.2 | 118 | 53 | 64 | 47 | 8 | .308 | .414 | 0 | 0 | SS-154 |
| 1933 | 152 | 587 | 159 | 25 | 5 | 1 | 0.2 | 78 | 37 | 56 | 46 | 6 | .271 | .336 | 0 | 0 | SS-152 |
| 1934 | 146 | 604 | 187 | 30 | 4 | 0 | 0.0 | 102 | 37 | 64 | 59 | 13 | .310 | .373 | 0 | 0 | SS-146 |
| 1935 NY N | 137 | 539 | 141 | 28 | 4 | 14 | 2.6 | 60 | 53 | 37 | 52 | 5 | .262 | .406 | 0 | 0 | SS-137 |
| 1936 | 145 | 510 | 152 | 31 | 3 | 8 | 1.6 | 71 | 42 | 40 | 36 | 6 | .298 | .418 | 0 | 0 | SS-144 |
| 1937 | 128 | 516 | 158 | 38 | 2 | 14 | 2.7 | 91 | 62 | 40 | 38 | 5 | .306 | .469 | 0 | 0 | SS-128 |
| 1938 | 127 | 481 | 126 | 26 | 1 | 9 | 1.9 | 67 | 49 | 55 | 60 | 4 | .262 | .376 | 0 | 0 | SS-127 |
| 1939 CHI N | 105 | 336 | 80 | 24 | 3 | 3 | 0.9 | 37 | 34 | 42 | 25 | 6 | .238 | .348 | 3 | 1 | SS-101, 3B-1 |
| 1940 DET A | 139 | 528 | 123 | 24 | 3 | 7 | 1.3 | 76 | 53 | 47 | 53 | 12 | .233 | .330 | 0 | 0 | SS-139 |

| | G | AB | H | 2B | 3B | HR | HR % | R | RBI | BB | SO | SB | BA | SA | Pinch Hit AB | H | G by POS |
|---|---|---|---|---|---|---|---|---|---|---|---|---|---|---|---|---|---|

## Dick Bartell continued

| | | | | | | | | | | | | | | | | | |
|---|---|---|---|---|---|---|---|---|---|---|---|---|---|---|---|---|---|
| 1941 2 teams | DET | A | (5G – | .167) | NY | N | (104G – .303) | | | | | | | | | | |
| " total | 109 | 385 | 115 | 21 | 0 | 5 | 1.3 | 44 | 36 | 54 | 31 | 6 | .299 | .392 | 3 | 0 | 3B-84, SS-26 |
| 1942 NY N | 90 | 316 | 77 | 10 | 3 | 5 | 1.6 | 53 | 24 | 44 | 34 | 4 | .244 | .342 | 8 | 1 | 3B-52, SS-31 |
| 1943 | 99 | 337 | 91 | 14 | 0 | 5 | 1.5 | 48 | 28 | 47 | 27 | 5 | .270 | .356 | 10 | 1 | 3B-54, SS-33 |
| 1946 | 5 | 2 | 0 | 0 | 0 | 0 | 0.0 | 0 | 0 | 0 | 0 | 0 | .000 | .000 | 0 | 0 | 3B-4, 2B-2 |
| 18 yrs. | 2016 | 7629 | 2165 | 442 | 71 | 79 | 1.0 | 1130 | 710 | 748 | 627 | 109 | .284 | .391 | 29 | 3 | SS-1702, 3B-196, 2B-114 |
| 1 yr. | 105 | 336 | 80 | 24 | 2 | 3 | 0.9 | 37 | 34 | 42 | 25 | 6 | .238 | .348 | 3 | 1 | SS-101, 3B-1 |
| WORLD SERIES | | | | | | | | | | | | | | | | | |
| 1936 NY N | 6 | 21 | 8 | 3 | 0 | 1 | 4.8 | 5 | 3 | 4 | 4 | 0 | .381 | .667 | 0 | 0 | SS-6 |
| 1937 | 5 | 21 | 5 | 1 | 0 | 0 | 0.0 | 3 | 1 | 0 | 3 | 0 | .238 | .286 | 0 | 0 | SS-5 |
| 1940 DET A | 7 | 26 | 7 | 2 | 0 | 0 | 0.0 | 2 | 3 | 3 | 3 | 0 | .269 | .346 | 0 | 0 | SS-7 |
| 3 yrs. | 18 | 68 | 20 | 6 | 0 | 1 | 1.5 | 10 | 7 | 7 | 10 | 0 | .294 | .426 | 0 | 0 | SS-18 |

## Vince Barton

**BARTON, VINCENT DAVID**                                   BL  TR  6'        180 lbs.
B. Feb. 1, 1908, Edmonton, Alta., Canada    D. Sept. 13, 1972, Toronto, Ont., Canada

| | | | | | | | | | | | | | | | | | |
|---|---|---|---|---|---|---|---|---|---|---|---|---|---|---|---|---|---|
| 1931 CHI N | 66 | 239 | 57 | 10 | 1 | 13 | 5.4 | 45 | 50 | 21 | 40 | 1 | .238 | .452 | 4 | 1 | OF-61 |
| 1932 | 36 | 134 | 30 | 2 | 3 | 3 | 2.2 | 19 | 15 | 8 | 22 | 0 | .224 | .351 | 2 | 0 | OF-34 |
| 2 yrs. | 102 | 373 | 87 | 12 | 4 | 16 | 4.3 | 64 | 65 | 29 | 62 | 1 | .233 | .416 | 6 | 1 | OF-95 |
| 2 yrs. | 102 | 373 | 87 | 12 | 4 | 16 | 4.3 | 64 | 65 | 29 | 62 | 1 | .233 | .416 | 6 | 1 | OF-95 |

## Charlie Bastian

**BASTIAN, CHARLES J.**                                     BR  TR  5'6½"      145 lbs.
B. July 4, 1860, Philadelphia, Pa.    D. Jan. 18, 1932, Pennsauken, N. J.

| | | | | | | | | | | | | | | | | | |
|---|---|---|---|---|---|---|---|---|---|---|---|---|---|---|---|---|---|
| 1884 2 teams | WIL | U | (17G – | .200) | KC | U | (11G – .196) | | | | | | | | | | |
| " total | 28 | 106 | 21 | 4 | 3 | 3 | 2.8 | 12 | | 7 | | | .198 | .377 | 0 | 0 | 2B-27, SS-1, P-1 |
| 1885 PHI N | 103 | 389 | 65 | 11 | 5 | 4 | 1.0 | 63 | | 35 | 82 | | .167 | .252 | 0 | 0 | SS-103 |
| 1886 | 105 | 373 | 81 | 9 | 11 | 2 | 0.5 | 46 | 38 | 33 | 73 | | .217 | .316 | 0 | 0 | 2B-87, SS-10, 3B-8 |
| 1887 | 60 | 221 | 47 | 11 | 1 | 1 | 0.5 | 33 | 21 | 19 | 29 | 11 | .213 | .285 | 0 | 0 | 2B-39, SS-18, 3B-4 |
| 1888 | 80 | 275 | 53 | 4 | 1 | 1 | 0.4 | 30 | 17 | 27 | 41 | 12 | .193 | .225 | 0 | 0 | 2B-65, 3B-14, SS-1 |
| 1889 CHI N | 46 | 155 | 21 | 0 | 0 | 0 | 0.0 | 19 | 10 | 25 | 46 | 1 | .135 | .135 | 0 | 0 | SS-45, 2B-1 |
| 1890 CHI P | 80 | 283 | 54 | 10 | 5 | 0 | 0.0 | 38 | 29 | 33 | 37 | 4 | .191 | .261 | 0 | 0 | SS-64, 2B-12, 3B-4 |
| 1891 2 teams | C-M | AA | (1G – | .000) | PHI | N | (1G – .000) | | | | | | | | | | |
| " total | 2 | 4 | 0 | 0 | 0 | 0 | 0.0 | 0 | 0 | 0 | 0 | 0 | .000 | .000 | 0 | 0 | SS-1, 2B-1 |
| 8 yrs. | 504 | 1806 | 342 | 49 | 26 | 11 | 0.6 | 241 | 114 | 179 | 308 | 28 | .189 | .264 | 0 | 0 | SS-243, 2B-232, 3B-30, P-1 |
| 1 yr. | 46 | 155 | 21 | 0 | 0 | 0 | 0.0 | 19 | 10 | 25 | 46 | 1 | .135 | .135 | 0 | 0 | SS-45, 2B-1 |

## Johnny Bates

**BATES, JOHN WILLIAM**                                     BL  TL  5'7"       168 lbs.
B. Jan. 10, 1882, Steubenville, Ohio    D. Feb. 10, 1949, Steubenville, Ohio

| | | | | | | | | | | | | | | | | | |
|---|---|---|---|---|---|---|---|---|---|---|---|---|---|---|---|---|---|
| 1906 BOS N | 140 | 504 | 127 | 21 | 5 | 6 | 1.2 | 52 | 54 | 36 | | 9 | .252 | .349 | 0 | 0 | OF-140 |
| 1907 | 126 | 447 | 116 | 18 | 12 | 2 | 0.4 | 52 | 49 | 39 | | 11 | .260 | .367 | 5 | 1 | OF-120 |
| 1908 | 127 | 445 | 115 | 14 | 6 | 1 | 0.2 | 48 | 29 | 35 | | 25 | .258 | .324 | 10 | 0 | OF-117 |
| 1909 2 teams | BOS | N | (63G – | .288) | PHI | N | (77G – .293) | | | | | | | | | | |
| " total | 140 | 502 | 146 | 26 | 4 | 2 | 0.4 | 70 | 38 | 48 | | 37 | .291 | .371 | 5 | 1 | OF-133 |
| 1910 PHI N | 135 | 498 | 152 | 26 | 11 | 3 | 0.6 | 91 | 61 | 61 | 49 | 31 | .305 | .420 | 4 | 0 | OF-131 |
| 1911 CIN N | 148 | 518 | 151 | 24 | 13 | 1 | 0.2 | 89 | 61 | 103 | 59 | 33 | .292 | .394 | 1 | 0 | OF-147 |
| 1912 | 81 | 239 | 69 | 12 | 7 | 1 | 0.4 | 45 | 29 | 47 | 16 | 10 | .289 | .410 | 12 | 3 | OF-65 |
| 1913 | 131 | 406 | 113 | 13 | 7 | 6 | 1.5 | 63 | 51 | 67 | 30 | 21 | .278 | .388 | 17 | 6 | OF-112 |
| 1914 3 teams | CIN | N | (67G – | .245) | CHI | N | (9G – .125) | BAL | F | (59G – | .305) | | | | | | |
| " total | 135 | 361 | 99 | 13 | 8 | 3 | 0.8 | 62 | 45 | 68 | 19 | 10 | .274 | .380 | 8 | 1 | OF-119 |
| 9 yrs. | 1163 | 3921 | 1088 | 167 | 73 | 25 | 0.6 | 572 | 417 | 504 | 173 | 187 | .277 | .376 | 62 | 12 | OF-1084 |
| 1 yr. | 9 | 8 | 1 | 0 | 0 | 0 | 0.0 | 2 | 1 | 1 | 1 | 0 | .125 | .125 | 4 | 0 | OF-3 |

## Frankie Baumholtz

**BAUMHOLTZ, FRANK CONRAD**                                 BL  TL  5'10½"     175 lbs.
B. Oct. 7, 1918, Midvale, Ohio

| | | | | | | | | | | | | | | | | | |
|---|---|---|---|---|---|---|---|---|---|---|---|---|---|---|---|---|---|
| 1947 CIN N | 151 | 643 | 182 | 32 | 9 | 5 | 0.8 | 96 | 45 | 56 | 53 | 6 | .283 | .384 | 1 | 1 | OF-150 |
| 1948 | 128 | 415 | 123 | 19 | 5 | 4 | 1.0 | 57 | 30 | 27 | 32 | 8 | .296 | .395 | 15 | 7 | OF-110 |
| 1949 2 teams | CIN | N | (27G – | .235) | CHI | N | (58G – .226) | | | | | | | | | | |
| " total | 85 | 245 | 56 | 9 | 5 | 2 | 0.8 | 27 | 23 | 15 | 29 | 2 | .229 | .331 | 20 | 6 | OF-63 |
| 1951 CHI N | 146 | 560 | 159 | 28 | 10 | 2 | 0.4 | 62 | 50 | 49 | 36 | 5 | .284 | .380 | 4 | 2 | OF-140 |
| 1952 | 103 | 409 | 133 | 17 | 4 | 4 | 1.0 | 59 | 35 | 27 | 27 | 5 | .325 | .416 | 2 | 0 | OF-101 |
| 1953 | 133 | 520 | 159 | 36 | 7 | 3 | 0.6 | 75 | 25 | 42 | 36 | 3 | .306 | .419 | 3 | 0 | OF-130 |
| 1954 | 90 | 303 | 90 | 12 | 6 | 4 | 1.3 | 38 | 20 | 20 | 15 | 1 | .297 | .416 | 17 | 2 | OF-71 |
| 1955 | 105 | 280 | 81 | 12 | 5 | 1 | 0.4 | 23 | 27 | 16 | 24 | 0 | .289 | .379 | 37 | 15 | OF-67 |
| 1956 PHI N | 76 | 100 | 27 | 0 | 0 | 0 | 0.0 | 13 | 9 | 6 | 6 | 0 | .270 | .270 | 52 | 14 | OF-15 |
| 1957 | 2 | 0 | 0 | 0 | 0 | 0 | 0.0 | 0 | 0 | 0 | 0 | 0 | .000 | .000 | 2 | 0 | |
| 10 yrs. | 1019 | 3477 | 1010 | 165 | 51 | 25 | 0.7 | 450 | 272 | 258 | 258 | 30 | .290 | .389 | 153 | 47 | OF-843 |
| 6 yrs. | 635 | 2236 | 659 | 109 | 34 | 15 | 0.7 | 272 | 180 | 163 | 159 | 16 | .295 | .394 | 78 | 24 | OF-548 |

## Tommy Beals

**BEALS, THOMAS L.**                                        BR      5'5"       144 lbs.
B. Hartford, Conn.    D. Oct. 2, 1915, San Francisco, Calif.

| | | | | | | | | | | | | | | | | | |
|---|---|---|---|---|---|---|---|---|---|---|---|---|---|---|---|---|---|
| 1880 CHI N | 13 | 46 | 7 | 0 | 0 | 0 | 0.0 | 4 | 3 | 1 | 6 | | .152 | .152 | 0 | 0 | OF-10, 2B-3 |

## Ginger Beaumont

**BEAUMONT, CLARENCE HOWETH**                               BL  TR  5'8"       190 lbs.
B. July 23, 1876, Rochester, Wis.    D. Apr. 10, 1956, Burlington, Wis.

| | | | | | | | | | | | | | | | | | |
|---|---|---|---|---|---|---|---|---|---|---|---|---|---|---|---|---|---|
| 1899 PIT N | 111 | 437 | 154 | 15 | 8 | 3 | 0.7 | 90 | 38 | 41 | | 31 | .352 | .444 | 6 | 3 | OF-102, 1B-2 |
| 1900 | 138 | 567 | 158 | 14 | 9 | 4 | 0.7 | 107 | 50 | 40 | | 27 | .279 | .356 | 0 | 0 | OF-138 |
| 1901 | 133 | 558 | 185 | 14 | 6 | 8 | 1.4 | 120 | 72 | 44 | | 36 | .332 | .421 | 0 | 0 | OF-133 |
| 1902 | 131 | 544 | 194 | 21 | 6 | 0 | 0.0 | 101 | 67 | 39 | | 33 | .357 | .417 | 0 | 0 | OF-130 |
| 1903 | 141 | 613 | 209 | 30 | 6 | 7 | 1.1 | 137 | 68 | 44 | | 23 | .341 | .444 | 0 | 0 | OF-141 |
| 1904 | 153 | 615 | 185 | 12 | 12 | 3 | 0.5 | 97 | 54 | 34 | | 28 | .301 | .374 | 0 | 0 | OF-153 |

| | G | AB | H | 2B | 3B | HR | HR % | R | RBI | BB | SO | SB | BA | SA | Pinch Hit AB | Pinch Hit H | G by POS |
|---|---|---|---|---|---|---|---|---|---|---|---|---|---|---|---|---|---|

## Ginger Beaumont continued

| | G | AB | H | 2B | 3B | HR | HR% | R | RBI | BB | SO | SB | BA | SA | AB | H | G by POS |
|---|---|---|---|---|---|---|---|---|---|---|---|---|---|---|---|---|---|
| 1905 | 103 | 384 | 126 | 12 | 8 | 3 | 0.8 | 60 | 40 | 22 | | 21 | .328 | .424 | 4 | 1 | OF-97 |
| 1906 | 80 | 310 | 82 | 9 | 3 | 2 | 0.6 | 48 | 32 | 19 | | 1 | .265 | .332 | 1 | 0 | OF-78 |
| 1907 BOS N | 150 | 580 | **187** | 19 | 14 | 4 | 0.7 | 67 | 62 | 37 | | 25 | .322 | .424 | 1 | 1 | OF-149 |
| 1908 | 125 | 476 | 127 | 20 | 6 | 2 | 0.4 | 66 | 52 | 42 | | 13 | .267 | .347 | 4 | 1 | OF-121 |
| 1909 | 123 | 407 | 107 | 11 | 4 | 0 | 0.0 | 35 | 60 | 35 | | 12 | .263 | .310 | 14 | 5 | OF-111 |
| 1910 CHI N | 56 | 172 | 46 | 5 | 1 | 2 | 1.2 | 30 | 22 | 28 | 14 | 4 | .267 | .343 | 13 | 3 | OF-56 |
| 12 yrs. | 1444 | 5663 | 1760 | 182 | 83 | 38 | 0.7 | 958 | 617 | 425 | 14 | 254 | .311 | .392 | 43 | 14 | OF-1409, 1B-2 |
| 1 yr. | 56 | 172 | 46 | 5 | 1 | 2 | 1.2 | 30 | 22 | 28 | 14 | 4 | .267 | .343 | 13 | 3 | OF-56 |

WORLD SERIES

| | G | AB | H | 2B | 3B | HR | HR% | R | RBI | BB | SO | SB | BA | SA | AB | H | G by POS |
|---|---|---|---|---|---|---|---|---|---|---|---|---|---|---|---|---|---|
| 1903 PIT N | 8 | 34 | 9 | 0 | 1 | 0 | 0.0 | 6 | 0 | 2 | | 4 | 2 | .265 | .324 | 0 | 0 | OF-8 |
| 1910 CHI N | 3 | 2 | 0 | 0 | 0 | 0 | 0.0 | 1 | 0 | 1 | 1 | 0 | .000 | .000 | 2 | 0 | |
| 2 yrs. | 11 | 36 | 9 | 0 | 1 | 0 | 0.0 | 7 | 0 | 3 | 5 | 2 | .250 | .306 | 2 | 0 | OF-8 |

## Clyde Beck

**BECK, CLYDE EUGENE (Jersey)**
B. Jan. 6, 1902, Bassett, Calif.

BR TR 5'10" 150 lbs.

| | G | AB | H | 2B | 3B | HR | HR% | R | RBI | BB | SO | SB | BA | SA | AB | H | G by POS |
|---|---|---|---|---|---|---|---|---|---|---|---|---|---|---|---|---|---|
| 1926 CHI N | 30 | 81 | 16 | 0 | 0 | 1 | 1.2 | 10 | 4 | 7 | 15 | 0 | .198 | .235 | 0 | 0 | 2B-27 |
| 1927 | 117 | 391 | 101 | 20 | 5 | 2 | 0.5 | 44 | 44 | 43 | 37 | 0 | .258 | .350 | 0 | 0 | 2B-99, 3B-17, SS-1 |
| 1928 | 131 | 483 | 124 | 18 | 4 | 3 | 0.6 | 72 | 52 | 58 | 58 | 3 | .257 | .329 | 1 | 1 | 3B-87, SS-47, 2B-1 |
| 1929 | 54 | 190 | 40 | 7 | 0 | 0 | 0.0 | 28 | 9 | 19 | 24 | 3 | .211 | .247 | 5 | 1 | 3B-33, SS-14 |
| 1930 | 83 | 244 | 52 | 7 | 0 | 6 | 2.5 | 32 | 34 | 36 | 32 | 2 | .213 | .316 | 0 | 0 | SS-57, 2B-24, 3B-2 |
| 1931 CIN N | 53 | 136 | 21 | 4 | 2 | 0 | 0.0 | 17 | 19 | 21 | 14 | 1 | .154 | .213 | 8 | 2 | 2B-38, SS-6 |
| 6 yrs. | 468 | 1525 | 354 | 56 | 11 | 12 | 0.8 | 203 | 162 | 184 | 180 | 9 | .232 | .307 | 14 | 4 | 3B-177, 2B-151, SS-125 |
| 5 yrs. | 415 | 1389 | 333 | 52 | 9 | 12 | 0.9 | 186 | 143 | 163 | 166 | 8 | .240 | .316 | 6 | 2 | 2B-151, 3B-139, SS-119 |

## Heinz Becker

**BECKER, HEINZ REINHARD (Dutch)**
B. Aug. 26, 1915, Berlin, Germany

BB TR 6'2" 200 lbs.
BL 1947

| | G | AB | H | 2B | 3B | HR | HR% | R | RBI | BB | SO | SB | BA | SA | AB | H | G by POS |
|---|---|---|---|---|---|---|---|---|---|---|---|---|---|---|---|---|---|
| 1943 CHI N | 24 | 69 | 10 | 0 | 0 | 0 | 0.0 | 5 | 2 | 9 | 6 | 0 | .145 | .145 | 3 | 0 | 1B-18 |
| 1945 | 67 | 133 | 38 | 8 | 2 | 2 | 1.5 | 25 | 27 | 17 | 16 | 0 | .286 | .421 | 36 | 5 | 1B-28 |
| 1946 2 teams | CHI N (9G – .286) | | | CLE A (50G – .299) | | | | | | | | | | | | | |
| " total | 59 | 154 | 46 | 10 | 1 | 0 | 0.0 | 15 | 18 | 24 | 19 | 1 | .299 | .377 | 11 | 3 | 1B-44 |
| 1947 CLE A | 2 | 2 | 0 | 0 | 0 | 0 | 0.0 | 0 | 0 | 0 | 1 | 0 | .000 | .000 | 2 | 0 | |
| 4 yrs. | 152 | 358 | 94 | 18 | 3 | 2 | 0.6 | 45 | 47 | 50 | 42 | 1 | .263 | .346 | 52 | 8 | 1B-90 |
| 3 yrs. | 100 | 209 | 50 | 8 | 2 | 2 | 1.0 | 30 | 30 | 27 | 23 | 0 | .239 | .325 | 46 | 7 | 1B-46 |

WORLD SERIES

| | G | AB | H | 2B | 3B | HR | HR% | R | RBI | BB | SO | SB | BA | SA | AB | H | G by POS |
|---|---|---|---|---|---|---|---|---|---|---|---|---|---|---|---|---|---|
| 1945 CHI N | 3 | 2 | 1 | 0 | 0 | 0 | 0.0 | 0 | 0 | 1 | 1 | 0 | .500 | .500 | 2 | 1 | |

## Glenn Beckert

**BECKERT, GLENN ALFRED**
B. Oct. 12, 1940, Pittsburgh, Pa.

BR TR 6'1" 190 lbs.

| | G | AB | H | 2B | 3B | HR | HR% | R | RBI | BB | SO | SB | BA | SA | AB | H | G by POS |
|---|---|---|---|---|---|---|---|---|---|---|---|---|---|---|---|---|---|
| 1965 CHI N | 154 | 614 | 147 | 21 | 3 | 3 | 0.5 | 73 | 30 | 28 | 52 | 6 | .239 | .298 | 2 | 2 | 2B-153 |
| 1966 | 153 | 656 | 188 | 23 | 7 | 1 | 0.2 | 73 | 59 | 26 | 36 | 10 | .287 | .348 | 1 | 0 | 2B-152, SS-1 |
| 1967 | 146 | 597 | 167 | 32 | 3 | 5 | 0.8 | 91 | 40 | 30 | 25 | 10 | .280 | .369 | 1 | 0 | 2B-144 |
| 1968 | 155 | 643 | 189 | 28 | 4 | 4 | 0.6 | **98** | 37 | 31 | 20 | 8 | .294 | .369 | 0 | 0 | 2B-155 |
| 1969 | 131 | 543 | 158 | 22 | 1 | 1 | 0.2 | 69 | 37 | 24 | 24 | 6 | .291 | .341 | 1 | 0 | 2B-129 |
| 1970 | 143 | 591 | 170 | 15 | 6 | 3 | 0.5 | 99 | 36 | 32 | 22 | 4 | .288 | .349 | 3 | 0 | 2B-138, OF-1 |
| 1971 | 131 | 530 | 181 | 18 | 5 | 2 | 0.4 | 80 | 42 | 24 | 24 | 3 | .342 | .406 | 2 | 1 | 2B-129 |
| 1972 | 120 | 474 | 128 | 22 | 2 | 3 | 0.6 | 51 | 43 | 23 | 17 | 2 | .270 | .344 | 2 | 1 | 2B-118 |
| 1973 | 114 | 372 | 95 | 13 | 0 | 0 | 0.0 | 38 | 29 | 30 | 15 | 0 | .255 | .290 | 25 | 6 | 2B-88 |
| 1974 SD N | 64 | 172 | 44 | 1 | 0 | 0 | 0.0 | 11 | 7 | 11 | 8 | 0 | .256 | .262 | 26 | 4 | 2B-36, 3B-1 |
| 1975 | 9 | 16 | 6 | 1 | 0 | 0 | 0.0 | 2 | 0 | 1 | 0 | 0 | .375 | .438 | 5 | 1 | 3B-4 |
| 11 yrs. | 1320 | 5208 | 1473 | 196 | 31 | 22 | 0.4 | 685 | 360 | 260 | 243 | 49 | .283 | .345 | 68 | 15 | 2B-1242, 3B-5, OF-1, SS-1 |
| 9 yrs. | 1247 | 5020 | 1423 | 194 | 31 | 22 | 0.4 | 672 | 353 | 248 | 235 | 49 | .283 | .348 | 37 | 10 | 2B-1206, OF-1, SS-1 |

## Les Bell

**BELL, LESTER ROWLAND**
B. Dec. 14, 1901, Harrisburg, Pa.

BR TR 5'11" 165 lbs.

| | G | AB | H | 2B | 3B | HR | HR% | R | RBI | BB | SO | SB | BA | SA | AB | H | G by POS |
|---|---|---|---|---|---|---|---|---|---|---|---|---|---|---|---|---|---|
| 1923 STL N | 15 | 51 | 19 | 2 | 1 | 0 | 0.0 | 5 | 9 | 9 | 7 | 1 | .373 | .451 | 0 | 0 | SS-15 |
| 1924 | 17 | 57 | 14 | 3 | 2 | 1 | 1.8 | 5 | 5 | 3 | 7 | 0 | .246 | .421 | 0 | 0 | SS-17 |
| 1925 | 153 | 586 | 167 | 29 | 9 | 11 | 1.9 | 80 | 88 | 43 | 47 | 4 | .285 | .422 | 0 | 0 | 3B-153, SS-1 |
| 1926 | 155 | 581 | 189 | 33 | 14 | 17 | 2.9 | 85 | 100 | 54 | 62 | 9 | .325 | .518 | 0 | 0 | 3B-155 |
| 1927 | 115 | 390 | 101 | 26 | 6 | 9 | 2.3 | 48 | 65 | 34 | 63 | 5 | .259 | .426 | 5 | 0 | 3B-100, SS-10 |
| 1928 BOS N | 153 | 591 | 164 | 36 | 7 | 10 | 1.7 | 58 | 91 | 40 | 45 | 1 | .277 | .413 | 0 | 0 | 3B-153 |
| 1929 | 139 | 483 | 144 | 23 | 5 | 9 | 1.9 | 58 | 72 | 50 | 42 | 4 | .298 | .422 | 9 | 2 | 3B-127, SS-1, 2B-1 |
| 1930 CHI N | 74 | 248 | 69 | 15 | 4 | 5 | 2.0 | 35 | 47 | 24 | 27 | 1 | .278 | .431 | 2 | 0 | 3B-70, 1B-2 |
| 1931 | 75 | 252 | 71 | 17 | 1 | 4 | 1.6 | 30 | 32 | 19 | 22 | 0 | .282 | .405 | 5 | 1 | 3B-70 |
| 9 yrs. | 896 | 3239 | 938 | 184 | 49 | 66 | 2.0 | 404 | 509 | 276 | 322 | 25 | .290 | .438 | 21 | 3 | 3B-828, SS-44, 1B-2, 2B-1 |
| 2 yrs. | 149 | 500 | 140 | 32 | 5 | 9 | 1.8 | 65 | 79 | 43 | 49 | 1 | .280 | .418 | 7 | 1 | 3B-140, 1B-2 |

WORLD SERIES

| | G | AB | H | 2B | 3B | HR | HR% | R | RBI | BB | SO | SB | BA | SA | AB | H | G by POS |
|---|---|---|---|---|---|---|---|---|---|---|---|---|---|---|---|---|---|
| 1926 STL N | 7 | 27 | 7 | 1 | 0 | 1 | 3.7 | 4 | 6 | 2 | 5 | 0 | .259 | .407 | 0 | 0 | 3B-7 |

## Butch Benton

**BENTON, ALFRED LEE**
B. Aug. 24, 1957, Tampa, Fla.

BR TR 6'2" 190 lbs.

| | G | AB | H | 2B | 3B | HR | HR% | R | RBI | BB | SO | SB | BA | SA | AB | H | G by POS |
|---|---|---|---|---|---|---|---|---|---|---|---|---|---|---|---|---|---|
| 1978 NY N | 4 | 4 | 2 | 0 | 0 | 0 | 0.0 | 1 | 2 | 0 | 0 | 0 | .500 | .500 | 1 | 0 | C-1 |
| 1980 | 12 | 21 | 1 | 0 | 0 | 0 | 0.0 | 0 | 0 | 2 | 4 | 0 | .048 | .048 | 4 | 0 | C-8 |
| 1982 CHI N | 4 | 7 | 1 | 0 | 0 | 0 | 0.0 | 0 | 0 | 0 | 1 | 0 | .143 | .143 | 0 | 0 | C-4 |
| 1985 CLE A | 31 | 67 | 12 | 4 | 0 | 0 | 0.0 | 5 | 7 | 3 | 9 | 0 | .179 | .239 | 4 | 1 | C-26 |
| 4 yrs. | 51 | 99 | 16 | 4 | 0 | 0 | 0.0 | 6 | 10 | 5 | 14 | 0 | .162 | .202 | 9 | 1 | C-39 |
| 1 yr. | 4 | 7 | 1 | 0 | 0 | 0 | 0.0 | 0 | 0 | 0 | 1 | 0 | .143 | .143 | 0 | 0 | C-4 |

| | G | AB | H | 2B | 3B | HR | HR % | R | RBI | BB | SO | SB | BA | SA | Pinch Hit AB | Pinch Hit H | G by POS |
|---|---|---|---|---|---|---|---|---|---|---|---|---|---|---|---|---|---|

# Dick Bertell

**BERTELL, RICHARD GEORGE**
B. Nov. 21, 1935, Oak Park, Ill.     BR TR 6'½" 200 lbs.

| | G | AB | H | 2B | 3B | HR | HR % | R | RBI | BB | SO | SB | BA | SA | PH AB | PH H | G by POS |
|---|---|---|---|---|---|---|---|---|---|---|---|---|---|---|---|---|---|
| 1960 CHI N | 5 | 15 | 2 | 0 | 0 | 0 | 0.0 | 0 | 2 | 3 | 1 | 0 | .133 | .133 | 0 | 0 | C-5 |
| 1961 | 92 | 267 | 73 | 7 | 1 | 2 | 0.7 | 20 | 33 | 15 | 33 | 0 | .273 | .330 | 6 | 2 | C-90 |
| 1962 | 77 | 215 | 65 | 6 | 2 | 2 | 0.9 | 19 | 18 | 13 | 30 | 0 | .302 | .377 | 5 | 1 | C-76 |
| 1963 | 100 | 322 | 75 | 7 | 2 | 2 | 0.6 | 15 | 14 | 24 | 41 | 0 | .233 | .286 | 1 | 0 | C-99 |
| 1964 | 112 | 353 | 84 | 11 | 3 | 4 | 1.1 | 29 | 35 | 33 | 67 | 2 | .238 | .320 | 3 | 0 | C-110 |
| 1965 2 teams | | CHI N (34G – .214) | | | SF N (22G – .188) | | | | | | | | | | | | |
| "   total | 56 | 132 | 27 | 3 | 0 | 0 | 0.0 | 7 | 10 | 18 | 15 | 0 | .205 | .227 | 0 | 0 | C-56 |
| 1967 CHI N | 2 | 6 | 1 | 0 | 0 | 0 | 0.0 | 1 | 0 | 0 | 1 | 0 | .167 | .500 | 0 | 0 | C-2 |
| 7 yrs. | 444 | 1310 | 327 | 34 | 9 | 10 | 0.8 | 91 | 112 | 106 | 188 | 2 | .250 | .312 | 15 | 3 | C-438 |
| 7 yrs. | 422 | 1262 | 318 | 33 | 9 | 10 | 0.8 | 90 | 109 | 99 | 183 | 2 | .252 | .316 | 15 | 3 | C-416 |

# Oscar Bielaski

**BIELASKI, OSCAR**
B. Mar. 21, 1847, Washington, D. C.    D. Nov. 8, 1911, Washington, D. C.     BR TR

| | G | AB | H | 2B | 3B | HR | HR % | R | RBI | BB | SO | SB | BA | SA | PH AB | PH H | G by POS |
|---|---|---|---|---|---|---|---|---|---|---|---|---|---|---|---|---|---|
| 1876 CHI N | 32 | 139 | 29 | 3 | 0 | 0 | 0.0 | 24 | 10 | 2 | 3 | | .209 | .230 | 0 | 0 | OF-32 |

# Larry Biittner

**BIITTNER, LARRY DAVID**
B. July 27, 1946, Pocahontas, Iowa     BL TL 6'2" 205 lbs.

| | G | AB | H | 2B | 3B | HR | HR % | R | RBI | BB | SO | SB | BA | SA | PH AB | PH H | G by POS |
|---|---|---|---|---|---|---|---|---|---|---|---|---|---|---|---|---|---|
| 1970 WAS A | 2 | 2 | 0 | 0 | 0 | 0 | 0.0 | 0 | 0 | 0 | 0 | 0 | .000 | .000 | 2 | 0 | |
| 1971 | 66 | 171 | 44 | 4 | 1 | 0 | 0.0 | 12 | 16 | 16 | 20 | 1 | .257 | .292 | 19 | 7 | OF-41, 1B-3 |
| 1972 TEX A | 137 | 382 | 99 | 18 | 1 | 3 | 0.8 | 34 | 31 | 29 | 37 | 1 | .259 | .335 | 17 | 4 | OF-65, 1B-65 |
| 1973 | 83 | 258 | 65 | 8 | 2 | 1 | 0.4 | 19 | 12 | 20 | 21 | 1 | .252 | .310 | 7 | 1 | OF-57, 1B-20, DH-3 |
| 1974 MON N | 18 | 26 | 7 | 1 | 0 | 0 | 0.0 | 2 | 3 | 0 | 2 | 0 | .269 | .308 | 15 | 4 | 1B-4 |
| 1975 | 121 | 346 | 109 | 13 | 5 | 3 | 0.9 | 34 | 28 | 34 | 33 | 2 | .315 | .408 | 27 | 8 | OF-93 |
| 1976 2 teams | | MON N (11G – .188) | | | CHI N (78G – .245) | | | | | | | | | | | | |
| "   total | 89 | 224 | 53 | 14 | 1 | 0 | 0.0 | 23 | 18 | 10 | 9 | 0 | .237 | .308 | 32 | 6 | 1B-33, OF-31 |
| 1977 CHI N | 138 | 493 | 147 | 28 | 1 | 12 | 2.4 | 74 | 62 | 35 | 36 | 2 | .298 | .432 | 15 | 5 | 1B-80, OF-52, P-1 |
| 1978 | 120 | 343 | 88 | 15 | 1 | 4 | 1.2 | 32 | 50 | 23 | 37 | 0 | .257 | .341 | 33 | 11 | 1B-62, OF-29 |
| 1979 | 111 | 272 | 79 | 13 | 3 | 3 | 1.1 | 35 | 50 | 21 | 23 | 1 | .290 | .393 | 42 | 13 | OF-44, 1B-32 |
| 1980 | 127 | 273 | 68 | 12 | 2 | 1 | 0.4 | 21 | 34 | 18 | 33 | 1 | .249 | .319 | 52 | 11 | 1B-41, OF-38 |
| 1981 CIN N | 42 | 61 | 13 | 4 | 0 | 0 | 0.0 | 1 | 8 | 4 | 4 | 0 | .213 | .279 | 29 | 7 | 1B-8, OF-3 |
| 1982 | 97 | 184 | 57 | 9 | 2 | 2 | 1.1 | 18 | 24 | 17 | 16 | 1 | .310 | .413 | 49 | 10 | OF-31, 1B-15 |
| 1983 TEX A | 66 | 116 | 32 | 5 | 1 | 0 | 0.0 | 5 | 18 | 9 | 16 | 0 | .276 | .336 | 31 | 8 | 1B-22, DH-9, OF-2 |
| 14 yrs. | 1217 | 3151 | 861 | 144 | 20 | 29 | 0.9 | 310 | 354 | 236 | 287 | 10 | .273 | .359 | 370 | 95 | OF-486, 1B-385, DH-12, P-1 |
| 5 yrs. | 574 | 1573 | 429 | 81 | 8 | 20 | 1.3 | 183 | 213 | 107 | 135 | 4 | .273 | .373 | 170 3rd | 46 1st | 1B-248, OF-187, P-1 |

# Steve Bilko

**BILKO, STEVEN THOMAS**
B. Nov. 13, 1928, Nanticoke, Pa.    D. Mar. 7, 1978, Wilkes Barre, Pa.     BR TR 6'1" 230 lbs.

| | G | AB | H | 2B | 3B | HR | HR % | R | RBI | BB | SO | SB | BA | SA | PH AB | PH H | G by POS |
|---|---|---|---|---|---|---|---|---|---|---|---|---|---|---|---|---|---|
| 1949 STL N | 6 | 17 | 5 | 2 | 0 | 0 | 0.0 | 3 | 2 | 5 | 6 | 0 | .294 | .412 | 1 | 0 | 1B-5 |
| 1950 | 10 | 33 | 6 | 1 | 0 | 0 | 0.0 | 1 | 2 | 4 | 10 | 0 | .182 | .212 | 1 | 1 | 1B-9 |
| 1951 | 21 | 72 | 16 | 4 | 0 | 2 | 2.8 | 5 | 12 | 9 | 10 | 0 | .222 | .361 | 2 | 1 | 1B-19 |
| 1952 | 20 | 72 | 19 | 6 | 1 | 1 | 1.4 | 7 | 6 | 4 | 15 | 0 | .264 | .417 | 0 | 0 | 1B-20 |
| 1953 | 154 | 570 | 143 | 23 | 3 | 21 | 3.7 | 72 | 84 | 70 | 125 | 0 | .251 | .412 | 0 | 0 | 1B-154 |
| 1954 2 teams | | STL N (8G – .143) | | | CHI N (47G – .239) | | | | | | | | | | | | |
| "   total | 55 | 106 | 24 | 8 | 1 | 4 | 3.8 | 12 | 13 | 14 | 25 | 0 | .226 | .434 | 24 | 6 | 1B-28 |
| 1958 2 teams | | CIN N (31G – .264) | | | LA N (47G – .208) | | | | | | | | | | | | |
| "   total | 78 | 188 | 44 | 5 | 4 | 11 | 5.9 | 25 | 35 | 18 | 57 | 0 | .234 | .479 | 27 | 5 | 1B-46 |
| 1960 DET A | 78 | 222 | 46 | 11 | 2 | 9 | 4.1 | 20 | 25 | 27 | 31 | 0 | .207 | .396 | 17 | 1 | 1B-62 |
| 1961 LA A | 114 | 294 | 82 | 16 | 1 | 20 | 6.8 | 49 | 59 | 58 | 81 | 1 | .279 | .544 | 24 | 8 | 1B-86, OF-3 |
| 1962 | 64 | 164 | 47 | 9 | 1 | 8 | 4.9 | 26 | 38 | 25 | 35 | 1 | .287 | .500 | 14 | 3 | 1B-50 |
| 10 yrs. | 600 | 1738 | 432 | 85 | 13 | 76 | 4.4 | 220 | 276 | 234 | 395 | 2 | .249 | .444 | 110 | 25 | 1B-479, OF-3 |
| 1 yr. | 47 | 92 | 22 | 8 | 1 | 4 | 4.3 | 11 | 12 | 11 | 24 | 0 | .239 | .478 | 23 | 6 | 1B-22 |

# Earl Blackburn

**BLACKBURN, EARL STUART**
B. Nov. 1, 1892, Leesville, Ohio    D. Aug. 3, 1966, Mansfield, Ohio     BR TR 5'11" 180 lbs.

| | G | AB | H | 2B | 3B | HR | HR % | R | RBI | BB | SO | SB | BA | SA | PH AB | PH H | G by POS |
|---|---|---|---|---|---|---|---|---|---|---|---|---|---|---|---|---|---|
| 1912 2 teams | | PIT N (1G – .000) | | | CIN N (1G – .000) | | | | | | | | | | | | |
| "   total | 2 | 0 | 0 | 0 | 0 | 0 | | 0 | 0 | 1 | 0 | 0 | – | – | 0 | 0 | C-2 |
| 1913 CIN N | 17 | 27 | 7 | 0 | 0 | 0 | 0.0 | 1 | 3 | 2 | 5 | 2 | .259 | .259 | 5 | 1 | C-12 |
| 1915 BOS N | 3 | 6 | 1 | 0 | 0 | 0 | 0.0 | 0 | 0 | 2 | 1 | 0 | .167 | .167 | 0 | 0 | C-3 |
| 1916 | 47 | 110 | 30 | 4 | 4 | 0 | 0.0 | 12 | 7 | 9 | 21 | 2 | .273 | .382 | 3 | 1 | C-44 |
| 1917 CHI N | 2 | 2 | 0 | 0 | 0 | 0 | 0.0 | 0 | 0 | 0 | 0 | 0 | .000 | .000 | 2 | 0 | |
| 5 yrs. | 71 | 145 | 38 | 4 | 4 | 0 | 0.0 | 13 | 10 | 14 | 27 | 4 | .262 | .345 | 10 | 2 | C-61 |
| 1 yr. | 2 | 2 | 0 | 0 | 0 | 0 | 0.0 | 0 | 0 | 0 | 0 | 0 | .000 | .000 | 2 | 0 | |

# Tim Blackwell

**BLACKWELL, TIMOTHY P.**
B. Aug. 19, 1952, San Diego, Calif.     BB TR 5'11" 170 lbs.

| | G | AB | H | 2B | 3B | HR | HR % | R | RBI | BB | SO | SB | BA | SA | PH AB | PH H | G by POS |
|---|---|---|---|---|---|---|---|---|---|---|---|---|---|---|---|---|---|
| 1974 BOS A | 44 | 122 | 30 | 1 | 1 | 0 | 0.0 | 9 | 8 | 10 | 21 | 1 | .246 | .270 | 0 | 0 | C-44 |
| 1975 | 59 | 132 | 26 | 3 | 2 | 0 | 0.0 | 15 | 6 | 19 | 13 | 0 | .197 | .250 | 0 | 0 | C-57, DH-2 |
| 1976 PHI N | 4 | 8 | 2 | 0 | 0 | 0 | 0.0 | 1 | 0 | 1 | 1 | 0 | .250 | .250 | 2 | 1 | C-4 |
| 1977 2 teams | | PHI N (1G – .000) | | | MON N (16G – .091) | | | | | | | | | | | | |
| "   total | 17 | 22 | 2 | 0 | 0 | 0 | 0.0 | 4 | 0 | 2 | 7 | 0 | .091 | .136 | 2 | 0 | C-15 |
| 1978 CHI N | 49 | 103 | 23 | 3 | 0 | 0 | 0.0 | 8 | 7 | 23 | 17 | 0 | .223 | .252 | 2 | 0 | C-49 |
| 1979 | 63 | 122 | 20 | 3 | 1 | 0 | 0.0 | 8 | 12 | 32 | 25 | 0 | .164 | .205 | 1 | 0 | C-63 |
| 1980 | 103 | 320 | 87 | 16 | 4 | 5 | 1.6 | 24 | 30 | 41 | 62 | 0 | .272 | .394 | 0 | 0 | C-103 |
| 1981 | 58 | 158 | 37 | 10 | 2 | 1 | 0.6 | 21 | 11 | 23 | 23 | 2 | .234 | .342 | 2 | 0 | C-56 |
| 1982 MON N | 23 | 42 | 8 | 1 | 0 | 0 | 0.0 | 2 | 3 | 3 | 11 | 0 | .190 | .286 | 6 | 1 | C-18 |
| 1983 | 6 | 15 | 3 | 1 | 0 | 0 | 0.0 | 0 | 2 | 1 | 3 | 0 | .200 | .267 | 0 | 0 | C-5 |
| 10 yrs. | 426 | 1044 | 238 | 40 | 11 | 6 | 0.6 | 91 | 80 | 154 | 183 | 3 | .228 | .305 | 14 | 2 | C-414, DH-2 |
| 4 yrs. | 273 | 703 | 167 | 32 | 7 | 6 | 0.9 | 61 | 60 | 119 | 127 | 2 | .238 | .329 | 3 | 0 | C-271 |

| | G | AB | H | 2B | 3B | HR | HR % | R | RBI | BB | SO | SB | BA | SA | Pinch Hit AB | Pinch Hit H | G by POS |
|---|---|---|---|---|---|---|---|---|---|---|---|---|---|---|---|---|---|

## Rick Bladt

**BLADT, RICHARD ALAN**
B. Dec. 9, 1946, Santa Cruz, Calif.    BR TR 6'1"    160 lbs.

| | G | AB | H | 2B | 3B | HR | HR % | R | RBI | BB | SO | SB | BA | SA | AB | H | G by POS |
|---|---|---|---|---|---|---|---|---|---|---|---|---|---|---|---|---|---|
| 1969 CHI N | 10 | 13 | 2 | 0 | 0 | 0 | 0.0 | 1 | 1 | 0 | 5 | 0 | .154 | .154 | 1 | 0 | 1B-7 |
| 1975 NY A | 52 | 117 | 26 | 3 | 1 | 1 | 0.9 | 13 | 11 | 11 | 8 | 6 | .222 | .291 | 1 | 1 | OF-51 |
| 2 yrs. | 62 | 130 | 28 | 3 | 1 | 1 | 0.8 | 14 | 12 | 11 | 13 | 6 | .215 | .277 | 2 | 1 | OF-51, 1B-7 |
| 1 yr. | 10 | 13 | 2 | 0 | 0 | 0 | 0.0 | 1 | 1 | 0 | 5 | 0 | .154 | .154 | 1 | 0 | 1B-7 |

## Footsie Blair

**BLAIR, CLARENCE VICK**
B. July 13, 1900, Interprise, Okla.    D. July 1, 1982, Texarkana, Tex.    BL TR 6'1"    180 lbs.

| | G | AB | H | 2B | 3B | HR | HR % | R | RBI | BB | SO | SB | BA | SA | AB | H | G by POS |
|---|---|---|---|---|---|---|---|---|---|---|---|---|---|---|---|---|---|
| 1929 CHI N | 26 | 72 | 23 | 5 | 0 | 1 | 1.4 | 10 | 8 | 3 | 4 | 1 | .319 | .431 | 3 | 2 | 3B-8, 1B-7, 2B-2 |
| 1930 | 134 | 578 | 158 | 24 | 12 | 6 | 1.0 | 97 | 59 | 20 | 58 | 9 | .273 | .388 | 6 | 1 | 2B-115, 3B-13 |
| 1931 | 86 | 240 | 62 | 19 | 5 | 2 | 0.8 | 31 | 29 | 14 | 26 | 1 | .258 | .404 | 16 | 2 | 2B-44, 1B-23, 3B-1 |
| 3 yrs. | 246 | 890 | 243 | 48 | 17 | 9 | 1.0 | 138 | 96 | 37 | 88 | 11 | .273 | .396 | 25 | 5 | 2B-161, 1B-30, 3B-22 |
| 3 yrs. | 246 | 890 | 243 | 48 | 17 | 9 | 1.0 | 138 | 96 | 37 | 88 | 11 | .273 | .396 | 25 | 5 | 2B-161, 1B-30, 3B-22 |

WORLD SERIES

| | G | AB | H | 2B | 3B | HR | HR % | R | RBI | BB | SO | SB | BA | SA | AB | H | G by POS |
|---|---|---|---|---|---|---|---|---|---|---|---|---|---|---|---|---|---|
| 1929 CHI N | 1 | 1 | 0 | 0 | 0 | 0 | 0.0 | 0 | 0 | 0 | 0 | 0 | .000 | .000 | 1 | 0 | |

## Cy Block

**BLOCK, SEYMOUR**
B. May 4, 1919, Brooklyn, N. Y.    BR TR 6'    180 lbs.

| | G | AB | H | 2B | 3B | HR | HR % | R | RBI | BB | SO | SB | BA | SA | AB | H | G by POS |
|---|---|---|---|---|---|---|---|---|---|---|---|---|---|---|---|---|---|
| 1942 CHI N | 9 | 33 | 12 | 1 | 1 | 0 | 0.0 | 6 | 4 | 3 | 3 | 2 | .364 | .455 | 0 | 0 | 3B-8, 2B-1 |
| 1945 | 2 | 7 | 1 | 0 | 0 | 0 | 0.0 | 1 | 1 | 0 | 0 | 0 | .143 | .143 | 0 | 0 | 3B-1, 2B-1 |
| 1946 | 6 | 13 | 3 | 0 | 0 | 0 | 0.0 | 2 | 0 | 4 | 0 | 0 | .231 | .231 | 1 | 0 | 3B-4 |
| 3 yrs. | 17 | 53 | 16 | 1 | 1 | 0 | 0.0 | 9 | 5 | 7 | 3 | 2 | .302 | .358 | 1 | 0 | 3B-13, 2B-2 |
| 3 yrs. | 17 | 53 | 16 | 1 | 1 | 0 | 0.0 | 9 | 5 | 7 | 3 | 2 | .302 | .358 | 1 | 0 | 3B-13, 2B-2 |

WORLD SERIES

| | G | AB | H | 2B | 3B | HR | HR % | R | RBI | BB | SO | SB | BA | SA | AB | H | G by POS |
|---|---|---|---|---|---|---|---|---|---|---|---|---|---|---|---|---|---|
| 1945 CHI N | 1 | 0 | 0 | 0 | 0 | 0 | — | 0 | 0 | 0 | 0 | 0 | — | — | 0 | 0 | |

## Randy Bobb

**BOBB, MARK RANDALL**
B. Jan. 1, 1948, Los Angeles, Calif.    D. June 13, 1982, Carnelian Bay, Calif.    BR TR 6'1"    195 lbs.

| | G | AB | H | 2B | 3B | HR | HR % | R | RBI | BB | SO | SB | BA | SA | AB | H | G by POS |
|---|---|---|---|---|---|---|---|---|---|---|---|---|---|---|---|---|---|
| 1968 CHI N | 7 | 8 | 1 | 0 | 0 | 0 | 0.0 | 0 | 0 | 1 | 2 | 0 | .125 | .125 | 0 | 0 | C-7 |
| 1969 | 3 | 2 | 0 | 0 | 0 | 0 | 0.0 | 0 | 0 | 0 | 1 | 0 | .000 | .000 | 0 | 0 | C-2 |
| 2 yrs. | 10 | 10 | 1 | 0 | 0 | 0 | 0.0 | 0 | 0 | 1 | 3 | 0 | .100 | .100 | 0 | 0 | C-9 |
| 2 yrs. | 10 | 10 | 1 | 0 | 0 | 0 | 0.0 | 0 | 0 | 1 | 3 | 0 | .100 | .100 | 0 | 0 | C-9 |

## John Boccabella

**BOCCABELLA, JOHN DOMINIC**
B. June 29, 1941, San Francisco, Calif.    BR TR 6'1"    195 lbs.

| | G | AB | H | 2B | 3B | HR | HR % | R | RBI | BB | SO | SB | BA | SA | AB | H | G by POS |
|---|---|---|---|---|---|---|---|---|---|---|---|---|---|---|---|---|---|
| 1963 CHI N | 24 | 74 | 14 | 4 | 1 | 1 | 1.4 | 7 | 5 | 6 | 21 | 0 | .189 | .311 | 1 | 0 | 1B-24 |
| 1964 | 9 | 23 | 9 | 2 | 1 | 0 | 0.0 | 4 | 6 | 0 | 3 | 0 | .391 | .565 | 3 | 1 | 1B-5, OF-2 |
| 1965 | 6 | 12 | 4 | 0 | 0 | 2 | 16.7 | 2 | 4 | 1 | 2 | 0 | .333 | .833 | 2 | 1 | 1B-2, OF-1 |
| 1966 | 75 | 206 | 47 | 9 | 0 | 6 | 2.9 | 22 | 25 | 14 | 39 | 0 | .228 | .359 | 16 | 2 | OF-33, 1B-30, C-5 |
| 1967 | 25 | 35 | 6 | 1 | 1 | 0 | 0.0 | 0 | 8 | 3 | 7 | 0 | .171 | .257 | 11 | 2 | OF-9, 1B-3, C-1 |
| 1968 | 7 | 14 | 1 | 0 | 0 | 0 | 0.0 | 0 | 0 | 2 | 2 | 0 | .071 | .071 | 2 | 0 | C-4, OF-1 |
| 1969 MON N | 40 | 86 | 9 | 2 | 0 | 1 | 1.2 | 4 | 6 | 6 | 30 | 1 | .105 | .163 | 7 | 1 | C-32 |
| 1970 | 61 | 145 | 39 | 3 | 1 | 5 | 3.4 | 18 | 17 | 11 | 24 | 0 | .269 | .407 | 8 | 2 | 1B-33, C-24, 3B-1 |
| 1971 | 74 | 177 | 39 | 11 | 0 | 3 | 1.7 | 15 | 15 | 14 | 26 | 0 | .220 | .333 | 5 | 0 | 1B-37, C-37, 3B-2 |
| 1972 | 83 | 207 | 47 | 8 | 1 | 1 | 0.5 | 14 | 10 | 9 | 29 | 1 | .227 | .290 | 3 | 0 | C-73, 1B-7, 3B-1 |
| 1973 | 118 | 403 | 94 | 13 | 0 | 7 | 1.7 | 25 | 46 | 26 | 57 | 1 | .233 | .318 | 1 | 0 | C-117, 1B-1 |
| 1974 SF N | 29 | 80 | 11 | 3 | 0 | 0 | 0.0 | 6 | 5 | 4 | 6 | 0 | .138 | .175 | 4 | 0 | C-26 |
| 12 yrs. | 551 | 1462 | 320 | 56 | 5 | 26 | 1.8 | 117 | 148 | 96 | 246 | 3 | .219 | .317 | 63 | 9 | C-319, 1B-142, OF-46, 3B-4 |
| 6 yrs. | 146 | 364 | 81 | 16 | 3 | 9 | 2.5 | 35 | 49 | 26 | 74 | 0 | .223 | .357 | 35 | 6 | 1B-64, OF-46, C-10 |

## Jim Bolger

**BOLGER, JAMES CYRIL (Dutch)**
B. Feb. 23, 1932, Cincinnati, Ohio    BR TR 6'2"    180 lbs.

| | G | AB | H | 2B | 3B | HR | HR % | R | RBI | BB | SO | SB | BA | SA | AB | H | G by POS |
|---|---|---|---|---|---|---|---|---|---|---|---|---|---|---|---|---|---|
| 1950 CIN N | 2 | 1 | 0 | 0 | 0 | 0 | 0.0 | 0 | 0 | 0 | 0 | 0 | .000 | .000 | 0 | 0 | OF-2 |
| 1951 | 2 | 0 | 0 | 0 | 0 | 0 | — | 1 | 0 | 0 | 0 | 1 | — | — | 0 | 0 | |
| 1954 | 5 | 3 | 1 | 0 | 0 | 0 | 0.0 | 1 | 0 | 0 | 1 | 0 | .333 | .333 | 2 | 0 | OF-2 |
| 1955 CHI N | 64 | 160 | 33 | 5 | 4 | 0 | 0.0 | 19 | 7 | 9 | 17 | 2 | .206 | .288 | 1 | 0 | OF-51 |
| 1957 | 112 | 273 | 75 | 4 | 1 | 5 | 1.8 | 28 | 29 | 10 | 36 | 0 | .275 | .352 | 48 | 17 | OF-63, 3B-3 |
| 1958 | 84 | 120 | 27 | 4 | 1 | 1 | 0.8 | 15 | 11 | 9 | 20 | 0 | .225 | .300 | 51 | 10 | OF-37 |
| 1959 2 teams | CLE A (8G – .000) | | | PHI N (35G – .083) | | | | | | | | | | | | | |
| " total | 43 | 55 | 4 | 1 | 0 | 0 | 0.0 | 0 | 1 | 4 | 9 | 0 | .073 | .091 | 32 | 4 | OF-9 |
| 7 yrs. | 312 | 612 | 140 | 14 | 6 | 6 | 1.0 | 65 | 48 | 32 | 83 | 3 | .229 | .301 | 134 | 32 | OF-164, 3B-3 |
| 3 yrs. | 260 | 553 | 135 | 13 | 6 | 6 | 1.1 | 62 | 47 | 28 | 73 | 2 | .244 | .322 | 100 | 28 | OF-151, 3B-3 |

## Bobby Bonds

**BONDS, BOBBY LEE**
B. Mar. 15, 1946, Riverside, Calif.    BR TR 6'1"    190 lbs.

| | G | AB | H | 2B | 3B | HR | HR % | R | RBI | BB | SO | SB | BA | SA | AB | H | G by POS |
|---|---|---|---|---|---|---|---|---|---|---|---|---|---|---|---|---|---|
| 1968 SF N | 81 | 307 | 78 | 10 | 5 | 9 | 2.9 | 55 | 35 | 38 | 84 | 16 | .254 | .407 | 0 | 0 | OF-80 |
| 1969 | 158 | 622 | 161 | 25 | 6 | 32 | 5.1 | 120 | 90 | 81 | 187 | 45 | .259 | .473 | 1 | 0 | OF-155 |
| 1970 | 157 | 663 | 200 | 36 | 10 | 26 | 3.9 | 134 | 78 | 77 | 189 | 48 | .302 | .504 | 2 | 0 | OF-157 |
| 1971 | 155 | 619 | 178 | 32 | 4 | 33 | 5.3 | 110 | 102 | 62 | 137 | 26 | .288 | .512 | 3 | 1 | OF-154 |
| 1972 | 153 | 626 | 162 | 29 | 5 | 26 | 4.2 | 118 | 80 | 60 | 137 | 44 | .259 | .446 | 0 | 0 | OF-153 |
| 1973 | 160 | 643 | 182 | 34 | 4 | 39 | 6.1 | 131 | 96 | 87 | 148 | 43 | .283 | .530 | 2 | 1 | OF-158 |
| 1974 | 150 | 567 | 145 | 22 | 8 | 21 | 3.7 | 97 | 71 | 95 | 134 | 41 | .256 | .434 | 3 | 1 | OF-148 |
| 1975 NY A | 145 | 529 | 143 | 26 | 3 | 32 | 6.0 | 93 | 85 | 89 | 137 | 30 | .270 | .512 | 4 | 1 | OF-129, DH-12 |
| 1976 CAL A | 99 | 378 | 100 | 10 | 3 | 10 | 2.6 | 48 | 54 | 41 | 90 | 30 | .265 | .386 | 1 | 0 | OF-98, DH-1 |
| 1977 | 158 | 592 | 156 | 23 | 9 | 37 | 6.3 | 103 | 115 | 74 | 141 | 41 | .264 | .520 | 1 | 0 | OF-140, DH-18 |
| 1978 2 teams | CHI A (130G – .278) | | | TEX A (130G – .265) | | | | | | | | | | | | | |
| " total | 156 | 565 | 151 | 19 | 4 | 31 | 5.5 | 93 | 90 | 79 | 120 | 43 | .267 | .480 | 2 | 1 | OF-133, DH-21 |
| 1979 CLE A | 146 | 538 | 148 | 24 | 1 | 25 | 4.6 | 93 | 85 | 74 | 135 | 34 | .275 | .463 | 1 | 0 | OF-116, DH-29 |

| | G | AB | H | 2B | 3B | HR | HR % | R | RBI | BB | SO | SB | BA | SA | Pinch Hit AB | Pinch Hit H | G by POS |
|---|---|---|---|---|---|---|---|---|---|---|---|---|---|---|---|---|---|

## Bobby Bonds continued

| | G | AB | H | 2B | 3B | HR | HR% | R | RBI | BB | SO | SB | BA | SA | AB | H | G by POS |
|---|---|---|---|---|---|---|---|---|---|---|---|---|---|---|---|---|---|
| 1980 STL N | 86 | 231 | 47 | 5 | 3 | 5 | 2.2 | 37 | 24 | 33 | 74 | 15 | .203 | .316 | 15 | 2 | OF-70 |
| 1981 CHI N | 45 | 163 | 35 | 7 | 1 | 6 | 3.7 | 26 | 19 | 24 | 44 | 5 | .215 | .380 | 0 | 0 | OF-45 |
| 14 yrs. | 1849 | 7043 | 1886 | 302 | 66 | 332 | 4.7 | 1258 | 1024 | 914 | 1757 **4th** | 461 | .268 | .471 | 35 | 7 | OF-1736, DH-81 |
| 1 yr. | 45 | 163 | 35 | 7 | 1 | 6 | 3.7 | 26 | 19 | 24 | 44 | 5 | .215 | .380 | 0 | 0 | OF-45 |

LEAGUE CHAMPIONSHIP SERIES

| | G | AB | H | 2B | 3B | HR | HR% | R | RBI | BB | SO | SB | BA | SA | AB | H | G by POS |
|---|---|---|---|---|---|---|---|---|---|---|---|---|---|---|---|---|---|
| 1971 SF N | 3 | 8 | 2 | 0 | 0 | 0 | 0.0 | 0 | 0 | 2 | 4 | 0 | .250 | .250 | 0 | 0 | OF-3 |

## Zeke Bonura

**BONURA, HENRY JOHN**
B. Sept. 20, 1908, New Orleans, La.                                    BR  TR  6'          210 lbs.

| | G | AB | H | 2B | 3B | HR | HR% | R | RBI | BB | SO | SB | BA | SA | AB | H | G by POS |
|---|---|---|---|---|---|---|---|---|---|---|---|---|---|---|---|---|---|
| 1934 CHI A | 127 | 510 | 154 | 35 | 4 | 27 | 5.3 | 86 | 110 | 64 | 31 | 0 | .302 | .545 | 0 | 0 | 1B-127 |
| 1935 | 138 | 550 | 162 | 34 | 4 | 21 | 3.8 | 107 | 92 | 57 | 28 | 4 | .295 | .485 | 0 | 0 | 1B-138 |
| 1936 | 148 | 587 | 194 | 39 | 7 | 12 | 2.0 | 120 | 138 | 94 | 29 | 4 | .330 | .482 | 1 | 0 | 1B-146 |
| 1937 | 116 | 447 | 154 | 41 | 2 | 19 | 4.3 | 79 | 100 | 49 | 24 | 5 | .345 | .573 | 1 | 0 | 1B-115 |
| 1938 WAS A | 137 | 540 | 156 | 27 | 3 | 22 | 4.1 | 72 | 114 | 44 | 29 | 2 | .289 | .472 | 8 | 2 | 1B-129 |
| 1939 NY N | 123 | 455 | 146 | 26 | 6 | 11 | 2.4 | 75 | 85 | 46 | 22 | 1 | .321 | .477 | 0 | 0 | 1B-122 |
| 1940 2 teams | | | WAS | A | (79G — | .273) | | CHI | N | (49G — | .264) | | | | | | |
| " total | 128 | 493 | 133 | 30 | 3 | 7 | 1.4 | 61 | 65 | 50 | 17 | 3 | .270 | .385 | 5 | 1 | 1B-123 |
| 7 yrs. | 917 | 3582 | 1099 | 232 | 29 | 119 | 3.3 | 600 | 704 | 404 | 180 | 19 | .307 | .487 | 15 | 3 | 1B-900 |
| 1 yr. | 49 | 182 | 48 | 14 | 0 | 4 | 2.2 | 20 | 20 | 10 | 4 | 1 | .264 | .407 | 5 | 1 | 1B-44 |

## Bob Borkowski

**BORKOWSKI, ROBERT VILARIAN (Bush)**
B. Jan. 27, 1926, Dayton, Ohio                                         BR  TR  6'          182 lbs.

| | G | AB | H | 2B | 3B | HR | HR% | R | RBI | BB | SO | SB | BA | SA | AB | H | G by POS |
|---|---|---|---|---|---|---|---|---|---|---|---|---|---|---|---|---|---|
| 1950 CHI N | 85 | 256 | 70 | 7 | 4 | 4 | 1.6 | 27 | 29 | 16 | 30 | 1 | .273 | .379 | 14 | 2 | OF-65, 1B-1 |
| 1951 | 58 | 89 | 14 | 1 | 0 | 0 | 0.0 | 9 | 10 | 3 | 16 | 0 | .157 | .169 | 23 | 3 | OF-25 |
| 1952 CIN N | 126 | 377 | 95 | 11 | 4 | 4 | 1.1 | 42 | 24 | 26 | 53 | 1 | .252 | .334 | 18 | 3 | OF-103, 1B-5 |
| 1953 | 94 | 249 | 67 | 11 | 1 | 7 | 2.8 | 32 | 29 | 21 | 41 | 0 | .269 | .406 | 27 | 9 | OF-67, 1B-2 |
| 1954 | 73 | 162 | 43 | 12 | 1 | 1 | 0.6 | 13 | 19 | 8 | 18 | 0 | .265 | .370 | 33 | 8 | OF-36, 1B-3 |
| 1955 2 teams | | | CIN | N | (25G — | .167) | | BKN | N | (9G — | .105) | | | | | | |
| " total | 34 | 37 | 5 | 1 | 0 | 0 | 0.0 | 3 | 1 | 2 | 8 | 0 | .135 | .162 | 9 | 2 | OF-20, 1B-1 |
| 6 yrs. | 470 | 1170 | 294 | 43 | 10 | 16 | 1.4 | 126 | 112 | 76 | 166 | 2 | .251 | .346 | 124 | 27 | OF-316, 1B-12 |
| 2 yrs. | 143 | 345 | 84 | 8 | 4 | 4 | 1.2 | 36 | 39 | 19 | 46 | 1 | .243 | .325 | 37 | 5 | OF-90, 1B-1 |

## Steve Boros

**BOROS, STEPHEN**
B. Sept. 3, 1936, Flint, Mich.                                         BR  TR  6'          185 lbs.
Manager 1983-84.

| | G | AB | H | 2B | 3B | HR | HR% | R | RBI | BB | SO | SB | BA | SA | AB | H | G by POS |
|---|---|---|---|---|---|---|---|---|---|---|---|---|---|---|---|---|---|
| 1957 DET A | 24 | 41 | 6 | 1 | 0 | 0 | 0.0 | 4 | 2 | 1 | 8 | 0 | .146 | .171 | 4 | 0 | 3B-9, SS-5 |
| 1958 | 6 | 2 | 0 | 0 | 0 | 0 | 0.0 | 0 | 0 | 0 | 0 | 0 | .000 | .000 | 0 | 0 | 2B-1 |
| 1961 | 116 | 396 | 107 | 18 | 2 | 5 | 1.3 | 51 | 62 | 68 | 42 | 4 | .270 | .364 | 0 | 0 | 3B-116 |
| 1962 | 116 | 356 | 81 | 14 | 1 | 16 | 4.5 | 46 | 47 | 53 | 62 | 3 | .228 | .407 | 8 | 0 | 3B-105, 2B-6 |
| 1963 CHI N | 41 | 90 | 19 | 5 | 1 | 3 | 3.3 | 9 | 7 | 12 | 19 | 0 | .211 | .389 | 17 | 2 | 1B-14, OF-11 |
| 1964 CIN N | 117 | 370 | 95 | 12 | 3 | 2 | 0.5 | 31 | 31 | 47 | 43 | 4 | .257 | .322 | 1 | 0 | 3B-114 |
| 1965 | 2 | 0 | 0 | 0 | 0 | 0 | — | 0 | 0 | 0 | 0 | 0 | — | — | 0 | 0 | 3B-2 |
| 7 yrs. | 422 | 1255 | 308 | 50 | 7 | 26 | 2.1 | 141 | 149 | 181 | 174 | 11 | .245 | .359 | 30 | 2 | 3B-346, 1B-14, OF-11, 2B-7, SS-5 |
| 1 yr. | 41 | 90 | 19 | 5 | 1 | 3 | 3.3 | 9 | 7 | 12 | 19 | 0 | .211 | .389 | 17 | 2 | 1B-14, OF-11 |

## Thad Bosley

**BOSLEY, THADDIS**
B. Sept. 17, 1956, Oceanside, Calif.                                    BL  TL  6'3"        175 lbs.

| | G | AB | H | 2B | 3B | HR | HR% | R | RBI | BB | SO | SB | BA | SA | AB | H | G by POS |
|---|---|---|---|---|---|---|---|---|---|---|---|---|---|---|---|---|---|
| 1977 CAL A | 58 | 212 | 63 | 10 | 2 | 0 | 0.0 | 19 | 19 | 16 | 32 | 5 | .297 | .363 | 4 | 2 | OF-55 |
| 1978 CHI A | 66 | 219 | 59 | 5 | 1 | 2 | 0.9 | 25 | 13 | 13 | 32 | 12 | .269 | .329 | 1 | 0 | OF-64 |
| 1979 | 36 | 77 | 24 | 1 | 1 | 1 | 1.3 | 13 | 8 | 9 | 14 | 4 | .312 | .390 | 7 | 1 | OF-28, DH-1 |
| 1980 | 70 | 147 | 33 | 2 | 0 | 2 | 1.4 | 12 | 14 | 10 | 27 | 3 | .224 | .279 | 25 | 8 | OF-52 |
| 1981 MIL A | 42 | 105 | 24 | 2 | 0 | 0 | 0.0 | 11 | 3 | 6 | 13 | 2 | .229 | .248 | 4 | 0 | OF-37, DH-1 |
| 1982 SEA A | 22 | 46 | 8 | 1 | 0 | 0 | 0.0 | 3 | 2 | 4 | 8 | 3 | .174 | .196 | 3 | 0 | OF-19 |
| 1983 CHI N | 43 | 72 | 21 | 4 | 1 | 2 | 2.8 | 12 | 12 | 10 | 12 | 1 | .292 | .458 | 18 | 4 | OF-20 |
| 1984 | 55 | 98 | 29 | 2 | 2 | 2 | 2.0 | 17 | 14 | 13 | 22 | 5 | .296 | .418 | 23 | 6 | OF-33 |
| 1985 | 108 | 180 | 59 | 6 | 3 | 7 | 3.9 | 25 | 27 | 20 | 29 | 5 | .328 | .511 | 60 | **20** | OF-55 |
| 9 yrs. | 500 | 1156 | 320 | 33 | 10 | 16 | 1.4 | 137 | 112 | 101 | 189 | 40 | .277 | .364 | 145 | 41 | OF-363, DH-2 |
| 3 yrs. | 206 | 350 | 109 | 12 | 6 | 11 | 3.1 | 54 | 53 | 43 | 63 | 11 | .311 | .474 | 101 **7th** | 30 | OF-108 |

DIVISIONAL PLAYOFF SERIES

| | G | AB | H | 2B | 3B | HR | HR% | R | RBI | BB | SO | SB | BA | SA | AB | H | G by POS |
|---|---|---|---|---|---|---|---|---|---|---|---|---|---|---|---|---|---|
| 1981 MIL A | 1 | 0 | 0 | 0 | 0 | 0 | — | 0 | 0 | 0 | 0 | 0 | — | — | 0 | 0 | DH-1 |

LEAGUE CHAMPIONSHIP SERIES

| | G | AB | H | 2B | 3B | HR | HR% | R | RBI | BB | SO | SB | BA | SA | AB | H | G by POS |
|---|---|---|---|---|---|---|---|---|---|---|---|---|---|---|---|---|---|
| 1984 CHI N | 2 | 2 | 0 | 0 | 0 | 0 | 0.0 | 0 | 0 | 0 | 2 | 0 | .000 | .000 | 2 | 0 | |

## John Bottarini

**BOTTARINI, JOHN CHARLES**
B. Sept. 14, 1908, Crockett, Calif.   D. Oct. 8, 1976, Jemez Springs, N. M.          BR  TR  6'          190 lbs.

| | G | AB | H | 2B | 3B | HR | HR% | R | RBI | BB | SO | SB | BA | SA | AB | H | G by POS |
|---|---|---|---|---|---|---|---|---|---|---|---|---|---|---|---|---|---|
| 1937 CHI N | 26 | 40 | 11 | 3 | 0 | 1 | 2.5 | 3 | 7 | 5 | 10 | 0 | .275 | .425 | 7 | 2 | C-18, OF-1 |

## Ed Bouchee

**BOUCHEE, EDWARD FRANCIS**
B. Mar. 7, 1933, Livingston, Mont.                                     BL  TL  6'          200 lbs.

| | G | AB | H | 2B | 3B | HR | HR% | R | RBI | BB | SO | SB | BA | SA | AB | H | G by POS |
|---|---|---|---|---|---|---|---|---|---|---|---|---|---|---|---|---|---|
| 1956 PHI N | 9 | 22 | 6 | 2 | 0 | 0 | 0.0 | 0 | 1 | 5 | 6 | 0 | .273 | .364 | 2 | 0 | 1B-6 |
| 1957 | 154 | 574 | 168 | 35 | 8 | 17 | 3.0 | 78 | 76 | 84 | 91 | 1 | .293 | .470 | 0 | 0 | 1B-154 |
| 1958 | 89 | 334 | 86 | 19 | 5 | 9 | 2.7 | 55 | 39 | 51 | 74 | 1 | .257 | .425 | 0 | 0 | 1B-89 |
| 1959 | 136 | 499 | 142 | 29 | 4 | 15 | 3.0 | 75 | 74 | 70 | 74 | 0 | .285 | .449 | 2 | 1 | 1B-134 |
| 1960 2 teams | | | PHI | N | (22G — | .262) | | CHI | N | (98G — | .237) | | | | | | |
| " total | 120 | 364 | 88 | 15 | 1 | 5 | 1.4 | 34 | 52 | 54 | 62 | 2 | .242 | .330 | 17 | 1 | 1B-102 |
| 1961 CHI N | 112 | 319 | 79 | 12 | 3 | 12 | 3.8 | 49 | 38 | 58 | 77 | 1 | .248 | .417 | 12 | 1 | 1B-107 |

| | G | AB | H | 2B | 3B | HR | HR % | R | RBI | BB | SO | SB | BA | SA | Pinch Hit AB | Pinch Hit H | G by POS |
|---|---|---|---|---|---|---|---|---|---|---|---|---|---|---|---|---|---|

## Ed Bouchee continued

| | G | AB | H | 2B | 3B | HR | HR % | R | RBI | BB | SO | SB | BA | SA | AB | H | G by POS |
|---|---|---|---|---|---|---|---|---|---|---|---|---|---|---|---|---|---|
| 1962 NY N | 50 | 87 | 14 | 2 | 0 | 3 | 3.4 | 7 | 10 | 18 | 17 | 0 | .161 | .287 | 28 | 5 | 1B-19 |
| 7 yrs. | 670 | 2199 | 583 | 114 | 21 | 61 | 2.8 | 298 | 290 | 340 | 401 | 5 | .265 | .419 | 61 | 8 | 1B-611 |
| 2 yrs. | 210 | 618 | 150 | 23 | 4 | 17 | 2.8 | 82 | 82 | 103 | 128 | 3 | .243 | .375 | 28 | 2 | 1B-187 |

## Pat Bourque

**BOURQUE, PATRICK DANIEL** BL TL 6' 210 lbs.
B. Mar. 23, 1947, Worcester, Mass.

| | G | AB | H | 2B | 3B | HR | HR % | R | RBI | BB | SO | SB | BA | SA | AB | H | G by POS |
|---|---|---|---|---|---|---|---|---|---|---|---|---|---|---|---|---|---|
| 1971 CHI N | 14 | 37 | 7 | 0 | 1 | 1 | 2.7 | 3 | 3 | 3 | 9 | 0 | .189 | .324 | 3 | 1 | 1B-11 |
| 1972 | 11 | 27 | 7 | 1 | 0 | 0 | 0.0 | 3 | 5 | 2 | 2 | 0 | .259 | .296 | 4 | 0 | 1B-7 |
| 1973 2 teams | | CHI | N (57G – | .209) | | OAK | A | (23G – | .190) | | | | | | | | |
| " total | 80 | 181 | 37 | 10 | 1 | 9 | 5.0 | 19 | 29 | 31 | 31 | 1 | .204 | .420 | 20 | 4 | 1B-43, DH-15 |
| 1974 2 teams | | OAK | A (73G – | .229) | | MIN | A | (23G – | .219) | | | | | | | | |
| " total | 96 | 160 | 36 | 6 | 0 | 2 | 1.3 | 11 | 24 | 22 | 31 | 0 | .225 | .300 | 35 | 7 | 1B-60, DH-8 |
| 4 yrs. | 201 | 405 | 87 | 17 | 2 | 12 | 3.0 | 36 | 61 | 58 | 73 | 1 | .215 | .356 | 62 | 12 | 1B-121, DH-23 |
| 3 yrs. | 82 | 203 | 43 | 7 | 1 | 8 | 3.9 | 17 | 28 | 21 | 32 | 1 | .212 | .374 | 24 | 5 | 1B-56 |

LEAGUE CHAMPIONSHIP SERIES

| | G | AB | H | 2B | 3B | HR | HR % | R | RBI | BB | SO | SB | BA | SA | AB | H | G by POS |
|---|---|---|---|---|---|---|---|---|---|---|---|---|---|---|---|---|---|
| 1973 OAK A | 2 | 1 | 0 | 0 | 0 | 0 | 0.0 | 0 | 0 | 1 | 1 | 0 | .000 | .000 | 0 | 0 | DH-2 |

WORLD SERIES

| | G | AB | H | 2B | 3B | HR | HR % | R | RBI | BB | SO | SB | BA | SA | AB | H | G by POS |
|---|---|---|---|---|---|---|---|---|---|---|---|---|---|---|---|---|---|
| 1973 OAK A | 2 | 2 | 1 | 0 | 0 | 0 | 0.0 | 0 | 0 | 0 | 0 | 0 | .500 | .500 | 1 | 0 | 1B-2 |

## Larry Bowa

**BOWA, LAWRENCE ROBERT** BB TR 5'10" 155 lbs.
B. Dec. 6, 1945, Sacramento, Calif.

| | G | AB | H | 2B | 3B | HR | HR % | R | RBI | BB | SO | SB | BA | SA | AB | H | G by POS |
|---|---|---|---|---|---|---|---|---|---|---|---|---|---|---|---|---|---|
| 1970 PHI N | 145 | 547 | 137 | 17 | 6 | 0 | 0.0 | 50 | 34 | 21 | 48 | 24 | .250 | .303 | 0 | 0 | SS-143, 2B-1 |
| 1971 | 159 | 650 | 162 | 18 | 5 | 0 | 0.0 | 74 | 25 | 36 | 61 | 28 | .249 | .292 | 0 | 0 | SS-157 |
| 1972 | 152 | 579 | 145 | 11 | 13 | 1 | 0.2 | 67 | 31 | 32 | 51 | 17 | .250 | .320 | 0 | 0 | SS-150 |
| 1973 | 122 | 446 | 94 | 11 | 3 | 0 | 0.0 | 42 | 23 | 24 | 31 | 10 | .211 | .249 | 0 | 0 | SS-122 |
| 1974 | 162 | 669 | 184 | 19 | 10 | 1 | 0.1 | 97 | 36 | 23 | 52 | 39 | .275 | .338 | 0 | 0 | SS-162 |
| 1975 | 136 | 583 | 178 | 18 | 9 | 2 | 0.3 | 79 | 38 | 24 | 32 | 24 | .305 | .377 | 0 | 0 | SS-135 |
| 1976 | 156 | 624 | 155 | 15 | 9 | 0 | 0.0 | 71 | 49 | 32 | 31 | 30 | .248 | .301 | 0 | 0 | SS-156 |
| 1977 | 154 | 624 | 175 | 19 | 3 | 4 | 0.6 | 93 | 41 | 32 | 32 | 32 | .280 | .340 | 0 | 0 | SS-154 |
| 1978 | 156 | 654 | 192 | 31 | 5 | 3 | 0.5 | 78 | 43 | 24 | 40 | 27 | .294 | .370 | 0 | 0 | SS-156 |
| 1979 | 147 | 539 | 130 | 17 | 11 | 0 | 0.0 | 74 | 31 | 61 | 32 | 20 | .241 | .314 | 0 | 0 | SS-146 |
| 1980 | 147 | 540 | 144 | 16 | 4 | 2 | 0.4 | 57 | 39 | 24 | 28 | 21 | .267 | .322 | 0 | 0 | SS-147 |
| 1981 | 103 | 360 | 102 | 14 | 3 | 0 | 0.0 | 34 | 31 | 26 | 17 | 16 | .283 | .339 | 1 | 0 | SS-102 |
| 1982 CHI N | 142 | 499 | 123 | 15 | 7 | 0 | 0.0 | 50 | 29 | 39 | 38 | 8 | .246 | .305 | 2 | 1 | SS-140 |
| 1983 | 147 | 499 | 133 | 20 | 5 | 2 | 0.4 | 73 | 43 | 35 | 30 | 7 | .267 | .339 | 4 | 1 | SS-145 |
| 1984 | 133 | 391 | 87 | 14 | 2 | 0 | 0.0 | 33 | 17 | 28 | 24 | 10 | .223 | .269 | 2 | 1 | SS-132 |
| 1985 2 teams | | CHI | N (72G – | .246) | | NY | N | (14G – | .105) | | | | | | | | |
| " total | 86 | 214 | 50 | 7 | 4 | 0 | 0.0 | 15 | 15 | 13 | 22 | 5 | .234 | .304 | 3 | 0 | SS-75, 2B-4 |
| 16 yrs. | 2247 | 8418 | 2191 | 262 | 99 | 15 | 0.2 | 987 | 525 | 474 | 569 | 318 | .260 | .320 | 12 | 3 | SS-2222, 2B-5 |
| 4 yrs. | 494 | 1584 | 391 | 55 | 18 | 2 | 0.1 | 169 | 102 | 113 | 112 | 30 | .247 | .308 | 10 | 3 | SS-483 |

DIVISIONAL PLAYOFF SERIES

| | G | AB | H | 2B | 3B | HR | HR % | R | RBI | BB | SO | SB | BA | SA | AB | H | G by POS |
|---|---|---|---|---|---|---|---|---|---|---|---|---|---|---|---|---|---|
| 1981 PHI N | 5 | 17 | 3 | 1 | 0 | 0 | 0.0 | 0 | 1 | 0 | 0 | 0 | .176 | .235 | 0 | 0 | SS-5 |

LEAGUE CHAMPIONSHIP SERIES

| | G | AB | H | 2B | 3B | HR | HR % | R | RBI | BB | SO | SB | BA | SA | AB | H | G by POS |
|---|---|---|---|---|---|---|---|---|---|---|---|---|---|---|---|---|---|
| 1976 PHI N | 3 | 8 | 1 | 1 | 0 | 0 | 0.0 | 1 | 1 | 3 | 0 | 0 | .125 | .250 | 0 | 0 | SS-3 |
| 1977 | 4 | 17 | 2 | 0 | 0 | 0 | 0.0 | 2 | 1 | 1 | 0 | 0 | .118 | .118 | 0 | 0 | SS-4 |
| 1978 | 4 | 18 | 6 | 0 | 0 | 0 | 0.0 | 2 | 0 | 1 | 2 | 0 | .333 | .333 | 0 | 0 | SS-4 |
| 1980 | 5 | 19 | 6 | 0 | 0 | 0 | 0.0 | 2 | 3 | 3 | 3 | 1 | .316 | .316 | 0 | 0 | SS-5 |
| 1984 CHI N | 5 | 15 | 3 | 1 | 0 | 0 | 0.0 | 1 | 1 | 1 | 0 | 0 | .200 | .267 | 0 | 0 | SS-5 |
| 5 yrs. | 21 | 77 | 18 | 2 | 0 | 0 | 0.0 | 8 | 3 | 9 | 5 | 1 | .234 | .260 | 0 | 0 | SS-21 |

WORLD SERIES

| | G | AB | H | 2B | 3B | HR | HR % | R | RBI | BB | SO | SB | BA | SA | AB | H | G by POS |
|---|---|---|---|---|---|---|---|---|---|---|---|---|---|---|---|---|---|
| 1980 PHI N | 6 | 24 | 9 | 1 | 0 | 0 | 0.0 | 3 | 2 | 0 | 0 | 3 | .375 | .417 | 0 | 0 | SS-6 |

## Bill Bowman

**BOWMAN, WILLIAM GEORGE** 5'11" 180 lbs.
B. 1869, Chicago, Ill. D. Apr. 6, 1918, Arlington Heights, Ill.

| | G | AB | H | 2B | 3B | HR | HR % | R | RBI | BB | SO | SB | BA | SA | AB | H | G by POS |
|---|---|---|---|---|---|---|---|---|---|---|---|---|---|---|---|---|---|
| 1891 CHI N | 15 | 45 | 4 | 1 | 0 | 0 | 0.0 | 2 | 5 | 5 | 9 | 0 | .089 | .111 | 0 | 0 | C-15 |

## Bill Bradley

**BRADLEY, WILLIAM JOSEPH** BR TR 6' 185 lbs.
B. Feb. 13, 1878, Cleveland, Ohio   D. Mar. 11, 1954, Cleveland, Ohio
Manager 1914.

| | G | AB | H | 2B | 3B | HR | HR % | R | RBI | BB | SO | SB | BA | SA | AB | H | G by POS |
|---|---|---|---|---|---|---|---|---|---|---|---|---|---|---|---|---|---|
| 1899 CHI N | 35 | 129 | 40 | 6 | 1 | 2 | 1.6 | 26 | 18 | 12 | | 4 | .310 | .419 | 0 | 0 | 3B-30, SS-5 |
| 1900 | 122 | 444 | 125 | 21 | 8 | 5 | 1.1 | 63 | 49 | 27 | | 14 | .282 | .399 | 1 | 1 | 3B-106, 1B-15 |
| 1901 CLE A | 133 | 516 | 151 | 28 | 13 | 1 | 0.2 | 95 | 55 | 26 | | 15 | .293 | .403 | 0 | 0 | 3B-133, P-1 |
| 1902 | 137 | 550 | 187 | 39 | 12 | 11 | 2.0 | 104 | 77 | 27 | | 11 | .340 | .515 | 0 | 0 | 3B-137 |
| 1903 | 137 | 543 | 171 | 36 | 22 | 6 | 1.1 | 103 | 68 | 25 | | 21 | .315 | .495 | 0 | 0 | 3B-137 |
| 1904 | 154 | 607 | 182 | 31 | 8 | 5 | 0.8 | 94 | 83 | 26 | | 27 | .300 | .402 | 0 | 0 | 3B-154 |
| 1905 | 145 | 537 | 144 | 34 | 6 | 0 | 0.0 | 63 | 51 | 27 | | 22 | .268 | .354 | 0 | 0 | 3B-145 |
| 1906 | 82 | 302 | 83 | 15 | 2 | 2 | 0.7 | 32 | 25 | 18 | | 13 | .275 | .358 | 0 | 0 | 3B-82 |
| 1907 | 139 | 498 | 111 | 20 | 1 | 0 | 0.0 | 48 | 34 | 35 | | 20 | .223 | .267 | 0 | 0 | 3B-139 |
| 1908 | 148 | 548 | 133 | 24 | 7 | 1 | 0.2 | 70 | 46 | 29 | | 18 | .243 | .318 | 0 | 0 | 3B-116, SS-32 |
| 1909 | 95 | 334 | 62 | 6 | 3 | 0 | 0.0 | 30 | 22 | 19 | | 8 | .186 | .222 | 2 | 1 | 3B-87, 2B-3, 1B-3 |
| 1910 | 61 | 214 | 42 | 3 | 0 | 0 | 0.0 | 12 | 12 | 10 | | 6 | .196 | .210 | 0 | 0 | 3B-61 |
| 1914 BKN F | 7 | 6 | 3 | 1 | 0 | 0 | 0.0 | 1 | 3 | 0 | | 0 | .500 | .667 | 6 | 3 | |
| 1915 KC F | 66 | 203 | 38 | 9 | 1 | 0 | 0.0 | 15 | 9 | 9 | | 6 | .187 | .241 | 5 | 0 | 3B-61 |
| 14 yrs. | 1461 | 5431 | 1472 | 273 | 84 | 33 | 0.6 | 756 | 552 | 290 | | 185 | .271 | .370 | 14 | 5 | 3B-1388, SS-37, 1B-18, 2B-3, P-1 |
| 2 yrs. | 157 | 573 | 165 | 27 | 9 | 7 | 1.2 | 89 | 67 | 39 | | 18 | .288 | .403 | 1 | 1 | 3B-136, 1B-15, SS-5 |

| | G | AB | H | 2B | 3B | HR | HR % | R | RBI | BB | SO | SB | BA | SA | Pinch Hit AB | Pinch Hit H | G by POS |
|---|---|---|---|---|---|---|---|---|---|---|---|---|---|---|---|---|---|

## George Bradley

**BRADLEY, GEORGE WASHINGTON (Grin)**　　　　　BR TR 5'10½" 175 lbs.
B. July 13, 1852, Reading, Pa.　　D. Oct. 2, 1931, Philadelphia, Pa.

| | G | AB | H | 2B | 3B | HR | HR % | R | RBI | BB | SO | SB | BA | SA | PH AB | PH H | G by POS |
|---|---|---|---|---|---|---|---|---|---|---|---|---|---|---|---|---|---|
| 1876 STL N | 64 | 265 | 66 | 7 | 6 | 0 | 0.0 | 29 | 28 | 3 | 12 | | .249 | .321 | 0 | 0 | P-64 |
| 1877 CHI N | 55 | 214 | 52 | 7 | 3 | 0 | 0.0 | 31 | 12 | 6 | 19 | | .243 | .304 | 0 | 0 | P-50, 3B-16, 1B-3, OF-1 |
| 1879 TRO N | 63 | 251 | 62 | 9 | 5 | 0 | 0.0 | 36 | 23 | 1 | 20 | | .247 | .323 | 0 | 0 | P-54, 3B-5, 1B-3, OF-1, SS-1 |
| 1880 PRO N | 82 | 309 | 70 | 7 | 6 | 0 | 0.0 | 32 | 23 | 5 | 38 | | .227 | .288 | 0 | 0 | 3B-57, P-28, OF-7, 1B-2 |
| 1881 2 teams | | DET | N | (1G – | .000) | | CLE | N | (60G – | .249) | | | | | | | |
| " total | 61 | 245 | 60 | 10 | 1 | 2 | 0.8 | 21 | 18 | 4 | 25 | | .245 | .318 | 0 | 0 | 3B-48, SS-7, P-6, OF-1 |
| 1882 CLE N | 30 | 115 | 21 | 5 | 0 | 0 | 0.0 | 16 | 6 | 4 | 16 | | .183 | .226 | 0 | 0 | P-18, OF-9, 1B-6 |
| 1883 2 teams | | CLE | N | (4G – | .313) | | PHI | AA | (76G – | .234) | | | | | | | |
| " total | 80 | 328 | 78 | 8 | 6 | 1 | 0.3 | 47 | | 8 | 1 | | .238 | .308 | 0 | 0 | 3B-44, P-26, OF-11, SS-4, 1B-2 |
| 1884 CIN U | 58 | 226 | 43 | 4 | 7 | 0 | 0.0 | 31 | | 7 | | | .190 | .270 | 0 | 0 | P-41, OF-16, SS-5, 1B-2 |
| 1886 PHI AA | 13 | 48 | 4 | 0 | 1 | 0 | 0.0 | 1 | | 1 | | | .083 | .125 | 0 | 0 | SS-13 |
| 1888 BAL AA | 1 | 3 | 0 | 0 | 0 | 0 | 0.0 | 0 | 0 | 0 | | 0 | .000 | .000 | 0 | 0 | SS-1 |
| 10 yrs. | 507 | 2004 | 456 | 57 | 35 | 3 | 0.1 | 244 | 110 | 39 | 131 | 0 | .228 | .295 | 0 | 0 | P-287, 3B-170, OF-46, SS-31, 1B-18 |
| 1 yr. | 55 | 214 | 52 | 7 | 3 | 0 | 0.0 | 31 | 12 | 6 | 19 | | .243 | .304 | 0 | 0 | P-50, 3B-16, 1B-3, OF-1 |

## Kitty Bransfield

**BRANSFIELD, WILLIAM EDWARD**　　　　　BR TR 5'11" 207 lbs.
B. Jan. 7, 1875, Worcester, Mass.　　D. May 1, 1947, Worcester, Mass.

| | G | AB | H | 2B | 3B | HR | HR % | R | RBI | BB | SO | SB | BA | SA | PH AB | PH H | G by POS |
|---|---|---|---|---|---|---|---|---|---|---|---|---|---|---|---|---|---|
| 1898 BOS N | 5 | 9 | 2 | 0 | 1 | 0 | 0.0 | 2 | 1 | 0 | | 0 | .222 | .444 | 0 | 0 | C-4, 1B-1 |
| 1901 PIT N | 139 | 566 | 167 | 26 | 17 | 0 | 0.0 | 92 | 91 | 29 | | 23 | .295 | .401 | 0 | 0 | 1B-139 |
| 1902 | 102 | 417 | 127 | 21 | 7 | 1 | 0.2 | 50 | 69 | 17 | | 23 | .305 | .396 | 1 | 0 | 1B-101 |
| 1903 | 127 | 505 | 134 | 23 | 7 | 2 | 0.4 | 69 | 57 | 33 | | 13 | .265 | .350 | 0 | 0 | 1B-127 |
| 1904 | 139 | 520 | 116 | 17 | 9 | 0 | 0.0 | 47 | 60 | 22 | | 11 | .223 | .290 | 0 | 0 | 1B-139 |
| 1905 PHI N | 151 | 580 | 150 | 23 | 9 | 3 | 0.5 | 55 | 76 | 27 | | 27 | .259 | .345 | 0 | 0 | 1B-151 |
| 1906 | 140 | 524 | 144 | 28 | 5 | 1 | 0.2 | 47 | 60 | 16 | | 12 | .275 | .353 | 1 | 0 | 1B-139 |
| 1907 | 94 | 348 | 81 | 15 | 2 | 0 | 0.0 | 25 | 38 | 14 | | 8 | .233 | .287 | 2 | 0 | 1B-92 |
| 1908 | 144 | 527 | 160 | 25 | 7 | 3 | 0.6 | 53 | 71 | 23 | | 30 | .304 | .395 | 1 | 1 | 1B-143 |
| 1909 | 140 | 527 | 154 | 27 | 6 | 1 | 0.2 | 47 | 59 | 18 | | 17 | .292 | .372 | 2 | 0 | 1B-138 |
| 1910 | 123 | 427 | 102 | 17 | 4 | 3 | 0.7 | 39 | 52 | 20 | 34 | 10 | .239 | .319 | 12 | 2 | 1B-110 |
| 1911 2 teams | | PHI | N | (23G – | .256) | | CHI | N | (3G – | .400) | | | | | | | |
| " total | 26 | 53 | 15 | 3 | 1 | 0 | 0.0 | 4 | 3 | 2 | 7 | 1 | .283 | .377 | 15 | 1 | 1B-11 |
| 12 yrs. | 1330 | 5003 | 1352 | 225 | 75 | 14 | 0.3 | 530 | 637 | 221 | 41 | 175 | .270 | .354 | 34 | 4 | 1B-1291, C-4 |
| 1 yr. | 3 | 10 | 4 | 2 | 0 | 0 | 0.0 | 0 | 0 | 2 | 2 | 0 | .400 | .600 | 0 | 0 | 1B-3 |

WORLD SERIES

| | G | AB | H | 2B | 3B | HR | HR % | R | RBI | BB | SO | SB | BA | SA | PH AB | PH H | G by POS |
|---|---|---|---|---|---|---|---|---|---|---|---|---|---|---|---|---|---|
| 1903 PIT N | 8 | 30 | 6 | 0 | 2 | 0 | 0.0 | 3 | 1 | 1 | 6 | 1 | .200 | .333 | 0 | 0 | 1B-8 |

## Danny Breeden

**BREEDEN, DANIEL RICHARD.**　　　　　BR TR 5'11½" 185 lbs.
Brother of Hal Breeden.
B. June 27, 1942, Albany, Ga.

| | G | AB | H | 2B | 3B | HR | HR % | R | RBI | BB | SO | SB | BA | SA | PH AB | PH H | G by POS |
|---|---|---|---|---|---|---|---|---|---|---|---|---|---|---|---|---|---|
| 1969 CIN N | 3 | 8 | 1 | 0 | 0 | 0 | 0.0 | 0 | 1 | 0 | 3 | 0 | .125 | .125 | 0 | 0 | C-3 |
| 1971 CHI N | 25 | 65 | 10 | 1 | 0 | 0 | 0.0 | 3 | 4 | 9 | 18 | 0 | .154 | .169 | 0 | 0 | C-25 |
| 2 yrs. | 28 | 73 | 11 | 1 | 0 | 0 | 0.0 | 3 | 5 | 9 | 21 | 0 | .151 | .164 | 0 | 0 | C-28 |
| 1 yr. | 25 | 65 | 10 | 1 | 0 | 0 | 0.0 | 3 | 4 | 9 | 18 | 0 | .154 | .169 | 0 | 0 | C-25 |

## Hal Breeden

**BREEDEN, HAROLD NOEL**　　　　　BR TL 6'2" 200 lbs.
Brother of Danny Breeden.
B. June 28, 1944, Albany, Ga.

| | G | AB | H | 2B | 3B | HR | HR % | R | RBI | BB | SO | SB | BA | SA | PH AB | PH H | G by POS |
|---|---|---|---|---|---|---|---|---|---|---|---|---|---|---|---|---|---|
| 1971 CHI N | 23 | 36 | 5 | 1 | 0 | 1 | 2.8 | 1 | 2 | 2 | 7 | 0 | .139 | .250 | 14 | 0 | 1B-8 |
| 1972 MON N | 42 | 87 | 20 | 2 | 0 | 3 | 3.4 | 6 | 10 | 7 | 15 | 0 | .230 | .356 | 17 | 5 | 1B-26, OF-10 |
| 1973 | 105 | 258 | 71 | 10 | 6 | 15 | 5.8 | 36 | 43 | 29 | 45 | 0 | .275 | .535 | 43 | 12 | 1B-66 |
| 1974 | 79 | 190 | 47 | 13 | 0 | 2 | 1.1 | 14 | 20 | 24 | 35 | 0 | .247 | .347 | 25 | 6 | 1B-56 |
| 1975 | 24 | 37 | 5 | 2 | 0 | 0 | 0.0 | 4 | 1 | 7 | 5 | 0 | .135 | .189 | 12 | 3 | 1B-12 |
| 5 yrs. | 273 | 608 | 148 | 28 | 6 | 21 | 3.5 | 61 | 76 | 69 | 107 | 0 | .243 | .413 | 111 | 26 | 1B-168, OF-10 |
| 1 yr. | 23 | 36 | 5 | 1 | 0 | 1 | 2.8 | 1 | 2 | 2 | 7 | 0 | .139 | .250 | 14 | 0 | 1B-8 |

## Roger Bresnahan

**BRESNAHAN, ROGER PHILIP (The Duke of Tralee)**　　　　　BR TR 5'9" 200 lbs.
B. June 11, 1879, Toledo, Ohio　　D. Dec. 4, 1944, Toledo, Ohio
Manager 1909-12, 1915.
Hall of Fame 1945.

| | G | AB | H | 2B | 3B | HR | HR % | R | RBI | BB | SO | SB | BA | SA | PH AB | PH H | G by POS |
|---|---|---|---|---|---|---|---|---|---|---|---|---|---|---|---|---|---|
| 1897 WAS N | 6 | 16 | 6 | 0 | 0 | 0 | 0.0 | 1 | 3 | 1 | | 0 | .375 | .375 | 0 | 0 | P-6, OF-1 |
| 1900 CHI N | 2 | 2 | 0 | 0 | 0 | 0 | 0.0 | 0 | 0 | 0 | | 0 | .000 | .000 | 0 | 0 | C-1 |
| 1901 BAL A | 86 | 293 | 77 | 9 | 9 | 1 | 0.3 | 40 | 32 | 23 | | 10 | .263 | .365 | 1 | 0 | C-69, OF-8, 3B-4, 2B-2, P-2 |
| 1902 2 teams | | BAL | A | (65G – | .272) | | NY | N | (51G – | .292) | | | | | | | |
| " total | 116 | 413 | 116 | 22 | 9 | 5 | 1.2 | 47 | 56 | 37 | | 18 | .281 | .414 | 2 | 2 | OF-42, C-38, 3B-31, SS-4, 1B-4 |
| 1903 NY N | 113 | 406 | 142 | 30 | 8 | 4 | 1.0 | 87 | 55 | 61 | | 34 | .350 | .493 | 1 | 1 | OF-84, 1B-13, C-11, 3B-4 |
| 1904 | 109 | 402 | 114 | 22 | 7 | 5 | 1.2 | 81 | 33 | 58 | | 13 | .284 | .410 | 3 | 1 | OF-93, 1B-10, SS-4, 3B-1, 2B-1 |
| 1905 | 104 | 331 | 100 | 18 | 3 | 0 | 0.0 | 58 | 46 | 50 | | 11 | .302 | .375 | 6 | 0 | C-87, OF-8 |
| 1906 | 124 | 405 | 114 | 22 | 4 | 0 | 0.0 | 69 | 43 | 81 | | 25 | .281 | .356 | 0 | 0 | C-82, OF-40 |
| 1907 | 110 | 328 | 83 | 9 | 7 | 4 | 1.2 | 57 | 38 | 61 | | 15 | .253 | .360 | 6 | 2 | C-95, 1B-6, OF-2, 3B-1 |
| 1908 | 140 | 449 | 127 | 25 | 3 | 1 | 0.2 | 70 | 54 | 83 | | 14 | .283 | .359 | 1 | 1 | C-139 |
| 1909 STL N | 72 | 234 | 57 | 4 | 1 | 0 | 0.0 | 27 | 23 | 46 | | 11 | .244 | .269 | 2 | 0 | C-59, 2B-9, 3B-1 |
| 1910 | 88 | 234 | 65 | 15 | 3 | 0 | 0.0 | 35 | 27 | 55 | 17 | 13 | .278 | .368 | 5 | 0 | C-77, OF-2, P-1 |
| 1911 | 81 | 227 | 63 | 17 | 8 | 3 | 1.3 | 22 | 41 | 45 | 19 | 4 | .278 | .463 | 3 | 1 | C-77, 2B-2 |
| 1912 | 48 | 108 | 36 | 7 | 2 | 1 | 0.9 | 8 | 15 | 14 | 9 | 4 | .333 | .463 | 14 | 7 | C-28 |
| 1913 CHI N | 68 | 161 | 37 | 5 | 2 | 1 | 0.6 | 20 | 21 | 21 | 11 | 7 | .230 | .304 | 9 | 4 | C-58 |
| 1914 | 86 | 248 | 69 | 10 | 4 | 0 | 0.0 | 42 | 26 | 49 | 20 | 20 | .278 | .351 | 4 | 1 | C-85, 2B-14, OF-1 |

| | G | AB | H | 2B | 3B | HR | HR % | R | RBI | BB | SO | SB | BA | SA | Pinch Hit AB | Pinch Hit H | G by POS |
|---|---|---|---|---|---|---|---|---|---|---|---|---|---|---|---|---|---|

## Roger Bresnahan continued

| | G | AB | H | 2B | 3B | HR | HR% | R | RBI | BB | SO | SB | BA | SA | AB | H | G by POS |
|---|---|---|---|---|---|---|---|---|---|---|---|---|---|---|---|---|---|
| 1915 | 77 | 221 | 45 | 8 | 1 | 1 | 0.5 | 19 | 19 | 29 | 23 | 19 | .204 | .262 | 6 | 0 | C-68 |
| 17 yrs. | 1430 | 4478 | 1251 | 223 | 71 | 26 | 0.6 | 683 | 530 | 714 | 99 | 212 | .279 | .378 | 63 | 20 | C-974, OF-281, 3B-42, 1B-33, 2B-28, P-9, SS-8 |
| 4 yrs. | 233 | 632 | 151 | 23 | 7 | 2 | 0.3 | 81 | 64 | 99 | 54 | 40 | .239 | .307 | 19 | 5 | C-212, 2B-14, OF-1 |
| WORLD SERIES | | | | | | | | | | | | | | | | | |
| 1905 NY N | 5 | 16 | 5 | 2 | 0 | 0 | 0.0 | 3 | 1 | 4 | 0 | 1 | .313 | .438 | 0 | 0 | C-5 |

## Charlie Brewster

**BREWSTER, CHARLES LAWRENCE**
B. Dec. 27, 1916, Marthaville, La.
BR TR 5'8½" 175 lbs.

| | G | AB | H | 2B | 3B | HR | HR% | R | RBI | BB | SO | SB | BA | SA | AB | H | G by POS |
|---|---|---|---|---|---|---|---|---|---|---|---|---|---|---|---|---|---|
| 1943 2 teams | CIN | N (7G – | .125) | | PHI | N (49G – | .220) | | | | | | | | | | |
| " total | 56 | 167 | 36 | 2 | 0 | 0 | 0.0 | 13 | 12 | 10 | 20 | 1 | .216 | .228 | 2 | 0 | SS-46, 2B-2 |
| 1944 CHI N | 10 | 44 | 11 | 2 | 0 | 0 | 0.0 | 4 | 2 | 5 | 7 | 0 | .250 | .295 | 0 | 0 | SS-10 |
| 1946 CLE A | 3 | 2 | 0 | 0 | 0 | 0 | 0.0 | 0 | 0 | 1 | 1 | 0 | .000 | .000 | 1 | 0 | SS-1 |
| 3 yrs. | 69 | 213 | 47 | 4 | 0 | 0 | 0.0 | 17 | 14 | 16 | 28 | 1 | .221 | .239 | 3 | 0 | SS-57, 2B-2 |
| 1 yr. | 10 | 44 | 11 | 2 | 0 | 0 | 0.0 | 4 | 2 | 5 | 7 | 0 | .250 | .295 | 0 | 0 | SS-10 |

## Al Bridwell

**BRIDWELL, ALBERT HENRY**
B. Jan. 4, 1884, Friendship, Ohio    D. Jan. 23, 1969, Portsmouth, Ohio
BL TR 5'9" 150 lbs.

| | G | AB | H | 2B | 3B | HR | HR% | R | RBI | BB | SO | SB | BA | SA | AB | H | G by POS |
|---|---|---|---|---|---|---|---|---|---|---|---|---|---|---|---|---|---|
| 1905 CIN N | 82 | 254 | 64 | 3 | 1 | 0 | 0.0 | 17 | 17 | 19 | | 8 | .252 | .272 | 7 | 3 | 3B-43, OF-18, 2B-7, SS-5, 1B-1 |
| 1906 BOS N | 120 | 459 | 104 | 9 | 1 | 0 | 0.0 | 41 | 22 | 44 | | 6 | .227 | .251 | 0 | 0 | SS-119, OF-1 |
| 1907 | 140 | 509 | 111 | 8 | 2 | 0 | 0.0 | 49 | 26 | 61 | | 17 | .218 | .242 | 0 | 0 | SS-140 |
| 1908 NY N | 147 | 467 | 133 | 14 | 1 | 0 | 0.0 | 53 | 46 | 52 | | 20 | .285 | .319 | 0 | 0 | SS-147 |
| 1909 | 145 | 476 | 140 | 11 | 5 | 0 | 0.0 | 59 | 55 | 67 | | 32 | .294 | .338 | 0 | 0 | SS-144 |
| 1910 | 142 | 492 | 136 | 15 | 7 | 0 | 0.0 | 74 | 48 | 73 | 23 | 14 | .276 | .335 | 1 | 0 | SS-141 |
| 1911 2 teams | NY | N (76G – | .270) | | BOS | N (51G – | .291) | | | | | | | | | | |
| " total | 127 | 445 | 124 | 15 | 1 | 0 | 0.0 | 57 | 41 | 66 | 18 | 10 | .279 | .317 | 0 | 0 | SS-127 |
| 1912 BOS N | 31 | 106 | 25 | 5 | 1 | 0 | 0.0 | 6 | 14 | 7 | 6 | 2 | .236 | .302 | 0 | 0 | SS-31 |
| 1913 CHI N | 135 | 405 | 97 | 6 | 6 | 1 | 0.2 | 35 | 37 | 74 | 28 | 12 | .240 | .291 | 0 | 0 | SS-135 |
| 1914 STL F | 117 | 381 | 90 | 6 | 5 | 1 | 0.3 | 46 | 33 | 71 | | 9 | .236 | .286 | 3 | 0 | SS-103, 2B-11 |
| 1915 | 65 | 175 | 40 | 3 | 2 | 0 | 0.0 | 20 | 9 | 25 | | 6 | .229 | .269 | 6 | 2 | 2B-42, 3B-15, 1B-1 |
| 11 yrs. | 1251 | 4169 | 1064 | 95 | 32 | 2 | 0.0 | 457 | 348 | 559 | 75 | 136 | .255 | .295 | 17 | 5 | SS-1092, 2B-60, 3B-58, OF-19, 1B-2 |
| 1 yr. | 135 | 405 | 97 | 6 | 6 | 1 | 0.2 | 35 | 37 | 74 | 28 | 12 | .240 | .291 | 0 | 0 | SS-135 |

## Dan Briggs

**BRIGGS, DANIEL LEE**
B. Nov. 18, 1952, Scotia, Calif.
BL TL 6' 180 lbs.

| | G | AB | H | 2B | 3B | HR | HR% | R | RBI | BB | SO | SB | BA | SA | AB | H | G by POS |
|---|---|---|---|---|---|---|---|---|---|---|---|---|---|---|---|---|---|
| 1975 CAL A | 13 | 31 | 7 | 1 | 0 | 1 | 3.2 | 3 | 3 | 2 | 6 | 0 | .226 | .355 | 1 | 0 | 1B-6, OF-5, DH-2 |
| 1976 | 77 | 248 | 53 | 13 | 2 | 1 | 0.4 | 19 | 14 | 13 | 47 | 0 | .214 | .294 | 4 | 2 | 1B-44, OF-40, DH-1 |
| 1977 | 59 | 74 | 12 | 2 | 0 | 1 | 1.4 | 6 | 4 | 8 | 14 | 0 | .162 | .230 | 3 | 0 | 1B-45, OF-13 |
| 1978 CLE A | 15 | 49 | 8 | 0 | 1 | 1 | 2.0 | 4 | 1 | 4 | 9 | 0 | .163 | .265 | 0 | 0 | OF-15 |
| 1979 SD N | 104 | 227 | 47 | 4 | 3 | 8 | 3.5 | 34 | 30 | 18 | 45 | 2 | .207 | .357 | 29 | 3 | 1B-50, OF-44 |
| 1981 MON N | 9 | 11 | 1 | 0 | 0 | 0 | 0.0 | 0 | 0 | 0 | 3 | 0 | .091 | .091 | 3 | 0 | OF-3, 1B-3 |
| 1982 CHI N | 48 | 48 | 6 | 0 | 0 | 0 | 0.0 | 1 | 1 | 0 | 9 | 0 | .125 | .125 | 37 | 4 | OF-10, 1B-4 |
| 7 yrs. | 325 | 688 | 134 | 20 | 6 | 12 | 1.7 | 67 | 53 | 45 | 133 | 2 | .195 | .294 | 77 | 9 | 1B-152, OF-130, DH-3 |
| 1 yr. | 48 | 48 | 6 | 0 | 0 | 0 | 0.0 | 1 | 1 | 0 | 9 | 0 | .125 | .125 | 37 | 4 | OF-10, 1B-4 |

## Harry Bright

**BRIGHT, HARRY JAMES**
B. Sept. 22, 1929, Kansas City, Mo.
BR TR 6' 190 lbs.

| | G | AB | H | 2B | 3B | HR | HR% | R | RBI | BB | SO | SB | BA | SA | AB | H | G by POS |
|---|---|---|---|---|---|---|---|---|---|---|---|---|---|---|---|---|---|
| 1958 PIT N | 15 | 24 | 6 | 1 | 0 | 1 | 4.2 | 4 | 3 | 1 | 6 | 0 | .250 | .417 | 4 | 1 | 3B-7 |
| 1959 | 40 | 48 | 12 | 1 | 0 | 3 | 6.3 | 4 | 8 | 5 | 10 | 0 | .250 | .458 | 31 | 7 | OF-4, 3B-3, 2B-1 |
| 1960 | 4 | 4 | 0 | 0 | 0 | 0 | 0.0 | 0 | 0 | 0 | 2 | 0 | .000 | .000 | 4 | 0 | |
| 1961 WAS A | 72 | 183 | 44 | 6 | 0 | 4 | 2.2 | 20 | 21 | 19 | 23 | 0 | .240 | .339 | 23 | 3 | 3B-40, C-8, 2B-1 |
| 1962 | 113 | 392 | 107 | 15 | 4 | 17 | 4.3 | 55 | 67 | 26 | 51 | 2 | .273 | .462 | 15 | 4 | 1B-99, C-3, 3B-1 |
| 1963 2 teams | CIN | N (1G – | .000) | | NY | A (60G – | .236) | | | | | | | | | | |
| " total | 61 | 158 | 37 | 7 | 0 | 7 | 4.4 | 15 | 23 | 13 | 32 | 0 | .234 | .411 | 12 | 2 | 1B-36, 3B-12 |
| 1964 NY A | 4 | 5 | 1 | 0 | 0 | 0 | 0.0 | 0 | 0 | 1 | 1 | 0 | .200 | .200 | 1 | 0 | 1B-2 |
| 1965 CHI N | 27 | 25 | 7 | 1 | 0 | 0 | 0.0 | 1 | 4 | 0 | 8 | 0 | .280 | .320 | 25 | 7 | |
| 8 yrs. | 336 | 839 | 214 | 31 | 4 | 32 | 3.8 | 99 | 126 | 65 | 133 | 2 | .255 | .416 | 115 | 24 | 1B-137, 3B-63, C-11, OF-4, 2B-2 |
| 1 yr. | 27 | 25 | 7 | 1 | 0 | 0 | 0.0 | 1 | 4 | 0 | 8 | 0 | .280 | .320 | 25 | 7 | |
| WORLD SERIES | | | | | | | | | | | | | | | | | |
| 1963 NY A | 2 | 2 | 0 | 0 | 0 | 0 | 0.0 | 0 | 0 | 0 | 2 | 0 | .000 | .000 | 2 | 0 | |

## Leon Brinkopf

**BRINKOPF, LEON CLARENCE**
B. Oct. 20, 1926, Cape Girardeau, Mo.
BR TR 5'11½" 185 lbs.

| | G | AB | H | 2B | 3B | HR | HR% | R | RBI | BB | SO | SB | BA | SA | AB | H | G by POS |
|---|---|---|---|---|---|---|---|---|---|---|---|---|---|---|---|---|---|
| 1952 CHI N | 9 | 22 | 4 | 0 | 0 | 0 | 0.0 | 1 | 2 | 4 | 5 | 0 | .182 | .182 | 2 | 1 | SS-6 |

## Lou Brock

**BROCK, LOUIS CLARK**
B. June 18, 1939, El Dorado, Ark.
Hall of Fame 1985.
BL TL 5'11½" 170 lbs.

| | G | AB | H | 2B | 3B | HR | HR% | R | RBI | BB | SO | SB | BA | SA | AB | H | G by POS |
|---|---|---|---|---|---|---|---|---|---|---|---|---|---|---|---|---|---|
| 1961 CHI N | 4 | 11 | 1 | 0 | 0 | 0 | 0.0 | 1 | 0 | 1 | 3 | 0 | .091 | .091 | 0 | 0 | OF-3 |
| 1962 | 123 | 434 | 114 | 24 | 7 | 9 | 2.1 | 73 | 35 | 35 | 96 | 16 | .263 | .412 | 15 | 2 | OF-106 |
| 1963 | 148 | 547 | 141 | 19 | 11 | 9 | 1.6 | 79 | 37 | 31 | 122 | 24 | .258 | .382 | 10 | 2 | OF-140 |
| 1964 2 teams | CHI | N (52G – | .251) | | STL | N (103G – | .348) | | | | | | | | | | |
| " total | 155 | 634 | 200 | 30 | 11 | 14 | 2.2 | 111 | 58 | 40 | 127 | 43 | .315 | .464 | 1 | 0 | OF-154 |
| 1965 STL N | 155 | 631 | 182 | 35 | 8 | 16 | 2.5 | 107 | 69 | 45 | 116 | 63 | .288 | .445 | 1 | 0 | OF-153 |
| 1966 | 156 | 643 | 183 | 24 | 12 | 15 | 2.3 | 94 | 46 | 31 | 134 | 74 | .285 | .429 | 1 | 0 | OF-154 |
| 1967 | 159 | 689 | 206 | 32 | 12 | 21 | 3.0 | 113 | 76 | 24 | 109 | 52 | .299 | .472 | 4 | 0 | OF-157 |
| 1968 | 159 | 660 | 184 | 46 | 14 | 6 | 0.9 | 92 | 51 | 46 | 124 | 62 | .279 | .418 | 3 | 1 | OF-156 |

| | G | AB | H | 2B | 3B | HR | HR % | R | RBI | BB | SO | SB | BA | SA | Pinch Hit AB | Pinch Hit H | G by POS |
|---|---|---|---|---|---|---|---|---|---|---|---|---|---|---|---|---|---|

## Lou Brock continued

| | G | AB | H | 2B | 3B | HR | HR % | R | RBI | BB | SO | SB | BA | SA | PH AB | PH H | G by POS |
|---|---|---|---|---|---|---|---|---|---|---|---|---|---|---|---|---|---|
| 1969 | 157 | 655 | 195 | 33 | 10 | 12 | 1.8 | 97 | 47 | 50 | 115 | 53 | .298 | .434 | 2 | 1 | OF-157 |
| 1970 | 155 | 664 | 202 | 29 | 5 | 13 | 2.0 | 114 | 57 | 60 | 99 | 51 | .304 | .422 | 3 | 2 | OF-152 |
| 1971 | 157 | 640 | 200 | 37 | 7 | 7 | 1.1 | 126 | 61 | 76 | 107 | 64 | .313 | .425 | 2 | 1 | OF-157 |
| 1972 | 153 | 621 | 193 | 26 | 8 | 3 | 0.5 | 81 | 42 | 47 | 93 | 63 | .311 | .393 | 4 | 1 | OF-149 |
| 1973 | 160 | 650 | 193 | 29 | 8 | 7 | 1.1 | 110 | 63 | 71 | 112 | 70 | .297 | .398 | 1 | 0 | OF-159 |
| 1974 | 153 | 635 | 194 | 25 | 7 | 3 | 0.5 | 105 | 48 | 61 | 88 | 118 | .306 | .381 | 3 | 1 | OF-152 |
| 1975 | 136 | 528 | 163 | 27 | 6 | 3 | 0.6 | 78 | 47 | 38 | 64 | 56 | .309 | .400 | 8 | 3 | OF-128 |
| 1976 | 133 | 498 | 150 | 24 | 5 | 4 | 0.8 | 73 | 67 | 35 | 75 | 56 | .301 | .394 | 12 | 3 | OF-123 |
| 1977 | 141 | 489 | 133 | 22 | 6 | 2 | 0.4 | 69 | 46 | 30 | 74 | 35 | .272 | .354 | 18 | 7 | OF-130 |
| 1978 | 92 | 298 | 66 | 9 | 0 | 0 | 0.0 | 31 | 12 | 17 | 29 | 17 | .221 | .252 | 15 | 4 | OF-79 |
| 1979 | 120 | 405 | 123 | 15 | 4 | 5 | 1.2 | 56 | 38 | 23 | 43 | 21 | .304 | .398 | 22 | 5 | OF-98 |
| 19 yrs. | 2616 | 10332 | 3023 | 486 | 141 | 149 | 1.4 | 1610 | 900 | 761 | 1730 | 938 | .293 | .410 | 125 | 33 | OF-2507 |
| | | | 9th | | | | | | | | | 5th | 1st | | | | |
| 4 yrs. | 327 | 1207 | 310 | 52 | 20 | 20 | 1.7 | 183 | 86 | 80 | 261 | 50 | .257 | .383 | 25 | 4 | OF-301 |

WORLD SERIES

| | G | AB | H | 2B | 3B | HR | HR % | R | RBI | BB | SO | SB | BA | SA | PH AB | PH H | G by POS |
|---|---|---|---|---|---|---|---|---|---|---|---|---|---|---|---|---|---|
| 1964 STL N | 7 | 30 | 9 | 2 | 0 | 1 | 3.3 | 2 | 5 | 0 | 3 | 0 | .300 | .467 | 0 | 0 | OF-7 |
| 1967 " | 7 | 29 | 12 | 2 | 1 | 1 | 3.4 | 8 | 3 | 2 | 3 | 7 | .414 | .655 | 0 | 0 | OF-7 |
| 1968 " | 7 | 28 | 13 | 3 | 1 | 2 | 7.1 | 6 | 5 | 3 | 4 | 7 | .464 | .857 | 0 | 0 | OF-7 |
| 3 yrs. | 21 | 87 | 34 | 7 | 2 | 4 | 4.6 | 16 | 13 | 5 | 10 | 14 | .391 | .655 | 0 | 0 | OF-21 |
| | | | 9th | | | | | | | | | 1st | 2nd | 5th | | | |

## Herman Bronkie

**BRONKIE, HERMAN CHARLES (Dutch)**      BR TR 5'9"   165 lbs.
B. Mar. 30, 1885, S. Manchester, Conn.    D. May 27, 1968, Somers, Conn.

| | G | AB | H | 2B | 3B | HR | HR % | R | RBI | BB | SO | SB | BA | SA | PH AB | PH H | G by POS |
|---|---|---|---|---|---|---|---|---|---|---|---|---|---|---|---|---|---|
| 1910 CLE A | 4 | 9 | 2 | 0 | 0 | 0 | 0.0 | 1 | 0 | 1 | | 1 | .222 | .222 | 0 | 0 | 3B-3, SS-1 |
| 1911 " | 2 | 6 | 1 | 0 | 0 | 0 | 0.0 | 0 | 0 | 0 | | 0 | .167 | .167 | 0 | 0 | 3B-2 |
| 1912 " | 6 | 16 | 0 | 0 | 0 | 0 | 0.0 | 1 | 0 | 1 | | 0 | .000 | .000 | 0 | 0 | 3B-6 |
| 1914 CHI N | 1 | 1 | 1 | 1 | 0 | 0 | 0.0 | 1 | 1 | 0 | 0 | 0 | 1.000 | 1.000 | 0 | 0 | 3B-1 |
| 1918 STL N | 18 | 68 | 15 | 3 | 0 | 1 | 1.5 | 7 | 7 | 2 | 4 | 0 | .221 | .309 | 0 | 0 | 3B-18 |
| 1919 STL A | 67 | 196 | 50 | 6 | 4 | 0 | 0.0 | 23 | 14 | 23 | 23 | 2 | .255 | .327 | 12 | 3 | 3B-34, 2B-16, 1B-2 |
| 1922 " | 23 | 64 | 18 | 4 | 1 | 0 | 0.0 | 7 | 2 | 6 | 7 | 0 | .281 | .375 | 4 | 1 | 3B-18 |
| 7 yrs. | 121 | 360 | 87 | 14 | 5 | 1 | 0.3 | 40 | 24 | 33 | 34 | 3 | .242 | .317 | 16 | 4 | 3B-82, 2B-16, 1B-2, SS-1 |
| 1 yr. | 1 | 1 | 1 | 1 | 0 | 0 | 0.0 | 1 | 1 | 0 | 0 | 0 | 1.000 | 1.000 | 0 | 0 | 3B-1 |

## Mandy Brooks

**BROOKS, JONATHAN JOSEPH**
Born Jonathan Joseph Brozek.      BR TR 5'9"   165 lbs.
B. Aug. 18, 1898, Milwaukee, Wis.    D. June 17, 1962, Kirkwood, Mo.

| | G | AB | H | 2B | 3B | HR | HR % | R | RBI | BB | SO | SB | BA | SA | PH AB | PH H | G by POS |
|---|---|---|---|---|---|---|---|---|---|---|---|---|---|---|---|---|---|
| 1925 CHI N | 90 | 349 | 98 | 25 | 7 | 13 | 3.7 | 55 | 72 | 19 | 28 | 10 | .281 | .504 | 1 | 0 | OF-89 |
| 1926 " | 26 | 48 | 9 | 1 | 0 | 1 | 2.1 | 7 | 6 | 5 | 5 | 0 | .188 | .271 | 6 | 1 | OF-18 |
| 2 yrs. | 116 | 397 | 107 | 26 | 7 | 14 | 3.5 | 62 | 78 | 24 | 33 | 10 | .270 | .476 | 7 | 1 | OF-107 |
| 2 yrs. | 116 | 397 | 107 | 26 | 7 | 14 | 3.5 | 62 | 78 | 24 | 33 | 10 | .270 | .476 | 7 | 1 | OF-107 |

## Lew Brown

**BROWN, LEWIS J. (Blower)**      BR TR 5'10½" 185 lbs.
B. Feb. 1, 1858, Leominster, Mass.    D. Jan. 16, 1889, Boston, Mass.

| | G | AB | H | 2B | 3B | HR | HR % | R | RBI | BB | SO | SB | BA | SA | PH AB | PH H | G by POS |
|---|---|---|---|---|---|---|---|---|---|---|---|---|---|---|---|---|---|
| 1876 BOS N | 45 | 195 | 41 | 6 | 6 | 2 | 1.0 | 23 | 21 | 3 | 22 | | .210 | .333 | 0 | 0 | C-45, OF-1 |
| 1877 " | 58 | 221 | 56 | 12 | 8 | 1 | 0.5 | 27 | 31 | 6 | 33 | | .253 | .394 | 0 | 0 | C-55, 1B-4 |
| 1878 PRO N | 58 | 243 | 74 | 21 | 6 | 1 | 0.4 | 44 | 43 | 7 | 37 | | .305 | .453 | 0 | 0 | C-45, 1B-15, OF-1, P-1 |
| 1879 2 teams | PRO | N (53G – .258) | | | CHI | N (6G – .286) | | | | | | | | | | | |
| " total | 59 | 250 | 65 | 14 | 4 | 2 | 0.8 | 25 | 41 | 5 | 28 | | .260 | .372 | 0 | 0 | C-48, OF-6, 1B-6 |
| 1881 2 teams | DET | N (27G – .241) | | | PRO | N (18G – .240) | | | | | | | | | | | |
| " total | 45 | 183 | 44 | 6 | 3 | 1.6 | | 25 | 24 | 7 | 29 | | .240 | .344 | 0 | 0 | 1B-32, OF-13 |
| 1883 2 teams | BOS | N (14G – .241) | | | LOU | AA (14G – .183) | | | | | | | | | | | |
| " total | 28 | 114 | 24 | 6 | 2 | 0 | 0.0 | 11 | 9 | 4 | 6 | | .211 | .298 | 0 | 0 | 1B-28, C-1 |
| 1884 BOS U | 85 | 325 | 75 | 18 | 3 | 1 | 0.3 | 50 | | 13 | | | .231 | .314 | 0 | 0 | C-54, 1B-33, OF-2, P-1 |
| 7 yrs. | 378 | 1531 | 379 | 83 | 31 | 10 | 0.7 | 205 | 169 | 45 | 155 | | .248 | .362 | 0 | 0 | C-248, 1B-118, OF-23, P-2 |
| 1 yr. | 6 | 21 | 6 | 1 | 0 | 0 | 0.0 | 2 | 1 | 1 | 4 | | .286 | .333 | 0 | 0 | 1B-6 |

## Tommy Brown

**BROWN, THOMAS MICHAEL (Buckshot)**      BR TR 6'1"   170 lbs.
B. Dec. 6, 1927, Brooklyn, N. Y.

| | G | AB | H | 2B | 3B | HR | HR % | R | RBI | BB | SO | SB | BA | SA | PH AB | PH H | G by POS |
|---|---|---|---|---|---|---|---|---|---|---|---|---|---|---|---|---|---|
| 1944 BKN N | 46 | 146 | 24 | 4 | 0 | 0 | 0.0 | 17 | 8 | 8 | 17 | 0 | .164 | .192 | 0 | 0 | SS-46 |
| 1945 " | 57 | 196 | 48 | 3 | 4 | 2 | 1.0 | 13 | 19 | 6 | 16 | 3 | .245 | .332 | 1 | 0 | SS-55, OF-1 |
| 1947 " | 15 | 34 | 8 | 1 | 0 | 0 | 0.0 | 3 | 2 | 1 | 6 | 0 | .235 | .265 | 4 | 1 | 3B-6, OF-3, SS-1 |
| 1948 " | 54 | 145 | 35 | 4 | 0 | 2 | 1.4 | 18 | 20 | 7 | 17 | 1 | .241 | .310 | 9 | 1 | 3B-43, 1B-1 |
| 1949 " | 41 | 89 | 27 | 2 | 0 | 3 | 3.4 | 14 | 18 | 6 | 8 | 0 | .303 | .427 | 13 | 4 | OF-27 |
| 1950 BKN N | 48 | 86 | 25 | 2 | 1 | 8 | 9.3 | 15 | 20 | 11 | 9 | 0 | .291 | .616 | 29 | 7 | OF-16 |
| 1951 2 teams | BKN | N (11G – .160) | | | PHI | N (78G – .219) | | | | | | | | | | | |
| " total | 89 | 221 | 47 | 4 | 1 | 10 | 4.5 | 26 | 33 | 17 | 25 | 1 | .213 | .376 | 26 | 4 | OF-37, 2B-14, 1B-12, 3B-1 |
| 1952 2 teams | PHI | N (18G – .160) | | | CHI | N (61G – .320) | | | | | | | | | | | |
| " total | 79 | 225 | 68 | 12 | 0 | 4 | 1.8 | 26 | 26 | 16 | 27 | 1 | .302 | .409 | 15 | 3 | SS-39, 2B-10, 1B-8, OF-3 |
| 1953 CHI N | 65 | 138 | 27 | 7 | 1 | 2 | 1.4 | 19 | 13 | 13 | 17 | 1 | .196 | .304 | 30 | 5 | SS-25, OF-6 |
| 9 yrs. | 494 | 1280 | 309 | 39 | 7 | 31 | 2.4 | 151 | 159 | 85 | 142 | 7 | .241 | .355 | 127 | 25 | SS-166, OF-93, 3B-50, 2B-24, 1B-21 |
| 2 yrs. | 126 | 338 | 91 | 18 | 1 | 5 | 1.5 | 43 | 37 | 25 | 41 | 2 | .269 | .373 | 35 | 6 | SS-64, 2B-10, OF-6, 1B-5 |

WORLD SERIES

| | G | AB | H | 2B | 3B | HR | HR % | R | RBI | BB | SO | SB | BA | SA | PH AB | PH H | G by POS |
|---|---|---|---|---|---|---|---|---|---|---|---|---|---|---|---|---|---|
| 1949 BKN N | 2 | 2 | 0 | 0 | 0 | 0 | 0.0 | 0 | 0 | 0 | 1 | 0 | .000 | .000 | 2 | 0 | |

## Byron Browne

**BROWNE, BYRON ELLIS**      BR TR 6'2"   190 lbs.
B. Dec. 27, 1942, St. Joseph, Mo.

| | G | AB | H | 2B | 3B | HR | HR % | R | RBI | BB | SO | SB | BA | SA | PH AB | PH H | G by POS |
|---|---|---|---|---|---|---|---|---|---|---|---|---|---|---|---|---|---|
| 1965 CHI N | 4 | 6 | 0 | 0 | 0 | 0 | 0.0 | 0 | 0 | 0 | 2 | 0 | .000 | .000 | 1 | 0 | OF-4 |
| 1966 " | 120 | 419 | 102 | 15 | 7 | 16 | 3.8 | 46 | 51 | 40 | 143 | 3 | .243 | .427 | 5 | 0 | OF-114 |
| 1967 " | 10 | 19 | 3 | 2 | 0 | 0 | 0.0 | 3 | 2 | 4 | 5 | 1 | .158 | .263 | 2 | 0 | OF-8 |

| | G | AB | H | 2B | 3B | HR | HR % | R | RBI | BB | SO | SB | BA | SA | Pinch Hit AB | Pinch Hit H | G by POS |
|---|---|---|---|---|---|---|---|---|---|---|---|---|---|---|---|---|---|

## Byron Browne continued

| | G | AB | H | 2B | 3B | HR | HR% | R | RBI | BB | SO | SB | BA | SA | PH AB | PH H | G by POS |
|---|---|---|---|---|---|---|---|---|---|---|---|---|---|---|---|---|---|
| 1968 HOU N | 10 | 13 | 3 | 0 | 0 | 0 | 0.0 | 0 | 1 | 4 | 6 | 0 | .231 | .231 | 6 | 1 | OF-2 |
| 1969 STL N | 22 | 53 | 12 | 0 | 1 | 1 | 1.9 | 9 | 7 | 11 | 14 | 0 | .226 | .321 | 7 | 0 | OF-16 |
| 1970 PHI N | 104 | 270 | 67 | 17 | 2 | 10 | 3.7 | 29 | 36 | 33 | 72 | 1 | .248 | .437 | 18 | 4 | OF-88 |
| 1971 | 58 | 68 | 14 | 3 | 0 | 3 | 4.4 | 5 | 5 | 8 | 23 | 0 | .206 | .382 | 27 | 7 | OF-30 |
| 1972 | 21 | 21 | 4 | 0 | 0 | 0 | 0.0 | 2 | 0 | 1 | 8 | 0 | .190 | .190 | 14 | 3 | OF-9 |
| 8 yrs. | 349 | 869 | 205 | 37 | 10 | 30 | 3.5 | 94 | 102 | 101 | 273 | 5 | .236 | .405 | 80 | 15 | OF-271 |
| 3 yrs. | 134 | 444 | 105 | 17 | 7 | 16 | 3.6 | 49 | 53 | 44 | 150 | 4 | .236 | .414 | 8 | 0 | OF-126 |

## George Browne

**BROWNE, GEORGE EDWARD**  BL TR 5'10½" 160 lbs.
B. Jan. 12, 1876, Richmond, Va.    D. Dec. 9, 1920, Hyde Park, N. Y.

| | G | AB | H | 2B | 3B | HR | HR% | R | RBI | BB | SO | SB | BA | SA | PH AB | PH H | G by POS |
|---|---|---|---|---|---|---|---|---|---|---|---|---|---|---|---|---|---|
| 1901 PHI N | 8 | 26 | 5 | 1 | 0 | 0 | 0.0 | 2 | 4 | 1 | | 2 | .192 | .231 | 0 | 0 | OF-8 |
| 1902 2 teams | | PHI | N (70G – | .260) | | NY | N (53G – | .319) | | | | | | | | | |
| " total | 123 | 497 | 142 | 16 | 6 | 0 | 0.0 | 71 | 40 | 25 | | 24 | .286 | .342 | 0 | 0 | OF-123 |
| 1903 NY N | 141 | 591 | 185 | 20 | 3 | 3 | 0.5 | 105 | 45 | 43 | | 27 | .313 | .372 | 0 | 0 | OF-141 |
| 1904 | 150 | 596 | 169 | 16 | 5 | 4 | 0.7 | 99 | 39 | 39 | | 24 | .284 | .347 | 1 | 0 | OF-149 |
| 1905 | 127 | 536 | 157 | 16 | 14 | 4 | 0.7 | 95 | 43 | 20 | | 26 | .293 | .397 | 0 | 0 | OF-127 |
| 1906 | 122 | 477 | 126 | 10 | 4 | 0 | 0.0 | 61 | 38 | 27 | | 32 | .264 | .302 | 1 | 0 | OF-121 |
| 1907 | 127 | 458 | 119 | 11 | 10 | 5 | 1.1 | 54 | 37 | 31 | | 15 | .260 | .360 | 4 | 0 | OF-121 |
| 1908 BOS N | 138 | 536 | 122 | 10 | 6 | 1 | 0.2 | 61 | 34 | 36 | | 17 | .228 | .274 | 3 | 1 | OF-138 |
| 1909 2 teams | | CHI | N (12G – | .205) | | WAS | A (103G – | .272) | | | | | | | | | |
| " total | 115 | 432 | 115 | 15 | 6 | 1 | 0.2 | 47 | 17 | 22 | | 16 | .266 | .336 | 2 | 0 | OF-113 |
| 1910 2 teams | | WAS | A (7G – | .182) | | CHI | A (30G – | .241) | | | | | | | | | |
| " total | 37 | 134 | 31 | 4 | 1 | 0 | 0.0 | 18 | 4 | 13 | | 5 | .231 | .276 | 3 | 0 | OF-34 |
| 1911 BKN N | 8 | 12 | 4 | 0 | 0 | 0 | 0.0 | 1 | 2 | 1 | 1 | 2 | .333 | .333 | 4 | 0 | OF-2 |
| 1912 PHI N | 6 | 5 | 1 | 0 | 0 | 0 | 0.0 | 0 | 0 | 1 | | 0 | .200 | .200 | 4 | 1 | 3B-1 |
| 12 yrs. | 1102 | 4300 | 1176 | 119 | 55 | 18 | 0.4 | 614 | 303 | 259 | 1 | 190 | .273 | .339 | 22 | 2 | OF-1077, 3B-1 |
| 1 yr. | 12 | 39 | 8 | 0 | 1 | 0 | 0.0 | 7 | 1 | 5 | | 3 | .205 | .256 | 0 | 0 | OF-12 |

WORLD SERIES

| | G | AB | H | 2B | 3B | HR | HR% | R | RBI | BB | SO | SB | BA | SA | PH AB | PH H | G by POS |
|---|---|---|---|---|---|---|---|---|---|---|---|---|---|---|---|---|---|
| 1905 NY N | 5 | 22 | 4 | 0 | 0 | 0 | 0.0 | 2 | 1 | 0 | 2 | 2 | .182 | .182 | 0 | 0 | OF-5 |

## Don Bryant

**BRYANT, DONALD RAY**  BR TR 6'5" 200 lbs.
B. July 13, 1941, Jasper, Fla.

| | G | AB | H | 2B | 3B | HR | HR% | R | RBI | BB | SO | SB | BA | SA | PH AB | PH H | G by POS |
|---|---|---|---|---|---|---|---|---|---|---|---|---|---|---|---|---|---|
| 1966 CHI N | 13 | 26 | 8 | 2 | 0 | 0 | 0.0 | 2 | 4 | 1 | 4 | 1 | .308 | .385 | 3 | 0 | C-10 |
| 1969 HOU N | 31 | 59 | 11 | 1 | 0 | 1 | 1.7 | 2 | 6 | 4 | 13 | 0 | .186 | .254 | 2 | 1 | C-28 |
| 1970 | 15 | 24 | 5 | 0 | 0 | 0 | 0.0 | 2 | 3 | 1 | 8 | 0 | .208 | .208 | 3 | 0 | C-13 |
| 3 yrs. | 59 | 109 | 24 | 3 | 0 | 1 | 0.9 | 6 | 13 | 6 | 25 | 1 | .220 | .275 | 8 | 1 | C-51 |
| 1 yr. | 13 | 26 | 8 | 2 | 0 | 0 | 0.0 | 2 | 4 | 1 | 4 | 1 | .308 | .385 | 3 | 0 | C-10 |

## Bill Buckner

**BUCKNER, WILLIAM JOSEPH**  BL TL 6' 185 lbs.
B. Dec. 14, 1949, Vallejo, Calif.

| | G | AB | H | 2B | 3B | HR | HR% | R | RBI | BB | SO | SB | BA | SA | PH AB | PH H | G by POS |
|---|---|---|---|---|---|---|---|---|---|---|---|---|---|---|---|---|---|
| 1969 LA N | 1 | 1 | 0 | 0 | 0 | 0 | 0.0 | 0 | 0 | 0 | 0 | 0 | .000 | .000 | 1 | 0 | |
| 1970 | 28 | 68 | 13 | 3 | 1 | 0 | 0.0 | 6 | 4 | 3 | 7 | 0 | .191 | .265 | 8 | 2 | OF-20, 1B-1 |
| 1971 | 108 | 358 | 99 | 15 | 1 | 5 | 1.4 | 37 | 41 | 11 | 18 | 4 | .277 | .366 | 17 | 3 | OF-86, 1B-11 |
| 1972 | 105 | 383 | 122 | 14 | 3 | 5 | 1.3 | 47 | 37 | 17 | 13 | 10 | .319 | .410 | 11 | 3 | OF-61, 1B-35 |
| 1973 | 140 | 575 | 158 | 20 | 0 | 8 | 1.4 | 68 | 46 | 17 | 34 | 12 | .275 | .351 | 9 | 2 | 1B-93, OF-48 |
| 1974 | 145 | 580 | 182 | 30 | 4 | 7 | 1.2 | 83 | 58 | 30 | 24 | 31 | .314 | .412 | 9 | 1 | OF-137, 1B-6 |
| 1975 | 92 | 288 | 70 | 11 | 2 | 6 | 2.1 | 30 | 31 | 17 | 15 | 8 | .243 | .358 | 19 | 4 | OF-72 |
| 1976 | 154 | 642 | 193 | 28 | 4 | 7 | 1.1 | 76 | 60 | 26 | 26 | 28 | .301 | .389 | 1 | 1 | OF-153, 1B-1 |
| 1977 CHI N | 122 | 426 | 121 | 27 | 0 | 11 | 2.6 | 40 | 60 | 21 | 23 | 7 | .284 | .425 | 22 | 7 | 1B-99 |
| 1978 | 117 | 446 | 144 | 26 | 1 | 5 | 1.1 | 47 | 74 | 18 | 17 | 7 | .323 | .419 | 12 | 2 | 1B-105 |
| 1979 | 149 | 591 | 168 | 34 | 7 | 14 | 2.4 | 72 | 66 | 30 | 28 | 9 | .284 | .437 | 8 | 3 | 1B-140 |
| 1980 | 145 | 578 | 187 | 41 | 3 | 10 | 1.7 | 69 | 68 | 30 | 18 | 1 | .324 | .457 | 6 | 0 | 1B-94, OF-50 |
| 1981 | 106 | 421 | 131 | 35 | 3 | 10 | 2.4 | 45 | 75 | 26 | 16 | 5 | .311 | .480 | 2 | 1 | 1B-105 |
| 1982 | 161 | 657 | 201 | 34 | 5 | 15 | 2.3 | 93 | 105 | 36 | 26 | 15 | .306 | .441 | 0 | 0 | 1B-161 |
| 1983 | 153 | 626 | 175 | 38 | 6 | 16 | 2.6 | 79 | 66 | 25 | 30 | 12 | .280 | .436 | 2 | 1 | 1B-144, OF-15 |
| 1984 2 teams | | CHI | N (21G – | .209) | | BOS | A (114G – | .278) | | | | | | | | | |
| " total | 135 | 482 | 131 | 21 | 2 | 11 | 2.3 | 54 | 69 | 25 | 39 | 2 | .272 | .392 | 12 | 3 | 1B-120, OF-2 |
| 1985 BOS A | 162 | 673 | 201 | 46 | 3 | 16 | 2.4 | 89 | 110 | 30 | 36 | 18 | .299 | .447 | 0 | 0 | 1B-162 |
| 17 yrs. | 2023 | 7795 | 2296 | 423 | 44 | 146 | 1.9 | 935 | 970 | 362 | 370 | 169 | .295 | .416 | 139 | 32 | 1B-1277, OF-644 |
| 8 yrs. | 974 | 3788 | 1136 | 235 | 25 | 81 | 2.1 | 448 | 516 | 187 | 159 | 56 | .300 | .439 | 64 | 17 | 1B-855, OF-67 |

LEAGUE CHAMPIONSHIP SERIES

| | G | AB | H | 2B | 3B | HR | HR% | R | RBI | BB | SO | SB | BA | SA | PH AB | PH H | G by POS |
|---|---|---|---|---|---|---|---|---|---|---|---|---|---|---|---|---|---|
| 1974 LA N | 4 | 18 | 3 | 1 | 0 | 0 | 0.0 | 0 | 0 | 0 | 2 | 0 | .167 | .222 | 0 | 0 | OF-4 |

WORLD SERIES

| | G | AB | H | 2B | 3B | HR | HR% | R | RBI | BB | SO | SB | BA | SA | PH AB | PH H | G by POS |
|---|---|---|---|---|---|---|---|---|---|---|---|---|---|---|---|---|---|
| 1974 LA N | 5 | 20 | 5 | 1 | 0 | 1 | 5.0 | 1 | 1 | 0 | 1 | 0 | .250 | .450 | 0 | 0 | OF-5 |

## Art Bues

**BUES, ARTHUR FREDERICK**  BR TR 5'11" 184 lbs.
B. Mar. 3, 1888, Milwaukee, Wis.    D. Nov. 7, 1954, Whitefish Bay, Wis.

| | G | AB | H | 2B | 3B | HR | HR% | R | RBI | BB | SO | SB | BA | SA | PH AB | PH H | G by POS |
|---|---|---|---|---|---|---|---|---|---|---|---|---|---|---|---|---|---|
| 1913 BOS N | 2 | 1 | 0 | 0 | 0 | 0 | 0.0 | 0 | 0 | 0 | 0 | 0 | .000 | .000 | 0 | 0 | 3B-1, 2B-1 |
| 1914 CHI N | 14 | 45 | 10 | 1 | 1 | 0 | 0.0 | 3 | 4 | 5 | 6 | 1 | .222 | .289 | 2 | 0 | 3B-12 |
| 2 yrs. | 16 | 46 | 10 | 1 | 1 | 0 | 0.0 | 3 | 4 | 5 | 7 | 1 | .217 | .283 | 2 | 0 | 3B-13, 2B-1 |
| 1 yr. | 14 | 45 | 10 | 1 | 1 | 0 | 0.0 | 3 | 4 | 5 | 6 | 1 | .222 | .289 | 2 | 0 | 3B-12 |

## Smoky Burgess

**BURGESS, FORREST HARRILL**  BL TR 5'8½" 185 lbs.
B. Feb. 6, 1927, Caroleen, N. C.

| | G | AB | H | 2B | 3B | HR | HR% | R | RBI | BB | SO | SB | BA | SA | PH AB | PH H | G by POS |
|---|---|---|---|---|---|---|---|---|---|---|---|---|---|---|---|---|---|
| 1949 CHI N | 46 | 56 | 15 | 0 | 0 | 1 | 1.8 | 4 | 12 | 4 | 4 | 0 | .268 | .321 | 37 | 12 | C-8 |
| 1951 | 94 | 219 | 55 | 4 | 2 | 2 | 0.9 | 21 | 20 | 21 | 12 | 2 | .251 | .315 | 30 | 5 | C-64 |
| 1952 PHI N | 110 | 371 | 110 | 27 | 2 | 6 | 1.6 | 49 | 56 | 49 | 21 | 3 | .296 | .429 | 6 | 3 | C-104 |
| 1953 | 102 | 312 | 91 | 17 | 5 | 4 | 1.3 | 31 | 36 | 37 | 17 | 3 | .292 | .417 | 9 | 3 | C-95 |
| 1954 | 108 | 345 | 127 | 27 | 5 | 4 | 1.2 | 41 | 46 | 42 | 11 | 1 | .368 | .510 | 17 | 6 | C-91 |

Present at the creation: Albert G. Spalding *(below)* was Chicago's manager and only pitcher in the National League's inaugural season. Their starting third baseman that year, soon to shift to first where he would spend nineteen years, all but two as a .300 hitter, was Adrian "Cap" Anson *(left)*.

These two men hold the modern National League single-season records in the Triple Crown statistics. Short, barrel-chested Hack Wilson *(left)* carried 190 pounds on his 5'6" frame, but put it all behind his 56 homers, good for 190 RBIs, in 1930. Rogers Hornsby *(right),* who managed that '30 club, also helped the Cubs into the Series in 1929 with his 39 homers and .380 batting average. (His .424 for the Cardinals in 1924 is this century's high-water mark.)

| | G | AB | H | 2B | 3B | HR | HR % | R | RBI | BB | SO | SB | BA | SA | Pinch Hit AB | Pinch Hit H | G by POS |
|---|---|---|---|---|---|---|---|---|---|---|---|---|---|---|---|---|---|

# Smoky Burgess continued

| | | | | | | | | | | | | | | | | | |
|---|---|---|---|---|---|---|---|---|---|---|---|---|---|---|---|---|---|
| 1955 2 teams | PHI | N | (7G – | .190) | | CIN | N | (116G – | .306) | | | | | | | | |
| " total | 123 | 442 | 133 | 17 | 3 | 21 | 4.8 | 71 | 78 | 50 | 36 | 1 | .301 | .495 | 9 | 3 | C-113 |
| 1956 CIN N | 90 | 229 | 63 | 10 | 0 | 12 | 5.2 | 28 | 39 | 26 | 18 | 0 | .275 | .476 | 29 | 7 | C-55 |
| 1957 | 90 | 205 | 58 | 14 | 1 | 14 | 6.8 | 29 | 39 | 24 | 16 | 0 | .283 | .566 | 39 | 11 | C-45 |
| 1958 | 99 | 251 | 71 | 12 | 1 | 6 | 2.4 | 28 | 31 | 22 | 20 | 0 | .283 | .410 | 40 | 11 | C-58 |
| 1959 PIT N | 114 | 377 | 112 | 28 | 5 | 11 | 2.9 | 41 | 59 | 31 | 16 | 0 | .297 | .485 | 17 | 7 | C-101 |
| 1960 | 110 | 337 | 99 | 15 | 2 | 7 | 2.1 | 33 | 39 | 35 | 13 | 0 | .294 | .412 | 20 | 9 | C-89 |
| 1961 | 100 | 323 | 98 | 17 | 3 | 12 | 3.7 | 37 | 52 | 30 | 16 | 1 | .303 | .486 | 14 | 4 | C-92 |
| 1962 | 130 | 360 | 118 | 19 | 2 | 13 | 3.6 | 38 | 61 | 31 | 19 | 0 | .328 | .500 | 5 | 1 | C-101 |
| 1963 | 91 | 264 | 74 | 10 | 1 | 6 | 2.3 | 20 | 37 | 24 | 14 | 0 | .280 | .394 | 18 | 6 | C-72 |
| 1964 2 teams | PIT | N | (68G – | .246) | | CHI | A | (7G – | .200) | | | | | | | | |
| " total | 75 | 176 | 43 | 3 | 1 | 3 | 1.7 | 10 | 18 | 15 | 14 | 2 | .244 | .324 | 26 | 8 | C-44 |
| 1965 CHI A | 80 | 77 | 22 | 4 | 0 | 2 | 2.6 | 2 | 24 | 11 | 7 | 0 | .286 | .416 | 65 | 20 | C-5 |
| 1966 | 79 | 67 | 21 | 5 | 0 | 0 | 0.0 | 0 | 15 | 11 | 8 | 0 | .313 | .388 | 66 | 21 | C-2 |
| 1967 | 77 | 60 | 8 | 1 | 0 | 2 | 3.3 | 2 | 11 | 14 | 8 | 0 | .133 | .250 | 60 | 8 | |
| 18 yrs. | 1718 | 4471 | 1318 | 230 | 33 | 126 | 2.8 | 485 | 673 | 477 | 270 | 13 | .295 | .446 | 507 | 145 | C-1139 |
| | | | | | | | | | | | | | | | 1st | 2nd | |
| 2 yrs. | 140 | 275 | 70 | 4 | 2 | 3 | 1.1 | 25 | 32 | 25 | 16 | 2 | .255 | .316 | 67 | 17 | C-72 |

WORLD SERIES

| | G | AB | H | 2B | 3B | HR | HR % | R | RBI | BB | SO | SB | BA | SA | AB | H | G by POS |
|---|---|---|---|---|---|---|---|---|---|---|---|---|---|---|---|---|---|
| 1960 PIT N | 5 | 18 | 6 | 1 | 0 | 0 | 0.0 | 2 | 0 | 2 | 1 | 0 | .333 | .389 | 0 | 0 | C-5 |

# Leo Burke

**BURKE, LEO PATRICK**       BR TR 5'11" 185 lbs.
B. May 6, 1934, Hagerstown, Md.

| | G | AB | H | 2B | 3B | HR | HR % | R | RBI | BB | SO | SB | BA | SA | AB | H | G by POS |
|---|---|---|---|---|---|---|---|---|---|---|---|---|---|---|---|---|---|
| 1958 BAL A | 7 | 11 | 5 | 1 | 0 | 1 | 9.1 | 4 | 4 | 1 | 2 | 0 | .455 | .818 | 3 | 1 | OF-3, 3B-1 |
| 1959 | 5 | 10 | 2 | 0 | 0 | 0 | 0.0 | 0 | 1 | 0 | 5 | 0 | .200 | .200 | 2 | 0 | 3B-2, 2B-2 |
| 1961 LA A | 6 | 5 | 0 | 0 | 0 | 0 | 0.0 | 0 | 0 | 0 | 1 | 0 | .000 | .000 | 5 | 0 | |
| 1962 | 19 | 64 | 17 | 1 | 0 | 4 | 6.3 | 8 | 14 | 5 | 11 | 0 | .266 | .469 | 2 | 0 | OF-12, 3B-4, SS-1 |
| 1963 2 teams | STL | N | (30G – | .204) | | CHI | N | (27G – | .184) | | | | | | | | |
| " total | 57 | 98 | 19 | 2 | 1 | 3 | 3.1 | 10 | 12 | 8 | 25 | 0 | .194 | .327 | 28 | 8 | OF-11, 2B-10, 3B-5, 1B-4 |
| 1964 CHI N | 59 | 103 | 27 | 3 | 1 | 1 | 1.0 | 11 | 14 | 7 | 31 | 0 | .262 | .340 | 34 | 10 | OF-18, 2B-5, 3B-4, 1B-2, C-1 |
| 1965 | 12 | 10 | 2 | 0 | 0 | 0 | 0.0 | 0 | 0 | 0 | 4 | 0 | .200 | .200 | 9 | 1 | C-2, OF-1 |
| 7 yrs. | 165 | 301 | 72 | 7 | 2 | 9 | 3.0 | 33 | 45 | 21 | 79 | 0 | .239 | .365 | 83 | 20 | OF-45, 2B-17, 3B-16, 1B-6, C-3, SS-1 |
| 3 yrs. | 98 | 162 | 38 | 3 | 1 | 3 | 1.9 | 15 | 21 | 11 | 48 | 0 | .235 | .321 | 55 | 15 | OF-19, 2B-15, 1B-6, 3B-4, C-3 |

# Tom Burns

**BURNS, THOMAS EVERETT**       BL TR 5'7" 152 lbs.
B. Mar. 30, 1857, Honesdale, Pa.    D. Mar. 19, 1902, Jersey City, N. J.
Manager 1892, 1898-99.

| | G | AB | H | 2B | 3B | HR | HR % | R | RBI | BB | SO | SB | BA | SA | AB | H | G by POS |
|---|---|---|---|---|---|---|---|---|---|---|---|---|---|---|---|---|---|
| 1880 CHI N | 85 | 333 | 103 | 17 | 3 | 0 | 0.0 | 47 | 43 | 12 | 23 | | .309 | .378 | 0 | 0 | SS-79, 3B-9, C-2 |
| 1881 | 84 | 342 | 95 | 20 | 3 | 4 | 1.2 | 41 | 42 | 14 | 22 | | .278 | .389 | 0 | 0 | SS-80, 3B-3, 2B-3 |
| 1882 | 84 | 355 | 88 | 23 | 6 | 0 | 0.0 | 55 | 48 | 15 | 28 | | .248 | .346 | 0 | 0 | 2B-43, SS-41 |
| 1883 | 97 | 405 | 119 | 37 | 7 | 2 | 0.5 | 69 | | 13 | 31 | | .294 | .435 | 0 | 0 | SS-79, 2B-19, OF-1 |
| 1884 | 83 | 343 | 84 | 14 | 2 | 7 | 2.0 | 54 | | 13 | 50 | | .245 | .359 | 0 | 0 | SS-80, 3B-3 |
| 1885 | 111 | 445 | 121 | 23 | 9 | 7 | 1.6 | 82 | 70 | 16 | 48 | | .272 | .411 | 0 | 0 | SS-111, 2B-1 |
| 1886 | 112 | 445 | 123 | 18 | 10 | 3 | 0.7 | 64 | 65 | 14 | 40 | | .276 | .382 | 0 | 0 | 3B-112 |
| 1887 | 115 | 424 | 112 | 20 | 10 | 3 | 0.7 | 57 | 60 | 34 | 32 | 32 | .264 | .380 | 0 | 0 | 3B-107, OF-8 |
| 1888 | 134 | 483 | 115 | 12 | 6 | 3 | 0.6 | 60 | 70 | 26 | 49 | 34 | .238 | .306 | 0 | 0 | 3B-134 |
| 1889 | 136 | 525 | 127 | 27 | 6 | 4 | 0.8 | 64 | 66 | 32 | 57 | 18 | .242 | .339 | 0 | 0 | 3B-136 |
| 1890 | 139 | 538 | 149 | 16 | 6 | 6 | 1.1 | 86 | 86 | 57 | 45 | 44 | .277 | .362 | 0 | 0 | 3B-139 |
| 1891 | 59 | 243 | 55 | 8 | 1 | 1 | 0.4 | 36 | 17 | 21 | 21 | 18 | .226 | .280 | 0 | 0 | 3B-53, SS-4, OF-2 |
| 1892 PIT N | 12 | 39 | 8 | 0 | 0 | 0 | 0.0 | 7 | 4 | 3 | 8 | 1 | .205 | .205 | 1 | 0 | 3B-8, OF-3 |
| 13 yrs. | 1251 | 4920 | 1299 | 235 | 69 | 40 | 0.8 | 722 | 571 | 270 | 454 | 147 | .264 | .364 | 1 | 0 | 3B-704, SS-474, 2B-66, OF-14, C-2 |
| 12 yrs. | 1239 | 4881 | 1291 | 235 | 69 | 40 | 0.8 | 715 | 567 | 267 | 446 | 146 | .264 | .365 | 0 | 0 | 3B-696, SS-474, 2B-66, OF-11, C-2 |

# Ellis Burton

**BURTON, ELLIS NARRINGTON**       BB TR 5'11" 160 lbs.
B. Aug. 12, 1936, Los Angeles, Calif.

| | G | AB | H | 2B | 3B | HR | HR % | R | RBI | BB | SO | SB | BA | SA | AB | H | G by POS |
|---|---|---|---|---|---|---|---|---|---|---|---|---|---|---|---|---|---|
| 1958 STL N | 8 | 30 | 7 | 0 | 1 | 2 | 6.7 | 5 | 4 | 3 | 8 | 0 | .233 | .500 | 1 | 0 | OF-7 |
| 1960 | 29 | 28 | 6 | 1 | 0 | 0 | 0.0 | 5 | 2 | 4 | 14 | 0 | .214 | .250 | 5 | 2 | OF-23 |
| 1963 2 teams | CLE | A | (26G – | .194) | | CHI | N | (93G – | .230) | | | | | | | | |
| " total | 119 | 353 | 80 | 19 | 4 | 13 | 3.7 | 51 | 42 | 40 | 63 | 6 | .227 | .397 | 9 | 2 | OF-106 |
| 1964 CHI N | 42 | 105 | 20 | 3 | 2 | 2 | 1.9 | 12 | 7 | 17 | 22 | 4 | .190 | .314 | 12 | 2 | OF-29 |
| 1965 | 17 | 40 | 7 | 1 | 0 | 0 | 0.0 | 6 | 4 | 1 | 10 | 1 | .175 | .200 | 8 | 2 | OF-12 |
| 5 yrs. | 215 | 556 | 120 | 24 | 4 | 17 | 3.1 | 79 | 59 | 65 | 117 | 11 | .216 | .365 | 35 | 8 | OF-177 |
| 3 yrs. | 152 | 467 | 101 | 23 | 4 | 14 | 3.0 | 63 | 52 | 54 | 91 | 11 | .216 | .362 | 23 | 4 | OF-131 |

# Johnny Butler

**BUTLER, JOHN STEPHEN (Trolley Line)**       BR TR 6' 175 lbs.
B. Mar. 20, 1894, Eureka, Kans.    D. Apr. 29, 1967, Long Beach, Calif.

| | G | AB | H | 2B | 3B | HR | HR % | R | RBI | BB | SO | SB | BA | SA | AB | H | G by POS |
|---|---|---|---|---|---|---|---|---|---|---|---|---|---|---|---|---|---|
| 1926 BKN N | 147 | 501 | 135 | 27 | 5 | 1 | 0.2 | 54 | 68 | 54 | 44 | 6 | .269 | .349 | 0 | 0 | SS-102, 3B-42, 2B-8 |
| 1927 | 149 | 521 | 124 | 13 | 6 | 2 | 0.4 | 39 | 57 | 34 | 33 | 9 | .238 | .298 | 1 | 0 | SS-90, 3B-60 |
| 1928 CHI N | 62 | 174 | 47 | 7 | 0 | 0 | 0.0 | 17 | 16 | 19 | 7 | 2 | .270 | .310 | 1 | 0 | 3B-59, SS-2 |
| 1929 STL N | 17 | 55 | 9 | 1 | 1 | 0 | 0.0 | 5 | 5 | 4 | 5 | 0 | .164 | .218 | 0 | 0 | 3B-9, SS-8 |
| 4 yrs. | 375 | 1251 | 315 | 48 | 12 | 3 | 0.2 | 115 | 146 | 111 | 89 | 17 | .252 | .317 | 2 | 0 | SS-202, 3B-170, 2B-8 |
| 1 yr. | 62 | 174 | 47 | 7 | 0 | 0 | 0.0 | 17 | 16 | 19 | 7 | 2 | .270 | .310 | 1 | 0 | 3B-59, SS-2 |

# Marty Callaghan

**CALLAGHAN, MARTIN FRANCIS**       BL TL 5'10" 157 lbs.
B. June 9, 1900, Norwood, Mass.    D. June 23, 1975, Norwood, Kans.

| | G | AB | H | 2B | 3B | HR | HR % | R | RBI | BB | SO | SB | BA | SA | AB | H | G by POS |
|---|---|---|---|---|---|---|---|---|---|---|---|---|---|---|---|---|---|
| 1922 CHI N | 74 | 175 | 45 | 7 | 4 | 0 | 0.0 | 31 | 20 | 17 | 17 | 2 | .257 | .343 | 17 | 3 | OF-53 |

| | G | AB | H | 2B | 3B | HR | HR % | R | RBI | BB | SO | SB | BA | SA | Pinch Hit AB | Pinch Hit H | G by POS |
|---|---|---|---|---|---|---|---|---|---|---|---|---|---|---|---|---|---|

## Marty Callaghan continued

| | G | AB | H | 2B | 3B | HR | HR% | R | RBI | BB | SO | SB | BA | SA | AB | H | G by POS |
|---|---|---|---|---|---|---|---|---|---|---|---|---|---|---|---|---|---|
| 1923 | 61 | 129 | 29 | 1 | 3 | 0 | 0.0 | 18 | 14 | 8 | 18 | 2 | .225 | .279 | 16 | 3 | OF-38 |
| 1928 **CIN N** | 81 | 238 | 69 | 11 | 4 | 0 | 0.0 | 29 | 24 | 27 | 10 | 5 | .290 | .370 | 7 | 1 | OF-69 |
| 1930 | 79 | 225 | 62 | 9 | 2 | 0 | 0.0 | 28 | 16 | 19 | 25 | 1 | .276 | .333 | 23 | 3 | OF-54 |
| 4 yrs. | 295 | 767 | 205 | 28 | 13 | 0 | 0.0 | 106 | 74 | 71 | 70 | 10 | .267 | .338 | 63 | 10 | OF-214 |
| 2 yrs. | 135 | 304 | 74 | 8 | 7 | 0 | 0.0 | 49 | 34 | 25 | 35 | 4 | .243 | .316 | 33 | 6 | OF-91 |

## Nixey Callahan

**CALLAHAN, JAMES JOSEPH**     BR TR 5'10½" 180 lbs.
B. Mar. 18, 1874, Fitchburg, Mass.    D. Oct. 4, 1934, Boston, Mass.
Manager 1903-04, 1912-14, 1916-17.

| | G | AB | H | 2B | 3B | HR | HR% | R | RBI | BB | SO | SB | BA | SA | AB | H | G by POS |
|---|---|---|---|---|---|---|---|---|---|---|---|---|---|---|---|---|---|
| 1894 **PHI N** | 9 | 21 | 5 | 0 | 0 | 0 | 0.0 | 4 | 0 | 0 | 7 | 0 | .238 | .238 | 0 | 0 | P-9 |
| 1897 **CHI N** | 94 | 360 | 105 | 18 | 6 | 3 | 0.8 | 60 | 47 | 10 | | 12 | .292 | .400 | 2 | 0 | 2B-30, P-23, OF-21, SS-18, 3B-2 |
| 1898 | 43 | 164 | 43 | 7 | 5 | 0 | 0.0 | 27 | 22 | 4 | | 3 | .262 | .366 | 0 | 0 | P-31, OF-9, SS-1, 2B-1, 1B-1 |
| 1899 | 47 | 150 | 39 | 4 | 3 | 0 | 0.0 | 21 | 18 | 8 | | 9 | .260 | .327 | 1 | 0 | P-35, OF-9, SS-2, 2B-1 |
| 1900 | 32 | 115 | 27 | 3 | 2 | 0 | 0.0 | 16 | 9 | 6 | | 5 | .235 | .296 | 0 | 0 | P-32 |
| 1901 **CHI A** | 45 | 118 | 39 | 7 | 3 | 1 | 0.8 | 15 | 19 | 10 | | 10 | .331 | .466 | 10 | 3 | P-27, 3B-6, 2B-2 |
| 1902 | 70 | 218 | 51 | 7 | 2 | 0 | 0.0 | 27 | 13 | 6 | | 4 | .234 | .284 | 12 | 2 | P-35, OF-23, SS-1 |
| 1903 | 118 | 439 | 128 | 26 | 5 | 2 | 0.5 | 47 | 56 | 20 | | 24 | .292 | .387 | 5 | 3 | 3B-102, OF-8, P-3 |
| 1904 | 132 | 482 | 126 | 23 | 2 | 0 | 0.0 | 64 | 54 | 39 | | 29 | .261 | .317 | 1 | 0 | OF-104, 2B-28 |
| 1905 | 96 | 345 | 94 | 18 | 6 | 1 | 0.3 | 50 | 43 | 29 | | 26 | .272 | .368 | 3 | 1 | OF-93 |
| 1911 | 120 | 466 | 131 | 13 | 5 | 3 | 0.6 | 64 | 60 | 15 | | 45 | .281 | .350 | 5 | 1 | OF-114 |
| 1912 | 111 | 408 | 111 | 9 | 7 | 1 | 0.2 | 45 | 52 | 12 | | 19 | .272 | .336 | 4 | 1 | OF-107 |
| 1913 | 6 | 9 | 2 | 0 | 0 | 0 | 0.0 | 1 | 0 | 1 | | 2 | .222 | .222 | 5 | 1 | OF-1 |
| 13 yrs. | 923 | 3295 | 901 | 135 | 46 | 11 | 0.3 | 442 | 394 | 159 | 9 | 186 | .273 | .352 | 48 | 12 | OF-489, P-195, 3B-110, 2B-62, SS-22, 1B-1 |
| 4 yrs. | 216 | 789 | 214 | 32 | 16 | 3 | 0.4 | 124 | 96 | 28 | | 29 | .271 | .364 | 3 | 0 | P-121, OF-39, 2B-32, SS-21, 3B-2, 1B-1 |

## Johnny Callison

**CALLISON, JOHN WESLEY**     BL TR 5'10" 175 lbs.
B. Mar. 12, 1939, Qualls, Okla.

| | G | AB | H | 2B | 3B | HR | HR% | R | RBI | BB | SO | SB | BA | SA | AB | H | G by POS |
|---|---|---|---|---|---|---|---|---|---|---|---|---|---|---|---|---|---|
| 1958 **CHI A** | 18 | 64 | 19 | 4 | 2 | 1 | 1.6 | 10 | 12 | 6 | 14 | 1 | .297 | .469 | 0 | 0 | OF-18 |
| 1959 | 49 | 104 | 18 | 3 | 0 | 3 | 2.9 | 12 | 12 | 13 | 20 | 0 | .173 | .288 | 4 | 0 | OF-41 |
| 1960 **PHI N** | 99 | 288 | 75 | 11 | 5 | 9 | 3.1 | 36 | 30 | 45 | 70 | 0 | .260 | .427 | 15 | 3 | OF-86 |
| 1961 | 138 | 455 | 121 | 20 | 11 | 9 | 2.0 | 74 | 47 | 69 | 76 | 10 | .266 | .418 | 14 | 3 | OF-124 |
| 1962 | 157 | 603 | 181 | 26 | 10 | 23 | 3.8 | 107 | 83 | 54 | 96 | 10 | .300 | .491 | 9 | 4 | OF-152 |
| 1963 | 157 | 626 | 178 | 36 | 11 | 26 | 4.2 | 96 | 78 | 50 | 111 | 8 | .284 | .502 | 2 | 0 | OF-157 |
| 1964 | 162 | 654 | 179 | 30 | 10 | 31 | 4.7 | 101 | 104 | 36 | 95 | 6 | .274 | .492 | 2 | 1 | OF-162 |
| 1965 | 160 | 619 | 162 | 25 | 16 | 32 | 5.2 | 93 | 101 | 57 | 117 | 6 | .262 | .509 | 6 | 0 | OF-159 |
| 1966 | 155 | 612 | 169 | 40 | 7 | 11 | 1.8 | 93 | 55 | 56 | 83 | 8 | .276 | .418 | 3 | 1 | OF-154 |
| 1967 | 149 | 556 | 145 | 30 | 5 | 14 | 2.5 | 62 | 64 | 55 | 63 | 6 | .261 | .408 | 3 | 0 | OF-147 |
| 1968 | 121 | 398 | 97 | 18 | 4 | 14 | 3.5 | 46 | 40 | 42 | 70 | 4 | .244 | .415 | 11 | 3 | OF-109 |
| 1969 | 134 | 495 | 131 | 29 | 5 | 16 | 3.2 | 66 | 64 | 49 | 73 | 2 | .265 | .440 | 6 | 1 | OF-129 |
| 1970 **CHI N** | 147 | 477 | 126 | 23 | 2 | 19 | 4.0 | 65 | 68 | 60 | 63 | 7 | .264 | .440 | 3 | 1 | OF-144 |
| 1971 | 103 | 290 | 61 | 12 | 1 | 8 | 2.8 | 27 | 38 | 36 | 55 | 2 | .210 | .341 | 14 | 1 | OF-89 |
| 1972 **NY A** | 92 | 275 | 71 | 10 | 0 | 9 | 3.3 | 28 | 34 | 18 | 34 | 3 | .258 | .393 | 19 | 4 | OF-74 |
| 1973 | 45 | 136 | 24 | 4 | 0 | 1 | 0.7 | 10 | 10 | 4 | 24 | 1 | .176 | .228 | 5 | 2 | OF-32, DH-10 |
| 16 yrs. | 1886 | 6652 | 1757 | 321 | 89 | 226 | 3.4 | 926 | 840 | 650 | 1064 | 74 | .264 | .441 | 116 | 24 | OF-1777, DH-10 |
| 2 yrs. | 250 | 767 | 187 | 35 | 3 | 27 | 3.5 | 92 | 106 | 96 | 118 | 9 | .244 | .403 | 17 | 2 | OF-233 |

## Dolf Camilli

**CAMILLI, ADOLF LOUIS**     BL TL 5'10" 185 lbs.
Father of Doug Camilli.
B. Apr. 23, 1907, San Francisco, Calif.

| | G | AB | H | 2B | 3B | HR | HR% | R | RBI | BB | SO | SB | BA | SA | AB | H | G by POS |
|---|---|---|---|---|---|---|---|---|---|---|---|---|---|---|---|---|---|
| 1933 **CHI N** | 16 | 58 | 13 | 2 | 1 | 2 | 3.4 | 8 | 7 | 4 | 11 | 3 | .224 | .397 | 0 | 0 | 1B-16 |
| 1934 **2 teams** | | **CHI N** (32G – .275) | | | | | **PHI N** (102G – .265) | | | | | | | | | | |
| " total | 134 | 498 | 133 | 28 | 3 | 16 | 3.2 | 69 | 87 | 53 | 94 | 4 | .267 | .432 | 0 | 0 | 1B-134 |
| 1935 **PHI N** | 156 | 602 | 157 | 23 | 5 | 25 | 4.2 | 88 | 83 | 65 | 113 | 9 | .261 | .440 | 0 | 0 | 1B-156 |
| 1936 | 151 | 530 | 167 | 29 | 13 | 28 | 5.3 | 106 | 102 | 116 | 84 | 5 | .315 | .577 | 1 | 1 | 1B-150 |
| 1937 | 131 | 475 | 161 | 23 | 7 | 27 | 5.7 | 101 | 80 | 90 | 82 | 6 | .339 | .587 | 0 | 0 | 1B-131 |
| 1938 **BKN N** | 146 | 509 | 128 | 25 | 11 | 24 | 4.7 | 106 | 100 | 119 | 101 | 6 | .251 | .485 | 0 | 0 | 1B-145 |
| 1939 | 157 | 565 | 164 | 30 | 12 | 26 | 4.6 | 105 | 104 | 110 | 107 | 1 | .290 | .524 | 0 | 0 | 1B-157 |
| 1940 | 142 | 512 | 147 | 29 | 13 | 23 | 4.5 | 92 | 96 | 89 | 83 | 9 | .287 | .529 | 1 | 0 | 1B-140 |
| 1941 | 149 | 529 | 151 | 29 | 6 | 34 | 6.4 | 92 | 120 | 104 | 115 | 3 | .285 | .556 | 1 | 0 | 1B-148 |
| 1942 | 150 | 524 | 132 | 23 | 7 | 26 | 5.0 | 89 | 109 | 97 | 85 | 10 | .252 | .471 | 0 | 0 | 1B-150 |
| 1943 | 95 | 353 | 87 | 15 | 6 | 6 | 1.7 | 56 | 43 | 65 | 48 | 2 | .246 | .374 | 0 | 0 | 1B-95 |
| 1945 **BOS A** | 63 | 198 | 42 | 5 | 2 | 2 | 1.0 | 24 | 19 | 35 | 38 | 2 | .212 | .288 | 8 | 1 | 1B-54 |
| 12 yrs. | 1490 | 5353 | 1482 | 261 | 86 | 239 | 4.5 | 936 | 950 | 947 | 961 | 60 | .277 | .492 | 11 | 2 | 1B-1476 |
| 2 yrs. | 48 | 178 | 46 | 10 | 1 | 6 | 3.4 | 25 | 26 | 9 | 36 | 4 | .258 | .427 | 0 | 0 | 1B-48 |

**WORLD SERIES**

| | G | AB | H | 2B | 3B | HR | HR% | R | RBI | BB | SO | SB | BA | SA | AB | H | G by POS |
|---|---|---|---|---|---|---|---|---|---|---|---|---|---|---|---|---|---|
| 1941 **BKN N** | 5 | 18 | 3 | 1 | 0 | 0 | 0.0 | 1 | 1 | 1 | 6 | 0 | .167 | .222 | 0 | 0 | 1B-5 |

## Llewellan Camp

**CAMP, LLEWELLAN ROBERT**     BL TR 6'1½" 165 lbs.
Brother of Kid Camp.
B. Feb. 22, 1868, Columbus, Ohio    D. Oct. 1, 1948, Omaha, Neb.

| | G | AB | H | 2B | 3B | HR | HR% | R | RBI | BB | SO | SB | BA | SA | AB | H | G by POS |
|---|---|---|---|---|---|---|---|---|---|---|---|---|---|---|---|---|---|
| 1892 **STL N** | 42 | 145 | 30 | 3 | 1 | 2 | 1.4 | 19 | 13 | 17 | 27 | 12 | .207 | .283 | 0 | 0 | 3B-39, OF-3 |
| 1893 **CHI N** | 38 | 156 | 41 | 7 | 7 | 2 | 1.3 | 37 | 17 | 19 | 19 | 30 | .263 | .436 | 0 | 0 | 3B-16, OF-11, 2B-9, SS-3 |
| 1894 | 8 | 33 | 6 | 2 | 0 | 0 | 0.0 | 1 | 1 | 1 | 6 | 0 | .182 | .242 | 0 | 0 | 2B-8 |
| 3 yrs. | 88 | 334 | 77 | 12 | 8 | 4 | 1.2 | 57 | 31 | 37 | 52 | 42 | .231 | .350 | 0 | 0 | 3B-55, 2B-17, OF-14, SS-3 |
| 2 yrs. | 46 | 189 | 47 | 9 | 7 | 2 | 1.1 | 38 | 18 | 20 | 25 | 30 | .249 | .402 | 0 | 0 | 2B-17, 3B-16, OF-11, SS-3 |

| | G | AB | H | 2B | 3B | HR | HR % | R | RBI | BB | SO | SB | BA | SA | Pinch Hit AB | Pinch Hit H | G by POS |
|---|---|---|---|---|---|---|---|---|---|---|---|---|---|---|---|---|---|

**illy Campbell**

CAMPBELL, WILLIAM GILTHORPE      BL TR 5'11" 176 lbs.
B. Feb. 13, 1908, Kansas City, Kans.    D. Feb. 21, 1973, Los Angeles, Calif.

| | G | AB | H | 2B | 3B | HR | HR % | R | RBI | BB | SO | SB | BA | SA | AB | H | G by POS |
|---|---|---|---|---|---|---|---|---|---|---|---|---|---|---|---|---|---|
| 43 CHI N | 46 | 89 | 25 | 3 | 1 | 1 | 1.1 | 11 | 10 | 7 | 4 | 0 | .281 | .371 | 23 | 6 | C-20 |
| 45 CIN N | 88 | 218 | 56 | 7 | 0 | 3 | 1.4 | 26 | 30 | 42 | 7 | 3 | .257 | .330 | 15 | 4 | C-66, 1B-5, OF-1 |
| 6 | 89 | 235 | 63 | 13 | 1 | 1 | 0.4 | 28 | 40 | 43 | 14 | 2 | .268 | .345 | 14 | 3 | C-71, 1B-1 |
| 7 | 18 | 40 | 11 | 2 | 0 | 0 | 0.0 | 3 | 2 | 5 | 1 | 0 | .275 | .325 | 1 | 0 | C-17 |
| 8 BKN N | 54 | 126 | 31 | 5 | 0 | 0 | 0.0 | 10 | 11 | 19 | 9 | 0 | .246 | .286 | 10 | 2 | C-44 |
| 5 yrs. | 295 | 708 | 186 | 30 | 2 | 5 | 0.7 | 78 | 93 | 116 | 35 | 5 | .263 | .332 | 63 | 15 | C-218, 1B-6, OF-1 |
| 1 yr. | 46 | 89 | 25 | 3 | 1 | 1 | 1.1 | 11 | 10 | 7 | 4 | 0 | .281 | .371 | 23 | 6 | C-20 |

**oe Campbell**

CAMPBELL, JOSEPH EARL      BR TR 6'1" 175 lbs.
B. Mar. 10, 1944, Louisville, Ky.

| | G | AB | H | 2B | 3B | HR | HR % | R | RBI | BB | SO | SB | BA | SA | AB | H | G by POS |
|---|---|---|---|---|---|---|---|---|---|---|---|---|---|---|---|---|---|
| 7 CHI N | 1 | 3 | 0 | 0 | 0 | 0 | 0.0 | 0 | 0 | 0 | 3 | 0 | .000 | .000 | 0 | 0 | OF-1 |

**on Campbell**

CAMPBELL, RONALD THOMAS      BR TR 6'1" 180 lbs.
B. Apr. 5, 1940, Chattanooga, Tenn.

| | G | AB | H | 2B | 3B | HR | HR % | R | RBI | BB | SO | SB | BA | SA | AB | H | G by POS |
|---|---|---|---|---|---|---|---|---|---|---|---|---|---|---|---|---|---|
| 4 CHI N | 26 | 92 | 25 | 6 | 1 | 1 | 1.1 | 7 | 10 | 1 | 21 | 0 | .272 | .391 | 0 | 0 | 2B-26 |
| 5 | 2 | 2 | 0 | 0 | 0 | 0 | 0.0 | 0 | 0 | 0 | 0 | 0 | .000 | .000 | 2 | 0 | |
| 6 | 24 | 60 | 13 | 1 | 0 | 0 | 0.0 | 4 | 4 | 6 | 5 | 1 | .217 | .233 | 5 | 1 | SS-11, 3B-7 |
| 3 yrs. | 52 | 154 | 38 | 7 | 1 | 1 | 0.6 | 11 | 14 | 7 | 26 | 1 | .247 | .325 | 7 | 1 | 2B-26, SS-11, 3B-7 |
| 3 yrs. | 52 | 154 | 38 | 7 | 1 | 1 | 0.6 | 11 | 14 | 7 | 26 | 1 | .247 | .325 | 7 | 1 | 2B-26, SS-11, 3B-7 |

**in Campbell**

CAMPBELL, ARTHUR VINCENT      BL TR
B. Jan. 30, 1888, St. Louis, Mo.    D. Nov. 16, 1969, Towson, Md.

| | G | AB | H | 2B | 3B | HR | HR % | R | RBI | BB | SO | SB | BA | SA | AB | H | G by POS |
|---|---|---|---|---|---|---|---|---|---|---|---|---|---|---|---|---|---|
| 8 CHI N | 1 | 1 | 0 | 0 | 0 | 0 | 0.0 | 0 | 0 | 0 | | 0 | .000 | .000 | 1 | 0 | |
| 0 PIT N | 97 | 282 | 92 | 9 | 5 | 4 | 1.4 | 42 | 21 | 26 | 23 | 17 | .326 | .436 | 18 | 5 | OF-74 |
| 1 | 42 | 93 | 29 | 3 | 1 | 0 | 0.0 | 12 | 10 | 8 | 7 | 6 | .312 | .366 | 17 | 4 | OF-21 |
| 2 BOS N | 145 | 624 | 185 | 32 | 9 | 3 | 0.5 | 102 | 48 | 32 | 44 | 19 | .296 | .391 | 1 | 0 | OF-144 |
| 4 IND F | 134 | 544 | 173 | 23 | 11 | 7 | 1.3 | 92 | 44 | 37 | | 26 | .318 | .439 | 1 | 0 | OF-132 |
| 5 NWK F | 127 | 525 | 163 | 18 | 10 | 1 | 0.2 | 78 | 44 | 29 | | 24 | .310 | .389 | 1 | 0 | OF-126 |
| 6 yrs. | 546 | 2069 | 642 | 85 | 36 | 15 | 0.7 | 326 | 167 | 132 | 74 | 92 | .310 | .408 | 39 | 9 | OF-497 |
| 1 yr. | 1 | 1 | 0 | 0 | 0 | 0 | 0.0 | 0 | 0 | 0 | | 0 | .000 | .000 | 1 | 0 | |

**mmy Canavan**

CANAVAN, JAMES EDWARD      BR TR 5'8" 160 lbs.
B. Nov. 26, 1866, New Bedford, Mass.    D. May 26, 1949, New Bedford, Mass.

| | G | AB | H | 2B | 3B | HR | HR % | R | RBI | BB | SO | SB | BA | SA | AB | H | G by POS |
|---|---|---|---|---|---|---|---|---|---|---|---|---|---|---|---|---|---|
| 1 C-M AA | 136 | 568 | 135 | 15 | 18 | 10 | 1.8 | 107 | 87 | 43 | 54 | 28 | .238 | .380 | 0 | 0 | SS-112, 2B-24 |
| 2 CHI N | 118 | 439 | 73 | 10 | 11 | 0 | 0.0 | 48 | 32 | 48 | 48 | 33 | .166 | .239 | 0 | 0 | 2B-112, OF-4, SS-2 |
| 3 CIN N | 121 | 461 | 104 | 13 | 7 | 5 | 1.1 | 65 | 64 | 51 | 20 | 31 | .226 | .317 | 1 | 0 | OF-116, 2B-5, 3B-1 |
| 4 | 101 | 356 | 97 | 16 | 9 | 13 | 3.7 | 77 | 70 | 62 | 25 | 13 | .272 | .478 | 1 | 0 | OF-95, SS-3, 3B-2, 2B-1, 1B-1 |
| 7 BKN N | 63 | 240 | 52 | 9 | 3 | 2 | 0.8 | 25 | 34 | 26 | | 9 | .217 | .304 | 0 | 0 | 2B-63 |
| 5 yrs. | 539 | 2064 | 461 | 63 | 48 | 30 | 1.5 | 322 | 287 | 230 | 147 | 114 | .223 | .344 | 2 | 0 | OF-215, 2B-205, SS-117, 3B-3, 1B-1 |
| 1 yr. | 118 | 439 | 73 | 10 | 11 | 0 | 0.0 | 48 | 32 | 48 | 48 | 33 | .166 | .239 | 0 | 0 | 2B-112, OF-4, SS-2 |

**hris Cannizzaro**

CANNIZZARO, CHRISTOPHER JOHN      BR TR 6' 190 lbs.
B. May 3, 1938, Oakland, Calif.

| | G | AB | H | 2B | 3B | HR | HR % | R | RBI | BB | SO | SB | BA | SA | AB | H | G by POS |
|---|---|---|---|---|---|---|---|---|---|---|---|---|---|---|---|---|---|
| 0 STL N | 7 | 9 | 2 | 0 | 0 | 0 | 0.0 | 0 | 1 | 1 | 3 | 0 | .222 | .222 | 0 | 0 | C-6 |
| 1 | 6 | 2 | 1 | 0 | 0 | 0 | 0.0 | 0 | 0 | 0 | 0 | 0 | .500 | .500 | 1 | 1 | C-5 |
| 2 NY N | 59 | 133 | 32 | 2 | 1 | 0 | 0.0 | 9 | 9 | 19 | 26 | 1 | .241 | .271 | 3 | 1 | C-56, OF-1 |
| 3 | 16 | 33 | 8 | 1 | 0 | 0 | 0.0 | 4 | 4 | 1 | 8 | 0 | .242 | .273 | 1 | 1 | C-15 |
| 4 | 60 | 164 | 51 | 10 | 0 | 0 | 0.0 | 11 | 10 | 14 | 28 | 0 | .311 | .372 | 5 | 1 | C-53 |
| 5 | 114 | 251 | 46 | 8 | 2 | 0 | 0.0 | 17 | 7 | 28 | 60 | 1 | .183 | .231 | 2 | 0 | C-112 |
| 8 PIT N | 25 | 58 | 14 | 2 | 1 | 1 | 1.7 | 5 | 7 | 9 | 13 | 0 | .241 | .397 | 0 | 0 | C-25 |
| 9 SD N | 134 | 418 | 92 | 14 | 3 | 4 | 1.0 | 23 | 33 | 42 | 81 | 0 | .220 | .297 | 2 | 0 | C-132 |
| 0 | 111 | 341 | 95 | 13 | 3 | 5 | 1.5 | 27 | 42 | 48 | 49 | 2 | .279 | .378 | 2 | 0 | C-110 |
| 1 2 teams | SD | N | (21G — | .190) | | CHI | N | (71G — | .213) | | | | | | | | |
| total | 92 | 260 | 54 | 9 | 1 | 6 | 2.3 | 20 | 31 | 39 | 34 | 0 | .208 | .319 | 2 | 0 | C-89 |
| 2 LA N | 73 | 200 | 48 | 6 | 0 | 2 | 1.0 | 14 | 18 | 31 | 38 | 0 | .240 | .300 | 5 | 2 | C-72 |
| 3 | 17 | 21 | 4 | 0 | 0 | 0 | 0.0 | 3 | 3 | 3 | 3 | 0 | .190 | .190 | 3 | 0 | C-13 |
| 4 SD N | 26 | 60 | 11 | 1 | 0 | 0 | 0.0 | 2 | 4 | 6 | 11 | 0 | .183 | .200 | 0 | 0 | C-26 |
| 3 yrs. | 740 | 1950 | 458 | 66 | 12 | 18 | 0.9 | 132 | 169 | 241 | 354 | 3 | .235 | .309 | 26 | 6 | C-714, OF-1 |
| 1 yr. | 71 | 197 | 42 | 8 | 1 | 5 | 2.5 | 18 | 23 | 28 | 24 | 0 | .213 | .340 | 0 | 0 | C-70 |

**ose Cardenal**

CARDENAL, JOSE DOMEC      BR TR 5'10" 150 lbs.
B. Oct. 7, 1943, Matanzas, Cuba

| | G | AB | H | 2B | 3B | HR | HR % | R | RBI | BB | SO | SB | BA | SA | AB | H | G by POS |
|---|---|---|---|---|---|---|---|---|---|---|---|---|---|---|---|---|---|
| 3 SF N | 9 | 5 | 1 | 0 | 0 | 0 | 0.0 | 1 | 2 | 1 | 1 | 0 | .200 | .200 | 4 | 1 | OF-2 |
| 4 | 20 | 15 | 0 | 0 | 0 | 0 | 0.0 | 3 | 0 | 2 | 3 | 2 | .000 | .000 | 2 | 0 | OF-16 |
| 5 CAL A | 134 | 512 | 128 | 23 | 2 | 11 | 2.1 | 58 | 57 | 27 | 72 | 37 | .250 | .367 | 1 | 1 | OF-129, 3B-2, 2B-1 |
| 6 | 154 | 561 | 155 | 15 | 3 | 16 | 2.9 | 67 | 48 | 34 | 69 | 24 | .276 | .399 | 10 | 2 | OF-146 |
| 7 | 108 | 381 | 90 | 13 | 5 | 6 | 1.6 | 40 | 27 | 15 | 63 | 10 | .236 | .344 | 8 | 0 | OF-101 |
| 8 CLE A | 157 | 583 | 150 | 21 | 7 | 7 | 1.2 | 78 | 44 | 39 | 74 | 40 | .257 | .353 | 7 | 1 | OF-153 |
| 9 | 146 | 557 | 143 | 26 | 3 | 11 | 2.0 | 75 | 45 | 49 | 58 | 36 | .257 | .373 | 4 | 1 | OF-142, 3B-5 |
| 0 STL N | 148 | 552 | 162 | 32 | 6 | 10 | 1.8 | 73 | 74 | 45 | 70 | 26 | .293 | .428 | 16 | 8 | OF-134 |
| 1 2 teams | STL | N | (89G — | .243) | | MIL | A | (53G — | .258) | | | | | | | | |
| total | 142 | 499 | 124 | 22 | 4 | 10 | 2.0 | 57 | 80 | 42 | 55 | 21 | .248 | .369 | 9 | 5 | OF-135 |
| 2 CHI N | 143 | 533 | 155 | 24 | 6 | 17 | 3.2 | 96 | 70 | 55 | 58 | 25 | .291 | .454 | 5 | 2 | OF-137 |
| 3 | 145 | 522 | 158 | 33 | 2 | 11 | 2.1 | 80 | 68 | 58 | 62 | 19 | .303 | .437 | 2 | 1 | OF-142 |
| 4 | 143 | 542 | 159 | 35 | 3 | 13 | 2.4 | 75 | 72 | 56 | 67 | 23 | .293 | .441 | 8 | 2 | OF-136 |
| 5 | 154 | 574 | 182 | 30 | 2 | 9 | 1.6 | 85 | 68 | 77 | 50 | 34 | .317 | .423 | 5 | 1 | OF-151 |
| 6 | 136 | 521 | 156 | 25 | 2 | 8 | 1.5 | 64 | 47 | 32 | 39 | 23 | .299 | .401 | 8 | 1 | OF-128 |

| | G | AB | H | 2B | 3B | HR | HR % | R | RBI | BB | SO | SB | BA | SA | Pinch Hit AB | Pinch Hit H | G by POS |
|---|---|---|---|---|---|---|---|---|---|---|---|---|---|---|---|---|---|

## Jose Cardenal continued

| | | G | AB | H | 2B | 3B | HR | HR % | R | RBI | BB | SO | SB | BA | SA | AB | H | G by POS |
|---|---|---|---|---|---|---|---|---|---|---|---|---|---|---|---|---|---|---|
| 1977 | | 100 | 226 | 54 | 12 | 1 | 3 | 1.3 | 33 | 18 | 28 | 30 | 5 | .239 | .341 | 31 | 10 | OF-62, 3B-1, 2B-1 |
| 1978 | PHI N | 87 | 201 | 50 | 12 | 0 | 4 | 2.0 | 27 | 33 | 23 | 16 | 2 | .249 | .368 | 33 | 9 | 1B-50, OF-13 |
| 1979 | 2 teams | PHI | N | (29G – .208) | | NY | N | (11G – .297) | | | | | | | | | | |
| " | total | 40 | 85 | 21 | 7 | 0 | 2 | 2.4 | 12 | 13 | 14 | 11 | 2 | .247 | .400 | 17 | 4 | OF-21, 1B-3 |
| 1980 | 2 teams | NY | N | (26G – .167) | | KC | A | (25G – .340) | | | | | | | | | | |
| " | total | 51 | 95 | 25 | 3 | 0 | 0 | 0.0 | 12 | 9 | 11 | 9 | 0 | .263 | .295 | 17 | 1 | OF-29, 1B-5 |
| 18 yrs. | | 2017 | 6964 | 1913 | 333 | 46 | 138 | 2.0 | 936 | 775 | 608 | 807 | 329 | .275 | .395 | 187 | 50 | OF-1777, 1B-58, 3B-8, 2B-2 |
| 6 yrs. | | 821 | 2918 | 864 | 159 | 16 | 61 | 2.1 | 433 | 343 | 306 | 306 | 129 | .296 | .424 | 59 | 17 | OF-756, 3B-1, 2B-1 |

LEAGUE CHAMPIONSHIP SERIES

| | | G | AB | H | 2B | 3B | HR | HR % | R | RBI | BB | SO | SB | BA | SA | AB | H | G by POS |
|---|---|---|---|---|---|---|---|---|---|---|---|---|---|---|---|---|---|---|
| 1978 | PHI N | 2 | 6 | 1 | 0 | 0 | 0 | 0.0 | 0 | 0 | 1 | 1 | 0 | .167 | .167 | 0 | 0 | 1B-2 |

WORLD SERIES

| | | G | AB | H | 2B | 3B | HR | HR % | R | RBI | BB | SO | SB | BA | SA | AB | H | G by POS |
|---|---|---|---|---|---|---|---|---|---|---|---|---|---|---|---|---|---|---|
| 1980 | KC A | 4 | 10 | 2 | 0 | 0 | 0 | 0.0 | 0 | 0 | 0 | 0 | 3 | .200 | .200 | 1 | 0 | OF-4 |

## Bill Carney

**CARNEY, WILLIAM JOHN**  BB TR 5'10"
B. Mar. 25, 1874, St. Paul, Minn.  D. July 31, 1938, Hopkins, Minn.

| | | G | AB | H | 2B | 3B | HR | HR % | R | RBI | BB | SO | SB | BA | SA | AB | H | G by POS |
|---|---|---|---|---|---|---|---|---|---|---|---|---|---|---|---|---|---|---|
| 1904 | CHI N | 2 | 7 | 0 | 0 | 0 | 0 | 0.0 | 0 | 0 | 1 | | 0 | .000 | .000 | 0 | 0 | OF-2 |

## Cliff Carroll

**CARROLL, SAMUEL CLIFFORD**  BB TR 5'8"  163 lbs
B. Oct. 18, 1859, Clay Grove, Iowa  D. June 12, 1923, Portland, Ore.

| | | G | AB | H | 2B | 3B | HR | HR % | R | RBI | BB | SO | SB | BA | SA | AB | H | G by POS |
|---|---|---|---|---|---|---|---|---|---|---|---|---|---|---|---|---|---|---|
| 1882 | PRO N | 10 | 41 | 5 | 0 | 0 | 0 | 0.0 | 4 | | 0 | 4 | | .122 | .122 | 0 | 0 | OF-10 |
| 1883 | | 58 | 238 | 63 | 12 | 3 | 1 | 0.4 | 37 | | 4 | 28 | | .265 | .353 | 0 | 0 | OF-58 |
| 1884 | | 113 | 452 | 118 | 16 | 4 | 3 | 0.7 | 90 | | 29 | 39 | | .261 | .334 | 0 | 0 | OF-113 |
| 1885 | | 104 | 426 | 99 | 12 | 3 | 1 | 0.2 | 62 | 40 | 29 | 29 | | .232 | .282 | 0 | 0 | OF-104 |
| 1886 | WAS N | 111 | 433 | 99 | 11 | 6 | 2 | 0.5 | 73 | 22 | 44 | 26 | | .229 | .296 | 0 | 0 | OF-111 |
| 1887 | | 103 | 420 | 104 | 17 | 4 | 4 | 1.0 | 79 | 37 | 17 | 30 | 40 | .248 | .336 | 0 | 0 | OF-103 |
| 1888 | PIT N | 5 | 20 | 0 | 0 | 0 | 0 | 0.0 | 1 | 0 | 0 | 8 | 2 | .000 | .000 | 0 | 0 | OF-5 |
| 1890 | CHI N | 136 | 582 | 166 | 16 | 6 | 7 | 1.2 | 134 | 65 | 53 | 34 | 34 | .285 | .369 | 0 | 0 | OF-136 |
| 1891 | | 130 | 515 | 132 | 20 | 8 | 7 | 1.4 | 87 | 80 | 50 | 42 | 31 | .256 | .367 | 0 | 0 | OF-130 |
| 1892 | STL N | 101 | 407 | 111 | 14 | 8 | 4 | 1.0 | 82 | 49 | 47 | 22 | 30 | .273 | .376 | 0 | 0 | OF-101 |
| 1893 | BOS N | 120 | 438 | 98 | 7 | 5 | 3 | 0.7 | 80 | 54 | 88 | 28 | 29 | .224 | .276 | 0 | 0 | OF-120 |
| 11 yrs. | | 991 | 3972 | 995 | 125 | 47 | 31 | 0.8 | 729 | 346 | 361 | 290 | 166 | .251 | .329 | 0 | 0 | OF-991 |
| 2 yrs. | | 266 | 1097 | 298 | 36 | 14 | 14 | 1.3 | 221 | 145 | 103 | 76 | 65 | .272 | .368 | 0 | 0 | OF-266 |

## Joe Carter

**CARTER, JOSEPH CHRIS**  BR TR 6'3"  210 lbs
B. Mar. 7, 1960, Oklahoma City, Okla.

| | | G | AB | H | 2B | 3B | HR | HR % | R | RBI | BB | SO | SB | BA | SA | AB | H | G by POS |
|---|---|---|---|---|---|---|---|---|---|---|---|---|---|---|---|---|---|---|
| 1983 | CHI N | 23 | 51 | 9 | 1 | 1 | 0 | 0.0 | 6 | 1 | 0 | 21 | 1 | .176 | .235 | 5 | 1 | OF-16 |
| 1984 | CLE A | 66 | 244 | 67 | 6 | 1 | 13 | 5.3 | 32 | 41 | 11 | 48 | 2 | .275 | .467 | 7 | 5 | OF-59, 1B-7 |
| 1985 | | 143 | 489 | 128 | 27 | 0 | 15 | 3.1 | 64 | 59 | 25 | 74 | 24 | .262 | .409 | 4 | 0 | OF-135, 1B-11, DH-7, 3B-1, 2B-1 |
| 3 yrs. | | 232 | 784 | 204 | 34 | 2 | 28 | 3.6 | 102 | 101 | 36 | 143 | 27 | .260 | .416 | 16 | 6 | OF-210, 1B-18, DH-7, 3B-1, 2B-1 |
| 1 yr. | | 23 | 51 | 9 | 1 | 1 | 0 | 0.0 | 6 | 1 | 0 | 21 | 1 | .176 | .235 | 5 | 1 | OF-16 |

## Rico Carty

**CARTY, RICARDO ADOLFO JACABO**  BR TR 6'3"  200 lbs
B. Sept. 1, 1941, San Pedro de Macoris, Dominican Republic

| | | G | AB | H | 2B | 3B | HR | HR % | R | RBI | BB | SO | SB | BA | SA | AB | H | G by POS |
|---|---|---|---|---|---|---|---|---|---|---|---|---|---|---|---|---|---|---|
| 1963 | MIL N | 2 | 2 | 0 | 0 | 0 | 0 | 0.0 | 0 | 0 | 0 | 2 | 0 | .000 | .000 | 2 | 0 | |
| 1964 | | 133 | 455 | 150 | 28 | 4 | 22 | 4.8 | 72 | 88 | 43 | 78 | 1 | .330 | .554 | 12 | 3 | OF-121 |
| 1965 | | 83 | 271 | 84 | 18 | 1 | 10 | 3.7 | 37 | 35 | 17 | 44 | 1 | .310 | .494 | 11 | 3 | OF-73 |
| 1966 | ATL N | 151 | 521 | 170 | 25 | 2 | 15 | 2.9 | 73 | 76 | 60 | 74 | 4 | .326 | .468 | 12 | 2 | OF-126, C-17, 1B-2, 3B-1 |
| 1967 | | 134 | 444 | 113 | 16 | 2 | 15 | 3.4 | 41 | 64 | 49 | 70 | 4 | .255 | .401 | 14 | 2 | OF-112, 1B-9 |
| 1969 | | 104 | 304 | 104 | 15 | 0 | 16 | 5.3 | 47 | 58 | 32 | 28 | 0 | .342 | .549 | 22 | 9 | OF-79 |
| 1970 | | 136 | 478 | 175 | 23 | 3 | 25 | 5.2 | 84 | 101 | 77 | 46 | 1 | .366 | .584 | 3 | 1 | OF-133 |
| 1972 | | 86 | 271 | 75 | 12 | 2 | 6 | 2.2 | 31 | 29 | 44 | 33 | 0 | .277 | .402 | 8 | 2 | OF-78 |
| 1973 | 3 teams | TEX | N | (86G – .232) | | CHI | N | (22G – .214) | | OAK | A | (7G – .250) | | | | | | |
| " | total | 115 | 384 | 88 | 13 | 0 | 5 | 1.3 | 29 | 42 | 44 | 50 | 2 | .229 | .302 | 7 | 2 | OF-72, DH-32 |
| 1974 | CLE A | 33 | 91 | 33 | 5 | 0 | 1 | 1.1 | 6 | 16 | 5 | 9 | 0 | .363 | .451 | 11 | 2 | DH-14, 1B-8 |
| 1975 | | 118 | 383 | 118 | 19 | 1 | 18 | 4.7 | 57 | 64 | 45 | 31 | 2 | .308 | .504 | 8 | 6 | DH-72, 1B-26, OF-12 |
| 1976 | | 152 | 552 | 171 | 34 | 0 | 13 | 2.4 | 67 | 83 | 67 | 45 | 1 | .310 | .442 | 1 | 1 | DH-137, 1B-12, OF-1 |
| 1977 | | 127 | 461 | 129 | 23 | 1 | 15 | 3.3 | 50 | 80 | 56 | 51 | 1 | .280 | .432 | 2 | 1 | DH-123, 1B-2 |
| 1978 | 2 teams | TOR | A | (104G – .284) | | OAK | A | (41G – .277) | | | | | | | | | | |
| " | total | 145 | 528 | 149 | 21 | 1 | 31 | 5.9 | 70 | 99 | 57 | 57 | 1 | .282 | .502 | 4 | 0 | DH-142 |
| 1979 | TOR A | 132 | 461 | 118 | 26 | 0 | 12 | 2.6 | 48 | 55 | 46 | 45 | 3 | .256 | .390 | 9 | 4 | DH-129 |
| 15 yrs. | | 1651 | 5606 | 1677 | 278 | 17 | 204 | 3.6 | 712 | 890 | 642 | 663 | 21 | .299 | .464 | 126 | 38 | OF-807, DH-649, 1B-59, C-17, 3B-1 |
| 1 yr. | | 22 | 70 | 15 | 0 | 0 | 1 | 1.4 | 4 | 8 | 6 | 10 | 0 | .214 | .257 | 2 | 0 | OF-19 |

LEAGUE CHAMPIONSHIP SERIES

| | | G | AB | H | 2B | 3B | HR | HR % | R | RBI | BB | SO | SB | BA | SA | AB | H | G by POS |
|---|---|---|---|---|---|---|---|---|---|---|---|---|---|---|---|---|---|---|
| 1969 | ATL N | 3 | 10 | 3 | 2 | 0 | 0 | 0.0 | 4 | 0 | 3 | 1 | 0 | .300 | .500 | 0 | 0 | OF-3 |

## Bob Caruthers

**CARUTHERS, ROBERT LEE (Parisian Bob)**  BL TR 5'7"  138 lbs.
B. Jan. 5, 1864, Memphis, Tenn.  D. Aug. 5, 1911, Peoria, Ill.

| | | G | AB | H | 2B | 3B | HR | HR % | R | RBI | BB | SO | SB | BA | SA | AB | H | G by POS |
|---|---|---|---|---|---|---|---|---|---|---|---|---|---|---|---|---|---|---|
| 1884 | STL AA | 23 | 82 | 21 | 2 | 0 | 2 | 2.4 | 15 | | 4 | | | .256 | .354 | 0 | 0 | OF-16, P-13 |
| 1885 | | 60 | 222 | 50 | 10 | 2 | 1 | 0.5 | 37 | | 20 | | | .225 | .302 | 0 | 0 | P-53, OF-7 |
| 1886 | | 87 | 317 | 106 | 21 | 14 | 4 | 1.3 | 91 | | 64 | | | .334 | .527 | 0 | 0 | P-44, OF-43, 2B-2 |
| 1887 | BKN AA | 98 | 364 | 130 | 23 | 11 | 8 | 2.2 | 102 | | 66 | | 49 | .357 | .547 | 0 | 0 | OF-54, P-39, 1B-7 |
| 1888 | | 94 | 335 | 77 | 10 | 5 | 5 | 1.5 | 58 | 53 | 45 | | 23 | .230 | .334 | 0 | 0 | OF-51, P-44 |
| 1889 | | 59 | 172 | 43 | 8 | 3 | 2 | 1.2 | 45 | 31 | 44 | 17 | 9 | .250 | .366 | 0 | 0 | P-56, OF-3, 1B-2 |
| 1890 | BKN N | 71 | 238 | 63 | 7 | 4 | 1 | 0.4 | 46 | 29 | 47 | 18 | 13 | .265 | .340 | 0 | 0 | OF-39, P-37 |
| 1891 | | 56 | 171 | 48 | 5 | 3 | 2 | 1.2 | 24 | 23 | 25 | 13 | 4 | .281 | .380 | 1 | 0 | P-38, OF-17, 2B-1 |
| 1892 | STL N | 143 | 513 | 142 | 16 | 8 | 3 | 0.6 | 74 | 69 | 86 | 29 | 24 | .277 | .357 | 0 | 0 | OF-122, P-16, 2B-6, 1B-4 |

| | G | AB | H | 2B | 3B | HR | HR % | R | RBI | BB | SO | SB | BA | SA | Pinch Hit AB | Pinch Hit H | G by POS |
|---|---|---|---|---|---|---|---|---|---|---|---|---|---|---|---|---|---|

## Bob Caruthers  continued

| | G | AB | H | 2B | 3B | HR | HR % | R | RBI | BB | SO | SB | BA | SA | AB | H | G by POS |
|---|---|---|---|---|---|---|---|---|---|---|---|---|---|---|---|---|---|
| 1893 **2 teams** | | CHI | **N** | (1G – | .000) | | **CIN** | **N** | (13G – | .292) | | | | | | | OF-14 |
| " total | 14 | 51 | 14 | 2 | 0 | 1 | 2.0 | 14 | 8 | 16 | 2 | 4 | .275 | .373 | 0 | 0 | OF-14 |
| 10 yrs. | 705 | 2465 | 694 | 104 | 50 | 29 | 1.2 | 508 | 212 | 417 | 79 | 126 | .282 | .400 | 1 | 0 | OF-366, P-340, 1B-13, 2B-9 |
| 1 yr. | 1 | 3 | 0 | 0 | 0 | 0 | 0.0 | 0 | 0 | 1 | 0 | 0 | .000 | .000 | 0 | 0 | OF-1 |

## Doc Casey

**CASEY, JAMES PETER**                                                BL  TR
B. Mar. 15, 1871, Lawrence, Mass.    D. Dec. 30, 1936, Detroit, Mich.

| | G | AB | H | 2B | 3B | HR | HR % | R | RBI | BB | SO | SB | BA | SA | AB | H | G by POS |
|---|---|---|---|---|---|---|---|---|---|---|---|---|---|---|---|---|---|
| 1898 **WAS N** | 28 | 112 | 31 | 2 | 0 | 0 | 0.0 | 13 | 15 | 3 | | 15 | .277 | .295 | 0 | 0 | 3B-22, SS-4, C-3 |
| 1899 **2 teams** | | WAS | **N** | (9G – | .118) | | **BKN** | **N** | (134G – | .269) | | | | | | | 3B-143 |
| " total | 143 | 559 | 145 | 16 | 8 | 1 | 0.2 | 78 | 45 | 27 | | 28 | .259 | .322 | 0 | 0 | 3B-143 |
| 1900 **BKN N** | 1 | 3 | 1 | 0 | 0 | 0 | 0.0 | 0 | 1 | 0 | | 0 | .333 | .333 | 0 | 0 | 3B-1 |
| 1901 **DET A** | 128 | 540 | 153 | 16 | 9 | 2 | 0.4 | 105 | 46 | 32 | | 34 | .283 | .357 | 1 | 0 | 3B-127 |
| 1902 | 132 | 520 | 142 | 18 | 7 | 3 | 0.6 | 69 | 55 | 44 | | 22 | .273 | .352 | 0 | 0 | 3B-132 |
| 1903 **CHI N** | 112 | 435 | 126 | 8 | 3 | 1 | 0.2 | 56 | 40 | 19 | | 11 | .290 | .329 | 0 | 0 | 3B-112 |
| 1904 | 136 | 548 | 147 | 20 | 4 | 1 | 0.2 | 71 | 43 | 18 | | 21 | .268 | .325 | 0 | 0 | 3B-134, C-2 |
| 1905 | 144 | 526 | 122 | 21 | 10 | 1 | 0.2 | 66 | 56 | 41 | | 22 | .232 | .316 | 2 | 0 | 3B-142, SS-1 |
| 1906 **BKN N** | 149 | 571 | 133 | 17 | 8 | 0 | 0.0 | 71 | 34 | 52 | | 22 | .233 | .291 | 0 | 0 | 3B-149 |
| 1907 | 141 | 527 | 122 | 19 | 3 | 0 | 0.0 | 55 | 19 | 34 | | 16 | .231 | .279 | 3 | 0 | 3B-138 |
| 10 yrs. | 1114 | 4341 | 1122 | 137 | 52 | 9 | 0.2 | 584 | 354 | 270 | | 191 | .258 | .320 | 6 | 0 | 3B-1100, SS-5, C-5 |
| 3 yrs. | 392 | 1509 | 395 | 49 | 17 | 3 | 0.2 | 193 | 139 | 78 | | 54 | .262 | .323 | 2 | 0 | 3B-388, C-2, SS-1 |

## John Cassidy

**CASSIDY, JOHN P.**                                                BR  TL  5'8"   168 lbs.
B. 1857, Brooklyn, N. Y.    D. July 2, 1891, Brooklyn, N. Y.

| | G | AB | H | 2B | 3B | HR | HR % | R | RBI | BB | SO | SB | BA | SA | AB | H | G by POS |
|---|---|---|---|---|---|---|---|---|---|---|---|---|---|---|---|---|---|
| 1876 **HAR N** | 12 | 47 | 13 | 2 | 0 | 0 | 0.0 | 6 | 8 | 1 | 0 | | .277 | .319 | 0 | 0 | OF-8, 1B-4 |
| 1877 | 60 | 251 | 95 | 10 | 5 | 0 | 0.0 | 43 | 27 | 3 | 3 | | .378 | .458 | 0 | 0 | OF-58, P-2 |
| 1878 **CHI N** | 60 | 256 | 68 | 7 | 1 | 0 | 0.0 | 33 | 29 | 9 | 11 | | .266 | .301 | 0 | 0 | OF-60, C-1 |
| 1879 **TRO N** | 9 | 37 | 7 | 1 | 0 | 0 | 0.0 | 4 | 1 | 2 | 4 | | .189 | .216 | 0 | 0 | OF-8, 1B-2 |
| 1880 | 83 | 352 | 89 | 14 | 8 | 0 | 0.0 | 40 | | 12 | 34 | | .253 | .338 | 0 | 0 | OF-82, 2B-1 |
| 1881 | 85 | 370 | 82 | 13 | 3 | 1 | 0.3 | 57 | 11 | 18 | 21 | | .222 | .281 | 0 | 0 | OF-84, SS-1 |
| 1882 | 29 | 121 | 21 | 3 | 1 | 0 | 0.0 | 14 | 9 | 3 | 16 | | .174 | .215 | 0 | 0 | OF-16, 3B-13 |
| 1883 **PRO N** | 89 | 366 | 87 | 16 | 5 | 0 | 0.0 | 46 | | 9 | 38 | | .238 | .309 | 0 | 0 | OF-88, 2B-1, 1B-1 |
| 1884 **BKN AA** | 106 | 433 | 109 | 11 | 6 | 2 | 0.5 | 57 | | 19 | | | .252 | .319 | 0 | 0 | OF-100, 3B-5, SS-1 |
| 1885 | 54 | 221 | 47 | 6 | 2 | 1 | 0.5 | 36 | | 8 | | | .213 | .271 | 0 | 0 | OF-54 |
| 10 yrs. | 587 | 2454 | 618 | 83 | 31 | 4 | 0.2 | 336 | 85 | 84 | 127 | | .252 | .316 | 0 | 0 | OF-558, 3B-18, 1B-7, SS-2, 2B-2, P-2, C-1 |
| 1 yr. | 60 | 256 | 68 | 7 | 1 | 0 | 0.0 | 33 | 29 | 9 | 11 | | .266 | .301 | 0 | 0 | OF-60, C-1 |

## Phil Cavarretta

**CAVARRETTA, PHILIP JOSEPH**                                        BL  TL  5'11½"  175 lbs.
B. July 19, 1916, Chicago, Ill.
Manager 1951-53.

| | G | AB | H | 2B | 3B | HR | HR % | R | RBI | BB | SO | SB | BA | SA | AB | H | G by POS |
|---|---|---|---|---|---|---|---|---|---|---|---|---|---|---|---|---|---|
| 1934 **CHI N** | 7 | 21 | 8 | 0 | 1 | 1 | 4.8 | 5 | 6 | 2 | 3 | 1 | .381 | .619 | 2 | 0 | 1B-5 |
| 1935 | 146 | 589 | 162 | 28 | 12 | 8 | 1.4 | 85 | 82 | 39 | 61 | 4 | .275 | .404 | 1 | 0 | 1B-145 |
| 1936 | 124 | 458 | 125 | 18 | 1 | 9 | 2.0 | 55 | 56 | 17 | 36 | 8 | .273 | .376 | 8 | 4 | 1B-115 |
| 1937 | 106 | 329 | 94 | 18 | 7 | 5 | 1.5 | 43 | 56 | 32 | 35 | 7 | .286 | .429 | 11 | 4 | OF-53, 1B-43 |
| 1938 | 92 | 268 | 64 | 11 | 4 | 1 | 0.4 | 29 | 28 | 14 | 27 | 4 | .239 | .321 | 13 | 1 | OF-52, 1B-28 |
| 1939 | 22 | 55 | 15 | 3 | 1 | 0 | 0.0 | 4 | 0 | 4 | 3 | 2 | .273 | .364 | 7 | 3 | 1B-13, OF-1 |
| 1940 | 65 | 193 | 54 | 11 | 4 | 2 | 1.0 | 34 | 22 | 31 | 18 | 3 | .280 | .409 | 10 | 0 | 1B-52 |
| 1941 | 107 | 346 | 99 | 18 | 4 | 6 | 1.7 | 46 | 40 | 53 | 28 | 2 | .286 | .413 | 5 | 2 | OF-66, 1B-33 |
| 1942 | 136 | 482 | 130 | 28 | 4 | 3 | 0.6 | 59 | 54 | 71 | 42 | 7 | .270 | .363 | 6 | 0 | OF-70, 1B-61 |
| 1943 | 143 | 530 | 154 | 27 | 9 | 8 | 1.5 | 93 | 73 | 75 | 42 | 3 | .291 | .421 | 2 | 0 | 1B-134, OF-7 |
| 1944 | 152 | 614 | 197 | 35 | 15 | 5 | 0.8 | 106 | 82 | 67 | 42 | 4 | .321 | .451 | 0 | 0 | 1B-139, OF-13 |
| 1945 | 132 | 498 | 177 | 34 | 10 | 6 | 1.2 | 94 | 97 | 81 | 34 | 5 | .355 | .500 | 0 | 0 | 1B-120, OF-11 |
| 1946 | 139 | 510 | 150 | 28 | 10 | 8 | 1.6 | 89 | 78 | 88 | 54 | 2 | .294 | .435 | 2 | 0 | OF-86, 1B-51 |
| 1947 | 127 | 459 | 144 | 22 | 5 | 2 | 0.4 | 56 | 63 | 58 | 35 | 2 | .314 | .397 | 3 | 2 | OF-100, 1B-24 |
| 1948 | 111 | 334 | 93 | 16 | 5 | 3 | 0.9 | 41 | 40 | 35 | 29 | 4 | .278 | .383 | 23 | 9 | 1B-41, OF-40 |
| 1949 | 105 | 360 | 106 | 22 | 4 | 8 | 2.2 | 46 | 49 | 45 | 31 | 2 | .294 | .444 | 9 | 2 | 1B-70, OF-25 |
| 1950 | 82 | 256 | 70 | 11 | 1 | 10 | 3.9 | 49 | 31 | 40 | 31 | 1 | .273 | .441 | 9 | 2 | 1B-67, OF-3 |
| 1951 | 89 | 206 | 64 | 7 | 1 | 6 | 2.9 | 24 | 28 | 27 | 28 | 0 | .311 | .442 | 33 | 12 | 1B-53 |
| 1952 | 41 | 63 | 15 | 1 | 1 | 1 | 1.6 | 7 | 8 | 9 | 3 | 0 | .238 | .333 | 26 | 5 | 1B-13 |
| 1953 | 27 | 21 | 6 | 3 | 0 | 0 | 0.0 | 3 | 3 | 6 | 3 | 0 | .286 | .429 | 21 | 6 | |
| 1954 **CHI A** | 71 | 158 | 50 | 6 | 0 | 3 | 1.9 | 21 | 24 | 26 | 12 | 4 | .316 | .411 | 16 | 2 | 1B-44, OF-9 |
| 1955 | 6 | 4 | 0 | 0 | 0 | 0 | 0.0 | 0 | 0 | 0 | 0 | 0 | .000 | .000 | 2 | 0 | 1B-3 |
| 22 yrs. | 2030 | 6754 | 1977 | 347 | 99 | 95 | 1.4 | 990 | 920 | 820 | 598 | 65 | .293 | .416 | 209 | 48 | 1B-1254, OF-536 |
| 20 yrs. | 1953 | 6592 | 1927 | 341 | 99 | 92 | 1.4 | 968 | 896 | 794 | 585 | 61 | .292 | .416 | 191 | 46 | 1B-1207, OF-527 |
| | 5th | 7th | 7th | 9th | 5th | | | 7th | 7th | 5th | 7th | | | | 2nd | 1st | |
| WORLD SERIES | | | | | | | | | | | | | | | | | |
| 1935 **CHI N** | 6 | 24 | 3 | 0 | 0 | 0 | 0.0 | 1 | 0 | 0 | 5 | 0 | .125 | .125 | 0 | 0 | 1B-6 |
| 1938 | 4 | 13 | 6 | 1 | 0 | 0 | 0.0 | 1 | 0 | 0 | 1 | 0 | .462 | .538 | 1 | 1 | OF-3 |
| 1945 | 7 | 26 | 11 | 2 | 0 | 1 | 3.8 | 7 | 5 | 4 | 3 | 0 | .423 | .615 | 0 | 0 | 1B-7 |
| 3 yrs. | 17 | 63 | 20 | 3 | 0 | 1 | 1.6 | 9 | 5 | 4 | 9 | 0 | .317 | .413 | 1 | 1 | 1B-13, OF-3 |

## Ron Cey

**CEY, RONALD CHARLES (Penguin)**                                    BR  TR  5'10"   185 lbs.
B. Feb. 15, 1948, Tacoma, Wash.

| | G | AB | H | 2B | 3B | HR | HR % | R | RBI | BB | SO | SB | BA | SA | AB | H | G by POS |
|---|---|---|---|---|---|---|---|---|---|---|---|---|---|---|---|---|---|
| 1971 **LA N** | 2 | 2 | 0 | 0 | 0 | 0 | 0.0 | 0 | 0 | 0 | 2 | 0 | .000 | .000 | 2 | 0 | |
| 1972 | 11 | 37 | 10 | 1 | 0 | 1 | 2.7 | 3 | 3 | 7 | 10 | 0 | .270 | .378 | 0 | 0 | 3B-11 |
| 1973 | 152 | 507 | 124 | 18 | 4 | 15 | 3.0 | 60 | 80 | 74 | 77 | 1 | .245 | .385 | 7 | 1 | 3B-146 |
| 1974 | 159 | 577 | 151 | 20 | 2 | 18 | 3.1 | 88 | 97 | 76 | 68 | 1 | .262 | .397 | 0 | 0 | 3B-158 |
| 1975 | 158 | 566 | 160 | 29 | 2 | 25 | 4.4 | 72 | 101 | 78 | 74 | 5 | .283 | .473 | 0 | 0 | 3B-158 |
| 1976 | 145 | 502 | 139 | 18 | 3 | 23 | 4.6 | 69 | 80 | 89 | 74 | 0 | .277 | .462 | 1 | 0 | 3B-144 |
| 1977 | 153 | 564 | 136 | 22 | 3 | 30 | 5.3 | 77 | 110 | 93 | 106 | 3 | .241 | .450 | 0 | 0 | 3B-153 |

| | G | AB | H | 2B | 3B | HR | HR % | R | RBI | BB | SO | SB | BA | SA | Pinch Hit AB | H | G by POS |
|---|---|---|---|---|---|---|---|---|---|---|---|---|---|---|---|---|---|

## Ron Cey continued

| | G | AB | H | 2B | 3B | HR | HR % | R | RBI | BB | SO | SB | BA | SA | AB | H | G by POS |
|---|---|---|---|---|---|---|---|---|---|---|---|---|---|---|---|---|---|
| 1978 | 159 | 555 | 150 | 32 | 0 | 23 | 4.1 | 84 | 84 | 96 | 96 | 2 | .270 | .452 | 1 | 0 | 3B-158 |
| 1979 | 150 | 487 | 137 | 20 | 1 | 28 | 5.7 | 77 | 81 | 86 | 85 | 3 | .281 | .499 | 0 | 0 | 3B-150 |
| 1980 | 157 | 551 | 140 | 25 | 0 | 28 | 5.1 | 81 | 77 | 69 | 92 | 2 | .254 | .452 | 0 | 0 | 3B-157 |
| 1981 | 85 | 312 | 90 | 15 | 2 | 13 | 4.2 | 42 | 50 | 40 | 55 | 0 | .288 | .474 | 1 | 1 | 3B-84 |
| 1982 | 150 | 556 | 141 | 23 | 1 | 24 | 4.3 | 62 | 79 | 57 | 99 | 3 | .254 | .428 | 1 | 0 | 3B-149 |
| 1983 CHI N | 159 | 581 | 160 | 33 | 1 | 24 | 4.1 | 73 | 90 | 62 | 85 | 0 | .275 | .460 | 1 | 0 | 3B-157 |
| 1984 | 146 | 505 | 121 | 27 | 0 | 25 | 5.0 | 71 | 97 | 61 | 108 | 3 | .240 | .442 | 2 | 1 | 3B-144 |
| 1985 | 145 | 500 | 116 | 18 | 2 | 22 | 4.4 | 58 | 63 | 58 | 106 | 1 | .232 | .408 | 7 | 2 | 3B-140 |
| 15 yrs. | 1931 | 6802 | 1775 | 301 | 21 | 299 | 4.4 | 923 | 1092 | 946 | 1137 | 24 | .261 | .443 | 23 | 5 | 3B-1909 |
| 3 yrs. | 450 | 1586 | 397 | 78 | 3 | 71 | 4.5 6th | 208 | 250 | 181 | 299 | 4 | .250 | .438 | 10 | 3 | 3B-441 |

### LEAGUE CHAMPIONSHIP SERIES

| | G | AB | H | 2B | 3B | HR | HR % | R | RBI | BB | SO | SB | BA | SA | AB | H | G by POS |
|---|---|---|---|---|---|---|---|---|---|---|---|---|---|---|---|---|---|
| 1974 LA N | 4 | 16 | 5 | 3 | 0 | 1 | 6.3 | 2 | 1 | 3 | 2 | 0 | .313 | .688 | 0 | 0 | 3B-4 |
| 1977 | 4 | 13 | 4 | 1 | 0 | 1 | 7.7 | 4 | 4 | 2 | 4 | 1 | .308 | .615 | 0 | 0 | 3B-4 |
| 1978 | 4 | 16 | 5 | 1 | 0 | 1 | 6.3 | 4 | 3 | 2 | 4 | 0 | .313 | .563 | 0 | 0 | 3B-4 |
| 1981 | 5 | 18 | 5 | 1 | 0 | 0 | 0.0 | 1 | 3 | 3 | 2 | 0 | .278 | .333 | 0 | 0 | 3B-5 |
| 1984 CHI N | 5 | 19 | 3 | 1 | 0 | 1 | 5.3 | 3 | 3 | 3 | 3 | 0 | .158 | .368 | 0 | 0 | 3B-5 |
| 5 yrs. | 22 | 82 | 22 | 7 | 0 | 4 | 4.9 | 14 | 14 | 13 | 15 | 1 | .268 | .500 | 0 | 0 | 3B-22 |

### WORLD SERIES

| | G | AB | H | 2B | 3B | HR | HR % | R | RBI | BB | SO | SB | BA | SA | AB | H | G by POS |
|---|---|---|---|---|---|---|---|---|---|---|---|---|---|---|---|---|---|
| 1974 LA N | 5 | 17 | 3 | 0 | 0 | 0 | 0.0 | 1 | 0 | 3 | 3 | 0 | .176 | .176 | 0 | 0 | 3B-5 |
| 1977 | 6 | 21 | 4 | 1 | 0 | 1 | 4.8 | 2 | 3 | 3 | 5 | 0 | .190 | .381 | 0 | 0 | 3B-6 |
| 1978 | 6 | 21 | 6 | 0 | 0 | 1 | 4.8 | 2 | 4 | 3 | 3 | 0 | .286 | .429 | 0 | 0 | 3B-6 |
| 1981 | 6 | 20 | 7 | 0 | 0 | 1 | 5.0 | 3 | 6 | 3 | 3 | 0 | .350 | .500 | 0 | 0 | 3B-6 |
| 4 yrs. | 23 | 79 | 20 | 1 | 0 | 3 | 3.8 | 8 | 13 | 12 | 14 | 0 | .253 | .380 | 0 | 0 | 3B-23 |

## Frank Chance

**CHANCE, FRANK LEROY (Husk, The Peerless Leader)**     BR TR 6'    190 lbs.
B. Sept. 9, 1877, Fresno, Calif.    D. Sept. 14, 1924, Los Angeles, Calif.
Manager 1905-14, 1923.
Hall of Fame 1946.

| | G | AB | H | 2B | 3B | HR | HR % | R | RBI | BB | SO | SB | BA | SA | AB | H | G by POS |
|---|---|---|---|---|---|---|---|---|---|---|---|---|---|---|---|---|---|
| 1898 CHI N | 53 | 147 | 42 | 4 | 3 | 1 | 0.7 | 32 | 14 | 7 | | 7 | .286 | .374 | 2 | 1 | C-33, OF-17, 1B-3 |
| 1899 | 64 | 192 | 55 | 6 | 2 | 1 | 0.5 | 37 | 22 | 15 | | 10 | .286 | .354 | 3 | 0 | C-57, OF-1, 1B-1 |
| 1900 | 56 | 151 | 46 | 8 | 4 | 0 | 0.0 | 26 | 13 | 15 | | 8 | .305 | .411 | 4 | 1 | C-51, 1B-1 |
| 1901 | 69 | 241 | 67 | 12 | 4 | 0 | 0.0 | 38 | 36 | 29 | | 30 | .278 | .361 | 2 | 1 | OF-50, C-13, 1B-6 |
| 1902 | 75 | 236 | 67 | 9 | 4 | 1 | 0.4 | 40 | 31 | 35 | | 28 | .284 | .369 | 4 | 1 | 1B-38, C-29, OF-4 |
| 1903 | 125 | 441 | 144 | 24 | 10 | 2 | 0.5 | 83 | 81 | 78 | | 67 | .327 | .440 | 2 | 1 | 1B-121, C-2 |
| 1904 | 124 | 451 | 140 | 16 | 10 | 6 | 1.3 | 89 | 49 | 36 | | 42 | .310 | .430 | 0 | 0 | 1B-123, C-1 |
| 1905 | 118 | 392 | 124 | 16 | 12 | 2 | 0.5 | 92 | 70 | 78 | | 38 | .316 | .434 | 0 | 0 | 1B-115 |
| 1906 | 136 | 474 | 151 | 24 | 10 | 3 | 0.6 | 103 | 71 | 70 | | 57 | .319 | .430 | 0 | 0 | 1B-136 |
| 1907 | 111 | 382 | 112 | 19 | 2 | 1 | 0.3 | 58 | 49 | 51 | | 35 | .293 | .361 | 2 | 1 | 1B-109 |
| 1908 | 129 | 452 | 123 | 27 | 4 | 2 | 0.4 | 65 | 55 | 37 | | 27 | .272 | .363 | 4 | 2 | 1B-126 |
| 1909 | 93 | 324 | 88 | 16 | 4 | 0 | 0.0 | 53 | 46 | 30 | | 29 | .272 | .346 | 0 | 0 | 1B-92 |
| 1910 | 88 | 295 | 88 | 12 | 8 | 0 | 0.0 | 54 | 36 | 37 | 15 | 16 | .298 | .393 | 1 | 0 | 1B-87 |
| 1911 | 31 | 88 | 21 | 6 | 3 | 1 | 1.1 | 23 | 17 | 25 | 13 | 9 | .239 | .409 | 1 | 0 | 1B-29 |
| 1912 | 2 | 5 | 1 | 0 | 0 | 0 | 0.0 | 2 | 0 | 3 | 0 | 1 | .200 | .200 | 0 | 0 | 1B-2 |
| 1913 NY A | 11 | 24 | 5 | 0 | 0 | 0 | 0.0 | 3 | 6 | 8 | 1 | 1 | .208 | .208 | 3 | 1 | 1B-8 |
| 1914 | 1 | 0 | 0 | 0 | 0 | 0 | — | 0 | 0 | 0 | 0 | 0 | — | — | 0 | 0 | 1B-1 |
| 17 yrs. | 1286 | 4295 | 1274 | 199 | 80 | 20 | 0.5 | 798 | 596 | 554 | 29 | 405 | .297 | .394 | 31 | 8 | 1B-998, C-186, OF-72 |
| 15 yrs. | 1274 | 4271 | 1269 | 199 | 80 | 20 | 0.5 10th | 795 | 590 | 546 | 28 | 404 1st | .297 | .395 | 28 | 8 | 1B-989, C-186, OF-72 |

### WORLD SERIES

| | G | AB | H | 2B | 3B | HR | HR % | R | RBI | BB | SO | SB | BA | SA | AB | H | G by POS |
|---|---|---|---|---|---|---|---|---|---|---|---|---|---|---|---|---|---|
| 1906 CHI N | 6 | 21 | 5 | 1 | 0 | 0 | 0.0 | 3 | 0 | 2 | 1 | 2 | .238 | .286 | 0 | 0 | 1B-6 |
| 1907 | 4 | 14 | 3 | 1 | 0 | 0 | 0.0 | 3 | 0 | 3 | 2 | 3 | .214 | .286 | 0 | 0 | 1B-4 |
| 1908 | 5 | 19 | 8 | 1 | 0 | 0 | 0.0 | 4 | 2 | 3 | 1 | 5 | .421 | .421 | 0 | 0 | 1B-5 |
| 1910 | 5 | 17 | 6 | 1 | 1 | 0 | 0.0 | 1 | 4 | 0 | 2 | 0 | .353 | .529 | 0 | 0 | 1B-5 |
| 4 yrs. | 20 | 71 | 22 | 3 | 1 | 0 | 0.0 | 11 | 6 | 8 | 6 | 10 3rd | .310 | .380 | 0 | 0 | 1B-20 |

## Harry Chapman

**CHAPMAN, HARRY E.**     BR TR 5'11"    160 lbs.
B. Oct. 26, 1887, Severance, Kans.    D. Oct. 21, 1918, Nevada, Mo.

| | G | AB | H | 2B | 3B | HR | HR % | R | RBI | BB | SO | SB | BA | SA | AB | H | G by POS |
|---|---|---|---|---|---|---|---|---|---|---|---|---|---|---|---|---|---|
| 1912 CHI N | 1 | 4 | 1 | 0 | 1 | 0 | 0.0 | 1 | 0 | 0 | 0 | 1 | .250 | .750 | 0 | 0 | C-1 |
| 1913 CIN N | 2 | 2 | 1 | 0 | 0 | 0 | 0.0 | 0 | 0 | 0 | 1 | 0 | .500 | .500 | 2 | 1 | |
| 1914 STL F | 64 | 181 | 38 | 2 | 1 | 0 | 0.0 | 16 | 14 | 13 | | 2 | .210 | .232 | 4 | 1 | C-51, OF-1, 2B-1, 1B-1 |
| 1915 | 62 | 186 | 37 | 6 | 3 | 1 | 0.5 | 19 | 29 | 22 | | 4 | .199 | .280 | 8 | 1 | C-53 |
| 1916 STL A | 18 | 31 | 3 | 0 | 0 | 0 | 0.0 | 2 | 1 | 2 | | 0 | .097 | .097 | 3 | 0 | C-14 |
| 5 yrs. | 147 | 404 | 80 | 8 | 5 | 1 | 0.2 | 38 | 44 | 37 | 6 | 7 | .198 | .250 | 17 | 3 | C-119, OF-1, 2B-1, 1B-1 |
| 1 yr. | 1 | 4 | 1 | 0 | 1 | 0 | 0.0 | 1 | 0 | 0 | 0 | 1 | .250 | .750 | 0 | 0 | C-1 |

## Cupid Childs

**CHILDS, CLARENCE ALGERNON**     BL TR 5'8"    185 lbs.
B. Aug. 14, 1868, County, Md.    D. Nov. 8, 1912, Baltimore, Md.

| | G | AB | H | 2B | 3B | HR | HR % | R | RBI | BB | SO | SB | BA | SA | AB | H | G by POS |
|---|---|---|---|---|---|---|---|---|---|---|---|---|---|---|---|---|---|
| 1888 PHI N | 2 | 4 | 0 | 0 | 0 | 0 | 0.0 | 0 | 0 | 0 | 0 | 0 | .000 | .000 | 0 | 0 | 2B-2 |
| 1890 SYR AA | 136 | 493 | 170 | 33 | 14 | 2 | 0.4 | 109 | | 72 | | 56 | .345 | .481 | 0 | 0 | 2B-125, SS-1 |
| 1891 CLE N | 141 | 551 | 155 | 21 | 12 | 2 | 0.4 | 120 | 83 | 97 | 32 | 39 | .281 | .374 | 0 | 0 | 2B-141 |
| 1892 | 145 | 558 | 177 | 14 | 11 | 3 | 0.5 | 136 | 53 | 117 | 20 | 26 | .317 | .398 | 0 | 0 | 2B-145 |
| 1893 | 124 | 485 | 158 | 19 | 10 | 3 | 0.6 | 145 | 65 | 120 | 12 | 23 | .326 | .425 | 0 | 0 | 2B-123 |
| 1894 | 118 | 479 | 169 | 21 | 12 | 2 | 0.4 | 143 | 52 | 107 | 11 | 17 | .353 | .459 | 0 | 0 | 2B-118 |
| 1895 | 119 | 462 | 133 | 15 | 3 | 4 | 0.9 | 96 | 90 | 74 | 24 | 20 | .288 | .359 | 0 | 0 | 2B-119 |
| 1896 | 132 | 498 | 177 | 24 | 9 | 1 | 0.2 | 106 | 106 | 100 | 18 | 25 | .355 | .446 | 0 | 0 | 2B-132 |
| 1897 | 114 | 444 | 150 | 15 | 9 | 1 | 0.2 | 105 | 61 | 74 | | 25 | .338 | .419 | 0 | 0 | 2B-114 |
| 1898 | 110 | 422 | 122 | 9 | 4 | 1 | 0.2 | 91 | 31 | 69 | | 9 | .289 | .336 | 0 | 0 | 2B-110 |
| 1899 STL N | 125 | 465 | 124 | 11 | 11 | 1 | 0.2 | 73 | 48 | 74 | | 11 | .267 | .344 | 0 | 0 | 2B-125 |
| 1900 CHI N | 138 | 538 | 131 | 14 | 5 | 1 | 0.2 | 70 | 44 | 57 | | 15 | .243 | .288 | 0 | 0 | 2B-137 |

| | G | AB | H | 2B | 3B | HR | HR % | R | RBI | BB | SO | SB | BA | SA | Pinch Hit AB | Pinch Hit H | G by POS |
|---|---|---|---|---|---|---|---|---|---|---|---|---|---|---|---|---|---|

## Cupid Childs  continued

| | G | AB | H | 2B | 3B | HR | HR % | R | RBI | BB | SO | SB | BA | SA | AB | H | G by POS |
|---|---|---|---|---|---|---|---|---|---|---|---|---|---|---|---|---|---|
| 1901 | 63 | 237 | 61 | 9 | 0 | 0 | 0.0 | 24 | 21 | 29 | | 3 | .257 | .295 | 0 | 0 | 2B-62 |
| 13 yrs. | 1467 | 5636 | 1727 | 205 | 100 | 20 | 0.4 | 1218 | 653 | 990 | 117 | 269 | .306 | .389 | 0 | 0 | 2B-1453, SS-1 |
| 2 yrs. | 201 | 775 | 192 | 23 | 5 | 0 | 0.0 | 94 | 65 | 86 | | 18 | .248 | .290 | 0 | 0 | 2B-199 |

## Pete Childs

**CHILDS, PETER PIERRE**  TR
B. Nov. 15, 1871, Philadelphia, Pa.  D. Feb. 15, 1922, Philadelphia, Pa.

| | G | AB | H | 2B | 3B | HR | HR % | R | RBI | BB | SO | SB | BA | SA | AB | H | G by POS |
|---|---|---|---|---|---|---|---|---|---|---|---|---|---|---|---|---|---|
| 1901 2 teams | STL N (29G – .266) | | | | | | | CHI N (61G – .225) | | | | | | | | | |
| " total | 90 | 292 | 69 | 6 | 1 | 0 | 0.0 | 35 | 22 | 41 | | 4 | .236 | .264 | 6 | 1 | 2B-80, OF-2, SS-1 |
| 1902 PHI N | 123 | 403 | 78 | 5 | 0 | 0 | 0.0 | 25 | 25 | 34 | | 6 | .194 | .206 | 0 | 0 | 2B-123 |
| 2 yrs. | 213 | 695 | 147 | 11 | 1 | 0 | 0.0 | 60 | 47 | 75 | | 10 | .212 | .230 | 6 | 1 | 2B-203, OF-2, SS-1 |
| 1 yr. | 61 | 213 | 48 | 5 | 1 | 0 | 0.0 | 23 | 14 | 27 | | 4 | .225 | .258 | 0 | 0 | 2B-61 |

## Harry Chiti

**CHITI, HARRY DOMINICK**  BR TR 6'2½" 221 lbs.
B. Nov. 16, 1932, Kincaid, Ill.

| | G | AB | H | 2B | 3B | HR | HR % | R | RBI | BB | SO | SB | BA | SA | AB | H | G by POS |
|---|---|---|---|---|---|---|---|---|---|---|---|---|---|---|---|---|---|
| 1950 CHI N | 3 | 6 | 2 | 0 | 0 | 0 | 0.0 | 0 | 0 | 0 | 0 | 0 | .333 | .333 | 2 | 0 | C-1 |
| 1951 | 9 | 31 | 11 | 2 | 0 | 0 | 0.0 | 1 | 5 | 2 | 2 | 0 | .355 | .419 | 1 | 0 | C-8 |
| 1952 | 32 | 113 | 31 | 5 | 0 | 5 | 4.4 | 14 | 13 | 5 | 8 | 0 | .274 | .451 | 0 | 0 | C-32 |
| 1955 | 113 | 338 | 78 | 6 | 1 | 11 | 3.3 | 24 | 41 | 25 | 68 | 0 | .231 | .352 | 1 | 0 | C-113 |
| 1956 | 72 | 203 | 43 | 6 | 4 | 4 | 2.0 | 17 | 18 | 19 | 35 | 0 | .212 | .340 | 5 | 2 | C-67 |
| 1958 KC A | 103 | 295 | 79 | 11 | 3 | 9 | 3.1 | 32 | 44 | 18 | 48 | 3 | .268 | .417 | 19 | 3 | C-83 |
| 1959 | 55 | 162 | 44 | 11 | 1 | 5 | 3.1 | 20 | 25 | 17 | 26 | 0 | .272 | .444 | 8 | 4 | C-47 |
| 1960 2 teams | KC A (58G – .221) | | | | | | | DET A (37G – .163) | | | | | | | | | |
| " total | 95 | 294 | 59 | 7 | 0 | 7 | 2.4 | 25 | 33 | 27 | 45 | 1 | .201 | .296 | 8 | 2 | C-88 |
| 1961 DET A | 5 | 12 | 1 | 0 | 0 | 0 | 0.0 | 0 | 0 | 1 | 2 | 0 | .083 | .083 | 0 | 0 | C-5 |
| 1962 NY N | 15 | 41 | 8 | 1 | 0 | 0 | 0.0 | 2 | 0 | 1 | 8 | 0 | .195 | .220 | 2 | 0 | C-14 |
| 10 yrs. | 502 | 1495 | 356 | 49 | 9 | 41 | 2.7 | 135 | 179 | 115 | 242 | 4 | .238 | .365 | 46 | 11 | C-458 |
| 5 yrs. | 229 | 691 | 165 | 19 | 5 | 20 | 2.9 | 56 | 77 | 51 | 113 | 0 | .239 | .368 | 9 | 2 | C-221 |

## Lloyd Christopher

**CHRISTOPHER, LLOYD EUGENE**  BR TR 6'2" 190 lbs.
Brother of Russ Christopher.
B. Dec. 31, 1919, Richmond, Calif.

| | G | AB | H | 2B | 3B | HR | HR % | R | RBI | BB | SO | SB | BA | SA | AB | H | G by POS |
|---|---|---|---|---|---|---|---|---|---|---|---|---|---|---|---|---|---|
| 1945 2 teams | BOS A (8G – .286) | | | | | | | CHI N (1G – .000) | | | | | | | | | |
| " total | 9 | 14 | 4 | 0 | 0 | 0 | 0.0 | 4 | 4 | 3 | 2 | 0 | .286 | .286 | 3 | 0 | OF-4 |
| 1947 CHI A | 7 | 23 | 5 | 0 | 1 | 0 | 0.0 | 1 | 0 | 2 | 4 | 0 | .217 | .304 | 0 | 0 | OF-7 |
| 2 yrs. | 16 | 37 | 9 | 0 | 1 | 0 | 0.0 | 5 | 4 | 5 | 6 | 0 | .243 | .297 | 3 | 0 | OF-11 |
| 1 yr. | 1 | 0 | 0 | 0 | 0 | 0 | – | 0 | 0 | 0 | 0 | 0 | | | 0 | 0 | OF-1 |

## John Churry

**CHURRY, JOHN**  BR TR 5'9" 172 lbs.
B. Nov. 26, 1900, Johnstown, Pa.  D. Feb. 8, 1970, Zanesville, Ohio

| | G | AB | H | 2B | 3B | HR | HR % | R | RBI | BB | SO | SB | BA | SA | AB | H | G by POS |
|---|---|---|---|---|---|---|---|---|---|---|---|---|---|---|---|---|---|
| 1924 CHI N | 6 | 7 | 1 | 1 | 0 | 0 | 0.0 | 0 | 0 | 2 | 0 | 0 | .143 | .286 | 2 | 0 | C-3 |
| 1925 | 3 | 6 | 3 | 0 | 0 | 0 | 0.0 | 1 | 1 | 0 | 0 | 0 | .500 | .500 | 0 | 0 | C-3 |
| 1926 | 2 | 4 | 0 | 0 | 0 | 0 | 0.0 | 0 | 0 | 1 | 2 | 0 | .000 | .000 | 1 | 0 | C-1 |
| 1927 | 1 | 1 | 1 | 0 | 0 | 0 | 0.0 | 1 | 0 | 0 | 0 | 0 | 1.000 | 1.000 | 0 | 0 | C-1 |
| 4 yrs. | 12 | 18 | 5 | 1 | 0 | 0 | 0.0 | 1 | 1 | 3 | 2 | 0 | .278 | .333 | 3 | 0 | C-8 |
| 4 yrs. | 12 | 18 | 5 | 1 | 0 | 0 | 0.0 | 1 | 1 | 3 | 2 | 0 | .278 | .333 | 3 | 0 | C-8 |

## Fred Clark

**CLARK, ALFRED ROBERT**  TL
B. July 16, 1873, San Francisco, Calif.  D. July 26, 1956, Ogden, Utah

| | G | AB | H | 2B | 3B | HR | HR % | R | RBI | BB | SO | SB | BA | SA | AB | H | G by POS |
|---|---|---|---|---|---|---|---|---|---|---|---|---|---|---|---|---|---|
| 1902 CHI N | 12 | 43 | 8 | 1 | 0 | 0 | 0.0 | 1 | 2 | 4 | | 1 | .186 | .209 | 0 | 0 | 1B-12 |

## Sumpter Clarke

**CLARKE, SUMPTER MILLS**  BR TR 5'11" 170 lbs.
Brother of Rufe Clarke.
B. Oct. 18, 1897, Savannah, Ga.  D. Mar. 16, 1962, Knoxville, Tenn.

| | G | AB | H | 2B | 3B | HR | HR % | R | RBI | BB | SO | SB | BA | SA | AB | H | G by POS |
|---|---|---|---|---|---|---|---|---|---|---|---|---|---|---|---|---|---|
| 1920 CHI N | 1 | 3 | 1 | 0 | 0 | 0 | 0.0 | 0 | 0 | 0 | 1 | 0 | .333 | .333 | 0 | 0 | 3B-1 |
| 1923 CLE A | 1 | 3 | 0 | 0 | 0 | 0 | 0.0 | 0 | 0 | 0 | 0 | 0 | .000 | .000 | 0 | 0 | OF-1 |
| 1924 | 45 | 104 | 24 | 6 | 1 | 0 | 0.0 | 17 | 11 | 6 | 12 | 0 | .231 | .308 | 2 | 1 | OF-66 |
| 3 yrs. | 47 | 110 | 25 | 6 | 1 | 0 | 0.0 | 17 | 11 | 6 | 13 | 0 | .227 | .300 | 2 | 1 | OF-67, 3B-1 |
| 1 yr. | 1 | 3 | 1 | 0 | 0 | 0 | 0.0 | 0 | 0 | 0 | 1 | 0 | .333 | .333 | 0 | 0 | 3B-1 |

## Tommy Clarke

**CLARKE, THOMAS ALOYSIUS**  BR TR 5'11" 175 lbs.
B. May 9, 1888, New York, N.Y.  D. Aug. 14, 1945, Corona, N.Y.

| | G | AB | H | 2B | 3B | HR | HR % | R | RBI | BB | SO | SB | BA | SA | AB | H | G by POS |
|---|---|---|---|---|---|---|---|---|---|---|---|---|---|---|---|---|---|
| 1909 CIN N | 18 | 52 | 13 | 3 | 2 | 0 | 0.0 | 8 | 10 | 6 | | 3 | .250 | .385 | 1 | 0 | C-17 |
| 1910 | 64 | 151 | 42 | 6 | 5 | 1 | 0.7 | 19 | 20 | 19 | 17 | 1 | .278 | .404 | 7 | 0 | C-56 |
| 1911 | 86 | 203 | 49 | 6 | 7 | 1 | 0.5 | 20 | 25 | 25 | 22 | 4 | .241 | .355 | 4 | 0 | C-81, 1B-1 |
| 1912 | 72 | 146 | 41 | 7 | 2 | 0 | 0.0 | 19 | 22 | 28 | 14 | 9 | .281 | .356 | 7 | 1 | C-63 |
| 1913 | 114 | 330 | 87 | 11 | 8 | 1 | 0.3 | 29 | 38 | 39 | 40 | 2 | .264 | .355 | 13 | 5 | C-100 |
| 1914 | 113 | 313 | 82 | 13 | 7 | 2 | 0.6 | 30 | 25 | 31 | 30 | 6 | .262 | .367 | 6 | 1 | C-108 |
| 1915 | 96 | 226 | 65 | 7 | 2 | 0 | 0.0 | 23 | 21 | 33 | 22 | 7 | .288 | .336 | 20 | 5 | C-72 |
| 1916 | 78 | 177 | 42 | 10 | 1 | 0 | 0.0 | 10 | 17 | 24 | 20 | 8 | .237 | .305 | 25 | 5 | C-51 |
| 1917 | 29 | 110 | 32 | 3 | 3 | 1 | 0.9 | 11 | 13 | 11 | 12 | 2 | .291 | .400 | 27 | 9 | C-29 |
| 1918 CHI N | 1 | 0 | 0 | 0 | 0 | 0 | – | 0 | 0 | 0 | 0 | 0 | | | 0 | 0 | C-1 |
| 10 yrs. | 671 | 1708 | 453 | 66 | 37 | 6 | 0.4 | 169 | 191 | 216 | 177 | 42 | .265 | .358 | 110 | 26 | C-578, 1B-1 |
| 1 yr. | 1 | 0 | 0 | 0 | 0 | 0 | – | 0 | 0 | 0 | 0 | 0 | | | 0 | 0 | C-1 |

## John Clarkson

**CLARKSON, JOHN GIBSON**  BR TR 5'10" 155 lbs.
Brother of Dad Clarkson.  Brother of Walter Clarkson.
B. July 1, 1861, Cambridge, Mass.  D. Feb. 4, 1909, Cambridge, Mass.
Hall of Fame 1963.

| | G | AB | H | 2B | 3B | HR | HR % | R | RBI | BB | SO | SB | BA | SA | AB | H | G by POS |
|---|---|---|---|---|---|---|---|---|---|---|---|---|---|---|---|---|---|
| 1882 WOR N | 3 | 11 | 4 | 2 | 0 | 0 | 0.0 | 0 | 2 | 0 | 3 | | .364 | .545 | 0 | 0 | P-3, 1B-1 |

| | G | AB | H | 2B | 3B | HR | HR % | R | RBI | BB | SO | SB | BA | SA | Pinch Hit AB | Pinch Hit H | G by POS |
|---|---|---|---|---|---|---|---|---|---|---|---|---|---|---|---|---|---|

## John Clarkson continued

| | | G | AB | H | 2B | 3B | HR | HR% | R | RBI | BB | SO | SB | BA | SA | PH AB | PH H | G by POS |
|---|---|---|---|---|---|---|---|---|---|---|---|---|---|---|---|---|---|---|
| 1884 | CHI N | 21 | 84 | 22 | 6 | 2 | 3 | 3.6 | 16 | | 2 | 16 | | .262 | .488 | 0 | 0 | P-14, OF-8, 3B-2, 1B-1 |
| 1885 | | 72 | 283 | 61 | 11 | 5 | 4 | 1.4 | 34 | 31 | 3 | 44 | | .216 | .332 | 0 | 0 | P-70, OF-3, 3B-1 |
| 1886 | | 55 | 210 | 49 | 9 | 1 | 3 | 1.4 | 21 | 23 | 0 | 38 | | .233 | .329 | 0 | 0 | P-55, OF-5 |
| 1887 | | 63 | 215 | 52 | 5 | 5 | 6 | 2.8 | 40 | 25 | 11 | 25 | 6 | .242 | .395 | 0 | 0 | P-60, OF-5 |
| 1888 | BOS N | 55 | 205 | 40 | 9 | 1 | 1 | 0.5 | 20 | 17 | 7 | 48 | 5 | .195 | .263 | 0 | 0 | P-54, OF-1 |
| 1889 | | 73 | 262 | 54 | 9 | 3 | 2 | 0.8 | 36 | 23 | 11 | 59 | 8 | .206 | .286 | 0 | 0 | P-73, OF-2, 3B-1 |
| 1890 | | 45 | 173 | 43 | 6 | 3 | 2 | 1.2 | 18 | 26 | 8 | 31 | 2 | .249 | .353 | 0 | 0 | P-44, OF-1 |
| 1891 | | 55 | 187 | 42 | 7 | 4 | 0 | 0.0 | 28 | 26 | 18 | 51 | 2 | .225 | .305 | 0 | 0 | P-55, OF-1 |
| 1892 | 2 teams | 45 | BOS | N (16G – .228) | | | CLE | N (29G – .139) | | | | | | | | | | |
| " | total | 45 | 158 | 27 | 3 | 0 | 1 | 0.6 | 15 | 17 | 11 | 39 | 3 | .171 | .209 | 0 | 0 | P-45 |
| 1893 | CLE N | 37 | 131 | 27 | 6 | 2 | 1 | 0.8 | 18 | 17 | 4 | 20 | 2 | .206 | .305 | 0 | 0 | P-36, OF-1 |
| 1894 | | 22 | 55 | 11 | 0 | 0 | 1 | 1.8 | 8 | 7 | 6 | 9 | 1 | .200 | .255 | 0 | 0 | P-22 |
| | 12 yrs. | 546 | 1974 | 432 | 73 | 26 | 24 | 1.2 | 254 | 214 | 81 | 383 | 29 | .219 | .319 | 0 | 0 | P-531, OF-27, 3B-4, 1B-1 |
| | 4 yrs. | 211 | 792 | 184 | 31 | 13 | 16 | 2.0 | 111 | 79 | 16 | 123 | 6 | .232 | .365 | 0 | 0 | P-199, OF-21, 3B-3, 1B-1 |

## Clem Clemens

**CLEMENS, CLEMENT LAMBERT**  BR  TR  5'11"  176 lbs.
Born Clement Lambert Ulatowski.
B. Nov. 21, 1886, Chicago, Ill.   D. Nov. 2, 1967, St. Petersburg, Fla.

| | | G | AB | H | 2B | 3B | HR | HR% | R | RBI | BB | SO | SB | BA | SA | PH AB | PH H | G by POS |
|---|---|---|---|---|---|---|---|---|---|---|---|---|---|---|---|---|---|---|
| 1914 | CHI F | 13 | 27 | 4 | 0 | 0 | 0 | 0.0 | 4 | 2 | 3 | | 0 | .148 | .148 | 5 | 0 | C-8 |
| 1915 | | 11 | 22 | 3 | 1 | 0 | 0 | 0.0 | 3 | 3 | 1 | | 0 | .136 | .182 | 0 | 0 | C-9, 2B-2 |
| 1916 | CHI N | 10 | 15 | 0 | 0 | 0 | 0 | 0.0 | 0 | 0 | 1 | 6 | 0 | .000 | .000 | 1 | 0 | C-9 |
| | 3 yrs. | 34 | 64 | 7 | 1 | 0 | 0 | 0.0 | 7 | 5 | 5 | 6 | 0 | .109 | .125 | 6 | 0 | C-26, 2B-2 |
| | 1 yr. | 10 | 15 | 0 | 0 | 0 | 0 | 0.0 | 0 | 0 | 1 | 6 | 0 | .000 | .000 | 1 | 0 | C-9 |

## Doug Clemens

**CLEMENS, DOUGLAS HORACE**  BL  TR  6'  180 lbs.
B. June 9, 1939, Leesport, Pa.

| | | G | AB | H | 2B | 3B | HR | HR% | R | RBI | BB | SO | SB | BA | SA | PH AB | PH H | G by POS |
|---|---|---|---|---|---|---|---|---|---|---|---|---|---|---|---|---|---|---|
| 1960 | STL N | 1 | 0 | 0 | 0 | 0 | 0 | – | 0 | 0 | 0 | 0 | 0 | – | – | 0 | 0 | OF-1 |
| 1961 | | 6 | 12 | 2 | 1 | 0 | 0 | 0.0 | 1 | 0 | 3 | 1 | 0 | .167 | .250 | 3 | 1 | OF-3 |
| 1962 | | 48 | 93 | 22 | 1 | 1 | 1 | 1.1 | 12 | 12 | 17 | 19 | 0 | .237 | .301 | 15 | 5 | OF-34 |
| 1963 | | 5 | 6 | 1 | 0 | 0 | 1 | 16.7 | 1 | 2 | 1 | 2 | 0 | .167 | .667 | 1 | 0 | OF-3 |
| 1964 | 2 teams | 87 | STL | N (33G – .205) | | | CHI | N (54G – .279) | | | | | | | | | | |
| " | total | 87 | 218 | 55 | 14 | 5 | 3 | 1.4 | 31 | 24 | 24 | 38 | 0 | .252 | .404 | 19 | 3 | OF-62 |
| 1965 | CHI N | 128 | 340 | 75 | 11 | 0 | 4 | 1.2 | 36 | 26 | 38 | 53 | 5 | .221 | .288 | 25 | 6 | OF-105 |
| 1966 | PHI N | 79 | 121 | 31 | 1 | 0 | 1 | 0.8 | 10 | 15 | 16 | 25 | 1 | .256 | .289 | 49 | 12 | OF-28, 1B-1 |
| 1967 | | 69 | 73 | 13 | 5 | 0 | 0 | 0.0 | 2 | 4 | 8 | 15 | 0 | .178 | .247 | 54 | 11 | OF-10 |
| 1968 | | 29 | 57 | 12 | 1 | 1 | 2 | 3.5 | 6 | 8 | 7 | 13 | 0 | .211 | .368 | 13 | 3 | OF-17 |
| | 9 yrs. | 452 | 920 | 211 | 34 | 7 | 12 | 1.3 | 99 | 88 | 114 | 166 | 6 | .229 | .321 | 179 | 41 | OF-263, 1B-1 |
| | 2 yrs. | 182 | 480 | 114 | 21 | 2 | 6 | 1.3 | 59 | 38 | 56 | 75 | 5 | .238 | .327 | 36 | 7 | OF-145 |

## Ty Cline

**CLINE, TYRONE ALEXANDER**  BL  TL  6'½"  170 lbs.
B. June 15, 1939, Hampton, S. C.

| | | G | AB | H | 2B | 3B | HR | HR% | R | RBI | BB | SO | SB | BA | SA | PH AB | PH H | G by POS |
|---|---|---|---|---|---|---|---|---|---|---|---|---|---|---|---|---|---|---|
| 1960 | CLE A | 7 | 26 | 8 | 1 | 1 | 0 | 0.0 | 2 | 2 | 0 | 4 | 0 | .308 | .423 | 1 | 0 | OF-6 |
| 1961 | | 12 | 43 | 9 | 2 | 1 | 0 | 0.0 | 9 | 1 | 6 | 1 | 0 | .209 | .302 | 0 | 0 | OF-12 |
| 1962 | | 118 | 375 | 93 | 15 | 5 | 2 | 0.5 | 53 | 28 | 28 | 50 | 5 | .248 | .331 | 10 | 1 | OF-107 |
| 1963 | MIL N | 72 | 174 | 41 | 2 | 1 | 0 | 0.0 | 17 | 10 | 10 | 31 | 2 | .236 | .259 | 7 | 3 | OF-62 |
| 1964 | | 101 | 116 | 35 | 4 | 2 | 1 | 0.9 | 22 | 13 | 8 | 22 | 0 | .302 | .397 | 40 | 14 | OF-54, 1B-6 |
| 1965 | | 123 | 220 | 42 | 5 | 3 | 0 | 0.0 | 27 | 10 | 16 | 50 | 2 | .191 | .241 | 29 | 6 | OF-86, 1B-5 |
| 1966 | 2 teams | 49 | CHI | N (7G – .353) | | | ATL | N (42G – .254) | | | | | | | | | | |
| " | total | 49 | 88 | 24 | 0 | 0 | 0 | 0.0 | 15 | 8 | 3 | 13 | 3 | .273 | .273 | 22 | 6 | OF-24, 1B-6 |
| 1967 | 2 teams | 74 | ATL | N (10G – .000) | | | SF | N (64G – .270) | | | | | | | | | | |
| " | total | 74 | 130 | 33 | 5 | 5 | 0 | 0.0 | 18 | 4 | 9 | 16 | 2 | .254 | .369 | 24 | 4 | OF-38 |
| 1968 | SF N | 116 | 291 | 65 | 6 | 3 | 1 | 0.3 | 37 | 28 | 11 | 26 | 0 | .223 | .275 | 26 | 5 | OF-70, 1B-24 |
| 1969 | MON N | 101 | 209 | 50 | 5 | 3 | 2 | 1.0 | 26 | 12 | 32 | 22 | 4 | .239 | .321 | 42 | 9 | OF-41, 1B-17 |
| 1970 | 2 teams | 50 | MON | N (2G – .500) | | | CIN | N (48G – .270) | | | | | | | | | | |
| " | total | 50 | 65 | 18 | 7 | 1 | 0 | 0.0 | 13 | 8 | 12 | 11 | 1 | .277 | .415 | 26 | 7 | OF-20, 1B-2 |
| 1971 | CIN N | 69 | 97 | 19 | 1 | 0 | 0 | 0.0 | 12 | 1 | 18 | 16 | 2 | .196 | .206 | 39 | 5 | OF-28, 1B-2 |
| | 12 yrs. | 892 | 1834 | 437 | 53 | 25 | 6 | 0.3 | 251 | 125 | 153 | 262 | 22 | .238 | .304 | 266 | 60 | OF-548, 1B-62 |
| | 1 yr. | 7 | 17 | 6 | 0 | 0 | 0 | 0.0 | 3 | 2 | 0 | 2 | 1 | .353 | .353 | 4 | 0 | OF-5 |

LEAGUE CHAMPIONSHIP SERIES

| | | G | AB | H | 2B | 3B | HR | HR% | R | RBI | BB | SO | SB | BA | SA | PH AB | PH H | G by POS |
|---|---|---|---|---|---|---|---|---|---|---|---|---|---|---|---|---|---|---|
| 1970 | CIN N | 2 | 1 | 1 | 1 | 0 | 0 | 0.0 | 2 | 0 | 1 | 0 | 0 | 1.000 | 3.000 | 1 | 1 | OF-1 |

WORLD SERIES

| | | G | AB | H | 2B | 3B | HR | HR% | R | RBI | BB | SO | SB | BA | SA | PH AB | PH H | G by POS |
|---|---|---|---|---|---|---|---|---|---|---|---|---|---|---|---|---|---|---|
| 1970 | CIN N | 3 | 3 | 1 | 0 | 0 | 0 | 0.0 | 0 | 0 | 0 | 0 | 0 | .333 | .333 | 3 | 1 | |

## Gene Clines

**CLINES, EUGENE**  BR  TR  5'9"  170 lbs.
B. Oct. 6, 1946, San Pablo, Calif.

| | | G | AB | H | 2B | 3B | HR | HR% | R | RBI | BB | SO | SB | BA | SA | PH AB | PH H | G by POS |
|---|---|---|---|---|---|---|---|---|---|---|---|---|---|---|---|---|---|---|
| 1970 | PIT N | 31 | 37 | 15 | 2 | 0 | 0 | 0.0 | 4 | 3 | 2 | 5 | 2 | .405 | .459 | 20 | 8 | OF-7 |
| 1971 | | 97 | 273 | 84 | 12 | 4 | 1 | 0.4 | 52 | 24 | 22 | 36 | 15 | .308 | .392 | 19 | 7 | OF-74 |
| 1972 | | 107 | 311 | 104 | 15 | 6 | 0 | 0.0 | 52 | 17 | 16 | 47 | 12 | .334 | .421 | 19 | 2 | OF-83 |
| 1973 | | 110 | 304 | 80 | 11 | 3 | 1 | 0.3 | 42 | 23 | 26 | 36 | 8 | .263 | .329 | 35 | 10 | OF-77 |
| 1974 | | 107 | 276 | 62 | 5 | 1 | 0 | 0.0 | 29 | 14 | 30 | 40 | 14 | .225 | .250 | 27 | 6 | OF-78 |
| 1975 | NY N | 82 | 203 | 46 | 6 | 3 | 0 | 0.0 | 25 | 10 | 11 | 21 | 4 | .227 | .286 | 18 | 2 | OF-60 |
| 1976 | TEX A | 116 | 446 | 123 | 12 | 3 | 0 | 0.0 | 52 | 38 | 16 | 52 | 11 | .276 | .316 | 5 | 2 | OF-103, DH-10 |
| 1977 | CHI N | 101 | 239 | 70 | 12 | 2 | 3 | 1.3 | 27 | 41 | 25 | 25 | 1 | .293 | .397 | 39 | 10 | OF-63 |
| 1978 | | 109 | 229 | 59 | 10 | 2 | 0 | 0.0 | 31 | 17 | 21 | 28 | 4 | .258 | .319 | 43 | 10 | OF-66 |
| 1979 | | 10 | 10 | 2 | 0 | 0 | 0 | 0.0 | 0 | 0 | 0 | 1 | 0 | .200 | .200 | 10 | 2 | |
| | 10 yrs. | 870 | 2328 | 645 | 85 | 24 | 5 | 0.2 | 314 | 187 | 169 | 291 | 71 | .277 | .341 | 235 | 59 | OF-611, DH-10 |
| | 3 yrs. | 220 | 478 | 131 | 22 | 4 | 3 | 0.6 | 58 | 58 | 46 | 54 | 5 | .274 | .356 | 92 | 22 | OF-129 |

LEAGUE CHAMPIONSHIP SERIES

| | | G | AB | H | 2B | 3B | HR | HR% | R | RBI | BB | SO | SB | BA | SA | PH AB | PH H | G by POS |
|---|---|---|---|---|---|---|---|---|---|---|---|---|---|---|---|---|---|---|
| 1971 | PIT N | 1 | 3 | 1 | 0 | 0 | 1 | 33.3 | 1 | 1 | 0 | 1 | 0 | .333 | 1.333 | 0 | 0 | OF-1 |
| 1972 | | 2 | 2 | 0 | 0 | 0 | 0 | 0.0 | 0 | 0 | 1 | 0 | 0 | .000 | .000 | 2 | 0 | |

| | G | AB | H | 2B | 3B | HR | HR % | R | RBI | BB | SO | SB | BA | SA | Pinch Hit AB | Pinch Hit H | G by POS |
|---|---|---|---|---|---|---|---|---|---|---|---|---|---|---|---|---|---|

## Gene Clines continued

| | G | AB | H | 2B | 3B | HR | HR % | R | RBI | BB | SO | SB | BA | SA | PH AB | PH H | G by POS |
|---|---|---|---|---|---|---|---|---|---|---|---|---|---|---|---|---|---|
| 1974 | 2 | 1 | 0 | 0 | 0 | 0 | 0.0 | 1 | 0 | 0 | 0 | 0 | .000 | .000 | 0 | 0 | OF-2 |
| 3 yrs. | 5 | 6 | 1 | 0 | 0 | 1 | 16.7 | 3 | 1 | 0 | 2 | 0 | .167 | .667 | 2 | 0 | OF-3 |

WORLD SERIES

| | G | AB | H | 2B | 3B | HR | HR % | R | RBI | BB | SO | SB | BA | SA | PH AB | PH H | G by POS |
|---|---|---|---|---|---|---|---|---|---|---|---|---|---|---|---|---|---|
| 1971 PIT N | 3 | 11 | 1 | 0 | 1 | 0 | 0.0 | 2 | 0 | 1 | 1 | 1 | .091 | .273 | 0 | 0 | OF-3 |

## Billy Clingman

**CLINGMAN, WILLIAM FREDERICK**
B. Nov. 21, 1869, Cincinnati, Ohio    D. May 14, 1958, Cincinnati, Ohio
BB TR 5'11" 150 lbs.

| | G | AB | H | 2B | 3B | HR | HR % | R | RBI | BB | SO | SB | BA | SA | PH AB | PH H | G by POS |
|---|---|---|---|---|---|---|---|---|---|---|---|---|---|---|---|---|---|
| 1890 CIN N | 7 | 27 | 7 | 1 | 0 | 0 | 0.0 | 2 | 5 | 1 | 0 | 0 | .259 | .296 | 0 | 0 | SS-6, 2B-1 |
| 1891 C-M AA | 1 | 5 | 1 | 1 | 0 | 0 | 0.0 | 0 | 0 | 0 | 0 | 0 | .200 | .400 | 0 | 0 | 2B-1 |
| 1895 PIT N | 106 | 382 | 99 | 16 | 4 | 0 | 0.0 | 69 | 45 | 41 | 43 | 19 | .259 | .322 | 0 | 0 | 3B-106 |
| 1896 LOU N | 121 | 423 | 99 | 10 | 2 | 2 | 0.5 | 57 | 37 | 57 | 51 | 19 | .234 | .281 | 0 | 0 | 3B-121 |
| 1897 | 113 | 395 | 90 | 14 | 7 | 2 | 0.5 | 59 | 47 | 37 | | 14 | .228 | .314 | 0 | 0 | 3B-113 |
| 1898 | 154 | 538 | 138 | 12 | 6 | 0 | 0.0 | 65 | 50 | 51 | | 15 | .257 | .301 | 0 | 0 | 3B-79, SS-74, OF-1, 2B-1 |
| 1899 | 109 | 366 | 96 | 15 | 4 | 2 | 0.5 | 67 | 44 | 46 | | 13 | .262 | .342 | 0 | 0 | SS-109 |
| 1900 CHI N | 47 | 159 | 33 | 6 | 0 | 0 | 0.0 | 15 | 11 | 17 | | 6 | .208 | .245 | 0 | 0 | SS-47 |
| 1901 WAS A | 137 | 480 | 116 | 10 | 7 | 2 | 0.4 | 66 | 55 | 42 | | 10 | .242 | .304 | 0 | 0 | SS-137 |
| 1903 CLE A | 21 | 64 | 18 | 1 | 1 | 0 | 0.0 | 10 | 7 | 11 | | 2 | .281 | .328 | 0 | 0 | 2B-11, SS-7, 3B-3 |
| 10 yrs. | 816 | 2839 | 697 | 86 | 31 | 8 | 0.3 | 410 | 301 | 303 | 94 | 98 | .246 | .306 | 0 | 0 | 3B-422, SS-380, 2B-14, OF-1 |
| 1 yr. | 47 | 159 | 33 | 6 | 0 | 0 | 0.0 | 15 | 11 | 17 | | 6 | .208 | .245 | 0 | 0 | SS-47 |

## Otis Clymer

**CLYMER, OTIS EDGAR (Gump)**
B. Jan. 27, 1876, Pine Grove, Pa.    D. Feb. 27, 1926, St. Paul, Minn.
BB TR 6' 175 lbs.

| | G | AB | H | 2B | 3B | HR | HR % | R | RBI | BB | SO | SB | BA | SA | PH AB | PH H | G by POS |
|---|---|---|---|---|---|---|---|---|---|---|---|---|---|---|---|---|---|
| 1905 PIT N | 96 | 365 | 108 | 11 | 5 | 0 | 0.0 | 74 | 23 | 19 | | 23 | .296 | .353 | 6 | 2 | OF-89, 1B-1 |
| 1906 | 11 | 45 | 11 | 0 | 1 | 0 | 0.0 | 7 | 1 | 3 | | 1 | .244 | .289 | 0 | 0 | OF-11 |
| 1907 2 teams | | | PIT | N | (22G | – | .227) | WAS | A | (57G | – | .316) | | | | | |
| " total | 79 | 272 | 80 | 7 | 5 | 1 | 0.4 | 38 | 20 | 23 | | 22 | .294 | .368 | 9 | 3 | OF-66, 1B-2 |
| 1908 WAS A | 110 | 368 | 93 | 11 | 4 | 1 | 0.3 | 32 | 35 | 20 | | 19 | .253 | .313 | 9 | 3 | OF-82, 2B-13, 3B-2 |
| 1909 | 45 | 138 | 27 | 5 | 2 | 0 | 0.0 | 11 | 6 | 17 | | 7 | .196 | .261 | 2 | 0 | OF-41 |
| 1913 2 teams | | | CHI | N | (30G | – | .229) | BOS | N | (14G | – | .324) | | | | | |
| " total | 44 | 142 | 36 | 8 | 2 | 0 | 0.0 | 20 | 13 | 17 | 21 | 11 | .254 | .338 | 6 | 2 | OF-37 |
| 6 yrs. | 385 | 1330 | 355 | 42 | 19 | 2 | 0.2 | 182 | 98 | 99 | 21 | 83 | .267 | .332 | 32 | 10 | OF-326, 2B-13, 1B-3, 3B-2 |
| 1 yr. | 30 | 105 | 24 | 5 | 1 | 0 | 0.0 | 16 | 7 | 14 | 18 | 9 | .229 | .295 | 3 | 0 | OF-26 |

## Frank Coggins

**COGGINS, FRANKLIN (Swish)**
B. May 22, 1944, Griffin, Ga.
BB TR 6'2" 187 lbs.

| | G | AB | H | 2B | 3B | HR | HR % | R | RBI | BB | SO | SB | BA | SA | PH AB | PH H | G by POS |
|---|---|---|---|---|---|---|---|---|---|---|---|---|---|---|---|---|---|
| 1967 WAS A | 19 | 75 | 23 | 3 | 0 | 1 | 1.3 | 9 | 8 | 2 | 17 | 1 | .307 | .387 | 0 | 0 | 2B-19 |
| 1968 | 62 | 171 | 30 | 6 | 1 | 0 | 0.0 | 15 | 7 | 9 | 33 | 1 | .175 | .222 | 8 | 0 | 2B-52 |
| 1972 CHI N | 6 | 1 | 0 | 0 | 0 | 0 | 0.0 | 1 | 0 | 1 | 0 | 0 | .000 | .000 | 1 | 0 | |
| 3 yrs. | 87 | 247 | 53 | 9 | 1 | 1 | 0.4 | 25 | 15 | 12 | 50 | 2 | .215 | .271 | 9 | 0 | 2B-71 |
| 1 yr. | 6 | 1 | 0 | 0 | 0 | 0 | 0.0 | 1 | 0 | 1 | 0 | 0 | .000 | .000 | 1 | 0 | |

## Bill Collins

**COLLINS, WILLIAM SHIRLEY**
B. Mar. 27, 1882, Chestertown, Ind.    D. June 26, 1961, San Bernardino, Calif.
BR TR

| | G | AB | H | 2B | 3B | HR | HR % | R | RBI | BB | SO | SB | BA | SA | PH AB | PH H | G by POS |
|---|---|---|---|---|---|---|---|---|---|---|---|---|---|---|---|---|---|
| 1910 BOS N | 151 | 584 | 141 | 6 | 7 | 3 | 0.5 | 67 | 40 | 43 | 48 | 36 | .241 | .291 | 0 | 0 | OF-151 |
| 1911 2 teams | | | BOS | N | (17G | – | .136) | CHI | N | (7G | – | .200) | | | | | |
| " total | 24 | 49 | 7 | 2 | 1 | 0 | 0.0 | 10 | 8 | 2 | 11 | 4 | .143 | .224 | 1 | 1 | OF-17, 3B-1 |
| 1913 BKN N | 32 | 95 | 18 | 1 | 0 | 0 | 0.0 | 8 | 4 | 8 | 11 | 2 | .189 | .200 | 4 | 0 | OF-27 |
| 1914 BUF F | 21 | 47 | 7 | 2 | 2 | 0 | 0.0 | 6 | 2 | 1 | | 0 | .149 | .277 | 4 | 0 | OF-15 |
| 4 yrs. | 228 | 775 | 173 | 11 | 10 | 3 | 0.4 | 91 | 54 | 54 | 70 | 42 | .223 | .275 | 9 | 1 | OF-210, 3B-1 |
| 1 yr. | 7 | 5 | 1 | 1 | 0 | 0 | 0.0 | 2 | 0 | 1 | 3 | 0 | .200 | .400 | 1 | 1 | OF-4 |

## Bob Collins

**COLLINS, ROBERT JOSEPH**
B. Sept. 18, 1909, Pittsburgh, Pa.    D. Apr. 19, 1969, Pittsburgh, Pa.
BR TR 5'11" 176 lbs.

| | G | AB | H | 2B | 3B | HR | HR % | R | RBI | BB | SO | SB | BA | SA | PH AB | PH H | G by POS |
|---|---|---|---|---|---|---|---|---|---|---|---|---|---|---|---|---|---|
| 1940 CHI N | 47 | 120 | 25 | 3 | 0 | 1 | 0.8 | 11 | 14 | 14 | 18 | 4 | .208 | .258 | 4 | 1 | C-42 |
| 1944 NY A | 3 | 3 | 1 | 0 | 0 | 0 | 0.0 | 0 | 0 | 1 | 0 | 0 | .333 | .333 | 0 | 0 | C-3 |
| 2 yrs. | 50 | 123 | 26 | 3 | 0 | 1 | 0.8 | 11 | 14 | 15 | 18 | 4 | .211 | .260 | 4 | 1 | C-45 |
| 1 yr. | 47 | 120 | 25 | 3 | 0 | 1 | 0.8 | 11 | 14 | 14 | 18 | 4 | .208 | .258 | 4 | 1 | C-42 |

## Ripper Collins

**COLLINS, JAMES ANTHONY**
B. Mar. 30, 1904, Altoona, Pa.    D. Apr. 16, 1970, New Haven, N. Y.
BB TL 5'9" 165 lbs.

| | G | AB | H | 2B | 3B | HR | HR % | R | RBI | BB | SO | SB | BA | SA | PH AB | PH H | G by POS |
|---|---|---|---|---|---|---|---|---|---|---|---|---|---|---|---|---|---|
| 1931 STL N | 89 | 279 | 84 | 20 | 10 | 4 | 1.4 | 34 | 59 | 18 | 24 | 1 | .301 | .487 | 16 | 2 | 1B-68, OF-3 |
| 1932 | 149 | 549 | 153 | 28 | 8 | 21 | 3.8 | 82 | 91 | 38 | 67 | 4 | .279 | .474 | 8 | 2 | 1B-81, OF-60 |
| 1933 | 132 | 493 | 153 | 26 | 7 | 10 | 2.0 | 66 | 68 | 38 | 49 | 7 | .310 | .452 | 8 | 3 | 1B-123 |
| 1934 | 154 | 600 | 200 | 40 | 12 | 35 | 5.8 | 116 | 128 | 57 | 50 | 2 | .333 | .615 | 0 | 0 | 1B-154 |
| 1935 | 150 | 578 | 181 | 36 | 10 | 23 | 4.0 | 109 | 122 | 65 | 45 | 0 | .313 | .529 | 0 | 0 | 1B-150 |
| 1936 | 103 | 277 | 81 | 15 | 3 | 13 | 4.7 | 48 | 48 | 48 | 30 | 1 | .292 | .509 | 26 | 8 | 1B-61, OF-9 |
| 1937 CHI N | 115 | 456 | 125 | 16 | 5 | 16 | 3.5 | 77 | 71 | 32 | 46 | 2 | .274 | .436 | 4 | 0 | 1B-111 |
| 1938 | 143 | 490 | 131 | 22 | 8 | 13 | 2.7 | 78 | 61 | 54 | 48 | 1 | .267 | .424 | 7 | 0 | 1B-135 |
| 1941 PIT N | 49 | 62 | 13 | 2 | 2 | 0 | 0.0 | 5 | 11 | 6 | 14 | 0 | .210 | .306 | 32 | 4 | 1B-11, OF-3 |
| 9 yrs. | 1084 | 3784 | 1121 | 205 | 65 | 135 | 3.6 | 615 | 659 | 356 | 373 | 18 | .296 | .492 | 101 | 19 | 1B-894, OF-75 |
| 2 yrs. | 258 | 946 | 256 | 38 | 13 | 29 | 3.1 | 155 | 132 | 86 | 94 | 3 | .271 | .430 | 11 | 0 | 1B-246 |

WORLD SERIES

| | G | AB | H | 2B | 3B | HR | HR % | R | RBI | BB | SO | SB | BA | SA | PH AB | PH H | G by POS |
|---|---|---|---|---|---|---|---|---|---|---|---|---|---|---|---|---|---|
| 1931 STL N | 2 | 2 | 0 | 0 | 0 | 0 | 0.0 | 0 | 0 | 0 | 1 | 0 | .000 | .000 | 2 | 0 | |
| 1934 | 7 | 30 | 11 | 1 | 0 | 0 | 0.0 | 4 | 4 | 1 | 2 | 0 | .367 | .400 | 0 | 0 | 1B-7 |
| 1938 CHI N | 4 | 15 | 2 | 0 | 0 | 0 | 0.0 | 1 | 0 | 0 | 3 | 0 | .133 | .133 | 0 | 0 | 1B-4 |
| 3 yrs. | 13 | 47 | 13 | 1 | 0 | 0 | 0.0 | 5 | 4 | 1 | 6 | 0 | .277 | .298 | 2 | 0 | 1B-11 |

| | G | AB | H | 2B | 3B | HR | HR % | R | RBI | BB | SO | SB | BA | SA | Pinch Hit AB | Pinch Hit H | G by POS |
|---|---|---|---|---|---|---|---|---|---|---|---|---|---|---|---|---|---|

## Bunk Congalton

**CONGALTON, WILLIAM MILLAR**  BL TL 5'11"  190 lbs.
B. Jan. 24, 1875, Guelph, Ont., Canada    D. Aug. 19, 1937, Cleveland, Ohio

| | G | AB | H | 2B | 3B | HR | HR % | R | RBI | BB | SO | SB | BA | SA | PH AB | PH H | G by POS |
|---|---|---|---|---|---|---|---|---|---|---|---|---|---|---|---|---|---|
| 1902 CHI N | 45 | 179 | 40 | 3 | 0 | 1 | 0.6 | 14 | 24 | 7 | | 3 | .223 | .257 | 0 | 0 | OF-45 |
| 1905 CLE A | 12 | 47 | 17 | 0 | 0 | 0 | 0.0 | 4 | 5 | 2 | | 3 | .362 | .362 | 0 | 0 | OF-12 |
| 1906 | 117 | 419 | 134 | 13 | 5 | 2 | 0.5 | 51 | 50 | 24 | | 12 | .320 | .389 | 3 | 0 | OF-114 |
| 1907 2 teams | | CLE | A | (9G – | .182) | | | BOS | A | (127G – | .286) | | | | | | |
| " total | 136 | 518 | 146 | 11 | 8 | 2 | 0.4 | 46 | 49 | 24 | | 13 | .282 | .346 | 4 | 0 | OF-132 |
| 4 yrs. | 310 | 1163 | 337 | 27 | 13 | 5 | 0.4 | 115 | 128 | 57 | | 31 | .290 | .348 | 7 | 0 | OF-303 |
| 1 yr. | 45 | 179 | 40 | 3 | 0 | 1 | 0.6 | 14 | 24 | 7 | | 3 | .223 | .257 | 0 | 0 | OF-45 |

## Fritz Connally

**CONNALLY, FRITZIE LEE**  BR TR 6'4"  210 lbs.
B. May 19, 1958, Bryan, Tex.

| | G | AB | H | 2B | 3B | HR | HR % | R | RBI | BB | SO | SB | BA | SA | PH AB | PH H | G by POS |
|---|---|---|---|---|---|---|---|---|---|---|---|---|---|---|---|---|---|
| 1983 CHI N | 8 | 10 | 1 | 0 | 0 | 0 | 0.0 | 0 | 0 | 0 | 5 | 0 | .100 | .100 | 7 | 1 | 3B-3 |
| 1985 BAL A | 50 | 112 | 26 | 4 | 0 | 3 | 2.7 | 16 | 15 | 19 | 21 | 0 | .232 | .348 | 16 | 5 | 3B-46, 1B-2, DH-1 |
| 2 yrs. | 58 | 122 | 27 | 4 | 0 | 3 | 2.5 | 16 | 15 | 19 | 26 | 0 | .221 | .328 | 23 | 6 | 3B-49, 1B-2, DH-1 |
| 1 yr. | 8 | 10 | 1 | 0 | 0 | 0 | 0.0 | 0 | 0 | 0 | 5 | 0 | .100 | .100 | 7 | 1 | 3B-3 |

## Jim Connor

**CONNOR, JAMES MATTHEW**
Born James Matthew O'Connor.
B. May 11, 1865, Port Jervis, N. Y.    D. Sept. 4, 1950, Providence, R. I.

| | G | AB | H | 2B | 3B | HR | HR % | R | RBI | BB | SO | SB | BA | SA | PH AB | PH H | G by POS |
|---|---|---|---|---|---|---|---|---|---|---|---|---|---|---|---|---|---|
| 1892 CHI N | 9 | 34 | 2 | 0 | 0 | 0 | 0.0 | 0 | 1 | 7 | | 0 | .059 | .059 | 0 | 0 | 2B-9 |
| 1897 | 77 | 285 | 83 | 10 | 5 | 3 | 1.1 | 40 | 38 | 24 | | 10 | .291 | .393 | 2 | 1 | 2B-76 |
| 1898 | 138 | 505 | 114 | 9 | 9 | 0 | 0.0 | 51 | 67 | 42 | | 11 | .226 | .279 | 0 | 0 | 2B-138 |
| 1899 | 69 | 234 | 48 | 7 | 1 | 0 | 0.0 | 26 | 24 | 18 | | 6 | .205 | .244 | 0 | 0 | 2B-44, 3B-25 |
| 4 yrs. | 293 | 1058 | 247 | 26 | 15 | 3 | 0.3 | 117 | 129 | 85 | 7 | 27 | .233 | .295 | 2 | 1 | 2B-267, 3B-25 |
| 4 yrs. | 293 | 1058 | 247 | 26 | 15 | 3 | 0.3 | 117 | 129 | 85 | 7 | 27 | .233 | .295 | 2 | 1 | 2B-267, 3B-25 |

## Chuck Connors

**CONNORS, KEVIN JOSEPH**  BL TL 6'5"  190 lbs.
B. Apr. 10, 1921, Brooklyn, N. Y.

| | G | AB | H | 2B | 3B | HR | HR % | R | RBI | BB | SO | SB | BA | SA | PH AB | PH H | G by POS |
|---|---|---|---|---|---|---|---|---|---|---|---|---|---|---|---|---|---|
| 1949 BKN N | 1 | 1 | 0 | 0 | 0 | 0 | 0.0 | 0 | 0 | 0 | 0 | 0 | .000 | .000 | 1 | 0 | |
| 1951 CHI N | 66 | 201 | 48 | 5 | 1 | 2 | 1.0 | 16 | 18 | 12 | 25 | 4 | .239 | .303 | 10 | 1 | 1B-57 |
| 2 yrs. | 67 | 202 | 48 | 5 | 1 | 2 | 1.0 | 16 | 18 | 12 | 25 | 4 | .238 | .302 | 11 | 1 | 1B-57 |
| 1 yr. | 66 | 201 | 48 | 5 | 1 | 2 | 1.0 | 16 | 18 | 12 | 25 | 4 | .239 | .303 | 10 | 1 | 1B-57 |

## Jim Cook

**COOK, JAMES FITCHIE**  TR 5'9"  163 lbs.
B. Nov. 10, 1879, Dundee, Ill.    D. June 17, 1949, St. Louis, Mo.

| | G | AB | H | 2B | 3B | HR | HR % | R | RBI | BB | SO | SB | BA | SA | PH AB | PH H | G by POS |
|---|---|---|---|---|---|---|---|---|---|---|---|---|---|---|---|---|---|
| 1903 CHI N | 8 | 26 | 4 | 1 | 0 | 0 | 0.0 | 3 | 2 | 2 | | 1 | .154 | .192 | 0 | 0 | OF-5, 2B-2, 1B-1 |

## Jimmy Cooney

**COONEY, JAMES EDWARD (Scoops)**  BR TR 5'11"  160 lbs.
Son of Jimmy Cooney.   Brother of Johnny Cooney.
B. Aug. 24, 1894, Cranston, R. I.

| | G | AB | H | 2B | 3B | HR | HR % | R | RBI | BB | SO | SB | BA | SA | PH AB | PH H | G by POS |
|---|---|---|---|---|---|---|---|---|---|---|---|---|---|---|---|---|---|
| 1917 BOS A | 11 | 36 | 8 | 1 | 0 | 0 | 0.0 | 4 | 3 | 6 | 2 | 0 | .222 | .250 | 0 | 0 | 2B-10, SS-1 |
| 1919 NY N | 5 | 14 | 3 | 0 | 0 | 0 | 0.0 | 3 | 1 | 0 | 0 | 0 | .214 | .214 | 0 | 0 | SS-4, 2B-1 |
| 1924 STL N | 110 | 383 | 113 | 20 | 8 | 1 | 0.3 | 44 | 57 | 20 | 20 | 12 | .295 | .397 | 0 | 0 | SS-99, 3B-7, 2B-1 |
| 1925 | 54 | 187 | 51 | 11 | 2 | 0 | 0.0 | 27 | 18 | 4 | 5 | 1 | .273 | .353 | 1 | 0 | SS-37, 2B-15, OF-1 |
| 1926 CHI N | 141 | 513 | 129 | 18 | 5 | 1 | 0.2 | 52 | 47 | 23 | 10 | 11 | .251 | .312 | 0 | 0 | SS-141 |
| 1927 2 teams | | CHI | N | (33G – | .242) | | | PHI | N | (76G – | .270) | | | | | | |
| " total | 109 | 391 | 102 | 14 | 1 | 0 | 0.0 | 49 | 21 | 21 | 16 | 5 | .261 | .302 | 1 | 0 | SS-107 |
| 1928 BOS N | 18 | 51 | 7 | 0 | 0 | 0 | 0.0 | 2 | 3 | 2 | 5 | 1 | .137 | .137 | 4 | 0 | SS-11, 2B-4 |
| 7 yrs. | 448 | 1575 | 413 | 64 | 16 | 2 | 0.1 | 181 | 150 | 76 | 58 | 30 | .262 | .327 | 6 | 0 | SS-400, 2B-31, 3B-7, OF-1 |
| 2 yrs. | 174 | 645 | 161 | 20 | 5 | 1 | 0.2 | 68 | 53 | 31 | 17 | 12 | .250 | .301 | 0 | 0 | SS-174 |

## Jimmy Cooney

**COONEY, JAMES JOSEPH**  BR TR 5'9"  155 lbs.
Father of Jimmy Cooney.   Father of Johnny Cooney.
B. July 9, 1865, Cranston, R. I.    D. July 1, 1903, Cranston, R. I.

| | G | AB | H | 2B | 3B | HR | HR % | R | RBI | BB | SO | SB | BA | SA | PH AB | PH H | G by POS |
|---|---|---|---|---|---|---|---|---|---|---|---|---|---|---|---|---|---|
| 1890 CHI N | 135 | 574 | 156 | 19 | 10 | 4 | 0.7 | 114 | 52 | 73 | 23 | 45 | .272 | .361 | 0 | 0 | SS-135, C-1 |
| 1891 | 118 | 465 | 114 | 15 | 3 | 0 | 0.0 | 84 | 42 | 48 | 17 | 21 | .245 | .290 | 0 | 0 | SS-118 |
| 1892 2 teams | | CHI | N | (65G – | .172) | | | WAS | N | (6G – | .160) | | | | | | |
| " total | 71 | 263 | 45 | 1 | 1 | 0 | 0.0 | 23 | 24 | 27 | 8 | 11 | .171 | .183 | 0 | 0 | SS-71 |
| 3 yrs. | 324 | 1302 | 315 | 35 | 14 | 4 | 0.3 | 221 | 118 | 148 | 48 | 77 | .242 | .300 | 0 | 0 | SS-324, C-1 |
| 3 yrs. | 318 | 1277 | 311 | 35 | 13 | 4 | 0.3 | 216 | 114 | 144 | 45 | 76 | .244 | .301 | 0 | 0 | SS-318, C-1 |

## Walker Cooper

**COOPER, WILLIAM WALKER**  BR TR 6'3"  210 lbs.
Brother of Mort Cooper.
B. Jan. 8, 1915, Atherton, Mo.

| | G | AB | H | 2B | 3B | HR | HR % | R | RBI | BB | SO | SB | BA | SA | PH AB | PH H | G by POS |
|---|---|---|---|---|---|---|---|---|---|---|---|---|---|---|---|---|---|
| 1940 STL N | 6 | 19 | 6 | 1 | 0 | 0 | 0.0 | 3 | 2 | 2 | 2 | 1 | .316 | .368 | 0 | 0 | C-6 |
| 1941 | 68 | 200 | 49 | 9 | 1 | 1 | 0.5 | 19 | 20 | 13 | 14 | 1 | .245 | .315 | 5 | 2 | C-63 |
| 1942 | 125 | 438 | 123 | 32 | 7 | 7 | 1.6 | 58 | 65 | 29 | 29 | 4 | .281 | .434 | 10 | 5 | C-115 |
| 1943 | 122 | 449 | 143 | 30 | 4 | 9 | 2.0 | 52 | 81 | 19 | 19 | 1 | .318 | .463 | 10 | 1 | C-112 |
| 1944 | 112 | 397 | 126 | 25 | 5 | 13 | 3.3 | 56 | 72 | 20 | 19 | 4 | .317 | .504 | 15 | 5 | C-97 |
| 1945 | 4 | 18 | 7 | 0 | 0 | 0 | 0.0 | 3 | 1 | 0 | 1 | 0 | .389 | .389 | 0 | 0 | C-4 |
| 1946 NY N | 87 | 280 | 75 | 10 | 1 | 8 | 2.9 | 29 | 46 | 17 | 12 | 0 | .268 | .396 | 13 | 3 | C-73 |
| 1947 | 140 | 515 | 157 | 24 | 8 | 35 | 6.8 | 79 | 122 | 24 | 43 | 2 | .305 | .586 | 6 | 1 | C-132 |
| 1948 | 91 | 290 | 77 | 12 | 0 | 16 | 5.5 | 40 | 54 | 28 | 29 | 1 | .266 | .472 | 12 | 2 | C-79 |
| 1949 2 teams | | NY | N | (42G – | .211) | | | CIN | N | (82G – | .280) | | | | | | |
| " total | 124 | 454 | 117 | 13 | 4 | 20 | 4.4 | 48 | 83 | 28 | 32 | 0 | .258 | .436 | 5 | 1 | C-117 |
| 1950 2 teams | | CIN | N | (15G – | .191) | | | BOS | N | (102G – | .329) | | | | | | |
| " total | 117 | 384 | 120 | 22 | 3 | 14 | 3.6 | 55 | 64 | 30 | 31 | 1 | .313 | .495 | 12 | 6 | C-101 |
| 1951 BOS N | 109 | 342 | 107 | 14 | 1 | 18 | 5.3 | 42 | 59 | 28 | 18 | 1 | .313 | .518 | 18 | 2 | C-90 |
| 1952 | 102 | 349 | 82 | 12 | 1 | 10 | 2.9 | 33 | 55 | 22 | 32 | 1 | .235 | .361 | 13 | 4 | C-89 |

| | G | AB | H | 2B | 3B | HR | HR % | R | RBI | BB | SO | SB | BA | SA | Pinch Hit AB | Pinch Hit H | G by POS |
|---|---|---|---|---|---|---|---|---|---|---|---|---|---|---|---|---|---|

## Walker Cooper continued

| | G | AB | H | 2B | 3B | HR | HR % | R | RBI | BB | SO | SB | BA | SA | PH AB | PH H | G by POS |
|---|---|---|---|---|---|---|---|---|---|---|---|---|---|---|---|---|---|
| 1953 MIL N | 53 | 137 | 30 | 6 | 0 | 3 | 2.2 | 12 | 16 | 12 | 15 | 1 | .219 | .328 | 17 | 3 | C-35 |
| 1954 2 teams | PIT N (14G – .200) | | | | CHI N (57G – .310) | | | | | | | | | | | | |
| " total | 71 | 173 | 52 | 12 | 2 | 7 | 4.0 | 21 | 33 | 23 | 24 | 0 | .301 | .514 | 23 | 5 | C-50 |
| 1955 CHI N | 54 | 111 | 31 | 8 | 1 | 7 | 6.3 | 11 | 15 | 6 | 19 | 0 | .279 | .559 | 28 | 6 | C-31 |
| 1956 STL N | 40 | 68 | 18 | 5 | 1 | 2 | 2.9 | 5 | 14 | 3 | 8 | 0 | .265 | .456 | 22 | 3 | C-16 |
| 1957 | 48 | 78 | 21 | 5 | 1 | 3 | 3.8 | 7 | 10 | 5 | 10 | 0 | .269 | .474 | 30 | 7 | C-13 |
| 18 yrs. | 1473 | 4702 | 1341 | 240 | 40 | 173 | 3.7 | 573 | 812 | 309 | 357 | 18 | .285 | .464 | 239 | 56 | C-1223 |
| 2 yrs. | 111 | 269 | 80 | 18 | 3 | 14 | 5.2 | 32 | 47 | 27 | 42 | 0 | .297 | .543 | 39 | 8 | C-79 |
| WORLD SERIES | | | | | | | | | | | | | | | | | |
| 1942 STL N | 5 | 21 | 6 | 1 | 0 | 0 | 0.0 | 3 | 4 | 0 | 1 | 0 | .286 | .333 | 0 | 0 | C-5 |
| 1943 | 5 | 17 | 5 | 0 | 0 | 0 | 0.0 | 1 | 0 | 0 | 1 | 0 | .294 | .294 | 0 | 0 | C-5 |
| 1944 | 6 | 22 | 7 | 2 | 1 | 0 | 0.0 | 1 | 2 | 3 | 2 | 0 | .318 | .500 | 0 | 0 | C-6 |
| 3 yrs. | 16 | 60 | 18 | 3 | 1 | 0 | 0.0 | 5 | 6 | 3 | 4 | 0 | .300 | .383 | 0 | 0 | C-16 |

## Larry Corcoran

**CORCORAN, LAWRENCE J.**                                                  TR
Brother of Mike Corcoran.
B. Aug. 10, 1859, Brooklyn, N. Y.   D. Oct. 14, 1891, Newark, N. J.

| | G | AB | H | 2B | 3B | HR | HR % | R | RBI | BB | SO | SB | BA | SA | PH AB | PH H | G by POS |
|---|---|---|---|---|---|---|---|---|---|---|---|---|---|---|---|---|---|
| 1880 CHI N | 72 | 286 | 66 | 11 | 1 | 0 | 0.0 | 41 | 25 | 10 | 33 | | .231 | .276 | 0 | 0 | P-63, OF-8, SS-8 |
| 1881 | 47 | 189 | 42 | 8 | 0 | 0 | 0.0 | 25 | 9 | 5 | 22 | | .222 | .265 | 0 | 0 | P-45, SS-2, OF-1 |
| 1882 | 40 | 169 | 35 | 10 | 2 | 1 | 0.6 | 23 | 24 | 6 | 18 | | .207 | .308 | 0 | 0 | P-39, 3B-1 |
| 1883 | 68 | 263 | 55 | 12 | 7 | 0 | 0.0 | 40 | | 6 | 62 | | .209 | .308 | 0 | 0 | P-56, OF-13, SS-3, 2B-1 |
| 1884 | 64 | 251 | 61 | 3 | 4 | 1 | 0.4 | 43 | | 10 | 33 | | .243 | .299 | 0 | 0 | P-60, OF-4, SS-2 |
| 1885 2 teams | CHI N (7G – .273) | | | | NY N (3G – .357) | | | | | | | | | | | | |
| " total | 10 | 36 | 11 | 1 | 0 | 0 | 0.0 | 9 | 4 | 6 | 2 | | .306 | .333 | 0 | 0 | P-10, SS-1 |
| 1886 2 teams | NY N (1G – .000) | | | | WAS N (21G – .185) | | | | | | | | | | | | |
| " total | 22 | 85 | 15 | 2 | 1 | 0 | 0.0 | 9 | 3 | 7 | 16 | | .176 | .224 | 0 | 0 | OF-12, SS-9, P-2 |
| 1887 IND N | 3 | 10 | 2 | 0 | 0 | 0 | 0.0 | 2 | 0 | 2 | 1 | 2 | .200 | .200 | 0 | 0 | OF-2, P-2 |
| 8 yrs. | 326 | 1289 | 287 | 47 | 15 | 2 | 0.2 | 192 | 65 | 52 | 187 | 2 | .223 | .287 | 0 | 0 | P-277, OF-40, SS-25, 3B-1, 2B-1 |
| 6 yrs. | 298 | 1180 | 265 | 45 | 14 | 2 | 0.2 | 178 | 62 | 43 | 169 | | .225 | .292 | 0 | 0 | P-270, OF-26, SS-16, 3B-1, 2B-1 |

## Red Corriden

**CORRIDEN, JOHN MICHAEL, SR.**                                  BR TR 5'9"   165 lbs.
Father of John Corriden.
B. Sept. 4, 1887, Logansport, Ind.   D. Sept. 28, 1959, Indianapolis, Ind.
Manager 1950.

| | G | AB | H | 2B | 3B | HR | HR % | R | RBI | BB | SO | SB | BA | SA | PH AB | PH H | G by POS |
|---|---|---|---|---|---|---|---|---|---|---|---|---|---|---|---|---|---|
| 1910 STL A | 26 | 84 | 13 | 3 | 0 | 1 | 1.2 | 19 | 4 | 13 | | 5 | .155 | .226 | 0 | 0 | SS-14, 3B-12 |
| 1912 DET A | 38 | 138 | 28 | 6 | 0 | 0 | 0.0 | 22 | 5 | 15 | | 4 | .203 | .246 | 3 | 0 | 3B-25, 2B-7, SS-3 |
| 1913 CHI N | 45 | 97 | 17 | 3 | 0 | 2 | 2.1 | 13 | 9 | 9 | 14 | 4 | .175 | .268 | 4 | 1 | SS-36, 2B-2, 3B-1 |
| 1914 | 107 | 318 | 73 | 9 | 5 | 3 | 0.9 | 42 | 29 | 35 | 33 | 13 | .230 | .318 | 6 | 2 | SS-96, 3B-8, 2B-3 |
| 1915 | 6 | 3 | 0 | 0 | 0 | 0 | 0.0 | 1 | 0 | 2 | 1 | 0 | .000 | .000 | 2 | 0 | OF-1, 3B-1 |
| 5 yrs. | 222 | 640 | 131 | 21 | 5 | 6 | 0.9 | 97 | 47 | 74 | 48 | 26 | .205 | .281 | 15 | 3 | SS-149, 3B-47, 2B-12, OF-1 |
| 3 yrs. | 158 | 418 | 90 | 12 | 5 | 5 | 1.2 | 56 | 38 | 46 | 48 | 17 | .215 | .304 | 12 | 3 | SS-132, 3B-10, 2B-5, OF-1 |

## Dick Cotter

**COTTER, RICHARD RAPHAEL**                                        BR TR 5'11"   172 lbs.
B. Oct. 12, 1889, Manchester, N. H.   D. Apr. 4, 1945, Brooklyn, N. Y.

| | G | AB | H | 2B | 3B | HR | HR % | R | RBI | BB | SO | SB | BA | SA | PH AB | PH H | G by POS |
|---|---|---|---|---|---|---|---|---|---|---|---|---|---|---|---|---|---|
| 1911 PHI N | 20 | 46 | 13 | 0 | 0 | 0 | 0.0 | 5 | 5 | 5 | 7 | 1 | .283 | .283 | 2 | 0 | C-17 |
| 1912 CHI N | 26 | 54 | 15 | 0 | 2 | 0 | 0.0 | 6 | 10 | 6 | 13 | 1 | .278 | .352 | 1 | 0 | C-24 |
| 2 yrs. | 46 | 100 | 28 | 0 | 2 | 0 | 0.0 | 8 | 15 | 11 | 20 | 2 | .280 | .320 | 3 | 0 | C-41 |
| 1 yr. | 26 | 54 | 15 | 0 | 2 | 0 | 0.0 | 6 | 10 | 6 | 13 | 1 | .278 | .352 | 1 | 0 | C-24 |

## Harvey Cotter

**COTTER, HARVEY LOUIS (Hooks)**                                   BL TL 5'10"   160 lbs.
B. May 22, 1900, Holden, Mo.   D. Aug. 6, 1955, Los Angeles, Calif.

| | G | AB | H | 2B | 3B | HR | HR % | R | RBI | BB | SO | SB | BA | SA | PH AB | PH H | G by POS |
|---|---|---|---|---|---|---|---|---|---|---|---|---|---|---|---|---|---|
| 1922 CHI N | 1 | 1 | 1 | 1 | 0 | 0 | 0.0 | 0 | 0 | 0 | 0 | 0 | 1.000 | 2.000 | 1 | 1 | |
| 1924 | 98 | 310 | 81 | 16 | 4 | 4 | 1.3 | 39 | 33 | 36 | 31 | 3 | .261 | .377 | 7 | 2 | 1B-90 |
| 2 yrs. | 99 | 311 | 82 | 17 | 4 | 4 | 1.3 | 39 | 33 | 36 | 31 | 3 | .264 | .383 | 8 | 3 | 1B-90 |
| 2 yrs. | 99 | 311 | 82 | 17 | 4 | 4 | 1.3 | 39 | 33 | 36 | 31 | 3 | .264 | .383 | 8 | 3 | 1B-90 |

## Henry Cotto

**COTTO, HENRY**                                                     BR TR 6'2"   180 lbs.
B. Jan. 5, 1961, New York, N. Y.

| | G | AB | H | 2B | 3B | HR | HR % | R | RBI | BB | SO | SB | BA | SA | PH AB | PH H | G by POS |
|---|---|---|---|---|---|---|---|---|---|---|---|---|---|---|---|---|---|
| 1984 CHI N | 105 | 146 | 40 | 5 | 0 | 0 | 0.0 | 24 | 8 | 10 | 23 | 9 | .274 | .308 | 13 | 3 | OF-88 |
| 1985 NY A | 34 | 56 | 17 | 1 | 0 | 1 | 1.8 | 4 | 6 | 3 | 12 | 1 | .304 | .375 | 4 | 1 | OF-30 |
| 2 yrs. | 139 | 202 | 57 | 6 | 0 | 1 | 0.5 | 28 | 14 | 13 | 35 | 10 | .282 | .327 | 17 | 4 | OF-118 |
| 1 yr. | 105 | 146 | 40 | 5 | 0 | 0 | 0.0 | 24 | 8 | 10 | 23 | 9 | .274 | .308 | 13 | 3 | OF-88 |

| LEAGUE CHAMPIONSHIP SERIES | | | | | | | | | | | | | | | | | |
|---|---|---|---|---|---|---|---|---|---|---|---|---|---|---|---|---|---|
| 1984 CHI N | 3 | 1 | 1 | 0 | 0 | 0 | 0.0 | 1 | 0 | 0 | 0 | 0 | 1.000 | 1.000 | 0 | 0 | OF-3 |

## Wes Covington

**COVINGTON, JOHN WESLEY**                                          BL TR 6'1"   205 lbs.
B. Mar. 27, 1932, Laurinburg, N. C.

| | G | AB | H | 2B | 3B | HR | HR % | R | RBI | BB | SO | SB | BA | SA | PH AB | PH H | G by POS |
|---|---|---|---|---|---|---|---|---|---|---|---|---|---|---|---|---|---|
| 1956 MIL N | 75 | 138 | 39 | 4 | 0 | 2 | 1.4 | 17 | 16 | 16 | 20 | 1 | .283 | .355 | 31 | 10 | OF-35 |
| 1957 | 96 | 328 | 93 | 8 | 1 | 21 | 6.4 | 51 | 65 | 29 | 44 | 4 | .284 | .537 | 8 | 1 | OF-89 |
| 1958 | 90 | 294 | 97 | 12 | 1 | 24 | 8.2 | 43 | 74 | 20 | 35 | 0 | .330 | .622 | 7 | 0 | OF-82 |
| 1959 | 103 | 373 | 104 | 17 | 3 | 7 | 1.9 | 38 | 45 | 26 | 41 | 0 | .279 | .397 | 9 | 2 | OF-94 |
| 1960 | 95 | 281 | 70 | 16 | 1 | 10 | 3.6 | 25 | 29 | 15 | 37 | 1 | .249 | .420 | 22 | 5 | OF-72 |
| 1961 4 teams | MIL N (9G – .190) | | | | CHI A (22G – .288) | | | | KC A (17G – .159) | | | | PHI N (57G – .303) | | | | |
| " total | 105 | 289 | 78 | 11 | 0 | 12 | 4.2 | 34 | 47 | 25 | 33 | 0 | .270 | .433 | 28 | 6 | OF-76 |
| 1962 PHI N | 116 | 304 | 86 | 12 | 1 | 9 | 3.0 | 36 | 44 | 19 | 44 | 0 | .283 | .418 | 30 | 9 | OF-88 |
| 1963 | 119 | 353 | 107 | 24 | 1 | 17 | 4.8 | 46 | 64 | 26 | 56 | 1 | .303 | .521 | 25 | 8 | OF-101 |
| 1964 | 129 | 339 | 95 | 18 | 0 | 13 | 3.8 | 37 | 58 | 38 | 50 | 0 | .280 | .448 | 31 | 5 | OF-108 |

| | G | AB | H | 2B | 3B | HR | HR % | R | RBI | BB | SO | SB | BA | SA | Pinch Hit AB | H | G by POS |
|---|---|---|---|---|---|---|---|---|---|---|---|---|---|---|---|---|---|

## Wes Covington continued

| | G | AB | H | 2B | 3B | HR | HR % | R | RBI | BB | SO | SB | BA | SA | AB | H | G by POS |
|---|---|---|---|---|---|---|---|---|---|---|---|---|---|---|---|---|---|
| 1965 | 101 | 235 | 58 | 10 | 1 | 15 | 6.4 | 27 | 45 | 26 | 47 | 0 | .247 | .489 | 35 | 7 | OF-64 |
| 1966 2 teams | CHI | N (9G – .091) | | | | LA | N (37G – .121) | | | | | | | | | | |
| " total | 46 | 44 | 5 | 0 | 1 | 1 | 2.3 | 1 | 6 | 7 | 7 | 0 | .114 | .227 | 34 | 4 | OF-3 |
| 11 yrs. | 1075 | 2978 | 832 | 128 | 17 | 131 | 4.4 | 355 | 499 | 247 | 414 | 7 | .279 | .466 | 260 | 57 | OF-812 |
| 1 yr. | 9 | 11 | 1 | 0 | 0 | 0 | 0.0 | 0 | 0 | 1 | 2 | 0 | .091 | .091 | 7 | 0 | OF-1 |
| WORLD SERIES | | | | | | | | | | | | | | | | | |
| 1957 MIL N | 7 | 24 | 5 | 1 | 0 | 0 | 0.0 | 1 | 1 | 2 | 6 | 1 | .208 | .250 | 0 | 0 | OF-7 |
| 1958 | 7 | 26 | 7 | 0 | 0 | 0 | 0.0 | 2 | 4 | 2 | 4 | 0 | .269 | .269 | 0 | 0 | OF-7 |
| 1966 LA N | 1 | 1 | 0 | 0 | 0 | 0 | 0.0 | 0 | 0 | 0 | 1 | 0 | .000 | .000 | 1 | 0 | |
| 3 yrs. | 15 | 51 | 12 | 1 | 0 | 0 | 0.0 | 3 | 5 | 4 | 11 | 1 | .235 | .255 | 1 | 0 | OF-14 |

## Billy Cowan

COWAN, BILLY ROLAND
B. Aug. 28, 1938, Calhoun City, Miss.

BR TR 6' 170 lbs.

| | G | AB | H | 2B | 3B | HR | HR % | R | RBI | BB | SO | SB | BA | SA | AB | H | G by POS |
|---|---|---|---|---|---|---|---|---|---|---|---|---|---|---|---|---|---|
| 1963 CHI N | 14 | 36 | 9 | 1 | 1 | 1 | 2.8 | 1 | 2 | 0 | 11 | 0 | .250 | .417 | 4 | 1 | OF-10 |
| 1964 | 139 | 497 | 120 | 16 | 4 | 19 | 3.8 | 52 | 50 | 18 | 128 | 12 | .241 | .404 | 4 | 2 | OF-134 |
| 1965 2 teams | NY | N (82G – .179) | | | | MIL | N (19G – .185) | | | | | | | | | | |
| " total | 101 | 183 | 33 | 9 | 2 | 3 | 1.6 | 20 | 9 | 4 | 54 | 3 | .180 | .301 | 20 | 2 | OF-71, 2B-2, SS-1 |
| 1967 PHI N | 34 | 59 | 9 | 0 | 0 | 3 | 5.1 | 11 | 6 | 4 | 14 | 1 | .153 | .305 | 5 | 0 | OF-20, 3B-1, 2B-1 |
| 1969 2 teams | NY | A (32G – .167) | | | | CAL | A (28G – .304) | | | | | | | | | | |
| " total | 60 | 104 | 25 | 1 | 0 | 5 | 4.8 | 15 | 13 | 6 | 18 | 0 | .240 | .394 | 33 | 9 | OF-27, 1B-6 |
| 1970 CAL A | 68 | 134 | 37 | 9 | 1 | 5 | 3.7 | 20 | 25 | 11 | 29 | 0 | .276 | .470 | 39 | 11 | OF-27, 1B-14, 3B-2 |
| 1971 | 74 | 174 | 48 | 8 | 0 | 4 | 2.3 | 12 | 20 | 7 | 41 | 1 | .276 | .391 | 34 | 8 | OF-40, 1B-5 |
| 1972 | 3 | 3 | 0 | 0 | 0 | 0 | 0.0 | 0 | 0 | 0 | 2 | 0 | .000 | .000 | 3 | 0 | |
| 8 yrs. | 493 | 1190 | 281 | 44 | 8 | 40 | 3.4 | 131 | 125 | 50 | 297 | 17 | .236 | .387 | 142 | 33 | OF-329, 1B-25, 3B-3, 2B-3, SS-1 |
| 2 yrs. | 153 | 533 | 129 | 17 | 5 | 20 | 3.8 | 53 | 52 | 18 | 139 | 12 | .242 | .405 | 8 | 3 | OF-144 |

## Larry Cox

COX, LARRY EUGENE
B. Sept. 11, 1947, Bluffton, Ohio

BR TR 5'10" 178 lbs.

| | G | AB | H | 2B | 3B | HR | HR % | R | RBI | BB | SO | SB | BA | SA | AB | H | G by POS |
|---|---|---|---|---|---|---|---|---|---|---|---|---|---|---|---|---|---|
| 1973 PHI N | 1 | 0 | 0 | 0 | 0 | 0 | – | 0 | 0 | 0 | 0 | 0 | – | – | 0 | 0 | C-1 |
| 1974 | 30 | 53 | 9 | 2 | 0 | 0 | 0.0 | 5 | 4 | 4 | 9 | 0 | .170 | .208 | 2 | 1 | C-29 |
| 1975 | 11 | 5 | 1 | 0 | 0 | 0 | 0.0 | 0 | 1 | 1 | 0 | 1 | .200 | .200 | 1 | 0 | C-10 |
| 1977 SEA A | 35 | 93 | 23 | 6 | 0 | 2 | 2.2 | 6 | 6 | 10 | 12 | 1 | .247 | .376 | 0 | 0 | C-35 |
| 1978 CHI N | 59 | 121 | 34 | 5 | 0 | 2 | 1.7 | 10 | 18 | 12 | 16 | 0 | .281 | .372 | 0 | 0 | C-58 |
| 1979 SEA A | 100 | 293 | 63 | 11 | 3 | 4 | 1.4 | 32 | 36 | 22 | 39 | 2 | .215 | .314 | 8 | 0 | C-99 |
| 1980 | 105 | 243 | 49 | 6 | 2 | 4 | 1.6 | 18 | 20 | 19 | 36 | 1 | .202 | .292 | 2 | 0 | C-104 |
| 1981 TEX A | 5 | 13 | 3 | 1 | 0 | 0 | 0.0 | 1 | 0 | 0 | 4 | 0 | .231 | .308 | 0 | 0 | C-5 |
| 1982 CHI N | 2 | 4 | 0 | 0 | 0 | 0 | 0.0 | 0 | 0 | 1 | 0 | 0 | .000 | .000 | 0 | 0 | C-2 |
| 9 yrs. | 348 | 825 | 182 | 31 | 5 | 12 | 1.5 | 72 | 85 | 70 | 117 | 5 | .221 | .314 | 13 | 1 | C-343 |
| 2 yrs. | 61 | 125 | 34 | 5 | 0 | 2 | 1.6 | 11 | 18 | 14 | 17 | 0 | .272 | .360 | 0 | 0 | C-60 |

## Harry Croft

CROFT, HENRY T.
B. Aug. 1, 1875, Chicago, Ill.   D. Dec. 11, 1933, Oak Park, Ill.

| | G | AB | H | 2B | 3B | HR | HR % | R | RBI | BB | SO | SB | BA | SA | AB | H | G by POS |
|---|---|---|---|---|---|---|---|---|---|---|---|---|---|---|---|---|---|
| 1899 2 teams | LOU | N (2G – .000) | | | | PHI | N (2G – .143) | | | | | | | | | | |
| " total | 4 | 9 | 1 | 0 | 0 | 0 | 0.0 | 0 | 1 | 0 | | 0 | .111 | .111 | 2 | 0 | 2B-2 |
| 1901 CHI N | 3 | 12 | 4 | 0 | 0 | 0 | 0.0 | 1 | 4 | 0 | | 0 | .333 | .333 | 0 | 0 | OF-3 |
| 2 yrs. | 7 | 21 | 5 | 0 | 0 | 0 | 0.0 | 1 | 4 | 0 | | 0 | .238 | .238 | 2 | 0 | OF-3, 2B-2 |
| 1 yr. | 3 | 12 | 4 | 0 | 0 | 0 | 0.0 | 1 | 4 | 0 | | 0 | .333 | .333 | 0 | 0 | OF-3 |

## Jeff Cross

CROSS, JOFFRE JAMES
B. Aug. 28, 1918, Tulsa, Okla.

BR TR 5'11" 160 lbs.

| | G | AB | H | 2B | 3B | HR | HR % | R | RBI | BB | SO | SB | BA | SA | AB | H | G by POS |
|---|---|---|---|---|---|---|---|---|---|---|---|---|---|---|---|---|---|
| 1942 STL N | 1 | 4 | 1 | 0 | 0 | 0 | 0.0 | 0 | 1 | 0 | 0 | 0 | .250 | .250 | 0 | 0 | SS-1 |
| 1946 | 49 | 69 | 15 | 3 | 0 | 0 | 0.0 | 17 | 6 | 10 | 8 | 4 | .217 | .261 | 3 | 0 | SS-17, 2B-8, 3B-1 |
| 1947 | 51 | 49 | 5 | 1 | 0 | 0 | 0.0 | 4 | 3 | 10 | 6 | 0 | .102 | .122 | 1 | 0 | 3B-15, SS-14, 2B-2 |
| 1948 2 teams | STL | N (2G – .000) | | | | CHI | N (16G – .100) | | | | | | | | | | |
| " total | 18 | 20 | 2 | 0 | 0 | 0 | 0.0 | 1 | 0 | 0 | 4 | 0 | .100 | .100 | 4 | 0 | SS-9, 2B-1 |
| 4 yrs. | 119 | 142 | 23 | 4 | 0 | 0 | 0.0 | 22 | 10 | 20 | 18 | 4 | .162 | .190 | 8 | 0 | SS-41, 3B-16, 2B-11 |
| 1 yr. | 16 | 20 | 2 | 0 | 0 | 0 | 0.0 | 1 | 0 | 0 | 4 | 0 | .100 | .100 | 4 | 0 | SS-9, 2B-1 |

## Hector Cruz

CRUZ, HECTOR (Heity)
Born Hector Cruz Dilan.  Brother of Jose Cruz.
Brother of Tommy Cruz.
B. Apr. 2, 1953, Arroyo, Puerto Rico

BR TR 5'11" 170 lbs.

| | G | AB | H | 2B | 3B | HR | HR % | R | RBI | BB | SO | SB | BA | SA | AB | H | G by POS |
|---|---|---|---|---|---|---|---|---|---|---|---|---|---|---|---|---|---|
| 1973 STL N | 11 | 11 | 0 | 0 | 0 | 0 | 0.0 | 0 | 0 | 0 | 3 | 0 | .000 | .000 | 4 | 0 | OF-5 |
| 1975 | 23 | 48 | 7 | 2 | 0 | 0 | 0.0 | 7 | 6 | 2 | 4 | 0 | .146 | .271 | 6 | 0 | 3B-12, OF-6 |
| 1976 | 151 | 526 | 120 | 17 | 1 | 13 | 2.5 | 54 | 71 | 42 | 119 | 1 | .228 | .338 | 3 | 0 | 3B-148 |
| 1977 | 118 | 339 | 80 | 19 | 2 | 6 | 1.8 | 50 | 42 | 46 | 56 | 2 | .236 | .357 | 15 | 2 | OF-106, 3B-2 |
| 1978 2 teams | CHI | N (30G – .237) | | | | SF | N (79G – .223) | | | | | | | | | | |
| " total | 109 | 273 | 62 | 13 | 4 | 8 | 2.9 | 27 | 33 | 24 | 45 | 0 | .227 | .370 | 30 | 7 | OF-67, 3B-21 |
| 1979 2 teams | SF | N (16G – .120) | | | | CIN | N (74G – .242) | | | | | | | | | | |
| " total | 90 | 207 | 47 | 10 | 2 | 4 | 1.9 | 26 | 28 | 34 | 46 | 0 | .227 | .353 | 16 | 2 | OF-75, 3B-2 |
| 1980 CIN N | 52 | 75 | 16 | 4 | 1 | 1 | 1.3 | 5 | 5 | 8 | 16 | 0 | .213 | .333 | 22 | 1 | OF-29 |
| 1981 CHI N | 53 | 109 | 25 | 5 | 0 | 7 | 6.4 | 15 | 15 | 17 | 24 | 2 | .229 | .468 | 17 | 3 | 3B-18, OF-16 |
| 1982 | 19 | 19 | 4 | 1 | 0 | 0 | 0.0 | 1 | 0 | 2 | 4 | 0 | .211 | .263 | 15 | 3 | OF-4 |
| 9 yrs. | 624 | 1607 | 361 | 71 | 9 | 39 | 2.4 | 186 | 200 | 176 | 317 | 5 | .225 | .353 | 128 | 19 | OF-308, 3B-203 |
| 3 yrs. | 100 | 204 | 47 | 11 | 2 | 9 | 4.4 | 24 | 24 | 22 | 34 | 2 | .230 | .417 | 42 | 8 | OF-34, 3B-25 |
| LEAGUE CHAMPIONSHIP SERIES | | | | | | | | | | | | | | | | | |
| 1979 CIN N | 2 | 5 | 1 | 1 | 0 | 0 | 0.0 | 0 | 0 | 0 | 1 | 0 | .200 | .400 | 1 | 1 | OF-1 |

| | G | AB | H | 2B | 3B | HR | HR % | R | RBI | BB | SO | SB | BA | SA | Pinch Hit AB | Pinch Hit H | G by POS |
|---|---|---|---|---|---|---|---|---|---|---|---|---|---|---|---|---|---|

## Dick Culler

**CULLER, RICHARD BROADUS**
B. Jan. 25, 1915, High Point, N. C.     D. June 16, 1964, Chapel Hill, N. C.
BR  TR  5'9½"  155 lbs.

| | G | AB | H | 2B | 3B | HR | HR % | R | RBI | BB | SO | SB | BA | SA | PH AB | PH H | G by POS |
|---|---|---|---|---|---|---|---|---|---|---|---|---|---|---|---|---|---|
| 1936 PHI A | 9 | 38 | 9 | 0 | 0 | 0 | 0.0 | 3 | 1 | 1 | 3 | 0 | .237 | .237 | 0 | 0 | 2B-7, SS-2 |
| 1943 CHI A | 53 | 148 | 32 | 5 | 1 | 0 | 0.0 | 9 | 11 | 16 | 11 | 4 | .216 | .264 | 0 | 0 | 3B-26, 2B-19, SS-3 |
| 1944 BOS N | 8 | 28 | 2 | 0 | 0 | 0 | 0.0 | 2 | 0 | 4 | 2 | 0 | .071 | .071 | 0 | 0 | SS-8 |
| 1945 | 136 | 527 | 138 | 12 | 1 | 2 | 0.4 | 87 | 30 | 50 | 35 | 7 | .262 | .300 | 1 | 0 | SS-126, 3B-6 |
| 1946 | 134 | 482 | 123 | 15 | 3 | 0 | 0.0 | 70 | 33 | 62 | 18 | 7 | .255 | .299 | 2 | 1 | SS-132 |
| 1947 | 77 | 214 | 53 | 5 | 1 | 0 | 0.0 | 20 | 19 | 19 | 15 | 1 | .248 | .280 | 1 | 1 | SS-75 |
| 1948 CHI N | 48 | 89 | 15 | 2 | 0 | 0 | 0.0 | 4 | 5 | 13 | 3 | 0 | .169 | .191 | 1 | 0 | SS-43, 2B-2 |
| 1949 NY N | 7 | 1 | 0 | 0 | 0 | 0 | 0.0 | 0 | 0 | 1 | 0 | 0 | .000 | .000 | 0 | 0 | SS-7 |
| 8 yrs. | 472 | 1527 | 372 | 39 | 6 | 2 | 0.1 | 195 | 99 | 166 | 87 | 19 | .244 | .281 | 5 | 2 | SS-396, 3B-32, 2B-28 |
| 1 yr. | 48 | 89 | 15 | 2 | 0 | 0 | 0.0 | 4 | 5 | 13 | 3 | 0 | .169 | .191 | 1 | 0 | SS-43, 2B-2 |

## Doc Curley

**CURLEY, WALTER JAMES**
B. Mar. 12, 1874, Upton, Mass.     D. Sept. 23, 1920, Worcester, Mass.
BR  TR

| | G | AB | H | 2B | 3B | HR | HR % | R | RBI | BB | SO | SB | BA | SA | PH AB | PH H | G by POS |
|---|---|---|---|---|---|---|---|---|---|---|---|---|---|---|---|---|---|
| 1899 CHI N | 10 | 37 | 4 | 0 | 1 | 0 | 0.0 | 7 | 2 | 3 | | 0 | .108 | .162 | 0 | 0 | 2B-10 |

## Jack Cusick

**CUSICK, JOHN PETER**
B. June 12, 1928, Weehawken, N. J.
BR  TR  6'  170 lbs.

| | G | AB | H | 2B | 3B | HR | HR % | R | RBI | BB | SO | SB | BA | SA | PH AB | PH H | G by POS |
|---|---|---|---|---|---|---|---|---|---|---|---|---|---|---|---|---|---|
| 1951 CHI N | 65 | 164 | 29 | 3 | 2 | 2 | 1.2 | 16 | 16 | 17 | 29 | 2 | .177 | .256 | 3 | 1 | SS-56 |
| 1952 BOS N | 49 | 78 | 13 | 1 | 0 | 0 | 0.0 | 5 | 6 | 6 | 9 | 0 | .167 | .179 | 9 | 1 | SS-28, 3B-3 |
| 2 yrs. | 114 | 242 | 42 | 4 | 2 | 2 | 0.8 | 21 | 22 | 23 | 38 | 2 | .174 | .231 | 12 | 2 | SS-84, 3B-3 |
| 1 yr. | 65 | 164 | 29 | 3 | 2 | 2 | 1.2 | 16 | 16 | 17 | 29 | 2 | .177 | .256 | 3 | 1 | SS-56 |

## Kiki Cuyler

**CUYLER, HAZEN SHIRLEY**
B. Aug. 30, 1899, Harrisville, Mich.     D. Feb. 11, 1950, Ann Arbor, Mich.
Hall of Fame 1968.
BR  TR  5'10½"  180 lbs.

| | G | AB | H | 2B | 3B | HR | HR % | R | RBI | BB | SO | SB | BA | SA | PH AB | PH H | G by POS |
|---|---|---|---|---|---|---|---|---|---|---|---|---|---|---|---|---|---|
| 1921 PIT N | 1 | 3 | 0 | 0 | 0 | 0 | 0.0 | 0 | 0 | 0 | 1 | 0 | .000 | .000 | 0 | 0 | OF-1 |
| 1922 | 1 | 0 | 0 | 0 | 0 | 0 | – | 0 | 0 | 0 | 0 | 0 | – | – | 0 | 0 | |
| 1923 | 11 | 40 | 10 | 1 | 1 | 0 | 0.0 | 4 | 2 | 5 | 3 | 2 | .250 | .325 | 0 | 0 | OF-11 |
| 1924 | 117 | 466 | 165 | 27 | 16 | 9 | 1.9 | 94 | 85 | 30 | 62 | 32 | .354 | .539 | 3 | 1 | OF-114 |
| 1925 | 153 | 617 | 220 | 43 | 26 | 17 | 2.8 | 144 | 102 | 58 | 56 | 41 | .357 | .593 | 0 | 0 | OF-153 |
| 1926 | 157 | 614 | 197 | 31 | 15 | 8 | 1.3 | 113 | 92 | 50 | 66 | 35 | .321 | .459 | 0 | 0 | OF-157 |
| 1927 | 85 | 285 | 88 | 13 | 7 | 3 | 1.1 | 60 | 31 | 37 | 36 | 20 | .309 | .435 | 11 | 2 | OF-73 |
| 1928 CHI N | 133 | 499 | 142 | 25 | 9 | 17 | 3.4 | 92 | 79 | 51 | 61 | 37 | .285 | .473 | 5 | 0 | OF-127 |
| 1929 | 139 | 509 | 183 | 29 | 7 | 15 | 2.9 | 111 | 102 | 66 | 56 | 43 | .360 | .532 | 9 | 4 | OF-129 |
| 1930 | 156 | 642 | 228 | 50 | 17 | 13 | 2.0 | 155 | 134 | 72 | 49 | 37 | .355 | .547 | 0 | 0 | OF-156 |
| 1931 | 154 | 613 | 202 | 37 | 12 | 9 | 1.5 | 110 | 88 | 72 | 54 | 13 | .330 | .473 | 1 | 0 | OF-153 |
| 1932 | 110 | 446 | 130 | 19 | 9 | 10 | 2.2 | 58 | 77 | 29 | 43 | 9 | .291 | .442 | 1 | 0 | OF-109 |
| 1933 | 70 | 262 | 83 | 13 | 3 | 5 | 1.9 | 37 | 35 | 21 | 29 | 4 | .317 | .447 | 1 | 0 | OF-69 |
| 1934 | 142 | 559 | 189 | 42 | 8 | 6 | 1.1 | 80 | 69 | 31 | 62 | 15 | .338 | .474 | 0 | 0 | OF-142 |
| 1935 2 teams | CHI | N (45G – | .268) | | CIN | N | (62G – | .251) | | | | | | | | | |
| " total | 107 | 380 | 98 | 13 | 4 | 6 | 1.6 | 58 | 40 | 37 | 34 | 8 | .258 | .361 | 6 | 2 | OF-99 |
| 1936 CIN N | 144 | 567 | 185 | 29 | 11 | 7 | 1.2 | 96 | 74 | 47 | 67 | 16 | .326 | .453 | 4 | 2 | OF-140 |
| 1937 | 117 | 406 | 110 | 12 | 4 | 0 | 0.0 | 48 | 32 | 36 | 50 | 10 | .271 | .320 | 10 | 2 | OF-106 |
| 1938 BKN N | 82 | 253 | 69 | 10 | 8 | 2 | 0.8 | 45 | 23 | 34 | 23 | 6 | .273 | .399 | 11 | 1 | OF-68 |
| 18 yrs. | 1879 | 7161 | 2299 | 394 | 157 | 127 | 1.8 | 1305 | 1065 | 676 | 752 | 328 | .321 | .473 | 62 | 14 | OF-1807 |
| 8 yrs. | 949 | 3687 | 1199 | 220 | 66 | 79 | 2.1 | 665 | 602 | 352 | 370 | 161 | .325 | .485 | 20 | 6 | OF-927 |
| | | | | | | | | | | | | 8th | 4th | 7th | | | |

**WORLD SERIES**

| | G | AB | H | 2B | 3B | HR | HR % | R | RBI | BB | SO | SB | BA | SA | PH AB | PH H | G by POS |
|---|---|---|---|---|---|---|---|---|---|---|---|---|---|---|---|---|---|
| 1925 PIT N | 7 | 26 | 7 | 3 | 0 | 1 | 3.8 | 3 | 6 | 1 | 4 | 0 | .269 | .500 | 0 | 0 | OF-7 |
| 1929 CHI N | 5 | 20 | 6 | 1 | 0 | 0 | 0.0 | 4 | 4 | 1 | 7 | 0 | .300 | .350 | 0 | 0 | OF-5 |
| 1932 | 4 | 18 | 5 | 1 | 1 | 1 | 5.6 | 2 | 2 | 0 | 3 | 1 | .278 | .611 | 0 | 0 | OF-4 |
| 3 yrs. | 16 | 64 | 18 | 5 | 1 | 2 | 3.1 | 9 | 12 | 2 | 14 | 1 | .281 | .484 | 0 | 0 | OF-16 |

## Bill Dahlen

**DAHLEN, WILLIAM FREDERICK (Bad Bill)**
B. Jan. 5, 1870, Nelliston, N. Y.     D. Dec. 5, 1950, Brooklyn, N. Y.
Manager 1910-13.
BR  TR  5'9"  180 lbs.

| | G | AB | H | 2B | 3B | HR | HR % | R | RBI | BB | SO | SB | BA | SA | PH AB | PH H | G by POS |
|---|---|---|---|---|---|---|---|---|---|---|---|---|---|---|---|---|---|
| 1891 CHI N | 135 | 551 | 145 | 20 | 13 | 9 | 1.6 | 116 | 76 | 67 | 60 | 29 | .263 | .396 | 0 | 0 | 3B-84, OF-37, SS-15 |
| 1892 | 143 | 587 | 173 | 23 | 19 | 5 | 0.9 | 116 | 58 | 45 | 56 | 60 | .295 | .424 | 0 | 0 | SS-72, 3B-68, OF-2, 2B-1 |
| 1893 | 116 | 485 | 146 | 28 | 15 | 5 | 1.0 | 113 | 64 | 58 | 30 | 31 | .301 | .452 | 0 | 0 | SS-88, OF-17, 2B-10, 3B-3 |
| 1894 | 121 | 508 | 184 | 32 | 14 | 15 | 3.0 | 150 | 107 | 76 | 33 | 42 | .362 | .569 | 0 | 0 | SS-66, 3B-55 |
| 1895 | 129 | 509 | 139 | 19 | 10 | 7 | 1.4 | 107 | 62 | 61 | 51 | 38 | .273 | .391 | 0 | 0 | SS-129, OF-1 |
| 1896 | 125 | 476 | 172 | 30 | 19 | 9 | 1.9 | 153 | 74 | 64 | 36 | 51 | .361 | .561 | 0 | 0 | SS-125 |
| 1897 | 75 | 277 | 82 | 18 | 8 | 6 | 2.2 | 67 | 40 | 43 | | 15 | .296 | .484 | 0 | 0 | SS-75 |
| 1898 | 142 | 524 | 152 | 35 | 8 | 1 | 0.2 | 96 | 79 | 58 | | 27 | .290 | .393 | 0 | 0 | SS-142 |
| 1899 BKN N | 121 | 428 | 121 | 22 | 7 | 4 | 0.9 | 87 | 76 | 67 | | 29 | .283 | .395 | 0 | 0 | SS-110, 3B-11 |
| 1900 | 133 | 483 | 125 | 16 | 11 | 1 | 0.2 | 87 | 69 | 73 | | 31 | .259 | .344 | 0 | 0 | SS-133 |
| 1901 | 131 | 513 | 134 | 17 | 10 | 4 | 0.8 | 69 | 82 | 30 | | 23 | .261 | .357 | 0 | 0 | SS-129, 2B-2 |
| 1902 | 138 | 527 | 139 | 26 | 7 | 2 | 0.4 | 67 | 74 | 43 | | 20 | .264 | .351 | 0 | 0 | SS-138 |
| 1903 | 138 | 474 | 124 | 17 | 9 | 1 | 0.2 | 71 | 64 | 82 | | 34 | .262 | .342 | 0 | 0 | SS-138 |
| 1904 NY N | 145 | 523 | 140 | 26 | 2 | 2 | 0.4 | 70 | 80 | 44 | | 47 | .268 | .337 | 0 | 0 | SS-145 |
| 1905 | 148 | 520 | 126 | 20 | 4 | 7 | 1.3 | 67 | 81 | 62 | | 37 | .242 | .337 | 0 | 0 | SS-147, OF-1 |
| 1906 | 143 | 471 | 113 | 18 | 3 | 1 | 0.2 | 63 | 49 | 76 | | 16 | .240 | .297 | 0 | 0 | SS-143 |
| 1907 | 143 | 464 | 96 | 20 | 1 | 0 | 0.0 | 40 | 34 | 51 | | 11 | .207 | .254 | 0 | 0 | SS-143 |
| 1908 BOS N | 144 | 524 | 125 | 23 | 2 | 3 | 0.6 | 50 | 48 | 35 | | 10 | .239 | .307 | 0 | 0 | SS-144 |
| 1909 | 69 | 197 | 46 | 6 | 1 | 2 | 1.0 | 22 | 16 | 29 | | 4 | .234 | .305 | 8 | 2 | SS-49, 2B-6, 3B-2 |
| 1910 BKN N | 3 | 2 | 0 | 0 | 0 | 0 | 0.0 | 0 | 0 | 0 | 0 | 0 | .000 | .000 | 2 | 0 | |

| | G | AB | H | 2B | 3B | HR | HR % | R | RBI | BB | SO | SB | BA | SA | Pinch Hit AB | H | G by POS |
|---|---|---|---|---|---|---|---|---|---|---|---|---|---|---|---|---|---|

## Bill Dahlen continued

| | G | AB | H | 2B | 3B | HR | HR % | R | RBI | BB | SO | SB | BA | SA | AB | H | G by POS |
|---|---|---|---|---|---|---|---|---|---|---|---|---|---|---|---|---|---|
| 1911 | 1 | 3 | 0 | 0 | 0 | 0 | 0.0 | 0 | 0 | 0 | 3 | 0 | .000 | .000 | 0 | 0 | SS-1 |
| 21 yrs. | 2443 | 9046 | 2482 | 416 | 163 | 84 | 0.9 | 1611 | 1233 | 1064 | 269 | 555 | .274 | .384 | 10 | 2 | SS-2132, 3B-223, OF-5, 2B-19 |
| 8 yrs. | 986 | 3917 | 1193 | 205 | 106 | 57 | 1.5 | 918 | 560 | 472 | 266 | 293 | .305 | .455 | 0 | 0 | SS-712, 3B-210, OF-57, 2B-11 |
| | | | | | 4th | | | 8th | | | | | | | | | |

WORLD SERIES

| | G | AB | H | 2B | 3B | HR | HR % | R | RBI | BB | SO | SB | BA | SA | AB | H | G by POS |
|---|---|---|---|---|---|---|---|---|---|---|---|---|---|---|---|---|---|
| 1905 NY N | 5 | 15 | 0 | 0 | 0 | 0 | 0.0 | 1 | 1 | 3 | 2 | 2 | .000 | .000 | 0 | 0 | SS-5 |

## Babe Dahlgren

**DAHLGREN, ELLSWORTH TENNEY**     BR TR 6'   190 lbs

B. June 15, 1912, San Francisco, Calif.

| | G | AB | H | 2B | 3B | HR | HR % | R | RBI | BB | SO | SB | BA | SA | AB | H | G by POS |
|---|---|---|---|---|---|---|---|---|---|---|---|---|---|---|---|---|---|
| 1935 BOS A | 149 | 525 | 138 | 27 | 7 | 9 | 1.7 | 77 | 63 | 56 | 67 | 6 | .263 | .392 | 0 | 0 | 1B-149 |
| 1936 | 16 | 57 | 16 | 3 | 1 | 1 | 1.8 | 6 | 7 | 7 | 1 | 2 | .281 | .421 | 0 | 0 | 1B-16 |
| 1937 NY A | 1 | 1 | 0 | 0 | 0 | 0 | 0.0 | 0 | 0 | 0 | 0 | 0 | .000 | .000 | 1 | 0 | |
| 1938 | 29 | 43 | 8 | 1 | 0 | 0 | 0.0 | 8 | 1 | 1 | 7 | 0 | .186 | .209 | 6 | 0 | 3B-8, 1B-6 |
| 1939 | 144 | 531 | 125 | 18 | 6 | 15 | 2.8 | 71 | 89 | 57 | 54 | 2 | .235 | .377 | 0 | 0 | 1B-144 |
| 1940 | 155 | 568 | 150 | 24 | 4 | 12 | 2.1 | 51 | 73 | 46 | 54 | 1 | .264 | .384 | 0 | 0 | 1B-155 |
| 1941 2 teams | | BOS | N | (44G – | .235) | | CHI | N | (99G – | .281) | | | | | | | |
| " total | 143 | 525 | 140 | 28 | 2 | 23 | 4.4 | 70 | 89 | 59 | 52 | 2 | .267 | .459 | 1 | 0 | 1B-137, 3B-5 |
| 1942 3 teams | | CHI | N | (17G – | .214) | | STL | A | (2G – | .000) | | BKN | N | (17G – | .053) | | |
| " total | 36 | 77 | 13 | 1 | 0 | 0 | 0.0 | 6 | 6 | 8 | 7 | 0 | .169 | .182 | 8 | 0 | 1B-24 |
| 1943 PHI N | 136 | 508 | 146 | 19 | 2 | 5 | 1.0 | 55 | 56 | 50 | 39 | 2 | .287 | .362 | 3 | 2 | 1B-73, 3B-35, SS-25, C- |
| 1944 PIT N | 158 | 599 | 173 | 28 | 7 | 12 | 2.0 | 67 | 101 | 47 | 56 | 2 | .289 | .419 | 0 | 0 | 1B-158 |
| 1945 | 144 | 531 | 133 | 24 | 8 | 5 | 0.9 | 57 | 75 | 51 | 51 | 1 | .250 | .354 | 2 | 0 | 1B-142 |
| 1946 STL A | 28 | 80 | 14 | 1 | 0 | 0 | 0.0 | 2 | 9 | 8 | 13 | 0 | .175 | .188 | 4 | 1 | 1B-24 |
| 12 yrs. | 1139 | 4045 | 1056 | 174 | 37 | 82 | 2.0 | 470 | 569 | 390 | 401 | 18 | .261 | .383 | 25 | 3 | 1B-1028, 3B-48, SS-25, C-1 |
| 2 yrs. | 116 | 415 | 113 | 21 | 1 | 16 | 3.9 | 54 | 65 | 47 | 41 | 2 | .272 | .443 | 2 | 0 | 1B-112 |

WORLD SERIES

| | G | AB | H | 2B | 3B | HR | HR % | R | RBI | BB | SO | SB | BA | SA | AB | H | G by POS |
|---|---|---|---|---|---|---|---|---|---|---|---|---|---|---|---|---|---|
| 1939 NY A | 4 | 14 | 3 | 2 | 0 | 1 | 7.1 | 2 | 2 | 0 | 4 | 0 | .214 | .571 | 0 | 0 | 1B-4 |

## Con Daily

**DAILY, CORNELIUS F.**     BL   6'   192 lbs

Brother of Ed Daily.

B. Sept. 11, 1864, Blackstone, Mass.    D. June 14, 1928, Brooklyn, N. Y.

| | G | AB | H | 2B | 3B | HR | HR % | R | RBI | BB | SO | SB | BA | SA | AB | H | G by POS |
|---|---|---|---|---|---|---|---|---|---|---|---|---|---|---|---|---|---|
| 1884 PHI U | 2 | 8 | 0 | 0 | 0 | 0 | 0.0 | 0 | | 0 | | | .000 | .000 | 0 | 0 | C-2 |
| 1885 PRO N | 60 | 223 | 58 | 6 | 1 | 0 | 0.0 | 20 | 19 | 12 | 20 | | .260 | .296 | 0 | 0 | C-48, 1B-7, OF-6 |
| 1886 BOS N | 50 | 180 | 43 | 4 | 2 | 0 | 0.0 | 25 | 21 | 19 | 29 | | .239 | .283 | 0 | 0 | C-49 |
| 1887 | 36 | 120 | 19 | 5 | 0 | 0 | 0.0 | 12 | 13 | 9 | 8 | 7 | .158 | .200 | 0 | 0 | C-36 |
| 1888 IND N | 57 | 202 | 44 | 6 | 1 | 0 | 0.0 | 14 | 14 | 10 | 28 | 15 | .218 | .257 | 0 | 0 | C-42, OF-5, 3B-5, 1B-5, 2B-1 |
| 1889 | 62 | 219 | 55 | 6 | 2 | 0 | 0.0 | 35 | 26 | 28 | 21 | 14 | .251 | .297 | 0 | 0 | C-51, OF-6, 1B-6, 3B-1 |
| 1890 BKN P | 46 | 168 | 42 | 6 | 3 | 0 | 0.0 | 20 | 35 | 15 | 14 | 6 | .250 | .321 | 0 | 0 | C-40, 1B-6, OF-1 |
| 1891 BKN N | 60 | 206 | 66 | 10 | 1 | 0 | 0.0 | 25 | 30 | 15 | 13 | 7 | .320 | .379 | 0 | 0 | C-55, OF-3, SS-2, 1B-1 |
| 1892 | 80 | 278 | 65 | 10 | 1 | 0 | 0.0 | 38 | 28 | 38 | 21 | 18 | .234 | .277 | 0 | 0 | C-68, OF-13 |
| 1893 | 61 | 215 | 57 | 4 | 2 | 1 | 0.5 | 33 | 32 | 20 | 12 | 13 | .265 | .316 | 1 | 1 | C-51, OF-9 |
| 1894 | 67 | 234 | 60 | 14 | 7 | 0 | 0.0 | 40 | 32 | 31 | 22 | 8 | .256 | .376 | 0 | 0 | C-60, 1B-7 |
| 1895 | 40 | 142 | 30 | 3 | 2 | 1 | 0.7 | 17 | 11 | 10 | 18 | 3 | .211 | .282 | 0 | 0 | C-39, OF-1 |
| 1896 CHI N | 9 | 27 | 2 | 0 | 0 | 0 | 0.0 | 1 | 1 | 1 | 2 | 1 | .074 | .074 | 0 | 0 | C-9 |
| 13 yrs. | 630 | 2222 | 541 | 74 | 22 | 2 | 0.1 | 280 | 261 | 208 | 208 | 92 | .243 | .299 | 1 | 1 | C-550, OF-44, 1B-32, 3B-6, SS-2, 2B-1 |
| 1 yr. | 9 | 27 | 2 | 0 | 0 | 0 | 0.0 | 1 | 1 | 1 | 2 | 1 | .074 | .074 | 0 | 0 | C-9 |

## Dom Dallessandro

**DALLESSANDRO, NICHOLAS DOMINIC (Dim Dom)**     BL TL 5'6"   168 lbs.

B. Oct. 3, 1913, Reading, Pa.

| | G | AB | H | 2B | 3B | HR | HR % | R | RBI | BB | SO | SB | BA | SA | AB | H | G by POS |
|---|---|---|---|---|---|---|---|---|---|---|---|---|---|---|---|---|---|
| 1937 BOS A | 68 | 147 | 34 | 7 | 1 | 0 | 0.0 | 18 | 11 | 27 | 16 | 2 | .231 | .293 | 26 | 7 | OF-35 |
| 1940 CHI N | 107 | 287 | 77 | 19 | 6 | 1 | 0.3 | 33 | 36 | 34 | 13 | 4 | .268 | .387 | 29 | 10 | OF-74 |
| 1941 | 140 | 486 | 132 | 36 | 2 | 6 | 1.2 | 73 | 85 | 68 | 37 | 3 | .272 | .391 | 7 | 1 | OF-131 |
| 1942 | 96 | 264 | 69 | 12 | 4 | 4 | 1.5 | 30 | 43 | 36 | 18 | 4 | .261 | .383 | 26 | 9 | OF-66 |
| 1943 | 87 | 176 | 39 | 8 | 3 | 1 | 0.6 | 13 | 31 | 40 | 14 | 1 | .222 | .318 | 32 | 8 | OF-45 |
| 1944 | 117 | 381 | 116 | 19 | 4 | 8 | 2.1 | 53 | 74 | 61 | 29 | 1 | .304 | .438 | 11 | 3 | OF-106 |
| 1946 | 65 | 89 | 20 | 2 | 2 | 1 | 1.1 | 4 | 9 | 23 | 12 | 1 | .225 | .326 | 29 | 6 | OF-20 |
| 1947 | 66 | 115 | 33 | 7 | 1 | 1 | 0.9 | 18 | 14 | 21 | 11 | 0 | .287 | .391 | 32 | 8 | OF-28 |
| 8 yrs. | 746 | 1945 | 520 | 110 | 23 | 22 | 1.1 | 242 | 303 | 310 | 150 | 16 | .267 | .381 | 192 | 52 | OF-505 |
| 7 yrs. | 678 | 1798 | 486 | 103 | 22 | 22 | 1.2 | 224 | 292 | 283 | 134 | 14 | .270 | .389 | 166 | 45 | OF-470 |
| | | | | | | | | | | | | | | | 4th | 4th | |

## Abner Dalrymple

**DALRYMPLE, ABNER FRANK**     BL TR 5'10½" 175 lbs.

B. Sept. 9, 1857, Warren, Ill.    D. Jan. 25, 1939, Warren, Ill.

| | G | AB | H | 2B | 3B | HR | HR % | R | RBI | BB | SO | SB | BA | SA | AB | H | G by POS |
|---|---|---|---|---|---|---|---|---|---|---|---|---|---|---|---|---|---|
| 1878 MIL N | 61 | 271 | 96 | 10 | 4 | 0 | 0.0 | 52 | 15 | 6 | 29 | | .354 | .421 | 0 | 0 | OF-61 |
| 1879 CHI N | 71 | 333 | 97 | 25 | 1 | 0 | 0.0 | 47 | 23 | 4 | 29 | | .291 | .372 | 0 | 0 | OF-71 |
| 1880 | 86 | 382 | 126 | 25 | 12 | 0 | 0.0 | 91 | 36 | 3 | 18 | | .330 | .458 | 0 | 0 | OF-86 |
| 1881 | 82 | 362 | 117 | 22 | 4 | 1 | 0.3 | 72 | 37 | 15 | 22 | | .323 | .414 | 0 | 0 | OF-82 |
| 1882 | 84 | 397 | 117 | 25 | 11 | 1 | 0.3 | 96 | 36 | 14 | 18 | | .295 | .421 | 0 | 0 | OF-84 |
| 1883 | 80 | 363 | 108 | 24 | 4 | 2 | 0.6 | 78 | | 11 | 29 | | .298 | .402 | 0 | 0 | OF-80 |
| 1884 | 111 | 521 | 161 | 18 | 9 | 22 | 4.2 | 111 | | 14 | 39 | | .309 | .505 | 0 | 0 | OF-111 |
| 1885 | 113 | 492 | 135 | 27 | 12 | 11 | 2.2 | 109 | 58 | 46 | 42 | | .274 | .445 | 0 | 0 | OF-113 |
| 1886 | 82 | 331 | 77 | 12 | 3 | 3 | 0.9 | 62 | 26 | 33 | 44 | | .233 | .353 | 0 | 0 | OF-82 |
| 1887 PIT N | 92 | 358 | 76 | 18 | 5 | 2 | 0.6 | 45 | 31 | 45 | 43 | 29 | .212 | .307 | 0 | 0 | OF-92 |
| 1888 | 57 | 227 | 50 | 9 | 2 | 0 | 0.0 | 19 | 14 | 6 | 28 | 7 | .220 | .278 | 0 | 0 | OF-57 |

| | G | AB | H | 2B | 3B | HR | HR % | R | RBI | BB | SO | SB | BA | SA | Pinch Hit AB | Pinch Hit H | G by POS |
|---|---|---|---|---|---|---|---|---|---|---|---|---|---|---|---|---|---|

## Abner Dalrymple continued

| | G | AB | H | 2B | 3B | HR | HR% | R | RBI | BB | SO | SB | BA | SA | AB | H | G by POS |
|---|---|---|---|---|---|---|---|---|---|---|---|---|---|---|---|---|---|
| 1891 C-M AA | 32 | 135 | 42 | 7 | 5 | 1 | 0.7 | 31 | 22 | 7 | 18 | 6 | .311 | .459 | 0 | 0 | OF-32 |
| 12 yrs. | 951 | 4172 | 1202 | 217 | 81 | 43 | 1.0 | 813 | 298 | 204 | 359 | 42 | .288 | .410 | 0 | 0 | OF-951 |
| 8 yrs. | 709 | 3181 | 938 | 173 | 65 | 40 | 1.3 | 666 | 216 | 140 | 241 | | .295 | .428 | 0 | 0 | OF-709 |

## Tom Daly

**DALY, THOMAS DANIEL**　　　　　　　　　BR TR 5'11½" 171 lbs.
B. Dec. 12, 1891, St. John, N. B., Canada　　D. Nov. 7, 1946, Bedford, Mass.

| | G | AB | H | 2B | 3B | HR | HR% | R | RBI | BB | SO | SB | BA | SA | AB | H | G by POS |
|---|---|---|---|---|---|---|---|---|---|---|---|---|---|---|---|---|---|
| 1913 CHI A | 1 | 3 | 0 | 0 | 0 | 0 | 0.0 | 0 | 0 | 0 | 0 | 0 | .000 | .000 | 0 | 0 | C-1 |
| 1914 | 61 | 133 | 31 | 2 | 0 | 0 | 0.0 | 13 | 8 | 7 | 13 | 3 | .233 | .248 | 24 | 6 | OF-23, 3B-5, C-4, 1B-2 |
| 1915 | 29 | 47 | 9 | 1 | 0 | 0 | 0.0 | 5 | 3 | 5 | 9 | 0 | .191 | .213 | 9 | 1 | C-19, 1B-1 |
| 1916 CLE A | 31 | 73 | 16 | 1 | 1 | 0 | 0.0 | 3 | 8 | 1 | 2 | 0 | .219 | .260 | 5 | 1 | C-25, OF-1 |
| 1918 CHI N | 1 | 1 | 0 | 0 | 0 | 0 | 0.0 | 0 | 0 | 0 | 0 | 0 | .000 | .000 | 0 | 0 | C-1 |
| 1919 | 25 | 50 | 11 | 0 | 1 | 0 | 0.0 | 4 | 1 | 2 | 5 | 0 | .220 | .260 | 6 | 0 | C-18 |
| 1920 | 44 | 90 | 28 | 6 | 0 | 0 | 0.0 | 12 | 13 | 2 | 6 | 1 | .311 | .378 | 14 | 4 | C-29 |
| 1921 | 51 | 143 | 34 | 7 | 1 | 0 | 0.0 | 12 | 22 | 8 | 8 | 1 | .238 | .301 | 4 | 1 | C-47 |
| 8 yrs. | 243 | 540 | 129 | 17 | 3 | 0 | 0.0 | 49 | 55 | 25 | 43 | 5 | .239 | .281 | 62 | 13 | C-144, OF-24, 3B-5, 1B-3 |
| 4 yrs. | 121 | 284 | 73 | 13 | 2 | 0 | 0.0 | 28 | 36 | 12 | 19 | 2 | .257 | .317 | 24 | 5 | C-95 |

## Tom Daly

**DALY, THOMAS PETER (Tido)**　　　　　　　BB TR 5'7" 170 lbs.
Brother of Joe Daly.
B. Feb. 7, 1866, Philadelphia, Pa.　　D. Oct. 29, 1939, Brooklyn, N. Y.

| | G | AB | H | 2B | 3B | HR | HR% | R | RBI | BB | SO | SB | BA | SA | AB | H | G by POS |
|---|---|---|---|---|---|---|---|---|---|---|---|---|---|---|---|---|---|
| 1887 CHI N | 74 | 256 | 53 | 10 | 4 | 2 | 0.8 | 45 | 17 | 22 | 25 | 29 | .207 | .301 | 0 | 0 | C-64, OF-8, SS-2, 2B-2, 1B-2 |
| 1888 | 65 | 219 | 42 | 2 | 6 | 0 | 0.0 | 34 | 29 | 10 | 26 | 10 | .192 | .256 | 0 | 0 | C-62, OF-4 |
| 1889 WAS N | 71 | 250 | 75 | 13 | 5 | 1 | 0.4 | 39 | 40 | 38 | 28 | 18 | .300 | .404 | 0 | 0 | C-57, 1B-8, 2B-4, OF-3, SS-1 |
| 1890 BKN N | 82 | 292 | 71 | 9 | 4 | 5 | 1.7 | 55 | 43 | 32 | 43 | 20 | .243 | .353 | 0 | 0 | C-69, 1B-12, OF-1 |
| 1891 | 58 | 200 | 50 | 11 | 5 | 2 | 1.0 | 29 | 27 | 21 | 34 | 7 | .250 | .385 | 0 | 0 | C-26, 1B-15, SS-11, OF-7 |
| 1892 | 124 | 446 | 114 | 15 | 6 | 4 | 0.9 | 76 | 51 | 64 | 61 | 34 | .256 | .343 | 0 | 0 | 3B-57, OF-30, C-27, 2B-10 |
| 1893 | 126 | 470 | 136 | 21 | 14 | 8 | 1.7 | 94 | 70 | 76 | 65 | 32 | .289 | .445 | 0 | 0 | 2B-82, 3B-45 |
| 1894 | 123 | 492 | 168 | 22 | 10 | 8 | 1.6 | 135 | 82 | 77 | 42 | 51 | .341 | .476 | 0 | 0 | 2B-123 |
| 1895 | 120 | 455 | 128 | 17 | 8 | 2 | 0.4 | 89 | 68 | 52 | 52 | 28 | .281 | .367 | 0 | 0 | 2B-120 |
| 1896 | 67 | 224 | 63 | 13 | 6 | 3 | 1.3 | 43 | 29 | 33 | 25 | 19 | .281 | .433 | 0 | 0 | 2B-66, C-1 |
| 1898 | 23 | 73 | 24 | 3 | 1 | 0 | 0.0 | 11 | 11 | 14 | | 6 | .329 | .397 | 0 | 0 | 2B-23 |
| 1899 | 141 | 498 | 156 | 24 | 9 | 5 | 1.0 | 95 | 88 | 69 | | 43 | .313 | .428 | 0 | 0 | 2B-141 |
| 1900 | 97 | 343 | 107 | 17 | 3 | 4 | 1.2 | 70 | 55 | 46 | | 27 | .312 | .414 | 0 | 0 | 2B-93, 1B-3, OF-2 |
| 1901 | 133 | 520 | 164 | 38 | 10 | 3 | 0.6 | 88 | 90 | 42 | | 31 | .315 | .444 | 0 | 0 | 2B-133 |
| 1902 CHI A | 137 | 489 | 110 | 22 | 4 | 1 | 0.2 | 57 | 54 | 55 | | 19 | .225 | .288 | 0 | 0 | 2B-137 |
| 1903 2 teams | | CHI | A | (43G – | .207) | | CIN | N | (80G – | .293) | | | | | | | |
| " total | 123 | 457 | 121 | 25 | 9 | 1 | 0.2 | 62 | 57 | 36 | | 11 | .265 | .365 | 1 | 0 | 2B-122 |
| 16 yrs. | 1564 | 5684 | 1582 | 262 | 103 | 49 | 0.9 | 1022 | 811 | 687 | 401 | 385 | .278 | .387 | 1 | 0 | 2B-1056, C-306, 3B-102, OF-55, 1B-40, SS-14 |
| 2 yrs. | 139 | 475 | 95 | 12 | 10 | 2 | 0.4 | 79 | 46 | 32 | 51 | 39 | .200 | .280 | 0 | 0 | C-126, OF-12, SS-2, 2B-2, 1B-2 |

## Alvin Dark

**DARK, ALVIN RALPH (Blackie)**　　　　　　BR TR 5'11" 185 lbs.
B. Jan. 7, 1922, Comanche, Okla.
Manager 1961-64, 1966-71, 1974-75, 1977.

| | G | AB | H | 2B | 3B | HR | HR% | R | RBI | BB | SO | SB | BA | SA | AB | H | G by POS |
|---|---|---|---|---|---|---|---|---|---|---|---|---|---|---|---|---|---|
| 1946 BOS N | 15 | 13 | 3 | 3 | 0 | 0 | 0.0 | 0 | 1 | 0 | 3 | 0 | .231 | .462 | 0 | 0 | SS-12, OF-1 |
| 1948 | 137 | 543 | 175 | 39 | 6 | 3 | 0.6 | 85 | 48 | 24 | 36 | 4 | .322 | .433 | 4 | 3 | SS-133 |
| 1949 | 130 | 529 | 146 | 23 | 5 | 3 | 0.6 | 74 | 53 | 31 | 43 | 5 | .276 | .355 | 0 | 0 | SS-125, 3B-4 |
| 1950 NY N | 154 | 587 | 164 | 36 | 5 | 16 | 2.7 | 79 | 67 | 39 | 60 | 9 | .279 | .440 | 0 | 0 | SS-154 |
| 1951 | 156 | 646 | 196 | 41 | 7 | 14 | 2.2 | 114 | 69 | 42 | 39 | 12 | .303 | .454 | 0 | 0 | SS-156 |
| 1952 | 151 | 589 | 177 | 29 | 3 | 14 | 2.4 | 92 | 73 | 47 | 39 | 6 | .301 | .431 | 1 | 0 | SS-150 |
| 1953 | 155 | 647 | 194 | 41 | 6 | 23 | 3.6 | 126 | 88 | 28 | 34 | 7 | .300 | .488 | 1 | 0 | SS-110, 2B-26, OF-17, 3B-8, P-1 |
| 1954 | 154 | 644 | 189 | 26 | 6 | 20 | 3.1 | 98 | 70 | 27 | 40 | 5 | .293 | .446 | 0 | 0 | SS-154 |
| 1955 | 115 | 475 | 134 | 20 | 3 | 9 | 1.9 | 77 | 45 | 22 | 32 | 2 | .282 | .394 | 1 | 0 | SS-115 |
| 1956 2 teams | | NY | N | (48G – | .252) | | STL | N | (100G – | .286) | | | | | | | |
| " total | 148 | 619 | 170 | 26 | 7 | 6 | 1.0 | 73 | 54 | 29 | 46 | 3 | .275 | .368 | 1 | 0 | SS-147 |
| 1957 STL N | 140 | 583 | 169 | 25 | 8 | 4 | 0.7 | 80 | 64 | 29 | 56 | 3 | .290 | .381 | 1 | 0 | SS-139, 3B-1 |
| 1958 2 teams | | STL | N | (18G – | .297) | | CHI | N | (114G – | .295) | | | | | | | |
| " total | 132 | 528 | 156 | 16 | 4 | 4 | 0.8 | 61 | 48 | 31 | 29 | 1 | .295 | .364 | 8 | 5 | 3B-119, SS-8 |
| 1959 CHI N | 136 | 477 | 126 | 22 | 9 | 6 | 1.3 | 60 | 45 | 55 | 50 | 1 | .264 | .386 | 1 | 0 | 3B-131, 1B-4, SS-1 |
| 1960 2 teams | | PHI | N | (55G – | .242) | | MIL | N | (50G – | .298) | | | | | | | |
| " total | 105 | 339 | 90 | 11 | 3 | 4 | 1.2 | 45 | 32 | 26 | 27 | 1 | .265 | .351 | 17 | 3 | 3B-57, OF-25, 1B-11, 2B-3 |
| 14 yrs. | 1828 | 7219 | 2089 | 358 | 72 | 126 | 1.7 | 1064 | 757 | 430 | 534 | 59 | .289 | .411 | 35 | 11 | SS-1404, 3B-320, OF-43, 2B-29, 1B-15, P-1 |
| 2 yrs. | 250 | 941 | 263 | 38 | 13 | 9 | 1.0 | 114 | 88 | 84 | 73 | 2 | .279 | .376 | 4 | 1 | 3B-242, 1B-4, SS-1 |
| WORLD SERIES | | | | | | | | | | | | | | | | | |
| 1948 BOS N | 6 | 24 | 4 | 1 | 0 | 0 | 0.0 | 2 | 0 | 0 | 2 | 0 | .167 | .208 | 0 | 0 | SS-6 |
| 1951 NY N | 6 | 24 | 10 | 3 | 0 | 1 | 4.2 | 5 | 4 | 2 | 3 | 0 | .417 | .667 | 0 | 0 | SS-6 |
| 1954 | 4 | 17 | 7 | 0 | 0 | 0 | 0.0 | 2 | 0 | 1 | 1 | 0 | .412 | .412 | 0 | 0 | SS-4 |
| 3 yrs. | 16 | 65 | 21 | 4 | 0 | 1 | 1.5 | 9 | 4 | 3 | 6 | 0 | .323 | .431 | 0 | 0 | SS-16 |

## Dell Darling

**DARLING, DELL CONRAD**　　　　　　　　BR TR 5'8" 170 lbs.
B. Dec. 21, 1861, Erie, Pa.　　D. Nov. 20, 1904, Erie, Pa.

| | G | AB | H | 2B | 3B | HR | HR% | R | RBI | BB | SO | SB | BA | SA | AB | H | G by POS |
|---|---|---|---|---|---|---|---|---|---|---|---|---|---|---|---|---|---|
| 1883 BUF N | 6 | 18 | 3 | 0 | 0 | 0 | 0.0 | 1 | | 2 | 5 | | .167 | .167 | 0 | 0 | C-6 |
| 1887 CHI N | 38 | 141 | 45 | 7 | 4 | 3 | 2.1 | 28 | 20 | 22 | 18 | 19 | .319 | .489 | 0 | 0 | OF-20, C-20 |
| 1888 | 20 | 75 | 16 | 3 | 1 | 2 | 2.7 | 12 | 7 | 3 | 12 | 0 | .213 | .360 | 0 | 0 | C-20 |
| 1889 | 36 | 120 | 23 | 1 | 1 | 0 | 0.0 | 14 | 7 | 25 | 22 | 5 | .192 | .217 | 0 | 0 | C-36 |
| 1890 CHI P | 58 | 221 | 57 | 12 | 4 | 2 | 0.9 | 45 | 39 | 29 | 28 | 5 | .258 | .376 | 0 | 0 | 1B-29, SS-15, C-9, OF-7, 2B-3, 3B-2 |

| | G | AB | H | 2B | 3B | HR | HR % | R | RBI | BB | SO | SB | BA | SA | Pinch Hit AB | Pinch Hit H | G by POS |
|---|---|---|---|---|---|---|---|---|---|---|---|---|---|---|---|---|---|

## Dell Darling continued

| | G | AB | H | 2B | 3B | HR | HR% | R | RBI | BB | SO | SB | BA | SA | AB | H | G by POS |
|---|---|---|---|---|---|---|---|---|---|---|---|---|---|---|---|---|---|
| 1891 STL AA | 17 | 53 | 7 | 1 | 3 | 0 | 0.0 | 9 | 9 | 10 | 11 | 0 | .132 | .264 | 0 | 0 | C-17, 2B-2, SS-1 |
| 6 yrs. | 175 | 628 | 151 | 24 | 13 | 7 | 1.1 | 109 | 81 | 91 | 96 | 29 | .240 | .354 | 0 | 0 | C-108, 1B-29, OF-27, SS-16, 2B-5, 3B-2 |
| 3 yrs. | 94 | 336 | 84 | 11 | 6 | 5 | 1.5 | 54 | 34 | 50 | 52 | 24 | .250 | .363 | 0 | 0 | C-76, OF-20 |

## Bobby Darwin

**DARWIN, ARTHUR BOBBY LEE**
B. Feb. 16, 1943, Los Angeles, Calif.          BR TR 6'2" 190 lbs.

| | G | AB | H | 2B | 3B | HR | HR% | R | RBI | BB | SO | SB | BA | SA | AB | H | G by POS |
|---|---|---|---|---|---|---|---|---|---|---|---|---|---|---|---|---|---|
| 1962 LA A | 1 | 1 | 0 | 0 | 0 | 0 | 0.0 | 0 | 0 | 0 | 1 | 0 | .000 | .000 | 0 | 0 | P-1 |
| 1969 LA N | 6 | 0 | 0 | 0 | 0 | 0 | – | 1 | 0 | 0 | 0 | 0 | – | – | 0 | 0 | P-3 |
| 1971 | 11 | 20 | 5 | 1 | 0 | 1 | 5.0 | 2 | 4 | 2 | 9 | 0 | .250 | .450 | 7 | 2 | OF-4 |
| 1972 MIN A | 145 | 513 | 137 | 20 | 2 | 22 | 4.3 | 48 | 80 | 38 | **145** | 2 | .267 | .442 | 5 | 1 | OF-142 |
| 1973 | 145 | 560 | 141 | 20 | 2 | 18 | 3.2 | 69 | 90 | 46 | **137** | 5 | .252 | .391 | 6 | 0 | OF-140, DH-1 |
| 1974 | 152 | 575 | 152 | 13 | 7 | 25 | 4.3 | 67 | 94 | 37 | **127** | 1 | .264 | .442 | 9 | 4 | OF-142 |
| 1975 2 teams | | MIN A (48G – .219) | | | | MIL A (55G – .247) | | | | | | | | | | | |
| " total | 103 | 355 | 83 | 12 | 2 | 13 | 3.7 | 45 | 41 | 29 | 98 | 6 | .234 | .389 | 6 | 2 | OF-70, DH-28 |
| 1976 2 teams | | MIL A (25G – .247) | | | | BOS A (43G – .179) | | | | | | | | | | | |
| " total | 68 | 179 | 37 | 8 | 3 | 4 | 2.2 | 15 | 18 | 8 | 51 | 1 | .207 | .352 | 18 | 3 | OF-38, DH-17 |
| 1977 2 teams | | BOS A (4G – .222) | | | | CHI N (11G – .167) | | | | | | | | | | | |
| " total | 15 | 21 | 4 | 2 | 0 | 0 | 0.0 | 3 | 1 | 0 | 9 | 0 | .190 | .286 | 10 | 2 | DH-2, OF-2 |
| 9 yrs. | 646 | 2224 | 559 | 76 | 16 | 83 | 3.7 | 250 | 328 | 160 | 577 | 15 | .251 | .412 | 61 | 14 | OF-538, DH-48, P-4 |
| 1 yr. | 11 | 12 | 2 | 1 | 0 | 0 | 0.0 | 2 | 0 | 0 | 5 | 0 | .167 | .250 | 8 | 2 | OF-1 |

## Bill Davidson

**DAVIDSON, WILLIAM SIMPSON**
B. May 10, 1884, Lafayette, Ind.    D. May 23, 1954, Lincoln, Neb.          BR TR

| | G | AB | H | 2B | 3B | HR | HR% | R | RBI | BB | SO | SB | BA | SA | AB | H | G by POS |
|---|---|---|---|---|---|---|---|---|---|---|---|---|---|---|---|---|---|
| 1909 CHI N | 2 | 7 | 1 | 0 | 0 | 0 | 0.0 | 2 | 0 | 1 | | 0 | .143 | .143 | 0 | 0 | OF-2 |
| 1910 BKN N | 136 | 509 | 121 | 13 | 7 | 0 | 0.0 | 48 | 34 | 24 | 54 | 27 | .238 | .291 | 4 | 0 | OF-131 |
| 1911 | 87 | 292 | 68 | 3 | 4 | 1 | 0.3 | 33 | 26 | 16 | 21 | 18 | .233 | .281 | 8 | 2 | OF-74 |
| 3 yrs. | 225 | 808 | 190 | 16 | 11 | 1 | 0.1 | 83 | 60 | 41 | 75 | 46 | .235 | .286 | 12 | 2 | OF-207 |
| 1 yr. | 2 | 7 | 1 | 0 | 0 | 0 | 0.0 | 2 | 0 | 1 | | 1 | .143 | .143 | 0 | 0 | OF-2 |

## Brock Davis

**DAVIS, BRYSHEAR BARNETT**
B. Oct. 19, 1943, Oakland, Calif.          BL TL 5'10" 160 lbs.

| | G | AB | H | 2B | 3B | HR | HR% | R | RBI | BB | SO | SB | BA | SA | AB | H | G by POS |
|---|---|---|---|---|---|---|---|---|---|---|---|---|---|---|---|---|---|
| 1963 HOU N | 34 | 55 | 11 | 2 | 0 | 1 | 1.8 | 7 | 2 | 4 | 10 | 0 | .200 | .291 | 17 | 3 | OF-14 |
| 1964 | 1 | 3 | 0 | 0 | 0 | 0 | 0.0 | 0 | 0 | 1 | 1 | 0 | .000 | .000 | 0 | 0 | OF-1 |
| 1966 | 10 | 27 | 4 | 1 | 0 | 0 | 0.0 | 2 | 1 | 5 | 4 | 1 | .148 | .185 | 3 | 1 | OF-7 |
| 1970 CHI N | 6 | 3 | 0 | 0 | 0 | 0 | 0.0 | 0 | 0 | 0 | 1 | 0 | .000 | .000 | 3 | 0 | OF-1 |
| 1971 | 106 | 301 | 77 | 7 | 5 | 0 | 0.0 | 22 | 28 | 35 | 34 | 0 | .256 | .312 | 10 | 1 | OF-93 |
| 1972 MIL A | 85 | 154 | 49 | 2 | 0 | 0 | 0.0 | 17 | 12 | 12 | 23 | 6 | .318 | .331 | 36 | 8 | OF-43 |
| 6 yrs. | 242 | 543 | 141 | 12 | 5 | 1 | 0.2 | 48 | 43 | 57 | 73 | 7 | .260 | .306 | 69 | 13 | OF-159 |
| 2 yrs. | 112 | 304 | 77 | 7 | 5 | 0 | 0.0 | 22 | 28 | 35 | 35 | 0 | .253 | .309 | 13 | 1 | OF-94 |

## Jody Davis

**DAVIS, JODY RICHARD**
B. Nov. 12, 1956, Gainesville, Ga.          BR TR 6'4" 192 lbs.

| | G | AB | H | 2B | 3B | HR | HR% | R | RBI | BB | SO | SB | BA | SA | AB | H | G by POS |
|---|---|---|---|---|---|---|---|---|---|---|---|---|---|---|---|---|---|
| 1981 CHI N | 56 | 180 | 46 | 5 | 1 | 4 | 2.2 | 14 | 21 | 21 | 28 | 0 | .256 | .361 | 0 | 0 | C-56 |
| 1982 | 130 | 418 | 109 | 20 | 2 | 12 | 2.9 | 41 | 52 | 36 | 92 | 0 | .261 | .404 | 1 | 0 | C-129 |
| 1983 | 151 | 510 | 138 | 31 | 2 | 24 | 4.7 | 56 | 84 | 33 | 93 | 0 | .271 | .480 | 2 | 0 | C-150 |
| 1984 | 150 | 523 | 134 | 24 | 2 | 19 | 3.6 | 55 | 94 | 47 | 99 | 5 | .256 | .419 | 4 | 1 | C-146 |
| 1985 | 142 | 482 | 112 | 30 | 0 | 17 | 3.5 | 47 | 58 | 48 | 83 | 1 | .232 | .400 | 11 | 2 | C-138 |
| 5 yrs. | 629 | 2113 | 539 | 110 | 7 | 76 | 3.6 | 213 | 309 | 185 | 395 | 6 | .255 | .422 | 18 | 3 | C-619 |
| 5 yrs. | 629 | 2113 | 539 | 110 | 7 | 76 | 3.6 | 213 | 309 | 185 | 395 | 6 | .255 | .422 | 18 | 3 | C-619 |

LEAGUE CHAMPIONSHIP SERIES

| | G | AB | H | 2B | 3B | HR | HR% | R | RBI | BB | SO | SB | BA | SA | AB | H | G by POS |
|---|---|---|---|---|---|---|---|---|---|---|---|---|---|---|---|---|---|
| 1984 CHI N | 5 | 18 | 7 | 2 | 0 | 2 | 11.1 | 3 | 6 | 0 | 3 | 0 | .389 | .833 | 0 | 0 | C-5 |

## Steve Davis

**DAVIS, STEVEN MICHAEL**
B. Dec. 30, 1953, Oakland, Calif.          BR TR 6'1" 200 lbs.

| | G | AB | H | 2B | 3B | HR | HR% | R | RBI | BB | SO | SB | BA | SA | AB | H | G by POS |
|---|---|---|---|---|---|---|---|---|---|---|---|---|---|---|---|---|---|
| 1979 CHI N | 3 | 4 | 0 | 0 | 0 | 0 | 0.0 | 0 | 1 | 0 | 0 | 0 | .000 | .000 | 0 | 0 | 2B-2, 3B-1 |

## Tommy Davis

**DAVIS, HERMAN THOMAS**
B. Mar. 21, 1939, Brooklyn, N.Y.          BR TR 6'2" 195 lbs.

| | G | AB | H | 2B | 3B | HR | HR% | R | RBI | BB | SO | SB | BA | SA | AB | H | G by POS |
|---|---|---|---|---|---|---|---|---|---|---|---|---|---|---|---|---|---|
| 1959 LA N | 1 | 1 | 0 | 0 | 0 | 0 | 0.0 | 0 | 0 | 0 | 1 | 0 | .000 | .000 | 1 | 0 | |
| 1960 | 110 | 352 | 97 | 18 | 1 | 11 | 3.1 | 43 | 44 | 13 | 35 | 6 | .276 | .426 | 21 | 7 | OF-87, 3B-5 |
| 1961 | 132 | 460 | 128 | 13 | 2 | 15 | 3.3 | 60 | 58 | 32 | 53 | 10 | .278 | .413 | 10 | 3 | OF-86, 3B-59 |
| 1962 | 163 | 665 | **230** | 27 | 9 | 27 | 4.1 | 120 | **153** | 33 | 65 | 18 | **.346** | .535 | 2 | 0 | OF-146, 3B-39 |
| 1963 | 146 | 556 | 181 | 19 | 3 | 16 | 2.9 | 69 | 88 | 29 | 59 | 15 | **.326** | .457 | 3 | 0 | OF-129, 3B-40 |
| 1964 | 152 | 592 | 163 | 20 | 5 | 14 | 2.4 | 70 | 86 | 29 | 68 | 11 | .275 | .397 | 4 | 2 | OF-148 |
| 1965 | 17 | 60 | 15 | 1 | 0 | 1 | 1.7 | 0 | 9 | 2 | 4 | 2 | .250 | .300 | 1 | 0 | OF-16 |
| 1966 | 100 | 313 | 98 | 11 | 1 | 3 | 1.0 | 27 | 27 | 16 | 36 | 3 | .313 | .383 | 22 | 5 | OF-79, 3B-2 |
| 1967 NY N | 154 | 577 | 174 | 32 | 0 | 16 | 2.8 | 72 | 73 | 31 | 71 | 9 | .302 | .440 | 4 | 1 | OF-149, 1B-1 |
| 1968 CHI A | 132 | 456 | 122 | 5 | 3 | 8 | 1.8 | 30 | 50 | 16 | 48 | 4 | .268 | .344 | 12 | 4 | OF-116, 1B-6 |
| 1969 2 teams | | SEA A (123G – .271) | | | | HOU N (24G – .241) | | | | | | | | | | | |
| " total | 147 | 533 | 142 | 32 | 1 | 7 | 1.3 | 54 | 89 | 38 | 55 | 20 | .266 | .370 | 16 | 7 | OF-133, 1B-1 |
| 1970 3 teams | | HOU N (57G – .282) | | | OAK A (66G – .290) | | | CHI N (11G – .262) | | | | | | | | | |
| " total | 134 | 455 | 129 | 23 | 3 | 6 | 1.3 | 45 | 65 | 16 | 44 | 10 | .284 | .387 | 23 | 5 | OF-108, 1B-8 |
| 1971 OAK A | 79 | 219 | 71 | 8 | 1 | 3 | 1.4 | 26 | 42 | 15 | 19 | 7 | .324 | .411 | 28 | 13 | 1B-35, OF-16, 2B-3, 3B-2 |
| 1972 2 teams | | CHI N (15G – .269) | | | | BAL A (26G – .256) | | | | | | | | | | | |
| " total | 41 | 108 | 28 | 4 | 0 | 0 | 0.0 | 12 | 12 | 8 | 21 | 2 | .259 | .296 | 15 | 3 | OF-20, 1B-6 |
| 1973 BAL A | 137 | 552 | 169 | 20 | 3 | 7 | 1.3 | 53 | 89 | 30 | 56 | 11 | .306 | .391 | 6 | 4 | DH-127, 1B-4 |
| 1974 | 158 | 626 | 181 | 20 | 1 | 11 | 1.8 | 67 | 84 | 34 | 49 | 6 | .289 | .377 | 4 | 1 | DH-155 |
| 1975 | 116 | 460 | 130 | 14 | 1 | 6 | 1.3 | 43 | 57 | 23 | 52 | 2 | .283 | .357 | 4 | 1 | DH-111 |

| | G | AB | H | 2B | 3B | HR | HR % | R | RBI | BB | SO | SB | BA | SA | Pinch Hit AB | Pinch Hit H | G by POS |
|---|---|---|---|---|---|---|---|---|---|---|---|---|---|---|---|---|---|

## Tommy Davis continued

| | G | AB | H | 2B | 3B | HR | HR% | R | RBI | BB | SO | SB | BA | SA | PH AB | PH H | G by POS |
|---|---|---|---|---|---|---|---|---|---|---|---|---|---|---|---|---|---|
| 1976 2 teams | CAL A (72G – .265) | | | | | KC A (8G – .263) | | | | | | | | | | | |
| " total | 80 | 238 | 63 | 5 | 0 | 3 | 1.3 | 17 | 26 | 16 | 18 | 0 | .265 | .324 | 21 | 8 | DH-56, 1B-1 |
| 18 yrs. | 1999 | 7223 | 2121 | 272 | 35 | 153 | 2.1 | 811 | 1052 | 381 | 754 | 136 | .294 | .405 | 197 | 63 | OF-1233, DH-449, 3B-147, 1B-62, 2B-3 |
| 2 yrs. | 26 | 68 | 18 | 3 | 0 | 2 | 2.9 | 7 | 14 | 3 | 4 | 0 | .265 | .397 | 10 | 2 | OF-12, 1B-3 |
| LEAGUE CHAMPIONSHIP SERIES | | | | | | | | | | | | | | | | | |
| 1971 OAK A | 3 | 8 | 3 | 1 | 0 | 0 | 0.0 | 1 | 0 | 0 | 0 | 0 | .375 | .500 | 1 | 0 | 1B-2 |
| 1973 BAL A | 5 | 21 | 6 | 1 | 0 | 0 | 0.0 | 1 | 2 | 1 | 0 | 0 | .286 | .333 | 0 | 0 | DH-5 |
| 1974 | 4 | 15 | 4 | 0 | 0 | 0 | 0.0 | 0 | 1 | 0 | 1 | 0 | .267 | .267 | 0 | 0 | DH-4 |
| 3 yrs. | 12 | 44 | 13 | 2 | 0 | 0 | 0.0 | 2 | 3 | 1 | 1 | 0 | .295 | .341 | 1 | 0 | DH-9, 1B-2 |
| WORLD SERIES | | | | | | | | | | | | | | | | | |
| 1963 LA N | 4 | 15 | 6 | 0 | 2 | 0 | 0.0 | 0 | 2 | 0 | 2 | 1 | .400 | .667 | 0 | 0 | OF-4 |
| 1966 | 4 | 8 | 2 | 0 | 0 | 0 | 0.0 | 0 | 1 | 0 | 1 | 0 | .250 | .250 | 2 | 2 | OF-3 |
| 2 yrs. | 8 | 23 | 8 | 0 | 2 | 0 | 0.0 | 0 | 2 | 1 | 3 | 1 | .348 | .522 | 2 | 2 | OF-7 |

## Boots Day

DAY, CHARLES FREDERICK  B. Aug. 31, 1947, Ilion, N. Y.  BL TL 5'9" 160 lbs.

| | G | AB | H | 2B | 3B | HR | HR% | R | RBI | BB | SO | SB | BA | SA | PH AB | PH H | G by POS |
|---|---|---|---|---|---|---|---|---|---|---|---|---|---|---|---|---|---|
| 1969 STL N | 11 | 6 | 0 | 0 | 0 | 0 | 0.0 | 1 | 1 | 1 | 1 | 0 | .000 | .000 | 5 | 0 | OF-1 |
| 1970 2 teams | CHI N (11G – .250) | | | | | MON N (41G – .269) | | | | | | | | | | | |
| " total | 52 | 116 | 31 | 4 | 0 | 0 | 0.0 | 16 | 5 | 6 | 21 | 3 | .267 | .302 | 13 | 4 | OF-42 |
| 1971 MON N | 127 | 371 | 105 | 10 | 2 | 4 | 1.1 | 53 | 33 | 33 | 39 | 9 | .283 | .353 | 15 | 5 | OF-120 |
| 1972 | 128 | 386 | 90 | 7 | 4 | 0 | 0.0 | 32 | 30 | 29 | 44 | 3 | .233 | .272 | 17 | 5 | OF-117 |
| 1973 | 101 | 207 | 57 | 7 | 0 | 4 | 1.9 | 36 | 28 | 21 | 28 | 0 | .275 | .367 | 48 | 13 | OF-51 |
| 1974 | 52 | 65 | 12 | 0 | 0 | 0 | 0.0 | 8 | 2 | 5 | 8 | 0 | .185 | .185 | 31 | 3 | OF-16 |
| 6 yrs. | 471 | 1151 | 295 | 28 | 6 | 8 | 0.7 | 146 | 98 | 95 | 141 | 15 | .256 | .312 | 129 | 30 | OF-347 |
| 1 yr. | 11 | 8 | 2 | 0 | 0 | 0 | 0.0 | 2 | 0 | 0 | 3 | 0 | .250 | .250 | 2 | 1 | OF-7 |

## Brian Dayett

DAYETT, BRIAN KELLY  B. Jan. 22, 1957, New London, Conn.  BR TR 5'10" 180 lbs.

| | G | AB | H | 2B | 3B | HR | HR% | R | RBI | BB | SO | SB | BA | SA | PH AB | PH H | G by POS |
|---|---|---|---|---|---|---|---|---|---|---|---|---|---|---|---|---|---|
| 1983 NY A | 11 | 29 | 6 | 0 | 1 | 0 | 0.0 | 3 | 5 | 2 | 4 | 0 | .207 | .276 | 3 | 1 | OF-9 |
| 1984 | 64 | 127 | 31 | 9 | 0 | 4 | 3.1 | 14 | 23 | 9 | 14 | 0 | .244 | .409 | 7 | 3 | OF-62, DH-1 |
| 1985 CHI N | 22 | 26 | 6 | 0 | 0 | 1 | 3.8 | 1 | 4 | 0 | 6 | 0 | .231 | .346 | 14 | 4 | OF-10 |
| 3 yrs. | 97 | 182 | 43 | 9 | 1 | 5 | 2.7 | 18 | 32 | 11 | 24 | 0 | .236 | .379 | 24 | 8 | OF-81, DH-1 |
| 1 yr. | 22 | 26 | 6 | 0 | 0 | 1 | 3.8 | 1 | 4 | 0 | 6 | 0 | .231 | .346 | 14 | 4 | OF-10 |

## Charlie Deal

DEAL, CHARLES ALBERT  B. Oct. 30, 1891, Wilkinsburg, Pa.  D. Sept. 16, 1979, Covina, Calif.  BR TR 5'11" 160 lbs.

| | G | AB | H | 2B | 3B | HR | HR% | R | RBI | BB | SO | SB | BA | SA | PH AB | PH H | G by POS |
|---|---|---|---|---|---|---|---|---|---|---|---|---|---|---|---|---|---|
| 1912 DET A | 41 | 142 | 32 | 4 | 2 | 0 | 0.0 | 13 | 11 | 9 | | 4 | .225 | .282 | 0 | 0 | 3B-41 |
| 1913 2 teams | DET A (16G – .220) | | | | | BOS N (10G – .306) | | | | | | | | | | | |
| " total | 26 | 86 | 22 | 1 | 2 | 0 | 0.0 | 9 | 6 | 3 | 8 | 3 | .256 | .314 | 1 | 0 | 3B-15, 2B-10 |
| 1914 BOS N | 79 | 257 | 54 | 13 | 2 | 0 | 0.0 | 17 | 23 | 20 | 23 | 4 | .210 | .276 | 4 | 0 | 3B-74, SS-1 |
| 1915 STL F | 65 | 223 | 72 | 12 | 4 | 1 | 0.4 | 21 | 27 | 12 | | 10 | .323 | .426 | 0 | 0 | 3B-65 |
| 1916 2 teams | STL A (23G – .135) | | | | | CHI N (2G – .250) | | | | | | | | | | | |
| " total | 25 | 82 | 12 | 2 | 0 | 0 | 0.0 | 9 | 13 | 6 | 8 | 4 | .146 | .171 | 1 | 0 | 3B-24, 2B-1 |
| 1917 CHI N | 135 | 449 | 114 | 11 | 3 | 0 | 0.0 | 46 | 47 | 19 | 18 | 10 | .254 | .292 | 5 | 1 | 3B-130 |
| 1918 | 119 | 414 | 99 | 9 | 3 | 0 | 0.0 | 43 | 34 | 21 | 13 | 11 | .239 | .290 | 1 | 0 | 3B-118 |
| 1919 | 116 | 405 | 117 | 23 | 5 | 2 | 0.5 | 37 | 52 | 12 | 12 | 11 | .289 | .385 | 0 | 0 | 3B-116 |
| 1920 | 129 | 450 | 108 | 10 | 5 | 3 | 0.7 | 48 | 39 | 20 | 14 | 5 | .240 | .304 | 1 | 1 | 3B-128 |
| 1921 | 115 | 422 | 122 | 19 | 8 | 3 | 0.7 | 52 | 66 | 13 | 9 | 3 | .289 | .393 | 2 | 0 | 3B-113 |
| 10 yrs. | 850 | 2930 | 752 | 104 | 34 | 11 | 0.4 | 295 | 318 | 135 | 105 | 65 | .257 | .327 | 14 | 2 | 3B-824, 2B-11, SS-1 |
| 6 yrs. | 616 | 2148 | 562 | 73 | 24 | 10 | 0.5 | 228 | 241 | 85 | 66 | 40 | .262 | .332 | 9 | 2 | 3B-607 |
| WORLD SERIES | | | | | | | | | | | | | | | | | |
| 1914 BOS N | 4 | 16 | 2 | 2 | 0 | 0 | 0.0 | 1 | 0 | 0 | 0 | 2 | .125 | .250 | 0 | 0 | 3B-4 |
| 1918 CHI N | 6 | 17 | 3 | 0 | 0 | 0 | 0.0 | 0 | 0 | 0 | 1 | 0 | .176 | .176 | 0 | 0 | 3B-6 |
| 2 yrs. | 10 | 33 | 5 | 2 | 0 | 0 | 0.0 | 1 | 0 | 0 | 1 | 2 | .152 | .212 | 0 | 0 | 3B-10 |

## Wayland Dean

DEAN, WAYLAND OGDEN  B. June 20, 1903, Richwood, W. Va.  D. Apr. 10, 1930, Huntington, W. Va.  BB TR 6'2" 178 lbs.  BL 1926-27

| | G | AB | H | 2B | 3B | HR | HR% | R | RBI | BB | SO | SB | BA | SA | PH AB | PH H | G by POS |
|---|---|---|---|---|---|---|---|---|---|---|---|---|---|---|---|---|---|
| 1924 NY N | 26 | 40 | 8 | 0 | 0 | 2 | 5.0 | 4 | 1 | 9 | | 0 | .200 | .350 | 0 | 0 | P-26 |
| 1925 | 33 | 51 | 12 | 2 | 1 | 1 | 2.0 | 7 | 7 | 3 | 12 | 0 | .235 | .373 | 0 | 0 | P-33 |
| 1926 PHI N | 63 | 102 | 27 | 4 | 0 | 3 | 2.9 | 11 | 19 | 5 | 26 | 0 | .265 | .392 | 26 | 6 | P-33 |
| 1927 2 teams | PHI N (3G – .667) | | | | | CHI N (2G – .000) | | | | | | | | | | | |
| " total | 5 | 3 | 2 | 0 | 0 | 0 | 0.0 | 1 | 1 | 0 | 0 | 0 | .667 | 1.333 | 1 | 0 | P-4 |
| 4 yrs. | 127 | 196 | 49 | 6 | 2 | 6 | 3.1 | 24 | 31 | 9 | 47 | 0 | .250 | .393 | 27 | 6 | P-96 |
| 1 yr. | 2 | 0 | 0 | 0 | 0 | 0 | – | 0 | 0 | 0 | 0 | 0 | – | – | 0 | 0 | P-2 |
| WORLD SERIES | | | | | | | | | | | | | | | | | |
| 1924 NY N | 1 | 0 | 0 | 0 | 0 | 0 | – | 0 | 0 | 0 | 0 | 0 | – | – | 0 | 0 | P-1 |

## George Decker

DECKER, GEORGE A.  B. June 1, 1869, York, Pa.  D. June 9, 1909, Compton, Calif.  6'1" 180 lbs.

| | G | AB | H | 2B | 3B | HR | HR% | R | RBI | BB | SO | SB | BA | SA | PH AB | PH H | G by POS |
|---|---|---|---|---|---|---|---|---|---|---|---|---|---|---|---|---|---|
| 1892 CHI N | 78 | 291 | 66 | 6 | 7 | 1 | 0.3 | 32 | 28 | 20 | 49 | 9 | .227 | .306 | 0 | 0 | OF-62, 2B-16 |
| 1893 | 81 | 328 | 89 | 9 | 8 | 2 | 0.6 | 57 | 48 | 24 | 22 | 22 | .271 | .366 | 0 | 0 | OF-33, 1B-27, 2B-20, SS-2 |
| 1894 | 91 | 384 | 120 | 17 | 6 | 8 | 2.1 | 74 | 92 | 24 | 17 | 23 | .313 | .451 | 4 | 1 | 1B-48, OF-29, 3B-7, 2B-2, SS-1 |
| 1895 | 73 | 297 | 82 | 9 | 7 | 2 | 0.7 | 51 | 41 | 17 | 22 | 11 | .276 | .374 | 0 | 0 | OF-57, 1B-11, 3B-3, SS-1, 2B-1 |
| 1896 | 107 | 421 | 118 | 23 | 11 | 5 | 1.2 | 68 | 61 | 23 | 14 | 20 | .280 | .423 | 0 | 0 | OF-71, 1B-36 |
| 1897 | 111 | 428 | 124 | 12 | 7 | 5 | 1.2 | 72 | 63 | 24 | | 11 | .290 | .386 | 1 | 0 | OF-75, 1B-38, 2B-1 |

| | G | AB | H | 2B | 3B | HR | HR % | R | RBI | BB | SO | SB | BA | SA | Pinch Hit AB | Pinch Hit H | G by POS |
|---|---|---|---|---|---|---|---|---|---|---|---|---|---|---|---|---|---|

## George Decker continued

| | | G | AB | H | 2B | 3B | HR | HR% | R | RBI | BB | SO | SB | BA | SA | PH AB | PH H | G by POS |
|---|---|---|---|---|---|---|---|---|---|---|---|---|---|---|---|---|---|---|
| 1898 **2 teams** | **STL N** (76G – .259) | | | **LOU N** (42G – .297) | | | | | | | | | | | | | | |
| " total | 118 | 434 | 118 | 14 | 3 | 1 | 0.2 | 53 | 64 | 29 | | 13 | .272 | .325 | 5 | 2 | 1B-107, OF-6 |
| 1899 **2 teams** | **LOU N** (38G – .267) | | | **WAS N** (4G – .000) | | | | | | | | | | | | | | |
| " total | 42 | 144 | 36 | 8 | 0 | 0 | 0.7 | 13 | 18 | 12 | | 3 | .250 | .326 | 1 | 0 | 1B-40, OF-1 |
| 8 yrs. | 701 | 2727 | 753 | 98 | 49 | 25 | 0.9 | 420 | 415 | 173 | 124 | 112 | .276 | .376 | 11 | 3 | OF-334, 1B-307, 2B-40, 3B-10, SS-4 |
| 6 yrs. | 541 | 2149 | 599 | 76 | 46 | 23 | 1.1 | 354 | 333 | 132 | 124 | 96 | .279 | .389 | 5 | 1 | OF-327, 1B-160, 2B-40, 3B-10, SS-4 |

## Ivan DeJesus

**DeJESUS, IVAN**
Born Ivan DeJesus Alvarez.
B. Jan. 9, 1953, Santurce, Puerto Rico

BR TR 5'11" 175 lbs.

| | | G | AB | H | 2B | 3B | HR | HR% | R | RBI | BB | SO | SB | BA | SA | PH AB | PH H | G by POS |
|---|---|---|---|---|---|---|---|---|---|---|---|---|---|---|---|---|---|---|
| 1974 **LA N** | | 3 | 3 | 1 | 0 | 0 | 0 | 0.0 | 1 | 0 | 0 | 2 | 0 | .333 | .333 | 1 | 0 | SS-2 |
| 1975 | | 63 | 87 | 16 | 2 | 1 | 0 | 0.0 | 10 | 2 | 11 | 15 | 1 | .184 | .230 | 2 | 0 | SS-63 |
| 1976 | | 22 | 41 | 7 | 2 | 1 | 0 | 0.0 | 4 | 2 | 4 | 9 | 0 | .171 | .268 | 1 | 0 | SS-13, 3B-7 |
| 1977 **CHI N** | | 155 | 624 | 166 | 31 | 7 | 3 | 0.5 | 91 | 40 | 56 | 90 | 24 | .266 | .353 | 0 | 0 | SS-154 |
| 1978 | | 160 | 619 | 172 | 24 | 7 | 3 | 0.5 | 104 | 35 | 74 | 78 | 41 | .278 | .354 | 0 | 0 | SS-160 |
| 1979 | | 160 | 636 | 180 | 26 | 10 | 5 | 0.8 | 92 | 52 | 59 | 82 | 24 | .283 | .379 | 0 | 0 | SS-160 |
| 1980 | | 157 | 618 | 160 | 26 | 3 | 3 | 0.5 | 78 | 33 | 60 | 81 | 44 | .259 | .325 | 0 | 0 | SS-156 |
| 1981 | | 106 | 403 | 78 | 8 | 4 | 0 | 0.0 | 49 | 13 | 46 | 61 | 21 | .194 | .233 | 0 | 0 | SS-106 |
| 1982 **PHI N** | | 161 | 536 | 128 | 21 | 5 | 3 | 0.6 | 53 | 59 | 54 | 70 | 14 | .239 | .313 | 0 | 0 | SS-154, 3B-7 |
| 1983 | | 158 | 497 | 126 | 15 | 7 | 4 | 0.8 | 60 | 45 | 53 | 77 | 11 | .254 | .336 | 0 | 0 | SS-158 |
| 1984 | | 144 | 435 | 112 | 15 | 3 | 0 | 0.0 | 40 | 35 | 43 | 76 | 12 | .257 | .306 | 2 | 0 | SS-141 |
| 1985 **STL N** | | 59 | 72 | 16 | 5 | 0 | 0 | 0.0 | 11 | 7 | 4 | 16 | 2 | .222 | .292 | 24 | 6 | 3B-20, SS-13 |
| 12 yrs. | | 1348 | 4571 | 1162 | 175 | 48 | 21 | 0.5 | 593 | 323 | 464 | 657 | 194 | .254 | .327 | 30 | 6 | SS-1280, 3B-34 |
| 5 yrs. | | 738 | 2900 | 756 | 115 | 31 | 14 | 0.5 | 414 | 173 | 295 | 392 | 154 | .261 | .336 | 0 | 0 | SS-736 |

LEAGUE CHAMPIONSHIP SERIES

| | | G | AB | H | 2B | 3B | HR | HR% | R | RBI | BB | SO | SB | BA | SA | PH AB | PH H | G by POS |
|---|---|---|---|---|---|---|---|---|---|---|---|---|---|---|---|---|---|---|
| 1983 **PHI N** | | 4 | 12 | 3 | 0 | 0 | 0 | 0.0 | 0 | 1 | 3 | 3 | 0 | .250 | .250 | 0 | 0 | SS-4 |

WORLD SERIES

| | | G | AB | H | 2B | 3B | HR | HR% | R | RBI | BB | SO | SB | BA | SA | PH AB | PH H | G by POS |
|---|---|---|---|---|---|---|---|---|---|---|---|---|---|---|---|---|---|---|
| 1983 **PHI N** | | 5 | 16 | 2 | 0 | 0 | 0 | 0.0 | 0 | 1 | 2 | 0 | .125 | .125 | 0 | 0 | SS-5 |
| 1985 **STL N** | | 1 | 1 | 0 | 0 | 0 | 0 | 0.0 | 0 | 0 | 0 | 0 | 0 | .000 | .000 | 1 | 0 | |
| 2 yrs. | | 6 | 17 | 2 | 0 | 0 | 0 | 0.0 | 0 | 1 | 2 | 0 | .118 | .118 | 1 | 0 | SS-5 |

## Jim Delahanty

**DELAHANTY, JAMES CHRISTOPHER**
Brother of Ed Delahanty.  Brother of Frank Delahanty.
Brother of Tom Delahanty.  Brother of Joe Delahanty.
B. June 20, 1879, Cleveland, Ohio  D. Oct. 17, 1953, Cleveland, Ohio

BR TR 5'10½" 170 lbs.

| | | G | AB | H | 2B | 3B | HR | HR% | R | RBI | BB | SO | SB | BA | SA | PH AB | PH H | G by POS |
|---|---|---|---|---|---|---|---|---|---|---|---|---|---|---|---|---|---|---|
| 1901 **CHI N** | | 17 | 63 | 12 | 2 | 0 | 0 | 0.0 | 4 | 4 | 3 | | 5 | | .190 | .222 | 0 | 0 | 3B-17, 2B-1 |
| 1902 **NY N** | | 7 | 26 | 6 | 1 | 0 | 0 | 0.0 | 3 | 3 | 1 | | 0 | | .231 | .269 | 0 | 0 | OF-7 |
| 1904 **BOS N** | | 142 | 499 | 142 | 27 | 8 | 3 | 0.6 | 56 | 60 | 27 | | 16 | | .285 | .389 | 0 | 0 | 3B-113, 2B-18, OF-9, P-1 |
| 1905 | | 125 | 461 | 119 | 11 | 8 | 5 | 1.1 | 50 | 55 | 28 | | 12 | | .258 | .349 | 1 | 0 | OF-124, P-1 |
| 1906 **CIN N** | | 115 | 379 | 106 | 21 | 4 | 1 | 0.3 | 63 | 39 | 45 | | 21 | | .280 | .364 | 3 | 1 | 3B-105, SS-5, OF-2 |
| 1907 **2 teams** | **STL A** (33G – .221) | | | **WAS A** (109G – .292) | | | | | | | | | | | | | | |
| " total | 142 | 499 | 139 | 21 | 7 | 2 | 0.4 | 52 | 60 | 41 | | 24 | | .279 | .361 | 8 | 0 | 2B-70, 3B-48, OF-13, 1B-4 |
| 1908 **WAS A** | | 83 | 287 | 91 | 11 | 4 | 1 | 0.3 | 33 | 30 | 24 | | 16 | | .317 | .394 | 2 | 0 | 2B-79 |
| 1909 **2 teams** | **WAS A** (90G – .222) | | | **DET A** (46G – .253) | | | | | | | | | | | | | | |
| " total | 136 | 452 | 105 | 23 | 6 | 1 | 0.2 | 47 | 41 | 40 | | 13 | | .232 | .316 | 5 | 0 | 2B-131 |
| 1910 **DET A** | | 106 | 378 | 111 | 16 | 3 | 2 | 0.5 | 67 | 45 | 43 | | 15 | | .294 | .368 | 0 | 0 | 2B-106 |
| 1911 | | 144 | 542 | 184 | 30 | 14 | 3 | 0.6 | 83 | 94 | 56 | | 15 | | .339 | .463 | 1 | 0 | 1B-72, 2B-59, 3B-12 |
| 1912 | | 78 | 266 | 76 | 14 | 1 | 0 | 0.0 | 34 | 41 | 42 | | 9 | | .286 | .346 | 1 | 0 | 2B-44, OF-33 |
| 1914 **BKN F** | | 74 | 214 | 62 | 13 | 5 | 0 | 0.0 | 28 | 15 | 25 | | 4 | | .290 | .397 | 13 | 2 | 2B-55, 1B-5 |
| 1915 | | 17 | 25 | 6 | 1 | 0 | 0 | 0.0 | 0 | 2 | 3 | | 1 | | .240 | .280 | 11 | 1 | 2B-4 |
| 13 yrs. | | 1186 | 4091 | 1159 | 191 | 60 | 18 | 0.4 | 520 | 489 | 378 | | 151 | | .283 | .373 | 45 | 4 | 2B-567, 3B-295, OF-188, 1B-81, SS-5, P-2 |
| 1 yr. | | 17 | 63 | 12 | 2 | 0 | 0 | 0.0 | 4 | 4 | 3 | | 5 | | .190 | .222 | 0 | 0 | 3B-17, 2B-1 |

WORLD SERIES

| | | G | AB | H | 2B | 3B | HR | HR% | R | RBI | BB | SO | SB | BA | SA | PH AB | PH H | G by POS |
|---|---|---|---|---|---|---|---|---|---|---|---|---|---|---|---|---|---|---|
| 1909 **DET A** | | 7 | 26 | 9 | 4 | 0 | 0 | 0.0 | 2 | 4 | 2 | | 5 | | .346 | .500 | 0 | 0 | 2B-7 |

## Bobby Del Greco

**DEL GRECO, ROBERT GEORGE**
B. Apr. 7, 1933, Pittsburgh, Pa.

BR TR 5'10½" 185 lbs.

| | | G | AB | H | 2B | 3B | HR | HR% | R | RBI | BB | SO | SB | BA | SA | PH AB | PH H | G by POS |
|---|---|---|---|---|---|---|---|---|---|---|---|---|---|---|---|---|---|---|
| 1952 **PIT N** | | 99 | 341 | 74 | 14 | 2 | 1 | 0.3 | 34 | 20 | 38 | 70 | 6 | .217 | .279 | 4 | 1 | OF-93 |
| 1956 **2 teams** | **PIT N** (14G – .200) | | | **STL N** (102G – .215) | | | | | | | | | | | | | | |
| " total | 116 | 290 | 62 | 16 | 2 | 7 | 2.4 | 33 | 21 | 35 | 53 | 1 | .214 | .355 | 7 | 0 | OF-107, 3B-3 |
| 1957 **2 teams** | **CHI N** (20G – .200) | | | **NY A** (8G – .429) | | | | | | | | | | | | | | |
| " total | 28 | 47 | 11 | 2 | 0 | 0 | 0.0 | 5 | 3 | 12 | 19 | 2 | .234 | .277 | 6 | 1 | OF-22 |
| 1958 **NY A** | | 12 | 5 | 1 | 0 | 0 | 0 | 0.0 | 1 | 0 | 1 | 1 | 0 | .200 | .200 | 0 | 0 | OF-12 |
| 1960 **PHI N** | | 100 | 300 | 71 | 16 | 4 | 10 | 3.3 | 48 | 26 | 54 | 64 | 1 | .237 | .417 | 11 | 3 | OF-89 |
| 1961 **2 teams** | **PHI N** (41G – .259) | | | **KC A** (74G – .230) | | | | | | | | | | | | | | |
| " total | 115 | 351 | 84 | 19 | 1 | 7 | 2.0 | 48 | 32 | 42 | 48 | 1 | .239 | .359 | 9 | 1 | OF-105, 3B-1, 2B-1 |
| 1962 **KC A** | | 132 | 338 | 86 | 21 | 1 | 9 | 2.7 | 61 | 38 | 49 | 62 | 4 | .254 | .402 | 6 | 1 | OF-124 |
| 1963 | | 121 | 306 | 65 | 7 | 1 | 8 | 2.6 | 40 | 29 | 40 | 52 | 1 | .212 | .320 | 8 | 2 | OF-110, 3B-2 |
| 1965 **PHI N** | | 8 | 4 | 0 | 0 | 0 | 0 | 0.0 | 1 | 0 | 0 | 3 | 0 | .000 | .000 | 2 | 0 | OF-4 |
| 9 yrs. | | 731 | 1982 | 454 | 95 | 11 | 42 | 2.1 | 271 | 169 | 271 | 372 | 16 | .229 | .352 | 53 | 9 | OF-666, 3B-6, 2B-1 |
| 1 yr. | | 20 | 40 | 8 | 2 | 0 | 0 | 0.0 | 2 | 3 | 10 | 17 | 1 | .200 | .250 | 6 | 1 | OF-16 |

## Frank Demaree

**DEMAREE, JOSEPH FRANKLIN**
Born Joseph Franklin Dimaria.
B. June 10, 1910, Winters, Calif.  D. Aug. 30, 1958, Los Angeles, Calif.

BR TR 5'11½" 185 lbs.

| | | G | AB | H | 2B | 3B | HR | HR% | R | RBI | BB | SO | SB | BA | SA | PH AB | PH H | G by POS |
|---|---|---|---|---|---|---|---|---|---|---|---|---|---|---|---|---|---|---|
| 1932 **CHI N** | | 23 | 56 | 14 | 3 | 0 | 0 | 0.0 | 4 | 6 | 2 | 7 | 0 | .250 | .304 | 5 | 1 | OF-17 |
| 1933 | | 134 | 515 | 140 | 24 | 6 | 6 | 1.2 | 68 | 51 | 22 | 42 | 4 | .272 | .377 | 0 | 0 | OF-133 |
| 1935 | | 107 | 385 | 125 | 19 | 4 | 2 | 0.5 | 60 | 66 | 26 | 23 | 0 | .325 | .410 | 8 | 2 | OF-98 |
| 1936 | | 154 | 605 | 212 | 34 | 3 | 16 | 2.6 | 93 | 96 | 49 | 30 | 4 | .350 | .496 | 0 | 0 | OF-154 |

| | G | AB | H | 2B | 3B | HR | HR % | R | RBI | BB | SO | SB | BA | SA | Pinch Hit AB | Pinch Hit H | G by POS |
|---|---|---|---|---|---|---|---|---|---|---|---|---|---|---|---|---|---|

## Frank Demaree continued

| | | G | AB | H | 2B | 3B | HR | HR% | R | RBI | BB | SO | SB | BA | SA | AB | H | G by POS |
|---|---|---|---|---|---|---|---|---|---|---|---|---|---|---|---|---|---|---|
| 1937 | | 154 | 615 | 199 | 36 | 6 | 17 | 2.8 | 104 | 115 | 57 | 31 | 6 | .324 | .485 | 0 | 0 | OF-154 |
| 1938 | | 129 | 476 | 130 | 15 | 7 | 8 | 1.7 | 63 | 62 | 45 | 34 | 1 | .273 | .384 | 4 | 1 | OF-125 |
| 1939 NY N | | 150 | 560 | 170 | 27 | 2 | 11 | 2.0 | 68 | 79 | 66 | 40 | 2 | .304 | .418 | 0 | 0 | OF-150 |
| 1940 | | 121 | 460 | 139 | 18 | 6 | 7 | 1.5 | 68 | 61 | 45 | 39 | 5 | .302 | .413 | 2 | 1 | OF-119 |
| 1941 2 teams | | 64 | NY | N (16G – | .171) | | BOS | N | (48G – | .230) | | | | | | | | |
| " total | | 64 | 148 | 32 | 5 | 2 | 2 | 1.4 | 23 | 16 | 16 | 6 | 2 | .216 | .318 | 22 | 3 | OF-38 |
| 1942 BOS N | | 64 | 187 | 42 | 5 | 0 | 3 | 1.6 | 18 | 24 | 17 | 10 | 2 | .225 | .299 | 13 | 1 | OF-49 |
| 1943 STL N | | 39 | 86 | 25 | 2 | 0 | 0 | 0.0 | 5 | 9 | 8 | 4 | 1 | .291 | .314 | 13 | 1 | OF-23 |
| 1944 STL A | | 16 | 51 | 13 | 2 | 0 | 0 | 0.0 | 4 | 6 | 6 | 3 | 0 | .255 | .294 | 0 | 0 | OF-16 |
| 12 yrs. | | 1155 | 4144 | 1241 | 190 | 36 | 72 | 1.7 | 578 | 591 | 359 | 269 | 33 | .299 | .415 | 67 | 10 | OF-1076 |
| 6 yrs. | | 701 | 2652 | 820 | 131 | 26 | 49 | 1.8 | 392 | 396 | 201 | 167 | 21 | .309 | .434 | 17 | 4 | OF-681 |
| | | | | | | | | | | | | | | 10th | | | | |
| **WORLD SERIES** | | | | | | | | | | | | | | | | | | |
| 1932 CHI N | | 2 | 7 | 2 | 0 | 0 | 1 | 14.3 | 1 | 4 | 1 | 0 | 0 | .286 | .714 | 0 | 0 | OF-2 |
| 1935 | | 6 | 24 | 6 | 1 | 0 | 2 | 8.3 | 2 | 2 | 1 | 4 | 0 | .250 | .542 | 0 | 0 | OF-6 |
| 1938 | | 3 | 10 | 1 | 0 | 0 | 0 | 0.0 | 1 | 0 | 1 | 2 | 0 | .100 | .100 | 0 | 0 | OF-3 |
| 1943 STL N | | 1 | 1 | 0 | 0 | 0 | 0 | 0.0 | 0 | 0 | 0 | 0 | 0 | .000 | .000 | 1 | 0 | |
| 4 yrs. | | 12 | 42 | 9 | 1 | 0 | 3 | 7.1 | 4 | 6 | 3 | 6 | 0 | .214 | .452 | 1 | 0 | OF-11 |

## Gene DeMontreville

**DeMONTREVILLE, EUGENE**    BR TR  5'8"    165 lbs.
Also appeared in box score as Demont    Brother of Lee DeMontreville.
B. Mar. 26, 1874, St. Paul, Minn.    D. Feb. 18, 1935, Memphis, Tenn.

| | | G | AB | H | 2B | 3B | HR | HR% | R | RBI | BB | SO | SB | BA | SA | AB | H | G by POS |
|---|---|---|---|---|---|---|---|---|---|---|---|---|---|---|---|---|---|---|---|
| 1894 PIT N | | 2 | 8 | 2 | 0 | 0 | 0 | 0.0 | 0 | 0 | 1 | 4 | 0 | .250 | .250 | 0 | 0 | SS-2 |
| 1895 WAS N | | 12 | 46 | 10 | 1 | 3 | 0 | 0.0 | 7 | 9 | 3 | 4 | 5 | .217 | .370 | 0 | 0 | SS-12 |
| 1896 | | 133 | 533 | 183 | 24 | 5 | 8 | 1.5 | 94 | 77 | 29 | 27 | 28 | .343 | .452 | 0 | 0 | SS-133 |
| 1897 | | 133 | 566 | 197 | 27 | 8 | 3 | 0.5 | 92 | 93 | 21 | | 30 | .348 | .440 | 1 | 1 | SS-99, 2B-33 |
| 1898 BAL N | | 151 | 567 | 186 | 19 | 2 | 0 | 0.0 | 93 | 86 | 52 | | 49 | .328 | .369 | 0 | 0 | 2B-123, SS-28 |
| 1899 2 teams | | 142 | CHI | N (82G – | .281) | | BAL | N | (60G – | .279) | | | | | | | | |
| " total | | 142 | 550 | 154 | 19 | 7 | 1 | 0.2 | 83 | 76 | 27 | | 47 | .280 | .345 | 0 | 0 | SS-82, 2B-60 |
| 1900 BKN N | | 69 | 234 | 57 | 8 | 1 | 0 | 0.0 | 32 | 28 | 10 | | 21 | .244 | .286 | 1 | 0 | 2B-48, SS-12, 3B-7, OF-1, 1B-1 |
| 1901 BOS N | | 140 | 570 | 173 | 14 | 4 | 5 | 0.9 | 83 | 72 | 17 | | 25 | .304 | .368 | 0 | 0 | 2B-120, 3B-20 |
| 1902 | | 124 | 481 | 129 | 16 | 5 | 0 | 0.0 | 51 | 53 | 12 | | 23 | .268 | .322 | 2 | 0 | 2B-112, SS-10 |
| 1903 WAS A | | 12 | 44 | 12 | 2 | 0 | 0 | 0.0 | 0 | 3 | 0 | | 0 | .273 | .318 | 0 | 0 | 2B-11, SS-1 |
| 1904 STL A | | 4 | 9 | 1 | 0 | 0 | 0 | 0.0 | 0 | 0 | 2 | | 0 | .111 | .111 | 0 | 0 | 2B-3 |
| 11 yrs. | | 922 | 3608 | 1104 | 130 | 35 | 17 | 0.5 | 535 | 497 | 174 | 35 | 228 | .306 | .376 | 5 | 1 | 2B-510, SS-379, 3B-27, OF-1, 1B-1 |
| 1 yr. | | 82 | 310 | 87 | 6 | 3 | 0 | 0.0 | 43 | 40 | 17 | | 26 | .281 | .319 | 0 | 0 | SS-82 |

## Bob Dernier

**DERNIER, ROBERT EUGENE**    BR TR  6'    160 lbs.
B. Jan. 5, 1957, Kansas City, Mo.

| | | G | AB | H | 2B | 3B | HR | HR% | R | RBI | BB | SO | SB | BA | SA | AB | H | G by POS |
|---|---|---|---|---|---|---|---|---|---|---|---|---|---|---|---|---|---|---|---|
| 1980 PHI N | | 10 | 7 | 4 | 0 | 0 | 0 | 0.0 | 5 | 1 | 1 | 0 | 3 | .571 | .571 | 0 | 0 | OF-3 |
| 1981 | | 10 | 4 | 3 | 0 | 0 | 0 | 0.0 | 0 | 0 | 0 | 0 | 2 | .750 | .750 | 0 | 0 | OF-5 |
| 1982 | | 122 | 370 | 92 | 10 | 2 | 4 | 1.1 | 56 | 21 | 36 | 69 | 42 | .249 | .319 | 1 | 0 | OF-119 |
| 1983 | | 122 | 221 | 51 | 10 | 0 | 1 | 0.5 | 41 | 15 | 18 | 21 | 35 | .231 | .290 | 3 | 0 | OF-107 |
| 1984 CHI N | | 143 | 536 | 149 | 26 | 5 | 3 | 0.6 | 94 | 32 | 63 | 60 | 45 | .278 | .362 | 2 | 0 | OF-140 |
| 1985 | | 121 | 469 | 119 | 20 | 3 | 1 | 0.2 | 63 | 21 | 40 | 44 | 31 | .254 | .316 | 4 | 0 | OF-116 |
| 6 yrs. | | 528 | 1607 | 418 | 66 | 10 | 9 | 0.6 | 259 | 90 | 158 | 194 | 158 | .260 | .330 | 10 | 0 | OF-490 |
| 2 yrs. | | 264 | 1005 | 268 | 46 | 8 | 4 | 0.4 | 157 | 53 | 103 | 104 | 76 | .267 | .340 | 6 | 0 | OF-256 |
| **LEAGUE CHAMPIONSHIP SERIES** | | | | | | | | | | | | | | | | | | |
| 1983 PHI N | | 1 | 0 | 0 | 0 | 0 | 0 | – | 0 | 0 | 0 | 0 | 0 | – | – | 0 | 0 | OF-1 |
| 1984 CHI N | | 5 | 17 | 4 | 2 | 0 | 1 | 5.9 | 5 | 1 | 5 | 4 | 2 | .235 | .529 | 0 | 0 | OF-5 |
| 2 yrs. | | 6 | 17 | 4 | 2 | 0 | 1 | 5.9 | 5 | 1 | 5 | 4 | 2 | .235 | .529 | 0 | 0 | OF-6 |
| **WORLD SERIES** | | | | | | | | | | | | | | | | | | |
| 1983 PHI N | | 1 | 0 | 0 | 0 | 0 | 0 | – | 1 | 0 | 0 | 0 | 0 | – | – | 0 | 0 | |

## Claud Derrick

**DERRICK, CLAUD LESTER (Deek)**    BR TR  6'    175 lbs.
B. June 11, 1886, Burton, Ga.    D. July 15, 1974, Clayton, Ga.

| | | G | AB | H | 2B | 3B | HR | HR% | R | RBI | BB | SO | SB | BA | SA | AB | H | G by POS |
|---|---|---|---|---|---|---|---|---|---|---|---|---|---|---|---|---|---|---|---|
| 1910 PHI A | | 1 | 1 | 0 | 0 | 0 | 0 | 0.0 | 0 | 0 | 0 | | 0 | .000 | .000 | 0 | 0 | SS-1 |
| 1911 | | 36 | 100 | 23 | 1 | 2 | 0 | 0.0 | 14 | 5 | 7 | | 7 | .230 | .280 | 1 | 0 | 2B-20, SS-6, 1B-3, 3B-2 |
| 1912 | | 21 | 58 | 14 | 0 | 1 | 0 | 0.0 | 7 | 7 | 5 | | 1 | .241 | .276 | 3 | 0 | SS-18 |
| 1913 NY A | | 22 | 65 | 19 | 1 | 0 | 1 | 1.5 | 7 | 7 | 5 | 8 | 2 | .292 | .354 | 2 | 0 | SS-14, 3B-4, 2B-1 |
| 1914 2 teams | | 30 | CIN | N (2G – | .333) | | CHI | N | (28G – | .219) | | | | | | | | |
| " total | | 30 | 102 | 23 | 4 | 1 | 0 | 0.0 | 7 | 14 | 5 | 13 | 3 | .225 | .284 | 1 | 0 | SS-30 |
| 5 yrs. | | 110 | 326 | 79 | 6 | 4 | 1 | 0.3 | 35 | 33 | 22 | 21 | 13 | .242 | .294 | 7 | 0 | SS-69, 2B-21, 3B-6, 1B-3 |
| 1 yr. | | 28 | 96 | 21 | 1 | 0 | 0 | 0.0 | 5 | 13 | 5 | 13 | 1 | .219 | .271 | 0 | 0 | SS-28 |

## Charlie Dexter

**DEXTER, CHARLES DANA**    TR  5'7"    155 lbs.
B. June 15, 1876, Evansville, Ind.    D. June 9, 1934, Cedar Rapids, Iowa

| | | G | AB | H | 2B | 3B | HR | HR% | R | RBI | BB | SO | SB | BA | SA | AB | H | G by POS |
|---|---|---|---|---|---|---|---|---|---|---|---|---|---|---|---|---|---|---|---|
| 1896 LOU N | | 107 | 402 | 112 | 18 | 7 | 3 | 0.7 | 65 | 37 | 17 | 34 | 21 | .279 | .381 | 5 | 4 | C-55, OF-47 |
| 1897 | | 76 | 257 | 72 | 12 | 5 | 2 | 0.8 | 43 | 46 | 21 | | 12 | .280 | .389 | 5 | 0 | OF-32, C-23, 3B-14, SS-2 |
| 1898 | | 112 | 421 | 132 | 13 | 5 | 1 | 0.2 | 76 | 66 | 26 | | 44 | .314 | .375 | 3 | 1 | OF-95, 2B-8, C-7 |
| 1899 | | 80 | 295 | 76 | 7 | 1 | 1 | 0.3 | 47 | 33 | 21 | | 21 | .258 | .298 | 3 | 0 | OF-71, SS-6 |
| 1900 CHI N | | 40 | 125 | 25 | 5 | 0 | 2 | 1.6 | 7 | 20 | 1 | | 2 | .200 | .288 | 4 | 1 | C-22, OF-13, 2B-1 |
| 1901 | | 116 | 460 | 123 | 9 | 5 | 1 | 0.2 | 46 | 66 | 16 | | 22 | .267 | .315 | 2 | 0 | 1B-54, 3B-25, OF-21, 2B-13, C-3 |
| 1902 2 teams | | 117 | CHI | N (69G – | .226) | | BOS | N | (48G – | .257) | | | | | | | | |
| " total | | 117 | 449 | 107 | 15 | 0 | 3 | 0.7 | 63 | 44 | 35 | | 29 | .238 | .292 | 0 | 0 | 3B-40, SS-22, 1B-22, 2B-19, OF-17 |
| 1903 BOS N | | 123 | 457 | 102 | 15 | 1 | 3 | 0.7 | 82 | 34 | 61 | | 32 | .223 | .280 | 2 | 0 | OF-106, SS-9, C-6 |
| 8 yrs. | | 771 | 2866 | 749 | 94 | 24 | 16 | 0.6 | 429 | 346 | 198 | 34 | 183 | .261 | .328 | 24 | 3 | OF-402, C-116, 3B-79, 1B-76, 2B-41, SS-39 |
| 3 yrs. | | 225 | 851 | 208 | 26 | 5 | 6 | 0.6 | 83 | 112 | 36 | | 37 | .244 | .304 | 6 | 1 | 1B-76, 3B-64, OF-44, C-25, 2B-14 |

| | G | AB | H | 2B | 3B | HR | HR % | R | RBI | BB | SO | SB | BA | SA | Pinch Hit AB | Pinch Hit H | G by POS |
|---|---|---|---|---|---|---|---|---|---|---|---|---|---|---|---|---|---|

## Mike Diaz

**DIAZ, MICHAEL ANTHONY**
B. Apr. 15, 1960, San Francisco, Calif.  BR TR 6'2" 205 lbs.

| | G | AB | H | 2B | 3B | HR | HR % | R | RBI | BB | SO | SB | BA | SA | PH AB | PH H | G by POS |
|---|---|---|---|---|---|---|---|---|---|---|---|---|---|---|---|---|---|
| 1983 CHI N | 6 | 7 | 2 | 1 | 0 | 0 | 0.0 | 2 | 1 | 0 | 0 | 0 | .286 | .429 | 3 | 1 | C-3 |

## Steve Dillard

**DILLARD, STEPHEN BRADLEY**
B. Dec. 8, 1951, Memphis, Tenn.  BR TR 6'1" 171 lbs.

| | G | AB | H | 2B | 3B | HR | HR % | R | RBI | BB | SO | SB | BA | SA | PH AB | PH H | G by POS |
|---|---|---|---|---|---|---|---|---|---|---|---|---|---|---|---|---|---|
| 1975 BOS A | 1 | 5 | 2 | 0 | 0 | 0 | 0.0 | 0 | 0 | 0 | 1 | 0 | .400 | .400 | 0 | 0 | 2B-1 |
| 1976 | 57 | 167 | 46 | 14 | 0 | 1 | 0.6 | 22 | 15 | 17 | 20 | 6 | .275 | .377 | 3 | 1 | 3B-18, 2B-17, SS-12, DH-7 |
| 1977 | 66 | 141 | 34 | 7 | 0 | 1 | 0.7 | 22 | 13 | 7 | 13 | 4 | .241 | .312 | 7 | 1 | 2B-45, SS-9, DH-6 |
| 1978 DET A | 56 | 130 | 29 | 5 | 2 | 0 | 0.0 | 21 | 7 | 6 | 11 | 1 | .223 | .292 | 1 | 0 | 2B-41, DH-4 |
| 1979 CHI N | 89 | 166 | 47 | 6 | 1 | 5 | 3.0 | 31 | 24 | 17 | 24 | 1 | .283 | .422 | 17 | 6 | 2B-60, 3B-9 |
| 1980 | 100 | 244 | 55 | 8 | 1 | 4 | 1.6 | 31 | 24 | 20 | 54 | 2 | .225 | .316 | 13 | 3 | 3B-51, 2B-38, SS-2 |
| 1981 | 53 | 119 | 26 | 7 | 1 | 2 | 1.7 | 18 | 11 | 8 | 20 | 1 | .218 | .345 | 11 | 3 | 2B-32, 3B-7, SS-2 |
| 1982 CHI A | 16 | 41 | 7 | 3 | 1 | 0 | 0.0 | 1 | 5 | 1 | 5 | 0 | .171 | .293 | 0 | 0 | 2B-16 |
| 8 yrs. | 438 | 1013 | 246 | 50 | 6 | 13 | 1.3 | 148 | 102 | 76 | 147 | 15 | .243 | .343 | 52 | 14 | 2B-250, 3B-85, SS-25, DH-17 |
| 3 yrs. | 242 | 529 | 128 | 21 | 3 | 11 | 2.1 | 80 | 62 | 45 | 98 | 3 | .242 | .355 | 41 | 12 | 2B-130, 3B-67, SS-4 |

## Pickles Dillhoefer

**DILLHOEFER, WILLIAM MARTIN**
B. Oct. 13, 1894, Cleveland, Ohio.  D. Feb. 22, 1922, St. Louis, Mo.  BR TR 5'7" 154 lbs.

| | G | AB | H | 2B | 3B | HR | HR % | R | RBI | BB | SO | SB | BA | SA | PH AB | PH H | G by POS |
|---|---|---|---|---|---|---|---|---|---|---|---|---|---|---|---|---|---|
| 1917 CHI N | 42 | 95 | 12 | 1 | 1 | 0 | 0.0 | 3 | 8 | 2 | 9 | 1 | .126 | .158 | 4 | 0 | C-37 |
| 1918 PHI N | 8 | 11 | 1 | 0 | 0 | 0 | 0.0 | 0 | 0 | 1 | 1 | 2 | .091 | .091 | 2 | 0 | C-6 |
| 1919 STL N | 45 | 108 | 23 | 3 | 2 | 0 | 0.0 | 11 | 12 | 8 | 6 | 5 | .213 | .278 | 1 | 1 | C-39 |
| 1920 | 76 | 224 | 59 | 8 | 3 | 0 | 0.0 | 26 | 13 | 13 | 7 | 2 | .263 | .326 | 2 | 0 | C-73 |
| 1921 | 76 | 162 | 39 | 4 | 4 | 0 | 0.0 | 19 | 15 | 11 | 7 | 2 | .241 | .315 | 4 | 0 | C-69 |
| 5 yrs. | 247 | 600 | 134 | 16 | 10 | 0 | 0.0 | 59 | 48 | 35 | 30 | 12 | .223 | .283 | 13 | 1 | C-224 |
| 1 yr. | 42 | 95 | 12 | 1 | 1 | 0 | 0.0 | 3 | 8 | 2 | 9 | 1 | .126 | .158 | 4 | 0 | C-37 |

## Miguel Dilone

**DILONE, MIGUEL ANGEL**
Born Miguel Angel Dilone Reyes.
B. Nov. 1, 1954, Santiago, Dominican Republic  BB TR 6' 160 lbs.

| | G | AB | H | 2B | 3B | HR | HR % | R | RBI | BB | SO | SB | BA | SA | PH AB | PH H | G by POS |
|---|---|---|---|---|---|---|---|---|---|---|---|---|---|---|---|---|---|
| 1974 PIT N | 12 | 2 | 0 | 0 | 0 | 0 | 0.0 | | | 0 | 1 | 2 | .000 | .000 | 2 | 0 | OF-2 |
| 1975 | 18 | 6 | 0 | 0 | 0 | 0 | 0.0 | 8 | 0 | 0 | 1 | 2 | .000 | .000 | 1 | 0 | OF-2 |
| 1976 | 16 | 17 | 4 | 0 | 0 | 0 | 0.0 | 7 | 0 | 0 | 5 | 5 | .235 | .235 | 4 | 0 | OF-3 |
| 1977 | 29 | 44 | 6 | 0 | 0 | 0 | 0.0 | 5 | 0 | 2 | 3 | 12 | .136 | .136 | 10 | 1 | OF-17 |
| 1978 OAK A | 135 | 258 | 59 | 8 | 0 | 1 | 0.4 | 34 | 14 | 23 | 30 | 50 | .229 | .271 | 1 | 0 | OF-99, 3B-3, DH-1 |
| 1979 2 teams | OAK A (30G – .187) | | CHI N (43G – .306) | | | | | | | | | | | | | | |
| " total | 73 | 127 | 28 | 1 | 2 | 1 | 0.8 | 29 | 7 | 8 | 12 | 21 | .220 | .283 | 2 | 1 | OF-47 |
| 1980 CLE A | 132 | 528 | 180 | 30 | 9 | 0 | 0.0 | 82 | 40 | 28 | 45 | 61 | .341 | .432 | 3 | 0 | OF-118, DH-11 |
| 1981 | 72 | 269 | 78 | 5 | 5 | 0 | 0.0 | 33 | 19 | 18 | 28 | 29 | .290 | .346 | 4 | 2 | OF-56, DH-11 |
| 1982 | 104 | 379 | 89 | 12 | 3 | 3 | 0.8 | 50 | 25 | 25 | 36 | 33 | .235 | .306 | 12 | 1 | OF-97, DH-1 |
| 1983 3 teams | CLE A (32G – .191) | | CHI A (4G – .000) | | PIT N (7G – .000) | | | | | | | | | | | | |
| " total | 43 | 71 | 13 | 3 | 1 | 0 | 0.0 | 7 | 10 | 5 | 8 | | .183 | .254 | 4 | 0 | OF-21, DH-2 |
| 1984 MON N | 88 | 169 | 47 | 8 | 2 | 1 | 0.6 | 28 | 10 | 17 | 18 | 27 | .278 | .367 | 37 | 9 | OF-41 |
| 1985 2 teams | MON N (51G – .190) | | SD N (27G – .217) | | | | | | | | | | | | | | |
| " total | 78 | 130 | 26 | 0 | 3 | 0 | 0.0 | 18 | 7 | 10 | 19 | 17 | .200 | .246 | 29 | 4 | OF-36 |
| 12 yrs. | 800 | 2000 | 530 | 67 | 25 | 6 | 0.3 | 314 | 129 | 142 | 197 | 267 | .265 | .333 | 109 | 18 | OF-539, DH-26, 3B-3 |
| 1 yr. | 43 | 36 | 11 | 0 | 0 | 0 | 0.0 | 14 | 1 | 2 | 5 | 15 | .306 | .306 | 0 | 0 | OF-22 |

## John Dobbs

**DOBBS, JOHN L.**
B. June 3, 1876, Chattanooga, Tenn.  D. Sept. 9, 1934, Charlotte, N. C.  BL TR 5'9½" 170 lbs.

| | G | AB | H | 2B | 3B | HR | HR % | R | RBI | BB | SO | SB | BA | SA | PH AB | PH H | G by POS |
|---|---|---|---|---|---|---|---|---|---|---|---|---|---|---|---|---|---|
| 1901 CIN N | 109 | 435 | 119 | 17 | 4 | 2 | 0.5 | 71 | 27 | 36 | | 19 | .274 | .345 | 1 | 0 | OF-100, 3B-8 |
| 1902 2 teams | CIN N (63G – .297) | | CHI N (59G – .302) | | | | | | | | | | | | | | |
| " total | 122 | 491 | 147 | 16 | 5 | 1 | 0.2 | 70 | 51 | 37 | | 10 | .299 | .358 | 0 | 0 | OF-122 |
| 1903 2 teams | CHI N (16G – .230) | | BKN N (111G – .237) | | | | | | | | | | | | | | |
| " total | 127 | 475 | 112 | 16 | 8 | 2 | 0.4 | 69 | 63 | 55 | | 23 | .236 | .316 | 1 | 1 | OF-126 |
| 1904 BKN N | 101 | 363 | 90 | 16 | 2 | 0 | 0.0 | 36 | 30 | 28 | | 11 | .248 | .303 | 3 | 0 | OF-92, SS-2, 2B-2 |
| 1905 | 123 | 460 | 117 | 21 | 4 | 2 | 0.4 | 59 | 36 | 31 | | 15 | .254 | .330 | 0 | 0 | OF-123 |
| 5 yrs. | 582 | 2224 | 585 | 86 | 23 | 7 | 0.3 | 305 | 207 | 187 | | 78 | .263 | .332 | 5 | 1 | OF-563, 3B-8, SS-2, 2B-2 |
| 2 yrs. | 75 | 296 | 85 | 9 | 3 | 0 | 0.0 | 39 | 39 | 25 | | 3 | .287 | .338 | 0 | 0 | OF-75 |

## Cozy Dolan

**DOLAN, PATRICK HENRY**
B. Dec. 3, 1872, Cambridge, Mass.  D. Mar. 29, 1907, Louisville, Ky.  BL TL 5'10" 160 lbs.

| | G | AB | H | 2B | 3B | HR | HR % | R | RBI | BB | SO | SB | BA | SA | PH AB | PH H | G by POS |
|---|---|---|---|---|---|---|---|---|---|---|---|---|---|---|---|---|---|
| 1895 BOS N | 26 | 83 | 20 | 4 | 1 | 0 | 0.0 | 12 | 7 | 6 | 7 | 3 | .241 | .313 | 0 | 0 | P-25, OF-1 |
| 1896 | 6 | 14 | 2 | 0 | 0 | 0 | 0.0 | 4 | 0 | 0 | 1 | 0 | .143 | .143 | 0 | 0 | P-6 |
| 1900 CHI N | 13 | 48 | 13 | 1 | 0 | 0 | 0.0 | 5 | 2 | 2 | | | .271 | .292 | 0 | 0 | OF-13 |
| 1901 2 teams | CHI N (43G – .263) | | BKN N (66G – .261) | | | | | | | | | | | | | | |
| " total | 109 | 424 | 111 | 12 | 3 | 0 | 0.0 | 62 | 45 | 24 | | 10 | .262 | .304 | 4 | 1 | OF-105 |
| 1902 BKN N | 141 | 592 | 166 | 16 | 7 | 1 | 0.2 | 72 | 54 | 33 | | 24 | .280 | .336 | 0 | 0 | OF-141 |
| 1903 2 teams | CHI A (27G – .260) | | CIN N (93G – .288) | | | | | | | | | | | | | | |
| " total | 120 | 489 | 138 | 25 | 4 | 0 | 0.0 | 80 | 65 | 34 | | 16 | .282 | .350 | 4 | 0 | OF-97, 1B-19 |
| 1904 CIN N | 129 | 465 | 132 | 8 | 10 | 6 | 1.3 | 88 | 51 | 39 | | 19 | .284 | .383 | 3 | 0 | OF-102, 1B-24 |
| 1905 2 teams | CIN N (22G – .234) | | BOS N (112G – .275) | | | | | | | | | | | | | | |
| " total | 134 | 510 | 137 | 13 | 8 | 3 | 0.6 | 51 | 52 | 34 | | 23 | .269 | .343 | 0 | 0 | OF-120, 1B-15, P-2 |
| 1906 BOS N | 152 | 549 | 136 | 20 | 4 | 0 | 0.0 | 54 | 39 | 55 | | 17 | .248 | .299 | 0 | 0 | OF-144, 2B-7, P-2, 1B-1 |
| 9 yrs. | 830 | 3174 | 855 | 99 | 37 | 10 | 0.3 | 428 | 315 | 227 | 8 | 114 | .269 | .333 | 11 | 1 | OF-723, 1B-59, P-35, 2B-7 |
| 2 yrs. | 56 | 219 | 58 | 2 | 2 | 0 | 0.0 | 34 | 18 | 9 | | 5 | .265 | .292 | 2 | 0 | OF-54 |

## Tom Dolan

**DOLAN, THOMAS J.**
B. Jan. 10, 1859, New York, N. Y.  D. Jan. 16, 1913, St. Louis, Mo.  BR TR

| | G | AB | H | 2B | 3B | HR | HR % | R | RBI | BB | SO | SB | BA | SA | PH AB | PH H | G by POS |
|---|---|---|---|---|---|---|---|---|---|---|---|---|---|---|---|---|---|
| 1879 CHI N | 1 | 4 | 0 | 0 | 0 | 0 | 0.0 | 0 | 0 | | 0 | 2 | .000 | .000 | 0 | 0 | C-1 |
| 1882 BUF N | 22 | 89 | 14 | 0 | 1 | 0 | 0.0 | 12 | | 0 | 2 | 11 | .157 | .180 | 0 | 0 | C-18, OF-4, 3B-2 |

| | G | AB | H | 2B | 3B | HR | HR % | R | RBI | BB | SO | SB | BA | SA | Pinch Hit AB | Pinch Hit H | G by POS |
|---|---|---|---|---|---|---|---|---|---|---|---|---|---|---|---|---|---|

# Tom Dolan continued

| | G | AB | H | 2B | 3B | HR | HR % | R | RBI | BB | SO | SB | BA | SA | AB | H | G by POS |
|---|---|---|---|---|---|---|---|---|---|---|---|---|---|---|---|---|---|
| 883 STL AA | 81 | 295 | 63 | 9 | 2 | 1 | 0.3 | 32 | | 9 | | | .214 | .268 | 0 | 0 | OF-82, P-1 |
| 884 2 teams | STL | AA (35G – | .263) | | | STL | U (19G – | .188) | | | | | | | | | |
| " total | 54 | 206 | 49 | 9 | 2 | 0 | 0.0 | 28 | | 10 | | | .238 | .301 | 0 | 0 | C-48, OF-4, 3B-3 |
| 885 STL N | 9 | 9 | 2 | 0 | 0 | 0 | 0.0 | 1 | 0 | 2 | 1 | | .222 | .222 | 0 | 0 | C-3 |
| 886 2 teams | STL | N (15G – | .250) | | | BAL | AA (38G – | .152) | | | | | | | | | |
| " total | 53 | 169 | 30 | 6 | 2 | 0 | 0.0 | 21 | 1 | 15 | 9 | | .178 | .237 | 0 | 0 | C-50, OF-3 |
| 888 STL AA | 11 | 36 | 7 | 1 | 0 | 0 | 0.0 | 1 | 1 | 1 | | 1 | .194 | .222 | 0 | 0 | C-11 |
| 7 yrs. | 225 | 808 | 165 | 25 | 7 | 1 | 0.1 | 95 | 1 | 39 | 23 | 1 | .204 | .256 | 0 | 0 | C-131, OF-93, 3B-5, P-1 |
| 1 yr. | 1 | 4 | 0 | 0 | 0 | 0 | 0.0 | 0 | | 0 | 2 | | .000 | .000 | 0 | 0 | C-1 |

# Tim Donahue

**DONAHUE, TIMOTHY CORNELIUS**                  BL  TR  5'11"   180 lbs.
B. June 8, 1870, Raynham, Mass.   D. June 12, 1902, Taunton, Mass.

| | G | AB | H | 2B | 3B | HR | HR % | R | RBI | BB | SO | SB | BA | SA | AB | H | G by POS |
|---|---|---|---|---|---|---|---|---|---|---|---|---|---|---|---|---|---|
| 891 BOS AA | 4 | 7 | 0 | 0 | 0 | 0 | 0.0 | 0 | | 0 | 5 | 0 | .000 | .000 | 0 | 0 | C-4 |
| 895 CHI N | 63 | 219 | 59 | 9 | 1 | 2 | 0.9 | 29 | 36 | 20 | 25 | 5 | .269 | .347 | 0 | 0 | C-63 |
| 896 | 57 | 188 | 41 | 10 | 1 | 0 | 0.0 | 27 | 20 | 11 | 15 | 11 | .218 | .282 | 0 | 0 | C-57 |
| 897 | 58 | 188 | 45 | 7 | 3 | 0 | 0.0 | 28 | 21 | 9 | | 3 | .239 | .309 | 1 | 1 | C-55, SS-2, 1B-1 |
| 898 | 122 | 396 | 87 | 12 | 3 | 0 | 0.0 | 52 | 39 | 49 | | 17 | .220 | .265 | 0 | 0 | C-122 |
| 1899 | 92 | 278 | 69 | 9 | 3 | 0 | 0.0 | 39 | 29 | 34 | | 10 | .248 | .302 | 0 | 0 | C-91, 1B-1 |
| 1900 | 67 | 216 | 51 | 10 | 1 | 0 | 0.0 | 21 | 17 | 19 | | 8 | .236 | .292 | 0 | 0 | C-66, 2B-1 |
| 1902 WAS A | 3 | 8 | 2 | 0 | 0 | 0 | 0.0 | 0 | 1 | 0 | | 0 | .250 | .250 | 0 | 0 | C-3 |
| 8 yrs. | 466 | 1500 | 354 | 57 | 12 | 2 | 0.1 | 196 | 163 | 142 | 45 | 54 | .236 | .294 | 1 | 1 | C-461, SS-2, 1B-2, 2B-1 |
| 6 yrs. | 459 | 1485 | 352 | 57 | 12 | 2 | 0.1 | 196 | 162 | 142 | 40 | 54 | .237 | .296 | 1 | 1 | C-454, SS-2, 1B-2, 2B-1 |

# Mickey Doolan

**DOOLAN, MICHAEL JOSEPH**                      BR  TR  5'10½" 170 lbs.
Born Michael Joseph Doolittle.
B. May 7, 1880, Ashland, Pa.   D. Nov. 1, 1951, Orlando, Fla.

| | G | AB | H | 2B | 3B | HR | HR % | R | RBI | BB | SO | SB | BA | SA | AB | H | G by POS |
|---|---|---|---|---|---|---|---|---|---|---|---|---|---|---|---|---|---|
| 1905 PHI N | 136 | 492 | 125 | 27 | 11 | 1 | 0.2 | 53 | 48 | 24 | | 17 | .254 | .360 | 1 | 0 | SS-135 |
| 1906 | 154 | 535 | 123 | 19 | 7 | 1 | 0.2 | 41 | 55 | 27 | | 16 | .230 | .297 | 0 | 0 | SS-154 |
| 1907 | 145 | 509 | 104 | 19 | 7 | 1 | 0.2 | 33 | 47 | 25 | | 18 | .204 | .275 | 0 | 0 | SS-145 |
| 1908 | 129 | 445 | 104 | 25 | 4 | 2 | 0.4 | 29 | 49 | 17 | | 5 | .234 | .321 | 0 | 0 | SS-129 |
| 1909 | 147 | 493 | 108 | 12 | 10 | 1 | 0.2 | 39 | 35 | 37 | | 10 | .219 | .290 | 0 | 0 | SS-147 |
| 1910 | 148 | 536 | 141 | 31 | 6 | 2 | 0.4 | 58 | 57 | 35 | 56 | 16 | .263 | .354 | 0 | 0 | SS-148 |
| 1911 | 146 | 512 | 122 | 23 | 6 | 1 | 0.2 | 51 | 49 | 44 | 65 | 14 | .238 | .313 | 1 | 0 | SS-145 |
| 1912 | 146 | 532 | 137 | 26 | 6 | 1 | 0.2 | 47 | 62 | 34 | 59 | 6 | .258 | .335 | 0 | 0 | SS-146 |
| 1913 | 151 | 518 | 113 | 12 | 6 | 1 | 0.2 | 32 | 43 | 29 | 68 | 17 | .218 | .270 | 0 | 0 | SS-148, 2B-3 |
| 1914 BAL F | 145 | 486 | 119 | 23 | 6 | 1 | 0.2 | 58 | 53 | 40 | | 30 | .245 | .323 | 0 | 0 | SS-145 |
| 1915 2 teams | BAL | F (119G – | .186) | | | CHI | F (24G – | .267) | | | | | | | | | |
| " total | 143 | 490 | 98 | 14 | 8 | 2 | 0.4 | 50 | 30 | 26 | | 15 | .200 | .273 | 0 | 0 | SS-143 |
| 1916 2 teams | CHI | N (28G – | .214) | | | NY | N (18G – | .235) | | | | | | | | | |
| " total | 46 | 121 | 27 | 5 | 2 | 1 | 0.8 | 8 | 8 | 10 | 11 | 1 | .223 | .322 | 3 | 0 | SS-40, 2B-2 |
| 1918 BKN N | 92 | 308 | 55 | 8 | 2 | 0 | 0.0 | 14 | 18 | 22 | 24 | 8 | .179 | .218 | 0 | 0 | 2B-91 |
| 13 yrs. | 1728 | 5977 | 1376 | 244 | 81 | 15 | 0.3 | 513 | 554 | 370 | 283 | 173 | .230 | .306 | 5 | 0 | SS-1625, 2B-96 |
| 1 yr. | 28 | 70 | 15 | 2 | 1 | 0 | 0.0 | 4 | 5 | 8 | 7 | 0 | .214 | .271 | 3 | 0 | SS-24 |

# Herm Doscher

**DOSCHER, JOHN HENRY, SR.**                    5'10"   182 lbs.
Father of John Doscher.
B. Dec. 20, 1852, New York, N. Y.   D. Mar. 30, 1934, Buffalo, N. Y.

| | G | AB | H | 2B | 3B | HR | HR % | R | RBI | BB | SO | SB | BA | SA | AB | H | G by POS |
|---|---|---|---|---|---|---|---|---|---|---|---|---|---|---|---|---|---|
| 1879 2 teams | TRO | N (47G – | .220) | | | CHI | N (3G – | .182) | | | | | | | | | |
| " total | 50 | 202 | 44 | 8 | 0 | 0 | 0.0 | 17 | 19 | 2 | 13 | | .218 | .257 | 0 | 0 | 3B-50 |
| 1881 CLE N | 5 | 19 | 4 | 0 | 0 | 0 | 0.0 | 2 | 0 | 0 | 2 | | .211 | .211 | 0 | 0 | 3B-5 |
| 1882 | 25 | 104 | 25 | 2 | 0 | 0 | 0.0 | 7 | 10 | 0 | 11 | | .240 | .260 | 0 | 0 | 3B-22, OF-2, SS-1 |
| 3 yrs. | 80 | 325 | 73 | 10 | 0 | 0 | 0.0 | 26 | 29 | 2 | 26 | | .225 | .255 | 0 | 0 | 3B-77, OF-2, SS-1 |
| 1 yr. | 3 | 11 | 2 | 0 | 0 | 0 | 0.0 | 1 | 1 | 0 | 3 | | .182 | .182 | 0 | 0 | 3B-3 |

# Taylor Douthit

**DOUTHIT, TAYLOR LEE**                         BR  TR  5'11½" 175 lbs.
B. Apr. 22, 1901, Little Rock, Ark.

| | G | AB | H | 2B | 3B | HR | HR % | R | RBI | BB | SO | SB | BA | SA | AB | H | G by POS |
|---|---|---|---|---|---|---|---|---|---|---|---|---|---|---|---|---|---|
| 1923 STL N | 9 | 27 | 5 | 0 | 2 | 0 | 0.0 | 3 | 0 | 0 | 4 | 1 | .185 | .333 | 2 | 0 | OF-7 |
| 1924 | 53 | 173 | 48 | 13 | 1 | 0 | 0.0 | 24 | 13 | 16 | 19 | 4 | .277 | .364 | 1 | 0 | OF-50 |
| 1925 | 30 | 73 | 20 | 3 | 1 | 1 | 1.4 | 13 | 8 | 2 | 6 | 0 | .274 | .384 | 9 | 5 | OF-21 |
| 1926 | 139 | 530 | 163 | 20 | 4 | 3 | 0.6 | 96 | 52 | 55 | 46 | 23 | .308 | .377 | 1 | 0 | OF-138 |
| 1927 | 130 | 488 | 128 | 29 | 6 | 5 | 1.0 | 81 | 50 | 52 | 45 | 6 | .262 | .377 | 4 | 2 | OF-125 |
| 1928 | 154 | 648 | 191 | 35 | 3 | 3 | 0.5 | 111 | 43 | 84 | 36 | 11 | .295 | .372 | 0 | 0 | OF-154 |
| 1929 | 150 | 613 | 206 | 42 | 7 | 9 | 1.5 | 128 | 62 | 79 | 49 | 8 | .336 | .471 | 0 | 0 | OF-150 |
| 1930 | 154 | 664 | 201 | 41 | 10 | 7 | 1.1 | 109 | 93 | 60 | 38 | 4 | .303 | .426 | 0 | 0 | OF-154 |
| 1931 2 teams | STL | N (36G – | .331) | | | CIN | N (95G – | .262) | | | | | | | | | |
| " total | 131 | 507 | 142 | 20 | 3 | 1 | 0.2 | 63 | 45 | 53 | 33 | 5 | .280 | .337 | 0 | 0 | OF-131 |
| 1932 CIN N | 96 | 333 | 81 | 12 | 1 | 0 | 0.0 | 28 | 25 | 31 | 29 | 3 | .243 | .285 | 2 | 0 | OF-88 |
| 1933 2 teams | CIN | N (1G – | .000) | | | CHI | N (27G – | .225) | | | | | | | | | |
| " total | 28 | 71 | 16 | 5 | 0 | 0 | 0.0 | 9 | 5 | 11 | 7 | 2 | .225 | .296 | 1 | 0 | OF-18 |
| 11 yrs. | 1074 | 4127 | 1201 | 220 | 38 | 29 | 0.7 | 665 | 396 | 443 | 312 | 67 | .291 | .384 | 20 | 7 | OF-1036 |
| 1 yr. | 27 | 71 | 16 | 5 | 0 | 0 | 0.0 | 8 | 5 | 11 | 7 | 2 | .225 | .296 | 1 | 0 | OF-18 |

| WORLD SERIES | | | | | | | | | | | | | | | | | |
|---|---|---|---|---|---|---|---|---|---|---|---|---|---|---|---|---|---|
| 1926 STL N | 4 | 15 | 4 | 2 | 0 | 0 | 0.0 | 3 | 1 | 3 | 2 | 0 | .267 | .400 | 0 | 0 | OF-4 |
| 1928 | 3 | 11 | 1 | 0 | 0 | 0 | 0.0 | 1 | 0 | 1 | 1 | 0 | .091 | .091 | 0 | 0 | OF-3 |
| 1930 | 6 | 24 | 2 | 0 | 0 | 1 | 4.2 | 1 | 2 | 0 | 2 | 0 | .083 | .208 | 0 | 0 | OF-6 |
| 3 yrs. | 13 | 50 | 7 | 2 | 0 | 1 | 2.0 | 5 | 3 | 4 | 5 | 0 | .140 | .240 | 0 | 0 | OF-13 |

# Tom Downey

**DOWNEY, THOMAS EDWARD**                       BR  TR  6'   170 lbs.
B. Jan. 1, 1884, Lewiston, Me.   D. Aug. 3, 1961, Passaic, N. J.

| | G | AB | H | 2B | 3B | HR | HR % | R | RBI | BB | SO | SB | BA | SA | AB | H | G by POS |
|---|---|---|---|---|---|---|---|---|---|---|---|---|---|---|---|---|---|
| 1909 CIN N | 119 | 416 | 96 | 9 | 6 | 1 | 0.2 | 39 | 32 | 32 | | 16 | .231 | .288 | 0 | 0 | SS-119, C-1 |
| 1910 | 111 | 378 | 102 | 9 | 3 | 2 | 0.5 | 43 | 32 | 34 | 28 | 12 | .270 | .325 | 0 | 0 | SS-68, 3B-41 |

| | G | AB | H | 2B | 3B | HR | HR % | R | RBI | BB | SO | SB | BA | SA | Pinch Hit AB | Pinch Hit H | G by POS |
|---|---|---|---|---|---|---|---|---|---|---|---|---|---|---|---|---|---|

## Tom Downey continued

| | G | AB | H | 2B | 3B | HR | HR% | R | RBI | BB | SO | SB | BA | SA | AB | H | G by POS |
|---|---|---|---|---|---|---|---|---|---|---|---|---|---|---|---|---|---|
| 1911 | 111 | 360 | 94 | 16 | 7 | 0 | 0.0 | 50 | 36 | 44 | 38 | 10 | .261 | .344 | 4 | 0 | SS-93, 2B-6, 3B-5, 1B-2, OF-1 |
| 1912 2 teams | PHI | N | (54G – | .292) | | CHI | N | (13G – | .182) | | | | | | | | |
| " total | 67 | 193 | 54 | 6 | 5 | 1 | 0.5 | 31 | 27 | 22 | 25 | 3 | .280 | .378 | 7 | 2 | 3B-49, SS-8, 2B-1 |
| 1914 BUF F | 151 | 541 | 118 | 20 | 3 | 2 | 0.4 | 69 | 42 | 40 | | 35 | .218 | .277 | 1 | 0 | 2B-129, SS-16, 3B-5 |
| 1915 | 92 | 282 | 56 | 9 | 1 | 1 | 0.4 | 24 | 19 | 26 | | 11 | .199 | .248 | 5 | 1 | 2B-48, 3B-35, SS-2, 1B-1 |
| 6 yrs. | 651 | 2170 | 520 | 69 | 25 | 7 | 0.3 | 256 | 188 | 198 | 91 | 87 | .240 | .304 | 17 | 3 | SS-306, 2B-184, 3B-135, 1B-3, OF-1, C-1 |
| 1 yr. | 13 | 22 | 4 | 0 | 2 | 0 | 0.0 | 4 | 4 | 1 | 5 | 0 | .182 | .364 | 3 | 0 | SS-5, 3B-3, 2B-1 |

## Red Downs

**DOWNS, JEROME WILLIS**     BR TR 5'11"   155 lbs.
B. Aug. 22, 1883, Neola, Iowa     D. Oct. 19, 1939, Council Bluffs, Iowa

| | G | AB | H | 2B | 3B | HR | HR% | R | RBI | BB | SO | SB | BA | SA | AB | H | G by POS |
|---|---|---|---|---|---|---|---|---|---|---|---|---|---|---|---|---|---|
| 1907 DET A | 105 | 374 | 82 | 13 | 5 | 1 | 0.3 | 28 | 42 | 13 | | 3 | .219 | .289 | 4 | 1 | 2B-80, OF-20, SS-1, 3B- |
| 1908 | 84 | 289 | 64 | 10 | 3 | 1 | 0.3 | 29 | 35 | 5 | | 2 | .221 | .287 | 1 | 0 | 2B-82, 3B-1 |
| 1912 2 teams | BKN | N | (9G – | .250) | | CHI | N | (43G – | .263) | | | | | | | | |
| " total | 52 | 127 | 33 | 7 | 3 | 1 | 0.8 | 11 | 17 | 10 | 22 | 8 | .260 | .386 | 11 | 2 | 2B-25, SS-9, 3B-5 |
| 3 yrs. | 241 | 790 | 179 | 30 | 11 | 3 | 0.4 | 68 | 94 | 28 | 22 | 13 | .227 | .304 | 16 | 3 | 2B-187, OF-20, SS-10, 3B-7 |
| 1 yr. | 43 | 95 | 25 | 4 | 3 | 1 | 1.1 | 9 | 14 | 9 | 17 | 5 | .263 | .400 | 11 | 2 | 2B-16, SS-9, 3B-5 |

**WORLD SERIES**

| | G | AB | H | 2B | 3B | HR | HR% | R | RBI | BB | SO | SB | BA | SA | AB | H | G by POS |
|---|---|---|---|---|---|---|---|---|---|---|---|---|---|---|---|---|---|
| 1908 DET A | 2 | 6 | 1 | 1 | 0 | 0 | 0.0 | 1 | 1 | 1 | 2 | 0 | .167 | .333 | 0 | 0 | 2B-2 |

## Jack Doyle

**DOYLE, JOHN JOSEPH (Dirty Jack)**     BR TR 5'9"   155 lbs.
B. Oct. 25, 1869, Killorgin, Ireland   D. Dec. 31, 1958, Holyoke, Mass.
Manager 1895, 1898.

| | G | AB | H | 2B | 3B | HR | HR% | R | RBI | BB | SO | SB | BA | SA | AB | H | G by POS |
|---|---|---|---|---|---|---|---|---|---|---|---|---|---|---|---|---|---|
| 1889 COL AA | 11 | 36 | 10 | 1 | 1 | 0 | 0.0 | 6 | 3 | 6 | 6 | 9 | .278 | .361 | 0 | 0 | C-7, OF-3, 2B-2 |
| 1890 | 77 | 298 | 80 | 17 | 7 | 2 | 0.7 | 48 | | 13 | | 27 | .268 | .393 | 0 | 0 | C-38, SS-25, OF-9, 2B-6, 3B-3 |
| 1891 CLE N | 69 | 250 | 69 | 14 | 4 | 0 | 0.0 | 43 | 43 | 26 | 44 | 24 | .276 | .364 | 0 | 0 | C-29, OF-21, 3B-20, SS- |
| 1892 2 teams | CLE | N | (24G – | .295) | | NY | N | (90G – | .298) | | | | | | | | |
| " total | 114 | 454 | 135 | 26 | 2 | 6 | 1.3 | 78 | 69 | 24 | 40 | 47 | .297 | .403 | 1 | 1 | C-35, 2B-31, OF-29, 3B-13, SS-8, 1B-1 |
| 1893 NY N | 82 | 318 | 102 | 17 | 5 | 1 | 0.3 | 56 | 51 | 27 | 12 | 40 | .321 | .415 | 0 | 0 | C-48, OF-29, SS-4, 3B-3, 1B-1 |
| 1894 | 105 | 425 | 157 | 30 | 8 | 3 | 0.7 | 94 | 100 | 35 | 3 | 42 | .369 | .499 | 0 | 0 | 1B-99, C-6 |
| 1895 | 82 | 319 | 100 | 21 | 3 | 1 | 0.3 | 52 | 66 | 24 | 12 | 35 | .313 | .408 | 0 | 0 | 1B-58, 2B-13, 3B-6, C-4 |
| 1896 BAL N | 118 | 487 | 168 | 29 | 4 | 1 | 0.2 | 116 | 101 | 42 | 15 | 73 | .345 | .427 | 0 | 0 | 1B-118, 2B-1 |
| 1897 | 114 | 463 | 165 | 29 | 4 | 1 | 0.2 | 93 | 87 | 29 | | 62 | .356 | .443 | 0 | 0 | 1B-114 |
| 1898 2 teams | WAS | N | (43G – | .305) | | NY | N | (82G – | .283) | | | | | | | | |
| " total | 125 | 474 | 138 | 17 | 5 | 3 | 0.6 | 68 | 69 | 19 | | 23 | .291 | .367 | 1 | 1 | 1B-62, OF-38, SS-15, 3B-5, 2B-5, C-2 |
| 1899 NY N | 118 | 454 | 140 | 15 | 7 | 3 | 0.7 | 57 | 76 | 33 | | 35 | .308 | .392 | 0 | 0 | 1B-113, C-5 |
| 1900 | 133 | 505 | 138 | 24 | 1 | 1 | 0.2 | 69 | 66 | 34 | | 34 | .273 | .331 | 0 | 0 | 1B-133 |
| 1901 CHI N | 75 | 285 | 66 | 9 | 2 | 0 | 0.0 | 21 | 39 | 7 | | 8 | .232 | .277 | 0 | 0 | 1B-75 |
| 1902 2 teams | NY | N | (49G – | .301) | | WAS | A | (78G – | .247) | | | | | | | | |
| " total | 127 | 498 | 133 | 27 | 2 | 2 | 0.4 | 73 | 39 | 39 | | 18 | .267 | .341 | 0 | 0 | 2B-68, 1B-56, OF-4, C-1 |
| 1903 BKN N | 139 | 524 | 164 | 27 | 4 | 0 | 0.0 | 84 | 91 | 54 | | 34 | .313 | .387 | 0 | 0 | 1B-139 |
| 1904 2 teams | BKN | N | (8G – | .227) | | PHI | N | (66G – | .220) | | | | | | | | |
| " total | 74 | 258 | 57 | 11 | 3 | 0 | 0.0 | 4 | 22 | 24 | 25 | | 5 | .221 | .298 | 0 | 0 | 1B-73, 2B-1 |
| 1905 NY A | 1 | 3 | 0 | 0 | 0 | 0 | 0.0 | 0 | 0 | 0 | | 0 | .000 | .000 | 0 | 0 | 1B-1 |
| 17 yrs. | 1564 | 6051 | 1822 | 314 | 64 | 25 | 0.4 | 980 | 924 | 437 | 132 | 516 | .301 | .387 | 5 | 3 | 1B-1043, C-175, OF-133, 2B-127, SS-53, 3B-50 |
| 1 yr. | 75 | 285 | 66 | 9 | 2 | 0 | 0.0 | 21 | 39 | 7 | | 8 | .232 | .277 | 0 | 0 | 1B-75 |

## Jim Doyle

**DOYLE, JAMES FRANCIS**     BR TR 5'10"   168 lbs.
B. Dec. 25, 1881, Detroit, Mich.   D. Feb. 1, 1912, Syracuse, N. Y.

| | G | AB | H | 2B | 3B | HR | HR% | R | RBI | BB | SO | SB | BA | SA | AB | H | G by POS |
|---|---|---|---|---|---|---|---|---|---|---|---|---|---|---|---|---|---|
| 1910 CIN N | 7 | 13 | 2 | 2 | 0 | 0 | 0.0 | 1 | | 0 | 2 | 0 | .154 | .308 | 1 | 0 | 3B-3, OF-1 |
| 1911 CHI N | 130 | 472 | 133 | 23 | 12 | 5 | 1.1 | 69 | 62 | 40 | 54 | 19 | .282 | .413 | 3 | 1 | 3B-127 |
| 2 yrs. | 137 | 485 | 135 | 25 | 12 | 5 | 1.0 | 70 | 63 | 40 | 56 | 19 | .278 | .410 | 4 | 1 | 3B-130, OF-1 |
| 1 yr. | 130 | 472 | 133 | 23 | 12 | 5 | 1.1 | 69 | 62 | 40 | 54 | 19 | .282 | .413 | 3 | 1 | 3B-127 |

## Larry Doyle

**DOYLE, LAWRENCE JOSEPH (Laughing Larry)**     BL TR 5'10"   165 lbs.
B. July 31, 1886, Caseyville, Ill.   D. Mar. 1, 1974, Saranac Lake, N. Y.

| | G | AB | H | 2B | 3B | HR | HR% | R | RBI | BB | SO | SB | BA | SA | AB | H | G by POS |
|---|---|---|---|---|---|---|---|---|---|---|---|---|---|---|---|---|---|
| 1907 NY N | 69 | 227 | 59 | 3 | 0 | 0 | 0.0 | 16 | 16 | 20 | | 3 | .260 | .273 | 0 | 0 | 2B-69 |
| 1908 | 104 | 377 | 116 | 16 | 9 | 0 | 0.0 | 65 | 33 | 22 | | 17 | .308 | .398 | 3 | 1 | 2B-102 |
| 1909 | 146 | 570 | 172 | 27 | 11 | 6 | 1.1 | 86 | 49 | 45 | | 30 | .302 | .419 | 3 | 2 | 2B-143 |
| 1910 | 151 | 575 | 164 | 21 | 14 | 8 | 1.4 | 97 | 69 | 71 | 26 | 39 | .285 | .412 | 0 | 0 | 2B-151 |
| 1911 | 143 | 526 | 163 | 25 | 25 | 13 | 2.5 | 102 | 77 | 71 | 39 | 38 | .310 | .527 | 2 | 1 | 2B-141 |
| 1912 | 143 | 558 | 184 | 33 | 8 | 10 | 1.8 | 98 | 90 | 56 | 20 | 36 | .330 | .471 | 0 | 0 | 2B-143 |
| 1913 | 132 | 482 | 135 | 25 | 6 | 5 | 1.0 | 67 | 73 | 59 | 29 | 38 | .280 | .388 | 2 | 1 | 2B-130 |
| 1914 | 145 | 539 | 140 | 19 | 8 | 5 | 0.9 | 87 | 63 | 58 | 25 | 17 | .260 | .353 | 0 | 0 | 2B-145 |
| 1915 | 150 | 591 | 189 | 40 | 10 | 4 | 0.7 | 86 | 70 | 32 | 28 | 22 | **.320** | .442 | 0 | 0 | 2B-150 |
| 1916 2 teams | NY | N | (113G – | .268) | | CHI | N | (9G – | .395) | | | | | | | | |
| " total | 122 | 479 | 133 | 29 | 11 | 3 | 0.6 | 61 | 54 | 28 | 24 | 19 | .278 | .403 | 2 | 0 | 2B-122 |
| 1917 CHI N | 135 | 476 | 121 | 19 | 5 | 6 | 1.3 | 48 | 61 | 48 | 28 | 5 | .254 | .353 | 7 | 3 | 2B-128 |
| 1918 NY N | 75 | 257 | 67 | 7 | 4 | 3 | 1.2 | 38 | 36 | 37 | 10 | 10 | .261 | .354 | 2 | 0 | 2B-73 |
| 1919 | 113 | 381 | 110 | 14 | 10 | 7 | 1.8 | 61 | 52 | 31 | 17 | 12 | .289 | .433 | 11 | 1 | 2B-100 |
| 1920 | 137 | 471 | 134 | 21 | 4 | 4 | 0.8 | 48 | 50 | 47 | 28 | 11 | .285 | .363 | 4 | 0 | 2B-133 |
| 14 yrs. | 1765 | 6509 | 1887 | 299 | 123 | 74 | 1.1 | 960 | 793 | 625 | 274 | 297 | .290 | .408 | 37 | 9 | 2B-1730 |
| 2 yrs. | 144 | 514 | 136 | 24 | 6 | 1 | 1.4 | 54 | 68 | 49 | 29 | 7 | .265 | .375 | 7 | 3 | 2B-137 |

**WORLD SERIES**

| | G | AB | H | 2B | 3B | HR | HR% | R | RBI | BB | SO | SB | BA | SA | AB | H | G by POS |
|---|---|---|---|---|---|---|---|---|---|---|---|---|---|---|---|---|---|
| 1911 NY N | 6 | 23 | 7 | 3 | 1 | 0 | 0.0 | 3 | 1 | 2 | 1 | 2 | .304 | .522 | 0 | 0 | 2B-6 |
| 1912 | 8 | 33 | 8 | 1 | 0 | 1 | 3.0 | 5 | 2 | 3 | 2 | 2 | .242 | .364 | 0 | 0 | 2B-8 |

| | G | AB | H | 2B | 3B | HR | HR % | R | RBI | BB | SO | SB | BA | SA | Pinch Hit AB | Pinch Hit H | G by POS |
|---|---|---|---|---|---|---|---|---|---|---|---|---|---|---|---|---|---|

## Larry Doyle continued

| | G | AB | H | 2B | 3B | HR | HR % | R | RBI | BB | SO | SB | BA | SA | AB | H | G by POS |
|---|---|---|---|---|---|---|---|---|---|---|---|---|---|---|---|---|---|
| 1913 | 5 | 20 | 3 | 0 | 0 | 0 | 0.0 | 1 | 2 | 0 | 1 | 0 | .150 | .150 | 0 | 0 | 2B-5 |
| 3 yrs. | 19 | 76 | 18 | 4 | 1 | 1 | 1.3 | 9 | 5 | 5 | 4 | 4 | .237 | .355 | 0 | 0 | 2B-19 |

## Sammy Drake

**DRAKE, SAMUEL HARRISON**      BB TR 5'11" 175 lbs.
Brother of Solly Drake.
B. Oct. 7, 1934, Little Rock, Ark.

| | | G | AB | H | 2B | 3B | HR | HR % | R | RBI | BB | SO | SB | BA | SA | AB | H | G by POS |
|---|---|---|---|---|---|---|---|---|---|---|---|---|---|---|---|---|---|---|
| 1960 | CHI N | 15 | 15 | 1 | 0 | 0 | 0 | 0.0 | 5 | 0 | 1 | 4 | 0 | .067 | .067 | 4 | 1 | 3B-6, 2B-2 |
| 1961 | | 13 | 5 | 0 | 0 | 0 | 0 | 0.0 | 1 | 0 | 1 | 1 | 0 | .000 | .000 | 2 | 0 | OF-1 |
| 1962 | NY N | 25 | 52 | 10 | 0 | 0 | 0 | 0.0 | 2 | 7 | 6 | 12 | 0 | .192 | .192 | 6 | 3 | 2B-10, 3B-6 |
| 3 yrs. | | 53 | 72 | 11 | 0 | 0 | 0 | 0.0 | 8 | 7 | 8 | 17 | 0 | .153 | .153 | 12 | 4 | 3B-12, 2B-12, OF-1 |
| 2 yrs. | | 28 | 20 | 1 | 0 | 0 | 0 | 0.0 | 6 | 0 | 2 | 5 | 0 | .050 | .050 | 6 | 1 | 3B-6, 2B-2, OF-1 |

## Solly Drake

**DRAKE, SOLOMON LOUIS**      BB TR 6' 170 lbs.
Brother of Sammy Drake.
B. Oct. 23, 1930, Little Rock, Ark.

| | | G | AB | H | 2B | 3B | HR | HR % | R | RBI | BB | SO | SB | BA | SA | AB | H | G by POS |
|---|---|---|---|---|---|---|---|---|---|---|---|---|---|---|---|---|---|---|
| 1956 | CHI N | 65 | 215 | 55 | 9 | 1 | 2 | 0.9 | 29 | 15 | 23 | 35 | 9 | .256 | .335 | 8 | 3 | OF-53 |
| 1959 | 2 teams | LA | N (9G – .250) | | PHI | N (67G – .145) | | | | | | | | | | | | |
| " | total | 76 | 70 | 11 | 1 | 0 | 0 | 0.0 | 12 | 3 | 9 | 18 | 6 | .157 | .171 | 22 | 0 | OF-41 |
| 2 yrs. | | 141 | 285 | 66 | 10 | 1 | 2 | 0.7 | 41 | 18 | 32 | 53 | 15 | .232 | .295 | 30 | 3 | OF-94 |
| 1 yr. | | 65 | 215 | 55 | 9 | 1 | 2 | 0.9 | 29 | 15 | 23 | 35 | 9 | .256 | .335 | 8 | 3 | OF-53 |

## Paddy Driscoll

**DRISCOLL, JOHN LEO**      BR TR 5'8½" 155 lbs.
B. Jan. 11, 1895, Evanston, Ill.    D. June 29, 1968, Chicago, Ill.

| | | G | AB | H | 2B | 3B | HR | HR % | R | RBI | BB | SO | SB | BA | SA | AB | H | G by POS |
|---|---|---|---|---|---|---|---|---|---|---|---|---|---|---|---|---|---|---|
| 1917 | CHI N | 13 | 28 | 3 | 1 | 0 | 0 | 0.0 | 2 | 3 | 2 | 6 | 2 | .107 | .143 | 0 | 0 | 2B-8, 3B-2, SS-1 |

## Hugh Duffy

**DUFFY, HUGH**      BR TR 5'7" 168 lbs.
B. Nov. 26, 1866, Cranston, R. I.    D. Oct. 19, 1954, Boston, Mass.
Manager 1901, 1904-06, 1910-11, 1921-22.
Hall of Fame 1945.

| | | G | AB | H | 2B | 3B | HR | HR % | R | RBI | BB | SO | SB | BA | SA | AB | H | G by POS |
|---|---|---|---|---|---|---|---|---|---|---|---|---|---|---|---|---|---|---|
| 1888 | CHI N | 71 | 298 | 84 | 10 | 4 | 7 | 2.3 | 60 | 41 | 9 | 32 | 13 | .282 | .413 | 0 | 0 | OF-67, SS-3, 3B-1 |
| 1889 | | 136 | 584 | 182 | 21 | 7 | 12 | 2.1 | 144 | 89 | 46 | 30 | 52 | .312 | .433 | 0 | 0 | OF-126, SS-10 |
| 1890 | CHI P | 137 | 596 | 194 | 36 | 16 | 7 | 1.2 | 161 | 82 | 59 | 20 | 79 | .326 | .475 | 0 | 0 | OF-137 |
| 1891 | BOS AA | 127 | 536 | 180 | 20 | 8 | 8 | 1.5 | 134 | 108 | 61 | 29 | 85 | .336 | .448 | 0 | 0 | OF-124, 3B-3, SS-1 |
| 1892 | BOS N | 147 | 612 | 184 | 28 | 12 | 5 | 0.8 | 125 | 81 | 60 | 37 | 61 | .301 | .410 | 0 | 0 | OF-146, 3B-2 |
| 1893 | | 131 | 560 | 203 | 23 | 7 | 6 | 1.1 | 147 | 118 | 50 | 13 | 50 | .363 | .461 | 0 | 0 | OF-131 |
| 1894 | | 124 | 539 | 236 | 50 | 13 | 18 | 3.3 | 160 | 145 | 66 | 15 | 49 | .438¹ | .679 | 0 | 0 | OF-124, SS-2 |
| 1895 | | 131 | 540 | 190 | 30 | 6 | 9 | 1.7 | 113 | 100 | 63 | 16 | 42 | .352 | .480 | 0 | 0 | OF-130 |
| 1896 | | 131 | 533 | 161 | 16 | 8 | 5 | 0.9 | 93 | 112 | 52 | 19 | 45 | .302 | .390 | 0 | 0 | OF-126, 2B-9, SS-2 |
| 1897 | | 134 | 554 | 189 | 25 | 10 | 11 | 2.0 | 131 | 129 | 52 | | 45 | .341 | .482 | 0 | 0 | OF-129, 2B-6, SS-2 |
| 1898 | | 152 | 568 | 179 | 13 | 3 | 8 | 1.4 | 97 | 108 | 59 | | 32 | .315 | .391 | 0 | 0 | OF-152, 3B-1, 1B-1, C-1 |
| 1899 | | 147 | 588 | 164 | 29 | 7 | 3 | 0.5 | 103 | 102 | 39 | | 18 | .279 | .367 | 0 | 0 | OF-147 |
| 1900 | | 55 | 181 | 55 | 5 | 4 | 2 | 1.1 | 28 | 31 | 16 | | 12 | .304 | .409 | 4 | 1 | OF-49, 2B-1 |
| 1901 | MIL N | 79 | 286 | 88 | 15 | 9 | 2 | 0.7 | 41 | 45 | 16 | | 13 | .308 | .444 | 2 | 0 | OF-77 |
| 1904 | PHI N | 18 | 46 | 13 | 1 | 1 | 0 | 0.0 | 10 | 5 | 13 | | 3 | .283 | .348 | 4 | 1 | OF-14 |
| 1905 | | 15 | 40 | 12 | 2 | 1 | 0 | 0.0 | 7 | 3 | 1 | | 0 | .300 | .400 | 7 | 3 | OF-8 |
| 1906 | | 1 | 1 | 0 | 0 | 0 | 0 | 0.0 | 0 | 0 | 0 | | 0 | .000 | .000 | 1 | 0 | |
| 17 yrs. | | 1736 | 7062 | 2314 | 324 | 116 | 103 | 1.5 | 1554 | 1299 | 662 | 211 | 599 | .328 | .450 | 18 | 5 | OF-1687, SS-20, 2B-16, 3B-7, 1B-1, C-1 |
| 2 yrs. | | 207 | 882 | 266 | 31 | 11 | 19 | 2.2 | 204 | 130 | 55 | 62 | 65 | .302 | .426 | 0 | 0 | OF-193, SS-13, 3B-1 |

## Sam Dungan

**DUNGAN, SAMUEL MORRISON**      BR 5'11" 180 lbs.
B. Jan. 29, 1866, Ferndale, Calif.    D. Mar. 16, 1939, Santa Ana, Calif.

| | | G | AB | H | 2B | 3B | HR | HR % | R | RBI | BB | SO | SB | BA | SA | AB | H | G by POS |
|---|---|---|---|---|---|---|---|---|---|---|---|---|---|---|---|---|---|---|
| 1892 | CHI N | 113 | 433 | 123 | 19 | 7 | 0 | 0.0 | 46 | 53 | 35 | 19 | 15 | .284 | .360 | 0 | 0 | OF-113 |
| 1893 | | 107 | 465 | 138 | 23 | 7 | 2 | 0.4 | 86 | 64 | 29 | 8 | 11 | .297 | .389 | 0 | 0 | OF-107 |
| 1894 | 2 teams | CHI | N (10G – .231) | | LOU | N (8G – .344) | | | | | | | | | | | | |
| " | total | 18 | 71 | 20 | 3 | 0 | 0 | 0.0 | 11 | 6 | 11 | 2 | 3 | .282 | .324 | 0 | 0 | OF-18 |
| 1900 | CHI N | 6 | 15 | 4 | 0 | 0 | 0 | 0.0 | 1 | 1 | 1 | | 0 | .267 | .267 | 3 | 1 | OF-3 |
| 1901 | WAS A | 138 | 559 | 179 | 26 | 12 | 1 | 0.2 | 70 | 73 | 40 | | 9 | .320 | .415 | 0 | 0 | OF-104, 1B-35 |
| 5 yrs. | | 382 | 1543 | 464 | 71 | 26 | 3 | 0.2 | 214 | 197 | 116 | 29 | 38 | .301 | .386 | 3 | 1 | OF-345, 1B-35 |
| 4 yrs. | | 236 | 952 | 274 | 44 | 14 | 2 | 0.2 | 138 | 121 | 72 | 28 | 27 | .288 | .370 | 3 | 1 | OF-233 |

## Ron Dunn

**DUNN, RONALD RAY**      BR TR 5'11" 180 lbs.
B. Jan. 24, 1950, Oklahoma City, Okla.

| | | G | AB | H | 2B | 3B | HR | HR % | R | RBI | BB | SO | SB | BA | SA | AB | H | G by POS |
|---|---|---|---|---|---|---|---|---|---|---|---|---|---|---|---|---|---|---|
| 1974 | CHI N | 23 | 68 | 20 | 7 | 0 | 2 | 2.9 | 6 | 15 | 12 | 8 | 0 | .294 | .485 | 1 | 0 | 2B-21, 3B-6 |
| 1975 | | 32 | 44 | 7 | 3 | 0 | 1 | 2.3 | 2 | 6 | 6 | 17 | 0 | .159 | .295 | 17 | 3 | 3B-11, OF-2, 2B-1 |
| 2 yrs. | | 55 | 112 | 27 | 10 | 0 | 3 | 2.7 | 8 | 21 | 18 | 25 | 0 | .241 | .411 | 18 | 3 | 2B-22, 3B-17, OF-2 |
| 2 yrs. | | 55 | 112 | 27 | 10 | 0 | 3 | 2.7 | 8 | 21 | 18 | 25 | 0 | .241 | .411 | 18 | 3 | 2B-22, 3B-17, OF-2 |

## Shawon Dunston

**DUNSTON, SHAWON DONNELL**      BR TR 6'1" 175 lbs.
B. Mar. 21, 1963, Brooklyn, N. Y.

| | | G | AB | H | 2B | 3B | HR | HR % | R | RBI | BB | SO | SB | BA | SA | AB | H | G by POS |
|---|---|---|---|---|---|---|---|---|---|---|---|---|---|---|---|---|---|---|
| 1985 | CHI N | 74 | 250 | 65 | 12 | 4 | 4 | 1.6 | 40 | 18 | 19 | 42 | 11 | .260 | .388 | 0 | 0 | SS-73 |

## Kid Durbin

**DURBIN, BLAINE ALPHONSUS**      BL TL 5'8" 155 lbs.
B. Sept. 10, 1886, Lamar, Kans.    D. Sept. 11, 1943, Kirkwood, Mo.

| | | G | AB | H | 2B | 3B | HR | HR % | R | RBI | BB | SO | SB | BA | SA | AB | H | G by POS |
|---|---|---|---|---|---|---|---|---|---|---|---|---|---|---|---|---|---|---|
| 1907 | CHI N | 11 | 18 | 6 | 0 | 0 | 0 | 0.0 | 0 | 1 | | | 0 | .333 | .333 | 1 | 0 | OF-5, P-5 |
| 1908 | | 14 | 28 | 7 | 1 | 0 | 0 | 0.0 | 2 | 0 | 2 | | 0 | .250 | .286 | 2 | 0 | OF-11 |

| | G | AB | H | 2B | 3B | HR | HR % | R | RBI | BB | SO | SB | BA | SA | Pinch Hit AB | H | G by POS |
|---|---|---|---|---|---|---|---|---|---|---|---|---|---|---|---|---|---|

## Kid Durbin continued

| | | G | AB | H | 2B | 3B | HR | HR% | R | RBI | BB | SO | SB | BA | SA | AB | H | G by POS |
|---|---|---|---|---|---|---|---|---|---|---|---|---|---|---|---|---|---|---|
| 1909 | **2 teams** | | | **CIN** | **N** (6G – .200) | | **PIT** | **N** (1G – .000) | | | | | | | | | | |
| " | total | 7 | 5 | 1 | 0 | 0 | 0 | 0.0 | 1 | 0 | 1 | | 0 | .200 | .200 | 5 | 1 | |
| 3 yrs. | | 32 | 51 | 14 | 1 | 0 | 0 | 0.0 | 6 | 0 | 4 | | 0 | .275 | .294 | 8 | 1 | OF-16, P-5 |
| 2 yrs. | | 25 | 46 | 13 | 1 | 0 | 0 | 0.0 | 5 | 0 | 3 | | 0 | .283 | .304 | 3 | 0 | OF-16, P-5 |

## Leon Durham

**DURHAM, LEON (Bull)**     BL TL 6'1"    185 lbs.
B. July 31, 1957, Cincinnati, Ohio

| | | G | AB | H | 2B | 3B | HR | HR% | R | RBI | BB | SO | SB | BA | SA | AB | H | G by POS |
|---|---|---|---|---|---|---|---|---|---|---|---|---|---|---|---|---|---|---|
| 1980 | **STL N** | 96 | 303 | 82 | 15 | 4 | 8 | 2.6 | 42 | 42 | 18 | 55 | 8 | .271 | .426 | 16 | 5 | OF-78, 1B-8 |
| 1981 | **CHI N** | 87 | 328 | 95 | 14 | 6 | 10 | 3.0 | 42 | 35 | 27 | 53 | 25 | .290 | .460 | 3 | 1 | OF-83, 1B-3 |
| 1982 | | 148 | 539 | 168 | 33 | 7 | 22 | 4.1 | 84 | 90 | 66 | 77 | 28 | .312 | .521 | 5 | 2 | OF-143, 1B-1 |
| 1983 | | 100 | 337 | 87 | 18 | 8 | 12 | 3.6 | 58 | 55 | 66 | 83 | 12 | .258 | .466 | 1 | 0 | OF-95, 1B-6 |
| 1984 | | 137 | 473 | 132 | 30 | 4 | 23 | 4.9 | 86 | 96 | 69 | 86 | 16 | .279 | .505 | 8 | 2 | 1B-130 |
| 1985 | | 153 | 542 | 153 | 32 | 2 | 21 | 3.9 | 58 | 75 | 64 | 99 | 7 | .282 | .465 | 2 | 0 | 1B-151 |
| 6 yrs. | | 721 | 2522 | 717 | 142 | 31 | 96 | 3.8 | 370 | 393 | 310 | 453 | 96 | .284 | .479 | 35 | 10 | OF-399, 1B-299 |
| 5 yrs. | | 625 | 2219 | 635 | 127 | 27 | 88 | 4.0 | 328 | 351 | 292 | 398 | 88 | .286 | .487 | 19 | 5 | OF-321, 1B-291 |
| | | | | | | | | | | | | **6th** | | | | | | |

### LEAGUE CHAMPIONSHIP SERIES

| | | G | AB | H | 2B | 3B | HR | HR% | R | RBI | BB | SO | SB | BA | SA | AB | H | G by POS |
|---|---|---|---|---|---|---|---|---|---|---|---|---|---|---|---|---|---|---|
| 1984 | **CHI N** | 5 | 20 | 3 | 0 | 0 | 2 | 10.0 | 2 | 4 | 1 | 4 | 0 | .150 | .450 | 0 | 0 | 1B-5 |

## Frank Dwyer

**DWYER, JOHN FRANCIS**     BR TR 5'8"    145 lbs.
B. Mar. 25, 1868, Lee, Mass.    D. Feb. 4, 1943, Pittsfield, Mass.
Manager 1902.

| | | G | AB | H | 2B | 3B | HR | HR% | R | RBI | BB | SO | SB | BA | SA | AB | H | G by POS |
|---|---|---|---|---|---|---|---|---|---|---|---|---|---|---|---|---|---|---|
| 1888 | **CHI N** | 5 | 21 | 4 | 1 | 0 | 0 | 0.0 | 2 | 2 | 0 | 5 | 0 | .190 | .238 | 0 | 0 | P-5 |
| 1889 | | 36 | 135 | 27 | 1 | 1 | 1 | 0.7 | 14 | 6 | 4 | 8 | 0 | .200 | .244 | 0 | 0 | P-32, OF-3, SS-2 |
| 1890 | **CHI P** | 16 | 53 | 14 | 2 | 0 | 0 | 0.0 | 10 | 11 | 0 | 2 | 1 | .264 | .302 | 0 | 0 | P-12, OF-4 |
| 1891 | **C-M AA** | 48 | 181 | 49 | 5 | 3 | 0 | 0.0 | 25 | 20 | 6 | 16 | 5 | .271 | .331 | 0 | 0 | P-45, OF-4, 2B-2 |
| 1892 | **2 teams** | 50 | 154 | **STL** | 23 | **N** (10G – .080) | 0 | 2 | **CIN** | 0 | **N** (40G – .163) | | | | | | | |
| " | total | 50 | 154 | 23 | 0 | 2 | 0 | 0.0 | 19 | 6 | 8 | 11 | 2 | .149 | .175 | 1 | 0 | P-43, OF-6 |
| 1893 | **CIN N** | 38 | 120 | 24 | 1 | 2 | 1 | 0.8 | 22 | 17 | 9 | 5 | 2 | .200 | .267 | 0 | 0 | P-37, OF-1, 1B-1 |
| 1894 | | 54 | 172 | 46 | 9 | 2 | 2 | 1.2 | 31 | 28 | 15 | 13 | 0 | .267 | .378 | 1 | 0 | P-45, OF-10, SS-2 |
| 1895 | | 37 | 113 | 30 | 3 | 5 | 1 | 0.9 | 14 | 16 | 5 | 5 | 2 | .265 | .407 | 0 | 0 | P-37 |
| 1896 | | 36 | 110 | 29 | 4 | 4 | 0 | 0.0 | 17 | 15 | 11 | 15 | 3 | .264 | .373 | 0 | 0 | P-36 |
| 1897 | | 37 | 94 | 25 | 1 | 1 | 0 | 0.0 | 13 | 10 | 5 | | 0 | .266 | .298 | 0 | 0 | P-37 |
| 1898 | | 31 | 85 | 12 | 1 | 1 | 0 | 0.0 | 11 | 5 | 7 | | 1 | .141 | .176 | 0 | 0 | P-31 |
| 1899 | | 5 | 11 | 4 | 0 | 0 | 0 | 0.0 | 0 | 0 | 0 | | 0 | .364 | .364 | 0 | 0 | P-5 |
| 12 yrs. | | 393 | 1249 | 287 | 28 | 21 | 5 | 0.4 | 178 | 136 | 70 | 80 | 16 | .230 | .298 | 2 | 0 | P-365, OF-28, SS-4, 2B-2, 1B-1 |
| 2 yrs. | | 41 | 156 | 31 | 2 | 1 | 1 | 0.6 | 16 | 8 | 4 | 13 | 0 | .199 | .244 | 0 | 0 | P-37, OF-3, SS-2 |

## Don Eaddy

**EADDY, DONALD JOHNSON**     BR TR 5'11"    165 lbs.
B. Feb. 16, 1934, Grand Rapids, Mich.

| | | G | AB | H | 2B | 3B | HR | HR% | R | RBI | BB | SO | SB | BA | SA | AB | H | G by POS |
|---|---|---|---|---|---|---|---|---|---|---|---|---|---|---|---|---|---|---|
| 1959 | **CHI N** | 15 | 1 | 0 | 0 | 0 | 0 | 0.0 | 3 | 0 | 0 | 1 | 0 | .000 | .000 | 0 | 0 | 3B-1 |

## Bad Bill Eagan

**EAGAN, WILLIAM**    
B. June 1, 1869, Camden, N. J.    D. Feb. 14, 1905, Denver, Colo.

| | | G | AB | H | 2B | 3B | HR | HR% | R | RBI | BB | SO | SB | BA | SA | AB | H | G by POS |
|---|---|---|---|---|---|---|---|---|---|---|---|---|---|---|---|---|---|---|
| 1891 | **STL AA** | 83 | 302 | 65 | 11 | 4 | 4 | 1.3 | 49 | 43 | 44 | 54 | 21 | .215 | .318 | 0 | 0 | 2B-83 |
| 1893 | **CHI N** | 6 | 19 | 5 | 0 | 0 | 0 | 0.0 | 3 | 2 | 5 | 5 | 4 | .263 | .263 | 0 | 0 | 2B-6 |
| 1898 | **PIT N** | 19 | 61 | 20 | 2 | 3 | 0 | 0.0 | 14 | 5 | 8 | | 1 | .328 | .459 | 0 | 0 | 2B-17 |
| 3 yrs. | | 108 | 382 | 90 | 13 | 7 | 4 | 1.0 | 66 | 50 | 57 | 59 | 26 | .236 | .338 | 0 | 0 | 2B-106 |
| 1 yr. | | 6 | 19 | 5 | 0 | 0 | 0 | 0.0 | 3 | 2 | 5 | 5 | 4 | .263 | .263 | 0 | 0 | 2B-6 |

## Howard Earl

**EARL, HOWARD J. (Slim Jim)**     6'1"
B. Feb. 27, 1869, Massachusetts    D. Dec. 22, 1916, North Bay, N. Y.

| | | G | AB | H | 2B | 3B | HR | HR% | R | RBI | BB | SO | SB | BA | SA | AB | H | G by POS |
|---|---|---|---|---|---|---|---|---|---|---|---|---|---|---|---|---|---|---|
| 1890 | **CHI N** | 92 | 384 | 95 | 10 | 3 | 6 | 1.6 | 57 | 51 | 18 | 47 | 17 | .247 | .336 | 0 | 0 | OF-49, 2B-39, SS-4, 1B-3 |
| 1891 | **C-M AA** | 31 | 129 | 32 | 5 | 2 | 1 | 0.8 | 21 | 17 | 5 | 13 | 3 | .248 | .341 | 0 | 0 | OF-30, 1B-2 |
| 2 yrs. | | 123 | 513 | 127 | 15 | 5 | 7 | 1.4 | 78 | 68 | 23 | 60 | 20 | .248 | .337 | 0 | 0 | OF-79, 2B-39, 1B-5, SS-4 |
| 1 yr. | | 92 | 384 | 95 | 10 | 3 | 6 | 1.6 | 57 | 51 | 18 | 47 | 17 | .247 | .336 | 0 | 0 | OF-49, 2B-39, SS-4, 1B-3 |

## Roy Easterwood

**EASTERWOOD, ROY CHARLES (Shag)**     BR TR 6½"    196 lbs.
B. Jan. 12, 1915, Waxahachie, Tex.

| | | G | AB | H | 2B | 3B | HR | HR% | R | RBI | BB | SO | SB | BA | SA | AB | H | G by POS |
|---|---|---|---|---|---|---|---|---|---|---|---|---|---|---|---|---|---|---|
| 1944 | **CHI N** | 17 | 33 | 7 | 2 | 0 | 1 | 3.0 | 1 | 2 | 1 | 11 | 0 | .212 | .364 | 5 | 1 | C-12 |

## Charlie Eden

**EDEN, CHARLES M.**     BR TR
B. Jan. 18, 1855, Lexington, Ky.    D. Sept. 17, 1920, Cincinnati, Ohio

| | | G | AB | H | 2B | 3B | HR | HR% | R | RBI | BB | SO | SB | BA | SA | AB | H | G by POS |
|---|---|---|---|---|---|---|---|---|---|---|---|---|---|---|---|---|---|---|
| 1877 | **CHI N** | 15 | 55 | 12 | 0 | 1 | 0 | 0.0 | 9 | 5 | 3 | 6 | | .218 | .255 | 0 | 0 | OF-15 |
| 1879 | **CLE N** | 81 | 353 | 96 | 31 | 7 | 3 | 0.8 | 40 | 34 | 6 | 20 | | .272 | .425 | 0 | 0 | OF-80, 1B-3, C-1 |
| 1884 | **PIT AA** | 32 | 122 | 33 | 7 | 4 | 1 | 0.8 | 12 | | 7 | | | .270 | .418 | 0 | 0 | OF-31, P-2 |
| 1885 | | 98 | 405 | 103 | 18 | 6 | 0 | 0.0 | 57 | | 17 | | | .254 | .328 | 0 | 0 | OF-96, P-4, 3B-2 |
| 4 yrs. | | 226 | 935 | 244 | 56 | 18 | 4 | 0.4 | 118 | 39 | 33 | 26 | | .261 | .372 | 0 | 0 | OF-222, P-6, 1B-3, 3B-2, C-1 |
| 1 yr. | | 15 | 55 | 12 | 0 | 1 | 0 | 0.0 | 9 | 5 | 3 | 6 | | .218 | .255 | 0 | 0 | OF-15 |

## Bruce Edwards

**EDWARDS, CHARLES BRUCE (Bull)**     BR TR 5'8"    180 lbs.
B. July 15, 1923, Quincy, Ill.    D. Apr. 25, 1975, Sacramento, Calif.

| | | G | AB | H | 2B | 3B | HR | HR% | R | RBI | BB | SO | SB | BA | SA | AB | H | G by POS |
|---|---|---|---|---|---|---|---|---|---|---|---|---|---|---|---|---|---|---|
| 1946 | **BKN N** | 92 | 292 | 78 | 13 | 5 | 1 | 0.3 | 24 | 25 | 34 | 20 | 1 | .267 | .356 | 0 | 0 | C-91 |
| 1947 | | 130 | 471 | 139 | 15 | 8 | 9 | 1.9 | 53 | 80 | 49 | 55 | 2 | .295 | .418 | 2 | 0 | C-128 |
| 1948 | | 96 | 286 | 79 | 17 | 2 | 8 | 2.8 | 36 | 54 | 26 | 28 | 4 | .276 | .434 | 9 | 2 | C-48, OF-21, 3B-14, 1B-1 |
| 1949 | | 64 | 148 | 31 | 3 | 0 | 8 | 5.4 | 24 | 25 | 25 | 15 | 0 | .209 | .392 | 17 | 3 | C-41, OF-4, 3B-1 |

| | G | AB | H | 2B | 3B | HR | HR% | R | RBI | BB | SO | SB | BA | SA | Pinch Hit AB | Pinch Hit H | G by POS |
|---|---|---|---|---|---|---|---|---|---|---|---|---|---|---|---|---|---|

# Bruce Edwards continued

| | G | AB | H | 2B | 3B | HR | HR% | R | RBI | BB | SO | SB | BA | SA | AB | H | G by POS |
|---|---|---|---|---|---|---|---|---|---|---|---|---|---|---|---|---|---|
| 1950 | 50 | 142 | 26 | 4 | 1 | 8 | 5.6 | 16 | 16 | 13 | 22 | 1 | .183 | .394 | 8 | 1 | C-38, 1B-2 |
| 1951 2 teams | | | | BKN N (17G – .250) | | CHI N (51G – .234) | | | | | | | | | | | |
| " total | 68 | 177 | 42 | 11 | 2 | 4 | 2.3 | 25 | 25 | 17 | 17 | 1 | .237 | .390 | 22 | 8 | C-42, 1B-9 |
| 1952 CHI N | 50 | 94 | 23 | 2 | 2 | 1 | 1.1 | 7 | 12 | 8 | 12 | 0 | .245 | .340 | 24 | 7 | C-22, 2B-1 |
| 1954 | 4 | 3 | 0 | 0 | 0 | 0 | 0.0 | 1 | 1 | 2 | 2 | 0 | .000 | .000 | 3 | 0 | |
| 1955 WAS A | 30 | 57 | 10 | 2 | 0 | 0 | 0.0 | 5 | 3 | 16 | 6 | 0 | .175 | .211 | 1 | 0 | C-22, 3B-5 |
| 1956 CIN N | 7 | 5 | 1 | 0 | 0 | 0 | 0.0 | 0 | 0 | 0 | 2 | 0 | .200 | .200 | 5 | 1 | C-2, 3B-1, 2B-1 |
| 10 yrs. | 591 | 1675 | 429 | 67 | 20 | 39 | 2.3 | 191 | 241 | 190 | 179 | 9 | .256 | .390 | 91 | 22 | C-434, OF-25, 3B-21, 1B-12, 2B-2 |
| 3 yrs. | 105 | 238 | 56 | 11 | 4 | 4 | 1.7 | 27 | 30 | 26 | 28 | 1 | .235 | .366 | 40 | 12 | C-50, 1B-9, 2B-1 |
| WORLD SERIES | | | | | | | | | | | | | | | | | |
| 1947 BKN N | 7 | 27 | 6 | 1 | 0 | 0 | 0.0 | 3 | 2 | 2 | 7 | 0 | .222 | .259 | 0 | 0 | C-7 |
| 1949 | 2 | 2 | 1 | 0 | 0 | 0 | 0.0 | 0 | 0 | 0 | 1 | 0 | .500 | .500 | 2 | 1 | |
| 2 yrs. | 9 | 29 | 7 | 1 | 0 | 0 | 0.0 | 3 | 2 | 2 | 8 | 0 | .241 | .276 | 2 | 1 | C-7 |

# Hank Edwards

**EDWARDS, HENRY ALBERT**     BL TL 6'   190 lbs.
B. Jan. 29, 1919, Elmwood Place, Ohio

| | G | AB | H | 2B | 3B | HR | HR% | R | RBI | BB | SO | SB | BA | SA | AB | H | G by POS |
|---|---|---|---|---|---|---|---|---|---|---|---|---|---|---|---|---|---|
| 1941 CLE A | 16 | 68 | 15 | 1 | 1 | 1 | 1.5 | 10 | 6 | 2 | 4 | 0 | .221 | .309 | 0 | 0 | OF-16 |
| 1942 | 13 | 48 | 12 | 2 | 1 | 0 | 0.0 | 6 | 7 | 5 | 8 | 2 | .250 | .333 | 1 | 0 | OF-12 |
| 1943 | 92 | 297 | 82 | 18 | 6 | 3 | 1.0 | 38 | 28 | 30 | 34 | 4 | .276 | .407 | 15 | 4 | OF-74 |
| 1946 | 124 | 458 | 138 | 33 | 16 | 10 | 2.2 | 62 | 54 | 43 | 48 | 1 | .301 | .509 | 2 | 1 | OF-123 |
| 1947 | 108 | 393 | 102 | 12 | 3 | 15 | 3.8 | 54 | 59 | 31 | 55 | 1 | .260 | .420 | 8 | 3 | OF-100 |
| 1948 | 55 | 160 | 43 | 9 | 2 | 3 | 1.9 | 27 | 18 | 18 | 18 | 1 | .269 | .406 | 12 | 2 | OF-41 |
| 1949 2 teams | | | | CLE A (5G – .267) | | CHI N (58G – .290) | | | | | | | | | | | |
| " total | 63 | 191 | 55 | 8 | 4 | 8 | 4.2 | 28 | 22 | 20 | 24 | 0 | .288 | .497 | 6 | 1 | OF-56 |
| 1950 CHI N | 41 | 110 | 40 | 11 | 1 | 2 | 1.8 | 13 | 21 | 10 | 13 | 0 | .364 | .536 | 10 | 0 | OF-29 |
| 1951 2 teams | | | | BKN N (35G – .226) | | CIN N (41G – .315) | | | | | | | | | | | |
| " total | 76 | 158 | 47 | 12 | 1 | 3 | 1.9 | 15 | 23 | 17 | 26 | 0 | .297 | .443 | 37 | 8 | OF-34 |
| 1952 2 teams | | | | CIN N (74G – .283) | | CHI A (8G – .333) | | | | | | | | | | | |
| " total | 82 | 202 | 58 | 7 | 6 | 6 | 3.0 | 26 | 29 | 19 | 24 | 0 | .287 | .470 | 26 | 4 | OF-54 |
| 1953 STL A | 65 | 106 | 21 | 3 | 0 | 0 | 0.0 | 6 | 9 | 13 | 10 | 0 | .198 | .226 | 40 | 12 | OF-21 |
| 11 yrs. | 735 | 2191 | 613 | 116 | 41 | 51 | 2.3 | 285 | 276 | 208 | 264 | 9 | .280 | .440 | 157 | 35 | OF-560 |
| 2 yrs. | 99 | 286 | 91 | 19 | 5 | 9 | 3.1 | 38 | 42 | 29 | 35 | 0 | .318 | .514 | 16 | 1 | OF-80 |

# Dave Eggler

**EGGLER, DAVID DANIEL**     BR TR 5'9"   165 lbs.
B. Apr. 30, 1851, Brooklyn, N. Y.    D. Apr. 5, 1902, Buffalo, N. Y.

| | G | AB | H | 2B | 3B | HR | HR% | R | RBI | BB | SO | SB | BA | SA | AB | H | G by POS |
|---|---|---|---|---|---|---|---|---|---|---|---|---|---|---|---|---|---|
| 1876 PHI N | 39 | 174 | 52 | 4 | 0 | 0 | 0.0 | 28 | 19 | 2 | 4 | | .299 | .322 | 0 | 0 | OF-39 |
| 1877 CHI N | 33 | 136 | 36 | 3 | 0 | 0 | 0.0 | 20 | 20 | 1 | 5 | | .265 | .287 | 0 | 0 | OF-33 |
| 1879 BUF N | 78 | 317 | 66 | 5 | 7 | 0 | 0.0 | 41 | 27 | 11 | 41 | | .208 | .268 | 0 | 0 | OF-78 |
| 1883 2 teams | | | | BAL AA (53G – .188) | | BUF N (38G – .248) | | | | | | | | | | | |
| " total | 91 | 355 | 76 | 4 | 1 | 0 | 0.0 | 28 | | 3 | 29 | | .214 | .231 | 0 | 0 | OF-91 |
| 1884 BUF N | 63 | 241 | 47 | 3 | 1 | 0 | 0.0 | 25 | | 6 | 54 | | .195 | .216 | 0 | 0 | OF-63 |
| 1885 | 6 | 24 | 2 | 0 | 0 | 0 | 0.0 | 0 | 0 | 2 | 4 | | .083 | .083 | 0 | 0 | OF-6 |
| 6 yrs. | 310 | 1247 | 279 | 19 | 9 | 0 | 0.0 | 142 | 66 | 25 | 137 | | .224 | .253 | 0 | 0 | OF-310 |
| 1 yr. | 33 | 136 | 36 | 3 | 0 | 0 | 0.0 | 20 | 20 | 1 | 5 | | .265 | .287 | 0 | 0 | OF-33 |

# Lee Elia

**ELIA, LEE CONSTANTINE**     BR TR 5'11"   175 lbs.
B. July 16, 1937, Philadelphia, Pa.
Manager 1982-83.

| | G | AB | H | 2B | 3B | HR | HR% | R | RBI | BB | SO | SB | BA | SA | AB | H | G by POS |
|---|---|---|---|---|---|---|---|---|---|---|---|---|---|---|---|---|---|
| 1966 CHI A | 80 | 195 | 40 | 5 | 2 | 3 | 1.5 | 16 | 22 | 15 | 39 | 0 | .205 | .297 | 1 | 0 | SS-75 |
| 1968 CHI N | 15 | 17 | 3 | 0 | 0 | 0 | 0.0 | 1 | 3 | 0 | 6 | 0 | .176 | .176 | 10 | 2 | SS-2, 3B-1, 2B-1 |
| 2 yrs. | 95 | 212 | 43 | 5 | 2 | 3 | 1.4 | 17 | 25 | 15 | 45 | 0 | .203 | .288 | 11 | 2 | SS-77, 3B-1, 2B-1 |
| 1 yr. | 15 | 17 | 3 | 0 | 0 | 0 | 0.0 | 1 | 3 | 0 | 6 | 0 | .176 | .176 | 10 | 2 | SS-2, 3B-1, 2B-1 |

# Pete Elko

**ELKO, PETER (Piccolo Pete)**     BR TR 5'11"   185 lbs.
B. June 17, 1918, Wilkes-Barre, Pa.

| | G | AB | H | 2B | 3B | HR | HR% | R | RBI | BB | SO | SB | BA | SA | AB | H | G by POS |
|---|---|---|---|---|---|---|---|---|---|---|---|---|---|---|---|---|---|
| 1943 CHI N | 9 | 30 | 4 | 0 | 0 | 0 | 0.0 | 1 | 0 | 4 | 5 | 0 | .133 | .133 | 0 | 0 | 3B-9 |
| 1944 | 7 | 22 | 5 | 1 | 0 | 0 | 0.0 | 2 | 0 | 0 | 1 | 0 | .227 | .273 | 1 | 1 | 3B-6 |
| 2 yrs. | 16 | 52 | 9 | 1 | 0 | 0 | 0.0 | 3 | 0 | 4 | 6 | 0 | .173 | .192 | 1 | 1 | 3B-15 |
| 2 yrs. | 16 | 52 | 9 | 1 | 0 | 0 | 0.0 | 3 | 0 | 4 | 6 | 0 | .173 | .192 | 1 | 1 | 3B-15 |

# Allen Elliott

**ELLIOTT, ALLEN CLIFFORD (Ace)**     BL TR 6'   170 lbs.
B. Dec. 25, 1897, St. Louis, Mo.    D. May 6, 1979, St. Louis, Mo.

| | G | AB | H | 2B | 3B | HR | HR% | R | RBI | BB | SO | SB | BA | SA | AB | H | G by POS |
|---|---|---|---|---|---|---|---|---|---|---|---|---|---|---|---|---|---|
| 1923 CHI N | 53 | 168 | 42 | 8 | 2 | 2 | 1.2 | 21 | 29 | 2 | 12 | 3 | .250 | .357 | 0 | 0 | 1B-52 |
| 1924 | 10 | 14 | 2 | 0 | 0 | 0 | 0.0 | 0 | 0 | 0 | 1 | 0 | .143 | .143 | 0 | 0 | 1B-10 |
| 2 yrs. | 63 | 182 | 44 | 8 | 2 | 2 | 1.1 | 21 | 29 | 2 | 13 | 3 | .242 | .341 | 0 | 0 | 1B-62 |
| 2 yrs. | 63 | 182 | 44 | 8 | 2 | 2 | 1.1 | 21 | 29 | 2 | 13 | 3 | .242 | .341 | 0 | 0 | 1B-62 |

# Carter Elliott

**ELLIOTT, CARTER WARD**     BL TR 5'11"   165 lbs.
B. Nov. 29, 1893, Atchison, Kans.    D. May 21, 1959, Palm Springs, Calif.

| | G | AB | H | 2B | 3B | HR | HR% | R | RBI | BB | SO | SB | BA | SA | AB | H | G by POS |
|---|---|---|---|---|---|---|---|---|---|---|---|---|---|---|---|---|---|
| 1921 CHI N | 12 | 28 | 7 | 2 | 0 | 0 | 0.0 | 5 | 0 | 5 | 3 | 0 | .250 | .321 | 0 | 0 | SS-10 |

# Rowdy Elliott

**ELLIOTT, HAROLD B.**     BR TR 5'9½"   160 lbs.
B. July 8, 1890, Kokomo, Ind.    D. Feb. 12, 1934, San Francisco, Calif.

| | G | AB | H | 2B | 3B | HR | HR% | R | RBI | BB | SO | SB | BA | SA | AB | H | G by POS |
|---|---|---|---|---|---|---|---|---|---|---|---|---|---|---|---|---|---|
| 1910 BOS N | 3 | 2 | 0 | 0 | 0 | 0 | 0.0 | 0 | 0 | 0 | 0 | 0 | .000 | .000 | 2 | 0 | C-1 |
| 1916 CHI N | 23 | 55 | 14 | 3 | 0 | 0 | 0.0 | 5 | 3 | 3 | 5 | 1 | .255 | .309 | 4 | 0 | C-18 |
| 1917 | 85 | 223 | 56 | 8 | 5 | 0 | 0.0 | 18 | 28 | 11 | 11 | 4 | .251 | .332 | 12 | 2 | C-73 |
| 1918 | 5 | 10 | 0 | 0 | 0 | 0 | 0.0 | 0 | 0 | 2 | 1 | 0 | .000 | .000 | 0 | 0 | C-5 |

| | G | AB | H | 2B | 3B | HR | HR % | R | RBI | BB | SO | SB | BA | SA | Pinch Hit AB | Pinch Hit H | G by POS |
|---|---|---|---|---|---|---|---|---|---|---|---|---|---|---|---|---|---|

## Rowdy Elliott continued

| | G | AB | H | 2B | 3B | HR | HR % | R | RBI | BB | SO | SB | BA | SA | AB | H | G by POS |
|---|---|---|---|---|---|---|---|---|---|---|---|---|---|---|---|---|---|
| 1920 **BKN N** | 41 | 112 | 27 | 4 | 0 | 1 | 0.9 | 13 | 13 | 3 | 6 | 0 | .241 | .304 | 2 | 0 | C-39 |
| 5 yrs. | 157 | 402 | 97 | 15 | 5 | 1 | 0.2 | 36 | 44 | 19 | 23 | 5 | .241 | .311 | 20 | 2 | C-136 |
| 3 yrs. | 113 | 288 | 70 | 11 | 5 | 0 | 0.0 | 23 | 31 | 16 | 17 | 5 | .243 | .316 | 16 | 2 | C-96 |

## Woody English

**ENGLISH, ELWOOD GEORGE**
B. Mar. 2, 1907, Fredonia, Ohio

BR TR 5'10" 155 lbs.

| | G | AB | H | 2B | 3B | HR | HR % | R | RBI | BB | SO | SB | BA | SA | AB | H | G by POS |
|---|---|---|---|---|---|---|---|---|---|---|---|---|---|---|---|---|---|
| 1927 **CHI N** | 87 | 334 | 97 | 14 | 4 | 1 | 0.3 | 46 | 28 | 16 | 26 | 1 | .290 | .365 | 0 | 0 | SS-84, 3B-1 |
| 1928 | 116 | 475 | 142 | 22 | 4 | 2 | 0.4 | 68 | 34 | 30 | 28 | 4 | .299 | .375 | 0 | 0 | SS-114, 3B-2 |
| 1929 | 144 | 608 | 168 | 29 | 3 | 1 | 0.2 | 131 | 52 | 68 | 50 | 13 | .276 | .339 | 0 | 0 | SS-144 |
| 1930 | 156 | 638 | 214 | 36 | 17 | 14 | 2.2 | 152 | 59 | 100 | 72 | 3 | .335 | .511 | 0 | 0 | 3B-83, SS-78 |
| 1931 | 156 | 634 | 202 | 38 | 8 | 2 | 0.3 | 117 | 53 | 68 | 80 | 12 | .319 | .413 | 0 | 0 | SS-138, 3B-18 |
| 1932 | 127 | 522 | 142 | 23 | 7 | 3 | 0.6 | 70 | 47 | 55 | 73 | 5 | .272 | .360 | 1 | 0 | 3B-93, SS-38 |
| 1933 | 105 | 398 | 104 | 19 | 2 | 3 | 0.8 | 54 | 41 | 53 | 44 | 5 | .261 | .342 | 0 | 0 | 3B-103, SS-1 |
| 1934 | 109 | 421 | 117 | 26 | 5 | 3 | 0.7 | 65 | 31 | 48 | 65 | 6 | .278 | .385 | 0 | 0 | SS-56, 3B-46, 2B-7 |
| 1935 | 34 | 84 | 17 | 2 | 0 | 2 | 2.4 | 11 | 8 | 20 | 4 | 1 | .202 | .298 | 4 | 2 | 3B-16, SS-12 |
| 1936 | 64 | 182 | 45 | 9 | 0 | 0 | 0.0 | 33 | 20 | 40 | 28 | 1 | .247 | .297 | 5 | 0 | SS-42, 3B-17, 2B-1 |
| 1937 **BKN N** | 129 | 378 | 90 | 16 | 2 | 1 | 0.3 | 45 | 42 | 65 | 55 | 4 | .238 | .299 | 2 | 0 | SS-116, 2B-11 |
| 1938 | 34 | 72 | 18 | 2 | 0 | 0 | 0.0 | 9 | 7 | 8 | 11 | 2 | .250 | .278 | 7 | 1 | 3B-21, SS-3, 2B-3 |
| 12 yrs. | 1261 | 4746 | 1356 | 236 | 52 | 32 | 0.7 | 801 | 422 | 571 | 536 | 57 | .286 | .378 | 19 | 3 | SS-826, 3B-400, 2B-22 |
| 10 yrs. | 1098 | 4296 | 1248 | 218 | 50 | 31 | 0.7 | 747 | 373 | 498 | 470 | 51 | .291 | .386 | 12 | 2 | SS-707, 3B-379, 2B-8 |
| WORLD SERIES | | | | | | | | | | | | | | | | | |
| 1929 **CHI N** | 5 | 21 | 4 | 2 | 0 | 0 | 0.0 | 1 | 0 | 1 | 6 | 0 | .190 | .286 | 0 | 0 | SS-5 |
| 1932 | 4 | 17 | 3 | 0 | 0 | 0 | 0.0 | 2 | 1 | 2 | 2 | 0 | .176 | .176 | 0 | 0 | 3B-4 |
| 2 yrs. | 9 | 38 | 7 | 2 | 0 | 0 | 0.0 | 3 | 1 | 3 | 8 | 0 | .184 | .237 | 0 | 0 | SS-5, 3B-4 |

## Frank Ernaga

**ERNAGA, FRANK JOHN**
B. Aug. 22, 1930, Susanville, Calif.

BR TR 6'1" 195 lbs.

| | G | AB | H | 2B | 3B | HR | HR % | R | RBI | BB | SO | SB | BA | SA | AB | H | G by POS |
|---|---|---|---|---|---|---|---|---|---|---|---|---|---|---|---|---|---|
| 1957 **CHI N** | 20 | 35 | 11 | 3 | 2 | 2 | 5.7 | 9 | 7 | 9 | 14 | 0 | .314 | .686 | 7 | 1 | OF-10 |
| 1958 | 9 | 8 | 1 | 0 | 0 | 0 | 0.0 | 0 | 0 | 0 | 2 | 0 | .125 | .125 | 8 | 1 | |
| 2 yrs. | 29 | 43 | 12 | 3 | 2 | 2 | 4.7 | 9 | 7 | 9 | 16 | 0 | .279 | .581 | 15 | 2 | OF-10 |
| 2 yrs. | 29 | 43 | 12 | 3 | 2 | 2 | 4.7 | 9 | 7 | 9 | 16 | 0 | .279 | .581 | 15 | 2 | OF-10 |

## Bill Everett

**EVERETT, WILLIAM L.**
B. Dec. 13, 1868, Fort Wayne, Ind.    D. Jan. 19, 1938, Denver, Colo.

BL TR 6'½" 188 lbs.

| | G | AB | H | 2B | 3B | HR | HR % | R | RBI | BB | SO | SB | BA | SA | AB | H | G by POS |
|---|---|---|---|---|---|---|---|---|---|---|---|---|---|---|---|---|---|
| 1895 **CHI N** | 133 | 550 | 197 | 16 | 10 | 3 | 0.5 | 129 | 88 | 33 | 42 | 47 | .358 | .440 | 0 | 0 | 3B-130, 2B-3 |
| 1896 | 132 | 575 | 184 | 16 | 13 | 2 | 0.3 | 130 | 46 | 41 | 43 | 46 | .320 | .403 | 0 | 0 | 3B-97, OF-35 |
| 1897 | 92 | 379 | 119 | 14 | 7 | 5 | 1.3 | 63 | 39 | 36 | | 26 | .314 | .427 | 1 | 0 | 3B-83, OF-8 |
| 1898 | 149 | 596 | 190 | 15 | 6 | 0 | 0.0 | 102 | 69 | 53 | | 28 | .319 | .364 | 0 | 0 | 1B-149 |
| 1899 | 136 | 536 | 166 | 17 | 5 | 1 | 0.2 | 87 | 74 | 31 | | 30 | .310 | .366 | 0 | 0 | 1B-136 |
| 1900 | 23 | 91 | 24 | 4 | 0 | 0 | 0.0 | 10 | 17 | 3 | | 2 | .264 | .308 | 0 | 0 | 1B-23 |
| 1901 **WAS A** | 33 | 115 | 22 | 3 | 2 | 0 | 0.0 | 14 | 8 | 15 | | 7 | .191 | .252 | 0 | 0 | 1B-33 |
| 7 yrs. | 698 | 2842 | 902 | 85 | 43 | 11 | 0.4 | 535 | 341 | 212 | 85 | 186 | .317 | .389 | 1 | 0 | 1B-341, 3B-310, OF-43, 2B-3 |
| 6 yrs. | 665 | 2727 | 880 | 82 | 41 | 11 | 0.4 | 521 | 333 | 197 | 85 | 179 | .323 5th | .395 | 1 | 0 | 3B-310, 1B-308, OF-43, 2B-3 |

## Johnny Evers

**EVERS, JOHN JOSEPH (The Trojan, The Crab)**
Brother of Joe Evers.
B. July 21, 1881, Troy, N. Y.    D. Mar. 28, 1947, Albany, N. Y.
Manager 1913, 1921, 1924.
Hall of Fame 1946.

BL TR 5'9" 125 lbs.

| | G | AB | H | 2B | 3B | HR | HR % | R | RBI | BB | SO | SB | BA | SA | AB | H | G by POS |
|---|---|---|---|---|---|---|---|---|---|---|---|---|---|---|---|---|---|
| 1902 **CHI N** | 26 | 89 | 20 | 0 | 0 | 0 | 0.0 | 7 | 2 | 3 | | 1 | .225 | .225 | 0 | 0 | 2B-18, SS-8 |
| 1903 | 124 | 464 | 136 | 27 | 7 | 0 | 0.0 | 70 | 52 | 19 | | 25 | .293 | .381 | 0 | 0 | 2B-110, SS-11, 3B-2 |
| 1904 | 152 | 532 | 141 | 14 | 7 | 0 | 0.0 | 49 | 47 | 28 | | 26 | .265 | .318 | 0 | 0 | 2B-152 |
| 1905 | 99 | 340 | 94 | 11 | 2 | 1 | 0.3 | 44 | 37 | 27 | | 19 | .276 | .329 | 0 | 0 | 2B-99 |
| 1906 | 154 | 533 | 136 | 17 | 6 | 1 | 0.2 | 65 | 51 | 36 | | 49 | .255 | .315 | 0 | 0 | 2B-153, 3B-1 |
| 1907 | 151 | 508 | 127 | 18 | 4 | 2 | 0.4 | 66 | 51 | 38 | | 46 | .250 | .313 | 0 | 0 | 2B-151 |
| 1908 | 126 | 416 | 125 | 19 | 6 | 0 | 0.0 | 83 | 37 | 66 | | 36 | .300 | .375 | 2 | 1 | 2B-123 |
| 1909 | 127 | 463 | 122 | 19 | 6 | 1 | 0.2 | 88 | 24 | 73 | | 28 | .263 | .337 | 0 | 0 | 2B-126 |
| 1910 | 125 | 433 | 114 | 11 | 7 | 0 | 0.0 | 87 | 28 | 108 | 18 | 28 | .263 | .321 | 0 | 0 | 2B-125 |
| 1911 | 46 | 155 | 35 | 4 | 3 | 0 | 0.0 | 29 | 7 | 34 | 10 | 6 | .226 | .290 | 2 | 0 | 2B-33, 3B-11 |
| 1912 | 143 | 478 | 163 | 23 | 11 | 1 | 0.2 | 73 | 63 | 74 | 18 | 16 | .341 | .441 | 0 | 0 | 2B-143 |
| 1913 | 135 | 444 | 126 | 20 | 5 | 3 | 0.7 | 81 | 49 | 50 | 14 | 11 | .284 | .372 | 0 | 0 | 2B-135 |
| 1914 **BOS N** | 139 | 491 | 137 | 20 | 3 | 1 | 0.2 | 81 | 40 | 87 | 26 | 12 | .279 | .338 | 0 | 0 | 2B-139 |
| 1915 | 83 | 278 | 73 | 4 | 1 | 1 | 0.4 | 38 | 22 | 50 | 16 | 7 | .263 | .295 | 0 | 0 | 2B-83 |
| 1916 | 71 | 241 | 52 | 4 | 1 | 0 | 0.0 | 33 | 15 | 40 | 19 | 5 | .216 | .241 | 0 | 0 | 2B-71 |
| 1917 2 teams | **BOS N** (24G – .193) | | | | | **PHI N** (56G – .224) | | | | | | | | | | | |
| " total | 80 | 266 | 57 | 5 | 1 | 0 | 0.0 | 25 | 12 | 43 | 21 | 9 | .214 | .252 | 0 | 0 | 2B-73, 3B-7 |
| 1922 **CHI A** | 1 | 3 | 0 | 0 | 0 | 0 | 0.0 | 0 | 1 | 2 | 0 | 0 | .000 | .000 | 0 | 0 | 2B-1 |
| 1929 **BOS N** | 1 | 0 | 0 | 0 | 0 | 0 | – | 0 | 0 | 0 | 0 | 0 | – | – | 0 | 0 | 2B-1 |
| 18 yrs. | 1783 | 6134 | 1658 | 216 | 70 | 12 | 0.2 | 919 | 538 | 778 | 142 | 324 | .270 | .334 | 4 | 1 | 2B-1736, 3B-21, SS-19 |
| 12 yrs. | 1408 | 4855 | 1339 | 183 | 64 | 9 | 0.2 | 742 | 448 | 556 | 60 | 291 | .276 3rd | .345 | 4 | 1 | 2B-1368, SS-19, 3B-14 |
| WORLD SERIES | | | | | | | | | | | | | | | | | |
| 1906 **CHI N** | 6 | 20 | 3 | 1 | 0 | 0 | 0.0 | 2 | 1 | 1 | 3 | 2 | .150 | .200 | 0 | 0 | 2B-6 |
| 1907 | 5 | 20 | 7 | 2 | 0 | 0 | 0.0 | 2 | 1 | 0 | 1 | 3 | .350 | .450 | 0 | 0 | 2B-5 |
| 1908 | 5 | 20 | 7 | 1 | 0 | 0 | 0.0 | 5 | 2 | 1 | 2 | 2 | .350 | .400 | 0 | 0 | 2B-5 |
| 1914 **BOS N** | 4 | 16 | 7 | 0 | 0 | 0 | 0.0 | 2 | 2 | 2 | 2 | 1 | .438 | .438 | 0 | 0 | 2B-4 |
| 4 yrs. | 20 | 76 | 24 | 4 | 0 | 0 | 0.0 | 11 | 6 | 4 | 8 | 8 | .316 | .368 8th | | 0 | 0 | 2B-20 |

| | G | AB | H | 2B | 3B | HR | HR % | R | RBI | BB | SO | SB | BA | SA | Pinch Hit AB | H | G by POS |
|---|---|---|---|---|---|---|---|---|---|---|---|---|---|---|---|---|---|

# im Fanning

**FANNING, WILLIAM JAMES**
B. Sept. 14, 1927, Chicago, Ill.
Manager 1981-82, 1984.                                   BR  TR  5'11"   180 lbs.

| | G | AB | H | 2B | 3B | HR | HR % | R | RBI | BB | SO | SB | BA | SA | AB | H | G by POS |
|---|---|---|---|---|---|---|---|---|---|---|---|---|---|---|---|---|---|
| '54 CHI N | 11 | 38 | 7 | 0 | 0 | 0 | 0.0 | 2 | 1 | 1 | 7 | 0 | .184 | .184 | 0 | 0 | C-11 |
| 55 | 5 | 10 | 0 | 0 | 0 | 0 | 0.0 | 0 | 0 | 1 | 2 | 0 | .000 | .000 | 0 | 0 | C-5 |
| 56 | 1 | 4 | 1 | 0 | 0 | 0 | 0.0 | 0 | 0 | 0 | 0 | 0 | .250 | .250 | 0 | 0 | C-1 |
| 57 | 47 | 89 | 16 | 2 | 0 | 0 | 0.0 | 3 | 4 | 4 | 17 | 0 | .180 | .202 | 12 | 1 | C-35 |
| 4 yrs. | 64 | 141 | 24 | 2 | 0 | 0 | 0.0 | 5 | 5 | 6 | 26 | 0 | .170 | .184 | 12 | 1 | C-52 |
| 4 yrs. | 64 | 141 | 24 | 2 | 0 | 0 | 0.0 | 5 | 5 | 6 | 26 | 0 | .170 | .184 | 12 | 1 | C-52 |

# Carmen Fanzone

**FANZONE, CARMEN RONALD**
B. Aug. 30, 1941, Detroit, Mich.                           BR  TR  6'   200 lbs.

| | G | AB | H | 2B | 3B | HR | HR % | R | RBI | BB | SO | SB | BA | SA | AB | H | G by POS |
|---|---|---|---|---|---|---|---|---|---|---|---|---|---|---|---|---|---|
| 70 BOS A | 10 | 15 | 3 | 1 | 0 | 0 | 0.0 | 0 | 3 | 2 | 2 | 0 | .200 | .267 | 4 | 0 | 3B-5 |
| 71 CHI N | 12 | 43 | 8 | 2 | 0 | 2 | 4.7 | 5 | 5 | 2 | 7 | 0 | .186 | .372 | 2 | 1 | OF-6, 3B-3, 1B-2 |
| 72 | 86 | 222 | 50 | 11 | 0 | 8 | 3.6 | 26 | 42 | 35 | 45 | 2 | .225 | .383 | 15 | 4 | 3B-36, 1B-21, 2B-13, OF-1, SS-1 |
| 73 | 64 | 150 | 41 | 7 | 0 | 6 | 4.0 | 22 | 22 | 20 | 38 | 1 | .273 | .440 | 15 | 5 | 3B-25, 1B-24, OF-6 |
| 74 | 65 | 158 | 30 | 6 | 0 | 4 | 2.5 | 13 | 22 | 15 | 27 | 0 | .190 | .304 | 15 | 4 | 3B-35, 2B-10, 1B-7, OF-1 |
| 5 yrs. | 237 | 588 | 132 | 27 | 0 | 20 | 3.4 | 66 | 94 | 74 | 119 | 3 | .224 | .372 | 51 | 14 | 3B-104, 1B-54, 2B-23, OF-14, SS-1 |
| 4 yrs. | 227 | 573 | 129 | 26 | 0 | 20 | 3.5 | 66 | 91 | 72 | 117 | 3 | .225 | .375 | 47 | 14 | 3B-99, 1B-54, 2B-23, OF-14, SS-1 |

# Doc Farrell

**FARRELL, EDWARD STEPHEN**
B. Dec. 26, 1901, Johnson City, N. Y.    D. Dec. 20, 1966, Livingston, N. J.    BR  TR  5'8"   160 lbs.

| | G | AB | H | 2B | 3B | HR | HR % | R | RBI | BB | SO | SB | BA | SA | AB | H | G by POS |
|---|---|---|---|---|---|---|---|---|---|---|---|---|---|---|---|---|---|
| 25 NY N | 27 | 56 | 12 | 1 | 0 | 0 | 0.0 | 6 | 4 | 4 | 6 | 0 | .214 | .232 | 3 | 0 | SS-13, 3B-7, 2B-1 |
| 26 | 67 | 171 | 49 | 10 | 1 | 2 | 1.2 | 19 | 23 | 12 | 17 | 4 | .287 | .392 | 8 | 2 | SS-53, 2B-3 |
| 27 2 teams | NY | N (42G – .387) | | | | | | BOS | N (110G – .292) | | | | | | | | |
| total | 152 | 566 | 179 | 23 | 3 | 4 | 0.7 | 57 | 92 | 26 | 32 | 4 | .316 | .389 | 4 | 2 | SS-93, 2B-40, 3B-20 |
| 28 BOS N | 134 | 483 | 104 | 14 | 2 | 3 | 0.6 | 36 | 43 | 26 | 26 | 3 | .215 | .271 | 1 | 0 | SS-132, 2B-1 |
| 29 2 teams | BOS | N (5G – .125) | | | | | | NY | N (63G – .213) | | | | | | | | |
| total | 68 | 186 | 39 | 6 | 0 | 0 | 0.0 | 18 | 18 | 9 | 18 | 2 | .210 | .242 | 8 | 1 | 3B-28, 2B-26, SS-5 |
| 30 2 teams | STL | N (23G – .213) | | | | | | CHI | N (46G – .292) | | | | | | | | |
| total | 69 | 174 | 46 | 7 | 1 | 1 | 0.6 | 24 | 22 | 13 | 7 | 1 | .264 | .333 | 2 | 0 | SS-53, 2B-7, 1B-1 |
| 32 NY A | 26 | 63 | 11 | 1 | 1 | 0 | 0.0 | 4 | 4 | 2 | 8 | 0 | .175 | .222 | 0 | 0 | 2B-16, SS-5, 1B-2, 3B-1 |
| 33 | 44 | 93 | 25 | 0 | 0 | 0 | 0.0 | 16 | 6 | 16 | 6 | 0 | .269 | .269 | 0 | 0 | SS-22, 2B-20 |
| 35 BOS A | 4 | 7 | 2 | 1 | 0 | 0 | 0.0 | 1 | 1 | 1 | 0 | 0 | .286 | .429 | 0 | 0 | 2B-4 |
| 9 yrs. | 591 | 1799 | 467 | 63 | 8 | 10 | 0.6 | 181 | 213 | 109 | 120 | 14 | .260 | .320 | 26 | 5 | SS-376, 2B-118, 3B-56, 1B-3 |
| 1 yr. | 46 | 113 | 33 | 6 | 0 | 1 | 0.9 | 21 | 16 | 9 | 5 | 0 | .292 | .372 | 1 | 0 | SS-38, 2B-1 |

# Duke Farrell

**FARRELL, CHARLES ANDREW**
B. Aug. 31, 1866, Oakdale, Mass.    D. Feb. 15, 1925, Boston, Mass.    BB  TR  6'2"   180 lbs.

| | G | AB | H | 2B | 3B | HR | HR % | R | RBI | BB | SO | SB | BA | SA | AB | H | G by POS |
|---|---|---|---|---|---|---|---|---|---|---|---|---|---|---|---|---|---|
| 88 CHI N | 64 | 241 | 56 | 6 | 3 | 3 | 1.2 | 34 | 19 | 4 | 41 | 8 | .232 | .320 | 0 | 0 | C-33, OF-31, 1B-1 |
| 89 | 101 | 407 | 101 | 19 | 7 | 11 | 2.7 | 66 | 75 | 41 | 21 | 13 | .248 | .410 | 0 | 0 | C-76, OF-25 |
| 90 CHI P | 117 | 451 | 131 | 21 | 12 | 2 | 0.4 | 79 | 84 | 42 | 28 | 8 | .290 | .404 | 0 | 0 | C-90, 1B-22, OF-10 |
| 91 BOS AA | 122 | 473 | 143 | 19 | 13 | 12 | 2.5 | 108 | 110 | 59 | 48 | 21 | .302 | .474 | 0 | 0 | 3B-66, C-37, OF-23, 1B-4 |
| 92 PIT N | 152 | 605 | 130 | 10 | 13 | 8 | 1.3 | 96 | 77 | 46 | 53 | 20 | .215 | .314 | 0 | 0 | 3B-133, OF-20 |
| 93 WAS N | 124 | 511 | 143 | 13 | 13 | 4 | 0.8 | 84 | 75 | 47 | 12 | 11 | .280 | .380 | 0 | 0 | C-81, 3B-41, 1B-3 |
| 94 NY N | 114 | 401 | 114 | 20 | 12 | 4 | 1.0 | 47 | 66 | 35 | 15 | 9 | .284 | .424 | 1 | 0 | C-104, 3B-5, 1B-4 |
| 95 | 90 | 312 | 90 | 16 | 9 | 1 | 0.3 | 38 | 58 | 38 | 18 | 11 | .288 | .407 | 2 | 1 | C-62, 3B-24, 1B-2 |
| 96 2 teams | NY | N (58G – .283) | | | | | | WAS | N (37G – .300) | | | | | | | | |
| total | 95 | 321 | 93 | 14 | 6 | 2 | 0.6 | 41 | 67 | 26 | 10 | 4 | .290 | .389 | 10 | 4 | C-52, 3B-21, SS-13 |
| 97 WAS N | 78 | 261 | 84 | 9 | 6 | 0 | 0.0 | 41 | 53 | 17 | | 8 | .322 | .402 | 14 | 8 | C-63, 1B-1 |
| 98 | 99 | 338 | 106 | 12 | 6 | 1 | 0.3 | 47 | 53 | 34 | | 12 | .314 | .393 | 10 | 5 | C-61, 1B-28 |
| 99 2 teams | WAS | N (5G – .333) | | | | | | BKN | N (80G – .299) | | | | | | | | |
| total | 85 | 266 | 80 | 11 | 7 | 2 | 0.8 | 42 | 56 | 37 | | 7 | .301 | .417 | 3 | 1 | C-82 |
| 00 BKN N | 76 | 273 | 75 | 11 | 5 | 0 | 0.0 | 33 | 39 | 11 | | 3 | .275 | .352 | 2 | 0 | C-74 |
| 01 | 80 | 284 | 84 | 10 | 6 | 1 | 0.4 | 38 | 31 | 7 | | 7 | .296 | .384 | 4 | 3 | C-59, 1B-17 |
| 02 | 74 | 264 | 64 | 5 | 2 | 0 | 0.0 | 14 | 24 | 12 | | 6 | .242 | .277 | 2 | 0 | C-49, 1B-24 |
| 03 BOS A | 17 | 52 | 21 | 5 | 1 | 0 | 0.0 | 5 | 8 | 5 | | 1 | .404 | .538 | 0 | 0 | C-17 |
| 04 | 68 | 198 | 42 | 9 | 2 | 0 | 0.0 | 11 | 15 | 15 | | 1 | .212 | .278 | 11 | 1 | C-56 |
| 05 | 7 | 21 | 6 | 1 | 0 | 0 | 0.0 | 2 | 2 | 1 | | 0 | .286 | .333 | 0 | 0 | C-7 |
| 18 yrs. | 1563 | 5679 | 1563 | 211 | 123 | 51 | 0.9 | 826 | 912 | 477 | 246 | 150 | .275 | .383 | 59 | 23 | C-1003, 3B-290, OF-109, 1B-106, SS-13 |
| 2 yrs. | 165 | 648 | 157 | 25 | 10 | 14 | 2.2 | 100 | 94 | 45 | 62 | 21 | .242 | .377 | 0 | 0 | C-109, OF-56, 1B-1 |
| **WORLD SERIES** | | | | | | | | | | | | | | | | | |
| 03 BOS A | 2 | 2 | 0 | 0 | 0 | 0 | 0.0 | 0 | 1 | 0 | 0 | 0 | .000 | .000 | 2 | 0 | |

# Marv Felderman

**FELDERMAN, MARVIN WILFRED**
B. Dec. 20, 1915, Bellevue, Iowa                          BR  TR  6'1"   187 lbs.

| | G | AB | H | 2B | 3B | HR | HR % | R | RBI | BB | SO | SB | BA | SA | AB | H | G by POS |
|---|---|---|---|---|---|---|---|---|---|---|---|---|---|---|---|---|---|
| 42 CHI N | 3 | 6 | 1 | 0 | 0 | 0 | 0.0 | 0 | 1 | 4 | 0 | .167 | .167 | 0 | 0 | C-2 |

# John Felske

**FELSKE, JOHN FREDRICK**
B. May 30, 1942, Chicago, Ill.
Manager 1985.                                             BR  TR  6'3"   195 lbs.

| | G | AB | H | 2B | 3B | HR | HR % | R | RBI | BB | SO | SB | BA | SA | AB | H | G by POS |
|---|---|---|---|---|---|---|---|---|---|---|---|---|---|---|---|---|---|
| 68 CHI N | 4 | 2 | 0 | 0 | 0 | 0 | 0.0 | 0 | 0 | 0 | 1 | 0 | .000 | .000 | 1 | 0 | C-3 |
| 72 MIL A | 37 | 80 | 11 | 3 | 0 | 1 | 1.3 | 6 | 5 | 8 | 23 | 0 | .138 | .213 | 8 | 2 | C-23, 1B-8 |
| 73 | 13 | 22 | 3 | 0 | 1 | 0 | 0.0 | 1 | 4 | 1 | 11 | 0 | .136 | .227 | 1 | 0 | C-7, 1B-6 |
| 3 yrs. | 54 | 104 | 14 | 3 | 1 | 1 | 1.0 | 7 | 9 | 9 | 35 | 0 | .135 | .212 | 10 | 2 | C-33, 1B-14 |
| 1 yr. | 4 | 2 | 0 | 0 | 0 | 0 | 0.0 | 0 | 0 | 0 | 1 | 0 | .000 | .000 | 1 | 0 | C-3 |

| | G | AB | H | 2B | 3B | HR | HR % | R | RBI | BB | SO | SB | BA | SA | Pinch Hit AB | Pinch Hit H | G by POS |
|---|---|---|---|---|---|---|---|---|---|---|---|---|---|---|---|---|---|

## Bob Ferguson

**FERGUSON, ROBERT V. (Death to Flying Things)**    BB TR 5'9½"   149 lbs.
B. Jan. 31, 1845, Brooklyn, N. Y.    D. May 3, 1894, Brooklyn, N. Y.
Manager 1871-84, 1886-87.

| | G | AB | H | 2B | 3B | HR | HR % | R | RBI | BB | SO | SB | BA | SA | PH AB | PH H | G by POS |
|---|---|---|---|---|---|---|---|---|---|---|---|---|---|---|---|---|---|
| 1876 HAR N | 69 | 310 | 82 | 8 | 5 | 0 | 0.0 | 48 | 32 | 2 | 11 | | .265 | .323 | 0 | 0 | 3B-69 |
| 1877 | 58 | 254 | 65 | 7 | 2 | 0 | 0.0 | 40 | 35 | 3 | 10 | | .256 | .299 | 0 | 0 | 3B-56, P-3 |
| 1878 CHI N | 61 | 259 | 91 | 10 | 2 | 0 | 0.0 | 44 | 39 | 10 | 12 | | .351 | .405 | 0 | 0 | SS-57, 2B-4, C-1 |
| 1879 TRO N | 30 | 123 | 31 | 5 | 2 | 0 | 0.0 | 18 | 4 | 4 | 3 | | .252 | .325 | 0 | 0 | 3B-24, 2B-6 |
| 1880 | 82 | 332 | 87 | 9 | 0 | 0 | 0.0 | 55 | | 24 | 24 | | .262 | .289 | 0 | 0 | 2B-82 |
| 1881 | 85 | 339 | 96 | 13 | 5 | 1 | 0.3 | 56 | 35 | 29 | 12 | | .283 | .360 | 0 | 0 | 2B-85 |
| 1882 | 81 | 319 | 82 | 15 | 2 | 0 | 0.0 | 44 | 33 | 23 | 21 | | .257 | .317 | 0 | 0 | 2B-79, SS-2 |
| 1883 PHI N | 86 | 329 | 85 | 9 | 2 | 0 | 0.0 | 39 | | 18 | 21 | | .258 | .298 | 0 | 0 | 2B-86, P-1 |
| 1884 PIT AA | 10 | 41 | 6 | 0 | 0 | 0 | 0.0 | 2 | | 0 | | | .146 | .146 | 0 | 0 | OF-6, 1B-3, 3B-1 |
| 9 yrs. | 562 | 2306 | 625 | 76 | 20 | 1 | 0.0 | 346 | 178 | 113 | 114 | | .271 | .323 | 0 | 0 | 2B-342, 3B-150, SS-59, OF-6, P-4, 1B-3, C-1 |
| 1 yr. | 61 | 259 | 91 | 10 | 2 | 0 | 0.0 | 44 | 39 | 10 | 12 | | .351 | .405 | 0 | 0 | SS-57, 2B-4, C-1 |

## Frank Fernandez

**FERNANDEZ, FRANK**    BR TR 6'   185 lbs.
B. Apr. 16, 1943, Staten Island, N. Y.

| | G | AB | H | 2B | 3B | HR | HR % | R | RBI | BB | SO | SB | BA | SA | PH AB | PH H | G by POS |
|---|---|---|---|---|---|---|---|---|---|---|---|---|---|---|---|---|---|
| 1967 NY A | 9 | 28 | 6 | 2 | 0 | 1 | 3.6 | 1 | 4 | 2 | 7 | 1 | .214 | .393 | 0 | 0 | C-7, OF-2 |
| 1968 | 51 | 135 | 23 | 6 | 1 | 7 | 5.2 | 15 | 30 | 35 | 50 | 1 | .170 | .385 | 1 | 0 | C-45, OF-4 |
| 1969 | 89 | 229 | 51 | 6 | 1 | 12 | 5.2 | 34 | 29 | 65 | 68 | 1 | .223 | .415 | 11 | 1 | C-65, OF-14 |
| 1970 OAK A | 94 | 252 | 54 | 5 | 0 | 15 | 6.0 | 30 | 44 | 40 | 76 | 1 | .214 | .413 | 14 | 5 | C-76, OF-1 |
| 1971 3 teams | OAK A (4G – .111) | | | WAS A (18G – .100) | | | | CHI N (17G – .171) | | | | | | | | | |
| " total | 39 | 80 | 11 | 2 | 0 | 4 | 5.0 | 12 | 9 | 22 | 28 | 0 | .138 | .313 | 14 | 1 | C-20, OF-6 |
| 1972 CHI N | 3 | 3 | 0 | 0 | 0 | 0 | 0.0 | 0 | 0 | 0 | 2 | 0 | .000 | .000 | 2 | 0 | C-1 |
| 6 yrs. | 285 | 727 | 145 | 21 | 2 | 39 | 5.4 | 92 | 116 | 164 | 231 | 4 | .199 | .395 | 42 | 7 | C-214, OF-27 |
| 2 yrs. | 20 | 44 | 7 | 1 | 0 | 4 | 9.1 | 11 | 4 | 17 | 17 | 0 | .159 | .455 | 4 | 0 | C-17 |

## Jesus Figueroa

**FIGUEROA, JESUS MARIA**    BL TL 5'10"   160 lbs.
Born Jesus Maria Figueroa Figueroa.
B. Feb. 20, 1957, Santo Domingo, Dominican Republic

| | G | AB | H | 2B | 3B | HR | HR % | R | RBI | BB | SO | SB | BA | SA | PH AB | PH H | G by POS |
|---|---|---|---|---|---|---|---|---|---|---|---|---|---|---|---|---|---|
| 1980 CHI N | 115 | 198 | 50 | 5 | 0 | 1 | 0.5 | 20 | 11 | 14 | 16 | 2 | .253 | .293 | 53 | 15 | OF-57 |

## Bill Fischer

**FISCHER, WILLIAM CHARLES**    BL TR 6'   174 lbs.
B. Mar. 2, 1891, New York, N. Y.    D. Sept. 4, 1945, Richmond, Va.

| | G | AB | H | 2B | 3B | HR | HR % | R | RBI | BB | SO | SB | BA | SA | PH AB | PH H | G by POS |
|---|---|---|---|---|---|---|---|---|---|---|---|---|---|---|---|---|---|
| 1913 BKN N | 62 | 165 | 44 | 9 | 4 | 1 | 0.6 | 16 | 12 | 10 | 5 | 0 | .267 | .388 | 1 | 0 | C-51 |
| 1914 | 43 | 105 | 27 | 1 | 2 | 0 | 0.0 | 12 | 8 | 8 | 12 | 1 | .257 | .305 | 12 | 5 | C-30 |
| 1915 CHI F | 105 | 292 | 96 | 15 | 4 | 4 | 1.4 | 30 | 50 | 24 | | 1 | .329 | .449 | 21 | 7 | C-80 |
| 1916 2 teams | CHI N (65G – .196) | | | PIT N (42G – .257) | | | | | | | | | | | | | |
| " total | 107 | 292 | 64 | 16 | 3 | 2 | 0.7 | 26 | 20 | 21 | 11 | 3 | .219 | .315 | 12 | 0 | C-91 |
| 1917 PIT N | 95 | 245 | 70 | 9 | 2 | 3 | 1.2 | 25 | 25 | 27 | 19 | 11 | .286 | .376 | 16 | 3 | C-69, 1B-2 |
| 5 yrs. | 412 | 1099 | 301 | 50 | 15 | 10 | 0.9 | 109 | 115 | 90 | 47 | 20 | .274 | .374 | 62 | 15 | C-321, 1B-2 |
| 1 yr. | 65 | 179 | 35 | 9 | 2 | 1 | 0.6 | 15 | 14 | 11 | 8 | 2 | .196 | .285 | 6 | 0 | C-56 |

## Bob Fisher

**FISHER, ROBERT TECUMSEH**    BR TR 5'9½"   170 lbs.
Brother of Newt Fisher.
B. Nov. 3, 1887, Nashville, Tenn.    D. Aug. 4, 1963, Jacksonville, Fla.

| | G | AB | H | 2B | 3B | HR | HR % | R | RBI | BB | SO | SB | BA | SA | PH AB | PH H | G by POS |
|---|---|---|---|---|---|---|---|---|---|---|---|---|---|---|---|---|---|
| 1912 BKN N | 82 | 257 | 60 | 10 | 3 | 0 | 0.0 | 27 | 26 | 14 | 32 | 7 | .233 | .296 | 4 | 0 | SS-74, 3B-1, 2B-1 |
| 1913 | 132 | 474 | 124 | 11 | 10 | 4 | 0.8 | 42 | 54 | 10 | 43 | 16 | .262 | .352 | 11 | 2 | SS-131 |
| 1914 CHI N | 15 | 50 | 15 | 2 | 2 | 0 | 0.0 | 5 | 5 | 3 | 4 | 2 | .300 | .420 | 0 | 0 | SS-15 |
| 1915 | 147 | 568 | 163 | 22 | 5 | 5 | 0.9 | 70 | 53 | 30 | 51 | 9 | .287 | .370 | 2 | 0 | SS-147 |
| 1916 CIN N | 61 | 136 | 37 | 4 | 3 | 0 | 0.0 | 9 | 11 | 8 | 14 | 7 | .272 | .346 | 25 | 6 | SS-29, 2B-6, OF-1 |
| 1918 STL N | 63 | 246 | 78 | 11 | 3 | 2 | 0.8 | 36 | 20 | 15 | 11 | 7 | .317 | .411 | 0 | 0 | 2B-63 |
| 1919 | 3 | 11 | 3 | 1 | 0 | 0 | 0.0 | 0 | 1 | 0 | 2 | 0 | .273 | .364 | 0 | 0 | 2B-3 |
| 7 yrs. | 503 | 1742 | 480 | 61 | 26 | 11 | 0.6 | 189 | 170 | 80 | 157 | 48 | .276 | .359 | 42 | 8 | SS-396, 2B-73, OF-1, 3B-1 |
| 2 yrs. | 162 | 618 | 178 | 24 | 7 | 5 | 0.8 | 75 | 58 | 33 | 55 | 11 | .288 | .374 | 2 | 0 | SS-162 |

## Howie Fitzgerald

**FITZGERALD, HOWARD CHUMNEY (Lefty)**    BL TL 5'11½" 163 lbs.
B. May 16, 1902, Eagle Lake, Tex.    D. Feb. 27, 1959, Eagle Falls, Tex.

| | G | AB | H | 2B | 3B | HR | HR % | R | RBI | BB | SO | SB | BA | SA | PH AB | PH H | G by POS |
|---|---|---|---|---|---|---|---|---|---|---|---|---|---|---|---|---|---|
| 1922 CHI N | 10 | 24 | 8 | 1 | 0 | 0 | 0.0 | 3 | 4 | 3 | 2 | 1 | .333 | .375 | 3 | 2 | OF-10 |
| 1924 | 7 | 19 | 3 | 0 | 0 | 0 | 0.0 | 1 | 2 | 0 | 2 | 0 | .158 | .158 | 2 | 0 | OF-5 |
| 1926 BOS A | 31 | 97 | 25 | 2 | 0 | 0 | 0.0 | 11 | 8 | 5 | 7 | 1 | .258 | .278 | 8 | 2 | OF-23 |
| 3 yrs. | 48 | 140 | 36 | 3 | 0 | 0 | 0.0 | 15 | 14 | 8 | 11 | 2 | .257 | .279 | 13 | 4 | OF-38 |
| 2 yrs. | 17 | 43 | 11 | 1 | 0 | 0 | 0.0 | 4 | 6 | 3 | 4 | 1 | .256 | .279 | 5 | 2 | OF-15 |

## Max Flack

**FLACK, MAX JOHN**    BL TL 5'7"   148 lbs.
B. Feb. 5, 1890, Belleville, Ill.    D. July 31, 1975, Belleville, Ill.

| | G | AB | H | 2B | 3B | HR | HR % | R | RBI | BB | SO | SB | BA | SA | PH AB | PH H | G by POS |
|---|---|---|---|---|---|---|---|---|---|---|---|---|---|---|---|---|---|
| 1914 CHI F | 134 | 502 | 124 | 15 | 3 | 2 | 0.4 | 66 | 39 | 51 | | 37 | .247 | .301 | 1 | 0 | OF-133 |
| 1915 | 141 | 523 | 164 | 20 | 14 | 3 | 0.6 | 88 | 45 | 40 | | 37 | .314 | .423 | 3 | 2 | OF-138 |
| 1916 CHI N | 141 | 465 | 120 | 14 | 3 | 3 | 0.6 | 65 | 20 | 42 | 40 | 24 | .258 | .320 | 3 | 0 | OF-136 |
| 1917 | 131 | 447 | 111 | 18 | 7 | 0 | 0.0 | 65 | 21 | 51 | 34 | 17 | .248 | .320 | 10 | 3 | OF-117 |
| 1918 | 123 | 478 | 123 | 17 | 10 | 4 | 0.8 | 74 | 41 | 56 | 19 | 17 | .257 | .360 | 2 | 0 | OF-121 |
| 1919 | 116 | 469 | 138 | 20 | 4 | 6 | 1.3 | 71 | 35 | 34 | 13 | 18 | .294 | .392 | 0 | 0 | OF-116 |
| 1920 | 135 | 520 | 157 | 30 | 6 | 4 | 0.8 | 85 | 49 | 52 | 15 | 13 | .302 | .406 | 2 | 0 | OF-132 |
| 1921 | 133 | 572 | 172 | 31 | 6 | 3 | 1.0 | 80 | 37 | 32 | 15 | 17 | .301 | .400 | 3 | 1 | OF-130 |
| 1922 2 teams | CHI N (17G – .222) | | | STL N (66G – .292) | | | | | | | | | | | | | |
| " total | 83 | 321 | 90 | 13 | 1 | 2 | 0.6 | 53 | 27 | 33 | 15 | 5 | .280 | .346 | 1 | 0 | OF-83 |
| 1923 STL N | 128 | 505 | 147 | 16 | 9 | 3 | 0.6 | 82 | 28 | 41 | 16 | 7 | .291 | .376 | 6 | 3 | OF-121 |
| 1924 | 67 | 209 | 55 | 11 | 3 | 1 | 0.5 | 31 | 21 | 21 | 5 | 3 | .263 | .373 | 13 | 3 | OF-52 |

| | G | AB | H | 2B | 3B | HR | HR % | R | RBI | BB | SO | SB | BA | SA | Pinch Hit AB | Pinch Hit H | G by POS |
|---|---|---|---|---|---|---|---|---|---|---|---|---|---|---|---|---|---|

## Max Flack continued

| | G | AB | H | 2B | 3B | HR | HR% | R | RBI | BB | SO | SB | BA | SA | AB | H | G by POS |
|---|---|---|---|---|---|---|---|---|---|---|---|---|---|---|---|---|---|
| 1925 | 79 | 241 | 60 | 7 | 8 | 0 | 0.0 | 23 | 28 | 21 | 9 | 5 | .249 | .344 | 19 | 3 | OF-59 |
| 12 yrs. | 1411 | 5252 | 1461 | 212 | 72 | 35 | 0.7 | 783 | 391 | 474 | 184 | 200 | .278 | .366 | 61 | 15 | OF-1338 |
| 7 yrs. | 796 | 3005 | 833 | 131 | 34 | 23 | 0.8 | 447 | 209 | 269 | 143 | 108 | .277 | .366 | 19 | 4 | OF-769 |

**WORLD SERIES**

| | G | AB | H | 2B | 3B | HR | HR% | R | RBI | BB | SO | SB | BA | SA | AB | H | G by POS |
|---|---|---|---|---|---|---|---|---|---|---|---|---|---|---|---|---|---|
| 1918 CHI N | 6 | 19 | 5 | 0 | 0 | 0 | 0.0 | 2 | 1 | 4 | 1 | 1 | .263 | .263 | 0 | 0 | OF-6 |

## Scott Fletcher

FLETCHER, SCOTT BRIAN      BR TR 5'11" 168 lbs.
B. July 30, 1958, Fort Walton Beach, Fla.

| | G | AB | H | 2B | 3B | HR | HR% | R | RBI | BB | SO | SB | BA | SA | AB | H | G by POS |
|---|---|---|---|---|---|---|---|---|---|---|---|---|---|---|---|---|---|
| 1981 CHI N | 19 | 46 | 10 | 4 | 0 | 0 | 0.0 | 6 | 1 | 2 | 4 | 0 | .217 | .304 | 0 | 0 | 2B-13, SS-4, 3B-1 |
| 1982 | 11 | 24 | 4 | 0 | 0 | 0 | 0.0 | 4 | 1 | 4 | 5 | 1 | .167 | .167 | 0 | 0 | SS-11 |
| 1983 CHI A | 114 | 262 | 62 | 16 | 5 | 3 | 1.1 | 42 | 31 | 29 | 22 | 5 | .237 | .370 | 0 | 0 | SS-100, 2B-12, 3B-7, DH-1 |
| 1984 | 149 | 456 | 114 | 13 | 3 | 3 | 0.7 | 46 | 35 | 46 | 46 | 10 | .250 | .311 | 0 | 0 | SS-134, 2B-28, 3B-3 |
| 1985 | 119 | 301 | 77 | 8 | 1 | 2 | 0.7 | 38 | 31 | 35 | 47 | 5 | .256 | .309 | 12 | 3 | 3B-55, SS-44, 2B-37, DH-2 |
| 5 yrs. | 412 | 1089 | 267 | 41 | 9 | 8 | 0.7 | 136 | 99 | 116 | 124 | 21 | .245 | .321 | 12 | 3 | SS-293, 2B-90, 3B-66, DH-3 |
| 2 yrs. | 30 | 70 | 14 | 4 | 0 | 0 | 0.0 | 10 | 2 | 6 | 9 | 1 | .200 | .257 | 0 | 0 | SS-15, 2B-13, 3B-1 |

**LEAGUE CHAMPIONSHIP SERIES**

| | G | AB | H | 2B | 3B | HR | HR% | R | RBI | BB | SO | SB | BA | SA | AB | H | G by POS |
|---|---|---|---|---|---|---|---|---|---|---|---|---|---|---|---|---|---|
| 1983 CHI A | 3 | 7 | 0 | 0 | 0 | 0 | 0.0 | 0 | 0 | 1 | 0 | 0 | .000 | .000 | 0 | 0 | SS-3 |

## Silver Flint

FLINT, FRANK SYLVESTER      BR TR 6' 180 lbs.
B. Aug. 3, 1856, Philadelphia, Pa.    D. Jan. 14, 1892, Chicago, Ill.

| | G | AB | H | 2B | 3B | HR | HR% | R | RBI | BB | SO | SB | BA | SA | AB | H | G by POS |
|---|---|---|---|---|---|---|---|---|---|---|---|---|---|---|---|---|---|
| 1878 IND N | 63 | 254 | 57 | 7 | 0 | 0 | 0.0 | 23 | 18 | 2 | 15 | | .224 | .252 | 0 | 0 | C-59, OF-9 |
| 1879 CHI N | 79 | 324 | 92 | 22 | 6 | 1 | 0.3 | 46 | 41 | 6 | 44 | | .284 | .398 | 0 | 0 | C-78, OF-1 |
| 1880 | 74 | 284 | 46 | 10 | 4 | 0 | 0.0 | 30 | 17 | 5 | 32 | | .162 | .225 | 0 | 0 | C-67, OF-13 |
| 1881 | 80 | 306 | 95 | 18 | 0 | 1 | 0.3 | 46 | 34 | 6 | 39 | | .310 | .379 | 0 | 0 | C-80, OF-8, 1B-1 |
| 1882 | 81 | 331 | 83 | 18 | 8 | 4 | 1.2 | 48 | 44 | 2 | 50 | | .251 | .390 | 0 | 0 | C-81, OF-10 |
| 1883 | 85 | 332 | 88 | 23 | 4 | 0 | 0.0 | 57 | | 3 | 69 | | .265 | .358 | 0 | 0 | C-83, OF-23 |
| 1884 | 73 | 279 | 57 | 5 | 2 | 9 | 3.2 | 35 | | 7 | 57 | | .204 | .333 | 0 | 0 | C-73 |
| 1885 | 68 | 249 | 52 | 8 | 2 | 1 | 0.4 | 27 | 19 | 2 | 52 | | .209 | .269 | 0 | 0 | C-68, OF-1 |
| 1886 | 54 | 173 | 35 | 6 | 2 | 1 | 0.6 | 30 | 13 | 12 | 36 | | .202 | .277 | 0 | 0 | C-54, 1B-3 |
| 1887 | 49 | 187 | 50 | 8 | 6 | 3 | 1.6 | 22 | 21 | 4 | 28 | 7 | .267 | .422 | 0 | 0 | C-47, 1B-2 |
| 1888 | 22 | 77 | 14 | 3 | 0 | 0 | 0.0 | 6 | 3 | 1 | 21 | 1 | .182 | .221 | 0 | 0 | C-22 |
| 1889 | 15 | 56 | 13 | 1 | 0 | 1 | 1.8 | 6 | 9 | 3 | 18 | 1 | .232 | .304 | 0 | 0 | C-15 |
| 12 yrs. | 743 | 2852 | 682 | 129 | 34 | 21 | 0.7 | 376 | 219 | 53 | 461 | 9 | .239 | .330 | 0 | 0 | C-727, OF-65, 1B-6 |
| 11 yrs. | 680 | 2598 | 625 | 122 | 34 | 21 | 0.8 | 353 | 201 | 51 | 446 | 9 | .241 | .338 | 0 | 0 | C-668, OF-56, 1B-6 |

## John Fluhrer

FLUHRER, JOHN L.      BR TR 5'9" 165 lbs.
Played as William Morris Part Of 1915.
B. Jan. 3, 1894, Adrian, Mich.    D. July 17, 1946, Columbus, Ohio

| | G | AB | H | 2B | 3B | HR | HR% | R | RBI | BB | SO | SB | BA | SA | AB | H | G by POS |
|---|---|---|---|---|---|---|---|---|---|---|---|---|---|---|---|---|---|
| 1915 CHI N | 6 | 6 | 2 | 0 | 0 | 0 | 0.0 | 0 | 0 | 1 | 0 | 1 | .333 | .333 | 3 | 0 | OF-2 |

## George Flynn

FLYNN, GEORGE A. (Dibby)     
B. May 24, 1871, Chicago, Ill.    D. Dec. 28, 1901, Chicago, Ill.

| | G | AB | H | 2B | 3B | HR | HR% | R | RBI | BB | SO | SB | BA | SA | AB | H | G by POS |
|---|---|---|---|---|---|---|---|---|---|---|---|---|---|---|---|---|---|
| 1896 CHI N | 29 | 106 | 27 | 1 | 2 | 0 | 0.0 | 15 | 4 | 11 | 9 | 12 | .255 | .302 | 0 | 0 | OF-29 |

## Jocko Flynn

FLYNN, JOHN A.      5'6½" 143 lbs.
B. June 30, 1864, Lawrence, Mass.    D. Dec. 30, 1907, Lawrence, Mass.

| | G | AB | H | 2B | 3B | HR | HR% | R | RBI | BB | SO | SB | BA | SA | AB | H | G by POS |
|---|---|---|---|---|---|---|---|---|---|---|---|---|---|---|---|---|---|
| 1886 CHI N | 57 | 205 | 41 | 6 | 2 | 4 | 2.0 | 40 | 19 | 18 | 45 | | .200 | .307 | 0 | 0 | P-32, OF-28 |
| 1887 | 1 | 0 | 0 | 0 | 0 | 0 | – | 0 | 0 | 0 | 0 | 0 | – | – | 0 | 0 | OF-1 |
| 2 yrs. | 58 | 205 | 41 | 6 | 2 | 4 | 2.0 | 40 | 19 | 18 | 45 | 0 | .200 | .307 | 0 | 0 | P-32, OF-29 |
| 2 yrs. | 58 | 205 | 41 | 6 | 2 | 4 | 2.0 | 40 | 19 | 18 | 45 | 0 | .200 | .307 | 0 | 0 | P-32, OF-29 |

## Dee Fondy

FONDY, DEE VIRGIL      BL TL 6'3" 195 lbs.
B. Oct. 31, 1924, Slaton, Tex.

| | G | AB | H | 2B | 3B | HR | HR% | R | RBI | BB | SO | SB | BA | SA | AB | H | G by POS |
|---|---|---|---|---|---|---|---|---|---|---|---|---|---|---|---|---|---|
| 1951 CHI N | 49 | 170 | 46 | 7 | 2 | 3 | 1.8 | 23 | 20 | 11 | 20 | 5 | .271 | .388 | 5 | 1 | 1B-44 |
| 1952 | 145 | 554 | 166 | 21 | 9 | 10 | 1.8 | 69 | 67 | 28 | 60 | 13 | .300 | .424 | 2 | 0 | 1B-143 |
| 1953 | 150 | 595 | 184 | 24 | 11 | 18 | 3.0 | 79 | 78 | 44 | 106 | 10 | .309 | .477 | 1 | 0 | 1B-149 |
| 1954 | 141 | 568 | 162 | 30 | 4 | 9 | 1.6 | 77 | 49 | 35 | 84 | 20 | .285 | .400 | 2 | 1 | 1B-138 |
| 1955 | 150 | 574 | 152 | 23 | 8 | 17 | 3.0 | 69 | 65 | 35 | 87 | 8 | .265 | .422 | 0 | 0 | 1B-147 |
| 1956 | 137 | 543 | 146 | 22 | 9 | 9 | 1.7 | 52 | 46 | 20 | 74 | 9 | .269 | .392 | 4 | 1 | 1B-133 |
| 1957 2 teams | | CHI | N (11G – | .314) | | PIT | N | (95G – | .313) | | | | | | | | |
| " total | 106 | 374 | 117 | 16 | 3 | 2 | 0.5 | 45 | 37 | 25 | 68 | 12 | .313 | .388 | 23 | 6 | 1B-84 |
| 1958 CIN N | 89 | 124 | 27 | 1 | 1 | 1 | 0.8 | 23 | 11 | 5 | 27 | 7 | .218 | .266 | 23 | 4 | 1B-36, OF-22 |
| 8 yrs. | 967 | 3502 | 1000 | 144 | 47 | 69 | 2.0 | 437 | 373 | 203 | 526 | 84 | .286 | .413 | 60 | 13 | 1B-874, OF-22 |
| 7 yrs. | 783 | 3055 | 872 | 130 | 44 | 66 | 2.2 | 372 | 327 | 173 | 440 | 66 | .285 | .422 | 14 | 3 | 1B-765 |

## Barry Foote

FOOTE, BARRY CLIFTON      BR TR 6'3" 205 lbs.
B. Feb. 16, 1952, Smithfield, N. C.

| | G | AB | H | 2B | 3B | HR | HR% | R | RBI | BB | SO | SB | BA | SA | AB | H | G by POS |
|---|---|---|---|---|---|---|---|---|---|---|---|---|---|---|---|---|---|
| 1973 MON N | 6 | 6 | 4 | 0 | 1 | 0 | 0.0 | 0 | 1 | 0 | 0 | 0 | .667 | 1.000 | 6 | 4 | |
| 1974 | 125 | 420 | 110 | 23 | 4 | 11 | 2.6 | 44 | 60 | 35 | 74 | 2 | .262 | .414 | 3 | 2 | C-122 |
| 1975 | 118 | 387 | 75 | 16 | 1 | 7 | 1.8 | 25 | 30 | 17 | 48 | 0 | .194 | .295 | 6 | 3 | C-115 |
| 1976 | 105 | 350 | 82 | 12 | 2 | 7 | 2.0 | 32 | 27 | 17 | 32 | 2 | .234 | .340 | 8 | 2 | C-96, 3B-2, 1B-1 |
| 1977 2 teams | | MON | N (15G – | .245) | | PHI | N | (18G – | .219) | | | | | | | | |
| " total | 33 | 81 | 19 | 4 | 1 | 3 | 3.7 | 7 | 11 | 7 | 16 | 0 | .235 | .420 | 4 | 0 | C-30 |
| 1978 PHI N | 39 | 57 | 9 | 0 | 0 | 1 | 1.8 | 4 | 4 | 1 | 11 | 0 | .158 | .211 | 13 | 1 | C-31 |
| 1979 CHI N | 132 | 429 | 109 | 26 | 0 | 16 | 3.7 | 47 | 56 | 34 | 49 | 5 | .254 | .427 | 5 | 0 | C-129 |

| | G | AB | H | 2B | 3B | HR | HR % | R | RBI | BB | SO | SB | BA | SA | Pinch Hit AB | Pinch Hit H | G by POS |
|---|---|---|---|---|---|---|---|---|---|---|---|---|---|---|---|---|---|

## Barry Foote continued

| | G | AB | H | 2B | 3B | HR | HR% | R | RBI | BB | SO | SB | BA | SA | PH AB | PH H | G by POS |
|---|---|---|---|---|---|---|---|---|---|---|---|---|---|---|---|---|---|
| 1980 | 63 | 202 | 48 | 13 | 1 | 6 | 3.0 | 16 | 28 | 13 | 18 | 1 | .238 | .401 | 9 | 2 | C-55 |
| 1981 2 teams | CHI | N (9G – .000) | | | NY | A (40G – .208) | | | | | | | | | | | |
| " total | 49 | 147 | 26 | 4 | 0 | 6 | 4.1 | 12 | 11 | 11 | 28 | 0 | .177 | .327 | 4 | 0 | C-42, DH-4, 1B-1 |
| 1982 NY A | 17 | 48 | 7 | 5 | 0 | 0 | 0.0 | 4 | 2 | 1 | 11 | 0 | .146 | .250 | 0 | 0 | C-17 |
| 10 yrs. | 687 | 2127 | 489 | 103 | 10 | 57 | 2.7 | 191 | 230 | 136 | 287 | 10 | .230 | .368 | 58 | 14 | C-637, DH-4, 3B-2, 1B-2 |
| 3 yrs. | 204 | 653 | 157 | 39 | 1 | 22 | 3.4 | 63 | 85 | 50 | 74 | 6 | .240 | .404 | 17 | 2 | C-192 |

### DIVISIONAL PLAYOFF SERIES

| | G | AB | H | 2B | 3B | HR | HR% | R | RBI | BB | SO | SB | BA | SA | PH AB | PH H | G by POS |
|---|---|---|---|---|---|---|---|---|---|---|---|---|---|---|---|---|---|
| 1981 NY A | 1 | 1 | 0 | 0 | 0 | 0 | – | 0 | 0 | 0 | 0 | 0 | – | – | 0 | 0 | |

### LEAGUE CHAMPIONSHIP SERIES

| | G | AB | H | 2B | 3B | HR | HR% | R | RBI | BB | SO | SB | BA | SA | PH AB | PH H | G by POS |
|---|---|---|---|---|---|---|---|---|---|---|---|---|---|---|---|---|---|
| 1978 PHI N | 1 | 1 | 0 | 0 | 0 | 0 | 0.0 | 0 | 0 | 0 | 1 | 0 | .000 | .000 | 1 | 0 | |
| 1981 NY A | 2 | 1 | 1 | 0 | 0 | 0 | 0.0 | 0 | 0 | 0 | 0 | 0 | 1.000 | 1.000 | 1 | 1 | C-1 |
| 2 yrs. | 3 | 2 | 1 | 0 | 0 | 0 | 0.0 | 0 | 0 | 0 | 1 | 0 | .500 | .500 | 2 | 1 | C-1 |

### WORLD SERIES

| | G | AB | H | 2B | 3B | HR | HR% | R | RBI | BB | SO | SB | BA | SA | PH AB | PH H | G by POS |
|---|---|---|---|---|---|---|---|---|---|---|---|---|---|---|---|---|---|
| 1981 NY A | 1 | 1 | 0 | 0 | 0 | 0 | 0.0 | 0 | 0 | 0 | 1 | 0 | .000 | .000 | 1 | 0 | |

## Elmer Foster

**FOSTER, ELMER E.**    BR TL
B. Aug. 15, 1861, Minneapolis, Minn.    D. July 22, 1946, Minneapolis, Minn.

| | G | AB | H | 2B | 3B | HR | HR% | R | RBI | BB | SO | SB | BA | SA | PH AB | PH H | G by POS |
|---|---|---|---|---|---|---|---|---|---|---|---|---|---|---|---|---|---|
| 1884 2 teams | PHI | AA (4G – .182) | | | PHI | U (1G – .333) | | | | | | | | | | | |
| " total | 5 | 14 | 3 | 0 | 1 | 0 | 0.0 | 4 | | 3 | | | .214 | .357 | 0 | 0 | C-5, OF-1 |
| 1886 NY AA | 35 | 125 | 23 | 0 | 1 | 0 | 0.0 | 16 | | 7 | | | .184 | .200 | 0 | 0 | 2B-21, OF-14 |
| 1888 NY N | 37 | 136 | 20 | 3 | 2 | 0 | 0.0 | 15 | 10 | 9 | 20 | 13 | .147 | .199 | 0 | 0 | OF-37, 3B-1 |
| 1889 | 2 | 4 | 0 | 0 | 0 | 0 | 0.0 | 2 | 0 | 3 | 1 | 2 | .000 | .000 | 0 | 0 | OF-2 |
| 1890 CHI N | 27 | 105 | 26 | 4 | 2 | 5 | 4.8 | 20 | 23 | 9 | 21 | 18 | .248 | .467 | 0 | 0 | OF-27 |
| 1891 | 4 | 16 | 3 | 0 | 0 | 1 | 6.3 | 3 | 1 | 1 | 2 | 1 | .188 | .375 | 0 | 0 | OF-4 |
| 6 yrs. | 110 | 400 | 75 | 7 | 6 | 6 | 1.5 | 60 | 33 | 32 | 44 | 34 | .188 | .280 | 0 | 0 | OF-85, 2B-21, C-5, 3B-1 |
| 2 yrs. | 31 | 121 | 29 | 4 | 2 | 6 | 5.0 | 23 | 24 | 10 | 23 | 19 | .240 | .455 | 0 | 0 | OF-31 |

## Jimmie Foxx

**FOXX, JAMES EMORY (Double X, The Beast)**    BR TR 6'    195 lbs.
B. Oct. 22, 1907, Sudlersville, Md.    D. July 21, 1967, Miami, Fla.
Hall of Fame 1951.

| | G | AB | H | 2B | 3B | HR | HR% | R | RBI | BB | SO | SB | BA | SA | PH AB | PH H | G by POS |
|---|---|---|---|---|---|---|---|---|---|---|---|---|---|---|---|---|---|
| 1925 PHI A | 10 | 9 | 6 | 1 | 0 | 0 | 0.0 | 2 | 0 | 0 | 1 | 0 | .667 | .778 | 9 | 6 | C-1 |
| 1926 | 26 | 32 | 10 | 2 | 1 | 0 | 0.0 | 8 | 5 | 1 | 6 | 1 | .313 | .438 | 8 | 0 | C-12, OF-3 |
| 1927 | 61 | 130 | 42 | 6 | 5 | 3 | 2.3 | 23 | 20 | 14 | 11 | 2 | .323 | .515 | 20 | 7 | 1B-32, C-5 |
| 1928 | 118 | 400 | 131 | 29 | 10 | 13 | 3.3 | 85 | 79 | 60 | 43 | 3 | .328 | .548 | 8 | 2 | 3B-61, 1B-30, C-20 |
| 1929 | 149 | 517 | 183 | 23 | 9 | 33 | 6.4 | 123 | 117 | 103 | 70 | 10 | .354 | .625 | 0 | 0 | 1B-142, 3B-7 |
| 1930 | 153 | 562 | 188 | 33 | 13 | 37 | 6.6 | 127 | 156 | 93 | 66 | 7 | .335 | .637 | 0 | 0 | 1B-153 |
| 1931 | 139 | 515 | 150 | 32 | 10 | 30 | 5.8 | 93 | 120 | 73 | 84 | 4 | .291 | .567 | 2 | 1 | 1B-112, 3B-20, OF-1 |
| 1932 | 154 | 585 | 213 | 33 | 9 | 58 | 9.9 | 151 | 169 | 116 | 96 | 3 | .364 | .749 | 0 | 0 | 1B-141, 3B-13 |
| 1933 | 149 | 573 | 204 | 37 | 9 | 48 | 8.4 | 125 | 163 | 96 | 93 | 2 | .356 | .703 | 0 | 0 | 1B-149, SS-1 |
| 1934 | 150 | 539 | 180 | 28 | 6 | 44 | 8.2 | 120 | 130 | 111 | 75 | 11 | .334 | .653 | 1 | 0 | 1B-140, 3B-9 |
| 1935 | 147 | 535 | 185 | 33 | 7 | 36 | 6.7 | 118 | 115 | 114 | 99 | 6 | .346 | .636 | 0 | 0 | 1B-121, C-26, 3B-2 |
| 1936 BOS A | 155 | 585 | 198 | 32 | 8 | 41 | 7.0 | 130 | 143 | 105 | 119 | 13 | .338 | .631 | 0 | 0 | 1B-139, OF-16, 3B-1 |
| 1937 | 150 | 569 | 162 | 24 | 6 | 36 | 6.3 | 111 | 127 | 99 | 96 | 10 | .285 | .538 | 0 | 0 | 1B-150, C-1 |
| 1938 | 149 | 565 | 197 | 33 | 9 | 50 | 8.8 | 139 | 175 | 119 | 76 | 5 | .349 | .704 | 0 | 0 | 1B-149 |
| 1939 | 124 | 467 | 168 | 31 | 10 | 35 | 7.5 | 130 | 105 | 89 | 72 | 4 | .360 | .694 | 1 | 0 | 1B-123, P-1 |
| 1940 | 144 | 515 | 153 | 30 | 4 | 36 | 7.0 | 106 | 119 | 101 | 87 | 4 | .297 | .581 | 4 | 1 | 1B-95, C-42, 3B-1 |
| 1941 | 135 | 487 | 146 | 27 | 8 | 19 | 3.9 | 87 | 105 | 93 | 103 | 2 | .300 | .505 | 4 | 2 | 1B-124, 3B-5, OF-1 |
| 1942 2 teams | BOS | A (30G – .270) | | | CHI | N (70G – .205) | | | | | | | | | | | |
| " total | 100 | 305 | 69 | 12 | 0 | 8 | 2.6 | 43 | 33 | 40 | 70 | 1 | .226 | .344 | 18 | 3 | 1B-79, C-1 |
| 1944 CHI N | 15 | 20 | 1 | 1 | 0 | 0 | 0.0 | 0 | 2 | 2 | 5 | 0 | .050 | .100 | 11 | 0 | 3B-2, C-1 |
| 1945 PHI N | 89 | 224 | 60 | 11 | 1 | 7 | 3.1 | 30 | 38 | 23 | 39 | 0 | .268 | .420 | 26 | 8 | 1B-40, 3B-14, P-9 |
| 20 yrs. | 2317 | 8134 | 2646 | 458 | 125 | 534 | 6.6 | 1751 | 1921 | 1452 | 1311 | 88 | .325 | .609 | 112 | 30 | 1B-1919, 3B-135, C-109, OF-21, P-10, SS-1 |
| | | | | | | | | 7th | 8th | | 6th | | | 4th | | | |
| 2 yrs. | 85 | 225 | 43 | 9 | 0 | 3 | 1.3 | 25 | 21 | 24 | 60 | 1 | .191 | .271 | 27 | 3 | 1B-52, 3B-2, C-2 |

### WORLD SERIES

| | G | AB | H | 2B | 3B | HR | HR% | R | RBI | BB | SO | SB | BA | SA | PH AB | PH H | G by POS |
|---|---|---|---|---|---|---|---|---|---|---|---|---|---|---|---|---|---|
| 1929 PHI A | 5 | 20 | 7 | 1 | 0 | 2 | 10.0 | 5 | 5 | 1 | 1 | 0 | .350 | .700 | 0 | 0 | 1B-5 |
| 1930 | 6 | 21 | 7 | 2 | 1 | 1 | 4.8 | 3 | 3 | 2 | 4 | 0 | .333 | .667 | 0 | 0 | 1B-6 |
| 1931 | 7 | 23 | 8 | 0 | 1 | 1 | 4.3 | 3 | 3 | 6 | 5 | 0 | .348 | .478 | 0 | 0 | 1B-7 |
| 3 yrs. | 18 | 64 | 22 | 3 | 2 | 4 | 6.3 | 11 | 11 | 9 | 10 | 0 | .344 | .609 | 0 | 0 | 1B-18 |
| | | | | | | | | | | | | | | 9th | | | |

## George Freese

**FREESE, GEORGE WALTER (Bud)**    BR TR 6'    190 lbs.
Brother of Gene Freese.
B. Sept. 12, 1926, Wheeling, W. Va.

| | G | AB | H | 2B | 3B | HR | HR% | R | RBI | BB | SO | SB | BA | SA | PH AB | PH H | G by POS |
|---|---|---|---|---|---|---|---|---|---|---|---|---|---|---|---|---|---|
| 1953 DET A | 1 | 1 | 0 | 0 | 0 | 0 | 0.0 | 0 | 0 | 0 | 0 | 0 | .000 | .000 | 1 | 0 | |
| 1955 PIT N | 51 | 179 | 46 | 8 | 2 | 3 | 1.7 | 17 | 22 | 17 | 18 | 1 | .257 | .374 | 1 | 0 | 3B-50 |
| 1961 CHI N | 9 | 7 | 2 | 0 | 0 | 0 | 0.0 | 0 | 1 | 1 | 4 | 0 | .286 | .286 | 7 | 2 | |
| 3 yrs. | 61 | 187 | 48 | 8 | 2 | 3 | 1.6 | 17 | 23 | 18 | 22 | 1 | .257 | .369 | 9 | 2 | 3B-50 |
| 1 yr. | 9 | 7 | 2 | 0 | 0 | 0 | 0.0 | 0 | 1 | 1 | 4 | 0 | .286 | .286 | 7 | 2 | |

## Howard Freigau

**FREIGAU, HOWARD EARL (Ty)**    BR TR 5'10½" 160 lbs.
B. Aug. 1, 1902, Dayton, Ohio    D. July 18, 1932, Chattanooga, Tenn.

| | G | AB | H | 2B | 3B | HR | HR% | R | RBI | BB | SO | SB | BA | SA | PH AB | PH H | G by POS |
|---|---|---|---|---|---|---|---|---|---|---|---|---|---|---|---|---|---|
| 1922 STL N | 3 | 1 | 0 | 0 | 0 | 0 | 0.0 | 0 | 0 | 0 | 0 | 0 | .000 | .000 | 0 | 0 | SS-2, 3B-1 |
| 1923 | 113 | 358 | 94 | 18 | 1 | 1 | 0.3 | 30 | 35 | 25 | 36 | 5 | .263 | .327 | 0 | 0 | SS-87, 2B-16, 1B-9, OF-1, 3B-1 |
| 1924 | 98 | 376 | 101 | 17 | 6 | 2 | 0.5 | 35 | 39 | 19 | 24 | 10 | .269 | .362 | 0 | 0 | 3B-98, SS-2 |
| 1925 2 teams | STL | N (9G – .154) | | | CHI | N (117G – .307) | | | | | | | | | | | |
| " total | 126 | 502 | 150 | 22 | 10 | 8 | 1.6 | 79 | 71 | 32 | 32 | 10 | .299 | .430 | 0 | 0 | 3B-96, SS-24, 1B-7, 2B-1 |
| 1926 CHI N | 140 | 508 | 137 | 27 | 7 | 3 | 0.6 | 51 | 51 | 43 | 42 | 6 | .270 | .368 | 4 | 2 | 3B-135, SS-2, OF-1 |
| 1927 | 30 | 86 | 20 | 5 | 0 | 0 | 0.0 | 12 | 10 | 9 | 10 | 0 | .233 | .291 | 0 | 0 | 3B-30 |

| | G | AB | H | 2B | 3B | HR | HR % | R | RBI | BB | SO | SB | BA | SA | Pinch Hit AB | Pinch Hit H | G by POS |
|---|---|---|---|---|---|---|---|---|---|---|---|---|---|---|---|---|---|

## Howard Freigau continued

| | G | AB | H | 2B | 3B | HR | HR% | R | RBI | BB | SO | SB | BA | SA | AB | H | G by POS |
|---|---|---|---|---|---|---|---|---|---|---|---|---|---|---|---|---|---|
| 1928 2 teams | BKN | N | (17G – | .206) | | BOS | N | (52G – | .257) | | | | | | | | |
| " total | 69 | 143 | 35 | 10 | 1 | 1 | 0.7 | 17 | 20 | 10 | 17 | 1 | .245 | .350 | 26 | 8 | SS-15, 2B-11, 3B-10 |
| 7 yrs. | 579 | 1974 | 537 | 99 | 25 | 15 | 0.8 | 224 | 226 | 138 | 161 | 32 | .272 | .370 | 30 | 10 | 3B-371, SS-132, 2B-28, 1B-16, OF-2 |
| 3 yrs. | 287 | 1070 | 303 | 54 | 17 | 11 | 1.0 | 140 | 132 | 82 | 83 | 16 | .283 | .396 | 4 | 2 | 3B-261, SS-19, 1B-7, OF-1 |

## Lonny Frey

**FREY, LINUS REINHARD (Junior)**
B. Aug. 23, 1910, St. Louis, Mo.

BL TR 5'10" 160 lbs.
BB 1933-38

| | G | AB | H | 2B | 3B | HR | HR% | R | RBI | BB | SO | SB | BA | SA | AB | H | G by POS |
|---|---|---|---|---|---|---|---|---|---|---|---|---|---|---|---|---|---|
| 1933 BKN N | 34 | 135 | 43 | 5 | 3 | 0 | 0.0 | 25 | 12 | 13 | 13 | 4 | .319 | .400 | 0 | 0 | SS-34 |
| 1934 | 125 | 490 | 139 | 24 | 5 | 8 | 1.6 | 77 | 57 | 52 | 54 | 11 | .284 | .402 | 2 | 0 | SS-109, 3B-13 |
| 1935 | 131 | 515 | 135 | 35 | 11 | 11 | 2.1 | 88 | 77 | 66 | 68 | 6 | .262 | .437 | 0 | 0 | SS-127, 2B-4 |
| 1936 | 148 | 524 | 146 | 29 | 4 | 4 | 0.8 | 63 | 60 | 71 | 56 | 7 | .279 | .372 | 3 | 0 | SS-117, 2B-30, OF-1 |
| 1937 CHI N | 78 | 198 | 55 | 9 | 3 | 1 | 0.5 | 33 | 22 | 33 | 15 | 6 | .278 | .369 | 14 | 2 | SS-30, 2B-13, 3B-9, OF-5 |
| 1938 CIN N | 124 | 501 | 133 | 26 | 6 | 4 | 0.8 | 76 | 36 | 49 | 50 | 4 | .265 | .365 | 0 | 0 | 2B-121, SS-3 |
| 1939 | 125 | 484 | 141 | 27 | 9 | 11 | 2.3 | 95 | 55 | 72 | 46 | 5 | .291 | .452 | 1 | 1 | 2B-123 |
| 1940 | 150 | 563 | 150 | 23 | 6 | 8 | 1.4 | 102 | 54 | 80 | 48 | 22 | .266 | .371 | 0 | 0 | 2B-150 |
| 1941 | 146 | 543 | 138 | 29 | 5 | 6 | 1.1 | 78 | 59 | 72 | 37 | 16 | .254 | .359 | 1 | 1 | 2B-145 |
| 1942 | 141 | 523 | 139 | 23 | 6 | 2 | 0.4 | 66 | 39 | 87 | 38 | 9 | .266 | .344 | 1 | 0 | 2B-140 |
| 1943 | 144 | 586 | 154 | 20 | 8 | 2 | 0.3 | 78 | 43 | 76 | 56 | 7 | .263 | .334 | 0 | 0 | 2B-144 |
| 1946 | 111 | 333 | 82 | 10 | 3 | 3 | 0.9 | 46 | 24 | 63 | 31 | 5 | .246 | .321 | 17 | 4 | 2B-65, OF-28 |
| 1947 2 teams | CHI | N | (24G – | .209) | | NY | A | (24G – | .179) | | | | | | | | |
| " total | 48 | 71 | 14 | 2 | 0 | 0 | 0.0 | 14 | 5 | 14 | 7 | 3 | .197 | .225 | 14 | 4 | 2B-32 |
| 1948 2 teams | NY | A | (1G – | .000) | | NY | N | (29G – | .255) | | | | | | | | |
| " total | 30 | 51 | 13 | 1 | 0 | 1 | 2.0 | 7 | 6 | 4 | 6 | 0 | .255 | .333 | 14 | 2 | 2B-13 |
| 14 yrs. | 1535 | 5517 | 1482 | 263 | 69 | 61 | 1.1 | 848 | 549 | 752 | 525 | 105 | .269 | .374 | 67 | 14 | 2B-980, SS-420, OF-34, 3B-22 |
| 2 yrs. | 102 | 241 | 64 | 9 | 3 | 1 | 0.4 | 37 | 25 | 37 | 21 | 6 | .266 | .340 | 25 | 5 | 2B-37, SS-30, 3B-9, OF-5 |
| WORLD SERIES | | | | | | | | | | | | | | | | | |
| 1939 CIN N | 4 | 17 | 0 | 0 | 0 | 0 | 0.0 | 0 | 0 | 1 | 4 | 0 | .000 | .000 | 0 | 0 | 2B-4 |
| 1940 | 3 | 2 | 0 | 0 | 0 | 0 | 0.0 | 0 | 0 | 0 | 0 | 0 | .000 | .000 | 2 | 0 | |
| 1947 NY A | 1 | 1 | 0 | 0 | 0 | 0 | 0.0 | 0 | 1 | 0 | 0 | 0 | .000 | .000 | 1 | 0 | |
| 3 yrs. | 8 | 20 | 0 | 0 | 0 | 0 | 0.0 | 0 | 1 | 1 | 4 | 0 | .000 | .000 | 3 | 0 | 2B-4 |

## Barney Friberg

**FRIBERG, AUGUSTAF BERNHARDT**
Also known as Bernard Albert Friberg.
B. Aug. 18, 1899, Manchester, N. H.    D. Dec. 8, 1958, Swampscott, Mass.

BR TR 5'11" 178 lbs.

| | G | AB | H | 2B | 3B | HR | HR% | R | RBI | BB | SO | SB | BA | SA | AB | H | G by POS |
|---|---|---|---|---|---|---|---|---|---|---|---|---|---|---|---|---|---|
| 1919 CHI N | 8 | 20 | 4 | 1 | 0 | 0 | 0.0 | 0 | 1 | 0 | 2 | 0 | .200 | .250 | 1 | 0 | OF-7 |
| 1920 | 50 | 114 | 24 | 5 | 1 | 0 | 0.0 | 11 | 7 | 6 | 20 | 2 | .211 | .272 | 2 | 0 | OF-24, 2B-24 |
| 1922 | 97 | 296 | 92 | 8 | 2 | 0 | 0.0 | 51 | 23 | 37 | 37 | 8 | .311 | .351 | 12 | 2 | OF-74, 1B-6, 3B-5, 2B-3 |
| 1923 | 146 | 547 | 174 | 27 | 11 | 12 | 2.2 | 91 | 88 | 45 | 49 | 13 | .318 | .473 | 0 | 0 | 3B-146 |
| 1924 | 142 | 495 | 138 | 19 | 3 | 5 | 1.0 | 67 | 82 | 66 | 53 | 19 | .279 | .360 | 0 | 0 | 3B-142 |
| 1925 2 teams | CHI | N | (44G – | .257) | | PHI | N | (91G – | .270) | | | | | | | | |
| " total | 135 | 456 | 121 | 17 | 4 | 6 | 1.3 | 53 | 38 | 53 | 57 | 1 | .265 | .360 | 2 | 0 | 2B-77, 3B-40, OF-12, 1B-6, SS-2, C-1, P-1 |
| 1926 PHI N | 144 | 478 | 128 | 21 | 3 | 1 | 0.2 | 38 | 51 | 57 | 77 | 2 | .268 | .331 | 0 | 0 | 2B-144 |
| 1927 | 111 | 335 | 78 | 8 | 2 | 1 | 0.3 | 31 | 28 | 41 | 49 | 3 | .233 | .278 | 4 | 2 | 3B-103, 2B-5 |
| 1928 | 52 | 94 | 19 | 3 | 0 | 1 | 1.1 | 11 | 7 | 12 | 16 | 0 | .202 | .266 | 6 | 1 | SS-31, 3B-5, OF-3, 2B-3, 1B-2 |
| 1929 | 128 | 455 | 137 | 21 | 10 | 7 | 1.5 | 74 | 55 | 49 | 54 | 5 | .301 | .437 | 5 | 2 | SS-73, OF-40, 2B-8, 1B-2 |
| 1930 | 105 | 331 | 113 | 21 | 1 | 4 | 1.2 | 62 | 42 | 47 | 35 | 1 | .341 | .447 | 7 | 3 | 2B-44, OF-35, SS-12, 3B-8 |
| 1931 | 103 | 353 | 92 | 19 | 5 | 1 | 0.3 | 33 | 26 | 33 | 25 | 1 | .261 | .351 | 3 | 0 | 2B-64, 3B-25, 1B-5, SS-3 |
| 1932 | 61 | 154 | 37 | 8 | 2 | 0 | 0.0 | 17 | 14 | 19 | 23 | 0 | .240 | .318 | 2 | 0 | 2B-56 |
| 1933 BOS A | 17 | 41 | 13 | 3 | 0 | 0 | 0.0 | 5 | 9 | 6 | 1 | 0 | .317 | .390 | 3 | 1 | 2B-6, 3B-5, SS-2 |
| 14 yrs. | 1299 | 4169 | 1170 | 181 | 44 | 38 | 0.9 | 544 | 471 | 471 | 498 | 51 | .281 | .373 | 47 | 11 | 3B-479, 2B-434, OF-195, SS-123, 1B-21, C-1, P-1 |
| 6 yrs. | 487 | 1624 | 471 | 65 | 20 | 18 | 1.1 | 232 | 217 | 168 | 183 | 42 | .290 | .388 | 17 | 2 | 3B-319, OF-117, 2B-27, 1B-12, SS-2 |

## Owen Friend

**FRIEND, OWEN LACEY (Red)**
B. Mar. 21, 1927, Granite City, Ill.

BR TR 6'1" 180 lbs.

| | G | AB | H | 2B | 3B | HR | HR% | R | RBI | BB | SO | SB | BA | SA | AB | H | G by POS |
|---|---|---|---|---|---|---|---|---|---|---|---|---|---|---|---|---|---|
| 1949 STL A | 2 | 8 | 3 | 0 | 0 | 0 | 0.0 | 1 | 1 | 0 | 0 | 0 | .375 | .375 | 0 | 0 | 2B-2 |
| 1950 | 119 | 372 | 88 | 15 | 2 | 8 | 2.2 | 48 | 50 | 40 | 68 | 2 | .237 | .352 | 1 | 1 | 2B-93, 3B-24, SS-3 |
| 1953 2 teams | DET | A | (31G – | .177) | | CLE | A | (34G – | .235) | | | | | | | | |
| " total | 65 | 164 | 33 | 6 | 0 | 5 | 3.0 | 17 | 23 | 11 | 25 | 0 | .201 | .329 | 2 | 1 | 2B-45, SS-8, 3B-1 |
| 1955 2 teams | BOS | A | (14G – | .262) | | CHI | N | (6G – | .100) | | | | | | | | |
| " total | 20 | 52 | 12 | 3 | 0 | 0 | 0.0 | 3 | 2 | 4 | 14 | 0 | .231 | .288 | 3 | 0 | SS-15, 3B-2, 2B-1 |
| 1956 CHI N | 2 | 2 | 0 | 0 | 0 | 0 | 0.0 | 0 | 0 | 0 | 2 | 0 | .000 | .000 | 2 | 0 | |
| 5 yrs. | 208 | 598 | 136 | 24 | 2 | 13 | 2.2 | 69 | 76 | 55 | 109 | 2 | .227 | .339 | 8 | 2 | 2B-141, 3B-27, SS-26 |
| 2 yrs. | 8 | 12 | 1 | 0 | 0 | 0 | 0.0 | 0 | 0 | 0 | 5 | 0 | .083 | .083 | 5 | 0 | 3B-2, SS-1 |

## Bill Gabler

**GABLER, WILLIAM LOUIS (Gabe)**
B. Aug. 4, 1930, St. Louis, Mo.

BL TL 6'1" 190 lbs.

| | G | AB | H | 2B | 3B | HR | HR% | R | RBI | BB | SO | SB | BA | SA | AB | H | G by POS |
|---|---|---|---|---|---|---|---|---|---|---|---|---|---|---|---|---|---|
| 1958 CHI N | 3 | 3 | 0 | 0 | 0 | 0 | 0.0 | 0 | 0 | 0 | 3 | 0 | .000 | .000 | 3 | 0 | |

## Len Gabrielson

**GABRIELSON, LEONARD GARY**
Son of Len Gabrielson.
B. Feb. 14, 1940, Oakland, Calif.

BL TR 6'4" 210 lbs.

| | G | AB | H | 2B | 3B | HR | HR% | R | RBI | BB | SO | SB | BA | SA | AB | H | G by POS |
|---|---|---|---|---|---|---|---|---|---|---|---|---|---|---|---|---|---|
| 1960 MIL N | 4 | 3 | 0 | 0 | 0 | 0 | 0.0 | 0 | 1 | 0 | 1 | 0 | .000 | .000 | 3 | 0 | OF-1 |
| 1963 | 46 | 120 | 26 | 5 | 0 | 3 | 2.5 | 14 | 15 | 8 | 23 | 1 | .217 | .333 | 12 | 4 | OF-22, 1B-16, 3B-3 |

| | G | AB | H | 2B | 3B | HR | HR % | R | RBI | BB | SO | SB | BA | SA | Pinch Hit AB | H | G by POS |
|---|---|---|---|---|---|---|---|---|---|---|---|---|---|---|---|---|---|

## Len Gabrielson continued

| | G | AB | H | 2B | 3B | HR | HR % | R | RBI | BB | SO | SB | BA | SA | PH AB | PH H | G by POS |
|---|---|---|---|---|---|---|---|---|---|---|---|---|---|---|---|---|---|
| 1964 2 teams | | MIL | N | (24G – | .184) | | CHI | N | (89G – | .246) | | | | | | | |
| " total | 113 | 310 | 74 | 13 | 2 | 5 | 1.6 | 22 | 24 | 20 | 45 | 10 | .239 | .342 | 25 | 8 | OF-70, 1B-20 |
| 1965 2 teams | | CHI | N | (28G – | .250) | | SF | N | (88G – | .301) | | | | | | | |
| " total | 116 | 317 | 93 | 6 | 5 | 7 | 2.2 | 40 | 31 | 33 | 64 | 4 | .293 | .410 | 22 | 4 | OF-91, 1B-6 |
| 1966 SF N | 94 | 240 | 52 | 7 | 0 | 4 | 1.7 | 27 | 16 | 21 | 51 | 0 | .217 | .296 | 25 | 5 | OF-67, 1B-6 |
| 1967 2 teams | | CAL | A | (11G – | .083) | | LA | N | (90G – | .261) | | | | | | | |
| " total | 101 | 250 | 63 | 10 | 3 | 7 | 2.8 | 22 | 31 | 17 | 45 | 3 | .252 | .400 | 34 | 6 | OF-69 |
| 1968 LA N | 108 | 304 | 82 | 16 | 1 | 10 | 3.3 | 38 | 35 | 32 | 47 | 1 | .270 | .428 | 27 | 7 | OF-86 |
| 1969 | 83 | 178 | 48 | 5 | 1 | 1 | 0.6 | 13 | 18 | 12 | 25 | 1 | .270 | .326 | 36 | 13 | OF-47, 1B-2 |
| 1970 | 43 | 42 | 8 | 2 | 0 | 0 | 0.0 | 1 | 6 | 1 | 15 | 0 | .190 | .238 | 38 | 8 | OF-2, 1B-1 |
| 9 yrs. | 708 | 1764 | 446 | 64 | 12 | 37 | 2.1 | 178 | 176 | 145 | 315 | 20 | .253 | .366 | 222 | 55 | OF-455, 1B-51, 3B-3 |
| 2 yrs. | 117 | 320 | 79 | 11 | 2 | 8 | 2.5 | 26 | 28 | 26 | 53 | 9 | .247 | .369 | 27 | 7 | OF-82, 1B-9 |

## Phil Gagliano

**GAGLIANO, PHILIP JOSEPH**
Brother of Ralph Gagliano.
B. Dec. 27, 1941, Memphis, Tenn.

BR TR 6'1" 180 lbs.

| | G | AB | H | 2B | 3B | HR | HR % | R | RBI | BB | SO | SB | BA | SA | PH AB | PH H | G by POS |
|---|---|---|---|---|---|---|---|---|---|---|---|---|---|---|---|---|---|
| 1963 STL N | 10 | 5 | 2 | 0 | 0 | 0 | 0.0 | 1 | 1 | 1 | 1 | 0 | .400 | .400 | 2 | 0 | 2B-3, 3B-1 |
| 1964 | 40 | 58 | 15 | 4 | 0 | 1 | 1.7 | 5 | 9 | 3 | 10 | 0 | .259 | .379 | 19 | 3 | 2B-12, OF-2, 3B-1, 1B-1 |
| 1965 | 122 | 363 | 87 | 14 | 2 | 8 | 2.2 | 46 | 53 | 40 | 45 | 2 | .240 | .355 | 26 | 5 | 2B-57, OF-25, 3B-19 |
| 1966 | 90 | 213 | 54 | 8 | 2 | 2 | 0.9 | 23 | 15 | 24 | 29 | 2 | .254 | .338 | 36 | 4 | 3B-41, 1B-8, OF-5, 2B-1 |
| 1967 | 73 | 217 | 48 | 7 | 0 | 2 | 0.9 | 20 | 21 | 19 | 26 | 0 | .221 | .281 | 17 | 0 | 2B-27, 3B-25, 1B-4, SS-3 |
| 1968 | 53 | 105 | 24 | 4 | 2 | 0 | 0.0 | 13 | 13 | 7 | 12 | 0 | .229 | .305 | 17 | 4 | 2B-17, 3B-10, OF-5 |
| 1969 | 62 | 128 | 29 | 2 | 0 | 1 | 0.8 | 7 | 10 | 14 | 12 | 0 | .227 | .266 | 21 | 2 | 2B-20, 3B-9, 1B-9, OF-2 |
| 1970 2 teams | | STL | N | (18G – | .188) | | CHI | N | (26G – | .150) | | | | | | | |
| " total | 44 | 72 | 12 | 0 | 0 | 0 | 0.0 | 5 | 7 | 6 | 8 | 0 | .167 | .167 | 16 | 3 | 2B-18, 3B-7, 1B-4 |
| 1971 BOS A | 47 | 68 | 22 | 5 | 0 | 0 | 0.0 | 11 | 13 | 11 | 5 | 0 | .324 | .397 | 22 | 8 | OF-11, 2B-7, 3B-4 |
| 1972 | 52 | 82 | 21 | 4 | 1 | 0 | 0.0 | 9 | 10 | 10 | 13 | 1 | .256 | .329 | 26 | 9 | OF-12, 3B-5, 2B-4, 1B-2 |
| 1973 CIN N | 63 | 69 | 20 | 2 | 0 | 0 | 0.0 | 8 | 7 | 13 | 16 | 0 | .290 | .319 | 41 | 15 | 2B-4, 3B-2, OF-1, 1B-1 |
| 1974 | 46 | 31 | 2 | 0 | 0 | 0 | 0.0 | 2 | 0 | 15 | 7 | 0 | .065 | .065 | 29 | 2 | 2B-2, 3B-1, 1B-1 |
| 12 yrs. | 702 | 1411 | 336 | 50 | 7 | 14 | 1.0 | 150 | 159 | 163 | 184 | 5 | .238 | .313 | 272 | 55 | 2B-172, 3B-125, OF-63, 1B-30, SS-2 |
| 1 yr. | 26 | 40 | 6 | 0 | 0 | 0 | 0.0 | 5 | 5 | 5 | 5 | 0 | .150 | .150 | 8 | 1 | 2B-16, 3B-1, 1B-1 |
| **LEAGUE CHAMPIONSHIP SERIES** | | | | | | | | | | | | | | | | | |
| 1973 CIN N | 3 | 3 | 0 | 0 | 0 | 0 | 0.0 | 0 | 0 | 0 | 2 | 0 | .000 | .000 | 3 | 0 | |
| **WORLD SERIES** | | | | | | | | | | | | | | | | | |
| 1967 STL N | 1 | 1 | 0 | 0 | 0 | 0 | 0.0 | 0 | 0 | 0 | 0 | 0 | .000 | .000 | 1 | 0 | |
| 1968 | 3 | 3 | 0 | 0 | 0 | 0 | 0.0 | 0 | 0 | 0 | 0 | 0 | .000 | .000 | 3 | 0 | |
| 2 yrs. | 4 | 4 | 0 | 0 | 0 | 0 | 0.0 | 0 | 0 | 0 | 0 | 0 | .000 | .000 | 4 | 0 | |

## Augie Galan

**GALAN, AUGUST JOHN**
B. May 25, 1912, Berkeley, Calif.

BB TR 6' 175 lbs.
BL 1945-49

| | G | AB | H | 2B | 3B | HR | HR % | R | RBI | BB | SO | SB | BA | SA | PH AB | PH H | G by POS |
|---|---|---|---|---|---|---|---|---|---|---|---|---|---|---|---|---|---|
| 1934 CHI N | 66 | 192 | 50 | 6 | 2 | 5 | 2.6 | 31 | 22 | 16 | 15 | 22 | .260 | .391 | 12 | 5 | 2B-43, 3B-3, SS-1 |
| 1935 | 154 | 646 | 203 | 41 | 11 | 12 | 1.9 | 133 | 79 | 87 | 53 | 22 | .314 | .467 | 0 | 0 | OF-154 |
| 1936 | 145 | 575 | 152 | 26 | 4 | 8 | 1.4 | 74 | 81 | 67 | 50 | 16 | .264 | .365 | 2 | 0 | OF-145 |
| 1937 | 147 | 611 | 154 | 24 | 10 | 18 | 2.9 | 104 | 78 | 79 | 48 | 23 | .252 | .412 | 0 | 0 | OF-140, 2B-8, SS-2 |
| 1938 | 110 | 395 | 113 | 16 | 9 | 6 | 1.5 | 52 | 69 | 49 | 17 | 8 | .286 | .418 | 6 | 0 | OF-103 |
| 1939 | 148 | 549 | 167 | 36 | 8 | 6 | 1.1 | 104 | 71 | 75 | 26 | 8 | .304 | .432 | 3 | 0 | OF-145 |
| 1940 | 68 | 209 | 48 | 14 | 2 | 3 | 1.4 | 33 | 22 | 37 | 23 | 9 | .230 | .359 | 9 | 2 | OF-54, 2B-2 |
| 1941 2 teams | | CHI | N | (65G – | .208) | | BKN | N | (17G – | .259) | | | | | | | |
| " total | 82 | 147 | 32 | 6 | 0 | 1 | 0.7 | 21 | 17 | 25 | 11 | 0 | .218 | .279 | 40 | 7 | OF-37 |
| 1942 BKN N | 69 | 209 | 55 | 16 | 0 | 0 | 0.0 | 24 | 22 | 24 | 12 | 2 | .263 | .340 | 9 | 3 | OF-55, 1B-4, 2B-3 |
| 1943 | 139 | 495 | 142 | 26 | 3 | 9 | 1.8 | 83 | 67 | 103 | 39 | 6 | .287 | .406 | 1 | 0 | OF-124, 1B-13 |
| 1944 | 151 | 547 | 174 | 43 | 9 | 12 | 2.2 | 96 | 93 | 101 | 23 | 4 | .318 | .495 | 4 | 2 | OF-147, 2B-2 |
| 1945 | 152 | 576 | 177 | 36 | 7 | 9 | 1.6 | 114 | 92 | 114 | 27 | 13 | .307 | .441 | 1 | 1 | 1B-66, OF-49, 3B-40 |
| 1946 | 99 | 274 | 85 | 22 | 5 | 3 | 1.1 | 53 | 38 | 68 | 21 | 8 | .310 | .460 | 7 | 1 | OF-60, 3B-19, 1B-12 |
| 1947 CIN N | 124 | 392 | 123 | 18 | 2 | 6 | 1.5 | 60 | 61 | 94 | 19 | 0 | .314 | .416 | 5 | 2 | OF-118 |
| 1948 | 54 | 77 | 22 | 3 | 2 | 2 | 2.6 | 18 | 16 | 26 | 4 | 0 | .286 | .455 | 26 | 3 | OF-18 |
| 1949 2 teams | | NY | N | (22G – | .059) | | PHI | A | (12G – | .308) | | | | | | | |
| " total | 34 | 43 | 9 | 3 | 0 | 0 | 0.0 | 4 | 2 | 14 | 5 | 0 | .209 | .279 | 18 | 2 | OF-10, 1B-3 |
| 16 yrs. | 1742 | 5937 | 1706 | 336 | 74 | 100 | 1.7 | 1004 | 830 | 979 | 393 | 123 | .287 | .419 | 143 | 28 | OF-1359, 1B-98, 3B-62, 2B-58, SS-3 |
| 8 yrs. | 903 | 3297 | 912 | 166 | 46 | 59 | 1.8 | 549 | 435 | 432 | 242 | 90 | .277 | .409 | 60 | 11 | OF-772, 2B-53, SS-3, 3B-3 |
| **WORLD SERIES** | | | | | | | | | | | | | | | | | |
| 1935 CHI N | 6 | 25 | 4 | 1 | 0 | 0 | 0.0 | 2 | 2 | 2 | 2 | 0 | .160 | .200 | 0 | 0 | OF-6 |
| 1938 | 2 | 2 | 0 | 0 | 0 | 0 | 0.0 | 0 | 0 | 0 | 1 | 0 | .000 | .000 | 2 | 0 | |
| 1941 BKN N | 2 | 2 | 0 | 0 | 0 | 0 | 0.0 | 0 | 0 | 0 | 1 | 0 | .000 | .000 | 2 | 0 | |
| 3 yrs. | 10 | 29 | 4 | 1 | 0 | 0 | 0.0 | 2 | 2 | 2 | 4 | 0 | .138 | .172 | 4 | 0 | OF-6 |

## Oscar Gamble

**GAMBLE, OSCAR CHARLES**
B. Dec. 20, 1949, Ramer, Ala.

BL TR 5'11" 160 lbs.

| | G | AB | H | 2B | 3B | HR | HR % | R | RBI | BB | SO | SB | BA | SA | PH AB | PH H | G by POS |
|---|---|---|---|---|---|---|---|---|---|---|---|---|---|---|---|---|---|
| 1969 CHI N | 24 | 71 | 16 | 1 | 1 | 1 | 1.4 | 6 | 5 | 10 | 12 | 0 | .225 | .310 | 0 | 0 | OF-24 |
| 1970 PHI N | 88 | 275 | 72 | 12 | 4 | 1 | 0.4 | 31 | 19 | 27 | 37 | 5 | .262 | .345 | 14 | 4 | OF-74 |
| 1971 | 92 | 280 | 62 | 11 | 1 | 6 | 2.1 | 24 | 23 | 21 | 35 | 5 | .221 | .332 | 13 | 4 | OF-80 |
| 1972 | 74 | 135 | 32 | 5 | 2 | 1 | 0.7 | 17 | 13 | 19 | 16 | 0 | .237 | .326 | 30 | 9 | OF-35, 1B-1 |
| 1973 CLE A | 113 | 390 | 104 | 11 | 3 | 20 | 5.1 | 56 | 44 | 34 | 37 | 1 | .267 | .464 | 8 | 2 | DH-70, OF-37 |
| 1974 | 135 | 454 | 132 | 16 | 4 | 19 | 4.2 | 74 | 59 | 48 | 51 | 5 | .291 | .469 | 7 | 0 | DH-115, OF-13 |
| 1975 | 121 | 348 | 91 | 16 | 3 | 15 | 4.3 | 60 | 45 | 53 | 39 | 11 | .261 | .454 | 11 | 2 | OF-82, DH-29 |
| 1976 NY A | 110 | 340 | 79 | 13 | 1 | 17 | 5.0 | 43 | 57 | 38 | 38 | 5 | .232 | .426 | 16 | 6 | OF-104, DH-1 |
| 1977 CHI A | 137 | 408 | 121 | 22 | 2 | 31 | 7.6 | 75 | 83 | 54 | 54 | 1 | .297 | .588 | 18 | 8 | DH-79, OF-49 |
| 1978 SD N | 126 | 375 | 103 | 15 | 3 | 7 | 1.9 | 46 | 47 | 51 | 45 | 1 | .275 | .387 | 13 | 6 | OF-107 |

| | G | AB | H | 2B | 3B | HR | HR % | R | RBI | BB | SO | SB | BA | SA | Pinch Hit AB | Pinch Hit H | G by POS |
|---|---|---|---|---|---|---|---|---|---|---|---|---|---|---|---|---|---|

## Oscar Gamble continued

| | G | AB | H | 2B | 3B | HR | HR % | R | RBI | BB | SO | SB | BA | SA | AB | H | G by POS |
|---|---|---|---|---|---|---|---|---|---|---|---|---|---|---|---|---|---|
| 1979 2 teams | | TEX A | (64G – | .335) | | NY | A | (36G – | .389) | | | | | | | | |
| " total | 100 | 274 | 98 | 10 | 1 | 19 | 6.9 | 48 | 64 | 50 | 28 | 2 | .358 | .609 | 18 | 5 | OF-48, DH-43 |
| 1980 NY A | 78 | 194 | 54 | 10 | 2 | 14 | 7.2 | 40 | 50 | 28 | 21 | 2 | .278 | .567 | 17 | 4 | OF-49, DH-20 |
| 1981 | 80 | 189 | 45 | 8 | 0 | 10 | 5.3 | 24 | 27 | 35 | 23 | 0 | .238 | .439 | 15 | 5 | OF-43, DH-33 |
| 1982 | 108 | 316 | 86 | 21 | 2 | 18 | 5.7 | 49 | 57 | 58 | 47 | 6 | .272 | .522 | 18 | 2 | DH-74, OF-29 |
| 1983 | 74 | 180 | 47 | 10 | 2 | 7 | 3.9 | 26 | 26 | 25 | 23 | 0 | .261 | .456 | 20 | 6 | OF-32, DH-21 |
| 1984 | 54 | 125 | 23 | 2 | 0 | 10 | 8.0 | 17 | 27 | 25 | 18 | 1 | .184 | .440 | 13 | 1 | DH-26, OF-12 |
| 1985 CHI A | 70 | 148 | 30 | 5 | 0 | 4 | 2.7 | 20 | 20 | 34 | 22 | 0 | .203 | .318 | 24 | 3 | DH-48 |
| 17 yrs. | 1584 | 4502 | 1195 | 188 | 31 | 200 | 4.4 | 656 | 666 | 610 | 546 | 47 | .265 | .454 | 255 | 67 | OF-818, DH-559, 1B-1 |
| 1 yr. | 24 | 71 | 16 | 1 | 1 | 1 | 1.4 | 6 | 5 | 10 | 12 | 0 | .225 | .310 | 0 | 0 | OF-24 |

DIVISIONAL PLAYOFF SERIES

| | G | AB | H | 2B | 3B | HR | HR % | R | RBI | BB | SO | SB | BA | SA | AB | H | G by POS |
|---|---|---|---|---|---|---|---|---|---|---|---|---|---|---|---|---|---|
| 1981 NY A | 4 | 9 | 5 | 1 | 0 | 2 | 22.2 | 2 | 3 | 1 | 2 | 0 | .556 | 1.333 | 1 | 1 | DH-4 |

LEAGUE CHAMPIONSHIP SERIES

| | G | AB | H | 2B | 3B | HR | HR % | R | RBI | BB | SO | SB | BA | SA | AB | H | G by POS |
|---|---|---|---|---|---|---|---|---|---|---|---|---|---|---|---|---|---|
| 1976 NY A | 3 | 8 | 2 | 1 | 0 | 0 | 0.0 | 1 | 1 | 1 | 1 | 0 | .250 | .375 | 1 | 1 | OF-3 |
| 1980 | 2 | 5 | 1 | 0 | 0 | 0 | 0.0 | 1 | 0 | 1 | 1 | 0 | .200 | .200 | 1 | 1 | OF-1 |
| 1981 | 3 | 6 | 1 | 0 | 0 | 0 | 0.0 | 2 | 1 | 5 | 3 | 0 | .167 | .167 | 0 | 0 | OF-1 |
| 3 yrs. | 8 | 19 | 4 | 1 | 0 | 0 | 0.0 | 4 | 2 | 7 | 5 | 0 | .211 | .263 | 2 | 2 | OF-5 |

WORLD SERIES

| | G | AB | H | 2B | 3B | HR | HR % | R | RBI | BB | SO | SB | BA | SA | AB | H | G by POS |
|---|---|---|---|---|---|---|---|---|---|---|---|---|---|---|---|---|---|
| 1976 NY A | 3 | 8 | 1 | 0 | 0 | 0 | 0.0 | 0 | 1 | 0 | 0 | 0 | .125 | .125 | 1 | 0 | OF-2 |
| 1981 | 3 | 6 | 2 | 0 | 0 | 0 | 0.0 | 1 | 1 | 1 | 0 | 0 | .333 | .333 | 0 | 0 | OF-2 |
| 2 yrs. | 6 | 14 | 3 | 0 | 0 | 0 | 0.0 | 1 | 2 | 1 | 0 | 0 | .214 | .214 | 1 | 0 | OF-4 |

# Bill Gannon

**GANNON, WILLIAM G.**
B. 1876, New Haven, Conn.    D. Apr. 26, 1927, Ft. Worth, Tex.

| | G | AB | H | 2B | 3B | HR | HR % | R | RBI | BB | SO | SB | BA | SA | AB | H | G by POS |
|---|---|---|---|---|---|---|---|---|---|---|---|---|---|---|---|---|---|
| 1898 STL N | 1 | 3 | 0 | 0 | 0 | 0 | 0.0 | 0 | 0 | 0 | | 0 | .000 | .000 | 0 | 0 | P-1 |
| 1901 CHI N | 15 | 61 | 9 | 0 | 0 | 0 | 0.0 | 2 | 0 | 1 | | 5 | .148 | .148 | 0 | 0 | OF-15 |
| 2 yrs. | 16 | 64 | 9 | 0 | 0 | 0 | 0.0 | 2 | 0 | 1 | | 5 | .141 | .141 | 0 | 0 | OF-15, P-1 |
| 1 yr. | 15 | 61 | 9 | 0 | 0 | 0 | 0.0 | 2 | 0 | 1 | | 5 | .148 | .148 | 0 | 0 | OF-15 |

# John Ganzel

**GANZEL, JOHN HENRY**      BR TR 6'½"   195 lbs.
Brother of Charlie Ganzel.
B. Apr. 7, 1874, Kalamazoo, Mich.    D. Jan. 14, 1959, Orlando, Fla.
Manager 1908, 1915.

| | G | AB | H | 2B | 3B | HR | HR % | R | RBI | BB | SO | SB | BA | SA | AB | H | G by POS |
|---|---|---|---|---|---|---|---|---|---|---|---|---|---|---|---|---|---|
| 1898 PIT N | 15 | 45 | 6 | 0 | 0 | 0 | 0.0 | 5 | 2 | 4 | | 0 | .133 | .133 | 2 | 0 | 1B-12 |
| 1900 CHI N | 78 | 284 | 78 | 14 | 4 | 4 | 1.4 | 29 | 32 | 10 | | 5 | .275 | .394 | 0 | 0 | 1B-78 |
| 1901 NY N | 138 | 526 | 113 | 13 | 3 | 2 | 0.4 | 42 | 66 | 20 | | 6 | .215 | .262 | 0 | 0 | 1B-138 |
| 1903 NY A | 129 | 476 | 132 | 25 | 7 | 3 | 0.6 | 62 | 71 | 30 | | 9 | .277 | .378 | 0 | 0 | 1B-129 |
| 1904 | 130 | 465 | 121 | 16 | 10 | 6 | 1.3 | 50 | 48 | 24 | | 13 | .260 | .376 | 4 | 2 | 1B-118, 2B-9, SS-1 |
| 1907 CIN N | 145 | 531 | 135 | 20 | 16 | 2 | 0.4 | 61 | 64 | 29 | | 9 | .254 | .363 | 2 | 0 | 1B-143 |
| 1908 | 112 | 388 | 97 | 16 | 10 | 1 | 0.3 | 32 | 53 | 19 | | 6 | .250 | .351 | 5 | 1 | 1B-108 |
| 7 yrs. | 747 | 2715 | 682 | 104 | 50 | 18 | 0.7 | 281 | 336 | 136 | | 48 | .251 | .346 | 13 | 3 | 1B-726, 2B-9, SS-1 |
| 1 yr. | 78 | 284 | 78 | 14 | 4 | 4 | 1.4 | 29 | 32 | 10 | | 5 | .275 | .394 | 0 | 0 | 1B-78 |

# Joe Garagiola

**GARAGIOLA, JOSEPH HENRY**      BL TR 6'   190 lbs.
B. Feb. 12, 1926, St. Louis, Mo.

| | G | AB | H | 2B | 3B | HR | HR % | R | RBI | BB | SO | SB | BA | SA | AB | H | G by POS |
|---|---|---|---|---|---|---|---|---|---|---|---|---|---|---|---|---|---|
| 1946 STL N | 74 | 211 | 50 | 4 | 1 | 3 | 1.4 | 21 | 22 | 23 | 25 | 0 | .237 | .308 | 4 | 2 | C-70 |
| 1947 | 77 | 183 | 47 | 10 | 2 | 5 | 2.7 | 20 | 25 | 40 | 14 | 0 | .257 | .415 | 4 | 1 | C-74 |
| 1948 | 24 | 56 | 6 | 1 | 0 | 2 | 3.6 | 9 | 7 | 12 | 9 | 0 | .107 | .232 | 1 | 0 | C-23 |
| 1949 | 81 | 241 | 63 | 14 | 0 | 3 | 1.2 | 25 | 26 | 31 | 19 | 0 | .261 | .357 | 2 | 1 | C-80 |
| 1950 | 34 | 88 | 28 | 6 | 1 | 2 | 2.3 | 8 | 20 | 10 | 7 | 0 | .318 | .477 | 4 | 0 | C-30 |
| 1951 2 teams | 99 | | STL | N | (27G – | .194) | | PIT | N | (72G – | .255) | | | | | | |
| " total | 99 | 284 | 68 | 11 | 4 | 11 | 3.9 | 33 | 44 | 41 | 27 | 4 | .239 | .423 | 12 | 0 | C-84 |
| 1952 PIT N | 118 | 344 | 94 | 15 | 4 | 8 | 2.3 | 35 | 54 | 50 | 24 | 0 | .273 | .410 | 12 | 4 | C-105 |
| 1953 2 teams | | | PIT | N | (27G – | .233) | | CHI | N | (74G – | .272) | | | | | | |
| " total | 101 | 301 | 79 | 14 | 4 | 3 | 1.0 | 30 | 35 | 31 | 34 | 1 | .262 | .365 | 13 | 3 | C-90 |
| 1954 2 teams | | | CHI | N | (63G – | .281) | | NY | N | (5G – | .273) | | | | | | |
| " total | 68 | 164 | 46 | 7 | 0 | 5 | 3.0 | 17 | 22 | 29 | 14 | 0 | .280 | .415 | 11 | 2 | C-58 |
| 9 yrs. | 676 | 1872 | 481 | 82 | 16 | 42 | 2.2 | 198 | 255 | 267 | 173 | 5 | .257 | .385 | 63 | 13 | C-614 |
| 2 yrs. | 137 | 381 | 105 | 14 | 4 | 6 | 1.6 | 37 | 42 | 49 | 35 | 0 | .276 | .381 | 16 | 4 | C-123 |

WORLD SERIES

| | G | AB | H | 2B | 3B | HR | HR % | R | RBI | BB | SO | SB | BA | SA | AB | H | G by POS |
|---|---|---|---|---|---|---|---|---|---|---|---|---|---|---|---|---|---|
| 1946 STL N | 5 | 19 | 6 | 2 | 0 | 0 | 0.0 | 2 | 4 | 0 | 3 | 0 | .316 | .421 | 0 | 0 | C-5 |

# Bob Garbark

**GARBARK, ROBERT MICHAEL**      BR TR 5'11"   178 lbs.
Also known as Robert Michael Garbach.   Brother of Mike Garbark.
B. Nov. 13, 1909, Houston, Tex.

| | G | AB | H | 2B | 3B | HR | HR % | R | RBI | BB | SO | SB | BA | SA | AB | H | G by POS |
|---|---|---|---|---|---|---|---|---|---|---|---|---|---|---|---|---|---|
| 1934 CLE A | 5 | 11 | 0 | 0 | 0 | 0 | 0.0 | 1 | 0 | 1 | 3 | 0 | .000 | .000 | 0 | 0 | C-5 |
| 1935 | 6 | 18 | 6 | 1 | 0 | 0 | 0.0 | 4 | 4 | 5 | 1 | 0 | .333 | .389 | 0 | 0 | C-6 |
| 1937 CHI A | 1 | 1 | 0 | 0 | 0 | 0 | 0.0 | 0 | 0 | 0 | 0 | 0 | .000 | .000 | 1 | 0 | |
| 1938 | 23 | 54 | 14 | 0 | 0 | 0 | 0.0 | 2 | 5 | 1 | 0 | 0 | .259 | .259 | 1 | 0 | C-20, 1B-1 |
| 1939 | 24 | 21 | 3 | 0 | 0 | 0 | 0.0 | 1 | 0 | 0 | 3 | 0 | .143 | .143 | 2 | 0 | C-21 |
| 1944 PHI A | 18 | 23 | 6 | 2 | 0 | 0 | 0.0 | 2 | 2 | 1 | 0 | 0 | .261 | .348 | 3 | 0 | C-15 |
| 1945 BOS A | 68 | 199 | 52 | 6 | 0 | 0 | 0.0 | 21 | 17 | 18 | 10 | 0 | .261 | .291 | 1 | 0 | C-67 |
| 7 yrs. | 145 | 327 | 81 | 9 | 0 | 0 | 0.0 | 31 | 28 | 26 | 17 | 0 | .248 | .275 | 8 | 0 | C-134, 1B-1 |
| 3 yrs. | 48 | 76 | 17 | 0 | 0 | 0 | 0.0 | 3 | 5 | 1 | 3 | 0 | .224 | .224 | 4 | 0 | C-41, 1B-1 |

# Adrian Garrett

**GARRETT, HENRY ADRIAN**      BL TR 6'3"   185 lbs.
Brother of Wayne Garrett.
B. Jan. 3, 1943, Brooksville, Fla.

| | G | AB | H | 2B | 3B | HR | HR % | R | RBI | BB | SO | SB | BA | SA | AB | H | G by POS |
|---|---|---|---|---|---|---|---|---|---|---|---|---|---|---|---|---|---|
| 1966 ATL N | 4 | 3 | 0 | 0 | 0 | 0 | 0.0 | 0 | 0 | 0 | 2 | 0 | .000 | .000 | 3 | 0 | OF-1 |
| 1970 CHI N | 3 | 3 | 0 | 0 | 0 | 0 | 0.0 | 0 | 0 | 0 | 3 | 0 | .000 | .000 | 3 | 0 | |

| | G | AB | H | 2B | 3B | HR | HR % | R | RBI | BB | SO | SB | BA | SA | Pinch Hit AB | Pinch Hit H | G by POS |
|---|---|---|---|---|---|---|---|---|---|---|---|---|---|---|---|---|---|

## Adrian Garrett continued

| | G | AB | H | 2B | 3B | HR | HR% | R | RBI | BB | SO | SB | BA | SA | AB | H | G by POS |
|---|---|---|---|---|---|---|---|---|---|---|---|---|---|---|---|---|---|
| 1971 OAK A | 14 | 21 | 3 | 0 | 0 | 1 | 4.8 | 1 | 2 | 5 | 7 | 0 | .143 | .286 | 7 | 0 | OF-5 |
| 1972 | 14 | 11 | 0 | 0 | 0 | 0 | 0.0 | 0 | 0 | 1 | 4 | 0 | .000 | .000 | 11 | 0 | OF-2 |
| 1973 CHI N | 36 | 54 | 12 | 0 | 0 | 3 | 5.6 | 7 | 8 | 4 | 18 | 1 | .222 | .389 | 21 | 6 | OF-7, C-6 |
| 1974 | 10 | 8 | 0 | 0 | 0 | 0 | 0.0 | 0 | 0 | 1 | 1 | 0 | .000 | .000 | 6 | 0 | C-3, OF-1, 1B-1 |
| 1975 2 teams | CHI N (16G – .095) | | | | CAL A (37G – .262) | | | | | | | | | | | | |
| " total | 53 | 128 | 30 | 5 | 0 | 7 | 5.5 | 18 | 24 | 15 | 36 | 3 | .234 | .438 | 9 | 0 | DH-23, 1B-14, OF-2, C-1 |
| 1976 CAL A | 29 | 48 | 6 | 3 | 0 | 0 | 0.0 | 4 | 3 | 5 | 16 | 0 | .125 | .188 | 12 | 2 | C-15, DH-4, 1B-1 |
| 8 yrs. | 163 | 276 | 51 | 8 | 0 | 11 | 4.0 | 30 | 37 | 31 | 87 | 4 | .185 | .333 | 72 | 8 | DH-27, C-25, OF-18, 1B-16 |
| 4 yrs. | 65 | 86 | 14 | 0 | 0 | 4 | 4.7 | 8 | 14 | 6 | 30 | 1 | .163 | .302 | 38 | 6 | C-9, OF-8, 1B-5 |

## Rabbit Garriott

**GARRIOTT, VIRGIL CECIL**
B. Aug. 15, 1916, Harristown, Ill.      BB  TR  5'8"      165 lbs.

| | G | AB | H | 2B | 3B | HR | HR% | R | RBI | BB | SO | SB | BA | SA | AB | H | G by POS |
|---|---|---|---|---|---|---|---|---|---|---|---|---|---|---|---|---|---|
| 1946 CHI N | 6 | 5 | 0 | 0 | 0 | 0 | 0.0 | 1 | 0 | 2 | 0 | .000 | .000 | 5 | 0 | |

## Ed Gastfield

**GASTFIELD, EDWARD**
B. Aug. 1, 1865, Chicago, Ill.      D. Dec. 1, 1899, Chicago, Ill.

| | G | AB | H | 2B | 3B | HR | HR% | R | RBI | BB | SO | SB | BA | SA | AB | H | G by POS |
|---|---|---|---|---|---|---|---|---|---|---|---|---|---|---|---|---|---|
| 1884 DET N | 23 | 82 | 6 | 1 | 0 | 0 | 0.0 | 6 | | 2 | 34 | | .073 | .085 | 0 | 0 | C-19, OF-2, 1B-2 |
| 1885 2 teams | DET N (1G – .000) | | | | CHI N (1G – .000) | | | | | | | | | | | | |
| " total | 2 | 6 | 0 | 0 | 0 | 0 | 0.0 | 0 | | 0 | 3 | | .000 | .000 | 0 | 0 | C-2 |
| 2 yrs. | 25 | 88 | 6 | 1 | 0 | 0 | 0.0 | 6 | | 2 | 37 | | .068 | .080 | 0 | 0 | C-21, OF-2, 1B-2 |
| 1 yr. | 1 | 3 | 0 | 0 | 0 | 0 | 0.0 | 0 | | 0 | 1 | | .000 | .000 | 0 | 0 | C-1 |

## Emil Geis

**GEIS, EMIL AUGUST**
Brother of Bill Geis.      BR
B. Mar. 20, 1867, Chicago, Ill.      D. Oct. 4, 1911, Chicago, Ill.

| | G | AB | H | 2B | 3B | HR | HR% | R | RBI | BB | SO | SB | BA | SA | AB | H | G by POS |
|---|---|---|---|---|---|---|---|---|---|---|---|---|---|---|---|---|---|
| 1887 CHI N | 3 | 12 | 1 | 0 | 0 | 0 | 0.0 | 0 | | 0 | 7 | 0 | .083 | .083 | 0 | 0 | 2B-1, 1B-1, P-1 |

## Greek George

**GEORGE, CHARLES PETER**
B. Dec. 25, 1912, Waycross, Ga.      BR  TR  6'2"      200 lbs.

| | G | AB | H | 2B | 3B | HR | HR% | R | RBI | BB | SO | SB | BA | SA | AB | H | G by POS |
|---|---|---|---|---|---|---|---|---|---|---|---|---|---|---|---|---|---|
| 1935 CLE A | 2 | 0 | 0 | 0 | 0 | 0 | | 0 | 0 | 0 | 0 | 0 | – | – | 0 | 0 | C-1 |
| 1936 | 23 | 77 | 15 | 3 | 0 | 0 | 0.0 | 3 | 5 | 9 | 16 | 0 | .195 | .234 | 1 | 0 | C-22 |
| 1938 BKN N | 7 | 20 | 4 | 0 | 1 | 0 | 0.0 | 0 | 2 | 0 | 4 | 0 | .200 | .300 | 0 | 0 | C-7 |
| 1941 CHI N | 35 | 64 | 10 | 2 | 0 | 0 | 0.0 | 4 | 6 | 2 | 10 | 0 | .156 | .188 | 17 | 0 | C-18 |
| 1945 PHI A | 51 | 138 | 24 | 4 | 1 | 0 | 0.0 | 8 | 11 | 17 | 29 | 0 | .174 | .217 | 5 | 0 | C-46 |
| 5 yrs. | 118 | 299 | 53 | 9 | 2 | 0 | 0.0 | 15 | 24 | 28 | 59 | 0 | .177 | .221 | 23 | 0 | C-94 |
| 1 yr. | 35 | 64 | 10 | 2 | 0 | 0 | 0.0 | 4 | 6 | 2 | 10 | 0 | .156 | .188 | 17 | 0 | C-18 |

## Dick Gernert

**GERNERT, RICHARD EDWARD**
B. Sept. 28, 1928, Reading, Pa.      BR  TR  6'3"      209 lbs.

| | G | AB | H | 2B | 3B | HR | HR% | R | RBI | BB | SO | SB | BA | SA | AB | H | G by POS |
|---|---|---|---|---|---|---|---|---|---|---|---|---|---|---|---|---|---|
| 1952 BOS A | 102 | 367 | 89 | 20 | 2 | 19 | 5.2 | 58 | 67 | 35 | 83 | 4 | .243 | .463 | 4 | 1 | 1B-99 |
| 1953 | 139 | 494 | 125 | 15 | 1 | 21 | 4.3 | 73 | 71 | 88 | 82 | 0 | .253 | .415 | 3 | 0 | 1B-136 |
| 1954 | 14 | 23 | 6 | 2 | 0 | 0 | 0.0 | 2 | 1 | 6 | 4 | 0 | .261 | .348 | 7 | 1 | 1B-6 |
| 1955 | 7 | 20 | 4 | 2 | 0 | 0 | 0.0 | 6 | 1 | 1 | 5 | 0 | .200 | .300 | 1 | 0 | 1B-5 |
| 1956 | 106 | 306 | 89 | 11 | 0 | 16 | 5.2 | 53 | 68 | 56 | 57 | 1 | .291 | .484 | 22 | 4 | OF-50, 1B-37 |
| 1957 | 99 | 316 | 75 | 13 | 3 | 14 | 4.4 | 45 | 58 | 39 | 62 | 1 | .237 | .430 | 18 | 6 | 1B-71, OF-16 |
| 1958 | 122 | 431 | 102 | 19 | 1 | 20 | 4.6 | 59 | 69 | 59 | 78 | 2 | .237 | .425 | 7 | 3 | 1B-114 |
| 1959 | 117 | 298 | 78 | 14 | 1 | 11 | 3.7 | 41 | 42 | 52 | 49 | 1 | .262 | .426 | 21 | 4 | 1B-75, OF-25 |
| 1960 2 teams | CHI N (52G – .250) | | | | DET A (21G – .300) | | | | | | | | | | | | |
| " total | 73 | 146 | 39 | 7 | 0 | 1 | 0.7 | 14 | 16 | 14 | 24 | 1 | .267 | .336 | 31 | 8 | 1B-31, OF-11 |
| 1961 2 teams | DET A (6G – .200) | | | | CIN N (40G – .302) | | | | | | | | | | | | |
| " total | 46 | 68 | 20 | 1 | 0 | 1 | 1.5 | 5 | 8 | 8 | 11 | 0 | .294 | .353 | 25 | 6 | 1B-21 |
| 1962 HOU N | 10 | 24 | 5 | 0 | 0 | 0 | 0.0 | 1 | 1 | 5 | 7 | 0 | .208 | .208 | 1 | 0 | 1B-9 |
| 11 yrs. | 835 | 2493 | 632 | 104 | 8 | 103 | 4.1 | 357 | 402 | 363 | 462 | 10 | .254 | .426 | 140 | 33 | 1B-604, OF-102 |
| 1 yr. | 52 | 96 | 24 | 3 | 0 | 0 | 0.0 | 8 | 11 | 10 | 19 | 1 | .250 | .281 | 27 | 7 | 1B-18, OF-5 |

**WORLD SERIES**

| | G | AB | H | 2B | 3B | HR | HR% | R | RBI | BB | SO | SB | BA | SA | AB | H | G by POS |
|---|---|---|---|---|---|---|---|---|---|---|---|---|---|---|---|---|---|
| 1961 CIN N | 4 | 4 | 0 | 0 | 0 | 0 | 0.0 | 0 | 0 | 0 | 1 | 0 | .000 | .000 | 4 | 0 | |

## Doc Gessler

**GESSLER, HARRY HOMER**
B. Dec. 23, 1880, Indiana, Pa.      D. Dec. 26, 1924, Indiana, Pa.      BL  TR
Manager 1914.

| | G | AB | H | 2B | 3B | HR | HR% | R | RBI | BB | SO | SB | BA | SA | AB | H | G by POS |
|---|---|---|---|---|---|---|---|---|---|---|---|---|---|---|---|---|---|
| 1903 2 teams | DET A (29G – .238) | | | | BKN N (49G – .247) | | | | | | | | | | | | |
| " total | 78 | 259 | 63 | 13 | 7 | 0 | 0.0 | 29 | 30 | 20 | | 10 | .243 | .347 | 4 | 1 | OF-71 |
| 1904 BKN N | 104 | 341 | 99 | 18 | 4 | 2 | 0.6 | 41 | 28 | 30 | | 13 | .290 | .384 | 12 | 2 | OF-88, 2B-1, 1B-1 |
| 1905 | 126 | 431 | 125 | 17 | 4 | 3 | 0.7 | 44 | 46 | 38 | | 26 | .290 | .369 | 7 | 2 | 1B-107, OF-12 |
| 1906 2 teams | BKN N (9G – .242) | | | | CHI N (34G – .253) | | | | | | | | | | | | |
| " total | 43 | 116 | 29 | 4 | 0 | 0 | 0.0 | 11 | 14 | 15 | | 7 | .250 | .319 | 11 | 2 | OF-21, 1B-10 |
| 1908 BOS A | 128 | 435 | 134 | 13 | 14 | 3 | 0.7 | 55 | 63 | 51 | | 19 | .308 | .423 | 2 | 2 | OF-126 |
| 1909 2 teams | BOS A (111G – .298) | | | | WAS A (17G – .241) | | | | | | | | | | | | |
| " total | 128 | 440 | 128 | 26 | 2 | 0 | 0.0 | 66 | 54 | 43 | | 20 | .291 | .359 | 1 | 0 | OF-127, 1B-2 |
| 1910 WAS A | 145 | 487 | 126 | 17 | 11 | 2 | 0.4 | 58 | 50 | 62 | | 18 | .259 | .351 | 1 | 0 | OF-144 |
| 1911 | 128 | 450 | 127 | 19 | 5 | 4 | 0.9 | 65 | 78 | 74 | | 29 | .282 | .373 | 1 | 0 | OF-126, 1B-1 |
| 8 yrs. | 880 | 2959 | 831 | 127 | 49 | 14 | 0.5 | 369 | 363 | 333 | | 142 | .281 | .371 | 39 | 9 | OF-715, 1B-121, 2B-1 |
| 1 yr. | 34 | 83 | 21 | 3 | 0 | 0 | 0.0 | 8 | 10 | 12 | | 4 | .253 | .289 | 11 | 2 | OF-21, 1B-1 |

**WORLD SERIES**

| | G | AB | H | 2B | 3B | HR | HR% | R | RBI | BB | SO | SB | BA | SA | AB | H | G by POS |
|---|---|---|---|---|---|---|---|---|---|---|---|---|---|---|---|---|---|
| 1906 CHI N | 2 | 1 | 0 | 0 | 0 | 0 | 0.0 | 0 | 0 | 1 | | 0 | .000 | .000 | 1 | 0 | |

| | G | AB | H | 2B | 3B | HR | HR % | R | RBI | BB | SO | SB | BA | SA | Pinch Hit AB | Pinch Hit H | G by POS |
|---|---|---|---|---|---|---|---|---|---|---|---|---|---|---|---|---|---|

## Norm Gigon

**GIGON, NORMAN PHILLIP**
B. May 12, 1938, Teaneck, N. J.                                        BR TR 6'          195 lbs.

| | G | AB | H | 2B | 3B | HR | HR % | R | RBI | BB | SO | SB | BA | SA | AB | H | G by POS |
|---|---|---|---|---|---|---|---|---|---|---|---|---|---|---|---|---|---|
| 1967 CHI N | 34 | 70 | 12 | 3 | 1 | 1 | 1.4 | 8 | 6 | 4 | 14 | 0 | .171 | .286 | 15 | 2 | 2B-12, OF-4, 3B-1 |

## Charlie Gilbert

**GILBERT, CHARLES MADER**
Son of Larry Gilbert.  Brother of Tookie Gilbert.
B. July 8, 1919, New Orleans, La.   D. Aug. 13, 1983, New Orleans, La.                BL TL 5'9"          165 lbs.

| | G | AB | H | 2B | 3B | HR | HR % | R | RBI | BB | SO | SB | BA | SA | AB | H | G by POS |
|---|---|---|---|---|---|---|---|---|---|---|---|---|---|---|---|---|---|
| 1940 BKN N | 57 | 142 | 35 | 9 | 1 | 2 | 1.4 | 23 | 8 | 8 | 13 | 0 | .246 | .366 | 8 | 1 | OF-43 |
| 1941 CHI N | 39 | 86 | 24 | 2 | 1 | 0 | 0.0 | 11 | 12 | 11 | 6 | 1 | .279 | .326 | 14 | 2 | OF-22 |
| 1942 | 74 | 179 | 33 | 6 | 3 | 0 | 0.0 | 18 | 7 | 25 | 24 | 1 | .184 | .251 | 23 | 2 | OF-47 |
| 1943 | 8 | 20 | 3 | 0 | 0 | 0 | 0.0 | 1 | 0 | 3 | 3 | 1 | .150 | .150 | 2 | 0 | OF-6 |
| 1946 2 teams | | CHI | N | (15G – | .077) | | PHI | N | (88G – | .242) | | | | | | | |
| " total | 103 | 273 | 64 | 5 | 2 | 1 | 0.4 | 36 | 18 | 26 | 22 | 3 | .234 | .278 | 28 | 0 | OF-71 |
| 1947 PHI N | 83 | 152 | 36 | 5 | 2 | 2 | 1.3 | 20 | 10 | 13 | 14 | 1 | .237 | .336 | 40 | 9 | OF-37 |
| 6 yrs. | 364 | 852 | 195 | 27 | 9 | 5 | 0.6 | 109 | 55 | 86 | 82 | 7 | .229 | .299 | 115 | 14 | OF-226 |
| 4 yrs. | 136 | 298 | 61 | 8 | 4 | 0 | 0.0 | 32 | 20 | 40 | 37 | 3 | .205 | .258 | 51 | 4 | OF-77 |

## Johnny Gill

**GILL, JOHN WESLEY (Patcheye)**
B. Mar. 27, 1905, Nashville, Tenn.   D. Dec. 26, 1984, Nashville, Tenn.               BL TR 6'2"          190 lbs.

| | G | AB | H | 2B | 3B | HR | HR % | R | RBI | BB | SO | SB | BA | SA | AB | H | G by POS |
|---|---|---|---|---|---|---|---|---|---|---|---|---|---|---|---|---|---|
| 1927 CLE A | 21 | 60 | 13 | 3 | 0 | 1 | 1.7 | 8 | 4 | 7 | 13 | 1 | .217 | .317 | 2 | 2 | OF-17 |
| 1928 | 2 | 2 | 0 | 0 | 0 | 0 | 0.0 | 0 | 0 | 0 | 1 | 0 | .000 | .000 | 2 | 0 | |
| 1931 WAS A | 8 | 30 | 8 | 2 | 1 | 0 | 0.0 | 2 | 5 | 1 | 6 | 0 | .267 | .400 | 0 | 0 | OF-8 |
| 1934 | 13 | 53 | 13 | 3 | 0 | 2 | 3.8 | 7 | 7 | 2 | 3 | 0 | .245 | .415 | 0 | 0 | OF-13 |
| 1935 CHI N | 3 | 3 | 1 | 1 | 0 | 0 | 0.0 | 2 | 1 | 0 | 1 | 0 | .333 | .667 | 3 | 1 | |
| 1936 | 71 | 174 | 44 | 8 | 0 | 7 | 4.0 | 20 | 28 | 13 | 19 | 0 | .253 | .420 | 25 | 6 | OF-41 |
| 6 yrs. | 118 | 322 | 79 | 17 | 1 | 10 | 3.1 | 39 | 45 | 23 | 43 | 1 | .245 | .398 | 32 | 9 | OF-79 |
| 2 yrs. | 74 | 177 | 45 | 9 | 0 | 7 | 4.0 | 22 | 29 | 13 | 20 | 0 | .254 | .424 | 28 | 7 | OF-41 |

## Paul Gillespie

**GILLESPIE, PAUL ALLEN**
B. Sept. 18, 1920, Sugar Valley, Ga.   D. Aug. 11, 1970, Anniston, Ala.               BL TR 6'2"          180 lbs.

| | G | AB | H | 2B | 3B | HR | HR % | R | RBI | BB | SO | SB | BA | SA | AB | H | G by POS |
|---|---|---|---|---|---|---|---|---|---|---|---|---|---|---|---|---|---|
| 1942 CHI N | 5 | 16 | 4 | 0 | 0 | 2 | 12.5 | 3 | 4 | 1 | 2 | 0 | .250 | .625 | 1 | 0 | C-4 |
| 1944 | 9 | 26 | 7 | 1 | 0 | 1 | 3.8 | 2 | 2 | 3 | 3 | 0 | .269 | .423 | 2 | 0 | C-7 |
| 1945 | 75 | 163 | 47 | 6 | 0 | 3 | 1.8 | 12 | 25 | 18 | 9 | 2 | .288 | .380 | 24 | 7 | C-45, OF-1 |
| 3 yrs. | 89 | 205 | 58 | 7 | 0 | 6 | 2.9 | 17 | 31 | 22 | 14 | 2 | .283 | .405 | 27 | 7 | C-56, OF-1 |
| 3 yrs. | 89 | 205 | 58 | 7 | 0 | 6 | 2.9 | 17 | 31 | 22 | 14 | 2 | .283 | .405 | 27 | 7 | C-56, OF-1 |
| WORLD SERIES | | | | | | | | | | | | | | | | | |
| 1945 CHI N | 3 | 6 | 0 | 0 | 0 | 0 | 0.0 | 0 | 0 | 0 | 0 | 0 | .000 | .000 | 2 | 0 | C-1 |

## Jim Gleeson

**GLEESON, JAMES JOSEPH (Gee Gee)**
B. Mar. 5, 1912, Kansas City, Mo.                                     BB TR 6'1"          191 lbs.

| | G | AB | H | 2B | 3B | HR | HR % | R | RBI | BB | SO | SB | BA | SA | AB | H | G by POS |
|---|---|---|---|---|---|---|---|---|---|---|---|---|---|---|---|---|---|
| 1936 CLE A | 41 | 139 | 36 | 9 | 2 | 4 | 2.9 | 26 | 12 | 18 | 17 | 2 | .259 | .439 | 7 | 0 | OF-33 |
| 1939 CHI N | 111 | 332 | 74 | 19 | 6 | 4 | 1.2 | 43 | 45 | 39 | 46 | 7 | .223 | .352 | 17 | 4 | OF-91 |
| 1940 | 129 | 485 | 152 | 39 | 11 | 5 | 1.0 | 76 | 61 | 54 | 52 | 4 | .313 | .470 | 5 | 1 | OF-123 |
| 1941 CIN N | 102 | 301 | 70 | 10 | 0 | 3 | 1.0 | 47 | 34 | 45 | 30 | 7 | .233 | .296 | 14 | 3 | OF-84 |
| 1942 | 9 | 20 | 4 | 0 | 0 | 0 | 0.0 | 3 | 2 | 2 | 2 | 0 | .200 | .200 | 3 | 0 | OF-5 |
| 5 yrs. | 392 | 1277 | 336 | 77 | 19 | 16 | 1.3 | 195 | 154 | 158 | 147 | 20 | .263 | .391 | 46 | 8 | OF-336 |
| 2 yrs. | 240 | 817 | 226 | 58 | 17 | 9 | 1.1 | 119 | 106 | 93 | 98 | 11 | .277 | .422 | 22 | 5 | OF-214 |

## Bob Glenalvin

**GLENALVIN, ROBERT J.**
Born Rodney J. Dowling.
B. Jan. 17, 1867, Kalamazoo, Mich.   D. Mar. 24, 1944, Detroit, Mich.                 TR

| | G | AB | H | 2B | 3B | HR | HR % | R | RBI | BB | SO | SB | BA | SA | AB | H | G by POS |
|---|---|---|---|---|---|---|---|---|---|---|---|---|---|---|---|---|---|
| 1890 CHI N | 66 | 250 | 67 | 10 | 3 | 4 | 1.6 | 43 | 26 | 19 | 31 | 30 | .268 | .380 | 0 | 0 | 2B-66 |
| 1893 | 16 | 61 | 21 | 3 | 1 | 0 | 0.0 | 11 | 12 | 7 | 3 | 7 | .344 | .426 | 0 | 0 | 2B-16 |
| 2 yrs. | 82 | 311 | 88 | 13 | 4 | 4 | 1.3 | 54 | 38 | 26 | 34 | 37 | .283 | .389 | 0 | 0 | 2B-82 |
| 2 yrs. | 82 | 311 | 88 | 13 | 4 | 4 | 1.3 | 54 | 38 | 26 | 34 | 37 | .283 | .389 | 0 | 0 | 2B-82 |

## Ed Glenn

**GLENN, EDWARD D.**
B. 1874, Ludlow, Ky.   D. Dec. 6, 1911, Ludlow, Ky.

| | G | AB | H | 2B | 3B | HR | HR % | R | RBI | BB | SO | SB | BA | SA | AB | H | G by POS |
|---|---|---|---|---|---|---|---|---|---|---|---|---|---|---|---|---|---|
| 1898 2 teams | | WAS | N | (1G – | .000) | | NY | N | (2G – | .250) | | | | | | | |
| " total | 3 | 8 | 1 | 0 | 0 | 0 | 0.0 | 1 | 0 | 3 | | 1 | .125 | .125 | 0 | 0 | SS-3 |
| 1902 CHI N | 2 | 7 | 0 | 0 | 0 | 0 | 0.0 | 0 | 0 | 1 | | 0 | .000 | .000 | 0 | 0 | SS-2 |
| 2 yrs. | 5 | 15 | 1 | 0 | 0 | 0 | 0.0 | 1 | 0 | 4 | | 1 | .067 | .067 | 0 | 0 | SS-5 |
| 1 yr. | 2 | 7 | 0 | 0 | 0 | 0 | 0.0 | 0 | 0 | 1 | | 0 | .000 | .000 | 0 | 0 | SS-2 |

## John Glenn

**GLENN, JOHN W.**
B. 1849, Rochester, N. Y.   D. Nov. 10, 1888, Sandy Hill, N. Y.                       BR TR 5'8½"          169 lbs.

| | G | AB | H | 2B | 3B | HR | HR % | R | RBI | BB | SO | SB | BA | SA | AB | H | G by POS |
|---|---|---|---|---|---|---|---|---|---|---|---|---|---|---|---|---|---|
| 1876 CHI N | 66 | 276 | 84 | 9 | 2 | 0 | 0.0 | 55 | 32 | 12 | 6 | | .304 | .351 | 0 | 0 | OF-56, 1B-15 |
| 1877 | 50 | 202 | 46 | 6 | 1 | 0 | 0.0 | 31 | 20 | 8 | 16 | | .228 | .267 | 0 | 0 | OF-36, 1B-14 |
| 2 yrs. | 116 | 478 | 130 | 15 | 3 | 0 | 0.0 | 86 | 52 | 20 | 22 | | .272 | .316 | 0 | 0 | OF-92, 1B-29 |
| 2 yrs. | 116 | 478 | 130 | 15 | 3 | 0 | 0.0 | 86 | 52 | 20 | 22 | | .272 | .316 | 0 | 0 | OF-92, 1B-29 |

## Al Glossop

**GLOSSOP, ALBAN**
B. July 23, 1912, Christopher, Ill.                                   BB TR 6'          170 lbs.

| | G | AB | H | 2B | 3B | HR | HR % | R | RBI | BB | SO | SB | BA | SA | AB | H | G by POS |
|---|---|---|---|---|---|---|---|---|---|---|---|---|---|---|---|---|---|
| 1939 NY N | 10 | 32 | 6 | 0 | 0 | 1 | 3.1 | 3 | 3 | 4 | 2 | 0 | .188 | .281 | 0 | 0 | 2B-10 |
| 1940 2 teams | | NY | N | (27G – | .209) | | BOS | N | (60G – | .236) | | | | | | | |
| " total | 87 | 239 | 54 | 5 | 1 | 7 | 2.9 | 33 | 22 | 27 | 38 | 2 | .226 | .343 | 25 | 5 | 2B-42, 3B-18, SS-10 |
| 1942 PHI N | 121 | 454 | 102 | 15 | 1 | 4 | 0.9 | 33 | 40 | 29 | 35 | 3 | .225 | .289 | 3 | 1 | 2B-118, 3B-1 |
| 1943 BKN N | 87 | 217 | 37 | 9 | 0 | 3 | 1.4 | 28 | 21 | 28 | 27 | 0 | .171 | .253 | 11 | 0 | SS-33, 2B-24, 3B-17 |

| | G | AB | H | 2B | 3B | HR | HR % | R | RBI | BB | SO | SB | BA | SA | Pinch Hit AB | Pinch Hit H | G by POS |
|---|---|---|---|---|---|---|---|---|---|---|---|---|---|---|---|---|---|

## Al Glossop continued

| | G | AB | H | 2B | 3B | HR | HR % | R | RBI | BB | SO | SB | BA | SA | PH AB | PH H | G by POS |
|---|---|---|---|---|---|---|---|---|---|---|---|---|---|---|---|---|---|
| 1946 CHI N | 4 | 10 | 0 | 0 | 0 | 0 | 0.0 | 2 | 0 | 1 | 3 | 0 | .000 | .000 | 0 | 0 | SS-2, 2B-2 |
| 5 yrs. | 309 | 952 | 199 | 29 | 2 | 15 | 1.6 | 99 | 86 | 89 | 105 | 5 | .209 | .291 | 39 | 6 | 2B-196, SS-45, 3B-36 |
| 1 yr. | 4 | 10 | 0 | 0 | 0 | 0 | 0.0 | 2 | 0 | 1 | 3 | 0 | .000 | .000 | 0 | 0 | SS-2, 2B-2 |

## Fred Goldsmith

**GOLDSMITH, FRED ERNEST**                                    BR TR 6'1"    195 lbs.
B. May 15, 1852, New Haven, Conn.    D. Mar. 28, 1939, Berkley, Mich.

| | G | AB | H | 2B | 3B | HR | HR % | R | RBI | BB | SO | SB | BA | SA | PH AB | PH H | G by POS |
|---|---|---|---|---|---|---|---|---|---|---|---|---|---|---|---|---|---|
| 1879 TRO N | 9 | 38 | 9 | 1 | 0 | 0 | 0.0 | 6 | 2 | 1 | 3 | | .237 | .263 | 0 | 0 | P-8, OF-2, 1B-1 |
| 1880 CHI N | 35 | 142 | 37 | 4 | 2 | 0 | 0.0 | 24 | 15 | 2 | 15 | | .261 | .317 | 0 | 0 | P-26, OF-10, 1B-4 |
| 1881 | 42 | 158 | 38 | 3 | 4 | 0 | 0.0 | 24 | 16 | 6 | 17 | | .241 | .310 | 0 | 0 | P-39, OF-3 |
| 1882 | 45 | 183 | 42 | 11 | 1 | 0 | 0.0 | 23 | 19 | 4 | 29 | | .230 | .301 | 0 | 0 | P-45, 1B-1 |
| 1883 | 60 | 235 | 52 | 12 | 3 | 1 | 0.4 | 38 | | 4 | 35 | | .221 | .311 | 0 | 0 | P-46, OF-16, 1B-2 |
| 1884 2 teams | | CHI | N | (22G – | .136) | | BAL | AA | (4G – | .143) | | | | | | | |
| " total | 26 | 95 | 13 | 2 | 0 | 2 | 2.1 | 13 | | 9 | 26 | | .137 | .221 | 0 | 0 | P-25, OF-2, 1B-1 |
| 6 yrs. | 217 | 851 | 191 | 33 | 10 | 3 | 0.4 | 128 | 52 | 26 | 125 | | .224 | .297 | 0 | 0 | P-189, OF-33, 1B-9 |
| 5 yrs. | 204 | 799 | 180 | 32 | 10 | 3 | 0.4 | 120 | 50 | 23 | 122 | | .225 | .302 | 0 | 0 | P-177, OF-31, 1B-7 |

## Walt Golvin

**GOLVIN, WALTER GEORGE**                                     BL TL 6'    165 lbs.
B. Feb. 1, 1894, Hershey, Neb.    D. June 11, 1973, Gardinia, Calif.

| | G | AB | H | 2B | 3B | HR | HR % | R | RBI | BB | SO | SB | BA | SA | PH AB | PH H | G by POS |
|---|---|---|---|---|---|---|---|---|---|---|---|---|---|---|---|---|---|
| 1922 CHI N | 2 | 2 | 0 | 0 | 0 | 0 | 0.0 | 0 | 1 | 0 | 0 | 0 | .000 | .000 | 0 | 0 | 1B-2 |

## Mike Gonzalez

**GONZALEZ, MIGUEL ANGEL**                                    BR TR 6'1"    200 lbs.
B. Sept. 24, 1890, Havana, Cuba    D. Feb. 19, 1977, Havana, Cuba
Manager 1938, 1940.

| | G | AB | H | 2B | 3B | HR | HR % | R | RBI | BB | SO | SB | BA | SA | PH AB | PH H | G by POS |
|---|---|---|---|---|---|---|---|---|---|---|---|---|---|---|---|---|---|
| 1912 BOS N | 1 | 2 | 0 | 0 | 0 | 0 | 0.0 | 0 | 0 | 1 | 1 | 0 | .000 | .000 | 0 | 0 | C-1 |
| 1914 CIN N | 95 | 176 | 41 | 6 | 0 | 0 | 0.0 | 19 | 10 | 13 | 16 | 2 | .233 | .267 | 9 | 2 | C-83 |
| 1915 STL N | 51 | 97 | 22 | 2 | 2 | 0 | 0.0 | 12 | 10 | 8 | 9 | 4 | .227 | .289 | 6 | 1 | C-31, 1B-8 |
| 1916 | 118 | 331 | 79 | 15 | 4 | 0 | 0.0 | 33 | 29 | 28 | 18 | 5 | .239 | .308 | 10 | 0 | C-93, 1B-13 |
| 1917 | 106 | 290 | 76 | 8 | 1 | 1 | 0.3 | 28 | 28 | 22 | 24 | 12 | .262 | .307 | 17 | 2 | C-68, 1B-18, OF-1 |
| 1918 | 117 | 349 | 88 | 13 | 4 | 3 | 0.9 | 33 | 20 | 39 | 30 | 14 | .252 | .338 | 8 | 1 | C-100, OF-5, 1B-2 |
| 1919 NY N | 58 | 158 | 30 | 6 | 0 | 0 | 0.0 | 18 | 8 | 20 | 9 | 3 | .190 | .228 | 3 | 0 | C-52, 1B-4 |
| 1920 | 11 | 13 | 3 | 0 | 0 | 0 | 0.0 | 1 | 0 | 3 | 1 | 1 | .231 | .231 | 2 | 0 | C-8 |
| 1921 | 13 | 24 | 9 | 1 | 0 | 0 | 0.0 | 3 | 0 | 1 | 0 | 0 | .375 | .417 | 4 | 1 | 1B-6, C-2 |
| 1924 STL N | 120 | 402 | 119 | 27 | 1 | 3 | 0.7 | 34 | 53 | 24 | 22 | 1 | .296 | .391 | 1 | 1 | C-119 |
| 1925 2 teams | | STL | N | (22G – | .310) | | CHI | N | (70G – | .264) | | | | | | | |
| " total | 92 | 268 | 74 | 16 | 1 | 3 | 1.1 | 35 | 22 | 19 | 17 | 3 | .276 | .377 | 9 | 2 | C-72, 1B-9 |
| 1926 CHI N | 80 | 253 | 63 | 13 | 3 | 1 | 0.4 | 24 | 23 | 13 | 17 | 3 | .249 | .336 | 2 | 0 | C-78 |
| 1927 | 39 | 108 | 26 | 4 | 1 | 1 | 0.9 | 15 | 15 | 10 | 8 | 1 | .241 | .324 | 3 | 1 | C-36 |
| 1928 | 49 | 158 | 43 | 9 | 2 | 1 | 0.6 | 12 | 21 | 12 | 7 | 2 | .272 | .373 | 4 | 0 | C-45 |
| 1929 | 60 | 167 | 40 | 3 | 0 | 0 | 0.0 | 15 | 18 | 18 | 14 | 1 | .240 | .257 | 0 | 0 | C-60 |
| 1931 STL N | 15 | 19 | 2 | 0 | 0 | 0 | 0.0 | 1 | 3 | 0 | 3 | 0 | .105 | .105 | 3 | 0 | C-12 |
| 1932 | 17 | 14 | 2 | 0 | 0 | 0 | 0.0 | 0 | 3 | 0 | 2 | 0 | .143 | .143 | 10 | 2 | C-7 |
| 17 yrs. | 1042 | 2829 | 717 | 123 | 19 | 13 | 0.5 | 283 | 263 | 231 | 198 | 52 | .253 | .324 | 91 | 13 | C-867, 1B-60, OF-6 |
| 5 yrs. | 298 | 883 | 224 | 42 | 7 | 6 | 0.7 | 92 | 95 | 66 | 61 | 9 | .254 | .337 | 18 | 3 | C-269, 1B-9 |

**WORLD SERIES**

| | G | AB | H | 2B | 3B | HR | HR % | R | RBI | BB | SO | SB | BA | SA | PH AB | PH H | G by POS |
|---|---|---|---|---|---|---|---|---|---|---|---|---|---|---|---|---|---|
| 1929 CHI N | 2 | 1 | 0 | 0 | 0 | 0 | 0.0 | 0 | 0 | 0 | 1 | 0 | .000 | .000 | 1 | 0 | C-1 |

## Wilbur Good

**GOOD, WILBUR DAVID (Lefty)**                                BL TL 5'6"    165 lbs.
B. Sept. 28, 1885, Punxsutawney, Pa.    D. Dec. 30, 1963, Brooksville, Fla.

| | G | AB | H | 2B | 3B | HR | HR % | R | RBI | BB | SO | SB | BA | SA | PH AB | PH H | G by POS |
|---|---|---|---|---|---|---|---|---|---|---|---|---|---|---|---|---|---|
| 1905 NY A | 6 | 8 | 3 | 0 | 0 | 0 | 0.0 | 0 | 0 | 0 | | 0 | .375 | .375 | 0 | 0 | P-5 |
| 1908 CLE N | 46 | 154 | 43 | 1 | 3 | 1 | 0.6 | 23 | 14 | 13 | | 7 | .279 | .344 | 2 | 1 | OF-42 |
| 1909 | 94 | 318 | 68 | 6 | 5 | 0 | 0.0 | 33 | 17 | 28 | | 13 | .214 | .264 | 10 | 1 | OF-80 |
| 1910 BOS N | 23 | 86 | 29 | 5 | 4 | 0 | 0.0 | 15 | 11 | 6 | 13 | 5 | .337 | .488 | 0 | 0 | OF-23 |
| 1911 2 teams | | BOS | N | (43G – | .267) | | CHI | N | (58G – | .269) | | | | | | | |
| " total | 101 | 310 | 83 | 14 | 7 | 2 | 0.6 | 48 | 36 | 23 | 39 | 13 | .268 | .377 | 12 | 1 | OF-83 |
| 1912 CHI N | 39 | 35 | 5 | 0 | 0 | 0 | 0.0 | 7 | 1 | 3 | 7 | 3 | .143 | .143 | 21 | 3 | OF-10 |
| 1913 | 49 | 91 | 23 | 3 | 2 | 1 | 1.1 | 11 | 12 | 11 | 16 | 5 | .253 | .363 | 16 | 4 | OF-26 |
| 1914 | 154 | 580 | 158 | 24 | 7 | 2 | 0.3 | 70 | 43 | 53 | 74 | 31 | .272 | .348 | 0 | 0 | OF-154 |
| 1915 | 128 | 498 | 126 | 18 | 9 | 2 | 0.4 | 66 | 27 | 34 | 65 | 19 | .253 | .337 | 2 | 1 | OF-125 |
| 1916 PHI N | 75 | 136 | 34 | 4 | 3 | 1 | 0.7 | 25 | 15 | 8 | 13 | 7 | .250 | .346 | 22 | 3 | OF-46 |
| 1918 CHI A | 35 | 148 | 37 | 9 | 4 | 0 | 0.0 | 24 | 11 | 11 | 16 | 1 | .250 | .365 | 0 | 0 | OF-35 |
| 11 yrs. | 750 | 2364 | 609 | 84 | 44 | 9 | 0.4 | 322 | 187 | 190 | 243 | 104 | .258 | .342 | 85 | 14 | OF-624, P-5 |
| 5 yrs. | 428 | 1349 | 351 | 50 | 22 | 7 | 0.5 | 181 | 104 | 112 | 179 | 68 | .260 | .345 | 51 | 9 | OF-355 |

## Ival Goodman

**GOODMAN, IVAL RICHARD (Goodie)**                            BL TR 5'11"    170 lbs.
B. July 23, 1908, Northview, Mo.    D. Nov. 25, 1984, Cincinnati, Ohio

| | G | AB | H | 2B | 3B | HR | HR % | R | RBI | BB | SO | SB | BA | SA | PH AB | PH H | G by POS |
|---|---|---|---|---|---|---|---|---|---|---|---|---|---|---|---|---|---|
| 1935 CIN N | 148 | 592 | 159 | 23 | 18 | 12 | 2.0 | 86 | 72 | 35 | 50 | 14 | .269 | .429 | 2 | 0 | OF-146 |
| 1936 | 136 | 489 | 139 | 15 | 14 | 17 | 3.5 | 81 | 71 | 38 | 53 | 6 | .284 | .476 | 15 | 5 | OF-120 |
| 1937 | 147 | 549 | 150 | 25 | 12 | 12 | 2.2 | 86 | 55 | 55 | 58 | 10 | .273 | .428 | 3 | 1 | OF-141 |
| 1938 | 145 | 568 | 166 | 27 | 10 | 30 | 5.3 | 103 | 92 | 53 | 51 | 3 | .292 | .533 | 3 | 1 | OF-142 |
| 1939 | 124 | 470 | 152 | 37 | 16 | 7 | 1.5 | 85 | 84 | 54 | 32 | 2 | .323 | .515 | 1 | 1 | OF-123 |
| 1940 | 136 | 519 | 134 | 20 | 6 | 12 | 2.3 | 78 | 63 | 60 | 54 | 9 | .258 | .389 | 0 | 0 | OF-135 |
| 1941 | 42 | 149 | 40 | 5 | 2 | 1 | 0.7 | 14 | 12 | 16 | 15 | 1 | .268 | .349 | 1 | 0 | OF-40 |
| 1942 | 87 | 226 | 55 | 18 | 1 | 0 | 0.0 | 21 | 15 | 24 | 32 | 0 | .243 | .332 | 23 | 6 | OF-57 |
| 1943 CHI N | 80 | 225 | 72 | 10 | 5 | 3 | 1.3 | 31 | 45 | 24 | 20 | 4 | .320 | .449 | 17 | 5 | OF-61 |
| 1944 | 62 | 141 | 37 | 8 | 1 | 1 | 0.7 | 24 | 16 | 23 | 15 | 0 | .262 | .355 | 23 | 6 | OF-35 |
| 10 yrs. | 1107 | 3928 | 1104 | 188 | 85 | 95 | 2.4 | 609 | 525 | 382 | 380 | 49 | .281 | .445 | 88 | 25 | OF-1000 |
| 2 yrs. | 142 | 366 | 109 | 18 | 6 | 4 | 1.1 | 55 | 61 | 47 | 35 | 4 | .298 | .413 | 40 | 11 | OF-96 |

**WORLD SERIES**

| | G | AB | H | 2B | 3B | HR | HR % | R | RBI | BB | SO | SB | BA | SA | PH AB | PH H | G by POS |
|---|---|---|---|---|---|---|---|---|---|---|---|---|---|---|---|---|---|
| 1939 CIN N | 4 | 15 | 5 | 1 | 0 | 0 | 0.0 | 3 | 1 | 1 | 2 | 1 | .333 | .400 | 0 | 0 | OF-4 |

| | G | AB | H | 2B | 3B | HR | HR % | R | RBI | BB | SO | SB | BA | SA | Pinch Hit AB | Pinch Hit H | G by POS |
|---|---|---|---|---|---|---|---|---|---|---|---|---|---|---|---|---|---|

## Ival Goodman   continued

| | G | AB | H | 2B | 3B | HR | HR% | R | RBI | BB | SO | SB | BA | SA | AB | H | G by POS |
|---|---|---|---|---|---|---|---|---|---|---|---|---|---|---|---|---|---|
| 1940 | 7 | 29 | 8 | 2 | 0 | 0 | 0.0 | 5 | 5 | 0 | 3 | 0 | .276 | .345 | 0 | 0 | OF-7 |
| 2 yrs. | 11 | 44 | 13 | 3 | 0 | 0 | 0.0 | 8 | 6 | 1 | 5 | 1 | .295 | .364 | 0 | 0 | OF-11 |

## Mike Gordon

**GORDON, MICHAEL WILLIAM**
B. Sept. 11, 1953, Leominister, Mass.    BB  TR  6'3"    215 lbs.

| | G | AB | H | 2B | 3B | HR | HR% | R | RBI | BB | SO | SB | BA | SA | AB | H | G by POS |
|---|---|---|---|---|---|---|---|---|---|---|---|---|---|---|---|---|---|
| 1977 CHI N | 8 | 23 | 1 | 0 | 0 | 0 | 0.0 | 0 | 2 | 2 | 8 | 0 | .043 | .043 | 0 | 0 | C-8 |
| 1978 | 4 | 5 | 1 | 0 | 0 | 0 | 0.0 | 0 | 0 | 3 | 2 | 0 | .200 | .200 | 0 | 0 | C-4 |
| 2 yrs. | 12 | 28 | 2 | 0 | 0 | 0 | 0.0 | 0 | 2 | 5 | 10 | 0 | .071 | .071 | 0 | 0 | C-12 |
| 2 yrs. | 12 | 28 | 2 | 0 | 0 | 0 | 0.0 | 0 | 2 | 5 | 10 | 0 | .071 | .071 | 0 | 0 | C-12 |

## George Gore

**GORE, GEORGE F.**
B. 1855, Hartland, Me.    D. Sept. 16, 1933, Utica, N. Y.    BL  TR  5'11"    195 lbs.

| | G | AB | H | 2B | 3B | HR | HR% | R | RBI | BB | SO | SB | BA | SA | AB | H | G by POS |
|---|---|---|---|---|---|---|---|---|---|---|---|---|---|---|---|---|---|
| 1879 CHI N | 63 | 266 | 70 | 17 | 4 | 0 | 0.0 | 43 | 32 | 8 | 30 | | .263 | .357 | 0 | 0 | OF-54, 1B-9 |
| 1880 | 77 | 322 | 116 | 23 | 2 | 2 | 0.6 | 70 | 47 | 21 | 10 | | **.360** | **.463** | 0 | 0 | OF-74, 1B-7 |
| 1881 | 73 | 309 | 92 | 18 | 9 | 1 | 0.3 | **86** | 44 | 27 | 23 | | .298 | .424 | 0 | 0 | OF-72, 3B-1, 1B-1 |
| 1882 | 84 | 367 | 117 | 15 | 7 | 3 | 0.8 | **99** | 51 | **29** | 19 | | .319 | .422 | 0 | 0 | OF-84 |
| 1883 | 92 | 392 | 131 | 30 | 9 | 2 | 0.5 | 105 | | 27 | 13 | | .334 | .472 | 0 | 0 | OF-92 |
| 1884 | 103 | 422 | 134 | 18 | 4 | 5 | 1.2 | 104 | | **61** | 26 | | .318 | .415 | 0 | 0 | OF-103 |
| 1885 | 109 | 441 | 138 | 21 | 13 | 5 | 1.1 | 115 | 51 | 68 | 25 | | .313 | .454 | 0 | 0 | OF-109 |
| 1886 | 118 | 444 | 135 | 20 | 12 | 6 | 1.4 | 150 | 63 | **102** | 30 | | .304 | .444 | 0 | 0 | OF-118 |
| 1887 NY N | 111 | 459 | 133 | 16 | 5 | 1 | 0.2 | 95 | 49 | 42 | 18 | 39 | .290 | .353 | 0 | 0 | OF-111 |
| 1888 | 64 | 254 | 56 | 4 | 4 | 2 | 0.8 | 37 | 17 | 30 | 31 | 11 | .220 | .291 | 0 | 0 | OF-64 |
| 1889 | 120 | 488 | 149 | 21 | 7 | 7 | 1.4 | 132 | 54 | 84 | 28 | 28 | .305 | .420 | 0 | 0 | OF-120 |
| 1890 NY P | 93 | 399 | 127 | 26 | 8 | 10 | 2.5 | 132 | 55 | 77 | 23 | 28 | .318 | .499 | 0 | 0 | OF-93 |
| 1891 NY N | 130 | 528 | 150 | 22 | 7 | 2 | 0.4 | 103 | 48 | 74 | 34 | 19 | .284 | .364 | 0 | 0 | OF-130 |
| 1892 2 teams | | NY | N (53G – .254) | | | STL | N (20G – .205) | | | | | | | | | | |
| " total | 73 | 266 | 64 | 11 | 3 | 0 | 0.0 | 56 | 15 | 67 | 22 | 22 | .241 | .305 | 0 | 0 | OF-73 |
| 14 yrs. | 1310 | 5357 | 1612 | 262 | 94 | 46 | 0.9 | 1327 | 526 | 717 | 332 | 147 | .301 | .411 | 0 | 0 | OF-1297, 1B-17, 3B-1 |
| 8 yrs. | 719 | 2963 | 933 | 162 | 60 | 24 | 0.8 | 772 | 288 | 343 | 176 | | .315 | .434 | 0 | 0 | OF-706, 1B-17, 3B-1 |
| | | | | | | | | | | | | | | **8th** | | | |

## John Goryl

**GORYL, JOHN ALBERT**
B. Oct. 21, 1933, Cumberland, R. I.
Manager 1980-81.    BR  TR  5'10"    175 lbs.

| | G | AB | H | 2B | 3B | HR | HR% | R | RBI | BB | SO | SB | BA | SA | AB | H | G by POS |
|---|---|---|---|---|---|---|---|---|---|---|---|---|---|---|---|---|---|
| 1957 CHI N | 9 | 38 | 8 | 2 | 0 | 0 | 0.0 | 7 | 1 | 5 | 9 | 0 | .211 | .263 | 0 | 0 | 3B-9 |
| 1958 | 83 | 219 | 53 | 9 | 3 | 4 | 1.8 | 27 | 14 | 27 | 34 | 0 | .242 | .365 | 10 | 3 | 3B-44, 2B-35 |
| 1959 | 25 | 48 | 9 | 3 | 1 | 1 | 2.1 | 1 | 6 | 5 | 3 | 1 | .188 | .354 | 8 | 1 | 2B-11, 3B-4 |
| 1962 MIN A | 37 | 26 | 5 | 0 | 1 | 2 | 7.7 | 6 | 2 | 2 | 6 | 0 | .192 | .500 | 19 | 3 | 2B-4, SS-1 |
| 1963 | 64 | 150 | 43 | 5 | 3 | 9 | 6.0 | 29 | 24 | 15 | 29 | 0 | .287 | .540 | 12 | 2 | 2B-34, 3B-11, SS-7 |
| 1964 | 58 | 114 | 16 | 0 | 2 | 0 | 0.0 | 9 | 1 | 10 | 25 | 1 | .140 | .175 | 22 | 4 | 2B-28, 3B-13 |
| 6 yrs. | 276 | 595 | 134 | 19 | 10 | 16 | 2.7 | 79 | 48 | 64 | 106 | 2 | .225 | .371 | 71 | 13 | 2B-112, 3B-81, SS-8 |
| 3 yrs. | 117 | 305 | 70 | 14 | 4 | 5 | 1.6 | 35 | 21 | 37 | 46 | 1 | .230 | .351 | 18 | 4 | 3B-57, 2B-46 |

## Billy Grabarkewitz

**GRABARKEWITZ, BILLY CORDELL**
B. Jan. 18, 1946, Lockhart, Tex.    BR  TR  5'10"    165 lbs.

| | G | AB | H | 2B | 3B | HR | HR% | R | RBI | BB | SO | SB | BA | SA | AB | H | G by POS |
|---|---|---|---|---|---|---|---|---|---|---|---|---|---|---|---|---|---|
| 1969 LA N | 34 | 65 | 6 | 1 | 1 | 0 | 0.0 | 4 | 5 | 4 | 19 | 1 | .092 | .138 | 3 | 0 | SS-18, 3B-6, 2B-3 |
| 1970 | 156 | 529 | 153 | 20 | 8 | 17 | 3.2 | 92 | 84 | 95 | 149 | 19 | .289 | .454 | 2 | 1 | 3B-97, SS-50, 2B-20 |
| 1971 | 44 | 71 | 16 | 5 | 0 | 0 | 0.0 | 9 | 6 | 19 | 16 | 1 | .225 | .296 | 11 | 3 | 2B-13, 3B-10, SS-1 |
| 1972 | 53 | 144 | 24 | 4 | 0 | 4 | 2.8 | 17 | 16 | 18 | 53 | 3 | .167 | .278 | 5 | 1 | 3B-24, 2B-19, SS-2 |
| 1973 2 teams | | CAL | A (61G – .163) | | | PHI | N (25G – .288) | | | | | | | | | | |
| " total | 86 | 195 | 40 | 8 | 1 | 5 | 2.6 | 39 | 16 | 40 | 45 | 5 | .205 | .333 | 16 | 6 | 2B-38, 3B-14, OF-2, SS-1 |
| 1974 2 teams | | PHI | N (34G – .133) | | | CHI | N (53G – .248) | | | | | | | | | | |
| " total | 87 | 155 | 35 | 3 | 2 | 2 | 1.3 | 28 | 14 | 26 | 38 | 4 | .226 | .310 | 14 | 2 | 2B-45, SS-7, 3B-7, OF-5 |
| 1975 OAK A | 6 | 2 | 0 | 0 | 0 | 0 | 0.0 | 0 | 0 | 0 | 1 | 0 | .000 | .000 | 2 | 0 | 2B-4, DH-1 |
| 7 yrs. | 466 | 1161 | 274 | 41 | 12 | 28 | 2.4 | 189 | 141 | 202 | 321 | 33 | .236 | .364 | 53 | 13 | 3B-158, 2B-142, SS-79, OF-7, DH-1 |
| 1 yr. | 53 | 125 | 31 | 3 | 2 | 1 | 0.8 | 21 | 12 | 21 | 28 | 1 | .248 | .328 | 0 | 0 | 2B-45, SS-7, 3B-6 |

## Earl Grace

**GRACE, ROBERT EARL**
B. Feb. 24, 1907, Barlow, Ky.    D. Dec. 22, 1980, Phoenix, Ariz.    BL  TR  6'    175 lbs.

| | G | AB | H | 2B | 3B | HR | HR% | R | RBI | BB | SO | SB | BA | SA | AB | H | G by POS |
|---|---|---|---|---|---|---|---|---|---|---|---|---|---|---|---|---|---|
| 1929 CHI N | 27 | 80 | 20 | 1 | 0 | 2 | 2.5 | 7 | 17 | 9 | 7 | 0 | .250 | .338 | 0 | 0 | C-27 |
| 1931 2 teams | | CHI | N (7G – .111) | | | PIT | N (47G – .280) | | | | | | | | | | |
| " total | 54 | 159 | 43 | 6 | 1 | 1 | 0.6 | 10 | 21 | 17 | 6 | 0 | .270 | .340 | 6 | 0 | C-47 |
| 1932 PIT N | 115 | 390 | 107 | 17 | 5 | 7 | 1.8 | 41 | 55 | 14 | 23 | 0 | .274 | .397 | 1 | 0 | C-114 |
| 1933 | 93 | 291 | 84 | 13 | 1 | 3 | 1.0 | 22 | 44 | 26 | 23 | 0 | .289 | .371 | 4 | 0 | C-88 |
| 1934 | 95 | 289 | 78 | 17 | 1 | 4 | 1.4 | 27 | 24 | 20 | 19 | 0 | .270 | .377 | 10 | 5 | C-83, 1B-1 |
| 1935 | 77 | 224 | 59 | 8 | 1 | 3 | 1.3 | 19 | 29 | 32 | 17 | 1 | .263 | .348 | 8 | 3 | C-69 |
| 1936 PHI N | 86 | 221 | 55 | 11 | 0 | 4 | 1.8 | 24 | 32 | 34 | 20 | 0 | .249 | .353 | 19 | 2 | C-65 |
| 1937 | 80 | 223 | 47 | 10 | 1 | 6 | 2.7 | 19 | 29 | 33 | 15 | 0 | .211 | .345 | 13 | 0 | C-64 |
| 8 yrs. | 627 | 1877 | 493 | 83 | 10 | 30 | 1.6 | 169 | 251 | 185 | 130 | 1 | .263 | .365 | 61 | 10 | C-557, 1B-1 |
| 2 yrs. | 34 | 89 | 21 | 1 | 0 | 2 | 2.2 | 9 | 18 | 13 | 8 | 0 | .236 | .315 | 4 | 0 | C-29 |

## Peaches Graham

**GRAHAM, GEORGE FREDERICK**
Father of Jack Graham.
B. Mar. 23, 1880, Aledo, Ill.    D. July 25, 1939, Long Beach, Calif.    BR  TR  5'9"    180 lbs.

| | G | AB | H | 2B | 3B | HR | HR% | R | RBI | BB | SO | SB | BA | SA | AB | H | G by POS |
|---|---|---|---|---|---|---|---|---|---|---|---|---|---|---|---|---|---|
| 1902 CLE A | 2 | 6 | 2 | 0 | 0 | 0 | 0.0 | 1 | | 1 | | 0 | .333 | .333 | 1 | 0 | 2B-1 |
| 1903 CHI N | 1 | 2 | 0 | 0 | 0 | 0 | 0.0 | 0 | 0 | 0 | | 0 | .000 | .000 | 0 | 0 | P-1 |
| 1908 BOS N | 75 | 215 | 59 | 5 | 0 | 0 | 0.0 | 22 | 22 | 23 | | 4 | .274 | .298 | 8 | 2 | C-62, 2B-5 |
| 1909 | 92 | 267 | 64 | 6 | 3 | 0 | 0.0 | 27 | 17 | 24 | | 7 | .240 | .285 | 10 | 1 | C-76, OF-6, SS-1, 3B-1 |
| 1910 | 110 | 291 | 82 | 13 | 2 | 0 | 0.0 | 31 | 21 | 33 | 15 | 5 | .282 | .340 | 20 | 7 | C-87, 3B-2, OF-1, 1B-1 |

| | G | AB | H | 2B | 3B | HR | HR % | R | RBI | BB | SO | SB | BA | SA | Pinch Hit AB | Pinch Hit H | G by POS |
|---|---|---|---|---|---|---|---|---|---|---|---|---|---|---|---|---|---|

## Peaches Graham continued

| | G | AB | H | 2B | 3B | HR | HR % | R | RBI | BB | SO | SB | BA | SA | P.H. AB | P.H. H | G by POS |
|---|---|---|---|---|---|---|---|---|---|---|---|---|---|---|---|---|---|
| 1911 2 teams | BOS N (33G – .273) | | | | | CHI N (36G – .239) | | | | | | | | | | | |
| " total | 69 | 159 | 41 | 9 | 1 | 0 | 0.0 | 13 | 20 | 25 | 13 | 4 | .258 | .327 | 13 | 3 | C-54 |
| 1912 PHI N | 24 | 59 | 17 | 1 | 0 | 1 | 1.7 | 6 | 4 | 8 | 5 | 1 | .288 | .356 | 2 | 2 | C-19 |
| 7 yrs. | 373 | 999 | 265 | 34 | 6 | 1 | 0.1 | 99 | 85 | 114 | 33 | 21 | .265 | .314 | 54 | 15 | C-298, OF-7, 2B-6, 3B-3, SS-1, 1B-1, P-1 |
| 2 yrs. | 37 | 73 | 17 | 3 | 0 | 0 | 0.0 | 6 | 8 | 11 | 8 | 2 | .233 | .274 | 8 | 2 | C-28, P-1 |

## Alex Grammas

**GRAMMAS, ALEXANDER PETER**  BR TR 6' 175 lbs.
B. Apr. 3, 1926, Birmingham, Ala.
Manager 1969, 1976-77.

| | G | AB | H | 2B | 3B | HR | HR % | R | RBI | BB | SO | SB | BA | SA | P.H. AB | P.H. H | G by POS |
|---|---|---|---|---|---|---|---|---|---|---|---|---|---|---|---|---|---|
| 1954 STL N | 142 | 401 | 106 | 17 | 4 | 2 | 0.5 | 57 | 29 | 40 | 29 | 6 | .264 | .342 | 0 | 0 | SS-142, 3B-1 |
| 1955 | 128 | 366 | 88 | 19 | 2 | 3 | 0.8 | 32 | 25 | 33 | 36 | 4 | .240 | .328 | 1 | 0 | SS-126 |
| 1956 2 teams | STL N (6G – .250) | | | | | CIN N (77G – .243) | | | | | | | | | | | |
| " total | 83 | 152 | 37 | 11 | 0 | 0 | 0.0 | 18 | 17 | 17 | 20 | 0 | .243 | .316 | 2 | 1 | 3B-58, SS-17, 2B-5 |
| 1957 CIN N | 73 | 99 | 30 | 4 | 0 | 0 | 0.0 | 14 | 8 | 10 | 6 | 1 | .303 | .343 | 2 | 0 | SS-42, 2B-20, 3B-9 |
| 1958 | 105 | 216 | 47 | 8 | 0 | 0 | 0.0 | 25 | 12 | 34 | 24 | 2 | .218 | .255 | 1 | 0 | SS-61, 3B-38, 2B-14 |
| 1959 STL N | 131 | 368 | 99 | 14 | 2 | 3 | 0.8 | 43 | 30 | 38 | 26 | 3 | .269 | .342 | 1 | 1 | SS-130 |
| 1960 | 102 | 196 | 48 | 4 | 1 | 4 | 2.0 | 20 | 17 | 12 | 15 | 0 | .245 | .337 | 7 | 2 | SS-40, 2B-38, 3B-13 |
| 1961 | 89 | 170 | 36 | 10 | 1 | 0 | 0.0 | 23 | 21 | 19 | 21 | 0 | .212 | .282 | 5 | 1 | SS-65, 2B-5, 3B-3 |
| 1962 2 teams | STL N (21G – .111) | | | | | CHI N (23G – .233) | | | | | | | | | | | |
| " total | 44 | 78 | 16 | 3 | 0 | 0 | 0.0 | 3 | 4 | 3 | 13 | 1 | .205 | .244 | 4 | 0 | SS-29, 2B-5, 3B-1 |
| 1963 CHI N | 16 | 27 | 5 | 0 | 0 | 0 | 0.0 | 1 | 0 | 0 | 3 | 0 | .185 | .185 | 3 | 0 | SS-13 |
| 10 yrs. | 913 | 2073 | 512 | 90 | 10 | 12 | 0.6 | 236 | 163 | 206 | 193 | 17 | .247 | .317 | 26 | 5 | SS-665, 3B-123, 2B-100 |
| 2 yrs. | 39 | 87 | 19 | 3 | 0 | 0 | 0.0 | 4 | 3 | 2 | 10 | 1 | .218 | .253 | 6 | 0 | SS-26, 2B-3, 3B-1 |

## Tom Grant

**GRANT, THOMAS RAYMOND**  BL TR 6'2" 185 lbs.
B. May 28, 1957, Worcester, Mass.

| | G | AB | H | 2B | 3B | HR | HR % | R | RBI | BB | SO | SB | BA | SA | P.H. AB | P.H. H | G by POS |
|---|---|---|---|---|---|---|---|---|---|---|---|---|---|---|---|---|---|
| 1983 CHI N | 16 | 20 | 3 | 1 | 0 | 0 | 0.0 | 2 | 3 | | 4 | 0 | .150 | .200 | 5 | 0 | OF-10 |

## George Grantham

**GRANTHAM, GEORGE FARLEY (Boots)**  BL TR 5'10" 170 lbs.
B. May 20, 1900, Galena, Kans.  D. Mar. 16, 1954, Kingman, Ariz.

| | G | AB | H | 2B | 3B | HR | HR % | R | RBI | BB | SO | SB | BA | SA | P.H. AB | P.H. H | G by POS |
|---|---|---|---|---|---|---|---|---|---|---|---|---|---|---|---|---|---|
| 1922 CHI N | 7 | 23 | 4 | 1 | 1 | 0 | 0.0 | 3 | 3 | 1 | 3 | 2 | .174 | .304 | 1 | 0 | 3B-5 |
| 1923 | 152 | 570 | 160 | 36 | 8 | 8 | 1.4 | 81 | 70 | 71 | 92 | 43 | .281 | .414 | 2 | 0 | 2B-150 |
| 1924 | 127 | 469 | 148 | 19 | 6 | 12 | 2.6 | 85 | 60 | 55 | 63 | 21 | .316 | .458 | 2 | 0 | 2B-118, 3B-6 |
| 1925 PIT N | 114 | 359 | 117 | 24 | 6 | 8 | 2.2 | 74 | 52 | 50 | 29 | 14 | .326 | .493 | 9 | 1 | 1B-102 |
| 1926 | 141 | 449 | 143 | 27 | 13 | 8 | 1.8 | 66 | 70 | 60 | 42 | 6 | .318 | .490 | 6 | 2 | 1B-132 |
| 1927 | 151 | 531 | 162 | 33 | 11 | 8 | 1.5 | 96 | 66 | 74 | 39 | 9 | .305 | .454 | 0 | 0 | 2B-124, 1B-29 |
| 1928 | 124 | 440 | 142 | 24 | 9 | 10 | 2.3 | 93 | 85 | 59 | 37 | 9 | .323 | .486 | 4 | 0 | 1B-119, 3B-1, 2B-1 |
| 1929 | 110 | 349 | 107 | 23 | 10 | 12 | 3.4 | 85 | 90 | 93 | 38 | 10 | .307 | .533 | 5 | 0 | 2B-76, OF-19, 1B-12 |
| 1930 | 146 | 552 | 179 | 34 | 14 | 18 | 3.3 | 120 | 99 | 81 | 66 | 5 | .324 | .534 | 1 | 0 | 2B-141, 1B-4 |
| 1931 | 127 | 465 | 142 | 26 | 6 | 10 | 2.2 | 91 | 46 | 71 | 50 | 5 | .305 | .452 | 4 | 0 | 1B-78, 2B-51 |
| 1932 CIN N | 126 | 493 | 144 | 29 | 6 | 6 | 1.2 | 81 | 39 | 56 | 40 | 4 | .292 | .412 | 0 | 0 | 2B-115, 1B-10 |
| 1933 | 87 | 260 | 53 | 14 | 3 | 4 | 1.5 | 32 | 28 | 38 | 21 | 4 | .204 | .327 | 7 | 2 | 2B-72, 1B-17 |
| 1934 NY N | 32 | 29 | 7 | 2 | 0 | 1 | 3.4 | 5 | 4 | 8 | 6 | 0 | .241 | .414 | 21 | 6 | 1B-4, 3B-2 |
| 13 yrs. | 1444 | 4989 | 1508 | 292 | 93 | 105 | 2.1 | 912 | 712 | 717 | 526 | 132 | .302 | .461 | 62 | 11 | 2B-848, 1B-507, OF-19, 3B-14 |
| 3 yrs. | 286 | 1062 | 312 | 56 | 15 | 20 | 1.9 | 169 | 133 | 127 | 158 | 66 | .294 | .431 | 5 | 0 | 2B-268, 3B-11 |

WORLD SERIES

| | G | AB | H | 2B | 3B | HR | HR % | R | RBI | BB | SO | SB | BA | SA | P.H. AB | P.H. H | G by POS |
|---|---|---|---|---|---|---|---|---|---|---|---|---|---|---|---|---|---|
| 1925 PIT N | 5 | 15 | 2 | 0 | 0 | 0 | 0.0 | 0 | 0 | 0 | 3 | 1 | .133 | .133 | 1 | 0 | 1B-4 |
| 1927 | 3 | 11 | 4 | 1 | 0 | 0 | 0.0 | 0 | 0 | 1 | 1 | 0 | .364 | .455 | 0 | 0 | 2B-3 |
| 2 yrs. | 8 | 26 | 6 | 1 | 0 | 0 | 0.0 | 0 | 0 | 1 | 4 | 1 | .231 | .269 | 1 | 0 | 1B-4, 2B-3 |

## Joe Graves

**GRAVES, JOSEPH EBENEZER**  BL TR 5'10" 160 lbs.
Brother of Sid Graves.
B. Feb. 27, 1906, Marblehead, Mass.  D. Dec. 22, 1980, Salem, Mass.

| | G | AB | H | 2B | 3B | HR | HR % | R | RBI | BB | SO | SB | BA | SA | P.H. AB | P.H. H | G by POS |
|---|---|---|---|---|---|---|---|---|---|---|---|---|---|---|---|---|---|
| 1926 CHI N | 2 | 5 | 0 | 0 | 0 | 0 | 0.0 | 0 | 0 | 0 | 1 | 0 | .000 | .000 | 0 | 0 | 3B-2 |

## Danny Green

**GREEN, EDWARD**  BL
B. Nov. 6, 1876, Burlington, N. J.  D. Nov. 9, 1914, Camden, N. J.

| | G | AB | H | 2B | 3B | HR | HR % | R | RBI | BB | SO | SB | BA | SA | P.H. AB | P.H. H | G by POS |
|---|---|---|---|---|---|---|---|---|---|---|---|---|---|---|---|---|---|
| 1898 CHI N | 47 | 188 | 59 | 4 | 3 | 4 | 2.1 | 26 | 27 | 7 | | 12 | .314 | .431 | 0 | 0 | OF-47 |
| 1899 | 117 | 475 | 140 | 12 | 11 | 6 | 1.3 | 90 | 56 | 35 | | 18 | .295 | .404 | 2 | 0 | OF-115 |
| 1900 | 103 | 389 | 116 | 21 | 5 | 5 | 1.3 | 63 | 49 | 17 | | 28 | .298 | .416 | 2 | 0 | OF-101 |
| 1901 | 133 | 537 | 168 | 16 | 12 | 6 | 1.1 | 82 | 60 | 40 | | 31 | .313 | .421 | 0 | 0 | OF-133 |
| 1902 CHI A | 129 | 481 | 150 | 16 | 11 | 0 | 0.0 | 77 | 62 | 53 | | 35 | .312 | .391 | 0 | 0 | OF-129 |
| 1903 | 135 | 499 | 154 | 26 | 7 | 6 | 1.2 | 75 | 62 | 47 | | 29 | .309 | .425 | 2 | 0 | OF-133 |
| 1904 | 147 | 536 | 142 | 16 | 10 | 2 | 0.4 | 83 | 62 | 63 | | 28 | .265 | .343 | 1 | 0 | OF-146 |
| 1905 | 112 | 379 | 92 | 13 | 6 | 0 | 0.0 | 56 | 44 | 53 | | 11 | .243 | .309 | 5 | 0 | OF-107 |
| 8 yrs. | 923 | 3484 | 1021 | 124 | 65 | 29 | 0.8 | 552 | 422 | 315 | | 192 | .293 | .391 | 12 | 2 | OF-911 |
| 4 yrs. | 400 | 1589 | 483 | 53 | 31 | 21 | 1.3 | 261 | 192 | 99 | | 89 | .304 | .416 | 4 | 1 | OF-396 |

## Clark Griffith

**GRIFFITH, CLARK CALVIN (The Old Fox)**  BR TR 5'6½" 156 lbs.
B. Nov. 20, 1869, Clear Creek, Mo.  D. Oct. 27, 1955, Washington, D. C.
Manager 1901-20.
Hall of Fame 1946.

| | G | AB | H | 2B | 3B | HR | HR % | R | RBI | BB | SO | SB | BA | SA | P.H. AB | P.H. H | G by POS |
|---|---|---|---|---|---|---|---|---|---|---|---|---|---|---|---|---|---|
| 1891 2 teams | STL AA (27G – .156) | | | | | BOS AA (10G – .174) | | | | | | | | | | | |
| " total | 37 | 100 | 16 | 2 | 1 | 2 | 2.0 | 17 | 11 | 14 | 20 | 3 | .160 | .260 | 1 | 0 | P-34, OF-3 |
| 1893 CHI N | 4 | 11 | 2 | 0 | 0 | 0 | 0.0 | 1 | 2 | 0 | 1 | 0 | .182 | .182 | 0 | 0 | P-4 |
| 1894 | 46 | 142 | 33 | 5 | 4 | 0 | 0.0 | 27 | 15 | 23 | 9 | 6 | .232 | .324 | 2 | 1 | P-36, OF-7, SS-1 |
| 1895 | 43 | 144 | 46 | 3 | 0 | 1 | 0.7 | 20 | 27 | 16 | 9 | 2 | .319 | .361 | 0 | 0 | P-42, OF-1 |

| | G | AB | H | 2B | 3B | HR | HR % | R | RBI | BB | SO | SB | BA | SA | Pinch Hit AB | Pinch Hit H | G by POS |
|---|---|---|---|---|---|---|---|---|---|---|---|---|---|---|---|---|---|

## Clark Griffith continued

| | G | AB | H | 2B | 3B | HR | HR% | R | RBI | BB | SO | SB | BA | SA | PH AB | PH H | G by POS |
|---|---|---|---|---|---|---|---|---|---|---|---|---|---|---|---|---|---|
| 1896 | 38 | 135 | 36 | 5 | 2 | 1 | 0.7 | 22 | 16 | 9 | 7 | 3 | .267 | .356 | 2 | 0 | P-36 |
| 1897 | 46 | 162 | 38 | 8 | 4 | 0 | 0.0 | 27 | 21 | 18 | | 2 | .235 | .333 | 0 | 0 | P-41, OF-2, SS-2, 3B-1, 1B-1 |
| 1898 | 38 | 122 | 20 | 2 | 3 | 0 | 0.0 | 15 | 15 | 13 | | 1 | .164 | .230 | 0 | 0 | P-38 |
| 1899 | 39 | 120 | 31 | 5 | 0 | 0 | 0.0 | 15 | 14 | 14 | | 2 | .258 | .300 | 0 | 0 | P-38, SS-1 |
| 1900 | 30 | 95 | 24 | 4 | 1 | 1 | 1.1 | 16 | 7 | 8 | | 2 | .253 | .347 | 0 | 0 | P-30 |
| 1901 CHI A | 35 | 89 | 27 | 3 | 1 | 2 | 2.2 | 21 | 14 | 23 | | 0 | .303 | .427 | 0 | 0 | P-35 |
| 1902 | 35 | 92 | 20 | 3 | 0 | 0 | 0.0 | 11 | 8 | 7 | | 0 | .217 | .250 | 4 | 0 | P-28, OF-3 |
| 1903 NY A | 25 | 69 | 11 | 4 | 0 | 1 | 1.4 | 5 | 7 | 11 | | 1 | .159 | .261 | 0 | 0 | P-25 |
| 1904 | 16 | 42 | 6 | 2 | 0 | 0 | 0.0 | 2 | 1 | 4 | | 0 | .143 | .190 | 0 | 0 | P-16 |
| 1905 | 26 | 32 | 7 | 1 | 1 | 0 | 0.0 | 2 | 5 | 3 | | 0 | .219 | .313 | 0 | 0 | P-25, OF-1 |
| 1906 | 17 | 18 | 2 | 0 | 0 | 0 | 0.0 | 0 | 1 | 3 | | 0 | .111 | .111 | 0 | 0 | P-17 |
| 1907 | 4 | 2 | 0 | 0 | 0 | 0 | 0.0 | 0 | 0 | 0 | | 0 | .000 | .000 | 0 | 0 | P-4 |
| 1909 CIN N | 1 | 2 | 0 | 0 | 0 | 0 | 0.0 | 0 | 0 | 0 | | 0 | .000 | .000 | 0 | 0 | P-1 |
| 1910 | 1 | 0 | 0 | 0 | 0 | 0 | – | 1 | 0 | 0 | 0 | 0 | – | – | 0 | 0 | |
| 1912 WAS A | 1 | 1 | 0 | 0 | 0 | 0 | 0.0 | 0 | 0 | 0 | | 0 | .000 | .000 | 0 | 0 | 2B-1, P-1 |
| 1913 | 1 | 1 | 1 | 1 | 0 | 0 | 0.0 | 0 | 1 | 0 | 0 | 0 | 1.000 | 2.000 | 0 | 0 | OF-1, P-1 |
| 1914 | 1 | 1 | 1 | 1 | 0 | 0 | 0.0 | 0 | 1 | 0 | 0 | 0 | 1.000 | 2.000 | 0 | 0 | P-1 |
| 21 yrs. | 484 | 1380 | 321 | 49 | 17 | 8 | 0.6 | 202 | 166 | 166 | 46 | 22 | .233 | .310 | 9 | 1 | P-453, OF-18, SS-4, 3B-1, 2B-1, 1B-1 |
| 8 yrs. | 284 | 931 | 230 | 32 | 14 | 3 | 0.3 | 143 | 117 | 101 | 26 | 18 | .247 | .321 | 4 | 1 | P-265, OF-10, SS-4, 3B-1, 1B-1 |

# Tommy Griffith

**GRIFFITH, THOMAS HERMAN**   BL TR 5'10"   175 lbs.
B. Oct. 26, 1889, Prospect, Ohio   D. Apr. 13, 1967, Cincinnati, Ohio

| | G | AB | H | 2B | 3B | HR | HR% | R | RBI | BB | SO | SB | BA | SA | PH AB | PH H | G by POS |
|---|---|---|---|---|---|---|---|---|---|---|---|---|---|---|---|---|---|
| 1913 BOS N | 37 | 127 | 32 | 4 | 1 | 1 | 0.8 | 16 | 12 | 9 | 8 | 1 | .252 | .323 | 1 | 0 | OF-35 |
| 1914 | 16 | 48 | 5 | 0 | 0 | 0 | 0.0 | 3 | 1 | 2 | 6 | 0 | .104 | .104 | 2 | 2 | OF-14 |
| 1915 CIN N | 160 | 583 | 179 | 31 | 16 | 4 | 0.7 | 59 | 85 | 41 | 34 | 6 | .307 | .436 | 0 | 0 | OF-160 |
| 1916 | 155 | 595 | 158 | 28 | 7 | 2 | 0.3 | 50 | 61 | 36 | 37 | 16 | .266 | .346 | 0 | 0 | OF-155 |
| 1917 | 115 | 363 | 98 | 18 | 7 | 1 | 0.3 | 45 | 45 | 19 | 23 | 5 | .270 | .366 | 13 | 4 | OF-100 |
| 1918 | 118 | 427 | 113 | 10 | 4 | 2 | 0.5 | 47 | 48 | 39 | 30 | 10 | .265 | .321 | 0 | 0 | OF-118 |
| 1919 BKN N | 125 | 484 | 136 | 18 | 4 | 6 | 1.2 | 65 | 57 | 23 | 32 | 8 | .281 | .372 | 0 | 0 | OF-125 |
| 1920 | 93 | 334 | 87 | 9 | 4 | 2 | 0.6 | 41 | 30 | 15 | 18 | 3 | .260 | .329 | 1 | 1 | OF-92 |
| 1921 | 129 | 455 | 142 | 21 | 6 | 12 | 2.6 | 66 | 71 | 36 | 13 | 3 | .312 | .464 | 4 | 1 | OF-124 |
| 1922 | 99 | 329 | 104 | 17 | 8 | 4 | 1.2 | 44 | 49 | 23 | 10 | 7 | .316 | .453 | 14 | 4 | OF-82 |
| 1923 | 131 | 481 | 141 | 21 | 9 | 8 | 1.7 | 70 | 66 | 50 | 19 | 8 | .293 | .424 | 2 | 0 | OF-128 |
| 1924 | 140 | 482 | 121 | 19 | 5 | 3 | 0.6 | 43 | 67 | 34 | 19 | 0 | .251 | .330 | 0 | 0 | OF-139 |
| 1925 2 teams | | | | BKN | N | (7G – | .000) | | | CHI | N | (76G – | .285) | | | | |
| " total | 83 | 239 | 67 | 12 | 1 | 7 | 2.9 | 40 | 27 | 24 | 13 | 3 | .280 | .427 | 16 | 3 | OF-62 |
| 13 yrs. | 1401 | 4947 | 1383 | 208 | 72 | 52 | 1.1 | 589 | 619 | 351 | 262 | 70 | .280 | .382 | 53 | 15 | OF-1334 |
| 1 yr. | 76 | 235 | 67 | 12 | 1 | 7 | 3.0 | 38 | 27 | 21 | 11 | 2 | .285 | .434 | 13 | 3 | OF-60 |

**WORLD SERIES**

| | G | AB | H | 2B | 3B | HR | HR% | R | RBI | BB | SO | SB | BA | SA | PH AB | PH H | G by POS |
|---|---|---|---|---|---|---|---|---|---|---|---|---|---|---|---|---|---|
| 1920 BKN N | 7 | 21 | 4 | 2 | 0 | 0 | 0.0 | 1 | 3 | 0 | 2 | 0 | .190 | .286 | 0 | 0 | OF-7 |

# Denver Grigsby

**GRIGSBY, DENVER CLARENCE**   BL TR 5'9"   155 lbs.
B. Mar. 24, 1901, Jackson, Ky.   D. Nov. 10, 1973, Sapulpa, Okla.

| | G | AB | H | 2B | 3B | HR | HR% | R | RBI | BB | SO | SB | BA | SA | PH AB | PH H | G by POS |
|---|---|---|---|---|---|---|---|---|---|---|---|---|---|---|---|---|---|
| 1923 CHI N | 24 | 72 | 21 | 5 | 2 | 0 | 0.0 | 8 | 5 | 7 | 5 | 1 | .292 | .417 | 1 | 1 | OF-22 |
| 1924 | 124 | 411 | 123 | 18 | 2 | 3 | 0.7 | 58 | 48 | 31 | 47 | 10 | .299 | .375 | 2 | 0 | OF-121 |
| 1925 | 51 | 137 | 35 | 5 | 0 | 0 | 0.0 | 20 | 20 | 19 | 12 | 1 | .255 | .292 | 8 | 1 | OF-39 |
| 3 yrs. | 199 | 620 | 179 | 28 | 4 | 3 | 0.5 | 86 | 73 | 57 | 64 | 12 | .289 | .361 | 11 | 1 | OF-182 |
| 3 yrs. | 199 | 620 | 179 | 28 | 4 | 3 | 0.5 | 86 | 73 | 57 | 64 | 12 | .289 | .361 | 11 | 1 | OF-182 |

# Ray Grimes

**GRIMES, OSCAR RAY, SR.**   BR TR 5'11"   168 lbs.
Father of Oscar Grimes.   Brother of Roy Grimes.
B. Sept. 11, 1893, Bergholz, Ohio   D. May 25, 1953, Minerva, Ohio

| | G | AB | H | 2B | 3B | HR | HR% | R | RBI | BB | SO | SB | BA | SA | PH AB | PH H | G by POS |
|---|---|---|---|---|---|---|---|---|---|---|---|---|---|---|---|---|---|
| 1920 BOS A | 1 | 4 | 1 | 0 | 0 | 0 | 0.0 | 1 | 0 | 1 | 0 | 0 | .250 | .250 | 0 | 0 | 1B-1 |
| 1921 CHI N | 147 | 530 | 170 | 38 | 6 | 6 | 1.1 | 91 | 79 | 70 | 55 | 5 | .321 | .449 | 0 | 0 | 1B-147 |
| 1922 | 138 | 509 | 180 | 45 | 12 | 14 | 2.8 | 99 | 99 | 75 | 33 | 7 | .354 | .572 | 0 | 0 | 1B-138 |
| 1923 | 64 | 216 | 71 | 7 | 2 | 2 | 0.9 | 32 | 36 | 24 | 17 | 5 | .329 | .407 | 2 | 0 | 1B-62 |
| 1924 | 51 | 177 | 53 | 6 | 5 | 5 | 2.8 | 33 | 34 | 28 | 15 | 4 | .299 | .475 | 1 | 0 | 1B-50 |
| 1926 PHI N | 32 | 101 | 30 | 5 | 0 | 0 | 0.0 | 13 | 15 | 6 | 13 | 0 | .297 | .347 | 3 | 0 | 1B-28 |
| 6 yrs. | 433 | 1537 | 505 | 101 | 25 | 27 | 1.8 | 269 | 263 | 204 | 133 | 21 | .329 | .480 | 6 | 0 | 1B-426 |
| 4 yrs. | 400 | 1432 | 474 | 96 | 25 | 27 | 1.9 | 255 | 248 | 197 | 120 | 21 | .331 | .490 | 3 | 0 | 1B-397 |

# Charlie Grimm

**GRIMM, CHARLES JOHN (Jolly Cholly)**   BL TL 5'11½" 173 lbs.
B. Aug. 28, 1898, St. Louis, Mo.   D. Nov. 15, 1983, Scottsdale, Ariz.
Manager 1932-38, 1944-49, 1952-56, 1960.

| | G | AB | H | 2B | 3B | HR | HR% | R | RBI | BB | SO | SB | BA | SA | PH AB | PH H | G by POS |
|---|---|---|---|---|---|---|---|---|---|---|---|---|---|---|---|---|---|
| 1916 PHI A | 12 | 22 | 2 | 0 | 0 | 0 | 0.0 | 0 | 0 | 2 | 4 | 0 | .091 | .091 | 4 | 0 | OF-7 |
| 1918 STL N | 50 | 141 | 31 | 7 | 0 | 0 | 0.0 | 11 | 12 | 6 | 15 | 2 | .220 | .270 | 5 | 0 | 1B-42, OF-2, 3B-1 |
| 1919 PIT N | 12 | 44 | 14 | 1 | 3 | 0 | 0.0 | 6 | 6 | 2 | 4 | 1 | .318 | .477 | 0 | 0 | 1B-11 |
| 1920 | 148 | 533 | 121 | 13 | 7 | 2 | 0.4 | 38 | 54 | 30 | 40 | 7 | .227 | .289 | 0 | 0 | 1B-148 |
| 1921 | 151 | 562 | 154 | 21 | 17 | 7 | 1.2 | 62 | 71 | 31 | 38 | 6 | .274 | .409 | 1 | 0 | 1B-150 |
| 1922 | 154 | 593 | 173 | 28 | 13 | 0 | 0.0 | 64 | 76 | 43 | 15 | 6 | .292 | .383 | 0 | 0 | 1B-154 |
| 1923 | 152 | 563 | 194 | 29 | 7 | 7 | 1.2 | 78 | 99 | 41 | 43 | 6 | .345 | .480 | 0 | 0 | 1B-152 |
| 1924 | 151 | 542 | 156 | 25 | 12 | 2 | 0.4 | 53 | 63 | 37 | 22 | 3 | .288 | .389 | 0 | 0 | 1B-151 |
| 1925 CHI N | 141 | 519 | 159 | 29 | 5 | 10 | 1.9 | 73 | 76 | 38 | 25 | 4 | .306 | .439 | 2 | 0 | 1B-139 |
| 1926 | 147 | 524 | 145 | 30 | 6 | 8 | 1.5 | 58 | 82 | 49 | 25 | 3 | .277 | .403 | 0 | 0 | 1B-147 |
| 1927 | 147 | 543 | 169 | 29 | 6 | 2 | 0.4 | 68 | 74 | 45 | 21 | 3 | .311 | .398 | 0 | 0 | 1B-147 |
| 1928 | 147 | 547 | 161 | 25 | 5 | 5 | 0.9 | 67 | 62 | 39 | 20 | 7 | .294 | .386 | 0 | 0 | 1B-147 |
| 1929 | 120 | 463 | 138 | 28 | 3 | 10 | 2.2 | 66 | 91 | 42 | 25 | 3 | .298 | .436 | 0 | 0 | 1B-120 |
| 1930 | 114 | 429 | 124 | 27 | 2 | 6 | 1.4 | 58 | 66 | 41 | 26 | 1 | .289 | .403 | 0 | 0 | 1B-113 |

| | G | AB | H | 2B | 3B | HR | HR % | R | RBI | BB | SO | SB | BA | SA | Pinch Hit AB | Pinch Hit H | G by POS |
|---|---|---|---|---|---|---|---|---|---|---|---|---|---|---|---|---|---|

## Charlie Grimm continued

| Year | G | AB | H | 2B | 3B | HR | HR% | R | RBI | BB | SO | SB | BA | SA | PH AB | PH H | G by POS |
|---|---|---|---|---|---|---|---|---|---|---|---|---|---|---|---|---|---|
| 1931 | 146 | 531 | 176 | 33 | 11 | 4 | 0.8 | 65 | 66 | 53 | 29 | 1 | .331 | .458 | 1 | 0 | 1B-144 |
| 1932 | 149 | 570 | 175 | 42 | 2 | 7 | 1.2 | 66 | 80 | 35 | 22 | 2 | .307 | .425 | 0 | 0 | 1B-149 |
| 1933 | 107 | 384 | 95 | 15 | 2 | 3 | 0.8 | 38 | 37 | 23 | 15 | 1 | .247 | .320 | 2 | 0 | 1B-104 |
| 1934 | 75 | 267 | 79 | 8 | 1 | 5 | 1.9 | 24 | 47 | 16 | 12 | 1 | .296 | .390 | 1 | 0 | 1B-74 |
| 1935 | 2 | 8 | 0 | 0 | 0 | 0 | 0.0 | 0 | 0 | 0 | 1 | 0 | .000 | .000 | 0 | 0 | 1B-2 |
| 1936 | 39 | 132 | 33 | 4 | 0 | 1 | 0.8 | 13 | 16 | 5 | 8 | 0 | .250 | .303 | 4 | 1 | 1B-35 |
| 20 yrs. | 2164 | 7917 | 2299 | 394 | 108 | 79 | 1.0 | 908 | 1078 | 578 | 410 | 57 | .290 | .397 | 21 | 1 | 1B-2129, OF-9, 3B-1 |
| 12 yrs. | 1334 | 4917 | 1454 | 270 10th | 43 | 61 | 1.2 | 596 | 697 | 386 | 229 | 26 | .296 | .405 | 11 | 1 | 1B-1321 |

WORLD SERIES

| Year | G | AB | H | 2B | 3B | HR | HR% | R | RBI | BB | SO | SB | BA | SA | PH AB | PH H | G by POS |
|---|---|---|---|---|---|---|---|---|---|---|---|---|---|---|---|---|---|
| 1929 CHI N | 5 | 18 | 7 | 0 | 0 | 1 | 5.6 | 2 | 4 | 1 | 2 | 0 | .389 | .556 | 0 | 0 | 1B-5 |
| 1932 | 4 | 15 | 5 | 2 | 0 | 0 | 0.0 | 2 | 1 | 2 | 2 | 0 | .333 | .467 | 0 | 0 | 1B-4 |
| 2 yrs. | 9 | 33 | 12 | 2 | 0 | 1 | 3.0 | 4 | 5 | 3 | 4 | 0 | .364 | .515 | 0 | 0 | 1B-9 |

## Greg Gross

**GROSS, GREGORY EUGENE**  
B. Aug. 1, 1952, York, Pa.  
BL TL 5'10" 160 lbs.

| Year | G | AB | H | 2B | 3B | HR | HR% | R | RBI | BB | SO | SB | BA | SA | PH AB | PH H | G by POS |
|---|---|---|---|---|---|---|---|---|---|---|---|---|---|---|---|---|---|
| 1973 HOU N | 14 | 39 | 9 | 2 | 1 | 0 | 0.0 | 5 | 1 | 4 | 4 | 2 | .231 | .333 | 4 | 0 | OF-9 |
| 1974 | 156 | 589 | 185 | 21 | 8 | 0 | 0.0 | 78 | 36 | 76 | 39 | 12 | .314 | .377 | 5 | 2 | OF-151 |
| 1975 | 132 | 483 | 142 | 14 | 10 | 0 | 0.0 | 67 | 41 | 63 | 37 | 2 | .294 | .364 | 8 | 1 | OF-121 |
| 1976 | 128 | 426 | 122 | 12 | 3 | 0 | 0.0 | 52 | 27 | 64 | 39 | 2 | .286 | .329 | 13 | 1 | OF-115 |
| 1977 CHI N | 115 | 239 | 77 | 10 | 4 | 5 | 2.1 | 43 | 32 | 33 | 19 | 0 | .322 | .460 | 39 | 10 | OF-71 |
| 1978 | 124 | 347 | 92 | 12 | 7 | 1 | 0.3 | 34 | 39 | 33 | 19 | 3 | .265 | .349 | 20 | 5 | OF-111 |
| 1979 PHI N | 111 | 174 | 58 | 6 | 3 | 0 | 0.0 | 21 | 15 | 29 | 5 | 5 | .333 | .402 | 51 | 14 | OF-73 |
| 1980 | 127 | 154 | 37 | 7 | 2 | 0 | 0.0 | 19 | 12 | 24 | 7 | 1 | .240 | .312 | 39 | 10 | OF-91, 1B-1 |
| 1981 | 83 | 102 | 23 | 6 | 1 | 0 | 0.0 | 14 | 7 | 15 | 5 | 2 | .225 | .304 | 39 | 6 | OF-55 |
| 1982 | 119 | 134 | 40 | 4 | 0 | 0 | 0.0 | 14 | 10 | 19 | 8 | 4 | .299 | .328 | 53 | 19 | OF-71 |
| 1983 | 136 | 245 | 74 | 12 | 3 | 0 | 0.0 | 25 | 29 | 34 | 16 | 3 | .302 | .376 | 33 | 7 | OF-110, 1B-1 |
| 1984 | 112 | 202 | 65 | 9 | 1 | 0 | 0.0 | 19 | 16 | 24 | 11 | 1 | .322 | .376 | 46 | 13 | OF-48, 1B-28 |
| 1985 | 93 | 169 | 44 | 5 | 2 | 0 | 0.0 | 21 | 14 | 32 | 9 | 1 | .260 | .314 | 41 | 7 | OF-52, 1B-8 |
| 13 yrs. | 1450 | 3303 | 968 | 120 | 45 | 6 | 0.2 | 412 | 279 | 450 | 218 | 38 | .293 | .362 | 391 | 95 | OF-1078, 1B-38 |
| 2 yrs. | 239 | 586 | 169 | 22 | 11 | 6 | 1.0 | 77 | 71 | 66 | 38 | 3 | .288 | .394 | 59 | 15 | OF-182 |

DIVISIONAL PLAYOFF SERIES

| Year | G | AB | H | 2B | 3B | HR | HR% | R | RBI | BB | SO | SB | BA | SA | PH AB | PH H | G by POS |
|---|---|---|---|---|---|---|---|---|---|---|---|---|---|---|---|---|---|
| 1981 PHI N | 4 | 4 | 0 | 0 | 0 | 0 | 0.0 | 0 | 0 | 0 | 0 | 0 | .000 | .000 | 3 | 0 | OF-2 |

LEAGUE CHAMPIONSHIP SERIES

| Year | G | AB | H | 2B | 3B | HR | HR% | R | RBI | BB | SO | SB | BA | SA | PH AB | PH H | G by POS |
|---|---|---|---|---|---|---|---|---|---|---|---|---|---|---|---|---|---|
| 1980 PHI N | 4 | 4 | 3 | 0 | 0 | 0 | 0.0 | 2 | 1 | 0 | 0 | 0 | .750 | .750 | 2 | 2 | OF-1 |
| 1983 | 4 | 5 | 0 | 0 | 0 | 0 | 0.0 | 1 | 0 | 2 | 2 | 0 | .000 | .000 | 0 | 0 | OF-3 |
| 2 yrs. | 8 | 9 | 3 | 0 | 0 | 0 | 0.0 | 3 | 1 | 2 | 2 | 0 | .333 | .333 | 2 | 2 | OF-4 |

WORLD SERIES

| Year | G | AB | H | 2B | 3B | HR | HR% | R | RBI | BB | SO | SB | BA | SA | PH AB | PH H | G by POS |
|---|---|---|---|---|---|---|---|---|---|---|---|---|---|---|---|---|---|
| 1980 PHI N | 4 | 2 | 0 | 0 | 0 | 0 | 0.0 | 0 | 0 | 0 | 0 | 0 | .000 | .000 | 1 | 0 | OF-3 |
| 1983 | 2 | 6 | 0 | 0 | 0 | 0 | 0.0 | 0 | 0 | 0 | 0 | 0 | .000 | .000 | 0 | 0 | OF-2 |
| 2 yrs. | 6 | 8 | 0 | 0 | 0 | 0 | 0.0 | 0 | 0 | 0 | 0 | 0 | .000 | .000 | 1 | 0 | OF-5 |

## Marv Gudat

**GUDAT, MARVIN JOHN**  
B. Aug. 27, 1905, Goliad, Tex.   D. Mar. 1, 1954, Los Angeles, Calif.  
BL TL 5'11" 176 lbs.

| Year | G | AB | H | 2B | 3B | HR | HR% | R | RBI | BB | SO | SB | BA | SA | PH AB | PH H | G by POS |
|---|---|---|---|---|---|---|---|---|---|---|---|---|---|---|---|---|---|
| 1929 CIN N | 9 | 10 | 2 | 0 | 0 | 0 | 0.0 | 0 | 0 | 0 | 0 | 0 | .200 | .200 | 2 | 0 | P-7 |
| 1932 CHI N | 60 | 94 | 24 | 4 | 1 | 1 | 1.1 | 15 | 15 | 16 | 10 | 0 | .255 | .351 | 30 | 10 | OF-14, 1B-8, P-1 |
| 2 yrs. | 69 | 104 | 26 | 4 | 1 | 1 | 1.0 | 15 | 15 | 16 | 10 | 0 | .250 | .337 | 32 | 10 | OF-14, 1B-8, P-8 |
| 1 yr. | 60 | 94 | 24 | 4 | 1 | 1 | 1.1 | 15 | 15 | 16 | 10 | 0 | .255 | .351 | 30 | 10 | OF-14, 1B-8, P-1 |

WORLD SERIES

| Year | G | AB | H | 2B | 3B | HR | HR% | R | RBI | BB | SO | SB | BA | SA | PH AB | PH H | G by POS |
|---|---|---|---|---|---|---|---|---|---|---|---|---|---|---|---|---|---|
| 1932 CHI N | 2 | 2 | 0 | 0 | 0 | 0 | 0.0 | 0 | 0 | 0 | 1 | 0 | .000 | .000 | 2 | 0 | |

## Ad Gumbert

**GUMBERT, ADDISON COURTNEY**  
Brother of Billy Gumbert.  
B. Oct. 10, 1868, Pittsburgh, Pa.   D. Apr. 23, 1925, Pittsburgh, Pa.  
BR TR 5'10" 200 lbs.

| Year | G | AB | H | 2B | 3B | HR | HR% | R | RBI | BB | SO | SB | BA | SA | PH AB | PH H | G by POS |
|---|---|---|---|---|---|---|---|---|---|---|---|---|---|---|---|---|---|
| 1888 CHI N | 7 | 24 | 8 | 0 | 1 | 0 | 0.0 | 3 | 2 | 0 | 2 | 0 | .333 | .417 | 0 | 0 | P-6, OF-2 |
| 1889 | 41 | 153 | 44 | 3 | 2 | 7 | 4.6 | 30 | 29 | 11 | 36 | 2 | .288 | .471 | 0 | 0 | P-31, OF-13 |
| 1890 BOS P | 44 | 145 | 35 | 7 | 1 | 3 | 2.1 | 23 | 20 | 18 | 26 | 5 | .241 | .366 | 0 | 0 | P-39, OF-7 |
| 1891 CHI N | 34 | 105 | 32 | 7 | 4 | 0 | 0.0 | 18 | 16 | 13 | 14 | 4 | .305 | .448 | 0 | 0 | P-32, OF-1, 1B-1 |
| 1892 | 52 | 178 | 42 | 1 | 2 | 1 | 0.6 | 18 | 18 | 8 | 14 | 5 | .236 | .281 | 0 | 0 | P-46, OF-7 |
| 1893 PIT N | 29 | 95 | 21 | 3 | 3 | 0 | 0.0 | 17 | 10 | 10 | 16 | 0 | .221 | .316 | 0 | 0 | P-22, OF-7 |
| 1894 | 38 | 113 | 33 | 4 | 5 | 1 | 0.9 | 18 | 19 | 6 | 20 | 1 | .292 | .442 | 1 | 0 | P-37 |
| 1895 BKN N | 34 | 97 | 35 | 6 | 0 | 2 | 2.1 | 21 | 13 | 7 | 10 | 0 | .361 | .485 | 0 | 0 | P-33, OF-1 |
| 1896 2 teams | BKN | N | (5G – | .182) | | PHI | N | (11G – | .265) | | | | | | | | |
| " total | 16 | 45 | 11 | 2 | 1 | 1 | 2.2 | 7 | 7 | 1 | 5 | 1 | .244 | .400 | 0 | 0 | P-16 |
| 9 yrs. | 295 | 955 | 261 | 33 | 19 | 15 | 1.6 | 155 | 124 | 80 | 153 | 18 | .273 | .395 | 1 | 0 | P-262, OF-38, 1B-1 |
| 4 yrs. | 134 | 460 | 126 | 11 | 9 | 8 | 1.7 | 69 | 55 | 38 | 76 | 11 | .274 | .389 | 0 | 0 | P-115, OF-23, 1B-1 |

## Frankie Gustine

**GUSTINE, FRANK WILLIAM**  
B. Feb. 20, 1920, Hoopeston, Ill.  
BR TR 6' 175 lbs.

| Year | G | AB | H | 2B | 3B | HR | HR% | R | RBI | BB | SO | SB | BA | SA | PH AB | PH H | G by POS |
|---|---|---|---|---|---|---|---|---|---|---|---|---|---|---|---|---|---|
| 1939 PIT N | 22 | 70 | 13 | 3 | 0 | 0 | 0.0 | 5 | 3 | 9 | 4 | 0 | .186 | .229 | 0 | 0 | 3B-22 |
| 1940 | 133 | 524 | 147 | 32 | 7 | 1 | 0.2 | 59 | 55 | 35 | 39 | 7 | .281 | .374 | 3 | 1 | 2B-130 |
| 1941 | 121 | 463 | 125 | 24 | 7 | 1 | 0.2 | 46 | 46 | 28 | 38 | 5 | .270 | .359 | 2 | 0 | 2B-104, 3B-15 |
| 1942 | 115 | 388 | 89 | 11 | 4 | 2 | 0.5 | 34 | 35 | 29 | 27 | 5 | .229 | .294 | 3 | 0 | 2B-108, SS-2, 3B-2, C-1 |
| 1943 | 112 | 414 | 120 | 21 | 3 | 0 | 0.0 | 40 | 43 | 32 | 36 | 12 | .290 | .355 | 5 | 1 | SS-68, 2B-40, 1B-1 |
| 1944 | 127 | 405 | 93 | 18 | 3 | 2 | 0.5 | 42 | 42 | 33 | 41 | 8 | .230 | .304 | 1 | 0 | SS-116, 2B-11, 3B-1 |
| 1945 | 128 | 478 | 134 | 27 | 5 | 2 | 0.4 | 67 | 66 | 37 | 33 | 8 | .280 | .370 | 1 | 0 | SS-104, 2B-29, C-1 |
| 1946 | 131 | 495 | 128 | 23 | 6 | 8 | 1.6 | 60 | 52 | 40 | 52 | 2 | .259 | .378 | 1 | 0 | 2B-113, SS-13, 3B-7 |
| 1947 | 156 | 616 | 183 | 30 | 6 | 9 | 1.5 | 102 | 67 | 63 | 65 | 5 | .297 | .409 | 0 | 0 | 3B-156 |
| 1948 | 131 | 449 | 120 | 19 | 2 | 9 | 2.0 | 68 | 42 | 42 | 62 | 5 | .267 | .379 | 10 | 2 | 3B-119 |
| 1949 CHI N | 76 | 261 | 59 | 13 | 4 | 4 | 1.5 | 29 | 27 | 18 | 22 | 3 | .226 | .352 | 5 | 0 | 3B-55, 2B-16 |

| | G | AB | H | 2B | 3B | HR | HR % | R | RBI | BB | SO | SB | BA | SA | Pinch Hit AB | Pinch Hit H | G by POS |
|---|---|---|---|---|---|---|---|---|---|---|---|---|---|---|---|---|---|

## Frankie Gustine continued

| | G | AB | H | 2B | 3B | HR | HR % | R | RBI | BB | SO | SB | BA | SA | PH AB | PH H | G by POS |
|---|---|---|---|---|---|---|---|---|---|---|---|---|---|---|---|---|---|
| 1950 STL A | 9 | 19 | 3 | 1 | 0 | 0 | 0.0 | 1 | 2 | 3 | 8 | 0 | .158 | .211 | 1 | 0 | 3B-6 |
| 12 yrs. | 1261 | 4582 | 1214 | 222 | 47 | 38 | 0.8 | 553 | 480 | 369 | 427 | 60 | .265 | .359 | 32 | 4 | 2B-551, 3B-383, SS-303, C-2, 1B-1 |
| 1 yr. | 76 | 261 | 59 | 13 | 4 | 4 | 1.5 | 29 | 27 | 18 | 22 | 3 | .226 | .352 | 5 | 0 | 3B-55, 2B-16 |

## Eddie Haas

**HAAS, GEORGE EDWIN**
B. May 26, 1935, Paducah, Ky.
Manager 1985.

BL  TR  5'11"  178 lbs.

| | G | AB | H | 2B | 3B | HR | HR % | R | RBI | BB | SO | SB | BA | SA | PH AB | PH H | G by POS |
|---|---|---|---|---|---|---|---|---|---|---|---|---|---|---|---|---|---|
| 1957 CHI N | 14 | 24 | 5 | 1 | 0 | 0 | 0.0 | 1 | 4 | 1 | 5 | 0 | .208 | .250 | 8 | 2 | OF-4 |
| 1958 MIL N | 9 | 14 | 5 | 0 | 0 | 0 | 0.0 | 2 | 1 | 2 | 1 | 0 | .357 | .357 | 4 | 3 | OF-3 |
| 1960 | 32 | 32 | 7 | 2 | 0 | 1 | 3.1 | 4 | 5 | 5 | 14 | 0 | .219 | .375 | 25 | 6 | OF-2 |
| 3 yrs. | 55 | 70 | 17 | 3 | 0 | 1 | 1.4 | 7 | 10 | 8 | 20 | 0 | .243 | .329 | 37 | 11 | OF-9 |
| 1 yr. | 14 | 24 | 5 | 1 | 0 | 0 | 0.0 | 1 | 4 | 1 | 5 | 0 | .208 | .250 | 8 | 2 | OF-4 |

## Stan Hack

**HACK, STANLEY CAMFIELD (Smiling Stan)**
B. Dec. 6, 1909, Sacramento, Calif.   D. Dec. 15, 1979, Dickson, Ill.
Manager 1954-56, 1958.

BL  TR  6'   170 lbs.

| | G | AB | H | 2B | 3B | HR | HR % | R | RBI | BB | SO | SB | BA | SA | PH AB | PH H | G by POS |
|---|---|---|---|---|---|---|---|---|---|---|---|---|---|---|---|---|---|
| 1932 CHI N | 72 | 178 | 42 | 5 | 6 | 2 | 1.1 | 32 | 19 | 17 | 16 | 5 | .236 | .365 | 14 | 2 | 3B-51 |
| 1933 | 20 | 60 | 21 | 3 | 1 | 1 | 1.7 | 10 | 2 | 8 | 3 | 4 | .350 | .483 | 0 | 0 | 3B-17 |
| 1934 | 111 | 402 | 116 | 16 | 6 | 1 | 0.2 | 54 | 21 | 45 | 42 | 11 | .289 | .366 | 2 | 0 | 3B-109 |
| 1935 | 124 | 427 | 133 | 23 | 9 | 4 | 0.9 | 75 | 64 | 65 | 17 | 14 | .311 | .436 | 5 | 2 | 3B-111, 1B-7 |
| 1936 | 149 | 561 | 167 | 27 | 4 | 6 | 1.1 | 102 | 78 | 89 | 39 | 17 | .298 | .392 | 0 | 0 | 3B-140, 1B-11 |
| 1937 | 154 | 582 | 173 | 27 | 6 | 2 | 0.3 | 106 | 63 | 83 | 42 | 16 | .297 | .375 | 1 | 0 | 3B-150, 1B-4 |
| 1938 | 152 | 609 | 195 | 34 | 11 | 4 | 0.7 | 109 | 67 | 94 | 39 | 16 | .320 | .432 | 0 | 0 | 3B-152 |
| 1939 | 156 | 641 | 191 | 28 | 6 | 8 | 1.2 | 112 | 56 | 65 | 35 | 17 | .298 | .398 | 0 | 0 | 3B-156 |
| 1940 | 149 | 603 | **191** | 38 | 6 | 8 | 1.3 | 101 | 40 | 75 | 24 | 21 | .317 | .439 | 0 | 0 | 3B-148, 1B-1 |
| 1941 | 151 | 586 | **186** | 33 | 5 | 7 | 1.2 | 111 | 45 | 99 | 40 | 10 | .317 | .427 | 0 | 0 | 3B-150, 1B-1 |
| 1942 | 140 | 553 | 166 | 36 | 3 | 6 | 1.1 | 91 | 39 | 94 | 40 | 9 | .300 | .409 | 0 | 0 | 3B-139 |
| 1943 | 144 | 533 | 154 | 24 | 4 | 3 | 0.6 | 78 | 35 | 82 | 27 | 5 | .289 | .366 | 7 | 0 | 3B-136 |
| 1944 | 98 | 383 | 108 | 16 | 1 | 3 | 0.8 | 65 | 32 | 53 | 21 | 5 | .282 | .352 | 4 | 1 | 3B-75, 1B-18 |
| 1945 | 150 | 597 | 193 | 29 | 7 | 2 | 0.3 | 110 | 43 | 99 | 30 | 12 | .323 | .405 | 0 | 0 | 3B-146, 1B-5 |
| 1946 | 92 | 323 | 92 | 13 | 4 | 0 | 0.0 | 55 | 26 | 83 | 32 | 3 | .285 | .350 | 2 | 0 | 3B-90 |
| 1947 | 76 | 240 | 65 | 11 | 2 | 0 | 0.0 | 28 | 12 | 41 | 19 | 0 | .271 | .333 | 10 | 2 | 3B-66 |
| 16 yrs. | 1938 | 7278 | 2193 | 363 | 81 | 57 | 0.8 | 1239 | 642 | 1092 | 466 | 165 | .301 | .397 | 45 | 7 | 3B-1836, 1B-47 |
| 16 yrs. | 1938 | 7278 | 2193 | 363 | 81 | 57 | 0.8 | 1239 | 642 | 1092 | 466 | 165 | .301 | .397 | 45 | 7 | 3B-1836, 1B-47 |
| | 6th | 5th | 4th | 5th | 9th | | | 5th | | 1st | | 6th | | | | | |

### WORLD SERIES

| | G | AB | H | 2B | 3B | HR | HR % | R | RBI | BB | SO | SB | BA | SA | PH AB | PH H | G by POS |
|---|---|---|---|---|---|---|---|---|---|---|---|---|---|---|---|---|---|
| 1932 CHI N | 1 | 0 | 0 | 0 | 0 | 0 | – | 0 | 0 | 0 | 0 | 0 | – | – | 0 | 0 | SS-1 |
| 1935 | 6 | 22 | 5 | 1 | 1 | 0 | 0.0 | 2 | 0 | 2 | 2 | 1 | .227 | .364 | 0 | 0 | 3B-4 |
| 1938 | 4 | 17 | 8 | 1 | 0 | 0 | 0.0 | 3 | 1 | 1 | 2 | 0 | .471 | .529 | 0 | 0 | 3B-7 |
| 1945 | 7 | 30 | 11 | 3 | 0 | 0 | 0.0 | 1 | 4 | 4 | 2 | 0 | .367 | .467 | 0 | 0 | 3B-7 |
| 4 yrs. | 18 | 69 | 24 | 5 | 1 | 0 | 0.0 | 6 | 5 | 7 | 6 | 1 | .348 | .449 | 0 | 0 | 3B-11, SS-1 |

## John Hairston

**HAIRSTON, JOHN LOUIS**
Son of Sam Hairston.   Brother of Jerry Hairston.
B. Aug. 29, 1945, Birmingham, Ala.

BR  TR  6'2"  200 lbs.

| | G | AB | H | 2B | 3B | HR | HR % | R | RBI | BB | SO | SB | BA | SA | PH AB | PH H | G by POS |
|---|---|---|---|---|---|---|---|---|---|---|---|---|---|---|---|---|---|
| 1969 CHI N | 3 | 4 | 1 | 0 | 0 | 0 | 0.0 | 0 | 0 | 0 | 2 | 0 | .250 | .250 | 1 | 1 | OF-1, C-1 |

## Jimmie Hall

**HALL, JIMMIE RANDOLPH**
B. Mar. 17, 1938, Mt. Holly, N. C.

BL  TR  6'   175 lbs.

| | G | AB | H | 2B | 3B | HR | HR % | R | RBI | BB | SO | SB | BA | SA | PH AB | PH H | G by POS |
|---|---|---|---|---|---|---|---|---|---|---|---|---|---|---|---|---|---|
| 1963 MIN A | 156 | 497 | 129 | 21 | 5 | 33 | 6.6 | 88 | 80 | 63 | 101 | 3 | .260 | .521 | 13 | 5 | OF-143 |
| 1964 | 149 | 510 | 144 | 20 | 3 | 25 | 4.9 | 61 | 75 | 44 | 112 | 5 | .282 | .480 | 10 | 3 | OF-137 |
| 1965 | 148 | 522 | 149 | 25 | 4 | 20 | 3.8 | 81 | 86 | 51 | 79 | 14 | .285 | .464 | 10 | 2 | OF-141 |
| 1966 | 120 | 356 | 85 | 7 | 4 | 20 | 5.6 | 52 | 47 | 33 | 66 | 1 | .239 | .449 | 21 | 4 | OF-103 |
| 1967 CAL A | 129 | 401 | 100 | 8 | 3 | 16 | 4.0 | 54 | 55 | 42 | 65 | 4 | .249 | .404 | 14 | 8 | OF-120 |
| 1968 2 teams | | CAL A (46G – .214) | | | | | | CLE A (58G – .198) | | | | | | | | | |
| " total | 104 | 237 | 49 | 7 | 0 | 2 | 0.8 | 19 | 16 | 26 | 38 | 2 | .207 | .262 | 35 | 6 | OF-68 |
| 1969 3 teams | | CLE A (4G – .000) | | | | | | NY A (80G – .236) | | | | CHI N (11G – .208) | | | | | |
| " total | 95 | 246 | 55 | 9 | 5 | 3 | 1.2 | 23 | 27 | 22 | 42 | 9 | .224 | .337 | 22 | 5 | OF-58, 1B-7 |
| 1970 2 teams | | CHI N (28G – .094) | | | | | | ATL N (39G – .213) | | | | | | | | | |
| " total | 67 | 79 | 13 | 3 | 0 | 2 | 2.5 | 9 | 5 | 6 | 26 | 0 | .165 | .278 | 29 | 4 | OF-36 |
| 8 yrs. | 968 | 2848 | 724 | 100 | 24 | 121 | 4.2 | 387 | 391 | 287 | 529 | 38 | .254 | .434 | 154 | 37 | OF-806, 1B-7 |
| 2 yrs. | 39 | 56 | 8 | 2 | 0 | 0 | 0.0 | 3 | 2 | 5 | 17 | 0 | .143 | .179 | 20 | 3 | OF-13 |

### WORLD SERIES

| | G | AB | H | 2B | 3B | HR | HR % | R | RBI | BB | SO | SB | BA | SA | PH AB | PH H | G by POS |
|---|---|---|---|---|---|---|---|---|---|---|---|---|---|---|---|---|---|
| 1965 MIN A | 2 | 7 | 1 | 0 | 0 | 0 | 0.0 | 0 | 0 | 1 | 5 | 0 | .143 | .143 | 0 | 0 | OF-2 |

## Mel Hall

**HALL, MELVIN, JR.**
B. Sept. 16, 1960, Lyons, N. Y.

BL  TL  6'   185 lbs.

| | G | AB | H | 2B | 3B | HR | HR % | R | RBI | BB | SO | SB | BA | SA | PH AB | PH H | G by POS |
|---|---|---|---|---|---|---|---|---|---|---|---|---|---|---|---|---|---|
| 1981 CHI N | 10 | 11 | 1 | 0 | 0 | 1 | 9.1 | 1 | 2 | 1 | 4 | 0 | .091 | .364 | 7 | 1 | OF-3 |
| 1982 | 24 | 80 | 21 | 3 | 2 | 0 | 0.0 | 6 | 4 | 5 | 17 | 0 | .263 | .350 | 1 | 0 | OF-22 |
| 1983 | 112 | 410 | 116 | 23 | 5 | 17 | 4.1 | 60 | 56 | 42 | 101 | 6 | .283 | .488 | 2 | 1 | OF-112 |
| 1984 2 teams | | CHI N (48G – .280) | | | | | | CLE A (83G – .257) | | | | | | | | | |
| " total | 131 | 407 | 108 | 24 | 4 | 11 | 2.7 | 68 | 52 | 47 | 78 | 3 | .265 | .425 | 14 | 3 | OF-115, DH-9 |
| 1985 CLE A | 23 | 66 | 21 | 6 | 0 | 0 | 0.0 | 7 | 12 | 8 | 12 | 0 | .318 | .409 | 6 | 2 | OF-15, DH-5 |
| 5 yrs. | 300 | 974 | 267 | 56 | 11 | 29 | 3.0 | 142 | 126 | 103 | 212 | 9 | .274 | .444 | 30 | 7 | OF-267, DH-14 |
| 4 yrs. | 194 | 651 | 180 | 37 | 10 | 22 | 3.4 | 92 | 84 | 60 | 145 | 8 | .276 | .465 | 14 | 4 | OF-183 |

## Jimmy Hallinan

**HALLINAN, JAMES H.**
B. May 27, 1849, Ireland   D. Oct. 28, 1879, Chicago, Ill.

BL  TL  5'9"  172 lbs.

| | G | AB | H | 2B | 3B | HR | HR % | R | RBI | BB | SO | SB | BA | SA | PH AB | PH H | G by POS |
|---|---|---|---|---|---|---|---|---|---|---|---|---|---|---|---|---|---|
| 1876 NY N | 54 | 240 | 67 | 7 | 6 | 2 | 0.8 | 45 | 36 | 2 | 4 | | .279 | .383 | 0 | 0 | SS-50, 2B-4, OF-2 |

| | G | AB | H | 2B | 3B | HR | HR % | R | RBI | BB | SO | SB | BA | SA | Pinch Hit AB | Pinch Hit H | G by POS |
|---|---|---|---|---|---|---|---|---|---|---|---|---|---|---|---|---|---|

## Jimmy Hallinan continued

| | | G | AB | H | 2B | 3B | HR | HR% | R | RBI | BB | SO | SB | BA | SA | PH AB | PH H | G by POS |
|---|---|---|---|---|---|---|---|---|---|---|---|---|---|---|---|---|---|---|
| 1877 | 2 teams | **CIN N** (16G – .370) | | | | | **CHI N** (19G – .281) | | | | | | | | | | | |
| " | total | 35 | 162 | 52 | 5 | 2 | 0 | 0.0 | 35 | 18 | 5 | 3 | | .321 | .377 | 0 | 0 | OF-19, 2B-16 |
| 1878 | 2 teams | **CHI N** (16G – .284) | | | | | **IND N** (3G – .250) | | | | | | | | | | | |
| " | total | 19 | 79 | 22 | 5 | 0 | 0 | 0.0 | 14 | 3 | 5 | 8 | | .278 | .342 | 0 | 0 | OF-14, 2B-5 |
| | 3 yrs. | 108 | 481 | 141 | 17 | 8 | 2 | 0.4 | 94 | 57 | 12 | 15 | | .293 | .374 | 0 | 0 | SS-50, OF-35, 2B-25 |
| | 2 yrs. | 35 | 156 | 44 | 7 | 1 | 0 | 0.0 | 31 | 13 | 9 | 8 | | .282 | .340 | 0 | 0 | OF-30, 2B-5 |

## Fred Haney

**HANEY, FRED GIRARD (Pudge)**     BR TR 5'6"   170 lbs.
B. Apr. 25, 1898, Albuquerque, N. M.    D. Nov. 9, 1977, Beverly Hills, Calif.
Manager 1939-41, 1953-59.

| | | G | AB | H | 2B | 3B | HR | HR% | R | RBI | BB | SO | SB | BA | SA | PH AB | PH H | G by POS |
|---|---|---|---|---|---|---|---|---|---|---|---|---|---|---|---|---|---|---|
| 1922 | DET A | 81 | 213 | 75 | 7 | 4 | 0 | 0.0 | 41 | 25 | 32 | 14 | 3 | .352 | .423 | 9 | 3 | 3B-42, 1B-11, SS-2 |
| 1923 | | 142 | 503 | 142 | 13 | 4 | 4 | 0.8 | 85 | 67 | 45 | 23 | 12 | .282 | .348 | 0 | 0 | 2B-69, 3B-55, SS-16 |
| 1924 | | 86 | 256 | 79 | 11 | 1 | 1 | 0.4 | 54 | 30 | 39 | 13 | 7 | .309 | .371 | 13 | 4 | 3B-59, SS-4, 2B-3 |
| 1925 | | 114 | 398 | 111 | 15 | 3 | 0 | 0.0 | 84 | 40 | 66 | 29 | 11 | .279 | .332 | 5 | 1 | 3B-107 |
| 1926 | BOS A | 138 | 462 | 102 | 15 | 7 | 0 | 0.0 | 47 | 52 | 74 | 28 | 13 | .221 | .284 | 1 | 0 | 3B-137 |
| 1927 | 2 teams | **BOS A** (47G – .276) | | | | | **CHI N** (4G – .000) | | | | | | | | | | | |
| " | total | 51 | 119 | 32 | 4 | 1 | 3 | 2.5 | 23 | 12 | 25 | 14 | 4 | .269 | .395 | 14 | 4 | 3B-34, OF-1 |
| 1929 | STL N | 10 | 26 | 3 | 1 | 1 | 0 | 0.0 | 4 | 2 | 1 | 2 | 0 | .115 | .231 | 2 | 1 | 3B-6 |
| | 7 yrs. | 622 | 1977 | 544 | 66 | 21 | 8 | 0.4 | 338 | 228 | 282 | 123 | 50 | .275 | .342 | 44 | 13 | 3B-440, 2B-72, SS-22, 1B-11, OF-1 |
| | 1 yr. | 4 | 3 | 0 | 0 | 0 | 0 | 0.0 | 0 | 0 | 0 | 0 | 0 | .000 | .000 | 3 | 0 | |

## Frank Hankinson

**HANKINSON, FRANK EDWARD**     BR TR 5'11"   168 lbs.
B. Apr. 29, 1856, New York, N. Y.    D. Apr. 5, 1911, Palisades Park, N. J.

| | | G | AB | H | 2B | 3B | HR | HR% | R | RBI | BB | SO | SB | BA | SA | PH AB | PH H | G by POS |
|---|---|---|---|---|---|---|---|---|---|---|---|---|---|---|---|---|---|---|
| 1878 | CHI N | 58 | 240 | 64 | 8 | 3 | 1 | 0.4 | 38 | 27 | 5 | 36 | | .267 | .338 | 0 | 0 | 3B-57, P-1 |
| 1879 | | 44 | 171 | 31 | 4 | 0 | 0 | 0.0 | 14 | 8 | 2 | 14 | | .181 | .205 | 0 | 0 | P-26, OF-14, 3B-5 |
| 1880 | CLE N | 69 | 263 | 55 | 7 | 4 | 1 | 0.4 | 32 | | 1 | 23 | | .209 | .278 | 0 | 0 | 3B-56, OF-12, P-4 |
| 1881 | TRO N | 85 | 321 | 62 | 15 | 0 | 1 | 0.3 | 34 | 19 | 10 | 41 | | .193 | .249 | 0 | 0 | 3B-84, SS-1 |
| 1883 | NY N | 94 | 337 | 74 | 13 | 6 | 2 | 0.6 | 40 | | 19 | 38 | | .220 | .312 | 0 | 0 | 3B-93, OF-1 |
| 1884 | | 105 | 389 | 90 | 16 | 7 | 2 | 0.5 | 44 | | 23 | 59 | | .231 | .324 | 0 | 0 | 3B-105, OF-1 |
| 1885 | NY AA | 94 | 362 | 81 | 12 | 2 | 2 | 0.6 | 43 | | 12 | | | .224 | .285 | 0 | 0 | 3B-94, P-1 |
| 1886 | | 136 | 522 | 126 | 14 | 5 | 2 | 0.4 | 66 | | 49 | | 19 | .241 | .299 | 0 | 0 | 3B-136 |
| 1887 | | 127 | 512 | 137 | 29 | 11 | 1 | 0.2 | 79 | | 38 | | | .268 | .373 | 0 | 0 | 3B-127 |
| 1888 | KC AA | 37 | 155 | 27 | 4 | 1 | 1 | 0.6 | 20 | 20 | 11 | | 2 | .174 | .232 | 0 | 0 | 2B-13, SS-9, OF-7, 3B-7, 1B-2 |
| | 10 yrs. | 849 | 3272 | 747 | 122 | 39 | 13 | 0.4 | 410 | 74 | 170 | 211 | 21 | .228 | .301 | 0 | 0 | 3B-764, OF-35, P-32, 2B-13, SS-10, 1B-2 |
| | 2 yrs. | 102 | 411 | 95 | 12 | 3 | 1 | 0.2 | 52 | 35 | 7 | 50 | | .231 | .282 | 0 | 0 | 3B-62, P-27, OF-14 |

## Bill Hanlon

**HANLON, WILLIAM HENRY (Big Bill)**
B. Mar. 16, 1865, Sacramento, Calif.    D. Mar. 18, 1951, Sacramento, Calif.

| | | G | AB | H | 2B | 3B | HR | HR% | R | RBI | BB | SO | SB | BA | SA | PH AB | PH H | G by POS |
|---|---|---|---|---|---|---|---|---|---|---|---|---|---|---|---|---|---|---|
| 1903 | CHI N | 8 | 21 | 2 | 0 | 0 | 0 | 0.0 | 4 | 2 | 6 | | 1 | .095 | .095 | 0 | 0 | 1B-8 |

## Bill Harbidge

**HARBIDGE, WILLIAM ARTHUR**     BL TL   162 lbs.
B. Mar. 29, 1855, Philadelphia, Pa.    D. Mar. 17, 1924, Philadelphia, Pa.

| | | G | AB | H | 2B | 3B | HR | HR% | R | RBI | BB | SO | SB | BA | SA | PH AB | PH H | G by POS |
|---|---|---|---|---|---|---|---|---|---|---|---|---|---|---|---|---|---|---|
| 1876 | HAR N | 30 | 106 | 23 | 2 | 1 | 0 | 0.0 | 11 | 6 | 3 | 2 | | .217 | .255 | 0 | 0 | C-24, OF-6, 1B-2 |
| 1877 | | 41 | 167 | 37 | 5 | 2 | 0 | 0.0 | 18 | 6 | 3 | 6 | | .222 | .275 | 0 | 0 | C-32, OF-5, 2B-4, 3B-1 |
| 1878 | CHI N | 54 | 240 | 71 | 12 | 0 | 0 | 0.0 | 32 | 37 | 6 | 13 | | .296 | .346 | 0 | 0 | C-50, OF-8 |
| 1879 | | 4 | 18 | 2 | 0 | 0 | 0 | 0.0 | 2 | 1 | 0 | 5 | | .111 | .111 | 0 | 0 | OF-4 |
| 1880 | TRO N | 9 | 27 | 10 | 0 | 1 | 0 | 0.0 | 3 | | 0 | | | .370 | .444 | 0 | 0 | C-9, OF-1 |
| 1882 | | 32 | 123 | 23 | 1 | 1 | 0 | 0.0 | 11 | 13 | 10 | 17 | | .187 | .211 | 0 | 0 | OF-23, 1B-6, C-3 |
| 1883 | PHI N | 73 | 280 | 62 | 12 | 3 | 0 | 0.0 | 32 | | 24 | 20 | | .221 | .286 | 0 | 0 | OF-44, SS-11, 2B-9, C-7, 3B-5 |
| 1884 | CIN U | 82 | 341 | 95 | 12 | 5 | 2 | 0.6 | 59 | | 25 | | | .279 | .361 | 0 | 0 | OF-80, SS-3, 1B-2 |
| | 8 yrs. | 325 | 1302 | 323 | 44 | 13 | 2 | 0.2 | 168 | 65 | 71 | 66 | | .248 | .306 | 0 | 0 | OF-171, C-125, SS-14, 2B-13, 1B-10, 3B-6 |
| | 2 yrs. | 58 | 258 | 73 | 12 | 0 | 0 | 0.0 | 34 | 38 | 6 | 18 | | .283 | .329 | 0 | 0 | C-50, OF-12 |

## Lew Hardie

**HARDIE, LOUIS W.**     5'11"   180 lbs.
B. Aug. 24, 1864, New York, N. Y.    D. Mar. 5, 1929, Oakland, Calif.

| | | G | AB | H | 2B | 3B | HR | HR% | R | RBI | BB | SO | SB | BA | SA | PH AB | PH H | G by POS |
|---|---|---|---|---|---|---|---|---|---|---|---|---|---|---|---|---|---|---|
| 1884 | PHI N | 3 | 8 | 3 | 2 | 0 | 0 | 0.0 | 4 | | 0 | 2 | | .375 | .625 | 0 | 0 | C-3 |
| 1886 | CHI N | 16 | 51 | 9 | 0 | 0 | 0 | 0.0 | 4 | 3 | 4 | 10 | | .176 | .176 | 0 | 0 | C-13, OF-2, 3B-1 |
| 1890 | BOS N | 47 | 185 | 42 | 8 | 0 | 3 | 1.6 | 17 | 17 | 18 | 36 | 4 | .227 | .319 | 0 | 0 | C-25, OF-15, 3B-7, SS-1, 1B-1 |
| 1891 | BAL AA | 15 | 56 | 13 | 0 | 3 | 0 | 0.0 | 7 | 1 | 8 | 8 | 3 | .232 | .339 | 0 | 0 | OF-15 |
| | 4 yrs. | 81 | 300 | 67 | 10 | 3 | 3 | 1.0 | 28 | 20 | 30 | 56 | 7 | .223 | .307 | 0 | 0 | C-41, OF-32, 3B-8, SS-1, 1B-1 |
| | 1 yr. | 16 | 51 | 9 | 0 | 0 | 0 | 0.0 | 4 | 3 | 4 | 10 | | .176 | .176 | 0 | 0 | C-13, OF-2, 3B-1 |

## Bud Hardin

**HARDIN, WILLIAM EDGAR**     BR TR 5'10"   165 lbs.
B. June 14, 1922, Shelby, N. C.

| | | G | AB | H | 2B | 3B | HR | HR% | R | RBI | BB | SO | SB | BA | SA | PH AB | PH H | G by POS |
|---|---|---|---|---|---|---|---|---|---|---|---|---|---|---|---|---|---|---|
| 1952 | CHI N | 3 | 7 | 1 | 0 | 0 | 0 | 0.0 | 1 | 0 | 0 | 0 | 0 | .143 | .143 | 1 | 0 | SS-2, 2B-1 |

## Jack Hardy

**HARDY, JOHN DOOLITTLE**     BR TR 6'   185 lbs.
B. June 23, 1877, Cleveland, Ohio    D. Oct. 20, 1921, Cleveland, Ohio

| | | G | AB | H | 2B | 3B | HR | HR% | R | RBI | BB | SO | SB | BA | SA | PH AB | PH H | G by POS |
|---|---|---|---|---|---|---|---|---|---|---|---|---|---|---|---|---|---|---|
| 1903 | CLE A | 5 | 19 | 3 | 1 | 0 | 0 | 0.0 | 1 | 1 | 1 | | 1 | .158 | .211 | 0 | 0 | OF-5 |
| 1907 | CHI N | 1 | 4 | 1 | 0 | 0 | 0 | 0.0 | 1 | | 0 | | 0 | .250 | .250 | 0 | 0 | C-1 |
| 1909 | WAS A | 10 | 24 | 4 | 0 | 0 | 0 | 0.0 | 3 | 4 | 1 | | 0 | .167 | .167 | 0 | 0 | C-9, 2B-1 |

| | G | AB | H | 2B | 3B | HR | HR % | R | RBI | BB | SO | SB | BA | SA | Pinch Hit AB | Pinch Hit H | G by POS |
|---|---|---|---|---|---|---|---|---|---|---|---|---|---|---|---|---|---|

# Jack Hardy continued

| | G | AB | H | 2B | 3B | HR | HR% | R | RBI | BB | SO | SB | BA | SA | AB | H | G by POS |
|---|---|---|---|---|---|---|---|---|---|---|---|---|---|---|---|---|---|
| 1910 | 7 | 8 | 2 | 0 | 0 | 0 | 0.0 | 1 | 0 | 0 | | 0 | .250 | .250 | 2 | 0 | C-4, OF-1 |
| 4 yrs. | 23 | 55 | 10 | 1 | 0 | 0 | 0.0 | 5 | 5 | 2 | | 1 | .182 | .200 | 2 | 0 | C-14, OF-6, 2B-1 |
| 1 yr. | 1 | 4 | 1 | 0 | 0 | 0 | 0.0 | 0 | 0 | 0 | | 0 | .250 | .250 | 0 | 0 | C-1 |

# Bubbles Hargrave

**HARGRAVE, EUGENE FRANKLIN**                                    BR  TR  5'10½" 174 lbs.
Brother of Pinky Hargrave.
B. July 15, 1892, New Haven, Ind.    D. Feb. 23, 1969, Cincinnati, Ohio

| | G | AB | H | 2B | 3B | HR | HR% | R | RBI | BB | SO | SB | BA | SA | AB | H | G by POS |
|---|---|---|---|---|---|---|---|---|---|---|---|---|---|---|---|---|---|
| 1913 CHI N | 3 | 3 | 1 | 0 | 0 | 0 | 0.0 | 0 | 1 | 0 | 0 | 0 | .333 | .333 | 1 | 0 | C-2 |
| 1914 | 23 | 36 | 8 | 2 | 0 | 0 | 0.0 | 3 | 2 | 0 | 4 | 2 | .222 | .278 | 7 | 1 | C-16 |
| 1915 | 15 | 19 | 3 | 0 | 1 | 0 | 0.0 | 2 | 2 | 1 | 5 | 0 | .158 | .263 | 6 | 1 | C-9 |
| 1921 CIN N | 93 | 263 | 76 | 17 | 8 | 1 | 0.4 | 28 | 38 | 12 | 15 | 4 | .289 | .426 | 19 | 3 | C-73 |
| 1922 | 98 | 320 | 101 | 22 | 10 | 7 | 2.2 | 49 | 57 | 26 | 18 | 7 | .316 | .513 | 10 | 0 | C-87 |
| 1923 | 118 | 378 | 126 | 23 | 9 | 10 | 2.6 | 54 | 78 | 44 | 22 | 4 | .333 | .521 | 7 | 1 | C-109 |
| 1924 | 98 | 312 | 94 | 19 | 10 | 3 | 1.0 | 42 | 33 | 30 | 20 | 2 | .301 | .455 | 6 | 2 | C-91 |
| 1925 | 87 | 273 | 82 | 13 | 6 | 2 | 0.7 | 28 | 33 | 25 | 23 | 4 | .300 | .414 | 3 | 0 | C-84 |
| 1926 | 105 | 326 | 115 | 22 | 8 | 6 | 1.8 | 42 | 62 | 25 | 17 | 2 | .353 | .525 | 11 | 3 | C-93 |
| 1927 | 102 | 305 | 94 | 18 | 3 | 0 | 0.0 | 36 | 35 | 31 | 18 | 0 | .308 | .387 | 9 | 1 | C-92 |
| 1928 | 65 | 190 | 56 | 12 | 3 | 0 | 0.0 | 19 | 23 | 13 | 14 | 4 | .295 | .389 | 6 | 2 | C-57 |
| 1930 NY A | 45 | 108 | 30 | 7 | 0 | 0 | 0.0 | 11 | 12 | 10 | 9 | 0 | .278 | .343 | 11 | 0 | C-34 |
| 12 yrs. | 852 | 2533 | 786 | 155 | 58 | 29 | 1.1 | 314 | 376 | 217 | 165 | 29 | .310 | .452 | 96 | 14 | C-747 |
| 3 yrs. | 41 | 58 | 12 | 2 | 1 | 0 | 0.0 | 5 | 5 | 1 | 9 | 2 | .207 | .276 | 14 | 2 | C-27 |

# Dick Harley

**HARLEY, RICHARD JOSEPH**                                    BL  TR  5'10½" 150 lbs.
B. Sept. 25, 1872, Blue Bell, Pa.    D. Apr. 3, 1952, Philadelphia, Pa.

| | G | AB | H | 2B | 3B | HR | HR% | R | RBI | BB | SO | SB | BA | SA | AB | H | G by POS |
|---|---|---|---|---|---|---|---|---|---|---|---|---|---|---|---|---|---|
| 1897 STL N | 89 | 330 | 96 | 6 | 4 | 3 | 0.9 | 43 | 35 | 36 | | 23 | .291 | .361 | 0 | 0 | OF-89 |
| 1898 | 142 | 549 | 135 | 6 | 5 | 0 | 0.0 | 74 | 42 | 34 | | 13 | .246 | .275 | 1 | 1 | OF-141 |
| 1899 CLE N | 142 | 567 | 142 | 15 | 7 | 1 | 0.2 | 70 | 50 | 40 | | 15 | .250 | .307 | 0 | 0 | OF-143 |
| 1900 CIN N | 5 | 21 | 9 | 1 | 0 | 0 | 0.0 | 2 | 5 | 1 | | 4 | .429 | .476 | 0 | 0 | OF-5 |
| 1901 | 133 | 535 | 146 | 13 | 2 | 4 | 0.7 | 69 | 27 | 31 | | 37 | .273 | .327 | 0 | 0 | OF-133 |
| 1902 DET A | 125 | 491 | 138 | 9 | 8 | 2 | 0.4 | 59 | 44 | 36 | | 20 | .281 | .344 | 0 | 0 | OF-125 |
| 1903 CHI N | 104 | 386 | 89 | 9 | 1 | 0 | 0.0 | 72 | 33 | 45 | | 27 | .231 | .259 | 2 | 2 | OF-103 |
| 7 yrs. | 740 | 2879 | 755 | 59 | 27 | 10 | 0.3 | 389 | 236 | 223 | | 139 | .262 | .312 | 3 | 3 | OF-739 |
| 1 yr. | 104 | 386 | 89 | 9 | 1 | 0 | 0.0 | 72 | 33 | 45 | | 27 | .231 | .259 | 2 | 2 | OF-103 |

# Vic Harris

**HARRIS, VICTOR LANIER**                                    BB  TR  5'11"  165 lbs.
B. Mar. 27, 1950, Los Angeles, Calif.

| | G | AB | H | 2B | 3B | HR | HR% | R | RBI | BB | SO | SB | BA | SA | AB | H | G by POS |
|---|---|---|---|---|---|---|---|---|---|---|---|---|---|---|---|---|---|
| 1972 TEX A | 61 | 186 | 26 | 5 | 1 | 0 | 0.0 | 8 | 10 | 12 | 39 | 7 | .140 | .177 | 4 | 0 | 2B-58, SS-1 |
| 1973 | 152 | 555 | 138 | 14 | 7 | 8 | 1.4 | 71 | 44 | 55 | 81 | 13 | .249 | .342 | 1 | 0 | OF-113, 3B-25, 2B-18 |
| 1974 CHI N | 62 | 200 | 39 | 6 | 3 | 0 | 0.0 | 18 | 11 | 11 | 26 | 9 | .195 | .255 | 4 | 0 | 2B-56 |
| 1975 | 51 | 56 | 10 | 0 | 0 | 0 | 0.0 | 6 | 5 | 6 | 7 | 0 | .179 | .179 | 24 | 4 | OF-11, 3B-7, 2B-5 |
| 1976 STL N | 97 | 259 | 59 | 12 | 3 | 1 | 0.4 | 21 | 19 | 16 | 55 | 1 | .228 | .309 | 23 | 4 | 2B-37, OF-35, 3B-12, SS-1 |
| 1977 SF N | 69 | 165 | 43 | 12 | 0 | 2 | 1.2 | 28 | 14 | 19 | 36 | 2 | .261 | .370 | 25 | 3 | 2B-27, SS-11, 3B-9, OF-3 |
| 1978 | 53 | 100 | 15 | 4 | 0 | 1 | 1.0 | 8 | 11 | 11 | 24 | 0 | .150 | .220 | 16 | 1 | SS-22, 2B-10, OF-6 |
| 1980 MIL A | 34 | 89 | 19 | 4 | 1 | 1 | 1.1 | 8 | 7 | 12 | 13 | 4 | .213 | .315 | 1 | 0 | OF-31, 3B-2, 2B-1 |
| 8 yrs. | 579 | 1610 | 349 | 57 | 15 | 13 | 0.8 | 168 | 121 | 160 | 281 | 36 | .217 | .295 | 98 | 12 | 2B-212, OF-199, 3B-55, SS-35 |
| 2 yrs. | 113 | 256 | 49 | 6 | 3 | 0 | 0.0 | 24 | 16 | 35 | 33 | 9 | .191 | .238 | 28 | 4 | 2B-61, OF-11, 3B-7 |

# Gabby Hartnett

**HARTNETT, CHARLES LEO**                                    BR  TR  6'1"  195 lbs.
B. Dec. 20, 1900, Woonsocket, R. I.    D. Dec. 20, 1972, Park Ridge, Ill.
Manager 1938-40.
Hall of Fame 1955.

| | G | AB | H | 2B | 3B | HR | HR% | R | RBI | BB | SO | SB | BA | SA | AB | H | G by POS |
|---|---|---|---|---|---|---|---|---|---|---|---|---|---|---|---|---|---|
| 1922 CHI N | 31 | 72 | 14 | 1 | 0 | 0 | 0.0 | 4 | 4 | 6 | 8 | 1 | .194 | .236 | 4 | 1 | C-27 |
| 1923 | 85 | 231 | 62 | 12 | 2 | 8 | 3.5 | 28 | 39 | 25 | 22 | 4 | .268 | .442 | 15 | 2 | C-39, 1B-31 |
| 1924 | 111 | 354 | 106 | 17 | 7 | 16 | 4.5 | 56 | 67 | 39 | 37 | 10 | .299 | .523 | 4 | 0 | C-105 |
| 1925 | 117 | 398 | 115 | 28 | 3 | 24 | 6.0 | 61 | 67 | 36 | 77 | 1 | .289 | .555 | 6 | 2 | C-110 |
| 1926 | 93 | 284 | 78 | 25 | 3 | 8 | 2.8 | 35 | 41 | 32 | 37 | 0 | .275 | .468 | 3 | 1 | C-88 |
| 1927 | 127 | 449 | 132 | 32 | 5 | 10 | 2.2 | 56 | 80 | 44 | 42 | 2 | .294 | .454 | 2 | 1 | C-125 |
| 1928 | 120 | 388 | 117 | 26 | 9 | 14 | 3.6 | 61 | 57 | 65 | 32 | 3 | .302 | .523 | 2 | 0 | C-118 |
| 1929 | 25 | 22 | 6 | 2 | 1 | 1 | 4.5 | 2 | 9 | 5 | 5 | 1 | .273 | .591 | 20 | 6 | C-1 |
| 1930 | 141 | 508 | 172 | 31 | 3 | 37 | 7.3 | 84 | 122 | 55 | 62 | 0 | .339 | .630 | 3 | 2 | C-136 |
| 1931 | 116 | 380 | 107 | 32 | 1 | 8 | 2.1 | 53 | 70 | 52 | 48 | 3 | .282 | .434 | 10 | 0 | C-105 |
| 1932 | 121 | 406 | 110 | 25 | 3 | 12 | 3.0 | 52 | 52 | 51 | 59 | 0 | .271 | .436 | 2 | 1 | C-117, 1B-1 |
| 1933 | 140 | 490 | 135 | 21 | 4 | 16 | 3.3 | 55 | 88 | 37 | 51 | 1 | .276 | .433 | 0 | 0 | C-140 |
| 1934 | 130 | 438 | 131 | 21 | 1 | 22 | 5.0 | 58 | 90 | 37 | 46 | 0 | .299 | .502 | 1 | 0 | C-129 |
| 1935 | 116 | 413 | 142 | 32 | 6 | 13 | 3.1 | 67 | 91 | 41 | 46 | 1 | .344 | .545 | 6 | 1 | C-110 |
| 1936 | 121 | 424 | 130 | 25 | 6 | 7 | 1.7 | 49 | 64 | 30 | 36 | 0 | .307 | .443 | 7 | 0 | C-114 |
| 1937 | 110 | 356 | 126 | 21 | 6 | 12 | 3.4 | 47 | 82 | 43 | 19 | 0 | .354 | .548 | 8 | 2 | C-101 |
| 1938 | 88 | 299 | 82 | 19 | 1 | 10 | 3.3 | 40 | 59 | 48 | 17 | 1 | .274 | .445 | 4 | 2 | C-83 |
| 1939 | 97 | 306 | 85 | 18 | 2 | 12 | 3.9 | 36 | 59 | 37 | 32 | 0 | .278 | .467 | 8 | 3 | C-86 |
| 1940 | 37 | 64 | 17 | 3 | 0 | 1 | 1.6 | 3 | 12 | 8 | 7 | 0 | .266 | .359 | 13 | 5 | C-22, 1B-1 |
| 1941 NY N | 64 | 150 | 45 | 5 | 0 | 5 | 3.3 | 20 | 26 | 12 | 14 | 0 | .300 | .433 | 26 | 8 | C-34 |
| 20 yrs. | 1990 | 6432 | 1912 | 396 | 64 | 236 | 3.7 | 867 | 1179 | 703 | 697 | 28 | .297 | .489 | 144 | 37 | C-1790, 1B-33 |
| 19 yrs. | 1926 | 6282 | 1867 | 391 | 64 | 231 | 3.7 | 847 | 1153 | 691 | 683 | 28 | .297 | .490 | 118 | 29 | C-1756, 1B-33 |
| | 7th | 9th | 8th | 4th | | 4th | | | 10th | 5th | 8th | 4th | | 5th | 9th | 9th | |

| WORLD SERIES | G | AB | H | 2B | 3B | HR | HR% | R | RBI | BB | SO | SB | BA | SA | AB | H | G by POS |
|---|---|---|---|---|---|---|---|---|---|---|---|---|---|---|---|---|---|
| 1929 CHI N | 3 | 3 | 0 | 0 | 0 | 0 | 0.0 | 0 | 0 | 0 | 3 | 0 | .000 | .000 | 3 | 0 | |
| 1932 | 4 | 16 | 5 | 2 | 0 | 1 | 6.3 | 2 | 1 | 1 | 3 | 0 | .313 | .625 | 0 | 0 | C-4 |
| 1935 | 6 | 24 | 7 | 0 | 0 | 1 | 4.2 | 1 | 2 | 1 | 0 | 0 | .292 | .417 | 0 | 0 | C-6 |

| | G | AB | H | 2B | 3B | HR | HR % | R | RBI | BB | SO | SB | BA | SA | Pinch Hit AB | Pinch Hit H | G by POS |
|---|---|---|---|---|---|---|---|---|---|---|---|---|---|---|---|---|---|

## Gabby Hartnett continued

| | G | AB | H | 2B | 3B | HR | HR% | R | RBI | BB | SO | SB | BA | SA | AB | H | G by POS |
|---|---|---|---|---|---|---|---|---|---|---|---|---|---|---|---|---|---|
| 1938 | 3 | 11 | 1 | 0 | 1 | 0 | 0.0 | 0 | 0 | 0 | 2 | 0 | .091 | .273 | 0 | 0 | C-3 |
| 4 yrs. | 16 | 54 | 13 | 2 | 1 | 2 | 3.7 | 3 | 3 | 1 | 11 | 0 | .241 | .426 | 3 | 0 | C-13 |

## Topsy Hartsel

**HARTSEL, TULLY FREDERICK**  
B. June 26, 1874, Polk, Ohio   D. Oct. 14, 1944, Toledo, Ohio      BL TL 5'5" 155 lbs.

| | G | AB | H | 2B | 3B | HR | HR% | R | RBI | BB | SO | SB | BA | SA | AB | H | G by POS |
|---|---|---|---|---|---|---|---|---|---|---|---|---|---|---|---|---|---|
| 1898 LOU N | 22 | 71 | 23 | 0 | 0 | 0 | 0.0 | 11 | 9 | 11 | | 2 | .324 | .324 | 0 | 0 | OF-21 |
| 1899 | 30 | 75 | 18 | 1 | 1 | 1 | 1.3 | 8 | 7 | 11 | | 1 | .240 | .320 | 6 | 2 | OF-22 |
| 1900 CIN N | 18 | 64 | 21 | 2 | 1 | 2 | 3.1 | 10 | 5 | 8 | | 7 | .328 | .484 | 0 | 0 | OF-18 |
| 1901 CHI N | 140 | 558 | 187 | 25 | 16 | 7 | 1.3 | 111 | 54 | 74 | | 41 | .335 | .475 | 0 | 0 | OF-140 |
| 1902 PHI A | 137 | 545 | 154 | 20 | 12 | 5 | 0.9 | 109 | 58 | 87 | | 47 | .283 | .391 | 0 | 0 | OF-137 |
| 1903 | 98 | 373 | 116 | 19 | 14 | 5 | 1.3 | 65 | 26 | 49 | | 13 | .311 | .477 | 1 | 0 | OF-96 |
| 1904 | 147 | 534 | 135 | 17 | 12 | 2 | 0.4 | 79 | 25 | 75 | | 19 | .253 | .341 | 0 | 0 | OF-147 |
| 1905 | 148 | 533 | 147 | 22 | 8 | 0 | 0.0 | 88 | 28 | 121 | | 36 | .276 | .347 | 1 | 0 | OF-147 |
| 1906 | 144 | 533 | 136 | 21 | 9 | 1 | 0.2 | 96 | 30 | 88 | | 31 | .255 | .334 | 0 | 0 | OF-144 |
| 1907 | 143 | 507 | 142 | 23 | 6 | 3 | 0.6 | 93 | 29 | 106 | | 20 | .280 | .367 | 0 | 0 | OF-143 |
| 1908 | 129 | 460 | 112 | 16 | 6 | 4 | 0.9 | 73 | 29 | 93 | | 15 | .243 | .330 | 0 | 0 | OF-129 |
| 1909 | 83 | 267 | 72 | 4 | 5 | 0 | 0.0 | 30 | 18 | 48 | | 3 | .270 | .322 | 8 | 2 | OF-74 |
| 1910 | 90 | 285 | 63 | 10 | 3 | 0 | 0.0 | 45 | 22 | 58 | | 11 | .221 | .277 | 4 | 0 | OF-83 |
| 1911 | 25 | 38 | 9 | 2 | 0 | 0 | 0.0 | 8 | 1 | 8 | | 0 | .237 | .289 | 11 | 2 | OF-10 |
| 14 yrs. | 1354 | 4843 | 1335 | 182 | 93 | 30 | 0.6 | 826 | 341 | 837 | | 246 | .276 | .370 | 31 | 6 | OF-1311 |
| 1 yr. | 140 | 558 | 187 | 25 | 16 | 7 | 1.3 | 111 | 54 | 74 | | 41 | .335 | .475 | 0 | 0 | OF-140 |

**WORLD SERIES**

| | G | AB | H | 2B | 3B | HR | HR% | R | RBI | BB | SO | SB | BA | SA | AB | H | G by POS |
|---|---|---|---|---|---|---|---|---|---|---|---|---|---|---|---|---|---|
| 1905 PHI A | 5 | 17 | 5 | 1 | 0 | 0 | 0.0 | 1 | 0 | 2 | 1 | 2 | .294 | .353 | 0 | 0 | OF-5 |
| 1910 | 1 | 5 | 1 | 0 | 0 | 0 | 0.0 | 2 | 0 | 0 | 1 | 2 | .200 | .200 | 0 | 0 | OF-1 |
| 2 yrs. | 6 | 22 | 6 | 1 | 0 | 0 | 0.0 | 3 | 0 | 2 | 2 | 4 | .273 | .318 | 0 | 0 | OF-6 |

## Ervin Harvey

**HARVEY, ERVIN KING (Zaza)**  
B. Jan. 5, 1879, Saratoga, Calif.   D. June 3, 1954, Santa Monica, Calif.      BL TL

| | G | AB | H | 2B | 3B | HR | HR% | R | RBI | BB | SO | SB | BA | SA | AB | H | G by POS |
|---|---|---|---|---|---|---|---|---|---|---|---|---|---|---|---|---|---|
| 1900 CHI N | 2 | 3 | 0 | 0 | 0 | 0 | 0.0 | 0 | 0 | 0 | | 0 | .000 | .000 | 1 | 0 | P-1 |
| 1901 2 teams | | | CHI A | (17G – | .250) | | | CLE A | (45G – | .353) | | | | | | | |
| " total | 62 | 210 | 70 | 8 | 6 | 1 | 0.5 | 32 | 27 | 11 | | 16 | .333 | .443 | 1 | 0 | OF-45, P-16 |
| 1902 CLE A | 12 | 46 | 16 | 2 | 0 | 0 | 0.0 | 5 | 5 | 3 | | 1 | .348 | .391 | 0 | 0 | OF-12 |
| 3 yrs. | 76 | 259 | 86 | 10 | 6 | 1 | 0.4 | 37 | 32 | 14 | | 17 | .332 | .429 | 2 | 0 | OF-57, P-17 |
| 1 yr. | 2 | 3 | 0 | 0 | 0 | 0 | 0.0 | 0 | 0 | 0 | | 0 | .000 | .000 | 1 | 0 | P-1 |

## Ron Hassey

**HASSEY, RONALD WILLIAM**  
B. Feb. 27, 1953, Tucson, Ariz.      BL TR 6'2" 200 lbs.

| | G | AB | H | 2B | 3B | HR | HR% | R | RBI | BB | SO | SB | BA | SA | AB | H | G by POS |
|---|---|---|---|---|---|---|---|---|---|---|---|---|---|---|---|---|---|
| 1978 CLE A | 25 | 74 | 15 | 0 | 0 | 2 | 2.7 | 5 | 9 | 5 | 7 | 2 | .203 | .284 | 1 | 0 | C-24 |
| 1979 | 75 | 223 | 64 | 14 | 0 | 4 | 1.8 | 20 | 32 | 19 | 19 | 1 | .287 | .404 | 7 | 2 | C-68, 1B-2, DH-1 |
| 1980 | 130 | 390 | 124 | 18 | 4 | 8 | 2.1 | 43 | 65 | 49 | 51 | 0 | .318 | .446 | 18 | 6 | C-113, DH-7, 1B-3 |
| 1981 | 61 | 190 | 44 | 4 | 0 | 1 | 0.5 | 8 | 25 | 17 | 11 | 0 | .232 | .268 | 4 | 2 | C-56, 1B-5, DH-1 |
| 1982 | 113 | 323 | 81 | 18 | 0 | 5 | 1.5 | 33 | 34 | 53 | 32 | 3 | .251 | .353 | 10 | 3 | C-105, DH-2, 1B-2 |
| 1983 | 117 | 341 | 92 | 21 | 0 | 6 | 1.8 | 48 | 42 | 38 | 35 | 2 | .270 | .384 | 9 | 3 | C-113, DH-1 |
| 1984 2 teams | | | CLE A | (48G – | .255) | | | CHI N | (19G – | .333) | | | | | | | |
| " total | 67 | 182 | 49 | 5 | 1 | 2 | 1.1 | 16 | 24 | 19 | 32 | 1 | .269 | .341 | 9 | 2 | C-50, 1B-5, DH-1 |
| 1985 NY A | 92 | 267 | 79 | 16 | 1 | 13 | 4.9 | 31 | 42 | 28 | 21 | 0 | .296 | .509 | 20 | 5 | C-69, DH-2, 1B-2 |
| 8 yrs. | 680 | 1990 | 548 | 96 | 6 | 41 | 2.1 | 204 | 273 | 228 | 208 | 9 | .275 | .391 | 78 | 23 | C-598, 1B-19, DH-15 |
| 1 yr. | 19 | 33 | 11 | 0 | 0 | 2 | 6.1 | 5 | 5 | 4 | 6 | 0 | .333 | .515 | 8 | 2 | C-6, 1B-4 |

## Billy Hatcher

**HATCHER, WILLIAM AUGUSTUS**  
B. Oct. 4, 1960, Williams, Ariz.      BR TR 5'9" 175 lbs.

| | G | AB | H | 2B | 3B | HR | HR% | R | RBI | BB | SO | SB | BA | SA | AB | H | G by POS |
|---|---|---|---|---|---|---|---|---|---|---|---|---|---|---|---|---|---|
| 1984 CHI N | 8 | 9 | 1 | 0 | 0 | 0 | 0.0 | 1 | 0 | 1 | 0 | 2 | .111 | .111 | 3 | 0 | OF-4 |
| 1985 | 53 | 163 | 40 | 12 | 1 | 2 | 1.2 | 24 | 10 | 8 | 12 | 2 | .245 | .368 | 9 | 1 | OF-44 |
| 2 yrs. | 61 | 172 | 41 | 12 | 1 | 2 | 1.2 | 25 | 10 | 9 | 12 | 4 | .238 | .355 | 12 | 1 | OF-48 |
| 2 yrs. | 61 | 172 | 41 | 12 | 1 | 2 | 1.2 | 25 | 10 | 9 | 12 | 4 | .238 | .355 | 12 | 1 | OF-48 |

## Grady Hatton

**HATTON, GRADY EDGEBERT**  
B. Oct. 7, 1922, Beaumont, Tex.  
Manager 1966-68.      BL TR 5'8½" 170 lbs.

| | G | AB | H | 2B | 3B | HR | HR% | R | RBI | BB | SO | SB | BA | SA | AB | H | G by POS |
|---|---|---|---|---|---|---|---|---|---|---|---|---|---|---|---|---|---|
| 1946 CIN N | 116 | 436 | 118 | 18 | 3 | 14 | 3.2 | 56 | 69 | 66 | 53 | 6 | .271 | .422 | 0 | 0 | 3B-116, OF-2 |
| 1947 | 146 | 524 | 147 | 24 | 8 | 16 | 3.1 | 91 | 77 | 81 | 50 | 7 | .281 | .448 | 7 | 2 | 3B-136 |
| 1948 | 133 | 458 | 110 | 17 | 2 | 9 | 2.0 | 58 | 44 | 72 | 50 | 7 | .240 | .345 | 3 | 1 | 3B-123, 2B-3, SS-2, OF-1 |
| 1949 | 137 | 537 | 141 | 38 | 5 | 11 | 2.0 | 71 | 69 | 62 | 48 | 4 | .263 | .413 | 1 | 0 | 3B-136 |
| 1950 | 130 | 438 | 114 | 17 | 1 | 11 | 2.5 | 67 | 54 | 70 | 39 | 6 | .260 | .379 | 4 | 1 | 3B-126, SS-1, 2B-1 |
| 1951 | 96 | 331 | 84 | 9 | 3 | 4 | 1.2 | 41 | 37 | 33 | 32 | 4 | .254 | .335 | 7 | 2 | 3B-87, OF-2 |
| 1952 | 128 | 433 | 92 | 14 | 1 | 9 | 2.1 | 48 | 57 | 66 | 60 | 5 | .212 | .312 | 7 | 1 | 2B-120 |
| 1953 | 83 | 159 | 37 | 3 | 1 | 7 | 4.4 | 22 | 22 | 29 | 24 | 0 | .233 | .396 | 38 | 7 | 2B-35, 1B-10, 3B-5 |
| 1954 3 teams | | | CIN N | (1G – | .000) | | | CHI A | (13G – | .167) | | | BOS A | (99G – | .281) | | |
| " total | 113 | 333 | 90 | 13 | 3 | 5 | 1.5 | 43 | 36 | 63 | 28 | 2 | .270 | .372 | 8 | 0 | 3B-103, 1B-4, SS-1 |
| 1955 BOS A | 126 | 380 | 93 | 11 | 4 | 11 | 4.1 | 48 | 49 | 76 | 28 | 0 | .245 | .326 | 12 | 1 | 3B-111, 2B-1 |
| 1956 3 teams | | | BOS A | (5G – | .400) | | | STL N | (44G – | .247) | | | BAL A | (27G – | .148) | | |
| " total | 76 | 139 | 29 | 2 | 2 | 1 | 0.7 | 14 | 12 | 26 | 13 | 1 | .209 | .273 | 35 | 9 | 2B-28, 3B-13 |
| 1960 CHI N | 28 | 38 | 13 | 0 | 0 | 0 | 0.0 | 3 | 7 | 2 | 5 | 0 | .342 | .342 | 16 | 3 | 2B-8 |
| 12 yrs. | 1312 | 4206 | 1068 | 166 | 33 | 91 | 2.2 | 562 | 533 | 646 | 430 | 42 | .254 | .374 | 138 | 27 | 3B-956, 2B-196, 1B-14, OF-5, SS-4 |
| 1 yr. | 28 | 38 | 13 | 0 | 0 | 0 | 0.0 | 3 | 7 | 2 | 5 | 0 | .342 | .342 | 16 | 3 | 2B-8 |

| | G | AB | H | 2B | 3B | HR | HR % | R | RBI | BB | SO | SB | BA | SA | Pinch Hit AB | Pinch Hit H | G by POS |
|---|---|---|---|---|---|---|---|---|---|---|---|---|---|---|---|---|---|

## Jack Hayden

**HAYDEN, JOHN FRANCIS**
B. Oct. 21, 1880, Bryn Mawr, Pa.    D. Aug. 3, 1942, Haverford, Pa.    BR TL 5'9"

| | G | AB | H | 2B | 3B | HR | HR % | R | RBI | BB | SO | SB | BA | SA | AB | H | G by POS |
|---|---|---|---|---|---|---|---|---|---|---|---|---|---|---|---|---|---|
| 1901 PHI A | 51 | 211 | 56 | 6 | 4 | 0 | 0.0 | 35 | 17 | 18 | | 4 | .265 | .332 | 1 | 0 | OF-50 |
| 1906 BOS A | 85 | 322 | 90 | 6 | 4 | 1 | 0.3 | 22 | 13 | 17 | | 6 | .280 | .332 | 0 | 0 | OF-85 |
| 1908 CHI N | 11 | 45 | 9 | 2 | 0 | 0 | 0.0 | 3 | 2 | 1 | | 1 | .200 | .244 | 0 | 0 | OF-11 |
| 3 yrs. | 147 | 578 | 155 | 14 | 8 | 1 | 0.2 | 60 | 32 | 36 | | 11 | .268 | .325 | 1 | 0 | OF-146 |
| 1 yr. | 11 | 45 | 9 | 2 | 0 | 0 | 0.0 | 3 | 2 | 1 | | 1 | .200 | .244 | 0 | 0 | OF-11 |

## Bill Hayes

**HAYES, WILLIAM ERNEST**
B. Oct. 24, 1957, Cheverly, Md.    BR TR 6'    195 lbs.

| | G | AB | H | 2B | 3B | HR | HR % | R | RBI | BB | SO | SB | BA | SA | AB | H | G by POS |
|---|---|---|---|---|---|---|---|---|---|---|---|---|---|---|---|---|---|
| 1980 CHI N | 4 | 9 | 2 | 1 | 0 | 0 | 0.0 | 0 | 0 | 0 | 3 | 0 | .222 | .333 | 1 | 0 | C-3 |
| 1981 | 1 | 0 | 0 | 0 | 0 | 0 | — | 0 | 0 | 0 | 0 | 0 | — | — | 0 | 0 | C-1 |
| 2 yrs. | 5 | 9 | 2 | 1 | 0 | 0 | 0.0 | 0 | 0 | 0 | 3 | 0 | .222 | .333 | 1 | 0 | C-4 |
| 2 yrs. | 5 | 9 | 2 | 1 | 0 | 0 | 0.0 | 0 | 0 | 0 | 3 | 0 | .222 | .333 | 1 | 0 | C-4 |

## Bill Heath

**HEATH, WILLIAM CHRIS**
B. Mar. 10, 1939, Yuba City, Calif.    BL TR 5'8"    175 lbs.

| | G | AB | H | 2B | 3B | HR | HR % | R | RBI | BB | SO | SB | BA | SA | AB | H | G by POS |
|---|---|---|---|---|---|---|---|---|---|---|---|---|---|---|---|---|---|
| 1965 CHI A | 1 | 1 | 0 | 0 | 0 | 0 | 0.0 | 0 | 0 | 0 | 0 | 0 | .000 | .000 | 1 | 0 | |
| 1966 HOU N | 55 | 123 | 37 | 6 | 0 | 0 | 0.0 | 12 | 8 | 9 | 11 | 1 | .301 | .350 | 16 | 4 | C-37 |
| 1967 2 teams | | HOU N (9G – .091) | | | | DET A (20G – .125) | | | | | | | | | | | |
| " total | 29 | 43 | 5 | 0 | 0 | 0 | 0.0 | 0 | 4 | 5 | 7 | 0 | .116 | .116 | 19 | 2 | C-12 |
| 1969 CHI N | 27 | 32 | 5 | 0 | 1 | 0 | 0.0 | 1 | 1 | 12 | 4 | 0 | .156 | .219 | 12 | 2 | C-9 |
| 4 yrs. | 112 | 199 | 47 | 6 | 1 | 0 | 0.0 | 13 | 13 | 26 | 22 | 1 | .236 | .276 | 48 | 8 | C-58 |
| 1 yr. | 27 | 32 | 5 | 0 | 1 | 0 | 0.0 | 1 | 1 | 12 | 4 | 0 | .156 | .219 | 12 | 2 | C-9 |

## Cliff Heathcote

**HEATHCOTE, CLIFTON EARL**
B. Jan. 24, 1898, Glen Rock, Pa.    D. Jan. 19, 1939, York, Pa.    BL TL 5'10½" 160 lbs.

| | G | AB | H | 2B | 3B | HR | HR % | R | RBI | BB | SO | SB | BA | SA | AB | H | G by POS |
|---|---|---|---|---|---|---|---|---|---|---|---|---|---|---|---|---|---|
| 1918 STL N | 88 | 348 | 90 | 12 | 3 | 4 | 1.1 | 37 | 32 | 20 | 40 | 12 | .259 | .345 | 0 | 0 | OF-88 |
| 1919 | 114 | 401 | 112 | 13 | 4 | 1 | 0.2 | 53 | 29 | 20 | 41 | 26 | .279 | .339 | 9 | 3 | OF-101, 1B-2 |
| 1920 | 133 | 489 | 139 | 18 | 8 | 3 | 0.6 | 55 | 56 | 25 | 31 | 21 | .284 | .372 | 3 | 0 | OF-129 |
| 1921 | 62 | 156 | 38 | 6 | 2 | 0 | 0.0 | 18 | 9 | 10 | 9 | 7 | .244 | .308 | 7 | 1 | OF-51 |
| 1922 2 teams | | STL N (34G – .245) | | | | CHI N (76G – .280) | | | | | | | | | | | |
| " total | 110 | 341 | 92 | 13 | 9 | 1 | 0.3 | 48 | 48 | 27 | 19 | 5 | .270 | .370 | 12 | 3 | OF-92 |
| 1923 CHI N | 117 | 393 | 98 | 14 | 3 | 1 | 0.3 | 48 | 27 | 25 | 22 | 32 | .249 | .308 | 2 | 0 | OF-112 |
| 1924 | 113 | 392 | 121 | 19 | 7 | 0 | 0.0 | 66 | 30 | 28 | 28 | 26 | .309 | .393 | 1 | 0 | OF-111 |
| 1925 | 109 | 380 | 100 | 14 | 5 | 5 | 1.3 | 57 | 39 | 39 | 26 | 15 | .263 | .366 | 10 | 1 | OF-99 |
| 1926 | 139 | 510 | 141 | 33 | 3 | 10 | 2.0 | 98 | 53 | 58 | 30 | 18 | .276 | .412 | 3 | 1 | OF-133 |
| 1927 | 83 | 228 | 67 | 12 | 4 | 2 | 0.9 | 28 | 25 | 20 | 16 | 6 | .294 | .408 | 17 | 0 | OF-57 |
| 1928 | 67 | 137 | 39 | 8 | 0 | 3 | 2.2 | 26 | 18 | 17 | 12 | 6 | .285 | .409 | 21 | 5 | OF-39 |
| 1929 | 82 | 224 | 70 | 17 | 0 | 2 | 0.9 | 45 | 31 | 25 | 17 | 9 | .313 | .415 | 22 | 7 | OF-52 |
| 1930 | 70 | 150 | 39 | 10 | 1 | 9 | 6.0 | 30 | 18 | 18 | 15 | 4 | .260 | .520 | 31 | 5 | OF-35 |
| 1931 CIN N | 90 | 252 | 65 | 15 | 6 | 0 | 0.0 | 24 | 28 | 32 | 16 | 3 | .258 | .365 | 25 | 6 | OF-59 |
| 1932 2 teams | | CIN N (8G – .000) | | | | PHI N (30G – .282) | | | | | | | | | | | |
| " total | 38 | 42 | 11 | 2 | 0 | 1 | 2.4 | 10 | 5 | 3 | 3 | 0 | .262 | .381 | 20 | 4 | 1B-7 |
| 15 yrs. | 1415 | 4443 | 1222 | 206 | 55 | 42 | 0.9 | 643 | 448 | 367 | 325 | 190 | .275 | .375 | 183 | 36 | OF-1158, 1B-9 |
| 9 yrs. | 856 | 2657 | 743 | 135 | 30 | 33 | 1.2 | 435 | 275 | 248 | 181 | 121 | .280 | .390 | 119 | 22 | OF-698 |
| | | | | | | | | | | | | | | | 7th | | |

WORLD SERIES

| | G | AB | H | 2B | 3B | HR | HR % | R | RBI | BB | SO | SB | BA | SA | AB | H | G by POS |
|---|---|---|---|---|---|---|---|---|---|---|---|---|---|---|---|---|---|
| 1929 CHI N | 2 | 1 | 0 | 0 | 0 | 0 | 0.0 | 0 | 0 | 0 | 0 | 0 | .000 | .000 | 1 | 0 | |

## Richie Hebner

**HEBNER, RICHARD JOSEPH**
B. Nov. 26, 1947, Brighton, Mass.    BL TR 6'1"    195 lbs.

| | G | AB | H | 2B | 3B | HR | HR % | R | RBI | BB | SO | SB | BA | SA | AB | H | G by POS |
|---|---|---|---|---|---|---|---|---|---|---|---|---|---|---|---|---|---|
| 1968 PIT N | 2 | 1 | 0 | 0 | 0 | 0 | 0.0 | 0 | 0 | 0 | 0 | 0 | .000 | .000 | 1 | 0 | |
| 1969 | 129 | 459 | 138 | 23 | 4 | 8 | 1.7 | 72 | 47 | 53 | 53 | 4 | .301 | .420 | 4 | 1 | 3B-124, 1B-1 |
| 1970 | 120 | 420 | 122 | 24 | 8 | 11 | 2.6 | 60 | 46 | 42 | 48 | 2 | .290 | .464 | 6 | 2 | 3B-117 |
| 1971 | 112 | 388 | 105 | 17 | 8 | 17 | 4.4 | 50 | 67 | 32 | 68 | 2 | .271 | .487 | 7 | 2 | 3B-108 |
| 1972 | 124 | 427 | 128 | 24 | 4 | 19 | 4.4 | 63 | 72 | 52 | 54 | 0 | .300 | .508 | 5 | 1 | 3B-121 |
| 1973 | 144 | 509 | 138 | 28 | 1 | 25 | 4.9 | 73 | 74 | 56 | 60 | 0 | .271 | .477 | 7 | 1 | 3B-139 |
| 1974 | 146 | 550 | 160 | 21 | 6 | 18 | 3.3 | 97 | 68 | 60 | 53 | 0 | .291 | .449 | 7 | 1 | 3B-141 |
| 1975 | 128 | 472 | 116 | 16 | 4 | 15 | 3.2 | 65 | 57 | 43 | 48 | 0 | .246 | .392 | 7 | 3 | 3B-126 |
| 1976 | 132 | 434 | 108 | 21 | 3 | 8 | 1.8 | 60 | 51 | 47 | 39 | 1 | .249 | .366 | 7 | 0 | 3B-126 |
| 1977 PHI N | 118 | 397 | 113 | 17 | 4 | 18 | 4.5 | 67 | 62 | 61 | 46 | 7 | .285 | .484 | 10 | 3 | 1B-103, 3B-13, 2B-1 |
| 1978 | 137 | 435 | 123 | 22 | 4 | 17 | 3.9 | 61 | 71 | 53 | 58 | 4 | .283 | .464 | 9 | 5 | 1B-117, 3B-19, 2B-1 |
| 1979 NY N | 136 | 473 | 127 | 25 | 2 | 10 | 2.1 | 54 | 79 | 59 | 59 | 3 | .268 | .393 | 4 | 1 | 3B-134, 1B-6 |
| 1980 DET A | 104 | 341 | 99 | 10 | 7 | 12 | 3.5 | 48 | 82 | 38 | 45 | 0 | .290 | .466 | 11 | 6 | 1B-61, 3B-32, DH-5 |
| 1981 | 78 | 226 | 51 | 8 | 2 | 5 | 2.2 | 19 | 28 | 27 | 28 | 1 | .226 | .345 | 11 | 1 | 1B-61, DH-11 |
| 1982 2 teams | | DET A (68G – .274) | | | | PIT N (25G – .300) | | | | | | | | | | | |
| " total | 93 | 249 | 70 | 8 | 0 | 10 | 4.0 | 31 | 30 | 30 | 24 | 5 | .281 | .434 | 17 | 3 | 1B-44, OF-21, DH-20, 3B-1 |
| 1983 PIT N | 78 | 162 | 43 | 4 | 1 | 5 | 3.1 | 23 | 26 | 17 | 28 | 8 | .265 | .395 | 27 | 7 | 3B-40, OF-7, 1B-7 |
| 1984 CHI N | 44 | 81 | 27 | 3 | 0 | 2 | 2.5 | 12 | 8 | 10 | 15 | 1 | .333 | .444 | 26 | 8 | 3B-14, OF-3, 1B-3 |
| 1985 | 83 | 120 | 26 | 2 | 0 | 3 | 2.5 | 10 | 22 | 7 | 15 | 0 | .217 | .308 | 59 | 12 | 1B-12, 3B-7, OF-1 |
| 18 yrs. | 1908 | 6144 | 1694 | 273 | 57 | 203 | 3.3 | 865 | 890 | 687 | 741 | 38 | .276 | .438 | 221 | 55 | 3B-1262, 1B-415, DH-36, OF-32, 2B-2 |
| 2 yrs. | 127 | 201 | 53 | 5 | 0 | 5 | 2.5 | 22 | 30 | 17 | 30 | 1 | .264 | .363 | 85 | 20 | 3B-21, 1B-15, OF-4 |

LEAGUE CHAMPIONSHIP SERIES

| | G | AB | H | 2B | 3B | HR | HR % | R | RBI | BB | SO | SB | BA | SA | AB | H | G by POS |
|---|---|---|---|---|---|---|---|---|---|---|---|---|---|---|---|---|---|
| 1970 PIT N | 2 | 6 | 4 | 2 | 0 | 0 | 0.0 | 0 | 0 | 2 | 1 | 0 | .667 | 1.000 | 0 | 0 | 3B-2 |
| 1971 | 4 | 17 | 5 | 1 | 0 | 2 | 11.8 | 3 | 4 | 0 | 4 | 0 | .294 | .706 | 1 | 0 | 3B-4 |
| 1972 | 5 | 16 | 3 | 1 | 0 | 0 | 0.0 | 2 | 1 | 1 | 3 | 0 | .188 | .250 | 0 | 0 | 3B-5 |
| 1974 | 4 | 13 | 3 | 0 | 0 | 1 | 7.7 | 1 | 4 | 1 | 4 | 0 | .231 | .462 | 0 | 0 | 3B-4 |
| 1975 | 3 | 12 | 4 | 1 | 0 | 0 | 0.0 | 2 | 2 | 1 | 1 | 0 | .333 | .417 | 0 | 0 | 3B-3 |
| 1977 PHI N | 4 | 14 | 5 | 2 | 0 | 0 | 0.0 | 2 | 1 | 0 | 1 | 0 | .357 | .500 | 0 | 0 | 1B-3 |
| 1978 | 3 | 9 | 1 | 0 | 0 | 0 | 0.0 | 0 | 1 | 0 | 0 | 0 | .111 | .111 | 0 | 0 | 1B-2 |

| | G | AB | H | 2B | 3B | HR | HR % | R | RBI | BB | SO | SB | BA | SA | Pinch Hit AB | Pinch Hit H | G by POS |
|---|---|---|---|---|---|---|---|---|---|---|---|---|---|---|---|---|---|

## Richie Hebner continued

| | G | AB | H | 2B | 3B | HR | HR % | R | RBI | BB | SO | SB | BA | SA | AB | H | G by POS |
|---|---|---|---|---|---|---|---|---|---|---|---|---|---|---|---|---|---|
| 1984 CHI N | 1 | 1 | 0 | 0 | 0 | 0 | 0.0 | 0 | 0 | 0 | 0 | 0 | .000 | .000 | 1 | 0 | |
| 8 yrs. | 26 | 88 | 25 | 7 | 0 | 3 | 3.4 | 10 | 12 | 5 | 14 | 0 | .284 | .466 | 4 | 0 | 3B-18, 1B-5 |

WORLD SERIES

| | G | AB | H | 2B | 3B | HR | HR % | R | RBI | BB | SO | SB | BA | SA | AB | H | G by POS |
|---|---|---|---|---|---|---|---|---|---|---|---|---|---|---|---|---|---|
| 1971 PIT N | 3 | 12 | 2 | 0 | 0 | 1 | 8.3 | 2 | 3 | 3 | 3 | 0 | .167 | .417 | 0 | 0 | 3B-3 |

## Mike Hechinger

**HECHINGER, MICHAEL VINCENT**    BR TR 6'   175 lbs.
B. Feb. 14, 1890, Chicago, Ill.   D. Aug. 13, 1967, Chicago, Ill.

| | G | AB | H | 2B | 3B | HR | HR % | R | RBI | BB | SO | SB | BA | SA | AB | H | G by POS |
|---|---|---|---|---|---|---|---|---|---|---|---|---|---|---|---|---|---|
| 1912 CHI N | 2 | 3 | 0 | 0 | 0 | 0 | 0.0 | 0 | 0 | 2 | 0 | 0 | .000 | .000 | 0 | 0 | C-2 |
| 1913 2 teams | | CHI N (2G – .000) | | | | BKN N (9G – .182) | | | | | | | | | | | |
| " total | 11 | 13 | 2 | 1 | 0 | 0 | 0.0 | 1 | 0 | 0 | 2 | 0 | .154 | .231 | 7 | 1 | C-4 |
| 2 yrs. | 13 | 16 | 2 | 1 | 0 | 0 | 0.0 | 1 | 0 | 2 | 2 | 0 | .125 | .188 | 7 | 1 | C-6 |
| 2 yrs. | 4 | 5 | 0 | 0 | 0 | 0 | 0.0 | 0 | 0 | 2 | 0 | 0 | .000 | .000 | 2 | 0 | C-2 |

## Jim Hegan

**HEGAN, JAMES EDWARD**    BR TR 6'2"   195 lbs.
Father of Mike Hegan.
B. Aug. 3, 1920, Lynn, Mass.   D. June 17, 1984, Swampscott, Mass.

| | G | AB | H | 2B | 3B | HR | HR % | R | RBI | BB | SO | SB | BA | SA | AB | H | G by POS |
|---|---|---|---|---|---|---|---|---|---|---|---|---|---|---|---|---|---|
| 1941 CLE A | 16 | 47 | 15 | 2 | 0 | 1 | 2.1 | 4 | 5 | 4 | 7 | 0 | .319 | .426 | 0 | 0 | C-16 |
| 1942 | 68 | 170 | 33 | 5 | 0 | 0 | 0.0 | 10 | 11 | 11 | 31 | 1 | .194 | .224 | 2 | 1 | C-66 |
| 1946 | 88 | 271 | 64 | 11 | 5 | 0 | 0.0 | 29 | 17 | 17 | 44 | 1 | .236 | .314 | 0 | 0 | C-87 |
| 1947 | 135 | 378 | 94 | 14 | 5 | 4 | 1.1 | 38 | 42 | 41 | 49 | 3 | .249 | .344 | 1 | 0 | C-133 |
| 1948 | 144 | 472 | 117 | 21 | 6 | 14 | 3.0 | 60 | 61 | 48 | 74 | 6 | .248 | .407 | 3 | 0 | C-142 |
| 1949 | 152 | 468 | 105 | 19 | 5 | 8 | 1.7 | 54 | 55 | 49 | 89 | 1 | .224 | .338 | 0 | 0 | C-152 |
| 1950 | 131 | 415 | 91 | 16 | 5 | 14 | 3.4 | 53 | 58 | 42 | 52 | 1 | .219 | .383 | 0 | 0 | C-129 |
| 1951 | 133 | 416 | 99 | 17 | 5 | 6 | 1.4 | 60 | 43 | 38 | 72 | 0 | .238 | .346 | 2 | 0 | C-129 |
| 1952 | 112 | 333 | 75 | 17 | 2 | 4 | 1.2 | 39 | 41 | 29 | 47 | 0 | .225 | .324 | 3 | 0 | C-107 |
| 1953 | 112 | 299 | 65 | 10 | 1 | 9 | 3.0 | 37 | 37 | 25 | 41 | 1 | .217 | .348 | 0 | 0 | C-106 |
| 1954 | 139 | 423 | 99 | 12 | 7 | 11 | 2.6 | 56 | 40 | 34 | 48 | 0 | .234 | .374 | 2 | 0 | C-137 |
| 1955 | 116 | 304 | 67 | 5 | 2 | 9 | 3.0 | 30 | 40 | 34 | 33 | 0 | .220 | .339 | 2 | 0 | C-111 |
| 1956 | 122 | 315 | 70 | 15 | 2 | 6 | 1.9 | 42 | 34 | 49 | 54 | 1 | .222 | .340 | 3 | 1 | C-118 |
| 1957 | 58 | 148 | 32 | 7 | 0 | 4 | 2.7 | 14 | 15 | 16 | 23 | 0 | .216 | .345 | 0 | 0 | C-58 |
| 1958 2 teams | | DET A (45G – .192) | | | | PHI N (25G – .220) | | | | | | | | | | | |
| " total | 70 | 189 | 38 | 12 | 0 | 1 | 0.5 | 19 | 13 | 14 | 48 | 0 | .201 | .280 | 0 | 0 | C-70 |
| 1959 2 teams | | PHI N (25G – .196) | | | | SF N (21G – .133) | | | | | | | | | | | |
| " total | 46 | 81 | 14 | 2 | 0 | 0 | 0.0 | 1 | 8 | 4 | 20 | 0 | .173 | .198 | 0 | 0 | C-46 |
| 1960 CHI N | 24 | 43 | 9 | 2 | 1 | 1 | 2.3 | 4 | 5 | 1 | 10 | 0 | .209 | .372 | 0 | 0 | C-22 |
| 17 yrs. | 1666 | 4772 | 1087 | 187 | 46 | 92 | 1.9 | 550 | 525 | 456 | 742 | 15 | .228 | .344 | 20 | 2 | C-1629 |
| 1 yr. | 24 | 43 | 9 | 2 | 1 | 1 | 2.3 | 4 | 5 | 1 | 10 | 0 | .209 | .372 | 2 | 0 | C-22 |

WORLD SERIES

| | G | AB | H | 2B | 3B | HR | HR % | R | RBI | BB | SO | SB | BA | SA | AB | H | G by POS |
|---|---|---|---|---|---|---|---|---|---|---|---|---|---|---|---|---|---|
| 1948 CLE A | 6 | 19 | 4 | 0 | 0 | 1 | 5.3 | 2 | 5 | 1 | 4 | 1 | .211 | .368 | 0 | 0 | C-6 |
| 1954 | 4 | 13 | 2 | 1 | 0 | 0 | 0.0 | 1 | 0 | 1 | 1 | 0 | .154 | .231 | 0 | 0 | C-4 |
| 2 yrs. | 10 | 32 | 6 | 1 | 0 | 1 | 3.1 | 3 | 5 | 2 | 5 | 1 | .188 | .313 | 0 | 0 | C-10 |

## Al Heist

**HEIST, ALFRED MICHAEL**    BR TR 6'2"   185 lbs.
B. Oct. 5, 1927, Brooklyn, N. Y.

| | G | AB | H | 2B | 3B | HR | HR % | R | RBI | BB | SO | SB | BA | SA | AB | H | G by POS |
|---|---|---|---|---|---|---|---|---|---|---|---|---|---|---|---|---|---|
| 1960 CHI N | 41 | 102 | 28 | 5 | 3 | 1 | 1.0 | 11 | 6 | 10 | 12 | 3 | .275 | .412 | 10 | 2 | OF-33 |
| 1961 | 109 | 321 | 82 | 14 | 3 | 7 | 2.2 | 48 | 37 | 39 | 51 | 3 | .255 | .383 | 8 | 1 | OF-99 |
| 1962 HOU N | 27 | 72 | 16 | 1 | 0 | 0 | 0.0 | 4 | 3 | 3 | 9 | 0 | .222 | .236 | 4 | 0 | OF-23 |
| 3 yrs. | 177 | 495 | 126 | 20 | 6 | 8 | 1.6 | 63 | 46 | 52 | 72 | 6 | .255 | .368 | 22 | 3 | OF-155 |
| 2 yrs. | 150 | 423 | 110 | 19 | 6 | 8 | 1.9 | 59 | 43 | 49 | 63 | 6 | .260 | .390 | 18 | 3 | OF-132 |

## Rollie Hemsley

**HEMSLEY, RALSTON BURDETT**    BR TR 5'10"   170 lbs.
B. June 24, 1907, Syracuse, Ohio   D. July 31, 1972, Washington, D. C.

| | G | AB | H | 2B | 3B | HR | HR % | R | RBI | BB | SO | SB | BA | SA | AB | H | G by POS |
|---|---|---|---|---|---|---|---|---|---|---|---|---|---|---|---|---|---|
| 1928 PIT N | 50 | 133 | 36 | 2 | 3 | 0 | 0.0 | 14 | 18 | 4 | 10 | 1 | .271 | .331 | 1 | 0 | C-49 |
| 1929 | 88 | 235 | 68 | 13 | 7 | 0 | 0.0 | 31 | 37 | 11 | 22 | 1 | .289 | .404 | 6 | 0 | C-80 |
| 1930 | 104 | 324 | 82 | 19 | 6 | 2 | 0.6 | 45 | 45 | 22 | 21 | 3 | .253 | .367 | 5 | 1 | C-98 |
| 1931 2 teams | | PIT N (10G – .171) | | | | CHI N (66G – .309) | | | | | | | | | | | |
| " total | 76 | 239 | 69 | 20 | 4 | 3 | 1.3 | 31 | 32 | 20 | 33 | 4 | .289 | .444 | 9 | 3 | C-75 |
| 1932 CHI N | 60 | 151 | 36 | 10 | 3 | 4 | 2.6 | 27 | 20 | 10 | 16 | 2 | .238 | .424 | 8 | 3 | C-47, OF-1 |
| 1933 2 teams | | CIN N (49G – .190) | | | | STL A (32G – .242) | | | | | | | | | | | |
| " total | 81 | 211 | 45 | 10 | 1 | 1 | 0.5 | 16 | 22 | 17 | 20 | 1 | .213 | .284 | 7 | 1 | C-68 |
| 1934 STL A | 123 | 431 | 133 | 31 | 7 | 2 | 0.5 | 47 | 52 | 29 | 37 | 6 | .309 | .427 | 5 | 2 | C-114, OF-6 |
| 1935 | 144 | 504 | 146 | 32 | 7 | 0 | 0.0 | 57 | 48 | 44 | 41 | 3 | .290 | .381 | 6 | 1 | C-141 |
| 1936 | 116 | 377 | 99 | 24 | 2 | 2 | 0.5 | 43 | 39 | 46 | 30 | 2 | .263 | .353 | 8 | 2 | C-114 |
| 1937 | 100 | 334 | 74 | 12 | 3 | 3 | 0.9 | 30 | 28 | 25 | 29 | 0 | .222 | .302 | 3 | 2 | C-94, 1B-2 |
| 1938 CLE A | 66 | 203 | 60 | 11 | 3 | 2 | 1.0 | 27 | 28 | 23 | 14 | 1 | .296 | .409 | 6 | 0 | C-58 |
| 1939 | 107 | 395 | 104 | 17 | 4 | 2 | 0.5 | 58 | 36 | 26 | 26 | 2 | .263 | .342 | 0 | 0 | C-106 |
| 1940 | 119 | 416 | 111 | 20 | 5 | 4 | 1.0 | 46 | 42 | 22 | 25 | 1 | .267 | .368 | 2 | 0 | C-117 |
| 1941 | 98 | 288 | 69 | 10 | 5 | 2 | 0.7 | 29 | 24 | 18 | 19 | 2 | .240 | .330 | 2 | 0 | C-96 |
| 1942 2 teams | | CIN N (36G – .113) | | | | NY A (31G – .294) | | | | | | | | | | | |
| " total | 67 | 200 | 38 | 4 | 3 | 0 | 0.0 | 19 | 22 | 9 | 20 | 1 | .190 | .240 | 2 | 0 | C-63 |
| 1943 NY A | 62 | 180 | 43 | 6 | 3 | 2 | 1.1 | 12 | 24 | 13 | 9 | 0 | .239 | .339 | 10 | 1 | C-52 |
| 1944 | 81 | 284 | 76 | 12 | 2 | 2 | 0.7 | 23 | 26 | 9 | 13 | 0 | .268 | .366 | 6 | 1 | C-76 |
| 1946 PHI N | 49 | 139 | 31 | 4 | 1 | 0 | 0.0 | 7 | 11 | 9 | 10 | 0 | .223 | .266 | 3 | 1 | C-45 |
| 1947 | 2 | 3 | 1 | 0 | 0 | 0 | 0.0 | 1 | 0 | 1 | 0 | 0 | .333 | .333 | 0 | 0 | C-2 |
| 19 yrs. | 1593 | 5047 | 1321 | 257 | 72 | 31 | 0.6 | 562 | 555 | 357 | 395 | 29 | .262 | .360 | 89 | 18 | C-1495, OF-7, 1B-2 |
| 2 yrs. | 126 | 355 | 99 | 27 | 7 | 2 | 2.0 | 55 | 51 | 27 | 46 | 6 | .279 | .454 | 17 | 6 | C-113, OF-1 |

WORLD SERIES

| | G | AB | H | 2B | 3B | HR | HR % | R | RBI | BB | SO | SB | BA | SA | AB | H | G by POS |
|---|---|---|---|---|---|---|---|---|---|---|---|---|---|---|---|---|---|
| 1932 CHI N | 3 | 3 | 0 | 0 | 0 | 0 | 0.0 | 0 | 0 | 0 | 3 | 0 | .000 | .000 | 3 | 0 | C-1 |

| | G | AB | H | 2B | 3B | HR | HR% | R | RBI | BB | SO | SB | BA | SA | Pinch Hit AB | Pinch Hit H | G by POS |
|---|---|---|---|---|---|---|---|---|---|---|---|---|---|---|---|---|---|

# Ken Henderson

**HENDERSON, KENNETH JOSEPH**
B. June 15, 1946, Carroll, Iowa
BB TR 6'2" 180 lbs.
BL 1967

| | G | AB | H | 2B | 3B | HR | HR% | R | RBI | BB | SO | SB | BA | SA | PH AB | PH H | G by POS |
|---|---|---|---|---|---|---|---|---|---|---|---|---|---|---|---|---|---|
| 1965 SF N | 63 | 73 | 14 | 1 | 1 | 0 | 0.0 | 10 | 7 | 9 | 19 | 1 | .192 | .233 | 7 | 0 | OF-48 |
| 1966 | 11 | 29 | 9 | 1 | 1 | 1 | 3.4 | 4 | 1 | 2 | 3 | 0 | .310 | .517 | 1 | 0 | OF-10 |
| 1967 | 65 | 179 | 34 | 3 | 0 | 4 | 2.2 | 15 | 14 | 19 | 52 | 0 | .190 | .274 | 11 | 3 | OF-52 |
| 1968 | 3 | 3 | 1 | 0 | 0 | 0 | 0.0 | 1 | 0 | 2 | 1 | 0 | .333 | .333 | 0 | 0 | OF-2 |
| 1969 | 113 | 374 | 84 | 14 | 4 | 6 | 1.6 | 42 | 44 | 42 | 64 | 6 | .225 | .332 | 1 | 0 | OF-111, 3B-3 |
| 1970 | 148 | 554 | 163 | 35 | 3 | 17 | 3.1 | 104 | 88 | 87 | 78 | 20 | .294 | .460 | 4 | 1 | OF-140 |
| 1971 | 141 | 504 | 133 | 26 | 6 | 15 | 3.0 | 80 | 65 | 84 | 76 | 18 | .264 | .429 | 2 | 0 | OF-138, 1B-1 |
| 1972 | 130 | 439 | 113 | 21 | 2 | 18 | 4.1 | 60 | 51 | 38 | 66 | 14 | .257 | .437 | 7 | 1 | OF-123 |
| 1973 CHI A | 73 | 262 | 68 | 13 | 0 | 6 | 2.3 | 31 | 32 | 27 | 49 | 3 | .260 | .378 | 1 | 1 | OF-44, DH-26 |
| 1974 | 162 | 602 | 176 | 35 | 4 | 20 | 3.3 | 76 | 95 | 66 | 112 | 12 | .292 | .467 | 0 | 0 | OF-162 |
| 1975 | 140 | 513 | 129 | 20 | 3 | 9 | 1.8 | 65 | 53 | 74 | 65 | 5 | .251 | .355 | 3 | 1 | OF-137, DH-1 |
| 1976 ATL N | 133 | 435 | 114 | 19 | 0 | 13 | 3.0 | 52 | 61 | 62 | 68 | 5 | .262 | .395 | 10 | 2 | OF-122 |
| 1977 TEX A | 75 | 244 | 63 | 14 | 0 | 5 | 2.0 | 23 | 23 | 18 | 37 | 2 | .258 | .377 | 9 | 2 | OF-65, DH-3 |
| 1978 2 teams | NY N (7G – .227) | | | | CIN N (64G – .167) | | | | | | | | | | | | |
| " total | 71 | 166 | 29 | 8 | 1 | 4 | 2.4 | 12 | 23 | 27 | 36 | 0 | .175 | .307 | 28 | 6 | OF-45 |
| 1979 2 teams | CIN N (10G – .231) | | | | CHI N (62G – .235) | | | | | | | | | | | | |
| " total | 72 | 94 | 22 | 3 | 0 | 2 | 2.1 | 12 | 10 | 15 | 18 | 0 | .234 | .330 | 50 | 9 | OF-25 |
| 1980 CHI N | 44 | 82 | 16 | 3 | 0 | 2 | 2.4 | 7 | 9 | 17 | 19 | 0 | .195 | .305 | 19 | 3 | OF-22 |
| 16 yrs. | 1444 | 4553 | 1168 | 216 | 26 | 122 | 2.7 | 594 | 576 | 589 | 763 | 86 | .257 | .396 | 153 | 29 | OF-1246, DH-30, 3B-3, 1B-1 |
| 2 yrs. | 106 | 163 | 35 | 5 | 0 | 4 | 2.5 | 18 | 17 | 32 | 35 | 0 | .215 | .319 | 63 | 11 | OF-45 |

LEAGUE CHAMPIONSHIP SERIES

| | G | AB | H | 2B | 3B | HR | HR% | R | RBI | BB | SO | SB | BA | SA | PH AB | PH H | G by POS |
|---|---|---|---|---|---|---|---|---|---|---|---|---|---|---|---|---|---|
| 1971 SF N | 4 | 16 | 5 | 1 | 0 | 0 | 0.0 | 3 | 2 | 2 | 1 | 1 | .313 | .375 | 0 | 0 | OF-4 |

# Steve Henderson

**HENDERSON, STEPHEN CURTIS**
B. Nov. 18, 1952, Houston, Tex.
BR TR 6'2" 190 lbs.

| | G | AB | H | 2B | 3B | HR | HR% | R | RBI | BB | SO | SB | BA | SA | PH AB | PH H | G by POS |
|---|---|---|---|---|---|---|---|---|---|---|---|---|---|---|---|---|---|
| 1977 NY N | 99 | 350 | 104 | 16 | 6 | 12 | 3.4 | 67 | 65 | 43 | 79 | 6 | .297 | .480 | 2 | 0 | OF-97 |
| 1978 | 157 | 587 | 156 | 30 | 9 | 10 | 1.7 | 83 | 65 | 60 | 109 | 13 | .266 | .399 | 4 | 4 | OF-155 |
| 1979 | 98 | 350 | 107 | 16 | 8 | 5 | 1.4 | 42 | 39 | 38 | 58 | 13 | .306 | .440 | 3 | 2 | OF-94 |
| 1980 | 143 | 513 | 149 | 17 | 8 | 8 | 1.6 | 75 | 58 | 62 | 90 | 23 | .290 | .402 | 8 | 1 | OF-136 |
| 1981 CHI N | 82 | 287 | 84 | 9 | 5 | 5 | 1.7 | 32 | 35 | 42 | 61 | 5 | .293 | .411 | 4 | 0 | OF-77 |
| 1982 | 92 | 257 | 60 | 12 | 4 | 2 | 0.8 | 23 | 29 | 22 | 64 | 6 | .233 | .335 | 25 | 6 | OF-70 |
| 1983 SEA A | 121 | 436 | 128 | 32 | 3 | 10 | 2.3 | 50 | 54 | 44 | 82 | 10 | .294 | .450 | 6 | 1 | OF-112, DH-6 |
| 1984 | 109 | 325 | 85 | 12 | 3 | 10 | 3.1 | 42 | 35 | 38 | 62 | 2 | .262 | .409 | 15 | 4 | OF-53, DH-51 |
| 1985 OAK A | 85 | 193 | 58 | 8 | 3 | 3 | 1.6 | 25 | 31 | 18 | 34 | 0 | .301 | .420 | 27 | 8 | OF-58, DH-1 |
| 9 yrs. | 986 | 3298 | 931 | 152 | 49 | 65 | 2.0 | 439 | 411 | 367 | 639 | 78 | .282 | .417 | 94 | 26 | OF-852, DH-58 |
| 2 yrs. | 174 | 544 | 144 | 21 | 9 | 7 | 1.3 | 55 | 64 | 64 | 125 | 11 | .265 | .375 | 29 | 6 | OF-147 |

# Harvey Hendrick

**HENDRICK, HARVEY LEE (Gink)**
B. Nov. 9, 1897, Mason, Tenn. D. Oct. 29, 1941, Covington, Tenn.
BL TR 6'2" 190 lbs.

| | G | AB | H | 2B | 3B | HR | HR% | R | RBI | BB | SO | SB | BA | SA | PH AB | PH H | G by POS |
|---|---|---|---|---|---|---|---|---|---|---|---|---|---|---|---|---|---|
| 1923 NY A | 37 | 66 | 18 | 3 | 1 | 3 | 4.5 | 9 | 12 | 2 | 8 | 3 | .273 | .485 | 24 | 6 | OF-12 |
| 1924 | 40 | 76 | 20 | 0 | 0 | 1 | 1.3 | 7 | 11 | 2 | 7 | 1 | .263 | .303 | 21 | 4 | OF-17 |
| 1925 CLE A | 25 | 28 | 8 | 1 | 2 | 0 | 0.0 | 2 | 9 | 3 | 5 | 0 | .286 | .464 | 16 | 6 | 1B-3 |
| 1927 BKN N | 128 | 458 | 142 | 18 | 11 | 4 | 0.9 | 55 | 50 | 24 | 40 | 29 | .310 | .424 | 10 | 3 | OF-64, 1B-53, 2B-1 |
| 1928 | 126 | 425 | 135 | 15 | 10 | 11 | 2.6 | 83 | 59 | 54 | 34 | 16 | .318 | .478 | 13 | 5 | 3B-91, OF-17 |
| 1929 | 110 | 384 | 136 | 25 | 6 | 14 | 3.6 | 69 | 82 | 31 | 20 | 14 | .354 | .560 | 13 | 7 | OF-42, 1B-39, 3B-7, SS-4 |
| 1930 | 68 | 167 | 43 | 10 | 1 | 5 | 3.0 | 29 | 28 | 20 | 19 | 2 | .257 | .419 | 16 | 4 | OF-42, 1B-7 |
| 1931 2 teams | BKN N (1G – .000) | | | | CIN N (137G – .315) | | | | | | | | | | | | |
| " total | 138 | 531 | 167 | 32 | 9 | 1 | 0.2 | 74 | 75 | 53 | 40 | 3 | .315 | .414 | 1 | 0 | 1B-137 |
| 1932 2 teams | STL N (28G – .250) | | | | CIN N (94G – .302) | | | | | | | | | | | | |
| " total | 122 | 470 | 138 | 32 | 3 | 5 | 1.1 | 64 | 45 | 28 | 38 | 3 | .294 | .406 | 9 | 3 | 1B-94, 3B-12, OF-5 |
| 1933 CHI N | 69 | 189 | 55 | 13 | 3 | 4 | 2.1 | 30 | 23 | 13 | 17 | 4 | .291 | .455 | 19 | 6 | 1B-38, OF-8, 3B-1 |
| 1934 PHI N | 59 | 116 | 34 | 8 | 0 | 0 | 0.0 | 12 | 19 | 9 | 15 | 0 | .293 | .362 | 31 | 7 | OF-12, 3B-7, 1B-7 |
| 11 yrs. | 922 | 2910 | 896 | 157 | 46 | 48 | 1.6 | 434 | 413 | 239 | 243 | 75 | .308 | .443 | 173 | 51 | 1B-378, OF-219, 3B-118, SS-4, 2B-1 |
| 1 yr. | 69 | 189 | 55 | 13 | 3 | 4 | 2.1 | 30 | 23 | 13 | 17 | 4 | .291 | .455 | 19 | 6 | 1B-38, OF-8, 3B-1 |

WORLD SERIES

| | G | AB | H | 2B | 3B | HR | HR% | R | RBI | BB | SO | SB | BA | SA | PH AB | PH H | G by POS |
|---|---|---|---|---|---|---|---|---|---|---|---|---|---|---|---|---|---|
| 1923 NY A | 1 | 1 | 0 | 0 | 0 | 0 | 0.0 | 0 | 0 | 0 | 0 | 0 | .000 | .000 | 1 | 0 | |

# Ellie Hendricks

**HENDRICKS, ELROD JEROME**
B. Dec. 22, 1940, St. Thomas, Virgin Islands
BL TR 6'1" 175 lbs.

| | G | AB | H | 2B | 3B | HR | HR% | R | RBI | BB | SO | SB | BA | SA | PH AB | PH H | G by POS |
|---|---|---|---|---|---|---|---|---|---|---|---|---|---|---|---|---|---|
| 1968 BAL A | 79 | 183 | 37 | 8 | 1 | 7 | 3.8 | 19 | 23 | 19 | 51 | 0 | .202 | .372 | 27 | 4 | C-53 |
| 1969 | 105 | 295 | 72 | 5 | 0 | 12 | 4.1 | 36 | 38 | 39 | 44 | 0 | .244 | .383 | 16 | 5 | C-87, 1B-4 |
| 1970 | 106 | 322 | 78 | 9 | 0 | 12 | 3.7 | 32 | 41 | 33 | 44 | 1 | .242 | .382 | 16 | 3 | C-95 |
| 1971 | 101 | 316 | 79 | 14 | 1 | 9 | 2.8 | 33 | 42 | 39 | 38 | 0 | .250 | .386 | 11 | 3 | C-90, 1B-3 |
| 1972 2 teams | BAL A (33G – .155) | | | | CHI N (17G – .116) | | | | | | | | | | | | |
| " total | 50 | 127 | 18 | 5 | 0 | 2 | 1.6 | 13 | 10 | 25 | 27 | 0 | .142 | .228 | 4 | 0 | C-44 |
| 1973 BAL A | 41 | 101 | 18 | 5 | 1 | 3 | 3.0 | 9 | 15 | 10 | 22 | 0 | .178 | .337 | 2 | 0 | C-38 |
| 1974 | 66 | 159 | 33 | 8 | 2 | 3 | 1.9 | 18 | 8 | 17 | 25 | 0 | .208 | .340 | 14 | 5 | C-54, DH-1, 1B-1 |
| 1975 | 85 | 223 | 48 | 8 | 2 | 8 | 3.6 | 32 | 38 | 34 | 40 | 0 | .215 | .377 | 8 | 1 | C-83 |
| 1976 2 teams | BAL A (28G – .139) | | | | NY A (26G – .226) | | | | | | | | | | | | |
| " total | 54 | 132 | 23 | 2 | 0 | 4 | 3.0 | 8 | 9 | 10 | 23 | 0 | .174 | .280 | 12 | 2 | C-45 |
| 1977 NY A | 10 | 11 | 3 | 1 | 0 | 1 | 9.1 | 1 | 5 | 0 | 2 | 0 | .273 | .636 | 3 | 1 | C-6 |
| 1978 BAL A | 13 | 18 | 6 | 1 | 0 | 1 | 5.6 | 4 | 1 | 3 | 3 | 0 | .333 | .556 | 6 | 1 | C-6, DH-1, P-1 |
| 1979 | 1 | 1 | 0 | 0 | 0 | 0 | 0.0 | 0 | 0 | 0 | 0 | 0 | .000 | .000 | 0 | 0 | C-1 |
| 12 yrs. | 711 | 1888 | 415 | 66 | 7 | 62 | 3.3 | 205 | 230 | 229 | 319 | 1 | .220 | .361 | 119 | 25 | C-602, 1B-8, DH-2, P-1 |
| 1 yr. | 17 | 43 | 5 | 1 | 0 | 2 | 4.7 | 7 | 6 | 13 | 17 | 0 | .116 | .279 | 6 | 0 | C-16 |

LEAGUE CHAMPIONSHIP SERIES

| | G | AB | H | 2B | 3B | HR | HR% | R | RBI | BB | SO | SB | BA | SA | PH AB | PH H | G by POS |
|---|---|---|---|---|---|---|---|---|---|---|---|---|---|---|---|---|---|
| 1969 BAL A | 3 | 8 | 2 | 2 | 0 | 0 | 0.0 | 2 | 3 | 1 | 3 | 0 | .250 | .500 | 0 | 0 | C-3 |
| 1970 | 2 | 5 | 2 | 0 | 0 | 0 | 0.0 | 2 | 0 | 0 | 1 | 0 | .400 | .400 | 0 | 0 | C-2 |
| 1971 | 2 | 4 | 2 | 0 | 0 | 1 | 25.0 | 1 | 2 | 1 | 1 | 0 | .500 | 1.250 | 0 | 0 | C-2 |
| 1974 | 3 | 6 | 1 | 0 | 0 | 0 | 0.0 | 0 | 1 | 0 | 0 | 0 | .167 | .167 | 0 | 0 | C-3 |

| | G | AB | H | 2B | 3B | HR | HR % | R | RBI | BB | SO | SB | BA | SA | Pinch Hit AB | Pinch Hit H | G by POS |
|---|---|---|---|---|---|---|---|---|---|---|---|---|---|---|---|---|---|

## Ellie Hendricks continued

| | G | AB | H | 2B | 3B | HR | HR % | R | RBI | BB | SO | SB | BA | SA | AB | H | G by POS |
|---|---|---|---|---|---|---|---|---|---|---|---|---|---|---|---|---|---|
| 1976 NY A | 1 | 1 | 1 | 0 | 0 | 0 | 0.0 | 0 | 0 | 0 | 0 | 0 | 1.000 | 1.000 | 1 | 0 | |
| 5 yrs. | 10 | 24 | 8 | 2 | 0 | 1 | 4.2 | 6 | 5 | 3 | 8 | 0 | .333 | .542 | 1 | 0 | C-9 |
| WORLD SERIES | | | | | | | | | | | | | | | | | |
| 1969 BAL A | 3 | 10 | 1 | 0 | 0 | 0 | 0.0 | 1 | 0 | 1 | 0 | 0 | .100 | .100 | 0 | 0 | C-3 |
| 1970 | 3 | 11 | 4 | 1 | 0 | 1 | 9.1 | 1 | 4 | 1 | 2 | 0 | .364 | .727 | 0 | 0 | C-3 |
| 1971 | 6 | 19 | 5 | 1 | 0 | 0 | 0.0 | 3 | 1 | 3 | 3 | 0 | .263 | .316 | 0 | 0 | C-6 |
| 1976 NY A | 2 | 2 | 0 | 0 | 0 | 0 | 0.0 | 0 | 0 | 0 | 0 | 0 | .000 | .000 | 2 | 0 | |
| 4 yrs. | 14 | 42 | 10 | 2 | 0 | 1 | 2.4 | 5 | 5 | 5 | 5 | 0 | .238 | .357 | 2 | 0 | C-12 |

## Jack Hendricks

**HENDRICKS, JOHN CHARLES**
B. Apr. 9, 1875, Joliet, Ill.    D. May 13, 1943, Chicago, Ill.
Manager 1918, 1924-29.

BL TL 5'11½" 160 lbs.

| | G | AB | H | 2B | 3B | HR | HR % | R | RBI | BB | SO | SB | BA | SA | AB | H | G by POS |
|---|---|---|---|---|---|---|---|---|---|---|---|---|---|---|---|---|---|
| 1902 2 teams | NY N (8G – .231) | | | | CHI N | | (2G – .571) | | | | | | | | | | |
| " total | 10 | 33 | 10 | 2 | 1 | 0 | 0.0 | 1 | 0 | 2 | | 2 | .303 | .424 | 1 | 0 | OF-9 |
| 1903 WAS A | 32 | 112 | 20 | 1 | 3 | 0 | 0.0 | 10 | 4 | 13 | | 3 | .179 | .241 | 0 | 0 | OF-32 |
| 2 yrs. | 42 | 145 | 30 | 3 | 4 | 0 | 0.0 | 11 | 4 | 15 | | 5 | .207 | .283 | 1 | 0 | OF-41 |
| 1 yr. | 2 | 7 | 4 | 0 | 1 | 0 | 0.0 | 0 | 0 | 0 | | 0 | .571 | .857 | 0 | 0 | OF-2 |

## Claude Hendrix

**HENDRIX, CLAUDE RAYMOND**
B. Apr. 13, 1889, Olathe, Kans.    D. Mar. 22, 1944, Allentown, Pa.

BR TR 6' 195 lbs.

| | G | AB | H | 2B | 3B | HR | HR % | R | RBI | BB | SO | SB | BA | SA | AB | H | G by POS |
|---|---|---|---|---|---|---|---|---|---|---|---|---|---|---|---|---|---|
| 1911 PIT N | 22 | 41 | 4 | 1 | 1 | 0 | 0.0 | 2 | 2 | 1 | 15 | 0 | .098 | .171 | 0 | 0 | P-22 |
| 1912 | 39 | 121 | 39 | 10 | 6 | 1 | 0.8 | 25 | 15 | 3 | 18 | 1 | .322 | .529 | 5 | 2 | P-39 |
| 1913 | 53 | 99 | 27 | 5 | 4 | 1 | 1.0 | 13 | 8 | 3 | 16 | 0 | .273 | .434 | 8 | 0 | P-42 |
| 1914 CHI F | 52 | 130 | 30 | 3 | 0 | 2 | 1.5 | 15 | 13 | 7 | | 3 | .231 | .300 | 2 | 1 | P-49 |
| 1915 | 50 | 113 | 30 | 7 | 2 | 4 | 3.5 | 22 | 18 | 5 | | 1 | .265 | .469 | 9 | 2 | P-40 |
| 1916 CHI N | 45 | 80 | 16 | 3 | 0 | 1 | 1.3 | 4 | 5 | 6 | 24 | 0 | .200 | .275 | 7 | 1 | P-36 |
| 1917 | 48 | 86 | 22 | 3 | 1 | 0 | 0.0 | 7 | 7 | 5 | 20 | 1 | .256 | .314 | 5 | 1 | P-40, OF-2 |
| 1918 | 35 | 91 | 24 | 3 | 3 | 3 | 3.3 | 14 | 17 | 4 | 11 | 1 | .264 | .462 | 3 | 1 | P-32 |
| 1919 | 36 | 78 | 15 | 1 | 0 | 1 | 1.3 | 6 | 6 | 2 | 19 | 0 | .192 | .244 | 3 | 1 | P-33 |
| 1920 | 34 | 83 | 15 | 3 | 0 | 0 | 0.0 | 10 | 6 | 3 | 11 | 2 | .181 | .217 | 7 | 1 | P-27 |
| 10 yrs. | 414 | 922 | 222 | 39 | 17 | 13 | 1.4 | 118 | 97 | 39 | 134 | 9 | .241 | .362 | 49 | 10 | P-360, OF-2 |
| 5 yrs. | 198 | 418 | 92 | 13 | 4 | 5 | 1.2 | 41 | 41 | 20 | 85 | 4 | .220 | .306 | 25 | 5 | P-168, OF-2 |
| WORLD SERIES | | | | | | | | | | | | | | | | | |
| 1918 CHI N | 2 | 1 | 1 | 0 | 0 | 0 | 0.0 | 0 | 0 | 0 | 0 | 0 | 1.000 | 1.000 | 1 | 1 | P-1 |

## Babe Herman

**HERMAN, FLOYD CAVES**
B. June 26, 1903, Buffalo, N. Y.

BL TL 6'4" 190 lbs.

| | G | AB | H | 2B | 3B | HR | HR % | R | RBI | BB | SO | SB | BA | SA | AB | H | G by POS |
|---|---|---|---|---|---|---|---|---|---|---|---|---|---|---|---|---|---|
| 1926 BKN N | 137 | 496 | 158 | 35 | 11 | 11 | 2.2 | 64 | 81 | 44 | 53 | 8 | .319 | .500 | 6 | 2 | 1B-101, OF-35 |
| 1927 | 130 | 412 | 112 | 26 | 9 | 14 | 3.4 | 65 | 73 | 39 | 41 | 4 | .272 | .481 | 20 | 7 | 1B-105, OF-1 |
| 1928 | 134 | 486 | 165 | 37 | 6 | 12 | 2.5 | 64 | 91 | 38 | 36 | 1 | .340 | .514 | 6 | 1 | OF-127 |
| 1929 | 146 | 569 | 217 | 42 | 13 | 21 | 3.7 | 105 | 113 | 55 | 45 | 21 | .381 | .612 | 3 | 2 | OF-141, 1B-2 |
| 1930 | 153 | 614 | 241 | 48 | 11 | 35 | 5.7 | 143 | 130 | 66 | 56 | 18 | .393 | .678 | 0 | 0 | OF-153 |
| 1931 | 151 | 610 | 191 | 43 | 16 | 18 | 3.0 | 93 | 97 | 50 | 65 | 17 | .313 | .525 | 0 | 0 | OF-150 |
| 1932 CIN N | 148 | 577 | 188 | 38 | 19 | 16 | 2.8 | 87 | 87 | 60 | 45 | 7 | .326 | .541 | 2 | 1 | OF-146 |
| 1933 CHI N | 137 | 508 | 147 | 36 | 12 | 16 | 3.1 | 77 | 93 | 50 | 57 | 6 | .289 | .502 | 5 | 4 | OF-131 |
| 1934 | 125 | 467 | 142 | 34 | 5 | 14 | 3.0 | 65 | 84 | 35 | 71 | 1 | .304 | .488 | 6 | 2 | OF-113, 1B-7 |
| 1935 2 teams | PIT N (26G – .235) | | | | CIN N | | (92G – .335) | | | | | | | | | | |
| " total | 118 | 430 | 136 | 31 | 6 | 10 | 2.3 | 52 | 65 | 38 | 35 | 5 | .316 | .486 | 10 | 0 | OF-91, 1B-17 |
| 1936 CIN N | 119 | 380 | 106 | 25 | 2 | 13 | 3.4 | 59 | 71 | 39 | 36 | 4 | .279 | .458 | 19 | 4 | OF-92, 1B-4 |
| 1937 DET A | 17 | 20 | 6 | 3 | 0 | 0 | 0.0 | 2 | 3 | 1 | 6 | 2 | .300 | .450 | 14 | 3 | OF-2 |
| 1945 BKN N | 37 | 34 | 9 | 1 | 0 | 1 | 2.9 | 6 | 9 | 5 | 7 | 0 | .265 | .382 | 29 | 6 | OF-3 |
| 13 yrs. | 1552 | 5603 | 1818 | 399 | 110 | 181 | 3.2 | 882 | 997 | 520 | 553 | 94 | .324 | .532 | 120 | 32 | OF-1185, 1B-236 |
| 2 yrs. | 262 | 975 | 289 | 70 | 17 | 30 | 3.1 | 142 | 177 | 85 | 128 | 7 | .296 | .495 | 11 | 6 | OF-244, 1B-7 |

## Billy Herman

**HERMAN, WILLIAM JENNINGS (Bryan)**
B. July 7, 1909, New Albany, Ind.
Manager 1947, 1964-66.
Hall of Fame 1975.

BR TR 5'11" 180 lbs.

| | G | AB | H | 2B | 3B | HR | HR % | R | RBI | BB | SO | SB | BA | SA | AB | H | G by POS |
|---|---|---|---|---|---|---|---|---|---|---|---|---|---|---|---|---|---|
| 1931 CHI N | 25 | 98 | 32 | 7 | 0 | 0 | 0.0 | 14 | 16 | 13 | 6 | 2 | .327 | .398 | 0 | 0 | 2B-25 |
| 1932 | 154 | 656 | 206 | 42 | 7 | 1 | 0.2 | 102 | 51 | 40 | 33 | 14 | .314 | .404 | 0 | 0 | 2B-154 |
| 1933 | 153 | 619 | 173 | 35 | 2 | 0 | 0.0 | 82 | 44 | 45 | 34 | 5 | .279 | .342 | 0 | 0 | 2B-153 |
| 1934 | 113 | 456 | 138 | 21 | 6 | 3 | 0.7 | 79 | 42 | 34 | 31 | 6 | .303 | .395 | 1 | 0 | 2B-111 |
| 1935 | 154 | 666 | 227 | 57 | 6 | 7 | 1.1 | 113 | 83 | 42 | 29 | 6 | .341 | .476 | 0 | 0 | 2B-154 |
| 1936 | 153 | 632 | 211 | 57 | 7 | 5 | 0.8 | 101 | 93 | 59 | 30 | 5 | .334 | .470 | 0 | 0 | 2B-153 |
| 1937 | 138 | 564 | 189 | 35 | 11 | 8 | 1.4 | 106 | 65 | 56 | 22 | 1 | .335 | .479 | 1 | 0 | 2B-137 |
| 1938 | 152 | 624 | 173 | 34 | 7 | 1 | 0.2 | 86 | 56 | 59 | 31 | 3 | .277 | .359 | 1 | 0 | 2B-151 |
| 1939 | 156 | 623 | 191 | 34 | 18 | 7 | 1.1 | 111 | 70 | 66 | 31 | 9 | .307 | .453 | 0 | 0 | 2B-156 |
| 1940 | 135 | 558 | 163 | 24 | 4 | 5 | 0.9 | 77 | 57 | 47 | 30 | 1 | .292 | .376 | 0 | 0 | 2B-135 |
| 1941 2 teams | CHI N (11G – .194) | | | | BKN N | | (133G – .291) | | | | | | | | | | |
| " total | 144 | 572 | 163 | 30 | 5 | 3 | 0.5 | 81 | 41 | 67 | 43 | 1 | .285 | .371 | 0 | 0 | 2B-144 |
| 1942 BKN N | 155 | 571 | 146 | 34 | 2 | 2 | 0.4 | 76 | 65 | 72 | 52 | 6 | .256 | .333 | 0 | 0 | 2B-153, 1B-3 |
| 1943 | 153 | 585 | 193 | 41 | 2 | 2 | 0.3 | 76 | 100 | 66 | 26 | 4 | .330 | .417 | 0 | 0 | 2B-117, 3B-37 |
| 1946 2 teams | BKN N (47G – .288) | | | | BOS N | | (75G – .306) | | | | | | | | | | |
| " total | 122 | 436 | 130 | 31 | 5 | 3 | 0.7 | 56 | 50 | 69 | 23 | 3 | .298 | .413 | 4 | 1 | 2B-76, 3B-63, 1B-22 |
| 1947 PIT N | 15 | 47 | 10 | 4 | 0 | 0 | 0.0 | 3 | 6 | 2 | 7 | 0 | .213 | .298 | 1 | 0 | 2B-10, 1B-2 |
| 15 yrs. | 1922 | 7707 | 2345 | 486 | 82 | 47 | 0.6 | 1163 | 839 | 737 | 428 | 67 | .304 | .407 | 8 | 1 | 2B-1829, 3B-100, 1B-27 |
| 11 yrs. | 1344 | 5532 | 1710 | 346 | 69 | 37 | 0.7 | 875 | 577 | 470 | 282 | 53 | .309 | .417 | 3 | 0 | 2B-1340 |
| | | | 9th | 8th | | | | 9th | | | | | | | | | |
| WORLD SERIES | | | | | | | | | | | | | | | | | |
| 1932 CHI N | 4 | 18 | 4 | 1 | 0 | 0 | 0.0 | 5 | 1 | 1 | 3 | 0 | .222 | .278 | 0 | 0 | 2B-4 |
| 1935 | 6 | 24 | 8 | 2 | 1 | 1 | 4.2 | 3 | 6 | 0 | 2 | 0 | .333 | .625 | 0 | 0 | 2B-6 |
| 1938 | 4 | 16 | 3 | 0 | 0 | 0 | 0.0 | 1 | 0 | 1 | 4 | 0 | .188 | .188 | 0 | 0 | 2B-4 |

| | G | AB | H | 2B | 3B | HR | HR % | R | RBI | BB | SO | SB | BA | SA | Pinch Hit AB | Pinch Hit H | G by POS |
|---|---|---|---|---|---|---|---|---|---|---|---|---|---|---|---|---|---|

## Billy Herman continued

| | G | AB | H | 2B | 3B | HR | HR% | R | RBI | BB | SO | SB | BA | SA | PH AB | PH H | G by POS |
|---|---|---|---|---|---|---|---|---|---|---|---|---|---|---|---|---|---|
| 1941 BKN N | 4 | 8 | 1 | 0 | 0 | 0 | 0.0 | 0 | 0 | 2 | 0 | 0 | .125 | .125 | 0 | 0 | 2B-4 |
| 4 yrs. | 18 | 66 | 16 | 3 | 1 | 1 | 1.5 | 9 | 7 | 4 | 9 | 0 | .242 | .364 | 0 | 0 | 2B-18 |

## Gene Hermanski

**HERMANSKI, EUGENE VICTOR**
B. May 11, 1920, Pittsfield, Mass.      BL TR 5'11½" 185 lbs.

| | G | AB | H | 2B | 3B | HR | HR% | R | RBI | BB | SO | SB | BA | SA | PH AB | PH H | G by POS |
|---|---|---|---|---|---|---|---|---|---|---|---|---|---|---|---|---|---|
| 1943 BKN N | 18 | 60 | 18 | 2 | 1 | 0 | 0.0 | 6 | 12 | 11 | 7 | 1 | .300 | .367 | 0 | 0 | OF-18 |
| 1946 | 64 | 110 | 22 | 2 | 2 | 0 | 0.0 | 15 | 8 | 17 | 10 | 2 | .200 | .255 | 24 | 2 | OF-34 |
| 1947 | 79 | 189 | 52 | 7 | 1 | 7 | 3.7 | 36 | 39 | 28 | 7 | 5 | .275 | .434 | 12 | 4 | OF-66 |
| 1948 | 133 | 400 | 116 | 22 | 7 | 15 | 3.8 | 63 | 60 | 64 | 46 | 15 | .290 | .493 | 12 | 3 | OF-119 |
| 1949 | 87 | 224 | 67 | 12 | 3 | 8 | 3.6 | 48 | 42 | 47 | 21 | 12 | .299 | .487 | 13 | 5 | OF-77 |
| 1950 | 94 | 289 | 86 | 17 | 3 | 7 | 2.4 | 36 | 34 | 36 | 26 | 2 | .298 | .450 | 12 | 3 | OF-78 |
| 1951 2 teams | | BKN N | (31G – | .250) | | CHI N | (75G – | .281) | | | | | | | | | |
| " total | 106 | 311 | 85 | 16 | 1 | 4 | 1.3 | 36 | 25 | 45 | 42 | 3 | .273 | .370 | 20 | 7 | OF-94 |
| 1952 CHI N | 99 | 275 | 70 | 6 | 0 | 4 | 1.5 | 28 | 34 | 29 | 32 | 2 | .255 | .320 | 21 | 10 | OF-76 |
| 1953 2 teams | | CHI N | (18G – | .150) | | PIT N | (41G – | .177) | | | | | | | | | |
| " total | 59 | 102 | 17 | 1 | 0 | 1 | 1.0 | 8 | 5 | 12 | 21 | 1 | .167 | .206 | 29 | 4 | OF-26 |
| 9 yrs. | 739 | 1960 | 533 | 85 | 18 | 46 | 2.3 | 276 | 259 | 289 | 212 | 43 | .272 | .404 | 143 | 38 | OF-588 |
| 3 yrs. | 192 | 546 | 141 | 19 | 1 | 7 | 1.3 | 57 | 55 | 68 | 69 | 6 | .258 | .335 | 37 | 15 | OF-164 |

WORLD SERIES

| | G | AB | H | 2B | 3B | HR | HR% | R | RBI | BB | SO | SB | BA | SA | PH AB | PH H | G by POS |
|---|---|---|---|---|---|---|---|---|---|---|---|---|---|---|---|---|---|
| 1947 BKN N | 7 | 19 | 3 | 0 | 1 | 0 | 0.0 | 4 | 1 | 3 | 3 | 0 | .158 | .263 | 0 | 0 | OF-7 |
| 1949 | 4 | 13 | 4 | 0 | 1 | 0 | 0.0 | 1 | 2 | 3 | 3 | 0 | .308 | .462 | 0 | 0 | OF-4 |
| 2 yrs. | 11 | 32 | 7 | 0 | 2 | 0 | 0.0 | 5 | 3 | 6 | 6 | 0 | .219 | .344 | 0 | 0 | OF-11 |

## Chico Hernandez

**HERNANDEZ, SALVADOR JOSE RAMOS**
B. Jan. 3, 1916, Havana, Cuba      BR TR 6'1" 195 lbs.

| | G | AB | H | 2B | 3B | HR | HR% | R | RBI | BB | SO | SB | BA | SA | PH AB | PH H | G by POS |
|---|---|---|---|---|---|---|---|---|---|---|---|---|---|---|---|---|---|
| 1942 CHI N | 47 | 118 | 27 | 5 | 0 | 0 | 0.0 | 6 | 7 | 11 | 13 | 0 | .229 | .271 | 3 | 1 | C-43 |
| 1943 | 43 | 126 | 34 | 4 | 0 | 0 | 0.0 | 10 | 9 | 9 | 9 | 0 | .270 | .302 | 2 | 0 | C-41 |
| 2 yrs. | 90 | 244 | 61 | 9 | 0 | 0 | 0.0 | 16 | 16 | 20 | 22 | 0 | .250 | .287 | 5 | 1 | C-84 |
| 2 yrs. | 90 | 244 | 61 | 9 | 0 | 0 | 0.0 | 16 | 16 | 20 | 22 | 0 | .250 | .287 | 5 | 1 | C-84 |

## Tom Hernon

**HERNON, THOMAS H.**
B. Nov. 4, 1866, E. Bridgewater, Mass.     D. Feb. 4, 1902, New Bedford, Mass.

| | G | AB | H | 2B | 3B | HR | HR% | R | RBI | BB | SO | SB | BA | SA | PH AB | PH H | G by POS |
|---|---|---|---|---|---|---|---|---|---|---|---|---|---|---|---|---|---|
| 1897 CHI N | 4 | 16 | 1 | 0 | 0 | 0 | 0.0 | 2 | 2 | 0 | | 1 | .063 | .063 | 0 | 0 | OF-4 |

## John Herrnstein

**HERRNSTEIN, JOHN ELLETT**
B. Mar. 31, 1938, Hampton, Va.      BL TL 6'3" 215 lbs.

| | G | AB | H | 2B | 3B | HR | HR% | R | RBI | BB | SO | SB | BA | SA | PH AB | PH H | G by POS |
|---|---|---|---|---|---|---|---|---|---|---|---|---|---|---|---|---|---|
| 1962 PHI N | 6 | 5 | 1 | 0 | 0 | 0 | 0.0 | 0 | 1 | 1 | 3 | 0 | .200 | .200 | 5 | 1 | OF-1 |
| 1963 | 15 | 12 | 2 | 0 | 0 | 1 | 8.3 | 1 | 1 | 1 | 5 | 0 | .167 | .417 | 10 | 1 | OF-2, 1B-1 |
| 1964 | 125 | 303 | 71 | 12 | 4 | 6 | 2.0 | 38 | 25 | 22 | 67 | 1 | .234 | .360 | 21 | 7 | OF-69, 1B-68 |
| 1965 | 63 | 85 | 17 | 2 | 0 | 1 | 1.2 | 8 | 5 | 2 | 18 | 0 | .200 | .259 | 30 | 5 | 1B-18, OF-14 |
| 1966 3 teams | | PHI N | (4G – | .100) | | CHI N | (9G – | .176) | | ATL N | (17G – | .222) | | | | | |
| " total | 30 | 45 | 8 | 0 | 0 | 0 | 0.0 | 5 | 2 | 3 | 22 | 0 | .178 | .178 | 20 | 4 | OF-8, 1B-4 |
| 5 yrs. | 239 | 450 | 99 | 14 | 4 | 8 | 1.8 | 52 | 34 | 29 | 115 | 1 | .220 | .322 | 86 | 18 | OF-94, 1B-91 |
| 1 yr. | 9 | 17 | 3 | 0 | 0 | 0 | 0.0 | 3 | 0 | 3 | 8 | 0 | .176 | .176 | 5 | 0 | 1B-4, OF-1 |

## Buck Herzog

**HERZOG, CHARLES LINCOLN**
B. July 9, 1885, Baltimore, Md.    D. Sept. 4, 1953, Baltimore, Md.      BR TR 5'11" 160 lbs.
Manager 1914-16.

| | G | AB | H | 2B | 3B | HR | HR% | R | RBI | BB | SO | SB | BA | SA | PH AB | PH H | G by POS |
|---|---|---|---|---|---|---|---|---|---|---|---|---|---|---|---|---|---|
| 1908 NY N | 64 | 160 | 48 | 6 | 2 | 0 | 0.0 | 38 | 11 | 36 | | 16 | .300 | .363 | 3 | 0 | 2B-42, SS-11, 3B-3, OF-1 |
| 1909 | 42 | 130 | 24 | 2 | 0 | 0 | 0.0 | 16 | 8 | 13 | | 2 | .185 | .200 | 1 | 0 | OF-29, 3B-4, 2B-4, SS-1 |
| 1910 BOS N | 106 | 380 | 95 | 20 | 3 | 3 | 0.8 | 51 | 32 | 30 | 34 | 13 | .250 | .342 | 1 | 0 | 3B-105 |
| 1911 2 teams | | BOS N | (79G – | .310) | | NY N | (69G – | .267) | | | | | | | | | |
| " total | 148 | 541 | 157 | 33 | 9 | 6 | 1.1 | 90 | 67 | 47 | 40 | 48 | .290 | .418 | 1 | 0 | SS-75, 3B-69, 2B-3 |
| 1912 NY N | 140 | 482 | 127 | 20 | 9 | 2 | 0.4 | 72 | 47 | 57 | 34 | 37 | .263 | .355 | 0 | 0 | 3B-140 |
| 1913 | 96 | 290 | 83 | 15 | 3 | 3 | 1.0 | 46 | 31 | 22 | 12 | 23 | .286 | .390 | 2 | 1 | 3B-84, 2B-2 |
| 1914 CIN N | 138 | 498 | 140 | 14 | 8 | 1 | 0.2 | 54 | 40 | 42 | 27 | 46 | .281 | .347 | 0 | 0 | SS-137, 1B-2 |
| 1915 | 155 | 579 | 153 | 14 | 10 | 1 | 0.2 | 61 | 42 | 34 | 21 | 35 | .264 | .328 | 0 | 0 | SS-153, 1B-2 |
| 1916 2 teams | | CIN N | (79G – | .267) | | NY N | (77G – | .261) | | | | | | | | | |
| " total | 156 | 561 | 148 | 24 | 6 | 1 | 0.2 | 70 | 49 | 43 | 36 | 34 | .264 | .333 | 1 | 0 | SS-74, 2B-44, 3B-39, OF-1 |
| 1917 NY N | 114 | 417 | 98 | 10 | 8 | 2 | 0.5 | 69 | 31 | 31 | 36 | 12 | .235 | .312 | 0 | 0 | 2B-113 |
| 1918 BOS N | 118 | 473 | 108 | 12 | 6 | 0 | 0.0 | 57 | 26 | 29 | 28 | 10 | .228 | .279 | 0 | 0 | 2B-99, 1B-12, SS-7 |
| 1919 2 teams | | BOS N | (73G – | .280) | | CHI N | (52G – | .275) | | | | | | | | | |
| " total | 125 | 468 | 130 | 12 | 9 | 1 | 0.2 | 42 | 42 | 23 | 18 | 28 | .278 | .348 | 2 | 1 | 2B-122, 1B-1 |
| 1920 CHI N | 91 | 305 | 59 | 9 | 2 | 0 | 0.0 | 39 | 19 | 20 | 21 | 8 | .193 | .236 | 2 | 0 | 2B-59, 3B-28, 1B-1 |
| 13 yrs. | 1493 | 5284 | 1370 | 191 | 75 | 20 | 0.4 | 705 | 445 | 427 | 307 | 312 | .259 | .335 | 13 | 3 | 2B-488, 3B-472, SS-458, OF-31, 1B-18 |
| 2 yrs. | 143 | 498 | 112 | 13 | 6 | 0 | 0.0 | 54 | 36 | 30 | 28 | 20 | .225 | .275 | 2 | 0 | 2B-111, 3B-28, 1B-1 |

WORLD SERIES

| | G | AB | H | 2B | 3B | HR | HR% | R | RBI | BB | SO | SB | BA | SA | PH AB | PH H | G by POS |
|---|---|---|---|---|---|---|---|---|---|---|---|---|---|---|---|---|---|
| 1911 NY N | 6 | 21 | 4 | 2 | 0 | 0 | 0.0 | 3 | 0 | 2 | 3 | 2 | .190 | .286 | 0 | 0 | 3B-6 |
| 1912 | 8 | 30 | 12 | 4 | 1 | 0 | 0.0 | 6 | 4 | 1 | 3 | 2 | .400 | .600 | 0 | 0 | 3B-8 |
| 1913 | 5 | 19 | 1 | 0 | 0 | 0 | 0.0 | 1 | 0 | 1 | 0 | 0 | .053 | .053 | 0 | 0 | 3B-5 |
| 1917 | 6 | 24 | 6 | 0 | 1 | 0 | 0.0 | 1 | 2 | 0 | 4 | 0 | .250 | .333 | 0 | 0 | 2B-6 |
| 4 yrs. | 25 | 94 | 23 | 6 | 2 | 0 | 0.0 | 11 | 6 | 3 | 11 | 4 | .245 | .351 | 0 | 0 | 3B-19, 2B-6 |

## Jack Hiatt

**HIATT, JACK E.**
B. July 27, 1942, Bakersfield, Calif.      BR TR 6'2" 190 lbs.

| | G | AB | H | 2B | 3B | HR | HR% | R | RBI | BB | SO | SB | BA | SA | PH AB | PH H | G by POS |
|---|---|---|---|---|---|---|---|---|---|---|---|---|---|---|---|---|---|
| 1964 LA A | 9 | 16 | 6 | 0 | 0 | 0 | 0.0 | 2 | 2 | 2 | 3 | 0 | .375 | .375 | 4 | 3 | C-3, 1B-2 |
| 1965 SF N | 40 | 67 | 19 | 4 | 0 | 1 | 1.5 | 5 | 7 | 12 | 14 | 0 | .284 | .388 | 16 | 6 | C-21, 1B-7 |
| 1966 | 18 | 23 | 7 | 2 | 0 | 0 | 0.0 | 2 | 1 | 4 | 5 | 0 | .304 | .391 | 9 | 3 | 1B-7 |

| | G | AB | H | 2B | 3B | HR | HR % | R | RBI | BB | SO | SB | BA | SA | Pinch Hit AB | Pinch Hit H | G by POS |
|---|---|---|---|---|---|---|---|---|---|---|---|---|---|---|---|---|---|

## Jack Hiatt continued

| | G | AB | H | 2B | 3B | HR | HR% | R | RBI | BB | SO | SB | BA | SA | AB | H | G by POS |
|---|---|---|---|---|---|---|---|---|---|---|---|---|---|---|---|---|---|
| 1967 | 73 | 153 | 42 | 6 | 0 | 6 | 3.9 | 24 | 26 | 27 | 37 | 0 | .275 | .431 | 31 | 8 | 1B-36, C-3, OF-2 |
| 1968 | 90 | 224 | 52 | 10 | 2 | 4 | 1.8 | 14 | 34 | 41 | 61 | 0 | .232 | .348 | 21 | 6 | C-58, 1B-10 |
| 1969 | 69 | 194 | 38 | 4 | 0 | 7 | 3.6 | 18 | 34 | 48 | 58 | 0 | .196 | .325 | 2 | 0 | C-60, 1B-3 |
| 1970 2 teams | | MON | N | (17G – | .326) | | CHI | N | (66G – | .242) | | | | | | | |
| " total | 83 | 221 | 57 | 14 | 1 | 2 | 0.9 | 23 | 29 | 45 | 62 | 0 | .258 | .357 | 7 | 0 | C-75, 1B-4 |
| 1971 HOU N | 69 | 174 | 48 | 8 | 1 | 1 | 0.6 | 16 | 16 | 35 | 39 | 0 | .276 | .351 | 4 | 2 | C-65, 1B-1 |
| 1972 2 teams | 32 | HOU | N | (10G – | .200) | | CAL | A | (22G – | .289) | | | | | | | |
| " total | 32 | 70 | 18 | 3 | 1 | 1 | 1.4 | 6 | 5 | 10 | 16 | 0 | .257 | .371 | 7 | 2 | C-27 |
| 9 yrs. | 483 | 1142 | 287 | 51 | 5 | 22 | 1.9 | 110 | 154 | 224 | 295 | 0 | .251 | .363 | 101 | 30 | C-312, 1B-70, OF-2 |
| 1 yr. | 66 | 178 | 43 | 12 | 1 | 2 | 1.1 | 19 | 22 | 31 | 48 | 0 | .242 | .354 | 2 | 0 | C-63, 1B-2 |

## Mike Hickey

**HICKEY, MICHAEL EDWARD**    BR TR 5'10½" 150 lbs.
B. Dec. 25, 1871, Chicopee, Mass.    D. June 11, 1918, Springfield, Mass.

| | G | AB | H | 2B | 3B | HR | HR% | R | RBI | BB | SO | SB | BA | SA | AB | H | G by POS |
|---|---|---|---|---|---|---|---|---|---|---|---|---|---|---|---|---|---|
| 1899 BOS N | 1 | 3 | 1 | 0 | 0 | 0 | 0.0 | 0 | 0 | 0 | | 0 | .333 | .333 | 0 | 0 | 2B-1 |
| 1901 CHI N | 10 | 37 | 6 | 0 | 0 | 0 | 0.0 | 4 | 3 | 2 | | 1 | .162 | .162 | 0 | 0 | 3B-10 |
| 2 yrs. | 11 | 40 | 7 | 0 | 0 | 0 | 0.0 | 4 | 3 | 2 | | 1 | .175 | .175 | 0 | 0 | 3B-10, 2B-1 |
| 1 yr. | 10 | 37 | 6 | 0 | 0 | 0 | 0.0 | 4 | 3 | 2 | | 1 | .162 | .162 | 0 | 0 | 3B-10 |

## Jim Hickman

**HICKMAN, JAMES LUCIUS**    BR TR 6'3" 192 lbs.
B. May 10, 1937, Henning, Tenn.

| | G | AB | H | 2B | 3B | HR | HR% | R | RBI | BB | SO | SB | BA | SA | AB | H | G by POS |
|---|---|---|---|---|---|---|---|---|---|---|---|---|---|---|---|---|---|
| 1962 NY N | 140 | 392 | 96 | 18 | 2 | 13 | 3.3 | 54 | 46 | 47 | 96 | 4 | .245 | .401 | 13 | 3 | OF-124 |
| 1963 | 146 | 494 | 113 | 21 | 6 | 17 | 3.4 | 53 | 51 | 44 | 120 | 0 | .229 | .399 | 11 | 1 | OF-82, 3B-59 |
| 1964 | 139 | 409 | 105 | 14 | 1 | 11 | 2.7 | 48 | 57 | 36 | 90 | 0 | .257 | .377 | 31 | 8 | OF-113, 3B-1 |
| 1965 | 141 | 369 | 87 | 18 | 0 | 15 | 4.1 | 32 | 40 | 27 | 76 | 3 | .236 | .407 | 29 | 5 | OF-91, 1B-30, 3B-14 |
| 1966 | 58 | 160 | 38 | 7 | 0 | 4 | 2.5 | 15 | 16 | 13 | 34 | 1 | .238 | .356 | 11 | 1 | OF-45, 1B-17 |
| 1967 LA N | 65 | 98 | 16 | 6 | 1 | 0 | 0.0 | 7 | 10 | 14 | 28 | 1 | .163 | .245 | 25 | 3 | OF-37, 3B-2, 1B-2, P-1 |
| 1968 CHI N | 75 | 188 | 42 | 6 | 3 | 5 | 2.7 | 22 | 23 | 18 | 38 | 1 | .223 | .367 | 12 | 2 | OF-66 |
| 1969 | 134 | 338 | 80 | 11 | 2 | 21 | 6.2 | 38 | 54 | 47 | 74 | 2 | .237 | .467 | 18 | 5 | OF-125 |
| 1970 | 149 | 514 | 162 | 33 | 4 | 32 | 6.2 | 102 | 115 | 93 | 99 | 0 | .315 | .582 | 2 | 0 | OF-79, 1B-74 |
| 1971 | 117 | 383 | 98 | 13 | 2 | 19 | 5.0 | 50 | 60 | 50 | 61 | 0 | .256 | .449 | 12 | 2 | OF-69, 1B-44 |
| 1972 | 115 | 368 | 100 | 15 | 2 | 17 | 4.6 | 64 | 64 | 52 | 64 | 3 | .272 | .462 | 13 | 4 | 1B-77, OF-27 |
| 1973 | 92 | 201 | 49 | 9 | 1 | 3 | 1.5 | 27 | 20 | 42 | 42 | 1 | .244 | .313 | 34 | 6 | 1B-51, OF-13 |
| 1974 STL N | 50 | 60 | 16 | 0 | 0 | 2 | 3.3 | 5 | 4 | 8 | 10 | 1 | .267 | .367 | 30 | 6 | 1B-14, 3B-1 |
| 13 yrs. | 1421 | 3974 | 1002 | 163 | 25 | 159 | 4.0 | 518 | 560 | 491 | 832 | 17 | .252 | .426 | 241 | 45 | OF-871, 1B-309, 3B-77, P-1 |
| 6 yrs. | 682 | 1992 | 531 | 79 | 15 | 97 | 4.9 / 4th | 304 | 336 | 302 | 378 | 7 | .267 | .467 | 91 | 18 | OF-379, 1B-246 |

## R. E. Hildebrand

**HILDEBRAND, R. E.**
B. Unknown.    Deceased.

| | G | AB | H | 2B | 3B | HR | HR% | R | RBI | BB | SO | SB | BA | SA | AB | H | G by POS |
|---|---|---|---|---|---|---|---|---|---|---|---|---|---|---|---|---|---|
| 1902 CHI N | 1 | 4 | 0 | 0 | 0 | 0 | 0.0 | 1 | 0 | 1 | | 0 | .000 | .000 | 0 | 0 | OF-1 |

## Paul Hines

**HINES, PAUL A.**    BR TR 5'9½" 173 lbs.
B. Mar. 1, 1852, Washington, D. C.    D. July 10, 1935, Hyattsville, Md.

| | G | AB | H | 2B | 3B | HR | HR% | R | RBI | BB | SO | SB | BA | SA | AB | H | G by POS |
|---|---|---|---|---|---|---|---|---|---|---|---|---|---|---|---|---|---|
| 1876 CHI N | 64 | 305 | 101 | **21** | 3 | 2 | 0.7 | 62 | 59 | 1 | 3 | | .331 | .439 | 0 | 0 | OF-64, 2B-1 |
| 1877 | 60 | 261 | 73 | 11 | 7 | 0 | 0.0 | 44 | 23 | 1 | 8 | | .280 | .375 | 0 | 0 | OF-49, 1B-11 |
| 1878 PRO N | 62 | 257 | 92 | 13 | 4 | **4** | 1.6 | 42 | **50** | 2 | 10 | | **.358** | **.486** | 0 | 0 | OF-61, SS-1 |
| 1879 | 85 | **409** | **146** | 25 | 10 | 2 | 0.5 | 81 | 52 | 8 | 16 | | .357 | .482 | 0 | 0 | OF-85 |
| 1880 | 85 | 374 | 115 | 20 | 2 | 3 | 0.8 | 64 | 35 | 13 | 17 | | .307 | .396 | 0 | 0 | OF-75, 2B-6, 1B-4 |
| 1881 | 80 | 361 | 103 | **27** | 5 | 2 | 0.6 | 65 | 31 | 13 | 12 | | .285 | .404 | 0 | 0 | OF-78, 2B-4, 1B-1 |
| 1882 | 84 | 379 | 117 | 28 | 10 | 4 | 1.1 | 73 | | 10 | 14 | | .309 | .467 | 0 | 0 | OF-82, 1B-2 |
| 1883 | 97 | 442 | 132 | 32 | 4 | 4 | 0.9 | 94 | | 18 | 23 | | .299 | .416 | 0 | 0 | OF-89, 1B-9 |
| 1884 | 114 | 490 | 148 | **36** | 10 | 3 | 0.6 | 94 | | 44 | 28 | | .302 | .435 | 0 | 0 | OF-108, 1B-7, P-1 |
| 1885 | 98 | 411 | 111 | 20 | 4 | 1 | 0.2 | 63 | 35 | 19 | 18 | | .270 | .345 | 0 | 0 | OF-92, 1B-4, SS-1, 3B-1, 2B-1 |
| 1886 WAS N | 121 | 487 | 152 | 30 | 8 | 9 | 1.8 | 80 | 56 | 35 | 21 | | .312 | .462 | 0 | 0 | OF-92, 3B-15, 1B-10, SS-5, 2B-3 |
| 1887 | 123 | 478 | 147 | 32 | 5 | 10 | 2.1 | 83 | 72 | 48 | 24 | 46 | .308 | .458 | 0 | 0 | OF-109, 1B-7, 2B-5, SS-4 |
| 1888 IND N | 133 | 513 | 144 | 26 | 3 | 4 | 0.8 | 84 | 58 | 41 | 45 | 31 | .281 | .366 | 0 | 0 | OF-125, 1B-6, SS-2 |
| 1889 | 121 | 486 | 148 | 27 | 1 | 6 | 1.2 | 77 | 72 | 49 | 22 | 34 | .305 | .401 | 0 | 0 | 1B-109, OF-12 |
| 1890 2 teams | 100 | PIT | N | (31G – | .182) | | BOS | N | (69G – | .264) | | | | | | | |
| " total | 100 | 394 | 94 | 13 | 3 | 2 | 0.5 | 52 | 57 | 43 | 27 | 15 | .239 | .302 | 0 | 0 | OF-83, 1B-18 |
| 1891 WAS AA | 54 | 206 | 58 | 7 | 5 | 0 | 0.0 | 25 | 31 | 21 | 16 | 6 | .282 | .364 | 0 | 0 | OF-47, 1B-8 |
| 16 yrs. | 1481 | 6253 | 1881 | 368 | 84 | 56 | 0.9 | 1083 | 631 | 366 | 304 | 132 | .301 | .413 | 0 | 0 | OF-1251, 1B-185, 2B-31, 3B-16, SS-13, P-1 |
| 2 yrs. | 124 | 566 | 174 | 32 | 10 | 2 | 0.4 | 106 | 82 | 2 | 11 | | .307 | .410 | 0 | 0 | OF-113, 2B-12 |

## Gene Hiser

**HISER, GENE TAYLOR**    BL TL 5'11" 175 lbs.
B. Dec. 11, 1948, Baltimore, Md.

| | G | AB | H | 2B | 3B | HR | HR% | R | RBI | BB | SO | SB | BA | SA | AB | H | G by POS |
|---|---|---|---|---|---|---|---|---|---|---|---|---|---|---|---|---|---|
| 1971 CHI N | 17 | 29 | 6 | 0 | 0 | 0 | 0.0 | 4 | 1 | 4 | 8 | 1 | .207 | .207 | 5 | 1 | OF-9 |
| 1972 | 32 | 46 | 9 | 0 | 0 | 0 | 0.0 | 2 | 4 | 6 | 8 | 1 | .196 | .196 | 11 | 1 | OF-15 |
| 1973 | 100 | 109 | 19 | 3 | 0 | 1 | 0.9 | 15 | 6 | 11 | 17 | 4 | .174 | .229 | 37 | 6 | OF-64 |
| 1974 | 12 | 17 | 4 | 1 | 0 | 0 | 0.0 | 2 | 1 | 0 | 3 | 0 | .235 | .294 | 5 | 1 | OF-8 |
| 1975 | 45 | 62 | 15 | 3 | 0 | 0 | 0.0 | 11 | 6 | 11 | 7 | 0 | .242 | .290 | 24 | 8 | OF-18, 1B-1 |
| 5 yrs. | 206 | 263 | 53 | 7 | 0 | 1 | 0.4 | 34 | 18 | 32 | 43 | 6 | .202 | .240 | 82 | 17 | OF-114, 1B-1 |
| 5 yrs. | 206 | 263 | 53 | 7 | 0 | 1 | 0.4 | 34 | 18 | 32 | 43 | 6 | .202 | .240 | 82 | 17 | OF-114, 1B-1 |

## Don Hoak

**HOAK, DONALD ALBERT (Tiger)**    BR TR 6'1" 170 lbs.
B. Feb. 5, 1928, Roulette, Pa.    D. Oct. 9, 1969, Pittsburgh, Pa.

| | G | AB | H | 2B | 3B | HR | HR% | R | RBI | BB | SO | SB | BA | SA | AB | H | G by POS |
|---|---|---|---|---|---|---|---|---|---|---|---|---|---|---|---|---|---|
| 1954 BKN N | 88 | 261 | 64 | 9 | 5 | 7 | 2.7 | 41 | 26 | 25 | 39 | 8 | .245 | .398 | 11 | 2 | 3B-75 |

| | G | AB | H | 2B | 3B | HR | HR% | R | RBI | BB | SO | SB | BA | SA | Pinch Hit AB | Pinch Hit H | G by POS |
|---|---|---|---|---|---|---|---|---|---|---|---|---|---|---|---|---|---|

## Don Hoak continued

| | G | AB | H | 2B | 3B | HR | HR% | R | RBI | BB | SO | SB | BA | SA | AB | H | G by POS |
|---|---|---|---|---|---|---|---|---|---|---|---|---|---|---|---|---|---|
| 1955 | 94 | 279 | 67 | 13 | 3 | 5 | 1.8 | 50 | 19 | 46 | 50 | 9 | .240 | .362 | 4 | 1 | 3B-78 |
| 1956 CHI N | 121 | 424 | 91 | 18 | 4 | 5 | 1.2 | 51 | 37 | 41 | 46 | 8 | .215 | .311 | 5 | 1 | 3B-110 |
| 1957 CIN N | 149 | 529 | 155 | 39 | 2 | 19 | 3.6 | 78 | 89 | 74 | 54 | 8 | .293 | .482 | 0 | 0 | 3B-149, 2B-1 |
| 1958 | 114 | 417 | 109 | 30 | 0 | 6 | 1.4 | 51 | 50 | 43 | 36 | 6 | .261 | .376 | 1 | 0 | 3B-112, SS-1 |
| 1959 PIT N | 155 | 564 | 166 | 29 | 3 | 8 | 1.4 | 60 | 65 | 71 | 75 | 9 | .294 | .399 | 0 | 0 | 3B-155 |
| 1960 | 155 | 553 | 156 | 24 | 9 | 16 | 2.9 | 97 | 79 | 74 | 74 | 3 | .282 | .445 | 0 | 0 | 3B-155 |
| 1961 | 145 | 503 | 150 | 27 | 7 | 12 | 2.4 | 72 | 61 | 73 | 53 | 4 | .298 | .451 | 2 | 2 | 3B-143 |
| 1962 | 121 | 411 | 99 | 14 | 8 | 5 | 1.2 | 63 | 48 | 49 | 49 | 4 | .241 | .350 | 3 | 1 | 3B-116 |
| 1963 PHI N | 115 | 377 | 87 | 11 | 3 | 6 | 1.6 | 35 | 24 | 27 | 52 | 5 | .231 | .324 | 9 | 2 | 3B-106 |
| 1964 | 6 | 4 | 0 | 0 | 0 | 0 | 0.0 | 0 | 0 | 0 | 2 | 0 | .000 | .000 | 4 | 0 | |
| 11 yrs. | 1263 | 4322 | 1144 | 214 | 44 | 89 | 2.1 | 598 | 498 | 523 | 530 | 64 | .265 | .396 | 39 | 9 | 3B-1199, SS-1, 2B-1 |
| 1 yr. | 121 | 424 | 91 | 18 | 4 | 5 | 1.2 | 51 | 37 | 41 | 46 | 8 | .215 | .311 | 5 | 1 | 3B-110 |
| WORLD SERIES | | | | | | | | | | | | | | | | | |
| 1955 BKN N | 3 | 3 | 1 | 0 | 0 | 0 | 0.0 | 0 | 0 | 2 | 0 | 0 | .333 | .333 | 0 | 0 | 3B-1 |
| 1960 PIT N | 7 | 23 | 5 | 2 | 0 | 0 | 0.0 | 3 | 3 | 4 | 1 | 0 | .217 | .304 | 0 | 0 | 3B-7 |
| 2 yrs. | 10 | 26 | 6 | 2 | 0 | 0 | 0.0 | 3 | 3 | 6 | 1 | 0 | .231 | .308 | 0 | 0 | 3B-8 |

## Larry Hoffman

**HOFFMAN, LAWRENCE CHARLES**     BR TR
B. July 18, 1878, Chicago, Ill.    D. Dec. 29, 1948, Chicago, Ill.

| | G | AB | H | 2B | 3B | HR | HR% | R | RBI | BB | SO | SB | BA | SA | AB | H | G by POS |
|---|---|---|---|---|---|---|---|---|---|---|---|---|---|---|---|---|---|
| 1901 CHI N | 6 | 22 | 7 | 1 | 0 | 0 | 0.0 | 2 | 6 | 0 | | 1 | .318 | .364 | 0 | 0 | 3B-5, 2B-1 |

## Solly Hofman

**HOFMAN, ARTHUR FREDERICK (Circus Solly)**     BR TR 6'   160 lbs.
B. Oct. 29, 1882, St. Louis, Mo.    D. Mar. 10, 1956, St. Louis, Mo.

| | G | AB | H | 2B | 3B | HR | HR% | R | RBI | BB | SO | SB | BA | SA | AB | H | G by POS |
|---|---|---|---|---|---|---|---|---|---|---|---|---|---|---|---|---|---|
| 1903 PIT N | 3 | 2 | 0 | 0 | 0 | 0 | 0.0 | 1 | 0 | 1 | | 0 | .000 | .000 | 1 | 0 | OF-2 |
| 1904 CHI N | 7 | 26 | 7 | 0 | 0 | 1 | 3.8 | 7 | 4 | 1 | | 2 | .269 | .385 | 0 | 0 | OF-6, SS-1 |
| 1905 | 86 | 287 | 68 | 14 | 4 | 1 | 0.3 | 43 | 38 | 20 | | 15 | .237 | .324 | 1 | 0 | 2B-59, SS-9, 1B-9, OF-3, 3B-3 |
| 1906 | 64 | 195 | 50 | 2 | 3 | 2 | 1.0 | 30 | 20 | 20 | | 13 | .256 | .328 | 3 | 0 | OF-23, 1B-21, SS-9, 3B-4, 2B-4 |
| 1907 | 134 | 470 | 126 | 11 | 3 | 1 | 0.2 | 67 | 36 | 41 | | 29 | .268 | .311 | 0 | 0 | OF-68, SS-42, 1B-18, 3B-4, 2B-3 |
| 1908 | 120 | 411 | 100 | 15 | 5 | 2 | 0.5 | 55 | 42 | 33 | | 15 | .243 | .319 | 4 | 2 | OF-50, 1B-37, 2B-22, 3B-9 |
| 1909 | 153 | 527 | 150 | 21 | 4 | 2 | 0.4 | 60 | 58 | 53 | | 20 | .285 | .351 | 0 | 0 | OF-153 |
| 1910 | 136 | 477 | 155 | 24 | 16 | 3 | 0.6 | 83 | 86 | 65 | 34 | 29 | .325 | .461 | 0 | 0 | OF-110, 1B-24, 3B-1 |
| 1911 | 143 | 512 | 129 | 17 | 2 | 2 | 0.4 | 66 | 70 | 66 | 40 | 30 | .252 | .305 | 0 | 0 | OF-107, 1B-36 |
| 1912 2 teams | CHI N (36G – .272) | | | PIT N (17G – .283) | | | | | | | | | | | | | |
| " total | 53 | 178 | 49 | 15 | 1 | 0 | 0.0 | 35 | 20 | 27 | 19 | 5 | .275 | .371 | 2 | 0 | OF-42, 1B-9 |
| 1913 PIT N | 28 | 83 | 19 | 5 | 2 | 0 | 0.0 | 11 | 7 | 8 | 6 | 3 | .229 | .337 | 4 | 1 | OF-24 |
| 1914 BKN F | 147 | 515 | 148 | 25 | 12 | 5 | 1.0 | 65 | 83 | 54 | | 34 | .287 | .412 | 0 | 0 | 2B-108, 1B-22, OF-21, SS-1 |
| 1915 BUF F | 109 | 346 | 81 | 10 | 6 | 0 | 0.0 | 29 | 27 | 30 | | 12 | .234 | .298 | 13 | 5 | OF-82, 1B-11, 3B-4, 2B-2, SS-1 |
| 1916 2 teams | NY A (6G – .296) | | | CHI N (5G – .313) | | | | | | | | | | | | | |
| " total | 11 | 43 | 13 | 3 | 2 | 0 | 0.0 | 2 | 4 | 3 | 3 | 1 | .302 | .465 | 1 | 0 | OF-10 |
| 14 yrs. | 1194 | 4072 | 1095 | 162 | 60 | 19 | 0.5 | 554 | 495 | 421 | 102 | 208 | .269 | .352 | 29 | 9 | OF-701, 2B-198, 1B-187, SS-63, 3B-25 |
| 10 yrs. | 884 | 3046 | 824 | 117 | 38 | 14 | 0.5 | 441 | 374 | 323 | 89 | 158 9th | .271 | .348 | 9 | 5 | OF-551, 1B-154, 2B-88, SS-61, 3B-21 |
| WORLD SERIES | | | | | | | | | | | | | | | | | |
| 1906 CHI N | 6 | 23 | 7 | 1 | 0 | 0 | 0.0 | 3 | 2 | 3 | 4 | 1 | .304 | .348 | 0 | 0 | OF-6 |
| 1908 | 5 | 19 | 6 | 0 | 1 | 0 | 0.0 | 2 | 4 | 1 | 4 | 2 | .316 | .421 | 1 | 0 | OF-5 |
| 1910 | 5 | 15 | 4 | 0 | 0 | 0 | 0.0 | 2 | 2 | 4 | 3 | 0 | .267 | .267 | 0 | 0 | OF-5 |
| 3 yrs. | 16 | 57 | 17 | 1 | 1 | 0 | 0.0 | 7 | 8 | 8 | 11 | 3 | .298 | .351 | 1 | 0 | OF-16 |

## Charlie Hollocher

**HOLLOCHER, CHARLES JACOB**     BL TR 5'7½" 158 lbs.
B. June 11, 1896, St. Louis, Mo.    D. Aug. 14, 1940, Frontenac, Mo.

| | G | AB | H | 2B | 3B | HR | HR% | R | RBI | BB | SO | SB | BA | SA | AB | H | G by POS |
|---|---|---|---|---|---|---|---|---|---|---|---|---|---|---|---|---|---|
| 1918 CHI N | 131 | 509 | 161 | 23 | 6 | 2 | 0.4 | 72 | 38 | 47 | 30 | 26 | .316 | .397 | 0 | 0 | SS-131 |
| 1919 | 115 | 430 | 116 | 14 | 5 | 3 | 0.7 | 51 | 26 | 44 | 19 | 16 | .270 | .347 | 0 | 0 | SS-115 |
| 1920 | 80 | 301 | 96 | 17 | 2 | 0 | 0.0 | 53 | 22 | 41 | 15 | 20 | .319 | .389 | 0 | 0 | SS-80 |
| 1921 | 140 | 558 | 161 | 28 | 8 | 3 | 0.5 | 71 | 37 | 43 | 13 | 5 | .289 | .384 | 3 | 1 | SS-137 |
| 1922 | 152 | 592 | 201 | 37 | 8 | 3 | 0.5 | 90 | 69 | 58 | 5 | 19 | .340 | .444 | 0 | 0 | SS-152 |
| 1923 | 66 | 260 | 89 | 14 | 2 | 1 | 0.4 | 46 | 28 | 26 | 5 | 9 | .342 | .423 | 1 | 0 | SS-65 |
| 1924 | 76 | 286 | 70 | 12 | 4 | 2 | 0.7 | 28 | 21 | 18 | 7 | 4 | .245 | .336 | 5 | 1 | SS-71 |
| 7 yrs. | 760 | 2936 | 894 | 145 | 35 | 14 | 0.5 | 411 | 241 | 277 | 94 | 99 | .304 | .392 | 9 | 2 | SS-751 |
| 7 yrs. | 760 | 2936 | 894 | 145 | 35 | 14 | 0.5 | 411 | 241 | 277 | 94 | 99 | .304 | .392 | 9 | 2 | SS-751 |
| WORLD SERIES | | | | | | | | | | | | | | | | | |
| 1918 CHI N | 6 | 21 | 4 | 0 | 1 | 0 | 0.0 | 2 | 0 | 1 | 1 | 2 | .190 | .286 | 0 | 0 | SS-6 |

## Billy Holm

**HOLM, WILLIAM FREDERICK HENRY**     BR TR 5'10½" 168 lbs.
B. July 21, 1912, Chicago, Ill.    D. July 27, 1977, Portage, Ind.

| | G | AB | H | 2B | 3B | HR | HR% | R | RBI | BB | SO | SB | BA | SA | AB | H | G by POS |
|---|---|---|---|---|---|---|---|---|---|---|---|---|---|---|---|---|---|
| 1943 CHI N | 7 | 15 | 1 | 0 | 0 | 0 | 0.0 | 0 | 0 | 2 | 4 | 0 | .067 | .067 | 0 | 0 | C-7 |
| 1944 | 54 | 132 | 18 | 2 | 0 | 0 | 0.0 | 10 | 6 | 16 | 19 | 1 | .136 | .152 | 3 | 0 | C-50 |
| 1945 BOS A | 58 | 135 | 25 | 2 | 1 | 0 | 0.0 | 12 | 9 | 23 | 17 | 1 | .185 | .215 | 1 | 0 | C-57 |
| 3 yrs. | 119 | 282 | 44 | 4 | 1 | 0 | 0.0 | 22 | 15 | 41 | 40 | 2 | .156 | .177 | 4 | 0 | C-114 |
| 2 yrs. | 61 | 147 | 19 | 2 | 0 | 0 | 0.0 | 10 | 6 | 18 | 23 | 1 | .129 | .143 | 1 | 0 | C-57 |

## Fred Holmes

**HOLMES, FREDERICK**     BR TR
B. July 1, 1878, Chicago, Ill.    D. Feb. 13, 1956, Norwood Park Tnshp., Ill.

| | G | AB | H | 2B | 3B | HR | HR% | R | RBI | BB | SO | SB | BA | SA | AB | H | G by POS |
|---|---|---|---|---|---|---|---|---|---|---|---|---|---|---|---|---|---|
| 1903 NY A | 1 | 0 | 0 | 0 | 0 | 0 | – | 0 | 0 | 0 | | 0 | – | – | 0 | 0 | 1B-1 |

## Fred Holmes continued

| | G | AB | H | 2B | 3B | HR | HR% | R | RBI | BB | SO | SB | BA | SA | PH AB | PH H | G by POS |
|---|---|---|---|---|---|---|---|---|---|---|---|---|---|---|---|---|---|
| 1904 CHI N | 1 | 3 | 1 | 1 | 0 | 0 | 0.0 | 1 | 0 | 0 | | 0 | .333 | .667 | 0 | 0 | C-1 |
| 2 yrs. | 2 | 3 | 1 | 1 | 0 | 0 | 0.0 | 1 | 0 | 1 | | 0 | .333 | .667 | 0 | 0 | 1B-1, C-1 |
| 1 yr. | 1 | 3 | 1 | 1 | 0 | 0 | 0.0 | 1 | 0 | 0 | | 0 | .333 | .667 | 0 | 0 | C-1 |

## Marty Honan

**HONAN, MARTIN WELDON**
B. 1870, Chicago, Ill.  D. Aug. 20, 1908, Chicago, Ill.

| | G | AB | H | 2B | 3B | HR | HR% | R | RBI | BB | SO | SB | BA | SA | PH AB | PH H | G by POS |
|---|---|---|---|---|---|---|---|---|---|---|---|---|---|---|---|---|---|
| 1890 CHI N | 1 | 3 | 0 | 0 | 0 | 0 | 0.0 | 0 | 1 | 0 | 2 | 0 | .000 | .000 | 0 | 0 | C-1 |
| 1891 | 5 | 12 | 2 | 0 | 0 | 1 | 8.3 | 1 | 3 | 1 | 3 | 0 | .167 | .417 | 0 | 0 | C-5 |
| 2 yrs. | 6 | 15 | 2 | 0 | 0 | 1 | 6.7 | 1 | 4 | 1 | 5 | 0 | .133 | .333 | 0 | 0 | C-6 |
| 2 yrs. | 6 | 15 | 2 | 0 | 0 | 1 | 6.7 | 1 | 4 | 1 | 5 | 0 | .133 | .333 | 0 | 0 | C-6 |

## Rogers Hornsby

**HORNSBY, ROGERS (Rajah)**   BR TR 5'11" 175 lbs.
B. Apr. 27, 1896, Winters, Tex.   D. Jan. 5, 1963, Chicago, Ill.
Manager 1925-26, 1928, 1930-37, 1952-53.
Hall of Fame 1942.

| | G | AB | H | 2B | 3B | HR | HR% | R | RBI | BB | SO | SB | BA | SA | PH AB | PH H | G by POS |
|---|---|---|---|---|---|---|---|---|---|---|---|---|---|---|---|---|---|
| 1915 STL N | 18 | 57 | 14 | 2 | 0 | 0 | 0.0 | 5 | 4 | 2 | 6 | 0 | .246 | .281 | 0 | 0 | SS-18 |
| 1916 | 139 | 495 | 155 | 17 | 15 | 6 | 1.2 | 63 | 65 | 40 | 63 | 17 | .313 | .444 | 1 | 1 | 3B-83, SS-45, 1B-15, 2B-1 |
| 1917 | 145 | 523 | 171 | 24 | 17 | 8 | 1.5 | 86 | 66 | 45 | 34 | 17 | .327 | .484 | 1 | 0 | SS-144 |
| 1918 | 115 | 416 | 117 | 19 | 11 | 5 | 1.2 | 51 | 60 | 40 | 43 | 8 | .281 | .416 | 4 | 2 | SS-109, OF-2 |
| 1919 | 138 | 512 | 163 | 15 | 9 | 8 | 1.6 | 68 | 71 | 48 | 41 | 17 | .318 | .430 | 0 | 0 | 3B-72, SS-37, 2B-25, 1B-5 |
| 1920 | 149 | 589 | 218 | 44 | 20 | 9 | 1.5 | 96 | 94 | 60 | 50 | 12 | .370 | .559 | 0 | 0 | 2B-149 |
| 1921 | 154 | 592 | 235 | 44 | 18 | 21 | 3.5 | 131 | 126 | 60 | 48 | 13 | .397 | .639 | 0 | 0 | 2B-142, OF-6, SS-3, 3B-3, 1B-1 |
| 1922 | 154 | 623 | 250 | 46 | 14 | 42 | 6.7 | 141 | 152 | 65 | 50 | 17 | .401 | .722 | 0 | 0 | 2B-154 |
| 1923 | 107 | 424 | 163 | 32 | 10 | 17 | 4.0 | 89 | 83 | 55 | 29 | 3 | .384 | .627 | 1 | 0 | 2B-96, 1B-10 |
| 1924 | 143 | 536 | 227 | 43 | 14 | 25 | 4.7 | 121 | 94 | 89 | 32 | 5 | .424 | .696 | 0 | 0 | 2B-143 |
| 1925 | 138 | 504 | 203 | 41 | 10 | 39 | 7.7 | 133 | 143 | 83 | 39 | 5 | .403 | .756 | 0 | 0 | 2B-136 |
| 1926 | 134 | 527 | 167 | 34 | 5 | 11 | 2.1 | 96 | 93 | 61 | 39 | 3 | .317 | .463 | 0 | 0 | 2B-134 |
| 1927 NY N | 155 | 568 | 205 | 32 | 9 | 26 | 4.6 | 133 | 125 | 86 | 38 | 9 | .361 | .586 | 0 | 0 | 2B-155 |
| 1928 BOS N | 140 | 486 | 188 | 42 | 7 | 21 | 4.3 | 99 | 94 | 107 | 41 | 5 | .387 | .632 | 0 | 0 | 2B-140 |
| 1929 CHI N | 156 | 602 | 229 | 47 | 8 | 39 | 6.5 | 156 | 149 | 87 | 65 | 2 | .380 | .679 | 0 | 0 | 2B-156 |
| 1930 | 42 | 104 | 32 | 5 | 1 | 2 | 1.9 | 15 | 18 | 12 | 12 | 0 | .308 | .433 | 15 | 2 | 2B-25 |
| 1931 | 100 | 357 | 118 | 37 | 1 | 16 | 4.5 | 64 | 90 | 56 | 23 | 1 | .331 | .574 | 4 | 2 | 2B-69, 3B-26 |
| 1932 | 19 | 58 | 13 | 2 | 0 | 1 | 1.7 | 10 | 7 | 10 | 4 | 0 | .224 | .310 | 3 | 1 | OF-10, 3B-6 |
| 1933 2 teams | STL N (46G – .325) | | | STL A (11G – .333) | | | | | | | | | | | | | |
| " total | 57 | 92 | 30 | 7 | 0 | 3 | 3.3 | 11 | 23 | 14 | 7 | 1 | .326 | .500 | 35 | 11 | 2B-17 |
| 1934 STL A | 24 | 23 | 7 | 2 | 0 | 1 | 4.3 | 2 | 11 | 7 | 4 | 0 | .304 | .522 | 15 | 5 | OF-1, 3B-1 |
| 1935 | 10 | 24 | 5 | 3 | 0 | 0 | 0.0 | 1 | 3 | 3 | 6 | 0 | .208 | .333 | 3 | 1 | 1B-3, 2B-2, 3B-1 |
| 1936 | 2 | 5 | 2 | 0 | 0 | 0 | 0.0 | 1 | 2 | 1 | 0 | 0 | .400 | .400 | 1 | 1 | 1B-1 |
| 1937 | 20 | 56 | 18 | 3 | 0 | 1 | 1.8 | 7 | 11 | 7 | 5 | 0 | .321 | .429 | 3 | 0 | 2B-17 |
| 23 yrs. | 2259 | 8173 | 2930 | 541 | 169 | 301 | 3.7 | 1579 | 1584 | 1038 | 679 | 135 | .358 | .577 | 86 | 26 | 2B-1561, SS-356, 3B-192, 1B-35, OF-19 |
| | | | | | | | | | | | | | 2nd | 7th | | | |
| 4 yrs. | 317 | 1121 | 392 | 91 | 10 | 58 | 5.2 | 245 | 264 | 165 | 104 | 3 | .350 | .604 | 22 | 5 | 2B-250, 3B-32, OF-10 |

WORLD SERIES

| | G | AB | H | 2B | 3B | HR | HR% | R | RBI | BB | SO | SB | BA | SA | PH AB | PH H | G by POS |
|---|---|---|---|---|---|---|---|---|---|---|---|---|---|---|---|---|---|
| 1926 STL N | 7 | 28 | 7 | 1 | 0 | 0 | 0.0 | 2 | 4 | 2 | 2 | 1 | .250 | .286 | 0 | 0 | 2B-7 |
| 1929 CHI N | 5 | 21 | 5 | 1 | 1 | 0 | 0.0 | 4 | 1 | 1 | 8 | 0 | .238 | .381 | 0 | 0 | 2B-5 |
| 2 yrs. | 12 | 49 | 12 | 2 | 1 | 0 | 0.0 | 6 | 5 | 3 | 10 | 1 | .245 | .327 | 0 | 0 | 2B-12 |

## Tim Hosley

**HOSLEY, TIMOTHY KENNETH**   BR TR 5'11" 185 lbs.
B. May 10, 1947, Spartanburg, S. C.

| | G | AB | H | 2B | 3B | HR | HR% | R | RBI | BB | SO | SB | BA | SA | PH AB | PH H | G by POS |
|---|---|---|---|---|---|---|---|---|---|---|---|---|---|---|---|---|---|
| 1970 DET A | 7 | 12 | 2 | 0 | 0 | 1 | 8.3 | 1 | 2 | 0 | 6 | 0 | .167 | .417 | 4 | 1 | C-4 |
| 1971 | 7 | 16 | 3 | 0 | 0 | 2 | 12.5 | 2 | 6 | 0 | 1 | 0 | .188 | .563 | 4 | 2 | C-4, 1B-1 |
| 1973 OAK A | 13 | 14 | 3 | 0 | 0 | 0 | 0.0 | 3 | 2 | 2 | 3 | 0 | .214 | .214 | 4 | 1 | C-12 |
| 1974 | 11 | 7 | 2 | 0 | 0 | 0 | 0.0 | 0 | 1 | 1 | 2 | 0 | .286 | .286 | 4 | 1 | C-8, 1B-1 |
| 1975 CHI N | 62 | 141 | 36 | 7 | 0 | 6 | 4.3 | 22 | 20 | 27 | 25 | 1 | .255 | .433 | 10 | 2 | C-53 |
| 1976 2 teams | CHI N (1G – .000) | | | OAK A (37G – .164) | | | | | | | | | | | | | |
| " total | 38 | 56 | 9 | 2 | 0 | 1 | 1.8 | 4 | 4 | 8 | 12 | 0 | .161 | .250 | 12 | 2 | C-37 |
| 1977 OAK A | 39 | 78 | 15 | 0 | 0 | 1 | 1.3 | 5 | 10 | 16 | 13 | 0 | .192 | .231 | 5 | 1 | C-19, DH-12, 1B-3 |
| 1978 | 13 | 23 | 7 | 2 | 0 | 0 | 0.0 | 1 | 3 | 1 | 6 | 0 | .304 | .391 | 7 | 2 | C-2, DH-1 |
| 1981 | 18 | 21 | 2 | 0 | 0 | 1 | 4.8 | 2 | 5 | 2 | 5 | 0 | .095 | .238 | 14 | 1 | DH-4, 1B-1 |
| 9 yrs. | 208 | 368 | 79 | 11 | 0 | 12 | 3.3 | 43 | 53 | 57 | 73 | 1 | .215 | .342 | 64 | 11 | C-139, DH-17, 1B-6 |
| 2 yrs. | 63 | 142 | 36 | 7 | 0 | 6 | 4.2 | 22 | 20 | 27 | 25 | 1 | .254 | .430 | 11 | 2 | C-53 |

## John Houseman

**HOUSEMAN, JOHN FRANKLIN**   160 lbs.
B. Jan. 10, 1870, Holland   D. Nov. 4, 1922, Chicago, Ill.

| | G | AB | H | 2B | 3B | HR | HR% | R | RBI | BB | SO | SB | BA | SA | PH AB | PH H | G by POS |
|---|---|---|---|---|---|---|---|---|---|---|---|---|---|---|---|---|---|
| 1894 CHI N | 4 | 15 | 6 | 3 | 1 | 0 | 0.0 | 5 | 4 | 5 | | 3 | 2 | .400 | .733 | 0 | SS-3, 2B-1 |
| 1897 STL N | 80 | 278 | 68 | 6 | 6 | 0 | 0.0 | 34 | 21 | 28 | | 16 | | .245 | .309 | 2 | 1 | 2B-41, OF-33, SS-5, 3B-3 |
| 2 yrs. | 84 | 293 | 74 | 9 | 7 | 0 | 0.0 | 39 | 25 | 33 | 3 | 18 | .253 | .331 | 2 | 1 | 2B-42, OF-33, SS-8, 3B-3 |
| 1 yr. | 4 | 15 | 6 | 3 | 1 | 0 | 0.0 | 5 | 4 | 5 | 3 | 2 | .400 | .733 | 0 | 0 | SS-3, 2B-1 |

## Del Howard

**HOWARD, GEORGE ELMER**   BL TR 6' 180 lbs.
Brother of Ivan Howard.
B. Dec. 24, 1877, Kenney, Ill.   D. Dec. 24, 1956, Seattle, Wash.

| | G | AB | H | 2B | 3B | HR | HR% | R | RBI | BB | SO | SB | BA | SA | PH AB | PH H | G by POS |
|---|---|---|---|---|---|---|---|---|---|---|---|---|---|---|---|---|---|
| 1905 PIT N | 123 | 435 | 127 | 18 | 5 | 2 | 0.5 | 56 | 63 | 27 | | 19 | .292 | .370 | 3 | 0 | 1B-90, OF-28, P-1 |
| 1906 BOS N | 147 | 545 | 142 | 19 | 8 | 1 | 0.2 | 46 | 54 | 26 | | 17 | .261 | .330 | 0 | 0 | OF-87, 2B-45, SS-14, 1B-2 |
| 1907 2 teams | BOS N (50G – .273) | | | CHI N (51G – .230) | | | | | | | | | | | | | |
| " total | 101 | 335 | 85 | 6 | 4 | 1 | 0.3 | 30 | 26 | 17 | | 14 | .254 | .304 | 11 | 3 | OF-53, 1B-33, 2B-3 |
| 1908 CHI N | 96 | 315 | 88 | 7 | 3 | 1 | 0.3 | 42 | 26 | 23 | | 11 | .279 | .330 | 6 | 2 | OF-81, 1B-5 |

| | G | AB | H | 2B | 3B | HR | HR % | R | RBI | BB | SO | SB | BA | SA | Pinch Hit AB | Pinch Hit H | G by POS |
|---|---|---|---|---|---|---|---|---|---|---|---|---|---|---|---|---|---|

## Del Howard continued

| | G | AB | H | 2B | 3B | HR | HR % | R | RBI | BB | SO | SB | BA | SA | AB | H | G by POS |
|---|---|---|---|---|---|---|---|---|---|---|---|---|---|---|---|---|---|
| 1909 | 69 | 203 | 40 | 4 | 2 | 1 | 0.5 | 25 | 24 | 18 | | 6 | .197 | .251 | 8 | 0 | 1B-57 |
| 5 yrs. | 536 | 1833 | 482 | 54 | 22 | 6 | 0.3 | 199 | 193 | 111 | | 67 | .263 | .326 | 28 | 5 | OF-249, 1B-187, 2B-48, SS-14, P-1 |
| 3 yrs. | 216 | 666 | 162 | 13 | 7 | 2 | 0.3 | 77 | 63 | 47 | | 20 | .243 | .293 | 23 | 4 | 1B-95, OF-89 |

WORLD SERIES

| | G | AB | H | 2B | 3B | HR | HR % | R | RBI | BB | SO | SB | BA | SA | AB | H | G by POS |
|---|---|---|---|---|---|---|---|---|---|---|---|---|---|---|---|---|---|
| 1907 CHI N | 2 | 5 | 1 | 0 | 0 | 0 | 0.0 | 0 | 0 | 0 | 2 | 1 | .200 | .200 | 1 | 0 | 1B-1 |
| 1908 | 1 | 1 | 0 | 0 | 0 | 0 | 0.0 | 0 | 0 | 0 | 0 | 0 | .000 | .000 | 1 | 0 | |
| 2 yrs. | 3 | 6 | 1 | 0 | 0 | 0 | 0.0 | 0 | 0 | 0 | 2 | 1 | .167 | .167 | 2 | 0 | 1B-1 |

## Ken Hubbs

**HUBBS, KENNETH DOUGLASS**  BR  TR  6'2"  175 lbs.
B. Dec. 23, 1941, Riverside, Calif.  D. Feb. 15, 1964, Utah Lake, Utah

| | G | AB | H | 2B | 3B | HR | HR % | R | RBI | BB | SO | SB | BA | SA | AB | H | G by POS |
|---|---|---|---|---|---|---|---|---|---|---|---|---|---|---|---|---|---|
| 1961 CHI N | 10 | 28 | 5 | 1 | 1 | 1 | 3.6 | 4 | 2 | 0 | 8 | 0 | .179 | .393 | 2 | 0 | 2B-8 |
| 1962 | 160 | 661 | 172 | 24 | 9 | 5 | 0.8 | 90 | 49 | 35 | 129 | 3 | .260 | .346 | 1 | 0 | 2B-159 |
| 1963 | 154 | 566 | 133 | 19 | 3 | 8 | 1.4 | 54 | 47 | 39 | 93 | 8 | .235 | .322 | 2 | 1 | 2B-152 |
| 3 yrs. | 324 | 1255 | 310 | 44 | 13 | 14 | 1.1 | 148 | 98 | 74 | 230 | 11 | .247 | .336 | 5 | 1 | 2B-319 |
| 3 yrs. | 324 | 1255 | 310 | 44 | 13 | 14 | 1.1 | 148 | 98 | 74 | 230 | 11 | .247 | .336 | 5 | 1 | 2B-319 |

## Johnny Hudson

**HUDSON, JOHN WILSON**  BR  TR  5'10"  160 lbs.
B. June 30, 1912, Bryan, Tex.  D. Nov. 7, 1970, Bryan, Tex.

| | G | AB | H | 2B | 3B | HR | HR % | R | RBI | BB | SO | SB | BA | SA | AB | H | G by POS |
|---|---|---|---|---|---|---|---|---|---|---|---|---|---|---|---|---|---|
| 1936 BKN N | 6 | 12 | 2 | 0 | 0 | 0 | 0.0 | 1 | 0 | 2 | 1 | 0 | .167 | .167 | 0 | 0 | SS-4, 2B-1 |
| 1937 | 13 | 27 | 5 | 4 | 0 | 0 | 0.0 | 3 | 2 | 3 | 9 | 0 | .185 | .333 | 1 | 0 | SS-11, 2B-1 |
| 1938 | 135 | 498 | 130 | 21 | 5 | 2 | 0.4 | 59 | 37 | 39 | 76 | 7 | .261 | .335 | 1 | 0 | 2B-132, SS-3 |
| 1939 | 109 | 343 | 87 | 17 | 3 | 2 | 0.6 | 46 | 32 | 30 | 36 | 5 | .254 | .338 | 12 | 3 | SS-50, 2B-45, 3B-1 |
| 1940 | 85 | 179 | 39 | 4 | 3 | 0 | 0.0 | 13 | 19 | 9 | 26 | 2 | .218 | .274 | 4 | 2 | SS-38, 2B-27, 3B-1 |
| 1941 CHI N | 50 | 99 | 20 | 4 | 0 | 0 | 0.0 | 8 | 6 | 3 | 15 | 3 | .202 | .242 | 11 | 0 | SS-17, 2B-13, 3B-10 |
| 1945 NY N | 28 | 11 | 0 | 0 | 0 | 0 | 0.0 | 0 | 1 | 1 | 1 | 0 | .000 | .000 | 4 | 0 | 3B-5, 2B-2 |
| 7 yrs. | 426 | 1169 | 283 | 50 | 11 | 4 | 0.3 | 138 | 96 | 87 | 164 | 17 | .242 | .314 | 33 | 5 | 2B-221, SS-123, 3B-17 |
| 1 yr. | 50 | 99 | 20 | 4 | 0 | 0 | 0.0 | 8 | 6 | 3 | 15 | 3 | .202 | .242 | 11 | 0 | SS-17, 2B-13, 3B-10 |

## Ed Hughes

**HUGHES, EDWARD**
B. Unknown.  D. Oct. 24, 1933, Chicago, Ill.

| | G | AB | H | 2B | 3B | HR | HR % | R | RBI | BB | SO | SB | BA | SA | AB | H | G by POS |
|---|---|---|---|---|---|---|---|---|---|---|---|---|---|---|---|---|---|
| 1902 CHI N | 1 | 3 | 0 | 0 | 0 | 0 | 0.0 | 0 | 0 | 0 | | 0 | .000 | .000 | 0 | 0 | OF-1 |

## Roy Hughes

**HUGHES, ROY JOHN (Sage, Jeep)**  BR  TR  5'10½"  167 lbs.
B. Jan. 11, 1911, Cincinnati, Ohio

| | G | AB | H | 2B | 3B | HR | HR % | R | RBI | BB | SO | SB | BA | SA | AB | H | G by POS |
|---|---|---|---|---|---|---|---|---|---|---|---|---|---|---|---|---|---|
| 1935 CLE A | 82 | 266 | 78 | 15 | 3 | 0 | 0.0 | 40 | 14 | 18 | 17 | 13 | .293 | .372 | 6 | 0 | 2B-40, SS-29, 3B-1 |
| 1936 | 152 | 638 | 188 | 35 | 9 | 0 | 0.0 | 112 | 63 | 57 | 40 | 20 | .295 | .378 | 0 | 0 | 2B-152 |
| 1937 | 104 | 346 | 96 | 12 | 6 | 1 | 0.3 | 57 | 40 | 40 | 22 | 11 | .277 | .355 | 11 | 4 | 3B-58, 2B-32 |
| 1938 STL A | 58 | 96 | 27 | 3 | 0 | 2 | 2.1 | 16 | 13 | 12 | 11 | 3 | .281 | .375 | 30 | 6 | 2B-21, 3B-5, SS-2 |
| 1939 2 teams | | STL | A (17G – .087) | | PHI | N | (65G – .228) | | | | | | | | | | |
| " total | 82 | 260 | 56 | 5 | 1 | 1 | 0.4 | 28 | 17 | 25 | 22 | 4 | .215 | .254 | 5 | 1 | 2B-71, SS-1 |
| 1944 CHI N | 126 | 478 | 137 | 16 | 6 | 1 | 0.2 | 86 | 28 | 35 | 30 | 16 | .287 | .351 | 7 | 4 | 3B-66, SS-52 |
| 1945 | 69 | 222 | 58 | 8 | 1 | 0 | 0.0 | 34 | 8 | 16 | 18 | 6 | .261 | .306 | 5 | 1 | SS-36, 2B-21, 3B-9, 1B-2 |
| 1946 PHI N | 89 | 276 | 65 | 11 | 1 | 0 | 0.0 | 23 | 22 | 19 | 15 | 7 | .236 | .283 | 12 | 3 | SS-34, 3B-31, 2B-7, 1B-1 |
| 8 yrs. | 762 | 2582 | 705 | 105 | 27 | 5 | 0.2 | 396 | 205 | 222 | 175 | 80 | .273 | .340 | 76 | 19 | 2B-344, 3B-170, SS-154, 1B-3 |
| 2 yrs. | 195 | 700 | 195 | 24 | 7 | 1 | 0.1 | 120 | 36 | 51 | 48 | 22 | .279 | .337 | 12 | 5 | SS-88, 3B-75, 2B-21, 1B-2 |

WORLD SERIES

| | G | AB | H | 2B | 3B | HR | HR % | R | RBI | BB | SO | SB | BA | SA | AB | H | G by POS |
|---|---|---|---|---|---|---|---|---|---|---|---|---|---|---|---|---|---|
| 1945 CHI N | 6 | 17 | 5 | 1 | 0 | 0 | 0.0 | 1 | 3 | 4 | 5 | 0 | .294 | .353 | 0 | 0 | SS-6 |

## Terry Hughes

**HUGHES, TERRY WAYNE**  BR  TR  6'1"  185 lbs.
B. May 13, 1949, Spartanburg, S. C.

| | G | AB | H | 2B | 3B | HR | HR % | R | RBI | BB | SO | SB | BA | SA | AB | H | G by POS |
|---|---|---|---|---|---|---|---|---|---|---|---|---|---|---|---|---|---|
| 1970 CHI N | 2 | 3 | 1 | 0 | 0 | 0 | 0.0 | 0 | 0 | 0 | 0 | 0 | .333 | .333 | 1 | 1 | OF-1, 3B-1 |
| 1973 STL N | 11 | 14 | 3 | 1 | 0 | 0 | 0.0 | 1 | 1 | 1 | 4 | 0 | .214 | .286 | 4 | 1 | 3B-5, 1B-1 |
| 1974 BOS A | 41 | 69 | 14 | 2 | 0 | 1 | 1.4 | 5 | 6 | 6 | 18 | 0 | .203 | .275 | 1 | 0 | 3B-36, DH-1 |
| 3 yrs. | 54 | 86 | 18 | 3 | 0 | 1 | 1.2 | 6 | 7 | 7 | 22 | 0 | .209 | .279 | 6 | 2 | 3B-42, DH-1, OF-1, 1B-1 |
| 1 yr. | 2 | 3 | 1 | 0 | 0 | 0 | 0.0 | 0 | 0 | 0 | 0 | 0 | .333 | .333 | 1 | 1 | OF-1, 3B-1 |

## Randy Hundley

**HUNDLEY, CECIL RANDOLPH**  BR  TR  5'11"  170 lbs.
B. June 1, 1942, Martinsville, Va.

| | G | AB | H | 2B | 3B | HR | HR % | R | RBI | BB | SO | SB | BA | SA | AB | H | G by POS |
|---|---|---|---|---|---|---|---|---|---|---|---|---|---|---|---|---|---|
| 1964 SF N | 2 | 1 | 0 | 0 | 0 | 0 | 0.0 | 1 | 0 | 0 | 1 | 0 | .000 | .000 | 0 | 0 | C-2 |
| 1965 | 6 | 15 | 1 | 0 | 0 | 0 | 0.0 | 0 | 0 | 0 | 4 | 0 | .067 | .067 | 0 | 0 | C-6 |
| 1966 CHI N | 149 | 526 | 124 | 22 | 3 | 19 | 3.6 | 50 | 63 | 35 | 113 | 1 | .236 | .397 | 0 | 0 | C-149 |
| 1967 | 152 | 539 | 144 | 25 | 3 | 14 | 2.6 | 68 | 60 | 44 | 75 | 2 | .267 | .403 | 2 | 0 | C-152 |
| 1968 | 160 | 553 | 125 | 18 | 4 | 7 | 1.3 | 41 | 65 | 39 | 69 | 1 | .226 | .311 | 0 | 0 | C-160 |
| 1969 | 151 | 522 | 133 | 15 | 1 | 18 | 3.4 | 67 | 64 | 61 | 90 | 2 | .255 | .391 | 1 | 0 | C-151 |
| 1970 | 73 | 250 | 61 | 5 | 0 | 7 | 2.8 | 13 | 36 | 16 | 52 | 0 | .244 | .348 | 0 | 0 | C-73 |
| 1971 | 9 | 21 | 7 | 1 | 0 | 0 | 0.0 | 1 | 2 | 0 | 2 | 0 | .333 | .381 | 1 | 0 | C-8 |
| 1972 | 114 | 357 | 78 | 12 | 0 | 5 | 1.4 | 23 | 30 | 22 | 62 | 1 | .218 | .294 | 2 | 1 | C-113 |
| 1973 | 124 | 368 | 83 | 11 | 1 | 10 | 2.7 | 35 | 43 | 30 | 51 | 5 | .226 | .342 | 3 | 1 | C-122 |
| 1974 MIN A | 32 | 88 | 17 | 2 | 0 | 0 | 0.0 | 2 | 3 | 4 | 12 | 0 | .193 | .216 | 3 | 0 | C-28 |
| 1975 SD N | 74 | 180 | 37 | 5 | 1 | 2 | 1.1 | 7 | 14 | 19 | 29 | 0 | .206 | .278 | 18 | 4 | C-51 |
| 1976 CHI N | 13 | 18 | 3 | 2 | 0 | 0 | 0.0 | 3 | 1 | 1 | 4 | 0 | .167 | .278 | 4 | 0 | C-9 |
| 1977 | 2 | 4 | 0 | 0 | 0 | 0 | 0.0 | 0 | 0 | 0 | 1 | 0 | .000 | .000 | 0 | 0 | C-2 |
| 14 yrs. | 1061 | 3442 | 813 | 118 | 13 | 82 | 2.4 | 311 | 381 | 271 | 565 | 12 | .236 | .350 | 34 | 6 | C-1026 |
| 10 yrs. | 947 | 3158 | 758 | 111 | 12 | 80 | 2.5 | 301 | 364 | 248 | 519 | 12 | .240 | .359 | 13 | 2 | C-939 |

9th

| | G | AB | H | 2B | 3B | HR | HR % | R | RBI | BB | SO | SB | BA | SA | Pinch Hit AB | Pinch Hit H | G by POS |
|---|---|---|---|---|---|---|---|---|---|---|---|---|---|---|---|---|---|

## Herb Hunter

**HUNTER, HERBERT HARRISON**  BL TR 6'½"  165 lbs.
B. Dec. 25, 1895, Boston, Mass.  D. July 25, 1970, Orlando, Fla.

| | G | AB | H | 2B | 3B | HR | HR % | R | RBI | BB | SO | SB | BA | SA | AB | H | G by POS |
|---|---|---|---|---|---|---|---|---|---|---|---|---|---|---|---|---|---|
| 1916 **2 teams** | | NY | N (21G – .250) | | | CHI | N (2G – .000) | | | | | | | | | | |
| " total | 23 | 32 | 7 | 0 | 0 | 1 | 3.1 | 3 | 4 | 0 | 5 | 0 | .219 | .313 | 11 | 2 | 3B-7, 1B-2 |
| 1917 **CHI N** | 3 | 3 | 0 | 0 | 0 | 0 | 0.0 | 0 | 0 | 0 | 0 | 0 | .000 | .000 | 1 | 0 | 3B-1, 2B-1 |
| 1920 **BOS A** | 4 | 12 | 1 | 0 | 0 | 0 | 0.0 | 2 | 0 | 1 | 1 | 0 | .083 | .083 | 0 | 0 | OF-4 |
| 1921 **STL N** | 9 | 2 | 0 | 0 | 0 | 0 | 0.0 | 3 | 0 | 1 | 0 | 0 | .000 | .000 | 1 | 0 | 1B-1 |
| 4 yrs. | 39 | 49 | 8 | 0 | 0 | 1 | 2.0 | 8 | 4 | 2 | 6 | 0 | .163 | .224 | 13 | 2 | 3B-8, OF-4, 1B-3, 2B-1 |
| 2 yrs. | 5 | 7 | 0 | 0 | 0 | 0 | 0.0 | 0 | 0 | 0 | 0 | 0 | .000 | .000 | 2 | 0 | 3B-2, 2B-1 |

## Don Hurst

**HURST, FRANK O'DONNELL**  BL TL 6'  215 lbs.
B. Aug. 12, 1905, Maysville, Ky.  D. Dec. 6, 1952, Los Angeles, Calif.

| | G | AB | H | 2B | 3B | HR | HR % | R | RBI | BB | SO | SB | BA | SA | AB | H | G by POS |
|---|---|---|---|---|---|---|---|---|---|---|---|---|---|---|---|---|---|
| 1928 **PHI N** | 107 | 396 | 113 | 23 | 4 | 19 | 4.8 | 73 | 64 | 68 | 40 | 3 | .285 | .508 | 3 | 0 | 1B-104 |
| 1929 | 154 | 589 | 179 | 29 | 4 | 31 | 5.3 | 100 | 125 | 80 | 36 | 10 | .304 | .525 | 0 | 0 | 1B-154 |
| 1930 | 119 | 391 | 128 | 19 | 3 | 17 | 4.3 | 78 | 78 | 46 | 22 | 6 | .327 | .522 | 13 | 3 | 1B-96, OF-7 |
| 1931 | 137 | 489 | 149 | 37 | 5 | 11 | 2.2 | 63 | 91 | 64 | 28 | 8 | .305 | .468 | 2 | 0 | 1B-135 |
| 1932 | 150 | 579 | 196 | 41 | 4 | 24 | 4.1 | 109 | 143 | 65 | 27 | 10 | .339 | .547 | 0 | 0 | 1B-150 |
| 1933 | 147 | 550 | 147 | 27 | 8 | 8 | 1.5 | 58 | 76 | 48 | 32 | 3 | .267 | .389 | 5 | 1 | 1B-142 |
| 1934 **2 teams** | | PHI | N (40G – .262) | | | CHI | N (51G – .199) | | | | | | | | | | |
| " total | 91 | 281 | 64 | 14 | 0 | 5 | 1.8 | 29 | 33 | 20 | 25 | 1 | .228 | .331 | 9 | 2 | 1B-87 |
| 7 yrs. | 905 | 3275 | 976 | 190 | 28 | 115 | 3.5 | 510 | 610 | 391 | 210 | 41 | .298 | .478 | 32 | 6 | 1B-868, OF-7 |
| 1 yr. | 51 | 151 | 30 | 5 | 0 | 3 | 2.0 | 13 | 12 | 8 | 18 | 0 | .199 | .291 | 3 | 1 | 1B-47 |

## Ed Hutchinson

**HUTCHINSON, EDWARD F.**  BL  5'11"  163 lbs.
B. 1870, Pittsburgh, Pa.  D. California

| | G | AB | H | 2B | 3B | HR | HR % | R | RBI | BB | SO | SB | BA | SA | AB | H | G by POS |
|---|---|---|---|---|---|---|---|---|---|---|---|---|---|---|---|---|---|
| 1890 **CHI N** | 4 | 17 | 1 | 1 | 0 | 0 | 0.0 | 0 | 0 | 0 | 0 | 0 | .059 | .118 | 0 | 0 | 2B-4 |

## Monte Irvin

**IRVIN, MONFORD MERRILL**  BR TR 6'1"  195 lbs.
B. Feb. 25, 1919, Columbia, Ala.
Hall of Fame 1973.

| | G | AB | H | 2B | 3B | HR | HR % | R | RBI | BB | SO | SB | BA | SA | AB | H | G by POS |
|---|---|---|---|---|---|---|---|---|---|---|---|---|---|---|---|---|---|
| 1949 **NY N** | 36 | 76 | 17 | 3 | 2 | 0 | 0.0 | 7 | 7 | 17 | 11 | 0 | .224 | .316 | 13 | 0 | OF-10, 3B-5, 1B-5 |
| 1950 | 110 | 374 | 112 | 19 | 5 | 15 | 4.0 | 61 | 66 | 52 | 41 | 3 | .299 | .497 | 4 | 1 | 1B-59, OF-40, 3B-1 |
| 1951 | 151 | 558 | 174 | 19 | 11 | 24 | 4.3 | 94 | 121 | 89 | 44 | 12 | .312 | .514 | 1 | 1 | OF-112, 1B-39 |
| 1952 | 46 | 126 | 39 | 2 | 1 | 4 | 3.2 | 10 | 21 | 10 | 11 | 0 | .310 | .437 | 14 | 2 | OF-32 |
| 1953 | 124 | 444 | 146 | 21 | 5 | 21 | 4.7 | 72 | 97 | 55 | 34 | 2 | .329 | .541 | 8 | 2 | OF-113 |
| 1954 | 135 | 432 | 113 | 13 | 3 | 19 | 4.4 | 62 | 64 | 70 | 23 | 7 | .262 | .438 | 9 | 3 | OF-128, 3B-1, 1B-1 |
| 1955 | 51 | 150 | 38 | 7 | 1 | 1 | 0.7 | 16 | 17 | 17 | 15 | 3 | .253 | .333 | 6 | 1 | OF-45 |
| 1956 **CHI N** | 111 | 339 | 92 | 13 | 3 | 15 | 4.4 | 44 | 50 | 41 | 41 | 1 | .271 | .460 | 18 | 7 | OF-96 |
| 8 yrs. | 764 | 2499 | 731 | 97 | 31 | 99 | 4.0 | 366 | 443 | 351 | 220 | 28 | .293 | .475 | 73 | 17 | OF-585, 1B-104, 3B-7 |
| 1 yr. | 111 | 339 | 92 | 13 | 3 | 15 | 4.4 | 44 | 50 | 41 | 41 | 1 | .271 | .460 | 18 | 7 | OF-96 |
| WORLD SERIES | | | | | | | | | | | | | | | | | |
| 1951 **NY N** | 6 | 24 | 11 | 0 | 1 | 0 | 0.0 | 4 | 2 | 2 | 1 | 2 | .458 | .542 | 0 | 0 | OF-6 |
| 1954 | 4 | 9 | 2 | 1 | 0 | 0 | 0.0 | 1 | 2 | 0 | 3 | 0 | .222 | .333 | 0 | 0 | OF-4 |
| 2 yrs. | 10 | 33 | 13 | 1 | 1 | 0 | 0.0 | 5 | 4 | 2 | 4 | 2 | .394 | .485 | 0 | 0 | OF-10 |

## Charlie Irwin

**IRWIN, CHARLES EDWIN**  BR TR 5'10"  160 lbs.
B. Feb. 15, 1869, Clinton, Ill.  D. Sept. 21, 1925, Chicago, Ill.

| | G | AB | H | 2B | 3B | HR | HR % | R | RBI | BB | SO | SB | BA | SA | AB | H | G by POS |
|---|---|---|---|---|---|---|---|---|---|---|---|---|---|---|---|---|---|
| 1893 **CHI N** | 21 | 82 | 25 | 6 | 2 | 0 | 0.0 | 14 | 13 | 10 | 1 | 4 | .305 | .427 | 0 | 0 | SS-21 |
| 1894 | 128 | 498 | 144 | 24 | 9 | 8 | 1.6 | 84 | 95 | 63 | 23 | 35 | .289 | .422 | 0 | 0 | 3B-67, SS-61 |
| 1895 | 3 | 10 | 2 | 0 | 0 | 0 | 0.0 | 4 | 0 | 2 | 1 | 0 | .200 | .200 | 0 | 0 | SS-3 |
| 1896 **CIN N** | 127 | 476 | 141 | 16 | 6 | 1 | 0.2 | 77 | 67 | 26 | 17 | 31 | .296 | .361 | 0 | 0 | 3B-127 |
| 1897 | 134 | 505 | 146 | 26 | 6 | 0 | 0.0 | 89 | 74 | 47 | | 27 | .289 | .364 | 0 | 0 | 3B-134 |
| 1898 | 136 | 501 | 120 | 14 | 5 | 3 | 0.6 | 77 | 55 | 31 | | 18 | .240 | .305 | 0 | 0 | 3B-136 |
| 1899 | 90 | 314 | 73 | 4 | 8 | 1 | 0.3 | 42 | 52 | 26 | | 26 | .232 | .306 | 2 | 1 | 3B-78, SS-6, 2B-3, 1B-1 |
| 1900 | 87 | 333 | 91 | 15 | 6 | 1 | 0.3 | 59 | 44 | 14 | | 9 | .273 | .363 | 2 | 0 | 3B-61, SS-16, OF-6, 2B-3 |
| 1901 **2 teams** | | CIN | N (67G – .238) | | | BKN | N (65G – .215) | | | | | | | | | | |
| " total | 132 | 502 | 114 | 25 | 4 | 0 | 0.0 | 50 | 45 | 28 | | 17 | .227 | .293 | 0 | 0 | 3B-132 |
| 1902 **BKN N** | 131 | 458 | 125 | 14 | 0 | 2 | 0.4 | 59 | 43 | 39 | | 13 | .273 | .317 | 0 | 0 | 3B-130, SS-1 |
| 10 yrs. | 989 | 3679 | 981 | 144 | 46 | 16 | 0.4 | 555 | 488 | 286 | 42 | 180 | .267 | .344 | 4 | 1 | 3B-865, SS-108, OF-6, 2B-6, 1B-1 |
| 3 yrs. | 152 | 590 | 171 | 30 | 11 | 8 | 1.4 | 102 | 108 | 75 | 25 | 39 | .290 | .419 | 0 | 0 | SS-85, 3B-67 |

## Frank Isbell

**ISBELL, WILLIAM FRANK (Bald Eagle)**  BL TR 5'11"  190 lbs.
B. Aug. 21, 1875, Delevan, N. Y.  D. July 15, 1941, Wichita, Kans.

| | G | AB | H | 2B | 3B | HR | HR % | R | RBI | BB | SO | SB | BA | SA | AB | H | G by POS |
|---|---|---|---|---|---|---|---|---|---|---|---|---|---|---|---|---|---|
| 1898 **CHI N** | 45 | 159 | 37 | 4 | 0 | 0 | 0.0 | 17 | 8 | 3 | | 3 | .233 | .258 | 0 | 0 | OF-28, P-13, 3B-3, 2B-3, SS-2 |
| 1901 **CHI A** | 137 | 556 | 143 | 15 | 8 | 3 | 0.5 | 93 | 70 | 36 | | 52 | .257 | .329 | 0 | 0 | 1B-137, 2B-2, SS-1, 3B-1, P-1 |
| 1902 | 137 | 515 | 130 | 14 | 4 | 4 | 0.8 | 62 | 59 | 14 | | 38 | .252 | .318 | 0 | 0 | 1B-133, SS-4, C-1, P-1 |
| 1903 | 138 | 546 | 132 | 25 | 9 | 2 | 0.4 | 52 | 59 | 12 | | 26 | .242 | .332 | 0 | 0 | 1B-117, 3B-19, 2B-2, OF-1, SS-1 |
| 1904 | 96 | 314 | 66 | 10 | 3 | 1 | 0.3 | 27 | 34 | 16 | | 19 | .210 | .271 | 3 | 0 | 1B-57, 2B-27, OF-5, SS-4 |
| 1905 | 94 | 341 | 101 | 21 | 11 | 2 | 0.6 | 55 | 45 | 15 | | 15 | .296 | .440 | 0 | 0 | 2B-42, OF-40, 1B-9, SS-2 |
| 1906 | 143 | 549 | 153 | 18 | 11 | 0 | 0.0 | 71 | 57 | 30 | | 37 | .279 | .352 | 0 | 0 | 2B-132, OF-14, C-1, P-1 |
| 1907 | 125 | 486 | 118 | 19 | 7 | 0 | 0.0 | 60 | 41 | 22 | | 22 | .243 | .311 | 1 | 0 | 2B-109, OF-5, SS-1, P-1 |
| 1908 | 84 | 320 | 79 | 15 | 3 | 1 | 0.3 | 31 | 49 | 19 | | 18 | .247 | .322 | 1 | 0 | 1B-65, 2B-18 |
| 1909 | 120 | 433 | 97 | 17 | 6 | 0 | 0.0 | 33 | 33 | 23 | | 23 | .224 | .291 | 5 | 2 | 1B-101, OF-9, 2B-5 |
| 10 yrs. | 1119 | 4219 | 1056 | 158 | 62 | 13 | 0.3 | 501 | 455 | 190 | | 253 | .250 | .326 | 10 | 2 | 1B-619, 2B-350, OF-102, 3B-23, P-17, SS-15, C-2 |
| 1 yr. | 45 | 159 | 37 | 4 | 0 | 0 | 0.0 | 17 | 8 | 3 | | 3 | .233 | .258 | 0 | 0 | OF-28, P-13, 3B-3, 2B-3, SS-2 |
| WORLD SERIES | | | | | | | | | | | | | | | | | |
| 1906 **CHI A** | 6 | 26 | 8 | 4 | 0 | 0 | 0.0 | 4 | 4 | 0 | | 6 | 1 | .308 | .462 | 0 | 0 | 2B-6 |

| | G | AB | H | 2B | 3B | HR | HR % | R | RBI | BB | SO | SB | BA | SA | Pinch Hit AB | Pinch Hit H | G by POS |
|---|---|---|---|---|---|---|---|---|---|---|---|---|---|---|---|---|---|

## Darrin Jackson

**JACKSON, DARRIN JAY**
B. Aug. 22, 1962, Los Angeles, Calif.                    BR  TR  6'        170 lbs.

| | G | AB | H | 2B | 3B | HR | HR % | R | RBI | BB | SO | SB | BA | SA | AB | H | G by POS |
|---|---|---|---|---|---|---|---|---|---|---|---|---|---|---|---|---|---|
| 1985 CHI N | 5 | 11 | 1 | 0 | 0 | 0 | 0.0 | 0 | 0 | 0 | 3 | 0 | .091 | .091 | 1 | 0 | OF-4 |

## Lou Jackson

**JACKSON, LOUIS CLARENCE**
B. July 26, 1935, Riverton, La.    D. May 27, 1969, Tokyo, Japan    BL  TR  5'10"   168 lbs.

| | G | AB | H | 2B | 3B | HR | HR % | R | RBI | BB | SO | SB | BA | SA | AB | H | G by POS |
|---|---|---|---|---|---|---|---|---|---|---|---|---|---|---|---|---|---|
| 1958 CHI N | 24 | 35 | 6 | 2 | 1 | 1 | 2.9 | 5 | 6 | 1 | 9 | 0 | .171 | .371 | 11 | 1 | OF-12 |
| 1959 | 6 | 4 | 1 | 0 | 0 | 0 | 0.0 | 2 | 1 | 0 | 2 | 0 | .250 | .250 | 4 | 1 | |
| 1964 BAL A | 4 | 8 | 3 | 0 | 0 | 0 | 0.0 | 0 | 0 | 0 | 2 | 0 | .375 | .375 | 3 | 0 | OF-1 |
| 3 yrs. | 34 | 47 | 10 | 2 | 1 | 1 | 2.1 | 7 | 7 | 1 | 13 | 0 | .213 | .362 | 18 | 2 | OF-13 |
| 2 yrs. | 30 | 39 | 7 | 2 | 1 | 1 | 2.6 | 7 | 7 | 1 | 11 | 0 | .179 | .359 | 15 | 2 | OF-12 |

## Randy Jackson

**JACKSON, RANSOM JOSEPH (Handsome Ransom)**
B. Feb. 10, 1926, Little Rock, Ark.                    BR  TR  6'1½"   180 lbs.

| | G | AB | H | 2B | 3B | HR | HR % | R | RBI | BB | SO | SB | BA | SA | AB | H | G by POS |
|---|---|---|---|---|---|---|---|---|---|---|---|---|---|---|---|---|---|
| 1950 CHI N | 34 | 111 | 25 | 4 | 3 | 3 | 2.7 | 13 | 6 | 7 | 25 | 4 | .225 | .396 | 7 | 0 | 3B-27 |
| 1951 | 145 | 557 | 153 | 24 | 6 | 16 | 2.9 | 78 | 76 | 47 | 44 | 14 | .275 | .425 | 2 | 1 | 3B-143 |
| 1952 | 116 | 379 | 88 | 8 | 5 | 9 | 2.4 | 44 | 34 | 27 | 42 | 6 | .232 | .351 | 10 | 2 | 3B-104, OF-1 |
| 1953 | 139 | 498 | 142 | 22 | 8 | 19 | 3.8 | 61 | 66 | 42 | 61 | 8 | .285 | .476 | 7 | 0 | 3B-133 |
| 1954 | 126 | 484 | 132 | 17 | 6 | 19 | 3.9 | 77 | 67 | 44 | 55 | 2 | .273 | .450 | 2 | 0 | 3B-124 |
| 1955 | 138 | 499 | 132 | 13 | 7 | 21 | 4.2 | 73 | 70 | 58 | 58 | 0 | .265 | .445 | 3 | 1 | 3B-134 |
| 1956 BKN N | 101 | 307 | 84 | 15 | 7 | 8 | 2.6 | 37 | 53 | 28 | 38 | 2 | .274 | .446 | 21 | 5 | 3B-80 |
| 1957 | 48 | 131 | 26 | 1 | 0 | 2 | 1.5 | 7 | 16 | 9 | 20 | 0 | .198 | .252 | 4 | 2 | 3B-34 |
| 1958 2 teams | LA N (35G – .185) | | | CLE A (29G – .242) | | | | | | | | | | | | | |
| " total | 64 | 156 | 34 | 6 | 1 | 5 | 3.2 | 15 | 17 | 8 | 28 | 0 | .218 | .365 | 21 | 4 | 3B-41 |
| 1959 2 teams | CLE A (3G – .143) | | | CHI N (41G – .243) | | | | | | | | | | | | | |
| " total | 44 | 81 | 19 | 5 | 1 | 1 | 1.2 | 7 | 10 | 11 | 11 | 0 | .235 | .358 | 16 | 1 | 3B-24, OF-1 |
| 10 yrs. | 955 | 3203 | 835 | 115 | 44 | 103 | 3.2 | 412 | 415 | 281 | 382 | 36 | .261 | .421 | 93 | 16 | 3B-844, OF-2 |
| 7 yrs. | 739 | 2602 | 690 | 93 | 36 | 88 | 3.4 | 353 | 329 | 236 | 295 | 34 | .265 | .430 | 46 | 5 | 3B-687, OF-2 |

**WORLD SERIES**

| | G | AB | H | 2B | 3B | HR | HR % | R | RBI | BB | SO | SB | BA | SA | AB | H | G by POS |
|---|---|---|---|---|---|---|---|---|---|---|---|---|---|---|---|---|---|
| 1956 BKN N | 3 | 3 | 0 | 0 | 0 | 0 | 0.0 | 0 | 0 | 0 | 2 | 0 | .000 | .000 | 3 | 0 | |

## Mike Jacobs

**JACOBS, MORRIS ELMORE**
B. 1877    D. Mar. 26, 1949, Louisville, Ky.

| | G | AB | H | 2B | 3B | HR | HR % | R | RBI | BB | SO | SB | BA | SA | AB | H | G by POS |
|---|---|---|---|---|---|---|---|---|---|---|---|---|---|---|---|---|---|
| 1902 CHI N | 5 | 19 | 4 | 0 | 0 | 0 | 0.0 | 1 | 2 | 0 | | 0 | .211 | .211 | 0 | 0 | SS-5 |

## Ray Jacobs

**JACOBS, RAYMOND F.**
B. Jan. 2, 1902, Salt Lake City, Utah    D. Apr. 5, 1952, Los Angeles, Calif.    BR  TR  6'     160 lbs.

| | G | AB | H | 2B | 3B | HR | HR % | R | RBI | BB | SO | SB | BA | SA | AB | H | G by POS |
|---|---|---|---|---|---|---|---|---|---|---|---|---|---|---|---|---|---|
| 1928 CHI N | 2 | 2 | 0 | 0 | 0 | 0 | 0.0 | 0 | 0 | 0 | 1 | 0 | .000 | .000 | 2 | 0 | |

## Merwin Jacobson

**JACOBSON, MERWIN JOHN WILLIAM (Jake)**
B. Mar. 7, 1894, New Britain, Conn.    D. Jan. 13, 1978, Baltimore, Md.    BL  TL  5'11½"  165 lbs.

| | G | AB | H | 2B | 3B | HR | HR % | R | RBI | BB | SO | SB | BA | SA | AB | H | G by POS |
|---|---|---|---|---|---|---|---|---|---|---|---|---|---|---|---|---|---|
| 1915 NY N | 8 | 24 | 2 | 0 | 0 | 0 | 0.0 | 0 | 0 | 1 | 5 | 0 | .083 | .083 | 2 | 0 | OF-5 |
| 1916 CHI N | 4 | 13 | 3 | 0 | 0 | 0 | 0.0 | 2 | 0 | 1 | 4 | 2 | .231 | .231 | 0 | 0 | OF-4 |
| 1926 BKN N | 110 | 288 | 71 | 9 | 2 | 0 | 0.0 | 41 | 23 | 36 | 24 | 5 | .247 | .292 | 17 | 5 | OF-86 |
| 1927 | 11 | 6 | 0 | 0 | 0 | 0 | 0.0 | 4 | 1 | 0 | 1 | 0 | .000 | .000 | 5 | 0 | OF-3 |
| 4 yrs. | 133 | 331 | 76 | 9 | 2 | 0 | 0.0 | 47 | 24 | 38 | 34 | 7 | .230 | .269 | 24 | 5 | OF-98 |
| 1 yr. | 4 | 13 | 3 | 0 | 0 | 0 | 0.0 | 2 | 0 | 1 | 4 | 2 | .231 | .231 | 0 | 0 | OF-4 |

## Art Jahn

**JAHN, ARTHUR CHARLES**
B. Dec. 5, 1895, Struble, Iowa    D. Jan. 9, 1948, Little Rock, Ark.    BR  TR  6'     180 lbs.

| | G | AB | H | 2B | 3B | HR | HR % | R | RBI | BB | SO | SB | BA | SA | AB | H | G by POS |
|---|---|---|---|---|---|---|---|---|---|---|---|---|---|---|---|---|---|
| 1925 CHI N | 58 | 226 | 68 | 10 | 8 | 0 | 0.0 | 30 | 37 | 11 | 20 | 2 | .301 | .416 | 0 | 0 | OF-58 |
| 1928 2 teams | NY N (10G – .276) | | | PHI N (36G – .223) | | | | | | | | | | | | | |
| " total | 46 | 123 | 29 | 5 | 0 | 1 | 0.8 | 15 | 18 | 6 | 16 | 0 | .236 | .301 | 8 | 1 | OF-39 |
| 2 yrs. | 104 | 349 | 97 | 15 | 8 | 1 | 0.3 | 45 | 55 | 17 | 36 | 2 | .278 | .375 | 8 | 1 | OF-97 |
| 1 yr. | 58 | 226 | 68 | 10 | 8 | 0 | 0.0 | 30 | 37 | 11 | 20 | 2 | .301 | .416 | 0 | 0 | OF-58 |

## Cleo James

**JAMES, CLEO JOEL**
B. Aug. 31, 1940, Clarksdale, Mich.                    BR  TR  5'10"   176 lbs.

| | G | AB | H | 2B | 3B | HR | HR % | R | RBI | BB | SO | SB | BA | SA | AB | H | G by POS |
|---|---|---|---|---|---|---|---|---|---|---|---|---|---|---|---|---|---|
| 1968 LA N | 10 | 10 | 2 | 1 | 0 | 0 | 0.0 | 2 | 0 | 0 | 6 | 0 | .200 | .300 | 6 | 1 | OF-2 |
| 1970 CHI N | 100 | 176 | 37 | 7 | 2 | 3 | 1.7 | 33 | 14 | 17 | 24 | 5 | .210 | .324 | 6 | 0 | OF-90 |
| 1971 | 54 | 150 | 43 | 7 | 0 | 2 | 1.3 | 25 | 13 | 10 | 16 | 6 | .287 | .373 | 3 | 1 | OF-48, 3B-2 |
| 1973 | 44 | 45 | 5 | 0 | 0 | 0 | 0.0 | 9 | 0 | 1 | 6 | 5 | .111 | .111 | 10 | 1 | OF-22 |
| 4 yrs. | 208 | 381 | 87 | 15 | 2 | 5 | 1.3 | 69 | 27 | 28 | 52 | 16 | .228 | .318 | 25 | 3 | OF-162, 3B-2 |
| 3 yrs. | 198 | 371 | 85 | 14 | 2 | 5 | 1.3 | 67 | 27 | 28 | 46 | 16 | .229 | .318 | 19 | 2 | OF-160, 3B-2 |

## Hal Jeffcoat

**JEFFCOAT, HAROLD BENTLEY**
Brother of George Jeffcoat.
B. Sept. 6, 1924, West Columbia, S. C.                    BR  TR  5'10½"  185 lbs.

| | G | AB | H | 2B | 3B | HR | HR % | R | RBI | BB | SO | SB | BA | SA | AB | H | G by POS |
|---|---|---|---|---|---|---|---|---|---|---|---|---|---|---|---|---|---|
| 1948 CHI N | 134 | 473 | 132 | 16 | 4 | 4 | 0.8 | 53 | 42 | 24 | 68 | 8 | .279 | .355 | 14 | 6 | OF-119 |
| 1949 | 108 | 363 | 89 | 18 | 6 | 2 | 0.6 | 43 | 26 | 20 | 48 | 12 | .245 | .344 | 5 | 2 | OF-101 |
| 1950 | 66 | 179 | 42 | 13 | 1 | 2 | 1.1 | 21 | 18 | 6 | 23 | 7 | .235 | .352 | 8 | 1 | OF-53 |
| 1951 | 113 | 278 | 76 | 20 | 2 | 4 | 1.4 | 44 | 27 | 16 | 23 | 8 | .273 | .403 | 9 | 3 | OF-87 |
| 1952 | 102 | 297 | 65 | 17 | 2 | 4 | 1.3 | 29 | 30 | 15 | 40 | 7 | .219 | .330 | 1 | 1 | OF-95 |
| 1953 | 106 | 183 | 43 | 3 | 1 | 4 | 2.2 | 22 | 22 | 21 | 26 | 5 | .235 | .328 | 2 | 0 | OF-100 |
| 1954 | 56 | 31 | 8 | 2 | 1 | 1 | 3.2 | 13 | 6 | 1 | 7 | 2 | .258 | .484 | 0 | 0 | P-43, OF-3 |
| 1955 | 52 | 23 | 4 | 0 | 0 | 1 | 4.3 | 3 | 1 | 2 | 9 | 0 | .174 | .304 | 0 | 0 | P-50 |
| 1956 CIN N | 49 | 54 | 8 | 2 | 0 | 0 | 0.0 | 5 | 5 | 3 | 20 | 0 | .148 | .185 | 0 | 0 | P-38 |
| 1957 | 53 | 69 | 14 | 3 | 1 | 4 | 5.8 | 13 | 11 | 5 | 20 | 0 | .203 | .449 | 0 | 0 | P-37 |

| | G | AB | H | 2B | 3B | HR | HR % | R | RBI | BB | SO | SB | BA | SA | Pinch Hit AB | H | G by POS |
|---|---|---|---|---|---|---|---|---|---|---|---|---|---|---|---|---|---|

### Hal Jeffcoat continued

| | | G | AB | H | 2B | 3B | HR | HR % | R | RBI | BB | SO | SB | BA | SA | PH AB | H | G by POS |
|---|---|---|---|---|---|---|---|---|---|---|---|---|---|---|---|---|---|---|
| 1958 | | 50 | 9 | 5 | 0 | 0 | 0 | 0.0 | 2 | 0 | 1 | 2 | 0 | .556 | .556 | 0 | 0 | P-49, OF-1 |
| 1959 | 2 teams | CIN N (17G – 1.000) | | | | | STL N (12G – .000) | | | | | | | | | | | |
| " | total | 29 | 4 | 1 | 0 | 0 | 0 | 0.0 | 1 | 0 | 0 | 3 | 0 | .250 | .500 | 0 | 0 | P-28 |
| 12 yrs. | | 918 | 1963 | 487 | 95 | 18 | 26 | 1.3 | 249 | 188 | 114 | 289 | 49 | .248 | .355 | 39 | 12 | OF-559, P-245 |
| 8 yrs. | | 737 | 1827 | 459 | 89 | 17 | 22 | 1.2 | 228 | 172 | 105 | 244 | 49 | .251 | .355 | 39 | 12 | OF-558, P-93 |

### Frank Jelincich

JELINCICH, FRANK ANTHONY (Jelly)  
B. Sept. 3, 1919, San Jose, Calif.  
BR TR 6'2" 198 lbs.

| | | G | AB | H | 2B | 3B | HR | HR % | R | RBI | BB | SO | SB | BA | SA | PH AB | H | G by POS |
|---|---|---|---|---|---|---|---|---|---|---|---|---|---|---|---|---|---|---|
| 1941 | CHI N | 4 | 8 | 1 | 0 | 0 | 0 | 0.0 | 0 | 2 | 1 | 2 | 0 | .125 | .125 | 2 | 0 | OF-2 |

### Garry Jestadt

JESTADT, GARRY ARTHUR  
B. Mar. 19, 1947, Chicago, Ill.  
BR TR 6'2" 188 lbs.

| | | G | AB | H | 2B | 3B | HR | HR % | R | RBI | BB | SO | SB | BA | SA | PH AB | H | G by POS |
|---|---|---|---|---|---|---|---|---|---|---|---|---|---|---|---|---|---|---|
| 1969 | MON N | 6 | 6 | 0 | 0 | 0 | 0 | 0.0 | 1 | 1 | 0 | 0 | 0 | .000 | .000 | 4 | 0 | SS-1 |
| 1971 | 2 teams | CHI N (3G – .000) | | | | | SD N (75G – .291) | | | | | | | | | | | |
| " | total | 78 | 192 | 55 | 13 | 0 | 0 | 0.0 | 17 | 13 | 11 | 24 | 1 | .286 | .354 | 4 | 1 | 3B-50, 2B-23, SS-1 |
| 1972 | SD N | 92 | 256 | 63 | 5 | 1 | 6 | 2.3 | 15 | 22 | 13 | 21 | 0 | .246 | .344 | 23 | 5 | 2B-48, 3B-25, SS-3 |
| 3 yrs. | | 176 | 454 | 118 | 18 | 1 | 6 | 1.3 | 33 | 36 | 24 | 45 | 1 | .260 | .344 | 31 | 6 | 3B-75, 2B-71, SS-5 |
| 1 yr. | | 3 | 3 | 0 | 0 | 0 | 0 | 0.0 | 0 | 0 | 0 | 0 | 0 | .000 | .000 | 2 | 0 | 3B-1 |

### Manny Jimenez

JIMENEZ, MANUEL EMILIO  
Brother of Elvio Jimenez.  
B. Nov. 19, 1938, San Pedro de Macoris, Dominican Republic  
BL TR 6'1" 185 lbs.

| | | G | AB | H | 2B | 3B | HR | HR % | R | RBI | BB | SO | SB | BA | SA | PH AB | H | G by POS |
|---|---|---|---|---|---|---|---|---|---|---|---|---|---|---|---|---|---|---|
| 1962 | KC A | 139 | 479 | 144 | 24 | 2 | 11 | 2.3 | 48 | 69 | 31 | 34 | 0 | .301 | .428 | 17 | 7 | OF-122 |
| 1963 | | 60 | 157 | 44 | 9 | 0 | 0 | 0.0 | 12 | 15 | 16 | 14 | 0 | .280 | .338 | 15 | 2 | OF-40 |
| 1964 | | 95 | 204 | 46 | 7 | 0 | 12 | 5.9 | 19 | 38 | 15 | 24 | 0 | .225 | .436 | 41 | 9 | OF-49 |
| 1966 | | 13 | 35 | 4 | 0 | 1 | 0 | 0.0 | 1 | 1 | 6 | 4 | 0 | .114 | .171 | 2 | 0 | OF-12 |
| 1967 | PIT N | 50 | 56 | 14 | 2 | 0 | 2 | 3.6 | 3 | 10 | 1 | 4 | 0 | .250 | .393 | 42 | 12 | OF-6 |
| 1968 | | 66 | 66 | 20 | 1 | 1 | 1 | 1.5 | 7 | 11 | 6 | 15 | 0 | .303 | .394 | 53 | 10 | OF-5 |
| 1969 | CHI N | 6 | 6 | 1 | 0 | 0 | 0 | 0.0 | 0 | 0 | 0 | 2 | 0 | .167 | .167 | 6 | 1 | |
| 7 yrs. | | 429 | 1003 | 273 | 43 | 4 | 26 | 2.6 | 90 | 144 | 75 | 97 | 0 | .272 | .401 | 176 | 41 | OF-234 |
| 1 yr. | | 6 | 6 | 1 | 0 | 0 | 0 | 0.0 | 0 | 0 | 0 | 2 | 0 | .167 | .167 | 6 | 1 | |

### Cliff Johnson

JOHNSON, CLIFFORD, JR. (Heathcliff)  
B. July 22, 1947, San Antonio, Tex.  
BR TR 6'4" 215 lbs.

| | | G | AB | H | 2B | 3B | HR | HR % | R | RBI | BB | SO | SB | BA | SA | PH AB | H | G by POS |
|---|---|---|---|---|---|---|---|---|---|---|---|---|---|---|---|---|---|---|
| 1972 | HOU N | 5 | 4 | 1 | 0 | 0 | 0 | 0.0 | 0 | 0 | 2 | 0 | 0 | .250 | .250 | 3 | 0 | C-1 |
| 1973 | | 7 | 20 | 6 | 2 | 0 | 2 | 10.0 | 6 | 6 | 1 | 7 | 0 | .300 | .700 | 2 | 0 | 1B-5 |
| 1974 | | 83 | 171 | 39 | 4 | 1 | 10 | 5.8 | 26 | 29 | 33 | 45 | 0 | .228 | .439 | 38 | 13 | C-28, 1B-21 |
| 1975 | | 122 | 340 | 94 | 16 | 1 | 20 | 5.9 | 52 | 65 | 46 | 64 | 1 | .276 | .506 | 33 | 5 | 1B-47, C-41, OF-1 |
| 1976 | | 108 | 318 | 72 | 21 | 2 | 10 | 3.1 | 36 | 49 | 62 | 59 | 0 | .226 | .399 | 9 | 2 | C-66, OF-20, 1B-16 |
| 1977 | 2 teams | HOU N (51G – .299) | | | | | NY A (56G – .296) | | | | | | | | | | | |
| " | total | 107 | 286 | 85 | 16 | 0 | 22 | 7.7 | 46 | 54 | 43 | 53 | 0 | .297 | .584 | 22 | 8 | OF-34, DH-25, 1B-21, C-15 |
| 1978 | NY A | 76 | 174 | 32 | 9 | 1 | 6 | 3.4 | 20 | 19 | 30 | 32 | 0 | .184 | .351 | 15 | 2 | DH-39, C-22, 1B-1 |
| 1979 | 2 teams | NY A (28G – .266) | | | | | CLE A (72G – .271) | | | | | | | | | | | |
| " | total | 100 | 304 | 82 | 16 | 0 | 20 | 6.6 | 48 | 67 | 34 | 46 | 2 | .270 | .520 | 17 | 4 | DH-82, C-5 |
| 1980 | 2 teams | CLE A (54G – .230) | | | | | CHI A (68G – .235) | | | | | | | | | | | |
| " | total | 122 | 370 | 86 | 11 | 1 | 16 | 4.3 | 53 | 62 | 54 | 65 | 0 | .232 | .397 | 23 | 4 | 1B-46, DH-45, OF-3, C-1 |
| 1981 | OAK A | 84 | 273 | 71 | 8 | 0 | 17 | 6.2 | 40 | 59 | 28 | 60 | 5 | .260 | .476 | 17 | 2 | DH-68, 1B-9 |
| 1982 | | 73 | 214 | 51 | 10 | 0 | 7 | 3.3 | 19 | 31 | 26 | 41 | 1 | .238 | .383 | 20 | 5 | DH-48, 1B-11 |
| 1983 | TOR A | 142 | 407 | 108 | 23 | 1 | 22 | 5.4 | 59 | 76 | 67 | 69 | 0 | .265 | .489 | 24 | 4 | DH-130, 1B-6 |
| 1984 | | 127 | 359 | 109 | 23 | 1 | 16 | 4.5 | 51 | 61 | 50 | 62 | 0 | .304 | .507 | 34 | 11 | DH-109, 1B-2 |
| 1985 | 2 teams | TEX A (82G – .257) | | | | | TOR A (24G – .274) | | | | | | | | | | | |
| " | total | 106 | 369 | 96 | 17 | 1 | 13 | 3.5 | 35 | 66 | 40 | 59 | 0 | .260 | .417 | 8 | 3 | DH-103, 1B-3 |
| 14 yrs. | | 1262 | 3609 | 932 | 176 | 9 | 181 | 5.0 | 491 | 644 | 516 | 662 | 9 | .258 | .462 | 265 | 63 | DH-649, 1B-188, C-179, OF-58 |
| 1 yr. | | 68 | 196 | 46 | 8 | 0 | 10 | 5.1 | 28 | 34 | 29 | 35 | 0 | .235 | .429 | 17 | 2 | 1B-46, OF-3, C-1 |

DIVISIONAL PLAYOFF SERIES

| | | G | AB | H | 2B | 3B | HR | HR % | R | RBI | BB | SO | SB | BA | SA | PH AB | H | G by POS |
|---|---|---|---|---|---|---|---|---|---|---|---|---|---|---|---|---|---|---|
| 1981 | OAK A | 2 | 7 | 2 | 1 | 0 | 0 | 0.0 | 0 | 0 | 0 | 1 | 0 | .286 | .429 | 0 | 0 | DH-2 |

LEAGUE CHAMPIONSHIP SERIES

| | | G | AB | H | 2B | 3B | HR | HR % | R | RBI | BB | SO | SB | BA | SA | PH AB | H | G by POS |
|---|---|---|---|---|---|---|---|---|---|---|---|---|---|---|---|---|---|---|
| 1977 | NY A | 5 | 15 | 6 | 2 | 0 | 1 | 6.7 | 2 | 2 | 1 | 2 | 0 | .400 | .733 | 1 | 0 | DH-4 |
| 1978 | | 1 | 1 | 0 | 0 | 0 | 0 | 0.0 | 0 | 0 | 0 | 0 | 0 | .000 | .000 | 1 | 0 | |
| 1981 | OAK A | 2 | 6 | 0 | 0 | 0 | 0 | 0.0 | 0 | 0 | 2 | 2 | 0 | .000 | .000 | 0 | 0 | DH-2 |
| 1985 | TOR A | 7 | 19 | 7 | 2 | 0 | 0 | 0.0 | 1 | 2 | 1 | 4 | 0 | .368 | .474 | 3 | 2 | DH-7 |
| 4 yrs. | | 15 | 41 | 13 | 4 | 0 | 1 | 2.4 | 3 | 4 | 4 | 8 | 0 | .317 | .488 | 5 | 2 | DH-13 |

WORLD SERIES

| | | G | AB | H | 2B | 3B | HR | HR % | R | RBI | BB | SO | SB | BA | SA | PH AB | H | G by POS |
|---|---|---|---|---|---|---|---|---|---|---|---|---|---|---|---|---|---|---|
| 1977 | NY A | 2 | 1 | 0 | 0 | 0 | 0 | 0.0 | 0 | 0 | 0 | 0 | 0 | .000 | .000 | 1 | 0 | C-1 |
| 1978 | | 2 | 2 | 0 | 0 | 0 | 0 | 0.0 | 0 | 0 | 0 | 1 | 0 | .000 | .000 | 2 | 0 | |
| 2 yrs. | | 4 | 3 | 0 | 0 | 0 | 0 | 0.0 | 0 | 0 | 0 | 1 | 0 | .000 | .000 | 3 | 0 | C-1 |

### Davy Johnson

JOHNSON, DAVID ALLEN  
B. Jan. 30, 1943, Orlando, Fla.  
Manager 1984-85.  
BR TR 6'1" 170 lbs.

| | | G | AB | H | 2B | 3B | HR | HR % | R | RBI | BB | SO | SB | BA | SA | PH AB | H | G by POS |
|---|---|---|---|---|---|---|---|---|---|---|---|---|---|---|---|---|---|---|
| 1965 | BAL A | 20 | 47 | 8 | 3 | 0 | 0 | 0.0 | 5 | 1 | 5 | 6 | 3 | .170 | .234 | 4 | 1 | 3B-9, 2B-3, SS-2 |
| 1966 | | 131 | 501 | 129 | 20 | 3 | 7 | 1.4 | 47 | 56 | 31 | 64 | 3 | .257 | .351 | 2 | 0 | 2B-126, SS-3 |
| 1967 | | 148 | 510 | 126 | 30 | 3 | 10 | 2.0 | 62 | 64 | 59 | 82 | 4 | .247 | .376 | 2 | 0 | 2B-144, 3B-3 |
| 1968 | | 145 | 504 | 122 | 24 | 4 | 9 | 1.8 | 50 | 56 | 44 | 80 | 7 | .242 | .359 | 2 | 1 | 2B-127, SS-34 |
| 1969 | | 142 | 511 | 143 | 34 | 1 | 7 | 1.4 | 52 | 57 | 57 | 52 | 3 | .280 | .391 | 0 | 0 | 2B-142, SS-2 |
| 1970 | | 149 | 530 | 149 | 27 | 1 | 10 | 1.9 | 68 | 53 | 66 | 68 | 2 | .281 | .392 | 0 | 0 | 2B-149, SS-2 |
| 1971 | | 142 | 510 | 144 | 26 | 1 | 18 | 3.5 | 67 | 72 | 51 | 55 | 3 | .282 | .443 | 1 | 0 | 2B-140 |
| 1972 | | 118 | 376 | 83 | 22 | 3 | 5 | 1.3 | 31 | 32 | 52 | 68 | 1 | .221 | .335 | 2 | 1 | 2B-116 |
| 1973 | ATL N | 157 | 559 | 151 | 25 | 0 | 43 | 7.7 | 84 | 99 | 81 | 93 | 5 | .270 | .546 | 2 | 1 | 2B-155 |

| | G | AB | H | 2B | 3B | HR | HR % | R | RBI | BB | SO | SB | BA | SA | Pinch Hit AB | Pinch Hit H | G by POS |
|---|---|---|---|---|---|---|---|---|---|---|---|---|---|---|---|---|---|

## Davy Johnson  continued

| | G | AB | H | 2B | 3B | HR | HR % | R | RBI | BB | SO | SB | BA | SA | AB | H | G by POS |
|---|---|---|---|---|---|---|---|---|---|---|---|---|---|---|---|---|---|
| 1974 | 136 | 454 | 114 | 18 | 0 | 15 | 3.3 | 56 | 62 | 75 | 59 | 1 | .251 | .390 | 4 | 2 | 1B-73, 2B-71 |
| 1975 | 1 | 1 | 1 | 1 | 0 | 0 | 0.0 | 0 | 1 | 0 | 0 | 0 | 1.000 | 2.000 | 1 | 1 | |
| 1977 PHI N | 78 | 156 | 50 | 9 | 1 | 8 | 5.1 | 23 | 36 | 23 | 20 | 1 | .321 | .545 | 26 | 9 | 1B-43, 2B-9, 3B-6 |
| 1978 2 teams | | | PHI | N | (44G – | .191) | | CHI | N | (24G – | .306) | | | | | | |
| " total | 68 | 138 | 32 | 3 | 1 | 4 | 2.9 | 19 | 20 | 15 | 28 | 0 | .232 | .355 | 30 | 10 | 3B-21, 2B-15, 1B-7 |
| 13 yrs. | 1435 | 4797 | 1252 | 242 | 18 | 136 | 2.8 | 564 | 609 | 559 | 675 | 33 | .261 | .404 | 76 | 26 | 2B-1197, 1B-123, SS-43, 3B-39 |
| 1 yr. | 24 | 49 | 15 | 1 | 1 | 2 | 4.1 | 5 | 6 | 5 | 9 | 0 | .306 | .490 | 11 | 4 | 3B-12 |

LEAGUE CHAMPIONSHIP SERIES

| | G | AB | H | 2B | 3B | HR | HR % | R | RBI | BB | SO | SB | BA | SA | AB | H | G by POS |
|---|---|---|---|---|---|---|---|---|---|---|---|---|---|---|---|---|---|
| 1969 BAL A | 3 | 13 | 3 | 0 | 0 | 0 | 0.0 | 2 | 0 | 2 | 1 | 0 | .231 | .231 | 0 | 0 | 2B-3 |
| 1970 | 3 | 11 | 4 | 0 | 0 | 2 | 18.2 | 4 | 4 | 1 | 1 | 0 | .364 | .909 | 0 | 0 | 2B-3 |
| 1971 | 3 | 10 | 3 | 2 | 0 | 0 | 0.0 | 2 | 0 | 3 | 1 | 0 | .300 | .500 | 0 | 0 | 2B-3 |
| 1977 PHI N | 1 | 4 | 1 | 0 | 0 | 0 | 0.0 | 0 | 2 | 0 | 1 | 0 | .250 | .250 | 0 | 0 | 1B-1 |
| 4 yrs. | 10 | 38 | 11 | 2 | 0 | 2 | 5.3 | 8 | 6 | 6 | 4 | 0 | .289 | .500 | 0 | 0 | 2B-9, 1B-1 |

WORLD SERIES

| | G | AB | H | 2B | 3B | HR | HR % | R | RBI | BB | SO | SB | BA | SA | AB | H | G by POS |
|---|---|---|---|---|---|---|---|---|---|---|---|---|---|---|---|---|---|
| 1966 BAL A | 4 | 14 | 4 | 1 | 0 | 0 | 0.0 | 1 | 1 | 0 | 1 | 0 | .286 | .357 | 0 | 0 | 2B-4 |
| 1969 | 5 | 16 | 1 | 0 | 0 | 0 | 0.0 | 1 | 0 | 2 | 1 | 0 | .063 | .063 | 0 | 0 | 2B-5 |
| 1970 | 5 | 16 | 5 | 2 | 0 | 0 | 0.0 | 2 | 2 | 5 | 2 | 0 | .313 | .438 | 0 | 0 | 2B-5 |
| 1971 | 7 | 27 | 4 | 0 | 0 | 0 | 0.0 | 1 | 3 | 0 | 1 | 0 | .148 | .148 | 0 | 0 | 2B-7 |
| 4 yrs. | 21 | 73 | 14 | 3 | 0 | 0 | 0.0 | 5 | 6 | 7 | 5 | 0 | .192 | .233 | 0 | 0 | 2B-21 |

## Dick Johnson

**JOHNSON, RICHARD ALLAN (Footer, Treads)**
B. Feb. 15, 1932, Dayton, Ohio
BL  TL  5'11"  175 lbs.

| | G | AB | H | 2B | 3B | HR | HR % | R | RBI | BB | SO | SB | BA | SA | AB | H | G by POS |
|---|---|---|---|---|---|---|---|---|---|---|---|---|---|---|---|---|---|
| 1958 CHI N | 8 | 5 | 0 | 0 | 0 | 0 | 0.0 | 1 | 0 | 0 | 1 | 0 | .000 | .000 | 5 | 0 | |

## Don Johnson

**JOHNSON, DONALD SPORE (Pep)**
Son of Ernie Johnson.
B. Dec. 7, 1911, Chicago, Ill.
BR  TR  6'  170 lbs.

| | G | AB | H | 2B | 3B | HR | HR % | R | RBI | BB | SO | SB | BA | SA | AB | H | G by POS |
|---|---|---|---|---|---|---|---|---|---|---|---|---|---|---|---|---|---|
| 1943 CHI N | 10 | 42 | 8 | 2 | 0 | 0 | 0.0 | 5 | 1 | 2 | 4 | 0 | .190 | .238 | 0 | 0 | 2B-10 |
| 1944 | 154 | 608 | 169 | 37 | 1 | 2 | 0.3 | 50 | 71 | 28 | 48 | 8 | .278 | .352 | 0 | 0 | 2B-154 |
| 1945 | 138 | 557 | 168 | 23 | 2 | 2 | 0.4 | 94 | 58 | 32 | 34 | 9 | .302 | .361 | 0 | 0 | 2B-138 |
| 1946 | 83 | 314 | 76 | 10 | 1 | 1 | 0.3 | 37 | 19 | 26 | 39 | 6 | .242 | .290 | 0 | 0 | 2B-83 |
| 1947 | 120 | 402 | 104 | 17 | 2 | 3 | 0.7 | 33 | 26 | 24 | 45 | 2 | .259 | .333 | 5 | 1 | 2B-108, 3B-6 |
| 1948 | 6 | 12 | 3 | 0 | 0 | 0 | 0.0 | 0 | 0 | 0 | 1 | 1 | .250 | .250 | 2 | 0 | 3B-2, 2B-2 |
| 6 yrs. | 511 | 1935 | 528 | 89 | 6 | 8 | 0.4 | 219 | 175 | 112 | 171 | 26 | .273 | .337 | 7 | 1 | 2B-495, 3B-8 |
| 6 yrs. | 511 | 1935 | 528 | 89 | 6 | 8 | 0.4 | 219 | 175 | 112 | 171 | 26 | .273 | .337 | 7 | 1 | 2B-495, 3B-8 |

WORLD SERIES

| | G | AB | H | 2B | 3B | HR | HR % | R | RBI | BB | SO | SB | BA | SA | AB | H | G by POS |
|---|---|---|---|---|---|---|---|---|---|---|---|---|---|---|---|---|---|
| 1945 CHI N | 7 | 29 | 5 | 2 | 1 | 0 | 0.0 | 4 | 0 | 0 | 8 | 0 | .172 | .310 | 0 | 0 | 2B-7 |

## Lou Johnson

**JOHNSON, LOUIS BROWN (Slick, Sweet Lou)**
B. Sept. 22, 1934, Lexington, Ky.
BR  TR  5'11"  170 lbs.

| | G | AB | H | 2B | 3B | HR | HR % | R | RBI | BB | SO | SB | BA | SA | AB | H | G by POS |
|---|---|---|---|---|---|---|---|---|---|---|---|---|---|---|---|---|---|
| 1960 CHI N | 34 | 68 | 14 | 2 | 1 | 0 | 0.0 | 6 | 1 | 5 | 19 | 3 | .206 | .265 | 6 | 0 | OF-25 |
| 1961 LA A | 1 | 0 | 0 | 0 | 0 | 0 | – | 0 | 0 | 0 | 0 | 0 | – | – | 0 | 0 | OF-1 |
| 1962 MIL N | 61 | 117 | 33 | 4 | 5 | 2 | 1.7 | 22 | 13 | 11 | 27 | 6 | .282 | .453 | 9 | 1 | OF-55 |
| 1965 LA N | 131 | 468 | 121 | 24 | 1 | 12 | 2.6 | 57 | 58 | 24 | 81 | 15 | .259 | .391 | 2 | 0 | OF-128 |
| 1966 | 152 | 526 | 143 | 20 | 2 | 17 | 3.2 | 71 | 73 | 21 | 75 | 8 | .272 | .414 | 1 | 0 | OF-148 |
| 1967 | 104 | 330 | 89 | 14 | 1 | 11 | 3.3 | 39 | 41 | 24 | 52 | 4 | .270 | .418 | 16 | 5 | OF-91 |
| 1968 2 teams | | | CHI | N | (62G – | .244) | | CLE | A | (65G – | .257) | | | | | | |
| " total | 127 | 407 | 102 | 25 | 4 | 6 | 1.5 | 39 | 37 | 15 | 47 | 9 | .251 | .376 | 14 | 7 | OF-114 |
| 1969 CAL A | 67 | 133 | 27 | 8 | 0 | 0 | 0.0 | 10 | 9 | 10 | 19 | 5 | .203 | .263 | 22 | 3 | OF-44 |
| 8 yrs. | 677 | 2049 | 529 | 97 | 14 | 48 | 2.3 | 244 | 232 | 110 | 320 | 50 | .258 | .389 | 70 | 16 | OF-606 |
| 2 yrs. | 96 | 273 | 64 | 16 | 4 | 1 | 0.4 | 20 | 15 | 11 | 42 | 6 | .234 | .333 | 10 | 1 | OF-82 |

WORLD SERIES

| | G | AB | H | 2B | 3B | HR | HR % | R | RBI | BB | SO | SB | BA | SA | AB | H | G by POS |
|---|---|---|---|---|---|---|---|---|---|---|---|---|---|---|---|---|---|
| 1965 LA N | 7 | 27 | 8 | 2 | 0 | 2 | 7.4 | 3 | 4 | 1 | 3 | 0 | .296 | .593 | 0 | 0 | OF-7 |
| 1966 | 4 | 15 | 4 | 1 | 0 | 0 | 0.0 | 1 | 0 | 1 | 1 | 0 | .267 | .333 | 0 | 0 | OF-4 |
| 2 yrs. | 11 | 42 | 12 | 3 | 0 | 2 | 4.8 | 4 | 4 | 2 | 4 | 0 | .286 | .500 | 0 | 0 | OF-11 |

## Jimmy Johnston

**JOHNSTON, JAMES HARLE**
Brother of Doc Johnston.
B. Dec. 10, 1889, Cleveland, Tenn.    D. Feb. 14, 1967, Chattanooga, Tenn.
BR  TR  5'10"  160 lbs.

| | G | AB | H | 2B | 3B | HR | HR % | R | RBI | BB | SO | SB | BA | SA | AB | H | G by POS |
|---|---|---|---|---|---|---|---|---|---|---|---|---|---|---|---|---|---|
| 1911 CHI A | 1 | 2 | 0 | 0 | 0 | 0 | 0.0 | 0 | 2 | 0 | | 0 | .000 | .000 | 0 | 0 | OF-1 |
| 1914 CHI N | 50 | 101 | 23 | 3 | 2 | 1 | 1.0 | 9 | 8 | 4 | 9 | 3 | .228 | .327 | 11 | 2 | OF-28, 2B-4 |
| 1916 BKN N | 118 | 425 | 107 | 13 | 8 | 1 | 0.2 | 58 | 26 | 35 | 38 | 22 | .252 | .327 | 1 | 1 | OF-106 |
| 1917 | 103 | 330 | 89 | 10 | 4 | 0 | 0.0 | 33 | 25 | 23 | 28 | 16 | .270 | .324 | 8 | 1 | OF-92, 1B-14, SS-4, 3B-3, 2B-3 |
| 1918 | 123 | 484 | 136 | 16 | 8 | 0 | 0.0 | 54 | 27 | 33 | 31 | 22 | .281 | .347 | 1 | 0 | OF-96, 1B-21, 3B-4, 2B-1 |
| 1919 | 117 | 405 | 114 | 11 | 4 | 1 | 0.2 | 56 | 23 | 29 | 26 | 11 | .281 | .336 | 9 | 1 | 2B-87, OF-14, 1B-2, SS-1 |
| 1920 | 155 | 635 | 185 | 17 | 12 | 1 | 0.2 | 87 | 52 | 43 | 23 | 19 | .291 | .361 | 0 | 0 | 3B-146, OF-7, SS-3 |
| 1921 | 152 | 624 | 203 | 41 | 14 | 5 | 0.8 | 104 | 56 | 45 | 26 | 28 | .325 | .460 | 0 | 0 | 3B-150, SS-3 |
| 1922 | 138 | 567 | 181 | 20 | 7 | 4 | 0.7 | 110 | 49 | 38 | 17 | 18 | .319 | .400 | 0 | 0 | 2B-62, SS-50, 3B-26 |
| 1923 | 151 | 625 | 203 | 29 | 11 | 4 | 0.6 | 111 | 60 | 53 | 15 | 16 | .325 | .426 | 1 | 0 | 2B-84, SS-52, 3B-14 |
| 1924 | 86 | 315 | 94 | 11 | 2 | 2 | 0.6 | 51 | 29 | 27 | 10 | 5 | .298 | .365 | 7 | 4 | SS-63, 3B-10, 1B-4, OF-1 |
| 1925 | 123 | 431 | 128 | 13 | 3 | 2 | 0.5 | 63 | 43 | 45 | 15 | 7 | .297 | .355 | 12 | 4 | 3B-81, OF-20, 1B-8, SS-2 |
| 1926 2 teams | | | BOS | N | (23G – | .246) | | NY | N | (37G – | .232) | | | | | | |
| " total | 60 | 126 | 30 | 1 | 0 | 0 | 0.0 | 18 | 10 | 16 | 8 | 2 | .238 | .270 | 25 | 5 | OF-15, 3B-14, 2B-2 |
| 13 yrs. | 1377 | 5070 | 1493 | 185 | 75 | 22 | 0.4 | 754 | 410 | 391 | 246 | 169 | .294 | .374 | 75 | 18 | 3B-448, OF-380, 2B-243, SS-178, 1B-49 |
| 1 yr. | 50 | 101 | 23 | 3 | 2 | 1 | 1.0 | 9 | 8 | 4 | 9 | 3 | .228 | .327 | 11 | 2 | OF-28, 2B-4 |

WORLD SERIES

| | G | AB | H | 2B | 3B | HR | HR % | R | RBI | BB | SO | SB | BA | SA | AB | H | G by POS |
|---|---|---|---|---|---|---|---|---|---|---|---|---|---|---|---|---|---|
| 1916 BKN N | 3 | 10 | 3 | 1 | 0 | 0 | 0.0 | 0 | 1 | 0 | 0 | 0 | .300 | .500 | 1 | 1 | OF-2 |

| | G | AB | H | 2B | 3B | HR | HR % | R | RBI | BB | SO | SB | BA | SA | Pinch Hit AB | Pinch Hit H | G by POS |
|---|---|---|---|---|---|---|---|---|---|---|---|---|---|---|---|---|---|

## Jimmy Johnston continued

| | G | AB | H | 2B | 3B | HR | HR % | R | RBI | BB | SO | SB | BA | SA | AB | H | G by POS |
|---|---|---|---|---|---|---|---|---|---|---|---|---|---|---|---|---|---|
| 1920 | 4 | 14 | 3 | 0 | 0 | 0 | 0.0 | 2 | 0 | 0 | 2 | 1 | .214 | .214 | 0 | 0 | 3B-4 |
| 2 yrs. | 7 | 24 | 6 | 0 | 1 | 0 | 0.0 | 3 | 0 | 1 | 2 | 1 | .250 | .333 | 1 | 1 | 3B-4, OF-2 |

## Jay Johnstone

**JOHNSTONE, JOHN WILLIAM**    BL TR 6'1" 175 lbs.
B. Nov. 20, 1945, Manchester, Conn.    BB 1966

| | | G | AB | H | 2B | 3B | HR | HR % | R | RBI | BB | SO | SB | BA | SA | AB | H | G by POS |
|---|---|---|---|---|---|---|---|---|---|---|---|---|---|---|---|---|---|---|
| 1966 | CAL A | 61 | 254 | 67 | 12 | 4 | 3 | 1.2 | 35 | 17 | 11 | 36 | 3 | .264 | .378 | 0 | 0 | OF-61 |
| 1967 | | 79 | 230 | 48 | 7 | 1 | 2 | 0.9 | 19 | 10 | 5 | 37 | 3 | .209 | .274 | 21 | 5 | OF-63 |
| 1968 | | 41 | 115 | 30 | 4 | 1 | 0 | 0.0 | 11 | 3 | 7 | 15 | 2 | .261 | .313 | 8 | 0 | OF-29 |
| 1969 | | 148 | 540 | 146 | 20 | 5 | 10 | 1.9 | 64 | 59 | 38 | 75 | 3 | .270 | .381 | 4 | 1 | OF-144 |
| 1970 | | 119 | 320 | 76 | 10 | 5 | 11 | 3.4 | 34 | 39 | 24 | 53 | 1 | .238 | .403 | 23 | 5 | OF-100 |
| 1971 | CHI A | 124 | 388 | 101 | 14 | 1 | 16 | 4.1 | 53 | 40 | 38 | 50 | 10 | .260 | .425 | 11 | 3 | OF-119 |
| 1972 | | 113 | 261 | 49 | 9 | 0 | 4 | 1.5 | 27 | 17 | 25 | 42 | 2 | .188 | .268 | 19 | 6 | OF-97 |
| 1973 | OAK A | 23 | 28 | 3 | 1 | 0 | 0 | 0.0 | 1 | 3 | 2 | 4 | 0 | .107 | .143 | 11 | 0 | OF-7, DH-4, 2B-2 |
| 1974 | PHI N | 64 | 200 | 59 | 10 | 4 | 6 | 3.0 | 30 | 30 | 24 | 28 | 5 | .295 | .475 | 6 | 4 | OF-59 |
| 1975 | | 122 | 350 | 115 | 19 | 2 | 7 | 2.0 | 50 | 54 | 42 | 39 | 7 | .329 | .454 | 25 | 10 | OF-101 |
| 1976 | | 129 | 440 | 140 | 38 | 4 | 5 | 1.1 | 62 | 53 | 41 | 39 | 5 | .318 | .457 | 12 | 2 | OF-122, 1B-6 |
| 1977 | | 112 | 363 | 103 | 18 | 4 | 15 | 4.1 | 64 | 59 | 38 | 38 | 3 | .284 | .479 | 14 | 5 | OF-91, 1B-19 |
| 1978 2 teams | | 71 | 121 | 27 | 2 | 0 | 1 | 0.8 | 9 | 10 | 10 | 19 | 0 | .223 | .264 | 28 | 2 | OF-29, 1B-8, DH-5 |
| " total | PHI N (35G – .179) NY A (36G – .262) | | | | | | | | | | | | | | | | | |
| 1979 2 teams | | 98 | 249 | 69 | 9 | 2 | 1 | 0.4 | 17 | 39 | 20 | 28 | 2 | .277 | .341 | 25 | 6 | OF-64, 1B-22, DH-3 |
| " total | NY A (23G – .208) SD N (75G – .294) | | | | | | | | | | | | | | | | | |
| 1980 | LA N | 109 | 251 | 77 | 15 | 2 | 2 | 0.8 | 31 | 20 | 24 | 29 | 3 | .307 | .406 | 41 | 11 | OF-61 |
| 1981 | LA N | 61 | 83 | 17 | 3 | 0 | 3 | 3.6 | 8 | 6 | 7 | 13 | 0 | .205 | .349 | 38 | 11 | OF-16, 1B-2 |
| 1982 2 teams | | 119 | 282 | 68 | 14 | 1 | 10 | 3.5 | 40 | 45 | 45 | 43 | 0 | .241 | .404 | 26 | 3 | OF-86 |
| " total | LA N (21G – .077) CHI N (98G – .249) | | | | | | | | | | | | | | | | | |
| 1983 | CHI N | 86 | 140 | 36 | 7 | 0 | 6 | 4.3 | 16 | 22 | 20 | 24 | 1 | .257 | .436 | 38 | 6 | OF-44 |
| 1984 | | 52 | 73 | 21 | 2 | 2 | 0 | 0.0 | 8 | 3 | 7 | 18 | 0 | .288 | .370 | 39 | 10 | OF-15 |
| 1985 | LA N | 17 | 15 | 2 | 1 | 0 | 0 | 0.0 | 0 | 2 | 1 | 2 | 0 | .133 | .200 | 15 | 2 | |
| 20 yrs. | | 1748 | 4703 | 1254 | 215 | 38 | 102 | 2.2 | 578 | 531 | 429 | 632 | 50 | .267 | .394 | 404 9th | 92 | OF-1308, 1B-57, DH-12, 2B-2 |
| 3 yrs. | | 236 | 482 | 124 | 22 | 3 | 16 | 3.3 | 63 | 68 | 67 | 83 | 1 | .257 | .415 | 90 | 18 | OF-145 |

DIVISIONAL PLAYOFF SERIES

| | | G | AB | H | 2B | 3B | HR | HR % | R | RBI | BB | SO | SB | BA | SA | AB | H | G by POS |
|---|---|---|---|---|---|---|---|---|---|---|---|---|---|---|---|---|---|---|
| 1981 | LA N | 1 | 1 | 0 | 0 | 0 | 0 | 0.0 | 0 | 0 | 0 | 0 | 0 | .000 | .000 | 1 | 0 | |

LEAGUE CHAMPIONSHIP SERIES

| | | G | AB | H | 2B | 3B | HR | HR % | R | RBI | BB | SO | SB | BA | SA | AB | H | G by POS |
|---|---|---|---|---|---|---|---|---|---|---|---|---|---|---|---|---|---|---|
| 1976 | PHI N | 3 | 9 | 7 | 1 | 1 | 0 | 0.0 | 1 | 2 | 1 | 0 | 0 | .778 | 1.111 | 1 | 1 | OF-2 |
| 1977 | | 2 | 5 | 1 | 0 | 0 | 0 | 0.0 | 0 | 0 | 0 | 1 | 0 | .200 | .200 | 1 | 0 | OF-2 |
| 1981 | LA N | 2 | 2 | 0 | 0 | 0 | 0 | 0.0 | 0 | 0 | 0 | 0 | 0 | .000 | .000 | 2 | 0 | |
| 1985 | | 1 | 1 | 0 | 0 | 0 | 0 | 0.0 | 0 | 0 | 0 | 0 | 0 | .000 | .000 | 1 | 0 | |
| 4 yrs. | | 8 | 17 | 8 | 1 | 1 | 0 | 0.0 | 1 | 2 | 1 | 1 | 0 | .471 | .647 | 5 | 1 | OF-4 |

WORLD SERIES

| | | G | AB | H | 2B | 3B | HR | HR % | R | RBI | BB | SO | SB | BA | SA | AB | H | G by POS |
|---|---|---|---|---|---|---|---|---|---|---|---|---|---|---|---|---|---|---|
| 1978 | NY A | 2 | 0 | 0 | 0 | 0 | 0 | – | 0 | 0 | 0 | 0 | 0 | – | – | 0 | 0 | OF-2 |
| 1981 | LA N | 3 | 3 | 2 | 0 | 0 | 1 | 33.3 | 1 | 3 | 0 | 0 | 0 | .667 | 1.667 | 3 | 2 | OF-2 |
| 2 yrs. | | 5 | 3 | 2 | 0 | 0 | 1 | 33.3 | 1 | 3 | 0 | 0 | 0 | .667 | 1.667 | 3 | 2 | OF-2 |

## Charley Jones

**JONES, CHARLES WESLEY**    BR TR 5'11½" 202 lbs.
Also known as Benjamin Wesley Rippay.
B. Apr. 3, 1850, County, N. C.    Deceased.

| | | G | AB | H | 2B | 3B | HR | HR % | R | RBI | BB | SO | SB | BA | SA | AB | H | G by POS |
|---|---|---|---|---|---|---|---|---|---|---|---|---|---|---|---|---|---|---|
| 1876 | CIN N | 64 | 276 | 79 | 17 | 4 | 4 | 1.4 | 40 | 38 | 7 | 17 | | .286 | .420 | 0 | 0 | OF-64 |
| 1877 3 teams | | 57 | 240 | 75 | 12 | 10 | 2 | 0.8 | 53 | 38 | 15 | 25 | 0 | .313 | .471 | 0 | 0 | OF-94, 1B-10 |
| " total | CIN N (17G – .304) CHI N (2G – .375) CIN N (38G – .313) | | | | | | | | | | | | | | | | | |
| 1878 | CIN N | 61 | 261 | 81 | 11 | 7 | 3 | 1.1 | 50 | 39 | 4 | 17 | | .310 | .441 | 0 | 0 | OF-61 |
| 1879 | BOS N | 83 | 355 | 112 | 22 | 10 | 9 | 2.5 | 85 | 62 | 29 | 38 | | .315 | .510 | 0 | 0 | OF-83 |
| 1880 | | 66 | 280 | 84 | 15 | 3 | 5 | 1.8 | 44 | 37 | 11 | 27 | | .300 | .429 | 0 | 0 | OF-66 |
| 1883 | CIN AA | 90 | 391 | 115 | 15 | 11 | 11 | 2.8 | 84 | | 20 | | | .294 | .473 | 0 | 0 | OF-90 |
| 1884 | | 113 | 472 | 148 | 19 | 17 | 7 | 1.5 | 117 | | 37 | | | .314 | .470 | 0 | 0 | OF-113 |
| 1885 | | 112 | 487 | 157 | 19 | 17 | 4 | 0.8 | 108 | | 21 | | | .322 | .456 | 0 | 0 | OF-112 |
| 1886 | | 127 | 500 | 135 | 22 | 11 | 5 | 1.0 | 87 | | 61 | | | .270 | .388 | 0 | 0 | OF-127 |
| 1887 2 teams | | 103 | 400 | 111 | 18 | 7 | 5 | 1.3 | 58 | | 31 | | 15 | .278 | .395 | 0 | 0 | OF-103, P-2, 1B-1 |
| " total | CIN AA (41G – .314) NY AA (62G – .255) | | | | | | | | | | | | | | | | | |
| 1888 | KC AA | 6 | 25 | 4 | 0 | 1 | 0 | 0.0 | 2 | 5 | 1 | | 1 | .160 | .240 | 0 | 0 | OF-6 |
| 11 yrs. | | 882 | 3687 | 1101 | 170 | 98 | 55 | 1.5 | 728 | 219 | 237 | 124 | 16 | .299 | .443 | 0 | 0 | OF-919, 1B-11, P-2 |
| 1 yr. | | 2 | 8 | 3 | 1 | 0 | 0 | 0.0 | 1 | 2 | 1 | 0 | | .375 | .500 | 0 | 0 | OF-2 |

## Clarence Jones

**JONES, CLARENCE WOODROW**    BL TL 6'2" 185 lbs.
B. Nov. 7, 1942, Zanesville, Ohio

| | | G | AB | H | 2B | 3B | HR | HR % | R | RBI | BB | SO | SB | BA | SA | AB | H | G by POS |
|---|---|---|---|---|---|---|---|---|---|---|---|---|---|---|---|---|---|---|
| 1967 | CHI N | 53 | 135 | 34 | 7 | 0 | 2 | 1.5 | 13 | 16 | 14 | 33 | 0 | .252 | .348 | 9 | 3 | OF-31, 1B-13 |
| 1968 | | 5 | 2 | 0 | 0 | 0 | 0 | 0.0 | 0 | 0 | 2 | 1 | 0 | .000 | .000 | 2 | 0 | 1B-1 |
| 2 yrs. | | 58 | 137 | 34 | 7 | 0 | 2 | 1.5 | 13 | 16 | 16 | 34 | 0 | .248 | .343 | 11 | 3 | OF-31, 1B-14 |
| 2 yrs. | | 58 | 137 | 34 | 7 | 0 | 2 | 1.5 | 13 | 16 | 16 | 34 | 0 | .248 | .343 | 11 | 3 | OF-31, 1B-14 |

## Davy Jones

**JONES, DAVID JEFFERSON (Kangaroo)**    BL TR 5'10" 165 lbs.
B. June 30, 1880, Cambria, Wis.    D. Mar. 30, 1972, Mankato, Minn.

| | | G | AB | H | 2B | 3B | HR | HR % | R | RBI | BB | SO | SB | BA | SA | AB | H | G by POS |
|---|---|---|---|---|---|---|---|---|---|---|---|---|---|---|---|---|---|---|
| 1901 | MIL A | 14 | 52 | 9 | 0 | 0 | 3 | 5.8 | 12 | 5 | 11 | | 4 | .173 | .346 | 0 | 0 | OF-14 |
| 1902 2 teams | | 79 | 292 | 85 | 13 | 4 | 0 | 0.0 | 45 | 17 | 44 | | 17 | .291 | .363 | 0 | 0 | OF-79 |
| " total | STL A (15G – .224) CHI N (64G – .305) | | | | | | | | | | | | | | | | | |
| 1903 | CHI N | 130 | 497 | 140 | 18 | 3 | 1 | 0.2 | 64 | 62 | 53 | | 15 | .282 | .336 | 0 | 0 | OF-130 |
| 1904 | | 98 | 336 | 82 | 11 | 5 | 3 | 0.9 | 44 | 39 | 41 | | 14 | .244 | .333 | 0 | 0 | OF-97 |
| 1906 | DET A | 84 | 323 | 84 | 12 | 2 | 0 | 0.0 | 41 | 24 | 41 | | 21 | .260 | .310 | 0 | 0 | OF-84 |
| 1907 | | 126 | 491 | 134 | 10 | 6 | 0 | 0.0 | 101 | 27 | 60 | | 30 | .273 | .318 | 0 | 0 | OF-126 |
| 1908 | | 56 | 121 | 25 | 2 | 1 | 0 | 0.0 | 17 | 10 | 13 | | 11 | .207 | .240 | 21 | 3 | OF-32 |
| 1909 | | 69 | 204 | 57 | 2 | 2 | 0 | 0.0 | 44 | 10 | 28 | | 12 | .279 | .309 | 10 | 1 | OF-57 |

| | G | AB | H | 2B | 3B | HR | HR % | R | RBI | BB | SO | SB | BA | SA | Pinch Hit AB | Pinch Hit H | G by POS |
|---|---|---|---|---|---|---|---|---|---|---|---|---|---|---|---|---|---|

## Davy Jones continued

| | G | AB | H | 2B | 3B | HR | HR% | R | RBI | BB | SO | SB | BA | SA | AB | H | G by POS |
|---|---|---|---|---|---|---|---|---|---|---|---|---|---|---|---|---|---|
| 1910 | 113 | 377 | 100 | 6 | 6 | 0 | 0.0 | 77 | 24 | 51 | | 25 | .265 | .313 | 9 | 0 | OF-101 |
| 1911 | 98 | 341 | 93 | 10 | 0 | 0 | 0.0 | 78 | 19 | 41 | | 25 | .273 | .302 | 4 | 1 | OF-92 |
| 1912 | 97 | 316 | 93 | 5 | 2 | 0 | 0.0 | 54 | 24 | 38 | | 16 | .294 | .323 | 15 | 4 | OF-81 |
| 1913 CHI A | 10 | 21 | 6 | 0 | 0 | 0 | 0.0 | 2 | 0 | 9 | 0 | 1 | .286 | .286 | 1 | 0 | OF-8 |
| 1914 PIT F | 97 | 352 | 96 | 9 | 8 | 2 | 0.6 | 58 | 24 | 42 | | 15 | .273 | .361 | 4 | 2 | OF-93 |
| 1915 | 14 | 49 | 16 | 0 | 1 | 0 | 0.0 | 6 | 4 | 6 | | 1 | .327 | .367 | 0 | 0 | OF-13 |
| 14 yrs. | 1085 | 3772 | 1020 | 98 | 40 | 9 | 0.2 | 643 | 289 | 478 | | 207 | .270 | .325 | 64 | 11 | OF-1007 |
| 3 yrs. | 292 | 1076 | 296 | 41 | 11 | 4 | 0.4 | 149 | 115 | 132 | | 41 | .275 | .345 | 0 | 0 | OF-291 |

| WORLD SERIES | | | | | | | | | | | | | | | | | |
|---|---|---|---|---|---|---|---|---|---|---|---|---|---|---|---|---|---|
| 1907 DET A | 5 | 17 | 6 | 0 | 0 | 0 | 0.0 | 1 | 0 | 4 | 0 | 3 | .353 | .353 | 0 | 0 | OF-5 |
| 1908 | 3 | 2 | 0 | 0 | 0 | 0 | 0.0 | 1 | 0 | 1 | 1 | 0 | .000 | .000 | 2 | 0 | |
| 1909 | 7 | 30 | 7 | 0 | 0 | 1 | 3.3 | 6 | 2 | 2 | 1 | 1 | .233 | .333 | 0 | 0 | OF-7 |
| 3 yrs. | 15 | 49 | 13 | 0 | 0 | 1 | 2.0 | 8 | 2 | 7 | 2 | 4 | .265 | .327 | 2 | 0 | OF-12 |

## Bill Jurges

**JURGES, WILLIAM FREDERICK**
B. May 9, 1908, Bronx, N. Y.
Manager 1959-60.

BR  TR  5'11"  175 lbs.

| | G | AB | H | 2B | 3B | HR | HR% | R | RBI | BB | SO | SB | BA | SA | AB | H | G by POS |
|---|---|---|---|---|---|---|---|---|---|---|---|---|---|---|---|---|---|
| 1931 CHI N | 88 | 293 | 59 | 15 | 5 | 0 | 0.0 | 34 | 23 | 25 | 41 | 2 | .201 | .287 | 1 | 0 | 3B-54, 2B-33, SS-3 |
| 1932 | 115 | 396 | 100 | 24 | 4 | 2 | 0.5 | 40 | 52 | 19 | 26 | 1 | .253 | .348 | 1 | 0 | SS-103, 3B-5 |
| 1933 | 143 | 487 | 131 | 17 | 6 | 5 | 1.0 | 49 | 50 | 26 | 39 | 3 | .269 | .359 | 0 | 0 | SS-143 |
| 1934 | 100 | 358 | 88 | 15 | 2 | 8 | 2.2 | 43 | 33 | 19 | 34 | 1 | .246 | .366 | 2 | 1 | SS-98 |
| 1935 | 146 | 519 | 125 | 33 | 1 | 1 | 0.2 | 69 | 59 | 42 | 39 | 3 | .241 | .314 | 0 | 0 | SS-146 |
| 1936 | 118 | 429 | 120 | 25 | 1 | 1 | 0.2 | 51 | 42 | 23 | 25 | 4 | .280 | .350 | 0 | 0 | SS-116 |
| 1937 | 129 | 450 | 134 | 18 | 10 | 1 | 0.2 | 53 | 65 | 42 | 41 | 2 | .298 | .389 | 0 | 0 | SS-128 |
| 1938 | 137 | 465 | 114 | 18 | 3 | 1 | 0.2 | 53 | 47 | 58 | 53 | 3 | .245 | .303 | 0 | 0 | SS-136 |
| 1939 NY N | 138 | 543 | 155 | 21 | 11 | 6 | 1.1 | 84 | 63 | 47 | 34 | 3 | .285 | .398 | 0 | 0 | SS-137 |
| 1940 | 63 | 214 | 54 | 3 | 3 | 2 | 0.9 | 23 | 36 | 25 | 14 | 2 | .252 | .322 | 0 | 0 | SS-63 |
| 1941 | 134 | 471 | 138 | 25 | 2 | 5 | 1.1 | 50 | 61 | 47 | 36 | 0 | .293 | .386 | 0 | 0 | SS-134 |
| 1942 | 127 | 464 | 119 | 7 | 1 | 2 | 0.4 | 45 | 30 | 43 | 42 | 1 | .256 | .289 | 3 | 1 | SS-124 |
| 1943 | 136 | 481 | 110 | 8 | 2 | 4 | 0.8 | 46 | 29 | 53 | 38 | 2 | .229 | .279 | 8 | 3 | SS-99, 3B-28 |
| 1944 | 85 | 246 | 52 | 2 | 1 | 1 | 0.4 | 28 | 23 | 23 | 20 | 4 | .211 | .240 | 14 | 2 | 3B-61, SS-10, 2B-1 |
| 1945 | 61 | 176 | 57 | 3 | 1 | 3 | 1.7 | 22 | 24 | 24 | 11 | 2 | .324 | .403 | 7 | 2 | 3B-44, SS-8 |
| 1946 CHI N | 82 | 221 | 49 | 9 | 2 | 0 | 0.0 | 26 | 17 | 43 | 28 | 3 | .222 | .281 | 0 | 0 | SS-73, 3B-7, 2B-2 |
| 1947 | 14 | 40 | 8 | 2 | 0 | 1 | 2.5 | 5 | 2 | 9 | 9 | 0 | .200 | .325 | 0 | 0 | SS-14 |
| 17 yrs. | 1816 | 6253 | 1613 | 245 | 55 | 43 | 0.7 | 721 | 656 | 568 | 530 | 36 | .258 | .335 | 36 | 9 | SS-1535, 3B-199, 2B-36 |
| 10 yrs. | 1072 | 3658 | 928 | 176 | 34 | 20 | 0.5 | 423 | 390 | 306 | 335 | 22 | .254 | .337 | 4 | 1 | SS-960, 3B-66, 2B-35 |

| WORLD SERIES | | | | | | | | | | | | | | | | | |
|---|---|---|---|---|---|---|---|---|---|---|---|---|---|---|---|---|---|
| 1932 CHI N | 3 | 11 | 4 | 1 | 0 | 0 | 0.0 | 1 | 1 | 0 | 1 | 1 | .364 | .455 | 0 | 0 | SS-3 |
| 1935 | 6 | 16 | 4 | 0 | 0 | 0 | 0.0 | 3 | 1 | 4 | 4 | 0 | .250 | .250 | 0 | 0 | SS-6 |
| 1938 | 4 | 13 | 3 | 1 | 0 | 0 | 0.0 | 0 | 0 | 1 | 3 | 0 | .231 | .308 | 0 | 0 | SS-4 |
| 3 yrs. | 13 | 40 | 11 | 2 | 0 | 0 | 0.0 | 4 | 2 | 5 | 8 | 1 | .275 | .325 | 0 | 0 | SS-13 |

## Mike Kahoe

**KAHOE, MICHAEL JOSEPH**
B. Sept. 3, 1873, Yellow Springs, Ohio   D. May 14, 1949, Akron, Ohio

BR  TR  6'  185 lbs.

| | G | AB | H | 2B | 3B | HR | HR% | R | RBI | BB | SO | SB | BA | SA | AB | H | G by POS |
|---|---|---|---|---|---|---|---|---|---|---|---|---|---|---|---|---|---|
| 1895 CIN N | 3 | 4 | 0 | 0 | 0 | 0 | 0.0 | 0 | 0 | 0 | 0 | 0 | .000 | .000 | 0 | 0 | C-3 |
| 1899 | 14 | 42 | 7 | 1 | 1 | 0 | 0.0 | 2 | 4 | 0 | | 1 | .167 | .238 | 1 | 0 | C-13 |
| 1900 | 52 | 175 | 33 | 3 | 1 | 1 | 0.6 | 18 | 9 | 4 | | 3 | .189 | .257 | 0 | 0 | C-51, SS-1 |
| 1901 2 teams | | CIN | N | (4G – | .308) | | CHI | N | (67G – | .224) | | | | | | | |
| " total | 71 | 250 | 57 | 12 | 2 | 1 | 0.4 | 21 | 21 | 9 | | 5 | .228 | .304 | 0 | 0 | C-67, 1B-6 |
| 1902 2 teams | | CHI | N | (7G – | .222) | | STL | A | (55G – | .244) | | | | | | | |
| " total | 62 | 215 | 52 | 10 | 2 | 2 | 0.9 | 21 | 30 | 6 | | 4 | .242 | .335 | 2 | 1 | C-57, 3B-2, SS-1 |
| 1903 STL A | 77 | 244 | 46 | 7 | 5 | 0 | 0.0 | 26 | 23 | 11 | | 1 | .189 | .258 | 4 | 0 | C-71, OF-2 |
| 1904 | 72 | 236 | 51 | 6 | 1 | 0 | 0.0 | 9 | 12 | 8 | | 4 | .216 | .250 | 2 | 0 | C-69 |
| 1905 PHI N | 16 | 51 | 13 | 2 | 0 | 0 | 0.0 | 2 | 4 | 1 | | 1 | .255 | .294 | 1 | 0 | C-15 |
| 1907 2 teams | | CHI | N | (5G – | .400) | | WAS | A | (17G – | .191) | | | | | | | |
| " total | 22 | 57 | 13 | 1 | 0 | 0 | 0.0 | 3 | 2 | 0 | | 0 | .228 | .246 | 3 | 1 | C-18, 1B-1 |
| 1908 WAS A | 17 | 27 | 5 | 1 | 0 | 0 | 0.0 | 1 | 0 | 0 | | 0 | .185 | .222 | 6 | 1 | C-11 |
| 1909 | 4 | 8 | 1 | 0 | 0 | 0 | 0.0 | 0 | 0 | 0 | | 2 | .125 | .125 | 1 | 0 | C-3 |
| 11 yrs. | 410 | 1309 | 278 | 43 | 14 | 4 | 0.3 | 103 | 105 | 39 | | 21 | .212 | .276 | 20 | 3 | C-378, 1B-7, OF-2, SS-2, 3B-2 |
| 3 yrs. | 79 | 265 | 61 | 13 | 2 | 1 | 0.4 | 21 | 24 | 8 | | 5 | .230 | .306 | 1 | 1 | C-70, 1B-7, 3B-2, SS-1 |

## Al Kaiser

**KAISER, ALFRED EDWARD (Deerfoot)**
B. Aug. 3, 1886, Cincinnati, Ohio   D. Apr. 11, 1969, Cincinnati, Ohio

BR  TR  5'9"  165 lbs.

| | G | AB | H | 2B | 3B | HR | HR% | R | RBI | BB | SO | SB | BA | SA | AB | H | G by POS |
|---|---|---|---|---|---|---|---|---|---|---|---|---|---|---|---|---|---|
| 1911 2 teams | | CHI | N | (27G – | .250) | | BOS | N | (65G – | .203) | | | | | | | |
| " total | 92 | 281 | 61 | 5 | 2 | 0.7 | | 36 | 22 | 17 | 38 | 10 | .217 | .306 | 10 | 2 | OF-81 |
| 1912 BOS N | 4 | 13 | 0 | 0 | 0 | 0 | 0.0 | 0 | 0 | 0 | 3 | 0 | .000 | .000 | 0 | 0 | OF-4 |
| 1914 IND F | 59 | 187 | 43 | 10 | 0 | 1 | 0.5 | 22 | 16 | 17 | | 6 | .230 | .299 | 7 | 2 | OF-50, 1B-1 |
| 3 yrs. | 155 | 481 | 104 | 15 | 7 | 3 | 0.6 | 58 | 38 | 34 | 41 | 16 | .216 | .295 | 17 | 4 | OF-135, 1B-1 |
| 1 yr. | 27 | 84 | 21 | 0 | 5 | 0 | 0.0 | 16 | 7 | 7 | 12 | 6 | .250 | .369 | 4 | 1 | OF-23 |

## John Kane

**KANE, JOHN FRANCIS**
B. Sept. 24, 1882, Chicago, Ill.   D. Jan. 28, 1934, St. Anthony, Ida.

BR  TR  5'6"  138 lbs.

| | G | AB | H | 2B | 3B | HR | HR% | R | RBI | BB | SO | SB | BA | SA | AB | H | G by POS |
|---|---|---|---|---|---|---|---|---|---|---|---|---|---|---|---|---|---|
| 1907 CIN N | 79 | 262 | 65 | 9 | 4 | 3 | 1.1 | 40 | 19 | 22 | | 20 | .248 | .347 | 2 | 1 | OF-42, 3B-25, SS-6, 2B-2 |
| 1908 | 130 | 455 | 97 | 11 | 7 | 3 | 0.7 | 61 | 23 | 43 | | 30 | .213 | .288 | 1 | 0 | OF-127, 2B-1 |
| 1909 CHI N | 20 | 45 | 4 | 1 | 0 | 0 | 0.0 | 6 | 5 | 2 | | 1 | .089 | .111 | 2 | 0 | OF-8, SS-3, 3B-3, 2B-2 |
| 1910 | 32 | 62 | 15 | 0 | 0 | 1 | 1.6 | 11 | 12 | 9 | 10 | 2 | .242 | .290 | 0 | 0 | OF-18, 2B-6, 3B-4, SS-2 |
| 4 yrs. | 261 | 824 | 181 | 21 | 11 | 7 | 0.8 | 118 | 59 | 76 | 10 | 53 | .220 | .297 | 5 | 1 | OF-195, 3B-32, SS-11, 2B-11 |
| 2 yrs. | 52 | 107 | 19 | 1 | 0 | 1 | 0.9 | 17 | 17 | 11 | 10 | 3 | .178 | .215 | 2 | 0 | OF-26, 2B-8, 3B-7, SS-5 |

| WORLD SERIES | | | | | | | | | | | | | | | | | |
|---|---|---|---|---|---|---|---|---|---|---|---|---|---|---|---|---|---|
| 1910 CHI N | 1 | 0 | 0 | 0 | 0 | 0 | – | 0 | 0 | 0 | 0 | 0 | – | – | 0 | 0 | |

| | G | AB | H | 2B | 3B | HR | HR % | R | RBI | BB | SO | SB | BA | SA | Pinch Hit AB | H | G by POS |
|---|---|---|---|---|---|---|---|---|---|---|---|---|---|---|---|---|---|

## Ted Kearns

**KEARNS, EDWARD JOSEPH**   BR TR 5'11" 185 lbs.
B. Jan. 1, 1900, Trenton, N. J.   D. Dec. 21, 1949, Trenton, N. J.

| | G | AB | H | 2B | 3B | HR | HR % | R | RBI | BB | SO | SB | BA | SA | AB | H | G by POS |
|---|---|---|---|---|---|---|---|---|---|---|---|---|---|---|---|---|---|
| 1924 CHI N | 4 | 16 | 4 | 0 | 1 | 0 | 0.0 | 0 | 1 | 1 | 1 | 0 | .250 | .375 | 0 | 0 | 1B-4 |
| 1925 | 3 | 2 | 1 | 0 | 0 | 0 | 0.0 | 0 | 0 | 0 | 0 | 0 | .500 | .500 | 0 | 0 | 1B-3 |
| 2 yrs. | 7 | 18 | 5 | 0 | 1 | 0 | 0.0 | 0 | 1 | 1 | 1 | 0 | .278 | .389 | 0 | 0 | 1B-7 |
| 2 yrs. | 7 | 18 | 5 | 0 | 1 | 0 | 0.0 | 0 | 1 | 1 | 1 | 0 | .278 | .389 | 0 | 0 | 1B-7 |

## Chick Keating

**KEATING, WALTER FRANCIS**   BR TR 5'9½" 155 lbs.
B. Aug. 8, 1891, Philadelphia, Pa.   D. July 13, 1959, Philadelphia, Pa.

| | G | AB | H | 2B | 3B | HR | HR % | R | RBI | BB | SO | SB | BA | SA | AB | H | G by POS |
|---|---|---|---|---|---|---|---|---|---|---|---|---|---|---|---|---|---|
| 1913 CHI N | 2 | 5 | 1 | 1 | 0 | 0 | 0.0 | 1 | 0 | 0 | 1 | 0 | .200 | .400 | 0 | 0 | SS-2 |
| 1914 | 20 | 30 | 3 | 0 | 1 | 0 | 0.0 | 3 | 0 | 6 | 9 | 0 | .100 | .167 | 0 | 0 | SS-16 |
| 1915 | 4 | 8 | 0 | 0 | 0 | 0 | 0.0 | 1 | 0 | 0 | 3 | 1 | .000 | .000 | 1 | 0 | SS-2 |
| 1926 PHI N | 4 | 2 | 0 | 0 | 0 | 0 | 0.0 | 0 | 0 | 0 | 0 | 0 | .000 | .000 | 0 | 0 | SS-2, 2B-2, 3B-1 |
| 4 yrs. | 30 | 45 | 4 | 1 | 1 | 0 | 0.0 | 5 | 0 | 6 | 13 | 1 | .089 | .156 | 1 | 0 | SS-22, 2B-2, 3B-1 |
| 3 yrs. | 26 | 43 | 4 | 1 | 1 | 0 | 0.0 | 5 | 0 | 6 | 13 | 1 | .093 | .163 | 1 | 0 | SS-20 |

## John Kelleher

**KELLEHER, JOHN PATRICK**   BR TR 5'11" 150 lbs.
B. Sept. 13, 1893, Brookline, Mass.   D. Aug. 21, 1960, Boston, Mass.

| | G | AB | H | 2B | 3B | HR | HR % | R | RBI | BB | SO | SB | BA | SA | AB | H | G by POS |
|---|---|---|---|---|---|---|---|---|---|---|---|---|---|---|---|---|---|
| 1912 STL N | 8 | 12 | 4 | 1 | 0 | 0 | 0.0 | 0 | 1 | 0 | 2 | 0 | .333 | .417 | 4 | 1 | 3B-3 |
| 1916 BKN N | 2 | 3 | 0 | 0 | 0 | 0 | 0.0 | 0 | 0 | 0 | 0 | 0 | .000 | .000 | 0 | 0 | SS-1, 3B-1 |
| 1921 CHI N | 95 | 301 | 93 | 11 | 7 | 4 | 1.3 | 31 | 47 | 16 | 16 | 2 | .309 | .432 | 9 | 5 | 3B-37, 2B-27, SS-11, 1B-11, OF-1 |
| 1922 | 63 | 193 | 50 | 7 | 1 | 0 | 0.0 | 23 | 20 | 15 | 14 | 5 | .259 | .306 | 6 | 0 | 3B-46, SS-7, 1B-4 |
| 1923 | 66 | 193 | 59 | 10 | 0 | 6 | 3.1 | 27 | 21 | 14 | 9 | 2 | .306 | .451 | 15 | 6 | 1B-22, SS-14, 3B-11, 2B-6 |
| 1924 BOS N | 1 | 1 | 0 | 0 | 0 | 0 | 0.0 | 0 | 0 | 0 | 1 | 0 | .000 | .000 | 1 | 0 | |
| 6 yrs. | 235 | 703 | 206 | 29 | 8 | 10 | 1.4 | 81 | 89 | 45 | 42 | 9 | .293 | .400 | 35 | 12 | 3B-98, 1B-37, SS-33, 2B-33, OF-1 |
| 3 yrs. | 224 | 687 | 202 | 28 | 8 | 10 | 1.5 | 81 | 88 | 45 | 39 | 9 | .294 | .402 | 30 | 11 | 3B-94, 1B-37, 2B-33, SS-32, OF-1 |

## Mick Kelleher

**KELLEHER, MICHAEL DENNIS**   BR TR 5'9" 176 lbs.
B. July 25, 1947, Seattle, Wash.

| | G | AB | H | 2B | 3B | HR | HR % | R | RBI | BB | SO | SB | BA | SA | AB | H | G by POS |
|---|---|---|---|---|---|---|---|---|---|---|---|---|---|---|---|---|---|
| 1972 STL N | 23 | 63 | 10 | 2 | 1 | 0 | 0.0 | 5 | 1 | 6 | 15 | 0 | .159 | .222 | 0 | 0 | SS-23 |
| 1973 | 43 | 38 | 7 | 2 | 0 | 0 | 0.0 | 4 | 2 | 4 | 11 | 0 | .184 | .237 | 0 | 0 | SS-42 |
| 1974 HOU N | 19 | 57 | 9 | 0 | 0 | 0 | 0.0 | 4 | 2 | 5 | 10 | 1 | .158 | .158 | 0 | 0 | SS-18 |
| 1975 STL N | 7 | 4 | 0 | 0 | 0 | 0 | 0.0 | 0 | 0 | 0 | 1 | 0 | .000 | .000 | 0 | 0 | SS-7 |
| 1976 CHI N | 124 | 337 | 77 | 12 | 1 | 0 | 0.0 | 28 | 22 | 15 | 32 | 0 | .228 | .270 | 3 | 1 | SS-101, 3B-22, 2B-5 |
| 1977 | 63 | 122 | 28 | 5 | 2 | 0 | 0.0 | 14 | 11 | 9 | 12 | 0 | .230 | .303 | 0 | 0 | 2B-40, SS-14, 3B-1 |
| 1978 | 68 | 95 | 24 | 1 | 0 | 0 | 0.0 | 8 | 6 | 7 | 11 | 4 | .253 | .263 | 3 | 1 | 3B-37, 2B-17, SS-10 |
| 1979 | 73 | 142 | 36 | 4 | 1 | 0 | 0.0 | 14 | 10 | 7 | 9 | 2 | .254 | .296 | 0 | 0 | 3B-32, 2B-29, SS-14 |
| 1980 | 105 | 96 | 14 | 1 | 1 | 0 | 0.0 | 12 | 4 | 9 | 17 | 1 | .146 | .177 | 3 | 1 | 2B-57, 3B-31, SS-17 |
| 1981 DET A | 61 | 77 | 17 | 4 | 0 | 0 | 0.0 | 10 | 6 | 7 | 10 | 0 | .221 | .273 | 3 | 1 | 3B-39, 2B-11, SS-9 |
| 1982 2 teams | | | | | DET A (2G – .000) | | | CAL A (34G – .163) | | | | | | | | | |
| " total | 36 | 50 | 8 | 1 | 0 | 0 | 0.0 | 9 | 1 | 5 | 5 | 1 | .160 | .180 | 1 | 0 | SS-28, 3B-7, 2B-1 |
| 11 yrs. | 622 | 1081 | 230 | 32 | 6 | 0 | 0.0 | 108 | 65 | 74 | 133 | 9 | .213 | .253 | 13 | 4 | SS-283, 3B-169, 2B-160 |
| 5 yrs. | 433 | 792 | 179 | 23 | 5 | 0 | 0.0 | 76 | 53 | 47 | 81 | 7 | .226 | .268 | 9 | 3 | SS-156, 2B-148, 3B-123 |

## Frank Kellert

**KELLERT, FRANK WILLIAM**   BR TR 6'2½" 185 lbs.
B. July 6, 1924, Oklahoma City, Okla.   D. Nov. 19, 1976, Oklahoma City, Okla.

| | G | AB | H | 2B | 3B | HR | HR % | R | RBI | BB | SO | SB | BA | SA | AB | H | G by POS |
|---|---|---|---|---|---|---|---|---|---|---|---|---|---|---|---|---|---|
| 1953 STL A | 2 | 4 | 0 | 0 | 0 | 0 | 0.0 | 0 | 0 | 0 | 0 | 0 | .000 | .000 | 1 | 0 | 1B-1 |
| 1954 BAL A | 10 | 34 | 7 | 2 | 0 | 0 | 0.0 | 3 | 1 | 5 | 4 | 0 | .206 | .265 | 1 | 0 | 1B-9 |
| 1955 BKN N | 39 | 80 | 26 | 4 | 2 | 4 | 5.0 | 12 | 19 | 9 | 10 | 0 | .325 | .575 | 13 | 3 | 1B-22 |
| 1956 CHI N | 71 | 129 | 24 | 3 | 1 | 4 | 3.1 | 10 | 17 | 12 | 22 | 0 | .186 | .318 | 41 | 10 | 1B-27 |
| 4 yrs. | 122 | 247 | 57 | 9 | 3 | 8 | 3.2 | 25 | 37 | 26 | 36 | 0 | .231 | .389 | 56 | 13 | 1B-59 |
| 1 yr. | 71 | 129 | 24 | 3 | 1 | 4 | 3.1 | 10 | 17 | 12 | 22 | 0 | .186 | .318 | 41 | 10 | 1B-27 |

WORLD SERIES
| 1955 BKN N | 3 | 3 | 1 | 0 | 0 | 0 | 0.0 | 0 | 0 | 0 | 0 | 0 | .333 | .333 | 3 | 1 | |

## George Kelly

**KELLY, GEORGE LANGE (Highpockets)**   BR TR 6'4" 190 lbs.
Brother of Ren Kelly.
B. Sept. 10, 1895, San Francisco, Calif.   D. Oct. 13, 1984, Burlingame, Calif.
Hall of Fame 1973.

| | G | AB | H | 2B | 3B | HR | HR % | R | RBI | BB | SO | SB | BA | SA | AB | H | G by POS |
|---|---|---|---|---|---|---|---|---|---|---|---|---|---|---|---|---|---|
| 1915 NY N | 17 | 38 | 6 | 0 | 0 | 1 | 2.6 | 2 | 4 | 1 | 9 | 0 | .158 | .237 | 2 | 0 | 1B-9, OF-4 |
| 1916 | 49 | 76 | 12 | 2 | 1 | 0 | 0.0 | 4 | 3 | 6 | 24 | 0 | .158 | .211 | 23 | 5 | 1B-13, OF-12, 3B-1 |
| 1917 2 teams | | | | | NY N (11G – .000) | | | PIT N (8G – .087) | | | | | | | | | |
| " total | 19 | 30 | 2 | 0 | 1 | 0 | 0.0 | 2 | 0 | 1 | 12 | 0 | .067 | .133 | 3 | 0 | 1B-9, OF-3, 2B-1, P-1 |
| 1919 NY N | 32 | 107 | 31 | 6 | 2 | 1 | 0.9 | 12 | 14 | 3 | 15 | 1 | .290 | .411 | 0 | 0 | 1B-32 |
| 1920 | 155 | 590 | 157 | 22 | 11 | 11 | 1.9 | 69 | 94 | 41 | 92 | 6 | .266 | .397 | 0 | 0 | 1B-155 |
| 1921 | 149 | 587 | 181 | 42 | 9 | 23 | 3.9 | 95 | 122 | 40 | 73 | 4 | .308 | .528 | 0 | 0 | 1B-149 |
| 1922 | 151 | 592 | 194 | 33 | 8 | 17 | 2.9 | 96 | 107 | 30 | 65 | 12 | .328 | .497 | 0 | 0 | 1B-151 |
| 1923 | 145 | 560 | 172 | 23 | 5 | 16 | 2.9 | 82 | 103 | 47 | 64 | 14 | .307 | .452 | 0 | 0 | 1B-145 |
| 1924 | 144 | 571 | 185 | 37 | 9 | 21 | 3.7 | 91 | 136 | 38 | 52 | 7 | .324 | .531 | 2 | 0 | 1B-125, OF-14, 2B-5, 3B-1 |
| 1925 | 147 | 586 | 181 | 29 | 3 | 20 | 3.4 | 87 | 99 | 35 | 54 | 5 | .309 | .471 | 0 | 0 | 2B-108, 1B-25, OF-17 |
| 1926 | 136 | 499 | 151 | 24 | 4 | 13 | 2.6 | 70 | 80 | 36 | 52 | 4 | .303 | .445 | 5 | 0 | 1B-114, 2B-18 |
| 1927 CIN N | 61 | 222 | 60 | 16 | 4 | 5 | 2.3 | 27 | 21 | 11 | 23 | 1 | .270 | .446 | 1 | 0 | 1B-49, 2B-13, OF-2 |
| 1928 | 116 | 402 | 119 | 33 | 7 | 3 | 0.7 | 46 | 58 | 28 | 35 | 2 | .296 | .435 | 2 | 0 | 1B-99, OF-13 |
| 1929 | 147 | 577 | 169 | 45 | 9 | 5 | 0.9 | 73 | 103 | 33 | 61 | 7 | .293 | .428 | 0 | 0 | 1B-147 |
| 1930 2 teams | | | | | CIN N (51G – .287) | | | CHI N (39G – .331) | | | | | | | | | |
| " total | 90 | 354 | 109 | 16 | 2 | 8 | 2.3 | 40 | 54 | 14 | 36 | 1 | .308 | .432 | 1 | 0 | 1B-89 |

| | G | AB | H | 2B | 3B | HR | HR % | R | RBI | BB | SO | SB | BA | SA | Pinch Hit AB | Pinch Hit H | G by POS |
|---|---|---|---|---|---|---|---|---|---|---|---|---|---|---|---|---|---|

## George Kelly continued

| | G | AB | H | 2B | 3B | HR | HR % | R | RBI | BB | SO | SB | BA | SA | AB | H | G by POS |
|---|---|---|---|---|---|---|---|---|---|---|---|---|---|---|---|---|---|
| 1932 **BKN N** | 64 | 202 | 49 | 9 | 1 | 4 | 2.0 | 23 | 22 | 22 | 27 | 0 | .243 | .356 | 1 | 0 | 1B-62, OF-1 |
| 16 yrs. | 1622 | 5993 | 1778 | 337 | 76 | 148 | 2.5 | 819 | 1020 | 386 | 694 | 65 | .297 | .452 | 40 | 5 | 1B-1373, 2B-145, OF-66, 3B-2, P-1 |
| 1 yr. | 39 | 166 | 55 | 6 | 1 | 3 | 1.8 | 22 | 19 | 7 | 16 | 0 | .331 | .434 | 0 | 0 | 1B-39 |
| WORLD SERIES | | | | | | | | | | | | | | | | | |
| 1921 **NY N** | 8 | 30 | 7 | 1 | 0 | 0 | 0.0 | 3 | 3 | 3 | 10 | 0 | .233 | .267 | 0 | 0 | 1B-8 |
| 1922 | 5 | 18 | 5 | 0 | 0 | 0 | 0.0 | 0 | 2 | 0 | 3 | 0 | .278 | .278 | 0 | 0 | 1B-5 |
| 1923 | 6 | 22 | 4 | 0 | 0 | 0 | 0.0 | 1 | 1 | 1 | 2 | 0 | .182 | .182 | 0 | 0 | 1B-6 |
| 1924 | 7 | 31 | 9 | 1 | 0 | 1 | 3.2 | 7 | 4 | 1 | 8 | 0 | .290 | .419 | 0 | 0 | 1B-4 |
| 4 yrs. | 26 | 101 | 25 | 2 | 0 | 1 | 1.0 | 11 | 10 | 5 | 23 | 0 | .248 | .297 | 0 | 0 | 1B-23 |
| | | | | | | | | | | | 10th | | | | | | |

## Joe Kelly

**KELLY, JOSEPH HENRY**      BR TR 5'9"   172 lbs.
B. Sept. 23, 1886, Weir City, Kans.   D. Aug. 16, 1977, St. Joseph, Mo.

| | G | AB | H | 2B | 3B | HR | HR % | R | RBI | BB | SO | SB | BA | SA | AB | H | G by POS |
|---|---|---|---|---|---|---|---|---|---|---|---|---|---|---|---|---|---|
| 1914 **PIT N** | 141 | 508 | 113 | 19 | 9 | 1 | 0.2 | 47 | 48 | 39 | 59 | 21 | .222 | .301 | 2 | 0 | OF-138 |
| 1916 **CHI N** | 54 | 169 | 43 | 7 | 1 | 2 | 1.2 | 18 | 15 | 9 | 16 | 10 | .254 | .343 | 8 | 1 | OF-46 |
| 1917 **BOS N** | 116 | 445 | 99 | 9 | 8 | 3 | 0.7 | 41 | 36 | 26 | 45 | 21 | .222 | .299 | 0 | 0 | OF-116 |
| 1918 | 47 | 155 | 36 | 2 | 4 | 0 | 0.0 | 20 | 15 | 6 | 12 | 12 | .232 | .297 | 2 | 1 | OF-45 |
| 1919 | 18 | 64 | 9 | 1 | 0 | 0 | 0.0 | 3 | 3 | 0 | 11 | 2 | .141 | .156 | 2 | 1 | OF-16 |
| 5 yrs. | 376 | 1341 | 300 | 38 | 22 | 6 | 0.4 | 129 | 117 | 80 | 143 | 66 | .224 | .298 | 14 | 3 | OF-361 |
| 1 yr. | 54 | 169 | 43 | 7 | 1 | 2 | 1.2 | 18 | 15 | 9 | 16 | 10 | .254 | .343 | 8 | 1 | OF-46 |

## Joe Kelly

**KELLY, JOSEPH JAMES**      BL TL 6'   180 lbs.
B. Apr. 23, 1900, New York, N. Y.   D. Nov. 24, 1967, Lynbrook, N. Y.

| | G | AB | H | 2B | 3B | HR | HR % | R | RBI | BB | SO | SB | BA | SA | AB | H | G by POS |
|---|---|---|---|---|---|---|---|---|---|---|---|---|---|---|---|---|---|
| 1926 **CHI N** | 65 | 176 | 59 | 15 | 3 | 0 | 0.0 | 16 | 32 | 7 | 11 | 0 | .335 | .455 | 24 | 9 | OF-39 |
| 1928 | 32 | 52 | 11 | 1 | 0 | 1 | 1.9 | 3 | 7 | 1 | 3 | 0 | .212 | .288 | 21 | 3 | 1B-10 |
| 2 yrs. | 97 | 228 | 70 | 16 | 3 | 1 | 0.4 | 19 | 39 | 8 | 14 | 0 | .307 | .417 | 45 | 12 | OF-39, 1B-10 |
| 2 yrs. | 97 | 228 | 70 | 16 | 3 | 1 | 0.4 | 19 | 39 | 8 | 14 | 0 | .307 | .417 | 45 | 12 | OF-39, 1B-10 |

## King Kelly

**KELLY, MICHAEL JOSEPH**      BR TR 5'10"   170 lbs.
B. Dec. 31, 1857, Troy, N. Y.   D. Nov. 8, 1894, Boston, Mass.
Manager 1890-91.
Hall of Fame 1945.

| | G | AB | H | 2B | 3B | HR | HR % | R | RBI | BB | SO | SB | BA | SA | AB | H | G by POS |
|---|---|---|---|---|---|---|---|---|---|---|---|---|---|---|---|---|---|
| 1878 **CIN N** | 60 | 237 | 67 | 7 | 1 | 0 | 0.0 | 29 | 27 | 7 | 7 | | .283 | .321 | 0 | 0 | OF-47, C-17, 3B-2 |
| 1879 | 77 | 345 | 120 | 20 | 12 | 2 | 0.6 | 78 | 47 | 8 | 14 | | .348 | .493 | 0 | 0 | 3B-33, OF-29, C-21, 2B-1 |
| 1880 **CHI N** | 84 | 344 | 100 | 17 | 9 | 1 | 0.3 | 72 | 60 | 12 | 22 | | .291 | .401 | 0 | 0 | OF-64, C-17, 3B-14, SS-1, 2B-1, P-1 |
| 1881 | 82 | 353 | 114 | **27** | 3 | 2 | 0.6 | 84 | 55 | 16 | 14 | | .323 | .433 | 0 | 0 | OF-72, C-11, 3B-8 |
| 1882 | 84 | 377 | 115 | **37** | 4 | 1 | 0.3 | 81 | 55 | 10 | 27 | | .305 | .432 | 0 | 0 | SS-42, OF-38, C-12, 3B-3, 1B-1 |
| 1883 | 98 | 428 | 109 | 28 | 10 | 3 | 0.7 | 92 | | 16 | 35 | | .255 | .388 | 0 | 0 | OF-82, C-38, 2B-3, 3B-2, P-1 |
| 1884 | 108 | 452 | 160 | 28 | 5 | 13 | 2.9 | 120 | | 46 | 24 | | **.354** | .524 | 0 | 0 | OF-63, C-28, SS-12, 3B-10, 1B-2, P-2 |
| 1885 | 107 | 438 | 126 | 24 | 7 | 9 | 2.1 | 124 | 74 | 46 | 24 | | .288 | .436 | 0 | 0 | OF-69, C-37, 2B-6, 3B-2, 1B-2 |
| 1886 | 118 | 451 | 175 | 32 | 11 | 4 | 0.9 | 155 | 79 | 83 | 33 | | **.388** | .534 | 0 | 0 | OF-56, C-53, 1B-9, 3B-8, 2B-6, SS-5 |
| 1887 **BOS N** | 116 | 484 | 156 | 34 | 11 | 8 | 1.7 | 120 | 63 | 55 | 40 | 84 | .322 | .488 | 0 | 0 | OF-61, 2B-30, C-24, P-3, SS-2, 3B-2 |
| 1888 | 107 | 440 | 140 | 22 | 11 | 9 | 2.0 | 85 | 71 | 31 | 39 | 56 | .318 | .480 | 0 | 0 | C-76, OF-34 |
| 1889 | 125 | 507 | 149 | **41** | 5 | 9 | 1.8 | 120 | 78 | 65 | 40 | 68 | .294 | .448 | 0 | 0 | OF-113, C-23 |
| 1890 **BOS P** | 89 | 340 | 111 | 18 | 6 | 4 | 1.2 | 83 | 66 | 52 | 22 | 51 | .326 | .450 | 0 | 0 | C-56, SS-27, OF-6, 1B-4, 3B-2, P-1 |
| 1891 3 teams | **C-M** | **AA** (82G – .297) | | | **BOS** | **AA** (4G – .267) | | | **BOS** | **N** (24G – .235) | | | | | | | |
| " total | 110 | 379 | 107 | 17 | 7 | 2 | 0.5 | 71 | 63 | 58 | 43 | 29 | .282 | .380 | 0 | 0 | C-80, OF-22, 3B-8, 2B-6, 1B-5, P-3, SS-1 |
| 1892 **BOS N** | 78 | 281 | 53 | 7 | 0 | 2 | 0.7 | 40 | 41 | 39 | 31 | 24 | .189 | .235 | 0 | 0 | C-72, OF-2, 3B-2, 1B-2, P-1 |
| 1893 **NY N** | 20 | 67 | 18 | 1 | 0 | 0 | 0.0 | 9 | 15 | 6 | 5 | 3 | .269 | .284 | 2 | 0 | C-17, OF-1 |
| 16 yrs. | 1463 | 5923 | 1820 | 360 | 102 | 69 | 1.2 | 1363 | 794 | 550 | 420 | 315 | .307 | .437 | 2 | 0 | OF-759, C-582, 3B-96, SS-90, 2B-53, 1B-25, P-12 |
| 7 yrs. | 681 | 2843 | 899 | 193 | 49 | 33 | 1.2 | 728 | 323 | 229 | 179 | | .316 | .453 | 0 | 0 | OF-444, C-196, SS-60, 3B-47, 2B-16, 1B-14, P-4 |
| | | | | | | | | | | | 7th | | | | | | |

## Junior Kennedy

**KENNEDY, JUNIOR RAYMOND**      BR TR 5'11"   175 lbs.
Brother of Jim Kennedy.
B. Aug. 9, 1950, Fort Gibson, Okla.

| | G | AB | H | 2B | 3B | HR | HR % | R | RBI | BB | SO | SB | BA | SA | AB | H | G by POS |
|---|---|---|---|---|---|---|---|---|---|---|---|---|---|---|---|---|---|
| 1974 **CIN N** | 22 | 19 | 3 | 0 | 0 | 0 | 0.0 | 6 | 4 | 0 | .158 | .158 | 2 | 0 | 2B-17, 3B-5 | | |
| 1978 | 89 | 157 | 40 | 2 | 2 | 0 | 0.0 | 22 | 11 | 31 | 28 | 4 | .255 | .293 | 13 | 2 | 2B-71, 3B-4 |
| 1979 | 83 | 220 | 60 | 7 | 0 | 1 | 0.5 | 29 | 17 | 28 | 31 | 4 | .273 | .318 | 17 | 4 | 2B-59, SS-5, 3B-4 |
| 1980 | 104 | 337 | 88 | 16 | 3 | 1 | 0.3 | 31 | 34 | 36 | 34 | 3 | .261 | .335 | 1 | 0 | 2B-103 |
| 1981 | 27 | 44 | 11 | 1 | 0 | 0 | 0.0 | 5 | 5 | 1 | 5 | 0 | .250 | .273 | 6 | 1 | 2B-16, 3B-5 |
| 1982 **CHI N** | 105 | 242 | 53 | 3 | 1 | 2 | 0.8 | 22 | 25 | 21 | 34 | 1 | .219 | .264 | 4 | 0 | 2B-71, SS-28, 3B-7 |
| 1983 | 17 | 22 | 3 | 0 | 0 | 0 | 0.0 | 3 | 3 | 1 | 6 | 0 | .136 | .136 | 2 | 0 | 2B-7, 3B-4, SS-1 |
| 7 yrs. | 447 | 1041 | 258 | 29 | 6 | 4 | 0.4 | 114 | 95 | 124 | 142 | 12 | .248 | .299 | 45 | 7 | 2B-344, SS-34, 3B-29 |
| 2 yrs. | 122 | 264 | 56 | 3 | 1 | 2 | 0.8 | 25 | 28 | 22 | 40 | 1 | .212 | .254 | 6 | 0 | 2B-78, SS-29, 3B-11 |

## Snapper Kennedy

**KENNEDY, SHERMAN MONTGOMERY**      BB TR 5'10"   165 lbs.
B. Nov. 1, 1878, Conneaut, Ohio   D. Aug. 15, 1945, Pasadena, Tex.

| | G | AB | H | 2B | 3B | HR | HR % | R | RBI | BB | SO | SB | BA | SA | AB | H | G by POS |
|---|---|---|---|---|---|---|---|---|---|---|---|---|---|---|---|---|---|
| 1902 **CHI N** | 1 | 5 | 0 | 0 | 0 | 0 | 0.0 | 0 | 0 | 0 | | 0 | .000 | .000 | 0 | 0 | OF-1 |

| | G | AB | H | 2B | 3B | HR | HR % | R | RBI | BB | SO | SB | BA | SA | Pinch Hit AB | Pinch Hit H | G by POS |
|---|---|---|---|---|---|---|---|---|---|---|---|---|---|---|---|---|---|

## Marty Keough

**KEOUGH, RICHARD MARTIN**
Father of Matt Keough.    Brother of Joe Keough.
B. Apr. 14, 1935, Oakland, Calif.

BL  TL  6'      180 lbs.

| | G | AB | H | 2B | 3B | HR | HR% | R | RBI | BB | SO | SB | BA | SA | PH AB | PH H | G by POS |
|---|---|---|---|---|---|---|---|---|---|---|---|---|---|---|---|---|---|
| 1956 BOS A | 3 | 2 | 0 | 0 | 0 | 0 | 0.0 | 1 | 1 | 1 | 0 | 0 | .000 | .000 | 2 | 0 | |
| 1957 | 9 | 17 | 1 | 0 | 0 | 0 | 0.0 | 1 | 0 | 4 | 3 | 0 | .059 | .059 | 1 | 0 | OF-7 |
| 1958 | 68 | 118 | 26 | 3 | 3 | 1 | 0.8 | 9 | 7 | 9 | 29 | 1 | .220 | .322 | 34 | 5 | OF-25, 1B-2 |
| 1959 | 96 | 251 | 61 | 13 | 5 | 7 | 2.8 | 40 | 27 | 26 | 40 | 3 | .243 | .418 | 27 | 7 | OF-69, 1B-3 |
| 1960 2 teams | | BOS A | (38G – | .248) | | CLE A | (65G – | .248) | | | | | | | | | |
| " total | 103 | 254 | 63 | 11 | 1 | 4 | 1.6 | 34 | 20 | 17 | 31 | 4 | .248 | .346 | 32 | 5 | OF-71 |
| 1961 WAS A | 135 | 390 | 97 | 18 | 9 | 9 | 2.3 | 57 | 34 | 32 | 60 | 12 | .249 | .410 | 17 | 4 | OF-100, 1B-10 |
| 1962 CIN N | 111 | 230 | 64 | 8 | 2 | 7 | 3.0 | 34 | 27 | 21 | 31 | 3 | .278 | .422 | 20 | 4 | OF-71, 1B-29 |
| 1963 | 95 | 172 | 39 | 8 | 1 | 6 | 3.5 | 21 | 21 | 25 | 37 | 1 | .227 | .401 | 24 | 4 | 1B-46, OF-28 |
| 1964 | 109 | 276 | 71 | 9 | 1 | 9 | 3.3 | 29 | 28 | 22 | 58 | 1 | .257 | .395 | 34 | 9 | OF-81, 1B-4 |
| 1965 | 62 | 43 | 5 | 0 | 0 | 0 | 0.0 | 14 | 3 | 3 | 14 | 0 | .116 | .116 | 21 | 4 | 1B-32, OF-4 |
| 1966 2 teams | | ATL N | (17G – | .059) | | CHI N | (33G – | .231) | | | | | | | | | |
| " total | 50 | 43 | 7 | 1 | 0 | 0 | 0.0 | 4 | 6 | 6 | 15 | 1 | .163 | .186 | 31 | 5 | OF-8, 1B-4 |
| 11 yrs. | 841 | 1796 | 434 | 71 | 23 | 43 | 2.4 | 256 | 176 | 164 | 318 | 26 | .242 | .379 | 243 | 47 | OF-464, 1B-130 |
| 1 yr. | 33 | 26 | 6 | 1 | 0 | 0 | 0.0 | 3 | 5 | 5 | 9 | 1 | .231 | .269 | 21 | 5 | OF-5 |

## Mel Kerr

**KERR, JOHN MELVILLE**
B. May 22, 1903, Souris, Man., Canada    D. Aug. 9, 1980, Vero Beach, Fla.

BL  TL  5'11½"  155 lbs.

| | G | AB | H | 2B | 3B | HR | HR% | R | RBI | BB | SO | SB | BA | SA | PH AB | PH H | G by POS |
|---|---|---|---|---|---|---|---|---|---|---|---|---|---|---|---|---|---|
| 1925 CHI N | 1 | 0 | 0 | 0 | 0 | 0 | – | 1 | 0 | 0 | 0 | 0 | – | – | 0 | 0 | |

## Don Kessinger

**KESSINGER, DONALD EULON**
B. July 17, 1942, Forrest City, Ark.
Manager 1979.

BB  TR  6'1"      170 lbs.

BR 1964-65

| | G | AB | H | 2B | 3B | HR | HR% | R | RBI | BB | SO | SB | BA | SA | PH AB | PH H | G by POS |
|---|---|---|---|---|---|---|---|---|---|---|---|---|---|---|---|---|---|
| 1964 CHI N | 4 | 12 | 2 | 0 | 0 | 0 | 0.0 | 1 | 0 | 0 | 1 | 0 | .167 | .167 | 2 | 0 | SS-4 |
| 1965 | 106 | 309 | 62 | 4 | 3 | 0 | 0.0 | 19 | 14 | 20 | 44 | 1 | .201 | .233 | 0 | 0 | SS-105 |
| 1966 | 150 | 533 | 146 | 8 | 2 | 1 | 0.2 | 50 | 43 | 26 | 46 | 13 | .274 | .302 | 0 | 0 | SS-148 |
| 1967 | 145 | 580 | 134 | 10 | 7 | 0 | 0.0 | 61 | 42 | 33 | 80 | 6 | .231 | .272 | 0 | 0 | SS-143 |
| 1968 | 160 | 655 | 157 | 14 | 7 | 1 | 0.2 | 63 | 32 | 38 | 86 | 9 | .240 | .287 | 1 | 0 | SS-159 |
| 1969 | 158 | 664 | 181 | 38 | 6 | 4 | 0.6 | 109 | 53 | 61 | 70 | 11 | .273 | .366 | 1 | 0 | SS-157 |
| 1970 | 154 | 631 | 168 | 21 | 14 | 1 | 0.2 | 100 | 39 | 66 | 59 | 12 | .266 | .349 | 0 | 0 | SS-154 |
| 1971 | 155 | 617 | 159 | 18 | 6 | 2 | 0.3 | 77 | 38 | 52 | 54 | 15 | .258 | .316 | 2 | 0 | SS-154 |
| 1972 | 149 | 577 | 158 | 20 | 6 | 1 | 0.2 | 77 | 39 | 67 | 44 | 8 | .274 | .334 | 3 | 0 | SS-146 |
| 1973 | 160 | 577 | 151 | 22 | 3 | 0 | 0.0 | 52 | 43 | 57 | 44 | 6 | .262 | .310 | 2 | 0 | SS-158 |
| 1974 | 153 | 599 | 155 | 20 | 7 | 1 | 0.2 | 83 | 42 | 62 | 54 | 7 | .259 | .321 | 3 | 0 | SS-150 |
| 1975 | 154 | 601 | 146 | 26 | 10 | 0 | 0.0 | 77 | 46 | 68 | 47 | 4 | .243 | .319 | 2 | 0 | SS-140, 3B-13 |
| 1976 STL N | 145 | 502 | 120 | 22 | 6 | 1 | 0.2 | 55 | 40 | 61 | 51 | 3 | .239 | .313 | 1 | 0 | SS-113, 2B-31, 3B-2 |
| 1977 2 teams | | STL N | (59G – | .239) | | CHI A | (39G – | .235) | | | | | | | | | |
| " total | 98 | 253 | 60 | 7 | 2 | 0 | 0.0 | 26 | 18 | 27 | 33 | 2 | .237 | .281 | 15 | 0 | SS-47, 2B-37, 3B-13 |
| 1978 CHI A | 131 | 431 | 110 | 18 | 1 | 1 | 0.2 | 35 | 31 | 36 | 34 | 2 | .255 | .309 | 1 | 0 | SS-123, 2B-9 |
| 1979 | 56 | 110 | 22 | 6 | 0 | 1 | 0.9 | 14 | 7 | 10 | 12 | 1 | .200 | .282 | 0 | 0 | SS-54, 2B-1, 1B-1 |
| 16 yrs. | 2078 | 7651 | 1931 | 254 | 80 | 14 | 0.2 | 899 | 527 | 684 | 759 | 100 | .252 | .312 | 33 | 0 | SS-1955, 2B-78, 3B-28, 1B-1 |
| 12 yrs. | 1648 | 6355 | 1619 | 201 | 71 | 11 | 0.2 | 769 | 431 | 550 | 629 | 92 | .255 | .314 | 16 | 0 | SS-1618, 3B-13 |
| | 9th | 8th | 10th | | | | | | | | 6th | | | | | | |

## Pete Kilduff

**KILDUFF, PETER JOHN**
B. Apr. 4, 1893, Weir City, Kans.    D. Feb. 14, 1930, Pittsburg, Kans.

BR  TR  5'7"      155 lbs.

| | G | AB | H | 2B | 3B | HR | HR% | R | RBI | BB | SO | SB | BA | SA | PH AB | PH H | G by POS |
|---|---|---|---|---|---|---|---|---|---|---|---|---|---|---|---|---|---|
| 1917 2 teams | | NY N | (31G – | .205) | | CHI N | (56G – | .277) | | | | | | | | | |
| " total | 87 | 280 | 72 | 12 | 5 | 1 | 0.4 | 35 | 27 | 16 | 30 | 13 | .257 | .346 | 0 | 0 | SS-56, 2B-26, 3B-1 |
| 1918 CHI N | 30 | 93 | 19 | 2 | 2 | 0 | 0.0 | 7 | 13 | 7 | 7 | 1 | .204 | .269 | 0 | 0 | 2B-30 |
| 1919 2 teams | | CHI N | (31G – | .273) | | BKN N | (32G – | .301) | | | | | | | | | |
| " total | 63 | 161 | 46 | 7 | 3 | 0 | 0.0 | 14 | 16 | 22 | 16 | 6 | .286 | .366 | 2 | 1 | 3B-40, 2B-9, SS-7 |
| 1920 BKN N | 141 | 478 | 130 | 26 | 8 | 0 | 0.0 | 62 | 58 | 58 | 43 | 2 | .272 | .360 | 2 | 1 | 2B-134, 3B-5 |
| 1921 | 107 | 372 | 107 | 15 | 10 | 3 | 0.8 | 45 | 45 | 31 | 36 | 6 | .288 | .406 | 1 | 0 | 2B-105, 3B-1 |
| 5 yrs. | 428 | 1384 | 374 | 62 | 28 | 4 | 0.3 | 163 | 159 | 134 | 132 | 28 | .270 | .364 | 5 | 2 | 2B-304, SS-63, 3B-47 |
| 3 yrs. | 117 | 383 | 99 | 15 | 9 | 0 | 0.0 | 35 | 36 | 29 | 31 | 13 | .258 | .345 | 1 | 1 | SS-58, 2B-43, 3B-14 |

WORLD SERIES

| 1920 BKN N | 7 | 21 | 2 | 0 | 0 | 0 | 0.0 | 0 | 0 | 1 | 4 | 0 | .095 | .095 | 0 | 0 | 2B-7 |
|---|---|---|---|---|---|---|---|---|---|---|---|---|---|---|---|---|---|

## Bill Killefer

**KILLEFER, WILLIAM LAVIER (Reindeer Bill)**
Brother of Red Killefer.
B. Oct. 10, 1887, Bloomingdale, Mich.    D. July 2, 1960, Elsmere, Del.
Manager 1921-25, 1930-33.

BR  TR  5'10½"  200 lbs.

| | G | AB | H | 2B | 3B | HR | HR% | R | RBI | BB | SO | SB | BA | SA | PH AB | PH H | G by POS |
|---|---|---|---|---|---|---|---|---|---|---|---|---|---|---|---|---|---|
| 1909 STL A | 11 | 29 | 4 | 0 | 0 | 0 | 0.0 | 0 | 1 | 0 | | 2 | .138 | .138 | 0 | 0 | C-11 |
| 1910 | 74 | 193 | 24 | 2 | 2 | 0 | 0.0 | 14 | 7 | 12 | | 0 | .124 | .155 | 1 | 0 | C-73 |
| 1911 PHI N | 6 | 16 | 3 | 0 | 0 | 0 | 0.0 | 3 | 2 | 0 | 2 | 0 | .188 | .188 | 0 | 0 | C-6 |
| 1912 | 85 | 268 | 60 | 6 | 3 | 1 | 0.4 | 18 | 21 | 4 | 14 | 6 | .224 | .280 | 0 | 0 | C-85 |
| 1913 | 120 | 360 | 88 | 14 | 3 | 0 | 0.0 | 25 | 24 | 4 | 17 | 2 | .244 | .300 | 1 | 0 | C-118, 1B-1 |
| 1914 | 98 | 299 | 70 | 10 | 1 | 0 | 0.0 | 27 | 27 | 8 | 17 | 3 | .234 | .274 | 8 | 3 | C-90 |
| 1915 | 105 | 320 | 76 | 9 | 2 | 0 | 0.0 | 26 | 24 | 18 | 14 | 5 | .238 | .278 | 1 | 0 | C-105 |
| 1916 | 97 | 286 | 62 | 5 | 4 | 3 | 1.0 | 22 | 27 | 8 | 14 | 2 | .217 | .294 | 4 | 0 | C-91 |
| 1917 | 125 | 409 | 112 | 12 | 0 | 0 | 0.0 | 28 | 31 | 15 | 21 | 4 | .274 | .303 | 4 | 0 | C-120 |
| 1918 CHI N | 104 | 331 | 77 | 10 | 3 | 0 | 0.0 | 30 | 22 | 17 | 10 | 5 | .233 | .281 | 0 | 0 | C-104 |
| 1919 | 103 | 315 | 90 | 10 | 2 | 0 | 0.0 | 17 | 22 | 15 | 8 | 5 | .286 | .330 | 3 | 0 | C-100 |
| 1920 | 62 | 191 | 42 | 7 | 1 | 0 | 0.0 | 16 | 16 | 8 | 5 | 2 | .220 | .267 | 1 | 0 | C-61 |
| 1921 | 45 | 133 | 43 | 1 | 0 | 0 | 0.0 | 11 | 16 | 4 | 4 | 3 | .323 | .331 | 3 | 1 | C-42 |
| 13 yrs. | 1035 | 3150 | 751 | 86 | 21 | 4 | 0.1 | 237 | 240 | 113 | 126 | 39 | .238 | .283 | 26 | 4 | C-1006, 1B-1 |
| 4 yrs. | 314 | 970 | 252 | 28 | 6 | 0 | 0.0 | 74 | 76 | 44 | 27 | 15 | .260 | .301 | 7 | 1 | C-307 |

WORLD SERIES

| 1915 PHI N | 1 | 1 | 0 | 0 | 0 | 0 | 0.0 | 0 | 0 | 0 | 0 | 0 | .000 | .000 | 1 | 0 | |
|---|---|---|---|---|---|---|---|---|---|---|---|---|---|---|---|---|---|

| | G | AB | H | 2B | 3B | HR | HR % | R | RBI | BB | SO | SB | BA | SA | Pinch Hit AB | Pinch Hit H | G by POS |
|---|---|---|---|---|---|---|---|---|---|---|---|---|---|---|---|---|---|

# Bill Killefer continued

| | G | AB | H | 2B | 3B | HR | HR% | R | RBI | BB | SO | SB | BA | SA | AB | H | G by POS |
|---|---|---|---|---|---|---|---|---|---|---|---|---|---|---|---|---|---|
| 1918 **CHI N** | 6 | 17 | 2 | 1 | 0 | 0 | 0.0 | 2 | 2 | 2 | 0 | 0 | .118 | .176 | 0 | 0 | C-6 |
| 2 yrs. | 7 | 18 | 2 | 1 | 0 | 0 | 0.0 | 2 | 2 | 2 | 0 | 0 | .111 | .167 | 1 | 0 | C-6 |

# Matt Kilroy

**KILROY, MATTHEW ALOYSIUS (Matches)**
Brother of Mike Kilroy.
B. June 21, 1866, Philadelphia, Pa.    D. Mar. 2, 1940, Philadelphia, Pa.

BL   TL   5'9"     175 lbs.

| | G | AB | H | 2B | 3B | HR | HR% | R | RBI | BB | SO | SB | BA | SA | AB | H | G by POS |
|---|---|---|---|---|---|---|---|---|---|---|---|---|---|---|---|---|---|
| 1886 **BAL AA** | 68 | 218 | 38 | 3 | 1 | 0 | 0.0 | 33 | | 21 | | | .174 | .197 | 0 | 0 | P-68, OF-2 |
| 1887 | 72 | 239 | 59 | 5 | 6 | 0 | 0.0 | 46 | | 31 | | 12 | .247 | .318 | 0 | 0 | P-69, OF-4, SS-1 |
| 1888 | 43 | 145 | 26 | 5 | 2 | 0 | 0.0 | 13 | 19 | 11 | | 10 | .179 | .241 | 0 | 0 | P-40, OF-7 |
| 1889 | 65 | 208 | 57 | 3 | 6 | 1 | 0.5 | 32 | 26 | 23 | 26 | 13 | .274 | .361 | 0 | 0 | P-59, OF-8 |
| 1890 **BOS P** | 31 | 93 | 20 | 1 | 1 | 0 | 0.0 | 11 | 8 | 12 | 9 | 11 | .215 | .247 | 0 | 0 | P-30, OF-2, SS-1, 3B-1 |
| 1891 **C-M AA** | 8 | 20 | 3 | 0 | 0 | 0 | 0.0 | 2 | 0 | 4 | 2 | 0 | .150 | .150 | 0 | 0 | P-7, OF-1 |
| 1892 **WAS N** | 4 | 10 | 2 | 0 | 0 | 0 | 0.0 | 1 | 0 | 1 | 0 | 0 | .200 | .200 | 0 | 0 | P-4 |
| 1893 **LOU N** | 5 | 16 | 7 | 3 | 0 | 0 | 0.0 | 4 | 3 | 1 | 3 | 0 | .438 | .625 | 0 | 0 | P-5 |
| 1894 | 8 | 17 | 2 | 0 | 0 | 0 | 0.0 | 2 | 1 | 1 | 6 | 1 | .118 | .118 | 0 | 0 | P-8 |
| 1898 **CHI N** | 26 | 96 | 22 | 4 | 1 | 0 | 0.0 | 20 | 10 | 13 | | 0 | .229 | .292 | 1 | 0 | P-13, OF-12 |
| 10 yrs. | 330 | 1062 | 236 | 24 | 17 | 1 | 0.1 | 163 | 66 | 118 | 46 | 47 | .222 | .280 | 1 | 0 | P-303, OF-36, SS-2, 3B-1 |
| 1 yr. | 26 | 96 | 22 | 4 | 1 | 0 | 0.0 | 20 | 10 | 13 | | 0 | .229 | .292 | 1 | 0 | P-13, OF-12 |

# Bruce Kimm

**KIMM, BRUCE EDWARD**
B. June 29, 1951, Norway, Iowa

BR   TR   5'11"     175 lbs.

| | G | AB | H | 2B | 3B | HR | HR% | R | RBI | BB | SO | SB | BA | SA | AB | H | G by POS |
|---|---|---|---|---|---|---|---|---|---|---|---|---|---|---|---|---|---|
| 1976 **DET A** | 63 | 152 | 40 | 8 | 0 | 1 | 0.7 | 13 | 6 | 15 | 20 | 4 | .263 | .336 | 0 | 0 | C-61, DH-2 |
| 1977 | 14 | 25 | 2 | 1 | 0 | 0 | 0.0 | 2 | 1 | 0 | 4 | 0 | .080 | .120 | 0 | 0 | C-12, DH-2 |
| 1979 **CHI N** | 9 | 11 | 1 | 0 | 0 | 0 | 0.0 | 0 | 0 | 0 | 2 | 0 | .091 | .091 | 0 | 0 | C-9 |
| 1980 **CHI A** | 100 | 251 | 61 | 10 | 1 | 0 | 0.0 | 20 | 19 | 17 | 26 | 1 | .243 | .291 | 3 | 0 | C-98 |
| 4 yrs. | 186 | 439 | 104 | 19 | 1 | 1 | 0.2 | 35 | 26 | 32 | 50 | 5 | .237 | .292 | 3 | 0 | C-180, DH-4 |
| 1 yr. | 9 | 11 | 1 | 0 | 0 | 0 | 0.0 | 0 | 0 | 0 | 0 | 0 | .091 | .091 | 0 | 0 | C-9 |

# Jerry Kindall

**KINDALL, GERALD DONALD (Slim)**
B. May 27, 1935, St. Paul, Minn.

BR   TR   6'2½"     175 lbs.
BB 1960

| | G | AB | H | 2B | 3B | HR | HR% | R | RBI | BB | SO | SB | BA | SA | AB | H | G by POS |
|---|---|---|---|---|---|---|---|---|---|---|---|---|---|---|---|---|---|
| 1956 **CHI N** | 32 | 55 | 9 | 1 | 1 | 0 | 0.0 | 7 | 0 | 6 | 17 | 1 | .164 | .218 | 0 | 0 | SS-18 |
| 1957 | 72 | 181 | 29 | 3 | 0 | 6 | 3.3 | 18 | 12 | 8 | 48 | 1 | .160 | .276 | 10 | 2 | 2B-28, 3B-19, SS-9 |
| 1958 | 3 | 6 | 1 | 1 | 0 | 0 | 0.0 | 0 | 0 | 0 | 3 | 0 | .167 | .333 | 0 | 0 | 2B-3 |
| 1960 | 89 | 246 | 59 | 16 | 2 | 2 | 0.8 | 17 | 23 | 5 | 52 | 4 | .240 | .346 | 3 | 0 | 2B-82, SS-2 |
| 1961 | 96 | 310 | 75 | 22 | 3 | 9 | 2.9 | 37 | 44 | 18 | 89 | 2 | .242 | .419 | 7 | 1 | 2B-50, SS-47 |
| 1962 **CLE A** | 154 | 530 | 123 | 21 | 1 | 13 | 2.5 | 51 | 55 | 45 | 107 | 4 | .232 | .349 | 0 | 0 | 2B-154 |
| 1963 | 86 | 234 | 48 | 4 | 1 | 5 | 2.1 | 27 | 20 | 18 | 71 | 3 | .205 | .295 | 3 | 1 | SS-46, 2B-37, 1B-4 |
| 1964 2 teams | | CLE A | (23G – | .360) | | MIN A | (62G – | .148) | | | | | | | | | |
| " total | 85 | 153 | 28 | 3 | 0 | 3 | 2.0 | 13 | 8 | 9 | 51 | 0 | .183 | .261 | 0 | 0 | 2B-51, 1B-24, SS-7 |
| 1965 **MIN A** | 125 | 342 | 67 | 12 | 1 | 6 | 1.8 | 41 | 36 | 36 | 97 | 2 | .196 | .289 | 2 | 1 | 2B-106, 3B-10, SS-7 |
| 9 yrs. | 742 | 2057 | 439 | 83 | 9 | 44 | 2.1 | 211 | 198 | 145 | 535 | 17 | .213 | .327 | 25 | 5 | 2B-511, SS-136, 3B-29, 1B-28 |
| 5 yrs. | 292 | 798 | 173 | 43 | 6 | 17 | 2.1 | 79 | 79 | 37 | 209 | 8 | .217 | .350 | 20 | 3 | 2B-163, SS-76, 3B-19 |

# Ralph Kiner

**KINER, RALPH McPHERRAN**
B. Oct. 27, 1922, Santa Rita, N. M.
Hall of Fame 1975.

BR   TR   6'2"     195 lbs.

| | G | AB | H | 2B | 3B | HR | HR% | R | RBI | BB | SO | SB | BA | SA | AB | H | G by POS |
|---|---|---|---|---|---|---|---|---|---|---|---|---|---|---|---|---|---|
| 1946 **PIT N** | 144 | 502 | 124 | 17 | 3 | **23** | 4.6 | 63 | 81 | 74 | **109** | 3 | .247 | .430 | 3 | 0 | OF-140 |
| 1947 | 152 | 565 | 177 | 23 | 4 | **51** | **9.0** | 118 | 127 | 98 | 81 | 1 | .313 | **.639** | 0 | 0 | OF-152 |
| 1948 | 156 | 555 | 147 | 19 | 5 | **40** | 7.2 | 104 | 123 | 112 | 61 | 1 | .265 | .533 | 1 | 1 | OF-154 |
| 1949 | 152 | 549 | 170 | 19 | 5 | **54** | 9.8 | 116 | **127** | **117** | 61 | 6 | .310 | **.658** | 0 | 0 | OF-152 |
| 1950 | 150 | 547 | 149 | 21 | 6 | **47** | 8.6 | 112 | 118 | 122 | 79 | 2 | .272 | .590 | 0 | 0 | OF-150 |
| 1951 | 151 | 531 | 164 | 31 | 6 | **42** | 7.9 | **124** | 109 | **137** | 57 | 2 | .309 | **.627** | 0 | 0 | OF-94, 1B-58 |
| 1952 | 149 | 516 | 126 | 17 | 2 | **37** | 7.2 | 90 | 87 | **110** | 77 | 3 | .244 | .500 | 0 | 0 | OF-149 |
| 1953 2 teams | | PIT | N (41G – | .270) | | CHI | N (117G – | .283) | | | | | | | | | |
| " total | 158 | 562 | 157 | 20 | 3 | 35 | 6.2 | 100 | 116 | 100 | 88 | 2 | .279 | .512 | 1 | 0 | OF-157 |
| 1954 **CHI N** | 147 | 557 | 159 | 36 | 5 | 22 | 3.9 | 88 | 73 | 76 | 90 | 2 | .285 | .487 | 0 | 0 | OF-147 |
| 1955 **CLE A** | 113 | 321 | 78 | 13 | 0 | 18 | 5.6 | 56 | 54 | 65 | 46 | 0 | .243 | .452 | 28 | 11 | OF-87 |
| 10 yrs. | 1472 | 5205 | 1451 | 216 | 39 | 369 | 7.1 | 971 | 1015 | 1011 | 749 | 22 | .279 | .548 | 33 | 12 | OF-1382, 1B-58 |
| | | | | | | | **2nd** | | | | | | | | | | |
| 2 yrs. | 264 | 971 | 276 | 50 | 7 | 85 | 5.1 | 161 | 160 | 151 | 157 | 3 | .284 | .505 | 1 | 0 | OF-263 |

# Charlie King

**KING, CHARLES GILBERT (Chick)**
B. Nov. 10, 1930, Paris, Tenn.

BR   TR   6'2"     190 lbs.

| | G | AB | H | 2B | 3B | HR | HR% | R | RBI | BB | SO | SB | BA | SA | AB | H | G by POS |
|---|---|---|---|---|---|---|---|---|---|---|---|---|---|---|---|---|---|
| 1954 **DET A** | 11 | 28 | 6 | 0 | 1 | 0 | 0.0 | 4 | 3 | 3 | 8 | 0 | .214 | .286 | 4 | 0 | OF-7 |
| 1955 | 7 | 21 | 5 | 0 | 0 | 0 | 0.0 | 3 | 0 | 1 | 2 | 0 | .238 | .238 | 0 | 0 | OF-6 |
| 1956 | 7 | 9 | 2 | 0 | 0 | 0 | 0.0 | 0 | 0 | 1 | 4 | 0 | .222 | .222 | 2 | 0 | OF-4 |
| 1958 **CHI N** | 8 | 8 | 2 | 0 | 0 | 0 | 0.0 | 1 | 1 | 3 | 1 | 0 | .250 | .250 | 1 | 0 | OF-7 |
| 1959 2 teams | | CHI | N (7G – | .000) | | STL | N (5G – | .429) | | | | | | | | | |
| " total | 12 | 10 | 3 | 0 | 0 | 0 | 0.0 | 3 | 1 | 0 | 3 | 0 | .300 | .300 | 0 | 0 | OF-5 |
| 5 yrs. | 45 | 76 | 18 | 0 | 1 | 0 | 0.0 | 11 | 5 | 8 | 18 | 0 | .237 | .263 | 7 | 0 | OF-29 |
| 2 yrs. | 15 | 11 | 2 | 0 | 0 | 0 | 0.0 | 4 | 1 | 3 | 2 | 0 | .182 | .182 | 1 | 0 | OF-8 |

# Jim King

**KING, JAMES HUBERT**
B. Aug. 27, 1932, Elkins, Ark.

BL   TR   6'     185 lbs.

| | G | AB | H | 2B | 3B | HR | HR% | R | RBI | BB | SO | SB | BA | SA | AB | H | G by POS |
|---|---|---|---|---|---|---|---|---|---|---|---|---|---|---|---|---|---|
| 1955 **CHI N** | 113 | 301 | 77 | 12 | 3 | 11 | 3.7 | 43 | 45 | 24 | 39 | 2 | .256 | .425 | 18 | 4 | OF-93 |
| 1956 | 118 | 317 | 79 | 13 | 2 | 15 | 4.7 | 32 | 54 | 30 | 40 | 1 | .249 | .445 | 34 | 6 | OF-82 |
| 1957 **STL N** | 22 | 35 | 11 | 0 | 0 | 0 | 0.0 | 1 | 2 | 4 | 2 | 0 | .314 | .314 | 16 | 4 | OF-8 |
| 1958 **SF N** | 34 | 56 | 12 | 2 | 1 | 2 | 3.6 | 8 | 8 | 10 | 8 | 0 | .214 | .393 | 14 | 3 | OF-15 |
| 1961 **WAS A** | 110 | 263 | 71 | 12 | 1 | 11 | 4.2 | 43 | 46 | 38 | 45 | 4 | .270 | .449 | 17 | 1 | OF-91, C-1 |

| | G | AB | H | 2B | 3B | HR | HR % | R | RBI | BB | SO | SB | BA | SA | Pinch Hit AB | Pinch Hit H | G by POS |
|---|---|---|---|---|---|---|---|---|---|---|---|---|---|---|---|---|---|

## Jim King continued

| | G | AB | H | 2B | 3B | HR | HR % | R | RBI | BB | SO | SB | BA | SA | AB | H | G by POS |
|---|---|---|---|---|---|---|---|---|---|---|---|---|---|---|---|---|---|
| 1962 | 132 | 333 | 81 | 15 | 0 | 11 | 3.3 | 39 | 35 | 55 | 37 | 4 | .243 | .387 | 31 | 8 | OF-101 |
| 1963 | 136 | 459 | 106 | 16 | 5 | 24 | 5.2 | 61 | 62 | 45 | 43 | 3 | .231 | .444 | 22 | 4 | OF-123 |
| 1964 | 134 | 415 | 100 | 15 | 1 | 18 | 4.3 | 46 | 56 | 55 | 65 | 3 | .241 | .412 | 22 | 7 | OF-121 |
| 1965 | 120 | 258 | 55 | 10 | 2 | 14 | 5.4 | 46 | 49 | 44 | 50 | 1 | .213 | .430 | 37 | 8 | OF-88 |
| 1966 | 117 | 310 | 77 | 14 | 2 | 10 | 3.2 | 41 | 30 | 38 | 41 | 4 | .248 | .403 | 34 | 7 | OF-85 |
| 1967 3 teams | 89 | WAS A | (47G – | .210) | | CHI A | (23G – | .120) | | CLE A | (19G – | .143) | | | | | |
| " total | 89 | 171 | 30 | 3 | 2 | 1 | 0.6 | 14 | 14 | 20 | 31 | 1 | .175 | .234 | 42 | 11 | OF-44, C-1 |
| 11 yrs. | 1125 | 2918 | 699 | 112 | 19 | 117 | 4.0 | 374 | 401 | 363 | 401 | 23 | .240 | .411 | 287 | 63 | OF-851, C-2 |
| 2 yrs. | 231 | 618 | 156 | 25 | 5 | 26 | 4.2 | 75 | 99 | 54 | 79 | 3 | .252 | .435 | 52 | 10 | OF-175 |

## Dave Kingman

**KINGMAN, DAVID ARTHUR (Kong)**
B. Dec. 21, 1948, Pendleton, Ore.                                   BR TR 6'6''    210 lbs.

| | G | AB | H | 2B | 3B | HR | HR % | R | RBI | BB | SO | SB | BA | SA | AB | H | G by POS |
|---|---|---|---|---|---|---|---|---|---|---|---|---|---|---|---|---|---|
| 1971 SF N | 41 | 115 | 32 | 10 | 2 | 6 | 5.2 | 17 | 24 | 9 | 35 | 5 | .278 | .557 | 7 | 1 | 1B-20, OF-14 |
| 1972 | 135 | 472 | 106 | 17 | 4 | 29 | 6.1 | 65 | 83 | 51 | 140 | 16 | .225 | .462 | 5 | 0 | 3B-59, 1B-56, OF-22 |
| 1973 | 112 | 305 | 62 | 10 | 1 | 24 | 7.9 | 54 | 55 | 41 | 122 | 8 | .203 | .479 | 7 | 1 | 3B-60, 1B-46, P-2 |
| 1974 | 121 | 350 | 78 | 18 | 2 | 18 | 5.1 | 41 | 55 | 37 | 125 | 8 | .223 | .440 | 11 | 3 | 1B-91, 3B-21, OF-2 |
| 1975 NY N | 134 | 502 | 116 | 22 | 1 | 36 | 7.2 | 65 | 88 | 34 | 153 | 7 | .231 | .494 | 5 | 0 | OF-71, 1B-58, 3B-12 |
| 1976 | 123 | 474 | 113 | 14 | 0 | 37 | 7.8 | 70 | 86 | 28 | 135 | 7 | .238 | .506 | 1 | 0 | OF-111, 1B-16 |
| 1977 4 teams | | NY | N | (58G – | .209) | | SD | N | (56G – | .238) | | CAL | A | (10G – | .194) | | NY | A | (8G – | .250) |
| " total | 132 | 439 | 97 | 20 | 0 | 26 | 5.9 | 47 | 78 | 28 | 143 | 5 | .221 | .444 | 23 | 4 | OF-75, 1B-38, DH-6, 3B-2 |
| 1978 CHI N | 119 | 395 | 105 | 17 | 4 | 28 | 7.1 | 65 | 79 | 39 | 111 | 3 | .266 | .542 | 8 | 1 | OF-100, 1B-6 |
| 1979 | 145 | 532 | 153 | 19 | 5 | 48 | 9.0 | 97 | 115 | 45 | 131 | 4 | .288 | .613 | 5 | 3 | OF-139 |
| 1980 | 81 | 255 | 71 | 8 | 0 | 18 | 7.1 | 31 | 57 | 21 | 44 | 2 | .278 | .522 | 16 | 6 | OF-61, 1B-2 |
| 1981 NY N | 100 | 353 | 78 | 11 | 3 | 22 | 6.2 | 40 | 59 | 55 | 105 | 6 | .221 | .456 | 1 | 0 | 1B-56, OF-48 |
| 1982 | 149 | 535 | 109 | 9 | 1 | 37 | 6.9 | 80 | 99 | 59 | 156 | 4 | .204 | .432 | 5 | 0 | 1B-143 |
| 1983 | 100 | 248 | 49 | 7 | 0 | 13 | 5.2 | 25 | 29 | 22 | 57 | 2 | .198 | .383 | 39 | 7 | 1B-50, OF-5 |
| 1984 OAK A | 147 | 549 | 147 | 23 | 4 | 35 | 6.4 | 68 | 118 | 44 | 119 | 2 | .268 | .505 | 0 | 0 | DH-139, 1B-9 |
| 1985 | 158 | 592 | 141 | 16 | 0 | 30 | 5.1 | 66 | 91 | 62 | 114 | 3 | .238 | .417 | 2 | 1 | DH-149, 1B-9 |
| 15 yrs. | 1797 | 6116 | 1457 | 221 | 25 | 407 | 6.7 6th | 831 | 1116 | 575 | 1690 8th | 82 | .238 | .482 | 135 | 27 | OF-648, 1B-600, DH-294, 3B-154, P-2 |
| 3 yrs. | 345 | 1182 | 329 | 44 | 9 | 94 | 8.0 | 193 | 251 | 105 | 286 | 9 | .278 | .569 | 29 | 10 | OF-300, 1B-8 |

LEAGUE CHAMPIONSHIP SERIES

| | G | AB | H | 2B | 3B | HR | HR % | R | RBI | BB | SO | SB | BA | SA | AB | H | G by POS |
|---|---|---|---|---|---|---|---|---|---|---|---|---|---|---|---|---|---|
| 1971 SF N | 4 | 9 | 1 | 0 | 0 | 0 | 0.0 | 0 | 0 | 1 | 3 | 0 | .111 | .111 | 1 | 0 | OF-2 |

## Walt Kinzie

**KINZIE, WALTER H.**
B. Mar., 1857, Kansas    D. Nov. 5, 1909                                    5'10½'' 161 lbs.

| | G | AB | H | 2B | 3B | HR | HR % | R | RBI | BB | SO | SB | BA | SA | AB | H | G by POS |
|---|---|---|---|---|---|---|---|---|---|---|---|---|---|---|---|---|---|
| 1882 DET N | 13 | 53 | 5 | 0 | 1 | 0 | 0.0 | 5 | 2 | 0 | 8 | | .094 | .132 | 0 | 0 | SS-13 |
| 1884 2 teams | | CHI | N | (19G – | .159) | | STL | AA | (2G – | .111) | | | | | | | |
| " total | 21 | 91 | 14 | 3 | 0 | 2 | 2.2 | 4 | | 0 | 13 | | .154 | .253 | 0 | 0 | SS-17, 3B-2, 2B-2 |
| 2 yrs. | 34 | 144 | 19 | 3 | 1 | 2 | 1.4 | 9 | 2 | 0 | 21 | | .132 | .208 | 0 | 0 | SS-30, 3B-2, 2B-2 |
| 1 yr. | 19 | 82 | 13 | 3 | 0 | 2 | 2.4 | 4 | | 0 | 13 | | .159 | .268 | 0 | 0 | SS-17, 3B-2 |

## Jim Kirby

**KIRBY, JAMES HERSCHEL**
B. May 5, 1923, Nashville, Tenn.                                     BR TR 5'11''   175 lbs.

| | G | AB | H | 2B | 3B | HR | HR % | R | RBI | BB | SO | SB | BA | SA | AB | H | G by POS |
|---|---|---|---|---|---|---|---|---|---|---|---|---|---|---|---|---|---|
| 1949 CHI N | 3 | 2 | 1 | 0 | 0 | 0 | 0.0 | 0 | 0 | 0 | 0 | 0 | .500 | .500 | 2 | 1 | |

## Chris Kitsos

**KITSOS, CHRISTOPHER ANESTOS**
B. Feb. 11, 1928, New York, N. Y.                                    BB TR 5'9''    165 lbs.

| | G | AB | H | 2B | 3B | HR | HR % | R | RBI | BB | SO | SB | BA | SA | AB | H | G by POS |
|---|---|---|---|---|---|---|---|---|---|---|---|---|---|---|---|---|---|
| 1954 CHI N | 1 | 0 | 0 | 0 | 0 | 0 | – | 0 | 0 | 0 | 0 | 0 | – | – | 0 | 0 | SS-1 |

## Malachi Kittredge

**KITTREDGE, MALACHI J.**
B. Oct. 12, 1869, Clinton, Mass.    D. June 23, 1928, Gary, Ind.         BR TR 5'7''    170 lbs.
Manager 1904.

| | G | AB | H | 2B | 3B | HR | HR % | R | RBI | BB | SO | SB | BA | SA | AB | H | G by POS |
|---|---|---|---|---|---|---|---|---|---|---|---|---|---|---|---|---|---|
| 1890 CHI N | 96 | 333 | 67 | 8 | 3 | 3 | 0.9 | 46 | 35 | 39 | 53 | 7 | .201 | .270 | 0 | 0 | C-96 |
| 1891 | 79 | 296 | 62 | 8 | 5 | 2 | 0.7 | 26 | 27 | 17 | 28 | 4 | .209 | .291 | 0 | 0 | C-79 |
| 1892 | 69 | 229 | 41 | 5 | 0 | 0 | 0.0 | 19 | 10 | 11 | 27 | 2 | .179 | .201 | 0 | 0 | C-69 |
| 1893 | 70 | 255 | 59 | 9 | 5 | 2 | 0.8 | 32 | 30 | 17 | 15 | 3 | .231 | .329 | 0 | 0 | C-70 |
| 1894 | 51 | 168 | 53 | 8 | 2 | 0 | 0.0 | 36 | 23 | 26 | 20 | 2 | .315 | .387 | 0 | 0 | C-51 |
| 1895 | 60 | 212 | 48 | 6 | 3 | 3 | 1.4 | 30 | 29 | 16 | 9 | 6 | .226 | .325 | 0 | 0 | C-59 |
| 1896 | 65 | 215 | 48 | 4 | 1 | 1 | 0.5 | 17 | 19 | 14 | 14 | 6 | .223 | .265 | 0 | 0 | C-64, P-1 |
| 1897 | 79 | 262 | 53 | 5 | 5 | 1 | 0.4 | 25 | 30 | 22 | | 9 | .202 | .271 | 0 | 0 | C-79 |
| 1898 LOU N | 86 | 287 | 70 | 8 | 5 | 1 | 0.3 | 27 | 31 | 15 | | 9 | .244 | .317 | 0 | 0 | C-86 |
| 1899 2 teams | | LOU | N | (45G – | .202) | | WAS | N | (44G – | .150) | | | | | | | |
| " total | 89 | 262 | 46 | 5 | 1 | 0 | 0.0 | 25 | 23 | 36 | | 5 | .176 | .202 | 3 | 1 | C-86 |
| 1901 BOS N | 114 | 381 | 96 | 14 | 0 | 2 | 0.5 | 24 | 40 | 32 | | 2 | .252 | .304 | 0 | 0 | C-113 |
| 1902 | 80 | 255 | 60 | 7 | 0 | 2 | 0.8 | 18 | 30 | 24 | | 4 | .235 | .286 | 7 | 1 | C-72 |
| 1903 2 teams | | BOS | N | (32G – | .212) | | WAS | A | (60G – | .214) | | | | | | | |
| " total | 92 | 291 | 62 | 6 | 1 | 0 | 0.0 | 18 | 22 | 21 | | 2 | .213 | .241 | 2 | 0 | C-90 |
| 1904 WAS A | 81 | 265 | 64 | 7 | 0 | 0 | 0.0 | 11 | 24 | 8 | | 2 | .242 | .268 | 2 | 0 | C-79 |
| 1905 | 76 | 238 | 39 | 8 | 0 | 0 | 0.0 | 13 | 14 | 15 | | 1 | .164 | .197 | 0 | 0 | C-75 |
| 1906 2 teams | | WAS | A | (27G – | .179) | | CLE | A | (1G – | .000) | | | | | | | |
| " total | 28 | 81 | 14 | 0 | 0 | 0 | 0.0 | 5 | 3 | 1 | | 0 | .173 | .173 | 0 | 0 | C-28 |
| 16 yrs. | 1215 | 4030 | 882 | 108 | 31 | 17 | 0.4 | 372 | 390 | 314 | 166 | 64 | .219 | .274 | 14 | 2 | C-1196, P-1 |
| 8 yrs. | 569 | 1970 | 431 | 53 | 24 | 12 | 0.6 | 231 | 203 | 162 | 166 | 39 | .219 | .288 | 0 | 0 | C-567, P-1 |

## Chuck Klein

**KLEIN, CHARLES HERBERT**
B. Oct. 7, 1904, Indianapolis, Ind.    D. Mar. 28, 1958, Indianapolis, Ind.     BL TR 6'    185 lbs.
Hall of Fame 1980.

| | G | AB | H | 2B | 3B | HR | HR % | R | RBI | BB | SO | SB | BA | SA | AB | H | G by POS |
|---|---|---|---|---|---|---|---|---|---|---|---|---|---|---|---|---|---|
| 1928 PHI N | 64 | 253 | 91 | 14 | 4 | 11 | 4.3 | 41 | 34 | 14 | 22 | 0 | .360 | .577 | 1 | 0 | OF-63 |
| 1929 | 149 | 616 | 219 | 45 | 6 | 43 | 7.0 | 126 | 145 | 54 | 61 | 5 | .356 | .657 | 0 | 0 | OF-149 |

| | G | AB | H | 2B | 3B | HR | HR % | R | RBI | BB | SO | SB | BA | SA | Pinch Hit AB | Pinch Hit H | G by POS |
|---|---|---|---|---|---|---|---|---|---|---|---|---|---|---|---|---|---|

## Chuck Klein continued

| | G | AB | H | 2B | 3B | HR | HR % | R | RBI | BB | SO | SB | BA | SA | AB | H | G by POS |
|---|---|---|---|---|---|---|---|---|---|---|---|---|---|---|---|---|---|
| 1930 | 156 | 648 | 250 | 59 | 8 | 40 | 6.2 | 158 | 170 | 54 | 50 | 4 | .386 | .687 | 0 | 0 | OF-156 |
| 1931 | 148 | 594 | 200 | 34 | 10 | 31 | 5.2 | 121 | 121 | 59 | 49 | 7 | .337 | .584 | 0 | 0 | OF-148 |
| 1932 | 154 | 650 | 226 | 50 | 15 | 38 | 5.8 | 152 | 137 | 60 | 49 | 20 | .348 | .646 | 0 | 0 | OF-154 |
| 1933 | 152 | 606 | 223 | 44 | 7 | 28 | 4.6 | 101 | 120 | 56 | 36 | 15 | .368 | .602 | 0 | 0 | OF-152 |
| 1934 CHI N | 115 | 435 | 131 | 27 | 2 | 20 | 4.6 | 78 | 80 | 47 | 38 | 3 | .301 | .510 | 5 | 2 | OF-110 |
| 1935 | 119 | 434 | 127 | 14 | 4 | 21 | 4.8 | 71 | 73 | 41 | 42 | 4 | .293 | .488 | 6 | 1 | OF-111 |
| 1936 2 teams | CHI | N | (29G – | .294) | | PHI | N | (117G – | .309) | | | | | | | | |
| " total | 146 | 601 | 184 | 35 | 7 | 25 | 4.2 | 102 | 104 | 49 | 59 | 6 | .306 | .512 | 0 | 0 | OF-146 |
| 1937 PHI N | 115 | 406 | 132 | 20 | 2 | 15 | 3.7 | 74 | 57 | 39 | 21 | 3 | .325 | .495 | 13 | 3 | OF-102 |
| 1938 | 129 | 458 | 113 | 22 | 2 | 8 | 1.7 | 53 | 61 | 38 | 30 | 7 | .247 | .356 | 10 | 1 | OF-119 |
| 1939 2 teams | PHI | N | (25G – | .191) | | PIT | N | (85G – | .300) | | | | | | | | |
| " total | 110 | 317 | 90 | 18 | 5 | 12 | 3.8 | 45 | 56 | 36 | 21 | 2 | .284 | .486 | 26 | 11 | OF-77, 1B-1 |
| 1940 PHI N | 116 | 354 | 77 | 16 | 2 | 7 | 2.0 | 39 | 37 | 44 | 30 | 2 | .218 | .333 | 18 | 2 | OF-116 |
| 1941 | 50 | 73 | 9 | 0 | 0 | 1 | 1.4 | 6 | 3 | 10 | 6 | 0 | .123 | .164 | 31 | 5 | OF-14 |
| 1942 | 14 | 14 | 1 | 0 | 0 | 0 | 0.0 | 0 | 0 | 0 | 2 | 0 | .071 | .071 | 14 | 1 | |
| 1943 | 12 | 20 | 2 | 0 | 0 | 0 | 0.0 | 0 | 3 | 0 | 3 | 1 | .100 | .100 | 10 | 1 | OF-2 |
| 1944 | 4 | 7 | 1 | 0 | 0 | 0 | 0.0 | 1 | 0 | 2 | 1 | 0 | .143 | .143 | 3 | 1 | OF-1 |
| 17 yrs. | 1753 | 6486 | 2076 | 398 | 74 | 300 | 4.6 | 1168 | 1201 | 601 | 521 | 79 | .320 | .543 | 137 | 28 | OF-1620, 1B-1 |
| 3 yrs. | 263 | 978 | 290 | 46 | 6 | 46 | 4.7 | 168 | 171 | 104 | 94 | 7 | .297 | .497 | 11 | 3 | OF-250 |

WORLD SERIES

| | G | AB | H | 2B | 3B | HR | HR % | R | RBI | BB | SO | SB | BA | SA | AB | H | G by POS |
|---|---|---|---|---|---|---|---|---|---|---|---|---|---|---|---|---|---|
| 1935 CHI N | 5 | 12 | 4 | 0 | 0 | 1 | 8.3 | 2 | 2 | 0 | 2 | 0 | .333 | .583 | 3 | 1 | OF-3 |

## Johnny Kling

KLING, JOHN (Noisy)
Brother of Bill Kling.
B. Feb. 25, 1875, Kansas City, Mo.    D. Jan. 31, 1947, Kansas City, Mo.
Manager 1912.

BR  TR  5'9½"  160 lbs.

| | G | AB | H | 2B | 3B | HR | HR % | R | RBI | BB | SO | SB | BA | SA | AB | H | G by POS |
|---|---|---|---|---|---|---|---|---|---|---|---|---|---|---|---|---|---|
| 1900 CHI N | 15 | 51 | 15 | 3 | 1 | 0 | 0.0 | 8 | 7 | 2 | | 0 | .294 | .392 | 0 | 0 | C-15 |
| 1901 | 74 | 253 | 70 | 6 | 3 | 0 | 0.0 | 26 | 21 | 9 | | 7 | .277 | .324 | 4 | 1 | C-69, OF-1, 1B-1 |
| 1902 | 114 | 434 | 124 | 19 | 3 | 0 | 0.0 | 50 | 57 | 29 | | 23 | .286 | .343 | 1 | 0 | C-112, SS-1 |
| 1903 | 132 | 491 | 146 | 29 | 13 | 3 | 0.6 | 67 | 68 | 22 | | 23 | .297 | .428 | 0 | 0 | C-132 |
| 1904 | 123 | 452 | 110 | 18 | 0 | 2 | 0.4 | 41 | 46 | 16 | | 7 | .243 | .296 | 2 | 0 | C-104, OF-10, 1B-6 |
| 1905 | 111 | 380 | 83 | 8 | 6 | 1 | 0.3 | 26 | 52 | 28 | | 13 | .218 | .279 | 1 | 0 | C-106, OF-4, 1B-1 |
| 1906 | 107 | 343 | 107 | 15 | 8 | 2 | 0.6 | 45 | 46 | 23 | | 14 | .312 | .420 | 7 | 2 | C-96, OF-3 |
| 1907 | 104 | 334 | 95 | 15 | 8 | 1 | 0.3 | 44 | 43 | 27 | | 9 | .284 | .386 | 3 | 0 | C-98, 1B-2 |
| 1908 | 126 | 424 | 117 | 23 | 5 | 4 | 0.9 | 51 | 59 | 21 | | 16 | .276 | .382 | 2 | 0 | C-117, OF-6, 1B-2 |
| 1910 | 91 | 297 | 80 | 17 | 2 | 2 | 0.7 | 31 | 32 | 37 | 27 | 3 | .269 | .360 | 4 | 0 | C-86 |
| 1911 2 teams | CHI | N | (27G – | .175) | | BOS | N | (75G – | .224) | | | | | | | | |
| " total | 102 | 321 | 68 | 11 | 3 | 3 | 0.9 | 40 | 29 | 38 | 43 | 1 | .212 | .293 | 4 | 1 | C-96, 3B-1 |
| 1912 BOS N | 81 | 252 | 80 | 10 | 3 | 2 | 0.8 | 26 | 30 | 15 | 30 | 3 | .317 | .405 | 7 | 2 | C-74 |
| 1913 CIN N | 80 | 209 | 57 | 7 | 6 | 0 | 0.0 | 20 | 23 | 14 | 14 | 2 | .273 | .364 | 15 | 3 | C-63 |
| 13 yrs. | 1260 | 4241 | 1152 | 181 | 61 | 20 | 0.5 | 475 | 513 | 281 | 114 | 121 | .272 | .357 | 50 | 9 | C-1168, OF-24, 1B-12, SS-1, 3B-1 |
| 11 yrs. | 1024 | 3539 | 961 | 156 | 51 | 16 | 0.5 | 397 | 436 | 222 | 41 | 116 | .272 | .358 | 26 | 3 | C-960, OF-24, 1B-12, SS-1 |

WORLD SERIES

| | G | AB | H | 2B | 3B | HR | HR % | R | RBI | BB | SO | SB | BA | SA | AB | H | G by POS |
|---|---|---|---|---|---|---|---|---|---|---|---|---|---|---|---|---|---|
| 1906 CHI N | 6 | 17 | 3 | 1 | 0 | 0 | 0.0 | 2 | 0 | 4 | 3 | 0 | .176 | .235 | 0 | 0 | C-6 |
| 1907 | 5 | 19 | 4 | 0 | 0 | 0 | 0.0 | 2 | 1 | 1 | 4 | 0 | .211 | .211 | 0 | 0 | C-5 |
| 1908 | 5 | 16 | 4 | 1 | 0 | 0 | 0.0 | 2 | 1 | 2 | 2 | 0 | .250 | .313 | 0 | 0 | C-5 |
| 1910 | 5 | 13 | 1 | 0 | 0 | 0 | 0.0 | 0 | 1 | 1 | 2 | 0 | .077 | .077 | 2 | 0 | C-3 |
| 4 yrs. | 21 | 65 | 12 | 2 | 0 | 0 | 0.0 | 6 | 3 | 8 | 11 | 0 | .185 | .215 | 2 | 0 | C-19 |

## Joe Klugman

KLUGMAN, JOSIE
B. Mar. 26, 1895, St. Louis, Mo.    D. July 18, 1951, Moberly, Mo.

BR  TR  5'11"  175 lbs.

| | G | AB | H | 2B | 3B | HR | HR % | R | RBI | BB | SO | SB | BA | SA | AB | H | G by POS |
|---|---|---|---|---|---|---|---|---|---|---|---|---|---|---|---|---|---|
| 1921 CHI N | 6 | 21 | 6 | 0 | 0 | 0 | 0.0 | 3 | 2 | 1 | 2 | 0 | .286 | .286 | 1 | 1 | 2B-5 |
| 1922 | 2 | 2 | 0 | 0 | 0 | 0 | 0.0 | 0 | 0 | 0 | 0 | 0 | .000 | .000 | 0 | 0 | 2B-2 |
| 1924 BKN N | 31 | 79 | 13 | 2 | 1 | 0 | 0.0 | 7 | 3 | 2 | 9 | 0 | .165 | .215 | 1 | 0 | 2B-28, SS-1 |
| 1925 CLE A | 38 | 85 | 28 | 9 | 2 | 0 | 0.0 | 12 | 12 | 8 | 4 | 3 | .329 | .482 | 3 | 1 | 2B-29, 1B-4, 3B-2 |
| 4 yrs. | 77 | 187 | 47 | 11 | 3 | 0 | 0.0 | 22 | 17 | 11 | 15 | 3 | .251 | .342 | 5 | 2 | 2B-64, 1B-4, 3B-2, SS-1 |
| 2 yrs. | 8 | 23 | 6 | 0 | 0 | 0 | 0.0 | 3 | 2 | 1 | 2 | 0 | .261 | .261 | 1 | 1 | 2B-7 |

## Otto Knabe

KNABE, FRANZ OTTO (Dutch)
B. June 12, 1884, Carrick, Pa.    D. May 17, 1961, Philadelphia, Pa.
Manager 1914-15.

BR  TR  5'8"  175 lbs.

| | G | AB | H | 2B | 3B | HR | HR % | R | RBI | BB | SO | SB | BA | SA | AB | H | G by POS |
|---|---|---|---|---|---|---|---|---|---|---|---|---|---|---|---|---|---|
| 1905 PIT N | 3 | 10 | 3 | 1 | 0 | 0 | 0.0 | 0 | 2 | 3 | | 0 | .300 | .400 | 0 | 0 | 3B-3 |
| 1907 PHI N | 129 | 444 | 113 | 16 | 9 | 1 | 0.2 | 67 | 34 | 52 | | 18 | .255 | .338 | 2 | 0 | 2B-121, OF-5 |
| 1908 | 151 | 555 | 121 | 26 | 8 | 0 | 0.0 | 63 | 27 | 49 | | 27 | .218 | .294 | 0 | 0 | 2B-151 |
| 1909 | 114 | 402 | 94 | 13 | 3 | 0 | 0.0 | 40 | 33 | 35 | | 9 | .234 | .281 | 2 | 0 | 2B-109, OF-1 |
| 1910 | 137 | 510 | 133 | 18 | 6 | 1 | 0.2 | 73 | 44 | 47 | 42 | 15 | .261 | .325 | 1 | 0 | 2B-136 |
| 1911 | 142 | 528 | 125 | 15 | 6 | 1 | 0.2 | 99 | 42 | 94 | 35 | 23 | .237 | .294 | 0 | 0 | 2B-142 |
| 1912 | 126 | 426 | 120 | 11 | 4 | 0 | 0.0 | 56 | 46 | 55 | 20 | 16 | .282 | .326 | 3 | 1 | 2B-123 |
| 1913 | 148 | 571 | 150 | 25 | 7 | 2 | 0.4 | 70 | 53 | 45 | 26 | 14 | .263 | .342 | 0 | 0 | 2B-148 |
| 1914 BAL F | 147 | 469 | 106 | 26 | 2 | 2 | 0.4 | 45 | 42 | 53 | | 10 | .226 | .303 | 3 | 1 | 2B-144 |
| 1915 | 103 | 320 | 81 | 16 | 2 | 1 | 0.3 | 38 | 25 | 37 | | 7 | .253 | .325 | 8 | 2 | 2B-94, OF-1 |
| 1916 2 teams | PIT | N | (28G – | .191) | | CHI | N | (57G – | .276) | | | | | | | | |
| " total | 85 | 234 | 57 | 11 | 2 | 0 | 0.0 | 21 | 16 | 15 | 24 | 4 | .244 | .299 | 5 | 2 | 2B-70, OF-1, SS-1, 3B-1 |
| 11 yrs. | 1285 | 4469 | 1103 | 178 | 48 | 8 | 0.2 | 572 | 364 | 485 | 147 | 143 | .247 | .313 | 24 | 6 | 2B-1238, OF-8, 3B-4, SS-1 |
| 1 yr. | 57 | 145 | 40 | 8 | 0 | 0 | 0.0 | 17 | 7 | 9 | 18 | 3 | .276 | .331 | 5 | 2 | 2B-42, OF-1, SS-1, 3B-1 |

## Pete Knisely

KNISELY, PETER COLE
B. Aug. 11, 1883, Waynesburg, Pa.    D. July 1, 1948, Brownsville, Pa.

BR  TR  5'9"  185 lbs.

| | G | AB | H | 2B | 3B | HR | HR % | R | RBI | BB | SO | SB | BA | SA | AB | H | G by POS |
|---|---|---|---|---|---|---|---|---|---|---|---|---|---|---|---|---|---|
| 1912 CIN N | 21 | 67 | 22 | 7 | 3 | 0 | 0.0 | 10 | 7 | 4 | 5 | 3 | .328 | .522 | 3 | 0 | OF-13, 2B-3, SS-1 |

| | G | AB | H | 2B | 3B | HR | HR % | R | RBI | BB | SO | SB | BA | SA | Pinch Hit AB | Pinch Hit H | G by POS |
|---|---|---|---|---|---|---|---|---|---|---|---|---|---|---|---|---|---|

## Pete Knisely continued

| | G | AB | H | 2B | 3B | HR | HR % | R | RBI | BB | SO | SB | BA | SA | AB | H | G by POS |
|---|---|---|---|---|---|---|---|---|---|---|---|---|---|---|---|---|---|
| 1913 CHI N | 2 | 2 | 0 | 0 | 0 | 0 | 0.0 | 0 | 0 | 0 | 1 | 0 | .000 | .000 | 2 | 0 | |
| 1914 | 37 | 69 | 9 | 0 | 1 | 0 | 0.0 | 5 | 5 | 5 | 6 | 0 | .130 | .159 | 19 | 4 | OF-16 |
| 1915 | 64 | 134 | 33 | 9 | 0 | 0 | 0.0 | 12 | 17 | 15 | 18 | 1 | .246 | .313 | 17 | 4 | OF-34, 2B-9 |
| 4 yrs. | 124 | 272 | 64 | 16 | 4 | 0 | 0.0 | 27 | 29 | 24 | 30 | 4 | .235 | .324 | 41 | 8 | OF-63, 2B-12, SS-1 |
| 3 yrs. | 103 | 205 | 42 | 9 | 1 | 0 | 0.0 | 17 | 22 | 20 | 25 | 1 | .205 | .259 | 38 | 8 | OF-50, 2B-9 |

## Mark Koenig

KOENIG, MARK ANTHONY
B. July 19, 1902, San Francisco, Calif.

BB  TR  6'  180 lbs.
BL 1928

| | G | AB | H | 2B | 3B | HR | HR % | R | RBI | BB | SO | SB | BA | SA | AB | H | G by POS |
|---|---|---|---|---|---|---|---|---|---|---|---|---|---|---|---|---|---|
| 1925 NY A | 28 | 110 | 23 | 6 | 1 | 0 | 0.0 | 14 | 4 | 5 | 4 | 0 | .209 | .282 | 0 | 0 | SS-28 |
| 1926 | 147 | 617 | 167 | 26 | 8 | 5 | 0.8 | 93 | 62 | 43 | 37 | 4 | .271 | .363 | 6 | 1 | SS-141 |
| 1927 | 123 | 526 | 150 | 20 | 11 | 3 | 0.6 | 99 | 62 | 25 | 21 | 3 | .285 | .382 | 1 | 0 | SS-122 |
| 1928 | 132 | 533 | 170 | 19 | 10 | 4 | 0.8 | 89 | 63 | 32 | 19 | 3 | .319 | .415 | 7 | 3 | SS-125 |
| 1929 | 116 | 373 | 109 | 27 | 5 | 3 | 0.8 | 44 | 41 | 23 | 17 | 1 | .292 | .416 | 16 | 1 | SS-61, 3B-37, 2B-1 |
| 1930 2 teams | | NY | A (21G – | .230) | | DET | A (76G – | .240) | | | | | | | | | |
| " total | 97 | 341 | 81 | 14 | 2 | 1 | 0.3 | 46 | 25 | 26 | 20 | 2 | .238 | .299 | 4 | 0 | SS-89, 3B-2, P-2, OF-1 |
| 1931 DET A | 106 | 364 | 92 | 24 | 4 | 1 | 0.3 | 33 | 39 | 14 | 12 | 8 | .253 | .349 | 15 | 4 | 2B-55, SS-35, P-3 |
| 1932 CHI N | 33 | 102 | 36 | 5 | 1 | 3 | 2.9 | 15 | 11 | 3 | 5 | 0 | .353 | .510 | 2 | 0 | SS-33 |
| 1933 | 80 | 218 | 62 | 12 | 1 | 3 | 1.4 | 32 | 25 | 15 | 9 | 5 | .284 | .390 | 15 | 4 | 3B-37, SS-26, 2B-2 |
| 1934 CIN N | 151 | 633 | 172 | 26 | 6 | 1 | 0.2 | 60 | 67 | 15 | 24 | 5 | .272 | .336 | 2 | 0 | 3B-64, SS-58, 2B-26, 1B-4 |
| 1935 NY N | 107 | 396 | 112 | 12 | 0 | 3 | 0.8 | 40 | 37 | 13 | 18 | 0 | .283 | .336 | 9 | 1 | 2B-64, SS-21, 3B-15 |
| 1936 | 42 | 58 | 16 | 4 | 0 | 1 | 1.7 | 7 | 7 | 8 | 4 | 0 | .276 | .397 | 17 | 4 | SS-10, 2B-8, 3B-3 |
| 12 yrs. | 1162 | 4271 | 1190 | 195 | 49 | 28 | 0.7 | 572 | 443 | 222 | 190 | 31 | .279 | .367 | 94 | 18 | SS-749, 3B-158, 2B-156, P-5, 1B-4, OF-1 |
| 2 yrs. | 113 | 320 | 98 | 17 | 2 | 6 | 1.9 | 47 | 36 | 18 | 14 | 5 | .306 | .428 | 17 | 4 | SS-59, 3B-37, 2B-2 |

WORLD SERIES

| | G | AB | H | 2B | 3B | HR | HR % | R | RBI | BB | SO | SB | BA | SA | AB | H | G by POS |
|---|---|---|---|---|---|---|---|---|---|---|---|---|---|---|---|---|---|
| 1926 NY A | 7 | 32 | 4 | 1 | 0 | 0 | 0.0 | 2 | 2 | 0 | 6 | 0 | .125 | .156 | 0 | 0 | SS-7 |
| 1927 | 4 | 18 | 9 | 2 | 0 | 0 | 0.0 | 5 | 2 | 0 | 2 | 0 | .500 | .611 | 0 | 0 | SS-4 |
| 1928 | 4 | 19 | 3 | 0 | 0 | 0 | 0.0 | 1 | 0 | 0 | 1 | 0 | .158 | .158 | 0 | 0 | SS-4 |
| 1932 CHI N | 2 | 4 | 1 | 0 | 1 | 0 | 0.0 | 1 | 1 | 1 | 0 | 0 | .250 | .750 | 0 | 0 | SS-1 |
| 1936 NY N | 3 | 3 | 1 | 0 | 0 | 0 | 0.0 | 0 | 0 | 0 | 1 | 0 | .333 | .333 | 3 | 1 | 2B-1 |
| 5 yrs. | 20 | 76 | 18 | 3 | 1 | 0 | 0.0 | 9 | 5 | 1 | 10 | 0 | .237 | .303 | 3 | 1 | SS-16, 2B-1 |

## Mike Kreevich

KREEVICH, MICHAEL ANDREAS
B. June 10, 1908, Mount Olive, Ill.

BR  TR  5'7½"  168 lbs.

| | G | AB | H | 2B | 3B | HR | HR % | R | RBI | BB | SO | SB | BA | SA | AB | H | G by POS |
|---|---|---|---|---|---|---|---|---|---|---|---|---|---|---|---|---|---|
| 1931 CHI N | 5 | 12 | 2 | 0 | 0 | 0 | 0.0 | 0 | 0 | 0 | 6 | 1 | .167 | .167 | 1 | 0 | OF-4 |
| 1935 CHI A | 6 | 23 | 10 | 2 | 0 | 0 | 0.0 | 3 | 2 | 1 | 0 | 1 | .435 | .522 | 0 | 0 | 3B-6 |
| 1936 | 137 | 550 | 169 | 32 | 11 | 5 | 0.9 | 99 | 69 | 61 | 46 | 10 | .307 | .433 | 3 | 2 | OF-133 |
| 1937 | 144 | 583 | 176 | 29 | 16 | 12 | 2.1 | 94 | 73 | 43 | 45 | 10 | .302 | .468 | 3 | 1 | OF-138 |
| 1938 | 129 | 489 | 145 | 26 | 12 | 6 | 1.2 | 73 | 73 | 55 | 23 | 13 | .297 | .436 | 3 | 0 | OF-127 |
| 1939 | 145 | 541 | 175 | 30 | 8 | 5 | 0.9 | 85 | 77 | 59 | 40 | 23 | .323 | .436 | 3 | 0 | OF-139, 3B-4 |
| 1940 | 144 | 582 | 154 | 27 | 10 | 8 | 1.4 | 86 | 55 | 34 | 49 | 15 | .265 | .387 | 0 | 0 | OF-144 |
| 1941 | 121 | 436 | 101 | 16 | 8 | 0 | 0.0 | 44 | 37 | 35 | 26 | 17 | .232 | .305 | 7 | 4 | OF-113 |
| 1942 PHI A | 116 | 444 | 113 | 19 | 1 | 1 | 0.2 | 57 | 30 | 47 | 31 | 7 | .255 | .309 | 6 | 2 | OF-107 |
| 1943 STL A | 60 | 161 | 41 | 6 | 0 | 0 | 0.0 | 24 | 10 | 26 | 13 | 4 | .255 | .292 | 7 | 1 | OF-51 |
| 1944 | 105 | 402 | 121 | 15 | 6 | 5 | 1.2 | 55 | 44 | 27 | 24 | 3 | .301 | .405 | 5 | 0 | OF-100 |
| 1945 2 teams | | STL | A (81G – | .237) | | WAS | A (45G – | .278) | | | | | | | | | |
| " total | 126 | 453 | 114 | 19 | 3 | 3 | 0.7 | 56 | 44 | 58 | 38 | 11 | .252 | .327 | 7 | 2 | OF-118 |
| 12 yrs. | 1238 | 4676 | 1321 | 221 | 75 | 45 | 1.0 | 676 | 514 | 446 | 341 | 115 | .283 | .391 | 45 | 12 | OF-1174, 3B-10 |
| 1 yr. | 5 | 12 | 2 | 0 | 0 | 0 | 0.0 | 0 | 0 | 0 | 6 | 1 | .167 | .167 | 1 | 0 | OF-4 |

WORLD SERIES

| | G | AB | H | 2B | 3B | HR | HR % | R | RBI | BB | SO | SB | BA | SA | AB | H | G by POS |
|---|---|---|---|---|---|---|---|---|---|---|---|---|---|---|---|---|---|
| 1944 STL A | 6 | 26 | 6 | 3 | 0 | 0 | 0.0 | 0 | 0 | 0 | 5 | 0 | .231 | .346 | 0 | 0 | OF-6 |

## Bill Krieg

KRIEG, WILLIAM FREDERICK
B. Jan. 29, 1859, Petersburg, Ill.   D. Mar. 25, 1930, Chillicothe, Ill.

BR  TR  5'8"  180 lbs.

| | G | AB | H | 2B | 3B | HR | HR % | R | RBI | BB | SO | SB | BA | SA | AB | H | G by POS |
|---|---|---|---|---|---|---|---|---|---|---|---|---|---|---|---|---|---|
| 1884 C-P U | 71 | 279 | 69 | 15 | 4 | 0 | 0.0 | 35 | | 11 | | | | .247 | .330 | 0 | 0 | C-52, OF-20, SS-1, 1B-1 |
| 1885 2 teams | | CHI | N (1G – | .000) | | BKN | AA (17G – | .150) | | | | | | | | | |
| " total | 18 | 63 | 9 | 4 | 0 | 1 | 1.6 | 7 | | 2 | 2 | | .143 | .254 | 0 | 0 | C-12, 1B-5, OF-1 |
| 1886 WAS N | 27 | 98 | 25 | 6 | 3 | 1 | 1.0 | 11 | 15 | 3 | 12 | | .255 | .408 | 0 | 0 | 1B-27 |
| 1887 | 25 | 95 | 24 | 4 | 1 | 2 | 2.1 | 9 | 17 | 7 | 5 | 2 | .253 | .379 | 0 | 0 | 1B-16, OF-9 |
| 4 yrs. | 141 | 535 | 127 | 29 | 8 | 4 | 0.7 | 62 | 31 | 23 | 19 | 2 | .237 | .344 | 0 | 0 | C-64, 1B-49, OF-30, SS-1 |
| 1 yr. | 1 | 3 | 0 | 0 | 0 | 0 | 0.0 | 0 | 0 | 0 | 0 | 2 | .000 | .000 | 0 | 0 | OF-1 |

## Mickey Krietner

KRIETNER, ALBERT JOSEPH
B. Oct. 10, 1922, Nashville, Tenn.

BR  TR  6'3"  190 lbs.

| | G | AB | H | 2B | 3B | HR | HR % | R | RBI | BB | SO | SB | BA | SA | AB | H | G by POS |
|---|---|---|---|---|---|---|---|---|---|---|---|---|---|---|---|---|---|
| 1943 CHI N | 3 | 8 | 3 | 0 | 0 | 0 | 0.0 | 0 | 2 | 1 | 2 | 0 | .375 | .375 | 0 | 0 | C-3 |
| 1944 | 39 | 85 | 13 | 2 | 0 | 0 | 0.0 | 3 | 1 | 8 | 16 | 0 | .153 | .176 | 0 | 0 | C-39 |
| 2 yrs. | 42 | 93 | 16 | 2 | 0 | 0 | 0.0 | 3 | 3 | 9 | 18 | 0 | .172 | .194 | 0 | 0 | C-42 |
| 2 yrs. | 42 | 93 | 16 | 2 | 0 | 0 | 0.0 | 3 | 3 | 9 | 18 | 0 | .172 | .194 | 0 | 0 | C-42 |

## Chris Krug

KRUG, EVERETT BEN
B. Dec. 25, 1939, Los Angeles, Calif.

BR  TR  6'4"  200 lbs.

| | G | AB | H | 2B | 3B | HR | HR % | R | RBI | BB | SO | SB | BA | SA | AB | H | G by POS |
|---|---|---|---|---|---|---|---|---|---|---|---|---|---|---|---|---|---|
| 1965 CHI N | 60 | 169 | 34 | 5 | 0 | 5 | 3.0 | 16 | 24 | 13 | 52 | 0 | .201 | .320 | 3 | 0 | C-58 |
| 1966 | 11 | 28 | 6 | 1 | 0 | 0 | 0.0 | 1 | 1 | 1 | 8 | 0 | .214 | .250 | 1 | 0 | C-10 |
| 1969 SD N | 8 | 17 | 1 | 0 | 0 | 0 | 0.0 | 0 | 0 | 1 | 6 | 0 | .059 | .059 | 1 | 0 | C-7 |
| 3 yrs. | 79 | 214 | 41 | 6 | 0 | 5 | 2.3 | 17 | 25 | 15 | 66 | 0 | .192 | .290 | 5 | 0 | C-75 |
| 2 yrs. | 71 | 197 | 40 | 6 | 0 | 5 | 2.5 | 17 | 25 | 14 | 60 | 0 | .203 | .310 | 4 | 0 | C-68 |

| | G | AB | H | 2B | 3B | HR | HR % | R | RBI | BB | SO | SB | BA | SA | Pinch Hit AB | Pinch Hit H | G by POS |
|---|---|---|---|---|---|---|---|---|---|---|---|---|---|---|---|---|---|

## Gary Krug

**KRUG, GARY EUGENE**
B. Feb. 12, 1955, Garden City, Kans.

BL TL 6'4"    225 lbs.

| | G | AB | H | 2B | 3B | HR | HR% | R | RBI | BB | SO | SB | BA | SA | PH AB | PH H | G by POS |
|---|---|---|---|---|---|---|---|---|---|---|---|---|---|---|---|---|---|
| 1981 CHI N | 7 | 5 | 2 | 0 | 0 | 0 | 0.0 | 0 | 0 | 1 | 1 | 0 | .400 | .400 | 5 | 2 | |

## Marty Krug

**KRUG, MARTIN JOHN**
B. Sept. 10, 1888, Coblenz, Germany    D. June 27, 1966, Glendale, Calif.

BR TR 5'9"    165 lbs.

| | G | AB | H | 2B | 3B | HR | HR% | R | RBI | BB | SO | SB | BA | SA | PH AB | PH H | G by POS |
|---|---|---|---|---|---|---|---|---|---|---|---|---|---|---|---|---|---|
| 1912 BOS A | 16 | 39 | 12 | 2 | 1 | 0 | 0.0 | 6 | 7 | 5 | | 2 | .308 | .410 | 2 | 0 | SS-9, 2B-4 |
| 1922 CHI N | 127 | 450 | 124 | 23 | 4 | 4 | 0.9 | 67 | 60 | 43 | 43 | 7 | .276 | .371 | 0 | 0 | 3B-104, 2B-23, SS-1 |
| 2 yrs. | 143 | 489 | 136 | 25 | 5 | 4 | 0.8 | 73 | 67 | 48 | 43 | 9 | .278 | .374 | 2 | 0 | 3B-104, 2B-27, SS-10 |
| 1 yr. | 127 | 450 | 124 | 23 | 4 | 4 | 0.9 | 67 | 60 | 43 | 43 | 7 | .276 | .371 | 0 | 0 | 3B-104, 2B-23, SS-1 |

## Harvey Kuenn

**KUENN, HARVEY EDWARD**
B. Dec. 4, 1930, Milwaukee, Wis.
Manager 1975, 1982-83.

BR TR 6'2"    187 lbs.

| | G | AB | H | 2B | 3B | HR | HR% | R | RBI | BB | SO | SB | BA | SA | PH AB | PH H | G by POS |
|---|---|---|---|---|---|---|---|---|---|---|---|---|---|---|---|---|---|
| 1952 DET A | 19 | 80 | 26 | 2 | 2 | 0 | 0.0 | 2 | 8 | 2 | 1 | 2 | .325 | .400 | 0 | 0 | SS-19 |
| 1953 | 155 | 679 | 209 | 33 | 7 | 2 | 0.3 | 94 | 48 | 50 | 31 | 6 | .308 | .386 | 0 | 0 | SS-155 |
| 1954 | 155 | 656 | 201 | 28 | 6 | 5 | 0.8 | 81 | 48 | 29 | 13 | 9 | .306 | .390 | 0 | 0 | SS-155 |
| 1955 | 145 | 620 | 190 | 38 | 5 | 8 | 1.3 | 101 | 62 | 40 | 27 | 8 | .306 | .423 | 4 | 1 | SS-141 |
| 1956 | 146 | 591 | 196 | 32 | 7 | 12 | 2.0 | 96 | 88 | 55 | 34 | 9 | .332 | .470 | 6 | 1 | SS-141, OF-1 |
| 1957 | 151 | 624 | 173 | 30 | 6 | 9 | 1.4 | 74 | 44 | 47 | 28 | 5 | .277 | .388 | 1 | 0 | SS-136, 3B-17, 1B-1 |
| 1958 | 139 | 561 | 179 | 39 | 3 | 8 | 1.4 | 73 | 54 | 51 | 34 | 5 | .319 | .442 | 1 | 1 | OF-138 |
| 1959 | 139 | 561 | 198 | 42 | 7 | 9 | 1.6 | 99 | 71 | 48 | 37 | 7 | .353 | .501 | 1 | 0 | OF-137 |
| 1960 CLE A | 126 | 474 | 146 | 24 | 0 | 9 | 1.9 | 65 | 54 | 55 | 25 | 3 | .308 | .416 | 4 | 1 | OF-119, 3B-5 |
| 1961 SF N | 131 | 471 | 125 | 22 | 4 | 5 | 1.1 | 60 | 46 | 47 | 34 | 5 | .265 | .361 | 10 | 4 | OF-93, 3B-32, SS-1 |
| 1962 | 130 | 487 | 148 | 23 | 5 | 10 | 2.1 | 73 | 68 | 49 | 37 | 9 | .304 | .433 | 9 | 2 | OF-105, 3B-30 |
| 1963 | 120 | 417 | 121 | 13 | 2 | 6 | 1.4 | 61 | 31 | 44 | 38 | 2 | .290 | .384 | 14 | 2 | OF-64, 3B-53 |
| 1964 | 111 | 351 | 92 | 16 | 2 | 4 | 1.1 | 42 | 22 | 35 | 32 | 0 | .262 | .353 | 17 | 5 | OF-88, 1B-11, 3B-2 |
| 1965 2 teams | SF | N (23G – | .237) | | CHI | N | (54G – | .217) | | | | | | | | | |
| " total | 77 | 179 | 40 | 5 | 0 | 0 | 0.0 | 15 | 12 | 32 | 16 | 4 | .223 | .251 | 25 | 7 | OF-49, 1B-8 |
| 1966 2 teams | CHI | N (3G – | .333) | | PHI | N | (86G – | .296) | | | | | | | | | |
| " total | 89 | 162 | 48 | 9 | 0 | 0 | 0.0 | 15 | 15 | 10 | 17 | 0 | .296 | .352 | 48 | 11 | OF-32, 1B-13, 3B-1 |
| 15 yrs. | 1833 | 6913 | 2092 | 356 | 56 | 87 | 1.3 | 951 | 671 | 594 | 404 | 68 | .303 | .408 | 141 | 35 | OF-826, SS-748, 3B-140, 1B-33 |
| 2 yrs. | 57 | 123 | 27 | 5 | 0 | 0 | 0.0 | 11 | 6 | 22 | 14 | 1 | .220 | .260 | 25 | 6 | OF-36, 1B-1 |
| WORLD SERIES | | | | | | | | | | | | | | | | | |
| 1962 SF N | 4 | 12 | 1 | 0 | 0 | 0 | 0.0 | 1 | 0 | 1 | 1 | 0 | .083 | .083 | 0 | 0 | OF-4 |

## Pete LaCock

**LaCOCK, RALPH PIERRE II**
B. Jan. 17, 1952, Burbank, Calif.

BL TL 6'2"    200 lbs.

| | G | AB | H | 2B | 3B | HR | HR% | R | RBI | BB | SO | SB | BA | SA | PH AB | PH H | G by POS |
|---|---|---|---|---|---|---|---|---|---|---|---|---|---|---|---|---|---|
| 1972 CHI N | 5 | 6 | 3 | 0 | 0 | 0 | 0.0 | 3 | 4 | 0 | 1 | 1 | .500 | .500 | 1 | 1 | OF-3 |
| 1973 | 11 | 16 | 4 | 1 | 0 | 0 | 0.0 | 1 | 3 | 1 | 2 | 0 | .250 | .313 | 7 | 3 | OF-5 |
| 1974 | 35 | 110 | 20 | 4 | 1 | 1 | 0.9 | 9 | 8 | 12 | 16 | 0 | .182 | .264 | 4 | 1 | OF-22, 1B-11 |
| 1975 | 106 | 249 | 57 | 8 | 1 | 6 | 2.4 | 30 | 30 | 37 | 27 | 0 | .229 | .341 | 26 | 9 | 1B-53, OF-26 |
| 1976 | 106 | 244 | 54 | 9 | 2 | 8 | 3.3 | 34 | 28 | 42 | 37 | 1 | .221 | .373 | 39 | 7 | 1B-54, OF-19 |
| 1977 KC A | 88 | 218 | 66 | 12 | 1 | 3 | 1.4 | 25 | 29 | 15 | 25 | 2 | .303 | .408 | 22 | 8 | 1B-29, DH-26, OF-12 |
| 1978 | 118 | 322 | 95 | 21 | 2 | 5 | 1.6 | 44 | 48 | 21 | 27 | 1 | .295 | .419 | 23 | 3 | 1B-106 |
| 1979 | 132 | 408 | 113 | 25 | 4 | 3 | 0.7 | 54 | 56 | 37 | 26 | 2 | .277 | .380 | 18 | 3 | 1B-108, DH-16 |
| 1980 | 114 | 156 | 32 | 6 | 0 | 1 | 0.6 | 14 | 18 | 17 | 10 | 1 | .205 | .263 | 12 | 5 | 1B-86, OF-29 |
| 9 yrs. | 715 | 1729 | 444 | 86 | 11 | 27 | 1.6 | 214 | 224 | 182 | 171 | 8 | .257 | .366 | 152 | 40 | 1B-447, OF-116, DH-42 |
| 5 yrs. | 263 | 625 | 138 | 22 | 4 | 15 | 2.4 | 77 | 73 | 92 | 83 | 2 | .221 | .341 | 77 | 21 | 1B-118, OF-75 |
| LEAGUE CHAMPIONSHIP SERIES | | | | | | | | | | | | | | | | | |
| 1977 KC A | 1 | 1 | 0 | 0 | 0 | 0 | 0.0 | 0 | 0 | 1 | 1 | 0 | .000 | .000 | 1 | 0 | 1B-1 |
| 1978 | 4 | 11 | 4 | 2 | 1 | 0 | 0.0 | 1 | 1 | 3 | 1 | 1 | .364 | .727 | 1 | 0 | 1B-3 |
| 1980 | 1 | 0 | 0 | 0 | 0 | – | | 0 | 0 | 0 | 0 | 0 | – | – | 0 | 0 | 1B-1 |
| 3 yrs. | 6 | 12 | 4 | 2 | 1 | 0 | 0.0 | 1 | 1 | 4 | 2 | 1 | .333 | .667 | 2 | 0 | 1B-5 |
| WORLD SERIES | | | | | | | | | | | | | | | | | |
| 1980 KC A | 1 | 0 | 0 | 0 | 0 | 0 | – | 0 | 0 | 0 | 0 | 0 | – | – | 0 | 0 | 1B-1 |

## Steve Lake

**LAKE, STEVEN MICHAEL**
B. Mar. 14, 1957, Inglewood, Calif.

BR TR 6'1"    180 lbs.

| | G | AB | H | 2B | 3B | HR | HR% | R | RBI | BB | SO | SB | BA | SA | PH AB | PH H | G by POS |
|---|---|---|---|---|---|---|---|---|---|---|---|---|---|---|---|---|---|
| 1983 CHI N | 38 | 85 | 22 | 4 | 1 | 1 | 1.2 | 9 | 7 | 2 | 6 | 0 | .259 | .365 | 5 | 0 | C-32 |
| 1984 | 25 | 54 | 12 | 4 | 0 | 2 | 3.7 | 4 | 7 | 0 | 7 | 0 | .222 | .407 | 1 | 0 | C-24 |
| 1985 | 58 | 119 | 18 | 2 | 0 | 1 | 0.8 | 5 | 11 | 3 | 21 | 1 | .151 | .193 | 4 | 1 | C-55 |
| 3 yrs. | 121 | 258 | 52 | 10 | 1 | 4 | 1.6 | 18 | 25 | 5 | 34 | 1 | .202 | .295 | 10 | 1 | C-111 |
| 3 yrs. | 121 | 258 | 52 | 10 | 1 | 4 | 1.6 | 18 | 25 | 5 | 34 | 1 | .202 | .295 | 10 | 1 | C-111 |
| LEAGUE CHAMPIONSHIP SERIES | | | | | | | | | | | | | | | | | |
| 1984 CHI N | 1 | 1 | 1 | 0 | 0 | 0 | 0.0 | 0 | 0 | 0 | 0 | 0 | 1.000 | 2.000 | 0 | 0 | C-1 |

## Pete Lamer

**LAMER, PIERRE**
B. 1874, Hoboken, N. J.    D. Oct. 24, 1931, Brooklyn, N. Y.

TR

| | G | AB | H | 2B | 3B | HR | HR% | R | RBI | BB | SO | SB | BA | SA | PH AB | PH H | G by POS |
|---|---|---|---|---|---|---|---|---|---|---|---|---|---|---|---|---|---|
| 1902 CHI N | 2 | 9 | 2 | 0 | 0 | 0 | 0.0 | 2 | 0 | 0 | | 0 | .222 | .222 | 0 | 0 | C-2 |
| 1907 CIN N | 1 | 2 | 0 | 0 | 0 | 0 | 0.0 | 0 | 0 | 0 | | 0 | .000 | .000 | 0 | 0 | C-1 |
| 2 yrs. | 3 | 11 | 2 | 0 | 0 | 0 | 0.0 | 2 | 0 | 0 | | 0 | .182 | .182 | 0 | 0 | C-3 |
| 1 yr. | 2 | 9 | 2 | 0 | 0 | 0 | 0.0 | 2 | 0 | 0 | | 0 | .222 | .222 | 0 | 0 | C-2 |

## Hobie Landrith

**LANDRITH, HOBERT NEAL**
B. Mar. 16, 1930, Decatur, Ill.

BL TR 5'10"    170 lbs.

| | G | AB | H | 2B | 3B | HR | HR% | R | RBI | BB | SO | SB | BA | SA | PH AB | PH H | G by POS |
|---|---|---|---|---|---|---|---|---|---|---|---|---|---|---|---|---|---|
| 1950 CIN N | 4 | 14 | 3 | 0 | 0 | 0 | 0.0 | 1 | 1 | 2 | 1 | 0 | .214 | .214 | 0 | 0 | C-4 |
| 1951 | 4 | 13 | 5 | 1 | 0 | 0 | 0.0 | 3 | 0 | 1 | 1 | 0 | .385 | .462 | 0 | 0 | C-4 |

| | G | AB | H | 2B | 3B | HR | HR % | R | RBI | BB | SO | SB | BA | SA | Pinch Hit AB | Pinch Hit H | G by POS |
|---|---|---|---|---|---|---|---|---|---|---|---|---|---|---|---|---|---|

## Hobie Landrith continued

| | | G | AB | H | 2B | 3B | HR | HR % | R | RBI | BB | SO | SB | BA | SA | AB | H | G by POS |
|---|---|---|---|---|---|---|---|---|---|---|---|---|---|---|---|---|---|---|
| 1952 | | 15 | 50 | 13 | 4 | 0 | 0 | 0.0 | 1 | 4 | 0 | 4 | 0 | .260 | .340 | 1 | 1 | C-14 |
| 1953 | | 52 | 154 | 37 | 3 | 1 | 3 | 1.9 | 15 | 16 | 12 | 8 | 2 | .240 | .331 | 4 | 2 | C-47 |
| 1954 | | 48 | 81 | 16 | 0 | 0 | 5 | 6.2 | 12 | 14 | 18 | 9 | 1 | .198 | .383 | 5 | 2 | C-42 |
| 1955 | | 43 | 87 | 22 | 3 | 0 | 4 | 4.6 | 9 | 7 | 10 | 14 | 0 | .253 | .425 | 16 | 3 | C-27 |
| 1956 CHI N | | 111 | 312 | 69 | 10 | 3 | 4 | 1.3 | 22 | 32 | 39 | 38 | 0 | .221 | .311 | 15 | 4 | C-99 |
| 1957 STL N | | 75 | 214 | 52 | 6 | 0 | 3 | 1.4 | 18 | 26 | 25 | 27 | 1 | .243 | .313 | 10 | 1 | C-67 |
| 1958 | | 70 | 144 | 31 | 4 | 0 | 3 | 2.1 | 9 | 13 | 26 | 21 | 0 | .215 | .306 | 24 | 5 | C-45 |
| 1959 SF N | | 109 | 283 | 71 | 14 | 0 | 3 | 1.1 | 30 | 29 | 43 | 23 | 0 | .251 | .332 | 2 | 1 | C-109 |
| 1960 | | 71 | 190 | 46 | 10 | 0 | 1 | 0.5 | 18 | 20 | 23 | 11 | 1 | .242 | .311 | 2 | 0 | C-70 |
| 1961 | | 43 | 71 | 17 | 4 | 0 | 2 | 2.8 | 11 | 10 | 12 | 7 | 0 | .239 | .380 | 13 | 2 | C-30 |
| 1962 2 teams | | NY | N (23G – .289) | | | BAL | A | (60G – .222) | | | | | | | | | | |
| " total | | 83 | 212 | 50 | 7 | 1 | 5 | 2.4 | 24 | 24 | 27 | 12 | 0 | .236 | .349 | 2 | 0 | C-81 |
| 1963 2 teams | | BAL | A (2G – .000) | | | WAS | A | (42G – .175) | | | | | | | | | | |
| " total | | 44 | 104 | 18 | 3 | 0 | 1 | 1.0 | 6 | 7 | 15 | 12 | 0 | .173 | .231 | 7 | 0 | C-38 |
| 14 yrs. | | 772 | 1929 | 450 | 69 | 5 | 34 | 1.8 | 179 | 203 | 253 | 188 | 5 | .233 | .327 | 101 | 21 | C-677 |
| 1 yr. | | 111 | 312 | 69 | 10 | 3 | 4 | 1.3 | 22 | 32 | 39 | 38 | 0 | .221 | .311 | 15 | 4 | C-99 |

## Don Landrum

**LANDRUM, DONALD LeROY**
B. Feb. 16, 1936, Santa Rosa, Calif.

BL TR 6'  180 lbs.

| | | G | AB | H | 2B | 3B | HR | HR % | R | RBI | BB | SO | SB | BA | SA | AB | H | G by POS |
|---|---|---|---|---|---|---|---|---|---|---|---|---|---|---|---|---|---|---|
| 1957 PHI N | | 2 | 7 | 1 | 1 | 0 | 0 | 0.0 | 1 | 0 | 2 | 1 | 0 | .143 | .286 | 0 | 0 | OF-2 |
| 1960 STL N | | 13 | 49 | 12 | 0 | 1 | 2 | 4.1 | 7 | 3 | 4 | 6 | 3 | .245 | .408 | 0 | 0 | OF-13 |
| 1961 | | 28 | 66 | 11 | 2 | 0 | 1 | 1.5 | 5 | 3 | 5 | 14 | 1 | .167 | .242 | 1 | 0 | OF-25, 2B-1 |
| 1962 2 teams | | STL | N (32G – .314) | | | CHI | N | (83G – .282) | | | | | | | | | | |
| " total | | 115 | 273 | 78 | 5 | 2 | 1 | 0.4 | 40 | 18 | 34 | 33 | 11 | .286 | .330 | 20 | 2 | OF-85 |
| 1963 CHI N | | 84 | 227 | 55 | 4 | 1 | 1 | 0.4 | 27 | 10 | 13 | 42 | 6 | .242 | .282 | 24 | 3 | OF-57 |
| 1964 | | 11 | 11 | 0 | 0 | 0 | 0 | 0.0 | 2 | 0 | 1 | 2 | 0 | .000 | .000 | 8 | 0 | OF-1 |
| 1965 | | 131 | 425 | 96 | 20 | 4 | 6 | 1.4 | 60 | 34 | 36 | 84 | 14 | .226 | .334 | 15 | 2 | OF-115 |
| 1966 SF N | | 72 | 102 | 19 | 4 | 0 | 1 | 1.0 | 9 | 7 | 9 | 18 | 1 | .186 | .255 | 18 | 2 | OF-54 |
| 8 yrs. | | 456 | 1160 | 272 | 36 | 8 | 12 | 1.0 | 151 | 75 | 104 | 200 | 36 | .234 | .310 | 86 | 9 | OF-352, 2B-1 |
| 4 yrs. | | 309 | 901 | 218 | 29 | 7 | 8 | 0.9 | 118 | 59 | 80 | 159 | 29 | .242 | .316 | 64 | 7 | OF-232 |

## Bill Lange

**LANGE, WILLIAM ALEXANDER (Little Eva)**
B. June 6, 1871, San Francisco, Calif.    D. July 23, 1950, San Francisco, Calif.

BR TR 6'1"  180 lbs.

| | | G | AB | H | 2B | 3B | HR | HR % | R | RBI | BB | SO | SB | BA | SA | AB | H | G by POS |
|---|---|---|---|---|---|---|---|---|---|---|---|---|---|---|---|---|---|---|
| 1893 CHI N | | 117 | 469 | 132 | 8 | 7 | 8 | 1.7 | 92 | 88 | 52 | 20 | 47 | .281 | .380 | 0 | 0 | 2B-57, OF-40, 3B-8, SS-7, C-7 |
| 1894 | | 111 | 442 | 145 | 16 | 9 | 6 | 1.4 | 84 | 90 | 56 | 18 | 65 | .328 | .446 | 0 | 0 | OF-109, SS-2, 3B-1 |
| 1895 | | 123 | 478 | 186 | 27 | 16 | 10 | 2.1 | 120 | 98 | 55 | 24 | 67 | .389 | .575 | 0 | 0 | OF-123 |
| 1896 | | 122 | 469 | 153 | 21 | 16 | 4 | 0.9 | 114 | 92 | 65 | 24 | 84 | .326 | .465 | 0 | 0 | OF-121, C-1 |
| 1897 | | 118 | 479 | 163 | 24 | 14 | 5 | 1.0 | 119 | 83 | 48 | | 73 | .340 | .480 | 0 | 0 | OF-118 |
| 1898 | | 113 | 442 | 141 | 16 | 10 | 6 | 1.4 | 79 | 69 | 36 | | 22 | .319 | .441 | 0 | 0 | OF-111, 1B-2 |
| 1899 | | 107 | 416 | 135 | 21 | 7 | 1 | 0.2 | 81 | 58 | 38 | | 41 | .325 | .416 | 0 | 0 | OF-94, 1B-14 |
| 7 yrs. | | 811 | 3195 | 1055 | 133 | 79 | 40 | 1.3 | 689 | 578 | 350 | 86 | 399 | .330 | .459 | 0 | 0 | OF-716, 2B-57, 1B-16, SS-9, 3B-9, C-8 |
| 7 yrs. | | 811 | 3195 | 1055 | 133 | 79 | 40 | 1.3 | 689 | 578 | 350 | 86 | 399 | .330 **3rd** | .459 | 0 | 0 | OF-716, 2B-57, 1B-16, SS-9, 3B-9, C-8 |

## Terry Larkin

**LARKIN, FRANK S.**
B. New York, N. Y.    D. Sept. 16, 1894, Brooklyn, N. Y.

BR TR

| | | G | AB | H | 2B | 3B | HR | HR % | R | RBI | BB | SO | SB | BA | SA | AB | H | G by POS |
|---|---|---|---|---|---|---|---|---|---|---|---|---|---|---|---|---|---|---|
| 1876 NY N | | 1 | 4 | 0 | 0 | 0 | 0 | 0.0 | 0 | 0 | 0 | 0 | | .000 | .000 | 0 | 0 | P-1 |
| 1877 HAR N | | 58 | 228 | 52 | 6 | 5 | 1 | 0.4 | 28 | 18 | 5 | 23 | | .228 | .311 | 0 | 0 | P-56, 3B-2, 2B-1 |
| 1878 CHI N | | 58 | 226 | 65 | 9 | 4 | 0 | 0.0 | 33 | 32 | 17 | 17 | | .288 | .363 | 0 | 0 | P-56, OF-1, 3B-1 |
| 1879 | | 60 | 228 | 50 | 12 | 2 | 0 | 0.0 | 26 | 18 | 8 | 24 | | .219 | .289 | 0 | 0 | P-58, OF-3 |
| 1880 TRO N | | 6 | 20 | 3 | 1 | 0 | 0 | 0.0 | 1 | | 3 | 4 | | .150 | .200 | 0 | 0 | P-5, OF-2, SS-1 |
| 1884 2 teams | | WAS | U (17G – .243) | | | RIC | AA | (40G – .201) | | | | | | | | | | |
| " total | | 57 | 209 | 45 | 1 | 4 | 0 | 0.0 | 28 | | 13 | | | .215 | .258 | 0 | 0 | 2B-40, 3B-17 |
| 6 yrs. | | 240 | 915 | 215 | 29 | 15 | 1 | 0.1 | 116 | 68 | 46 | 68 | | .235 | .303 | 0 | 0 | P-176, 2B-41, 3B-20, OF-6, SS-1 |
| 2 yrs. | | 118 | 454 | 115 | 21 | 6 | 0 | 0.0 | 59 | 50 | 25 | 41 | | .253 | .326 | 0 | 0 | P-114, OF-4, 3B-1 |

## Vic LaRose

**LaROSE, VICTOR RAYMOND**
B. Dec. 23, 1944, Los Angeles, Calif.

BR TR 5'11"  180 lbs.

| | | G | AB | H | 2B | 3B | HR | HR % | R | RBI | BB | SO | SB | BA | SA | AB | H | G by POS |
|---|---|---|---|---|---|---|---|---|---|---|---|---|---|---|---|---|---|---|
| 1968 CHI N | | 4 | 2 | 0 | 0 | 0 | 0 | 0.0 | 0 | 0 | 0 | 1 | 0 | .000 | .000 | 0 | 0 | SS-2, 2B-2 |

## Don Larsen

**LARSEN, DONALD JAMES**
B. Aug. 7, 1929, Michigan City, Ind.

BR TR 6'4"  215 lbs.

| | | G | AB | H | 2B | 3B | HR | HR % | R | RBI | BB | SO | SB | BA | SA | AB | H | G by POS |
|---|---|---|---|---|---|---|---|---|---|---|---|---|---|---|---|---|---|---|
| 1953 STL A | | 50 | 81 | 23 | 3 | 1 | 3 | 3.7 | 11 | 10 | 4 | 14 | 0 | .284 | .457 | 10 | 1 | P-38, OF-1 |
| 1954 BAL A | | 44 | 88 | 22 | 5 | 3 | 1 | 1.1 | 6 | 4 | 5 | 15 | 0 | .250 | .409 | 15 | 0 | P-29 |
| 1955 NY A | | 21 | 41 | 6 | 1 | 0 | 2 | 4.9 | 4 | 7 | 4 | 13 | 0 | .146 | .317 | 3 | 1 | P-19 |
| 1956 | | 45 | 79 | 19 | 5 | 0 | 2 | 2.5 | 10 | 12 | 6 | 17 | 0 | .241 | .380 | 7 | 2 | P-38 |
| 1957 | | 31 | 56 | 14 | 5 | 0 | 0 | 0.0 | 6 | 5 | 6 | 11 | 0 | .250 | .339 | 1 | 0 | P-27 |
| 1958 | | 28 | 49 | 15 | 1 | 0 | 4 | 8.2 | 9 | 13 | 5 | 9 | 0 | .306 | .571 | 7 | 2 | P-19 |
| 1959 | | 29 | 47 | 12 | 2 | 0 | 0 | 0.0 | 8 | 8 | 7 | 15 | 0 | .255 | .298 | 3 | 1 | P-25 |
| 1960 KC A | | 23 | 29 | 6 | 1 | 0 | 0 | 0.0 | 3 | 3 | 0 | 11 | 0 | .207 | .241 | 1 | 0 | P-22 |
| 1961 2 teams | | KC | A (18G – .300) | | | CHI | A | (25G – .320) | | | | | | | | | | |
| " total | | 43 | 45 | 14 | 0 | 0 | 2 | 4.4 | 4 | 8 | 1 | 10 | 0 | .311 | .444 | 12 | 5 | P-33, OF-1 |
| 1962 SF N | | 52 | 25 | 5 | 0 | 1 | 0 | 0.0 | 3 | 1 | 1 | 7 | 0 | .200 | .280 | 4 | 0 | P-49 |
| 1963 | | 46 | 11 | 2 | 0 | 0 | 0 | 0.0 | 1 | 0 | 1 | 1 | 0 | .182 | .182 | 0 | 0 | P-46 |
| 1964 2 teams | | SF | N (6G – .000) | | | HOU | N | (31G – .097) | | | | | | | | | | |
| " total | | 37 | 32 | 3 | 1 | 0 | 0 | 0.0 | 0 | 0 | 4 | 10 | 0 | .094 | .125 | 3 | 0 | P-36 |
| 1965 2 teams | | HOU | N (1G – .000) | | | BAL | A | (27G – .273) | | | | | | | | | | |
| " total | | 28 | 13 | 3 | 1 | 0 | 0 | 0.0 | 1 | 1 | 0 | 5 | 0 | .231 | .308 | 0 | 0 | P-28 |

| | G | AB | H | 2B | 3B | HR | HR % | R | RBI | BB | SO | SB | BA | SA | Pinch Hit AB | Pinch Hit H | G by POS |
|---|---|---|---|---|---|---|---|---|---|---|---|---|---|---|---|---|---|

## Don Larsen  continued

| | G | AB | H | 2B | 3B | HR | HR % | R | RBI | BB | SO | SB | BA | SA | PH AB | PH H | G by POS |
|---|---|---|---|---|---|---|---|---|---|---|---|---|---|---|---|---|---|
| 1967 CHI N | 3 | 0 | 0 | 0 | 0 | 0 | – | 0 | 0 | 0 | 0 | 0 | – | – | 0 | 0 | P-3 |
| 14 yrs. | 480 | 596 | 144 | 25 | 5 | 14 | 2.3 | 65 | 72 | 43 | 138 | 0 | .242 | .371 | 66 | 12 | P-412, OF-2 |
| 1 yr. | 3 | 0 | 0 | 0 | 0 | 0 | – | 0 | 0 | 0 | 0 | 0 | – | – | 0 | 0 | P-3 |
| **WORLD SERIES** | | | | | | | | | | | | | | | | | |
| 1955 NY A | 1 | 2 | 0 | 0 | 0 | 0 | 0.0 | 0 | 0 | 0 | 0 | 0 | .000 | .000 | 0 | 0 | P-1 |
| 1956 | 2 | 3 | 1 | 0 | 0 | 0 | 0.0 | 1 | 1 | 0 | 1 | 0 | .333 | .333 | 0 | 0 | P-2 |
| 1957 | 2 | 2 | 0 | 0 | 0 | 0 | 0.0 | 1 | 0 | 2 | 1 | 0 | .000 | .000 | 0 | 0 | P-2 |
| 1958 | 2 | 2 | 0 | 0 | 0 | 0 | 0.0 | 0 | 0 | 1 | 0 | 0 | .000 | .000 | 0 | 0 | P-2 |
| 1962 SF N | 3 | 0 | 0 | 0 | 0 | 0 | – | 0 | 0 | 0 | 0 | 0 | – | – | 0 | 0 | P-3 |
| 5 yrs. | 10 | 9 | 1 | 0 | 0 | 0 | 0.0 | 2 | 1 | 3 | 2 | 0 | .111 | .111 | 0 | 0 | P-10 |

## Tony LaRussa

**LaRUSSA, ANTHONY**
B. Oct. 4, 1944, Tampa, Fla.
Manager 1979-85.

BR TR 6'          175 lbs.

| | G | AB | H | 2B | 3B | HR | HR % | R | RBI | BB | SO | SB | BA | SA | PH AB | PH H | G by POS |
|---|---|---|---|---|---|---|---|---|---|---|---|---|---|---|---|---|---|
| 1963 KC A | 34 | 44 | 11 | 1 | 1 | 0 | 0.0 | 4 | 1 | 7 | 12 | 0 | .250 | .318 | 1 | 1 | SS-14, 2B-3 |
| 1968 OAK A | 5 | 3 | 1 | 0 | 0 | 0 | 0.0 | 0 | 0 | 0 | 0 | 0 | .333 | .333 | 3 | 1 | |
| 1969 | 8 | 8 | 0 | 0 | 0 | 0 | 0.0 | 0 | 0 | 0 | 1 | 0 | .000 | .000 | 8 | 0 | |
| 1970 | 52 | 106 | 21 | 4 | 1 | 0 | 0.0 | 6 | 6 | 15 | 19 | 0 | .198 | .255 | 11 | 2 | 2B-44 |
| 1971 2 teams | | | OAK A (23G – .000) | | | | ATL N (9G – .286) | | | | | | | | | | |
| " total | 32 | 15 | 2 | 0 | 0 | 0 | 0.0 | 4 | 0 | 1 | 5 | 0 | .133 | .133 | 6 | 0 | 2B-16, SS-4, 3B-2 |
| 1973 CHI N | 1 | 0 | 0 | 0 | 0 | 0 | – | 1 | 0 | 0 | 0 | 0 | – | – | 0 | 0 | |
| 6 yrs. | 132 | 176 | 35 | 5 | 2 | 0 | 0.0 | 15 | 7 | 23 | 37 | 0 | .199 | .250 | 29 | 4 | 2B-63, SS-18, 3B-2 |
| 1 yr. | 1 | 0 | 0 | 0 | 0 | 0 | – | 1 | 0 | 0 | 0 | 0 | – | – | 0 | 0 | |

## Chuck Lauer

**LAUER, JOHN CHARLES**
B. 1865, Pittsburgh, Pa.    Deceased.

TR

| | G | AB | H | 2B | 3B | HR | HR % | R | RBI | BB | SO | SB | BA | SA | PH AB | PH H | G by POS |
|---|---|---|---|---|---|---|---|---|---|---|---|---|---|---|---|---|---|
| 1884 PIT AA | 13 | 44 | 5 | 0 | 0 | 0 | 0.0 | 5 | | 0 | | | .114 | .114 | 0 | 0 | OF-10, P-3, 1B-1 |
| 1889 PIT N | 4 | 16 | 3 | 0 | 0 | 0 | 0.0 | 2 | 1 | 0 | 5 | 0 | .188 | .188 | 0 | 0 | C-3, OF-1 |
| 1890 CHI N | 2 | 8 | 2 | 1 | 0 | 0 | 0.0 | 1 | 1 | 0 | 0 | 0 | .250 | .375 | 0 | 0 | C-2 |
| 3 yrs. | 19 | 68 | 10 | 1 | 0 | 0 | 0.0 | 8 | 2 | 0 | 5 | 0 | .147 | .162 | 0 | 0 | OF-11, C-5, P-3, 1B-1 |
| 1 yr. | 2 | 8 | 2 | 1 | 0 | 0 | 0.0 | 1 | 2 | 0 | 0 | 0 | .250 | .375 | 0 | 0 | C-2 |

## Tony Lazzeri

**LAZZERI, ANTHONY MICHAEL (Poosh 'Em Up)**
B. Dec. 6, 1903, San Francisco, Calif.   D. Aug. 6, 1946, San Francisco, Calif.

BR TR 5'11½" 170 lbs.

| | G | AB | H | 2B | 3B | HR | HR % | R | RBI | BB | SO | SB | BA | SA | PH AB | PH H | G by POS |
|---|---|---|---|---|---|---|---|---|---|---|---|---|---|---|---|---|---|
| 1926 NY A | 155 | 589 | 162 | 28 | 14 | 18 | 3.1 | 79 | 114 | 54 | 96 | 16 | .275 | .462 | 0 | 0 | 2B-149, SS-5, 3B-1 |
| 1927 | 153 | 570 | 176 | 29 | 8 | 18 | 3.2 | 92 | 102 | 69 | 82 | 22 | .309 | .482 | 0 | 0 | 2B-113, SS-38, 3B-9 |
| 1928 | 116 | 404 | 134 | 30 | 11 | 10 | 2.5 | 62 | 82 | 43 | 50 | 15 | .332 | .535 | 4 | 1 | 2B-116 |
| 1929 | 147 | 545 | 193 | 37 | 11 | 18 | 3.3 | 101 | 106 | 69 | 45 | 9 | .354 | .561 | 0 | 0 | 2B-147, SS-61 |
| 1930 | 143 | 571 | 173 | 34 | 15 | 9 | 1.6 | 109 | 121 | 60 | 62 | 4 | .303 | .462 | 1 | 0 | 2B-77, 3B-60, SS-8, OF-1, 1B-1 |
| 1931 | 135 | 484 | 129 | 27 | 7 | 8 | 1.7 | 67 | 83 | 79 | 80 | 18 | .267 | .401 | 7 | 5 | 2B-90, 3B-39 |
| 1932 | 141 | 510 | 153 | 28 | 16 | 15 | 2.9 | 79 | 113 | 82 | 64 | 11 | .300 | .506 | 3 | 1 | 2B-133, 3B-5 |
| 1933 | 139 | 523 | 154 | 22 | 12 | 18 | 3.4 | 94 | 104 | 73 | 62 | 15 | .294 | .486 | 1 | 0 | 2B-138 |
| 1934 | 123 | 438 | 117 | 24 | 6 | 14 | 3.2 | 59 | 67 | 71 | 64 | 11 | .267 | .445 | 1 | 1 | 2B-92, 3B-30 |
| 1935 | 130 | 477 | 130 | 18 | 6 | 13 | 2.7 | 72 | 83 | 63 | 75 | 11 | .273 | .417 | 3 | 1 | 2B-118, SS-9 |
| 1936 | 150 | 537 | 154 | 29 | 6 | 14 | 2.6 | 82 | 109 | 97 | 65 | 8 | .287 | .441 | 0 | 0 | 2B-148, SS-2 |
| 1937 | 126 | 446 | 109 | 21 | 3 | 14 | 3.1 | 56 | 70 | 71 | 76 | 7 | .244 | .399 | 1 | 0 | 2B-125 |
| 1938 CHI N | 54 | 120 | 32 | 5 | 0 | 5 | 4.2 | 21 | 23 | 22 | 30 | 0 | .267 | .433 | 14 | 2 | SS-25, 3B-7, 2B-4, OF-1 |
| 1939 2 teams | | | BKN N (14G – .282) | | | | NY N (13G – .295) | | | | | | | | | | |
| " total | 27 | 83 | 24 | 2 | 0 | 4 | 4.8 | 13 | 14 | 17 | 13 | 1 | .289 | .458 | 1 | 0 | 3B-15, 2B-11 |
| 14 yrs. | 1739 | 6297 | 1840 | 334 | 115 | 178 | 2.8 | 986 | 1191 | 870 | 864 | 148 | .292 | .467 | 38 | 13 | 2B-1461, 3B-166, SS-148, OF-2, 1B-1 |
| 1 yr. | 54 | 120 | 32 | 5 | 0 | 5 | 4.2 | 21 | 23 | 22 | 30 | 0 | .267 | .433 | 14 | 2 | SS-25, 3B-7, 2B-4, OF-1 |
| **WORLD SERIES** | | | | | | | | | | | | | | | | | |
| 1926 NY A | 7 | 26 | 5 | 1 | 0 | 0 | 0.0 | 2 | 3 | 1 | 6 | 0 | .192 | .231 | 0 | 0 | 2B-7 |
| 1927 | 4 | 15 | 4 | 1 | 0 | 0 | 0.0 | 1 | 2 | 1 | 4 | 0 | .267 | .333 | 0 | 0 | 2B-4 |
| 1928 | 4 | 12 | 3 | 1 | 0 | 0 | 0.0 | 2 | 0 | 1 | 0 | 2 | .250 | .333 | 0 | 0 | 2B-4 |
| 1932 | 4 | 17 | 5 | 0 | 0 | 2 | 11.8 | 4 | 5 | 2 | 1 | 0 | .294 | .647 | 0 | 0 | 2B-4 |
| 1936 | 6 | 20 | 5 | 0 | 0 | 1 | 5.0 | 4 | 7 | 4 | 4 | 0 | .250 | .400 | 0 | 0 | 2B-6 |
| 1937 | 5 | 15 | 6 | 0 | 1 | 1 | 6.7 | 3 | 2 | 3 | 3 | 0 | .400 | .733 | 0 | 0 | 2B-5 |
| 1938 CHI N | 2 | 2 | 0 | 0 | 0 | 0 | 0.0 | 0 | 0 | 0 | 1 | 0 | .000 | .000 | 2 | 0 | |
| 7 yrs. | 32 | 107 | 28 | 3 | 1 | 4 | 3.7 | 16 | 19 | 12 | 19 | 2 | .262 | .421 | 2 | 0 | 2B-30 |

## Tommy Leach

**LEACH, THOMAS WILLIAM**
B. Nov. 4, 1877, French Creek, N. Y.   D. Sept. 29, 1969, Haines City, Fla.

BR TR 5'6½" 150 lbs.

| | G | AB | H | 2B | 3B | HR | HR % | R | RBI | BB | SO | SB | BA | SA | PH AB | PH H | G by POS |
|---|---|---|---|---|---|---|---|---|---|---|---|---|---|---|---|---|---|
| 1898 LOU N | 3 | 10 | 3 | 0 | 0 | 0 | 0.0 | 0 | | | 0 | | .300 | .300 | 0 | 0 | 3B-3, 1B-1 |
| 1899 | 106 | 406 | 117 | 10 | 6 | 5 | 1.2 | 75 | 57 | 37 | | 19 | .288 | .379 | 0 | 0 | 3B-80, SS-25, 2B-2 |
| 1900 PIT N | 51 | 160 | 34 | 1 | 2 | 1 | 0.6 | 20 | 16 | 21 | | 8 | .213 | .263 | 1 | 0 | 3B-31, SS-8, 2B-7, OF-4 |
| 1901 | 98 | 374 | 112 | 13 | 13 | 1 | 0.3 | 64 | 44 | 20 | | 16 | .299 | .412 | 2 | 1 | 3B-92, SS-4 |
| 1902 | 135 | 514 | 144 | 21 | 22 | 6 | 1.2 | 97 | 85 | 45 | | 25 | .280 | .442 | 1 | 0 | 3B-134 |
| 1903 | 127 | 507 | 151 | 16 | 17 | 7 | 1.4 | 97 | 87 | 40 | | 22 | .298 | .438 | 0 | 0 | 3B-127 |
| 1904 | 146 | 579 | 149 | 15 | 12 | 2 | 0.3 | 92 | 56 | 45 | | 23 | .257 | .335 | 0 | 0 | 3B-146 |
| 1905 | 131 | 499 | 128 | 10 | 14 | 2 | 0.4 | 71 | 53 | 37 | | 17 | .257 | .345 | 0 | 0 | OF-71, 3B-58, SS-2, 2B-2 |
| 1906 | 133 | 476 | 136 | 10 | 7 | 1 | 0.2 | 66 | 39 | 33 | | 21 | .286 | .342 | 6 | 3 | 3B-65, OF-60, SS-1 |
| 1907 | 149 | 547 | 166 | 19 | 12 | 4 | 0.7 | 102 | 43 | 40 | | 21 | .303 | .404 | 0 | 0 | OF-111, 3B-33, SS-6, 2B-1 |
| 1908 | 152 | 583 | 151 | 24 | 16 | 5 | 0.9 | 93 | 43 | 54 | | 24 | .259 | .381 | 0 | 0 | 3B-150, OF-2 |
| 1909 | 151 | 587 | 153 | 29 | 8 | 6 | 1.0 | 126 | 43 | 66 | | 27 | .261 | .368 | 0 | 0 | OF-138, 3B-13 |
| 1910 | 135 | 529 | 143 | 24 | 5 | 4 | 0.8 | 83 | 52 | 38 | 62 | 18 | .270 | .357 | 1 | 0 | OF-131, SS-2, 3B-1 |
| 1911 | 108 | 386 | 92 | 12 | 6 | 3 | 0.8 | 60 | 43 | 46 | 50 | 19 | .238 | .324 | 4 | 0 | OF-89, SS-13, 3B-1 |
| 1912 2 teams | | | PIT N (28G – .299) | | | | CHI N (82G – .242) | | | | | | | | | | |
| " total | 110 | 362 | 93 | 14 | 5 | 2 | 0.6 | 74 | 67 | 29 | 20 | | .257 | .340 | 4 | 2 | OF-97, 3B-4 |
| 1913 CHI N | 130 | 454 | 131 | 23 | 10 | 6 | 1.3 | 99 | 32 | 77 | 44 | 21 | .289 | .423 | 7 | 3 | OF-119, 3B-2 |

| | G | AB | H | 2B | 3B | HR | HR % | R | RBI | BB | SO | SB | BA | SA | Pinch Hit AB | Pinch Hit H | G by POS |
|---|---|---|---|---|---|---|---|---|---|---|---|---|---|---|---|---|---|

## Tommy Leach continued

| | G | AB | H | 2B | 3B | HR | HR% | R | RBI | BB | SO | SB | BA | SA | PH AB | PH H | G by POS |
|---|---|---|---|---|---|---|---|---|---|---|---|---|---|---|---|---|---|
| 1914 | 153 | 577 | 152 | 24 | 9 | 7 | 1.2 | 80 | 46 | 79 | 50 | 16 | .263 | .373 | 1 | 0 | OF-137, 3B-16 |
| 1915 CIN N | 107 | 335 | 75 | 7 | 5 | 0 | 0.0 | 42 | 17 | 56 | 38 | 20 | .224 | .275 | 9 | 1 | OF-96 |
| 1918 PIT N | 30 | 72 | 14 | 2 | 3 | 0 | 0.0 | 14 | 5 | 19 | 5 | 2 | .194 | .306 | 2 | 0 | OF-23, SS-3 |
| 19 yrs. | 2155 | 7957 | 2144 | 274 | 172 | 62 | 0.8 | 1355 | 810 | 820 | 278 | 361 | .269 | .370 | 38 | 10 | OF-1078, 3B-955, SS-64, 2B-14 |
| 3 yrs. | 365 | 1296 | 347 | 57 | 22 | 15 | 1.2 | 229 | 110 | 211 | 114 | 51 | .268 | .380 | 9 | 4 | OF-329, 3B-22 |
| WORLD SERIES | | | | | | | | | | | | | | | | | |
| 1903 PIT N | 8 | 33 | 9 | 0 | 4 | 0 | 0.0 | 3 | 7 | 1 | 4 | 2 | .273 | .515 | 0 | 0 | 3B-8 |
| 1909 | 7 | 25 | 8 | 4 | 0 | 0 | 0.0 | 8 | 2 | 2 | 1 | 1 | .320 | .480 | 0 | 0 | OF-6 |
| 2 yrs. | 15 | 58 | 17 | 4 | 4 | 0 | 0.0 | 11 | 9 | 3 | 5 | 3 | .293 | .500 | 0 | 0 | 3B-8, OF-6 |

1st

## Fred Lear

LEAR, FREDRICK FRANCIS (King)
B. Apr. 7, 1894, New York, N.Y.   D. Oct. 13, 1955, East Orange, N.J.   BR TR 6'½" 180 lbs.

| | G | AB | H | 2B | 3B | HR | HR% | R | RBI | BB | SO | SB | BA | SA | PH AB | PH H | G by POS |
|---|---|---|---|---|---|---|---|---|---|---|---|---|---|---|---|---|---|
| 1915 PHI A | 2 | 2 | 0 | 0 | 0 | 0 | 0.0 | 0 | 0 | 0 | 2 | 0 | .000 | .000 | 0 | 0 | 3B-2 |
| 1918 CHI N | 2 | 1 | 0 | 0 | 0 | 0 | 0.0 | 0 | 0 | 1 | 0 | 0 | .000 | .000 | 1 | 0 | |
| 1919 | 40 | 76 | 17 | 3 | 1 | 1 | 1.3 | 8 | 11 | 8 | 11 | 2 | .224 | .329 | 14 | 2 | 2B-9, 1B-9, SS-3 |
| 1920 NY N | 31 | 87 | 22 | 0 | 1 | 1 | 1.1 | 12 | 7 | 8 | 15 | 0 | .253 | .310 | 4 | 1 | 3B-24, 2B-1 |
| 4 yrs. | 75 | 166 | 39 | 3 | 2 | 2 | 1.2 | 20 | 18 | 17 | 28 | 2 | .235 | .313 | 19 | 3 | 3B-26, 2B-10, 1B-9, SS-3 |
| 2 yrs. | 42 | 77 | 17 | 3 | 1 | 1 | 1.3 | 8 | 11 | 9 | 11 | 2 | .221 | .325 | 15 | 2 | 2B-9, 1B-9, SS-3 |

## Hal Leathers

LEATHERS, HAROLD LANGFORD
B. Dec. 2, 1898, Los Angeles, Calif.   D. Apr. 12, 1977, Modesto, Calif.   BL TR 5'7" 152 lbs.

| | G | AB | H | 2B | 3B | HR | HR% | R | RBI | BB | SO | SB | BA | SA | PH AB | PH H | G by POS |
|---|---|---|---|---|---|---|---|---|---|---|---|---|---|---|---|---|---|
| 1920 CHI N | 9 | 23 | 7 | 1 | 0 | 1 | 4.3 | 1 | 1 | 1 | 1 | 1 | .304 | .478 | 1 | 0 | SS-6, 2B-3 |

## Hank Leiber

LEIBER, HENRY EDWARD
B. Jan. 17, 1911, Phoenix, Ariz.   BR TR 6'1½" 205 lbs.

| | G | AB | H | 2B | 3B | HR | HR% | R | RBI | BB | SO | SB | BA | SA | PH AB | PH H | G by POS |
|---|---|---|---|---|---|---|---|---|---|---|---|---|---|---|---|---|---|
| 1933 NY N | 6 | 10 | 2 | 0 | 0 | 0 | 0.0 | 1 | 0 | 0 | 2 | 0 | .200 | .200 | 5 | 0 | OF-1 |
| 1934 | 63 | 187 | 45 | 5 | 3 | 2 | 1.1 | 17 | 25 | 4 | 13 | 1 | .241 | .332 | 12 | 2 | OF-51 |
| 1935 | 154 | 613 | 203 | 37 | 4 | 22 | 3.6 | 110 | 107 | 48 | 29 | 0 | .331 | .512 | 0 | 0 | OF-154 |
| 1936 | 101 | 337 | 94 | 19 | 7 | 9 | 2.7 | 44 | 67 | 37 | 41 | 1 | .279 | .457 | 12 | 1 | OF-86, 1B-1 |
| 1937 | 51 | 184 | 54 | 7 | 3 | 4 | 2.2 | 24 | 32 | 15 | 27 | 1 | .293 | .429 | 5 | 1 | OF-46 |
| 1938 | 98 | 360 | 97 | 18 | 4 | 12 | 3.3 | 50 | 65 | 31 | 45 | 0 | .269 | .442 | 8 | 3 | OF-89 |
| 1939 CHI N | 112 | 365 | 113 | 16 | 1 | 24 | 6.6 | 65 | 88 | 59 | 42 | 1 | .310 | .556 | 8 | 1 | OF-98 |
| 1940 | 117 | 440 | 133 | 24 | 2 | 17 | 3.9 | 68 | 86 | 45 | 68 | 1 | .302 | .482 | 3 | 0 | OF-103, 1B-12 |
| 1941 | 53 | 162 | 35 | 5 | 0 | 7 | 4.3 | 20 | 25 | 16 | 25 | 0 | .216 | .377 | 9 | 0 | OF-29, 1B-15 |
| 1942 NY N | 58 | 147 | 32 | 6 | 0 | 4 | 2.7 | 11 | 23 | 19 | 27 | 0 | .218 | .340 | 14 | 4 | OF-41, P-1 |
| 10 yrs. | 813 | 2805 | 808 | 137 | 24 | 101 | 3.6 | 410 | 518 | 274 | 319 | 5 | .288 | .462 | 76 | 12 | OF-698, 1B-28, P-1 |
| 3 yrs. | 282 | 967 | 281 | 45 | 3 | 48 | 5.0 | 153 | 199 | 120 | 135 | 2 | .291 | .492 | 20 | 1 | OF-230, 1B-27 |
| WORLD SERIES | | | | | | | | | | | | | | | | | |
| 1936 NY N | 2 | 6 | 0 | 0 | 0 | 0 | 0.0 | 0 | | 2 | 2 | 0 | .000 | .000 | 0 | 0 | OF-2 |
| 1937 | 3 | 11 | 4 | 0 | 0 | 0 | 0.0 | 2 | 2 | 1 | 1 | 0 | .364 | .364 | 0 | 0 | OF-3 |
| 2 yrs. | 5 | 17 | 4 | 0 | 0 | 0 | 0.0 | 2 | 2 | 3 | 3 | 0 | .235 | .235 | 0 | 0 | OF-5 |

## Bob Lennon

LENNON, ROBERT ALBERT (Arch)
B. Sept. 15, 1928, Brooklyn, N.Y.   BL TL 6' 200 lbs.

| | G | AB | H | 2B | 3B | HR | HR% | R | RBI | BB | SO | SB | BA | SA | PH AB | PH H | G by POS |
|---|---|---|---|---|---|---|---|---|---|---|---|---|---|---|---|---|---|
| 1954 NY N | 3 | 3 | 0 | 0 | 0 | 0 | 0.0 | 0 | 0 | 0 | 0 | 0 | .000 | .000 | 3 | 0 | |
| 1956 | 26 | 55 | 10 | 1 | 0 | 0 | 0.0 | 3 | 1 | 4 | 17 | 0 | .182 | .200 | 3 | 0 | OF-21 |
| 1957 CHI N | 9 | 21 | 3 | 1 | 0 | 1 | 4.8 | 2 | 3 | 1 | 9 | 0 | .143 | .333 | 5 | 0 | OF-4 |
| 3 yrs. | 38 | 79 | 13 | 2 | 0 | 1 | 1.3 | 5 | 4 | 5 | 26 | 0 | .165 | .228 | 11 | 0 | OF-25 |
| 1 yr. | 9 | 21 | 3 | 1 | 0 | 1 | 4.8 | 2 | 3 | 1 | 9 | 0 | .143 | .333 | 5 | 0 | OF-4 |

## Ed Lennox

LENNOX, JAMES EDGAR (Eggie)
B. Nov. 3, 1885, Camden, N.J.   D. Oct. 26, 1939, Camden, N.J.   BR TR 5'10" 174 lbs.

| | G | AB | H | 2B | 3B | HR | HR% | R | RBI | BB | SO | SB | BA | SA | PH AB | PH H | G by POS |
|---|---|---|---|---|---|---|---|---|---|---|---|---|---|---|---|---|---|
| 1906 PHI A | 6 | 17 | 1 | 1 | 0 | 0 | 0.0 | 1 | 0 | 1 | | 0 | .059 | .118 | 0 | 0 | 3B-6 |
| 1909 BKN N | 126 | 435 | 114 | 18 | 9 | 2 | 0.5 | 33 | 44 | 47 | | 11 | .262 | .359 | 5 | 1 | 3B-121 |
| 1910 | 110 | 367 | 95 | 19 | 4 | 3 | 0.8 | 19 | 32 | 36 | 39 | 7 | .259 | .357 | 10 | 1 | 3B-100 |
| 1912 CHI N | 27 | 81 | 19 | 4 | 1 | 1 | 1.2 | 13 | 16 | 12 | 10 | 1 | .235 | .346 | 2 | 1 | 3B-24 |
| 1914 PIT F | 124 | 430 | 134 | 25 | 10 | 11 | 2.6 | 71 | 84 | 71 | | 19 | .312 | .493 | 1 | 0 | 3B-123 |
| 1915 | 55 | 53 | 16 | 3 | 1 | 1 | 1.9 | 1 | 9 | 7 | | 0 | .302 | .453 | 45 | 14 | 3B-3 |
| 6 yrs. | 448 | 1383 | 379 | 70 | 25 | 18 | 1.3 | 138 | 185 | 174 | 49 | 38 | .274 | .400 | 63 | 17 | 3B-377 |
| 1 yr. | 27 | 81 | 19 | 4 | 1 | 1 | 1.2 | 13 | 16 | 12 | 10 | 1 | .235 | .346 | 2 | 1 | 3B-24 |

## Roy Leslie

LESLIE, ROY REID
B. Aug. 23, 1894, Bailey, Tex.   D. Apr. 10, 1972, Sherman, Tex.   BR TR 6'1" 175 lbs.

| | G | AB | H | 2B | 3B | HR | HR% | R | RBI | BB | SO | SB | BA | SA | PH AB | PH H | G by POS |
|---|---|---|---|---|---|---|---|---|---|---|---|---|---|---|---|---|---|
| 1917 CHI N | 7 | 19 | 4 | 0 | 0 | 0 | 0.0 | 1 | 1 | 1 | 5 | 1 | .211 | .211 | 1 | 0 | 1B-6 |
| 1919 STL N | 12 | 24 | 5 | 1 | 0 | 0 | 0.0 | 2 | 4 | 4 | 3 | 0 | .208 | .250 | 1 | 0 | 1B-9 |
| 1922 PHI N | 141 | 513 | 139 | 23 | 2 | 6 | 1.2 | 44 | 50 | 37 | 49 | 3 | .271 | .359 | 2 | 2 | 1B-139 |
| 3 yrs. | 160 | 556 | 148 | 24 | 2 | 6 | 1.1 | 47 | 55 | 42 | 57 | 4 | .266 | .349 | 4 | 2 | 1B-154 |
| 1 yr. | 7 | 19 | 4 | 0 | 0 | 0 | 0.0 | 1 | 1 | 1 | 5 | 1 | .211 | .211 | 1 | 0 | 1B-6 |

## Carlos Lezcano

LEZCANO, CARLOS MANUEL
B. Sept. 30, 1955, Arecibo, Puerto Rico   BR TR 6'2" 185 lbs.

| | G | AB | H | 2B | 3B | HR | HR% | R | RBI | BB | SO | SB | BA | SA | PH AB | PH H | G by POS |
|---|---|---|---|---|---|---|---|---|---|---|---|---|---|---|---|---|---|
| 1980 CHI N | 42 | 88 | 18 | 4 | 1 | 3 | 3.4 | 15 | 12 | 11 | 29 | 1 | .205 | .375 | 2 | 0 | OF-39 |
| 1981 | 7 | 14 | 1 | 0 | 0 | 0 | 0.0 | 1 | 2 | 0 | 4 | 0 | .071 | .071 | 2 | 0 | OF-5 |
| 2 yrs. | 49 | 102 | 19 | 4 | 1 | 3 | 2.9 | 16 | 14 | 11 | 33 | 1 | .186 | .333 | 4 | 0 | OF-44 |
| 2 yrs. | 49 | 102 | 19 | 4 | 1 | 3 | 2.9 | 16 | 14 | 11 | 33 | 1 | .186 | .333 | 4 | 0 | OF-44 |

| | G | AB | H | 2B | 3B | HR | HR % | R | RBI | BB | SO | SB | BA | SA | Pinch Hit AB | Pinch Hit H | G by POS |
|---|---|---|---|---|---|---|---|---|---|---|---|---|---|---|---|---|---|

## Gene Lillard

**LILLARD, ROBERT EUGENE**     BR TR 5'10½" 178 lbs.
Brother of Bill Lillard.
B. Nov. 12, 1913, Santa Barbara, Calif.

| | G | AB | H | 2B | 3B | HR | HR % | R | RBI | BB | SO | SB | BA | SA | PH AB | PH H | G by POS |
|---|---|---|---|---|---|---|---|---|---|---|---|---|---|---|---|---|---|
| 1936 CHI N | 19 | 34 | 7 | 1 | 0 | 0 | 0.0 | 6 | 2 | 3 | 8 | 0 | .206 | .235 | 10 | 3 | SS-4, 3B-3 |
| 1939 | 23 | 10 | 1 | 0 | 0 | 0 | 0.0 | 3 | 0 | 6 | 3 | 0 | .100 | .100 | 0 | 0 | P-20 |
| 1940 STL N | 2 | 0 | 0 | 0 | 0 | 0 | — | 0 | 0 | 0 | 0 | 0 | — | — | 0 | 0 | P-2 |
| 3 yrs. | 44 | 44 | 8 | 1 | 0 | 0 | 0.0 | 9 | 2 | 9 | 11 | 0 | .182 | .205 | 10 | 3 | P-22, SS-4, 3B-3 |
| 2 yrs. | 42 | 44 | 8 | 1 | 0 | 0 | 0.0 | 9 | 2 | 9 | 11 | 0 | .182 | .205 | 10 | 3 | P-20, SS-4, 3B-3 |

## Freddie Lindstrom

**LINDSTROM, FRED CHARLES (Lindy)**     BR TR 5'11" 170 lbs.
Born Frederick Anthony Lindstrom. Father of Charlie Lindstrom.
B. Nov. 21, 1905, Chicago, Ill. D. Oct. 4, 1981, Chicago, Ill.
Hall of Fame 1976.

| | G | AB | H | 2B | 3B | HR | HR % | R | RBI | BB | SO | SB | BA | SA | PH AB | PH H | G by POS |
|---|---|---|---|---|---|---|---|---|---|---|---|---|---|---|---|---|---|
| 1924 NY N | 52 | 79 | 20 | 3 | 1 | 0 | 0.0 | 19 | 4 | 6 | 10 | 3 | .253 | .316 | 6 | 2 | 2B-23, 3B-11 |
| 1925 | 104 | 356 | 102 | 15 | 12 | 4 | 1.1 | 43 | 33 | 22 | 20 | 5 | .287 | .430 | 2 | 1 | 3B-96, SS-1, 2B-1 |
| 1926 | 140 | 543 | 164 | 19 | 9 | 9 | 1.7 | 90 | 76 | 39 | 21 | 11 | .302 | .420 | 1 | 1 | 3B-138, OF-1 |
| 1927 | 138 | 562 | 172 | 36 | 8 | 7 | 1.2 | 107 | 58 | 40 | 40 | 10 | .306 | .436 | 1 | 0 | 3B-87, OF-51 |
| 1928 | 153 | 646 | **231** | 39 | 9 | 14 | 2.2 | 99 | 107 | 25 | 21 | 15 | .358 | .511 | 0 | 0 | 3B-153 |
| 1929 | 130 | 549 | 175 | 23 | 6 | 15 | 2.7 | 99 | 91 | 30 | 28 | 10 | .319 | .464 | 2 | 0 | 3B-128 |
| 1930 | 148 | 609 | 231 | 39 | 7 | 22 | 3.6 | 127 | 106 | 48 | 33 | 15 | .379 | .575 | 0 | 0 | 3B-148 |
| 1931 | 78 | 303 | 91 | 12 | 6 | 5 | 1.7 | 38 | 36 | 26 | 12 | 5 | .300 | .429 | 1 | 0 | OF-73, 2B-4 |
| 1932 | 144 | 595 | 161 | 26 | 5 | 15 | 2.5 | 83 | 92 | 27 | 28 | 6 | .271 | .407 | 0 | 0 | OF-128, 3B-15 |
| 1933 PIT N | 138 | 538 | 167 | 39 | 10 | 5 | 0.9 | 70 | 55 | 33 | 22 | 1 | .310 | .448 | 8 | 3 | OF-130 |
| 1934 | 97 | 383 | 111 | 24 | 4 | 4 | 1.0 | 59 | 49 | 23 | 21 | 1 | .290 | .405 | 4 | 1 | OF-92 |
| 1935 CHI N | 90 | 342 | 94 | 22 | 4 | 3 | 0.9 | 49 | 62 | 10 | 13 | 1 | .275 | .389 | 6 | 1 | OF-50, 3B-33 |
| 1936 BKN N | 26 | 106 | 28 | 4 | 0 | 0 | 0.0 | 12 | 10 | 5 | 7 | 1 | .264 | .302 | 0 | 0 | OF-26 |
| 13 yrs. | 1438 | 5611 | 1747 | 301 | 81 | 103 | 1.8 | 895 | 779 | 334 | 276 | 84 | .311 | .449 | 31 | 9 | 3B-809, OF-551, 2B-28, SS-1 |
| 1 yr. | 90 | 342 | 94 | 22 | 4 | 3 | 0.9 | 49 | 62 | 10 | 13 | 1 | .275 | .389 | 6 | 1 | OF-50, 3B-33 |

WORLD SERIES

| | G | AB | H | 2B | 3B | HR | HR % | R | RBI | BB | SO | SB | BA | SA | PH AB | PH H | G by POS |
|---|---|---|---|---|---|---|---|---|---|---|---|---|---|---|---|---|---|
| 1924 NY N | 7 | 30 | 10 | 2 | 0 | 0 | 0.0 | 1 | 4 | 3 | 6 | 0 | .333 | .400 | 0 | 0 | 3B-7 |
| 1935 CHI N | 4 | 15 | 3 | 1 | 0 | 0 | 0.0 | 0 | 0 | 1 | 1 | 0 | .200 | .267 | 0 | 0 | 3B-1 |
| 2 yrs. | 11 | 45 | 13 | 3 | 0 | 0 | 0.0 | 1 | 4 | 4 | 7 | 0 | .289 | .356 | 0 | 0 | 3B-8 |

## Jack Littrell

**LITTRELL, JACK NAPIER**     BR TR 6' 179 lbs.
B. Jan. 22, 1929, Louisville, Ky.

| | G | AB | H | 2B | 3B | HR | HR % | R | RBI | BB | SO | SB | BA | SA | PH AB | PH H | G by POS |
|---|---|---|---|---|---|---|---|---|---|---|---|---|---|---|---|---|---|
| 1952 PHI A | 4 | 2 | 0 | 0 | 0 | 0 | 0.0 | 0 | 1 | 0 | 1 | 2 | 0 | .000 | .000 | 1 | 0 | SS-2, 3B-1 |
| 1954 | 9 | 30 | 9 | 2 | 0 | 1 | 3.3 | 7 | 3 | 6 | 3 | 1 | .300 | .467 | 0 | 0 | SS-9 |
| 1955 KC A | 37 | 70 | 14 | 0 | 1 | 0 | 0.0 | 7 | 1 | 4 | 12 | 0 | .200 | .229 | 6 | 0 | SS-22, 1B-6, 2B-4 |
| 1957 CHI N | 61 | 153 | 29 | 4 | 2 | 1 | 0.7 | 8 | 13 | 9 | 43 | 0 | .190 | .261 | 2 | 1 | SS-47, 2B-6, 3B-5 |
| 4 yrs. | 111 | 255 | 52 | 6 | 3 | 2 | 0.8 | 22 | 17 | 20 | 60 | 1 | .204 | .275 | 9 | 1 | SS-80, 2B-10, 3B-6, 1B-6 |
| 1 yr. | 61 | 153 | 29 | 4 | 2 | 1 | 0.7 | 8 | 13 | 9 | 43 | 0 | .190 | .261 | 2 | 1 | SS-47, 2B-6, 3B-5 |

## Mickey Livingston

**LIVINGSTON, THOMPSON ORVILLE**     BR TR 6'1½" 185 lbs.
B. Nov. 15, 1914, Newberry, S. C. D. Apr. 3, 1983, Newberry, S. C.

| | G | AB | H | 2B | 3B | HR | HR % | R | RBI | BB | SO | SB | BA | SA | PH AB | PH H | G by POS |
|---|---|---|---|---|---|---|---|---|---|---|---|---|---|---|---|---|---|
| 1938 WAS A | 2 | 4 | 3 | 2 | 0 | 0 | 0.0 | 0 | 1 | 0 | 1 | 0 | .750 | 1.250 | 0 | 0 | C-2 |
| 1941 PHI N | 95 | 207 | 42 | 6 | 1 | 0 | 0.0 | 16 | 18 | 20 | 38 | 2 | .203 | .242 | 18 | 4 | C-71, 1B-1 |
| 1942 | 89 | 239 | 49 | 6 | 1 | 2 | 0.8 | 20 | 22 | 25 | 20 | 0 | .205 | .264 | 6 | 2 | C-78, 1B-6 |
| 1943 2 teams | PHI | N (84G – .249) | | | CHI | N (36G – .261) | | | | | | | | | | | |
| " total | 120 | 376 | 95 | 14 | 3 | 7 | 1.9 | 36 | 34 | 31 | 26 | 2 | .253 | .362 | 2 | 0 | C-115, 1B-6 |
| 1945 CHI N | 71 | 224 | 57 | 4 | 2 | 2 | 0.9 | 19 | 23 | 19 | 6 | 2 | .254 | .317 | 2 | 0 | C-68, 1B-1 |
| 1946 | 66 | 176 | 45 | 14 | 0 | 2 | 1.1 | 14 | 20 | 20 | 19 | 0 | .256 | .369 | 8 | 1 | C-56 |
| 1947 2 teams | CHI | N (19G – .212) | | | NY | N (5G – .167) | | | | | | | | | | | |
| " total | 24 | 39 | 8 | 2 | 0 | 0 | 0.0 | 2 | 3 | 2 | 7 | 0 | .205 | .256 | 14 | 5 | C-9 |
| 1948 NY N | 45 | 99 | 21 | 4 | 1 | 2 | 2.0 | 9 | 12 | 21 | 11 | 1 | .212 | .333 | 3 | 1 | C-42 |
| 1949 2 teams | NY | N (19G – .298) | | | BOS | N (28G – .234) | | | | | | | | | | | |
| " total | 47 | 121 | 32 | 4 | 1 | 4 | 3.3 | 12 | 18 | 5 | 13 | 0 | .264 | .413 | 6 | 0 | C-41 |
| 1951 BKN N | 2 | 5 | 2 | 0 | 0 | 0 | 0.0 | 0 | 2 | 1 | 0 | 0 | .400 | .400 | 0 | 0 | C-2 |
| 10 yrs. | 561 | 1490 | 354 | 56 | 9 | 19 | 1.3 | 128 | 153 | 144 | 141 | 7 | .238 | .326 | 59 | 13 | C-484, 1B-14 |
| 4 yrs. | 192 | 544 | 138 | 25 | 3 | 8 | 1.5 | 46 | 62 | 52 | 38 | 3 | .254 | .355 | 23 | 1 | C-162, 1B-5 |

WORLD SERIES

| | G | AB | H | 2B | 3B | HR | HR % | R | RBI | BB | SO | SB | BA | SA | PH AB | PH H | G by POS |
|---|---|---|---|---|---|---|---|---|---|---|---|---|---|---|---|---|---|
| 1945 CHI N | 6 | 22 | 8 | 3 | 0 | 0 | 0.0 | 3 | 4 | 1 | 1 | 0 | .364 | .500 | 0 | 0 | C-6 |

## Hans Lobert

**LOBERT, JOHN BERNARD (Honus)**     BR TR 5'9" 170 lbs.
Brother of Frank Lobert.
B. Oct. 18, 1881, Wilmington, Del. D. Sept. 14, 1968, Philadelphia, Pa.
Manager 1938, 1942.

| | G | AB | H | 2B | 3B | HR | HR % | R | RBI | BB | SO | SB | BA | SA | PH AB | PH H | G by POS |
|---|---|---|---|---|---|---|---|---|---|---|---|---|---|---|---|---|---|
| 1903 PIT N | 5 | 13 | 1 | 1 | 0 | 0 | 0.0 | 0 | 1 | 0 | | 1 | .077 | .154 | 0 | 0 | 3B-3, SS-1, 2B-1 |
| 1905 CHI N | 14 | 46 | 9 | 2 | 0 | 0 | 0.0 | 7 | 1 | 3 | | 4 | .196 | .239 | 0 | 0 | 3B-13, OF-1 |
| 1906 CIN N | 79 | 268 | 83 | 5 | 5 | 0 | 0.0 | 39 | 19 | 19 | | 20 | .310 | .366 | 4 | 1 | 3B-35, SS-31, 2B-10, OF-1 |
| 1907 | 148 | 537 | 132 | 9 | 12 | 1 | 0.2 | 61 | 41 | 37 | | 30 | .246 | .313 | 1 | 0 | SS-142, 3B-5 |
| 1908 | 155 | 570 | 167 | 17 | 18 | 4 | 0.7 | 71 | 63 | 46 | | 47 | .293 | .407 | 0 | 0 | 3B-99, SS-35, OF-21 |
| 1909 | 122 | 425 | 90 | 13 | 5 | 4 | 0.9 | 50 | 52 | 48 | | 30 | .212 | .294 | 0 | 0 | 3B-122 |
| 1910 | 93 | 314 | 97 | 6 | 6 | 3 | 1.0 | 43 | 40 | 30 | 9 | 41 | .309 | .395 | 0 | 0 | 3B-90 |
| 1911 PHI N | 147 | 541 | 154 | 20 | 9 | 9 | 1.7 | 94 | 72 | 66 | 31 | 40 | .285 | .405 | 0 | 0 | 3B-147 |
| 1912 | 65 | 257 | 84 | 12 | 5 | 2 | 0.8 | 37 | 33 | 19 | 13 | 13 | .327 | .436 | 1 | 0 | 3B-64 |
| 1913 | 150 | 573 | 172 | 28 | 11 | 7 | 1.2 | 98 | 55 | 42 | 34 | 41 | .300 | .424 | 1 | 0 | 3B-145, SS-3, 2B-1 |
| 1914 | 135 | 505 | 139 | 24 | 5 | 1 | 0.2 | 83 | 52 | 49 | 32 | 31 | .275 | .349 | 0 | 0 | 3B-133, SS-2 |
| 1915 NY N | 106 | 386 | 97 | 18 | 4 | 0 | 0.0 | 46 | 38 | 25 | 24 | 14 | .251 | .319 | 3 | 1 | 3B-106 |
| 1916 | 48 | 76 | 17 | 3 | 2 | 0 | 0.0 | 6 | 11 | 5 | 8 | 2 | .224 | .316 | 24 | 4 | 3B-20 |

| | G | AB | H | 2B | 3B | HR | HR % | R | RBI | BB | SO | SB | BA | SA | Pinch Hit AB | Pinch Hit H | G by POS |
|---|---|---|---|---|---|---|---|---|---|---|---|---|---|---|---|---|---|

## Hans Lobert continued

| | G | AB | H | 2B | 3B | HR | HR% | R | RBI | BB | SO | SB | BA | SA | AB | H | G by POS |
|---|---|---|---|---|---|---|---|---|---|---|---|---|---|---|---|---|---|
| 1917 | 50 | 52 | 10 | 1 | 0 | 1 | 1.9 | 4 | 5 | 5 | 5 | 2 | .192 | .269 | 24 | 3 | 3B-21 |
| 14 yrs. | 1317 | 4563 | 1252 | 159 | 82 | 32 | 0.7 | 640 | 482 | 395 | 156 | 316 | .274 | .366 | 58 | 11 | 3B-1003, SS-214, OF-23, 2B-12 |
| 1 yr. | 14 | 46 | 9 | 2 | 0 | 0 | 0.0 | 7 | 1 | 3 | | 4 | .196 | .239 | 0 | 0 | 3B-13, OF-1 |

## Dale Long

**LONG, RICHARD DALE**     BL TL 6'4"    205 lbs.
B. Feb. 6, 1926, Springfield, Mo.

| | G | AB | H | 2B | 3B | HR | HR% | R | RBI | BB | SO | SB | BA | SA | AB | H | G by POS |
|---|---|---|---|---|---|---|---|---|---|---|---|---|---|---|---|---|---|
| 1951 2 teams | | PIT N (10G – .167) | | | | STL A (34G – .238) | | | | | | | | | | | |
| " total | 44 | 117 | 27 | 5 | 1 | 3 | 2.6 | 12 | 12 | 10 | 25 | 0 | .231 | .368 | 13 | 1 | 1B-29, OF-1 |
| 1955 PIT N | 131 | 419 | 122 | 19 | 13 | 16 | 3.8 | 59 | 79 | 48 | 72 | 0 | .291 | .513 | 13 | 4 | 1B-119 |
| 1956 | 148 | 517 | 136 | 20 | 7 | 27 | 5.2 | 64 | 91 | 54 | 85 | 1 | .263 | .485 | 12 | 2 | 1B-138 |
| 1957 2 teams | | PIT N (7G – .182) | | | | CHI N (123G – .305) | | | | | | | | | | | |
| " total | 130 | 419 | 125 | 20 | 0 | 21 | 5.0 | 55 | 67 | 56 | 73 | 1 | .298 | .496 | 18 | 6 | 1B-111 |
| 1958 CHI N | 142 | 480 | 130 | 26 | 4 | 20 | 4.2 | 68 | 75 | 66 | 64 | 2 | .271 | .467 | 5 | 2 | 1B-137, C-2 |
| 1959 | 110 | 296 | 70 | 10 | 3 | 14 | 4.7 | 34 | 37 | 31 | 53 | 0 | .236 | .432 | 27 | 6 | 1B-85 |
| 1960 2 teams | | SF N (37G – .167) | | | | NY A (26G – .366) | | | | | | | | | | | |
| " total | 63 | 95 | 24 | 3 | 1 | 6 | 6.3 | 10 | 16 | 12 | 13 | 0 | .253 | .495 | 39 | 11 | 1B-21 |
| 1961 WAS A | 123 | 377 | 94 | 20 | 4 | 17 | 4.5 | 52 | 49 | 39 | 41 | 0 | .249 | .459 | 24 | 3 | 1B-95 |
| 1962 2 teams | | WAS A (67G – .241) | | | | NY A (41G – .298) | | | | | | | | | | | |
| " total | 108 | 285 | 74 | 12 | 0 | 8 | 2.8 | 29 | 41 | 36 | 31 | 6 | .260 | .386 | 28 | 3 | 1B-82 |
| 1963 NY A | 14 | 15 | 3 | 0 | 0 | 0 | 0.0 | 1 | 0 | 1 | 3 | 0 | .200 | .200 | 11 | 2 | 1B-2 |
| 10 yrs. | 1013 | 3020 | 805 | 135 | 33 | 132 | 4.4 | 384 | 467 | 353 | 460 | 10 | .267 | .464 | 190 | 40 | 1B-819, C-2, OF-1 |
| 3 yrs. | 375 | 1173 | 321 | 55 | 7 | 55 | 4.7 | 157 | 174 | 149 | 180 | 3 | .274 | .473 | 49 | 13 | 1B-326, C-2 |

WORLD SERIES

| | G | AB | H | 2B | 3B | HR | HR% | R | RBI | BB | SO | SB | BA | SA | AB | H | G by POS |
|---|---|---|---|---|---|---|---|---|---|---|---|---|---|---|---|---|---|
| 1960 NY A | 3 | 3 | 1 | 0 | 0 | 0 | 0.0 | 0 | 0 | 0 | 0 | 0 | .333 | .333 | 3 | 1 | |
| 1962 | 2 | 5 | 1 | 0 | 0 | 0 | 0.0 | 0 | 1 | 0 | 1 | 0 | .200 | .200 | 0 | 0 | 1B-2 |
| 2 yrs. | 5 | 8 | 2 | 0 | 0 | 0 | 0.0 | 0 | 1 | 0 | 1 | 0 | .250 | .250 | 3 | 1 | 1B-2 |

## Davey Lopes

**LOPES, DAVID EARL**     BR TR 5'9"    170 lbs.
B. May 3, 1946, Providence, R. I.

| | G | AB | H | 2B | 3B | HR | HR% | R | RBI | BB | SO | SB | BA | SA | AB | H | G by POS |
|---|---|---|---|---|---|---|---|---|---|---|---|---|---|---|---|---|---|
| 1972 LA N | 11 | 42 | 9 | 4 | 0 | 0 | 0.0 | 6 | 1 | 7 | 6 | 4 | .214 | .310 | 0 | 0 | 2B-11 |
| 1973 | 142 | 535 | 147 | 13 | 5 | 6 | 1.1 | 77 | 37 | 62 | 77 | 36 | .275 | .351 | 1 | 0 | 2B-135, OF-5, SS-2, 3B-1 |
| 1974 | 145 | 530 | 141 | 26 | 3 | 10 | 1.9 | 95 | 35 | 66 | 71 | 59 | .266 | .383 | 0 | 0 | 2B-143 |
| 1975 | 155 | 618 | 162 | 24 | 6 | 8 | 1.3 | 108 | 41 | 91 | 93 | 77 | .262 | .359 | 0 | 0 | 2B-137, OF-24, SS-14 |
| 1976 | 117 | 427 | 103 | 17 | 7 | 4 | 0.9 | 72 | 20 | 56 | 49 | 63 | .241 | .342 | 0 | 0 | 2B-100, OF-19 |
| 1977 | 134 | 502 | 142 | 19 | 5 | 11 | 2.2 | 85 | 53 | 73 | 69 | 47 | .283 | .406 | 1 | 0 | 2B-130 |
| 1978 | 151 | 587 | 163 | 25 | 4 | 17 | 2.9 | 93 | 58 | 71 | 70 | 45 | .278 | .421 | 1 | 1 | 2B-147, OF-2 |
| 1979 | 153 | 582 | 154 | 20 | 6 | 28 | 4.8 | 109 | 73 | 97 | 88 | 44 | .265 | .464 | 1 | 0 | 2B-152 |
| 1980 | 141 | 553 | 139 | 15 | 3 | 10 | 1.8 | 79 | 49 | 58 | 71 | 23 | .251 | .344 | 0 | 0 | 2B-140 |
| 1981 | 58 | 214 | 44 | 2 | 0 | 5 | 2.3 | 35 | 17 | 22 | 35 | 20 | .206 | .285 | 3 | 0 | 2B-55 |
| 1982 OAK A | 128 | 450 | 109 | 19 | 3 | 11 | 2.4 | 58 | 42 | 40 | 51 | 28 | .242 | .371 | 0 | 0 | 2B-125, OF-6 |
| 1983 | 147 | 494 | 137 | 13 | 4 | 17 | 3.4 | 64 | 67 | 51 | 61 | 22 | .277 | .423 | 10 | 3 | 2B-123, DH-12, OF-7, 3B-5 |
| 1984 2 teams | | OAK A (72G – .257) | | | | CHI N (16G – .235) | | | | | | | | | | | |
| " total | 88 | 247 | 63 | 12 | 1 | 9 | 3.6 | 37 | 36 | 37 | 41 | 15 | .255 | .421 | 7 | 2 | OF-51, 2B-19, DH-9, 3B-5 |
| 1985 CHI N | 99 | 275 | 78 | 11 | 0 | 11 | 4.0 | 52 | 44 | 46 | 37 | 47 | .284 | .444 | 22 | 4 | OF-79, 3B-4, 2B-1 |
| 14 yrs. | 1669 | 6056 | 1591 | 220 | 47 | 147 | 2.4 | 970 | 573 | 777 | 819 | 530 | .263 | .387 | 46 | 11 | 2B-1418, OF-193, DH-21, SS-16, 3B-15 |
| 2 yrs. | 115 | 292 | 82 | 12 | 0 | 11 | 3.8 | 57 | 44 | 52 | 42 | 50 | .281 | .435 | 27 | 5 | OF-88, 3B-4, 2B-3 |

DIVISIONAL PLAYOFF SERIES

| | G | AB | H | 2B | 3B | HR | HR% | R | RBI | BB | SO | SB | BA | SA | AB | H | G by POS |
|---|---|---|---|---|---|---|---|---|---|---|---|---|---|---|---|---|---|
| 1981 LA N | 5 | 20 | 4 | 1 | 0 | 0 | 0.0 | 1 | 0 | 3 | 7 | 1 | .200 | .250 | 0 | 0 | 2B-5 |

LEAGUE CHAMPIONSHIP SERIES

| | G | AB | H | 2B | 3B | HR | HR% | R | RBI | BB | SO | SB | BA | SA | AB | H | G by POS |
|---|---|---|---|---|---|---|---|---|---|---|---|---|---|---|---|---|---|
| 1974 LA N | 4 | 15 | 4 | 0 | 1 | 0 | 0.0 | 4 | 3 | 5 | 1 | 3 | .267 | .400 | 0 | 0 | 2B-4 |
| 1977 | 4 | 17 | 4 | 0 | 0 | 0 | 0.0 | 2 | 3 | 2 | 0 | 0 | .235 | .235 | 0 | 0 | 2B-4 |
| 1978 | 4 | 18 | 7 | 1 | 1 | 2 | 11.1 | 3 | 5 | 0 | 1 | 1 | .389 | .889 | 0 | 0 | 2B-4 |
| 1981 | 5 | 18 | 5 | 0 | 0 | 0 | 0.0 | 0 | 0 | 1 | 3 | 5 | .278 | .278 | 0 | 0 | 2B-5 |
| 1984 CHI N | 2 | 1 | 0 | 0 | 0 | 0 | 0.0 | 0 | 0 | 0 | 0 | 0 | .000 | .000 | 1 | 0 | OF-1 |
| 5 yrs. | 19 | 69 | 20 | 1 | 2 | 2 | 2.9 | 9 | 11 | 8 | 5 | 9 | .290 | .449 | 1 | 0 | 2B-17, OF-1 |

WORLD SERIES

| | G | AB | H | 2B | 3B | HR | HR% | R | RBI | BB | SO | SB | BA | SA | AB | H | G by POS |
|---|---|---|---|---|---|---|---|---|---|---|---|---|---|---|---|---|---|
| 1974 LA N | 5 | 18 | 2 | 0 | 0 | 0 | 0.0 | 2 | 0 | 3 | 4 | 2 | .111 | .111 | 0 | 0 | 2B-5 |
| 1977 | 6 | 24 | 4 | 0 | 1 | 1 | 4.2 | 3 | 2 | 4 | 3 | 2 | .167 | .375 | 0 | 0 | 2B-6 |
| 1978 | 6 | 26 | 8 | 0 | 0 | 3 | 11.5 | 7 | 7 | 2 | 1 | 2 | .308 | .654 | 0 | 0 | 2B-6 |
| 1981 | 6 | 22 | 5 | 1 | 0 | 0 | 0.0 | 6 | 2 | 4 | 3 | 4 | .227 | .273 | 0 | 0 | 2B-6 |
| 4 yrs. | 23 | 90 | 19 | 1 | 1 | 4 | 4.4 | 18 | 11 | 13 | 11 | 10 | .211 | .378 | 0 | 0 | 2B-23 |
| | | | | | | | | | | | **3rd** | | | | | | |

## Jay Loviglio

**LOVIGLIO, JOHN PAUL**     BR TR 5'9"    160 lbs.
B. May 30, 1956, Freeport, N. Y.

| | G | AB | H | 2B | 3B | HR | HR% | R | RBI | BB | SO | SB | BA | SA | AB | H | G by POS |
|---|---|---|---|---|---|---|---|---|---|---|---|---|---|---|---|---|---|
| 1980 PHI N | 16 | 5 | 0 | 0 | 0 | 0 | 0.0 | 7 | 0 | 1 | 0 | 1 | .000 | .000 | 0 | 0 | 2B-1 |
| 1981 CHI A | 14 | 15 | 4 | 0 | 0 | 0 | 0.0 | 5 | 2 | 1 | 1 | 2 | .267 | .267 | 0 | 0 | 3B-4, 2B-3, DH-2 |
| 1982 | 15 | 31 | 6 | 0 | 0 | 0 | 0.0 | 5 | 2 | 1 | 4 | 2 | .194 | .194 | 0 | 0 | 2B-13, DH-2 |
| 1983 CHI N | 1 | 1 | 0 | 0 | 0 | 0 | 0.0 | 0 | 0 | 0 | 1 | 0 | .000 | .000 | 1 | 0 | |
| 4 yrs. | 46 | 52 | 10 | 0 | 0 | 0 | 0.0 | 17 | 4 | 3 | 6 | 5 | .192 | .192 | 1 | 0 | 2B-17, DH-4, 3B-4 |
| 1 yr. | 1 | 1 | 0 | 0 | 0 | 0 | 0.0 | 0 | 0 | 0 | 1 | 0 | .000 | .000 | 1 | 0 | |

## Bobby Lowe

**LOWE, ROBERT LINCOLN (Link)**     BR TR 5'10"    150 lbs.
B. July 10, 1868, Pittsburgh, Pa.    D. Dec. 8, 1951, Detroit, Mich.
Manager 1904.

| | G | AB | H | 2B | 3B | HR | HR% | R | RBI | BB | SO | SB | BA | SA | AB | H | G by POS |
|---|---|---|---|---|---|---|---|---|---|---|---|---|---|---|---|---|---|
| 1890 BOS N | 52 | 207 | 58 | 13 | 2 | 2 | 1.0 | 35 | 21 | 26 | 32 | 15 | .280 | .391 | 0 | 0 | SS-24, OF-15, 3B-12 |
| 1891 | 125 | 497 | 129 | 19 | 5 | 6 | 1.2 | 92 | 74 | 53 | 54 | 43 | .260 | .354 | 1 | 0 | OF-107, 2B-17, SS-2, 3B-1, P-1 |
| 1892 | 124 | 475 | 115 | 16 | 7 | 3 | 0.6 | 79 | 57 | 37 | 46 | 36 | .242 | .324 | 0 | 0 | OF-90, 3B-14, SS-13, 2B-10 |

| | G | AB | H | 2B | 3B | HR | HR % | R | RBI | BB | SO | SB | BA | SA | Pinch Hit AB | Pinch Hit H | G by POS |
|---|---|---|---|---|---|---|---|---|---|---|---|---|---|---|---|---|---|

## Bobby Lowe continued

| | G | AB | H | 2B | 3B | HR | HR % | R | RBI | BB | SO | SB | BA | SA | AB | H | G by POS |
|---|---|---|---|---|---|---|---|---|---|---|---|---|---|---|---|---|---|
| 1893 | 126 | 526 | 157 | 19 | 5 | 13 | 2.5 | 130 | 89 | 55 | 29 | 22 | .298 | .428 | 0 | 0 | 2B-121, SS-5 |
| 1894 | 133 | 613 | 212 | 34 | 11 | 17 | 2.8 | 158 | 115 | 50 | 25 | 23 | .346 | .520 | 0 | 0 | 2B-130, SS-2, 3B-1 |
| 1895 | 99 | 412 | 122 | 12 | 7 | 7 | 1.7 | 101 | 62 | 40 | 16 | 24 | .296 | .410 | 0 | 0 | 2B-99 |
| 1896 | 73 | 305 | 98 | 11 | 4 | 2 | 0.7 | 59 | 48 | 20 | 11 | 15 | .321 | .403 | 0 | 0 | 2B-73 |
| 1897 | 123 | 499 | 154 | 24 | 8 | 5 | 1.0 | 87 | 106 | 32 | | 16 | .309 | .419 | 0 | 0 | 2B-123 |
| 1898 | 149 | 566 | 154 | 13 | 7 | 4 | 0.7 | 69 | 94 | 29 | | 12 | .272 | .341 | 0 | 0 | 2B-145, SS-2 |
| 1899 | 152 | 559 | 152 | 5 | 9 | 4 | 0.7 | 81 | 88 | 35 | | 17 | .272 | .335 | 0 | 0 | 2B-148, SS-4 |
| 1900 | 127 | 474 | 132 | 11 | 5 | 3 | 0.6 | 65 | 71 | 26 | | 15 | .278 | .342 | 0 | 0 | 2B-127 |
| 1901 | 129 | 491 | 125 | 11 | 1 | 3 | 0.6 | 47 | 47 | 17 | | 22 | .255 | .299 | 0 | 0 | 3B-111, 2B-18 |
| 1902 CHI N | 121 | 472 | 116 | 13 | 3 | 0 | 0.0 | 41 | 31 | 11 | | 16 | .246 | .286 | 0 | 0 | 2B-117, 3B-2 |
| 1903 | 32 | 105 | 28 | 5 | 3 | 0 | 0.0 | 14 | 15 | 4 | | 5 | .267 | .371 | 1 | 1 | 2B-22, 1B-6, 3B-1 |
| 1904 2 teams | PIT | N (1G – | .000) | | DET | A (140G – | .208) | | | | | | | | | | |
| " total | 141 | 507 | 105 | 14 | 6 | 0 | 0.0 | 47 | 40 | 17 | | 15 | .207 | .258 | 1 | 0 | 2B-140 |
| 1905 DET A | 60 | 181 | 35 | 7 | 2 | 0 | 0.0 | 17 | 9 | 13 | | 3 | .193 | .254 | 2 | 0 | OF-25, 3B-22, 2B-6, SS-4, 1B-1 |
| 1906 | 41 | 145 | 30 | 3 | 0 | 1 | 0.7 | 11 | 12 | 4 | | 3 | .207 | .248 | 2 | 0 | SS-19, 2B-17, 3B-5 |
| 1907 | 17 | 37 | 9 | 2 | 0 | 0 | 0.0 | 2 | 5 | 4 | | 0 | .243 | .297 | 2 | 0 | 3B-10, OF-4, SS-2 |
| 18 yrs. | 1824 | 7071 | 1931 | 232 | 85 | 70 | 1.0 | 1135 | 984 | 473 | 213 | 302 | .273 | .360 | 9 | 1 | 2B-1313, OF-241, 3B-179, SS-77, 1B-7, P-1 |
| 2 yrs. | 153 | 577 | 144 | 18 | 6 | 0 | 0.0 | 55 | 46 | 15 | | 21 | .250 | .302 | 1 | 1 | 2B-139, 1B-6, 3B-3 |

## Peanuts Lowrey

**LOWREY, HARRY LEE**
B. Aug. 27, 1918, Culver City, Calif.

BR TR 5'8½" 170 lbs.

| | G | AB | H | 2B | 3B | HR | HR % | R | RBI | BB | SO | SB | BA | SA | AB | H | G by POS |
|---|---|---|---|---|---|---|---|---|---|---|---|---|---|---|---|---|---|
| 1942 CHI N | 27 | 58 | 11 | 0 | 0 | 1 | 1.7 | 4 | 4 | 4 | 4 | 0 | .190 | .241 | 3 | 0 | OF-19 |
| 1943 | 130 | 480 | 140 | 25 | 12 | 1 | 0.2 | 59 | 63 | 35 | 24 | 13 | .292 | .400 | 4 | 1 | OF-113, SS-16, 2B-3 |
| 1945 | 143 | 523 | 148 | 22 | 7 | 7 | 1.3 | 72 | 89 | 48 | 27 | 11 | .283 | .392 | 5 | 1 | OF-138, SS-2 |
| 1946 | 144 | 540 | 139 | 24 | 5 | 4 | 0.7 | 75 | 54 | 56 | 22 | 10 | .257 | .343 | 0 | 0 | OF-126, 3B-20 |
| 1947 | 115 | 448 | 126 | 17 | 5 | 5 | 1.1 | 56 | 37 | 38 | 26 | 2 | .281 | .375 | 1 | 0 | 3B-91, OF-25, 2B-6 |
| 1948 | 129 | 435 | 128 | 12 | 2 | 2 | 0.5 | 47 | 54 | 34 | 31 | 2 | .294 | .349 | 13 | 3 | OF-103, 3B-9, 2B-2, SS-1 |
| 1949 2 teams | CHI | N (38G – | .270) | | CIN | N (89G – | .275) | | | | | | | | | | |
| " total | 127 | 420 | 115 | 21 | 2 | 4 | 1.0 | 66 | 35 | 46 | 19 | 4 | .274 | .362 | 16 | 6 | OF-109, 3B-1 |
| 1950 2 teams | CIN | N (91G – | .227) | | STL | N (17G – | .268) | | | | | | | | | | |
| " total | 108 | 320 | 75 | 14 | 0 | 2 | 0.6 | 44 | 15 | 42 | 8 | 0 | .234 | .297 | 14 | 2 | OF-76, 2B-7, 3B-5 |
| 1951 STL N | 114 | 370 | 112 | 19 | 5 | 5 | 1.4 | 52 | 40 | 35 | 12 | 0 | .303 | .422 | 19 | 5 | OF-85, 3B-11, 2B-3 |
| 1952 | 132 | 374 | 107 | 18 | 2 | 1 | 0.3 | 48 | 48 | 34 | 13 | 3 | .286 | .353 | 27 | 13 | OF-106, 3B-6 |
| 1953 | 104 | 182 | 49 | 9 | 2 | 5 | 2.7 | 26 | 27 | 15 | 21 | 1 | .269 | .423 | 59 | 22 | OF-38, 2B-10, 3B-1 |
| 1954 | 74 | 61 | 7 | 1 | 0 | 0 | 0.0 | 6 | 5 | 9 | 9 | 0 | .115 | .197 | 53 | 7 | OF-12 |
| 1955 PHI N | 54 | 106 | 20 | 4 | 0 | 0 | 0.0 | 9 | 8 | 7 | 10 | 2 | .189 | .226 | 16 | 4 | OF-28, 2B-2, 1B-1 |
| 13 yrs. | 1401 | 4317 | 1177 | 186 | 45 | 37 | 0.9 | 564 | 479 | 403 | 226 | 48 | .273 | .362 | 230 | 62 | OF-978, 3B-144, 2B-33, SS-19, 1B-1 |
| 7 yrs. | 726 | 2595 | 722 | 105 | 32 | 22 | 0.8 | 331 | 311 | 224 | 142 | 41 | .278 | .369 | 31 | 8 | OF-555, 3B-121, SS-19, 2B-11 |

**WORLD SERIES**

| | G | AB | H | 2B | 3B | HR | HR % | R | RBI | BB | SO | SB | BA | SA | AB | H | G by POS |
|---|---|---|---|---|---|---|---|---|---|---|---|---|---|---|---|---|---|
| 1945 CHI N | 7 | 29 | 9 | 1 | 0 | 0 | 0.0 | 4 | 0 | 1 | 2 | 1 | .310 | .345 | 0 | 0 | OF-7 |

## Pat Luby

**LUBY, JOHN PERKINS**
B. 1868, Charleston, S. C.    D. Apr. 24, 1899, Charleston, S. C.

TR 6'    185 lbs.

| | G | AB | H | 2B | 3B | HR | HR % | R | RBI | BB | SO | SB | BA | SA | AB | H | G by POS |
|---|---|---|---|---|---|---|---|---|---|---|---|---|---|---|---|---|---|
| 1890 CHI N | 36 | 116 | 31 | 5 | 3 | 3 | 2.6 | 27 | 17 | 9 | 6 | 3 | .267 | .440 | 0 | 0 | P-34, 1B-2 |
| 1891 | 32 | 98 | 24 | 2 | 4 | 2 | 2.0 | 19 | 24 | 8 | 16 | 3 | .245 | .408 | 0 | 0 | P-30, OF-2, 1B-1 |
| 1892 | 45 | 163 | 31 | 3 | 2 | 2 | 1.2 | 14 | 20 | 12 | 27 | 3 | .190 | .270 | 0 | 0 | P-31, OF-16 |
| 1895 LOU N | 19 | 53 | 15 | 2 | 2 | 0 | 0.0 | 6 | 9 | 8 | 3 | 2 | .283 | .396 | 0 | 0 | P-11, 1B-5, OF-2 |
| 4 yrs. | 132 | 430 | 101 | 12 | 11 | 7 | 1.6 | 66 | 70 | 37 | 52 | 11 | .235 | .363 | 0 | 0 | P-106, OF-20, 1B-8 |
| 3 yrs. | 113 | 377 | 86 | 10 | 9 | 7 | 1.9 | 60 | 61 | 29 | 49 | 9 | .228 | .358 | 0 | 0 | P-95, OF-18, 1B-3 |

## Fred Luderus

**LUDERUS, FREDERICK WILLIAM**
B. Sept. 12, 1885, Milwaukee, Wis.    D. Jan. 4, 1961, Milwaukee, Wis.

BL TR 5'11½" 185 lbs.

| | G | AB | H | 2B | 3B | HR | HR % | R | RBI | BB | SO | SB | BA | SA | AB | H | G by POS |
|---|---|---|---|---|---|---|---|---|---|---|---|---|---|---|---|---|---|
| 1909 CHI N | 11 | 37 | 11 | 1 | 1 | 1 | 2.7 | 9 | 8 | 3 | | 0 | .297 | .459 | 0 | 0 | 1B-11 |
| 1910 2 teams | CHI | N (24G – | .204) | | PHI | N (21G – | .294) | | | | | | | | | | |
| " total | 45 | 122 | 31 | 6 | 3 | 0 | 0.0 | 15 | 17 | 13 | 8 | 2 | .254 | .352 | 8 | 2 | 1B-36 |
| 1911 PHI N | 146 | 551 | 166 | 24 | 11 | 16 | 2.9 | 69 | 99 | 40 | 76 | 6 | .301 | .472 | 0 | 0 | 1B-146 |
| 1912 | 148 | 572 | 147 | 31 | 5 | 10 | 1.7 | 77 | 69 | 44 | 65 | 8 | .257 | .381 | 2 | 0 | 1B-146 |
| 1913 | 155 | 588 | 154 | 32 | 7 | 18 | 3.1 | 67 | 86 | 34 | 51 | 5 | .262 | .432 | 0 | 0 | 1B-155 |
| 1914 | 121 | 443 | 110 | 16 | 5 | 12 | 2.7 | 55 | 55 | 33 | 31 | 2 | .248 | .388 | 0 | 0 | 1B-121 |
| 1915 | 141 | 499 | 157 | 36 | 7 | 7 | 1.4 | 55 | 62 | 42 | 36 | 9 | .315 | .457 | 0 | 0 | 1B-141 |
| 1916 | 146 | 508 | 143 | 26 | 3 | 5 | 1.0 | 52 | 53 | 41 | 32 | 8 | .281 | .374 | 0 | 0 | 1B-146 |
| 1917 | 154 | 522 | 136 | 24 | 4 | 5 | 1.0 | 57 | 72 | 65 | 35 | 5 | .261 | .351 | 0 | 0 | 1B-154 |
| 1918 | 125 | 468 | 135 | 23 | 2 | 5 | 1.1 | 54 | 67 | 42 | 33 | 4 | .288 | .378 | 0 | 0 | 1B-125 |
| 1919 | 138 | 509 | 149 | 30 | 6 | 5 | 1.0 | 60 | 54 | 54 | 48 | 6 | .293 | .405 | 0 | 0 | 1B-138 |
| 1920 | 16 | 32 | 5 | 2 | 0 | 0 | 0.0 | 1 | 4 | 3 | 6 | 0 | .156 | .219 | 9 | 2 | 1B-7 |
| 12 yrs. | 1346 | 4851 | 1344 | 251 | 54 | 84 | 1.7 | 570 | 647 | 414 | 421 | 55 | .277 | .403 | 19 | 4 | 1B-1326 |
| 2 yrs. | 35 | 91 | 22 | 2 | 1 | 1 | 1.1 | 13 | 12 | 7 | 3 | 0 | .242 | .341 | 6 | 2 | 1B-28 |

**WORLD SERIES**

| | G | AB | H | 2B | 3B | HR | HR % | R | RBI | BB | SO | SB | BA | SA | AB | H | G by POS |
|---|---|---|---|---|---|---|---|---|---|---|---|---|---|---|---|---|---|
| 1915 PHI N | 5 | 16 | 7 | 2 | 0 | 1 | 6.3 | 1 | 6 | 1 | 4 | 0 | .438 | .750 | 0 | 0 | 1B-5 |

## Mike Lum

**LUM, MICHAEL KEN-WAI**
B. Oct. 27, 1945, Honolulu, Hawaii

BL TL 6'    180 lbs.

| | G | AB | H | 2B | 3B | HR | HR % | R | RBI | BB | SO | SB | BA | SA | AB | H | G by POS |
|---|---|---|---|---|---|---|---|---|---|---|---|---|---|---|---|---|---|
| 1967 ATL N | 9 | 26 | 6 | 0 | 0 | 0 | 0.0 | 1 | 1 | 1 | 4 | 0 | .231 | .231 | 3 | 1 | OF-6 |
| 1968 | 122 | 232 | 52 | 7 | 3 | 3 | 1.3 | 22 | 21 | 14 | 35 | 3 | .224 | .319 | 27 | 8 | OF-95 |
| 1969 | 121 | 168 | 45 | 8 | 0 | 1 | 0.6 | 20 | 22 | 16 | 18 | 0 | .268 | .333 | 31 | 9 | OF-89 |
| 1970 | 123 | 291 | 74 | 17 | 2 | 7 | 2.4 | 25 | 28 | 17 | 43 | 3 | .254 | .399 | 28 | 9 | OF-98 |
| 1971 | 145 | 454 | 122 | 14 | 1 | 13 | 2.9 | 56 | 55 | 47 | 43 | 0 | .269 | .390 | 14 | 2 | OF-125, 1B-1 |
| 1972 | 123 | 369 | 84 | 14 | 2 | 9 | 2.4 | 40 | 38 | 50 | 52 | 1 | .228 | .350 | 15 | 6 | OF-109, 1B-2 |

| | G | AB | H | 2B | 3B | HR | HR % | R | RBI | BB | SO | SB | BA | SA | Pinch Hit AB | Pinch Hit H | G by POS |
|---|---|---|---|---|---|---|---|---|---|---|---|---|---|---|---|---|---|

## Mike Lum continued

| | G | AB | H | 2B | 3B | HR | HR % | R | RBI | BB | SO | SB | BA | SA | P.H. AB | P.H. H | G by POS |
|---|---|---|---|---|---|---|---|---|---|---|---|---|---|---|---|---|---|
| 1973 | 138 | 513 | 151 | 26 | 6 | 16 | 3.1 | 74 | 82 | 41 | 89 | 2 | .294 | .462 | 9 | 0 | 1B-84, OF-64 |
| 1974 | 106 | 361 | 84 | 11 | 2 | 11 | 3.0 | 50 | 50 | 45 | 49 | 0 | .233 | .366 | 10 | 1 | 1B-60, OF-50 |
| 1975 | 124 | 364 | 83 | 8 | 2 | 8 | 2.2 | 32 | 36 | 39 | 38 | 2 | .228 | .327 | 26 | 4 | 1B-60, OF-38 |
| 1976 CIN N | 84 | 136 | 31 | 5 | 1 | 3 | 2.2 | 15 | 20 | 22 | 24 | 0 | .228 | .346 | 39 | 10 | OF-38 |
| 1977 | 81 | 125 | 20 | 1 | 0 | 5 | 4.0 | 14 | 16 | 9 | 33 | 2 | .160 | .288 | 47 | 5 | OF-24, 1B-8 |
| 1978 | 86 | 146 | 39 | 7 | 1 | 6 | 4.1 | 15 | 23 | 22 | 18 | 0 | .267 | .452 | 36 | 11 | OF-43, 1B-7 |
| 1979 ATL N | 111 | 217 | 54 | 6 | 0 | 6 | 2.8 | 27 | 27 | 18 | 34 | 0 | .249 | .359 | 52 | 17 | 1B-51, OF-3 |
| 1980 | 93 | 83 | 17 | 3 | 0 | 0 | 0.0 | 7 | 5 | 18 | 19 | 0 | .205 | .241 | 50 | 12 | OF-19, 1B-10 |
| 1981 2 teams | ATL | N (10G – .091) | | | | CHI | N (41G – .241) | | | | | | | | | | |
| " total | 51 | 69 | 15 | 1 | 0 | 2 | 2.9 | 6 | 7 | 7 | 7 | 0 | .217 | .319 | 31 | 8 | OF-15, 1B-1 |
| 15 yrs. | 1517 | 3554 | 877 | 128 | 20 | 90 | 2.5 | 404 | 431 | 366 | 506 | 13 | .247 | .370 | 418 | 103 | OF-816, 1B-284 |
| | | | | | | | | | | | | | | | 7th | 9th | |
| 1 yr. | 41 | 58 | 14 | 1 | 0 | 2 | 3.4 | 5 | 7 | 5 | 5 | 0 | .241 | .362 | 24 | 7 | OF-14, 1B-1 |
| LEAGUE CHAMPIONSHIP SERIES | | | | | | | | | | | | | | | | | |
| 1969 ATL N | 2 | 2 | 2 | 1 | 0 | 0 | 0.0 | 0 | 0 | 0 | 0 | 0 | 1.000 | 1.500 | 1 | 1 | OF-1 |
| 1976 CIN N | 1 | 1 | 0 | 0 | 0 | 0 | 0.0 | 0 | 0 | 0 | 0 | 0 | .000 | .000 | 1 | 0 | |
| 2 yrs. | 3 | 3 | 2 | 1 | 0 | 0 | 0.0 | 0 | 0 | 0 | 0 | 0 | .667 | 1.000 | 2 | 1 | OF-1 |

## Tom Lundstedt

**LUNDSTEDT, THOMAS ROBERT**
B. Apr. 10, 1949, Davenport, Iowa
BR TR 6'4" 195 lbs.

| | G | AB | H | 2B | 3B | HR | HR % | R | RBI | BB | SO | SB | BA | SA | P.H. AB | P.H. H | G by POS |
|---|---|---|---|---|---|---|---|---|---|---|---|---|---|---|---|---|---|
| 1973 CHI N | 4 | 5 | 0 | 0 | 0 | 0 | 0.0 | 0 | 0 | 0 | 1 | 0 | .000 | .000 | 0 | 0 | C-4 |
| 1974 | 22 | 32 | 3 | 0 | 0 | 0 | 0.0 | 1 | 0 | 5 | 7 | 0 | .094 | .094 | 0 | 0 | C-22 |
| 1975 MIN A | 18 | 28 | 3 | 0 | 0 | 0 | 0.0 | 2 | 1 | 4 | 5 | 0 | .107 | .107 | 3 | 1 | C-14, DH-2 |
| 3 yrs. | 44 | 65 | 6 | 0 | 0 | 0 | 0.0 | 3 | 1 | 9 | 13 | 0 | .092 | .092 | 3 | 1 | C-40, DH-2 |
| 2 yrs. | 26 | 37 | 3 | 0 | 0 | 0 | 0.0 | 1 | 0 | 5 | 8 | 0 | .081 | .081 | 0 | 0 | C-26 |

## Dummy Lynch

**LYNCH, MATTHEW DANIEL**
B. Feb. 7, 1927, Dallas, Tex.   D. June 30, 1978, Plano, Tex.
BR TR 5'11" 174 lbs.

| | G | AB | H | 2B | 3B | HR | HR % | R | RBI | BB | SO | SB | BA | SA | P.H. AB | P.H. H | G by POS |
|---|---|---|---|---|---|---|---|---|---|---|---|---|---|---|---|---|---|
| 1948 CHI N | 7 | 7 | 2 | 0 | 0 | 1 | 14.3 | 3 | 1 | 1 | 1 | 0 | .286 | .714 | 4 | 1 | 2B-1 |

## Henry Lynch

**LYNCH, HENRY W.**
B. 1866, Worcester, Mass.   D. Nov. 23, 1925, Worcester, Mass.
5'7" 143 lbs.

| | G | AB | H | 2B | 3B | HR | HR % | R | RBI | BB | SO | SB | BA | SA | P.H. AB | P.H. H | G by POS |
|---|---|---|---|---|---|---|---|---|---|---|---|---|---|---|---|---|---|
| 1893 CHI N | 4 | 14 | 3 | 2 | 0 | 0 | 0.0 | 0 | 2 | 1 | 1 | 0 | .214 | .357 | 0 | 0 | OF-4 |

## Mike Lynch

**LYNCH, MICHAEL JOSEPH**
B. Sept. 10, 1876, St. Paul, Minn.   D. Apr. 1, 1947, Jennings Lodge, Ore.
TR 6'2" 170 lbs.

| | G | AB | H | 2B | 3B | HR | HR % | R | RBI | BB | SO | SB | BA | SA | P.H. AB | P.H. H | G by POS |
|---|---|---|---|---|---|---|---|---|---|---|---|---|---|---|---|---|---|
| 1902 CHI N | 7 | 28 | 4 | 0 | 0 | 0 | 0.0 | 4 | 0 | 2 | | 0 | .143 | .143 | 0 | 0 | OF-7 |

## Pop Lytle

**LYTLE, EDWARD BENSON (Dad)**
B. Mar. 10, 1862, Racine, Wis.   D. Dec. 21, 1950, Long Beach, Calif.
BR TR 5'11" 160 lbs.

| | G | AB | H | 2B | 3B | HR | HR % | R | RBI | BB | SO | SB | BA | SA | P.H. AB | P.H. H | G by POS |
|---|---|---|---|---|---|---|---|---|---|---|---|---|---|---|---|---|---|
| 1890 2 teams | CHI | N (1G – .000) | | | | PIT | N (15G – .145) | | | | | | | | | | |
| " total | 16 | 59 | 8 | 1 | 0 | 0 | 0.0 | 3 | 0 | 8 | 10 | 0 | .136 | .153 | 0 | 0 | OF-8, 2B-8 |

## Ray Mack

**MACK, RAYMOND JAMES**
Born Raymond James Mickovsky.
B. Aug. 31, 1916, Cleveland, Ohio   D. May 7, 1969, Columbus, Ohio
BR TR 6' 200 lbs.

| | G | AB | H | 2B | 3B | HR | HR % | R | RBI | BB | SO | SB | BA | SA | P.H. AB | P.H. H | G by POS |
|---|---|---|---|---|---|---|---|---|---|---|---|---|---|---|---|---|---|
| 1938 CLE A | 2 | 6 | 2 | 0 | 1 | 0 | 0.0 | 2 | 2 | 0 | 1 | 0 | .333 | .667 | 0 | 0 | 2B-2 |
| 1939 | 36 | 112 | 17 | 4 | 0 | 1 | 0.9 | 12 | 6 | 12 | 19 | 0 | .152 | .232 | 2 | 0 | 2B-34, 3B-1 |
| 1940 | 146 | 530 | 150 | 21 | 5 | 12 | 2.3 | 60 | 69 | 51 | 77 | 4 | .283 | .409 | 0 | 0 | 2B-146 |
| 1941 | 145 | 501 | 114 | 22 | 4 | 9 | 1.8 | 54 | 44 | 54 | 69 | 8 | .228 | .341 | 0 | 0 | 2B-145 |
| 1942 | 143 | 481 | 108 | 14 | 6 | 2 | 0.4 | 43 | 45 | 41 | 51 | 9 | .225 | .291 | 0 | 0 | 2B-143 |
| 1943 | 153 | 545 | 120 | 25 | 2 | 7 | 1.3 | 56 | 62 | 47 | 61 | 8 | .220 | .312 | 0 | 0 | 2B-153 |
| 1944 | 83 | 284 | 66 | 15 | 3 | 0 | 0.0 | 24 | 29 | 28 | 45 | 4 | .232 | .306 | 0 | 0 | 2B-83 |
| 1946 | 61 | 171 | 35 | 6 | 2 | 1 | 0.6 | 13 | 9 | 23 | 27 | 2 | .205 | .281 | 0 | 0 | 2B-61 |
| 1947 2 teams | NY | A (1G – .000) | | | | CHI | N (21G – .218) | | | | | | | | | | |
| " total | 22 | 78 | 17 | 6 | 0 | 2 | 2.6 | 9 | 12 | 5 | 15 | 0 | .218 | .372 | 0 | 0 | 2B-21 |
| 9 yrs. | 791 | 2708 | 629 | 113 | 24 | 34 | 1.3 | 273 | 278 | 261 | 365 | 35 | .232 | .329 | 2 | 0 | 2B-788, 3B-1 |
| 1 yr. | 21 | 78 | 17 | 6 | 0 | 2 | 2.6 | 9 | 12 | 5 | 15 | 0 | .218 | .372 | 0 | 0 | 2B-21 |

## Steve Macko

**MACKO, STEVEN JOSEPH**
B. Sept. 6, 1954, Burlington, Iowa   D. Nov. 15, 1981, Arlington, Tex.
BL TR 5'10" 160 lbs.

| | G | AB | H | 2B | 3B | HR | HR % | R | RBI | BB | SO | SB | BA | SA | P.H. AB | P.H. H | G by POS |
|---|---|---|---|---|---|---|---|---|---|---|---|---|---|---|---|---|---|
| 1979 CHI N | 19 | 40 | 9 | 1 | 0 | 0 | 0.0 | 2 | 3 | 4 | 8 | 0 | .225 | .250 | 5 | 0 | 2B-10, 3B-4 |
| 1980 | 6 | 20 | 6 | 2 | 0 | 0 | 0.0 | 2 | 2 | 0 | 3 | 0 | .300 | .400 | 0 | 0 | SS-3, 3B-2, 2B-1 |
| 2 yrs. | 25 | 60 | 15 | 3 | 0 | 0 | 0.0 | 4 | 5 | 4 | 11 | 0 | .250 | .300 | 5 | 0 | 2B-11, 3B-6, SS-3 |
| 2 yrs. | 25 | 60 | 15 | 3 | 0 | 0 | 0.0 | 4 | 5 | 4 | 11 | 0 | .250 | .300 | 5 | 0 | 2B-11, 3B-6, SS-3 |

## Clarence Maddern

**MADDERN, CLARENCE JAMES**
B. Sept. 26, 1921, Bisbee, Ariz.
BR TR 6'1" 185 lbs.

| | G | AB | H | 2B | 3B | HR | HR % | R | RBI | BB | SO | SB | BA | SA | P.H. AB | P.H. H | G by POS |
|---|---|---|---|---|---|---|---|---|---|---|---|---|---|---|---|---|---|
| 1946 CHI N | 3 | 3 | 0 | 0 | 0 | 0 | 0.0 | 0 | 0 | 0 | 0 | 0 | .000 | .000 | 1 | 0 | OF-2 |
| 1948 | 80 | 214 | 54 | 12 | 1 | 4 | 1.9 | 16 | 27 | 10 | 25 | 0 | .252 | .374 | 23 | 5 | OF-55 |
| 1949 | 10 | 9 | 3 | 0 | 0 | 1 | 11.1 | 1 | 2 | 2 | 0 | 0 | .333 | .667 | 7 | 1 | 1B-1 |
| 1951 CLE A | 11 | 12 | 2 | 0 | 0 | 0 | 0.0 | 0 | 0 | 0 | 1 | 0 | .167 | .167 | 9 | 1 | OF-1 |
| 4 yrs. | 104 | 238 | 59 | 12 | 1 | 5 | 2.1 | 17 | 29 | 12 | 26 | 0 | .248 | .370 | 40 | 7 | OF-58, 1B-1 |
| 3 yrs. | 93 | 226 | 57 | 12 | 1 | 5 | 2.2 | 17 | 29 | 12 | 25 | 0 | .252 | .381 | 31 | 6 | OF-57, 1B-1 |

| | G | AB | H | 2B | 3B | HR | HR % | R | RBI | BB | SO | SB | BA | SA | Pinch Hit AB | Pinch Hit H | G by POS |
|---|---|---|---|---|---|---|---|---|---|---|---|---|---|---|---|---|---|

# Bill Madlock

**MADLOCK, BILL JR. (Mad Dog)**      BR TR 5'11" 185 lbs.
B. Jan. 12, 1951, Memphis, Tenn.

| Year Team | G | AB | H | 2B | 3B | HR | HR% | R | RBI | BB | SO | SB | BA | SA | PH AB | PH H | G by POS |
|---|---|---|---|---|---|---|---|---|---|---|---|---|---|---|---|---|---|
| 1973 TEX A | 21 | 77 | 27 | 5 | 3 | 1 | 1.3 | 16 | 5 | 7 | 9 | 3 | .351 | .532 | 0 | 0 | 3B-21 |
| 1974 CHI N | 128 | 453 | 142 | 21 | 5 | 9 | 2.0 | 65 | 54 | 42 | 39 | 11 | .313 | .442 | 8 | 4 | 3B-121 |
| 1975 | 130 | 514 | 182 | 29 | 7 | 7 | 1.4 | 77 | 64 | 42 | 34 | 9 | .354 | .479 | 0 | 0 | 3B-128 |
| 1976 | 142 | 514 | 174 | 36 | 1 | 15 | 2.9 | 68 | 84 | 56 | 27 | 15 | .339 | .500 | 5 | 1 | 3B-136 |
| 1977 SF N | 140 | 533 | 161 | 28 | 1 | 12 | 2.3 | 70 | 46 | 43 | 33 | 13 | .302 | .426 | 8 | 1 | 3B-126, 2B-6 |
| 1978 | 122 | 447 | 138 | 26 | 3 | 15 | 3.4 | 76 | 44 | 48 | 39 | 16 | .309 | .481 | 8 | 1 | 2B-114, 1B-3 |
| 1979 2 teams | | | SF N (69G – .261) | | | PIT N (85G – .328) | | | | | | | | | | | |
| " total | 154 | 560 | 167 | 26 | 5 | 14 | 2.5 | 85 | 85 | 52 | 41 | 32 | .298 | .438 | 5 | 2 | 3B-85, 2B-63, 1B-5 |
| 1980 PIT N | 137 | 494 | 137 | 22 | 4 | 10 | 2.0 | 62 | 53 | 45 | 33 | 16 | .277 | .399 | 3 | 1 | 3B-127, 1B-12 |
| 1981 | 82 | 279 | 95 | 23 | 1 | 6 | 2.2 | 35 | 45 | 34 | 17 | 18 | .341 | .495 | 4 | 0 | 3B-78 |
| 1982 | 154 | 568 | 181 | 33 | 3 | 19 | 3.3 | 92 | 95 | 48 | 39 | 18 | .319 | .488 | 7 | 2 | 3B-146, 1B-3 |
| 1983 | 130 | 473 | 153 | 21 | 0 | 12 | 2.5 | 68 | 68 | 49 | 24 | 3 | .323 | .444 | 4 | 1 | 3B-126 |
| 1984 | 103 | 403 | 102 | 16 | 0 | 4 | 1.0 | 38 | 44 | 26 | 29 | 3 | .253 | .323 | 3 | 0 | 3B-98, 1B-1 |
| 1985 2 teams | | | PIT N (110G – .251) | | | LA N (34G – .360) | | | | | | | | | | | |
| " total | 144 | 513 | 141 | 27 | 1 | 12 | 2.3 | 69 | 56 | 49 | 53 | 10 | .275 | .402 | 5 | 4 | 3B-130, 1B-12 |
| 13 yrs. | 1587 | 5828 | 1800 | 313 | 34 | 136 | 2.3 | 821 | 743 | 541 | 417 | 167 | .309 | .444 | 60 | 17 | 3B-1322, 2B-183, 1B-36 |
| 3 yrs. | 400 | 1481 | 498 | 86 | 13 | 31 | 2.1 | 210 | 202 | 140 | 100 | 35 | .336 | .475 | 13 | 5 | 3B-385 |

LEAGUE CHAMPIONSHIP SERIES

| Year Team | G | AB | H | 2B | 3B | HR | HR% | R | RBI | BB | SO | SB | BA | SA | PH AB | PH H | G by POS |
|---|---|---|---|---|---|---|---|---|---|---|---|---|---|---|---|---|---|
| 1979 PIT N | 3 | 12 | 3 | 0 | 0 | 1 | 8.3 | 1 | 2 | 2 | 0 | 2 | .250 | .500 | 0 | 0 | 3B-3 |
| 1985 LA N | 6 | 24 | 8 | 1 | 0 | 3 | 12.5 | 5 | 7 | 0 | 2 | 1 | .333 | .750 | 0 | 0 | 3B-6 |
| 2 yrs. | 9 | 36 | 11 | 1 | 0 | 4 | 11.1 | 6 | 9 | 2 | 2 | 3 | .306 | .667 | 0 | 0 | 3B-9 |

WORLD SERIES

| Year Team | G | AB | H | 2B | 3B | HR | HR% | R | RBI | BB | SO | SB | BA | SA | PH AB | PH H | G by POS |
|---|---|---|---|---|---|---|---|---|---|---|---|---|---|---|---|---|---|
| 1979 PIT N | 9 | 24 | 9 | 1 | 0 | 0 | 0.0 | 3 | 5 | 1 | | 0 | .375 | .417 | 0 | 0 | 3B-7 |

# Sal Madrid

**MADRID, SALVADOR**      BR TR 5'9" 165 lbs.
B. June 19, 1920, El Paso, Tex.    D. Feb. 24, 1977, Fort Wayne, Ind.

| Year Team | G | AB | H | 2B | 3B | HR | HR% | R | RBI | BB | SO | SB | BA | SA | PH AB | PH H | G by POS |
|---|---|---|---|---|---|---|---|---|---|---|---|---|---|---|---|---|---|
| 1947 CHI N | 8 | 24 | 3 | 1 | 0 | 0 | 0.0 | 0 | 1 | 1 | 6 | 0 | .125 | .167 | 0 | 0 | SS-8 |

# Lee Magee

**MAGEE, LEO CHRISTOPHER**      BB TR 5'11" 165 lbs.
Born Leopold Christopher Hoernschemeyer.
B. June 4, 1889, Cincinnati, Ohio    D. Mar. 14, 1966, Columbus, Ohio
Manager 1915.

| Year Team | G | AB | H | 2B | 3B | HR | HR% | R | RBI | BB | SO | SB | BA | SA | PH AB | PH H | G by POS |
|---|---|---|---|---|---|---|---|---|---|---|---|---|---|---|---|---|---|
| 1911 STL N | 26 | 69 | 18 | 1 | 1 | 0 | 0.0 | 9 | 8 | 8 | 8 | 4 | .261 | .304 | 2 | 0 | 2B-18, SS-3 |
| 1912 | 128 | 458 | 133 | 13 | 8 | 0 | 0.0 | 60 | 40 | 39 | 29 | 16 | .290 | .354 | 8 | 3 | OF-85, 2B-23, 1B-6, SS-1 |
| 1913 | 136 | 529 | 140 | 13 | 7 | 2 | 0.4 | 53 | 31 | 34 | 30 | 23 | .265 | .327 | 0 | 0 | OF-107, 2B-21, 1B-6, SS-2 |
| 1914 | 162 | 529 | 150 | 23 | 4 | 2 | 0.4 | 59 | 40 | 42 | 24 | 36 | .284 | .353 | 0 | 0 | OF-102, 1B-40, 2B-6 |
| 1915 BKN F | 121 | 452 | 146 | 19 | 10 | 4 | 0.9 | 87 | 49 | 22 | | 34 | .323 | .436 | 4 | 0 | 2B-115, 1B-2 |
| 1916 NY A | 131 | 510 | 131 | 18 | 4 | 3 | 0.6 | 57 | 45 | 50 | 31 | 29 | .257 | .325 | 1 | 0 | OF-128, 2B-2 |
| 1917 2 teams | | | NY A (51G – .220) | | | STL A (36G – .170) | | | | | | | | | | | |
| " total | 87 | 285 | 57 | 5 | 1 | 0 | 0.0 | 28 | 12 | 19 | 24 | 6 | .200 | .225 | 3 | 1 | OF-51, 3B-20, 2B-6, 1B-5 |
| 1918 CIN N | 119 | 459 | 133 | 22 | 13 | 0 | 0.0 | 62 | 28 | 28 | 19 | 19 | .290 | .394 | 1 | 0 | 2B-114, 3B-3 |
| 1919 2 teams | | | BKN N (45G – .238) | | | CHI N (79G – .292) | | | | | | | | | | | |
| " total | 124 | 448 | 121 | 19 | 6 | 1 | 0.2 | 52 | 24 | 23 | 24 | 19 | .270 | .346 | 7 | 2 | OF-44, 2B-43, 3B-19, SS-13 |
| 9 yrs. | 1034 | 3739 | 1029 | 133 | 54 | 12 | 0.3 | 467 | 277 | 265 | 189 | 186 | .275 | .349 | 26 | 6 | OF-517, 2B-348, 1B-59, 3B-42, SS-19 |
| 1 yr. | 79 | 267 | 78 | 12 | 4 | 1 | 0.4 | 36 | 17 | 18 | 16 | 14 | .292 | .378 | 7 | 2 | OF-44, SS-13, 3B-10, 2B-7 |

# George Magoon

**MAGOON, GEORGE HENRY (Topsy Maggie)**      BR TR 5'9" 165 lbs.
B. Mar. 27, 1875, St. Albans, Me.    D. Dec. 6, 1943, Rochester, N. H.

| Year Team | G | AB | H | 2B | 3B | HR | HR% | R | RBI | BB | SO | SB | BA | SA | PH AB | PH H | G by POS |
|---|---|---|---|---|---|---|---|---|---|---|---|---|---|---|---|---|---|
| 1898 BKN N | 93 | 343 | 77 | 7 | 0 | 1 | 0.3 | 35 | 39 | 30 | | 7 | .224 | .254 | 0 | 0 | SS-93 |
| 1899 2 teams | | | BAL N (62G – .256) | | | CHI N (59G – .228) | | | | | | | | | | | |
| " total | 121 | 396 | 96 | 13 | 4 | 0 | 0.0 | 50 | 52 | 50 | | 12 | .242 | .295 | 0 | 0 | SS-121 |
| 1901 CIN N | 127 | 460 | 116 | 16 | 7 | 1 | 0.2 | 47 | 53 | 52 | | 15 | .252 | .324 | 0 | 0 | SS-112, 2B-15 |
| 1902 | 45 | 162 | 44 | 9 | 2 | 0 | 0.0 | 29 | 23 | 13 | | 7 | .272 | .352 | 1 | 0 | 2B-41, SS-3 |
| 1903 2 teams | | | CIN A (42G – .216) | | | CHI A (94G – .228) | | | | | | | | | | | |
| " total | 136 | 473 | 106 | 17 | 3 | 0 | 0.0 | 38 | 34 | 49 | | 6 | .224 | .273 | 1 | 0 | 2B-126, 3B-9 |
| 5 yrs. | 522 | 1834 | 439 | 62 | 16 | 2 | 0.1 | 199 | 201 | 194 | | 47 | .239 | .294 | 2 | 0 | SS-329, 2B-182, 3B-9 |
| 1 yr. | 59 | 189 | 43 | 5 | 1 | 0 | 0.0 | 24 | 21 | 24 | | 5 | .228 | .265 | 0 | 0 | SS-59 |

# Freddie Maguire

**MAGUIRE, FRED EDWARD**      BR TR 5'11" 155 lbs.
B. May 10, 1899, Roxbury, Mass.    D. Nov. 3, 1961, Brighton, Mass.

| Year Team | G | AB | H | 2B | 3B | HR | HR% | R | RBI | BB | SO | SB | BA | SA | PH AB | PH H | G by POS |
|---|---|---|---|---|---|---|---|---|---|---|---|---|---|---|---|---|---|
| 1922 NY N | 5 | 12 | 4 | 0 | 0 | 0 | 0.0 | 1 | 0 | 1 | 0 | 1 | .333 | .333 | 1 | 0 | 2B-3 |
| 1923 | 41 | 30 | 6 | 1 | 0 | 0 | 0.0 | 11 | 2 | 2 | 4 | 1 | .200 | .233 | 1 | 0 | 2B-16, 3B-1 |
| 1928 CHI N | 140 | 574 | 160 | 24 | 7 | 1 | 0.2 | 67 | 41 | 25 | 38 | 6 | .279 | .350 | 2 | 1 | 2B-138 |
| 1929 BOS N | 138 | 496 | 125 | 26 | 8 | 0 | 0.0 | 54 | 41 | 19 | 40 | 8 | .252 | .337 | 0 | 0 | 2B-138, SS-1 |
| 1930 | 146 | 516 | 138 | 21 | 5 | 0 | 0.0 | 54 | 52 | 20 | 22 | 4 | .267 | .328 | 0 | 0 | 2B-146 |
| 1931 | 148 | 492 | 112 | 18 | 2 | 0 | 0.0 | 36 | 26 | 16 | 26 | 3 | .228 | .272 | 0 | 0 | 2B-148 |
| 6 yrs. | 618 | 2120 | 545 | 90 | 22 | 1 | 0.0 | 226 | 163 | 82 | 131 | 23 | .257 | .322 | 4 | 1 | 2B-589, SS-1, 3B-1 |
| 1 yr. | 140 | 574 | 160 | 24 | 7 | 1 | 0.2 | 67 | 41 | 25 | 38 | 6 | .279 | .350 | 2 | 1 | 2B-138 |

WORLD SERIES

| Year Team | G | AB | H | 2B | 3B | HR | HR% | R | RBI | BB | SO | SB | BA | SA | PH AB | PH H | G by POS |
|---|---|---|---|---|---|---|---|---|---|---|---|---|---|---|---|---|---|
| 1923 NY N | 2 | 0 | 0 | 0 | 0 | 0 | – | 1 | 0 | 0 | 0 | 0 | – | – | 0 | 0 | |

# George Maisel

**MAISEL, GEORGE JOHN**      BR TR 5'10½" 180 lbs.
Brother of Fritz Maisel.
B. Mar. 12, 1892, Catonsville, Md.    D. Nov. 20, 1968, Baltimore, Md.

| Year Team | G | AB | H | 2B | 3B | HR | HR% | R | RBI | BB | SO | SB | BA | SA | PH AB | PH H | G by POS |
|---|---|---|---|---|---|---|---|---|---|---|---|---|---|---|---|---|---|
| 1913 STL A | 11 | 18 | 3 | 2 | 0 | 0 | 0.0 | 2 | 1 | 1 | 7 | 0 | .167 | .278 | 5 | 1 | OF-5 |
| 1916 DET A | 7 | 5 | 0 | 0 | 0 | 0 | 0.0 | 2 | 0 | 0 | 2 | 0 | .000 | .000 | 0 | 0 | 3B-3 |

| | G | AB | H | 2B | 3B | HR | HR % | R | RBI | BB | SO | SB | BA | SA | Pinch Hit AB | Pinch Hit H | G by POS |
|---|---|---|---|---|---|---|---|---|---|---|---|---|---|---|---|---|---|

## George Maisel continued

| | G | AB | H | 2B | 3B | HR | HR % | R | RBI | BB | SO | SB | BA | SA | AB | H | G by POS |
|---|---|---|---|---|---|---|---|---|---|---|---|---|---|---|---|---|---|
| 1921 CHI N | 111 | 393 | 122 | 7 | 2 | 0 | 0.0 | 54 | 43 | 11 | 13 | 17 | .310 | .338 | 1 | 1 | OF-108 |
| 1922 | 38 | 84 | 16 | 1 | 1 | 0 | 0.0 | 9 | 6 | 8 | 2 | 1 | .190 | .226 | 5 | 1 | OF-38 |
| 4 yrs. | 167 | 500 | 141 | 10 | 3 | 0 | 0.0 | 67 | 50 | 20 | 24 | 18 | .282 | .314 | 11 | 3 | OF-151, 3B-3 |
| 2 yrs. | 149 | 477 | 138 | 8 | 3 | 0 | 0.0 | 63 | 49 | 19 | 15 | 18 | .289 | .319 | 6 | 2 | OF-146 |

## Billy Maloney

**MALONEY, WILLIAM ALPHONSE**    BL TR 5'10" 177 lbs.
B. June 5, 1878, Lewiston, Me.    D. Sept. 2, 1960, Breckenridge, Tex.

| | G | AB | H | 2B | 3B | HR | HR % | R | RBI | BB | SO | SB | BA | SA | AB | H | G by POS |
|---|---|---|---|---|---|---|---|---|---|---|---|---|---|---|---|---|---|
| 1901 MIL A | 86 | 290 | 85 | 3 | 4 | 0 | 0.0 | 42 | 22 | 7 | | 11 | .293 | .331 | 5 | 2 | C-72, OF-8 |
| 1902 2 teams | | STL | A (30G – | .205) | | CIN | N | (27G – | .247) | | | | | | | | |
| " total | 57 | 201 | 45 | 7 | 0 | 1 | 0.5 | 21 | 18 | 8 | | 8 | .224 | .274 | 3 | 0 | OF-41, C-14 |
| 1905 CHI N | 145 | 558 | 145 | 17 | 14 | 2 | 0.4 | 78 | 56 | 43 | | 59 | .260 | .351 | 0 | 0 | OF-145 |
| 1906 BKN N | 151 | 566 | 125 | 15 | 7 | 0 | 0.0 | 71 | 32 | 49 | | 38 | .221 | .272 | 0 | 0 | OF-151 |
| 1907 | 144 | 502 | 115 | 7 | 10 | 0 | 0.0 | 51 | 32 | 31 | | 25 | .229 | .283 | 0 | 0 | OF-144 |
| 1908 | 113 | 359 | 70 | 5 | 7 | 3 | 0.8 | 31 | 17 | 24 | | 14 | .195 | .273 | 6 | 1 | OF-103, C-4 |
| 6 yrs. | 696 | 2476 | 585 | 54 | 42 | 6 | 0.2 | 294 | 177 | 162 | | 155 | .236 | .299 | 14 | 3 | OF-592, C-90 |
| 1 yr. | 145 | 558 | 145 | 17 | 14 | 2 | 0.4 | 78 | 56 | 43 | | 59 | .260 | .351 | 0 | 0 | OF-145 |

## Gus Mancuso

**MANCUSO, AUGUST RODNEY (Blackie)**    BR TR 5'10" 185 lbs.
Brother of Frank Mancuso.
B. Dec. 5, 1905, Galveston, Tex.    D. Oct. 26, 1984, Houston, Tex.

| | G | AB | H | 2B | 3B | HR | HR % | R | RBI | BB | SO | SB | BA | SA | AB | H | G by POS |
|---|---|---|---|---|---|---|---|---|---|---|---|---|---|---|---|---|---|
| 1928 STL N | 11 | 38 | 7 | 0 | 1 | 0 | 0.0 | 2 | 3 | 0 | 5 | 0 | .184 | .237 | 0 | 0 | C-11 |
| 1930 | 76 | 227 | 83 | 17 | 2 | 7 | 3.1 | 39 | 59 | 18 | 16 | 1 | .366 | .551 | 12 | 3 | C-61 |
| 1931 | 67 | 187 | 49 | 16 | 1 | 1 | 0.5 | 13 | 23 | 18 | 13 | 2 | .262 | .374 | 10 | 1 | C-56 |
| 1932 | 103 | 310 | 88 | 23 | 1 | 5 | 1.6 | 25 | 43 | 30 | 15 | 0 | .284 | .413 | 19 | 6 | C-82 |
| 1933 NY N | 144 | 481 | 127 | 17 | 2 | 6 | 1.2 | 39 | 56 | 48 | 21 | 0 | .264 | .345 | 2 | 1 | C-142 |
| 1934 | 122 | 383 | 94 | 14 | 0 | 7 | 1.8 | 32 | 46 | 27 | 19 | 0 | .245 | .337 | 0 | 0 | C-122 |
| 1935 | 128 | 447 | 133 | 18 | 2 | 5 | 1.1 | 33 | 56 | 30 | 16 | 1 | .298 | .380 | 2 | 0 | C-126 |
| 1936 | 139 | 519 | 156 | 21 | 3 | 9 | 1.7 | 55 | 63 | 39 | 28 | 0 | .301 | .405 | 1 | 0 | C-138 |
| 1937 | 86 | 287 | 80 | 17 | 1 | 4 | 1.4 | 30 | 39 | 17 | 20 | 1 | .279 | .387 | 5 | 0 | C-81 |
| 1938 | 52 | 158 | 55 | 8 | 0 | 2 | 1.3 | 19 | 15 | 17 | 13 | 0 | .348 | .437 | 8 | 2 | C-44 |
| 1939 CHI N | 80 | 251 | 58 | 10 | 0 | 2 | 0.8 | 17 | 17 | 24 | 19 | 0 | .231 | .295 | 3 | 0 | C-76 |
| 1940 BKN N | 60 | 144 | 33 | 8 | 0 | 0 | 0.0 | 16 | 16 | 13 | 7 | 0 | .229 | .285 | 4 | 1 | C-56 |
| 1941 STL N | 106 | 328 | 75 | 13 | 1 | 2 | 0.6 | 25 | 37 | 37 | 19 | 0 | .229 | .293 | 1 | 0 | C-105 |
| 1942 2 teams | | STL | N (5G – | .077) | | NY | N | (39G – | .193) | | | | | | | | |
| " total | 44 | 122 | 22 | 1 | 1 | 0 | 0.0 | 4 | 9 | 14 | 7 | 1 | .180 | .205 | 3 | 0 | C-41 |
| 1943 NY N | 94 | 252 | 50 | 5 | 0 | 2 | 0.8 | 11 | 20 | 28 | 16 | 0 | .198 | .242 | 15 | 3 | C-77 |
| 1944 | 78 | 195 | 49 | 4 | 1 | 1 | 0.5 | 15 | 25 | 30 | 20 | 0 | .251 | .297 | 4 | 2 | C-72 |
| 1945 PHI N | 70 | 176 | 35 | 5 | 0 | 0 | 0.0 | 11 | 16 | 28 | 10 | 2 | .199 | .227 | 0 | 0 | C-70 |
| 17 yrs. | 1460 | 4505 | 1194 | 197 | 16 | 53 | 1.2 | 386 | 543 | 418 | 264 | 8 | .265 | .351 | 89 | 19 | C-1360 |
| 1 yr. | 80 | 251 | 58 | 10 | 0 | 2 | 0.8 | 17 | 17 | 24 | 19 | 0 | .231 | .295 | 3 | 0 | C-76 |

WORLD SERIES

| | G | AB | H | 2B | 3B | HR | HR % | R | RBI | BB | SO | SB | BA | SA | AB | H | G by POS |
|---|---|---|---|---|---|---|---|---|---|---|---|---|---|---|---|---|---|
| 1930 STL N | 2 | 7 | 2 | 0 | 0 | 0 | 0.0 | 1 | 0 | 1 | 2 | 0 | .286 | .286 | 0 | 0 | C-2 |
| 1931 | 2 | 1 | 0 | 0 | 0 | 0 | 0.0 | 0 | 0 | 0 | 0 | 0 | .000 | .000 | 1 | 0 | C-1 |
| 1933 NY N | 5 | 17 | 2 | 1 | 0 | 0 | 0.0 | 2 | 2 | 3 | 0 | 0 | .118 | .176 | 0 | 0 | C-5 |
| 1936 | 6 | 19 | 5 | 2 | 0 | 0 | 0.0 | 3 | 1 | 3 | 3 | 0 | .263 | .368 | 0 | 0 | C-6 |
| 1937 | 3 | 8 | 0 | 0 | 0 | 0 | 0.0 | 0 | 1 | 0 | 1 | 0 | .000 | .000 | 1 | 0 | C-2 |
| 5 yrs. | 18 | 52 | 9 | 3 | 0 | 0 | 0.0 | 6 | 4 | 7 | 6 | 0 | .173 | .231 | 2 | 0 | C-16 |

## Ben Mann

**MANN, BEN GARTH (Red)**    BR TR 6' 155 lbs.
B. Nov. 16, 1915, Brandon, Tex.

| | G | AB | H | 2B | 3B | HR | HR % | R | RBI | BB | SO | SB | BA | SA | AB | H | G by POS |
|---|---|---|---|---|---|---|---|---|---|---|---|---|---|---|---|---|---|
| 1944 CHI N | 1 | 0 | 0 | 0 | 0 | 0 | – | 1 | 0 | 0 | 0 | 0 | – | – | 0 | 0 | |

## Les Mann

**MANN, LESLIE**    BR TR 5'9" 172 lbs.
B. Nov. 18, 1893, Lincoln, Neb.    D. Jan. 14, 1962, Pasadena, Calif.

| | G | AB | H | 2B | 3B | HR | HR % | R | RBI | BB | SO | SB | BA | SA | AB | H | G by POS |
|---|---|---|---|---|---|---|---|---|---|---|---|---|---|---|---|---|---|
| 1913 BOS N | 120 | 407 | 103 | 24 | 7 | 3 | 0.7 | 54 | 51 | 18 | 73 | 7 | .253 | .369 | 0 | 0 | OF-120 |
| 1914 | 126 | 389 | 96 | 16 | 11 | 4 | 1.0 | 44 | 40 | 24 | 50 | 9 | .247 | .375 | 3 | 0 | OF-123 |
| 1915 CHI F | 135 | 470 | 144 | 12 | 19 | 4 | 0.9 | 74 | 58 | 36 | | 18 | .306 | .438 | 4 | 2 | OF-130, SS-1 |
| 1916 CHI N | 127 | 415 | 113 | 13 | 9 | 2 | 0.5 | 46 | 29 | 19 | 31 | 11 | .272 | .361 | 9 | 1 | OF-115 |
| 1917 | 117 | 444 | 121 | 19 | 10 | 1 | 0.2 | 63 | 44 | 27 | 46 | 14 | .273 | .367 | 1 | 0 | OF-116 |
| 1918 | 129 | 489 | 141 | 27 | 7 | 2 | 0.4 | 69 | 55 | 38 | 45 | 21 | .288 | .384 | 0 | 0 | OF-129 |
| 1919 2 teams | | CHI | N (80G – | .227) | | BOS | N | (40G – | .283) | | | | | | | | |
| " total | 120 | 444 | 109 | 14 | 12 | 4 | 0.9 | 46 | 42 | 20 | 43 | 19 | .245 | .358 | 1 | 0 | OF-118 |
| 1920 BOS N | 110 | 424 | 117 | 7 | 8 | 3 | 0.7 | 48 | 32 | 38 | 42 | 7 | .276 | .351 | 3 | 0 | OF-110 |
| 1921 STL N | 97 | 256 | 84 | 12 | 7 | 7 | 2.7 | 57 | 30 | 23 | 28 | 5 | .328 | .512 | 5 | 1 | OF-79 |
| 1922 | 84 | 147 | 51 | 14 | 1 | 2 | 1.4 | 42 | 20 | 16 | 12 | 0 | .347 | .497 | 2 | 0 | OF-57 |
| 1923 2 teams | | STL | N (38G – | .371) | | CIN | N | (8G – | .000) | | | | | | | | |
| " total | 46 | 90 | 33 | 5 | 2 | 5 | 5.6 | 21 | 11 | 9 | 5 | 0 | .367 | .633 | 1 | 0 | OF-26 |
| 1924 BOS N | 32 | 102 | 28 | 7 | 4 | 0 | 0.0 | 13 | 10 | 8 | 10 | 1 | .275 | .422 | 3 | 1 | OF-28 |
| 1925 | 60 | 184 | 63 | 11 | 4 | 2 | 1.1 | 27 | 20 | 5 | 11 | 6 | .342 | .478 | 2 | 1 | OF-57 |
| 1926 | 50 | 129 | 39 | 8 | 2 | 1 | 0.8 | 23 | 20 | 9 | 9 | 5 | .302 | .419 | 3 | 0 | OF-46 |
| 1927 2 teams | | BOS | N (29G – | .258) | | NY | N | (29G – | .328) | | | | | | | | |
| " total | 58 | 133 | 39 | 7 | 2 | 2 | 1.5 | 21 | 16 | 16 | 10 | 4 | .293 | .421 | 5 | 1 | OF-46 |
| 1928 NY N | 82 | 193 | 51 | 7 | 1 | 2 | 1.0 | 29 | 25 | 18 | 9 | 2 | .264 | .342 | 1 | 0 | OF-68 |
| 16 yrs. | 1493 | 4716 | 1332 | 203 | 106 | 44 | 0.9 | 677 | 503 | 324 | 424 | 129 | .282 | .398 | 43 | 7 | OF-1368, SS-1 |
| 4 yrs. | 453 | 1647 | 443 | 67 | 34 | 6 | 0.4 | 209 | 150 | 95 | 151 | 58 | .269 | .362 | 11 | 1 | OF-438 |

WORLD SERIES

| | G | AB | H | 2B | 3B | HR | HR % | R | RBI | BB | SO | SB | BA | SA | AB | H | G by POS |
|---|---|---|---|---|---|---|---|---|---|---|---|---|---|---|---|---|---|
| 1914 BOS N | 3 | 7 | 2 | 0 | 0 | 0 | 0.0 | 1 | 1 | 0 | 1 | 0 | .286 | .286 | 0 | 0 | OF-3 |
| 1918 CHI N | 6 | 22 | 5 | 2 | 0 | 0 | 0.0 | 0 | 2 | 0 | 0 | 0 | .227 | .318 | 0 | 0 | OF-6 |
| 2 yrs. | 9 | 29 | 7 | 2 | 0 | 0 | 0.0 | 1 | 3 | 0 | 1 | 0 | .241 | .310 | 1 | 0 | OF-8 |

| | G | AB | H | 2B | 3B | HR | HR % | R | RBI | BB | SO | SB | BA | SA | Pinch Hit AB | Pinch Hit H | G by POS |
|---|---|---|---|---|---|---|---|---|---|---|---|---|---|---|---|---|---|

## Rabbit Maranville

**MARANVILLE, WALTER JAMES VINCENT**  BR TR 5'5" 155 lbs.
B. Nov. 11, 1891, Springfield, Mass.   D. Jan. 5, 1954, New York, N. Y.
Manager 1925.
Hall of Fame 1954.

| | G | AB | H | 2B | 3B | HR | HR % | R | RBI | BB | SO | SB | BA | SA | PH AB | PH H | G by POS |
|---|---|---|---|---|---|---|---|---|---|---|---|---|---|---|---|---|---|
| 1912 BOS N | 26 | 86 | 18 | 2 | 0 | 0 | 0.0 | 8 | 8 | 9 | 14 | 1 | .209 | .233 | 0 | 0 | SS-26 |
| 1913 | 143 | 571 | 141 | 13 | 8 | 2 | 0.4 | 68 | 48 | 68 | 62 | 25 | .247 | .308 | 0 | 0 | SS-143 |
| 1914 | 156 | 586 | 144 | 23 | 6 | 4 | 0.7 | 74 | 78 | 45 | 56 | 28 | .246 | .326 | 0 | 0 | SS-156 |
| 1915 | 149 | 509 | 124 | 23 | 6 | 2 | 0.4 | 51 | 43 | 45 | 65 | 18 | .244 | .324 | 0 | 0 | SS-149 |
| 1916 | 155 | 604 | 142 | 16 | 13 | 4 | 0.7 | 79 | 38 | 50 | 69 | 32 | .235 | .325 | 0 | 0 | SS-155 |
| 1917 | 142 | 561 | 146 | 19 | 13 | 3 | 0.5 | 69 | 43 | 40 | 47 | 27 | .260 | .357 | 0 | 0 | SS-142 |
| 1918 | 11 | 38 | 12 | 0 | 1 | 0 | 0.0 | 3 | 3 | 4 | 0 | 0 | .316 | .368 | 0 | 0 | SS-11 |
| 1919 | 131 | 480 | 128 | 18 | 10 | 5 | 1.0 | 44 | 43 | 36 | 23 | 12 | .267 | .377 | 0 | 0 | SS-131 |
| 1920 | 134 | 493 | 131 | 19 | 15 | 1 | 0.2 | 48 | 43 | 28 | 24 | 14 | .266 | .371 | 0 | 0 | SS-133 |
| 1921 PIT N | 153 | 612 | 180 | 25 | 12 | 1 | 0.2 | 90 | 70 | 47 | 38 | 25 | .294 | .379 | 0 | 0 | SS-153 |
| 1922 | 155 | **672** | 198 | 26 | 15 | 0 | 0.0 | 115 | 63 | 61 | 43 | 24 | .295 | .378 | 0 | 0 | SS-138, 2B-18 |
| 1923 | 141 | 581 | 161 | 19 | 9 | 1 | 0.2 | 78 | 41 | 42 | 34 | 14 | .277 | .346 | 0 | 0 | SS-141 |
| 1924 | 152 | 594 | 158 | 33 | 20 | 2 | 0.3 | 62 | 71 | 35 | 53 | 18 | .266 | .399 | 0 | 0 | 2B-152 |
| 1925 CHI N | 75 | 266 | 62 | 10 | 3 | 0 | 0.0 | 37 | 23 | 29 | 20 | 6 | .233 | .293 | 1 | 0 | SS-74 |
| 1926 BKN N | 78 | 234 | 55 | 8 | 5 | 0 | 0.0 | 32 | 24 | 26 | 24 | 7 | .235 | .312 | 0 | 0 | SS-60, 2B-18 |
| 1927 STL N | 9 | 29 | 7 | 1 | 0 | 0 | 0.0 | 0 | 0 | 2 | 2 | 0 | .241 | .276 | 0 | 0 | SS-9 |
| 1928 | 112 | 366 | 88 | 14 | 10 | 1 | 0.3 | 40 | 34 | 36 | 27 | 3 | .240 | .342 | 0 | 0 | SS-112, 2B-2 |
| 1929 BOS N | 146 | 560 | 159 | 26 | 10 | 0 | 0.0 | 87 | 55 | 47 | 33 | 13 | .284 | .366 | 0 | 0 | SS-146, 2B-1 |
| 1930 | 142 | 558 | 157 | 26 | 8 | 2 | 0.4 | 85 | 43 | 48 | 23 | 9 | .281 | .367 | 0 | 0 | SS-138, 3B-4 |
| 1931 | 145 | 562 | 146 | 22 | 5 | 0 | 0.0 | 69 | 33 | 56 | 34 | 9 | .260 | .317 | 1 | 0 | SS-137, 2B-11 |
| 1932 | 149 | 571 | 134 | 20 | 4 | 0 | 0.0 | 67 | 37 | 46 | 28 | 4 | .235 | .284 | 0 | 0 | 2B-149 |
| 1933 | 143 | 478 | 104 | 15 | 4 | 0 | 0.0 | 46 | 38 | 36 | 34 | 2 | .218 | .266 | 1 | 1 | 2B-142 |
| 1935 | 23 | 67 | 10 | 2 | 0 | 0 | 0.0 | 3 | 3 | 5 | 3 | 0 | .149 | .179 | 3 | 1 | 2B-20 |
| 23 yrs. | 2670 | 10078 | 2605 | 380 | 177 | 28 | 0.3 | 1255 | 884 | 839 | 756 | 291 | .258 | .340 | 7 | 1 | SS-2154, 2B-513, 3B-4 |
| 1 yr. | 75 | 266 | 62 | 10 | 3 | 0 | 0.0 | 37 | 23 | 29 | 20 | 6 | .233 | .293 | 1 | 0 | SS-74 |
| **WORLD SERIES** | | | | | | | | | | | | | | | | | |
| 1914 BOS N | 4 | 13 | 4 | 0 | 0 | 0 | 0.0 | 1 | 3 | 1 | 1 | 2 | .308 | .308 | 0 | 0 | SS-4 |
| 1928 STL N | 4 | 13 | 4 | 1 | 0 | 0 | 0.0 | 2 | 0 | 1 | 1 | 1 | .308 | .385 | 0 | 0 | SS-4 |
| 2 yrs. | 8 | 26 | 8 | 1 | 0 | 0 | 0.0 | 3 | 3 | 2 | 2 | 3 | .308 | .346 | 0 | 0 | SS-8 |

## Gonzalo Marquez

**MARQUEZ, GONZALO ENRIQUE**  BL TL 5'11" 180 lbs.
Born Gonzalo Enrique Marquez Moya.
B. Mar. 31, 1946, Carupano, Venezuela   D. Dec. 20, 1984, Valencia, Venezuela

| | G | AB | H | 2B | 3B | HR | HR % | R | RBI | BB | SO | SB | BA | SA | PH AB | PH H | G by POS |
|---|---|---|---|---|---|---|---|---|---|---|---|---|---|---|---|---|---|
| 1972 OAK A | 23 | 21 | 8 | 0 | 0 | 0 | 0.0 | 2 | 4 | 3 | 4 | 1 | .381 | .381 | 16 | 7 | 1B-2 |
| 1973 2 teams | OAK A (23G – .240) | | | | | | CHI N (19G – .224) | | | | | | | | | | |
| " total | 42 | 83 | 19 | 3 | 0 | 1 | 1.2 | 6 | 6 | 3 | 8 | 0 | .229 | .301 | 20 | 5 | 1B-19, 2B-2 |
| 1974 CHI N | 11 | 11 | 0 | 0 | 0 | 0 | 0.0 | 1 | 0 | 1 | 2 | 0 | .000 | .000 | 10 | 0 | 1B-1 |
| 3 yrs. | 76 | 115 | 27 | 3 | 0 | 1 | 0.9 | 9 | 10 | 7 | 14 | 1 | .235 | .287 | 46 | 12 | 1B-22, 2B-2 |
| 2 yrs. | 30 | 69 | 13 | 2 | 0 | 1 | 1.4 | 6 | 4 | 4 | 6 | 0 | .188 | .261 | 12 | 1 | 1B-19 |
| **LEAGUE CHAMPIONSHIP SERIES** | | | | | | | | | | | | | | | | | |
| 1972 OAK A | 3 | 3 | 2 | 0 | 0 | 0 | 0.0 | 1 | 1 | 0 | 0 | 0 | .667 | .667 | 3 | 2 | |
| **WORLD SERIES** | | | | | | | | | | | | | | | | | |
| 1972 OAK A | 5 | 5 | 3 | 0 | 0 | 0 | 0.0 | 0 | 1 | 0 | 0 | 0 | .600 | .600 | 5 | 3 **1st** | |

## Luis Marquez

**MARQUEZ, LUIS ANGEL (Canena)**  BR TR 5'10½" 174 lbs.
B. Oct. 28, 1925, Aguadilla, Puerto Rico

| | G | AB | H | 2B | 3B | HR | HR % | R | RBI | BB | SO | SB | BA | SA | PH AB | PH H | G by POS |
|---|---|---|---|---|---|---|---|---|---|---|---|---|---|---|---|---|---|
| 1951 BOS N | 68 | 122 | 24 | 5 | 1 | 0 | 0.0 | 19 | 11 | 10 | 20 | 4 | .197 | .254 | 9 | 2 | OF-43 |
| 1954 2 teams | CHI N (17G – .083) | | | | | | PIT N (14G – .111) | | | | | | | | | | |
| " total | 31 | 21 | 2 | 0 | 0 | 0 | 0.0 | 5 | 0 | 6 | 4 | 3 | .095 | .095 | 5 | 1 | OF-18 |
| 2 yrs. | 99 | 143 | 26 | 5 | 1 | 0 | 0.0 | 24 | 11 | 16 | 24 | 7 | .182 | .231 | 14 | 3 | OF-61 |
| 1 yr. | 17 | 12 | 1 | 0 | 0 | 0 | 0.0 | 2 | 0 | 2 | 4 | 3 | .083 | .083 | 0 | 0 | OF-14 |

## Bill Marriott

**MARRIOTT, WILLIAM EARL**  BL TR 6' 170 lbs.
B. Apr. 18, 1893, Pratt, Kans.   D. Aug. 11, 1969, Berkeley, Calif.

| | G | AB | H | 2B | 3B | HR | HR % | R | RBI | BB | SO | SB | BA | SA | PH AB | PH H | G by POS |
|---|---|---|---|---|---|---|---|---|---|---|---|---|---|---|---|---|---|
| 1917 CHI N | 2 | 6 | 0 | 0 | 0 | 0 | 0.0 | 0 | 0 | 1 | 0 | 0 | .000 | .000 | 2 | 0 | OF-1 |
| 1920 | 14 | 43 | 12 | 4 | 2 | 0 | 0.0 | 7 | 5 | 6 | 5 | 1 | .279 | .465 | 0 | 0 | 2B-14 |
| 1921 | 30 | 38 | 12 | 1 | 1 | 0 | 0.0 | 3 | 7 | 4 | 1 | 0 | .316 | .395 | 20 | 4 | 2B-6, OF-1, SS-1, 3B-1 |
| 1925 BOS N | 103 | 370 | 99 | 9 | 1 | 1 | 0.3 | 37 | 40 | 28 | 26 | 3 | .268 | .305 | 8 | 1 | 3B-89, OF-1 |
| 1926 BKN N | 109 | 360 | 96 | 13 | 9 | 3 | 0.8 | 39 | 42 | 17 | 20 | 12 | .267 | .378 | 4 | 0 | 3B-104 |
| 1927 | 6 | 9 | 1 | 0 | 1 | 0 | 0.0 | 0 | 1 | 2 | 2 | 0 | .111 | .333 | 4 | 0 | 3B-2 |
| 6 yrs. | 264 | 826 | 220 | 27 | 14 | 4 | 0.5 | 86 | 95 | 57 | 55 | 16 | .266 | .347 | 38 | 5 | 3B-196, 2B-20, OF-3, SS-1 |
| 3 yrs. | 46 | 87 | 24 | 5 | 3 | 0 | 0.0 | 10 | 12 | 10 | 7 | 1 | .276 | .402 | 22 | 4 | 2B-20, OF-2, SS-1, 3B-1 |

## Doc Marshall

**MARSHALL, WILLIAM RIDDLE**  BR TR 6'1" 185 lbs.
B. Sept. 22, 1875, Butler, Pa.   D. Dec. 11, 1959, Clinton, Ill.

| | G | AB | H | 2B | 3B | HR | HR % | R | RBI | BB | SO | SB | BA | SA | PH AB | PH H | G by POS |
|---|---|---|---|---|---|---|---|---|---|---|---|---|---|---|---|---|---|
| 1904 3 teams | PHI N (8G – .100) | | | NY N (11G – .353) | | | BOS N (13G – .209) | | | | | | | | | | |
| " total | 32 | 80 | 17 | 1 | 1 | 0 | 0.0 | 7 | 5 | 3 | | 2 | .213 | .250 | 7 | 0 | C-20, OF-3, 2B-1 |
| 1906 2 teams | NY N (38G – .167) | | | STL N (39G – .276) | | | | | | | | | | | | | |
| " total | 77 | 225 | 51 | 7 | 3 | 0 | 0.0 | 14 | 17 | 13 | | 8 | .227 | .284 | 9 | 1 | C-51, OF-16, 1B-2 |
| 1907 STL N | 84 | 268 | 54 | 8 | 2 | 1 | 0.7 | 19 | 18 | 12 | | 2 | .201 | .269 | 1 | 0 | C-83 |
| 1908 2 teams | STL N (6G – .071) | | | CHI N (12G – .300) | | | | | | | | | | | | | |
| " total | 18 | 34 | 7 | 0 | 1 | 0 | 0.0 | 4 | 4 | 0 | | 0 | .206 | .265 | 2 | 1 | C-10, OF-3 |
| 1909 BKN N | 50 | 149 | 30 | 7 | 1 | 0 | 0.0 | 7 | 10 | 6 | | 3 | .201 | .262 | 1 | 0 | C-49, OF-3 |
| 5 yrs. | 261 | 756 | 159 | 23 | 8 | 2 | 0.3 | 51 | 54 | 34 | | 15 | .210 | .270 | 20 | 2 | C-213, OF-23, 1B-2, 2B-1 |
| 1 yr. | 12 | 20 | 6 | 0 | 1 | 0 | 0.0 | 4 | 3 | 0 | | 0 | .300 | .400 | 2 | 1 | C-4, OF-3 |

| | G | AB | H | 2B | 3B | HR | HR % | R | RBI | BB | SO | SB | BA | SA | Pinch Hit AB | Pinch Hit H | G by POS |
|---|---|---|---|---|---|---|---|---|---|---|---|---|---|---|---|---|---|

## Jim Marshall

**MARSHALL, RUFUS JAMES**
B. May 25, 1932, Danville, Ill.
Manager 1974-76, 1979.

BL TL 6'1" 190 lbs.

| | G | AB | H | 2B | 3B | HR | HR % | R | RBI | BB | SO | SB | BA | SA | AB | H | G by POS |
|---|---|---|---|---|---|---|---|---|---|---|---|---|---|---|---|---|---|
| 1958 2 teams | | BAL A (85G – .215) | | | | CHI N (26G – .272) | | | | | | | | | | | |
| " total | 111 | 272 | 63 | 6 | 3 | 10 | 3.7 | 29 | 30 | 30 | 43 | 4 | .232 | .386 | 36 | 6 | 1B-67, OF-19 |
| 1959 CHI N | 108 | 294 | 74 | 10 | 1 | 11 | 3.7 | 39 | 40 | 33 | 39 | 0 | .252 | .405 | 33 | 8 | 1B-72, OF-8 |
| 1960 SF N | 75 | 118 | 28 | 2 | 2 | 2 | 1.7 | 19 | 13 | 17 | 24 | 0 | .237 | .339 | 38 | 8 | 1B-28, OF-6 |
| 1961 | 44 | 36 | 8 | 0 | 0 | 1 | 2.8 | 5 | 7 | 3 | 8 | 0 | .222 | .306 | 32 | 7 | 1B-4, OF-2 |
| 1962 2 teams | | NY N (17G – .344) | | | | PIT N (55G – .220) | | | | | | | | | | | |
| " total | 72 | 132 | 33 | 6 | 1 | 5 | 3.8 | 19 | 16 | 18 | 25 | 1 | .250 | .424 | 32 | 6 | 1B-31, OF-5 |
| 5 yrs. | 410 | 852 | 206 | 24 | 7 | 29 | 3.4 | 111 | 106 | 101 | 139 | 5 | .242 | .388 | 171 | 35 | 1B-202, OF-36 |
| 2 yrs. | 134 | 375 | 96 | 12 | 1 | 16 | 4.3 | 51 | 51 | 45 | 52 | 1 | .256 | .421 | 34 | 8 | 1B-87, OF-19 |

## Frank Martin

**MARTIN, FRANK**
B. 1877, Chicago, Ill. Deceased.

| | G | AB | H | 2B | 3B | HR | HR % | R | RBI | BB | SO | SB | BA | SA | AB | H | G by POS |
|---|---|---|---|---|---|---|---|---|---|---|---|---|---|---|---|---|---|
| 1897 LOU N | 2 | 8 | 2 | 0 | 0 | 0 | 0.0 | 1 | 0 | 0 | | 0 | .250 | .250 | 0 | 0 | 2B-2 |
| 1898 CHI N | 1 | 4 | 0 | 0 | 0 | 0 | 0.0 | 0 | 0 | 0 | | 0 | .000 | .000 | 0 | 0 | 2B-1 |
| 1899 NY N | 17 | 54 | 14 | 2 | 0 | 0 | 0.0 | 5 | 1 | 2 | | 0 | .259 | .296 | 0 | 0 | 3B-17 |
| 3 yrs. | 20 | 66 | 16 | 2 | 0 | 0 | 0.0 | 6 | 1 | 2 | | 0 | .242 | .273 | 0 | 0 | 3B-17, 2B-3 |
| 1 yr. | 1 | 4 | 0 | 0 | 0 | 0 | 0.0 | 0 | 0 | 0 | | 0 | .000 | .000 | 0 | 0 | 2B-1 |

## J. C. Martin

**MARTIN, JOSEPH CLIFTON**
B. Dec. 13, 1936, Axton, Va.

BL TR 6'2" 188 lbs.

| | G | AB | H | 2B | 3B | HR | HR % | R | RBI | BB | SO | SB | BA | SA | AB | H | G by POS |
|---|---|---|---|---|---|---|---|---|---|---|---|---|---|---|---|---|---|
| 1959 CHI A | 3 | 4 | 1 | 0 | 0 | 0 | 0.0 | 0 | 1 | 0 | 1 | 0 | .250 | .250 | 1 | 0 | 3B-2 |
| 1960 | 4 | 20 | 2 | 1 | 0 | 0 | 0.0 | 0 | 2 | 0 | 6 | 0 | .100 | .150 | 0 | 0 | 3B-5, 1B-1 |
| 1961 | 110 | 274 | 63 | 8 | 3 | 5 | 1.8 | 26 | 32 | 21 | 31 | 1 | .230 | .336 | 11 | 2 | 1B-60, 3B-36 |
| 1962 | 18 | 26 | 2 | 0 | 0 | 0 | 0.0 | 0 | 2 | 0 | 3 | 0 | .077 | .077 | 11 | 0 | C-6, 3B-1, 1B-1 |
| 1963 | 105 | 259 | 53 | 11 | 1 | 5 | 1.9 | 25 | 28 | 26 | 35 | 0 | .205 | .313 | 12 | 3 | C-98, 1B-3, 3B-1 |
| 1964 | 122 | 294 | 58 | 10 | 1 | 4 | 1.4 | 23 | 22 | 16 | 30 | 0 | .197 | .279 | 6 | 0 | C-120 |
| 1965 | 119 | 230 | 60 | 12 | 0 | 2 | 0.9 | 21 | 21 | 24 | 29 | 2 | .261 | .339 | 15 | 3 | C-112, 1B-4, 3B-2 |
| 1966 | 67 | 157 | 40 | 5 | 3 | 2 | 1.3 | 13 | 20 | 14 | 24 | 0 | .255 | .363 | 4 | 1 | C-63 |
| 1967 | 101 | 252 | 59 | 12 | 1 | 4 | 1.6 | 22 | 22 | 30 | 41 | 4 | .234 | .337 | 6 | 1 | C-96, 1B-1 |
| 1968 NY N | 78 | 244 | 55 | 9 | 2 | 3 | 1.2 | 20 | 31 | 21 | 31 | 0 | .225 | .316 | 8 | 1 | C-53, 1B-14 |
| 1969 | 66 | 177 | 37 | 5 | 1 | 4 | 2.3 | 12 | 21 | 12 | 32 | 0 | .209 | .316 | 18 | 3 | C-48, 1B-2 |
| 1970 CHI N | 40 | 77 | 12 | 1 | 0 | 1 | 1.3 | 11 | 4 | 20 | 11 | 0 | .156 | .208 | 3 | 0 | C-36, 1B-3 |
| 1971 | 47 | 125 | 33 | 5 | 0 | 2 | 1.6 | 13 | 17 | 12 | 16 | 1 | .264 | .352 | 5 | 0 | C-43, OF-1 |
| 1972 | 25 | 50 | 12 | 3 | 0 | 0 | 0.0 | 3 | 7 | 5 | 9 | 1 | .240 | .300 | 9 | 2 | C-17 |
| 14 yrs. | 905 | 2189 | 487 | 82 | 12 | 32 | 1.5 | 189 | 230 | 201 | 299 | 9 | .222 | .315 | 109 | 16 | C-692, 1B-89, 3B-47, OF-1 |
| 3 yrs. | 112 | 252 | 57 | 9 | 0 | 3 | 1.2 | 27 | 28 | 37 | 36 | 2 | .226 | .298 | 17 | 2 | C-96, 1B-3, OF-1 |

**LEAGUE CHAMPIONSHIP SERIES**

| | G | AB | H | 2B | 3B | HR | HR % | R | RBI | BB | SO | SB | BA | SA | AB | H | G by POS |
|---|---|---|---|---|---|---|---|---|---|---|---|---|---|---|---|---|---|
| 1969 NY N | 2 | 2 | 1 | 0 | 0 | 0 | 0.0 | 0 | 2 | 0 | 0 | 0 | .500 | .500 | 2 | 1 | |

**WORLD SERIES**

| | G | AB | H | 2B | 3B | HR | HR % | R | RBI | BB | SO | SB | BA | SA | AB | H | G by POS |
|---|---|---|---|---|---|---|---|---|---|---|---|---|---|---|---|---|---|
| 1969 NY N | 1 | 0 | 0 | 0 | 0 | 0 | – | 0 | 0 | 0 | 0 | 0 | – | – | 0 | 0 | |

## Jerry Martin

**MARTIN, JERRY LINDSEY**
Son of Barney Martin.
B. May 11, 1949, Columbia, S. C.

BR TR 6'1" 195 lbs.

| | G | AB | H | 2B | 3B | HR | HR % | R | RBI | BB | SO | SB | BA | SA | AB | H | G by POS |
|---|---|---|---|---|---|---|---|---|---|---|---|---|---|---|---|---|---|
| 1974 PHI N | 13 | 14 | 3 | 1 | 0 | 0 | 0.0 | 2 | 1 | 1 | 5 | 0 | .214 | .286 | 4 | 1 | OF-11 |
| 1975 | 57 | 113 | 24 | 7 | 1 | 2 | 1.8 | 15 | 11 | 11 | 16 | 2 | .212 | .345 | 9 | 1 | OF-49 |
| 1976 | 130 | 121 | 30 | 7 | 0 | 2 | 1.7 | 30 | 15 | 7 | 28 | 3 | .248 | .355 | 22 | 6 | OF-110, 1B-1 |
| 1977 | 116 | 215 | 56 | 16 | 3 | 6 | 2.8 | 34 | 28 | 18 | 42 | 6 | .260 | .447 | 18 | 5 | OF-106, 1B-1 |
| 1978 | 128 | 266 | 72 | 13 | 4 | 9 | 3.4 | 40 | 36 | 28 | 65 | 9 | .271 | .451 | 24 | 5 | OF-112 |
| 1979 CHI N | 150 | 534 | 145 | 34 | 3 | 19 | 3.6 | 74 | 73 | 38 | 85 | 2 | .272 | .453 | 8 | 1 | OF-144 |
| 1980 | 141 | 494 | 112 | 22 | 2 | 23 | 4.7 | 57 | 73 | 38 | 107 | 8 | .227 | .419 | 11 | 2 | OF-129 |
| 1981 SF N | 72 | 241 | 58 | 5 | 3 | 4 | 1.7 | 23 | 25 | 21 | 52 | 6 | .241 | .336 | 7 | 0 | OF-64 |
| 1982 KC A | 147 | 519 | 138 | 22 | 1 | 15 | 2.9 | 52 | 65 | 38 | 138 | 1 | .266 | .399 | 7 | 2 | OF-142, DH-3 |
| 1983 | 13 | 44 | 14 | 2 | 0 | 2 | 4.5 | 4 | 13 | 1 | 7 | 1 | .318 | .500 | 0 | 0 | OF-13 |
| 1984 NY N | 51 | 91 | 14 | 1 | 0 | 3 | 3.3 | 6 | 5 | 6 | 29 | 0 | .154 | .264 | 24 | 3 | OF-30, 1B-3 |
| 11 yrs. | 1018 | 2652 | 666 | 130 | 17 | 85 | 3.2 | 337 | 345 | 207 | 574 | 38 | .251 | .409 | 134 | 26 | OF-910, 1B-5, DH-3 |
| 2 yrs. | 291 | 1028 | 257 | 56 | 5 | 42 | 4.1 | 131 | 146 | 76 | 192 | 10 | .250 | .437 | 19 | 3 | OF-273 |

**LEAGUE CHAMPIONSHIP SERIES**

| | G | AB | H | 2B | 3B | HR | HR % | R | RBI | BB | SO | SB | BA | SA | AB | H | G by POS |
|---|---|---|---|---|---|---|---|---|---|---|---|---|---|---|---|---|---|
| 1976 PHI N | 1 | 1 | 0 | 0 | 0 | 0 | 0.0 | 1 | 0 | 0 | 0 | 0 | .000 | .000 | 0 | 0 | OF-1 |
| 1977 | 3 | 4 | 0 | 0 | 0 | 0 | 0.0 | 0 | 0 | 0 | 2 | 0 | .000 | .000 | 1 | 0 | OF-1 |
| 1978 | 4 | 9 | 2 | 1 | 0 | 1 | 11.1 | 1 | 2 | 1 | 3 | 0 | .222 | .667 | 2 | 1 | OF-3 |
| 3 yrs. | 8 | 14 | 2 | 1 | 0 | 1 | 7.1 | 2 | 2 | 1 | 5 | 0 | .143 | .429 | 3 | 1 | OF-5 |

## Stu Martin

**MARTIN, STUART McGUIRE**
B. Nov. 17, 1913, Rich Square, N. C.

BL TR 6' 155 lbs.

| | G | AB | H | 2B | 3B | HR | HR % | R | RBI | BB | SO | SB | BA | SA | AB | H | G by POS |
|---|---|---|---|---|---|---|---|---|---|---|---|---|---|---|---|---|---|
| 1936 STL N | 92 | 332 | 99 | 21 | 4 | 6 | 1.8 | 63 | 41 | 29 | 27 | 17 | .298 | .440 | 4 | 0 | 2B-83, SS-3 |
| 1937 | 90 | 223 | 58 | 6 | 1 | 1 | 0.4 | 34 | 17 | 32 | 18 | 3 | .260 | .309 | 28 | 6 | 2B-48, 1B-9, SS-1 |
| 1938 | 114 | 417 | 116 | 26 | 2 | 1 | 0.2 | 54 | 27 | 30 | 28 | 4 | .278 | .357 | 15 | 3 | 2B-99 |
| 1939 | 120 | 425 | 114 | 26 | 7 | 3 | 0.7 | 60 | 30 | 33 | 40 | 4 | .268 | .384 | 11 | 0 | 2B-107, 1B-1 |
| 1940 | 112 | 369 | 88 | 12 | 6 | 4 | 1.1 | 45 | 32 | 33 | 35 | 4 | .238 | .336 | 9 | 1 | 3B-73, 2B-33 |
| 1941 PIT N | 88 | 233 | 71 | 13 | 2 | 0 | 0.0 | 37 | 19 | 10 | 17 | 2 | .305 | .378 | 28 | 6 | 2B-53, 3B-2, 1B-1 |
| 1942 | 42 | 120 | 27 | 4 | 2 | 1 | 0.8 | 16 | 12 | 8 | 10 | 1 | .225 | .317 | 10 | 0 | 2B-30, SS-1, 1B-1 |
| 1943 CHI N | 64 | 118 | 26 | 4 | 0 | 0 | 0.0 | 13 | 5 | 15 | 10 | 1 | .220 | .254 | 25 | 5 | 2B-22, 3B-8, 1B-2 |
| 8 yrs. | 722 | 2237 | 599 | 112 | 24 | 16 | 0.7 | 322 | 183 | 190 | 185 | 36 | .268 | .361 | 130 | 21 | 2B-475, 3B-83, 1B-14, SS-5 |
| 1 yr. | 64 | 118 | 26 | 4 | 0 | 0 | 0.0 | 13 | 5 | 15 | 10 | 1 | .220 | .254 | 25 | 5 | 2B-22, 3B-8, 1B-2 |

| | G | AB | H | 2B | 3B | HR | HR % | R | RBI | BB | SO | SB | BA | SA | Pinch Hit AB | Pinch Hit H | G by POS |
|---|---|---|---|---|---|---|---|---|---|---|---|---|---|---|---|---|---|

## Carmelo Martinez

**MARTINEZ, CARMELO**
Born Carmelo Martinez Salgado.
B. July 28, 1960, Dorado, puerto Rico

BR  TR  6'2"    185 lbs.

| | G | AB | H | 2B | 3B | HR | HR % | R | RBI | BB | SO | SB | BA | SA | AB | H | G by POS |
|---|---|---|---|---|---|---|---|---|---|---|---|---|---|---|---|---|---|
| 1983 CHI N | 29 | 89 | 23 | 3 | 0 | 6 | 6.7 | 8 | 16 | 4 | 19 | 0 | .258 | .494 | 4 | 1 | 1B-26, OF-1, 3B-1 |
| 1984 SD N | 149 | 488 | 122 | 28 | 2 | 13 | 2.7 | 64 | 66 | 68 | 82 | 1 | .250 | .395 | 4 | 0 | OF-142, 1B-2 |
| 1985 | 150 | 514 | 130 | 28 | 1 | 21 | 4.1 | 64 | 72 | 87 | 82 | 0 | .253 | .434 | 0 | 0 | OF-150, 1B-3 |
| 3 yrs. | 328 | 1091 | 275 | 59 | 3 | 40 | 3.7 | 136 | 154 | 159 | 183 | 1 | .252 | .422 | 8 | 1 | OF-293, 1B-31, 3B-1 |
| 1 yr. | 29 | 89 | 23 | 3 | 0 | 6 | 6.7 | 8 | 16 | 4 | 19 | 0 | .258 | .494 | 4 | 1 | 1B-26, OF-1, 3B-1 |

LEAGUE CHAMPIONSHIP SERIES

| | G | AB | H | 2B | 3B | HR | HR % | R | RBI | BB | SO | SB | BA | SA | AB | H | G by POS |
|---|---|---|---|---|---|---|---|---|---|---|---|---|---|---|---|---|---|
| 1984 SD N | 5 | 17 | 3 | 0 | 0 | 0 | 0.0 | 1 | 0 | 2 | 4 | 0 | .176 | .176 | 0 | 0 | OF-5 |

WORLD SERIES

| | G | AB | H | 2B | 3B | HR | HR % | R | RBI | BB | SO | SB | BA | SA | AB | H | G by POS |
|---|---|---|---|---|---|---|---|---|---|---|---|---|---|---|---|---|---|
| 1984 SD N | 5 | 17 | 3 | 0 | 0 | 0 | 0.0 | 0 | 0 | 1 | 9 | 0 | .176 | .176 | 0 | 0 | OF-5 |

## Joe Marty

**MARTY, JOSEPH ANTON**
B. Sept. 1, 1913, Sacramento, Calif.    D. Oct. 4, 1984, Sacramento, Calif.

BR  TR  6'    182 lbs.

| | G | AB | H | 2B | 3B | HR | HR % | R | RBI | BB | SO | SB | BA | SA | AB | H | G by POS |
|---|---|---|---|---|---|---|---|---|---|---|---|---|---|---|---|---|---|
| 1937 CHI N | 88 | 290 | 84 | 17 | 2 | 5 | 1.7 | 41 | 44 | 28 | 30 | 3 | .290 | .414 | 3 | 2 | OF-84 |
| 1938 | 76 | 235 | 57 | 8 | 3 | 7 | 3.0 | 32 | 35 | 18 | 26 | 0 | .243 | .391 | 7 | 0 | OF-68 |
| 1939 2 teams | | CHI | N | (23G – | .132) | | PHI | N | (91G – | .254) | | | | | | | |
| " total | 114 | 375 | 86 | 13 | 6 | 11 | 2.9 | 38 | 54 | 28 | 40 | 3 | .229 | .384 | 12 | 3 | OF-100, P-1 |
| 1940 PHI N | 123 | 455 | 123 | 21 | 8 | 13 | 2.9 | 52 | 50 | 17 | 50 | 2 | .270 | .437 | 4 | 1 | OF-118 |
| 1941 | 137 | 477 | 128 | 19 | 3 | 8 | 1.7 | 60 | 39 | 51 | 41 | 6 | .268 | .371 | 5 | 0 | OF-132 |
| 5 yrs. | 538 | 1832 | 478 | 78 | 22 | 44 | 2.4 | 223 | 222 | 142 | 187 | 14 | .261 | .400 | 31 | 6 | OF-502, P-1 |
| 3 yrs. | 187 | 601 | 151 | 26 | 5 | 14 | 2.3 | 79 | 89 | 50 | 69 | 5 | .251 | .381 | 12 | 2 | OF-173 |

WORLD SERIES

| | G | AB | H | 2B | 3B | HR | HR % | R | RBI | BB | SO | SB | BA | SA | AB | H | G by POS |
|---|---|---|---|---|---|---|---|---|---|---|---|---|---|---|---|---|---|
| 1938 CHI N | 3 | 12 | 6 | 1 | 0 | 1 | 8.3 | 1 | 5 | 0 | 2 | 0 | .500 | .833 | 0 | 0 | OF-3 |

## Gordon Massa

**MASSA, GORDON RICHARD (Moose, Duke)**
B. Sept. 2, 1935, Cincinnati, Ohio

BL  TR  6'3"    210 lbs.

| | G | AB | H | 2B | 3B | HR | HR % | R | RBI | BB | SO | SB | BA | SA | AB | H | G by POS |
|---|---|---|---|---|---|---|---|---|---|---|---|---|---|---|---|---|---|
| 1957 CHI N | 6 | 15 | 7 | 1 | 0 | 0 | 0.0 | 2 | 3 | 4 | 3 | 0 | .467 | .533 | 0 | 0 | C-6 |
| 1958 | 2 | 2 | 0 | 0 | 0 | 0 | 0.0 | 0 | 0 | 0 | 2 | 0 | .000 | .000 | 2 | 0 | |
| 2 yrs. | 8 | 17 | 7 | 1 | 0 | 0 | 0.0 | 2 | 3 | 4 | 5 | 0 | .412 | .471 | 2 | 0 | C-6 |
| 2 yrs. | 8 | 17 | 7 | 1 | 0 | 0 | 0.0 | 2 | 3 | 4 | 5 | 0 | .412 | .471 | 2 | 0 | C-6 |

## Nelson Mathews

**MATHEWS, NELSON ELMER**
B. July 21, 1941, Columbia, Ill.

BR  TR  6'4"    195 lbs.

| | G | AB | H | 2B | 3B | HR | HR % | R | RBI | BB | SO | SB | BA | SA | AB | H | G by POS |
|---|---|---|---|---|---|---|---|---|---|---|---|---|---|---|---|---|---|
| 1960 CHI N | 3 | 8 | 2 | 0 | 0 | 0 | 0.0 | 1 | 0 | 0 | 2 | 0 | .250 | .250 | 1 | 1 | OF-2 |
| 1961 | 3 | 9 | 1 | 0 | 0 | 0 | 0.0 | 0 | 0 | 0 | 2 | 0 | .111 | .111 | 1 | 0 | OF-2 |
| 1962 | 15 | 49 | 15 | 2 | 0 | 2 | 4.1 | 5 | 13 | 5 | 4 | 3 | .306 | .469 | 1 | 0 | OF-14 |
| 1963 | 61 | 155 | 24 | 3 | 2 | 4 | 2.6 | 12 | 10 | 16 | 48 | 3 | .155 | .277 | 8 | 0 | OF-46 |
| 1964 KC A | 157 | 573 | 137 | 27 | 5 | 14 | 2.4 | 58 | 60 | 43 | 143 | 1 | .239 | .377 | 1 | 0 | OF-154 |
| 1965 | 67 | 184 | 39 | 7 | 7 | 2 | 1.1 | 17 | 15 | 24 | 49 | 0 | .212 | .359 | 10 | 1 | OF-57 |
| 6 yrs. | 306 | 978 | 218 | 39 | 14 | 22 | 2.2 | 93 | 98 | 88 | 248 | 8 | .223 | .359 | 22 | 2 | OF-275 |
| 4 yrs. | 82 | 221 | 42 | 5 | 2 | 6 | 2.7 | 18 | 23 | 21 | 56 | 6 | .190 | .312 | 11 | 1 | OF-64 |

## Gary Matthews

**MATTHEWS, GARY NATHANIEL**
B. July 5, 1950, San Fernando, Calif.

BR  TR  6'2"    185 lbs.

| | G | AB | H | 2B | 3B | HR | HR % | R | RBI | BB | SO | SB | BA | SA | AB | H | G by POS |
|---|---|---|---|---|---|---|---|---|---|---|---|---|---|---|---|---|---|
| 1972 SF N | 20 | 62 | 18 | 1 | 1 | 4 | 6.5 | 11 | 14 | 7 | 13 | 0 | .290 | .532 | 1 | 0 | OF-19 |
| 1973 | 148 | 540 | 162 | 22 | 10 | 12 | 2.2 | 74 | 58 | 58 | 83 | 17 | .300 | .444 | 1 | 1 | OF-145 |
| 1974 | 154 | 561 | 161 | 27 | 6 | 16 | 2.9 | 87 | 82 | 70 | 69 | 11 | .287 | .442 | 4 | 0 | OF-151 |
| 1975 | 116 | 425 | 119 | 22 | 3 | 12 | 2.8 | 67 | 58 | 65 | 53 | 13 | .280 | .431 | 3 | 1 | OF-113 |
| 1976 | 156 | 587 | 164 | 28 | 4 | 20 | 3.4 | 79 | 84 | 75 | 94 | 12 | .279 | .443 | 1 | 0 | OF-156 |
| 1977 ATL N | 148 | 555 | 157 | 25 | 5 | 17 | 3.1 | 89 | 64 | 67 | 90 | 22 | .283 | .438 | 2 | 1 | OF-145 |
| 1978 | 129 | 474 | 135 | 20 | 5 | 18 | 3.8 | 75 | 62 | 61 | 92 | 8 | .285 | .462 | 3 | 0 | OF-127 |
| 1979 | 156 | 631 | 192 | 34 | 5 | 27 | 4.3 | 97 | 90 | 60 | 75 | 18 | .304 | .502 | 0 | 0 | OF-156 |
| 1980 | 155 | 571 | 159 | 17 | 3 | 19 | 3.3 | 79 | 75 | 42 | 93 | 11 | .278 | .419 | 8 | 2 | OF-143 |
| 1981 PHI N | 101 | 359 | 108 | 21 | 3 | 9 | 2.5 | 62 | 67 | 59 | 42 | 15 | .301 | .451 | 2 | 0 | OF-100 |
| 1982 | 162 | 616 | 173 | 31 | 1 | 19 | 3.1 | 89 | 83 | 66 | 87 | 21 | .281 | .427 | 1 | 0 | OF-162 |
| 1983 | 132 | 446 | 115 | 18 | 2 | 10 | 2.2 | 66 | 50 | 69 | 81 | 13 | .258 | .374 | 9 | 2 | OF-122 |
| 1984 CHI N | 147 | 491 | 143 | 21 | 2 | 14 | 2.9 | 101 | 82 | 103 | 97 | 17 | .291 | .428 | 3 | 0 | OF-145 |
| 1985 | 97 | 298 | 70 | 12 | 0 | 13 | 4.4 | 45 | 40 | 59 | 64 | 2 | .235 | .406 | 11 | 2 | OF-85 |
| 14 yrs. | 1821 | 6616 | 1876 | 299 | 50 | 210 | 3.2 | 1021 | 909 | 861 | 1033 | 180 | .284 | .439 | 49 | 9 | OF-1769 |
| 2 yrs. | 244 | 789 | 213 | 33 | 2 | 27 | 3.4 | 146 | 122 | 162 | 161 | 19 | .270 | .420 | 14 | 2 | OF-230 |

DIVISIONAL PLAYOFF SERIES

| | G | AB | H | 2B | 3B | HR | HR % | R | RBI | BB | SO | SB | BA | SA | AB | H | G by POS |
|---|---|---|---|---|---|---|---|---|---|---|---|---|---|---|---|---|---|
| 1981 PHI N | 5 | 20 | 8 | 0 | 1 | 1 | 5.0 | 3 | 1 | 0 | 2 | 0 | .400 | .650 | 0 | 0 | OF-5 |

LEAGUE CHAMPIONSHIP SERIES

| | G | AB | H | 2B | 3B | HR | HR % | R | RBI | BB | SO | SB | BA | SA | AB | H | G by POS |
|---|---|---|---|---|---|---|---|---|---|---|---|---|---|---|---|---|---|
| 1983 PHI N | 4 | 14 | 6 | 0 | 0 | 3 | 21.4 | 4 | 8 | 2 | 1 | 1 | .429 | 1.071 | 0 | 0 | OF-4 |
| 1984 CHI N | 5 | 15 | 3 | 0 | 0 | 2 | 13.3 | 4 | 5 | 6 | 4 | 1 | .200 | .600 | 0 | 0 | OF-5 |
| 2 yrs. | 9 | 29 | 9 | 0 | 0 | 5 | 17.2 | 8 | 13 | 8 | 5 | 2 | .310 | .828 | 0 | 0 | OF-9 |

WORLD SERIES

| | G | AB | H | 2B | 3B | HR | HR % | R | RBI | BB | SO | SB | BA | SA | AB | H | G by POS |
|---|---|---|---|---|---|---|---|---|---|---|---|---|---|---|---|---|---|
| 1983 PHI N | 5 | 16 | 4 | 0 | 0 | 1 | 6.3 | 1 | 1 | 2 | 2 | 0 | .250 | .438 | 0 | 0 | OF-5 |

## Bobby Mattick

**MATTICK, ROBERT JAMES**
Son of Wally Mattick.
B. Dec. 5, 1915, Sioux City, Iowa
Manager 1980-81.

BR  TR  5'11"    178 lbs.

| | G | AB | H | 2B | 3B | HR | HR % | R | RBI | BB | SO | SB | BA | SA | AB | H | G by POS |
|---|---|---|---|---|---|---|---|---|---|---|---|---|---|---|---|---|---|
| 1938 CHI N | 1 | 1 | 1 | 0 | 0 | 0 | 0.0 | 0 | 1 | 0 | 0 | 0 | 1.000 | 1.000 | 0 | 0 | SS-1 |
| 1939 | 51 | 178 | 51 | 12 | 1 | 0 | 0.0 | 16 | 23 | 6 | 19 | 1 | .287 | .365 | 1 | 0 | SS-48 |
| 1940 | 128 | 441 | 96 | 15 | 0 | 0 | 0.0 | 30 | 33 | 19 | 33 | 5 | .218 | .252 | 1 | 0 | SS-126, 3B-1 |
| 1941 CIN N | 20 | 60 | 11 | 3 | 0 | 0 | 0.0 | 8 | 7 | 8 | 7 | 1 | .183 | .233 | 2 | 0 | SS-12, 3B-5, 2B-1 |

| | G | AB | H | 2B | 3B | HR | HR % | R | RBI | BB | SO | SB | BA | SA | Pinch Hit AB | Pinch Hit H | G by POS |
|---|---|---|---|---|---|---|---|---|---|---|---|---|---|---|---|---|---|

## Bobby Mattick continued

| | G | AB | H | 2B | 3B | HR | HR% | R | RBI | BB | SO | SB | BA | SA | AB | H | G by POS |
|---|---|---|---|---|---|---|---|---|---|---|---|---|---|---|---|---|---|
| 1942 | 6 | 10 | 2 | 1 | 0 | 0 | 0.0 | 0 | 0 | 0 | 1 | 0 | .200 | .300 | 0 | 0 | SS-3 |
| 5 yrs. | 206 | 690 | 161 | 31 | 1 | 0 | 0.0 | 54 | 64 | 33 | 60 | 7 | .233 | .281 | 4 | 0 | SS-190, 3B-6, 2B-1 |
| 3 yrs. | 180 | 620 | 148 | 27 | 1 | 0 | 0.0 | 46 | 57 | 25 | 52 | 6 | .239 | .285 | 2 | 0 | SS-175, 3B-1 |

## Gene Mauch

MAUCH, GENE WILLIAM (Skip)
B. Nov. 18, 1925, Salina, Kans.
Manager 1960-82, 1985.

BR TR 5'10" 165 lbs.

| | G | AB | H | 2B | 3B | HR | HR% | R | RBI | BB | SO | SB | BA | SA | AB | H | G by POS |
|---|---|---|---|---|---|---|---|---|---|---|---|---|---|---|---|---|---|
| 1944 BKN N | 5 | 15 | 2 | 1 | 0 | 0 | 0.0 | 2 | 2 | 2 | 3 | 0 | .133 | .200 | 0 | 0 | SS-5 |
| 1947 PIT N | 16 | 30 | 9 | 0 | 0 | 0 | 0.0 | 8 | 1 | 7 | 6 | 0 | .300 | .300 | 0 | 0 | 2B-6, SS-4 |
| 1948 2 teams | | BKN N | (12G – | .154) | | CHI N | (53G – | .203) | | | | | | | | | |
| " total | 65 | 151 | 30 | 3 | 2 | 1 | 0.7 | 19 | 7 | 27 | 14 | 1 | .199 | .265 | 11 | 0 | 2B-33, SS-20 |
| 1949 CHI N | 72 | 150 | 37 | 6 | 2 | 1 | 0.7 | 15 | 7 | 21 | 15 | 3 | .247 | .333 | 13 | 4 | 2B-25, SS-19, 3B-7 |
| 1950 BOS N | 48 | 121 | 28 | 5 | 0 | 1 | 0.8 | 17 | 15 | 14 | 9 | 1 | .231 | .298 | 3 | 2 | 2B-28, 3B-7, SS-5 |
| 1951 | 19 | 20 | 2 | 0 | 0 | 0 | 0.0 | 5 | 1 | 7 | 4 | 0 | .100 | .100 | 2 | 0 | SS-10, 3B-3, 2B-2 |
| 1952 STL N | 7 | 3 | 0 | 0 | 0 | 0 | 0.0 | 0 | 0 | 1 | 2 | 0 | .000 | .000 | 1 | 0 | SS-2 |
| 1956 BOS A | 7 | 25 | 8 | 0 | 0 | 0 | 0.0 | 4 | 1 | 3 | 3 | 0 | .320 | .320 | 1 | 0 | 2B-6 |
| 1957 | 65 | 222 | 60 | 10 | 3 | 2 | 0.9 | 23 | 28 | 22 | 26 | 1 | .270 | .369 | 7 | 3 | 2B-58 |
| 9 yrs. | 304 | 737 | 176 | 25 | 7 | 5 | 0.7 | 93 | 62 | 104 | 82 | 6 | .239 | .312 | 38 | 9 | 2B-158, SS-65, 3B-17 |
| 2 yrs. | 125 | 288 | 65 | 9 | 4 | 2 | 0.7 | 33 | 14 | 47 | 25 | 4 | .226 | .306 | 20 | 4 | 2B-51, SS-38, 3B-7 |

## Carmen Mauro

MAURO, CARMEN LOUIS
B. Nov. 10, 1926, St. Paul, Minn.

BL TR 6' 167 lbs.

| | G | AB | H | 2B | 3B | HR | HR% | R | RBI | BB | SO | SB | BA | SA | AB | H | G by POS |
|---|---|---|---|---|---|---|---|---|---|---|---|---|---|---|---|---|---|
| 1948 CHI N | 3 | 5 | 1 | 0 | 0 | 1 | 20.0 | 2 | 1 | 2 | 0 | 0 | .200 | .800 | 0 | 0 | OF-2 |
| 1950 | 62 | 185 | 42 | 4 | 3 | 1 | 0.5 | 19 | 10 | 13 | 31 | 3 | .227 | .297 | 9 | 1 | OF-49 |
| 1951 | 13 | 29 | 5 | 1 | 0 | 0 | 0.0 | 3 | 3 | 2 | 6 | 0 | .172 | .207 | 6 | 1 | OF-6 |
| 1953 3 teams | | BKN N | (8G – | .000) | | WAS A | (17G – | .174) | | PHI A | (64G – | .267) | | | | | |
| " total | 89 | 197 | 48 | 4 | 5 | 0 | 0.0 | 16 | 19 | 20 | 28 | 3 | .244 | .315 | 31 | 8 | OF-56, 3B-1 |
| 4 yrs. | 167 | 416 | 96 | 9 | 8 | 2 | 0.5 | 40 | 33 | 37 | 65 | 6 | .231 | .305 | 46 | 10 | OF-113, 3B-1 |
| 3 yrs. | 78 | 219 | 48 | 5 | 3 | 2 | 0.9 | 24 | 14 | 17 | 37 | 3 | .219 | .297 | 15 | 2 | OF-57 |

## Jack McAllister

**Playing record listed under Andy Coakley**

## Jim McAnany

McANANY, JAMES
B. Sept. 4, 1936, Los Angeles, Calif.

BR TR 5'10" 196 lbs.

| | G | AB | H | 2B | 3B | HR | HR% | R | RBI | BB | SO | SB | BA | SA | AB | H | G by POS |
|---|---|---|---|---|---|---|---|---|---|---|---|---|---|---|---|---|---|
| 1958 CHI A | 5 | 13 | 0 | 0 | 0 | 0 | 0.0 | 0 | 0 | 0 | 5 | 0 | .000 | .000 | 1 | 0 | OF-3 |
| 1959 | 67 | 210 | 58 | 9 | 3 | 0 | 0.0 | 22 | 27 | 19 | 26 | 2 | .276 | .348 | 6 | 0 | OF-67 |
| 1960 | 3 | 2 | 0 | 0 | 0 | 0 | 0.0 | 0 | 0 | 0 | 2 | 0 | .000 | .000 | 2 | 0 | |
| 1961 CHI N | 11 | 10 | 3 | 1 | 0 | 0 | 0.0 | 1 | 0 | 1 | 3 | 0 | .300 | .400 | 10 | 3 | OF-1 |
| 1962 | 7 | 6 | 0 | 0 | 0 | 0 | 0.0 | 0 | 0 | 1 | 2 | 0 | .000 | .000 | 6 | 0 | |
| 5 yrs. | 93 | 241 | 61 | 10 | 3 | 0 | 0.0 | 23 | 27 | 21 | 38 | 2 | .253 | .320 | 19 | 3 | OF-71 |
| 2 yrs. | 18 | 16 | 3 | 1 | 0 | 0 | 0.0 | 1 | 0 | 2 | 5 | 0 | .188 | .250 | 16 | 3 | OF-1 |
| WORLD SERIES | | | | | | | | | | | | | | | | | |
| 1959 CHI A | 3 | 5 | 0 | 0 | 0 | 0 | 0.0 | 0 | 0 | 1 | 0 | 0 | .000 | .000 | 0 | 0 | OF-3 |

## Ike McAuley

McAULEY, JAMES EARL
B. Aug. 19, 1891, Wichita, Kans. D. Apr. 6, 1928, Des Moines, Iowa

BR TR 5'9½" 150 lbs.

| | G | AB | H | 2B | 3B | HR | HR% | R | RBI | BB | SO | SB | BA | SA | AB | H | G by POS |
|---|---|---|---|---|---|---|---|---|---|---|---|---|---|---|---|---|---|
| 1914 PIT N | 15 | 24 | 3 | 0 | 0 | 0 | 0.0 | 3 | 0 | 0 | 8 | 0 | .125 | .125 | 1 | 0 | SS-5, 3B-3, 2B-2 |
| 1915 | 5 | 15 | 2 | 1 | 0 | 0 | 0.0 | 0 | 0 | 0 | 6 | 0 | .133 | .200 | 2 | 0 | SS-5 |
| 1916 | 4 | 8 | 2 | 0 | 0 | 0 | 0.0 | 1 | 1 | 0 | 1 | 0 | .250 | .250 | 0 | 0 | SS-4 |
| 1917 STL N | 3 | 7 | 2 | 0 | 0 | 0 | 0.0 | 0 | 1 | 0 | 1 | 0 | .286 | .286 | 0 | 0 | SS-3 |
| 1925 CHI N | 37 | 125 | 35 | 7 | 2 | 0 | 0.0 | 10 | 11 | 11 | 12 | 1 | .280 | .368 | 0 | 0 | SS-37 |
| 5 yrs. | 64 | 179 | 44 | 8 | 2 | 0 | 0.0 | 14 | 13 | 11 | 28 | 1 | .246 | .313 | 3 | 0 | SS-54, 3B-3, 2B-2 |
| 1 yr. | 37 | 125 | 35 | 7 | 2 | 0 | 0.0 | 10 | 11 | 11 | 12 | 1 | .280 | .368 | 0 | 0 | SS-37 |

## Algie McBride

McBRIDE, ALGERNON G.
B. May 23, 1869, Washington, D. C. D. Jan. 10, 1956, Georgetown, Ohio

BL TL 5'9" 152 lbs.

| | G | AB | H | 2B | 3B | HR | HR% | R | RBI | BB | SO | SB | BA | SA | AB | H | G by POS |
|---|---|---|---|---|---|---|---|---|---|---|---|---|---|---|---|---|---|
| 1896 CHI N | 9 | 29 | 7 | 1 | 1 | 1 | 3.4 | 2 | 7 | 7 | | 0 | .241 | .448 | 0 | 0 | OF-9 |
| 1898 CIN N | 120 | 486 | 147 | 14 | 12 | 2 | 0.4 | 94 | 43 | 51 | | 16 | .302 | .393 | 0 | 0 | OF-120 |
| 1899 | 64 | 251 | 87 | 12 | 5 | 1 | 0.4 | 57 | 23 | 30 | | 5 | .347 | .446 | 0 | 0 | OF-64 |
| 1900 | 112 | 436 | 120 | 15 | 8 | 4 | 0.9 | 57 | 59 | 25 | | 12 | .275 | .374 | 3 | 0 | OF-109 |
| 1901 2 teams | | CIN N | (30G – | .236) | | NY N | (68G – | .280) | | | | | | | | | |
| " total | 98 | 387 | 103 | 18 | 0 | 4 | 1.0 | 46 | 47 | 19 | | 3 | .266 | .344 | 5 | 2 | OF-93 |
| 5 yrs. | 403 | 1589 | 464 | 60 | 26 | 12 | 0.8 | 256 | 179 | 132 | 3 | 36 | .292 | .385 | 8 | 2 | OF-395 |
| 1 yr. | 9 | 29 | 7 | 1 | 1 | 1 | 3.4 | 2 | 7 | 7 | | 0 | .241 | .448 | 0 | 0 | OF-9 |

## Bill McCabe

McCABE, WILLIAM FRANCIS
B. Oct. 28, 1892, Chicago, Ill. D. July 2, 1968, Chicago, Ill.

BB TR 5'9½" 180 lbs.

| | G | AB | H | 2B | 3B | HR | HR% | R | RBI | BB | SO | SB | BA | SA | AB | H | G by POS |
|---|---|---|---|---|---|---|---|---|---|---|---|---|---|---|---|---|---|
| 1918 CHI N | 29 | 45 | 8 | 0 | 1 | 0 | 0.0 | 9 | 5 | 4 | 7 | 2 | .178 | .222 | 6 | 1 | 2B-13, OF-4 |
| 1919 | 33 | 84 | 13 | 3 | 1 | 0 | 0.0 | 8 | 5 | 9 | 15 | 3 | .155 | .214 | 3 | 0 | OF-19, SS-4, 3B-1 |
| 1920 2 teams | | CHI N | (3G – | .500) | | BKN N | (41G – | .147) | | | | | | | | | |
| " total | 44 | 70 | 11 | 0 | 0 | 0 | 0.0 | 11 | 3 | 2 | 6 | 1 | .157 | .157 | 4 | 1 | SS-13, OF-6, 2B-4, 3B-3 |
| 3 yrs. | 106 | 199 | 32 | 3 | 2 | 0 | 0.0 | 28 | 13 | 15 | 28 | 6 | .161 | .196 | 13 | 2 | OF-29, SS-17, 2B-17, 3B-4 |
| 3 yrs. | 65 | 131 | 22 | 3 | 2 | 0 | 0.0 | 18 | 10 | 13 | 22 | 5 | .168 | .221 | 11 | 2 | OF-23, 2B-13, SS-4, 3B-1 |
| WORLD SERIES | | | | | | | | | | | | | | | | | |
| 1918 CHI N | 3 | 1 | 0 | 0 | 0 | 0 | 0.0 | 1 | 0 | 0 | 0 | 0 | .000 | .000 | 1 | 0 | |

| | G | AB | H | 2B | 3B | HR | HR % | R | RBI | BB | SO | SB | BA | SA | Pinch Hit AB | Pinch Hit H | G by POS |
|---|---|---|---|---|---|---|---|---|---|---|---|---|---|---|---|---|---|

## Bill McCabe continued

| | G | AB | H | 2B | 3B | HR | HR% | R | RBI | BB | SO | SB | BA | SA | PH AB | PH H | G by POS |
|---|---|---|---|---|---|---|---|---|---|---|---|---|---|---|---|---|---|
| 1920 BKN N | 1 | 0 | 0 | 0 | 0 | 0 | – | 0 | 0 | 0 | 0 | 0 | – | – | 0 | 0 | |
| 2 yrs. | 4 | 1 | 0 | 0 | 0 | 0 | 0.0 | 1 | 0 | 0 | 0 | 0 | .000 | .000 | 1 | 0 | |

## Alex McCarthy

**McCARTHY, ALEXANDER GEORGE**          BR TR 5'9"     150 lbs.
B. May 12, 1888, Chicago, Ill.    D. Mar. 12, 1978, Salisbury, Md.

| | G | AB | H | 2B | 3B | HR | HR% | R | RBI | BB | SO | SB | BA | SA | PH AB | PH H | G by POS |
|---|---|---|---|---|---|---|---|---|---|---|---|---|---|---|---|---|---|
| 1910 PIT N | 3 | 12 | 1 | 0 | 0 | 0 | 0.0 | 1 | 0 | 0 | 2 | 0 | .083 | .250 | 0 | 0 | SS-3 |
| 1911 | 50 | 150 | 36 | 5 | 1 | 2 | 1.3 | 18 | 31 | 14 | 24 | 4 | .240 | .327 | 2 | 0 | SS-33, 2B-11, OF-1, 3B-1 |
| 1912 | 111 | 401 | 111 | 12 | 4 | 1 | 0.2 | 53 | 41 | 30 | 36 | 8 | .277 | .334 | 2 | 0 | 2B-105, 3B-4 |
| 1913 | 31 | 74 | 15 | 5 | 0 | 0 | 0.0 | 7 | 10 | 7 | 7 | 1 | .203 | .270 | 1 | 0 | SS-12, 3B-12, 2B-6 |
| 1914 | 57 | 173 | 26 | 0 | 1 | 1 | 0.6 | 14 | 14 | 6 | 17 | 2 | .150 | .179 | 1 | 0 | 3B-36, 2B-10, SS-6 |
| 1915 2 teams | | PIT N (21G – .204) | | | | CHI N (23G – .264) | | | | | | | | | | | |
| " total | 44 | 121 | 29 | 3 | 1 | 1 | 0.8 | 7 | 9 | 10 | 17 | 3 | .240 | .306 | 2 | 1 | 2B-21, 3B-16, SS-6, 1B-1 |
| 1916 2 teams | | CHI N (37G – .243) | | | | PIT N (50G – .199) | | | | | | | | | | | |
| " total | 87 | 253 | 55 | 5 | 3 | 0 | 0.0 | 21 | 9 | 26 | 17 | 4 | .217 | .261 | 2 | 0 | SS-42, 2B-41, 3B-5 |
| 1917 PIT N | 49 | 151 | 33 | 4 | 0 | 0 | 0.0 | 15 | 8 | 11 | 13 | 1 | .219 | .245 | 0 | 0 | 3B-26, 2B-13, SS-9 |
| 8 yrs. | 432 | 1335 | 306 | 34 | 11 | 5 | 0.4 | 136 | 122 | 104 | 133 | 23 | .229 | .282 | 10 | 1 | 2B-207, SS-111, 3B-100, OF-1, 1B-1 |
| 2 yrs. | 60 | 179 | 45 | 5 | 3 | 1 | 0.6 | 14 | 12 | 16 | 14 | 3 | .251 | .330 | 1 | 0 | 2B-46, 3B-12, SS-4 |

## Jack McCarthy

**McCARTHY, JOHN A.**          BL TL 5'9"     155 lbs.
B. Mar. 26, 1869, Gilbertville, Mass.    D. Sept. 11, 1931, Chicago, Ill.

| | G | AB | H | 2B | 3B | HR | HR% | R | RBI | BB | SO | SB | BA | SA | PH AB | PH H | G by POS |
|---|---|---|---|---|---|---|---|---|---|---|---|---|---|---|---|---|---|
| 1893 CIN N | 49 | 195 | 55 | 8 | 3 | 0 | 0.0 | 28 | 22 | 22 | 7 | 6 | .282 | .354 | 0 | 0 | OF-47, 1B-2 |
| 1894 | 40 | 167 | 45 | 9 | 1 | 0 | 0.0 | 29 | 21 | 17 | 6 | 3 | .269 | .335 | 0 | 0 | OF-25, 1B-15 |
| 1898 PIT N | 137 | 537 | 155 | 13 | 12 | 4 | 0.7 | 75 | 78 | 34 | | 28 | .289 | .380 | 0 | 0 | OF-137 |
| 1899 | 138 | 560 | 171 | 22 | 17 | 3 | 0.5 | 108 | 67 | 39 | | 28 | .305 | .421 | 0 | 0 | OF-138 |
| 1900 CHI N | 124 | 503 | 148 | 16 | 7 | 0 | 0.0 | 68 | 48 | 24 | | 22 | .294 | .354 | 1 | 0 | OF-123 |
| 1901 CLE A | 86 | 343 | 110 | 14 | 7 | 0 | 0.0 | 60 | 32 | 30 | | 9 | .321 | .402 | 0 | 0 | OF-86 |
| 1902 | 95 | 359 | 102 | 31 | 5 | 0 | 0.0 | 45 | 41 | 24 | | 12 | .284 | .398 | 0 | 0 | OF-95 |
| 1903 2 teams | | CLE A (108G – .265) | | | | CHI N (24G – .277) | | | | | | | | | | | |
| " total | 132 | 516 | 138 | 25 | 8 | 0 | 0.0 | 58 | 57 | 23 | | 23 | .267 | .347 | 0 | 0 | OF-132 |
| 1904 CHI N | 115 | 432 | 114 | 14 | 2 | 0 | 0.0 | 36 | 51 | 23 | | 14 | .264 | .306 | 0 | 0 | OF-115 |
| 1905 | 59 | 170 | 47 | 4 | 3 | 0 | 0.0 | 16 | 14 | 10 | | 8 | .276 | .335 | 15 | 6 | OF-37, 1B-6 |
| 1906 BKN N | 91 | 322 | 98 | 13 | 1 | 0 | 0.0 | 23 | 35 | 20 | | 9 | .304 | .351 | 5 | 1 | OF-86 |
| 1907 | 25 | 91 | 20 | 2 | 0 | 0 | 0.0 | 4 | 8 | 2 | | 4 | .220 | .242 | 0 | 0 | OF-25 |
| 12 yrs. | 1091 | 4195 | 1203 | 171 | 66 | 7 | 0.2 | 550 | 474 | 268 | 13 | 145 | .287 | .364 | 21 | 7 | OF-1046, 1B-23 |
| 4 yrs. | 322 | 1206 | 337 | 39 | 12 | 0 | 0.0 | 131 | 127 | 61 | | 52 | .279 | .332 | 16 | 6 | OF-299, 1B-6 |

## Jim McCauley

**McCAULEY, JAMES A.**          6'     180 lbs.
B. Mar. 24, 1863, Stanley, N. Y.    D. Sept. 14, 1930, Canandaigua, N. Y.

| | G | AB | H | 2B | 3B | HR | HR% | R | RBI | BB | SO | SB | BA | SA | PH AB | PH H | G by POS |
|---|---|---|---|---|---|---|---|---|---|---|---|---|---|---|---|---|---|
| 1884 STL AA | 1 | 2 | 0 | 0 | 0 | 0 | 0.0 | 0 | | | | | .000 | .000 | 0 | 0 | C-1 |
| 1885 2 teams | | BUF N (24G – .179) | | | | CHI N (3G – .167) | | | | | | | | | | | |
| " total | 27 | 90 | 16 | 2 | 1 | 0 | 0.0 | 5 | 7 | 13 | 15 | | .178 | .222 | 0 | 0 | C-23, OF-6 |
| 1886 BKN AA | 11 | 30 | 7 | 1 | 0 | 0 | 0.0 | 5 | | 11 | | | .233 | .267 | 0 | 0 | C-11 |
| 3 yrs. | 39 | 122 | 23 | 3 | 1 | 0 | 0.0 | 10 | 6 | 24 | 15 | | .189 | .230 | 0 | 0 | C-35, OF-6 |
| 1 yr. | 3 | 6 | 1 | 0 | 0 | 0 | 0.0 | 1 | 0 | 2 | 3 | | .167 | .167 | 0 | 0 | OF-2, C-2 |

## Harry McChesney

**McCHESNEY, HARRY VINCENT (Pud)**          BR TR 5'9"     165 lbs.
B. June 1, 1880, Pittsburgh, Pa.    D. Aug. 11, 1960, Pittsburgh, Pa.

| | G | AB | H | 2B | 3B | HR | HR% | R | RBI | BB | SO | SB | BA | SA | PH AB | PH H | G by POS |
|---|---|---|---|---|---|---|---|---|---|---|---|---|---|---|---|---|---|
| 1904 CHI N | 22 | 88 | 23 | 6 | 2 | 0 | 0.0 | 9 | 11 | 4 | | 2 | .261 | .375 | 0 | 0 | OF-22 |

## Bill McClellan

**McCLELLAN, WILLIAM HENRY**          BL TL     156 lbs.
B. Mar. 22, 1856, Chicago, Ill.    D. July 2, 1929, Chicago, Ill.

| | G | AB | H | 2B | 3B | HR | HR% | R | RBI | BB | SO | SB | BA | SA | PH AB | PH H | G by POS |
|---|---|---|---|---|---|---|---|---|---|---|---|---|---|---|---|---|---|
| 1878 CHI N | 48 | 205 | 46 | 6 | 1 | 0 | 0.0 | 26 | 29 | 2 | 13 | | .224 | .263 | 0 | 0 | 2B-42, SS-5, OF-1 |
| 1881 PRO N | 68 | 259 | 43 | 3 | 1 | 0 | 0.0 | 30 | 16 | 15 | 21 | | .166 | .185 | 0 | 0 | SS-50, OF-17, 2B-1 |
| 1883 PHI N | 80 | 326 | 75 | 21 | 4 | 1 | 0.3 | 42 | | 19 | 18 | | .230 | .328 | 0 | 0 | SS-78, OF-2, 3B-1 |
| 1884 | 111 | 450 | 116 | 13 | 2 | 3 | 0.7 | 71 | | 28 | 43 | | .258 | .316 | 0 | 0 | SS-111, OF-1 |
| 1885 BKN AA | 112 | 464 | 124 | 22 | 7 | 0 | 0.0 | 85 | | 28 | | | .267 | .345 | 0 | 0 | 3B-57, 2B-55 |
| 1886 | 141 | 595 | 152 | 33 | 9 | 1 | 0.2 | 131 | | 56 | | | .255 | .346 | 0 | 0 | 2B-141 |
| 1887 | 136 | 548 | 144 | 24 | 6 | 1 | 0.2 | 109 | | 80 | | 70 | .263 | .334 | 0 | 0 | 2B-136 |
| 1888 2 teams | | BKN AA (74G – .205) | | | | CLE AA (22G – .222) | | | | | | | | | | | |
| " total | 96 | 350 | 73 | 7 | 3 | 0 | 0.0 | 39 | 26 | 46 | | 19 | .209 | .246 | 0 | 0 | 2B-61, OF-33, SS-2 |
| 8 yrs. | 792 | 3197 | 773 | 129 | 33 | 6 | 0.2 | 533 | 71 | 274 | 95 | 89 | .242 | .308 | 0 | 0 | 2B-436, SS-246, 3B-58, OF-54 |
| 1 yr. | 48 | 205 | 46 | 6 | 1 | 0 | 0.0 | 26 | 29 | 2 | 13 | | .224 | .263 | 0 | 0 | 2B-42, SS-5, OF-1 |

## George McConnell

**McCONNELL, GEORGE NEELY**          BR TR 6'3"     190 lbs.
B. Sept. 16, 1877, Shelbyville, Tenn.    D. May 10, 1964, Chattanooga, Tenn.

| | G | AB | H | 2B | 3B | HR | HR% | R | RBI | BB | SO | SB | BA | SA | PH AB | PH H | G by POS |
|---|---|---|---|---|---|---|---|---|---|---|---|---|---|---|---|---|---|
| 1909 NY A | 13 | 43 | 9 | 0 | 1 | 0 | 0.0 | 4 | 5 | 1 | | 1 | .209 | .256 | 0 | 0 | 1B-11, P-2 |
| 1912 | 42 | 91 | 27 | 4 | 2 | 0 | 0.0 | 11 | 8 | 4 | | 0 | .297 | .385 | 17 | 6 | P-23, 1B-2 |
| 1913 | 39 | 67 | 12 | 2 | 0 | 0 | 0.0 | 4 | 2 | 0 | 11 | 0 | .179 | .209 | 3 | 0 | P-35, 1B-1 |
| 1914 CHI N | 1 | 2 | 0 | 0 | 0 | 0 | 0.0 | 0 | 0 | 0 | | 0 | .000 | .000 | 0 | 0 | P-1 |
| 1915 CHI F | 53 | 125 | 31 | 6 | 2 | 1 | 0.8 | 14 | 18 | 0 | | 2 | .248 | .352 | 8 | 2 | P-44 |
| 1916 CHI N | 48 | 57 | 9 | 0 | 0 | 0 | 0.0 | 2 | 0 | 2 | | 4 | .158 | .158 | 0 | 0 | P-28 |
| 6 yrs. | 196 | 385 | 88 | 12 | 5 | 1 | 0.3 | 35 | 33 | 7 | 16 | 3 | .229 | .294 | 28 | 8 | P-133, 1B-14 |
| 2 yrs. | 49 | 59 | 9 | 0 | 0 | 0 | 0.0 | 2 | 0 | 2 | | 5 | .153 | .153 | 0 | 0 | P-29 |

## Barry McCormick

**McCORMICK, WILLIAM J.**          TR 5'9"
B. Dec. 25, 1874, Maysville, Ky.    D. Jan. 28, 1956, Cincinnati, Ohio

| | G | AB | H | 2B | 3B | HR | HR% | R | RBI | BB | SO | SB | BA | SA | PH AB | PH H | G by POS |
|---|---|---|---|---|---|---|---|---|---|---|---|---|---|---|---|---|---|
| 1895 LOU N | 3 | 12 | 3 | 0 | 1 | 0 | 0.0 | 2 | 0 | 0 | | 1 | .250 | .417 | 0 | 0 | SS-2, 2B-1 |

| | G | AB | H | 2B | 3B | HR | HR % | R | RBI | BB | SO | SB | BA | SA | Pinch Hit AB | Pinch Hit H | G by POS |
|---|---|---|---|---|---|---|---|---|---|---|---|---|---|---|---|---|---|

## Barry McCormick continued

| | G | AB | H | 2B | 3B | HR | HR % | R | RBI | BB | SO | SB | BA | SA | AB | H | G by POS |
|---|---|---|---|---|---|---|---|---|---|---|---|---|---|---|---|---|---|
| 1896 CHI N | 45 | 168 | 37 | 3 | 1 | 1 | 0.6 | 22 | 23 | 14 | 30 | 9 | .220 | .268 | 0 | 0 | 3B-35, SS-6, 2B-3, OF-1 |
| 1897 | 101 | 419 | 112 | 8 | 10 | 2 | 0.5 | 87 | 55 | 33 | | 44 | .267 | .348 | 0 | 0 | 3B-56, SS-46, 2B-1 |
| 1898 | 137 | 530 | 131 | 15 | 9 | 2 | 0.4 | 76 | 78 | 47 | | 15 | .247 | .321 | 0 | 0 | 3B-136, SS-1, 2B-1 |
| 1899 | 102 | 376 | 97 | 15 | 2 | 2 | 0.5 | 48 | 52 | 25 | | 14 | .258 | .324 | 0 | 0 | 2B-99, SS-3 |
| 1900 | 110 | 379 | 83 | 13 | 5 | 3 | 0.8 | 35 | 48 | 38 | | 8 | .219 | .303 | 0 | 0 | SS-84, 3B-21, 2B-5 |
| 1901 | 115 | 427 | 100 | 15 | 6 | 1 | 0.2 | 45 | 32 | 31 | | 12 | .234 | .304 | 0 | 0 | SS-112, 3B-3 |
| 1902 STL A | 139 | 504 | 124 | 14 | 4 | 3 | 0.6 | 55 | 51 | 37 | | 10 | .246 | .308 | 0 | 0 | 3B-132, SS-7, OF-1 |
| 1903 2 teams | | STL A | (61G – | .217) | | WAS A | (63G – | .215) | | | | | | | | | |
| " total | 124 | 426 | 92 | 16 | 3 | 2 | 0.5 | 27 | 40 | 28 | | 8 | .216 | .282 | 0 | 0 | 2B-91, 3B-28, SS-4 |
| 1904 WAS A | 113 | 404 | 88 | 11 | 1 | 0 | 0.0 | 36 | 39 | 27 | | 9 | .218 | .250 | 0 | 0 | 2B-113 |
| 10 yrs. | 989 | 3645 | 867 | 110 | 42 | 16 | 0.4 | 433 | 418 | 280 | 30 | 130 | .238 | .304 | 0 | 0 | 3B-411, 2B-314, SS-265, OF-2 |
| 6 yrs. | 610 | 2299 | 560 | 69 | 33 | 11 | 0.5 | 313 | 288 | 188 | 30 | 102 | .244 | .317 | 0 | 0 | SS-252, 3B-251, 2B-109, OF-1 |

## Jim McCormick

**McCORMICK, JAMES**　　　　　　　　BR TR 5'10½" 195 lbs.
B. 1856, Glasgow, Scotland　　D. Mar. 10, 1918, Paterson, N. J.
Manager 1879-80.

| | G | AB | H | 2B | 3B | HR | HR % | R | RBI | BB | SO | SB | BA | SA | AB | H | G by POS |
|---|---|---|---|---|---|---|---|---|---|---|---|---|---|---|---|---|---|
| 1878 IND N | 15 | 56 | 8 | 1 | 0 | 0 | 0.0 | 5 | 0 | 0 | 2 | | .143 | .161 | 0 | 0 | P-14, OF-3 |
| 1879 CLE N | 75 | 282 | 62 | 10 | 2 | 0 | 0.0 | 35 | 20 | 1 | 9 | | .220 | .270 | 0 | 0 | P-62, OF-13, 1B-4 |
| 1880 | 78 | 289 | 71 | 11 | 0 | 0 | 0.0 | 34 | | 5 | 5 | | .246 | .284 | 0 | 0 | P-74, OF-5 |
| 1881 | 70 | 309 | 79 | 9 | 4 | 0 | 0.0 | 45 | 26 | 5 | 16 | | .256 | .311 | 0 | 0 | P-59, OF-10, 3B-1, 2B-1 |
| 1882 | 70 | 262 | 57 | 7 | 3 | 2 | 0.8 | 35 | 15 | 2 | 22 | | .218 | .290 | 0 | 0 | P-68, OF-4 |
| 1883 | 43 | 157 | 37 | 2 | 2 | 0 | 0.0 | 21 | | 2 | 14 | | .236 | .274 | 0 | 0 | P-42, OF-1, 1B-1 |
| 1884 2 teams | 76 | CLE N | (49G – | .263) | | CIN U | (27G – | .245) | | | | | | | | | |
| " total | 76 | 300 | 77 | 8 | 5 | 0 | 0.0 | 27 | 23 | 1 | 11 | | .257 | .317 | 0 | 0 | P-66, OF-11 |
| 1885 2 teams | | PRO N | (4G – | .214) | | CHI N | (25G – | .223) | | | | | | | | | |
| " total | 29 | 117 | 26 | 2 | 4 | 0 | 0.0 | 15 | 16 | 2 | 18 | | .222 | .308 | 0 | 0 | P-28, OF-1 |
| 1886 CHI N | 42 | 174 | 41 | 9 | 2 | 2 | 1.1 | 17 | 21 | 2 | 30 | | .236 | .345 | 0 | 0 | P-42, OF-4 |
| 1887 PIT N | 36 | 136 | 33 | 7 | 0 | 0 | 0.0 | 12 | 18 | 2 | 0 | 9 | .243 | .294 | 0 | 0 | P-36 |
| 10 yrs. | 534 | 2082 | 491 | 66 | 22 | 4 | 0.2 | 246 | 139 | 22 | 127 | 9 | .236 | .294 | 0 | 0 | P-491, OF-52, 1B-5, 3B-1, 2B-1 |
| 2 yrs. | 67 | 277 | 64 | 10 | 6 | 2 | 0.7 | 30 | 37 | 3 | 48 | | .231 | .332 | 0 | 0 | P-66, OF-5 |

## Clyde McCullough

**McCULLOUGH, CLYDE EDWARD**　　　　　BR TR 5'11½" 180 lbs.
B. Mar. 4, 1917, Nashville, Tenn.　　D. Sept. 18, 1982, San Francisco, Calif.

| | G | AB | H | 2B | 3B | HR | HR % | R | RBI | BB | SO | SB | BA | SA | AB | H | G by POS |
|---|---|---|---|---|---|---|---|---|---|---|---|---|---|---|---|---|---|
| 1940 CHI N | 9 | 26 | 4 | 1 | 0 | 0 | 0.0 | 4 | 1 | 5 | 5 | 0 | .154 | .192 | 2 | 0 | C-7 |
| 1941 | 125 | 418 | 95 | 9 | 2 | 9 | 2.2 | 41 | 53 | 34 | 67 | 5 | .227 | .323 | 5 | 1 | C-119 |
| 1942 | 109 | 337 | 95 | 22 | 1 | 5 | 1.5 | 39 | 31 | 25 | 47 | 7 | .282 | .398 | 8 | 2 | C-97 |
| 1943 | 87 | 266 | 63 | 5 | 2 | 2 | 0.8 | 20 | 23 | 24 | 33 | 6 | .237 | .293 | 4 | 0 | C-81 |
| 1946 | 95 | 307 | 88 | 18 | 5 | 4 | 1.3 | 38 | 34 | 22 | 39 | 2 | .287 | .417 | 5 | 0 | C-89 |
| 1947 | 86 | 234 | 59 | 12 | 4 | 3 | 1.3 | 25 | 30 | 20 | 20 | 1 | .252 | .376 | 17 | 3 | C-64 |
| 1948 | 69 | 172 | 36 | 4 | 2 | 1 | 0.6 | 10 | 7 | 15 | 25 | 0 | .209 | .273 | 15 | 2 | C-51 |
| 1949 PIT N | 91 | 241 | 57 | 9 | 3 | 4 | 1.7 | 30 | 21 | 24 | 30 | 1 | .237 | .349 | 0 | 0 | C-90 |
| 1950 | 103 | 279 | 71 | 16 | 4 | 6 | 2.2 | 28 | 34 | 31 | 35 | 3 | .254 | .405 | 2 | 0 | C-100 |
| 1951 | 92 | 259 | 77 | 9 | 2 | 8 | 3.1 | 26 | 39 | 27 | 31 | 2 | .297 | .440 | 7 | 4 | C-86 |
| 1952 | 66 | 172 | 40 | 5 | 1 | 1 | 0.6 | 10 | 15 | 10 | 18 | 0 | .233 | .291 | 5 | 1 | C-61, 1B-1 |
| 1953 CHI N | 77 | 229 | 59 | 3 | 2 | 6 | 2.6 | 21 | 23 | 15 | 23 | 0 | .258 | .367 | 4 | 1 | C-73 |
| 1954 | 31 | 81 | 21 | 7 | 0 | 3 | 3.7 | 9 | 17 | 5 | 5 | 0 | .259 | .457 | 2 | 0 | C-26, 3B-3 |
| 1955 | 44 | 81 | 16 | 0 | 0 | 0 | 0.0 | 7 | 10 | 8 | 15 | 0 | .198 | .198 | 7 | 3 | C-37 |
| 1956 | 14 | 19 | 4 | 1 | 0 | 0 | 0.0 | 0 | 1 | 0 | 5 | 0 | .211 | .263 | 7 | 1 | C-7 |
| 15 yrs. | 1098 | 3121 | 785 | 121 | 28 | 52 | 1.7 | 308 | 339 | 265 | 398 | 27 | .252 | .358 | 90 | 18 | C-988, 3B-3, 1B-1 |
| 11 yrs. | 746 | 2170 | 540 | 82 | 18 | 33 | 1.5 | 214 | 230 | 173 | 284 | 21 | .249 | .349 | 76 | 13 | C-651, 3B-3 |

## Ed McDonald

**McDONALD, EDWARD C.**　　　　　　　BR TR 6'　180 lbs.
B. Oct. 28, 1886, Albany, N. Y.　　D. Mar. 11, 1946, Albany, N. Y.

| | G | AB | H | 2B | 3B | HR | HR % | R | RBI | BB | SO | SB | BA | SA | AB | H | G by POS |
|---|---|---|---|---|---|---|---|---|---|---|---|---|---|---|---|---|---|
| 1911 BOS N | 54 | 175 | 36 | 7 | 3 | 1 | 0.6 | 28 | 21 | 40 | 39 | 11 | .206 | .297 | 0 | 0 | 3B-53, SS-1 |
| 1912 | 121 | 459 | 119 | 23 | 6 | 2 | 0.4 | 70 | 34 | 70 | 91 | 22 | .259 | .349 | 3 | 1 | 3B-118 |
| 1913 CHI N | 1 | 0 | 0 | 0 | 0 | 0 | – | 0 | 0 | 0 | 0 | 0 | – | – | 0 | 0 | |
| 3 yrs. | 176 | 634 | 155 | 30 | 9 | 3 | 0.5 | 98 | 55 | 110 | 130 | 33 | .244 | .334 | 3 | 1 | 3B-171, SS-1 |
| 1 yr. | 1 | 0 | 0 | 0 | 0 | 0 | – | 0 | 0 | 0 | 0 | 0 | – | – | 0 | 0 | |

## Jim McKnight

**McKNIGHT, JAMES ARTHUR**　　　　　BR TR 6'1"　185 lbs.
B. July 1, 1936, Bee Branch, Ark.

| | G | AB | H | 2B | 3B | HR | HR % | R | RBI | BB | SO | SB | BA | SA | AB | H | G by POS |
|---|---|---|---|---|---|---|---|---|---|---|---|---|---|---|---|---|---|
| 1960 CHI N | 3 | 6 | 2 | 0 | 0 | 0 | 0.0 | 0 | 1 | 0 | 1 | 0 | .333 | .333 | 1 | 0 | OF-1, 2B-1 |
| 1962 | 60 | 85 | 19 | 0 | 1 | 0 | 0.0 | 6 | 5 | 2 | 13 | 0 | .224 | .247 | 49 | 11 | 3B-9, OF-5, 2B-2 |
| 2 yrs. | 63 | 91 | 21 | 0 | 1 | 0 | 0.0 | 6 | 6 | 2 | 14 | 0 | .231 | .253 | 50 | 11 | 3B-9, OF-6, 2B-3 |
| 2 yrs. | 63 | 91 | 21 | 0 | 1 | 0 | 0.0 | 6 | 6 | 2 | 14 | 0 | .231 | .253 | 50 | 11 | 3B-9, OF-6, 2B-3 |

## Polly McLarry

**McLARRY, HOWARD BELL**　　　　　　BL TR 6'　185 lbs.
B. Mar. 25, 1891, Leonard, Tex.　　D. Nov. 4, 1971, Bonham, Tex.

| | G | AB | H | 2B | 3B | HR | HR % | R | RBI | BB | SO | SB | BA | SA | AB | H | G by POS |
|---|---|---|---|---|---|---|---|---|---|---|---|---|---|---|---|---|---|
| 1912 CHI A | 2 | 2 | 0 | 0 | 0 | 0 | 0.0 | 0 | 0 | 0 | 0 | 0 | .000 | .000 | 2 | 0 | |
| 1915 CHI N | 68 | 127 | 25 | 3 | 0 | 1 | 0.8 | 16 | 12 | 14 | 20 | 2 | .197 | .244 | 21 | 2 | 1B-25, 2B-20 |
| 2 yrs. | 70 | 129 | 25 | 3 | 0 | 1 | 0.8 | 16 | 12 | 14 | 20 | 2 | .194 | .240 | 23 | 2 | 1B-25, 2B-20 |
| 1 yr. | 68 | 127 | 25 | 3 | 0 | 1 | 0.8 | 16 | 12 | 14 | 20 | 2 | .197 | .244 | 21 | 2 | 1B-25, 2B-20 |

## Larry McLean

**McLEAN, JOHN BANNERMAN**　　　　　BR TR 6'5"　228 lbs.
B. July 18, 1881, Cambridge, Mass.　　D. Mar. 14, 1921, Boston, Mass.

| | G | AB | H | 2B | 3B | HR | HR % | R | RBI | BB | SO | SB | BA | SA | AB | H | G by POS |
|---|---|---|---|---|---|---|---|---|---|---|---|---|---|---|---|---|---|
| 1901 BOS A | 9 | 19 | 4 | 1 | 0 | 0 | 0.0 | 4 | 2 | 0 | | 1 | .211 | .263 | 4 | 2 | 1B-5 |
| 1903 CHI N | 1 | 4 | 0 | 0 | 0 | 0 | 0.0 | 0 | 1 | 1 | | 0 | .000 | .000 | 0 | 0 | C-1 |

| | G | AB | H | 2B | 3B | HR | HR % | R | RBI | BB | SO | SB | BA | SA | Pinch Hit AB | Pinch Hit H | G by POS |
|---|---|---|---|---|---|---|---|---|---|---|---|---|---|---|---|---|---|

## Larry McLean continued

| | G | AB | H | 2B | 3B | HR | HR % | R | RBI | BB | SO | SB | BA | SA | AB | H | G by POS |
|---|---|---|---|---|---|---|---|---|---|---|---|---|---|---|---|---|---|
| 1904 STL N | 27 | 84 | 14 | 2 | 1 | 0 | 0.0 | 5 | 4 | 4 | | 1 | .167 | .214 | 2 | 0 | C-24 |
| 1906 CIN N | 12 | 35 | 7 | 2 | 0 | 0 | 0.0 | 3 | 2 | 4 | | 0 | .200 | .257 | 0 | 0 | C-12 |
| 1907 | 113 | 374 | 108 | 9 | 9 | 0 | 0.0 | 35 | 54 | 13 | | 4 | .289 | .361 | 11 | 2 | C-89, 1B-13 |
| 1908 | 99 | 309 | 67 | 9 | 4 | 1 | 0.3 | 24 | 28 | 15 | | 2 | .217 | .282 | 10 | 2 | C-69, 1B-19 |
| 1909 | 95 | 324 | 83 | 12 | 2 | 2 | 0.6 | 26 | 36 | 21 | | 1 | .256 | .324 | 0 | 0 | C-95 |
| 1910 | 127 | 423 | 126 | 14 | 7 | 0 | 0.0 | 27 | 71 | 26 | 23 | 4 | .298 | .378 | 9 | 2 | C-119 |
| 1911 | 107 | 328 | 94 | 7 | 2 | 0 | 0.0 | 24 | 34 | 20 | 18 | 1 | .287 | .320 | 8 | 0 | C-98 |
| 1912 | 102 | 333 | 81 | 15 | 1 | 1 | 0.3 | 17 | 27 | 18 | 15 | 1 | .243 | .303 | 4 | 2 | C-98 |
| 1913 2 teams | STL | N | (48G – | .270) | | NY | N | (30G – | .320) | | | | | | | | |
| " total | 78 | 227 | 65 | 13 | 0 | 0 | 0.0 | 10 | 21 | 10 | 13 | 1 | .286 | .344 | 8 | 2 | C-70 |
| 1914 NY N | 79 | 154 | 40 | 6 | 0 | 0 | 0.0 | 8 | 14 | 4 | 9 | 4 | .260 | .299 | 4 | 0 | C-74 |
| 1915 | 13 | 33 | 5 | 0 | 0 | 0 | 0.0 | 0 | 4 | 0 | 1 | 0 | .152 | .152 | 1 | 0 | C-12 |
| 13 yrs. | 862 | 2647 | 694 | 90 | 26 | 6 | 0.2 | 183 | 298 | 136 | 79 | 20 | .262 | .323 | 61 | 12 | C-761, 1B-37 |
| 1 yr. | 1 | 4 | 0 | 0 | 0 | 0 | 0.0 | 0 | 1 | 1 | | 0 | .000 | .000 | 0 | 0 | C-1 |
| WORLD SERIES | | | | | | | | | | | | | | | | | |
| 1913 NY N | 5 | 12 | 6 | 0 | 0 | 0 | 0.0 | 0 | 2 | 0 | 0 | 0 | .500 | .500 | 1 | 0 | C-4 |

## Jimmy McMath

McMATH, JIMMY LEE  
B. Aug. 10, 1949, Tuscaloosa, Ala.  
BL TL 6'1½" 195 lbs.

| | G | AB | H | 2B | 3B | HR | HR % | R | RBI | BB | SO | SB | BA | SA | AB | H | G by POS |
|---|---|---|---|---|---|---|---|---|---|---|---|---|---|---|---|---|---|
| 1968 CHI N | 6 | 14 | 2 | 0 | 0 | 0 | 0.0 | 0 | 2 | 0 | 6 | 0 | .143 | .143 | 3 | 0 | OF-3 |

## Norm McMillan

McMILLAN, NORMAN ALEXIS (Bub)  
B. Oct. 5, 1895, Latta, S. C.    D. Sept. 28, 1969, Marion, S. C.  
BR TR 6' 175 lbs.

| | G | AB | H | 2B | 3B | HR | HR % | R | RBI | BB | SO | SB | BA | SA | AB | H | G by POS |
|---|---|---|---|---|---|---|---|---|---|---|---|---|---|---|---|---|---|
| 1922 NY A | 33 | 78 | 20 | 1 | 2 | 0 | 0.0 | 7 | 11 | 6 | 10 | 4 | .256 | .321 | 1 | 0 | OF-23, 3B-5 |
| 1923 BOS A | 131 | 459 | 116 | 24 | 5 | 0 | 0.0 | 37 | 42 | 28 | 44 | 13 | .253 | .327 | 2 | 0 | 3B-67, 2B-35, SS-28 |
| 1924 STL A | 76 | 201 | 56 | 12 | 2 | 0 | 0.0 | 25 | 27 | 12 | 17 | 6 | .279 | .358 | 8 | 4 | 2B-37, 3B-17, SS-6, 1B-2 |
| 1928 CHI N | 49 | 123 | 27 | 2 | 2 | 1 | 0.8 | 11 | 12 | 13 | 19 | 0 | .220 | .293 | 9 | 1 | 2B-19, 3B-18 |
| 1929 | 124 | 495 | 134 | 35 | 5 | 5 | 1.0 | 77 | 55 | 36 | 43 | 13 | .271 | .392 | 3 | 2 | 3B-120 |
| 5 yrs. | 413 | 1356 | 353 | 74 | 16 | 6 | 0.4 | 157 | 147 | 95 | 133 | 36 | .260 | .352 | 23 | 7 | 3B-227, 2B-91, SS-34, OF-23, 1B-2 |
| 2 yrs. | 173 | 618 | 161 | 37 | 7 | 6 | 1.0 | 88 | 67 | 49 | 62 | 13 | .261 | .372 | 12 | 3 | 3B-138, 2B-19 |
| WORLD SERIES | | | | | | | | | | | | | | | | | |
| 1922 NY A | 1 | 2 | 0 | 0 | 0 | 0 | 0.0 | 0 | 0 | 0 | 0 | 0 | .000 | .000 | 1 | 0 | OF-1 |
| 1929 CHI N | 5 | 20 | 2 | 0 | 0 | 0 | 0.0 | 0 | 0 | 2 | 6 | 1 | .100 | .100 | 0 | 0 | 3B-5 |
| 2 yrs. | 6 | 22 | 2 | 0 | 0 | 0 | 0.0 | 0 | 0 | 2 | 6 | 1 | .091 | .091 | 1 | 0 | 3B-5, OF-1 |

## Cal McVey

McVEY, CALVIN ALEXANDER  
B. Aug. 30, 1850, County, Iowa    D. Aug. 20, 1926, San Francisco, Calif.  
Manager 1873, 1878-79.  
BR TR 5'9" 170 lbs.

| | G | AB | H | 2B | 3B | HR | HR % | R | RBI | BB | SO | SB | BA | SA | AB | H | G by POS |
|---|---|---|---|---|---|---|---|---|---|---|---|---|---|---|---|---|---|
| 1876 CHI N | 63 | 308 | 107 | 15 | 0 | 1 | 0.3 | 62 | 53 | 2 | 4 | | .347 | .406 | 0 | 0 | 1B-55, P-11, C-6, OF-1, 3B-1 |
| 1877 | 60 | 266 | 98 | 9 | 7 | 0 | 0.0 | 58 | 36 | 8 | 11 | | .368 | .455 | 0 | 0 | C-40, 3B-17, P-17, 2B-1, 1B-1 |
| 1878 CIN N | 61 | 271 | 83 | 10 | 4 | 2 | 0.7 | 43 | 28 | 5 | 10 | | .306 | .395 | 0 | 0 | 3B-61, C-3 |
| 1879 | 81 | 354 | 105 | 18 | 6 | 0 | 0.0 | 64 | 55 | 8 | 13 | | .297 | .381 | 0 | 0 | 1B-72, OF-7, P-3, 3B-1, C-1 |
| 4 yrs. | 265 | 1199 | 393 | 52 | 17 | 3 | 0.3 | 227 | 172 | 23 | 38 | | .328 | .407 | 0 | 0 | 1B-128, 3B-80, C-50, P-31, OF-8, 2B-1 |
| 2 yrs. | 123 | 574 | 205 | 24 | 7 | 1 | 0.2 | 120 | 89 | 10 | 15 | | .357 | .429 | 0 | 0 | 1B-56, C-46, P-28, 3B-18, OF-1, 2B-1 |

## Sam Mejias

MEJIAS, SAMUEL ELIAS  
B. May 9, 1953, Santiago, Dominican Republic  
BR TR 6' 170 lbs.

| | G | AB | H | 2B | 3B | HR | HR % | R | RBI | BB | SO | SB | BA | SA | AB | H | G by POS |
|---|---|---|---|---|---|---|---|---|---|---|---|---|---|---|---|---|---|
| 1976 STL N | 18 | 21 | 3 | 1 | 0 | 0 | 0.0 | 1 | 0 | 2 | 2 | 2 | .143 | .190 | 1 | 0 | OF-17 |
| 1977 MON N | 74 | 101 | 23 | 4 | 1 | 3 | 3.0 | 14 | 8 | 2 | 17 | 1 | .228 | .376 | 20 | 4 | OF-56 |
| 1978 | 67 | 56 | 13 | 1 | 0 | 0 | 0.0 | 9 | 6 | 2 | 5 | 0 | .232 | .250 | 10 | 3 | OF-52, P-1 |
| 1979 2 teams | CHI | N | (31G – | .182) | | CIN | N | (7G – | .500) | | | | | | | | |
| " total | 38 | 13 | 3 | 0 | 0 | 0 | 0.0 | 5 | 0 | 2 | 5 | 0 | .231 | .231 | 7 | 1 | OF-28 |
| 1980 CIN N | 71 | 108 | 30 | 5 | 1 | 1 | 0.9 | 16 | 10 | 6 | 13 | 4 | .278 | .370 | 7 | 2 | OF-67 |
| 1981 | 66 | 49 | 14 | 2 | 0 | 0 | 0.0 | 6 | 7 | 2 | 9 | 1 | .286 | .327 | 8 | 2 | OF-58 |
| 6 yrs. | 334 | 348 | 86 | 13 | 2 | 4 | 1.1 | 51 | 31 | 16 | 51 | 8 | .247 | .330 | 53 | 12 | OF-278, P-1 |
| 1 yr. | 31 | 11 | 2 | 0 | 0 | 0 | 0.0 | 4 | 0 | 2 | 5 | 0 | .182 | .182 | 6 | 1 | OF-23 |

## Jock Menefee

MENEFEE, JOHN  
B. Jan. 16, 1868, West Virginia    D. Mar. 11, 1953, Belle Vernon, Pa.  
BR TR 6'

| | G | AB | H | 2B | 3B | HR | HR % | R | RBI | BB | SO | SB | BA | SA | AB | H | G by POS |
|---|---|---|---|---|---|---|---|---|---|---|---|---|---|---|---|---|---|
| 1892 PIT N | 2 | 3 | 0 | 0 | 0 | 0 | 0.0 | 0 | 0 | 0 | 0 | 0 | .000 | .000 | 0 | 0 | OF-1, P-1 |
| 1893 LOU N | 22 | 73 | 20 | 2 | 0 | 0 | 0.0 | 10 | 12 | 13 | 5 | 2 | .274 | .329 | 0 | 0 | P-15, OF-7 |
| 1894 2 teams | LOU | N | (29G – | .165) | | PIT | N | (13G – | .255) | | | | | | | | |
| " total | 42 | 126 | 25 | 2 | 0 | 0 | 0.0 | 13 | 11 | 11 | 10 | 4 | .198 | .246 | 0 | 0 | P-41, 2B-1 |
| 1895 PIT N | 2 | 0 | 0 | 0 | 0 | 0 | – | 0 | 0 | 0 | 0 | 0 | – | – | 0 | 0 | P-2 |
| 1898 NY N | 1 | 5 | 0 | 0 | 0 | 0 | 0.0 | 0 | 0 | 0 | | 0 | .000 | .000 | 0 | 0 | P-1 |
| 1900 CHI N | 17 | 46 | 5 | 0 | 0 | 0 | 0.0 | 5 | 4 | 2 | | 0 | .109 | .109 | 1 | 0 | P-16 |
| 1901 | 48 | 152 | 39 | 5 | 3 | 0 | 0.0 | 19 | 13 | 8 | | 4 | .257 | .329 | 1 | 0 | OF-24, P-21, 1B-2, 2B-1 |
| 1902 | 65 | 216 | 50 | 4 | 1 | 0 | 0.0 | 24 | 15 | 15 | | 4 | .231 | .259 | 0 | 0 | OF-23, P-22, 1B-18, 3B-2, 2B-1 |
| 1903 | 22 | 64 | 13 | 3 | 0 | 0 | 0.0 | 3 | 2 | 3 | | 0 | .203 | .250 | 0 | 0 | P-20, 1B-2 |
| 9 yrs. | 221 | 685 | 152 | 16 | 7 | 0 | 0.0 | 74 | 57 | 52 | 15 | 14 | .222 | .266 | 2 | 0 | P-139, OF-55, 1B-22, 2B-3, 3B-2 |
| 4 yrs. | 152 | 478 | 107 | 12 | 4 | 0 | 0.0 | 51 | 34 | 28 | | 8 | .224 | .266 | 2 | 0 | P-79, OF-47, 1B-22, 3B-2, 2B-2 |

# Rudi Meoli

**MEOLI, RUDOLPH BART**
B. May 1, 1951, Troy, N. Y.
BL TR 5'9"  165 lbs.

| | | G | AB | H | 2B | 3B | HR | HR % | R | RBI | BB | SO | SB | BA | SA | Pinch Hit AB | H | G by POS |
|---|---|---|---|---|---|---|---|---|---|---|---|---|---|---|---|---|---|---|
| 1971 | CAL A | 7 | 3 | 0 | 0 | 0 | 0 | 0.0 | 0 | 0 | 0 | 1 | 0 | .000 | .000 | 3 | 0 | |
| 1973 | | 120 | 305 | 68 | 12 | 1 | 2 | 0.7 | 36 | 23 | 31 | 38 | 2 | .223 | .289 | 1 | 1 | SS-95, 3B-13, 2B-8 |
| 1974 | | 36 | 90 | 22 | 2 | 0 | 0 | 0.0 | 9 | 3 | 8 | 10 | 2 | .244 | .267 | 5 | 0 | 3B-20, SS-8, 2B-1, 1B-1 |
| 1975 | | 70 | 126 | 27 | 2 | 1 | 0 | 0.0 | 12 | 6 | 15 | 20 | 3 | .214 | .246 | 8 | 1 | SS-28, 3B-15, 2B-11, DH-3 |
| 1978 | CHI N | 47 | 29 | 3 | 0 | 1 | 0 | 0.0 | 10 | 0 | 6 | 4 | 1 | .103 | .172 | 19 | 2 | 2B-6, 3B-5 |
| 1979 | PHI N | 30 | 73 | 13 | 4 | 1 | 0 | 0.0 | 2 | 6 | 9 | 15 | 2 | .178 | .260 | 2 | 0 | SS-16, 2B-15, 3B-1 |
| 6 yrs. | | 310 | 626 | 133 | 20 | 4 | 2 | 0.3 | 69 | 40 | 69 | 88 | 10 | .212 | .267 | 38 | 4 | SS-147, 3B-54, 2B-41, DH-3, 1B-1 |
| 1 yr. | | 47 | 29 | 3 | 0 | 1 | 0 | 0.0 | 10 | 2 | 6 | 4 | 1 | .103 | .172 | 19 | 2 | 2B-6, 3B-5 |

# Fred Merkle

**MERKLE, FREDERICK CHARLES**
B. Dec. 20, 1888, Watertown, Wis.   D. Mar. 2, 1956, Daytona Beach, Fla.
BR TR 6'1"  190 lbs.

| | | G | AB | H | 2B | 3B | HR | HR % | R | RBI | BB | SO | SB | BA | SA | Pinch Hit AB | H | G by POS |
|---|---|---|---|---|---|---|---|---|---|---|---|---|---|---|---|---|---|---|
| 1907 | NY N | 15 | 47 | 12 | 1 | 0 | 0 | 0.0 | 0 | 5 | 1 | | 0 | .255 | .277 | 0 | 0 | 1B-15 |
| 1908 | | 38 | 41 | 11 | 2 | 1 | 1 | 2.4 | 6 | 7 | 4 | | 0 | .268 | .439 | 16 | 2 | 1B-11, OF-5, 3B-1, 2B-1 |
| 1909 | | 78 | 236 | 45 | 9 | 1 | 0 | 0.0 | 15 | 20 | 16 | | 7 | .191 | .237 | 8 | 3 | 1B-69, 2B-1 |
| 1910 | | 144 | 506 | 148 | 35 | 14 | 4 | 0.8 | 75 | 70 | 44 | 59 | 23 | .292 | .441 | 0 | 0 | 1B-144 |
| 1911 | | 149 | 541 | 153 | 24 | 12 | 12 | 2.2 | 80 | 84 | 43 | 60 | 49 | .283 | .438 | 0 | 0 | 1B-148 |
| 1912 | | 129 | 479 | 148 | 22 | 6 | 11 | 2.3 | 82 | 84 | 42 | 70 | 37 | .309 | .449 | 0 | 0 | 1B-129 |
| 1913 | | 153 | 563 | 147 | 30 | 12 | 3 | 0.5 | 78 | 69 | 41 | 60 | 35 | .261 | .373 | 0 | 0 | 1B-153 |
| 1914 | | 146 | 512 | 132 | 25 | 7 | 7 | 1.4 | 71 | 63 | 52 | 80 | 23 | .258 | .375 | 0 | 0 | 1B-146 |
| 1915 | | 140 | 505 | 151 | 25 | 3 | 4 | 0.8 | 52 | 62 | 36 | 39 | 20 | .299 | .384 | 1 | 0 | 1B-111, OF-29 |
| 1916 | 2 teams | NY | N (112G – .237) | | | | BKN | N (23G – .232) | | | | | | | | | | |
| " | total | 135 | 470 | 111 | 20 | 3 | 7 | 1.5 | 51 | 46 | 40 | 50 | 19 | .236 | .336 | 5 | 2 | 1B-127, OF-4 |
| 1917 | 2 teams | BKN | N (2G – .125) | | | | CHI | N (146G – .266) | | | | | | | | | | |
| " | total | 148 | 557 | 147 | 31 | 9 | 3 | 0.5 | 66 | 57 | 42 | 61 | 13 | .264 | .368 | 1 | 0 | 1B-142, OF-6 |
| 1918 | CHI N | 129 | 482 | 143 | 25 | 5 | 3 | 0.6 | 55 | 65 | 35 | 36 | 21 | .297 | .388 | 0 | 0 | 1B-129 |
| 1919 | | 133 | 498 | 133 | 20 | 6 | 3 | 0.6 | 52 | 62 | 33 | 35 | 20 | .267 | .349 | 0 | 0 | 1B-132 |
| 1920 | | 92 | 330 | 94 | 20 | 4 | 3 | 0.9 | 33 | 38 | 24 | 32 | 3 | .285 | .397 | 6 | 0 | 1B-85, OF-1 |
| 1925 | NY A | 7 | 13 | 5 | 1 | 0 | 0 | 0.0 | 4 | 1 | 1 | 1 | 1 | .385 | .462 | 2 | 1 | 1B-5 |
| 1926 | | 1 | 2 | 0 | 0 | 0 | 0 | 0.0 | 0 | 0 | 0 | 0 | 0 | .000 | .000 | 0 | 0 | 1B-1 |
| 16 yrs. | | 1637 | 5782 | 1580 | 290 | 83 | 61 | 1.1 | 720 | 733 | 454 | 583 | 271 | .273 | .384 | 39 | 8 | 1B-1547, OF-45, 2B-2, 3B-1 |
| 4 yrs. | | 500 | 1859 | 516 | 95 | 24 | 12 | 0.6 | 205 | 222 | 134 | 163 | 57 | .278 | .374 | 7 | 0 | 1B-486, OF-7 |

**WORLD SERIES**

| | | G | AB | H | 2B | 3B | HR | HR % | R | RBI | BB | SO | SB | BA | SA | Pinch Hit AB | H | G by POS |
|---|---|---|---|---|---|---|---|---|---|---|---|---|---|---|---|---|---|---|
| 1911 | NY N | 6 | 20 | 3 | 1 | 0 | 0 | 0.0 | 1 | 1 | 2 | 6 | 0 | .150 | .200 | 0 | 0 | 1B-6 |
| 1912 | | 8 | 33 | 9 | 2 | 1 | 0 | 0.0 | 5 | 3 | 0 | 7 | 1 | .273 | .394 | 0 | 0 | 1B-8 |
| 1913 | | 4 | 13 | 3 | 0 | 0 | 1 | 7.7 | 3 | 3 | 1 | 2 | 0 | .231 | .462 | 0 | 0 | 1B-4 |
| 1916 | BKN N | 3 | 4 | 1 | 0 | 0 | 0 | 0.0 | 0 | 0 | 2 | 0 | 0 | .250 | .250 | 1 | 0 | 1B-1 |
| 1918 | CHI N | 6 | 18 | 5 | 0 | 0 | 0 | 0.0 | 1 | 1 | 4 | 3 | 0 | .278 | .278 | 0 | 0 | 1B-6 |
| 5 yrs. | | 27 | 88 | 21 | 3 | 1 | 1 | 1.1 | 10 | 8 | 9 | 18 | 1 | .239 | .330 | 1 | 0 | 1B-25 |

# Lloyd Merriman

**MERRIMAN, LLOYD ARCHER (Citation)**
B. Aug. 2, 1924, Clovis, Calif.
BL TL 6'  190 lbs.

| | | G | AB | H | 2B | 3B | HR | HR % | R | RBI | BB | SO | SB | BA | SA | Pinch Hit AB | H | G by POS |
|---|---|---|---|---|---|---|---|---|---|---|---|---|---|---|---|---|---|---|
| 1949 | CIN N | 103 | 287 | 66 | 12 | 5 | 4 | 1.4 | 35 | 26 | 21 | 36 | 2 | .230 | .348 | 11 | 1 | OF-86 |
| 1950 | | 92 | 298 | 77 | 15 | 3 | 2 | 0.7 | 44 | 31 | 30 | 23 | 6 | .258 | .349 | 4 | 1 | OF-84 |
| 1951 | | 114 | 359 | 87 | 23 | 2 | 5 | 1.4 | 34 | 36 | 31 | 34 | 8 | .242 | .359 | 14 | 4 | OF-102 |
| 1954 | | 73 | 112 | 30 | 8 | 1 | 0 | 0.0 | 12 | 16 | 23 | 10 | 3 | .268 | .357 | 38 | 11 | OF-25 |
| 1955 | 2 teams | CHI | A (1G – .000) | | | | CHI | N (72G – .214) | | | | | | | | | | |
| " | total | 73 | 146 | 31 | 6 | 1 | 1 | 0.7 | 15 | 8 | 21 | 21 | 1 | .212 | .288 | 20 | 4 | OF-49 |
| 5 yrs. | | 455 | 1202 | 291 | 64 | 12 | 12 | 1.0 | 140 | 117 | 126 | 124 | 20 | .242 | .345 | 87 | 21 | OF-346 |
| 1 yr. | | 72 | 145 | 31 | 6 | 1 | 1 | 0.7 | 15 | 8 | 21 | 21 | 1 | .214 | .290 | 19 | 4 | OF-49 |

# Bill Merritt

**MERRITT, WILLIAM HENRY**
B. July 30, 1870, Lowell, Mass.   D. Nov. 17, 1937, Lowell, Mass.
BR TR 5'7"  160 lbs.

| | | G | AB | H | 2B | 3B | HR | HR % | R | RBI | BB | SO | SB | BA | SA | Pinch Hit AB | H | G by POS |
|---|---|---|---|---|---|---|---|---|---|---|---|---|---|---|---|---|---|---|
| 1891 | CHI N | 11 | 42 | 9 | 1 | 0 | 0 | 0.0 | 4 | 4 | 2 | 2 | 0 | .214 | .238 | 0 | 0 | C-11, 1B-1 |
| 1892 | LOU N | 46 | 168 | 33 | 4 | 2 | 1 | 0.6 | 22 | 13 | 11 | 15 | 3 | .196 | .262 | 0 | 0 | C-46 |
| 1893 | BOS N | 39 | 141 | 49 | 6 | 3 | 3 | 2.1 | 30 | 26 | 13 | 13 | 3 | .348 | .496 | 0 | 0 | C-37, OF-2 |
| 1894 | 3 teams | BOS | N (10G – .231) | | | | PIT | N (36G – .275) | | | | CIN | N (29G – .327) | | | | | |
| " | total | 75 | 248 | 73 | 8 | 3 | 2 | 0.8 | 38 | 45 | 32 | 10 | 6 | .294 | .375 | 4 | 0 | C-60, 1B-5, OF-4, 3B-3 |
| 1895 | 2 teams | CIN | N (22G – .177) | | | | PIT | N (67G – .285) | | | | | | | | | | |
| " | total | 89 | 318 | 82 | 7 | 1 | 0 | 0.0 | 41 | 39 | 24 | 21 | 4 | .258 | .286 | 1 | 0 | C-83, 1B-2, 2B-1 |
| 1896 | PIT N | 77 | 282 | 82 | 8 | 2 | 1 | 0.4 | 26 | 42 | 18 | 10 | 3 | .291 | .344 | 3 | 1 | C-62, 3B-5, 2B-3, 1B-3, SS-2 |
| 1897 | | 62 | 209 | 55 | 6 | 1 | 1 | 0.5 | 21 | 26 | 9 | | 2 | .263 | .316 | 2 | 0 | C-53, 1B-7 |
| 1899 | BOS N | 1 | 2 | 0 | 0 | 0 | 0 | 0.0 | 0 | 0 | 0 | | 0 | .000 | .000 | 0 | 0 | C-1 |
| 8 yrs. | | 400 | 1410 | 383 | 40 | 12 | 8 | 0.6 | 182 | 195 | 109 | 71 | 21 | .272 | .334 | 10 | 1 | C-353, 1B-18, 3B-8, OF-6, 2B-4, SS-2 |
| 1 yr. | | 11 | 42 | 9 | 1 | 0 | 0 | 0.0 | 4 | 4 | 2 | 2 | 0 | .214 | .238 | 0 | 0 | C-11, 1B-1 |

# Sam Mertes

**MERTES, SAMUEL BLAIR (Sandow)**
B. Aug. 6, 1872, San Francisco, Calif.   D. Mar. 11, 1945, San Francisco, Calif.
BR TR 5'10"  185 lbs.

| | | G | AB | H | 2B | 3B | HR | HR % | R | RBI | BB | SO | SB | BA | SA | Pinch Hit AB | H | G by POS |
|---|---|---|---|---|---|---|---|---|---|---|---|---|---|---|---|---|---|---|
| 1896 | PHI N | 37 | 143 | 34 | 4 | 4 | 0 | 0.0 | 20 | 14 | 8 | 10 | 19 | .238 | .322 | 1 | 0 | OF-35, SS-1, 2B-1 |
| 1898 | CHI N | 83 | 269 | 80 | 4 | 8 | 1 | 0.4 | 45 | 47 | 34 | | 27 | .297 | .383 | 5 | 0 | OF-60, SS-14, 2B-4, 1B-2 |
| 1899 | | 117 | 426 | 127 | 13 | 16 | 9 | 2.1 | 83 | 81 | 33 | | 45 | .298 | .467 | 5 | 1 | OF-108, 1B-3, SS-1 |
| 1900 | | 127 | 481 | 142 | 25 | 4 | 7 | 1.5 | 72 | 60 | 42 | | 38 | .295 | .407 | 5 | 0 | OF-88, 1B-33, SS-7 |
| 1901 | CHI A | 137 | 545 | 151 | 16 | 17 | 5 | 0.9 | 94 | 98 | 52 | | 46 | .277 | .396 | 0 | 0 | 2B-132, OF-5 |
| 1902 | | 129 | 497 | 140 | 23 | 7 | 1 | 0.2 | 60 | 79 | 37 | | 46 | .282 | .362 | 0 | 0 | OF-120, SS-5, C-2, 3B-1, 2B-1, 1B-1, P-1 |
| 1903 | NY N | 138 | 517 | 145 | 32 | 14 | 7 | 1.4 | 100 | 104 | 61 | | 45 | .280 | .437 | 0 | 0 | OF-137, 1B-1, C-1 |
| 1904 | | 148 | 532 | 147 | 28 | 11 | 4 | 0.8 | 83 | 78 | 54 | | 47 | .276 | .393 | 0 | 0 | OF-147, SS-1 |
| 1905 | | 150 | 551 | 154 | 27 | 17 | 5 | 0.9 | 81 | 108 | 56 | | 52 | .279 | .417 | 0 | 0 | OF-150 |

| | G | AB | H | 2B | 3B | HR | HR % | R | RBI | BB | SO | SB | BA | SA | Pinch Hit AB | Pinch Hit H | G by POS |
|---|---|---|---|---|---|---|---|---|---|---|---|---|---|---|---|---|---|

## Sam Mertes continued

| | G | AB | H | 2B | 3B | HR | HR% | R | RBI | BB | SO | SB | BA | SA | AB | H | G by POS |
|---|---|---|---|---|---|---|---|---|---|---|---|---|---|---|---|---|---|
| 1906 2 teams | NY N (71G – .237) | | | STL N (53G – .246) | | | | | | | | | | | | | |
| " total | 124 | 444 | 107 | 16 | 10 | 1 | 0.2 | 57 | 52 | 45 | | 31 | .241 | .329 | 0 | 0 | OF-124 |
| 10 yrs. | 1190 | 4405 | 1227 | 188 | 108 | 40 | 0.9 | 695 | 721 | 422 | 10 | 396 | .279 | .398 | 11 | 1 | OF-974, 2B-138, 1B-40, SS-29, C-3, 3B-1, P-1 |
| 3 yrs. | 327 | 1176 | 349 | 42 | 28 | 17 | 1.4 | 200 | 188 | 109 | | 110 | .297 | .423 | 10 | 1 | OF-256, 1B-38, SS-22, 2B-4 |

**WORLD SERIES**

| | G | AB | H | 2B | 3B | HR | HR% | R | RBI | BB | SO | SB | BA | SA | AB | H | G by POS |
|---|---|---|---|---|---|---|---|---|---|---|---|---|---|---|---|---|---|
| 1905 NY N | 5 | 17 | 3 | 1 | 0 | 0 | 0.0 | 2 | 3 | 2 | 5 | 0 | .176 | .235 | 0 | 0 | OF-5 |

## Lennie Merullo

**MERULLO, LEONARD RICHARD**     BR   TR   5'11½" 166 lbs.
B. May 5, 1917, Boston, Mass.

| | G | AB | H | 2B | 3B | HR | HR% | R | RBI | BB | SO | SB | BA | SA | AB | H | G by POS |
|---|---|---|---|---|---|---|---|---|---|---|---|---|---|---|---|---|---|
| 1941 CHI N | 7 | 17 | 6 | 1 | 0 | 0 | 0.0 | 3 | 1 | 2 | 0 | 1 | .353 | .412 | 0 | 0 | SS-7 |
| 1942 | 143 | 515 | 132 | 23 | 3 | 2 | 0.4 | 53 | 37 | 35 | 45 | 14 | .256 | .324 | 0 | 0 | SS-143 |
| 1943 | 129 | 453 | 115 | 18 | 3 | 1 | 0.2 | 37 | 25 | 26 | 42 | 7 | .254 | .313 | 0 | 0 | SS-125, 3B-2, 2B-1 |
| 1944 | 66 | 193 | 41 | 8 | 1 | 1 | 0.5 | 20 | 16 | 16 | 18 | 3 | .212 | .280 | 6 | 1 | SS-56, 1B-1 |
| 1945 | 121 | 394 | 94 | 18 | 0 | 2 | 0.5 | 40 | 37 | 31 | 30 | 7 | .239 | .299 | 0 | 0 | SS-118 |
| 1946 | 65 | 126 | 19 | 8 | 0 | 0 | 0.0 | 14 | 7 | 11 | 13 | 2 | .151 | .214 | 1 | 0 | SS-44 |
| 1947 | 108 | 373 | 90 | 16 | 1 | 0 | 0.0 | 24 | 29 | 15 | 26 | 4 | .241 | .290 | 0 | 0 | SS-108 |
| 7 yrs. | 639 | 2071 | 497 | 92 | 8 | 6 | 0.3 | 191 | 152 | 136 | 174 | 38 | .240 | .301 | 7 | 1 | SS-601, 3B-2, 2B-1, 1B-1 |
| 7 yrs. | 639 | 2071 | 497 | 92 | 8 | 6 | 0.3 | 191 | 152 | 136 | 174 | 38 | .240 | .301 | 7 | 1 | SS-601, 3B-2, 2B-1, 1B-1 |

**WORLD SERIES**

| | G | AB | H | 2B | 3B | HR | HR% | R | RBI | BB | SO | SB | BA | SA | AB | H | G by POS |
|---|---|---|---|---|---|---|---|---|---|---|---|---|---|---|---|---|---|
| 1945 CHI N | 3 | 2 | 0 | 0 | 0 | 0 | 0.0 | 0 | 0 | 0 | 1 | 0 | .000 | .000 | 0 | 0 | SS-3 |

## Steve Mesner

**MESNER, STEPHEN MATHIAS**     BR   TR   5'9"    178 lbs.
B. Jan. 13, 1918, Los Angeles, Calif.    D. Apr. 6, 1981, San Diego, Calif.

| | G | AB | H | 2B | 3B | HR | HR% | R | RBI | BB | SO | SB | BA | SA | AB | H | G by POS |
|---|---|---|---|---|---|---|---|---|---|---|---|---|---|---|---|---|---|
| 1938 CHI N | 2 | 4 | 1 | 0 | 0 | 0 | 0.0 | 2 | 0 | 1 | 0 | 0 | .250 | .250 | 1 | 0 | SS-1 |
| 1939 | 17 | 43 | 12 | 4 | 0 | 0 | 0.0 | 7 | 6 | 3 | 4 | 0 | .279 | .372 | 3 | 0 | SS-12, 3B-1, 2B-1 |
| 1941 STL N | 24 | 69 | 10 | 1 | 0 | 0 | 0.0 | 8 | 10 | 5 | 6 | 0 | .145 | .159 | 1 | 0 | 3B-22 |
| 1943 CIN N | 137 | 504 | 137 | 26 | 1 | 0 | 0.0 | 53 | 52 | 26 | 20 | 6 | .272 | .327 | 7 | 4 | 3B-130 |
| 1944 | 121 | 414 | 100 | 17 | 4 | 1 | 0.2 | 31 | 47 | 34 | 20 | 1 | .242 | .309 | 1 | 0 | 3B-120 |
| 1945 | 150 | 540 | 137 | 19 | 1 | 1 | 0.2 | 52 | 52 | 52 | 18 | 4 | .254 | .298 | 0 | 0 | 3B-148, 2B-3 |
| 6 yrs. | 451 | 1574 | 397 | 67 | 6 | 2 | 0.1 | 153 | 167 | 121 | 69 | 11 | .252 | .306 | 13 | 4 | 3B-421, SS-13, 2B-4 |
| 2 yrs. | 19 | 47 | 13 | 4 | 0 | 0 | 0.0 | 9 | 6 | 4 | 5 | 0 | .277 | .340 | 4 | 0 | SS-13, 3B-1, 2B-1 |

## Catfish Metkovich

**METKOVICH, GEORGE MICHAEL**     BL   TL   6'1"    185 lbs.
B. Oct. 8, 1921, Angel's Camp, Calif.

| | G | AB | H | 2B | 3B | HR | HR% | R | RBI | BB | SO | SB | BA | SA | AB | H | G by POS |
|---|---|---|---|---|---|---|---|---|---|---|---|---|---|---|---|---|---|
| 1943 BOS A | 78 | 321 | 79 | 14 | 4 | 5 | 1.6 | 34 | 27 | 19 | 38 | 1 | .246 | .361 | 0 | 0 | OF-76, 1B-2 |
| 1944 | 134 | 549 | 152 | 28 | 8 | 9 | 1.6 | 94 | 59 | 31 | 57 | 13 | .277 | .406 | 2 | 1 | OF-82, 1B-50 |
| 1945 | 138 | 539 | 140 | 26 | 3 | 5 | 0.9 | 65 | 62 | 51 | 70 | 19 | .260 | .347 | 3 | 0 | 1B-97, OF-42 |
| 1946 | 86 | 281 | 69 | 15 | 2 | 4 | 1.4 | 42 | 25 | 36 | 39 | 8 | .246 | .356 | 3 | 0 | OF-81 |
| 1947 CLE A | 126 | 473 | 120 | 22 | 7 | 5 | 1.1 | 68 | 40 | 32 | 51 | 5 | .254 | .362 | 6 | 2 | OF-119, 1B-1 |
| 1949 CHI A | 93 | 338 | 80 | 9 | 4 | 5 | 1.5 | 50 | 45 | 41 | 24 | 5 | .237 | .331 | 5 | 1 | OF-87 |
| 1951 PIT N | 120 | 423 | 124 | 21 | 3 | 3 | 0.7 | 51 | 40 | 28 | 23 | 3 | .293 | .378 | 13 | 6 | OF-69, 1B-37 |
| 1952 | 125 | 373 | 101 | 18 | 3 | 7 | 1.9 | 41 | 41 | 32 | 29 | 5 | .271 | .391 | 20 | 4 | 1B-72, OF-33 |
| 1953 2 teams | PIT N (26G – .146) | | | CHI N (61G – .234) | | | | | | | | | | | | | |
| " total | 87 | 165 | 35 | 9 | 1 | 3 | 1.8 | 24 | 19 | 22 | 13 | 2 | .212 | .333 | 33 | 8 | OF-42, 1B-12 |
| 1954 MIL N | 68 | 123 | 34 | 5 | 1 | 1 | 0.8 | 7 | 15 | 15 | 15 | 0 | .276 | .358 | 31 | 9 | 1B-18, OF-13 |
| 10 yrs. | 1055 | 3585 | 934 | 167 | 36 | 47 | 1.3 | 476 | 373 | 307 | 359 | 61 | .261 | .367 | 116 | 31 | OF-644, 1B-289 |
| 1 yr. | 61 | 124 | 29 | 9 | 0 | 2 | 1.6 | 19 | 12 | 16 | 10 | 2 | .234 | .355 | 18 | 5 | OF-38, 1B-7 |

**WORLD SERIES**

| | G | AB | H | 2B | 3B | HR | HR% | R | RBI | BB | SO | SB | BA | SA | AB | H | G by POS |
|---|---|---|---|---|---|---|---|---|---|---|---|---|---|---|---|---|---|
| 1946 BOS A | 2 | 2 | 1 | 1 | 0 | 0 | 0.0 | 1 | 0 | 0 | 0 | 0 | .500 | 1.000 | 2 | 1 | |

## Roger Metzger

**METZGER, ROGER HENRY**     BB   TR   6'    165 lbs.
B. Oct. 10, 1947, Fredericksburg, Tex.

| | G | AB | H | 2B | 3B | HR | HR% | R | RBI | BB | SO | SB | BA | SA | AB | H | G by POS |
|---|---|---|---|---|---|---|---|---|---|---|---|---|---|---|---|---|---|
| 1970 CHI N | 1 | 2 | 0 | 0 | 0 | 0 | 0.0 | 0 | 0 | 0 | 0 | 0 | .000 | .000 | 0 | 0 | SS-1 |
| 1971 HOU N | 150 | 562 | 132 | 14 | 11 | 0 | 0.0 | 64 | 26 | 44 | 50 | 15 | .235 | .299 | 1 | 1 | SS-148 |
| 1972 | 153 | 641 | 142 | 12 | 3 | 2 | 0.3 | 84 | 38 | 60 | 71 | 23 | .222 | .259 | 0 | 0 | SS-153 |
| 1973 | 154 | 580 | 145 | 11 | 14 | 1 | 0.2 | 67 | 35 | 39 | 70 | 10 | .250 | .322 | 1 | 0 | SS-149 |
| 1974 | 143 | 572 | 145 | 18 | 10 | 0 | 0.0 | 66 | 30 | 37 | 73 | 9 | .253 | .320 | 0 | 0 | SS-143 |
| 1975 | 127 | 450 | 102 | 7 | 9 | 2 | 0.4 | 54 | 26 | 41 | 39 | 4 | .227 | .296 | 2 | 1 | SS-126 |
| 1976 | 152 | 481 | 101 | 13 | 8 | 0 | 0.0 | 37 | 29 | 52 | 63 | 1 | .210 | .270 | 0 | 0 | SS-150, 2B-2 |
| 1977 | 97 | 269 | 50 | 9 | 6 | 0 | 0.0 | 24 | 16 | 32 | 24 | 2 | .186 | .264 | 1 | 0 | SS-96, 2B-1 |
| 1978 2 teams | HOU N (45G – .220) | | | SF N (75G – .260) | | | | | | | | | | | | | |
| " total | 120 | 358 | 88 | 10 | 2 | 0 | 0.0 | 28 | 23 | 24 | 26 | 8 | .246 | .285 | 4 | 1 | SS-116, 2B-1 |
| 1979 SF N | 94 | 259 | 65 | 7 | 8 | 0 | 0.0 | 24 | 31 | 23 | 31 | 11 | .251 | .340 | 6 | 1 | SS-78, 2B-10, 3B-1 |
| 1980 | 28 | 27 | 2 | 0 | 0 | 0 | 0.0 | 5 | 0 | 3 | 2 | 0 | .074 | .074 | 8 | 1 | SS-13, 2B-1 |
| 11 yrs. | 1219 | 4201 | 972 | 101 | 71 | 5 | 0.1 | 453 | 254 | 355 | 449 | 83 | .231 | .293 | 23 | 5 | SS-1173, 2B-15, 3B-1 |
| 1 yr. | 1 | 2 | 0 | 0 | 0 | 0 | 0.0 | 0 | 0 | 0 | 0 | 0 | .000 | .000 | 0 | 0 | SS-1 |

## Alex Metzler

**METZLER, ALEXANDER**     BL   TR   5'9"    167 lbs.
B. Jan. 4, 1903, Fresno, Calif.    D. Nov. 30, 1973, Fresno, Calif.

| | G | AB | H | 2B | 3B | HR | HR% | R | RBI | BB | SO | SB | BA | SA | AB | H | G by POS |
|---|---|---|---|---|---|---|---|---|---|---|---|---|---|---|---|---|---|
| 1925 CHI N | 9 | 38 | 7 | 2 | 0 | 0 | 0.0 | 2 | 3 | 3 | 7 | 1 | .184 | .237 | 0 | 0 | OF-9 |
| 1926 PHI A | 20 | 67 | 16 | 3 | 0 | 0 | 0.0 | 8 | 12 | 7 | 5 | 1 | .239 | .284 | 3 | 1 | OF-17 |
| 1927 CHI A | 134 | 543 | 173 | 29 | 11 | 3 | 0.6 | 87 | 61 | 61 | 39 | 15 | .319 | .429 | 0 | 0 | OF-134 |
| 1928 | 139 | 464 | 141 | 18 | 14 | 3 | 0.6 | 71 | 55 | 77 | 30 | 16 | .304 | .422 | 6 | 2 | OF-134 |
| 1929 | 146 | 568 | 156 | 23 | 13 | 2 | 0.4 | 80 | 49 | 80 | 45 | 11 | .275 | .371 | 4 | 0 | OF-141 |
| 1930 2 teams | CHI A (56G – .184) | | | STL A (56G – .258) | | | | | | | | | | | | | |
| " total | 112 | 285 | 68 | 10 | 3 | 1 | 0.4 | 42 | 28 | 32 | 18 | 5 | .239 | .305 | 24 | 4 | OF-83 |
| 6 yrs. | 560 | 1965 | 561 | 85 | 41 | 9 | 0.5 | 290 | 207 | 260 | 144 | 48 | .285 | .384 | 37 | 7 | OF-518 |
| 1 yr. | 9 | 38 | 7 | 2 | 0 | 0 | 0.0 | 2 | 3 | 3 | 7 | 0 | .184 | .237 | 0 | 0 | OF-9 |

| | G | AB | H | 2B | 3B | HR | HR % | R | RBI | BB | SO | SB | BA | SA | Pinch Hit AB | Pinch Hit H | G by POS |
|---|---|---|---|---|---|---|---|---|---|---|---|---|---|---|---|---|---|

## Dutch Meyer

**MEYER, LAMBERT DANIEL**
B. Oct. 6, 1915, Waco, Tex.

BR TR 5'10½" 181 lbs.

| | G | AB | H | 2B | 3B | HR | HR% | R | RBI | BB | SO | SB | BA | SA | AB | H | G by POS |
|---|---|---|---|---|---|---|---|---|---|---|---|---|---|---|---|---|---|
| 1937 CHI N | 1 | 0 | 0 | 0 | 0 | 0 | – | 0 | 0 | 0 | 0 | 0 | – | – | 0 | 0 | |
| 1940 DET A | 23 | 58 | 15 | 3 | 0 | 0 | 0.0 | 12 | 6 | 4 | 10 | 2 | .259 | .310 | 3 | 0 | 2B-21 |
| 1941 | 46 | 153 | 29 | 9 | 1 | 1 | 0.7 | 12 | 14 | 8 | 13 | 1 | .190 | .281 | 6 | 2 | 2B-40 |
| 1942 | 14 | 52 | 17 | 3 | 0 | 2 | 3.8 | 5 | 9 | 4 | 4 | 0 | .327 | .500 | 0 | 0 | 2B-14 |
| 1945 CLE A | 130 | 524 | 153 | 29 | 8 | 7 | 1.3 | 71 | 48 | 40 | 32 | 2 | .292 | .418 | 0 | 0 | 2B-130 |
| 1946 | 72 | 207 | 48 | 5 | 3 | 0 | 0.0 | 13 | 16 | 26 | 16 | 0 | .232 | .285 | 7 | 1 | 2B-64 |
| 6 yrs. | 286 | 994 | 262 | 49 | 12 | 10 | 1.0 | 113 | 93 | 82 | 75 | 5 | .264 | .367 | 16 | 3 | 2B-269 |
| 1 yr. | 1 | 0 | 0 | 0 | 0 | 0 | – | 0 | 0 | 0 | 0 | 0 | – | – | 0 | 0 | |

## Ralph Michaels

**MICHAELS, RALPH JOSEPH**
B. May 3, 1902, Etna, Pa.

BR TR 5'10½" 178 lbs.

| | G | AB | H | 2B | 3B | HR | HR% | R | RBI | BB | SO | SB | BA | SA | AB | H | G by POS |
|---|---|---|---|---|---|---|---|---|---|---|---|---|---|---|---|---|---|
| 1924 CHI N | 8 | 11 | 4 | 0 | 0 | 0 | 0.0 | 1 | 2 | 0 | 1 | 0 | .364 | .364 | 3 | 1 | SS-4 |
| 1925 | 22 | 50 | 14 | 1 | 0 | 0 | 0.0 | 10 | 6 | 6 | 9 | 1 | .280 | .300 | 3 | 0 | 3B-15, SS-1, 2B-1, 1B-1 |
| 1926 | 2 | 0 | 0 | 0 | 0 | 0 | – | 1 | 0 | 0 | 0 | 0 | – | – | 0 | 0 | |
| 3 yrs. | 32 | 61 | 18 | 1 | 0 | 0 | 0.0 | 11 | 8 | 6 | 10 | 1 | .295 | .311 | 6 | 1 | 3B-15, SS-5, 2B-1, 1B-1 |
| 3 yrs. | 32 | 61 | 18 | 1 | 0 | 0 | 0.0 | 11 | 8 | 6 | 10 | 1 | .295 | .311 | 6 | 1 | 3B-15, SS-5, 2B-1, 1B-1 |

## Ed Mickelson

**MICKELSON, EDWARD ALLEN**
B. Sept. 9, 1926, Ottawa, Ill.

BR TR 6'3" 205 lbs.

| | G | AB | H | 2B | 3B | HR | HR% | R | RBI | BB | SO | SB | BA | SA | AB | H | G by POS |
|---|---|---|---|---|---|---|---|---|---|---|---|---|---|---|---|---|---|
| 1950 STL A | 5 | 10 | 1 | 0 | 0 | 0 | 0.0 | 1 | 2 | 2 | 3 | 0 | .100 | .100 | 1 | 0 | 1B-4 |
| 1953 STL A | 7 | 15 | 2 | 1 | 0 | 0 | 0.0 | 1 | 2 | 2 | 6 | 0 | .133 | .200 | 3 | 0 | 1B-3 |
| 1957 CHI N | 6 | 12 | 0 | 0 | 0 | 0 | 0.0 | 0 | 1 | 0 | 4 | 0 | .000 | .000 | 4 | 0 | 1B-2 |
| 3 yrs. | 18 | 37 | 3 | 1 | 0 | 0 | 0.0 | 2 | 3 | 4 | 13 | 0 | .081 | .108 | 8 | 0 | 1B-9 |
| 1 yr. | 6 | 12 | 0 | 0 | 0 | 0 | 0.0 | 0 | 1 | 0 | 4 | 0 | .000 | .000 | 4 | 0 | 1B-2 |

## Eddie Miksis

**MIKSIS, EDWARD THOMAS**
B. Sept. 11, 1926, Burlington, N. J.

BR TR 6'½" 185 lbs.

| | G | AB | H | 2B | 3B | HR | HR% | R | RBI | BB | SO | SB | BA | SA | AB | H | G by POS |
|---|---|---|---|---|---|---|---|---|---|---|---|---|---|---|---|---|---|
| 1944 BKN N | 26 | 91 | 20 | 2 | 0 | 0 | 0.0 | 12 | 6 | 6 | 11 | 4 | .220 | .242 | 1 | 0 | 3B-15, SS-10 |
| 1946 | 23 | 48 | 7 | 0 | 0 | 0 | 0.0 | 3 | 5 | 3 | 3 | 0 | .146 | .146 | 3 | 0 | 3B-13, 2B-1 |
| 1947 | 45 | 86 | 23 | 1 | 0 | 4 | 4.7 | 18 | 10 | 9 | 8 | 0 | .267 | .419 | 12 | 1 | 2B-13, OF-11, 3B-5, SS-2 |
| 1948 | 86 | 221 | 47 | 7 | 1 | 2 | 0.9 | 28 | 16 | 19 | 27 | 5 | .213 | .281 | 3 | 1 | 2B-54, 3B-22, SS-5 |
| 1949 | 50 | 113 | 25 | 5 | 0 | 1 | 0.9 | 17 | 6 | 7 | 8 | 3 | .221 | .292 | 8 | 0 | 3B-29, SS-4, 2B-3, 1B-1 |
| 1950 | 51 | 76 | 19 | 2 | 1 | 2 | 2.6 | 13 | 10 | 5 | 10 | 3 | .250 | .382 | 4 | 1 | SS-15, 2B-15, 3B-7 |
| 1951 2 teams | | BKN | N | (19G – | .200) | | CHI | N | (102G – | .266) | | | | | | | |
| " total | 121 | 431 | 114 | 14 | 3 | 4 | 0.9 | 54 | 35 | 34 | 38 | 11 | .265 | .339 | 5 | 1 | 2B-103, 3B-6 |
| 1952 CHI N | 93 | 383 | 89 | 20 | 1 | 2 | 0.5 | 44 | 19 | 20 | 32 | 4 | .232 | .305 | 1 | 0 | 2B-54, SS-40 |
| 1953 | 142 | 577 | 145 | 17 | 6 | 8 | 1.4 | 61 | 39 | 33 | 59 | 13 | .251 | .343 | 0 | 0 | 2B-92, SS-53 |
| 1954 | 38 | 99 | 20 | 3 | 0 | 2 | 2.0 | 9 | 3 | 3 | 9 | 1 | .202 | .293 | 10 | 0 | 2B-21, 3B-2, OF-1 |
| 1955 | 131 | 481 | 113 | 14 | 2 | 9 | 1.9 | 52 | 41 | 32 | 55 | 3 | .235 | .328 | 2 | 0 | OF-111, 3B-18 |
| 1956 | 114 | 356 | 85 | 10 | 3 | 9 | 2.5 | 54 | 27 | 32 | 40 | 4 | .239 | .360 | 13 | 6 | 3B-48, OF-33, 2B-19, SS-2 |
| 1957 2 teams | 50 | STL | N | (49G – | .211) | | BAL | A | (1G – | .000) | | | | | | | |
| " total | 50 | 39 | 8 | 0 | 0 | 1 | 2.6 | 9 | 2 | 7 | 7 | 0 | .205 | .282 | 15 | 3 | OF-31 |
| 1958 2 teams | 72 | BAL | A | (3G – | .000) | | CIN | N | (69G – | .140) | | | | | | | |
| " total | 72 | 52 | 7 | 0 | 0 | 0 | 0.0 | 15 | 4 | 5 | 6 | 1 | .135 | .135 | 5 | 0 | OF-32, 3B-14, 2B-7, SS-6, 1B-1 |
| 14 yrs. | 1042 | 3053 | 722 | 95 | 17 | 44 | 1.4 | 383 | 228 | 215 | 313 | 52 | .236 | .322 | 82 | 13 | 2B-382, OF-219, 3B-179, SS-137, 1B-2 |
| 6 yrs. | 620 | 2317 | 564 | 77 | 15 | 34 | 1.5 | 268 | 164 | 153 | 231 | 36 | .243 | .334 | 26 | 6 | 2B-288, OF-145, SS-95, 3B-68 |

WORLD SERIES

| | G | AB | H | 2B | 3B | HR | HR% | R | RBI | BB | SO | SB | BA | SA | AB | H | G by POS |
|---|---|---|---|---|---|---|---|---|---|---|---|---|---|---|---|---|---|
| 1947 BKN N | 5 | 4 | 1 | 0 | 0 | 0 | 0.0 | 1 | 0 | 0 | 1 | 0 | .250 | .250 | 3 | 0 | OF-2 |
| 1949 | 3 | 7 | 2 | 1 | 0 | 0 | 0.0 | 0 | 0 | 0 | 1 | 0 | .286 | .429 | 1 | 1 | 3B-2 |
| 2 yrs. | 8 | 11 | 3 | 1 | 0 | 0 | 0.0 | 1 | 0 | 0 | 2 | 0 | .273 | .364 | 4 | 1 | OF-2, 3B-2 |

## Dakin Miller

**MILLER, DAKIN EVANS**
B. Sept. 2, 1877, Malvern, Iowa    D. Apr. 20, 1950, Stockton, Calif.

BL TR 5'10" 175 lbs.

| | G | AB | H | 2B | 3B | HR | HR% | R | RBI | BB | SO | SB | BA | SA | AB | H | G by POS |
|---|---|---|---|---|---|---|---|---|---|---|---|---|---|---|---|---|---|
| 1902 CHI N | 51 | 187 | 46 | 4 | 1 | 0 | 0.0 | 17 | 13 | 7 | | 10 | .246 | .278 | 0 | 0 | OF-51 |

## Doc Miller

**MILLER, ROY OSCAR**
B. 1883, Chatham, Ont., Canada    D. July 31, 1938, Jersey City, N. J.

BL TL 5'10½" 170 lbs.

| | G | AB | H | 2B | 3B | HR | HR% | R | RBI | BB | SO | SB | BA | SA | AB | H | G by POS |
|---|---|---|---|---|---|---|---|---|---|---|---|---|---|---|---|---|---|
| 1910 2 teams | | CHI | N | (1G – | .000) | | BOS | N | (130G – | .286) | | | | | | | |
| " total | 131 | 483 | 138 | 27 | 4 | 3 | 0.6 | 48 | 55 | 33 | 52 | 17 | .286 | .377 | 1 | 0 | OF-130 |
| 1911 BOS N | 146 | 577 | 192 | 36 | 3 | 7 | 1.2 | 69 | 91 | 43 | 43 | 32 | .333 | .442 | 0 | 0 | OF-146 |
| 1912 2 teams | | BOS | N | (51G – | .234) | | PHI | N | (67G – | .288) | | | | | | | |
| " total | 118 | 378 | 98 | 20 | 6 | 2 | 0.5 | 50 | 45 | 23 | 30 | 9 | .259 | .360 | 28 | 7 | OF-90 |
| 1913 PHI N | 69 | 87 | 30 | 6 | 0 | 0 | 0.0 | 9 | 11 | 6 | 6 | 2 | .345 | .414 | 56 | 20 | OF-12 |
| 1914 CIN N | 47 | 192 | 49 | 7 | 2 | 0 | 0.0 | 8 | 33 | 16 | 18 | 4 | .255 | .313 | 35 | 12 | OF-47 |
| 5 yrs. | 511 | 1717 | 507 | 96 | 15 | 12 | 0.7 | 184 | 235 | 121 | 149 | 64 | .295 | .390 | 120 | 39 | OF-425 |
| 1 yr. | 1 | 1 | 0 | 0 | 0 | 0 | 0.0 | 0 | 0 | 0 | 0 | 0 | .000 | .000 | 1 | 0 | |

## Hack Miller

**MILLER, LAWRENCE H.**
B. Jan. 1, 1894, Chicago, Ill.    D. Sept. 17, 1971, Oakland, Calif.

BR TR 5'9" 195 lbs.

| | G | AB | H | 2B | 3B | HR | HR% | R | RBI | BB | SO | SB | BA | SA | AB | H | G by POS |
|---|---|---|---|---|---|---|---|---|---|---|---|---|---|---|---|---|---|
| 1916 BKN N | 3 | 3 | 1 | 0 | 0 | 0 | 0.0 | 0 | 1 | 1 | 1 | 0 | .333 | 1.000 | 0 | 0 | OF-3 |
| 1918 BOS A | 12 | 29 | 8 | 2 | 0 | 0 | 0.0 | 2 | 4 | 0 | 4 | 0 | .276 | .345 | 2 | 0 | OF-10 |
| 1922 CHI N | 122 | 466 | 164 | 28 | 5 | 12 | 2.6 | 61 | 78 | 26 | 39 | 3 | .352 | .511 | 6 | 2 | OF-116 |
| 1923 | 135 | 485 | 146 | 24 | 2 | 20 | 4.1 | 74 | 88 | 27 | 39 | 6 | .301 | .482 | 4 | 0 | OF-129 |
| 1924 | 53 | 131 | 44 | 8 | 1 | 4 | 3.1 | 17 | 25 | 8 | 11 | 1 | .336 | .504 | 20 | 7 | OF-32 |

| | G | AB | H | 2B | 3B | HR | HR % | R | RBI | BB | SO | SB | BA | SA | Pinch Hit AB | Pinch Hit H | G by POS |
|---|---|---|---|---|---|---|---|---|---|---|---|---|---|---|---|---|---|

## Hack Miller continued

| | G | AB | H | 2B | 3B | HR | HR % | R | RBI | BB | SO | SB | BA | SA | PH AB | PH H | G by POS |
|---|---|---|---|---|---|---|---|---|---|---|---|---|---|---|---|---|---|
| 1925 | 24 | 86 | 24 | 3 | 2 | 2 | 2.3 | 10 | 9 | 2 | 9 | 0 | .279 | .430 | 3 | 2 | OF-21 |
| 6 yrs. | 349 | 1200 | 387 | 65 | 11 | 38 | 3.2 | 164 | 205 | 64 | 103 | 10 | .323 | .490 | 35 | 15 | OF-311 |
| 4 yrs. | 334 | 1168 | 378 | 63 | 10 | 38 | 3.3 | 162 | 200 | 63 | 98 | 10 | .324 | .492 | 33 | 15 | OF-298 |

**WORLD SERIES**

| | G | AB | H | 2B | 3B | HR | HR % | R | RBI | BB | SO | SB | BA | SA | PH AB | PH H | G by POS |
|---|---|---|---|---|---|---|---|---|---|---|---|---|---|---|---|---|---|
| 1918 BOS A | 1 | 1 | 0 | 0 | 0 | 0 | 0.0 | 0 | 0 | 0 | 0 | 0 | .000 | .000 | 1 | 0 | |

## Ward Miller

**MILLER, WARD TAYLOR (Windy)**　　　　　　　　BL TR 5'11" 177 lbs.
B. July 5, 1884, Mt. Carroll, Ill.　　D. Sept. 4, 1958, Dixon, Ill.

| | G | AB | H | 2B | 3B | HR | HR % | R | RBI | BB | SO | SB | BA | SA | PH AB | PH H | G by POS |
|---|---|---|---|---|---|---|---|---|---|---|---|---|---|---|---|---|---|
| 1909 2 teams | | PIT | N | (15G – | .143) | | CIN | N | (43G – | .310) | | | | | | | |
| " total | 58 | 169 | 43 | 3 | 2 | 0 | 0.0 | 19 | 8 | 10 | | 11 | .254 | .296 | 13 | 1 | OF-40 |
| 1910 CIN N | 81 | 126 | 30 | 6 | 0 | 0 | 0.0 | 21 | 10 | 22 | 13 | 10 | .238 | .286 | 40 | 11 | OF-26 |
| 1912 CHI N | 86 | 241 | 74 | 11 | 4 | 0 | 0.0 | 45 | 22 | 26 | 18 | 11 | .307 | .386 | 15 | 6 | OF-64 |
| 1913 | 80 | 203 | 48 | 5 | 7 | 1 | 0.5 | 23 | 16 | 34 | 33 | 13 | .236 | .345 | 13 | 8 | OF-63 |
| 1914 STL F | 121 | 402 | 118 | 17 | 7 | 4 | 1.0 | 49 | 50 | 59 | | 18 | .294 | .400 | 8 | 3 | OF-111 |
| 1915 | 154 | 536 | 164 | 19 | 9 | 1 | 0.2 | 80 | 63 | 79 | | 33 | .306 | .381 | 0 | 0 | OF-154 |
| 1916 STL A | 146 | 485 | 129 | 17 | 5 | 1 | 0.2 | 72 | 50 | 72 | 76 | 22 | .266 | .328 | 9 | 3 | OF-135, 2B-1 |
| 1917 | 43 | 82 | 17 | 1 | 1 | 1 | 1.2 | 13 | 2 | 16 | 15 | 7 | .207 | .280 | 12 | 4 | OF-25 |
| 8 yrs. | 769 | 2244 | 623 | 79 | 35 | 8 | 0.4 | 322 | 221 | 318 | 155 | 128 | .278 | .355 | 110 | 36 | OF-618, 2B-1 |
| 2 yrs. | 166 | 444 | 122 | 16 | 11 | 1 | 0.2 | 68 | 38 | 60 | 51 | 24 | .275 | .367 | 28 | 4 | OF-127 |

## Fred Mitchell

**MITCHELL, FREDERICK FRANCIS**　　　　　　　　BR TR 5'9½" 185 lbs.
Born Frederick Francis Yapp.
B. June 5, 1878, Cambridge, Mass.　　D. Oct. 13, 1970, Newton, Mass.
Manager 1917-23.

| | G | AB | H | 2B | 3B | HR | HR % | R | RBI | BB | SO | SB | BA | SA | PH AB | PH H | G by POS |
|---|---|---|---|---|---|---|---|---|---|---|---|---|---|---|---|---|---|
| 1901 BOS A | 20 | 44 | 7 | 0 | 2 | 0 | 0.0 | 5 | 4 | 2 | | 0 | .159 | .250 | 0 | 0 | P-17, 2B-2, SS-1 |
| 1902 2 teams | | BOS | A | (1G – | .000) | | PHI | A | (20G – | .188) | | | | | | | |
| " total | 21 | 49 | 9 | 1 | 0 | 0 | 0.0 | 7 | 3 | 1 | | 1 | .184 | .245 | 1 | 0 | P-19, OF-1 |
| 1903 PHI N | 29 | 95 | 19 | 4 | 0 | 0 | 0.0 | 11 | 10 | 0 | | 0 | .200 | .242 | 1 | 1 | P-28 |
| 1904 2 teams | | PHI | N | (25G – | .207) | | BKN | N | (8G – | .292) | | | | | | | |
| " total | 33 | 106 | 24 | 4 | 2 | 0 | 0.0 | 12 | 9 | 6 | | 1 | .226 | .302 | 0 | 0 | P-21, 1B-9, 3B-2, OF-1 |
| 1905 BKN N | 27 | 79 | 15 | 0 | 0 | 0 | 0.0 | 4 | 8 | 4 | | 0 | .190 | .190 | 2 | 1 | P-12, 1B-7, 3B-4, OF-1, SS-1 |
| 1910 NY A | 68 | 196 | 45 | 7 | 2 | 0 | 0.0 | 16 | 18 | 9 | | 6 | .230 | .286 | 6 | 2 | C-68 |
| 1913 BOS N | 4 | 3 | 1 | 0 | 0 | 0 | 0.0 | 0 | 0 | 0 | 2 | 0 | .333 | .333 | 3 | 1 | |
| 7 yrs. | 202 | 572 | 120 | 16 | 7 | 0 | 0.0 | 55 | 52 | 22 | 2 | 8 | .210 | .262 | 13 | 5 | P-97, C-68, 1B-16, 3B-6, OF-3, SS-2, 2B-2 |

## Mike Mitchell

**MITCHELL, MICHAEL FRANCIS**　　　　　　　　BR TR 6'1" 185 lbs.
B. Dec. 12, 1879, Springfield, Ohio　　D. July 16, 1961, Phoenix, Ariz.

| | G | AB | H | 2B | 3B | HR | HR % | R | RBI | BB | SO | SB | BA | SA | PH AB | PH H | G by POS |
|---|---|---|---|---|---|---|---|---|---|---|---|---|---|---|---|---|---|
| 1907 CIN N | 148 | 558 | 163 | 17 | 12 | 3 | 0.5 | 64 | 47 | 37 | | 17 | .292 | .382 | 0 | 0 | OF-146, 1B-2 |
| 1908 | 119 | 406 | 90 | 9 | 6 | 1 | 0.2 | 41 | 37 | 46 | | 18 | .222 | .281 | 0 | 0 | OF-118, 1B-1 |
| 1909 | 145 | 523 | 162 | 17 | 17 | 4 | 0.8 | 83 | 86 | 57 | | 37 | .310 | .430 | 0 | 0 | OF-144, 1B-1 |
| 1910 | 156 | 583 | 167 | 16 | 18 | 5 | 0.9 | 79 | 88 | 59 | 56 | 35 | .286 | .401 | 0 | 0 | OF-149, 1B-7 |
| 1911 | 142 | 529 | 154 | 22 | 22 | 2 | 0.4 | 74 | 84 | 44 | 34 | 35 | .291 | .427 | 2 | 0 | OF-140 |
| 1912 | 157 | 552 | 156 | 14 | 13 | 4 | 0.7 | 60 | 78 | 41 | 43 | 23 | .283 | .377 | 2 | 1 | OF-144 |
| 1913 2 teams | | CHI | N | (81G – | .259) | | PIT | N | (54G – | .271) | | | | | | | |
| " total | 135 | 477 | 126 | 19 | 8 | 5 | 1.0 | 62 | 51 | 46 | 48 | 23 | .264 | .369 | 0 | 0 | OF-135 |
| 1914 2 teams | | PIT | N | (76G – | .234) | | WAS | A | (55G – | .285) | | | | | | | |
| " total | 131 | 466 | 119 | 16 | 8 | 3 | 0.6 | 51 | 43 | 38 | 35 | 14 | .255 | .343 | 2 | 0 | OF-129 |
| 8 yrs. | 1133 | 4094 | 1137 | 130 | 104 | 27 | 0.7 | 514 | 514 | 368 | 216 | 202 | .278 | .380 | 6 | 1 | OF-1105, 1B-11 |
| 1 yr. | 81 | 278 | 72 | 11 | 6 | 4 | 1.4 | 37 | 35 | 32 | 33 | 15 | .259 | .385 | 0 | 0 | OF-81 |

## George Mitterwald

**MITTERWALD, GEORGE EUGENE**　　　　　　　　BR TR 6'2" 195 lbs.
B. June 7, 1945, Berkeley, Calif.

| | G | AB | H | 2B | 3B | HR | HR % | R | RBI | BB | SO | SB | BA | SA | PH AB | PH H | G by POS |
|---|---|---|---|---|---|---|---|---|---|---|---|---|---|---|---|---|---|
| 1966 MIN A | 3 | 5 | 1 | 0 | 0 | 0 | 0.0 | 1 | 0 | 0 | 0 | 0 | .200 | .200 | 0 | 0 | C-3 |
| 1968 | 11 | 34 | 7 | 1 | 0 | 0 | 0.0 | 1 | 1 | 3 | 8 | 0 | .206 | .235 | 1 | 0 | C-10 |
| 1969 | 69 | 187 | 48 | 8 | 0 | 5 | 2.7 | 18 | 13 | 17 | 47 | 0 | .257 | .380 | 6 | 1 | C-63, OF-1 |
| 1970 | 117 | 369 | 82 | 12 | 2 | 15 | 4.1 | 36 | 46 | 34 | 84 | 3 | .222 | .388 | 1 | 0 | C-117 |
| 1971 | 125 | 388 | 97 | 13 | 1 | 13 | 3.4 | 38 | 44 | 39 | 104 | 1 | .250 | .389 | 2 | 2 | C-120 |
| 1972 | 64 | 163 | 30 | 4 | 1 | 1 | 0.6 | 12 | 8 | 9 | 37 | 0 | .184 | .239 | 4 | 1 | C-61 |
| 1973 | 125 | 432 | 112 | 15 | 0 | 16 | 3.7 | 50 | 64 | 39 | 111 | 3 | .259 | .405 | 3 | 0 | C-122, DH-3 |
| 1974 CHI N | 78 | 215 | 54 | 7 | 0 | 7 | 3.3 | 17 | 29 | 18 | 42 | 1 | .251 | .381 | 11 | 3 | C-68 |
| 1975 | 84 | 200 | 44 | 4 | 3 | 5 | 2.5 | 19 | 26 | 19 | 42 | 0 | .220 | .345 | 15 | 3 | C-59, 1B-10 |
| 1976 | 101 | 303 | 65 | 7 | 0 | 5 | 1.7 | 19 | 28 | 16 | 63 | 1 | .215 | .287 | 16 | 1 | C-64, 1B-25 |
| 1977 | 110 | 349 | 83 | 22 | 0 | 9 | 2.6 | 40 | 43 | 28 | 69 | 3 | .238 | .378 | 2 | 0 | C-109, 1B-1 |
| 11 yrs. | 887 | 2645 | 623 | 93 | 7 | 76 | 2.9 | 251 | 301 | 222 | 607 | 14 | .236 | .362 | 66 | 11 | C-796, 1B-36, DH-3, OF-1 |
| 4 yrs. | 373 | 1067 | 246 | 40 | 3 | 26 | 2.4 | 95 | 125 | 81 | 216 | 5 | .231 | .347 | 44 | 7 | C-300, 1B-36 |

**LEAGUE CHAMPIONSHIP SERIES**

| | G | AB | H | 2B | 3B | HR | HR % | R | RBI | BB | SO | SB | BA | SA | PH AB | PH H | G by POS |
|---|---|---|---|---|---|---|---|---|---|---|---|---|---|---|---|---|---|
| 1969 MIN A | 2 | 7 | 1 | 0 | 0 | 0 | 0.0 | 1 | 3 | 0 | 1 | 0 | .143 | .143 | 0 | 0 | C-2 |
| 1970 | 3 | 8 | 4 | 1 | 0 | 0 | 0.0 | 2 | 2 | 0 | 2 | 0 | .500 | .625 | 0 | 0 | C-2 |
| 2 yrs. | 5 | 15 | 5 | 1 | 0 | 0 | 0.0 | 3 | 5 | 0 | 3 | 0 | .333 | .400 | 0 | 0 | C-4 |

## Bob Molinaro

**MOLINARO, ROBERT JOSEPH (Molly)**　　　　　　　　BL TR 6' 180 lbs.
B. May 21, 1950, Newark, N. J.

| | G | AB | H | 2B | 3B | HR | HR % | R | RBI | BB | SO | SB | BA | SA | PH AB | PH H | G by POS |
|---|---|---|---|---|---|---|---|---|---|---|---|---|---|---|---|---|---|
| 1975 DET A | 6 | 19 | 5 | 0 | 1 | 0 | 0.0 | 1 | 1 | 0 | 0 | 0 | .263 | .368 | 0 | 0 | OF-6 |
| 1977 2 teams | | DET | A | (4G – | .250) | | CHI | A | (1G – | .500) | | | | | | | |
| " total | 5 | 6 | 2 | 1 | 0 | 0 | 0.0 | 0 | 0 | 0 | 3 | 1 | .333 | .500 | 4 | 1 | OF-1 |
| 1978 CHI A | 105 | 286 | 75 | 5 | 5 | 6 | 2.1 | 39 | 27 | 19 | 12 | 22 | .262 | .378 | 12 | 4 | OF-62, DH-32 |
| 1979 BAL A | 8 | 6 | 0 | 0 | 0 | 0 | 0.0 | 0 | 0 | 1 | 1 | 0 | .000 | .000 | 1 | 0 | OF-5 |
| 1980 CHI A | 119 | 344 | 100 | 16 | 4 | 5 | 1.5 | 48 | 36 | 26 | 29 | 18 | .291 | .404 | 21 | 7 | OF-49, DH-47 |
| 1981 | 47 | 42 | 11 | 1 | 1 | 1 | 2.4 | 7 | 9 | 8 | 1 | 1 | .262 | .405 | 35 | 9 | DH-4, OF-2 |

| | G | AB | H | 2B | 3B | HR | HR % | R | RBI | BB | SO | SB | BA | SA | Pinch Hit AB | Pinch Hit H | G by POS |
|---|---|---|---|---|---|---|---|---|---|---|---|---|---|---|---|---|---|

## Bob Molinaro continued

| | G | AB | H | 2B | 3B | HR | HR% | R | RBI | BB | SO | SB | BA | SA | PH AB | PH H | G by POS |
|---|---|---|---|---|---|---|---|---|---|---|---|---|---|---|---|---|---|
| 1982 2 teams | CHI N (65G – .197) | | | PHI N (19G – .286) | | | | | | | | | | | | | |
| " total | 84 | 80 | 17 | 1 | 0 | 1 | 1.3 | 6 | 14 | 9 | 6 | 2 | .213 | .263 | 67 | 14 | OF-4 |
| 1983 2 teams | PHI N (19G – .111) | | | DET A (8G – .000) | | | | | | | | | | | | | |
| " total | 27 | 20 | 2 | 1 | 0 | 1 | 5.0 | 4 | 3 | 1 | 3 | 1 | .100 | .300 | 20 | 2 | DH-1 |
| 8 yrs. | 401 | 803 | 212 | 25 | 11 | 14 | 1.7 | 106 | 90 | 65 | 57 | 46 | .264 | .375 | 160 | 37 | OF-129, DH-84 |
| 1 yr. | 65 | 66 | 13 | 1 | 0 | 1 | 1.5 | 6 | 12 | 6 | 5 | 1 | .197 | .258 | 53 | 10 | OF-4 |

## Fritz Mollwitz

**MOLLWITZ, FREDERICK AUGUST (Zip)**   BR TR 6'2''   170 lbs.
B. June 16, 1890, Kolberg, Germany   D. Oct. 3, 1967, Bradenton, Fla.

| | G | AB | H | 2B | 3B | HR | HR% | R | RBI | BB | SO | SB | BA | SA | PH AB | PH H | G by POS |
|---|---|---|---|---|---|---|---|---|---|---|---|---|---|---|---|---|---|
| 1913 CHI N | 2 | 7 | 3 | 0 | 0 | 0 | 0.0 | 1 | 0 | 0 | 0 | 0 | .429 | .429 | 0 | 0 | 1B-2 |
| 1914 2 teams | CHI N (13G – .150) | | | CIN N (32G – .162) | | | | | | | | | | | | | |
| " total | 45 | 131 | 21 | 2 | 0 | 0 | 0.0 | 12 | 6 | 3 | 12 | 3 | .160 | .176 | 6 | 0 | 1B-36, OF-1 |
| 1915 CIN N | 153 | 525 | 136 | 21 | 3 | 1 | 0.2 | 36 | 51 | 15 | 49 | 19 | .259 | .316 | 0 | 0 | 1B-153 |
| 1916 2 teams | CIN N (65G – .224) | | | CHI N (33G – .268) | | | | | | | | | | | | | |
| " total | 98 | 254 | 60 | 6 | 4 | 0 | 0.0 | 13 | 27 | 12 | 18 | 10 | .236 | .291 | 20 | 5 | 1B-73, OF-6 |
| 1917 PIT N | 36 | 140 | 36 | 4 | 1 | 0 | 0.0 | 15 | 12 | 8 | 8 | 4 | .257 | .300 | 0 | 0 | 1B-36, 2B-1 |
| 1918 | 119 | 432 | 116 | 12 | 7 | 0 | 0.0 | 43 | 45 | 23 | 24 | 23 | .269 | .329 | 0 | 0 | 1B-119 |
| 1919 2 teams | PIT N (56G – .173) | | | STL N (25G – .229) | | | | | | | | | | | | | |
| " total | 81 | 251 | 48 | 5 | 4 | 0 | 0.0 | 18 | 17 | 22 | 21 | 11 | .191 | .243 | 2 | 1 | 1B-77, OF-2 |
| 7 yrs. | 534 | 1740 | 420 | 50 | 19 | 1 | 0.1 | 138 | 158 | 83 | 132 | 70 | .241 | .294 | 28 | 6 | 1B-496, OF-9, 2B-1 |
| 3 yrs. | 48 | 98 | 25 | 2 | 0 | 0 | 0.0 | 2 | 12 | 7 | 9 | 5 | .255 | .276 | 15 | 2 | 1B-25, OF-7 |

## Rick Monday

**MONDAY, ROBERT JAMES**   BL TL 6'3''   195 lbs.
B. Nov. 20, 1945, Batesville, Ark.

| | G | AB | H | 2B | 3B | HR | HR% | R | RBI | BB | SO | SB | BA | SA | PH AB | PH H | G by POS |
|---|---|---|---|---|---|---|---|---|---|---|---|---|---|---|---|---|---|
| 1966 KC A | 17 | 41 | 4 | 1 | 1 | 0 | 0.0 | 4 | 2 | 6 | 16 | 1 | .098 | .171 | 1 | 0 | OF-15 |
| 1967 | 124 | 406 | 102 | 14 | 6 | 14 | 3.4 | 52 | 58 | 42 | 107 | 3 | .251 | .419 | 13 | 2 | OF-113 |
| 1968 OAK A | 148 | 482 | 132 | 24 | 7 | 8 | 1.7 | 56 | 49 | 72 | 143 | 14 | .274 | .402 | 6 | 2 | OF-144 |
| 1969 | 122 | 399 | 108 | 17 | 4 | 12 | 3.0 | 57 | 54 | 72 | 100 | 12 | .271 | .424 | 5 | 1 | OF-119 |
| 1970 | 112 | 376 | 109 | 19 | 7 | 10 | 2.7 | 63 | 37 | 58 | 99 | 17 | .290 | .457 | 1 | 0 | OF-109 |
| 1971 | 116 | 355 | 87 | 9 | 3 | 18 | 5.1 | 53 | 56 | 49 | 93 | 6 | .245 | .439 | 7 | 2 | OF-111 |
| 1972 CHI N | 138 | 434 | 108 | 22 | 5 | 11 | 2.5 | 68 | 42 | 78 | 102 | 12 | .249 | .399 | 3 | 0 | OF-134 |
| 1973 | 149 | 554 | 148 | 24 | 5 | 26 | 4.7 | 93 | 56 | 92 | 124 | 5 | .267 | .469 | 3 | 1 | OF-148 |
| 1974 | 142 | 538 | 158 | 19 | 7 | 20 | 3.7 | 84 | 58 | 70 | 94 | 7 | .294 | .467 | 4 | 0 | OF-139 |
| 1975 | 136 | 491 | 131 | 29 | 4 | 17 | 3.5 | 89 | 60 | 83 | 95 | 8 | .267 | .446 | 4 | 1 | OF-131 |
| 1976 | 137 | 534 | 145 | 20 | 5 | 32 | 6.0 | 107 | 77 | 60 | 125 | 5 | .272 | .507 | 4 | 1 | OF-103, 1B-32 |
| 1977 LA N | 118 | 392 | 90 | 13 | 1 | 15 | 3.8 | 47 | 48 | 60 | 109 | 1 | .230 | .383 | 6 | 0 | OF-115, 1B-3 |
| 1978 | 119 | 342 | 87 | 14 | 1 | 19 | 5.6 | 54 | 57 | 49 | 100 | 2 | .254 | .468 | 16 | 2 | OF-103, 1B-1 |
| 1979 | 12 | 33 | 10 | 0 | 0 | 0 | 0.0 | 3 | 5 | 6 | 6 | 0 | .303 | .303 | 1 | 1 | OF-10 |
| 1980 | 96 | 194 | 52 | 7 | 1 | 10 | 5.2 | 35 | 25 | 28 | 49 | 2 | .268 | .469 | 36 | 8 | OF-50 |
| 1981 | 66 | 130 | 41 | 1 | 2 | 11 | 8.5 | 24 | 25 | 24 | 42 | 1 | .315 | .608 | 23 | 8 | OF-41 |
| 1982 | 104 | 210 | 54 | 6 | 4 | 11 | 5.2 | 37 | 42 | 39 | 51 | 2 | .257 | .481 | 35 | 4 | OF-57, 1B-4 |
| 1983 | 99 | 178 | 44 | 7 | 1 | 6 | 3.4 | 21 | 20 | 29 | 42 | 0 | .247 | .399 | 42 | 8 | OF-44, 1B-4 |
| 1984 | 31 | 47 | 9 | 2 | 0 | 1 | 2.1 | 4 | 7 | 8 | 16 | 0 | .191 | .298 | 17 | 3 | 1B-10, OF-2 |
| 19 yrs. | 1986 | 6136 | 1619 | 248 | 64 | 241 | 3.9 | 950 | 775 | 924 | 1513 | 98 | .264 | .443 | 227 | 44 | OF-1688, 1B-54 |
| 5 yrs. | 702 | 2551 | 690 | 114 | 26 | 106 | 4.2 | 441 | 293 | 383 | 540 | 37 | .270 | .460 | 18 | 3 | OF-655, 1B-32 |
| | | | | 9th | 9th | | | | | | 8th | | | | | | |

### DIVISIONAL PLAYOFF SERIES

| | G | AB | H | 2B | 3B | HR | HR% | R | RBI | BB | SO | SB | BA | SA | PH AB | PH H | G by POS |
|---|---|---|---|---|---|---|---|---|---|---|---|---|---|---|---|---|---|
| 1981 LA N | 5 | 14 | 3 | 0 | 0 | 0 | 0.0 | 1 | 1 | 2 | 4 | 0 | .214 | .214 | 0 | 0 | OF-5 |

### LEAGUE CHAMPIONSHIP SERIES

| | G | AB | H | 2B | 3B | HR | HR% | R | RBI | BB | SO | SB | BA | SA | PH AB | PH H | G by POS |
|---|---|---|---|---|---|---|---|---|---|---|---|---|---|---|---|---|---|
| 1971 OAK A | 1 | 3 | 0 | 0 | 0 | 0 | 0.0 | 0 | 0 | 1 | 2 | 0 | .000 | .000 | 0 | 0 | OF-1 |
| 1977 LA N | 3 | 7 | 2 | 1 | 0 | 0 | 0.0 | 0 | 0 | 2 | 1 | 0 | .286 | .429 | 1 | 0 | OF-3 |
| 1978 | 3 | 10 | 2 | 1 | 0 | 0 | 0.0 | 2 | 0 | 1 | 5 | 0 | .200 | .400 | 1 | 0 | OF-3 |
| 1981 | 3 | 9 | 3 | 0 | 0 | 1 | 11.1 | 2 | 1 | 0 | 4 | 0 | .333 | .667 | 1 | 0 | OF-2 |
| 1983 | 1 | 0 | 0 | 0 | 0 | 0 | – | 0 | 0 | 0 | 0 | 0 | – | – | 0 | 0 | |
| 5 yrs. | 11 | 29 | 7 | 1 | 1 | 1 | 3.4 | 5 | 1 | 4 | 12 | 0 | .241 | .448 | 3 | 0 | OF-9 |

### WORLD SERIES

| | G | AB | H | 2B | 3B | HR | HR% | R | RBI | BB | SO | SB | BA | SA | PH AB | PH H | G by POS |
|---|---|---|---|---|---|---|---|---|---|---|---|---|---|---|---|---|---|
| 1977 LA N | 4 | 12 | 2 | 0 | 0 | 0 | 0.0 | 0 | 0 | 0 | 3 | 0 | .167 | .167 | 0 | 0 | OF-4 |
| 1978 | 5 | 13 | 2 | 1 | 0 | 0 | 0.0 | 2 | 0 | 4 | 3 | 0 | .154 | .231 | 0 | 0 | OF-4 |
| 1981 | 5 | 13 | 3 | 1 | 0 | 0 | 0.0 | 1 | 0 | 3 | 6 | 0 | .231 | .308 | 1 | 0 | OF-4 |
| 3 yrs. | 14 | 38 | 7 | 2 | 0 | 0 | 0.0 | 3 | 0 | 7 | 12 | 0 | .184 | .237 | 1 | 0 | OF-12 |

## Allan Montreuil

**MONTREUIL, ALLAN ARTHUR**   BR TR 5'5''   158 lbs.
B. Aug. 23, 1943, New Orleans, La.

| | G | AB | H | 2B | 3B | HR | HR% | R | RBI | BB | SO | SB | BA | SA | PH AB | PH H | G by POS |
|---|---|---|---|---|---|---|---|---|---|---|---|---|---|---|---|---|---|
| 1972 CHI N | 5 | 11 | 1 | 0 | 0 | 0 | 0.0 | 0 | 0 | 1 | 4 | 0 | .091 | .091 | 0 | 0 | 2B-5 |

## George Moolic

**MOOLIC, GEORGE HENRY (Prunes)**   BR TR 5'7''   145 lbs.
B. Mar. 12, 1865, Lawrence, Mass.   D. Feb. 19, 1915, Lawrence, Mass.

| | G | AB | H | 2B | 3B | HR | HR% | R | RBI | BB | SO | SB | BA | SA | PH AB | PH H | G by POS |
|---|---|---|---|---|---|---|---|---|---|---|---|---|---|---|---|---|---|
| 1886 CHI N | 16 | 56 | 8 | 3 | 0 | 0 | 0.0 | 9 | 2 | 2 | 17 | | .143 | .196 | 0 | 0 | C-15, OF-2 |

## Charley Moore

**MOORE, CHARLES WESLEY**   BR TR 5'10''   160 lbs.
B. Dec. 1, 1884, County, Ind.   D. July 29, 1970, Portland, Ore.

| | G | AB | H | 2B | 3B | HR | HR% | R | RBI | BB | SO | SB | BA | SA | PH AB | PH H | G by POS |
|---|---|---|---|---|---|---|---|---|---|---|---|---|---|---|---|---|---|
| 1912 CHI N | 5 | 9 | 2 | 0 | 1 | 0 | 0.0 | 2 | 2 | 0 | 1 | 0 | .222 | .444 | 0 | 0 | SS-2, 3B-1, 2B-1 |

## Johnny Moore

**MOORE, JOHN FRANCIS**   BL TR 5'10½''   175 lbs.
B. Mar. 23, 1902, Waterville, Conn.

| | G | AB | H | 2B | 3B | HR | HR% | R | RBI | BB | SO | SB | BA | SA | PH AB | PH H | G by POS |
|---|---|---|---|---|---|---|---|---|---|---|---|---|---|---|---|---|---|
| 1928 CHI N | 4 | 4 | 0 | 0 | 0 | 0 | 0.0 | 0 | 0 | 0 | 0 | 0 | .000 | .000 | 4 | 0 | |
| 1929 | 37 | 63 | 18 | 1 | 0 | 2 | 3.2 | 13 | 8 | 4 | 6 | 0 | .286 | .397 | 15 | 5 | OF-15 |
| 1931 | 39 | 104 | 25 | 3 | 1 | 2 | 1.9 | 19 | 16 | 7 | 5 | 1 | .240 | .346 | 15 | 3 | OF-22 |
| 1932 | 119 | 443 | 135 | 24 | 5 | 13 | 2.9 | 59 | 64 | 22 | 38 | 4 | .305 | .470 | 10 | 4 | OF-109 |

| | G | AB | H | 2B | 3B | HR | HR % | R | RBI | BB | SO | SB | BA | SA | Pinch Hit AB | Pinch Hit H | G by POS |
|---|---|---|---|---|---|---|---|---|---|---|---|---|---|---|---|---|---|

## Johnny Moore continued

| | | G | AB | H | 2B | 3B | HR | HR% | R | RBI | BB | SO | SB | BA | SA | AB | H | G by POS |
|---|---|---|---|---|---|---|---|---|---|---|---|---|---|---|---|---|---|---|
| 1933 | CIN N | 135 | 514 | 135 | 19 | 5 | 1 | 0.2 | 60 | 44 | 29 | 16 | 4 | .263 | .325 | 3 | 1 | OF-132 |
| 1934 | 2 teams | | CIN N | (16G – | .190) | | PHI N | (116G – | .343) | | | | | | | | | |
| " | total | 132 | 500 | 165 | 35 | 7 | 11 | 2.2 | 73 | 98 | 43 | 20 | 7 | .330 | .494 | 6 | 1 | OF-125 |
| 1935 | PHI N | 153 | 600 | 194 | 33 | 3 | 19 | 3.2 | 84 | 93 | 45 | 50 | 4 | .323 | .483 | 3 | 0 | OF-150 |
| 1936 | | 124 | 472 | 155 | 24 | 3 | 16 | 3.4 | 85 | 68 | 26 | 22 | 1 | .328 | .494 | 10 | 4 | OF-112 |
| 1937 | | 96 | 307 | 98 | 16 | 2 | 9 | 2.9 | 46 | 59 | 18 | 18 | 2 | .319 | .472 | 20 | 7 | OF-72 |
| 1945 | CHI N | 7 | 6 | 1 | 0 | 0 | 0 | 0.0 | 0 | 2 | 1 | 1 | 0 | .167 | .167 | 6 | 1 | |
| 10 yrs. | | 846 | 3013 | 926 | 155 | 26 | 73 | 2.4 | 439 | 452 | 195 | 176 | 23 | .307 | .449 | 92 | 26 | OF-737 |
| 5 yrs. | | 206 | 620 | 179 | 28 | 6 | 17 | 2.7 | 91 | 90 | 34 | 50 | 5 | .289 | .435 | 50 | 13 | OF-146 |

WORLD SERIES

| | | G | AB | H | 2B | 3B | HR | HR% | R | RBI | BB | SO | SB | BA | SA | AB | H | G by POS |
|---|---|---|---|---|---|---|---|---|---|---|---|---|---|---|---|---|---|---|
| 1932 | CHI N | 2 | 7 | 0 | 0 | 0 | 0 | 0.0 | 1 | 0 | 2 | 1 | 0 | .000 | .000 | 0 | 0 | OF-2 |

## Jerry Morales

**MORALES, JULIO RUBEN**  
B. Feb. 18, 1949, Yabucoa, Puerto Rico

BR  TR  5'10"  155 lbs.

| | | G | AB | H | 2B | 3B | HR | HR% | R | RBI | BB | SO | SB | BA | SA | AB | H | G by POS |
|---|---|---|---|---|---|---|---|---|---|---|---|---|---|---|---|---|---|---|
| 1969 | SD N | 19 | 41 | 8 | 2 | 0 | 1 | 2.4 | 5 | 6 | 5 | 7 | 0 | .195 | .317 | 0 | 0 | OF-19 |
| 1970 | | 28 | 58 | 9 | 0 | 1 | 1 | 1.7 | 6 | 4 | 3 | 11 | 0 | .155 | .241 | 2 | 0 | OF-26 |
| 1971 | | 12 | 17 | 2 | 0 | 0 | 0 | 0.0 | 1 | 1 | 2 | 2 | 1 | .118 | .118 | 2 | 0 | OF-7 |
| 1972 | | 115 | 347 | 83 | 15 | 7 | 4 | 1.2 | 38 | 18 | 35 | 54 | 4 | .239 | .357 | 19 | 3 | OF-96, 3B-4 |
| 1973 | | 122 | 388 | 109 | 23 | 2 | 9 | 2.3 | 47 | 34 | 27 | 55 | 6 | .281 | .420 | 22 | 9 | OF-100 |
| 1974 | CHI N | 151 | 534 | 146 | 21 | 7 | 15 | 2.8 | 70 | 82 | 46 | 63 | 2 | .273 | .423 | 8 | 2 | OF-143 |
| 1975 | | 153 | 578 | 156 | 21 | 0 | 12 | 2.1 | 62 | 91 | 50 | 65 | 3 | .270 | .369 | 2 | 2 | OF-151 |
| 1976 | | 140 | 537 | 147 | 17 | 0 | 16 | 3.0 | 66 | 67 | 41 | 49 | 3 | .274 | .395 | 5 | 1 | OF-136 |
| 1977 | | 136 | 490 | 142 | 34 | 5 | 11 | 2.2 | 56 | 69 | 43 | 75 | 0 | .290 | .447 | 11 | 3 | OF-128 |
| 1978 | STL N | 130 | 457 | 109 | 19 | 8 | 4 | 0.9 | 44 | 46 | 33 | 44 | 4 | .239 | .341 | 8 | 1 | OF-126 |
| 1979 | DET A | 129 | 440 | 93 | 23 | 1 | 14 | 3.2 | 50 | 56 | 30 | 56 | 10 | .211 | .364 | 7 | 0 | OF-119, DH-7 |
| 1980 | NY N | 94 | 193 | 49 | 7 | 1 | 3 | 1.6 | 19 | 30 | 13 | 31 | 2 | .254 | .347 | 30 | 7 | OF-63 |
| 1981 | CHI N | 84 | 245 | 70 | 6 | 2 | 1 | 0.4 | 27 | 25 | 22 | 29 | 1 | .286 | .339 | 12 | 3 | OF-72 |
| 1982 | | 65 | 116 | 33 | 2 | 2 | 4 | 3.4 | 14 | 30 | 9 | 7 | 1 | .284 | .440 | 30 | 10 | OF-41 |
| 1983 | | 63 | 87 | 17 | 9 | 0 | 0 | 0.0 | 11 | 11 | 7 | 19 | 0 | .195 | .299 | 41 | 8 | OF-29 |
| 15 yrs. | | 1441 | 4528 | 1173 | 199 | 36 | 95 | 2.1 | 516 | 570 | 366 | 567 | 37 | .259 | .382 | 199 | 49 | OF-1256, DH-7, 3B-4 |
| 7 yrs. | | 792 | 2587 | 711 | 110 | 16 | 59 | 2.3 | 306 | 375 | 218 | 307 | 10 | .275 | .398 | 109 | 29 | OF-700 |
| | | | | | | | | | | | | | | | | | **9th** | |

## Bill Moran

**MORAN, WILLIAM L.**  
B. Oct. 10, 1869, Joliet, Ill.     D. Apr. 8, 1916, Joliet, Ill.

175 lbs.

| | | G | AB | H | 2B | 3B | HR | HR% | R | RBI | BB | SO | SB | BA | SA | AB | H | G by POS |
|---|---|---|---|---|---|---|---|---|---|---|---|---|---|---|---|---|---|---|
| 1892 | STL N | 24 | 81 | 11 | 1 | 0 | 0 | 0.0 | 2 | 5 | 2 | 12 | 0 | .136 | .148 | 0 | 0 | C-22 |
| 1895 | CHI N | 15 | 55 | 9 | 2 | 1 | 1 | 1.8 | 8 | 9 | 3 | 2 | 2 | .164 | .291 | 0 | 0 | C-15 |
| 2 yrs. | | 39 | 136 | 20 | 3 | 1 | 1 | 0.7 | 10 | 14 | 5 | 14 | 2 | .147 | .206 | 0 | 0 | C-37 |
| 1 yr. | | 15 | 55 | 9 | 2 | 1 | 1 | 1.8 | 8 | 9 | 3 | 2 | 2 | .164 | .291 | 0 | 0 | C-15 |

## Pat Moran

**MORAN, PATRICK JOSEPH**  
B. Feb. 7, 1876, Fitchburg, Mass.     D. Mar. 7, 1924, Orlando, Fla.  
Manager 1915-23.

TR

| | | G | AB | H | 2B | 3B | HR | HR% | R | RBI | BB | SO | SB | BA | SA | AB | H | G by POS |
|---|---|---|---|---|---|---|---|---|---|---|---|---|---|---|---|---|---|---|
| 1901 | BOS N | 53 | 180 | 38 | 5 | 1 | 2 | 1.1 | 12 | 18 | 3 | | 3 | .211 | .283 | 0 | 0 | C-28, 1B-13, 3B-4, OF-3, SS-3, 2B-1 |
| 1902 | | 80 | 251 | 60 | 5 | 5 | 1 | 0.4 | 22 | 24 | 17 | | 6 | .239 | .311 | 6 | 1 | C-71, 1B-3, OF-1 |
| 1903 | | 109 | 389 | 102 | 25 | 5 | 7 | 1.8 | 40 | 54 | 29 | | 8 | .262 | .406 | 1 | 0 | C-107, 1B-1 |
| 1904 | | 113 | 398 | 90 | 11 | 3 | 4 | 1.0 | 26 | 34 | 18 | | 10 | .226 | .299 | 2 | 0 | C-72, 3B-39, 1B-2 |
| 1905 | | 85 | 267 | 64 | 11 | 5 | 2 | 0.7 | 22 | 22 | 8 | | 3 | .240 | .341 | 7 | 0 | C-78 |
| 1906 | CHI N | 70 | 226 | 57 | 13 | 1 | 0 | 0.0 | 22 | 35 | 7 | | 6 | .252 | .319 | 9 | 0 | C-61 |
| 1907 | | 65 | 198 | 45 | 5 | 1 | 1 | 0.5 | 8 | 19 | 10 | | 5 | .227 | .278 | 6 | 2 | C-59 |
| 1908 | | 50 | 150 | 39 | 5 | 1 | 0 | 0.0 | 12 | 12 | 13 | | 6 | .260 | .307 | 4 | 0 | C-45 |
| 1909 | | 77 | 246 | 54 | 11 | 1 | 1 | 0.4 | 18 | 23 | 16 | | 2 | .220 | .285 | 2 | 1 | C-74 |
| 1910 | PHI N | 68 | 199 | 47 | 7 | 1 | 0 | 0.0 | 13 | 11 | 17 | 16 | 6 | .236 | .281 | 11 | 1 | C-56 |
| 1911 | | 34 | 103 | 19 | 3 | 0 | 0 | 0.0 | 2 | 8 | 3 | 13 | 0 | .184 | .214 | 1 | 0 | C-32 |
| 1912 | | 13 | 26 | 3 | 1 | 0 | 0 | 0.0 | 1 | 1 | 1 | 7 | 0 | .115 | .154 | 4 | 1 | C-13 |
| 1913 | | 1 | 1 | 0 | 0 | 0 | 0 | 0.0 | 0 | 0 | 0 | 0 | 0 | .000 | .000 | 1 | 0 | |
| 1914 | | 1 | 0 | 0 | 0 | 0 | 0 | – | 0 | 1 | 0 | 0 | 0 | – | – | 0 | 0 | C-1 |
| 14 yrs. | | 819 | 2634 | 618 | 102 | 24 | 18 | 0.7 | 198 | 262 | 142 | 36 | 55 | .235 | .312 | 54 | 6 | C-697, 3B-43, 1B-19, OF-4, SS-3, 2B-1 |
| 4 yrs. | | 262 | 820 | 195 | 34 | 4 | 2 | 0.2 | 60 | 89 | 46 | | 19 | .238 | .296 | 21 | 1 | C-239 |

WORLD SERIES

| | | G | AB | H | 2B | 3B | HR | HR% | R | RBI | BB | SO | SB | BA | SA | AB | H | G by POS |
|---|---|---|---|---|---|---|---|---|---|---|---|---|---|---|---|---|---|---|
| 1906 | CHI N | 2 | 2 | 0 | 0 | 0 | 0 | 0.0 | 0 | 0 | 0 | 0 | 0 | .000 | .000 | 2 | 0 | |
| 1907 | | 1 | 0 | 0 | 0 | 0 | 0 | – | 0 | 0 | 0 | 0 | 0 | – | – | 0 | 0 | |
| 2 yrs. | | 3 | 2 | 0 | 0 | 0 | 0 | 0.0 | 0 | 0 | 0 | 0 | 0 | .000 | .000 | 2 | 0 | |

## Keith Moreland

**MORELAND, BOBBY KEITH**  
B. May 2, 1954, Dallas, Tex.

BR  TR  6'  190 lbs.

| | | G | AB | H | 2B | 3B | HR | HR% | R | RBI | BB | SO | SB | BA | SA | AB | H | G by POS |
|---|---|---|---|---|---|---|---|---|---|---|---|---|---|---|---|---|---|---|
| 1978 | PHI N | 1 | 2 | 0 | 0 | 0 | 0 | 0.0 | 0 | 0 | 0 | 0 | 0 | .000 | .000 | 0 | 0 | C-1 |
| 1979 | | 14 | 48 | 18 | 3 | 2 | 0 | 0.0 | 3 | 8 | 3 | 5 | 0 | .375 | .521 | 1 | 0 | C-13 |
| 1980 | | 62 | 159 | 50 | 8 | 0 | 4 | 2.5 | 13 | 29 | 8 | 14 | 3 | .314 | .440 | 17 | 7 | C-39, 3B-4, OF-2 |
| 1981 | | 61 | 196 | 50 | 7 | 0 | 6 | 3.1 | 16 | 37 | 15 | 13 | 1 | .255 | .383 | 5 | 1 | C-50, 3B-7, OF-2, 1B-2 |
| 1982 | CHI N | 138 | 476 | 124 | 17 | 2 | 15 | 3.2 | 50 | 68 | 46 | 71 | 0 | .261 | .399 | 6 | 1 | OF-86, C-44, 3B-2 |
| 1983 | | 154 | 533 | 161 | 30 | 3 | 16 | 3.0 | 76 | 70 | 68 | 73 | 0 | .302 | .460 | 2 | 0 | OF-151, C-3 |
| 1984 | | 140 | 495 | 138 | 17 | 3 | 16 | 3.2 | 59 | 80 | 34 | 71 | 1 | .279 | .422 | 15 | 2 | OF-103, 1B-29, 3B-8, C-3 |
| 1985 | | 161 | 587 | 180 | 30 | 3 | 14 | 2.4 | 74 | 106 | 68 | 58 | 12 | .307 | .440 | 2 | 1 | OF-148, 1B-12, 3B-11, C-2 |
| 8 yrs. | | 731 | 2496 | 721 | 112 | 13 | 71 | 2.8 | 291 | 398 | 242 | 305 | 17 | .289 | .429 | 48 | 12 | OF-492, C-155, 1B-43, 3B-32 |
| 4 yrs. | | 593 | 2091 | 603 | 94 | 11 | 61 | 2.9 | 259 | 324 | 216 | 273 | 13 | .288 | .431 | 25 | 4 | OF-488, C-52, 1B-41, 3B-21 |

| | G | AB | H | 2B | 3B | HR | HR % | R | RBI | BB | SO | SB | BA | SA | Pinch Hit AB | H | G by POS |
|---|---|---|---|---|---|---|---|---|---|---|---|---|---|---|---|---|---|

## Keith Moreland continued

**DIVISIONAL PLAYOFF SERIES**

| | G | AB | H | 2B | 3B | HR | HR% | R | RBI | BB | SO | SB | BA | SA | PH AB | H | G by POS |
|---|---|---|---|---|---|---|---|---|---|---|---|---|---|---|---|---|---|
| 1981 PHI N | 4 | 13 | 6 | 0 | 0 | 1 | 7.7 | 2 | 3 | 1 | 1 | 0 | .462 | .692 | 0 | 0 | C-4 |

**LEAGUE CHAMPIONSHIP SERIES**

| | G | AB | H | 2B | 3B | HR | HR% | R | RBI | BB | SO | SB | BA | SA | PH AB | H | G by POS |
|---|---|---|---|---|---|---|---|---|---|---|---|---|---|---|---|---|---|
| 1980 PHI N | 2 | 1 | 0 | 0 | 0 | 0 | 0.0 | 0 | 1 | 0 | 0 | 0 | .000 | .000 | 1 | 0 | C-1 |
| 1984 CHI N | 5 | 18 | 6 | 2 | 0 | 0 | 0.0 | 3 | 2 | 1 | 1 | 0 | .333 | .444 | 0 | 0 | OF-5 |
| 2 yrs. | 7 | 19 | 6 | 2 | 0 | 0 | | 3 | 3 | 1 | 1 | 0 | .316 | .421 | 1 | 0 | OF-5, C-1 |

**WORLD SERIES**

| | G | AB | H | 2B | 3B | HR | HR% | R | RBI | BB | SO | SB | BA | SA | PH AB | H | G by POS |
|---|---|---|---|---|---|---|---|---|---|---|---|---|---|---|---|---|---|
| 1980 PHI N | 3 | 12 | 4 | 0 | 0 | 0 | 0.0 | 1 | 1 | 0 | 1 | 0 | .333 | .333 | 0 | 0 | DH-3 |

## Bobby Morgan

**MORGAN, ROBERT MORRIS**   BR TR 5'9"  175 lbs.
B. June 29, 1926, Oklahoma City, Okla.

| | G | AB | H | 2B | 3B | HR | HR% | R | RBI | BB | SO | SB | BA | SA | PH AB | H | G by POS |
|---|---|---|---|---|---|---|---|---|---|---|---|---|---|---|---|---|---|
| 1950 BKN N | 67 | 199 | 45 | 10 | 3 | 7 | 3.5 | 38 | 21 | 32 | 43 | 0 | .226 | .412 | 5 | 1 | 3B-52, SS-10 |
| 1952 | 67 | 191 | 45 | 8 | 0 | 7 | 3.7 | 36 | 16 | 46 | 35 | 2 | .236 | .387 | 2 | 0 | 3B-60, 2B-5, SS-4 |
| 1953 | 69 | 196 | 51 | 6 | 2 | 7 | 3.6 | 35 | 33 | 33 | 47 | 2 | .260 | .418 | 9 | 0 | 3B-36, SS-21 |
| 1954 PHI N | 135 | 455 | 119 | 25 | 2 | 14 | 3.1 | 58 | 50 | 70 | 68 | 3 | .262 | .418 | 0 | 0 | SS-129, 3B-8, 2B-5 |
| 1955 | 136 | 483 | 112 | 20 | 2 | 10 | 2.1 | 61 | 49 | 73 | 72 | 6 | .232 | .344 | 6 | 2 | 2B-88, SS-41, 3B-6, 1B-1 |
| 1956 2 teams | | PHI | N (8G – .200) | | STL | N | (61G – | .195) | | | | | | | | | |
| " total | 69 | 138 | 27 | 7 | 0 | 3 | 2.2 | 15 | 21 | 21 | 28 | 0 | .196 | .312 | 29 | 5 | 3B-16, 2B-16, SS-6 |
| 1957 2 teams | | PHI | N (2G – | .000) | CHI | N | (125G – | .207) | | | | | | | | | |
| " total | 127 | 425 | 88 | 20 | 2 | 5 | 1.2 | 43 | 27 | 52 | 87 | 5 | .207 | .299 | 0 | 0 | 2B-118, 3B-12 |
| 1958 CHI N | 1 | 1 | 0 | 0 | 0 | 0 | 0.0 | 0 | 0 | 0 | 1 | 0 | .000 | .000 | 1 | 0 | |
| 8 yrs. | 671 | 2088 | 487 | 96 | 11 | 53 | 2.5 | 286 | 217 | 327 | 381 | 18 | .233 | .366 | 52 | 8 | 2B-232, SS-211, 3B-190, 1B-1 |
| 2 yrs. | 126 | 426 | 88 | 20 | 2 | 5 | 1.2 | 43 | 27 | 52 | 88 | 5 | .207 | .298 | 1 | 0 | 2B-116, 3B-12 |

**WORLD SERIES**

| | G | AB | H | 2B | 3B | HR | HR% | R | RBI | BB | SO | SB | BA | SA | PH AB | H | G by POS |
|---|---|---|---|---|---|---|---|---|---|---|---|---|---|---|---|---|---|
| 1952 BKN N | 2 | 1 | 0 | 0 | 0 | 0 | 0.0 | 0 | 0 | 0 | 0 | 0 | .000 | .000 | 1 | 0 | 3B-2 |
| 1953 | 1 | 1 | 0 | 0 | 0 | 0 | 0.0 | 0 | 0 | 0 | 0 | 0 | .000 | .000 | 1 | 0 | |
| 2 yrs. | 3 | 2 | 0 | 0 | 0 | 0 | | 0 | 0 | 0 | 0 | 0 | .000 | .000 | 2 | 0 | 3B-2 |

## Vern Morgan

**MORGAN, VERNON THOMAS**   BL TR 6'1"  190 lbs.
B. Aug. 8, 1928, Emporia, Va.   D. Nov. 8, 1975, Minneapolis, Minn.

| | G | AB | H | 2B | 3B | HR | HR% | R | RBI | BB | SO | SB | BA | SA | PH AB | H | G by POS |
|---|---|---|---|---|---|---|---|---|---|---|---|---|---|---|---|---|---|
| 1954 CHI N | 24 | 64 | 15 | 2 | 0 | 0 | 0.0 | 3 | 2 | 1 | 10 | 0 | .234 | .266 | 7 | 1 | 3B-15 |
| 1955 | 7 | 7 | 1 | 0 | 0 | 0 | 0.0 | 1 | 1 | 3 | 4 | 0 | .143 | .143 | 3 | 0 | 3B-2 |
| 2 yrs. | 31 | 71 | 16 | 2 | 0 | 0 | | 4 | 3 | 4 | 14 | 0 | .225 | .254 | 10 | 1 | 3B-17 |
| 2 yrs. | 31 | 71 | 16 | 2 | 0 | 0 | | 4 | 3 | 4 | 14 | 0 | .225 | .254 | 10 | 1 | 3B-17 |

## Moe Morhardt

**MORHARDT, MEREDITH GOODWIN**   BL TL 6'1"  185 lbs.
B. Jan. 16, 1937, Manchester, Conn.

| | G | AB | H | 2B | 3B | HR | HR% | R | RBI | BB | SO | SB | BA | SA | PH AB | H | G by POS |
|---|---|---|---|---|---|---|---|---|---|---|---|---|---|---|---|---|---|
| 1961 CHI N | 7 | 18 | 5 | 0 | 0 | 0 | 0.0 | 3 | 1 | 3 | 5 | 0 | .278 | .278 | 0 | 0 | 1B-7 |
| 1962 | 18 | 16 | 2 | 0 | 0 | 0 | 0.0 | 1 | 2 | 2 | 8 | 0 | .125 | .125 | 16 | 2 | |
| 2 yrs. | 25 | 34 | 7 | 0 | 0 | 0 | 0.0 | 4 | 3 | 5 | 13 | 0 | .206 | .206 | 16 | 2 | 1B-7 |
| 2 yrs. | 25 | 34 | 7 | 0 | 0 | 0 | 0.0 | 4 | 3 | 5 | 13 | 0 | .206 | .206 | 16 | 2 | 1B-7 |

## George Moriarty

**MORIARTY, GEORGE JOSEPH**   BR TR 6'  185 lbs.
Brother of Bill Moriarty.
B. July 7, 1884, Chicago, Ill.   D. Apr. 8, 1964, Miami, Fla.
Manager 1927-28.

| | G | AB | H | 2B | 3B | HR | HR% | R | RBI | BB | SO | SB | BA | SA | PH AB | H | G by POS |
|---|---|---|---|---|---|---|---|---|---|---|---|---|---|---|---|---|---|
| 1903 CHI N | 1 | 5 | 0 | 0 | 0 | 0 | 0.0 | 1 | 0 | 0 | | 0 | .000 | .000 | 0 | 0 | 3B-1 |
| 1904 | 4 | 13 | 0 | 0 | 0 | 0 | 0.0 | 0 | 0 | 1 | | 0 | .000 | .000 | 0 | 0 | OF-2, 3B-2 |
| 1906 NY A | 65 | 197 | 46 | 7 | 7 | 0 | 0.0 | 22 | 23 | 17 | | 8 | .234 | .340 | 4 | 1 | 3B-39, OF-15, 1B-5, 2B-1 |
| 1907 | 126 | 437 | 121 | 16 | 5 | 0 | 0.0 | 51 | 43 | 25 | | 28 | .277 | .336 | 1 | 0 | 3B-91, 1B-22, OF-9, 2B-8, SS-1 |
| 1908 | 101 | 348 | 82 | 12 | 1 | 0 | 0.0 | 25 | 27 | 11 | | 22 | .236 | .276 | 8 | 1 | 1B-52, 3B-28, OF-10, 2B-4 |
| 1909 DET A | 133 | 473 | 129 | 20 | 4 | 1 | 0.2 | 43 | 39 | 24 | | 34 | .273 | .338 | 3 | 1 | 3B-106, 1B-24 |
| 1910 | 136 | 490 | 123 | 24 | 3 | 2 | 0.4 | 53 | 60 | 33 | | 33 | .251 | .324 | 0 | 0 | 3B-134 |
| 1911 | 130 | 478 | 116 | 20 | 4 | 1 | 0.2 | 51 | 60 | 27 | | 28 | .243 | .308 | 0 | 0 | 3B-129, 1B-1 |
| 1912 | 105 | 375 | 93 | 23 | 1 | 0 | 0.0 | 38 | 54 | 26 | | 27 | .248 | .315 | 1 | 1 | 1B-71, 3B-33 |
| 1913 | 102 | 347 | 83 | 5 | 2 | 0 | 0.0 | 29 | 30 | 24 | 25 | 33 | .239 | .265 | 0 | 0 | 3B-93, OF-7 |
| 1914 | 130 | 465 | 118 | 19 | 5 | 1 | 0.2 | 56 | 40 | 39 | 27 | 34 | .254 | .323 | 0 | 0 | 3B-126, 1B-3 |
| 1915 | 31 | 38 | 8 | 0 | 0 | 0 | 0.0 | 2 | 0 | 5 | 7 | 1 | .211 | .237 | 10 | 2 | 3B-12, OF-1, 2B-1, 1B-1 |
| 1916 CHI A | 7 | 5 | 1 | 0 | 0 | 0 | 0.0 | 1 | 0 | 2 | 0 | 0 | .200 | .200 | 3 | 1 | 3B-1, 1B-1 |
| 13 yrs. | 1071 | 3671 | 920 | 147 | 32 | 5 | 0.1 | 372 | 376 | 234 | 59 | 248 | .251 | .312 | 31 | 8 | 3B-795, 1B-180, OF-44, 2B-14, SS-1 |
| 2 yrs. | 5 | 18 | 0 | 0 | 0 | 0 | 0.0 | 1 | 0 | 1 | | 0 | .000 | .000 | 0 | 0 | 3B-3, OF-2 |

**WORLD SERIES**

| | G | AB | H | 2B | 3B | HR | HR% | R | RBI | BB | SO | SB | BA | SA | PH AB | H | G by POS |
|---|---|---|---|---|---|---|---|---|---|---|---|---|---|---|---|---|---|
| 1909 DET A | 7 | 22 | 6 | 1 | 0 | 0 | 0.0 | 4 | 1 | 3 | 1 | 0 | .273 | .318 | 0 | 0 | 3B-7 |

## William Morris

Playing record listed under John Fluhrer

## Walt Moryn

**MORYN, WALTER JOSEPH (Moose)**   BL TR 6'2"  205 lbs.
B. Apr. 12, 1926, St. Paul, Minn.

| | G | AB | H | 2B | 3B | HR | HR% | R | RBI | BB | SO | SB | BA | SA | PH AB | H | G by POS |
|---|---|---|---|---|---|---|---|---|---|---|---|---|---|---|---|---|---|
| 1954 BKN N | 48 | 91 | 25 | 4 | 2 | 2 | 2.2 | 16 | 14 | 7 | 11 | 0 | .275 | .429 | 23 | 5 | OF-21 |
| 1955 | 11 | 19 | 5 | 1 | 0 | 1 | 5.3 | 3 | 3 | 5 | 4 | 0 | .263 | .474 | 4 | 0 | OF-7 |
| 1956 CHI N | 147 | 529 | 151 | 27 | 3 | 23 | 4.3 | 69 | 67 | 50 | 67 | 4 | .285 | .478 | 6 | 0 | OF-141 |
| 1957 | 149 | 568 | 164 | 33 | 0 | 19 | 3.3 | 76 | 88 | 50 | 90 | 0 | .289 | .447 | 4 | 1 | OF-147 |
| 1958 | 143 | 512 | 135 | 26 | 7 | 26 | 5.1 | 77 | 77 | 62 | 83 | 1 | .264 | .494 | 6 | 4 | OF-141 |
| 1959 | 117 | 381 | 89 | 14 | 1 | 14 | 3.7 | 41 | 48 | 44 | 66 | 0 | .234 | .386 | 13 | 5 | OF-104 |

| | G | AB | H | 2B | 3B | HR | HR % | R | RBI | BB | SO | SB | BA | SA | Pinch Hit AB | H | G by POS |
|---|---|---|---|---|---|---|---|---|---|---|---|---|---|---|---|---|---|

# Walt Moryn continued

| | | G | AB | H | 2B | 3B | HR | HR % | R | RBI | BB | SO | SB | BA | SA | PH AB | PH H | G by POS |
|---|---|---|---|---|---|---|---|---|---|---|---|---|---|---|---|---|---|---|
| 1960 | 2 teams | CHI N (38G – .294) | | | | STL N (75G – .245) | | | | | | | | | | | | |
| " | total | 113 | 309 | 81 | 8 | 3 | 13 | 4.2 | 36 | 46 | 30 | 57 | 2 | .262 | .434 | 22 | 3 | OF-92 |
| 1961 | 2 teams | STL N (17G – .125) | | | | PIT N (40G – .200) | | | | | | | | | | | | |
| " | total | 57 | 97 | 17 | 3 | 0 | 3 | 3.1 | 6 | 11 | 3 | 15 | 0 | .175 | .299 | 36 | 6 | OF-18 |
| 8 yrs. | | 785 | 2506 | 667 | 116 | 16 | 101 | 4.0 | 324 | 354 | 251 | 393 | 7 | .266 | .446 | 114 | 24 | OF-671 |
| 5 yrs. | | 594 | 2099 | 571 | 104 | 11 | 84 | 4.0 | 275 | 291 | 219 | 325 | 7 | .272 | .452 | 37 | 12 | OF-563 |
| | | | | | | | | 10th | | | | | | | | | | |

# Jim Mosolf

MOSOLF, JAMES FREDERICK      BL TR 5'10" 186 lbs.
B. Aug. 21, 1905, Puyallup, Wash.    D. Dec. 28, 1979, Salem, Ore.

| | | G | AB | H | 2B | 3B | HR | HR % | R | RBI | BB | SO | SB | BA | SA | PH AB | PH H | G by POS |
|---|---|---|---|---|---|---|---|---|---|---|---|---|---|---|---|---|---|---|
| 1929 | PIT N | 8 | 13 | 6 | 1 | 1 | 0 | 0.0 | 3 | 2 | 1 | 1 | 0 | .462 | .692 | 4 | 2 | OF-3 |
| 1930 | | 40 | 51 | 17 | 2 | 1 | 0 | 0.0 | 16 | 9 | 8 | 7 | 0 | .333 | .412 | 22 | 8 | OF-12, P-1 |
| 1931 | | 39 | 44 | 11 | 1 | 0 | 1 | 2.3 | 7 | 8 | 8 | 5 | 0 | .250 | .341 | 30 | 6 | OF-4 |
| 1933 | CHI N | 31 | 82 | 22 | 5 | 1 | 1 | 1.2 | 13 | 9 | 5 | 8 | 0 | .268 | .390 | 8 | 3 | OF-22 |
| 4 yrs. | | 118 | 190 | 56 | 9 | 3 | 2 | 1.1 | 39 | 28 | 22 | 21 | 0 | .295 | .405 | 64 | 19 | OF-41, P-1 |
| 1 yr. | | 31 | 82 | 22 | 5 | 1 | 1 | 1.2 | 13 | 9 | 5 | 8 | 0 | .268 | .390 | 8 | 3 | OF-22 |

# Eddie Mulligan

MULLIGAN, EDWARD JOSEPH      BR TR 5'9" 152 lbs.
B. Aug. 27, 1894, St. Louis, Mo.    D. Mar. 15, 1982, San Rafael, Calif.

| | | G | AB | H | 2B | 3B | HR | HR % | R | RBI | BB | SO | SB | BA | SA | PH AB | PH H | G by POS |
|---|---|---|---|---|---|---|---|---|---|---|---|---|---|---|---|---|---|---|
| 1915 | CHI N | 11 | 22 | 8 | 1 | 0 | 0 | 0.0 | 5 | 2 | 5 | 1 | 2 | .364 | .409 | 0 | 0 | SS-10, 3B-1 |
| 1916 | | 58 | 189 | 29 | 3 | 4 | 0 | 0.0 | 13 | 9 | 8 | 30 | 1 | .153 | .212 | 0 | 0 | SS-58 |
| 1921 | CHI A | 152 | 609 | 153 | 21 | 12 | 1 | 0.2 | 82 | 45 | 32 | 53 | 13 | .251 | .330 | 0 | 0 | 3B-152, SS-1 |
| 1922 | | 103 | 372 | 87 | 14 | 8 | 0 | 0.0 | 39 | 31 | 22 | 32 | 7 | .234 | .315 | 10 | 2 | 3B-86, SS-7 |
| 1928 | PIT N | 27 | 43 | 10 | 2 | 0 | 0 | 0.0 | 4 | 1 | 3 | 4 | 0 | .233 | .279 | 9 | 5 | 3B-6, 2B-4 |
| 5 yrs. | | 351 | 1235 | 287 | 41 | 24 | 1 | 0.1 | 143 | 88 | 70 | 120 | 23 | .232 | .307 | 19 | 7 | 3B-245, SS-76, 2B-4 |
| 2 yrs. | | 69 | 211 | 37 | 4 | 4 | 0 | 0.0 | 18 | 11 | 13 | 31 | 3 | .175 | .232 | 0 | 0 | SS-68, 3B-1 |

# Joe Munson

MUNSON, JOSEPH MARTIN NAPOLEON      BL TR 5'9" 184 lbs.
Born Joseph Martin Napoleon Carlson.
B. Nov. 6, 1899, Renovo, Pa.

| | | G | AB | H | 2B | 3B | HR | HR % | R | RBI | BB | SO | SB | BA | SA | PH AB | PH H | G by POS |
|---|---|---|---|---|---|---|---|---|---|---|---|---|---|---|---|---|---|---|
| 1925 | CHI N | 9 | 35 | 13 | 3 | 1 | 0 | 0.0 | 5 | 3 | 3 | 1 | 1 | .371 | .514 | 0 | 0 | OF-9 |
| 1926 | | 33 | 101 | 26 | 2 | 2 | 3 | 3.0 | 17 | 15 | 8 | 4 | 0 | .257 | .406 | 4 | 1 | OF-28 |
| 2 yrs. | | 42 | 136 | 39 | 5 | 3 | 3 | 2.2 | 22 | 18 | 11 | 5 | 1 | .287 | .434 | 4 | 1 | OF-37 |
| 2 yrs. | | 42 | 136 | 39 | 5 | 3 | 3 | 2.2 | 22 | 18 | 11 | 5 | 1 | .287 | .434 | 4 | 1 | OF-37 |

# Bobby Murcer

MURCER, BOBBY RAY      BL TR 5'11" 160 lbs.
B. May 20, 1946, Oklahoma City, Okla.

| | | G | AB | H | 2B | 3B | HR | HR % | R | RBI | BB | SO | SB | BA | SA | PH AB | PH H | G by POS |
|---|---|---|---|---|---|---|---|---|---|---|---|---|---|---|---|---|---|---|
| 1965 | NY A | 11 | 37 | 9 | 0 | 1 | 1 | 2.7 | 2 | 4 | 5 | 12 | 0 | .243 | .378 | 0 | 0 | SS-11 |
| 1966 | | 21 | 69 | 12 | 1 | 1 | 0 | 0.0 | 3 | 5 | 4 | 5 | 2 | .174 | .217 | 1 | 0 | SS-18 |
| 1969 | | 152 | 564 | 146 | 24 | 4 | 26 | 4.6 | 82 | 82 | 50 | 103 | 7 | .259 | .454 | 5 | 0 | OF-118, 3B-31 |
| 1970 | | 159 | 581 | 146 | 23 | 3 | 23 | 4.0 | 95 | 78 | 87 | 100 | 15 | .251 | .420 | 2 | 1 | OF-155 |
| 1971 | | 146 | 529 | 175 | 25 | 6 | 25 | 4.7 | 94 | 94 | 91 | 60 | 14 | .331 | .543 | 4 | 1 | OF-143 |
| 1972 | | 153 | 585 | 171 | 30 | 7 | 33 | 5.6 | 102 | 96 | 63 | 67 | 11 | .292 | .537 | 3 | 2 | OF-151 |
| 1973 | | 160 | 616 | 187 | 29 | 2 | 22 | 3.6 | 83 | 95 | 50 | 67 | 6 | .304 | .464 | 0 | 0 | OF-160 |
| 1974 | | 156 | 606 | 166 | 25 | 4 | 10 | 1.7 | 69 | 88 | 57 | 59 | 14 | .274 | .378 | 1 | 0 | OF-156 |
| 1975 | SF N | 147 | 526 | 157 | 29 | 4 | 11 | 2.1 | 80 | 91 | 91 | 45 | 9 | .298 | .432 | 3 | 2 | OF-144 |
| 1976 | | 147 | 533 | 138 | 20 | 2 | 23 | 4.3 | 73 | 90 | 84 | 78 | 12 | .259 | .433 | 2 | 0 | OF-146 |
| 1977 | CHI N | 154 | 554 | 147 | 18 | 3 | 27 | 4.9 | 90 | 89 | 80 | 77 | 16 | .265 | .455 | 5 | 2 | OF-150, SS-1, 2B-1 |
| 1978 | | 146 | 499 | 140 | 22 | 6 | 9 | 1.8 | 66 | 64 | 80 | 57 | 14 | .281 | .403 | 10 | 4 | OF-138 |
| 1979 | 2 teams | CHI N (58G – .258) | | | | NY A (74G – .273) | | | | | | | | | | | | |
| " | total | 132 | 454 | 121 | 16 | 1 | 15 | 3.3 | 64 | 55 | 61 | 52 | 3 | .267 | .405 | 5 | 1 | OF-124 |
| 1980 | NY A | 100 | 297 | 80 | 9 | 1 | 13 | 4.4 | 41 | 57 | 34 | 28 | 2 | .269 | .438 | 22 | 7 | OF-59, DH-33 |
| 1981 | | 50 | 117 | 31 | 6 | 0 | 6 | 5.1 | 14 | 24 | 12 | 15 | 0 | .265 | .470 | 22 | 6 | DH-33 |
| 1982 | | 65 | 141 | 32 | 6 | 0 | 7 | 5.0 | 12 | 30 | 12 | 15 | 2 | .227 | .418 | 30 | 6 | DH-47 |
| 1983 | | 9 | 22 | 4 | 2 | 0 | 1 | 4.5 | 2 | 1 | 1 | 1 | 0 | .182 | .409 | 4 | 0 | DH-5 |
| 17 yrs. | | 1908 | 6730 | 1862 | 285 | 45 | 252 | 3.7 | 972 | 1043 | 862 | 841 | 127 | .277 | .445 | 119 | 32 | OF-1644, DH-118, 3B-31, SS-30, 2B-1 |
| 3 yrs. | | 358 | 1243 | 336 | 44 | 10 | 43 | 3.5 | 178 | 175 | 196 | 154 | 32 | .270 | .426 | 18 | 7 | OF-342, SS-1, 2B-1 |

DIVISIONAL PLAYOFF SERIES

| | | G | AB | H | 2B | 3B | HR | HR % | R | RBI | BB | SO | SB | BA | SA | PH AB | PH H | G by POS |
|---|---|---|---|---|---|---|---|---|---|---|---|---|---|---|---|---|---|---|
| 1981 | NY A | 2 | 1 | 0 | 0 | 0 | 0 | 0.0 | 0 | 0 | 1 | 0 | 0 | .000 | .000 | 1 | 0 | |

LEAGUE CHAMPIONSHIP SERIES

| | | G | AB | H | 2B | 3B | HR | HR % | R | RBI | BB | SO | SB | BA | SA | PH AB | PH H | G by POS |
|---|---|---|---|---|---|---|---|---|---|---|---|---|---|---|---|---|---|---|
| 1980 | NY A | 1 | 4 | 0 | 0 | 0 | 0 | 0.0 | 0 | 0 | 0 | 2 | 0 | .000 | .000 | 0 | 0 | DH-1 |
| 1981 | | 1 | 3 | 1 | 0 | 0 | 0 | 0.0 | 0 | 0 | 1 | 1 | 0 | .333 | .333 | 0 | 0 | DH-1 |
| 2 yrs. | | 2 | 7 | 1 | 0 | 0 | 0 | 0.0 | 0 | 0 | 1 | 3 | 0 | .143 | .143 | 0 | 0 | DH-2 |

WORLD SERIES

| | | G | AB | H | 2B | 3B | HR | HR % | R | RBI | BB | SO | SB | BA | SA | PH AB | PH H | G by POS |
|---|---|---|---|---|---|---|---|---|---|---|---|---|---|---|---|---|---|---|
| 1981 | NY A | 4 | 3 | 0 | 0 | 0 | 0 | 0.0 | 0 | 0 | 0 | 0 | 0 | .000 | .000 | 3 | 0 | |

# Danny Murphy

MURPHY, DANIEL FRANCIS      BL TR 5'11" 185 lbs.
B. Aug. 23, 1942, Beverly, Mass.

| | | G | AB | H | 2B | 3B | HR | HR % | R | RBI | BB | SO | SB | BA | SA | PH AB | PH H | G by POS |
|---|---|---|---|---|---|---|---|---|---|---|---|---|---|---|---|---|---|---|
| 1960 | CHI N | 31 | 75 | 9 | 2 | 0 | 1 | 1.3 | 7 | 6 | 4 | 13 | 0 | .120 | .187 | 7 | 0 | OF-21 |
| 1961 | | 4 | 13 | 5 | 0 | 0 | 2 | 15.4 | 3 | 3 | 1 | 5 | 0 | .385 | .846 | 0 | 0 | OF-4 |
| 1962 | | 14 | 35 | 7 | 3 | 1 | 0 | 0.0 | 5 | 3 | 2 | 9 | 0 | .200 | .343 | 6 | 0 | OF-9 |
| 1969 | CHI A | 17 | 1 | 0 | 0 | 0 | 0 | 0.0 | 0 | 0 | 2 | 0 | 0 | .000 | .000 | 0 | 0 | P-17 |
| 1970 | | 51 | 6 | 2 | 0 | 0 | 1 | 16.7 | 3 | 1 | 2 | 2 | 0 | .333 | .833 | 0 | 0 | P-51 |
| 5 yrs. | | 117 | 130 | 23 | 5 | 1 | 4 | 3.1 | 18 | 13 | 11 | 29 | 0 | .177 | .323 | 13 | 0 | P-68, OF-34 |
| 3 yrs. | | 49 | 123 | 21 | 5 | 1 | 3 | 2.4 | 15 | 12 | 7 | 27 | 0 | .171 | .301 | 13 | 0 | OF-34 |

| | G | AB | H | 2B | 3B | HR | HR % | R | RBI | BB | SO | SB | BA | SA | Pinch Hit AB | Pinch Hit H | G by POS |
|---|---|---|---|---|---|---|---|---|---|---|---|---|---|---|---|---|---|

## Jim Murray

**MURRAY, JAMES OSCAR**　　　　　　　　　　　　　　　　BR　TL
B. Jan. 16, 1878, Galveston, Tex.　　D. Apr. 25, 1945, Galveston, Tex.

| | G | AB | H | 2B | 3B | HR | HR% | R | RBI | BB | SO | SB | BA | SA | PH AB | PH H | G by POS |
|---|---|---|---|---|---|---|---|---|---|---|---|---|---|---|---|---|---|
| 1902 CHI N | 12 | 47 | 8 | 0 | 0 | 0 | 0.0 | 3 | 1 | 2 | | 0 | .170 | .170 | 0 | 0 | OF-12 |
| 1911 STL A | 31 | 102 | 19 | 5 | 0 | 3 | 2.9 | 8 | 11 | 5 | | 0 | .186 | .324 | 6 | 1 | OF-25 |
| 1914 BOS N | 39 | 112 | 26 | 4 | 2 | 0 | 0.0 | 10 | 12 | 6 | 24 | 2 | .232 | .304 | 6 | 2 | OF-32 |
| 3 yrs. | 82 | 261 | 53 | 9 | 2 | 3 | 1.1 | 21 | 24 | 13 | 24 | 2 | .203 | .287 | 12 | 3 | OF-69 |
| 1 yr. | 12 | 47 | 8 | 0 | 0 | 0 | 0.0 | 3 | 1 | 2 | | 0 | .170 | .170 | 0 | 0 | OF-12 |

## Red Murray

**MURRAY, JOHN JOSEPH**　　　　　　　　　　　　　　BR　TR　5'10½"　190 lbs.
B. Mar. 4, 1884, Arnot, Pa.　　D. Dec. 4, 1958, Sayre, Pa.

| | G | AB | H | 2B | 3B | HR | HR% | R | RBI | BB | SO | SB | BA | SA | PH AB | PH H | G by POS |
|---|---|---|---|---|---|---|---|---|---|---|---|---|---|---|---|---|---|
| 1906 STL N | 46 | 144 | 37 | 9 | 7 | 1 | 0.7 | 18 | 16 | 9 | | 5 | .257 | .438 | 5 | 0 | OF-34, C-7 |
| 1907 | 132 | 485 | 127 | 10 | 10 | 7 | 1.4 | 46 | 46 | 24 | | 23 | .262 | .367 | 1 | 1 | OF-131 |
| 1908 | 154 | 593 | 167 | 19 | 15 | 7 | 1.2 | 64 | 62 | 37 | | 48 | .282 | .400 | 0 | 0 | OF-154 |
| 1909 NY N | 149 | 570 | 150 | 15 | 12 | 7 | 1.2 | 74 | 91 | 44 | | 48 | .263 | .368 | 0 | 0 | OF-148 |
| 1910 | 149 | 553 | 153 | 27 | 8 | 4 | 0.7 | 78 | 87 | 52 | 51 | 57 | .277 | .376 | 1 | 1 | OF-148 |
| 1911 | 140 | 488 | 142 | 27 | 15 | 3 | 0.6 | 70 | 78 | 43 | 37 | 48 | .291 | .426 | 6 | 1 | OF-131 |
| 1912 | 143 | 549 | 152 | 26 | 20 | 3 | 0.5 | 83 | 92 | 27 | 45 | 38 | .277 | .413 | 0 | 0 | OF-143 |
| 1913 | 147 | 520 | 139 | 21 | 3 | 2 | 0.4 | 70 | 59 | 34 | 28 | 35 | .267 | .331 | 0 | 0 | OF-147 |
| 1914 | 86 | 139 | 31 | 6 | 3 | 0 | 0.0 | 19 | 23 | 9 | 7 | 11 | .223 | .309 | 26 | 4 | OF-49 |
| 1915 2 teams | NY | N | (45G – | .220) | | CHI | N | (51G – | .299) | | | | | | | | |
| " total | 96 | 271 | 71 | 7 | 3 | 3 | 1.1 | 32 | 22 | 15 | 23 | 8 | .262 | .343 | 17 | 8 | OF-73, 2B-1 |
| 1917 NY N | 22 | 22 | 1 | 1 | 0 | 0 | 0.0 | 1 | 3 | 4 | 3 | 0 | .045 | .091 | 8 | 0 | OF-11, C-1 |
| 11 yrs. | 1264 | 4334 | 1170 | 168 | 96 | 37 | 0.9 | 555 | 579 | 298 | 194 | 321 | .270 | .379 | 64 | 15 | OF-1169, C-8, 2B-1 |
| 1 yr. | 51 | 144 | 43 | 6 | 1 | 0 | 0.0 | 20 | 11 | 8 | 8 | 6 | .299 | .354 | 9 | 5 | OF-39, 2B-1 |

| WORLD SERIES | | | | | | | | | | | | | | | | | |
|---|---|---|---|---|---|---|---|---|---|---|---|---|---|---|---|---|---|
| 1911 NY N | 6 | 21 | 0 | 0 | 0 | 0 | 0.0 | 0 | 0 | 2 | 5 | 0 | .000 | .000 | 0 | 0 | OF-6 |
| 1912 | 8 | 31 | 10 | 4 | 1 | 0 | 0.0 | 5 | 5 | 2 | 2 | 0 | .323 | .516 | 0 | 0 | OF-8 |
| 1913 | 5 | 16 | 4 | 0 | 0 | 0 | 0.0 | 2 | 1 | 2 | 2 | 2 | .250 | .250 | 0 | 0 | OF-5 |
| 3 yrs. | 19 | 68 | 14 | 4 | ·1 | 0 | 0.0 | 7 | 6 | 6 | 9 | 2 | .206 | .294 | 0 | 0 | OF-19 |

## Tony Murray

**MURRAY, ANTHONY JOSEPH**　　　　　　　　　　　BR　TR　5'10½"　154 lbs.
B. Apr. 30, 1904, Chicago, Ill.　　D. Mar. 19, 1974, Chicago, Ill.

| | G | AB | H | 2B | 3B | HR | HR% | R | RBI | BB | SO | SB | BA | SA | PH AB | PH H | G by POS |
|---|---|---|---|---|---|---|---|---|---|---|---|---|---|---|---|---|---|
| 1923 CHI N | 2 | 4 | 1 | 0 | 0 | 0 | 0.0 | 0 | 0 | 0 | 0 | 0 | .250 | .250 | 0 | 0 | OF-2 |

## Billy Myers

**MYERS, WILLIAM HARRISON**　　　　　　　　　　　BR　TR　5'8"　168 lbs.
Brother of Lynn Myers.
B. Aug. 14, 1910, Enola, Pa.

| | G | AB | H | 2B | 3B | HR | HR% | R | RBI | BB | SO | SB | BA | SA | PH AB | PH H | G by POS |
|---|---|---|---|---|---|---|---|---|---|---|---|---|---|---|---|---|---|
| 1935 CIN N | 117 | 445 | 119 | 15 | 10 | 5 | 1.1 | 60 | 36 | 29 | 81 | 10 | .267 | .380 | 0 | 0 | SS-112 |
| 1936 | 98 | 323 | 87 | 9 | 6 | 6 | 1.9 | 45 | 27 | 28 | 56 | 6 | .269 | .390 | 0 | 0 | SS-98 |
| 1937 | 124 | 335 | 84 | 13 | 3 | 7 | 2.1 | 35 | 43 | 44 | 57 | 0 | .251 | .370 | 0 | 0 | SS-121, 2B-6 |
| 1938 | 134 | 442 | 112 | 18 | 6 | 12 | 2.7 | 57 | 47 | 41 | 80 | 2 | .253 | .403 | 0 | 0 | SS-123, 2B-11 |
| 1939 | 151 | 509 | 143 | 18 | 6 | 9 | 1.8 | 79 | 56 | 71 | 90 | 4 | .281 | .393 | 0 | 0 | SS-151 |
| 1940 | 90 | 282 | 57 | 14 | 2 | 5 | 1.8 | 33 | 30 | 30 | 56 | 0 | .202 | .319 | 0 | 0 | SS-88 |
| 1941 CHI N | 24 | 63 | 14 | 1 | 0 | 1 | 1.6 | 10 | 4 | 7 | 25 | 1 | .222 | .286 | 0 | 0 | SS-19, 2B-1 |
| 7 yrs. | 738 | 2399 | 616 | 88 | 33 | 45 | 1.9 | 319 | 243 | 250 | 445 | 23 | .257 | .377 | 0 | 0 | SS-712, 2B-18 |
| 1 yr. | 24 | 63 | 14 | 1 | 0 | 1 | 1.6 | 10 | 4 | 7 | 25 | 1 | .222 | .286 | 0 | 0 | SS-19, 2B-1 |

| WORLD SERIES | | | | | | | | | | | | | | | | | |
|---|---|---|---|---|---|---|---|---|---|---|---|---|---|---|---|---|---|
| 1939 CIN N | 4 | 12 | 4 | 0 | 1 | 0 | 0.0 | 2 | 0 | 2 | 3 | 0 | .333 | .500 | 0 | 0 | SS-4 |
| 1940 | 7 | 23 | 3 | 0 | 0 | 0 | 0.0 | 0 | 2 | 2 | 5 | 0 | .130 | .130 | 0 | 0 | SS-7 |
| 2 yrs. | 11 | 35 | 7 | 0 | 1 | 0 | 0.0 | 2 | 2 | 4 | 8 | 0 | .200 | .257 | 0 | 0 | SS-11 |

## Richie Myers

**MYERS, RICHARD**　　　　　　　　　　　　　　　　　BR　TR　5'6"　150 lbs.
B. Apr. 7, 1930, Sacramento, Calif.

| | G | AB | H | 2B | 3B | HR | HR% | R | RBI | BB | SO | SB | BA | SA | PH AB | PH H | G by POS |
|---|---|---|---|---|---|---|---|---|---|---|---|---|---|---|---|---|---|
| 1956 CHI N | 4 | 1 | 0 | 0 | 0 | 0 | 0.0 | 1 | 0 | 0 | 0 | 0 | .000 | .000 | 1 | 0 | |

## Tom Nagle

**NAGLE, THOMAS EDWARD**　　　　　　　　　　　　BR　TR　5'10"　150 lbs.
B. Oct. 30, 1865, Milwaukee, Wis.　　D. Mar. 9, 1946, Milwaukee, Wis.

| | G | AB | H | 2B | 3B | HR | HR% | R | RBI | BB | SO | SB | BA | SA | PH AB | PH H | G by POS |
|---|---|---|---|---|---|---|---|---|---|---|---|---|---|---|---|---|---|
| 1890 CHI N | 38 | 144 | 39 | 5 | 1 | 1 | 0.7 | 21 | 11 | 7 | 24 | 4 | .271 | .340 | 0 | 0 | C-33, OF-6 |
| 1891 | 8 | 25 | 3 | 0 | 0 | 0 | 0.0 | 3 | 1 | 1 | 3 | 0 | .120 | .120 | 0 | 0 | C-7, OF-1 |
| 2 yrs. | 46 | 169 | 42 | 5 | 1 | 1 | 0.6 | 24 | 12 | 8 | 27 | 4 | .249 | .308 | 0 | 0 | C-40, OF-7 |
| 2 yrs. | 46 | 169 | 42 | 5 | 1 | 1 | 0.6 | 24 | 12 | 8 | 27 | 4 | .249 | .308 | 0 | 0 | C-40, OF-7 |

## Tom Needham

**NEEDHAM, THOMAS J. (Deerfoot)**　　　　　　　　BR　TR　5'10"　180 lbs.
B. Apr. 7, 1879, Ireland　　D. Dec. 13, 1926, Steubenville, Ohio

| | G | AB | H | 2B | 3B | HR | HR% | R | RBI | BB | SO | SB | BA | SA | PH AB | PH H | G by POS |
|---|---|---|---|---|---|---|---|---|---|---|---|---|---|---|---|---|---|
| 1904 BOS N | 84 | 269 | 70 | 12 | 3 | 4 | 1.5 | 18 | 19 | 11 | | 3 | .260 | .372 | 6 | 0 | C-77, OF-1 |
| 1905 | 83 | 271 | 59 | 6 | 1 | 2 | 0.7 | 21 | 17 | 24 | | 3 | .218 | .269 | 1 | 0 | C-77, OF-3, 1B-2 |
| 1906 | 83 | 285 | 54 | 8 | 2 | 1 | 0.4 | 11 | 12 | 13 | | 3 | .189 | .242 | 2 | 0 | C-76, 2B-5, 1B-2, OF-1, 3B-1 |
| 1907 | 86 | 260 | 51 | 6 | 2 | 1 | 0.4 | 19 | 19 | 18 | | 4 | .196 | .246 | 5 | 0 | C-78, 1B-1 |
| 1908 NY N | 54 | 91 | 19 | 3 | 0 | 0 | 0.0 | 8 | 11 | 12 | | 0 | .209 | .242 | 5 | 0 | C-47 |
| 1909 CHI N | 13 | 28 | 4 | 0 | 0 | 0 | 0.0 | 3 | 0 | 0 | | 0 | .143 | .143 | 6 | 2 | C-7 |
| 1910 | 31 | 76 | 14 | 3 | 1 | 0 | 0.0 | 9 | 10 | 10 | 10 | 1 | .184 | .250 | 2 | 0 | C-27, 1B-1 |
| 1911 | 27 | 62 | 12 | 2 | 0 | 0 | 0.0 | 4 | 5 | 9 | 14 | 2 | .194 | .226 | 3 | 0 | C-23 |
| 1912 | 33 | 90 | 16 | 5 | 0 | 0 | 0.0 | 12 | 10 | 7 | 13 | 3 | .178 | .233 | 1 | 0 | C-32 |
| 1913 | 20 | 42 | 10 | 4 | 1 | 0 | 0.0 | 5 | 11 | 4 | 8 | 0 | .238 | .381 | 4 | 0 | C-14, 1B-1 |
| 1914 | 9 | 17 | 2 | 1 | 0 | 0 | 0.0 | 3 | 3 | 1 | 4 | 1 | .118 | .176 | 2 | 0 | C-6 |
| 11 yrs. | 523 | 1491 | 311 | 50 | 10 | 8 | 0.5 | 113 | 117 | 109 | 49 | 20 | .209 | .272 | 38 | 2 | C-465, 1B-7, OF-5, 2B-5, 3B-1 |
| 6 yrs. | 133 | 315 | 58 | 15 | 2 | 0 | 0.0 | 36 | 39 | 31 | 49 | 7 | .184 | .244 | 19 | 2 | C-110, 1B-2 |

| WORLD SERIES | | | | | | | | | | | | | | | | | |
|---|---|---|---|---|---|---|---|---|---|---|---|---|---|---|---|---|---|
| 1910 CHI N | 1 | 1 | 0 | 0 | 0 | 0 | 0.0 | 0 | 0 | 0 | 0 | 0 | .000 | .000 | 1 | 0 | |

| | G | AB | H | 2B | 3B | HR | HR % | R | RBI | BB | SO | SB | BA | SA | Pinch Hit AB | Pinch Hit H | G by POS |
|---|---|---|---|---|---|---|---|---|---|---|---|---|---|---|---|---|---|

## Cal Neeman

**NEEMAN, CALVIN AMANDUS**       BR TR 6'1"    192 lbs.
B. Feb. 18, 1929, Valmeyer, Ill.

| | G | AB | H | 2B | 3B | HR | HR % | R | RBI | BB | SO | SB | BA | SA | AB | H | G by POS |
|---|---|---|---|---|---|---|---|---|---|---|---|---|---|---|---|---|---|
| 1957 CHI N | 122 | 415 | 107 | 17 | 1 | 10 | 2.4 | 37 | 39 | 22 | 87 | 0 | .258 | .376 | 4 | 0 | C-118 |
| 1958 | 76 | 201 | 52 | 7 | 0 | 12 | 6.0 | 30 | 29 | 21 | 41 | 0 | .259 | .473 | 8 | 0 | C-71 |
| 1959 | 44 | 105 | 17 | 2 | 0 | 3 | 2.9 | 7 | 9 | 11 | 23 | 0 | .162 | .267 | 5 | 0 | C-38 |
| 1960 2 teams | | | CHI | N | (9G – | .154) | | PHI | N | (59G – | .181) | | | | | | |
| "    total | 68 | 173 | 31 | 7 | 2 | 4 | 2.3 | 13 | 13 | 16 | 47 | 0 | .179 | .312 | 4 | 0 | C-61 |
| 1961 PHI N | 19 | 31 | 7 | 1 | 0 | 0 | 0.0 | 0 | 2 | 4 | 8 | 1 | .226 | .258 | 0 | 0 | C-19 |
| 1962 PIT N | 24 | 50 | 9 | 1 | 1 | 1 | 2.0 | 5 | 5 | 3 | 10 | 0 | .180 | .300 | 0 | 0 | C-24 |
| 1963 2 teams | | | CLE | A | (9G – | .000) | | WAS | A | (14G – | .056) | | | | | | |
| "    total | 23 | 27 | 1 | 0 | 0 | 0 | 0.0 | 1 | 0 | 2 | 5 | 0 | .037 | .037 | 2 | 0 | C-21 |
| 7 yrs. | 376 | 1002 | 224 | 35 | 4 | 30 | 3.0 | 93 | 97 | 79 | 221 | 1 | .224 | .356 | 23 | 0 | C-352 |
| 4 yrs. | 251 | 734 | 178 | 27 | 1 | 25 | 3.4 | 74 | 77 | 54 | 156 | 0 | .243 | .384 | 17 | 0 | C-236 |

## Lynn Nelson

**NELSON, LYNN BERNARD (Line Drive)**       BL TR 5'10½" 170 lbs.
B. Feb. 24, 1905, Sheldon, N. D.    D. Feb. 15, 1955, Kansas City, Mo.

| | G | AB | H | 2B | 3B | HR | HR % | R | RBI | BB | SO | SB | BA | SA | AB | H | G by POS |
|---|---|---|---|---|---|---|---|---|---|---|---|---|---|---|---|---|---|
| 1930 CHI N | 37 | 18 | 4 | 1 | 1 | 0 | 0.0 | 2 | 2 | 0 | 1 | 0 | .222 | .389 | 0 | 0 | P-37 |
| 1933 | 29 | 21 | 5 | 1 | 1 | 0 | 0.0 | 5 | 1 | 1 | 3 | 0 | .238 | .381 | 0 | 0 | P-24 |
| 1934 | 2 | 0 | 0 | 0 | 0 | 0 | – | 0 | 0 | 0 | 0 | 0 | – | – | 0 | 0 | P-2 |
| 1937 PHI A | 74 | 113 | 40 | 6 | 2 | 4 | 3.5 | 18 | 29 | 6 | 13 | 1 | .354 | .549 | 38 | 9 | P-30, OF-6 |
| 1938 | 67 | 112 | 31 | 0 | 0 | 0 | 0.0 | 12 | 15 | 7 | 12 | 0 | .277 | .277 | 32 | 6 | P-32 |
| 1939 | 40 | 80 | 15 | 2 | 0 | 0 | 0.0 | 3 | 5 | 2 | 13 | 0 | .188 | .213 | 5 | 1 | P-35 |
| 1940 DET A | 19 | 23 | 8 | 0 | 0 | 1 | 4.3 | 4 | 3 | 0 | 6 | 0 | .348 | .478 | 14 | 5 | P-6 |
| 7 yrs. | 268 | 367 | 103 | 10 | 4 | 5 | 1.4 | 42 | 55 | 16 | 48 | 1 | .281 | .371 | 89 | 21 | P-166, OF-6 |
| 3 yrs. | 68 | 39 | 9 | 2 | 2 | 0 | 0.0 | 5 | 3 | 1 | 4 | 0 | .231 | .385 | 0 | 0 | P-63 |

## Dick Nen

**NEN, RICHARD LeROY**       BL TL 6'2"    200 lbs.
B. Sept. 24, 1939, South Gate, Calif.

| | G | AB | H | 2B | 3B | HR | HR % | R | RBI | BB | SO | SB | BA | SA | AB | H | G by POS |
|---|---|---|---|---|---|---|---|---|---|---|---|---|---|---|---|---|---|
| 1963 LA N | 7 | 8 | 1 | 0 | 0 | 1 | 12.5 | 2 | 1 | 3 | 3 | 0 | .125 | .500 | 4 | 0 | 1B-5 |
| 1965 WAS A | 69 | 246 | 64 | 7 | 1 | 6 | 2.4 | 18 | 31 | 19 | 47 | 1 | .260 | .370 | 5 | 1 | 1B-65 |
| 1966 | 94 | 235 | 50 | 8 | 0 | 6 | 2.6 | 20 | 30 | 28 | 46 | 0 | .213 | .323 | 20 | 3 | 1B-76 |
| 1967 | 110 | 238 | 52 | 7 | 1 | 6 | 2.5 | 21 | 29 | 21 | 39 | 0 | .218 | .332 | 40 | 6 | 1B-65, OF-1 |
| 1968 CHI N | 81 | 94 | 17 | 1 | 1 | 2 | 2.1 | 8 | 16 | 6 | 17 | 0 | .181 | .277 | 28 | 4 | 1B-52 |
| 1970 WAS A | 6 | 5 | 1 | 0 | 0 | 0 | 0.0 | 1 | 0 | 0 | 0 | 0 | .200 | .200 | 5 | 1 | 1B-1 |
| 6 yrs. | 367 | 826 | 185 | 23 | 3 | 21 | 2.5 | 70 | 107 | 77 | 152 | 1 | .224 | .335 | 102 | 15 | 1B-264, OF-1 |
| 1 yr. | 81 | 94 | 17 | 1 | 1 | 2 | 2.1 | 8 | 16 | 6 | 17 | 0 | .181 | .277 | 28 | 4 | 1B-52 |

## Charlie Newman

**NEWMAN, CHARLES DECKER**       BR TR 5'11"    160 lbs.
B. Nov. 5, 1868, Juda, Wis.    D. Nov. 23, 1947, San Diego, Calif.

| | G | AB | H | 2B | 3B | HR | HR % | R | RBI | BB | SO | SB | BA | SA | AB | H | G by POS |
|---|---|---|---|---|---|---|---|---|---|---|---|---|---|---|---|---|---|
| 1892 2 teams | | | NY | N | (3G – | .333) | | CHI | N | (16G – | .164) | | | | | | |
| "    total | 19 | 73 | 14 | 0 | 0 | 0 | 0.0 | 5 | 3 | 3 | 6 | 5 | .192 | .192 | 0 | 0 | OF-19 |

## Art Nichols

**NICHOLS, ARTHUR FRANCIS**       BR TR 5'10"    175 lbs.
Born Arthur Francis Meikle.
B. July 14, 1871, Manchester, N. H.    D. Aug. 9, 1945, Willimantic, Conn.

| | G | AB | H | 2B | 3B | HR | HR % | R | RBI | BB | SO | SB | BA | SA | AB | H | G by POS |
|---|---|---|---|---|---|---|---|---|---|---|---|---|---|---|---|---|---|
| 1898 CHI N | 14 | 42 | 12 | 1 | 0 | 0 | 0.0 | 7 | 6 | 4 | | 6 | .286 | .310 | 0 | 0 | C-14 |
| 1899 | 17 | 47 | 12 | 2 | 0 | 1 | 2.1 | 5 | 11 | 0 | | 3 | .255 | .362 | 2 | 0 | C-15 |
| 1900 | 8 | 25 | 5 | 0 | 0 | 0 | 0.0 | 1 | 0 | 3 | | 1 | .200 | .200 | 1 | 0 | C-7 |
| 1901 STL N | 93 | 308 | 75 | 11 | 3 | 1 | 0.3 | 50 | 33 | 10 | | 14 | .244 | .308 | 6 | 1 | C-47, OF-40 |
| 1902 | 73 | 251 | 67 | 12 | 0 | 1 | 0.4 | 36 | 31 | 21 | | 18 | .267 | .327 | 2 | 0 | 1B-56, C-11, OF-4 |
| 1903 | 36 | 120 | 23 | 2 | 0 | 0 | 0.0 | 13 | 9 | 12 | | 9 | .192 | .208 | 1 | 0 | 1B-25, OF-7, C-2 |
| 6 yrs. | 241 | 793 | 194 | 28 | 3 | 3 | 0.4 | 112 | 90 | 50 | | 51 | .245 | .299 | 12 | 1 | C-96, 1B-81, OF-51 |
| 3 yrs. | 39 | 114 | 29 | 3 | 0 | 1 | 0.9 | 13 | 17 | 7 | | 10 | .254 | .307 | 3 | 0 | C-36 |

## Bill Nicholson

**NICHOLSON, WILLIAM BECK (Swish)**       BL TR 6'    205 lbs.
B. Dec. 11, 1914, Chestertown, Md.

| | G | AB | H | 2B | 3B | HR | HR % | R | RBI | BB | SO | SB | BA | SA | AB | H | G by POS |
|---|---|---|---|---|---|---|---|---|---|---|---|---|---|---|---|---|---|
| 1936 PHI A | 11 | 12 | 0 | 0 | 0 | 0 | 0.0 | 2 | 0 | 0 | 5 | 0 | .000 | .000 | 10 | 0 | OF-1 |
| 1939 CHI N | 58 | 220 | 65 | 12 | 5 | 5 | 2.3 | 37 | 38 | 20 | 29 | 0 | .295 | .464 | 0 | 0 | OF-58 |
| 1940 | 135 | 491 | 146 | 27 | 7 | 25 | 5.1 | 78 | 98 | 50 | 67 | 2 | .297 | .534 | 9 | 2 | OF-123 |
| 1941 | 147 | 532 | 135 | 26 | 1 | 26 | 4.9 | 74 | 98 | 82 | 91 | 1 | .254 | .453 | 4 | 0 | OF-143 |
| 1942 | 152 | 588 | 173 | 22 | 11 | 21 | 3.6 | 83 | 78 | 76 | 80 | 8 | .294 | .476 | 1 | 0 | OF-151 |
| 1943 | 154 | 608 | 188 | 30 | 9 | **29** | **4.8** | 95 | **128** | 71 | 78 | 4 | .309 | .531 | 0 | 0 | OF-154 |
| 1944 | 156 | 582 | 167 | 35 | 8 | **33** | 5.7 | **116** | **122** | 93 | 71 | 3 | .287 | .545 | 0 | 0 | OF-156 |
| 1945 | 151 | 559 | 136 | 28 | 4 | 13 | 2.3 | 82 | 88 | 92 | 73 | 4 | .243 | .377 | 0 | 0 | OF-151 |
| 1946 | 105 | 296 | 65 | 13 | 2 | 8 | 2.7 | 36 | 41 | 44 | 44 | 1 | .220 | .358 | 18 | 6 | OF-80 |
| 1947 | 148 | 487 | 119 | 28 | 1 | 26 | 5.3 | 69 | 75 | 87 | **83** | 1 | .244 | .466 | 7 | 0 | OF-140 |
| 1948 | 143 | 494 | 129 | 24 | 5 | 19 | 3.8 | 68 | 67 | 81 | 60 | 2 | .261 | .445 | 4 | 3 | OF-136 |
| 1949 PHI N | 98 | 299 | 70 | 8 | 3 | 11 | 3.7 | 42 | 40 | 45 | 53 | 1 | .234 | .391 | 7 | 0 | OF-91 |
| 1950 | 41 | 58 | 13 | 2 | 1 | 3 | 5.2 | 3 | 10 | 8 | 16 | 0 | .224 | .448 | 24 | 5 | OF-15 |
| 1951 | 85 | 170 | 41 | 9 | 2 | 8 | 4.7 | 23 | 30 | 25 | 24 | 0 | .241 | .459 | 36 | 11 | OF-41 |
| 1952 | 55 | 88 | 24 | 3 | 0 | 6 | 6.8 | 17 | 19 | 14 | 26 | 0 | .273 | .511 | 31 | 8 | OF-19 |
| 1953 | 38 | 62 | 13 | 5 | 1 | 2 | 3.2 | 12 | 16 | 12 | 20 | 0 | .210 | .419 | 23 | 2 | OF-12 |
| 16 yrs. | 1677 | 5546 | 1484 | 272 | 60 | 235 | 4.2 | 837 | 948 | 800 | 820 | 27 | .268 | .465 | 174 | 37 | OF-1471 |
| 10 yrs. | 1349 | 4857 | 1323 | 245 | 53 | 205 | 4.2 | 738 | 833 | 696 | 676 | 26 | .272 | .471 | 43 | 11 | OF-1292 |
| | | | | 5th | 8th | | | | 8th | 7th | 5th | | | 9th | | | |

WORLD SERIES
| | G | AB | H | 2B | 3B | HR | HR % | R | RBI | BB | SO | SB | BA | SA | AB | H | G by POS |
|---|---|---|---|---|---|---|---|---|---|---|---|---|---|---|---|---|---|
| 1945 CHI N | 7 | 28 | 6 | 1 | 1 | 0 | 0.0 | 1 | 8 | 2 | 5 | 0 | .214 | .321 | 0 | 0 | OF-7 |

## George Nicol

**NICOL, GEORGE EDWARD**       TL 5'7"    155 lbs.
B. Oct. 17, 1870, Barry, Ill.    D. Aug. 10, 1924, Milwaukee, Wis.

| | G | AB | H | 2B | 3B | HR | HR % | R | RBI | BB | SO | SB | BA | SA | AB | H | G by POS |
|---|---|---|---|---|---|---|---|---|---|---|---|---|---|---|---|---|---|
| 1890 STL AA | 3 | 7 | 2 | 1 | 0 | 0 | 0.0 | 4 | | 4 | | 0 | .286 | .429 | 0 | 0 | P-3 |

| | G | AB | H | 2B | 3B | HR | HR % | R | RBI | BB | SO | SB | BA | SA | Pinch Hit AB | Pinch Hit H | G by POS |
|---|---|---|---|---|---|---|---|---|---|---|---|---|---|---|---|---|---|

## George Nicol continued

| | G | AB | H | 2B | 3B | HR | HR% | R | RBI | BB | SO | SB | BA | SA | AB | H | G by POS |
|---|---|---|---|---|---|---|---|---|---|---|---|---|---|---|---|---|---|
| 1891 **CHI N** | 3 | 6 | 2 | 0 | 1 | 0 | 0.0 | 0 | 3 | 0 | 1 | 0 | .333 | .667 | 0 | 0 | P-3 |
| 1894 **2 teams** | PIT | N (8G – .450) | | LOU | N | (27G – .352) | | | | | | | | | | | |
| " total | 35 | 128 | 47 | 7 | 4 | 0 | 0.0 | 20 | 22 | 2 | 4 | 4 | .367 | .484 | 0 | 0 | OF-26, P-9 |
| 3 yrs. | 41 | 141 | 51 | 8 | 5 | 0 | 0.0 | 24 | 24 | 6 | 5 | 4 | .362 | .489 | 0 | 0 | OF-26, P-15 |
| 1 yr. | 3 | 6 | 2 | 0 | 1 | 0 | 0.0 | 0 | 3 | 0 | 1 | 0 | .333 | .667 | 0 | 0 | P-3 |

## Hugh Nicol

**NICOL, HUGH N.**
B. Jan. 1, 1858, Campsie, Scotland    D. June 27, 1921, Lafayette, Ind.
Manager 1897.
BR TR 5'4"    145 lbs.

| | G | AB | H | 2B | 3B | HR | HR% | R | RBI | BB | SO | SB | BA | SA | AB | H | G by POS |
|---|---|---|---|---|---|---|---|---|---|---|---|---|---|---|---|---|---|
| 1881 **CHI N** | 26 | 108 | 22 | 2 | 0 | 0 | 0.0 | 13 | 7 | 4 | 12 | | .204 | .222 | 0 | 0 | OF-26, SS-1 |
| 1882 | 47 | 186 | 37 | 9 | 1 | 1 | 0.5 | 19 | 16 | 7 | 29 | | .199 | .274 | 0 | 0 | OF-47, SS-8 |
| 1883 **STL AA** | 94 | 368 | 106 | 13 | 3 | 0 | 0.0 | 73 | | 18 | | | .288 | .340 | 0 | 0 | OF-84, 2B-11 |
| 1884 | 110 | 442 | 115 | 14 | 5 | 0 | 0.0 | 79 | | 22 | | | .260 | .314 | 0 | 0 | OF-87, 2B-23, SS-1, 3B-1 |
| 1885 | 112 | 425 | 88 | 11 | 1 | 0 | 0.0 | 59 | | 34 | | | .207 | .238 | 0 | 0 | OF-111, 3B-1 |
| 1886 | 67 | 253 | 52 | 6 | 3 | 0 | 0.0 | 44 | | 26 | | | .206 | .253 | 0 | 0 | OF-57, SS-8, 2B-4 |
| 1887 **CIN AA** | 125 | 475 | 102 | 18 | 2 | 1 | 0.2 | 122 | | 86 | | 138 | .215 | .267 | 0 | 0 | OF-125 |
| 1888 | 135 | 548 | 131 | 10 | 2 | 1 | 0.2 | 112 | 35 | 67 | | 103 | .239 | .270 | 0 | 0 | OF-125, 2B-12, SS-1 |
| 1889 | 122 | 474 | 121 | 7 | 8 | 2 | 0.4 | 82 | 58 | 54 | 35 | 80 | .255 | .316 | 0 | 0 | OF-115, 2B-7, 3B-3 |
| 1890 **CIN N** | 50 | 186 | 39 | 1 | 4 | 0 | 0.0 | 28 | 19 | 19 | 12 | 24 | .210 | .258 | 0 | 0 | OF-46, SS-3, 2B-1 |
| 10 yrs. | 888 | 3465 | 813 | 91 | 29 | 5 | 0.1 | 631 | 135 | 337 | 88 | 345 | .235 | .282 | 0 | 0 | OF-823, 2B-58, SS-22, 3B-5 |
| 2 yrs. | 73 | 294 | 59 | 11 | 1 | 1 | 0.3 | 32 | 23 | 11 | 41 | | .201 | .255 | 0 | 0 | OF-73, SS-9 |

## Pete Noonan

**NOONAN, PETER JOHN**
B. Nov. 24, 1881, W. Stockbridge, Mass.    D. Jan. 11, 1965, Pittsfield, Mass.
BR TR 6'    180 lbs.

| | G | AB | H | 2B | 3B | HR | HR% | R | RBI | BB | SO | SB | BA | SA | AB | H | G by POS |
|---|---|---|---|---|---|---|---|---|---|---|---|---|---|---|---|---|---|
| 1904 **PHI A** | 39 | 114 | 23 | 3 | 1 | 2 | 1.8 | 13 | 13 | 1 | | 1 | .202 | .298 | 6 | 1 | C-22, 1B-10 |
| 1906 **2 teams** | CHI | N (5G – .333) | | STL | N | (44G – .168) | | | | | | | | | | | |
| " total | 49 | 128 | 22 | 1 | 3 | 1 | 0.8 | 9 | 8 | 11 | | 1 | .172 | .250 | 8 | 2 | C-23, 1B-17 |
| 1907 **STL N** | 74 | 236 | 53 | 7 | 3 | 1 | 0.4 | 19 | 16 | 9 | | 3 | .225 | .292 | 5 | 1 | C-70 |
| 3 yrs. | 162 | 478 | 98 | 11 | 7 | 4 | 0.8 | 40 | 38 | 21 | | 5 | .205 | .282 | 19 | 4 | C-115, 1B-27 |
| 1 yr. | 5 | 3 | 1 | 0 | 0 | 0 | 0.0 | 0 | 0 | 0 | | 0 | .333 | .333 | 3 | 1 | 1B-1 |

## Wayne Nordhagen

**NORDHAGEN, WAYNE OREN**
B. July 4, 1948, Thief River Falls, Minn.
BR TR 6'2"    205 lbs.

| | G | AB | H | 2B | 3B | HR | HR% | R | RBI | BB | SO | SB | BA | SA | AB | H | G by POS |
|---|---|---|---|---|---|---|---|---|---|---|---|---|---|---|---|---|---|
| 1976 **CHI A** | 22 | 53 | 10 | 2 | 0 | 0 | 0.0 | 6 | 5 | 4 | 12 | 0 | .189 | .226 | 2 | 0 | OF-10, DH-6, C-5 |
| 1977 | 52 | 124 | 39 | 7 | 3 | 4 | 3.2 | 16 | 22 | 2 | 12 | 1 | .315 | .516 | 7 | 2 | OF-46, C-3, DH-2 |
| 1978 | 68 | 206 | 62 | 16 | 0 | 5 | 2.4 | 28 | 35 | 5 | 18 | 0 | .301 | .451 | 15 | 6 | OF-36, DH-16, C-12 |
| 1979 | 78 | 193 | 54 | 15 | 0 | 7 | 3.6 | 20 | 25 | 13 | 22 | 0 | .280 | .466 | 21 | 7 | DH-47, OF-12, C-5, P-2 |
| 1980 | 123 | 415 | 115 | 22 | 4 | 15 | 3.6 | 45 | 59 | 10 | 45 | 0 | .277 | .458 | 21 | 5 | OF-74, DH-32 |
| 1981 | 65 | 208 | 64 | 8 | 1 | 6 | 2.9 | 19 | 33 | 10 | 25 | 0 | .308 | .442 | 7 | 1 | OF-60 |
| 1982 **2 teams** | TOR | A (72G – .270) | | PIT | N | (1G – .500) | | | | | | | | | | | |
| " total | 73 | 189 | 52 | 6 | 0 | 1 | 0.5 | 12 | 22 | 10 | 23 | 0 | .275 | .323 | 26 | 11 | DH-60, 1B-10, OF-1 |
| 1983 **CHI N** | 21 | 35 | 5 | 1 | 0 | 1 | 2.9 | 1 | 4 | 0 | 5 | 0 | .143 | .257 | 15 | 2 | OF-7 |
| 8 yrs. | 502 | 1423 | 401 | 77 | 8 | 39 | 2.7 | 147 | 205 | 54 | 162 | 1 | .282 | .429 | 114 | 34 | OF-246, DH-163, C-25, 1B-10, P-2 |
| 1 yr. | 21 | 35 | 5 | 1 | 0 | 1 | 2.9 | 1 | 4 | 0 | 5 | 0 | .143 | .257 | 15 | 2 | OF-7 |

## Irv Noren

**NOREN, IRVING ARNOLD**
B. Nov. 29, 1924, Jamestown, N. Y.
BL TL 6'    190 lbs.

| | G | AB | H | 2B | 3B | HR | HR% | R | RBI | BB | SO | SB | BA | SA | AB | H | G by POS |
|---|---|---|---|---|---|---|---|---|---|---|---|---|---|---|---|---|---|
| 1950 **WAS A** | 138 | 542 | 160 | 27 | 10 | 14 | 2.6 | 80 | 98 | 67 | 77 | 5 | .295 | .459 | 0 | 0 | OF-121, 1B-17 |
| 1951 | 129 | 509 | 142 | 33 | 5 | 8 | 1.6 | 82 | 86 | 51 | 35 | 10 | .279 | .411 | 3 | 0 | OF-126 |
| 1952 **2 teams** | WAS | A (12G – .245) | | NY | A | (93G – .235) | | | | | | | | | | | |
| " total | 105 | 321 | 76 | 16 | 3 | 5 | 1.6 | 40 | 23 | 32 | 37 | 5 | .237 | .352 | 18 | 3 | OF-72, 1B-19 |
| 1953 **NY A** | 109 | 345 | 92 | 12 | 6 | 6 | 1.7 | 55 | 46 | 42 | 39 | 3 | .267 | .388 | 15 | 3 | OF-96 |
| 1954 | 125 | 426 | 136 | 21 | 6 | 12 | 2.8 | 70 | 66 | 43 | 38 | 4 | .319 | .481 | 12 | 5 | OF-116, 1B-1 |
| 1955 | 132 | 371 | 94 | 19 | 1 | 8 | 2.2 | 49 | 59 | 43 | 33 | 5 | .253 | .375 | 11 | 1 | OF-126 |
| 1956 | 29 | 37 | 8 | 1 | 0 | 0 | 0.0 | 4 | 6 | 12 | 7 | 0 | .216 | .243 | 13 | 4 | OF-10, 1B-1 |
| 1957 **2 teams** | KC | A (81G – .213) | | STL | N | (17G – .367) | | | | | | | | | | | |
| " total | 98 | 190 | 45 | 12 | 1 | 3 | 1.6 | 11 | 26 | 15 | 25 | 0 | .237 | .358 | 54 | 13 | 1B-25, OF-14 |
| 1958 **STL N** | 117 | 178 | 47 | 9 | 1 | 4 | 2.2 | 24 | 22 | 13 | 21 | 0 | .264 | .393 | 43 | 8 | OF-77 |
| 1959 **2 teams** | STL | N (8G – .125) | | CHI | N | (65G – .321) | | | | | | | | | | | |
| " total | 73 | 164 | 51 | 7 | 2 | 4 | 2.4 | 27 | 19 | 13 | 26 | 2 | .311 | .451 | 29 | 12 | OF-42, 1B-2 |
| 1960 **2 teams** | CHI | N (12G – .091) | | LA | N | (26G – .200) | | | | | | | | | | | |
| " total | 38 | 36 | 6 | 0 | 0 | 1 | 2.8 | 1 | 2 | 4 | 12 | 0 | .167 | .250 | 32 | 5 | OF-1, 1B-1 |
| 11 yrs. | 1093 | 3119 | 857 | 157 | 35 | 65 | 2.1 | 443 | 453 | 335 | 350 | 34 | .275 | .410 | 230 | 52 | OF-801, 1B-66 |
| 2 yrs. | 77 | 167 | 51 | 6 | 2 | 4 | 2.4 | 27 | 20 | 16 | 28 | 2 | .305 | .437 | 31 | 12 | OF-41, 1B-2 |
| WORLD SERIES | | | | | | | | | | | | | | | | | |
| 1952 **NY A** | 4 | 10 | 3 | 0 | 0 | 0 | 0.0 | 0 | 1 | 1 | 3 | 0 | .300 | .300 | 1 | 1 | OF-3 |
| 1953 | 2 | 1 | 0 | 0 | 0 | 0 | 0.0 | 0 | 0 | 1 | 0 | 0 | .000 | .000 | 1 | 0 | |
| 1955 | 5 | 16 | 1 | 0 | 0 | 0 | 0.0 | 0 | 1 | 1 | 1 | 0 | .063 | .063 | 0 | 0 | OF-5 |
| 3 yrs. | 11 | 27 | 4 | 0 | 0 | 0 | 0.0 | 0 | 2 | 3 | 4 | 0 | .148 | .148 | 2 | 1 | OF-8 |

## Billy North

**NORTH, WILLIAM ALEX**
B. May 15, 1948, Seattle, Wash.
BB TR 5'11"    185 lbs.

| | G | AB | H | 2B | 3B | HR | HR% | R | RBI | BB | SO | SB | BA | SA | AB | H | G by POS |
|---|---|---|---|---|---|---|---|---|---|---|---|---|---|---|---|---|---|
| 1971 **CHI N** | 8 | 16 | 6 | 0 | 0 | 0 | 0.0 | 4 | 0 | 4 | 6 | 1 | .375 | .375 | 0 | 0 | OF-6 |
| 1972 | 66 | 127 | 23 | 2 | 3 | 0 | 0.0 | 22 | 4 | 13 | 33 | 6 | .181 | .244 | 13 | 3 | OF-48 |
| 1973 **OAK A** | 146 | 554 | 158 | 10 | 5 | 5 | 0.9 | 98 | 34 | 78 | 89 | 53 | .285 | .348 | 2 | 0 | OF-138, DH-6 |
| 1974 | 149 | 543 | 141 | 20 | 5 | 4 | 0.7 | 79 | 33 | 69 | 86 | 54 | .260 | .337 | 1 | 1 | OF-138, DH-8 |
| 1975 | 140 | 524 | 143 | 17 | 5 | 1 | 0.2 | 74 | 43 | 81 | 80 | 30 | .273 | .330 | 1 | 1 | OF-138, DH-1 |
| 1976 | 154 | 590 | 163 | 20 | 5 | 2 | 0.3 | 91 | 31 | 73 | 95 | 75 | .276 | .337 | 1 | 0 | OF-144, DH-8 |
| 1977 | 56 | 184 | 48 | 3 | 3 | 1 | 0.5 | 32 | 9 | 32 | 25 | 17 | .261 | .326 | 4 | 0 | OF-52, DH-1 |

| | G | AB | H | 2B | 3B | HR | HR % | R | RBI | BB | SO | SB | BA | SA | Pinch Hit AB | Pinch Hit H | G by POS |
|---|---|---|---|---|---|---|---|---|---|---|---|---|---|---|---|---|---|

## Billy North continued

| | | G | AB | H | 2B | 3B | HR | HR% | R | RBI | BB | SO | SB | BA | SA | AB | H | G by POS |
|---|---|---|---|---|---|---|---|---|---|---|---|---|---|---|---|---|---|---|
| 1978 2 teams | OAK A (24G – .212) | | | | | LA N | | (110G – .234) | | | | | | | | | | |
| " total | | 134 | 356 | 82 | 14 | 0 | 0 | 0.0 | 59 | 15 | 74 | 61 | 30 | .230 | .270 | 9 | 4 | OF-120 |
| 1979 SF N | | 142 | 460 | 119 | 15 | 4 | 5 | 1.1 | 87 | 30 | 96 | 84 | 58 | .259 | .341 | 11 | 1 | OF-130 |
| 1980 | | 128 | 415 | 104 | 12 | 1 | 1 | 0.2 | 73 | 19 | 81 | 78 | 45 | .251 | .292 | 19 | 5 | OF-115 |
| 1981 | | 46 | 131 | 29 | 7 | 0 | 1 | 0.8 | 22 | 12 | 26 | 28 | 26 | .221 | .298 | 7 | 1 | OF-37 |
| 11 yrs. | | 1169 | 3900 | 1016 | 120 | 31 | 20 | 0.5 | 640 | 230 | 627 | 665 | 395 | .261 | .323 | 68 | 16 | OF-1066, DH-24 |
| 2 yrs. | | 74 | 143 | 29 | 2 | 3 | 0 | 0.0 | 25 | 4 | 17 | 39 | 7 | .203 | .259 | 13 | 3 | OF-54 |
| LEAGUE CHAMPIONSHIP SERIES | | | | | | | | | | | | | | | | | | |
| 1974 OAK A | | 4 | 16 | 1 | 1 | 0 | 0 | 0.0 | 3 | 0 | 2 | 1 | 1 | .063 | .125 | 0 | 0 | OF-4 |
| 1975 | | 3 | 10 | 0 | 0 | 0 | 0 | 0.0 | 0 | 1 | 2 | 0 | 0 | .000 | .000 | 0 | 0 | OF-3 |
| 1978 LA N | | 4 | 8 | 0 | 0 | 0 | 0 | 0.0 | 0 | 0 | 0 | 1 | 0 | .000 | .000 | 0 | 0 | OF-4 |
| 3 yrs. | | 11 | 34 | 1 | 1 | 0 | 0 | 0.0 | 3 | 1 | 4 | 2 | 1 | .029 | .059 | 0 | 0 | OF-11 |
| WORLD SERIES | | | | | | | | | | | | | | | | | | |
| 1974 OAK A | | 5 | 17 | 1 | 0 | 0 | 0 | 0.0 | 3 | 0 | 2 | 5 | 1 | .059 | .059 | 0 | 0 | OF-5 |
| 1978 LA N | | 4 | 8 | 1 | 1 | 0 | 0 | 0.0 | 2 | 2 | 1 | 0 | 1 | .125 | .250 | 1 | 1 | |
| 2 yrs. | | 9 | 25 | 2 | 1 | 0 | 0 | 0.0 | 5 | 2 | 3 | 5 | 2 | .080 | .120 | 1 | 1 | OF-5 |

## Ron Northey

**NORTHEY, RONALD JAMES (The Round Man)**          BL  TR  5'10"   195 lbs.
Father of Scott Northey.
B. Apr. 26, 1920, Mahanoy City, Pa.      D. Apr. 16, 1971, Pittsburgh, Pa.

| | | G | AB | H | 2B | 3B | HR | HR% | R | RBI | BB | SO | SB | BA | SA | AB | H | G by POS |
|---|---|---|---|---|---|---|---|---|---|---|---|---|---|---|---|---|---|---|---|
| 1942 PHI N | | 127 | 402 | 101 | 13 | 2 | 5 | 1.2 | 31 | 31 | 28 | 33 | 2 | .251 | .331 | 17 | 4 | OF-109 |
| 1943 | | 147 | 586 | 163 | 31 | 5 | 16 | 2.7 | 72 | 68 | 51 | 52 | 2 | .278 | .430 | 2 | 0 | OF-145 |
| 1944 | | 152 | 570 | 164 | 35 | 9 | 22 | 3.9 | 72 | 104 | 67 | 51 | 1 | .288 | .496 | 1 | 0 | OF-151 |
| 1946 | | 128 | 438 | 109 | 24 | 6 | 16 | 3.7 | 55 | 62 | 39 | 59 | 1 | .249 | .441 | 14 | 5 | OF-111 |
| 1947 2 teams | PHI N (13G – .255) | | | | | STL N | | (110G – .293) | | | | | | | | | | |
| " total | | 123 | 358 | 103 | 22 | 3 | 15 | 4.2 | 59 | 66 | 54 | 32 | 1 | .288 | .492 | 13 | 3 | OF-107, 3B-2 |
| 1948 STL N | | 96 | 246 | 79 | 10 | 1 | 13 | 5.3 | 40 | 64 | 38 | 25 | 0 | .321 | .528 | 25 | 11 | OF-67 |
| 1949 | | 90 | 265 | 69 | 18 | 2 | 7 | 2.6 | 28 | 50 | 31 | 15 | 0 | .260 | .423 | 12 | 0 | OF-73 |
| 1950 2 teams | CIN N (27G – .260) | | | | | CHI N | | (53G – .281) | | | | | | | | | | |
| " total | | 80 | 191 | 52 | 14 | 0 | 9 | 4.7 | 22 | 29 | 25 | 15 | 0 | .272 | .487 | 27 | 5 | OF-51 |
| 1952 CHI N | | 1 | 1 | 0 | 0 | 0 | 0 | 0.0 | 0 | 0 | 0 | 0 | 0 | .000 | .000 | 1 | 0 | |
| 1955 CHI A | | 14 | 14 | 5 | 2 | 0 | 1 | 7.1 | 1 | 4 | 3 | 3 | 0 | .357 | .714 | 10 | 4 | OF-2 |
| 1956 | | 53 | 48 | 17 | 2 | 0 | 3 | 6.3 | 4 | 23 | 8 | 1 | 0 | .354 | .583 | 39 | 15 | OF-4 |
| 1957 2 teams | CHI A (40G – .185) | | | | | PHI N | | (33G – .269) | | | | | | | | | | |
| " total | | 73 | 53 | 12 | 1 | 0 | 1 | 1.9 | 1 | 12 | 17 | 11 | 0 | .226 | .302 | 53 | 12 | |
| 12 yrs. | | 1084 | 3172 | 874 | 172 | 28 | 108 | 3.4 | 385 | 513 | 361 | 297 | 7 | .276 | .450 | 214 | 59 | OF-820, 3B-2 |
| 2 yrs. | | 54 | 115 | 32 | 9 | 0 | 4 | 3.5 | 11 | 20 | 10 | 9 | 0 | .278 | .461 | 26 | 5 | OF-27 |

## Lou Novikoff

**NOVIKOFF, LOUIE ALEXANDER (The Mad Russian)**          BR  TR  5'10"   185 lbs.
B. Oct. 12, 1915, Glendale, Ariz.      D. Sept. 30, 1970, South Gate, Calif.

| | G | AB | H | 2B | 3B | HR | HR% | R | RBI | BB | SO | SB | BA | SA | AB | H | G by POS |
|---|---|---|---|---|---|---|---|---|---|---|---|---|---|---|---|---|---|---|
| 1941 CHI N | 62 | 203 | 49 | 8 | 0 | 5 | 2.5 | 22 | 24 | 11 | 15 | 0 | .241 | .355 | 8 | 3 | OF-54 |
| 1942 | 128 | 483 | 145 | 25 | 5 | 7 | 1.4 | 48 | 64 | 24 | 28 | 3 | .300 | .416 | 8 | 2 | OF-120 |
| 1943 | 78 | 233 | 65 | 7 | 3 | 0 | 0.0 | 22 | 28 | 18 | 15 | 0 | .279 | .335 | 15 | 6 | OF-61 |
| 1944 | 71 | 139 | 39 | 4 | 2 | 3 | 2.2 | 15 | 19 | 10 | 11 | 1 | .281 | .403 | 39 | 12 | OF-29 |
| 1946 PHI N | 17 | 23 | 7 | 1 | 0 | 0 | 0.0 | 0 | 3 | 1 | 2 | 0 | .304 | .348 | 14 | 6 | OF-3 |
| 5 yrs. | 356 | 1081 | 305 | 45 | 10 | 15 | 1.4 | 107 | 138 | 64 | 71 | 4 | .282 | .384 | 84 | 29 | OF-267 |
| 4 yrs. | 339 | 1058 | 298 | 44 | 10 | 15 | 1.4 | 107 | 135 | 63 | 69 | 4 | .282 | .385 | 70 | 23 | OF-264 |

## Rube Novotney

**NOVOTNEY, RALPH JOSEPH**          BR  TR  6'   187 lbs.
B. Aug. 5, 1924, Streator, Ill.

| | G | AB | H | 2B | 3B | HR | HR% | R | RBI | BB | SO | SB | BA | SA | AB | H | G by POS |
|---|---|---|---|---|---|---|---|---|---|---|---|---|---|---|---|---|---|---|
| 1949 CHI N | 22 | 67 | 18 | 2 | 1 | 0 | 0.0 | 4 | 6 | 3 | 11 | 0 | .269 | .328 | 2 | 1 | C-20 |

## Mike O'Berry

**O'BERRY, PRESTON MICHAEL**          BR  TR  6'2"   190 lbs.
B. Apr. 20, 1954, Birmingham, Ala.

| | G | AB | H | 2B | 3B | HR | HR% | R | RBI | BB | SO | SB | BA | SA | AB | H | G by POS |
|---|---|---|---|---|---|---|---|---|---|---|---|---|---|---|---|---|---|---|
| 1979 BOS A | 43 | 59 | 10 | 1 | 0 | 1 | 1.7 | 8 | 4 | 5 | 16 | 0 | .169 | .237 | 0 | 0 | C-43 |
| 1980 CHI N | 19 | 48 | 10 | 1 | 0 | 0 | 0.0 | 7 | 5 | 5 | 13 | 0 | .208 | .229 | 0 | 0 | C-19 |
| 1981 CIN N | 55 | 111 | 20 | 3 | 1 | 1 | 0.9 | 6 | 5 | 14 | 19 | 0 | .180 | .252 | 0 | 0 | C-55 |
| 1982 | 21 | 45 | 10 | 2 | 0 | 0 | 0.0 | 5 | 3 | 10 | 13 | 0 | .222 | .267 | 0 | 0 | C-21 |
| 1983 CAL A | 26 | 60 | 10 | 1 | 0 | 1 | 1.7 | 7 | 5 | 3 | 11 | 0 | .167 | .233 | 1 | 0 | C-26 |
| 1984 NY A | 13 | 32 | 8 | 2 | 0 | 0 | 0.0 | 3 | 5 | 2 | 2 | 0 | .250 | .313 | 1 | 0 | C-12, 3B-1 |
| 1985 MON N | 20 | 21 | 4 | 0 | 0 | 0 | 0.0 | 2 | 0 | 4 | 3 | 1 | .190 | .190 | 0 | 0 | C-20 |
| 7 yrs. | 197 | 376 | 72 | 10 | 1 | 3 | 0.8 | 38 | 27 | 43 | 77 | 1 | .191 | .247 | 2 | 0 | C-196, 3B-1 |
| 1 yr. | 19 | 48 | 10 | 1 | 0 | 0 | 0.0 | 7 | 5 | 5 | 13 | 0 | .208 | .229 | 0 | 0 | C-19 |

## John O'Brien

**O'BRIEN, JOHN J. (Chewing Gum)**          BL  TR   175 lbs.
B. July 14, 1870, St. John, N. B., Canada      D. May 13, 1913, Lewiston, Me.

| | | G | AB | H | 2B | 3B | HR | HR% | R | RBI | BB | SO | SB | BA | SA | AB | H | G by POS |
|---|---|---|---|---|---|---|---|---|---|---|---|---|---|---|---|---|---|---|---|
| 1891 BKN N | | 43 | 167 | 41 | 4 | 2 | 0 | 0.0 | 22 | 26 | 12 | 17 | 4 | .246 | .293 | 0 | 0 | 2B-43 |
| 1893 CHI N | | 4 | 14 | 5 | 0 | 1 | 0 | 0.0 | 3 | 1 | 2 | 2 | 0 | .357 | .500 | 0 | 0 | 2B-4 |
| 1895 LOU N | | 128 | 539 | 138 | 10 | 4 | 1 | 0.2 | 82 | 50 | 45 | 20 | 15 | .256 | .295 | 0 | 0 | 2B-125, 1B-3 |
| 1896 2 teams | LOU N (49G – .339) | | | | | WAS N | | (73G – .267) | | | | | | | | | | |
| " total | | 122 | 456 | 135 | 15 | 4 | 6 | 1.3 | 62 | 57 | 40 | 19 | 8 | .296 | .386 | 0 | 0 | 2B-122 |
| 1897 WAS N | | 86 | 320 | 78 | 12 | 2 | 3 | 0.9 | 37 | 45 | 19 | | 6 | .244 | .322 | 0 | 0 | 2B-86 |
| 1899 2 teams | BAL N (39G – .193) | | | | | PIT N | | (79G – .226) | | | | | | | | | | |
| " total | | 118 | 414 | 89 | 6 | 4 | 2 | 0.5 | 40 | 50 | 36 | | 12 | .215 | .263 | 0 | 0 | 2B-118 |
| 6 yrs. | | 501 | 1910 | 486 | 47 | 17 | 12 | 0.6 | 246 | 229 | 154 | 58 | 45 | .254 | .316 | 0 | 0 | 2B-498, 1B-3 |
| 1 yr. | | 4 | 14 | 5 | 0 | 1 | 0 | 0.0 | 3 | 1 | 2 | 2 | 0 | .357 | .500 | 0 | 0 | 2B-4 |

## Pete O'Brien

**O'BRIEN, PETER F.**
B. June 16, 1868, Chicago, Ill.      Deceased.

| | G | AB | H | 2B | 3B | HR | HR% | R | RBI | BB | SO | SB | BA | SA | AB | H | G by POS |
|---|---|---|---|---|---|---|---|---|---|---|---|---|---|---|---|---|---|---|
| 1890 CHI N | 27 | 106 | 30 | 7 | 0 | 3 | 2.8 | 15 | 16 | 5 | 10 | 4 | .283 | .434 | 0 | 0 | 2B-27 |

| | G | AB | H | 2B | 3B | HR | HR % | R | RBI | BB | SO | SB | BA | SA | Pinch Hit AB | Pinch Hit H | G by POS |
|---|---|---|---|---|---|---|---|---|---|---|---|---|---|---|---|---|---|

## John O'Connor

**O'CONNOR, JOHN J.**
B. Unknown.                                                    TR

| 1916 CHI N | 1 | 0 | 0 | 0 | 0 | 0 | – | 0 | 0 | 0 | 0 | 0 | – | – | 0 | 0 | C-1 |

## Ken O'Dea

**O'DEA, JAMES KENNETH**
B. Mar. 16, 1913, Lima, N. Y.                                 BL  TR  6'    180 lbs.

| 1935 CHI N | 76 | 202 | 52 | 13 | 2 | 6 | 3.0 | 30 | 38 | 26 | 18 | 0 | .257 | .431 | 9 | 1 | C-63 |
| 1936 | 80 | 189 | 58 | 10 | 3 | 2 | 1.1 | 36 | 38 | 38 | 18 | 0 | .307 | .423 | 22 | 7 | C-55 |
| 1937 | 83 | 219 | 66 | 7 | 5 | 4 | 1.8 | 31 | 32 | 24 | 26 | 1 | .301 | .434 | 13 | 3 | C-64 |
| 1938 | 86 | 247 | 65 | 12 | 1 | 3 | 1.2 | 22 | 33 | 12 | 18 | 1 | .263 | .356 | 13 | 2 | C-71 |
| 1939 NY N | 52 | 97 | 17 | 1 | 0 | 3 | 3.1 | 7 | 11 | 10 | 16 | 0 | .175 | .278 | 26 | 3 | C-30 |
| 1940 | 48 | 96 | 23 | 4 | 1 | 0 | 0 | 9 | 12 | 16 | 15 | 0 | .240 | .302 | 14 | 2 | C-31 |
| 1941 | 59 | 89 | 19 | 5 | 1 | 3 | 3.4 | 13 | 17 | 8 | 20 | 0 | .213 | .393 | 42 | 9 | C-14 |
| 1942 STL N | 58 | 192 | 45 | 7 | 1 | 5 | 2.6 | 22 | 32 | 17 | 23 | 0 | .234 | .359 | 9 | 1 | C-49 |
| 1943 | 71 | 203 | 57 | 11 | 2 | 3 | 1.5 | 15 | 25 | 19 | 25 | 0 | .281 | .399 | 14 | 4 | C-56 |
| 1944 | 85 | 265 | 66 | 11 | 2 | 6 | 2.3 | 35 | 37 | 37 | 29 | 1 | .249 | .374 | 14 | 4 | C-69 |
| 1945 | 100 | 307 | 78 | 18 | 2 | 4 | 1.3 | 36 | 43 | 50 | 31 | 0 | .254 | .365 | 8 | 0 | C-91 |
| 1946 2 teams | STL | N | (22G – | .123) | | BOS | N | (12G – | .219) | | | | | | | | |
| " total | 34 | 89 | 14 | 2 | 0 | 1 | 1.1 | 6 | 5 | 16 | 12 | 0 | .157 | .213 | 0 | 0 | C-34 |
| 12 yrs. | 832 | 2195 | 560 | 101 | 20 | 40 | 1.8 | 262 | 323 | 273 | 251 | 3 | .255 | .374 | 184 | 36 | C-627 |
| 4 yrs. | 325 | 857 | 241 | 42 | 11 | 15 | 1.8 | 119 | 141 | 100 | 80 | 2 | .281 | .408 | 57 | 13 | C-253 |
| WORLD SERIES | | | | | | | | | | | | | | | | | |
| 1935 CHI N | 1 | 1 | 1 | 0 | 0 | 0 | 0.0 | 0 | 1 | 0 | 0 | 0 | 1.000 | 1.000 | 1 | 1 | |
| 1938 | 3 | 5 | 1 | 0 | 0 | 1 | 20.0 | 1 | 2 | 1 | 0 | 0 | .200 | .800 | 2 | 0 | C-1 |
| 1942 STL N | 1 | 1 | 1 | 0 | 0 | 0 | 0.0 | 0 | 1 | 0 | 0 | 0 | 1.000 | 1.000 | 1 | 1 | |
| 1943 | 2 | 3 | 2 | 0 | 0 | 0 | 0.0 | 0 | 0 | 0 | 0 | 0 | .667 | .667 | 1 | 0 | C-1 |
| 1944 | 3 | 3 | 1 | 0 | 0 | 0 | 0.0 | 0 | 2 | 0 | 0 | 0 | .333 | .333 | 3 | 1 | |
| 5 yrs. | 10 | 13 | 6 | 0 | 0 | 1 | 7.7 | 1 | 6 | 1 | 0 | 0 | .462 | .692 | 8 | 3 | C-2 |
| | | | | | | | | | | | | | 3rd | 1st | | | |

## Bob O'Farrell

**O'FARRELL, ROBERT ARTHUR**
B. Oct. 19, 1896, Waukegan, Ill.                              BR  TR  5'9½"  180 lbs.
Manager 1927, 1934.

| 1915 CHI N | 2 | 3 | 1 | 0 | 0 | 0 | 0.0 | 0 | 0 | 0 | 0 | 0 | .333 | .333 | 0 | 0 | C-2 |
| 1916 | 1 | 0 | 0 | 0 | 0 | 0 | – | 0 | 0 | 0 | 0 | 0 | – | – | 0 | 0 | C-1 |
| 1917 | 3 | 8 | 3 | 2 | 0 | 0 | 0.0 | 1 | 1 | 1 | 0 | 1 | .375 | .625 | 0 | 0 | C-3 |
| 1918 | 52 | 113 | 32 | 7 | 3 | 1 | 0.9 | 9 | 14 | 10 | 15 | 0 | .283 | .425 | 7 | 2 | C-45 |
| 1919 | 49 | 125 | 27 | 4 | 2 | 0 | 0.0 | 11 | 9 | 7 | 10 | 2 | .216 | .280 | 9 | 1 | C-38 |
| 1920 | 94 | 270 | 67 | 11 | 4 | 3 | 1.1 | 29 | 19 | 34 | 23 | 1 | .248 | .352 | 8 | 0 | C-86 |
| 1921 | 96 | 260 | 65 | 12 | 4 | 4 | 1.5 | 32 | 32 | 18 | 14 | 2 | .250 | .396 | 6 | 1 | C-90 |
| 1922 | 128 | 392 | 127 | 18 | 8 | 4 | 1.0 | 68 | 60 | 79 | 34 | 5 | .324 | .441 | 2 | 1 | C-125 |
| 1923 | 131 | 452 | 144 | 25 | 4 | 12 | 2.7 | 73 | 84 | 67 | 38 | 10 | .319 | .471 | 6 | 3 | C-124 |
| 1924 | 71 | 183 | 44 | 6 | 2 | 3 | 1.6 | 25 | 28 | 30 | 13 | 2 | .240 | .344 | 10 | 3 | C-57 |
| 1925 2 teams | CHI | N | (17G – | .182) | | STL | N | (94G – | .278) | | | | | | | | |
| " total | 111 | 339 | 92 | 13 | 3 | 3 | 0.9 | 39 | 35 | 48 | 31 | 0 | .271 | .354 | 14 | 4 | C-95 |
| 1926 STL N | 147 | 492 | 144 | 30 | 9 | 7 | 1.4 | 63 | 68 | 61 | 44 | 1 | .293 | .433 | 1 | 1 | C-146 |
| 1927 | 61 | 178 | 47 | 10 | 1 | 0 | 0 | 19 | 18 | 23 | 22 | 3 | .264 | .331 | 6 | 2 | C-53 |
| 1928 2 teams | STL | N | (16G – | .212) | | NY | N | (75G – | .195) | | | | | | | | |
| " total | 91 | 185 | 37 | 7 | 0 | 2 | 1.1 | 29 | 24 | 47 | 25 | 4 | .200 | .270 | 9 | 1 | C-77 |
| 1929 NY N | 91 | 248 | 76 | 14 | 3 | 4 | 1.6 | 35 | 42 | 28 | 30 | 3 | .306 | .435 | 4 | 2 | C-84 |
| 1930 | 94 | 249 | 75 | 16 | 4 | 4 | 1.6 | 37 | 54 | 31 | 21 | 0 | .301 | .446 | 23 | 6 | C-69 |
| 1931 | 85 | 174 | 39 | 8 | 3 | 1 | 0.6 | 11 | 19 | 21 | 23 | 0 | .224 | .322 | 5 | 0 | C-80 |
| 1932 | 50 | 67 | 16 | 3 | 0 | 0 | 0 | 7 | 8 | 11 | 10 | 0 | .239 | .284 | 5 | 1 | C-41 |
| 1933 STL N | 55 | 163 | 39 | 4 | 2 | 2 | 1.2 | 16 | 20 | 15 | 25 | 0 | .239 | .325 | 4 | 1 | C-50 |
| 1934 2 teams | CIN | N | (44G – | .244) | | CHI | N | (22G – | .224) | | | | | | | | |
| " total | 66 | 190 | 45 | 11 | 3 | 1 | 0.5 | 13 | 14 | 14 | 30 | 0 | .237 | .342 | 2 | 0 | C-64 |
| 1935 STL N | 14 | 10 | 0 | 0 | 0 | 0 | 0 | 0 | 0 | 2 | 0 | 0 | .000 | .000 | 4 | 0 | C-8 |
| 21 yrs. | 1492 | 4101 | 1120 | 201 | 58 | 51 | 1.2 | 517 | 549 | 547 | 408 | 35 | .273 | .388 | 125 | 29 | C-1338 |
| 12 yrs. | 666 | 1895 | 529 | 88 | 31 | 27 | 1.4 | 253 | 255 | 251 | 163 | 23 | .279 | .401 | 60 | 15 | C-596 |
| WORLD SERIES | | | | | | | | | | | | | | | | | |
| 1918 CHI N | 3 | 3 | 0 | 0 | 0 | 0 | 0.0 | 0 | 0 | 0 | 0 | 0 | .000 | .000 | 3 | 0 | C-1 |
| 1926 STL N | 7 | 23 | 7 | 1 | 0 | 0 | 0.0 | 2 | 2 | 2 | 2 | 0 | .304 | .348 | 0 | 0 | C-7 |
| 2 yrs. | 10 | 26 | 7 | 1 | 0 | 0 | 0.0 | 2 | 2 | 2 | 2 | 0 | .269 | .308 | 3 | 0 | C-8 |

## Hal O'Hagan

**O'HAGAN, HAROLD P.**
B. Sept. 30, 1873, Washington, D. C.   D. Jan. 14, 1913, Newark, N. J.    6'    173 lbs.

| 1892 WAS N | 1 | 4 | 1 | 0 | 0 | 0 | 0.0 | 1 | 0 | 0 | 2 | 0 | .250 | .250 | 0 | 0 | C-1 |
| 1902 3 teams | CHI | N | (31G – | .194) | | NY | N | (26G – | .143) | | CLE | A | (3G – | .385) | | | |
| " total | 60 | 205 | 38 | 5 | 4 | 0 | 0.0 | 17 | 19 | 13 | | 13 | .185 | .249 | 0 | 0 | 1B-52, OF-8 |
| 2 yrs. | 61 | 209 | 39 | 5 | 4 | 0 | 0.0 | 18 | 19 | 13 | 2 | 13 | .187 | .249 | 0 | 0 | 1B-52, OF-8, C-1 |
| 1 yr. | 31 | 108 | 21 | 1 | 0 | 0 | 0.0 | 10 | 10 | 11 | | 8 | .194 | .259 | 0 | 0 | 1B-31 |

## Dick Oliver

**Playing record listed under Dick Barrett**

## Gene Oliver

**OLIVER, EUGENE GEORGE**
B. Mar. 22, 1936, Moline, Ill.                                BR  TR  6'2"  225 lbs.

| 1959 STL N | 68 | 172 | 42 | 9 | 0 | 6 | 3.5 | 14 | 28 | 7 | 41 | 3 | .244 | .401 | 18 | 4 | OF-42, C-9, 1B-5 |
| 1961 | 22 | 52 | 14 | 2 | 0 | 4 | 7.7 | 8 | 9 | 6 | 10 | 0 | .269 | .538 | 5 | 1 | C-15, OF-1 |
| 1962 | 122 | 345 | 89 | 19 | 1 | 14 | 4.1 | 42 | 45 | 50 | 59 | 5 | .258 | .441 | 19 | 6 | C-98, OF-8, 1B-3 |

| | G | AB | H | 2B | 3B | HR | HR % | R | RBI | BB | SO | SB | BA | SA | Pinch Hit AB | H | G by POS |
|---|---|---|---|---|---|---|---|---|---|---|---|---|---|---|---|---|---|

## Gene Oliver continued

| | | G | AB | H | 2B | 3B | HR | HR% | R | RBI | BB | SO | SB | BA | SA | AB | H | G by POS |
|---|---|---|---|---|---|---|---|---|---|---|---|---|---|---|---|---|---|---|
| 1963 2 teams | STL N (39G – .225) | | | | | | | MIL N (95G – .250) | | | | | | | | | | |
| " total | | 134 | 398 | 97 | 16 | 2 | 17 | 4.3 | 44 | 65 | 40 | 78 | 4 | .244 | .422 | 16 | 2 | 1B-55, C-37, OF-35 |
| 1964 MIL N | | 93 | 279 | 77 | 15 | 1 | 13 | 4.7 | 45 | 49 | 17 | 41 | 3 | .276 | .477 | 23 | 3 | 1B-76, C-1 |
| 1965 | | 122 | 392 | 106 | 20 | 0 | 21 | 5.4 | 56 | 58 | 36 | 61 | 5 | .270 | .482 | 12 | 5 | C-64, 1B-52, OF-1 |
| 1966 ATL N | | 76 | 191 | 37 | 9 | 1 | 8 | 4.2 | 19 | 24 | 16 | 43 | 2 | .194 | .377 | 24 | 5 | C-48, 1B-5, OF-2 |
| 1967 2 teams | ATL N (17G – .196) | | | | | | | PHI N (85G – .224) | | | | | | | | | | |
| " total | | 102 | 314 | 69 | 18 | 0 | 10 | 3.2 | 37 | 40 | 35 | 64 | 2 | .220 | .373 | 11 | 0 | C-93, 1B-2 |
| 1968 2 teams | BOS A (16G – .143) | | | | | | | CHI N (8G – .364) | | | | | | | | | | |
| " total | | 24 | 46 | 9 | 0 | 0 | 0 | 0.0 | 3 | 2 | 7 | 14 | 0 | .196 | .196 | 10 | 3 | C-11, OF-2, 1B-2 |
| 1969 CHI N | | 23 | 27 | 6 | 3 | 0 | 0 | 0.0 | 0 | 1 | 1 | 9 | 0 | .222 | .333 | 14 | 4 | C-6 |
| 10 yrs. | | 786 | 2216 | 546 | 111 | 5 | 93 | 4.2 | 268 | 320 | 215 | 420 | 24 | .246 | .427 | 152 | 31 | C-382, 1B-200, OF-91 |
| 2 yrs. | | 31 | 38 | 10 | 3 | 0 | 0 | 0.0 | 1 | 1 | 4 | 11 | 0 | .263 | .342 | 16 | 5 | C-7, 1B-2, OF-1 |

## Nate Oliver

**OLIVER, NATHANIEL (Pee Wee)**          BR TR 5'10"  160 lbs.
B. Dec. 13, 1940, St. Petersburg, Fla.

| | | G | AB | H | 2B | 3B | HR | HR% | R | RBI | BB | SO | SB | BA | SA | AB | H | G by POS |
|---|---|---|---|---|---|---|---|---|---|---|---|---|---|---|---|---|---|---|
| 1963 LA N | | 65 | 163 | 39 | 2 | 3 | 1 | 0.6 | 23 | 9 | 13 | 25 | 3 | .239 | .307 | 6 | 0 | 2B-57, SS-2 |
| 1964 | | 99 | 321 | 78 | 9 | 0 | 0 | 0.0 | 28 | 21 | 31 | 57 | 7 | .243 | .271 | 1 | 0 | 2B-98, SS-1 |
| 1965 | | 8 | 1 | 1 | 0 | 0 | 0 | 0.0 | 3 | 0 | 0 | 0 | 1 | 1.000 | 1.000 | 0 | 0 | 2B-2 |
| 1966 | | 80 | 119 | 23 | 2 | 0 | 0 | 0.0 | 17 | 3 | 13 | 17 | 3 | .193 | .210 | 3 | 1 | 2B-68, SS-2, 3B-1 |
| 1967 | | 77 | 232 | 55 | 6 | 2 | 0 | 0.0 | 18 | 7 | 13 | 50 | 3 | .237 | .280 | 12 | 3 | 2B-39, SS-32, OF-1 |
| 1968 SF N | | 36 | 73 | 13 | 2 | 0 | 0 | 0.0 | 3 | 1 | 1 | 13 | 0 | .178 | .205 | 3 | 0 | 2B-14, SS-13, 3B-1 |
| 1969 2 teams | NY A (1G – .000) | | | | | | | CHI N (44G – .159) | | | | | | | | | | |
| " total | | 45 | 45 | 7 | 3 | 0 | 1 | 2.2 | 15 | 4 | 1 | 10 | 0 | .156 | .289 | 4 | 0 | 2B-13 |
| 7 yrs. | | 410 | 954 | 216 | 24 | 5 | 2 | 0.2 | 107 | 45 | 72 | 172 | 17 | .226 | .268 | 29 | 4 | 2B-291, SS-50, 3B-2, OF-1 |
| 1 yr. | | 44 | 44 | 7 | 3 | 0 | 1 | 2.3 | 15 | 4 | 1 | 10 | 0 | .159 | .295 | 3 | 0 | 2B-13 |

WORLD SERIES

| | | G | AB | H | 2B | 3B | HR | HR% | R | RBI | BB | SO | SB | BA | SA | AB | H | G by POS |
|---|---|---|---|---|---|---|---|---|---|---|---|---|---|---|---|---|---|---|
| 1966 LA N | | 1 | 0 | 0 | 0 | 0 | 0 | – | 0 | 0 | 0 | 0 | 0 | – | – | 0 | 0 | |

## Barney Olsen

**OLSEN, BERNARD CHARLES**          BR TR 5'11"  179 lbs.
B. Sept. 11, 1919, Everett, Mass.   D. Mar. 30, 1977, Everett, Mass.

| | | G | AB | H | 2B | 3B | HR | HR% | R | RBI | BB | SO | SB | BA | SA | AB | H | G by POS |
|---|---|---|---|---|---|---|---|---|---|---|---|---|---|---|---|---|---|---|
| 1941 CHI N | | 24 | 73 | 21 | 6 | 1 | 1 | 1.4 | 13 | 4 | 4 | 11 | 0 | .288 | .438 | 1 | 1 | OF-23 |

## Jack O'Neill

**O'NEILL, JOHN JOSEPH**          BR TR 6'  165 lbs.
Brother of Jim O'Neill.   Brother of Steve O'Neill.
Brother of Mike O'Neill.
B. Jan. 10, 1882, Galway, Ireland   D. June 29, 1935, Scranton, Pa.

| | | G | AB | H | 2B | 3B | HR | HR% | R | RBI | BB | SO | SB | BA | SA | AB | H | G by POS |
|---|---|---|---|---|---|---|---|---|---|---|---|---|---|---|---|---|---|---|
| 1902 STL N | | 63 | 192 | 27 | 1 | 1 | 0 | 0.0 | 13 | 12 | 13 | | 2 | .141 | .156 | 4 | 0 | C-59 |
| 1903 | | 75 | 246 | 58 | 9 | 1 | 0 | 0.0 | 23 | 27 | 13 | | 11 | .236 | .280 | 1 | 0 | C-74 |
| 1904 CHI N | | 51 | 168 | 36 | 5 | 0 | 1 | 0.6 | 8 | 19 | 6 | | 1 | .214 | .262 | 2 | 0 | C-49 |
| 1905 | | 53 | 172 | 34 | 4 | 2 | 0 | 0.0 | 16 | 12 | 8 | | 6 | .198 | .244 | 3 | 0 | C-50 |
| 1906 BOS N | | 61 | 167 | 30 | 5 | 1 | 0 | 0.0 | 14 | 4 | 12 | | 0 | .180 | .222 | 7 | 2 | C-48, 1B-2, OF-1 |
| 5 yrs. | | 303 | 945 | 185 | 24 | 5 | 1 | 0.1 | 74 | 74 | 52 | | 20 | .196 | .235 | 17 | 2 | C-280, 1B-2, OF-1 |
| 2 yrs. | | 104 | 340 | 70 | 9 | 2 | 1 | 0.3 | 24 | 31 | 14 | | 7 | .206 | .253 | 5 | 0 | C-99 |

## Steve Ontiveros

**ONTIVEROS, STEVEN ROBERT**          BB TR 6'  185 lbs.
B. Oct. 26, 1951, Bakersfield, Calif.

| | | G | AB | H | 2B | 3B | HR | HR% | R | RBI | BB | SO | SB | BA | SA | AB | H | G by POS |
|---|---|---|---|---|---|---|---|---|---|---|---|---|---|---|---|---|---|---|
| 1973 SF N | | 24 | 33 | 8 | 0 | 0 | 1 | 3.0 | 3 | 5 | 4 | 7 | 0 | .242 | .333 | 17 | 5 | 1B-5, OF-1 |
| 1974 | | 120 | 343 | 91 | 15 | 1 | 4 | 1.2 | 45 | 33 | 57 | 41 | 0 | .265 | .350 | 23 | 4 | 3B-75, 1B-19, OF-2 |
| 1975 | | 108 | 325 | 94 | 16 | 0 | 3 | 0.9 | 21 | 31 | 55 | 44 | 2 | .289 | .366 | 11 | 2 | 3B-89, OF-8, 1B-4 |
| 1976 | | 59 | 74 | 13 | 3 | 0 | 0 | 0.0 | 8 | 5 | 6 | 11 | 0 | .176 | .216 | 44 | 8 | OF-7, 3B-7, 1B-4 |
| 1977 CHI N | | 156 | 546 | 163 | 32 | 3 | 10 | 1.8 | 54 | 68 | 81 | 69 | 3 | .299 | .423 | 3 | 1 | 3B-155 |
| 1978 | | 82 | 276 | 67 | 14 | 4 | 1 | 0.4 | 34 | 22 | 34 | 33 | 0 | .243 | .333 | 4 | 2 | 3B-77, 1B-1 |
| 1979 | | 152 | 519 | 148 | 28 | 2 | 4 | 0.8 | 58 | 57 | 58 | 68 | 0 | .285 | .370 | 9 | 3 | 3B-142, 1B-1 |
| 1980 | | 31 | 77 | 16 | 3 | 0 | 1 | 1.3 | 7 | 3 | 14 | 17 | 0 | .208 | .286 | 6 | 0 | 3B-24 |
| 8 yrs. | | 732 | 2193 | 600 | 111 | 10 | 24 | 1.1 | 230 | 224 | 309 | 290 | 5 | .274 | .366 | 117 | 25 | 3B-569, 1B-34, OF-18 |
| 4 yrs. | | 421 | 1418 | 394 | 77 | 9 | 16 | 1.1 | 153 | 150 | 187 | 187 | 3 | .278 | .379 | 22 | 6 | 3B-398, 1B-2 |

## Jose Ortiz

**ORTIZ, JOSE LUIS**          BR TR 5'9½"  155 lbs.
B. June 25, 1947, Ponce, Puerto Rico

| | | G | AB | H | 2B | 3B | HR | HR% | R | RBI | BB | SO | SB | BA | SA | AB | H | G by POS |
|---|---|---|---|---|---|---|---|---|---|---|---|---|---|---|---|---|---|---|
| 1969 CHI A | | 16 | 11 | 3 | 1 | 0 | 0 | 0.0 | 0 | 2 | 1 | 0 | 0 | .273 | .364 | 1 | 0 | OF-8 |
| 1970 | | 15 | 24 | 8 | 1 | 0 | 0 | 0.0 | 4 | 1 | 2 | 2 | 1 | .333 | .375 | 1 | 0 | OF-8 |
| 1971 CHI N | | 36 | 88 | 26 | 7 | 1 | 0 | 0.0 | 10 | 3 | 4 | 10 | 2 | .295 | .398 | 1 | 0 | OF-20 |
| 3 yrs. | | 67 | 123 | 37 | 9 | 1 | 0 | 0.0 | 14 | 6 | 7 | 12 | 3 | .301 | .390 | 3 | 0 | OF-36 |
| 1 yr. | | 36 | 88 | 26 | 7 | 1 | 0 | 0.0 | 10 | 3 | 4 | 10 | 2 | .295 | .398 | 1 | 0 | OF-20 |

## John Ostrowski

**OSTROWSKI, JOHN THADDEUS**          BR TR 5'10½"  170 lbs.
B. Oct. 17, 1917, Chicago, Ill.

| | | G | AB | H | 2B | 3B | HR | HR% | R | RBI | BB | SO | SB | BA | SA | AB | H | G by POS |
|---|---|---|---|---|---|---|---|---|---|---|---|---|---|---|---|---|---|---|
| 1943 CHI N | | 10 | 29 | 6 | 0 | 1 | 0 | 0.0 | 2 | 3 | 3 | 8 | 0 | .207 | .276 | 0 | 0 | OF-5, 3B-4 |
| 1944 | | 8 | 13 | 2 | 1 | 0 | 0 | 0.0 | 2 | 2 | 1 | 4 | 0 | .154 | .231 | 5 | 2 | OF-2 |
| 1945 | | 7 | 10 | 3 | 2 | 0 | 0 | 0.0 | 4 | 1 | 0 | 0 | 0 | .300 | .500 | 2 | 0 | 3B-4 |
| 1946 | | 64 | 160 | 34 | 4 | 2 | 3 | 1.9 | 20 | 12 | 20 | 31 | 1 | .213 | .319 | 10 | 0 | 3B-50, 2B-1 |
| 1948 BOS A | | 1 | 1 | 0 | 0 | 0 | 0 | 0.0 | 0 | 0 | 0 | 1 | 0 | .000 | .000 | 1 | 0 | |
| 1949 CHI A | | 49 | 158 | 42 | 9 | 4 | 5 | 3.2 | 19 | 31 | 15 | 41 | 4 | .266 | .468 | 6 | 1 | OF-41, 3B-8 |
| 1950 2 teams | CHI A (22G – .245) | | | | | | | WAS A (55G – .227) | | | | | | | | | | |
| " total | | 77 | 190 | 44 | 4 | 2 | 6 | 3.2 | 26 | 25 | 29 | 40 | 2 | .232 | .368 | 16 | 0 | OF-61 |
| 7 yrs. | | 216 | 561 | 131 | 20 | 9 | 14 | 2.5 | 73 | 74 | 68 | 125 | 7 | .234 | .376 | 40 | 3 | OF-109, 3B-66, 2B-1 |
| 4 yrs. | | 89 | 212 | 45 | 7 | 3 | 3 | 1.4 | 28 | 18 | 24 | 43 | 1 | .212 | .316 | 17 | 2 | 3B-58, OF-7, 2B-1 |

| | G | AB | H | 2B | 3B | HR | HR % | R | RBI | BB | SO | SB | BA | SA | Pinch Hit AB | Pinch Hit H | G by POS |
|---|---|---|---|---|---|---|---|---|---|---|---|---|---|---|---|---|---|

## Reggie Otero

**OTERO, REGINO JOSEPH GOMEZ**
B. Sept. 7, 1915, Havana, Cuba

BL TR 5'11" 160 lbs.

| | G | AB | H | 2B | 3B | HR | HR % | R | RBI | BB | SO | SB | BA | SA | AB | H | G by POS |
|---|---|---|---|---|---|---|---|---|---|---|---|---|---|---|---|---|---|
| 1945 CHI N | 14 | 23 | 9 | 0 | 0 | 0 | 0.0 | 1 | 5 | 2 | 2 | 0 | .391 | .391 | 6 | 0 | 1B-8 |

## Billy Ott

**OTT, WILLIAM JOSEPH**
B. Nov. 23, 1940, New York, N. Y.

BB TR 6'1" 180 lbs.

| | G | AB | H | 2B | 3B | HR | HR % | R | RBI | BB | SO | SB | BA | SA | AB | H | G by POS |
|---|---|---|---|---|---|---|---|---|---|---|---|---|---|---|---|---|---|
| 1962 CHI N | 12 | 28 | 4 | 0 | 0 | 1 | 3.6 | 3 | 2 | 2 | 10 | 0 | .143 | .250 | 5 | 1 | OF-7 |
| 1964 | 20 | 39 | 7 | 3 | 0 | 0 | 0.0 | 4 | 1 | 3 | 10 | 0 | .179 | .256 | 10 | 2 | OF-10 |
| 2 yrs. | 32 | 67 | 11 | 3 | 0 | 1 | 1.5 | 7 | 3 | 5 | 20 | 0 | .164 | .254 | 15 | 3 | OF-17 |
| 2 yrs. | 32 | 67 | 11 | 3 | 0 | 1 | 1.5 | 7 | 3 | 5 | 20 | 0 | .164 | .254 | 15 | 3 | OF-17 |

## Dave Owen

**OWEN, DAVE**
Brother of Spike Owen.
B. Apr. 25, 1958, Cleburne, Tex.

BB TR 6'1" 175 lbs.

| | G | AB | H | 2B | 3B | HR | HR % | R | RBI | BB | SO | SB | BA | SA | AB | H | G by POS |
|---|---|---|---|---|---|---|---|---|---|---|---|---|---|---|---|---|---|
| 1983 CHI N | 16 | 22 | 2 | 0 | 1 | 0 | 0.0 | 1 | 2 | 2 | 7 | 1 | .091 | .182 | 0 | 0 | SS-14, 3B-3 |
| 1984 | 47 | 93 | 18 | 2 | 2 | 1 | 1.1 | 8 | 10 | 8 | 15 | 1 | .194 | .290 | 3 | 2 | SS-35, 3B-6, 2B-4 |
| 1985 | 22 | 19 | 7 | 0 | 0 | 0 | 0.0 | 6 | 4 | 1 | 5 | 1 | .368 | .368 | 3 | 0 | SS-7, 3B-7, 2B-4 |
| 3 yrs. | 85 | 134 | 27 | 2 | 3 | 1 | 0.7 | 15 | 16 | 11 | 27 | 3 | .201 | .284 | 6 | 2 | SS-56, 3B-16, 2B-8 |
| 3 yrs. | 85 | 134 | 27 | 2 | 3 | 1 | 0.7 | 15 | 16 | 11 | 27 | 3 | .201 | .284 | 6 | 2 | SS-56, 3B-16, 2B-8 |

## Mickey Owen

**OWEN, ARNOLD MALCOLM**
B. Apr. 4, 1916, Nixa, Mo.

BR TR 5'10" 190 lbs.

| | G | AB | H | 2B | 3B | HR | HR % | R | RBI | BB | SO | SB | BA | SA | AB | H | G by POS |
|---|---|---|---|---|---|---|---|---|---|---|---|---|---|---|---|---|---|
| 1937 STL N | 80 | 234 | 54 | 4 | 2 | 0 | 0.0 | 17 | 20 | 15 | 13 | 1 | .231 | .265 | 2 | 0 | C-78 |
| 1938 | 122 | 397 | 106 | 25 | 2 | 4 | 1.0 | 45 | 36 | 32 | 14 | 2 | .267 | .370 | 5 | 1 | C-116 |
| 1939 | 131 | 344 | 89 | 18 | 2 | 3 | 0.9 | 32 | 35 | 43 | 28 | 6 | .259 | .349 | 5 | 0 | C-126 |
| 1940 | 117 | 307 | 81 | 16 | 2 | 0 | 0.0 | 27 | 27 | 34 | 13 | 4 | .264 | .329 | 4 | 2 | C-113 |
| 1941 BKN N | 128 | 386 | 89 | 15 | 2 | 1 | 0.3 | 32 | 44 | 34 | 14 | 1 | .231 | .288 | 0 | 0 | C-128 |
| 1942 | 133 | 421 | 109 | 16 | 3 | 0 | 0.0 | 53 | 44 | 44 | 17 | 10 | .259 | .311 | 0 | 0 | C-133 |
| 1943 | 106 | 365 | 95 | 11 | 2 | 0 | 0.0 | 31 | 54 | 25 | 15 | 4 | .260 | .301 | 5 | 1 | C-100, 3B-3, SS-1 |
| 1944 | 130 | 461 | 126 | 20 | 3 | 1 | 0.2 | 43 | 42 | 36 | 17 | 4 | .273 | .336 | 4 | 1 | C-125, 2B-1 |
| 1945 | 24 | 84 | 24 | 9 | 0 | 0 | 0.0 | 5 | 11 | 10 | 2 | 0 | .286 | .393 | 0 | 0 | C-24 |
| 1949 CHI N | 62 | 198 | 54 | 9 | 3 | 2 | 1.0 | 15 | 18 | 12 | 13 | 1 | .273 | .379 | 3 | 1 | C-59 |
| 1950 | 86 | 259 | 63 | 11 | 0 | 2 | 0.8 | 22 | 21 | 13 | 16 | 2 | .243 | .309 | 1 | 0 | C-86 |
| 1951 | 58 | 125 | 23 | 6 | 0 | 0 | 0.0 | 10 | 15 | 19 | 13 | 1 | .184 | .232 | 1 | 0 | C-57 |
| 1954 BOS A | 32 | 68 | 16 | 3 | 0 | 1 | 1.5 | 6 | 11 | 9 | 6 | 0 | .235 | .324 | 1 | 0 | C-30 |
| 13 yrs. | 1209 | 3649 | 929 | 163 | 21 | 14 | 0.4 | 338 | 378 | 326 | 181 | 36 | .255 | .322 | 31 | 7 | C-1175, 3B-3, SS-1, 2B-1 |
| 3 yrs. | 206 | 582 | 140 | 26 | 3 | 4 | 0.7 | 47 | 54 | 44 | 42 | 4 | .241 | .316 | 5 | 1 | C-202 |

WORLD SERIES

| | G | AB | H | 2B | 3B | HR | HR % | R | RBI | BB | SO | SB | BA | SA | AB | H | G by POS |
|---|---|---|---|---|---|---|---|---|---|---|---|---|---|---|---|---|---|
| 1941 BKN N | 5 | 12 | 2 | 1 | 0 | 0 | 0.0 | 1 | 2 | 3 | 0 | 0 | .167 | .333 | 0 | 0 | C-5 |

## Andy Pafko

**PAFKO, ANDREW (Pruschka, Handy Andy)**
B. Feb. 25, 1921, Boyceville, Wis.

BR TR 6' 190 lbs.

| | G | AB | H | 2B | 3B | HR | HR % | R | RBI | BB | SO | SB | BA | SA | AB | H | G by POS |
|---|---|---|---|---|---|---|---|---|---|---|---|---|---|---|---|---|---|
| 1943 CHI N | 13 | 58 | 22 | 3 | 0 | 0 | 0.0 | 7 | 10 | 2 | 5 | 1 | .379 | .431 | 0 | 0 | OF-13 |
| 1944 | 128 | 469 | 126 | 16 | 2 | 6 | 1.3 | 47 | 62 | 28 | 23 | 2 | .269 | .350 | 5 | 1 | OF-123 |
| 1945 | 144 | 534 | 159 | 24 | 12 | 12 | 2.2 | 64 | 110 | 45 | 36 | 5 | .298 | .455 | 4 | 1 | OF-140 |
| 1946 | 65 | 234 | 66 | 6 | 4 | 3 | 1.3 | 18 | 39 | 27 | 15 | 4 | .282 | .380 | 1 | 0 | OF-64 |
| 1947 | 129 | 513 | 155 | 25 | 7 | 13 | 2.5 | 68 | 66 | 31 | 39 | 4 | .302 | .454 | 2 | 0 | OF-127 |
| 1948 | 142 | 548 | 171 | 30 | 2 | 26 | 4.7 | 82 | 101 | 50 | 50 | 3 | .312 | .516 | 2 | 1 | 3B-139 |
| 1949 | 144 | 519 | 146 | 29 | 2 | 18 | 3.5 | 79 | 69 | 63 | 33 | 4 | .281 | .449 | 1 | 1 | OF-98, 3B-49 |
| 1950 | 146 | 514 | 156 | 24 | 8 | 36 | 7.0 | 95 | 92 | 69 | 32 | 4 | .304 | .591 | 2 | 0 | OF-144 |
| 1951 2 teams | CHI N (49G – .264) | | | | BKN N | (84G – .249) | | | | | | | | | | | |
| " total | 133 | 455 | 116 | 16 | 3 | 30 | 6.6 | 68 | 93 | 52 | 37 | 2 | .255 | .501 | 6 | 1 | OF-126 |
| 1952 BKN N | 150 | 551 | 158 | 17 | 5 | 19 | 3.4 | 76 | 85 | 64 | 48 | 4 | .287 | .439 | 4 | 1 | OF-139, 3B-13 |
| 1953 MIL N | 140 | 516 | 153 | 23 | 4 | 17 | 3.3 | 70 | 72 | 37 | 33 | 2 | .297 | .455 | 1 | 0 | OF-139 |
| 1954 | 138 | 510 | 146 | 22 | 4 | 14 | 2.7 | 61 | 69 | 37 | 36 | 1 | .286 | .427 | 0 | 0 | OF-138 |
| 1955 | 86 | 252 | 67 | 3 | 5 | 5 | 2.0 | 29 | 34 | 7 | 23 | 1 | .266 | .377 | 22 | 3 | OF-58, 3B-12 |
| 1956 | 45 | 93 | 24 | 5 | 0 | 2 | 2.2 | 15 | 9 | 10 | 13 | 0 | .258 | .376 | 12 | 3 | OF-37 |
| 1957 | 83 | 220 | 61 | 6 | 1 | 8 | 3.6 | 31 | 27 | 10 | 22 | 1 | .277 | .423 | 22 | 3 | OF-69 |
| 1958 | 95 | 164 | 39 | 7 | 1 | 3 | 1.8 | 17 | 23 | 15 | 17 | 0 | .238 | .348 | 13 | 3 | OF-93 |
| 1959 | 71 | 142 | 31 | 4 | 2 | 1 | 0.7 | 17 | 15 | 14 | 15 | 0 | .218 | .324 | 13 | 2 | OF-64 |
| 17 yrs. | 1852 | 6292 | 1796 | 264 | 62 | 213 | 3.4 | 844 | 976 | 561 | 477 | 38 | .285 | .449 | 110 | 20 | OF-1572, 3B-213 |
| 9 yrs. | 960 | 3567 | 1048 | 162 | 40 | 126 | 3.5 | 486 | 584 | 332 | 243 | 28 | .294 | .468 | 17 | 4 | OF-757, 3B-188 |
| | | | | | | | **8th** | | | | | | | | | | |

WORLD SERIES

| | G | AB | H | 2B | 3B | HR | HR % | R | RBI | BB | SO | SB | BA | SA | AB | H | G by POS |
|---|---|---|---|---|---|---|---|---|---|---|---|---|---|---|---|---|---|
| 1945 CHI N | 7 | 28 | 6 | 2 | 1 | 0 | 0.0 | 5 | 2 | 2 | 5 | 0 | .214 | .357 | 0 | 0 | OF-7 |
| 1952 BKN N | 7 | 21 | 4 | 0 | 0 | 0 | 0.0 | 0 | 2 | 0 | 4 | 0 | .190 | .190 | 2 | 0 | OF-5 |
| 1957 MIL N | 6 | 14 | 3 | 0 | 0 | 0 | 0.0 | 1 | 0 | 0 | 1 | 0 | .214 | .214 | 1 | 0 | OF-5 |
| 1958 | 4 | 9 | 3 | 1 | 0 | 0 | 0.0 | 0 | 1 | 0 | 0 | 0 | .333 | .444 | 0 | 0 | OF-4 |
| 4 yrs. | 24 | 72 | 16 | 3 | 1 | 0 | 0.0 | 6 | 5 | 2 | 10 | 0 | .222 | .292 | 3 | 0 | OF-21 |

## Karl Pagel

**PAGEL, KARL DOUGLAS**
B. Mar. 29, 1955, Madison, Wis.

BL TL 6'2" 188 lbs.

| | G | AB | H | 2B | 3B | HR | HR % | R | RBI | BB | SO | SB | BA | SA | AB | H | G by POS |
|---|---|---|---|---|---|---|---|---|---|---|---|---|---|---|---|---|---|
| 1978 CHI N | 2 | 2 | 0 | 0 | 0 | 0 | 0.0 | 0 | 0 | 0 | 2 | 0 | .000 | .000 | 2 | 0 | |
| 1979 | 1 | 1 | 0 | 0 | 0 | 0 | 0.0 | 0 | 0 | 0 | 1 | 0 | .000 | .000 | 1 | 0 | |
| 1981 CLE A | 14 | 15 | 4 | 0 | 2 | 1 | 6.7 | 3 | 4 | 4 | 1 | 0 | .267 | .733 | 5 | 1 | 1B-6, DH-1 |
| 1982 | 23 | 18 | 3 | 0 | 0 | 0 | 0.0 | 3 | 2 | 7 | 11 | 0 | .167 | .167 | 8 | 2 | 1B-10, DH-1 |
| 1983 | 8 | 20 | 6 | 0 | 0 | 0 | 0.0 | 1 | 1 | 0 | 5 | 0 | .300 | .300 | 3 | 1 | DH-5, OF-1 |
| 5 yrs. | 48 | 56 | 13 | 0 | 2 | 1 | 1.8 | 7 | 7 | 11 | 20 | 0 | .232 | .357 | 19 | 4 | 1B-16, DH-7, OF-1 |
| 2 yrs. | 3 | 3 | 0 | 0 | 0 | 0 | 0.0 | 0 | 0 | 0 | 3 | 0 | .000 | .000 | 3 | 0 | |

| | G | AB | H | 2B | 3B | HR | HR % | R | RBI | BB | SO | SB | BA | SA | Pinch Hit AB | Pinch Hit H | G by POS |
|---|---|---|---|---|---|---|---|---|---|---|---|---|---|---|---|---|---|

## Jiggs Parrott

**PARROTT, WALTER EDWARD**       5'11"   160 lbs.
Brother of Tom Parrott.
B. July 14, 1871, Portland, Ore.    D. Apr. 16, 1898, Phoenix, Ariz.

| | G | AB | H | 2B | 3B | HR | HR% | R | RBI | BB | SO | SB | BA | SA | PH AB | PH H | G by POS |
|---|---|---|---|---|---|---|---|---|---|---|---|---|---|---|---|---|---|
| 1892 CHI N | 78 | 335 | 72 | 9 | 5 | 2 | 0.6 | 40 | 22 | 8 | 30 | 7 | .215 | .290 | 0 | 0 | 3B-78 |
| 1893 | 110 | 455 | 111 | 10 | 9 | 1 | 0.2 | 54 | 65 | 13 | 25 | 25 | .244 | .312 | 0 | 0 | 3B-99, 2B-7, OF-4 |
| 1894 | 127 | 532 | 139 | 17 | 9 | 3 | 0.6 | 83 | 64 | 16 | 35 | 30 | .261 | .344 | 0 | 0 | 2B-123, 3B-1 |
| 1895 | 3 | 4 | 1 | 0 | 0 | 0 | 0.0 | 0 | 0 | 0 | 0 | 0 | .250 | .250 | 0 | 0 | OF-1, SS-1, 1B-1 |
| 4 yrs. | 318 | 1326 | 323 | 36 | 23 | 6 | 0.5 | 177 | 151 | 37 | 90 | 62 | .244 | .319 | 0 | 0 | 3B-178, 2B-130, OF-5, SS-1, 1B-1 |
| 4 yrs. | 318 | 1326 | 323 | 36 | 23 | 6 | 0.5 | 177 | 151 | 37 | 90 | 62 | .244 | .319 | 0 | 0 | 3B-178, 2B-130, OF-5, SS-1, 1B-1 |

## Tom Parrott

**PARROTT, THOMAS WILLIAM (Tacky Tom)**      BR TR 6'2"   170 lbs.
Brother of Jiggs Parrott.
B. Apr. 10, 1868, Portland, Ore.    D. Jan. 1, 1932, Dundee, Ore.

| | G | AB | H | 2B | 3B | HR | HR% | R | RBI | BB | SO | SB | BA | SA | PH AB | PH H | G by POS |
|---|---|---|---|---|---|---|---|---|---|---|---|---|---|---|---|---|---|
| 1893 2 teams | CHI | N (7G – | .259) | | CIN | N | (24G – | .191) | | | | | | | | | |
| " total | 31 | 95 | 20 | 2 | 1 | 1 | 1.1 | 9 | 12 | 2 | 11 | 0 | .211 | .284 | 1 | 0 | P-26, 3B-2, OF-1, 2B-1 |
| 1894 CIN N | 68 | 229 | 74 | 12 | 6 | 4 | 1.7 | 51 | 40 | 17 | 10 | 4 | .323 | .480 | 3 | 2 | P-41, OF-13, 1B-12, SS-1, 3B-1, 2B-1 |
| 1895 | 64 | 201 | 69 | 13 | 7 | 3 | 1.5 | 35 | 41 | 11 | 8 | 10 | .343 | .522 | 0 | 0 | P-41, 1B-14, OF-9 |
| 1896 STL N | 118 | 474 | 138 | 13 | 12 | 7 | 1.5 | 62 | 70 | 11 | 24 | 12 | .291 | .414 | 0 | 0 | OF-108, P-7, 1B-6 |
| 4 yrs. | 281 | 999 | 301 | 40 | 26 | 15 | 1.5 | 157 | 163 | 41 | 53 | 26 | .301 | .438 | 4 | 2 | OF-131, P-115, 1B-32, 3B-3, 2B-2, SS-1 |
| 1 yr. | 7 | 27 | 7 | 1 | 0 | 0 | 0.0 | 4 | 3 | 1 | 2 | 0 | .259 | .296 | 0 | 0 | P-4, 3B-2, 2B-1 |

## Dode Paskert

**PASKERT, GEORGE HENRY**      BR TR 5'11"   165 lbs.
B. Aug. 28, 1881, Cleveland, Ohio    D. Feb. 12, 1959, Cleveland, Ohio

| | G | AB | H | 2B | 3B | HR | HR% | R | RBI | BB | SO | SB | BA | SA | PH AB | PH H | G by POS |
|---|---|---|---|---|---|---|---|---|---|---|---|---|---|---|---|---|---|
| 1907 CIN N | 16 | 50 | 14 | 4 | 0 | 1 | 2.0 | 10 | 8 | 2 | | 2 | .280 | .420 | 0 | 0 | OF-16 |
| 1908 | 118 | 395 | 96 | 14 | 4 | 1 | 0.3 | 40 | 36 | 27 | | 25 | .243 | .306 | 3 | 1 | OF-116 |
| 1909 | 104 | 322 | 81 | 7 | 4 | 0 | 0.0 | 49 | 33 | 34 | | 23 | .252 | .298 | 16 | 3 | OF-82, 1B-6 |
| 1910 | 144 | 506 | 152 | 21 | 5 | 2 | 0.4 | 63 | 46 | 70 | 60 | 51 | .300 | .374 | 2 | 0 | OF-139, 1B-2 |
| 1911 PHI N | 153 | 560 | 153 | 18 | 5 | 4 | 0.7 | 96 | 47 | 70 | 70 | 28 | .273 | .345 | 0 | 0 | OF-153 |
| 1912 | 145 | 540 | 170 | 37 | 5 | 2 | 0.4 | 102 | 43 | 91 | 67 | 36 | .315 | .413 | 0 | 0 | OF-141, 2B-2, 3B-1 |
| 1913 | 124 | 454 | 119 | 21 | 9 | 4 | 0.9 | 83 | 29 | 65 | 69 | 12 | .262 | .374 | 4 | 0 | OF-120 |
| 1914 | 132 | 451 | 119 | 25 | 6 | 3 | 0.7 | 59 | 44 | 56 | 68 | 23 | .264 | .366 | 3 | 0 | OF-128, SS-4 |
| 1915 | 109 | 328 | 80 | 17 | 4 | 3 | 0.9 | 51 | 39 | 35 | 38 | 9 | .244 | .348 | 10 | 3 | OF-104, 1B-5 |
| 1916 | 149 | 555 | 155 | 30 | 7 | 8 | 1.4 | 82 | 46 | 54 | 76 | 22 | .279 | .402 | 2 | 1 | OF-146, SS-1 |
| 1917 | 141 | 546 | 137 | 27 | 11 | 4 | 0.7 | 78 | 43 | 62 | 63 | 19 | .251 | .363 | 1 | 1 | OF-138 |
| 1918 CHI N | 127 | 461 | 132 | 24 | 3 | 3 | 0.7 | 69 | 59 | 53 | 49 | 20 | .286 | .371 | 0 | 0 | OF-121, 3B-6 |
| 1919 | 87 | 270 | 53 | 11 | 3 | 2 | 0.7 | 21 | 29 | 28 | 33 | 7 | .196 | .281 | 8 | 1 | OF-80 |
| 1920 | 139 | 487 | 136 | 22 | 10 | 5 | 1.0 | 57 | 71 | 64 | 58 | 16 | .279 | .396 | 1 | 0 | OF-137 |
| 1921 CIN N | 27 | 92 | 16 | 1 | 1 | 0 | 0.0 | 8 | 4 | 4 | 8 | 0 | .174 | .207 | 1 | 0 | OF-24 |
| 15 yrs. | 1715 | 6017 | 1613 | 279 | 77 | 42 | 0.7 | 868 | 577 | 715 | 659 | 293 | .268 | .361 | 51 | 10 | OF-1645, 1B-13, 3B-7, SS-5, 2B-2 |
| 3 yrs. | 353 | 1218 | 321 | 57 | 16 | 10 | 0.8 | 147 | 159 | 145 | 140 | 43 | .264 | .361 | 9 | 1 | OF-338, 3B-6 |

**WORLD SERIES**

| | G | AB | H | 2B | 3B | HR | HR% | R | RBI | BB | SO | SB | BA | SA | PH AB | PH H | G by POS |
|---|---|---|---|---|---|---|---|---|---|---|---|---|---|---|---|---|---|
| 1915 PHI N | 5 | 19 | 3 | 0 | 0 | 0 | 0.0 | 2 | 0 | 1 | 2 | 0 | .158 | .158 | 0 | 0 | OF-5 |
| 1918 CHI N | 6 | 21 | 4 | 1 | 0 | 0 | 0.0 | 0 | 2 | 2 | 2 | 0 | .190 | .238 | 0 | 0 | OF-6 |
| 2 yrs. | 11 | 40 | 7 | 1 | 0 | 0 | 0.0 | 2 | 2 | 3 | 4 | 0 | .175 | .200 | 0 | 0 | OF-11 |

## Ted Pawelek

**PAWELEK, THEODORE JOHN (Porky)**      BL TR 5'10½" 202 lbs.
B. Aug. 15, 1919, Chicago Heights, Ill.    D. Feb. 12, 1964, Chicago Heights, Ill.

| | G | AB | H | 2B | 3B | HR | HR% | R | RBI | BB | SO | SB | BA | SA | PH AB | PH H | G by POS |
|---|---|---|---|---|---|---|---|---|---|---|---|---|---|---|---|---|---|
| 1946 CHI N | 4 | 4 | 1 | 1 | 0 | 0 | 0.0 | 0 | 0 | 0 | 0 | 0 | .250 | .500 | 3 | 1 | C-1 |

## Charlie Pechous

**PECHOUS, CHARLES EDWARD**      BR TR 6'   170 lbs.
B. Oct. 5, 1896, Chicago, Ill.    D. Sept. 13, 1980, Kenosha, Wis.

| | G | AB | H | 2B | 3B | HR | HR% | R | RBI | BB | SO | SB | BA | SA | PH AB | PH H | G by POS |
|---|---|---|---|---|---|---|---|---|---|---|---|---|---|---|---|---|---|
| 1915 CHI F | 18 | 51 | 9 | 3 | 0 | 0 | 0.0 | 4 | 4 | 4 | | 1 | .176 | .235 | 0 | 0 | 3B-18 |
| 1916 CHI N | 22 | 69 | 10 | 1 | 1 | 0 | 0.0 | 5 | 4 | 3 | 21 | 1 | .145 | .188 | 0 | 0 | 3B-22 |
| 1917 | 13 | 41 | 10 | 0 | 0 | 0 | 0.0 | 2 | 1 | 2 | 9 | 1 | .244 | .244 | 0 | 0 | 3B-7, SS-5 |
| 3 yrs. | 53 | 161 | 29 | 4 | 1 | 0 | 0.0 | 11 | 9 | 9 | 30 | 3 | .180 | .217 | 0 | 0 | 3B-47, SS-5 |
| 2 yrs. | 35 | 110 | 20 | 1 | 1 | 0 | 0.0 | 7 | 5 | 5 | 30 | 2 | .182 | .209 | 0 | 0 | 3B-29, SS-5 |

## Chick Pedroes

**PEDROES, CHARLES P.**      
B. Oct. 27, 1869, Chicago, Ill.    D. Aug. 6, 1927, Chicago, Ill.

| | G | AB | H | 2B | 3B | HR | HR% | R | RBI | BB | SO | SB | BA | SA | PH AB | PH H | G by POS |
|---|---|---|---|---|---|---|---|---|---|---|---|---|---|---|---|---|---|
| 1902 CHI N | 2 | 6 | 0 | 0 | 0 | 0 | 0.0 | 0 | 0 | 0 | | 0 | .000 | .000 | 0 | 0 | OF-2 |

## Roberto Pena

**PENA, RAMIREZ ROBERTO**      BR TR 5'8"   175 lbs.
B. Apr. 17, 1940, Santo Domingo, Dominican Republic

| | G | AB | H | 2B | 3B | HR | HR% | R | RBI | BB | SO | SB | BA | SA | PH AB | PH H | G by POS |
|---|---|---|---|---|---|---|---|---|---|---|---|---|---|---|---|---|---|
| 1965 CHI N | 51 | 170 | 37 | 5 | 1 | 2 | 1.2 | 17 | 12 | 16 | 19 | 1 | .218 | .294 | 1 | 0 | SS-50 |
| 1966 | 6 | 17 | 3 | 2 | 0 | 0 | 0.0 | 0 | 1 | 0 | 4 | 0 | .176 | .294 | 2 | 0 | SS-5 |
| 1968 PHI N | 138 | 500 | 130 | 13 | 2 | 1 | 0.2 | 56 | 38 | 34 | 63 | 3 | .260 | .300 | 1 | 1 | SS-133 |
| 1969 SD N | 139 | 472 | 118 | 16 | 3 | 4 | 0.8 | 44 | 30 | 21 | 63 | 0 | .250 | .322 | 18 | 5 | SS-65, 2B-33, 3B-27, 1B-12 |
| 1970 2 teams | OAK | A | (19G – | .259) | | MIL | A | (121G – | .238) | | | | | | | | |
| " total | 140 | 474 | 114 | 20 | 1 | 3 | 0.6 | 40 | 45 | 28 | 49 | 4 | .241 | .306 | 11 | 5 | SS-111, 2B-15, 1B-7, 3B-5 |
| 1971 MIL A | 113 | 274 | 65 | 9 | 3 | 3 | 1.1 | 17 | 28 | 15 | 37 | 2 | .237 | .325 | 29 | 5 | 1B-50, 3B-37, SS-23, 2B-1 |
| 6 yrs. | 587 | 1907 | 467 | 65 | 10 | 13 | 0.7 | 174 | 154 | 114 | 235 | 10 | .245 | .310 | 62 | 13 | SS-387, 3B-69, 1B-69, 2B-49 |
| 2 yrs. | 57 | 187 | 40 | 7 | 1 | 2 | 1.1 | 17 | 13 | 16 | 23 | 1 | .214 | .294 | 3 | 0 | SS-55 |

| | G | AB | H | 2B | 3B | HR | HR % | R | RBI | BB | SO | SB | BA | SA | Pinch Hit AB | H | G by POS |
|---|---|---|---|---|---|---|---|---|---|---|---|---|---|---|---|---|---|

## Joe Pepitone

**PEPITONE, JOSEPH ANTHONY (Pepi)**
B. Oct. 9, 1940, Brooklyn, N. Y.                    BL TL 6'2"    185 lbs.

| | G | AB | H | 2B | 3B | HR | HR % | R | RBI | BB | SO | SB | BA | SA | AB | H | G by POS |
|---|---|---|---|---|---|---|---|---|---|---|---|---|---|---|---|---|---|
| 1962 NY A | 63 | 138 | 33 | 3 | 2 | 7 | 5.1 | 14 | 17 | 3 | 21 | 1 | .239 | .442 | 19 | 5 | OF-32, 1B-16 |
| 1963 | 157 | 580 | 157 | 16 | 3 | 27 | 4.7 | 79 | 89 | 23 | 63 | 3 | .271 | .448 | 9 | 1 | 1B-143, OF-16 |
| 1964 | 160 | 613 | 154 | 12 | 3 | 28 | 4.6 | 71 | 100 | 24 | 63 | 2 | .251 | .418 | 3 | 1 | 1B-155, OF-30 |
| 1965 | 143 | 531 | 131 | 18 | 3 | 18 | 3.4 | 51 | 62 | 43 | 59 | 4 | .247 | .394 | 2 | 0 | 1B-115, OF-41 |
| 1966 | 152 | 585 | 149 | 21 | 4 | 31 | 5.3 | 85 | 83 | 29 | 58 | 4 | .255 | .463 | 1 | 0 | 1B-119, OF-55 |
| 1967 | 133 | 501 | 126 | 18 | 3 | 13 | 2.6 | 45 | 64 | 34 | 62 | 1 | .251 | .377 | 4 | 1 | OF-123, 1B-6 |
| 1968 | 108 | 380 | 93 | 9 | 3 | 15 | 3.9 | 41 | 56 | 37 | 45 | 8 | .245 | .403 | 4 | 0 | OF-92, 1B-12 |
| 1969 | 135 | 513 | 124 | 16 | 3 | 27 | 5.3 | 49 | 70 | 30 | 42 | 8 | .242 | .442 | 4 | 2 | 1B-132 |
| 1970 2 teams | | HOU N | (75G – | .251) | | CHI N | (56G – | .268) | | | | | | | | | |
| " total | 131 | 492 | 127 | 18 | 7 | 26 | 5.3 | 82 | 79 | 33 | 43 | 5 | .258 | .482 | 2 | 0 | OF-84, 1B-63 |
| 1971 CHI N | 115 | 427 | 131 | 19 | 4 | 16 | 3.7 | 50 | 61 | 24 | 41 | 1 | .307 | .482 | 2 | 1 | 1B-95, OF-23 |
| 1972 | 66 | 214 | 56 | 5 | 0 | 8 | 3.7 | 23 | 21 | 13 | 22 | 1 | .262 | .397 | 5 | 1 | 1B-66 |
| 1973 2 teams | | CHI N | (31G – | .268) | | ATL N | (3G – | .364) | | | | | | | | | |
| " total | 34 | 123 | 34 | 3 | 0 | 3 | 2.4 | 16 | 19 | 9 | 7 | 3 | .276 | .374 | 3 | 1 | 1B-31 |
| 12 yrs. | 1397 | 5097 | 1315 | 158 | 35 | 219 | 4.3 | 606 | 721 | 302 | 526 | 41 | .258 | .432 | 58 | 13 | 1B-953, OF-496 |
| 4 yrs. | 268 | 966 | 274 | 36 | 6 | 39 | 4.0 | 127 | 144 | 60 | 84 | 5 | .284 | .454 | 10 | 3 | 1B-202, OF-79 |
| **WORLD SERIES** | | | | | | | | | | | | | | | | | |
| 1963 NY A | 4 | 13 | 2 | 0 | 0 | 0 | 0.0 | 0 | 0 | 1 | 3 | 0 | .154 | .154 | 0 | 0 | 1B-4 |
| 1964 | 7 | 26 | 4 | 1 | 0 | 1 | 3.8 | 1 | 5 | 2 | 3 | 0 | .154 | .308 | 0 | 0 | 1B-7 |
| 2 yrs. | 11 | 39 | 6 | 1 | 0 | 1 | 2.6 | 1 | 5 | 3 | 6 | 0 | .154 | .256 | 0 | 0 | 1B-11 |

## Johnny Peters

**PETERS, JOHN PAUL**
B. Apr. 8, 1850, Louisiana, Mo.      D. Jan. 4, 1924, St. Louis, Mo.                    BR TR    180 lbs.

| | G | AB | H | 2B | 3B | HR | HR % | R | RBI | BB | SO | SB | BA | SA | AB | H | G by POS |
|---|---|---|---|---|---|---|---|---|---|---|---|---|---|---|---|---|---|
| 1876 CHI N | 66 | 316 | 111 | 14 | 2 | 1 | 0.3 | 70 | 47 | 3 | 2 | | .351 | .418 | 0 | 0 | SS-66, P-1 |
| 1877 | 60 | 265 | 84 | 10 | 3 | 0 | 0.0 | 45 | 41 | 1 | 7 | | .317 | .377 | 0 | 0 | SS-60 |
| 1878 MIL N | 55 | 246 | 76 | 6 | 1 | 0 | 0.0 | 33 | 22 | 5 | 8 | | .309 | .341 | 0 | 0 | 2B-34, SS-22 |
| 1879 CHI N | 83 | 379 | 93 | 13 | 2 | 1 | 0.3 | 45 | 31 | 1 | 19 | | .245 | .298 | 0 | 0 | SS-83 |
| 1880 PRO N | 86 | 359 | 82 | 5 | 0 | 0 | 0.0 | 30 | 24 | 5 | 15 | | .228 | .242 | 0 | 0 | SS-86 |
| 1881 BUF N | 54 | 229 | 49 | 8 | 1 | 0 | 0.0 | 21 | 25 | 3 | 12 | | .214 | .258 | 0 | 0 | SS-53, OF-1 |
| 1882 PIT AA | 78 | 333 | 96 | 10 | 1 | 0 | 0.0 | 46 | | 4 | | | .288 | .324 | 0 | 0 | SS-77, 2B-1 |
| 1883 | 8 | 28 | 3 | 0 | 0 | 0 | 0.0 | 3 | | 0 | | | .107 | .107 | 0 | 0 | SS-8 |
| 1884 | 1 | 4 | 0 | 0 | 0 | 0 | 0.0 | 0 | | 0 | | | .000 | .000 | 0 | 0 | SS-1 |
| 9 yrs. | 491 | 2159 | 594 | 66 | 10 | 2 | 0.1 | 293 | 190 | 22 | 63 | | .275 | .318 | 0 | 0 | SS-456, 2B-35, OF-1, P-1 |
| 3 yrs. | 209 | 960 | 288 | 37 | 7 | 2 | 0.2 | 160 | 119 | 5 | 28 | | .300 | .359 | 0 | 0 | SS-209, P-1 |

## Bob Pettit

**PETTIT, ROBERT HENRY**
B. July 19, 1861, Williamstown, Mass.      D. Nov. 1, 1910, Derby, Conn.                    BL    5'9"    160 lbs.

| | G | AB | H | 2B | 3B | HR | HR % | R | RBI | BB | SO | SB | BA | SA | AB | H | G by POS |
|---|---|---|---|---|---|---|---|---|---|---|---|---|---|---|---|---|---|
| 1887 CHI N | 32 | 138 | 36 | 3 | 3 | 2 | 1.4 | 29 | 12 | 8 | 15 | 16 | .261 | .370 | 0 | 0 | OF-32, C-1, P-1 |
| 1888 | 43 | 169 | 43 | 1 | 4 | 4 | 2.4 | 23 | 23 | 7 | 9 | 7 | .254 | .379 | 0 | 0 | OF-43 |
| 1891 C-M AA | 21 | 80 | 14 | 4 | 0 | 1 | 1.3 | 10 | 5 | 7 | 7 | 2 | .175 | .263 | 0 | 0 | 2B-9, OF-7, 3B-6 |
| 3 yrs. | 96 | 387 | 93 | 8 | 7 | 7 | 1.8 | 62 | 40 | 22 | 31 | 25 | .240 | .351 | 0 | 0 | OF-82, 2B-9, 3B-6, C-1, P-1 |
| 2 yrs. | 75 | 307 | 79 | 4 | 7 | 6 | 2.0 | 52 | 35 | 15 | 24 | 23 | .257 | .375 | 0 | 0 | OF-75, C-1, P-1 |

## Big Jeff Pfeffer

**PFEFFER, FRANCIS XAVIER**
Brother of Jeff Pfeffer.
B. Mar. 31, 1882, Champaign, Ill.      D. Dec. 19, 1954, Kankakee, Ill.                    BR TR

| | G | AB | H | 2B | 3B | HR | HR % | R | RBI | BB | SO | SB | BA | SA | AB | H | G by POS |
|---|---|---|---|---|---|---|---|---|---|---|---|---|---|---|---|---|---|
| 1905 CHI N | 15 | 40 | 8 | 3 | 0 | 0 | 0.0 | 4 | 3 | 0 | | 2 | .200 | .275 | 0 | 0 | P-15 |
| 1906 BOS N | 60 | 158 | 31 | 3 | 3 | 1 | 0.6 | 10 | 11 | 5 | | 2 | .196 | .272 | 8 | 0 | P-35, OF-14 |
| 1907 | 21 | 60 | 15 | 3 | 0 | 0 | 0.0 | 1 | 6 | 2 | | 0 | .250 | .300 | 2 | 0 | P-19 |
| 1908 | 4 | 2 | 0 | 0 | 0 | 0 | 0.0 | 0 | 0 | 0 | | 0 | .000 | .000 | 0 | 0 | P-4 |
| 1910 CHI N | 14 | 17 | 3 | 1 | 1 | 0 | 0.0 | 1 | 2 | 1 | 1 | 0 | .176 | .353 | 0 | 0 | P-13, OF-1 |
| 1911 BOS N | 33 | 46 | 9 | 2 | 0 | 1 | 2.2 | 4 | 6 | 5 | 7 | 0 | .196 | .304 | 3 | 0 | P-26, OF-3, 1B-1 |
| 6 yrs. | 147 | 323 | 66 | 12 | 4 | 2 | 0.6 | 20 | 28 | 13 | 8 | 4 | .204 | .285 | 13 | 0 | P-112, OF-18, 1B-1 |
| 2 yrs. | 29 | 57 | 11 | 4 | 1 | 0 | 0.0 | 5 | 5 | 1 | 1 | 2 | .193 | .298 | 0 | 0 | P-28, OF-1 |

## Fred Pfeffer

**PFEFFER, NATHANIEL FREDERICK (Dandelion Fritz)**      BR TR  5'10½" 184 lbs.
B. Mar. 17, 1860, Louisville, Ky.      D. Apr. 10, 1932, Chicago, Ill.
Manager 1892.

| | G | AB | H | 2B | 3B | HR | HR % | R | RBI | BB | SO | SB | BA | SA | AB | H | G by POS |
|---|---|---|---|---|---|---|---|---|---|---|---|---|---|---|---|---|---|
| 1882 TRO N | 85 | 330 | 72 | 7 | 4 | 1 | 0.3 | 26 | 31 | 1 | 24 | | .218 | .273 | 0 | 0 | SS-83, 2B-2 |
| 1883 CHI N | 96 | 371 | 87 | 22 | 7 | 1 | 0.3 | 41 | | 8 | 50 | | .235 | .340 | 0 | 0 | 2B-79, SS-18, 3B-1, 1B-1 |
| 1884 | 112 | 467 | 135 | 10 | 10 | 25 | 5.4 | 105 | | 25 | 47 | | .289 | .514 | 0 | 0 | 2B-112 |
| 1885 | 112 | 469 | 113 | 12 | 6 | 6 | 1.3 | 90 | 71 | 26 | 47 | | .241 | .330 | 0 | 0 | 2B-109, P-5, OF-1 |
| 1886 | 118 | 474 | 125 | 17 | 8 | 7 | 1.5 | 88 | 95 | 36 | 46 | | .264 | .378 | 0 | 0 | 2B-118, 1B-1 |
| 1887 | 123 | 479 | 133 | 21 | 6 | 16 | 3.3 | 95 | 89 | 34 | 20 | 51 | .278 | .447 | 0 | 0 | 2B-123, OF-2 |
| 1888 | 135 | 517 | 129 | 22 | 10 | 8 | 1.5 | 90 | 57 | 32 | 38 | 64 | .250 | .377 | 0 | 0 | 2B-135 |
| 1889 | 134 | 531 | 121 | 15 | 7 | 7 | 1.3 | 85 | 77 | 53 | 51 | 45 | .228 | .322 | 0 | 0 | 2B-134 |
| 1890 CHI P | 124 | 499 | 128 | 21 | 8 | 5 | 1.0 | 86 | 80 | 44 | 23 | 27 | .257 | .361 | 0 | 0 | 2B-124 |
| 1891 CHI N | 137 | 498 | 123 | 12 | 9 | 7 | 1.4 | 93 | 77 | 79 | 60 | 40 | .247 | .349 | 0 | 0 | 2B-137 |
| 1892 LOU N | 124 | 470 | 121 | 14 | 9 | 2 | 0.4 | 78 | 76 | 67 | 36 | 27 | .257 | .338 | 0 | 0 | 2B-116, 1B-10, OF-1, P-1 |
| 1893 | 125 | 508 | 129 | 29 | 12 | 3 | 0.6 | 85 | 75 | 51 | 18 | 32 | .254 | .376 | 0 | 0 | 2B-125 |
| 1894 | 104 | 409 | 126 | 12 | 14 | 5 | 1.2 | 68 | 59 | 30 | 14 | 31 | .308 | .443 | 0 | 0 | 2B-90, SS-15, P-1 |
| 1895 | 11 | 45 | 13 | 1 | 0 | 0 | 0.0 | 8 | 5 | 5 | 3 | 2 | .289 | .311 | 0 | 0 | SS-5, 2B-3, 1B-3 |
| 1896 2 teams | | NY | N | (4G – | .143) | | CHI | N | (94G – | .244) | | | | | | | |
| " total | 98 | 374 | 90 | 16 | 7 | 2 | 0.5 | 46 | 56 | 24 | 21 | 22 | .241 | .337 | 0 | 0 | 2B-98 |
| 1897 CHI N | 32 | 114 | 26 | 0 | 1 | 0 | 0.0 | 10 | 11 | 12 | | 5 | .228 | .246 | 0 | 0 | 2B-32 |
| 16 yrs. | 1670 | 6555 | 1671 | 231 | 118 | 95 | 1.4 | 1094 | 859 | 527 | 498 | 352 | .255 | .370 | 0 | 0 | 2B-1537, SS-121, 1B-15, P-7, OF-4, 3B-1 |
| 10 yrs. | 1093 | 4280 | 1080 | 147 | 71 | 79 | 1.8 | 742 | 529 | 328 | 379 | 233 | .252 | .375 | 0 | 0 | 2B-1073, SS-18, P-5, OF-3, 1B-2, 3B-1 |

| | G | AB | H | 2B | 3B | HR | HR % | R | RBI | BB | SO | SB | BA | SA | Pinch Hit AB | Pinch Hit H | G by POS |
|---|---|---|---|---|---|---|---|---|---|---|---|---|---|---|---|---|---|

## Art Phelan

**PHELAN, ARTHUR THOMAS (Dugan)**
B. Aug. 14, 1887, Niantic, Ill.   D. Dec. 27, 1964, Fort Worth, Tex.                BR  TR  5'8"    160 lbs.

| | G | AB | H | 2B | 3B | HR | HR % | R | RBI | BB | SO | SB | BA | SA | Pinch Hit AB | Pinch Hit H | G by POS |
|---|---|---|---|---|---|---|---|---|---|---|---|---|---|---|---|---|---|
| 1910 CIN N | 23 | 42 | 9 | 0 | 0 | 0 | 0.0 | 7 | 4 | 7 | 6 | 5 | .214 | .214 | 2 | 0 | 3B-8, 2B-5, OF-3, SS-1 |
| 1912 | 130 | 461 | 112 | 9 | 11 | 3 | 0.7 | 56 | 54 | 46 | 37 | 25 | .243 | .330 | 0 | 0 | 3B-127, 2B-3 |
| 1913 CHI N | 90 | 259 | 65 | 11 | 6 | 2 | 0.8 | 41 | 35 | 29 | 25 | 8 | .251 | .363 | 7 | 3 | 2B-46, 3B-38, SS-1 |
| 1914 | 25 | 46 | 13 | 2 | 1 | 0 | 0.0 | 5 | 3 | 4 | 3 | 0 | .283 | .370 | 13 | 6 | 3B-7, 2B-3, SS-2 |
| 1915 | 133 | 448 | 98 | 16 | 7 | 3 | 0.7 | 41 | 35 | 55 | 42 | 12 | .219 | .306 | 0 | 0 | 3B-110, 2B-24 |
| 5 yrs. | 401 | 1256 | 297 | 38 | 25 | 8 | 0.6 | 150 | 131 | 141 | 113 | 50 | .236 | .326 | 22 | 9 | 3B-290, 2B-81, SS-4, OF-3 |
| 3 yrs. | 248 | 753 | 176 | 29 | 14 | 5 | 0.7 | 87 | 73 | 88 | 70 | 20 | .234 | .329 | 20 | 9 | 3B-155, 2B-73, SS-3 |

## Babe Phelps

**PHELPS, ERNEST GORDON (Blimp)**
B. Apr. 19, 1908, Odenton, Md.                                                      BL  TR  6'2"    225 lbs.

| | G | AB | H | 2B | 3B | HR | HR % | R | RBI | BB | SO | SB | BA | SA | Pinch Hit AB | Pinch Hit H | G by POS |
|---|---|---|---|---|---|---|---|---|---|---|---|---|---|---|---|---|---|
| 1931 WAS A | 3 | 3 | 1 | 0 | 0 | 0 | 0.0 | 0 | 0 | 0 | 0 | 0 | .333 | .333 | 3 | 1 | |
| 1933 CHI N | 3 | 7 | 2 | 0 | 0 | 0 | 0.0 | 0 | 2 | 0 | 1 | 0 | .286 | .286 | 1 | 0 | C-2 |
| 1934 | 44 | 70 | 20 | 5 | 2 | 2 | 2.9 | 7 | 12 | 1 | 8 | 0 | .286 | .500 | 26 | 9 | C-18 |
| 1935 BKN N | 47 | 121 | 44 | 7 | 2 | 5 | 4.1 | 17 | 22 | 9 | 10 | 0 | .364 | .579 | 12 | 6 | C-34 |
| 1936 | 115 | 319 | 117 | 23 | 2 | 5 | 1.6 | 36 | 57 | 27 | 18 | 1 | .367 | .498 | 15 | 5 | C-98, OF-1 |
| 1937 | 121 | 409 | 128 | 37 | 3 | 7 | 1.7 | 42 | 58 | 25 | 28 | 2 | .313 | .469 | 8 | 1 | C-111 |
| 1938 | 66 | 208 | 64 | 12 | 2 | 5 | 2.4 | 33 | 46 | 23 | 15 | 2 | .308 | .457 | 9 | 1 | C-55 |
| 1939 | 98 | 323 | 92 | 21 | 2 | 6 | 1.9 | 33 | 42 | 24 | 24 | 0 | .285 | .418 | 6 | 1 | C-92 |
| 1940 | 118 | 370 | 109 | 24 | 5 | 13 | 3.5 | 47 | 61 | 30 | 27 | 2 | .295 | .492 | 16 | 2 | C-99, 1B-1 |
| 1941 | 16 | 30 | 7 | 3 | 0 | 2 | 6.7 | 3 | 4 | 1 | 2 | 0 | .233 | .533 | 5 | 1 | C-11 |
| 1942 PIT N | 95 | 257 | 73 | 11 | 1 | 9 | 3.5 | 21 | 41 | 20 | 21 | 2 | .284 | .440 | 22 | 7 | C-72 |
| 11 yrs. | 726 | 2117 | 657 | 143 | 19 | 54 | 2.6 | 239 | 345 | 160 | 154 | 9 | .310 | .472 | 123 | 34 | C-592, OF-1, 1B-1 |
| 2 yrs. | 47 | 77 | 22 | 5 | 2 | 2 | 2.6 | 7 | 14 | 1 | 9 | 0 | .286 | .481 | 27 | 9 | C-20 |

## Adolfo Phillips

**PHILLIPS, ADOLFO EMILIO**
B. Dec. 16, 1941, Bethania, Panama                                                  BR  TR  6'1"    175 lbs.

| | G | AB | H | 2B | 3B | HR | HR % | R | RBI | BB | SO | SB | BA | SA | Pinch Hit AB | Pinch Hit H | G by POS |
|---|---|---|---|---|---|---|---|---|---|---|---|---|---|---|---|---|---|
| 1964 PHI N | 13 | 13 | 3 | 0 | 0 | 0 | 0.0 | 4 | 0 | 3 | 3 | 0 | .231 | .231 | 6 | 2 | OF-4 |
| 1965 | 41 | 87 | 20 | 4 | 0 | 3 | 3.4 | 5 | 5 | 5 | 34 | 3 | .230 | .379 | 6 | 1 | OF-32 |
| 1966 2 teams | | | | PHI | N | (2G – | .000) | | CHI | N | (116G – | .262) | | | | | |
| " total | 118 | 419 | 109 | 29 | 1 | 16 | 3.8 | 69 | 36 | 43 | 135 | 32 | .260 | .449 | 4 | 0 | OF-112 |
| 1967 CHI N | 144 | 448 | 120 | 20 | 7 | 17 | 3.8 | 66 | 70 | 80 | 93 | 24 | .268 | .458 | 2 | 1 | OF-141 |
| 1968 | 143 | 439 | 106 | 20 | 5 | 13 | 3.0 | 49 | 33 | 47 | 90 | 9 | .241 | .399 | 2 | 0 | OF-141 |
| 1969 2 teams | | | | CHI | N | (28G – | .224) | | MON | N | (58G – | .216) | | | | | |
| " total | 86 | 248 | 54 | 7 | 5 | 4 | 1.6 | 30 | 8 | 35 | 77 | 7 | .218 | .335 | 4 | 0 | OF-78 |
| 1970 MON N | 92 | 214 | 51 | 6 | 3 | 6 | 2.8 | 36 | 21 | 36 | 51 | 7 | .238 | .379 | 18 | 3 | OF-75 |
| 1972 CLE A | 12 | 7 | 0 | 0 | 0 | 0 | 0.0 | 2 | 0 | 2 | 2 | 0 | .000 | .000 | 3 | 0 | OF-10 |
| 8 yrs. | 649 | 1875 | 463 | 86 | 21 | 59 | 3.1 | 270 | 173 | 251 | 485 | 82 | .247 | .410 | 45 | 7 | OF-593 |
| 4 yrs. | 431 | 1352 | 346 | 72 | 14 | 46 | 3.4 | 188 | 140 | 186 | 333 | 66 | .256 | .432 | 9 | 1 | OF-418 |

## Charlie Pick

**PICK, CHARLES THOMAS**
B. Apr. 10, 1888, Brookneal, Va.   D. June 26, 1954, Lynchburg, Va.                 BL  TR  5'10"    160 lbs.

| | G | AB | H | 2B | 3B | HR | HR % | R | RBI | BB | SO | SB | BA | SA | Pinch Hit AB | Pinch Hit H | G by POS |
|---|---|---|---|---|---|---|---|---|---|---|---|---|---|---|---|---|---|
| 1914 WAS A | 10 | 23 | 9 | 0 | 0 | 0 | 0.0 | 0 | 1 | 4 | 4 | 1 | .391 | .391 | 2 | 1 | OF-7 |
| 1915 | 3 | 2 | 0 | 0 | 0 | 0 | 0.0 | 0 | 0 | 0 | 0 | 0 | .000 | .000 | 2 | 0 | |
| 1916 PHI A | 121 | 398 | 96 | 10 | 3 | 0 | 0.0 | 29 | 20 | 40 | 24 | 25 | .241 | .281 | 5 | 1 | 3B-108, OF-8 |
| 1918 CHI N | 29 | 89 | 29 | 4 | 1 | 0 | 0.0 | 13 | 12 | 14 | 4 | 7 | .326 | .393 | 0 | 0 | 2B-20, 3B-8 |
| 1919 2 teams | | | | CHI | N | (75G – | .242) | | BOS | N | (34G – | .254) | | | | | |
| " total | 109 | 383 | 94 | 9 | 7 | 1 | 0.3 | 39 | 25 | 21 | 17 | 21 | .245 | .313 | 3 | 1 | 2B-92, 3B-8, OF-3, 1B-2 |
| 1920 BOS N | 95 | 383 | 105 | 16 | 6 | 2 | 0.5 | 34 | 28 | 23 | 11 | 10 | .274 | .363 | 1 | 1 | 2B-94 |
| 6 yrs. | 367 | 1278 | 333 | 39 | 17 | 3 | 0.2 | 115 | 86 | 102 | 60 | 64 | .261 | .325 | 13 | 4 | 2B-206, 3B-124, OF-18, 1B-2 |
| 2 yrs. | 104 | 358 | 94 | 12 | 7 | 0 | 0.0 | 40 | 30 | 28 | 16 | 24 | .263 | .335 | 0 | 0 | 2B-91, 3B-11 |

**WORLD SERIES**

| | G | AB | H | 2B | 3B | HR | HR % | R | RBI | BB | SO | SB | BA | SA | Pinch Hit AB | Pinch Hit H | G by POS |
|---|---|---|---|---|---|---|---|---|---|---|---|---|---|---|---|---|---|
| 1918 CHI N | 6 | 18 | 7 | 1 | 0 | 0 | 0.0 | 2 | 0 | 1 | 1 | 0 | .389 | .444 | 0 | 0 | 2B-6 |

## Eddie Pick

**PICK, EDGAR EVERETT**
B. May 7, 1899, Attleboro, Mass.   D. May 13, 1967, Santa Monica, Calif.            BB  TR  6'    185 lbs.

| | G | AB | H | 2B | 3B | HR | HR % | R | RBI | BB | SO | SB | BA | SA | Pinch Hit AB | Pinch Hit H | G by POS |
|---|---|---|---|---|---|---|---|---|---|---|---|---|---|---|---|---|---|
| 1923 CIN N | 9 | 8 | 3 | 0 | 0 | 0 | 0.0 | 2 | 0 | 3 | 3 | 0 | .375 | .375 | 2 | 0 | OF-4 |
| 1924 | 3 | 2 | 0 | 0 | 0 | 0 | 0.0 | 0 | 2 | 0 | 1 | 0 | .000 | .000 | 1 | 0 | OF-1 |
| 1927 CHI N | 54 | 181 | 31 | 5 | 2 | 2 | 1.1 | 23 | 15 | 20 | 26 | 0 | .171 | .254 | 0 | 0 | 3B-49, OF-1, 2B-1 |
| 3 yrs. | 66 | 191 | 34 | 5 | 2 | 2 | 1.0 | 25 | 17 | 23 | 30 | 0 | .178 | .257 | 3 | 0 | 3B-49, OF-6, 2B-1 |
| 1 yr. | 54 | 181 | 31 | 5 | 2 | 2 | 1.1 | 23 | 15 | 20 | 26 | 0 | .171 | .254 | 0 | 0 | 3B-49, OF-1, 2B-1 |

## Andy Piercy

**PIERCY, ANDREW J.**
B. Aug., 1856, San Jose, Calif.   D. Dec. 27, 1932, San Jose, Calif.                TR

| | G | AB | H | 2B | 3B | HR | HR % | R | RBI | BB | SO | SB | BA | SA | Pinch Hit AB | Pinch Hit H | G by POS |
|---|---|---|---|---|---|---|---|---|---|---|---|---|---|---|---|---|---|
| 1881 CHI N | 2 | 8 | 2 | 0 | 0 | 0 | 0.0 | 1 | 0 | 0 | 1 | | .250 | .250 | 0 | 0 | 3B-1, 2B-1 |

## Pinky Pittenger

**PITTENGER, CLARKE ALONZO**
B. Feb. 24, 1899, Hudson, Mich.   D. Nov. 4, 1977, Ft. Lauderdale, Fla.              BR  TR  5'10"    160 lbs.

| | G | AB | H | 2B | 3B | HR | HR % | R | RBI | BB | SO | SB | BA | SA | Pinch Hit AB | Pinch Hit H | G by POS |
|---|---|---|---|---|---|---|---|---|---|---|---|---|---|---|---|---|---|
| 1921 BOS A | 40 | 91 | 18 | 1 | 0 | 0 | 0.0 | 6 | 5 | 4 | 13 | 3 | .198 | .209 | 6 | 1 | OF-27, 3B-3, SS-2, 2B-1 |
| 1922 | 66 | 186 | 48 | 3 | 0 | 0 | 0.0 | 16 | 7 | 9 | 10 | 2 | .258 | .274 | 0 | 0 | 3B-31, SS-29 |
| 1923 | 60 | 177 | 38 | 5 | 0 | 0 | 0.0 | 15 | 15 | 5 | 10 | 3 | .215 | .243 | 2 | 0 | 2B-42, SS-10, 3B-3 |
| 1925 CHI N | 59 | 173 | 54 | 7 | 2 | 0 | 0.0 | 21 | 15 | 12 | 7 | 5 | .312 | .376 | 0 | 0 | SS-24, 3B-24 |
| 1927 CIN N | 31 | 84 | 23 | 5 | 0 | 1 | 1.2 | 17 | 10 | 2 | 5 | 4 | .274 | .369 | 0 | 0 | 2B-20, SS-9, 3B-2 |
| 1928 | 40 | 38 | 9 | 0 | 1 | 0 | 0.0 | 12 | 4 | 0 | 1 | 2 | .237 | .289 | 3 | 0 | SS-12, 3B-4, 2B-4 |
| 1929 | 77 | 210 | 62 | 11 | 0 | 0 | 0.0 | 31 | 27 | 5 | 4 | 8 | .295 | .348 | 4 | 1 | SS-50, 3B-8, 2B-4 |
| 7 yrs. | 373 | 959 | 252 | 32 | 3 | 1 | 0.1 | 118 | 83 | 37 | 50 | 27 | .263 | .306 | 18 | 2 | SS-136, 3B-75, 2B-71, OF-27 |
| 1 yr. | 59 | 173 | 54 | 7 | 2 | 0 | 0.0 | 21 | 15 | 12 | 7 | 5 | .312 | .376 | 6 | 1 | SS-24, 3B-24 |

| | G | AB | H | 2B | 3B | HR | HR % | R | RBI | BB | SO | SB | BA | SA | Pinch Hit AB | H | G by POS |
|---|---|---|---|---|---|---|---|---|---|---|---|---|---|---|---|---|---|

## Whitey Platt

**PLATT, MIZELL GEORGE**
B. Aug. 21, 1920, West Palm Beach, Fla.    D. July 27, 1970, West Palm Beach, Fla.
BR  TR  6'1½"  190 lbs.

| | G | AB | H | 2B | 3B | HR | HR % | R | RBI | BB | SO | SB | BA | SA | AB | H | G by POS |
|---|---|---|---|---|---|---|---|---|---|---|---|---|---|---|---|---|---|
| 1942 CHI N | 4 | 16 | 1 | 0 | 0 | 0 | 0.0 | 1 | 2 | 0 | 3 | 0 | .063 | .063 | 0 | 0 | OF-4 |
| 1943 | 20 | 41 | 7 | 3 | 0 | 0 | 0.0 | 2 | 2 | 1 | 7 | 0 | .171 | .244 | 4 | 1 | OF-14 |
| 1946 CHI A | 84 | 247 | 62 | 8 | 5 | 3 | 1.2 | 28 | 32 | 17 | 34 | 1 | .251 | .360 | 24 | 6 | OF-61 |
| 1948 STL A | 123 | 454 | 123 | 22 | 10 | 7 | 1.5 | 57 | 82 | 39 | 51 | 1 | .271 | .410 | 8 | 2 | OF-114 |
| 1949 | 102 | 244 | 63 | 8 | 2 | 3 | 1.2 | 29 | 29 | 24 | 27 | 0 | .258 | .344 | 34 | 7 | OF-59, 1B-2 |
| 5 yrs. | 333 | 1002 | 256 | 41 | 17 | 13 | 1.3 | 117 | 147 | 81 | 122 | 2 | .255 | .369 | 70 | 16 | OF-252, 1B-2 |
| 2 yrs. | 24 | 57 | 8 | 3 | 0 | 0 | 0.0 | 3 | 4 | 1 | 10 | 0 | .140 | .193 | 4 | 1 | OF-18 |

## Bill Plummer

**PLUMMER, WILLIAM FRANCIS**
B. Mar. 21, 1947, Anderson, Calif.
BR  TR  6'1"  190 lbs.

| | G | AB | H | 2B | 3B | HR | HR % | R | RBI | BB | SO | SB | BA | SA | AB | H | G by POS |
|---|---|---|---|---|---|---|---|---|---|---|---|---|---|---|---|---|---|
| 1968 CHI N | 2 | 2 | 0 | 0 | 0 | 0 | 0.0 | 0 | 0 | 0 | 1 | 0 | .000 | .000 | 1 | 0 | C-1 |
| 1970 CIN N | 4 | 8 | 1 | 0 | 0 | 0 | 0.0 | 0 | 0 | 0 | 2 | 0 | .125 | .125 | 0 | 0 | C-4 |
| 1971 | 10 | 19 | 0 | 0 | 0 | 0 | 0.0 | 0 | 0 | 0 | 4 | 0 | .000 | .000 | 3 | 0 | C-4, 3B-2 |
| 1972 | 38 | 102 | 19 | 4 | 0 | 2 | 2.0 | 8 | 9 | 4 | 20 | 0 | .186 | .284 | 0 | 0 | C-35, 3B-1, 1B-1 |
| 1973 | 50 | 119 | 18 | 3 | 0 | 2 | 1.7 | 8 | 11 | 18 | 26 | 1 | .151 | .227 | 2 | 0 | C-42, 3B-5 |
| 1974 | 50 | 120 | 27 | 7 | 0 | 2 | 1.7 | 7 | 10 | 6 | 21 | 1 | .225 | .333 | 1 | 0 | C-49, 3B-1 |
| 1975 | 65 | 159 | 29 | 7 | 0 | 1 | 0.6 | 17 | 19 | 24 | 28 | 1 | .182 | .245 | 4 | 1 | C-63 |
| 1976 | 56 | 153 | 38 | 6 | 1 | 4 | 2.6 | 16 | 19 | 14 | 36 | 0 | .248 | .379 | 3 | 2 | C-54 |
| 1977 | 51 | 117 | 16 | 5 | 0 | 1 | 0.9 | 10 | 7 | 17 | 34 | 1 | .137 | .205 | 2 | 0 | C-50 |
| 1978 SEA A | 41 | 93 | 20 | 5 | 0 | 2 | 2.2 | 6 | 7 | 12 | 19 | 0 | .215 | .333 | 1 | 0 | C-40 |
| 10 yrs. | 367 | 892 | 168 | 37 | 1 | 14 | 1.6 | 72 | 82 | 95 | 191 | 4 | .188 | .279 | 17 | 3 | C-342, 3B-9, 1B-1 |
| 1 yr. | 2 | 2 | 0 | 0 | 0 | 0 | 0.0 | 0 | 0 | 0 | 1 | 0 | .000 | .000 | 1 | 0 | C-1 |

## Tom Poorman

**POORMAN, THOMAS IVERSON**
B. Oct. 14, 1857, Lock Haven, Pa.    D. Feb. 18, 1905, Lock Haven, Pa.
BL  TR  5'10½"  170 lbs.

| | G | AB | H | 2B | 3B | HR | HR % | R | RBI | BB | SO | SB | BA | SA | AB | H | G by POS |
|---|---|---|---|---|---|---|---|---|---|---|---|---|---|---|---|---|---|
| 1880 2 teams | | BUF N (19G – .157) | | | | | CHI N (7G – .200) | | | | | | | | | | |
| "   total | 26 | 95 | 16 | 2 | 2 | 0 | 0.0 | 8 | 1 | 0 | 15 | | .168 | .232 | 0 | 0 | OF-17, P-13 |
| 1884 TOL AA | 94 | 382 | 89 | 8 | 7 | 0 | 0.0 | 56 | | 10 | | | .233 | .291 | 0 | 0 | OF-93, P-1 |
| 1885 BOS N | 56 | 227 | 54 | 5 | 3 | 3 | 1.3 | 44 | 25 | 7 | 32 | | .238 | .326 | 0 | 0 | OF-56 |
| 1886 | 96 | 371 | 97 | 16 | 6 | 3 | 0.8 | 72 | 41 | 19 | 52 | | .261 | .361 | 0 | 0 | OF-96 |
| 1887 PHI AA | 135 | 585 | 155 | 18 | 19 | 4 | 0.7 | 140 | | 35 | | 88 | .265 | .381 | 0 | 0 | OF-135, 2B-2, P-1 |
| 1888 | 97 | 383 | 87 | 16 | 6 | 2 | 0.5 | 76 | 44 | 31 | | 46 | .227 | .316 | 0 | 0 | OF-97 |
| 6 yrs. | 504 | 2043 | 498 | 65 | 43 | 12 | 0.6 | 396 | 111 | 102 | 99 | 134 | .244 | .335 | 0 | 0 | OF-494, P-15, 2B-2 |
| 1 yr. | 7 | 25 | 5 | 1 | 2 | 0 | 0.0 | 3 | 0 | 0 | 2 | | .200 | .400 | 0 | 0 | OF-7, P-2 |

## Paul Popovich

**POPOVICH, PAUL EDWARD**
B. Aug. 18, 1940, Flemington, W. Va.
BR  TR  6'  175 lbs.
BB 1968

| | G | AB | H | 2B | 3B | HR | HR % | R | RBI | BB | SO | SB | BA | SA | AB | H | G by POS |
|---|---|---|---|---|---|---|---|---|---|---|---|---|---|---|---|---|---|
| 1964 CHI N | 1 | 1 | 1 | 0 | 0 | 0 | 0.0 | 0 | 0 | 0 | 0 | 0 | 1.000 | 1.000 | 1 | 1 | |
| 1966 | 2 | 6 | 0 | 0 | 0 | 0 | 0.0 | 0 | 0 | 0 | 2 | 0 | .000 | .000 | 0 | 0 | 2B-2 |
| 1967 | 49 | 159 | 34 | 4 | 0 | 0 | 0.0 | 18 | 2 | 9 | 12 | 0 | .214 | .239 | 5 | 0 | SS-31, 2B-17, 3B-2 |
| 1968 LA N | 134 | 418 | 97 | 8 | 1 | 2 | 0.5 | 35 | 25 | 29 | 37 | 1 | .232 | .270 | 4 | 0 | 2B-89, SS-45, 3B-7 |
| 1969 2 teams | | LA N (28G – .200) | | | | | CHI N (60G – .312) | | | | | | | | | | |
| "   total | 88 | 204 | 58 | 6 | 0 | 1 | 0.5 | 31 | 18 | 19 | 18 | 0 | .284 | .328 | 25 | 8 | 2B-48, SS-10, 3B-6, OF-1 |
| 1970 CHI N | 78 | 186 | 47 | 5 | 1 | 4 | 2.2 | 22 | 20 | 18 | 18 | 0 | .253 | .355 | 26 | 2 | 2B-22, SS-17, 3B-16 |
| 1971 | 89 | 226 | 49 | 7 | 1 | 4 | 1.8 | 24 | 28 | 14 | 17 | 0 | .217 | .310 | 30 | 2 | 2B-40, 3B-16, SS-1 |
| 1972 | 58 | 129 | 25 | 3 | 2 | 1 | 0.8 | 8 | 11 | 12 | 8 | 0 | .194 | .271 | 12 | 2 | 2B-36, SS-8, 3B-1 |
| 1973 | 99 | 280 | 66 | 6 | 3 | 2 | 0.7 | 24 | 24 | 18 | 27 | 3 | .236 | .300 | 9 | 1 | 2B-84, SS-9, 3B-1 |
| 1974 PIT N | 59 | 83 | 18 | 2 | 1 | 0 | 0.0 | 9 | 5 | 5 | 10 | 0 | .217 | .265 | 38 | 9 | 2B-12, SS-10 |
| 1975 | 25 | 40 | 8 | 1 | 0 | 0 | 0.0 | 5 | 1 | 3 | 2 | 0 | .200 | .225 | 15 | 3 | SS-8, 2B-8 |
| 11 yrs. | 682 | 1732 | 403 | 42 | 9 | 14 | 0.8 | 176 | 134 | 127 | 151 | 4 | .233 | .292 | 165 | 28 | 2B-358, SS-139, 3B-49, OF-1 |
| 8 yrs. | 436 | 1141 | 270 | 31 | 7 | 12 | 1.1 | 122 | 99 | 89 | 98 | 3 | .237 | .308 | 105 | 15 | 2B-226, SS-73, 3B-42, OF-1 |

LEAGUE CHAMPIONSHIP SERIES

| | G | AB | H | 2B | 3B | HR | HR % | R | RBI | BB | SO | SB | BA | SA | AB | H | G by POS |
|---|---|---|---|---|---|---|---|---|---|---|---|---|---|---|---|---|---|
| 1974 PIT N | 3 | 5 | 3 | 0 | 0 | 0 | 0.0 | 1 | 0 | 0 | 0 | 0 | .600 | .600 | 3 | 3 | SS-3 |

## Phil Powers

**POWERS, PHILIP J. (Grandmother)**
B. July 26, 1854, New York, N. Y.    D. Dec. 22, 1914, New York, N. Y.
BR  TR

| | G | AB | H | 2B | 3B | HR | HR % | R | RBI | BB | SO | SB | BA | SA | AB | H | G by POS |
|---|---|---|---|---|---|---|---|---|---|---|---|---|---|---|---|---|---|
| 1878 CHI N | 8 | 31 | 5 | 1 | 1 | 0 | 0.0 | 2 | 2 | 1 | 5 | | .161 | .258 | 0 | 0 | C-8 |
| 1880 BOS N | 37 | 126 | 18 | 5 | 0 | 0 | 0.0 | 11 | 10 | 5 | 15 | | .143 | .183 | 0 | 0 | C-37, OF-2 |
| 1881 CLE N | 5 | 15 | 1 | 0 | 0 | 0 | 0.0 | 0 | | 0 | 2 | | .067 | .067 | 0 | 0 | C-4, 3B-1 |
| 1882 CIN AA | 16 | 60 | 13 | 1 | 1 | 0 | 0.0 | 4 | | 3 | | | .217 | .267 | 0 | 0 | C-10, 1B-5, OF-1 |
| 1883 | 30 | 114 | 28 | 1 | 4 | 0 | 0.0 | 16 | | 3 | | | .246 | .325 | 0 | 0 | C-17, OF-13 |
| 1884 | 34 | 130 | 18 | 1 | 0 | 0 | 0.0 | 10 | | 5 | | | .138 | .146 | 0 | 0 | C-31, OF-2, 1B-2 |
| 1885 2 teams | | CIN AA (15G – .267) | | | | | BAL AA (9G – .118) | | | | | | | | | | |
| "   total | 24 | 94 | 20 | 3 | 0 | 0 | 0.0 | 12 | | 1 | | | .213 | .245 | 0 | 0 | C-23, OF-1 |
| 7 yrs. | 154 | 570 | 103 | 12 | 6 | 0 | 0.0 | 56 | 12 | 19 | 22 | | .181 | .223 | 0 | 0 | C-130, OF-19, 1B-7, 3B-1 |
| 1 yr. | 8 | 31 | 5 | 1 | 1 | 0 | 0.0 | 2 | 2 | 1 | 5 | | .161 | .258 | 0 | 0 | C-8 |

## Johnny Pramesa

**PRAMESA, JOHN STEVEN**
B. Aug. 28, 1925, Barton, Ohio
BR  TR  6'2"  210 lbs.

| | G | AB | H | 2B | 3B | HR | HR % | R | RBI | BB | SO | SB | BA | SA | AB | H | G by POS |
|---|---|---|---|---|---|---|---|---|---|---|---|---|---|---|---|---|---|
| 1949 CIN N | 17 | 25 | 6 | 1 | 0 | 1 | 4.0 | 2 | 2 | 3 | 5 | 0 | .240 | .400 | 4 | 1 | C-13 |
| 1950 | 74 | 228 | 70 | 10 | 1 | 5 | 2.2 | 14 | 30 | 19 | 15 | 0 | .307 | .425 | 1 | 0 | C-73 |
| 1951 | 72 | 227 | 52 | 5 | 2 | 6 | 2.6 | 12 | 22 | 5 | 17 | 0 | .229 | .348 | 9 | 2 | C-63 |
| 1952 CHI N | 22 | 46 | 13 | 1 | 0 | 1 | 2.2 | 1 | 5 | 4 | 4 | 0 | .283 | .370 | 5 | 2 | C-17 |
| 4 yrs. | 185 | 526 | 141 | 17 | 3 | 13 | 2.5 | 29 | 59 | 31 | 41 | 0 | .268 | .386 | 19 | 5 | C-166 |
| 1 yr. | 22 | 46 | 13 | 1 | 0 | 1 | 2.2 | 1 | 5 | 4 | 4 | 0 | .283 | .370 | 5 | 2 | C-17 |

| | G | AB | H | 2B | 3B | HR | HR % | R | RBI | BB | SO | SB | BA | SA | Pinch Hit AB | H | G by POS |
|---|---|---|---|---|---|---|---|---|---|---|---|---|---|---|---|---|---|

## Ed Putman

**PUTMAN, EDDIE WILLIAM**
B. Sept. 25, 1953, Los Angeles, Calif.     BR TR 6'1"    190 lbs.

| | G | AB | H | 2B | 3B | HR | HR % | R | RBI | BB | SO | SB | BA | SA | PH AB | H | G by POS |
|---|---|---|---|---|---|---|---|---|---|---|---|---|---|---|---|---|---|
| 1976 CHI N | 5 | 7 | 3 | 0 | 0 | 0 | 0.0 | 0 | 0 | 0 | 0 | 0 | .429 | .429 | 2 | 1 | C-3, 1B-1 |
| 1978 | 17 | 25 | 5 | 0 | 0 | 0 | 0.0 | 2 | 3 | 4 | 6 | 0 | .200 | .200 | 5 | 2 | 3B-8, 1B-3, C-2 |
| 1979 DET A | 21 | 39 | 9 | 3 | 0 | 2 | 5.1 | 4 | 4 | 4 | 12 | 0 | .231 | .462 | 3 | 0 | C-16, 1B-5 |
| 3 yrs. | 43 | 71 | 17 | 3 | 0 | 2 | 2.8 | 6 | 7 | 8 | 18 | 0 | .239 | .366 | 10 | 3 | C-21, 1B-9, 3B-8 |
| 2 yrs. | 22 | 32 | 8 | 0 | 0 | 0 | 0.0 | 2 | 3 | 4 | 6 | 0 | .250 | .250 | 7 | 3 | 3B-8, C-5, 1B-4 |

## Jim Qualls

**QUALLS, JAMES ROBERT**
B. Oct. 9, 1946, Exeter, Calif.     BB TR 5'10"    158 lbs.

| | G | AB | H | 2B | 3B | HR | HR % | R | RBI | BB | SO | SB | BA | SA | PH AB | H | G by POS |
|---|---|---|---|---|---|---|---|---|---|---|---|---|---|---|---|---|---|
| 1969 CHI N | 43 | 120 | 30 | 5 | 3 | 0 | 0.0 | 12 | 9 | 2 | 14 | 2 | .250 | .342 | 4 | 2 | OF-35, 2B-4 |
| 1970 MON N | 9 | 9 | 1 | 0 | 0 | 0 | 0.0 | 1 | 1 | 0 | 0 | 0 | .111 | .111 | 5 | 1 | OF-2, 2B-2 |
| 1972 CHI A | 11 | 10 | 0 | 0 | 0 | 0 | 0.0 | 0 | 0 | 0 | 2 | 0 | .000 | .000 | 7 | 0 | OF-1 |
| 3 yrs. | 63 | 139 | 31 | 5 | 3 | 0 | 0.0 | 13 | 10 | 2 | 16 | 2 | .223 | .302 | 16 | 3 | OF-38, 2B-6 |
| 1 yr. | 43 | 120 | 30 | 5 | 3 | 0 | 0.0 | 12 | 9 | 2 | 14 | 2 | .250 | .342 | 4 | 2 | OF-35, 2B-4 |

## Joe Quest

**QUEST, JOSEPH L.**
B. 1852, New Castle, Pa.   Deceased.     BR TR 5'6"    150 lbs.

| | G | AB | H | 2B | 3B | HR | HR % | R | RBI | BB | SO | SB | BA | SA | PH AB | H | G by POS |
|---|---|---|---|---|---|---|---|---|---|---|---|---|---|---|---|---|---|
| 1878 IND N | 62 | 278 | 57 | 3 | 2 | 0 | 0.0 | 45 | 13 | 12 | 24 | | .205 | .230 | 0 | 0 | 2B-62 |
| 1879 CHI N | 83 | 334 | 69 | 16 | 1 | 0 | 0.0 | 38 | 22 | 9 | 33 | | .207 | .260 | 0 | 0 | 2B-83 |
| 1880 | 82 | 300 | 71 | 12 | 1 | 0 | 0.0 | 37 | 27 | 8 | 16 | | .237 | .283 | 0 | 0 | 2B-80, SS-2, 3B-1 |
| 1881 | 78 | 293 | 72 | 6 | 0 | 1 | 0.3 | 35 | 26 | 2 | 29 | | .246 | .276 | 0 | 0 | 2B-77, SS-1 |
| 1882 | 42 | 159 | 32 | 5 | 2 | 0 | 0.0 | 24 | 15 | 8 | 16 | | .201 | .258 | 0 | 0 | 2B-41, SS-1 |
| 1883 2 teams | DET | N (37G – | .234) | | STL | AA (19G – | .256) | | | | | | | | | | |
| " total | 56 | 215 | 52 | 11 | 3 | 0 | 0.0 | 34 | | 11 | 18 | | .242 | .321 | 0 | 0 | 2B-56 |
| 1884 2 teams | STL | AA (81G – | .206) | | PIT | AA (12G – | .209) | | | | | | | | | | |
| " total | 93 | 353 | 73 | 12 | 5 | 0 | 0.0 | 48 | | 19 | | | .207 | .269 | 0 | 0 | 2B-87, SS-5, OF-1 |
| 1885 DET N | 55 | 200 | 39 | 8 | 2 | 0 | 0.0 | 24 | 21 | 14 | 25 | | .195 | .255 | 0 | 0 | 2B-39, SS-15, OF-1 |
| 1886 PHI AA | 42 | 150 | 31 | 4 | 1 | 0 | 0.0 | 14 | | 20 | | | .207 | .247 | 0 | 0 | SS-41, 2B-2 |
| 9 yrs. | 593 | 2282 | 496 | 77 | 17 | 1 | 0.0 | 299 | 124 | 103 | 161 | | .217 | .267 | 0 | 0 | 2B-527, SS-65, OF-2, 3B-1 |
| 4 yrs. | 285 | 1086 | 244 | 39 | 4 | 1 | 0.1 | 134 | 90 | 27 | 94 | | .225 | .271 | 0 | 0 | 2B-281, SS-4, 3B-1 |

## Frank Quinn

**QUINN, FRANK J.**
B. Grand Rapids, Mich.   D. Feb. 17, 1920, Camden, Ind.     5'8"

| | G | AB | H | 2B | 3B | HR | HR % | R | RBI | BB | SO | SB | BA | SA | PH AB | H | G by POS |
|---|---|---|---|---|---|---|---|---|---|---|---|---|---|---|---|---|---|
| 1899 CHI N | 12 | 34 | 6 | 0 | 1 | 0 | 0.0 | 6 | 1 | 6 | | 1 | .176 | .235 | 1 | 0 | OF-10, 2B-1 |

## Joe Quinn

**QUINN, JOSEPH C.**
B. 1851, Chicago, Ill.   D. Jan. 2, 1909, Chicago, Ill.     5'8½"   148 lbs.

| | G | AB | H | 2B | 3B | HR | HR % | R | RBI | BB | SO | SB | BA | SA | PH AB | H | G by POS |
|---|---|---|---|---|---|---|---|---|---|---|---|---|---|---|---|---|---|
| 1877 CHI N | 4 | 14 | 1 | 0 | 0 | 0 | 0.0 | 1 | 0 | 1 | 0 | | .071 | .071 | 0 | 0 | OF-4 |

## Dave Rader

**RADER, DAVID MARTIN**
B. Dec. 26, 1948, Claremore, Okla.     BL TR 5'11"    165 lbs.

| | G | AB | H | 2B | 3B | HR | HR % | R | RBI | BB | SO | SB | BA | SA | PH AB | H | G by POS |
|---|---|---|---|---|---|---|---|---|---|---|---|---|---|---|---|---|---|
| 1971 SF N | 3 | 4 | 0 | 0 | 0 | 0 | 0.0 | 0 | 0 | 0 | 0 | 0 | .000 | .000 | 3 | 0 | C-1 |
| 1972 | 133 | 459 | 119 | 14 | 1 | 6 | 1.3 | 44 | 41 | 29 | 31 | 1 | .259 | .333 | 9 | 2 | C-127 |
| 1973 | 148 | 462 | 106 | 15 | 4 | 9 | 1.9 | 59 | 41 | 63 | 22 | 0 | .229 | .338 | 4 | 3 | C-148 |
| 1974 | 113 | 323 | 94 | 16 | 2 | 1 | 0.3 | 26 | 26 | 31 | 21 | 1 | .291 | .362 | 13 | 4 | C-109 |
| 1975 | 98 | 292 | 85 | 15 | 0 | 5 | 1.7 | 39 | 31 | 32 | 30 | 1 | .291 | .394 | 7 | 1 | C-94 |
| 1976 | 88 | 255 | 67 | 15 | 0 | 1 | 0.4 | 25 | 22 | 27 | 21 | 2 | .263 | .333 | 12 | 2 | C-81 |
| 1977 STL N | 66 | 114 | 30 | 7 | 1 | 1 | 0.9 | 15 | 16 | 9 | 10 | 3 | .263 | .368 | 28 | 9 | C-38 |
| 1978 CHI N | 116 | 305 | 62 | 13 | 3 | 3 | 1.0 | 29 | 36 | 34 | 26 | 1 | .203 | .295 | 13 | 4 | C-114 |
| 1979 PHI N | 31 | 54 | 11 | 1 | 1 | 1 | 1.9 | 3 | 5 | 6 | 7 | 0 | .204 | .315 | 7 | 1 | C-25 |
| 1980 BOS A | 50 | 137 | 45 | 11 | 0 | 3 | 2.2 | 14 | 17 | 14 | 12 | 1 | .328 | .474 | 9 | 2 | C-34, DH-9 |
| 10 yrs. | 846 | 2405 | 619 | 107 | 12 | 30 | 1.2 | 254 | 235 | 245 | 180 | 10 | .257 | .349 | 105 | 28 | C-771, DH-9 |
| 1 yr. | 116 | 305 | 62 | 13 | 3 | 3 | 1.0 | 29 | 36 | 34 | 26 | 1 | .203 | .295 | 13 | 4 | C-114 |

## Bob Ramazzotti

**RAMAZZOTTI, ROBERT LOUIS**
B. Jan. 16, 1917, Elanora, Pa.     BR TR 5'8½"    175 lbs.

| | G | AB | H | 2B | 3B | HR | HR % | R | RBI | BB | SO | SB | BA | SA | PH AB | H | G by POS |
|---|---|---|---|---|---|---|---|---|---|---|---|---|---|---|---|---|---|
| 1946 BKN N | 62 | 120 | 25 | 4 | 0 | 0 | 0.0 | 10 | 7 | 9 | 13 | 0 | .208 | .242 | 15 | 1 | 3B-30, 2B-16 |
| 1948 | 4 | 3 | 0 | 0 | 0 | 0 | 0.0 | 0 | 0 | 0 | 1 | 0 | .000 | .000 | 2 | 0 | 3B-2, 1B-1 |
| 1949 2 teams | BKN | N (5G – | .154) | | CHI | N (65G – | .179) | | | | | | | | | | |
| " total | 70 | 203 | 36 | 3 | 1 | 1 | 0.5 | 15 | 9 | 5 | 36 | 9 | .177 | .217 | 11 | 2 | 3B-39, SS-12, 2B-4 |
| 1950 CHI N | 61 | 145 | 38 | 3 | 3 | 1 | 0.7 | 19 | 6 | 4 | 16 | 3 | .262 | .345 | 6 | 2 | 2B-31, 3B-10, SS-3 |
| 1951 | 73 | 158 | 39 | 5 | 2 | 1 | 0.6 | 13 | 15 | 10 | 23 | 0 | .247 | .323 | 9 | 2 | SS-51, 2B-6, 3B-1 |
| 1952 | 50 | 183 | 52 | 5 | 3 | 1 | 0.5 | 26 | 12 | 14 | 14 | 3 | .284 | .361 | 0 | 0 | 2B-50 |
| 1953 | 26 | 39 | 6 | 2 | 0 | 0 | 0.0 | 3 | 4 | 3 | 4 | 0 | .154 | .205 | 3 | 0 | 2B-18 |
| 7 yrs. | 346 | 851 | 196 | 22 | 9 | 4 | 0.5 | 86 | 53 | 45 | 107 | 15 | .230 | .291 | 46 | 7 | 2B-126, 3B-82, SS-66 |
| 5 yrs. | 275 | 715 | 169 | 18 | 9 | 3 | 0.4 | 75 | 43 | 36 | 90 | 15 | .236 | .299 | 27 | 6 | 2B-109, SS-66, 3B-47 |

## Newt Randall

**RANDALL, NEWTON J.**
B. Feb. 3, 1880, New Lowell, Ont., Canada   D. May 3, 1955, Duluth, Minn.     BR TR 5'10"

| | G | AB | H | 2B | 3B | HR | HR % | R | RBI | BB | SO | SB | BA | SA | PH AB | H | G by POS |
|---|---|---|---|---|---|---|---|---|---|---|---|---|---|---|---|---|---|
| 1907 2 teams | CHI | N (22G – | .205) | | BOS | N (75G – | .213) | | | | | | | | | | |
| " total | 97 | 336 | 71 | 10 | 5 | 0 | 0.0 | 22 | 19 | 27 | | 6 | .211 | .271 | 3 | 0 | OF-94 |

## Lenny Randle

**RANDLE, LEONARD SHENOFF**
B. Feb. 12, 1949, Long Beach, Calif.     BR TR 5'10"    169 lbs.

| | G | AB | H | 2B | 3B | HR | HR % | R | RBI | BB | SO | SB | BA | SA | PH AB | H | G by POS |
|---|---|---|---|---|---|---|---|---|---|---|---|---|---|---|---|---|---|
| 1971 WAS A | 75 | 215 | 47 | 11 | 0 | 2 | 0.9 | 27 | 13 | 24 | 56 | 1 | .219 | .298 | 6 | 0 | 2B-66 |
| 1972 TEX A | 74 | 249 | 48 | 13 | 0 | 2 | 0.8 | 23 | 21 | 13 | 51 | 4 | .193 | .269 | 4 | 0 | 2B-65, SS-4, OF-2 |
| 1973 | 10 | 29 | 6 | 1 | 1 | 1 | 3.4 | 3 | 1 | 0 | 2 | 0 | .207 | .414 | 0 | 0 | 2B-5, OF-2 |

| | G | AB | H | 2B | 3B | HR | HR % | R | RBI | BB | SO | SB | BA | SA | Pinch Hit AB | Pinch Hit H | G by POS |
|---|---|---|---|---|---|---|---|---|---|---|---|---|---|---|---|---|---|

## Lenny Randle continued

| | G | AB | H | 2B | 3B | HR | HR% | R | RBI | BB | SO | SB | BA | SA | AB | H | G by POS |
|---|---|---|---|---|---|---|---|---|---|---|---|---|---|---|---|---|---|
| 1974 | 151 | 520 | 157 | 17 | 4 | 1 | 0.2 | 65 | 49 | 29 | 43 | 26 | .302 | .356 | 2 | 2 | 3B-89, 2B-40, OF-21, DH-2, SS-1 |
| 1975 | 156 | 601 | 166 | 24 | 7 | 4 | 0.7 | 85 | 57 | 57 | 80 | 16 | .276 | .359 | 4 | 1 | 2B-79, OF-66, 3B-17, DH-3, SS-1, C-1 |
| 1976 | 142 | 539 | 121 | 11 | 6 | 1 | 0.2 | 53 | 51 | 46 | 63 | 30 | .224 | .273 | 2 | 0 | 2B-113, OF-30, 3B-2, DH-1 |
| 1977 NY N | 136 | 513 | 156 | 22 | 7 | 5 | 1.0 | 78 | 27 | 65 | 70 | 33 | .304 | .404 | 5 | 0 | 3B-110, 2B-20, OF-6, SS-1 |
| 1978 | 132 | 437 | 102 | 16 | 8 | 2 | 0.5 | 53 | 35 | 64 | 57 | 14 | .233 | .320 | 15 | 5 | 3B-124, 2B-5 |
| 1979 NY A | 20 | 39 | 7 | 0 | 0 | 0 | 0.0 | 2 | 3 | 3 | 2 | 0 | .179 | .179 | 5 | 1 | OF-11, DH-2 |
| 1980 CHI N | 130 | 489 | 135 | 19 | 6 | 5 | 1.0 | 67 | 39 | 50 | 55 | 19 | .276 | .370 | 8 | 4 | 3B-111, 2B-17, OF-6 |
| 1981 SEA A | 82 | 273 | 63 | 9 | 1 | 4 | 1.5 | 22 | 25 | 17 | 22 | 11 | .231 | .315 | 5 | 0 | 3B-59, 2B-21, OF-5, SS-3 |
| 1982 | 30 | 46 | 8 | 2 | 0 | 0 | 0.0 | 10 | 1 | 4 | 4 | 2 | .174 | .217 | 1 | 1 | DH-13, 3B-9, 2B-6 |
| 12 yrs. | 1138 | 3950 | 1016 | 145 | 40 | 27 | 0.7 | 488 | 322 | 372 | 505 | 156 | .257 | .335 | 57 | 14 | 3B-521, 2B-437, OF-149, DH-21, SS-10, C-1 |
| 1 yr. | 130 | 489 | 135 | 19 | 6 | 5 | 1.0 | 67 | 39 | 50 | 55 | 19 | .276 | .370 | 8 | 4 | 3B-111, 2B-17, OF-6 |

## Merritt Ranew

**RANEW, MERRITT THOMAS**
B. May 10, 1938, Albany, Ga.
BL TR 5'11" 170 lbs.

| | G | AB | H | 2B | 3B | HR | HR% | R | RBI | BB | SO | SB | BA | SA | AB | H | G by POS |
|---|---|---|---|---|---|---|---|---|---|---|---|---|---|---|---|---|---|
| 1962 HOU N | 71 | 218 | 51 | 6 | 8 | 4 | 1.8 | 26 | 24 | 14 | 43 | 2 | .234 | .390 | 15 | 1 | C-58 |
| 1963 CHI N | 78 | 154 | 52 | 8 | 1 | 3 | 1.9 | 18 | 15 | 9 | 32 | 1 | .338 | .461 | 41 | 17 | C-37, 1B-7 |
| 1964 2 teams | CHI N (16G – .091) | | | | MIL N (9G – .118) | | | | | | | | | | | | |
| " total | 25 | 50 | 5 | 0 | 0 | 0 | 0.0 | 1 | 1 | 2 | 9 | 0 | .100 | .100 | 11 | 2 | C-12 |
| 1965 CAL A | 41 | 91 | 19 | 4 | 0 | 1 | 1.1 | 12 | 10 | 7 | 22 | 0 | .209 | .286 | 17 | 2 | C-24 |
| 1969 SEA A | 54 | 81 | 20 | 2 | 0 | 0 | 0.0 | 11 | 4 | 10 | 14 | 0 | .247 | .272 | 31 | 6 | C-13, OF-3, 3B-1 |
| 5 yrs. | 269 | 594 | 147 | 20 | 9 | 8 | 1.3 | 68 | 54 | 42 | 120 | 3 | .247 | .352 | 115 | 28 | C-144, 1B-7, OF-3, 3B-1 |
| 2 yrs. | 94 | 187 | 55 | 8 | 1 | 3 | 1.6 | 18 | 16 | 11 | 38 | 1 | .294 | .396 | 46 | 18 | C-46, 1B-7 |

## Tommy Raub

**RAUB, THOMAS JEFFERSON**
B. Dec. 1, 1870, Raubsville, Pa.    D. Feb. 16, 1949, Phillipsburg, N. J.
BR TR 5'10" 155 lbs.

| | G | AB | H | 2B | 3B | HR | HR% | R | RBI | BB | SO | SB | BA | SA | AB | H | G by POS |
|---|---|---|---|---|---|---|---|---|---|---|---|---|---|---|---|---|---|
| 1903 CHI N | 36 | 84 | 19 | 3 | 2 | 0 | 0.0 | 6 | 7 | 5 | | 3 | .226 | .310 | 8 | 3 | C-12, 1B-6, OF-5, 3B-4 |
| 1906 STL N | 24 | 78 | 22 | 2 | 4 | 0 | 0.0 | 9 | 2 | 4 | | 2 | .282 | .410 | 0 | 0 | C-22 |
| 2 yrs. | 60 | 162 | 41 | 5 | 6 | 0 | 0.0 | 15 | 9 | 9 | | 5 | .253 | .358 | 8 | 3 | C-34, 1B-6, OF-5, 3B-4 |
| 1 yr. | 36 | 84 | 19 | 3 | 2 | 0 | 0.0 | 6 | 7 | 5 | | 3 | .226 | .310 | 8 | 3 | C-12, 1B-6, OF-5, 3B-4 |

## Bob Raudman

**RAUDMAN, ROBERT JOYCE (Shorty)**
B. Mar. 14, 1942, Erie, Pa.
BL TL 5'9½" 185 lbs.

| | G | AB | H | 2B | 3B | HR | HR% | R | RBI | BB | SO | SB | BA | SA | AB | H | G by POS |
|---|---|---|---|---|---|---|---|---|---|---|---|---|---|---|---|---|---|
| 1966 CHI N | 8 | 29 | 7 | 2 | 0 | 0 | 0.0 | 1 | 1 | 1 | 4 | 0 | .241 | .310 | 0 | 0 | OF-8 |
| 1967 | 8 | 26 | 4 | 0 | 0 | 0 | 0.0 | 0 | 2 | 1 | 4 | 0 | .154 | .154 | 0 | 0 | OF-8 |
| 2 yrs. | 16 | 55 | 11 | 2 | 0 | 0 | 0.0 | 1 | 3 | 2 | 8 | 0 | .200 | .236 | 0 | 0 | OF-16 |
| 2 yrs. | 16 | 55 | 11 | 2 | 0 | 0 | 0.0 | 1 | 3 | 2 | 8 | 0 | .200 | .236 | 0 | 0 | OF-16 |

## Fred Raymer

**RAYMER, FREDERICK CHARLES**
B. Nov. 12, 1875, Leavenworth, Kans.    D. June 11, 1957, Los Angeles, Calif.
TR

| | G | AB | H | 2B | 3B | HR | HR% | R | RBI | BB | SO | SB | BA | SA | AB | H | G by POS |
|---|---|---|---|---|---|---|---|---|---|---|---|---|---|---|---|---|---|
| 1901 CHI N | 120 | 463 | 108 | 14 | 2 | 0 | 0.0 | 41 | 43 | 11 | | 18 | .233 | .272 | 1 | 1 | 3B-82, SS-29, 1B-5, 2B-3 |
| 1904 BOS N | 114 | 419 | 88 | 12 | 3 | 1 | 0.2 | 28 | 27 | 13 | | 17 | .210 | .260 | 0 | 0 | 2B-114 |
| 1905 | 137 | 498 | 105 | 14 | 2 | 0 | 0.0 | 26 | 31 | 8 | | 15 | .211 | .247 | 1 | 0 | 2B-134, OF-1, 1B-1 |
| 3 yrs. | 371 | 1380 | 301 | 40 | 7 | 1 | 0.1 | 95 | 101 | 32 | | 50 | .218 | .259 | 2 | 1 | 2B-251, 3B-82, SS-29, 1B-6, OF-1 |
| 1 yr. | 120 | 463 | 108 | 14 | 2 | 0 | 0.0 | 41 | 43 | 11 | | 18 | .233 | .272 | 1 | 1 | 3B-82, SS-29, 1B-5, 2B-3 |

## Herm Reich

**REICH, HERMAN CHARLES**
B. Nov. 23, 1917, Bell, Calif.
BR TL 6'2" 200 lbs.

| | G | AB | H | 2B | 3B | HR | HR% | R | RBI | BB | SO | SB | BA | SA | AB | H | G by POS |
|---|---|---|---|---|---|---|---|---|---|---|---|---|---|---|---|---|---|
| 1949 3 teams | WAS A (2G – .000) | | | CLE A (1G – .500) | | | | CHI N (108G – .280) | | | | | | | | | |
| " total | 111 | 390 | 109 | 18 | 2 | 3 | 0.8 | 43 | 34 | 14 | 33 | 4 | .279 | .359 | 10 | 1 | 1B-85, OF-17 |

## Hal Reilly

**REILLY, HAROLD J.**
B. Unknown.

| | G | AB | H | 2B | 3B | HR | HR% | R | RBI | BB | SO | SB | BA | SA | AB | H | G by POS |
|---|---|---|---|---|---|---|---|---|---|---|---|---|---|---|---|---|---|
| 1919 CHI N | 1 | 3 | 0 | 0 | 0 | 0 | 0.0 | 0 | 0 | 0 | 1 | 0 | .000 | .000 | 0 | 0 | OF-1 |

## Josh Reilly

**REILLY, CHARLES**
B. 1868, San Francisco, Calif.    D. June 13, 1938, San Francisco, Calif.

| | G | AB | H | 2B | 3B | HR | HR% | R | RBI | BB | SO | SB | BA | SA | AB | H | G by POS |
|---|---|---|---|---|---|---|---|---|---|---|---|---|---|---|---|---|---|
| 1896 CHI N | 9 | 42 | 9 | 1 | 0 | 0 | 0.0 | 6 | 2 | 1 | 1 | 2 | .214 | .238 | 0 | 0 | 2B-8, SS-1 |

## Ken Reitz

**REITZ, KENNETH JOHN**
B. June 24, 1951, San Francisco, Calif.
BR TR 6' 180 lbs.

| | G | AB | H | 2B | 3B | HR | HR% | R | RBI | BB | SO | SB | BA | SA | AB | H | G by POS |
|---|---|---|---|---|---|---|---|---|---|---|---|---|---|---|---|---|---|
| 1972 STL N | 21 | 78 | 28 | 4 | 0 | 0 | 0.0 | 5 | 10 | 2 | 4 | 0 | .359 | .410 | 1 | 0 | 3B-20 |
| 1973 | 147 | 426 | 100 | 20 | 2 | 6 | 1.4 | 40 | 42 | 9 | 25 | 0 | .235 | .333 | 12 | 2 | 3B-135, SS-1 |
| 1974 | 154 | 579 | 157 | 28 | 2 | 7 | 1.2 | 48 | 54 | 23 | 63 | 0 | .271 | .363 | 3 | 1 | 3B-151, SS-2 |
| 1975 | 161 | 592 | 159 | 25 | 1 | 5 | 0.8 | 43 | 63 | 22 | 54 | 1 | .269 | .340 | 1 | 0 | 3B-160 |
| 1976 SF N | 155 | 577 | 154 | 21 | 1 | 5 | 0.9 | 40 | 66 | 24 | 48 | 5 | .267 | .333 | 0 | 0 | 3B-155, SS-1 |
| 1977 STL N | 157 | 587 | 153 | 36 | 1 | 17 | 2.9 | 58 | 79 | 19 | 74 | 2 | .261 | .412 | 0 | 0 | 3B-157 |
| 1978 | 150 | 540 | 133 | 26 | 2 | 10 | 1.9 | 41 | 75 | 23 | 61 | 1 | .246 | .357 | 4 | 4 | 3B-150 |
| 1979 | 159 | 605 | 162 | 41 | 2 | 8 | 1.3 | 42 | 73 | 25 | 85 | 1 | .268 | .382 | 2 | 0 | 3B-158 |
| 1980 | 151 | 523 | 141 | 33 | 0 | 8 | 1.5 | 39 | 58 | 22 | 44 | 0 | .270 | .379 | 1 | 0 | 3B-150 |
| 1981 CHI N | 82 | 260 | 56 | 9 | 1 | 2 | 0.8 | 10 | 28 | 15 | 56 | 0 | .215 | .281 | 1 | 0 | 3B-81 |

| | G | AB | H | 2B | 3B | HR | HR % | R | RBI | BB | SO | SB | BA | SA | Pinch Hit AB | Pinch Hit H | G by POS |
|---|---|---|---|---|---|---|---|---|---|---|---|---|---|---|---|---|---|

## Ken Reitz continued

| | G | AB | H | 2B | 3B | HR | HR % | R | RBI | BB | SO | SB | BA | SA | AB | H | G by POS |
|---|---|---|---|---|---|---|---|---|---|---|---|---|---|---|---|---|---|
| 1982 PIT N | 7 | 10 | 0 | 0 | 0 | 0 | 0.0 | 0 | 0 | 0 | 4 | 0 | .000 | .000 | 3 | 0 | 3B-4 |
| 11 yrs. | 1344 | 4777 | 1243 | 243 | 12 | 68 | 1.4 | 366 | 548 | 184 | 518 | 10 | .260 | .359 | 28 | 7 | 3B-1321, SS-4 |
| 1 yr. | 82 | 260 | 56 | 9 | 1 | 2 | 0.8 | 10 | 28 | 15 | 56 | 0 | .215 | .281 | 1 | 0 | 3B-81 |

## Jack Remsen

REMSEN, JOHN J.          BR  TR  5'11½" 170 lbs.
B. Apr., 1851, Brooklyn, N. Y.   Deceased.

| | G | AB | H | 2B | 3B | HR | HR % | R | RBI | BB | SO | SB | BA | SA | AB | H | G by POS |
|---|---|---|---|---|---|---|---|---|---|---|---|---|---|---|---|---|---|
| 1876 HAR N | 69 | 324 | 89 | 12 | 5 | 1 | 0.3 | 62 | 30 | 1 | 15 | | .275 | .352 | 0 | 0 | OF-69 |
| 1877 STL N | 33 | 123 | 32 | 3 | 4 | 0 | 0.0 | 14 | 13 | 4 | 3 | | .260 | .350 | 0 | 0 | OF-33 |
| 1878 CHI N | 56 | 224 | 52 | 11 | 1 | 1 | 0.4 | 32 | 19 | 17 | 33 | | .232 | .304 | 0 | 0 | OF-56 |
| 1879 | 42 | 152 | 33 | 4 | 2 | 0 | 0.0 | 14 | 8 | 2 | 23 | | .217 | .270 | 0 | 0 | OF-31, 1B-11 |
| 1881 CLE N | 48 | 172 | 30 | 4 | 3 | 0 | 0.0 | 14 | 13 | 9 | 31 | | .174 | .233 | 0 | 0 | OF-48 |
| 1884 2 teams | | PHI | N (12G – | .209) | | BKN | AA (81G – | .223) | | | | | | | | | |
| "   total | 93 | 344 | 76 | 8 | 6 | 3 | 0.9 | 54 | | 29 | 9 | | .221 | .305 | 0 | 0 | OF-93 |
| 6 yrs. | 341 | 1339 | 312 | 42 | 21 | 5 | 0.4 | 190 | 83 | 62 | 114 | | .233 | .307 | 0 | 0 | OF-330, 1B-11 |
| 2 yrs. | 98 | 376 | 85 | 15 | 3 | 1 | 0.3 | 46 | 27 | 19 | 56 | | .226 | .290 | 0 | 0 | OF-87, 1B-11 |

## Carl Reynolds

REYNOLDS, CARL NETTLES          BR  TR  6'    194 lbs.
B. Feb. 1, 1903, LaRue, Tex.    D. May 29, 1978, Houston, Tex.

| | G | AB | H | 2B | 3B | HR | HR % | R | RBI | BB | SO | SB | BA | SA | AB | H | G by POS |
|---|---|---|---|---|---|---|---|---|---|---|---|---|---|---|---|---|---|
| 1927 CHI A | 14 | 42 | 9 | 3 | 0 | 1 | 2.4 | 5 | 7 | 5 | 7 | 1 | .214 | .357 | 0 | 0 | OF-13 |
| 1928 | 84 | 291 | 94 | 21 | 11 | 2 | 0.7 | 51 | 36 | 17 | 13 | 15 | .323 | .491 | 10 | 6 | OF-74 |
| 1929 | 131 | 517 | 164 | 24 | 12 | 11 | 2.1 | 81 | 67 | 20 | 37 | 19 | .317 | .474 | 0 | 0 | OF-131 |
| 1930 | 138 | 563 | 202 | 25 | 18 | 22 | 3.9 | 103 | 100 | 20 | 39 | 16 | .359 | .584 | 5 | 0 | OF-132 |
| 1931 | 118 | 462 | 134 | 24 | 14 | 6 | 1.3 | 71 | 77 | 24 | 26 | 17 | .290 | .442 | 9 | 3 | OF-109 |
| 1932 WAS A | 102 | 406 | 124 | 28 | 7 | 9 | 2.2 | 53 | 63 | 14 | 19 | 8 | .305 | .475 | 5 | 1 | OF-95 |
| 1933 STL A | 135 | 475 | 136 | 26 | 14 | 8 | 1.7 | 81 | 71 | 50 | 25 | 5 | .286 | .451 | 13 | 3 | OF-124 |
| 1934 BOS A | 113 | 413 | 125 | 26 | 9 | 4 | 1.0 | 61 | 86 | 27 | 28 | 5 | .303 | .438 | 14 | 3 | OF-100 |
| 1935 | 78 | 244 | 66 | 13 | 4 | 6 | 2.5 | 33 | 35 | 24 | 20 | 4 | .270 | .430 | 11 | 2 | OF-64 |
| 1936 WAS A | 89 | 293 | 81 | 18 | 2 | 4 | 1.4 | 41 | 41 | 21 | 22 | 8 | .276 | .392 | 15 | 3 | OF-72 |
| 1937 CHI N | 7 | 11 | 3 | 1 | 0 | 0 | 0.0 | 0 | 1 | 2 | 2 | 0 | .273 | .364 | 4 | 1 | OF-2 |
| 1938 | 125 | 497 | 150 | 28 | 10 | 3 | 0.6 | 59 | 67 | 22 | 32 | 9 | .302 | .416 | 0 | 0 | OF-125 |
| 1939 | 88 | 281 | 69 | 10 | 6 | 4 | 1.4 | 33 | 44 | 16 | 38 | 5 | .246 | .367 | 14 | 3 | OF-72 |
| 13 yrs. | 1222 | 4495 | 1357 | 247 | 107 | 80 | 1.8 | 672 | 695 | 262 | 308 | 112 | .302 | .458 | 100 | 25 | OF-1113 |
| 3 yrs. | 220 | 789 | 222 | 39 | 16 | 7 | 0.9 | 92 | 112 | 40 | 72 | 14 | .281 | .398 | 18 | 4 | OF-199 |

WORLD SERIES
| 1938 CHI N | 4 | 12 | 0 | 0 | 0 | 0 | 0.0 | 0 | 0 | 1 | 3 | 0 | .000 | .000 | 1 | 0 | OF-3 |

## Del Rice

RICE, DELBERT W.          BR  TR  6'2"  190 lbs.
B. Oct. 27, 1922, Portsmouth, Ohio    D. Jan. 26, 1983, Buena Park, Calif.
Manager 1972.

| | G | AB | H | 2B | 3B | HR | HR % | R | RBI | BB | SO | SB | BA | SA | AB | H | G by POS |
|---|---|---|---|---|---|---|---|---|---|---|---|---|---|---|---|---|---|
| 1945 STL N | 83 | 253 | 66 | 17 | 3 | 1 | 0.4 | 27 | 28 | 16 | 33 | 0 | .261 | .364 | 6 | 1 | C-77 |
| 1946 | 55 | 139 | 38 | 8 | 1 | 1 | 0.7 | 10 | 12 | 8 | 16 | 0 | .273 | .367 | 2 | 0 | C-53 |
| 1947 | 97 | 261 | 57 | 7 | 3 | 12 | 4.6 | 28 | 44 | 36 | 40 | 1 | .218 | .406 | 3 | 0 | C-94 |
| 1948 | 100 | 290 | 57 | 10 | 1 | 4 | 1.4 | 24 | 34 | 37 | 46 | 1 | .197 | .279 | 0 | 0 | C-99 |
| 1949 | 92 | 284 | 67 | 16 | 1 | 4 | 1.4 | 25 | 29 | 30 | 40 | 0 | .236 | .342 | 0 | 0 | C-92 |
| 1950 | 130 | 414 | 101 | 20 | 3 | 9 | 2.2 | 39 | 54 | 43 | 65 | 0 | .244 | .372 | 0 | 0 | C-130 |
| 1951 | 122 | 374 | 94 | 13 | 1 | 9 | 2.4 | 34 | 47 | 34 | 26 | 0 | .251 | .364 | 3 | 0 | C-120 |
| 1952 | 147 | 495 | 128 | 27 | 2 | 11 | 2.2 | 43 | 65 | 33 | 38 | 0 | .259 | .388 | 1 | 0 | C-147 |
| 1953 | 135 | 419 | 99 | 22 | 1 | 6 | 1.4 | 32 | 37 | 48 | 49 | 0 | .236 | .337 | 0 | 0 | C-135 |
| 1954 | 56 | 147 | 37 | 10 | 1 | 2 | 1.4 | 13 | 16 | 16 | 21 | 0 | .252 | .374 | 4 | 2 | C-52 |
| 1955 2 teams | | STL | N (20G – | .203) | | MIL | N (27G – | .197) | | | | | | | | | |
| "   total | 47 | 130 | 26 | 3 | 1 | 3 | 2.3 | 11 | 14 | 13 | 18 | 0 | .200 | .308 | 7 | 0 | C-40 |
| 1956 MIL N | 71 | 188 | 40 | 9 | 1 | 3 | 1.6 | 15 | 17 | 18 | 34 | 0 | .213 | .319 | 5 | 1 | C-65 |
| 1957 | 54 | 144 | 33 | 1 | 1 | 9 | 6.3 | 15 | 20 | 17 | 37 | 0 | .229 | .438 | 6 | 1 | C-48 |
| 1958 | 43 | 121 | 27 | 7 | 0 | 1 | 0.8 | 10 | 8 | 8 | 30 | 0 | .223 | .306 | 6 | 2 | C-38 |
| 1959 | 13 | 29 | 6 | 0 | 0 | 0 | 0.0 | 3 | 1 | 2 | 3 | 0 | .207 | .207 | 4 | 1 | C-9 |
| 1960 3 teams | | CHI | N (18G – | .231) | | STL | N (1G – | .000) | | BAL | A (1G – | .000) | | | | | |
| "   total | 20 | 55 | 12 | 3 | 0 | 0 | 0.0 | 2 | 4 | 3 | 7 | 0 | .218 | .273 | 0 | 0 | C-20 |
| 1961 LA A | 44 | 83 | 20 | 4 | 0 | 4 | 4.8 | 11 | 11 | 20 | 19 | 0 | .241 | .434 | 15 | 4 | C-30 |
| 17 yrs. | 1309 | 3826 | 908 | 177 | 20 | 79 | 2.1 | 342 | 441 | 382 | 522 | 2 | .237 | .356 | 62 | 12 | C-1249 |
| 1 yr. | 18 | 52 | 12 | 3 | 0 | 0 | 0.0 | 2 | 4 | 2 | 7 | 0 | .231 | .288 | 0 | 0 | C-18 |

WORLD SERIES
| 1946 STL N | 3 | 6 | 3 | 1 | 0 | 0 | 0.0 | 0 | 0 | 0 | 0 | 0 | .500 | .667 | 0 | 0 | C-3 |
| 1957 MIL N | 2 | 6 | 1 | 0 | 0 | 0 | 0.0 | 0 | 0 | 1 | 2 | 0 | .167 | .167 | 0 | 0 | C-2 |
| 2 yrs. | 5 | 12 | 4 | 1 | 0 | 0 | 0.0 | 0 | 0 | 3 | 2 | 0 | .333 | .417 | 0 | 0 | C-5 |

## Hal Rice

RICE, HAROLD HOUSTEN (Hoot)          BL  TR  6'1"  195 lbs.
B. Feb. 11, 1924, Morganette, W. Va.

| | G | AB | H | 2B | 3B | HR | HR % | R | RBI | BB | SO | SB | BA | SA | AB | H | G by POS |
|---|---|---|---|---|---|---|---|---|---|---|---|---|---|---|---|---|---|
| 1948 STL N | 8 | 31 | 10 | 1 | 2 | 0 | 0.0 | 3 | 3 | 2 | 4 | 0 | .323 | .484 | 0 | 0 | OF-8 |
| 1949 | 40 | 46 | 9 | 2 | 1 | 1 | 2.2 | 3 | 9 | 3 | 7 | 0 | .196 | .348 | 27 | 6 | OF-10 |
| 1950 | 44 | 128 | 27 | 3 | 1 | 2 | 1.6 | 12 | 11 | 10 | 10 | 0 | .211 | .297 | 6 | 1 | OF-37 |
| 1951 | 69 | 236 | 60 | 12 | 1 | 4 | 1.7 | 20 | 38 | 24 | 22 | 0 | .254 | .364 | 5 | 1 | OF-63 |
| 1952 | 98 | 295 | 85 | 14 | 5 | 7 | 2.4 | 37 | 45 | 16 | 26 | 1 | .288 | .441 | 19 | 3 | OF-81 |
| 1953 2 teams | | STL | N (8G – | .250) | | PIT | N (78G – | .311) | | | | | | | | | |
| "   total | 86 | 294 | 91 | 16 | | 4 | 1.4 | 39 | 42 | 17 | 25 | 0 | .310 | .412 | 17 | 3 | OF-70 |
| 1954 2 teams | | PIT | N (28G – | .173) | | CHI | N (51G – | .153) | | | | | | | | | |
| "   total | 79 | 153 | 25 | 4 | 1 | 1 | 0.7 | 15 | 14 | 22 | 39 | 0 | .163 | .222 | 29 | 2 | OF-48 |
| 7 yrs. | 424 | 1183 | 307 | 52 | 12 | 19 | 1.6 | 129 | 162 | 94 | 133 | 1 | .260 | .372 | 103 | 16 | OF-317 |
| 1 yr. | 51 | 72 | 11 | 0 | 0 | 0 | 0.0 | 5 | 5 | 8 | 15 | 0 | .153 | .153 | 24 | 2 | OF-24 |

| | G | AB | H | 2B | 3B | HR | HR % | R | RBI | BB | SO | SB | BA | SA | Pinch Hit AB | Pinch Hit H | G by POS |
|---|---|---|---|---|---|---|---|---|---|---|---|---|---|---|---|---|---|

## Len Rice

**RICE, LEONARD OLIVER**
B. Sept. 2, 1918, Lead, S. D.
BR TR 6' 180 lbs.

| | G | AB | H | 2B | 3B | HR | HR% | R | RBI | BB | SO | SB | BA | SA | AB | H | G by POS |
|---|---|---|---|---|---|---|---|---|---|---|---|---|---|---|---|---|---|
| 1944 CIN N | 10 | 4 | 0 | 0 | 0 | 0 | 0.0 | 1 | 0 | 0 | 0 | 0 | .000 | .000 | 1 | 0 | C-5 |
| 1945 CHI N | 32 | 99 | 23 | 3 | 0 | 0 | 0.0 | 10 | 7 | 5 | 8 | 2 | .232 | .263 | 2 | 0 | C-29 |
| 2 yrs. | 42 | 103 | 23 | 3 | 0 | 0 | 0.0 | 11 | 7 | 5 | 8 | 2 | .223 | .252 | 3 | 0 | C-34 |
| 1 yr. | 32 | 99 | 23 | 3 | 0 | 0 | 0.0 | 10 | 7 | 5 | 8 | 2 | .232 | .263 | 2 | 0 | C-29 |

## Fred Richards

**RICHARDS, FRED CHARLES (Fuzzy)**
B. Nov. 3, 1927, Warren, Ohio
BL TL 6'1½" 185 lbs.

| | G | AB | H | 2B | 3B | HR | HR% | R | RBI | BB | SO | SB | BA | SA | AB | H | G by POS |
|---|---|---|---|---|---|---|---|---|---|---|---|---|---|---|---|---|---|
| 1951 CHI N | 10 | 27 | 8 | 2 | 0 | 0 | 0.0 | 1 | 4 | 2 | 3 | 0 | .296 | .370 | 1 | 0 | 1B-9 |

## Lance Richbourg

**RICHBOURG, LANCE CLAYTON**
B. Dec. 18, 1897, DeFuniak Springs, Fla.    D. Sept. 10, 1975, Crestview, Fla.
BL TR 5'10½" 160 lbs.

| | G | AB | H | 2B | 3B | HR | HR% | R | RBI | BB | SO | SB | BA | SA | AB | H | G by POS |
|---|---|---|---|---|---|---|---|---|---|---|---|---|---|---|---|---|---|
| 1921 PHI N | 10 | 5 | 1 | 1 | 0 | 0 | 0.0 | 2 | 0 | 0 | 3 | 1 | .200 | .400 | 2 | 0 | 2B-4 |
| 1924 WAS A | 15 | 32 | 9 | 2 | 1 | 0 | 0.0 | 3 | 1 | 2 | 6 | 0 | .281 | .406 | 6 | 4 | OF-7 |
| 1927 BOS N | 115 | 450 | 139 | 12 | 9 | 2 | 0.4 | 57 | 34 | 22 | 30 | 24 | .309 | .389 | 4 | 1 | OF-110 |
| 1928 | 148 | 612 | 206 | 26 | 12 | 2 | 0.3 | 105 | 52 | 62 | 39 | 11 | .337 | .428 | 0 | 0 | OF-148 |
| 1929 | 139 | 557 | 170 | 24 | 13 | 3 | 0.5 | 76 | 56 | 42 | 26 | 7 | .305 | .411 | 3 | 0 | OF-134 |
| 1930 | 130 | 529 | 161 | 23 | 8 | 3 | 0.6 | 81 | 54 | 19 | 31 | 13 | .304 | .395 | 2 | 1 | OF-128 |
| 1931 | 97 | 286 | 82 | 11 | 6 | 2 | 0.7 | 32 | 29 | 19 | 14 | 9 | .287 | .388 | 22 | 5 | OF-71 |
| 1932 CHI N | 44 | 148 | 38 | 2 | 2 | 1 | 0.7 | 22 | 21 | 8 | 4 | 0 | .257 | .318 | 10 | 3 | OF-33 |
| 8 yrs. | 698 | 2619 | 806 | 101 | 51 | 13 | 0.5 | 378 | 247 | 174 | 153 | 65 | .308 | .400 | 49 | 14 | OF-631, 2B-4 |
| 1 yr. | 44 | 148 | 38 | 2 | 2 | 1 | 0.7 | 22 | 21 | 8 | 4 | 0 | .257 | .318 | 10 | 3 | OF-33 |

## Marv Rickert

**RICKERT, MARVIN AUGUST (Twitch)**
B. Jan. 8, 1921, Long Branch, Wash.    D. June 3, 1978, Oakville, Wash.
BL TR 6'2" 195 lbs.

| | G | AB | H | 2B | 3B | HR | HR% | R | RBI | BB | SO | SB | BA | SA | AB | H | G by POS |
|---|---|---|---|---|---|---|---|---|---|---|---|---|---|---|---|---|---|
| 1942 CHI N | 8 | 26 | 7 | 0 | 0 | 0 | 0.0 | 5 | 1 | 1 | 5 | 0 | .269 | .269 | 1 | 0 | OF-6 |
| 1946 | 111 | 392 | 103 | 18 | 3 | 7 | 1.8 | 44 | 47 | 28 | 54 | 3 | .263 | .378 | 6 | 0 | OF-104 |
| 1947 | 71 | 137 | 20 | 0 | 2 | 1.5 | | 7 | 15 | 15 | 17 | 0 | .146 | .190 | 27 | 6 | OF-30, 1B-7 |
| 1948 2 teams | | | | CIN N (8G – .167) | | | | BOS N (3G – .231) | | | | | | | | | |
| " total | 11 | 19 | 4 | 1 | 0 | 0 | 0.0 | 1 | 2 | 0 | 1 | 0 | .211 | .316 | 6 | 1 | OF-3 |
| 1949 BOS N | 100 | 277 | 81 | 18 | 3 | 6 | 2.2 | 44 | 49 | 23 | 38 | 1 | .292 | .444 | 12 | 3 | OF-75, 1B-12 |
| 1950 2 teams | | | | PIT N (17G – .150) | | | | CHI A (84G – .237) | | | | | | | | | |
| " total | 101 | 298 | 69 | 9 | 2 | 4 | 1.3 | 38 | 31 | 21 | 46 | 0 | .232 | .315 | 20 | 1 | OF-81, 1B-1 |
| 6 yrs. | 402 | 1149 | 284 | 45 | 9 | 19 | 1.7 | 139 | 145 | 88 | 161 | 4 | .247 | .352 | 72 | 11 | OF-299, 1B-20 |
| 3 yrs. | 190 | 555 | 130 | 18 | 3 | 9 | 1.6 | 56 | 63 | 44 | 76 | 3 | .234 | .326 | 34 | 6 | OF-140, 1B-7 |

WORLD SERIES

| | G | AB | H | 2B | 3B | HR | HR% | R | RBI | BB | SO | SB | BA | SA | AB | H | G by POS |
|---|---|---|---|---|---|---|---|---|---|---|---|---|---|---|---|---|---|
| 1948 BOS N | 5 | 19 | 4 | 0 | 0 | 1 | 5.3 | 2 | 2 | 0 | 4 | 0 | .211 | .368 | 0 | 0 | OF-5 |

## Mel Roach

**ROACH, MELVIN EARL**
B. Jan. 25, 1933, Richmond, Va.
BR TR 6'1" 190 lbs.

| | G | AB | H | 2B | 3B | HR | HR% | R | RBI | BB | SO | SB | BA | SA | AB | H | G by POS |
|---|---|---|---|---|---|---|---|---|---|---|---|---|---|---|---|---|---|
| 1953 MIL N | 5 | 2 | 0 | 0 | 0 | 0 | 0.0 | 0 | 1 | 0 | 1 | 0 | .000 | .000 | 1 | 0 | 2B-1 |
| 1954 | 3 | 4 | 0 | 0 | 0 | 0 | 0.0 | 0 | 0 | 1 | 0 | 0 | .000 | .000 | 2 | 0 | 1B-1 |
| 1957 | 7 | 6 | 1 | 0 | 0 | 0 | 0.0 | 1 | 0 | 0 | 3 | 0 | .167 | .167 | 3 | 0 | 2B-5 |
| 1958 | 44 | 136 | 42 | 7 | 0 | 3 | 2.2 | 14 | 10 | 6 | 15 | 0 | .309 | .426 | 12 | 3 | 2B-27, OF-7, 1B-3 |
| 1959 | 19 | 31 | 3 | 0 | 0 | 0 | 0.0 | 1 | 0 | 2 | 4 | 0 | .097 | .097 | 5 | 0 | 2B-8, OF-4, 3B-1 |
| 1960 | 48 | 140 | 42 | 12 | 0 | 3 | 2.1 | 12 | 18 | 6 | 19 | 0 | .300 | .450 | 10 | 3 | OF-21, 2B-20, 3B-1, 1B-1 |
| 1961 2 teams | | | | MIL N (13G – .167) | | | | CHI N (23G – .128) | | | | | | | | | |
| " total | 36 | 75 | 11 | 2 | 0 | 1 | 1.3 | 4 | 7 | 5 | 13 | 1 | .147 | .213 | 13 | 3 | OF-9, 1B-9, 2B-7 |
| 1962 PHI N | 65 | 105 | 20 | 4 | 0 | 0 | 0.0 | 9 | 8 | 5 | 19 | 0 | .190 | .229 | 28 | 4 | 3B-26, 2B-9, 1B-4, OF-3 |
| 8 yrs. | 227 | 499 | 119 | 25 | 0 | 7 | 1.4 | 42 | 43 | 24 | 75 | 1 | .238 | .331 | 74 | 13 | 2B-77, OF-44, 3B-28, 1B-16 |
| 1 yr. | 23 | 39 | 5 | 2 | 0 | 0 | 0.0 | 1 | 1 | 3 | 9 | 1 | .128 | .179 | 11 | 2 | 2B-7, 1B-7 |

## Fred Roat

**ROAT, FREDERICK**
B. Feb. 10, 1868, Oregon, Ill.    D. Sept. 24, 1918, Oregon, Ill.
TR

| | G | AB | H | 2B | 3B | HR | HR% | R | RBI | BB | SO | SB | BA | SA | AB | H | G by POS |
|---|---|---|---|---|---|---|---|---|---|---|---|---|---|---|---|---|---|
| 1890 PIT N | 57 | 215 | 48 | 2 | 0 | 2 | 0.9 | 18 | 17 | 16 | 22 | 7 | .223 | .260 | 0 | 0 | 3B-44, 1B-9, OF-4 |
| 1892 CHI N | 8 | 31 | 6 | 0 | 1 | 0 | 0.0 | 4 | 2 | 2 | 3 | 2 | .194 | .258 | 0 | 0 | 2B-8 |
| 2 yrs. | 65 | 246 | 54 | 2 | 1 | 2 | 0.8 | 22 | 19 | 18 | 25 | 9 | .220 | .260 | 0 | 0 | 3B-44, 1B-9, 2B-8, OF-4 |
| 1 yr. | 8 | 31 | 6 | 0 | 1 | 0 | 0.0 | 4 | 2 | 2 | 3 | 2 | .194 | .258 | 0 | 0 | 2B-8 |

## Daryl Robertson

**ROBERTSON, DARYL BERDINE**
B. Jan. 5, 1936, Cripple Creek, Colo.
BR TR 6' 184 lbs.

| | G | AB | H | 2B | 3B | HR | HR% | R | RBI | BB | SO | SB | BA | SA | AB | H | G by POS |
|---|---|---|---|---|---|---|---|---|---|---|---|---|---|---|---|---|---|
| 1962 CHI N | 9 | 19 | 2 | 0 | 0 | 0 | 0.0 | 0 | 2 | 2 | 10 | 0 | .105 | .105 | 2 | 0 | SS-6, 3B-1 |

## Dave Robertson

**ROBERTSON, DAVIS AYDELOTTE**
B. Sept. 25, 1889, Portsmouth, Va.    D. Nov. 5, 1970, Virginia Beach, Va.
BL TL 6' 186 lbs.

| | G | AB | H | 2B | 3B | HR | HR% | R | RBI | BB | SO | SB | BA | SA | AB | H | G by POS |
|---|---|---|---|---|---|---|---|---|---|---|---|---|---|---|---|---|---|
| 1912 NY N | 3 | 2 | 1 | 0 | 0 | 0 | 0.0 | 1 | 0 | 1 | 1 | 0 | .500 | .500 | 0 | 0 | 1B-1 |
| 1914 | 82 | 256 | 68 | 12 | 3 | 2 | 0.8 | 25 | 32 | 10 | 26 | 9 | .266 | .359 | 10 | 0 | OF-71 |
| 1915 | 138 | 544 | 160 | 17 | 10 | 3 | 0.6 | 72 | 58 | 22 | 52 | 22 | .294 | .379 | 0 | 0 | OF-138 |
| 1916 | 150 | 587 | 180 | 18 | 8 | 12 | 2.0 | 88 | 69 | 14 | 56 | 21 | .307 | .426 | 5 | 2 | OF-144 |
| 1917 | 142 | 532 | 138 | 16 | 9 | 12 | 2.3 | 64 | 54 | 10 | 47 | 17 | .259 | .391 | 1 | 1 | OF-140 |
| 1919 2 teams | | | | NY N (1G – .000) | | | | CHI N (27G – .208) | | | | | | | | | |
| " total | 28 | 96 | 20 | 2 | 0 | 1 | 1.0 | 8 | 10 | 1 | 10 | 3 | .208 | .260 | 2 | 0 | OF-25 |
| 1920 CHI N | 134 | 500 | 150 | 29 | 11 | 10 | 2.0 | 68 | 75 | 40 | 44 | 17 | .300 | .462 | 0 | 0 | OF-134 |
| 1921 2 teams | | | | CHI N (22G – .222) | | | | PIT N (60G – .322) | | | | | | | | | |
| " total | 82 | 266 | 82 | 21 | 3 | 6 | 2.3 | 36 | 62 | 13 | 19 | 4 | .308 | .477 | 15 | 4 | OF-65 |

| | G | AB | H | 2B | 3B | HR | HR % | R | RBI | BB | SO | SB | BA | SA | Pinch Hit AB | Pinch Hit H | G by POS |
|---|---|---|---|---|---|---|---|---|---|---|---|---|---|---|---|---|---|

## Dave Robertson continued

| | G | AB | H | 2B | 3B | HR | HR% | R | RBI | BB | SO | SB | BA | SA | AB | H | G by POS |
|---|---|---|---|---|---|---|---|---|---|---|---|---|---|---|---|---|---|
| 1922 NY N | 42 | 47 | 13 | 2 | 0 | 1 | 2.1 | 5 | 3 | 3 | 7 | 0 | .277 | .383 | 30 | 7 | OF-8 |
| 9 yrs. | 801 | 2830 | 812 | 117 | 44 | 47 | 1.7 | 366 | 364 | 113 | 262 | 94 | .287 | .409 | 66 | 14 | OF-725, 1B-1 |
| 3 yrs. | 183 | 632 | 178 | 34 | 11 | 11 | 1.7 | 83 | 99 | 42 | 57 | 20 | .282 | .422 | 15 | 4 | OF-166 |

WORLD SERIES
| 1917 NY N | 6 | 22 | 11 | 1 | 1 | 0 | 0.0 | 3 | 1 | 0 | 0 | 2 | .500 | .636 | 0 | 0 | OF-6 |

## Don Robertson

**ROBERTSON, DONALD ALEXANDER**       BL  TL  5'10"  180 lbs.
B. Oct. 15, 1930, Harvey, Ill.

| | G | AB | H | 2B | 3B | HR | HR% | R | RBI | BB | SO | SB | BA | SA | AB | H | G by POS |
|---|---|---|---|---|---|---|---|---|---|---|---|---|---|---|---|---|---|
| 1954 CHI N | 14 | 6 | 0 | 0 | 0 | 0 | 0.0 | 2 | 0 | 0 | 2 | 0 | .000 | .000 | 4 | 0 | OF-6 |

## Andre Rodgers

**RODGERS, KENNETH ANDRE IAN (Andy)**       BR  TR  6'3"  200 lbs.
B. Dec. 2, 1934, Nassau, Bahamas

| | G | AB | H | 2B | 3B | HR | HR% | R | RBI | BB | SO | SB | BA | SA | AB | H | G by POS |
|---|---|---|---|---|---|---|---|---|---|---|---|---|---|---|---|---|---|
| 1957 NY N | 32 | 86 | 21 | 2 | 1 | 3 | 3.5 | 8 | 9 | 9 | 21 | 0 | .244 | .395 | 2 | 0 | SS-20, 3B-8 |
| 1958 SF N | 22 | 63 | 13 | 3 | 1 | 2 | 3.2 | 7 | 11 | 4 | 14 | 0 | .206 | .381 | 4 | 1 | SS-18 |
| 1959 | 71 | 228 | 57 | 12 | 1 | 6 | 2.6 | 32 | 24 | 32 | 50 | 2 | .250 | .390 | 2 | 1 | SS-66 |
| 1960 | 81 | 217 | 53 | 8 | 5 | 2 | 0.9 | 22 | 22 | 24 | 44 | 1 | .244 | .355 | 16 | 7 | SS-41, 3B-21, 1B-6, OF-2 |
| 1961 CHI N | 73 | 214 | 57 | 17 | 0 | 6 | 2.8 | 27 | 23 | 25 | 54 | 1 | .266 | .430 | 7 | 1 | 1B-42, SS-24, OF-2, 2B-1 |
| 1962 | 138 | 461 | 128 | 20 | 8 | 5 | 1.1 | 40 | 44 | 44 | 93 | 5 | .278 | .388 | 6 | 0 | SS-133, 1B-1 |
| 1963 | 150 | 516 | 118 | 17 | 4 | 5 | 1.0 | 51 | 33 | 65 | 90 | 5 | .229 | .306 | 0 | 0 | SS-150 |
| 1964 | 129 | 448 | 107 | 17 | 3 | 12 | 2.7 | 50 | 46 | 53 | 88 | 5 | .239 | .371 | 3 | 0 | SS-126 |
| 1965 PIT N | 75 | 178 | 51 | 12 | 0 | 2 | 1.1 | 17 | 25 | 18 | 28 | 2 | .287 | .388 | 26 | 8 | SS-33, 3B-15, 1B-6, 2B-1 |
| 1966 | 36 | 49 | 9 | 1 | 0 | 0 | 0.0 | 6 | 4 | 8 | 7 | 0 | .184 | .204 | 23 | 6 | SS-5, OF-3, 3B-3, 1B-2 |
| 1967 | 47 | 61 | 14 | 3 | 0 | 2 | 3.3 | 8 | 4 | 8 | 18 | 1 | .230 | .377 | 22 | 4 | 1B-9, 3B-5, SS-3, 2B-2 |
| 11 yrs. | 854 | 2521 | 628 | 112 | 23 | 45 | 1.8 | 268 | 245 | 290 | 507 | 22 | .249 | .365 | 111 | 28 | SS-619, 1B-66, 3B-52, OF-7, 2B-4 |
| 4 yrs. | 490 | 1639 | 410 | 71 | 15 | 28 | 1.7 | 168 | 146 | 187 | 325 | 16 | .250 | .363 | 16 | 1 | SS-433, 1B-43, OF-2, 2B-1 |

## Billy Rogell

**ROGELL, WILLIAM GEORGE**       BB  TR  5'10½"  163 lbs.
B. Nov. 24, 1904, Springfield, Ill.

| | G | AB | H | 2B | 3B | HR | HR% | R | RBI | BB | SO | SB | BA | SA | AB | H | G by POS |
|---|---|---|---|---|---|---|---|---|---|---|---|---|---|---|---|---|---|
| 1925 BOS A | 58 | 169 | 33 | 5 | 1 | 0 | 0.0 | 12 | 17 | 11 | 17 | 0 | .195 | .237 | 2 | 0 | 2B-49, SS-6 |
| 1927 | 82 | 207 | 55 | 14 | 6 | 2 | 1.0 | 35 | 28 | 24 | 28 | 3 | .266 | .420 | 15 | 3 | 3B-53, OF-2, 2B-2 |
| 1928 | 102 | 296 | 69 | 10 | 4 | 0 | 0.0 | 33 | 29 | 22 | 47 | 2 | .233 | .294 | 7 | 1 | SS-67, 2B-22, OF-6, 3B-3 |
| 1930 DET A | 54 | 144 | 24 | 4 | 2 | 0 | 0.0 | 20 | 9 | 15 | 23 | 1 | .167 | .222 | 2 | 0 | SS-33, 3B-13, OF-1 |
| 1931 | 48 | 185 | 56 | 12 | 3 | 2 | 1.1 | 21 | 24 | 24 | 17 | 8 | .303 | .432 | 0 | 0 | SS-48 |
| 1932 | 143 | 554 | 150 | 29 | 6 | 9 | 1.6 | 88 | 61 | 50 | 38 | 14 | .271 | .394 | 0 | 0 | SS-139, 3B-4 |
| 1933 | 155 | 587 | 173 | 42 | 11 | 0 | 0.0 | 67 | 57 | 79 | 33 | 6 | .295 | .404 | 0 | 0 | SS-155 |
| 1934 | 154 | 592 | 175 | 32 | 8 | 3 | 0.5 | 114 | 100 | 74 | 36 | 13 | .296 | .392 | 0 | 0 | SS-154 |
| 1935 | 150 | 560 | 154 | 23 | 11 | 6 | 1.1 | 88 | 71 | 80 | 29 | 3 | .275 | .388 | 0 | 0 | SS-150 |
| 1936 | 146 | 585 | 160 | 27 | 5 | 6 | 1.0 | 85 | 68 | 73 | 41 | 14 | .274 | .368 | 1 | 0 | SS-146, 3B-1 |
| 1937 | 146 | 536 | 148 | 30 | 7 | 8 | 1.5 | 85 | 64 | 83 | 48 | 5 | .276 | .403 | 0 | 0 | SS-146 |
| 1938 | 136 | 501 | 130 | 22 | 8 | 3 | 0.6 | 76 | 55 | 86 | 37 | 9 | .259 | .353 | 2 | 0 | SS-134 |
| 1939 | 74 | 174 | 40 | 6 | 3 | 2 | 1.1 | 24 | 23 | 26 | 14 | 3 | .230 | .333 | 3 | 0 | SS-43, 3B-21, 2B-2 |
| 1940 CHI N | 33 | 59 | 8 | 0 | 0 | 1 | 1.7 | 7 | 3 | 2 | 8 | 1 | .136 | .186 | 6 | 1 | SS-14, 3B-9, 2B-3 |
| 14 yrs. | 1481 | 5149 | 1375 | 256 | 75 | 42 | 0.8 | 755 | 609 | 649 | 416 | 82 | .267 | .370 | 38 | 5 | SS-1235, 3B-104, 2B-78, OF-9 |
| 1 yr. | 33 | 59 | 8 | 0 | 0 | 1 | 1.7 | 7 | 3 | 2 | 8 | 1 | .136 | .186 | 6 | 1 | SS-14, 3B-9, 2B-3 |

WORLD SERIES
| 1934 DET A | 7 | 29 | 8 | 1 | 0 | 0 | 0.0 | 3 | 4 | 1 | 4 | 0 | .276 | .310 | 0 | 0 | SS-7 |
| 1935 | 6 | 24 | 7 | 2 | 0 | 0 | 0.0 | 1 | 1 | 2 | 5 | 0 | .292 | .375 | 0 | 0 | SS-6 |
| 2 yrs. | 13 | 53 | 15 | 3 | 0 | 0 | 0.0 | 4 | 5 | 3 | 9 | 0 | .283 | .340 | 0 | 0 | SS-13 |

## Dan Rohn

**ROHN, DANIEL JAY**       BL  TR  5'8"  165 lbs.
B. Jan. 10, 1956, Alpena, Mich.

| | G | AB | H | 2B | 3B | HR | HR% | R | RBI | BB | SO | SB | BA | SA | AB | H | G by POS |
|---|---|---|---|---|---|---|---|---|---|---|---|---|---|---|---|---|---|
| 1983 CHI N | 23 | 31 | 12 | 3 | 2 | 0 | 0.0 | 3 | 6 | 2 | 2 | 1 | .387 | .613 | 17 | 6 | 2B-6, SS-1 |
| 1984 | 25 | 31 | 4 | 0 | 0 | 1 | 3.2 | 1 | 3 | 1 | 6 | 0 | .129 | .226 | 13 | 2 | 3B-7, SS-5, 2B-5 |
| 2 yrs. | 48 | 62 | 16 | 3 | 2 | 1 | 1.6 | 4 | 9 | 3 | 8 | 1 | .258 | .419 | 30 | 8 | 2B-11, 3B-7, SS-6 |
| 2 yrs. | 48 | 62 | 16 | 3 | 2 | 1 | 1.6 | 4 | 9 | 3 | 8 | 1 | .258 | .419 | 30 | 8 | 2B-11, 3B-7, SS-6 |

## Dave Rosello

**ROSELLO, DAVID**       BR  TR  5'11"  160 lbs.
Born David Rosello Rodriguez.
B. June 25, 1950, Mayaguez, Puerto Rico

| | G | AB | H | 2B | 3B | HR | HR% | R | RBI | BB | SO | SB | BA | SA | AB | H | G by POS |
|---|---|---|---|---|---|---|---|---|---|---|---|---|---|---|---|---|---|
| 1972 CHI N | 5 | 12 | 3 | 0 | 0 | 1 | 8.3 | 2 | 3 | 3 | 2 | 0 | .250 | .500 | 0 | 0 | SS-5 |
| 1973 | 16 | 38 | 10 | 2 | 0 | 0 | 0.0 | 4 | 2 | 2 | 4 | 2 | .263 | .316 | 1 | 0 | 2B-13, SS-1 |
| 1974 | 62 | 148 | 30 | 7 | 0 | 0 | 0.0 | 9 | 10 | 10 | 28 | 1 | .203 | .250 | 2 | 1 | 2B-49, SS-12 |
| 1975 | 19 | 58 | 15 | 2 | 0 | 1 | 1.7 | 9 | 8 | 9 | 8 | 0 | .259 | .345 | 0 | 0 | SS-19 |
| 1976 | 91 | 227 | 55 | 5 | 1 | 1 | 0.4 | 27 | 11 | 41 | 33 | 1 | .242 | .286 | 1 | 0 | SS-86, 2B-1 |
| 1977 | 56 | 82 | 18 | 2 | 1 | 1 | 1.2 | 18 | 9 | 12 | 12 | 0 | .220 | .305 | 22 | 7 | 3B-21, SS-10, 2B-3 |
| 1979 CLE A | 59 | 107 | 26 | 6 | 1 | 3 | 2.8 | 20 | 14 | 15 | 27 | 1 | .243 | .402 | 3 | 1 | 2B-33, 3B-14, SS-11 |
| 1980 | 71 | 117 | 29 | 3 | 0 | 2 | 1.7 | 16 | 12 | 9 | 19 | 0 | .248 | .325 | 1 | 0 | 2B-43, 3B-22, SS-3, DH-1 |
| 1981 | 43 | 84 | 20 | 4 | 0 | 1 | 1.2 | 11 | 7 | 7 | 12 | 0 | .238 | .321 | 10 | 1 | 2B-26, 3B-8, DH-4, SS-4 |
| 9 yrs. | 422 | 873 | 206 | 31 | 3 | 10 | 1.1 | 114 | 76 | 108 | 145 | 5 | .236 | .313 | 40 | 10 | 2B-168, SS-151, 3B-65, DH-5 |
| 6 yrs. | 249 | 565 | 131 | 18 | 2 | 4 | 0.7 | 67 | 43 | 77 | 87 | 4 | .232 | .292 | 26 | 8 | SS-133, 2B-66, 3B-21 |

## Dave Rowe

**ROWE, DAVID**       BR  TR  5'9"  180 lbs.
Brother of Jack Rowe.
B. Feb., 1856, Jacksonville, Ill.  Deceased.
Manager 1886, 1888.

| | G | AB | H | 2B | 3B | HR | HR% | R | RBI | BB | SO | SB | BA | SA | AB | H | G by POS |
|---|---|---|---|---|---|---|---|---|---|---|---|---|---|---|---|---|---|
| 1877 CHI N | 2 | 7 | 2 | 0 | 0 | 0 | 0.0 | 0 | 0 | 0 | 0 | 3 | .286 | .286 | 0 | 0 | OF-2, P-1 |

| | G | AB | H | 2B | 3B | HR | HR % | R | RBI | BB | SO | SB | BA | SA | Pinch Hit AB | Pinch Hit H | G by POS |
|---|---|---|---|---|---|---|---|---|---|---|---|---|---|---|---|---|---|

## Dave Rowe continued

| | G | AB | H | 2B | 3B | HR | HR % | R | RBI | BB | SO | SB | BA | SA | AB | H | G by POS |
|---|---|---|---|---|---|---|---|---|---|---|---|---|---|---|---|---|---|
| 1882 CLE N | 24 | 97 | 25 | 4 | 3 | 1 | 1.0 | 13 | 17 | 4 | | 9 | .258 | .392 | 0 | 0 | OF-23, P-1 |
| 1883 BAL AA | 59 | 256 | 80 | 11 | 6 | 0 | 0.0 | 40 | | 2 | | | .313 | .402 | 0 | 0 | OF-50, SS-7, 1B-3, P-1 |
| 1884 STL U | 109 | **485** | 142 | 32 | 11 | 3 | 0.6 | 95 | | 10 | | | .293 | .423 | 0 | 0 | OF-92, SS-14, 2B-2, 1B-2, P-1 |
| 1885 STL N | 16 | 62 | 10 | 3 | 0 | 0 | 0.0 | 8 | 3 | 5 | | 8 | .161 | .210 | 0 | 0 | OF-16 |
| 1886 KC N | 105 | 429 | 103 | 24 | 8 | 3 | 0.7 | 53 | 57 | 15 | | 43 | .240 | .354 | 0 | 0 | OF-90, SS-11, 2B-4 |
| 1888 KC AA | 32 | 122 | 21 | 3 | 4 | 0 | 0.0 | 14 | 13 | 6 | | 2 | .172 | .262 | 0 | 0 | OF-32 |
| 7 yrs. | 347 | 1458 | 383 | 77 | 32 | 7 | 0.5 | 223 | 90 | 42 | 63 | 2 | .263 | .374 | 0 | 0 | OF-305, SS-32, 2B-6, 1B-5, P-4 |
| 1 yr. | 2 | 7 | 2 | 0 | 0 | 0 | 0.0 | 0 | 0 | 0 | 3 | | .286 | .286 | 0 | 0 | OF-2, P-1 |

## Vic Roznovsky

**ROZNOVSKY, VICTOR JOSEPH**     BL TR 6'   170 lbs.
B. Oct. 19, 1938, Shiner, Tex.

| | G | AB | H | 2B | 3B | HR | HR % | R | RBI | BB | SO | SB | BA | SA | AB | H | G by POS |
|---|---|---|---|---|---|---|---|---|---|---|---|---|---|---|---|---|---|
| 1964 CHI N | 35 | 76 | 15 | 1 | 0 | 0 | 0.0 | 2 | 2 | 5 | 18 | 0 | .197 | .211 | 16 | 1 | C-26 |
| 1965 | 71 | 172 | 38 | 4 | 1 | 3 | 1.7 | 9 | 15 | 16 | 30 | 1 | .221 | .308 | 11 | 4 | C-63 |
| 1966 BAL A | 41 | 97 | 23 | 5 | 0 | 1 | 1.0 | 4 | 10 | 9 | 11 | 0 | .237 | .320 | 5 | 2 | C-34 |
| 1967 | 45 | 97 | 20 | 5 | 0 | 0 | 0.0 | 7 | 10 | 1 | 20 | 0 | .206 | .258 | 20 | 6 | C-23 |
| 1969 PHI N | 13 | 13 | 3 | 0 | 0 | 0 | 0.0 | 0 | 1 | 1 | 4 | 0 | .231 | .231 | 12 | 3 | C-2 |
| 5 yrs. | 205 | 455 | 99 | 15 | 1 | 4 | 0.9 | 22 | 38 | 32 | 83 | 1 | .218 | .281 | 64 | 16 | C-148 |
| 2 yrs. | 106 | 248 | 53 | 5 | 1 | 3 | 1.2 | 11 | 17 | 21 | 48 | 1 | .214 | .278 | 27 | 5 | C-89 |

## Dutch Rudolph

**RUDOLPH, JOHN HERMAN**     BL TL 5'10"   160 lbs.
B. July 10, 1882, Natrona, Pa.    D. Apr. 17, 1967, Natrona, Pa.

| | G | AB | H | 2B | 3B | HR | HR % | R | RBI | BB | SO | SB | BA | SA | AB | H | G by POS |
|---|---|---|---|---|---|---|---|---|---|---|---|---|---|---|---|---|---|
| 1903 PHI N | 1 | 1 | 0 | 0 | 0 | 0 | 0.0 | 0 | 0 | 0 | | 0 | .000 | .000 | 1 | 0 | |
| 1904 CHI N | 2 | 3 | 1 | 0 | 0 | 0 | 0.0 | 0 | 0 | 0 | | 0 | .333 | .333 | 0 | 0 | OF-2 |
| 2 yrs. | 3 | 4 | 1 | 0 | 0 | 0 | 0.0 | 0 | 0 | 0 | | 0 | .250 | .250 | 1 | 0 | OF-2 |
| 1 yr. | 2 | 3 | 1 | 0 | 0 | 0 | 0.0 | 0 | 0 | 0 | | 0 | .333 | .333 | 0 | 0 | OF-2 |

## Ken Rudolph

**RUDOLPH, KENNETH VICTOR**     BR TR 6'1"   180 lbs.
B. Dec. 29, 1946, Rockford, Ill.

| | G | AB | H | 2B | 3B | HR | HR % | R | RBI | BB | SO | SB | BA | SA | AB | H | G by POS |
|---|---|---|---|---|---|---|---|---|---|---|---|---|---|---|---|---|---|
| 1969 CHI N | 27 | 34 | 7 | 1 | 0 | 1 | 2.9 | 7 | 6 | 6 | 11 | 0 | .206 | .324 | 10 | 3 | C-11, OF-3 |
| 1970 | 20 | 40 | 4 | 1 | 0 | 0 | 0.0 | 1 | 2 | 1 | 12 | 0 | .100 | .125 | 3 | 0 | C-16 |
| 1971 | 25 | 76 | 15 | 3 | 0 | 0 | 0.0 | 5 | 7 | 6 | 20 | 0 | .197 | .237 | 0 | 0 | C-25 |
| 1972 | 42 | 106 | 25 | 1 | 1 | 2 | 1.9 | 10 | 9 | 6 | 14 | 1 | .236 | .321 | 1 | 0 | C-41 |
| 1973 | 64 | 170 | 35 | 8 | 1 | 2 | 1.2 | 12 | 17 | 7 | 25 | 0 | .206 | .300 | 1 | 0 | C-64 |
| 1974 SF N | 57 | 158 | 41 | 3 | 0 | 0 | 0.0 | 11 | 10 | 21 | 15 | 0 | .259 | .278 | 0 | 0 | C-56 |
| 1975 STL N | 44 | 80 | 16 | 2 | 0 | 1 | 1.3 | 5 | 6 | 3 | 10 | 0 | .200 | .263 | 14 | 1 | C-31 |
| 1976 | 27 | 50 | 8 | 3 | 0 | 0 | 0.0 | 1 | 5 | 1 | 7 | 0 | .160 | .220 | 13 | 4 | C-14 |
| 1977 2 teams | 22 | SF | N (11G – .200) | | | BAL | A | (11G – .286) | | | | | | | | | |
| " total | 22 | 29 | 7 | 1 | 0 | 0 | 0.0 | 3 | 2 | 1 | 7 | 0 | .241 | .276 | 5 | 0 | C-22 |
| 9 yrs. | 328 | 743 | 158 | 23 | 2 | 6 | 0.8 | 55 | 64 | 52 | 121 | 2 | .213 | .273 | 46 | 8 | C-280, OF-3 |
| 5 yrs. | 178 | 426 | 86 | 14 | 2 | 5 | 1.2 | 35 | 41 | 26 | 82 | 2 | .202 | .279 | 14 | 3 | C-157, OF-3 |

## Dutch Ruether

**RUETHER, WALTER HENRY**     BL TL 6'1½"   180 lbs.
B. Sept. 13, 1893, Alameda, Calif.    D. May 16, 1970, Phoenix, Ariz.

| | G | AB | H | 2B | 3B | HR | HR % | R | RBI | BB | SO | SB | BA | SA | AB | H | G by POS |
|---|---|---|---|---|---|---|---|---|---|---|---|---|---|---|---|---|---|
| 1917 2 teams | 50 | CHI | N (31G – .273) | | | CIN | N | (19G – .208) | | | | | | | | | |
| " total | 50 | 68 | 17 | 3 | 3 | 0 | 0.0 | 4 | 12 | 11 | 17 | 1 | .250 | .382 | 22 | 6 | P-17, 1B-5 |
| 1918 CIN N | 2 | 3 | 0 | 0 | 0 | 0 | 0.0 | 0 | 0 | 0 | 2 | 0 | .000 | .000 | 0 | 0 | P-2 |
| 1919 | 42 | 92 | 24 | 2 | 3 | 0 | 0.0 | 8 | 6 | 4 | 18 | 1 | .261 | .348 | 7 | 2 | P-33 |
| 1920 | 45 | 104 | 20 | 4 | 0 | 0 | 0.0 | 3 | 10 | 5 | 24 | 0 | .192 | .231 | 7 | 0 | P-37, 1B-1 |
| 1921 BKN N | 49 | 97 | 34 | 5 | 2 | 2 | 2.1 | 12 | 13 | 4 | 9 | 1 | .351 | .505 | 11 | 3 | P-36 |
| 1922 | 67 | 125 | 26 | 6 | 1 | 2 | 1.6 | 12 | 20 | 12 | 11 | 0 | .208 | .320 | 27 | 6 | P-35 |
| 1923 | 49 | 117 | 32 | 1 | 0 | 0 | 0.0 | 6 | 10 | 12 | 12 | 0 | .274 | .282 | 12 | 3 | P-34, 1B-1 |
| 1924 | 34 | 62 | 15 | 1 | 1 | 0 | 0.0 | 4 | 5 | 4 | 2 | 0 | .242 | .290 | 4 | 0 | P-30 |
| 1925 WAS A | 55 | 108 | 36 | 3 | 2 | 1 | 0.9 | 18 | 15 | 10 | 8 | 0 | .333 | .426 | 19 | 6 | P-30, 1B-1 |
| 1926 2 teams | 60 | WAS | A (47G – .250) | | | NY | A | (13G – .095) | | | | | | | | | |
| " total | 60 | 113 | 25 | 2 | 0 | 1 | 0.9 | 8 | 11 | 6 | 11 | 0 | .221 | .265 | 30 | 6 | P-28 |
| 1927 NY A | 35 | 80 | 21 | 3 | 0 | 1 | 1.3 | 7 | 10 | 8 | 15 | 0 | .263 | .338 | 6 | 2 | P-27 |
| 11 yrs. | 488 | 969 | 250 | 30 | 12 | 7 | 0.7 | 83 | 111 | 77 | 129 | 3 | .258 | .335 | 145 | 34 | P-309, 1B-8 |
| 1 yr. | 31 | 44 | 12 | 1 | 3 | 0 | 0.0 | 3 | 11 | 8 | 11 | 0 | .273 | .432 | 13 | 4 | P-10, 1B-5 |

WORLD SERIES

| | G | AB | H | 2B | 3B | HR | HR % | R | RBI | BB | SO | SB | BA | SA | AB | H | G by POS |
|---|---|---|---|---|---|---|---|---|---|---|---|---|---|---|---|---|---|
| 1919 CIN N | 3 | 6 | 4 | 1 | 2 | 0 | 0.0 | 2 | 4 | 1 | 0 | 0 | .667 | 1.500 | 1 | 0 | P-2 |
| 1925 WAS A | 1 | 1 | 0 | 0 | 0 | 0 | 0.0 | 0 | 0 | 0 | 0 | 0 | .000 | .000 | 1 | 0 | |
| 1926 NY A | 3 | 4 | 0 | 0 | 0 | 0 | 0.0 | 0 | 0 | 0 | 0 | 0 | .000 | .000 | 2 | 0 | P-1 |
| 3 yrs. | 7 | 11 | 4 | 1 | 2 | 0 | 0.0 | 2 | 4 | 1 | 0 | 0 | .364 | .818 | 4 | 0 | P-3 |

## Rip Russell

**RUSSELL, GLEN DAVID**     BR TR 6'1"   180 lbs.
B. Jan. 26, 1915, Los Angeles, Calif.    D. Sept. 26, 1976, Los Alamitos, Calif.

| | G | AB | H | 2B | 3B | HR | HR % | R | RBI | BB | SO | SB | BA | SA | AB | H | G by POS |
|---|---|---|---|---|---|---|---|---|---|---|---|---|---|---|---|---|---|
| 1939 CHI N | 143 | 542 | 148 | 24 | 5 | 9 | 1.7 | 55 | 79 | 36 | 56 | 2 | .273 | .386 | 0 | 0 | 1B-143 |
| 1940 | 68 | 215 | 53 | 7 | 2 | 5 | 2.3 | 15 | 33 | 8 | 23 | 1 | .247 | .367 | 15 | 5 | 1B-51, 3B-3 |
| 1941 | 6 | 17 | 5 | 1 | 0 | 0 | 0.0 | 1 | 1 | 1 | 5 | 0 | .294 | .353 | 0 | 0 | 1B-5 |
| 1942 | 102 | 302 | 73 | 9 | 0 | 8 | 2.6 | 32 | 41 | 17 | 21 | 0 | .242 | .351 | 31 | 5 | 1B-35, 2B-24, 3B-10, OF-3 |
| 1946 BOS A | 80 | 274 | 57 | 10 | 1 | 6 | 2.2 | 22 | 35 | 13 | 30 | 1 | .208 | .318 | 9 | 2 | 3B-70, 2B-3 |
| 1947 | 26 | 52 | 8 | 1 | 0 | 1 | 1.9 | 8 | 3 | 8 | 7 | 0 | .154 | .231 | 12 | 1 | 3B-13 |
| 6 yrs. | 425 | 1402 | 344 | 52 | 8 | 29 | 2.1 | 133 | 192 | 83 | 142 | 4 | .245 | .356 | 67 | 13 | 1B-234, 3B-96, 2B-27, OF-3 |
| 4 yrs. | 319 | 1076 | 279 | 41 | 7 | 22 | 2.0 | 103 | 154 | 62 | 105 | 3 | .259 | .372 | 46 | 10 | 1B-234, 2B-24, 3B-13, OF-3 |

WORLD SERIES

| | G | AB | H | 2B | 3B | HR | HR % | R | RBI | BB | SO | SB | BA | SA | AB | H | G by POS |
|---|---|---|---|---|---|---|---|---|---|---|---|---|---|---|---|---|---|
| 1946 BOS A | 2 | 2 | 2 | 0 | 0 | 0 | 0.0 | 1 | 0 | 0 | 0 | 0 | 1.000 | 1.000 | 2 | 2 | 3B-1 |

| | G | AB | H | 2B | 3B | HR | HR % | R | RBI | BB | SO | SB | BA | SA | Pinch Hit AB | Pinch Hit H | G by POS |
|---|---|---|---|---|---|---|---|---|---|---|---|---|---|---|---|---|---|

# Jimmy Ryan

**RYAN, JAMES E.**  BR TL 5'9" 162 lbs.
B. Feb. 11, 1863, Clinton, Mass.   D. Oct. 26, 1923, Chicago, Ill.

| | G | AB | H | 2B | 3B | HR | HR % | R | RBI | BB | SO | SB | BA | SA | PH AB | PH H | G by POS |
|---|---|---|---|---|---|---|---|---|---|---|---|---|---|---|---|---|---|
| 1885 CHI N | 3 | 13 | 6 | 1 | 0 | 0 | 0.0 | 2 | 2 | 1 | 1 | | .462 | .538 | 0 | 0 | SS-2, OF-1 |
| 1886 | 84 | 327 | 100 | 17 | 6 | 4 | 1.2 | 58 | 53 | 12 | 28 | | .306 | .431 | 0 | 0 | OF-70, SS-6, 3B-6, 2B-5, P-5 |
| 1887 | 126 | 508 | 145 | 23 | 10 | 11 | 2.2 | 117 | 74 | 53 | 19 | 50 | .285 | .435 | 0 | 0 | OF-122, P-8, 2B-3 |
| 1888 | 129 | 549 | **182** | **33** | 10 | **16** | **2.9** | 115 | 64 | 35 | 50 | 60 | .332 | **.515** | 0 | 0 | OF-128, P-8 |
| 1889 | 135 | 576 | 187 | 31 | 14 | 17 | 3.0 | 140 | 72 | 70 | 62 | 45 | .325 | .516 | 0 | 0 | OF-106, SS-29 |
| 1890 CHI P | 118 | 486 | 165 | 32 | 5 | 6 | 1.2 | 99 | 89 | 60 | 36 | 30 | .340 | .463 | 0 | 0 | OF-118 |
| 1891 CHI N | 118 | 505 | 145 | 22 | 15 | 9 | 1.8 | 110 | 66 | 53 | 38 | 27 | .287 | .444 | 0 | 0 | OF-117, SS-2, P-2 |
| 1892 | 128 | 505 | 148 | 21 | 11 | 10 | 2.0 | 105 | 65 | 61 | 41 | 27 | .293 | .438 | 0 | 0 | OF-120, SS-9 |
| 1893 | 83 | 341 | 102 | 21 | 7 | 3 | 0.9 | 82 | 30 | 59 | 25 | 8 | .299 | .428 | 0 | 0 | OF-73, SS-10, P-1 |
| 1894 | 108 | 481 | 173 | 37 | 7 | 3 | 0.6 | 133 | 62 | 50 | 23 | 11 | .360 | .484 | 0 | 0 | OF-108 |
| 1895 | 108 | 443 | 143 | 22 | 8 | 6 | 1.4 | 83 | 49 | 48 | 22 | 18 | .323 | .449 | 0 | 0 | OF-108 |
| 1896 | 128 | 490 | 153 | 24 | 10 | 3 | 0.6 | 83 | 86 | 46 | 16 | 29 | .312 | .420 | 0 | 0 | OF-128 |
| 1897 | 136 | 520 | 160 | 33 | 17 | 5 | 1.0 | 103 | 85 | 50 | | 27 | .308 | .465 | 0 | 0 | OF-136 |
| 1898 | 144 | 572 | 185 | 32 | 13 | 4 | 0.7 | 122 | 79 | 73 | | 29 | .323 | .446 | 0 | 0 | OF-144 |
| 1899 | 125 | 525 | 158 | 20 | 10 | 3 | 0.6 | 91 | 68 | 43 | | 9 | .301 | .394 | 0 | 0 | OF-125 |
| 1900 | 105 | 415 | 115 | 25 | 4 | 5 | 1.2 | 66 | 59 | 29 | | 19 | .277 | .393 | 0 | 0 | OF-105 |
| 1902 WAS A | 120 | 484 | 155 | 32 | 6 | 6 | 1.2 | 92 | 44 | 43 | | 10 | .320 | .448 | 0 | 0 | OF-120 |
| 1903 | 114 | 437 | 107 | 25 | 4 | 7 | 1.6 | 42 | 46 | 17 | | 9 | .245 | .368 | 0 | 0 | OF-114 |
| 18 yrs. | 2012 | 8177 | 2529 | 451 | 157 | 118 | 1.4 | 1643 | 1093 | 803 | 361 | 408 | .309 | .446 | 0 | 0 | OF-1943, SS-58, P-24, 2B-8, 3B-6 |
| 15 yrs. | 1660 | 6770 | 2102 | 362 | 142 | 99 | 1.5 | 1410 | 914 | 683 | 325 | 359 | .310 | .450 | 0 | 0 | OF-1591, SS-58, P-24, 2B-8, 3B-6 |
| | **8th** | **6th** | **6th** | **6th** | **1st** | | | **2nd** | **6th** | **9th** | | **9th** | | | | | |

# Vic Saier

**SAIER, VICTOR SYLVESTER**  BL TR 5'11" 185 lbs.
B. May 4, 1891, Lansing, Mich.   D. May 14, 1967, East Lansing, Mich.

| | G | AB | H | 2B | 3B | HR | HR % | R | RBI | BB | SO | SB | BA | SA | PH AB | PH H | G by POS |
|---|---|---|---|---|---|---|---|---|---|---|---|---|---|---|---|---|---|
| 1911 CHI N | 86 | 259 | 67 | 15 | 1 | 1 | 0.4 | 42 | 37 | 25 | 37 | 11 | .259 | .336 | 12 | 4 | 1B-73 |
| 1912 | 122 | 451 | 130 | 25 | 14 | 2 | 0.4 | 74 | 61 | 34 | 65 | 11 | .288 | .419 | 1 | 0 | 1B-120 |
| 1913 | 148 | 518 | 149 | 14 | **21** | 14 | 2.7 | 93 | 92 | 62 | 62 | 26 | .288 | .477 | 1 | 0 | 1B-148 |
| 1914 | 153 | 537 | 129 | 24 | 8 | 18 | 3.4 | 87 | 72 | 94 | 61 | 19 | .240 | .415 | 0 | 0 | 1B-153 |
| 1915 | 144 | 497 | 131 | 35 | 11 | 11 | 2.2 | 74 | 64 | 64 | 62 | 29 | .264 | .445 | 4 | 1 | 1B-139 |
| 1916 | 147 | 498 | 126 | 25 | 3 | 7 | 1.4 | 60 | 50 | 79 | 68 | 20 | .253 | .357 | 0 | 0 | 1B-147 |
| 1917 | 6 | 21 | 5 | 1 | 0 | 0 | 0.0 | 5 | 2 | 2 | 1 | 0 | .238 | .286 | 0 | 0 | 1B-6 |
| 1919 PIT N | 58 | 166 | 37 | 3 | 3 | 2 | 1.2 | 19 | 17 | 18 | 13 | 5 | .223 | .313 | 7 | 3 | 1B-51 |
| 8 yrs. | 864 | 2947 | 774 | 142 | 61 | 55 | 1.9 | 454 | 395 | 378 | 369 | 121 | .263 | .408 | 25 | 8 | 1B-837 |
| 7 yrs. | 806 | 2781 | 737 | 139 | 58 | 53 | 1.9 | 435 | 378 | 360 | 356 | 116 | .265 | .414 | 18 | 5 | 1B-786 |

# Ryne Sandberg

**SANDBERG, RYNE DEE**  BR TR 6'1" 175 lbs.
B. Sept. 18, 1959, Spokane, Wash.

| | G | AB | H | 2B | 3B | HR | HR % | R | RBI | BB | SO | SB | BA | SA | PH AB | PH H | G by POS |
|---|---|---|---|---|---|---|---|---|---|---|---|---|---|---|---|---|---|
| 1981 PHI N | 13 | 6 | 1 | 0 | 0 | 0 | 0.0 | 2 | 0 | 0 | 1 | 0 | .167 | .167 | 0 | 0 | SS-5, 2B-1 |
| 1982 CHI N | 156 | 635 | 172 | 33 | 5 | 7 | 1.1 | 103 | 54 | 36 | 90 | 32 | .271 | .372 | 1 | 0 | 3B-133, 2B-24 |
| 1983 | 158 | 633 | 165 | 25 | 4 | 8 | 1.3 | 94 | 48 | 51 | 79 | 37 | .261 | .351 | 4 | 2 | 2B-157, SS-1 |
| 1984 | 156 | 636 | 200 | 36 | **19** | 19 | 3.0 | **114** | 84 | 52 | 101 | 32 | .314 | .520 | 0 | 0 | 2B-156 |
| 1985 | 153 | 609 | 186 | 31 | 6 | 26 | 4.3 | 113 | 83 | 57 | 97 | 54 | .305 | .504 | 1 | 0 | 2B-153, SS-1 |
| 5 yrs. | 636 | 2519 | 724 | 125 | 34 | 60 | 2.4 | 426 | 269 | 196 | 368 | 155 | .287 | .435 | 6 | 2 | 2B-491, 3B-133, SS-7 |
| 4 yrs. | 623 | 2513 | 723 | 125 | 34 | 60 | 2.4 | 424 | 269 | 196 | 367 | 155 | .288 | .436 | 6 | 2 | 2B-490, 3B-133, SS-2 |
| | | | | | | | | | | | | **10th** | | | | | |

**LEAGUE CHAMPIONSHIP SERIES**

| | G | AB | H | 2B | 3B | HR | HR % | R | RBI | BB | SO | SB | BA | SA | PH AB | PH H | G by POS |
|---|---|---|---|---|---|---|---|---|---|---|---|---|---|---|---|---|---|
| 1984 CHI N | 5 | 19 | 7 | 2 | 0 | 0 | 0.0 | 3 | 2 | 3 | 2 | 3 | .368 | .474 | 0 | 0 | 2B-5 |

# Ron Santo

**SANTO, RONALD EDWARD**  BR TR 6' 190 lbs.
B. Feb. 25, 1940, Seattle, Wash.

| | G | AB | H | 2B | 3B | HR | HR % | R | RBI | BB | SO | SB | BA | SA | PH AB | PH H | G by POS |
|---|---|---|---|---|---|---|---|---|---|---|---|---|---|---|---|---|---|
| 1960 CHI N | 95 | 347 | 87 | 24 | 2 | 9 | 2.6 | 44 | 44 | 31 | 44 | 0 | .251 | .409 | 1 | 0 | 3B-94 |
| 1961 | 154 | 578 | 164 | 32 | 6 | 23 | 4.0 | 84 | 83 | 73 | 77 | 2 | .284 | .479 | 1 | 1 | 3B-153 |
| 1962 | 162 | 604 | 137 | 20 | 4 | 17 | 2.8 | 44 | 83 | 65 | 94 | 4 | .227 | .358 | 2 | 0 | 3B-157, SS-8 |
| 1963 | 162 | 630 | 187 | 29 | 6 | 25 | 4.0 | 79 | 99 | 42 | 92 | 6 | .297 | .481 | 0 | 0 | 3B-162 |
| 1964 | 161 | 592 | 185 | 33 | **13** | 30 | 5.1 | 94 | 114 | **86** | 96 | 3 | .313 | .564 | 0 | 0 | 3B-161 |
| 1965 | 164 | 608 | 173 | 30 | 4 | 33 | 5.4 | 88 | 101 | 88 | 109 | 3 | .285 | .510 | 0 | 0 | 3B-164 |
| 1966 | 155 | 561 | 175 | 21 | 8 | 30 | 5.3 | 93 | **95** | 78 | 4 | | .312 | .538 | 0 | 0 | 3B-152, SS-8 |
| 1967 | 161 | 586 | 176 | 23 | 4 | 31 | 5.3 | 107 | 98 | **96** | 103 | 1 | .300 | .512 | 0 | 0 | 3B-161 |
| 1968 | 162 | 577 | 142 | 17 | 3 | 26 | 4.5 | 86 | 98 | **96** | 106 | 3 | .246 | .421 | 0 | 0 | 3B-162 |
| 1969 | 160 | 575 | 166 | 18 | 4 | 29 | 5.0 | 97 | 123 | 96 | 97 | 1 | .289 | .485 | 1 | 0 | 3B-160 |
| 1970 | 154 | 555 | 148 | 30 | 4 | 26 | 4.7 | 83 | 114 | 92 | 108 | 2 | .267 | .476 | 2 | 1 | 3B-152, OF-1 |
| 1971 | 154 | 555 | 148 | 22 | 1 | 21 | 3.8 | 77 | 88 | 79 | 95 | 4 | .267 | .423 | 1 | 0 | 3B-149, OF-6 |
| 1972 | 133 | 464 | 140 | 25 | 5 | 17 | 3.7 | 68 | 74 | 69 | 75 | 1 | .302 | .487 | 1 | 1 | 3B-129, 2B-3, OF-1, SS-1 |
| 1973 | 149 | 536 | 143 | 29 | 2 | 20 | 3.7 | 65 | 77 | 63 | 97 | 1 | .267 | .440 | 2 | 0 | 3B-146 |
| 1974 CHI A | 117 | 375 | 83 | 12 | 1 | 5 | 1.3 | 29 | 41 | 37 | 72 | 0 | .221 | .299 | 5 | 3 | DH-47, 2B-39, 3B-28, 1B-3, SS-1 |
| 15 yrs. | 2243 | 8143 | 2254 | 365 | 67 | 342 | 4.2 | 1138 | 1331 | 1108 | 1343 | 35 | .277 | .464 | 16 | 6 | 3B-2130, DH-47, 2B-42, SS-18, OF-8, 1B-3 |
| 14 yrs. | 2126 | 7768 | 2171 | 353 | 66 | 337 | 4.3 | 1109 | 1290 | 1071 | 1271 | 35 | .279 | .472 | 11 | 3 | 3B-2102, SS-17, OF-8, 2B-3 |
| | **4th** | **4th** | **5th** | **7th** | | **3rd** | **7th** | | **6th** | **4th** | **2nd** | **1st** | | **8th** | | | |

# Ed Sauer

**SAUER, EDWARD (Horn)**  BR TR 6'1" 188 lbs.
Brother of Hank Sauer.
B. Jan. 3, 1920, Pittsburgh, Pa.

| | G | AB | H | 2B | 3B | HR | HR % | R | RBI | BB | SO | SB | BA | SA | PH AB | PH H | G by POS |
|---|---|---|---|---|---|---|---|---|---|---|---|---|---|---|---|---|---|
| 1943 CHI N | 14 | 55 | 15 | 3 | 0 | 0 | 0.0 | 3 | 9 | 3 | 6 | 1 | .273 | .327 | 0 | 0 | OF-13, 3B-1 |
| 1944 | 23 | 50 | 11 | 4 | 0 | 0 | 0.0 | 3 | 5 | 2 | 6 | 0 | .220 | .300 | 9 | 2 | OF-12 |
| 1945 | 49 | 93 | 24 | 4 | 1 | 2 | 2.2 | 8 | 11 | 8 | 23 | 2 | .258 | .387 | 15 | 3 | OF-26 |

| | G | AB | H | 2B | 3B | HR | HR % | R | RBI | BB | SO | SB | BA | SA | Pinch Hit AB | Pinch Hit H | G by POS |
|---|---|---|---|---|---|---|---|---|---|---|---|---|---|---|---|---|---|

### Ed Sauer continued

| | | G | AB | H | 2B | 3B | HR | HR% | R | RBI | BB | SO | SB | BA | SA | PH AB | PH H | G by POS |
|---|---|---|---|---|---|---|---|---|---|---|---|---|---|---|---|---|---|---|
| 1949 | 2 teams | STL N (24G – .222) | | | | | BOS N (79G – .266) | | | | | | | | | | | |
| " | total | 103 | 259 | 67 | 14 | 1 | 3 | 1.2 | 31 | 32 | 20 | 42 | 0 | .259 | .355 | 19 | 4 | OF-81, 3B-2 |
| | 4 yrs. | 189 | 457 | 117 | 25 | 2 | 5 | 1.1 | 45 | 57 | 33 | 77 | 3 | .256 | .352 | 43 | 9 | OF-132, 3B-3 |
| | 3 yrs. | 86 | 198 | 50 | 11 | 1 | 2 | 1.0 | 14 | 25 | 13 | 35 | 3 | .253 | .348 | 24 | 5 | OF-51, 3B-1 |

WORLD SERIES

| | | G | AB | H | 2B | 3B | HR | HR% | R | RBI | BB | SO | SB | BA | SA | PH AB | PH H | G by POS |
|---|---|---|---|---|---|---|---|---|---|---|---|---|---|---|---|---|---|---|
| 1945 | CHI N | 2 | 2 | 0 | 0 | 0 | 0 | 0.0 | 0 | 0 | 0 | 2 | 0 | .000 | .000 | 2 | 0 | |

### Hank Sauer

SAUER, HENRY JOHN
Brother of Ed Sauer.
B. Mar. 17, 1919, Pittsburgh, Pa.                   BR TR 6'2"  198 lbs.

| | | G | AB | H | 2B | 3B | HR | HR% | R | RBI | BB | SO | SB | BA | SA | PH AB | PH H | G by POS |
|---|---|---|---|---|---|---|---|---|---|---|---|---|---|---|---|---|---|---|
| 1941 | CIN N | 9 | 33 | 10 | 4 | 0 | 0 | 0.0 | 4 | 5 | 1 | 4 | 0 | .303 | .424 | 1 | 1 | OF-8 |
| 1942 | | 7 | 20 | 5 | 0 | 0 | 2 | 10.0 | 4 | 4 | 2 | 2 | 0 | .250 | .550 | 3 | 1 | 1B-4 |
| 1945 | | 31 | 116 | 34 | 1 | 0 | 5 | 4.3 | 18 | 20 | 6 | 16 | 2 | .293 | .431 | 1 | 0 | OF-28, 1B-3 |
| 1948 | | 145 | 530 | 138 | 22 | 1 | 35 | 6.6 | 78 | 97 | 60 | 85 | 2 | .260 | .504 | 2 | 0 | OF-132, 1B-12 |
| 1949 | 2 teams | CIN N (42G – .237) | | | | | CHI N (96G – .291) | | | | | | | | | | | |
| " | total | 138 | 509 | 140 | 23 | 1 | 31 | 6.1 | 81 | 99 | 55 | 66 | 0 | .275 | .507 | 3 | 1 | OF-135, 1B-1 |
| 1950 | CHI N | 145 | 540 | 148 | 32 | 2 | 32 | 5.9 | 85 | 103 | 60 | 67 | 1 | .274 | .519 | 3 | 2 | OF-125, 1B-18 |
| 1951 | | 141 | 525 | 138 | 19 | 4 | 30 | 5.7 | 77 | 89 | 45 | 77 | 2 | .263 | .486 | 8 | 1 | OF-132 |
| 1952 | | 151 | 567 | 153 | 31 | 3 | 37 | 6.5 | 89 | 121 | 77 | 92 | 1 | .270 | .531 | 0 | 0 | OF-151 |
| 1953 | | 108 | 395 | 104 | 16 | 5 | 19 | 4.8 | 61 | 60 | 50 | 56 | 0 | .263 | .473 | 5 | 1 | OF-105 |
| 1954 | | 142 | 520 | 150 | 18 | 1 | 41 | 7.9 | 98 | 103 | 70 | 68 | 2 | .288 | .563 | 1 | 0 | OF-141 |
| 1955 | | 79 | 261 | 55 | 8 | 1 | 12 | 4.6 | 29 | 28 | 26 | 47 | 0 | .211 | .387 | 10 | 0 | OF-68 |
| 1956 | STL N | 75 | 151 | 45 | 4 | 0 | 5 | 3.3 | 11 | 24 | 25 | 31 | 0 | .298 | .424 | 31 | 6 | OF-37 |
| 1957 | NY N | 127 | 378 | 98 | 14 | 1 | 26 | 6.9 | 46 | 76 | 49 | 59 | 1 | .259 | .508 | 24 | 7 | OF-98 |
| 1958 | SF N | 88 | 236 | 59 | 8 | 0 | 12 | 5.1 | 27 | 46 | 35 | 37 | 0 | .250 | .436 | 19 | 2 | OF-67 |
| 1959 | | 13 | 15 | 1 | 0 | 0 | 1 | 6.7 | 1 | 1 | 0 | 7 | 0 | .067 | .267 | 12 | 1 | OF-1 |
| | 15 yrs. | 1399 | 4796 | 1278 | 200 | 19 | 288 | 6.0 | 709 | 876 | 561 | 714 | 11 | .266 | .496 | 123 | 22 | OF-1228, 1B-38 |
| | 7 yrs. | 862 | 3165 | 852 | 141 | 17 | 198 | 6.3 | 498 | 587 | 365 | 454 | 6 | .269 | .512 | 27 | 4 | OF-818, 1B-18 |
| | | | | | | | 6th | 1st | | | | | | | 2nd | | | |

### Ted Savage

SAVAGE, THEODORE EDMUND
B. Feb. 21, 1937, Venice, Ill.                   BR TR 6'1"  185 lbs.

| | | G | AB | H | 2B | 3B | HR | HR% | R | RBI | BB | SO | SB | BA | SA | PH AB | PH H | G by POS |
|---|---|---|---|---|---|---|---|---|---|---|---|---|---|---|---|---|---|---|
| 1962 | PHI N | 127 | 335 | 89 | 11 | 2 | 7 | 2.1 | 54 | 39 | 40 | 66 | 16 | .266 | .373 | 21 | 3 | OF-109 |
| 1963 | PIT N | 85 | 149 | 29 | 2 | 1 | 5 | 3.4 | 22 | 14 | 14 | 31 | 4 | .195 | .322 | 33 | 5 | OF-47 |
| 1965 | STL N | 30 | 63 | 10 | 3 | 0 | 1 | 1.6 | 7 | 4 | 6 | 9 | 1 | .159 | .254 | 7 | 2 | OF-20 |
| 1966 | | 16 | 29 | 5 | 2 | 1 | 0 | 0.0 | 4 | 3 | 4 | 7 | 4 | .172 | .310 | 9 | 2 | OF-7 |
| 1967 | 2 teams | STL N (9G – .125) | | | | | CHI N (96G – .218) | | | | | | | | | | | |
| " | total | 105 | 233 | 50 | 10 | 1 | 5 | 2.1 | 41 | 33 | 41 | 57 | 7 | .215 | .330 | 17 | 4 | OF-86, 3B-1 |
| 1968 | 2 teams | CHI N (3G – .250) | | | | | LA N (61G – .206) | | | | | | | | | | | |
| " | total | 64 | 134 | 28 | 6 | 1 | 2 | 1.5 | 7 | 7 | 10 | 21 | 1 | .209 | .313 | 21 | 3 | OF-41 |
| 1969 | CIN N | 68 | 110 | 25 | 7 | 0 | 2 | 1.8 | 20 | 11 | 20 | 27 | 3 | .227 | .345 | 27 | 5 | OF-17, 2B-1 |
| 1970 | MIL A | 114 | 276 | 77 | 10 | 5 | 12 | 4.3 | 43 | 50 | 57 | 44 | 10 | .279 | .482 | 31 | 6 | OF-82, 1B-1 |
| 1971 | 2 teams | MIL A (14G – .176) | | | | | KC A (19G – .172) | | | | | | | | | | | |
| " | total | 33 | 46 | 8 | 0 | 0 | 0 | 0.0 | 4 | 2 | 8 | 10 | 3 | .174 | .174 | 18 | 2 | OF-15 |
| | 9 yrs. | 642 | 1375 | 321 | 51 | 11 | 34 | 2.5 | 202 | 163 | 200 | 272 | 49 | .233 | .361 | 184 | 32 | OF-424, 3B-1, 2B-1, 1B-1 |
| | 2 yrs. | 99 | 233 | 51 | 10 | 1 | 5 | 2.1 | 40 | 33 | 40 | 55 | 7 | .219 | .335 | 12 | 4 | OF-88, 3B-1 |

### Carl Sawatski

SAWATSKI, CARL ERNEST (Swats)
B. Nov. 4, 1927, Shickshinny, Pa.                   BL TR 5'10"  210 lbs.

| | | G | AB | H | 2B | 3B | HR | HR% | R | RBI | BB | SO | SB | BA | SA | PH AB | PH H | G by POS |
|---|---|---|---|---|---|---|---|---|---|---|---|---|---|---|---|---|---|---|
| 1948 | CHI N | 2 | 2 | 0 | 0 | 0 | 0 | 0.0 | 0 | 0 | 0 | 0 | 0 | .000 | .000 | 2 | 0 | |
| 1950 | | 38 | 103 | 18 | 1 | 0 | 1 | 1.0 | 4 | 7 | 11 | 19 | 0 | .175 | .214 | 7 | 0 | C-32 |
| 1953 | | 43 | 59 | 13 | 3 | 0 | 1 | 1.7 | 5 | 5 | 7 | 7 | 0 | .220 | .322 | 29 | 6 | C-15 |
| 1954 | CHI A | 43 | 109 | 20 | 3 | 3 | 1 | 0.9 | 6 | 12 | 15 | 20 | 0 | .183 | .294 | 8 | 1 | C-33 |
| 1957 | MIL N | 58 | 105 | 25 | 4 | 0 | 6 | 5.7 | 13 | 17 | 10 | 15 | 0 | .238 | .448 | 31 | 6 | C-28 |
| 1958 | 2 teams | MIL N (10G – .100) | | | | | PHI N (60G – .230) | | | | | | | | | | | |
| " | total | 70 | 193 | 43 | 4 | 1 | 5 | 2.6 | 13 | 13 | 18 | 47 | 0 | .223 | .332 | 13 | 4 | C-56 |
| 1959 | PHI N | 74 | 198 | 58 | 10 | 0 | 9 | 4.5 | 15 | 43 | 32 | 36 | 0 | .293 | .480 | 7 | 1 | C-69 |
| 1960 | STL N | 78 | 179 | 41 | 4 | 0 | 6 | 3.4 | 16 | 27 | 22 | 24 | 0 | .229 | .352 | 27 | 7 | C-67 |
| 1961 | | 86 | 174 | 52 | 8 | 0 | 10 | 5.7 | 23 | 33 | 25 | 17 | 0 | .299 | .517 | 39 | 10 | C-60, OF-1 |
| 1962 | | 85 | 222 | 56 | 9 | 1 | 13 | 5.9 | 26 | 42 | 36 | 38 | 0 | .252 | .477 | 15 | 2 | C-70 |
| 1963 | | 56 | 105 | 25 | 0 | 0 | 6 | 5.7 | 12 | 14 | 15 | 28 | 2 | .238 | .410 | 31 | 4 | C-27 |
| | 11 yrs. | 633 | 1449 | 351 | 46 | 5 | 58 | 4.0 | 133 | 213 | 191 | 251 | 2 | .242 | .401 | 209 | 41 | C-457, OF-1 |
| | 3 yrs. | 83 | 164 | 31 | 4 | 0 | 2 | 1.2 | 9 | 12 | 18 | 26 | 0 | .189 | .250 | 38 | 6 | C-47 |

WORLD SERIES

| | | G | AB | H | 2B | 3B | HR | HR% | R | RBI | BB | SO | SB | BA | SA | PH AB | PH H | G by POS |
|---|---|---|---|---|---|---|---|---|---|---|---|---|---|---|---|---|---|---|
| 1957 | MIL N | 2 | 2 | 0 | 0 | 0 | 0 | 0.0 | 0 | 0 | 0 | 2 | 0 | .000 | .000 | 2 | 0 | |

### Germany Schaefer

SCHAEFER, HERMAN A.
B. Feb. 4, 1878, Chicago, Ill.   D. May 16, 1919, Saranac Lake, N. Y.                   BR TR

| | | G | AB | H | 2B | 3B | HR | HR% | R | RBI | BB | SO | SB | BA | SA | PH AB | PH H | G by POS |
|---|---|---|---|---|---|---|---|---|---|---|---|---|---|---|---|---|---|---|
| 1901 | CHI N | 2 | 5 | 3 | 1 | 0 | 0 | 0.0 | 0 | 0 | 2 | | 0 | .600 | .800 | 0 | 0 | 3B-1, 2B-1 |
| 1902 | | 81 | 291 | 57 | 2 | 3 | 0 | 0.0 | 32 | 14 | 19 | | 12 | .196 | .223 | 0 | 0 | 3B-75, 1B-3, OF-2, SS-1 |
| 1905 | DET A | 153 | 554 | 135 | 17 | 9 | 2 | 0.4 | 64 | 47 | 45 | | 19 | .244 | .318 | 0 | 0 | 2B-151, SS-3 |
| 1906 | | 124 | 446 | 106 | 14 | 3 | 2 | 0.4 | 48 | 42 | 32 | | 31 | .238 | .296 | 2 | 1 | 2B-114, SS-7 |
| 1907 | | 109 | 372 | 96 | 12 | 3 | 1 | 0.3 | 45 | 32 | 30 | | 21 | .258 | .315 | 2 | 0 | 2B-74, SS-18, 3B-14, OF-1 |
| 1908 | | 153 | 584 | 151 | 20 | 10 | 3 | 0.5 | 96 | 52 | 37 | | 40 | .259 | .342 | 0 | 0 | SS-68, 2B-58, 3B-29 |
| 1909 | 2 teams | DET A (87G – .250) | | | | | WAS A (37G – .242) | | | | | | | | | | | |
| " | total | 124 | 408 | 101 | 17 | 1 | 0 | 0.2 | 39 | 26 | 20 | | 14 | .248 | .301 | 4 | 0 | 2B-118, OF-1, 3B-1 |
| 1910 | WAS A | 74 | 229 | 63 | 6 | 5 | 0 | 0.0 | 27 | 14 | 25 | | 17 | .275 | .345 | 10 | 2 | 2B-35, OF-26, 3B-2 |
| 1911 | | 125 | 440 | 147 | 14 | 7 | 0 | 0.0 | 74 | 45 | 57 | | 22 | .334 | .398 | 9 | 3 | 1B-108, OF-7 |
| 1912 | | 60 | 166 | 41 | 7 | 3 | 0 | 0.0 | 21 | 19 | 23 | | 11 | .247 | .325 | 11 | 2 | OF-19, 2B-15, 1B-15, P-1 |
| 1913 | | 52 | 100 | 32 | 1 | 1 | 0 | 0.0 | 17 | 7 | 15 | 12 | 6 | .320 | .350 | 21 | 11 | 2B-17, 1B-5, 3B-2, OF-1, P-1 |
| 1914 | | 25 | 29 | 7 | 1 | 0 | 0 | 0.0 | 6 | 2 | 3 | 5 | 4 | .241 | .276 | 14 | 3 | OF-3, 2B-3 |

| | G | AB | H | 2B | 3B | HR | HR % | R | RBI | BB | SO | SB | BA | SA | Pinch Hit AB | Pinch Hit H | G by POS |
|---|---|---|---|---|---|---|---|---|---|---|---|---|---|---|---|---|---|

## Germany Schaefer continued

| | G | AB | H | 2B | 3B | HR | HR% | R | RBI | BB | SO | SB | BA | SA | AB | H | G by POS |
|---|---|---|---|---|---|---|---|---|---|---|---|---|---|---|---|---|---|
| 1915 NWK F | 59 | 154 | 33 | 5 | 3 | 0 | 0.0 | 26 | 8 | 25 | | 3 | .214 | .286 | 15 | 2 | OF-17, 1B-13, 3B-9, 2B-2 |
| 1916 NY A | 1 | 0 | 0 | 0 | 0 | 0 | – | 0 | 0 | 0 | 0 | 0 | – | – | 0 | 0 | OF-1 |
| 1918 CLE A | 1 | 5 | 0 | 0 | 0 | 0 | 0.0 | 2 | 0 | 0 | 0 | 1 | .000 | .000 | 0 | 0 | 2B-1 |
| 15 yrs. | 1143 | 3783 | 972 | 117 | 48 | 9 | 0.2 | 497 | 308 | 333 | 17 | 201 | .257 | .320 | 88 | 24 | 2B-589, 1B-144, 3B-133, SS-97, OF-78, P-2 |
| 2 yrs. | 83 | 296 | 60 | 3 | 3 | 0 | 0.0 | 32 | 14 | 21 | | 12 | .203 | .233 | 0 | 0 | 3B-76, 1B-3, OF-2, SS-1, 2B-1 |

| WORLD SERIES | | | | | | | | | | | | | | | | | |
|---|---|---|---|---|---|---|---|---|---|---|---|---|---|---|---|---|---|
| 1907 DET A | 5 | 21 | 3 | 0 | 0 | 0 | 0.0 | 1 | 0 | 0 | 3 | 1 | .143 | .143 | 0 | 0 | 2B-5 |
| 1908 | 5 | 16 | 2 | 0 | 0 | 0 | 0.0 | 0 | 0 | 1 | 4 | 0 | .125 | .125 | 0 | 0 | 3B-2 |
| 2 yrs. | 10 | 37 | 5 | 0 | 0 | 0 | 0.0 | 1 | 0 | 1 | 7 | 1 | .135 | .135 | 0 | 0 | 2B-5, 3B-2 |

## Jimmie Schaffer

**SCHAFFER, JIMMIE RONALD**      BR TR 5'9" 170 lbs.
B. Apr. 5, 1936, Limeport, Pa.

| | G | AB | H | 2B | 3B | HR | HR% | R | RBI | BB | SO | SB | BA | SA | AB | H | G by POS |
|---|---|---|---|---|---|---|---|---|---|---|---|---|---|---|---|---|---|
| 1961 STL N | 68 | 153 | 39 | 7 | 0 | 1 | 0.7 | 15 | 16 | 9 | 29 | 0 | .255 | .320 | 1 | 1 | C-68 |
| 1962 | 70 | 66 | 16 | 2 | 1 | 0 | 0.0 | 7 | 6 | 6 | 16 | 1 | .242 | .303 | 1 | 0 | C-69 |
| 1963 CHI N | 57 | 142 | 34 | 7 | 0 | 7 | 4.9 | 17 | 19 | 11 | 35 | 0 | .239 | .437 | 1 | 0 | C-54 |
| 1964 | 54 | 122 | 25 | 6 | 1 | 2 | 1.6 | 9 | 9 | 17 | 17 | 2 | .205 | .320 | 9 | 3 | C-43 |
| 1965 2 teams | CHI A (17G – .194) | | | | NY N (24G – .135) | | | | | | | | | | | | |
| " total | 41 | 68 | 11 | 5 | 1 | 0 | 0.0 | 2 | 1 | 4 | 19 | 0 | .162 | .265 | 7 | 0 | C-35 |
| 1966 PHI N | 18 | 15 | 2 | 1 | 0 | 1 | 6.7 | 2 | 4 | 1 | 7 | 0 | .133 | .400 | 2 | 0 | C-6 |
| 1967 | 2 | 2 | 0 | 0 | 0 | 0 | 0.0 | 1 | 0 | 1 | 1 | 0 | .000 | .000 | 0 | 0 | C-1 |
| 1968 CIN N | 4 | 6 | 1 | 0 | 0 | 0 | 0.0 | 0 | 1 | 0 | 3 | 0 | .167 | .167 | 2 | 0 | C-2 |
| 8 yrs. | 314 | 574 | 128 | 28 | 3 | 11 | 1.9 | 53 | 56 | 49 | 127 | 3 | .223 | .340 | 23 | 4 | C-278 |
| 2 yrs. | 111 | 264 | 59 | 13 | 1 | 9 | 3.4 | 26 | 28 | 28 | 52 | 2 | .223 | .383 | 10 | 3 | C-97 |

## Bob Scheffing

**SCHEFFING, ROBERT BODEN**      BR TR 6'2" 180 lbs.
B. Aug. 11, 1915, Overland, Mo.    D. Oct. 26, 1985, Scottsdale, Ariz.
Manager 1957-59, 1961-63.

| | G | AB | H | 2B | 3B | HR | HR% | R | RBI | BB | SO | SB | BA | SA | AB | H | G by POS |
|---|---|---|---|---|---|---|---|---|---|---|---|---|---|---|---|---|---|
| 1941 CHI N | 51 | 132 | 32 | 8 | 0 | 1 | 0.8 | 9 | 20 | 5 | 19 | 2 | .242 | .326 | 17 | 3 | C-34 |
| 1942 | 44 | 102 | 20 | 3 | 0 | 2 | 2.0 | 7 | 12 | 7 | 11 | 2 | .196 | .284 | 12 | 1 | C-32 |
| 1946 | 63 | 115 | 32 | 4 | 1 | 0 | 0.0 | 8 | 18 | 12 | 18 | 0 | .278 | .330 | 19 | 7 | C-43 |
| 1947 | 110 | 363 | 96 | 11 | 5 | 5 | 1.4 | 33 | 50 | 25 | 25 | 2 | .264 | .364 | 13 | 5 | C-97 |
| 1948 | 102 | 293 | 88 | 18 | 2 | 5 | 1.7 | 23 | 45 | 22 | 27 | 0 | .300 | .427 | 24 | 9 | C-78 |
| 1949 | 55 | 149 | 40 | 6 | 1 | 3 | 2.0 | 12 | 19 | 9 | 9 | 0 | .268 | .383 | 14 | 4 | C-40 |
| 1950 2 teams | CHI N (12G – .188) | | | | CIN N (21G – .277) | | | | | | | | | | | | |
| " total | 33 | 63 | 16 | 1 | 0 | 2 | 3.2 | 4 | 7 | 4 | 4 | 0 | .254 | .365 | 19 | 5 | C-14 |
| 1951 2 teams | CIN N (47G – .254) | | | | STL N (12G – .111) | | | | | | | | | | | | |
| " total | 59 | 140 | 33 | 2 | 0 | 2 | 1.4 | 9 | 16 | 19 | 14 | 0 | .236 | .293 | 7 | 3 | C-52 |
| 8 yrs. | 517 | 1357 | 357 | 53 | 9 | 20 | 1.5 | 105 | 187 | 103 | 127 | 6 | .263 | .360 | 124 | 33 | C-390 |
| 7 yrs. | 437 | 1170 | 311 | 51 | 9 | 16 | 1.4 | 92 | 165 | 80 | 111 | 6 | .266 | .366 | 107 | 28 | C-327 |

## Hank Schenz

**SCHENZ, HENRY LEONARD**      BR TR 5'9½" 175 lbs.
B. Apr. 11, 1919, New Richmond, Ohio

| | G | AB | H | 2B | 3B | HR | HR% | R | RBI | BB | SO | SB | BA | SA | AB | H | G by POS |
|---|---|---|---|---|---|---|---|---|---|---|---|---|---|---|---|---|---|
| 1946 CHI N | 6 | 11 | 2 | 0 | 0 | 0 | 0.0 | 0 | 1 | 0 | 0 | 1 | .182 | .182 | 0 | 0 | 3B-5 |
| 1947 | 7 | 14 | 1 | 0 | 0 | 0 | 0.0 | 2 | 0 | 2 | 1 | 0 | .071 | .071 | 0 | 0 | 3B-5 |
| 1948 | 96 | 337 | 88 | 17 | 1 | 1 | 0.3 | 43 | 14 | 18 | 15 | 3 | .261 | .326 | 10 | 1 | 2B-78, 3B-5 |
| 1949 | 7 | 14 | 6 | 0 | 0 | 0 | 0.0 | 2 | 1 | 1 | 0 | 2 | .429 | .429 | 0 | 0 | 3B-5 |
| 1950 PIT N | 58 | 101 | 23 | 4 | 2 | 1 | 1.0 | 17 | 5 | 6 | 7 | 0 | .228 | .337 | 14 | 5 | 2B-21, 3B-12, SS-4 |
| 1951 2 teams | PIT N (25G – .213) | | | | NY N (8G – .000) | | | | | | | | | | | | |
| " total | 33 | 61 | 13 | 1 | 0 | 0 | 0.0 | 6 | 3 | 0 | 2 | 0 | .213 | .230 | 1 | 0 | 2B-19, 3B-2 |
| 6 yrs. | 207 | 538 | 133 | 22 | 3 | 2 | 0.4 | 70 | 24 | 27 | 25 | 6 | .247 | .310 | 25 | 6 | 2B-118, 3B-34, SS-4 |
| 4 yrs. | 116 | 376 | 97 | 17 | 1 | 1 | 0.3 | 47 | 16 | 21 | 16 | 6 | .258 | .316 | 10 | 1 | 2B-78, 3B-20 |

| WORLD SERIES | | | | | | | | | | | | | | | | | |
|---|---|---|---|---|---|---|---|---|---|---|---|---|---|---|---|---|---|
| 1951 NY N | 1 | 0 | 0 | 0 | 0 | 0 | – | 0 | 0 | 0 | 0 | 0 | – | – | 0 | 0 | |

## Morrie Schick

**SCHICK, MAURICE FRANCIS**      BR TR 5'11" 170 lbs.
B. Apr. 17, 1892, Chicago, Ill.    D. Oct. 25, 1979, Hazel Crest, Ill.

| | G | AB | H | 2B | 3B | HR | HR% | R | RBI | BB | SO | SB | BA | SA | AB | H | G by POS |
|---|---|---|---|---|---|---|---|---|---|---|---|---|---|---|---|---|---|
| 1917 CHI N | 14 | 34 | 5 | 0 | 0 | 0 | 0.0 | 3 | 3 | 3 | 10 | 0 | .147 | .147 | 0 | 0 | OF-12 |

## Larry Schlafly

**SCHLAFLY, HARRY LAWRENCE**      BR TR
B. Sept. 20, 1878, Port Washington, Ohio    D. June 27, 1919, Beach City, Ohio
Manager 1914-15.

| | G | AB | H | 2B | 3B | HR | HR% | R | RBI | BB | SO | SB | BA | SA | AB | H | G by POS |
|---|---|---|---|---|---|---|---|---|---|---|---|---|---|---|---|---|---|
| 1902 CHI N | 10 | 31 | 10 | 0 | 3 | 0 | 0.0 | 5 | 5 | 6 | | 2 | .323 | .516 | 0 | 0 | OF-5, 2B-4, 3B-2 |
| 1906 WAS A | 123 | 426 | 105 | 13 | 8 | 2 | 0.5 | 60 | 30 | 50 | | 29 | .246 | .329 | 0 | 0 | 2B-123 |
| 1907 | 24 | 74 | 10 | 0 | 0 | 2 | 2.7 | 10 | 4 | 22 | | 7 | .135 | .216 | 0 | 0 | 2B-24 |
| 1914 BUF F | 51 | 127 | 33 | 7 | 1 | 2 | 1.6 | 16 | 19 | 12 | | 3 | .260 | .378 | 14 | 5 | 2B-23, 1B-7, OF-1, 3B-1, C-1 |
| 4 yrs. | 208 | 658 | 158 | 20 | 12 | 6 | 0.9 | 91 | 58 | 90 | | 41 | .240 | .334 | 14 | 5 | 2B-174, 1B-7, OF-6, 3B-3, C-1 |
| 1 yr. | 10 | 31 | 10 | 0 | 3 | 0 | 0.0 | 5 | 5 | 6 | | 2 | .323 | .516 | 0 | 0 | OF-5, 2B-4, 3B-2 |

## Paul Schramka

**SCHRAMKA, PAUL EDWARD**      BL TL 6' 185 lbs.
B. Mar. 22, 1928, Milwaukee, Wis.

| | G | AB | H | 2B | 3B | HR | HR% | R | RBI | BB | SO | SB | BA | SA | AB | H | G by POS |
|---|---|---|---|---|---|---|---|---|---|---|---|---|---|---|---|---|---|
| 1953 CHI N | 2 | 0 | 0 | 0 | 0 | 0 | – | 0 | 0 | 0 | 0 | 0 | – | – | 0 | 0 | OF-1 |

## Hank Schreiber

**SCHREIBER, HENRY WALTER**      BR TR 5'11" 165 lbs.
B. July 12, 1891, Cleveland, Ohio    D. Feb. 21, 1968, Indianapolis, Ind.

| | G | AB | H | 2B | 3B | HR | HR% | R | RBI | BB | SO | SB | BA | SA | AB | H | G by POS |
|---|---|---|---|---|---|---|---|---|---|---|---|---|---|---|---|---|---|
| 1914 CHI A | 1 | 2 | 0 | 0 | 0 | 0 | 0.0 | 0 | 0 | 0 | 1 | 0 | .000 | .000 | 0 | 0 | OF-1 |

| | G | AB | H | 2B | 3B | HR | HR % | R | RBI | BB | SO | SB | BA | SA | Pinch Hit AB | Pinch Hit H | G by POS |
|---|---|---|---|---|---|---|---|---|---|---|---|---|---|---|---|---|---|

## Hank Schreiber continued

| | G | AB | H | 2B | 3B | HR | HR % | R | RBI | BB | SO | SB | BA | SA | AB | H | G by POS |
|---|---|---|---|---|---|---|---|---|---|---|---|---|---|---|---|---|---|
| 1917 BOS N | 2 | 7 | 2 | 0 | 0 | 0 | 0.0 | 1 | 0 | 0 | 1 | 0 | .286 | .286 | 0 | 0 | SS-1, 3B-1 |
| 1919 CIN N | 19 | 58 | 13 | 4 | 0 | 0 | 0.0 | 5 | 4 | 0 | 12 | 0 | .224 | .293 | 0 | 0 | 3B-17, SS-2 |
| 1921 NY N | 4 | 6 | 2 | 0 | 0 | 0 | 0.0 | 2 | 2 | 1 | 1 | 0 | .333 | .333 | 0 | 0 | SS-2, 2B-2, 3B-1 |
| 1926 CHI N | 10 | 18 | 1 | 1 | 0 | 0 | 0.0 | 2 | 0 | 0 | 1 | 0 | .056 | .111 | 0 | 0 | SS-3, 3B-3, 2B-1 |
| 5 yrs. | 36 | 91 | 18 | 5 | 0 | 0 | 0.0 | 10 | 6 | 1 | 16 | 0 | .198 | .253 | 0 | 0 | 3B-22, SS-8, 2B-3, OF-1 |
| 1 yr. | 10 | 18 | 1 | 1 | 0 | 0 | 0.0 | 2 | 0 | 0 | 1 | 0 | .056 | .111 | 0 | 0 | SS-3, 3B-3, 2B-1 |

## Pop Schriver

**SCHRIVER, WILLIAM FREDERICK**
B. June 11, 1866, Brooklyn, N. Y.   D. Dec. 27, 1932, Brooklyn, N. Y.   BR TR 5'10" 185 lbs.

| | G | AB | H | 2B | 3B | HR | HR % | R | RBI | BB | SO | SB | BA | SA | AB | H | G by POS |
|---|---|---|---|---|---|---|---|---|---|---|---|---|---|---|---|---|---|
| 1886 BKN AA | 8 | 21 | 1 | 0 | 0 | 0 | 0.0 | 2 | | 2 | | | .048 | .048 | 0 | 0 | OF-5, C-3 |
| 1888 PHI N | 40 | 134 | 26 | 5 | 2 | 1 | 0.7 | 15 | 23 | 7 | 21 | 2 | .194 | .284 | 0 | 0 | C-27, SS-6, 3B-6, OF-1 |
| 1889 | 55 | 211 | 56 | 10 | 0 | 1 | 0.5 | 24 | 19 | 16 | 8 | 5 | .265 | .327 | 0 | 0 | C-48, 2B-6, 3B-1 |
| 1890 | 57 | 223 | 61 | 9 | 6 | 0 | 0.0 | 37 | 35 | 22 | 15 | 9 | .274 | .368 | 0 | 0 | C-34, 1B-10, 3B-8, 2B-3, OF-2 |
| 1891 CHI N | 27 | 90 | 30 | 1 | 4 | 1 | 1.1 | 15 | 21 | 10 | 9 | 1 | .333 | .467 | 0 | 0 | C-27, 1B-2 |
| 1892 | 92 | 326 | 73 | 10 | 6 | 1 | 0.3 | 40 | 34 | 27 | 25 | 4 | .224 | .301 | 0 | 0 | C-82, OF-10 |
| 1893 | 64 | 229 | 65 | 8 | 3 | 4 | 1.7 | 49 | 34 | 14 | 9 | 4 | .284 | .397 | 3 | 0 | C-56, OF-5 |
| 1894 | 96 | 349 | 96 | 12 | 3 | 3 | 0.9 | 55 | 47 | 29 | 21 | 9 | .275 | .352 | 1 | 0 | C-88, SS-3, 3B-3, 1B-3 |
| 1895 NY N | 24 | 92 | 29 | 2 | 1 | 1 | 1.1 | 16 | 16 | 9 | 10 | 3 | .315 | .391 | 0 | 0 | C-18, 1B-6 |
| 1897 CIN N | 61 | 178 | 54 | 12 | 4 | 1 | 0.6 | 29 | 30 | 19 | | 3 | .303 | .433 | 5 | 1 | C-53 |
| 1898 PIT N | 95 | 315 | 72 | 15 | 3 | 0 | 0.0 | 25 | 32 | 23 | | 4 | .229 | .295 | 2 | 0 | C-92, 1B-1 |
| 1899 | 91 | 301 | 85 | 19 | 5 | 1 | 0.3 | 31 | 49 | 23 | | 4 | .282 | .389 | 5 | 1 | C-78, 1B-8 |
| 1900 | 37 | 92 | 27 | 7 | 0 | 1 | 1.1 | 11 | 12 | 10 | | 0 | .293 | .402 | 9 | 3 | C-24, 1B-1 |
| 1901 STL N | 53 | 166 | 45 | 7 | 3 | 1 | 0.6 | 17 | 23 | 12 | | 2 | .271 | .367 | 9 | 3 | C-24, 1B-19 |
| 14 yrs. | 800 | 2727 | 720 | 117 | 40 | 16 | 0.6 | 366 | 374 | 223 | 118 | 46 | .264 | .354 | 34 | 8 | C-654, 1B-49, OF-23, 3B-18, SS-9, 2B-9 |
| 4 yrs. | 279 | 994 | 264 | 31 | 16 | 9 | 0.9 | 159 | 136 | 80 | 64 | 18 | .266 | .356 | 4 | 0 | C-253, OF-15, 1B-4, SS-3, 3B-3 |

## Art Schult

**SCHULT, ARTHUR WILLIAM (Dutch)**
B. June 20, 1928, Brooklyn, N. Y.   BR TR 6'3" 210 lbs.

| | G | AB | H | 2B | 3B | HR | HR % | R | RBI | BB | SO | SB | BA | SA | AB | H | G by POS |
|---|---|---|---|---|---|---|---|---|---|---|---|---|---|---|---|---|---|
| 1953 NY A | 7 | 0 | 0 | 0 | 0 | 0 | — | 3 | | 0 | 0 | 0 | — | — | 0 | 0 | |
| 1956 CIN N | 5 | 7 | 3 | 0 | 0 | 0 | 0.0 | 3 | 2 | 1 | 1 | 0 | .429 | .429 | 3 | 2 | OF-1 |
| 1957 2 teams | | | CIN N | (21G – | .265) | | WAS A | (77G – | .263) | | | | | | | | |
| " total | 98 | 281 | 74 | 16 | 0 | 4 | 1.4 | 34 | 39 | 14 | 32 | 0 | .263 | .363 | 26 | 5 | OF-36, 1B-35 |
| 1959 CHI N | 42 | 118 | 32 | 7 | 0 | 2 | 1.7 | 17 | 14 | 7 | 14 | 0 | .271 | .381 | 9 | 2 | 1B-23, OF-15 |
| 1960 | 12 | 15 | 2 | 1 | 0 | 0 | 0.0 | 1 | 1 | 1 | 3 | 0 | .133 | .200 | 7 | 1 | OF-4, 1B-1 |
| 5 yrs. | 164 | 421 | 111 | 24 | 0 | 6 | 1.4 | 58 | 56 | 23 | 50 | 0 | .264 | .363 | 45 | 10 | 1B-59, OF-56 |
| 2 yrs. | 54 | 133 | 34 | 8 | 0 | 2 | 1.5 | 18 | 15 | 8 | 17 | 0 | .256 | .361 | 16 | 3 | 1B-24, OF-19 |

## Johnny Schulte

**SCHULTE, JOHN CLEMENT**
B. Sept. 8, 1896, Fredericktown, Mo.   D. June 28, 1978, St. Louis, Mo.   BL TR 5'11" 190 lbs.

| | G | AB | H | 2B | 3B | HR | HR % | R | RBI | BB | SO | SB | BA | SA | AB | H | G by POS |
|---|---|---|---|---|---|---|---|---|---|---|---|---|---|---|---|---|---|
| 1923 STL A | 7 | 3 | 0 | 0 | 0 | 0 | 0.0 | 1 | 1 | 4 | 0 | 0 | .000 | .000 | 2 | 0 | 1B-1, C-1 |
| 1927 STL N | 64 | 156 | 45 | 8 | 2 | 9 | 5.8 | 35 | 32 | 47 | 19 | 1 | .288 | .538 | 3 | 1 | C-59 |
| 1928 PHI N | 65 | 113 | 28 | 2 | 2 | 4 | 3.5 | 14 | 17 | 15 | 12 | 0 | .248 | .407 | 26 | 6 | C-34 |
| 1929 CHI N | 31 | 69 | 18 | 3 | 0 | 0 | 0.0 | 6 | 9 | 7 | 11 | 0 | .261 | .304 | 1 | 1 | C-30 |
| 1932 2 teams | | | STL A | (15G – | .208) | | BOS N | (10G – | .222) | | | | | | | | |
| " total | 25 | 33 | 7 | 2 | 0 | 1 | 3.0 | 3 | 5 | 3 | 7 | 0 | .212 | .364 | 8 | 1 | C-16 |
| 5 yrs. | 192 | 374 | 98 | 15 | 4 | 14 | 3.7 | 59 | 64 | 76 | 49 | 1 | .262 | .436 | 40 | 9 | C-140, 1B-1 |
| 1 yr. | 31 | 69 | 18 | 3 | 0 | 0 | 0.0 | 6 | 9 | 7 | 11 | 0 | .261 | .304 | 1 | 1 | C-30 |

## Wildfire Schulte

**SCHULTE, FRANK**
B. Sept. 17, 1882, Cohocton, N. Y.   D. Aug. 17, 1975, Roseville, Mich.   BL TR 5'11" 170 lbs.

| | G | AB | H | 2B | 3B | HR | HR % | R | RBI | BB | SO | SB | BA | SA | AB | H | G by POS |
|---|---|---|---|---|---|---|---|---|---|---|---|---|---|---|---|---|---|
| 1904 CHI N | 20 | 84 | 24 | 4 | 3 | 2 | 2.4 | 16 | 13 | 2 | | 1 | .286 | .476 | 0 | 0 | OF-20 |
| 1905 | 123 | 493 | 135 | 15 | 14 | 1 | 0.2 | 67 | 47 | 32 | | 16 | .274 | .367 | 0 | 0 | OF-123 |
| 1906 | 146 | 563 | 158 | 18 | 13 | 7 | 1.2 | 77 | 60 | 31 | | 25 | .281 | .396 | 0 | 0 | OF-146 |
| 1907 | 97 | 342 | 98 | 14 | 7 | 2 | 0.6 | 44 | 32 | 22 | | 7 | .287 | .386 | 5 | 1 | OF-91 |
| 1908 | 102 | 386 | 91 | 20 | 2 | 1 | 0.3 | 42 | 43 | 29 | | 15 | .236 | .306 | 0 | 0 | OF-102 |
| 1909 | 140 | 538 | 142 | 16 | 11 | 4 | 0.7 | 57 | 60 | 24 | | 23 | .264 | .357 | 0 | 0 | OF-140 |
| 1910 | 151 | 559 | 168 | 29 | 15 | 10 | 1.8 | 93 | 68 | 39 | 57 | 22 | .301 | .460 | 1 | 0 | OF-150 |
| 1911 | 154 | 577 | 173 | 30 | 21 | 21 | 3.6 | 105 | 121 | 76 | 68 | 23 | .300 | .534 | 0 | 0 | OF-154 |
| 1912 | 139 | 553 | 146 | 27 | 11 | 13 | 2.4 | 90 | 70 | 53 | 70 | 17 | .264 | .423 | 0 | 0 | OF-139 |
| 1913 | 132 | 495 | 138 | 28 | 6 | 9 | 1.8 | 85 | 72 | 39 | 68 | 21 | .279 | .414 | 2 | 1 | OF-129 |
| 1914 | 137 | 465 | 112 | 22 | 7 | 5 | 1.1 | 54 | 61 | 39 | 55 | 16 | .241 | .351 | 3 | 1 | OF-134 |
| 1915 | 151 | 550 | 137 | 20 | 6 | 12 | 2.2 | 66 | 69 | 49 | 68 | 19 | .249 | .373 | 3 | 1 | OF-147 |
| 1916 2 teams | | | CHI N | (72G – | .296) | | PIT N | (55G – | .254) | | | | | | | | |
| " total | 127 | 407 | 113 | 16 | 4 | 5 | 1.2 | 43 | 41 | 37 | 54 | 14 | .278 | .373 | 9 | 1 | OF-113 |
| 1917 2 teams | | | PIT N | (30G – | .214) | | PHI N | (64G – | .215) | | | | | | | | |
| " total | 94 | 252 | 54 | 15 | 1 | 1 | 0.4 | 32 | 22 | 26 | 36 | 9 | .214 | .294 | 21 | 5 | OF-70 |
| 1918 WAS A | 93 | 267 | 77 | 14 | 3 | 0 | 0.0 | 35 | 44 | 47 | 36 | 5 | .288 | .363 | 16 | 5 | OF-75 |
| 15 yrs. | 1806 | 6531 | 1766 | 288 | 124 | 93 | 1.4 | 906 | 823 | 545 | 512 | 233 | .270 | .395 | 60 | 15 | OF-1733 |
| 13 yrs. | 1564 | 5835 | 1590 | 254 | 117 | 92 | 1.6 | 827 | 743 | 455 | 421 | 214 | .272 | .403 | 19 | 4 | OF-1540 |
| | 10th | 10th | | | 3rd | | | | 10th | | | 4th | | | | | |

### WORLD SERIES

| | G | AB | H | 2B | 3B | HR | HR % | R | RBI | BB | SO | SB | BA | SA | AB | H | G by POS |
|---|---|---|---|---|---|---|---|---|---|---|---|---|---|---|---|---|---|
| 1906 CHI N | 6 | 26 | 7 | 3 | 0 | 0 | 0.0 | 1 | 3 | 1 | 3 | 0 | .269 | .385 | 0 | 0 | OF-6 |
| 1907 | 5 | 20 | 5 | 0 | 0 | 0 | 0.0 | 3 | 2 | 1 | 2 | 1 | .250 | .250 | 0 | 0 | OF-5 |
| 1908 | 5 | 18 | 7 | 0 | 1 | 0 | 0.0 | 4 | 2 | 2 | 1 | 1 | .389 | .500 | 0 | 0 | OF-5 |
| 1910 | 5 | 17 | 6 | 3 | 0 | 0 | 0.0 | 3 | 2 | 2 | 3 | 0 | .353 | .529 | 0 | 0 | OF-5 |
| 4 yrs. | 21 | 81 | 25 | 6 | 1 | 0 | 0.0 | 11 | 9 | 6 | 9 | 3 | .309 | .407 | 0 | 0 | OF-21 |

| | G | AB | H | 2B | 3B | HR | HR % | R | RBI | BB | SO | SB | BA | SA | Pinch Hit AB | Pinch Hit H | G by POS |
|---|---|---|---|---|---|---|---|---|---|---|---|---|---|---|---|---|---|

## Joe Schultz

**SCHULTZ, JOSEPH CHARLES (Germany)**    BR TR 5'11½" 172 lbs.
Father of Joe Schultz.
B. July 24, 1893, Pittsburgh, Pa.    D. Apr. 13, 1941, Columbia, S. C.

| | G | AB | H | 2B | 3B | HR | HR % | R | RBI | BB | SO | SB | BA | SA | Pinch Hit AB | Pinch Hit H | G by POS |
|---|---|---|---|---|---|---|---|---|---|---|---|---|---|---|---|---|---|
| 1912 BOS N | 4 | 12 | 3 | 1 | 0 | 0 | 0.0 | 1 | 4 | 0 | 2 | 0 | .250 | .333 | 0 | 0 | 2B-4 |
| 1913 | 9 | 18 | 4 | 0 | 0 | 0 | 0.0 | 2 | 1 | 2 | 7 | 0 | .222 | .222 | 1 | 0 | OF-5, 2B-1 |
| 1915 2 teams | | BKN | N | (56G – | .292) | | CHI | N | (7G – | .250) | | | | | | | |
| " total | 63 | 128 | 37 | 3 | 2 | 0 | 0.0 | 14 | 7 | 10 | 20 | 3 | .289 | .344 | 29 | 8 | 3B-55, 2B-2, SS-1 |
| 1916 PIT N | 77 | 204 | 53 | 8 | 2 | 0 | 0.0 | 18 | 22 | 7 | 14 | 6 | .260 | .319 | 20 | 5 | 3B-24, 2B-24, OF-6, SS-1 |
| 1919 STL N | 88 | 229 | 58 | 9 | 1 | 2 | 0.9 | 24 | 21 | 11 | 7 | 4 | .253 | .328 | 31 | 8 | OF-49, 2B-5 |
| 1920 | 99 | 320 | 84 | 5 | 5 | 0 | 0.0 | 38 | 32 | 21 | 11 | 5 | .263 | .309 | 14 | 2 | OF-80 |
| 1921 | 92 | 275 | 85 | 20 | 3 | 6 | 2.2 | 37 | 45 | 15 | 11 | 4 | .309 | .469 | 18 | 6 | OF-67, 3B-3, 1B-2 |
| 1922 | 112 | 344 | 108 | 13 | 4 | 2 | 0.6 | 50 | 64 | 19 | 10 | 3 | .314 | .392 | 22 | 8 | OF-89 |
| 1923 | 2 | 7 | 2 | 0 | 0 | 0 | 0.0 | 0 | 1 | 1 | 0 | 0 | .286 | .286 | 0 | 0 | OF-2 |
| 1924 2 teams | | STL | N | (12G – | .167) | | PHI | N | (88G – | .282) | | | | | | | |
| " total | 100 | 296 | 82 | 15 | 1 | 5 | 1.7 | 35 | 31 | 23 | 18 | 6 | .277 | .385 | 17 | 6 | OF-78 |
| 1925 2 teams | | PHI | N | (24G – | .344) | | CIN | N | (33G – | .323) | | | | | | | |
| " total | 57 | 126 | 42 | 9 | 1 | 0 | 0.0 | 16 | 21 | 7 | 2 | 4 | .333 | .421 | 18 | 3 | OF-35, 2B-1 |
| 11 yrs. | 703 | 1959 | 558 | 83 | 19 | 15 | 0.8 | 235 | 249 | 116 | 102 | 35 | .285 | .370 | 170 | 46 | OF-411, 3B-82, 2B-37, SS-2, 1B-2 |
| 1 yr. | 7 | 8 | 2 | 0 | 0 | 0 | 0.0 | 1 | 3 | 0 | 2 | 0 | .250 | .250 | 4 | 1 | 2B-2 |

## Bill Schuster

**SCHUSTER, WILLIAM CHARLES (Broadway)**    BR TR 5'9" 164 lbs.
B. Aug. 4, 1914, Buffalo, N. Y.

| | G | AB | H | 2B | 3B | HR | HR % | R | RBI | BB | SO | SB | BA | SA | Pinch Hit AB | Pinch Hit H | G by POS |
|---|---|---|---|---|---|---|---|---|---|---|---|---|---|---|---|---|---|
| 1937 PIT N | 3 | 6 | 3 | 0 | 0 | 0 | 0.0 | 2 | 1 | 1 | 0 | 0 | .500 | .500 | 0 | 0 | SS-2 |
| 1939 BOS N | 2 | 3 | 0 | 0 | 0 | 0 | 0.0 | 0 | 0 | 0 | 1 | 0 | .000 | .000 | 0 | 0 | SS-1, 3B-1 |
| 1943 CHI N | 13 | 51 | 15 | 2 | 1 | 0 | 0.0 | 3 | 0 | 3 | 2 | 0 | .294 | .373 | 0 | 0 | SS-13 |
| 1944 | 60 | 154 | 34 | 7 | 1 | 1 | 0.6 | 14 | 14 | 12 | 16 | 4 | .221 | .299 | 11 | 3 | 2B-66, SS-38 |
| 1945 | 45 | 47 | 9 | 2 | 1 | 0 | 0.0 | 8 | 2 | 7 | 4 | 2 | .191 | .277 | 2 | 0 | SS-22, 2B-3, 3B-1 |
| 5 yrs. | 123 | 261 | 61 | 11 | 3 | 1 | 0.4 | 27 | 17 | 23 | 23 | 6 | .234 | .310 | 13 | 3 | SS-76, 2B-69, 3B-2 |
| 3 yrs. | 118 | 252 | 58 | 11 | 3 | 1 | 0.4 | 25 | 16 | 22 | 22 | 6 | .230 | .310 | 13 | 3 | SS-73, 2B-69, 3B-1 |

**WORLD SERIES**

| | G | AB | H | 2B | 3B | HR | HR % | R | RBI | BB | SO | SB | BA | SA | Pinch Hit AB | Pinch Hit H | G by POS |
|---|---|---|---|---|---|---|---|---|---|---|---|---|---|---|---|---|---|
| 1945 CHI N | 2 | 1 | 0 | 0 | 0 | 0 | 0.0 | 1 | 0 | 0 | 0 | 0 | .000 | .000 | 0 | 0 | SS-1 |

## Milt Scott

**SCOTT, MILTON PARKER (Mikado Milt)**    5'9" 160 lbs.
B. Jan. 17, 1866, Chicago, Ill.    D. Nov. 3, 1938, Baltimore, Md.

| | G | AB | H | 2B | 3B | HR | HR % | R | RBI | BB | SO | SB | BA | SA | Pinch Hit AB | Pinch Hit H | G by POS |
|---|---|---|---|---|---|---|---|---|---|---|---|---|---|---|---|---|---|
| 1882 CHI N | 1 | 5 | 2 | 0 | 0 | 0 | 0.0 | 1 | | 0 | 0 | | .400 | .400 | 0 | 0 | 1B-1 |
| 1884 DET N | 110 | 438 | 108 | 17 | 5 | 3 | 0.7 | 29 | | 9 | 62 | | .247 | .329 | 0 | 0 | 1B-110 |
| 1885 2 teams | | DET | N | (38G – | .264) | | PIT | AA | (55G – | .248) | | | | | | | |
| " total | 93 | 358 | 91 | 14 | 1 | 0 | 0.0 | 29 | 12 | 9 | 16 | | .254 | .299 | 0 | 0 | 1B-93 |
| 1886 BAL AA | 137 | 484 | 92 | 11 | 4 | 2 | 0.4 | 48 | | 22 | | | .190 | .242 | 0 | 0 | 1B-137, P-1 |
| 4 yrs. | 341 | 1285 | 293 | 42 | 10 | 5 | 0.4 | 107 | 11 | 40 | 78 | | .228 | .288 | 0 | 0 | 1B-341, P-1 |
| 1 yr. | 1 | 5 | 2 | 0 | 0 | 0 | 0.0 | 1 | 0 | 0 | 0 | | .400 | .400 | 0 | 0 | 1B-1 |

## Pete Scott

**SCOTT, FLOYD JOHN**    BR TR 5'11½" 175 lbs.
B. Dec. 21, 1898, Woodland, Calif.    D. May 3, 1953, Daly City, Calif.

| | G | AB | H | 2B | 3B | HR | HR % | R | RBI | BB | SO | SB | BA | SA | Pinch Hit AB | Pinch Hit H | G by POS |
|---|---|---|---|---|---|---|---|---|---|---|---|---|---|---|---|---|---|
| 1926 CHI N | 77 | 189 | 54 | 13 | 1 | 3 | 1.6 | 34 | 34 | 22 | 31 | 1 | .286 | .413 | 4 | 1 | OF-59, 3B-1 |
| 1927 | 71 | 156 | 49 | 18 | 1 | 0 | 0.0 | 28 | 21 | 19 | 18 | 1 | .314 | .442 | 31 | 7 | OF-36 |
| 1928 PIT N | 60 | 177 | 55 | 10 | 4 | 5 | 2.8 | 33 | 33 | 18 | 14 | 1 | .311 | .497 | 6 | 2 | OF-42, 1B-8 |
| 3 yrs. | 208 | 522 | 158 | 41 | 6 | 8 | 1.5 | 95 | 88 | 59 | 63 | 5 | .303 | .450 | 41 | 10 | OF-137, 1B-8, 3B-1 |
| 2 yrs. | 148 | 345 | 103 | 31 | 2 | 3 | 0.9 | 62 | 55 | 41 | 49 | 4 | .299 | .426 | 35 | 8 | OF-95, 3B-1 |

## Rodney Scott

**SCOTT, RODNEY DARRELL**    BR TR 6' 160 lbs.
B. Oct. 16, 1953, Indianapolis, Ind.

| | G | AB | H | 2B | 3B | HR | HR % | R | RBI | BB | SO | SB | BA | SA | Pinch Hit AB | Pinch Hit H | G by POS |
|---|---|---|---|---|---|---|---|---|---|---|---|---|---|---|---|---|---|
| 1975 KC A | 48 | 15 | 1 | 0 | 0 | 0 | 0.0 | 13 | 0 | 1 | 3 | 4 | .067 | .067 | 1 | 0 | DH-22, 2B-9, SS-8 |
| 1976 MON N | 7 | 10 | 4 | 0 | 0 | 0 | 0.0 | 3 | 0 | 1 | 1 | 2 | .400 | .400 | 0 | 0 | 2B-6, SS-3 |
| 1977 OAK A | 133 | 364 | 95 | 4 | 4 | 0 | 0.0 | 56 | 20 | 43 | 50 | 33 | .261 | .294 | 8 | 3 | 2B-71, SS-70, 3B-5, DH-1, OF-1 |
| 1978 CHI N | 78 | 227 | 64 | 5 | 1 | 0 | 0.0 | 41 | 15 | 43 | 41 | 27 | .282 | .313 | 3 | 0 | 3B-60, OF-10, SS-6, 2B-6 |
| 1979 MON N | 151 | 562 | 134 | 12 | 5 | 3 | 0.5 | 69 | 42 | 66 | 82 | 39 | .238 | .294 | 1 | 1 | 2B-113, SS-39 |
| 1980 | 154 | 567 | 127 | 13 | 13 | 0 | 0.0 | 84 | 46 | 70 | 75 | 63 | .224 | .294 | 3 | 2 | 2B-129, SS-21 |
| 1981 | 95 | 336 | 69 | 9 | 3 | 0 | 0.0 | 43 | 26 | 50 | 35 | 30 | .205 | .250 | 0 | 0 | 2B-93 |
| 1982 2 teams | | MON | N | (14G – | .200) | | NY | A | (10G – | .192) | | | | | | | |
| " total | 24 | 51 | 10 | 0 | 0 | 0 | 0.0 | 7 | 1 | 7 | 4 | 7 | .196 | .196 | 2 | 0 | 2B-16, SS-6 |
| 8 yrs. | 690 | 2132 | 504 | 43 | 26 | 3 | 0.1 | 316 | 150 | 281 | 291 | 205 | .236 | .285 | 18 | 6 | 2B-443, SS-153, 3B-65, DH-23, OF-11 |
| 1 yr. | 78 | 227 | 64 | 5 | 1 | 0 | 0.0 | 41 | 15 | 43 | 41 | 27 | .282 | .313 | 3 | 0 | 3B-60, OF-10, SS-6, 2B-6 |

**LEAGUE CHAMPIONSHIP SERIES**

| | G | AB | H | 2B | 3B | HR | HR % | R | RBI | BB | SO | SB | BA | SA | Pinch Hit AB | Pinch Hit H | G by POS |
|---|---|---|---|---|---|---|---|---|---|---|---|---|---|---|---|---|---|
| 1981 MON N | 5 | 18 | 3 | 0 | 0 | 0 | 0.0 | 0 | 1 | 3 | 1 | 1 | .167 | .167 | 0 | 0 | 2B-5 |

## Frank Secory

**SECORY, FRANK EDWARD**    BR TR 6'1" 200 lbs.
B. Aug. 24, 1912, Mason City, Iowa

| | G | AB | H | 2B | 3B | HR | HR % | R | RBI | BB | SO | SB | BA | SA | Pinch Hit AB | Pinch Hit H | G by POS |
|---|---|---|---|---|---|---|---|---|---|---|---|---|---|---|---|---|---|
| 1940 DET A | 1 | 1 | 0 | 0 | 0 | 0 | 0.0 | 0 | 0 | 0 | 1 | 0 | .000 | .000 | 1 | 0 | |
| 1942 CIN N | 2 | 5 | 0 | 0 | 0 | 0 | 0.0 | 1 | 1 | 3 | 2 | 0 | .000 | .000 | 0 | 0 | OF-2 |
| 1944 CHI N | 22 | 56 | 18 | 1 | 0 | 4 | 7.1 | 10 | 17 | 6 | 8 | 1 | .321 | .554 | 4 | 0 | OF-17 |
| 1945 | 35 | 57 | 9 | 1 | 0 | 0 | 0.0 | 4 | 6 | 2 | 7 | 0 | .158 | .175 | 21 | 2 | OF-12 |
| 1946 | 33 | 43 | 10 | 3 | 0 | 3 | 7.0 | 6 | 12 | 6 | 6 | 0 | .233 | .512 | 22 | 4 | OF-9 |
| 5 yrs. | 93 | 162 | 37 | 5 | 0 | 7 | 4.3 | 21 | 36 | 17 | 24 | 1 | .228 | .389 | 48 | 6 | OF-40 |
| 3 yrs. | 90 | 156 | 37 | 5 | 0 | 7 | 4.5 | 20 | 35 | 14 | 21 | 1 | .237 | .404 | 47 | 6 | OF-38 |

**WORLD SERIES**

| | G | AB | H | 2B | 3B | HR | HR % | R | RBI | BB | SO | SB | BA | SA | Pinch Hit AB | Pinch Hit H | G by POS |
|---|---|---|---|---|---|---|---|---|---|---|---|---|---|---|---|---|---|
| 1945 CHI N | 5 | 5 | 2 | 0 | 0 | 0 | 0.0 | 0 | 0 | 0 | 2 | 0 | .400 | .400 | 5 | 2 | |

| | G | AB | H | 2B | 3B | HR | HR % | R | RBI | BB | SO | SB | BA | SA | Pinch Hit AB | Pinch Hit H | G by POS |
|---|---|---|---|---|---|---|---|---|---|---|---|---|---|---|---|---|---|

## Kurt Seibert

**SEIBERT, KURT ELLIOTT**
B. Oct. 16, 1955, Cheverly, Md.

BB TR 6' 165 lbs.

| | G | AB | H | 2B | 3B | HR | HR % | R | RBI | BB | SO | SB | BA | SA | AB | H | G by POS |
|---|---|---|---|---|---|---|---|---|---|---|---|---|---|---|---|---|---|
| 1979 CHI N | 7 | 2 | 0 | 0 | 0 | 0 | 0.0 | 2 | 0 | 0 | 1 | 0 | .000 | .000 | 1 | 0 | 3B-1 |

## Mike Sember

**SEMBER, MICHAEL DAVID**
B. Feb. 24, 1953, Hammond, Ind.

BR TR 6' 185 lbs.

| | G | AB | H | 2B | 3B | HR | HR % | R | RBI | BB | SO | SB | BA | SA | AB | H | G by POS |
|---|---|---|---|---|---|---|---|---|---|---|---|---|---|---|---|---|---|
| 1977 CHI N | 3 | 4 | 1 | 0 | 0 | 0 | 0.0 | 0 | 0 | 0 | 2 | 0 | .250 | .250 | 2 | 0 | 3B-1 |
| 1978 | 9 | 3 | 1 | 0 | 0 | 0 | 0.0 | 2 | 0 | 1 | 1 | 0 | .333 | .333 | 2 | 1 | 3B-7, SS-1 |
| 2 yrs. | 12 | 7 | 2 | 0 | 0 | 0 | 0.0 | 2 | 0 | 1 | 3 | 0 | .286 | .286 | 4 | 1 | 3B-7, SS-1, 2B-1 |
| 2 yrs. | 12 | 7 | 2 | 0 | 0 | 0 | 0.0 | 2 | 0 | 1 | 3 | 0 | .286 | .286 | 4 | 1 | 3B-7, SS-1, 2B-1 |

## Bill Serena

**SERENA, WILLIAM ROBERT**
B. Oct. 2, 1924, Alameda, Calif.

BR TR 5'9½" 175 lbs.

| | G | AB | H | 2B | 3B | HR | HR % | R | RBI | BB | SO | SB | BA | SA | AB | H | G by POS |
|---|---|---|---|---|---|---|---|---|---|---|---|---|---|---|---|---|---|
| 1949 CHI N | 12 | 37 | 8 | 3 | 0 | 1 | 2.7 | 3 | 7 | 7 | 9 | 0 | .216 | .378 | 1 | 0 | 3B-11 |
| 1950 | 127 | 435 | 104 | 20 | 4 | 17 | 3.9 | 56 | 61 | 65 | 75 | 1 | .239 | .421 | 2 | 1 | 3B-125 |
| 1951 | 13 | 39 | 13 | 3 | 1 | 1 | 2.6 | 8 | 4 | 11 | 4 | 0 | .333 | .538 | 0 | 0 | 3B-12 |
| 1952 | 122 | 390 | 107 | 21 | 5 | 15 | 3.8 | 49 | 61 | 39 | 83 | 1 | .274 | .469 | 14 | 4 | 3B-58, 2B-49 |
| 1953 | 93 | 275 | 69 | 10 | 5 | 10 | 3.6 | 30 | 52 | 41 | 46 | 0 | .251 | .433 | 13 | 4 | 2B-49, 3B-28 |
| 1954 | 41 | 63 | 10 | 0 | 1 | 4 | 6.3 | 8 | 13 | 14 | 18 | 0 | .159 | .381 | 22 | 4 | 3B-12, 2B-2 |
| 6 yrs. | 408 | 1239 | 311 | 57 | 16 | 48 | 3.9 | 154 | 198 | 177 | 235 | 2 | .251 | .439 | 52 | 13 | 3B-246, 2B-100 |
| 6 yrs. | 408 | 1239 | 311 | 57 | 16 | 48 | 3.9 | 154 | 198 | 177 | 235 | 2 | .251 | .439 | 52 | 13 | 3B-246, 2B-100 |

## Tommy Sewell

**SEWELL, THOMAS WESLEY**
Brother of Joe Sewell. Brother of Luke Sewell.
B. Apr. 16, 1906, Titus, Ala. D. July 30, 1956, Montgomery, Ala.

BL TR 5'7½" 155 lbs.

| | G | AB | H | 2B | 3B | HR | HR % | R | RBI | BB | SO | SB | BA | SA | AB | H | G by POS |
|---|---|---|---|---|---|---|---|---|---|---|---|---|---|---|---|---|---|
| 1927 CHI N | 1 | 1 | 0 | 0 | 0 | 0 | 0.0 | 0 | 0 | 0 | 0 | 0 | .000 | .000 | 1 | 0 | |

## Orator Shaffer

**SHAFFER, GEORGE**
Brother of Taylor Shaffer.
B. 1852, Philadelphia, Pa. Deceased.

BL TR 5'9" 165 lbs.

| | G | AB | H | 2B | 3B | HR | HR % | R | RBI | BB | SO | SB | BA | SA | AB | H | G by POS |
|---|---|---|---|---|---|---|---|---|---|---|---|---|---|---|---|---|---|
| 1877 LOU N | 61 | 260 | 74 | 9 | 5 | 3 | 1.2 | 38 | 34 | 9 | 17 | | .285 | .392 | 0 | 0 | OF-60, 1B-1 |
| 1878 IND N | 63 | 266 | 90 | 19 | 6 | 0 | 0.0 | 48 | 30 | 13 | 20 | | .338 | .455 | 0 | 0 | OF-63 |
| 1879 CHI N | 73 | 316 | 96 | 13 | 0 | 0 | 0.0 | 53 | 35 | 6 | 28 | | .304 | .345 | 0 | 0 | OF-72, 3B-1 |
| 1880 CLE N | 83 | 338 | 90 | 14 | 9 | 0 | 0.0 | 62 | | 17 | 36 | | .266 | .361 | 0 | 0 | OF-83 |
| 1881 | 85 | 343 | 88 | 13 | 6 | 1 | 0.3 | 48 | 34 | 23 | 20 | | .257 | .338 | 0 | 0 | OF-85 |
| 1882 | 84 | 313 | 67 | 14 | 2 | 3 | 1.0 | 37 | 28 | 27 | 20 | | .214 | .300 | 0 | 0 | OF-84 |
| 1883 BUF N | 95 | 401 | 117 | 11 | 3 | 0 | 0.0 | 67 | | 27 | 39 | | .292 | .334 | 0 | 0 | OF-95 |
| 1884 STL U | 106 | 467 | 168 | 40 | 10 | 2 | 0.4 | 130 | | 30 | | | .360 | .501 | 0 | 0 | OF-100, 2B-7, 1B-1 |
| 1885 2 teams | | STL N (69G – .195) | | | | PHI AA (2G – .222) | | | | | | | | | | | |
| " total | 71 | 266 | 52 | 11 | 3 | 0 | 0.0 | 31 | 18 | 20 | 31 | | .195 | .259 | 0 | 0 | OF-71 |
| 1886 PHI AA | 21 | 82 | 22 | 3 | 3 | 0 | 0.0 | 15 | | 8 | | | .268 | .378 | 0 | 0 | OF-12 |
| 1890 | 100 | 390 | 110 | 15 | 5 | 1 | 0.3 | 55 | 47 | | | 29 | .282 | .354 | 0 | 0 | OF-98, 1B-3 |
| 11 yrs. | 842 | 3442 | 974 | 162 | 52 | 10 | 0.3 | 584 | 179 | 227 | 218 | 29 | .283 | .369 | 0 | 0 | OF-833, 2B-7, 1B-5, 3B-1 |
| 1 yr. | 73 | 316 | 96 | 13 | 0 | 0 | 0.0 | 53 | 35 | 6 | 28 | | .304 | .345 | 0 | 0 | OF-72, 3B-1 |

## Art Shamsky

**SHAMSKY, ARTHUR LEWIS**
B. Oct. 14, 1941, St. Louis, Mo.

BL TL 6'1" 168 lbs.

| | G | AB | H | 2B | 3B | HR | HR % | R | RBI | BB | SO | SB | BA | SA | AB | H | G by POS |
|---|---|---|---|---|---|---|---|---|---|---|---|---|---|---|---|---|---|
| 1965 CIN N | 64 | 96 | 25 | 4 | 3 | 2 | 2.1 | 13 | 10 | 10 | 29 | 1 | .260 | .427 | 45 | 13 | OF-18, 1B-1 |
| 1966 | 96 | 234 | 54 | 5 | 0 | 21 | 9.0 | 41 | 47 | 32 | 45 | 0 | .231 | .521 | 24 | 5 | OF-74 |
| 1967 | 76 | 147 | 29 | 3 | 1 | 3 | 2.0 | 6 | 13 | 15 | 34 | 0 | .197 | .293 | 34 | 10 | OF-40 |
| 1968 NY N | 116 | 345 | 82 | 14 | 4 | 12 | 3.5 | 30 | 48 | 21 | 58 | 1 | .238 | .406 | 23 | 1 | OF-82, 1B-17 |
| 1969 | 100 | 303 | 91 | 9 | 3 | 14 | 4.6 | 42 | 47 | 36 | 32 | 1 | .300 | .488 | 13 | 5 | OF-78, 1B-9 |
| 1970 | 122 | 403 | 118 | 19 | 2 | 11 | 2.7 | 48 | 49 | 49 | 33 | 1 | .293 | .432 | 11 | 2 | OF-58, 1B-56 |
| 1971 | 68 | 135 | 25 | 6 | 2 | 5 | 3.7 | 13 | 18 | 21 | 18 | 1 | .185 | .370 | 24 | 3 | OF-38, 1B-1 |
| 1972 2 teams | | CHI N (15G – .125) | | | | OAK A (8G – .000) | | | | | | | | | | | |
| " total | 23 | 23 | 2 | 0 | 0 | 0 | 0.0 | 1 | 1 | 4 | 5 | 0 | .087 | .087 | 15 | 1 | 1B-4 |
| 8 yrs. | 665 | 1686 | 426 | 60 | 15 | 68 | 4.0 | 194 | 233 | 188 | 254 | 5 | .253 | .427 | 189 | 41 | OF-388, 1B-88 |
| 1 yr. | 15 | 16 | 2 | 0 | 0 | 0 | 0.0 | 1 | 1 | 3 | 3 | 0 | .125 | .125 | 8 | 2 | 1B-4 |
| LEAGUE CHAMPIONSHIP SERIES | | | | | | | | | | | | | | | | | |
| 1969 NY N | 3 | 13 | 7 | 0 | 0 | 0 | 0.0 | 3 | 1 | 0 | 3 | 0 | .538 | .538 | 0 | 0 | OF-3 |
| WORLD SERIES | | | | | | | | | | | | | | | | | |
| 1969 NY N | 3 | 6 | 0 | 0 | 0 | 0 | 0.0 | 0 | 0 | 0 | 0 | 0 | .000 | .000 | 2 | 0 | OF-1 |

## Red Shannon

**SHANNON, MAURICE JOSEPH**
Brother of Joe Shannon.
B. Feb. 11, 1895, Jersey City, N. J. D. Apr. 12, 1970, Jersey City, N. J.

BB TR 5'11" 170 lbs.

| | G | AB | H | 2B | 3B | HR | HR % | R | RBI | BB | SO | SB | BA | SA | AB | H | G by POS |
|---|---|---|---|---|---|---|---|---|---|---|---|---|---|---|---|---|---|
| 1915 BOS N | 1 | 3 | 0 | 0 | 0 | 0 | 0.0 | 0 | 0 | 0 | 0 | 0 | .000 | .000 | 0 | 0 | 2B-1 |
| 1917 PHI A | 11 | 35 | 10 | 0 | 0 | 0 | 0.0 | 8 | 7 | 6 | 9 | 0 | .286 | .286 | 1 | 0 | SS-10 |
| 1918 | 72 | 225 | 54 | 6 | 5 | 0 | 0.0 | 23 | 16 | 42 | 52 | 5 | .240 | .311 | 0 | 0 | SS-45, 2B-26 |
| 1919 2 teams | | PHI A (39G – .271) | | | | BOS A (80G – .259) | | | | | | | | | | | |
| " total | 119 | 445 | 117 | 18 | 9 | 0 | 0.0 | 50 | 31 | 29 | 70 | 11 | .263 | .344 | 3 | 1 | 2B-116 |
| 1920 2 teams | | WAS A (62G – .288) | | | | PHI A (25G – .170) | | | | | | | | | | | |
| " total | 87 | 310 | 79 | 9 | 8 | 0 | 0.0 | 34 | 33 | 26 | 44 | 3 | .255 | .335 | 1 | 0 | SS-55, 2B-16, 3B-15 |
| 1921 PHI A | 1 | 1 | 0 | 0 | 0 | 0 | 0.0 | 0 | 0 | 0 | 0 | 0 | .000 | .000 | 1 | 0 | |
| 1926 CHI N | 19 | 51 | 17 | 5 | 0 | 0 | 0.0 | 9 | 4 | 6 | 3 | 0 | .333 | .431 | 5 | 2 | SS-13 |
| 7 yrs. | 310 | 1070 | 277 | 38 | 22 | 0 | 0.0 | 124 | 91 | 109 | 178 | 21 | .259 | .336 | 11 | 3 | 2B-159, SS-123, 3B-15 |
| 1 yr. | 19 | 51 | 17 | 5 | 0 | 0 | 0.0 | 9 | 4 | 6 | 3 | 0 | .333 | .431 | 5 | 2 | SS-13 |

| | G | AB | H | 2B | 3B | HR | HR % | R | RBI | BB | SO | SB | BA | SA | Pinch Hit AB | Pinch Hit H | G by POS |
|---|---|---|---|---|---|---|---|---|---|---|---|---|---|---|---|---|---|

# Marty Shay

**SHAY, ARTHUR JOSEPH**     BR TR 5'7½" 148 lbs.
B. Apr. 25, 1896, Boston, Mass.   D. Feb. 20, 1951, Worcester, Mass.

| | G | AB | H | 2B | 3B | HR | HR% | R | RBI | BB | SO | SB | BA | SA | PH AB | PH H | G by POS |
|---|---|---|---|---|---|---|---|---|---|---|---|---|---|---|---|---|---|
| 1916 CHI N | 2 | 7 | 2 | 0 | 0 | 0 | 0.0 | 0 | 0 | 0 | 1 | 0 | .286 | .286 | 0 | 0 | SS-2 |
| 1924 BOS N | 19 | 68 | 16 | 3 | 1 | 0 | 0.0 | 4 | 2 | 5 | 5 | 2 | .235 | .309 | 0 | 0 | 2B-19, SS-1 |
| 2 yrs. | 21 | 75 | 18 | 3 | 1 | 0 | 0.0 | 4 | 2 | 5 | 6 | 2 | .240 | .307 | 0 | 0 | 2B-19, SS-3 |
| 1 yr. | 2 | 7 | 2 | 0 | 0 | 0 | 0.0 | 0 | 0 | 0 | 1 | 0 | .286 | .286 | 0 | 0 | SS-2 |

# Dave Shean

**SHEAN, DAVID WILLIAM**     BR TR 5'11" 175 lbs.
B. May 23, 1878, Ware, Mass.   D. May 22, 1963, Boston, Mass.

| | G | AB | H | 2B | 3B | HR | HR% | R | RBI | BB | SO | SB | BA | SA | PH AB | PH H | G by POS |
|---|---|---|---|---|---|---|---|---|---|---|---|---|---|---|---|---|---|
| 1906 PHI A | 22 | 75 | 16 | 3 | 2 | 0 | 0.0 | 7 | 3 | 5 | | 6 | .213 | .307 | 0 | 0 | 2B-22 |
| 1908 PHI N | 14 | 48 | 7 | 2 | 0 | 0 | 0.0 | 2 | 1 | 1 | | 1 | .146 | .188 | 0 | 0 | SS-14 |
| 1909 2 teams | | | | | PHI N (36G – .232) | | | | BOS N (75G – .247) | | | | | | | | |
| " total | 111 | 379 | 92 | 13 | 6 | 1 | 0.3 | 46 | 33 | 31 | | 17 | .243 | .317 | 10 | 3 | 2B-86, 1B-11, OF-3, SS-1 |
| 1910 BOS N | 150 | 543 | 130 | 12 | 7 | 3 | 0.6 | 52 | 36 | 42 | 45 | 16 | .239 | .304 | 2 | 1 | 2B-148 |
| 1911 CHI N | 54 | 145 | 28 | 4 | 0 | 0 | 0.0 | 17 | 15 | 8 | 15 | 4 | .193 | .221 | 9 | 1 | 2B-23, SS-19, 3B-1 |
| 1912 BOS N | 4 | 10 | 3 | 0 | 0 | 0 | 0.0 | 1 | 0 | 1 | 2 | 0 | .300 | .300 | 1 | 0 | SS-4 |
| 1917 CIN N | 131 | 442 | 93 | 9 | 5 | 2 | 0.5 | 36 | 35 | 22 | 39 | 10 | .210 | .267 | 0 | 0 | 2B-131 |
| 1918 BOS A | 115 | 425 | 112 | 16 | 3 | 0 | 0.0 | 58 | 34 | 40 | 25 | 11 | .264 | .315 | 0 | 0 | 2B-115 |
| 1919 | 29 | 100 | 14 | 0 | 0 | 0 | 0.0 | 4 | 8 | 5 | 7 | 1 | .140 | .140 | 0 | 0 | 2B-29 |
| 9 yrs. | 630 | 2167 | 495 | 59 | 23 | 6 | 0.3 | 225 | 166 | 155 | 133 | 66 | .228 | .285 | 22 | 5 | 2B-554, SS-38, 1B-11, OF-3, 3B-1 |
| 1 yr. | 54 | 145 | 28 | 4 | 0 | 0 | 0.0 | 17 | 15 | 8 | 15 | 4 | .193 | .221 | 9 | 1 | 2B-23, SS-19, 3B-1 |

WORLD SERIES

| | G | AB | H | 2B | 3B | HR | HR% | R | RBI | BB | SO | SB | BA | SA | PH AB | PH H | G by POS |
|---|---|---|---|---|---|---|---|---|---|---|---|---|---|---|---|---|---|
| 1918 BOS A | 6 | 19 | 4 | 1 | 0 | 0 | 0.0 | 2 | 0 | 4 | 3 | 1 | .211 | .263 | 0 | 0 | 2B-6 |

# Jimmy Sheckard

**SHECKARD, SAMUEL JAMES TILDEN**     BL TR 5'9" 175 lbs.
B. Nov. 23, 1878, Upper Chanceford, Pa.   D. Jan. 15, 1947, Lancaster, Pa.

| | G | AB | H | 2B | 3B | HR | HR% | R | RBI | BB | SO | SB | BA | SA | PH AB | PH H | G by POS |
|---|---|---|---|---|---|---|---|---|---|---|---|---|---|---|---|---|---|
| 1897 BKN N | 13 | 49 | 16 | 3 | 2 | 3 | 6.1 | 12 | 14 | 6 | | 5 | .327 | .653 | 0 | 0 | SS-11, OF-2 |
| 1898 | 105 | 409 | 119 | 17 | 9 | 4 | 1.0 | 51 | 64 | 37 | | 8 | .291 | .406 | 0 | 0 | OF-105, 3B-1 |
| 1899 BAL N | 147 | 536 | 158 | 18 | 10 | 3 | 0.6 | 104 | 75 | 56 | | 77 | .295 | .382 | 0 | 0 | OF-146, 1B-1 |
| 1900 BKN N | 85 | 273 | 82 | 19 | 10 | 1 | 0.4 | 74 | 39 | 42 | | 30 | .300 | .454 | 6 | 1 | OF-78 |
| 1901 | 133 | 558 | 197 | 31 | 19 | 11 | 2.0 | 116 | 104 | 47 | | 35 | .353 | .536 | 0 | 0 | OF-121, 3B-12 |
| 1902 2 teams | | | | | BAL A (4G – .267) | | | | BKN N (123G – .270) | | | | | | | | |
| " total | 127 | 501 | 135 | 21 | 10 | 4 | 0.8 | 89 | 37 | 58 | | 25 | .269 | .375 | 0 | 0 | OF-127 |
| 1903 BKN N | 139 | 515 | 171 | 29 | 9 | 9 | 1.7 | 99 | 75 | 75 | | 67 | .332 | .476 | 0 | 0 | OF-139 |
| 1904 | 143 | 507 | 121 | 23 | 6 | 1 | 0.2 | 70 | 46 | 56 | | 21 | .239 | .314 | 0 | 0 | OF-141, 2B-2 |
| 1905 | 130 | 480 | 140 | 20 | 11 | 3 | 0.6 | 58 | 41 | 61 | | 23 | .292 | .398 | 0 | 0 | OF-129 |
| 1906 CHI N | 149 | 549 | 144 | 27 | 10 | 1 | 0.2 | 90 | 45 | 67 | | 30 | .262 | .353 | 0 | 0 | OF-149 |
| 1907 | 142 | 484 | 129 | 23 | 1 | 1 | 0.2 | 76 | 36 | 76 | | 31 | .267 | .324 | 1 | 0 | OF-142 |
| 1908 | 115 | 403 | 93 | 18 | 3 | 2 | 0.5 | 54 | 22 | 62 | | 18 | .231 | .305 | 0 | 0 | OF-115 |
| 1909 | 148 | 525 | 134 | 29 | 5 | 1 | 0.2 | 81 | 43 | 72 | | 15 | .255 | .335 | 0 | 0 | OF-148 |
| 1910 | 144 | 507 | 130 | 27 | 6 | 5 | 1.0 | 82 | 51 | 83 | 53 | 32 | .256 | .363 | 1 | 1 | OF-143 |
| 1911 | 156 | 539 | 149 | 26 | 11 | 4 | 0.7 | 121 | 50 | 147 | 58 | 32 | .276 | .388 | 0 | 0 | OF-156 |
| 1912 | 146 | 523 | 128 | 22 | 10 | 3 | 0.6 | 85 | 47 | 122 | 81 | 15 | .245 | .342 | 0 | 0 | OF-146 |
| 1913 2 teams | | | | | STL N (52G – .199) | | | | CIN N (47G – .190) | | | | | | | | |
| " total | 99 | 252 | 49 | 3 | 4 | 0 | 0.0 | 34 | 24 | 68 | 41 | 11 | .194 | .238 | 12 | 2 | OF-84 |
| 17 yrs. | 2121 | 7610 | 2095 | 356 | 136 | 56 | 0.7 | 1296 | 813 | 1135 | 233 | 465 | .275 | .380 | 20 | 4 | OF-2071, 3B-13, SS-11, 2B-2, 1B-1 |
| 7 yrs. | 1000 | 3530 | 907 | 172 | 46 | 17 | 0.5 | 589 | 294 | 629 10th | 192 7th | 163 | .257 | .346 | 2 | 1 | OF-999 |

WORLD SERIES

| | G | AB | H | 2B | 3B | HR | HR% | R | RBI | BB | SO | SB | BA | SA | PH AB | PH H | G by POS |
|---|---|---|---|---|---|---|---|---|---|---|---|---|---|---|---|---|---|
| 1906 CHI N | 6 | 21 | 0 | 0 | 0 | 0 | 0.0 | 0 | 1 | 2 | 4 | 1 | .000 | .000 | 0 | 0 | OF-6 |
| 1907 | 5 | 21 | 5 | 2 | 0 | 0 | 0.0 | 0 | 2 | 0 | 1 | 1 | .238 | .333 | 0 | 0 | OF-5 |
| 1908 | 5 | 21 | 5 | 2 | 0 | 0 | 0.0 | 2 | 1 | 2 | 3 | 1 | .238 | .333 | 0 | 0 | OF-5 |
| 1910 | 5 | 14 | 4 | 2 | 0 | 0 | 0.0 | 5 | 1 | 7 | 2 | 1 | .286 | .429 | 0 | 0 | OF-5 |
| 4 yrs. | 21 | 77 | 14 | 6 | 0 | 0 | 0.0 | 7 | 5 | 11 | 10 | 4 | .182 | .260 | 0 | 0 | OF-21 |

# Eddie Sicking

**SICKING, EDWARD JOSEPH**     BB TR 5'9½" 165 lbs.
B. Mar. 30, 1897, St. Bernard, Ohio   D. Aug. 30, 1978, Cincinnati, Ohio

| | G | AB | H | 2B | 3B | HR | HR% | R | RBI | BB | SO | SB | BA | SA | PH AB | PH H | G by POS |
|---|---|---|---|---|---|---|---|---|---|---|---|---|---|---|---|---|---|
| 1916 CHI N | 1 | 1 | 0 | 0 | 0 | 0 | 0.0 | 0 | 0 | 0 | 0 | 0 | .000 | .000 | 1 | 0 | |
| 1918 NY N | 46 | 132 | 33 | 4 | 0 | 0 | 0.0 | 9 | 12 | 6 | 11 | 2 | .250 | .280 | 3 | 0 | 3B-24, 2B-18, SS-2 |
| 1919 2 teams | | | | | NY N (6G – .333) | | | | PHI N (61G – .216) | | | | | | | | |
| " total | 67 | 200 | 45 | 2 | 1 | 0 | 0.0 | 18 | 18 | 9 | 17 | 4 | .225 | .245 | 3 | 0 | SS-41, 2B-21 |
| 1920 2 teams | | | | | NY N (46G – .172) | | | | CIN N (37G – .268) | | | | | | | | |
| " total | 83 | 257 | 56 | 6 | 1 | 0 | 0.0 | 23 | 26 | 23 | 15 | 8 | .218 | .249 | 1 | 0 | 2B-40, 3B-30, SS-12 |
| 1927 PIT N | 6 | 7 | 1 | 0 | 0 | 0 | 0.0 | 1 | 3 | 1 | 0 | 0 | .143 | .286 | 0 | 0 | 2B-5 |
| 5 yrs. | 203 | 597 | 135 | 13 | 2 | 0 | 0.0 | 51 | 59 | 39 | 43 | 14 | .226 | .255 | 8 | 0 | 2B-84, SS-55, 3B-54 |
| 1 yr. | 1 | 1 | 0 | 0 | 0 | 0 | 0.0 | 0 | 0 | 0 | 0 | 0 | .000 | .000 | 1 | 0 | |

# Charlie Silvera

**SILVERA, CHARLES ANTHONY RYAN (Swede)**     BR TR 5'10" 175 lbs.
B. Oct. 13, 1924, San Francisco, Calif.

| | G | AB | H | 2B | 3B | HR | HR% | R | RBI | BB | SO | SB | BA | SA | PH AB | PH H | G by POS |
|---|---|---|---|---|---|---|---|---|---|---|---|---|---|---|---|---|---|
| 1948 NY A | 4 | 14 | 8 | 0 | 1 | 0 | 0.0 | 1 | 0 | 1 | 0 | 0 | .571 | .714 | 0 | 0 | C-4 |
| 1949 | 58 | 130 | 41 | 2 | 0 | 0 | 0.0 | 8 | 13 | 18 | 5 | 2 | .315 | .331 | 6 | 3 | C-51 |
| 1950 | 18 | 25 | 4 | 0 | 0 | 0 | 0.0 | 2 | 1 | 1 | 2 | 0 | .160 | .160 | 3 | 1 | C-15 |
| 1951 | 18 | 51 | 14 | 0 | 0 | 1 | 2.0 | 5 | 7 | 5 | 3 | 0 | .275 | .392 | 0 | 0 | C-18 |
| 1952 | 20 | 55 | 18 | 3 | 0 | 0 | 0.0 | 4 | 11 | 5 | 2 | 0 | .327 | .382 | 0 | 0 | C-20 |
| 1953 | 42 | 82 | 23 | 3 | 1 | 0 | 0.0 | 11 | 12 | 9 | 5 | 0 | .280 | .341 | 2 | 1 | C-39, 3B-1 |
| 1954 | 20 | 37 | 10 | 1 | 0 | 0 | 0.0 | 1 | 4 | 3 | 2 | 0 | .270 | .297 | 2 | 0 | C-18 |
| 1955 | 14 | 52 | 10 | 0 | 0 | 0 | 0.0 | 1 | 1 | 6 | 4 | 0 | .192 | .192 | 2 | 0 | C-11 |
| 1956 | 7 | 9 | 2 | 0 | 0 | 0 | 0.0 | 0 | 0 | 2 | 3 | 0 | .222 | .222 | 0 | 0 | C-7 |

| | G | AB | H | 2B | 3B | HR | HR % | R | RBI | BB | SO | SB | BA | SA | Pinch Hit AB | Pinch Hit H | G by POS |
|---|---|---|---|---|---|---|---|---|---|---|---|---|---|---|---|---|---|

## Charlie Silvera continued

| | G | AB | H | 2B | 3B | HR | HR % | R | RBI | BB | SO | SB | BA | SA | PH AB | PH H | G by POS |
|---|---|---|---|---|---|---|---|---|---|---|---|---|---|---|---|---|---|
| 1957 CHI N | 26 | 53 | 11 | 3 | 0 | 0 | 0.0 | 1 | 2 | 4 | 5 | 0 | .208 | .264 | 0 | 0 | C-26 |
| 10 yrs. | 227 | 482 | 136 | 15 | 2 | 1 | 0.2 | 34 | 52 | 53 | 32 | 2 | .282 | .328 | 15 | 5 | C-209, 3B-1 |
| 1 yr. | 26 | 53 | 11 | 3 | 0 | 0 | 0.0 | 1 | 2 | 4 | 5 | 0 | .208 | .264 | 0 | 0 | C-26 |

WORLD SERIES

| | G | AB | H | 2B | 3B | HR | HR % | R | RBI | BB | SO | SB | BA | SA | PH AB | PH H | G by POS |
|---|---|---|---|---|---|---|---|---|---|---|---|---|---|---|---|---|---|
| 1949 NY A | 1 | 2 | 0 | 0 | 0 | 0 | 0.0 | 0 | 0 | 0 | 0 | 0 | .000 | .000 | 0 | 0 | C-1 |

## Ted Sizemore

**SIZEMORE, TED CRAWFORD**
B. Apr. 15, 1946, Gadsden, Ala.   BR TR 5'10" 165 lbs.

| | G | AB | H | 2B | 3B | HR | HR % | R | RBI | BB | SO | SB | BA | SA | PH AB | PH H | G by POS |
|---|---|---|---|---|---|---|---|---|---|---|---|---|---|---|---|---|---|
| 1969 LA N | 159 | 590 | 160 | 20 | 5 | 4 | 0.7 | 69 | 46 | 45 | 40 | 5 | .271 | .342 | 0 | 0 | 2B-118, SS-46, OF-1 |
| 1970 | 96 | 340 | 104 | 10 | 1 | 1 | 0.3 | 40 | 34 | 34 | 19 | 5 | .306 | .350 | 3 | 2 | 2B-86, OF-9, SS-2 |
| 1971 STL N | 135 | 478 | 126 | 14 | 5 | 3 | 0.6 | 53 | 42 | 42 | 26 | 4 | .264 | .333 | 6 | 3 | 2B-93, SS-39, OF-15, 3B-1 |
| 1972 | 120 | 439 | 116 | 17 | 4 | 2 | 0.5 | 53 | 38 | 37 | 36 | 8 | .264 | .335 | 13 | 1 | 2B-111 |
| 1973 | 142 | 521 | 147 | 22 | 1 | 1 | 0.2 | 69 | 54 | 68 | 34 | 6 | .282 | .334 | 1 | 0 | 2B-139, 3B-3 |
| 1974 | 129 | 504 | 126 | 17 | 0 | 2 | 0.4 | 68 | 47 | 70 | 37 | 8 | .250 | .296 | 2 | 0 | 2B-128, OF-1, SS-1 |
| 1975 | 153 | 562 | 135 | 23 | 1 | 3 | 0.5 | 56 | 49 | 45 | 37 | 1 | .240 | .301 | 1 | 1 | 2B-153 |
| 1976 LA N | 84 | 266 | 64 | 8 | 1 | 0 | 0.0 | 18 | 18 | 15 | 22 | 2 | .241 | .278 | 13 | 5 | 2B-71, 3B-3, C-2 |
| 1977 PHI N | 152 | 519 | 146 | 20 | 3 | 4 | 0.8 | 64 | 47 | 52 | 40 | 8 | .281 | .355 | 1 | 0 | 2B-152 |
| 1978 | 108 | 351 | 77 | 12 | 0 | 0 | 0.0 | 38 | 25 | 25 | 29 | 8 | .219 | .254 | 1 | 0 | 2B-107 |
| 1979 2 teams | | | CHI N (98G – .248) | | | BOS A (26G – .261) | | | | | | | | | | | |
| " total | 124 | 418 | 105 | 24 | 0 | 3 | 0.7 | 48 | 30 | 36 | 30 | 4 | .251 | .330 | 3 | 0 | 2B-122, C-2 |
| 1980 BOS A | 9 | 23 | 5 | 1 | 0 | 0 | 0.0 | 1 | 0 | 0 | 0 | 0 | .217 | .261 | 1 | 0 | 2B-8 |
| 12 yrs. | 1411 | 5011 | 1311 | 188 | 21 | 23 | 0.5 | 577 | 430 | 469 | 350 | 59 | .262 | .321 | 45 | 12 | 2B-1288, SS-88, OF-26, 3B-7, C-4 |
| 1 yr. | 98 | 330 | 82 | 17 | 0 | 2 | 0.6 | 36 | 24 | 32 | 25 | 3 | .248 | .318 | 2 | 0 | 2B-96 |

LEAGUE CHAMPIONSHIP SERIES

| | G | AB | H | 2B | 3B | HR | HR % | R | RBI | BB | SO | SB | BA | SA | PH AB | PH H | G by POS |
|---|---|---|---|---|---|---|---|---|---|---|---|---|---|---|---|---|---|
| 1977 PHI N | 4 | 13 | 3 | 0 | 0 | 0 | 0.0 | 1 | 0 | 2 | 0 | 0 | .231 | .231 | 0 | 0 | 2B-4 |
| 1978 | 4 | 13 | 5 | 0 | 1 | 0 | 0.0 | 3 | 1 | 1 | 0 | 0 | .385 | .538 | 0 | 0 | 2B-4 |
| 2 yrs. | 8 | 26 | 8 | 0 | 1 | 0 | 0.0 | 4 | 1 | 3 | 0 | 0 | .308 | .385 | 0 | 0 | 2B-8 |

## Roe Skidmore

**SKIDMORE, ROBERT ROE**
B. Oct. 30, 1945, Decatur, Ill.   BR TL 6'3" 188 lbs.

| | G | AB | H | 2B | 3B | HR | HR % | R | RBI | BB | SO | SB | BA | SA | PH AB | PH H | G by POS |
|---|---|---|---|---|---|---|---|---|---|---|---|---|---|---|---|---|---|
| 1970 CHI N | 1 | 1 | 1 | 0 | 0 | 0 | 0.0 | 0 | 0 | 0 | 0 | 0 | 1.000 | 1.000 | 1 | 1 | |

## Jimmy Slagle

**SLAGLE, JAMES FRANKLIN (Rabbit, Shorty, The Human Mosquito)**
B. July 11, 1873, Worthville, Pa.   D. May 10, 1956, Chicago, Ill.   BL TR 5'7"

| | G | AB | H | 2B | 3B | HR | HR % | R | RBI | BB | SO | SB | BA | SA | PH AB | PH H | G by POS |
|---|---|---|---|---|---|---|---|---|---|---|---|---|---|---|---|---|---|
| 1899 WAS N | 147 | 599 | 163 | 15 | 8 | 0 | 0.0 | 92 | 41 | 55 | | 22 | .272 | .324 | 1 | 0 | OF-146 |
| 1900 PHI N | 141 | 574 | 165 | 16 | 9 | 0 | 0.0 | 115 | 45 | 60 | | 34 | .287 | .347 | 0 | 0 | OF-141 |
| 1901 2 teams | | | PHI N (48G – .202) | | | BOS N (66G – .271) | | | | | | | | | | | |
| " total | 114 | 438 | 106 | 13 | 2 | 1 | 0.2 | 55 | 27 | 50 | | 19 | .242 | .288 | 0 | 0 | OF-114 |
| 1902 CHI N | 115 | 454 | 143 | 11 | 4 | 0 | 0.0 | 64 | 28 | 53 | | 40 | .315 | .357 | 2 | 1 | OF-113 |
| 1903 | 139 | 543 | 162 | 20 | 6 | 0 | 0.0 | 104 | 44 | 81 | | 33 | .298 | .357 | 0 | 0 | OF-139 |
| 1904 | 120 | 481 | 125 | 12 | 10 | 1 | 0.2 | 73 | 31 | 41 | | 28 | .260 | .333 | 0 | 0 | OF-120 |
| 1905 | 155 | 568 | 153 | 19 | 4 | 0 | 0.0 | 96 | 37 | 97 | | 27 | .269 | .317 | 0 | 0 | OF-155 |
| 1906 | 127 | 498 | 119 | 8 | 6 | 0 | 0.0 | 71 | 33 | 63 | | 25 | .239 | .279 | 0 | 0 | OF-127 |
| 1907 | 136 | 489 | 126 | 6 | 6 | 0 | 0.0 | 71 | 32 | 76 | | 28 | .258 | .294 | 0 | 0 | OF-135 |
| 1908 | 104 | 352 | 78 | 4 | 1 | 0 | 0.0 | 38 | 26 | 43 | | 17 | .222 | .239 | 2 | 0 | OF-101 |
| 10 yrs. | 1298 | 4996 | 1340 | 124 | 56 | 2 | 0.0 | 779 | 344 | 619 | | 273 | .268 | .317 | 5 | 1 | OF-1291 |
| 7 yrs. | 896 | 3385 | 906 | 80 | 37 | 1 | 0.0 | 517 | 231 | 454 | | 198 5th | .268 | .314 | 4 | 1 | OF-890 |

WORLD SERIES

| | G | AB | H | 2B | 3B | HR | HR % | R | RBI | BB | SO | SB | BA | SA | PH AB | PH H | G by POS |
|---|---|---|---|---|---|---|---|---|---|---|---|---|---|---|---|---|---|
| 1907 CHI N | 5 | 22 | 6 | 0 | 0 | 0 | 0.0 | 3 | 4 | 2 | 5 | 6 | .273 | .273 | 0 | 0 | OF-5 |

## Roy Smalley

**SMALLEY, ROY FREDERICK**
Father of Roy Smalley.
B. June 9, 1926, Springfield, Mo.   BR TR 6'3" 190 lbs.

| | G | AB | H | 2B | 3B | HR | HR % | R | RBI | BB | SO | SB | BA | SA | PH AB | PH H | G by POS |
|---|---|---|---|---|---|---|---|---|---|---|---|---|---|---|---|---|---|
| 1948 CHI N | 124 | 361 | 78 | 11 | 4 | 4 | 1.1 | 25 | 36 | 23 | 76 | 0 | .216 | .302 | 0 | 0 | SS-124 |
| 1949 | 135 | 477 | 117 | 21 | 10 | 8 | 1.7 | 57 | 35 | 36 | 77 | 2 | .245 | .382 | 3 | 1 | SS-132 |
| 1950 | 154 | 557 | 128 | 21 | 9 | 21 | 3.8 | 58 | 85 | 49 | 114 | 2 | .230 | .413 | 0 | 0 | SS-154 |
| 1951 | 79 | 238 | 55 | 7 | 4 | 8 | 3.4 | 24 | 31 | 25 | 53 | 0 | .231 | .395 | 4 | 2 | SS-74 |
| 1952 | 87 | 261 | 58 | 14 | 1 | 5 | 1.9 | 36 | 30 | 29 | 58 | 0 | .222 | .341 | 5 | 1 | SS-82 |
| 1953 | 82 | 253 | 63 | 9 | 0 | 6 | 2.4 | 20 | 25 | 28 | 57 | 0 | .249 | .356 | 5 | 1 | SS-77 |
| 1954 MIL N | 25 | 36 | 8 | 0 | 0 | 1 | 2.8 | 5 | 7 | 4 | 9 | 0 | .222 | .306 | 8 | 2 | SS-9, 2B-7, 1B-2 |
| 1955 PHI N | 92 | 260 | 51 | 11 | 1 | 7 | 2.7 | 33 | 39 | 39 | 58 | 0 | .196 | .327 | 3 | 1 | SS-87, 3B-1, 2B-1 |
| 1956 | 65 | 168 | 38 | 9 | 3 | 0 | 0.0 | 14 | 16 | 23 | 29 | 0 | .226 | .315 | 4 | 0 | SS-60 |
| 1957 | 28 | 31 | 5 | 0 | 1 | 1 | 3.2 | 5 | 1 | 1 | 9 | 0 | .161 | .323 | 6 | 0 | SS-20 |
| 1958 | 1 | 2 | 0 | 0 | 0 | 0 | 0.0 | 0 | 0 | 0 | 1 | 0 | .000 | .000 | 0 | 0 | SS-1 |
| 11 yrs. | 872 | 2644 | 601 | 103 | 33 | 61 | 2.3 | 277 | 305 | 257 | 541 | 4 | .227 | .360 | 38 | 8 | SS-820, 2B-8, 1B-2, 3B-1 |
| 6 yrs. | 661 | 2147 | 499 | 83 | 28 | 52 | 2.4 | 220 | 242 | 190 | 435 | 4 | .232 | .370 | 17 | 5 | SS-643 |

## Bob Smith

**SMITH, ROBERT ELDRIDGE**
B. Apr. 22, 1898, Rogersville, Tenn.   BR TR 5'10" 175 lbs.

| | G | AB | H | 2B | 3B | HR | HR % | R | RBI | BB | SO | SB | BA | SA | PH AB | PH H | G by POS |
|---|---|---|---|---|---|---|---|---|---|---|---|---|---|---|---|---|---|
| 1923 BOS N | 115 | 375 | 94 | 16 | 3 | 0 | 0.0 | 30 | 40 | 17 | 35 | 4 | .251 | .309 | 3 | 1 | SS-101, 2B-8 |
| 1924 | 106 | 347 | 79 | 12 | 3 | 2 | 0.6 | 32 | 38 | 15 | 26 | 5 | .228 | .297 | 2 | 0 | SS-80, 3B-23 |
| 1925 | 58 | 174 | 49 | 9 | 4 | 0 | 0.0 | 17 | 23 | 5 | 6 | 2 | .282 | .379 | 8 | 0 | SS-21, 2B-15, P-13, OF-1 |
| 1926 | 40 | 84 | 25 | 6 | 2 | 0 | 0.0 | 10 | 13 | 2 | 4 | 0 | .298 | .417 | 7 | 4 | P-33 |
| 1927 | 54 | 109 | 27 | 3 | 1 | 1 | 0.9 | 10 | 10 | 2 | 4 | 0 | .248 | .321 | 13 | 2 | P-41 |
| 1928 | 39 | 92 | 23 | 2 | 0 | 1 | 1.1 | 11 | 8 | 1 | 6 | 2 | .250 | .304 | 1 | 0 | P-38 |
| 1929 | 39 | 99 | 17 | 4 | 2 | 1 | 1.0 | 12 | 8 | 2 | 8 | 1 | .172 | .283 | 0 | 0 | P-34, SS-5 |
| 1930 | 39 | 81 | 19 | 2 | 0 | 0 | 0.0 | 7 | 4 | 0 | 5 | 0 | .235 | .259 | 1 | 0 | P-38 |

| | G | AB | H | 2B | 3B | HR | HR % | R | RBI | BB | SO | SB | BA | SA | Pinch Hit AB | Pinch Hit H | G by POS |
|---|---|---|---|---|---|---|---|---|---|---|---|---|---|---|---|---|---|

## Bob Smith  continued

| | G | AB | H | 2B | 3B | HR | HR% | R | RBI | BB | SO | SB | BA | SA | PH AB | PH H | G by POS |
|---|---|---|---|---|---|---|---|---|---|---|---|---|---|---|---|---|---|
| 1931 CHI N | 36 | 87 | 19 | 2 | 0 | 0 | 0.0 | 7 | 4 | 5 | 2 | 0 | .218 | .241 | 0 | 0 | P-36 |
| 1932 | 36 | 42 | 10 | 4 | 1 | 0 | 0.0 | 5 | 4 | 0 | 2 | 1 | .238 | .381 | 0 | 0 | P-34, 2B-2 |
| 1933 2 teams | CIN | N (23G – | .200) | | BOS | N (14G – | .200) | | | | | | | | | | |
| " total | 37 | 45 | 9 | 1 | 1 | 0 | 0.0 | 3 | 3 | 1 | 1 | 1 | .200 | .267 | 1 | 1 | P-30, SS-1 |
| 1934 BOS N | 42 | 36 | 9 | 1 | 0 | 0 | 0.0 | 5 | 3 | 1 | 0 | 1 | .250 | .278 | 0 | 0 | P-39 |
| 1935 | 47 | 63 | 17 | 0 | 0 | 0 | 0.0 | 3 | 4 | 1 | 5 | 0 | .270 | .270 | 1 | 1 | P-46 |
| 1936 | 35 | 45 | 10 | 2 | 0 | 0 | 0.0 | 1 | 4 | 0 | 4 | 0 | .222 | .267 | 0 | 0 | P-35 |
| 1937 | 19 | 10 | 2 | 0 | 0 | 0 | 0.0 | 1 | 0 | 1 | 1 | 0 | .200 | .200 | 0 | 0 | P-18 |
| 15 yrs. | 742 | 1689 | 409 | 64 | 17 | 5 | 0.3 | 154 | 166 | 52 | 110 | 16 | .242 | .309 | 37 | 9 | P-435, SS-208, 2B-25, 3B-23, OF-1 |
| 2 yrs. | 72 | 129 | 29 | 6 | 1 | 0 | 0.0 | 12 | 8 | 5 | 4 | 1 | .225 | .287 | 0 | 0 | P-70, 2B-2 |
| WORLD SERIES | | | | | | | | | | | | | | | | | |
| 1932 CHI N | 1 | 0 | 0 | 0 | 0 | 0 | – | 0 | 0 | 0 | 0 | 0 | – | – | 0 | 0 | P-1 |

## Bobby Gene Smith

**SMITH, BOBBY GENE**  
B. May 28, 1934, Hood River, Ore.    BR TR 5'11" 180 lbs.

| | G | AB | H | 2B | 3B | HR | HR% | R | RBI | BB | SO | SB | BA | SA | PH AB | PH H | G by POS |
|---|---|---|---|---|---|---|---|---|---|---|---|---|---|---|---|---|---|
| 1957 STL N | 93 | 185 | 39 | 7 | 1 | 3 | 1.6 | 24 | 18 | 13 | 35 | 1 | .211 | .308 | 11 | 1 | OF-79 |
| 1958 | 28 | 88 | 25 | 3 | 0 | 2 | 2.3 | 8 | 5 | 2 | 18 | 1 | .284 | .386 | 1 | 0 | OF-27 |
| 1959 | 43 | 60 | 13 | 1 | 1 | 1 | 1.7 | 11 | 7 | 1 | 9 | 0 | .217 | .317 | 7 | 2 | OF-32 |
| 1960 PHI N | 98 | 217 | 62 | 5 | 2 | 4 | 1.8 | 24 | 27 | 10 | 28 | 2 | .286 | .382 | 35 | 11 | OF-70, 3B-1 |
| 1961 | 79 | 174 | 44 | 7 | 0 | 2 | 1.1 | 16 | 18 | 15 | 32 | 0 | .253 | .328 | 31 | 6 | OF-47 |
| 1962 3 teams | NY | N (8G – | .136) | | CHI | N (13G – | .172) | | STL | N (91G – | .231) | | | | | | |
| " total | 112 | 181 | 38 | 9 | 1 | 1 | 0.6 | 17 | 16 | 12 | 22 | 1 | .210 | .287 | 18 | 2 | OF-93 |
| 1965 CAL A | 23 | 57 | 13 | 3 | 0 | 0 | 0.0 | 1 | 5 | 2 | 10 | 0 | .228 | .281 | 7 | 2 | OF-15 |
| 7 yrs. | 476 | 962 | 234 | 35 | 5 | 13 | 1.4 | 101 | 96 | 55 | 154 | 5 | .243 | .331 | 110 | 24 | OF-363, 3B-1 |
| 1 yr. | 13 | 29 | 5 | 0 | 0 | 1 | 3.4 | 3 | 2 | 2 | 6 | 0 | .172 | .276 | 6 | 1 | OF-7 |

## Broadway Aleck Smith

**SMITH, ALEXANDER BENJAMIN**  
B. 1871, New York, N. Y.   D. July 9, 1919, New York, N. Y.    TR

| | G | AB | H | 2B | 3B | HR | HR% | R | RBI | BB | SO | SB | BA | SA | PH AB | PH H | G by POS |
|---|---|---|---|---|---|---|---|---|---|---|---|---|---|---|---|---|---|
| 1897 BKN N | 66 | 237 | 71 | 13 | 1 | 1 | 0.4 | 36 | 39 | 4 | | 12 | .300 | .376 | 0 | 0 | C-43, OF-18, 1B-6 |
| 1898 | 52 | 199 | 52 | 6 | 5 | 0 | 0.0 | 25 | 23 | 3 | | 7 | .261 | .342 | 2 | 0 | OF-26, C-20, 3B-2, 2B-2, 1B-1 |
| 1899 2 teams | BKN | N (17G – | .180) | | BAL | N (41G – | .383) | | | | | | | | | | |
| " total | 58 | 181 | 57 | 6 | 5 | 0 | 0.0 | 23 | 31 | 6 | | 7 | .315 | .403 | 1 | 0 | C-53, OF-2, 1B-1 |
| 1900 BKN N | 7 | 25 | 6 | 0 | 0 | 0 | 0.0 | 2 | 3 | 1 | | 2 | .240 | .240 | 0 | 0 | 3B-6, C-1 |
| 1901 NY N | 26 | 78 | 11 | 0 | 1 | 0 | 0.0 | 5 | 6 | 0 | | 3 | .141 | .167 | 1 | 0 | C-25 |
| 1902 BAL A | 41 | 145 | 34 | 3 | 0 | 0 | 0.0 | 10 | 21 | 8 | | 5 | .234 | .255 | 0 | 0 | C-27, 1B-7, OF-4, 2B-3, 3B-1 |
| 1903 BOS A | 11 | 33 | 10 | 1 | 0 | 0 | 0.0 | 4 | 4 | 0 | | 1 | .303 | .333 | 1 | 0 | C-10 |
| 1904 CHI N | 10 | 29 | 6 | 1 | 0 | 0 | 0.0 | 2 | 1 | 3 | | 1 | .207 | .241 | 2 | 0 | OF-6, 3B-1, C-1 |
| 1906 NY N | 16 | 28 | 5 | 0 | 0 | 0 | 0.0 | 0 | 2 | 1 | | 1 | .179 | .179 | 4 | 1 | C-8, 1B-3, OF-1 |
| 9 yrs. | 287 | 955 | 252 | 30 | 12 | 1 | 0.1 | 107 | 130 | 26 | | 38 | .264 | .324 | 11 | | C-188, OF-57, 1B-18, 3B-10, 2B-5 |
| 1 yr. | 10 | 29 | 6 | 1 | 0 | 0 | 0.0 | 2 | 1 | 3 | | 1 | .207 | .241 | 2 | 0 | OF-6, 3B-1, C-1 |

## Bull Smith

**SMITH, LEWIS OSCAR**  
B. Aug. 20, 1880, Plum, W. Va.   D. May 1, 1928, Charlestown, W. Va.    BR TR 6' 180 lbs.

| | G | AB | H | 2B | 3B | HR | HR% | R | RBI | BB | SO | SB | BA | SA | PH AB | PH H | G by POS |
|---|---|---|---|---|---|---|---|---|---|---|---|---|---|---|---|---|---|
| 1904 PIT N | 13 | 42 | 6 | 0 | 1 | 0 | 0.0 | 2 | 0 | 1 | | 0 | .143 | .190 | 0 | 0 | OF-13 |
| 1906 CHI N | 1 | 1 | 0 | 0 | 0 | 0 | 0.0 | 0 | 0 | 0 | | 0 | .000 | .000 | 1 | 0 | |
| 1911 WAS A | 1 | 0 | 0 | 0 | 0 | 0 | – | 0 | 0 | 0 | | 0 | – | – | 0 | 0 | |
| 3 yrs. | 15 | 43 | 6 | 0 | 1 | 0 | 0.0 | 2 | 0 | 1 | | 0 | .140 | .186 | 1 | 0 | OF-13 |
| 1 yr. | 1 | 1 | 0 | 0 | 0 | 0 | 0.0 | 0 | 0 | 0 | | 0 | .000 | .000 | 1 | 0 | |

## Charley Smith

**SMITH, CHARLES WILLIAM**  
B. Sept. 15, 1937, Charleston, S. C.    BR TR 6'1" 170 lbs.

| | G | AB | H | 2B | 3B | HR | HR% | R | RBI | BB | SO | SB | BA | SA | PH AB | PH H | G by POS |
|---|---|---|---|---|---|---|---|---|---|---|---|---|---|---|---|---|---|
| 1960 LA N | 18 | 60 | 10 | 1 | 0 | 0 | 0.0 | 2 | 5 | 1 | 15 | 0 | .167 | .217 | 0 | 0 | 3B-18 |
| 1961 2 teams | LA | N (9G – | .250) | | PHI | N (112G – | .248) | | | | | | | | | | |
| " total | 121 | 435 | 108 | 14 | 4 | 11 | 2.5 | 47 | 50 | 24 | 82 | 3 | .248 | .375 | 5 | 1 | 3B-98, SS-17 |
| 1962 CHI N | 65 | 145 | 30 | 4 | 0 | 2 | 1.4 | 11 | 17 | 9 | 32 | 0 | .207 | .276 | 13 | 2 | 3B-54 |
| 1963 | 4 | 7 | 2 | 0 | 1 | 0 | 0.0 | 0 | 1 | 0 | 2 | 0 | .286 | .571 | 3 | 1 | SS-1 |
| 1964 2 teams | CHI | A (2G – | .143) | | NY | N (127G – | .239) | | | | | | | | | | |
| " total | 129 | 450 | 107 | 12 | 1 | 20 | 4.4 | 45 | 58 | 20 | 102 | 2 | .238 | .402 | 7 | 2 | 3B-87, SS-36, OF-13 |
| 1965 NY N | 135 | 499 | 122 | 20 | 3 | 16 | 3.2 | 49 | 62 | 17 | 123 | 2 | .244 | .393 | 3 | 0 | 3B-131, SS-6, 2B-1 |
| 1966 STL N | 116 | 391 | 104 | 13 | 4 | 10 | 2.6 | 34 | 43 | 22 | 81 | 0 | .266 | .396 | 8 | 3 | 3B-107, SS-1 |
| 1967 NY A | 135 | 425 | 95 | 15 | 3 | 9 | 2.1 | 38 | 38 | 32 | 110 | 0 | .224 | .336 | 20 | 6 | 3B-115 |
| 1968 | 46 | 70 | 16 | 4 | 1 | 1 | 1.4 | 2 | 7 | 5 | 18 | 0 | .229 | .357 | 31 | 10 | 3B-13 |
| 1969 CHI N | 2 | 2 | 0 | 0 | 0 | 0 | 0.0 | 0 | 0 | 0 | 0 | 0 | .000 | .000 | 2 | 0 | |
| 10 yrs. | 771 | 2484 | 594 | 83 | 18 | 69 | 2.8 | 228 | 281 | 130 | 565 | 7 | .239 | .370 | 92 | 25 | 3B-623, SS-61, OF-13, 2B-1 |
| 1 yr. | 2 | 2 | 0 | 0 | 0 | 0 | 0.0 | 0 | 0 | 0 | 0 | 0 | .000 | .000 | 2 | 0 | |

## Earl Smith

**SMITH, EARL LEONARD**  
B. Jan. 20, 1891, Oak Hill, Ohio   D. Mar. 14, 1943, Portsmouth, Ohio    BL TR 5'11" 170 lbs.

| | G | AB | H | 2B | 3B | HR | HR% | R | RBI | BB | SO | SB | BA | SA | PH AB | PH H | G by POS |
|---|---|---|---|---|---|---|---|---|---|---|---|---|---|---|---|---|---|
| 1916 CHI N | 14 | 27 | 7 | 1 | 1 | 0 | 0.0 | 2 | 4 | 2 | 5 | 1 | .259 | .370 | 7 | 1 | OF-7 |
| 1917 STL A | 52 | 199 | 56 | 7 | 7 | 0 | 0.0 | 31 | 10 | 15 | 21 | 5 | .281 | .387 | 1 | 1 | OF-51 |
| 1918 | 89 | 286 | 77 | 10 | 5 | 0 | 0.0 | 28 | 32 | 13 | 16 | 13 | .269 | .339 | 8 | 4 | OF-81 |
| 1919 | 88 | 252 | 63 | 12 | 5 | 1 | 0.4 | 21 | 36 | 18 | 27 | 1 | .250 | .349 | 14 | 5 | OF-68 |
| 1920 | 103 | 353 | 108 | 21 | 8 | 3 | 0.8 | 45 | 55 | 13 | 18 | 11 | .306 | .436 | 16 | 2 | 3B-70, OF-15 |
| 1921 2 teams | STL | A (25G – | .333) | | WAS | A (59G – | .217) | | | | | | | | | | |
| " total | 84 | 258 | 65 | 9 | 4 | 4 | 1.6 | 27 | 26 | 13 | 23 | 1 | .252 | .364 | 20 | 6 | OF-47, 3B-14 |

| | G | AB | H | 2B | 3B | HR | HR % | R | RBI | BB | SO | SB | BA | SA | Pinch Hit AB | Pinch Hit H | G by POS |
|---|---|---|---|---|---|---|---|---|---|---|---|---|---|---|---|---|---|

## Earl Smith continued

| | G | AB | H | 2B | 3B | HR | HR% | R | RBI | BB | SO | SB | BA | SA | AB | H | G by POS |
|---|---|---|---|---|---|---|---|---|---|---|---|---|---|---|---|---|---|
| 1922 **WAS A** | 65 | 205 | 53 | 12 | 2 | 1 | 0.5 | 22 | 23 | 8 | 17 | 4 | .259 | .351 | 10 | 2 | OF-49, 3B-1 |
| 7 yrs. | 495 | 1580 | 429 | 72 | 32 | 9 | 0.6 | 176 | 186 | 82 | 127 | 36 | .272 | .375 | 76 | 21 | OF-318, 3B-85 |
| 1 yr. | 14 | 27 | 7 | 1 | 1 | 0 | 0.0 | 2 | 4 | 2 | 5 | 1 | .259 | .370 | 7 | 1 | OF-7 |

## Harry Smith

**SMITH, HARRY W.**
B. Feb. 5, 1856, N. Vernon, Ind.   D. June 4, 1898, N. Vernon, Ind.
BR  TR  6'    175 lbs.

| | G | AB | H | 2B | 3B | HR | HR% | R | RBI | BB | SO | SB | BA | SA | AB | H | G by POS |
|---|---|---|---|---|---|---|---|---|---|---|---|---|---|---|---|---|---|
| 1877 **2 teams** | | | CHI | N | (24G – | .202) | | CIN | N | (10G – | .250) | | | | | | |
| " total | 34 | 130 | 28 | 3 | 1 | 0 | 0.0 | 11 | 6 | 5 | 11 | | .215 | .254 | 0 | 0 | 2B-17, OF-13, C-8 |
| 1889 **LOU AA** | 1 | 2 | 1 | 0 | 0 | 0 | 0.0 | 0 | 1 | 0 | 1 | 0 | .500 | .500 | 0 | 0 | OF-1, C-1 |
| 2 yrs. | 35 | 132 | 29 | 3 | 1 | 0 | 0.0 | 11 | 7 | 5 | 12 | 0 | .220 | .258 | 0 | 0 | 2B-17, OF-14, C-9 |
| 1 yr. | 24 | 94 | 19 | 1 | 0 | 0 | 0.0 | 7 | 3 | 4 | 6 | | .202 | .213 | 0 | 0 | 2B-14, OF-10 |

## Paul Smith

**SMITH, PAUL LESLIE**
B. Mar. 19, 1931, New Castle, Pa.
BL  TL  5'8"    165 lbs.

| | G | AB | H | 2B | 3B | HR | HR% | R | RBI | BB | SO | SB | BA | SA | AB | H | G by POS |
|---|---|---|---|---|---|---|---|---|---|---|---|---|---|---|---|---|---|
| 1953 **PIT N** | 118 | 389 | 110 | 12 | 7 | 4 | 1.0 | 41 | 44 | 24 | 23 | 3 | .283 | .380 | 23 | 8 | 1B-74, OF-19 |
| 1957 | 81 | 150 | 38 | 4 | 0 | 3 | 2.0 | 12 | 11 | 12 | 17 | 0 | .253 | .340 | 45 | 9 | OF-33, 1B-1 |
| 1958 **2 teams** | 24 | | PIT | N | (6G – | .333) | | CHI | N | (18G – | .150) | | | | | | |
| " total | 24 | 23 | 4 | 0 | 0 | 0 | 0.0 | 1 | 1 | 6 | 4 | 0 | .174 | .174 | 13 | 3 | 1B-4 |
| 3 yrs. | 223 | 562 | 152 | 16 | 7 | 7 | 1.2 | 54 | 56 | 42 | 44 | 3 | .270 | .361 | 81 | 20 | 1B-79, OF-52 |
| 1 yr. | 18 | 20 | 3 | 0 | 0 | 0 | 0.0 | 1 | 1 | 3 | 4 | 0 | .150 | .150 | 10 | 2 | 1B-4 |

## Willie Smith

**SMITH, WILLIE (Wonderful Willie)**
B. Feb. 11, 1939, Anniston, Ala.
BL  TL  6'    182 lbs.

| | G | AB | H | 2B | 3B | HR | HR% | R | RBI | BB | SO | SB | BA | SA | AB | H | G by POS |
|---|---|---|---|---|---|---|---|---|---|---|---|---|---|---|---|---|---|
| 1963 **DET A** | 17 | 8 | 1 | 0 | 0 | 0 | 0.0 | 2 | 0 | | 1 | 0 | .125 | .125 | 2 | 0 | P-11 |
| 1964 **LA A** | 118 | 359 | 108 | 14 | 6 | 11 | 3.1 | 46 | 51 | 8 | 39 | 7 | .301 | .465 | 23 | 10 | OF-87, P-15 |
| 1965 **CAL A** | 136 | 459 | 120 | 14 | 9 | 14 | 3.1 | 52 | 57 | 32 | 60 | 9 | .261 | .423 | 21 | 4 | OF-123, 1B-2 |
| 1966 | 90 | 195 | 36 | 3 | 2 | 1 | 0.5 | 18 | 20 | 12 | 37 | 1 | .185 | .236 | 41 | 5 | OF-52 |
| 1967 **CLE A** | 21 | 32 | 7 | 2 | 0 | 0 | 0.0 | 0 | 2 | 1 | 10 | 0 | .219 | .281 | 16 | 4 | OF-4, 1B-3 |
| 1968 **2 teams** | | | CLE | A | (33G – | .143) | | CHI | N | (55G – | .275) | | | | | | |
| " total | 88 | 184 | 45 | 10 | 2 | 5 | 2.7 | 14 | 28 | 15 | 47 | 0 | .245 | .402 | 36 | 10 | OF-39, 1B-11, P-3 |
| 1969 **CHI N** | 103 | 195 | 48 | 9 | 1 | 9 | 4.6 | 21 | 25 | 25 | 49 | 1 | .246 | .441 | 40 | 12 | OF-33, 1B-24 |
| 1970 | 87 | 167 | 36 | 9 | 1 | 5 | 3.0 | 15 | 24 | 11 | 32 | 2 | .216 | .371 | 40 | 9 | 1B-43, OF-1 |
| 1971 **CIN N** | 31 | 55 | 9 | 2 | 0 | 1 | 1.8 | 3 | 4 | 3 | 9 | 0 | .164 | .255 | 20 | 0 | 1B-10 |
| 9 yrs. | 691 | 1654 | 410 | 63 | 21 | 46 | 2.8 | 171 | 211 | 107 | 284 | 20 | .248 | .395 | 239 | 54 | OF-339, 1B-93, P-29 |
| 3 yrs. | 245 | 504 | 123 | 26 | 4 | 19 | 3.8 | 49 | 74 | 48 | 114 | 3 | .244 | .425 | 95 | 26 | OF-72, 1B-71, P-1 |

## Pete Sommers

**SOMMERS, JOSEPH ANDREWS**
B. Oct. 26, 1866, Cleveland, Ohio   D. July 22, 1908, Cleveland, Ohio
BR

| | G | AB | H | 2B | 3B | HR | HR% | R | RBI | BB | SO | SB | BA | SA | AB | H | G by POS |
|---|---|---|---|---|---|---|---|---|---|---|---|---|---|---|---|---|---|
| 1887 **NY AA** | 33 | 116 | 21 | 3 | 0 | 1 | 0.9 | 9 | | 7 | | 6 | .181 | .233 | 0 | 0 | C-31, OF-1, 1B-1 |
| 1888 **BOS N** | 4 | 13 | 3 | 1 | 0 | 0 | 0.0 | 1 | 0 | | 3 | 0 | .231 | .308 | 0 | 0 | C-4 |
| 1889 **2 teams** | | | CHI | N | (12G – | .222) | | IND | N | (23G – | .250) | | | | | | |
| " total | 35 | 129 | 31 | 7 | 2 | 1 | 0.8 | 17 | 22 | 3 | 24 | 2 | .240 | .372 | 0 | 0 | C-32, OF-3 |
| 1890 **2 teams** | | | NY | N | (17G – | .106) | | CLE | N | (9G – | .206) | | | | | | |
| " total | 26 | 81 | 12 | 2 | 2 | 0 | 0.0 | 8 | 2 | 6 | 15 | 0 | .148 | .222 | 0 | 0 | C-19, 1B-5, OF-3 |
| 4 yrs. | 98 | 339 | 67 | 13 | 4 | 3 | 0.9 | 35 | 23 | 16 | 42 | 8 | .198 | .286 | 0 | 0 | C-86, OF-7, 1B-6 |
| 1 yr. | 12 | 45 | 10 | 5 | 0 | 0 | 0.0 | 5 | 8 | 2 | 8 | 0 | .222 | .333 | 0 | 0 | C-11, OF-1 |

## Al Spalding

**SPALDING, ALBERT GOODWILL**
B. Sept. 2, 1850, Byron, Ill.   D. Sept. 9, 1915, Point Loma, Calif.
Manager 1876-77.
Hall of Fame 1939.
BR  TR  6'1"    170 lbs.

| | G | AB | H | 2B | 3B | HR | HR% | R | RBI | BB | SO | SB | BA | SA | AB | H | G by POS |
|---|---|---|---|---|---|---|---|---|---|---|---|---|---|---|---|---|---|
| 1876 **CHI N** | 66 | 292 | 91 | 14 | 2 | 0 | 0.0 | 54 | 44 | 6 | 3 | | .312 | .373 | 0 | 0 | P-61, OF-10, 1B-3 |
| 1877 | 60 | 254 | 65 | 7 | 6 | 0 | 0.0 | 29 | 35 | 3 | 16 | | .256 | .331 | 0 | 0 | 1B-45, 2B-13, P-4, 3B-2 |
| 1878 | 1 | 4 | 2 | 0 | 0 | 0 | 0.0 | 0 | 0 | 0 | 0 | | .500 | .500 | 0 | 0 | 2B-1 |
| 3 yrs. | 127 | 550 | 158 | 21 | 8 | 0 | 0.0 | 83 | 79 | 9 | 19 | | .287 | .355 | 0 | 0 | P-65, 1B-48, 2B-14, OF-10, 3B-2 |
| 3 yrs. | 127 | 550 | 158 | 21 | 8 | 0 | 0.0 | 83 | 79 | 9 | 19 | | .287 | .355 | 0 | 0 | P-65, 1B-48, 2B-14, OF-10, 3B-2 |

## Al Spangler

**SPANGLER, ALBERT DONALD**
B. July 8, 1933, Philadelphia, Pa.
BL  TL  6'    175 lbs.

| | G | AB | H | 2B | 3B | HR | HR% | R | RBI | BB | SO | SB | BA | SA | AB | H | G by POS |
|---|---|---|---|---|---|---|---|---|---|---|---|---|---|---|---|---|---|
| 1959 **MIL N** | 6 | 12 | 5 | 0 | 1 | 0 | 0.0 | 3 | 0 | 1 | 1 | 1 | .417 | .583 | 1 | 1 | OF-4 |
| 1960 | 101 | 105 | 28 | 5 | 2 | 0 | 0.0 | 26 | 6 | 14 | 17 | 6 | .267 | .352 | 4 | 0 | OF-92 |
| 1961 | 68 | 97 | 26 | 2 | 0 | 0 | 0.0 | 23 | 6 | 28 | 9 | 4 | .268 | .289 | 16 | 3 | OF-44 |
| 1962 **HOU N** | 129 | 418 | 119 | 10 | 9 | 5 | 1.2 | 51 | 35 | 70 | 46 | 7 | .285 | .388 | 8 | 1 | OF-121 |
| 1963 | 120 | 430 | 121 | 25 | 4 | 4 | 0.9 | 52 | 27 | 50 | 38 | 5 | .281 | .386 | 7 | 3 | OF-113 |
| 1964 | 135 | 449 | 110 | 18 | 5 | 4 | 0.9 | 51 | 38 | 41 | 43 | 7 | .245 | .334 | 10 | 2 | OF-127 |
| 1965 **2 teams** | | | HOU | N | (38G – | .214) | | CAL | A | (51G – | .260) | | | | | | |
| " total | 89 | 208 | 49 | 2 | 1 | 1 | 0.5 | 35 | 8 | 22 | 17 | 5 | .236 | .269 | 26 | 4 | OF-57 |
| 1966 **CAL A** | 6 | 9 | 6 | 0 | 0 | 0 | 0.0 | 2 | 0 | 2 | 2 | 0 | .667 | .667 | 3 | 3 | OF-3 |
| 1967 **CHI N** | 62 | 130 | 33 | 7 | 0 | 0 | 0.0 | 18 | 13 | 23 | 17 | 2 | .254 | .308 | 23 | 4 | OF-41 |
| 1968 | 88 | 177 | 48 | 9 | 3 | 2 | 1.1 | 21 | 18 | 20 | 24 | 0 | .271 | .390 | 41 | 10 | OF-48 |
| 1969 | 82 | 213 | 45 | 8 | 1 | 4 | 1.9 | 23 | 23 | 21 | 16 | 0 | .211 | .315 | 26 | 1 | OF-58 |
| 1970 | 21 | 14 | 2 | 1 | 0 | 1 | 7.1 | 2 | 1 | 3 | 3 | 0 | .143 | .429 | 11 | 2 | OF-6 |
| 1971 | 5 | 5 | 2 | 0 | 0 | 0 | 0.0 | 0 | 0 | 0 | 1 | 0 | .400 | .400 | 5 | 2 | |
| 13 yrs. | 912 | 2267 | 594 | 87 | 26 | 21 | 0.9 | 307 | 175 | 295 | 234 | 37 | .262 | .351 | 181 | 36 | OF-714 |
| 5 yrs. | 258 | 539 | 130 | 25 | 4 | 7 | 1.3 | 64 | 55 | 67 | 61 | 2 | .241 | .341 | 106 | 19 | OF-153 |

| | G | AB | H | 2B | 3B | HR | HR % | R | RBI | BB | SO | SB | BA | SA | Pinch Hit AB | Pinch Hit H | G by POS |
|---|---|---|---|---|---|---|---|---|---|---|---|---|---|---|---|---|---|

## Bob Speake

**SPEAKE, ROBERT CHARLES (Spook)**
B. Aug. 22, 1930, Springfield, Mo.                    BL TL 6'1"   178 lbs.

| | G | AB | H | 2B | 3B | HR | HR% | R | RBI | BB | SO | SB | BA | SA | PH AB | PH H | G by POS |
|---|---|---|---|---|---|---|---|---|---|---|---|---|---|---|---|---|---|
| 1955 CHI N | 95 | 261 | 57 | 9 | 5 | 12 | 4.6 | 36 | 43 | 28 | 71 | 3 | .218 | .429 | 24 | 5 | OF-55, 1B-8 |
| 1957 | 129 | 418 | 97 | 14 | 5 | 16 | 3.8 | 65 | 50 | 38 | 68 | 5 | .232 | .404 | 23 | 9 | OF-60, 1B-39 |
| 1958 SF N | 66 | 71 | 15 | 3 | 0 | 3 | 4.2 | 9 | 10 | 13 | 15 | 0 | .211 | .380 | 41 | 7 | OF-10 |
| 1959 | 15 | 11 | 1 | 0 | 0 | 0 | 0.0 | 0 | 1 | 1 | 4 | 0 | .091 | .091 | 11 | 1 | |
| 4 yrs. | 305 | 761 | 170 | 26 | 10 | 31 | 4.1 | 110 | 104 | 80 | 158 | 8 | .223 | .406 | 99 | 22 | OF-125, 1B-47 |
| 2 yrs. | 224 | 679 | 154 | 23 | 10 | 28 | 4.1 | 101 | 93 | 66 | 139 | 8 | .227 | .414 | 47 | 14 | OF-115, 1B-47 |

## Chris Speier

**SPEIER, CHRIS EDWARD**
B. June 28, 1950, Alameda, Calif.                    BR TR 6'1"   175 lbs.

| | G | AB | H | 2B | 3B | HR | HR% | R | RBI | BB | SO | SB | BA | SA | PH AB | PH H | G by POS |
|---|---|---|---|---|---|---|---|---|---|---|---|---|---|---|---|---|---|
| 1971 SF N | 157 | 601 | 141 | 17 | 6 | 8 | 1.3 | 74 | 46 | 56 | 90 | 4 | .235 | .323 | 2 | 1 | SS-156 |
| 1972 | 150 | 562 | 151 | 25 | 2 | 15 | 2.7 | 74 | 71 | 82 | 92 | 9 | .269 | .400 | 0 | 0 | SS-150 |
| 1973 | 153 | 542 | 135 | 17 | 4 | 11 | 2.0 | 58 | 71 | 66 | 69 | 4 | .249 | .356 | 3 | 2 | SS-150, 2B-1 |
| 1974 | 141 | 501 | 125 | 19 | 5 | 9 | 1.8 | 55 | 53 | 62 | 64 | 3 | .250 | .361 | 4 | 0 | SS-135, 2B-4 |
| 1975 | 141 | 487 | 132 | 30 | 5 | 10 | 2.1 | 60 | 69 | 70 | 50 | 4 | .271 | .415 | 4 | 0 | SS-136, 3B-1 |
| 1976 | 145 | 495 | 112 | 18 | 4 | 5 | 1.0 | 51 | 40 | 60 | 52 | 2 | .226 | .297 | 5 | 1 | SS-135, 2B-7, 3B-5, 1B-1 |
| 1977 2 teams | | | | SF N (6G – .176) | | MON N (139G – .235) | | | | | | | | | | | |
| " total | 145 | 548 | 128 | 31 | 6 | 5 | 0.9 | 59 | 38 | 67 | 81 | 1 | .234 | .339 | 2 | 0 | SS-143 |
| 1978 MON N | 150 | 501 | 126 | 18 | 3 | 5 | 1.0 | 47 | 51 | 60 | 75 | 1 | .251 | .329 | 2 | 0 | SS-148 |
| 1979 | 113 | 344 | 78 | 13 | 1 | 7 | 2.0 | 31 | 26 | 43 | 45 | 0 | .227 | .331 | 0 | 0 | SS-112 |
| 1980 | 128 | 388 | 103 | 14 | 4 | 1 | 0.3 | 35 | 32 | 52 | 38 | 0 | .265 | .330 | 0 | 0 | SS-127, 2B-1 |
| 1981 | 96 | 307 | 69 | 10 | 2 | 2 | 0.7 | 33 | 25 | 38 | 29 | 1 | .225 | .290 | 0 | 0 | SS-96 |
| 1982 | 156 | 530 | 136 | 26 | 4 | 7 | 1.3 | 41 | 60 | 47 | 67 | 1 | .257 | .360 | 1 | 0 | SS-155 |
| 1983 | 88 | 261 | 67 | 12 | 2 | 2 | 0.8 | 31 | 22 | 29 | 37 | 2 | .257 | .341 | 5 | 1 | SS-74, 3B-12, 2B-2 |
| 1984 3 teams | | | | MON N (25G – .150) | | STL N (38G – .178) | | MIN A (12G – .212) | | | | | | | | | |
| " total | 75 | 191 | 34 | 7 | 1 | 3 | 1.6 | 12 | 10 | 13 | 34 | 0 | .178 | .272 | 16 | 3 | SS-59, 3B-6 |
| 1985 CHI N | 106 | 218 | 53 | 11 | 0 | 4 | 1.8 | 16 | 24 | 17 | 34 | 1 | .243 | .349 | 12 | 5 | SS-58, 3B-31, 2B-13 |
| 15 yrs. | 1944 | 6476 | 1590 | 268 | 49 | 92 | 1.4 | 677 | 638 | 762 | 857 | 33 | .246 | .345 | 56 | 15 | SS-1834, 3B-55, 2B-28, 1B-1 |
| 1 yr. | 106 | 218 | 53 | 11 | 0 | 4 | 1.8 | 16 | 24 | 17 | 34 | 1 | .243 | .349 | 12 | 5 | SS-58, 3B-31, 2B-13 |

**DIVISIONAL PLAYOFF SERIES**

| | G | AB | H | 2B | 3B | HR | HR% | R | RBI | BB | SO | SB | BA | SA | PH AB | PH H | G by POS |
|---|---|---|---|---|---|---|---|---|---|---|---|---|---|---|---|---|---|
| 1981 MON N | 5 | 15 | 6 | 2 | 0 | 0 | 0.0 | 4 | 3 | 4 | 2 | 0 | .400 | .533 | 0 | 0 | SS-5 |

**LEAGUE CHAMPIONSHIP SERIES**

| | G | AB | H | 2B | 3B | HR | HR% | R | RBI | BB | SO | SB | BA | SA | PH AB | PH H | G by POS |
|---|---|---|---|---|---|---|---|---|---|---|---|---|---|---|---|---|---|
| 1971 SF N | 4 | 14 | 5 | 1 | 0 | 1 | 7.1 | 4 | 1 | 1 | 0 | 0 | .357 | .643 | 0 | 0 | SS-4 |
| 1981 MON N | 5 | 16 | 3 | 0 | 0 | 0 | 0.0 | 0 | 0 | 2 | 0 | 0 | .188 | .188 | 0 | 0 | SS-5 |
| 2 yrs. | 9 | 30 | 8 | 1 | 0 | 1 | 3.3 | 4 | 1 | 3 | 0 | 0 | .267 | .400 | 0 | 0 | SS-9 |

## Rob Sperring

**SPERRING, ROBERT WALTER**
B. Oct. 10, 1949, San Francisco, Calif.                    BR TR 6'1"   185 lbs.

| | G | AB | H | 2B | 3B | HR | HR% | R | RBI | BB | SO | SB | BA | SA | PH AB | PH H | G by POS |
|---|---|---|---|---|---|---|---|---|---|---|---|---|---|---|---|---|---|
| 1974 CHI N | 42 | 107 | 22 | 3 | 0 | 1 | 0.9 | 9 | 5 | 9 | 28 | 1 | .206 | .262 | 1 | 0 | 2B-35, SS-8 |
| 1975 | 65 | 144 | 30 | 4 | 1 | 1 | 0.7 | 25 | 9 | 16 | 31 | 0 | .208 | .271 | 1 | 0 | 3B-22, 2B-17, SS-16, OF-8 |
| 1976 | 43 | 93 | 24 | 3 | 0 | 0 | 0.0 | 8 | 7 | 9 | 25 | 0 | .258 | .290 | 1 | 0 | 3B-20, SS-15, 2B-4, OF-3 |
| 1977 HOU N | 58 | 129 | 24 | 3 | 0 | 1 | 0.8 | 6 | 9 | 12 | 23 | 0 | .186 | .233 | 10 | 3 | SS-22, 2B-20, 3B-11 |
| 4 yrs. | 208 | 473 | 100 | 13 | 1 | 3 | 0.6 | 48 | 30 | 46 | 107 | 1 | .211 | .262 | 13 | 3 | 2B-76, SS-61, 3B-53, OF-11 |
| 3 yrs. | 150 | 344 | 76 | 10 | 1 | 2 | 0.6 | 42 | 21 | 34 | 84 | 1 | .221 | .273 | 3 | 0 | 2B-56, 3B-42, SS-39, OF-11 |

## Charlie Sprague

**SPRAGUE, CHARLES WELLINGTON**
B. Oct. 10, 1864, Cleveland, Ohio   D. Dec. 31, 1912, Des Moines, Iowa       BL TL 5'11"   150 lbs.

| | G | AB | H | 2B | 3B | HR | HR% | R | RBI | BB | SO | SB | BA | SA | PH AB | PH H | G by POS |
|---|---|---|---|---|---|---|---|---|---|---|---|---|---|---|---|---|---|
| 1887 CHI N | 3 | 13 | 2 | 0 | 0 | 0 | 0.0 | 0 | 0 | 0 | 2 | 0 | .154 | .154 | 0 | 0 | P-3, OF-1 |
| 1889 CLE N | 2 | 7 | 1 | 0 | 0 | 0 | 0.0 | 2 | 1 | 1 | 0 | 1 | .143 | .143 | 0 | 0 | P-2 |
| 1890 TOL AA | 55 | 199 | 47 | 5 | 6 | 1 | 0.5 | 25 | | 16 | | 10 | .236 | .337 | 0 | 0 | OF-40, P-19 |
| 3 yrs. | 60 | 219 | 50 | 5 | 6 | 1 | 0.5 | 27 | 1 | 17 | 2 | 11 | .228 | .320 | 0 | 0 | OF-41, P-24 |
| 1 yr. | 3 | 13 | 2 | 0 | 0 | 0 | 0.0 | 0 | 0 | 0 | 2 | 0 | .154 | .154 | 0 | 0 | P-3, OF-1 |

## Tuck Stainback

**STAINBACK, GEORGE TUCKER**
B. Aug. 4, 1910, Los Angeles, Calif.                    BR TR 5'11½"   175 lbs.

| | G | AB | H | 2B | 3B | HR | HR% | R | RBI | BB | SO | SB | BA | SA | PH AB | PH H | G by POS |
|---|---|---|---|---|---|---|---|---|---|---|---|---|---|---|---|---|---|
| 1934 CHI N | 104 | 359 | 110 | 14 | 3 | 2 | 0.6 | 47 | 46 | 8 | 42 | 7 | .306 | .379 | 8 | 3 | OF-96, 3B-1 |
| 1935 | 47 | 94 | 24 | 4 | 0 | 3 | 3.2 | 16 | 11 | 0 | 13 | 1 | .255 | .394 | 10 | 3 | OF-28 |
| 1936 | 44 | 75 | 13 | 3 | 0 | 1 | 1.3 | 13 | 5 | 6 | 14 | 1 | .173 | .253 | 9 | 1 | OF-26 |
| 1937 | 72 | 160 | 37 | 7 | 4 | 0 | 0.0 | 18 | 14 | 7 | 16 | 3 | .231 | .288 | 10 | 2 | OF-49 |
| 1938 3 teams | | | | STL N (6G – .000) | | PHI N (30G – .259) | | BKN N (35G – .327) | | | | | | | | | |
| " total | 71 | 195 | 55 | 9 | 3 | 1 | 0.5 | 26 | 31 | 5 | 10 | 2 | .282 | .374 | 17 | 4 | OF-50 |
| 1939 BKN N | 168 | 201 | 54 | 7 | 0 | 3 | 1.5 | 22 | 19 | 4 | 23 | 0 | .269 | .348 | 10 | 2 | OF-55 |
| 1940 DET A | 15 | 40 | 9 | 2 | 0 | 0 | 0.0 | 4 | 1 | 1 | 9 | 0 | .225 | .275 | 5 | 1 | OF-9 |
| 1941 | 94 | 200 | 49 | 8 | 1 | 2 | 1.0 | 19 | 10 | 3 | 21 | 6 | .245 | .325 | 8 | 1 | OF-80 |
| 1942 NY A | 15 | 10 | 2 | 0 | 0 | 0 | 0.0 | 0 | 0 | 0 | 2 | 0 | .200 | .200 | 1 | 0 | OF-3 |
| 1943 | 71 | 231 | 60 | 11 | 2 | 0 | 0.0 | 31 | 10 | 7 | 16 | 3 | .260 | .325 | 5 | 3 | OF-61 |
| 1944 | 30 | 78 | 17 | 3 | 0 | 0 | 0.0 | 13 | 5 | 3 | 7 | 1 | .218 | .256 | 5 | 1 | OF-24 |
| 1945 | 95 | 327 | 84 | 12 | 2 | 5 | 1.5 | 40 | 32 | 13 | 20 | 0 | .257 | .352 | 9 | 2 | OF-83 |
| 1946 PHI A | 91 | 291 | 71 | 10 | 2 | 0 | 0.0 | 35 | 20 | 7 | 20 | 3 | .244 | .292 | 23 | 5 | OF-66 |
| 13 yrs. | 917 | 2261 | 585 | 90 | 14 | 17 | 0.8 | 284 | 204 | 64 | 213 | 27 | .259 | .333 | 120 | 28 | OF-630, 3B-1 |
| 4 yrs. | 267 | 688 | 184 | 28 | 4 | 6 | 0.9 | 94 | 76 | 21 | 85 | 12 | .267 | .346 | 37 | 9 | OF-199, 3B-1 |

**WORLD SERIES**

| | G | AB | H | 2B | 3B | HR | HR% | R | RBI | BB | SO | SB | BA | SA | PH AB | PH H | G by POS |
|---|---|---|---|---|---|---|---|---|---|---|---|---|---|---|---|---|---|
| 1942 NY A | 2 | 0 | 0 | 0 | 0 | 0 | – | 0 | 0 | 0 | 0 | 0 | – | – | 0 | 0 | |
| 1943 | 5 | 17 | 3 | 0 | 0 | 0 | 0.0 | 0 | 0 | 0 | 2 | 0 | .176 | .176 | 0 | 0 | OF-5 |
| 2 yrs. | 7 | 17 | 3 | 0 | 0 | 0 | 0.0 | 0 | 0 | 0 | 2 | 0 | .176 | .176 | 0 | 0 | OF-5 |

| | G | AB | H | 2B | 3B | HR | HR % | R | RBI | BB | SO | SB | BA | SA | Pinch Hit AB | Pinch Hit H | G by POS |
|---|---|---|---|---|---|---|---|---|---|---|---|---|---|---|---|---|---|

## Gale Staley

**STALEY, GEORGE GAYLORD**
B. May 2, 1899, De Pere, Wis.
BL TR 5'8½" 167 lbs.

| | G | AB | H | 2B | 3B | HR | HR % | R | RBI | BB | SO | SB | BA | SA | AB | H | G by POS |
|---|---|---|---|---|---|---|---|---|---|---|---|---|---|---|---|---|---|
| 1925 CHI N | 7 | 26 | 11 | 2 | 0 | 0 | 0.0 | 2 | 3 | 2 | 1 | 0 | .423 | .500 | 0 | 0 | 2B-7 |

## Eddie Stanky

**STANKY, EDWARD RAYMOND (The Brat, Muggsy)**
B. Sept. 3, 1916, Philadelphia, Pa.
Manager 1952-55, 1966-68, 1977.
BR TR 5'8" 170 lbs.

| | G | AB | H | 2B | 3B | HR | HR % | R | RBI | BB | SO | SB | BA | SA | AB | H | G by POS |
|---|---|---|---|---|---|---|---|---|---|---|---|---|---|---|---|---|---|
| 1943 CHI N | 142 | 510 | 125 | 15 | 1 | 0 | 0.0 | 92 | 47 | 92 | 42 | 4 | .245 | .278 | 0 | 0 | 2B-131, SS-12, 3B-2 |
| 1944 2 teams | CHI | N | (13G – | .240) | | BKN | N | (89G – | .276) | | | | | | | | |
| " total | 102 | 286 | 78 | 9 | 3 | 0 | 0.0 | 36 | 16 | 46 | 15 | 4 | .273 | .325 | 5 | 0 | 2B-61, SS-38, 3B-4 |
| 1945 BKN N | 153 | 555 | 143 | 29 | 5 | 1 | 0.2 | 128 | 39 | 148 | 42 | 6 | .258 | .333 | 0 | 0 | 2B-153, SS-1 |
| 1946 | 144 | 483 | 132 | 24 | 7 | 0 | 0.0 | 98 | 36 | 137 | 56 | 8 | .273 | .352 | 2 | 0 | 2B-141 |
| 1947 | 146 | 559 | 141 | 24 | 5 | 3 | 0.5 | 97 | 53 | 103 | 39 | 3 | .252 | .329 | 0 | 0 | 2B-146 |
| 1948 BOS N | 67 | 247 | 79 | 14 | 2 | 2 | 0.8 | 49 | 29 | 61 | 13 | 3 | .320 | .417 | 1 | 1 | 2B-66 |
| 1949 | 138 | 506 | 144 | 24 | 5 | 1 | 0.2 | 90 | 42 | 113 | 41 | 3 | .285 | .358 | 3 | 0 | 2B-135 |
| 1950 NY N | 152 | 527 | 158 | 25 | 5 | 8 | 1.5 | 115 | 51 | 144 | 50 | 9 | .300 | .412 | 0 | 0 | 2B-151 |
| 1951 | 145 | 515 | 127 | 17 | 2 | 14 | 2.7 | 88 | 43 | 127 | 63 | 8 | .247 | .369 | 4 | 0 | 2B-140 |
| 1952 STL N | 53 | 83 | 19 | 4 | 0 | 0 | 0.0 | 13 | 7 | 19 | 9 | 0 | .229 | .277 | 26 | 9 | 2B-20 |
| 1953 | 17 | 30 | 8 | 0 | 0 | 0 | 0.0 | 5 | 1 | 6 | 4 | 0 | .267 | .267 | 5 | 0 | 2B-8 |
| 11 yrs. | 1259 | 4301 | 1154 | 185 | 35 | 29 | 0.7 | 811 | 364 | 996 | 374 | 48 | .268 | .348 | 46 | 10 | 2B-1152, SS-51, 3B-6 |
| 2 yrs. | 155 | 535 | 131 | 15 | 2 | 0 | 0.0 | 96 | 47 | 94 | 44 | 5 | .245 | .280 | 4 | 0 | 2B-134, SS-15, 3B-5 |
| **WORLD SERIES** | | | | | | | | | | | | | | | | | |
| 1947 BKN N | 7 | 25 | 6 | 1 | 0 | 0 | 0.0 | 4 | 2 | 3 | 2 | 0 | .240 | .280 | 0 | 0 | 2B-7 |
| 1948 BOS N | 6 | 14 | 4 | 1 | 0 | 0 | 0.0 | 0 | 1 | 7 | 1 | 0 | .286 | .357 | 0 | 0 | 2B-6 |
| 1951 NY N | 6 | 22 | 3 | 0 | 0 | 0 | 0.0 | 3 | 1 | 3 | 2 | 0 | .136 | .136 | 0 | 0 | 2B-6 |
| 3 yrs. | 19 | 61 | 13 | 2 | 0 | 0 | 0.0 | 7 | 4 | 13 | 5 | 0 | .213 | .246 | 0 | 0 | 2B-19 |

## Joe Stanley

**STANLEY, JOSEPH BERNARD**
Brother of Buck Stanley.
B. Apr. 2, 1881, Washington, D. C.   D. Sept. 13, 1967, Detroit, Mich.
BB TR 5'9½" 150 lbs.

| | G | AB | H | 2B | 3B | HR | HR % | R | RBI | BB | SO | SB | BA | SA | AB | H | G by POS |
|---|---|---|---|---|---|---|---|---|---|---|---|---|---|---|---|---|---|
| 1897 WAS N | 1 | 1 | 0 | 0 | 0 | 0 | 0.0 | 0 | 0 | 0 | | 0 | .000 | .000 | 0 | 0 | P-1 |
| 1902 WAS A | 3 | 12 | 4 | 0 | 0 | 0 | 0.0 | 2 | 1 | 0 | | 0 | .333 | .333 | 0 | 0 | OF-3 |
| 1903 BOS N | 86 | 308 | 77 | 12 | 5 | 1 | 0.3 | 40 | 47 | 18 | | 10 | .250 | .331 | 5 | 0 | OF-77, SS-1, P-1 |
| 1904 | 3 | 8 | 0 | 0 | 0 | 0 | 0.0 | 0 | 0 | 0 | | 0 | .000 | .000 | 0 | 0 | OF-3 |
| 1905 WAS A | 28 | 92 | 24 | 2 | 1 | 1 | 1.1 | 13 | 17 | 7 | | 4 | .261 | .337 | 1 | 0 | OF-27 |
| 1906 | 73 | 221 | 36 | 0 | 4 | 0 | 0.0 | 18 | 9 | 20 | | 6 | .163 | .199 | 10 | 1 | OF-64, P-1 |
| 1909 CHI N | 22 | 52 | 7 | 1 | 0 | 0 | 0.0 | 4 | 2 | 6 | | 0 | .135 | .154 | 6 | 0 | OF-16 |
| 7 yrs. | 216 | 694 | 148 | 15 | 10 | 2 | 0.3 | 77 | 76 | 51 | | 20 | .213 | .272 | 22 | 1 | OF-190, P-3, SS-1 |
| 1 yr. | 22 | 52 | 7 | 1 | 0 | 0 | 0.0 | 4 | 2 | 6 | | 0 | .135 | .154 | 6 | 0 | OF-16 |

## Tom Stanton

**STANTON, THOMAS PATRICK**
B. Oct. 25, 1874, St. Louis, Mo.   D. Jan. 17, 1957, St. Louis, Mo.
BB TR 5'10" 175 lbs.

| | G | AB | H | 2B | 3B | HR | HR % | R | RBI | BB | SO | SB | BA | SA | AB | H | G by POS |
|---|---|---|---|---|---|---|---|---|---|---|---|---|---|---|---|---|---|
| 1904 CHI N | 1 | 3 | 0 | 0 | 0 | 0 | 0.0 | 0 | 0 | 0 | | 0 | .000 | .000 | 0 | 0 | C-1 |

## Joe Start

**START, JOSEPH (Old Reliable)**
B. Oct. 14, 1842, New York, N. Y.   D. Mar. 27, 1927, Providence, R. I.
BL TL 5'9" 165 lbs.

| | G | AB | H | 2B | 3B | HR | HR % | R | RBI | BB | SO | SB | BA | SA | AB | H | G by POS |
|---|---|---|---|---|---|---|---|---|---|---|---|---|---|---|---|---|---|
| 1876 NY N | 56 | 264 | 73 | 6 | 0 | 0 | 0.0 | 40 | 21 | 1 | 2 | | .277 | .299 | 0 | 0 | 1B-56 |
| 1877 HAR N | 60 | 271 | 90 | 3 | 6 | 1 | 0.4 | 55 | 21 | 6 | 2 | | .332 | .399 | 0 | 0 | 1B-60 |
| 1878 CHI N | 61 | 285 | 100 | 12 | 5 | 1 | 0.4 | 58 | 27 | 2 | 3 | | .351 | .439 | 0 | 0 | 1B-61 |
| 1879 PRO N | 66 | 317 | 101 | 11 | 5 | 2 | 0.6 | 70 | 37 | 7 | 4 | | .319 | .404 | 0 | 0 | 1B-65, OF-1 |
| 1880 | 82 | 345 | 96 | 14 | 6 | 0 | 0.0 | 53 | 27 | 13 | 20 | | .278 | .354 | 0 | 0 | 1B-82 |
| 1881 | 79 | 348 | 114 | 12 | 6 | 0 | 0.0 | 56 | 29 | 9 | 7 | | .328 | .397 | 0 | 0 | 1B-79 |
| 1882 | 82 | 356 | 117 | 8 | 10 | 0 | 0.0 | 58 | | 11 | 7 | | .329 | .407 | 0 | 0 | 1B-82 |
| 1883 | 87 | 370 | 105 | 16 | 7 | 1 | 0.3 | 63 | | 22 | 16 | | .284 | .373 | 0 | 0 | 1B-87 |
| 1884 | 93 | 381 | 105 | 10 | 5 | 2 | 0.5 | 80 | | 35 | 25 | | .276 | .344 | 0 | 0 | 1B-93 |
| 1885 | 101 | 374 | 103 | 11 | 4 | 0 | 0.0 | 47 | 41 | 39 | 10 | | .275 | .326 | 0 | 0 | 1B-101 |
| 1886 WAS N | 31 | 122 | 27 | 4 | 1 | 0 | 0.0 | 10 | 17 | 5 | 13 | | .221 | .270 | 0 | 0 | 1B-31 |
| 11 yrs. | 798 | 3433 | 1031 | 107 | 55 | 7 | 0.2 | 590 | 220 | 150 | 109 | | .300 | .370 | 0 | 0 | 1B-797, OF-1 |
| 1 yr. | 61 | 285 | 100 | 12 | 5 | 1 | 0.4 | 58 | 27 | 2 | 3 | | .351 | .439 | 0 | 0 | 1B-61 |

## Jigger Statz

**STATZ, ARNOLD JOHN**
B. Oct. 20, 1897, Waukegan, Ill.
BR TR 5'7½" 150 lbs.
BB 1922

| | G | AB | H | 2B | 3B | HR | HR % | R | RBI | BB | SO | SB | BA | SA | AB | H | G by POS |
|---|---|---|---|---|---|---|---|---|---|---|---|---|---|---|---|---|---|
| 1919 NY N | 21 | 60 | 18 | 2 | 1 | 0 | 0.0 | 7 | 6 | 3 | 8 | 2 | .300 | .367 | 0 | 0 | OF-18, 2B-5 |
| 1920 2 teams | NY | N | (16G – | .133) | | BOS | A | (2G – | .000) | | | | | | | | |
| " total | 18 | 33 | 4 | 0 | 1 | 0 | 0.0 | 5 | | 2 | 9 | 0 | .121 | .182 | 3 | 0 | OF-14 |
| 1922 CHI N | 110 | 462 | 137 | 19 | 5 | 1 | 0.2 | 77 | 34 | 41 | 31 | 16 | .297 | .366 | 0 | 0 | OF-110 |
| 1923 | 154 | 655 | 209 | 33 | 8 | 10 | 1.5 | 110 | 70 | 56 | 42 | 29 | .319 | .440 | 0 | 0 | OF-154 |
| 1924 | 135 | 549 | 152 | 22 | 5 | 3 | 0.5 | 69 | 49 | 37 | 50 | 13 | .277 | .352 | 2 | 1 | OF-131, 2B-1 |
| 1925 | 38 | 148 | 38 | 6 | 3 | 2 | 1.4 | 21 | 14 | 11 | 16 | 4 | .257 | .378 | 1 | 0 | OF-37 |
| 1927 BKN N | 130 | 507 | 139 | 24 | 7 | 1 | 0.2 | 64 | 21 | 26 | 43 | 10 | .274 | .355 | 4 | 0 | OF-122, 2B-1 |
| 1928 | 77 | 171 | 40 | 8 | 1 | 0 | 0.0 | 28 | 16 | 18 | 12 | 3 | .234 | .292 | 5 | 2 | OF-77, 2B-1 |
| 8 yrs. | 683 | 2585 | 737 | 114 | 31 | 17 | 0.7 | 376 | 215 | 194 | 211 | 77 | .285 | .373 | 15 | 3 | OF-663, 2B-8 |
| 4 yrs. | 437 | 1814 | 536 | 80 | 21 | 16 | 0.9 | 277 | 167 | 145 | 139 | 62 | .295 | .389 | 3 | 1 | OF-432, 2B-1 |

## Stedronsky

**STEDRONSKY,**
B. Troy, N. Y.   Deceased.

| | G | AB | H | 2B | 3B | HR | HR % | R | RBI | BB | SO | SB | BA | SA | AB | H | G by POS |
|---|---|---|---|---|---|---|---|---|---|---|---|---|---|---|---|---|---|
| 1879 CHI N | 4 | 12 | 1 | 0 | 0 | 0 | 0.0 | 0 | 0 | 0 | | 3 | .083 | .083 | 0 | 0 | 3B-4 |

| | G | AB | H | 2B | 3B | HR | HR % | R | RBI | BB | SO | SB | BA | SA | Pinch Hit AB | Pinch Hit H | G by POS |
|---|---|---|---|---|---|---|---|---|---|---|---|---|---|---|---|---|---|

## Harry Steinfeldt

**STEINFELDT, HARRY M.**
B. Sept. 29, 1877, St. Louis, Mo.  D. Aug. 17, 1914, Bellevue, Ky.  BR TR 5'9½" 180 lbs.

| | G | AB | H | 2B | 3B | HR | HR% | R | RBI | BB | SO | SB | BA | SA | PH AB | PH H | G by POS |
|---|---|---|---|---|---|---|---|---|---|---|---|---|---|---|---|---|---|
| 1898 CIN N | 88 | 308 | 91 | 18 | 6 | 0 | 0.0 | 47 | 43 | 27 | | 9 | .295 | .393 | 0 | 0 | 2B-31, OF-29, 3B-22, SS-5, 1B-4 |
| 1899 | 107 | 386 | 94 | 16 | 8 | 0 | 0.0 | 62 | 43 | 40 | | 19 | .244 | .326 | 0 | 0 | 3B-59, 2B-40, SS-8, OF-2 |
| 1900 | 136 | 513 | 127 | 29 | 7 | 2 | 0.4 | 58 | 66 | 27 | | 14 | .248 | .343 | 0 | 0 | 3B-67, 2B-64, OF-2, SS-2 |
| 1901 | 105 | 382 | 95 | 18 | 7 | 6 | 1.6 | 40 | 47 | 28 | | 10 | .249 | .380 | 0 | 0 | 3B-55, 2B-50 |
| 1902 | 129 | 479 | 133 | 20 | 7 | 1 | 0.2 | 53 | 49 | 24 | | 12 | .278 | .355 | 0 | 0 | 3B-129, OF-1 |
| 1903 | 118 | 439 | 137 | 32 | 12 | 6 | 1.4 | 71 | 83 | 47 | | 6 | .312 | .481 | 0 | 0 | 3B-104, SS-14 |
| 1904 | 99 | 349 | 85 | 11 | 6 | 1 | 0.3 | 35 | 52 | 29 | | 16 | .244 | .318 | 1 | 0 | 3B-98 |
| 1905 | 114 | 384 | 104 | 16 | 9 | 1 | 0.3 | 49 | 39 | 30 | | 15 | .271 | .367 | 8 | 1 | 3B-103, OF-1, 2B-1, 1B-1 |
| 1906 CHI N | 151 | 539 | **176** | 27 | 10 | 3 | 0.6 | 81 | **83** | 47 | | 29 | .327 | .430 | 0 | 0 | 3B-150, 2B-1 |
| 1907 | 152 | 542 | 144 | 25 | 5 | 1 | 0.2 | 52 | 70 | 37 | | 19 | .266 | .336 | 1 | 0 | 3B-151 |
| 1908 | 150 | 539 | 130 | 20 | 6 | 1 | 0.2 | 63 | 62 | 36 | | 12 | .241 | .306 | 1 | 0 | 3B-150 |
| 1909 | 151 | 528 | 133 | 27 | 6 | 2 | 0.4 | 73 | 59 | 57 | | 22 | .252 | .337 | 0 | 0 | 3B-151 |
| 1910 | 129 | 448 | 113 | 21 | 1 | 2 | 0.4 | 70 | 58 | 36 | 29 | 10 | .252 | .317 | 1 | 0 | 3B-128 |
| 1911 BOS N | 19 | 63 | 16 | 4 | 0 | 1 | 1.6 | 5 | 8 | 6 | 3 | 1 | .254 | .365 | 0 | 0 | 3B-19 |
| 14 yrs. | 1648 | 5899 | 1578 | 284 | 90 | 27 | 0.5 | 759 | 762 | 471 | 32 | 194 | .268 | .360 | 12 | 1 | 3B-1386, 2B-187, OF-35, SS-29, 1B-5 |
| 5 yrs. | 733 | 2596 | 696 | 120 | 28 | 9 | 0.3 | 339 | 332 | 213 | 29 | 92 | .268 | .346 | 3 | 0 | 3B-730, 2B-1 |
| WORLD SERIES | | | | | | | | | | | | | | | | | |
| 1906 CHI N | 6 | 20 | 5 | 1 | 0 | 0 | 0.0 | 2 | 2 | 1 | 0 | 0 | .250 | .300 | 0 | 0 | 3B-6 |
| 1907 | 5 | 17 | 8 | 1 | 1 | 0 | 0.0 | 2 | 2 | 1 | 2 | 1 | .471 | .647 | 0 | 0 | 3B-5 |
| 1908 | 5 | 16 | 4 | 0 | 0 | 0 | 0.0 | 3 | 3 | 2 | 5 | 1 | .250 | .250 | 0 | 0 | 3B-5 |
| 1910 | 5 | 20 | 2 | 1 | 0 | 0 | 0.0 | 0 | 1 | 0 | 4 | 0 | .100 | .150 | 0 | 0 | 3B-5 |
| 4 yrs. | 21 | 73 | 19 | 3 | 1 | 0 | 0.0 | 7 | 8 | 4 | 11 | 2 | .260 | .329 | 0 | 0 | 3B-21 |

## Rick Stelmaszek

**STELMASZEK, RICHARD FRANCIS**
B. Oct. 8, 1948, Chicago, Ill.  BL TR 6'1" 195 lbs.

| | G | AB | H | 2B | 3B | HR | HR% | R | RBI | BB | SO | SB | BA | SA | PH AB | PH H | G by POS |
|---|---|---|---|---|---|---|---|---|---|---|---|---|---|---|---|---|---|
| 1971 WAS A | 6 | 9 | 0 | 0 | 0 | 0 | 0.0 | 0 | 0 | 3 | 0 | 0 | .000 | .000 | 3 | 0 | C-3 |
| 1973 2 teams | | | TEX A (7G – .111) | | | CAL A (22G – .154) | | | | | | | | | | | |
| " total | 29 | 35 | 5 | 1 | 0 | 0 | 0.0 | 2 | 3 | 7 | 9 | 0 | .143 | .171 | 0 | 0 | C-29 |
| 1974 CHI N | 25 | 44 | 10 | 2 | 0 | 1 | 2.3 | 2 | 7 | 10 | 6 | 0 | .227 | .341 | 10 | 2 | C-16 |
| 3 yrs. | 60 | 88 | 15 | 3 | 0 | 1 | 1.1 | 4 | 10 | 17 | 18 | 0 | .170 | .239 | 13 | 2 | C-48 |
| 1 yr. | 25 | 44 | 10 | 2 | 0 | 1 | 2.3 | 2 | 7 | 10 | 6 | 0 | .227 | .341 | 10 | 2 | C-16 |

## Jake Stenzel

**STENZEL, JACOB CHARLES**
Born Jacob Charles Stelzle.
B. June 24, 1867, Cincinnati, Ohio  D. Jan. 6, 1919, Cincinnati, Ohio  BR TR 5'10" 168 lbs.

| | G | AB | H | 2B | 3B | HR | HR% | R | RBI | BB | SO | SB | BA | SA | PH AB | PH H | G by POS |
|---|---|---|---|---|---|---|---|---|---|---|---|---|---|---|---|---|---|
| 1890 CHI N | 11 | 41 | 11 | 1 | 0 | 0 | 0.0 | 3 | 3 | 1 | 0 | 0 | .268 | .293 | 0 | 0 | OF-6, C-6 |
| 1892 PIT N | 3 | 9 | 0 | 0 | 0 | 0 | 0.0 | 0 | 0 | 1 | 3 | 1 | .000 | .000 | 0 | 0 | OF-2, C-1 |
| 1893 | 60 | 224 | 81 | 13 | 4 | 4 | 1.8 | 57 | 37 | 24 | 17 | 16 | .362 | .509 | 6 | 1 | OF-45, C-12, SS-1, 2B-1 |
| 1894 | 131 | 522 | 185 | 39 | 20 | 13 | 2.5 | 148 | 121 | 75 | 13 | 61 | .354 | .580 | 0 | 0 | OF-131 |
| 1895 | 129 | 514 | 192 | 38 | 13 | 7 | 1.4 | 114 | 97 | 57 | 25 | 53 | .374 | .539 | 0 | 0 | OF-129 |
| 1896 | 114 | 479 | 173 | 26 | 14 | 2 | 0.4 | 104 | 82 | 32 | 13 | 57 | .361 | .486 | 0 | 0 | OF-114, 1B-1 |
| 1897 BAL N | 131 | 536 | 189 | **43** | 7 | 5 | 0.9 | 113 | 116 | 36 | | 69 | .353 | .487 | 0 | 0 | OF-131 |
| 1898 2 teams | | | BAL N (35G – .254) | | | STL N (108G – .282) | | | | | | | | | | | |
| " total | 143 | 542 | 149 | 20 | 13 | 1 | 0.2 | 97 | 55 | 53 | | 25 | .275 | .365 | 0 | 0 | OF-143 |
| 1899 2 teams | | | STL N (35G – .273) | | | CIN N (9G – .310) | | | | | | | | | | | |
| " total | 44 | 157 | 44 | 10 | 0 | 1 | 0.6 | 26 | 22 | 20 | | 10 | .280 | .363 | 3 | 0 | OF-40 |
| 9 yrs. | 766 | 3024 | 1024 | 190 | 71 | 33 | 1.1 | 662 | 533 | 299 | 71 | 292 | .339 | .481 | 9 | 1 | OF-741, C-19, SS-1, 2B-1, 1B-1 |
| 1 yr. | 11 | 41 | 11 | 1 | 0 | 0 | 0.0 | 3 | 3 | 1 | 0 | 0 | .268 | .293 | 0 | 0 | OF-6, C-6 |

## Joe Stephenson

**STEPHENSON, JOSEPH CHESTER**
Father of Jerry Stephenson.
B. June 30, 1921, Detroit, Mich.  BR TR 6'2" 185 lbs.

| | G | AB | H | 2B | 3B | HR | HR% | R | RBI | BB | SO | SB | BA | SA | PH AB | PH H | G by POS |
|---|---|---|---|---|---|---|---|---|---|---|---|---|---|---|---|---|---|
| 1943 NY N | 9 | 24 | 6 | 1 | 0 | 0 | 0.0 | 4 | 1 | 0 | 5 | 0 | .250 | .292 | 1 | 0 | C-6 |
| 1944 CHI N | 4 | 8 | 1 | 0 | 0 | 0 | 0.0 | 1 | 0 | 1 | 3 | 1 | .125 | .125 | 1 | 0 | C-3 |
| 1947 CHI A | 16 | 35 | 5 | 0 | 0 | 0 | 0.0 | 3 | 3 | 1 | 7 | 0 | .143 | .143 | 1 | 0 | C-13 |
| 3 yrs. | 29 | 67 | 12 | 1 | 0 | 0 | 0.0 | 8 | 4 | 2 | 15 | 1 | .179 | .194 | 3 | 0 | C-22 |
| 1 yr. | 4 | 8 | 1 | 0 | 0 | 0 | 0.0 | 1 | 0 | 1 | 3 | 1 | .125 | .125 | 1 | 0 | C-3 |

## Johnny Stephenson

**STEPHENSON, JOHN HERMAN**
B. Apr. 13, 1941, South Portsmouth, Ky.  BL TR 5'11" 180 lbs.

| | G | AB | H | 2B | 3B | HR | HR% | R | RBI | BB | SO | SB | BA | SA | PH AB | PH H | G by POS |
|---|---|---|---|---|---|---|---|---|---|---|---|---|---|---|---|---|---|
| 1964 NY N | 37 | 57 | 9 | 0 | 0 | 1 | 1.8 | 2 | 2 | 4 | 18 | 0 | .158 | .211 | 21 | 2 | 3B-14, OF-8 |
| 1965 | 62 | 121 | 26 | 5 | 0 | 4 | 3.3 | 9 | 15 | 8 | 19 | 0 | .215 | .355 | 29 | 6 | C-47, OF-2 |
| 1966 | 63 | 143 | 28 | 1 | 1 | 1 | 0.7 | 17 | 11 | 8 | 28 | 0 | .196 | .238 | 25 | 4 | C-52, OF-1 |
| 1967 CHI N | 18 | 49 | 11 | 3 | 1 | 0 | 0.0 | 3 | 5 | 1 | 6 | 0 | .224 | .327 | 3 | 1 | C-13 |
| 1968 | 2 | 2 | 0 | 0 | 0 | 0 | 0.0 | 0 | 0 | 0 | 0 | 0 | .000 | .000 | 2 | 0 | |
| 1969 SF N | 22 | 27 | 6 | 2 | 0 | 0 | 0.0 | 2 | 3 | 0 | 4 | 0 | .222 | .296 | 15 | 4 | C-9, 3B-1 |
| 1970 | 23 | 43 | 3 | 1 | 0 | 0 | 0.0 | 3 | 6 | 2 | 7 | 0 | .070 | .093 | 14 | 3 | C-9, OF-1 |
| 1971 CAL A | 98 | 279 | 61 | 17 | 0 | 3 | 1.1 | 24 | 25 | 22 | 21 | 0 | .219 | .312 | 16 | 1 | C-88 |
| 1972 | 66 | 146 | 40 | 3 | 1 | 2 | 1.4 | 14 | 17 | 11 | 8 | 0 | .274 | .349 | 21 | 8 | C-56 |
| 1973 | 60 | 122 | 30 | 5 | 0 | 1 | 0.8 | 9 | 9 | 7 | 7 | 0 | .246 | .311 | 10 | 4 | C-56 |
| 10 yrs. | 451 | 989 | 214 | 37 | 3 | 12 | 1.2 | 83 | 93 | 63 | 118 | 0 | .216 | .296 | 156 | 33 | C-330, 3B-15, OF-12 |
| 2 yrs. | 20 | 51 | 11 | 3 | 0 | 0 | 0.0 | 3 | 5 | 1 | 6 | 0 | .216 | .314 | 5 | 1 | C-13 |

## Riggs Stephenson

**STEPHENSON, JACKSON RIGGS (Old Hoss)**
B. Jan. 5, 1898, Akron, Ala.  D. Nov. 15, 1985, Tuscaloosa, Ala.  BR TR 5'10" 185 lbs.

| | G | AB | H | 2B | 3B | HR | HR% | R | RBI | BB | SO | SB | BA | SA | PH AB | PH H | G by POS |
|---|---|---|---|---|---|---|---|---|---|---|---|---|---|---|---|---|---|
| 1921 CLE A | 65 | 206 | 68 | 17 | 2 | 2 | 1.0 | 45 | 34 | 23 | 15 | 4 | .330 | .461 | 6 | 0 | 2B-54, 3B-2 |
| 1922 | 86 | 233 | 79 | 24 | 5 | 2 | 0.9 | 47 | 32 | 27 | 18 | 3 | .339 | .511 | 24 | 6 | 3B-34, 2B-25, OF-3 |

| | G | AB | H | 2B | 3B | HR | HR % | R | RBI | BB | SO | SB | BA | SA | Pinch Hit AB | H | G by POS |
|---|---|---|---|---|---|---|---|---|---|---|---|---|---|---|---|---|---|

## Riggs Stephenson continued

| | G | AB | H | 2B | 3B | HR | HR % | R | RBI | BB | SO | SB | BA | SA | AB | H | G by POS |
|---|---|---|---|---|---|---|---|---|---|---|---|---|---|---|---|---|---|
| 1923 | 91 | 301 | 96 | 20 | 6 | 5 | 1.7 | 48 | 65 | 15 | 25 | 6 | .319 | .475 | 21 | 4 | 2B-66, OF-3, 3B-1 |
| 1924 | 71 | 240 | 89 | 20 | 0 | 4 | 1.7 | 33 | 44 | 27 | 10 | 1 | .371 | .504 | 6 | 1 | 2B-58, OF-7 |
| 1925 | 19 | 54 | 16 | 3 | 1 | 1 | 1.9 | 8 | 9 | 7 | 3 | 1 | .296 | .444 | 3 | 2 | OF-16 |
| 1926 CHI N | 82 | 281 | 95 | 18 | 3 | 3 | 1.1 | 40 | 44 | 31 | 16 | 2 | .338 | .456 | 6 | 2 | OF-74 |
| 1927 | 152 | 579 | 199 | 46 | 9 | 7 | 1.2 | 101 | 82 | 65 | 28 | 8 | .344 | .491 | 0 | 0 | OF-146, 3B-6 |
| 1928 | 137 | 512 | 166 | 36 | 9 | 8 | 1.6 | 75 | 90 | 68 | 29 | 8 | .324 | .477 | 2 | 1 | OF-135 |
| 1929 | 136 | 495 | 179 | 36 | 6 | 17 | 3.4 | 91 | 110 | 67 | 21 | 10 | .362 | .562 | 5 | 3 | OF-130 |
| 1930 | 109 | 341 | 125 | 21 | 1 | 5 | 1.5 | 56 | 68 | 32 | 20 | 2 | .367 | .478 | 27 | 11 | OF-80 |
| 1931 | 80 | 263 | 84 | 14 | 4 | 1 | 0.4 | 34 | 52 | 37 | 14 | 1 | .319 | .414 | 14 | 2 | OF-80 |
| 1932 | 147 | 583 | 189 | 44 | 4 | 4 | 0.7 | 86 | 85 | 54 | 27 | 3 | .324 | .443 | 0 | 0 | OF-147 |
| 1933 | 97 | 346 | 114 | 17 | 4 | 4 | 1.2 | 45 | 51 | 34 | 16 | 5 | .329 | .436 | 3 | 0 | OF-91 |
| 1934 | 38 | 74 | 16 | 0 | 0 | 0 | 0.0 | 5 | 7 | 7 | 5 | 0 | .216 | .216 | 22 | 5 | OF-15 |
| 14 yrs. | 1310 | 4508 | 1515 | 321 | 54 | 63 | 1.4 | 714 | 773 | 494 | 247 | 54 | .336 | .473 | 139 | 37 | OF-927, 2B-203, 3B-43 |
| 9 yrs. | 978 | 3474 | 1167 | 237 | 40 | 49 | 1.4 | 533 | 589 | 395 | 176 | 39 | .336 1st | .469 10th | 79 | 24 | OF-898, 3B-6 |

WORLD SERIES

| | G | AB | H | 2B | 3B | HR | HR % | R | RBI | BB | SO | SB | BA | SA | AB | H | G by POS |
|---|---|---|---|---|---|---|---|---|---|---|---|---|---|---|---|---|---|
| 1929 CHI N | 5 | 19 | 6 | 1 | 0 | 0 | 0.0 | 3 | 3 | 2 | 2 | 0 | .316 | .368 | 0 | 0 | OF-5 |
| 1932 | 4 | 18 | 8 | 1 | 0 | 0 | 0.0 | 2 | 4 | 0 | 0 | 0 | .444 | .500 | 0 | 0 | OF-4 |
| 2 yrs. | 9 | 37 | 14 | 2 | 0 | 0 | 0.0 | 5 | 7 | 2 | 2 | 0 | .378 | .432 | 0 | 0 | OF-9 |

## Walter Stephenson

STEPHENSON, WALTER McQUEEN (Tarzan)  BR  TR  6'  180 lbs.
B. Mar. 27, 1911, Saluda, N. C.

| | G | AB | H | 2B | 3B | HR | HR % | R | RBI | BB | SO | SB | BA | SA | AB | H | G by POS |
|---|---|---|---|---|---|---|---|---|---|---|---|---|---|---|---|---|---|
| 1935 CHI N | 16 | 26 | 10 | 1 | 1 | 0 | 0.0 | 2 | 2 | 1 | 5 | 0 | .385 | .500 | 9 | 2 | C-6 |
| 1936 | 6 | 12 | 1 | 0 | 0 | 0 | 0.0 | 0 | 1 | 0 | 5 | 0 | .083 | .083 | 2 | 0 | C-4 |
| 1937 PHI N | 10 | 23 | 6 | 0 | 0 | 0 | 0.0 | 1 | 2 | 2 | 3 | 0 | .261 | .261 | 2 | 0 | C-7 |
| 3 yrs. | 32 | 61 | 17 | 1 | 1 | 0 | 0.0 | 3 | 5 | 3 | 13 | 0 | .279 | .328 | 13 | 2 | C-17 |
| 2 yrs. | 22 | 38 | 11 | 1 | 1 | 0 | 0.0 | 2 | 3 | 1 | 10 | 0 | .289 | .368 | 11 | 2 | C-10 |

WORLD SERIES

| | G | AB | H | 2B | 3B | HR | HR % | R | RBI | BB | SO | SB | BA | SA | AB | H | G by POS |
|---|---|---|---|---|---|---|---|---|---|---|---|---|---|---|---|---|---|
| 1935 CHI N | 1 | 1 | 0 | 0 | 0 | 0 | 0.0 | 0 | 0 | 0 | 1 | 0 | .000 | .000 | 1 | 0 | |

## Ace Stewart

STEWART, ASA  BR  TR  5'10"  176 lbs.
B. Feb. 14, 1869, Terre Haute, Ind.  D. Apr. 17, 1912, Terre Haute, Ind.

| | G | AB | H | 2B | 3B | HR | HR % | R | RBI | BB | SO | SB | BA | SA | AB | H | G by POS |
|---|---|---|---|---|---|---|---|---|---|---|---|---|---|---|---|---|---|
| 1895 CHI N | 97 | 365 | 88 | 8 | 10 | 8 | 2.2 | 52 | 76 | 39 | 40 | 14 | .241 | .384 | 0 | 0 | 2B-97 |

## Jimmy Stewart

STEWART, JOHN FRANKLIN  BB  TR  6'  165 lbs.
B. June 11, 1939, Opelika, Ala.  D. Dec. 30, 1980, Lake City, Fla.

| | G | AB | H | 2B | 3B | HR | HR % | R | RBI | BB | SO | SB | BA | SA | AB | H | G by POS |
|---|---|---|---|---|---|---|---|---|---|---|---|---|---|---|---|---|---|
| 1963 CHI N | 13 | 37 | 11 | 2 | 0 | 0 | 0.0 | 1 | 1 | 1 | 7 | 1 | .297 | .351 | 5 | 1 | SS-9, 2B-1 |
| 1964 | 132 | 415 | 105 | 17 | 0 | 3 | 0.7 | 59 | 33 | 49 | 61 | 10 | .253 | .316 | 31 | 9 | 2B-61, SS-45, OF-4, 3B-1 |
| 1965 | 116 | 282 | 63 | 9 | 4 | 0 | 0.0 | 26 | 19 | 30 | 53 | 13 | .223 | .284 | 41 | 6 | OF-55, SS-48 |
| 1966 | 57 | 90 | 16 | 4 | 1 | 0 | 0.0 | 4 | 4 | 7 | 12 | 1 | .178 | .244 | 31 | 6 | OF-15, 2B-4, SS-2, 3B-2 |
| 1967 2 teams | | CHI N (6G – .167) | | | CHI A (24G – .167) | | | | | | | | | | | | |
| " total | 30 | 24 | 4 | 0 | 0 | 0 | 0.0 | 6 | 2 | 1 | 6 | 1 | .167 | .167 | 13 | 1 | OF-66, 2B-5, SS-2 |
| 1969 CIN N | 119 | 221 | 56 | 3 | 4 | 4 | 1.8 | 26 | 24 | 19 | 33 | 4 | .253 | .357 | 38 | 9 | OF-48, 2B-18, 3B-9, 1B-1, C-1 |
| 1970 | 101 | 105 | 28 | 3 | 1 | 1 | 1.0 | 15 | 8 | 8 | 13 | 5 | .267 | .343 | 39 | 13 | OF-48, 2B-18, 3B-9, 1B-1, C-1 |
| 1971 | 80 | 82 | 19 | 2 | 2 | 0 | 0.0 | 7 | 9 | 7 | 9 | 3 | .232 | .305 | 48 | 11 | OF-19, 2B-9, 2B-6 |
| 1972 HOU N | 68 | 96 | 21 | 5 | 2 | 0 | 0.0 | 14 | 9 | 6 | 9 | 0 | .219 | .313 | 40 | 7 | OF-11, 1B-9, 2B-8, 3B-2 |
| 1973 | 61 | 68 | 13 | 0 | 0 | 0 | 0.0 | 6 | 3 | 9 | 12 | 0 | .191 | .191 | 44 | 8 | 3B-8, OF-3, 2B-1 |
| 10 yrs. | 777 | 1420 | 336 | 45 | 14 | 8 | 0.6 | 164 | 112 | 139 | 218 | 38 | .237 | .305 | 330 | 71 | OF-227, 2B-122, SS-107, 3B-37, 1B-10, C-1 |
| 5 yrs. | 324 | 830 | 196 | 32 | 5 | 3 | 0.4 | 91 | 58 | 87 | 133 | 25 | .236 | .298 10th | 114 | 23 | SS-104, OF-74, 2B-66, 3B-3 |

LEAGUE CHAMPIONSHIP SERIES

| | G | AB | H | 2B | 3B | HR | HR % | R | RBI | BB | SO | SB | BA | SA | AB | H | G by POS |
|---|---|---|---|---|---|---|---|---|---|---|---|---|---|---|---|---|---|
| 1970 CIN N | 1 | 2 | 0 | 0 | 0 | 0 | 0.0 | 0 | 0 | 0 | 0 | 0 | .000 | .000 | 0 | 0 | OF-1 |

WORLD SERIES

| | G | AB | H | 2B | 3B | HR | HR % | R | RBI | BB | SO | SB | BA | SA | AB | H | G by POS |
|---|---|---|---|---|---|---|---|---|---|---|---|---|---|---|---|---|---|
| 1970 CIN N | 2 | 2 | 0 | 0 | 0 | 0 | 0.0 | 0 | 0 | 0 | 1 | 0 | .000 | .000 | 2 | 0 | |

## Tuffy Stewart

STEWART, CHARLES EUGENE  BL  TL  5'10"  167 lbs.
B. July 31, 1883, Chicago, Ill.  D. Nov. 18, 1934, Chicago, Ill.

| | G | AB | H | 2B | 3B | HR | HR % | R | RBI | BB | SO | SB | BA | SA | AB | H | G by POS |
|---|---|---|---|---|---|---|---|---|---|---|---|---|---|---|---|---|---|
| 1913 CHI N | 9 | 8 | 1 | 1 | 0 | 0 | 0.0 | 1 | 2 | 2 | 5 | 1 | .125 | .250 | 5 | 0 | OF-1 |
| 1914 | 2 | 1 | 0 | 0 | 0 | 0 | 0.0 | 0 | 0 | 0 | 0 | 0 | .000 | .000 | 1 | 0 | |
| 2 yrs. | 11 | 9 | 1 | 1 | 0 | 0 | 0.0 | 1 | 2 | 2 | 5 | 1 | .111 | .222 | 6 | 0 | OF-1 |
| 2 yrs. | 11 | 9 | 1 | 1 | 0 | 0 | 0.0 | 1 | 2 | 2 | 5 | 1 | .111 | .222 | 6 | 0 | OF-1 |

## Joe Strain

STRAIN, JOSEPH ALLAN, JR.  BR  TR  5'10"  169 lbs.
B. Apr. 30, 1954, Denver, Colo.

| | G | AB | H | 2B | 3B | HR | HR % | R | RBI | BB | SO | SB | BA | SA | AB | H | G by POS |
|---|---|---|---|---|---|---|---|---|---|---|---|---|---|---|---|---|---|
| 1979 SF N | 67 | 257 | 62 | 8 | 1 | 1 | 0.4 | 27 | 12 | 13 | 21 | 8 | .241 | .292 | 0 | 0 | 2B-67, 3B-1 |
| 1980 | 77 | 189 | 54 | 6 | 0 | 0 | 0.0 | 26 | 16 | 10 | 10 | 1 | .286 | .317 | 30 | 8 | 2B-42, 3B-6, SS-1 |
| 1981 CHI N | 25 | 74 | 14 | 1 | 0 | 0 | 0.0 | 7 | 1 | 5 | 7 | 0 | .189 | .203 | 3 | 2 | 2B-20 |
| 3 yrs. | 169 | 520 | 130 | 15 | 1 | 1 | 0.2 | 60 | 29 | 28 | 38 | 9 | .250 | .288 | 33 | 10 | 2B-129, 3B-7, SS-1 |
| 1 yr. | 25 | 74 | 14 | 1 | 0 | 0 | 0.0 | 7 | 1 | 5 | 7 | 0 | .189 | .203 | 3 | 2 | 2B-20 |

## Sammy Strang

STRANG, SAMUEL NICKLIN (The Dixie Thrush)  BB  TR  5'8"  160 lbs.
Also known as Samuel Strang Nicklin.
B. Dec. 16, 1876, Chattanooga, Tenn.  D. Mar. 13, 1932, Chattanooga, Tenn.

| | G | AB | H | 2B | 3B | HR | HR % | R | RBI | BB | SO | SB | BA | SA | AB | H | G by POS |
|---|---|---|---|---|---|---|---|---|---|---|---|---|---|---|---|---|---|
| 1896 LOU N | 14 | 46 | 12 | 0 | 0 | 0 | 0.0 | 6 | 7 | 6 | | 4 | .261 | .261 | 0 | 0 | SS-14 |
| 1900 CHI N | 27 | 102 | 29 | 3 | 0 | 0 | 0.0 | 15 | 9 | 8 | | 1 | .284 | .314 | 0 | 0 | 3B-16, SS-9, 2B-2 |
| 1901 NY N | 135 | 493 | 139 | 14 | 6 | 1 | 0.2 | 55 | 34 | 59 | | 40 | .282 | .341 | 0 | 0 | 3B-91, 2B-37, OF-5, SS-4 |

| | G | AB | H | 2B | 3B | HR | HR % | R | RBI | BB | SO | SB | BA | SA | Pinch Hit AB | Pinch Hit H | G by POS |
|---|---|---|---|---|---|---|---|---|---|---|---|---|---|---|---|---|---|

## Sammy Strang continued

| | G | AB | H | 2B | 3B | HR | HR% | R | RBI | BB | SO | SB | BA | SA | PH AB | PH H | G by POS |
|---|---|---|---|---|---|---|---|---|---|---|---|---|---|---|---|---|---|
| 1902 2 teams | | CHI A (137G – .295) | | | CHI N (3G – .364) | | | | | | | | | | | | |
| " total | 140 | 547 | 162 | 18 | 5 | 3 | 0.5 | 109 | 46 | 76 | | 39 | .296 | .364 | 0 | 0 | 3B-139, 2B-2 |
| 1903 BKN N | 135 | 508 | 138 | 21 | 5 | 0 | 0.0 | 101 | 38 | 75 | | 46 | .272 | .333 | 0 | 0 | 3B-124, OF-8, 2B-3 |
| 1904 | 77 | 271 | 52 | 11 | 0 | 1 | 0.4 | 28 | 9 | 45 | | 16 | .192 | .244 | 0 | 0 | 2B-63, 3B-12, SS-1 |
| 1905 NY N | 111 | 294 | 76 | 9 | 4 | 3 | 1.0 | 51 | 29 | 58 | | 23 | .259 | .347 | 14 | 8 | 2B-47, OF-38, SS-9, 3B-1, 1B-1 |
| 1906 | 113 | 313 | 100 | 16 | 4 | 4 | 1.3 | 50 | 49 | 54 | | 21 | .319 | .435 | 9 | 1 | 2B-57, OF-39, SS-4, 3B-3, 1B-1 |
| 1907 | 123 | 306 | 77 | 20 | 4 | 4 | 1.3 | 56 | 30 | 60 | | 21 | .252 | .382 | 19 | 4 | OF-70, 2B-13, 3B-7, 1B-5, SS-1 |
| 1908 | 28 | 53 | 5 | 0 | 0 | 0 | 0.0 | 8 | 2 | 23 | | 5 | .094 | .094 | 4 | 2 | 2B-14, OF-5, SS-3 |
| 10 yrs. | 903 | 2933 | 790 | 112 | 28 | 16 | 0.5 | 479 | 253 | 464 | 6 | 216 | .269 | .343 | 46 | 15 | 3B-393, 2B-238, OF-165, SS-45, 1B-7 |
| 2 yrs. | 30 | 113 | 33 | 3 | 0 | 0 | 0.0 | 16 | 9 | 8 | | 2 | .292 | .319 | 0 | 0 | 3B-18, SS-9, 2B-4 |
| WORLD SERIES | | | | | | | | | | | | | | | | | |
| 1905 NY N | 1 | 1 | 0 | 0 | 0 | 0 | 0.0 | 0 | 0 | 0 | 1 | 0 | .000 | .000 | 1 | 0 | |

## Scott Stratton

STRATTON, C. SCOTT    BL  TR  6'    180 lbs.
B. Oct. 2, 1869, Campbellsburg, Ky.    D. Mar. 8, 1939, Louisville, Ky.

| | G | AB | H | 2B | 3B | HR | HR% | R | RBI | BB | SO | SB | BA | SA | PH AB | PH H | G by POS |
|---|---|---|---|---|---|---|---|---|---|---|---|---|---|---|---|---|---|
| 1888 LOU AA | 67 | 249 | 64 | 8 | 1 | 1 | 0.4 | 35 | 29 | 12 | | 10 | .257 | .309 | 0 | 0 | OF-38, P-33 |
| 1889 | 62 | 229 | 66 | 7 | 5 | 4 | 1.7 | 30 | 34 | 13 | 36 | 10 | .288 | .415 | 0 | 0 | OF-29, P-19, 1B-17 |
| 1890 | 55 | 189 | 61 | 3 | 5 | 0 | 0.0 | 29 | | 16 | | 8 | .323 | .392 | 0 | 0 | P-50, OF-5 |
| 1891 2 teams | | PIT N (2G – .125) | | | LOU AA (34G – .235) | | | | | | | | | | | | |
| " total | 36 | 123 | 28 | 2 | 0 | 0 | 0.0 | 10 | 8 | 11 | 16 | 8 | .228 | .244 | 0 | 0 | P-22, 1B-8, OF-6 |
| 1892 LOU N | 63 | 219 | 56 | 2 | 9 | 0 | 0.0 | 22 | 23 | 17 | 21 | 9 | .256 | .347 | 0 | 0 | P-42, OF-17, 1B-6 |
| 1893 | 61 | 221 | 50 | 8 | 5 | 0 | 0.0 | 34 | 16 | 25 | 15 | 6 | .226 | .308 | 0 | 0 | P-38, OF-23, 1B-1 |
| 1894 2 teams | | LOU N (13G – .324) | | | CHI N (23G – .375) | | | | | | | | | | | | |
| " total | 36 | 133 | 48 | 6 | 6 | 3 | 2.3 | 38 | 27 | 10 | 3 | 4 | .361 | .564 | 2 | 0 | P-22, OF-10, 1B-2 |
| 1895 CHI N | 10 | 24 | 7 | 1 | 1 | 0 | 0.0 | 3 | 2 | 4 | 2 | 1 | .292 | .417 | 1 | 0 | P-5, OF-4 |
| 8 yrs. | 390 | 1387 | 380 | 37 | 32 | 8 | 0.6 | 201 | 139 | 108 | 93 | 56 | .274 | .364 | 3 | 0 | P-231, OF-132, 1B-34 |
| 2 yrs. | 33 | 120 | 43 | 6 | 5 | 3 | 2.5 | 32 | 25 | 10 | 3 | 4 | .358 | .567 | 2 | 0 | P-20, OF-9, 1B-2 |

## Lou Stringer

STRINGER, LOUIS BERNARD    BR  TR  5'11"  173 lbs.
B. May 13, 1917, Grand Rapids, Mich.

| | G | AB | H | 2B | 3B | HR | HR% | R | RBI | BB | SO | SB | BA | SA | PH AB | PH H | G by POS |
|---|---|---|---|---|---|---|---|---|---|---|---|---|---|---|---|---|---|
| 1941 CHI N | 145 | 512 | 126 | 31 | 4 | 5 | 1.0 | 59 | 53 | 59 | 86 | 3 | .246 | .352 | 0 | 0 | 2B-137, SS-7 |
| 1942 | 121 | 406 | 96 | 10 | 5 | 9 | 2.2 | 45 | 41 | 31 | 55 | 3 | .236 | .352 | 7 | 3 | 2B-113, 3B-1 |
| 1946 | 80 | 209 | 51 | 3 | 1 | 3 | 1.4 | 26 | 19 | 26 | 34 | 0 | .244 | .311 | 5 | 0 | 2B-62, SS-1, 3B-1 |
| 1948 BOS A | 4 | 11 | 1 | 0 | 0 | 1 | 9.1 | 1 | 1 | 0 | 3 | 0 | .091 | .364 | 2 | 0 | 2B-2 |
| 1949 | 35 | 41 | 11 | 4 | 0 | 1 | 2.4 | 10 | 6 | 5 | 10 | 0 | .268 | .439 | 9 | 1 | 2B-9 |
| 1950 | 24 | 17 | 5 | 1 | 0 | 0 | 0.0 | 7 | 2 | 0 | 4 | 1 | .294 | .353 | 9 | 2 | 3B-3, SS-1, 2B-1 |
| 6 yrs. | 409 | 1196 | 290 | 49 | 10 | 19 | 1.6 | 148 | 122 | 121 | 192 | 7 | .242 | .348 | 32 | 6 | 2B-324, SS-9, 3B-5 |
| 3 yrs. | 346 | 1127 | 273 | 44 | 10 | 17 | 1.5 | 130 | 113 | 116 | 175 | 6 | .242 | .344 | 12 | 3 | 2B-312, SS-8, 3B-2 |

## Bobby Sturgeon

STURGEON, ROBERT HARWOOD    BR  TR  6'    175 lbs.
B. Aug. 6, 1919, Clinton, Ind.

| | G | AB | H | 2B | 3B | HR | HR% | R | RBI | BB | SO | SB | BA | SA | PH AB | PH H | G by POS |
|---|---|---|---|---|---|---|---|---|---|---|---|---|---|---|---|---|---|
| 1940 CHI N | 7 | 21 | 4 | 1 | 0 | 0 | 0.0 | 1 | 2 | 0 | 1 | 0 | .190 | .238 | 0 | 0 | SS-7 |
| 1941 | 129 | 433 | 106 | 15 | 3 | 0 | 0.0 | 45 | 25 | 9 | 30 | 5 | .245 | .293 | 0 | 0 | SS-126, 3B-1, 2B-1 |
| 1942 | 63 | 162 | 40 | 7 | 1 | 0 | 0.0 | 8 | 7 | 4 | 13 | 2 | .247 | .302 | 2 | 0 | 2B-32, SS-29, 3B-2 |
| 1946 | 100 | 294 | 87 | 12 | 2 | 1 | 0.3 | 26 | 21 | 10 | 18 | 0 | .296 | .361 | 7 | 3 | SS-72, 2B-21 |
| 1947 | 87 | 232 | 59 | 10 | 5 | 0 | 0.0 | 16 | 21 | 7 | 12 | 0 | .254 | .341 | 10 | 3 | SS-45, 2B-30, 3B-5 |
| 1948 BOS N | 34 | 78 | 17 | 3 | 1 | 0 | 0.0 | 10 | 4 | 4 | 5 | 0 | .218 | .282 | 4 | 2 | 2B-18, SS-4, 3B-4 |
| 6 yrs. | 420 | 1220 | 313 | 48 | 12 | 1 | 0.1 | 106 | 80 | 34 | 79 | 7 | .257 | .318 | 23 | 8 | SS-283, 2B-102, 3B-12 |
| 5 yrs. | 386 | 1142 | 296 | 45 | 11 | 1 | 0.1 | 96 | 76 | 30 | 74 | 7 | .259 | .320 | 19 | 6 | SS-279, 2B-84, 3B-8 |

## Bill Sullivan

SULLIVAN, WILLIAM
B. July 4, 1853, Holyoke, Mass.    D. Nov. 13, 1884, Holyoke, Mass.

| | G | AB | H | 2B | 3B | HR | HR% | R | RBI | BB | SO | SB | BA | SA | PH AB | PH H | G by POS |
|---|---|---|---|---|---|---|---|---|---|---|---|---|---|---|---|---|---|
| 1878 CHI N | 2 | 6 | 1 | 0 | 0 | 0 | 0.0 | 0 | 0 | 0 | | | .167 | .167 | 0 | 0 | OF-2 |

## John Sullivan

SULLIVAN, JOHN LAWRENCE    BR  TR  5'11"  180 lbs.
B. Mar. 21, 1890, Williamsport, Pa.    D. Apr. 1, 1966, Milton, Pa.

| | G | AB | H | 2B | 3B | HR | HR% | R | RBI | BB | SO | SB | BA | SA | PH AB | PH H | G by POS |
|---|---|---|---|---|---|---|---|---|---|---|---|---|---|---|---|---|---|
| 1920 BOS N | 82 | 250 | 74 | 14 | 4 | 1 | 0.4 | 36 | 28 | 29 | 29 | 3 | .296 | .396 | 6 | 3 | OF-66, 1B-6 |
| 1921 2 teams | | BOS N (5G – .000) | | | CHI N (76G – .329) | | | | | | | | | | | | |
| " total | 81 | 245 | 79 | 14 | 4 | 4 | 1.6 | 28 | 41 | 19 | 26 | 3 | .322 | .461 | 14 | 3 | OF-65 |
| 2 yrs. | 163 | 495 | 153 | 28 | 8 | 5 | 1.0 | 64 | 69 | 48 | 55 | 6 | .309 | .428 | 20 | 6 | OF-131, 1B-6 |
| 1 yr. | 76 | 240 | 79 | 14 | 4 | 4 | 1.7 | 28 | 41 | 19 | 26 | 3 | .329 | .471 | 9 | 3 | OF-65 |

## Marty Sullivan

SULLIVAN, MARTIN C.    BR  TR
B. Oct. 20, 1862, Lowell, Mass.    D. Jan. 6, 1894, Lowell, Mass.

| | G | AB | H | 2B | 3B | HR | HR% | R | RBI | BB | SO | SB | BA | SA | PH AB | PH H | G by POS |
|---|---|---|---|---|---|---|---|---|---|---|---|---|---|---|---|---|---|
| 1887 CHI N | 115 | 472 | 134 | 13 | 16 | 7 | 1.5 | 98 | 77 | 36 | 53 | 35 | .284 | .424 | 0 | 0 | OF-115, P-1 |
| 1888 | 75 | 314 | 74 | 12 | 6 | 7 | 2.2 | 40 | 39 | 15 | 32 | 9 | .236 | .379 | 0 | 0 | OF-75 |
| 1889 IND N | 69 | 256 | 73 | 11 | 3 | 4 | 1.6 | 45 | 35 | 50 | 31 | 15 | .285 | .398 | 0 | 0 | OF-64, 1B-5 |
| 1890 BOS N | 121 | 505 | 144 | 19 | 7 | 6 | 1.2 | 82 | 61 | 56 | 48 | 33 | .285 | .386 | 0 | 0 | OF-120, 3B-1 |
| 1891 2 teams | | BOS N (17G – .224) | | | CLE N (1G – .250) | | | | | | | | | | | | |
| " total | 18 | 71 | 16 | 1 | 2 | 2 | 2.8 | 15 | 8 | 5 | 4 | 7 | .225 | .324 | 0 | 0 | OF-18 |
| 5 yrs. | 398 | 1618 | 441 | 56 | 32 | 26 | 1.6 | 280 | 220 | 162 | 168 | 99 | .273 | .395 | 0 | 0 | OF-392, 1B-5, 3B-1, P-1 |
| 2 yrs. | 190 | 786 | 208 | 25 | 22 | 14 | 1.8 | 138 | 116 | 51 | 85 | 44 | .265 | .406 | 0 | 0 | OF-190, P-1 |

## Champ Summers

SUMMERS, JOHN JUNIOR II    BL  TR  6'2"  205 lbs.
B. June 15, 1946, Bremerton, Wash.

| | G | AB | H | 2B | 3B | HR | HR% | R | RBI | BB | SO | SB | BA | SA | PH AB | PH H | G by POS |
|---|---|---|---|---|---|---|---|---|---|---|---|---|---|---|---|---|---|
| 1974 OAK A | 20 | 24 | 3 | 1 | 0 | 0 | 0.0 | 2 | 3 | 1 | 5 | 0 | .125 | .167 | 7 | 1 | OF-12, DH-2 |

| | G | AB | H | 2B | 3B | HR | HR % | R | RBI | BB | SO | SB | BA | SA | Pinch Hit AB | Pinch Hit H | G by POS |
|---|---|---|---|---|---|---|---|---|---|---|---|---|---|---|---|---|---|

## Champm Summers continued

| | G | AB | H | 2B | 3B | HR | HR % | R | RBI | BB | SO | SB | BA | SA | AB | H | G by POS |
|---|---|---|---|---|---|---|---|---|---|---|---|---|---|---|---|---|---|
| 1975 CHI N | 76 | 91 | 21 | 5 | 1 | 1 | 1.1 | 14 | 16 | 10 | 13 | 0 | .231 | .341 | 46 | 14 | OF-18 |
| 1976 | 83 | 126 | 26 | 2 | 0 | 3 | 2.4 | 11 | 13 | 13 | 31 | 1 | .206 | .294 | 47 | 12 | OF-26, 1B-10, C-1 |
| 1977 CIN N | 59 | 76 | 13 | 4 | 0 | 3 | 3.9 | 11 | 6 | 6 | 16 | 0 | .171 | .342 | 38 | 6 | OF-16, 3B-1 |
| 1978 | 13 | 35 | 9 | 2 | 0 | 1 | 2.9 | 4 | 3 | 7 | 4 | 2 | .257 | .400 | 0 | 0 | OF-12 |
| 1979 2 teams | | CIN | N | (27G – | .200) | | DET | A | (90G – | .313) | | | | | | | |
| " total | 117 | 306 | 89 | 14 | 2 | 21 | 6.9 | 57 | 62 | 53 | 48 | 7 | .291 | .556 | 23 | 5 | OF-82, DH-10, 1B-10 |
| 1980 DET A | 120 | 347 | 103 | 19 | 1 | 17 | 4.9 | 61 | 60 | 52 | 52 | 4 | .297 | .504 | 26 | 7 | DH-64, OF-47, 1B-1 |
| 1981 | 64 | 165 | 42 | 8 | 0 | 3 | 1.8 | 16 | 21 | 19 | 35 | 1 | .255 | .358 | 14 | 3 | DH-37, OF-18 |
| 1982 SF N | 70 | 125 | 31 | 5 | 0 | 4 | 3.2 | 15 | 19 | 16 | 17 | 0 | .248 | .384 | 31 | 10 | OF-31, 1B-3 |
| 1983 | 29 | 22 | 3 | 0 | 0 | 0 | 0.0 | 3 | 3 | 7 | 8 | 0 | .136 | .136 | 20 | 3 | OF-1 |
| 1984 SD N | 47 | 54 | 10 | 3 | 0 | 1 | 1.9 | 5 | 12 | 4 | 15 | 0 | .185 | .296 | 36 | 7 | 1B-8 |
| 11 yrs. | 698 | 1371 | 350 | 63 | 4 | 54 | 3.9 | 199 | 218 | 188 | 244 | 15 | .255 | .425 | 288 | 68 | OF-263, DH-113, 1B-32, 3B-1, C-1 |
| 2 yrs. | 159 | 217 | 47 | 7 | 1 | 4 | 1.8 | 25 | 29 | 23 | 44 | 1 | .217 | .313 | 93 | 26 | OF-44, 1B-10, C-1 |

LEAGUE CHAMPIONSHIP SERIES

| | G | AB | H | 2B | 3B | HR | HR % | R | RBI | BB | SO | SB | BA | SA | AB | H | G by POS |
|---|---|---|---|---|---|---|---|---|---|---|---|---|---|---|---|---|---|
| 1984 SD N | 2 | 2 | 0 | 0 | 0 | 0 | 0.0 | 0 | 0 | 0 | 1 | 0 | .000 | .000 | 0 | 0 | |

WORLD SERIES

| | G | AB | H | 2B | 3B | HR | HR % | R | RBI | BB | SO | SB | BA | SA | AB | H | G by POS |
|---|---|---|---|---|---|---|---|---|---|---|---|---|---|---|---|---|---|
| 1984 SD N | 1 | 1 | 0 | 0 | 0 | 0 | 0.0 | 0 | 0 | 0 | 0 | 0 | .000 | .000 | 1 | 0 | |

## Billy Sunday

**SUNDAY, WILLIAM ASHLEY (The Evangelist)**    BL TR 5'10"   160 lbs.
B. Nov. 19, 1862, Ames, Iowa    D. Nov. 6, 1935, Chicago, Ill.

| | G | AB | H | 2B | 3B | HR | HR % | R | RBI | BB | SO | SB | BA | SA | AB | H | G by POS |
|---|---|---|---|---|---|---|---|---|---|---|---|---|---|---|---|---|---|
| 1883 CHI N | 14 | 54 | 13 | 4 | 0 | 0 | 0.0 | 6 | | 1 | 18 | | .241 | .315 | 0 | 0 | OF-14 |
| 1884 | 43 | 176 | 39 | 4 | 1 | 4 | 2.3 | 25 | | 4 | 36 | | .222 | .324 | 0 | 0 | OF-43 |
| 1885 | 46 | 172 | 44 | 3 | 3 | 2 | 1.2 | 36 | 20 | 12 | 33 | | .256 | .343 | 0 | 0 | OF-46 |
| 1886 | 28 | 103 | 25 | 2 | 2 | 0 | 0.0 | 16 | 6 | 7 | 26 | | .243 | .301 | 0 | 0 | OF-28 |
| 1887 | 50 | 199 | 58 | 6 | 6 | 3 | 1.5 | 41 | 32 | 21 | 20 | 34 | .291 | .427 | 0 | 0 | OF-50 |
| 1888 PIT N | 120 | 505 | 119 | 14 | 3 | 0 | 0.0 | 69 | 15 | 12 | 36 | 71 | .236 | .275 | 0 | 0 | OF-120 |
| 1889 | 81 | 321 | 77 | 10 | 6 | 2 | 0.6 | 62 | 25 | 27 | 33 | 47 | .240 | .327 | 0 | 0 | OF-81 |
| 1890 2 teams | | PIT | N | (86G – | .257) | | PHI | N | (31G – | .261) | | | | | | | |
| " total | 117 | 477 | 123 | 12 | 3 | 1 | 0.2 | 84 | 39 | 50 | 27 | 84 | .258 | .302 | 0 | 0 | OF-117, P-1 |
| 8 yrs. | 499 | 2007 | 498 | 55 | 24 | 12 | 0.6 | 339 | 136 | 134 | 229 | 236 | .248 | .317 | 0 | 0 | OF-499, P-1 |
| 5 yrs. | 181 | 704 | 179 | 19 | 12 | 9 | 1.3 | 124 | 58 | 45 | 133 | 34 | .254 | .354 | 0 | 0 | OF-181 |

## Sy Sutcliffe

**SUTCLIFFE, EDWARD ELMER**    BL   6'2"   170 lbs.
B. Apr. 15, 1863, Wheaton, Ill.    D. Feb. 13, 1893, Wheaton, Ill.

| | G | AB | H | 2B | 3B | HR | HR % | R | RBI | BB | SO | SB | BA | SA | AB | H | G by POS |
|---|---|---|---|---|---|---|---|---|---|---|---|---|---|---|---|---|---|
| 1884 CHI N | 4 | 15 | 3 | 1 | 0 | 0 | 0.0 | 4 | | 2 | 4 | | .200 | .267 | 0 | 0 | C-4 |
| 1885 2 teams | | CHI | N | (11G – | .186) | | STL | N | (16G – | .122) | | | | | | | |
| " total | 27 | 92 | 14 | 2 | 1 | 0 | 0.0 | 7 | 8 | 7 | 15 | | .152 | .196 | 0 | 0 | C-25, OF-3 |
| 1888 DET N | 49 | 191 | 49 | 5 | 3 | 0 | 0.0 | 17 | 23 | 5 | 14 | 6 | .257 | .314 | 0 | 0 | SS-24, C-14, 1B-5, OF-4, 2B-2 |
| 1889 CLE N | 46 | 161 | 40 | 3 | 2 | 1 | 0.6 | 17 | 21 | 14 | 6 | 5 | .248 | .311 | 0 | 0 | C-37, 1B-8, OF-1 |
| 1890 CLE P | 99 | 386 | 127 | 14 | 8 | 2 | 0.5 | 62 | 60 | 33 | 16 | 10 | .329 | .422 | 0 | 0 | C-84, OF-15, SS-4, 3B-2 |
| 1891 WAS AA | 53 | 201 | 71 | 8 | 3 | 2 | 1.0 | 29 | 33 | 17 | 17 | 8 | .353 | .453 | 0 | 0 | OF-35, C-22, SS-3, 3B-1 |
| 1892 BAL N | 66 | 276 | 77 | 10 | 7 | 1 | 0.4 | 41 | 27 | 14 | 15 | 12 | .279 | .377 | 0 | 0 | 1B-66 |
| 7 yrs. | 344 | 1322 | 381 | 43 | 24 | 6 | 0.5 | 177 | 171 | 92 | 87 | 41 | .288 | .371 | 0 | 0 | C-186, 1B-79, OF-58, SS-31, 3B-3, 2B-2 |
| 2 yrs. | 15 | 58 | 11 | 2 | 1 | 0 | 0.0 | 9 | 4 | 4 | 9 | | .190 | .259 | 0 | 0 | C-15, OF-1 |

## Bill Sweeney

**SWEENEY, WILLIAM JOHN**    BR TR 5'11"   175 lbs.
B. Mar. 6, 1886, Covington, Ky.    D. May 26, 1948, Cambridge, Mass.

| | G | AB | H | 2B | 3B | HR | HR % | R | RBI | BB | SO | SB | BA | SA | AB | H | G by POS |
|---|---|---|---|---|---|---|---|---|---|---|---|---|---|---|---|---|---|
| 1907 2 teams | | CHI | N | (3G – | .100) | | BOS | N | (58G – | .262) | | | | | | | |
| " total | 61 | 201 | 51 | 2 | 0 | 0 | 0.0 | 25 | 19 | 16 | | 9 | .254 | .264 | 2 | 0 | 3B-23, SS-18, OF-11, 2B-5, 1B-1 |
| 1908 BOS N | 127 | 418 | 102 | 15 | 3 | 0 | 0.0 | 44 | 40 | 45 | | 17 | .244 | .294 | 3 | 2 | 3B-123, SS-2, 2B-1 |
| 1909 | 138 | 493 | 120 | 19 | 3 | 1 | 0.2 | 45 | 36 | 37 | | 25 | .243 | .300 | 0 | 0 | 3B-112, SS-26 |
| 1910 | 150 | 499 | 133 | 22 | 4 | 5 | 1.0 | 43 | 46 | 61 | 28 | 25 | .267 | .357 | 4 | 3 | SS-110, 3B-21, 1B-17 |
| 1911 | 137 | 523 | 164 | 33 | 6 | 3 | 0.6 | 92 | 63 | 77 | 26 | 33 | .314 | .417 | 1 | 1 | 2B-136 |
| 1912 | 153 | 593 | 204 | 31 | 13 | 1 | 0.2 | 84 | 100 | 68 | 34 | 27 | .344 | .445 | 0 | 0 | 2B-153 |
| 1913 | 139 | 502 | 129 | 17 | 6 | 0 | 0.0 | 65 | 47 | 66 | 50 | 18 | .257 | .315 | 2 | 1 | 2B-137 |
| 1914 CHI N | 134 | 463 | 101 | 14 | 5 | 1 | 0.2 | 45 | 38 | 53 | 15 | 18 | .218 | .276 | 0 | 0 | 2B-134 |
| 8 yrs. | 1039 | 3692 | 1004 | 153 | 40 | 11 | 0.3 | 443 | 389 | 423 | 153 | 172 | .272 | .344 | 12 | 7 | 2B-566, 3B-279, SS-156, 1B-18, OF-11 |
| 2 yrs. | 137 | 473 | 102 | 14 | 5 | 1 | 0.2 | 46 | 39 | 54 | 15 | 19 | .216 | .273 | 0 | 0 | 2B-134, SS-3 |

## Steve Swisher

**SWISHER, STEVEN EUGENE**    BR TR 6'2"   205 lbs.
B. Aug. 9, 1951, Parkersburg, W. Va.

| | G | AB | H | 2B | 3B | HR | HR % | R | RBI | BB | SO | SB | BA | SA | AB | H | G by POS |
|---|---|---|---|---|---|---|---|---|---|---|---|---|---|---|---|---|---|
| 1974 CHI N | 90 | 280 | 60 | 5 | 0 | 5 | 1.8 | 21 | 27 | 37 | 63 | 0 | .214 | .286 | 0 | 0 | C-90 |
| 1975 | 93 | 254 | 54 | 16 | 2 | 1 | 0.4 | 20 | 22 | 30 | 57 | 1 | .213 | .303 | 0 | 0 | C-93 |
| 1976 | 109 | 377 | 89 | 13 | 3 | 5 | 1.3 | 25 | 42 | 20 | 82 | 2 | .236 | .326 | 4 | 1 | C-107 |
| 1977 | 74 | 205 | 39 | 7 | 0 | 5 | 2.4 | 21 | 15 | 9 | 47 | 0 | .190 | .298 | 4 | 1 | C-72 |
| 1978 STL N | 45 | 115 | 32 | 5 | 1 | 1 | 0.9 | 11 | 10 | 8 | 14 | 1 | .278 | .365 | 3 | 1 | C-42 |
| 1979 | 38 | 73 | 11 | 1 | 1 | 1 | 1.4 | 4 | 3 | 6 | 17 | 0 | .151 | .233 | 5 | 0 | C-33 |
| 1980 | 18 | 24 | 6 | 1 | 0 | 0 | 0.0 | 2 | 2 | 1 | 7 | 0 | .250 | .292 | 9 | 2 | C-8 |
| 1981 SD N | 16 | 28 | 4 | 0 | 0 | 0 | 0.0 | 2 | 3 | 2 | 11 | 0 | .143 | .143 | 7 | 1 | C-10 |
| 1982 | 26 | 58 | 10 | 1 | 0 | 2 | 3.4 | 2 | 3 | 5 | 24 | 0 | .172 | .293 | 0 | 0 | C-26 |
| 9 yrs. | 509 | 1414 | 305 | 49 | 7 | 20 | 1.4 | 108 | 124 | 118 | 322 | 4 | .216 | .303 | 32 | 6 | C-481 |
| 4 yrs. | 366 | 1116 | 242 | 41 | 5 | 16 | 1.4 | 87 | 106 | 96 | 249 | 3 | .217 | .306 | 8 | 2 | C-362 |

## Jerry Tabb

**TABB, JERRY LYNN**    BL TR 6'2"   195 lbs.
B. Mar. 17, 1952, Altus, Okla.

| | G | AB | H | 2B | 3B | HR | HR % | R | RBI | BB | SO | SB | BA | SA | AB | H | G by POS |
|---|---|---|---|---|---|---|---|---|---|---|---|---|---|---|---|---|---|
| 1976 CHI N | 11 | 24 | 7 | 0 | 0 | 0 | 0.0 | 2 | 0 | 3 | 2 | 0 | .292 | .292 | 6 | 1 | 1B-6 |

| | G | AB | H | 2B | 3B | HR | HR% | R | RBI | BB | SO | SB | BA | SA | Pinch Hit AB | Pinch Hit H | G by POS |
|---|---|---|---|---|---|---|---|---|---|---|---|---|---|---|---|---|---|

## Jerry Tabb  continued

| | G | AB | H | 2B | 3B | HR | HR% | R | RBI | BB | SO | SB | BA | SA | AB | H | G by POS |
|---|---|---|---|---|---|---|---|---|---|---|---|---|---|---|---|---|---|
| 1977 OAK A | 51 | 144 | 32 | 3 | 0 | 6 | 4.2 | 8 | 19 | 10 | 26 | 0 | .222 | .368 | 10 | 2 | 1B-36, DH-5 |
| 1978 | 12 | 9 | 1 | 0 | 0 | 0 | 0.0 | 0 | 1 | 2 | 5 | 0 | .111 | .111 | 9 | 1 | DH-2, 1B-2 |
| 3 yrs. | 74 | 177 | 40 | 3 | 0 | 6 | 3.4 | 10 | 20 | 15 | 33 | 0 | .226 | .345 | 25 | 4 | 1B-44, DH-7 |
| 1 yr. | 11 | 24 | 7 | 0 | 0 | 0 | 0.0 | 2 | 0 | 3 | 2 | 0 | .292 | .292 | 6 | 1 | 1B-6 |

## Pat Tabler

**TABLER, PATRICK SEAN**
B. Feb. 2, 1958, Hamilton, Ohio　　　　　　　　　BR TR 6'3"　175 lbs.

| | G | AB | H | 2B | 3B | HR | HR% | R | RBI | BB | SO | SB | BA | SA | AB | H | G by POS |
|---|---|---|---|---|---|---|---|---|---|---|---|---|---|---|---|---|---|
| 1981 CHI N | 35 | 101 | 19 | 3 | 1 | 1 | 1.0 | 11 | 5 | 13 | 26 | 0 | .188 | .267 | 0 | 0 | 2B-35 |
| 1982 | 25 | 85 | 20 | 4 | 2 | 1 | 1.2 | 9 | 7 | 6 | 20 | 0 | .235 | .365 | 0 | 0 | 3B-25 |
| 1983 CLE A | 124 | 430 | 125 | 23 | 5 | 6 | 1.4 | 56 | 65 | 56 | 63 | 2 | .291 | .409 | 5 | 2 | OF-80, 3B-25, DH-6, 2B-2 |
| 1984 | 144 | 473 | 137 | 21 | 3 | 10 | 2.1 | 66 | 68 | 47 | 62 | 3 | .290 | .410 | 6 | 1 | 1B-67, OF-43, 3B-36, DH-1, 2B-1 |
| 1985 | 117 | 404 | 111 | 18 | 3 | 5 | 1.2 | 47 | 59 | 27 | 55 | 0 | .275 | .371 | 8 | 4 | 1B-92, DH-18, 3B-4, 2B-1 |
| 5 yrs. | 445 | 1493 | 412 | 69 | 14 | 23 | 1.5 | 189 | 204 | 149 | 226 | 5 | .276 | .387 | 19 | 7 | 1B-159, OF-123, 3B-90, 2B-39, DH-25 |
| 2 yrs. | 60 | 186 | 39 | 7 | 3 | 2 | 1.1 | 20 | 12 | 19 | 46 | 0 | .210 | .312 | 0 | 0 | 2B-35, 3B-25 |

## Dale Talbot

**TALBOT, ROBERT DALE**
B. June 6, 1927, Visalia, Calif.　　　　　　　　　BR TR 6'　170 lbs.

| | G | AB | H | 2B | 3B | HR | HR% | R | RBI | BB | SO | SB | BA | SA | AB | H | G by POS |
|---|---|---|---|---|---|---|---|---|---|---|---|---|---|---|---|---|---|
| 1953 CHI N | 8 | 30 | 10 | 0 | 1 | 0 | 0.0 | 5 | 0 | 0 | 4 | 1 | .333 | .400 | 0 | 0 | OF-7 |
| 1954 | 114 | 403 | 97 | 15 | 4 | 1 | 0.2 | 45 | 19 | 16 | 25 | 3 | .241 | .305 | 1 | 0 | OF-110 |
| 2 yrs. | 122 | 433 | 107 | 15 | 5 | 1 | 0.2 | 50 | 19 | 16 | 29 | 4 | .247 | .312 | 1 | 0 | OF-117 |
| 2 yrs. | 122 | 433 | 107 | 15 | 5 | 1 | 0.2 | 50 | 19 | 16 | 29 | 4 | .247 | .312 | 1 | 0 | OF-117 |

## Chuck Tanner

**TANNER, CHARLES WILLIAM**
Father of Bruce Tanner.
B. July 4, 1929, New Castle, Pa.
Manager 1970-85.　　　　　　　　　　　　　　BL TL 6'　185 lbs.

| | G | AB | H | 2B | 3B | HR | HR% | R | RBI | BB | SO | SB | BA | SA | AB | H | G by POS |
|---|---|---|---|---|---|---|---|---|---|---|---|---|---|---|---|---|---|
| 1955 MIL N | 97 | 243 | 60 | 9 | 3 | 6 | 2.5 | 27 | 27 | 27 | 32 | 0 | .247 | .383 | 32 | 7 | OF-62 |
| 1956 | 60 | 63 | 15 | 2 | 0 | 1 | 1.6 | 6 | 4 | 10 | 10 | 0 | .238 | .317 | 44 | 10 | OF-8 |
| 1957 2 teams | | | MIL | N | (22G – | .246) | | CHI | N | (95G – | .286) | | | | | | |
| " total | 117 | 387 | 108 | 19 | 2 | 9 | 2.3 | 47 | 48 | 28 | 24 | 0 | .279 | .408 | 16 | 4 | OF-100 |
| 1958 CHI N | 73 | 103 | 27 | 6 | 0 | 4 | 3.9 | 10 | 17 | 9 | 10 | 1 | .262 | .437 | 53 | 12 | OF-15 |
| 1959 CLE A | 14 | 48 | 12 | 2 | 0 | 1 | 2.1 | 6 | 5 | 2 | 9 | 0 | .250 | .354 | 4 | 0 | OF-10 |
| 1960 | 21 | 25 | 7 | 1 | 0 | 0 | 0.0 | 2 | 4 | 4 | 6 | 1 | .280 | .320 | 15 | 3 | OF-4 |
| 1961 LA A | 7 | 8 | 1 | 0 | 0 | 0 | 0.0 | 0 | 2 | 2 | 2 | 0 | .125 | .125 | 4 | 1 | OF-1 |
| 1962 | 7 | 8 | 1 | 0 | 0 | 0 | 0.0 | 0 | 0 | 0 | 0 | 0 | .125 | .125 | 6 | 1 | OF-2 |
| 8 yrs. | 396 | 885 | 231 | 39 | 5 | 21 | 2.4 | 98 | 105 | 82 | 93 | 2 | .261 | .388 | 174 | 38 | OF-202 |
| 2 yrs. | 168 | 421 | 118 | 22 | 2 | 11 | 2.6 | 52 | 59 | 32 | 30 | 1 | .280 | .420 | 65 | 15 | OF-97 |

## El Tappe

**TAPPE, ELVIN WALTER**
B. May 21, 1927, Quincy, Ill.
Manager 1961-62.　　　　　　　　　　　　　　BR TR 5'11"　180 lbs.

| | G | AB | H | 2B | 3B | HR | HR% | R | RBI | BB | SO | SB | BA | SA | AB | H | G by POS |
|---|---|---|---|---|---|---|---|---|---|---|---|---|---|---|---|---|---|
| 1954 CHI N | 46 | 119 | 22 | 3 | 0 | 0 | 0.0 | 5 | 4 | 10 | 9 | 0 | .185 | .210 | 0 | 0 | C-46 |
| 1955 | 2 | 0 | 0 | 0 | 0 | 0 | – | 0 | 0 | 0 | 0 | 0 | – | – | 0 | 0 | C-2 |
| 1956 | 3 | 1 | 0 | 0 | 0 | 0 | 0.0 | 0 | 0 | 1 | 0 | 0 | .000 | .000 | 0 | 0 | C-3 |
| 1958 | 17 | 28 | 6 | 0 | 0 | 0 | 0.0 | 2 | 4 | 3 | 1 | 0 | .214 | .214 | 1 | 0 | C-16 |
| 1960 | 51 | 103 | 24 | 7 | 0 | 0 | 0.0 | 11 | 3 | 11 | 12 | 0 | .233 | .301 | 2 | 0 | C-49 |
| 1962 | 26 | 53 | 11 | 0 | 0 | 0 | 0.0 | 3 | 6 | 4 | 3 | 0 | .208 | .208 | 0 | 0 | C-26 |
| 6 yrs. | 145 | 304 | 63 | 10 | 0 | 0 | 0.0 | 21 | 17 | 29 | 25 | 0 | .207 | .240 | 3 | 0 | C-142 |
| 6 yrs. | 145 | 304 | 63 | 10 | 0 | 0 | 0.0 | 21 | 17 | 29 | 25 | 0 | .207 | .240 | 3 | 0 | C-142 |

## Ted Tappe

**TAPPE, THEODORE NASH**
B. Feb. 2, 1931, Seattle, Wash.　　　　　　　　　BL TR 6'3"　185 lbs.

| | G | AB | H | 2B | 3B | HR | HR% | R | RBI | BB | SO | SB | BA | SA | AB | H | G by POS |
|---|---|---|---|---|---|---|---|---|---|---|---|---|---|---|---|---|---|
| 1950 CIN N | 7 | 5 | 1 | 0 | 0 | 1 | 20.0 | 1 | 1 | 1 | 1 | 0 | .200 | .800 | 5 | 1 | |
| 1951 | 4 | 3 | 1 | 0 | 0 | 0 | 0.0 | 0 | 0 | 0 | 0 | 0 | .333 | .333 | 3 | 1 | |
| 1955 CHI N | 23 | 50 | 13 | 2 | 0 | 4 | 8.0 | 12 | 10 | 11 | 11 | 0 | .260 | .540 | 8 | 2 | OF-15 |
| 3 yrs. | 34 | 58 | 15 | 2 | 0 | 5 | 8.6 | 13 | 11 | 12 | 12 | 0 | .259 | .552 | 16 | 4 | OF-15 |
| 1 yr. | 23 | 50 | 13 | 2 | 0 | 4 | 8.0 | 12 | 10 | 11 | 11 | 0 | .260 | .540 | 8 | 2 | OF-15 |

## Bennie Tate

**TATE, HENRY BENNETT**
B. Dec. 3, 1901, Whitwell, Tenn.　　D. Oct. 27, 1973, W. Frankfort, Ill.　　BL TR 5'8"　165 lbs.

| | G | AB | H | 2B | 3B | HR | HR% | R | RBI | BB | SO | SB | BA | SA | AB | H | G by POS |
|---|---|---|---|---|---|---|---|---|---|---|---|---|---|---|---|---|---|
| 1924 WAS A | 21 | 43 | 13 | 2 | 0 | 0 | 0.0 | 2 | 7 | 1 | 2 | 0 | .302 | .349 | 6 | 3 | C-14 |
| 1925 | 16 | 27 | 13 | 3 | 0 | 0 | 0.0 | 0 | 7 | 2 | 2 | 0 | .481 | .593 | 2 | 1 | C-14 |
| 1926 | 59 | 142 | 38 | 5 | 2 | 1 | 0.7 | 17 | 13 | 15 | 1 | 0 | .268 | .352 | 9 | 2 | C-45 |
| 1927 | 61 | 131 | 41 | 5 | 1 | 1 | 0.8 | 12 | 24 | 8 | 4 | 0 | .313 | .389 | 16 | 5 | C-39 |
| 1928 | 57 | 122 | 30 | 6 | 0 | 0 | 0.0 | 10 | 15 | 10 | 4 | 0 | .246 | .295 | 25 | 9 | C-30 |
| 1929 | 81 | 265 | 78 | 12 | 3 | 0 | 0.0 | 26 | 30 | 16 | 8 | 2 | .294 | .362 | 6 | 3 | C-74 |
| 1930 2 teams | | | WAS | A | (14G – | .250) | | CHI | A | (72G – | .317) | | | | | | |
| " total | 86 | 250 | 78 | 11 | 2 | 0 | 0.0 | 27 | 29 | 18 | 11 | 2 | .312 | .372 | 5 | 2 | C-79 |
| 1931 CHI A | 89 | 273 | 73 | 12 | 3 | 0 | 0.0 | 27 | 22 | 26 | 10 | 1 | .267 | .333 | 4 | 1 | C-85 |
| 1932 2 teams | | | CHI | A | (4G – | .100) | | BOS | A | (81G – | .245) | | | | | | |
| " total | 85 | 283 | 68 | 12 | 5 | 2 | 0.7 | 22 | 26 | 21 | 6 | 0 | .240 | .339 | 5 | 3 | C-80 |
| 1934 CHI N | 11 | 24 | 3 | 0 | 0 | 0 | 0.0 | 1 | 0 | 1 | 3 | 0 | .125 | .125 | 3 | 0 | C-8 |
| 10 yrs. | 566 | 1560 | 435 | 68 | 16 | 4 | 0.3 | 144 | 173 | 118 | 51 | 5 | .279 | .351 | 81 | 29 | C-468 |
| 1 yr. | 11 | 24 | 3 | 0 | 0 | 0 | 0.0 | 1 | 0 | 1 | 3 | 0 | .125 | .125 | 3 | 0 | C-8 |

WORLD SERIES

| | G | AB | H | 2B | 3B | HR | HR% | R | RBI | BB | SO | SB | BA | SA | AB | H | G by POS |
|---|---|---|---|---|---|---|---|---|---|---|---|---|---|---|---|---|---|
| 1924 WAS A | 3 | 0 | 0 | 0 | 0 | 0 | – | 0 | 1 | 3 | 0 | 0 | – | – | 0 | 0 | |

| | G | AB | H | 2B | 3B | HR | HR % | R | RBI | BB | SO | SB | BA | SA | Pinch Hit AB | Pinch Hit H | G by POS |
|---|---|---|---|---|---|---|---|---|---|---|---|---|---|---|---|---|---|

## Chink Taylor

**TAYLOR, C. L.**
B. Feb. 9, 1898, Burnet, Tex.   D. July 7, 1980, Temple, Tex.
BR TR 5'9"   160 lbs.

| | G | AB | H | 2B | 3B | HR | HR% | R | RBI | BB | SO | SB | BA | SA | PH AB | PH H | G by POS |
|---|---|---|---|---|---|---|---|---|---|---|---|---|---|---|---|---|---|
| 1925 CHI N | 8 | 6 | 0 | 0 | 0 | 0 | 0.0 | 2 | 0 | 0 | 0 | 0 | .000 | .000 | 2 | 0 | OF-2 |

## Danny Taylor

**TAYLOR, DANIEL TURNEY**
B. Dec. 23, 1900, Lash, Pa.   D. Oct. 13, 1972, Latrobe, Pa.
BR TR 5'10"   190 lbs.

| | G | AB | H | 2B | 3B | HR | HR% | R | RBI | BB | SO | SB | BA | SA | PH AB | PH H | G by POS |
|---|---|---|---|---|---|---|---|---|---|---|---|---|---|---|---|---|---|
| 1926 WAS A | 21 | 50 | 15 | 0 | 1 | 1 | 2.0 | 10 | 5 | 5 | 7 | 1 | .300 | .400 | 5 | 2 | OF-12 |
| 1929 CHI N | 2 | 3 | 0 | 0 | 0 | 0 | 0.0 | 0 | 0 | 1 | 1 | 0 | .000 | .000 | 1 | 0 | OF-1 |
| 1930 | 74 | 219 | 62 | 14 | 3 | 2 | 0.9 | 43 | 37 | 27 | 34 | 6 | .283 | .402 | 14 | 7 | OF-52 |
| 1931 | 88 | 270 | 81 | 13 | 6 | 5 | 1.9 | 48 | 41 | 31 | 46 | 4 | .300 | .448 | 18 | 6 | OF-67 |
| 1932 2 teams | | CHI | N | (6G – | .227) | | BKN | N | (105G – | .324) | | | | | | | | |
| " total | 111 | 417 | 133 | 24 | 7 | 11 | 2.6 | 87 | 51 | 36 | 42 | 14 | .319 | .489 | 3 | 0 | OF-102 |
| 1933 BKN N | 103 | 358 | 102 | 21 | 9 | 9 | 2.5 | 75 | 40 | 47 | 45 | 11 | .285 | .469 | 11 | 3 | OF-91 |
| 1934 | 120 | 405 | 121 | 24 | 6 | 7 | 1.7 | 62 | 57 | 63 | 47 | 12 | .299 | .440 | 10 | 2 | OF-108 |
| 1935 | 112 | 352 | 102 | 19 | 5 | 7 | 2.0 | 51 | 59 | 46 | 32 | 6 | .290 | .432 | 9 | 4 | OF-99 |
| 1936 | 43 | 116 | 34 | 6 | 0 | 2 | 1.7 | 12 | 15 | 11 | 14 | 2 | .293 | .397 | 8 | 1 | OF-31 |
| 9 yrs. | 674 | 2190 | 650 | 121 | 37 | 44 | 2.0 | 388 | 305 | 267 | 268 | 56 | .297 | .446 | 79 | 25 | OF-563 |
| 4 yrs. | 170 | 514 | 148 | 29 | 9 | 7 | 1.4 | 94 | 81 | 62 | 82 | 11 | .288 | .420 | 33 | 13 | OF-126 |

## Harry Taylor

**TAYLOR, HARRY WARREN (Handsome Harry)**
B. Dec. 26, 1907, McKeesport, Pa.   D. Apr. 27, 1969, Toledo, Ohio
BL TL 6'1½"   185 lbs.

| | G | AB | H | 2B | 3B | HR | HR% | R | RBI | BB | SO | SB | BA | SA | PH AB | PH H | G by POS |
|---|---|---|---|---|---|---|---|---|---|---|---|---|---|---|---|---|---|
| 1932 CHI N | 10 | 8 | 1 | 0 | 0 | 0 | 0.0 | 1 | 0 | 1 | 1 | 0 | .125 | .125 | 7 | 1 | 1B-1 |

## Jack Taylor

**TAYLOR, JOHN W.**
B. Jan. 14, 1874, Straightville, Ohio   D. Mar. 4, 1938, Columbus, Ohio
BR TR 5'10"   170 lbs.

| | G | AB | H | 2B | 3B | HR | HR% | R | RBI | BB | SO | SB | BA | SA | PH AB | PH H | G by POS |
|---|---|---|---|---|---|---|---|---|---|---|---|---|---|---|---|---|---|
| 1898 CHI N | 5 | 15 | 3 | 2 | 0 | 0 | 0.0 | 4 | 2 | 3 | | 0 | .200 | .333 | 0 | 0 | P-5 |
| 1899 | 42 | 139 | 37 | 9 | 2 | 0 | 0.0 | 25 | 17 | 16 | | 0 | .266 | .360 | 1 | 1 | P-41 |
| 1900 | 28 | 81 | 19 | 3 | 1 | 1 | 1.2 | 7 | 6 | 3 | | 1 | .235 | .333 | 0 | 0 | P-28 |
| 1901 | 35 | 106 | 23 | 6 | 0 | 0 | 0.0 | 12 | 2 | 4 | | 0 | .217 | .274 | 2 | 0 | P-33 |
| 1902 | 55 | 186 | 44 | 6 | 1 | 0 | 0.0 | 18 | 17 | 8 | | 6 | .237 | .280 | 1 | 0 | P-36, 3B-12, OF-3, 1B-2, 2B-1 |
| 1903 | 40 | 126 | 28 | 3 | 4 | 0 | 0.0 | 13 | 17 | 6 | | 3 | .222 | .310 | 0 | 0 | P-37, 3B-1, 2B-1 |
| 1904 STL N | 42 | 133 | 28 | 3 | 3 | 1 | 0.8 | 9 | 8 | 4 | | 3 | .211 | .301 | 0 | 0 | P-41 |
| 1905 | 39 | 121 | 23 | 5 | 2 | 0 | 0.0 | 11 | 12 | 8 | | 4 | .190 | .264 | 0 | 0 | P-37, 3B-2 |
| 1906 2 teams | | STL | N | (17G – | .208) | | CHI | N | (17G – | .208) | | | | | | | | |
| " total | 34 | 106 | 22 | 3 | 0 | 0 | 0.0 | 9 | 5 | 14 | | 1 | .208 | .236 | 0 | 0 | P-34 |
| 1907 CHI N | 18 | 47 | 9 | 2 | 0 | 0 | 0.0 | 2 | 1 | 0 | | 0 | .191 | .234 | 0 | 0 | P-18 |
| 10 yrs. | 338 | 1060 | 236 | 42 | 13 | 2 | 0.2 | 110 | 87 | 66 | | 18 | .223 | .292 | 4 | 1 | P-310, 3B-15, OF-3, 2B-2, 1B-2 |
| 8 yrs. | 240 | 753 | 174 | 34 | 8 | 1 | 0.1 | 86 | 65 | 44 | | 10 | .231 | .301 | 4 | 1 | P-215, 3B-13, OF-3, 2B-2, 1B-2 |

## Sammy Taylor

**TAYLOR, SAMUEL DOUGLAS**
B. Feb. 27, 1933, Woodruff, S. C.
BL TR 6'2"   185 lbs.

| | G | AB | H | 2B | 3B | HR | HR% | R | RBI | BB | SO | SB | BA | SA | PH AB | PH H | G by POS |
|---|---|---|---|---|---|---|---|---|---|---|---|---|---|---|---|---|---|
| 1958 CHI N | 96 | 301 | 78 | 12 | 2 | 6 | 2.0 | 30 | 36 | 27 | 46 | 2 | .259 | .372 | 12 | 4 | C-87 |
| 1959 | 110 | 353 | 95 | 13 | 2 | 13 | 3.7 | 41 | 43 | 35 | 47 | 1 | .269 | .428 | 9 | 1 | C-109 |
| 1960 | 74 | 150 | 31 | 9 | 0 | 3 | 2.0 | 14 | 17 | 6 | 18 | 0 | .207 | .327 | 36 | 6 | C-43 |
| 1961 | 89 | 235 | 56 | 8 | 2 | 8 | 3.4 | 26 | 23 | 23 | 39 | 0 | .238 | .391 | 14 | 0 | C-75 |
| 1962 2 teams | | CHI | N | (7G – | .133) | | NY | N | (68G – | .222) | | | | | | | | |
| " total | 75 | 173 | 37 | 5 | 2 | 3 | 1.7 | 12 | 21 | 26 | 20 | 0 | .214 | .318 | 16 | 3 | C-56 |
| 1963 3 teams | | NY | N | (22G – | .257) | | CIN | N | (3G – | .000) | | CLE | A | (4G – | .300) | | | |
| " total | 29 | 51 | 12 | 0 | 1 | 0 | 0.0 | 4 | 7 | 5 | 11 | 0 | .235 | .275 | 14 | 5 | C-17 |
| 6 yrs. | 473 | 1263 | 309 | 47 | 9 | 33 | 2.6 | 127 | 147 | 122 | 181 | 3 | .245 | .375 | 101 | 19 | C-387 |
| 5 yrs. | 376 | 1054 | 262 | 43 | 6 | 30 | 2.8 | 111 | 120 | 94 | 153 | 3 | .249 | .386 | 71 | 11 | C-320 |

## Tony Taylor

**TAYLOR, ANTONIO SANCHEZ**
B. Dec. 19, 1935, Central Alara, Cuba
BR TR 5'9"   170 lbs.

| | G | AB | H | 2B | 3B | HR | HR% | R | RBI | BB | SO | SB | BA | SA | PH AB | PH H | G by POS |
|---|---|---|---|---|---|---|---|---|---|---|---|---|---|---|---|---|---|
| 1958 CHI N | 140 | 497 | 117 | 15 | 3 | 6 | 1.2 | 63 | 27 | 40 | 93 | 21 | .235 | .314 | 0 | 0 | 2B-137, 3B-1 |
| 1959 | 150 | 624 | 175 | 30 | 8 | 8 | 1.3 | 96 | 38 | 45 | 86 | 23 | .280 | .393 | 0 | 0 | 2B-149, SS-2 |
| 1960 2 teams | | CHI | N | (19G – | .263) | | PHI | N | (127G – | .287) | | | | | | | | |
| " total | 146 | 581 | 165 | 25 | 7 | 5 | 0.9 | 80 | 44 | 41 | 98 | 26 | .284 | .377 | 2 | 0 | 2B-142, 3B-4 |
| 1961 PHI N | 106 | 400 | 100 | 17 | 3 | 2 | 0.5 | 47 | 26 | 29 | 59 | 11 | .250 | .323 | 14 | 3 | 2B-91, 3B-3 |
| 1962 | 152 | 625 | 162 | 21 | 5 | 7 | 1.1 | 87 | 43 | 68 | 82 | 20 | .259 | .342 | 2 | 1 | 2B-150, SS-2 |
| 1963 | 157 | 640 | 180 | 20 | 10 | 5 | 0.8 | 102 | 49 | 42 | 99 | 23 | .281 | .367 | 4 | 0 | 2B-149, 3B-13 |
| 1964 | 154 | 570 | 143 | 13 | 6 | 4 | 0.7 | 62 | 46 | 46 | 74 | 13 | .251 | .316 | 3 | 1 | 2B-150 |
| 1965 | 106 | 323 | 74 | 14 | 3 | 3 | 0.9 | 41 | 27 | 22 | 58 | 5 | .229 | .319 | 14 | 1 | 2B-86, 3B-5 |
| 1966 | 125 | 434 | 105 | 14 | 8 | 5 | 1.2 | 47 | 40 | 31 | 56 | 8 | .242 | .346 | 8 | 1 | 2B-68, 3B-52 |
| 1967 | 132 | 462 | 110 | 16 | 6 | 2 | 0.4 | 55 | 34 | 42 | 74 | 10 | .238 | .312 | 8 | 3 | 1B-58, 3B-44, 2B-42, SS-5 |
| 1968 | 145 | 547 | 137 | 20 | 2 | 3 | 0.5 | 59 | 38 | 39 | 60 | 22 | .250 | .311 | 3 | 0 | 3B-138, 2B-5, 1B-1 |
| 1969 | 138 | 557 | 146 | 24 | 5 | 3 | 0.5 | 68 | 30 | 42 | 62 | 19 | .262 | .339 | 5 | 2 | 3B-71, 2B-57, 1B-19 |
| 1970 | 124 | 439 | 132 | 26 | 6 | 9 | 2.1 | 74 | 55 | 50 | 67 | 9 | .301 | .462 | 14 | 4 | 2B-59, 3B-38, OF-18, SS-1 |
| 1971 2 teams | | PHI | N | (36G – | .234) | | DET | A | (55G – | .287) | | | | | | | | |
| " total | 91 | 288 | 77 | 12 | 3 | 4 | 1.4 | 36 | 24 | 21 | 21 | 7 | .267 | .372 | 18 | 5 | 2B-65, 3B-14, 1B-2 |
| 1972 DET A | 78 | 228 | 69 | 12 | 4 | 1 | 0.4 | 33 | 20 | 14 | 34 | 5 | .303 | .404 | 20 | 6 | 2B-67, 3B-8, 1B-1 |
| 1973 | 84 | 275 | 63 | 9 | 3 | 5 | 1.8 | 35 | 24 | 17 | 29 | 9 | .229 | .338 | 9 | 0 | 2B-72, 1B-6, 3B-4, DH-1 |
| 1974 PHI N | 62 | 64 | 21 | 4 | 0 | 2 | 3.1 | 5 | 13 | 6 | 6 | 0 | .328 | .484 | 46 | 17 | 1B-7, 3B-5, 2B-3 |
| 1975 | 79 | 103 | 25 | 5 | 1 | 1 | 1.0 | 13 | 14 | 17 | 18 | 3 | .243 | .340 | 54 | 12 | 3B-16, 1B-4, 2B-3 |
| 1976 | 26 | 23 | 6 | 1 | 0 | 0 | 0.0 | 2 | 3 | 1 | 7 | 0 | .261 | .304 | 21 | 5 | 2B-3, 1B-1 |
| 19 yrs. | 2195 | 7680 | 2007 | 298 | 86 | 75 | 1.0 | 1005 | 598 | 613 | 1083 | 234 | .261 | .352 | 245 | 63 | 2B-1498, 3B-417, 1B-89, OF-18, SS-8, DH-1 |
| 3 yrs. | 309 | 1197 | 312 | 48 | 14 | 15 | 1.3 | 173 | 74 | 93 | 191 | 46 | .261 | .362 | 0 | 0 | 2B-305, SS-2, 3B-1 |

LEAGUE CHAMPIONSHIP SERIES

| | G | AB | H | 2B | 3B | HR | HR% | R | RBI | BB | SO | SB | BA | SA | PH AB | PH H | G by POS |
|---|---|---|---|---|---|---|---|---|---|---|---|---|---|---|---|---|---|
| 1972 DET A | 4 | 15 | 2 | 2 | 0 | 0 | 0.0 | 0 | 0 | 0 | 2 | 0 | .133 | .267 | 0 | 0 | 2B-4 |

| | G | AB | H | 2B | 3B | HR | HR % | R | RBI | BB | SO | SB | BA | SA | Pinch Hit AB | Pinch Hit H | G by POS |
|---|---|---|---|---|---|---|---|---|---|---|---|---|---|---|---|---|---|

## Zack Taylor

**TAYLOR, JAMES WREN**     BR TR 5'11½" 180 lbs.
B. July 27, 1898, Yulee, Fla.     D. July 6, 1974, Orlando, Fla.
Manager 1946, 1948-51.

| | G | AB | H | 2B | 3B | HR | HR % | R | RBI | BB | SO | SB | BA | SA | AB | H | G by POS |
|---|---|---|---|---|---|---|---|---|---|---|---|---|---|---|---|---|---|
| 1920 BKN N | 9 | 13 | 5 | 2 | 0 | 0 | 0.0 | 3 | 5 | 0 | 2 | 0 | .385 | .538 | 0 | 0 | C-9 |
| 1921 | 30 | 102 | 20 | 0 | 2 | 0 | 0.0 | 6 | 8 | 1 | 8 | 2 | .196 | .235 | 0 | 0 | C-30 |
| 1922 | 7 | 14 | 3 | 0 | 0 | 0 | 0.0 | 0 | 2 | 1 | 1 | 0 | .214 | .214 | 1 | 0 | C-7 |
| 1923 | 96 | 337 | 97 | 11 | 6 | 0 | 0.0 | 29 | 46 | 9 | 13 | 2 | .288 | .356 | 11 | 4 | C-84 |
| 1924 | 99 | 345 | 100 | 9 | 4 | 1 | 0.3 | 36 | 39 | 14 | 14 | 0 | .290 | .348 | 6 | 2 | C-93 |
| 1925 | 109 | 352 | 109 | 16 | 4 | 3 | 0.9 | 33 | 44 | 17 | 19 | 0 | .310 | .403 | 12 | 2 | C-96 |
| 1926 BOS N | 125 | 432 | 110 | 22 | 3 | 0 | 0.0 | 36 | 42 | 28 | 27 | 1 | .255 | .319 | 1 | 0 | C-123 |
| 1927 2 teams | | BOS | N | (30G – | .240) | | NY | N | (83G – | .233) | | | | | | | |
| " total | 113 | 354 | 83 | 9 | 4 | 1 | 0.3 | 26 | 35 | 25 | 25 | 2 | .234 | .291 | 5 | 1 | C-108 |
| 1928 BOS N | 125 | 399 | 100 | 15 | 1 | 2 | 0.5 | 36 | 30 | 33 | 29 | 2 | .251 | .308 | 1 | 0 | C-124 |
| 1929 2 teams | | BOS | N | (34G – | .248) | | CHI | N | (64G – | .274) | | | | | | | |
| " total | 98 | 316 | 84 | 23 | 3 | 1 | 0.3 | 37 | 41 | 26 | 27 | 0 | .266 | .367 | 3 | 0 | C-95 |
| 1930 CHI N | 32 | 95 | 22 | 2 | 1 | 1 | 1.1 | 12 | 11 | 2 | 12 | 0 | .232 | .305 | 2 | 0 | C-28 |
| 1931 | 8 | 4 | 1 | 0 | 0 | 0 | 0.0 | 0 | 0 | 2 | 1 | 0 | .250 | .250 | 1 | 0 | C-5 |
| 1932 | 21 | 30 | 6 | 1 | 0 | 0 | 0.0 | 2 | 3 | 1 | 4 | 0 | .200 | .233 | 7 | 1 | C-14 |
| 1933 | 16 | 11 | 0 | 0 | 0 | 0 | 0.0 | 0 | 0 | 0 | 1 | 0 | .000 | .000 | 4 | 0 | C-12 |
| 1934 NY A | 4 | 7 | 1 | 0 | 0 | 0 | 0.0 | 0 | 0 | 0 | 1 | 0 | .143 | .143 | 1 | 0 | C-3 |
| 1935 BKN N | 26 | 54 | 7 | 3 | 0 | 0 | 0.0 | 2 | 5 | 2 | 8 | 0 | .130 | .185 | 0 | 0 | C-26 |
| 16 yrs. | 918 | 2865 | 748 | 113 | 28 | 9 | 0.3 | 258 | 311 | 161 | 192 | 9 | .261 | .329 | 55 | 10 | C-857 |
| 5 yrs. | 141 | 355 | 88 | 19 | 4 | 2 | 0.6 | 43 | 45 | 24 | 36 | 0 | .248 | .341 | 14 | 1 | C-123 |
| WORLD SERIES | | | | | | | | | | | | | | | | | |
| 1929 CHI N | 5 | 17 | 3 | 0 | 0 | 0 | 0.0 | 0 | 3 | 0 | 3 | 0 | .176 | .176 | 0 | 0 | C-5 |

## Patsy Tebeau

**TEBEAU, OLIVER WENDELL**     BR TR 5'8" 163 lbs.
Brother of White Wings Tebeau.
B. Dec. 5, 1864, St. Louis, Mo.     D. May 15, 1918, St. Louis, Mo.
Manager 1890-1900.

| | G | AB | H | 2B | 3B | HR | HR % | R | RBI | BB | SO | SB | BA | SA | AB | H | G by POS |
|---|---|---|---|---|---|---|---|---|---|---|---|---|---|---|---|---|---|
| 1887 CHI N | 20 | 68 | 11 | 3 | 0 | 0 | 0.0 | 8 | 10 | 4 | 4 | 8 | .162 | .206 | 0 | 0 | 3B-20 |
| 1889 CLE N | 136 | 521 | 147 | 20 | 6 | 8 | 1.5 | 72 | 76 | 37 | 41 | 26 | .282 | .390 | 0 | 0 | 3B-136 |
| 1890 CLE P | 110 | 450 | 135 | 26 | 6 | 5 | 1.1 | 86 | 74 | 34 | 20 | 14 | .300 | .418 | 0 | 0 | 3B-110 |
| 1891 CLE N | 61 | 249 | 65 | 8 | 3 | 1 | 0.4 | 38 | 41 | 16 | 13 | 12 | .261 | .329 | 0 | 0 | 3B-61, OF-1 |
| 1892 | 86 | 340 | 83 | 13 | 3 | 2 | 0.6 | 47 | 49 | 23 | 34 | 6 | .244 | .318 | 0 | 0 | 3B-74, 2B-5, 1B-4, SS-3 |
| 1893 | 116 | 486 | 160 | 32 | 8 | 2 | 0.4 | 90 | 102 | 32 | 11 | 19 | .329 | .440 | 0 | 0 | 1B-57, 3B-56, 2B-3 |
| 1894 | 125 | 523 | 158 | 23 | 7 | 3 | 0.6 | 82 | 89 | 35 | 35 | 30 | .302 | .390 | 0 | 0 | 1B-115, 2B-10, 3B-2, SS-1 |
| 1895 | 63 | 264 | 84 | 13 | 2 | 2 | 0.8 | 50 | 52 | 16 | 18 | 8 | .318 | .405 | 0 | 0 | 1B-49, 2B-9, 3B-6 |
| 1896 | 132 | 543 | 146 | 22 | 6 | 2 | 0.4 | 56 | 94 | 21 | 22 | 20 | .269 | .343 | 0 | 0 | 1B-122, 3B-7, 2B-5, SS-1, P-1 |
| 1897 | 109 | 412 | 110 | 15 | 9 | 0 | 0.0 | 62 | 59 | 30 | | 11 | .267 | .347 | 0 | 0 | 1B-92, 2B-18, 3B-2, SS-1 |
| 1898 | 131 | 477 | 123 | 11 | 4 | 1 | 0.2 | 53 | 63 | 53 | | 5 | .258 | .304 | 0 | 0 | 1B-91, 2B-34, SS-7, 3B-3 |
| 1899 STL N | 77 | 281 | 69 | 10 | 3 | 1 | 0.4 | 27 | 26 | 18 | | 5 | .246 | .313 | 0 | 0 | 1B-65, SS-11, 3B-1, 2B-1 |
| 1900 | 1 | 4 | 0 | 0 | 0 | 0 | 0.0 | 0 | 0 | 0 | | 0 | .000 | .000 | 0 | 0 | SS-1 |
| 13 yrs. | 1167 | 4618 | 1291 | 196 | 57 | 27 | 0.6 | 671 | 735 | 319 | 198 | 164 | .280 | .364 | 0 | 0 | 1B-595, 3B-478, 2B-85, SS-25, OF-1, P-1 |
| 1 yr. | 20 | 68 | 11 | 3 | 0 | 0 | 0.0 | 8 | 10 | 4 | 4 | 8 | .162 | .206 | 0 | 0 | 3B-20 |

## Adonis Terry

**TERRY, WILLIAM H**     BR TR 168 lbs.
B. Aug. 7, 1864, Westfield, Mass.     D. Feb. 24, 1915, Milwaukee, Wis.

| | G | AB | H | 2B | 3B | HR | HR % | R | RBI | BB | SO | SB | BA | SA | AB | H | G by POS |
|---|---|---|---|---|---|---|---|---|---|---|---|---|---|---|---|---|---|
| 1884 BKN AA | 68 | 240 | 56 | 10 | 3 | 0 | 0.0 | 16 | | 8 | | | .233 | .300 | 0 | 0 | P-57, OF-13 |
| 1885 | 71 | 264 | 45 | 1 | 3 | 1 | 0.4 | 23 | | 10 | | | .170 | .208 | 0 | 0 | OF-47, P-25, 3B-1 |
| 1886 | 75 | 299 | 71 | 8 | 9 | 2 | 0.7 | 34 | | 10 | | | .237 | .344 | 0 | 0 | P-34, OF-32, SS-13 |
| 1887 | 86 | 352 | 103 | 6 | 10 | 3 | 0.9 | 56 | | 16 | | 27 | .293 | .392 | 0 | 0 | OF-49, P-40, SS-2 |
| 1888 | 30 | 115 | 29 | 6 | 0 | 0 | 0.0 | 13 | 8 | 5 | | 7 | .252 | .304 | 0 | 0 | P-23, OF-7, 1B-2 |
| 1889 | 49 | 160 | 48 | 6 | 6 | 2 | 1.3 | 29 | 26 | 14 | 14 | 8 | .300 | .450 | 0 | 0 | P-41, 1B-10 |
| 1890 BKN N | 99 | 363 | 101 | 17 | 9 | 4 | 1.1 | 63 | 59 | 40 | 34 | 32 | .278 | .408 | 0 | 0 | OF-54, P-46, 1B-1 |
| 1891 | 30 | 91 | 19 | 7 | 1 | 0 | 0.0 | 10 | 6 | 9 | 26 | 4 | .209 | .308 | 0 | 0 | P-25, OF-5 |
| 1892 2 teams | | BAL | N | (1G – | .000) | | PIT | N | (31G – | .160) | | | | | | | |
| " total | 32 | 104 | 16 | 0 | 4 | 2 | 1.9 | 10 | 11 | 10 | 12 | 2 | .154 | .288 | 0 | 0 | P-31, OF-1 |
| 1893 PIT N | 26 | 71 | 18 | 4 | 3 | 0 | 0.0 | 9 | 11 | 3 | 11 | 1 | .254 | .394 | 0 | 0 | P-26 |
| 1894 2 teams | | PIT | N | (1G – | .000) | | CHI | N | (30G – | .347) | | | | | | | |
| " total | 31 | 95 | 33 | 4 | 2 | 0 | 0.0 | 19 | 17 | 11 | 12 | 3 | .347 | .432 | 0 | 0 | P-24, OF-7, 1B-2 |
| 1895 CHI N | 40 | 137 | 30 | 3 | 2 | 1 | 0.7 | 18 | 10 | 2 | 17 | 1 | .219 | .292 | 0 | 0 | P-38, OF-1, SS-1 |
| 1896 | 30 | 99 | 26 | 4 | 2 | 0 | 0.0 | 14 | 15 | 8 | 12 | 4 | .263 | .343 | 0 | 0 | P-30 |
| 1897 | 1 | 3 | 0 | 0 | 0 | 0 | 0.0 | 1 | 0 | 0 | | 0 | .000 | .000 | 0 | 0 | P-1 |
| 14 yrs. | 668 | 2393 | 595 | 76 | 54 | 15 | 0.6 | 315 | 162 | 146 | 138 | 89 | .249 | .344 | 0 | 0 | P-441, OF-216, SS-16, 1B-15, 3B-1 |
| 4 yrs. | 101 | 334 | 89 | 11 | 6 | 1 | 0.3 | 52 | 42 | 21 | 41 | 8 | .266 | .344 | 0 | 0 | P-92, OF-8, 1B-2, SS-1 |

## Zeb Terry

**TERRY, ZEBULON ALEXANDER**     BR TR 5'8" 129 lbs.
B. June 17, 1891, Denison, Tex.

| | G | AB | H | 2B | 3B | HR | HR % | R | RBI | BB | SO | SB | BA | SA | AB | H | G by POS |
|---|---|---|---|---|---|---|---|---|---|---|---|---|---|---|---|---|---|
| 1916 CHI A | 94 | 269 | 51 | 8 | 4 | 0 | 0.0 | 20 | 17 | 33 | 36 | 4 | .190 | .249 | 1 | 1 | SS-93 |
| 1917 | 2 | 1 | 0 | 0 | 0 | 0 | 0.0 | 0 | 2 | 0 | 0 | 0 | .000 | .000 | 0 | 0 | SS-1 |
| 1918 BOS N | 28 | 105 | 32 | 2 | 0 | 0 | 0.0 | 17 | 8 | 8 | 14 | 1 | .305 | .362 | 0 | 0 | SS-27 |
| 1919 PIT N | 129 | 472 | 107 | 12 | 6 | 0 | 0.0 | 46 | 27 | 31 | 26 | 12 | .227 | .278 | 2 | 1 | SS-127 |
| 1920 CHI N | 133 | 496 | 139 | 26 | 9 | 0 | 0.0 | 56 | 52 | 44 | 22 | 12 | .280 | .369 | 0 | 0 | SS-70, 2B-63 |
| 1921 | 123 | 488 | 134 | 18 | 1 | 2 | 0.4 | 59 | 45 | 27 | 19 | 1 | .275 | .328 | 1 | 0 | 2B-123 |
| 1922 | 131 | 496 | 142 | 24 | 2 | 0 | 0.0 | 56 | 67 | 34 | 16 | 2 | .286 | .343 | 0 | 0 | 2B-125, SS-4, 3B-3 |
| 7 yrs. | 640 | 2327 | 605 | 90 | 24 | 2 | 0.1 | 254 | 216 | 179 | 133 | 32 | .260 | .322 | 4 | 2 | SS-322, 2B-311, 3B-3 |
| 3 yrs. | 387 | 1480 | 415 | 68 | 12 | 2 | 0.1 | 171 | 164 | 105 | 57 | 15 | .280 | .347 | 1 | 0 | 2B-311, SS-74, 3B-3 |

| | G | AB | H | 2B | 3B | HR | HR % | R | RBI | BB | SO | SB | BA | SA | Pinch Hit AB | Pinch Hit H | G by POS |
|---|---|---|---|---|---|---|---|---|---|---|---|---|---|---|---|---|---|

## Wayne Terwilliger

**TERWILLIGER, WILLARD WAYNE (Twig)**
B. June 27, 1925, Clare, Mich.
BR TR 5'11" 165 lbs.

| | G | AB | H | 2B | 3B | HR | HR% | R | RBI | BB | SO | SB | BA | SA | AB | H | G by POS |
|---|---|---|---|---|---|---|---|---|---|---|---|---|---|---|---|---|---|
| 1949 CHI N | 36 | 112 | 25 | 2 | 1 | 2 | 1.8 | 11 | 10 | 16 | 22 | 0 | .223 | .313 | 1 | 0 | 2B-34 |
| 1950 | 133 | 480 | 116 | 22 | 3 | 10 | 2.1 | 63 | 32 | 43 | 63 | 13 | .242 | .363 | 4 | 1 | 2B-126, OF-1, 3B-1, 1B-1 |
| 1951 2 teams | CHI N (50G – .214) | | | | | BKN N (37G – .280) | | | | | | | | | | | |
| " total | 87 | 242 | 55 | 7 | 0 | 0 | 0.0 | 37 | 14 | 37 | 28 | 4 | .227 | .256 | 7 | 3 | 2B-73, 3B-1 |
| 1953 WAS A | 134 | 464 | 117 | 24 | 4 | 4 | 0.9 | 62 | 46 | 64 | 65 | 7 | .252 | .347 | 1 | 1 | 2B-133 |
| 1954 | 106 | 337 | 70 | 10 | 1 | 3 | 0.9 | 42 | 24 | 32 | 40 | 3 | .208 | .270 | 1 | 0 | 2B-90, 3B-10, SS-3 |
| 1955 NY N | 80 | 257 | 66 | 16 | 1 | 1 | 0.4 | 29 | 18 | 36 | 42 | 0 | .257 | .339 | 0 | 0 | 2B-78, SS-1, 3B-1 |
| 1956 | 14 | 18 | 4 | 1 | 0 | 0 | 0.0 | 0 | 0 | 0 | 5 | 0 | .222 | .278 | 4 | 0 | 2B-6 |
| 1959 KC A | 74 | 180 | 48 | 11 | 0 | 2 | 1.1 | 27 | 18 | 19 | 31 | 2 | .267 | .361 | 6 | 0 | 2B-63, SS-2, 3B-1 |
| 1960 | 2 | 1 | 0 | 0 | 0 | 0 | 0.0 | 0 | 0 | 0 | 0 | 0 | .000 | .000 | 0 | 0 | 2B-2 |
| 9 yrs. | 666 | 2091 | 501 | 93 | 10 | 22 | 1.1 | 271 | 162 | 247 | 296 | 31 | .240 | .325 | 24 | 5 | 2B-605, 3B-14, SS-6, OF-1, 1B-1 |
| 3 yrs. | 219 | 784 | 182 | 30 | 4 | 12 | 1.5 | 100 | 52 | 88 | 106 | 16 | .232 | .327 | 5 | 1 | 2B-209, OF-1, 3B-1, 1B-1 |

## Moe Thacker

**THACKER, MORRIS BENTON**
B. May 21, 1934, Louisville, Ky.
BR TR 6'3" 205 lbs.

| | G | AB | H | 2B | 3B | HR | HR% | R | RBI | BB | SO | SB | BA | SA | AB | H | G by POS |
|---|---|---|---|---|---|---|---|---|---|---|---|---|---|---|---|---|---|
| 1958 CHI N | 11 | 24 | 6 | 1 | 0 | 2 | 8.3 | 4 | 3 | 1 | 7 | 0 | .250 | .542 | 2 | 1 | C-9 |
| 1960 | 54 | 90 | 14 | 1 | 0 | 0 | 0.0 | 5 | 6 | 14 | 20 | 1 | .156 | .167 | 4 | 1 | C-50 |
| 1961 | 25 | 35 | 6 | 0 | 0 | 0 | 0.0 | 3 | 2 | 11 | 11 | 0 | .171 | .171 | 0 | 0 | C-25 |
| 1962 | 65 | 107 | 20 | 5 | 0 | 0 | 0.0 | 8 | 9 | 14 | 40 | 0 | .187 | .234 | 1 | 0 | C-65 |
| 1963 STL N | 3 | 4 | 0 | 0 | 0 | 0 | 0.0 | 0 | 0 | 0 | 3 | 0 | .000 | .000 | 0 | 0 | C-3 |
| 5 yrs. | 158 | 260 | 46 | 7 | 0 | 2 | 0.8 | 20 | 20 | 40 | 81 | 1 | .177 | .227 | 7 | 2 | C-152 |
| 4 yrs. | 155 | 256 | 46 | 7 | 0 | 2 | 0.8 | 20 | 20 | 40 | 78 | 1 | .180 | .230 | 7 | 2 | C-149 |

## Frank Thomas

**THOMAS, FRANK JOSEPH**
B. June 11, 1929, Pittsburgh, Pa.
BR TR 6'3" 200 lbs.

| | G | AB | H | 2B | 3B | HR | HR% | R | RBI | BB | SO | SB | BA | SA | AB | H | G by POS |
|---|---|---|---|---|---|---|---|---|---|---|---|---|---|---|---|---|---|
| 1951 PIT N | 39 | 148 | 39 | 9 | 2 | 2 | 1.4 | 21 | 16 | 9 | 15 | 0 | .264 | .392 | 3 | 1 | OF-37 |
| 1952 | 6 | 21 | 2 | 0 | 0 | 0 | 0.0 | 1 | 0 | 1 | 1 | 0 | .095 | .095 | 0 | 0 | OF-5 |
| 1953 | 128 | 455 | 116 | 22 | 1 | 30 | 6.6 | 68 | 102 | 50 | 93 | 1 | .255 | .505 | 9 | 1 | OF-118 |
| 1954 | 153 | 577 | 172 | 32 | 7 | 23 | 4.0 | 81 | 94 | 51 | 74 | 3 | .298 | .497 | 1 | 1 | OF-153 |
| 1955 | 142 | 510 | 125 | 16 | 2 | 25 | 4.9 | 72 | 72 | 60 | 76 | 2 | .245 | .431 | 3 | 1 | OF-139 |
| 1956 | 157 | 588 | 166 | 24 | 3 | 25 | 4.3 | 69 | 80 | 36 | 61 | 0 | .282 | .461 | 2 | 0 | 3B-111, OF-56, 2B-4 |
| 1957 | 151 | 594 | 172 | 30 | 1 | 23 | 3.9 | 72 | 89 | 44 | 66 | 3 | .290 | .460 | 0 | 0 | 1B-71, OF-59, 3B-31 |
| 1958 | 149 | 562 | 158 | 26 | 4 | 35 | 6.2 | 89 | 109 | 42 | 79 | 0 | .281 | .528 | 1 | 0 | 3B-139, OF-8, 1B-2 |
| 1959 CIN N | 108 | 374 | 84 | 18 | 2 | 12 | 3.2 | 41 | 47 | 27 | 56 | 0 | .225 | .380 | 8 | 1 | 3B-64, OF-33, 1B-14 |
| 1960 CHI N | 135 | 479 | 114 | 12 | 1 | 21 | 4.4 | 54 | 64 | 28 | 74 | 1 | .238 | .399 | 11 | 4 | 1B-50, OF-49, 3B-33 |
| 1961 2 teams | CHI N (15G – .260) | | | | | MIL N (124G – .284) | | | | | | | | | | | |
| " total | 139 | 473 | 133 | 15 | 3 | 27 | 5.7 | 65 | 73 | 31 | 78 | 2 | .281 | .497 | 11 | 1 | OF-119, 1B-17 |
| 1962 NY N | 156 | 571 | 152 | 23 | 3 | 34 | 6.0 | 69 | 94 | 48 | 95 | 2 | .266 | .496 | 11 | 4 | OF-126, 1B-11, 3B-10 |
| 1963 | 126 | 420 | 109 | 9 | 1 | 15 | 3.6 | 34 | 60 | 33 | 48 | 0 | .260 | .393 | 15 | 4 | OF-96, 1B-15, 3B-1 |
| 1964 2 teams | NY N (60G – .254) | | | | | PHI N (39G – .294) | | | | | | | | | | | |
| " total | 99 | 340 | 92 | 17 | 1 | 10 | 2.9 | 39 | 45 | 15 | 41 | 1 | .271 | .415 | 14 | 4 | 1B-58, OF-31, 3B-2 |
| 1965 3 teams | PHI N (35G – .260) | | | | | HOU N (23G – .172) | | | | MIL N (15G – .212) | | | | | | | |
| " total | 73 | 168 | 37 | 9 | 0 | 4 | 2.4 | 17 | 17 | 9 | 36 | 0 | .220 | .345 | 29 | 3 | 1B-33, OF-16, 3B-3 |
| 1966 CHI N | 5 | 5 | 0 | 0 | 0 | 0 | 0.0 | 0 | 0 | 0 | 1 | 0 | .000 | .000 | 5 | 0 | |
| 16 yrs. | 1766 | 6285 | 1671 | 262 | 31 | 286 | 4.6 | 792 | 962 | 484 | 894 | 15 | .266 | .454 | 123 | 25 | OF-1045, 3B-394, 1B-271, 2B-4 |
| 3 yrs. | 155 | 534 | 127 | 14 | 1 | 23 | 4.3 | 61 | 70 | 30 | 83 | 1 | .238 | .397 | 18 | 4 | OF-59, 1B-56, 3B-33 |

## Lee Thomas

**THOMAS, JAMES LEROY**
B. Feb. 5, 1936, Peoria, Ill.
BL TL 6'2" 195 lbs.

| | G | AB | H | 2B | 3B | HR | HR% | R | RBI | BB | SO | SB | BA | SA | AB | H | G by POS |
|---|---|---|---|---|---|---|---|---|---|---|---|---|---|---|---|---|---|
| 1961 2 teams | NY A (2G – .500) | | | | | LA A (130G – .284) | | | | | | | | | | | |
| " total | 132 | 452 | 129 | 11 | 5 | 24 | 5.3 | 77 | 70 | 47 | 74 | 0 | .285 | .491 | 18 | 5 | OF-86, 1B-34 |
| 1962 LA A | 160 | 583 | 169 | 21 | 2 | 26 | 4.5 | 88 | 104 | 55 | 74 | 6 | .290 | .467 | 3 | 0 | 1B-90, OF-74 |
| 1963 | 149 | 528 | 116 | 12 | 6 | 9 | 1.7 | 52 | 55 | 53 | 82 | 6 | .220 | .316 | 6 | 2 | 1B-104, OF-43 |
| 1964 2 teams | LA A (47G – .273) | | | | | BOS A (107G – .257) | | | | | | | | | | | |
| " total | 154 | 573 | 150 | 27 | 3 | 15 | 2.6 | 58 | 66 | 52 | 51 | 3 | .262 | .398 | 1 | 0 | OF-154, 1B-2 |
| 1965 BOS A | 151 | 521 | 141 | 27 | 4 | 22 | 4.2 | 74 | 75 | 72 | 42 | 6 | .271 | .464 | 9 | 1 | 1B-127, OF-20 |
| 1966 2 teams | ATL N (39G – .198) | | | | | CHI N (75G – .242) | | | | | | | | | | | |
| " total | 114 | 275 | 61 | 5 | 1 | 7 | 2.5 | 26 | 24 | 24 | 30 | 1 | .222 | .324 | 33 | 9 | 1B-56, OF-17 |
| 1967 CHI N | 77 | 191 | 42 | 4 | 1 | 2 | 1.0 | 16 | 23 | 15 | 22 | 1 | .220 | .283 | 22 | 4 | OF-43, 1B-10 |
| 1968 HOU N | 90 | 201 | 39 | 4 | 0 | 1 | 0.5 | 14 | 11 | 14 | 22 | 2 | .194 | .229 | 39 | 7 | OF-48, 1B-2 |
| 8 yrs. | 1027 | 3324 | 847 | 111 | 22 | 106 | 3.2 | 405 | 428 | 332 | 397 | 25 | .255 | .397 | 131 | 28 | OF-485, 1B-425 |
| 2 yrs. | 152 | 340 | 78 | 8 | 1 | 3 | 0.9 | 31 | 32 | 29 | 37 | 1 | .229 | .285 | 53 | 12 | OF-60, 1B-30 |

## Red Thomas

**THOMAS, ROBERT WILLIAM**
B. Apr. 25, 1898, Hargrove, Ala.   D. Mar. 29, 1962, Fremont, Ohio
BR TR 5'11" 165 lbs.

| | G | AB | H | 2B | 3B | HR | HR% | R | RBI | BB | SO | SB | BA | SA | AB | H | G by POS |
|---|---|---|---|---|---|---|---|---|---|---|---|---|---|---|---|---|---|
| 1921 CHI N | 8 | 30 | 8 | 3 | 0 | 1 | 3.3 | 5 | 5 | 4 | 5 | 0 | .267 | .467 | 0 | 0 | OF-8 |

## Scot Thompson

**THOMPSON, VERNON SCOT**
B. Dec. 7, 1955, Grove City, Pa.
BL TL 6'3" 195 lbs.

| | G | AB | H | 2B | 3B | HR | HR% | R | RBI | BB | SO | SB | BA | SA | AB | H | G by POS |
|---|---|---|---|---|---|---|---|---|---|---|---|---|---|---|---|---|---|
| 1978 CHI N | 19 | 36 | 15 | 3 | 0 | 0 | 0.0 | 7 | 2 | 2 | 4 | 0 | .417 | .500 | 12 | 6 | OF-5, 1B-2 |
| 1979 | 128 | 346 | 100 | 13 | 5 | 2 | 0.6 | 36 | 29 | 17 | 37 | 4 | .289 | .373 | 33 | 12 | OF-100 |
| 1980 | 102 | 226 | 48 | 10 | 1 | 2 | 0.9 | 26 | 13 | 28 | 31 | 6 | .212 | .292 | 21 | 6 | OF-66, 1B-12 |
| 1981 | 57 | 115 | 19 | 5 | 0 | 0 | 0.0 | 8 | 8 | 7 | 8 | 2 | .165 | .209 | 22 | 2 | OF-30, 1B-3 |
| 1982 | 49 | 74 | 27 | 5 | 1 | 0 | 0.0 | 11 | 7 | 5 | 4 | 0 | .365 | .459 | 27 | 7 | OF-23, 1B-4 |
| 1983 | 53 | 88 | 17 | 3 | 1 | 0 | 0.0 | 4 | 10 | 3 | 14 | 0 | .193 | .250 | 28 | 6 | OF-29, 1B-1 |
| 1984 SF N | 120 | 245 | 75 | 7 | 1 | 1 | 0.4 | 30 | 31 | 30 | 26 | 5 | .306 | .355 | 31 | 5 | 1B-87, OF-6 |
| 1985 2 teams | SF N (64G – .207) | | | | | MON N (34G – .281) | | | | | | | | | | | |
| " total | 98 | 143 | 32 | 6 | 0 | 0 | 0.0 | 10 | 10 | 5 | 17 | 0 | .224 | .266 | 62 | 9 | 1B-27, OF-3 |
| 8 yrs. | 626 | 1273 | 333 | 52 | 9 | 5 | 0.4 | 132 | 110 | 97 | 141 | 17 | .262 | .328 | 236 | 53 | OF-262, 1B-136 |
| 6 yrs. | 408 | 885 | 226 | 39 | 8 | 4 | 0.5 | 92 | 69 | 62 | 98 | 12 | .255 | .331 | 143 | 39 | OF-253, 1B-22 |
| | | | | | | | | | | | | | | | 5th | 5th | |

The pennant-winning clubs of the 1930s featured this trio: Billy Herman *(left),* who racked a club-record 57 doubles in '35, then did it again in '36; Stan Hack *(below left),* who guarded the hot corner at Wrigley for 16 seasons; and Lon Warneke *(below),* the Arkansas Humming Bird, whose league-leading figures in wins, winning percentage, ERA, and shutouts paced the '32 National League champs.

*(George Brace photo)*

Randy Hundley *(left)* was solid as a rock behind the plate; he set an all-time record by catching 160 games in 1968, averaged 153 games a year behind the plate from 1966 to 1969, and probably never recovered from the overwork. Ferguson Jenkins *(below)* bloomed on those teams, winning 20 or more for six straight seasons. His pitching was an awesome blend of power and control: he is the only pitcher in baseball history with more than three thousand strikeouts and fewer than one thousand walks.

*(George Brace photo)*

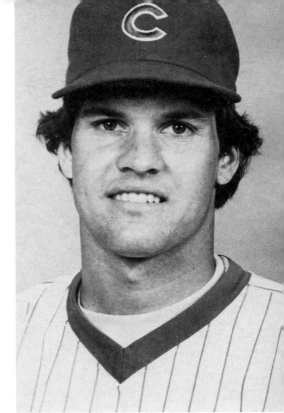

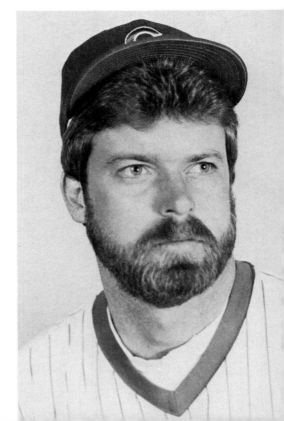

And then there was 1984. Leon Durham *(above)* hit 23 homers and drove in 96 runs, living up to the promise that led the Cubs to trade away Bruce Sutter to get him; Ryne Sandberg *(above right)* combined power, average, speed, and defense, winning the MVP and playing the game about as well as it can be played; Rick Sutcliffe *(right)* joined in June, went 16–1, and was all but unhittable down the stretch.

Baseball's crown jewel—one of the two places that still rates the appellation "ball park." Wrigley Field is that rarity today: you can see the players' faces, smell the fresh-mowed grass, and sense the long history, all under God's own sunshine. Long live Wrigley Field!

| | G | AB | H | 2B | 3B | HR | HR % | R | RBI | BB | SO | SB | BA | SA | Pinch Hit AB | Pinch Hit H | G by POS |
|---|---|---|---|---|---|---|---|---|---|---|---|---|---|---|---|---|---|

## Bobby Thomson

**THOMSON, ROBERT BROWN (The Staten Island Scot)**     BR TR 6'2"   180 lbs.
B. Oct. 25, 1923, Glasgow, Scotland

| | G | AB | H | 2B | 3B | HR | HR % | R | RBI | BB | SO | SB | BA | SA | AB | H | G by POS |
|---|---|---|---|---|---|---|---|---|---|---|---|---|---|---|---|---|---|
| 1946 NY N | 18 | 54 | 17 | 4 | 1 | 2 | 3.7 | 8 | 9 | 4 | 5 | 0 | .315 | .537 | 2 | 0 | 3B-16 |
| 1947 | 138 | 545 | 154 | 26 | 5 | 29 | 5.3 | 105 | 85 | 40 | 78 | 1 | .283 | .508 | 3 | 0 | OF-127, 2B-9 |
| 1948 | 138 | 471 | 117 | 20 | 2 | 16 | 3.4 | 75 | 63 | 30 | 77 | 2 | .248 | .401 | 9 | 3 | OF-125 |
| 1949 | 156 | 641 | 198 | 35 | 9 | 27 | 4.2 | 99 | 109 | 44 | 45 | 10 | .309 | .518 | 0 | 0 | OF-156 |
| 1950 | 149 | 563 | 142 | 22 | 7 | 25 | 4.4 | 79 | 85 | 55 | 45 | 3 | .252 | .449 | 0 | 0 | OF-149 |
| 1951 | 148 | 518 | 152 | 27 | 8 | 32 | 6.2 | 89 | 101 | 73 | 57 | 5 | .293 | .562 | 2 | 0 | OF-77, 3B-69 |
| 1952 | 153 | 608 | 164 | 29 | 14 | 24 | 3.9 | 89 | 108 | 52 | 74 | 5 | .270 | .482 | 0 | 0 | 3B-91, OF-63 |
| 1953 | 154 | 608 | 175 | 22 | 6 | 26 | 4.3 | 80 | 106 | 43 | 57 | 4 | .288 | .472 | 0 | 0 | OF-154 |
| 1954 MIL N | 43 | 99 | 23 | 3 | 0 | 2 | 2.0 | 7 | 15 | 12 | 29 | 0 | .232 | .323 | 14 | 5 | OF-26 |
| 1955 | 101 | 343 | 88 | 12 | 3 | 12 | 3.5 | 40 | 56 | 34 | 52 | 2 | .257 | .414 | 13 | 2 | OF-91 |
| 1956 | 142 | 451 | 106 | 10 | 4 | 20 | 4.4 | 59 | 74 | 43 | 75 | 2 | .235 | .408 | 5 | 0 | OF-136, 3B-3 |
| 1957 2 teams | | MIL N (41G – .236) | | | | NY N (81G – .242) | | | | | | | | | | | |
| " total | 122 | 363 | 87 | 12 | 7 | 12 | 3.3 | 39 | 61 | 27 | 66 | 3 | .240 | .410 | 13 | 2 | OF-109, 3B-1 |
| 1958 CHI N | 152 | 547 | 155 | 27 | 5 | 21 | 3.8 | 67 | 82 | 56 | 76 | 0 | .283 | .466 | 1 | 1 | OF-148, 3B-4 |
| 1959 | 122 | 374 | 97 | 15 | 2 | 11 | 2.9 | 55 | 52 | 35 | 50 | 1 | .259 | .398 | 9 | 4 | OF-116 |
| 1960 2 teams | | BOS A (40G – .263) | | | | BAL A (3G – .000) | | | | | | | | | | | |
| " total | 43 | 120 | 30 | 3 | 1 | 5 | 4.2 | 12 | 20 | 11 | 18 | 0 | .250 | .417 | 13 | 3 | OF-29, 1B-1 |
| 15 yrs. | 1779 | 6305 | 1705 | 267 | 74 | 264 | 4.2 | 903 | 1026 | 559 | 804 | 38 | .270 | .462 | 84 | 20 | OF-1506, 3B-184, 2B-9, 1B-1 |
| 2 yrs. | 274 | 921 | 252 | 42 | 7 | 32 | 3.5 | 122 | 134 | 91 | 126 | 1 | .274 | .439 | 10 | 5 | OF-264, 3B-4 |

**WORLD SERIES**

| | G | AB | H | 2B | 3B | HR | HR % | R | RBI | BB | SO | SB | BA | SA | AB | H | G by POS |
|---|---|---|---|---|---|---|---|---|---|---|---|---|---|---|---|---|---|
| 1951 NY N | 6 | 21 | 5 | 1 | 0 | 0 | 0.0 | 1 | 2 | 5 | 0 | 0 | .238 | .286 | 0 | 0 | 3B-6 |

## Andre Thornton

**THORNTON, ANDRE**     BR TR 6'3"   200 lbs.
B. Aug. 13, 1949, Tuskegee, Ala.

| | G | AB | H | 2B | 3B | HR | HR % | R | RBI | BB | SO | SB | BA | SA | AB | H | G by POS |
|---|---|---|---|---|---|---|---|---|---|---|---|---|---|---|---|---|---|
| 1973 CHI N | 17 | 35 | 7 | 3 | 0 | 0 | 0.0 | 3 | 2 | 7 | 9 | 0 | .200 | .286 | 9 | 3 | 1B-9 |
| 1974 | 107 | 303 | 79 | 16 | 4 | 10 | 3.3 | 41 | 46 | 48 | 50 | 2 | .261 | .439 | 19 | 6 | 1B-90, 3B-1 |
| 1975 | 120 | 372 | 109 | 21 | 4 | 18 | 4.8 | 70 | 60 | 88 | 63 | 3 | .293 | .516 | 9 | 1 | 1B-113, 3B-2 |
| 1976 2 teams | | CHI N (27G – .200) | | | | MON N (69G – .191) | | | | | | | | | | | |
| " total | 96 | 268 | 52 | 11 | 2 | 11 | 4.1 | 28 | 38 | 48 | 46 | 4 | .194 | .373 | 21 | 4 | 1B-68, OF-11 |
| 1977 CLE A | 131 | 433 | 114 | 20 | 5 | 28 | 6.5 | 77 | 70 | 70 | 82 | 3 | .263 | .527 | 7 | 1 | 1B-117, DH-9 |
| 1978 | 145 | 508 | 133 | 22 | 4 | 33 | 6.5 | 97 | 105 | 93 | 72 | 4 | .262 | .516 | 1 | 1 | 1B-145 |
| 1979 | 143 | 515 | 120 | 31 | 1 | 26 | 5.0 | 89 | 93 | 90 | 93 | 5 | .233 | .449 | 0 | 0 | 1B-130, DH-13 |
| 1981 | 69 | 226 | 54 | 12 | 0 | 6 | 2.7 | 22 | 30 | 23 | 37 | 3 | .239 | .372 | 6 | 3 | DH-53, 1B-11 |
| 1982 | 161 | 589 | 161 | 26 | 1 | 32 | 5.4 | 90 | 116 | 109 | 81 | 6 | .273 | .484 | 0 | 0 | DH-152, 1B-8 |
| 1983 | 141 | 508 | 143 | 27 | 1 | 17 | 3.3 | 78 | 77 | 87 | 72 | 4 | .281 | .439 | 2 | 0 | DH-114, 1B-27 |
| 1984 | 155 | 587 | 159 | 26 | 0 | 33 | 5.6 | 91 | 99 | 91 | 79 | 6 | .271 | .484 | 0 | 0 | DH-144, 1B-11 |
| 1985 | 124 | 461 | 109 | 13 | 0 | 22 | 4.8 | 49 | 88 | 47 | 75 | 3 | .236 | .408 | 2 | 1 | DH-122 |
| 12 yrs. | 1409 | 4805 | 1240 | 228 | 22 | 236 | 4.9 | 735 | 824 | 801 | 759 | 43 | .258 | .462 | 76 | 21 | 1B-729, DH-607, OF-11, 3B-3 |
| 4 yrs. | 271 | 795 | 212 | 46 | 8 | 30 | 3.8 | 122 | 122 | 163 | 136 | 7 | .267 | .458 | 41 | 11 | 1B-237, 3B-3 |

## Walter Thornton

**THORNTON, WALTER MILLER**     TL 6'1"   180 lbs.
B. Feb. 18, 1875, Lewiston, Me.    D. July 14, 1960, Los Angeles, Calif.

| | G | AB | H | 2B | 3B | HR | HR % | R | RBI | BB | SO | SB | BA | SA | AB | H | G by POS |
|---|---|---|---|---|---|---|---|---|---|---|---|---|---|---|---|---|---|
| 1895 CHI N | 8 | 22 | 7 | 1 | 0 | 1 | 4.5 | 4 | 7 | 3 | 1 | 0 | .318 | .500 | 0 | 0 | P-7, 1B-1 |
| 1896 | 9 | 22 | 8 | 0 | 1 | 0 | 0.0 | 6 | 1 | 5 | 2 | 2 | .364 | .455 | 1 | 0 | P-5, OF-3 |
| 1897 | 75 | 265 | 85 | 9 | 6 | 0 | 0.0 | 39 | 55 | 30 | | 13 | .321 | .400 | 1 | 0 | OF-59, P-16 |
| 1898 | 62 | 210 | 62 | 5 | 2 | 0 | 0.0 | 34 | 14 | 22 | | 8 | .295 | .338 | 2 | 0 | OF-34, P-28 |
| 4 yrs. | 154 | 519 | 162 | 15 | 9 | 1 | 0.2 | 83 | 77 | 60 | 3 | 23 | .312 | .382 | 4 | 0 | OF-96, P-56, 1B-1 |
| 4 yrs. | 154 | 519 | 162 | 15 | 9 | 1 | 0.2 | 83 | 77 | 60 | 3 | 23 | .312 | .382 | 4 | 0 | OF-96, P-56, 1B-1 |

## Joe Tinker

**TINKER, JOSEPH BERT**     BR TR 5'10"   160 lbs.
B. July 27, 1880, Muscotah, Kans.    D. July 27, 1948, Orlando, Fla.
Manager 1913-16.
Hall of Fame 1946.

| | G | AB | H | 2B | 3B | HR | HR % | R | RBI | BB | SO | SB | BA | SA | AB | H | G by POS |
|---|---|---|---|---|---|---|---|---|---|---|---|---|---|---|---|---|---|
| 1902 CHI N | 133 | 501 | 137 | 19 | 5 | 2 | 0.4 | 54 | 54 | 26 | | 27 | .273 | .343 | 0 | 0 | SS-124, 3B-8 |
| 1903 | 124 | 460 | 134 | 21 | 7 | 2 | 0.4 | 67 | 70 | 37 | | 27 | .291 | .380 | 0 | 0 | SS-107, 3B-17 |
| 1904 | 141 | 488 | 108 | 12 | 13 | 3 | 0.6 | 55 | 41 | 29 | | 41 | .221 | .318 | 0 | 0 | SS-140, OF-1 |
| 1905 | 149 | 547 | 135 | 18 | 8 | 2 | 0.4 | 70 | 66 | 34 | | 31 | .247 | .320 | 0 | 0 | SS-149 |
| 1906 | 148 | 523 | 122 | 18 | 4 | 1 | 0.2 | 75 | 64 | 43 | | 30 | .233 | .289 | 0 | 0 | SS-147, 3B-1 |
| 1907 | 117 | 402 | 89 | 11 | 3 | 1 | 0.2 | 36 | 36 | 25 | | 20 | .221 | .271 | 3 | 0 | SS-113 |
| 1908 | 157 | 548 | 146 | 23 | 14 | 6 | 1.1 | 67 | 68 | 32 | | 30 | .266 | .392 | 0 | 0 | SS-157 |
| 1909 | 143 | 516 | 132 | 26 | 11 | 4 | 0.8 | 56 | 57 | 17 | | 23 | .256 | .372 | 0 | 0 | SS-143 |
| 1910 | 133 | 473 | 136 | 25 | 9 | 3 | 0.6 | 48 | 69 | 24 | 35 | 20 | .288 | .397 | 2 | 0 | SS-131 |
| 1911 | 144 | 536 | 149 | 24 | 12 | 4 | 0.7 | 61 | 69 | 39 | 31 | 30 | .278 | .390 | 0 | 0 | SS-143 |
| 1912 | 142 | 550 | 155 | 24 | 7 | 0 | 0.0 | 80 | 75 | 38 | 21 | 25 | .282 | .351 | 0 | 0 | SS-142 |
| 1913 CIN N | 110 | 382 | 121 | 20 | 13 | 1 | 0.3 | 47 | 57 | 20 | 26 | 10 | .317 | .445 | 1 | 0 | SS-101, 3B-9 |
| 1914 CHI F | 126 | 438 | 112 | 21 | 7 | 2 | 0.5 | 50 | 46 | 38 | | 19 | .256 | .349 | 1 | 0 | SS-125 |
| 1915 | 31 | 67 | 18 | 2 | 1 | 0 | 0.0 | 7 | 9 | 13 | | 3 | .269 | .328 | 4 | 1 | SS-16, 2B-5, 3B-4 |
| 1916 CHI N | 7 | 10 | 1 | 0 | 0 | 0 | 0.0 | 0 | 1 | 1 | | 1 | .100 | .100 | 1 | 0 | SS-4, 3B-2 |
| 15 yrs. | 1805 | 6441 | 1695 | 264 | 114 | 31 | 0.5 | 773 | 782 | 416 | 114 | 336 | .263 | .354 | 12 | 0 | SS-1742, 3B-41, 2B-5, OF-1 |
| 12 yrs. | 1538 | 5554 | 1444 | 221 | 93 (6th) | 28 | 0.5 | 669 | 670 | 345 | 88 | 304 (2nd) | .260 | .348 | 6 | 0 | SS-1500, 3B-28, OF-1 |

**WORLD SERIES**

| | G | AB | H | 2B | 3B | HR | HR % | R | RBI | BB | SO | SB | BA | SA | AB | H | G by POS |
|---|---|---|---|---|---|---|---|---|---|---|---|---|---|---|---|---|---|
| 1906 CHI N | 6 | 18 | 3 | 0 | 0 | 0 | 0.0 | 4 | 1 | 2 | 2 | 2 | .167 | .167 | 0 | 0 | SS-6 |
| 1907 | 5 | 13 | 2 | 0 | 0 | 0 | 0.0 | 4 | 1 | 3 | 3 | 2 | .154 | .154 | 0 | 0 | SS-5 |
| 1908 | 5 | 19 | 5 | 0 | 1 | 0 | 5.3 | 2 | 5 | 0 | 2 | 1 | .263 | .421 | 0 | 0 | SS-5 |
| 1910 | 5 | 18 | 6 | 2 | 0 | 0 | 0.0 | 2 | 0 | 2 | 2 | 1 | .333 | .444 | 0 | 0 | SS-5 |
| 4 yrs. | 21 | 68 | 16 | 2 | 1 | 0 | 1.5 | 12 | 7 | 7 | 9 | 6 | .235 | .309 | 0 | 0 | SS-21 |

| | G | AB | H | 2B | 3B | HR | HR % | R | RBI | BB | SO | SB | BA | SA | Pinch Hit AB | Pinch Hit H | G by POS |
|---|---|---|---|---|---|---|---|---|---|---|---|---|---|---|---|---|---|

## Al Todd

**TODD, ALFRED CHESTER**
B. Jan. 7, 1904, Troy, N. Y.    D. Mar. 8, 1985, Elmira, N. Y.    BR TR 6'1"   198 lbs.

| | G | AB | H | 2B | 3B | HR | HR % | R | RBI | BB | SO | SB | BA | SA | PH AB | PH H | G by POS |
|---|---|---|---|---|---|---|---|---|---|---|---|---|---|---|---|---|---|
| 1932 PHI N | 33 | 70 | 16 | 5 | 0 | 0 | 0.0 | 8 | 9 | 1 | 9 | 1 | .229 | .300 | 7 | 1 | C-25 |
| 1933 | 73 | 136 | 28 | 4 | 0 | 0 | 0.0 | 13 | 10 | 4 | 18 | 1 | .206 | .235 | 34 | 7 | C-34, OF-2 |
| 1934 | 91 | 302 | 96 | 22 | 2 | 4 | 1.3 | 33 | 41 | 10 | 39 | 3 | .318 | .444 | 8 | 4 | C-82 |
| 1935 | 107 | 328 | 95 | 18 | 3 | 3 | 0.9 | 40 | 42 | 19 | 35 | 3 | .290 | .390 | 20 | 5 | C-87 |
| 1936 PIT N | 76 | 267 | 73 | 10 | 5 | 2 | 0.7 | 28 | 28 | 11 | 24 | 4 | .273 | .371 | 6 | 2 | C-70 |
| 1937 | 133 | 514 | 158 | 18 | 10 | 8 | 1.6 | 51 | 86 | 16 | 36 | 2 | .307 | .428 | 5 | 2 | C-128 |
| 1938 | 133 | 491 | 130 | 19 | 7 | 7 | 1.4 | 52 | 75 | 18 | 31 | 2 | .265 | .375 | 1 | 0 | C-132 |
| 1939 BKN N | 86 | 245 | 68 | 10 | 0 | 5 | 2.0 | 28 | 32 | 13 | 16 | 1 | .278 | .380 | 13 | 5 | C-73 |
| 1940 CHI N | 104 | 381 | 97 | 13 | 2 | 6 | 1.6 | 31 | 42 | 11 | 29 | 1 | .255 | .346 | 0 | 0 | C-104 |
| 1941 | 6 | 6 | 1 | 0 | 0 | 0 | 0.0 | 1 | 0 | 0 | 1 | 0 | .167 | .167 | 6 | 1 | |
| 1943 | 21 | 45 | 6 | 0 | 0 | 0 | 0.0 | 1 | 1 | 1 | 5 | 0 | .133 | .133 | 14 | 1 | C-17 |
| 11 yrs. | 863 | 2785 | 768 | 119 | 29 | 35 | 1.3 | 286 | 366 | 104 | 243 | 18 | .276 | .377 | 104 | 28 | C-752, OF-2 |
| 3 yrs. | 131 | 432 | 104 | 13 | 2 | 6 | 1.4 | 33 | 43 | 12 | 35 | 1 | .241 | .322 | 10 | 2 | C-121 |

## Chick Tolson

**TOLSON, CHARLES JULIUS (Slug)**
B. Nov. 6, 1898, Washington, D. C.    D. Apr. 16, 1965, Washington, D. C.    BR TR 6'   185 lbs.

| | G | AB | H | 2B | 3B | HR | HR % | R | RBI | BB | SO | SB | BA | SA | PH AB | PH H | G by POS |
|---|---|---|---|---|---|---|---|---|---|---|---|---|---|---|---|---|---|
| 1925 CLE A | 3 | 12 | 3 | 0 | 0 | 0 | 0.0 | 0 | 0 | 2 | 1 | 0 | .250 | .250 | 0 | 0 | 1B-3 |
| 1926 CHI N | 57 | 80 | 25 | 6 | 1 | 1 | 1.3 | 4 | 8 | 5 | 8 | 0 | .313 | .450 | 40 | 14 | 1B-13 |
| 1927 | 39 | 54 | 16 | 4 | 0 | 2 | 3.7 | 6 | 17 | 4 | 9 | 0 | .296 | .481 | 27 | 7 | 1B-8 |
| 1929 | 32 | 109 | 28 | 5 | 0 | 1 | 0.9 | 13 | 19 | 9 | 16 | 0 | .257 | .330 | 0 | 0 | 1B-32 |
| 1930 | 13 | 20 | 6 | 1 | 0 | 0 | 0.0 | 0 | 1 | 6 | 5 | 1 | .300 | .350 | 7 | 2 | 1B-5 |
| 5 yrs. | 144 | 275 | 78 | 16 | 1 | 4 | 1.5 | 23 | 45 | 26 | 39 | 1 | .284 | .393 | 74 | 23 | 1B-61 |
| 4 yrs. | 141 | 263 | 75 | 16 | 1 | 4 | 1.5 | 23 | 45 | 24 | 38 | 1 | .285 | .399 | 74 | 23 | 1B-58 |

**WORLD SERIES**

| | G | AB | H | 2B | 3B | HR | HR % | R | RBI | BB | SO | SB | BA | SA | PH AB | PH H | G by POS |
|---|---|---|---|---|---|---|---|---|---|---|---|---|---|---|---|---|---|
| 1929 CHI N | 1 | 1 | 0 | 0 | 0 | 0 | 0.0 | 0 | 0 | 0 | 1 | 0 | .000 | .000 | 1 | 0 | |

## Hector Torres

**TORRES, HECTOR EPITACIO**
B. Sept. 16, 1945, Monterrey, Mexico    BR TR 6'   175 lbs.

| | G | AB | H | 2B | 3B | HR | HR % | R | RBI | BB | SO | SB | BA | SA | PH AB | PH H | G by POS |
|---|---|---|---|---|---|---|---|---|---|---|---|---|---|---|---|---|---|
| 1968 HOU N | 128 | 466 | 104 | 11 | 1 | 1 | 0.2 | 44 | 24 | 18 | 64 | 2 | .223 | .258 | 0 | 0 | SS-127, 2B-1 |
| 1969 | 34 | 69 | 11 | 1 | 0 | 1 | 1.4 | 5 | 8 | 2 | 12 | 0 | .159 | .217 | 14 | 3 | SS-22 |
| 1970 | 31 | 65 | 16 | 1 | 2 | 0 | 0.0 | 6 | 5 | 6 | 8 | 0 | .246 | .323 | 4 | 1 | SS-22, 2B-6 |
| 1971 CHI N | 31 | 58 | 13 | 3 | 0 | 0 | 0.0 | 4 | 2 | 4 | 10 | 0 | .224 | .276 | 4 | 1 | SS-18, 2B-4 |
| 1972 MON N | 83 | 181 | 28 | 4 | 1 | 2 | 1.1 | 14 | 7 | 13 | 26 | 0 | .155 | .221 | 7 | 1 | 2B-60, SS-16, OF-2, 3B-1, P-1 |
| 1973 HOU N | 38 | 66 | 6 | 1 | 0 | 0 | 0.0 | 3 | 2 | 7 | 13 | 0 | .091 | .106 | 3 | 0 | SS-22, 2B-13 |
| 1975 SD N | 112 | 352 | 91 | 12 | 0 | 5 | 1.4 | 31 | 26 | 22 | 32 | 2 | .259 | .335 | 0 | 0 | SS-75, 3B-42, 2B-16 |
| 1976 | 74 | 215 | 42 | 6 | 0 | 4 | 1.9 | 8 | 15 | 16 | 31 | 2 | .195 | .279 | 8 | 0 | SS-63, 3B-4, 2B-3 |
| 1977 TOR A | 91 | 266 | 64 | 7 | 3 | 5 | 1.9 | 33 | 26 | 16 | 33 | 1 | .241 | .346 | 2 | 1 | SS-68, 2B-23, 3B-2 |
| 9 yrs. | 622 | 1738 | 375 | 46 | 7 | 18 | 1.0 | 148 | 115 | 104 | 229 | 7 | .216 | .281 | 43 | 7 | SS-433, 2B-126, 3B-49, OF-2, P-1 |
| 1 yr. | 31 | 58 | 13 | 3 | 0 | 0 | 0.0 | 4 | 2 | 4 | 10 | 0 | .224 | .276 | 4 | 1 | SS-18, 2B-4 |

## Jim Tracy

**TRACY, JAMES EDWIN**
B. Dec. 31, 1955, Hamilton, Ohio    BL TR 6'   185 lbs.

| | G | AB | H | 2B | 3B | HR | HR % | R | RBI | BB | SO | SB | BA | SA | PH AB | PH H | G by POS |
|---|---|---|---|---|---|---|---|---|---|---|---|---|---|---|---|---|---|
| 1980 CHI N | 42 | 122 | 31 | 3 | 3 | 3 | 2.5 | 12 | 9 | 13 | 37 | 2 | .254 | .402 | 12 | 2 | OF-31, 1B-1 |
| 1981 | 45 | 63 | 15 | 2 | 1 | 0 | 0.0 | 6 | 5 | 12 | 14 | 1 | .238 | .302 | 29 | 5 | OF-11 |
| 2 yrs. | 87 | 185 | 46 | 5 | 4 | 3 | 1.6 | 18 | 14 | 25 | 51 | 3 | .249 | .368 | 41 | 7 | OF-42, 1B-1 |
| 2 yrs. | 87 | 185 | 46 | 5 | 4 | 3 | 1.6 | 18 | 14 | 25 | 51 | 3 | .249 | .368 | 41 | 7 | OF-42, 1B-1 |

## Bill Traffley

**TRAFFLEY, WILLIAM F.**
Brother of John Traffley.
B. Dec. 21, 1859, Staten Island, N. Y.    D. June 24, 1908, Denver, Colo.    BR TR 5'11½" 185 lbs.

| | G | AB | H | 2B | 3B | HR | HR % | R | RBI | BB | SO | SB | BA | SA | PH AB | PH H | G by POS |
|---|---|---|---|---|---|---|---|---|---|---|---|---|---|---|---|---|---|
| 1878 CHI N | 2 | 9 | 1 | 0 | 0 | 0 | 0.0 | 1 | 1 | 0 | 1 | | .111 | .111 | 0 | 0 | C-2 |
| 1883 CIN AA | 30 | 105 | 21 | 5 | 0 | 0 | 0.0 | 17 | | 4 | | | .200 | .248 | 0 | 0 | C-29, SS-2 |
| 1884 BAL AA | 53 | 210 | 37 | 4 | 6 | 0 | 0.0 | 25 | | 3 | | | .176 | .252 | 0 | 0 | C-47, OF-6, 1B-1 |
| 1885 | 69 | 254 | 39 | 4 | 5 | 1 | 0.4 | 27 | | 17 | | | .154 | .220 | 0 | 0 | C-61, OF-10, 2B-3 |
| 1886 | 25 | 85 | 18 | 0 | 1 | 0 | 0.0 | 15 | | 10 | | | .212 | .235 | 0 | 0 | C-25 |
| 5 yrs. | 179 | 663 | 116 | 13 | 12 | 1 | 0.2 | 85 | 1 | 34 | 1 | | .175 | .235 | 0 | 0 | C-164, OF-16, 2B-3, SS-2, 1B-1 |
| 1 yr. | 2 | 9 | 1 | 0 | 0 | 0 | 0.0 | 1 | 1 | 0 | 1 | | .111 | .111 | 0 | 0 | C-2 |

## Manny Trillo

**TRILLO, JESUS MANUEL (Indio)**
Also known as Jesus Manuel Trillo Marcano.
B. Dec. 25, 1950, Edo Monagas, Venezuela    BR TR 6'1"   150 lbs.

| | G | AB | H | 2B | 3B | HR | HR % | R | RBI | BB | SO | SB | BA | SA | PH AB | PH H | G by POS |
|---|---|---|---|---|---|---|---|---|---|---|---|---|---|---|---|---|---|
| 1973 OAK A | 17 | 12 | 3 | 2 | 0 | 0 | 0.0 | 0 | 3 | 0 | 4 | 0 | .250 | .417 | 0 | 0 | 2B-16 |
| 1974 | 21 | 33 | 5 | 0 | 0 | 0 | 0.0 | 3 | 2 | 2 | 8 | 0 | .152 | .152 | 0 | 0 | 2B-21 |
| 1975 CHI N | 154 | 545 | 135 | 12 | 2 | 7 | 1.3 | 55 | 70 | 45 | 78 | 1 | .248 | .316 | 1 | 0 | 2B-153, SS-1 |
| 1976 | 158 | 582 | 139 | 24 | 3 | 4 | 0.7 | 42 | 59 | 53 | 70 | 17 | .239 | .311 | 1 | 0 | 2B-156, SS-1 |
| 1977 | 152 | 504 | 141 | 18 | 5 | 7 | 1.4 | 51 | 57 | 44 | 58 | 3 | .280 | .377 | 5 | 0 | 2B-149 |
| 1978 | 152 | 552 | 144 | 17 | 5 | 4 | 0.7 | 53 | 55 | 50 | 67 | 0 | .261 | .332 | 2 | 2 | 2B-149 |
| 1979 PHI N | 118 | 431 | 112 | 22 | 1 | 6 | 1.4 | 40 | 42 | 20 | 59 | 4 | .260 | .357 | 0 | 0 | 2B-118 |
| 1980 | 141 | 531 | 155 | 25 | 9 | 7 | 1.3 | 68 | 43 | 32 | 46 | 8 | .292 | .412 | 0 | 0 | 2B-140 |
| 1981 | 94 | 349 | 100 | 14 | 3 | 6 | 1.7 | 37 | 36 | 26 | 37 | 10 | .287 | .395 | 0 | 0 | 2B-94 |
| 1982 | 149 | 549 | 149 | 24 | 1 | 0 | 0.0 | 52 | 39 | 33 | 53 | 8 | .271 | .319 | 0 | 0 | 2B-149 |
| 1983 2 teams | CLE A | (88G – .272) | | | | MON N | (31G – .264) | | | | | | | | | | |
| " total | 119 | 441 | 119 | 21 | 1 | 3 | 0.7 | 49 | 45 | 31 | 64 | 1 | .270 | .342 | 1 | 0 | 2B-118 |
| 1984 SF N | 98 | 401 | 102 | 21 | 1 | 4 | 1.0 | .45 | 36 | 25 | 55 | 0 | .254 | .342 | 1 | 0 | 2B-96, 3B-4 |
| 1985 | 125 | 451 | 101 | 16 | 2 | 3 | 0.7 | 36 | 25 | 40 | 44 | 2 | .224 | .288 | 5 | 0 | 2B-120, 3B-1 |
| 13 yrs. | 1498 | 5381 | 1405 | 216 | 33 | 51 | 0.9 | 531 | 512 | 401 | 643 | 54 | .261 | .342 | 15 | 2 | 2B-1479, 3B-5, SS-2 |
| 4 yrs. | 616 | 2183 | 559 | 71 | 15 | 22 | 1.0 | 201 | 241 | 192 | 273 | 21 | .256 | .333 | 9 | 2 | 2B-607, SS-2 |

**DIVISIONAL PLAYOFF SERIES**

| | G | AB | H | 2B | 3B | HR | HR % | R | RBI | BB | SO | SB | BA | SA | PH AB | PH H | G by POS |
|---|---|---|---|---|---|---|---|---|---|---|---|---|---|---|---|---|---|
| 1981 PHI N | 5 | 16 | 3 | 0 | 0 | 0 | 0.0 | 1 | 1 | 4 | 0 | 0 | .188 | .188 | 0 | 0 | 2B-5 |

| | G | AB | H | 2B | 3B | HR | HR % | R | RBI | BB | SO | SB | BA | SA | Pinch Hit AB | H | G by POS |
|---|---|---|---|---|---|---|---|---|---|---|---|---|---|---|---|---|---|

## Manny Trillo continued

**LEAGUE CHAMPIONSHIP SERIES**

| | G | AB | H | 2B | 3B | HR | HR% | R | RBI | BB | SO | SB | BA | SA | PH AB | PH H | G by POS |
|---|---|---|---|---|---|---|---|---|---|---|---|---|---|---|---|---|---|
| 1974 OAK A | 1 | 0 | 0 | 0 | 0 | 0 | – | 1 | 0 | 0 | 0 | 0 | – | – | 0 | 0 | |
| 1980 PHI N | 5 | 21 | 8 | 2 | 1 | 0 | 0.0 | 1 | 4 | 0 | 2 | 0 | .381 | .571 | 0 | 0 | 2B-5 |
| 2 yrs. | 6 | 21 | 8 | 2 | 1 | 0 | 0.0 | 2 | 4 | 0 | 2 | 0 | .381 | .571 | 0 | 0 | 2B-5 |

**WORLD SERIES**

| | G | AB | H | 2B | 3B | HR | HR% | R | RBI | BB | SO | SB | BA | SA | PH AB | PH H | G by POS |
|---|---|---|---|---|---|---|---|---|---|---|---|---|---|---|---|---|---|
| 1980 PHI N | 6 | 23 | 5 | 2 | 0 | 0 | 0.0 | 4 | 2 | 0 | 0 | 0 | .217 | .304 | 0 | 0 | 2B-6 |

## Coaker Triplett

TRIPLETT, HERMAN COAKER    BR TR 5'11" 185 lbs.
B. Dec. 18, 1911, Boone, N. C.

| | G | AB | H | 2B | 3B | HR | HR% | R | RBI | BB | SO | SB | BA | SA | PH AB | PH H | G by POS |
|---|---|---|---|---|---|---|---|---|---|---|---|---|---|---|---|---|---|
| 1938 CHI N | 12 | 36 | 9 | 2 | 1 | 0 | 0.0 | 4 | 2 | 0 | 1 | 0 | .250 | .361 | 3 | 0 | OF-9 |
| 1941 STL N | 76 | 185 | 53 | 6 | 3 | 3 | 1.6 | 29 | 21 | 18 | 27 | 0 | .286 | .400 | 25 | 5 | OF-46 |
| 1942 | 64 | 154 | 42 | 7 | 4 | 1 | 0.6 | 18 | 23 | 17 | 15 | 1 | .273 | .390 | 16 | 2 | OF-46 |
| 1943 2 teams | | | STL | N | (9G | – | .080) | PHI | N | (105G | – | .272) | | | | | |
| " total | 114 | 385 | 100 | 16 | 4 | 15 | 3.9 | 46 | 56 | 29 | 34 | 2 | .260 | .439 | 16 | 4 | OF-96 |
| 1944 PHI N | 84 | 184 | 43 | 5 | 1 | 1 | 0.5 | 15 | 25 | 19 | 10 | 1 | .234 | .288 | 36 | 8 | OF-44 |
| 1945 | 120 | 363 | 87 | 11 | 1 | 7 | 1.9 | 36 | 46 | 40 | 27 | 6 | .240 | .333 | 28 | 5 | OF-92 |
| 6 yrs. | 470 | 1307 | 334 | 47 | 14 | 27 | 2.1 | 148 | 173 | 123 | 114 | 10 | .256 | .375 | 124 | 24 | OF-333 |
| 1 yr. | 12 | 36 | 9 | 2 | 1 | 0 | 0.0 | 4 | 2 | 0 | 1 | 0 | .250 | .361 | 3 | 0 | OF-9 |

## Harry Truby

TRUBY, HARRY GARVIN (Bird Eye)    TR 5'11" 185 lbs.
B. May 12, 1870, Ironton, Ohio    D. Mar. 21, 1953, Ironton, Ohio

| | G | AB | H | 2B | 3B | HR | HR% | R | RBI | BB | SO | SB | BA | SA | PH AB | PH H | G by POS |
|---|---|---|---|---|---|---|---|---|---|---|---|---|---|---|---|---|---|
| 1895 CHI N | 33 | 119 | 40 | 3 | 0 | 0 | 0.0 | 17 | 16 | 10 | 7 | 7 | .336 | .361 | 0 | 0 | 2B-33 |
| 1896 2 teams | | | CHI | N | (29G | – | .257) | PIT | N | (8G | – | .156) | | | | | |
| " total | 37 | 141 | 33 | 2 | 2 | 2 | 1.4 | 14 | 34 | 8 | 9 | 5 | .234 | .319 | 0 | 0 | 2B-36 |
| 2 yrs. | 70 | 260 | 73 | 5 | 2 | 2 | 0.8 | 31 | 50 | 18 | 16 | 12 | .281 | .338 | 0 | 0 | 2B-69 |
| 2 yrs. | 62 | 228 | 68 | 5 | 2 | 2 | 0.9 | 30 | 47 | 16 | 12 | 11 | .298 | .364 | 0 | 0 | 2B-61 |

## Pete Turgeon

TURGEON, EUGENE JOSEPH    BR TR 5'6" 145 lbs.
B. Jan. 3, 1897, Minneapolis, Minn.    D. Jan. 24, 1977, Wichita Falls, Tex.

| | G | AB | H | 2B | 3B | HR | HR% | R | RBI | BB | SO | SB | BA | SA | PH AB | PH H | G by POS |
|---|---|---|---|---|---|---|---|---|---|---|---|---|---|---|---|---|---|
| 1923 CHI N | 3 | 6 | 1 | 0 | 0 | 0 | 0.0 | 1 | 0 | 0 | 0 | 0 | .167 | .167 | 0 | 0 | SS-2 |

## Babe Twombly

TWOMBLY, CLARENCE EDWARD    BL TR 5'10" 165 lbs.
Brother of George Twombly.
B. Jan. 18, 1896, Jamaica Plain, Mass.    D. Nov. 23, 1974, San Clemente, Calif.

| | G | AB | H | 2B | 3B | HR | HR% | R | RBI | BB | SO | SB | BA | SA | PH AB | PH H | G by POS |
|---|---|---|---|---|---|---|---|---|---|---|---|---|---|---|---|---|---|
| 1920 CHI N | 78 | 183 | 43 | 1 | 1 | 2 | 1.1 | 25 | 14 | 17 | 20 | 5 | .235 | .284 | 22 | 4 | OF-45, 2B-2 |
| 1921 | 87 | 175 | 66 | 8 | 1 | 1 | 0.6 | 22 | 18 | 11 | 10 | 4 | .377 | .451 | 38 | 15 | OF-45 |
| 2 yrs. | 165 | 358 | 109 | 9 | 2 | 3 | 0.8 | 47 | 32 | 28 | 30 | 9 | .304 | .366 | 60 | 19 | OF-90, 2B-2 |
| 2 yrs. | 165 | 358 | 109 | 9 | 2 | 3 | 0.8 | 47 | 32 | 28 | 30 | 9 | .304 | .366 | 60 | 19 | OF-90, 2B-2 |

## Lefty Tyler

TYLER, GEORGE ALBERT    BL TL 6' 175 lbs.
Brother of Fred Tyler.
B. Dec. 14, 1889, Derry, N. H.    D. Sept. 29, 1953, Lowell, Mass.

| | G | AB | H | 2B | 3B | HR | HR% | R | RBI | BB | SO | SB | BA | SA | PH AB | PH H | G by POS |
|---|---|---|---|---|---|---|---|---|---|---|---|---|---|---|---|---|---|
| 1910 BOS N | 2 | 4 | 2 | 0 | 0 | 0 | 0.0 | 0 | 1 | 0 | 0 | 0 | .500 | .500 | 0 | 0 | P-2 |
| 1911 | 28 | 61 | 10 | 2 | 0 | 0 | 0.0 | 10 | 2 | 8 | 9 | 0 | .164 | .197 | 0 | 0 | P-28 |
| 1912 | 42 | 96 | 19 | 3 | 0 | 0 | 0.0 | 8 | 5 | 4 | 16 | 0 | .198 | .229 | 0 | 0 | P-42 |
| 1913 | 43 | 102 | 21 | 7 | 0 | 0 | 0.0 | 13 | 10 | 11 | 16 | 0 | .206 | .275 | 3 | 1 | P-39 |
| 1914 | 38 | 94 | 19 | 1 | 0 | 0 | 0.0 | 6 | 4 | 4 | 20 | 0 | .202 | .213 | 0 | 0 | P-38 |
| 1915 | 45 | 88 | 23 | 7 | 0 | 1 | 1.1 | 11 | 6 | 4 | 19 | 0 | .261 | .375 | 10 | 1 | P-32 |
| 1916 | 39 | 93 | 19 | 3 | 1 | 3 | 3.2 | 10 | 20 | 9 | 15 | 0 | .204 | .355 | 3 | 0 | P-34 |
| 1917 | 55 | 134 | 31 | 4 | 0 | 0 | 0.0 | 8 | 11 | 17 | 19 | 0 | .231 | .261 | 12 | 3 | P-32, 1B-11 |
| 1918 CHI N | 38 | 100 | 21 | 1 | 0 | 0 | 0.0 | 9 | 8 | 9 | 15 | 0 | .210 | .220 | 2 | 0 | P-33 |
| 1919 | 6 | 7 | 1 | 0 | 0 | 0 | 0.0 | 0 | 1 | 3 | 2 | 0 | .143 | .143 | 0 | 0 | P-6 |
| 1920 | 29 | 65 | 17 | 3 | 1 | 0 | 0.0 | 6 | 6 | 9 | 7 | 0 | .262 | .338 | 2 | 2 | P-27 |
| 1921 | 19 | 26 | 6 | 2 | 0 | 0 | 0.0 | 4 | 2 | 1 | 5 | 0 | .231 | .308 | 7 | 2 | P-10 |
| 12 yrs. | 384 | 870 | 189 | 33 | 2 | 4 | 0.5 | 85 | 75 | 80 | 143 | 0 | .217 | .274 | 39 | 9 | P-323, 1B-11 |
| 4 yrs. | 92 | 198 | 45 | 6 | 1 | 0 | 0.0 | 19 | 17 | 22 | 29 | 0 | .227 | .268 | 11 | 4 | P-76 |

**WORLD SERIES**

| | G | AB | H | 2B | 3B | HR | HR% | R | RBI | BB | SO | SB | BA | SA | PH AB | PH H | G by POS |
|---|---|---|---|---|---|---|---|---|---|---|---|---|---|---|---|---|---|
| 1914 BOS N | 1 | 3 | 0 | 0 | 0 | 0 | 0.0 | 0 | 0 | 0 | 1 | 0 | .000 | .000 | 0 | 0 | P-1 |
| 1918 CHI N | 3 | 5 | 1 | 0 | 0 | 0 | 0.0 | 0 | 2 | 2 | 0 | 0 | .200 | .200 | 0 | 0 | P-3 |
| 2 yrs. | 4 | 8 | 1 | 0 | 0 | 0 | 0.0 | 0 | 2 | 2 | 1 | 0 | .125 | .125 | 0 | 0 | P-4 |

## Earl Tyree

TYREE, EARL CARLTON    BR TR 5'8" 160 lbs.
B. Mar. 4, 1890, Huntsville, Ill.    D. May 17, 1954, Rushville, Ill.

| | G | AB | H | 2B | 3B | HR | HR% | R | RBI | BB | SO | SB | BA | SA | PH AB | PH H | G by POS |
|---|---|---|---|---|---|---|---|---|---|---|---|---|---|---|---|---|---|
| 1914 CHI N | 1 | 4 | 0 | 0 | 0 | 0 | 0.0 | 0 | 0 | 0 | 0 | 0 | .000 | .000 | 0 | 0 | C-1 |

## Jim Tyrone

TYRONE, JAMES VERNON    BR TR 6'1" 185 lbs.
Brother of Wayne Tyrone.
B. Jan. 29, 1949, Alice, Tex.

| | G | AB | H | 2B | 3B | HR | HR% | R | RBI | BB | SO | SB | BA | SA | PH AB | PH H | G by POS |
|---|---|---|---|---|---|---|---|---|---|---|---|---|---|---|---|---|---|
| 1972 CHI N | 13 | 8 | 0 | 0 | 0 | 0 | 0.0 | 1 | 0 | 0 | 3 | 1 | .000 | .000 | 3 | 0 | OF-4 |
| 1974 | 57 | 81 | 15 | 0 | 1 | 3 | 3.7 | 19 | 3 | 6 | 8 | 1 | .185 | .321 | 28 | 7 | OF-32, 3B-1 |
| 1975 | 11 | 22 | 5 | 0 | 1 | 0 | 0.0 | 0 | 3 | 1 | 4 | 1 | .227 | .318 | 5 | 1 | OF-8 |
| 1977 OAK A | 96 | 294 | 72 | 11 | 1 | 5 | 1.7 | 32 | 26 | 25 | 62 | 3 | .245 | .340 | 11 | 5 | OF-81, DH-4, SS-1, 1B-1 |
| 4 yrs. | 177 | 405 | 92 | 11 | 3 | 8 | 2.0 | 52 | 32 | 32 | 77 | 6 | .227 | .328 | 47 | 13 | OF-125, DH-4, SS-1, 3B-1, 1B-1 |
| 3 yrs. | 81 | 111 | 20 | 0 | 2 | 3 | 2.7 | 20 | 6 | 7 | 15 | 3 | .180 | .297 | 36 | 8 | OF-44, 3B-1 |

| | G | AB | H | 2B | 3B | HR | HR % | R | RBI | BB | SO | SB | BA | SA | Pinch Hit AB | Pinch Hit H | G by POS |
|---|---|---|---|---|---|---|---|---|---|---|---|---|---|---|---|---|---|

## Wayne Tyrone

**TYRONE, OSCAR WAYNE**
Brother of Jim Tyrone.
B. Aug. 1, 1950, Alice, Tex.　　BR TR 6'1" 185 lbs.

| | G | AB | H | 2B | 3B | HR | HR % | R | RBI | BB | SO | SB | BA | SA | PH AB | PH H | G by POS |
|---|---|---|---|---|---|---|---|---|---|---|---|---|---|---|---|---|---|
| 1976 CHI N | 30 | 57 | 13 | 1 | 0 | 1 | 1.8 | 3 | 8 | 3 | 21 | 0 | .228 | .298 | 14 | 4 | OF-7, 3B-5, 1B-5 |

## Mike Tyson

**TYSON, MICHAEL RAY**
B. Jan. 13, 1950, Rocky Mount, N. C.　　BR TR 5'9" 170 lbs.

| | G | AB | H | 2B | 3B | HR | HR % | R | RBI | BB | SO | SB | BA | SA | PH AB | PH H | G by POS |
|---|---|---|---|---|---|---|---|---|---|---|---|---|---|---|---|---|---|
| 1972 STL N | 13 | 37 | 7 | 1 | 0 | 0 | 0.0 | 1 | 0 | 1 | 9 | 0 | .189 | .216 | 0 | 0 | 2B-11, SS-2 |
| 1973 | 144 | 469 | 114 | 15 | 4 | 1 | 0.2 | 48 | 33 | 23 | 66 | 2 | .243 | .299 | 0 | 0 | SS-128, 2B-16 |
| 1974 | 151 | 422 | 94 | 14 | 5 | 1 | 0.2 | 35 | 37 | 22 | 70 | 4 | .223 | .287 | 0 | 0 | SS-143, 2B-12 |
| 1975 | 122 | 368 | 98 | 16 | 3 | 2 | 0.5 | 45 | 37 | 24 | 39 | 5 | .266 | .342 | 2 | 0 | SS-95, 2B-24, 3B-5 |
| 1976 | 76 | 245 | 70 | 12 | 9 | 3 | 1.2 | 26 | 28 | 16 | 34 | 3 | .286 | .445 | 1 | 0 | 2B-74 |
| 1977 | 138 | 418 | 103 | 15 | 2 | 7 | 1.7 | 42 | 57 | 30 | 48 | 3 | .246 | .342 | 2 | 0 | 2B-135 |
| 1978 | 125 | 377 | 88 | 16 | 0 | 3 | 0.8 | 26 | 26 | 24 | 41 | 2 | .233 | .300 | 4 | 1 | 2B-124 |
| 1979 | 75 | 190 | 42 | 8 | 2 | 5 | 2.6 | 18 | 20 | 13 | 28 | 2 | .221 | .363 | 9 | 2 | 2B-71 |
| 1980 CHI N | 123 | 341 | 81 | 19 | 3 | 3 | 0.9 | 34 | 23 | 15 | 61 | 1 | .238 | .337 | 6 | 2 | 2B-117 |
| 1981 | 50 | 92 | 17 | 2 | 0 | 2 | 2.2 | 6 | 8 | 7 | 15 | 1 | .185 | .272 | 13 | 4 | 2B-36, SS-1 |
| 10 yrs. | 1017 | 2959 | 714 | 118 | 28 | 27 | 0.9 | 281 | 269 | 175 | 411 | 23 | .241 | .327 | 37 | 9 | 2B-620, SS-369, 3B-5 |
| 2 yrs. | 173 | 433 | 98 | 21 | 3 | 5 | 1.2 | 40 | 31 | 22 | 76 | 2 | .226 | .323 | 19 | 6 | 2B-153, SS-1 |

## John Upham

**UPHAM, JOHN LESLIE**
B. Dec. 29, 1941, Windsor, Ont., Canada　　BL TL 6' 180 lbs.

| | G | AB | H | 2B | 3B | HR | HR % | R | RBI | BB | SO | SB | BA | SA | PH AB | PH H | G by POS |
|---|---|---|---|---|---|---|---|---|---|---|---|---|---|---|---|---|---|
| 1967 CHI N | 8 | 3 | 2 | 0 | 0 | 0 | 0.0 | 0 | 0 | 0 | 0 | 0 | .667 | .667 | 3 | 2 | P-5 |
| 1968 | 13 | 10 | 2 | 0 | 0 | 0 | 0.0 | 0 | 0 | 0 | 3 | 0 | .200 | .200 | 6 | 1 | OF-2, P-2 |
| 2 yrs. | 21 | 13 | 4 | 0 | 0 | 0 | 0.0 | 1 | 0 | 0 | 3 | 0 | .308 | .308 | 9 | 3 | P-7, OF-2 |
| 2 yrs. | 21 | 13 | 4 | 0 | 0 | 0 | 0.0 | 1 | 0 | 0 | 3 | 0 | .308 | .308 | 9 | 3 | P-7, OF-2 |

## Bob Usher

**USHER, ROBERT ROYCE**
B. Mar. 1, 1925, San Diego, Calif.　　BR TR 6'1½" 180 lbs.

| | G | AB | H | 2B | 3B | HR | HR % | R | RBI | BB | SO | SB | BA | SA | PH AB | PH H | G by POS |
|---|---|---|---|---|---|---|---|---|---|---|---|---|---|---|---|---|---|
| 1946 CIN N | 92 | 152 | 31 | 5 | 1 | 0 | 0.7 | 16 | 14 | 13 | 27 | 2 | .204 | .270 | 1 | 0 | OF-80, 3B-1 |
| 1947 | 9 | 22 | 4 | 0 | 0 | 1 | 4.5 | 2 | 1 | 2 | 2 | 0 | .182 | .318 | 0 | 0 | OF-8 |
| 1950 | 106 | 321 | 83 | 17 | 0 | 6 | 1.9 | 51 | 35 | 27 | 38 | 3 | .259 | .368 | 10 | 2 | OF-95 |
| 1951 | 114 | 303 | 63 | 12 | 2 | 5 | 1.7 | 27 | 25 | 19 | 36 | 4 | .208 | .310 | 13 | 2 | OF-98 |
| 1952 CHI N | 1 | 0 | 0 | 0 | 0 | 0 | – | 0 | 0 | 1 | 0 | 0 | – | – | 0 | 0 | |
| 1957 2 teams | CLE A (10G – .125) | | | | WAS A (96G – .261) | | | | | | | | | | | | |
| " total | 106 | 303 | 78 | 7 | 1 | 5 | 1.7 | 37 | 27 | 28 | 33 | 0 | .257 | .337 | 4 | 0 | OF-99, 3B-1 |
| 6 yrs. | 428 | 1101 | 259 | 41 | 4 | 18 | 1.6 | 133 | 102 | 90 | 136 | 9 | .235 | .329 | 28 | 4 | OF-380, 3B-2 |
| 1 yr. | 1 | 0 | 0 | 0 | 0 | 0 | – | 0 | 0 | 1 | 0 | 0 | – | – | 0 | 0 | |

## Mike Vail

**VAIL, MICHAEL LEWIS**
B. Nov. 10, 1951, San Francisco, Calif.　　BR TR 6'1" 180 lbs.

| | G | AB | H | 2B | 3B | HR | HR % | R | RBI | BB | SO | SB | BA | SA | PH AB | PH H | G by POS |
|---|---|---|---|---|---|---|---|---|---|---|---|---|---|---|---|---|---|
| 1975 NY N | 38 | 162 | 49 | 8 | 1 | 3 | 1.9 | 17 | 17 | 9 | 37 | 0 | .302 | .420 | 1 | 1 | OF-36 |
| 1976 | 53 | 143 | 31 | 5 | 1 | 0 | 0.0 | 8 | 9 | 6 | 19 | 0 | .217 | .266 | 17 | 4 | OF-35 |
| 1977 | 108 | 279 | 73 | 12 | 1 | 8 | 2.9 | 29 | 35 | 19 | 58 | 0 | .262 | .398 | 30 | 4 | OF-85 |
| 1978 2 teams | CLE A (14G – .235) | | | | CHI N (74G – .333) | | | | | | | | | | | | |
| " total | 88 | 214 | 68 | 8 | 3 | 4 | 1.9 | 17 | 35 | 4 | 33 | 1 | .318 | .439 | 35 | 13 | OF-54, DH-1, 3B-1 |
| 1979 CHI N | 87 | 179 | 60 | 8 | 2 | 7 | 3.9 | 28 | 35 | 14 | 27 | 0 | .335 | .520 | 44 | 12 | OF-39, 3B-2 |
| 1980 | 114 | 312 | 93 | 17 | 2 | 6 | 1.9 | 30 | 47 | 14 | 77 | 2 | .298 | .423 | 45 | 8 | OF-77 |
| 1981 CIN N | 31 | 31 | 5 | 0 | 0 | 0 | 0.0 | 1 | 3 | 0 | 9 | 0 | .161 | .161 | 28 | 5 | OF-3 |
| 1982 | 78 | 189 | 48 | 10 | 1 | 4 | 2.1 | 9 | 29 | 6 | 33 | 0 | .254 | .381 | 29 | 8 | OF-52 |
| 1983 2 teams | SF N (18G – .154) | | | | MON N (34G – .283) | | | | | | | | | | | | |
| " total | 52 | 79 | 19 | 3 | 0 | 2 | 2.5 | 6 | 7 | 8 | 17 | 0 | .241 | .354 | 25 | 5 | OF-17, 1B-5, 3B-1 |
| 1984 LA N | 16 | 16 | 1 | 0 | 0 | 0 | 0.0 | 1 | 2 | 1 | 7 | 0 | .063 | .063 | 13 | 1 | OF-1 |
| 10 yrs. | 665 | 1604 | 447 | 71 | 11 | 34 | 2.1 | 146 | 219 | 81 | 317 | 3 | .279 | .400 | 267 | 61 | OF-399, 1B-5, 3B-4, DH-1 |
| 3 yrs. | 275 | 671 | 213 | 31 | 6 | 17 | 2.5 | 73 | 115 | 31 | 128 | 2 | .317 | .458 | 119 7th | 31 6th | OF-161, 3B-3 |

## George Van Haltren

**VAN HALTREN, GEORGE EDWARD MARTIN**
B. Mar. 30, 1866, St. Louis, Mo.　　D. Sept. 29, 1945, Oakland, Calif.
Manager 1891-92.　　BL TL 5'11" 170 lbs.

| | G | AB | H | 2B | 3B | HR | HR % | R | RBI | BB | SO | SB | BA | SA | PH AB | PH H | G by POS |
|---|---|---|---|---|---|---|---|---|---|---|---|---|---|---|---|---|---|
| 1887 CHI N | 45 | 172 | 35 | 4 | 0 | 3 | 1.7 | 30 | 17 | 15 | 15 | 12 | .203 | .279 | 0 | 0 | OF-27, P-20 |
| 1888 | 81 | 318 | 90 | 9 | 14 | 4 | 1.3 | 46 | 34 | 22 | 34 | 21 | .283 | .437 | 0 | 0 | OF-57, P-30 |
| 1889 | 134 | 543 | 168 | 20 | 10 | 9 | 1.7 | 126 | 81 | 82 | 41 | 28 | .309 | .433 | 0 | 0 | OF-130, SS-3, 2B-1 |
| 1890 BKN P | 92 | 376 | 126 | 8 | 9 | 5 | 1.3 | 84 | 54 | 41 | 23 | 35 | .335 | .444 | 0 | 0 | OF-67, P-28, SS-3 |
| 1891 BAL AA | 139 | 566 | 180 | 14 | 15 | 9 | 1.6 | 136 | 83 | 71 | 46 | 75 | .318 | .443 | 0 | 0 | OF-81, SS-P, P-6, 2B-2 |
| 1892 2 teams | BAL N (135G – .302) | | | | PIT N (13G – .200) | | | | | | | | | | | | |
| " total | 148 | 611 | 179 | 22 | 14 | 7 | 1.1 | 115 | 62 | 76 | 34 | 55 | .293 | .409 | 0 | 0 | OF-142, P-4, 3B-3, SS-2, 1B-2 |
| 1893 PIT N | 124 | 529 | 179 | 14 | 11 | 3 | 0.6 | 129 | 79 | 75 | 25 | 37 | .338 | .423 | 1 | 0 | OF-111, SS-12, 2B-2 |
| 1894 NY N | 137 | 519 | 172 | 25 | 4 | 7 | 1.3 | 109 | 104 | 55 | 22 | 43 | .331 | .435 | 0 | 0 | OF-137 |
| 1895 | 131 | 521 | 177 | 23 | 19 | 8 | 1.5 | 113 | 103 | 57 | 29 | 32 | .340 | .503 | 0 | 0 | OF-131, P-1 |
| 1896 | 133 | 562 | 197 | 19 | 21 | 5 | 0.9 | 136 | 74 | 55 | 36 | 39 | .351 | .486 | 0 | 0 | OF-133, P-1 |
| 1897 | 129 | 564 | 186 | 22 | 9 | 3 | 0.5 | 117 | 64 | 40 | | 50 | .330 | .417 | 0 | 0 | OF-129 |
| 1898 | 156 | 654 | 204 | 28 | 16 | 2 | 0.3 | 129 | 68 | 59 | | 36 | .312 | .413 | 0 | 0 | OF-156 |
| 1899 | 151 | 604 | 182 | 21 | 3 | 2 | 0.3 | 117 | 58 | 74 | | 31 | .301 | .356 | 0 | 0 | OF-151 |
| 1900 | 141 | 571 | 180 | 7 | 7 | 1 | 0.2 | 114 | 51 | 50 | | 45 | .315 | .398 | 0 | 0 | OF-141, P-1 |
| 1901 | 135 | 544 | 186 | 22 | 7 | 1 | 0.2 | 82 | 47 | 51 | | 24 | .342 | .414 | 0 | 0 | OF-135, P-1 |
| 1902 | 24 | 88 | 23 | 1 | 2 | 0 | 0.0 | 14 | 7 | 17 | | 6 | .261 | .318 | 0 | 0 | OF-24 |
| 1903 | 84 | 280 | 72 | 6 | 1 | 0 | 0.0 | 42 | 28 | 28 | | 14 | .257 | .286 | 8 | 1 | OF-75 |
| 17 yrs. | 1984 | 8022 | 2536 | 288 | 162 | 69 | 0.9 | 1639 | 1014 | 868 | 305 | 583 | .316 | .418 | 9 | 1 | OF-1827, P-93, SS-79, 2B-5, 3B-3, 1B-2 |
| 3 yrs. | 260 | 1033 | 293 | 33 | 24 | 16 | 1.5 | 202 | 132 | 119 | 90 | 61 | .284 | .409 | 0 | 0 | OF-214, P-50, SS-3, 2B-1 |

| | G | AB | H | 2B | 3B | HR | HR % | R | RBI | BB | SO | SB | BA | SA | Pinch Hit AB | Pinch Hit H | G by POS |
|---|---|---|---|---|---|---|---|---|---|---|---|---|---|---|---|---|---|

# Ike Van Zandt

**VAN ZANDT, CHARLES ISAAC**   BL
B. 1877, Brooklyn, N. Y.   D. Sept. 14, 1908, Nashua, N. H.

| | G | AB | H | 2B | 3B | HR | HR % | R | RBI | BB | SO | SB | BA | SA | AB | H | G by POS |
|---|---|---|---|---|---|---|---|---|---|---|---|---|---|---|---|---|---|
| 1901 NY N | 3 | 6 | 1 | 0 | 0 | 0 | 0.0 | 1 | 0 | 0 | | 0 | .167 | .167 | 0 | 0 | P-2, OF-1 |
| 1904 CHI N | 3 | 11 | 0 | 0 | 0 | 0 | 0.0 | 0 | 0 | 0 | | 0 | .000 | .000 | 0 | 0 | OF-3 |
| 1905 STL A | 94 | 322 | 75 | 15 | 1 | 1 | 0.3 | 31 | 20 | 7 | | 7 | .233 | .295 | 18 | 4 | OF-74, 1B-1, P-1 |
| 3 yrs. | 100 | 339 | 76 | 15 | 1 | 1 | 0.3 | 32 | 20 | 7 | | 7 | .224 | .283 | 18 | 4 | OF-78, P-3, 1B-1 |
| 1 yr. | 3 | 11 | 0 | 0 | 0 | 0 | 0.0 | 0 | 0 | 0 | | 0 | .000 | .000 | 0 | 0 | OF-3 |

# Emil Verban

**VERBAN, EMIL MATTHEW (Dutch, The Antelope)**   BR TR 5'11" 165 lbs.
B. Aug. 27, 1915, Lincoln, Ill.

| | G | AB | H | 2B | 3B | HR | HR % | R | RBI | BB | SO | SB | BA | SA | AB | H | G by POS |
|---|---|---|---|---|---|---|---|---|---|---|---|---|---|---|---|---|---|
| 1944 STL N | 146 | 498 | 128 | 14 | 2 | 0 | 0.0 | 51 | 43 | 19 | 14 | 0 | .257 | .293 | 0 | 0 | 2B-146 |
| 1945 | 155 | 597 | 166 | 22 | 8 | 0 | 0.0 | 59 | 72 | 19 | 15 | 4 | .278 | .342 | 0 | 0 | 2B-155 |
| 1946 2 teams | STL N (1G – .000) | | | | | PHI N (138G – .275) | | | | | | | | | | | |
| " total | 139 | 474 | 130 | 17 | 5 | 0 | 0.0 | 44 | 34 | 21 | 18 | 5 | .274 | .331 | 1 | 0 | 2B-138 |
| 1947 PHI N | 155 | 540 | 154 | 14 | 8 | 0 | 0.0 | 50 | 42 | 23 | 8 | 5 | .285 | .341 | 0 | 0 | 2B-155 |
| 1948 2 teams | PHI N (55G – .231) | | | | | CHI N (56G – .294) | | | | | | | | | | | |
| " total | 111 | 417 | 112 | 20 | 2 | 1 | 0.2 | 51 | 27 | 15 | 12 | 4 | .269 | .333 | 1 | 0 | 2B-110 |
| 1949 CHI N | 98 | 343 | 99 | 11 | 1 | 0 | 0.0 | 38 | 22 | 8 | 2 | 3 | .289 | .327 | 7 | 1 | 2B-88 |
| 1950 2 teams | CHI N (45G – .108) | | | | | BOS N (4G – .000) | | | | | | | | | | | |
| " total | 49 | 42 | 4 | 1 | 0 | 0 | 0.0 | 8 | 1 | 3 | 5 | 0 | .095 | .119 | 13 | 1 | 2B-10, SS-3, OF-1, 3B-1 |
| 7 yrs. | 853 | 2911 | 793 | 99 | 26 | 1 | 0.0 | 301 | 241 | 108 | 74 | 21 | .272 | .325 | 22 | 2 | 2B-802, SS-3, OF-1, 3B-1 |
| 3 yrs. | 199 | 628 | 176 | 27 | 2 | 1 | 0.2 | 82 | 39 | 15 | 14 | 7 | .280 | .334 | 20 | 2 | 2B-152, SS-3, OF-1, 3B-1 |

**WORLD SERIES**

| | G | AB | H | 2B | 3B | HR | HR % | R | RBI | BB | SO | SB | BA | SA | AB | H | G by POS |
|---|---|---|---|---|---|---|---|---|---|---|---|---|---|---|---|---|---|
| 1944 STL N | 6 | 17 | 7 | 0 | 0 | 0 | 0.0 | 1 | 2 | 2 | 0 | 0 | .412 | .412 | 0 | 0 | 2B-6 |

# Tom Veryzer

**VERYZER, THOMAS MARTIN**   BR TR 6'1½" 175 lbs.
B. Feb. 11, 1953, Islip, N. Y.

| | G | AB | H | 2B | 3B | HR | HR % | R | RBI | BB | SO | SB | BA | SA | AB | H | G by POS |
|---|---|---|---|---|---|---|---|---|---|---|---|---|---|---|---|---|---|
| 1973 DET A | 18 | 20 | 6 | 0 | 1 | 0 | 0.0 | 1 | 2 | 2 | 4 | 0 | .300 | .400 | 0 | 0 | SS-18 |
| 1974 | 22 | 55 | 13 | 2 | 0 | 2 | 3.6 | 4 | 9 | 5 | 8 | 1 | .236 | .382 | 1 | 0 | SS-20 |
| 1975 | 128 | 404 | 102 | 13 | 1 | 5 | 1.2 | 37 | 48 | 23 | 76 | 2 | .252 | .327 | 0 | 0 | SS-128 |
| 1976 | 97 | 354 | 83 | 8 | 2 | 1 | 0.3 | 31 | 25 | 21 | 44 | 1 | .234 | .277 | 0 | 0 | SS-97 |
| 1977 | 125 | 350 | 69 | 12 | 1 | 2 | 0.6 | 31 | 28 | 16 | 44 | 0 | .197 | .254 | 0 | 0 | SS-124 |
| 1978 CLE A | 130 | 421 | 114 | 18 | 4 | 1 | 0.2 | 48 | 32 | 13 | 36 | 1 | .271 | .340 | 0 | 0 | SS-129 |
| 1979 | 149 | 449 | 99 | 9 | 3 | 0 | 0.0 | 41 | 34 | 34 | 54 | 2 | .220 | .254 | 0 | 0 | SS-148 |
| 1980 | 109 | 358 | 97 | 12 | 0 | 0 | 0.0 | 28 | 28 | 10 | 25 | 0 | .271 | .321 | 0 | 0 | SS-108 |
| 1981 | 75 | 221 | 54 | 4 | 0 | 0 | 0.0 | 13 | 14 | 10 | 10 | 1 | .244 | .262 | 0 | 0 | SS-75 |
| 1982 NY A | 40 | 54 | 18 | 2 | 0 | 0 | 0.0 | 6 | 4 | 3 | 4 | 1 | .333 | .370 | 0 | 0 | 2B-26, SS-16 |
| 1983 CHI N | 59 | 88 | 18 | 3 | 0 | 1 | 1.1 | 5 | 3 | 5 | 13 | 0 | .205 | .273 | 11 | 3 | SS-28, 3B-17 |
| 1984 | 44 | 74 | 14 | 1 | 0 | 0 | 0.0 | 5 | 4 | 3 | 11 | 0 | .189 | .203 | 0 | 0 | SS-36, 3B-5, 2B-4 |
| 12 yrs. | 996 | 2848 | 687 | 84 | 12 | 14 | 0.5 | 250 | 231 | 143 | 329 | 9 | .241 | .294 | 12 | 3 | SS-927, 2B-30, 3B-22 |
| 2 yrs. | 103 | 162 | 32 | 4 | 0 | 1 | 0.6 | 10 | 7 | 6 | 24 | 0 | .198 | .241 | 11 | 3 | SS-64, 3B-22, 2B-4 |

**LEAGUE CHAMPIONSHIP SERIES**

| | G | AB | H | 2B | 3B | HR | HR % | R | RBI | BB | SO | SB | BA | SA | AB | H | G by POS |
|---|---|---|---|---|---|---|---|---|---|---|---|---|---|---|---|---|---|
| 1984 CHI N | 3 | 1 | 0 | 0 | 0 | 0 | 0.0 | 0 | 0 | 0 | 0 | 0 | .000 | .000 | 0 | 0 | 3B-1 |

# Otto Vogel

**VOGEL, OTTO HENRY**   BR TR 6' 195 lbs.
B. Oct. 26, 1899, Mendota, Ill.   D. July 19, 1969, Iowa City, Iowa

| | G | AB | H | 2B | 3B | HR | HR % | R | RBI | BB | SO | SB | BA | SA | AB | H | G by POS |
|---|---|---|---|---|---|---|---|---|---|---|---|---|---|---|---|---|---|
| 1923 CHI N | 41 | 81 | 17 | 0 | 1 | 1 | 1.2 | 10 | 6 | 7 | 11 | 2 | .210 | .272 | 6 | 1 | OF-24, 3B-1 |
| 1924 | 70 | 172 | 46 | 11 | 2 | 1 | 0.6 | 28 | 24 | 10 | 26 | 4 | .267 | .372 | 9 | 2 | OF-53, 3B-2 |
| 2 yrs. | 111 | 253 | 63 | 11 | 3 | 2 | 0.8 | 38 | 30 | 17 | 37 | 6 | .249 | .340 | 15 | 3 | OF-77, 3B-3 |
| 2 yrs. | 111 | 253 | 63 | 11 | 3 | 2 | 0.8 | 38 | 30 | 17 | 37 | 6 | .249 | .340 | 15 | 3 | OF-77, 3B-3 |

# Gale Wade

**WADE, GALEARD LEE**   BL TR 6'1½" 185 lbs.
B. Jan. 20, 1929, Hollister, Mo.

| | G | AB | H | 2B | 3B | HR | HR % | R | RBI | BB | SO | SB | BA | SA | AB | H | G by POS |
|---|---|---|---|---|---|---|---|---|---|---|---|---|---|---|---|---|---|
| 1955 CHI N | 9 | 33 | 6 | 1 | 0 | 1 | 3.0 | 5 | 1 | 4 | 3 | 0 | .182 | .303 | 0 | 0 | OF-9 |
| 1956 | 10 | 12 | 0 | 0 | 0 | 0 | 0.0 | 0 | 0 | 1 | 0 | 0 | .000 | .000 | 3 | 0 | OF-3 |
| 2 yrs. | 19 | 45 | 6 | 1 | 0 | 1 | 2.2 | 5 | 1 | 5 | 3 | 0 | .133 | .222 | 3 | 0 | OF-12 |
| 2 yrs. | 19 | 45 | 6 | 1 | 0 | 1 | 2.2 | 5 | 1 | 5 | 3 | 0 | .133 | .222 | 3 | 0 | OF-12 |

# Eddie Waitkus

**WAITKUS, EDWARD STEPHEN**   BL TL 6' 170 lbs.
B. Sept. 4, 1919, Cambridge, Mass.   D. Sept. 15, 1972, Boston, Mass.

| | G | AB | H | 2B | 3B | HR | HR % | R | RBI | BB | SO | SB | BA | SA | AB | H | G by POS |
|---|---|---|---|---|---|---|---|---|---|---|---|---|---|---|---|---|---|
| 1941 CHI N | 12 | 28 | 5 | 0 | 0 | 0 | 0.0 | 1 | 0 | 0 | 3 | 0 | .179 | .179 | 3 | 1 | 1B-9 |
| 1946 | 113 | 441 | 134 | 24 | 5 | 4 | 0.9 | 50 | 55 | 23 | 14 | 3 | .304 | .408 | 5 | 2 | 1B-106 |
| 1947 | 130 | 514 | 150 | 28 | 6 | 2 | 0.4 | 60 | 35 | 32 | 17 | 3 | .292 | .381 | 2 | 0 | 1B-126 |
| 1948 | 139 | 562 | 166 | 27 | 10 | 7 | 1.2 | 87 | 44 | 43 | 19 | 11 | .295 | .416 | 2 | 0 | 1B-116, OF-20 |
| 1949 PHI N | 54 | 209 | 64 | 16 | 3 | 1 | 0.5 | 41 | 28 | 33 | 12 | 3 | .306 | .426 | 0 | 0 | 1B-54 |
| 1950 | 154 | 641 | 182 | 32 | 5 | 2 | 0.3 | 102 | 44 | 55 | 29 | 3 | .284 | .359 | 1 | 1 | 1B-154 |
| 1951 | 145 | 610 | 157 | 27 | 4 | 1 | 0.2 | 65 | 46 | 53 | 22 | 0 | .257 | .320 | 2 | 0 | 1B-144 |
| 1952 | 146 | 499 | 144 | 29 | 4 | 2 | 0.4 | 51 | 49 | 64 | 23 | 2 | .289 | .375 | 3 | 0 | 1B-143 |
| 1953 | 81 | 247 | 72 | 9 | 2 | 1 | 0.4 | 24 | 16 | 13 | 23 | 1 | .291 | .356 | 20 | 7 | 1B-78 |
| 1954 BAL A | 95 | 311 | 88 | 17 | 4 | 2 | 0.6 | 35 | 33 | 28 | 25 | 0 | .283 | .383 | 15 | 4 | 1B-78 |
| 1955 2 teams | BAL A (38G – .259) | | | | | PHI N (33G – .280) | | | | | | | | | | | |
| " total | 71 | 192 | 52 | 6 | 1 | 2 | 1.0 | 12 | 23 | 28 | 17 | 2 | .271 | .344 | 11 | 4 | 1B-57 |
| 11 yrs. | 1140 | 4254 | 1214 | 215 | 44 | 24 | 0.6 | 528 | 373 | 372 | 204 | 28 | .285 | .374 | 64 | 19 | 1B-1046, OF-20 |
| 4 yrs. | 394 | 1545 | 455 | 79 | 21 | 13 | 0.8 | 198 | 134 | 98 | 53 | 17 | .294 | .398 | 12 | 3 | 1B-357, OF-20 |

**WORLD SERIES**

| | G | AB | H | 2B | 3B | HR | HR % | R | RBI | BB | SO | SB | BA | SA | AB | H | G by POS |
|---|---|---|---|---|---|---|---|---|---|---|---|---|---|---|---|---|---|
| 1950 PHI N | 4 | 15 | 4 | 1 | 0 | 0 | 0.0 | 0 | 0 | 2 | 0 | 0 | .267 | .333 | 0 | 0 | 1B-4 |

# Charlie Waitt

**WAITT, CHARLES C.**   5'11" 165 lbs.
B. Oct. 14, 1853, Hallowell, Me.   D. Oct. 21, 1912, San Francisco, Calif.

| | G | AB | H | 2B | 3B | HR | HR % | R | RBI | BB | SO | SB | BA | SA | AB | H | G by POS |
|---|---|---|---|---|---|---|---|---|---|---|---|---|---|---|---|---|---|
| 1877 CHI N | 10 | 41 | 4 | 0 | 0 | 0 | 0.0 | 2 | 2 | 0 | 3 | | .098 | .098 | 0 | 0 | OF-10 |

| | G | AB | H | 2B | 3B | HR | HR % | R | RBI | BB | SO | SB | BA | SA | Pinch Hit AB | Pinch Hit H | G by POS |
|---|---|---|---|---|---|---|---|---|---|---|---|---|---|---|---|---|---|

## Charlie Waitt continued

| | G | AB | H | 2B | 3B | HR | HR% | R | RBI | BB | SO | SB | BA | SA | AB | H | G by POS |
|---|---|---|---|---|---|---|---|---|---|---|---|---|---|---|---|---|---|
| 1882 BAL AA | 72 | 250 | 39 | 4 | 0 | 0 | 0.0 | 19 | | 13 | | | .156 | .172 | 0 | 0 | OF-72 |
| 1883 PHI N | 1 | 3 | 1 | 0 | 0 | 0 | 0.0 | 0 | | 0 | | 1 | .333 | .333 | 0 | 0 | OF-1 |
| 3 yrs. | 83 | 294 | 44 | 4 | 0 | 0 | 0.0 | 21 | 2 | 13 | 4 | | .150 | .163 | 0 | 0 | OF-83 |
| 1 yr. | 10 | 41 | 4 | 0 | 0 | 0 | 0.0 | 2 | 2 | 0 | 3 | | .098 | .098 | 0 | 0 | OF-10 |

## Chico Walker

**WALKER, CLEOTHA**
B. Nov. 25, 1957, Jackson, Miss.

BB TR 5'9" 170 lbs.

| | G | AB | H | 2B | 3B | HR | HR% | R | RBI | BB | SO | SB | BA | SA | AB | H | G by POS |
|---|---|---|---|---|---|---|---|---|---|---|---|---|---|---|---|---|---|
| 1980 BOS A | 19 | 57 | 12 | 0 | 0 | 1 | 1.8 | 3 | 5 | 6 | 10 | 3 | .211 | .263 | 1 | 1 | 2B-11, DH-7 |
| 1981 | 6 | 17 | 6 | 0 | 0 | 0 | 0.0 | 3 | 2 | 1 | 2 | 0 | .353 | .353 | 1 | 0 | 2B-5 |
| 1983 | 4 | 5 | 2 | 0 | 2 | 0 | 0.0 | 2 | 1 | 0 | 0 | 0 | .400 | 1.200 | 1 | 0 | OF-3 |
| 1984 | 3 | 2 | 0 | 0 | 0 | 0 | 0.0 | 0 | 1 | 0 | 1 | 0 | .000 | .000 | 1 | 0 | 2B-1 |
| 1985 CHI N | 21 | 12 | 1 | 0 | 0 | 0 | 0.0 | 3 | 0 | 0 | 5 | 1 | .083 | .083 | 8 | 1 | OF-6, 2B-2 |
| 5 yrs. | 53 | 93 | 21 | 0 | 2 | 1 | 1.1 | 11 | 9 | 7 | 18 | 4 | .226 | .301 | 13 | 2 | 2B-19, OF-9, DH-7 |
| 1 yr. | 21 | 12 | 1 | 0 | 0 | 0 | 0.0 | 3 | 0 | 0 | 5 | 1 | .083 | .083 | 8 | 1 | OF-6, 2B-2 |

## Harry Walker

**WALKER, HARRY WILLIAM (The Hat)**
Son of Dixie Walker. Brother of Dixie Walker.
B. Oct. 22, 1918, Pascagoula, Miss.
Manager 1955, 1965-72.

BL TR 6'2" 175 lbs.

| | G | AB | H | 2B | 3B | HR | HR% | R | RBI | BB | SO | SB | BA | SA | AB | H | G by POS |
|---|---|---|---|---|---|---|---|---|---|---|---|---|---|---|---|---|---|
| 1940 STL N | 7 | 27 | 5 | 2 | 0 | 0 | 0.0 | 2 | 6 | 0 | 2 | 0 | .185 | .259 | 0 | 0 | OF-7 |
| 1941 | 7 | 15 | 4 | 1 | 0 | 0 | 0.0 | 3 | 1 | 2 | 1 | 0 | .267 | .333 | 0 | 0 | OF-5 |
| 1942 | 74 | 191 | 60 | 12 | 2 | 0 | 0.0 | 38 | 16 | 11 | 14 | 2 | .314 | .398 | 16 | 0 | OF-56, 2B-2 |
| 1943 | 148 | 564 | 166 | 28 | 6 | 2 | 0.4 | 76 | 53 | 40 | 24 | 5 | .294 | .376 | 4 | 1 | OF-144, 2B-1 |
| 1946 | 112 | 346 | 82 | 14 | 6 | 3 | 0.9 | 53 | 27 | 30 | 29 | 12 | .237 | .338 | 11 | 3 | OF-92, 1B-8 |
| 1947 2 teams | STL N (10G – .200) | | | | | PHI N (130G – .371) | | | | | | | | | | | |
| " total | 140 | 513 | 186 | 29 | 16 | 1 | 0.2 | 81 | 41 | 63 | 39 | 13 | **.363** | .487 | 2 | 0 | OF-136, 1B-4 |
| 1948 PHI N | 112 | 332 | 97 | 11 | 2 | 2 | 0.6 | 34 | 23 | 33 | 30 | 4 | .292 | .355 | 26 | 7 | OF-81, 1B-4, 3B-1 |
| 1949 2 teams | CHI N (42G – .264) | | | | | CIN N (86G – .318) | | | | | | | | | | | |
| " total | 128 | 473 | 142 | 21 | 5 | 2 | 0.4 | 73 | 37 | 45 | 23 | 6 | .300 | .378 | 11 | 2 | OF-116, 1B-1 |
| 1950 STL N | 60 | 150 | 31 | 5 | 0 | 0 | 0.0 | 17 | 7 | 18 | 12 | 0 | .207 | .240 | 6 | 0 | OF-46, 1B-2 |
| 1951 | 8 | 26 | 8 | 1 | 0 | 0 | 0.0 | 6 | 2 | 2 | 1 | 0 | .308 | .346 | 0 | 0 | OF-6, 1B-1 |
| 1955 | 11 | 14 | 5 | 2 | 0 | 0 | 0.0 | 2 | 1 | 1 | 0 | 0 | .357 | .500 | 9 | 4 | OF-1 |
| 11 yrs. | 807 | 2651 | 786 | 126 | 37 | 10 | 0.4 | 385 | 214 | 245 | 175 | 42 | .296 | .383 | 85 | 17 | OF-690, 1B-20, 2B-3, 3B-1 |
| 1 yr. | 42 | 159 | 42 | 6 | 3 | 1 | 0.6 | 20 | 14 | 11 | 6 | 2 | .264 | .358 | 3 | 0 | OF-39 |

WORLD SERIES

| | G | AB | H | 2B | 3B | HR | HR% | R | RBI | BB | SO | SB | BA | SA | AB | H | G by POS |
|---|---|---|---|---|---|---|---|---|---|---|---|---|---|---|---|---|---|
| 1942 STL N | 1 | 1 | 0 | 0 | 0 | 0 | 0.0 | 0 | 0 | 0 | 1 | 0 | .000 | .000 | 1 | 0 | |
| 1943 | 5 | 18 | 3 | 1 | 0 | 0 | 0.0 | 0 | 0 | 0 | 2 | 0 | .167 | .222 | 1 | 1 | OF-5 |
| 1946 | 7 | 17 | 7 | 2 | 0 | 0 | 0.0 | 3 | 6 | 4 | 2 | 0 | .412 | .529 | 1 | 0 | OF-7 |
| 3 yrs. | 13 | 36 | 10 | 3 | 0 | 0 | 0.0 | 3 | 6 | 4 | 5 | 0 | .278 | .361 | 3 | 1 | OF-12 |

## Rube Walker

**WALKER, ALBERT BLUFORD**
B. May 16, 1926, Lenoir, N. C.

BL TR 6' 175 lbs.

| | G | AB | H | 2B | 3B | HR | HR% | R | RBI | BB | SO | SB | BA | SA | AB | H | G by POS |
|---|---|---|---|---|---|---|---|---|---|---|---|---|---|---|---|---|---|
| 1948 CHI N | 79 | 171 | 47 | 8 | 0 | 5 | 2.9 | 17 | 26 | 24 | 17 | 0 | .275 | .409 | 32 | 7 | C-44 |
| 1949 | 56 | 172 | 42 | 4 | 1 | 3 | 1.7 | 11 | 22 | 9 | 18 | 0 | .244 | .331 | 12 | 3 | C-43 |
| 1950 | 74 | 213 | 49 | 7 | 1 | 6 | 2.8 | 19 | 16 | 18 | 34 | 0 | .230 | .357 | 14 | 1 | C-62 |
| 1951 2 teams | CHI N (37G – .234) | | | | | BKN N (36G – .243) | | | | | | | | | | | |
| " total | 73 | 181 | 43 | 8 | 0 | 4 | 2.2 | 15 | 14 | 18 | 27 | 0 | .238 | .348 | 17 | 3 | C-54 |
| 1952 BKN N | 46 | 139 | 36 | 8 | 0 | 1 | 0.7 | 9 | 19 | 8 | 17 | 0 | .259 | .338 | 6 | 1 | C-40 |
| 1953 | 43 | 95 | 23 | 6 | 0 | 3 | 3.2 | 5 | 9 | 7 | 11 | 0 | .242 | .400 | 14 | 5 | C-28 |
| 1954 | 50 | 155 | 28 | 7 | 0 | 5 | 3.2 | 12 | 23 | 24 | 17 | 0 | .181 | .323 | 3 | 0 | C-47 |
| 1955 | 48 | 103 | 26 | 5 | 0 | 2 | 1.9 | 6 | 13 | 15 | 11 | 1 | .252 | .359 | 10 | 2 | C-35 |
| 1956 | 54 | 146 | 31 | 6 | 1 | 3 | 2.1 | 5 | 20 | 7 | 18 | 0 | .212 | .329 | 9 | 2 | C-43 |
| 1957 | 60 | 166 | 30 | 8 | 0 | 2 | 1.2 | 12 | 23 | 15 | 33 | 2 | .181 | .265 | 10 | 3 | C-50 |
| 1958 LA N | 25 | 44 | 5 | 2 | 0 | 1 | 2.3 | 3 | 7 | 5 | 10 | 0 | .114 | .227 | 5 | 1 | C-20 |
| 11 yrs. | 608 | 1585 | 360 | 69 | 3 | 35 | 2.2 | 114 | 192 | 150 | 213 | 3 | .227 | .341 | 132 | 28 | C-466 |
| 4 yrs. | 246 | 663 | 163 | 23 | 2 | 16 | 2.4 | 56 | 69 | 63 | 82 | 0 | .246 | .359 | 63 | 12 | C-180 |

WORLD SERIES

| | G | AB | H | 2B | 3B | HR | HR% | R | RBI | BB | SO | SB | BA | SA | AB | H | G by POS |
|---|---|---|---|---|---|---|---|---|---|---|---|---|---|---|---|---|---|
| 1956 BKN N | 2 | 2 | 0 | 0 | 0 | 0 | 0.0 | 0 | 0 | 0 | 0 | 0 | .000 | .000 | 2 | 0 | |

## Jack Wallace

**WALLACE, CLARENCE EUGENE**
B. Aug. 6, 1890, Winnfield, La. D. Oct. 15, 1960, Winnfield, La.

BR TR 5'10½" 175 lbs.

| | G | AB | H | 2B | 3B | HR | HR% | R | RBI | BB | SO | SB | BA | SA | AB | H | G by POS |
|---|---|---|---|---|---|---|---|---|---|---|---|---|---|---|---|---|---|
| 1915 CHI N | 2 | 7 | 2 | 0 | 0 | 0 | 0.0 | 1 | 0 | 2 | 0 | 0 | .286 | .286 | 0 | 0 | C-2 |

## Ty Waller

**WALLER, ELLIOTT TYRONE**
B. Mar. 14, 1957, Fresno, Calif.

BR TR 6' 180 lbs.

| | G | AB | H | 2B | 3B | HR | HR% | R | RBI | BB | SO | SB | BA | SA | AB | H | G by POS |
|---|---|---|---|---|---|---|---|---|---|---|---|---|---|---|---|---|---|
| 1980 STL N | 5 | 12 | 1 | 0 | 0 | 0 | 0.0 | 3 | 0 | 1 | 5 | 0 | .083 | .083 | 0 | 0 | 3B-5 |
| 1981 CHI N | 30 | 71 | 19 | 2 | 1 | 3 | 4.2 | 10 | 13 | 4 | 18 | 2 | .268 | .451 | 1 | 1 | 3B-22, OF-3, 2B-3 |
| 1982 | 17 | 21 | 5 | 0 | 0 | 0 | 0.0 | 4 | 1 | 2 | 5 | 0 | .238 | .238 | 6 | 2 | OF-7, 3B-1 |
| 3 yrs. | 52 | 104 | 25 | 2 | 1 | 3 | 2.9 | 17 | 14 | 7 | 28 | 2 | .240 | .365 | 7 | 3 | 3B-28, OF-10, 2B-3 |
| 2 yrs. | 47 | 92 | 24 | 2 | 1 | 3 | 3.3 | 14 | 14 | 6 | 23 | 2 | .261 | .402 | 7 | 3 | 3B-23, OF-10, 2B-3 |

## Joe Wallis

**WALLIS, HAROLD JOSEPH**
B. Jan. 9, 1952, East St. Louis, Mo.

BL TR 5'10" 185 lbs.

| | G | AB | H | 2B | 3B | HR | HR% | R | RBI | BB | SO | SB | BA | SA | AB | H | G by POS |
|---|---|---|---|---|---|---|---|---|---|---|---|---|---|---|---|---|---|
| 1975 CHI N | 16 | 56 | 16 | 2 | 2 | 1 | 1.8 | 9 | 4 | 5 | 14 | 2 | .286 | .446 | 3 | 1 | OF-15 |
| 1976 | 121 | 338 | 86 | 11 | 5 | 5 | 1.5 | 51 | 29 | 33 | 62 | 3 | .254 | .361 | 26 | 4 | OF-90 |
| 1977 | 56 | 80 | 20 | 3 | 0 | 2 | 2.5 | 14 | 8 | 16 | 25 | 0 | .250 | .363 | 16 | 2 | OF-35 |
| 1978 2 teams | CHI N (28G – .309) | | | | | OAK A (85G – .237) | | | | | | | | | | | |
| " total | 113 | 334 | 83 | 18 | 2 | 7 | 2.1 | 35 | 32 | 31 | 55 | 1 | .249 | .377 | 10 | 2 | OF-105, DH-1 |

| | G | AB | H | 2B | 3B | HR | HR % | R | RBI | BB | SO | SB | BA | SA | Pinch Hit AB | Pinch Hit H | G by POS |
|---|---|---|---|---|---|---|---|---|---|---|---|---|---|---|---|---|---|

## Joe Wallis continued

| | G | AB | H | 2B | 3B | HR | HR % | R | RBI | BB | SO | SB | BA | SA | PH AB | PH H | G by POS |
|---|---|---|---|---|---|---|---|---|---|---|---|---|---|---|---|---|---|
| 1979 OAK A | 23 | 78 | 11 | 2 | 0 | 1 | 1.3 | 6 | 3 | 10 | 18 | 1 | .141 | .205 | 0 | 0 | OF-23 |
| 5 yrs. | 329 | 886 | 216 | 36 | 9 | 16 | 1.8 | 115 | 68 | 95 | 174 | 7 | .244 | .359 | 55 | 9 | OF-268, DH-1 |
| 4 yrs. | 221 | 529 | 139 | 18 | 8 | 9 | 1.7 | 81 | 39 | 59 | 114 | 5 | .263 | .378 | 49 | 9 | OF-165 |

## Lee Walls

**WALLS, RAY LEE**        BR TR 6'3"   205 lbs.
B. Jan. 6, 1933, San Diego, Calif.

| | G | AB | H | 2B | 3B | HR | HR % | R | RBI | BB | SO | SB | BA | SA | PH AB | PH H | G by POS |
|---|---|---|---|---|---|---|---|---|---|---|---|---|---|---|---|---|---|
| 1952 PIT N | 32 | 80 | 15 | 0 | 1 | 2 | 2.5 | 6 | 5 | 8 | 22 | 0 | .188 | .288 | 10 | 1 | OF-19 |
| 1956 | 143 | 474 | 130 | 20 | 11 | 11 | 2.3 | 72 | 54 | 50 | 83 | 3 | .274 | .432 | 10 | 1 | OF-134 |
| 1957 2 teams | | PIT | N (8G – | .182) | | CHI | N (117G – | .240) | | | | | | | | | |
| " total | 125 | 388 | 92 | 11 | 5 | 6 | 1.5 | 45 | 33 | 29 | 72 | 6 | .237 | .338 | 22 | 8 | OF-101, 3B-1 |
| 1958 CHI N | 136 | 513 | 156 | 19 | 3 | 24 | 4.7 | 80 | 72 | 47 | 62 | 4 | .304 | .493 | 4 | 2 | OF-132 |
| 1959 | 120 | 354 | 91 | 18 | 3 | 8 | 2.3 | 43 | 33 | 42 | 73 | 0 | .257 | .393 | 4 | 0 | OF-119 |
| 1960 2 teams | | CIN | N (29G – | .274) | | PHI | N (65G – | .199) | | | | | | | | | |
| " total | 94 | 265 | 59 | 9 | 3 | 4 | 1.5 | 31 | 26 | 31 | 52 | 5 | .223 | .325 | 20 | 5 | OF-37, 3B-34, 1B-9 |
| 1961 PHI N | 91 | 261 | 73 | 6 | 4 | 8 | 3.1 | 32 | 30 | 19 | 48 | 2 | .280 | .425 | 19 | 4 | 1B-28, 3B-26, OF-18 |
| 1962 LA N | 60 | 109 | 29 | 3 | 1 | 0 | 0.0 | 9 | 17 | 10 | 21 | 1 | .266 | .312 | 27 | 13 | OF-17, 1B-11, 3B-4 |
| 1963 | 64 | 86 | 20 | 1 | 0 | 3 | 3.5 | 12 | 11 | 7 | 25 | 0 | .233 | .349 | 39 | 7 | OF-18, 1B-5, 3B-2 |
| 1964 | 37 | 28 | 5 | 1 | 0 | 0 | 0.0 | 1 | 3 | 2 | 12 | 0 | .179 | .214 | 28 | 5 | OF-6, C-1 |
| 10 yrs. | 902 | 2558 | 670 | 88 | 31 | 66 | 2.6 | 331 | 284 | 245 | 470 | 21 | .262 | .398 | 183 | 46 | OF-601, 3B-67, 1B-53, C-1 |
| 3 yrs. | 373 | 1233 | 335 | 47 | 11 | 38 | 3.1 | 165 | 138 | 116 | 202 | 9 | .272 | .420 | 28 | 10 | OF-345, 3B-1 |

## Tom Walsh

**WALSH, THOMAS JOSEPH**      BR TR 5'11"   170 lbs.
B. Feb. 28, 1885, Davenport, Iowa     D. Mar. 16, 1963, Naples, Fla.

| | G | AB | H | 2B | 3B | HR | HR % | R | RBI | BB | SO | SB | BA | SA | PH AB | PH H | G by POS |
|---|---|---|---|---|---|---|---|---|---|---|---|---|---|---|---|---|---|
| 1906 CHI N | 2 | 1 | 0 | 0 | 0 | 0 | 0.0 | 0 | 0 | 0 | | 0 | .000 | .000 | 0 | 0 | C-2 |

## Chris Ward

**WARD, CHRIS GILBERT**      BL TL 6'   180 lbs.
B. May 18, 1949, Oakland, Calif.

| | G | AB | H | 2B | 3B | HR | HR % | R | RBI | BB | SO | SB | BA | SA | PH AB | PH H | G by POS |
|---|---|---|---|---|---|---|---|---|---|---|---|---|---|---|---|---|---|
| 1972 CHI N | 1 | 1 | 0 | 0 | 0 | 0 | 0.0 | 0 | 0 | 0 | 0 | 0 | .000 | .000 | 1 | 0 | |
| 1974 | 92 | 137 | 28 | 4 | 0 | 1 | 0.7 | 8 | 15 | 18 | 13 | 0 | .204 | .255 | 49 | 9 | OF-22, 1B-6 |
| 2 yrs. | 93 | 138 | 28 | 4 | 0 | 1 | 0.7 | 8 | 15 | 18 | 13 | 0 | .203 | .254 | 50 | 9 | OF-22, 1B-6 |
| 2 yrs. | 93 | 138 | 28 | 4 | 0 | 1 | 0.7 | 8 | 15 | 18 | 13 | 0 | .203 | .254 | 50 | 9 | OF-22, 1B-6 |

## Preston Ward

**WARD, PRESTON MEYER**      BL TR 6'4"   190 lbs.
B. July 24, 1927, Columbia, Mo.

| | G | AB | H | 2B | 3B | HR | HR % | R | RBI | BB | SO | SB | BA | SA | PH AB | PH H | G by POS |
|---|---|---|---|---|---|---|---|---|---|---|---|---|---|---|---|---|---|
| 1948 BKN N | 42 | 146 | 38 | 9 | 2 | 1 | 0.7 | 9 | 21 | 15 | 23 | 0 | .260 | .370 | 3 | 0 | 1B-38 |
| 1950 CHI N | 80 | 285 | 72 | 11 | 2 | 6 | 2.1 | 31 | 33 | 27 | 42 | 3 | .253 | .368 | 14 | 1 | 1B-76 |
| 1953 2 teams | | CHI | N (33G – | .230) | | PIT | N (88G – | .210) | | | | | | | | | |
| " total | 121 | 381 | 82 | 12 | 1 | 12 | 3.1 | 45 | 39 | 62 | 60 | 4 | .215 | .346 | 9 | 2 | 1B-85, OF-27 |
| 1954 PIT N | 117 | 360 | 97 | 16 | 2 | 7 | 1.9 | 37 | 48 | 39 | 61 | 0 | .269 | .383 | 18 | 4 | 1B-48, OF-42, 3B-11 |
| 1955 | 84 | 179 | 38 | 7 | 4 | 5 | 2.8 | 16 | 25 | 22 | 28 | 0 | .212 | .380 | 30 | 6 | 1B-48, OF-1 |
| 1956 2 teams | | PIT | N (16G – | .333) | | CLE | A (87G – | .253) | | | | | | | | | |
| " total | 103 | 180 | 48 | 10 | 1 | 7 | 3.9 | 21 | 32 | 22 | 24 | 0 | .267 | .450 | 26 | 8 | 1B-60, OF-22, 3B-5 |
| 1957 CLE A | 10 | 11 | 2 | 1 | 0 | 0 | 0.0 | 2 | 0 | 0 | 2 | 0 | .182 | .273 | 9 | 1 | 1B-1 |
| 1958 2 teams | | CLE | A (48G – | .338) | | KC | A (81G – | .254) | | | | | | | | | |
| " total | 129 | 416 | 118 | 13 | 2 | 10 | 2.4 | 50 | 45 | 37 | 63 | 0 | .284 | .397 | 18 | 4 | 1B-60, 3B-58, OF-2 |
| 1959 KC A | 58 | 109 | 27 | 4 | 1 | 2 | 1.8 | 8 | 19 | 7 | 12 | 0 | .248 | .358 | 32 | 8 | 1B-22, OF-1 |
| 9 yrs. | 744 | 2067 | 522 | 83 | 15 | 50 | 2.4 | 219 | 262 | 231 | 315 | 7 | .253 | .380 | 159 | 34 | 1B-438, OF-95, 3B-74 |
| 2 yrs. | 113 | 385 | 95 | 16 | 2 | 10 | 2.6 | 41 | 45 | 45 | 63 | 6 | .247 | .377 | 17 | 2 | 1B-83, OF-26 |

## Hooks Warner

**WARNER, HOKE HAYDEN**      BL TR 5'10½" 170 lbs.
B. May 22, 1894, Del Rio, Tex.     D. Feb. 19, 1947, San Francisco, Calif.

| | G | AB | H | 2B | 3B | HR | HR % | R | RBI | BB | SO | SB | BA | SA | PH AB | PH H | G by POS |
|---|---|---|---|---|---|---|---|---|---|---|---|---|---|---|---|---|---|
| 1916 PIT N | 44 | 168 | 40 | 1 | 1 | 2 | 1.2 | 12 | 14 | 6 | 19 | 6 | .238 | .292 | 0 | 0 | 3B-42, 2B-1 |
| 1917 | 3 | 5 | 1 | 0 | 0 | 0 | 0.0 | 0 | 0 | 0 | 1 | 0 | .200 | .200 | 1 | 1 | 3B-1 |
| 1919 | 6 | 8 | 1 | 0 | 0 | 0 | 0.0 | 0 | 2 | 3 | 1 | 0 | .125 | .125 | 1 | 1 | 3B-3 |
| 1921 CHI N | 14 | 38 | 8 | 1 | 0 | 0 | 0.0 | 4 | 3 | 2 | 1 | 1 | .211 | .237 | 3 | 0 | 3B-10 |
| 4 yrs. | 67 | 219 | 50 | 2 | 1 | 2 | 0.9 | 16 | 19 | 11 | 22 | 7 | .228 | .274 | 5 | 2 | 3B-56, 2B-1 |
| 1 yr. | 14 | 38 | 8 | 1 | 0 | 0 | 0.0 | 4 | 3 | 2 | 1 | 1 | .211 | .237 | 3 | 0 | 3B-10 |

## Rabbit Warstler

**WARSTLER, HAROLD BURTON**      BR TR 5'7½" 150 lbs.
B. Sept. 13, 1903, North Canton, Ohio     D. May 31, 1964, North Canton, Ohio

| | G | AB | H | 2B | 3B | HR | HR % | R | RBI | BB | SO | SB | BA | SA | PH AB | PH H | G by POS |
|---|---|---|---|---|---|---|---|---|---|---|---|---|---|---|---|---|---|
| 1930 BOS A | 55 | 162 | 30 | 2 | 3 | 1 | 0.6 | 16 | 13 | 20 | 21 | 0 | .185 | .253 | 0 | 0 | SS-54 |
| 1931 | 66 | 181 | 44 | 5 | 3 | 0 | 0.0 | 20 | 10 | 15 | 27 | 2 | .243 | .304 | 5 | 0 | 2B-42, SS-19 |
| 1932 | 115 | 388 | 82 | 15 | 5 | 0 | 0.0 | 26 | 34 | 22 | 43 | 9 | .211 | .276 | 3 | 0 | SS-107 |
| 1933 | 92 | 322 | 70 | 13 | 1 | 1 | 0.3 | 44 | 17 | 42 | 36 | 2 | .217 | .273 | 1 | 0 | SS-87 |
| 1934 PHI A | 117 | 419 | 99 | 19 | 3 | 1 | 0.2 | 56 | 36 | 51 | 30 | 9 | .236 | .303 | 4 | 0 | 2B-107, SS-2 |
| 1935 | 138 | 496 | 124 | 20 | 7 | 3 | 0.6 | 62 | 59 | 56 | 53 | 8 | .250 | .337 | 0 | 0 | 2B-136, 3B-2 |
| 1936 2 teams | | PHI | A (66G – | .250) | | BOS | N (74G – | .211) | | | | | | | | | |
| " total | 140 | 540 | 123 | 14 | 6 | 1 | 0.2 | 54 | 41 | 58 | 49 | 2 | .228 | .281 | 0 | 0 | SS-74, 2B-66 |
| 1937 BOS N | 149 | 555 | 124 | 20 | 3 | 0 | 0.5 | 57 | 36 | 51 | 62 | 4 | .223 | .276 | 0 | 0 | SS-149 |
| 1938 | 142 | 467 | 108 | 10 | 4 | 0 | 0.0 | 37 | 40 | 48 | 38 | 3 | .231 | .270 | 0 | 0 | SS-135, 2B-7 |
| 1939 | 114 | 342 | 83 | 11 | 3 | 0 | 0.0 | 34 | 24 | 24 | 31 | 2 | .243 | .292 | 1 | 0 | SS-49, 2B-43, 3B-21 |
| 1940 2 teams | | BOS | N (33G – | .211) | | CHI | N (45G – | .226) | | | | | | | | | |
| " total | 78 | 216 | 48 | 4 | 1 | 0 | 0.5 | 25 | 22 | 18 | 24 | 1 | .222 | .264 | 6 | 0 | 2B-41, SS-29, 3B-2 |
| 11 yrs. | 1206 | 4088 | 935 | 133 | 36 | 11 | 0.3 | 431 | 332 | 405 | 414 | 42 | .229 | .287 | 20 | 0 | SS-705, 2B-442, 3B-25 |
| 1 yr. | 45 | 159 | 36 | 4 | 1 | 1 | 0.6 | 19 | 18 | 8 | 19 | 1 | .226 | .283 | 0 | 0 | SS-28, 2B-17 |

| | G | AB | H | 2B | 3B | HR | HR% | R | RBI | BB | SO | SB | BA | SA | Pinch Hit AB | H | G by POS |
|---|---|---|---|---|---|---|---|---|---|---|---|---|---|---|---|---|---|

## Carl Warwick

**WARWICK, CARL WAYNE**
B. Feb. 27, 1937, Dallas, Tex.                                         BR TL 5'10" 170 lbs.

| | G | AB | H | 2B | 3B | HR | HR% | R | RBI | BB | SO | SB | BA | SA | Pinch Hit AB | H | G by POS |
|---|---|---|---|---|---|---|---|---|---|---|---|---|---|---|---|---|---|
| 1961 2 teams | LA | N | (19G – | .091) | | STL | N | (55G – | .250) | | | | | | | | |
| " total | 74 | 163 | 39 | 6 | 2 | 4 | 2.5 | 29 | 17 | 20 | 36 | 3 | .239 | .374 | 13 | 4 | OF-60 |
| 1962 2 teams | STL | N | (13G – | .348) | | HOU | N | (130G – | .260) | | | | | | | | |
| " total | 143 | 500 | 132 | 17 | 1 | 17 | 3.4 | 67 | 64 | 40 | 79 | 4 | .264 | .404 | 13 | 4 | OF-138 |
| 1963 HOU N | 150 | 528 | 134 | 19 | 5 | 7 | 1.3 | 49 | 47 | 49 | 70 | 3 | .254 | .348 | 10 | 2 | OF-141, 1B-2 |
| 1964 STL N | 88 | 158 | 41 | 7 | 1 | 3 | 1.9 | 14 | 15 | 11 | 30 | 2 | .259 | .373 | 43 | 11 | OF-49 |
| 1965 2 teams | STL | N | (50G – | .156) | | BAL | A | (9G – | .000) | | | | | | | | |
| " total | 59 | 91 | 12 | 2 | 1 | 0 | 0.0 | 6 | 6 | 7 | 20 | 1 | .132 | .176 | 36 | 4 | OF-24, 1B-4 |
| 1966 CHI N | 16 | 22 | 5 | 0 | 0 | 0 | 0.0 | 3 | 0 | 0 | 6 | 0 | .227 | .227 | 7 | 2 | OF-10 |
| 6 yrs. | 530 | 1462 | 363 | 51 | 10 | 31 | 2.1 | 168 | 149 | 127 | 241 | 13 | .248 | .360 | 122 | 27 | OF-422, 1B-6 |
| 1 yr. | 16 | 22 | 5 | 0 | 0 | 0 | 0.0 | 3 | 0 | 0 | 6 | 0 | .227 | .227 | 7 | 2 | OF-10 |
| WORLD SERIES | | | | | | | | | | | | | | | | | |
| 1964 STL N | 5 | 4 | 3 | 0 | 0 | 0 | 0.0 | 2 | 2 | 1 | 0 | 0 | .750 | .750 | 4 | 3 | |
| | | | | | | | | | | | | | | | | 1st | |

## Earl Webb

**WEBB, WILLIAM EARL**
B. Sept. 17, 1898, Bon Air, Tenn.    D. May 23, 1965, Jamestown, Tenn.     BL TR 6'1" 185 lbs.

| | G | AB | H | 2B | 3B | HR | HR% | R | RBI | BB | SO | SB | BA | SA | Pinch Hit AB | H | G by POS |
|---|---|---|---|---|---|---|---|---|---|---|---|---|---|---|---|---|---|
| 1925 NY N | 4 | 3 | 0 | 0 | 0 | 0 | 0.0 | 0 | 1 | 1 | 1 | 0 | .000 | .000 | 3 | 0 | |
| 1927 CHI N | 102 | 332 | 100 | 18 | 4 | 14 | 4.2 | 58 | 52 | 48 | 31 | 3 | .301 | .506 | 15 | 3 | OF-86 |
| 1928 | 62 | 140 | 35 | 7 | 3 | 3 | 2.1 | 22 | 23 | 14 | 17 | 0 | .250 | .407 | 24 | 8 | OF-31 |
| 1930 BOS A | 127 | 449 | 145 | 30 | 6 | 16 | 3.6 | 61 | 66 | 44 | 56 | 2 | .323 | .523 | 8 | 2 | OF-116 |
| 1931 | 151 | 589 | 196 | 67¹ | 3 | 14 | 2.4 | 96 | 103 | 70 | 51 | 2 | .333 | .528 | 0 | 0 | OF-151 |
| 1932 2 teams | BOS | A | (52G – | .281) | | DET | A | (87G – | .287) | | | | | | | | |
| " total | 139 | 530 | 151 | 28 | 9 | 8 | 1.5 | 72 | 78 | 64 | 33 | 1 | .285 | .417 | 1 | 0 | OF-134, 1B-2 |
| 1933 2 teams | DET | A | (6G – | .273) | | CHI | A | (58G – | .290) | | | | | | | | |
| " total | 64 | 118 | 34 | 5 | 0 | 1 | 0.8 | 17 | 11 | 19 | 13 | 0 | .288 | .356 | 30 | 8 | OF-18, 1B-10 |
| 7 yrs. | 649 | 2161 | 661 | 155 | 25 | 56 | 2.6 | 326 | 333 | 260 | 202 | 8 | .306 | .478 | 81 | 21 | OF-536, 1B-12 |
| 2 yrs. | 164 | 472 | 135 | 25 | 7 | 17 | 3.6 | 80 | 75 | 62 | 48 | 3 | .286 | .477 | 39 | 11 | OF-117 |

## Ramon Webster

**WEBSTER, RAMON ALBERTO**
B. Aug. 31, 1942, Colon, Panama                                         BL TL 6' 185 lbs.

| | G | AB | H | 2B | 3B | HR | HR% | R | RBI | BB | SO | SB | BA | SA | Pinch Hit AB | H | G by POS |
|---|---|---|---|---|---|---|---|---|---|---|---|---|---|---|---|---|---|
| 1967 KC A | 122 | 360 | 92 | 15 | 4 | 11 | 3.1 | 41 | 51 | 32 | 44 | 5 | .256 | .411 | 26 | 5 | 1B-83, OF-15 |
| 1968 OAK A | 66 | 196 | 42 | 11 | 1 | 3 | 1.5 | 17 | 23 | 12 | 24 | 3 | .214 | .327 | 11 | 6 | 1B-55 |
| 1969 | 64 | 77 | 20 | 0 | 0 | 1 | 1.3 | 5 | 13 | 12 | 8 | 0 | .260 | .325 | 39 | 10 | 1B-13 |
| 1970 SD N | 95 | 116 | 30 | 3 | 0 | 2 | 1.7 | 12 | 11 | 11 | 12 | 1 | .259 | .336 | 70 | 17 | 1B-15, OF-1 |
| 1971 3 teams | SD | N | (10G – | .125) | | CHI | N | (16G – | .313) | | OAK | A | (7G – | .000) | | | |
| " total | 33 | 29 | 6 | 2 | 0 | 0 | 0.0 | 1 | 0 | 3 | 6 | 0 | .207 | .276 | 27 | 4 | 1B-2 |
| 5 yrs. | 380 | 778 | 190 | 31 | 6 | 17 | 2.2 | 76 | 98 | 70 | 94 | 9 | .244 | .365 | 173 | 42 | 1B-168, OF-16 |
| 1 yr. | 16 | 16 | 5 | 2 | 0 | 0 | 0.0 | 1 | 0 | 1 | 3 | 0 | .313 | .438 | 14 | 3 | 1B-1 |

## Butch Weis

**WEIS, ARTHUR JOHN**
B. Mar. 2, 1903, St. Louis, Mo.                                         BL TL 5'11" 180 lbs.

| | G | AB | H | 2B | 3B | HR | HR% | R | RBI | BB | SO | SB | BA | SA | Pinch Hit AB | H | G by POS |
|---|---|---|---|---|---|---|---|---|---|---|---|---|---|---|---|---|---|
| 1922 CHI N | 2 | 2 | 1 | 0 | 0 | 0 | 0.0 | 2 | 0 | 0 | 0 | 0 | .500 | .500 | 2 | 1 | |
| 1923 | 22 | 26 | 6 | 1 | 0 | 0 | 0.0 | 2 | 2 | 5 | 8 | 0 | .231 | .269 | 13 | 3 | OF-6 |
| 1924 | 39 | 133 | 37 | 8 | 1 | 0 | 0.0 | 19 | 23 | 15 | 14 | 4 | .278 | .353 | 1 | 1 | OF-36 |
| 1925 | 67 | 180 | 48 | 5 | 3 | 2 | 1.1 | 16 | 25 | 23 | 22 | 2 | .267 | .361 | 20 | 3 | OF-46 |
| 4 yrs. | 130 | 341 | 92 | 14 | 4 | 2 | 0.6 | 39 | 50 | 43 | 44 | 6 | .270 | .352 | 36 | 8 | OF-88 |
| 4 yrs. | 130 | 341 | 92 | 14 | 4 | 2 | 0.6 | 39 | 50 | 43 | 44 | 6 | .270 | .352 | 36 | 8 | OF-88 |

## Pete Whisenant

**WHISENANT, THOMAS PETER**
B. Dec. 14, 1929, Asheville, N. C.                                         BR TR 6'2" 190 lbs.

| | G | AB | H | 2B | 3B | HR | HR% | R | RBI | BB | SO | SB | BA | SA | Pinch Hit AB | H | G by POS |
|---|---|---|---|---|---|---|---|---|---|---|---|---|---|---|---|---|---|
| 1952 BOS N | 24 | 52 | 10 | 2 | 0 | 0 | 0.0 | 3 | 7 | 4 | 13 | 1 | .192 | .231 | 9 | 1 | OF-14 |
| 1955 STL N | 58 | 115 | 22 | 5 | 1 | 2 | 1.7 | 10 | 9 | 5 | 29 | 2 | .191 | .304 | 20 | 5 | OF-40 |
| 1956 CHI N | 103 | 314 | 75 | 16 | 3 | 11 | 3.5 | 37 | 46 | 24 | 53 | 8 | .239 | .414 | 8 | 2 | OF-93 |
| 1957 CIN N | 67 | 90 | 19 | 3 | 2 | 5 | 5.6 | 18 | 11 | 5 | 24 | 0 | .211 | .456 | 20 | 8 | OF-43 |
| 1958 | 85 | 203 | 48 | 9 | 2 | 11 | 5.4 | 33 | 40 | 18 | 37 | 3 | .236 | .463 | 25 | 6 | OF-66, 2B-1 |
| 1959 | 36 | 71 | 17 | 2 | 0 | 5 | 7.0 | 11 | 13 | 8 | 18 | 0 | .239 | .479 | 14 | 1 | OF-21 |
| 1960 3 teams | CIN | N | (1G – | .000) | | CLE | A | (7G – | .167) | | WAS | A | (58G – | .226) | | | |
| " total | 66 | 122 | 27 | 9 | 0 | 3 | 2.5 | 19 | 9 | 19 | 16 | 2 | .221 | .369 | 15 | 2 | OF-49 |
| 1961 2 teams | MIN | A | (10G – | .000) | | CIN | N | (26G – | .200) | | | | | | | | |
| " total | 36 | 21 | 3 | 0 | 0 | 0 | 0.0 | 7 | 1 | 3 | 6 | 1 | .143 | .143 | 13 | 1 | OF-17, 3B-1, C-1 |
| 8 yrs. | 475 | 988 | 221 | 46 | 8 | 37 | 3.7 | 140 | 134 | 86 | 196 | 17 | .224 | .399 | 124 | 26 | OF-343, 3B-1, 2B-1, C-1 |
| 1 yr. | 103 | 314 | 75 | 16 | 3 | 11 | 3.5 | 37 | 46 | 24 | 53 | 8 | .239 | .414 | 8 | 2 | OF-93 |

## Deacon White

**WHITE, JAMES LAURIE**
Brother of Will White.
B. Dec. 7, 1847, Caton, N. Y.    D. July 7, 1939, Aurora, Ill.     BL TR 5'11" 175 lbs.
Manager 1879.

| | G | AB | H | 2B | 3B | HR | HR% | R | RBI | BB | SO | SB | BA | SA | Pinch Hit AB | H | G by POS |
|---|---|---|---|---|---|---|---|---|---|---|---|---|---|---|---|---|---|
| 1876 CHI N | 66 | 303 | 104 | 18 | 1 | 1 | 0.3 | 66 | 60 | 7 | 3 | | .343 | .419 | 0 | 0 | C-63, OF-3, 1B-3, 3B-1, P-1 |
| 1877 BOS N | 59 | 266 | 103 | 14 | 11 | 2 | 0.8 | 51 | 49 | 8 | 3 | | .387 | .545 | 0 | 0 | 1B-35, OF-19, C-7 |
| 1878 CIN N | 61 | 258 | 81 | 4 | 1 | 0 | 0.0 | 41 | 29 | 10 | 5 | | .314 | .337 | 0 | 0 | C-48, OF-16, 3B-1 |
| 1879 | 78 | 333 | 110 | 16 | 6 | 1 | 0.3 | 55 | 52 | 6 | 9 | | .330 | .423 | 0 | 0 | C-59, OF-21, 1B-2 |
| 1880 | 35 | 141 | 42 | 4 | 2 | 0 | 0.0 | 21 | 7 | 9 | 7 | | .298 | .355 | 0 | 0 | OF-33, 1B-3, 2B-1 |
| 1881 BUF N | 78 | 319 | 99 | 24 | 4 | 0 | 0.0 | 58 | 53 | 9 | 8 | | .310 | .411 | 0 | 0 | 1B-26, 2B-25, OF-17, 3B-7, C-4 |
| 1882 | 83 | 337 | 95 | 17 | 0 | 1 | 0.3 | 51 | | 15 | 16 | | .282 | .341 | 0 | 0 | 3B-63, C-20 |
| 1883 | 94 | 391 | 114 | 14 | 5 | 0 | 0.0 | 62 | | 23 | 18 | | .292 | .353 | 0 | 0 | 3B-77, C-22 |
| 1884 | 110 | 452 | 147 | 16 | 11 | 5 | 1.1 | 82 | | 32 | 13 | | .325 | .442 | 0 | 0 | 3B-108, C-3 |
| 1885 | 98 | 404 | 118 | 6 | 6 | 0 | 0.0 | 54 | 57 | 12 | 11 | | .292 | .337 | 0 | 0 | 3B-98 |
| 1886 DET N | 124 | 491 | 142 | 19 | 5 | 1 | 0.2 | 65 | 76 | 31 | 35 | | .289 | .354 | 0 | 0 | 3B-124 |
| 1887 | 111 | 449 | 136 | 20 | 11 | 3 | 0.7 | 71 | 75 | 26 | 15 | 20 | .303 | .416 | 0 | 0 | 3B-106, OF-3, 1B-2 |

| | G | AB | H | 2B | 3B | HR | HR % | R | RBI | BB | SO | SB | BA | SA | Pinch Hit AB | Pinch Hit H | G by POS |
|---|---|---|---|---|---|---|---|---|---|---|---|---|---|---|---|---|---|

## Deacon White continued

| | G | AB | H | 2B | 3B | HR | HR % | R | RBI | BB | SO | SB | BA | SA | AB | H | G by POS |
|---|---|---|---|---|---|---|---|---|---|---|---|---|---|---|---|---|---|
| 1888 | 125 | 527 | 157 | 22 | 5 | 4 | 0.8 | 75 | 71 | 21 | 24 | 12 | .298 | .381 | 0 | 0 | 3B-125 |
| 1889 PIT N | 55 | 225 | 57 | 10 | 1 | 0 | 0.0 | 35 | 26 | 16 | 18 | 2 | .253 | .307 | 0 | 0 | 3B-52, 1B-3 |
| 1890 BUF P | 122 | 439 | 114 | 13 | 4 | 0 | 0.0 | 62 | 47 | 67 | 30 | 3 | .260 | .308 | 0 | 0 | 3B-64, 1B-57, SS-1, P-1 |
| 15 yrs. | 1299 | 5335 | 1619 | 217 | 73 | 18 | 0.3 | 849 | 602 | 292 | 215 | 37 | .303 | .382 | 0 | 0 | 3B-826, C-226, 1B-131, OF-112, 2B-26, P-2, SS-1 |
| 1 yr. | 66 | 303 | 104 | 18 | 1 | 1 | 0.3 | 66 | 60 | 7 | 3 | | .343 | .419 | 0 | 0 | C-63, OF-3, 1B-3, 3B-1, P-1 |

## Elder White

**WHITE, ELDER LAFAYETTE**  BR  TR  5'11"  165 lbs.
B. Dec. 23, 1934, Colerain, N. C.

| | G | AB | H | 2B | 3B | HR | HR % | R | RBI | BB | SO | SB | BA | SA | AB | H | G by POS |
|---|---|---|---|---|---|---|---|---|---|---|---|---|---|---|---|---|---|
| 1962 CHI N | 23 | 53 | 8 | 2 | 0 | 0 | 0.0 | 4 | 1 | 8 | 11 | 3 | .151 | .189 | 6 | 1 | SS-15, 2B-1 |

## Jerry White

**WHITE, JEROME CARDELL**  BB  TR  5'10"  164 lbs.
B. Aug. 23, 1952, Shirley, Mass.

| | G | AB | H | 2B | 3B | HR | HR % | R | RBI | BB | SO | SB | BA | SA | AB | H | G by POS |
|---|---|---|---|---|---|---|---|---|---|---|---|---|---|---|---|---|---|
| 1974 MON N | 9 | 10 | 4 | 1 | 1 | 0 | 0.0 | 0 | 2 | 0 | 0 | 3 | .400 | .700 | 0 | 0 | OF-7 |
| 1975 | 39 | 97 | 29 | 4 | 1 | 2 | 2.1 | 14 | 7 | 10 | 7 | 5 | .299 | .423 | 3 | 0 | OF-30 |
| 1976 | 114 | 278 | 68 | 11 | 1 | 2 | 0.7 | 32 | 21 | 27 | 31 | 15 | .245 | .313 | 17 | 2 | OF-92 |
| 1977 | 16 | 21 | 4 | 0 | 0 | 0 | 0.0 | 4 | 1 | 1 | 3 | 1 | .190 | .190 | 10 | 2 | OF-8 |
| 1978 2 teams | | | | MON N (18G – .200) | | | | CHI N (59G – .272) | | | | | | | | | |
| " total | 77 | 146 | 39 | 6 | 0 | 1 | 0.7 | 24 | 10 | 24 | 19 | 5 | .267 | .329 | 12 | 3 | OF-57 |
| 1979 MON N | 88 | 138 | 41 | 7 | 1 | 3 | 2.2 | 30 | 18 | 21 | 23 | 8 | .297 | .428 | 38 | 12 | OF-43 |
| 1980 | 110 | 214 | 56 | 9 | 3 | 7 | 3.3 | 22 | 23 | 30 | 37 | 8 | .262 | .430 | 29 | 6 | OF-84 |
| 1981 | 59 | 119 | 26 | 5 | 1 | 3 | 2.5 | 11 | 11 | 13 | 17 | 5 | .218 | .353 | 18 | 5 | OF-39 |
| 1982 | 69 | 115 | 28 | 6 | 1 | 2 | 1.7 | 13 | 13 | 8 | 26 | 3 | .243 | .365 | 39 | 10 | OF-30 |
| 1983 | 40 | 34 | 5 | 1 | 0 | 0 | 0.0 | 4 | 0 | 12 | 8 | 4 | .147 | .176 | 23 | 2 | OF-13 |
| 10 yrs. | 621 | 1172 | 300 | 50 | 9 | 20 | 1.7 | 154 | 106 | 146 | 171 | 57 | .256 | .365 | 189 | 42 | OF-403 |
| 1 yr. | 59 | 136 | 37 | 6 | 0 | 1 | 0.7 | 22 | 10 | 23 | 16 | 4 | .272 | .338 | 4 | 2 | OF-54 |

DIVISIONAL PLAYOFF SERIES

| | G | AB | H | 2B | 3B | HR | HR % | R | RBI | BB | SO | SB | BA | SA | AB | H | G by POS |
|---|---|---|---|---|---|---|---|---|---|---|---|---|---|---|---|---|---|
| 1981 MON N | 5 | 18 | 3 | 1 | 0 | 0 | 0.0 | 3 | 1 | 2 | 2 | 3 | .167 | .222 | 0 | 0 | OF-5 |

LEAGUE CHAMPIONSHIP SERIES

| | G | AB | H | 2B | 3B | HR | HR % | R | RBI | BB | SO | SB | BA | SA | AB | H | G by POS |
|---|---|---|---|---|---|---|---|---|---|---|---|---|---|---|---|---|---|
| 1981 MON N | 5 | 16 | 5 | 1 | 0 | 1 | 6.3 | 2 | 3 | 3 | 1 | 1 | .313 | .563 | 0 | 0 | OF-5 |

## Bob Wicker

**WICKER, ROBERT KITRIDGE**  BR  TR  6'1"  195 lbs.
B. May 25, 1878, Bedford, Ind.    D. Jan. 22, 1955, Evanston, Ill.

| | G | AB | H | 2B | 3B | HR | HR % | R | RBI | BB | SO | SB | BA | SA | AB | H | G by POS |
|---|---|---|---|---|---|---|---|---|---|---|---|---|---|---|---|---|---|
| 1901 STL N | 3 | 3 | 1 | 0 | 0 | 0 | 0.0 | 1 | 0 | 0 | | 0 | .333 | .333 | 1 | 0 | P-1 |
| 1902 | 31 | 77 | 18 | 2 | 0 | 0 | 0.0 | 6 | 3 | 3 | | 2 | .234 | .260 | 6 | 1 | P-22, OF-3 |
| 1903 2 teams | | | | STL N (1G – .000) | | | | CHI N (32G – .245) | | | | | | | | | |
| " total | 33 | 100 | 24 | 5 | 2 | 0 | 0.0 | 19 | 8 | 4 | | 1 | .240 | .330 | 0 | 0 | P-33 |
| 1904 CHI N | 50 | 155 | 34 | 1 | 0 | 0 | 0.0 | 17 | 9 | 4 | | 4 | .219 | .226 | 0 | 0 | P-30, OF-20 |
| 1905 | 25 | 72 | 10 | 0 | 0 | 0 | 0.0 | 5 | 3 | 4 | | 1 | .139 | .139 | 0 | 0 | P-22, OF-3 |
| 1906 2 teams | | | | CHI N (10G – .100) | | | | CIN N (20G – .180) | | | | | | | | | |
| " total | 30 | 70 | 11 | 1 | 2 | 0 | 0.0 | 6 | 4 | 7 | | 2 | .157 | .229 | 0 | 0 | P-30 |
| 6 yrs. | 172 | 477 | 98 | 9 | 4 | 0 | 0.0 | 54 | 27 | 22 | | 10 | .205 | .241 | 7 | 1 | P-138, OF-26 |
| 4 yrs. | 117 | 345 | 70 | 6 | 2 | 0 | 0.0 | 41 | 21 | 14 | | 6 | .203 | .232 | 0 | 0 | P-94, OF-23 |

## Harry Wilke

**WILKE, HENRY JOSEPH**  BR  TR  5'10½"  171 lbs.
B. Dec. 14, 1900, Cincinnati, Ohio

| | G | AB | H | 2B | 3B | HR | HR % | R | RBI | BB | SO | SB | BA | SA | AB | H | G by POS |
|---|---|---|---|---|---|---|---|---|---|---|---|---|---|---|---|---|---|
| 1927 CHI N | 3 | 9 | 0 | 0 | 0 | 0 | 0.0 | 0 | 0 | 0 | 1 | 0 | .000 | .000 | 0 | 0 | 3B-3 |

## Bob Will

**WILL, ROBERT LEE (Butch)**  BL  TL  5'10½"  175 lbs.
B. July 15, 1931, Irwin, Ill.

| | G | AB | H | 2B | 3B | HR | HR % | R | RBI | BB | SO | SB | BA | SA | AB | H | G by POS |
|---|---|---|---|---|---|---|---|---|---|---|---|---|---|---|---|---|---|
| 1957 CHI N | 70 | 112 | 25 | 3 | 0 | 1 | 0.9 | 13 | 10 | 5 | 21 | 1 | .223 | .277 | 36 | 8 | OF-30 |
| 1958 | 6 | 4 | 1 | 0 | 0 | 0 | 0.0 | 1 | 0 | 2 | 0 | 0 | .250 | .250 | 4 | 1 | OF-1 |
| 1960 | 138 | 475 | 121 | 20 | 9 | 6 | 1.3 | 58 | 53 | 47 | 54 | 1 | .255 | .373 | 20 | 5 | OF-121 |
| 1961 | 86 | 113 | 29 | 9 | 0 | 0 | 0.0 | 9 | 8 | 15 | 19 | 0 | .257 | .336 | 52 | 11 | OF-30, 1B-1 |
| 1962 | 87 | 92 | 22 | 3 | 0 | 2 | 2.2 | 6 | 15 | 13 | 22 | 0 | .239 | .337 | 67 | 17 | OF-9 |
| 1963 | 23 | 23 | 4 | 0 | 0 | 0 | 0.0 | 0 | 1 | 1 | 3 | 0 | .174 | .174 | 20 | 4 | 1B-1 |
| 6 yrs. | 410 | 819 | 202 | 35 | 9 | 9 | 1.1 | 87 | 87 | 83 | 119 | 2 | .247 | .344 | 199 | 46 | OF-191, 1B-2 |
| 6 yrs. | 410 | 819 | 202 | 35 | 9 | 9 | 1.1 | 87 | 87 | 83 | 119 | 2 | .247 | .344 | 199 | 46 | OF-191, 1B-2 |
| | | | | | | | | | | | | | | | 1st | 1st | |

## Art Williams

**WILLIAMS, ARTHUR FRANKLIN**  TR
B. Aug. 26, 1877, Somerville, Mass.    D. May 16, 1941, Arlington, Va.

| | G | AB | H | 2B | 3B | HR | HR % | R | RBI | BB | SO | SB | BA | SA | AB | H | G by POS |
|---|---|---|---|---|---|---|---|---|---|---|---|---|---|---|---|---|---|
| 1902 CHI N | 47 | 160 | 37 | 3 | 0 | 0 | 0.0 | 17 | 14 | 15 | | 9 | .231 | .250 | 4 | 0 | OF-24, 1B-19 |

## Billy Williams

**WILLIAMS, BILLY LEO**  BL  TR  6'1"  175 lbs.
B. June 15, 1938, Whistler, Ala.

| | G | AB | H | 2B | 3B | HR | HR % | R | RBI | BB | SO | SB | BA | SA | AB | H | G by POS |
|---|---|---|---|---|---|---|---|---|---|---|---|---|---|---|---|---|---|
| 1959 CHI N | 18 | 33 | 5 | 0 | 1 | 0 | 0.0 | 0 | 2 | 1 | 7 | 0 | .152 | .212 | 6 | 0 | OF-10 |
| 1960 | 12 | 47 | 13 | 0 | 2 | 2 | 4.3 | 4 | 7 | 5 | 12 | 0 | .277 | .489 | 0 | 0 | OF-12 |
| 1961 | 146 | 529 | 147 | 20 | 7 | 25 | 4.7 | 75 | 86 | 45 | 70 | 6 | .278 | .484 | 13 | 6 | OF-135 |
| 1962 | 159 | 618 | 184 | 22 | 8 | 22 | 3.6 | 94 | 91 | 70 | 72 | 9 | .298 | .466 | 0 | 0 | OF-159 |
| 1963 | 161 | 612 | 175 | 36 | 9 | 25 | 4.1 | 87 | 95 | 68 | 78 | 7 | .286 | .497 | 1 | 0 | OF-160 |
| 1964 | 162 | 645 | 201 | 39 | 2 | 33 | 5.1 | 100 | 98 | 59 | 84 | 10 | .312 | .532 | 1 | 0 | OF-162 |
| 1965 | 164 | 645 | 203 | 39 | 6 | 34 | 5.3 | 115 | 108 | 65 | 76 | 10 | .315 | .552 | 0 | 0 | OF-164 |
| 1966 | 162 | 648 | 179 | 23 | 5 | 29 | 4.5 | 100 | 91 | 69 | 61 | 6 | .276 | .461 | 0 | 0 | OF-162 |
| 1967 | 162 | 634 | 176 | 21 | 12 | 28 | 4.4 | 92 | 84 | 68 | 67 | 6 | .278 | .481 | 0 | 0 | OF-162 |
| 1968 | 163 | 642 | 185 | 30 | 8 | 30 | 4.7 | 91 | 98 | 48 | 53 | 4 | .288 | .500 | 0 | 0 | OF-163 |
| 1969 | 163 | 642 | 188 | 33 | 10 | 21 | 3.3 | 103 | 95 | 59 | 70 | 3 | .293 | .474 | 2 | 0 | OF-159 |

| | G | AB | H | 2B | 3B | HR | HR % | R | RBI | BB | SO | SB | BA | SA | Pinch Hit AB | Pinch Hit H | G by POS |
|---|---|---|---|---|---|---|---|---|---|---|---|---|---|---|---|---|---|

## Billy Williams continued

| | G | AB | H | 2B | 3B | HR | HR% | R | RBI | BB | SO | SB | BA | SA | AB | H | G by POS |
|---|---|---|---|---|---|---|---|---|---|---|---|---|---|---|---|---|---|
| 1970 | 161 | 636 | **205** | 34 | 4 | 42 | 6.6 | **137** | 129 | 72 | 65 | 7 | .322 | .586 | 0 | 0 | OF-160 |
| 1971 | 157 | 594 | 179 | 27 | 5 | 28 | 4.7 | 86 | 93 | 77 | 44 | 7 | .301 | .505 | 5 | 1 | OF-154 |
| 1972 | 150 | 574 | 191 | 34 | 6 | 37 | 6.4 | 95 | 122 | 62 | 59 | 3 | **.333** | **.606** | 2 | 1 | OF-144, 1B-5 |
| 1973 | 156 | 576 | 166 | 22 | 2 | 20 | 3.5 | 72 | 86 | 76 | 72 | 4 | .288 | .438 | 3 | 1 | OF-138, 1B-19 |
| 1974 | 117 | 404 | 113 | 22 | 0 | 16 | 4.0 | 55 | 68 | 67 | 44 | 4 | .280 | .453 | 10 | 2 | 1B-65, OF-43 |
| 1975 OAK A | 155 | 520 | 127 | 20 | 1 | 23 | 4.4 | 68 | 81 | 76 | 68 | 0 | .244 | .419 | 3 | 1 | DH-145, 1B-7 |
| 1976 | 120 | 351 | 74 | 12 | 0 | 11 | 3.1 | 36 | 41 | 58 | 44 | 4 | .211 | .339 | 13 | 3 | DH-106, OF-1 |
| 18 yrs. | 2488 | 9350 | 2711 | 434 | 88 | 426 | 4.6 | 1410 | 1475 | 1045 | 1046 | 90 | .290 | .492 | 59 | 15 | OF-2088, DH-251, 1B-96 |
| 16 yrs. | 2213 | 8479 | 2510 | 402 | 87 | 392 | 4.6 | 1306 | 1353 | 911 | 934 | 86 | .296 | .503 | 43 | 11 | OF-2087, 1B-89 |
| | 3rd | 3rd | 3rd | 3rd | 8th | 2nd | 5th | 3rd | 3rd | 4th | 3rd | | | 3rd | | | |

LEAGUE CHAMPIONSHIP SERIES

| | G | AB | H | 2B | 3B | HR | HR% | R | RBI | BB | SO | SB | BA | SA | AB | H | G by POS |
|---|---|---|---|---|---|---|---|---|---|---|---|---|---|---|---|---|---|
| 1975 OAK A | 3 | 8 | 0 | 0 | 0 | 0 | 0.0 | 0 | 0 | 1 | 1 | 0 | .000 | .000 | 1 | 0 | DH-2 |

## Cy Williams

**WILLIAMS, FRED**
B. Dec. 21, 1887, Wadena, Ind.   D. Apr. 23, 1974, Eagle River, Wis.   BL TL 6'2"   180 lbs.

| | G | AB | H | 2B | 3B | HR | HR% | R | RBI | BB | SO | SB | BA | SA | AB | H | G by POS |
|---|---|---|---|---|---|---|---|---|---|---|---|---|---|---|---|---|---|
| 1912 CHI N | 28 | 62 | 15 | 1 | 1 | 0 | 0.0 | 3 | 1 | 6 | 14 | 2 | .242 | .290 | 5 | 0 | OF-22 |
| 1913 | 49 | 156 | 35 | 3 | 3 | 4 | 2.6 | 17 | 32 | 5 | 26 | 5 | .224 | .359 | 5 | 2 | OF-44 |
| 1914 | 55 | 94 | 19 | 2 | 2 | 0 | 0.0 | 12 | 5 | 13 | 13 | 2 | .202 | .266 | 22 | 4 | OF-27 |
| 1915 | 151 | 518 | 133 | 22 | 6 | 13 | 2.5 | 59 | 64 | 26 | 49 | 15 | .257 | .398 | 1 | 1 | OF-151 |
| 1916 | 118 | 405 | 113 | 19 | 9 | **12** | 3.0 | 55 | 66 | 51 | 64 | 6 | .279 | .459 | 2 | 0 | OF-116 |
| 1917 | 138 | 468 | 113 | 22 | 4 | 5 | 1.1 | 53 | 42 | 38 | **78** | 8 | .241 | .338 | 1 | 1 | OF-136 |
| 1918 PHI N | 94 | 351 | 97 | 14 | 1 | 6 | 1.7 | 49 | 39 | 27 | 30 | 10 | .276 | .373 | 1 | 0 | OF-91 |
| 1919 | 109 | 435 | 121 | 21 | 1 | 9 | 2.1 | 54 | 39 | 30 | 43 | 9 | .278 | .393 | 1 | 0 | OF-108 |
| 1920 | 148 | 590 | 192 | 36 | 10 | **15** | 2.5 | 88 | 72 | 32 | 45 | 18 | .325 | .497 | 1 | 0 | OF-147 |
| 1921 | 146 | 562 | 180 | 28 | 6 | 18 | 3.2 | 67 | 75 | 30 | 32 | 5 | .320 | .488 | 0 | 0 | OF-146 |
| 1922 | 151 | 584 | 180 | 30 | 6 | 26 | 4.5 | 98 | 92 | 74 | 49 | 11 | .308 | .514 | 1 | 0 | OF-150 |
| 1923 | 136 | 535 | 157 | 22 | 3 | **41** | 7.7 | 98 | 114 | 59 | 57 | 11 | .293 | .576 | 1 | 0 | OF-135 |
| 1924 | 148 | 558 | 183 | 31 | 11 | 24 | 4.3 | 101 | 93 | 67 | 49 | 7 | .328 | .552 | 3 | 0 | OF-145 |
| 1925 | 107 | 314 | 104 | 11 | 5 | 13 | 4.1 | 78 | 60 | 53 | 34 | 4 | .331 | .522 | 10 | 5 | OF-96 |
| 1926 | 107 | 336 | 116 | 13 | 4 | 18 | 5.4 | 63 | 53 | 38 | 35 | 2 | .345 | **.568** | 13 | 4 | OF-93 |
| 1927 | 131 | 492 | 135 | 18 | 2 | **30** | 6.1 | 86 | 98 | 61 | 57 | 0 | .274 | .502 | 1 | 0 | OF-130 |
| 1928 | 99 | 238 | 61 | 9 | 0 | 12 | 5.0 | 31 | 37 | 54 | 34 | 0 | .256 | .445 | 20 | 7 | OF-69 |
| 1929 | 66 | 65 | 19 | 2 | 0 | 5 | 7.7 | 11 | 21 | 22 | 9 | 0 | .292 | .554 | 38 | 6 | OF-11 |
| 1930 | 21 | 17 | 8 | 2 | 0 | 0 | 0.0 | 1 | 2 | 4 | 3 | 0 | .471 | .588 | 16 | 8 | OF-3 |
| 19 yrs. | 2002 | 6780 | 1981 | 306 | 74 | 251 | 3.7 | 1024 | 1005 | 690 | 721 | 115 | .292 | .470 | 142 | 41 | OF-1820 |
| 6 yrs. | 539 | 1703 | 428 | 69 | 25 | 34 | 2.0 | 199 | 210 | 139 | 244 | 38 | .251 | .381 | 36 | 8 | OF-496 |

## Dewey Williams

**WILLIAMS, DEWEY EDGAR (Dee)**
B. Feb. 5, 1916, Durham, N. C.   BR TR 6'   160 lbs.

| | G | AB | H | 2B | 3B | HR | HR% | R | RBI | BB | SO | SB | BA | SA | AB | H | G by POS |
|---|---|---|---|---|---|---|---|---|---|---|---|---|---|---|---|---|---|
| 1944 CHI N | 79 | 262 | 63 | 7 | 2 | 0 | 0.0 | 23 | 27 | 23 | 18 | 2 | .240 | .282 | 1 | 0 | C-77 |
| 1945 | 59 | 100 | 28 | 2 | 2 | 2 | 2.0 | 16 | 5 | 13 | 13 | 0 | .280 | .400 | 4 | 1 | C-54 |
| 1946 | 4 | 5 | 1 | 0 | 0 | 0 | 0.0 | 0 | 0 | 0 | 2 | 0 | .200 | .200 | 2 | 1 | C-2 |
| 1947 | 3 | 2 | 0 | 0 | 0 | 0 | 0.0 | 0 | 0 | 0 | 1 | 0 | .000 | .000 | 2 | 0 | C-1 |
| 1948 CIN N | 48 | 95 | 16 | 2 | 0 | 1 | 1.1 | 9 | 5 | 10 | 18 | 0 | .168 | .221 | 1 | 0 | C-47 |
| 5 yrs. | 193 | 464 | 108 | 11 | 4 | 3 | 0.6 | 48 | 37 | 46 | 52 | 2 | .233 | .293 | 10 | 2 | C-181 |
| 4 yrs. | 145 | 369 | 92 | 9 | 4 | 2 | 0.5 | 39 | 32 | 36 | 34 | 2 | .249 | .312 | 9 | 2 | C-134 |

WORLD SERIES

| | G | AB | H | 2B | 3B | HR | HR% | R | RBI | BB | SO | SB | BA | SA | AB | H | G by POS |
|---|---|---|---|---|---|---|---|---|---|---|---|---|---|---|---|---|---|
| 1945 CHI N | 2 | 2 | 0 | 0 | 0 | 0 | 0.0 | 0 | 0 | 0 | 1 | 0 | .000 | .000 | 1 | 0 | C-1 |

## Otto Williams

**WILLIAMS, OTTO GEORGE**
B. Nov. 2, 1877, Newark, N. J.   D. Mar. 19, 1937, Omaha, Neb.   BR TR 5'6"

| | G | AB | H | 2B | 3B | HR | HR% | R | RBI | BB | SO | SB | BA | SA | AB | H | G by POS |
|---|---|---|---|---|---|---|---|---|---|---|---|---|---|---|---|---|---|
| 1902 STL N | 2 | 5 | 2 | 0 | 0 | 0 | 0.0 | 0 | | 1 | | 1 | .400 | .400 | 0 | 0 | SS-2 |
| 1903 2 teams | STL N (53G – .203) | | | | | CHI N (38G – .223) | | | | | | | | | | | |
| " total | 91 | 317 | 67 | 9 | 2 | 0 | 0.0 | 24 | 22 | 13 | | 14 | .211 | .252 | 0 | 0 | SS-78, 2B-8, 1B-3, 3B-1 |
| 1904 CHI N | 57 | 185 | 37 | 4 | 1 | 0 | 0.0 | 21 | 8 | 13 | | 9 | .200 | .232 | 2 | 1 | OF-21, 1B-11, SS-10, 3B-6, 2B-6 |
| 1906 WAS A | 20 | 51 | 7 | 0 | 0 | 0 | 0.0 | 3 | 2 | 2 | | 0 | .137 | .137 | 3 | 0 | SS-8, 2B-6, 1B-2, 3B-1 |
| 4 yrs. | 170 | 558 | 113 | 13 | 3 | 0 | 0.0 | 48 | 34 | 29 | | 24 | .203 | .237 | 5 | 1 | SS-98, OF-21, 2B-20, 1B-16, 3B-8 |
| 2 yrs. | 95 | 315 | 66 | 9 | 1 | 0 | 0.0 | 35 | 21 | 17 | | 17 | .210 | .244 | 2 | 1 | SS-36, OF-21, 1B-14, 2B-13, 3B-7 |

## Wash Williams

**WILLIAMS, WASHINGTON J.**
B. Philadelphia, Pa.   D. Jan. 9, 1890, Philadelphia, Pa.   5'11"   180 lbs.

| | G | AB | H | 2B | 3B | HR | HR% | R | RBI | BB | SO | SB | BA | SA | AB | H | G by POS |
|---|---|---|---|---|---|---|---|---|---|---|---|---|---|---|---|---|---|
| 1884 RIC AA | 2 | 8 | 2 | 0 | 0 | 0 | 0.0 | 0 | | 0 | | | .250 | .250 | 0 | 0 | OF-2 |
| 1885 CHI N | 1 | 4 | 1 | 0 | 0 | 0 | 0.0 | 0 | | 0 | 0 | | .250 | .250 | 0 | 0 | OF-1, P-1 |
| 2 yrs. | 3 | 12 | 3 | 0 | 0 | 0 | 0.0 | 0 | | 0 | 0 | | .250 | .250 | 0 | 0 | OF-3, P-1 |
| 1 yr. | 1 | 4 | 1 | 0 | 0 | 0 | 0.0 | 0 | | 0 | 0 | | .250 | .250 | 0 | 0 | OF-1, P-1 |

## Ned Williamson

**WILLIAMSON, EDWARD NAGLE**
B. Oct. 24, 1857, Philadelphia, Pa.   D. Mar. 3, 1894, Hot Springs, Ark.   BR TR 5'11"   170 lbs.

| | G | AB | H | 2B | 3B | HR | HR% | R | RBI | BB | SO | SB | BA | SA | AB | H | G by POS |
|---|---|---|---|---|---|---|---|---|---|---|---|---|---|---|---|---|---|
| 1878 IND N | 63 | 250 | 58 | 10 | 2 | 1 | 0.4 | 31 | 19 | 5 | 15 | | .232 | .300 | 0 | 0 | 3B-63 |
| 1879 CHI N | 80 | 320 | 94 | 20 | 13 | 1 | 0.3 | 66 | 36 | 24 | 31 | | .294 | .444 | 0 | 0 | 3B-70, 1B-6, C-4 |
| 1880 | 75 | 311 | 78 | 20 | 2 | 0 | 0.0 | 65 | 31 | 15 | 26 | | .251 | .328 | 0 | 0 | 3B-63, C-11, 2B-3 |
| 1881 | 82 | 343 | 92 | 12 | 6 | 1 | 0.3 | 56 | 48 | 19 | 19 | | .268 | .347 | 0 | 0 | 3B-76, 2B-4, P-3, SS-2, C-1 |
| 1882 | 83 | 348 | 98 | 27 | 4 | 3 | 0.9 | 66 | 60 | 27 | 21 | | .282 | .408 | 0 | 0 | 3B-83, P-1 |
| 1883 | 98 | 402 | 111 | **49** | 5 | 2 | 0.5 | 83 | | 22 | 48 | | .276 | .438 | 0 | 0 | 3B-97, C-3, P-1 |
| 1884 | 107 | 417 | 116 | 18 | 8 | **27** | 6.5 | 84 | | 42 | 56 | | .278 | .554 | 0 | 0 | 3B-99, C-10, P-2 |
| 1885 | 113 | 407 | 97 | 16 | 5 | 3 | 0.7 | 87 | 64 | **75** | 60 | | .238 | .324 | 0 | 0 | 3B-113, P-2, C-1 |

| | G | AB | H | 2B | 3B | HR | HR % | R | RBI | BB | SO | SB | BA | SA | Pinch Hit AB | Pinch Hit H | G by POS |
|---|---|---|---|---|---|---|---|---|---|---|---|---|---|---|---|---|---|

## Ned Williamson  continued

| | G | AB | H | 2B | 3B | HR | HR % | R | RBI | BB | SO | SB | BA | SA | AB | H | G by POS |
|---|---|---|---|---|---|---|---|---|---|---|---|---|---|---|---|---|---|
| 1886 | 121 | 430 | 93 | 17 | 8 | 6 | 1.4 | 69 | 58 | 80 | 71 | | .216 | .335 | 0 | 0 | SS-121, C-4, P-2 |
| 1887 | 127 | 439 | 117 | 20 | 14 | 9 | 2.1 | 77 | 78 | 73 | 57 | 45 | .267 | .437 | 0 | 0 | SS-127, P-1 |
| 1888 | 132 | 452 | 113 | 9 | 14 | 8 | 1.8 | 75 | 73 | 65 | 71 | 25 | .250 | .385 | 0 | 0 | SS-132 |
| 1889 | 47 | 173 | 41 | 3 | 1 | 1 | 0.6 | 16 | 30 | 23 | 22 | 2 | .237 | .283 | 0 | 0 | SS-47 |
| 1890 CHI P | 73 | 261 | 51 | 7 | 4 | 1 | 0.4 | 34 | 26 | 36 | 35 | 3 | .195 | .264 | 0 | 0 | 3B-52, SS-21 |
| 13 yrs. | 1201 | 4553 | 1159 | 228 | 86 | 63 | 1.4 | 809 | 523 | 506 | 532 | 75 | .255 | .384 | 0 | 0 | 3B-716, SS-450, C-34, P-12, 2B-7, 1B-6 |
| 11 yrs. | 1065 | 4042 | 1050 | 211 | 80 | 61 | 1.5 | 744 | 478 | 465 | 482 | 72 | .260 | .397 | 0 | 0 | 3B-601, SS-429, C-34, P-12, 2B-7, 1B-6 |
| | | | | | **10th** | | | | | | **10th** | | | | | | |

## Bump Wills

**WILLS, ELLIOTT TAYLOR**
Son of Maury Wills.
B. July 27, 1952, Washington, D. C.      BB TR 5'9"  172 lbs.

| | G | AB | H | 2B | 3B | HR | HR % | R | RBI | BB | SO | SB | BA | SA | AB | H | G by POS |
|---|---|---|---|---|---|---|---|---|---|---|---|---|---|---|---|---|---|
| 1977 TEX A | 152 | 541 | 155 | 28 | 6 | 9 | 1.7 | 87 | 62 | 65 | 96 | 28 | .287 | .410 | 1 | 0 | 2B-150, SS-2, DH-1, 1B-1 |
| 1978 | 157 | 539 | 135 | 17 | 4 | 9 | 1.7 | 78 | 57 | 63 | 91 | 52 | .250 | .347 | 3 | 0 | 2B-156 |
| 1979 | 146 | 543 | 148 | 21 | 3 | 5 | 0.9 | 90 | 46 | 53 | 58 | 35 | .273 | .350 | 2 | 1 | 2B-146 |
| 1980 | 146 | 578 | 152 | 31 | 5 | 5 | 0.9 | 102 | 58 | 51 | 71 | 34 | .263 | .360 | 0 | 0 | 2B-144 |
| 1981 | 102 | 410 | 103 | 13 | 2 | 2 | 0.5 | 51 | 41 | 32 | 49 | 12 | .251 | .307 | 0 | 0 | 2B-101, DH-1 |
| 1982 CHI N | 128 | 419 | 114 | 18 | 4 | 6 | 1.4 | 64 | 38 | 46 | 76 | 35 | .272 | .377 | 21 | 6 | 2B-103 |
| 6 yrs. | 831 | 3030 | 807 | 128 | 24 | 36 | 1.2 | 472 | 302 | 310 | 441 | 196 | .266 | .360 | 27 | 7 | 2B-800, DH-2, SS-2, 1B-1 |
| 1 yr. | 128 | 419 | 114 | 18 | 4 | 6 | 1.4 | 64 | 38 | 46 | 76 | 35 | .272 | .377 | 21 | 6 | 2B-103 |

## Walt Wilmot

**WILMOT, WALTER R.**
B. Oct. 18, 1863, Plover, Wis.    D. Feb. 1, 1929, Chicago, Ill.      BB TL

| | G | AB | H | 2B | 3B | HR | HR % | R | RBI | BB | SO | SB | BA | SA | AB | H | G by POS |
|---|---|---|---|---|---|---|---|---|---|---|---|---|---|---|---|---|---|
| 1888 WAS N | 119 | 473 | 106 | 16 | 9 | 4 | 0.8 | 61 | 43 | 23 | 55 | 46 | .224 | .321 | 0 | 0 | OF-119 |
| 1889 | 108 | 432 | 125 | 19 | 19 | 9 | 2.1 | 88 | 57 | 51 | 32 | 40 | .289 | .484 | 0 | 0 | OF-108 |
| 1890 CHI N | 139 | 571 | 159 | 15 | 12 | 14 | 2.5 | 114 | 99 | 64 | 44 | 76 | .278 | .420 | 0 | 0 | OF-139 |
| 1891 | 121 | 498 | 139 | 14 | 10 | 11 | 2.2 | 102 | 71 | 55 | 21 | 42 | .279 | .414 | 0 | 0 | OF-121 |
| 1892 | 92 | 380 | 82 | 7 | 7 | 2 | 0.5 | 47 | 35 | 40 | 20 | 31 | .216 | .287 | 0 | 0 | OF-92 |
| 1893 | 94 | 392 | 118 | 14 | 14 | 3 | 0.8 | 69 | 61 | 40 | 8 | 39 | .301 | .431 | 1 | 0 | OF-93 |
| 1894 | 133 | 597 | 197 | 45 | 12 | 5 | 0.8 | 134 | 130 | 35 | 23 | 74 | .330 | .471 | 0 | 0 | OF-133 |
| 1895 | 108 | 466 | 132 | 16 | 6 | 8 | 1.7 | 86 | 72 | 30 | 19 | 28 | .283 | .395 | 0 | 0 | OF-108 |
| 1897 NY N | 11 | 34 | 9 | 2 | 0 | 1 | 2.9 | 8 | 4 | 2 | | 1 | .265 | .412 | 1 | 0 | OF-9 |
| 1898 | 35 | 138 | 33 | 4 | 2 | 2 | 1.4 | 16 | 22 | 14 | | 4 | .239 | .341 | 1 | 0 | OF-34 |
| 10 yrs. | 960 | 3981 | 1100 | 152 | 91 | 59 | 1.5 | 725 | 594 | 349 | 222 | 381 | .276 | .405 | 3 | 0 | OF-956 |
| 6 yrs. | 687 | 2904 | 827 | 111 | 61 | 43 | 1.5 | 552 | 468 | 264 | 135 | 290 | .285 | .409 | 1 | 0 | OF-686 |

## Art Wilson

**WILSON, ARTHUR EARL (Dutch)**
B. Dec. 11, 1885, Macon, Ill.    D. June 12, 1960, Chicago, Ill.      BR TR 5'8"  170 lbs.

| | G | AB | H | 2B | 3B | HR | HR % | R | RBI | BB | SO | SB | BA | SA | AB | H | G by POS |
|---|---|---|---|---|---|---|---|---|---|---|---|---|---|---|---|---|---|
| 1908 NY N | 1 | 0 | 0 | 0 | 0 | 0 | – | 0 | 0 | 0 | | 0 | – | – | 0 | 0 | C-18 |
| 1909 | 19 | 42 | 10 | 2 | 1 | 0 | 0.0 | 4 | 5 | 4 | | 0 | .238 | .333 | 1 | 0 | C-18 |
| 1910 | 26 | 52 | 14 | 4 | 1 | 0 | 0.0 | 10 | 5 | 9 | 6 | 2 | .269 | .385 | 0 | 0 | C-25, 1B-1 |
| 1911 | 66 | 109 | 33 | 9 | 1 | 1 | 0.9 | 17 | 17 | 19 | 12 | 6 | .303 | .431 | 2 | 0 | C-64 |
| 1912 | 65 | 121 | 35 | 6 | 0 | 3 | 2.5 | 17 | 19 | 13 | 14 | 2 | .289 | .413 | 3 | 1 | C-61 |
| 1913 | 54 | 79 | 15 | 0 | 1 | 0 | 0.0 | 5 | 8 | 11 | 11 | 1 | .190 | .215 | 2 | 1 | C-49, 1B-2 |
| 1914 CHI F | 137 | *440 | 128 | 31 | 8 | 10 | 2.3 | 78 | 64 | 70 | | 13 | .291 | .466 | 4 | 2 | C-132 |
| 1915 | 96 | 269 | 82 | 11 | 2 | 7 | 2.6 | 44 | 31 | 65 | | 8 | .305 | .439 | 7 | 2 | C-87 |
| 1916 2 teams | | PIT | N (53G – | .258) | | CHI | N (36G – | .193) | | | | | | | | | |
| " total | 89 | 242 | 55 | 8 | 3 | 1 | 0.4 | 16 | 17 | 19 | 41 | 5 | .227 | .298 | 14 | 2 | C-73 |
| 1917 CHI N | 81 | 211 | 45 | 9 | 2 | 2 | 0.9 | 17 | 25 | 32 | 36 | 6 | .213 | .303 | 4 | 2 | C-75 |
| 1918 BOS N | 89 | 280 | 69 | 8 | 2 | 0 | 0.0 | 15 | 19 | 24 | 31 | 5 | .246 | .289 | 2 | 0 | C-85 |
| 1919 | 71 | 191 | 49 | 8 | 1 | 0 | 0.0 | 14 | 16 | 25 | 19 | 2 | .257 | .309 | 5 | 1 | C-64, 1B-1 |
| 1920 | 16 | 19 | 1 | 0 | 0 | 0 | 0.0 | 0 | 0 | 1 | 0 | 1 | .053 | .053 | 7 | 0 | 3B-6, C-2 |
| 1921 CLE A | 2 | 1 | 0 | 0 | 0 | 0 | 0.0 | 0 | 0 | 0 | 0 | 0 | .000 | .000 | 0 | 0 | C-2 |
| 14 yrs. | 812 | 2056 | 536 | 96 | 22 | 24 | 1.2 | 237 | 226 | 292 | 171 | 50 | .261 | .364 | 51 | 11 | C-737, 3B-6, 1B-4 |
| 2 yrs. | 117 | 325 | 67 | 12 | 3 | 2 | 0.6 | 22 | 30 | 38 | 50 | 7 | .206 | .280 | 6 | 3 | C-109 |

| WORLD SERIES | | | | | | | | | | | | | | | | | |
|---|---|---|---|---|---|---|---|---|---|---|---|---|---|---|---|---|---|
| 1911 NY N | 1 | 1 | 0 | 0 | 0 | 0 | 0.0 | 0 | 0 | 0 | 0 | 0 | .000 | .000 | 0 | 0 | C-1 |
| 1912 | 2 | 1 | 1 | 0 | 0 | 0 | 0.0 | 0 | 0 | 0 | 0 | 0 | 1.000 | 1.000 | 0 | 0 | C-2 |
| 1913 | 3 | 3 | 0 | 0 | 0 | 0 | 0.0 | 0 | 0 | 0 | 2 | 0 | .000 | .000 | 0 | 0 | C-3 |
| 3 yrs. | 6 | 5 | 1 | 0 | 0 | 0 | 0.0 | 0 | 0 | 0 | 2 | 0 | .200 | .200 | 0 | 0 | C-6 |

## Hack Wilson

**WILSON, LEWIS ROBERT**
B. Apr. 26, 1900, Elwood City, Pa.    D. Nov. 23, 1948, Baltimore, Md.      BR TR 5'6"  190 lbs.
Hall of Fame 1979.

| | G | AB | H | 2B | 3B | HR | HR % | R | RBI | BB | SO | SB | BA | SA | AB | H | G by POS |
|---|---|---|---|---|---|---|---|---|---|---|---|---|---|---|---|---|---|
| 1923 NY N | 3 | 10 | 2 | 0 | 0 | 0 | 0.0 | 0 | 1 | 0 | 1 | 0 | .200 | .200 | 0 | 0 | OF-3 |
| 1924 | 107 | 383 | 113 | 19 | 12 | 10 | 2.6 | 62 | 57 | 44 | 46 | 4 | .295 | .486 | 4 | 0 | OF-103 |
| 1925 | 62 | 180 | 43 | 7 | 4 | 6 | 3.3 | 28 | 30 | 21 | 33 | 5 | .239 | .422 | 5 | 2 | OF-50 |
| 1926 CHI N | 142 | 529 | 170 | 36 | 8 | 21 | 4.0 | 97 | 109 | 69 | 61 | 10 | .321 | .539 | 2 | 1 | OF-140 |
| 1927 | 146 | 551 | 175 | 30 | 12 | 30 | 5.4 | 119 | 129 | 71 | 70 | 13 | .318 | .579 | 0 | 0 | OF-146 |
| 1928 | 145 | 520 | 163 | 32 | 9 | 31 | 6.0 | 89 | 120 | 77 | 94 | 4 | .313 | .588 | 2 | 0 | OF-143 |
| 1929 | 150 | 574 | 198 | 30 | 5 | 39 | 6.8 | 135 | 159 | 78 | 83 | 3 | .345 | .618 | 0 | 0 | OF-150 |
| 1930 | 155 | 585 | 208 | 35 | 6 | 56 | 9.6 | 146 | 190 | 105 | 84 | 3 | .356 | .723 | 0 | 0 | OF-155 |
| 1931 | 112 | 395 | 103 | 22 | 4 | 13 | 3.3 | 66 | 61 | 63 | 69 | 1 | .261 | .435 | 8 | 2 | OF-103 |
| 1932 BKN N | 135 | 481 | 143 | 37 | 5 | 23 | 4.8 | 77 | 123 | 51 | 85 | 7 | .297 | .538 | 7 | 1 | OF-125 |
| 1933 | 117 | 360 | 96 | 13 | 2 | 9 | 2.5 | 41 | 54 | 52 | 50 | 7 | .267 | .389 | 16 | 5 | OF-90, 2B-5 |
| 1934 2 teams | | BKN | N (67G – | .262) | | PHI | N (7G – | .100) | | | | | | | | | |
| " total | 74 | 192 | 47 | 5 | 0 | 6 | 3.1 | 24 | 30 | 43 | 37 | 0 | .245 | .365 | 20 | 5 | OF-49 |
| 12 yrs. | 1348 | 4760 | 1461 | 266 | 67 | 244 | 5.1 | 884 | 1062 | 674 | 713 | 52 | .307 | .545 | 64 | 16 | OF-1257, 2B-5 |
| 6 yrs. | 850 | 3154 | 1017 | 185 | 44 | 190 | 6.0 | 652 | 652 | 463 | 461 | 34 | .322 | .590 | 12 | 3 | OF-837 |
| | | | | | | **7th** | **2nd** | | **9th** | | | | **6th** | **1st** | | | |

| WORLD SERIES | | | | | | | | | | | | | | | | | |
|---|---|---|---|---|---|---|---|---|---|---|---|---|---|---|---|---|---|
| 1924 NY N | 7 | 30 | 7 | 1 | 0 | 0 | 0.0 | 3 | 1 | 3 | 1 | 9 | 0 | .233 | .267 | 0 | 0 | OF-7 |

| | G | AB | H | 2B | 3B | HR | HR % | R | RBI | BB | SO | SB | BA | SA | PH AB | PH H | G by POS |
|---|---|---|---|---|---|---|---|---|---|---|---|---|---|---|---|---|---|

## Hack Wilson continued

| | G | AB | H | 2B | 3B | HR | HR % | R | RBI | BB | SO | SB | BA | SA | PH AB | PH H | G by POS |
|---|---|---|---|---|---|---|---|---|---|---|---|---|---|---|---|---|---|
| 1929 CHI N | 5 | 17 | 8 | 0 | 1 | 0 | 0.0 | 2 | 0 | 4 | 3 | 0 | .471 | .588 | 0 | 0 | OF-5 |
| 2 yrs. | 12 | 47 | 15 | 1 | 1 | 0 | 0.0 | 3 | 3 | 5 | 12 | 0 | .319 | .383 | 0 | 0 | OF-12 |

## Ed Winceniak

WINCENIAK, EDWARD JOSEPH
B. Apr. 16, 1929, Chicago, Ill.    BR TR 5'9" 165 lbs.

| | G | AB | H | 2B | 3B | HR | HR % | R | RBI | BB | SO | SB | BA | SA | PH AB | PH H | G by POS |
|---|---|---|---|---|---|---|---|---|---|---|---|---|---|---|---|---|---|
| 1956 CHI N | 15 | 17 | 2 | 0 | 0 | 0 | 0.0 | 1 | 0 | 1 | 3 | 0 | .118 | .118 | 7 | 0 | 3B-4, 2B-1 |
| 1957 | 17 | 50 | 12 | 3 | 0 | 1 | 2.0 | 5 | 8 | 2 | 9 | 0 | .240 | .360 | 5 | 1 | SS-5, 3B-4, 2B-3 |
| 2 yrs. | 32 | 67 | 14 | 3 | 0 | 1 | 1.5 | 6 | 8 | 3 | 12 | 0 | .209 | .299 | 12 | 1 | 3B-8, SS-5, 2B-4 |
| 2 yrs. | 32 | 67 | 14 | 3 | 0 | 1 | 1.5 | 6 | 8 | 3 | 12 | 0 | .209 | .299 | 12 | 1 | 3B-8, SS-5, 2B-4 |

## Kettle Wirtz

WIRTZ, ELWOOD VERNON
B. Oct. 30, 1897, Edge Hill, Pa.    D. July 12, 1968, Sacramento, Calif.    BR TR 5'11" 170 lbs.

| | G | AB | H | 2B | 3B | HR | HR % | R | RBI | BB | SO | SB | BA | SA | PH AB | PH H | G by POS |
|---|---|---|---|---|---|---|---|---|---|---|---|---|---|---|---|---|---|
| 1921 CHI N | 7 | 11 | 2 | 0 | 0 | 0 | 0.0 | 0 | 1 | | 3 | 0 | .182 | .182 | 2 | 2 | C-5 |
| 1922 | 31 | 58 | 10 | 1 | 0 | 1 | 1.7 | 7 | 6 | 12 | 15 | 0 | .172 | .259 | 3 | 0 | C-27 |
| 1923 | 5 | 5 | 1 | 0 | 0 | 0 | 0.0 | 2 | 1 | 2 | 0 | 0 | .200 | .200 | 0 | 0 | C-3 |
| 1924 CHI A | 6 | 12 | 1 | 0 | 0 | 0 | 0.0 | 0 | 1 | 2 | 2 | 1 | .083 | .083 | 0 | 0 | C-5 |
| 4 yrs. | 49 | 86 | 14 | 2 | 0 | 1 | 1.2 | 9 | 8 | 16 | 20 | 1 | .163 | .221 | 5 | 5 | C-40 |
| 3 yrs. | 43 | 74 | 13 | 2 | 0 | 1 | 1.4 | 9 | 8 | 14 | 18 | 0 | .176 | .243 | 5 | 5 | C-35 |

## Casey Wise

WISE, KENDALL COLE
B. Sept. 8, 1932, Lafayette, Ind.    BB TR 6' 170 lbs.

| | G | AB | H | 2B | 3B | HR | HR % | R | RBI | BB | SO | SB | BA | SA | PH AB | PH H | G by POS |
|---|---|---|---|---|---|---|---|---|---|---|---|---|---|---|---|---|---|
| 1957 CHI N | 43 | 106 | 19 | 3 | 1 | 0 | 0.0 | 12 | 7 | 11 | 14 | 0 | .179 | .226 | 4 | 0 | 2B-31, SS-5 |
| 1958 MIL N | 31 | 71 | 14 | 1 | 0 | 0 | 0.0 | 8 | 0 | 4 | 8 | 1 | .197 | .211 | 8 | 0 | 2B-10, SS-7, 3B-1 |
| 1959 | 22 | 76 | 13 | 2 | 0 | 1 | 1.3 | 11 | 5 | 10 | 5 | 0 | .171 | .237 | 1 | 0 | 2B-20, SS-5 |
| 1960 DET A | 30 | 68 | 10 | 0 | 2 | 2 | 2.9 | 6 | 5 | 4 | 9 | 1 | .147 | .294 | 3 | 0 | 2B-17, SS-10, 3B-1 |
| 4 yrs. | 126 | 321 | 56 | 6 | 3 | 3 | 0.9 | 37 | 17 | 29 | 36 | 2 | .174 | .240 | 16 | 0 | 2B-78, SS-27, 3B-2 |
| 1 yr. | 43 | 106 | 19 | 3 | 1 | 0 | 0.0 | 12 | 7 | 11 | 14 | 0 | .179 | .226 | 4 | 0 | 2B-31, SS-5 |

WORLD SERIES

| | G | AB | H | 2B | 3B | HR | HR % | R | RBI | BB | SO | SB | BA | SA | PH AB | PH H | G by POS |
|---|---|---|---|---|---|---|---|---|---|---|---|---|---|---|---|---|---|
| 1958 MIL N | 2 | 1 | 0 | 0 | 0 | 0 | 0.0 | 0 | 0 | 0 | 1 | 0 | .000 | .000 | 1 | 0 | |

## Harry Wolfe

WOLFE, HAROLD (Whitey)
B. Nov. 24, 1890, Worcester, Mass.    D. July 28, 1971    BR TR 5'8" 160 lbs.

| | G | AB | H | 2B | 3B | HR | HR % | R | RBI | BB | SO | SB | BA | SA | PH AB | PH H | G by POS |
|---|---|---|---|---|---|---|---|---|---|---|---|---|---|---|---|---|---|
| 1917 2 teams | CHI N (9G – .400) | | | PIT N (3G – .000) | | | | | | | | | | | | | |
| " total | 12 | 10 | 2 | 0 | 0 | 0 | 0.0 | 1 | | 2 | 5 | 0 | .200 | .200 | 3 | 0 | OF-2, SS-2, 2B-1 |

## Harry Wolter

WOLTER, HARRY MEIGS
B. July 11, 1884, Monterey, Calif.    D. July 7, 1970, Palo Alto, Calif.    BL TL 5'10" 175 lbs.

| | G | AB | H | 2B | 3B | HR | HR % | R | RBI | BB | SO | SB | BA | SA | PH AB | PH H | G by POS |
|---|---|---|---|---|---|---|---|---|---|---|---|---|---|---|---|---|---|
| 1907 3 teams | CIN N (4G – .133) | | | PIT N (1G – .000) | | | STL N (16G – .340) | | | | | | | | | | |
| " total | 21 | 63 | 18 | 0 | 0 | 0 | 0.0 | 5 | 7 | 3 | | 1 | .286 | .286 | 4 | 0 | OF-13, P-4 |
| 1909 BOS A | 54 | 119 | 29 | 4 | 2 | 1 | 1.7 | 14 | 10 | 9 | | 2 | .244 | .378 | 13 | 1 | 1B-17, P-10, OF-9 |
| 1910 NY A | 135 | 479 | 128 | 15 | 9 | 4 | 0.8 | 84 | 42 | 66 | | 39 | .267 | .361 | 2 | 0 | OF-130 |
| 1911 | 122 | 434 | 132 | 17 | 15 | 4 | 0.9 | 78 | 36 | 62 | | 28 | .304 | .440 | 3 | 2 | OF-113, 1B-2 |
| 1912 | 12 | 32 | 11 | 2 | 1 | 0 | 0.0 | 8 | 1 | 10 | | 5 | .344 | .469 | 3 | 0 | OF-9 |
| 1913 | 126 | 425 | 108 | 18 | 6 | 2 | 0.5 | 53 | 43 | 80 | 50 | 13 | .254 | .339 | 3 | 1 | OF-121 |
| 1917 CHI N | 117 | 353 | 88 | 15 | 7 | 0 | 0.0 | 44 | 28 | 38 | 40 | 7 | .249 | .331 | 16 | 7 | OF-97, 1B-1 |
| 7 yrs. | 587 | 1905 | 514 | 69 | 42 | 12 | 0.6 | 286 | 167 | 268 | 90 | 95 | .270 | .369 | 44 | 11 | OF-492, 1B-20, P-14 |
| 1 yr. | 117 | 353 | 88 | 15 | 7 | 0 | 0.0 | 44 | 28 | 38 | 40 | 7 | .249 | .331 | 16 | 7 | OF-97, 1B-1 |

## Harry Wolverton

WOLVERTON, HARRY STERLING
B. Dec. 6, 1873, Mt. Vernon, Ohio    D. Feb. 4, 1937, Oakland, Calif.    BL TR
Manager 1912.

| | G | AB | H | 2B | 3B | HR | HR % | R | RBI | BB | SO | SB | BA | SA | PH AB | PH H | G by POS |
|---|---|---|---|---|---|---|---|---|---|---|---|---|---|---|---|---|---|
| 1898 CHI N | 13 | 49 | 16 | 1 | 0 | 0 | 0.0 | 4 | 2 | 1 | | 1 | .327 | .347 | 0 | 0 | 3B-13 |
| 1899 | 99 | 389 | 111 | 14 | 11 | 1 | 0.3 | 50 | 49 | 30 | | 14 | .285 | .386 | 0 | 0 | 3B-98, SS-1 |
| 1900 2 teams | CHI N (3G – .182) | | | PHI N (101G – .282) | | | | | | | | | | | | | |
| " total | 104 | 394 | 110 | 10 | 8 | 3 | 0.8 | 44 | 58 | 22 | | 5 | .279 | .368 | 0 | 0 | 3B-104 |
| 1901 PHI N | 93 | 379 | 117 | 15 | 4 | 3 | 0.8 | 42 | 43 | 22 | | 13 | .309 | .369 | 0 | 0 | 3B-93 |
| 1902 2 teams | WAS A (59G – .249) | | | PHI N (34G – .294) | | | | | | | | | | | | | |
| " total | 93 | 385 | 102 | 11 | 5 | 1 | 0.3 | 47 | 39 | 22 | | 11 | .265 | .327 | 0 | 0 | 3B-93 |
| 1903 PHI N | 123 | 494 | 152 | 13 | 12 | 1 | 0.2 | 72 | 53 | 18 | | 10 | .308 | .383 | 0 | 0 | 3B-123 |
| 1904 | 102 | 398 | 106 | 15 | 5 | 0 | 0.0 | 43 | 49 | 26 | | 18 | .266 | .329 | 0 | 0 | 3B-102 |
| 1905 BOS N | 122 | 463 | 104 | 15 | 7 | 2 | 0.4 | 38 | 55 | 23 | | 10 | .225 | .300 | 0 | 0 | 3B-122 |
| 1912 NY A | 33 | 50 | 15 | 1 | 1 | 0 | 0.0 | 6 | 4 | 2 | | 1 | .300 | .360 | 26 | 10 | 3B-7 |
| 9 yrs. | 782 | 3001 | 833 | 95 | 53 | 7 | 0.2 | 346 | 352 | 166 | | 83 | .278 | .352 | 26 | 10 | 3B-755, SS-1 |
| 3 yrs. | 115 | 449 | 129 | 15 | 11 | 1 | 0.2 | 56 | 51 | 33 | | 16 | .287 | .376 | 0 | 0 | 3B-114, SS-1 |

## Gary Woods

WOODS, GARY LEE
B. July 20, 1954, Santa Barbara, Calif.    BR TR 6'2" 185 lbs.

| | G | AB | H | 2B | 3B | HR | HR % | R | RBI | BB | SO | SB | BA | SA | PH AB | PH H | G by POS |
|---|---|---|---|---|---|---|---|---|---|---|---|---|---|---|---|---|---|
| 1976 OAK A | 6 | 8 | 1 | 0 | 0 | 0 | 0.0 | 0 | 0 | 0 | 3 | 0 | .125 | .125 | 2 | 0 | OF-4, DH-1 |
| 1977 TOR A | 60 | 227 | 49 | 9 | 1 | 0 | 0.0 | 21 | 17 | 7 | 38 | 5 | .216 | .264 | 1 | 1 | OF-60 |
| 1978 | 8 | 19 | 3 | 1 | 0 | 0 | 0.0 | 1 | 0 | 1 | 1 | 1 | .158 | .211 | 1 | 0 | OF-6 |
| 1980 HOU N | 19 | 53 | 20 | 5 | 0 | 2 | 3.8 | 8 | 15 | 2 | 9 | 1 | .377 | .585 | 5 | 3 | OF-14 |
| 1981 | 54 | 110 | 23 | 4 | 1 | 0 | 0.0 | 10 | 12 | 11 | 22 | 2 | .209 | .264 | 15 | 3 | OF-40 |
| 1982 CHI N | 117 | 245 | 66 | 15 | 1 | 4 | 1.6 | 28 | 30 | 21 | 48 | 3 | .269 | .388 | 22 | 4 | OF-103 |
| 1983 | 93 | 190 | 46 | 9 | 0 | 4 | 2.1 | 25 | 22 | 15 | 27 | 5 | .242 | .353 | 31 | 6 | OF-73, 2B-1 |
| 1984 | 87 | 98 | 23 | 4 | 1 | 3 | 3.1 | 13 | 10 | 15 | 21 | 2 | .235 | .388 | 31 | 7 | OF-62, 2B-3 |
| 1985 | 81 | 82 | 20 | 3 | 0 | 0 | 0.0 | 11 | 4 | 14 | 18 | 0 | .244 | .280 | 27 | 7 | OF-56 |
| 9 yrs. | 525 | 1032 | 251 | 50 | 4 | 13 | 1.3 | 117 | 110 | 86 | 187 | 19 | .243 | .337 | 135 | 31 | OF-418, 2B-4, DH-1 |
| 4 yrs. | 378 | 615 | 155 | 31 | 2 | 11 | 1.8 | 77 | 66 | 65 | 114 | 10 | .252 | .363 | 111 | 24 | OF-294, 2B-4 |

DIVISIONAL PLAYOFF SERIES

| | G | AB | H | 2B | 3B | HR | HR % | R | RBI | BB | SO | SB | BA | SA | PH AB | PH H | G by POS |
|---|---|---|---|---|---|---|---|---|---|---|---|---|---|---|---|---|---|
| 1981 HOU N | 2 | 2 | 0 | 0 | 0 | 0 | 0.0 | 0 | 0 | | 1 | 0 | .000 | .000 | 2 | 0 | |

| | G | AB | H | 2B | 3B | HR | HR % | R | RBI | BB | SO | SB | BA | SA | Pinch Hit AB | Pinch Hit H | G by POS |
|---|---|---|---|---|---|---|---|---|---|---|---|---|---|---|---|---|---|

## Gary Woods continued

LEAGUE CHAMPIONSHIP SERIES

| | G | AB | H | 2B | 3B | HR | HR % | R | RBI | BB | SO | SB | BA | SA | AB | H | G by POS |
|---|---|---|---|---|---|---|---|---|---|---|---|---|---|---|---|---|---|
| 1980 HOU N | 4 | 8 | 2 | 0 | 0 | 0 | 0.0 | 0 | 1 | 1 | 3 | 1 | .250 | .250 | 2 | 0 | OF-3 |
| 1984 CHI N | 1 | 1 | 0 | 0 | 0 | 0 | 0.0 | 0 | 0 | 0 | 1 | 0 | .000 | .000 | 1 | 0 | OF-1 |
| 2 yrs. | 5 | 9 | 2 | 0 | 0 | 0 | 0.0 | 0 | 1 | 1 | 4 | 1 | .222 | .222 | 3 | 0 | OF-4 |

## Jim Woods

**WOODS, JAMES JEROME (Woody)**
B. Sept. 17, 1939, Chicago, Ill.                BR  TR  6'        175 lbs.

| | G | AB | H | 2B | 3B | HR | HR % | R | RBI | BB | SO | SB | BA | SA | AB | H | G by POS |
|---|---|---|---|---|---|---|---|---|---|---|---|---|---|---|---|---|---|
| 1957 CHI N | 2 | 0 | 0 | 0 | 0 | 0 | – | 1 | 0 | 0 | 0 | 0 | – | – | 0 | 0 | |
| 1960 PHI N | 11 | 34 | 6 | 0 | 0 | 1 | 2.9 | 4 | 3 | 3 | 13 | 0 | .176 | .265 | 0 | 0 | 3B-11 |
| 1961 | 23 | 48 | 11 | 3 | 0 | 2 | 4.2 | 6 | 9 | 4 | 15 | 0 | .229 | .417 | 10 | 3 | 3B-15 |
| 3 yrs. | 36 | 82 | 17 | 3 | 0 | 3 | 3.7 | 11 | 12 | 7 | 28 | 0 | .207 | .354 | 10 | 3 | 3B-26 |
| 1 yr. | 2 | 0 | 0 | 0 | 0 | 0 | – | 1 | 0 | 0 | 0 | 0 | – | – | 0 | 0 | |

## Walt Woods

**WOODS, WALTER SYDNEY**
B. Apr. 28, 1875, Rye, N. H.    D. Oct. 30, 1951, Portsmouth, N. H.                TR  5'9½"  165 lbs.

| | G | AB | H | 2B | 3B | HR | HR % | R | RBI | BB | SO | SB | BA | SA | AB | H | G by POS |
|---|---|---|---|---|---|---|---|---|---|---|---|---|---|---|---|---|---|
| 1898 CHI N | 48 | 154 | 27 | 1 | 0 | 0 | 0.0 | 16 | 8 | 4 | | 3 | .175 | .182 | 0 | 0 | P-27, OF-11, 2B-6, SS-3, 3B-3 |
| 1899 LOU N | 42 | 126 | 19 | 1 | 1 | 1 | 0.8 | 15 | 14 | 10 | | 5 | .151 | .198 | 0 | 0 | P-26, 2B-11, SS-3, OF-2 |
| 1900 PIT N | 1 | 1 | 0 | 0 | 0 | 0 | 0.0 | 0 | 0 | 0 | | 0 | .000 | .000 | 0 | 0 | P-1 |
| 3 yrs. | 91 | 281 | 46 | 2 | 1 | 1 | 0.4 | 31 | 22 | 14 | | 8 | .164 | .189 | 0 | 0 | P-54, 2B-17, OF-13, SS-6, 3B-3 |
| 1 yr. | 48 | 154 | 27 | 1 | 0 | 0 | 0.0 | 16 | 8 | 4 | | 3 | .175 | .182 | 0 | 0 | P-27, OF-11, 2B-6, SS-3, 3B-3 |

## Chuck Wortman

**WORTMAN, WILLIAM LEWIS**
B. Jan. 5, 1892, Baltimore, Md.    D. Aug. 19, 1977, Las Vegas, Nev.                BR  TR  5'7"  150 lbs.

| | G | AB | H | 2B | 3B | HR | HR % | R | RBI | BB | SO | SB | BA | SA | AB | H | G by POS |
|---|---|---|---|---|---|---|---|---|---|---|---|---|---|---|---|---|---|
| 1916 CHI N | 69 | 234 | 47 | 4 | 2 | 2 | 0.9 | 17 | 16 | 18 | 22 | 4 | .201 | .261 | 0 | 0 | SS-69 |
| 1917 | 75 | 190 | 33 | 4 | 1 | 0 | 0.0 | 24 | 9 | 18 | 23 | 6 | .174 | .205 | 0 | 0 | SS-65, 3B-1, 2B-1 |
| 1918 | 17 | 17 | 2 | 0 | 0 | 1 | 5.9 | 4 | 3 | 1 | 2 | 3 | .118 | .294 | 0 | 0 | 2B-8, SS-4 |
| 3 yrs. | 161 | 441 | 82 | 8 | 3 | 3 | 0.7 | 45 | 28 | 37 | 47 | 13 | .186 | .238 | 0 | 0 | SS-138, 2B-9, 3B-1 |
| 3 yrs. | 161 | 441 | 82 | 8 | 3 | 3 | 0.7 | 45 | 28 | 37 | 47 | 13 | .186 | .238 | 0 | 0 | SS-138, 2B-9, 3B-1 |

WORLD SERIES

| | G | AB | H | 2B | 3B | HR | HR % | R | RBI | BB | SO | SB | BA | SA | AB | H | G by POS |
|---|---|---|---|---|---|---|---|---|---|---|---|---|---|---|---|---|---|
| 1918 CHI N | 1 | 1 | 0 | 0 | 0 | 0 | 0.0 | 0 | 0 | 0 | 0 | 0 | .000 | .000 | 0 | 0 | 2B-1 |

## Pat Wright

**WRIGHT, PATRICK FRANCIS**
B. July 5, 1865, Pottsville, Pa.    D. May 29, 1943, Springfield, Ill.                BB  TR  6'2"  190 lbs.

| | G | AB | H | 2B | 3B | HR | HR % | R | RBI | BB | SO | SB | BA | SA | AB | H | G by POS |
|---|---|---|---|---|---|---|---|---|---|---|---|---|---|---|---|---|---|
| 1890 CHI N | 1 | 2 | 0 | 0 | 0 | 0 | 0.0 | 0 | 0 | 1 | 0 | 0 | .000 | .000 | 0 | 0 | 2B-1 |

## George Yantz

**YANTZ, GEORGE WEBB**
B. July 27, 1886, Louisville, Ky.    D. Feb. 26, 1967, Louisville, Ky.                BR  TR  5'6½"  168 lbs.

| | G | AB | H | 2B | 3B | HR | HR % | R | RBI | BB | SO | SB | BA | SA | AB | H | G by POS |
|---|---|---|---|---|---|---|---|---|---|---|---|---|---|---|---|---|---|
| 1912 CHI N | 1 | 1 | 1 | 0 | 0 | 0 | 0.0 | 0 | 0 | 0 | 0 | 0 | 1.000 | 1.000 | 0 | 0 | C-1 |

## Steve Yerkes

**YERKES, STEPHEN DOUGLAS**
B. May 15, 1888, Hatboro, Pa.    D. Jan. 31, 1971, Lansdale, Pa.                BR  TR  5'9"  165 lbs.

| | G | AB | H | 2B | 3B | HR | HR % | R | RBI | BB | SO | SB | BA | SA | AB | H | G by POS |
|---|---|---|---|---|---|---|---|---|---|---|---|---|---|---|---|---|---|
| 1909 BOS A | 5 | 2 | 1 | 0 | 0 | 0 | 0.0 | 0 | 0 | 0 | | 0 | .500 | .500 | 2 | 1 | SS-3 |
| 1911 | 142 | 502 | 140 | 24 | 3 | 1 | 0.2 | 70 | 57 | 52 | | 14 | .279 | .345 | 0 | 0 | SS-116, 2B-14, 3B-11 |
| 1912 | 131 | 523 | 132 | 22 | 6 | 0 | 0.0 | 73 | 42 | 41 | | 4 | .252 | .317 | 0 | 0 | 2B-131 |
| 1913 | 137 | 487 | 130 | 30 | 6 | 1 | 0.2 | 67 | 48 | 50 | 32 | 11 | .267 | .359 | 7 | 1 | 2B-129 |
| 1914 2 teams | | BOS | A (92G – .218) | | | PIT | F (39G – .338) | | | | | | | | | | |
| " total | 131 | 435 | 112 | 26 | 7 | 2 | 0.5 | 41 | 48 | 25 | 23 | 7 | .257 | .363 | 0 | 0 | 2B-91, SS-39 |
| 1915 PIT F | 121 | 434 | 125 | 17 | 8 | 1 | 0.2 | 44 | 49 | 30 | | 17 | .288 | .371 | 0 | 0 | 2B-114, SS-8 |
| 1916 CHI N | 44 | 137 | 36 | 6 | 2 | 1 | 0.7 | 12 | 10 | 9 | 7 | 1 | .263 | .358 | 3 | 1 | 2B-41 |
| 7 yrs. | 711 | 2520 | 676 | 125 | 32 | 6 | 0.2 | 307 | 254 | 207 | 62 | 54 | .268 | .350 | 12 | 3 | 2B-520, SS-166, 3B-11 |
| 1 yr. | 44 | 137 | 36 | 6 | 2 | 1 | 0.7 | 12 | 10 | 9 | 7 | 1 | .263 | .358 | 3 | 1 | 2B-41 |

WORLD SERIES

| | G | AB | H | 2B | 3B | HR | HR % | R | RBI | BB | SO | SB | BA | SA | AB | H | G by POS |
|---|---|---|---|---|---|---|---|---|---|---|---|---|---|---|---|---|---|
| 1912 BOS A | 8 | 32 | 8 | 0 | 2 | 0 | 0.0 | 3 | 4 | 2 | 3 | 0 | .250 | .375 | 0 | 0 | 2B-8 |

## Tony York

**YORK, ANTHONY BATTON**
B. Nov. 27, 1912, Irene, Tex.    D. Apr. 18, 1970, Hillsboro, Tex.                BR  TR  5'10"  165 lbs.

| | G | AB | H | 2B | 3B | HR | HR % | R | RBI | BB | SO | SB | BA | SA | AB | H | G by POS |
|---|---|---|---|---|---|---|---|---|---|---|---|---|---|---|---|---|---|
| 1944 CHI N | 28 | 85 | 20 | 1 | 0 | 0 | 0.0 | 4 | 7 | 4 | 11 | 0 | .235 | .247 | 0 | 0 | SS-15, 3B-12 |

## Elmer Yoter

**YOTER, ELMER ELLSWORTH**
B. June 26, 1900, Carlisle, Pa.    D. July 26, 1966, Camp Hill, Pa.                BR  TR  5'7"  155 lbs.

| | G | AB | H | 2B | 3B | HR | HR % | R | RBI | BB | SO | SB | BA | SA | AB | H | G by POS |
|---|---|---|---|---|---|---|---|---|---|---|---|---|---|---|---|---|---|
| 1921 PHI A | 3 | 3 | 0 | 0 | 0 | 0 | 0.0 | 0 | 0 | 0 | 1 | 0 | .000 | .000 | 3 | 0 | |
| 1924 CLE A | 19 | 66 | 18 | 1 | 1 | 0 | 0.0 | 3 | 7 | 5 | 8 | 0 | .273 | .318 | 0 | 0 | 3B-19 |
| 1927 CHI N | 13 | 27 | 6 | 1 | 1 | 0 | 0.0 | 2 | 5 | 4 | 4 | 0 | .222 | .333 | 1 | 0 | 3B-11 |
| 1928 | 1 | 0 | 0 | 0 | 0 | 0 | – | 0 | 0 | 0 | 0 | 0 | – | – | 0 | 0 | 3B-1 |
| 4 yrs. | 36 | 96 | 24 | 2 | 2 | 0 | 0.0 | 5 | 12 | 9 | 13 | 0 | .250 | .313 | 4 | 0 | 3B-31 |
| 2 yrs. | 14 | 27 | 6 | 1 | 1 | 0 | 0.0 | 2 | 5 | 4 | 4 | 0 | .222 | .333 | 1 | 0 | 3B-12 |

## Don Young

**YOUNG, DONALD WAYNE**
B. Oct. 18, 1945, Houston, Tex.                BR  TR  6'2"  185 lbs.

| | G | AB | H | 2B | 3B | HR | HR % | R | RBI | BB | SO | SB | BA | SA | AB | H | G by POS |
|---|---|---|---|---|---|---|---|---|---|---|---|---|---|---|---|---|---|
| 1965 CHI N | 11 | 35 | 2 | 0 | 0 | 1 | 2.9 | 1 | 2 | 0 | 11 | 0 | .057 | .143 | 3 | 1 | OF-11 |

| | G | AB | H | 2B | 3B | HR | HR % | R | RBI | BB | SO | SB | BA | SA | Pinch Hit AB | Pinch Hit H | G by POS |
|---|---|---|---|---|---|---|---|---|---|---|---|---|---|---|---|---|---|

## Don Young continued

| | G | AB | H | 2B | 3B | HR | HR % | R | RBI | BB | SO | SB | BA | SA | AB | H | G by POS |
|---|---|---|---|---|---|---|---|---|---|---|---|---|---|---|---|---|---|
| 1969 | 101 | 272 | 65 | 12 | 3 | 6 | 2.2 | 36 | 27 | 38 | 74 | 1 | .239 | .371 | 0 | 0 | OF-100 |
| 2 yrs. | 112 | 307 | 67 | 12 | 3 | 7 | 2.3 | 37 | 29 | 38 | 85 | 1 | .218 | .345 | 3 | 1 | OF-111 |
| 2 yrs. | 112 | 307 | 67 | 12 | 3 | 7 | 2.3 | 37 | 29 | 38 | 85 | 1 | .218 | .345 | 3 | 1 | OF-111 |

## Rollie Zeider

**ZEIDER, ROLLIE HUBERT (Bunions)**     BR TR 5'10" 162 lbs.
B. Nov. 16, 1883, Auburn, Ind.    D. Sept. 12, 1967, Garrett, Ind.

| | G | AB | H | 2B | 3B | HR | HR % | R | RBI | BB | SO | SB | BA | SA | AB | H | G by POS |
|---|---|---|---|---|---|---|---|---|---|---|---|---|---|---|---|---|---|
| 1910 CHI A | 136 | 498 | 108 | 9 | 2 | 0 | 0.0 | 57 | 31 | 62 | | 49 | .217 | .243 | 0 | 0 | 2B-87, SS-45, 3B-4 |
| 1911 | 73 | 217 | 55 | 3 | 0 | 2 | 0.9 | 39 | 21 | 29 | | 28 | .253 | .295 | 8 | 4 | 1B-29, SS-17, 3B-10, 2B-9 |
| 1912 | 129 | 420 | 103 | 12 | 10 | 1 | 0.2 | 57 | 42 | 50 | | 47 | .245 | .329 | 3 | 1 | 1B-66, 3B-56, SS-1 |
| 1913 2 teams | | CHI | A (13G – .350) | | NY | A | (49G – .233) | | | | | | | | | | |
| " total | 62 | 179 | 44 | 2 | 0 | 0 | 0.0 | 19 | 14 | 29 | 10 | 6 | .246 | .257 | 2 | 0 | SS-23, 2B-20, 3B-8, 1B-7 |
| 1914 CHI F | 119 | 452 | 124 | 13 | 2 | 1 | 0.2 | 60 | 36 | 44 | | 35 | .274 | .319 | 1 | 0 | 3B-117, SS-1 |
| 1915 | 129 | 494 | 112 | 22 | 2 | 0 | 0.0 | 65 | 34 | 43 | | 16 | .227 | .279 | 0 | 0 | 2B-83, 3B-30, SS-21 |
| 1916 CHI N | 98 | 345 | 81 | 11 | 2 | 1 | 0.3 | 29 | 22 | 26 | 26 | 9 | .235 | .287 | 1 | 0 | 3B-55, 2B-33, OF-7, SS-5, 1B-2 |
| 1917 | 108 | 354 | 86 | 14 | 2 | 0 | 0.0 | 36 | 27 | 28 | 30 | 17 | .243 | .294 | 15 | 2 | SS-48, 3B-26, 2B-24, OF-1, 1B-1 |
| 1918 | 82 | 251 | 56 | 3 | 2 | 0 | 0.0 | 31 | 26 | 23 | 20 | 16 | .223 | .251 | 7 | 1 | 2B-79, 3B-1, 1B-1 |
| 9 yrs. | 936 | 3210 | 769 | 89 | 22 | 5 | 0.2 | 393 | 253 | 334 | 86 | 223 | .240 | .286 | 37 | 8 | 2B-335, 3B-307, SS-161, 1B-106, OF-8 |
| 3 yrs. | 288 | 950 | 223 | 28 | 6 | 1 | 0.1 | 96 | 75 | 77 | 76 | 42 | .235 | .280 | 23 | 3 | 2B-136, 3B-82, SS-53, OF-8, 1B-4 |

**WORLD SERIES**

| | G | AB | H | 2B | 3B | HR | HR % | R | RBI | BB | SO | SB | BA | SA | AB | H | G by POS |
|---|---|---|---|---|---|---|---|---|---|---|---|---|---|---|---|---|---|
| 1918 CHI N | 2 | 0 | 0 | 0 | 0 | 0 | – | 0 | 0 | 2 | 0 | 0 | – | – | 0 | 0 | 3B-2 |

## Don Zimmer

**ZIMMER, DONALD WILLIAM**     BR TR 5'9" 165 lbs.
B. Jan. 17, 1931, Cincinnati, Ohio
Manager 1972-73, 1976-82.

| | G | AB | H | 2B | 3B | HR | HR % | R | RBI | BB | SO | SB | BA | SA | AB | H | G by POS |
|---|---|---|---|---|---|---|---|---|---|---|---|---|---|---|---|---|---|
| 1954 BKN N | 24 | 33 | 6 | 0 | 1 | 0 | 0.0 | 3 | 0 | 3 | 8 | 2 | .182 | .242 | 2 | 0 | SS-13 |
| 1955 | 88 | 280 | 67 | 10 | 1 | 15 | 5.4 | 38 | 50 | 19 | 66 | 5 | .239 | .443 | 3 | 0 | 2B-62, SS-21, 3B-8 |
| 1956 | 17 | 20 | 6 | 1 | 0 | 0 | 0.0 | 4 | 2 | 0 | 7 | 0 | .300 | .350 | 0 | 0 | SS-8, 3B-3, 2B-1 |
| 1957 | 84 | 269 | 59 | 9 | 1 | 6 | 2.2 | 23 | 19 | 16 | 63 | 1 | .219 | .327 | 1 | 0 | 3B-39, SS-37, 2B-5 |
| 1958 LA N | 127 | 455 | 119 | 15 | 2 | 17 | 3.7 | 52 | 60 | 28 | 92 | 14 | .262 | .415 | 1 | 0 | SS-114, 3B-12, OF-1, 2B-1 |
| 1959 | 97 | 249 | 41 | 7 | 1 | 4 | 1.6 | 21 | 28 | 37 | 56 | 3 | .165 | .249 | 4 | 1 | SS-88, 3B-5, 2B-1 |
| 1960 CHI N | 132 | 368 | 95 | 16 | 7 | 6 | 1.6 | 37 | 35 | 27 | 56 | 8 | .258 | .389 | 13 | 3 | 2B-75, 3B-45, SS-5, OF-2 |
| 1961 | 128 | 477 | 120 | 25 | 4 | 13 | 2.7 | 57 | 40 | 25 | 70 | 5 | .252 | .403 | 8 | 1 | 2B-116, 3B-5, OF-1 |
| 1962 2 teams | | NY | N (14G – .077) | | CIN | N | (63G – .250) | | | | | | | | | | |
| " total | 77 | 244 | 52 | 12 | 2 | 2 | 0.8 | 19 | 17 | 17 | 40 | 1 | .213 | .303 | 9 | 4 | 3B-57, 2B-17, SS-1 |
| 1963 2 teams | | LA | N (22G – .217) | | WAS | A | (83G – .248) | | | | | | | | | | |
| " total | 105 | 321 | 79 | 13 | 1 | 14 | 4.4 | 41 | 46 | 21 | 67 | 3 | .246 | .424 | 14 | 5 | 3B-88, 2B-3, SS-1 |
| 1964 WAS A | 121 | 341 | 84 | 16 | 2 | 12 | 3.5 | 38 | 38 | 27 | 94 | 1 | .246 | .411 | 38 | 10 | 3B-87, OF-4, C-2, 2B-1 |
| 1965 | 95 | 226 | 45 | 6 | 0 | 2 | 0.9 | 20 | 17 | 26 | 59 | 2 | .199 | .252 | 27 | 5 | 3B-36, C-33, 2B-12 |
| 12 yrs. | 1095 | 3283 | 773 | 130 | 22 | 91 | 2.8 | 353 | 352 | 246 | 678 | 45 | .235 | .372 | 120 | 29 | 3B-385, 2B-294, SS-288, C-35, OF-8 |
| 2 yrs. | 260 | 845 | 215 | 41 | 11 | 19 | 2.2 | 94 | 75 | 52 | 126 | 13 | .254 | .396 | 21 | 4 | 2B-191, 3B-50, SS-5, OF-3 |

**WORLD SERIES**

| | G | AB | H | 2B | 3B | HR | HR % | R | RBI | BB | SO | SB | BA | SA | AB | H | G by POS |
|---|---|---|---|---|---|---|---|---|---|---|---|---|---|---|---|---|---|
| 1955 BKN N | 4 | 9 | 2 | 0 | 0 | 0 | 0.0 | 0 | 2 | 2 | 5 | 0 | .222 | .222 | 1 | 0 | 2B-4 |
| 1959 LA N | 1 | 1 | 0 | 0 | 0 | 0 | 0.0 | 0 | 0 | 0 | 0 | 0 | .000 | .000 | 0 | 0 | SS-1 |
| 2 yrs. | 5 | 10 | 2 | 0 | 0 | 0 | 0.0 | 0 | 2 | 2 | 5 | 0 | .200 | .200 | 1 | 0 | 2B-4, SS-1 |

## Heinie Zimmerman

**ZIMMERMAN, HENRY**     BR TR 5'11½" 176 lbs.
B. Feb. 9, 1887, New York, N.Y.    D. Mar. 14, 1969, New York, N.Y.

| | G | AB | H | 2B | 3B | HR | HR % | R | RBI | BB | SO | SB | BA | SA | AB | H | G by POS |
|---|---|---|---|---|---|---|---|---|---|---|---|---|---|---|---|---|---|
| 1907 CHI N | 5 | 9 | 2 | 1 | 0 | 0 | 0.0 | 0 | 1 | 0 | | 0 | .222 | .333 | 0 | 0 | 2B-4, OF-1, SS-1 |
| 1908 | 46 | 113 | 33 | 4 | 1 | 0 | 0.0 | 17 | 9 | 1 | | 2 | .292 | .345 | 15 | 2 | 2B-20, OF-8, SS-1, 3B-1 |
| 1909 | 65 | 183 | 50 | 9 | 2 | 0 | 0.0 | 23 | 21 | 3 | | 7 | .273 | .344 | 18 | 6 | 2B-27, 3B-16, SS-12 |
| 1910 | 99 | 335 | 95 | 16 | 6 | 3 | 0.9 | 35 | 38 | 20 | 36 | 7 | .284 | .394 | 12 | 3 | 2B-33, SS-26, 3B-22, OF-4, 1B-1 |
| 1911 | 143 | 535 | 164 | 22 | 17 | 9 | 1.7 | 80 | 85 | 25 | 50 | 23 | .307 | .462 | 4 | 1 | 2B-108, 3B-20, 1B-11 |
| 1912 | 145 | 557 | **207** | **41** | 14 | **14** | 2.5 | 95 | **103** | 38 | 60 | 23 | **.372** | **.571** | 2 | 0 | 3B-121, 1B-22 |
| 1913 | 127 | 447 | 140 | 28 | 12 | 9 | 2.0 | 69 | 95 | 41 | 40 | 18 | .313 | .490 | 1 | 0 | 3B-125 |
| 1914 | 146 | 564 | 167 | 36 | 12 | 4 | 0.7 | 75 | 87 | 20 | 46 | 17 | .296 | .424 | 1 | 1 | 3B-119, SS-15, 2B-12 |
| 1915 | 139 | 520 | 138 | 28 | 11 | 3 | 0.6 | 65 | 62 | 21 | 33 | 19 | .265 | .379 | 1 | 1 | 2B-100, 3B-36, SS-4 |
| 1916 2 teams | | CHI | N (107G – .291) | | NY | N | (40G – .272) | | | | | | | | | | |
| " total | 147 | 549 | 157 | 29 | 5 | 6 | 1.1 | 76 | **83** | 23 | 43 | 24 | .286 | .390 | 4 | 1 | 3B-115, 2B-14, SS-4 |
| 1917 NY N | 150 | 585 | 174 | 22 | 9 | 5 | 0.9 | 61 | **102** | 16 | 43 | 13 | .297 | .391 | 0 | 0 | 3B-149, 2B-5 |
| 1918 | 121 | 463 | 126 | 19 | 10 | 1 | 0.2 | 43 | 56 | 13 | 23 | 14 | .272 | .363 | 1 | 1 | 3B-100, 1B-19 |
| 1919 | 123 | 444 | 113 | 20 | 6 | 4 | 0.9 | 56 | 58 | 21 | 30 | 8 | .255 | .354 | 0 | 0 | 3B-123 |
| 13 yrs. | 1456 | 5304 | 1566 | 275 | 105 | 58 | 1.1 | 695 | 800 | 242 | 404 | 175 | .295 | .419 | 59 | 16 | 3B-947, 2B-323, SS-63, 1B-53, OF-13 |
| 10 yrs. | 1022 | 3661 | 1112 | 210 | 80 10th | 48 | 1.3 | 513 | 565 | 185 | 298 | 131 | .304 | .444 | 58 | 15 | 3B-535, 2B-318, SS-63, 1B-34, OF-13 |

**WORLD SERIES**

| | G | AB | H | 2B | 3B | HR | HR % | R | RBI | BB | SO | SB | BA | SA | AB | H | G by POS |
|---|---|---|---|---|---|---|---|---|---|---|---|---|---|---|---|---|---|
| 1907 CHI N | 1 | 1 | 0 | 0 | 0 | 0 | 0.0 | 0 | 0 | 0 | | 1 | .000 | .000 | 0 | 0 | 2B-1 |
| 1910 | 5 | 17 | 4 | 1 | 0 | 0 | 0.0 | 0 | 2 | 1 | 3 | 1 | .235 | .294 | 0 | 0 | 2B-5 |
| 1917 NY N | 6 | 25 | 3 | 0 | 1 | 0 | 0.0 | 1 | 0 | 0 | 0 | 0 | .120 | .200 | 0 | 0 | 3B-6 |
| 3 yrs. | 12 | 43 | 7 | 1 | 1 | 0 | 0.0 | 1 | 2 | 1 | 4 | 1 | .163 | .233 | 0 | 0 | 3B-6, 2B-6 |

## Dutch Zwilling

**ZWILLING, EDWARD HARRISON**     BL TL 5'6½" 160 lbs.
B. Nov. 2, 1888, St. Louis, Mo.    D. Mar. 27, 1978, La Crescenta, Calif.

| | G | AB | H | 2B | 3B | HR | HR % | R | RBI | BB | SO | SB | BA | SA | AB | H | G by POS |
|---|---|---|---|---|---|---|---|---|---|---|---|---|---|---|---|---|---|
| 1910 CHI A | 27 | 87 | 16 | 5 | 0 | 0 | 0.0 | 7 | 5 | 11 | | 1 | .184 | .241 | 0 | 0 | OF-27 |
| 1914 CHI F | 154 | 592 | 185 | 38 | 8 | 15 | 2.5 | 91 | 95 | 46 | | 21 | .313 | .480 | 0 | 0 | OF-154 |

| | G | AB | H | 2B | 3B | HR | HR % | R | RBI | BB | SO | SB | BA | SA | Pinch Hit AB | H | G by POS |
|---|---|---|---|---|---|---|---|---|---|---|---|---|---|---|---|---|---|

## Dutch Zwilling continued

| | G | AB | H | 2B | 3B | HR | HR % | R | RBI | BB | SO | SB | BA | SA | Pinch Hit AB | H | G by POS |
|---|---|---|---|---|---|---|---|---|---|---|---|---|---|---|---|---|---|
| 1915 | 150 | 548 | 157 | 32 | 7 | 13 | 2.4 | 65 | 94 | 67 | | 24 | .286 | .442 | 1 | 0 | OF-148, 1B-3 |
| 1916 CHI N | 35 | 53 | 6 | 1 | 0 | 1 | 1.9 | 4 | 8 | 4 | 6 | 0 | .113 | .189 | 23 | 4 | OF-10 |
| 4 yrs. | 366 | 1280 | 364 | 76 | 15 | 29 | 2.3 | 167 | 202 | 128 | 6 | 46 | .284 | .435 | 24 | 4 | OF-339, 1B-3 |
| 1 yr. | 35 | 53 | 6 | 1 | 0 | 1 | 1.9 | 4 | 8 | 4 | 6 | 0 | .113 | .189 | 23 | 4 | OF-10 |

# Pitcher Register

The Pitcher Register is an alphabetical list of every man who pitched in the major leagues and played or managed for the Chicago Cubs from 1876 through today. Included are lifetime totals of League Championship Series and World Series.

The player and team information for the Pitcher Register is the same as that for the Player Register explained on page 211.

| | | W | L | PCT | ERA | G | GS | CG | IP | H | BB | SO | ShO | Relief Pitching W | L | SV | BATTING AB | H | HR | BA |
|---|---|---|---|---|---|---|---|---|---|---|---|---|---|---|---|---|---|---|---|---|

**John Doe**

**DOE, JOHN LEE (Slim)**                     TR  6'2"   165 lbs.
Played as John Cherry part of 1900.
Born John Lee Doughnut.    Brother of Bill Doe.
B. Jan. 1,1850, New York, N. Y.    D. July 1, 1955, New York, N. Y.
Hall of Fame 1946.

| Year | Team | Lg | W | L | PCT | ERA | G | GS | CG | IP | H | BB | SO | ShO | RP W | L | SV | AB | H | HR | BA |
|---|---|---|---|---|---|---|---|---|---|---|---|---|---|---|---|---|---|---|---|---|---|
| 1884 | STL | U | 4 | 2 | .667 | 3.40 | 26 | 0 | 0 | 54.2 | 41 | 38 | 40 | 0 | 1 | 0 | 0 | 4 | 0 | 0 | .000 |
| 1885 | LOU | AA | 14 | 10 | .583 | 4.12 | 40 | 19 | 10 | 207.2 | 193 | 76 | 70 | 0 | 1 | 0 | 1 | 16 | 2 | 0 | .111 |
| 1886 | CLE | N | 10 | 5 | .667 | 4.08 | 40 | 8 | 4 | 117 | 110 | 55 | 77 | 0 | 0 | 1 | 0 | 10 | 0 | 0 | .000 |
| 1887 | BOS | N | 9 | 3 | .750 | 3.38 | 27 | 5 | 2 | 88 | 90 | 36 | 34 | 0 | 2 | 2 | 5 | 44 | 3 | 0 | .214 |
| 1888 | NY | N | 13 | 4 | .765 | 4.17 | 39 | 4 | 0 | 110 | 121 | 50 | **236** | 0 | 0 | 0 | 0 | 3 | 0 | 0 | – |
| 1889 | 3 teams | | | | DET N (10G 4–2) | | PIT N (2G 0–0) | | | PHI N (10G 4–0) | | | | | | | | | | | |
| " | total | | 8 | 2 | .800 | 4.25 | 22 | 2 | 2 | 91.1 | 90 | 41 | 43 | 0 | 2 | 1 | 10 | 37 | 1 | 0 | .036 |
| 1890 | NY | P | 13 | 6 | .684 | 4.43 | 38 | 0 | 0 | 61.1 | 57 | 28 | 30 | 0 | 4 | 4 | 8 | 45 | 0 | 0 | .000 |
| 1900 | CHI | A | 18 | 4 | .818 | 3.71 | 35 | 1 | 0 | 63.1 | 58 | 15 | 23 | 0 | 4 | 2 | 3 | 42 | 2 | 0 | .027 |
| 1901 | BAL | A | 18 | 4 | .818 | 1.98 | 35 | 0 | 0 | 77.1 | 68 | 40 | 29 | 0 | 0 | 2 | 0 | 38 | 10 | 0 | .132 |
| 1906 | CHI | N | 14 | 10 | .583 | 3.41 | 31 | 0 | 0 | 58 | 66 | 23 | 24 | 0 | 0 | 0 | 1 | 32 | 3 | 0 | .057 |
| 1907 | | | 13 | 4 | .765 | 2.51 | 22 | 1 | 0 | 68 | 44 | 30 | 31 | 0 | 0 | 1 | 0 | 31 | 1 | 0 | .500 |
| 1908 | | | 0 | 0 | – | 3.38 | 1 | 1 | 0 | 8 | 8 | 1 | 1 | 0 | 1 | 2 | 3 | 25 | 0 | 0 | .000 |
| 1914 | CHI | F | 3 | 1 | .750 | 2.78 | 6 | 0 | 0 | 54.2 | 41 | 28 | 9 | 0 | 1 | 0 | 1 | 41 | 2 | 0 | .400 |
| 13 | yrs. | | 137 | 55 | .714 | 3.50 | 377 | 40 | 18 | 1059.1 | 987 | 461 | 647 | 0 | 16 | 18 | 32 8th | | | | |
| 3 | yrs. | | 27 | 14 | .659 | 2.96 | 69 | 1 | 0 | 134 | 118 | 54 | 56 | 0 | 5 | 5 | 3 | 79 | 25 | 1 | .316 |

LEAGUE CHAMPIONSHIP SERIES

| 1901 | BAL | A | 1 | 1 | .500 | 4.76 | 4 | 0 | 0 | 22.2 | 26 | 8 | 16 | 8 | 0 | 0 | 0 | 0 | 0 | 0 | – |

WORLD SERIES

| 1901 | BAL | A | 2 | 0 | 1.000 | 1.00 | 2 | 2 | 2 | 18 | 14 | 7 | 31 | 0 | 0 | 0 | 1 | 7 | 1 | 0 | .143 |
| 1908 | STL | N | 2 | 0 | .500 | 2.30 | 4 | 4 | 3 | 30 | 20 | 3 | 24 | 0 | 0 | 0 | 0 | 4 | 1 | 0 | .250 |
| 2 | yrs. | | 4 | 0 | 1.000 | 1.15 | 6 | 6 | 5 | 48 | 34 | 10 | 55 9th | 0 | 0 | 0 | 1 | 11 | 2 | 0 | .182 |

## COLUMN HEADINGS INFORMATION

| | W | L | PCT | ERA | G | GS | CG | IP | H | BB | SO | ShO | Relief Pitching W | L | SV | BATTING AB | H | HR | BA |
|---|---|---|---|---|---|---|---|---|---|---|---|---|---|---|---|---|---|---|---|---|

*Total Pitching* (including all starting and relief appearances)

| W | Wins |
|---|---|
| L | Losses |
| PCT | Winning Percentage |
| ERA | Earned Run Average |
| G | Games Pitched |
| GS | Games Started |
| CG | Complete Games |
| IP | Innings Pitched |
| H | Hits Allowed |
| BB | Bases on Balls Allowed |
| SO | Strikeouts |
| ShO | Shutouts |

*Relief Pitching*

| W | Wins |
|---|---|
| L | Losses |
| SV | Saves |

*Batting*

| AB | At Bats |
|---|---|
| H | Hits |
| HR | Home Runs |
| BA | Batting Average |

427

*Partial Innings Pitched.* These are shown in the Innings Pitched column, and are indicated by a ".1" or ".2" after the total. Doe, for example, pitched 54⅔ innings in 1884.

*All-Time Single Season Leaders.* (Starts with 1893, the first year that the pitcher's box was moved to its present distance of 60 feet 6 inches.) Indicated by the small number that appears next to the statistic. Doe, for example, is shown by a small number "1" next to his earned run average in 1901. This means he is first on the all-time major league list for having the lowest earned run average in a single season. All pitchers who tied for first are also shown by the same number.

*Meaningless Averages.* Indicated by the use of a dash (—). In the case of Doe, a dash is shown for his 1908 winning percentage. This means that although he pitched in one game he never had a decision. A percentage of .000 would mean that he had at least one loss.

*Estimated Earned Run Averages.* Any time an earned run average appears in italics, it indicates that not all the earned runs allowed by the pitcher are known, and the information had to be estimated. Doe's 1885 earned run average, for example, appears in italics. It is known that Doe's team, Louisville, allowed 560 runs in 112 games. Of these games, it is known that in 90 of them Louisville allowed 420 runs of which 315 or 75% were earned. Doe pitched 207⅔ innings in 40 games and allowed 134 runs. In 35 of these games, it is known that he allowed 118 runs of which 83 were earned. By multiplying the team's known ratio of earned runs to total runs (75%), by Doe's 16 (134 minus 118) remaining runs allowed, a figure of 12 additional estimated earned runs is calculated. This means that Doe allowed an estimated total of 95 earned runs in 207⅔ innings, for an estimated earned run average of 4.12. In all cases at least 50% of the runs allowed by the team were "known" as a basis for estimating earned run averages. (Any time the symbol "infinity" (∞) is shown for a pitcher's earned run average, it means that the pitcher allowed one or more earned runs during a season without retiring a batter.)

*Batting Statistics.* Because a pitcher's batting statistics are of relatively minor importance—and the Designated Hitter rule may eliminate pitchers' batting entirely—only the most significant statistics are given; number of hits, home runs, and batting average.

*An asterisk (\*)* shown in the lifetime batting totals means that the pitcher's complete year-by-year and lifetime batting record is listed in the Player Register.

| | W | L | PCT | ERA | G | GS | CG | IP | H | BB | SO | ShO | Relief Pitching W | L | SV | BATTING AB | H | HR | BA |
|---|---|---|---|---|---|---|---|---|---|---|---|---|---|---|---|---|---|---|---|

## Bert Abbey

**ABBEY, BERT WOOD**
B. Nov. 29, 1869, Essex, Vt.    D. June 11, 1962, Essex Junction, Vt.
BR TR  5'11"  175 lbs.

| | W | L | PCT | ERA | G | GS | CG | IP | H | BB | SO | ShO | RP W | L | SV | AB | H | HR | BA |
|---|---|---|---|---|---|---|---|---|---|---|---|---|---|---|---|---|---|---|---|
| 1892 WAS N | 5 | 18 | .217 | 3.45 | 27 | 23 | 19 | 195.2 | 207 | 76 | 77 | 0 | 0 | 2 | 1 | 75 | 9 | 0 | .120 |
| 1893 CHI N | 2 | 4 | .333 | 5.46 | 7 | 7 | 5 | 56 | 74 | 20 | 6 | 0 | 0 | 0 | 0 | 26 | 6 | 0 | .231 |
| 1894 | 2 | 7 | .222 | 5.18 | 11 | 11 | 10 | 92 | 119 | 37 | 24 | 0 | 0 | 0 | 0 | 39 | 5 | 0 | .128 |
| 1895 2 teams | | | CHI | N (1G 0–1) | BKN | N | (8G 5–2) | | | | | | | | | | | | |
| " total | 5 | 3 | .625 | 4.35 | 9 | 7 | 6 | 60 | 76 | 11 | 17 | 0 | 1 | 0 | 0 | 22 | 6 | 0 | .273 |
| 1896 BKN N | 8 | 8 | .500 | 5.15 | 25 | 18 | 12 | 164.1 | 210 | 48 | 37 | 0 | 1 | 1 | 0 | 63 | 12 | 0 | .190 |
| 5 yrs. | 22 | 40 | .355 | 4.52 | 79 | 66 | 52 | 568 | 686 | 192 | 161 | 0 | 2 | 3 | 1 | 225 | 38 | 0 | .169 |
| 3 yrs. | 4 | 12 | .250 | 5.25 | 19 | 19 | 16 | 156 | 203 | 59 | 33 | 0 | 0 | 0 | 0 | 68 | 12 | 0 | .176 |

## Ted Abernathy

**ABERNATHY, THEODORE WADE**
B. Mar. 6, 1933, Stanley, N. C.
BR TR  6'4"  215 lbs.

| | W | L | PCT | ERA | G | GS | CG | IP | H | BB | SO | ShO | RP W | L | SV | AB | H | HR | BA |
|---|---|---|---|---|---|---|---|---|---|---|---|---|---|---|---|---|---|---|---|
| 1955 WAS A | 5 | 9 | .357 | 5.96 | 40 | 14 | 3 | 119.1 | 136 | 67 | 79 | 2 | 1 | 1 | 0 | 26 | 4 | 0 | .154 |
| 1956 | 1 | 3 | .250 | 4.15 | 5 | 4 | 2 | 30.1 | 35 | 10 | 18 | 0 | 0 | 0 | 0 | 11 | 2 | 0 | .182 |
| 1957 | 2 | 10 | .167 | 6.78 | 26 | 16 | 2 | 85 | 100 | 65 | 50 | 0 | 1 | 0 | 0 | 24 | 4 | 0 | .167 |
| 1960 | 0 | 0 | – | 12.00 | 2 | 0 | 0 | 3 | 4 | 4 | 1 | 0 | 0 | 0 | 0 | 1 | 1 | 0 | 1.000 |
| 1963 CLE A | 7 | 2 | .778 | 2.88 | 43 | 0 | 0 | 59.1 | 54 | 29 | 47 | 0 | 7 | 2 | 12 | 5 | 2 | 0 | .400 |
| 1964 | 2 | 6 | .250 | 4.33 | 53 | 0 | 0 | 72.2 | 66 | 46 | 57 | 0 | 2 | 6 | 11 | 6 | 0 | 0 | .000 |
| 1965 CHI N | 4 | 6 | .400 | 2.57 | 84 | 0 | 0 | 136.1 | 113 | 56 | 104 | 0 | 4 | 6 | 31 | 18 | 3 | 0 | .167 |
| 1966 2 teams | | | CHI | N (20G 1–3) | ATL | N | (38G 4–4) | | | | | | | | | | | | |
| " total | 5 | 7 | .417 | 4.55 | 58 | 0 | 0 | 93 | 84 | 53 | 60 | 0 | 5 | 7 | 8 | 12 | 2 | 0 | .167 |
| 1967 CIN N | 6 | 3 | .667 | 1.27 | 70 | 0 | 0 | 106.1 | 63 | 41 | 88 | 0 | 6 | 3 | 28 | 17 | 1 | 0 | .059 |
| 1968 | 10 | 7 | .588 | 2.46 | 78 | 0 | 0 | 135.1 | 111 | 55 | 64 | 0 | 10 | 7 | 13 | 17 | 0 | 0 | .000 |
| 1969 CHI N | 4 | 3 | .571 | 3.18 | 56 | 0 | 0 | 85 | 75 | 42 | 55 | 0 | 4 | 3 | 3 | 8 | 2 | 0 | .250 |
| 1970 3 teams | | | CHI | N (11G 0–0) | STL | N | (11G 1–0) | KC | A | (36G 9–3) | | | | | | | | | |
| " total | 10 | 3 | .769 | 2.59 | 58 | 0 | 0 | 83.1 | 65 | 55 | 59 | 0 | 10 | 3 | 14 | 17 | 3 | 0 | .176 |
| 1971 KC A | 4 | 6 | .400 | 2.56 | 63 | 0 | 0 | 81 | 60 | 50 | 55 | 0 | 4 | 6 | 23 | 13 | 1 | 0 | .077 |
| 1972 | 3 | 4 | .429 | 1.71 | 45 | 0 | 0 | 74 | 44 | 19 | 28 | 0 | 3 | 4 | 5 | 6 | 0 | 0 | .000 |
| 14 yrs. | 63 | 69 | .477 | 3.46 | 681 | 34 | 7 | 1148 | 1010 | 592 | 765 | 2 | 57 | 48 | 148 | 181 | 25 | 0 | .138 |
| 4 yrs. | 9 | 12 | .429 | 3.14 | 171 | 0 | 0 | 258 | 223 | 120 | 179 | 0 | 9 | 12 | 39 | 30 | 5 | 0 | .167 |
| | | | | | | | | | | | | | | | 6th | | | | |

## Johnny Abrego

**ABREGO, JOHNNY RAY**
B. July 4, 1962, Corpus Christi, Tex.
BR TR  6'  185 lbs.

| | W | L | PCT | ERA | G | GS | CG | IP | H | BB | SO | ShO | RP W | L | SV | AB | H | HR | BA |
|---|---|---|---|---|---|---|---|---|---|---|---|---|---|---|---|---|---|---|---|
| 1985 CHI N | 1 | 1 | .500 | 6.38 | 6 | 5 | 0 | 24 | 32 | 12 | 13 | 0 | 0 | 0 | 0 | 9 | 0 | 0 | .000 |

## Karl Adams

**ADAMS, KARL TUTWILER (Rebel)**
B. Aug. 11, 1891, Columbus, Ga.    D. Sept. 17, 1967, Everett, Wash.
BR TR  6'2"  170 lbs.

| | W | L | PCT | ERA | G | GS | CG | IP | H | BB | SO | ShO | RP W | L | SV | AB | H | HR | BA |
|---|---|---|---|---|---|---|---|---|---|---|---|---|---|---|---|---|---|---|---|
| 1914 CIN N | 0 | 0 | – | 9.00 | 4 | 0 | 0 | 8 | 14 | 5 | 5 | 0 | 0 | 0 | 0 | 2 | 1 | 0 | .500 |
| 1915 CHI N | 1 | 9 | .100 | 4.71 | 26 | 12 | 3 | 107 | 105 | 43 | 57 | 0 | 0 | 1 | 0 | 30 | 0 | 0 | .000 |
| 2 yrs. | 1 | 9 | .100 | 5.01 | 30 | 12 | 3 | 115 | 119 | 48 | 62 | 0 | 0 | 1 | 0 | 32 | 1 | 0 | .031 |
| 1 yr. | 1 | 9 | .100 | 4.71 | 26 | 12 | 3 | 107 | 105 | 43 | 57 | 0 | 0 | 1 | 0 | 30 | 0 | 0 | .000 |

## Red Adams

**ADAMS, CHARLES DWIGHT**
B. Oct. 7, 1921, Parlier, Calif.
BR TR  6'  185 lbs.

| | W | L | PCT | ERA | G | GS | CG | IP | H | BB | SO | ShO | RP W | L | SV | AB | H | HR | BA |
|---|---|---|---|---|---|---|---|---|---|---|---|---|---|---|---|---|---|---|---|
| 1946 CHI N | 0 | 1 | .000 | 8.25 | 8 | 0 | 0 | 12 | 18 | 7 | 8 | 0 | 0 | 1 | 0 | 1 | 0 | 0 | .000 |

## Dewey Adkins

**ADKINS, JOHN DEWEY**
B. May 11, 1918, Norcatur, Kans.
BR TR  6'2"  195 lbs.

| | W | L | PCT | ERA | G | GS | CG | IP | H | BB | SO | ShO | RP W | L | SV | AB | H | HR | BA |
|---|---|---|---|---|---|---|---|---|---|---|---|---|---|---|---|---|---|---|---|
| 1942 WAS A | 0 | 0 | – | 9.95 | 1 | 1 | 0 | 6.1 | 7 | 6 | 3 | 0 | 0 | 0 | 0 | 2 | 1 | 0 | .500 |
| 1943 | 0 | 0 | – | 2.61 | 7 | 0 | 0 | 10.1 | 9 | 5 | 1 | 0 | 0 | 0 | 0 | 0 | 0 | 0 | – |
| 1949 CHI N | 2 | 4 | .333 | 5.68 | 30 | 5 | 1 | 82.1 | 98 | 39 | 43 | 0 | 1 | 1 | 0 | 20 | 4 | 1 | .200 |
| 3 yrs. | 2 | 4 | .333 | 5.64 | 38 | 6 | 1 | 99 | 114 | 50 | 47 | 0 | 1 | 1 | 0 | 22 | 5 | 1 | .227 |
| 1 yr. | 2 | 4 | .333 | 5.68 | 30 | 5 | 1 | 82.1 | 98 | 39 | 43 | 0 | 1 | 1 | 0 | 20 | 4 | 1 | .200 |

## Hank Aguirre

**AGUIRRE, HENRY JOHN**
B. Jan. 31, 1932, Azusa, Calif.
BR TL  6'4"  205 lbs.
BB 1965–68

| | W | L | PCT | ERA | G | GS | CG | IP | H | BB | SO | ShO | RP W | L | SV | AB | H | HR | BA |
|---|---|---|---|---|---|---|---|---|---|---|---|---|---|---|---|---|---|---|---|
| 1955 CLE A | 2 | 0 | 1.000 | 1.42 | 4 | 1 | 1 | 12.2 | 6 | 12 | 6 | 1 | 1 | 0 | 0 | 4 | 0 | 0 | .000 |
| 1956 | 3 | 5 | .375 | 3.72 | 16 | 9 | 2 | 65.1 | 63 | 27 | 31 | 1 | 1 | 0 | 1 | 18 | 2 | 0 | .111 |
| 1957 | 1 | 1 | .500 | 5.75 | 10 | 1 | 0 | 20.1 | 26 | 13 | 9 | 0 | 0 | 1 | 0 | 4 | 0 | 0 | .000 |
| 1958 DET A | 3 | 4 | .429 | 3.75 | 44 | 3 | 0 | 69.2 | 67 | 27 | 38 | 0 | 2 | 2 | 5 | 14 | 3 | 0 | .214 |
| 1959 | 0 | 0 | – | 3.38 | 3 | 0 | 0 | 2.2 | 4 | 3 | 3 | 0 | 0 | 0 | 0 | 0 | 0 | 0 | – |
| 1960 | 5 | 3 | .625 | 2.85 | 37 | 6 | 1 | 94.2 | 75 | 30 | 80 | 0 | 2 | 1 | 10 | 28 | 1 | 0 | .036 |
| 1961 | 4 | 4 | .500 | 3.25 | 45 | 0 | 0 | 55.1 | 44 | 38 | 32 | 0 | 4 | 4 | 8 | 9 | 0 | 0 | .000 |
| 1962 | 16 | 8 | .667 | 2.21 | 42 | 22 | 11 | 216 | 162 | 65 | 156 | 2 | 4 | 2 | 3 | 75 | 2 | 0 | .027 |
| 1963 | 14 | 15 | .483 | 3.67 | 38 | 33 | 14 | 225.2 | 222 | 68 | 134 | 3 | 0 | 2 | 0 | 76 | 10 | 0 | .132 |
| 1964 | 5 | 10 | .333 | 3.79 | 32 | 27 | 3 | 161.2 | 134 | 59 | 88 | 0 | 0 | 0 | 0 | 53 | 3 | 0 | .057 |
| 1965 | 14 | 10 | .583 | 3.59 | 32 | 32 | 10 | 208.1 | 185 | 60 | 141 | 2 | 0 | 0 | 0 | 70 | 6 | 0 | .086 |
| 1966 | 3 | 9 | .250 | 3.82 | 30 | 14 | 2 | 103.2 | 104 | 26 | 50 | 0 | 0 | 3 | 0 | 25 | 3 | 0 | .120 |
| 1967 | 0 | 1 | .000 | 2.40 | 31 | 1 | 0 | 41.1 | 34 | 17 | 33 | 0 | 0 | 1 | 0 | 2 | 1 | 0 | .500 |
| 1968 LA N | 1 | 2 | .333 | 0.69 | 25 | 0 | 0 | 39 | 32 | 13 | 25 | 0 | 1 | 2 | 3 | 3 | 0 | 0 | .000 |
| 1969 CHI N | 1 | 0 | 1.000 | 2.60 | 41 | 0 | 0 | 45 | 45 | 12 | 19 | 0 | 1 | 0 | 1 | 5 | 2 | 0 | .400 |
| 1970 | 3 | 0 | 1.000 | 4.50 | 17 | 0 | 0 | 14 | 13 | 9 | 11 | 0 | 3 | 0 | 0 | 0 | 0 | 0 | .000 |
| 16 yrs. | 75 | 72 | .510 | 3.25 | 447 | 149 | 44 | 1375.1 | 1216 | 479 | 856 | 9 | 19 | 18 | 33 | 388 | 33 | 0 | .085 |
| 2 yrs. | 4 | 0 | 1.000 | 3.05 | 58 | 0 | 0 | 59 | 58 | 21 | 30 | 0 | 4 | 0 | 2 | 7 | 2 | 0 | .286 |

## Jack Aker

**AKER, JACK DELANE (Chief)**
B. July 13, 1940, Tulare, Calif.
BR TR  6'2"  190 lbs.

| | W | L | PCT | ERA | G | GS | CG | IP | H | BB | SO | ShO | RP W | L | SV | AB | H | HR | BA |
|---|---|---|---|---|---|---|---|---|---|---|---|---|---|---|---|---|---|---|---|
| 1964 KC A | 0 | 1 | .000 | 8.82 | 9 | 0 | 0 | 16.1 | 17 | 10 | 7 | 0 | 0 | 1 | 0 | 3 | 0 | 0 | .000 |

| | W | L | PCT | ERA | G | GS | CG | IP | H | BB | SO | ShO | W | L | SV | AB | H | HR | BA |
|---|---|---|---|---|---|---|---|---|---|---|---|---|---|---|---|---|---|---|---|
| | | | | | | | | | | | | | **Relief Pitching** | | | **BATTING** | | | |

## Jack Aker continued

| | W | L | PCT | ERA | G | GS | CG | IP | H | BB | SO | ShO | W | L | SV | AB | H | HR | BA |
|---|---|---|---|---|---|---|---|---|---|---|---|---|---|---|---|---|---|---|---|
| 1965 | 4 | 3 | .571 | 3.16 | 34 | 0 | 0 | 51.1 | 45 | 18 | 26 | 0 | 4 | 3 | 3 | 8 | 0 | 0 | .000 |
| 1966 | 8 | 4 | .667 | 1.99 | 66 | 0 | 0 | 113 | 81 | 28 | 68 | 0 | 8 | 4 | 32 | 21 | 2 | 0 | .095 |
| 1967 | 3 | 8 | .273 | 4.30 | 57 | 0 | 0 | 88 | 87 | 32 | 65 | 0 | 3 | 8 | 12 | 8 | 1 | 0 | .125 |
| 1968 OAK A | 4 | 4 | .500 | 4.10 | 54 | 0 | 0 | 74.2 | 72 | 33 | 44 | 0 | 4 | 4 | 11 | 7 | 1 | 0 | .143 |
| 1969 2 teams | | | SEA A | (15G 0–2) | | NY | A | (38G 8–4) | | | | | | | | | | | |
| " total | 8 | 6 | .571 | 3.17 | 53 | 0 | 0 | 82.1 | 76 | 35 | 47 | 0 | 8 | 6 | 14 | 10 | 1 | 0 | .100 |
| 1970 NY A | 4 | 2 | .667 | 2.06 | 41 | 0 | 0 | 70 | 57 | 20 | 36 | 0 | 4 | 2 | 16 | 16 | 1 | 0 | .063 |
| 1971 | 4 | 4 | .500 | 2.57 | 41 | 0 | 0 | 56 | 48 | 26 | 24 | 0 | 4 | 4 | 4 | 3 | 0 | 0 | .000 |
| 1972 2 teams | | | NY | A (4G 0–0) | | CHI | N | (48G 6–6) | | | | | | | | | | | |
| " total | 6 | 6 | .500 | 2.96 | 52 | 0 | 0 | 73 | 70 | 26 | 37 | 0 | 6 | 6 | 17 | 6 | 0 | 0 | .000 |
| 1973 CHI N | 4 | 5 | .444 | 4.08 | 47 | 0 | 0 | 64 | 76 | 23 | 25 | 0 | 4 | 5 | 12 | 7 | 0 | 0 | .000 |
| 1974 2 teams | | | ATL | N (17G 0–1) | | NY | N | (24G 2–1) | | | | | | | | | | | |
| " total | 2 | 2 | .500 | 3.57 | 41 | 0 | 0 | 58 | 50 | 23 | 25 | 0 | 2 | 2 | 2 | 3 | 1 | 0 | .333 |
| 11 yrs. | 47 | 45 | .511 | 3.28 | 495 | 0 | 0 | 746.2 | 679 | 274 | 404 | 0 | 47 | 45 | 123 | 92 | 7 | 0 | .076 |
| 2 yrs. | 10 | 11 | .476 | 3.50 | 95 | 0 | 0 | 131 | 141 | 46 | 61 | 0 | 10 | 11 | 29 (9th) | 13 | 0 | 0 | .000 |

## Dale Alderson

**ALDERSON, DALE LEONARD**     BR TR 5'10"   190 lbs.
B. Mar. 9, 1918, Belden, Neb.    D. Feb. 12, 1982, Garden Grove, Calif.

| | W | L | PCT | ERA | G | GS | CG | IP | H | BB | SO | ShO | W | L | SV | AB | H | HR | BA |
|---|---|---|---|---|---|---|---|---|---|---|---|---|---|---|---|---|---|---|---|
| 1943 CHI N | 0 | 1 | .000 | 6.43 | 4 | 2 | 0 | 14 | 21 | 3 | 4 | 0 | 0 | 0 | 0 | 3 | 0 | 0 | .000 |
| 1944 | 0 | 0 | – | 6.65 | 12 | 1 | 0 | 21.2 | 31 | 9 | 7 | 0 | 0 | 0 | 0 | 4 | 0 | 0 | .000 |
| 2 yrs. | 0 | 1 | .000 | 6.56 | 16 | 3 | 0 | 35.2 | 52 | 12 | 11 | 0 | 0 | 0 | 0 | 7 | 0 | 0 | .000 |
| 2 yrs. | 0 | 1 | .000 | 6.56 | 16 | 3 | 0 | 35.2 | 52 | 12 | 11 | 0 | 0 | 0 | 0 | 7 | 0 | 0 | .000 |

## Vic Aldridge

**ALDRIDGE, VICTOR EDDINGTON**     BR TR 5'9½"   175 lbs.
B. Oct. 25, 1893, Indian Springs, Ind.    D. Apr. 17, 1973, Terre Haute, Ind.

| | W | L | PCT | ERA | G | GS | CG | IP | H | BB | SO | ShO | W | L | SV | AB | H | HR | BA |
|---|---|---|---|---|---|---|---|---|---|---|---|---|---|---|---|---|---|---|---|
| 1917 CHI N | 6 | 6 | .500 | 3.12 | 30 | 6 | 1 | 106.2 | 100 | 37 | 44 | 1 | 5 | 1 | 2 | 29 | 4 | 0 | .138 |
| 1918 | 0 | 1 | .000 | 1.46 | 3 | 0 | 0 | 12.1 | 11 | 6 | 10 | 0 | 0 | 1 | 0 | 3 | 1 | 0 | .333 |
| 1922 | 16 | 15 | .516 | 3.52 | 36 | 34 | 20 | 258.1 | 287 | 56 | 66 | 2 | 1 | 0 | 0 | 100 | 26 | 0 | .260 |
| 1923 | 16 | 9 | .640 | 3.48 | 30 | 30 | 15 | 217 | 209 | 67 | 64 | 2 | 0 | 0 | 0 | 71 | 19 | 0 | .268 |
| 1924 | 15 | 12 | .556 | 3.50 | 32 | 32 | 20 | 244.1 | 261 | 80 | 74 | 0 | 0 | 0 | 0 | 85 | 15 | 0 | .176 |
| 1925 PIT N | 15 | 7 | .682 | 3.63 | 30 | 26 | 14 | 213.1 | 218 | 74 | 88 | 1 | 2 | 0 | 0 | 86 | 20 | 1 | .233 |
| 1926 | 10 | 13 | .435 | 4.07 | 30 | 26 | 12 | 190 | 204 | 73 | 61 | 1 | 0 | 1 | 1 | 71 | 16 | 0 | .225 |
| 1927 | 15 | 10 | .600 | 4.25 | 35 | 34 | 17 | 239.1 | 248 | 74 | 86 | 1 | 0 | 0 | 0 | 96 | 21 | 0 | .219 |
| 1928 NY N | 4 | 7 | .364 | 4.83 | 22 | 17 | 3 | 119.1 | 133 | 45 | 33 | 0 | 0 | 0 | 2 | 40 | 11 | 1 | .275 |
| 9 yrs. | 97 | 80 | .548 | 3.76 | 248 | 205 | 102 | 1600.2 | 1671 | 512 | 526 | 8 | 8 | 3 | 6 | 581 | 133 | 2 | .229 |
| 5 yrs. | 53 | 43 | .552 | 3.42 | 131 | 102 | 56 | 838.2 | 868 | 246 | 258 | 5 | 6 | 2 | 2 | 288 | 65 | 0 | .226 |

**WORLD SERIES**

| | W | L | PCT | ERA | G | GS | CG | IP | H | BB | SO | ShO | W | L | SV | AB | H | HR | BA |
|---|---|---|---|---|---|---|---|---|---|---|---|---|---|---|---|---|---|---|---|
| 1925 PIT N | 2 | 0 | 1.000 | 3.93 | 3 | 3 | 2 | 18.1 | 18 | 9 | 9 | 0 | 0 | 0 | 0 | 7 | 0 | 0 | .000 |
| 1927 | 0 | 1 | .000 | 7.36 | 1 | 1 | 0 | 7.1 | 10 | 4 | 4 | 0 | 0 | 0 | 0 | 2 | 0 | 0 | .000 |
| 2 yrs. | 2 | 1 | .667 | 4.91 | 4 | 4 | 2 | 25.2 | 28 | 13 | 13 | 0 | 0 | 0 | 0 | 9 | 0 | 0 | .000 |

## Grover Alexander

**ALEXANDER, GROVER CLEVELAND (Pete)**     BR TR 6'1"   185 lbs.
B. Feb. 26, 1887, Elba, Neb.    D. Nov. 4, 1950, St. Paul, Neb.
Hall of Fame 1938.

| | W | L | PCT | ERA | G | GS | CG | IP | H | BB | SO | ShO | W | L | SV | AB | H | HR | BA |
|---|---|---|---|---|---|---|---|---|---|---|---|---|---|---|---|---|---|---|---|
| 1911 PHI N | 28 | 13 | .683 | 2.57 | 48 | 37 | 31 | 367 | 285 | 129 | 227 | 7 | 4 | 2 | 3 | 138 | 24 | 0 | .174 |
| 1912 | 19 | 17 | .528 | 2.81 | 46 | 34 | 26 | 310.1 | 289 | 105 | 195 | 3 | 3 | 2 | 2 | 102 | 19 | 2 | .186 |
| 1913 | 22 | 8 | .733 | 2.79 | 47 | 35 | 23 | 306.1 | 288 | 75 | 159 | 9 | 4 | 2 | 2 | 103 | 13 | 0 | .126 |
| 1914 | 27 | 15 | .643 | 2.38 | 46 | 39 | 32 | 355 | 327 | 76 | 214 | 6 | 4 | 1 | 1 | 137 | 32 | 0 | .234 |
| 1915 | 31 | 10 | .756 | 1.22 | 49 | 42 | 36 | 376.1 | 253 | 64 | 241 | 12 | 1 | 1 | 3 | 130 | 22 | 1 | .169 |
| 1916 | 33 | 12 | .733 | 1.55 | 48 | 45 | 38 | 388.2 | 323 | 50 | 167 | 16[1] | 0 | 0 | 3 | 138 | 33 | 0 | .239 |
| 1917 | 30 | 13 | .698 | 1.86 | 45 | 44 | 35 | 387.2 | 336 | 58 | 201 | 8 | 0 | 0 | 0 | 139 | 30 | 1 | .216 |
| 1918 CHI N | 2 | 1 | .667 | 1.73 | 3 | 3 | 3 | 26 | 19 | 3 | 15 | 0 | 0 | 0 | 0 | 10 | 1 | 0 | .100 |
| 1919 | 16 | 11 | .593 | 1.72 | 30 | 27 | 20 | 235 | 180 | 38 | 121 | 9 | 0 | 1 | 1 | 70 | 12 | 0 | .171 |
| 1920 | 27 | 14 | .659 | 1.91 | 46 | 40 | 33 | 363.1 | 335 | 69 | 173 | 7 | 1 | 0 | 5 | 118 | 27 | 1 | .229 |
| 1921 | 15 | 13 | .536 | 3.39 | 31 | 29 | 21 | 252 | 286 | 33 | 77 | 3 | 0 | 0 | 1 | 95 | 29 | 1 | .305 |
| 1922 | 16 | 13 | .552 | 3.63 | 33 | 31 | 20 | 245.2 | 283 | 34 | 48 | 1 | 1 | 0 | 1 | 85 | 15 | 0 | .176 |
| 1923 | 22 | 12 | .647 | 3.19 | 39 | 36 | 26 | 305 | 308 | 30 | 72 | 3 | 0 | 0 | 2 | 111 | 24 | 1 | .216 |
| 1924 | 12 | 5 | .706 | 3.03 | 21 | 20 | 12 | 169.1 | 183 | 25 | 33 | 0 | 0 | 1 | 0 | 65 | 15 | 1 | .231 |
| 1925 | 15 | 11 | .577 | 3.39 | 32 | 30 | 20 | 236 | 270 | 29 | 63 | 1 | 0 | 1 | 0 | 79 | 19 | 2 | .241 |
| 1926 2 teams | | | CHI | N (7G 3–3) | | STL | N | (23G 9–7) | | | | | | | | | | | |
| " total | 12 | 10 | .545 | 3.05 | 30 | 23 | 15 | 200.1 | 191 | 31 | 47 | 2 | 2 | 1 | 2 | 65 | 13 | 0 | .200 |
| 1927 STL N | 21 | 10 | .677 | 2.52 | 37 | 30 | 22 | 268 | 261 | 38 | 48 | 2 | 2 | 1 | 3 | 94 | 23 | 0 | .245 |
| 1928 | 16 | 9 | .640 | 3.36 | 34 | 31 | 18 | 243.2 | 262 | 37 | 59 | 1 | 0 | 0 | 2 | 86 | 25 | 1 | .291 |
| 1929 | 9 | 8 | .529 | 3.89 | 22 | 19 | 8 | 132 | 149 | 23 | 33 | 0 | 1 | 0 | 0 | 41 | 2 | 0 | .000 |
| 1930 PHI N | 0 | 3 | .000 | 9.14 | 9 | 3 | 0 | 21.2 | 40 | 6 | 6 | 0 | 0 | 2 | 0 | 4 | 0 | 0 | .000 |
| 20 yrs. | 373 (3rd) | 208 | .642 | 2.56 | 696 | 598 | 439 | 5189.1 (6th) | 4868 | 953 | 2199 | 90 (2nd) | 23 | 17 | 31 | 1810 | 378 | 11 | .209 |
| 9 yrs. | 128 | 83 | .607 | 2.84 | 242 | 223 | 159 (10th) | 1884.1 | 1919 | 268 | 614 | 24 (7th) | 2 | 4 | 10 | 648 | 149 | 6 | .230 |

**WORLD SERIES**

| | W | L | PCT | ERA | G | GS | CG | IP | H | BB | SO | ShO | W | L | SV | AB | H | HR | BA |
|---|---|---|---|---|---|---|---|---|---|---|---|---|---|---|---|---|---|---|---|
| 1915 PHI N | 1 | 1 | .500 | 1.53 | 2 | 2 | 2 | 17.2 | 14 | 4 | 10 | 0 | 0 | 0 | 0 | 5 | 1 | 0 | .200 |
| 1926 STL N | 2 | 0 | 1.000 | 0.89 | 3 | 2 | 2 | 20.1 | 12 | 4 | 17 | 0 | 0 | 0 | 1 | 7 | 0 | 0 | .000 |
| 1928 | 0 | 1 | .000 | 19.80 | 2 | 1 | 0 | 5 | 10 | 4 | 2 | 0 | 0 | 0 | 0 | 1 | 0 | 0 | .000 |
| 3 yrs. | 3 | 2 | .600 | 3.35 | 7 | 5 | 4 | 43 | 36 | 12 | 29 | 0 | 0 | 0 | 1 | 13 | 1 | 0 | .077 |

## Porfirio Altamirano

**ALTAMIRANO, PORFIRIO**     BR TR 6'   175 lbs.
Born Porfirio Altamirano Ramirez.
B. May 17, 1952, Esteli, Nicaragua

| | W | L | PCT | ERA | G | GS | CG | IP | H | BB | SO | ShO | W | L | SV | AB | H | HR | BA |
|---|---|---|---|---|---|---|---|---|---|---|---|---|---|---|---|---|---|---|---|
| 1982 PHI N | 5 | 1 | .833 | 4.15 | 29 | 0 | 0 | 39 | 41 | 14 | 26 | 0 | 5 | 1 | 2 | 4 | 1 | 0 | .250 |
| 1983 | 2 | 3 | .400 | 3.70 | 31 | 0 | 0 | 41.1 | 38 | 15 | 24 | 0 | 2 | 3 | 0 | 2 | 0 | 0 | .000 |

| | W | L | PCT | ERA | G | GS | CG | IP | H | BB | SO | ShO | Relief Pitching W | L | SV | BATTING AB | H | HR | BA |
|---|---|---|---|---|---|---|---|---|---|---|---|---|---|---|---|---|---|---|---|

## Porfirio Altamirano continued

| | W | L | PCT | ERA | G | GS | CG | IP | H | BB | SO | ShO | W | L | SV | AB | H | HR | BA |
|---|---|---|---|---|---|---|---|---|---|---|---|---|---|---|---|---|---|---|---|
| 1984 CHI N | 0 | 0 | — | 4.76 | 5 | 0 | 0 | 11.1 | 8 | 1 | 7 | 0 | 0 | 0 | 0 | 2 | 0 | 0 | .000 |
| 3 yrs. | 7 | 4 | .636 | 4.03 | 65 | 0 | 0 | 91.2 | 87 | 30 | 57 | 0 | 7 | 4 | 2 | 8 | 1 | 0 | .125 |
| 1 yr. | 0 | 0 | — | 4.76 | 5 | 0 | 0 | 11.1 | 8 | 1 | 7 | 0 | 0 | 0 | 0 | 2 | 0 | 0 | .000 |

## Vincente Amor

**AMOR, VINCENTE ALVAREZ**                                       BR TR 6'3" 182 lbs.
B. Aug. 8, 1932, Havana, Cuba

| | W | L | PCT | ERA | G | GS | CG | IP | H | BB | SO | ShO | W | L | SV | AB | H | HR | BA |
|---|---|---|---|---|---|---|---|---|---|---|---|---|---|---|---|---|---|---|---|
| 1955 CHI N | 0 | 1 | .000 | 4.50 | 4 | 0 | 0 | 6 | 11 | 3 | 3 | 0 | 0 | 1 | 0 | 0 | 0 | 0 | — |
| 1957 CIN N | 1 | 2 | .333 | 5.93 | 9 | 4 | 1 | 27.1 | 39 | 10 | 9 | 0 | 0 | 1 | 0 | 6 | 1 | 0 | .167 |
| 2 yrs. | 1 | 3 | .250 | 5.67 | 13 | 4 | 1 | 33.1 | 50 | 13 | 12 | 0 | 0 | 2 | 0 | 6 | 1 | 0 | .167 |
| 1 yr. | 0 | 1 | .000 | 4.50 | 4 | 0 | 0 | 6 | 11 | 3 | 3 | 0 | 0 | 1 | 0 | 0 | 0 | 0 | — |

## Bob Anderson

**ANDERSON, ROBERT CARL**                                        BR TR 6'4½" 210 lbs.
B. Sept. 29, 1935, East Chicago, Ind.

| | W | L | PCT | ERA | G | GS | CG | IP | H | BB | SO | ShO | W | L | SV | AB | H | HR | BA |
|---|---|---|---|---|---|---|---|---|---|---|---|---|---|---|---|---|---|---|---|
| 1957 CHI N | 0 | 1 | .000 | 7.71 | 8 | 0 | 0 | 16.1 | 20 | 8 | 7 | 0 | 0 | 1 | 0 | 4 | 0 | 0 | .000 |
| 1958 | 3 | 3 | .500 | 3.97 | 17 | 8 | 2 | 65.2 | 61 | 29 | 51 | 0 | 0 | 0 | 0 | 17 | 2 | 0 | .118 |
| 1959 | 12 | 13 | .480 | 4.13 | 37 | 36 | 7 | 235.1 | 245 | 77 | 113 | 1 | 0 | 0 | 0 | 80 | 6 | 0 | .075 |
| 1960 | 9 | 11 | .450 | 4.11 | 38 | 30 | 5 | 203.2 | 201 | 68 | 115 | 0 | 0 | 1 | 1 | 71 | 12 | 0 | .169 |
| 1961 | 7 | 10 | .412 | 4.26 | 57 | 12 | 1 | 152 | 162 | 56 | 96 | 0 | 4 | 3 | 8 | 42 | 6 | 2 | .143 |
| 1962 | 2 | 7 | .222 | 5.02 | 57 | 4 | 0 | 107.2 | 111 | 60 | 82 | 0 | 1 | 6 | 4 | 23 | 3 | 0 | .130 |
| 1963 DET A | 3 | 1 | .750 | 3.30 | 32 | 3 | 0 | 60 | 58 | 21 | 38 | 0 | 2 | 0 | 0 | 9 | 4 | 0 | .444 |
| 7 yrs. | 36 | 46 | .439 | 4.26 | 246 | 93 | 15 | 840.2 | 858 | 319 | 502 | 1 | 7 | 11 | 13 | 246 | 33 | 2 | .134 |
| 6 yrs. | 33 | 45 | .423 | 4.33 | 214 | 90 | 15 | 780.2 | 800 | 298 | 464 | 1 | 5 | 11 | 13 | 237 | 29 | 2 | .122 |

## John Andre

**ANDRE, JOHN EDWARD (Long John)**                               BL TR 6'4" 200 lbs.
B. Jan. 3, 1923, Brockton, Mass.   D. Nov. 25, 1976, Centerville, Mass.

| | W | L | PCT | ERA | G | GS | CG | IP | H | BB | SO | ShO | W | L | SV | AB | H | HR | BA |
|---|---|---|---|---|---|---|---|---|---|---|---|---|---|---|---|---|---|---|---|
| 1955 CHI N | 0 | 1 | .000 | 5.80 | 22 | 3 | 0 | 45 | 45 | 28 | 19 | 0 | 0 | 1 | 1 | 9 | 1 | 0 | .111 |

## Fred Andrus

**ANDRUS, FREDERICK HOTHAM**                                     BR TR 6'2" 185 lbs.
B. Aug. 23, 1850, Washington, Mich.   D. Nov. 10, 1937, Detroit, Mich.

| | W | L | PCT | ERA | G | GS | CG | IP | H | BB | SO | ShO | W | L | SV | AB | H | HR | BA |
|---|---|---|---|---|---|---|---|---|---|---|---|---|---|---|---|---|---|---|---|
| 1884 CHI N | 1 | 0 | 1.000 | 2.00 | 1 | 1 | 1 | 9 | 11 | 2 | 2 | 0 | 0 | 0 | 0 | * | | |

## Cap Anson

**ANSON, ADRIAN CONSTANTINE (Pop)**                              BR TR 6'2" 202 lbs.
B. Apr. 17, 1852, Marshalltown, Iowa   D. Apr. 14, 1922, Chicago, Ill.
Manager 1879-98.
Hall of Fame 1939.

| | W | L | PCT | ERA | G | GS | CG | IP | H | BB | SO | ShO | W | L | SV | AB | H | HR | BA |
|---|---|---|---|---|---|---|---|---|---|---|---|---|---|---|---|---|---|---|---|
| 1883 CHI N | 0 | 0 | — | 0.00 | 2 | 0 | 0 | 3 | 1 | 1 | 0 | 0 | 0 | 0 | 0 | 413 | 127 | 0 | .308 |
| 1884 | 0 | 1 | .000 | 18.00 | 1 | 0 | 0 | 1 | 3 | 1 | 0 | 0 | 0 | 0 | 0 | 475 | 159 | 21 | .335 |
| 2 yrs. | 0 | 1 | .000 | 4.50 | 3 | 0 | 0 | 4 | 4 | 2 | 0 | 0 | 0 | 1 | 1 | * | | | |
| 2 yrs. | 0 | 1 | .000 | 4.50 | 3 | 0 | 0 | 4 | 4 | 2 | 1 | 0 | 0 | 1 | 1 | 9108 | 3041 | 96 | .334 |

## Fred Baczewski

**BACZEWSKI, FREDERIC JOHN (Lefty)**                             BL TL 6'2½" 185 lbs.
B. May 15, 1926, St. Paul, Minn.   D. Nov. 14, 1976, Culver City, Calif.

| | W | L | PCT | ERA | G | GS | CG | IP | H | BB | SO | ShO | W | L | SV | AB | H | HR | BA |
|---|---|---|---|---|---|---|---|---|---|---|---|---|---|---|---|---|---|---|---|
| 1953 2 teams | | | CHI N | (9G 0-0) | | | CIN N | (24G 11-4) | | | | | | | | | | | |
| " total | 11 | 4 | .733 | 3.64 | 33 | 18 | 10 | 148.1 | 145 | 58 | 61 | 1 | 1 | 0 | 1 | 47 | 9 | 1 | .191 |
| 1954 CIN N | 6 | 6 | .500 | 5.26 | 29 | 22 | 4 | 130 | 159 | 53 | 43 | 1 | 0 | 0 | 0 | 42 | 3 | 0 | .071 |
| 1955 | 0 | 0 | — | 18.00 | 1 | 0 | 0 | 1 | 2 | 0 | 0 | 0 | 0 | 0 | 0 | 0 | 0 | 0 | — |
| 3 yrs. | 17 | 10 | .630 | 4.45 | 63 | 40 | 14 | 279.1 | 306 | 111 | 104 | 2 | 1 | 0 | 1 | 89 | 12 | 1 | .135 |
| 1 yr. | 0 | 0 | — | 6.30 | 9 | 0 | 0 | 10 | 20 | 6 | 3 | 0 | 0 | 0 | 0 | 2 | 1 | 0 | .500 |

## Ed Baecht

**BAECHT, EDWARD JOSEPH**                                        BR TR 6'3" 195 lbs.
B. May 15, 1907, Baden, Okla.   D. Aug. 15, 1957, Quarry Township, Ill.

| | W | L | PCT | ERA | G | GS | CG | IP | H | BB | SO | ShO | W | L | SV | AB | H | HR | BA |
|---|---|---|---|---|---|---|---|---|---|---|---|---|---|---|---|---|---|---|---|
| 1926 PHI N | 2 | 0 | 1.000 | 6.11 | 28 | 1 | 1 | 56 | 73 | 28 | 14 | 0 | 1 | 0 | 0 | 14 | 2 | 0 | .143 |
| 1927 | 0 | 1 | .000 | 12.00 | 1 | 1 | 0 | 6 | 12 | 2 | 0 | 0 | 0 | 0 | 0 | 2 | 0 | 0 | .000 |
| 1928 | 1 | 1 | .500 | 6.00 | 9 | 1 | 0 | 24 | 37 | 9 | 10 | 0 | 1 | 0 | 0 | 7 | 1 | 0 | .143 |
| 1931 CHI N | 2 | 4 | .333 | 3.76 | 22 | 6 | 2 | 67 | 64 | 32 | 34 | 0 | 1 | 1 | 0 | 18 | 5 | 0 | .278 |
| 1932 | 0 | 0 | — | 0.00 | 1 | 0 | 0 | 1 | 1 | 1 | 0 | 0 | 0 | 0 | 0 | 0 | 0 | 0 | — |
| 1937 STL A | 0 | 0 | — | 12.79 | 3 | 0 | 0 | 6.1 | 13 | 6 | 3 | 0 | 0 | 0 | 0 | 1 | 0 | 0 | .000 |
| 6 yrs. | 5 | 6 | .455 | 5.56 | 64 | 9 | 3 | 160.1 | 200 | 78 | 61 | 0 | 3 | 1 | 0 | 42 | 8 | 0 | .190 |
| 2 yrs. | 2 | 4 | .333 | 3.71 | 23 | 6 | 2 | 68 | 65 | 33 | 34 | 0 | 1 | 1 | 0 | 18 | 5 | 0 | .278 |

## Sweetbreads Bailey

**BAILEY, ABRAHAM LINCOLN**                                      BR TR 6' 205 lbs.
B. Feb. 12, 1895, Joliet, Ill.   D. Sept. 27, 1939, Joliet, Ill.

| | W | L | PCT | ERA | G | GS | CG | IP | H | BB | SO | ShO | W | L | SV | AB | H | HR | BA |
|---|---|---|---|---|---|---|---|---|---|---|---|---|---|---|---|---|---|---|---|
| 1919 CHI N | 3 | 5 | .375 | 3.15 | 21 | 5 | 0 | 71.1 | 75 | 20 | 19 | 0 | 3 | 2 | 0 | 18 | 7 | 0 | .389 |
| 1920 | 1 | 2 | .333 | 7.12 | 21 | 1 | 0 | 36.2 | 38 | 11 | 8 | 0 | 0 | 1 | 0 | 7 | 1 | 0 | .143 |
| 1921 2 teams | | | CHI N | (3G 0-0) | | | BKN N | (7G 0-0) | | | | | | | | | | | |
| " total | 0 | 0 | — | 4.91 | 10 | 0 | 0 | 29.1 | 41 | 9 | 8 | 0 | 0 | 0 | 0 | 5 | 0 | 0 | .000 |
| 3 yrs. | 4 | 7 | .364 | 4.59 | 52 | 6 | 0 | 137.1 | 154 | 40 | 35 | 0 | 3 | 3 | 0 | 30 | 8 | 0 | .267 |
| 3 yrs. | 4 | 7 | .364 | 4.46 | 45 | 6 | 0 | 113 | 119 | 33 | 29 | 0 | 3 | 3 | 0 | 25 | 8 | 0 | .320 |

## Tom Baker

**BAKER, THOMAS HENRY**                                          BL TL 6' 195 lbs.
B. May 6, 1934, Port Townsend, Wash.   D. Mar. 9, 1980, Port Townsend, Wash.

| | W | L | PCT | ERA | G | GS | CG | IP | H | BB | SO | ShO | W | L | SV | AB | H | HR | BA |
|---|---|---|---|---|---|---|---|---|---|---|---|---|---|---|---|---|---|---|---|
| 1963 CHI N | 0 | 1 | .000 | 3.00 | 10 | 1 | 0 | 18 | 20 | 7 | 14 | 0 | 0 | 0 | 0 | 3 | 0 | 0 | .000 |

| | W | L | PCT | ERA | G | GS | CG | IP | H | BB | SO | ShO | Relief Pitching W | L | SV | BATTING AB | H | HR | BA |
|---|---|---|---|---|---|---|---|---|---|---|---|---|---|---|---|---|---|---|---|

## Mark Baldwin

**BALDWIN, MARCUS ELMORE (Fido)**
B. Oct. 29, 1865, Pittsburgh, Pa.    D. Nov. 10, 1929, Pittsburgh, Pa.
BR TR 6'    190 lbs.

| | W | L | PCT | ERA | G | GS | CG | IP | H | BB | SO | ShO | W | L | SV | AB | H | HR | BA |
|---|---|---|---|---|---|---|---|---|---|---|---|---|---|---|---|---|---|---|---|
| 1887 CHI N | 18 | 17 | .514 | 3.40 | 40 | 39 | 35 | 334 | 329 | 122 | 164 | 1 | 0 | 0 | 1 | 139 | 26 | 4 | .187 |
| 1888 | 13 | 15 | .464 | 2.76 | 30 | 30 | 27 | 251 | 241 | 99 | 157 | 2 | 0 | 0 | 0 | 106 | 16 | 1 | .151 |
| 1889 COL AA | 27 | 34 | .443 | 3.61 | 63 | 59 | 54 | 513.2 | 458 | 274 | 368 | 6 | 1 | 2 | 1 | 208 | 39 | 2 | .188 |
| 1890 CHI P | 32 | 24 | .571 | 3.31 | 59 | 57 | 54 | 501 | 498 | 249 | 211 | 1 | 2 | 0 | 0 | 215 | 45 | 1 | .209 |
| 1891 PIT N | 22 | 28 | .440 | 2.76 | 53 | 50 | 48 | 437.2 | 385 | 227 | 197 | 2 | 1 | 0 | 0 | 177 | 27 | 1 | .153 |
| 1892 | 26 | 27 | .491 | 3.47 | 56 | 53 | 45 | 440.1 | 447 | 194 | 157 | 0 | 2 | 0 | 0 | 178 | 18 | 1 | .101 |
| 1893 2 teams | | | | | | | PIT N | (1G 0–0) | | NY | N | (45G 16–20) | | | | | | | |
| " total | 16 | 20 | .444 | 4.15 | 46 | 40 | 33 | 333.2 | 341 | 142 | 100 | 2 | 2 | 1 | 2 | 135 | 17 | 0 | .126 |
| 7 yrs. | 154 | 165 | .483 | 3.36 | 347 | 328 | 296 | 2811.1 | 2699 | 1307 | 1354 | 14 | 8 | 3 | 4 | 1158 | 188 | 10 | .162 |
| 2 yrs. | 31 | 32 | .492 | 3.12 | 70 | 69 | 62 | 585 | 570 | 221 | 321 | 3 | 0 | 0 | 1 | 245 | 42 | 5 | .171 |

## Jay Baller

**BALLER, JAY SCOTT**
B. Oct. 6, 1960, Stayton, Ohio
BR TR 6'6"    215 lbs.

| | W | L | PCT | ERA | G | GS | CG | IP | H | BB | SO | ShO | W | L | SV | AB | H | HR | BA |
|---|---|---|---|---|---|---|---|---|---|---|---|---|---|---|---|---|---|---|---|
| 1982 PHI N | 0 | 0 | — | 3.38 | 4 | 1 | 0 | 8 | 7 | 2 | 7 | 0 | 0 | 0 | 0 | 0 | 0 | 0 | — |
| 1985 CHI N | 2 | 3 | .400 | 3.46 | 20 | 4 | 0 | 52 | 52 | 17 | 31 | 0 | 2 | 0 | 1 | 8 | 0 | 0 | .000 |
| 2 yrs. | 2 | 3 | .400 | 3.45 | 24 | 5 | 0 | 60 | 59 | 19 | 38 | 0 | 2 | 0 | 1 | 8 | 0 | 0 | .000 |
| 1 yr. | 2 | 3 | .400 | 3.46 | 20 | 4 | 0 | 52 | 52 | 17 | 31 | 0 | 2 | 0 | 1 | 8 | 0 | 0 | .000 |

## Tony Balsamo

**BALSAMO, ANTHONY FRED**
B. Nov. 21, 1937, Brooklyn, N. Y.
BR TR 6'2"    185 lbs.

| | W | L | PCT | ERA | G | GS | CG | IP | H | BB | SO | ShO | W | L | SV | AB | H | HR | BA |
|---|---|---|---|---|---|---|---|---|---|---|---|---|---|---|---|---|---|---|---|
| 1962 CHI N | 0 | 1 | .000 | 6.44 | 18 | 0 | 0 | 29.1 | 34 | 20 | 27 | 0 | 0 | 1 | 0 | 5 | 1 | 0 | .200 |

## Steve Barber

**BARBER, STEPHEN DAVID**
B. Feb. 22, 1939, Takoma Park, Md.
BL TL 6'    195 lbs.

| | W | L | PCT | ERA | G | GS | CG | IP | H | BB | SO | ShO | W | L | SV | AB | H | HR | BA |
|---|---|---|---|---|---|---|---|---|---|---|---|---|---|---|---|---|---|---|---|
| 1960 BAL A | 10 | 7 | .588 | 3.22 | 36 | 27 | 6 | 181.2 | 148 | 113 | 112 | 1 | 0 | 1 | 2 | 54 | 3 | 0 | .056 |
| 1961 | 18 | 12 | .600 | 3.33 | 37 | 34 | 14 | 248.1 | 194 | 130 | 150 | 8 | 0 | 0 | 1 | 80 | 13 | 2 | .163 |
| 1962 | 9 | 6 | .600 | 3.46 | 28 | 19 | 5 | 140.1 | 145 | 61 | 89 | 2 | 0 | 0 | 0 | 42 | 3 | 0 | .071 |
| 1963 | 20 | 13 | .606 | 2.75 | 39 | 36 | 11 | 258.2 | 253 | 92 | 180 | 2 | 0 | 1 | 0 | 87 | 12 | 1 | .138 |
| 1964 | 9 | 13 | .409 | 3.84 | 36 | 26 | 4 | 157 | 144 | 81 | 118 | 0 | 1 | 1 | 1 | 47 | 7 | 1 | .149 |
| 1965 | 15 | 10 | .600 | 2.69 | 37 | 32 | 7 | 220.2 | 177 | 81 | 130 | 2 | 1 | 1 | 0 | 65 | 5 | 1 | .077 |
| 1966 | 10 | 5 | .667 | 2.30 | 25 | 22 | 5 | 133.1 | 104 | 49 | 91 | 3 | 0 | 0 | 0 | 44 | 3 | 0 | .068 |
| 1967 2 teams | | | | | | | BAL | A | (15G 4–9) | | NY | A | (17G 6–9) | | | | | | |
| " total | 10 | 18 | .357 | 4.07 | 32 | 32 | 4 | 172.1 | 150 | 115 | 118 | 2 | 0 | 0 | 0 | 51 | 7 | 0 | .137 |
| 1968 NY A | 6 | 5 | .545 | 3.23 | 20 | 19 | 3 | 128.1 | 127 | 64 | 87 | 1 | 0 | 0 | 0 | 39 | 2 | 0 | .051 |
| 1969 SEA A | 4 | 7 | .364 | 4.80 | 25 | 16 | 0 | 86.1 | 99 | 48 | 69 | 0 | 0 | 0 | 0 | 25 | 5 | 0 | .200 |
| 1970 2 teams | | | | | | | CHI | N | (5G 0–1) | | ATL | N | (5G 0–1) | | | | | | |
| " total | 0 | 2 | .000 | 6.20 | 10 | 2 | 0 | 20.1 | 27 | 11 | 14 | 0 | 0 | 1 | 0 | 4 | 1 | 0 | .250 |
| 1971 ATL N | 3 | 1 | .750 | 4.80 | 39 | 3 | 0 | 75 | 92 | 25 | 40 | 0 | 3 | 0 | 2 | 13 | 2 | 0 | .154 |
| 1972 2 teams | | | | | | | ATL | N | (5G 0–0) | | CAL | A | (34G 4–4) | | | | | | |
| " total | 4 | 4 | .500 | 2.80 | 39 | 3 | 0 | 74 | 55 | 36 | 40 | 0 | 3 | 4 | 3 | 12 | 2 | 0 | .167 |
| 1973 CAL A | 3 | 2 | .600 | 3.53 | 50 | 1 | 0 | 89.1 | 90 | 32 | 58 | 0 | 3 | 2 | 4 | 0 | 0 | 0 | — |
| 1974 SF N | 0 | 1 | .000 | 5.14 | 13 | 0 | 0 | 14 | 13 | 12 | 13 | 0 | 0 | 1 | 1 | 0 | 0 | 0 | — |
| 15 yrs. | 121 | 106 | .533 | 3.36 | 466 | 272 | 59 | 1999.2 | 1818 | 950 | 1309 | 21 | 11 | 12 | 13 | 563 | 65 | 5 | .115 |
| 1 yr. | 0 | 1 | .000 | 9.53 | 5 | 0 | 0 | 5.2 | 10 | 6 | 3 | 0 | 0 | 1 | 0 | 0 | 0 | 0 | — |

## Ross Barnes

**BARNES, ROSCOE CHARLES**
B. May 8, 1850, New Jersey    D. Feb. 5, 1915, Chicago, Ill.
BR TR 5'8½"    145 lbs.

| | W | L | PCT | ERA | G | GS | CG | IP | H | BB | SO | ShO | W | L | SV | AB | H | HR | BA |
|---|---|---|---|---|---|---|---|---|---|---|---|---|---|---|---|---|---|---|---|
| 1876 CHI N | 0 | 0 | — | 20.25 | 1 | 0 | 0 | 1.1 | 7 | 0 | 0 | 0 | 0 | 0 | 0 | * | | | |

## Dick Barrett

**BARRETT, TRACEY SOUTER (Kewpie)**
Played as Dick Oliver 1933.
B. Sept. 28, 1906, Montoursville, Pa.    D. Oct. 30, 1966, Seattle, Wash.
BR TR 5'9"    175 lbs.

| | W | L | PCT | ERA | G | GS | CG | IP | H | BB | SO | ShO | W | L | SV | AB | H | HR | BA |
|---|---|---|---|---|---|---|---|---|---|---|---|---|---|---|---|---|---|---|---|
| 1933 PHI A | 4 | 4 | .500 | 5.76 | 15 | 7 | 3 | 70.1 | 74 | 49 | 26 | 0 | 0 | 0 | 0 | 21 | 6 | 0 | .286 |
| 1934 BOS N | 1 | 3 | .250 | 6.68 | 15 | 3 | 0 | 32.1 | 50 | 12 | 14 | 0 | 1 | 1 | 0 | 7 | 1 | 0 | .143 |
| 1943 2 teams | | | | | | | CHI | N | (15G 0–4) | | PHI | N | (23G 10–9) | | | | | | |
| " total | 10 | 13 | .435 | 2.90 | 38 | 24 | 10 | 214.1 | 189 | 79 | 85 | 2 | 0 | 0 | 1 | 58 | 8 | 0 | .138 |
| 1944 PHI N | 12 | 18 | .400 | 3.86 | 37 | 27 | 11 | 221.1 | 223 | 88 | 74 | 1 | 3 | 2 | 0 | 74 | 16 | 0 | .216 |
| 1945 | 7 | 20 | .259 | 5.43 | 36 | 30 | 8 | 190.2 | 216 | 92 | 72 | 0 | 1 | 2 | 1 | 62 | 9 | 0 | .145 |
| 5 yrs. | 34 | 58 | .370 | 4.30 | 141 | 91 | 32 | 729 | 752 | 320 | 271 | 3 | 5 | 5 | 2 | 222 | 40 | 0 | .180 |
| 1 yr. | 0 | 4 | .000 | 4.80 | 15 | 4 | 0 | 45 | 52 | 28 | 20 | 0 | 0 | 0 | 0 | 9 | 1 | 0 | .111 |

## Charlie Bastian

**BASTIAN, CHARLES J.**
B. July 4, 1860, Philadelphia, Pa.    D. Jan. 18, 1932, Pennsauken, N. J.
BR TR 5'6½"    145 lbs.

| | W | L | PCT | ERA | G | GS | CG | IP | H | BB | SO | ShO | W | L | SV | AB | H | HR | BA |
|---|---|---|---|---|---|---|---|---|---|---|---|---|---|---|---|---|---|---|---|
| 1884 2 teams | | | | | | | WIL | U | (1G 0–0) | | KC | U | (0G 0–0) | | | | | | |
| " total | 0 | 0 | — | 3.00 | 1 | 0 | 0 | 6 | 6 | 2 | 0 | 0 | 0 | 0 | 0 | * | | | |

## Russ Bauers

**BAUERS, RUSSELL LEE**
B. May 10, 1914, Townsend, Wis.
BL TR 6'3"    195 lbs.

| | W | L | PCT | ERA | G | GS | CG | IP | H | BB | SO | ShO | W | L | SV | AB | H | HR | BA |
|---|---|---|---|---|---|---|---|---|---|---|---|---|---|---|---|---|---|---|---|
| 1936 PIT N | 0 | 0 | — | 33.75 | 1 | 1 | 0 | 1.1 | 2 | 4 | 0 | 0 | 0 | 0 | 0 | 0 | 0 | 0 | — |
| 1937 | 13 | 6 | .684 | 2.88 | 34 | 19 | 11 | 187.2 | 174 | 80 | 118 | 2 | 3 | 1 | 1 | 69 | 15 | 0 | .217 |
| 1938 | 13 | 14 | .481 | 3.07 | 40 | 34 | 12 | 243 | 207 | 99 | 117 | 3 | 1 | 2 | 3 | 88 | 21 | 0 | .239 |
| 1939 | 2 | 4 | .333 | 3.35 | 15 | 8 | 1 | 53.2 | 46 | 25 | 12 | 0 | 1 | 1 | 1 | 19 | 4 | 0 | .211 |
| 1940 | 0 | 2 | .000 | 7.63 | 15 | 2 | 0 | 30.2 | 42 | 18 | 11 | 0 | 0 | 0 | 0 | 7 | 2 | 0 | .286 |
| 1941 | 1 | 3 | .250 | 5.54 | 8 | 5 | 1 | 37.1 | 40 | 25 | 20 | 0 | 0 | 0 | 0 | 14 | 5 | 0 | .357 |
| 1946 CHI N | 2 | 1 | .667 | 3.53 | 15 | 2 | 2 | 43.1 | 45 | 19 | 22 | 0 | 1 | 0 | 1 | 10 | 3 | 0 | .300 |

| | W | L | PCT | ERA | G | GS | CG | IP | H | BB | SO | ShO | Relief Pitching W | L | SV | BATTING AB | H | HR | BA |
|---|---|---|---|---|---|---|---|---|---|---|---|---|---|---|---|---|---|---|---|

## Russ Bauers continued

| | W | L | PCT | ERA | G | GS | CG | IP | H | BB | SO | ShO | W | L | SV | AB | H | HR | BA |
|---|---|---|---|---|---|---|---|---|---|---|---|---|---|---|---|---|---|---|---|
| 1950 STL A | 0 | 0 | — | 4.50 | 1 | 0 | 0 | 2 | 6 | 1 | 0 | 0 | 0 | 0 | 0 | 0 | 0 | 0 | — |
| 8 yrs. | 31 | 30 | .508 | 3.53 | 129 | 71 | 27 | 599 | 562 | 271 | 300 | 5 | 6 | 4 | 6 | 207 | 50 | 0 | .242 |
| 1 yr. | 2 | 1 | .667 | 3.53 | 15 | 2 | 2 | 43.1 | 45 | 19 | 22 | 0 | 1 | 0 | 1 | 10 | 3 | 0 | .300 |

## Frank Baumann

**BAUMANN, FRANK MATT (The Beau)**
B. July 1, 1933, St. Louis, Mo.
BL TL 6' 205 lbs.

| | W | L | PCT | ERA | G | GS | CG | IP | H | BB | SO | ShO | W | L | SV | AB | H | HR | BA |
|---|---|---|---|---|---|---|---|---|---|---|---|---|---|---|---|---|---|---|---|
| 1955 BOS A | 2 | 1 | .667 | 5.82 | 7 | 5 | 0 | 34 | 38 | 17 | 27 | 0 | 1 | 0 | 0 | 13 | 3 | 0 | .231 |
| 1956 | 2 | 1 | .667 | 3.28 | 7 | 1 | 0 | 24.2 | 22 | 14 | 18 | 0 | 1 | 1 | 0 | 9 | 3 | 0 | .333 |
| 1957 | 1 | 0 | 1.000 | 3.75 | 4 | 1 | 0 | 12 | 13 | 3 | 7 | 0 | 0 | 0 | 0 | 2 | 1 | 0 | .500 |
| 1958 | 2 | 2 | .500 | 4.47 | 10 | 7 | 2 | 52.1 | 56 | 27 | 31 | 0 | 0 | 0 | 0 | 14 | 3 | 0 | .214 |
| 1959 | 6 | 4 | .600 | 4.05 | 26 | 10 | 2 | 95.2 | 96 | 55 | 48 | 0 | 2 | 0 | 1 | 29 | 6 | 0 | .207 |
| 1960 CHI A | 13 | 6 | .684 | 2.67 | 44 | 20 | 7 | 185.1 | 169 | 53 | 71 | 2 | 6 | 2 | 3 | 52 | 8 | 0 | .154 |
| 1961 | 10 | 13 | .435 | 5.61 | 53 | 23 | 5 | 187.2 | 249 | 59 | 75 | 1 | 4 | 4 | 3 | 61 | 16 | 2 | .262 |
| 1962 | 7 | 6 | .538 | 3.38 | 40 | 10 | 3 | 119.2 | 117 | 36 | 55 | 1 | 4 | 2 | 4 | 30 | 8 | 0 | .267 |
| 1963 | 2 | 1 | .667 | 3.04 | 24 | 1 | 0 | 50.1 | 52 | 17 | 31 | 0 | 2 | 0 | 1 | 11 | 1 | 0 | .091 |
| 1964 | 0 | 3 | .000 | 6.19 | 22 | 0 | 0 | 32 | 40 | 16 | 19 | 0 | 0 | 3 | 1 | 4 | 0 | 0 | .000 |
| 1965 CHI N | 0 | 1 | .000 | 7.36 | 4 | 0 | 0 | 3.2 | 4 | 3 | 2 | 0 | 0 | 1 | 0 | 0 | 0 | 0 | — |
| 11 yrs. | 45 | 38 | .542 | 4.11 | 241 | 78 | 19 | 797.1 | 856 | 300 | 384 | 4 | 20 | 13 | 13 | 225 | 49 | 2 | .218 |
| 1 yr. | 0 | 1 | .000 | 7.36 | 4 | 0 | 0 | 3.2 | 4 | 3 | 2 | 0 | 0 | 1 | 0 | 0 | 0 | 0 | — |

## Dave Beard

**BEARD, CHARLES DAVID**
B. Oct. 2, 1959, Chamblee, Ga.
BL TR 6'5" 190 lbs.

| | W | L | PCT | ERA | G | GS | CG | IP | H | BB | SO | ShO | W | L | SV | AB | H | HR | BA |
|---|---|---|---|---|---|---|---|---|---|---|---|---|---|---|---|---|---|---|---|
| 1980 OAK A | 0 | 1 | .000 | 3.38 | 13 | 0 | 0 | 16 | 12 | 7 | 12 | 0 | 0 | 1 | 1 | 0 | 0 | 0 | — |
| 1981 | 1 | 1 | .500 | 2.77 | 8 | 0 | 0 | 13 | 9 | 4 | 15 | 0 | 1 | 1 | 3 | 0 | 0 | 0 | — |
| 1982 | 10 | 9 | .526 | 3.44 | 54 | 2 | 0 | 91.2 | 85 | 35 | 73 | 0 | 10 | 7 | 11 | 0 | 0 | 0 | — |
| 1983 | 5 | 5 | .500 | 5.61 | 43 | 0 | 0 | 61 | 55 | 36 | 40 | 0 | 5 | 5 | 10 | 0 | 0 | 0 | — |
| 1984 SEA A | 3 | 2 | .600 | 5.80 | 43 | 0 | 0 | 76 | 88 | 33 | 40 | 0 | 3 | 2 | 5 | 0 | 0 | 0 | — |
| 1985 CHI N | 0 | 0 | — | 6.39 | 9 | 0 | 0 | 12.2 | 16 | 7 | 4 | 0 | 0 | 0 | 0 | 0 | 0 | 0 | — |
| 6 yrs. | 19 | 18 | .514 | 4.69 | 170 | 2 | 0 | 270.1 | 265 | 122 | 184 | 0 | 19 | 16 | 30 | 0 | 0 | 0 | — |
| 1 yr. | 0 | 0 | — | 6.39 | 9 | 0 | 0 | 12.2 | 16 | 7 | 4 | 0 | 0 | 0 | 0 | 0 | 0 | 0 | — |

DIVISIONAL PLAYOFF SERIES

| | W | L | PCT | ERA | G | GS | CG | IP | H | BB | SO | ShO | W | L | SV | AB | H | HR | BA |
|---|---|---|---|---|---|---|---|---|---|---|---|---|---|---|---|---|---|---|---|
| 1981 OAK A | 0 | 0 | — | 0.00 | 1 | 0 | 0 | 1.1 | 0 | 0 | 2 | 0 | 0 | 0 | 0 | 0 | 0 | 0 | — |

LEAGUE CHAMPIONSHIP SERIES

| | W | L | PCT | ERA | G | GS | CG | IP | H | BB | SO | ShO | W | L | SV | AB | H | HR | BA |
|---|---|---|---|---|---|---|---|---|---|---|---|---|---|---|---|---|---|---|---|
| 1981 OAK A | 0 | 0 | — | 40.50 | 1 | 0 | 0 | .2 | 5 | 0 | 0 | 0 | 0 | 0 | 0 | 0 | 0 | 0 | — |

## Fred Beebe

**BEEBE, FREDERICK LEONARD**
B. Dec. 31, 1880, Lincoln, Neb.    D. Oct. 30, 1957, LaGrange, Ill.
BR TR 6'1" 190 lbs.

| | W | L | PCT | ERA | G | GS | CG | IP | H | BB | SO | ShO | W | L | SV | AB | H | HR | BA |
|---|---|---|---|---|---|---|---|---|---|---|---|---|---|---|---|---|---|---|---|
| 1906 2 teams | | | | | CHI | N | (14G 7–1) | | STL | N | (20G 9–9) | | | | | | | | |
| " total | 16 | 10 | .615 | 2.93 | 34 | 25 | 20 | 230.2 | 171 | 100 | 171 | 1 | 3 | 0 | 1 | 87 | 13 | 0 | .149 |
| 1907 STL N | 7 | 19 | .269 | 2.72 | 31 | 29 | 24 | 238.1 | 192 | 109 | 141 | 4 | 1 | 0 | 0 | 86 | 11 | 0 | .128 |
| 1908 | 5 | 13 | .278 | 2.63 | 29 | 19 | 12 | 174.1 | 134 | 66 | 72 | 0 | 0 | 1 | 0 | 56 | 7 | 0 | .125 |
| 1909 | 15 | 21 | .417 | 2.82 | 44 | 34 | 18 | 287.2 | 256 | 104 | 105 | 1 | 2 | 3 | 1 | 108 | 18 | 0 | .167 |
| 1910 CIN N | 12 | 15 | .444 | 3.07 | 35 | 26 | 11 | 214.1 | 193 | 94 | 93 | 2 | 3 | 0 | 0 | 73 | 12 | 0 | .164 |
| 1911 PHI N | 3 | 3 | .500 | 4.47 | 9 | 8 | 3 | 48.1 | 52 | 24 | 20 | 0 | 0 | 0 | 0 | 19 | 5 | 0 | .263 |
| 1916 CLE A | 5 | 3 | .625 | 2.41 | 20 | 12 | 5 | 100.2 | 92 | 37 | 32 | 1 | 0 | 0 | 2 | 28 | 6 | 0 | .214 |
| 7 yrs. | 63 | 84 | .429 | 2.86 | 202 | 153 | 93 | 1294.1 | 1090 | 534 | 634 | 9 | 9 | 4 | 4 | 457 | 72 | 0 | .158 |
| 1 yr. | 7 | 1 | .875 | 2.70 | 14 | 6 | 4 | 70 | 56 | 32 | 55 | 0 | 3 | 0 | 1 | 29 | 3 | 0 | .103 |

## Joe Berry

**BERRY, JONAS ARTHUR (Jittery Joe)**
B. Dec. 16, 1904, Huntsville, Ark.    D. Sept. 27, 1958, Anaheim, Calif.
BR TR 5'10½" 145 lbs.

| | W | L | PCT | ERA | G | GS | CG | IP | H | BB | SO | ShO | W | L | SV | AB | H | HR | BA |
|---|---|---|---|---|---|---|---|---|---|---|---|---|---|---|---|---|---|---|---|
| 1942 CHI N | 0 | 0 | — | 18.00 | 2 | 0 | 0 | 2 | 7 | 2 | 1 | 0 | 0 | 0 | 0 | 0 | 0 | 0 | — |
| 1944 PHI A | 10 | 8 | .556 | 1.94 | 53 | 0 | 0 | 111.1 | 78 | 23 | 44 | 0 | 10 | 8 | 12 | 25 | 3 | 0 | .120 |
| 1945 | 8 | 7 | .533 | 2.35 | 52 | 0 | 0 | 130.1 | 114 | 38 | 51 | 0 | 8 | 7 | 5 | 35 | 5 | 0 | .143 |
| 1946 2 teams | | | | | PHI | A | (5G 0–1) | | CLE | A | (21G 3–6) | | | | | | | | |
| " total | 3 | 7 | .300 | 3.22 | 26 | 0 | 0 | 50.1 | 47 | 24 | 21 | 0 | 3 | 7 | 1 | 10 | 3 | 0 | .300 |
| 4 yrs. | 21 | 22 | .488 | 2.45 | 133 | 0 | 0 | 294 | 246 | 87 | 117 | 0 | 21 | 22 | 18 | 70 | 11 | 0 | .157 |
| 1 yr. | 0 | 0 | — | 18.00 | 2 | 0 | 0 | 2 | 7 | 2 | 1 | 0 | 0 | 0 | 0 | 0 | 0 | 0 | — |

## Larry Biittner

**BIITTNER, LARRY DAVID**
B. July 27, 1946, Pocahontas, Iowa
BL TL 6'2" 205 lbs.

| | W | L | PCT | ERA | G | GS | CG | IP | H | BB | SO | ShO | W | L | SV | AB | H | HR | BA |
|---|---|---|---|---|---|---|---|---|---|---|---|---|---|---|---|---|---|---|---|
| 1977 CHI N | 0 | 0 | — | 54.00 | 1 | 0 | 0 | 1 | 5 | 1 | 3 | 0 | 0 | 0 | 0 | * | | | |

## Doug Bird

**BIRD, JAMES DOUGLAS**
B. Mar. 5, 1950, Corona, Calif.
BR TR 6'4" 180 lbs.

| | W | L | PCT | ERA | G | GS | CG | IP | H | BB | SO | ShO | W | L | SV | AB | H | HR | BA |
|---|---|---|---|---|---|---|---|---|---|---|---|---|---|---|---|---|---|---|---|
| 1973 KC A | 4 | 4 | .500 | 3.00 | 54 | 0 | 0 | 102 | 81 | 30 | 84 | 0 | 4 | 4 | 20 | 0 | 0 | 0 | — |
| 1974 | 7 | 6 | .538 | 2.74 | 55 | 1 | 1 | 92 | 100 | 27 | 62 | 0 | 7 | 5 | 10 | 0 | 0 | 0 | — |
| 1975 | 9 | 6 | .600 | 3.25 | 51 | 4 | 0 | 105.1 | 100 | 40 | 81 | 0 | 9 | 5 | 11 | 0 | 0 | 0 | — |
| 1976 | 12 | 10 | .545 | 3.36 | 39 | 27 | 2 | 198 | 191 | 31 | 107 | 1 | 3 | 0 | 2 | 0 | 0 | 0 | — |
| 1977 | 11 | 4 | .733 | 3.89 | 53 | 5 | 0 | 118 | 120 | 29 | 83 | 0 | 10 | 3 | 14 | 0 | 0 | 0 | — |
| 1978 | 6 | 6 | .500 | 5.29 | 40 | 6 | 0 | 98.2 | 110 | 31 | 48 | 0 | 5 | 3 | 1 | 0 | 0 | 0 | — |
| 1979 PHI N | 2 | 0 | 1.000 | 5.16 | 32 | 1 | 1 | 61 | 73 | 16 | 33 | 0 | 1 | 0 | 0 | 6 | 1 | 0 | .167 |
| 1980 NY A | 3 | 0 | 1.000 | 2.65 | 22 | 1 | 0 | 51 | 47 | 14 | 17 | 0 | 2 | 0 | 1 | 0 | 0 | 0 | — |
| 1981 2 teams | | | | | NY | A | (17G 5–1) | | CHI | N | (12G 4–5) | | | | | | | | |
| " total | 9 | 6 | .600 | 3.23 | 29 | 16 | 2 | 128 | 130 | 32 | 62 | 1 | 2 | 0 | 0 | 20 | 2 | 0 | .100 |
| 1982 CHI N | 9 | 14 | .391 | 5.14 | 35 | 33 | 2 | 191 | 230 | 30 | 71 | 1 | 0 | 0 | 0 | 56 | 8 | 0 | .143 |
| 1983 BOS A | 1 | 4 | .200 | 6.65 | 22 | 6 | 0 | 67.2 | 91 | 16 | 33 | 0 | 0 | 1 | 1 | 0 | 0 | 0 | — |
| 11 yrs. | 73 | 60 | .549 | 3.99 | 432 | 100 | 8 | 1212.2 | 1273 | 296 | 681 | 3 | 43 | 21 | 60 | 82 | 11 | 0 | .134 |
| 2 yrs. | 13 | 19 | .406 | 4.70 | 47 | 45 | 4 | 266 | 302 | 46 | 105 | 2 | 0 | 0 | 0 | 76 | 10 | 0 | .132 |

LEAGUE CHAMPIONSHIP SERIES

| | W | L | PCT | ERA | G | GS | CG | IP | H | BB | SO | ShO | W | L | SV | AB | H | HR | BA |
|---|---|---|---|---|---|---|---|---|---|---|---|---|---|---|---|---|---|---|---|
| 1976 KC A | 1 | 0 | 1.000 | 1.93 | 1 | 0 | 0 | 4.2 | 4 | 0 | 1 | 0 | 1 | 0 | 0 | 0 | 0 | 0 | — |

| | W | L | PCT | ERA | G | GS | CG | IP | H | BB | SO | ShO | Relief Pitching W | L | SV | BATTING AB | H | HR | BA |
|---|---|---|---|---|---|---|---|---|---|---|---|---|---|---|---|---|---|---|---|

## Doug Bird continued

| | W | L | PCT | ERA | G | GS | CG | IP | H | BB | SO | ShO | W | L | SV | AB | H | HR | BA |
|---|---|---|---|---|---|---|---|---|---|---|---|---|---|---|---|---|---|---|---|
| 1977 | 0 | 0 | – | 0.00 | 3 | 0 | 0 | 2 | 4 | 0 | 1 | 0 | 0 | 0 | 0 | 0 | 0 | 0 | – |
| 1978 | 0 | 1 | .000 | 9.00 | 2 | 0 | 0 | 1 | 2 | 0 | 1 | 0 | 0 | 1 | 0 | 0 | 0 | 0 | – |
| 3 yrs. | 1 | 1 | .500 | 2.35 | 6 | 0 | 0 | 7.2 | 10 | 0 | 3 | 0 | 1 | 1 | 0 | 0 | 0 | 0 | – |

## Bill Bishop

**BISHOP, WILLIAM ROBINSON**
B. Dec. 27, 1869, Adamsburg, Pa.     D. Dec. 15, 1932, Pittsburgh, Pa.

| | W | L | PCT | ERA | G | GS | CG | IP | H | BB | SO | ShO | W | L | SV | AB | H | HR | BA |
|---|---|---|---|---|---|---|---|---|---|---|---|---|---|---|---|---|---|---|---|
| 1886 PIT AA | 0 | 1 | .000 | *3.18* | 2 | 2 | 2 | 17 | 17 | 11 | 4 | 0 | 0 | 0 | 0 | 7 | 1 | 0 | .143 |
| 1887 PIT N | 0 | 3 | .000 | 13.33 | 3 | 3 | 3 | 27 | 45 | 22 | 4 | 0 | 0 | 0 | 0 | 9 | 0 | 0 | .000 |
| 1889 CHI N | 0 | 0 | – | 18.00 | 2 | 0 | 0 | 3 | 6 | 6 | 1 | 0 | 0 | 0 | 2 | 1 | 0 | 0 | .000 |
| 3 yrs. | 0 | 4 | .000 | 9.96 | 7 | 5 | 5 | 47 | 68 | 39 | 9 | 0 | 0 | 0 | 2 | 17 | 1 | 0 | .059 |
| 1 yr. | 0 | 0 | – | 18.00 | 2 | 0 | 0 | 3 | 6 | 6 | 1 | 0 | 0 | 0 | 2 | 1 | 0 | 0 | .000 |

## Hi Bithorn

**BITHORN, HIRAM GABRIEL**     BR  TR  6'1"     200 lbs.
B. Mar. 18, 1916, Santurce, Puerto Rico     D. Jan. 1, 1952, El Mante, Mexico

| | W | L | PCT | ERA | G | GS | CG | IP | H | BB | SO | ShO | W | L | SV | AB | H | HR | BA |
|---|---|---|---|---|---|---|---|---|---|---|---|---|---|---|---|---|---|---|---|
| 1942 CHI N | 9 | 14 | .391 | 3.68 | 38 | 16 | 9 | 171.1 | 191 | 81 | 65 | 0 | 3 | 5 | 2 | 57 | 7 | 0 | .123 |
| 1943 | 18 | 12 | .600 | 2.60 | 39 | 30 | 19 | 249.2 | 226 | 65 | 86 | 7 | 1 | 1 | 2 | 92 | 16 | 0 | .174 |
| 1946 | 6 | 5 | .545 | 3.84 | 26 | 7 | 2 | 86.2 | 97 | 25 | 34 | 1 | 4 | 2 | 1 | 28 | 5 | 0 | .179 |
| 1947 CHI A | 1 | 0 | 1.000 | 0.00 | 2 | 0 | 0 | 2 | 2 | 0 | 0 | 0 | 1 | 0 | 0 | 0 | 0 | 0 | – |
| 4 yrs. | 34 | 31 | .523 | 3.16 | 105 | 53 | 30 | 509.2 | 516 | 171 | 185 | 8 | 9 | 8 | 5 | 177 | 28 | 0 | .158 |
| 3 yrs. | 33 | 31 | .516 | 3.17 | 103 | 53 | 30 | 507.2 | 514 | 171 | 185 | 8 | 8 | 8 | 5 | 177 | 28 | 0 | .158 |

## Sheriff Blake

**BLAKE, JOHN FREDERICK**     BL  TR  6'     180 lbs.
B. Sept. 17, 1899, Ansted, W. Va.     BR 1920,1925-27, BB 1937

D. Oct. 31, 1982, Beckley, W. Va.

| | W | L | PCT | ERA | G | GS | CG | IP | H | BB | SO | ShO | W | L | SV | AB | H | HR | BA |
|---|---|---|---|---|---|---|---|---|---|---|---|---|---|---|---|---|---|---|---|
| 1920 PIT N | 0 | 0 | – | 8.10 | 6 | 0 | 0 | 13.1 | 21 | 6 | 7 | 0 | 0 | 0 | 0 | 4 | 1 | 0 | .250 |
| 1924 CHI N | 6 | 6 | .500 | 4.57 | 29 | 11 | 4 | 106.1 | 123 | 44 | 42 | 0 | 2 | 2 | 1 | 31 | 9 | 0 | .290 |
| 1925 | 10 | 18 | .357 | 4.86 | 36 | 31 | 14 | 231.1 | 260 | 114 | 93 | 0 | 0 | 1 | 2 | 79 | 12 | 0 | .152 |
| 1926 | 11 | 12 | .478 | 3.60 | 39 | 27 | 11 | 197.2 | 204 | 92 | 95 | 4 | 1 | 1 | 1 | 65 | 14 | 0 | .215 |
| 1927 | 13 | 14 | .481 | 3.29 | 32 | 27 | 13 | 224.1 | 238 | 82 | 64 | 2 | 0 | 3 | 0 | 83 | 16 | 0 | .193 |
| 1928 | 17 | 11 | .607 | 2.47 | 34 | 29 | 16 | 240.2 | 209 | 101 | 78 | 4 | 3 | 0 | 1 | 88 | 19 | 0 | .216 |
| 1929 | 14 | 13 | .519 | 4.29 | 35 | 30 | 13 | 218.1 | 244 | 103 | 70 | 1 | 0 | 0 | 1 | 81 | 14 | 0 | .173 |
| 1930 | 10 | 14 | .417 | 4.82 | 34 | 24 | 7 | 186.2 | 213 | 99 | 80 | 0 | 2 | 2 | 0 | 66 | 15 | 0 | .227 |
| 1931 2 teams | | | | CHI N (16G 0–4) | | | | PHI N (14G 4–5) | | | | | | | | | | | |
| " total | 4 | 9 | .308 | 5.43 | 30 | 14 | 1 | 121 | 154 | 61 | 60 | 0 | 0 | 3 | 1 | 41 | 14 | 0 | .341 |
| 1937 2 teams | | | | STL A (15G 2–2) | | | | STL N (14G 0–3) | | | | | | | | | | | |
| " total | 2 | 5 | .286 | 5.49 | 29 | 3 | 2 | 80.1 | 100 | 38 | 32 | 0 | 2 | 3 | 1 | 20 | 4 | 0 | .200 |
| 10 yrs. | 87 | 102 | .460 | 4.13 | 304 | 196 | 81 | 1620 | 1766 | 740 | 621 | 11 | 10 | 15 | 8 | 558 | 118 | 0 | .211 |
| 8 yrs. | 81 | 92 | .468 | 3.95 | 255 | 184 | 78 | 1455.1 | 1555 | 661 | 551 | 11 | 8 | 11 | 6 | 509 | 107 | 0 | .210 |
| | | | | | | | | | **6th** | | | | | | | | | | |

WORLD SERIES

| | W | L | PCT | ERA | G | GS | CG | IP | H | BB | SO | ShO | W | L | SV | AB | H | HR | BA |
|---|---|---|---|---|---|---|---|---|---|---|---|---|---|---|---|---|---|---|---|
| 1929 CHI N | 0 | 1 | .000 | 13.50 | 2 | 0 | 0 | 1.1 | 4 | 0 | 1 | 0 | 0 | 1 | 0 | 1 | 1 | 0 | 1.000 |

## Julio Bonetti

**BONETTI, JULIO G.**     BR  TR  6'     180 lbs.
B. July 14, 1911, Genoa, Italy     D. June 17, 1952, Belmont, Calif.

| | W | L | PCT | ERA | G | GS | CG | IP | H | BB | SO | ShO | W | L | SV | AB | H | HR | BA |
|---|---|---|---|---|---|---|---|---|---|---|---|---|---|---|---|---|---|---|---|
| 1937 STL A | 4 | 11 | .267 | 5.84 | 28 | 16 | 7 | 143.1 | 190 | 60 | 43 | 0 | 2 | 0 | 1 | 47 | 7 | 0 | .149 |
| 1938 | 2 | 3 | .400 | 6.35 | 17 | 0 | 0 | 28.1 | 41 | 13 | 7 | 0 | 2 | 3 | 0 | 8 | 0 | 0 | .000 |
| 1940 CHI N | 0 | 0 | – | 20.25 | 1 | 0 | 0 | 1.1 | 3 | 4 | 0 | 0 | 0 | 0 | 0 | 0 | 0 | 0 | – |
| 3 yrs. | 6 | 14 | .300 | 6.03 | 46 | 16 | 7 | 173 | 234 | 77 | 50 | 0 | 4 | 3 | 1 | 55 | 7 | 0 | .127 |
| 1 yr. | 0 | 0 | – | 20.25 | 1 | 0 | 0 | 1.1 | 3 | 4 | 0 | 0 | 0 | 0 | 0 | 0 | 0 | 0 | – |

## Bill Bonham

**BONHAM, WILLIAM GORDON**     BR  TR  6'3"     190 lbs.
B. Oct. 1, 1948, Glendale, Calif.

| | W | L | PCT | ERA | G | GS | CG | IP | H | BB | SO | ShO | W | L | SV | AB | H | HR | BA |
|---|---|---|---|---|---|---|---|---|---|---|---|---|---|---|---|---|---|---|---|
| 1971 CHI N | 2 | 1 | .667 | 4.65 | 33 | 2 | 0 | 60 | 63 | 36 | 41 | 0 | 2 | 0 | 0 | 12 | 2 | 0 | .167 |
| 1972 | 1 | 1 | .500 | 3.10 | 19 | 4 | 0 | 58 | 56 | 25 | 49 | 0 | 0 | 0 | 4 | 14 | 4 | 0 | .286 |
| 1973 | 7 | 5 | .583 | 3.02 | 44 | 15 | 3 | 152 | 126 | 64 | 121 | 0 | 3 | 0 | 6 | 43 | 4 | 0 | .093 |
| 1974 | 11 | 22 | .333 | 3.85 | 44 | 36 | 10 | 243 | 246 | 109 | 191 | 2 | 1 | 2 | 1 | 84 | 12 | 0 | .143 |
| 1975 | 13 | 15 | .464 | 4.72 | 38 | 36 | 7 | 229 | 254 | 109 | 165 | 2 | 0 | 1 | 0 | 82 | 15 | 0 | .183 |
| 1976 | 9 | 13 | .409 | 4.27 | 32 | 31 | 3 | 196 | 215 | 96 | 110 | 0 | 0 | 0 | 0 | 65 | 13 | 0 | .200 |
| 1977 | 10 | 13 | .435 | 4.35 | 34 | 34 | 1 | 215 | 207 | 82 | 134 | 0 | 0 | 0 | 0 | 65 | 15 | 0 | .231 |
| 1978 CIN N | 11 | 5 | .688 | 3.54 | 23 | 23 | 1 | 140 | 151 | 50 | 83 | 0 | 0 | 0 | 0 | 43 | 8 | 0 | .186 |
| 1979 | 9 | 7 | .563 | 3.78 | 29 | 29 | 2 | 176 | 173 | 60 | 78 | 0 | 0 | 0 | 0 | 57 | 8 | 0 | .140 |
| 1980 | 2 | 1 | .667 | 4.74 | 4 | 4 | 0 | 19 | 21 | 5 | 13 | 0 | 0 | 0 | 0 | 6 | 0 | 0 | .000 |
| 10 yrs. | 75 | 83 | .475 | 4.00 | 300 | 214 | 27 | 1488 | 1512 | 636 | 985 | 4 | 6 | 3 | 11 | 471 | 81 | 0 | .172 |
| 7 yrs. | 53 | 70 | .431 | 4.08 | 244 | 158 | 24 | 1153 | 1167 | 521 | 811 | 4 | 6 | 3 | 11 | 365 | 65 | 0 | .178 |

## George Borchers

**BORCHERS, GEORGE BERNARD**     5'10"     180 lbs.
B. Apr. 18, 1869, Sacramento, Calif.     D. Oct. 24, 1938, Sacramento, Calif.

| | W | L | PCT | ERA | G | GS | CG | IP | H | BB | SO | ShO | W | L | SV | AB | H | HR | BA |
|---|---|---|---|---|---|---|---|---|---|---|---|---|---|---|---|---|---|---|---|
| 1888 CHI N | 4 | 4 | .500 | 3.49 | 10 | 10 | 7 | 67 | 67 | 29 | 26 | 1 | 0 | 0 | 0 | 33 | 2 | 0 | .061 |
| 1895 LOU N | 0 | 1 | .000 | 27.00 | 1 | 1 | 0 | .2 | 1 | 3 | 0 | 0 | 0 | 0 | 0 | 0 | 0 | 0 | – |
| 2 yrs. | 4 | 5 | .444 | 3.72 | 11 | 11 | 7 | 67.2 | 68 | 32 | 26 | 1 | 0 | 0 | 0 | 33 | 2 | 0 | .061 |
| 1 yr. | 4 | 4 | .500 | 3.49 | 10 | 10 | 7 | 67 | 67 | 29 | 26 | 1 | 0 | 0 | 0 | 33 | 2 | 0 | .061 |

## Rich Bordi

**BORDI, RICHARD ALBERT**     BR  TR  6'7"     210 lbs.
B. Apr. 18, 1959, San Francisco, Calif.

| | W | L | PCT | ERA | G | GS | CG | IP | H | BB | SO | ShO | W | L | SV | AB | H | HR | BA |
|---|---|---|---|---|---|---|---|---|---|---|---|---|---|---|---|---|---|---|---|
| 1980 OAK A | 0 | 0 | – | 4.50 | 1 | 0 | 0 | 2 | 4 | 0 | 0 | 0 | 0 | 0 | 0 | 0 | 0 | 0 | – |
| 1981 | 0 | 0 | – | 0.00 | 2 | 0 | 0 | 2 | 1 | 1 | 1 | 0 | 0 | 0 | 0 | 0 | 0 | 0 | – |
| 1982 SEA A | 0 | 2 | .000 | 8.31 | 7 | 2 | 0 | 13 | 18 | 1 | 10 | 0 | 0 | 0 | 0 | 0 | 0 | 0 | – |
| 1983 CHI N | 0 | 2 | .000 | 4.97 | 11 | 0 | 0 | 25.1 | 34 | 12 | 20 | 0 | 0 | 1 | 1 | 4 | 0 | 0 | .000 |
| 1984 | 5 | 2 | .714 | 3.46 | 31 | 7 | 0 | 83.1 | 78 | 20 | 41 | 0 | 1 | 1 | 4 | 19 | 1 | 0 | .053 |

| | W | L | PCT | ERA | G | GS | CG | IP | H | BB | SO | ShO | Relief Pitching W | L | SV | BATTING AB | H | HR | BA |
|---|---|---|---|---|---|---|---|---|---|---|---|---|---|---|---|---|---|---|---|

# Rich Bordi  continued

| | | W | L | PCT | ERA | G | GS | CG | IP | H | BB | SO | ShO | W | L | SV | AB | H | HR | BA |
|---|---|---|---|---|---|---|---|---|---|---|---|---|---|---|---|---|---|---|---|---|
| 1985 NY | A | 6 | 8 | .429 | 3.21 | 51 | 3 | 0 | 98 | 95 | 29 | 64 | 0 | 4 | 7 | 2 | 0 | 0 | 0 | – |
| 6 yrs. | | 11 | 14 | .440 | 3.78 | 103 | 13 | 0 | 223.2 | 230 | 63 | 135 | 0 | 5 | 9 | 7 | 23 | 1 | 0 | .043 |
| 2 yrs. | | 5 | 4 | .556 | 3.81 | 42 | 8 | 0 | 108.2 | 112 | 32 | 61 | 0 | 1 | 2 | 5 | 23 | 1 | 0 | .043 |

# Hank Borowy

**BOROWY, HENRY LUDWIG**      BR  TR  6'      175 lbs.
B. May 12, 1916, Bloomfield, N. J.

| | | W | L | PCT | ERA | G | GS | CG | IP | H | BB | SO | ShO | W | L | SV | AB | H | HR | BA |
|---|---|---|---|---|---|---|---|---|---|---|---|---|---|---|---|---|---|---|---|---|
| 1942 NY | A | 15 | 4 | .789 | 2.52 | 25 | 21 | 13 | 178.1 | 157 | 66 | 85 | 4 | 1 | 0 | 1 | 70 | 11 | 0 | .157 |
| 1943 | | 14 | 9 | .609 | 2.82 | 29 | 27 | 14 | 217.1 | 195 | 72 | 113 | 3 | 1 | 0 | 0 | 74 | 15 | 0 | .203 |
| 1944 | | 17 | 12 | .586 | 2.64 | 35 | 30 | 19 | 252.2 | 224 | 88 | 107 | 3 | 0 | 0 | 2 | 90 | 12 | 0 | .133 |
| 1945 2 teams | | | | NY A (18G 10–5) | | | | CHI N (15G 11–2) | | | | | | | | | | | | |
| " total | | 21 | 7 | .750 | **2.65** | 33 | 32 | 18 | 254.2 | 212 | 105 | 82 | 2 | 0 | 0 | 1 | 91 | 18 | 0 | .198 |
| 1946 CHI | N | 12 | 10 | .545 | 3.76 | 32 | 28 | 8 | 201 | 220 | 61 | 95 | 1 | 1 | 0 | 0 | 72 | 13 | 0 | .181 |
| 1947 | | 8 | 12 | .400 | 4.38 | 40 | 25 | 7 | 183 | 190 | 63 | 75 | 1 | 1 | 1 | 2 | 56 | 7 | 0 | .125 |
| 1948 | | 5 | 10 | .333 | 4.89 | 39 | 17 | 2 | 127 | 156 | 49 | 50 | 1 | 1 | 0 | 1 | 36 | 8 | 0 | .222 |
| 1949 PHI | N | 12 | 12 | .500 | 4.19 | 28 | 28 | 12 | 193.1 | 188 | 63 | 43 | 2 | 0 | 0 | 0 | 61 | 13 | 0 | .213 |
| 1950 3 teams | | | | PHI N (3G 0–0) | | | | PIT N (11G 1–3) | | | | DET A (13G 1–1) | | | | | | | | |
| " total | | 2 | 4 | .333 | 4.83 | 27 | 5 | 1 | 63.1 | 60 | 29 | 24 | 0 | 2 | 1 | 0 | 13 | 2 | 0 | .154 |
| 1951 DET | A | 2 | 2 | .500 | 6.95 | 26 | 1 | 0 | 45.1 | 58 | 27 | 16 | 0 | 2 | 2 | 0 | 8 | 0 | 0 | .000 |
| 10 yrs. | | 108 | 82 | .568 | 3.50 | 314 | 214 | 94 | 1716 | 1660 | 623 | 690 | 17 | 9 | 4 | 7 | 571 | 99 | 0 | .173 |
| 4 yrs. | | 36 | 34 | .514 | 3.85 | 126 | 84 | 28 | 633.1 | 671 | 220 | 267 | 4 | 3 | 1 | 4 | 205 | 35 | 0 | .171 |
| WORLD SERIES | | | | | | | | | | | | | | | | | | | | |
| 1942 NY | A | 0 | 0 | – | 18.00 | 1 | 1 | 0 | 3 | 6 | 3 | 1 | 0 | 0 | 0 | 0 | 1 | 0 | 0 | .000 |
| 1943 | | 1 | 0 | 1.000 | 2.25 | 1 | 1 | 0 | 8 | 6 | 3 | 4 | 0 | 0 | 0 | 0 | 2 | 1 | 0 | .500 |
| 1945 CHI | N | 2 | 2 | .500 | 4.00 | 4 | 3 | 1 | 18 | 21 | 6 | 8 | 1 | 1 | 0 | 0 | 5 | 1 | 0 | .200 |
| 3 yrs. | | 3 | 2 | .600 | 4.97 | 6 | 5 | 1 | 29 | 33 | 12 | 13 | 1 | 1 | 0 | 0 | 8 | 2 | 0 | .250 |

# Derek Botelho

**BOTELHO, DEREK WAYNE**      BR  TR  6'2"      160 lbs.
B. Aug. 2, 1956, Long Beach, Calif.

| | | W | L | PCT | ERA | G | GS | CG | IP | H | BB | SO | ShO | W | L | SV | AB | H | HR | BA |
|---|---|---|---|---|---|---|---|---|---|---|---|---|---|---|---|---|---|---|---|---|
| 1982 KC | A | 2 | 1 | .667 | 4.13 | 8 | 4 | 0 | 24 | 25 | 8 | 12 | 0 | 0 | 0 | 0 | 0 | 0 | 0 | – |
| 1985 CHI | N | 1 | 3 | .250 | 5.32 | 11 | 7 | 1 | 44 | 52 | 23 | 23 | 0 | 0 | 0 | 0 | 14 | 2 | 0 | .143 |
| 2 yrs. | | 3 | 4 | .429 | 4.90 | 19 | 11 | 1 | 68 | 77 | 31 | 35 | 0 | 0 | 0 | 0 | 14 | 2 | 0 | .143 |
| 1 yr. | | 1 | 3 | .250 | 5.32 | 11 | 7 | 1 | 44 | 52 | 23 | 23 | 0 | 0 | 0 | 0 | 14 | 2 | 0 | .143 |

# Bob Bowman

**BOWMAN, ROBERT JAMES**      BR  TR  5'10½" 160 lbs.
B. Oct. 3, 1910, Keystone, W. Va.      D. Sept. 4, 1972, Bluefield, W. Va.

| | | W | L | PCT | ERA | G | GS | CG | IP | H | BB | SO | ShO | W | L | SV | AB | H | HR | BA |
|---|---|---|---|---|---|---|---|---|---|---|---|---|---|---|---|---|---|---|---|---|
| 1939 STL | N | 13 | 5 | .722 | 2.60 | 51 | 15 | 4 | 169.1 | 141 | 60 | 78 | 2 | 7 | 0 | 9 | 47 | 4 | 0 | .085 |
| 1940 | | 7 | 5 | .583 | 4.33 | 28 | 17 | 7 | 114.1 | 118 | 43 | 43 | 0 | 0 | 2 | 0 | 33 | 2 | 0 | .061 |
| 1941 NY | N | 6 | 7 | .462 | 5.71 | 29 | 6 | 2 | 80.1 | 100 | 36 | 25 | 0 | 4 | 4 | 1 | 21 | 1 | 1 | .048 |
| 1942 CHI | N | 0 | 0 | – | 0.00 | 1 | 0 | 0 | 1 | 1 | 0 | 0 | 0 | 0 | 0 | 0 | 0 | 0 | 0 | – |
| 4 yrs. | | 26 | 17 | .605 | 3.82 | 109 | 38 | 13 | 365 | 360 | 139 | 146 | 2 | 11 | 6 | 10 | 101 | 7 | 1 | .069 |
| 1 yr. | | 0 | 0 | – | 0.00 | 1 | 0 | 0 | 1 | 1 | 0 | 0 | 0 | 0 | 0 | 0 | 0 | 0 | 0 | – |

# Bill Bradley

**BRADLEY, WILLIAM JOSEPH**      BR  TR  6'      185 lbs.
B. Feb. 13, 1878, Cleveland, Ohio      D. Mar. 11, 1954, Cleveland, Ohio
Manager 1914.

| | | W | L | PCT | ERA | G | GS | CG | IP | H | BB | SO | ShO | W | L | SV | AB | H | HR | BA |
|---|---|---|---|---|---|---|---|---|---|---|---|---|---|---|---|---|---|---|---|---|
| 1901 CLE | A | 0 | 0 | – | 0.00 | 1 | 0 | 0 | 1 | 4 | 0 | 0 | 0 | 0 | 0 | 0 | * | | | |

# George Bradley

**BRADLEY, GEORGE WASHINGTON (Grin)**      BR  TR  5'10½" 175 lbs.
B. July 13, 1852, Reading, Pa.      D. Oct. 2, 1931, Philadelphia, Pa.

| | | W | L | PCT | ERA | G | GS | CG | IP | H | BB | SO | ShO | W | L | SV | AB | H | HR | BA |
|---|---|---|---|---|---|---|---|---|---|---|---|---|---|---|---|---|---|---|---|---|
| 1876 STL | N | 45 | 19 | .703 | **1.23** | 64 | 64 | 63 | 573 | 470 | 38 | 103 | **16** | 0 | 0 | 0 | 265 | 66 | 0 | .249 |
| 1877 CHI | N | 18 | 23 | .439 | 3.31 | 50 | 44 | 35 | 394 | 452 | 39 | 59 | 2 | 1 | 0 | 0 | 214 | 52 | 0 | .243 |
| 1879 TRO | N | 13 | 40 | .245 | 2.85 | 54 | 54 | 53 | 487 | 590 | 26 | 133 | 3 | 0 | 0 | 0 | 251 | 62 | 0 | .247 |
| 1880 PRO | N | 12 | 9 | .571 | 1.38 | 28 | 20 | 16 | 196 | 158 | 6 | 54 | 4 | 3 | 1 | 1 | 309 | 70 | 0 | .227 |
| 1881 CLE | N | 2 | 4 | .333 | 3.88 | 6 | 6 | 5 | 51 | 70 | 3 | 6 | 0 | 0 | 0 | 0 | 245 | 60 | 2 | .245 |
| 1882 | | 7 | 10 | .412 | **3.73** | 18 | 16 | 15 | 147 | 164 | 22 | 32 | 0 | 0 | 0 | 0 | 115 | 21 | 0 | .183 |
| 1883 2 teams | | | | CLE N (0G 0–0) | | | | PHI AA (26G 16–7) | | | | | | | | | | | | |
| " total | | 16 | 7 | .696 | *3.15* | 26 | 23 | 22 | 214.1 | 215 | 22 | 56 | 0 | 0 | 0 | 0 | 328 | 78 | 1 | .238 |
| 1884 CIN | U | 25 | 15 | .625 | 2.71 | 41 | 38 | 36 | 342 | 350 | 23 | 168 | 3 | 1 | 1 | 0 | 226 | 43 | 0 | .190 |
| 1886 PHI | AA | 0 | 0 | – | 0.00 | 0 | 0 | 0 | 0 | 0 | 0 | 0 | 0 | 0 | 0 | 0 | 48 | 4 | 0 | .083 |
| 1888 BAL | AA | 0 | 0 | – | 0.00 | 0 | 0 | 0 | 0 | 0 | 0 | 0 | 0 | 0 | 0 | 0 | 3 | 0 | 0 | .000 |
| 10 yrs. | | 138 | 127 | .521 | 2.50 | 287 | 265 | 245 | 2404.1 | 2469 | 179 | 611 | 28 | 5 | 2 | 1 | * | | | |
| 1 yr. | | 18 | 23 | .439 | 3.31 | 50 | 44 | 35 | 394 | 452 | 39 | 59 | 2 | 1 | 0 | 0 | 214 | 52 | 0 | .243 |

# Roger Bresnahan

**BRESNAHAN, ROGER PHILIP (The Duke of Tralee)**      BR  TR  5'9"      200 lbs.
B. June 11, 1879, Toledo, Ohio      D. Dec. 4, 1944, Toledo, Ohio
Manager 1909-12, 1915.
Hall of Fame 1945.

| | | W | L | PCT | ERA | G | GS | CG | IP | H | BB | SO | ShO | W | L | SV | AB | H | HR | BA |
|---|---|---|---|---|---|---|---|---|---|---|---|---|---|---|---|---|---|---|---|---|
| 1897 WAS | N | 4 | 0 | 1.000 | 3.95 | 6 | 5 | 3 | 41 | 52 | 10 | 12 | 1 | 0 | 0 | 0 | 16 | 6 | 0 | .375 |
| 1901 BAL | A | 0 | 1 | .000 | 6.00 | 2 | 1 | 0 | 6 | 10 | 4 | 3 | 0 | 0 | 0 | 0 | 293 | 77 | 1 | .263 |
| 1910 STL | N | 0 | 0 | – | 0.00 | 1 | 0 | 0 | 3.1 | 6 | 1 | 0 | 0 | 0 | 0 | 0 | 234 | 65 | 0 | .278 |
| 3 yrs. | | 4 | 1 | .800 | 3.93 | 9 | 6 | 3 | 50.1 | 68 | 15 | 15 | 1 | 0 | 0 | 0 | * | | | |

# Herb Brett

**BRETT, HERBERT JAMES (Duke)**      BR  TR  6'      175 lbs.
B. May 23, 1900, Lawrenceville, Va.      D. Nov. 25, 1974, St. Petersburg, Fla.

| | | W | L | PCT | ERA | G | GS | CG | IP | H | BB | SO | ShO | W | L | SV | AB | H | HR | BA |
|---|---|---|---|---|---|---|---|---|---|---|---|---|---|---|---|---|---|---|---|---|
| 1924 CHI | N | 0 | 0 | – | 5.06 | 1 | 1 | 0 | 5.1 | 6 | 7 | 1 | 0 | 0 | 0 | 0 | 2 | 0 | 0 | .000 |
| 1925 | | 1 | 1 | .500 | 3.63 | 10 | 1 | 0 | 17.1 | 12 | 3 | 6 | 0 | 1 | 0 | 0 | 1 | 0 | 0 | .000 |
| 2 yrs. | | 1 | 1 | .500 | 3.97 | 11 | 2 | 0 | 22.2 | 18 | 10 | 7 | 0 | 1 | 0 | 0 | 3 | 0 | 0 | .000 |
| 2 yrs. | | 1 | 1 | .500 | 3.97 | 11 | 2 | 0 | 22.2 | 18 | 10 | 7 | 0 | 1 | 0 | 0 | 3 | 0 | 0 | .000 |

| | W | L | PCT | ERA | G | GS | CG | IP | H | BB | SO | ShO | Relief Pitching W | L | SV | BATTING AB | H | HR | BA |
|---|---|---|---|---|---|---|---|---|---|---|---|---|---|---|---|---|---|---|---|

## Jim Brewer

**BREWER, JAMES THOMAS**
B. Nov. 14, 1937, Merced, Calif.

BL TL 6'1"  186 lbs.

| | W | L | PCT | ERA | G | GS | CG | IP | H | BB | SO | ShO | W | L | SV | AB | H | HR | BA |
|---|---|---|---|---|---|---|---|---|---|---|---|---|---|---|---|---|---|---|---|
| 1960 CHI N | 0 | 3 | .000 | 5.82 | 5 | 4 | 0 | 21.2 | 25 | 6 | 7 | 0 | 0 | 0 | 0 | 6 | 1 | 0 | .167 |
| 1961 | 1 | 7 | .125 | 5.82 | 36 | 11 | 0 | 86.2 | 116 | 21 | 57 | 0 | 0 | 1 | 0 | 22 | 4 | 0 | .182 |
| 1962 | 0 | 1 | .000 | 9.53 | 6 | 1 | 0 | 5.2 | 10 | 3 | 1 | 0 | 0 | 1 | 0 | 0 | 0 | 0 | — |
| 1963 | 3 | 2 | .600 | 4.89 | 29 | 1 | 0 | 49.2 | 59 | 15 | 35 | 0 | 3 | 1 | 0 | 6 | 0 | 0 | .000 |
| 1964 LA N | 4 | 3 | .571 | 3.00 | 34 | 5 | 1 | 93 | 79 | 25 | 63 | 1 | 2 | 2 | 1 | 22 | 6 | 0 | .273 |
| 1965 | 3 | 2 | .600 | 1.82 | 19 | 2 | 0 | 49.1 | 33 | 28 | 31 | 0 | 3 | 1 | 2 | 10 | 0 | 0 | .000 |
| 1966 | 0 | 2 | .000 | 3.68 | 13 | 0 | 0 | 22 | 17 | 11 | 8 | 0 | 0 | 2 | 2 | 0 | 0 | 0 | — |
| 1967 | 5 | 4 | .556 | 2.68 | 30 | 11 | 0 | 100.2 | 78 | 31 | 74 | 0 | 1 | 0 | 1 | 22 | 1 | 0 | .045 |
| 1968 | 8 | 3 | .727 | 2.49 | 54 | 0 | 0 | 76 | 59 | 33 | 75 | 0 | 8 | 3 | 14 | 9 | 2 | 0 | .222 |
| 1969 | 7 | 6 | .538 | 2.56 | 59 | 0 | 0 | 88 | 71 | 41 | 92 | 0 | 7 | 6 | 20 | 11 | 1 | 0 | .091 |
| 1970 | 7 | 6 | .538 | 3.13 | 58 | 0 | 0 | 89 | 66 | 33 | 91 | 0 | 7 | 6 | 24 | 12 | 1 | 0 | .083 |
| 1971 | 6 | 5 | .545 | 1.89 | 55 | 0 | 0 | 81 | 55 | 24 | 66 | 0 | 6 | 5 | 22 | 9 | 3 | 0 | .333 |
| 1972 | 8 | 7 | .533 | 1.26 | 51 | 0 | 0 | 78.1 | 41 | 25 | 69 | 0 | 8 | 7 | 17 | 1 | 0 | 0 | .000 |
| 1973 | 6 | 8 | .429 | 3.01 | 56 | 0 | 0 | 71.2 | 58 | 25 | 56 | 0 | 6 | 8 | 20 | 5 | 2 | 0 | .400 |
| 1974 | 4 | 4 | .500 | 2.54 | 24 | 0 | 0 | 39 | 29 | 10 | 26 | 0 | 4 | 4 | 0 | 2 | 0 | 0 | .000 |
| 1975 2 teams | | | LA | N | (21G | 3–1) | | CAL | A | (21G | 1–0) | | | | | | | | |
| " total | 4 | 1 | .800 | 3.46 | 42 | 0 | 0 | 67.2 | 82 | 23 | 43 | 0 | 4 | 1 | 7 | 3 | 0 | 0 | .000 |
| 1976 CAL A | 3 | 1 | .750 | 2.70 | 13 | 0 | 0 | 20 | 20 | 6 | 16 | 0 | 3 | 1 | 2 | 0 | 0 | 0 | — |
| 17 yrs. | 69 | 65 | .515 | 3.07 | 584 | 35 | 1 | 1039.1 | 898 | 360 | 810 | 1 | 62 | 49 | 132 | 140 | 21 | 0 | .150 |
| 4 yrs. | 4 | 13 | .235 | 5.66 | 76 | 17 | 0 | 163.2 | 210 | 45 | 100 | 0 | 3 | 3 | 0 | 34 | 5 | 0 | .147 |
| WORLD SERIES | | | | | | | | | | | | | | | | | | | |
| 1965 LA N | 0 | 0 | — | 4.50 | 1 | 0 | 0 | 2 | 3 | 0 | 1 | 0 | 0 | 0 | 0 | 0 | 0 | 0 | — |
| 1966 | 0 | 0 | — | 0.00 | 1 | 0 | 0 | 1 | 0 | 0 | 1 | 0 | 0 | 0 | 0 | 0 | 0 | 0 | — |
| 1974 | 0 | 0 | — | 0.00 | 1 | 0 | 0 | .1 | 0 | 0 | 1 | 0 | 0 | 0 | 0 | 0 | 0 | 0 | — |
| 3 yrs. | 0 | 0 | — | 2.70 | 3 | 0 | 0 | 3.1 | 3 | 0 | 3 | 0 | 0 | 0 | 0 | 0 | 0 | 0 | — |

## Buttons Briggs

**BRIGGS, HERBERT THEODORE**
B. July 8, 1875, Poughkeepsie, N. Y.   D. Feb. 18, 1911, Cleveland, Ohio

BR TR 6'1"  180 lbs.

| | W | L | PCT | ERA | G | GS | CG | IP | H | BB | SO | ShO | W | L | SV | AB | H | HR | BA |
|---|---|---|---|---|---|---|---|---|---|---|---|---|---|---|---|---|---|---|---|
| 1896 CHI N | 12 | 8 | .600 | 4.31 | 26 | 21 | 19 | 194 | 202 | 108 | 84 | 0 | 0 | 1 | 1 | 78 | 10 | 0 | .128 |
| 1897 | 4 | 17 | .190 | 5.26 | 22 | 22 | 21 | 186.2 | 246 | 85 | 60 | 0 | 0 | 0 | 0 | 81 | 13 | 0 | .160 |
| 1898 | 1 | 3 | .250 | 5.70 | 4 | 4 | 3 | 30 | 38 | 10 | 14 | 0 | 0 | 0 | 0 | 14 | 6 | 0 | .429 |
| 1904 | 19 | 11 | .633 | 2.05 | 34 | 30 | 28 | 277 | 252 | 77 | 112 | 3 | 1 | 0 | 2 | 94 | 16 | 1 | .170 |
| 1905 | 8 | 8 | .500 | 2.14 | 20 | 20 | 13 | 168 | 141 | 52 | 68 | 5 | 0 | 0 | 0 | 57 | 3 | 0 | .053 |
| 5 yrs. | 44 | 47 | .484 | 3.41 | 106 | 97 | 84 | 855.2 | 879 | 332 | 338 | 8 | 1 | 1 | 3 | 324 | 48 | 1 | .148 |
| 5 yrs. | 44 | 47 | .484 | 3.41 | 106 | 97 | 84 | 855.2 | 879 | 332 | 338 | 8 | 1 | 1 | 3 | 324 | 48 | 1 | .148 |

## Johnny Briggs

**BRIGGS, JONATHAN TIFT**
B. Jan. 24, 1934, Natoma, Calif.

BR TR 5'10"  175 lbs.

| | W | L | PCT | ERA | G | GS | CG | IP | H | BB | SO | ShO | W | L | SV | AB | H | HR | BA |
|---|---|---|---|---|---|---|---|---|---|---|---|---|---|---|---|---|---|---|---|
| 1956 CHI N | 0 | 0 | — | 1.69 | 3 | 0 | 0 | 5.1 | 5 | 4 | 1 | 0 | 0 | 0 | 0 | 0 | 0 | 0 | — |
| 1957 | 0 | 1 | .000 | 12.46 | 3 | 0 | 0 | 4.1 | 7 | 3 | 1 | 0 | 0 | 1 | 0 | 0 | 0 | 0 | — |
| 1958 | 5 | 5 | .500 | 4.52 | 20 | 17 | 3 | 95.2 | 99 | 45 | 46 | 1 | 0 | 0 | 0 | 35 | 9 | 0 | .257 |
| 1959 CLE A | 0 | 1 | .000 | 2.13 | 4 | 1 | 0 | 12.2 | 12 | 3 | 5 | 0 | 0 | 0 | 0 | 2 | 0 | 0 | .000 |
| 1960 2 teams | | | CLE | A | (21G | 4–2) | | KC | A | (8G | 0–2) | | | | | | | | |
| " total | 4 | 4 | .500 | 6.42 | 29 | 3 | 0 | 47.2 | 51 | 27 | 27 | 0 | 1 | 2 | 1 | 11 | 1 | 0 | .091 |
| 5 yrs. | 9 | 11 | .450 | 5.00 | 59 | 21 | 3 | 165.2 | 174 | 82 | 80 | 1 | 1 | 3 | 1 | 48 | 10 | 0 | .208 |
| 3 yrs. | 5 | 6 | .455 | 4.70 | 26 | 17 | 3 | 105.1 | 111 | 52 | 48 | 1 | 0 | 1 | 0 | 35 | 9 | 0 | .257 |

## Jim Brillheart

**BRILLHEART, JAMES BENSON (Buck)**
B. Sept. 28, 1903, Dublin, Va.   D. Sept. 2, 1972, Radford, Va.

BR TL 5'11"  170 lbs.

| | W | L | PCT | ERA | G | GS | CG | IP | H | BB | SO | ShO | W | L | SV | AB | H | HR | BA |
|---|---|---|---|---|---|---|---|---|---|---|---|---|---|---|---|---|---|---|---|
| 1922 WAS A | 4 | 6 | .400 | 3.61 | 31 | 10 | 3 | 119.2 | 120 | 72 | 47 | 0 | 0 | 2 | 1 | 36 | 3 | 0 | .083 |
| 1923 | 0 | 1 | .000 | 7.00 | 12 | 0 | 0 | 18 | 27 | 12 | 8 | 0 | 0 | 1 | 0 | 2 | 0 | 0 | .000 |
| 1927 CHI N | 4 | 2 | .667 | 4.13 | 32 | 12 | 4 | 128.2 | 140 | 38 | 36 | 0 | 0 | 0 | 0 | 44 | 1 | 0 | .023 |
| 1931 BOS A | 0 | 0 | — | 5.49 | 11 | 1 | 0 | 19.2 | 27 | 15 | 7 | 0 | 0 | 0 | 0 | 4 | 2 | 1 | .500 |
| 4 yrs. | 8 | 9 | .471 | 4.19 | 86 | 23 | 7 | 286 | 314 | 137 | 98 | 0 | 0 | 3 | 1 | 86 | 6 | 1 | .070 |
| 1 yr. | 4 | 2 | .667 | 4.13 | 32 | 12 | 4 | 128.2 | 140 | 38 | 36 | 0 | 0 | 0 | 0 | 44 | 1 | 0 | .023 |

## Pete Broberg

**BROBERG, PETER SVEN**
B. Mar. 2, 1950, West Palm Beach, Fla.

BR TR 6'3"  205 lbs.

| | W | L | PCT | ERA | G | GS | CG | IP | H | BB | SO | ShO | W | L | SV | AB | H | HR | BA |
|---|---|---|---|---|---|---|---|---|---|---|---|---|---|---|---|---|---|---|---|
| 1971 WAS A | 5 | 9 | .357 | 3.46 | 18 | 18 | 7 | 125 | 104 | 53 | 89 | 1 | 0 | 0 | 0 | 44 | 5 | 1 | .114 |
| 1972 TEX A | 5 | 12 | .294 | 4.30 | 39 | 25 | 3 | 175.2 | 153 | 85 | 133 | 2 | 0 | 0 | 1 | 51 | 4 | 0 | .078 |
| 1973 | 5 | 9 | .357 | 5.60 | 22 | 20 | 6 | 119 | 130 | 66 | 57 | 1 | 0 | 0 | 0 | 0 | 0 | 0 | — |
| 1974 | 0 | 4 | .000 | 8.07 | 12 | 2 | 0 | 29 | 29 | 13 | 15 | 0 | 0 | 2 | 0 | 0 | 0 | 0 | — |
| 1975 MIL A | 14 | 16 | .467 | 4.13 | 38 | 32 | 7 | 220.1 | 219 | 106 | 100 | 2 | 2 | 0 | 0 | 0 | 0 | 0 | — |
| 1976 | 1 | 7 | .125 | 4.97 | 20 | 11 | 1 | 92.1 | 99 | 72 | 28 | 0 | 0 | 0 | 0 | 0 | 0 | 0 | — |
| 1977 CHI N | 1 | 2 | .333 | 4.75 | 22 | 0 | 0 | 36 | 34 | 18 | 20 | 0 | 1 | 2 | 0 | 6 | 0 | 0 | .000 |
| 1978 OAK A | 10 | 12 | .455 | 4.62 | 35 | 26 | 2 | 165.2 | 174 | 65 | 94 | 0 | 2 | 1 | 0 | 0 | 0 | 0 | — |
| 8 yrs. | 41 | 71 | .366 | 4.56 | 206 | 134 | 26 | 963 | 942 | 478 | 536 | 6 | 5 | 5 | 1 | 101 | 9 | 1 | .089 |
| 1 yr. | 1 | 2 | .333 | 4.75 | 22 | 0 | 0 | 36 | 34 | 18 | 20 | 0 | 1 | 2 | 0 | 6 | 0 | 0 | .000 |

## Ernie Broglio

**BROGLIO, ERNEST GILBERT**
B. Aug. 27, 1935, Berkeley, Calif.

BR TR 6'2"  200 lbs.

| | W | L | PCT | ERA | G | GS | CG | IP | H | BB | SO | ShO | W | L | SV | AB | H | HR | BA |
|---|---|---|---|---|---|---|---|---|---|---|---|---|---|---|---|---|---|---|---|
| 1959 STL N | 7 | 12 | .368 | 4.72 | 35 | 25 | 6 | 181.1 | 174 | 89 | 133 | 3 | 0 | 1 | 0 | 61 | 6 | 0 | .098 |
| 1960 | 21 | 9 | .700 | 2.74 | 52 | 24 | 9 | 226.1 | 172 | 100 | 188 | 3 | 7 | 2 | 0 | 68 | 14 | 0 | .206 |
| 1961 | 9 | 12 | .429 | 4.12 | 29 | 26 | 7 | 174.2 | 166 | 75 | 113 | 2 | 0 | 1 | 0 | 62 | 9 | 0 | .145 |
| 1962 | 12 | 9 | .571 | 3.00 | 34 | 30 | 11 | 222.1 | 193 | 93 | 132 | 4 | 1 | 1 | 0 | 72 | 10 | 0 | .139 |
| 1963 | 18 | 8 | .692 | 2.99 | 39 | 35 | 11 | 250 | 202 | 90 | 145 | 5 | 2 | 1 | 0 | 89 | 10 | 0 | .112 |
| 1964 2 teams | | | STL | N | (11G | 3–5) | | CHI | N | (18G | 4–7) | | | | | | | | |
| " total | 7 | 12 | .368 | 3.82 | 29 | 27 | 6 | 169.2 | 176 | 56 | 82 | 1 | 0 | 0 | 1 | 56 | 12 | 0 | .214 |
| 1965 CHI N | 1 | 6 | .143 | 6.93 | 26 | 6 | 0 | 50.2 | 63 | 46 | 22 | 0 | 1 | 3 | 0 | 4 | 0 | 0 | .000 |

| | W | L | PCT | ERA | G | GS | CG | IP | H | BB | SO | ShO | Relief Pitching W | L | SV | BATTING AB | H | HR | BA |
|---|---|---|---|---|---|---|---|---|---|---|---|---|---|---|---|---|---|---|---|

## Ernie Broglio continued

| | W | L | PCT | ERA | G | GS | CG | IP | H | BB | SO | ShO | W | L | SV | AB | H | HR | BA |
|---|---|---|---|---|---|---|---|---|---|---|---|---|---|---|---|---|---|---|---|
| 1966 | 2 | 6 | .250 | 6.35 | 15 | 11 | 2 | 62.1 | 70 | 38 | 34 | 0 | 0 | 0 | 1 | 19 | 7 | 0 | .368 |
| 8 yrs. | 77 | 74 | .510 | 3.74 | 259 | 184 | 52 | 1337.1 | 1216 | 587 | 849 | 18 | 11 | 11 | 2 | 431 | 68 | 0 | .158 |
| 3 yrs. | 7 | 19 | .269 | 5.40 | 59 | 33 | 5 | 213.1 | 244 | 114 | 102 | 0 | 1 | 3 | 2 | 58 | 17 | 0 | .293 |

## Jim Brosnan

**BROSNAN, JAMES PATRICK (Professor)**     BR TR 6'4"    197 lbs.
B. Oct. 24, 1929, Cincinnati, Ohio

| | W | L | PCT | ERA | G | GS | CG | IP | H | BB | SO | ShO | W | L | SV | AB | H | HR | BA |
|---|---|---|---|---|---|---|---|---|---|---|---|---|---|---|---|---|---|---|---|
| 1954 CHI N | 1 | 0 | 1.000 | 9.45 | 18 | 0 | 0 | 33.1 | 44 | 18 | 17 | 0 | 1 | 0 | 0 | 8 | 1 | 0 | .125 |
| 1956 | 5 | 9 | .357 | 3.79 | 30 | 10 | 1 | 95 | 95 | 45 | 51 | 1 | 3 | 4 | 1 | 22 | 4 | 0 | .182 |
| 1957 | 5 | 5 | .500 | 3.38 | 41 | 5 | 1 | 98.2 | 79 | 46 | 73 | 0 | 4 | 4 | 0 | 20 | 5 | 0 | .250 |
| 1958 2 teams | | | CHI | N (8G 3–4) | | STL | N (33G 8–4) | | | | | | | | | | | | |
| " total | 11 | 8 | .579 | 3.35 | 41 | 20 | 4 | 166.2 | 148 | 79 | 89 | 0 | 4 | 1 | 7 | 50 | 5 | 0 | .100 |
| 1959 2 teams | | | STL | N (20G 1–3) | | CIN | N (26G 8–3) | | | | | | | | | | | | |
| " total | 9 | 6 | .600 | 3.79 | 46 | 10 | 1 | 116.1 | 113 | 41 | 74 | 1 | 5 | 3 | 4 | 30 | 3 | 0 | .100 |
| 1960 CIN N | 7 | 2 | .778 | 2.36 | 57 | 2 | 0 | 99 | 79 | 22 | 62 | 0 | 7 | 2 | 12 | 15 | 3 | 1 | .200 |
| 1961 | 10 | 4 | .714 | 3.04 | 53 | 0 | 0 | 80 | 77 | 18 | 40 | 0 | 10 | 4 | 16 | 13 | 2 | 0 | .154 |
| 1962 | 4 | 4 | .500 | 3.34 | 48 | 0 | 0 | 64.2 | 76 | 18 | 51 | 0 | 4 | 4 | 13 | 6 | 0 | 0 | .000 |
| 1963 2 teams | | | CIN | N (6G 0–1) | | CHI | A (45G 3–8) | | | | | | | | | | | | |
| " total | 3 | 9 | .250 | 3.13 | 51 | 0 | 0 | 77.2 | 79 | 25 | 50 | 0 | 3 | 9 | 14 | 13 | 4 | 0 | .308 |
| 9 yrs. | 55 | 47 | .539 | 3.54 | 385 | 47 | 7 | 831.1 | 790 | 312 | 507 | 2 | 41 | 31 | 67 | 177 | 27 | 1 | .153 |
| 4 yrs. | 14 | 18 | .438 | 4.20 | 97 | 23 | 4 | 278.2 | 259 | 138 | 165 | 1 | 8 | 8 | 1 | 69 | 12 | 0 | .174 |
| WORLD SERIES | | | | | | | | | | | | | | | | | | | |
| 1961 CIN N | 0 | 0 | — | 7.50 | 3 | 0 | 0 | 6 | 9 | 4 | 5 | 0 | 0 | 0 | 0 | 0 | 0 | 0 | — |

## Joe Brown

**BROWN, JOSEPH E.**
B. Apr. 4, 1859, Warren, Pa.    D. June 28, 1888, Warren, Pa.

| | W | L | PCT | ERA | G | GS | CG | IP | H | BB | SO | ShO | W | L | SV | AB | H | HR | BA |
|---|---|---|---|---|---|---|---|---|---|---|---|---|---|---|---|---|---|---|---|
| 1884 CHI N | 4 | 2 | .667 | 4.68 | 7 | 6 | 5 | 50 | 56 | 7 | 27 | 0 | 0 | 0 | 0 | 61 | 13 | 0 | .213 |
| 1885 BAL AA | 0 | 4 | .000 | 5.68 | 4 | 4 | 4 | 38 | 52 | 4 | 9 | 0 | 0 | 0 | 0 | 19 | 3 | 0 | .158 |
| 2 yrs. | 4 | 6 | .400 | 5.11 | 11 | 10 | 9 | 88 | 108 | 11 | 36 | 0 | 0 | 0 | 0 | 80 | 16 | 0 | .200 |
| 1 yr. | 4 | 2 | .667 | 4.68 | 7 | 6 | 5 | 50 | 56 | 7 | 27 | 0 | 0 | 0 | 0 | 61 | 13 | 0 | .213 |

## Jophery Brown

**BROWN, JOPHERY CLIFFORD**     BL TR 6'2"    190 lbs.
B. Jan. 22, 1945, Grambling, La.

| | W | L | PCT | ERA | G | GS | CG | IP | H | BB | SO | ShO | W | L | SV | AB | H | HR | BA |
|---|---|---|---|---|---|---|---|---|---|---|---|---|---|---|---|---|---|---|---|
| 1968 CHI N | 0 | 0 | — | 4.50 | 1 | 0 | 0 | 2 | 2 | 1 | 0 | 0 | 0 | 0 | 0 | 0 | 0 | 0 | — |

## Jumbo Brown

**BROWN, WALTER GEORGE**     BR TR 6'4"    295 lbs.
B. Apr. 30, 1907, Greene, R. I.    D. Oct. 2, 1966, Freeport, N. Y.

| | W | L | PCT | ERA | G | GS | CG | IP | H | BB | SO | ShO | W | L | SV | AB | H | HR | BA |
|---|---|---|---|---|---|---|---|---|---|---|---|---|---|---|---|---|---|---|---|
| 1925 CHI N | 0 | 0 | — | 3.00 | 2 | 0 | 0 | 6 | 5 | 4 | 0 | 0 | 0 | 0 | 0 | 1 | 0 | 0 | .000 |
| 1927 CLE A | 0 | 2 | .000 | 6.27 | 8 | 0 | 0 | 18.2 | 19 | 26 | 8 | 0 | 0 | 2 | 0 | 3 | 2 | 0 | .667 |
| 1928 | 0 | 1 | .000 | 6.75 | 5 | 0 | 0 | 14.2 | 19 | 15 | 12 | 0 | 0 | 1 | 0 | 3 | 2 | 0 | .667 |
| 1932 NY A | 5 | 2 | .714 | 4.45 | 19 | 3 | 3 | 56.2 | 58 | 30 | 31 | 1 | 2 | 2 | 1 | 23 | 4 | 0 | .174 |
| 1933 | 7 | 5 | .583 | 5.23 | 21 | 8 | 1 | 74 | 78 | 52 | 55 | 0 | 3 | 3 | 0 | 28 | 5 | 0 | .179 |
| 1935 | 6 | 5 | .545 | 3.61 | 20 | 8 | 3 | 87.1 | 94 | 37 | 41 | 0 | 2 | 1 | 0 | 32 | 10 | 0 | .313 |
| 1936 | 1 | 4 | .200 | 5.91 | 20 | 3 | 0 | 64 | 93 | 29 | 19 | 0 | 1 | 2 | 1 | 19 | 0 | 0 | .000 |
| 1937 2 teams | | | CIN | N (4G 1–0) | | NY | N (4G 1–0) | | | | | | | | | | | | |
| " total | 2 | 0 | 1.000 | 4.91 | 8 | 1 | 0 | 18.1 | 21 | 8 | 8 | 0 | 1 | 0 | 0 | 2 | 0 | 0 | .000 |
| 1938 NY N | 5 | 3 | .625 | 1.80 | 43 | 0 | 0 | 90 | 65 | 28 | 42 | 0 | 5 | 3 | 5 | 16 | 3 | 0 | .188 |
| 1939 | 4 | 0 | 1.000 | 4.15 | 31 | 0 | 0 | 56.1 | 69 | 25 | 24 | 0 | 4 | 0 | 7 | 11 | 4 | 0 | .364 |
| 1940 | 2 | 4 | .333 | 3.42 | 41 | 0 | 0 | 55.1 | 49 | 25 | 31 | 0 | 2 | 4 | 7 | 10 | 1 | 0 | .100 |
| 1941 | 1 | 5 | .167 | 3.32 | 31 | 0 | 0 | 57 | 49 | 21 | 30 | 0 | 1 | 5 | 8 | 9 | 1 | 0 | .111 |
| 12 yrs. | 33 | 31 | .516 | 4.06 | 249 | 23 | 7 | 598.1 | 619 | 300 | 301 | 1 | 21 | 23 | 29 | 157 | 32 | 0 | .204 |
| 1 yr. | 0 | 0 | — | 3.00 | 2 | 0 | 0 | 6 | 5 | 4 | 0 | 0 | 0 | 0 | 0 | 1 | 0 | 0 | .000 |

## Lew Brown

**BROWN, LEWIS J. (Blower)**     BR TR 5'10½" 185 lbs.
B. Feb. 1, 1858, Leominster, Mass.    D. Jan. 16, 1889, Boston, Mass.

| | W | L | PCT | ERA | G | GS | CG | IP | H | BB | SO | ShO | W | L | SV | AB | H | HR | BA |
|---|---|---|---|---|---|---|---|---|---|---|---|---|---|---|---|---|---|---|---|
| 1878 PRO N | 0 | 0 | — | 18.00 | 1 | 0 | 0 | 1 | 0 | 4 | 0 | 0 | 0 | 0 | 0 | 243 | 74 | 1 | .305 |
| 1884 BOS U | 0 | 0 | — | 36.00 | 1 | 0 | 0 | 1 | 6 | 1 | 0 | 0 | 0 | 0 | 1 | 325 | 75 | 1 | .231 |
| 2 yrs. | 0 | 0 | — | 27.00 | 2 | 0 | 0 | 2 | 6 | 5 | 0 | 0 | 0 | 0 | 1 | * | | | |

## Ray Brown

**BROWN, PAUL PERCIVAL**
B. Jan. 30, 1889, Chicago, Ill.    D. May 29, 1955, Los Angeles, Calif.

| | W | L | PCT | ERA | G | GS | CG | IP | H | BB | SO | ShO | W | L | SV | AB | H | HR | BA |
|---|---|---|---|---|---|---|---|---|---|---|---|---|---|---|---|---|---|---|---|
| 1909 CHI N | 1 | 0 | 1.000 | 2.00 | 1 | 1 | 1 | 9 | 5 | 4 | 2 | 0 | 0 | 0 | 0 | 3 | 0 | 0 | .000 |

## Three Finger Brown

**BROWN, MORDECAI PETER CENTENNIAL (Miner)**     BB TR 5'10"    175 lbs.
B. Oct. 19, 1876, Nyesville, Ind.    D. Feb. 14, 1948, Terre Haute, Ind.
Manager 1914.
Hall of Fame 1949.

| | W | L | PCT | ERA | G | GS | CG | IP | H | BB | SO | ShO | W | L | SV | AB | H | HR | BA |
|---|---|---|---|---|---|---|---|---|---|---|---|---|---|---|---|---|---|---|---|
| 1903 STL N | 9 | 13 | .409 | 2.60 | 26 | 24 | 19 | 201 | 231 | 59 | 83 | 1 | 0 | 0 | 0 | 77 | 15 | 0 | .195 |
| 1904 CHI N | 15 | 10 | .600 | 1.86 | 26 | 23 | 21 | 212.1 | 155 | 50 | 81 | 4 | 2 | 0 | 1 | 89 | 19 | 0 | .213 |
| 1905 | 18 | 12 | .600 | 2.17 | 30 | 24 | 24 | 249 | 219 | 44 | 89 | 4 | 2 | 2 | 0 | 93 | 13 | 1 | .140 |
| 1906 | 26 | 6 | .813 | 1.04 | 36 | 32 | 27 | 277.1 | 198 | 61 | 144 | 10 | 1 | 0 | 3 | 98 | 20 | 0 | .204 |
| 1907 | 20 | 6 | .769 | 1.39 | 34 | 27 | 20 | 233 | 180 | 40 | 107 | 6 | 1 | 0 | 3 | 85 | 13 | 1 | .153 |
| 1908 | 29 | 9 | .763 | 1.47 | 44 | 31 | 27 | 312.1 | 214 | 49 | 123 | 9 | 4 | 1 | 5 | 121 | 25 | 0 | .207 |
| 1909 | 27 | 9 | .750 | 1.31 | 50 | 34 | 32 | 342.2 | 246 | 53 | 172 | 8 | 1 | 1 | 7 | 125 | 22 | 0 | .176 |
| 1910 | 25 | 13 | .658 | 1.86 | 46 | 31 | 27 | 295.1 | 256 | 64 | 143 | 7 | 2 | 2 | 7 | 103 | 18 | 0 | .175 |
| 1911 | 21 | 11 | .656 | 2.80 | 53 | 27 | 21 | 270 | 267 | 55 | 129 | 0 | 5 | 3 | 13 | 91 | 23 | 0 | .253 |
| 1912 | 5 | 6 | .455 | 2.64 | 15 | 8 | 5 | 88.2 | 92 | 20 | 34 | 2 | 2 | 3 | 0 | 31 | 9 | 0 | .290 |
| 1913 CIN N | 11 | 12 | .478 | 2.91 | 39 | 16 | 11 | 173.1 | 174 | 44 | 41 | 1 | 4 | 3 | 6 | 54 | 11 | 0 | .204 |

| | W | L | PCT | ERA | G | GS | CG | IP | H | BB | SO | ShO | Relief Pitching W | L | SV | BATTING AB | H | HR | BA |
|---|---|---|---|---|---|---|---|---|---|---|---|---|---|---|---|---|---|---|---|

## Three Finger Brown continued

| | | | | | | | | | | | | | | | | | | | |
|---|---|---|---|---|---|---|---|---|---|---|---|---|---|---|---|---|---|---|---|
| 1914 2 teams | | STL F (26G 12–6) | | | | BKN F (9G 2–5) | | | | | | | | | | | | | |
| " total | 14 | 11 | .560 | 3.52 | 35 | 26 | 18 | 232.2 | 235 | 61 | 113 | 2 | 1 | 2 | 0 | 78 | 19 | 0 | .244 |
| 1915 CHI F | 17 | 8 | .680 | 2.09 | 35 | 25 | 18 | 236.1 | 189 | 64 | 95 | 3 | 3 | 2 | 3 | 82 | 24 | 0 | .293 |
| 1916 CHI N | 2 | 3 | .400 | 3.91 | 12 | 4 | 2 | 48.1 | 52 | 9 | 21 | 0 | 1 | 0 | 0 | 16 | 4 | 0 | .250 |
| 14 yrs. | 239 | 129 | .649 | 2.06 | 481 | 332 | 272 | 3172.1 | 2708 | 673 | 1375 | 57 | 29 | 19 | 48 | 1143 | 235 | 2 | .206 |
| | | | 3rd | | | | | | | | | 8th | | | | | | | |
| 10 yrs. | 188 | 85 | .689 | 1.80 | 346 | 241 | 206 | 2329 | 1879 | 445 | 1043 | 50 | 21 | 12 | 39 | 852 | 166 | 2 | .195 |
| | 2nd | | 2nd | 1st | 8th | | 4th | 5th | | | 8th | 1st | 10th | | 6th | | | | |

### WORLD SERIES

| | | | | | | | | | | | | | | | | | | | |
|---|---|---|---|---|---|---|---|---|---|---|---|---|---|---|---|---|---|---|---|
| 1906 CHI N | 1 | 2 | .333 | 3.66 | 3 | 3 | 2 | 19.2 | 14 | 4 | 12 | 1 | 0 | 0 | 0 | 6 | 2 | 0 | .333 |
| 1907 | 1 | 0 | 1.000 | 0.00 | 1 | 1 | 1 | 9 | 7 | 1 | 4 | 1 | 0 | 0 | 0 | 3 | 0 | 0 | .000 |
| 1908 | 2 | 0 | 1.000 | 0.00 | 2 | 1 | 1 | 11 | 6 | 1 | 5 | 1 | 1 | 0 | 0 | 4 | 0 | 0 | .000 |
| 1910 | 1 | 2 | .333 | 5.00 | 3 | 2 | 1 | 18 | 23 | 7 | 14 | 0 | 1 | 0 | 0 | 7 | 0 | 0 | .000 |
| 4 yrs. | 5 | 4 | .556 | 2.81 | 9 | 7 | 5 | 57.2 | 50 | 13 | 35 | 3 | 2 | 0 | 0 | 20 | 2 | 0 | .100 |
| | 8th | 7th | | | | | 10th | | | | | 2nd | 2nd | | | | | | |

## Warren Brusstar

**BRUSSTAR, WARREN SCOTT**
B. Feb. 2, 1952, Oakland, Calif.　　　　　BR TR 6'3" 200 lbs.

| | | | | | | | | | | | | | | | | | | | |
|---|---|---|---|---|---|---|---|---|---|---|---|---|---|---|---|---|---|---|---|
| 1977 PHI N | 7 | 2 | .778 | 2.66 | 46 | 0 | 0 | 71 | 64 | 24 | 46 | 0 | 7 | 2 | 3 | 6 | 0 | 0 | .000 |
| 1978 | 6 | 3 | .667 | 2.33 | 58 | 0 | 0 | 89 | 74 | 30 | 60 | 0 | 6 | 3 | 0 | 7 | 1 | 0 | .143 |
| 1979 | 1 | 0 | 1.000 | 7.07 | 13 | 0 | 0 | 14 | 23 | 4 | 3 | 0 | 1 | 0 | 1 | 0 | 0 | 0 | – |
| 1980 | 2 | 2 | .500 | 3.69 | 26 | 0 | 0 | 39 | 42 | 13 | 21 | 0 | 2 | 2 | 0 | 1 | 0 | 0 | .000 |
| 1981 | 0 | 1 | .000 | 4.50 | 14 | 0 | 0 | 12 | 12 | 10 | 8 | 0 | 0 | 1 | 0 | 0 | 0 | 0 | – |
| 1982 2 teams | | | PHI N (22G 2–3) | | | | CHI A (10G 2–0) | | | | | | | | | | | | |
| " total | 4 | 3 | .571 | 4.17 | 32 | 0 | 0 | 41 | 50 | 8 | 19 | 0 | 4 | 3 | 2 | 2 | 0 | 0 | .000 |
| 1983 CHI N | 3 | 1 | .750 | 2.35 | 59 | 0 | 0 | 80.1 | 67 | 37 | 46 | 0 | 3 | 1 | 1 | 4 | 0 | 0 | .000 |
| 1984 | 1 | 1 | .500 | 3.11 | 41 | 0 | 0 | 63.2 | 57 | 21 | 36 | 0 | 1 | 1 | 3 | 5 | 1 | 0 | .200 |
| 1985 | 4 | 3 | .571 | 6.05 | 51 | 0 | 0 | 74.1 | 87 | 36 | 34 | 0 | 4 | 3 | 4 | 7 | 1 | 0 | .143 |
| 9 yrs. | 28 | 16 | .636 | 3.51 | 340 | 0 | 0 | 484.1 | 476 | 183 | 273 | 0 | 28 | 16 | 14 | 32 | 3 | 0 | .094 |
| 3 yrs. | 8 | 5 | .615 | 3.83 | 151 | 0 | 0 | 218.1 | 211 | 94 | 116 | 0 | 8 | 5 | 8 | 16 | 2 | 0 | .125 |

### DIVISIONAL PLAYOFF SERIES

| | | | | | | | | | | | | | | | | | | | |
|---|---|---|---|---|---|---|---|---|---|---|---|---|---|---|---|---|---|---|---|
| 1981 PHI N | 0 | 0 | – | 4.91 | 2 | 0 | 0 | 3.2 | 5 | 1 | 3 | 0 | 0 | 0 | 0 | 0 | 0 | 0 | – |

### LEAGUE CHAMPIONSHIP SERIES

| | | | | | | | | | | | | | | | | | | | |
|---|---|---|---|---|---|---|---|---|---|---|---|---|---|---|---|---|---|---|---|
| 1977 PHI N | 0 | 0 | – | 3.38 | 2 | 0 | 0 | 2.2 | 1 | 2 | 0 | 0 | 0 | 0 | 0 | 0 | 0 | 0 | – |
| 1978 | 0 | 0 | – | 0.00 | 3 | 0 | 0 | 2.2 | 2 | 1 | 0 | 0 | 0 | 0 | 0 | 0 | 0 | 0 | – |
| 1980 | 1 | 0 | 1.000 | 3.38 | 2 | 0 | 0 | 2.2 | 1 | 1 | 0 | 0 | 1 | 0 | 0 | 1 | 0 | 0 | .000 |
| 1984 CHI N | 0 | 0 | – | 0.00 | 3 | 0 | 0 | 4.2 | 6 | 0 | 1 | 0 | 0 | 0 | 0 | 1 | 0 | 0 | .000 |
| 4 yrs. | 1 | 0 | 1.000 | 1.42 | 10 | 0 | 0 | 12.2 | 11 | 3 | 3 | 0 | 1 | 0 | 0 | 2 | 0 | 0 | .000 |

### WORLD SERIES

| | | | | | | | | | | | | | | | | | | | |
|---|---|---|---|---|---|---|---|---|---|---|---|---|---|---|---|---|---|---|---|
| 1980 PHI N | 0 | 0 | – | 0.00 | 1 | 0 | 0 | 2.1 | 0 | 1 | 0 | 0 | 0 | 0 | 0 | 0 | 0 | 0 | – |

## Clay Bryant

**BRYANT, CLAIBORNE HENRY**
B. Nov. 16, 1911, Madison Heights, Va.　　　　　BR TR 6'2½" 195 lbs.

| | | | | | | | | | | | | | | | | | | | |
|---|---|---|---|---|---|---|---|---|---|---|---|---|---|---|---|---|---|---|---|
| 1935 CHI N | 1 | 2 | .333 | 5.16 | 9 | 1 | 0 | 22.2 | 34 | 7 | 13 | 0 | 1 | 2 | 2 | 6 | 2 | 1 | .333 |
| 1936 | 1 | 2 | .333 | 3.30 | 26 | 0 | 0 | 57.1 | 57 | 24 | 35 | 0 | 1 | 2 | 0 | 12 | 5 | 0 | .417 |
| 1937 | 9 | 3 | .750 | 4.26 | 38 | 10 | 4 | 135.1 | 117 | 78 | 75 | 1 | 7 | 0 | 3 | 45 | 14 | 1 | .311 |
| 1938 | 19 | 11 | .633 | 3.10 | 44 | 30 | 17 | 270.1 | 235 | 125 | 135 | 3 | 4 | 1 | 2 | 106 | 24 | 3 | .226 |
| 1939 | 2 | 1 | .667 | 5.74 | 4 | 4 | 2 | 31.1 | 42 | 14 | 9 | 0 | 0 | 0 | 0 | 14 | 3 | 0 | .214 |
| 1940 | 0 | 1 | .000 | 4.78 | 8 | 0 | 0 | 26.1 | 26 | 14 | 5 | 0 | 0 | 1 | 0 | 9 | 3 | 0 | .333 |
| 6 yrs. | 32 | 20 | .615 | 3.73 | 129 | 45 | 23 | 543.1 | 511 | 262 | 272 | 4 | 13 | 6 | 7 | 192 | 51 | 5 | .266 |
| 6 yrs. | 32 | 20 | .615 | 3.73 | 129 | 45 | 23 | 543.1 | 511 | 262 | 272 | 4 | 13 | 6 | 7 | 192 | 51 | 5 | .266 |

### WORLD SERIES

| | | | | | | | | | | | | | | | | | | | |
|---|---|---|---|---|---|---|---|---|---|---|---|---|---|---|---|---|---|---|---|
| 1938 CHI N | 0 | 1 | .000 | 6.75 | 1 | 1 | 0 | 5.1 | 6 | 5 | 3 | 0 | 0 | 0 | 0 | 2 | 0 | 0 | .000 |

## Charlie Brynan

**BRYNAN, CHARLES RULEY (Tod)**　　　　　BR TR
B. July, 1863, Philadelphia, Pa.　　　D. May 10, 1925, Philadelphia, Pa.

| | | | | | | | | | | | | | | | | | | | |
|---|---|---|---|---|---|---|---|---|---|---|---|---|---|---|---|---|---|---|---|
| 1888 CHI N | 2 | 1 | .667 | 6.48 | 3 | 3 | 2 | 25 | 29 | 7 | 11 | 0 | 0 | 0 | 0 | 11 | 2 | 0 | .182 |
| 1891 BOS N | 0 | 1 | .000 | 54.00 | 1 | 1 | 0 | 1 | 4 | 3 | 0 | 0 | 0 | 0 | 0 | 0 | 0 | 0 | – |
| 2 yrs. | 2 | 2 | .500 | 8.31 | 4 | 4 | 2 | 26 | 33 | 10 | 11 | 0 | 0 | 0 | 0 | 11 | 2 | 0 | .182 |
| 1 yr. | 2 | 1 | .667 | 6.48 | 3 | 3 | 2 | 25 | 29 | 7 | 11 | 0 | 0 | 0 | 0 | 11 | 2 | 0 | .182 |

## Bob Buhl

**BUHL, ROBERT RAY**　　　　　BR TR 6'2" 180 lbs.
B. Aug. 12, 1928, Saginaw, Mich.　　　　　BB 1958-60,1966

| | | | | | | | | | | | | | | | | | | | |
|---|---|---|---|---|---|---|---|---|---|---|---|---|---|---|---|---|---|---|---|
| 1953 MIL N | 13 | 8 | .619 | 2.97 | 30 | 18 | 8 | 154.1 | 133 | 73 | 83 | 3 | 4 | 2 | 0 | 53 | 6 | 0 | .113 |
| 1954 | 2 | 7 | .222 | 4.00 | 31 | 14 | 2 | 110.1 | 117 | 65 | 57 | 1 | 0 | 2 | 3 | 31 | 1 | 0 | .032 |
| 1955 | 13 | 11 | .542 | 3.21 | 38 | 27 | 11 | 201.2 | 168 | 109 | 117 | 1 | 1 | 1 | 1 | 57 | 6 | 0 | .105 |
| 1956 | 18 | 8 | .692 | 3.32 | 38 | 33 | 13 | 216.2 | 190 | 105 | 86 | 2 | 1 | 0 | 0 | 73 | 7 | 0 | .096 |
| 1957 | 18 | 7 | .720 | 2.74 | 34 | 31 | 14 | 216.2 | 191 | 121 | 117 | 2 | 0 | 0 | 0 | 73 | 6 | 0 | .082 |
| 1958 | 5 | 2 | .714 | 3.45 | 11 | 10 | 3 | 73 | 74 | 30 | 27 | 0 | 0 | 0 | 0 | 25 | 5 | 0 | .200 |
| 1959 | 15 | 9 | .625 | 2.86 | 31 | 25 | 12 | 198 | 181 | 74 | 105 | 4 | 0 | 1 | 0 | 70 | 4 | 0 | .057 |
| 1960 | 16 | 9 | .640 | 3.09 | 36 | 33 | 11 | 238.2 | 202 | 103 | 121 | 2 | 1 | 0 | 0 | 89 | 14 | 0 | .157 |
| 1961 | 9 | 10 | .474 | 4.11 | 32 | 28 | 9 | 188.1 | 180 | 98 | 77 | 0 | 1 | 0 | 0 | 60 | 4 | 0 | .067 |
| 1962 2 teams | | | MIL N (1G 0–1) | | | | CHI N (34G 12–13) | | | | | | | | | | | | |
| " | 12 | 14 | .462 | 3.87 | 35 | 31 | 8 | 214 | 210 | 98 | 110 | 1 | 0 | 0 | 0 | 70 | 0 | 0 | .000 |
| 1963 CHI N | 11 | 14 | .440 | 3.38 | 37 | 34 | 6 | 226 | 219 | 62 | 108 | 0 | 0 | 0 | 0 | 74 | 8 | 0 | .108 |
| 1964 | 15 | 14 | .517 | 3.83 | 36 | 35 | 11 | 227.2 | 208 | 68 | 107 | 3 | 0 | 0 | 0 | 73 | 7 | 0 | .096 |
| 1965 | 13 | 11 | .542 | 4.39 | 32 | 31 | 2 | 184.1 | 207 | 57 | 92 | 0 | 0 | 0 | 0 | 67 | 4 | 0 | .060 |
| 1966 2 teams | | | CHI N (1G 0–0) | | | | PHI N (32G 6–8) | | | | | | | | | | | | |
| " total | 6 | 8 | .429 | 4.96 | 33 | 19 | 1 | 134.1 | 160 | 40 | 60 | 0 | 2 | 2 | 1 | 42 | 4 | 0 | .095 |

| | W | L | PCT | ERA | G | GS | CG | IP | H | BB | SO | ShO | Relief Pitching W | L | SV | BATTING AB | H | HR | BA |
|---|---|---|---|---|---|---|---|---|---|---|---|---|---|---|---|---|---|---|---|

## Bob Buhl continued

| | W | L | PCT | ERA | G | GS | CG | IP | H | BB | SO | ShO | W | L | SV | AB | H | HR | BA |
|---|---|---|---|---|---|---|---|---|---|---|---|---|---|---|---|---|---|---|---|
| 1967 PHI N | 0 | 0 | – | 13.50 | 3 | 0 | 0 | 2.2 | 6 | 2 | 1 | 0 | 0 | 0 | 0 | 0 | 0 | 0 | – |
| 15 yrs. | 166 | 132 | .557 | 3.55 | 457 | 369 | 111 | 2586.2 | 2446 | 1105 | 1268 | 20 | 9 | 8 | 6 | 857 | 76 | 0 | .089 |
| 5 yrs. | 51 | 52 | .495 | 3.83 | 140 | 131 | 27 | 852.1 | 842 | 282 | 417 | 4 | 0 | 0 | 0 | 284 | 19 | 0 | .067 |
| WORLD SERIES | | | | | | | | | | | | | | | | | | | |
| 1957 MIL N | 0 | 1 | .000 | 10.80 | 2 | 2 | 0 | 3.1 | 6 | 6 | 4 | 0 | 0 | 0 | 0 | 1 | 0 | 0 | .000 |

## Freddie Burdette

BURDETTE, FREDDIE THOMASON　　　　　　　BR TR 6'1"　　170 lbs.
B. Sept. 15, 1936, Moultrie, Ga.

| | W | L | PCT | ERA | G | GS | CG | IP | H | BB | SO | ShO | W | L | SV | AB | H | HR | BA |
|---|---|---|---|---|---|---|---|---|---|---|---|---|---|---|---|---|---|---|---|
| 1962 CHI N | 0 | 0 | – | 3.72 | 8 | 0 | 0 | 9.2 | 5 | 8 | 5 | 0 | 0 | 0 | 1 | 1 | 0 | 0 | .000 |
| 1963 | 0 | 0 | – | 3.86 | 4 | 0 | 0 | 4.2 | 5 | 2 | 1 | 0 | 0 | 0 | 0 | 0 | 0 | 0 | – |
| 1964 | 1 | 0 | 1.000 | 3.15 | 18 | 0 | 0 | 20 | 17 | 10 | 4 | 0 | 1 | 0 | 0 | 1 | 1 | 0 | 1.000 |
| 3 yrs. | 1 | 0 | 1.000 | 3.41 | 30 | 0 | 0 | 34.1 | 27 | 20 | 10 | 0 | 1 | 0 | 1 | 2 | 1 | 0 | .500 |
| 3 yrs. | 1 | 0 | 1.000 | 3.41 | 30 | 0 | 0 | 34.1 | 27 | 20 | 10 | 0 | 1 | 0 | 1 | 2 | 1 | 0 | .500 |

## Lew Burdette

BURDETTE, SELVA LEWIS　　　　　　　BR TR 6'2"　　180 lbs.
B. Nov. 22, 1926, Nitro, W. Va.

| | W | L | PCT | ERA | G | GS | CG | IP | H | BB | SO | ShO | W | L | SV | AB | H | HR | BA |
|---|---|---|---|---|---|---|---|---|---|---|---|---|---|---|---|---|---|---|---|
| 1950 NY A | 0 | 0 | – | 6.75 | 2 | 0 | 0 | 1.1 | 3 | 0 | 0 | 0 | 0 | 0 | 0 | 0 | 0 | 0 | – |
| 1951 BOS N | 0 | 0 | – | 6.23 | 3 | 0 | 0 | 4.1 | 6 | 5 | 1 | 0 | 0 | 0 | 0 | 1 | 0 | 0 | .000 |
| 1952 | 6 | 11 | .353 | 3.61 | 45 | 9 | 5 | 137 | 138 | 47 | 47 | 0 | 2 | 8 | 7 | 35 | 4 | 0 | .114 |
| 1953 MIL N | 15 | 5 | .750 | 3.24 | 46 | 13 | 6 | 175 | 177 | 56 | 58 | 1 | 8 | 0 | 8 | 53 | 9 | 0 | .170 |
| 1954 | 15 | 14 | .517 | 2.76 | 38 | 32 | 13 | 238 | 224 | 62 | 79 | 4 | 1 | 1 | 0 | 79 | 7 | 0 | .089 |
| 1955 | 13 | 8 | .619 | 4.03 | 42 | 33 | 11 | 230 | 253 | 73 | 70 | 2 | 2 | 1 | 0 | 86 | 20 | 0 | .233 |
| 1956 | 19 | 10 | .655 | 2.70 | 39 | 35 | 16 | 256.1 | 234 | 52 | 110 | 6 | 0 | 0 | 1 | 86 | 16 | 0 | .186 |
| 1957 | 17 | 9 | .654 | 3.72 | 37 | 33 | 14 | 256.2 | 260 | 59 | 78 | 1 | 2 | 1 | 0 | 88 | 13 | 2 | .148 |
| 1958 | 20 | 10 | .667 | 2.91 | 40 | 36 | 19 | 275.1 | 279 | 50 | 113 | 3 | 2 | 0 | 0 | 99 | 24 | 3 | .242 |
| 1959 | 21 | 15 | .583 | 4.07 | 41 | 39 | 20 | 289.2 | 312 | 38 | 105 | 4 | 0 | 0 | 1 | 104 | 21 | 0 | .202 |
| 1960 | 19 | 13 | .594 | 3.36 | 45 | 32 | 18 | 275.2 | 277 | 35 | 83 | 4 | 3 | 2 | 4 | 91 | 16 | 2 | .176 |
| 1961 | 18 | 11 | .621 | 4.00 | 40 | 36 | 14 | 272.1 | 295 | 33 | 92 | 3 | 2 | 0 | 0 | 103 | 21 | 3 | .204 |
| 1962 | 10 | 9 | .526 | 4.89 | 37 | 19 | 6 | 143.2 | 172 | 23 | 59 | 1 | 3 | 1 | 2 | 51 | 9 | 0 | .176 |
| 1963 2 teams | | | | MIL | N | (15G 6–5) | | STL | N | (21G 3–8) | | | | | | | | | |
| " total | 9 | 13 | .409 | 3.70 | 36 | 27 | 7 | 182.2 | 177 | 40 | 73 | 1 | 1 | 2 | 2 | 57 | 4 | 0 | .070 |
| 1964 2 teams | | | | STL | N | (8G 1–0) | | CHI | N | (28G 9–9) | | | | | | | | | |
| " total | 10 | 9 | .526 | 4.66 | 36 | 17 | 8 | 141 | 162 | 22 | 43 | 2 | 2 | 1 | 0 | 44 | 12 | 2 | .273 |
| 1965 2 teams | | | | CHI | N | (7G 0–2) | | PHI | N | (19G 3–3) | | | | | | | | | |
| " total | 3 | 5 | .375 | 5.44 | 26 | 12 | 1 | 91 | 121 | 21 | 28 | 1 | 0 | 0 | 0 | 26 | 8 | 0 | .308 |
| 1966 CAL A | 7 | 2 | .778 | 3.39 | 54 | 0 | 0 | 79.2 | 80 | 12 | 27 | 0 | 7 | 2 | 5 | 8 | 1 | 0 | .125 |
| 1967 | 1 | 0 | 1.000 | 4.91 | 19 | 0 | 0 | 18.1 | 16 | 0 | 8 | 0 | 1 | 0 | 0 | 0 | 0 | 0 | – |
| 18 yrs. | 203 | 144 | .585 | 3.66 | 626 | 373 | 158 | 3068 | 3186 | 628 | 1074 | 33 | 36 | 19 | 31 | 1011 | 185 | 12 | .183 |
| 2 yrs. | 9 | 11 | .450 | 4.94 | 35 | 20 | 8 | 151.1 | 178 | 23 | 45 | 2 | 1 | 1 | 0 | 49 | 14 | 2 | .286 |
| WORLD SERIES | | | | | | | | | | | | | | | | | | | |
| 1957 MIL N | 3 | 0 | 1.000 | 0.67 | 3 | 3 | 3 | 27 | 21 | 4 | 13 | 2 | 0 | 0 | 0 | 8 | 0 | 0 | .000 |
| 1958 | 1 | 2 | .333 | 5.64 | 3 | 3 | 1 | 22.1 | 22 | 4 | 12 | 0 | 0 | 0 | 0 | 9 | 1 | 1 | .111 |
| 2 yrs. | 4 | 2 | .667 | 2.92 | 6 | 6 | 4 | 49.1 | 43 | 8 | 25 | 2 4th | 0 | 0 | 0 | 17 | 1 | 1 | .059 |

## Tom Burns

BURNS, THOMAS EVERETT　　　　　　　BL TR 5'7"　　152 lbs.
B. Mar. 30, 1857, Honesdale, Pa.　　D. Mar. 19, 1902, Jersey City, N. J.
Manager 1892, 1898-99.

| | W | L | PCT | ERA | G | GS | CG | IP | H | BB | SO | ShO | W | L | SV | AB | H | HR | BA |
|---|---|---|---|---|---|---|---|---|---|---|---|---|---|---|---|---|---|---|---|
| 1880 CHI N | 0 | 0 | – | 0.00 | 1 | 0 | 0 | 1.1 | 2 | 2 | 1 | 0 | 0 | 0 | 0 | * | | | |

## Ray Burris

BURRIS, BERTRAM RAY　　　　　　　BR TR 6'5"　　200 lbs.
B. Aug. 22, 1950, Idabel, Okla.

| | W | L | PCT | ERA | G | GS | CG | IP | H | BB | SO | ShO | W | L | SV | AB | H | HR | BA |
|---|---|---|---|---|---|---|---|---|---|---|---|---|---|---|---|---|---|---|---|
| 1973 CHI N | 1 | 1 | .500 | 2.91 | 31 | 1 | 0 | 65 | 65 | 27 | 57 | 0 | 0 | 1 | 0 | 7 | 1 | 0 | .143 |
| 1974 | 3 | 5 | .375 | 6.60 | 40 | 5 | 0 | 75 | 91 | 26 | 40 | 0 | 3 | 1 | 1 | 13 | 1 | 0 | .077 |
| 1975 | 15 | 10 | .600 | 4.12 | 36 | 35 | 8 | 238 | 259 | 73 | 108 | 2 | 0 | 0 | 0 | 82 | 15 | 0 | .183 |
| 1976 | 15 | 13 | .536 | 3.11 | 37 | 36 | 10 | 249 | 251 | 70 | 112 | 4 | 0 | 0 | 0 | 81 | 9 | 0 | .111 |
| 1977 | 14 | 16 | .467 | 4.72 | 39 | 39 | 5 | 221 | 270 | 67 | 105 | 1 | 0 | 0 | 0 | 69 | 12 | 1 | .174 |
| 1978 | 7 | 13 | .350 | 4.75 | 40 | 32 | 4 | 199 | 210 | 79 | 94 | 1 | 1 | 1 | 1 | 61 | 7 | 0 | .115 |
| 1979 3 teams | | | | CHI | N | (14G 0–0) | | NY | A | (15G 1–3) | | NY | N | (4G 0–2) | | | | | |
| " total | 1 | 5 | .167 | 5.30 | 33 | 4 | 0 | 71.1 | 84 | 31 | 43 | 0 | 1 | 3 | 0 | 7 | 1 | 0 | .143 |
| 1980 NY N | 7 | 13 | .350 | 4.02 | 29 | 29 | 1 | 170 | 181 | 54 | 83 | 0 | 0 | 0 | 0 | 51 | 5 | 0 | .098 |
| 1981 MON N | 9 | 7 | .563 | 3.04 | 22 | 21 | 4 | 136 | 117 | 41 | 52 | 0 | 0 | 0 | 0 | 37 | 7 | 0 | .189 |
| 1982 | 4 | 14 | .222 | 4.73 | 37 | 15 | 2 | 123.2 | 143 | 53 | 55 | 0 | 4 | 3 | 2 | 28 | 5 | 0 | .179 |
| 1983 | 4 | 7 | .364 | 3.68 | 40 | 17 | 2 | 154 | 139 | 56 | 100 | 1 | 1 | 2 | 0 | 39 | 9 | 0 | .231 |
| 1984 OAK A | 13 | 10 | .565 | 3.15 | 34 | 28 | 5 | 211.2 | 193 | 90 | 93 | 1 | 0 | 0 | 0 | 0 | 0 | 0 | – |
| 1985 MIL A | 9 | 13 | .409 | 4.81 | 29 | 28 | 6 | 170.1 | 182 | 53 | 81 | 0 | 0 | 0 | 0 | 0 | 0 | 0 | – |
| 13 yrs. | 102 | 127 | .445 | 4.10 | 447 | 290 | 47 | 2084 | 2185 | 720 | 1023 | 10 | 11 | 11 | 4 | 475 | 72 | 1 | .152 |
| 7 yrs. | 55 | 58 | .487 | 4.27 | 237 | 148 | 27 | 1068.2 | 1169 | 357 | 530 | 8 | 4 | 3 | 2 | 314 | 45 | 1 | .143 |
| DIVISIONAL PLAYOFF SERIES | | | | | | | | | | | | | | | | | | | |
| 1981 MON N | 0 | 1 | .000 | 5.06 | 1 | 1 | 0 | 5.1 | 7 | 4 | 4 | 0 | 0 | 0 | 0 | 2 | 0 | 0 | .000 |
| LEAGUE CHAMPIONSHIP SERIES | | | | | | | | | | | | | | | | | | | |
| 1981 MON N | 1 | 0 | 1.000 | 0.53 | 2 | 2 | 1 | 17 | 10 | 3 | 4 | 1 | 0 | 0 | 0 | 6 | 0 | 0 | .000 |

## John Burrows

BURROWS, JOHN　　　　　　　BR TL 5'10"　　200 lbs.
B. Oct. 30, 1913, Winnfield, La.

| | W | L | PCT | ERA | G | GS | CG | IP | H | BB | SO | ShO | W | L | SV | AB | H | HR | BA |
|---|---|---|---|---|---|---|---|---|---|---|---|---|---|---|---|---|---|---|---|
| 1943 2 teams | | | | PHI | A | (4G 0–1) | | CHI | N | (23G 0–2) | | | | | | | | | |
| " total | 0 | 3 | .000 | 4.69 | 27 | 2 | 0 | 40.1 | 33 | 25 | 21 | 0 | 0 | 1 | 2 | 4 | 2 | 0 | .500 |

| | W | L | PCT | ERA | G | GS | CG | IP | H | BB | SO | ShO | Relief Pitching W | L | SV | BATTING AB | H | HR | BA |
|---|---|---|---|---|---|---|---|---|---|---|---|---|---|---|---|---|---|---|---|

## John Burrows continued

| | W | L | PCT | ERA | G | GS | CG | IP | H | BB | SO | ShO | W | L | SV | AB | H | HR | BA |
|---|---|---|---|---|---|---|---|---|---|---|---|---|---|---|---|---|---|---|---|
| 1944 CHI N | 0 | 0 | – | 18.00 | 3 | 0 | 0 | 3 | 7 | 3 | 1 | 0 | 0 | 0 | 0 | 0 | 0 | 0 | – |
| 2 yrs. | 0 | 3 | .000 | 5.61 | 30 | 2 | 0 | 43.1 | 40 | 28 | 22 | 0 | 0 | 1 | 2 | 4 | 2 | 0 | .500 |
| 2 yrs. | 0 | 2 | .000 | 5.05 | 26 | 1 | 0 | 35.2 | 32 | 19 | 19 | 0 | 0 | 1 | 2 | 3 | 2 | 0 | .667 |

## Dick Burwell

BURWELL, RICHARD MATTHEW
B. Jan. 23, 1940, Alton, Ill.
BR TR 6'1"   190 lbs.

| | W | L | PCT | ERA | G | GS | CG | IP | H | BB | SO | ShO | W | L | SV | AB | H | HR | BA |
|---|---|---|---|---|---|---|---|---|---|---|---|---|---|---|---|---|---|---|---|
| 1960 CHI N | 0 | 0 | – | 5.59 | 3 | 1 | 0 | 9.2 | 11 | 7 | 1 | 0 | 0 | 0 | 0 | 3 | 1 | 0 | .333 |
| 1961 | 0 | 0 | – | 9.00 | 2 | 0 | 0 | 4 | 6 | 4 | 0 | 0 | 0 | 0 | 0 | 1 | 0 | 0 | .000 |
| 2 yrs. | 0 | 0 | – | 6.59 | 5 | 1 | 0 | 13.2 | 17 | 11 | 1 | 0 | 0 | 0 | 0 | 4 | 1 | 0 | .250 |
| 2 yrs. | 0 | 0 | – | 6.59 | 5 | 1 | 0 | 13.2 | 17 | 11 | 1 | 0 | 0 | 0 | 0 | 4 | 1 | 0 | .250 |

## Guy Bush

BUSH, GUY TERRELL (The Mississippi Mudcat)
B. Aug. 23, 1901, Aberdeen, Miss.   D. July 2, 1985, Shannon, Miss.
BR TR 6'   175 lbs.

| | W | L | PCT | ERA | G | GS | CG | IP | H | BB | SO | ShO | W | L | SV | AB | H | HR | BA |
|---|---|---|---|---|---|---|---|---|---|---|---|---|---|---|---|---|---|---|---|
| 1923 CHI N | 0 | 0 | – | 0.00 | 1 | 0 | 0 | 1 | 0 | 0 | 2 | 0 | 0 | 0 | 0 | 0 | 0 | 0 | – |
| 1924 | 2 | 5 | .286 | 4.02 | 16 | 8 | 4 | 80.2 | 91 | 24 | 36 | 0 | 0 | 1 | 0 | 26 | 4 | 0 | .154 |
| 1925 | 6 | 13 | .316 | 4.30 | 42 | 15 | 5 | 182 | 213 | 52 | 76 | 0 | 4 | 2 | 4 | 57 | 11 | 0 | .193 |
| 1926 | 13 | 9 | .591 | 2.86 | 35 | 16 | 7 | 157.1 | 149 | 42 | 32 | 2 | 6 | 2 | 2 | 48 | 8 | 0 | .167 |
| 1927 | 10 | 10 | .500 | 3.03 | 36 | 22 | 9 | 193.1 | 177 | 79 | 62 | 1 | 3 | 0 | 2 | 65 | 8 | 0 | .123 |
| 1928 | 15 | 6 | .714 | 3.83 | 42 | 24 | 9 | 204.1 | 229 | 86 | 61 | 2 | 4 | 0 | 2 | 73 | 6 | 0 | .082 |
| 1929 | 18 | 7 | .720 | 3.66 | 50 | 29 | 18 | 270.2 | 277 | 107 | 82 | 2 | 2 | 1 | 8 | 91 | 15 | 0 | .165 |
| 1930 | 15 | 10 | .600 | 6.20 | 46 | 25 | 11 | 225 | 291 | 86 | 75 | 0 | 3 | 2 | 3 | 78 | 22 | 0 | .282 |
| 1931 | 16 | 8 | .667 | 4.49 | 39 | 24 | 14 | 180.1 | 190 | 66 | 54 | 1 | 4 | 0 | 2 | 57 | 7 | 0 | .123 |
| 1932 | 19 | 11 | .633 | 3.21 | 40 | 30 | 15 | 238.2 | 262 | 70 | 73 | 1 | 4 | 2 | 0 | 84 | 15 | 0 | .179 |
| 1933 | 20 | 12 | .625 | 2.75 | 41 | 32 | 20 | 258.2 | 261 | 68 | 84 | 4 | 1 | 1 | 2 | 88 | 11 | 0 | .125 |
| 1934 | 18 | 10 | .643 | 3.83 | 40 | 27 | 15 | 209.1 | 213 | 54 | 75 | 1 | 3 | 1 | 2 | 70 | 16 | 0 | .229 |
| 1935 PIT N | 11 | 11 | .500 | 4.32 | 41 | 25 | 8 | 204.1 | 237 | 40 | 42 | 1 | 5 | 1 | 2 | 63 | 8 | 0 | .127 |
| 1936 2 teams | PIT N | (16G 1–3) | | BOS | N | (15G 4–5) | | | | | | | | | | | | | |
| " total | 5 | 8 | .385 | 4.10 | 31 | 11 | 5 | 125 | 147 | 31 | 38 | 0 | 2 | 3 | 2 | 34 | 6 | 0 | .176 |
| 1937 BOS N | 8 | 15 | .348 | 3.54 | 32 | 20 | 11 | 180.2 | 201 | 48 | 56 | 1 | 2 | 3 | 1 | 54 | 6 | 0 | .111 |
| 1938 STL N | 0 | 1 | .000 | 5.06 | 6 | 0 | 0 | 5.1 | 6 | 3 | 1 | 0 | 0 | 1 | 1 | 0 | 0 | 0 | – |
| 1945 CIN N | 0 | 0 | – | 8.31 | 4 | 0 | 0 | 4.1 | 5 | 3 | 1 | 0 | 0 | 0 | 0 | 0 | 0 | 0 | – |
| 17 yrs. | 176 | 136 | .564 | 3.86 | 542 | 308 | 151 | 2721 | 2950 | 859 | 850 | 16 | 43 | 20 | 34 | 888 | 143 | 0 | .161 |
| 12 yrs. | 152 | 101 | .601 | 3.81 | 428 | 252 | 127 | 2201.1 | 2354 | 734 | 712 | 14 | 34 | 12 | 27 | 737 | 123 | 0 | .167 |
| | 6th | 9th | | | | | 3rd | | 9th | | 3rd | | 3rd | | | | | | |

WORLD SERIES

| | W | L | PCT | ERA | G | GS | CG | IP | H | BB | SO | ShO | W | L | SV | AB | H | HR | BA |
|---|---|---|---|---|---|---|---|---|---|---|---|---|---|---|---|---|---|---|---|
| 1929 CHI N | 1 | 0 | 1.000 | 0.82 | 2 | 1 | 1 | 11 | 12 | 2 | 4 | 0 | 0 | 0 | 0 | 3 | 0 | 0 | .000 |
| 1932 | 0 | 1 | .000 | 14.29 | 2 | 2 | 0 | 5.2 | 5 | 6 | 2 | 0 | 0 | 0 | 0 | 1 | 0 | 0 | .000 |
| 2 yrs. | 1 | 1 | .500 | 5.40 | 4 | 3 | 1 | 16.2 | 17 | 8 | 6 | 0 | 0 | 0 | 0 | 4 | 0 | 0 | .000 |

## John Buzhardt

BUZHARDT, JOHN WILLIAM
B. Aug. 15, 1936, Prosperity, S. C.
BR TR 6'2½" 195 lbs.

| | W | L | PCT | ERA | G | GS | CG | IP | H | BB | SO | ShO | W | L | SV | AB | H | HR | BA |
|---|---|---|---|---|---|---|---|---|---|---|---|---|---|---|---|---|---|---|---|
| 1958 CHI N | 3 | 0 | 1.000 | 1.85 | 6 | 2 | 1 | 24.1 | 16 | 7 | 9 | 0 | 1 | 0 | 0 | 8 | 1 | 0 | .125 |
| 1959 | 4 | 5 | .444 | 4.97 | 31 | 10 | 1 | 101.1 | 107 | 29 | 33 | 1 | 1 | 2 | 0 | 29 | 2 | 0 | .069 |
| 1960 PHI N | 5 | 16 | .238 | 3.86 | 30 | 29 | 5 | 200.1 | 198 | 68 | 73 | 0 | 0 | 0 | 0 | 62 | 10 | 0 | .161 |
| 1961 | 6 | 18 | .250 | 4.49 | 41 | 27 | 6 | 202.1 | 200 | 65 | 92 | 1 | 0 | 2 | 0 | 57 | 6 | 0 | .105 |
| 1962 CHI A | 8 | 12 | .400 | 4.19 | 28 | 25 | 8 | 152.1 | 156 | 59 | 64 | 2 | 1 | 0 | 0 | 51 | 6 | 0 | .118 |
| 1963 | 9 | 4 | .692 | 2.42 | 19 | 18 | 6 | 126.1 | 100 | 31 | 59 | 3 | 0 | 0 | 0 | 48 | 4 | 0 | .083 |
| 1964 | 10 | 8 | .556 | 2.98 | 31 | 25 | 8 | 160 | 150 | 35 | 97 | 3 | 0 | 0 | 0 | 54 | 11 | 0 | .204 |
| 1965 | 13 | 8 | .619 | 3.01 | 32 | 30 | 4 | 188.2 | 167 | 56 | 108 | 1 | 0 | 1 | 1 | 56 | 7 | 0 | .125 |
| 1966 | 6 | 11 | .353 | 3.83 | 33 | 22 | 5 | 150.1 | 144 | 30 | 66 | 4 | 1 | 2 | 1 | 43 | 5 | 0 | .116 |
| 1967 3 teams | CHI | A | (28G 3–9) | | BAL | A | (7G 0–1) | | HOU | N | (1G 0–0) | | | | | | | | |
| " total | 3 | 10 | .231 | 4.01 | 36 | 8 | 0 | 101 | 114 | 42 | 40 | 0 | 1 | 5 | 0 | 21 | 4 | 0 | .190 |
| 1968 HOU N | 4 | 4 | .500 | 3.12 | 39 | 4 | 0 | 83.2 | 73 | 35 | 37 | 0 | 3 | 3 | 5 | 16 | 4 | 0 | .250 |
| 11 yrs. | 71 | 96 | .425 | 3.66 | 326 | 200 | 44 | 1490.2 | 1425 | 457 | 678 | 15 | 8 | 15 | 7 | 445 | 60 | 0 | .135 |
| 2 yrs. | 7 | 5 | .583 | 4.37 | 37 | 12 | 2 | 125.2 | 123 | 36 | 42 | 1 | 2 | 2 | 0 | 37 | 3 | 0 | .081 |

## Nixey Callahan

CALLAHAN, JAMES JOSEPH
B. Mar. 18, 1874, Fitchburg, Mass.   D. Oct. 4, 1934, Boston, Mass.
Manager 1903-04, 1912-14, 1916-17.
BR TR 5'10½" 180 lbs.

| | W | L | PCT | ERA | G | GS | CG | IP | H | BB | SO | ShO | W | L | SV | AB | H | HR | BA |
|---|---|---|---|---|---|---|---|---|---|---|---|---|---|---|---|---|---|---|---|
| 1894 PHI N | 1 | 2 | .333 | 9.89 | 9 | 2 | 1 | 33.2 | 62 | 17 | 9 | 0 | 1 | 0 | 2 | 21 | 5 | 0 | .238 |
| 1897 CHI N | 12 | 9 | .571 | 4.03 | 23 | 22 | 21 | 189.2 | 221 | 55 | 52 | 1 | 0 | 1 | 0 | 360 | 105 | 3 | .292 |
| 1898 | 20 | 10 | .667 | 2.46 | 31 | 31 | 30 | 274.1 | 267 | 71 | 73 | 2 | 0 | 0 | 0 | 164 | 43 | 0 | .262 |
| 1899 | 21 | 12 | .636 | 3.06 | 35 | 34 | 33 | 294.1 | 327 | 76 | 77 | 3 | 1 | 0 | 0 | 150 | 39 | 0 | .260 |
| 1900 | 13 | 16 | .448 | 3.82 | 32 | 32 | 32 | 285.1 | 347 | 74 | 77 | 2 | 0 | 0 | 0 | 115 | 27 | 0 | .235 |
| 1901 CHI A | 15 | 8 | .652 | 2.42 | 27 | 22 | 20 | 215.1 | 195 | 50 | 70 | 1 | 1 | 2 | 0 | 118 | 39 | 1 | .331 |
| 1902 | 16 | 14 | .533 | 3.60 | 35 | 31 | 29 | 282.1 | 287 | 89 | 75 | 2 | 1 | 0 | 0 | 218 | 51 | 0 | .234 |
| 1903 | 1 | 2 | .333 | 4.50 | 3 | 3 | 3 | 28 | 42 | 5 | 12 | 0 | 0 | 0 | 0 | 439 | 128 | 2 | .292 |
| 8 yrs. | 99 | 73 | .576 | 3.39 | 195 | 177 | 169 | 1603 | 1748 | 437 | 445 | 11 | 4 | 3 | 2 | * | | | |
| 4 yrs. | 66 | 47 | .584 | 3.29 | 121 | 119 | 116 | 1043.2 | 1162 | 276 | 279 | 8 | 1 | 1 | 0 | 789 | 214 | 3 | .271 |

## Dick Calmus

CALMUS, RICHARD LEE
B. Jan. 7, 1944, Los Angeles, Calif.
BR TR 6'4" 187 lbs.

| | W | L | PCT | ERA | G | GS | CG | IP | H | BB | SO | ShO | W | L | SV | AB | H | HR | BA |
|---|---|---|---|---|---|---|---|---|---|---|---|---|---|---|---|---|---|---|---|
| 1963 LA N | 3 | 1 | .750 | 2.66 | 21 | 1 | 0 | 44 | 32 | 16 | 25 | 0 | 3 | 0 | 0 | 6 | 0 | 0 | .000 |
| 1967 CHI N | 0 | 0 | – | 8.31 | 1 | 1 | 0 | 4.1 | 5 | 0 | 1 | 0 | 0 | 0 | 0 | 2 | 1 | 0 | .500 |
| 2 yrs. | 3 | 1 | .750 | 3.17 | 22 | 2 | 0 | 48.1 | 37 | 16 | 26 | 0 | 3 | 0 | 0 | 8 | 1 | 0 | .125 |
| 1 yr. | 0 | 0 | – | 8.31 | 1 | 1 | 0 | 4.1 | 5 | 0 | 1 | 0 | 0 | 0 | 0 | 2 | 1 | 0 | .500 |

| | W | L | PCT | ERA | G | GS | CG | IP | H | BB | SO | ShO | Relief Pitching W | L | SV | BATTING AB | H | HR | BA |
|---|---|---|---|---|---|---|---|---|---|---|---|---|---|---|---|---|---|---|---|

## Kid Camp

**CAMP, WINFIELD SCOTT**
Brother of Llewellan Camp.
B. 1870, Columbus, Ohio    D. Mar. 2, 1895, Omaha, Neb.     6'    160 lbs.

| | W | L | PCT | ERA | G | GS | CG | IP | H | BB | SO | ShO | W | L | SV | AB | H | HR | BA |
|---|---|---|---|---|---|---|---|---|---|---|---|---|---|---|---|---|---|---|---|
| 1892 PIT N | 0 | 1 | .000 | 6.26 | 4 | 1 | 1 | 23 | 31 | 9 | 6 | 0 | 0 | 0 | 0 | 11 | 1 | 0 | .091 |
| 1894 CHI N | 0 | 1 | .000 | 6.55 | 3 | 2 | 2 | 22 | 34 | 12 | 6 | 0 | 0 | 0 | 0 | 11 | 0 | 0 | .000 |
| 2 yrs. | 0 | 2 | .000 | 6.40 | 7 | 3 | 3 | 45 | 65 | 21 | 12 | 0 | 0 | 0 | 0 | 22 | 1 | 0 | .045 |
| 1 yr. | 0 | 1 | .000 | 6.55 | 3 | 2 | 2 | 22 | 34 | 12 | 6 | 0 | 0 | 0 | 0 | 11 | 0 | 0 | .000 |

## Bill Campbell

**CAMPBELL, WILLIAM RICHARD**
B. Aug. 9, 1948, Highland Park, Mich.     BR TR 6'3"    185 lbs.

| | W | L | PCT | ERA | G | GS | CG | IP | H | BB | SO | ShO | W | L | SV | AB | H | HR | BA |
|---|---|---|---|---|---|---|---|---|---|---|---|---|---|---|---|---|---|---|---|
| 1973 MIN A | 3 | 3 | .500 | 3.14 | 28 | 2 | 0 | 51.2 | 44 | 20 | 42 | 0 | 3 | 1 | 7 | 0 | 0 | 0 | — |
| 1974 | 8 | 7 | .533 | 2.63 | 63 | 0 | 0 | 120 | 109 | 55 | 89 | 0 | 8 | 7 | 19 | 0 | 0 | 0 | — |
| 1975 | 4 | 6 | .400 | 3.79 | 47 | 7 | 2 | 121 | 119 | 46 | 76 | 1 | 1 | 4 | 5 | 1 | 0 | 0 | .000 |
| 1976 | 17 | 5 | .773 | 3.01 | 78 | 0 | 0 | 167.2 | 145 | 62 | 115 | 0 | 17 | 5 | 20 | 0 | 0 | 0 | — |
| 1977 BOS A | 13 | 9 | .591 | 2.96 | 69 | 0 | 0 | 140 | 112 | 60 | 114 | 0 | 13 | 9 | 31 | 0 | 0 | 0 | — |
| 1978 | 7 | 5 | .583 | 3.91 | 29 | 0 | 0 | 50.2 | 62 | 17 | 47 | 0 | 7 | 5 | 4 | 0 | 0 | 0 | — |
| 1979 | 3 | 4 | .429 | 4.25 | 41 | 0 | 0 | 55 | 55 | 23 | 25 | 0 | 3 | 4 | 9 | 0 | 0 | 0 | — |
| 1980 | 4 | 0 | 1.000 | 4.83 | 23 | 0 | 0 | 41 | 44 | 22 | 17 | 0 | 4 | 0 | 0 | 0 | 0 | 0 | — |
| 1981 | 1 | 1 | .500 | 3.19 | 30 | 0 | 0 | 48 | 45 | 20 | 37 | 0 | 1 | 1 | 7 | 0 | 0 | 0 | — |
| 1982 CHI N | 3 | 6 | .333 | 3.69 | 62 | 0 | 0 | 100 | 89 | 40 | 71 | 0 | 3 | 6 | 8 | 7 | 1 | 0 | .143 |
| 1983 | 6 | 8 | .429 | 4.49 | 82 | 0 | 0 | 122.1 | 128 | 49 | 97 | 0 | 6 | 8 | 8 | 10 | 1 | 0 | .100 |
| 1984 PHI N | 6 | 5 | .545 | 3.43 | 57 | 0 | 0 | 81.1 | 68 | 35 | 52 | 0 | 6 | 5 | 1 | 1 | 0 | 0 | .000 |
| 1985 STL N | 5 | 3 | .625 | 3.50 | 50 | 0 | 0 | 64.1 | 55 | 21 | 41 | 0 | 5 | 3 | 4 | 6 | 2 | 0 | .333 |
| 13 yrs. | 80 | 62 | .563 | 3.49 | 659 | 9 | 2 | 1163 | 1075 | 470 | 823 | 1 | 77 | 58 | 123 | 25 | 4 | 0 | .160 |
| 2 yrs. | 9 | 14 | .391 | 4.13 | 144 | 0 | 0 | 222.1 | 217 | 89 | 168 | 0 | 9 | 14 | 16 | 17 | 2 | 0 | .118 |

LEAGUE CHAMPIONSHIP SERIES

| | W | L | PCT | ERA | G | GS | CG | IP | H | BB | SO | ShO | W | L | SV | AB | H | HR | BA |
|---|---|---|---|---|---|---|---|---|---|---|---|---|---|---|---|---|---|---|---|
| 1985 STL N | 0 | 0 | — | 0.00 | 3 | 0 | 0 | 2.1 | 3 | 0 | 2 | 0 | 0 | 0 | 0 | 0 | 0 | 0 | — |

WORLD SERIES

| | W | L | PCT | ERA | G | GS | CG | IP | H | BB | SO | ShO | W | L | SV | AB | H | HR | BA |
|---|---|---|---|---|---|---|---|---|---|---|---|---|---|---|---|---|---|---|---|
| 1985 STL N | 0 | 0 | — | 2.25 | 3 | 0 | 0 | 4 | 4 | 2 | 5 | 0 | 0 | 0 | 0 | 0 | 0 | 0 | — |

## Doug Capilla

**CAPILLA, DOUGLAS EDMUND**
B. Jan. 7, 1952, Honolulu, Hawaii     BL TL 5'11"    160 lbs.

| | W | L | PCT | ERA | G | GS | CG | IP | H | BB | SO | ShO | W | L | SV | AB | H | HR | BA |
|---|---|---|---|---|---|---|---|---|---|---|---|---|---|---|---|---|---|---|---|
| 1976 STL N | 1 | 0 | 1.000 | 5.40 | 7 | 0 | 0 | 8.1 | 8 | 4 | 5 | 0 | 1 | 0 | 0 | 0 | 0 | 0 | — |
| 1977 2 teams | | | STL | N (2G 0–0) | | | | CIN | N | (22G 7–8) | | | | | | | | | |
| " total | 7 | 8 | .467 | 4.47 | 24 | 16 | 1 | 108.2 | 96 | 61 | 75 | 0 | 0 | 0 | 0 | 34 | 2 | 0 | .059 |
| 1978 CIN N | 0 | 1 | .000 | 9.82 | 6 | 3 | 0 | 11 | 14 | 11 | 9 | 0 | 0 | 0 | 0 | 2 | 0 | 0 | .000 |
| 1979 2 teams | | | CIN | N (5G 1–0) | | | | CHI | N | (13G 0–1) | | | | | | | | | |
| " total | 1 | 1 | .500 | 4.18 | 18 | 1 | 0 | 23.2 | 21 | 12 | 10 | 0 | 1 | 0 | 0 | 1 | 1 | 0 | 1.000 |
| 1980 CHI N | 2 | 8 | .200 | 4.10 | 39 | 11 | 0 | 90 | 82 | 51 | 51 | 0 | 1 | 0 | 0 | 21 | 4 | 0 | .190 |
| 1981 | 1 | 0 | 1.000 | 3.18 | 42 | 0 | 0 | 51 | 52 | 34 | 28 | 0 | 1 | 0 | 0 | 3 | 0 | 0 | .000 |
| 6 yrs. | 12 | 18 | .400 | 4.34 | 136 | 31 | 1 | 292.2 | 273 | 173 | 178 | 0 | 4 | 0 | 0 | 61 | 7 | 0 | .115 |
| 3 yrs. | 3 | 9 | .250 | 3.64 | 94 | 12 | 0 | 158.1 | 148 | 92 | 89 | 0 | 2 | 0 | 0 | 24 | 4 | 0 | .167 |

## Don Cardwell

**CARDWELL, DONALD EUGENE**
B. Dec. 7, 1935, Winston-Salem, N. C.     BR TR 6'4"    210 lbs.

| | W | L | PCT | ERA | G | GS | CG | IP | H | BB | SO | ShO | W | L | SV | AB | H | HR | BA |
|---|---|---|---|---|---|---|---|---|---|---|---|---|---|---|---|---|---|---|---|
| 1957 PHI N | 4 | 8 | .333 | 4.91 | 30 | 19 | 5 | 128.1 | 122 | 42 | 92 | 1 | 0 | 0 | 1 | 35 | 7 | 1 | .200 |
| 1958 | 3 | 6 | .333 | 4.51 | 16 | 14 | 3 | 107.2 | 99 | 37 | 77 | 0 | 0 | 0 | 0 | 38 | 8 | 0 | .211 |
| 1959 | 9 | 10 | .474 | 4.06 | 25 | 22 | 3 | 153 | 135 | 65 | 106 | 1 | 0 | 1 | 0 | 55 | 3 | 1 | .055 |
| 1960 2 teams | | | PHI | N (5G 1–2) | | | | CHI | N | (31G 8–14) | | | | | | | | | |
| " total | 9 | 16 | .360 | 4.38 | 36 | 30 | 6 | 205.1 | 194 | 79 | 150 | 1 | 1 | 2 | 0 | 77 | 16 | 5 | .208 |
| 1961 CHI N | 15 | 14 | .517 | 3.82 | 39 | 38 | 13 | 259.1 | 243 | 88 | 156 | 3 | 0 | 1 | 0 | 95 | 10 | 3 | .105 |
| 1962 | 7 | 16 | .304 | 4.92 | 41 | 29 | 6 | 195.2 | 205 | 60 | 104 | 1 | 1 | 0 | 4 | 61 | 9 | 0 | .148 |
| 1963 PIT N | 13 | 15 | .464 | 3.07 | 33 | 32 | 7 | 213.2 | 195 | 52 | 112 | 2 | 1 | 0 | 0 | 71 | 6 | 0 | .085 |
| 1964 | 1 | 2 | .333 | 2.79 | 4 | 4 | 1 | 19.1 | 15 | 7 | 10 | 1 | 0 | 0 | 0 | 7 | 1 | 0 | .143 |
| 1965 | 13 | 10 | .565 | 3.18 | 37 | 34 | 12 | 240.1 | 214 | 59 | 107 | 2 | 0 | 0 | 0 | 74 | 12 | 2 | .162 |
| 1966 | 6 | 6 | .500 | 4.60 | 32 | 14 | 1 | 101.2 | 112 | 27 | 60 | 0 | 3 | 1 | 1 | 29 | 3 | 0 | .103 |
| 1967 NY N | 5 | 9 | .357 | 3.57 | 26 | 16 | 3 | 118.1 | 112 | 39 | 71 | 3 | 1 | 0 | 0 | 38 | 6 | 1 | .158 |
| 1968 | 7 | 13 | .350 | 2.95 | 29 | 25 | 5 | 180 | 156 | 50 | 82 | 1 | 0 | 0 | 1 | 61 | 3 | 1 | .049 |
| 1969 | 8 | 10 | .444 | 3.01 | 30 | 21 | 4 | 152.1 | 145 | 47 | 60 | 0 | 1 | 1 | 0 | 47 | 8 | 1 | .170 |
| 1970 2 teams | | | NY | N (16G 0–2) | | | | ATL | N | (16G 2–1) | | | | | | | | | |
| " total | 2 | 3 | .400 | 7.69 | 32 | 3 | 1 | 48 | 62 | 19 | 24 | 1 | 1 | 1 | 0 | 10 | 2 | 0 | .200 |
| 14 yrs. | 102 | 138 | .425 | 3.92 | 410 | 301 | 72 | 2123 | 2009 | 671 | 1211 | 17 | 9 | 7 | 7 | 698 | 94 | 15 | .135 |
| 3 yrs. | 30 | 44 | .405 | 4.31 | 111 | 93 | 25 | 632 | 614 | 216 | 389 | 5 | 1 | 3 | 4 | 225 | 33 | 6 | .147 |

WORLD SERIES

| | W | L | PCT | ERA | G | GS | CG | IP | H | BB | SO | ShO | W | L | SV | AB | H | HR | BA |
|---|---|---|---|---|---|---|---|---|---|---|---|---|---|---|---|---|---|---|---|
| 1969 NY N | 0 | 0 | — | 0.00 | 1 | 0 | 0 | 1 | 0 | 0 | 0 | 0 | 0 | 0 | 0 | 0 | 0 | 0 | — |

## Tex Carleton

**CARLETON, JAMES OTTO**
B. Aug. 19, 1906, Comanche, Tex.
D. Jan. 11, 1977, Fort Worth, Tex.     BB TR 6'1½"    180 lbs.
BR 1933-34

| | W | L | PCT | ERA | G | GS | CG | IP | H | BB | SO | ShO | W | L | SV | AB | H | HR | BA |
|---|---|---|---|---|---|---|---|---|---|---|---|---|---|---|---|---|---|---|---|
| 1932 STL N | 10 | 13 | .435 | 4.08 | 44 | 22 | 9 | 196.1 | 198 | 70 | 113 | 3 | 3 | 2 | 0 | 60 | 9 | 1 | .150 |
| 1933 | 17 | 11 | .607 | 3.38 | 44 | 33 | 15 | 277 | 263 | 97 | 147 | 4 | 1 | 1 | 3 | 91 | 17 | 1 | .187 |
| 1934 | 16 | 11 | .593 | 4.26 | 40 | 31 | 16 | 240.2 | 260 | 52 | 103 | 0 | 0 | 1 | 2 | 88 | 17 | 1 | .193 |
| 1935 CHI N | 11 | 8 | .579 | 3.89 | 31 | 22 | 8 | 171 | 169 | 60 | 84 | 0 | 2 | 2 | 1 | 62 | 8 | 0 | .129 |
| 1936 | 14 | 10 | .583 | 3.65 | 35 | 26 | 12 | 197.1 | 204 | 67 | 88 | 4 | 2 | 1 | 1 | 60 | 14 | 3 | .233 |
| 1937 | 16 | 8 | .667 | 3.15 | 32 | 27 | 18 | 208.1 | 183 | 94 | 105 | 4 | 0 | 1 | 0 | 71 | 12 | 0 | .169 |
| 1938 | 10 | 9 | .526 | 5.42 | 33 | 24 | 9 | 167.2 | 213 | 74 | 80 | 0 | 2 | 1 | 0 | 65 | 15 | 0 | .231 |
| 1940 BKN N | 6 | 6 | .500 | 3.81 | 34 | 17 | 4 | 149 | 140 | 47 | 88 | 1 | 2 | 1 | 2 | 43 | 8 | 0 | .186 |
| 8 yrs. | 100 | 76 | .568 | 3.91 | 293 | 202 | 91 | 1607.1 | 1630 | 561 | 808 | 16 | 12 | 10 | 9 | 540 | 100 | 6 | .185 |
| 4 yrs. | 51 | 35 | .593 | 3.97 | 131 | 99 | 47 | 744.1 | 769 | 295 | 357 | 8 | 6 | 5 | 2 | 258 | 49 | 3 | .190 |

WORLD SERIES

| | W | L | PCT | ERA | G | GS | CG | IP | H | BB | SO | ShO | W | L | SV | AB | H | HR | BA |
|---|---|---|---|---|---|---|---|---|---|---|---|---|---|---|---|---|---|---|---|
| 1934 STL N | 0 | 0 | — | 7.36 | 2 | 1 | 0 | 3.2 | 5 | 2 | 2 | 0 | 0 | 0 | 0 | 1 | 0 | 0 | .000 |
| 1935 CHI N | 0 | 1 | .000 | 1.29 | 1 | 1 | 0 | 7 | 6 | 7 | 4 | 0 | 0 | 0 | 0 | 1 | 0 | 0 | .000 |

| | W | L | PCT | ERA | G | GS | CG | IP | H | BB | SO | ShO | Relief Pitching W | L | SV | BATTING AB | H | HR | BA |
|---|---|---|---|---|---|---|---|---|---|---|---|---|---|---|---|---|---|---|---|

## Tex Carleton continued

| | W | L | PCT | ERA | G | GS | CG | IP | H | BB | SO | ShO | W | L | SV | AB | H | HR | BA |
|---|---|---|---|---|---|---|---|---|---|---|---|---|---|---|---|---|---|---|---|
| 1938 | 0 | 0 | — | ∞ | 1 | 0 | 0 | 1 | 2 | 0 | 0 | 0 | 0 | 0 | 0 | 0 | 0 | 0 | — |
| 3 yrs. | 0 | 1 | .000 | 5.06 | 4 | 2 | 0 | 10.2 | 12 | 11 | 6 | 0 | 0 | 0 | 0 | 2 | 0 | 0 | .000 |

## Don Carlsen

CARLSEN, DONALD HERBERT     BR TR 6'1"   175 lbs.
B. Oct. 15, 1926, Chicago, Ill.

| | W | L | PCT | ERA | G | GS | CG | IP | H | BB | SO | ShO | W | L | SV | AB | H | HR | BA |
|---|---|---|---|---|---|---|---|---|---|---|---|---|---|---|---|---|---|---|---|
| 1948 CHI N | 0 | 0 | — | 36.00 | 1 | 0 | 0 | 1 | 5 | 2 | 1 | 0 | 0 | 0 | 0 | 0 | 0 | 0 | — |
| 1951 PIT N | 2 | 3 | .400 | 4.19 | 7 | 6 | 2 | 43 | 50 | 14 | 20 | 0 | 0 | 0 | 0 | 16 | 4 | 0 | .250 |
| 1952 | 0 | 1 | .000 | 10.80 | 5 | 1 | 0 | 10 | 20 | 5 | 2 | 0 | 0 | 0 | 0 | 3 | 1 | 0 | .333 |
| 3 yrs. | 2 | 4 | .333 | 6.00 | 13 | 7 | 2 | 54 | 75 | 21 | 23 | 0 | 0 | 0 | 0 | 19 | 5 | 0 | .263 |
| 1 yr. | 0 | 0 | — | 36.00 | 1 | 0 | 0 | 1 | 5 | 2 | 1 | 0 | 0 | 0 | 0 | 0 | 0 | 0 | — |

## Hal Carlson

CARLSON, HAROLD GUST     BR TR 6'   180 lbs.
B. May 17, 1892, Rockford, Ill.    D. May 28, 1930, Chicago, Ill.

| | W | L | PCT | ERA | G | GS | CG | IP | H | BB | SO | ShO | W | L | SV | AB | H | HR | BA |
|---|---|---|---|---|---|---|---|---|---|---|---|---|---|---|---|---|---|---|---|
| 1917 PIT N | 7 | 11 | .389 | 2.90 | 34 | 17 | 9 | 161.1 | 140 | 49 | 68 | 1 | 3 | 2 | 1 | 49 | 6 | 0 | .122 |
| 1918 | 0 | 1 | .000 | 3.75 | 3 | 2 | 0 | 12 | 12 | 5 | 5 | 0 | 0 | 0 | 0 | 5 | 1 | 0 | .200 |
| 1919 | 8 | 10 | .444 | 2.23 | 22 | 14 | 7 | 141 | 114 | 39 | 49 | 1 | 3 | 1 | 0 | 43 | 7 | 0 | .163 |
| 1920 | 14 | 13 | .519 | 3.36 | 39 | 31 | 16 | 246.2 | 262 | 63 | 62 | 3 | 1 | 0 | 3 | 85 | 23 | 0 | .271 |
| 1921 | 4 | 8 | .333 | 4.27 | 31 | 10 | 3 | 109.2 | 121 | 23 | 37 | 0 | 1 | 3 | 4 | 34 | 10 | 0 | .294 |
| 1922 | 9 | 12 | .429 | 5.70 | 39 | 18 | 6 | 145.1 | 193 | 58 | 64 | 0 | 2 | 4 | 2 | 56 | 15 | 1 | .268 |
| 1923 | 0 | 0 | — | 4.73 | 4 | 0 | 0 | 13.1 | 19 | 2 | 4 | 0 | 0 | 0 | 0 | 5 | 0 | 0 | .000 |
| 1924 PHI N | 8 | 17 | .320 | 4.86 | 38 | 24 | 12 | 203.2 | 267 | 55 | 66 | 1 | 1 | 3 | 2 | 76 | 21 | 2 | .276 |
| 1925 | 13 | 14 | .481 | 4.23 | 35 | 32 | 18 | 234 | 281 | 52 | 80 | 4 | 0 | 1 | 0 | 93 | 17 | 2 | .183 |
| 1926 | 17 | 12 | .586 | 3.23 | 35 | 34 | 20 | 267.1 | 293 | 47 | 55 | 3 | 0 | 0 | 0 | 96 | 23 | 0 | .240 |
| 1927 2 teams | | | PHI | N | (11G 4–5) | CHI | N | (27G 12–8) | | | | | | | | | | | |
| " total | 16 | 13 | .552 | 3.70 | 38 | 31 | 19 | 248 | 281 | 45 | 40 | 2 | 1 | 0 | 1 | 92 | 17 | 0 | .185 |
| 1928 CHI N | 3 | 2 | .600 | 5.91 | 20 | 5 | 2 | 56.1 | 74 | 15 | 11 | 0 | 1 | 0 | 4 | 19 | 5 | 0 | .263 |
| 1929 | 11 | 5 | .688 | 5.16 | 31 | 14 | 6 | 111.2 | 131 | 31 | 35 | 2 | 2 | 2 | 2 | 39 | 9 | 0 | .231 |
| 1930 | 4 | 2 | .667 | 5.05 | 8 | 6 | 3 | 51.2 | 68 | 14 | 14 | 0 | 1 | 0 | 0 | 20 | 5 | 0 | .250 |
| 14 yrs. | 114 | 120 | .487 | 3.97 | 377 | 238 | 121 | 2002 | 2256 | 498 | 590 | 17 | 16 | 16 | 19 | 712 | 159 | 5 | .223 |
| 4 yrs. | 30 | 17 | .638 | 4.34 | 86 | 47 | 26 | 404 | 474 | 87 | 87 | 4 | 5 | 2 | 6 | 145 | 30 | 0 | .207 |

WORLD SERIES

| | W | L | PCT | ERA | G | GS | CG | IP | H | BB | SO | ShO | W | L | SV | AB | H | HR | BA |
|---|---|---|---|---|---|---|---|---|---|---|---|---|---|---|---|---|---|---|---|
| 1929 CHI N | 0 | 0 | — | 6.75 | 2 | 0 | 0 | 4 | 7 | 1 | 3 | 0 | 0 | 0 | 0 | 0 | 0 | 0 | |

## Bob Carpenter

CARPENTER, ROBERT LOUIS     BR TR 6'3"   195 lbs.
B. Dec. 12, 1917, Chicago, Ill.

| | W | L | PCT | ERA | G | GS | CG | IP | H | BB | SO | ShO | W | L | SV | AB | H | HR | BA |
|---|---|---|---|---|---|---|---|---|---|---|---|---|---|---|---|---|---|---|---|
| 1940 NY N | 2 | 0 | 1.000 | 2.73 | 5 | 3 | 2 | 33 | 29 | 14 | 25 | 0 | 0 | 0 | 0 | 10 | 1 | 0 | .100 |
| 1941 | 11 | 6 | .647 | 3.83 | 29 | 19 | 8 | 131.2 | 138 | 42 | 42 | 1 | 1 | 0 | 2 | 45 | 7 | 0 | .156 |
| 1942 | 11 | 10 | .524 | 3.15 | 28 | 25 | 12 | 185.2 | 192 | 51 | 53 | 2 | 1 | 1 | 0 | 65 | 12 | 0 | .185 |
| 1946 | 1 | 3 | .250 | 4.85 | 12 | 6 | 1 | 39 | 37 | 18 | 13 | 1 | 0 | 0 | 0 | 10 | 1 | 0 | .100 |
| 1947 2 teams | | | NY | N | (2G 0–0) | CHI | N | (4G 0–1) | | | | | | | | | | | |
| " total | 0 | 1 | .000 | 6.97 | 6 | 1 | 0 | 10.1 | 15 | 7 | 1 | 0 | 0 | 0 | 0 | 1 | 1 | 0 | 1.000 |
| 5 yrs. | 25 | 20 | .556 | 3.60 | 80 | 54 | 23 | 399.2 | 411 | 132 | 134 | 4 | 2 | 1 | 2 | 131 | 22 | 0 | .168 |
| 1 yr. | 0 | 1 | .000 | 4.91 | 4 | 1 | 0 | 7.1 | 10 | 4 | 1 | 0 | 0 | 0 | 0 | 1 | 1 | 0 | 1.000 |

## Alex Carson

CARSON, ALBERT JAMES (Soldier)     TR
B. Aug. 22, 1882, Chicago, Ill.    D. Nov. 26, 1962, San Diego, Calif.

| | W | L | PCT | ERA | G | GS | CG | IP | H | BB | SO | ShO | W | L | SV | AB | H | HR | BA |
|---|---|---|---|---|---|---|---|---|---|---|---|---|---|---|---|---|---|---|---|
| 1910 CHI N | 0 | 0 | — | 4.05 | 2 | 0 | 0 | 6.2 | 6 | 1 | 2 | 0 | 0 | 0 | 0 | 1 | 0 | 0 | .000 |

## Paul Carter

CARTER, PAUL WARREN (Nick)     BL TR 6'3"   175 lbs.
B. May 1, 1894, Lake Park, Ga.    D. Sept. 11, 1984, Lake Park, Ga.

| | W | L | PCT | ERA | G | GS | CG | IP | H | BB | SO | ShO | W | L | SV | AB | H | HR | BA |
|---|---|---|---|---|---|---|---|---|---|---|---|---|---|---|---|---|---|---|---|
| 1914 CLE A | 1 | 3 | .250 | 2.92 | 5 | 4 | 1 | 24.2 | 35 | 5 | 9 | 0 | 0 | 0 | 0 | 7 | 0 | 0 | .000 |
| 1915 | 1 | 1 | .500 | 3.21 | 11 | 2 | 2 | 42 | 44 | 18 | 14 | 0 | 0 | 0 | 0 | 14 | 3 | 0 | .214 |
| 1916 CHI N | 2 | 2 | .500 | 2.75 | 8 | 5 | 2 | 36 | 26 | 17 | 14 | 0 | 0 | 0 | 0 | 12 | 2 | 0 | .167 |
| 1917 | 5 | 8 | .385 | 3.26 | 23 | 13 | 6 | 113.1 | 115 | 19 | 34 | 0 | 1 | 2 | 2 | 33 | 6 | 0 | .182 |
| 1918 | 4 | 1 | .800 | 2.71 | 21 | 4 | 2 | 73 | 78 | 19 | 13 | 0 | 3 | 0 | 1 | 25 | 6 | 0 | .240 |
| 1919 | 5 | 4 | .556 | 2.65 | 28 | 7 | 2 | 85 | 81 | 28 | 17 | 0 | 3 | 0 | 1 | 26 | 7 | 0 | .269 |
| 1920 | 3 | 6 | .333 | 4.67 | 31 | 8 | 2 | 106 | 131 | 36 | 14 | 0 | 1 | 2 | 2 | 35 | 6 | 0 | .171 |
| 7 yrs. | 21 | 25 | .457 | 3.32 | 127 | 43 | 16 | 480 | 510 | 142 | 115 | 0 | 8 | 4 | 6 | 152 | 30 | 0 | .197 |
| 5 yrs. | 19 | 21 | .475 | 3.35 | 111 | 37 | 13 | 413.1 | 431 | 119 | 92 | 0 | 8 | 4 | 6 | 131 | 27 | 0 | .206 |

## Bob Caruthers

CARUTHERS, ROBERT LEE (Parisian Bob)     BL TR 5'7"   138 lbs.
B. Jan. 5, 1864, Memphis, Tenn.    D. Aug. 5, 1911, Peoria, Ill.

| | W | L | PCT | ERA | G | GS | CG | IP | H | BB | SO | ShO | W | L | SV | AB | H | HR | BA |
|---|---|---|---|---|---|---|---|---|---|---|---|---|---|---|---|---|---|---|---|
| 1884 STL AA | 7 | 2 | .778 | 2.61 | 13 | 7 | 7 | 82.2 | 61 | 15 | 58 | 0 | 3 | 0 | 0 | 82 | 21 | 2 | .256 |
| 1885 | 40 | 13 | .755 | 2.07 | 53 | 53 | 53 | 482.1 | 430 | 57 | 190 | 6 | 0 | 0 | 0 | 222 | 50 | 1 | .225 |
| 1886 | 30 | 14 | .682 | 2.32 | 44 | 43 | 42 | 387.1 | 323 | 86 | 166 | 2 | 1 | 0 | 0 | 317 | 106 | 4 | .334 |
| 1887 | 29 | 9 | .763 | 3.30 | 39 | 39 | 39 | 341 | 337 | 61 | 74 | 2 | 0 | 0 | 0 | 364 | 130 | 8 | .357 |
| 1888 BKN AA | 29 | 15 | .659 | 2.39 | 44 | 43 | 42 | 391.2 | 337 | 53 | 140 | 4 | 1 | 0 | 0 | 335 | 77 | 5 | .230 |
| 1889 | 40 | 11 | .784 | 3.13 | 56 | 50 | 46 | 445 | 444 | 104 | 118 | 7 | 4 | 0 | 1 | 172 | 43 | 0 | .250 |
| 1890 BKN N | 23 | 11 | .676 | 3.09 | 37 | 33 | 30 | 300 | 292 | 87 | 64 | 2 | 1 | 0 | 1 | 238 | 63 | 1 | .265 |
| 1891 | 18 | 14 | .563 | 3.12 | 38 | 32 | 29 | 297 | 323 | 107 | 69 | 2 | 1 | 0 | 1 | 171 | 48 | 2 | .281 |
| 1892 STL N | 2 | 8 | .200 | 5.84 | 16 | 10 | 10 | 101.2 | 131 | 27 | 21 | 0 | 0 | 2 | 1 | 513 | 142 | 3 | .277 |
| 9 yrs. | 218 | 97 | .692 2nd | 2.83 | 340 | 310 | 298 | 2828.2 | 2678 | 597 | 900 | 25 | 11 | 2 | 3 | * | | | |

## Hugh Casey

CASEY, HUGH THOMAS     BR TR 6'1"   207 lbs.
B. Oct. 14, 1913, Atlanta, Ga.    D. July 3, 1951, Atlanta, Ga.

| | W | L | PCT | ERA | G | GS | CG | IP | H | BB | SO | ShO | W | L | SV | AB | H | HR | BA |
|---|---|---|---|---|---|---|---|---|---|---|---|---|---|---|---|---|---|---|---|
| 1935 CHI N | 0 | 0 | — | 3.86 | 13 | 0 | 0 | 25.2 | 29 | 14 | 10 | 0 | 0 | 0 | 0 | 6 | 1 | 0 | .167 |
| 1939 BKN N | 15 | 10 | .600 | 2.93 | 40 | 25 | 15 | 227.1 | 228 | 54 | 79 | 0 | 2 | 1 | 1 | 74 | 15 | 0 | .203 |

| | W | L | PCT | ERA | G | GS | CG | IP | H | BB | SO | ShO | Relief Pitching W | L | SV | BATTING AB | H | HR | BA |
|---|---|---|---|---|---|---|---|---|---|---|---|---|---|---|---|---|---|---|---|

## Hugh Casey continued

| | W | L | PCT | ERA | G | GS | CG | IP | H | BB | SO | ShO | W | L | SV | AB | H | HR | BA |
|---|---|---|---|---|---|---|---|---|---|---|---|---|---|---|---|---|---|---|---|
| 1940 | 11 | 8 | .579 | 3.62 | 44 | 10 | 5 | 154 | 136 | 51 | 53 | 2 | 6 | 5 | 2 | 36 | 9 | 0 | .250 |
| 1941 | 14 | 11 | .560 | 3.89 | 45 | 18 | 4 | 162 | 155 | 57 | 61 | 1 | 8 | 4 | 7 | 50 | 6 | 0 | .120 |
| 1942 | 6 | 3 | .667 | 2.25 | 50 | 2 | 0 | 112 | 91 | 44 | 54 | 0 | 6 | 1 | 13 | 27 | 4 | 0 | .148 |
| 1946 | 11 | 5 | .688 | 1.99 | 46 | 1 | 0 | 99.2 | 101 | 33 | 31 | 0 | 11 | 4 | 5 | 22 | 3 | 0 | .136 |
| 1947 | 10 | 4 | .714 | 3.99 | 46 | 0 | 0 | 76.2 | 75 | 29 | 40 | 0 | 10 | 4 | 18 | 18 | 1 | 0 | .056 |
| 1948 | 3 | 0 | 1.000 | 8.00 | 22 | 0 | 0 | 36 | 59 | 17 | 7 | 0 | 3 | 0 | 4 | 7 | 0 | 0 | .000 |
| 1949 2 teams | | | PIT | N | (33G | 4–1) | | NY | A | (4G | 1–0) | | | | | | | | |
| " total | 5 | 1 | .833 | 5.24 | 37 | 0 | 0 | 46.1 | 61 | 22 | 14 | 0 | 5 | 1 | 5 | 4 | 1 | 0 | .250 |
| 9 yrs. | 75 | 42 | .641 | 3.45 | 343 | 56 | 24 | 939.2 | 935 | 321 | 349 | 3 | 51 | 20 | 55 | 244 | 40 | 0 | .164 |
| 1 yr. | 0 | 0 | – | 3.86 | 13 | 0 | 0 | 25.2 | 29 | 14 | 10 | 0 | 0 | 0 | 0 | 6 | 1 | 0 | .167 |
| WORLD SERIES | | | | | | | | | | | | | | | | | | | |
| 1941 BKN N | 0 | 2 | .000 | 3.38 | 3 | 0 | 0 | 5.1 | 9 | 2 | 1 | 0 | 0 | 2 | 0 | 2 | 1 | 0 | .500 |
| 1947 | 2 | 0 | 1.000 | 0.87 | 6 | 0 | 0 | 10.1 | 5 | 1 | 3 | 0 | 2 | 0 | 1 | 1 | 0 | 0 | .000 |
| 2 yrs. | 2 | 2 | .500 | 1.72 | 9 | 0 | 0 | 15.2 | 14 | 3 | 4 | 0 | 2 | 2 | 1 | 3 | 1 | 0 | .333 |
| | | | | | | | | | | | | | 2nd | 2nd | | | | | |

## John Cassidy

**CASSIDY, JOHN P.**
B. 1857, Brooklyn, N. Y.    D. July 2, 1891, Brooklyn, N. Y.          BR TL 5'8"      168 lbs.

| | W | L | PCT | ERA | G | GS | CG | IP | H | BB | SO | ShO | W | L | SV | AB | H | HR | BA |
|---|---|---|---|---|---|---|---|---|---|---|---|---|---|---|---|---|---|---|---|
| 1877 HAR N | 1 | 1 | .500 | 5.00 | 2 | 2 | 2 | 18 | 24 | 1 | 2 | 0 | 0 | 0 | 0 | * | | | |

## Bill Caudill

**CAUDILL, WILLIAM HOLLAND**
B. July 13, 1956, Santa Monica, Calif.          BR TR 6'1"      190 lbs.

| | W | L | PCT | ERA | G | GS | CG | IP | H | BB | SO | ShO | W | L | SV | AB | H | HR | BA |
|---|---|---|---|---|---|---|---|---|---|---|---|---|---|---|---|---|---|---|---|
| 1979 CHI N | 1 | 7 | .125 | 4.80 | 29 | 12 | 0 | 90 | 89 | 41 | 104 | 0 | 1 | 0 | 0 | 17 | 1 | 0 | .059 |
| 1980 | 4 | 6 | .400 | 2.18 | 72 | 2 | 0 | 128 | 100 | 59 | 112 | 0 | 4 | 6 | 1 | 9 | 2 | 0 | .222 |
| 1981 | 1 | 5 | .167 | 5.83 | 30 | 10 | 0 | 71 | 87 | 31 | 45 | 0 | 0 | 0 | 0 | 14 | 2 | 0 | .143 |
| 1982 SEA A | 12 | 9 | .571 | 2.35 | 70 | 0 | 0 | 95.2 | 65 | 35 | 111 | 0 | 12 | 9 | 26 | 0 | 0 | 0 | – |
| 1983 | 2 | 8 | .200 | 4.71 | 63 | 0 | 0 | 72.2 | 70 | 38 | 73 | 0 | 2 | 8 | 26 | 0 | 0 | 0 | – |
| 1984 OAK A | 9 | 7 | .563 | 2.71 | 68 | 0 | 0 | 96.1 | 77 | 31 | 89 | 0 | 9 | 7 | 36 | 1 | 0 | 0 | .000 |
| 1985 TOR A | 4 | 6 | .400 | 2.99 | 67 | 0 | 0 | 69.1 | 53 | 35 | 46 | 0 | 4 | 6 | 14 | 0 | 0 | 0 | – |
| 7 yrs. | 33 | 48 | .407 | 3.47 | 399 | 24 | 0 | 623 | 541 | 270 | 580 | 0 | 32 | 36 | 103 | 41 | 5 | 0 | .122 |
| 3 yrs. | 6 | 18 | .250 | 3.89 | 131 | 24 | 0 | 289 | 276 | 131 | 261 | 0 | 5 | 6 | 1 | 40 | 5 | 0 | .125 |

## Art Ceccarelli

**CECCARELLI, ARTHUR EDWARD (Chic)**
B. Apr. 2, 1930, New Haven, Conn.          BR TL 6'      190 lbs.
BB 1957

| | W | L | PCT | ERA | G | GS | CG | IP | H | BB | SO | ShO | W | L | SV | AB | H | HR | BA |
|---|---|---|---|---|---|---|---|---|---|---|---|---|---|---|---|---|---|---|---|
| 1955 KC A | 4 | 7 | .364 | 5.31 | 31 | 16 | 3 | 123.2 | 123 | 71 | 68 | 1 | 1 | 0 | 0 | 38 | 3 | 0 | .079 |
| 1956 | 0 | 1 | .000 | 7.20 | 3 | 2 | 0 | 10 | 13 | 4 | 2 | 0 | 0 | 0 | 0 | 3 | 0 | 0 | .000 |
| 1957 BAL A | 0 | 5 | .000 | 4.50 | 20 | 8 | 1 | 58 | 62 | 31 | 30 | 0 | 0 | 0 | 0 | 14 | 0 | 0 | .000 |
| 1959 CHI N | 5 | 5 | .500 | 4.76 | 18 | 15 | 4 | 102 | 95 | 37 | 56 | 2 | 0 | 0 | 0 | 33 | 3 | 0 | .091 |
| 1960 | 0 | 0 | – | 5.54 | 7 | 1 | 0 | 13 | 16 | 4 | 10 | 0 | 0 | 0 | 0 | 0 | 0 | 0 | – |
| 5 yrs. | 9 | 18 | .333 | 5.05 | 79 | 42 | 8 | 306.2 | 309 | 147 | 166 | 3 | 1 | 0 | 0 | 88 | 6 | 0 | .068 |
| 2 yrs. | 5 | 5 | .500 | 4.85 | 25 | 16 | 4 | 115 | 111 | 41 | 66 | 2 | 0 | 0 | 0 | 33 | 3 | 0 | .091 |

## Cliff Chambers

**CHAMBERS, CLIFFORD DAY (Lefty)**
B. Jan. 10, 1922, Portland, Ore.          BL TL 6'3"      208 lbs.

| | W | L | PCT | ERA | G | GS | CG | IP | H | BB | SO | ShO | W | L | SV | AB | H | HR | BA |
|---|---|---|---|---|---|---|---|---|---|---|---|---|---|---|---|---|---|---|---|
| 1948 CHI N | 2 | 9 | .182 | 4.43 | 29 | 12 | 3 | 103.2 | 100 | 48 | 51 | 1 | 0 | 2 | 0 | 30 | 4 | 0 | .133 |
| 1949 PIT N | 13 | 7 | .650 | 3.96 | 34 | 21 | 10 | 177.1 | 186 | 58 | 93 | 1 | 1 | 0 | 0 | 55 | 13 | 0 | .236 |
| 1950 | 12 | 15 | .444 | 4.30 | 37 | 33 | 11 | 249.1 | 262 | 92 | 93 | 2 | 1 | 2 | 0 | 90 | 26 | 2 | .289 |
| 1951 2 teams | | | PIT | N | (10G | 3–6) | | STL | N | (21G | 11–6) | | | | | | | | |
| " total | 14 | 12 | .538 | 4.38 | 31 | 26 | 11 | 189 | 184 | 87 | 64 | 2 | 1 | 2 | 0 | 70 | 15 | 1 | .214 |
| 1952 STL N | 4 | 4 | .500 | 4.12 | 26 | 13 | 2 | 98.1 | 110 | 33 | 47 | 1 | 0 | 0 | 1 | 32 | 9 | 0 | .281 |
| 1953 | 3 | 6 | .333 | 4.86 | 32 | 8 | 0 | 79.2 | 82 | 43 | 26 | 0 | 2 | 2 | 0 | 17 | 2 | 0 | .118 |
| 6 yrs. | 48 | 53 | .475 | 4.29 | 189 | 113 | 37 | 897.1 | 924 | 361 | 374 | 7 | 5 | 8 | 1 | 294 | 69 | 3 | .235 |
| 1 yr. | 2 | 9 | .182 | 4.43 | 29 | 12 | 3 | 103.2 | 100 | 48 | 51 | 1 | 0 | 2 | 0 | 30 | 4 | 0 | .133 |

## Virgil Cheeves

**CHEEVES, VIRGIL EARL (Chief)**
B. Feb. 12, 1901, Oklahoma City, Okla.    D. May 5, 1979, Dallas, Tex.          BR TR 6'      195 lbs.

| | W | L | PCT | ERA | G | GS | CG | IP | H | BB | SO | ShO | W | L | SV | AB | H | HR | BA |
|---|---|---|---|---|---|---|---|---|---|---|---|---|---|---|---|---|---|---|---|
| 1920 CHI N | 0 | 0 | – | 3.50 | 5 | 2 | 0 | 18 | 16 | 7 | 3 | 0 | 0 | 0 | 0 | 4 | 0 | 0 | .000 |
| 1921 | 11 | 12 | .478 | 4.64 | 37 | 22 | 9 | 163 | 192 | 47 | 39 | 1 | 3 | 1 | 0 | 48 | 8 | 0 | .167 |
| 1922 | 12 | 11 | .522 | 4.09 | 39 | 23 | 9 | 182.2 | 195 | 76 | 40 | 1 | 3 | 3 | 2 | 62 | 13 | 1 | .210 |
| 1923 | 3 | 4 | .429 | 6.18 | 19 | 8 | 0 | 71.1 | 89 | 37 | 13 | 0 | 3 | 1 | 0 | 23 | 4 | 0 | .174 |
| 1924 CLE A | 0 | 0 | – | 7.79 | 8 | 1 | 0 | 17.1 | 26 | 17 | 2 | 0 | 0 | 0 | 0 | 4 | 1 | 0 | .250 |
| 1927 NY N | 0 | 0 | – | 4.26 | 3 | 0 | 0 | 6.1 | 8 | 4 | 1 | 0 | 0 | 0 | 0 | 0 | 0 | 0 | – |
| 6 yrs. | 26 | 27 | .491 | 4.73 | 111 | 56 | 18 | 458.2 | 526 | 188 | 98 | 2 | 9 | 5 | 2 | 141 | 26 | 1 | .184 |
| 4 yrs. | 26 | 27 | .491 | 4.61 | 100 | 55 | 18 | 435 | 492 | 167 | 95 | 2 | 9 | 5 | 2 | 137 | 25 | 1 | .182 |

## Larry Cheney

**CHENEY, LAURANCE RUSSELL**
B. May 2, 1886, Belleville, Kans.    D. Jan. 6, 1969, Daytona Beach, Fla.          BR TR 6'1½"      185 lbs.

| | W | L | PCT | ERA | G | GS | CG | IP | H | BB | SO | ShO | W | L | SV | AB | H | HR | BA |
|---|---|---|---|---|---|---|---|---|---|---|---|---|---|---|---|---|---|---|---|
| 1911 CHI N | 1 | 0 | 1.000 | 0.00 | 3 | 1 | 0 | 10 | 8 | 3 | 11 | 0 | 0 | 0 | 0 | 4 | 1 | 0 | .250 |
| 1912 | 26 | 10 | .722 | 2.85 | 42 | 37 | 28 | 303.1 | 262 | 111 | 140 | 4 | 2 | 0 | 0 | 106 | 24 | 1 | .226 |
| 1913 | 21 | 14 | .600 | 2.57 | 54 | 36 | 25 | 305 | 271 | 98 | 136 | 2 | 4 | 0 | 11 | 104 | 20 | 0 | .192 |
| 1914 | 20 | 18 | .526 | 2.54 | 50 | 40 | 18 | 311.1 | 239 | 140 | 157 | 6 | 3 | 0 | 5 | 100 | 18 | 0 | .180 |
| 1915 2 teams | | | CHI | N | (25G | 8–9) | | BKN | N | (5G | 0–2) | | | | | | | | |
| " total | 8 | 11 | .421 | 3.24 | 30 | 22 | 7 | 158.1 | 136 | 72 | 79 | 2 | 2 | 2 | 0 | 47 | 7 | 0 | .149 |
| 1916 BKN N | 18 | 12 | .600 | 1.92 | 41 | 32 | 15 | 253 | 178 | 105 | 166 | 5 | 2 | 3 | 0 | 79 | 9 | 0 | .114 |
| 1917 | 8 | 12 | .400 | 2.35 | 35 | 24 | 15 | 210.1 | 185 | 73 | 102 | 1 | 1 | 0 | 2 | 68 | 14 | 0 | .206 |
| 1918 | 11 | 13 | .458 | 2.42 | 35 | 21 | 15 | 200.2 | 177 | 74 | 83 | 0 | 3 | 2 | 1 | 66 | 16 | 0 | .242 |
| 1919 3 teams | | | BKN | N | (9G | 1–3) | | BOS | N | (8G | 0–2) | PHI | N | (9G | 2–5) | | | | |
| " total | 3 | 10 | .231 | 4.18 | 26 | 12 | 7 | 129.1 | 149 | 57 | 52 | 0 | 2 | 0 | 0 | 43 | 6 | 0 | .140 |
| 9 yrs. | 116 | 100 | .537 | 2.70 | 313 | 225 | 132 | 1881.1 | 1605 | 733 | 926 | 20 | 18 | 8 | 19 | 617 | 115 | 1 | .186 |
| 5 yrs. | 76 | 51 | .598 | 2.74 | 174 | 132 | 80 | 1061 | 900 | 407 | 512 | 14 | 11 | 2 | 16 | 354 | 69 | 1 | .195 |

| | W | L | PCT | ERA | G | GS | CG | IP | H | BB | SO | ShO | Relief Pitching W | L | SV | BATTING AB | H | HR | BA |
|---|---|---|---|---|---|---|---|---|---|---|---|---|---|---|---|---|---|---|---|

## Larry Cheney continued

**WORLD SERIES**

| 1916 BKN N | 0 | 0 | — | 3.00 | 1 | 0 | 0 | 3 | 4 | 1 | 5 | 0 | 0 | 0 | 0 | 0 | 0 | 0 | — |

## Bob Chipman

CHIPMAN, ROBERT HOWARD (Mr. Chips)  BL TL 6'2" 190 lbs.
B. Oct. 11, 1918, Brooklyn, N. Y.    D. Nov. 8, 1973, Huntington, N. Y.

| 1941 BKN N | 1 | 0 | 1.000 | 0.00 | 1 | 0 | 0 | 5 | 3 | 1 | 3 | 0 | 1 | 0 | 0 | 3 | 0 | 0 | .000 |
| 1942 | 0 | 0 | — | 0.00 | 2 | 0 | 0 | 1.1 | 1 | 2 | 1 | 0 | 0 | 0 | 0 | 0 | 0 | 0 | — |
| 1943 | 0 | 0 | — | 0.00 | 1 | 0 | 0 | 1.2 | 2 | 2 | 0 | 0 | 0 | 0 | 0 | 0 | 0 | 0 | — |
| 1944 2 teams | | | BKN | N | (11G 3–1) | CHI | N | (26G 9–9) | | | | | | | | | | | |
| " total | 12 | 10 | .545 | 3.65 | 37 | 24 | 9 | 165.1 | 185 | 64 | 61 | 1 | 2 | 3 | 2 | 59 | 7 | 0 | .119 |
| 1945 CHI N | 4 | 5 | .444 | 3.50 | 25 | 10 | 3 | 72 | 63 | 34 | 29 | 1 | 0 | 1 | 0 | 17 | 3 | 0 | .176 |
| 1946 | 6 | 5 | .545 | 3.13 | 34 | 10 | 5 | 109.1 | 103 | 54 | 42 | 3 | 1 | 0 | 2 | 33 | 2 | 0 | .061 |
| 1947 | 7 | 6 | .538 | 3.68 | 32 | 17 | 5 | 134.2 | 135 | 66 | 51 | 1 | 1 | 0 | 0 | 44 | 4 | 0 | .091 |
| 1948 | 2 | 1 | .667 | 3.58 | 34 | 3 | 0 | 60.1 | 73 | 24 | 16 | 0 | 2 | 0 | 4 | 16 | 4 | 0 | .250 |
| 1949 | 7 | 8 | .467 | 3.97 | 38 | 11 | 3 | 113.1 | 110 | 63 | 46 | 1 | 3 | 2 | 1 | 24 | 3 | 0 | .125 |
| 1950 BOS N | 7 | 7 | .500 | 4.43 | 27 | 12 | 4 | 124 | 127 | 37 | 40 | 0 | 2 | 1 | 1 | 39 | 6 | 0 | .154 |
| 1951 | 4 | 3 | .571 | 4.85 | 33 | 0 | 0 | 52 | 59 | 19 | 17 | 0 | 4 | 3 | 4 | 10 | 1 | 0 | .100 |
| 1952 | 1 | 1 | .500 | 2.81 | 29 | 0 | 0 | 41.2 | 28 | 20 | 16 | 0 | 1 | 1 | 0 | 5 | 2 | 0 | .400 |
| 12 yrs. | 51 | 46 | .526 | 3.72 | 293 | 87 | 29 | 880.2 | 889 | 386 | 322 | 7 | 17 | 11 | 14 | 250 | 32 | 0 | .128 |
| 6 yrs. | 35 | 34 | .507 | 3.56 | 189 | 72 | 24 | 618.2 | 631 | 281 | 225 | 7 | 7 | 5 | 9 | 182 | 21 | 0 | .115 |

**WORLD SERIES**

| 1945 CHI N | 0 | 0 | — | 0.00 | 1 | 0 | 0 | .1 | 0 | 1 | 0 | 0 | 0 | 0 | 0 | 0 | 0 | 0 | — |

## Bubba Church

CHURCH, EMORY NICHOLAS  BR TR 6' 180 lbs.
B. Sept. 12, 1924, Birmingham, Ala.

| 1950 PHI N | 8 | 6 | .571 | 2.73 | 31 | 18 | 8 | 142 | 113 | 56 | 50 | 2 | 0 | 0 | 1 | 44 | 8 | 0 | .182 |
| 1951 | 15 | 11 | .577 | 3.53 | 38 | 33 | 15 | 247 | 246 | 90 | 104 | 4 | 1 | 1 | 1 | 86 | 22 | 1 | .256 |
| 1952 2 teams | | | PHI | N | (2G 0–0) | CIN | N | (29G 5–9) | | | | | | | | | | | |
| " total | 5 | 9 | .357 | 4.55 | 31 | 23 | 5 | 158.1 | 184 | 49 | 50 | 1 | 0 | 0 | 0 | 51 | 12 | 1 | .235 |
| 1953 2 teams | | | CIN | N | (11G 3–3) | CHI | N | (27G 4–5) | | | | | | | | | | | |
| " total | 7 | 8 | .467 | 5.29 | 38 | 18 | 3 | 148 | 170 | 68 | 59 | 0 | 2 | 2 | 1 | 48 | 11 | 1 | .229 |
| 1954 CHI N | 1 | 3 | .250 | 9.82 | 7 | 3 | 1 | 14.2 | 21 | 13 | 8 | 0 | 0 | 1 | 0 | 5 | 0 | 0 | .000 |
| 1955 | 0 | 0 | — | 5.40 | 2 | 0 | 0 | 3.1 | 4 | 1 | 3 | 0 | 0 | 0 | 0 | 1 | 0 | 0 | .000 |
| 6 yrs. | 36 | 37 | .493 | 4.10 | 147 | 95 | 32 | 713.1 | 738 | 277 | 274 | 7 | 3 | 4 | 4 | 235 | 53 | 3 | .226 |
| 3 yrs. | 5 | 8 | .385 | 5.59 | 36 | 14 | 2 | 122.1 | 140 | 63 | 58 | 0 | 2 | 1 | 2 | 39 | 7 | 1 | .179 |

## Len Church

CHURCH, LEONARD  BB TR 6' 190 lbs.
B. Mar. 21, 1942, Chicago, Ill.

| 1966 CHI N | 0 | 1 | .000 | 7.50 | 4 | 0 | 0 | 6 | 10 | 7 | 3 | 0 | 0 | 1 | 0 | 1 | 0 | 0 | .000 |

## Dad Clarke

CLARKE, WILLIAM H.  BB TR
B. Jan. 7, 1865, Oswego, N. Y.    D. June 3, 1911, Lorain, Ohio

| 1888 CHI N | 1 | 0 | 1.000 | 5.06 | 2 | 2 | 1 | 16 | 23 | 6 | 6 | 0 | 0 | 0 | 0 | 7 | 2 | 1 | .286 |
| 1891 COL AA | 1 | 2 | .333 | 6.86 | 4 | 3 | 2 | 21 | 30 | 16 | 2 | 0 | 0 | 0 | 0 | 9 | 1 | 0 | .111 |
| 1894 NY N | 3 | 4 | .429 | 4.93 | 15 | 6 | 5 | 84 | 114 | 26 | 15 | 0 | 0 | 1 | 1 | 37 | 8 | 0 | .216 |
| 1895 | 18 | 15 | .545 | 3.39 | 37 | 30 | 27 | 281.2 | 336 | 60 | 67 | 1 | 1 | 4 | 1 | 121 | 29 | 0 | .240 |
| 1896 | 17 | 24 | .415 | 4.26 | 48 | 40 | 33 | 351 | 431 | 60 | 66 | 1 | 2 | 0 | 1 | 147 | 30 | 0 | .204 |
| 1897 2 teams | | | NY | N | (6G 2–1) | LOU | N | (4G 1–3) | | | | | | | | | | | |
| " total | 3 | 4 | .429 | 4.92 | 10 | 8 | 6 | 64 | 87 | 20 | 16 | 0 | 0 | 0 | 0 | 30 | 5 | 0 | .167 |
| 1898 LOU N | 0 | 1 | .000 | 5.00 | 1 | 1 | 1 | 9 | 10 | 2 | 1 | 0 | 0 | 0 | 0 | 3 | 0 | 0 | .000 |
| 7 yrs. | 43 | 50 | .462 | 4.17 | 117 | 90 | 75 | 826.2 | 1031 | 190 | 173 | 2 | 3 | 5 | 3 | 354 | 75 | 1 | .212 |
| 1 yr. | 1 | 0 | 1.000 | 5.06 | 2 | 2 | 1 | 16 | 23 | 6 | 6 | 0 | 0 | 0 | 0 | 7 | 2 | 1 | .286 |

## Henry Clarke

CLARKE, HENRY TEFFT  BR TR
B. Aug. 4, 1875, Bellevue, Neb.    D. Mar. 28, 1950, Colorado Springs, Colo.

| 1897 CLE N | 0 | 4 | .000 | 5.87 | 5 | 4 | 3 | 30.2 | 32 | 12 | 3 | 0 | 0 | 0 | 0 | 25 | 7 | 0 | .280 |
| 1898 CHI N | 1 | 0 | 1.000 | 2.00 | 1 | 1 | 1 | 9 | 8 | 5 | 1 | 0 | 0 | 0 | 0 | 4 | 1 | 0 | .250 |
| 2 yrs. | 1 | 4 | .200 | 4.99 | 6 | 5 | 4 | 39.2 | 40 | 17 | 4 | 0 | 0 | 0 | 0 | 29 | 8 | 0 | .276 |
| 1 yr. | 1 | 0 | 1.000 | 2.00 | 1 | 1 | 1 | 9 | 8 | 5 | 1 | 0 | 0 | 0 | 0 | 4 | 1 | 0 | .250 |

## John Clarkson

CLARKSON, JOHN GIBSON  BR TR 5'10" 155 lbs.
Brother of Dad Clarkson.    Brother of Walter Clarkson.
B. July 1, 1861, Cambridge, Mass.    D. Feb. 4, 1909, Cambridge, Mass.
Hall of Fame 1963.

| 1882 WOR N | 1 | 2 | .333 | 4.50 | 3 | 3 | 2 | 24 | 49 | 2 | 3 | 0 | 0 | 0 | 0 | 11 | 4 | 0 | .364 |
| 1884 CHI N | 10 | 3 | .769 | 2.14 | 14 | 13 | 12 | 118 | 94 | 25 | 102 | 0 | 0 | 0 | 0 | 84 | 22 | 3 | .262 |
| 1885 | 53 | 16 | .768 | 1.85 | 70 | 70 | 68 | 623 | 497 | 97 | 318 | 10 | 0 | 0 | 0 | 283 | 61 | 4 | .216 |
| 1886 | 35 | 17 | .673 | 2.41 | 55 | 55 | 50 | 466.2 | 419 | 86 | 340 | 3 | 0 | 0 | 0 | 210 | 49 | 3 | .233 |
| 1887 | 38 | 21 | .644 | 3.08 | 60 | 59 | 56 | 523 | 513 | 92 | 237 | 2 | 1 | 0 | 0 | 215 | 52 | 6 | .242 |
| 1888 BOS N | 33 | 20 | .623 | 2.76 | 54 | 54 | 53 | 483.1 | 448 | 119 | 223 | 3 | 0 | 0 | 0 | 205 | 40 | 1 | .195 |
| 1889 | 49 | 19 | .721 | 2.73 | 73 | 72 | 68 | 620 | 589 | 203 | 284 | 8 | 0 | 0 | 1 | 262 | 54 | 2 | .206 |
| 1890 | 25 | 18 | .581 | 3.27 | 44 | 44 | 43 | 383 | 370 | 140 | 138 | 2 | 0 | 0 | 0 | 173 | 43 | 2 | .249 |
| 1891 | 33 | 19 | .635 | 2.79 | 55 | 51 | 47 | 460.2 | 435 | 154 | 141 | 3 | 0 | 1 | 3 | 187 | 42 | 0 | .225 |
| 1892 2 teams | | | BOS | N | (16G 8–6) | CLE | N | (29G 17–10) | | | | | | | | | | | |
| " total | 25 | 16 | .610 | 2.48 | 45 | 44 | 42 | 389 | 350 | 132 | 139 | 5 | 0 | 0 | 1 | 158 | 27 | 1 | .171 |
| 1893 CLE N | 16 | 17 | .485 | 4.45 | 36 | 35 | 31 | 295 | 358 | 95 | 62 | 0 | 0 | 1 | 0 | 131 | 27 | 1 | .206 |
| 1894 | 8 | 9 | .471 | 4.42 | 22 | 18 | 13 | 150.2 | 173 | 46 | 28 | 1 | 0 | 2 | 0 | 55 | 11 | 1 | .200 |
| 12 yrs. | 326 | 177 | .648 | 2.81 | 531 | 518 | 485 | 4536.1 | 4295 | 1191 | 2015 | 37 | 1 | 4 | 5 | * | | | |
| | | 10th | | | | | 8th | | | | | | | | | | | | |
| 4 yrs. | 136 | 57 | .705 | 2.39 | 199 | 197 | 186 | 1730.2 | 1523 | 300 | 997 | 15 | 1 | 0 | 0 | 792 | 184 | 16 | .232 |
| | | 10th | | 1st | | | 9th | | | | | 6th | | | | | 9th | | | |

| | W | L | PCT | ERA | G | GS | CG | IP | H | BB | SO | ShO | Relief Pitching W | L | SV | BATTING AB | H | HR | BA |
|---|---|---|---|---|---|---|---|---|---|---|---|---|---|---|---|---|---|---|---|

## Fritz Clausen

**CLAUSEN, FREDERICK WILLIAM**                                      BR TL 5'11"   190 lbs.
B. Apr. 26, 1869, New York, N. Y.       D. Feb. 11, 1960, Memphis, Tenn.

| | W | L | PCT | ERA | G | GS | CG | IP | H | BB | SO | ShO | W | L | SV | AB | H | HR | BA |
|---|---|---|---|---|---|---|---|---|---|---|---|---|---|---|---|---|---|---|---|
| 1892 LOU N | 9 | 13 | .409 | 3.06 | 24 | 24 | 24 | 200 | 181 | 87 | 94 | 2 | 0 | 0 | 0 | 84 | 13 | 0 | .155 |
| 1893 2 teams | | | LOU | N (5G 1–4) | | | | CHI | N (10G 6–2) | | | | | | | | | | |
| " total | 7 | 6 | .538 | 3.96 | 15 | 14 | 11 | 109 | 112 | 61 | 35 | 0 | 0 | 0 | 1 | 47 | 7 | 0 | .149 |
| 1894 CHI N | 0 | 1 | .000 | 10.38 | 1 | 1 | 0 | 4.1 | 5 | 3 | 1 | 0 | 0 | 0 | 0 | 1 | 0 | 0 | .000 |
| 1896 LOU N | 0 | 2 | .000 | 6.55 | 2 | 2 | 1 | 11 | 17 | 6 | 4 | 0 | 0 | 0 | 0 | 4 | 0 | 0 | .000 |
| 4 yrs. | 16 | 22 | .421 | 3.58 | 42 | 41 | 36 | 324.1 | 315 | 157 | 134 | 2 | 0 | 0 | 1 | 136 | 20 | 0 | .147 |
| 2 yrs. | 6 | 3 | .667 | 3.47 | 11 | 10 | 8 | 80.1 | 76 | 42 | 32 | 0 | 0 | 0 | 1 | 34 | 4 | 0 | .118 |

## Andy Coakley

**COAKLEY, ANDREW JAMES**                                         BL TR 6'   165 lbs.
Played as Jack McAllister 1902.
B. Nov. 20, 1882, Providence, R. I.       D. Sept. 27, 1963, New York, N. Y.

| | W | L | PCT | ERA | G | GS | CG | IP | H | BB | SO | ShO | W | L | SV | AB | H | HR | BA |
|---|---|---|---|---|---|---|---|---|---|---|---|---|---|---|---|---|---|---|---|
| 1902 PHI A | 2 | 1 | .667 | 2.67 | 3 | 3 | 3 | 27 | 25 | 9 | 9 | 0 | 0 | 0 | 0 | 8 | 3 | 0 | .375 |
| 1903 | 0 | 3 | .000 | 5.50 | 6 | 3 | 2 | 37.2 | 48 | 11 | 20 | 0 | 0 | 0 | 0 | 15 | 3 | 0 | .200 |
| 1904 | 4 | 4 | .500 | 2.03 | 8 | 8 | 8 | 62 | 50 | 23 | 33 | 2 | 0 | 0 | 0 | 23 | 2 | 0 | .087 |
| 1905 | 20 | 7 | .741 | 1.84 | 35 | 31 | 22 | 255 | 227 | 73 | 145 | 3 | 1 | 0 | 0 | 90 | 13 | 0 | .144 |
| 1906 | 7 | 8 | .467 | 3.14 | 22 | 16 | 10 | 149 | 144 | 44 | 59 | 0 | 1 | 0 | 0 | 49 | 7 | 0 | .143 |
| 1907 CIN N | 17 | 16 | .515 | 2.34 | 37 | 30 | 21 | 265.1 | 269 | 79 | 89 | 1 | 4 | 1 | 1 | 84 | 6 | 0 | .071 |
| 1908 2 teams | | | CIN | N (32G 8–18) | | | | CHI | N (4G 2–0) | | | | | | | | | | |
| " total | 10 | 18 | .357 | 1.78 | 36 | 31 | 22 | 262.2 | 233 | 70 | 68 | 5 | 0 | 1 | 2 | 82 | 7 | 0 | .085 |
| 1909 CHI N | 0 | 1 | .000 | 18.00 | 1 | 1 | 0 | 2 | 7 | 3 | 1 | 0 | 0 | 0 | 0 | 0 | 0 | 0 | .000 |
| 1911 NY A | 0 | 1 | .000 | 5.40 | 2 | 1 | 1 | 11.2 | 20 | 2 | 4 | 0 | 0 | 0 | 0 | 4 | 1 | 0 | .250 |
| 9 yrs. | 60 | 59 | .504 | 2.36 | 150 | 124 | 89 | 1072.1 | 1023 | 314 | 428 | 11 | 6 | 2 | 3 | 355 | 42 | 0 | .118 |
| 2 yrs. | 2 | 1 | .667 | 2.42 | 5 | 4 | 2 | 22.1 | 21 | 9 | 8 | 1 | 0 | 0 | 0 | 6 | 0 | 0 | .000 |
| WORLD SERIES | | | | | | | | | | | | | | | | | | | |
| 1905 PHI A | 0 | 1 | .000 | 2.00 | 1 | 1 | 1 | 9 | 9 | 5 | 2 | 0 | 0 | 0 | 0 | 2 | 0 | 0 | .000 |

## Dick Cogan

**COGAN, RICHARD HENRY**                                          BR TR 5'7"   150 lbs.
B. Dec. 5, 1871, Paterson, N. J.       D. May 2, 1948, Paterson, N. J.

| | W | L | PCT | ERA | G | GS | CG | IP | H | BB | SO | ShO | W | L | SV | AB | H | HR | BA |
|---|---|---|---|---|---|---|---|---|---|---|---|---|---|---|---|---|---|---|---|
| 1897 BAL N | 0 | 0 | — | 13.50 | 1 | 0 | 0 | 2 | 4 | 2 | 0 | 0 | 0 | 0 | 0 | 1 | 0 | 0 | .000 |
| 1899 CHI N | 2 | 3 | .400 | 4.30 | 5 | 5 | 5 | 44 | 54 | 24 | 9 | 0 | 0 | 0 | 0 | 25 | 5 | 0 | .200 |
| 1900 NY N | 0 | 0 | — | 6.75 | 2 | 0 | 0 | 8 | 10 | 6 | 1 | 0 | 0 | 0 | 0 | 8 | 1 | 0 | .125 |
| 3 yrs. | 2 | 3 | .400 | 5.00 | 8 | 5 | 5 | 54 | 68 | 32 | 10 | 0 | 0 | 0 | 0 | 34 | 6 | 0 | .176 |
| 1 yr. | 2 | 3 | .400 | 4.30 | 5 | 5 | 5 | 44 | 54 | 24 | 9 | 0 | 0 | 0 | 0 | 25 | 5 | 0 | .200 |

## Hy Cohen

**COHEN, HYMAN**                                                   BR TR 6'5"   215 lbs.
B. Jan. 29, 1931, Brooklyn, N. Y.

| | W | L | PCT | ERA | G | GS | CG | IP | H | BB | SO | ShO | W | L | SV | AB | H | HR | BA |
|---|---|---|---|---|---|---|---|---|---|---|---|---|---|---|---|---|---|---|---|
| 1955 CHI N | 0 | 0 | — | 7.94 | 7 | 1 | 0 | 17 | 28 | 10 | 4 | 0 | 0 | 0 | 0 | 3 | 0 | 0 | .000 |

## Jim Colborn

**COLBORN, JAMES WILLIAM**                                         BR TR 6'   185 lbs.
B. May 22, 1946, Santa Paula, Calif.

| | W | L | PCT | ERA | G | GS | CG | IP | H | BB | SO | ShO | W | L | SV | AB | H | HR | BA |
|---|---|---|---|---|---|---|---|---|---|---|---|---|---|---|---|---|---|---|---|
| 1969 CHI N | 1 | 0 | 1.000 | 3.00 | 6 | 2 | 0 | 15 | 15 | 9 | 4 | 0 | 0 | 0 | 0 | 3 | 0 | 0 | .000 |
| 1970 | 3 | 1 | .750 | 3.58 | 34 | 5 | 0 | 73 | 88 | 23 | 50 | 0 | 2 | 0 | 4 | 15 | 1 | 0 | .067 |
| 1971 | 0 | 1 | .000 | 7.20 | 14 | 0 | 0 | 10 | 18 | 3 | 2 | 0 | 0 | 1 | 0 | 0 | 0 | 0 | — |
| 1972 MIL A | 7 | 7 | .500 | 3.10 | 39 | 12 | 4 | 148 | 135 | 43 | 97 | 1 | 2 | 0 | 0 | 37 | 3 | 0 | .081 |
| 1973 | 20 | 12 | .625 | 3.18 | 43 | 36 | 22 | 314.1 | 297 | 87 | 135 | 4 | 2 | 0 | 1 | 0 | 0 | 0 | — |
| 1974 | 10 | 13 | .435 | 4.06 | 33 | 31 | 10 | 224 | 230 | 60 | 83 | 1 | 1 | 0 | 0 | 0 | 0 | 0 | — |
| 1975 | 11 | 13 | .458 | 4.27 | 36 | 29 | 8 | 206.1 | 215 | 65 | 79 | 1 | 0 | 1 | 2 | 0 | 0 | 0 | — |
| 1976 | 9 | 15 | .375 | 3.71 | 32 | 32 | 7 | 225.2 | 232 | 54 | 101 | 0 | 0 | 0 | 0 | 0 | 0 | 0 | — |
| 1977 KC A | 18 | 14 | .563 | 3.62 | 36 | 35 | 6 | 239 | 233 | 81 | 103 | 1 | 0 | 0 | 0 | 0 | 0 | 0 | — |
| 1978 2 teams | | | KC | A (8G 1–2) | | | | SEA | A (20G 3–10) | | | | | | | | | | |
| " total | 4 | 12 | .250 | 5.26 | 28 | 22 | 3 | 142 | 156 | 50 | 34 | 0 | 0 | 0 | 0 | 0 | 0 | 0 | — |
| 10 yrs. | 83 | 88 | .485 | 3.80 | 301 | 204 | 60 | 1597.1 | 1619 | 475 | 688 | 8 | 7 | 2 | 7 | 55 | 4 | 0 | .073 |
| 3 yrs. | 4 | 2 | .667 | 3.86 | 54 | 7 | 0 | 98 | 121 | 35 | 56 | 0 | 2 | 1 | 4 | 18 | 1 | 0 | .056 |

## Dave Cole

**COLE, DAVID BRUCE**                                              BR TR 6'2"   175 lbs.
B. Aug. 29, 1930, Williamsport, Md.

| | W | L | PCT | ERA | G | GS | CG | IP | H | BB | SO | ShO | W | L | SV | AB | H | HR | BA |
|---|---|---|---|---|---|---|---|---|---|---|---|---|---|---|---|---|---|---|---|
| 1950 BOS N | 0 | 1 | .000 | 1.13 | 4 | 0 | 0 | 8 | 7 | 3 | 8 | 0 | 0 | 0 | 0 | 1 | 0 | 0 | .000 |
| 1951 | 2 | 4 | .333 | 4.26 | 23 | 7 | 1 | 67.2 | 64 | 64 | 33 | 0 | 2 | 0 | 0 | 17 | 6 | 1 | .353 |
| 1952 | 1 | 1 | .500 | 4.03 | 22 | 3 | 0 | 44.2 | 38 | 42 | 22 | 0 | 0 | 0 | 0 | 8 | 0 | 0 | .000 |
| 1953 MIL N | 0 | 1 | .000 | 8.59 | 10 | 0 | 0 | 14.2 | 17 | 14 | 13 | 0 | 0 | 1 | 0 | 2 | 1 | 1 | .500 |
| 1954 CHI N | 3 | 8 | .273 | 5.36 | 18 | 14 | 2 | 84 | 74 | 62 | 37 | 1 | 0 | 0 | 0 | 28 | 6 | 1 | .214 |
| 1955 PHI N | 0 | 3 | .000 | 6.38 | 7 | 3 | 0 | 18.1 | 21 | 14 | 6 | 0 | 0 | 0 | 0 | 5 | 1 | 0 | .200 |
| 6 yrs. | 6 | 18 | .250 | 4.93 | 84 | 27 | 3 | 237.1 | .221 | 199 | 119 | 1 | 0 | 4 | 0 | 61 | 14 | 3 | .230 |
| 1 yr. | 3 | 8 | .273 | 5.36 | 18 | 14 | 2 | 84 | 74 | 62 | 37 | 1 | 0 | 0 | 0 | 28 | 6 | 1 | .214 |

## King Cole

**COLE, LEONARD LESLIE**                                          BR TR
B. Apr. 15, 1886, Toledo, Iowa       D. Jan. 6, 1916, Bay City, Mich.

| | W | L | PCT | ERA | G | GS | CG | IP | H | BB | SO | ShO | W | L | SV | AB | H | HR | BA |
|---|---|---|---|---|---|---|---|---|---|---|---|---|---|---|---|---|---|---|---|
| 1909 CHI N | 1 | 0 | 1.000 | 0.00 | 1 | 1 | 1 | 9 | 6 | 3 | 1 | 1 | 0 | 0 | 0 | 4 | 3 | 0 | .750 |
| 1910 | 20 | 4 | .833 | 1.80 | 33 | 29 | 21 | 239.2 | 174 | 130 | 114 | 4 | 2 | 0 | 0 | 91 | 21 | 0 | .231 |
| 1911 | 18 | 7 | .720 | 3.13 | 32 | 27 | 13 | 221.1 | 188 | 99 | 101 | 2 | 1 | 1 | 0 | 79 | 12 | 0 | .152 |
| 1912 2 teams | | | CHI | N (8G 1–2) | | | | PIT | N (12G 2–2) | | | | | | | | | | |
| " total | 3 | 4 | .429 | 7.68 | 20 | 7 | 2 | 68 | 97 | 26 | 20 | 0 | 1 | 1 | 0 | 20 | 4 | 0 | .200 |
| 1914 NY A | 11 | 9 | .550 | 3.30 | 33 | 15 | 8 | 141.2 | 151 | 51 | 43 | 2 | 5 | 2 | 0 | 42 | 2 | 0 | .048 |
| 1915 | 3 | 3 | .500 | 3.18 | 10 | 6 | 2 | 51 | 41 | 22 | 19 | 0 | 1 | 0 | 1 | 13 | 1 | 0 | .077 |
| 6 yrs. | 56 | 27 | .675 | 3.12 | 129 | 85 | 47 | 730.2 | 657 | 331 | 298 | 9 | 10 | 4 | 1 | 249 | 43 | 0 | .173 |
| 4 yrs. | 40 | 13 | .755 | 2.72 | 74 | 60 | 35 | 489 | 404 | 240 | 225 | 7 | 4 | 1 | 0 | 179 | 38 | 0 | .212 |
| WORLD SERIES | | | | | | | | | | | | | | | | | | | |
| 1910 CHI N | 0 | 0 | — | 3.38 | 1 | 1 | 0 | 8 | 10 | 3 | 5 | 0 | 0 | 0 | 0 | 2 | 0 | 0 | .000 |

| | W | L | PCT | ERA | G | GS | CG | IP | H | BB | SO | ShO | Relief Pitching W | L | SV | BATTING AB | H | HR | BA |
|---|---|---|---|---|---|---|---|---|---|---|---|---|---|---|---|---|---|---|---|

## Joe Coleman

**COLEMAN, JOSEPH HOWARD**
Son of Joe Coleman.
B. Feb. 3, 1947, Boston, Mass.                                    BR TR 6'3"   175 lbs.

| | W | L | PCT | ERA | G | GS | CG | IP | H | BB | SO | ShO | W | L | SV | AB | H | HR | BA |
|---|---|---|---|---|---|---|---|---|---|---|---|---|---|---|---|---|---|---|---|
| 1965 **WAS A** | 2 | 0 | 1.000 | 1.50 | 2 | 2 | 2 | 18 | 9 | 8 | 7 | 0 | 0 | 0 | 0 | 6 | 0 | 0 | .000 |
| 1966 | 1 | 0 | 1.000 | 2.00 | 1 | 1 | 1 | 9 | 6 | 2 | 4 | 0 | 0 | 0 | 0 | 3 | 0 | 0 | .000 |
| 1967 | 8 | 9 | .471 | 4.63 | 28 | 22 | 3 | 134 | 154 | 47 | 77 | 0 | 0 | 1 | 0 | 36 | 2 | 0 | .056 |
| 1968 | 12 | 16 | .429 | 3.27 | 33 | 33 | 12 | 223 | 212 | 51 | 139 | 2 | 0 | 0 | 0 | 70 | 9 | 0 | .129 |
| 1969 | 12 | 13 | .480 | 3.27 | 40 | 36 | 12 | 247.2 | 222 | 100 | 182 | 4 | 0 | 0 | 1 | 84 | 9 | 0 | .107 |
| 1970 | 8 | 12 | .400 | 3.58 | 39 | 29 | 6 | 219 | 190 | 89 | 152 | 1 | 0 | 0 | 0 | 67 | 8 | 0 | .119 |
| 1971 **DET A** | 20 | 9 | .690 | 3.15 | 39 | 38 | 16 | 286 | 241 | 96 | 236 | 3 | 0 | 0 | 0 | 96 | 9 | 0 | .094 |
| 1972 | 19 | 14 | .576 | 2.80 | 40 | 39 | 9 | 279.2 | 216 | 110 | 222 | 3 | 0 | 0 | 0 | 82 | 9 | 0 | .110 |
| 1973 | 23 | 15 | .605 | 3.53 | 40 | 40 | 13 | 288 | 283 | 93 | 202 | 2 | 0 | 0 | 0 | 0 | 0 | 0 | – |
| 1974 | 14 | 12 | .538 | 4.31 | 41 | 41 | 11 | 286 | 272 | 158 | 177 | 2 | 0 | 0 | 0 | 0 | 0 | 0 | – |
| 1975 | 10 | 18 | .357 | 5.55 | 31 | 31 | 6 | 201 | 234 | 85 | 125 | 1 | 0 | 0 | 0 | 0 | 0 | 0 | – |
| 1976 2 teams | | | | | **DET** A (12G 2–5) | | | **CHI** N (39G 2–8) | | | | | | | | | | | |
| " total | 4 | 13 | .235 | 4.44 | 51 | 16 | 1 | 146 | 152 | 69 | 104 | 0 | 2 | 5 | 4 | 13 | 2 | 0 | .154 |
| 1977 **OAK A** | 4 | 4 | .500 | 2.95 | 43 | 12 | 2 | 128 | 114 | 49 | 55 | 0 | 0 | 0 | 2 | 0 | 0 | 0 | – |
| 1978 2 teams | | | | | **OAK** A (10G 3–0) | | | **TOR** A (31G 2–0) | | | | | | | | | | | |
| " total | 5 | 0 | 1.000 | 3.78 | 41 | 0 | 0 | 81 | 79 | 35 | 32 | 0 | 5 | 0 | 0 | 0 | 0 | 0 | – |
| 1979 2 teams | | | | | **SF** N (5G 0–0) | | | **PIT** N (10G 0–0) | | | | | | | | | | | |
| " total | 0 | 0 | | 5.18 | 15 | 0 | 0 | 24.1 | 32 | 11 | 14 | 0 | 0 | 0 | 0 | 5 | 1 | 0 | .200 |
| 15 yrs. | 142 | 135 | .513 | 3.69 | 484 | 340 | 94 | 2570.2 | 2416 | 1003 | 1728 | 18 | 7 | 6 | 7 | 462 | 49 | 0 | .106 |
| 1 yr. | 2 | 8 | .200 | 4.10 | 39 | 4 | 0 | 79 | 72 | 35 | 66 | 0 | 2 | 5 | 4 | 13 | 2 | 0 | .154 |
| LEAGUE CHAMPIONSHIP SERIES | | | | | | | | | | | | | | | | | | | |
| 1972 **DET A** | 1 | 0 | 1.000 | 0.00 | 1 | 1 | 1 | 9 | 7 | 3 | 14 | 1 | 0 | 0 | 0 | 2 | 1 | 0 | .500 |

## Phil Collins

**COLLINS, PHILIP EUGENE (Fidgety Phil)**
B. Aug. 27, 1901, Chicago, Ill.   D. Aug. 14, 1948, Chicago, Ill.      BR TR 6'   170 lbs.

| | W | L | PCT | ERA | G | GS | CG | IP | H | BB | SO | ShO | W | L | SV | AB | H | HR | BA |
|---|---|---|---|---|---|---|---|---|---|---|---|---|---|---|---|---|---|---|---|
| 1923 **CHI N** | 1 | 0 | 1.000 | 3.60 | 1 | 1 | 0 | 5 | 8 | 1 | 2 | 0 | 0 | 0 | 0 | 2 | 0 | 0 | .000 |
| 1929 **PHI N** | 9 | 7 | .563 | 5.75 | 43 | 11 | 3 | 153.1 | 172 | 83 | 61 | 0 | 7 | 2 | 5 | 58 | 11 | 1 | .190 |
| 1930 | 16 | 11 | .593 | 4.78 | 47 | 25 | 17 | 239 | 287 | 86 | 87 | 1 | 3 | 1 | 3 | 87 | 22 | 3 | .253 |
| 1931 | 12 | 16 | .429 | 3.86 | 42 | 27 | 16 | 240.1 | 268 | 83 | 73 | 2 | 0 | 2 | 4 | 95 | 16 | 0 | .168 |
| 1932 | 14 | 12 | .538 | 5.27 | 43 | 21 | 6 | 184.1 | 231 | 65 | 66 | 0 | 5 | 3 | 3 | 68 | 18 | 0 | .265 |
| 1933 | 8 | 13 | .381 | 4.11 | 42 | 13 | 5 | 151 | 178 | 57 | 40 | 1 | 3 | 6 | 6 | 53 | 7 | 0 | .132 |
| 1934 | 13 | 18 | .419 | 4.18 | 45 | 32 | 15 | 254 | 277 | 87 | 72 | 0 | 4 | 1 | 1 | 88 | 15 | 0 | .170 |
| 1935 2 teams | | | | | **PHI** N (3G 0–2) | | | **STL** N (26G 7–6) | | | | | | | | | | | |
| " total | 7 | 8 | .467 | 5.64 | 29 | 11 | 2 | 97.1 | 120 | 35 | 22 | 0 | 3 | 2 | 2 | 31 | 4 | 0 | .129 |
| 8 yrs. | 80 | 85 | .485 | 4.66 | 292 | 141 | 64 | 1324.1 | 1541 | 497 | 423 | 4 | 25 | 17 | 24 | 482 | 93 | 4 | .193 |
| 1 yr. | 1 | 0 | 1.000 | 3.60 | 1 | 1 | 0 | 5 | 8 | 1 | 2 | 0 | 0 | 0 | 0 | 2 | 0 | 0 | .000 |

## Jackie Collum

**COLLUM, JACK DEAN**
B. June 21, 1927, Victor, Iowa                               BL TL 5'7½"   160 lbs.

| | W | L | PCT | ERA | G | GS | CG | IP | H | BB | SO | ShO | W | L | SV | AB | H | HR | BA |
|---|---|---|---|---|---|---|---|---|---|---|---|---|---|---|---|---|---|---|---|
| 1951 **STL N** | 2 | 1 | .667 | 1.59 | 3 | 2 | 1 | 17 | 11 | 10 | 5 | 1 | 0 | 1 | 0 | 7 | 3 | 0 | .429 |
| 1952 | 0 | 0 | | 0.00 | 2 | 0 | 0 | 3 | 2 | 1 | 0 | 0 | 0 | 0 | 0 | 0 | 0 | 0 | – |
| 1953 2 teams | | | | | **STL** N (7G 0–0) | | | **CIN** N (30G 7–11) | | | | | | | | | | | |
| " total | 7 | 11 | .389 | 3.97 | 37 | 12 | 4 | 136 | 138 | 43 | 56 | 1 | 3 | 3 | 3 | 39 | 10 | 0 | .256 |
| 1954 **CIN N** | 7 | 3 | .700 | 3.74 | 36 | 2 | 1 | 79.1 | 86 | 32 | 28 | 0 | 7 | 2 | 0 | 13 | 3 | 1 | .231 |
| 1955 | 9 | 8 | .529 | 3.63 | 32 | 17 | 5 | 134 | 128 | 37 | 49 | 0 | 2 | 1 | 1 | 40 | 10 | 0 | .250 |
| 1956 **STL N** | 6 | 2 | .750 | 4.20 | 38 | 1 | 0 | 60 | 63 | 27 | 17 | 0 | 6 | 2 | 7 | 14 | 3 | 0 | .214 |
| 1957 2 teams | | | | | **CHI** N (9G 1–1) | | | **BKN** N (3G 0–0) | | | | | | | | | | | |
| " total | 1 | 1 | .500 | 7.20 | 12 | 0 | 0 | 15 | 15 | 10 | 10 | 0 | 1 | 1 | 1 | 0 | 0 | 0 | – |
| 1958 **LA N** | 0 | 0 | | 8.10 | 2 | 0 | 0 | 3.1 | 4 | 2 | 0 | 0 | 0 | 0 | 0 | 1 | 0 | 0 | .000 |
| 1962 2 teams | | | | | **MIN** A (8G 0–2) | | | **CLE** A (1G 0–0) | | | | | | | | | | | |
| " total | 0 | 2 | .000 | 11.34 | 9 | 3 | 0 | 16.2 | 33 | 11 | 6 | 0 | 0 | 0 | 0 | 4 | 0 | 0 | .000 |
| 9 yrs. | 32 | 28 | .533 | 4.15 | 171 | 37 | 11 | 464.1 | 480 | 173 | 171 | 2 | 19 | 10 | 12 | 118 | 29 | 1 | .246 |
| 1 yr. | 1 | 1 | .500 | 6.75 | 9 | 0 | 0 | 10.2 | 8 | 9 | 7 | 0 | 1 | 1 | 1 | 0 | 0 | 0 | – |

## Jorge Comellas

**COMELLAS, JORGE (Pancho)**
B. Dec. 7, 1916, Havana, Cuba                               BR TR 6'   185 lbs.

| | W | L | PCT | ERA | G | GS | CG | IP | H | BB | SO | ShO | W | L | SV | AB | H | HR | BA |
|---|---|---|---|---|---|---|---|---|---|---|---|---|---|---|---|---|---|---|---|
| 1945 **CHI N** | 0 | 2 | .000 | 4.50 | 7 | 1 | 0 | 12 | 11 | 6 | 6 | 0 | 0 | 0 | 0 | 3 | 0 | 0 | .000 |

## Clint Compton

**COMPTON, ROBERT CLINTON**
B. Nov. 1, 1950, Montgomery, Ala.                           BL TL 5'11"   185 lbs.

| | W | L | PCT | ERA | G | GS | CG | IP | H | BB | SO | ShO | W | L | SV | AB | H | HR | BA |
|---|---|---|---|---|---|---|---|---|---|---|---|---|---|---|---|---|---|---|---|
| 1972 **CHI N** | 0 | 0 | – | 9.00 | 1 | 0 | 0 | 2 | 2 | 2 | 0 | 0 | 0 | 0 | 0 | 0 | 0 | 0 | – |

## Bill Connors

**CONNORS, WILLIAM JOSEPH**
B. Nov. 2, 1941, Schenectady, N. Y.                         BR TR 6'1"   180 lbs.

| | W | L | PCT | ERA | G | GS | CG | IP | H | BB | SO | ShO | W | L | SV | AB | H | HR | BA |
|---|---|---|---|---|---|---|---|---|---|---|---|---|---|---|---|---|---|---|---|
| 1966 **CHI N** | 0 | 1 | .000 | 7.31 | 11 | 0 | 0 | 16 | 20 | 7 | 3 | 0 | 0 | 0 | 0 | 0 | 0 | 0 | – |
| 1967 **NY N** | 0 | 0 | – | 6.23 | 6 | 1 | 0 | 13 | 8 | 5 | 13 | 0 | 0 | 0 | 0 | 1 | 0 | 0 | .000 |
| 1968 | 0 | 1 | .000 | 9.00 | 9 | 0 | 0 | 14 | 21 | 7 | 8 | 0 | 0 | 1 | 0 | 1 | 1 | 0 | 1.000 |
| 3 yrs. | 0 | 2 | .000 | 7.53 | 26 | 1 | 0 | 43 | 49 | 19 | 24 | 0 | 0 | 2 | 0 | 2 | 1 | 0 | .500 |
| 1 yr. | 0 | 1 | .000 | 7.31 | 11 | 0 | 0 | 16 | 20 | 7 | 3 | 0 | 0 | 1 | 0 | 0 | 0 | 0 | – |

## Mort Cooper

**COOPER, MORTON CECIL**
Brother of Walker Cooper.
B. Mar. 2, 1913, Atherton, Mo.   D. Nov. 17, 1958, Little Rock, Ark.   BR TR 6'2"   210 lbs.

| | W | L | PCT | ERA | G | GS | CG | IP | H | BB | SO | ShO | W | L | SV | AB | H | HR | BA |
|---|---|---|---|---|---|---|---|---|---|---|---|---|---|---|---|---|---|---|---|
| 1938 **STL N** | 2 | 1 | .667 | 3.04 | 4 | 3 | 1 | 23.2 | 17 | 12 | 11 | 0 | 0 | 0 | 1 | 9 | 2 | 0 | .222 |
| 1939 | 12 | 6 | .667 | 3.25 | 45 | 26 | 7 | 210.2 | 208 | 97 | 130 | 2 | 2 | 0 | 4 | 69 | 16 | 2 | .232 |
| 1940 | 11 | 12 | .478 | 3.63 | 38 | 29 | 16 | 230.2 | 225 | 86 | 95 | 3 | 1 | 0 | 3 | 83 | 13 | 0 | .157 |
| 1941 | 13 | 9 | .591 | 3.91 | 29 | 25 | 12 | 186.2 | 175 | 69 | 118 | 0 | 1 | 0 | 0 | 70 | 13 | 0 | .186 |
| 1942 | **22** | 7 | .759 | **1.78** | 37 | 35 | 22 | 278.2 | 207 | 68 | 152 | **10** | 0 | 1 | 0 | 103 | 19 | 0 | .184 |

| | W | L | PCT | ERA | G | GS | CG | IP | H | BB | SO | ShO | Relief Pitching W | L | SV | BATTING AB | H | HR | BA |
|---|---|---|---|---|---|---|---|---|---|---|---|---|---|---|---|---|---|---|---|

## Mort Cooper continued

| | W | L | PCT | ERA | G | GS | CG | IP | H | BB | SO | ShO | W | L | SV | AB | H | HR | BA |
|---|---|---|---|---|---|---|---|---|---|---|---|---|---|---|---|---|---|---|---|
| 1943 | 21 | 8 | .724 | 2.30 | 37 | 32 | 24 | 274 | 228 | 79 | 141 | 6 | 1 | 1 | 3 | 100 | 17 | 1 | .170 |
| 1944 | 22 | 7 | .759 | 2.46 | 34 | 33 | 22 | 252.1 | 227 | 60 | 97 | 7 | 0 | 0 | 1 | 94 | 19 | 0 | .202 |
| 1945 2 teams | | | STL | N (4G 2-0) | | BOS | N (20G 7-4) | | | | | | | | | | | | |
| " total | 9 | 4 | .692 | 2.92 | 24 | 14 | 5 | 101.2 | 97 | 34 | 59 | 1 | 3 | 2 | 1 | 32 | 8 | 1 | .250 |
| 1946 BOS N | 13 | 11 | .542 | 3.12 | 28 | 27 | 15 | 199 | 181 | 39 | 83 | 4 | 0 | 0 | 1 | 67 | 14 | 1 | .209 |
| 1947 2 teams | | | BOS | N (10G 2-5) | | NY | N (8G 1-5) | | | | | | | | | | | | |
| " total | 3 | 10 | .231 | 5.40 | 18 | 15 | 4 | 83.1 | 99 | 26 | 27 | 0 | 1 | 0 | 0 | 27 | 6 | 1 | .222 |
| 1949 CHI N | 0 | 0 | – | ∞ | 1 | 0 | 0 | 0 | 2 | 1 | 0 | 0 | 0 | 0 | 0 | 0 | 0 | 0 | – |
| 11 yrs. | 128 | 75 | .631 | 2.97 | 295 | 239 | 128 | 1840.2 | 1666 | 571 | 913 | 33 | 9 | 4 | 14 | 654 | 127 | 6 | .194 |
| 1 yr. | 0 | 0 | – | ∞ | 1 | 0 | 0 | 0 | 2 | 1 | 0 | 0 | 0 | 0 | 0 | 0 | 0 | 0 | – |

| WORLD SERIES | | | | | | | | | | | | | | | | | | | |
|---|---|---|---|---|---|---|---|---|---|---|---|---|---|---|---|---|---|---|---|
| 1942 STL N | 0 | 1 | .000 | 5.54 | 2 | 2 | 0 | 13 | 17 | 4 | 9 | 0 | 0 | 0 | 0 | 5 | 1 | 0 | .200 |
| 1943 | 1 | 1 | .500 | 2.81 | 2 | 2 | 1 | 16 | 11 | 3 | 10 | 0 | 0 | 0 | 0 | 5 | 0 | 0 | .000 |
| 1944 | 1 | 1 | .500 | 1.13 | 2 | 2 | 1 | 16 | 9 | 5 | 16 | 1 | 0 | 0 | 0 | 4 | 0 | 0 | .000 |
| 3 yrs. | 2 | 3 | .400 | 3.00 | 6 | 6 | 2 | 45 | 37 | 12 | 35 | 1 | 0 | 0 | 0 | 14 | 1 | 0 | .071 |

## Wilbur Cooper

**COOPER, ARLEY WILBUR**                                                           BR TL 5'11½" 165 lbs.
B. Feb. 24, 1892, Bearsville, W. Va.     D. Aug. 7, 1973, Encino, Calif.

| | W | L | PCT | ERA | G | GS | CG | IP | H | BB | SO | ShO | W | L | SV | AB | H | HR | BA |
|---|---|---|---|---|---|---|---|---|---|---|---|---|---|---|---|---|---|---|---|
| 1912 PIT N | 3 | 0 | 1.000 | 1.66 | 6 | 4 | 3 | 38 | 32 | 15 | 30 | 2 | 0 | 0 | 0 | 13 | 2 | 0 | .154 |
| 1913 | 5 | 3 | .625 | 3.29 | 30 | 9 | 3 | 93 | 98 | 45 | 39 | 1 | 3 | 1 | 0 | 26 | 2 | 0 | .077 |
| 1914 | 16 | 15 | .516 | 2.13 | 40 | 34 | 19 | 266.2 | 246 | 79 | 102 | 0 | 0 | 1 | 0 | 92 | 19 | 0 | .207 |
| 1915 | 5 | 16 | .238 | 3.30 | 38 | 21 | 11 | 185.2 | 180 | 52 | 71 | 1 | 1 | 0 | 4 | 60 | 7 | 0 | .117 |
| 1916 | 12 | 11 | .522 | 1.87 | 42 | 23 | 16 | 246 | 189 | 74 | 111 | 2 | 4 | 0 | 2 | 79 | 17 | 0 | .215 |
| 1917 | 17 | 11 | .607 | 2.36 | 40 | 34 | 23 | 297.2 | 276 | 54 | 99 | 7 | 1 | 0 | 1 | 103 | 21 | 0 | .204 |
| 1918 | 19 | 14 | .576 | 2.11 | 38 | 29 | 26 | 273.1 | 219 | 65 | 117 | 3 | 4 | 1 | 3 | 95 | 23 | 0 | .242 |
| 1919 | 19 | 13 | .594 | 2.67 | 35 | 32 | 27 | 286.2 | 229 | 74 | 106 | 4 | 1 | 0 | 1 | 101 | 29 | 0 | .287 |
| 1920 | 24 | 15 | .615 | 2.39 | 44 | 37 | 28 | 327 | 307 | 52 | 114 | 3 | 2 | 1 | 2 | 113 | 25 | 0 | .221 |
| 1921 | 22 | 14 | .611 | 3.25 | 38 | 38 | 29 | 327 | 341 | 80 | 134 | 2 | 0 | 0 | 0 | 122 | 31 | 0 | .254 |
| 1922 | 23 | 14 | .622 | 3.18 | 41 | 37 | 27 | 294.2 | 330 | 61 | 129 | 4 | 0 | 1 | 0 | 108 | 29 | 4 | .269 |
| 1923 | 17 | 19 | .472 | 3.57 | 39 | 38 | 26 | 294.2 | 331 | 71 | 77 | 1 | 1 | 0 | 0 | 107 | 28 | 0 | .262 |
| 1924 | 20 | 14 | .588 | 3.28 | 38 | 35 | 25 | 268.2 | 296 | 40 | 62 | 4 | 1 | 0 | 1 | 104 | 36 | 0 | .346 |
| 1925 CHI N | 12 | 14 | .462 | 4.28 | 32 | 26 | 13 | 212.1 | 249 | 61 | 41 | 0 | 3 | 1 | 0 | 82 | 17 | 2 | .207 |
| 1926 2 teams | | | CHI | N (8G 2-1) | | DET | A (8G 0-4) | | | | | | | | | | | | |
| " total | 2 | 5 | .286 | 5.77 | 16 | 11 | 3 | 68.2 | 92 | 30 | 20 | 0 | 0 | 1 | 0 | 22 | 7 | 0 | .318 |
| 15 yrs. | 216 | 178 | .548 | 2.89 | 517 | 408 | 279 | 3480 | 3415 | 853 | 1252 | 36 | 21 | 7 | 14 | 1227 | 293 | 6 | .239 |
| 2 yrs. | 14 | 15 | .483 | 4.31 | 40 | 34 | 16 | 267.1 | 314 | 82 | 59 | 2 | 3 | 1 | 0 | 100 | 24 | 2 | .240 |

## Larry Corcoran

**CORCORAN, LAWRENCE J.**                                                                    TR
Brother of Mike Corcoran.
B. Aug. 10, 1859, Brooklyn, N. Y.     D. Oct. 14, 1891, Newark, N. J.

| | W | L | PCT | ERA | G | GS | CG | IP | H | BB | SO | ShO | W | L | SV | AB | H | HR | BA |
|---|---|---|---|---|---|---|---|---|---|---|---|---|---|---|---|---|---|---|---|
| 1880 CHI N | 43 | 14 | .754 | 1.95 | 63 | 60 | 57 | 536.1 | 404 | 99 | 268 | 5 | 0 | 0 | 2 | 286 | 66 | 0 | .231 |
| 1881 | 31 | 14 | .689 | 2.31 | 45 | 44 | 43 | 396.2 | 380 | 78 | 150 | 4 | 1 | 0 | 0 | 189 | 42 | 0 | .222 |
| 1882 | 27 | 13 | .675 | 1.95 | 40 | 40 | 39 | 355.2 | 281 | 63 | 170 | 3 | 0 | 0 | 0 | 169 | 35 | 1 | .207 |
| 1883 | 34 | 20 | .630 | 2.49 | 56 | 53 | 51 | 473.2 | 483 | 82 | 216 | 3 | 1 | 0 | 0 | 263 | 55 | 0 | .209 |
| 1884 | 35 | 23 | .603 | 2.40 | 60 | 59 | 57 | 516.2 | 473 | 116 | 272 | 7 | 0 | 1 | 0 | 251 | 61 | 1 | .243 |
| 1885 2 teams | | | CHI | N (7G 5-2) | | NY | N (3G 2-1) | | | | | | | | | | | | |
| " total | 7 | 3 | .700 | 3.42 | 10 | 10 | 8 | 84.1 | 87 | 35 | 20 | 1 | 0 | 0 | 0 | 36 | 11 | 0 | .306 |
| 1886 2 teams | | | NY | N (0G 0-0) | | WAS | N (2G 0-1) | | | | | | | | | | | | |
| " total | 0 | 1 | .000 | 5.79 | 2 | 1 | 1 | 14 | 16 | 4 | 3 | 0 | 0 | 0 | 0 | 85 | 15 | 0 | .176 |
| 1887 IND N | 0 | 2 | .000 | 12.60 | 2 | 2 | 1 | 15 | 23 | 19 | 4 | 0 | 0 | 0 | 0 | 10 | 2 | 0 | .200 |
| 8 yrs. | 177 | 90 | .663 | 2.36 | 278 | 269 | 257 | 2392.1 | 2147 | 496 | 1103 | 23 | 2 | 1 | 2 | * | | | .225 |
| | | | | 8th | | | | | | | | | | | | | | | |
| 6 yrs. | 175 | 86 | .670 | 2.26 | 271 | 263 | 253 | 2338.1 | 2084 | 462 | 1086 | 23 | 2 | 1 | 2 | 1180 | 265 | 2 | .225 |
| | | | 4th | 4th | | | 2nd | 4th | | | 6th | 8th | | | | | | | |

## Mike Corcoran

**CORCORAN, MICHAEL**
Brother of Larry Corcoran.
Deceased.

| | W | L | PCT | ERA | G | GS | CG | IP | H | BB | SO | ShO | W | L | SV | AB | H | HR | BA |
|---|---|---|---|---|---|---|---|---|---|---|---|---|---|---|---|---|---|---|---|
| 1884 CHI N | 0 | 1 | .000 | 4.00 | 1 | 1 | 1 | 9 | 16 | 7 | 2 | 0 | 0 | 0 | 0 | 3 | 0 | 0 | .000 |

## Frank Corridon

**CORRIDON, FRANK J. (Fiddler)**                                                         BR TR
B. Nov. 25, 1880, Newport, R. I.     D. Feb. 21, 1941, Syracuse, N. Y.

| | W | L | PCT | ERA | G | GS | CG | IP | H | BB | SO | ShO | W | L | SV | AB | H | HR | BA |
|---|---|---|---|---|---|---|---|---|---|---|---|---|---|---|---|---|---|---|---|
| 1904 2 teams | | | CHI | N (12G 5-5) | | PHI | N (12G 6-5) | | | | | | | | | | | | |
| " total | 11 | 10 | .524 | 2.64 | 24 | 21 | 20 | 194.2 | 176 | 65 | 78 | 1 | 1 | 1 | 0 | 93 | 19 | 0 | .204 |
| 1905 PHI N | 10 | 13 | .435 | 3.48 | 35 | 26 | 18 | 212 | 203 | 57 | 79 | 1 | 1 | 1 | 1 | 72 | 15 | 1 | .208 |
| 1907 | 18 | 14 | .563 | 2.46 | 37 | 32 | 23 | 274 | 228 | 89 | 131 | 3 | 0 | 1 | 1 | 97 | 16 | 0 | .165 |
| 1908 | 14 | 10 | .583 | 2.51 | 27 | 24 | 18 | 208.1 | 178 | 48 | 50 | 2 | 0 | 0 | 1 | 73 | 9 | 0 | .123 |
| 1909 | 11 | 7 | .611 | 2.11 | 27 | 19 | 11 | 171 | 147 | 61 | 69 | 3 | 1 | 1 | 0 | 59 | 11 | 0 | .186 |
| 1910 STL N | 6 | 14 | .300 | 3.81 | 30 | 18 | 9 | 156 | 168 | 55 | 51 | 0 | 1 | 2 | 2 | 51 | 10 | 0 | .196 |
| 6 yrs. | 70 | 68 | .507 | 2.80 | 180 | 140 | 99 | 1216 | 1100 | 375 | 458 | 10 | 4 | 6 | 5 | 445 | 80 | 1 | .180 |
| 1 yr. | 5 | 5 | .500 | 3.05 | 12 | 10 | 9 | 100.1 | 88 | 37 | 34 | 0 | 0 | 1 | 0 | 58 | 13 | 0 | .224 |

## Jim Cosman

**COSMAN, JAMES HENRY**                                                      BR TR 6'4½" 211 lbs.
B. Feb. 19, 1943, Brockport, N. Y.

| | W | L | PCT | ERA | G | GS | CG | IP | H | BB | SO | ShO | W | L | SV | AB | H | HR | BA |
|---|---|---|---|---|---|---|---|---|---|---|---|---|---|---|---|---|---|---|---|
| 1966 STL N | 1 | 0 | 1.000 | 0.00 | 1 | 1 | 1 | 9 | 2 | 2 | 5 | 1 | 0 | 0 | 0 | 3 | 0 | 0 | .000 |
| 1967 | 1 | 0 | 1.000 | 3.16 | 10 | 5 | 0 | 31.1 | 21 | 24 | 11 | 0 | 0 | 0 | 0 | 8 | 1 | 0 | .125 |
| 1970 CHI N | 0 | 0 | – | 27.00 | 1 | 0 | 0 | 1 | 3 | 1 | 0 | 0 | 0 | 0 | 0 | 0 | 0 | 0 | – |
| 3 yrs. | 2 | 0 | 1.000 | 3.05 | 12 | 6 | 1 | 41.1 | 26 | 27 | 16 | 1 | 0 | 0 | 0 | 11 | 1 | 0 | .091 |
| 1 yr. | 0 | 0 | | 27.00 | 1 | 0 | 0 | 1 | 3 | 1 | 0 | 0 | 0 | 0 | 0 | 0 | 0 | 0 | – |

| | W | L | PCT | ERA | G | GS | CG | IP | H | BB | SO | ShO | Relief Pitching W | L | SV | BATTING AB | H | HR | BA |
|---|---|---|---|---|---|---|---|---|---|---|---|---|---|---|---|---|---|---|---|

## Ensign Cottrell

**COTTRELL, ENSIGN STOVER**
B. Aug. 29, 1888, Hoosick Falls, N. Y.  D. Feb. 27, 1947, Syracuse, N. Y.  BL TL 5'9½" 173 lbs.

| | W | L | PCT | ERA | G | GS | CG | IP | H | BB | SO | ShO | W | L | SV | AB | H | HR | BA |
|---|---|---|---|---|---|---|---|---|---|---|---|---|---|---|---|---|---|---|---|
| 1911 PIT N | 0 | 0 | – | 9.00 | 1 | 0 | 0 | 1 | 4 | 1 | 0 | 0 | 0 | 0 | 0 | 0 | 0 | 0 | – |
| 1912 CHI N | 0 | 0 | – | 9.00 | 1 | 0 | 0 | 4 | 8 | 1 | 1 | 0 | 0 | 0 | 0 | 1 | 0 | 0 | .000 |
| 1913 PHI A | 1 | 0 | 1.000 | 5.40 | 2 | 1 | 1 | 10 | 15 | 2 | 3 | 0 | 0 | 0 | 0 | 4 | 1 | 0 | .250 |
| 1914 BOS N | 0 | 1 | .000 | 9.00 | 1 | 1 | 0 | 1 | 2 | 3 | 1 | 0 | 0 | 0 | 0 | 0 | 0 | 0 | – |
| 1915 NY A | 0 | 1 | .000 | 3.38 | 7 | 0 | 0 | 21.1 | 29 | 7 | 7 | 0 | 0 | 1 | 0 | 7 | 0 | 0 | .000 |
| 5 yrs. | 1 | 2 | .333 | 4.82 | 12 | 2 | 1 | 37.1 | 58 | 14 | 12 | 0 | 0 | 1 | 0 | 12 | 1 | 0 | .083 |
| 1 yr. | 0 | 0 | – | 9.00 | 1 | 0 | 0 | 4 | 8 | 1 | 1 | 0 | 0 | 0 | 0 | 1 | 0 | 0 | .000 |

## Roscoe Coughlin

**COUGHLIN, WILLIAM EDWARD**
B. Mar. 15, 1868, Walpole, Mass.  D. Mar. 20, 1951, Chelsea, Mass.  TR 5'10" 160 lbs.

| | W | L | PCT | ERA | G | GS | CG | IP | H | BB | SO | ShO | W | L | SV | AB | H | HR | BA |
|---|---|---|---|---|---|---|---|---|---|---|---|---|---|---|---|---|---|---|---|
| 1890 CHI N | 4 | 4 | .500 | 4.26 | 11 | 10 | 10 | 95 | 102 | 40 | 29 | 0 | 0 | 0 | 0 | 39 | 10 | 0 | .256 |
| 1891 NY N | 3 | 3 | .500 | 3.84 | 8 | 7 | 6 | 61 | 74 | 23 | 22 | 0 | 0 | 0 | 0 | 23 | 3 | 0 | .130 |
| 2 yrs. | 7 | 7 | .500 | 4.10 | 19 | 17 | 16 | 156 | 176 | 63 | 51 | 0 | 0 | 0 | 0 | 62 | 13 | 0 | .210 |
| 1 yr. | 4 | 4 | .500 | 4.26 | 11 | 10 | 10 | 95 | 102 | 40 | 29 | 0 | 0 | 0 | 0 | 39 | 10 | 0 | .256 |

## George Crosby

**CROSBY, GEORGE WASHINGTON**
B. 1860, Iowa  D. Jan. 9, 1913, San Francisco, Calif.

| | W | L | PCT | ERA | G | GS | CG | IP | H | BB | SO | ShO | W | L | SV | AB | H | HR | BA |
|---|---|---|---|---|---|---|---|---|---|---|---|---|---|---|---|---|---|---|---|
| 1884 CHI N | 1 | 2 | .333 | *3.54* | 3 | 3 | 3 | 28 | 27 | 12 | 11 | 0 | 0 | 0 | 0 | 13 | 4 | 1 | .308 |

## Ken Crosby

**CROSBY, KENNETH STEWART**
B. Dec. 16, 1947, New Denver, B. C., Canada  BR TR 6'2" 179 lbs.

| | W | L | PCT | ERA | G | GS | CG | IP | H | BB | SO | ShO | W | L | SV | AB | H | HR | BA |
|---|---|---|---|---|---|---|---|---|---|---|---|---|---|---|---|---|---|---|---|
| 1975 CHI N | 1 | 0 | 1.000 | 3.38 | 9 | 0 | 0 | 8 | 10 | 7 | 6 | 0 | 1 | 0 | 0 | 0 | 0 | 0 | – |
| 1976 | 0 | 0 | – | 12.00 | 7 | 1 | 0 | 12 | 20 | 8 | 5 | 0 | 0 | 0 | 0 | 2 | 1 | 0 | .500 |
| 2 yrs. | 1 | 0 | 1.000 | 8.55 | 16 | 1 | 0 | 20 | 30 | 15 | 11 | 0 | 1 | 0 | 0 | 2 | 1 | 0 | .500 |
| 2 yrs. | 1 | 0 | 1.000 | 8.55 | 16 | 1 | 0 | 20 | 30 | 15 | 11 | 0 | 1 | 0 | 0 | 2 | 1 | 0 | .500 |

## Ray Culp

**CULP, RAY LEONARD**
B. Aug. 6, 1941, Elgin, Tex.  BR TR 6' 200 lbs.

| | W | L | PCT | ERA | G | GS | CG | IP | H | BB | SO | ShO | W | L | SV | AB | H | HR | BA |
|---|---|---|---|---|---|---|---|---|---|---|---|---|---|---|---|---|---|---|---|
| 1963 PHI N | 14 | 11 | .560 | 2.97 | 34 | 30 | 10 | 203.1 | 148 | 102 | 176 | 5 | 2 | 1 | 0 | 66 | 9 | 0 | .136 |
| 1964 | 8 | 7 | .533 | 4.13 | 30 | 19 | 3 | 135 | 139 | 56 | 96 | 1 | 1 | 0 | 0 | 44 | 5 | 0 | .114 |
| 1965 | 14 | 10 | .583 | 3.22 | 33 | 30 | 11 | 204.1 | 188 | 78 | 134 | 2 | 1 | 1 | 0 | 68 | 6 | 0 | .088 |
| 1966 | 7 | 4 | .636 | 5.04 | 34 | 12 | 1 | 110.2 | 106 | 53 | 100 | 0 | 4 | 0 | 1 | 26 | 2 | 0 | .077 |
| 1967 CHI N | 8 | 11 | .421 | 3.89 | 30 | 22 | 4 | 152.2 | 138 | 59 | 111 | 1 | 1 | 1 | 0 | 51 | 5 | 0 | .098 |
| 1968 BOS A | 16 | 6 | .727 | 2.91 | 35 | 30 | 11 | 216.1 | 166 | 82 | 190 | 6 | 0 | 0 | 0 | 70 | 8 | 0 | .114 |
| 1969 | 17 | 8 | .680 | 3.81 | 32 | 32 | 9 | 227 | 195 | 79 | 172 | 2 | 0 | 0 | 0 | 79 | 12 | 1 | .152 |
| 1970 | 17 | 14 | .548 | 3.05 | 33 | 33 | 15 | 251 | 211 | 91 | 197 | 1 | 0 | 0 | 0 | 97 | 12 | 0 | .124 |
| 1971 | 14 | 16 | .467 | 3.61 | 35 | 35 | 12 | 242 | 236 | 67 | 151 | 3 | 0 | 0 | 0 | 68 | 8 | 0 | .118 |
| 1972 | 5 | 8 | .385 | 4.46 | 16 | 16 | 4 | 105 | 104 | 53 | 52 | 1 | 0 | 0 | 0 | 33 | 7 | 0 | .212 |
| 1973 | 2 | 6 | .250 | 4.50 | 10 | 9 | 0 | 50 | 46 | 32 | 32 | 0 | 0 | 0 | 0 | 0 | 0 | 0 | – |
| 11 yrs. | 122 | 101 | .547 | 3.58 | 322 | 268 | 80 | 1897.1 | 1677 | 752 | 1411 | 22 | 9 | 3 | 1 | 602 | 74 | 1 | .123 |
| 1 yr. | 8 | 11 | .421 | 3.89 | 30 | 22 | 4 | 152.2 | 138 | 59 | 111 | 1 | 1 | 1 | 0 | 51 | 5 | 0 | .098 |

## Bert Cunningham

**CUNNINGHAM, ELLSWORTH ELMER**
B. Nov. 25, 1866, Wilmington, Del.  D. May 14, 1952, Cragmere, Del.  BR TR

| | W | L | PCT | ERA | G | GS | CG | IP | H | BB | SO | ShO | W | L | SV | AB | H | HR | BA |
|---|---|---|---|---|---|---|---|---|---|---|---|---|---|---|---|---|---|---|---|
| 1887 BKN AA | 0 | 2 | .000 | *5.09* | 3 | 3 | 3 | 23 | 26 | 13 | 8 | 0 | 0 | 0 | 0 | 8 | 0 | 0 | .000 |
| 1888 BAL AA | 22 | 29 | .431 | 3.39 | 51 | 51 | 50 | 453.1 | 412 | 157 | 186 | 0 | 0 | 0 | 0 | 177 | 33 | 1 | .186 |
| 1889 | 16 | 19 | .457 | 4.87 | 39 | 33 | 29 | 279.1 | 306 | 141 | 140 | 0 | 2 | 0 | 1 | 131 | 27 | 0 | .206 |
| 1890 2 teams | | | | | | | PHI P (14G 3–9) | | | BUF P (25G 9–15) | | | | | | | | | |
| " total | 12 | 24 | .333 | 5.63 | 39 | 36 | 35 | 319.2 | 384 | 201 | 111 | 2 | 0 | 1 | 0 | 153 | 29 | 0 | .190 |
| 1891 BAL AA | 11 | 14 | .440 | 4.01 | 30 | 25 | 21 | 237.2 | 241 | 138 | 59 | 0 | 1 | 0 | 0 | 100 | 15 | 1 | .150 |
| 1895 LOU N | 11 | 16 | .407 | 4.75 | 31 | 28 | 24 | 231 | 299 | 104 | 49 | 1 | 0 | 0 | 0 | 100 | 30 | 0 | .300 |
| 1896 | 7 | 14 | .333 | 5.09 | 27 | 20 | 17 | 189.1 | 242 | 74 | 37 | 0 | 0 | 1 | 1 | 88 | 22 | 2 | .250 |
| 1897 | 14 | 13 | .519 | 4.14 | 29 | 27 | 25 | 234.2 | 286 | 72 | 49 | 0 | 2 | 0 | 0 | 93 | 22 | 2 | .237 |
| 1898 | 28 | 15 | .651 | 3.16 | 44 | 42 | 41 | 362 | 387 | 65 | 34 | 0 | 0 | 1 | 0 | 140 | 32 | 1 | .229 |
| 1899 | 17 | 17 | .500 | 3.84 | 39 | 37 | 33 | 323.2 | 385 | 75 | 36 | 1 | 0 | 1 | 0 | 154 | 40 | 2 | .260 |
| 1900 CHI N | 4 | 3 | .571 | 4.36 | 8 | 7 | 7 | 64 | 84 | 21 | 7 | 0 | 0 | 0 | 0 | 27 | 4 | 0 | .148 |
| 1901 | 0 | 1 | .000 | 5.00 | 1 | 1 | 1 | 9 | 11 | 3 | 2 | 0 | 0 | 0 | 0 | 1 | 0 | 0 | .000 |
| 12 yrs. | 142 | 167 | .460 | 4.22 | 341 | 310 | 286 | 2726.2 | 3063 | 1064 | 718 | 4 | 5 | 4 | 2 | 1172 | 254 | 9 | .217 |
| 2 yrs. | 4 | 4 | .500 | 4.44 | 9 | 8 | 8 | 73 | 95 | 24 | 9 | 0 | 0 | 0 | 0 | 28 | 4 | 0 | .143 |

## Clarence Currie

**CURRIE, CLARENCE F.**
B. Dec. 30, 1878, Glencoe, Ont., Canada  D. July 15, 1941, Little Chute, Wis.  BR TR

| | W | L | PCT | ERA | G | GS | CG | IP | H | BB | SO | ShO | W | L | SV | AB | H | HR | BA |
|---|---|---|---|---|---|---|---|---|---|---|---|---|---|---|---|---|---|---|---|
| 1902 2 teams | | | CIN N (10G 3–4) | | | | STL N (15G 6–5) | | | | | | | | | | | | |
| " total | 9 | 9 | .500 | 3.10 | 25 | 18 | 15 | 183 | 192 | 48 | 49 | 2 | 0 | 0 | 0 | 70 | 11 | 0 | .157 |
| 1903 2 teams | | | STL N (22G 4–12) | | | | CHI N (6G 1–2) | | | | | | | | | | | | |
| " total | 5 | 14 | .263 | 3.82 | 28 | 19 | 15 | 181.1 | 190 | 69 | 61 | 1 | 2 | 1 | 2 | 59 | 9 | 0 | .153 |
| 2 yrs. | 14 | 23 | .378 | 3.46 | 53 | 37 | 30 | 364.1 | 382 | 117 | 110 | 3 | 2 | 1 | 2 | 129 | 20 | 0 | .155 |
| 1 yr. | 1 | 2 | .333 | 2.97 | 6 | 3 | 2 | 33.1 | 35 | 9 | 9 | 0 | 1 | 0 | 1 | 12 | 5 | 0 | .417 |

## Cliff Curtis

**CURTIS, CLIFTON GARFIELD**
B. July 3, 1883, Delaware, Ohio  D. Apr. 23, 1943, Newark, Ohio  BR TR

| | W | L | PCT | ERA | G | GS | CG | IP | H | BB | SO | ShO | W | L | SV | AB | H | HR | BA |
|---|---|---|---|---|---|---|---|---|---|---|---|---|---|---|---|---|---|---|---|
| 1909 BOS N | 4 | 5 | .444 | 1.41 | 10 | 9 | 8 | 83 | 53 | 30 | 22 | 2 | 0 | 1 | 0 | 29 | 1 | 0 | .034 |
| 1910 | 6 | 24 | .200 | 3.55 | 43 | 37 | 12 | 251 | 251 | 124 | 75 | 2 | 0 | 1 | 2 | 82 | 12 | 0 | .146 |
| 1911 3 teams | | | BOS N (12G 1–8) | | | | CHI N (4G 1–2) | | | PHI N (8G 2–1) | | | | | | | | | |
| " total | 4 | 11 | .267 | 3.77 | 24 | 15 | 8 | 129 | 131 | 54 | 40 | 1 | 1 | 2 | 1 | 45 | 12 | 0 | .267 |
| 1912 2 teams | | | PHI N (10G 2–5) | | | | BKN N (19G 4–7) | | | | | | | | | | | | |
| " total | 6 | 12 | .333 | 3.67 | 29 | 17 | 5 | 130 | 127 | 54 | 42 | 0 | 1 | 2 | 0 | 41 | 8 | 0 | .195 |

| | W | L | PCT | ERA | G | GS | CG | IP | H | BB | SO | ShO | Relief Pitching W | L | SV | BATTING AB | H | HR | BA |
|---|---|---|---|---|---|---|---|---|---|---|---|---|---|---|---|---|---|---|---|

## Cliff Curtis continued

| | W | L | PCT | ERA | G | GS | CG | IP | H | BB | SO | ShO | W | L | SV | AB | H | HR | BA |
|---|---|---|---|---|---|---|---|---|---|---|---|---|---|---|---|---|---|---|---|
| 1913 BKN N | 8 | 9 | .471 | 3.26 | 30 | 16 | 5 | 151.2 | 145 | 55 | 57 | 0 | 3 | 1 | 1 | 49 | 6 | 0 | .122 |
| 5 yrs. | 28 | 61 | .315 | 3.31 | 136 | 94 | 38 | 744.2 | 707 | 317 | 236 | 5 | 5 | 7 | 4 | 246 | 39 | 0 | .159 |
| 1 yr. | 1 | 2 | .333 | 3.86 | 4 | 1 | 0 | 7 | 7 | 5 | 4 | 0 | 1 | 1 | 0 | 2 | 1 | 0 | .500 |

## Jack Curtis

CURTIS, JACK PATRICK     BL TL 5'10" 175 lbs.
B. Jan. 11, 1937, Rhodhiss, N. C.

| | W | L | PCT | ERA | G | GS | CG | IP | H | BB | SO | ShO | W | L | SV | AB | H | HR | BA |
|---|---|---|---|---|---|---|---|---|---|---|---|---|---|---|---|---|---|---|---|
| 1961 CHI N | 10 | 13 | .435 | 4.89 | 31 | 27 | 6 | 180.1 | 220 | 51 | 57 | 0 | 0 | 0 | 0 | 60 | 10 | 2 | .167 |
| 1962 2 teams | | | CHI | N (4G 0–2) | | | MIL | N (30G 4–4) | | | | | | | | | | | |
| " total | 4 | 6 | .400 | 4.04 | 34 | 8 | 0 | 93.2 | 100 | 33 | 48 | 0 | 4 | 3 | 1 | 22 | 5 | 0 | .227 |
| 1963 CLE A | 0 | 0 | — | 18.00 | 4 | 0 | 0 | 5 | 8 | 5 | 3 | 0 | 0 | 0 | 0 | 0 | 0 | 0 | — |
| 3 yrs. | 14 | 19 | .424 | 4.84 | 69 | 35 | 6 | 279 | 328 | 89 | 108 | 0 | 4 | 3 | 1 | 82 | 15 | 2 | .183 |
| 2 yrs. | 10 | 15 | .400 | 4.76 | 35 | 30 | 6 | 198.1 | 238 | 57 | 65 | 0 | 0 | 0 | 0 | 64 | 11 | 2 | .172 |

## Mike Cvengros

CVENGROS, MICHAEL JOHN     BL TL 5'8" 159 lbs.
B. Dec. 1, 1901, Hot Springs, Ark.    D. Aug. 2, 1970, Hot Springs, Ark.

| | W | L | PCT | ERA | G | GS | CG | IP | H | BB | SO | ShO | W | L | SV | AB | H | HR | BA |
|---|---|---|---|---|---|---|---|---|---|---|---|---|---|---|---|---|---|---|---|
| 1922 NY N | 0 | 1 | .000 | 4.00 | 1 | 1 | 1 | 9 | 6 | 3 | 3 | 0 | 0 | 0 | 0 | 3 | 0 | 0 | .000 |
| 1923 CHI A | 12 | 13 | .480 | 4.39 | 41 | 26 | 14 | 215.1 | 216 | 107 | 86 | 0 | 2 | 1 | 3 | 74 | 15 | 0 | .203 |
| 1924 | 3 | 12 | .200 | 5.88 | 26 | 15 | 2 | 105.2 | 119 | 67 | 36 | 0 | 1 | 3 | 0 | 30 | 6 | 0 | .200 |
| 1925 | 3 | 9 | .250 | 4.30 | 22 | 11 | 4 | 104.2 | 109 | 55 | 32 | 0 | 1 | 2 | 0 | 33 | 5 | 0 | .152 |
| 1927 PIT N | 2 | 1 | .667 | 3.35 | 23 | 4 | 0 | 53.2 | 55 | 24 | 21 | 0 | 2 | 0 | 1 | 19 | 3 | 0 | .158 |
| 1929 CHI N | 5 | 4 | .556 | 4.64 | 32 | 2 | 0 | 64 | 82 | 29 | 23 | 0 | 5 | 4 | 2 | 15 | 6 | 0 | .400 |
| 6 yrs. | 25 | 40 | .385 | 4.58 | 145 | 59 | 21 | 552.1 | 587 | 285 | 201 | 0 | 11 | 10 | 6 | 174 | 35 | 0 | .201 |
| 1 yr. | 5 | 4 | .556 | 4.64 | 32 | 2 | 0 | 64 | 82 | 29 | 23 | 0 | 5 | 4 | 2 | 15 | 6 | 0 | .400 |

WORLD SERIES

| | W | L | PCT | ERA | G | GS | CG | IP | H | BB | SO | ShO | W | L | SV | AB | H | HR | BA |
|---|---|---|---|---|---|---|---|---|---|---|---|---|---|---|---|---|---|---|---|
| 1927 PIT N | 0 | 0 | — | 3.86 | 2 | 0 | 0 | 2.1 | 3 | 0 | 2 | 0 | 0 | 0 | 0 | 0 | 0 | 0 | — |

## Alvin Dark

DARK, ALVIN RALPH (Blackie)     BR TR 5'11" 185 lbs.
B. Jan. 7, 1922, Comanche, Okla.
Manager 1961-64, 1966-71, 1974-75, 1977.

| | W | L | PCT | ERA | G | GS | CG | IP | H | BB | SO | ShO | W | L | SV | AB | H | HR | BA |
|---|---|---|---|---|---|---|---|---|---|---|---|---|---|---|---|---|---|---|---|
| 1953 NY N | 0 | 0 | — | 18.00 | 1 | 1 | 0 | 1 | 1 | 1 | 0 | 0 | 0 | 0 | 0 | * | | | |

## Bobby Darwin

DARWIN, ARTHUR BOBBY LEE     BR TR 6'2" 190 lbs.
B. Feb. 16, 1943, Los Angeles, Calif.

| | W | L | PCT | ERA | G | GS | CG | IP | H | BB | SO | ShO | W | L | SV | AB | H | HR | BA |
|---|---|---|---|---|---|---|---|---|---|---|---|---|---|---|---|---|---|---|---|
| 1962 LA A | 0 | 1 | .000 | 10.80 | 1 | 1 | 0 | 3.1 | 8 | 4 | 6 | 0 | 0 | 0 | 0 | 1 | 0 | 0 | .000 |
| 1969 LA N | 0 | 0 | — | 9.00 | 3 | 0 | 0 | 4 | 4 | 5 | 0 | 0 | 0 | 0 | 0 | 0 | 0 | 0 | |
| | 0 | 1 | .000 | 9.82 | 4 | 1 | 0 | 7.1 | 12 | 9 | 6 | 0 | 0 | 0 | 0 | * | | | |

## Curt Davis

DAVIS, CURTIS BENTON (Coonskin)     BR TR 6'2" 185 lbs.
B. Sept. 7, 1903, Greenfield, Mo.    D. Oct. 13, 1965, Covina, Calif.

| | W | L | PCT | ERA | G | GS | CG | IP | H | BB | SO | ShO | W | L | SV | AB | H | HR | BA |
|---|---|---|---|---|---|---|---|---|---|---|---|---|---|---|---|---|---|---|---|
| 1934 PHI N | 19 | 17 | .528 | 2.95 | 51 | 31 | 18 | 274.1 | 283 | 60 | 99 | 3 | 6 | 2 | 5 | 95 | 20 | 1 | .211 |
| 1935 | 16 | 14 | .533 | 3.66 | 44 | 27 | 19 | 231 | 264 | 47 | 74 | 3 | 2 | 2 | 2 | 75 | 13 | 1 | .173 |
| 1936 2 teams | | | PHI | N (10G 2–4) | | | CHI | N (24G 11–9) | | | | | | | | | | | |
| " total | 13 | 13 | .500 | 3.46 | 34 | 28 | 13 | 213.1 | 217 | 50 | 70 | 0 | 1 | 2 | 1 | 79 | 12 | 0 | .152 |
| 1937 CHI N | 10 | 5 | .667 | 4.08 | 28 | 14 | 8 | 123.2 | 138 | 30 | 32 | 0 | 1 | 1 | 1 | 40 | 12 | 1 | .300 |
| 1938 STL N | 12 | 8 | .600 | 3.63 | 40 | 21 | 8 | 173.1 | 187 | 27 | 36 | 2 | 4 | 0 | 3 | 57 | 13 | 3 | .228 |
| 1939 | 22 | 16 | .579 | 3.63 | 49 | 31 | 13 | 248 | 279 | 48 | 70 | 3 | 3 | 5 | 7 | 105 | 40 | 1 | .381 |
| 1940 2 teams | | | STL | N (14G 0–4) | | | BKN | N (22G 8–7) | | | | | | | | | | | |
| " total | 8 | 11 | .421 | 4.19 | 36 | 25 | 9 | 191 | 208 | 38 | 58 | 0 | 1 | 1 | 3 | 66 | 6 | 1 | .091 |
| 1941 BKN N | 13 | 7 | .650 | 2.97 | 28 | 16 | 10 | 154.1 | 141 | 27 | 50 | 5 | 2 | 3 | 2 | 59 | 11 | 2 | .186 |
| 1942 | 15 | 6 | .714 | 2.36 | 32 | 26 | 13 | 206 | 179 | 51 | 60 | 5 | 1 | 0 | 2 | 68 | 12 | 0 | .176 |
| 1943 | 10 | 13 | .435 | 3.78 | 31 | 21 | 8 | 164.1 | 182 | 39 | 47 | 2 | 3 | 1 | 3 | 55 | 9 | 0 | .164 |
| 1944 | 10 | 11 | .476 | 3.34 | 31 | 23 | 12 | 194 | 207 | 39 | 49 | 1 | 1 | 0 | 4 | 63 | 10 | 0 | .159 |
| 1945 | 10 | 10 | .500 | 3.25 | 24 | 18 | 10 | 149.2 | 171 | 21 | 39 | 0 | 0 | 2 | 0 | 51 | 7 | 1 | .137 |
| 1946 | 0 | 0 | — | 13.50 | 1 | 0 | 0 | 2 | 3 | 2 | 0 | 0 | 0 | 0 | 0 | 0 | 0 | 0 | — |
| 13 yrs. | 158 | 131 | .547 | 3.42 | 429 | 281 | 141 | 2325 | 2459 | 479 | 684 | 24 | 25 | 19 | 33 | 813 | 165 | 11 | .203 |
| 2 yrs. | 21 | 14 | .600 | 3.48 | 52 | 34 | 18 | 276.2 | 284 | 61 | 84 | 0 | 2 | 2 | 2 | 93 | 20 | 1 | .215 |

WORLD SERIES

| | W | L | PCT | ERA | G | GS | CG | IP | H | BB | SO | ShO | W | L | SV | AB | H | HR | BA |
|---|---|---|---|---|---|---|---|---|---|---|---|---|---|---|---|---|---|---|---|
| 1941 BKN N | 0 | 1 | .000 | 5.06 | 1 | 1 | 0 | 5.1 | 6 | 3 | 1 | 0 | 0 | 0 | 0 | 2 | 0 | 0 | .000 |

## Jim Davis

DAVIS, JAMES BENNETT     BB TL 6' 180 lbs.
B. Sept. 15, 1924, Red Bluff, Calif.

| | W | L | PCT | ERA | G | GS | CG | IP | H | BB | SO | ShO | W | L | SV | AB | H | HR | BA |
|---|---|---|---|---|---|---|---|---|---|---|---|---|---|---|---|---|---|---|---|
| 1954 CHI N | 11 | 7 | .611 | 3.52 | 46 | 12 | 2 | 127.2 | 114 | 51 | 58 | 0 | 6 | 4 | 2 | 32 | 2 | 0 | .063 |
| 1955 | 7 | 11 | .389 | 4.44 | 42 | 16 | 2 | 133.2 | 122 | 58 | 62 | 0 | 5 | 3 | 3 | 37 | 1 | 0 | .027 |
| 1956 | 5 | 7 | .417 | 3.66 | 46 | 11 | 2 | 120.1 | 116 | 59 | 66 | 1 | 3 | 2 | 2 | 28 | 5 | 0 | .179 |
| 1957 2 teams | | | STL | N (10G 0–1) | | | NY | N (10G 1–0) | | | | | | | | | | | |
| " total | 1 | 1 | .500 | 5.84 | 20 | 0 | 0 | 24.2 | 31 | 11 | 11 | 0 | 1 | 1 | 2 | 2 | 1 | 0 | .500 |
| 4 yrs. | 24 | 26 | .480 | 4.01 | 154 | 39 | 4 | 406.1 | 383 | 179 | 197 | 1 | 15 | 8 | 10 | 99 | 9 | 0 | .091 |
| 3 yrs. | 23 | 25 | .479 | 3.89 | 134 | 39 | 4 | 381.2 | 352 | 168 | 186 | 1 | 14 | 7 | 9 | 97 | 8 | 0 | .082 |

## Dizzy Dean

DEAN, JAY HANNA     BR TR 6'2" 182 lbs.
Brother of Paul Dean.
B. Jan. 16, 1911, Lucas, Ark.    D. July 17, 1974, Reno, Nev.
Hall of Fame 1953.

| | W | L | PCT | ERA | G | GS | CG | IP | H | BB | SO | ShO | W | L | SV | AB | H | HR | BA |
|---|---|---|---|---|---|---|---|---|---|---|---|---|---|---|---|---|---|---|---|
| 1930 STL N | 1 | 0 | 1.000 | 1.00 | 1 | 1 | 1 | 9 | 3 | 3 | 5 | 0 | 0 | 0 | 0 | 3 | 1 | 0 | .333 |
| 1932 | 18 | 15 | .545 | 3.30 | 46 | 33 | 16 | 286 | 280 | 102 | 191 | 4 | 0 | 3 | 2 | 97 | 25 | 2 | .258 |
| 1933 | 20 | 18 | .526 | 3.04 | 48 | 34 | 26 | 293 | 279 | 64 | 199 | 3 | 1 | 3 | 4 | 105 | 19 | 1 | .181 |
| 1934 | 30 | 7 | .811 | 2.66 | 50 | 33 | 24 | 311.2 | 288 | 75 | 195 | 7 | 4 | 2 | 7 | 118 | 29 | 2 | .246 |
| 1935 | 28 | 12 | .700 | 3.11 | 50 | 36 | 29 | 324.1 | 326 | 82 | 182 | 3 | 4 | 3 | 5 | 128 | 30 | 2 | .234 |
| 1936 | 24 | 13 | .649 | 3.17 | 51 | 34 | 28 | 315 | 310 | 53 | 195 | 2 | 2 | 3 | 11 | 121 | 27 | 0 | .223 |

| | W | L | PCT | ERA | G | GS | CG | IP | H | BB | SO | ShO | Relief Pitching W | L | SV | BATTING AB | H | HR | BA |
|---|---|---|---|---|---|---|---|---|---|---|---|---|---|---|---|---|---|---|---|

## Dizzy Dean continued

| | W | L | PCT | ERA | G | GS | CG | IP | H | BB | SO | ShO | W | L | SV | AB | H | HR | BA |
|---|---|---|---|---|---|---|---|---|---|---|---|---|---|---|---|---|---|---|---|
| 1937 | 13 | 10 | .565 | 2.69 | 27 | 25 | 17 | 197.1 | 206 | 33 | 120 | 4 | 0 | 1 | 1 | 66 | 15 | 1 | .227 |
| 1938 CHI N | 7 | 1 | .875 | 1.81 | 13 | 10 | 3 | 74.2 | 63 | 8 | 22 | 1 | 0 | 0 | 0 | 26 | 5 | 0 | .192 |
| 1939 | 6 | 4 | .600 | 3.36 | 19 | 13 | 7 | 96.1 | 98 | 17 | 27 | 2 | 0 | 1 | 0 | 34 | 5 | 0 | .147 |
| 1940 | 3 | 3 | .500 | 5.17 | 10 | 9 | 3 | 54 | 68 | 20 | 18 | 0 | 0 | 0 | 0 | 18 | 4 | 0 | .222 |
| 1941 | 0 | 0 | — | 18.00 | 1 | 1 | 0 | 1 | 3 | 0 | 1 | 0 | 0 | 0 | 0 | 0 | 0 | 0 | — |
| 1947 STL A | 0 | 0 | — | 0.00 | 1 | 1 | 0 | 4 | 3 | 1 | 0 | 0 | 0 | 0 | 0 | 1 | 1 | 0 | 1.000 |
| 12 yrs. | 150 | 83 | .644 | 3.03 | 317 | 230 | 154 | 1966.1 | 1927 | 458 | 1155 | 26 | 11 | 16 | 30 | 717 | 161 | 8 | .225 |
| 4 yrs. | 16 | 8 | .667 | 3.35 | 43 | 33 | 13 | 226 | 232 | 45 | 68 | 3 | 0 | 1 | 0 | 78 | 14 | 0 | .179 |

WORLD SERIES

| | W | L | PCT | ERA | G | GS | CG | IP | H | BB | SO | ShO | W | L | SV | AB | H | HR | BA |
|---|---|---|---|---|---|---|---|---|---|---|---|---|---|---|---|---|---|---|---|
| 1934 STL N | 2 | 1 | .667 | 1.73 | 3 | 3 | 2 | 26 | 20 | 5 | 17 | 1 | 0 | 0 | 0 | 12 | 3 | 0 | .250 |
| 1938 CHI N | 0 | 1 | .000 | 6.48 | 2 | 1 | 0 | 8.1 | 8 | 1 | 2 | 0 | 0 | 0 | 0 | 3 | 2 | 0 | .667 |
| 2 yrs. | 2 | 2 | .500 | 2.88 | 5 | 4 | 2 | 34.1 | 28 | 6 | 19 | 1 | 0 | 0 | 0 | 15 | 5 | 0 | .333 |

## Wayland Dean

**DEAN, WAYLAND OGDEN**
B. June 20, 1903, Richwood, W. Va.
D. Apr. 10, 1930, Huntington, W. Va.

BB TR 6'2"  178 lbs.
BL 1926-27

| | W | L | PCT | ERA | G | GS | CG | IP | H | BB | SO | ShO | W | L | SV | AB | H | HR | BA |
|---|---|---|---|---|---|---|---|---|---|---|---|---|---|---|---|---|---|---|---|
| 1924 NY N | 6 | 12 | .333 | 5.01 | 26 | 20 | 6 | 125.2 | 139 | 45 | 39 | 0 | 1 | 2 | 0 | 40 | 8 | 2 | .200 |
| 1925 | 10 | 7 | .588 | 4.64 | 33 | 14 | 6 | 151.1 | 169 | 50 | 53 | 1 | 5 | 1 | 1 | 51 | 12 | 1 | .235 |
| 1926 PHI N | 8 | 16 | .333 | 6.10 | 33 | 26 | 15 | 163.2 | 245 | 89 | 52 | 1 | 0 | 2 | 0 | 102 | 27 | 3 | .265 |
| 1927 2 teams | PHI N (2G 0–1) | | | CHI N (2G 0–0) | | | | | | | | | | | | | | | |
| " total | 0 | 1 | .000 | 7.20 | 4 | 0 | 0 | 5 | 6 | 4 | 3 | 0 | 0 | 1 | 0 | 3 | 2 | 0 | .667 |
| 4 yrs. | 24 | 36 | .400 | 5.31 | 96 | 60 | 27 | 445.2 | 559 | 188 | 147 | 2 | 6 | 6 | 1 | * | | | |
| 1 yr. | 0 | 0 | — | 0.00 | 2 | 0 | 0 | 2 | 0 | 2 | 2 | 0 | 0 | 0 | 0 | 0 | 0 | 0 | — |

WORLD SERIES

| | W | L | PCT | ERA | G | GS | CG | IP | H | BB | SO | ShO | W | L | SV | AB | H | HR | BA |
|---|---|---|---|---|---|---|---|---|---|---|---|---|---|---|---|---|---|---|---|
| 1924 NY N | 0 | 0 | — | 4.50 | 1 | 0 | 0 | 2 | 3 | 0 | 2 | 0 | 0 | 0 | 0 | 0 | 0 | 0 | — |

## Joe Decker

**DECKER, GEORGE HENRY**
B. June 16, 1947, Storm Lake, Iowa

BR TR 5'11"  183 lbs.

| | W | L | PCT | ERA | G | GS | CG | IP | H | BB | SO | ShO | W | L | SV | AB | H | HR | BA |
|---|---|---|---|---|---|---|---|---|---|---|---|---|---|---|---|---|---|---|---|
| 1969 CHI N | 1 | 0 | 1.000 | 3.00 | 4 | 1 | 0 | 12 | 10 | 6 | 13 | 0 | 0 | 0 | 0 | 2 | 0 | 0 | .000 |
| 1970 | 2 | 7 | .222 | 4.62 | 24 | 17 | 1 | 109 | 108 | 56 | 79 | 0 | 0 | 0 | 0 | 34 | 6 | 1 | .176 |
| 1971 | 3 | 2 | .600 | 4.70 | 21 | 4 | 0 | 46 | 62 | 25 | 37 | 0 | 2 | 0 | 0 | 8 | 2 | 0 | .250 |
| 1972 | 1 | 0 | 1.000 | 2.08 | 5 | 1 | 0 | 13 | 9 | 4 | 7 | 0 | 0 | 0 | 0 | 2 | 0 | 0 | .000 |
| 1973 MIN A | 10 | 10 | .500 | 4.17 | 29 | 24 | 6 | 170.1 | 167 | 88 | 109 | 3 | 0 | 0 | 0 | 0 | 0 | 0 | — |
| 1974 | 16 | 14 | .533 | 3.29 | 37 | 37 | 11 | 249 | 234 | 97 | 158 | 1 | 0 | 0 | 0 | 0 | 0 | 0 | — |
| 1975 | 1 | 3 | .250 | 8.54 | 10 | 7 | 1 | 26.1 | 25 | 36 | 8 | 0 | 0 | 0 | 0 | 0 | 0 | 0 | — |
| 1976 | 2 | 7 | .222 | 5.28 | 13 | 12 | 0 | 58 | 60 | 51 | 35 | 0 | 0 | 0 | 0 | 0 | 0 | 0 | — |
| 1979 SEA A | 0 | 1 | .000 | 4.33 | 9 | 2 | 0 | 27 | 27 | 14 | 12 | 0 | 0 | 0 | 0 | 0 | 0 | 0 | — |
| 9 yrs. | 36 | 44 | .450 | 4.17 | 152 | 105 | 19 | 710.2 | 702 | 377 | 458 | 4 | 2 | 0 | 0 | 46 | 8 | 1 | .174 |
| 4 yrs. | 7 | 9 | .438 | 4.35 | 54 | 23 | 1 | 180 | 189 | 91 | 136 | 0 | 2 | 0 | 0 | 46 | 8 | 1 | .174 |

## Jim Delahanty

**DELAHANTY, JAMES CHRISTOPHER**
Brother of Ed Delahanty.    Brother of Frank Delahanty.
Brother of Tom Delahanty.    Brother of Joe Delahanty.
B. June 20, 1879, Cleveland, Ohio    D. Oct. 17, 1953, Cleveland, Ohio

BR TR 5'10½" 170 lbs.

| | W | L | PCT | ERA | G | GS | CG | IP | H | BB | SO | ShO | W | L | SV | AB | H | HR | BA |
|---|---|---|---|---|---|---|---|---|---|---|---|---|---|---|---|---|---|---|---|
| 1904 BOS N | 0 | 0 | — | 0.00 | 1 | 0 | 0 | 3.1 | 5 | 1 | 0 | 0 | 0 | 0 | 0 | 499 | 142 | 3 | .285 |
| 1905 | 0 | 0 | — | 4.50 | 1 | 1 | 0 | 2 | 5 | 0 | 0 | 0 | 0 | 0 | 0 | 461 | 119 | 5 | .258 |
| 2 yrs. | 0 | 0 | — | 1.69 | 2 | 1 | 0 | 5.1 | 10 | 1 | 0 | 0 | 0 | 0 | 0 | * | | | |

## Al Demaree

**DEMAREE, ALBERT WENTWORTH**
B. Sept. 8, 1886, Quincy, Ill.    D. Apr. 30, 1962, Long Beach, Calif.

BL TR 6'  170 lbs.

| | W | L | PCT | ERA | G | GS | CG | IP | H | BB | SO | ShO | W | L | SV | AB | H | HR | BA |
|---|---|---|---|---|---|---|---|---|---|---|---|---|---|---|---|---|---|---|---|
| 1912 NY N | 1 | 0 | 1.000 | 1.69 | 2 | 2 | 1 | 16 | 17 | 2 | 11 | 1 | 0 | 0 | 0 | 5 | 0 | 0 | .000 |
| 1913 | 13 | 4 | .765 | 2.21 | 31 | 24 | 11 | 199.2 | 176 | 38 | 76 | 3 | 0 | 1 | 2 | 66 | 7 | 0 | .106 |
| 1914 | 10 | 17 | .370 | 3.09 | 38 | 30 | 13 | 224 | 219 | 77 | 89 | 2 | 0 | 2 | 0 | 68 | 9 | 0 | .132 |
| 1915 PHI N | 14 | 11 | .560 | 3.05 | 32 | 26 | 13 | 209.2 | 201 | 58 | 69 | 3 | 0 | 1 | 1 | 68 | 12 | 0 | .176 |
| 1916 | 19 | 14 | .576 | 2.62 | 39 | 35 | 25 | 285 | 252 | 48 | 130 | 4 | 2 | 0 | 1 | 101 | 11 | 0 | .109 |
| 1917 2 teams | CHI N (24G 5–9) | | | NY N (15G 4–5) | | | | | | | | | | | | | | | |
| " total | 9 | 14 | .391 | 2.58 | 39 | 29 | 7 | 219.2 | 195 | 54 | 66 | 1 | 2 | 0 | 1 | 59 | 7 | 0 | .119 |
| 1918 NY N | 8 | 6 | .571 | 2.47 | 26 | 14 | 8 | 142 | 143 | 25 | 39 | 2 | 0 | 1 | 1 | 47 | 6 | 0 | .128 |
| 1919 BOS N | 6 | 6 | .500 | 3.80 | 25 | 13 | 6 | 128 | 147 | 35 | 34 | 0 | 2 | 1 | 3 | 42 | 2 | 0 | .048 |
| 8 yrs. | 80 | 72 | .526 | 2.77 | 232 | 173 | 84 | 1424 | 1350 | 337 | 514 | 16 | 6 | 6 | 9 | 456 | 54 | 0 | .118 |
| 1 yr. | 5 | 9 | .357 | 2.55 | 24 | 18 | 6 | 141.1 | 125 | 37 | 43 | 1 | 0 | 0 | 1 | 41 | 5 | 0 | .122 |

WORLD SERIES

| | W | L | PCT | ERA | G | GS | CG | IP | H | BB | SO | ShO | W | L | SV | AB | H | HR | BA |
|---|---|---|---|---|---|---|---|---|---|---|---|---|---|---|---|---|---|---|---|
| 1913 NY N | 0 | 1 | .000 | 4.50 | 1 | 1 | 0 | 4 | 7 | 1 | 0 | 0 | 0 | 0 | 0 | 1 | 0 | 0 | .000 |

## Fred Demarris

**DEMARRIS, FRED**
B. 1865, Nashua, N. H.    Deceased.

TR

| | W | L | PCT | ERA | G | GS | CG | IP | H | BB | SO | ShO | W | L | SV | AB | H | HR | BA |
|---|---|---|---|---|---|---|---|---|---|---|---|---|---|---|---|---|---|---|---|
| 1890 CHI N | 0 | 0 | — | 0.00 | 1 | 0 | 0 | 2 | 1 | 1 | 1 | 0 | 0 | 0 | 0 | 2 | 0 | 0 | .000 |

## Harry DeMiller

**DeMILLER, HARRY**
B. Nov. 12, 1867, Wooster, Ohio    D. Oct. 19, 1928, Santa Ana, Calif.

| | W | L | PCT | ERA | G | GS | CG | IP | H | BB | SO | ShO | W | L | SV | AB | H | HR | BA |
|---|---|---|---|---|---|---|---|---|---|---|---|---|---|---|---|---|---|---|---|
| 1892 CHI N | 1 | 1 | .500 | 6.38 | 4 | 2 | 2 | 24 | 29 | 16 | 15 | 0 | 0 | 0 | 0 | 10 | 3 | 0 | .300 |

## Roger Denzer

**DENZER, ROGER (Peaceful Valley)**
B. Oct. 5, 1871, LeSeuer, Minn.    D. Sept. 18, 1949, LeSeuer, Minn.

BL TR 6'  180 lbs.

| | W | L | PCT | ERA | G | GS | CG | IP | H | BB | SO | ShO | W | L | SV | AB | H | HR | BA |
|---|---|---|---|---|---|---|---|---|---|---|---|---|---|---|---|---|---|---|---|
| 1897 CHI N | 2 | 8 | .200 | 5.13 | 12 | 10 | 8 | 94.2 | 125 | 34 | 17 | 0 | 1 | 1 | 0 | 39 | 6 | 0 | .154 |

| | W | L | PCT | ERA | G | GS | CG | IP | H | BB | SO | ShO | Relief Pitching W | L | SV | BATTING AB | H | HR | BA |
|---|---|---|---|---|---|---|---|---|---|---|---|---|---|---|---|---|---|---|---|

## Roger Denzer continued

| | W | L | PCT | ERA | G | GS | CG | IP | H | BB | SO | ShO | W | L | SV | AB | H | HR | BA |
|---|---|---|---|---|---|---|---|---|---|---|---|---|---|---|---|---|---|---|---|
| 1901 NY N | 2 | 5 | .286 | 3.36 | 11 | 9 | 3 | 61.2 | 69 | 5 | 22 | 1 | 0 | 0 | 0 | 22 | 2 | 0 | .091 |
| 2 yrs. | 4 | 13 | .235 | 4.43 | 23 | 19 | 11 | 156.1 | 194 | 39 | 39 | 1 | 1 | 1 | 0 | 61 | 8 | 0 | .131 |
| 1 yr. | 2 | 8 | .200 | 5.13 | 12 | 10 | 8 | 94.2 | 125 | 34 | 17 | 0 | 1 | 1 | 0 | 39 | 6 | 0 | .154 |

## Paul Derringer

**DERRINGER, PAUL (Duke, 'Oom Paul)**  BR TR 6'3½" 205 lbs.
B. Oct. 17, 1906, Springfield, Ky.

| | W | L | PCT | ERA | G | GS | CG | IP | H | BB | SO | ShO | W | L | SV | AB | H | HR | BA |
|---|---|---|---|---|---|---|---|---|---|---|---|---|---|---|---|---|---|---|---|
| 1931 STL N | 18 | 8 | **.692** | 3.36 | 35 | 23 | 15 | 211.2 | 225 | 65 | 134 | 4 | 4 | 0 | 2 | 72 | 7 | 0 | .097 |
| 1932 | 11 | 14 | .440 | 4.05 | 39 | 30 | 14 | 233.1 | 296 | 67 | 78 | 1 | 1 | 1 | 0 | 73 | 13 | 0 | .178 |
| 1933 2 teams | | | STL | N | (3G 0–2) | | | CIN | N | (33G 7–25) | | | | | | | | | |
| " total | 7 | 27 | .206 | 3.30 | 36 | 33 | 17 | 248 | 264 | 60 | 89 | 2 | 0 | 1 | 1 | 81 | 14 | 0 | .173 |
| 1934 CIN N | 15 | 21 | .417 | 3.59 | 47 | 31 | 18 | 261 | 297 | 59 | 122 | 1 | 2 | 4 | 4 | 92 | 18 | 0 | .196 |
| 1935 | 22 | 13 | .629 | 3.51 | 45 | 33 | 20 | 276.2 | 295 | 49 | 120 | 3 | 3 | 2 | 2 | 93 | 13 | 0 | .140 |
| 1936 | 19 | 19 | .500 | 4.02 | 51 | 37 | 13 | 282.1 | 331 | 42 | 121 | 2 | 1 | 3 | 5 | 90 | 18 | 0 | .200 |
| 1937 | 10 | 14 | .417 | 4.04 | 43 | 26 | 12 | 222.2 | 240 | 55 | 94 | 1 | 1 | 4 | 1 | 80 | 16 | 0 | .200 |
| 1938 | 21 | 14 | .600 | 2.93 | 41 | 37 | 26 | 307 | 315 | 49 | 132 | 4 | 0 | 0 | 3 | 119 | 21 | 2 | .176 |
| 1939 | 25 | 7 | **.781** | 2.93 | 38 | 35 | 28 | 301 | 321 | 35 | 128 | 5 | 1 | 0 | 0 | 110 | 23 | 0 | .209 |
| 1940 | 20 | 12 | .625 | 3.06 | 37 | 37 | 26 | 296.2 | 280 | 48 | 115 | 3 | 0 | 0 | 0 | 108 | 18 | 0 | .167 |
| 1941 | 12 | 14 | .462 | 3.31 | 29 | 28 | 17 | 228.1 | 233 | 54 | 76 | 2 | 0 | 0 | 1 | 84 | 13 | 0 | .155 |
| 1942 | 10 | 11 | .476 | 3.06 | 29 | 27 | 13 | 208.2 | 203 | 49 | 68 | 1 | 0 | 0 | 0 | 68 | 9 | 0 | .132 |
| 1943 CHI N | 10 | 14 | .417 | 3.57 | 32 | 22 | 10 | 174 | 184 | 39 | 75 | 2 | 1 | 2 | 3 | 58 | 13 | 0 | .224 |
| 1944 | 7 | 13 | .350 | 4.15 | 42 | 16 | 7 | 180 | 205 | 39 | 69 | 0 | 2 | 5 | 3 | 57 | 9 | 0 | .158 |
| 1945 | 16 | 11 | .593 | 3.45 | 35 | 30 | 15 | 213.2 | 223 | 51 | 86 | 1 | 1 | 0 | 4 | 75 | 15 | 0 | .200 |
| 15 yrs. | 223 | 212 | .513 | 3.46 | 579 | 445 | 251 | 3645 | 3912 | 761 | 1507 | 32 | 17 | 22 | 29 | 1260 | 220 | 2 | .175 |
| 3 yrs. | 33 | 38 | .465 | 3.71 | 109 | 68 | 32 | 567.2 | 612 | 129 | 230 | 3 | 4 | 7 | 10 | 190 | 37 | 0 | .195 |

WORLD SERIES

| | W | L | PCT | ERA | G | GS | CG | IP | H | BB | SO | ShO | W | L | SV | AB | H | HR | BA |
|---|---|---|---|---|---|---|---|---|---|---|---|---|---|---|---|---|---|---|---|
| 1931 STL N | 0 | 2 | .000 | 4.26 | 3 | 2 | 0 | 12.2 | 14 | 7 | 14 | 0 | 0 | 0 | 0 | 2 | 0 | 0 | .000 |
| 1939 CIN N | 0 | 1 | .000 | 2.35 | 2 | 2 | 1 | 15.1 | 9 | 3 | 9 | 0 | 0 | 0 | 0 | 5 | 1 | 0 | .200 |
| 1940 | 2 | 1 | .667 | 2.79 | 3 | 3 | 2 | 19.1 | 17 | 10 | 6 | 0 | 0 | 0 | 0 | 7 | 0 | 0 | .000 |
| 1945 CHI N | 0 | 0 | – | 6.75 | 3 | 0 | 0 | 5.1 | 5 | 7 | 1 | 0 | 0 | 0 | 0 | 0 | 0 | 0 | – |
| 4 yrs. | 2 | 4 | .333 | 3.42 | 11 | 7 | 3 | 52.2 | 45 | 27 | 30 | 0 | 0 | 0 | 0 | 14 | 1 | 0 | .071 |
| | | | 7th | | 10th | | | | | | 6th | | | | | | | | |

## Tom Dettore

**DETTORE, THOMAS ANTHONY**  BL TR 6'4" 200 lbs.
B. Nov. 17, 1947, Canonsburg, Pa.

| | W | L | PCT | ERA | G | GS | CG | IP | H | BB | SO | ShO | W | L | SV | AB | H | HR | BA |
|---|---|---|---|---|---|---|---|---|---|---|---|---|---|---|---|---|---|---|---|
| 1973 PIT N | 0 | 1 | .000 | 5.96 | 12 | 1 | 0 | 22.2 | 33 | 14 | 13 | 0 | 0 | 0 | 0 | 4 | 0 | 0 | .000 |
| 1974 CHI N | 3 | 5 | .375 | 4.15 | 16 | 9 | 0 | 65 | 64 | 31 | 43 | 0 | 1 | 0 | 0 | 20 | 5 | 0 | .250 |
| 1975 | 5 | 4 | .556 | 4.15 | 36 | 5 | 0 | 85 | 88 | 31 | 46 | 0 | 4 | 3 | 0 | 24 | 6 | 0 | .250 |
| 1976 | 0 | 1 | .000 | 10.29 | 4 | 0 | 0 | 7 | 11 | 2 | 4 | 0 | 0 | 1 | 0 | 0 | 0 | 0 | – |
| 4 yrs. | 8 | 11 | .421 | 5.21 | 68 | 15 | 0 | 179.2 | 196 | 78 | 106 | 0 | 5 | 4 | 0 | 48 | 11 | 0 | .229 |
| 3 yrs. | 8 | 10 | .444 | 5.10 | 56 | 14 | 0 | 157 | 163 | 64 | 93 | 0 | 5 | 4 | 0 | 44 | 11 | 0 | .250 |

## Alec Distaso

**DISTASO, ALEC JOHN**  BR TR 6'2" 200 lbs.
B. Dec. 23, 1948, Los Angeles, Calif.

| | W | L | PCT | ERA | G | GS | CG | IP | H | BB | SO | ShO | W | L | SV | AB | H | HR | BA |
|---|---|---|---|---|---|---|---|---|---|---|---|---|---|---|---|---|---|---|---|
| 1969 CHI N | 0 | 0 | – | 3.60 | 2 | 0 | 0 | 5 | 6 | 1 | 1 | 0 | 0 | 0 | 0 | 0 | 0 | 0 | – |

## Jess Dobernic

**DOBERNIC, ANDREW JOSEPH**  BR TR 5'10" 170 lbs.
B. Nov. 20, 1917, Mt. Olive, Ill.

| | W | L | PCT | ERA | G | GS | CG | IP | H | BB | SO | ShO | W | L | SV | AB | H | HR | BA |
|---|---|---|---|---|---|---|---|---|---|---|---|---|---|---|---|---|---|---|---|
| 1939 CHI A | 0 | 1 | .000 | 13.50 | 4 | 0 | 0 | 3.1 | 3 | 6 | 1 | 0 | 0 | 1 | 0 | 1 | 0 | 0 | .000 |
| 1948 CHI N | 7 | 2 | .778 | 3.15 | 54 | 0 | 0 | 85.2 | 67 | 40 | 48 | 0 | 7 | 2 | 1 | 10 | 2 | 0 | .200 |
| 1949 2 teams | | | CHI | N | (4G 0–0) | | | CIN | N | (14G 0–0) | | | | | | | | | |
| " total | 0 | 0 | – | 11.57 | 18 | 0 | 0 | 23.1 | 37 | 20 | 6 | 0 | 0 | 0 | 0 | 2 | 0 | 0 | .000 |
| 3 yrs. | 7 | 3 | .700 | 5.21 | 76 | 0 | 0 | 112.1 | 107 | 66 | 55 | 0 | 7 | 3 | 1 | 13 | 2 | 0 | .154 |
| 2 yrs. | 7 | 2 | .778 | 3.91 | 58 | 0 | 0 | 89.2 | 76 | 44 | 48 | 0 | 7 | 2 | 1 | 10 | 2 | 0 | .200 |

## Cozy Dolan

**DOLAN, PATRICK HENRY**  BL TL 5'10" 160 lbs.
B. Dec. 3, 1872, Cambridge, Mass.   D. Mar. 29, 1907, Louisville, Ky.

| | W | L | PCT | ERA | G | GS | CG | IP | H | BB | SO | ShO | W | L | SV | AB | H | HR | BA |
|---|---|---|---|---|---|---|---|---|---|---|---|---|---|---|---|---|---|---|---|
| 1895 BOS N | 11 | 7 | .611 | 4.27 | 25 | 21 | 18 | 198.1 | 215 | 67 | 47 | 3 | 0 | 0 | 1 | 83 | 20 | 0 | .241 |
| 1896 | 1 | 4 | .200 | 4.83 | 6 | 5 | 3 | 41 | 55 | 27 | 14 | 0 | 0 | 0 | 0 | 14 | 2 | 0 | .143 |
| 1905 | 0 | 1 | .000 | 9.00 | 2 | 0 | 0 | 4 | 7 | 1 | 1 | 0 | 0 | 1 | 0 | 510 | 137 | 3 | .269 |
| 1906 | 0 | 1 | .000 | 4.50 | 2 | 0 | 0 | 12 | 12 | 6 | 7 | 0 | 0 | 1 | 0 | 549 | 136 | 0 | .248 |
| 4 yrs. | 12 | 13 | .480 | 4.44 | 35 | 26 | 21 | 255.1 | 289 | 101 | 69 | 3 | 0 | 2 | 1 | * | | | |

## John Dolan

**DOLAN, JOHN**  TR 5'10" 170 lbs.
B. Sept. 12, 1867, Newport, Ky.   D. May 8, 1948, Springfield, Ohio

| | W | L | PCT | ERA | G | GS | CG | IP | H | BB | SO | ShO | W | L | SV | AB | H | HR | BA |
|---|---|---|---|---|---|---|---|---|---|---|---|---|---|---|---|---|---|---|---|
| 1890 CIN N | 1 | 1 | .500 | 4.50 | 2 | 2 | 2 | 18 | 17 | 10 | 9 | 0 | 0 | 0 | 0 | 8 | 1 | 0 | .125 |
| 1891 COL AA | 12 | 11 | .522 | 4.16 | 27 | 24 | 19 | 203.1 | 216 | 84 | 68 | 0 | 0 | 0 | 0 | 78 | 7 | 1 | .090 |
| 1892 WAS N | 2 | 2 | .500 | 4.38 | 5 | 4 | 3 | 37 | 39 | 15 | 8 | 0 | 0 | 1 | 0 | 13 | 3 | 0 | .231 |
| 1893 STL N | 0 | 2 | .000 | 4.15 | 3 | 1 | 1 | 17.1 | 26 | 7 | 1 | 0 | 0 | 0 | 1 | 7 | 1 | 1 | .143 |
| 1895 CHI N | 0 | 1 | .000 | 6.55 | 2 | 1 | 1 | 11 | 16 | 6 | 1 | 0 | 0 | 0 | 0 | 3 | 0 | 0 | .000 |
| 5 yrs. | 15 | 17 | .469 | 4.30 | 39 | 33 | 26 | 286.2 | 314 | 122 | 87 | 0 | 0 | 1 | 1 | 109 | 12 | 2 | .110 |
| 1 yr. | 0 | 1 | .000 | 6.55 | 2 | 1 | 1 | 11 | 16 | 6 | 1 | 0 | 0 | 0 | 0 | 3 | 0 | 0 | .000 |

## Tom Dolan

**DOLAN, THOMAS J.**  BR TR
B. Jan. 10, 1859, New York, N. Y.   D. Jan. 16, 1913, St. Louis, Mo.

| | W | L | PCT | ERA | G | GS | CG | IP | H | BB | SO | ShO | W | L | SV | AB | H | HR | BA |
|---|---|---|---|---|---|---|---|---|---|---|---|---|---|---|---|---|---|---|---|
| 1883 STL AA | 0 | 0 | – | 4.50 | 1 | 0 | 0 | 4 | 4 | 0 | 0 | 0 | 0 | 0 | 0 | * | | | |

## Ed Donnelly

**DONNELLY, EDWARD VINCENT**
B. Dec. 10, 1934, Allen, Mich.  BR TR 6'  175 lbs.

| | W | L | PCT | ERA | G | GS | CG | IP | H | BB | SO | ShO | Relief Pitching W | L | SV | Batting AB | H | HR | BA |
|---|---|---|---|---|---|---|---|---|---|---|---|---|---|---|---|---|---|---|---|
| 1959 CHI N | 1 | 1 | .500 | 3.14 | 9 | 0 | 0 | 14.1 | 18 | 9 | 6 | 0 | 1 | 1 | 0 | 0 | 0 | 0 | — |

## Frank Donnelly

**DONNELLY, FRANKLIN MARION**
B. Oct. 7, 1869, Tamaroa, Ill.  D. Feb. 3, 1953, Canton, Ill.  180 lbs.

| | W | L | PCT | ERA | G | GS | CG | IP | H | BB | SO | ShO | Relief Pitching W | L | SV | Batting AB | H | HR | BA |
|---|---|---|---|---|---|---|---|---|---|---|---|---|---|---|---|---|---|---|---|
| 1893 CHI N | 3 | 1 | .750 | 5.36 | 7 | 5 | 3 | 42 | 51 | 17 | 6 | 0 | 0 | 0 | 2 | 18 | 8 | 0 | .444 |

## John Doscher

**DOSCHER, JOHN HENRY**
Son of Herm Doscher.
B. July 27, 1880, Troy, N. Y.  D. May 27, 1971, Ridgefield Park, N. J.  BR TR 6'1"

| | W | L | PCT | ERA | G | GS | CG | IP | H | BB | SO | ShO | Relief Pitching W | L | SV | Batting AB | H | HR | BA |
|---|---|---|---|---|---|---|---|---|---|---|---|---|---|---|---|---|---|---|---|
| 1903 2 teams | | | CHI N (1G 0-1) | | BKN N (3G 0-0) | | | | | | | | | | | | | | |
| " total | 0 | 1 | .000 | 9.00 | 4 | 1 | 0 | 10 | 14 | 11 | 9 | 0 | 0 | 0 | 0 | 4 | 0 | 0 | .000 |
| 1904 BKN N | 0 | 1 | .000 | 0.00 | 2 | 0 | 0 | 6.1 | 1 | 1 | 2 | 0 | 0 | 0 | 0 | 2 | 1 | 0 | .500 |
| 1905 | 1 | 5 | .167 | 3.17 | 12 | 7 | 6 | 71 | 60 | 30 | 33 | 0 | 0 | 0 | 0 | 24 | 2 | 0 | .083 |
| 1906 | 0 | 1 | .000 | 1.29 | 2 | 1 | 1 | 14 | 12 | 4 | 10 | 0 | 0 | 0 | 0 | 5 | 0 | 0 | .000 |
| 1908 CIN N | 1 | 3 | .250 | 1.83 | 7 | 4 | 3 | 44.1 | 31 | 22 | 7 | 0 | 0 | 0 | 0 | 15 | 2 | 0 | .133 |
| 5 yrs. | 2 | 11 | .154 | 2.84 | 27 | 13 | 10 | 145.2 | 118 | 68 | 61 | 0 | 0 | 0 | 0 | 50 | 5 | 0 | .100 |
| 1 yr. | 0 | 1 | .000 | 12.00 | 1 | 1 | 0 | 3 | 6 | 2 | 5 | 0 | 0 | 0 | 0 | 1 | 0 | 0 | .000 |

## Phil Douglas

**DOUGLAS, PHILLIP BROOKS (Shufflin' Phil)**
B. June 17, 1890, Cedartown, Ga.  D. Aug. 1, 1952, Sequatchie Valley, Tenn.  BR TR 6'5"  210 lbs.

| | W | L | PCT | ERA | G | GS | CG | IP | H | BB | SO | ShO | Relief Pitching W | L | SV | Batting AB | H | HR | BA |
|---|---|---|---|---|---|---|---|---|---|---|---|---|---|---|---|---|---|---|---|
| 1912 CHI A | 0 | 1 | .000 | 7.30 | 3 | 1 | 0 | 12.1 | 21 | 6 | 7 | 0 | 0 | 0 | 0 | 2 | 0 | 0 | .000 |
| 1914 CIN N | 11 | 18 | .379 | 2.56 | 45 | 25 | 13 | 239.1 | 186 | 92 | 121 | 0 | 4 | 4 | 1 | 73 | 10 | 0 | .137 |
| 1915 3 teams | | | CIN N (8G 1-5) | | BKN N (20G 5-5) | | | CHI N (4G 1-1) | | | | | | | | | | | |
| " total | 7 | 11 | .389 | 3.25 | 32 | 24 | 7 | 188.1 | 174 | 47 | 110 | 2 | 0 | 0 | 0 | 64 | 8 | 0 | .125 |
| 1917 CHI N | 14 | 20 | .412 | 2.55 | 51 | 37 | 20 | 293.1 | 269 | 50 | 151 | 5 | 3 | 0 | 1 | 89 | 11 | 0 | .124 |
| 1918 | 9 | 9 | .500 | 2.13 | 25 | 19 | 11 | 156.2 | 145 | 31 | 51 | 2 | 1 | 1 | 2 | 55 | 14 | 0 | .255 |
| 1919 2 teams | | | CHI N (25G 10-6) | | NY N (8G 2-4) | | | | | | | | | | | | | | |
| " total | 12 | 10 | .545 | 2.03 | 33 | 25 | 12 | 213 | 186 | 40 | 84 | 4 | 2 | 0 | 0 | 66 | 8 | 0 | .121 |
| 1920 NY N | 14 | 10 | .583 | 2.71 | 46 | 21 | 10 | 226 | 225 | 55 | 71 | 3 | 4 | 5 | 2 | 73 | 11 | 0 | .151 |
| 1921 | 15 | 10 | .600 | 4.22 | 40 | 27 | 13 | 221.2 | 266 | 55 | 55 | 3 | 2 | 1 | 2 | 81 | 16 | 1 | .198 |
| 1922 | 11 | 4 | .733 | 2.63 | 24 | 21 | 9 | 157.2 | 154 | 35 | 33 | 1 | 1 | 0 | 0 | 58 | 12 | 1 | .207 |
| 9 yrs. | 93 | 93 | .500 | 2.80 | 299 | 200 | 95 | 1708.1 | 1626 | 411 | 683 | 20 | 17 | 11 | 8 | 561 | 90 | 2 | .160 |
| 4 yrs. | 34 | 36 | .486 | 2.29 | 105 | 79 | 41 | 636.2 | 564 | 122 | 283 | 12 | 6 | 1 | 3 | 203 | 33 | 0 | .163 |

WORLD SERIES

| | W | L | PCT | ERA | G | GS | CG | IP | H | BB | SO | ShO | Relief Pitching W | L | SV | Batting AB | H | HR | BA |
|---|---|---|---|---|---|---|---|---|---|---|---|---|---|---|---|---|---|---|---|
| 1918 CHI N | 0 | 1 | .000 | 0.00 | 1 | 0 | 0 | 1 | 1 | 0 | 0 | 0 | 0 | 0 | 0 | 0 | 0 | 0 | — |
| 1921 NY N | 2 | 1 | .667 | 2.08 | 3 | 3 | 2 | 26 | 24 | 5 | 17 | 0 | 0 | 0 | 0 | 7 | 0 | 0 | .000 |
| 2 yrs. | 2 | 2 | .500 | 2.00 | 4 | 3 | 2 | 27 | 25 | 5 | 17 | 0 | 0 | 0 | 0 | 7 | 0 | 0 | .000 |

## Dave Dowling

**DOWLING, DAVID BARCLAY**
B. Aug. 23, 1942, St. Louis, Mo.  BR TL 6'2"  181 lbs.

| | W | L | PCT | ERA | G | GS | CG | IP | H | BB | SO | ShO | Relief Pitching W | L | SV | Batting AB | H | HR | BA |
|---|---|---|---|---|---|---|---|---|---|---|---|---|---|---|---|---|---|---|---|
| 1964 STL N | 0 | 0 | — | 0.00 | 1 | 0 | 0 | 1 | 1 | 0 | 0 | 0 | 0 | 0 | 0 | 0 | 0 | 0 | — |
| 1966 CHI N | 1 | 0 | 1.000 | 2.00 | 1 | 1 | 1 | 9 | 10 | 0 | 3 | 0 | 0 | 0 | 0 | 2 | 0 | 0 | .000 |
| 2 yrs. | 1 | 0 | 1.000 | 1.80 | 2 | 1 | 1 | 10 | 12 | 0 | 3 | 0 | 0 | 0 | 0 | 2 | 0 | 0 | .000 |
| 1 yr. | 1 | 0 | 1.000 | 2.00 | 1 | 1 | 1 | 9 | 10 | 0 | 3 | 0 | 0 | 0 | 0 | 2 | 0 | 0 | .000 |

## Moe Drabowsky

**DRABOWSKY, MYRON WALTER**
B. July 21, 1935, Ozanna, Poland  BR TR 6'3"  190 lbs.

| | W | L | PCT | ERA | G | GS | CG | IP | H | BB | SO | ShO | Relief Pitching W | L | SV | Batting AB | H | HR | BA |
|---|---|---|---|---|---|---|---|---|---|---|---|---|---|---|---|---|---|---|---|
| 1956 CHI N | 2 | 4 | .333 | 2.47 | 9 | 7 | 3 | 51 | 37 | 39 | 36 | 0 | 0 | 0 | 0 | 16 | 4 | 0 | .250 |
| 1957 | 13 | 15 | .464 | 3.53 | 36 | 33 | 12 | 239.2 | 214 | 94 | 170 | 2 | 0 | 0 | 0 | 82 | 15 | 1 | .183 |
| 1958 | 9 | 11 | .450 | 4.51 | 22 | 20 | 4 | 125.2 | 118 | 73 | 77 | 1 | 1 | 1 | 0 | 45 | 7 | 0 | .156 |
| 1959 | 5 | 10 | .333 | 4.13 | 31 | 23 | 3 | 141.2 | 138 | 75 | 70 | 1 | 0 | 0 | 0 | 45 | 5 | 0 | .111 |
| 1960 | 3 | 1 | .750 | 6.44 | 32 | 7 | 0 | 50.1 | 71 | 23 | 26 | 0 | 2 | 0 | 1 | 6 | 0 | 0 | .000 |
| 1961 MIL N | 0 | 2 | .000 | 4.62 | 16 | 0 | 0 | 25.1 | 26 | 18 | 5 | 0 | 0 | 2 | 2 | 4 | 1 | 0 | .250 |
| 1962 2 teams | | | CIN N (23G 2-6) | | KC A (10G 1-1) | | | | | | | | | | | | | | |
| " total | 3 | 7 | .300 | 5.03 | 33 | 13 | 1 | 111 | 113 | 41 | 75 | 0 | 1 | 1 | 1 | 23 | 1 | 0 | .043 |
| 1963 KC A | 7 | 13 | .350 | 3.05 | 26 | 22 | 9 | 174.1 | 135 | 64 | 109 | 2 | 0 | 0 | 0 | 62 | 10 | 2 | .161 |
| 1964 | 5 | 13 | .278 | 5.29 | 53 | 21 | 0 | 168.1 | 176 | 72 | 119 | 0 | 1 | 2 | 1 | 43 | 1 | 0 | .023 |
| 1965 | 1 | 5 | .167 | 4.42 | 14 | 5 | 0 | 38.2 | 44 | 18 | 25 | 0 | 1 | 2 | 0 | 11 | 1 | 0 | .091 |
| 1966 BAL A | 6 | 0 | 1.000 | 2.81 | 44 | 3 | 0 | 96 | 62 | 29 | 98 | 0 | 5 | 0 | 7 | 22 | 8 | 0 | .364 |
| 1967 | 7 | 5 | .583 | 1.60 | 43 | 0 | 0 | 95.1 | 66 | 25 | 96 | 0 | 7 | 5 | 12 | 20 | 7 | 0 | .350 |
| 1968 | 4 | 4 | .500 | 1.91 | 45 | 0 | 0 | 61.1 | 35 | 25 | 46 | 0 | 4 | 4 | 7 | 7 | 2 | 0 | .286 |
| 1969 KC A | 11 | 9 | .550 | 2.94 | 52 | 0 | 0 | 98 | 68 | 30 | 76 | 0 | 11 | 9 | 11 | 17 | 4 | 0 | .235 |
| 1970 2 teams | | | KC A (24G 1-2) | | BAL A (21G 4-2) | | | | | | | | | | | | | | |
| " total | 5 | 4 | .556 | 3.52 | 45 | 0 | 0 | 69 | 58 | 27 | 59 | 0 | 5 | 4 | 3 | 9 | 1 | 0 | .111 |
| 1971 STL N | 6 | 1 | .857 | 3.45 | 51 | 0 | 0 | 60 | 45 | 33 | 49 | 0 | 6 | 1 | 8 | 6 | 1 | 0 | .167 |
| 1972 2 teams | | | STL N (30G 1-1) | | CHI A (7G 0-0) | | | | | | | | | | | | | | |
| " total | 1 | 1 | .500 | 2.57 | 37 | 0 | 0 | 35 | 35 | 16 | 26 | 0 | 1 | 1 | 2 | 2 | 0 | 0 | .000 |
| 17 yrs. | 88 | 105 | .456 | 3.71 | 589 | 154 | 33 | 1640.2 | 1441 | 702 | 1162 | 6 | 45 | 32 | 55 | 420 | 68 | 3 | .162 |
| 5 yrs. | 32 | 41 | .438 | 4.02 | 130 | 90 | 22 | 608.1 | 578 | 304 | 379 | 4 | 3 | 1 | 1 | 194 | 31 | 1 | .160 |

WORLD SERIES

| | W | L | PCT | ERA | G | GS | CG | IP | H | BB | SO | ShO | Relief Pitching W | L | SV | Batting AB | H | HR | BA |
|---|---|---|---|---|---|---|---|---|---|---|---|---|---|---|---|---|---|---|---|
| 1966 BAL A | 1 | 0 | 1.000 | 0.00 | 1 | 0 | 0 | 6.2 | 1 | 2 | 11 | 0 | 0 | 0 | 0 | 2 | 0 | 0 | .000 |
| 1970 | 0 | 0 | — | 2.70 | 2 | 0 | 0 | 3.1 | 2 | 1 | 1 | 0 | 0 | 0 | 0 | 1 | 0 | 0 | .000 |
| 2 yrs. | 1 | 0 | 1.000 | 0.90 | 3 | 0 | 0 | 10 | 3 | 3 | 12 | 0 | 1 | 0 | 0 | 3 | 0 | 0 | .000 |

## Dick Drott

**DROTT, RICHARD FRED (Hummer)**
B. July 1, 1936, Cincinnati, Ohio  D. Aug. 10, 1985, Glendale Heights, Ill.  BR TR 6'  185 lbs.

| | W | L | PCT | ERA | G | GS | CG | IP | H | BB | SO | ShO | Relief Pitching W | L | SV | Batting AB | H | HR | BA |
|---|---|---|---|---|---|---|---|---|---|---|---|---|---|---|---|---|---|---|---|
| 1957 CHI N | 15 | 11 | .577 | 3.58 | 38 | 32 | 7 | 229 | 200 | 129 | 170 | 3 | 2 | 0 | 0 | 80 | 8 | 0 | .100 |
| 1958 | 7 | 11 | .389 | 5.43 | 39 | 31 | 4 | 167.1 | 156 | 99 | 127 | 0 | 0 | 0 | 0 | 55 | 15 | 0 | .273 |
| 1959 | 1 | 2 | .333 | 5.93 | 8 | 6 | 1 | 27.1 | 25 | 26 | 15 | 1 | 0 | 0 | 0 | 8 | 1 | 0 | .125 |

| | W | L | PCT | ERA | G | GS | CG | IP | H | BB | SO | ShO | Relief Pitching W | L | SV | BATTING AB | H | HR | BA |
|---|---|---|---|---|---|---|---|---|---|---|---|---|---|---|---|---|---|---|---|

## Dick Drott continued

| | W | L | PCT | ERA | G | GS | CG | IP | H | BB | SO | ShO | W | L | SV | AB | H | HR | BA |
|---|---|---|---|---|---|---|---|---|---|---|---|---|---|---|---|---|---|---|---|
| 1960 | 0 | 6 | .000 | 7.16 | 23 | 9 | 0 | 55.1 | 63 | 42 | 32 | 0 | 0 | 0 | 0 | 10 | 1 | 0 | .100 |
| 1961 | 1 | 4 | .200 | 4.22 | 35 | 8 | 0 | 98 | 75 | 51 | 48 | 0 | 1 | 1 | 0 | 22 | 6 | 0 | .273 |
| 1962 HOU N | 1 | 0 | 1.000 | 7.62 | 6 | 1 | 0 | 13 | 12 | 9 | 10 | 0 | 0 | 0 | 0 | 4 | 0 | 0 | .000 |
| 1963 | 2 | 12 | .143 | 4.98 | 27 | 14 | 2 | 97.2 | 95 | 49 | 58 | 1 | 0 | 2 | 0 | 23 | 3 | 0 | .130 |
| 7 yrs. | 27 | 46 | .370 | 4.78 | 176 | 101 | 14 | 687.2 | 626 | 405 | 460 | 5 | 3 | 3 | 0 | 202 | 34 | 0 | .168 |
| 5 yrs. | 24 | 34 | .414 | 4.68 | 143 | 86 | 12 | 577 | 519 | 347 | 392 | 4 | 3 | 1 | 0 | 175 | 31 | 0 | .177 |

## Monk Dubiel

**DUBIEL, WALTER JOHN**            BR TR 6'      190 lbs.
B. Feb. 12, 1919, Hartford, Conn.    D. Oct. 25, 1969, Hartford, Conn.

| | W | L | PCT | ERA | G | GS | CG | IP | H | BB | SO | ShO | W | L | SV | AB | H | HR | BA |
|---|---|---|---|---|---|---|---|---|---|---|---|---|---|---|---|---|---|---|---|
| 1944 NY A | 13 | 13 | .500 | 3.38 | 30 | 28 | 19 | 232 | 217 | 86 | 79 | 3 | 1 | 0 | 0 | 83 | 15 | 0 | .181 |
| 1945 | 10 | 9 | .526 | 4.64 | 26 | 20 | 9 | 151.1 | 157 | 62 | 45 | 1 | 1 | 0 | 0 | 58 | 16 | 1 | .276 |
| 1948 PHI N | 8 | 10 | .444 | 3.89 | 37 | 17 | 6 | 150.1 | 139 | 58 | 42 | 2 | 1 | 3 | 4 | 42 | 7 | 0 | .167 |
| 1949 CHI N | 6 | 9 | .400 | 4.14 | 32 | 20 | 3 | 147.2 | 142 | 54 | 52 | 1 | 1 | 1 | 4 | 35 | 10 | 0 | .286 |
| 1950 | 6 | 10 | .375 | 4.16 | 39 | 12 | 4 | 142.2 | 152 | 67 | 51 | 2 | 3 | 3 | 2 | 45 | 9 | 0 | .200 |
| 1951 | 2 | 2 | .500 | 2.30 | 22 | 0 | 0 | 54.2 | 46 | 22 | 19 | 0 | 2 | 2 | 1 | 12 | 0 | 0 | .000 |
| 1952 | 0 | 0 | — | 0.00 | 1 | 0 | 0 | .2 | 1 | 0 | 1 | 0 | 0 | 0 | 0 | 0 | 0 | 0 | — |
| 7 yrs. | 45 | 53 | .459 | 3.87 | 187 | 97 | 41 | 879.1 | 854 | 349 | 289 | 9 | 9 | 10 | 11 | 275 | 57 | 1 | .207 |
| 4 yrs. | 14 | 21 | .400 | 3.85 | 94 | 32 | 7 | 345.2 | 341 | 143 | 123 | 3 | 6 | 6 | 7 | 92 | 19 | 0 | .207 |

## Nick Dumovich

**DUMOVICH, NICHOLAS MARTIN**        BL TL 6'     170 lbs.
B. Jan. 2, 1902, Sacramento, Calif.    D. Dec. 12, 1979, Laguna Hills, Calif.

| | W | L | PCT | ERA | G | GS | CG | IP | H | BB | SO | ShO | W | L | SV | AB | H | HR | BA |
|---|---|---|---|---|---|---|---|---|---|---|---|---|---|---|---|---|---|---|---|
| 1923 CHI N | 3 | 5 | .375 | 4.60 | 28 | 8 | 1 | 94 | 118 | 45 | 23 | 0 | 2 | 1 | 1 | 29 | 7 | 0 | .241 |

## Jim Dunegan

**DUNEGAN, JAMES WILLIAM JR**        BR TR 6'1"    205 lbs.
B. Aug. 6, 1947, Burlington, Iowa

| | W | L | PCT | ERA | G | GS | CG | IP | H | BB | SO | ShO | W | L | SV | AB | H | HR | BA |
|---|---|---|---|---|---|---|---|---|---|---|---|---|---|---|---|---|---|---|---|
| 1970 CHI N | 0 | 2 | .000 | 4.85 | 7 | 0 | 0 | 13 | 13 | 12 | 3 | 0 | 0 | 2 | 0 | 4 | 1 | 0 | .250 |

## Kid Durbin

**DURBIN, BLAINE ALPHONSUS**        BL TL 5'8"    155 lbs.
B. Sept. 10, 1886, Lamar, Kans.    D. Sept. 11, 1943, Kirkwood, Mo.

| | W | L | PCT | ERA | G | GS | CG | IP | H | BB | SO | ShO | W | L | SV | AB | H | HR | BA |
|---|---|---|---|---|---|---|---|---|---|---|---|---|---|---|---|---|---|---|---|
| 1907 CHI N | 0 | 1 | .000 | 5.40 | 5 | 1 | 1 | 16.2 | 14 | 10 | 5 | 0 | 0 | 0 | 1 | * | | | |

## Frank Dwyer

**DWYER, JOHN FRANCIS**        BR TR 5'8"    145 lbs.
B. Mar. 25, 1868, Lee, Mass.    D. Feb. 4, 1943, Pittsfield, Mass.
Manager 1902.

| | W | L | PCT | ERA | G | GS | CG | IP | H | BB | SO | ShO | W | L | SV | AB | H | HR | BA |
|---|---|---|---|---|---|---|---|---|---|---|---|---|---|---|---|---|---|---|---|
| 1888 CHI N | 4 | 1 | .800 | 1.07 | 5 | 5 | 5 | 42 | 32 | 9 | 17 | 1 | 0 | 0 | 0 | 21 | 4 | 0 | .190 |
| 1889 | 16 | 13 | .552 | 3.59 | 32 | 30 | 27 | 276 | 307 | 72 | 63 | 0 | 1 | 0 | 0 | 135 | 27 | 1 | .200 |
| 1890 CHI P | 3 | 6 | .333 | 6.23 | 12 | 6 | 6 | 69.1 | 98 | 25 | 17 | 0 | 2 | 1 | 1 | 53 | 14 | 0 | .264 |
| 1891 C-M AA | 19 | 23 | .452 | 3.98 | 45 | 41 | 39 | 375 | 424 | 145 | 128 | 1 | 0 | 1 | 0 | 181 | 49 | 0 | .271 |
| 1892 2 teams | | | STL | N | (10G | 2–8) | | CIN | N | (33G | 19–10) | | | | | | | | |
| " total | 21 | 18 | .538 | 2.98 | 43 | 37 | 30 | 323.1 | 341 | 73 | 61 | 3 | 2 | 1 | 1 | 154 | 23 | 0 | .149 |
| 1893 CIN N | 18 | 15 | .545 | 4.13 | 37 | 30 | 28 | 287.1 | 332 | 93 | 53 | 1 | 2 | 2 | 2 | 120 | 24 | 1 | .200 |
| 1894 | 19 | 22 | .463 | 5.07 | 45 | 40 | 34 | 348 | 471 | 106 | 49 | 1 | 1 | 1 | 1 | 172 | 46 | 2 | .267 |
| 1895 | 18 | 15 | .545 | 4.24 | 37 | 31 | 23 | 280.1 | 355 | 74 | 46 | 2 | 2 | 3 | 0 | 113 | 30 | 1 | .265 |
| 1896 | 24 | 11 | .686 | 3.15 | 36 | 34 | 30 | 288.2 | 321 | 60 | 57 | 3 | 1 | 0 | 1 | 110 | 29 | 0 | .264 |
| 1897 | 18 | 13 | .581 | 3.78 | 37 | 31 | 22 | 247.1 | 315 | 56 | 41 | 0 | 3 | 1 | 0 | 94 | 25 | 0 | .266 |
| 1898 | 16 | 10 | .615 | 3.04 | 31 | 28 | 24 | 240 | 257 | 42 | 29 | 0 | 1 | 0 | 0 | 85 | 12 | 0 | .141 |
| 1899 | 0 | 5 | .000 | 5.51 | 5 | 5 | 2 | 32.2 | 48 | 9 | 2 | 0 | 0 | 0 | 0 | 11 | 4 | 0 | .364 |
| 12 yrs. | 176 | 152 | .537 | 3.85 | 365 | 318 | 270 | 2810 | 3301 | 764 | 563 | 12 | 15 | 10 | 6 | * | | | .199 |
| 2 yrs. | 20 | 14 | .588 | 3.25 | 37 | 35 | 32 | 318 | 339 | 81 | 80 | 1 | 1 | 0 | 0 | 156 | 31 | 1 | .199 |

## Arnie Earley

**EARLEY, ARNOLD CARL**        BL TL 6'1"    195 lbs.
B. June 4, 1933, Lincoln Park, Mich.

| | W | L | PCT | ERA | G | GS | CG | IP | H | BB | SO | ShO | W | L | SV | AB | H | HR | BA |
|---|---|---|---|---|---|---|---|---|---|---|---|---|---|---|---|---|---|---|---|
| 1960 BOS A | 0 | 1 | .000 | 15.75 | 2 | 0 | 0 | 4 | 9 | 4 | 5 | 0 | 0 | 1 | 0 | 0 | 0 | 0 | .000 |
| 1961 | 2 | 4 | .333 | 3.99 | 33 | 0 | 0 | 49.2 | 42 | 34 | 44 | 0 | 2 | 4 | 7 | 6 | 0 | 0 | .000 |
| 1962 | 4 | 5 | .444 | 5.80 | 38 | 3 | 0 | 68.1 | 76 | 46 | 59 | 0 | 3 | 3 | 5 | 10 | 2 | 0 | .200 |
| 1963 | 3 | 7 | .300 | 4.75 | 53 | 4 | 0 | 115.2 | 124 | 43 | 97 | 0 | 1 | 5 | 1 | 18 | 5 | 0 | .278 |
| 1964 | 1 | 1 | .500 | 2.68 | 25 | 3 | 1 | 50.1 | 51 | 18 | 45 | 0 | 0 | 0 | 1 | 9 | 1 | 0 | .111 |
| 1965 | 0 | 1 | .000 | 3.63 | 57 | 0 | 0 | 74.1 | 79 | 29 | 47 | 0 | 0 | 1 | 0 | 1 | 0 | 0 | .000 |
| 1966 CHI N | 2 | 1 | .667 | 3.57 | 13 | 0 | 0 | 17.2 | 14 | 9 | 12 | 0 | 2 | 1 | 0 | 1 | 0 | 0 | .000 |
| 1967 HOU N | 0 | 0 | — | 27.00 | 2 | 0 | 0 | 1 | 5 | 1 | 1 | 0 | 0 | 0 | 0 | | | | |
| 8 yrs. | 12 | 20 | .375 | 4.48 | 223 | 10 | 1 | 381.1 | 400 | 184 | 310 | 0 | 8 | 15 | 14 | 51 | 8 | 0 | .157 |
| 1 yr. | 2 | 1 | .667 | 3.57 | 13 | 0 | 0 | 17.2 | 14 | 9 | 12 | 0 | 2 | 1 | 0 | 1 | 0 | 0 | .000 |

## Mal Eason

**EASON, MALCOLM WAYNE (Kid)**        TR
B. Mar. 13, 1879, Brookville, Pa.    D. Apr. 16, 1970, Douglas, Ariz.

| | W | L | PCT | ERA | G | GS | CG | IP | H | BB | SO | ShO | W | L | SV | AB | H | HR | BA |
|---|---|---|---|---|---|---|---|---|---|---|---|---|---|---|---|---|---|---|---|
| 1900 CHI N | 1 | 0 | 1.000 | 1.00 | 1 | 1 | 1 | 9 | 5 | 3 | 2 | 0 | 0 | 0 | 0 | 3 | 0 | 0 | .000 |
| 1901 | 8 | 17 | .320 | 3.59 | 27 | 25 | 23 | 220.2 | 246 | 60 | 68 | 1 | 0 | 0 | 0 | 87 | 12 | 0 | .138 |
| 1902 2 teams | | | CHI | N | (2G | 1–1) | | BOS | N | (27G | 9–14) | | | | | | | | |
| " total | 10 | 15 | .400 | 2.61 | 29 | 28 | 22 | 224.1 | 258 | 61 | 54 | 2 | 0 | 0 | 0 | 77 | 7 | 0 | .091 |
| 1903 DET A | 2 | 5 | .286 | 3.36 | 7 | 6 | 6 | 56.1 | 60 | 19 | 21 | 1 | 0 | 1 | 0 | 20 | 2 | 0 | .100 |
| 1905 BKN N | 5 | 21 | .192 | 4.30 | 27 | 27 | 20 | 207 | 230 | 72 | 64 | 3 | 0 | 0 | 0 | 81 | 14 | 0 | .173 |
| 1906 | 10 | 17 | .370 | 3.25 | 34 | 26 | 18 | 227 | 212 | 74 | 64 | 3 | 1 | 0 | 0 | 88 | 8 | 0 | .091 |
| 6 yrs. | 36 | 75 | .324 | 3.39 | 125 | 113 | 90 | 944.1 | 1015 | 289 | 273 | 10 | 1 | 1 | 0 | 356 | 43 | 0 | .121 |
| 3 yrs. | 10 | 18 | .357 | 3.31 | 30 | 28 | 26 | 247.2 | 276 | 65 | 74 | 1 | 0 | 0 | 0 | 95 | 13 | 0 | .137 |

| | W | L | PCT | ERA | G | GS | CG | IP | H | BB | SO | ShO | Relief Pitching W | L | SV | BATTING AB | H | HR | BA |
|---|---|---|---|---|---|---|---|---|---|---|---|---|---|---|---|---|---|---|---|

## Rawley Eastwick

**EASTWICK, RAWLINS JACKSON**
B. Oct. 24, 1950, Camden, N. J.　　　　　　　　　　　　　　BR TR 6'3" 180 lbs.

| | W | L | PCT | ERA | G | GS | CG | IP | H | BB | SO | ShO | W | L | SV | AB | H | HR | BA |
|---|---|---|---|---|---|---|---|---|---|---|---|---|---|---|---|---|---|---|---|
| 1974 CIN N | 0 | 0 | — | 2.00 | 8 | 0 | 0 | 18 | 12 | 5 | 14 | 0 | 0 | 0 | 2 | 1 | 0 | 0 | .000 |
| 1975 | 5 | 3 | .625 | 2.60 | 58 | 0 | 0 | 90 | 77 | 25 | 61 | 0 | 5 | 3 | 22 | 15 | 1 | 0 | .067 |
| 1976 | 11 | 5 | .688 | 2.08 | 71 | 0 | 0 | 108 | 93 | 27 | 70 | 0 | 11 | 5 | 26 | 17 | 0 | 0 | .000 |
| 1977 2 teams | | | CIN | N (23G 2–2) | | STL | N (41G 3–7) | | | | | | | | | | | | |
| " total | 5 | 9 | .357 | 3.90 | 64 | 1 | 0 | 97 | 114 | 29 | 47 | 0 | 4 | 7 | 11 | 11 | 3 | 0 | .273 |
| 1978 2 teams | | | NY | A (8G 2–1) | | PHI | N (22G 2–1) | | | | | | | | | | | | |
| " total | 4 | 2 | .667 | 3.76 | 30 | 0 | 0 | 64.2 | 53 | 22 | 27 | 0 | 4 | 2 | 0 | 3 | 0 | 0 | .000 |
| 1979 PHI N | 3 | 6 | .333 | 4.88 | 51 | 0 | 0 | 83 | 90 | 25 | 47 | 0 | 3 | 6 | 6 | 7 | 0 | 0 | .000 |
| 1980 KC A | 0 | 1 | .000 | 5.32 | 14 | 0 | 0 | 22 | 37 | 8 | 5 | 0 | 0 | 1 | 0 | 0 | 0 | 0 | — |
| 1981 CHI N | 0 | 1 | .000 | 2.30 | 30 | 0 | 0 | 43 | 43 | 15 | 24 | 0 | 0 | 1 | 1 | 2 | 0 | 0 | .000 |
| 8 yrs. | 28 | 27 | .509 | 3.30 | 326 | 1 | 0 | 525.2 | 519 | 156 | 295 | 0 | 27 | 25 | 68 | 56 | 4 | 0 | .071 |
| 1 yr. | 0 | 1 | .000 | 2.30 | 30 | 0 | 0 | 43 | 43 | 15 | 24 | 0 | 0 | 1 | 1 | 2 | 0 | 0 | .000 |
| LEAGUE CHAMPIONSHIP SERIES | | | | | | | | | | | | | | | | | | | |
| 1975 CIN N | 1 | 0 | 1.000 | 0.00 | 2 | 0 | 0 | 3.2 | 2 | 2 | 1 | 0 | 1 | 0 | 1 | 0 | 0 | 0 | — |
| 1976 | 1 | 0 | 1.000 | 12.00 | 2 | 0 | 0 | 3 | 7 | 2 | 1 | 0 | 1 | 0 | 0 | 0 | 0 | 0 | — |
| 1978 PHI N | 0 | 0 | — | 9.00 | 1 | 0 | 0 | 1 | 3 | 0 | 1 | 0 | 0 | 0 | 0 | 0 | 0 | 0 | — |
| 3 yrs. | 2 | 0 | 1.000 | 5.87 | 5 | 0 | 0 | 7.2 | 12 | 4 | 3 | 0 | 2 | 0 | 1 | 0 | 0 | 0 | — |
| WORLD SERIES | | | | | | | | | | | | | | | | | | | |
| 1975 CIN N | 2 | 0 | 1.000 | 2.25 | 5 | 0 | 0 | 8 | 6 | 3 | 4 | 0 | 2 | 0 | 1 | 1 | 0 | 0 | .000 |
| | | | | | | | | | | | | | **2nd** | | | | | | |

## Vallie Eaves

**EAVES, VALLIE ENNIS (Chief)**
B. Sept. 6, 1911, Allen, Okla.　　D. Apr. 19, 1960, Norman, Okla.　　BR TR 6'2½" 180 lbs.

| | W | L | PCT | ERA | G | GS | CG | IP | H | BB | SO | ShO | W | L | SV | AB | H | HR | BA |
|---|---|---|---|---|---|---|---|---|---|---|---|---|---|---|---|---|---|---|---|
| 1935 PHI A | 1 | 2 | .333 | 5.14 | 3 | 3 | 1 | 14 | 12 | 15 | 6 | 0 | 0 | 0 | 0 | 4 | 0 | 0 | .000 |
| 1939 CHI A | 0 | 1 | .000 | 4.63 | 2 | 1 | 1 | 11.2 | 11 | 8 | 5 | 0 | 0 | 0 | 0 | 6 | 2 | 0 | .333 |
| 1940 | 0 | 2 | .000 | 6.75 | 5 | 3 | 0 | 18.2 | 22 | 24 | 11 | 0 | 0 | 0 | 0 | 5 | 0 | 0 | .000 |
| 1941 CHI N | 3 | 3 | .500 | 3.53 | 12 | 7 | 4 | 58.2 | 56 | 21 | 24 | 0 | 1 | 0 | 0 | 20 | 2 | 0 | .100 |
| 1942 | 0 | 0 | — | 9.00 | 2 | 0 | 0 | 3 | 4 | 2 | 0 | 0 | 0 | 0 | 0 | 0 | 0 | 0 | — |
| 5 yrs. | 4 | 8 | .333 | 4.58 | 24 | 14 | 6 | 106 | 105 | 70 | 46 | 0 | 1 | 0 | 0 | 35 | 4 | 0 | .114 |
| 2 yrs. | 3 | 3 | .500 | 3.79 | 14 | 7 | 4 | 61.2 | 60 | 23 | 24 | 0 | 1 | 0 | 0 | 20 | 2 | 0 | .100 |

## Dennis Eckersley

**ECKERSLEY, DENNIS LEE**
B. Oct. 3, 1954, Oakland, Calif.　　　　　　　　　　　　　BR TR 6'2" 190 lbs.

| | W | L | PCT | ERA | G | GS | CG | IP | H | BB | SO | ShO | W | L | SV | AB | H | HR | BA |
|---|---|---|---|---|---|---|---|---|---|---|---|---|---|---|---|---|---|---|---|
| 1975 CLE A | 13 | 7 | .650 | 2.60 | 34 | 24 | 6 | 186.2 | 147 | 90 | 152 | 2 | 1 | 0 | 2 | 0 | 0 | 0 | — |
| 1976 | 13 | 12 | .520 | 3.44 | 36 | 30 | 9 | 199 | 155 | 78 | 200 | 3 | 0 | 1 | 1 | 0 | 0 | 0 | — |
| 1977 | 14 | 13 | .519 | 3.53 | 33 | 33 | 12 | 247 | 214 | 54 | 191 | 3 | 0 | 0 | 0 | 0 | 0 | 0 | — |
| 1978 BOS A | 20 | 8 | .714 | 2.99 | 35 | 35 | 16 | 268.1 | 258 | 71 | 162 | 3 | 0 | 0 | 0 | 0 | 0 | 0 | — |
| 1979 | 17 | 10 | .630 | 2.99 | 33 | 33 | 17 | 247 | 234 | 59 | 150 | 2 | 0 | 0 | 0 | 0 | 0 | 0 | — |
| 1980 | 12 | 14 | .462 | 4.27 | 30 | 30 | 8 | 198 | 188 | 44 | 121 | 0 | 0 | 0 | 0 | 0 | 0 | 0 | — |
| 1981 | 9 | 8 | .529 | 4.27 | 23 | 23 | 8 | 154 | 160 | 35 | 79 | 2 | 0 | 0 | 0 | 0 | 0 | 0 | — |
| 1982 | 13 | 13 | .500 | 3.73 | 33 | 33 | 11 | 224.1 | 228 | 43 | 127 | 3 | 0 | 0 | 0 | 0 | 0 | 0 | — |
| 1983 | 9 | 13 | .409 | 5.61 | 28 | 28 | 2 | 176.1 | 223 | 39 | 77 | 0 | 0 | 0 | 0 | 0 | 0 | 0 | — |
| 1984 2 teams | | | BOS | A (9G 4–4) | | CHI | N (24G 10–8) | | | | | | | | | | | | |
| " total | 14 | 12 | .538 | 3.60 | 33 | 33 | 4 | 225 | 223 | 49 | 114 | 0 | 0 | 0 | 0 | 55 | 6 | 0 | .109 |
| 1985 CHI N | 11 | 7 | .611 | 3.08 | 25 | 25 | 6 | 169.1 | 145 | 19 | 117 | 2 | 0 | 0 | 0 | 56 | 7 | 1 | .125 |
| 11 yrs. | 145 | 117 | .553 | 3.59 | 343 | 327 | 99 | 2295 | 2175 | 581 | 1490 | 20 | 1 | 1 | 3 | 111 | 13 | 1 | .117 |
| 2 yrs. | 21 | 15 | .583 | 3.06 | 49 | 49 | 8 | 329.2 | 297 | 55 | 198 | 2 | 0 | 0 | 0 | 111 | 13 | 1 | .117 |
| LEAGUE CHAMPIONSHIP SERIES | | | | | | | | | | | | | | | | | | | |
| 1984 CHI N | 0 | 1 | .000 | 8.44 | 1 | 1 | 0 | 5.1 | 9 | 0 | 0 | 0 | 0 | 0 | 0 | 2 | 0 | 0 | .000 |

## Charlie Eden

**EDEN, CHARLES M.**
B. Jan. 18, 1855, Lexington, Ky.　　D. Sept. 17, 1920, Cincinnati, Ohio　　BR TR

| | W | L | PCT | ERA | G | GS | CG | IP | H | BB | SO | ShO | W | L | SV | AB | H | HR | BA |
|---|---|---|---|---|---|---|---|---|---|---|---|---|---|---|---|---|---|---|---|
| 1884 PIT AA | 0 | 1 | .000 | 6.00 | 2 | 1 | 1 | 12 | 12 | 3 | 3 | 0 | 0 | 0 | 0 | 122 | 33 | 1 | .270 |
| 1885 | 1 | 2 | .333 | 5.17 | 4 | 1 | 0 | 15.2 | 22 | 3 | 5 | 0 | 1 | 1 | 0 | 405 | 103 | 0 | .254 |
| 2 yrs. | 1 | 3 | .250 | 5.53 | 6 | 2 | 1 | 27.2 | 34 | 6 | 8 | 0 | 1 | 1 | 0 | * | | | |

## Ed Eiteljorg

**EITELJORG, EDWARD HENRY**
B. Oct. 14, 1871, Berlin, Germany　　D. Dec. 7, 1942, Greencastle, Ind.　　BR TR 6'2" 190 lbs.

| | W | L | PCT | ERA | G | GS | CG | IP | H | BB | SO | ShO | W | L | SV | AB | H | HR | BA |
|---|---|---|---|---|---|---|---|---|---|---|---|---|---|---|---|---|---|---|---|
| 1890 CHI N | 0 | 1 | .000 | 22.50 | 1 | 1 | 0 | 2 | 5 | 1 | 1 | 0 | 0 | 0 | 0 | 1 | 0 | 0 | .000 |
| 1891 WAS AA | 1 | 5 | .167 | 6.16 | 8 | 7 | 6 | 61.1 | 79 | 41 | 23 | 0 | 0 | 0 | 0 | 26 | 5 | 0 | .192 |
| 2 yrs. | 1 | 6 | .143 | 6.68 | 9 | 8 | 6 | 63.1 | 84 | 42 | 24 | 0 | 0 | 0 | 0 | 27 | 5 | 0 | .185 |
| 1 yr. | 0 | 1 | .000 | 22.50 | 1 | 1 | 0 | 2 | 5 | 1 | 1 | 0 | 0 | 0 | 0 | 1 | 0 | 0 | .000 |

## Jim Ellis

**ELLIS, JAMES RUSSELL**
B. Mar. 25, 1945, Tulare, Calif.　　　　　　　　　　　　　BR TL 6'2" 185 lbs.

| | W | L | PCT | ERA | G | GS | CG | IP | H | BB | SO | ShO | W | L | SV | AB | H | HR | BA |
|---|---|---|---|---|---|---|---|---|---|---|---|---|---|---|---|---|---|---|---|
| 1967 CHI N | 1 | 1 | .500 | 3.24 | 8 | 1 | 0 | 16.2 | 20 | 9 | 8 | 0 | 0 | 1 | 0 | 5 | 1 | 0 | .200 |
| 1969 STL N | 0 | 0 | — | 1.80 | 2 | 1 | 0 | 5 | 7 | 3 | 0 | 0 | 0 | 0 | 0 | 0 | 0 | 0 | — |
| 2 yrs. | 1 | 1 | .500 | 2.91 | 10 | 2 | 0 | 21.2 | 27 | 12 | 8 | 0 | 0 | 1 | 0 | 5 | 1 | 0 | .200 |
| 1 yr. | 1 | 1 | .500 | 3.24 | 8 | 1 | 0 | 16.2 | 20 | 9 | 8 | 0 | 0 | 1 | 0 | 5 | 1 | 0 | .200 |

## Dick Ellsworth

**ELLSWORTH, RICHARD CLARK**
B. Mar. 22, 1940, Lusk, Wyo.　　　　　　　　　　　　　BL TL 6'3½" 180 lbs.

| | W | L | PCT | ERA | G | GS | CG | IP | H | BB | SO | ShO | W | L | SV | AB | H | HR | BA |
|---|---|---|---|---|---|---|---|---|---|---|---|---|---|---|---|---|---|---|---|
| 1958 CHI N | 0 | 1 | .000 | 15.43 | 1 | 1 | 0 | 2.1 | 4 | 3 | 0 | 0 | 0 | 0 | 0 | 1 | 0 | 0 | .000 |
| 1960 | 7 | 13 | .350 | 3.72 | 31 | 27 | 6 | 176.2 | 170 | 72 | 94 | 0 | 0 | 0 | 0 | 48 | 2 | 0 | .042 |
| 1961 | 10 | 11 | .476 | 3.86 | 37 | 31 | 7 | 186.2 | 213 | 48 | 91 | 1 | 1 | 0 | 0 | 56 | 2 | 0 | .036 |
| 1962 | 9 | 20 | .310 | 5.09 | 37 | 33 | 6 | 208.2 | 241 | 77 | 113 | 0 | 1 | 1 | 1 | 62 | 7 | 0 | .113 |
| 1963 | 22 | 10 | .688 | 2.11 | 37 | 37 | 19 | 290.2 | 223 | 75 | 185 | 4 | 0 | 0 | 0 | 94 | 9 | 0 | .096 |
| 1964 | 14 | 18 | .438 | 3.75 | 37 | 36 | 16 | 256.2 | 267 | 71 | 148 | 1 | 0 | 1 | 0 | 87 | 4 | 0 | .046 |

| | W | L | PCT | ERA | G | GS | CG | IP | H | BB | SO | ShO | Relief Pitching W | L | SV | BATTING AB | H | HR | BA |
|---|---|---|---|---|---|---|---|---|---|---|---|---|---|---|---|---|---|---|---|

## Dick Ellsworth continued

| | W | L | PCT | ERA | G | GS | CG | IP | H | BB | SO | ShO | W | L | SV | AB | H | HR | BA |
|---|---|---|---|---|---|---|---|---|---|---|---|---|---|---|---|---|---|---|---|
| 1965 | 14 | 15 | .483 | 3.81 | 36 | 34 | 8 | 222.1 | 227 | 57 | 130 | 0 | 1 | 0 | 1 | 73 | 7 | 0 | .096 |
| 1966 | 8 | 22 | .267 | 3.98 | 38 | 37 | 9 | 269.1 | 321 | 51 | 144 | 0 | 0 | 0 | 0 | 90 | 14 | 0 | .156 |
| 1967 PHI N | 6 | 7 | .462 | 4.38 | 32 | 21 | 3 | 125.1 | 152 | 36 | 45 | 1 | 0 | 0 | 0 | 37 | 4 | 0 | .108 |
| 1968 BOS A | 16 | 7 | .696 | 3.03 | 31 | 28 | 10 | 196 | 196 | 37 | 106 | 1 | 1 | 0 | 0 | 72 | 4 | 0 | .056 |
| 1969 2 teams | | | | BOS | A | (2G 0–0) | | CLE | A | (34G 6–9) | | | | | | | | | |
| " total | 6 | 9 | .400 | 4.10 | 36 | 24 | 3 | 147 | 178 | 44 | 52 | 1 | 0 | 0 | 0 | 48 | 6 | 0 | .125 |
| 1970 2 teams | | | | CLE | A | (29G 3–3) | | MIL | A | (14G 0–0) | | | | | | | | | |
| " total | 3 | 3 | .500 | 3.79 | 43 | 1 | 0 | 59.1 | 60 | 17 | 22 | 0 | 3 | 2 | 3 | 4 | 0 | 0 | .000 |
| 1971 MIL A | 0 | 1 | .000 | 4.80 | 11 | 0 | 0 | 15 | 22 | 7 | 10 | 0 | 0 | 1 | 0 | 1 | 0 | 0 | .000 |
| 13 yrs. | 115 | 137 | .456 | 3.72 | 407 | 310 | 87 | 2156 | 2274 | 595 | 1140 | 9 | 7 | 5 | 5 | 673 | 59 | 0 | .088 |
| 8 yrs. | 84 | 110 | .433 | 3.70 | 254 | 236 | 71 | 1613.1 | 1666 | 454 | 905 | 6 | 3 | 2 | 2 | 511 | 45 | 0 | .088 |
| | | | | 7th | | | | | | | | | | | | | | | |

## Don Elston

**ELSTON, DONALD RAY**
B. Apr. 26, 1929, Campbellstown, Ohio                      BR TR 6'      165 lbs.

| | W | L | PCT | ERA | G | GS | CG | IP | H | BB | SO | ShO | W | L | SV | AB | H | HR | BA |
|---|---|---|---|---|---|---|---|---|---|---|---|---|---|---|---|---|---|---|---|
| 1953 CHI N | 0 | 1 | .000 | 14.40 | 2 | 1 | 0 | 5 | 11 | 0 | 2 | 0 | 0 | 0 | 0 | 1 | 0 | 0 | .000 |
| 1957 2 teams | | | | BKN | N | (1G 0–0) | | CHI | N | (39G 6–7) | | | | | | | | | |
| " total | 6 | 7 | .462 | 3.54 | 40 | 14 | 2 | 145 | 140 | 55 | 103 | 0 | 3 | 1 | 8 | 37 | 4 | 0 | .108 |
| 1958 CHI N | 9 | 8 | .529 | 2.88 | 69 | 0 | 0 | 97 | 75 | 39 | 84 | 0 | 9 | 8 | 10 | 14 | 5 | 0 | .357 |
| 1959 | 10 | 8 | .556 | 3.32 | 65 | 0 | 0 | 97.2 | 77 | 46 | 82 | 0 | 10 | 8 | 13 | 19 | 4 | 0 | .211 |
| 1960 | 8 | 9 | .471 | 3.40 | 60 | 0 | 0 | 127 | 109 | 55 | 85 | 0 | 8 | 9 | 11 | 24 | 3 | 0 | .125 |
| 1961 | 6 | 7 | .462 | 5.59 | 58 | 0 | 0 | 93.1 | 108 | 45 | 59 | 0 | 6 | 7 | 8 | 11 | 2 | 0 | .182 |
| 1962 | 4 | 8 | .333 | 2.44 | 57 | 0 | 0 | 66.1 | 57 | 32 | 37 | 0 | 4 | 8 | 8 | 8 | 0 | 0 | .000 |
| 1963 | 4 | 1 | .800 | 2.83 | 51 | 0 | 0 | 70 | 57 | 21 | 41 | 0 | 4 | 1 | 4 | 4 | 0 | 0 | .000 |
| 1964 | 2 | 5 | .286 | 5.30 | 48 | 0 | 0 | 54.1 | 68 | 34 | 26 | 0 | 2 | 5 | 1 | 6 | 1 | 0 | .167 |
| 9 yrs. | 49 | 54 | .476 | 3.69 | 450 | 15 | 2 | 755.2 | 702 | 327 | 519 | 0 | 46 | 47 | 63 | 124 | 19 | 0 | .153 |
| 9 yrs. | 49 | 54 | .476 | 3.70 | 449 | 15 | 2 | 754.2 | 701 | 327 | 518 | 0 | 46 | 47 | 63 | 124 | 19 | 0 | .153 |
| | | | | 2nd | | | | | | | | | 1st | | 3rd | | | | |

## Steve Engel

**ENGEL, STEVEN MICHAEL**
B. Dec. 31, 1961, Cincinnati, Ohio                        BR TL 6'3"    210 lbs.

| | W | L | PCT | ERA | G | GS | CG | IP | H | BB | SO | ShO | W | L | SV | AB | H | HR | BA |
|---|---|---|---|---|---|---|---|---|---|---|---|---|---|---|---|---|---|---|---|
| 1985 CHI N | 1 | 5 | .167 | 5.57 | 11 | 8 | 1 | 51.2 | 61 | 26 | 29 | 0 | 0 | 0 | 1 | 16 | 3 | 1 | .188 |

## Al Epperly

**EPPERLY, ALBERT PAUL (Pard)**
B. May 7, 1918, Glidden, Iowa                             BL TR 6'2"    194 lbs.

| | W | L | PCT | ERA | G | GS | CG | IP | H | BB | SO | ShO | W | L | SV | AB | H | HR | BA |
|---|---|---|---|---|---|---|---|---|---|---|---|---|---|---|---|---|---|---|---|
| 1938 CHI N | 2 | 0 | 1.000 | 3.67 | 9 | 4 | 1 | 27 | 28 | 15 | 10 | 0 | 0 | 0 | 0 | 8 | 2 | 0 | .250 |
| 1950 BKN N | 0 | 0 | – | 5.00 | 5 | 0 | 0 | 9 | 14 | 5 | 3 | 0 | 0 | 0 | 0 | 0 | 0 | 0 | – |
| 2 yrs. | 2 | 0 | 1.000 | 4.00 | 14 | 4 | 1 | 36 | 42 | 20 | 13 | 0 | 0 | 0 | 0 | 8 | 2 | 0 | .250 |
| 1 yr. | 2 | 0 | 1.000 | 3.67 | 9 | 4 | 1 | 27 | 28 | 15 | 10 | 0 | 0 | 0 | 0 | 8 | 2 | 0 | .250 |

## Paul Erickson

**ERICKSON, PAUL WALFORD (Li'l Abner)**
B. Dec. 14, 1915, Zion, Ill.                              BR TR 6'2½"   200 lbs.

| | W | L | PCT | ERA | G | GS | CG | IP | H | BB | SO | ShO | W | L | SV | AB | H | HR | BA |
|---|---|---|---|---|---|---|---|---|---|---|---|---|---|---|---|---|---|---|---|
| 1941 CHI N | 5 | 7 | .417 | 3.70 | 32 | 15 | 7 | 141 | 126 | 64 | 85 | 1 | 0 | 0 | 1 | 46 | 7 | 1 | .152 |
| 1942 | 1 | 6 | .143 | 5.43 | 18 | 7 | 1 | 63 | 70 | 41 | 26 | 0 | 1 | 0 | 0 | 21 | 3 | 0 | .143 |
| 1943 | 1 | 3 | .250 | 6.12 | 15 | 4 | 0 | 42.2 | 47 | 22 | 24 | 0 | 1 | 0 | 1 | 15 | 3 | 0 | .200 |
| 1944 | 5 | 9 | .357 | 3.55 | 33 | 15 | 5 | 124.1 | 113 | 67 | 82 | 3 | 5 | 8 | 1 | 36 | 2 | 1 | .056 |
| 1945 | 7 | 4 | .636 | 3.32 | 28 | 9 | 3 | 108.1 | 94 | 48 | 53 | 0 | 2 | 2 | 3 | 32 | 5 | 0 | .156 |
| 1946 | 9 | 7 | .563 | 2.43 | 32 | 14 | 5 | 137 | 119 | 65 | 70 | 1 | 2 | 0 | 0 | 40 | 2 | 0 | .050 |
| 1947 | 7 | 12 | .368 | 4.34 | 40 | 20 | 6 | 177 | 179 | 93 | 82 | 0 | 3 | 1 | 1 | 60 | 15 | 1 | .250 |
| 1948 3 teams | | | | CHI | N | (3G 0–0) | | PHI | N | (4G 2–0) | | NY | N | (2G 0–0) | | | | |
| " total | 2 | 0 | 1.000 | 5.25 | 9 | 2 | 0 | 24 | 26 | 25 | 10 | 0 | 0 | 0 | 0 | 8 | 1 | 0 | .125 |
| 8 yrs. | 37 | 48 | .435 | 3.86 | 207 | 86 | 27 | 814.1 | 774 | 425 | 432 | 5 | 13 | 12 | 6 | 258 | 38 | 3 | .147 |
| 8 yrs. | 35 | 48 | .422 | 3.83 | 201 | 84 | 27 | 796 | 755 | 406 | 426 | 5 | 13 | 12 | 6 | 251 | 37 | 3 | .147 |
| WORLD SERIES | | | | | | | | | | | | | | | | | | | |
| 1945 CHI N | 0 | 0 | – | 3.86 | 4 | 0 | 0 | 7 | 8 | 3 | 5 | 0 | 0 | 0 | 0 | 0 | 0 | 0 | – |

## Dick Errickson

**ERRICKSON, RICHARD MERRIWELL (Lief)**
B. Mar. 4, 1914, Vineland, N. J.                          BL TR 6'1"    175 lbs.

| | W | L | PCT | ERA | G | GS | CG | IP | H | BB | SO | ShO | W | L | SV | AB | H | HR | BA |
|---|---|---|---|---|---|---|---|---|---|---|---|---|---|---|---|---|---|---|---|
| 1938 BOS N | 9 | 7 | .563 | 3.15 | 34 | 10 | 6 | 122.2 | 113 | 56 | 40 | 1 | 3 | 3 | 6 | 35 | 4 | 0 | .114 |
| 1939 | 6 | 9 | .400 | 4.00 | 28 | 11 | 3 | 128.1 | 143 | 54 | 33 | 0 | 1 | 3 | 1 | 44 | 10 | 0 | .227 |
| 1940 | 12 | 13 | .480 | 3.16 | 34 | 29 | 17 | 236.1 | 241 | 90 | 34 | 3 | 0 | 0 | 4 | 83 | 13 | 0 | .157 |
| 1941 | 6 | 12 | .333 | 4.78 | 38 | 23 | 5 | 165.2 | 192 | 62 | 45 | 2 | 1 | 1 | 1 | 45 | 8 | 0 | .178 |
| 1942 2 teams | | | | BOS | N | (21G 2–5) | | CHI | N | (13G 1–1) | | | | | | | | | |
| " total | 3 | 6 | .333 | 4.75 | 34 | 4 | 0 | 83.1 | 115 | 28 | 24 | 0 | 1 | 4 | 1 | 21 | 2 | 0 | .095 |
| 5 yrs. | 36 | 47 | .434 | 3.85 | 168 | 77 | 31 | 736.1 | 804 | 290 | 176 | 6 | 6 | 11 | 13 | 228 | 37 | 0 | .162 |
| 1 yr. | 1 | 1 | .500 | 4.13 | 13 | 0 | 0 | 24 | 39 | 8 | 9 | 0 | 1 | 1 | 0 | 5 | 0 | 0 | .000 |

## Chuck Estrada

**ESTRADA, CHARLES LEONARD**
B. Feb. 15, 1938, San Luis Obispo, Calif.                 BR TR 6'1"    185 lbs.

| | W | L | PCT | ERA | G | GS | CG | IP | H | BB | SO | ShO | W | L | SV | AB | H | HR | BA |
|---|---|---|---|---|---|---|---|---|---|---|---|---|---|---|---|---|---|---|---|
| 1960 BAL A | 18 | 11 | .621 | 3.58 | 36 | 25 | 12 | 208.2 | 162 | 101 | 144 | 1 | 5 | 2 | 2 | 64 | 9 | 0 | .141 |
| 1961 | 15 | 9 | .625 | 3.69 | 33 | 31 | 6 | 212 | 159 | 132 | 160 | 1 | 0 | 0 | 0 | 70 | 8 | 0 | .114 |
| 1962 | 9 | 17 | .346 | 3.83 | 34 | 33 | 6 | 223.1 | 199 | 121 | 165 | 0 | 0 | 0 | 0 | 66 | 10 | 0 | .152 |
| 1963 | 3 | 2 | .600 | 4.60 | 8 | 7 | 0 | 31.1 | 26 | 19 | 16 | 0 | 0 | 0 | 0 | 10 | 1 | 0 | .100 |
| 1964 | 3 | 2 | .600 | 5.27 | 17 | 6 | 0 | 54.2 | 62 | 21 | 32 | 0 | 1 | 2 | 0 | 14 | 2 | 0 | .143 |
| 1966 CHI N | 1 | 1 | .500 | 7.30 | 9 | 1 | 0 | 12.1 | 16 | 5 | 3 | 0 | 0 | 0 | 0 | 3 | 0 | 0 | .000 |
| 1967 NY N | 1 | 2 | .333 | 9.41 | 9 | 2 | 0 | 22 | 28 | 17 | 15 | 0 | 1 | 0 | 0 | 5 | 0 | 0 | .000 |
| 7 yrs. | 50 | 44 | .532 | 4.07 | 146 | 105 | 24 | 764.1 | 652 | 416 | 535 | 2 | 7 | 4 | 2 | 232 | 30 | 1 | .129 |
| 1 yr. | 1 | 1 | .500 | 7.30 | 9 | 1 | 0 | 12.1 | 16 | 5 | 3 | 0 | 0 | 0 | 0 | 3 | 0 | 0 | .000 |

| | W | L | PCT | ERA | G | GS | CG | IP | H | BB | SO | ShO | Relief Pitching W | L | SV | BATTING AB | H | HR | BA |
|---|---|---|---|---|---|---|---|---|---|---|---|---|---|---|---|---|---|---|---|

## Uel Eubanks

**EUBANKS, UEL MELVIN (Poss)**
B. Feb. 14, 1903, Quinlan, Tex.    D. Nov. 21, 1954, Dallas, Tex.    BR TR 6'3"    175 lbs.

| | W | L | PCT | ERA | G | GS | CG | IP | H | BB | SO | ShO | W | L | SV | AB | H | HR | BA |
|---|---|---|---|---|---|---|---|---|---|---|---|---|---|---|---|---|---|---|---|
| 1922 CHI N | 0 | 0 | – | 27.00 | 2 | 0 | 0 | 1.2 | 5 | 4 | 1 | 0 | 0 | 0 | 0 | 1 | 1 | 0 | 1.000 |

## Darcy Fast

**FAST, DARCY RAE**
B. Mar. 10, 1947, Dallas, Ore.    BL TL 6'3"    195 lbs.

| | | | | | | | | | | | | | | | | | | | |
|---|---|---|---|---|---|---|---|---|---|---|---|---|---|---|---|---|---|---|---|
| 1968 CHI N | 0 | 1 | .000 | 5.40 | 8 | 1 | 0 | 10 | 8 | 8 | 10 | 0 | 0 | 1 | 0 | 3 | 0 | 0 | .000 |

## Bill Faul

**FAUL, WILLIAM ALVAN**
B. Apr. 21, 1940, Cincinnati, Ohio    BR TR 5'10"    184 lbs.

| | | | | | | | | | | | | | | | | | | | |
|---|---|---|---|---|---|---|---|---|---|---|---|---|---|---|---|---|---|---|---|
| 1962 DET A | 0 | 0 | – | 32.40 | 1 | 0 | 0 | 1.2 | 4 | 3 | 2 | 0 | 0 | 0 | 0 | 0 | 0 | 0 | |
| 1963 | 5 | 6 | .455 | 4.64 | 28 | 10 | 2 | 97 | 93 | 48 | 64 | 0 | 1 | 1 | 1 | 27 | 4 | 0 | .148 |
| 1964 | 0 | 0 | – | 10.80 | 1 | 1 | 0 | 5 | 5 | 2 | 1 | 0 | 0 | 0 | 0 | 2 | 0 | 0 | .000 |
| 1965 CHI N | 6 | 6 | .500 | 3.54 | 17 | 16 | 5 | 96.2 | 83 | 18 | 59 | 3 | 0 | 0 | 0 | 30 | 3 | 0 | .100 |
| 1966 | 1 | 4 | .200 | 5.08 | 17 | 6 | 1 | 51.1 | 47 | 18 | 32 | 0 | 0 | 0 | 0 | 13 | 0 | 0 | .000 |
| 1970 SF N | 0 | 0 | – | 7.20 | 7 | 0 | 0 | 10 | 15 | 6 | 6 | 0 | 0 | 0 | 1 | 0 | 0 | 0 | |
| 6 yrs. | 12 | 16 | .429 | 4.71 | 71 | 33 | 8 | 261.2 | 247 | 95 | 164 | 3 | 1 | 1 | 2 | 72 | 7 | 0 | .097 |
| 2 yrs. | 7 | 10 | .412 | 4.07 | 34 | 22 | 6 | 148 | 130 | 36 | 91 | 3 | 0 | 0 | 0 | 43 | 3 | 0 | .070 |

## Vern Fear

**FEAR, LUVERN CARL**
B. Aug. 21, 1924, Everly, Iowa    D. Sept. 6, 1976, Spencer, Iowa    BB TR 6'    170 lbs.

| | | | | | | | | | | | | | | | | | | | |
|---|---|---|---|---|---|---|---|---|---|---|---|---|---|---|---|---|---|---|---|
| 1952 CHI N | 0 | 0 | – | 7.88 | 4 | 0 | 0 | 8 | 9 | 3 | 4 | 0 | 0 | 0 | 0 | 1 | 0 | 0 | .000 |

## Bob Ferguson

**FERGUSON, ROBERT V. (Death to Flying Things)**
B. Jan. 31, 1845, Brooklyn, N.Y.    D. May 3, 1894, Brooklyn, N.Y.    BB TR 5'9½"    149 lbs.
Manager 1871-84, 1886-87.

| | | | | | | | | | | | | | | | | | | | |
|---|---|---|---|---|---|---|---|---|---|---|---|---|---|---|---|---|---|---|---|
| 1877 HAR N | 1 | 1 | .500 | 3.96 | 3 | 2 | 2 | 25 | 38 | 2 | 1 | 0 | 0 | 0 | 0 | 254 | 65 | 0 | .256 |
| 1883 PHI N | 0 | 0 | – | 9.00 | 1 | 0 | 0 | 1 | 2 | 0 | 0 | 0 | 0 | 0 | 0 | 329 | 85 | 0 | .258 |
| 2 yrs. | 1 | 1 | .500 | 4.15 | 4 | 2 | 2 | 26 | 40 | 2 | 1 | 0 | 0 | 0 | 0 | * | | | |

## Charlie Ferguson

**FERGUSON, CHARLES AUGUSTUS**
B. May 10, 1875, Okemos, Mich.    D. May 17, 1931, Sault Ste. Marie, Mich.    TR 5'11"

| | | | | | | | | | | | | | | | | | | | |
|---|---|---|---|---|---|---|---|---|---|---|---|---|---|---|---|---|---|---|---|
| 1901 CHI N | 0 | 0 | – | 0.00 | 1 | 0 | 0 | 2 | 1 | 2 | 0 | 0 | 0 | 0 | 0 | 1 | 0 | 0 | .000 |

## Tom Filer

**FILER, THOMAS CARSON**
B. Dec. 1, 1956, Philadelphia, Pa.    BR TR 6'1"    195 lbs.

| | | | | | | | | | | | | | | | | | | | |
|---|---|---|---|---|---|---|---|---|---|---|---|---|---|---|---|---|---|---|---|
| 1982 CHI N | 1 | 2 | .333 | 5.53 | 8 | 8 | 0 | 40.2 | 50 | 18 | 15 | 0 | 0 | 0 | 0 | 12 | 1 | 0 | .083 |
| 1985 TOR A | 7 | 0 | 1.000 | 3.88 | 11 | 9 | 0 | 48.2 | 38 | 18 | 24 | 0 | 0 | 0 | 0 | 0 | 0 | 0 | – |
| 2 yrs. | 8 | 2 | .800 | 4.63 | 19 | 17 | 0 | 89.1 | 88 | 36 | 39 | 0 | 0 | 0 | 0 | 12 | 1 | 0 | .083 |
| 1 yr. | 1 | 2 | .333 | 5.53 | 8 | 8 | 0 | 40.2 | 50 | 18 | 15 | 0 | 0 | 0 | 0 | 12 | 1 | 0 | .083 |

## Cherokee Fisher

**FISHER, WILLIAM CHARLES**
B. Dec., 1845, Philadelphia, Pa.    D. Sept. 26, 1912, New York, N.Y.    BR TR 5'9"    164 lbs.

| | | | | | | | | | | | | | | | | | | | |
|---|---|---|---|---|---|---|---|---|---|---|---|---|---|---|---|---|---|---|---|
| 1876 CIN N | 4 | 20 | .167 | 3.02 | 28 | 24 | 22 | 229.1 | 294 | 6 | 29 | 0 | 0 | 0 | 0 | 129 | 32 | 0 | .248 |
| 1877 CHI N | 0 | 0 | – | 0.00 | 0 | 0 | 0 | 0 | 0 | 0 | 0 | 0 | 0 | 0 | 0 | 4 | 0 | 0 | .000 |
| 1878 PRO N | 0 | 1 | .000 | 4.00 | 1 | 1 | 1 | 9 | 14 | 0 | 2 | 0 | 0 | 0 | 0 | 3 | 0 | 0 | .000 |
| 3 yrs. | 4 | 21 | .160 | 3.06 | 29 | 25 | 23 | 238.1 | 308 | 6 | 31 | 0 | 0 | 0 | 0 | 136 | 32 | 0 | .235 |

## John Flavin

**FLAVIN, JOHN THOMAS**
B. May 7, 1942, Albany, Calif.    BL TL 6'2"    208 lbs.

| | | | | | | | | | | | | | | | | | | | |
|---|---|---|---|---|---|---|---|---|---|---|---|---|---|---|---|---|---|---|---|
| 1964 CHI N | 0 | 1 | .000 | 13.50 | 5 | 1 | 0 | 4.2 | 11 | 3 | 5 | 0 | 0 | 0 | 0 | 1 | 0 | 0 | .000 |

## Bill Fleming

**FLEMING, LESLIE FLETCHARD**
B. July 31, 1913, Rowland, Calif.    BR TR 6'    190 lbs.

| | | | | | | | | | | | | | | | | | | | |
|---|---|---|---|---|---|---|---|---|---|---|---|---|---|---|---|---|---|---|---|
| 1940 BOS A | 1 | 2 | .333 | 4.86 | 10 | 6 | 1 | 46.1 | 53 | 20 | 24 | 0 | 0 | 1 | 0 | 13 | 0 | 0 | .000 |
| 1941 | 1 | 1 | .500 | 3.92 | 16 | 1 | 0 | 41.1 | 32 | 24 | 20 | 0 | 1 | 1 | 1 | 9 | 2 | 0 | .222 |
| 1942 CHI N | 5 | 6 | .455 | 3.01 | 33 | 14 | 4 | 134.1 | 117 | 63 | 59 | 2 | 0 | 1 | 2 | 39 | 2 | 0 | .051 |
| 1943 | 0 | 1 | .000 | 6.40 | 11 | 0 | 0 | 32.1 | 40 | 12 | 12 | 0 | 0 | 1 | 0 | 8 | 0 | 0 | .000 |
| 1944 | 9 | 10 | .474 | 3.13 | 39 | 18 | 9 | 158.1 | 163 | 62 | 42 | 1 | 6 | 10 | 0 | 53 | 9 | 0 | .170 |
| 1946 | 0 | 1 | .000 | 6.14 | 14 | 1 | 0 | 29.1 | 37 | 12 | 10 | 0 | 0 | 0 | 0 | 3 | 0 | 0 | .000 |
| 6 yrs. | 16 | 21 | .432 | 3.79 | 123 | 40 | 14 | 442 | 442 | 193 | 167 | 3 | 7 | 14 | 3 | 125 | 13 | 0 | .104 |
| 4 yrs. | 14 | 18 | .438 | 3.63 | 97 | 33 | 13 | 354.1 | 357 | 149 | 123 | 3 | 6 | 12 | 2 | 103 | 11 | 0 | .107 |

## Jesse Flores

**FLORES, JESSE SANDOVAL**
B. Nov. 2, 1914, Guadalajara, Mexico    BR TR 5'10"    175 lbs.

| | | | | | | | | | | | | | | | | | | | |
|---|---|---|---|---|---|---|---|---|---|---|---|---|---|---|---|---|---|---|---|
| 1942 CHI N | 0 | 1 | .000 | 3.38 | 4 | 0 | 0 | 5.1 | 5 | 2 | 6 | 0 | 0 | 0 | 0 | 0 | 0 | 0 | |
| 1943 PHI A | 12 | 14 | .462 | 3.11 | 31 | 27 | 13 | 231.1 | 208 | 70 | 113 | 0 | 1 | 2 | 0 | 80 | 14 | 0 | .175 |
| 1944 | 9 | 11 | .450 | 3.39 | 27 | 25 | 11 | 185.2 | 172 | 49 | 65 | 2 | 0 | 0 | 0 | 64 | 11 | 0 | .172 |
| 1945 | 7 | 10 | .412 | 3.43 | 29 | 24 | 9 | 191.1 | 180 | 63 | 52 | 1 | 0 | 2 | 1 | 44 | 9 | 0 | .148 |
| 1946 | 9 | 7 | .563 | 2.32 | 29 | 15 | 8 | 155 | 147 | 38 | 48 | 4 | 0 | 0 | 0 | 44 | 11 | 0 | .250 |
| 1947 | 4 | 13 | .235 | 3.39 | 28 | 20 | 4 | 151.1 | 139 | 59 | 41 | 0 | 1 | 0 | 0 | 44 | 10 | 0 | .227 |
| 1950 CLE A | 3 | 3 | .500 | 3.74 | 28 | 2 | 1 | 53 | 53 | 25 | 27 | 1 | 0 | 0 | 4 | 11 | 0 | 0 | .000 |
| 7 yrs. | 44 | 59 | .427 | 3.18 | 176 | 113 | 46 | 973 | 904 | 306 | 352 | 11 | 2 | 5 | 6 | 304 | 55 | 0 | .181 |
| 1 yr. | 0 | 1 | .000 | 3.38 | 4 | 0 | 0 | 5.1 | 5 | 2 | 6 | 0 | 0 | 0 | 0 | 0 | 0 | 0 | |

| | W | L | PCT | ERA | G | GS | CG | IP | H | BB | SO | ShO | Relief Pitching W | L | SV | BATTING AB | H | HR | BA |
|---|---|---|---|---|---|---|---|---|---|---|---|---|---|---|---|---|---|---|---|

## Jocko Flynn

**FLYNN, JOHN A.**
B. June 30, 1864, Lawrence, Mass.   D. Dec. 30, 1907, Lawrence, Mass.   5'6½" 143 lbs.

| | W | L | PCT | ERA | G | GS | CG | IP | H | BB | SO | ShO | W | L | SV | AB | H | HR | BA |
|---|---|---|---|---|---|---|---|---|---|---|---|---|---|---|---|---|---|---|---|
| 1886 CHI N | 24 | 6 | .800 | 2.24 | 32 | 29 | 28 | 257 | 207 | 63 | 146 | 2 | 1 | 0 | 1 | 205 | 41 | 4 | .200 |
| 1887 | 0 | 0 | – | 0.00 | 0 | 0 | 0 | 0 | 0 | 0 | 0 | 0 | 0 | 0 | 0 | 0 | 0 | 0 | – |
| 2 yrs. | 24 | 6 | .800 | 2.24 | 32 | 29 | 28 | 257 | 207 | 63 | 146 | 2 | 1 | 0 | 1 | * | | | |
| 1 yr. | 24 | 6 | .800 | 2.24 | 32 | 29 | 28 | 257 | 207 | 63 | 146 | 2 | 1 | 0 | 1 | 205 | 41 | 4 | .200 |

## Gene Fodge

**FODGE, EUGENE ARLAN (Suds)**
B. July 9, 1931, South Bend, Ind.   BR TR 6' 175 lbs.

| | W | L | PCT | ERA | G | GS | CG | IP | H | BB | SO | ShO | W | L | SV | AB | H | HR | BA |
|---|---|---|---|---|---|---|---|---|---|---|---|---|---|---|---|---|---|---|---|
| 1958 CHI N | 1 | 1 | .500 | 4.76 | 16 | 4 | 1 | 39.2 | 47 | 11 | 15 | 0 | 0 | 0 | 0 | 7 | 0 | 0 | .000 |

## Ray Fontenot

**FONTENOT, SILTON RAY**
B. Aug. 8, 1957, Lake Charles, La.   BL TL 6' 175 lbs.

| | W | L | PCT | ERA | G | GS | CG | IP | H | BB | SO | ShO | W | L | SV | AB | H | HR | BA |
|---|---|---|---|---|---|---|---|---|---|---|---|---|---|---|---|---|---|---|---|
| 1983 NY A | 8 | 2 | .800 | 3.33 | 15 | 15 | 3 | 97.1 | 101 | 25 | 27 | 1 | 0 | 0 | 0 | 0 | 0 | 0 | – |
| 1984 | 8 | 9 | .471 | 3.61 | 33 | 24 | 0 | 169.1 | 189 | 58 | 85 | 0 | 1 | 0 | 0 | 0 | 0 | 0 | – |
| 1985 CHI N | 6 | 10 | .375 | 4.36 | 38 | 23 | 0 | 154.2 | 177 | 45 | 70 | 0 | 0 | 1 | 0 | 41 | 2 | 0 | .049 |
| 3 yrs. | 22 | 21 | .512 | 3.82 | 86 | 62 | 3 | 421.1 | 467 | 128 | 182 | 1 | 1 | 1 | 0 | 41 | 2 | 0 | .049 |
| 1 yr. | 6 | 10 | .375 | 4.36 | 38 | 23 | 0 | 154.2 | 177 | 45 | 70 | 0 | 0 | 1 | 0 | 41 | 2 | 0 | .049 |

## Bill Foxen

**FOXEN, WILLIAM ALOYSIUS**
B. May 31, 1884, Tenafly, N.J.   D. Apr. 17, 1937, Brooklyn, N.Y.   BL TL 5'11½" 165 lbs.

| | W | L | PCT | ERA | G | GS | CG | IP | H | BB | SO | ShO | W | L | SV | AB | H | HR | BA |
|---|---|---|---|---|---|---|---|---|---|---|---|---|---|---|---|---|---|---|---|
| 1908 PHI N | 7 | 7 | .500 | 1.95 | 22 | 16 | 10 | 147.1 | 126 | 53 | 52 | 2 | 0 | 0 | 0 | 53 | 5 | 0 | .094 |
| 1909 | 3 | 7 | .300 | 3.35 | 18 | 7 | 5 | 83.1 | 65 | 32 | 37 | 1 | 0 | 3 | 0 | 24 | 5 | 1 | .208 |
| 1910 2 teams | | | PHI | N (16G 5–5) | | CHI | N (2G 0–0) | | | | | | | | | | | | |
| " total | 5 | 5 | .500 | 2.94 | 18 | 9 | 5 | 82.2 | 80 | 43 | 35 | 0 | 2 | 0 | 0 | 25 | 4 | 0 | .160 |
| 1911 CHI N | 1 | 1 | .500 | 2.08 | 3 | 1 | 0 | 13 | 12 | 12 | 6 | 0 | 0 | 0 | 0 | 4 | 1 | 0 | .250 |
| 4 yrs. | 16 | 20 | .444 | 2.56 | 61 | 33 | 20 | 326.1 | 283 | 140 | 130 | 3 | 2 | 3 | 0 | 106 | 15 | 1 | .142 |
| 2 yrs. | 1 | 1 | .500 | 4.00 | 5 | 1 | 0 | 18 | 19 | 15 | 8 | 0 | 0 | 0 | 0 | 6 | 1 | 0 | .167 |

## Jimmie Foxx

**FOXX, JAMES EMORY (Double X, The Beast)**
B. Oct. 22, 1907, Sudlersville, Md.   D. July 21, 1967, Miami, Fla.
Hall of Fame 1951.   BR TR 6' 195 lbs.

| | W | L | PCT | ERA | G | GS | CG | IP | H | BB | SO | ShO | W | L | SV | AB | H | HR | BA |
|---|---|---|---|---|---|---|---|---|---|---|---|---|---|---|---|---|---|---|---|
| 1939 BOS A | 0 | 0 | – | 0.00 | 1 | 0 | 0 | 1 | 0 | 0 | 1 | 0 | 0 | 0 | 0 | 467 | 168 | 35 | .360 |
| 1945 PHI N | 1 | 0 | 1.000 | 1.59 | 9 | 2 | 0 | 22.2 | 13 | 14 | 10 | 0 | 0 | 0 | 0 | 224 | 60 | 7 | .268 |
| 2 yrs. | 1 | 0 | 1.000 | 1.52 | 10 | 2 | 0 | 23.2 | 13 | 14 | 11 | 0 | 0 | 0 | 0 | * | | | |

## Ken Frailing

**FRAILING, KENNETH DOUGLAS**
B. Jan. 19, 1948, Marion, Wis.   BL TL 6' 190 lbs.

| | W | L | PCT | ERA | G | GS | CG | IP | H | BB | SO | ShO | W | L | SV | AB | H | HR | BA |
|---|---|---|---|---|---|---|---|---|---|---|---|---|---|---|---|---|---|---|---|
| 1972 CHI A | 1 | 0 | 1.000 | 3.00 | 4 | 0 | 0 | 3 | 3 | 1 | 1 | 0 | 1 | 0 | 0 | 0 | 0 | 0 | – |
| 1973 | 0 | 0 | – | 1.96 | 10 | 0 | 0 | 18.1 | 18 | 7 | 15 | 0 | 0 | 0 | 0 | 0 | 0 | 0 | – |
| 1974 CHI N | 6 | 9 | .400 | 3.89 | 55 | 16 | 1 | 125 | 150 | 43 | 71 | 0 | 1 | 2 | 1 | 31 | 8 | 0 | .258 |
| 1975 | 2 | 5 | .286 | 5.43 | 41 | 0 | 0 | 53 | 61 | 26 | 39 | 0 | 2 | 5 | 1 | 7 | 1 | 0 | .143 |
| 1976 | 1 | 2 | .333 | 2.37 | 6 | 3 | 0 | 19 | 20 | 5 | 10 | 0 | 1 | 0 | 0 | 3 | 0 | 0 | .000 |
| 5 yrs. | 10 | 16 | .385 | 3.96 | 116 | 19 | 1 | 218.1 | 252 | 82 | 136 | 0 | 5 | 7 | 2 | 41 | 9 | 0 | .220 |
| 3 yrs. | 9 | 16 | .360 | 4.16 | 102 | 19 | 1 | 197 | 231 | 74 | 120 | 0 | 4 | 7 | 2 | 41 | 9 | 0 | .220 |

## Ossie France

**FRANCE, OSMAN B.**
B. Oct. 4, 1859, Greentown, Ohio   D. May 2, 1947, Akron, Ohio   BL

| | W | L | PCT | ERA | G | GS | CG | IP | H | BB | SO | ShO | W | L | SV | AB | H | HR | BA |
|---|---|---|---|---|---|---|---|---|---|---|---|---|---|---|---|---|---|---|---|
| 1890 CHI N | 0 | 0 | – | 13.50 | 1 | 0 | 0 | 2 | 3 | 2 | 0 | 0 | 0 | 0 | 0 | 1 | 0 | 0 | .000 |

## Chick Fraser

**FRASER, CHARLES CARROLTON**
B. Mar. 17, 1871, Chicago, Ill.   D. May 8, 1940, Wendell, Ida.   BR TR 5'10½" 188 lbs.

| | W | L | PCT | ERA | G | GS | CG | IP | H | BB | SO | ShO | W | L | SV | AB | H | HR | BA |
|---|---|---|---|---|---|---|---|---|---|---|---|---|---|---|---|---|---|---|---|
| 1896 LOU N | 13 | 25 | .342 | 4.87 | 43 | 38 | 36 | 349.1 | 396 | 166 | 91 | 0 | 0 | 2 | 1 | 146 | 22 | 0 | .151 |
| 1897 | 15 | 17 | .469 | 4.09 | 35 | 34 | 32 | 286.1 | 332 | 133 | 70 | 0 | 1 | 0 | 0 | 112 | 18 | 2 | .161 |
| 1898 2 teams | | | LOU | N (26G 7–19) | | CLE | N (6G 2–3) | | | | | | | | | | | | |
| " total | 9 | 22 | .290 | 5.36 | 32 | 32 | 26 | 245 | 279 | 112 | 77 | 0 | 0 | 0 | 0 | 94 | 17 | 0 | .181 |
| 1899 PHI N | 21 | 13 | .618 | 3.36 | 35 | 33 | 29 | 270.2 | 278 | 85 | 68 | 4 | 0 | 1 | 0 | 117 | 21 | 0 | .179 |
| 1900 | 16 | 10 | .615 | 3.14 | 29 | 26 | 22 | 223.1 | 250 | 93 | 58 | 1 | 0 | 0 | 0 | 85 | 22 | 0 | .259 |
| 1901 PHI A | 22 | 16 | .579 | 3.81 | 40 | 37 | 35 | 331 | 344 | 132 | 110 | 2 | 1 | 0 | 0 | 139 | 26 | 0 | .187 |
| 1902 PHI N | 12 | 13 | .480 | 3.42 | 27 | 26 | 24 | 224 | 238 | 74 | 97 | 3 | 0 | 1 | 0 | 86 | 15 | 0 | .174 |
| 1903 | 12 | 17 | .414 | 4.50 | 31 | 29 | 26 | 250 | 260 | 97 | 104 | 1 | 0 | 1 | 1 | 93 | 19 | 1 | .204 |
| 1904 | 14 | 24 | .368 | 3.25 | 42 | 36 | 32 | 302 | 287 | 100 | 127 | 2 | 2 | 1 | 1 | 110 | 17 | 0 | .155 |
| 1905 BOS N | 14 | 21 | .400 | 3.29 | 39 | 38 | 35 | 334 | 320 | 149 | 130 | 2 | 0 | 0 | 0 | 156 | 35 | 0 | .224 |
| 1906 CIN N | 10 | 20 | .333 | 2.67 | 31 | 28 | 25 | 236 | 221 | 80 | 58 | 2 | 1 | 2 | 0 | 82 | 14 | 0 | .171 |
| 1907 CHI N | 8 | 5 | .615 | 2.28 | 22 | 15 | 9 | 138.1 | 112 | 46 | 41 | 2 | 4 | 0 | 0 | 45 | 3 | 0 | .067 |
| 1908 | 11 | 9 | .550 | 2.27 | 26 | 17 | 11 | 162.2 | 141 | 61 | 66 | 2 | 3 | 0 | 2 | 50 | 6 | 0 | .120 |
| 1909 | 0 | 0 | – | 0.00 | 1 | 0 | 0 | 3 | 2 | 1 | 0 | 0 | 0 | 0 | 0 | 0 | 0 | 0 | .000 |
| 14 yrs. | 177 | 212 | .455 | 3.68 | 433 | 389 | 342 | 3355.2 | 3460 | 1332 | 1098 | 22 | 12 | 8 | 5 | 1316 | 235 | 3 | .179 |
| 3 yrs. | 19 | 14 | .576 | 2.25 | 49 | 32 | 20 | 304 | 255 | 111 | 108 | 4 | 7 | 0 | 2 | 96 | 9 | 0 | .094 |

## George Frazier

**FRAZIER, GEORGE ALLEN**
B. Oct. 13, 1954, Oklahoma City, Okla.   BR TR 6'5" 205 lbs.

| | W | L | PCT | ERA | G | GS | CG | IP | H | BB | SO | ShO | W | L | SV | AB | H | HR | BA |
|---|---|---|---|---|---|---|---|---|---|---|---|---|---|---|---|---|---|---|---|
| 1978 STL N | 0 | 3 | .000 | 4.09 | 14 | 0 | 0 | 22 | 22 | 6 | 8 | 0 | 0 | 0 | 0 | 3 | 1 | 0 | .333 |
| 1979 | 2 | 4 | .333 | 4.50 | 25 | 0 | 0 | 32 | 35 | 12 | 14 | 0 | 2 | 4 | 0 | 1 | 0 | 0 | .000 |
| 1980 | 4 | 2 | .200 | 2.74 | 22 | 0 | 0 | 23 | 24 | 7 | 11 | 0 | 1 | 4 | 3 | 0 | 0 | 0 | – |
| 1981 NY A | 0 | 1 | .000 | 1.61 | 16 | 0 | 0 | 28 | 26 | 11 | 17 | 0 | 0 | 1 | 3 | 0 | 0 | 0 | – |
| 1982 | 4 | 4 | .500 | 3.47 | 63 | 0 | 0 | 111.2 | 103 | 39 | 69 | 0 | 4 | 4 | 1 | 0 | 0 | 0 | – |
| 1983 | 4 | 4 | .500 | 3.43 | 61 | 0 | 0 | 115.1 | 94 | 45 | 78 | 0 | 4 | 4 | 8 | 0 | 0 | 0 | – |

| | W | L | PCT | ERA | G | GS | CG | IP | H | BB | SO | ShO | Relief Pitching W | L | SV | BATTING AB | H | HR | BA |
|---|---|---|---|---|---|---|---|---|---|---|---|---|---|---|---|---|---|---|---|

## George Frazier continued

| | W | L | PCT | ERA | G | GS | CG | IP | H | BB | SO | ShO | W | L | SV | AB | H | HR | BA |
|---|---|---|---|---|---|---|---|---|---|---|---|---|---|---|---|---|---|---|---|
| 1984 2 teams | | | CLE A (22G 3–2) | | CHI N (37G 6–3) | | | | | | | | | | | | | | |
| " total | 9 | 5 | .643 | 3.92 | 59 | 0 | 0 | 108 | 98 | 40 | 82 | 0 | 9 | 5 | 4 | 7 | 2 | 0 | .286 |
| 1985 CHI N | 7 | 8 | .467 | 6.39 | 51 | 0 | 0 | 76 | 88 | 52 | 46 | 0 | 7 | 8 | 2 | 6 | 0 | 0 | .000 |
| 8 yrs. | 27 | 33 | .450 | 3.94 | 311 | 0 | 0 | 516 | 490 | 212 | 325 | 0 | 27 | 33 | 21 | 17 | 3 | 0 | .176 |
| 2 yrs. | 13 | 11 | .542 | 5.35 | 88 | 0 | 0 | 139.2 | 141 | 78 | 104 | 0 | 13 | 11 | 5 | 13 | 2 | 0 | .154 |
| LEAGUE CHAMPIONSHIP SERIES | | | | | | | | | | | | | | | | | | | |
| 1981 NY A | 1 | 0 | 1.000 | 0.00 | 1 | 0 | 0 | 5.2 | 5 | 1 | 5 | 0 | 1 | 0 | 0 | 0 | 0 | 0 | – |
| 1984 CHI N | 0 | 0 | – | 10.80 | 1 | 0 | 0 | 1.2 | 2 | 0 | 1 | 0 | 0 | 0 | 0 | 0 | 0 | 0 | – |
| 2 yrs. | 1 | 0 | 1.000 | 2.45 | 2 | 0 | 0 | 7.1 | 7 | 1 | 6 | 0 | 1 | 0 | 0 | 0 | 0 | 0 | – |
| WORLD SERIES | | | | | | | | | | | | | | | | | | | |
| 1981 NY A | 0 | 3 | .000 | 17.18 | 3 | 0 | 0 | 3.2 | 9 | 3 | 2 | 0 | 0 | 3 | 0 | 2 | 0 | 0 | .000 |
| | | | | | | | | | | | | | | 1st | | | | | |

## Buck Freeman

**FREEMAN, ALEXANDER VERNON**
B. July 5, 1893, Mart, Tex.
D. Feb. 21, 1953, Fort Sam Houston, Tex.

BB TR 5'10" 167 lbs.
BR 1922

| | W | L | PCT | ERA | G | GS | CG | IP | H | BB | SO | ShO | W | L | SV | AB | H | HR | BA |
|---|---|---|---|---|---|---|---|---|---|---|---|---|---|---|---|---|---|---|---|
| 1921 CHI N | 9 | 10 | .474 | 4.11 | 38 | 20 | 6 | 177.1 | 189 | 70 | 42 | 0 | 4 | 2 | 3 | 53 | 11 | 0 | .208 |
| 1922 | 0 | 1 | .000 | 8.77 | 11 | 1 | 0 | 25.2 | 47 | 10 | 10 | 0 | 0 | 0 | 1 | 8 | 1 | 0 | .125 |
| 2 yrs. | 9 | 11 | .450 | 4.70 | 49 | 21 | 6 | 203 | 236 | 80 | 52 | 0 | 4 | 2 | 4 | 61 | 12 | 0 | .197 |
| 2 yrs. | 9 | 11 | .450 | 4.70 | 49 | 21 | 6 | 203 | 236 | 80 | 52 | 0 | 4 | 2 | 4 | 61 | 12 | 0 | .197 |

## Hersh Freeman

**FREEMAN, HERSHELL BASKIN (Buster)**
B. July 1, 1928, Gadsden, Ala.

BR TR 6'3" 220 lbs.

| | W | L | PCT | ERA | G | GS | CG | IP | H | BB | SO | ShO | W | L | SV | AB | H | HR | BA |
|---|---|---|---|---|---|---|---|---|---|---|---|---|---|---|---|---|---|---|---|
| 1952 BOS A | 1 | 0 | 1.000 | 3.29 | 4 | 1 | 1 | 13.2 | 13 | 5 | 5 | 0 | 0 | 0 | 0 | 4 | 2 | 0 | .500 |
| 1953 | 1 | 4 | .200 | 5.54 | 18 | 2 | 0 | 39 | 50 | 17 | 15 | 0 | 1 | 2 | 0 | 11 | 1 | 0 | .091 |
| 1955 2 teams | | | BOS A (2G 0–0) | | CIN N (52G 7–4) | | | | | | | | | | | | | | |
| " total | 7 | 4 | .636 | 2.12 | 54 | 0 | 0 | 93.1 | 95 | 31 | 38 | 0 | 7 | 4 | 11 | 18 | 3 | 1 | .167 |
| 1956 CIN N | 14 | 5 | .737 | 3.40 | 64 | 0 | 0 | 108.2 | 112 | 34 | 50 | 0 | 14 | 5 | 18 | 18 | 1 | 0 | .056 |
| 1957 | 7 | 2 | .778 | 4.52 | 52 | 0 | 0 | 83.2 | 90 | 14 | 36 | 0 | 7 | 2 | 8 | 10 | 2 | 0 | .200 |
| 1958 2 teams | | | CIN N (3G 0–0) | | CHI N (9G 0–1) | | | | | | | | | | | | | | |
| " total | 0 | 1 | .000 | 6.53 | 12 | 0 | 0 | 20.2 | 27 | 8 | 14 | 0 | 0 | 1 | 0 | 2 | 0 | 0 | .000 |
| 6 yrs. | 30 | 16 | .652 | 3.74 | 204 | 3 | 1 | 359 | 387 | 109 | 158 | 0 | 29 | 14 | 37 | 63 | 9 | 1 | .143 |
| 1 yr. | 0 | 1 | .000 | 8.31 | 9 | 0 | 0 | 13 | 23 | 3 | 7 | 0 | 0 | 1 | 0 | 1 | 0 | 0 | .000 |

## Mark Freeman

**FREEMAN, MARK PRICE**
B. Dec. 7, 1930, Memphis, Tenn.

BR TR 6'4" 220 lbs.

| | W | L | PCT | ERA | G | GS | CG | IP | H | BB | SO | ShO | W | L | SV | AB | H | HR | BA |
|---|---|---|---|---|---|---|---|---|---|---|---|---|---|---|---|---|---|---|---|
| 1959 2 teams | | | NY A (1G 0–0) | | KC A (3G 0–0) | | | | | | | | | | | | | | |
| " total | 0 | 0 | – | 5.06 | 4 | 1 | 0 | 10.2 | 12 | 5 | 5 | 0 | 0 | 0 | 0 | 2 | 0 | 0 | .000 |
| 1960 CHI N | 3 | 3 | .500 | 5.63 | 30 | 8 | 1 | 76.2 | 70 | 33 | 50 | 0 | 1 | 2 | 1 | 20 | 3 | 0 | .150 |
| 2 yrs. | 3 | 3 | .500 | 5.56 | 34 | 9 | 1 | 87.1 | 82 | 38 | 55 | 0 | 1 | 2 | 1 | 22 | 3 | 0 | .136 |
| 1 yr. | 3 | 3 | .500 | 5.63 | 30 | 8 | 1 | 76.2 | 70 | 33 | 50 | 0 | 1 | 2 | 1 | 20 | 3 | 0 | .150 |

## Larry French

**FRENCH, LAWRENCE ROBERT**
B. Nov. 1, 1907, Visalia, Calif.

BR TL 6'1" 195 lbs.
BB 1934,1940-42

| | W | L | PCT | ERA | G | GS | CG | IP | H | BB | SO | ShO | W | L | SV | AB | H | HR | BA |
|---|---|---|---|---|---|---|---|---|---|---|---|---|---|---|---|---|---|---|---|
| 1929 PIT N | 7 | 5 | .583 | 4.90 | 30 | 13 | 6 | 123 | 130 | 62 | 49 | 0 | 2 | 1 | 1 | 42 | 8 | 0 | .190 |
| 1930 | 17 | 18 | .486 | 4.36 | 42 | 35 | 21 | 274.2 | 325 | 89 | 90 | 3 | 1 | 1 | 1 | 91 | 22 | 0 | .242 |
| 1931 | 15 | 13 | .536 | 3.26 | 39 | 33 | 20 | 275.2 | 301 | 70 | 73 | 1 | 1 | 0 | 1 | 95 | 17 | 0 | .179 |
| 1932 | 18 | 16 | .529 | 3.02 | 47 | 33 | 20 | 274.1 | 301 | 62 | 72 | 3 | 2 | 2 | 4 | 92 | 19 | 0 | .207 |
| 1933 | 18 | 13 | .581 | 2.72 | 47 | 35 | 21 | 291.1 | 290 | 55 | 88 | 5 | 1 | 2 | 1 | 101 | 15 | 0 | .149 |
| 1934 | 12 | 18 | .400 | 3.58 | 49 | 35 | 16 | 263.2 | 299 | 59 | 103 | 3 | 1 | 4 | 1 | 84 | 16 | 0 | .190 |
| 1935 CHI N | 17 | 10 | .630 | 2.96 | 42 | 30 | 16 | 246.1 | 279 | 44 | 90 | 4 | 1 | 3 | 2 | 85 | 12 | 0 | .141 |
| 1936 | 18 | 9 | .667 | 3.39 | 43 | 28 | 16 | 252.1 | 262 | 54 | 104 | 4 | 3 | 2 | 3 | 85 | 18 | 0 | .212 |
| 1937 | 16 | 10 | .615 | 3.98 | 42 | 28 | 11 | 208 | 229 | 65 | 100 | 4 | 3 | 1 | 0 | 71 | 9 | 0 | .127 |
| 1938 | 10 | 19 | .345 | 3.80 | 43 | 27 | 10 | 201.1 | 210 | 62 | 83 | 3 | 2 | 4 | 0 | 62 | 13 | 0 | .210 |
| 1939 | 15 | 8 | .652 | 3.29 | 36 | 21 | 10 | 194 | 205 | 50 | 98 | 2 | 4 | 0 | 1 | 73 | 14 | 1 | .192 |
| 1940 | 14 | 14 | .500 | 3.29 | 40 | 33 | 18 | 246 | 240 | 64 | 107 | 3 | 1 | 1 | 2 | 85 | 14 | 0 | .165 |
| 1941 2 teams | | | CHI N (26G 5–14) | | BKN N (6G 0–0) | | | | | | | | | | | | | | |
| " total | 5 | 14 | .263 | 4.51 | 32 | 19 | 6 | 153.2 | 177 | 47 | 68 | 1 | 1 | 0 | 0 | 51 | 10 | 0 | .196 |
| 1942 BKN N | 15 | 4 | .789 | 1.83 | 38 | 14 | 8 | 147.2 | 127 | 36 | 62 | 4 | 7 | 1 | 0 | 40 | 12 | 0 | .300 |
| 14 yrs. | 197 | 171 | .535 | 3.44 | 570 | 384 | 199 | 3152 | 3375 | 819 | 1187 | 40 | 30 | 22 | 17 | 1057 | 199 | 1 | .188 |
| 7 yrs. | 95 | 84 | .531 | 3.54 | 272 | 185 | 87 | 1486 | 1586 | 382 | 642 | 21 | 15 | 11 | 8 | 508 | 89 | 1 | .175 |
| | | | | | | | | | | | | | | 10th | | | | | |
| WORLD SERIES | | | | | | | | | | | | | | | | | | | |
| 1935 CHI N | 0 | 2 | .000 | 3.38 | 2 | 1 | 1 | 10.2 | 15 | 2 | 8 | 0 | 0 | 1 | 0 | 4 | 1 | 0 | .250 |
| 1938 | 0 | 0 | – | 2.70 | 3 | 0 | 0 | 3.1 | 1 | 1 | 2 | 0 | 0 | 0 | 0 | 0 | 0 | 0 | – |
| 1941 BKN N | 0 | 0 | – | 0.00 | 2 | 0 | 0 | 1 | 0 | 0 | 0 | 0 | 0 | 0 | 0 | 0 | 0 | 0 | – |
| 3 yrs. | 0 | 2 | .000 | 3.00 | 7 | 1 | 1 | 15 | 16 | 3 | 10 | 0 | 0 | 1 | 0 | 4 | 1 | 0 | .250 |

## Barney Friberg

**FRIBERG, AUGUSTAF BERNHARDT**
Also known as Bernard Albert Friberg.
B. Aug. 18, 1899, Manchester, N. H.    D. Dec. 8, 1958, Swampscott, Mass.

BR TR 5'11" 178 lbs.

| | W | L | PCT | ERA | G | GS | CG | IP | H | BB | SO | ShO | W | L | SV | AB | H | HR | BA |
|---|---|---|---|---|---|---|---|---|---|---|---|---|---|---|---|---|---|---|---|
| 1925 2 teams | | | CHI N (0G 0–0) | | PHI N (1G 0–0) | | | | | | | | | | | | | | |
| " total | 0 | 0 | – | 4.50 | 1 | 0 | 0 | 4 | 4 | 3 | 1 | 0 | 0 | 0 | 0 | * | | | |

## Danny Friend

**FRIEND, DANIEL SEBASTIAN**
B. Apr. 18, 1873, Cincinnati, Ohio    D. June 1, 1942, Chillicothe, Ohio

TL 5'9" 175 lbs.

| | W | L | PCT | ERA | G | GS | CG | IP | H | BB | SO | ShO | W | L | SV | AB | H | HR | BA |
|---|---|---|---|---|---|---|---|---|---|---|---|---|---|---|---|---|---|---|---|
| 1895 CHI N | 2 | 2 | .500 | 5.27 | 5 | 5 | 5 | 41 | 50 | 14 | 10 | 0 | | | | 17 | 4 | 0 | .235 |
| 1896 | 18 | 14 | .563 | 4.74 | 36 | 33 | 28 | 290.2 | 298 | 139 | 86 | 1 | 1 | 1 | 0 | 126 | 30 | 1 | .238 |
| 1897 | 12 | 11 | .522 | 4.52 | 24 | 24 | 23 | 203 | 244 | 86 | 58 | 0 | 0 | 0 | 0 | 88 | 25 | 0 | .284 |

| | W | L | PCT | ERA | G | GS | CG | IP | H | BB | SO | ShO | Relief Pitching W | L | SV | BATTING AB | H | HR | BA |
|---|---|---|---|---|---|---|---|---|---|---|---|---|---|---|---|---|---|---|---|

## Danny Friend continued

| | W | L | PCT | ERA | G | GS | CG | IP | H | BB | SO | ShO | W | L | SV | AB | H | HR | BA |
|---|---|---|---|---|---|---|---|---|---|---|---|---|---|---|---|---|---|---|---|
| 1898 | 0 | 2 | .000 | 5.29 | 2 | 2 | 2 | 17 | 20 | 10 | 4 | 0 | 0 | 0 | 0 | 7 | 2 | 0 | .286 |
| 4 yrs. | 32 | 29 | .525 | 4.71 | 67 | 64 | 58 | 551.2 | 612 | 249 | 158 | 1 | 1 | 1 | 0 | 238 | 61 | 1 | .256 |
| 4 yrs. | 32 | 29 | .525 | 4.71 | 67 | 64 | 58 | 551.2 | 612 | 249 | 158 | 1 | 1 | 1 | 0 | 238 | 61 | 1 | .256 |

## Woodie Fryman

**FRYMAN, WOODROW THOMPSON**      BR TL 6'3"      197 lbs.
B. Apr. 12, 1940, Ewing, Ky.

| | W | L | PCT | ERA | G | GS | CG | IP | H | BB | SO | ShO | W | L | SV | AB | H | HR | BA |
|---|---|---|---|---|---|---|---|---|---|---|---|---|---|---|---|---|---|---|---|
| 1966 PIT N | 12 | 9 | .571 | 3.81 | 36 | 28 | 9 | 181.2 | 182 | 47 | 105 | 3 | 1 | 0 | 1 | 63 | 10 | 0 | .159 |
| 1967 | 3 | 8 | .273 | 4.05 | 28 | 18 | 3 | 113.1 | 121 | 44 | 74 | 1 | 0 | 0 | 1 | 34 | 4 | 0 | .118 |
| 1968 PHI N | 12 | 14 | .462 | 2.78 | 34 | 32 | 10 | 213.2 | 198 | 64 | 151 | 5 | 0 | 0 | 0 | 71 | 6 | 0 | .085 |
| 1969 | 12 | 15 | .444 | 4.42 | 36 | 35 | 10 | 228 | 243 | 89 | 150 | 1 | 0 | 0 | 0 | 76 | 9 | 1 | .118 |
| 1970 | 8 | 6 | .571 | 4.08 | 27 | 20 | 4 | 128 | 122 | 43 | 97 | 3 | 1 | 0 | 0 | 39 | 5 | 0 | .128 |
| 1971 | 10 | 7 | .588 | 3.38 | 37 | 17 | 3 | 149 | 133 | 46 | 104 | 2 | 3 | 2 | 2 | 37 | 7 | 0 | .189 |
| 1972 2 teams | | | PHI N | (23G 4–10) | | DET A | (16G 10–3) | | | | | | | | | | | | |
| " total | 14 | 13 | .519 | 3.24 | 39 | 31 | 9 | 233.2 | 224 | 70 | 141 | 3 | 0 | 0 | 1 | 73 | 10 | 1 | .137 |
| 1973 DET A | 6 | 13 | .316 | 5.35 | 34 | 29 | 1 | 170 | 200 | 64 | 119 | 0 | 0 | 0 | 0 | 0 | 0 | 0 | – |
| 1974 | 6 | 9 | .400 | 4.31 | 27 | 22 | 4 | 142 | 120 | 67 | 92 | 1 | 0 | 0 | 0 | 0 | 0 | 0 | – |
| 1975 MON N | 9 | 12 | .429 | 3.32 | 38 | 20 | 7 | 157 | 141 | 68 | 118 | 3 | 2 | 4 | 3 | 49 | 10 | 0 | .204 |
| 1976 | 13 | 13 | .500 | 3.37 | 34 | 32 | 4 | 216.1 | 218 | 76 | 123 | 2 | 0 | 0 | 2 | 64 | 7 | 0 | .109 |
| 1977 CIN N | 5 | 5 | .500 | 5.40 | 17 | 12 | 0 | 75 | 83 | 45 | 57 | 0 | 0 | 1 | 1 | 22 | 7 | 0 | .318 |
| 1978 2 teams | | | CHI N | (13G 2–4) | | MON N | (19G 5–7) | | | | | | | | | | | | |
| " total | 7 | 11 | .389 | 4.19 | 32 | 26 | 4 | 150.1 | 157 | 74 | 81 | 3 | 1 | 0 | 1 | 50 | 3 | 0 | .060 |
| 1979 MON N | 3 | 6 | .333 | 2.79 | 44 | 0 | 0 | 58 | 52 | 22 | 44 | 0 | 3 | 6 | 10 | 7 | 0 | 0 | .000 |
| 1980 | 7 | 4 | .636 | 2.25 | 61 | 0 | 0 | 80 | 61 | 30 | 59 | 0 | 7 | 4 | 17 | 12 | 2 | 0 | .167 |
| 1981 | 5 | 3 | .625 | 1.88 | 35 | 0 | 0 | 43 | 38 | 14 | 25 | 0 | 5 | 3 | 7 | 3 | 2 | 0 | .667 |
| 1982 | 9 | 4 | .692 | 3.75 | 60 | 0 | 0 | 69.2 | 66 | 26 | 46 | 0 | 9 | 4 | 12 | 9 | 2 | 0 | .222 |
| 1983 | 0 | 3 | .000 | 21.00 | 6 | 0 | 0 | 3 | 8 | 1 | 1 | 0 | 0 | 0 | 0 | 0 | 0 | 0 | – |
| 18 yrs. | 141 | 155 | .476 | 3.77 | 625 | 322 | 68 | 2411.2 | 2367 | 890 | 1587 | 27 | 32 | 27 | 58 | 609 | 84 | 2 | .138 |
| 1 yr. | 2 | 4 | .333 | 5.17 | 13 | 9 | 0 | 55.2 | 64 | 37 | 28 | 0 | 1 | 0 | 0 | 16 | 1 | 0 | .063 |

**DIVISIONAL PLAYOFF SERIES**

| | W | L | PCT | ERA | G | GS | CG | IP | H | BB | SO | ShO | W | L | SV | AB | H | HR | BA |
|---|---|---|---|---|---|---|---|---|---|---|---|---|---|---|---|---|---|---|---|
| 1981 MON N | 0 | 0 | – | 6.75 | 1 | 0 | 0 | 1.1 | 3 | 1 | 0 | 0 | 0 | 0 | 0 | 0 | 0 | 0 | – |

**LEAGUE CHAMPIONSHIP SERIES**

| | W | L | PCT | ERA | G | GS | CG | IP | H | BB | SO | ShO | W | L | SV | AB | H | HR | BA |
|---|---|---|---|---|---|---|---|---|---|---|---|---|---|---|---|---|---|---|---|
| 1972 DET A | 0 | 2 | .000 | 3.65 | 2 | 2 | 0 | 12.1 | 11 | 2 | 8 | 0 | 0 | 0 | 0 | 3 | 0 | 0 | .000 |
| 1981 MON N | 0 | 0 | – | 36.00 | 1 | 0 | 0 | 1 | 3 | 1 | 1 | 0 | 0 | 0 | 0 | 0 | 0 | 0 | – |
| 2 yrs. | 0 | 2 | .000 | 6.08 | 3 | 2 | 0 | 13.1 | 14 | 3 | 9 | 0 | 0 | 0 | 0 | 3 | 0 | 0 | .000 |

## Oscar Fuhr

**FUHR, OSCAR LAWRENCE**      BR TL 5'10"      170 lbs.
B. Aug. 22, 1893, Defiance, Mo.      D. Mar. 27, 1975, Dallas, Tex.

| | W | L | PCT | ERA | G | GS | CG | IP | H | BB | SO | ShO | W | L | SV | AB | H | HR | BA |
|---|---|---|---|---|---|---|---|---|---|---|---|---|---|---|---|---|---|---|---|
| 1921 CHI N | 0 | 0 | – | 9.00 | 1 | 0 | 0 | 4 | 11 | 0 | 2 | 0 | 0 | 0 | 0 | 1 | 0 | 0 | .000 |
| 1924 BOS A | 3 | 6 | .333 | 5.94 | 23 | 10 | 4 | 80.1 | 100 | 39 | 30 | 1 | 0 | 2 | 0 | 22 | 4 | 0 | .182 |
| 1925 | 0 | 6 | .000 | 6.60 | 39 | 6 | 0 | 91.1 | 138 | 30 | 27 | 0 | 0 | 2 | 0 | 20 | 5 | 0 | .250 |
| 3 yrs. | 3 | 12 | .200 | 6.35 | 63 | 16 | 4 | 175.2 | 249 | 69 | 59 | 1 | 0 | 4 | 0 | 43 | 9 | 0 | .209 |
| 1 yr. | 0 | 0 | – | 9.00 | 1 | 0 | 0 | 4 | 11 | 0 | 2 | 0 | 0 | 0 | 0 | 1 | 0 | 0 | .000 |

## Fred Fussell

**FUSSELL, FREDERICK MORRIS (Moonlight Ace)**      BL TL 5'10"      155 lbs.
B. Oct. 7, 1895, Sheridan, Mo.      D. Oct. 23, 1966, Syracuse, N. Y.

| | W | L | PCT | ERA | G | GS | CG | IP | H | BB | SO | ShO | W | L | SV | AB | H | HR | BA |
|---|---|---|---|---|---|---|---|---|---|---|---|---|---|---|---|---|---|---|---|
| 1922 CHI N | 1 | 1 | .500 | 4.74 | 3 | 2 | 1 | 19 | 24 | 8 | 4 | 0 | 0 | 0 | 0 | 6 | 0 | 0 | .000 |
| 1923 | 3 | 5 | .375 | 5.54 | 28 | 2 | 1 | 76.1 | 90 | 31 | 38 | 0 | 3 | 3 | 3 | 20 | 4 | 0 | .200 |
| 1928 PIT N | 8 | 9 | .471 | 3.61 | 28 | 20 | 9 | 159.2 | 183 | 41 | 43 | 2 | 1 | 1 | 1 | 58 | 7 | 0 | .121 |
| 1929 | 2 | 2 | .500 | 8.62 | 21 | 3 | 0 | 39.2 | 68 | 8 | 18 | 0 | 1 | 1 | 1 | 16 | 4 | 2 | .250 |
| 4 yrs. | 14 | 17 | .452 | 4.86 | 80 | 27 | 11 | 294.2 | 365 | 88 | 103 | 2 | 5 | 5 | 5 | 100 | 15 | 2 | .150 |
| 2 yrs. | 4 | 6 | .400 | 5.38 | 31 | 4 | 2 | 95.1 | 114 | 39 | 42 | 0 | 3 | 3 | 3 | 26 | 4 | 0 | .154 |

## Bill Gannon

**GANNON, WILLIAM G.**
B. 1876, New Haven, Conn.      D. Apr. 26, 1927, Ft. Worth, Tex.

| | W | L | PCT | ERA | G | GS | CG | IP | H | BB | SO | ShO | W | L | SV | AB | H | HR | BA |
|---|---|---|---|---|---|---|---|---|---|---|---|---|---|---|---|---|---|---|---|
| 1898 STL N | 0 | 1 | .000 | 11.00 | 1 | 1 | 1 | 9 | 13 | 5 | 2 | 0 | 0 | 0 | 0 | * | | | |

## John Ganzel

**GANZEL, JOHN HENRY**      BR TR 6'½"      195 lbs.
Brother of Charlie Ganzel.
B. Apr. 7, 1874, Kalamazoo, Mich.      D. Jan. 14, 1959, Orlando, Fla.
Manager 1908, 1915.

| | W | L | PCT | ERA | G | GS | CG | IP | H | BB | SO | ShO | W | L | SV | AB | H | HR | BA |
|---|---|---|---|---|---|---|---|---|---|---|---|---|---|---|---|---|---|---|---|
| 1898 PIT N | 0 | 0 | – | 0.00 | 1 | 0 | 0 | 0 | 0 | 0 | 0 | 0 | 0 | 0 | 0 | * | | | |

## Jim Gardner

**GARDNER, JAMES ANDERSON**      TR
B. Oct. 4, 1874, Pittsburgh, Pa.      D. Apr. 24, 1905, Pittsburgh, Pa.

| | W | L | PCT | ERA | G | GS | CG | IP | H | BB | SO | ShO | W | L | SV | AB | H | HR | BA |
|---|---|---|---|---|---|---|---|---|---|---|---|---|---|---|---|---|---|---|---|
| 1895 PIT N | 8 | 2 | .800 | 2.64 | 11 | 10 | 8 | 85.1 | 99 | 27 | 31 | 0 | 0 | 0 | 0 | 34 | 9 | 0 | .265 |
| 1897 | 5 | 5 | .500 | 5.19 | 14 | 11 | 8 | 95.1 | 115 | 32 | 35 | 0 | 1 | 0 | 0 | 76 | 12 | 1 | .158 |
| 1898 | 10 | 13 | .435 | 3.21 | 25 | 22 | 19 | 185.1 | 179 | 48 | 41 | 1 | 0 | 0 | 0 | 91 | 14 | 0 | .154 |
| 1899 | 1 | 0 | 1.000 | 7.52 | 6 | 3 | 0 | 32.1 | 52 | 13 | 2 | 0 | 0 | 0 | 0 | 13 | 3 | 0 | .231 |
| 1902 CHI N | 1 | 2 | .333 | 2.88 | 3 | 3 | 2 | 25 | 23 | 10 | 6 | 0 | 0 | 0 | 0 | 10 | 2 | 0 | .200 |
| 5 yrs. | 25 | 22 | .532 | 3.85 | 59 | 49 | 37 | 423.1 | 468 | 130 | 115 | 1 | 1 | 0 | 0 | 224 | 40 | 1 | .179 |
| 1 yr. | 1 | 2 | .333 | 2.88 | 3 | 3 | 2 | 25 | 23 | 10 | 6 | 0 | 0 | 0 | 0 | 10 | 2 | 0 | .200 |

## Rob Gardner

**GARDNER, RICHARD FRANK**      BR TL 6'1"      176 lbs.
B. Dec. 19, 1944, Binghamton, N. Y.

| | W | L | PCT | ERA | G | GS | CG | IP | H | BB | SO | ShO | W | L | SV | AB | H | HR | BA |
|---|---|---|---|---|---|---|---|---|---|---|---|---|---|---|---|---|---|---|---|
| 1965 NY N | 0 | 2 | .000 | 3.21 | 5 | 4 | 0 | 28 | 23 | 7 | 19 | 0 | 0 | 0 | 0 | 7 | 0 | 0 | .000 |
| 1966 | 4 | 8 | .333 | 5.12 | 41 | 17 | 3 | 133.2 | 147 | 64 | 74 | 0 | 1 | 1 | 1 | 41 | 7 | 0 | .171 |
| 1967 CHI N | 0 | 2 | .000 | 3.98 | 18 | 5 | 0 | 31.2 | 33 | 6 | 16 | 0 | 0 | 0 | 0 | 6 | 0 | 0 | .000 |
| 1968 CLE A | 0 | 0 | – | 6.75 | 5 | 0 | 0 | 2.2 | 5 | 2 | 6 | 0 | 0 | 0 | 0 | 0 | 0 | 0 | – |

| | | W | L | PCT | ERA | G | GS | CG | IP | H | BB | SO | ShO | Relief Pitching W | L | SV | Batting AB | H | HR | BA |
|---|---|---|---|---|---|---|---|---|---|---|---|---|---|---|---|---|---|---|---|---|

## Rob Gardner continued

| 1970 | NY A | 1 | 0 | 1.000 | 5.14 | 1 | 1 | 0 | 7 | 8 | 4 | 6 | 0 | 0 | 0 | 0 | 3 | 1 | 0 | .333 |
| 1971 | 2 teams | OAK | A | (4G 0–0) | | NY | A | (2G 0–0) | | | | | | | | | | | | |
| " | total | 0 | 0 | – | 2.53 | 6 | 1 | 0 | 10.2 | 11 | 5 | 7 | 0 | 0 | 0 | 0 | 2 | 1 | 0 | .500 |
| 1972 | NY A | 8 | 5 | .615 | 3.06 | 20 | 14 | 1 | 97 | 91 | 28 | 58 | 0 | 0 | 1 | 0 | 28 | 3 | 0 | .107 |
| 1973 | 2 teams | MIL | A | (10G 1–1) | | OAK | A | (3G 0–0) | | | | | | | | | | | | |
| " | total | 1 | 1 | .500 | 8.10 | 13 | 0 | 0 | 20 | 27 | 17 | 7 | 0 | 1 | 1 | 1 | 0 | 0 | 0 | – |
| | 8 yrs. | 14 | 18 | .438 | 4.35 | 109 | 42 | 4 | 330.2 | 345 | 133 | 193 | 0 | 2 | 3 | 2 | 87 | 12 | 0 | .138 |
| | 1 yr. | 0 | 2 | .000 | 3.98 | 18 | 5 | 0 | 31.2 | 33 | 6 | 16 | 0 | 0 | 0 | 0 | 6 | 0 | 0 | .000 |

## Mike Garman

GARMAN, MICHAEL DOUGLAS  BR TR 6'3" 195 lbs.
B. Sept. 16, 1949, Caldwell, Ida.

| 1969 | BOS A | 1 | 0 | 1.000 | 4.38 | 2 | 2 | 0 | 12.1 | 13 | 10 | 10 | 0 | 0 | 0 | 0 | 5 | 2 | 0 | .400 |
| 1971 | | 1 | 1 | .500 | 3.79 | 3 | 3 | 0 | 19 | 15 | 9 | 6 | 0 | 0 | 0 | 0 | 6 | 2 | 0 | .333 |
| 1972 | | 0 | 1 | .000 | 12.00 | 3 | 1 | 0 | 3 | 4 | 2 | 1 | 0 | 0 | 0 | 0 | 0 | 0 | 0 | – |
| 1973 | | 0 | 0 | – | 5.32 | 12 | 0 | 0 | 22 | 32 | 15 | 9 | 0 | 0 | 0 | 0 | 0 | 0 | 0 | – |
| 1974 | STL N | 7 | 2 | .778 | 2.63 | 64 | 0 | 0 | 82 | 66 | 27 | 45 | 0 | 7 | 2 | 6 | 10 | 1 | 0 | .100 |
| 1975 | | 3 | 8 | .273 | 2.39 | 66 | 0 | 0 | 79 | 73 | 48 | 48 | 0 | 3 | 8 | 10 | 2 | 0 | 0 | .000 |
| 1976 | CHI N | 2 | 4 | .333 | 4.97 | 47 | 2 | 0 | 76 | 79 | 35 | 37 | 0 | 2 | 2 | 1 | 7 | 0 | 0 | .000 |
| 1977 | LA N | 4 | 4 | .500 | 2.71 | 49 | 0 | 0 | 63 | 60 | 22 | 29 | 0 | 4 | 4 | 12 | 7 | 0 | 0 | .000 |
| 1978 | 2 teams | LA | N | (10G 0–1) | | MON | N | (47G 4–6) | | | | | | | | | | | | |
| " | total | 4 | 7 | .364 | 4.40 | 57 | 0 | 0 | 77.2 | 69 | 34 | 28 | 0 | 4 | 7 | 13 | 5 | 0 | 0 | .000 |
| | 9 yrs. | 22 | 27 | .449 | 3.63 | 303 | 8 | 0 | 434 | 411 | 202 | 213 | 0 | 20 | 23 | 42 | 42 | 5 | 0 | .119 |
| | 1 yr. | 2 | 4 | .333 | 4.97 | 47 | 2 | 0 | 76 | 79 | 35 | 37 | 0 | 2 | 2 | 1 | 7 | 0 | 0 | .000 |

LEAGUE CHAMPIONSHIP SERIES
| 1977 | LA N | 0 | 0 | – | 0.00 | 2 | 0 | 0 | 1.1 | 0 | 1 | 0 | 0 | 0 | 0 | 1 | 0 | 0 | 0 | – |

WORLD SERIES
| 1977 | LA N | 0 | 0 | – | 0.00 | 2 | 0 | 0 | 4 | 2 | 1 | 3 | 0 | 0 | 0 | 0 | 0 | 0 | 0 | – |

## Ned Garvin

GARVIN, VIRGIL LEE  TR 6'3½" 160 lbs.
B. Jan. 1, 1874, Navasota, Tex.  D. June 16, 1908, Fresno, Calif.

| 1896 | PHI N | 0 | 1 | .000 | 7.62 | 2 | 1 | 1 | 13 | 19 | 7 | 4 | 0 | | | | 6 | 0 | 0 | .000 |
| 1899 | CHI N | 9 | 13 | .409 | 2.85 | 24 | 23 | 22 | 199 | 202 | 42 | 69 | 4 | 0 | 0 | 0 | 71 | 11 | 0 | .155 |
| 1900 | | 10 | 18 | .357 | 2.41 | 30 | 28 | 25 | 246.1 | 225 | 63 | 107 | 1 | 0 | 1 | 0 | 91 | 14 | 0 | .154 |
| 1901 | MIL A | 7 | 20 | .259 | 3.46 | 37 | 27 | 22 | 257.1 | 258 | 90 | 122 | 1 | 0 | 0 | 2 | 93 | 10 | 0 | .108 |
| 1902 | 2 teams | CHI | A | (23G 10–10) | | BKN | N | (2G 1–1) | | | | | | | | | | | | |
| " | total | 11 | 11 | .500 | 2.09 | 25 | 21 | 18 | 193.1 | 184 | 47 | 62 | 3 | 1 | 0 | 0 | 66 | 10 | 0 | .152 |
| 1903 | BKN N | 15 | 18 | .455 | 3.08 | 38 | 34 | 30 | 298 | 277 | 84 | 154 | 2 | 0 | 1 | 2 | 106 | 8 | 0 | .075 |
| 1904 | 2 teams | BKN | N | (23G 5–15) | | NY | A | (2G 0–1) | | | | | | | | | | | | |
| " | total | 5 | 16 | .238 | 1.72 | 25 | 24 | 16 | 193.2 | 155 | 80 | 94 | 2 | 0 | 0 | 0 | 67 | 8 | 0 | .119 |
| | 7 yrs. | 57 | 97 | .370 | 2.72 | 181 | 158 | 134 | 1400.2 | 1320 | 413 | 612 | 13 | 1 | 2 | 4 | 500 | 61 | 0 | .122 |
| | 2 yrs. | 19 | 31 | .380 | 2.61 | 54 | 51 | 47 | 445.1 | 427 | 105 | 176 | 5 | 0 | 1 | 0 | 162 | 25 | 0 | .154 |

## Charlie Gassaway

GASSAWAY, CHARLES CASON (Sheriff)  BL TL 6'2½" 210 lbs.
B. Aug. 12, 1918, Gassaway, Tenn.

| 1944 | CHI N | 0 | 1 | .000 | 7.71 | 2 | 2 | 0 | 11.2 | 20 | 10 | 7 | 0 | 0 | 0 | 0 | 4 | 1 | 0 | .250 |
| 1945 | PHI A | 4 | 7 | .364 | 3.74 | 24 | 11 | 4 | 118 | 114 | 55 | 50 | 0 | 0 | 0 | 0 | 39 | 6 | 0 | .154 |
| 1946 | CLE A | 1 | 1 | .500 | 3.91 | 13 | 6 | 0 | 50.2 | 54 | 26 | 23 | 0 | 0 | 0 | 0 | 15 | 1 | 0 | .067 |
| | 3 yrs. | 5 | 9 | .357 | 4.04 | 39 | 19 | 4 | 180.1 | 188 | 91 | 80 | 0 | 0 | 0 | 0 | 58 | 8 | 0 | .138 |
| | 1 yr. | 0 | 1 | .000 | 7.71 | 2 | 2 | 0 | 11.2 | 20 | 10 | 7 | 0 | 0 | 0 | 0 | 4 | 1 | 0 | .250 |

## Chippy Gaw

GAW, GEORGE JOSEPH  BR TR 5'11" 180 lbs.
B. Mar. 13, 1892, West Newton, Mass.  D. May 26, 1968, Boston, Mass.

| 1920 | CHI N | 1 | 1 | .500 | 4.85 | 6 | 1 | 0 | 13 | 16 | 3 | 4 | 0 | 1 | 0 | 0 | 4 | 1 | 0 | .250 |

## Emil Geis

GEIS, EMIL AUGUST  BR
Brother of Bill Geis.
B. Mar. 20, 1867, Chicago, Ill.  D. Oct. 4, 1911, Chicago, Ill.

| 1887 | CHI N | 0 | 1 | .000 | 8.00 | 1 | 1 | 1 | 9 | 17 | 3 | 4 | 0 | 0 | 0 | 0 | * | | | |

## Dave Geisel

GEISEL, JOHN DAVID  BL TL 6'3" 210 lbs.
B. Jan. 18, 1955, Windber, Pa.

| 1978 | CHI N | 1 | 0 | 1.000 | 4.30 | 18 | 0 | 0 | 23 | 27 | 11 | 15 | 0 | 0 | 0 | 0 | 3 | 0 | 0 | .000 |
| 1979 | | 0 | 0 | – | 0.60 | 7 | 0 | 0 | 15 | 10 | 4 | 5 | 0 | 0 | 0 | 0 | 1 | 0 | 0 | .000 |
| 1981 | | 2 | 0 | 1.000 | 0.56 | 11 | 0 | 0 | 16 | 11 | 10 | 7 | 0 | 2 | 0 | 0 | 3 | 0 | 0 | .000 |
| 1982 | TOR A | 1 | 1 | .500 | 3.98 | 16 | 2 | 0 | 31.2 | 32 | 17 | 22 | 0 | 1 | 0 | 0 | 0 | 0 | 0 | – |
| 1983 | | 0 | 3 | .000 | 4.64 | 47 | 0 | 0 | 52.1 | 47 | 31 | 50 | 0 | 0 | 3 | 5 | 0 | 0 | 0 | – |
| 1984 | SEA A | 1 | 1 | .500 | 4.15 | 20 | 3 | 0 | 43.1 | 47 | 9 | 28 | 0 | 1 | 0 | 3 | 0 | 0 | 0 | – |
| 1985 | | 0 | 0 | – | 6.33 | 12 | 0 | 0 | 27 | 35 | 15 | 17 | 0 | 0 | 0 | 0 | 0 | 0 | 0 | – |
| | 7 yrs. | 5 | 5 | .500 | 4.02 | 131 | 8 | 0 | 208.1 | 209 | 97 | 144 | 0 | 4 | 3 | 8 | 7 | 0 | 0 | .000 |
| | 3 yrs. | 3 | 0 | 1.000 | 2.17 | 36 | 0 | 0 | 54 | 48 | 25 | 27 | 0 | 2 | 0 | 0 | 7 | 0 | 0 | .000 |

## Jug Gerard

GERARD, DAVID FREDERICK  BR TR 6'2" 205 lbs.
B. Aug. 6, 1936, New York, N. Y.

| 1962 | CHI N | 2 | 3 | .400 | 4.91 | 39 | 0 | 0 | 58.2 | 67 | 28 | 30 | 0 | 2 | 3 | 3 | 8 | 3 | 0 | .375 |

| | W | L | PCT | ERA | G | GS | CG | IP | H | BB | SO | ShO | Relief Pitching W | L | SV | BATTING AB | H | HR | BA |
|---|---|---|---|---|---|---|---|---|---|---|---|---|---|---|---|---|---|---|---|

## George Gerberman

**GERBERMAN, GEORGE ALOIS**  BR TR 6'  180 lbs.
B. Mar. 8, 1942, El Campo, Tex.

| | W | L | PCT | ERA | G | GS | CG | IP | H | BB | SO | ShO | W | L | SV | AB | H | HR | BA |
|---|---|---|---|---|---|---|---|---|---|---|---|---|---|---|---|---|---|---|---|
| 1962 CHI N | 0 | 0 | – | 1.69 | 1 | 1 | 0 | 5.1 | 3 | 5 | 1 | 0 | 0 | 0 | 0 | 1 | 0 | 0 | .000 |

## Bob Gibson

**GIBSON, ROBERT MURRAY**  BR TR 6'3"  185 lbs.
B. Aug. 20, 1869, Duncansville, Pa.    D. Dec. 19, 1949, Pittsburgh, Pa.

| | W | L | PCT | ERA | G | GS | CG | IP | H | BB | SO | ShO | W | L | SV | AB | H | HR | BA |
|---|---|---|---|---|---|---|---|---|---|---|---|---|---|---|---|---|---|---|---|
| 1890 2 teams | | | CHI N (1G 1–0) | | | PIT N (3G 0–3) | | | | | | | | | | | | | |
| " total | 1 | 3 | .250 | 9.86 | 4 | 4 | 3 | 21 | 30 | 25 | 4 | 0 | 0 | 0 | 0 | 17 | 3 | 0 | .176 |

## Dave Giusti

**GIUSTI, DAVID JOHN**  BR TR 5'10"  175 lbs.
B. Nov. 27, 1939, Seneca Falls, N. Y.

| | W | L | PCT | ERA | G | GS | CG | IP | H | BB | SO | ShO | W | L | SV | AB | H | HR | BA |
|---|---|---|---|---|---|---|---|---|---|---|---|---|---|---|---|---|---|---|---|
| 1962 HOU N | 2 | 3 | .400 | 5.62 | 22 | 5 | 0 | 73.2 | 82 | 30 | 43 | 0 | 2 | 0 | 0 | 24 | 7 | 0 | .292 |
| 1964 | 0 | 0 | – | 3.16 | 8 | 0 | 0 | 25.2 | 24 | 8 | 16 | 0 | 0 | 0 | 0 | 7 | 2 | 0 | .286 |
| 1965 | 8 | 7 | .533 | 4.32 | 38 | 13 | 4 | 131.1 | 132 | 46 | 92 | 1 | 4 | 3 | 3 | 35 | 6 | 1 | .171 |
| 1966 | 15 | 14 | .517 | 4.20 | 34 | 33 | 9 | 210 | 215 | 54 | 131 | 4 | 0 | 0 | 0 | 74 | 17 | 0 | .230 |
| 1967 | 11 | 15 | .423 | 4.18 | 37 | 33 | 8 | 221.2 | 231 | 58 | 157 | 1 | 0 | 1 | 1 | 84 | 13 | 3 | .155 |
| 1968 | 11 | 14 | .440 | 3.19 | 37 | 34 | 12 | 251 | 226 | 67 | 186 | 2 | 0 | 0 | 1 | 82 | 15 | 0 | .183 |
| 1969 STL N | 3 | 7 | .300 | 3.60 | 22 | 12 | 2 | 100 | 96 | 37 | 62 | 1 | 0 | 0 | 0 | 25 | 5 | 0 | .200 |
| 1970 PIT N | 9 | 3 | .750 | 3.06 | 66 | 1 | 0 | 103 | 98 | 39 | 85 | 0 | 9 | 3 | 26 | 16 | 3 | 0 | .188 |
| 1971 | 5 | 6 | .455 | 2.93 | 58 | 0 | 0 | 86 | 79 | 31 | 55 | 0 | 5 | 6 | 30 | 17 | 1 | 0 | .059 |
| 1972 | 7 | 4 | .636 | 1.93 | 54 | 0 | 0 | 74.2 | 59 | 20 | 54 | 0 | 7 | 4 | 22 | 10 | 0 | 0 | .000 |
| 1973 | 9 | 2 | .818 | 2.37 | 67 | 0 | 0 | 98.2 | 89 | 37 | 64 | 0 | 9 | 2 | 20 | 13 | 4 | 0 | .308 |
| 1974 | 7 | 5 | .583 | 3.31 | 64 | 2 | 0 | 106 | 101 | 40 | 53 | 0 | 6 | 5 | 12 | 9 | 1 | 0 | .111 |
| 1975 | 5 | 4 | .556 | 2.93 | 61 | 0 | 0 | 92 | 79 | 42 | 38 | 0 | 5 | 4 | 17 | 10 | 3 | 0 | .300 |
| 1976 | 5 | 4 | .556 | 4.32 | 40 | 0 | 0 | 58.1 | 59 | 27 | 24 | 0 | 5 | 4 | 6 | 4 | 0 | 0 | .000 |
| 1977 2 teams | | | CHI N (20G 0–2) | | | OAK A (40G 3–3) | | | | | | | | | | | | | |
| " total | 3 | 5 | .375 | 3.92 | 60 | 0 | 0 | 85 | 84 | 34 | 43 | 0 | 3 | 5 | 7 | 2 | 0 | 0 | .000 |
| 15 yrs. | 100 | 93 | .518 | 3.60 | 668 | 133 | 35 | 1717 | 1654 | 570 | 1103 | 9 | 55 | 37 | 145 | 412 | 77 | 4 | .187 |
| 1 yr. | 0 | 2 | .000 | 6.12 | 20 | 0 | 0 | 25 | 30 | 14 | 15 | 0 | 0 | 2 | 1 | 2 | 0 | 0 | .000 |

LEAGUE CHAMPIONSHIP SERIES

| | W | L | PCT | ERA | G | GS | CG | IP | H | BB | SO | ShO | W | L | SV | AB | H | HR | BA |
|---|---|---|---|---|---|---|---|---|---|---|---|---|---|---|---|---|---|---|---|
| 1970 PIT N | 0 | 0 | – | 3.86 | 2 | 0 | 0 | 2.1 | 3 | 1 | 1 | 0 | 0 | 0 | 0 | 0 | 0 | 0 | – |
| 1971 | 0 | 0 | – | 0.00 | 4 | 0 | 0 | 5.1 | 1 | 2 | 3 | 0 | 0 | 0 | 3 | 1 | 0 | 0 | .000 |
| 1972 | 0 | 1 | .000 | 6.75 | 3 | 0 | 0 | 2.2 | 5 | 0 | 3 | 0 | 0 | 1 | 1 | 1 | 0 | 0 | .000 |
| 1974 | 0 | 1 | .000 | 21.60 | 3 | 0 | 0 | 3.1 | 13 | 5 | 1 | 0 | 0 | 1 | 0 | 0 | 0 | 0 | – |
| 1975 | 0 | 0 | – | 0.00 | 1 | 0 | 0 | 1.1 | 0 | 1 | 0 | 0 | 0 | 0 | 0 | 0 | 0 | 0 | – |
| 5 yrs. | 0 | 2 | .000 | 6.60 | 13 | 0 | 0 | 15 | 22 | 8 | 9 | 0 | 0 | 2 | 4 | 2 | 0 | 0 | .000 |

WORLD SERIES

| | W | L | PCT | ERA | G | GS | CG | IP | H | BB | SO | ShO | W | L | SV | AB | H | HR | BA |
|---|---|---|---|---|---|---|---|---|---|---|---|---|---|---|---|---|---|---|---|
| 1971 PIT N | 0 | 0 | – | 0.00 | 3 | 0 | 0 | 5.1 | 3 | 2 | 4 | 0 | 0 | 0 | 0 | | | | |

## Fred Glade

**GLADE, FREDERICK MONROE**  BR TR 6'1"  200 lbs.
B. Jan. 25, 1876, Dubuque, Iowa    D. Nov. 21, 1934, Grand Island, Neb.

| | W | L | PCT | ERA | G | GS | CG | IP | H | BB | SO | ShO | W | L | SV | AB | H | HR | BA |
|---|---|---|---|---|---|---|---|---|---|---|---|---|---|---|---|---|---|---|---|
| 1902 CHI N | 0 | 1 | .000 | 9.00 | 1 | 1 | 1 | 8 | 13 | 3 | 3 | 0 | 0 | 0 | 0 | 3 | 1 | 0 | .333 |
| 1904 STL A | 18 | 15 | .545 | 2.27 | 35 | 34 | 30 | 289 | 248 | 58 | 156 | 6 | 0 | 0 | 1 | 102 | 19 | 0 | .186 |
| 1905 | 6 | 25 | .194 | 2.81 | 32 | 32 | 28 | 275 | 257 | 58 | 127 | 2 | 0 | 0 | 0 | 98 | 9 | 0 | .092 |
| 1906 | 15 | 14 | .517 | 2.36 | 35 | 32 | 28 | 266.2 | 215 | 59 | 96 | 4 | 0 | 0 | 1 | 95 | 13 | 0 | .137 |
| 1907 | 13 | 9 | .591 | 2.67 | 24 | 22 | 18 | 202 | 187 | 45 | 71 | 2 | 0 | 1 | 0 | 73 | 15 | 0 | .205 |
| 1908 NY A | 0 | 4 | .000 | 4.22 | 5 | 5 | 2 | 32 | 30 | 14 | 11 | 0 | 0 | 0 | 0 | 10 | 0 | 0 | .000 |
| 6 yrs. | 52 | 68 | .433 | 2.62 | 132 | 126 | 107 | 1072.2 | 950 | 237 | 464 | 14 | 0 | 1 | 2 | 381 | 57 | 0 | .150 |
| 1 yr. | 0 | 1 | .000 | 9.00 | 1 | 1 | 1 | 8 | 13 | 3 | 3 | 0 | 0 | 0 | 0 | 3 | 1 | 0 | .333 |

## John Goetz

**GOETZ, JOHN HARDY**  BR TR 6'  185 lbs.
B. Oct. 24, 1937, Goetzville, Mich.

| | W | L | PCT | ERA | G | GS | CG | IP | H | BB | SO | ShO | W | L | SV | AB | H | HR | BA |
|---|---|---|---|---|---|---|---|---|---|---|---|---|---|---|---|---|---|---|---|
| 1960 CHI N | 0 | 0 | – | 12.79 | 4 | 0 | 0 | 6.1 | 10 | 4 | 6 | 0 | 0 | 0 | 0 | 1 | 0 | 0 | .000 |

## Fred Goldsmith

**GOLDSMITH, FRED ERNEST**  BR TR 6'1"  195 lbs.
B. May 15, 1852, New Haven, Conn.    D. Mar. 28, 1939, Berkley, Mich.

| | W | L | PCT | ERA | G | GS | CG | IP | H | BB | SO | ShO | W | L | SV | AB | H | HR | BA |
|---|---|---|---|---|---|---|---|---|---|---|---|---|---|---|---|---|---|---|---|
| 1879 TRO N | 2 | 4 | .333 | 1.57 | 8 | 7 | 7 | 63 | 61 | 1 | 31 | 0 | 0 | 0 | 0 | 38 | 9 | 0 | .237 |
| 1880 CHI N | 21 | 3 | .875 | 1.75 | 26 | 24 | 22 | 210.1 | 189 | 18 | 90 | 4 | 0 | 0 | 1 | 142 | 37 | 0 | .261 |
| 1881 | 24 | 13 | .649 | 2.59 | 39 | 39 | 37 | 330 | 328 | 44 | 76 | 5 | 0 | 0 | 0 | 158 | 38 | 0 | .241 |
| 1882 | 28 | 16 | .636 | 2.42 | 44 | 44 | 44 | 405 | 377 | 38 | 109 | 4 | 0 | 0 | 0 | 183 | 42 | 0 | .230 |
| 1883 | 25 | 19 | .568 | 3.15 | 46 | 45 | 40 | 383.1 | 456 | 39 | 82 | 2 | 0 | 0 | 0 | 235 | 52 | 1 | .221 |
| 1884 2 teams | | | CHI N (21G 9–11) | | | BAL AA (4G 3–1) | | | | | | | | | | | | | |
| " total | 12 | 12 | .500 | 4.05 | 25 | 25 | 23 | 218 | 274 | 31 | 45 | 1 | 0 | 0 | 0 | 95 | 13 | 2 | .137 |
| 6 yrs. | 112 | 67 | .626 | 2.73 | 188 | 184 | 173 | 1609.2 | 1685 | 171 | 433 | 16 | 0 | 0 | 1 | * | | | |
| 5 yrs. | 107 | 62 | .633 | 2.78 | 176 | 173 | 163 | 1516.2 | 1595 | 168 | 391 | 16 | 0 | 0 | 1 | 799 | 180 | 3 | .225 |
| | | | | 7th | | | | | | | | | | | | | | | |
| | | | | | | | | | 9th | | | | | | | | | | |

## Wilbur Good

**GOOD, WILBUR DAVID (Lefty)**  BL TL 5'6"  165 lbs.
B. Sept. 28, 1885, Punxsutawney, Pa.    D. Dec. 30, 1963, Brooksville, Fla.

| | W | L | PCT | ERA | G | GS | CG | IP | H | BB | SO | ShO | W | L | SV | AB | H | HR | BA |
|---|---|---|---|---|---|---|---|---|---|---|---|---|---|---|---|---|---|---|---|
| 1905 NY A | 0 | 2 | .000 | 4.74 | 5 | 2 | 0 | 19 | 18 | 14 | 13 | 0 | 0 | 0 | 0 | * | | | |

## Hank Gornicki

**GORNICKI, FRANK TED**  BR TR 6'  145 lbs.
B. Jan. 14, 1911, Niagara Falls, N. Y.

| | W | L | PCT | ERA | G | GS | CG | IP | H | BB | SO | ShO | W | L | SV | AB | H | HR | BA |
|---|---|---|---|---|---|---|---|---|---|---|---|---|---|---|---|---|---|---|---|
| 1941 2 teams | | | STL N (4G 1–0) | | | CHI N (1G 0–0) | | | | | | | | | | | | | |
| " total | 1 | 0 | 1.000 | 3.38 | 5 | 1 | 1 | 13.1 | 9 | 9 | 8 | 1 | 0 | 0 | 0 | 4 | 1 | 0 | .250 |
| 1942 PIT N | 5 | 6 | .455 | 2.57 | 25 | 14 | 7 | 112 | 89 | 40 | 48 | 2 | 0 | 0 | 2 | 35 | 4 | 1 | .114 |
| 1943 | 9 | 13 | .409 | 3.98 | 42 | 18 | 4 | 147 | 165 | 47 | 63 | 1 | 3 | 3 | 4 | 40 | 7 | 0 | .175 |

| | W | L | PCT | ERA | G | GS | CG | IP | H | BB | SO | ShO | Relief Pitching W | L | SV | BATTING AB | H | HR | BA |
|---|---|---|---|---|---|---|---|---|---|---|---|---|---|---|---|---|---|---|---|

## Hank Gornicki continued

| | W | L | PCT | ERA | G | GS | CG | IP | H | BB | SO | ShO | W | L | SV | AB | H | HR | BA |
|---|---|---|---|---|---|---|---|---|---|---|---|---|---|---|---|---|---|---|---|
| 1946 | 0 | 0 | – | 3.55 | 7 | 0 | 0 | 12.2 | 12 | 11 | 4 | 0 | 0 | 0 | 0 | 3 | 0 | 0 | .000 |
| 4 yrs. | 15 | 19 | .441 | 3.38 | 79 | 33 | 12 | 285 | 275 | 107 | 123 | 4 | 3 | 3 | 6 | 82 | 12 | 1 | .146 |
| 1 yr. | 0 | 0 | – | 4.50 | 1 | 0 | 0 | 2 | 3 | 0 | 2 | 0 | 0 | 0 | 0 | 0 | 0 | 0 | |

## Peaches Graham

**GRAHAM, GEORGE FREDERICK**     BR TR 5'9"    180 lbs.
Father of Jack Graham.
B. Mar. 23, 1880, Aledo, Ill.     D. July 25, 1939, Long Beach, Calif.

| | W | L | PCT | ERA | G | GS | CG | IP | H | BB | SO | ShO | W | L | SV | AB | H | HR | BA |
|---|---|---|---|---|---|---|---|---|---|---|---|---|---|---|---|---|---|---|---|
| 1903 CHI N | 0 | 1 | .000 | 5.40 | 1 | 1 | 0 | 5 | 9 | 3 | 4 | 0 | 0 | 0 | 0 | * | | | |

## Henry Grampp

**GRAMPP, HENRY EKHARDT**     BR TR 6'1"    185 lbs.
B. Sept. 28, 1903, New York, N. Y.

| | W | L | PCT | ERA | G | GS | CG | IP | H | BB | SO | ShO | W | L | SV | AB | H | HR | BA |
|---|---|---|---|---|---|---|---|---|---|---|---|---|---|---|---|---|---|---|---|
| 1927 CHI N | 0 | 0 | | 9.00 | 2 | 0 | 0 | 3 | 4 | 1 | 3 | 0 | 0 | 0 | 0 | 0 | 0 | 0 | – |
| 1929 | 0 | 1 | .000 | 27.00 | 1 | 1 | 0 | 2 | 4 | 3 | 0 | 0 | 0 | 0 | 0 | 0 | 0 | 0 | – |
| 2 yrs. | 0 | 1 | .000 | 16.20 | 3 | 1 | 0 | 5 | 8 | 4 | 3 | 0 | 0 | 0 | 0 | 0 | 0 | 0 | – |
| 2 yrs. | 0 | 1 | .000 | 16.20 | 3 | 1 | 0 | 5 | 8 | 4 | 3 | 0 | 0 | 0 | 0 | 0 | 0 | 0 | – |

## Lee Gregory

**GREGORY, GROVER LeROY**     BL TL 6'1"    180 lbs.
B. June 2, 1938, Bakersfield, Calif.

| | W | L | PCT | ERA | G | GS | CG | IP | H | BB | SO | ShO | W | L | SV | AB | H | HR | BA |
|---|---|---|---|---|---|---|---|---|---|---|---|---|---|---|---|---|---|---|---|
| 1964 CHI N | 0 | 0 | – | 3.50 | 11 | 0 | 0 | 18 | 23 | 5 | 8 | 0 | 0 | 0 | 0 | 13 | 1 | 0 | .077 |

## Hank Griffin

**GRIFFIN, JAMES LINTON (Pepper)**     BR TR 6'    170 lbs.
B. July 11, 1886, Whitehouse, Tex.     D. Feb. 11, 1950, Terrell, Tex.

| | W | L | PCT | ERA | G | GS | CG | IP | H | BB | SO | ShO | W | L | SV | AB | H | HR | BA |
|---|---|---|---|---|---|---|---|---|---|---|---|---|---|---|---|---|---|---|---|
| 1911 2 teams | | | | | CHI | N | (1G 0–0) | | | BOS | N | (15G 0–6) | | | | | | | |
| " total | 0 | 6 | .000 | 5.38 | 16 | 7 | 1 | 83.2 | 97 | 37 | 31 | 0 | 0 | 1 | 0 | 30 | 7 | 0 | .233 |
| 1912 BOS N | 0 | 0 | | 27.00 | 3 | 0 | 0 | 1.2 | 3 | 3 | 0 | 0 | 0 | 0 | 0 | 0 | 0 | 0 | – |
| 2 yrs. | 0 | 6 | .000 | 5.80 | 19 | 7 | 1 | 85.1 | 100 | 40 | 31 | 0 | 0 | 1 | 0 | 30 | 7 | 0 | .233 |
| 1 yr. | 0 | 0 | – | 18.00 | 1 | 1 | 0 | 1 | 1 | 3 | 1 | 0 | 0 | 0 | 0 | 0 | 0 | 0 | |

## Mike Griffin

**GRIFFIN, MICHAEL LEROY**     BR TR 6'4"    195 lbs.
B. June 26, 1957, Colusa, Calif.

| | W | L | PCT | ERA | G | GS | CG | IP | H | BB | SO | ShO | W | L | SV | AB | H | HR | BA |
|---|---|---|---|---|---|---|---|---|---|---|---|---|---|---|---|---|---|---|---|
| 1979 NY A | 0 | 0 | – | 4.50 | 3 | 0 | 0 | 4 | 5 | 2 | 5 | 0 | 0 | 0 | 1 | 0 | 0 | 0 | – |
| 1980 | 2 | 4 | .333 | 4.83 | 13 | 9 | 0 | 54 | 64 | 23 | 25 | 0 | 0 | 1 | 0 | 0 | 0 | 0 | – |
| 1981 2 teams | | | | | NY | A | (2G 0–0) | | | CHI | N | (16G 2–5) | | | | | | | |
| " total | 2 | 5 | .286 | 4.34 | 18 | 9 | 0 | 56 | 69 | 9 | 24 | 0 | 0 | 1 | 0 | 13 | 2 | 0 | .154 |
| 1982 SD N | 0 | 1 | .000 | 3.48 | 7 | 0 | 0 | 10.1 | 9 | 3 | 4 | 0 | 0 | 1 | 0 | 1 | 0 | 0 | .000 |
| 4 yrs. | 4 | 10 | .286 | 4.49 | 41 | 18 | 0 | 124.1 | 147 | 37 | 58 | 0 | 0 | 2 | 2 | 14 | 2 | 0 | .143 |
| 1 yr. | 2 | 5 | .286 | 4.50 | 16 | 9 | 0 | 52 | 64 | 9 | 20 | 0 | 0 | 0 | 1 | 13 | 2 | 0 | .154 |

## Clark Griffith

**GRIFFITH, CLARK CALVIN (The Old Fox)**     BR TR 5'6½"    156 lbs.
B. Nov. 20, 1869, Clear Creek, Mo.     D. Oct. 27, 1955, Washington, D. C.
Manager 1901-20.
Hall of Fame 1946.

| | W | L | PCT | ERA | G | GS | CG | IP | H | BB | SO | ShO | W | L | SV | AB | H | HR | BA |
|---|---|---|---|---|---|---|---|---|---|---|---|---|---|---|---|---|---|---|---|
| 1891 2 teams | | | | | STL | AA | (27G 14–6) | | | BOS | AA | (7G 3–1) | | | | | | | |
| " total | 17 | 7 | .708 | 3.74 | 34 | 21 | 15 | 226.1 | 242 | 73 | 88 | 0 | 7 | 0 | 0 | 100 | 16 | 2 | .160 |
| 1893 CHI N | 1 | 1 | .500 | 5.03 | 4 | 2 | 2 | 19.2 | 24 | 5 | 9 | 0 | 0 | 1 | 0 | 11 | 2 | 0 | .182 |
| 1894 | 21 | 11 | .656 | 4.92 | 36 | 30 | 28 | 261.1 | 328 | 85 | 71 | 0 | 3 | 3 | 0 | 142 | 33 | 0 | .232 |
| 1895 | 25 | 13 | .658 | 3.93 | 42 | 41 | 39 | 353 | 434 | 91 | 79 | 0 | 1 | 0 | 0 | 144 | 46 | 1 | .319 |
| 1896 | 22 | 13 | .629 | 3.54 | 36 | 35 | 35 | 317.2 | 370 | 70 | 81 | 0 | 0 | 0 | 0 | 135 | 36 | 1 | .267 |
| 1897 | 21 | 19 | .525 | 3.72 | 41 | 38 | 38 | 343.2 | 410 | 86 | 102 | 1 | 1 | 0 | 1 | 162 | 38 | 0 | .235 |
| 1898 | 26 | 10 | .722 | 1.88 | 38 | 38 | 36 | 325.2 | 305 | 64 | 97 | 4 | 0 | 0 | 0 | 122 | 20 | 0 | .164 |
| 1899 | 22 | 13 | .629 | 2.79 | 38 | 38 | 35 | 319.2 | 329 | 65 | 73 | 0 | 0 | 0 | 0 | 120 | 31 | 0 | .258 |
| 1900 | 14 | 13 | .519 | 3.05 | 30 | 30 | 27 | 248 | 245 | 51 | 61 | 4 | 0 | 0 | 0 | 95 | 24 | 1 | .253 |
| 1901 CHI A | 24 | 7 | .774 | 2.67 | 35 | 30 | 26 | 266.2 | 275 | 50 | 67 | 5 | 3 | 0 | 1 | 89 | 27 | 2 | .303 |
| 1902 | 15 | 9 | .625 | 4.19 | 28 | 24 | 20 | 212.2 | 247 | 47 | 51 | 3 | 2 | 0 | 0 | 92 | 20 | 0 | .217 |
| 1903 NY A | 14 | 11 | .560 | 2.70 | 25 | 24 | 22 | 213 | 201 | 33 | 69 | 3 | 1 | 0 | 0 | 69 | 11 | 1 | .159 |
| 1904 | 7 | 5 | .583 | 2.87 | 16 | 11 | 8 | 100.1 | 91 | 16 | 36 | 1 | 1 | 0 | 0 | 42 | 6 | 0 | .143 |
| 1905 | 9 | 6 | .600 | 1.67 | 25 | 7 | 4 | 102.2 | 82 | 15 | 46 | 2 | 6 | 3 | 1 | 32 | 7 | 0 | .219 |
| 1906 | 2 | 2 | .500 | 3.02 | 17 | 2 | 1 | 59.2 | 58 | 15 | 16 | 0 | 1 | 2 | 2 | 18 | 2 | 0 | .111 |
| 1907 | 0 | 0 | – | 8.64 | 4 | 0 | 0 | 8.1 | 15 | 6 | 5 | 0 | 0 | 0 | 0 | 2 | 0 | 0 | .000 |
| 1909 CIN N | 0 | 1 | .000 | 6.00 | 1 | 1 | 1 | 6 | 11 | 2 | 3 | 0 | 0 | 0 | 0 | 2 | 0 | 0 | .000 |
| 1910 | 0 | 0 | – | 0.00 | 1 | 0 | 0 | 0 | 0 | 0 | 0 | 0 | 0 | 0 | 0 | 0 | 0 | 0 | – |
| 1912 WAS A | 0 | 0 | – | ∞ | 1 | 0 | 0 | 0 | 1 | 0 | 0 | 0 | 0 | 0 | 0 | 1 | 0 | 0 | .000 |
| 1913 | 0 | 0 | – | 0.00 | 1 | 0 | 0 | 1 | 0 | 0 | 0 | 0 | 0 | 0 | 0 | 1 | 1 | 0 | 1.000 |
| 1914 | 0 | 0 | – | 0.00 | 1 | 0 | 0 | 1 | 1 | 0 | 0 | 0 | 0 | 0 | 0 | 1 | 1 | 0 | 1.000 |
| 21 yrs. | 240 | 141 | .630 | 3.31 | 453 | 372 | 337 | 3386.1 | 3670 | 774 | 955 | 23 | 26 | 9 | 6 | * | | | |
| 8 yrs. | 152 | 93 | .620 | 3.40 | 265 | 252 | 240 | 2188.2 | 2445 | 517 | 573 | 9 | 5 | 4 | 1 | 931 | 230 | 3 | .247 |
| | **6th** | | **10th** | | | | **3rd** | **10th** | | | | | | | | | | | |

## Frank Griffith

**GRIFFITH, FRANK WESLEY**     BL TL    150 lbs.
B. Nov. 18, 1872, Gilman, Ill.     D. Dec. 13, 1908

| | W | L | PCT | ERA | G | GS | CG | IP | H | BB | SO | ShO | W | L | SV | AB | H | HR | BA |
|---|---|---|---|---|---|---|---|---|---|---|---|---|---|---|---|---|---|---|---|
| 1892 CHI N | 0 | 1 | .000 | 11.25 | 1 | 1 | 0 | 4 | 3 | 6 | 3 | 0 | 0 | 0 | 0 | 1 | 0 | 0 | .000 |
| 1894 CLE N | 1 | 2 | .333 | 9.99 | 7 | 6 | 3 | 42.1 | 64 | 37 | 15 | 0 | 0 | 0 | 0 | 24 | 8 | 0 | .333 |
| 2 yrs. | 1 | 3 | .250 | 10.10 | 8 | 7 | 3 | 46.1 | 67 | 43 | 18 | 0 | 0 | 0 | 0 | 25 | 8 | 0 | .320 |
| 1 yr. | 0 | 1 | .000 | 11.25 | 1 | 1 | 0 | 4 | 3 | 6 | 3 | 0 | 0 | 0 | 0 | 1 | 0 | 0 | .000 |

| | W | L | PCT | ERA | G | GS | CG | IP | H | BB | SO | ShO | Relief Pitching W | L | SV | BATTING AB | H | HR | BA |
|---|---|---|---|---|---|---|---|---|---|---|---|---|---|---|---|---|---|---|---|

# Burleigh Grimes

**GRIMES, BURLEIGH ARLAND (Ol' Stubblebeard)**          BR TR  5'10"   175 lbs.
B. Aug. 18, 1893, Clear Lake, Wis.     D. Dec. 6, 1985, Clear Lake, Wis.
Manager 1937-38.
Hall of Fame 1964.

| | W | L | PCT | ERA | G | GS | CG | IP | H | BB | SO | ShO | W | L | SV | AB | H | HR | BA |
|---|---|---|---|---|---|---|---|---|---|---|---|---|---|---|---|---|---|---|---|
| 1916 PIT N | 2 | 3 | .400 | 2.36 | 6 | 5 | 4 | 45.2 | 40 | 10 | 20 | 0 | 1 | 0 | 0 | 17 | 3 | 0 | .176 |
| 1917 | 3 | 16 | .158 | 3.53 | 37 | 17 | 8 | 194 | 186 | 70 | 72 | 1 | 1 | 4 | 0 | 69 | 16 | 0 | .232 |
| 1918 BKN N | 19 | 9 | .679 | 2.14 | 41 | 28 | 19 | 269.2 | 210 | 76 | 113 | 7 | 1 | 1 | 1 | 90 | 18 | 0 | .200 |
| 1919 | 10 | 11 | .476 | 3.47 | 25 | 21 | 13 | 181.1 | 179 | 60 | 82 | 1 | 1 | 1 | 0 | 69 | 17 | 0 | .246 |
| 1920 | 23 | 11 | .676 | 2.22 | 40 | 33 | 25 | 303.2 | 271 | 67 | 131 | 5 | 2 | 1 | 2 | 111 | 34 | 0 | .306 |
| 1921 | 22 | 13 | .629 | 2.83 | 37 | 35 | 30 | 302.1 | 313 | 76 | 136 | 2 | 0 | 1 | 0 | 114 | 27 | 1 | .237 |
| 1922 | 17 | 14 | .548 | 4.76 | 36 | 34 | 18 | 259 | 324 | 84 | 99 | 1 | 1 | 0 | 1 | 93 | 22 | 0 | .237 |
| 1923 | 21 | 18 | .538 | 3.58 | 39 | 38 | 33 | 327 | 356 | 100 | 119 | 2 | 0 | 1 | 0 | 126 | 30 | 0 | .238 |
| 1924 | 22 | 13 | .629 | 3.82 | 38 | 36 | 30 | 310.2 | 351 | 91 | 135 | 1 | 0 | 0 | 1 | 124 | 37 | 0 | .298 |
| 1925 | 12 | 19 | .387 | 5.04 | 33 | 31 | 19 | 246.2 | 305 | 102 | 73 | 0 | 1 | 0 | 0 | 96 | 24 | 1 | .250 |
| 1926 | 12 | 13 | .480 | 3.71 | 30 | 29 | 18 | 225.1 | 238 | 88 | 64 | 1 | 0 | 0 | 0 | 81 | 18 | 0 | .222 |
| 1927 NY N | 19 | 8 | .704 | 3.54 | 39 | 34 | 15 | 259.2 | 274 | 87 | 102 | 2 | 1 | 0 | 2 | 96 | 18 | 0 | .188 |
| 1928 PIT N | 25 | 14 | .641 | 2.99 | 48 | 37 | 28 | 330.2 | 311 | 77 | 97 | 4 | 4 | 1 | 3 | 131 | 42 | 0 | .321 |
| 1929 | 17 | 7 | .708 | 3.13 | 33 | 29 | 18 | 232.2 | 245 | 70 | 62 | 2 | 0 | 1 | 2 | 91 | 26 | 0 | .286 |
| 1930 2 teams | | | BOS | N | (11G 3-5) | | STL | N | (22G 13-6) | | | | | | | | | | |
| " total | 16 | 11 | .593 | 4.07 | 33 | 28 | 11 | 201.1 | 246 | 65 | 73 | 1 | 2 | 2 | 0 | 73 | 18 | 0 | .247 |
| 1931 STL N | 17 | 9 | .654 | 3.65 | 29 | 28 | 17 | 212.1 | 240 | 59 | 67 | 3 | 1 | 0 | 0 | 76 | 14 | 0 | .184 |
| 1932 CHI N | 6 | 11 | .353 | 4.78 | 30 | 18 | 5 | 141.1 | 174 | 50 | 36 | 1 | 0 | 2 | 1 | 44 | 11 | 0 | .250 |
| 1933 2 teams | | | CHI | N | (17G 3-6) | | STL | N | (4G 0-1) | | | | | | | | | | |
| " total | 3 | 7 | .300 | 3.78 | 21 | 10 | 3 | 83.1 | 86 | 37 | 16 | 1 | 1 | 1 | 4 | 25 | 4 | 0 | .160 |
| 1934 3 teams | | | STL | N | (4G 2-1) | | PIT | N | (8G 1-2) | | NY | A | (10G 1-2) | | | | | | |
| " total | 4 | 5 | .444 | 6.11 | 22 | 4 | 0 | 53 | 63 | 26 | 15 | 0 | 4 | 3 | 1 | 9 | 1 | 0 | .111 |
| 19 yrs. | 270 | 212 | .560 | 3.53 | 617 | 495 | 314 | 4179.2 | 4412 | 1295 | 1512 | 35 | 21 | 19 | 18 | 1535 | 380 | 2 | .248 |
| 2 yrs. | 9 | 17 | .346 | 4.35 | 47 | 25 | 8 | 211 | 245 | 79 | 48 | 2 | 1 | 3 | 4 | 64 | 14 | 0 | .219 |

| WORLD SERIES | | | | | | | | | | | | | | | | | | | |
|---|---|---|---|---|---|---|---|---|---|---|---|---|---|---|---|---|---|---|---|
| 1920 BKN N | 1 | 2 | .333 | 4.19 | 3 | 3 | 1 | 19.1 | 23 | 9 | 4 | 1 | 0 | 0 | 0 | 6 | 2 | 0 | .333 |
| 1930 STL N | 0 | 2 | .000 | 3.71 | 2 | 2 | 2 | 17 | 10 | 6 | 13 | 0 | 0 | 0 | 0 | 5 | 2 | 0 | .400 |
| 1931 | 2 | 0 | 1.000 | 2.04 | 2 | 2 | 1 | 17.2 | 9 | 9 | 11 | 0 | 0 | 0 | 0 | 7 | 2 | 0 | .286 |
| 1932 CHI N | 0 | 0 | — | 23.63 | 2 | 0 | 0 | 2.2 | 7 | 2 | 0 | 0 | 0 | 0 | 0 | 1 | 0 | 0 | .000 |
| 4 yrs. | 3 | 4 | .429 | 4.29 | 9 | 7 | 4 | 56.2 | 49 | 26 | 28 | 1 | 0 | 0 | 0 | 19 | 6 | 0 | .316 |
| | | | 7th | | | | | | | | 8th | | | | | | | | |

# Ed Groth

**GROTH, EDWARD JOHN**
B. Dec. 24, 1885, Cedarburg, Wis.     D. May 23, 1950, Milwaukee, Wis.

| | W | L | PCT | ERA | G | GS | CG | IP | H | BB | SO | ShO | W | L | SV | AB | H | HR | BA |
|---|---|---|---|---|---|---|---|---|---|---|---|---|---|---|---|---|---|---|---|
| 1904 CHI N | 0 | 2 | .000 | 5.63 | 3 | 2 | 1 | 16 | 22 | 6 | 9 | 0 | 0 | 0 | 1 | 6 | 0 | 0 | .000 |

# Marv Gudat

**GUDAT, MARVIN JOHN**          BL TL  5'11"   176 lbs.
B. Aug. 27, 1905, Goliad, Tex.     D. Mar. 1, 1954, Los Angeles, Calif.

| | W | L | PCT | ERA | G | GS | CG | IP | H | BB | SO | ShO | W | L | SV | AB | H | HR | BA |
|---|---|---|---|---|---|---|---|---|---|---|---|---|---|---|---|---|---|---|---|
| 1929 CIN N | 1 | 1 | .500 | 3.38 | 7 | 2 | 2 | 26.2 | 29 | 4 | 0 | 0 | 0 | 0 | 0 | 10 | 2 | 0 | .200 |
| 1932 CHI N | 0 | 0 | — | 0.00 | 1 | 0 | 0 | 1 | 1 | 0 | 2 | 0 | 0 | 0 | 0 | 94 | 24 | 1 | .255 |
| 2 yrs. | 1 | 1 | .500 | 3.25 | 8 | 2 | 2 | 27.2 | 30 | 4 | 2 | 0 | 0 | 0 | 0 | * | | | |
| 1 yr. | 0 | 0 | — | 0.00 | 1 | 0 | 0 | 1 | 1 | 0 | 2 | 0 | 0 | 0 | 0 | 94 | 24 | 1 | .255 |

# Ad Gumbert

**GUMBERT, ADDISON COURTNEY**          BR TR  5'10"   200 lbs.
Brother of Billy Gumbert.
B. Oct. 10, 1868, Pittsburgh, Pa.     D. Apr. 23, 1925, Pittsburgh, Pa.

| | W | L | PCT | ERA | G | GS | CG | IP | H | BB | SO | ShO | W | L | SV | AB | H | HR | BA |
|---|---|---|---|---|---|---|---|---|---|---|---|---|---|---|---|---|---|---|---|
| 1888 CHI N | 3 | 3 | .500 | 3.14 | 6 | 6 | 5 | 42.2 | 44 | 10 | 16 | 0 | 0 | 0 | 0 | 24 | 8 | 0 | .333 |
| 1889 | 16 | 13 | .552 | 3.62 | 31 | 28 | 25 | 246.1 | 258 | 76 | 91 | 2 | 2 | 0 | 0 | 153 | 44 | 7 | .288 |
| 1890 BOS P | 22 | 11 | .667 | 3.96 | 39 | 33 | 27 | 277.1 | 338 | 86 | 81 | 1 | 3 | 1 | 0 | 145 | 35 | 3 | .241 |
| 1891 CHI N | 17 | 11 | .607 | 3.58 | 32 | 31 | 24 | 256.1 | 282 | 90 | 73 | 1 | 0 | 0 | 0 | 105 | 32 | 0 | .305 |
| 1892 | 22 | 19 | .537 | 3.41 | 46 | 45 | 39 | 382.2 | 399 | 107 | 118 | 0 | 0 | 0 | 0 | 178 | 42 | 1 | .236 |
| 1893 PIT N | 11 | 7 | .611 | 5.15 | 22 | 20 | 16 | 162.2 | 207 | 78 | 40 | 2 | 1 | 0 | 0 | 95 | 21 | 0 | .221 |
| 1894 | 15 | 14 | .517 | 6.02 | 37 | 31 | 26 | 269 | 372 | 84 | 65 | 0 | 1 | 0 | 0 | 113 | 33 | 1 | .292 |
| 1895 BKN N | 11 | 14 | .407 | 5.08 | 33 | 26 | 20 | 234 | 288 | 69 | 45 | 0 | 1 | 1 | 1 | 97 | 35 | 2 | .361 |
| 1896 2 teams | | | BKN | N | (5G 0-4) | | PHI | N | (11G 5-3) | | | | | | | | | | |
| " total | 5 | 7 | .417 | 4.32 | 16 | 14 | 9 | 108.1 | 133 | 34 | 17 | 1 | 0 | 0 | 0 | 45 | 11 | 1 | .244 |
| 9 yrs. | 122 | 101 | .547 | 4.27 | 262 | 234 | 191 | 1985.1 | 2321 | 634 | 546 | 7 | 8 | 2 | 1 | * | | | |
| 4 yrs. | 58 | 46 | .558 | 3.50 | 115 | 110 | 93 | 934 | 983 | 283 | 298 | 3 | 2 | 0 | 0 | 460 | 126 | 8 | .274 |

# Dave Gumpert

**GUMPERT, DAVID LAWRENCE**          BR TR  6'3"   190 lbs.
B. May 5, 1958, South Haven, Mich.

| | W | L | PCT | ERA | G | GS | CG | IP | H | BB | SO | ShO | W | L | SV | AB | H | HR | BA |
|---|---|---|---|---|---|---|---|---|---|---|---|---|---|---|---|---|---|---|---|
| 1982 DET A | 0 | 0 | — | 27.00 | 5 | 1 | 0 | 2 | 7 | 2 | 0 | 0 | 0 | 0 | 1 | 0 | 0 | 0 | — |
| 1983 | 0 | 2 | .000 | 2.64 | 26 | 0 | 0 | 44.1 | 43 | 7 | 14 | 0 | 0 | 2 | 2 | 0 | 0 | 0 | — |
| 1985 CHI N | 1 | 0 | 1.000 | 3.48 | 9 | 0 | 0 | 10.1 | 12 | 7 | 4 | 0 | 1 | 0 | 0 | 0 | 0 | 0 | .000 |
| 3 yrs. | 1 | 2 | .333 | 3.65 | 40 | 1 | 0 | 56.2 | 62 | 16 | 18 | 0 | 1 | 2 | 3 | 1 | 0 | 0 | .000 |
| 1 yr. | 1 | 0 | 1.000 | 3.48 | 9 | 0 | 0 | 10.1 | 12 | 7 | 4 | 0 | 1 | 0 | 0 | 1 | 0 | 0 | .000 |

# Larry Gura

**GURA, LAWRENCE CYRIL**          BL TL  6'   170 lbs.
B. Nov. 26, 1947, Joliet, Ill.

| | W | L | PCT | ERA | G | GS | CG | IP | H | BB | SO | ShO | W | L | SV | AB | H | HR | BA |
|---|---|---|---|---|---|---|---|---|---|---|---|---|---|---|---|---|---|---|---|
| 1970 CHI N | 1 | 3 | .250 | 3.79 | 20 | 3 | 1 | 38 | 35 | 23 | 21 | 0 | 0 | 1 | 1 | 10 | 0 | 0 | .000 |
| 1971 | 0 | 0 | — | 6.00 | 6 | 0 | 0 | 3 | 6 | 1 | 2 | 0 | 0 | 0 | 1 | 1 | 0 | 0 | .000 |
| 1972 | 0 | 0 | — | 3.75 | 7 | 0 | 0 | 12 | 11 | 3 | 13 | 0 | 0 | 0 | 1 | 1 | 0 | 0 | — |
| 1973 | 2 | 4 | .333 | 4.85 | 21 | 7 | 0 | 65 | 79 | 11 | 43 | 0 | 0 | 0 | 0 | 15 | 3 | 0 | .200 |
| 1974 NY A | 5 | 1 | .833 | 2.41 | 8 | 8 | 4 | 56 | 54 | 12 | 17 | 0 | 0 | 0 | 0 | 0 | 0 | 0 | — |
| 1975 | 7 | 8 | .467 | 3.51 | 26 | 20 | 5 | 151.1 | 173 | 41 | 65 | 0 | 0 | 0 | 0 | 0 | 0 | 0 | — |
| 1976 KC A | 4 | 0 | 1.000 | 2.29 | 20 | 2 | 1 | 63 | 47 | 20 | 22 | 1 | 3 | 0 | 1 | 0 | 0 | 0 | — |
| 1977 | 8 | 5 | .615 | 3.14 | 52 | 6 | 1 | 106 | 108 | 28 | 46 | 1 | 5 | 3 | 10 | 0 | 0 | 0 | — |
| 1978 | 16 | 4 | .800 | 2.72 | 35 | 26 | 8 | 221.2 | 183 | 60 | 81 | 2 | 2 | 0 | 0 | 0 | 0 | 0 | — |

| | W | L | PCT | ERA | G | GS | CG | IP | H | BB | SO | ShO | Relief Pitching W | L | SV | BATTING AB | H | HR | BA |
|---|---|---|---|---|---|---|---|---|---|---|---|---|---|---|---|---|---|---|---|

### Larry Gura continued

| | W | L | PCT | ERA | G | GS | CG | IP | H | BB | SO | ShO | W | L | SV | AB | H | HR | BA |
|---|---|---|---|---|---|---|---|---|---|---|---|---|---|---|---|---|---|---|---|
| 1979 | 13 | 12 | .520 | 4.46 | 39 | 33 | 7 | 234 | 226 | 73 | 85 | 1 | 1 | 0 | 0 | 0 | 0 | 0 | – |
| 1980 | 18 | 10 | .643 | 2.96 | 36 | 36 | 16 | 283 | 272 | 76 | 113 | 4 | 0 | 0 | 0 | 0 | 0 | 0 | – |
| 1981 | 11 | 8 | .579 | 2.72 | 23 | 23 | 12 | 172 | 139 | 35 | 61 | 2 | 0 | 0 | 0 | 0 | 0 | 0 | – |
| 1982 | 18 | 12 | .600 | 4.03 | 37 | 37 | 8 | 248 | 251 | 64 | 98 | 3 | 0 | 0 | 0 | 0 | 0 | 0 | – |
| 1983 | 11 | 18 | .379 | 4.90 | 34 | 31 | 5 | 200.1 | 220 | 76 | 57 | 0 | 1 | 0 | 0 | 0 | 0 | 0 | – |
| 1984 | 12 | 9 | .571 | 5.18 | 31 | 25 | 3 | 168.2 | 175 | 67 | 68 | 0 | 1 | 0 | 0 | 0 | 0 | 0 | – |
| 1985 2 teams | | | | | KC | A | (3G 0–0) | CHI | N | (5G 0–3) | | | | | | | | | |
| " total | 0 | 3 | .000 | 9.12 | 8 | 4 | 0 | 24.2 | 41 | 10 | 9 | 0 | 0 | 0 | 1 | 6 | 0 | 0 | .000 |
| 16 yrs. | 126 | 97 | .565 | 3.76 | 403 | 261 | 71 | 2046.2 | 2020 | 600 | 801 | 14 | 13 | 4 | 14 | 33 | 3 | 0 | .091 |
| 5 yrs. | 3 | 10 | .231 | 5.01 | 59 | 14 | 1 | 138.1 | 165 | 44 | 86 | 0 | 0 | 1 | 2 | 33 | 3 | 0 | .091 |

DIVISIONAL PLAYOFF SERIES

| | W | L | PCT | ERA | G | GS | CG | IP | H | BB | SO | ShO | W | L | SV | AB | H | HR | BA |
|---|---|---|---|---|---|---|---|---|---|---|---|---|---|---|---|---|---|---|---|
| 1981 KC A | 0 | 1 | .000 | 7.36 | 1 | 1 | 0 | 3.2 | 7 | 3 | 3 | 0 | 0 | 0 | 0 | 0 | 0 | 0 | – |

LEAGUE CHAMPIONSHIP SERIES

| | W | L | PCT | ERA | G | GS | CG | IP | H | BB | SO | ShO | W | L | SV | AB | H | HR | BA |
|---|---|---|---|---|---|---|---|---|---|---|---|---|---|---|---|---|---|---|---|
| 1976 KC A | 0 | 1 | .000 | 4.22 | 2 | 2 | 0 | 10.2 | 18 | 1 | 4 | 0 | 0 | 0 | 0 | 0 | 0 | 0 | – |
| 1977 | 0 | 1 | .000 | 18.00 | 2 | 1 | 0 | 2 | 7 | 1 | 2 | 0 | 0 | 0 | 0 | 0 | 0 | 0 | – |
| 1978 | 1 | 0 | 1.000 | 2.84 | 1 | 1 | 0 | 6.1 | 8 | 2 | 2 | 0 | 0 | 0 | 0 | 0 | 0 | 0 | – |
| 1980 | 1 | 0 | 1.000 | 2.00 | 1 | 1 | 1 | 9 | 10 | 1 | 4 | 0 | 0 | 0 | 0 | 0 | 0 | 0 | – |
| 4 yrs. | 2 | 2 | .500 | 4.18 | 6 | 5 | 1 | 28 | 43 | 5 | 12 | 0 | 0 | 0 | 0 | 0 | 0 | 0 | – |

WORLD SERIES

| | W | L | PCT | ERA | G | GS | CG | IP | H | BB | SO | ShO | W | L | SV | AB | H | HR | BA |
|---|---|---|---|---|---|---|---|---|---|---|---|---|---|---|---|---|---|---|---|
| 1980 KC A | 0 | 0 | – | 2.19 | 2 | 2 | 0 | 12.1 | 8 | 3 | 4 | 0 | 0 | 0 | 0 | 0 | 0 | 0 | – |

### Charlie Guth

**GUTH, CHARLES J.**
B. 1856, Chicago, Ill.    D. July 5, 1883, Boston, Mass.

| | W | L | PCT | ERA | G | GS | CG | IP | H | BB | SO | ShO | W | L | SV | AB | H | HR | BA |
|---|---|---|---|---|---|---|---|---|---|---|---|---|---|---|---|---|---|---|---|
| 1880 CHI N | 1 | 0 | 1.000 | 5.00 | 1 | 1 | 1 | 9 | 12 | 1 | 7 | 0 | 0 | 0 | 0 | 4 | 1 | 0 | .250 |

### Warren Hacker

**HACKER, WARREN LOUIS**                BR TR 6'1"    185 lbs.
B. Nov. 21, 1924, Marissa, Ill.

| | W | L | PCT | ERA | G | GS | CG | IP | H | BB | SO | ShO | W | L | SV | AB | H | HR | BA |
|---|---|---|---|---|---|---|---|---|---|---|---|---|---|---|---|---|---|---|---|
| 1948 CHI N | 0 | 1 | .000 | 21.00 | 3 | 1 | 0 | 3 | 7 | 3 | 0 | 0 | 0 | 0 | 0 | 0 | 0 | 0 | – |
| 1949 | 5 | 8 | .385 | 4.23 | 30 | 12 | 3 | 125.2 | 141 | 53 | 40 | 0 | 3 | 1 | 0 | 38 | 7 | 0 | .184 |
| 1950 | 0 | 1 | .000 | 5.28 | 5 | 3 | 1 | 15.1 | 20 | 8 | 5 | 0 | 0 | 0 | 1 | 5 | 0 | 0 | .000 |
| 1951 | 0 | 0 | – | 13.50 | 2 | 0 | 0 | 1.1 | 3 | 0 | 2 | 0 | 0 | 0 | 0 | 0 | 0 | 0 | – |
| 1952 | 15 | 9 | .625 | 2.58 | 33 | 20 | 12 | 185 | 144 | 31 | 84 | 5 | 2 | 2 | 1 | 58 | 7 | 0 | .121 |
| 1953 | 12 | 19 | .387 | 4.38 | 39 | 32 | 9 | 221.2 | 225 | 54 | 106 | 0 | 1 | 2 | 2 | 78 | 17 | 0 | .218 |
| 1954 | 6 | 13 | .316 | 4.25 | 39 | 18 | 4 | 158.2 | 157 | 37 | 80 | 1 | 1 | 6 | 2 | 55 | 13 | 0 | .236 |
| 1955 | 11 | 15 | .423 | 4.27 | 35 | 30 | 13 | 213 | 202 | 43 | 80 | 0 | 1 | 0 | 3 | 72 | 18 | 0 | .250 |
| 1956 | 3 | 13 | .188 | 4.66 | 34 | 24 | 4 | 168 | 190 | 44 | 65 | 0 | 0 | 0 | 0 | 54 | 8 | 0 | .148 |
| 1957 2 teams | | | | | CIN | N | (15G 3–2) | PHI | N | (20G 4–4) | | | | | | | | | |
| " total | 7 | 6 | .538 | 4.76 | 35 | 16 | 1 | 117.1 | 122 | 31 | 51 | 0 | 1 | 0 | 0 | 31 | 7 | 0 | .226 |
| 1958 PHI N | 0 | 1 | .000 | 7.41 | 9 | 1 | 0 | 17 | 24 | 8 | 4 | 0 | 0 | 0 | 0 | 1 | 0 | 0 | .000 |
| 1961 CHI A | 3 | 3 | .500 | 3.77 | 42 | 0 | 0 | 57.1 | 62 | 8 | 40 | 0 | 3 | 3 | 8 | 9 | 1 | 0 | .111 |
| 12 yrs. | 62 | 89 | .411 | 4.21 | 306 | 157 | 47 | 1283.1 | 1297 | 320 | 557 | 6 | 12 | 14 | 17 | 401 | 78 | 0 | .195 |
| 9 yrs. | 52 | 79 | .397 | 4.13 | 220 | 140 | 46 | 1091.2 | 1089 | 273 | 462 | 6 | 8 | 11 | 9 | 360 | 70 | 0 | .194 |

### Casey Hageman

**HAGEMAN, KURT MORITZ**                BR TR 5'10½" 186 lbs.
B. May 12, 1887, Mt. Oliver, Pa.    D. Apr. 1, 1964, New Bedford, Pa.

| | W | L | PCT | ERA | G | GS | CG | IP | H | BB | SO | ShO | W | L | SV | AB | H | HR | BA |
|---|---|---|---|---|---|---|---|---|---|---|---|---|---|---|---|---|---|---|---|
| 1911 BOS A | 0 | 2 | .000 | 2.12 | 2 | 2 | 2 | 17 | 16 | 5 | 8 | 0 | 0 | 0 | 0 | 4 | 0 | 0 | .000 |
| 1912 | 0 | 0 | – | 27.00 | 2 | 1 | 0 | 1.1 | 5 | 3 | 1 | 0 | 0 | 0 | 0 | 0 | 0 | 0 | – |
| 1914 2 teams | | | | | STL | N | (12G 1–4) | CHI | N | (16G 2–1) | | | | | | | | | |
| " total | 3 | 5 | .375 | 2.91 | 28 | 8 | 1 | 102 | 87 | 32 | 38 | 0 | 2 | 1 | 1 | 31 | 9 | 0 | .290 |
| 3 yrs. | 3 | 7 | .300 | 3.07 | 32 | 11 | 3 | 120.1 | 108 | 40 | 47 | 0 | 2 | 1 | 1 | 35 | 9 | 0 | .257 |
| 1 yr. | 2 | 1 | .667 | 3.47 | 16 | 1 | 0 | 46.2 | 44 | 12 | 17 | 0 | 2 | 1 | 1 | 15 | 7 | 0 | .467 |

### Rip Hagerman

**HAGERMAN, ZERIAH ZEQUIEL**                BR TR
B. June 20, 1888, Linden, Kans.    D. Jan. 30, 1930, Albuquerque, N. M.

| | W | L | PCT | ERA | G | GS | CG | IP | H | BB | SO | ShO | W | L | SV | AB | H | HR | BA |
|---|---|---|---|---|---|---|---|---|---|---|---|---|---|---|---|---|---|---|---|
| 1909 CHI N | 4 | 4 | .500 | 1.82 | 13 | 7 | 4 | 79 | 64 | 28 | 32 | 1 | 1 | 0 | 0 | 23 | 3 | 0 | .130 |
| 1914 CLE A | 9 | 15 | .375 | 3.09 | 37 | 26 | 12 | 198 | 189 | 118 | 112 | 3 | 1 | 2 | 0 | 61 | 1 | 0 | .016 |
| 1915 | 6 | 14 | .300 | 3.52 | 29 | 22 | 7 | 151 | 156 | 77 | 69 | 0 | 1 | 1 | 0 | 38 | 4 | 0 | .105 |
| 1916 | 0 | 0 | – | 12.27 | 2 | 0 | 0 | 3.2 | 5 | 2 | 1 | 0 | 0 | 0 | 0 | 1 | 0 | 0 | .000 |
| 4 yrs. | 19 | 33 | .365 | 3.09 | 81 | 55 | 23 | 431.2 | 414 | 225 | 214 | 4 | 3 | 3 | 0 | 123 | 8 | 0 | .065 |
| 1 yr. | 4 | 4 | .500 | 1.82 | 13 | 7 | 4 | 79 | 64 | 28 | 32 | 1 | 1 | 0 | 0 | 23 | 3 | 0 | .130 |

### Steve Hamilton

**HAMILTON, STEVE ABSHER**                BL TL 6'6"    190 lbs.
B. Nov. 30, 1935, Columbia, Ky.

| | W | L | PCT | ERA | G | GS | CG | IP | H | BB | SO | ShO | W | L | SV | AB | H | HR | BA |
|---|---|---|---|---|---|---|---|---|---|---|---|---|---|---|---|---|---|---|---|
| 1961 CLE A | 0 | 0 | – | 2.70 | 2 | 0 | 0 | 3.1 | 2 | 3 | 4 | 0 | 0 | 0 | 0 | 1 | 1 | 0 | 1.000 |
| 1962 WAS A | 3 | 8 | .273 | 3.77 | 41 | 10 | 1 | 107.1 | 103 | 39 | 83 | 0 | 2 | 4 | 2 | 26 | 2 | 0 | .077 |
| 1963 2 teams | | | | | WAS | A | (3G 0–1) | NY | A | (34G 5–1) | | | | | | | | | |
| " total | 5 | 2 | .714 | 2.94 | 37 | 0 | 0 | 64.1 | 54 | 26 | 64 | 0 | 5 | 2 | 5 | 14 | 4 | 0 | .286 |
| 1964 NY A | 7 | 2 | .778 | 3.28 | 30 | 3 | 1 | 60.1 | 55 | 15 | 49 | 0 | 5 | 2 | 3 | 20 | 4 | 0 | .200 |
| 1965 | 3 | 1 | .750 | 1.39 | 46 | 1 | 0 | 58.1 | 47 | 16 | 51 | 0 | 3 | 1 | 5 | 6 | 1 | 0 | .167 |
| 1966 | 8 | 3 | .727 | 3.00 | 44 | 3 | 1 | 90 | 69 | 22 | 57 | 1 | 7 | 2 | 3 | 19 | 1 | 0 | .053 |
| 1967 | 2 | 4 | .333 | 3.48 | 44 | 0 | 0 | 62 | 57 | 23 | 55 | 0 | 2 | 4 | 4 | 9 | 1 | 0 | .111 |
| 1968 | 2 | 2 | .500 | 2.13 | 40 | 0 | 0 | 50.2 | 37 | 13 | 42 | 0 | 2 | 2 | 11 | 3 | 0 | 0 | .000 |
| 1969 | 2 | 4 | .429 | 3.32 | 38 | 0 | 0 | 57 | 39 | 21 | 39 | 0 | 3 | 4 | 2 | 5 | 0 | 0 | .000 |
| 1970 2 teams | | | | | NY | A | (35G 4–3) | CHI | A | (3G 0–0) | | | | | | | | | |
| " total | 4 | 3 | .571 | 2.98 | 38 | 0 | 0 | 48.1 | 40 | 17 | 36 | 0 | 4 | 3 | 3 | 6 | 0 | 0 | .000 |
| 1971 SF N | 2 | 2 | .500 | 3.00 | 39 | 0 | 0 | 45 | 29 | 11 | 38 | 0 | 2 | 2 | 4 | 2 | 0 | 0 | .000 |
| 1972 CHI N | 1 | 0 | 1.000 | 4.76 | 22 | 0 | 0 | 17 | 24 | 8 | 13 | 0 | 1 | 0 | 0 | 1 | 0 | 0 | .000 |
| 12 yrs. | 40 | 31 | .563 | 3.05 | 421 | 17 | 3 | 663.2 | 556 | 214 | 531 | 1 | 36 | 26 | 42 | 112 | 14 | 0 | .125 |
| 1 yr. | 1 | 0 | 1.000 | 4.76 | 22 | 0 | 0 | 17 | 24 | 8 | 13 | 0 | 1 | 0 | 0 | 1 | 0 | 0 | .000 |

LEAGUE CHAMPIONSHIP SERIES

| | W | L | PCT | ERA | G | GS | CG | IP | H | BB | SO | ShO | W | L | SV | AB | H | HR | BA |
|---|---|---|---|---|---|---|---|---|---|---|---|---|---|---|---|---|---|---|---|
| 1971 SF N | 0 | 0 | – | 9.00 | 1 | 0 | 0 | 1 | 1 | 0 | 3 | 0 | 0 | 0 | 0 | 0 | 0 | 0 | – |

| | W | L | PCT | ERA | G | GS | CG | IP | H | BB | SO | ShO | Relief Pitching W | L | SV | BATTING AB | H | HR | BA |
|---|---|---|---|---|---|---|---|---|---|---|---|---|---|---|---|---|---|---|---|

## Steve Hamilton continued

WORLD SERIES

| | W | L | PCT | ERA | G | GS | CG | IP | H | BB | SO | ShO | W | L | SV | AB | H | HR | BA |
|---|---|---|---|---|---|---|---|---|---|---|---|---|---|---|---|---|---|---|---|
| 1963 NY A | 0 | 0 | – | 0.00 | 1 | 0 | 0 | 1 | 0 | 0 | 1 | 0 | 0 | 0 | 0 | 0 | 0 | 0 | – |
| 1964 | 0 | 0 | – | 4.50 | 2 | 0 | 0 | 2 | 3 | 0 | 2 | 0 | 0 | 0 | 1 | 0 | 0 | 0 | – |
| 2 yrs. | 0 | 0 | – | 3.00 | 3 | 0 | 0 | 3 | 3 | 0 | 3 | 0 | 0 | 0 | 1 | 0 | 0 | 0 | – |

## Ralph Hamner

HAMNER, RALPH CONANT (Bruz)   BR TR 6'3"   165 lbs.
B. Sept. 12, 1916, Gibsland, La.

| | W | L | PCT | ERA | G | GS | CG | IP | H | BB | SO | ShO | W | L | SV | AB | H | HR | BA |
|---|---|---|---|---|---|---|---|---|---|---|---|---|---|---|---|---|---|---|---|
| 1946 CHI A | 2 | 7 | .222 | 4.42 | 25 | 7 | 1 | 71.1 | 80 | 39 | 29 | 0 | 0 | 0 | 1 | 18 | 3 | 0 | .167 |
| 1947 CHI N | 1 | 2 | .333 | 2.52 | 3 | 3 | 2 | 25 | 24 | 16 | 14 | 0 | 0 | 0 | 0 | 8 | 1 | 0 | .125 |
| 1948 | 5 | 9 | .357 | 4.69 | 27 | 17 | 5 | 111.1 | 110 | 69 | 53 | 0 | 0 | 1 | 0 | 33 | 6 | 1 | .182 |
| 1949 | 0 | 2 | .000 | 8.76 | 6 | 1 | 0 | 12.1 | 22 | 8 | 3 | 0 | 0 | 1 | 0 | 2 | 0 | 0 | .000 |
| 4 yrs. | 8 | 20 | .286 | 4.58 | 61 | 28 | 8 | 220 | 236 | 132 | 99 | 0 | 0 | 2 | 1 | 61 | 10 | 1 | .164 |
| 3 yrs. | 6 | 13 | .316 | 4.66 | 36 | 21 | 7 | 148.2 | 156 | 93 | 70 | 0 | 0 | 2 | 0 | 43 | 7 | 1 | .163 |

## Bill Hands

HANDS, WILLIAM ALFRED   BR TR 6'2"   185 lbs.
B. May 6, 1940, Rutherford, N. J.

| | W | L | PCT | ERA | G | GS | CG | IP | H | BB | SO | ShO | W | L | SV | AB | H | HR | BA |
|---|---|---|---|---|---|---|---|---|---|---|---|---|---|---|---|---|---|---|---|
| 1965 SF N | 0 | 2 | .000 | 16.50 | 4 | 2 | 0 | 6 | 13 | 6 | 5 | 0 | 0 | 0 | 0 | 1 | 0 | 0 | .000 |
| 1966 CHI N | 8 | 13 | .381 | 4.58 | 41 | 26 | 0 | 159 | 168 | 59 | 93 | 0 | 4 | 0 | 2 | 49 | 2 | 0 | .041 |
| 1967 | 7 | 8 | .467 | 2.46 | 49 | 11 | 3 | 150 | 134 | 48 | 84 | 1 | 3 | 6 | 6 | 38 | 4 | 0 | .105 |
| 1968 | 16 | 10 | .615 | 2.89 | 38 | 34 | 11 | 258.2 | 221 | 36 | 148 | 4 | 0 | 1 | 0 | 82 | 5 | 0 | .061 |
| 1969 | 20 | 14 | .588 | 2.49 | 41 | 41 | 18 | 300 | 268 | 73 | 181 | 3 | 0 | 0 | 0 | 98 | 9 | 0 | .092 |
| 1970 | 18 | 15 | .545 | 3.70 | 39 | 38 | 12 | 265 | 278 | 76 | 170 | 2 | 0 | 0 | 1 | 75 | 10 | 0 | .133 |
| 1971 | 12 | 18 | .400 | 3.42 | 36 | 35 | 14 | 242 | 248 | 50 | 128 | 1 | 0 | 0 | 0 | 72 | 6 | 0 | .083 |
| 1972 | 11 | 8 | .579 | 2.99 | 32 | 28 | 6 | 189.1 | 168 | 47 | 96 | 3 | 0 | 1 | 0 | 57 | 1 | 0 | .018 |
| 1973 MIN A | 7 | 10 | .412 | 3.49 | 39 | 15 | 3 | 142 | 138 | 41 | 78 | 1 | 2 | 3 | 2 | 0 | 0 | 0 | – |
| 1974 2 teams | | | MIN A | (35G 4–5) | | TEX A | (2G 2–0) | | | | | | | | | | | | |
| " total | 6 | 5 | .545 | 4.19 | 37 | 12 | 1 | 129 | 141 | 28 | 78 | 1 | 2 | 0 | 3 | 0 | 0 | 0 | – |
| 1975 TEX A | 6 | 7 | .462 | 4.02 | 18 | 18 | 4 | 109.2 | 118 | 28 | 67 | 1 | 0 | 0 | 0 | 0 | 0 | 0 | – |
| 11 yrs. | 111 | 110 | .502 | 3.35 | 374 | 260 | 72 | 1950.2 | 1895 | 492 | 1128 | 17 | 11 | 11 | 14 | 472 | 37 | 0 | .078 |
| 7 yrs. | 92 | 86 | .517 | 3.18 | 276 | 213 | 64 | 1564 | 1485 | 389 | 900 | 14 | 7 | 8 | 9 | 471 | 37 | 0 | .079 |

## Frank Hankinson

HANKINSON, FRANK EDWARD   BR TR 5'11"   168 lbs.
B. Apr. 29, 1856, New York, N. Y.   D. Apr. 5, 1911, Palisades Park, N. J.

| | W | L | PCT | ERA | G | GS | CG | IP | H | BB | SO | ShO | W | L | SV | AB | H | HR | BA |
|---|---|---|---|---|---|---|---|---|---|---|---|---|---|---|---|---|---|---|---|
| 1878 CHI N | 0 | 1 | .000 | 6.00 | 1 | 1 | 1 | 9 | 11 | 0 | 4 | 0 | 0 | 0 | 0 | 240 | 64 | 1 | .267 |
| 1879 | 15 | 10 | .600 | 2.50 | 26 | 25 | 25 | 230.2 | 248 | 27 | 69 | 2 | 1 | 0 | 0 | 171 | 31 | 0 | .181 |
| 1880 CLE N | 1 | 1 | .500 | 1.08 | 4 | 2 | 2 | 25 | 20 | 3 | 8 | 0 | 0 | 0 | 1 | 263 | 55 | 1 | .209 |
| 1885 NY AA | 0 | 0 | – | 4.50 | 1 | 0 | 0 | 2 | 2 | 1 | 0 | 0 | 0 | 0 | 0 | 362 | 81 | 2 | .224 |
| 4 yrs. | 16 | 12 | .571 | 2.50 | 32 | 28 | 28 | 266.2 | 281 | 31 | 81 | 2 | 1 | 0 | 1 | * | | | |
| 2 yrs. | 15 | 11 | .577 | 2.63 | 27 | 26 | 26 | 239.2 | 259 | 27 | 73 | 2 | 1 | 0 | 0 | 411 | 95 | 1 | .231 |

## Ollie Hanson

HANSON, EARL SYLVESTER   BR TR 5'11"   178 lbs.
B. Jan. 19, 1896, Holbrook, Mass.   D. Aug. 19, 1951, Clifton, N. J.

| | W | L | PCT | ERA | G | GS | CG | IP | H | BB | SO | ShO | W | L | SV | AB | H | HR | BA |
|---|---|---|---|---|---|---|---|---|---|---|---|---|---|---|---|---|---|---|---|
| 1921 CHI N | 0 | 2 | .000 | 7.00 | 2 | 2 | 1 | 9 | 9 | 6 | 2 | 0 | 0 | 0 | 0 | 3 | 0 | 0 | .000 |

## Ed Hanyzewski

HANYZEWSKI, EDWARD MICHAEL   BR TR 6'1"   200 lbs.
B. Sept. 18, 1920, Union Mills, Ind.

| | W | L | PCT | ERA | G | GS | CG | IP | H | BB | SO | ShO | W | L | SV | AB | H | HR | BA |
|---|---|---|---|---|---|---|---|---|---|---|---|---|---|---|---|---|---|---|---|
| 1942 CHI N | 1 | 1 | .500 | 3.79 | 6 | 1 | 0 | 19 | 17 | 8 | 6 | 0 | 1 | 0 | 0 | 5 | 1 | 0 | .200 |
| 1943 | 8 | 7 | .533 | 2.56 | 33 | 16 | 3 | 130 | 120 | 45 | 55 | 0 | 4 | 0 | 0 | 41 | 2 | 0 | .049 |
| 1944 | 2 | 5 | .286 | 4.47 | 14 | 7 | 3 | 58.1 | 61 | 20 | 19 | 0 | 0 | 1 | 0 | 17 | 1 | 0 | .059 |
| 1945 | 0 | 0 | – | 5.79 | 2 | 1 | 0 | 4.2 | 7 | 1 | 0 | 0 | 0 | 0 | 0 | 1 | 0 | 0 | .000 |
| 1946 | 1 | 0 | 1.000 | 4.50 | 3 | 0 | 0 | 6 | 8 | 5 | 1 | 0 | 1 | 0 | 0 | 1 | 0 | 0 | .000 |
| 5 yrs. | 12 | 13 | .480 | 3.30 | 58 | 25 | 6 | 218 | 213 | 79 | 81 | 0 | 6 | 1 | 0 | 65 | 4 | 0 | .062 |
| 5 yrs. | 12 | 13 | .480 | 3.30 | 58 | 25 | 6 | 218 | 213 | 79 | 81 | 0 | 6 | 1 | 0 | 65 | 4 | 0 | .062 |

## Alex Hardy

HARDY, DAVID ALEXANDER   TL
B. 1877, Toronto, Ont., Canada   D. Apr. 22, 1940, Toronto, Ont., Canada

| | W | L | PCT | ERA | G | GS | CG | IP | H | BB | SO | ShO | W | L | SV | AB | H | HR | BA |
|---|---|---|---|---|---|---|---|---|---|---|---|---|---|---|---|---|---|---|---|
| 1902 CHI N | 2 | 2 | .500 | 3.60 | 4 | 4 | 4 | 35 | 29 | 12 | 12 | 1 | 0 | 0 | 0 | 14 | 3 | 0 | .214 |
| 1903 | 2 | 1 | .667 | 6.39 | 3 | 3 | 1 | 12.2 | 21 | 7 | 4 | 0 | 0 | 0 | 0 | 6 | 1 | 0 | .167 |
| 2 yrs. | 4 | 3 | .571 | 4.34 | 7 | 7 | 5 | 47.2 | 50 | 19 | 16 | 1 | 0 | 0 | 0 | 20 | 4 | 0 | .200 |
| 2 yrs. | 4 | 3 | .571 | 4.34 | 7 | 7 | 5 | 47.2 | 50 | 19 | 16 | 1 | 0 | 0 | 0 | 20 | 4 | 0 | .200 |

## Alan Hargesheimer

HARGESHEIMER, ALAN ROBERT   BR TR 6'3"   195 lbs.
B. Nov. 21, 1956, Chicago, Ill.

| | W | L | PCT | ERA | G | GS | CG | IP | H | BB | SO | ShO | W | L | SV | AB | H | HR | BA |
|---|---|---|---|---|---|---|---|---|---|---|---|---|---|---|---|---|---|---|---|
| 1980 SF N | 4 | 6 | .400 | 4.32 | 15 | 13 | 0 | 75 | 82 | 32 | 40 | 0 | 0 | 0 | 0 | 22 | 4 | 0 | .182 |
| 1981 | 1 | 2 | .333 | 4.26 | 6 | 3 | 0 | 19 | 20 | 9 | 6 | 0 | 0 | 0 | 0 | 5 | 1 | 0 | .200 |
| 1983 CHI N | 0 | 0 | – | 9.00 | 5 | 0 | 0 | 4 | 6 | 2 | 5 | 0 | 0 | 0 | 0 | 0 | 0 | 0 | – |
| 3 yrs. | 5 | 8 | .385 | 4.50 | 26 | 16 | 0 | 98 | 108 | 43 | 51 | 0 | 0 | 0 | 0 | 27 | 5 | 0 | .185 |
| 1 yr. | 0 | 0 | – | 9.00 | 5 | 0 | 0 | 4 | 6 | 2 | 5 | 0 | 0 | 0 | 0 | 0 | 0 | 0 | – |

## Jack Harper

HARPER, CHARLES WILLIAM   BR TR 6'   178 lbs.
B. Apr. 2, 1878, Franklin, Pa.   D. Sept. 30, 1950, Jamestown, N. Y.

| | W | L | PCT | ERA | G | GS | CG | IP | H | BB | SO | ShO | W | L | SV | AB | H | HR | BA |
|---|---|---|---|---|---|---|---|---|---|---|---|---|---|---|---|---|---|---|---|
| 1899 CLE N | 1 | 4 | .200 | 3.89 | 5 | 5 | 5 | 37 | 44 | 12 | 14 | 0 | 0 | 0 | 0 | 11 | 2 | 0 | .182 |
| 1900 STL N | 0 | 1 | .000 | 12.00 | 1 | 1 | 0 | 3 | 4 | 2 | 0 | 0 | 0 | 0 | 0 | 1 | 0 | 0 | .000 |
| 1901 | 23 | 13 | .639 | 3.62 | 39 | 37 | 28 | 308.2 | 294 | 99 | 128 | 1 | 1 | 0 | 0 | 116 | 20 | 1 | .172 |
| 1902 STL A | 15 | 11 | .577 | 4.13 | 29 | 26 | 20 | 222.1 | 224 | 81 | 74 | 2 | 1 | 1 | 0 | 83 | 17 | 0 | .205 |
| 1903 CIN N | 6 | 8 | .429 | 4.33 | 17 | 15 | 13 | 135 | 143 | 70 | 45 | 0 | 0 | 2 | 0 | 56 | 14 | 0 | .250 |
| 1904 | 23 | 9 | .719 | 2.37 | 35 | 35 | 31 | 284.2 | 262 | 85 | 125 | 6 | 0 | 0 | 0 | 113 | 18 | 0 | .159 |
| 1905 | 10 | 13 | .435 | 3.87 | 26 | 23 | 15 | 179 | 189 | 69 | 70 | 1 | 1 | 0 | 0 | 60 | 10 | 0 | .167 |

| | W | L | PCT | ERA | G | GS | CG | IP | H | BB | SO | ShO | Relief Pitching W | L | SV | BATTING AB | H | HR | BA |
|---|---|---|---|---|---|---|---|---|---|---|---|---|---|---|---|---|---|---|---|

## Jack Harper continued

| | | | | | | | | | | | | | | | | | | | |
|---|---|---|---|---|---|---|---|---|---|---|---|---|---|---|---|---|---|---|---|
| 1906 2 teams | CIN | N | (5G 1–4) | | CHI | N | (1G 0–0) | | | | | | | | | | | | |
| " total | 1 | 4 | .200 | 4.06 | 6 | 6 | 3 | 37.2 | 38 | 20 | 10 | 0 | 0 | 0 | 0 | 11 | 3 | 0 | .273 |
| 8 yrs. | 79 | 63 | .556 | 3.58 | 158 | 148 | 115 | 1207.1 | 1198 | 438 | 466 | 10 | 3 | 3 | 0 | 451 | 84 | 1 | .186 |
| 1 yr. | 0 | 0 | — | 0.00 | 1 | 1 | 0 | 1 | 0 | 0 | 0 | 0 | 0 | 0 | 0 | 0 | 0 | 0 | — |

## Ray Harrell

HARRELL, RAYMOND JAMES (Cowboy)  BR TR 6'1" 185 lbs.
B. Feb. 16, 1912, Petrolia, Tex.  D. Jan. 28, 1984, Alexandria, La.

| | | | | | | | | | | | | | | | | | | | |
|---|---|---|---|---|---|---|---|---|---|---|---|---|---|---|---|---|---|---|---|
| 1935 STL N | 1 | 1 | .500 | 6.67 | 11 | 1 | 0 | 29.2 | 39 | 11 | 13 | 0 | 1 | 1 | 0 | 4 | 0 | 0 | .000 |
| 1937 | 3 | 7 | .300 | 5.87 | 35 | 15 | 1 | 96.2 | 99 | 59 | 41 | 1 | 1 | 0 | 1 | 22 | 1 | 0 | .045 |
| 1938 | 2 | 3 | .400 | 4.86 | 32 | 3 | 1 | 63 | 78 | 29 | 32 | 0 | 1 | 3 | 2 | 10 | 0 | 0 | .000 |
| 1939 2 teams | CHI | N | (4G 0–2) | | PHI | N | (22G 3–7) | | | | | | | | | | | | |
| " total | 3 | 9 | .250 | 5.87 | 26 | 12 | 4 | 112 | 127 | 62 | 40 | 0 | 1 | 0 | 0 | 31 | 3 | 0 | .097 |
| 1940 PIT N | 0 | 0 | — | 8.10 | 3 | 0 | 0 | 3.1 | 5 | 2 | 3 | 0 | 0 | 0 | 0 | 0 | 0 | 0 | — |
| 1945 NY N | 0 | 0 | — | 4.97 | 12 | 0 | 0 | 25.1 | 34 | 14 | 7 | 0 | 0 | 0 | 0 | 5 | 1 | 0 | .200 |
| 6 yrs. | 9 | 20 | .310 | 5.70 | 119 | 31 | 6 | 330 | 382 | 177 | 136 | 1 | 4 | 4 | 3 | 72 | 5 | 0 | .069 |
| 1 yr. | 0 | 2 | .000 | 8.31 | 4 | 2 | 0 | 17.1 | 26 | 6 | 5 | 0 | 0 | 0 | 0 | 5 | 0 | 0 | .000 |

## Chuck Hartenstein

HARTENSTEIN, CHARLES OSCAR (Twiggy)  BR TR 5'11" 165 lbs.
B. May 26, 1942, Seguin, Tex.

| | | | | | | | | | | | | | | | | | | | |
|---|---|---|---|---|---|---|---|---|---|---|---|---|---|---|---|---|---|---|---|
| 1965 CHI N | 0 | 0 | — | 0.00 | 0 | 0 | 0 | 0 | 0 | 0 | 0 | 0 | 0 | 0 | 0 | 0 | 0 | 0 | — |
| 1966 | 0 | 0 | — | 1.93 | 5 | 0 | 0 | 9.1 | 8 | 3 | 4 | 0 | 0 | 0 | 0 | 0 | 0 | 0 | — |
| 1967 | 9 | 5 | .643 | 3.08 | 45 | 0 | 0 | 73 | 74 | 17 | 20 | 0 | 9 | 5 | 10 | 16 | 1 | 0 | .063 |
| 1968 | 2 | 4 | .333 | 4.54 | 28 | 0 | 0 | 35.2 | 41 | 11 | 17 | 0 | 2 | 4 | 1 | 2 | 0 | 0 | .000 |
| 1969 PIT N | 5 | 4 | .556 | 3.94 | 56 | 0 | 0 | 96 | 84 | 27 | 44 | 0 | 5 | 4 | 10 | 14 | 1 | 0 | .071 |
| 1970 3 teams | PIT | N | (17G 1–1) | | STL | N | (6G 0–0) | | BOS | A | (17G 0–3) | | | | | | | | |
| " total | 1 | 4 | .200 | 6.75 | 40 | 0 | 0 | 56 | 70 | 25 | 35 | 0 | 1 | 4 | 2 | 5 | 0 | 0 | .000 |
| 1977 TOR A | 0 | 2 | .000 | 6.67 | 13 | 0 | 0 | 27 | 40 | 6 | 15 | 0 | 0 | 2 | 0 | 0 | 0 | 0 | — |
| 7 yrs. | 17 | 19 | .472 | 4.52 | 187 | 0 | 0 | 297 | 317 | 89 | 135 | 0 | 17 | 19 | 23 | 37 | 2 | 0 | .054 |
| 3 yrs. | 11 | 9 | .550 | 3.43 | 78 | 0 | 0 | 118 | 123 | 31 | 41 | 0 | 11 | 9 | 11 | 18 | 1 | 0 | .056 |

## Ervin Harvey

HARVEY, ERVIN KING (Zaza)  BL TL
B. Jan. 5, 1879, Saratoga, Calif.  D. June 3, 1954, Santa Monica, Calif.

| | | | | | | | | | | | | | | | | | | | |
|---|---|---|---|---|---|---|---|---|---|---|---|---|---|---|---|---|---|---|---|
| 1900 CHI N | 0 | 0 | — | 0.00 | 1 | 0 | 0 | 4 | 3 | 1 | 0 | 0 | 0 | 0 | 0 | 3 | 0 | 0 | .000 |
| 1901 CHI A | 3 | 6 | .333 | 3.62 | 16 | 9 | 5 | 92 | 91 | 34 | 27 | 0 | 2 | 0 | 1 | 210 | 70 | 1 | .333 |
| 2 yrs. | 3 | 6 | .333 | 3.47 | 17 | 9 | 5 | 96 | 94 | 35 | 27 | 0 | 2 | 0 | 1 | * | | | |
| 1 yr. | 0 | 0 | — | 0.00 | 1 | 0 | 0 | 4 | 3 | 1 | 0 | 0 | 0 | 0 | 0 | 3 | 0 | 0 | .000 |

## Joe Hatten

HATTEN, JOSEPH HILARIAN  BR TL 6' 176 lbs.
B. Nov. 7, 1916, Bancroft, Iowa

| | | | | | | | | | | | | | | | | | | | |
|---|---|---|---|---|---|---|---|---|---|---|---|---|---|---|---|---|---|---|---|
| 1946 BKN N | 14 | 11 | .560 | 2.84 | 42 | 30 | 13 | 222 | 207 | 110 | 85 | 1 | 1 | 1 | 2 | 79 | 6 | 0 | .076 |
| 1947 | 17 | 8 | .680 | 3.63 | 42 | 32 | 11 | 225.1 | 211 | 105 | 76 | 3 | 2 | 0 | 0 | 83 | 17 | 0 | .205 |
| 1948 | 13 | 10 | .565 | 3.58 | 42 | 30 | 11 | 208.2 | 228 | 94 | 73 | 1 | 0 | 1 | 0 | 63 | 13 | 0 | .206 |
| 1949 | 12 | 8 | .600 | 4.18 | 37 | 29 | 11 | 187.1 | 194 | 69 | 58 | 2 | 2 | 0 | 2 | 67 | 12 | 0 | .179 |
| 1950 | 2 | 2 | .500 | 4.59 | 23 | 8 | 2 | 68.2 | 82 | 31 | 29 | 1 | 0 | 0 | 0 | 18 | 2 | 0 | .111 |
| 1951 2 teams | BKN | N | (11G 1–0) | | CHI | N | (23G 2–6) | | | | | | | | | | | | |
| " total | 3 | 6 | .333 | 4.91 | 34 | 12 | 1 | 124.2 | 137 | 58 | 45 | 0 | 2 | 1 | 0 | 32 | 6 | 0 | .188 |
| 1952 CHI N | 4 | 4 | .500 | 6.08 | 13 | 8 | 2 | 50.1 | 65 | 25 | 15 | 0 | 2 | 0 | 0 | 15 | 1 | 0 | .067 |
| 7 yrs. | 65 | 49 | .570 | 3.87 | 233 | 149 | 51 | 1087 | 1124 | 492 | 381 | 8 | 9 | 3 | 4 | 357 | 57 | 0 | .160 |
| 2 yrs. | 6 | 10 | .375 | 5.51 | 36 | 14 | 3 | 125.2 | 147 | 62 | 38 | 0 | 4 | 1 | 0 | 32 | 5 | 0 | .156 |

**WORLD SERIES**

| | | | | | | | | | | | | | | | | | | | |
|---|---|---|---|---|---|---|---|---|---|---|---|---|---|---|---|---|---|---|---|
| 1947 BKN N | 0 | 0 | — | 7.00 | 4 | 1 | 0 | 9 | 12 | 7 | 5 | 0 | 0 | 0 | 0 | 3 | 1 | 0 | .333 |
| 1949 | 0 | 0 | — | 16.20 | 2 | 0 | 0 | 1.2 | 4 | 2 | 0 | 0 | 0 | 0 | 0 | 0 | 0 | 0 | — |
| 2 yrs. | 0 | 0 | — | 8.44 | 6 | 1 | 0 | 10.2 | 16 | 9 | 5 | 0 | 0 | 0 | 0 | 3 | 1 | 0 | .333 |

## Egyptian Healy

HEALY, JOHN J. (Long John)  BR TR 6'2"
B. Oct. 27, 1866, Cairo, Ill.  D. Mar. 16, 1899, St. Louis, Mo.

| | | | | | | | | | | | | | | | | | | | |
|---|---|---|---|---|---|---|---|---|---|---|---|---|---|---|---|---|---|---|---|
| 1885 STL N | 1 | 7 | .125 | 3.00 | 8 | 8 | 8 | 66 | 54 | 20 | 32 | 0 | 0 | 0 | 0 | 24 | 1 | 0 | .042 |
| 1886 | 17 | 23 | .425 | 2.88 | 42 | 41 | 39 | 353.2 | 314 | 118 | 213 | 3 | 1 | 0 | 0 | 145 | 14 | 0 | .097 |
| 1887 IND N | 12 | 29 | .293 | 5.17 | 41 | 41 | 40 | 341 | 415 | 108 | 75 | 3 | 0 | 0 | 0 | 138 | 24 | 3 | .174 |
| 1888 | 12 | 24 | .333 | 3.89 | 37 | 37 | 36 | 321.1 | 347 | 87 | 124 | 1 | 0 | 0 | 0 | 131 | 30 | 0 | .229 |
| 1889 2 teams | WAS | N | (13G 1–11) | | CHI | N | (5G 1–4) | | | | | | | | | | | | |
| " total | 2 | 15 | .118 | 5.69 | 18 | 17 | 15 | 147 | 187 | 56 | 71 | 0 | 0 | 0 | 0 | 65 | 12 | 1 | .185 |
| 1890 TOL AA | 22 | 21 | .512 | 2.89 | 46 | 46 | 44 | 389 | 326 | 127 | 225 | 2 | 0 | 0 | 0 | 156 | 34 | 1 | .218 |
| 1891 BAL AA | 9 | 10 | .474 | 3.75 | 23 | 22 | 19 | 170.1 | 179 | 57 | 54 | 0 | 0 | 0 | 0 | 64 | 9 | 0 | .141 |
| 1892 2 teams | BAL | N | (9G 3–6) | | LOU | N | (2G 1–1) | | | | | | | | | | | | |
| " total | 4 | 7 | .364 | 4.15 | 11 | 10 | 7 | 86.2 | 97 | 26 | 28 | 0 | 1 | 0 | 0 | 34 | 8 | 0 | .235 |
| 8 yrs. | 79 | 136 | .367 | 3.84 | 226 | 222 | 208 | 1875 | 1920 | 599 | 822 | 9 | 2 | 0 | 0 | 757 | 132 | 5 | .174 |
| 1 yr. | 1 | 4 | .200 | 4.50 | 5 | 5 | 5 | 46 | 48 | 18 | 22 | 0 | 0 | 0 | 0 | 20 | 2 | 0 | .100 |

## Bob Hendley

HENDLEY, CHARLES ROBERT  BR TL 6'2" 190 lbs.
B. Apr. 30, 1939, Macon, Ga.

| | | | | | | | | | | | | | | | | | | | |
|---|---|---|---|---|---|---|---|---|---|---|---|---|---|---|---|---|---|---|---|
| 1961 MIL N | 5 | 7 | .417 | 3.90 | 19 | 13 | 3 | 97 | 96 | 39 | 44 | 0 | 1 | 0 | 0 | 31 | 1 | 0 | .032 |
| 1962 | 11 | 13 | .458 | 3.60 | 35 | 29 | 7 | 200 | 188 | 59 | 112 | 2 | 0 | 1 | 1 | 59 | 7 | 1 | .119 |
| 1963 | 9 | 9 | .500 | 3.93 | 41 | 24 | 7 | 169.1 | 153 | 64 | 105 | 3 | 0 | 2 | 3 | 47 | 5 | 0 | .106 |
| 1964 SF N | 10 | 11 | .476 | 3.64 | 30 | 29 | 4 | 163.1 | 161 | 59 | 104 | 1 | 0 | 0 | 0 | 47 | 5 | 0 | .106 |
| 1965 2 teams | SF | N | (8G 0–0) | | CHI | N | (18G 4–4) | | | | | | | | | | | | |
| " total | 4 | 4 | .500 | 5.96 | 26 | 12 | 2 | 77 | 86 | 38 | 46 | 0 | 1 | 0 | 0 | 17 | 0 | 0 | .000 |
| 1966 CHI N | 4 | 5 | .444 | 3.91 | 43 | 6 | 0 | 89.2 | 98 | 39 | 65 | 0 | 4 | 3 | 7 | 18 | 3 | 0 | .167 |
| 1967 2 teams | CHI | N | (7G 2–0) | | NY | N | (15G 3–3) | | | | | | | | | | | | |
| " total | 5 | 3 | .625 | 3.90 | 22 | 13 | 2 | 83 | 82 | 31 | 46 | 0 | 2 | 0 | 1 | 24 | 2 | 0 | .083 |
| 7 yrs. | 48 | 52 | .480 | 3.97 | 216 | 126 | 25 | 879.1 | 864 | 329 | 522 | 6 | 8 | 7 | 12 | 243 | 23 | 1 | .095 |
| 3 yrs. | 10 | 9 | .526 | 4.28 | 68 | 16 | 2 | 164 | 174 | 67 | 113 | 0 | 7 | 4 | 8 | 38 | 3 | 0 | .079 |

| | W | L | PCT | ERA | G | GS | CG | IP | H | BB | SO | ShO | Relief Pitching W | L | SV | BATTING AB | H | HR | BA |
|---|---|---|---|---|---|---|---|---|---|---|---|---|---|---|---|---|---|---|---|

## Ellie Hendricks

**HENDRICKS, ELROD JEROME**
B. Dec. 22, 1940, St. Thomas, Virgin Islands
BL TR 6'1" 175 lbs.

| | W | L | PCT | ERA | G | GS | CG | IP | H | BB | SO | ShO | W | L | SV | AB | H | HR | BA |
|---|---|---|---|---|---|---|---|---|---|---|---|---|---|---|---|---|---|---|---|
| 1978 BAL A | 0 | 0 | – | 0.00 | 1 | 0 | 0 | 2.1 | 1 | 1 | 0 | 0 | 0 | 0 | 0 | * | | | |

## Claude Hendrix

**HENDRIX, CLAUDE RAYMOND**
B. Apr. 13, 1889, Olathe, Kans.   D. Mar. 22, 1944, Allentown, Pa.
BR TR 6' 195 lbs.

| | W | L | PCT | ERA | G | GS | CG | IP | H | BB | SO | ShO | W | L | SV | AB | H | HR | BA |
|---|---|---|---|---|---|---|---|---|---|---|---|---|---|---|---|---|---|---|---|
| 1911 PIT N | 4 | 6 | .400 | 2.73 | 22 | 12 | 6 | 118.2 | 85 | 53 | 57 | 1 | 0 | 1 | 1 | 41 | 4 | 0 | .098 |
| 1912 | 24 | 9 | **.727** | 2.59 | 39 | 32 | 25 | 288.2 | 256 | 105 | 176 | 4 | 3 | 1 | 1 | 121 | 39 | 1 | .322 |
| 1913 | 14 | 15 | .483 | 2.84 | 42 | 25 | 17 | 241 | 216 | 89 | 138 | 2 | 4 | 2 | 3 | 99 | 27 | 1 | .273 |
| 1914 CHI F | 29 | 11 | .725 | 1.69 | 49 | 37 | 34 | 362 | 262 | 77 | 189 | 6 | 3 | 2 | 5 | 130 | 30 | 2 | .231 |
| 1915 | 16 | 15 | .516 | 3.00 | 40 | 31 | 26 | 285 | 256 | 84 | 107 | 5 | 2 | 0 | 4 | 113 | 30 | 4 | .265 |
| 1916 CHI N | 8 | 16 | .333 | 2.68 | 36 | 24 | 15 | 218 | 193 | 67 | 117 | 3 | 1 | 1 | 2 | 80 | 16 | 1 | .200 |
| 1917 | 10 | 12 | .455 | 2.60 | 40 | 21 | 13 | 215 | 202 | 72 | 81 | 1 | 3 | 2 | 1 | 86 | 22 | 0 | .256 |
| 1918 | 19 | 7 | **.731** | 2.78 | 32 | 27 | 21 | 233 | 229 | 54 | 86 | 3 | 1 | 0 | 0 | 91 | 24 | 3 | .264 |
| 1919 | 10 | 14 | .417 | 2.62 | 33 | 25 | 15 | 206.1 | 208 | 42 | 69 | 2 | 1 | 1 | 0 | 78 | 15 | 1 | .192 |
| 1920 | 9 | 12 | .429 | 3.58 | 27 | 23 | 12 | 203.2 | 216 | 54 | 72 | 0 | 1 | 0 | 0 | 83 | 15 | 0 | .181 |
| 10 yrs. | 143 | 117 | .550 | 2.65 | 360 | 257 | 184 | 2371.1 | 2123 | 697 | 1092 | 27 | 19 | 10 | 17 | * | | | .220 |
| 5 yrs. | 56 | 61 | .479 | 2.84 | 168 | 120 | 76 | 1076 | 1048 | 289 | 425 | 9 | 7 | 4 | 3 | 418 | 92 | 5 | .220 |

WORLD SERIES

| 1918 CHI N | 0 | 0 | – | 0.00 | 1 | 0 | 0 | 1 | 0 | 0 | 0 | 0 | 0 | 0 | 0 | 1 | 1 | 0 | 1.000 |
|---|---|---|---|---|---|---|---|---|---|---|---|---|---|---|---|---|---|---|---|

## George Hennessey

**HENNESSEY, GEORGE (Three Star)**
B. Oct. 28, 1907, Slatington, Pa.
BR TR 5'10" 168 lbs.

| | W | L | PCT | ERA | G | GS | CG | IP | H | BB | SO | ShO | W | L | SV | AB | H | HR | BA |
|---|---|---|---|---|---|---|---|---|---|---|---|---|---|---|---|---|---|---|---|
| 1937 STL A | 0 | 1 | .000 | 10.29 | 5 | 0 | 0 | 7 | 15 | 6 | 4 | 0 | 0 | 1 | 0 | 0 | 0 | 0 | – |
| 1942 PHI N | 1 | 1 | .500 | 2.65 | 5 | 1 | 0 | 17 | 11 | 10 | 2 | 0 | 1 | 0 | 0 | 5 | 0 | 0 | .000 |
| 1945 CHI N | 0 | 0 | – | 7.36 | 2 | 0 | 0 | 3.2 | 7 | 1 | 2 | 0 | 0 | 0 | 0 | 0 | 0 | 0 | – |
| 3 yrs. | 1 | 2 | .333 | 5.20 | 12 | 1 | 0 | 27.2 | 33 | 17 | 8 | 0 | 1 | 1 | 0 | 5 | 0 | 0 | .000 |
| 1 yr. | 0 | 0 | – | 7.36 | 2 | 0 | 0 | 3.2 | 7 | 1 | 2 | 0 | 0 | 0 | 0 | 0 | 0 | 0 | – |

## Bill Henry

**HENRY, WILLIAM RODMAN**
B. Oct. 15, 1927, Alice, Tex.
BL TL 6'2" 180 lbs.

| | W | L | PCT | ERA | G | GS | CG | IP | H | BB | SO | ShO | W | L | SV | AB | H | HR | BA |
|---|---|---|---|---|---|---|---|---|---|---|---|---|---|---|---|---|---|---|---|
| 1952 BOS A | 5 | 4 | .556 | 3.87 | 13 | 10 | 5 | 76.2 | 75 | 36 | 23 | 0 | 0 | 0 | 0 | 31 | 8 | 0 | .258 |
| 1953 | 5 | 5 | .500 | 3.26 | 21 | 12 | 4 | 85.2 | 86 | 33 | 56 | 1 | 1 | 0 | 1 | 32 | 6 | 0 | .188 |
| 1954 | 3 | 7 | .300 | 4.52 | 24 | 13 | 3 | 95.2 | 104 | 49 | 38 | 1 | 0 | 1 | 0 | 34 | 4 | 0 | .118 |
| 1955 | 2 | 4 | .333 | 3.32 | 17 | 7 | 0 | 59.2 | 56 | 21 | 23 | 0 | 1 | 1 | 0 | 19 | 2 | 0 | .105 |
| 1958 CHI N | 5 | 4 | .556 | 2.88 | 44 | 0 | 0 | 81.1 | 63 | 17 | 58 | 0 | 5 | 4 | 6 | 17 | 4 | 0 | .235 |
| 1959 | 9 | 8 | .529 | 2.68 | 65 | 0 | 0 | 134.1 | 111 | 26 | 115 | 0 | 9 | 8 | 12 | 31 | 6 | 0 | .194 |
| 1960 CIN N | 1 | 5 | .167 | 3.19 | 51 | 0 | 0 | 67.2 | 62 | 20 | 58 | 0 | 1 | 5 | 17 | 8 | 0 | 0 | .000 |
| 1961 | 2 | 1 | .667 | 2.19 | 47 | 0 | 0 | 53.1 | 50 | 15 | 53 | 0 | 2 | 1 | 16 | 5 | 0 | 0 | .000 |
| 1962 | 4 | 2 | .667 | 4.58 | 40 | 0 | 0 | 37.1 | 40 | 20 | 35 | 0 | 4 | 2 | 11 | 3 | 1 | 0 | .333 |
| 1963 | 1 | 3 | .250 | 4.15 | 47 | 0 | 0 | 52 | 55 | 11 | 45 | 0 | 1 | 3 | 14 | 6 | 1 | 0 | .167 |
| 1964 | 2 | 2 | .500 | 0.87 | 37 | 0 | 0 | 52 | 31 | 12 | 28 | 0 | 2 | 2 | 6 | 6 | 3 | 0 | .500 |
| 1965 2 teams | | | CIN N | (3G 2–0) | | | SF N | (35G 2–2) | | | | | | | | | | | |
| " total | 4 | 2 | .667 | 3.26 | 38 | 0 | 0 | 47 | 43 | 9 | 40 | 0 | 4 | 2 | 4 | 5 | 1 | 0 | .200 |
| 1966 SF N | 1 | 1 | .500 | 2.49 | 35 | 0 | 0 | 21.2 | 15 | 10 | 15 | 0 | 1 | 1 | 1 | 2 | 0 | 0 | .000 |
| 1967 | 2 | 0 | 1.000 | 2.05 | 28 | 1 | 0 | 22 | 16 | 9 | 23 | 0 | 2 | 0 | 2 | 1 | 0 | 0 | .000 |
| 1968 2 teams | | | SF N | (7G 0–2) | | | PIT N | (10G 0–0) | | | | | | | | | | | |
| " total | 0 | 2 | .000 | 7.48 | 17 | 1 | 0 | 21.2 | 33 | 6 | 9 | 0 | 0 | 1 | 0 | 3 | 0 | 0 | .000 |
| 1969 HOU N | 0 | 0 | – | 0.00 | 3 | 0 | 0 | 5 | 2 | 2 | 2 | 0 | 0 | 0 | 0 | 0 | 0 | 0 | – |
| 16 yrs. | 46 | 50 | .479 | 3.26 | 527 | 44 | 12 | 913 | 842 | 296 | 621 | 2 | 33 | 31 | 90 | 203 | 36 | 0 | .177 |
| 2 yrs. | 14 | 12 | .538 | 2.75 | 109 | 0 | 0 | 215.2 | 174 | 43 | 173 | 0 | 14 | 12 | 18 | 48 | 10 | 0 | .208 |

WORLD SERIES

| 1961 CIN N | 0 | 0 | – | 19.29 | 2 | 0 | 0 | 2.1 | 4 | 2 | 3 | 0 | 0 | 0 | 0 | 0 | 0 | 0 | – |
|---|---|---|---|---|---|---|---|---|---|---|---|---|---|---|---|---|---|---|---|

## Roy Henshaw

**HENSHAW, ROY KNICKELBINE**
B. July 29, 1911, Chicago, Ill.
BR TL 5'8" 155 lbs.

| | W | L | PCT | ERA | G | GS | CG | IP | H | BB | SO | ShO | W | L | SV | AB | H | HR | BA |
|---|---|---|---|---|---|---|---|---|---|---|---|---|---|---|---|---|---|---|---|
| 1933 CHI N | 2 | 1 | .667 | 4.19 | 21 | 0 | 0 | 38.2 | 32 | 20 | 16 | 0 | 2 | 1 | 0 | 10 | 2 | 0 | .200 |
| 1935 | 13 | 5 | .722 | 3.28 | 31 | 18 | 7 | 142.2 | 135 | 68 | 53 | 3 | 4 | 0 | 1 | 51 | 13 | 0 | .255 |
| 1936 | 6 | 5 | .545 | 3.97 | 39 | 14 | 6 | 129.1 | 152 | 56 | 69 | 2 | 1 | 3 | 1 | 44 | 6 | 0 | .136 |
| 1937 BKN N | 5 | 12 | .294 | 5.07 | 42 | 16 | 5 | 156.1 | 176 | 69 | 98 | 0 | 1 | 3 | 2 | 48 | 8 | 0 | .167 |
| 1938 STL N | 5 | 11 | .313 | 4.02 | 27 | 15 | 4 | 130 | 132 | 48 | 34 | 0 | 2 | 1 | 0 | 41 | 9 | 0 | .220 |
| 1942 DET A | 4 | 8 | .333 | 4.09 | 23 | 2 | 0 | 61.2 | 63 | 27 | 24 | 0 | 2 | 3 | 1 | 12 | 1 | 0 | .083 |
| 1943 | 0 | 2 | .000 | 3.79 | 26 | 3 | 0 | 71.1 | 75 | 33 | 33 | 0 | 0 | 1 | 2 | 18 | 2 | 0 | .111 |
| 1944 | 0 | 0 | – | 8.76 | 7 | 1 | 0 | 12.1 | 17 | 6 | 10 | 0 | 0 | 0 | 0 | 5 | 0 | 0 | .000 |
| 8 yrs. | 33 | 40 | .452 | 4.16 | 216 | 69 | 22 | 742.1 | 782 | 327 | 337 | 5 | 12 | 12 | 7 | 229 | 41 | 0 | .179 |
| 3 yrs. | 21 | 11 | .656 | 3.68 | 91 | 32 | 13 | 310.2 | 319 | 144 | 138 | 5 | 7 | 4 | 2 | 105 | 21 | 0 | .200 |

WORLD SERIES

| 1935 CHI N | 0 | 0 | – | 7.36 | 1 | 0 | 0 | 3.2 | 2 | 5 | 2 | 0 | 0 | 0 | 0 | 1 | 0 | 0 | .000 |
|---|---|---|---|---|---|---|---|---|---|---|---|---|---|---|---|---|---|---|---|

## Ramon Hernandez

**HERNANDEZ, RAMON GONZALEZ**
B. Aug. 31, 1940, Carolina, Puerto Rico
BB TL 5'11" 165 lbs.

| | W | L | PCT | ERA | G | GS | CG | IP | H | BB | SO | ShO | W | L | SV | AB | H | HR | BA |
|---|---|---|---|---|---|---|---|---|---|---|---|---|---|---|---|---|---|---|---|
| 1967 ATL N | 0 | 2 | .000 | 4.18 | 46 | 0 | 0 | 51.2 | 60 | 14 | 28 | 0 | 0 | 2 | 5 | 4 | 0 | 0 | .000 |
| 1968 CHI N | 0 | 0 | – | 9.00 | 8 | 0 | 0 | 9 | 14 | 0 | 3 | 0 | 0 | 0 | 0 | 0 | 0 | 0 | – |
| 1971 PIT N | 0 | 1 | .000 | 0.75 | 10 | 0 | 0 | 12 | 5 | 2 | 7 | 0 | 0 | 1 | 4 | 2 | 1 | 0 | .500 |
| 1972 | 5 | 0 | 1.000 | 1.67 | 53 | 0 | 0 | 70 | 50 | 22 | 47 | 0 | 5 | 0 | 14 | 12 | 2 | 0 | .167 |
| 1973 | 4 | 5 | .444 | 2.41 | 59 | 0 | 0 | 89.2 | 71 | 25 | 64 | 0 | 4 | 5 | 11 | 8 | 1 | 0 | .125 |
| 1974 | 5 | 2 | .714 | 2.74 | 58 | 0 | 0 | 69 | 68 | 18 | 33 | 0 | 5 | 2 | 2 | 4 | 1 | 0 | .250 |
| 1975 | 7 | 2 | .778 | 2.95 | 46 | 0 | 0 | 64 | 62 | 28 | 43 | 0 | 7 | 2 | 5 | 6 | 0 | 0 | .000 |

| | W | L | PCT | ERA | G | GS | CG | IP | H | BB | SO | ShO | W | L | SV | AB | H | HR | BA |
|---|---|---|---|---|---|---|---|---|---|---|---|---|---|---|---|---|---|---|---|
| | | | | | | | | | | | | | **Relief Pitching** | | | **BATTING** | | | |

## Ramon Hernandez continued

| | W | L | PCT | ERA | G | GS | CG | IP | H | BB | SO | ShO | W | L | SV | AB | H | HR | BA |
|---|---|---|---|---|---|---|---|---|---|---|---|---|---|---|---|---|---|---|---|
| 1976 **2 teams** | | | **PIT N** (37G 2–2) | | **CHI N** (2G 0–0) | | | | | | | | | | | | | | |
| " total | 2 | 2 | .500 | 3.43 | 39 | 0 | 0 | 44.2 | 44 | 16 | 18 | 0 | 2 | 2 | 3 | 3 | 0 | 0 | .000 |
| 1977 **2 teams** | | | **CHI N** (6G 0–0) | | **BOS A** (12G 0–1) | | | | | | | | | | | | | | |
| " total | 0 | 1 | .000 | 6.53 | 18 | 0 | 0 | 20.2 | 25 | 10 | 12 | 0 | 0 | 1 | 2 | 1 | 0 | 0 | .000 |
| 9 yrs. | 23 | 15 | .605 | 3.03 | 337 | 0 | 0 | 430.2 | 399 | 135 | 255 | 0 | 23 | 15 | 46 | 40 | 5 | 0 | .125 |
| 3 yrs. | 0 | 0 | — | 7.71 | 16 | 0 | 0 | 18.2 | 27 | 3 | 8 | 0 | 0 | 0 | 1 | 1 | 0 | 0 | .000 |

### LEAGUE CHAMPIONSHIP SERIES

| | W | L | PCT | ERA | G | GS | CG | IP | H | BB | SO | ShO | W | L | SV | AB | H | HR | BA |
|---|---|---|---|---|---|---|---|---|---|---|---|---|---|---|---|---|---|---|---|
| 1972 **PIT N** | 0 | 0 | — | 2.70 | 3 | 0 | 0 | 3.1 | 1 | 0 | 3 | 0 | 0 | 0 | 1 | 0 | 0 | 0 | — |
| 1974 | 0 | 0 | — | 0.00 | 2 | 0 | 0 | 4.1 | 3 | 1 | 2 | 0 | 0 | 0 | 0 | 1 | 0 | 0 | .000 |
| 1975 | 0 | 1 | .000 | 27.00 | 1 | 0 | 0 | .2 | 3 | 0 | 0 | 0 | 0 | 1 | 0 | 0 | 0 | 0 | — |
| 3 yrs. | 0 | 1 | .000 | 3.24 | 6 | 0 | 0 | 8.1 | 7 | 1 | 5 | 0 | 0 | 1 | 1 | 1 | 0 | 0 | .000 |

## Willie Hernandez

**HERNANDEZ, GUILLERMO**  BL TL 6'3" 180 lbs.
Born Guillermo Hernandez Villanueva.
B. Nov. 14, 1955, Aguada, Puerto Rico

| | W | L | PCT | ERA | G | GS | CG | IP | H | BB | SO | ShO | W | L | SV | AB | H | HR | BA |
|---|---|---|---|---|---|---|---|---|---|---|---|---|---|---|---|---|---|---|---|
| 1977 **CHI N** | 8 | 7 | .533 | 3.03 | 67 | 1 | 0 | 110 | 94 | 28 | 78 | 0 | 8 | 6 | 4 | 16 | 1 | 0 | .063 |
| 1978 | 8 | 2 | .800 | 3.75 | 54 | 0 | 0 | 60 | 57 | 35 | 38 | 0 | 8 | 2 | 3 | 1 | 0 | 0 | .000 |
| 1979 | 4 | 4 | .500 | 5.01 | 51 | 2 | 0 | 79 | 85 | 39 | 53 | 0 | 4 | 3 | 0 | 8 | 2 | 0 | .250 |
| 1980 | 1 | 9 | .100 | 4.42 | 53 | 7 | 0 | 108 | 115 | 45 | 75 | 0 | 1 | 3 | 0 | 19 | 4 | 0 | .211 |
| 1981 | 0 | 0 | — | 3.86 | 12 | 0 | 0 | 14 | 14 | 8 | 13 | 0 | 0 | 0 | 2 | 0 | 0 | 0 | — |
| 1982 | 4 | 6 | .400 | 3.00 | 75 | 0 | 0 | 75 | 74 | 24 | 54 | 0 | 4 | 6 | 10 | 3 | 0 | 0 | .000 |
| 1983 **2 teams** | | | **CHI N** (11G 1–0) | | **PHI N** (63G 8–4) | | | | | | | | | | | | | | |
| " total | 9 | 4 | .692 | 3.28 | 74 | 1 | 0 | 115.1 | 109 | 32 | 93 | 0 | 9 | 4 | 8 | 15 | 6 | 0 | .400 |
| 1984 **DET A** | 9 | 3 | .750 | 1.92 | 80 | 0 | 0 | 140.1 | 96 | 36 | 112 | 0 | 9 | 3 | 32 | 0 | 0 | 0 | — |
| 1985 | 8 | 10 | .444 | 2.70 | 74 | 0 | 0 | 106.2 | 82 | 14 | 76 | 0 | 8 | 10 | 31 | 1 | 0 | 0 | .000 |
| 9 yrs. | 51 | 45 | .531 | 3.27 | 540 | 11 | 0 | 808.1 | 726 | 261 | 592 | 0 | 51 | 37 | 90 | 63 | 13 | 0 | .206 |
| 7 yrs. | 26 | 28 | .481 | 3.81 | 323 | 11 | 0 | 465.2 | 455 | 185 | 329 | 0 | 26 | 20 | 20 | 49 | 8 | 0 | .163 |
| | | | | | | | | | | | | | **8th** | | | | | | |

### LEAGUE CHAMPIONSHIP SERIES

| | W | L | PCT | ERA | G | GS | CG | IP | H | BB | SO | ShO | W | L | SV | AB | H | HR | BA |
|---|---|---|---|---|---|---|---|---|---|---|---|---|---|---|---|---|---|---|---|
| 1984 **DET A** | 0 | 0 | — | 2.25 | 3 | 0 | 0 | 4 | 3 | 1 | 3 | 0 | 0 | 0 | 1 | 0 | 0 | 0 | — |

### WORLD SERIES

| | W | L | PCT | ERA | G | GS | CG | IP | H | BB | SO | ShO | W | L | SV | AB | H | HR | BA |
|---|---|---|---|---|---|---|---|---|---|---|---|---|---|---|---|---|---|---|---|
| 1983 **PHI N** | 0 | 0 | — | 0.00 | 3 | 0 | 0 | 4 | 0 | 1 | 4 | 0 | 0 | 0 | 0 | 0 | 0 | 0 | — |
| 1984 **DET A** | 0 | 0 | — | 1.69 | 3 | 0 | 0 | 5.1 | 4 | 0 | 0 | 0 | 0 | 0 | 2 | 0 | 0 | 0 | — |
| 2 yrs. | 0 | 0 | — | 0.96 | 6 | 0 | 0 | 9.1 | 4 | 1 | 4 | 0 | 0 | 0 | 2 | 0 | 0 | 0 | — |
| | | | | | | | | | | | | | **10th** | | | | | | |

## LeRoy Herrmann

**HERRMANN, LeROY GEORGE**  BR TR 5'10" 185 lbs.
B. Feb. 27, 1906, Steward, Ill.    D. July 3, 1972, Escalon, Calif.

| | W | L | PCT | ERA | G | GS | CG | IP | H | BB | SO | ShO | W | L | SV | AB | H | HR | BA |
|---|---|---|---|---|---|---|---|---|---|---|---|---|---|---|---|---|---|---|---|
| 1932 **CHI N** | 2 | 1 | .667 | 6.39 | 7 | 0 | 0 | 12.2 | 18 | 9 | 5 | 0 | 2 | 1 | 0 | 2 | 1 | 0 | .500 |
| 1933 | 0 | 1 | .000 | 5.57 | 9 | 1 | 0 | 21 | 26 | 8 | 4 | 0 | 0 | 0 | 1 | 6 | 1 | 0 | .167 |
| 1935 **CIN N** | 3 | 5 | .375 | 3.58 | 29 | 8 | 2 | 108 | 124 | 31 | 30 | 0 | 1 | 0 | 0 | 30 | 8 | 0 | .267 |
| 3 yrs. | 5 | 7 | .417 | 4.13 | 45 | 9 | 2 | 141.2 | 168 | 48 | 39 | 0 | 3 | 1 | 1 | 38 | 10 | 0 | .263 |
| 2 yrs. | 2 | 2 | .500 | 5.88 | 16 | 1 | 0 | 33.2 | 44 | 17 | 9 | 0 | 2 | 1 | 1 | 8 | 2 | 0 | .250 |

## John Hibbard

**HIBBARD, JOHN DENISON**
B. Dec. 2, 1864, Chicago, Ill.    D. Nov. 17, 1937, Los Angeles, Calif.

| | W | L | PCT | ERA | G | GS | CG | IP | H | BB | SO | ShO | W | L | SV | AB | H | HR | BA |
|---|---|---|---|---|---|---|---|---|---|---|---|---|---|---|---|---|---|---|---|
| 1884 **CHI N** | 1 | 1 | .500 | 2.65 | 2 | 2 | 2 | 17 | 18 | 9 | 4 | 1 | 0 | 0 | 0 | 7 | 0 | 0 | .000 |

## Jim Hickman

**HICKMAN, JAMES LUCIUS**  BR TR 6'3" 192 lbs.
B. May 10, 1937, Henning, Tenn.

| | W | L | PCT | ERA | G | GS | CG | IP | H | BB | SO | ShO | W | L | SV | AB | H | HR | BA |
|---|---|---|---|---|---|---|---|---|---|---|---|---|---|---|---|---|---|---|---|
| 1967 **LA N** | 0 | 0 | — | 4.50 | 1 | 0 | 0 | 2 | 2 | 0 | 0 | 0 | 0 | 0 | 0 | * | | | |

## Kirby Higbe

**HIGBE, WALTER KIRBY**  BR TR 5'11" 190 lbs.
B. Apr. 8, 1915, Columbia, S. C.    D. May 6, 1985, Columbia, S. C.

| | W | L | PCT | ERA | G | GS | CG | IP | H | BB | SO | ShO | W | L | SV | AB | H | HR | BA |
|---|---|---|---|---|---|---|---|---|---|---|---|---|---|---|---|---|---|---|---|
| 1937 **CHI N** | 1 | 0 | 1.000 | 5.40 | 1 | 0 | 0 | 5 | 4 | 1 | 2 | 0 | 1 | 0 | 0 | 3 | 0 | 0 | .000 |
| 1938 | 0 | 0 | — | 5.40 | 2 | 2 | 0 | 10 | 10 | 6 | 4 | 0 | 0 | 0 | 0 | 3 | 0 | 0 | .000 |
| 1939 **2 teams** | | | **CHI N** (9G 2–1) | | **PHI N** (34G 10–14) | | | | | | | | | | | | | | |
| " total | 12 | 15 | .444 | 4.67 | 43 | 28 | 14 | 210 | 220 | **123** | 95 | 1 | 1 | 1 | 2 | 73 | 13 | 0 | .178 |
| 1940 **PHI N** | 14 | 19 | .424 | 3.72 | 41 | 36 | 20 | 283 | 242 | **121** | **137** | 1 | 1 | 0 | 1 | 103 | 17 | 0 | .165 |
| 1941 **BKN N** | **22** | 9 | .710 | 3.14 | **48** | **39** | 19 | 298 | 244 | **132** | 121 | 2 | 1 | 2 | 3 | 112 | 21 | 0 | .188 |
| 1942 | 16 | 11 | .593 | 3.25 | 38 | 32 | 13 | 221.2 | 180 | 106 | 115 | 2 | 1 | 2 | 0 | 77 | 8 | 0 | .104 |
| 1943 | 13 | 10 | .565 | 3.70 | 35 | 27 | 8 | 185 | 189 | 95 | 108 | 1 | 1 | 2 | 0 | 65 | 9 | 1 | .138 |
| 1946 | 17 | 8 | .680 | 3.03 | 42 | 29 | 11 | 210.2 | 178 | 107 | 134 | 3 | 2 | 2 | 1 | 77 | 10 | 0 | .130 |
| 1947 **2 teams** | | | **BKN N** (4G 2–0) | | **PIT N** (46G 11–17) | | | | | | | | | | | | | | |
| " total | 13 | 17 | .433 | 3.81 | 50 | 33 | 10 | 240.2 | 222 | **122** | 109 | 1 | 2 | 1 | 5 | 77 | 11 | 1 | .143 |
| 1948 **PIT N** | 8 | 7 | .533 | 3.36 | 56 | 8 | 3 | 158 | 140 | 83 | 86 | 0 | 6 | 4 | 10 | 48 | 10 | 1 | .208 |
| 1949 **2 teams** | | | **PIT N** (7G 0–2) | | **NY N** (37G 2–0) | | | | | | | | | | | | | | |
| " total | 2 | 2 | .500 | 5.08 | 44 | 3 | 0 | 95.2 | 97 | 53 | 43 | 0 | 2 | 1 | 2 | 18 | 1 | 0 | .056 |
| 1950 **NY N** | 0 | 3 | .000 | 4.93 | 18 | 1 | 0 | 34.2 | 37 | 30 | 17 | 0 | 0 | 2 | 0 | 4 | 1 | 0 | .250 |
| 12 yrs. | 118 | 101 | .539 | 3.69 | 418 | 238 | 98 | 1952.1 | 1763 | 979 | 971 | 11 | 18 | 17 | 24 | 660 | 101 | 3 | .153 |
| 3 yrs. | 3 | 1 | .750 | 4.06 | 12 | 4 | 0 | 37.2 | 26 | 29 | 22 | 0 | 2 | 0 | 0 | 13 | 2 | 0 | .154 |

### WORLD SERIES

| | W | L | PCT | ERA | G | GS | CG | IP | H | BB | SO | ShO | W | L | SV | AB | H | HR | BA |
|---|---|---|---|---|---|---|---|---|---|---|---|---|---|---|---|---|---|---|---|
| 1941 **BKN N** | 0 | 0 | — | 7.36 | 1 | 1 | 0 | 3.2 | 6 | 2 | 1 | 0 | 0 | 0 | 0 | 1 | 1 | 0 | 1.000 |

## Irv Higginbotham

**HIGGINBOTHAM, IRVING CLINTON**  BR TR
B. Apr. 26, 1882, Homer, Neb.    D. June 12, 1959, Seattle, Wash.

| | W | L | PCT | ERA | G | GS | CG | IP | H | BB | SO | ShO | W | L | SV | AB | H | HR | BA |
|---|---|---|---|---|---|---|---|---|---|---|---|---|---|---|---|---|---|---|---|
| 1906 **STL N** | 1 | 4 | .200 | 3.23 | 7 | 6 | 4 | 47.1 | 50 | 11 | 14 | 0 | 0 | 0 | 0 | 18 | 4 | 0 | .222 |
| 1908 | 3 | 8 | .273 | 3.20 | 19 | 11 | 7 | 107 | 113 | 33 | 38 | 1 | 0 | 1 | 0 | 38 | 5 | 0 | .132 |

| | W | L | PCT | ERA | G | GS | CG | IP | H | BB | SO | ShO | Relief Pitching W | L | SV | BATTING AB | H | HR | BA |
|---|---|---|---|---|---|---|---|---|---|---|---|---|---|---|---|---|---|---|---|

## Irv Higginbotham continued

| | W | L | PCT | ERA | G | GS | CG | IP | H | BB | SO | ShO | W | L | SV | AB | H | HR | BA |
|---|---|---|---|---|---|---|---|---|---|---|---|---|---|---|---|---|---|---|---|
| 1909 2 teams | STL | N | (3G 1–0) | | CHI | N | (19G 5–2) | | | | | | | | | | | | |
| " total | 6 | 2 | .750 | 2.12 | 22 | 7 | 5 | 89.1 | 69 | 22 | 34 | 0 | 3 | 1 | 0 | 29 | 6 | 0 | .207 |
| 3 yrs. | 10 | 14 | .417 | 2.81 | 48 | 24 | 16 | 243.2 | 232 | 66 | 86 | 1 | 3 | 2 | 0 | 85 | 15 | 0 | .176 |
| 1 yr. | 5 | 2 | .714 | 2.19 | 19 | 6 | 4 | 78 | 64 | 20 | 32 | 0 | 3 | 1 | 0 | 26 | 6 | 0 | .231 |

## Frank Hiller

**HILLER, FRANK WALTER (Dutch)**
B. July 13, 1920, Newark, N. J.                   BR TR 6'    200 lbs.

| | W | L | PCT | ERA | G | GS | CG | IP | H | BB | SO | ShO | W | L | SV | AB | H | HR | BA |
|---|---|---|---|---|---|---|---|---|---|---|---|---|---|---|---|---|---|---|---|
| 1946 NY A | 0 | 2 | .000 | 4.76 | 3 | 1 | 0 | 11.1 | 13 | 6 | 4 | 0 | 0 | 0 | 0 | 4 | 1 | 0 | .250 |
| 1948 | 5 | 2 | .714 | 4.04 | 22 | 5 | 1 | 62.1 | 59 | 30 | 25 | 0 | 3 | 1 | 0 | 16 | 6 | 0 | .375 |
| 1949 | 0 | 2 | .000 | 5.87 | 4 | 0 | 0 | 7.2 | 9 | 7 | 3 | 0 | 0 | 2 | 1 | 2 | 1 | 0 | .500 |
| 1950 CHI N | 12 | 5 | .706 | 3.53 | 38 | 17 | 9 | 153 | 153 | 32 | 55 | 2 | 2 | 1 | 1 | 44 | 5 | 0 | .114 |
| 1951 | 6 | 12 | .333 | 4.28 | 24 | 21 | 6 | 141.1 | 147 | 31 | 50 | 2 | 0 | 0 | 1 | 48 | 6 | 0 | .125 |
| 1952 CIN N | 5 | 8 | .385 | 4.63 | 28 | 15 | 6 | 124.1 | 129 | 37 | 50 | 1 | 0 | 3 | 1 | 30 | 5 | 0 | .167 |
| 1953 NY N | 2 | 1 | .667 | 6.15 | 19 | 1 | 0 | 33.2 | 43 | 15 | 10 | 0 | 2 | 0 | 0 | 4 | 2 | 0 | .500 |
| 7 yrs. | 30 | 32 | .484 | 4.42 | 138 | 60 | 22 | 533.2 | 553 | 158 | 197 | 5 | 7 | 7 | 4 | 148 | 26 | 0 | .176 |
| 2 yrs. | 18 | 17 | .514 | 4.16 | 62 | 38 | 15 | 294.1 | 300 | 63 | 105 | 4 | 2 | 1 | 2 | 92 | 11 | 0 | .120 |

## Dave Hillman

**HILLMAN, DARIUS DUTTON**
B. Sept. 14, 1927, Dungannon, Va.                 BR TR 5'11"    168 lbs.

| | W | L | PCT | ERA | G | GS | CG | IP | H | BB | SO | ShO | W | L | SV | AB | H | HR | BA |
|---|---|---|---|---|---|---|---|---|---|---|---|---|---|---|---|---|---|---|---|
| 1955 CHI N | 0 | 0 | – | 5.31 | 25 | 3 | 0 | 57.2 | 63 | 25 | 23 | 0 | 0 | 0 | 0 | 10 | 1 | 0 | .100 |
| 1956 | 0 | 2 | .000 | 2.19 | 2 | 2 | 0 | 12.1 | 11 | 5 | 6 | 0 | 0 | 0 | 0 | 4 | 0 | 0 | .000 |
| 1957 | 6 | 11 | .353 | 4.35 | 32 | 14 | 1 | 103.1 | 115 | 37 | 53 | 0 | 3 | 3 | 1 | 24 | 0 | 0 | .000 |
| 1958 | 4 | 8 | .333 | 3.15 | 31 | 16 | 3 | 125.2 | 132 | 31 | 65 | 0 | 0 | 1 | 1 | 41 | 6 | 0 | .146 |
| 1959 | 8 | 11 | .421 | 3.53 | 39 | 24 | 4 | 191 | 178 | 43 | 88 | 1 | 3 | 1 | 0 | 60 | 9 | 0 | .150 |
| 1960 BOS A | 0 | 3 | .000 | 5.65 | 16 | 3 | 0 | 36.2 | 41 | 12 | 14 | 0 | 0 | 1 | 0 | 6 | 0 | 0 | .000 |
| 1961 | 3 | 2 | .600 | 2.77 | 28 | 1 | 0 | 78 | 70 | 23 | 39 | 0 | 3 | 2 | 0 | 17 | 0 | 0 | .000 |
| 1962 2 teams | | | CIN | N | (2G 0–0) | | | NY | N | (13G 0–0) | | | | | | | | | |
| " total | 0 | 0 | – | 6.98 | 15 | 1 | 0 | 19.1 | 29 | 9 | 8 | 0 | 0 | 0 | 1 | 1 | 0 | 0 | .000 |
| 8 yrs. | 21 | 37 | .362 | 3.87 | 188 | 64 | 8 | 624 | 639 | 185 | 296 | 1 | 9 | 8 | 3 | 163 | 16 | 0 | .098 |
| 5 yrs. | 18 | 32 | .360 | 3.78 | 129 | 59 | 8 | 490 | 499 | 141 | 235 | 1 | 6 | 5 | 2 | 139 | 16 | 0 | .115 |

## Paul Hines

**HINES, PAUL A.**
B. Mar. 1, 1852, Washington, D. C.    D. July 10, 1935, Hyattsville, Md.    BR TR 5'9½"  173 lbs.

| | W | L | PCT | ERA | G | GS | CG | IP | H | BB | SO | ShO | W | L | SV | AB | H | HR | BA |
|---|---|---|---|---|---|---|---|---|---|---|---|---|---|---|---|---|---|---|---|
| 1884 PRO N | 0 | 0 | – | 0.00 | 1 | 0 | 0 | 1 | 3 | 0 | 0 | 0 | 0 | 0 | 0 | * | | | |

## Glen Hobbie

**HOBBIE, GLEN FREDERICK**
B. Apr. 24, 1936, Witt, Ill.                   BR TR 6'2"    195 lbs.

| | W | L | PCT | ERA | G | GS | CG | IP | H | BB | SO | ShO | W | L | SV | AB | H | HR | BA |
|---|---|---|---|---|---|---|---|---|---|---|---|---|---|---|---|---|---|---|---|
| 1957 CHI N | 0 | 0 | – | 10.38 | 2 | 0 | 0 | 4.1 | 6 | 5 | 3 | 0 | 0 | 0 | 0 | 2 | 0 | 0 | .000 |
| 1958 | 10 | 6 | .625 | 3.74 | 55 | 16 | 2 | 168.1 | 163 | 93 | 91 | 1 | 6 | 1 | 2 | 48 | 7 | 0 | .146 |
| 1959 | 16 | 13 | .552 | 3.69 | 46 | 33 | 10 | 234 | 204 | 106 | 138 | 3 | 0 | 1 | 0 | 79 | 9 | 0 | .114 |
| 1960 | 16 | 20 | .444 | 3.97 | 46 | 36 | 16 | 258.2 | 253 | 101 | 134 | 4 | 2 | 3 | 1 | 86 | 13 | 1 | .151 |
| 1961 | 7 | 13 | .350 | 4.26 | 36 | 29 | 7 | 198.2 | 207 | 54 | 103 | 2 | 1 | 0 | 2 | 66 | 11 | 2 | .167 |
| 1962 | 5 | 14 | .263 | 5.22 | 42 | 23 | 5 | 162 | 198 | 62 | 87 | 0 | 0 | 2 | 0 | 49 | 6 | 0 | .122 |
| 1963 | 7 | 10 | .412 | 3.92 | 36 | 24 | 4 | 165.1 | 172 | 49 | 94 | 1 | 1 | 0 | 0 | 50 | 4 | 0 | .080 |
| 1964 2 teams | | | CHI | N | (8G 0–3) | | | STL | N | (13G 1–2) | | | | | | | | | |
| " total | 1 | 5 | .167 | 5.65 | 21 | 9 | 1 | 71.2 | 80 | 25 | 32 | 0 | 0 | 0 | 1 | 18 | 2 | 1 | .111 |
| 8 yrs. | 62 | 81 | .434 | 4.20 | 284 | 170 | 45 | 1263 | 1283 | 495 | 682 | 11 | 10 | 7 | 6 | 398 | 52 | 4 | .131 |
| 8 yrs. | 61 | 79 | .436 | 4.20 | 271 | 165 | 44 | 1218.2 | 1242 | 480 | 664 | 11 | 10 | 7 | 5 | 385 | 50 | 3 | .130 |

## Billy Hoeft

**HOEFT, WILLIAM FREDERICK**
B. May 17, 1932, Oshkosh, Wis.                   BL TL 6'3"    180 lbs.

| | W | L | PCT | ERA | G | GS | CG | IP | H | BB | SO | ShO | W | L | SV | AB | H | HR | BA |
|---|---|---|---|---|---|---|---|---|---|---|---|---|---|---|---|---|---|---|---|
| 1952 DET A | 2 | 7 | .222 | 4.32 | 34 | 10 | 1 | 125 | 123 | 63 | 67 | 0 | 0 | 2 | 4 | 40 | 6 | 0 | .150 |
| 1953 | 9 | 14 | .391 | 4.83 | 29 | 27 | 9 | 197.2 | 223 | 58 | 90 | 0 | 0 | 0 | 2 | 64 | 11 | 0 | .172 |
| 1954 | 7 | 15 | .318 | 4.58 | 34 | 25 | 10 | 175 | 180 | 59 | 114 | 4 | 1 | 1 | 1 | 52 | 10 | 0 | .192 |
| 1955 | 16 | 7 | .696 | 2.99 | 32 | 29 | 17 | 220 | 187 | 75 | 133 | 7 | 0 | 1 | 0 | 82 | 17 | 0 | .207 |
| 1956 | 20 | 14 | .588 | 4.06 | 38 | 34 | 18 | 248 | 276 | 104 | 172 | 4 | 2 | 0 | 0 | 80 | 20 | 0 | .250 |
| 1957 | 9 | 11 | .450 | 3.48 | 34 | 28 | 10 | 207 | 188 | 69 | 111 | 1 | 0 | 0 | 1 | 67 | 10 | 3 | .149 |
| 1958 | 10 | 9 | .526 | 4.15 | 36 | 21 | 6 | 143 | 148 | 49 | 94 | 0 | 1 | 2 | 3 | 44 | 12 | 0 | .273 |
| 1959 3 teams | DET | A | (2G 1–1) | | BOS | A | (5G 0–3) | | BAL | A | (16G 1–1) | | | | | | | | |
| " total | 2 | 5 | .286 | 5.59 | 23 | 8 | 0 | 67.2 | 78 | 31 | 40 | 0 | 0 | 0 | 0 | 18 | 4 | 0 | .222 |
| 1960 BAL A | 2 | 1 | .667 | 4.34 | 19 | 0 | 0 | 18.2 | 18 | 14 | 14 | 0 | 2 | 1 | 0 | 1 | 0 | 0 | .000 |
| 1961 | 7 | 4 | .636 | 2.02 | 35 | 12 | 3 | 138 | 106 | 55 | 100 | 1 | 2 | 1 | 3 | 39 | 7 | 0 | .179 |
| 1962 | 4 | 8 | .333 | 4.59 | 57 | 4 | 0 | 113.2 | 103 | 43 | 73 | 0 | 4 | 6 | 7 | 19 | 3 | 0 | .158 |
| 1963 SF N | 2 | 0 | 1.000 | 4.44 | 23 | 0 | 0 | 24.1 | 26 | 10 | 8 | 0 | 2 | 0 | 4 | 1 | 1 | 0 | 1.000 |
| 1964 MIL N | 4 | 0 | 1.000 | 3.80 | 42 | 0 | 0 | 73.1 | 76 | 18 | 47 | 0 | 4 | 0 | 4 | 9 | 2 | 0 | .222 |
| 1965 CHI N | 4 | 2 | .500 | 2.81 | 29 | 2 | 1 | 51.1 | 41 | 20 | 44 | 0 | 1 | 1 | 1 | 11 | 3 | 0 | .273 |
| 1966 2 teams | | | CHI | N | (36G 1–2) | | | SF | N | (4G 0–2) | | | | | | | | | |
| " total | 1 | 4 | .200 | 4.84 | 40 | 0 | 0 | 44.2 | 47 | 17 | 33 | 0 | 1 | 4 | 3 | 4 | 1 | 0 | .250 |
| 15 yrs. | 97 | 101 | .490 | 3.94 | 505 | 200 | 75 | 1847.1 | 1820 | 685 | 1140 | 17 | 20 | 19 | 33 | 531 | 107 | 3 | .202 |
| 2 yrs. | 3 | 4 | .429 | 3.61 | 65 | 2 | 1 | 92.1 | 84 | 34 | 74 | 0 | 3 | 4 | 3 | 15 | 4 | 0 | .267 |

## Brad Hogg

**HOGG, CARTER BRADLEY**
B. Mar. 26, 1888, Buena Vista, Ga.    D. Apr. 2, 1935, Buena Vista, Ga.    BL TR 6'    185 lbs.

| | W | L | PCT | ERA | G | GS | CG | IP | H | BB | SO | ShO | W | L | SV | AB | H | HR | BA |
|---|---|---|---|---|---|---|---|---|---|---|---|---|---|---|---|---|---|---|---|
| 1911 BOS N | 0 | 3 | .000 | 6.66 | 8 | 3 | 2 | 25.2 | 33 | 14 | 8 | 0 | 0 | 1 | 0 | 9 | 4 | 0 | .444 |
| 1912 | 1 | 1 | .500 | 6.97 | 10 | 1 | 0 | 31 | 37 | 16 | 12 | 0 | 1 | 1 | 0 | 11 | 1 | 0 | .091 |
| 1915 CHI N | 1 | 0 | 1.000 | 2.08 | 2 | 2 | 1 | 13 | 12 | 6 | 0 | 1 | 0 | 0 | 0 | 3 | 0 | 0 | .000 |
| 1918 PHI N | 13 | 13 | .500 | 2.53 | 29 | 25 | 17 | 228 | 201 | 61 | 81 | 3 | 1 | 0 | 1 | 79 | 18 | 0 | .228 |

| | W | L | PCT | ERA | G | GS | CG | IP | H | BB | SO | ShO | Relief Pitching W | L | SV | BATTING AB | H | HR | BA |
|---|---|---|---|---|---|---|---|---|---|---|---|---|---|---|---|---|---|---|---|

## Brad Hogg continued

| | W | L | PCT | ERA | G | GS | CG | IP | H | BB | SO | ShO | W | L | SV | AB | H | HR | BA |
|---|---|---|---|---|---|---|---|---|---|---|---|---|---|---|---|---|---|---|---|
| 1919 | 5 | 12 | .294 | 4.43 | 22 | 19 | 13 | 150.1 | 163 | 55 | 48 | 0 | 0 | 1 | 0 | 60 | 17 | 0 | .283 |
| 5 yrs. | 20 | 29 | .408 | 3.70 | 71 | 50 | 33 | 448 | 446 | 152 | 149 | 4 | 2 | 3 | 1 | 162 | 40 | 0 | .247 |
| 1 yr. | 1 | 0 | 1.000 | 2.08 | 2 | 2 | 1 | 13 | 12 | 6 | 0 | 1 | 0 | 0 | 0 | 3 | 0 | 0 | .000 |

## Ed Holley

**HOLLEY, EDWARD EDGAR**      BR TR 6'1½" 195 lbs.
B. July 23, 1901, Benton, Ky.    D. Williamsport, Pa.

| | W | L | PCT | ERA | G | GS | CG | IP | H | BB | SO | ShO | W | L | SV | AB | H | HR | BA |
|---|---|---|---|---|---|---|---|---|---|---|---|---|---|---|---|---|---|---|---|
| 1928 CHI N | 0 | 0 | — | 3.77 | 13 | 1 | 0 | 31 | 16 | 10 | 10 | 0 | 0 | 0 | 0 | 5 | 0 | 0 | .000 |
| 1932 PHI N | 11 | 14 | .440 | 3.95 | 34 | 30 | 16 | 228 | 247 | 55 | 87 | 2 | 0 | 0 | 0 | 91 | 12 | 0 | .132 |
| 1933 | 13 | 15 | .464 | 3.53 | 30 | 28 | 12 | 206.2 | 219 | 62 | 56 | 3 | 0 | 1 | 0 | 74 | 12 | 0 | .162 |
| 1934 2 teams | | | PHI N | (15G 1–8) | | PIT N | (5G 0–3) | | | | | | | | | | | | |
| "   total | 1 | 11 | .083 | 8.12 | 20 | 17 | 2 | 82 | 105 | 37 | 16 | 0 | 0 | 0 | 0 | 26 | 7 | 0 | .269 |
| 4 yrs. | 25 | 40 | .385 | 4.40 | 97 | 76 | 30 | 547.2 | 602 | 170 | 169 | 5 | 0 | 1 | 0 | 196 | 31 | 0 | .158 |
| 1 yr. | 0 | 0 | — | 3.77 | 13 | 1 | 0 | 31 | 31 | 16 | 10 | 0 | 0 | 0 | 0 | 5 | 0 | 0 | .000 |

## John Hollison

**HOLLISON, JOHN HENRY (Swede)**      BR TL 5'8" 162 lbs.
B. May 3, 1870, Chicago, Ill.    D. Aug. 19, 1969, Chicago, Ill.

| | W | L | PCT | ERA | G | GS | CG | IP | H | BB | SO | ShO | W | L | SV | AB | H | HR | BA |
|---|---|---|---|---|---|---|---|---|---|---|---|---|---|---|---|---|---|---|---|
| 1892 CHI N | 0 | 0 | — | 2.25 | 1 | 0 | 0 | 4 | 1 | 0 | 2 | 0 | 0 | 0 | 0 | 3 | 0 | 0 | .000 |

## Ken Holtzman

**HOLTZMAN, KENNETH DALE**      BR TL 6'2" 175 lbs.
B. Nov. 3, 1945, St. Louis, Mo.

| | W | L | PCT | ERA | G | GS | CG | IP | H | BB | SO | ShO | W | L | SV | AB | H | HR | BA |
|---|---|---|---|---|---|---|---|---|---|---|---|---|---|---|---|---|---|---|---|
| 1965 CHI N | 0 | 0 | — | 2.25 | 3 | 0 | 0 | 4 | 2 | 3 | 3 | 0 | 0 | 0 | 0 | 0 | 0 | 0 | — |
| 1966 | 11 | 16 | .407 | 3.79 | 34 | 33 | 9 | 220.2 | 194 | 68 | 171 | 0 | 0 | 0 | 0 | 73 | 9 | 0 | .123 |
| 1967 | 9 | 0 | 1.000 | 2.53 | 12 | 12 | 3 | 92.2 | 76 | 44 | 62 | 0 | 0 | 0 | 0 | 35 | 7 | 0 | .200 |
| 1968 | 11 | 14 | .440 | 3.35 | 34 | 32 | 6 | 215 | 201 | 76 | 151 | 3 | 0 | 0 | 1 | 80 | 10 | 0 | .125 |
| 1969 | 17 | 13 | .567 | 3.59 | 39 | 39 | 12 | 261 | 248 | 93 | 176 | 6 | 0 | 0 | 0 | 100 | 15 | 1 | .150 |
| 1970 | 17 | 11 | .607 | 3.38 | 39 | 38 | 15 | 288 | 271 | 94 | 202 | 1 | 0 | 0 | 0 | 105 | 21 | 0 | .200 |
| 1971 | 9 | 15 | .375 | 4.48 | 30 | 29 | 9 | 195 | 213 | 64 | 143 | 3 | 0 | 0 | 0 | 69 | 9 | 1 | .130 |
| 1972 OAK A | 19 | 11 | .633 | 2.51 | 39 | 37 | 16 | 265 | 232 | 52 | 134 | 4 | 1 | 0 | 0 | 90 | 16 | 0 | .178 |
| 1973 | 21 | 13 | .618 | 2.97 | 40 | 40 | 16 | 297.1 | 275 | 66 | 157 | 4 | 0 | 0 | 0 | 0 | 0 | 0 | — |
| 1974 | 19 | 17 | .528 | 3.07 | 39 | 38 | 9 | 255 | 273 | 51 | 117 | 3 | 0 | 1 | 0 | 0 | 0 | 0 | — |
| 1975 | 18 | 14 | .563 | 3.14 | 39 | 38 | 13 | 266.1 | 217 | 108 | 122 | 2 | 1 | 0 | 0 | 2 | 0 | 0 | .000 |
| 1976 2 teams | | | BAL A | (13G 5–4) | | NY A | (21G 9–7) | | | | | | | | | | | | |
| "   total | 14 | 11 | .560 | 3.65 | 34 | 34 | 16 | 246.2 | 265 | 70 | 66 | 3 | 0 | 0 | 0 | 0 | 0 | 0 | — |
| 1977 NY A | 2 | 3 | .400 | 5.75 | 18 | 11 | 0 | 72 | 105 | 24 | 14 | 0 | 0 | 0 | 0 | 0 | 0 | 0 | — |
| 1978 2 teams | | | NY A | (5G 1–0) | | CHI N | (23G 0–3) | | | | | | | | | | | | |
| "   total | 1 | 3 | .250 | 5.60 | 28 | 9 | 0 | 70.2 | 82 | 44 | 39 | 0 | 0 | 0 | 0 | 10 | 2 | 0 | .200 |
| 1979 CHI N | 6 | 9 | .400 | 4.58 | 23 | 20 | 3 | 118 | 133 | 53 | 44 | 2 | 0 | 0 | 0 | 43 | 10 | 0 | .233 |
| 15 yrs. | 174 | 150 | .537 | 3.49 | 451 | 410 | 127 | 2867.1 | 2787 | 910 | 1601 | 31 | 2 | 1 | 3 | 607 | 99 | 2 | .163 |
| 9 yrs. | 80 | 81 | .497 | 3.76 | 237 | 209 | 57 | 1447.1 | 1399 | 530 | 988 | 15 | 0 | 0 | 3 | 515 | 83 | 2 | .161 |
| | | | | | | | | | | | **10th** | | | | | | | | |

**LEAGUE CHAMPIONSHIP SERIES**

| | W | L | PCT | ERA | G | GS | CG | IP | H | BB | SO | ShO | W | L | SV | AB | H | HR | BA |
|---|---|---|---|---|---|---|---|---|---|---|---|---|---|---|---|---|---|---|---|
| 1972 OAK A | 0 | 1 | .000 | 4.50 | 1 | 1 | 0 | 4 | 4 | 2 | 2 | 0 | 0 | 0 | 0 | 1 | 0 | 0 | .000 |
| 1973 | 1 | 0 | 1.000 | 0.82 | 1 | 1 | 1 | 11 | 3 | 1 | 7 | 0 | 0 | 0 | 0 | 0 | 0 | 0 | — |
| 1974 | 1 | 0 | 1.000 | 0.00 | 1 | 1 | 1 | 9 | 5 | 2 | 3 | 1 | 0 | 0 | 0 | 0 | 0 | 0 | — |
| 1975 | 0 | 2 | .000 | 4.09 | 2 | 2 | 0 | 11 | 12 | 1 | 7 | 0 | 0 | 0 | 0 | 0 | 0 | 0 | — |
| 4 yrs. | 2 | 3 | .400 | 2.06 | 5 | 5 | 2 | 35 | 24 | 6 | 19 | 1 | 0 | 0 | 0 | 1 | 0 | 0 | .000 |

**WORLD SERIES**

| | W | L | PCT | ERA | G | GS | CG | IP | H | BB | SO | ShO | W | L | SV | AB | H | HR | BA |
|---|---|---|---|---|---|---|---|---|---|---|---|---|---|---|---|---|---|---|---|
| 1972 OAK A | 1 | 0 | 1.000 | 2.13 | 3 | 2 | 0 | 12.2 | 11 | 3 | 4 | 0 | 0 | 0 | 0 | 5 | 0 | 0 | .000 |
| 1973 | 2 | 1 | .667 | 4.22 | 3 | 3 | 0 | 10.2 | 13 | 5 | 6 | 0 | 0 | 0 | 0 | 3 | 2 | 0 | .667 |
| 1974 | 1 | 0 | 1.000 | 1.50 | 2 | 2 | 0 | 12 | 13 | 4 | 10 | 0 | 0 | 0 | 0 | 4 | 2 | 1 | .500 |
| 3 yrs. | 4 | 1 | .800 | 2.55 | 8 | 7 | 0 | 35.1 | 37 | 12 | 20 | 0 | 0 | 0 | 0 | 12 | 4 | 1 | .333 |

## Burt Hooton

**HOOTON, BURT CARLTON (Happy)**      BR TR 6'1" 210 lbs.
B. Feb. 7, 1950, Greenville, Tex.

| | W | L | PCT | ERA | G | GS | CG | IP | H | BB | SO | ShO | W | L | SV | AB | H | HR | BA |
|---|---|---|---|---|---|---|---|---|---|---|---|---|---|---|---|---|---|---|---|
| 1971 CHI N | 2 | 0 | 1.000 | 2.14 | 3 | 3 | 2 | 21 | 8 | 10 | 22 | 1 | 0 | 0 | 0 | 7 | 0 | 0 | .000 |
| 1972 | 11 | 14 | .440 | 2.80 | 33 | 31 | 9 | 218.1 | 201 | 81 | 132 | 3 | 1 | 0 | 0 | 72 | 9 | 1 | .125 |
| 1973 | 14 | 17 | .452 | 3.68 | 42 | 34 | 9 | 240 | 248 | 73 | 134 | 2 | 1 | 2 | 0 | 70 | 9 | 0 | .129 |
| 1974 | 7 | 11 | .389 | 4.81 | 48 | 21 | 3 | 176 | 214 | 51 | 94 | 1 | 1 | 2 | 1 | 50 | 3 | 0 | .060 |
| 1975 2 teams | | | CHI N | (3G 0–2) | | LA N | (31G 18–7) | | | | | | | | | | | | |
| "   total | 18 | 9 | .667 | 3.07 | 34 | 33 | 12 | 234.2 | 190 | 68 | 153 | 4 | 0 | 1 | 0 | 73 | 9 | 0 | .123 |
| 1976 LA N | 11 | 15 | .423 | 3.26 | 33 | 33 | 8 | 226.2 | 203 | 60 | 116 | 4 | 0 | 0 | 0 | 62 | 6 | 0 | .097 |
| 1977 | 12 | 7 | .632 | 2.62 | 32 | 31 | 6 | 223 | 184 | 60 | 153 | 2 | 0 | 0 | 1 | 67 | 11 | 0 | .164 |
| 1978 | 19 | 10 | .655 | 2.71 | 32 | 32 | 10 | 236 | 196 | 61 | 104 | 3 | 0 | 0 | 0 | 67 | 10 | 0 | .149 |
| 1979 | 11 | 10 | .524 | 2.97 | 29 | 29 | 12 | 212 | 191 | 63 | 129 | 1 | 0 | 0 | 0 | 75 | 11 | 0 | .147 |
| 1980 | 14 | 8 | .636 | 3.65 | 34 | 33 | 4 | 207 | 194 | 64 | 118 | 2 | 0 | 0 | 0 | 64 | 4 | 1 | .063 |
| 1981 | 11 | 6 | .647 | 2.28 | 23 | 23 | 5 | 142 | 124 | 33 | 74 | 4 | 0 | 0 | 0 | 42 | 8 | 0 | .190 |
| 1982 | 4 | 7 | .364 | 4.03 | 21 | 21 | 2 | 120.2 | 130 | 33 | 51 | 2 | 0 | 0 | 0 | 35 | 3 | 1 | .086 |
| 1983 | 9 | 8 | .529 | 4.22 | 33 | 27 | 2 | 160 | 156 | 59 | 87 | 0 | 0 | 0 | 0 | 50 | 8 | 0 | .160 |
| 1984 | 3 | 6 | .333 | 3.44 | 54 | 6 | 0 | 110 | 109 | 43 | 62 | 0 | 3 | 4 | 4 | 14 | 1 | 0 | .071 |
| 1985 TEX A | 5 | 8 | .385 | 5.23 | 29 | 20 | 2 | 124 | 149 | 40 | 62 | 0 | 0 | 0 | 0 | 0 | 0 | 0 | — |
| 15 yrs. | 151 | 136 | .526 | 3.38 | 480 | 377 | 86 | 2651.1 | 2497 | 799 | 1491 | 29 | 6 | 9 | 7 | 748 | 92 | 4 | .123 |
| 5 yrs. | 34 | 44 | .436 | 3.71 | 129 | 92 | 23 | 666.1 | 689 | 219 | 387 | 7 | 3 | 5 | 1 | 202 | 21 | 1 | .104 |

**DIVISIONAL PLAYOFF SERIES**

| | W | L | PCT | ERA | G | GS | CG | IP | H | BB | SO | ShO | W | L | SV | AB | H | HR | BA |
|---|---|---|---|---|---|---|---|---|---|---|---|---|---|---|---|---|---|---|---|
| 1981 LA N | 1 | 0 | 1.000 | 1.29 | 1 | 1 | 0 | 7 | 3 | 3 | 2 | 0 | 0 | 0 | 0 | 3 | 0 | 0 | .000 |

**LEAGUE CHAMPIONSHIP SERIES**

| | W | L | PCT | ERA | G | GS | CG | IP | H | BB | SO | ShO | W | L | SV | AB | H | HR | BA |
|---|---|---|---|---|---|---|---|---|---|---|---|---|---|---|---|---|---|---|---|
| 1977 LA N | 0 | 0 | — | 16.20 | 1 | 1 | 0 | 1.2 | 2 | 4 | 1 | 0 | 0 | 0 | 0 | 1 | 1 | 0 | 1.000 |
| 1978 | 0 | 0 | — | 7.71 | 1 | 1 | 0 | 4.2 | 10 | 0 | 5 | 0 | 0 | 0 | 0 | 2 | 0 | 0 | .000 |
| 1981 | 2 | 0 | 1.000 | 0.00 | 2 | 2 | 0 | 14.2 | 11 | 6 | 7 | 0 | 0 | 0 | 0 | 5 | 0 | 0 | .000 |
| 3 yrs. | 2 | 0 | 1.000 | 3.00 | 4 | 4 | 0 | 21 | 23 | 10 | 13 | 0 | 0 | 0 | 0 | 8 | 1 | 0 | .125 |

**WORLD SERIES**

| | W | L | PCT | ERA | G | GS | CG | IP | H | BB | SO | ShO | W | L | SV | AB | H | HR | BA |
|---|---|---|---|---|---|---|---|---|---|---|---|---|---|---|---|---|---|---|---|
| 1977 LA N | 1 | 1 | .500 | 3.75 | 2 | 2 | 1 | 12 | 8 | 2 | 9 | 0 | 0 | 0 | 0 | 5 | 0 | 0 | .000 |

| | W | L | PCT | ERA | G | GS | CG | IP | H | BB | SO | ShO | Relief Pitching W | L | SV | BATTING AB | H | HR | BA |
|---|---|---|---|---|---|---|---|---|---|---|---|---|---|---|---|---|---|---|---|

## Burt Hooton continued

| | W | L | PCT | ERA | G | GS | CG | IP | H | BB | SO | ShO | W | L | SV | AB | H | HR | BA |
|---|---|---|---|---|---|---|---|---|---|---|---|---|---|---|---|---|---|---|---|
| 1978 | 1 | 1 | .500 | 6.48 | 2 | 2 | 0 | 8.1 | 13 | 3 | 6 | 0 | 0 | 0 | 0 | 0 | 0 | 0 | – |
| 1981 | 1 | 1 | .500 | 1.59 | 2 | 2 | 0 | 11.1 | 8 | 9 | 3 | 0 | 0 | 0 | 0 | 4 | 0 | 0 | .000 |
| 3 yrs. | 3 | 3 | .500 | 3.69 | 6 | 6 | 1 | 31.2 | 29 | 14 | 18 | 0 | 0 | 0 | 0 | 9 | 0 | 0 | .000 |

## Trader Horne

**HORNE, BERLYN DALE (Sonny)**  BR  TR  5'9"  155 lbs.
B. Apr. 12, 1899, Bachman, Ohio    D. Feb. 3, 1983, Franklin, Ohio

| | W | L | PCT | ERA | G | GS | CG | IP | H | BB | SO | ShO | W | L | SV | AB | H | HR | BA |
|---|---|---|---|---|---|---|---|---|---|---|---|---|---|---|---|---|---|---|---|
| 1929 CHI N | 1 | 1 | .500 | 5.09 | 11 | 1 | 0 | 23 | 24 | 21 | 6 | 0 | 1 | 1 | 0 | 5 | 2 | | .400 |

## Del Howard

**HOWARD, GEORGE ELMER**  BL  TR  6'  180 lbs.
Brother of Ivan Howard.
B. Dec. 24, 1877, Kenney, Ill.    D. Dec. 24, 1956, Seattle, Wash.

| | W | L | PCT | ERA | G | GS | CG | IP | H | BB | SO | ShO | W | L | SV | AB | H | HR | BA |
|---|---|---|---|---|---|---|---|---|---|---|---|---|---|---|---|---|---|---|---|
| 1905 PIT N | 0 | 0 | – | 0.00 | 1 | 0 | 0 | 6 | 4 | 1 | 0 | 0 | 0 | 0 | 0 | * | | | |

## Cal Howe

**HOWE, CALVIN EARL**  BL  TL  6'3"  205 lbs.
B. Nov. 27, 1924, Rock Falls, Ill.

| | W | L | PCT | ERA | G | GS | CG | IP | H | BB | SO | ShO | W | L | SV | AB | H | HR | BA |
|---|---|---|---|---|---|---|---|---|---|---|---|---|---|---|---|---|---|---|---|
| 1952 CHI N | 0 | 0 | – | 0.00 | 1 | 0 | 0 | 2 | 0 | 1 | 2 | 0 | 0 | 0 | 0 | 0 | 0 | 0 | – |

## Jay Howell

**HOWELL, JAY CANFIELD**  BR  TR  6'3"  200 lbs.
B. Nov. 26, 1955, Miami, Fla.

| | W | L | PCT | ERA | G | GS | CG | IP | H | BB | SO | ShO | W | L | SV | AB | H | HR | BA |
|---|---|---|---|---|---|---|---|---|---|---|---|---|---|---|---|---|---|---|---|
| 1980 CIN N | 0 | 0 | – | 15.00 | 5 | 0 | 0 | 3 | 8 | 0 | 1 | 0 | 0 | 0 | 0 | 0 | 0 | 0 | – |
| 1981 CHI N | 2 | 0 | 1.000 | 4.91 | 10 | 0 | 0 | 22 | 23 | 10 | 10 | 0 | 0 | 0 | 0 | 2 | 0 | 0 | .000 |
| 1982 NY A | 2 | 3 | .400 | 7.71 | 6 | 6 | 0 | 28 | 42 | 13 | 21 | 0 | 0 | 0 | 0 | 0 | 0 | 0 | – |
| 1983 | 1 | 5 | .167 | 5.38 | 19 | 12 | 2 | 82 | 89 | 35 | 61 | 0 | 0 | 0 | 0 | 0 | 0 | 0 | – |
| 1984 | 9 | 4 | .692 | 2.69 | 61 | 1 | 0 | 103.2 | 86 | 34 | 109 | 0 | 8 | 4 | 7 | 0 | 0 | 0 | – |
| 1985 OAK A | 9 | 8 | .529 | 2.85 | 63 | 0 | 0 | 98 | 98 | 31 | 68 | 0 | 9 | 8 | 29 | 0 | 0 | 0 | – |
| 6 yrs. | 23 | 20 | .535 | 4.06 | 164 | 21 | 2 | 336.2 | 346 | 123 | 270 | 0 | 17 | 12 | 36 | 2 | 0 | 0 | .000 |
| 1 yr. | 2 | 0 | 1.000 | 4.91 | 10 | 0 | 0 | 22 | 23 | 10 | 10 | 0 | 0 | 0 | 0 | 2 | 0 | 0 | .000 |

## Jim Hughes

**HUGHES, JAMES ROBERT**  BR  TR  6'1½"  200 lbs.
B. Mar. 21, 1923, Chicago, Ill.

| | W | L | PCT | ERA | G | GS | CG | IP | H | BB | SO | ShO | W | L | SV | AB | H | HR | BA |
|---|---|---|---|---|---|---|---|---|---|---|---|---|---|---|---|---|---|---|---|
| 1952 BKN N | 2 | 1 | .667 | 1.45 | 6 | 0 | 0 | 18.2 | 16 | 11 | 8 | 0 | 2 | 1 | 0 | 4 | 0 | 0 | .000 |
| 1953 | 4 | 3 | .571 | 3.47 | 48 | 0 | 0 | 85.2 | 80 | 41 | 49 | 0 | 4 | 3 | 9 | 14 | 4 | 0 | .286 |
| 1954 | 8 | 4 | .667 | 3.22 | 60 | 0 | 0 | 86.2 | 76 | 44 | 58 | 0 | 8 | 4 | 24 | 16 | 3 | 0 | .188 |
| 1955 | 0 | 2 | .000 | 4.22 | 24 | 0 | 0 | 42.2 | 41 | 19 | 20 | 0 | 0 | 2 | 6 | 10 | 0 | 0 | .000 |
| 1956 2 teams | | | BKN | N (5G 0–0) | | | CHI | N (25G 1–3) | | | | | | | | | | | |
| " total | 1 | 3 | .250 | 5.18 | 30 | 1 | 0 | 57.1 | 53 | 34 | 28 | 0 | 1 | 2 | 0 | 9 | 2 | 0 | .222 |
| 1957 CHI A | 0 | 0 | – | 10.80 | 4 | 0 | 0 | 5 | 12 | 3 | 2 | 0 | 0 | 0 | 0 | 0 | 0 | 0 | – |
| 6 yrs. | 15 | 13 | .536 | 3.83 | 172 | 1 | 0 | 296 | 278 | 152 | 165 | 0 | 15 | 12 | 39 | 53 | 9 | 0 | .170 |
| 1 yr. | 1 | 3 | .250 | 5.16 | 25 | 1 | 0 | 45.1 | 43 | 30 | 20 | 0 | 1 | 2 | 0 | 7 | 2 | 0 | .286 |

WORLD SERIES
| | W | L | PCT | ERA | G | GS | CG | IP | H | BB | SO | ShO | W | L | SV | AB | H | HR | BA |
|---|---|---|---|---|---|---|---|---|---|---|---|---|---|---|---|---|---|---|---|
| 1953 BKN N | 0 | 0 | – | 2.25 | 1 | 0 | 0 | 4 | 3 | 1 | 3 | 0 | 0 | 0 | 0 | 1 | 0 | 0 | .000 |

## Long Tom Hughes

**HUGHES, THOMAS JAMES**  BR  TR  6'1"
Brother of Ed Hughes.
B. Nov. 29, 1878, Chicago, Ill.    D. Feb. 8, 1956, Chicago, Ill.

| | W | L | PCT | ERA | G | GS | CG | IP | H | BB | SO | ShO | W | L | SV | AB | H | HR | BA |
|---|---|---|---|---|---|---|---|---|---|---|---|---|---|---|---|---|---|---|---|
| 1900 CHI N | 1 | 1 | .500 | 5.14 | 3 | 3 | 3 | 21 | 31 | 7 | 12 | 0 | 0 | 0 | 0 | 6 | 0 | 0 | .000 |
| 1901 | 11 | 21 | .344 | 3.24 | 37 | 35 | 32 | 308.1 | 309 | 115 | 225 | 1 | 1 | 0 | 0 | 118 | 14 | 0 | .119 |
| 1902 2 teams | | | BAL | A (13G 7–6) | | | BOS | A (9G 3–3) | | | | | | | | | | | |
| " total | 10 | 9 | .526 | 3.71 | 22 | 21 | 16 | 157.2 | 171 | 56 | 60 | 1 | 0 | 0 | 0 | 73 | 17 | 0 | .233 |
| 1903 BOS A | 20 | 7 | .741 | 2.57 | 33 | 31 | 25 | 244.2 | 232 | 60 | 112 | 5 | 0 | 1 | 0 | 93 | 26 | 1 | .280 |
| 1904 2 teams | | | NY | A (19G 7–11) | | | WAS | A (16G 2–13) | | | | | | | | | | | |
| " total | 9 | 24 | .273 | 3.59 | 35 | 32 | 26 | 260.2 | 274 | 82 | 123 | 2 | 0 | 2 | 1 | 111 | 26 | 1 | .234 |
| 1905 WAS A | 16 | 20 | .444 | 2.35 | 39 | 35 | 26 | 291.1 | 239 | 79 | 149 | 5 | 2 | 1 | 1 | 104 | 22 | 1 | .212 |
| 1906 | 7 | 17 | .292 | 3.62 | 30 | 24 | 18 | 204 | 230 | 81 | 90 | 1 | 1 | 1 | 0 | 66 | 14 | 1 | .212 |
| 1907 | 7 | 14 | .333 | 3.11 | 34 | 23 | 18 | 211 | 206 | 47 | 102 | 2 | 0 | 0 | 4 | 80 | 19 | 1 | .238 |
| 1908 | 18 | 15 | .545 | 2.21 | 43 | 31 | 24 | 276.1 | 224 | 77 | 165 | 3 | 3 | 1 | 4 | 87 | 17 | 0 | .195 |
| 1909 | 4 | 7 | .364 | 2.69 | 22 | 13 | 7 | 120.1 | 113 | 33 | 77 | 2 | 0 | 1 | 1 | 36 | 3 | 0 | .083 |
| 1911 | 11 | 17 | .393 | 3.47 | 34 | 27 | 17 | 223 | 251 | 77 | 86 | 2 | 2 | 1 | 0 | 81 | 15 | 1 | .185 |
| 1912 | 13 | 10 | .565 | 2.94 | 31 | 26 | 11 | 196 | 201 | 78 | 108 | 1 | 3 | 1 | 0 | 67 | 13 | 0 | .194 |
| 1913 | 4 | 12 | .250 | 4.30 | 36 | 13 | 4 | 129.2 | 129 | 61 | 59 | 0 | 2 | 3 | 6 | 36 | 4 | 0 | .111 |
| 13 yrs. | 131 | 174 | .430 | 3.09 | 399 | 314 | 227 | 2644 | 2610 | 853 | 1368 | 25 | 14 | 12 | 17 | 958 | 190 | 6 | .198 |
| 2 yrs. | 12 | 22 | .353 | 3.36 | 40 | 38 | 35 | 329.1 | 340 | 122 | 237 | 1 | 1 | 0 | 0 | 124 | 14 | 0 | .113 |

WORLD SERIES
| | W | L | PCT | ERA | G | GS | CG | IP | H | BB | SO | ShO | W | L | SV | AB | H | HR | BA |
|---|---|---|---|---|---|---|---|---|---|---|---|---|---|---|---|---|---|---|---|
| 1903 BOS A | 0 | 1 | .000 | 9.00 | 1 | 1 | 0 | 2 | 4 | 2 | 0 | 0 | 0 | 0 | 0 | 0 | 0 | 0 | – |

## Jim Hughey

**HUGHEY, JAMES ULYSSES (Cold Water Jim)**  TR  6'
B. Mar. 8, 1869, Coldwater, Mich.    D. Mar. 29, 1945, Coldwater, Mich.

| | W | L | PCT | ERA | G | GS | CG | IP | H | BB | SO | ShO | W | L | SV | AB | H | HR | BA |
|---|---|---|---|---|---|---|---|---|---|---|---|---|---|---|---|---|---|---|---|
| 1891 C-M AA | 1 | 0 | 1.000 | 3.00 | 2 | 1 | 1 | 15 | 18 | 3 | 9 | 0 | 0 | 0 | 0 | 7 | 1 | 0 | .143 |
| 1893 CHI N | 0 | 1 | .000 | 11.00 | 2 | 2 | 1 | 9 | 14 | 3 | 4 | 0 | 0 | 0 | 0 | 2 | 0 | 0 | .000 |
| 1896 PIT N | 6 | 8 | .429 | 4.99 | 25 | 14 | 11 | 155 | 171 | 67 | 48 | 0 | 2 | 0 | 0 | 65 | 14 | 0 | .215 |
| 1897 | 6 | 10 | .375 | 5.06 | 25 | 17 | 13 | 149.1 | 193 | 45 | 38 | 0 | 1 | 1 | 1 | 63 | 8 | 0 | .127 |
| 1898 STL N | 7 | 24 | .226 | 3.93 | 35 | 33 | 31 | 283.2 | 325 | 71 | 74 | 0 | 0 | 0 | 0 | 97 | 11 | 1 | .113 |
| 1899 CLE N | 4 | 30 | .118 | 5.41 | 36 | 34 | 32 | 283 | 403 | 88 | 54 | 0 | 0 | 2 | 0 | 111 | 18 | 0 | .162 |
| 1900 STL N | 5 | 7 | .417 | 5.20 | 20 | 12 | 11 | 112.2 | 147 | 40 | 23 | 0 | 0 | 0 | 0 | 41 | 7 | 0 | .171 |
| 7 yrs. | 29 | 80 | .266 | 4.87 | 145 | 113 | 100 | 1007.2 | 1271 | 317 | 250 | 0 | 3 | 3 | 1 | 386 | 59 | 1 | .153 |
| 1 yr. | 0 | 1 | .000 | 11.00 | 2 | 2 | 1 | 9 | 14 | 3 | 4 | 0 | 0 | 0 | 0 | 2 | 0 | 0 | .000 |

| | W | L | PCT | ERA | G | GS | CG | IP | H | BB | SO | ShO | Relief Pitching W | L | SV | BATTING AB | H | HR | BA |
|---|---|---|---|---|---|---|---|---|---|---|---|---|---|---|---|---|---|---|---|

## Bob Humphreys

**HUMPHREYS, ROBERT WILLIAM**
B. Aug. 18, 1935, Covington, Va.　　　BR TR 5'11" 165 lbs.

| Year | Tm | W | L | PCT | ERA | G | GS | CG | IP | H | BB | SO | ShO | RP W | RP L | SV | AB | H | HR | BA |
|---|---|---|---|---|---|---|---|---|---|---|---|---|---|---|---|---|---|---|---|---|
| 1962 | DET A | 0 | 1 | .000 | 7.20 | 4 | 0 | 0 | 5 | 8 | 2 | 3 | 0 | 0 | 1 | 1 | 0 | 0 | 0 | — |
| 1963 | STL N | 0 | 1 | .000 | 5.06 | 9 | 0 | 0 | 10.2 | 11 | 7 | 8 | 0 | 0 | 1 | 0 | 0 | 0 | 0 | — |
| 1964 | | 2 | 0 | 1.000 | 2.53 | 28 | 0 | 0 | 42.2 | 32 | 15 | 36 | 0 | 2 | 0 | 2 | 4 | 1 | 0 | .250 |
| 1965 | CHI N | 2 | 0 | 1.000 | 3.15 | 41 | 0 | 0 | 65.2 | 59 | 27 | 38 | 0 | 2 | 0 | 0 | 3 | 0 | 0 | .000 |
| 1966 | WAS A | 7 | 3 | .700 | 2.82 | 58 | 1 | 0 | 111.2 | 91 | 28 | 88 | 0 | 6 | 3 | 3 | 12 | 2 | 0 | .167 |
| 1967 | | 6 | 2 | .750 | 4.17 | 48 | 2 | 0 | 105.2 | 93 | 41 | 54 | 0 | 5 | 1 | 4 | 15 | 2 | 0 | .133 |
| 1968 | | 5 | 7 | .417 | 3.69 | 56 | 0 | 0 | 92.2 | 78 | 30 | 56 | 0 | 5 | 7 | 2 | 5 | 2 | 0 | .400 |
| 1969 | | 3 | 3 | .500 | 3.05 | 47 | 0 | 0 | 79.2 | 69 | 38 | 43 | 0 | 3 | 3 | 5 | 13 | 1 | 0 | .077 |
| 1970 | 2 teams | WAS A (5G 0-0) | | MIL A (23G 2-4) | | | | | | | | | | | | | | | | |
| " | total | 2 | 4 | .333 | 2.92 | 28 | 1 | 0 | 52.1 | 41 | 31 | 38 | 0 | 2 | 4 | 3 | 9 | 0 | 0 | .000 |
| | 9 yrs. | 27 | 21 | .563 | 3.36 | 319 | 4 | 0 | 566 | 482 | 219 | 364 | 0 | 25 | 20 | 20 | 61 | 8 | 0 | .131 |
| | 1 yr. | 2 | 0 | 1.000 | 3.15 | 41 | 0 | 0 | 65.2 | 59 | 27 | 38 | 0 | 2 | 0 | 0 | 3 | 0 | 0 | .000 |

WORLD SERIES

| 1964 | STL N | 0 | 0 | — | 0.00 | 1 | 0 | 0 | 1 | 0 | 0 | 1 | 0 | 0 | 0 | 0 | 0 | 0 | 0 | — |

## Bert Humphries

**HUMPHRIES, ALBERT**
B. Sept. 26, 1880, California, Pa.　　　D. Sept. 21, 1945, Orlando, Fla.　　　BR TR 5'11½" 182 lbs.

| Year | Tm | W | L | PCT | ERA | G | GS | CG | IP | H | BB | SO | ShO | RP W | RP L | SV | AB | H | HR | BA |
|---|---|---|---|---|---|---|---|---|---|---|---|---|---|---|---|---|---|---|---|---|
| 1910 | PHI N | 0 | 0 | — | 4.66 | 5 | 0 | 0 | 9.2 | 13 | 3 | 3 | 0 | 0 | 0 | 0 | 2 | 0 | 0 | .000 |
| 1911 | 2 teams | PHI N (11G 3-1) | | CIN N (14G 4-3) | | | | | | | | | | | | | | | | |
| " | total | 7 | 4 | .636 | 3.06 | 25 | 12 | 5 | 106 | 118 | 28 | 29 | 0 | 0 | 1 | 1 | 31 | 6 | 0 | .194 |
| 1912 | CIN N | 9 | 11 | .450 | 3.23 | 30 | 15 | 9 | 158.2 | 162 | 36 | 58 | 1 | 4 | 3 | 2 | 51 | 7 | 0 | .137 |
| 1913 | CHI N | 16 | 4 | .800 | 2.69 | 28 | 20 | 13 | 181 | 169 | 24 | 61 | 2 | 2 | 1 | 0 | 62 | 12 | 0 | .194 |
| 1914 | | 10 | 11 | .476 | 2.68 | 34 | 22 | 8 | 171 | 162 | 37 | 62 | 2 | 2 | 2 | 0 | 55 | 13 | 0 | .236 |
| 1915 | | 8 | 13 | .381 | 2.31 | 31 | 22 | 10 | 171.2 | 183 | 23 | 45 | 4 | 1 | 1 | 2 | 46 | 8 | 0 | .174 |
| | 6 yrs. | 50 | 43 | .538 | 2.79 | 153 | 91 | 45 | 798 | 807 | 151 | 258 | 9 | 9 | 8 | 6 | 247 | 46 | 0 | .186 |
| | 3 yrs. | 34 | 28 | .548 | 2.56 | 93 | 64 | 31 | 523.2 | 514 | 84 | 168 | 8 | 5 | 4 | 2 | 163 | 33 | 0 | .202 |

## Walter Huntzinger

**HUNTZINGER, WALTER HENRY (Shakes)**
B. Feb. 6, 1899, Pottsville, Pa.　　　D. Aug. 11, 1981, Upper Darby, Pa.　　　BR TR 6' 150 lbs.

| Year | Tm | W | L | PCT | ERA | G | GS | CG | IP | H | BB | SO | ShO | RP W | RP L | SV | AB | H | HR | BA |
|---|---|---|---|---|---|---|---|---|---|---|---|---|---|---|---|---|---|---|---|---|
| 1923 | NY N | 0 | 1 | .000 | 7.88 | 2 | 1 | 0 | 8 | 9 | 1 | 2 | 0 | 0 | 0 | 0 | 2 | 0 | 0 | .000 |
| 1924 | | 1 | 1 | .500 | 4.45 | 12 | 2 | 0 | 32.1 | 41 | 9 | 6 | 0 | 0 | 0 | 1 | 8 | 4 | 0 | .500 |
| 1925 | | 5 | 1 | .833 | 3.50 | 26 | 1 | 0 | 64.1 | 68 | 17 | 19 | 0 | 5 | 1 | 0 | 11 | 1 | 0 | .091 |
| 1926 | 2 teams | STL N (9G 0-4) | | CHI N (11G 1-1) | | | | | | | | | | | | | | | | |
| " | total | 1 | 5 | .167 | 2.73 | 20 | 4 | 2 | 62.2 | 61 | 22 | 13 | 0 | 1 | 2 | 2 | 15 | 1 | 0 | .067 |
| | 4 yrs. | 7 | 8 | .467 | 3.60 | 60 | 8 | 2 | 167.1 | 179 | 49 | 40 | 0 | 6 | 4 | 3 | 36 | 6 | 0 | .167 |
| | 1 yr. | 1 | 1 | .500 | 0.94 | 11 | 0 | 0 | 28.2 | 26 | 8 | 4 | 0 | 1 | 1 | 2 | 7 | 1 | 0 | .143 |

## Bill Hutchison

**HUTCHISON, WILLIAM FORREST (Wild Bill)**
B. Dec. 17, 1859, New Haven, Conn.　　　D. Mar. 19, 1926, Kansas City, Mo.　　　BR TR 5'9" 175 lbs.

| Year | Tm | W | L | PCT | ERA | G | GS | CG | IP | H | BB | SO | ShO | RP W | RP L | SV | AB | H | HR | BA |
|---|---|---|---|---|---|---|---|---|---|---|---|---|---|---|---|---|---|---|---|---|
| 1889 | CHI N | 16 | 17 | .485 | 3.54 | 37 | 36 | 33 | 318 | 306 | 117 | 136 | 3 | 0 | 0 | 0 | 133 | 21 | 1 | .158 |
| 1890 | | 42 | 25 | .627 | 2.70 | 71 | 66 | 65 | 603 | 505 | 199 | 289 | 5 | 1 | 1 | 2 | 261 | 53 | 2 | .203 |
| 1891 | | 43 | 19 | .694 | 2.81 | 66 | 58 | 56 | 561 | 508 | 178 | 261 | 4 | 7 | 0 | 1 | 243 | 45 | 2 | .185 |
| 1892 | | 37 | 34 | .521 | 2.74 | 75 | 71 | 67 | 627 | 572 | 187 | 316 | 5 | 1 | 2 | 0 | 263 | 57 | 1 | .217 |
| 1893 | | 16 | 23 | .410 | 4.75 | 44 | 40 | 38 | 348.1 | 420 | 156 | 80 | 2 | 0 | 1 | 0 | 162 | 41 | 0 | .253 |
| 1894 | | 14 | 15 | .483 | 6.06 | 36 | 34 | 28 | 277.2 | 373 | 140 | 59 | 0 | 1 | 0 | 0 | 136 | 42 | 6 | .309 |
| 1895 | | 13 | 21 | .382 | 4.73 | 38 | 35 | 30 | 291 | 371 | 129 | 85 | 2 | 0 | 0 | 0 | 126 | 25 | 0 | .198 |
| 1897 | STL N | 1 | 4 | .200 | 6.08 | 6 | 5 | 2 | 40 | 55 | 22 | 5 | 0 | 0 | 0 | 0 | 18 | 5 | 0 | .278 |
| | 8 yrs. | 182 | 158 | .535 | 3.59 | 373 | 345 | 319 | 3066 | 3110 | 1128 | 1231 | 21 | 10 | 4 | 3 | 1342 | 289 | 12 | .215 |
| | 7 yrs. | 181 | 154 | .540 | 3.56 | 367 | 340 | 317 | 3026 | 3055 | 1106 | 1226 | 21 | 10 | 4 | 3 | 1324 | 284 | 12 | .215 |
| | | | 3rd | 2nd | | | 5th | | 1st | 2nd | | 1st | 4th 10th | | | | | | | |

## Herb Hutson

**HUTSON, GEORGE HERBERT**
B. July 17, 1949, Savannah, Ga.　　　BR TR 6'2" 205 lbs.

| Year | Tm | W | L | PCT | ERA | G | GS | CG | IP | H | BB | SO | ShO | RP W | RP L | SV | AB | H | HR | BA |
|---|---|---|---|---|---|---|---|---|---|---|---|---|---|---|---|---|---|---|---|---|
| 1974 | CHI N | 0 | 2 | .000 | 3.41 | 20 | 2 | 0 | 29 | 24 | 15 | 22 | 0 | 0 | 0 | 0 | 2 | 0 | 0 | .000 |

## Frank Isbell

**ISBELL, WILLIAM FRANK (Bald Eagle)**
B. Aug. 21, 1875, Delevan, N.Y.　　　D. July 15, 1941, Wichita, Kans.　　　BL TR 5'11" 190 lbs.

| Year | Tm | W | L | PCT | ERA | G | GS | CG | IP | H | BB | SO | ShO | RP W | RP L | SV | AB | H | HR | BA |
|---|---|---|---|---|---|---|---|---|---|---|---|---|---|---|---|---|---|---|---|---|
| 1898 | CHI N | 4 | 7 | .364 | 3.56 | 13 | 9 | 7 | 81 | 86 | 42 | 16 | 0 | 1 | 1 | 0 | 159 | 37 | 0 | .233 |
| 1901 | CHI A | 0 | 0 | — | 9.00 | 1 | 0 | 0 | 1 | 2 | 0 | 0 | 0 | 0 | 0 | 0 | 556 | 143 | 3 | .257 |
| 1902 | | 0 | 0 | — | 9.00 | 1 | 1 | 0 | 1 | 3 | 1 | 1 | 0 | 0 | 0 | 0 | 515 | 130 | 4 | .252 |
| 1906 | | 0 | 0 | — | 0.00 | 1 | 0 | 0 | 2 | 1 | 0 | 2 | 0 | 0 | 0 | 0 | 549 | 153 | 0 | .279 |
| 1907 | | 0 | 0 | — | 0.00 | 1 | 0 | 0 | .1 | 0 | 0 | 0 | 0 | 0 | 0 | 0 | 486 | 118 | 0 | .243 |
| | 5 yrs. | 4 | 7 | .364 | 3.59 | 17 | 10 | 7 | 85.1 | 92 | 43 | 19 | 0 | 1 | 1 | 0 | * | | | |
| | 1 yr. | 4 | 7 | .364 | 3.56 | 13 | 9 | 7 | 81 | 86 | 42 | 16 | 0 | 1 | 1 | 0 | 159 | 37 | 0 | .233 |

## Larry Jackson

**JACKSON, LAWRENCE CURTIS**
B. June 2, 1931, Nampa, Ida.　　　BR TR 6'1½" 175 lbs.

| Year | Tm | W | L | PCT | ERA | G | GS | CG | IP | H | BB | SO | ShO | RP W | RP L | SV | AB | H | HR | BA |
|---|---|---|---|---|---|---|---|---|---|---|---|---|---|---|---|---|---|---|---|---|
| 1955 | STL N | 9 | 14 | .391 | 4.31 | 37 | 25 | 4 | 177.1 | 189 | 72 | 88 | 1 | 4 | 2 | 2 | 57 | 3 | 0 | .053 |
| 1956 | | 2 | 2 | .500 | 4.11 | 51 | 1 | 0 | 85.1 | 75 | 45 | 50 | 0 | 2 | 1 | 9 | 11 | 1 | 0 | .091 |
| 1957 | | 15 | 9 | .625 | 3.47 | 41 | 22 | 6 | 210.1 | 196 | 57 | 96 | 2 | 7 | 2 | 1 | 72 | 13 | 0 | .181 |
| 1958 | | 13 | 13 | .500 | 3.68 | 49 | 23 | 11 | 198 | 211 | 51 | 124 | 1 | 2 | 5 | 8 | 60 | 9 | 0 | .150 |
| 1959 | | 14 | 13 | .519 | 3.30 | 40 | 37 | 12 | 256 | 271 | 64 | 145 | 3 | 0 | 1 | 0 | 80 | 9 | 0 | .113 |
| 1960 | | 18 | 13 | .581 | 3.48 | 43 | 38 | 14 | 282 | 277 | 70 | 171 | 3 | 0 | 2 | 0 | 95 | 20 | 0 | .211 |
| 1961 | | 14 | 11 | .560 | 3.75 | 33 | 28 | 12 | 211 | 203 | 56 | 113 | 0 | 0 | 1 | 0 | 74 | 13 | 0 | .176 |
| 1962 | | 16 | 11 | .593 | 3.75 | 36 | 35 | 11 | 252.1 | 267 | 64 | 112 | 0 | 0 | 0 | 0 | 89 | 15 | 0 | .169 |
| 1963 | CHI N | 14 | 18 | .438 | 2.55 | 37 | 37 | 13 | 275 | 256 | 54 | 153 | 4 | 0 | 0 | 0 | 87 | 17 | 0 | .195 |
| 1964 | | 24 | 11 | .686 | 3.14 | 40 | 38 | 19 | 297.2 | 265 | 58 | 148 | 3 | 0 | 1 | 0 | 114 | 20 | 0 | .175 |
| 1965 | | 14 | 21 | .400 | 3.85 | 39 | 39 | 12 | 257.1 | 268 | 57 | 131 | 4 | 0 | 0 | 0 | 86 | 11 | 1 | .128 |

| | W | L | PCT | ERA | G | GS | CG | IP | H | BB | SO | ShO | Relief Pitching W | L | SV | BATTING AB | H | HR | BA |
|---|---|---|---|---|---|---|---|---|---|---|---|---|---|---|---|---|---|---|---|

## Larry Jackson continued

| | | W | L | PCT | ERA | G | GS | CG | IP | H | BB | SO | ShO | W | L | SV | AB | H | HR | BA |
|---|---|---|---|---|---|---|---|---|---|---|---|---|---|---|---|---|---|---|---|---|
| 1966 2 teams | CHI N (3G 0–2) | | | | | PHI N (35G 15–13) | | | | | | | | | | | | | | |
| " total | 15 | 15 | .500 | 3.32 | 38 | 35 | 12 | 255 | 257 | 62 | 112 | 5 | 1 | 0 | 0 | 92 | 13 | 1 | .141 |
| 1967 PHI N | 13 | 15 | .464 | 3.10 | 40 | 37 | 11 | 261.2 | 242 | 54 | 139 | 4 | 1 | 0 | 0 | 87 | 14 | 0 | .161 |
| 1968 | 13 | 17 | .433 | 2.77 | 34 | 34 | 12 | 243.2 | 229 | 60 | 127 | 2 | 0 | 0 | 0 | 85 | 12 | 0 | .141 |
| 14 yrs. | 194 | 183 | .515 | 3.40 | 558 | 429 | 149 | 3262.2 | 3206 | 824 | 1709 | 37 | 17 | 15 | 20 | 1089 | 170 | 2 | .156 |
| 4 yrs. | 52 | 52 | .500 | 3.26 | 119 | 116 | 44 | 838 | 803 | 173 | 437 | 11 | 0 | 1 | 0 | 290 | 48 | 1 | .166 |

## Elmer Jacobs

**JACOBS, WILLIAM ELMER**
B. Aug. 10, 1892, Salem, Mo.   D. Feb. 10, 1958, Salem, Mo.                    BR TR 6'        165 lbs.

| | | W | L | PCT | ERA | G | GS | CG | IP | H | BB | SO | ShO | W | L | SV | AB | H | HR | BA |
|---|---|---|---|---|---|---|---|---|---|---|---|---|---|---|---|---|---|---|---|---|
| 1914 PHI N | | 1 | 3 | .250 | 4.80 | 14 | 7 | 1 | 50.2 | 65 | 20 | 17 | 0 | 0 | 0 | 0 | 14 | 0 | 0 | .000 |
| 1916 PIT N | | 6 | 10 | .375 | 2.94 | 34 | 17 | 8 | 153 | 151 | 38 | 46 | 0 | 2 | 1 | 0 | 40 | 3 | 0 | .075 |
| 1917 | | 6 | 19 | .240 | 2.81 | 38 | 25 | 10 | 227.1 | 214 | 76 | 58 | 1 | 1 | 3 | 2 | 67 | 12 | 0 | .179 |
| 1918 2 teams | PIT N (8G 0–1) | | | | | PHI N (18G 9–5) | | | | | | | | | | | | | | |
| " total | | 9 | 6 | .600 | 2.95 | 26 | 18 | 12 | 146.1 | 122 | 56 | 35 | 4 | 0 | 1 | 1 | 45 | 8 | 0 | .178 |
| 1919 2 teams | PHI N (17G 6–10) | | | | | STL N (17G 3–6) | | | | | | | | | | | | | | |
| " total | | 9 | 16 | .360 | 3.32 | 34 | 23 | 17 | 214 | 231 | 69 | 68 | 1 | 2 | 1 | 1 | 68 | 16 | 0 | .235 |
| 1920 STL N | | 4 | 8 | .333 | 5.21 | 23 | 9 | 1 | 77.2 | 91 | 33 | 21 | 0 | 2 | 2 | 1 | 26 | 5 | 0 | .192 |
| 1924 CHI N | | 11 | 12 | .478 | 3.74 | 38 | 22 | 13 | 190.1 | 181 | 72 | 50 | 1 | 2 | 2 | 1 | 54 | 6 | 0 | .111 |
| 1925 | | 2 | 3 | .400 | 5.17 | 18 | 4 | 1 | 55.2 | 63 | 22 | 19 | 1 | 1 | 2 | 1 | 13 | 3 | 0 | .231 |
| 1927 CHI A | | 2 | 4 | .333 | 4.60 | 25 | 8 | 2 | 74.1 | 105 | 37 | 22 | 1 | 0 | 0 | 0 | 20 | 3 | 0 | .150 |
| 9 yrs. | | 50 | 81 | .382 | 3.55 | 250 | 133 | 65 | 1189.1 | 1223 | 423 | 336 | 9 | 10 | 12 | 7 | 347 | 56 | 0 | .161 |
| 2 yrs. | | 13 | 15 | .464 | 4.06 | 56 | 26 | 14 | 246 | 244 | 94 | 69 | 2 | 3 | 4 | 2 | 67 | 9 | 0 | .134 |

## Tony Jacobs

**JACOBS, ANTHONY ROBERT**
B. Aug. 5, 1925, Dixmoor, Ill.   D. Dec. 21, 1980, Nashville, Tenn.            BB TR 5'9"       150 lbs.

| | | W | L | PCT | ERA | G | GS | CG | IP | H | BB | SO | ShO | W | L | SV | AB | H | HR | BA |
|---|---|---|---|---|---|---|---|---|---|---|---|---|---|---|---|---|---|---|---|---|
| 1948 CHI N | | 0 | 0 | — | 4.50 | 1 | 0 | 0 | 2 | 3 | 0 | 2 | 0 | 0 | 0 | 0 | 0 | 0 | 0 | — |
| 1955 STL N | | 0 | 0 | — | 18.00 | 1 | 0 | 0 | 2 | 6 | 1 | 1 | 0 | 0 | 0 | 0 | 1 | 0 | 0 | .000 |
| 2 yrs. | | 0 | 0 | — | 11.25 | 2 | 0 | 0 | 4 | 9 | 1 | 3 | 0 | 0 | 0 | 0 | 1 | 0 | 0 | .000 |
| 1 yr. | | 0 | 0 | — | 4.50 | 1 | 0 | 0 | 2 | 3 | 0 | 2 | 0 | 0 | 0 | 0 | 0 | 0 | 0 | — |

## Paul Jaeckel

**JAECKEL, PAUL HENRY (Jake)**
B. Apr. 1, 1942, East Los Angeles, Calif.                                    BR TR 5'10"      170 lbs.

| | | W | L | PCT | ERA | G | GS | CG | IP | H | BB | SO | ShO | W | L | SV | AB | H | HR | BA |
|---|---|---|---|---|---|---|---|---|---|---|---|---|---|---|---|---|---|---|---|---|
| 1964 CHI N | | 1 | 0 | 1.000 | 0.00 | 4 | 0 | 0 | 8 | 4 | 3 | 2 | 0 | 1 | 0 | 1 | 1 | 0 | 0 | .000 |

## Joe Jaeger

**JAEGER, JOSEPH PETER (Zip)**
B. Mar. 3, 1895, St. Cloud, Minn.   D. Dec. 13, 1963, Hampton, Iowa           BR TR 6'3"       180 lbs.

| | | W | L | PCT | ERA | G | GS | CG | IP | H | BB | SO | ShO | W | L | SV | AB | H | HR | BA |
|---|---|---|---|---|---|---|---|---|---|---|---|---|---|---|---|---|---|---|---|---|
| 1920 CHI N | | 0 | 0 | — | 12.00 | 2 | 0 | 0 | 3 | 6 | 4 | 0 | 0 | 0 | 0 | 0 | 1 | 0 | 0 | .000 |

## Rick James

**JAMES, RICHARD LEE**
B. Oct. 11, 1947, Sheffield, Ala.                                            BR TR 6'2½" 205 lbs.

| | | W | L | PCT | ERA | G | GS | CG | IP | H | BB | SO | ShO | W | L | SV | AB | H | HR | BA |
|---|---|---|---|---|---|---|---|---|---|---|---|---|---|---|---|---|---|---|---|---|
| 1967 CHI N | | 0 | 1 | .000 | 13.50 | 3 | 1 | 0 | 4.2 | 9 | 2 | 2 | 0 | 0 | 0 | 0 | 1 | 0 | 0 | .000 |

## Hal Jeffcoat

**JEFFCOAT, HAROLD BENTLEY**
Brother of George Jeffcoat.
B. Sept. 6, 1924, West Columbia, S. C.                                       BR TR 5'10½" 185 lbs.

| | | W | L | PCT | ERA | G | GS | CG | IP | H | BB | SO | ShO | W | L | SV | AB | H | HR | BA |
|---|---|---|---|---|---|---|---|---|---|---|---|---|---|---|---|---|---|---|---|---|
| 1954 CHI N | | 5 | 6 | .455 | 5.19 | 43 | 3 | 1 | 104 | 110 | 58 | 35 | 0 | 4 | 4 | 7 | 31 | 8 | 1 | .258 |
| 1955 | | 8 | 6 | .571 | 2.95 | 50 | 1 | 0 | 100.2 | 107 | 53 | 32 | 0 | 8 | 6 | 6 | 23 | 4 | 1 | .174 |
| 1956 CIN N | | 8 | 2 | .800 | 3.84 | 38 | 16 | 2 | 171 | 189 | 55 | 55 | 0 | 2 | 0 | 2 | 54 | 8 | 0 | .148 |
| 1957 | | 12 | 13 | .480 | 4.52 | 37 | 31 | 10 | 207 | 236 | 46 | 63 | 1 | 0 | 1 | 0 | 69 | 14 | 4 | .203 |
| 1958 | | 6 | 8 | .429 | 3.72 | 49 | 0 | 0 | 75 | 76 | 26 | 35 | 0 | 6 | 8 | 9 | 9 | 5 | 0 | .556 |
| 1959 2 teams | CIN N (17G 0–1) | | | | | STL N (11G 0–1) | | | | | | | | | | | | | | |
| " total | | 0 | 2 | .000 | 5.95 | 28 | 0 | 0 | 39.1 | 54 | 19 | 19 | 0 | 0 | 2 | 1 | 4 | 1 | 0 | .250 |
| 6 yrs. | | 39 | 37 | .513 | 4.22 | 245 | 51 | 13 | 697 | 772 | 257 | 239 | 1 | 20 | 21 | 25 | * | | | |
| 2 yrs. | | 13 | 12 | .520 | 4.09 | 93 | 4 | 1 | 204.2 | 217 | 111 | 67 | 0 | 12 | 10 | 13 | 1827 | 459 | 22 | .251 |

## Ferguson Jenkins

**JENKINS, FERGUSON ARTHUR**
B. Dec. 13, 1943, Chatham, Ont., Canada                                      BR TR 6'5"       205 lbs.

| | | W | L | PCT | ERA | G | GS | CG | IP | H | BB | SO | ShO | W | L | SV | AB | H | HR | BA |
|---|---|---|---|---|---|---|---|---|---|---|---|---|---|---|---|---|---|---|---|---|
| 1965 PHI N | | 2 | 1 | .667 | 2.19 | 7 | 0 | 0 | 12.1 | 7 | 2 | 10 | 0 | 2 | 1 | 1 | 1 | 0 | 0 | .000 |
| 1966 2 teams | PHI N (1G 0–0) | | | | | CHI N (60G 6–8) | | | | | | | | | | | | | | |
| " total | | 6 | 8 | .429 | 3.32 | 61 | 12 | 2 | 184.1 | 150 | 52 | 150 | 1 | 2 | 5 | 5 | 51 | 7 | 1 | .137 |
| 1967 CHI N | | 20 | 13 | .606 | 2.80 | 38 | 38 | 20 | 289.1 | 230 | 83 | 236 | 3 | 0 | 0 | 0 | 93 | 14 | 0 | .151 |
| 1968 | | 20 | 15 | .571 | 2.63 | 40 | 40 | 20 | 308 | 255 | 65 | 260 | 3 | 0 | 0 | 0 | 100 | 16 | 1 | .160 |
| 1969 | | 21 | 15 | .583 | 3.21 | 43 | 42 | 23 | 311 | 284 | 71 | 273 | 7 | 0 | 0 | 1 | 108 | 15 | 1 | .139 |
| 1970 | | 22 | 16 | .579 | 3.39 | 40 | 39 | 24 | 313 | 265 | 60 | 274 | 3 | 0 | 0 | 0 | 113 | 14 | 3 | .124 |
| 1971 | | 24 | 13 | .649 | 2.77 | 39 | 39 | 30 | 325 | 304 | 37 | 263 | 3 | 0 | 0 | 0 | 115 | 28 | 6 | .243 |
| 1972 | | 20 | 12 | .625 | 3.21 | 36 | 36 | 23 | 289 | 253 | 62 | 184 | 5 | 0 | 0 | 0 | 109 | 20 | 1 | .183 |
| 1973 | | 14 | 16 | .467 | 3.89 | 38 | 38 | 7 | 271 | 267 | 57 | 170 | 2 | 0 | 0 | 0 | 84 | 10 | 0 | .119 |
| 1974 TEX A | | 25 | 12 | .676 | 2.83 | 41 | 41 | 29 | 328 | 286 | 45 | 225 | 6 | 0 | 0 | 0 | 2 | 1 | 0 | .500 |
| 1975 | | 17 | 18 | .486 | 3.93 | 37 | 37 | 22 | 270 | 261 | 56 | 157 | 4 | 0 | 0 | 0 | 0 | 0 | 0 | — |
| 1976 BOS A | | 12 | 11 | .522 | 3.27 | 30 | 29 | 8 | 209 | 201 | 43 | 142 | 1 | 2 | 1 | 0 | 0 | 0 | 0 | — |
| 1977 | | 10 | 10 | .500 | 3.68 | 28 | 28 | 11 | 193 | 190 | 36 | 105 | 1 | 0 | 0 | 0 | 0 | 0 | 0 | — |
| 1978 TEX A | | 18 | 8 | .692 | 3.04 | 34 | 30 | 16 | 249 | 228 | 41 | 157 | 4 | 0 | 1 | 0 | 0 | 0 | 0 | — |
| 1979 | | 16 | 14 | .533 | 4.07 | 37 | 37 | 10 | 259 | 252 | 81 | 164 | 3 | 0 | 0 | 0 | 0 | 0 | 0 | — |
| 1980 | | 12 | 12 | .500 | 3.77 | 29 | 29 | 12 | 198 | 190 | 52 | 129 | 0 | 0 | 0 | 0 | 0 | 0 | 0 | — |
| 1981 | | 5 | 8 | .385 | 4.50 | 19 | 16 | 1 | 106 | 122 | 40 | 63 | 0 | 0 | 1 | 0 | 0 | 0 | 0 | — |
| 1982 CHI N | | 14 | 15 | .483 | 3.15 | 34 | 34 | 4 | 217.1 | 221 | 68 | 134 | 1 | 0 | 0 | 0 | 67 | 10 | 0 | .149 |

| | W | L | PCT | ERA | G | GS | CG | IP | H | BB | SO | ShO | Relief Pitching W | L | SV | BATTING AB | H | HR | BA |
|---|---|---|---|---|---|---|---|---|---|---|---|---|---|---|---|---|---|---|---|

### Ferguson Jenkins continued

| | | | | | | | | | | | | | | | | | | | |
|---|---|---|---|---|---|---|---|---|---|---|---|---|---|---|---|---|---|---|---|
| 1983 | 6 | 9 | .400 | 4.30 | 33 | 29 | 1 | 167.1 | 176 | 46 | 96 | 1 | 0 | 0 | 0 | 53 | 13 | 0 | .245 |
| 19 yrs. | 284 | 226 | .557 | 3.34 | 664 | 594 | 267 | 4499.2 | 4142 | 997 | 3192 | 49 | 5 | 8 | 7 | 896 | 148 | 13 | .165 |
| | | | | | | | | | | | 8th | | | | | | | | |
| 10 yrs. | 167 | 132 | .559 | 3.21 | 401 | 347 | 154 | 2673 | 2402 | 600 | 2038 | 29 | 2 | 5 | 6 | 893 | 147 | 13 | .165 |
| | 5th | 4th | | | | | | 4th | | 3rd | | 10th | 1st | 4th | | | | | |

## Abe Johnson

**JOHNSON, ABRAHAM**
B. London, Ont., Canada    Deceased.

| | | | | | | | | | | | | | | | | | | | |
|---|---|---|---|---|---|---|---|---|---|---|---|---|---|---|---|---|---|---|---|
| 1893 CHI N | 0 | 0 | – | 36.00 | 1 | 0 | 0 | 1 | 2 | 2 | 0 | 0 | 0 | 0 | 1 | 0 | 0 | 0 | – |

## Ben Johnson

**JOHNSON, BENJAMIN FRANKLIN**    BR TR 6'2" 190 lbs.
B. May 16, 1931, Greenwood, S. C.

| | | | | | | | | | | | | | | | | | | | |
|---|---|---|---|---|---|---|---|---|---|---|---|---|---|---|---|---|---|---|---|
| 1959 CHI N | 0 | 0 | – | 2.16 | 4 | 2 | 0 | 16.2 | 17 | 4 | 6 | 0 | 0 | 0 | 0 | 4 | 0 | 0 | .000 |
| 1960 | 2 | 1 | .667 | 4.91 | 17 | 0 | 0 | 29.1 | 39 | 11 | 9 | 0 | 2 | 1 | 1 | 2 | 0 | 0 | .000 |
| 2 yrs. | 2 | 1 | .667 | 3.91 | 21 | 2 | 0 | 46 | 56 | 15 | 15 | 0 | 2 | 1 | 1 | 6 | 0 | 0 | .000 |
| 2 yrs. | 2 | 1 | .667 | 3.91 | 21 | 2 | 0 | 46 | 56 | 15 | 15 | 0 | 2 | 1 | 1 | 6 | 0 | 0 | .000 |

## Bill Johnson

**JOHNSON, WILLIAM CHARLES**    BR TR 6'5" 205 lbs.
B. Oct. 6, 1960, Wilmington, Del.

| | | | | | | | | | | | | | | | | | | | |
|---|---|---|---|---|---|---|---|---|---|---|---|---|---|---|---|---|---|---|---|
| 1983 CHI N | 1 | 0 | 1.000 | 4.38 | 10 | 0 | 0 | 12.1 | 17 | 3 | 4 | 0 | 1 | 0 | 0 | 0 | 0 | 0 | – |
| 1984 | 0 | 0 | – | 1.69 | 4 | 0 | 0 | 5.1 | 4 | 1 | 3 | 0 | 0 | 0 | 0 | 0 | 0 | 0 | – |
| 2 yrs. | 1 | 0 | 1.000 | 3.57 | 14 | 0 | 0 | 17.2 | 21 | 4 | 7 | 0 | 1 | 0 | 0 | 0 | 0 | 0 | – |
| 2 yrs. | 1 | 0 | 1.000 | 3.57 | 14 | 0 | 0 | 17.2 | 21 | 4 | 7 | 0 | 1 | 0 | 0 | 0 | 0 | 0 | – |

## Ken Johnson

**JOHNSON, KENNETH TRAVIS**    BR TR 6'4" 210 lbs.
B. June 16, 1933, West Palm Beach, Fla.

| | | | | | | | | | | | | | | | | | | | |
|---|---|---|---|---|---|---|---|---|---|---|---|---|---|---|---|---|---|---|---|
| 1958 KC A | 0 | 0 | – | 27.00 | 2 | 0 | 0 | 2.1 | 6 | 3 | 1 | 0 | 0 | 0 | 0 | 0 | 0 | 0 | – |
| 1959 | 1 | 1 | .500 | 4.09 | 2 | 2 | 0 | 11 | 11 | 5 | 8 | 0 | 0 | 0 | 0 | 3 | 0 | 0 | .000 |
| 1960 | 5 | 10 | .333 | 4.26 | 42 | 6 | 2 | 120.1 | 120 | 45 | 83 | 0 | 3 | 6 | 3 | 30 | 5 | 0 | .167 |
| 1961 2 teams | | | | KC | A | (15G 6–2) | | CIN | N | (6G 0–4) | | | | | | | | | |
| " total | 6 | 6 | .500 | 4.00 | 21 | 12 | 3 | 92.1 | 82 | 29 | 46 | 1 | 0 | 3 | 1 | 26 | 6 | 0 | .231 |
| 1962 HOU N | 7 | 16 | .304 | 3.84 | 33 | 33 | 5 | 197 | 195 | 46 | 178 | 1 | 0 | 0 | 0 | 52 | 4 | 0 | .077 |
| 1963 | 11 | 17 | .393 | 2.65 | 37 | 32 | 6 | 224 | 204 | 50 | 148 | 1 | 1 | 1 | 1 | 74 | 5 | 0 | .068 |
| 1964 | 11 | 16 | .407 | 3.63 | 35 | 35 | 7 | 218 | 209 | 44 | 117 | 1 | 0 | 0 | 0 | 76 | 6 | 1 | .079 |
| 1965 2 teams | | | | HOU | N | (8G 3–2) | | MIL | N | (29G 13–8) | | | | | | | | | |
| " total | 16 | 10 | .615 | 3.42 | 37 | 34 | 9 | 231.1 | 217 | 48 | 151 | 1 | 0 | 0 | 2 | 79 | 9 | 0 | .114 |
| 1966 ATL N | 14 | 8 | .636 | 3.30 | 32 | 31 | 11 | 215.2 | 213 | 46 | 105 | 2 | 0 | 0 | 0 | 70 | 10 | 1 | .143 |
| 1967 | 13 | 9 | .591 | 2.74 | 29 | 29 | 6 | 210.1 | 191 | 38 | 85 | 0 | 0 | 0 | 0 | 71 | 9 | 0 | .127 |
| 1968 | 5 | 8 | .385 | 3.47 | 31 | 16 | 1 | 135 | 145 | 25 | 57 | 0 | 1 | 2 | 0 | 40 | 7 | 0 | .175 |
| 1969 3 teams | | | ATL | N | (9G 0–1) | | NY | A | (12G 1–2) | | CHI | N | (9G 1–2) | | | | | | |
| " total | 2 | 5 | .286 | 3.89 | 30 | 3 | 0 | 74 | 68 | 33 | 59 | 0 | 1 | 2 | 2 | 13 | 0 | 0 | .000 |
| 1970 MON N | 0 | 0 | – | 7.50 | 3 | 0 | 0 | 6 | 9 | 1 | 4 | 0 | 0 | 0 | 0 | 0 | 0 | 0 | – |
| 13 yrs. | 91 | 106 | .462 | 3.46 | 334 | 231 | 50 | 1737.1 | 1670 | 413 | 1042 | 7 | 6 | 14 | 9 | 534 | 61 | 2 | .114 |
| 1 yr. | 1 | 2 | .333 | 2.84 | 9 | 1 | 0 | 19 | 17 | 13 | 18 | 0 | 0 | 0 | 1 | 4 | 0 | 0 | .000 |

**WORLD SERIES**

| | | | | | | | | | | | | | | | | | | | |
|---|---|---|---|---|---|---|---|---|---|---|---|---|---|---|---|---|---|---|---|
| 1961 CIN N | 0 | 0 | – | 0.00 | 1 | 0 | 0 | .2 | 0 | 0 | 0 | 0 | 0 | 0 | 0 | 0 | 0 | 0 | – |

## Roy Joiner

**JOINER, ROY MERRILL (Pop)**    BL TL 6' 170 lbs.
B. Oct. 30, 1906, Red Bluff, Calif.

| | | | | | | | | | | | | | | | | | | | |
|---|---|---|---|---|---|---|---|---|---|---|---|---|---|---|---|---|---|---|---|
| 1934 CHI N | 0 | 1 | .000 | 8.21 | 20 | 2 | 0 | 34 | 61 | 8 | 9 | 0 | 0 | 0 | 0 | 10 | 2 | 0 | .200 |
| 1935 | 0 | 0 | – | 5.40 | 2 | 2 | 0 | 3.1 | 6 | 2 | 0 | 0 | 0 | 0 | 0 | 1 | 0 | 0 | .000 |
| 1940 NY N | 3 | 2 | .600 | 3.40 | 30 | 2 | 0 | 53 | 66 | 17 | 25 | 0 | 2 | 1 | 1 | 11 | 3 | 0 | .273 |
| 3 yrs. | 3 | 3 | .500 | 5.28 | 52 | 4 | 0 | 90.1 | 133 | 27 | 34 | 0 | 2 | 1 | 1 | 22 | 5 | 0 | .227 |
| 2 yrs. | 0 | 1 | .000 | 7.96 | 22 | 2 | 0 | 37.1 | 67 | 10 | 9 | 0 | 0 | 0 | 0 | 11 | 2 | 0 | .182 |

## Charley Jones

**JONES, CHARLES WESLEY**    BR TR 5'11½" 202 lbs.
Also known as Benjamin Wesley Rippay.
B. Apr. 3, 1850, County, N. C.    Deceased.

| | | | | | | | | | | | | | | | | | | | |
|---|---|---|---|---|---|---|---|---|---|---|---|---|---|---|---|---|---|---|---|
| 1887 CIN AA | 0 | 0 | – | 3.00 | 2 | 0 | 0 | 3 | 2 | 4 | 0 | 0 | 0 | 0 | 0 | * | | | |

## Percy Jones

**JONES, PERCY LEE**    BR TL 5'11½" 175 lbs.
B. Oct. 28, 1899, Harwood, Tex.

| | | | | | | | | | | | | | | | | | | | |
|---|---|---|---|---|---|---|---|---|---|---|---|---|---|---|---|---|---|---|---|
| 1920 CHI N | 0 | 0 | – | 11.57 | 4 | 0 | 0 | 7 | 15 | 3 | 0 | 0 | 0 | 0 | 0 | 2 | 0 | 0 | .000 |
| 1921 | 3 | 5 | .375 | 4.56 | 32 | 5 | 1 | 98.2 | 116 | 39 | 46 | 0 | 2 | 3 | 0 | 27 | 6 | 0 | .222 |
| 1922 | 8 | 9 | .471 | 4.72 | 44 | 26 | 7 | 164 | 197 | 69 | 46 | 2 | 2 | 0 | 1 | 47 | 4 | 0 | .085 |
| 1925 | 6 | 6 | .500 | 4.65 | 28 | 13 | 6 | 124 | 123 | 71 | 60 | 1 | 2 | 1 | 0 | 39 | 6 | 0 | .154 |
| 1926 | 12 | 7 | .632 | 3.09 | 30 | 20 | 10 | 160.1 | 151 | 90 | 80 | 2 | 4 | 0 | 2 | 50 | 13 | 0 | .260 |
| 1927 | 7 | 8 | .467 | 4.07 | 30 | 11 | 5 | 112.2 | 123 | 72 | 37 | 1 | 3 | 1 | 0 | 40 | 14 | 0 | .350 |
| 1928 | 10 | 6 | .625 | 4.03 | 39 | 18 | 9 | 154 | 164 | 56 | 41 | 1 | 3 | 0 | 3 | 56 | 11 | 0 | .196 |
| 1929 BOS N | 7 | 15 | .318 | 4.64 | 35 | 22 | 11 | 188.1 | 219 | 84 | 69 | 1 | 2 | 1 | 0 | 61 | 9 | 0 | .148 |
| 1930 PIT N | 0 | 1 | .000 | 6.63 | 9 | 2 | 0 | 19 | 26 | 11 | 3 | 0 | 0 | 0 | 0 | 2 | 0 | 0 | .000 |
| 9 yrs. | 53 | 57 | .482 | 4.33 | 251 | 117 | 49 | 1028 | 1134 | 495 | 382 | 8 | 18 | 6 | 6 | 324 | 63 | 0 | .194 |
| 7 yrs. | 46 | 41 | .529 | 4.21 | 207 | 93 | 38 | 820.2 | 889 | 400 | 310 | 5 | 16 | 5 | 6 | 261 | 54 | 0 | .207 |

## Sam Jones

**JONES, SAMUEL (Toothpick Sam, Sad Sam)**    BR TR 6'4" 192 lbs.
B. Dec. 14, 1925, Stewartsville, Ohio    D. Nov. 5, 1971, Morgantown, W. Va.

| | | | | | | | | | | | | | | | | | | | |
|---|---|---|---|---|---|---|---|---|---|---|---|---|---|---|---|---|---|---|---|
| 1951 CLE A | 0 | 1 | .000 | 2.08 | 2 | 1 | 0 | 8.2 | 4 | 5 | 4 | 0 | 0 | 0 | 0 | 2 | 0 | 0 | .000 |
| 1952 | 2 | 3 | .400 | 7.25 | 14 | 4 | 0 | 36 | 38 | 37 | 28 | 0 | 1 | 0 | 1 | 10 | 1 | 0 | .100 |

| | W | L | PCT | ERA | G | GS | CG | IP | H | BB | SO | ShO | Relief Pitching W | L | SV | BATTING AB | H | HR | BA |
|---|---|---|---|---|---|---|---|---|---|---|---|---|---|---|---|---|---|---|---|

## Sam Jones continued

| | W | L | PCT | ERA | G | GS | CG | IP | H | BB | SO | ShO | W | L | SV | AB | H | HR | BA |
|---|---|---|---|---|---|---|---|---|---|---|---|---|---|---|---|---|---|---|---|
| 1955 CHI N | 14 | 20 | .412 | 4.10 | 36 | 34 | 12 | 241.2 | 175 | **185** | **198** | 4 | 1 | 1 | 0 | 77 | 14 | 0 | .182 |
| 1956 | 9 | 14 | .391 | 3.91 | 33 | 28 | 8 | 188.2 | 155 | **115** | 176 | 2 | 1 | 0 | 0 | 57 | 10 | 0 | .175 |
| 1957 STL N | 12 | 9 | .571 | 3.60 | 28 | 27 | 10 | 182.2 | 164 | 71 | 154 | 2 | 1 | 0 | 0 | 63 | 10 | 0 | .159 |
| 1958 | 14 | 13 | .519 | 2.88 | 35 | 35 | 14 | 250 | 204 | 107 | **225** | 2 | 0 | 0 | 0 | 90 | 9 | 0 | .100 |
| 1959 SF N | 21 | 15 | .583 | **2.83** | 50 | 35 | 16 | 270.2 | 232 | **109** | 209 | 4 | 4 | 1 | 4 | 85 | 11 | 0 | .129 |
| 1960 | 18 | 14 | .563 | 3.19 | 39 | 35 | 13 | 234 | 200 | 91 | 190 | 3 | 2 | 1 | 0 | 80 | 16 | 0 | .200 |
| 1961 | 8 | 8 | .500 | 4.49 | 37 | 17 | 2 | 128.1 | 134 | 57 | 105 | 0 | 2 | 1 | 1 | 36 | 5 | 0 | .139 |
| 1962 DET A | 2 | 4 | .333 | 3.65 | 30 | 6 | 1 | 81.1 | 77 | 35 | 73 | 0 | 1 | 1 | 1 | 21 | 2 | 1 | .095 |
| 1963 STL N | 2 | 0 | 1.000 | 9.00 | 11 | 0 | 0 | 11 | 15 | 5 | 8 | 0 | 2 | 0 | 2 | 11 | 0 | 0 | .000 |
| 1964 BAL A | 0 | 0 | — | 2.61 | 7 | 0 | 0 | 10.1 | 5 | 5 | 6 | 0 | 0 | 0 | 0 | 0 | 0 | 0 | — |
| 12 yrs. | 102 | 101 | .502 | 3.59 | 322 | 222 | 76 | 1643.1 | 1403 | 822 | 1376 | 17 | 15 | 5 | 9 | 522 | 78 | 1 | .149 |
| 2 yrs. | 23 | 34 | .404 | 4.02 | 69 | 62 | 20 | 430.1 | 330 | 300 | 374 | 6 | 2 | 1 | 0 | 134 | 24 | 0 | .179 |

## Sheldon Jones

**JONES, SHELDON LESLIE (Available)**     BR TR 6'     180 lbs.
B. Feb. 2, 1922, Tecumseh, Neb.

| | W | L | PCT | ERA | G | GS | CG | IP | H | BB | SO | ShO | W | L | SV | AB | H | HR | BA |
|---|---|---|---|---|---|---|---|---|---|---|---|---|---|---|---|---|---|---|---|
| 1946 NY N | 1 | 2 | .333 | 3.21 | 6 | 4 | 1 | 28 | 21 | 17 | 24 | 0 | 0 | 0 | 0 | 8 | 2 | 0 | .250 |
| 1947 | 2 | 2 | .500 | 3.88 | 15 | 6 | 0 | 55.2 | 51 | 29 | 24 | 0 | 2 | 0 | 0 | 16 | 2 | 0 | .125 |
| 1948 | 16 | 8 | .667 | 3.35 | 55 | 21 | 8 | 201.1 | 204 | 90 | 82 | 2 | 5 | 4 | 5 | 64 | 13 | 0 | .203 |
| 1949 | 15 | 12 | .556 | 3.34 | 42 | 27 | 11 | 207.1 | 198 | 88 | 79 | 1 | 5 | 0 | 0 | 66 | 8 | 0 | .121 |
| 1950 | 13 | 16 | .448 | 4.61 | 40 | 28 | 11 | 199 | 188 | 90 | 97 | 2 | 2 | 3 | 2 | 57 | 6 | 0 | .105 |
| 1951 | 6 | 11 | .353 | 4.26 | 41 | 12 | 2 | 120.1 | 119 | 52 | 58 | 0 | 4 | 4 | 4 | 31 | 3 | 0 | .097 |
| 1952 BOS N | 1 | 4 | .200 | 4.76 | 39 | 1 | 0 | 70 | 81 | 31 | 40 | 0 | 1 | 3 | 1 | 8 | 1 | 0 | .125 |
| 1953 CHI N | 0 | 2 | .000 | 5.40 | 22 | 2 | 0 | 38.1 | 47 | 16 | 9 | 0 | 0 | 1 | 0 | 7 | 0 | 0 | .000 |
| 8 yrs. | 54 | 57 | .486 | 3.96 | 260 | 101 | 33 | 920 | 909 | 413 | 413 | 5 | 19 | 15 | 12 | 257 | 35 | 0 | .136 |
| 1 yr. | 0 | 2 | .000 | 5.40 | 22 | 2 | 0 | 38.1 | 47 | 16 | 9 | 0 | 0 | 1 | 0 | 7 | 0 | 0 | .000 |

WORLD SERIES
| 1951 NY N | 0 | 0 | — | 2.08 | 2 | 0 | 0 | 4.1 | 5 | 1 | 2 | 0 | 0 | 0 | 1 | 0 | 0 | 0 | — |

## Claude Jonnard

**JONNARD, CLAUDE ALFRED**     BR TR 6'1"     165 lbs.
Brother of Bubber Jonnard.
B. Nov. 23, 1897, Nashville, Tenn.     D. Aug. 27, 1959, Nashville, Tenn.

| | W | L | PCT | ERA | G | GS | CG | IP | H | BB | SO | ShO | W | L | SV | AB | H | HR | BA |
|---|---|---|---|---|---|---|---|---|---|---|---|---|---|---|---|---|---|---|---|
| 1921 NY N | 0 | 0 | — | 0.00 | 1 | 0 | 0 | 4 | 7 | 0 | 7 | 0 | 0 | 0 | 0 | 1 | 0 | 0 | .000 |
| 1922 | 6 | 1 | .857 | 3.84 | 33 | 0 | 0 | 96 | 96 | 28 | 44 | 0 | 6 | 1 | 5 | 24 | 1 | 0 | .042 |
| 1923 | 4 | 3 | .571 | 3.28 | 45 | 1 | 1 | 96 | 105 | 35 | 45 | 0 | 3 | 3 | 5 | 26 | 1 | 0 | .038 |
| 1924 | 4 | 5 | .444 | 2.41 | 34 | 3 | 1 | 89.2 | 80 | 24 | 40 | 0 | 4 | 3 | 5 | 22 | 1 | 0 | .045 |
| 1926 STL A | 0 | 2 | .000 | 6.00 | 12 | 3 | 0 | 36 | 46 | 24 | 13 | 0 | 0 | 0 | 0 | 7 | 0 | 0 | .000 |
| 1929 CHI N | 0 | 1 | .000 | 7.48 | 12 | 2 | 0 | 27.2 | 41 | 11 | 11 | 0 | 0 | 0 | 0 | 10 | 2 | 0 | .200 |
| 6 yrs. | 14 | 12 | .538 | 3.79 | 137 | 9 | 2 | 349.1 | 372 | 122 | 160 | 0 | 13 | 7 | 17 | 90 | 5 | 0 | .056 |
| 1 yr. | 0 | 1 | .000 | 7.48 | 12 | 2 | 0 | 27.2 | 41 | 11 | 11 | 0 | 0 | 0 | 0 | 10 | 2 | 0 | .200 |

WORLD SERIES
| 1923 NY N | 0 | 0 | — | 0.00 | 2 | 0 | 0 | 2 | 1 | 1 | 1 | 0 | 0 | 0 | 0 | 0 | 0 | 0 | — |
| 1924 | 0 | 0 | — | 0.00 | 1 | 0 | 0 | 0 | 0 | 1 | 0 | 0 | 0 | 0 | 0 | 0 | 0 | 0 | — |
| 2 yrs. | 0 | 0 | — | 0.00 | 3 | 0 | 0 | 2 | 1 | 2 | 1 | 0 | 0 | 0 | 0 | 0 | 0 | 0 | — |

## Don Kaiser

**KAISER, CLYDE DONALD (Tiger)**     BR TR 6'5"     195 lbs.
B. Feb. 3, 1935, Byng, Okla.

| | W | L | PCT | ERA | G | GS | CG | IP | H | BB | SO | ShO | W | L | SV | AB | H | HR | BA |
|---|---|---|---|---|---|---|---|---|---|---|---|---|---|---|---|---|---|---|---|
| 1955 CHI N | 0 | 0 | — | 5.40 | 11 | 0 | 0 | 18.1 | 20 | 5 | 11 | 0 | 0 | 0 | 0 | 2 | 0 | 0 | .000 |
| 1956 | 4 | 9 | .308 | 3.59 | 27 | 22 | 5 | 150.1 | 144 | 52 | 74 | 1 | 0 | 0 | 0 | 47 | 2 | 0 | .043 |
| 1957 | 2 | 6 | .250 | 5.00 | 20 | 13 | 1 | 72 | 91 | 28 | 23 | 0 | 0 | 0 | 0 | 19 | 2 | 0 | .105 |
| 3 yrs. | 6 | 15 | .286 | 4.15 | 58 | 35 | 6 | 240.2 | 255 | 85 | 108 | 1 | 0 | 0 | 0 | 68 | 4 | 0 | .059 |
| 3 yrs. | 6 | 15 | .286 | 4.15 | 58 | 35 | 6 | 240.2 | 255 | 85 | 108 | 1 | 0 | 0 | 0 | 68 | 4 | 0 | .059 |

## John Katoll

**KATOLL, JOHN (Big Jack)**     BR TR 6'4"     200 lbs.
B. June 24, 1872, Germany     D. June 18, 1955, Hartland, Ill.

| | W | L | PCT | ERA | G | GS | CG | IP | H | BB | SO | ShO | W | L | SV | AB | H | HR | BA |
|---|---|---|---|---|---|---|---|---|---|---|---|---|---|---|---|---|---|---|---|
| 1898 CHI N | 0 | 1 | .000 | 0.82 | 2 | 1 | 1 | 11 | 8 | 1 | 3 | 0 | 0 | 0 | 0 | 4 | 0 | 0 | .000 |
| 1899 | 1 | 1 | .500 | 6.00 | 2 | 2 | 2 | 18 | 17 | 4 | 1 | 0 | 0 | 0 | 0 | 7 | 0 | 0 | .000 |
| 1901 CHI A | 11 | 10 | .524 | 2.81 | 27 | 25 | 19 | 208 | 231 | 53 | 59 | 0 | 0 | 0 | 0 | 80 | 10 | 1 | .125 |
| 1902 2 teams | | | | | CHI | A (1G 0–0) | | | | BAL | A (15G 5–10) | | | | | | | | |
| " total | 5 | 10 | .333 | 3.99 | 16 | 13 | 13 | 124 | 176 | 32 | 27 | 0 | 2 | 0 | 0 | 58 | 10 | 0 | .172 |
| 4 yrs. | 17 | 22 | .436 | 3.32 | 47 | 41 | 35 | 361 | 432 | 90 | 90 | 0 | 2 | 0 | 0 | 149 | 20 | 1 | .134 |
| 2 yrs. | 1 | 2 | .333 | 4.03 | 4 | 3 | 3 | 29 | 25 | 5 | 4 | 0 | 0 | 0 | 0 | 11 | 0 | 0 | .000 |

## Tony Kaufmann

**KAUFMANN, ANTHONY CHARLES**     BR TR 5'11"     165 lbs.
B. Dec. 16, 1900, Chicago, Ill.     D. June 4, 1982, Elgin, Ill.

| | W | L | PCT | ERA | G | GS | CG | IP | H | BB | SO | ShO | W | L | SV | AB | H | HR | BA |
|---|---|---|---|---|---|---|---|---|---|---|---|---|---|---|---|---|---|---|---|
| 1921 CHI N | 1 | 0 | 1.000 | 4.15 | 2 | 1 | 1 | 13 | 12 | 3 | 6 | 0 | 0 | 0 | 1 | 5 | 2 | 0 | .400 |
| 1922 | 7 | 13 | .350 | 4.06 | 37 | 9 | 4 | 153 | 161 | 57 | 45 | 1 | 1 | 6 | 3 | 45 | 9 | 1 | .200 |
| 1923 | 14 | 10 | .583 | 3.10 | 33 | 24 | 18 | 206.1 | 209 | 67 | 72 | 2 | 1 | 0 | 3 | 74 | 16 | 2 | .216 |
| 1924 | 16 | 11 | .593 | 4.02 | 34 | 26 | 16 | 208.1 | 218 | 66 | 79 | 3 | 1 | 2 | 0 | 76 | 24 | 1 | .316 |
| 1925 | 13 | 13 | .500 | 4.50 | 31 | 23 | 14 | 196 | 221 | 77 | 49 | 2 | 2 | 3 | 2 | 78 | 15 | 2 | .192 |
| 1926 | 9 | 7 | .563 | 3.02 | 26 | 21 | 14 | 169.2 | 169 | 44 | 52 | 1 | 0 | 0 | 2 | 60 | 15 | 1 | .250 |
| 1927 3 teams | | | | | CHI | N (9G 3–3) | | | | PHI | N (5G 0–3) | | | STL | N (1G 0–0) | | | | |
| " total | 3 | 6 | .333 | 7.84 | 15 | 11 | 4 | 72.1 | 116 | 28 | 25 | 0 | 0 | 0 | 0 | 23 | 6 | 2 | .261 |
| 1928 STL N | 0 | 0 | — | 9.64 | 4 | 1 | 0 | 4.2 | 8 | 4 | 2 | 0 | 0 | 0 | 0 | 0 | 0 | 0 | — |
| 1929 NY N | 0 | 0 | — | 0.00 | 0 | 0 | 0 | 0 | 0 | 0 | 0 | 0 | 0 | 0 | 0 | 32 | 1 | 0 | .031 |
| 1930 STL N | 0 | 1 | .000 | 7.84 | 2 | 1 | 0 | 10.1 | 15 | 4 | 2 | 0 | 0 | 0 | 0 | 3 | 1 | 0 | .333 |
| 1931 | 1 | 1 | .500 | 6.06 | 15 | 1 | 0 | 49 | 65 | 17 | 13 | 0 | 1 | 1 | 1 | 18 | 2 | 0 | .111 |
| 1935 | 0 | 0 | — | 2.45 | 3 | 0 | 0 | 3.2 | 4 | 1 | 0 | 0 | 0 | 0 | 0 | 0 | 0 | 0 | — |
| 12 yrs. | 64 | 62 | .508 | 4.18 | 202 | 118 | 71 | 1086.1 | 1198 | 368 | 345 | 9 | 6 | 12 | 12 | 414 | 91 | 9 | .220 |
| 7 yrs. | 63 | 57 | .525 | 3.89 | 172 | 110 | 70 | 999.2 | 1065 | 333 | 324 | 9 | 5 | 11 | 11 | 354 | 86 | 8 | .243 |

| | W | L | PCT | ERA | G | GS | CG | IP | H | BB | SO | ShO | Relief Pitching W | L | SV | BATTING AB | H | HR | BA |
|---|---|---|---|---|---|---|---|---|---|---|---|---|---|---|---|---|---|---|---|

## Vic Keen

**KEEN, HOWARD VICTOR**
B. Mar. 16, 1899, Bel Air, Md.   D. Dec. 10, 1976, Salisbury, Md.          BR TR 5'9"   165 lbs.

| | W | L | PCT | ERA | G | GS | CG | IP | H | BB | SO | ShO | W | L | SV | AB | H | HR | BA |
|---|---|---|---|---|---|---|---|---|---|---|---|---|---|---|---|---|---|---|---|
| 1918 PHI A | 0 | 1 | .000 | 3.38 | 1 | 1 | 0 | 8 | 9 | 1 | 1 | 0 | 0 | 0 | 0 | 1 | 0 | 0 | .000 |
| 1921 CHI N | 0 | 3 | .000 | 4.68 | 5 | 4 | 1 | 25 | 29 | 9 | 9 | 0 | 0 | 0 | 0 | 5 | 0 | 0 | .000 |
| 1922 | 1 | 2 | .333 | 3.89 | 7 | 3 | 2 | 34.2 | 36 | 10 | 11 | 0 | 0 | 1 | 1 | 12 | 4 | 0 | .333 |
| 1923 | 12 | 8 | .600 | 3.00 | 35 | 17 | 10 | 177 | 169 | 57 | 46 | 0 | 3 | 2 | 1 | 53 | 8 | 0 | .151 |
| 1924 | 15 | 14 | .517 | 3.80 | 40 | 28 | 15 | 234.2 | 242 | 80 | 75 | 0 | 2 | 1 | 3 | 77 | 12 | 0 | .156 |
| 1925 | 2 | 6 | .250 | 6.26 | 30 | 8 | 1 | 83.1 | 125 | 41 | 19 | 0 | 2 | 1 | 1 | 25 | 6 | 0 | .240 |
| 1926 STL N | 10 | 9 | .526 | 4.56 | 26 | 21 | 12 | 152 | 179 | 42 | 29 | 1 | 0 | 1 | 0 | 53 | 3 | 0 | .057 |
| 1927 | 2 | 1 | .667 | 4.81 | 21 | 0 | 0 | 33.2 | 39 | 8 | 12 | 0 | 2 | 1 | 0 | 4 | 1 | 0 | .250 |
| 8 yrs. | 42 | 44 | .488 | 4.11 | 165 | 82 | 41 | 748.1 | 828 | 248 | 202 | 1 | 9 | 7 | 6 | 230 | 34 | 0 | .148 |
| 5 yrs. | 30 | 33 | .476 | 3.96 | 117 | 60 | 29 | 554.2 | 601 | 197 | 160 | 0 | 7 | 5 | 6 | 172 | 30 | 0 | .174 |
| WORLD SERIES | | | | | | | | | | | | | | | | | | | |
| 1926 STL N | 0 | 0 | — | 0.00 | 1 | 0 | 0 | 1 | 0 | 0 | 0 | 0 | 0 | 0 | 0 | 0 | 0 | 0 | .000 |

## Bob Kelly

**KELLY, ROBERT EDWARD**
B. Oct. 4, 1927, Cleveland, Ohio          BR TR 6'   180 lbs.

| | W | L | PCT | ERA | G | GS | CG | IP | H | BB | SO | ShO | W | L | SV | AB | H | HR | BA |
|---|---|---|---|---|---|---|---|---|---|---|---|---|---|---|---|---|---|---|---|
| 1951 CHI N | 7 | 4 | .636 | 4.66 | 35 | 11 | 4 | 123.2 | 130 | 55 | 46 | 0 | 2 | 0 | 0 | 31 | 5 | 0 | .161 |
| 1952 | 4 | 9 | .308 | 3.59 | 31 | 15 | 3 | 125.1 | 114 | 46 | 50 | 2 | 0 | 3 | 0 | 37 | 8 | 0 | .216 |
| 1953 2 teams | | | CHI | N | (14G 0–1) | | CIN | N | (28G 1–2) | | | | | | | | | | |
| " total | 1 | 3 | .250 | 5.40 | 42 | 5 | 0 | 83.1 | 98 | 35 | 35 | 0 | 0 | 2 | 2 | 18 | 2 | 0 | .111 |
| 1958 2 teams | | | CIN | N | (2G 0–0) | | CLE | A | (13G 0–2) | | | | | | | | | | |
| " total | 0 | 2 | .000 | 5.16 | 15 | 4 | 0 | 29.2 | 32 | 16 | 13 | 0 | 0 | 1 | 0 | 4 | 1 | 0 | .250 |
| 4 yrs. | 12 | 18 | .400 | 4.50 | 123 | 35 | 7 | 362 | 374 | 152 | 146 | 2 | 2 | 6 | 2 | 90 | 16 | 0 | .178 |
| 3 yrs. | 11 | 14 | .440 | 4.47 | 80 | 26 | 7 | 266 | 271 | 110 | 104 | 2 | 2 | 4 | 0 | 69 | 13 | 0 | .188 |

## George Kelly

**KELLY, GEORGE LANGE (Highpockets)**
Brother of Ren Kelly.
B. Sept. 10, 1895, San Francisco, Calif.   D. Oct. 13, 1984, Burlingame, Calif.          BR TR 6'4"   190 lbs.
Hall of Fame 1973.

| | W | L | PCT | ERA | G | GS | CG | IP | H | BB | SO | ShO | W | L | SV | AB | H | HR | BA |
|---|---|---|---|---|---|---|---|---|---|---|---|---|---|---|---|---|---|---|---|
| 1917 NY N | 1 | 0 | 1.000 | 0.00 | 1 | 0 | 0 | 5 | 4 | 1 | 2 | 0 | 1 | 0 | 0 | * | | | |

## King Kelly

**KELLY, MICHAEL JOSEPH**
B. Dec. 31, 1857, Troy, N.Y.   D. Nov. 8, 1894, Boston, Mass.
Manager 1890-91.          BR TR 5'10"   170 lbs.
Hall of Fame 1945.

| | W | L | PCT | ERA | G | GS | CG | IP | H | BB | SO | ShO | W | L | SV | AB | H | HR | BA |
|---|---|---|---|---|---|---|---|---|---|---|---|---|---|---|---|---|---|---|---|
| 1880 CHI N | 0 | 0 | — | 0.00 | 1 | 0 | 0 | 3 | 3 | 1 | 1 | 0 | 0 | 0 | 0 | 344 | 100 | 1 | .291 |
| 1883 | 0 | 0 | — | 0.00 | 1 | 0 | 0 | 1 | 1 | 0 | 0 | 0 | 0 | 0 | 0 | 428 | 109 | 3 | .255 |
| 1884 | 0 | 1 | .000 | 8.44 | 2 | 0 | 0 | 5.1 | 12 | 2 | 1 | 0 | 0 | 1 | 0 | 452 | 160 | 13 | .354 |
| 1887 BOS N | 1 | 0 | 1.000 | 3.46 | 3 | 0 | 0 | 13 | 17 | 14 | 0 | 0 | 1 | 0 | 0 | 484 | 156 | 8 | .322 |
| 1890 BOS P | 1 | 0 | 1.000 | 4.50 | 1 | 0 | 0 | 4 | 1 | 2 | 0 | 0 | 1 | 0 | 0 | 340 | 111 | 4 | .326 |
| 1891 3 teams | | | C-M | AA | (3G 0–1) | | BOS | AA | (0G 0–0) | | BOS | N | (0G 0–0) | | | | | | |
| " total | 0 | 1 | .000 | 5.28 | 3 | 0 | 0 | 15.1 | 21 | 7 | 0 | 0 | 0 | 1 | 0 | 379 | 107 | 2 | .282 |
| 1892 BOS N | 0 | 0 | — | 1.50 | 1 | 0 | 0 | 6 | 8 | 4 | 0 | 0 | 0 | 0 | 0 | 281 | 53 | 2 | .189 |
| 7 yrs. | 2 | 2 | .500 | 4.14 | 12 | 0 | 0 | 45.2 | 63 | 30 | 4 | 0 | 2 | 2 | 0 | * | | | |
| 3 yrs. | 0 | 1 | .000 | 4.82 | 4 | 0 | 0 | 9.1 | 16 | 3 | 2 | 0 | 0 | 1 | 0 | 2843 | 899 | 33 | .316 |

## Ted Kennedy

**KENNEDY, THEODORE A.**
B. Feb., 1865, Henry, Ill.   D. Oct. 31, 1907, St. Louis, Mo.          BL

| | W | L | PCT | ERA | G | GS | CG | IP | H | BB | SO | ShO | W | L | SV | AB | H | HR | BA |
|---|---|---|---|---|---|---|---|---|---|---|---|---|---|---|---|---|---|---|---|
| 1885 CHI N | 7 | 2 | .778 | 3.43 | 9 | 8 | 8 | 78.2 | 91 | 28 | 36 | 0 | 0 | 0 | 0 | 36 | 3 | 0 | .083 |
| 1886 2 teams | | | PHI | AA | (20G 5–15) | | LOU | AA | (4G 0–4) | | | | | | | | | | |
| " total | 5 | 19 | .208 | 4.66 | 24 | 23 | 23 | 204.2 | 249 | 81 | 82 | 0 | 0 | 1 | 0 | 81 | 4 | 0 | .049 |
| 2 yrs. | 12 | 21 | .364 | 4.32 | 33 | 32 | 31 | 283.1 | 340 | 109 | 118 | 0 | 0 | 1 | 0 | 117 | 7 | 0 | .060 |
| 1 yr. | 7 | 2 | .778 | 3.43 | 9 | 8 | 8 | 78.2 | 91 | 28 | 36 | 0 | 0 | 0 | 0 | 36 | 3 | 0 | .083 |

## Frank Killen

**KILLEN, FRANK BISSELL (Lefty)**
B. Nov. 30, 1870, Pittsburgh, Pa.   D. Dec. 4, 1939, Pittsburgh, Pa.          BL TL 6'1"   200 lbs.

| | W | L | PCT | ERA | G | GS | CG | IP | H | BB | SO | ShO | W | L | SV | AB | H | HR | BA |
|---|---|---|---|---|---|---|---|---|---|---|---|---|---|---|---|---|---|---|---|
| 1891 C-M AA | 7 | 4 | .636 | 1.68 | 11 | 11 | 11 | 96.2 | 73 | 51 | 38 | 2 | 0 | 0 | 0 | 35 | 8 | 0 | .229 |
| 1892 WAS N | 29 | 26 | .527 | 3.31 | 60 | 52 | 46 | 459.2 | 448 | 182 | 147 | 2 | 1 | 3 | 0 | 186 | 37 | 4 | .199 |
| 1893 PIT N | 34 | 10 | .773 | 3.64 | 55 | 48 | 38 | 415 | 401 | 140 | 99 | 2 | 5 | 1 | 0 | 171 | 47 | 4 | .275 |
| 1894 | 14 | 11 | .560 | 4.50 | 28 | 28 | 20 | 204 | 261 | 86 | 62 | 1 | 0 | 0 | 0 | 80 | 21 | 0 | .263 |
| 1895 | 5 | 5 | .500 | 5.49 | 13 | 11 | 6 | 95 | 113 | 57 | 25 | 0 | 1 | 1 | 0 | 38 | 13 | 0 | .342 |
| 1896 | 29 | 15 | .659 | 3.41 | 52 | 50 | 44 | 432.1 | 476 | 119 | 134 | 5 | 1 | 0 | 0 | 173 | 40 | 2 | .231 |
| 1897 | 17 | 23 | .425 | 4.46 | 42 | 41 | 38 | 337.1 | 417 | 76 | 99 | 1 | 0 | 1 | 0 | 129 | 32 | 1 | .248 |
| 1898 2 teams | | | PIT | N | (23G 10–11) | | WAS | N | (17G 6–9) | | | | | | | | | | |
| " total | 16 | 20 | .444 | 3.68 | 40 | 39 | 32 | 306 | 350 | 70 | 91 | 0 | 0 | 0 | 0 | 120 | 32 | 0 | .267 |
| 1899 2 teams | | | WAS | N | (2G 0–2) | | BOS | N | (12G 7–5) | | | | | | | | | | |
| " total | 7 | 7 | .500 | 4.45 | 14 | 14 | 12 | 111.1 | 126 | 30 | 26 | 0 | 0 | 0 | 0 | 46 | 8 | 0 | .174 |
| 1900 CHI N | 3 | 3 | .500 | 4.67 | 6 | 6 | 6 | 54 | 65 | 11 | 4 | 0 | 0 | 0 | 0 | 20 | 3 | 0 | .150 |
| 10 yrs. | 161 | 124 | .565 | 3.78 | 321 | 300 | 253 | 2511.1 | 2730 | 822 | 725 | 13 | 8 | 6 | 0 | 998 | 241 | 11 | .241 |
| 1 yr. | 3 | 3 | .500 | 4.67 | 6 | 6 | 6 | 54 | 65 | 11 | 4 | 0 | 0 | 0 | 0 | 20 | 3 | 0 | .150 |

## Matt Kilroy

**KILROY, MATTHEW ALOYSIUS (Matches)**
Brother of Mike Kilroy.
B. June 21, 1866, Philadelphia, Pa.   D. Mar. 2, 1940, Philadelphia, Pa.          BL TL 5'9"   175 lbs.

| | W | L | PCT | ERA | G | GS | CG | IP | H | BB | SO | ShO | W | L | SV | AB | H | HR | BA |
|---|---|---|---|---|---|---|---|---|---|---|---|---|---|---|---|---|---|---|---|
| 1886 BAL AA | 29 | 34 | .460 | 3.37 | 68 | 68 | 66 | 583 | 476 | 182 | 513 | 5 | 0 | 0 | 0 | 218 | 38 | 0 | .174 |
| 1887 | 46 | 20 | .697 | 3.07 | 69 | 69 | 66 | 589.1 | 585 | 157 | 217 | 6 | 0 | 0 | 0 | 239 | 59 | 0 | .247 |
| 1888 | 17 | 21 | .447 | 4.04 | 40 | 40 | 35 | 321 | 347 | 79 | 135 | 2 | 0 | 0 | 0 | 145 | 26 | 0 | .179 |
| 1889 | 29 | 25 | .537 | 2.85 | 59 | 56 | 55 | 480.2 | 476 | 142 | 217 | 5 | 0 | 0 | 0 | 208 | 57 | 1 | .274 |
| 1890 BOS P | 10 | 15 | .400 | 4.26 | 30 | 27 | 18 | 217.2 | 268 | 87 | 48 | 0 | 2 | 1 | 0 | 93 | 20 | 0 | .215 |
| 1891 C-M AA | 1 | 4 | .200 | 2.98 | 7 | 6 | 4 | 45.1 | 51 | 19 | 6 | 0 | 0 | 0 | 0 | 20 | 3 | 0 | .150 |

| | W | L | PCT | ERA | G | GS | CG | IP | H | BB | SO | ShO | Relief Pitching | | | BATTING | | | BA |
|---|---|---|---|---|---|---|---|---|---|---|---|---|---|---|---|---|---|---|---|
| | | | | | | | | | | | | | W | L | SV | AB | H | HR | |

## Matt Kilroy continued

| | W | L | PCT | ERA | G | GS | CG | IP | H | BB | SO | ShO | W | L | SV | AB | H | HR | BA |
|---|---|---|---|---|---|---|---|---|---|---|---|---|---|---|---|---|---|---|---|
| 1892 WAS N | 1 | 1 | .500 | 2.39 | 4 | 3 | 2 | 26.1 | 20 | 15 | 1 | 0 | 0 | 0 | 0 | 10 | 2 | 0 | .200 |
| 1893 LOU N | 3 | 2 | .600 | 9.00 | 5 | 5 | 5 | 35 | 57 | 23 | 4 | 1 | 0 | 0 | 0 | 16 | 7 | 0 | .438 |
| 1894 | 0 | 5 | .000 | 3.89 | 8 | 7 | 3 | 37 | 46 | 20 | 11 | 0 | 0 | 0 | 0 | 17 | 2 | 0 | .118 |
| 1898 CHI N | 6 | 7 | .462 | 4.31 | 13 | 11 | 10 | 100.1 | 119 | 30 | 18 | 0 | 1 | 1 | 0 | 96 | 22 | 0 | .229 |
| 10 yrs. | 142 | 134 | .514 | 3.47 | 303 | 292 | 264 | 2435.2 | 2445 | 754 | 1170 | 19 | 3 | 2 | 0 | * | | | |
| 1 yr. | 6 | 7 | .462 | 4.31 | 13 | 11 | 10 | 100.1 | 119 | 30 | 18 | 0 | 1 | 1 | 0 | 96 | 22 | 0 | .229 |

## Newt Kimball    KIMBALL, NEWELL W.    BR TR 6'2½" 190 lbs.
B. Mar. 27, 1915, Logan, Utah

| | W | L | PCT | ERA | G | GS | CG | IP | H | BB | SO | ShO | W | L | SV | AB | H | HR | BA |
|---|---|---|---|---|---|---|---|---|---|---|---|---|---|---|---|---|---|---|---|
| 1937 CHI N | 0 | 0 | – | 10.80 | 2 | 0 | 0 | 5 | 12 | 1 | 0 | 0 | 0 | 0 | 0 | 1 | 0 | 0 | .000 |
| 1938 | 0 | 0 | – | 9.00 | 1 | 0 | 0 | 1 | 3 | 0 | 1 | 0 | 0 | 0 | 0 | 0 | 0 | 0 | – |
| 1940 2 teams | | | BKN | N | (21G 3–1) | | STL | N | (2G 1–0) | | | | | | | | | | |
| " total | 4 | 1 | .800 | 3.02 | 23 | 1 | 1 | 47.2 | 40 | 21 | 27 | 0 | 3 | 1 | 1 | 11 | 2 | 0 | .182 |
| 1941 BKN N | 3 | 1 | .750 | 3.63 | 15 | 5 | 1 | 52 | 43 | 29 | 17 | 0 | 1 | 0 | 1 | 14 | 3 | 0 | .214 |
| 1942 | 2 | 0 | 1.000 | 3.68 | 14 | 1 | 0 | 29.1 | 27 | 19 | 8 | 0 | 1 | 0 | 0 | 5 | 1 | 0 | .200 |
| 1943 2 teams | | | BKN | N | (5G 1–1) | | PHI | N | (34G 1–6) | | | | | | | | | | |
| " total | 2 | 7 | .222 | 3.84 | 39 | 6 | 2 | 100.2 | 94 | 47 | 35 | 0 | 1 | 4 | 3 | 19 | 3 | 0 | .158 |
| 6 yrs. | 11 | 9 | .550 | 3.78 | 94 | 13 | 4 | 235.2 | 219 | 117 | 88 | 0 | 6 | 5 | 5 | 50 | 9 | 0 | .180 |
| 2 yrs. | 0 | 0 | – | 10.50 | 3 | 0 | 0 | 6 | 15 | 1 | 1 | 0 | 0 | 0 | 0 | 1 | 0 | 0 | .000 |

## Dave Kingman    KINGMAN, DAVID ARTHUR (Kong)    BR TR 6'6" 210 lbs.
B. Dec. 21, 1948, Pendleton, Ore.

| | W | L | PCT | ERA | G | GS | CG | IP | H | BB | SO | ShO | W | L | SV | AB | H | HR | BA |
|---|---|---|---|---|---|---|---|---|---|---|---|---|---|---|---|---|---|---|---|
| 1973 SF N | 0 | 0 | – | 9.00 | 2 | 0 | 0 | 4 | 3 | 6 | 4 | 0 | 0 | 0 | 0 | * | | | |

## Malachi Kittredge    KITTREDGE, MALACHI J.    BR TR 5'7" 170 lbs.
B. Oct. 12, 1869, Clinton, Mass.    D. June 23, 1928, Gary, Ind.
Manager 1904.

| | W | L | PCT | ERA | G | GS | CG | IP | H | BB | SO | ShO | W | L | SV | AB | H | HR | BA |
|---|---|---|---|---|---|---|---|---|---|---|---|---|---|---|---|---|---|---|---|
| 1896 CHI N | 0 | 0 | – | 5.40 | 1 | 0 | 0 | 1.2 | 2 | 1 | 0 | 0 | 0 | 0 | 0 | * | | | |

## Johnny Klippstein    KLIPPSTEIN, JOHN CALVIN    BR TR 6'1" 173 lbs.
B. Oct. 17, 1927, Washington, D. C.

| | W | L | PCT | ERA | G | GS | CG | IP | H | BB | SO | ShO | W | L | SV | AB | H | HR | BA |
|---|---|---|---|---|---|---|---|---|---|---|---|---|---|---|---|---|---|---|---|
| 1950 CHI N | 2 | 9 | .182 | 5.25 | 33 | 11 | 3 | 104.2 | 112 | 64 | 51 | 0 | 1 | 1 | 1 | 33 | 11 | 1 | .333 |
| 1951 | 6 | 6 | .500 | 4.29 | 35 | 11 | 1 | 123.2 | 121 | 53 | 56 | 1 | 4 | 0 | 2 | 37 | 4 | 1 | .108 |
| 1952 | 9 | 14 | .391 | 4.44 | 41 | 25 | 7 | 202.2 | 208 | 89 | 110 | 2 | 4 | 0 | 3 | 63 | 11 | 1 | .175 |
| 1953 | 10 | 11 | .476 | 4.83 | 48 | 20 | 5 | 167.2 | 169 | 107 | 113 | 0 | 2 | 4 | 6 | 58 | 9 | 1 | .155 |
| 1954 | 4 | 11 | .267 | 5.29 | 36 | 21 | 4 | 148 | 155 | 96 | 69 | 0 | 0 | 2 | 1 | 45 | 6 | 0 | .133 |
| 1955 CIN N | 9 | 10 | .474 | 3.39 | 39 | 14 | 3 | 138 | 120 | 60 | 68 | 2 | 4 | 2 | 0 | 31 | 2 | 0 | .065 |
| 1956 | 12 | 11 | .522 | 4.09 | 37 | 29 | 11 | 211 | 219 | 82 | 86 | 0 | 2 | 0 | 1 | 71 | 7 | 0 | .099 |
| 1957 | 8 | 11 | .421 | 5.05 | 46 | 18 | 3 | 146 | 146 | 68 | 99 | 1 | 3 | 2 | 3 | 41 | 3 | 0 | .073 |
| 1958 2 teams | | | CIN | N | (12G 3–2) | | LA | N | (45G 3–5) | | | | | | | | | | |
| " total | 6 | 7 | .462 | 4.10 | 57 | 4 | 0 | 123 | 118 | 58 | 95 | 0 | 5 | 6 | 10 | 28 | 2 | 0 | .071 |
| 1959 LA N | 4 | 0 | 1.000 | 5.91 | 28 | 0 | 0 | 45.2 | 48 | 33 | 30 | 0 | 4 | 0 | 2 | 7 | 1 | 0 | .143 |
| 1960 CLE A | 5 | 5 | .500 | 2.91 | 49 | 0 | 0 | 74.1 | 53 | 35 | 46 | 0 | 5 | 5 | 14 | 14 | 2 | 0 | .143 |
| 1961 WAS A | 2 | 2 | .500 | 6.78 | 42 | 1 | 0 | 71.2 | 83 | 43 | 41 | 0 | 2 | 1 | 0 | 7 | 1 | 0 | .143 |
| 1962 CIN N | 7 | 6 | .538 | 4.47 | 40 | 7 | 0 | 108.2 | 113 | 64 | 67 | 0 | 6 | 3 | 4 | 24 | 3 | 1 | .125 |
| 1963 PHI N | 5 | 6 | .455 | 1.93 | 49 | 1 | 0 | 112 | 80 | 46 | 86 | 0 | 5 | 5 | 8 | 26 | 1 | 0 | .038 |
| 1964 2 teams | | | PHI | N | (11G 2–1) | | MIN | A | (33G 0–4) | | | | | | | | | | |
| " total | 2 | 5 | .286 | 2.65 | 44 | 0 | 0 | 68 | 66 | 28 | 52 | 0 | 2 | 5 | 3 | 6 | 0 | 0 | .000 |
| 1965 MIN A | 9 | 3 | .750 | 2.24 | 56 | 0 | 0 | 76.1 | 59 | 31 | 59 | 0 | 9 | 3 | 5 | 8 | 0 | 0 | .000 |
| 1966 | 1 | 1 | .500 | 3.40 | 26 | 0 | 0 | 39.2 | 35 | 20 | 26 | 0 | 1 | 1 | 3 | 3 | 0 | 0 | .000 |
| 1967 DET A | 0 | 0 | – | 5.40 | 5 | 0 | 0 | 6.2 | 6 | 1 | 4 | 0 | 0 | 0 | 0 | 0 | 0 | 0 | – |
| 18 yrs. | 101 | 118 | .461 | 4.24 | 711 | 162 | 37 | 1967.2 | 1911 | 978 | 1158 | 6 | 59 | 40 | 66 | 502 | 63 | 5 | .125 |
| 5 yrs. | 31 | 51 | .378 | 4.79 | 193 | 88 | 20 | 746.2 | 765 | 409 | 399 | 3 | 11 | 7 | 13 | 236 | 41 | 4 | .174 |

WORLD SERIES

| | W | L | PCT | ERA | G | GS | CG | IP | H | BB | SO | ShO | W | L | SV | AB | H | HR | BA |
|---|---|---|---|---|---|---|---|---|---|---|---|---|---|---|---|---|---|---|---|
| 1959 LA N | 0 | 0 | – | 0.00 | 1 | 0 | 0 | 2 | 1 | 0 | 2 | 0 | 0 | 0 | 0 | 0 | 0 | 0 | – |
| 1965 MIN A | 0 | 0 | – | 0.00 | 2 | 0 | 0 | 2.2 | 2 | 2 | 3 | 0 | 0 | 0 | 0 | 0 | 0 | 0 | – |
| 2 yrs. | 0 | 0 | – | 0.00 | 3 | 0 | 0 | 4.2 | 3 | 2 | 5 | 0 | 0 | 0 | 0 | 0 | 0 | 0 | – |

## Darold Knowles    KNOWLES, DAROLD DUANE    BL TL 6' 180 lbs.
B. Dec. 9, 1941, Brunswick, Mo.

| | W | L | PCT | ERA | G | GS | CG | IP | H | BB | SO | ShO | W | L | SV | AB | H | HR | BA |
|---|---|---|---|---|---|---|---|---|---|---|---|---|---|---|---|---|---|---|---|
| 1965 BAL A | 0 | 1 | .000 | 9.20 | 5 | 1 | 0 | 14.2 | 14 | 10 | 12 | 0 | 0 | 0 | 0 | 4 | 0 | 0 | .000 |
| 1966 PHI N | 6 | 5 | .545 | 3.05 | 69 | 1 | 0 | 100.1 | 98 | 46 | 88 | 0 | 6 | 5 | 13 | 16 | 4 | 0 | .250 |
| 1967 WAS A | 6 | 8 | .429 | 2.70 | 61 | 1 | 0 | 113.1 | 91 | 52 | 85 | 0 | 6 | 7 | 14 | 16 | 1 | 0 | .063 |
| 1968 | 1 | 1 | .500 | 2.18 | 32 | 0 | 0 | 41.1 | 38 | 12 | 37 | 0 | 1 | 1 | 4 | 4 | 1 | 0 | .250 |
| 1969 | 9 | 2 | .818 | 2.24 | 53 | 0 | 0 | 84.1 | 73 | 31 | 59 | 0 | 9 | 2 | 13 | 13 | 1 | 0 | .077 |
| 1970 | 2 | 14 | .125 | 2.04 | 71 | 0 | 0 | 119 | 100 | 58 | 71 | 0 | 2 | 14 | 27 | 20 | 1 | 0 | .050 |
| 1971 2 teams | | | WAS | A | (12G 2–2) | | OAK | A | (43G 5–2) | | | | | | | | | | |
| " total | 7 | 4 | .636 | 3.57 | 55 | 0 | 0 | 68 | 57 | 22 | 56 | 0 | 7 | 4 | 9 | 10 | 1 | 0 | .100 |
| 1972 OAK A | 5 | 1 | .833 | 1.36 | 54 | 0 | 0 | 66 | 49 | 37 | 36 | 0 | 5 | 1 | 11 | 12 | 3 | 0 | .250 |
| 1973 | 6 | 8 | .429 | 3.09 | 52 | 5 | 1 | 99 | 87 | 49 | 46 | 1 | 4 | 5 | 9 | 0 | 0 | – | |
| 1974 | 3 | 3 | .500 | 4.25 | 45 | 1 | 0 | 53 | 61 | 35 | 18 | 0 | 2 | 3 | 3 | 0 | 0 | 0 | – |
| 1975 CHI N | 6 | 9 | .400 | 5.83 | 58 | 0 | 0 | 88 | 107 | 36 | 63 | 0 | 6 | 9 | 15 | 15 | 1 | 0 | .067 |
| 1976 | 5 | 7 | .417 | 2.88 | 58 | 0 | 0 | 72 | 61 | 22 | 39 | 0 | 5 | 7 | 9 | 7 | 1 | 0 | .143 |
| 1977 TEX A | 5 | 2 | .714 | 3.24 | 42 | 0 | 0 | 50 | 50 | 23 | 14 | 0 | 5 | 2 | 4 | 0 | 0 | 0 | – |
| 1978 MON N | 3 | 3 | .500 | 2.38 | 60 | 0 | 0 | 72 | 63 | 30 | 34 | 0 | 3 | 3 | 6 | 6 | 1 | 0 | .167 |
| 1979 STL N | 2 | 5 | .286 | 4.04 | 48 | 0 | 0 | 49 | 54 | 17 | 22 | 0 | 2 | 5 | 6 | 2 | 0 | 0 | .000 |
| 1980 | 0 | 1 | .000 | 9.00 | 2 | 0 | 0 | 2 | 3 | 0 | 1 | 0 | 0 | 1 | 0 | 0 | 0 | 0 | – |
| 16 yrs. | 66 | 74 | .471 | 3.12 | 765 | 8 | 1 | 1092 | 1006 | 480 | 681 | 1 | 63 | 69 | 143 | 125 | 15 | 0 | .120 |
| 2 yrs. | 11 | 16 | .407 | 4.50 | 116 | 0 | 0 | 160 | 168 | 58 | 102 | 0 | 11 | 16 | 24 | 22 | 2 | 0 | .091 |

LEAGUE CHAMPIONSHIP SERIES

| | W | L | PCT | ERA | G | GS | CG | IP | H | BB | SO | ShO | W | L | SV | AB | H | HR | BA |
|---|---|---|---|---|---|---|---|---|---|---|---|---|---|---|---|---|---|---|---|
| 1971 OAK A | 0 | 0 | – | 0.00 | 1 | 0 | 0 | .1 | 1 | 1 | 0 | 0 | 0 | 0 | 0 | 0 | 0 | 0 | – |

| | W | L | PCT | ERA | G | GS | CG | IP | H | BB | SO | ShO | Relief Pitching W | L | SV | BATTING AB | H | HR | BA |
|---|---|---|---|---|---|---|---|---|---|---|---|---|---|---|---|---|---|---|---|

## Darold Knowles continued

WORLD SERIES

| | W | L | PCT | ERA | G | GS | CG | IP | H | BB | SO | ShO | W | L | SV | AB | H | HR | BA |
|---|---|---|---|---|---|---|---|---|---|---|---|---|---|---|---|---|---|---|---|
| 1973 **OAK A** | 0 | 0 | – | 0.00 | 7 | 0 | 0 | 6.1 | 4 | 5 | 5 | 0 | 0 | 0 | 2 | 0 | 0 | 0 | – |
| | | | | | | | | | | | | | | | 10th | | | | |

## Mark Koenig

**KOENIG, MARK ANTHONY**
B. July 19, 1902, San Francisco, Calif.

BB TR 6' 180 lbs.
BL 1928

| | W | L | PCT | ERA | G | GS | CG | IP | H | BB | SO | ShO | W | L | SV | AB | H | HR | BA |
|---|---|---|---|---|---|---|---|---|---|---|---|---|---|---|---|---|---|---|---|
| 1930 **DET A** | 0 | 1 | .000 | 10.00 | 2 | 1 | 0 | 9 | 11 | 8 | 6 | 0 | 0 | 0 | 0 | 341 | 81 | 1 | .238 |
| 1931 | 0 | 0 | – | 6.43 | 3 | 0 | 0 | 7 | 7 | 11 | 3 | 0 | 0 | 0 | 0 | 364 | 92 | 1 | .253 |
| 2 yrs. | 0 | 1 | .000 | 8.44 | 5 | 1 | 0 | 16 | 18 | 19 | 9 | 0 | 0 | 0 | 0 | * | | | |

## Elmer Koestner

**KOESTNER, ELMER JOSEPH (Bob)**
B. Nov. 30, 1885, Piper City, Ill.   D. Oct. 27, 1959, Fairbury, Ill.

BR TR 6'1½" 175 lbs.

| | W | L | PCT | ERA | G | GS | CG | IP | H | BB | SO | ShO | W | L | SV | AB | H | HR | BA |
|---|---|---|---|---|---|---|---|---|---|---|---|---|---|---|---|---|---|---|---|
| 1910 **CLE A** | 5 | 10 | .333 | 3.04 | 27 | 13 | 8 | 145 | 145 | 63 | 44 | 1 | 2 | 4 | 2 | 48 | 15 | 0 | .313 |
| 1914 **2 teams** | | | **CHI N** (4G 0–0) | | | **CIN N** (5G 0–0) | | | | | | | | | | | | | |
| " total | 0 | 0 | – | 4.01 | 9 | 1 | 0 | 24.2 | 24 | 13 | 12 | 0 | 0 | 0 | 0 | 6 | 2 | 0 | .333 |
| 2 yrs. | 5 | 10 | .333 | 3.18 | 36 | 14 | 8 | 169.2 | 169 | 76 | 56 | 1 | 2 | 4 | 2 | 54 | 17 | 0 | .315 |
| 1 yr. | 0 | 0 | – | 2.84 | 4 | 0 | 0 | 6.1 | 6 | 4 | 6 | 0 | 0 | 0 | 0 | 1 | 0 | 0 | .000 |

## Cal Koonce

**KOONCE, CALVIN LEE**
B. Nov. 18, 1940, Fayetteville, N. C.

BR TR 6'1" 185 lbs.

| | W | L | PCT | ERA | G | GS | CG | IP | H | BB | SO | ShO | W | L | SV | AB | H | HR | BA |
|---|---|---|---|---|---|---|---|---|---|---|---|---|---|---|---|---|---|---|---|
| 1962 **CHI N** | 10 | 10 | .500 | 3.97 | 35 | 30 | 3 | 190.2 | 200 | 86 | 84 | 1 | 0 | 0 | 0 | 64 | 6 | 0 | .094 |
| 1963 | 2 | 6 | .250 | 4.58 | 21 | 13 | 0 | 72.2 | 75 | 32 | 44 | 0 | 0 | 0 | 0 | 19 | 2 | 0 | .105 |
| 1964 | 3 | 0 | 1.000 | 2.03 | 6 | 2 | 0 | 31 | 30 | 7 | 17 | 0 | 1 | 0 | 0 | 10 | 0 | 0 | .000 |
| 1965 | 7 | 9 | .438 | 3.69 | 38 | 23 | 3 | 173 | 181 | 52 | 88 | 1 | 0 | 0 | 0 | 49 | 5 | 0 | .102 |
| 1966 | 5 | 5 | .500 | 3.81 | 45 | 5 | 0 | 108.2 | 113 | 35 | 65 | 0 | 4 | 4 | 2 | 23 | 3 | 0 | .130 |
| 1967 **2 teams** | | | **CHI N** (34G 2–2) | | | **NY N** (11G 3–3) | | | | | | | | | | | | | |
| " total | 5 | 5 | .500 | 3.75 | 45 | 6 | 2 | 96 | 97 | 28 | 52 | 1 | 2 | 2 | 2 | 20 | 2 | 0 | .100 |
| 1968 **NY N** | 6 | 4 | .600 | 2.42 | 55 | 2 | 0 | 96.2 | 80 | 32 | 50 | 0 | 5 | 4 | 11 | 14 | 0 | 0 | .000 |
| 1969 | 6 | 3 | .667 | 4.99 | 40 | 0 | 0 | 83 | 85 | 42 | 48 | 0 | 6 | 3 | 7 | 17 | 4 | 0 | .235 |
| 1970 **2 teams** | | | **NY N** (13G 0–2) | | | **BOS A** (23G 3–4) | | | | | | | | | | | | | |
| " total | 3 | 6 | .333 | 3.49 | 36 | 8 | 1 | 98 | 89 | 43 | 47 | 0 | 0 | 2 | 2 | 22 | 2 | 0 | .091 |
| 1971 **BOS A** | 0 | 1 | .000 | 5.57 | 13 | 1 | 0 | 21 | 22 | 11 | 9 | 0 | 0 | 0 | 0 | 1 | 0 | 0 | .000 |
| 10 yrs. | 47 | 49 | .490 | 3.78 | 334 | 90 | 9 | 970.2 | 972 | 368 | 504 | 3 | 18 | 15 | 24 | 239 | 24 | 0 | .100 |
| 6 yrs. | 29 | 32 | .475 | 3.89 | 179 | 73 | 6 | 627 | 651 | 233 | 326 | 2 | 7 | 6 | 4 | 172 | 16 | 0 | .093 |

## Jim Korwan

**KORWAN, JAMES**
B. Mar. 4, 1874, Brooklyn, N. Y.   D. Aug., 1899, Brooklyn, N. Y.

| | W | L | PCT | ERA | G | GS | CG | IP | H | BB | SO | ShO | W | L | SV | AB | H | HR | BA |
|---|---|---|---|---|---|---|---|---|---|---|---|---|---|---|---|---|---|---|---|
| 1894 **BKN N** | 0 | 0 | – | 14.40 | 1 | 0 | 0 | 5 | 9 | 5 | 2 | 0 | 0 | 0 | 0 | 2 | 0 | 0 | .000 |
| 1897 **CHI N** | 1 | 2 | .333 | 5.82 | 5 | 4 | 3 | 34 | 47 | 28 | 12 | 0 | 0 | 0 | 0 | 12 | 0 | 0 | .000 |
| 2 yrs. | 1 | 2 | .333 | 6.92 | 6 | 4 | 3 | 39 | 56 | 33 | 14 | 0 | 0 | 0 | 0 | 14 | 0 | 0 | .000 |
| 1 yr. | 1 | 2 | .333 | 5.82 | 5 | 4 | 3 | 34 | 47 | 28 | 12 | 0 | 0 | 0 | 0 | 12 | 0 | 0 | .000 |

## Fabian Kowalik

**KOWALIK, FABIAN LORENZ**
B. Apr. 22, 1908, Falls City, Tex.

D. Aug. 14, 1954, Karnes City, Tex.

BR TR 5'11" 185 lbs.
BL 1932,
BB 1935

| | W | L | PCT | ERA | G | GS | CG | IP | H | BB | SO | ShO | W | L | SV | AB | H | HR | BA |
|---|---|---|---|---|---|---|---|---|---|---|---|---|---|---|---|---|---|---|---|
| 1932 **CHI A** | 0 | 1 | .000 | 6.97 | 2 | 1 | 0 | 10.1 | 16 | 4 | 2 | 0 | 0 | 0 | 0 | 13 | 5 | 0 | .385 |
| 1935 **CHI N** | 2 | 2 | .500 | 4.42 | 20 | 2 | 1 | 55 | 60 | 19 | 20 | 0 | 2 | 0 | 1 | 15 | 3 | 0 | .200 |
| 1936 **3 teams** | | | **CHI N** (6G 0–2) | | | **PHI N** (22G 1–5) | | | **BOS N** (1G 0–1) | | | | | | | | | | |
| " total | 1 | 8 | .111 | 5.82 | 29 | 9 | 3 | 102 | 142 | 40 | 20 | 0 | 0 | 2 | 1 | 67 | 15 | 0 | .224 |
| 3 yrs. | 3 | 11 | .214 | 5.43 | 51 | 12 | 4 | 167.1 | 218 | 63 | 42 | 0 | 2 | 2 | 2 | 95 | 23 | 0 | .242 |
| 2 yrs. | 2 | 4 | .333 | 4.94 | 26 | 2 | 1 | 71 | 84 | 26 | 21 | 0 | 2 | 2 | 2 | 20 | 3 | 0 | .150 |

WORLD SERIES

| | W | L | PCT | ERA | G | GS | CG | IP | H | BB | SO | ShO | W | L | SV | AB | H | HR | BA |
|---|---|---|---|---|---|---|---|---|---|---|---|---|---|---|---|---|---|---|---|
| 1935 **CHI N** | 0 | 0 | – | 2.08 | 1 | 0 | 0 | 4.1 | 3 | 1 | 1 | 0 | 0 | 0 | 0 | 2 | 1 | 0 | .500 |

## Ken Kravec

**KRAVEC, KENNETH PETER**
B. July 29, 1951, Cleveland, Ohio

BL TL 6'2" 185 lbs.

| | W | L | PCT | ERA | G | GS | CG | IP | H | BB | SO | ShO | W | L | SV | AB | H | HR | BA |
|---|---|---|---|---|---|---|---|---|---|---|---|---|---|---|---|---|---|---|---|
| 1975 **CHI A** | 0 | 1 | .000 | 6.23 | 2 | 1 | 0 | 4.1 | 4 | 8 | 1 | 0 | 0 | 0 | 0 | 0 | 0 | 0 | – |
| 1976 | 1 | 5 | .167 | 4.86 | 9 | 8 | 1 | 50 | 49 | 32 | 38 | 0 | 0 | 0 | 0 | 0 | 0 | 0 | – |
| 1977 | 11 | 8 | .579 | 4.10 | 26 | 25 | 6 | 167 | 161 | 57 | 125 | 1 | 0 | 0 | 0 | 0 | 0 | 0 | – |
| 1978 | 11 | 16 | .407 | 4.08 | 30 | 30 | 7 | 203 | 188 | 95 | 154 | 2 | 0 | 0 | 0 | 0 | 0 | 0 | – |
| 1979 | 15 | 13 | .536 | 3.74 | 36 | 35 | 10 | 250 | 208 | 111 | 132 | 3 | 0 | 0 | 0 | 0 | 0 | 0 | – |
| 1980 | 3 | 6 | .333 | 6.91 | 20 | 15 | 0 | 82 | 100 | 44 | 37 | 0 | 0 | 0 | 0 | 0 | 0 | 0 | – |
| 1981 **CHI N** | 1 | 6 | .143 | 5.08 | 24 | 12 | 0 | 78 | 80 | 39 | 50 | 0 | 0 | 1 | 0 | 15 | 0 | 0 | .000 |
| 1982 | 1 | 1 | .500 | 6.12 | 13 | 2 | 0 | 25 | 27 | 18 | 20 | 0 | 1 | 1 | 0 | 3 | 0 | 0 | .000 |
| 8 yrs. | 43 | 56 | .434 | 4.46 | 160 | 128 | 24 | 859.1 | 814 | 404 | 557 | 6 | 1 | 2 | 1 | 18 | 0 | 0 | .000 |
| 2 yrs. | 2 | 7 | .222 | 5.33 | 37 | 14 | 0 | 103 | 107 | 57 | 70 | 0 | 1 | 2 | 0 | 18 | 0 | 0 | .000 |

## Jim Kremmel

**KREMMEL, DOUGLAS JAMES**
B. Feb. 28, 1949, Columbia, Ill.

BL TL 6' 175 lbs.

| | W | L | PCT | ERA | G | GS | CG | IP | H | BB | SO | ShO | W | L | SV | AB | H | HR | BA |
|---|---|---|---|---|---|---|---|---|---|---|---|---|---|---|---|---|---|---|---|
| 1973 **TEX A** | 0 | 2 | .000 | 9.00 | 4 | 2 | 0 | 9 | 15 | 6 | 6 | 0 | 0 | 0 | 0 | 0 | 0 | 0 | – |
| 1974 **CHI N** | 0 | 2 | .000 | 5.23 | 23 | 2 | 0 | 31 | 37 | 18 | 22 | 0 | 0 | 1 | 0 | 3 | 0 | 0 | .000 |
| 2 yrs. | 0 | 4 | .000 | 6.08 | 27 | 4 | 0 | 40 | 52 | 24 | 28 | 0 | 0 | 1 | 0 | 3 | 0 | 0 | .000 |
| 1 yr. | 0 | 2 | .000 | 5.23 | 23 | 2 | 0 | 31 | 37 | 18 | 22 | 0 | 0 | 1 | 0 | 3 | 0 | 0 | .000 |

## Gus Krock

**KROCK, AUGUST H.**
B. May 9, 1866, Milwaukee, Wis.   D. Mar. 22, 1905, Pasadena, Calif.

TL 6' 196 lbs.

| | W | L | PCT | ERA | G | GS | CG | IP | H | BB | SO | ShO | W | L | SV | AB | H | HR | BA |
|---|---|---|---|---|---|---|---|---|---|---|---|---|---|---|---|---|---|---|---|
| 1888 **CHI N** | 24 | 14 | .632 | 2.44 | 39 | 39 | 39 | 339.2 | 295 | 45 | 161 | 4 | 0 | 0 | 0 | 134 | 22 | 1 | .164 |

| | W | L | PCT | ERA | G | GS | CG | IP | H | BB | SO | ShO | Relief Pitching W | L | SV | BATTING AB | H | HR | BA |
|---|---|---|---|---|---|---|---|---|---|---|---|---|---|---|---|---|---|---|---|

## Gus Krock continued

| | W | L | PCT | ERA | G | GS | CG | IP | H | BB | SO | ShO | W | L | SV | AB | H | HR | BA |
|---|---|---|---|---|---|---|---|---|---|---|---|---|---|---|---|---|---|---|---|
| 1889 3 teams | CHI | N | (7G 3–3) | **IND** | **N** | (4G 2–2) | **WAS** | **N** | (6G 2–4) | | | | | | | | | | |
| " total | 7 | 9 | .438 | 5.57 | 17 | 17 | 14 | 140.2 | 199 | 50 | 43 | 0 | 0 | 0 | 0 | 61 | 11 | 0 | .180 |
| 1890 **BUF P** | 0 | 3 | .000 | 6.12 | 4 | 3 | 3 | 25 | 43 | 15 | 5 | 0 | 0 | 0 | 0 | 12 | 1 | 0 | .083 |
| 3 yrs. | 31 | 26 | .544 | 3.49 | 60 | 59 | 56 | 505.1 | 537 | 110 | 209 | 4 | 0 | 0 | 0 | 207 | 34 | 1 | .164 |
| 2 yrs. | 27 | 17 | .614 | 2.81 | 46 | 46 | 44 | 400.1 | 381 | 59 | 177 | 4 | 0 | 0 | 0 | 158 | 26 | 1 | .165 |

## Rube Kroh

**KROH, FLOYD MYRON**                               BL TL 6'2"  186 lbs.
B. Aug. 25, 1886, Friendship, N. Y.   D. Mar. 17, 1944, New Orleans, La.

| | W | L | PCT | ERA | G | GS | CG | IP | H | BB | SO | ShO | W | L | SV | AB | H | HR | BA |
|---|---|---|---|---|---|---|---|---|---|---|---|---|---|---|---|---|---|---|---|
| 1906 **BOS A** | 1 | 0 | 1.000 | 0.00 | 1 | 1 | 1 | 9 | 2 | 4 | 5 | 1 | 0 | 0 | 0 | 3 | 0 | 0 | .000 |
| 1907 | 1 | 4 | .200 | 2.62 | 7 | 5 | 1 | 34.1 | 33 | 8 | 8 | 0 | 0 | 0 | 0 | 11 | 3 | 0 | .273 |
| 1908 **CHI N** | 0 | 0 | – | 1.50 | 2 | 1 | 0 | 12 | 9 | 4 | 11 | 0 | 0 | 0 | 0 | 4 | 0 | 0 | .000 |
| 1909 | 9 | 4 | .692 | 1.65 | 17 | 13 | 10 | 120.1 | 97 | 30 | 51 | 2 | 0 | 0 | 0 | 40 | 6 | 0 | .150 |
| 1910 | 3 | 1 | .750 | 4.46 | 6 | 4 | 1 | 34.1 | 33 | 15 | 16 | 0 | 2 | 0 | 0 | 12 | 3 | 0 | .250 |
| 1912 **BOS N** | 0 | 0 | – | 5.68 | 3 | 1 | 0 | 6.1 | 8 | 6 | 1 | 0 | 0 | 0 | 0 | 2 | 1 | 0 | .500 |
| 6 yrs. | 14 | 9 | .609 | 2.29 | 36 | 25 | 13 | 216.1 | 182 | 67 | 92 | 3 | 2 | 0 | 0 | 72 | 13 | 0 | .181 |
| 3 yrs. | 12 | 5 | .706 | 2.21 | 25 | 18 | 11 | 166.2 | 139 | 49 | 78 | 2 | 2 | 0 | 0 | 56 | 9 | 0 | .161 |

## Mike Krukow

**KRUKOW, MICHAEL EDWARD**                          BR TR 6'5"  205 lbs.
B. Jan. 21, 1952, Long Beach, Calif.

| | W | L | PCT | ERA | G | GS | CG | IP | H | BB | SO | ShO | W | L | SV | AB | H | HR | BA |
|---|---|---|---|---|---|---|---|---|---|---|---|---|---|---|---|---|---|---|---|
| 1976 **CHI N** | 0 | 0 | – | 9.00 | 2 | 0 | 0 | 4 | 6 | 2 | 1 | 0 | 0 | 0 | 0 | 1 | 0 | 0 | .000 |
| 1977 | 8 | 14 | .364 | 4.40 | 34 | 33 | 1 | 172 | 195 | 61 | 106 | 1 | 0 | 0 | 0 | 55 | 11 | 0 | .200 |
| 1978 | 9 | 3 | .750 | 3.91 | 27 | 20 | 3 | 138 | 125 | 53 | 81 | 1 | 0 | 0 | 0 | 45 | 11 | 0 | .244 |
| 1979 | 9 | 9 | .500 | 4.20 | 28 | 28 | 0 | 165 | 172 | 81 | 119 | 0 | 0 | 0 | 0 | 51 | 16 | 1 | .314 |
| 1980 | 10 | 15 | .400 | 4.39 | 34 | 34 | 3 | 205 | 200 | 80 | 130 | 0 | 0 | 0 | 0 | 65 | 16 | 1 | .246 |
| 1981 | 9 | 9 | .500 | 3.69 | 25 | 25 | 2 | 144 | 146 | 55 | 101 | 1 | 0 | 0 | 0 | 50 | 9 | 0 | .180 |
| 1982 **PHI N** | 13 | 11 | .542 | 3.12 | 33 | 33 | 7 | 208 | 211 | 82 | 138 | 2 | 0 | 0 | 0 | 72 | 13 | 0 | .181 |
| 1983 **SF N** | 11 | 11 | .500 | 3.95 | 31 | 31 | 2 | 184.1 | 189 | 76 | 136 | 1 | 0 | 0 | 0 | 63 | 16 | 1 | .254 |
| 1984 | 11 | 12 | .478 | 4.56 | 35 | 33 | 3 | 199 | **234** | 78 | 141 | 1 | 0 | 0 | 0 | 72 | 10 | 1 | .139 |
| 1985 | 8 | 11 | .421 | 3.38 | 28 | 28 | 6 | 194.2 | 176 | 49 | 150 | 1 | 0 | 0 | 1 | 55 | 12 | 1 | .218 |
| 10 yrs. | 88 | 95 | .481 | 3.96 | 277 | 265 | 27 | 1614.1 | 1654 | 611 | 1103 | 8 | 0 | 0 | 1 | 529 | 114 | 4 | .216 |
| 6 yrs. | 45 | 50 | .474 | 4.17 | 150 | 140 | 9 | 828 | 844 | 332 | 538 | 3 | 0 | 0 | 0 | 267 | 63 | 2 | .236 |

## Emil Kush

**KUSH, EMIL BENEDICT (Moe)**                        BR TR 5'11"  185 lbs.
B. Nov. 4, 1916, Chicago, Ill.   D. Nov. 25, 1969, River Grove, Ill.

| | W | L | PCT | ERA | G | GS | CG | IP | H | BB | SO | ShO | W | L | SV | AB | H | HR | BA |
|---|---|---|---|---|---|---|---|---|---|---|---|---|---|---|---|---|---|---|---|
| 1941 **CHI N** | 0 | 0 | – | 2.25 | 2 | 0 | 0 | 4 | 2 | 0 | 2 | 0 | 0 | 0 | 0 | 1 | 0 | 0 | .000 |
| 1942 | 0 | 0 | – | 0.00 | 1 | 0 | 0 | 2 | 1 | 1 | 1 | 0 | 0 | 0 | 0 | 1 | 0 | 0 | .000 |
| 1946 | 9 | 2 | .818 | 3.05 | 40 | 6 | 1 | 129.2 | 120 | 43 | 50 | 1 | 8 | 0 | 2 | 38 | 8 | 0 | .211 |
| 1947 | 8 | 3 | .727 | 3.36 | 47 | 1 | 1 | 91 | 80 | 53 | 44 | 0 | 7 | 2 | 5 | 20 | 5 | 0 | .250 |
| 1948 | 1 | 4 | .200 | 4.38 | 34 | 1 | 0 | 72 | 70 | 37 | 31 | 0 | 1 | 3 | 3 | 13 | 2 | 0 | .154 |
| 1949 | 3 | 3 | .500 | 3.78 | 26 | 0 | 0 | 47.2 | 51 | 24 | 22 | 0 | 3 | 3 | 2 | 9 | 3 | 0 | .333 |
| 6 yrs. | 21 | 12 | .636 | 3.48 | 150 | 8 | 2 | 346.1 | 324 | 158 | 150 | 1 | 19 | 8 | 12 | 82 | 18 | 0 | .220 |
| 6 yrs. | 21 | 12 | .636 | 3.48 | 150 | 8 | 2 | 346.1 | 324 | 158 | 150 | 1 | 19 | 8 | 12 | 82 | 18 | 0 | .220 |

## Doyle Lade

**LADE, DOYLE MARION (Porky)**                       BR TR 5'10"  183 lbs.
B. Feb. 17, 1921, Fairbury, Neb.                     BB 1946–47

| | W | L | PCT | ERA | G | GS | CG | IP | H | BB | SO | ShO | W | L | SV | AB | H | HR | BA |
|---|---|---|---|---|---|---|---|---|---|---|---|---|---|---|---|---|---|---|---|
| 1946 **CHI N** | 0 | 2 | .000 | 4.11 | 3 | 2 | 0 | 15.1 | 15 | 3 | 8 | 0 | 0 | 1 | 0 | 5 | 1 | 0 | .200 |
| 1947 | 11 | 10 | .524 | 3.94 | 34 | 25 | 7 | 187.1 | 202 | 79 | 62 | 1 | 0 | 0 | 0 | 60 | 13 | 0 | .217 |
| 1948 | 5 | 6 | .455 | 4.02 | 19 | 12 | 6 | 87.1 | 99 | 31 | 29 | 0 | 0 | 0 | 0 | 32 | 5 | 0 | .156 |
| 1949 | 4 | 5 | .444 | 5.00 | 36 | 13 | 5 | 129.2 | 141 | 58 | 43 | 1 | 0 | 0 | 1 | 32 | 7 | 0 | .219 |
| 1950 | 5 | 6 | .455 | 4.74 | 34 | 12 | 2 | 117.2 | 126 | 50 | 36 | 0 | 2 | 1 | 2 | 35 | 10 | 0 | .286 |
| 5 yrs. | 25 | 29 | .463 | 4.39 | 126 | 64 | 20 | 537.1 | 583 | 221 | 178 | 2 | 2 | 2 | 3 | 164 | 36 | 0 | .220 |
| 5 yrs. | 25 | 29 | .463 | 4.39 | 126 | 64 | 20 | 537.1 | 583 | 221 | 178 | 2 | 2 | 2 | 3 | 164 | 36 | 0 | .220 |

## Jack Lamabe

**LAMABE, JOHN ALEXANDER**                           BR TR 6'1"  198 lbs.
B. Oct. 3, 1936, Farmingdale, N. Y.

| | W | L | PCT | ERA | G | GS | CG | IP | H | BB | SO | ShO | W | L | SV | AB | H | HR | BA |
|---|---|---|---|---|---|---|---|---|---|---|---|---|---|---|---|---|---|---|---|
| 1962 **PIT N** | 3 | 1 | .750 | 2.88 | 46 | 0 | 0 | 78 | 70 | 40 | 56 | 0 | 3 | 1 | 2 | 9 | 0 | 0 | .000 |
| 1963 **BOS A** | 7 | 4 | .636 | 3.15 | 65 | 2 | 0 | 151.1 | 139 | 46 | 93 | 0 | 7 | 3 | 6 | 32 | 3 | 1 | .094 |
| 1964 | 9 | 13 | .409 | 5.89 | 39 | 25 | 3 | 177.1 | 235 | 57 | 109 | 0 | 1 | 2 | 1 | 52 | 6 | 0 | .115 |
| 1965 2 teams | **BOS** | **A** | (14G 0–3) | **HOU** | **N** | (3G 0–2) | | | | | | | | | | | | |
| " total | 2 | 5 | .000 | 6.87 | 17 | 2 | 0 | 38 | 51 | 17 | 23 | 0 | 3 | 0 | 0 | 8 | 1 | 0 | .125 |
| 1966 **CHI A** | 7 | 9 | .438 | 3.93 | 34 | 17 | 3 | 121.1 | 116 | 35 | 67 | 2 | 2 | 0 | 0 | 35 | 2 | 0 | .057 |
| 1967 3 teams | CHI | A | (3G 1–0) | NY | N | (16G 0–3) | **STL** | **N** | (23G 3–4) | | | | | | | | | | |
| " total | 4 | 7 | .364 | 3.20 | 42 | 3 | 1 | 84.1 | 74 | 19 | 56 | 0 | 3 | 5 | 5 | 15 | 2 | 0 | .133 |
| 1968 **CHI N** | 3 | 2 | .600 | 4.30 | 42 | 0 | 0 | 60.2 | 68 | 24 | 30 | 0 | 3 | 2 | 1 | 5 | 1 | 0 | .200 |
| 7 yrs. | 33 | 41 | .446 | 4.24 | 285 | 49 | 7 | 711 | 753 | 238 | 434 | 3 | 19 | 16 | 15 | 156 | 15 | 1 | .096 |
| 1 yr. | 3 | 2 | .600 | 4.30 | 42 | 0 | 0 | 60.2 | 68 | 24 | 30 | 0 | 3 | 2 | 1 | 5 | 1 | 0 | .200 |
| WORLD SERIES | | | | | | | | | | | | | | | | | | | |
| 1967 **STL N** | 0 | 1 | .000 | 6.75 | 3 | 0 | 0 | 2.2 | 5 | 0 | 4 | 0 | 0 | 1 | 0 | 0 | 0 | 0 | – |

## Dennis Lamp

**LAMP, DENNIS PATRICK**                             BR TR 6'4"  200 lbs.
B. Sept. 23, 1952, Los Angeles, Calif.

| | W | L | PCT | ERA | G | GS | CG | IP | H | BB | SO | ShO | W | L | SV | AB | H | HR | BA |
|---|---|---|---|---|---|---|---|---|---|---|---|---|---|---|---|---|---|---|---|
| 1977 **CHI N** | 0 | 2 | .000 | 6.30 | 11 | 3 | 0 | 30 | 43 | 8 | 12 | 0 | 0 | 0 | 0 | 8 | 3 | 0 | .375 |
| 1978 | 7 | 15 | .318 | 3.29 | 37 | 36 | 6 | 224 | 221 | 56 | 73 | 3 | 0 | 0 | 0 | 73 | 15 | 0 | .205 |
| 1979 | 11 | 10 | .524 | 3.51 | 38 | 32 | 6 | 200 | 223 | 46 | 86 | 1 | 0 | 0 | 0 | 58 | 9 | 0 | .155 |
| 1980 | 10 | 14 | .417 | 5.19 | 41 | 37 | 2 | 203 | 259 | 82 | 83 | 1 | 1 | 0 | 0 | 61 | 6 | 0 | .098 |
| 1981 **CHI A** | 7 | 6 | .538 | 2.41 | 27 | 10 | 3 | 127 | 103 | 43 | 71 | 0 | 3 | 1 | 0 | 0 | 0 | 0 | – |
| 1982 | 11 | 8 | .579 | 3.99 | 44 | 27 | 3 | 189.2 | 206 | 59 | 78 | 2 | 1 | 1 | 5 | 0 | 0 | 0 | – |
| 1983 | 7 | 7 | .500 | 3.71 | 49 | 5 | 1 | 116.1 | 123 | 29 | 44 | 0 | 4 | 5 | 15 | 0 | 0 | 0 | – |
| 1984 **TOR A** | 8 | 8 | .500 | 4.55 | 56 | 4 | 0 | 85 | 97 | 38 | 45 | 0 | 5 | 7 | 9 | 0 | 0 | 0 | – |

| | W | L | PCT | ERA | G | GS | CG | IP | H | BB | SO | ShO | Relief Pitching W | L | SV | BATTING AB | H | HR | BA |
|---|---|---|---|---|---|---|---|---|---|---|---|---|---|---|---|---|---|---|---|

## Dennis Lamp continued

| | W | L | PCT | ERA | G | GS | CG | IP | H | BB | SO | ShO | W | L | SV | AB | H | HR | BA |
|---|---|---|---|---|---|---|---|---|---|---|---|---|---|---|---|---|---|---|---|
| 1985 | 11 | 0 | 1.000 | 3.32 | 53 | 1 | 0 | 105.2 | 96 | 27 | 68 | 0 | 11 | 0 | 2 | 0 | 0 | 0 | — |
| 9 yrs. | 72 | 70 | .507 | 3.84 | 356 | 155 | 21 | 1280.2 | 1371 | 388 | 560 | 7 | 25 | 16 | 31 | 200 | 33 | 0 | .165 |
| 4 yrs. | 28 | 41 | .406 | 4.08 | 127 | 108 | 14 | 657 | 746 | 192 | 254 | 5 | 1 | 2 | 0 | 200 | 33 | 0 | .165 |

LEAGUE CHAMPIONSHIP SERIES

| | W | L | PCT | ERA | G | GS | CG | IP | H | BB | SO | ShO | W | L | SV | AB | H | HR | BA |
|---|---|---|---|---|---|---|---|---|---|---|---|---|---|---|---|---|---|---|---|
| 1983 CHI A | 0 | 0 | — | 0.00 | 3 | 0 | 0 | 2 | 0 | 2 | 1 | 0 | 0 | 0 | 0 | 0 | 0 | 0 | — |
| 1985 TOR A | 0 | 0 | — | 0.00 | 3 | 0 | 0 | 9.1 | 2 | 1 | 10 | 0 | 0 | 0 | 0 | 0 | 0 | 0 | — |
| 2 yrs. | 0 | 0 | — | 0.00 | 6 | 0 | 0 | 11.1 | 2 | 3 | 11 | 0 | 0 | 0 | 0 | 0 | 0 | 0 | — |

## Walt Lanfranconi

**LANFRANCONI, WALTER OSWALD**
B. Nov. 9, 1916, Barre, Vt.  BR TR 5'7½" 155 lbs.

| | W | L | PCT | ERA | G | GS | CG | IP | H | BB | SO | ShO | W | L | SV | AB | H | HR | BA |
|---|---|---|---|---|---|---|---|---|---|---|---|---|---|---|---|---|---|---|---|
| 1941 CHI N | 0 | 1 | .000 | 3.00 | 2 | 1 | 0 | 6 | 7 | 2 | 1 | 0 | 0 | 0 | 0 | 1 | 0 | 0 | .000 |
| 1947 BOS N | 4 | 4 | .500 | 2.95 | 36 | 4 | 1 | 64 | 65 | 27 | 18 | 0 | 3 | 0 | 1 | 10 | 0 | 0 | .000 |
| 2 yrs. | 4 | 5 | .444 | 2.96 | 38 | 5 | 1 | 70 | 72 | 29 | 19 | 0 | 3 | 0 | 1 | 11 | 0 | 0 | .000 |
| 1 yr. | 0 | 1 | .000 | 3.00 | 2 | 1 | 0 | 6 | 7 | 2 | 1 | 0 | 0 | 0 | 0 | 1 | 0 | 0 | .000 |

## Terry Larkin

**LARKIN, FRANK S.**
B. New York, N. Y.   D. Sept. 16, 1894, Brooklyn, N. Y.  BR TR

| | W | L | PCT | ERA | G | GS | CG | IP | H | BB | SO | ShO | W | L | SV | AB | H | HR | BA |
|---|---|---|---|---|---|---|---|---|---|---|---|---|---|---|---|---|---|---|---|
| 1876 NY N | 0 | 1 | .000 | 3.00 | 1 | 1 | 1 | 9 | 9 | 0 | 0 | 0 | 0 | 0 | 0 | 4 | 0 | 0 | .000 |
| 1877 HAR N | 29 | 25 | .537 | 2.14 | 56 | 56 | 55 | 501 | 510 | 53 | 96 | 4 | 0 | 0 | 0 | 228 | 52 | 1 | .228 |
| 1878 CHI N | 29 | 26 | .527 | 2.24 | 56 | 56 | 56 | 506 | 511 | 31 | 163 | 4 | 0 | 0 | 0 | 226 | 65 | 0 | .288 |
| 1879 | 31 | 23 | .574 | 2.44 | 58 | 58 | 57 | 513.1 | 514 | 30 | 142 | 3 | 0 | 0 | 0 | 228 | 50 | 0 | .219 |
| 1880 TRO N | 0 | 5 | .000 | 8.76 | 5 | 5 | 3 | 38 | 83 | 10 | 5 | 0 | 0 | 0 | 0 | 20 | 3 | 0 | .150 |
| 1884 RIC AA | 0 | 0 | — | 0.00 | 0 | 0 | 0 | 0 | 0 | 0 | 0 | 0 | 0 | 0 | 0 | 209 | 45 | 0 | .215 |
| 6 yrs. | 89 | 80 | .527 | 2.43 | 176 | 176 | 172 | 1567.1 | 1627 | 124 | 406 | 8 | 0 | 0 | 0 | * | | | |
| 2 yrs. | 60 | 49 | .550 | 2.34 8th | 114 | 114 | 113 | 1019.1 | 1025 | 61 | 305 | 4 | 0 | 0 | 0 | 454 | 115 | 0 | .253 |

## Dave LaRoche

**LaROCHE, DAVID EUGENE**
B. May 14, 1948, Colorado Springs, Colo.  BL TL 6'2" 200 lbs.

| | W | L | PCT | ERA | G | GS | CG | IP | H | BB | SO | ShO | W | L | SV | AB | H | HR | BA |
|---|---|---|---|---|---|---|---|---|---|---|---|---|---|---|---|---|---|---|---|
| 1970 CAL A | 4 | 1 | .800 | 3.42 | 38 | 0 | 0 | 50 | 41 | 21 | 44 | 0 | 4 | 1 | 4 | 8 | 2 | 0 | .250 |
| 1971 | 5 | 1 | .833 | 2.50 | 56 | 0 | 0 | 72 | 55 | 27 | 63 | 0 | 5 | 1 | 9 | 11 | 1 | 0 | .091 |
| 1972 MIN A | 5 | 7 | .417 | 2.84 | 62 | 0 | 0 | 95 | 72 | 39 | 79 | 0 | 5 | 7 | 10 | 11 | 1 | 0 | .091 |
| 1973 CHI N | 4 | 1 | .800 | 5.83 | 45 | 0 | 0 | 54 | 55 | 29 | 34 | 0 | 4 | 1 | 4 | 4 | 2 | 0 | .500 |
| 1974 | 5 | 6 | .455 | 4.79 | 49 | 4 | 0 | 92 | 103 | 47 | 49 | 0 | 4 | 5 | 5 | 27 | 9 | 0 | .333 |
| 1975 CLE A | 5 | 3 | .625 | 2.19 | 61 | 0 | 0 | 82.1 | 61 | 57 | 94 | 0 | 5 | 3 | 17 | 0 | 0 | 0 | — |
| 1976 | 1 | 4 | .200 | 2.25 | 61 | 0 | 0 | 96 | 57 | 49 | 104 | 0 | 1 | 4 | 21 | 0 | 0 | 0 | — |
| 1977 2 teams | | | | | CLE A (13G 2–2) | | | | CAL A (46G 6–5) | | | | | | | | | | |
| " total | 8 | 7 | .533 | 3.51 | 59 | 0 | 0 | 100 | 79 | 44 | 79 | 0 | 8 | 7 | 17 | 0 | 0 | 0 | — |
| 1978 CAL A | 10 | 9 | .526 | 2.81 | 59 | 0 | 0 | 96 | 73 | 48 | 70 | 0 | 10 | 9 | 25 | 0 | 0 | 0 | — |
| 1979 | 7 | 11 | .389 | 5.55 | 53 | 1 | 0 | 86 | 107 | 32 | 59 | 0 | 6 | 11 | 10 | 0 | 0 | 0 | — |
| 1980 | 3 | 5 | .375 | 4.08 | 52 | 9 | 1 | 128 | 122 | 39 | 89 | 0 | 2 | 0 | 4 | 0 | 0 | 0 | — |
| 1981 NY A | 4 | 1 | .800 | 2.49 | 26 | 1 | 0 | 47 | 38 | 16 | 24 | 0 | 4 | 1 | 0 | 0 | 0 | 0 | — |
| 1982 | 4 | 2 | .667 | 3.42 | 25 | 0 | 0 | 50 | 54 | 11 | 31 | 0 | 4 | 2 | 0 | 0 | 0 | 0 | — |
| 1983 | 0 | 0 | — | 18.00 | 1 | 0 | 0 | 1 | 2 | 1 | 0 | 0 | 0 | 0 | 0 | 0 | 0 | 0 | — |
| 14 yrs. | 65 | 58 | .528 | 3.53 | 647 | 15 | 1 | 1049.1 | 919 | 459 | 819 | 0 | 62 | 52 | 126 | 61 | 15 | 0 | .246 |
| 2 yrs. | 9 | 7 | .563 | 5.18 | 94 | 4 | 0 | 146 | 158 | 76 | 83 | 0 | 8 | 6 | 9 | 31 | 11 | 0 | .355 |

LEAGUE CHAMPIONSHIP SERIES

| | W | L | PCT | ERA | G | GS | CG | IP | H | BB | SO | ShO | W | L | SV | AB | H | HR | BA |
|---|---|---|---|---|---|---|---|---|---|---|---|---|---|---|---|---|---|---|---|
| 1979 CAL A | 0 | 0 | — | 6.75 | 1 | 0 | 0 | 1.1 | 2 | 1 | 1 | 0 | 0 | 0 | 0 | 0 | 0 | 0 | — |

WORLD SERIES

| | W | L | PCT | ERA | G | GS | CG | IP | H | BB | SO | ShO | W | L | SV | AB | H | HR | BA |
|---|---|---|---|---|---|---|---|---|---|---|---|---|---|---|---|---|---|---|---|
| 1981 NY A | 0 | 0 | — | 0.00 | 1 | 0 | 0 | 1 | 0 | 2 | 2 | 0 | 0 | 0 | 0 | 0 | 0 | 0 | — |

## Don Larsen

**LARSEN, DONALD JAMES**
B. Aug. 7, 1929, Michigan City, Ind.  BR TR 6'4" 215 lbs.

| | W | L | PCT | ERA | G | GS | CG | IP | H | BB | SO | ShO | W | L | SV | AB | H | HR | BA |
|---|---|---|---|---|---|---|---|---|---|---|---|---|---|---|---|---|---|---|---|
| 1953 STL A | 7 | 12 | .368 | 4.16 | 38 | 22 | 7 | 192.2 | 201 | 64 | 96 | 2 | 1 | 2 | 2 | 81 | 23 | 3 | .284 |
| 1954 BAL A | 3 | 21 | .125 | 4.37 | 29 | 28 | 12 | 201.2 | 213 | 89 | 80 | 1 | 0 | 1 | 0 | 88 | 22 | 1 | .250 |
| 1955 NY A | 9 | 2 | .818 | 3.06 | 19 | 13 | 5 | 97 | 81 | 51 | 44 | 1 | 1 | 1 | 2 | 41 | 6 | 2 | .146 |
| 1956 | 11 | 5 | .688 | 3.26 | 38 | 20 | 6 | 179.2 | 133 | 96 | 107 | 1 | 2 | 0 | 1 | 79 | 19 | 2 | .241 |
| 1957 | 10 | 4 | .714 | 3.74 | 27 | 20 | 4 | 139.2 | 113 | 87 | 81 | 1 | 2 | 0 | 0 | 56 | 14 | 0 | .250 |
| 1958 | 9 | 6 | .600 | 3.07 | 19 | 19 | 5 | 114.1 | 100 | 52 | 55 | 3 | 0 | 0 | 0 | 49 | 15 | 4 | .306 |
| 1959 | 6 | 7 | .462 | 4.33 | 25 | 18 | 3 | 124.2 | 122 | 76 | 69 | 0 | 0 | 0 | 0 | 47 | 12 | 0 | .255 |
| 1960 KC A | 1 | 10 | .091 | 5.38 | 22 | 15 | 0 | 83.2 | 97 | 42 | 43 | 0 | 0 | 1 | 0 | 29 | 6 | 0 | .207 |
| 1961 2 teams | | | | | KC A (8G 1–0) | | | | CHI A (25G 7–2) | | | | | | | | | | |
| " total | 8 | 2 | .800 | 4.13 | 33 | 2 | 0 | 89.1 | 85 | 40 | 66 | 0 | 6 | 1 | 2 | 45 | 14 | 2 | .311 |
| 1962 SF N | 5 | 4 | .556 | 4.38 | 49 | 0 | 0 | 86.1 | 83 | 47 | 58 | 0 | 5 | 4 | 11 | 25 | 5 | 0 | .200 |
| 1963 | 7 | 7 | .500 | 3.05 | 46 | 0 | 0 | 62 | 46 | 30 | 44 | 0 | 7 | 7 | 3 | 11 | 2 | 0 | .182 |
| 1964 2 teams | | | | | SF N (30G 4–8) | | | | HOU N (6G 0–1) | | | | | | | | | | |
| " total | 4 | 9 | .308 | 2.45 | 36 | 10 | 2 | 113.2 | 102 | 26 | 64 | 1 | 1 | 4 | 1 | 32 | 3 | 0 | .094 |
| 1965 2 teams | | | | | HOU N (1G 0–0) | | | | BAL A (27G 1–2) | | | | | | | | | | |
| " total | 1 | 2 | .333 | 2.88 | 28 | 2 | 0 | 59.1 | 61 | 23 | 41 | 0 | 1 | 1 | 1 | 13 | 3 | 0 | .231 |
| 1967 CHI N | 0 | 0 | — | 9.00 | 3 | 0 | 0 | 4 | 5 | 2 | 1 | 0 | 0 | 0 | 0 | 0 | 0 | 0 | — |
| 14 yrs. | 81 | 91 | .471 | 3.78 | 412 | 171 | 44 | 1548 | 1442 | 725 | 849 | 11 | 26 | 23 | 23 | * | | | |
| 1 yr. | 0 | 0 | — | 9.00 | 3 | 0 | 0 | 4 | 5 | 2 | 1 | 0 | 0 | 0 | 0 | 0 | 0 | 0 | — |

WORLD SERIES

| | W | L | PCT | ERA | G | GS | CG | IP | H | BB | SO | ShO | W | L | SV | AB | H | HR | BA |
|---|---|---|---|---|---|---|---|---|---|---|---|---|---|---|---|---|---|---|---|
| 1955 NY A | 0 | 1 | .000 | 11.25 | 1 | 1 | 0 | 4 | 5 | 2 | 2 | 0 | 0 | 0 | 0 | 2 | 0 | 0 | .000 |
| 1956 | 1 | 0 | 1.000 | 0.00 | 2 | 2 | 1 | 10.2 | 4 | 7 | 1 | 1 | 0 | 0 | 0 | 3 | 1 | 0 | .333 |
| 1957 | 1 | 1 | .500 | 3.72 | 2 | 1 | 0 | 9.2 | 8 | 5 | 6 | 0 | 0 | 0 | 0 | 2 | 0 | 0 | .000 |
| 1958 | 1 | 0 | 1.000 | 0.96 | 2 | 2 | 0 | 9.1 | 9 | 6 | 9 | 0 | 0 | 0 | 0 | 2 | 0 | 0 | .000 |
| 1962 SF N | 1 | 0 | 1.000 | 3.86 | 3 | 0 | 0 | 2.1 | 1 | 2 | 0 | 0 | 1 | 0 | 0 | 0 | 0 | 0 | — |
| 5 yrs. | 4 | 2 | .667 | 2.75 | 10 | 6 | 1 | 36 | 24 | 19 | 24 | 1 | 2 | 0 | 0 | 9 | 1 | 0 | .111 |

2nd

| | W | L | PCT | ERA | G | GS | CG | IP | H | BB | SO | ShO | Relief Pitching W | L | SV | BATTING AB | H | HR | BA |
|---|---|---|---|---|---|---|---|---|---|---|---|---|---|---|---|---|---|---|---|

## Dan Larson

**LARSON, DANIEL JAMES**                                    BR TR 6'        175 lbs.
B. July 4, 1954, Los Angeles, Calif.

| | W | L | PCT | ERA | G | GS | CG | IP | H | BB | SO | ShO | W | L | SV | AB | H | HR | BA |
|---|---|---|---|---|---|---|---|---|---|---|---|---|---|---|---|---|---|---|---|
| 1976 HOU N | 5 | 8 | .385 | 3.03 | 13 | 13 | 5 | 92 | 81 | 28 | 42 | 0 | 0 | 0 | 0 | 31 | 9 | 0 | .290 |
| 1977 | 1 | 7 | .125 | 5.79 | 32 | 10 | 1 | 98 | 108 | 45 | 44 | 0 | 1 | 2 | 1 | 28 | 6 | 0 | .214 |
| 1978 PHI N | 0 | 0 | — | 9.00 | 1 | 0 | 0 | 1 | 1 | 1 | 2 | 0 | 0 | 0 | 0 | 0 | 0 | 0 | — |
| 1979 | 1 | 1 | .500 | 4.26 | 3 | 3 | 0 | 19 | 17 | 9 | 9 | 0 | 0 | 0 | 0 | 5 | 0 | 0 | .000 |
| 1980 | 0 | 5 | .000 | 3.13 | 12 | 7 | 0 | 46 | 46 | 24 | 17 | 0 | 0 | 0 | 0 | 13 | 2 | 0 | .154 |
| 1981 | 3 | 0 | 1.000 | 4.18 | 5 | 4 | 1 | 28 | 27 | 15 | 15 | 0 | 0 | 0 | 0 | 9 | 1 | 0 | .111 |
| 1982 CHI N | 0 | 4 | .000 | 5.67 | 12 | 6 | 0 | 39.2 | 51 | 18 | 22 | 0 | 0 | 0 | 0 | 11 | 3 | 0 | .273 |
| 7 yrs. | 10 | 25 | .286 | 4.39 | 78 | 43 | 7 | 323.2 | 331 | 140 | 151 | 0 | 1 | 2 | 1 | 97 | 21 | 0 | .216 |
| 1 yr. | 0 | 4 | .000 | 5.67 | 12 | 6 | 0 | 39.2 | 51 | 18 | 22 | 0 | 0 | 0 | 0 | 11 | 3 | 0 | .273 |

## Al Lary

**LARY, ALFRED ALLEN**                                      BR TR 6'3"      185 lbs.
Brother of Frank Lary.
B. Sept. 26, 1929, Northport, Ala.

| | W | L | PCT | ERA | G | GS | CG | IP | H | BB | SO | ShO | W | L | SV | AB | H | HR | BA |
|---|---|---|---|---|---|---|---|---|---|---|---|---|---|---|---|---|---|---|---|
| 1954 CHI N | 0 | 0 | — | 3.00 | 1 | 1 | 0 | 6 | 3 | 7 | 4 | 0 | 0 | 0 | 0 | 2 | 1 | 0 | .500 |
| 1955 | 0 | 0 | — | 0.00 | 0 | 0 | 0 | 0 | 0 | 0 | 0 | 0 | 0 | 0 | 0 | 0 | 0 | 0 | — |
| 1962 | 0 | 1 | .000 | 7.15 | 15 | 3 | 0 | 34 | 42 | 15 | 18 | 0 | 0 | 0 | 0 | 6 | 1 | 0 | .167 |
| 3 yrs. | 0 | 1 | .000 | 6.53 | 16 | 4 | 0 | 40 | 45 | 22 | 22 | 0 | 0 | 0 | 0 | 8 | 2 | 0 | .250 |
| 2 yrs. | 0 | 1 | .000 | 6.53 | 16 | 4 | 0 | 40 | 45 | 22 | 22 | 0 | 0 | 0 | 0 | 8 | 2 | 0 | .250 |

## Chuck Lauer

**LAUER, JOHN CHARLES**                                     TR
B. 1865, Pittsburgh, Pa.    Deceased.

| | W | L | PCT | ERA | G | GS | CG | IP | H | BB | SO | ShO | W | L | SV | AB | H | HR | BA |
|---|---|---|---|---|---|---|---|---|---|---|---|---|---|---|---|---|---|---|---|
| 1884 PIT AA | 0 | 2 | .000 | 7.58 | 3 | 3 | 2 | 19 | 23 | 9 | 8 | 0 | 0 | 0 | 0 | * | | | |

## Jimmy Lavender

**LAVENDER, JAMES SANFORD**                                 BR TR 5'11"     165 lbs.
B. Mar. 25, 1884, Barnesville, Ga.    D. Jan. 12, 1960, Cartersville, Ga.

| | W | L | PCT | ERA | G | GS | CG | IP | H | BB | SO | ShO | W | L | SV | AB | H | HR | BA |
|---|---|---|---|---|---|---|---|---|---|---|---|---|---|---|---|---|---|---|---|
| 1912 CHI N | 16 | 13 | .552 | 3.04 | 42 | 31 | 15 | 251.2 | 240 | 89 | 109 | 3 | 1 | 1 | 3 | 87 | 13 | 0 | .149 |
| 1913 | 10 | 14 | .417 | 3.66 | 40 | 20 | 10 | 204 | 206 | 98 | 91 | 0 | 3 | 2 | 2 | 68 | 8 | 0 | .118 |
| 1914 | 11 | 11 | .500 | 3.07 | 37 | 28 | 11 | 214.1 | 191 | 87 | 87 | 2 | 1 | 2 | 0 | 63 | 11 | 0 | .175 |
| 1915 | 10 | 16 | .385 | 2.58 | 41 | 24 | 13 | 220 | 178 | 67 | 117 | 1 | 2 | 4 | 3 | 67 | 9 | 0 | .134 |
| 1916 | 10 | 14 | .417 | 2.82 | 36 | 25 | 9 | 188 | 163 | 62 | 91 | 4 | 1 | 1 | 2 | 53 | 8 | 0 | .151 |
| 1917 PHI N | 5 | 8 | .385 | 3.55 | 28 | 14 | 7 | 129.1 | 119 | 44 | 52 | 0 | 1 | 0 | 1 | 36 | 5 | 0 | .139 |
| 6 yrs. | 62 | 76 | .449 | 3.09 | 224 | 142 | 65 | 1207.1 | 1097 | 447 | 547 | 10 | 9 | 10 | 11 | 374 | 54 | 0 | .144 |
| 5 yrs. | 57 | 68 | .456 | 3.03 | 196 | 128 | 58 | 1078 | 978 | 403 | 495 | 10 | 8 | 10 | 10 | 338 | 49 | 0 | .145 |

## Bill Lee

**LEE, WILLIAM CRUTCHER (Big Bill)**                        BR TR 6'3"      195 lbs.
B. Oct. 21, 1909, Plaquemine, La.    D. June 15, 1977, Plaquemine, La.

| | W | L | PCT | ERA | G | GS | CG | IP | H | BB | SO | ShO | W | L | SV | AB | H | HR | BA |
|---|---|---|---|---|---|---|---|---|---|---|---|---|---|---|---|---|---|---|---|
| 1934 CHI N | 13 | 14 | .481 | 3.40 | 35 | 29 | 16 | 214.1 | 218 | 74 | 104 | 4 | 0 | 0 | 1 | 76 | 10 | 0 | .132 |
| 1935 | 20 | 6 | .769 | 2.96 | 39 | 32 | 18 | 252 | 241 | 84 | 100 | 3 | 2 | 0 | 1 | 102 | 24 | 0 | .235 |
| 1936 | 18 | 11 | .621 | 3.31 | 43 | 33 | 20 | 258.2 | 238 | 93 | 102 | 4 | 1 | 2 | 1 | 87 | 12 | 1 | .138 |
| 1937 | 14 | 15 | .483 | 3.54 | 42 | 33 | 17 | 272.1 | 289 | 73 | 108 | 2 | 0 | 1 | 3 | 87 | 15 | 1 | .172 |
| 1938 | 22 | 9 | .710 | 2.66 | 44 | 37 | 19 | 291 | 281 | 74 | 121 | 9 | 1 | 1 | 2 | 101 | 20 | 0 | .198 |
| 1939 | 19 | 15 | .559 | 3.44 | 37 | 36 | 20 | 282.1 | 295 | 85 | 105 | 1 | 0 | 1 | 0 | 103 | 13 | 1 | .126 |
| 1940 | 9 | 17 | .346 | 5.03 | 37 | 30 | 9 | 211.1 | 246 | 70 | 70 | 1 | 1 | 1 | 0 | 76 | 10 | 0 | .132 |
| 1941 | 8 | 14 | .364 | 3.76 | 28 | 22 | 12 | 167.1 | 179 | 43 | 62 | 0 | 1 | 0 | 1 | 59 | 11 | 2 | .186 |
| 1942 | 13 | 13 | .500 | 3.85 | 32 | 30 | 18 | 219.2 | 221 | 67 | 75 | 1 | 0 | 0 | 0 | 69 | 11 | 0 | .159 |
| 1943 2 teams | | | CHI N (13G 3–7) | | | PHI N (13G 1–5) | | | | | | | | | | | | | |
| " total | 4 | 12 | .250 | 4.01 | 26 | 19 | 6 | 139 | 153 | 48 | 35 | 0 | 0 | 0 | 3 | 43 | 8 | 0 | .186 |
| 1944 PHI N | 10 | 11 | .476 | 3.15 | 31 | 28 | 11 | 208.1 | 199 | 57 | 50 | 3 | 0 | 0 | 1 | 72 | 14 | 0 | .194 |
| 1945 2 teams | | | PHI N (13G 3–6) | | | BOS N (16G 6–3) | | | | | | | | | | | | | |
| " total | 9 | 9 | .500 | 3.58 | 29 | 26 | 8 | 183.2 | 219 | 66 | 25 | 1 | 0 | 0 | 0 | 55 | 8 | 0 | .145 |
| 1946 BOS N | 10 | 9 | .526 | 4.18 | 25 | 21 | 8 | 140 | 148 | 45 | 32 | 0 | 1 | 0 | 0 | 47 | 8 | 0 | .170 |
| 1947 CHI N | 0 | 2 | .000 | 4.50 | 14 | 2 | 0 | 24 | 26 | 14 | 9 | 0 | 0 | 0 | 0 | 3 | 1 | 0 | .333 |
| 14 yrs. | 169 | 157 | .518 | 3.54 | 462 | 378 | 182 | 2864 | 2953 | 893 | 998 | 29 | 6 | 7 | 13 | 980 | 165 | 5 | .168 |
| 11 yrs. | 139 | 123 | .531 | 3.51 | 364 | 296 | 153 | 2271.1 | 2317 | 704 | 874 | 25 | 5 | 7 | 9 | 789 | 134 | 5 | .170 |
| | 9th | 6th | | | | 6th | | | 7th | | | 5th | | 6th | | | | | |

| WORLD SERIES | | | | | | | | | | | | | | | | | | | |
|---|---|---|---|---|---|---|---|---|---|---|---|---|---|---|---|---|---|---|---|
| 1935 CHI N | 0 | 0 | — | 3.48 | 2 | 1 | 0 | 10.1 | 11 | 5 | 5 | 0 | 0 | 0 | 1 | 1 | 0 | 0 | .000 |
| 1938 | 0 | 2 | .000 | 2.45 | 2 | 2 | 0 | 11 | 15 | 1 | 8 | 0 | 0 | 0 | 0 | 3 | 0 | 0 | .000 |
| 2 yrs. | 0 | 2 | .000 | 2.95 | 4 | 3 | 0 | 21.1 | 26 | 6 | 13 | 0 | 0 | 0 | 1 | 4 | 0 | 0 | .000 |

## Don Lee

**LEE, DONALD EDWARD**                                      BR TR 6'4"      205 lbs.
Son of Thornton Lee.
B. Feb. 26, 1934, Globe, Ariz.

| | W | L | PCT | ERA | G | GS | CG | IP | H | BB | SO | ShO | W | L | SV | AB | H | HR | BA |
|---|---|---|---|---|---|---|---|---|---|---|---|---|---|---|---|---|---|---|---|
| 1957 DET A | 1 | 3 | .250 | 4.66 | 11 | 6 | 0 | 38.2 | 48 | 18 | 19 | 0 | 0 | 0 | 0 | 12 | 2 | 0 | .167 |
| 1958 | 0 | 0 | — | 9.00 | 2 | 1 | 0 | 2 | 1 | 1 | 0 | 0 | 0 | 0 | 0 | 0 | 0 | 0 | — |
| 1960 WAS A | 8 | 7 | .533 | 3.44 | 44 | 20 | 1 | 165 | 160 | 64 | 88 | 0 | 3 | 2 | 3 | 43 | 5 | 1 | .116 |
| 1961 MIN A | 3 | 6 | .333 | 3.52 | 37 | 10 | 4 | 115 | 93 | 35 | 65 | 0 | 1 | 0 | 3 | 30 | 2 | 0 | .067 |
| 1962 2 teams | | | MIN A (9G 3–3) | | | LA A (27G 8–8) | | | | | | | | | | | | | |
| " total | 11 | 11 | .500 | 3.46 | 36 | 31 | 5 | 205.1 | 204 | 63 | 102 | 2 | 0 | 1 | 2 | 68 | 13 | 0 | .191 |
| 1963 LA A | 8 | 11 | .421 | 3.68 | 40 | 22 | 3 | 154 | 148 | 51 | 89 | 2 | 2 | 0 | 1 | 45 | 7 | 0 | .156 |
| 1964 | 5 | 4 | .556 | 2.72 | 33 | 8 | 0 | 89.1 | 99 | 24 | 73 | 0 | 3 | 1 | 2 | 23 | 6 | 0 | .261 |
| 1965 2 teams | | | CAL A (10G 0–1) | | | HOU N (7G 0–0) | | | | | | | | | | | | | |
| " total | 0 | 1 | .000 | 5.32 | 17 | 0 | 0 | 22 | 29 | 8 | 15 | 0 | 0 | 1 | 0 | 4 | 1 | 0 | .250 |
| 1966 2 teams | | | HOU N (9G 2–0) | | | CHI N (16G 2–1) | | | | | | | | | | | | | |
| " total | 4 | 1 | .800 | 4.86 | 25 | 0 | 0 | 37 | 45 | 16 | 16 | 0 | 4 | 0 | 1 | 1 | 1 | 0 | 1.000 |
| 9 yrs. | 40 | 44 | .476 | 3.61 | 244 | 97 | 13 | 828.1 | 827 | 281 | 467 | 4 | 13 | 7 | 11 | 226 | 37 | 1 | .164 |
| 1 yr. | 2 | 1 | .667 | 7.11 | 16 | 0 | 0 | 19 | 28 | 12 | 7 | 0 | 2 | 1 | 0 | 0 | 0 | 0 | — |

| | W | L | PCT | ERA | G | GS | CG | IP | H | BB | SO | ShO | Relief Pitching W | L | SV | BATTING AB | H | HR | BA |
|---|---|---|---|---|---|---|---|---|---|---|---|---|---|---|---|---|---|---|---|

## Tom Lee

**LEE, THOMAS F.**
B. June 9, 1864, Milwaukee, Wis.  D. Mar. 4, 1886, Milwaukee, Wis.

| | W | L | PCT | ERA | G | GS | CG | IP | H | BB | SO | ShO | W | L | SV | AB | H | HR | BA |
|---|---|---|---|---|---|---|---|---|---|---|---|---|---|---|---|---|---|---|---|
| 1884 2 teams | | | | | CHI N (5G 1–4) | | | BAL U (15G 5–8) | | | | | | | | | | | |
| " total | 6 | 12 | .333 | 3.50 | 20 | 19 | 17 | 167.1 | 176 | 44 | 95 | 0 | 0 | 0 | 0 | 106 | 26 | 0 | .245 |

## Craig Lefferts

**LEFFERTS, CRAIG LINDSAY**  BL TL 6'1"  180 lbs.
B. Sept. 29, 1957, Munich, West Germany

| | W | L | PCT | ERA | G | GS | CG | IP | H | BB | SO | ShO | W | L | SV | AB | H | HR | BA |
|---|---|---|---|---|---|---|---|---|---|---|---|---|---|---|---|---|---|---|---|
| 1983 CHI N | 3 | 4 | .429 | 3.13 | 56 | 5 | 0 | 89 | 80 | 29 | 60 | 0 | 2 | 3 | 1 | 18 | 2 | 0 | .111 |
| 1984 SD N | 3 | 4 | .429 | 2.13 | 62 | 0 | 0 | 105.2 | 88 | 24 | 56 | 0 | 3 | 4 | 10 | 17 | 5 | 0 | .294 |
| 1985 | 7 | 6 | .538 | 3.35 | 60 | 0 | 0 | 83.1 | 75 | 30 | 48 | 0 | 7 | 6 | 2 | 4 | 1 | 0 | .250 |
| 3 yrs. | 13 | 14 | .481 | 2.82 | 178 | 5 | 0 | 278 | 243 | 83 | 164 | 0 | 12 | 13 | 13 | 39 | 8 | 0 | .205 |
| 1 yr. | 3 | 4 | .429 | 3.13 | 56 | 5 | 0 | 89 | 80 | 29 | 60 | 0 | 2 | 3 | 1 | 18 | 2 | 0 | .111 |

LEAGUE CHAMPIONSHIP SERIES

| | W | L | PCT | ERA | G | GS | CG | IP | H | BB | SO | ShO | W | L | SV | AB | H | HR | BA |
|---|---|---|---|---|---|---|---|---|---|---|---|---|---|---|---|---|---|---|---|
| 1984 SD N | 2 | 0 | 1.000 | 0.00 | 3 | 0 | 0 | 4 | 1 | 1 | 1 | 0 | 2 | 0 | 0 | 0 | 0 | 0 | – |

WORLD SERIES

| | W | L | PCT | ERA | G | GS | CG | IP | H | BB | SO | ShO | W | L | SV | AB | H | HR | BA |
|---|---|---|---|---|---|---|---|---|---|---|---|---|---|---|---|---|---|---|---|
| 1984 SD N | 0 | 0 | – | 0.00 | 3 | 0 | 0 | 6 | 2 | 1 | 7 | 0 | 0 | 0 | 1 | 0 | 0 | 0 | – |

## Hank Leiber

**LEIBER, HENRY EDWARD**  BR TR 6'1½"  205 lbs.
B. Jan. 17, 1911, Phoenix, Ariz.

| | W | L | PCT | ERA | G | GS | CG | IP | H | BB | SO | ShO | W | L | SV | AB | H | HR | BA |
|---|---|---|---|---|---|---|---|---|---|---|---|---|---|---|---|---|---|---|---|
| 1942 NY N | 0 | 1 | .000 | 6.00 | 1 | 1 | 1 | 9 | 9 | 5 | 5 | 0 | 0 | 0 | 0 | * | | | |

## Lefty Leifield

**LEIFIELD, ALBERT PETER**  BL TL 6'1"  165 lbs.
B. Sept. 5, 1883, Trenton, Ill.  D. Oct. 10, 1970, Alexandria, Va.

| | W | L | PCT | ERA | G | GS | CG | IP | H | BB | SO | ShO | W | L | SV | AB | H | HR | BA |
|---|---|---|---|---|---|---|---|---|---|---|---|---|---|---|---|---|---|---|---|
| 1905 PIT N | 5 | 2 | .714 | 2.89 | 8 | 7 | 6 | 56 | 52 | 14 | 10 | 1 | 0 | 0 | 0 | 20 | 7 | 0 | .350 |
| 1906 | 18 | 13 | .581 | 1.87 | 37 | 31 | 24 | 255.2 | 214 | 68 | 111 | 8 | 3 | 0 | 1 | 88 | 11 | 0 | .125 |
| 1907 | 20 | 16 | .556 | 2.33 | 40 | 33 | 24 | 286 | 270 | 100 | 112 | 6 | 3 | 2 | 0 | 102 | 15 | 0 | .147 |
| 1908 | 15 | 14 | .517 | 2.10 | 34 | 26 | 18 | 218.2 | 168 | 86 | 87 | 5 | 2 | 1 | 2 | 75 | 17 | 0 | .227 |
| 1909 | 19 | 8 | .704 | 2.37 | 32 | 27 | 13 | 201.2 | 172 | 54 | 43 | 3 | 3 | 1 | 0 | 73 | 14 | 0 | .192 |
| 1910 | 15 | 12 | .556 | 2.64 | 40 | 30 | 13 | 218.1 | 197 | 67 | 64 | 3 | 5 | 0 | 1 | 60 | 11 | 0 | .183 |
| 1911 | 16 | 16 | .500 | 2.63 | 42 | 37 | 26 | 318 | 301 | 82 | 111 | 2 | 0 | 0 | 1 | 102 | 24 | 0 | .235 |
| 1912 2 teams | | | | | PIT N (6G 1–2) | | | CHI N (13G 7–2) | | | | | | | | | | | |
| " total | 8 | 4 | .667 | 2.86 | 19 | 10 | 5 | 94.1 | 97 | 31 | 31 | 1 | 3 | 1 | 0 | 33 | 4 | 0 | .121 |
| 1913 CHI N | 0 | 1 | .000 | 5.48 | 6 | 1 | 0 | 21.1 | 28 | 5 | 4 | 0 | 0 | 1 | 0 | 7 | 0 | 0 | .000 |
| 1918 STL A | 2 | 6 | .250 | 2.55 | 15 | 6 | 3 | 67 | 61 | 19 | 22 | 1 | 1 | 1 | 0 | 19 | 1 | 0 | .053 |
| 1919 | 6 | 4 | .600 | 2.93 | 19 | 9 | 6 | 92 | 96 | 25 | 18 | 2 | 1 | 1 | 0 | 30 | 3 | 0 | .100 |
| 1920 | 0 | 0 | – | 7.00 | 4 | 0 | 0 | 9 | 17 | 3 | 3 | 0 | 0 | 0 | 0 | 2 | 0 | 0 | .000 |
| 12 yrs. | 124 | 96 | .564 | 2.47 | 296 | 217 | 138 | 1838 | 1673 | 554 | 616 | 32 | 21 | 8 | 5 | 611 | 107 | 0 | .175 |
| 2 yrs. | 7 | 3 | .700 | 3.13 | 19 | 10 | 4 | 92 | 96 | 26 | 27 | 1 | 2 | 1 | 0 | 33 | 3 | 0 | .091 |

WORLD SERIES

| | W | L | PCT | ERA | G | GS | CG | IP | H | BB | SO | ShO | W | L | SV | AB | H | HR | BA |
|---|---|---|---|---|---|---|---|---|---|---|---|---|---|---|---|---|---|---|---|
| 1909 PIT N | 0 | 1 | .000 | 11.25 | 1 | 1 | 0 | 4 | 7 | 1 | 0 | 0 | 0 | 0 | 0 | 1 | 0 | 0 | .000 |

## Dick LeMay

**LeMAY, RICHARD PAUL**  BL TL 6'3"  190 lbs.
B. Aug. 28, 1938, Cincinnati, Ohio

| | W | L | PCT | ERA | G | GS | CG | IP | H | BB | SO | ShO | W | L | SV | AB | H | HR | BA |
|---|---|---|---|---|---|---|---|---|---|---|---|---|---|---|---|---|---|---|---|
| 1961 SF N | 3 | 6 | .333 | 3.56 | 27 | 5 | 1 | 83.1 | 65 | 36 | 54 | 0 | 2 | 6 | 3 | 26 | 2 | 0 | .077 |
| 1962 | 0 | 1 | .000 | 7.71 | 9 | 0 | 0 | 9.1 | 9 | 9 | 5 | 0 | 0 | 1 | 1 | 2 | 0 | 0 | – |
| 1963 CHI N | 0 | 1 | .000 | 5.28 | 9 | 1 | 0 | 15.1 | 26 | 4 | 10 | 0 | 0 | 1 | 0 | 2 | 0 | 0 | .000 |
| 3 yrs. | 3 | 8 | .273 | 4.17 | 45 | 6 | 1 | 108 | 100 | 49 | 69 | 0 | 2 | 8 | 4 | 28 | 2 | 0 | .071 |
| 1 yr. | 0 | 1 | .000 | 5.28 | 9 | 1 | 0 | 15.1 | 26 | 4 | 10 | 0 | 0 | 1 | 0 | 2 | 0 | 0 | .000 |

## Dave Lemonds

**LEMONDS, DAVID LEE**  BL TL 6'1½"  180 lbs.
B. July 5, 1948, Charlotte, N. C.

| | W | L | PCT | ERA | G | GS | CG | IP | H | BB | SO | ShO | W | L | SV | AB | H | HR | BA |
|---|---|---|---|---|---|---|---|---|---|---|---|---|---|---|---|---|---|---|---|
| 1969 CHI N | 0 | 1 | .000 | 3.60 | 2 | 1 | 0 | 5 | 5 | 5 | 0 | 0 | 0 | 0 | 0 | 1 | 0 | 0 | .000 |
| 1972 CHI A | 4 | 7 | .364 | 2.95 | 31 | 18 | 0 | 94.2 | 87 | 38 | 69 | 0 | 1 | 1 | 0 | 25 | 3 | 0 | .120 |
| 2 yrs. | 4 | 8 | .333 | 2.98 | 33 | 19 | 0 | 99.2 | 92 | 43 | 69 | 0 | 1 | 1 | 0 | 26 | 3 | 0 | .115 |
| 1 yr. | 0 | 1 | .000 | 3.60 | 2 | 1 | 0 | 5 | 5 | 5 | 0 | 0 | 0 | 0 | 0 | 1 | 0 | 0 | .000 |

## Dutch Leonard

**LEONARD, EMIL JOHN**  BR TR 6'  175 lbs.
B. Mar. 25, 1909, Auburn, Ill.  D. Apr. 17, 1983, Springfield, Ill.

| | W | L | PCT | ERA | G | GS | CG | IP | H | BB | SO | ShO | W | L | SV | AB | H | HR | BA |
|---|---|---|---|---|---|---|---|---|---|---|---|---|---|---|---|---|---|---|---|
| 1933 BKN N | 2 | 3 | .400 | 2.93 | 10 | 3 | 2 | 40 | 42 | 10 | 6 | 0 | 1 | 1 | 0 | 11 | 0 | 0 | .000 |
| 1934 | 14 | 11 | .560 | 3.28 | 44 | 20 | 11 | 183.2 | 210 | 34 | 58 | 2 | 5 | 3 | 5 | 67 | 12 | 0 | .179 |
| 1935 | 2 | 9 | .182 | 3.92 | 43 | 11 | 4 | 137.2 | 152 | 29 | 41 | 0 | 0 | 4 | 8 | 39 | 1 | 0 | .026 |
| 1936 | 0 | 0 | – | 3.66 | 16 | 0 | 0 | 32 | 34 | 5 | 8 | 0 | 0 | 0 | 1 | 5 | 2 | 0 | .400 |
| 1938 WAS A | 12 | 15 | .444 | 3.43 | 33 | 31 | 15 | 223.1 | 221 | 53 | 68 | 3 | 1 | 0 | 0 | 82 | 19 | 0 | .232 |
| 1939 | 20 | 8 | .714 | 3.54 | 34 | 34 | 21 | 269.1 | 273 | 59 | 88 | 2 | 1 | 0 | 0 | 95 | 21 | 0 | .221 |
| 1940 | 14 | 19 | .424 | 3.49 | 35 | 35 | 23 | 289 | 328 | 78 | 124 | 2 | 0 | 0 | 0 | 101 | 16 | 0 | .158 |
| 1941 | 18 | 13 | .581 | 3.45 | 34 | 33 | 19 | 256 | 271 | 54 | 91 | 4 | 0 | 0 | 0 | 88 | 9 | 0 | .102 |
| 1942 | 2 | 2 | .500 | 4.11 | 6 | 5 | 1 | 35 | 28 | 5 | 15 | 1 | 0 | 0 | 0 | 10 | 1 | 0 | .100 |
| 1943 | 11 | 13 | .458 | 3.28 | 31 | 30 | 15 | 219.2 | 218 | 46 | 51 | 2 | 0 | 0 | 1 | 67 | 7 | 0 | .104 |
| 1944 | 14 | 14 | .500 | 3.06 | 32 | 31 | 17 | 229.1 | 222 | 37 | 62 | 3 | 0 | 0 | 1 | 79 | 18 | 0 | .228 |
| 1945 | 17 | 7 | .708 | 2.13 | 31 | 29 | 12 | 216 | 208 | 35 | 96 | 4 | 1 | 0 | 1 | 78 | 18 | 0 | .231 |
| 1946 | 10 | 10 | .500 | 3.56 | 26 | 23 | 7 | 161.2 | 182 | 36 | 62 | 2 | 0 | 0 | 0 | 53 | 9 | 0 | .170 |
| 1947 PHI N | 17 | 12 | .586 | 2.68 | 32 | 29 | 19 | 235 | 224 | 57 | 103 | 3 | 1 | 1 | 0 | 80 | 14 | 0 | .175 |
| 1948 | 12 | 17 | .414 | 2.51 | 34 | 31 | 16 | 225.2 | 226 | 54 | 92 | 1 | 1 | 1 | 0 | 83 | 12 | 0 | .145 |
| 1949 CHI N | 7 | 16 | .304 | 4.15 | 33 | 28 | 10 | 180 | 198 | 43 | 83 | 1 | 0 | 0 | 0 | 59 | 12 | 0 | .203 |
| 1950 | 5 | 1 | .833 | 3.77 | 35 | 1 | 0 | 74 | 70 | 27 | 28 | 0 | 4 | 1 | 6 | 16 | 1 | 0 | .063 |
| 1951 | 10 | 6 | .625 | 2.64 | 41 | 1 | 0 | 81.2 | 69 | 28 | 30 | 0 | 10 | 5 | 3 | 21 | 0 | 0 | .000 |
| 1952 | 2 | 2 | .500 | 2.16 | 45 | 1 | 0 | 66.2 | 56 | 24 | 37 | 0 | 2 | 1 | 11 | 10 | 2 | 0 | .200 |

| | W | L | PCT | ERA | G | GS | CG | IP | H | BB | SO | ShO | Relief Pitching W | L | SV | BATTING AB | H | HR | BA |
|---|---|---|---|---|---|---|---|---|---|---|---|---|---|---|---|---|---|---|---|

## Dutch Leonard continued

| | | | | | | | | | | | | | | | | | | | |
|---|---|---|---|---|---|---|---|---|---|---|---|---|---|---|---|---|---|---|---|
| 1953 | 2 | 3 | .400 | 4.60 | 45 | 0 | 0 | 62.2 | 72 | 24 | 27 | 0 | 2 | 3 | 8 | 10 | 3 | 0 | .300 |
| 20 yrs. | 191 | 181 | .513 | 3.25 | 640 | 375 | 192 | 3218.1 | 3304 | 738 | 1170 | 30 | 28 | 22 | 44 | 1054 | 177 | 0 | .168 |
| 5 yrs. | 26 | 28 | .481 | 3.60 | 199 | 30 | 10 | 465 | 465 | 146 | 205 | 1 | 18 | 11 | 28 | 116 | 18 | 0 | .155 |
| | | | | | | | | | | | | | | | 10th | | | | |

## Gene Lillard

**LILLARD, ROBERT EUGENE**                 BR  TR  5'10½" 178 lbs.
Brother of Bill Lillard.
B. Nov. 12, 1913, Santa Barbara, Calif.

| | | | | | | | | | | | | | | | | | | | |
|---|---|---|---|---|---|---|---|---|---|---|---|---|---|---|---|---|---|---|---|
| 1939 CHI N | 3 | 5 | .375 | 6.55 | 20 | 7 | 2 | 55 | 68 | 36 | 31 | 0 | 1 | 1 | 0 | 10 | 1 | 0 | .100 |
| 1940 STL N | 0 | 1 | .000 | 13.50 | 2 | 1 | 0 | 4.2 | 8 | 4 | 2 | 0 | 0 | 1 | 0 | 0 | 0 | 0 | — |
| 2 yrs. | 3 | 6 | .333 | 7.09 | 22 | 8 | 2 | 59.2 | 76 | 40 | 33 | 0 | 1 | 2 | 0 | 44 | 8 | 0 | .182 |
| 1 yr. | 3 | 5 | .375 | 6.55 | 20 | 7 | 2 | 55 | 68 | 36 | 31 | 0 | 1 | 1 | 0 | 44 | 8 | 0 | .182 |

## Dick Littlefield

**LITTLEFIELD, RICHARD BERNARD**              BL  TL  6'  180 lbs.
B. Mar. 18, 1926, Detroit, Mich.

| | | | | | | | | | | | | | | | | | | | |
|---|---|---|---|---|---|---|---|---|---|---|---|---|---|---|---|---|---|---|---|
| 1950 BOS A | 2 | 2 | .500 | 9.26 | 15 | 2 | 0 | 23.1 | 27 | 24 | 13 | 0 | 2 | 0 | 1 | 4 | 0 | 0 | .000 |
| 1951 CHI A | 1 | 1 | .500 | 8.38 | 4 | 2 | 0 | 9.2 | 9 | 17 | 7 | 0 | 1 | 0 | 0 | 1 | 0 | 0 | .000 |
| 1952 2 teams | | | DET | A | (28G 0–3) | | STL | A | (7G 2–3) | | | | | | | | | | |
| " total | 2 | 6 | .250 | 3.54 | 35 | 6 | 3 | 94 | 81 | 42 | 66 | 0 | 1 | 3 | 1 | 23 | 2 | 0 | .087 |
| 1953 STL A | 7 | 12 | .368 | 5.08 | 36 | 22 | 2 | 152.1 | 153 | 84 | 104 | 0 | 2 | 1 | 0 | 42 | 8 | 0 | .190 |
| 1954 2 teams | | | BAL | A | (3G 0–0) | | PIT | N | (23G 10–11) | | | | | | | | | | |
| " total | 10 | 11 | .476 | 3.86 | 26 | 21 | 7 | 161 | 148 | 91 | 97 | 1 | 1 | 0 | 0 | 50 | 8 | 0 | .160 |
| 1955 PIT N | 5 | 12 | .294 | 5.12 | 35 | 17 | 4 | 130 | 148 | 68 | 70 | 1 | 1 | 3 | 0 | 34 | 6 | 0 | .176 |
| 1956 3 teams | | | PIT | N | (6G 0–0) | | STL | N | (3G 0–2) | | NY | N | (31G 4–4) | | | | | | |
| " total | 4 | 6 | .400 | 4.37 | 40 | 11 | 0 | 119.1 | 101 | 49 | 80 | 0 | 1 | 2 | 2 | 28 | 2 | 0 | .071 |
| 1957 CHI N | 2 | 3 | .400 | 5.35 | 48 | 2 | 0 | 65.2 | 76 | 37 | 51 | 0 | 2 | 1 | 4 | 11 | 2 | 0 | .182 |
| 1958 MIL N | 0 | 1 | .000 | 4.26 | 4 | 0 | 0 | 6.1 | 7 | 1 | 7 | 0 | 0 | 1 | 1 | 0 | 0 | 0 | — |
| 9 yrs. | 33 | 54 | .379 | 4.71 | 243 | 83 | 16 | 761.2 | 750 | 413 | 495 | 2 | 11 | 11 | 9 | 193 | 28 | 0 | .145 |
| 1 yr. | 2 | 3 | .400 | 5.35 | 48 | 2 | 0 | 65.2 | 76 | 37 | 51 | 0 | 2 | 1 | 4 | 11 | 2 | 0 | .182 |

## Bob Locker

**LOCKER, ROBERT AWTRY**             BR  TR  6'3"  200 lbs.
B. Mar. 15, 1938, Hull, Iowa          BB 1968

| | | | | | | | | | | | | | | | | | | | |
|---|---|---|---|---|---|---|---|---|---|---|---|---|---|---|---|---|---|---|---|
| 1965 CHI A | 5 | 2 | .714 | 3.15 | 51 | 0 | 0 | 91.1 | 71 | 30 | 69 | 0 | 5 | 2 | 2 | 14 | 0 | 0 | .000 |
| 1966 | 9 | 8 | .529 | 2.46 | 56 | 0 | 0 | 95 | 73 | 23 | 70 | 0 | 9 | 8 | 12 | 16 | 4 | 0 | .250 |
| 1967 | 7 | 5 | .583 | 2.09 | 77 | 0 | 0 | 124.2 | 102 | 23 | 80 | 0 | 7 | 5 | 20 | 10 | 0 | 0 | .000 |
| 1968 | 5 | 4 | .556 | 2.29 | 70 | 0 | 0 | 90.1 | 78 | 27 | 62 | 0 | 5 | 4 | 10 | 8 | 0 | 0 | .000 |
| 1969 2 teams | | | CHI | A | (17G 2–3) | | SEA | A | (51G 3–3) | | | | | | | | | | |
| " total | 5 | 6 | .455 | 3.14 | 68 | 0 | 0 | 100.1 | 95 | 32 | 61 | 0 | 5 | 6 | 10 | 13 | 1 | 0 | .077 |
| 1970 2 teams | | | MIL | A | (28G 0–1) | | OAK | A | (38G 3–3) | | | | | | | | | | |
| " total | 3 | 4 | .429 | 3.07 | 66 | 0 | 0 | 88 | 86 | 29 | 52 | 0 | 3 | 4 | 7 | 7 | 1 | 0 | .143 |
| 1971 OAK A | 7 | 2 | .778 | 2.88 | 47 | 0 | 0 | 72 | 68 | 19 | 46 | 0 | 7 | 2 | 6 | 6 | 0 | 0 | .000 |
| 1972 | 6 | 1 | .857 | 2.65 | 56 | 0 | 0 | 78 | 69 | 16 | 47 | 0 | 6 | 1 | 10 | 6 | 0 | 0 | .000 |
| 1973 CHI N | 10 | 6 | .625 | 2.55 | 63 | 0 | 0 | 106 | 96 | 42 | 76 | 0 | 10 | 6 | 18 | 15 | 1 | 0 | .067 |
| 1975 | 0 | 1 | .000 | 4.91 | 22 | 0 | 0 | 33 | 38 | 16 | 14 | 0 | 0 | 1 | 0 | 0 | 0 | 0 | — |
| 10 yrs. | 57 | 39 | .594 | 2.76 | 576 | 0 | 0 | 878.2 | 776 | 257 | 577 | 0 | 57 | 39 | 95 | 95 | 7 | 0 | .074 |
| 2 yrs. | 10 | 7 | .588 | 3.11 | 85 | 0 | 0 | 139 | 134 | 58 | 90 | 0 | 10 | 7 | 18 | 15 | 1 | 0 | .067 |

**LEAGUE CHAMPIONSHIP SERIES**

| | | | | | | | | | | | | | | | | | | | |
|---|---|---|---|---|---|---|---|---|---|---|---|---|---|---|---|---|---|---|---|
| 1971 OAK A | 0 | 0 | — | 0.00 | 1 | 0 | 0 | .2 | 0 | 2 | 0 | 0 | 0 | 0 | 0 | 0 | 0 | 0 | — |
| 1972 | 0 | 0 | — | 13.50 | 2 | 0 | 0 | 2 | 4 | 0 | 1 | 0 | 0 | 0 | 0 | 0 | 0 | 0 | — |
| 2 yrs. | 0 | 0 | — | 10.13 | 3 | 0 | 0 | 2.2 | 4 | 2 | 1 | 0 | 0 | 0 | 0 | 0 | 0 | 0 | — |

**WORLD SERIES**

| | | | | | | | | | | | | | | | | | | | |
|---|---|---|---|---|---|---|---|---|---|---|---|---|---|---|---|---|---|---|---|
| 1972 OAK A | 0 | 0 | — | 0.00 | 1 | 0 | 0 | .1 | 1 | 0 | 0 | 0 | 0 | 0 | 0 | 0 | 0 | 0 | — |

## Bob Logan

**LOGAN, ROBERT DEAN (Lefty)**        BR  TL  5'10"  170 lbs.
B. Feb. 10, 1910, Thompson, Neb.     D. May 20, 1978, Indianapolis, Ind.

| | | | | | | | | | | | | | | | | | | | |
|---|---|---|---|---|---|---|---|---|---|---|---|---|---|---|---|---|---|---|---|
| 1935 BKN N | 0 | 1 | .000 | 3.38 | 2 | 0 | 0 | 2.2 | 2 | 1 | 1 | 0 | 0 | 1 | 0 | 0 | 0 | 0 | — |
| 1937 2 teams | | | DET | A | (1G 0–0) | | CHI | N | (4G 0–0) | | | | | | | | | | |
| " total | 0 | 0 | — | 1.29 | 5 | 0 | 0 | 7 | 7 | 5 | 3 | 0 | 0 | 0 | 1 | 1 | 0 | 0 | .000 |
| 1938 CHI N | 2 | 0 | 1.000 | 2.78 | 14 | 0 | 0 | 22.2 | 18 | 17 | 10 | 0 | 0 | 0 | 2 | 3 | 0 | 0 | .000 |
| 1941 CIN N | 0 | 1 | .000 | 8.10 | 2 | 0 | 0 | 3.1 | 5 | 5 | 0 | 0 | 0 | 1 | 0 | 0 | 0 | 0 | — |
| 1945 BOS N | 7 | 11 | .389 | 3.18 | 34 | 25 | 5 | 187 | 213 | 53 | 53 | 1 | 0 | 2 | 1 | 61 | 13 | 0 | .213 |
| 5 yrs. | 7 | 15 | .318 | 3.15 | 57 | 25 | 5 | 222.2 | 245 | 81 | 67 | 1 | 0 | 6 | 4 | 65 | 13 | 0 | .200 |
| 2 yrs. | 0 | 2 | .000 | 2.48 | 18 | 0 | 0 | 29 | 24 | 21 | 12 | 0 | 0 | 2 | 3 | 4 | 0 | 0 | .000 |

## Grover Lowdermilk

**LOWDERMILK, GROVER CLEVELAND (Slim)**     BR  TR  6'4"  190 lbs.
Brother of Lou Lowdermilk.
B. Jan. 15, 1885, Sandborn, Ind.     D. Mar. 31, 1968, Odin, Ill.

| | | | | | | | | | | | | | | | | | | | |
|---|---|---|---|---|---|---|---|---|---|---|---|---|---|---|---|---|---|---|---|
| 1909 STL N | 0 | 2 | .000 | 6.21 | 7 | 3 | 1 | 29 | 28 | 30 | 14 | 0 | 0 | 0 | 0 | 10 | 1 | 0 | .100 |
| 1911 | 0 | 1 | .000 | 7.29 | 11 | 2 | 1 | 33.1 | 37 | 33 | 15 | 0 | 0 | 0 | 0 | 9 | 1 | 0 | .111 |
| 1912 CHI N | 0 | 1 | .000 | 9.69 | 2 | 1 | 1 | 13 | 17 | 14 | 8 | 0 | 0 | 0 | 0 | 4 | 0 | 0 | .000 |
| 1915 2 teams | | | STL | A | (38G 9–17) | | DET | A | (7G 4–1) | | | | | | | | | | |
| " total | 13 | 18 | .419 | 3.24 | 45 | 34 | 14 | 250.1 | 200 | 157 | 148 | 1 | 3 | 2 | 0 | 80 | 10 | 0 | .125 |
| 1916 2 teams | | | DET | A | (1G 0–0) | | CLE | A | (10G 1–5) | | | | | | | | | | |
| " total | 1 | 5 | .167 | 3.14 | 11 | 9 | 2 | 51.2 | 52 | 48 | 28 | 0 | 0 | 0 | 0 | 18 | 3 | 0 | .167 |
| 1917 STL A | 2 | 1 | .667 | 1.42 | 3 | 2 | 2 | 19 | 16 | 4 | 9 | 1 | 0 | 1 | 0 | 7 | 0 | 0 | .000 |
| 1918 | 2 | 6 | .250 | 3.15 | 13 | 11 | 4 | 80 | 74 | 38 | 25 | 0 | 0 | 0 | 0 | 28 | 7 | 0 | .250 |
| 1919 2 teams | | | STL | A | (7G 0–0) | | CHI | A | (20G 5–5) | | | | | | | | | | |
| " total | 5 | 5 | .500 | 2.57 | 27 | 11 | 5 | 108.2 | 101 | 47 | 49 | 0 | 0 | 0 | 0 | 35 | 3 | 0 | .086 |
| 1920 CHI A | 0 | 0 | — | 6.75 | 3 | 0 | 0 | 5.1 | 9 | 5 | 0 | 0 | 0 | 0 | 0 | 0 | 0 | 0 | — |
| 9 yrs. | 23 | 39 | .371 | 3.58 | 122 | 73 | 30 | 590.1 | 534 | 376 | 296 | 2 | 3 | 5 | 0 | 191 | 25 | 0 | .131 |
| 1 yr. | 0 | 1 | .000 | 9.69 | 2 | 1 | 1 | 13 | 17 | 14 | 8 | 0 | 0 | 0 | 0 | 4 | 0 | 0 | .000 |

**WORLD SERIES**

| | | | | | | | | | | | | | | | | | | | |
|---|---|---|---|---|---|---|---|---|---|---|---|---|---|---|---|---|---|---|---|
| 1919 CHI A | 0 | 0 | — | 9.00 | 1 | 0 | 0 | 1 | 2 | 1 | 0 | 0 | 0 | 0 | 0 | 0 | 0 | 0 | — |

| | W | L | PCT | ERA | G | GS | CG | IP | H | BB | SO | ShO | Relief Pitching W | L | SV | BATTING AB | H | HR | BA |
|---|---|---|---|---|---|---|---|---|---|---|---|---|---|---|---|---|---|---|---|

## Bobby Lowe

**LOWE, ROBERT LINCOLN (Link)**
B. July 10, 1868, Pittsburgh, Pa.   D. Dec. 8, 1951, Detroit, Mich.   BR TR 5'10" 150 lbs.
Manager 1904.

| | W | L | PCT | ERA | G | GS | CG | IP | H | BB | SO | ShO | W | L | SV | AB | H | HR | BA |
|---|---|---|---|---|---|---|---|---|---|---|---|---|---|---|---|---|---|---|---|
| 1891 BOS N | 0 | 0 | — | 9.00 | 1 | 0 | 0 | 1 | 3 | 1 | 0 | 0 | 0 | 0 | 0 | * | | | |

## Turk Lown

**LOWN, OMAR JOSEPH**
B. May 30, 1924, Brooklyn, N. Y.   BR TR 6' 180 lbs.

| | W | L | PCT | ERA | G | GS | CG | IP | H | BB | SO | ShO | W | L | SV | AB | H | HR | BA |
|---|---|---|---|---|---|---|---|---|---|---|---|---|---|---|---|---|---|---|---|
| 1951 CHI N | 4 | 9 | .308 | 5.46 | 31 | 18 | 3 | 127 | 80 | 90 | 39 | 1 | 1 | 2 | 0 | 39 | 8 | 0 | .205 |
| 1952 | 4 | 11 | .267 | 4.37 | 33 | 19 | 5 | 156.2 | 154 | 93 | 73 | 0 | 1 | 2 | 0 | 50 | 7 | 0 | .140 |
| 1953 | 8 | 7 | .533 | 5.16 | 49 | 12 | 2 | 148.1 | 166 | 84 | 76 | 0 | 7 | 3 | 3 | 48 | 6 | 0 | .125 |
| 1954 | 0 | 2 | .000 | 6.14 | 15 | 0 | 0 | 22 | 23 | 15 | 16 | 0 | 0 | 2 | 0 | 0 | 0 | 0 | — |
| 1956 | 9 | 8 | .529 | 3.58 | 61 | 0 | 0 | 110.2 | 95 | 78 | 74 | 0 | 9 | 8 | 13 | 23 | 5 | 1 | .217 |
| 1957 | 5 | 7 | .417 | 3.77 | 67 | 0 | 0 | 93 | 74 | 51 | 51 | 0 | 5 | 7 | 12 | 10 | 2 | 0 | .200 |
| 1958 3 teams | | | CHI N (4G 0-0) | | | | CIN N (11G 0-2) | | | CHI A (27G 3-3) | | | | | | | | | |
| " total | 3 | 5 | .375 | 4.31 | 42 | 0 | 0 | 56.1 | 63 | 43 | 53 | 0 | 3 | 5 | 8 | 10 | 3 | 0 | .300 |
| 1959 CHI A | 9 | 2 | .818 | 2.89 | 60 | 0 | 0 | 93.1 | 73 | 42 | 63 | 0 | 9 | 2 | 15 | 12 | 3 | 0 | .250 |
| 1960 | 2 | 3 | .400 | 3.88 | 45 | 0 | 0 | 67.1 | 60 | 34 | 39 | 0 | 2 | 3 | 5 | 5 | 1 | 0 | .200 |
| 1961 | 7 | 5 | .583 | 2.76 | 59 | 0 | 0 | 101 | 87 | 35 | 50 | 0 | 7 | 5 | 11 | 14 | 0 | 0 | .000 |
| 1962 | 4 | 2 | .667 | 3.04 | 42 | 0 | 0 | 56.1 | 58 | 25 | 40 | 0 | 4 | 2 | 6 | 3 | 0 | 0 | .000 |
| 11 yrs. | 55 | 61 | .474 | 4.12 | 504 | 49 | 10 | 1032 | 933 | 590 | 574 | 1 | 48 | 41 | 73 | 214 | 35 | 1 | .164 |
| 7 yrs. | 30 | 44 | .405 | 4.60 | 260 | 49 | 10 | 661.2 | 594 | 414 | 333 | 1 | 23 | 24 | 28 | 170 | 28 | 1 | .165 |
| | | | | | | | | | | | | | 9th | | 10th | | | | |

WORLD SERIES

| | W | L | PCT | ERA | G | GS | CG | IP | H | BB | SO | ShO | W | L | SV | AB | H | HR | BA |
|---|---|---|---|---|---|---|---|---|---|---|---|---|---|---|---|---|---|---|---|
| 1959 CHI A | 0 | 0 | — | 0.00 | 3 | 0 | 0 | 3.1 | 2 | 1 | 3 | 0 | 0 | 0 | 0 | 0 | 0 | 0 | — |

## Pat Luby

**LUBY, JOHN PERKINS**
B. 1868, Charleston, S. C.   D. Apr. 24, 1899, Charleston, S. C.   TR 6' 185 lbs.

| | W | L | PCT | ERA | G | GS | CG | IP | H | BB | SO | ShO | W | L | SV | AB | H | HR | BA |
|---|---|---|---|---|---|---|---|---|---|---|---|---|---|---|---|---|---|---|---|
| 1890 CHI N | 20 | 9 | .690 | 3.19 | 34 | 31 | 26 | 267.2 | 226 | 95 | 85 | 0 | 0 | 0 | 1 | 116 | 31 | 3 | .267 |
| 1891 | 8 | 11 | .421 | 4.76 | 30 | 24 | 18 | 206 | 221 | 94 | 52 | 0 | 1 | 0 | 1 | 98 | 24 | 2 | .245 |
| 1892 | 10 | 17 | .370 | 3.13 | 31 | 26 | 24 | 247.1 | 247 | 106 | 64 | 1 | 2 | 0 | 1 | 163 | 31 | 2 | .190 |
| 1895 LOU N | 1 | 5 | .167 | 6.81 | 11 | 6 | 5 | 71.1 | 115 | 19 | 12 | 0 | 0 | 0 | 0 | 53 | 15 | 0 | .283 |
| 4 yrs. | 39 | 42 | .481 | 3.91 | 106 | 87 | 73 | 792.1 | 809 | 314 | 213 | 1 | 3 | 0 | 3 | * | | | |
| 3 yrs. | 38 | 37 | .507 | 3.62 | 95 | 81 | 68 | 721 | 694 | 295 | 201 | 1 | 3 | 0 | 3 | 377 | 86 | 7 | .228 |

## Carl Lundgren

**LUNDGREN, CARL LEONARD**
B. Feb. 16, 1880, Marengo, Ill.   D. Aug. 21, 1934, Marengo, Ill.   BR TR 5'11½" 175 lbs.

| | W | L | PCT | ERA | G | GS | CG | IP | H | BB | SO | ShO | W | L | SV | AB | H | HR | BA |
|---|---|---|---|---|---|---|---|---|---|---|---|---|---|---|---|---|---|---|---|
| 1902 CHI N | 9 | 9 | .500 | 1.97 | 18 | 18 | 17 | 160 | 158 | 45 | 68 | 1 | 0 | 0 | 0 | 66 | 7 | 0 | .106 |
| 1903 | 10 | 9 | .526 | 2.94 | 27 | 20 | 16 | 193 | 191 | 60 | 67 | 0 | 1 | 0 | 3 | 61 | 7 | 0 | .115 |
| 1904 | 17 | 10 | .630 | 2.60 | 31 | 27 | 25 | 242 | 203 | 77 | 106 | 2 | 0 | 0 | 1 | 90 | 20 | 0 | .222 |
| 1905 | 13 | 4 | .765 | 2.24 | 23 | 19 | 16 | 169 | 132 | 53 | 69 | 3 | 0 | 0 | 1 | 61 | 11 | 0 | .180 |
| 1906 | 17 | 6 | .739 | 2.21 | 27 | 24 | 21 | 207.2 | 160 | 89 | 103 | 5 | 0 | 0 | 2 | 67 | 12 | 0 | .179 |
| 1907 | 18 | 7 | .720 | 1.17 | 28 | 25 | 21 | 207 | 130 | 92 | 84 | 7 | 3 | 0 | 0 | 66 | 7 | 0 | .106 |
| 1908 | 6 | 9 | .400 | 4.22 | 23 | 15 | 9 | 138.2 | 149 | 56 | 38 | 1 | 1 | 0 | 0 | 47 | 7 | 0 | .149 |
| 1909 | 0 | 1 | .000 | 4.15 | 2 | 1 | 0 | 4.1 | 6 | 4 | 0 | 0 | 0 | 0 | 0 | 2 | 1 | 0 | .500 |
| 8 yrs. | 90 | 55 | .621 | 2.42 | 179 | 149 | 125 | 1321.2 | 1129 | 476 | 535 | 19 | 6 | 0 | 6 | 460 | 72 | 0 | .157 |
| 8 yrs. | 90 | 55 | .621 | 2.42 | 179 | 149 | 125 | 1321.2 | 1129 | 476 | 535 | 19 | 6 | 0 | 6 | 460 | 72 | 0 | .157 |
| | | | | 9th | | | | | | | | | | | | | | | |
| | | | | 10th | | | | | | | | | | | | | | | |

## Thomas Lynch

**LYNCH, THOMAS S.**
B. 1862, Peru, Ill.   D. May 13, 1923, Peru, Ill.   BL 5'11" 175 lbs.

| | W | L | PCT | ERA | G | GS | CG | IP | H | BB | SO | ShO | W | L | SV | AB | H | HR | BA |
|---|---|---|---|---|---|---|---|---|---|---|---|---|---|---|---|---|---|---|---|
| 1884 CHI N | 0 | 0 | — | 2.57 | 1 | 1 | 0 | 7 | 7 | 3 | 2 | 0 | 0 | 0 | 0 | 4 | 0 | 0 | .000 |

## Red Lynn

**LYNN, JAPHET MONROE**
B. Dec. 27, 1913, Kenney, Tex.   D. Oct. 27, 1977, Bellville, Tex.   BR TR 6' 162 lbs.

| | W | L | PCT | ERA | G | GS | CG | IP | H | BB | SO | ShO | W | L | SV | AB | H | HR | BA |
|---|---|---|---|---|---|---|---|---|---|---|---|---|---|---|---|---|---|---|---|
| 1939 2 teams | | | DET A (4G 0-1) | | | | NY N (26G 1-0) | | | | | | | | | | | | |
| " total | 1 | 1 | .500 | 3.88 | 30 | 0 | 0 | 58 | 55 | 24 | 25 | 0 | 1 | 1 | 3 | 8 | 0 | 0 | .000 |
| 1940 NY N | 4 | 3 | .571 | 3.83 | 33 | 0 | 0 | 42.1 | 40 | 24 | 25 | 0 | 4 | 3 | 3 | 4 | 0 | 0 | .000 |
| 1944 CHI N | 5 | 4 | .556 | 4.06 | 22 | 7 | 4 | 84.1 | 80 | 37 | 35 | 1 | 0 | 2 | 1 | 29 | 6 | 0 | .207 |
| 3 yrs. | 10 | 8 | .556 | 3.95 | 85 | 7 | 4 | 184.2 | 175 | 85 | 85 | 1 | 5 | 6 | 5 | 41 | 6 | 0 | .146 |
| 1 yr. | 5 | 4 | .556 | 4.06 | 22 | 7 | 4 | 84.1 | 80 | 37 | 35 | 1 | 0 | 2 | 1 | 29 | 6 | 0 | .207 |

## Bill Mack

**MACK, WILLIAM FRANCIS**
B. Feb. 12, 1885, Elmira, N. Y.   D. Sept. 30, 1971, Elmira, N. Y.   BL TL 6'1" 155 lbs.

| | W | L | PCT | ERA | G | GS | CG | IP | H | BB | SO | ShO | W | L | SV | AB | H | HR | BA |
|---|---|---|---|---|---|---|---|---|---|---|---|---|---|---|---|---|---|---|---|
| 1908 CHI N | 0 | 0 | — | 2.84 | 2 | 0 | 0 | 6.1 | 5 | 1 | 2 | 0 | 0 | 0 | 0 | 3 | 2 | 0 | .667 |

## Len Madden

**MADDEN, LEONARD JOSEPH (Lefty)**
B. July 2, 1890, Toledo, Ohio   D. Sept. 9, 1949, Toledo, Ohio   BL TL 6'2" 165 lbs.

| | W | L | PCT | ERA | G | GS | CG | IP | H | BB | SO | ShO | W | L | SV | AB | H | HR | BA |
|---|---|---|---|---|---|---|---|---|---|---|---|---|---|---|---|---|---|---|---|
| 1912 CHI N | 0 | 1 | .000 | 2.92 | 6 | 2 | 0 | 12.1 | 16 | 9 | 5 | 0 | 0 | 0 | 0 | 4 | 1 | 0 | .250 |

## Willard Mains

**MAINS, WILLARD EBEN (Grasshopper)**
B. July 7, 1868, North Windham, Me.   D. May 23, 1923, Bridgton, Me.   TR 6'2" 190 lbs.

| | W | L | PCT | ERA | G | GS | CG | IP | H | BB | SO | ShO | W | L | SV | AB | H | HR | BA |
|---|---|---|---|---|---|---|---|---|---|---|---|---|---|---|---|---|---|---|---|
| 1888 CHI N | 1 | 1 | .500 | 4.91 | 2 | 2 | 1 | 11 | 8 | 6 | 5 | 0 | 0 | 0 | 0 | 7 | 1 | 0 | .143 |
| 1891 C-M AA | 12 | 14 | .462 | 3.07 | 32 | 25 | 20 | 214 | 210 | 117 | 78 | 0 | 1 | 2 | 0 | 95 | 25 | 1 | .263 |
| 1896 BOS N | 3 | 2 | .600 | 5.48 | 8 | 5 | 3 | 42.2 | 43 | 31 | 13 | 0 | 0 | 0 | 0 | 22 | 6 | 0 | .273 |
| 3 yrs. | 16 | 17 | .485 | 3.53 | 42 | 32 | 24 | 267.2 | 261 | 154 | 96 | 0 | 1 | 2 | 1 | 124 | 32 | 1 | .258 |
| 1 yr. | 1 | 1 | .500 | 4.91 | 2 | 2 | 1 | 11 | 8 | 6 | 5 | 0 | 0 | 0 | 0 | 7 | 1 | 0 | .143 |

| | W | L | PCT | ERA | G | GS | CG | IP | H | BB | SO | ShO | Relief Pitching W | L | SV | BATTING AB | H | HR | BA |
|---|---|---|---|---|---|---|---|---|---|---|---|---|---|---|---|---|---|---|---|

## John Malarkey

MALARKEY, JOHN S.
B. May 4, 1872, Springfield, Ohio    D. Oct. 29, 1949, Cincinnati, Ohio     TR 5'11" 155 lbs.

| | W | L | PCT | ERA | G | GS | CG | IP | H | BB | SO | ShO | W | L | SV | AB | H | HR | BA |
|---|---|---|---|---|---|---|---|---|---|---|---|---|---|---|---|---|---|---|---|
| 1894 WAS N | 2 | 1 | .667 | 4.15 | 3 | 3 | 3 | 26 | 42 | 5 | 3 | 0 | 0 | 0 | 0 | 14 | 1 | 0 | .071 |
| 1895 | 0 | 8 | .000 | 5.99 | 22 | 8 | 5 | 100.2 | 135 | 60 | 32 | 0 | 0 | 1 | 2 | 37 | 5 | 0 | .135 |
| 1896 | 0 | 1 | .000 | 1.29 | 1 | 1 | 0 | 7 | 9 | 3 | 0 | 0 | 0 | 0 | 0 | 2 | 1 | 0 | .500 |
| 1899 CHI N | 0 | 1 | .000 | 13.00 | 1 | 1 | 1 | 9 | 19 | 5 | 7 | 0 | 0 | 0 | 0 | 5 | 1 | 0 | .200 |
| 1902 BOS N | 8 | 11 | .421 | 2.59 | 21 | 19 | 18 | 170.1 | 158 | 58 | 39 | 1 | 1 | 0 | 1 | 62 | 13 | 1 | .210 |
| 1903 | 11 | 16 | .407 | 3.09 | 32 | 27 | 25 | 253 | 266 | 96 | 98 | 2 | 0 | 2 | 0 | 87 | 14 | 0 | .161 |
| 6 yrs. | 21 | 38 | .356 | 3.64 | 80 | 59 | 52 | 566 | 629 | 227 | 179 | 3 | 1 | 3 | 3 | 207 | 35 | 1 | .169 |
| 1 yr. | 0 | 1 | .000 | 13.00 | 1 | 1 | 1 | 9 | 19 | 5 | 7 | 0 | 0 | 0 | 0 | 5 | 1 | 0 | .200 |

## Pat Malone

MALONE, PERCE LEIGH
B. Sept. 25, 1902, Altoona, Pa.
D. May 13, 1943, Altoona, Pa.     BL TR 6' 200 lbs.   BB 1935-37

| | W | L | PCT | ERA | G | GS | CG | IP | H | BB | SO | ShO | W | L | SV | AB | H | HR | BA |
|---|---|---|---|---|---|---|---|---|---|---|---|---|---|---|---|---|---|---|---|
| 1928 CHI N | 18 | 13 | .581 | 2.84 | 42 | 25 | 16 | 250.2 | 218 | 99 | 155 | 2 | 2 | 4 | 2 | 95 | 18 | 1 | .189 |
| 1929 | 22 | 10 | .688 | 3.57 | 40 | 30 | 19 | 267 | 283 | 102 | 166 | 5 | 4 | 1 | 2 | 105 | 22 | 2 | .210 |
| 1930 | 20 | 9 | .690 | 3.94 | 45 | 35 | 22 | 271.2 | 290 | 96 | 142 | 2 | 1 | 1 | 4 | 105 | 26 | 4 | .248 |
| 1931 | 16 | 9 | .640 | 3.90 | 36 | 30 | 12 | 228.1 | 229 | 88 | 112 | 2 | 3 | 0 | 0 | 79 | 17 | 1 | .215 |
| 1932 | 15 | 17 | .469 | 3.38 | 37 | 33 | 17 | 237 | 222 | 78 | 120 | 2 | 1 | 1 | 0 | 78 | 14 | 1 | .179 |
| 1933 | 10 | 14 | .417 | 3.91 | 31 | 26 | 13 | 186.1 | 186 | 59 | 72 | 2 | 2 | 0 | 0 | 63 | 10 | 0 | .159 |
| 1934 | 14 | 7 | .667 | 3.53 | 34 | 21 | 8 | 191 | 200 | 55 | 111 | 1 | 2 | 0 | 0 | 64 | 11 | 0 | .172 |
| 1935 NY A | 3 | 5 | .375 | 5.43 | 29 | 2 | 0 | 56.1 | 53 | 33 | 25 | 0 | 3 | 4 | 3 | 15 | 0 | 0 | .000 |
| 1936 | 12 | 4 | .750 | 3.81 | 35 | 9 | 5 | 134.2 | 144 | 60 | 72 | 0 | 8 | 2 | 9 | 51 | 10 | 0 | .196 |
| 1937 | 4 | 4 | .500 | 5.48 | 28 | 9 | 3 | 92 | 109 | 35 | 49 | 0 | 1 | 3 | 6 | 33 | 1 | 0 | .030 |
| 10 yrs. | 134 | 92 | .593 | 3.74 | 357 | 220 | 115 | 1915 | 1934 | 705 | 1024 | 16 | 27 | 16 | 26 | 688 | 129 | 9 | .188 |
| 7 yrs. | 115 | 79 | .593 | 3.57 | 265 | 200 | 107 | 1632 | 1628 | 577 | 878 | 16 | 15 | 7 | 8 | 589 | 118 | 9 | .200 |
| WORLD SERIES | | | | | | | | | | | | | | | | | | | |
| 1929 CHI N | 0 | 2 | .000 | 4.15 | 3 | 2 | 1 | 13 | 12 | 7 | 11 | 0 | 0 | 0 | 0 | 4 | 1 | 0 | .250 |
| 1932 | 0 | 0 | — | 0.00 | 1 | 0 | 0 | 2.2 | 1 | 4 | 4 | 0 | 0 | 0 | 0 | 0 | 0 | 0 | — |
| 1936 NY A | 0 | 1 | .000 | 1.80 | 2 | 0 | 0 | 5 | 2 | 1 | 2 | 0 | 0 | 1 | 1 | 1 | 1 | 0 | 1.000 |
| 3 yrs. | 0 | 3 | .000 | 3.05 | 6 | 2 | 1 | 20.2 | 15 | 12 | 17 | 0 | 0 | 1 | 1 | 5 | 2 | 0 | .400 |

## Hal Manders

MANDERS, HAROLD CARL
B. June 14, 1917, Waukee, Iowa     BR TR 6' 187 lbs.

| | W | L | PCT | ERA | G | GS | CG | IP | H | BB | SO | ShO | W | L | SV | AB | H | HR | BA |
|---|---|---|---|---|---|---|---|---|---|---|---|---|---|---|---|---|---|---|---|
| 1941 DET A | 1 | 0 | 1.000 | 2.35 | 8 | 0 | 0 | 15.1 | 13 | 8 | 7 | 0 | 1 | 0 | 0 | 4 | 0 | 0 | .000 |
| 1942 | 2 | 0 | 1.000 | 4.09 | 18 | 0 | 0 | 33 | 39 | 15 | 14 | 0 | 2 | 0 | 0 | 4 | 1 | 0 | .250 |
| 1946 2 teams | DET A (2G 0-0) | | CHI N (2G 0-1) | | | | | | | | | | | | | | | | |
| " total | 0 | 1 | .000 | 9.75 | 4 | 1 | 0 | 12 | 19 | 5 | 7 | 0 | 0 | 0 | 0 | 4 | 1 | 0 | .250 |
| 3 yrs. | 3 | 1 | .750 | 4.77 | 30 | 1 | 0 | 60.1 | 71 | 28 | 28 | 0 | 3 | 0 | 0 | 12 | 2 | 0 | .167 |
| 1 yr. | 0 | 1 | .000 | 9.00 | 2 | 1 | 0 | 6 | 11 | 3 | 4 | 0 | 0 | 0 | 0 | 2 | 0 | 0 | .000 |

## Dick Manville

MANVILLE, RICHARD WESLEY
B. Dec. 25, 1926, Des Moines, Iowa     BR TR 6'5" 200 lbs.

| | W | L | PCT | ERA | G | GS | CG | IP | H | BB | SO | ShO | W | L | SV | AB | H | HR | BA |
|---|---|---|---|---|---|---|---|---|---|---|---|---|---|---|---|---|---|---|---|
| 1950 BOS N | 0 | 0 | — | 0.00 | 1 | 0 | 0 | 2 | 0 | 3 | 2 | 0 | 0 | 0 | 0 | 0 | 0 | 0 | — |
| 1952 CHI N | 0 | 0 | — | 7.94 | 11 | 0 | 0 | 17 | 25 | 12 | 6 | 0 | 0 | 0 | 0 | 2 | 1 | 0 | .500 |
| 2 yrs. | 0 | 0 | — | 7.11 | 12 | 0 | 0 | 19 | 25 | 15 | 8 | 0 | 0 | 0 | 0 | 2 | 1 | 0 | .500 |
| 1 yr. | 0 | 0 | — | 7.94 | 11 | 0 | 0 | 17 | 25 | 12 | 6 | 0 | 0 | 0 | 0 | 2 | 1 | 0 | .500 |

## Jim Maroney

MARONEY, JAMES FRANCIS
B. Dec. 4, 1885, Boston, Mass.    D. Feb. 26, 1929, Philadelphia, Pa.     BL TL 6'1" 175 lbs.

| | W | L | PCT | ERA | G | GS | CG | IP | H | BB | SO | ShO | W | L | SV | AB | H | HR | BA |
|---|---|---|---|---|---|---|---|---|---|---|---|---|---|---|---|---|---|---|---|
| 1906 BOS N | 0 | 3 | .000 | 5.33 | 3 | 3 | 3 | 27 | 28 | 12 | 11 | 0 | 0 | 0 | 0 | 10 | 1 | 0 | .100 |
| 1910 PHI N | 1 | 2 | .333 | 2.14 | 12 | 2 | 1 | 42 | 43 | 11 | 13 | 0 | 1 | 0 | 1 | 10 | 0 | 0 | .000 |
| 1912 CHI N | 1 | 1 | .500 | 4.56 | 10 | 3 | 1 | 23.2 | 25 | 17 | 5 | 0 | 0 | 0 | 1 | 6 | 3 | 0 | .500 |
| 3 yrs. | 2 | 6 | .250 | 3.69 | 25 | 8 | 5 | 92.2 | 96 | 40 | 29 | 0 | 1 | 0 | 2 | 26 | 4 | 0 | .154 |
| 1 yr. | 1 | 1 | .500 | 4.56 | 10 | 3 | 1 | 23.2 | 25 | 17 | 5 | 0 | 0 | 0 | 1 | 6 | 3 | 0 | .500 |

## Morrie Martin

MARTIN, MORRIS WEBSTER
B. Sept. 3, 1922, Dixon, Mo.     BL TL 6' 173 lbs.

| | W | L | PCT | ERA | G | GS | CG | IP | H | BB | SO | ShO | W | L | SV | AB | H | HR | BA |
|---|---|---|---|---|---|---|---|---|---|---|---|---|---|---|---|---|---|---|---|
| 1949 BKN N | 1 | 3 | .250 | 7.04 | 10 | 4 | 0 | 30.2 | 39 | 15 | 15 | 0 | 1 | 0 | 0 | 10 | 2 | 0 | .200 |
| 1951 PHI A | 11 | 4 | .733 | 3.78 | 35 | 13 | 3 | 138 | 139 | 63 | 35 | 1 | 5 | 0 | 0 | 50 | 11 | 0 | .220 |
| 1952 | 0 | 2 | .000 | 6.39 | 5 | 5 | 0 | 25.1 | 32 | 15 | 13 | 0 | 0 | 0 | 0 | 9 | 1 | 0 | .111 |
| 1953 | 10 | 12 | .455 | 4.43 | 58 | 11 | 2 | 156.1 | 158 | 59 | 64 | 0 | 8 | 5 | 7 | 42 | 4 | 0 | .095 |
| 1954 2 teams | PHI A (13G 2-4) | | CHI A (35G 5-4) | | | | | | | | | | | | | | | | |
| " total | 7 | 8 | .467 | 3.52 | 48 | 8 | 3 | 122.2 | 109 | 43 | 55 | 0 | 4 | 5 | 5 | 32 | 6 | 0 | .188 |
| 1955 CHI A | 2 | 3 | .400 | 3.63 | 37 | 0 | 0 | 52 | 50 | 22 | 22 | 0 | 2 | 3 | 2 | 10 | 3 | 0 | .300 |
| 1956 2 teams | CHI A (10G 1-0) | | BAL A (9G 1-1) | | | | | | | | | | | | | | | | |
| " total | 2 | 1 | .667 | 6.17 | 19 | 0 | 0 | 23.1 | 31 | 9 | 12 | 0 | 2 | 1 | 0 | 5 | 1 | 0 | .200 |
| 1957 STL N | 0 | 0 | — | 2.53 | 4 | 1 | 0 | 10.2 | 5 | 4 | 7 | 0 | 0 | 0 | 0 | 2 | 0 | 0 | .000 |
| 1958 2 teams | STL N (17G 3-1) | | CLE A (14G 2-0) | | | | | | | | | | | | | | | | |
| " total | 5 | 1 | .833 | 3.74 | 31 | 0 | 0 | 43.1 | 39 | 20 | 21 | 0 | 5 | 1 | 1 | 5 | 0 | 0 | .000 |
| 1959 CHI N | 0 | 0 | — | 19.29 | 3 | 0 | 0 | 2.1 | 5 | 1 | 1 | 0 | 0 | 0 | 0 | 0 | 0 | 0 | — |
| 10 yrs. | 38 | 34 | .528 | 4.29 | 250 | 42 | 8 | 604.2 | 607 | 251 | 245 | 1 | 27 | 15 | 15 | 165 | 28 | 0 | .170 |
| 1 yr. | 0 | 0 | — | 19.29 | 3 | 0 | 0 | 2.1 | 5 | 1 | 1 | 0 | 0 | 0 | 0 | 0 | 0 | 0 | — |

## Speed Martin

MARTIN, ELWOOD GOODE
B. Sept. 15, 1893, Wawawai, Wash.    D. June 14, 1983, Lemon Grove, Ga.     BR TR 6' 165 lbs.

| | W | L | PCT | ERA | G | GS | CG | IP | H | BB | SO | ShO | W | L | SV | AB | H | HR | BA |
|---|---|---|---|---|---|---|---|---|---|---|---|---|---|---|---|---|---|---|---|
| 1917 STL A | 0 | 2 | .000 | 5.74 | 9 | 2 | 0 | 15.2 | 20 | 5 | 5 | 0 | 0 | 0 | 0 | 2 | 0 | 0 | .000 |
| 1918 CHI N | 6 | 2 | .750 | 1.84 | 9 | 5 | 4 | 53.2 | 47 | 14 | 16 | 1 | 3 | 0 | 0 | 16 | 3 | 0 | .188 |
| 1919 | 8 | 8 | .500 | 2.47 | 35 | 14 | 7 | 163.2 | 158 | 52 | 54 | 2 | 2 | 1 | 2 | 44 | 8 | 0 | .182 |
| 1920 | 4 | 15 | .211 | 4.83 | 35 | 13 | 6 | 136 | 165 | 50 | 44 | 0 | 1 | 5 | 2 | 44 | 7 | 1 | .159 |
| 1921 | 11 | 15 | .423 | 4.35 | 37 | 28 | 13 | 217.1 | 245 | 68 | 86 | 1 | 2 | 1 | 1 | 73 | 17 | 0 | .233 |

| | W | L | PCT | ERA | G | GS | CG | IP | H | BB | SO | ShO | Relief Pitching W | L | SV | Batting AB | H | HR | BA |
|---|---|---|---|---|---|---|---|---|---|---|---|---|---|---|---|---|---|---|---|

## Speed Martin continued

| | W | L | PCT | ERA | G | GS | CG | IP | H | BB | SO | ShO | W | L | SV | AB | H | HR | BA |
|---|---|---|---|---|---|---|---|---|---|---|---|---|---|---|---|---|---|---|---|
| 1922 | 1 | 0 | 1.000 | 7.50 | 1 | 1 | 0 | 6 | 10 | 2 | 2 | 0 | 0 | 0 | 0 | 1 | 0 | 0 | .000 |
| 6 yrs. | 30 | 42 | .417 | 3.78 | 126 | 63 | 30 | 592.1 | 645 | 191 | 207 | 4 | 8 | 7 | 5 | 180 | 35 | 1 | .194 |
| 5 yrs. | 30 | 40 | .429 | 3.73 | 117 | 61 | 30 | 576.2 | 625 | 186 | 202 | 4 | 8 | 7 | 5 | 178 | 35 | 1 | .197 |

## Joe Marty

**MARTY, JOSEPH ANTON**   BR TR 6'   182 lbs.
B. Sept. 1, 1913, Sacramento, Calif.   D. Oct. 4, 1984, Sacramento, Calif.

| | W | L | PCT | ERA | G | GS | CG | IP | H | BB | SO | ShO | W | L | SV | AB | H | HR | BA |
|---|---|---|---|---|---|---|---|---|---|---|---|---|---|---|---|---|---|---|---|
| 1939 2 teams | | | CHI N (0G 0–0) | | | PHI N (1G 0–0) | | | | | | | | | | | | | |
| " total | 0 | 0 | – | 4.50 | 1 | 0 | 0 | 4 | 2 | 3 | 1 | 0 | 0 | 0 | 0 | * | | | |

## Randy Martz

**MARTZ, RANDY CARL**   BL TR 6'4"   210 lbs.
B. May 28, 1956, Harrisburg, Pa.

| | W | L | PCT | ERA | G | GS | CG | IP | H | BB | SO | ShO | W | L | SV | AB | H | HR | BA |
|---|---|---|---|---|---|---|---|---|---|---|---|---|---|---|---|---|---|---|---|
| 1980 CHI N | 1 | 2 | .333 | 2.10 | 6 | 6 | 0 | 30 | 28 | 11 | 5 | 0 | 0 | 0 | 0 | 9 | 1 | 0 | .111 |
| 1981 | 5 | 7 | .417 | 3.67 | 33 | 14 | 1 | 108 | 103 | 49 | 32 | 0 | 2 | 0 | 6 | 28 | 6 | 0 | .214 |
| 1982 | 11 | 10 | .524 | 4.21 | 28 | 24 | 1 | 147.2 | 157 | 36 | 40 | 0 | 1 | 1 | 1 | 42 | 6 | 0 | .143 |
| 1983 CHI A | 0 | 0 | – | 3.60 | 1 | 1 | 0 | 5 | 4 | 4 | 1 | 0 | 0 | 0 | 0 | 0 | 0 | 0 | – |
| 4 yrs. | 17 | 19 | .472 | 3.78 | 68 | 45 | 2 | 290.2 | 292 | 100 | 78 | 0 | 3 | 1 | 7 | 79 | 13 | 0 | .165 |
| 3 yrs. | 17 | 19 | .472 | 3.78 | 67 | 44 | 2 | 285.2 | 288 | 96 | 77 | 0 | 3 | 1 | 7 | 79 | 13 | 0 | .165 |

## Hal Mauck

**MAUCK, ALFRED MARIS**
B. Mar. 6, 1869, Princeton, Ind.   D. Apr. 27, 1921, Princeton, Ind.

| | W | L | PCT | ERA | G | GS | CG | IP | H | BB | SO | ShO | W | L | SV | AB | H | HR | BA |
|---|---|---|---|---|---|---|---|---|---|---|---|---|---|---|---|---|---|---|---|
| 1893 CHI N | 8 | 10 | .444 | 4.41 | 23 | 18 | 12 | 143 | 168 | 60 | 23 | 1 | 2 | 1 | 0 | 61 | 9 | 0 | .148 |

## Jakie May

**MAY, FRANK SPRUIELL**   BR TL 5'8"   178 lbs.
B. Nov. 25, 1895, Youngville, N. C.   D. June 3, 1970, Wendell, N. C.

| | W | L | PCT | ERA | G | GS | CG | IP | H | BB | SO | ShO | W | L | SV | AB | H | HR | BA |
|---|---|---|---|---|---|---|---|---|---|---|---|---|---|---|---|---|---|---|---|
| 1917 STL N | 0 | 0 | – | 3.38 | 15 | 1 | 0 | 29.1 | 29 | 11 | 18 | 0 | 0 | 0 | 0 | 4 | 0 | 0 | .000 |
| 1918 | 5 | 6 | .455 | 3.83 | 29 | 16 | 6 | 152.2 | 149 | 69 | 61 | 0 | 2 | 0 | 0 | 45 | 3 | 1 | .067 |
| 1919 | 3 | 12 | .200 | 3.22 | 28 | 19 | 8 | 125.2 | 99 | 87 | 58 | 1 | 0 | 1 | 0 | 37 | 6 | 0 | .162 |
| 1920 | 1 | 4 | .200 | 3.06 | 16 | 5 | 3 | 70.2 | 65 | 37 | 33 | 0 | 0 | 1 | 0 | 22 | 5 | 0 | .227 |
| 1921 | 1 | 3 | .250 | 4.71 | 5 | 5 | 1 | 21 | 29 | 12 | 5 | 0 | 0 | 0 | 0 | 6 | 2 | 0 | .333 |
| 1924 CIN N | 3 | 3 | .500 | 3.00 | 38 | 4 | 2 | 99 | 104 | 29 | 59 | 0 | 2 | 2 | 6 | 27 | 3 | 1 | .111 |
| 1925 | 8 | 9 | .471 | 3.87 | 36 | 12 | 7 | 137.1 | 146 | 45 | 74 | 1 | 2 | 4 | 2 | 43 | 8 | 0 | .186 |
| 1926 | 13 | 9 | .591 | 3.22 | 45 | 15 | 9 | 167.2 | 175 | 44 | 103 | 1 | 5 | 4 | 3 | 48 | 7 | 0 | .146 |
| 1927 | 15 | 12 | .556 | 3.51 | 44 | 28 | 17 | 235.2 | 242 | 70 | 121 | 2 | 4 | 1 | 0 | 76 | 14 | 0 | .184 |
| 1928 | 3 | 5 | .375 | 4.42 | 21 | 11 | 1 | 79.1 | 99 | 35 | 39 | 1 | 2 | 1 | 0 | 27 | 8 | 0 | .296 |
| 1929 | 10 | 14 | .417 | 4.61 | 41 | 24 | 10 | 199 | 219 | 75 | 92 | 0 | 4 | 1 | 3 | 64 | 13 | 0 | .203 |
| 1930 | 3 | 11 | .214 | 5.77 | 26 | 18 | 5 | 112.1 | 147 | 41 | 44 | 1 | 0 | 1 | 0 | 39 | 5 | 0 | .128 |
| 1931 CHI N | 5 | 5 | .500 | 3.87 | 31 | 4 | 1 | 79 | 81 | 43 | 38 | 0 | 3 | 4 | 2 | 22 | 5 | 0 | .227 |
| 1932 | 2 | 2 | .500 | 4.36 | 35 | 0 | 0 | 53.2 | 61 | 19 | 20 | 0 | 2 | 2 | 1 | 8 | 1 | 0 | .125 |
| 14 yrs. | 72 | 95 | .431 | 3.88 | 410 | 162 | 70 | 1562.1 | 1645 | 617 | 765 | 7 | 24 | 22 | 19 | 468 | 80 | 2 | .171 |
| 2 yrs. | 7 | 7 | .500 | 4.07 | 66 | 4 | 1 | 132.2 | 142 | 62 | 58 | 0 | 5 | 6 | 3 | 30 | 6 | 0 | .200 |

WORLD SERIES

| | W | L | PCT | ERA | G | GS | CG | IP | H | BB | SO | ShO | W | L | SV | AB | H | HR | BA |
|---|---|---|---|---|---|---|---|---|---|---|---|---|---|---|---|---|---|---|---|
| 1932 CHI N | 0 | 1 | .000 | 11.57 | 2 | 0 | 0 | 4.2 | 9 | 3 | 4 | 0 | 0 | 1 | 0 | 2 | 0 | 0 | .000 |

## Ed Mayer

**MAYER, EDWIN DAVID**   BL TL 6'2"   185 lbs.
B. Nov. 30, 1931, San Francisco, Calif.

| | W | L | PCT | ERA | G | GS | CG | IP | H | BB | SO | ShO | W | L | SV | AB | H | HR | BA |
|---|---|---|---|---|---|---|---|---|---|---|---|---|---|---|---|---|---|---|---|
| 1957 CHI N | 0 | 0 | – | 5.87 | 3 | 1 | 0 | 7.2 | 8 | 2 | 3 | 0 | 0 | 0 | 0 | 2 | 1 | 0 | .500 |
| 1958 | 2 | 2 | .500 | 3.80 | 19 | 0 | 0 | 23.2 | 15 | 16 | 14 | 0 | 2 | 2 | 1 | 5 | 1 | 0 | .200 |
| 2 yrs. | 2 | 2 | .500 | 4.31 | 22 | 1 | 0 | 31.1 | 23 | 18 | 17 | 0 | 2 | 2 | 1 | 7 | 2 | 0 | .286 |
| 2 yrs. | 2 | 2 | .500 | 4.31 | 22 | 1 | 0 | 31.1 | 23 | 18 | 17 | 0 | 2 | 2 | 1 | 7 | 2 | 0 | .286 |

## Bill McAfee

**McAFEE, WILLIAM FORT**   BR TR 6'2"   186 lbs.
B. Sept. 7, 1907, Smithville, Ga.   D. July 8, 1958, Culpeper, Va.

| | W | L | PCT | ERA | G | GS | CG | IP | H | BB | SO | ShO | W | L | SV | AB | H | HR | BA |
|---|---|---|---|---|---|---|---|---|---|---|---|---|---|---|---|---|---|---|---|
| 1930 CHI N | 0 | 0 | – | 0.00 | 2 | 0 | 0 | 3 | 2 | 0 | 0 | 0 | 0 | 0 | 0 | 0 | 0 | 0 | – |
| 1931 BOS N | 0 | 1 | .000 | 6.37 | 18 | 1 | 0 | 29.2 | 39 | 10 | 9 | 0 | 0 | 0 | 0 | 3 | 0 | 0 | .000 |
| 1932 WAS A | 6 | 1 | .857 | 3.92 | 8 | 5 | 2 | 41.1 | 47 | 22 | 10 | 0 | 3 | 0 | 0 | 18 | 2 | 0 | .111 |
| 1933 | 3 | 2 | .600 | 6.62 | 27 | 1 | 0 | 53 | 64 | 21 | 14 | 0 | 3 | 2 | 5 | 15 | 4 | 1 | .267 |
| 1934 STL A | 1 | 0 | 1.000 | 5.84 | 28 | 0 | 0 | 61.2 | 84 | 26 | 11 | 0 | 1 | 0 | 0 | 16 | 3 | 0 | .188 |
| 5 yrs. | 10 | 4 | .714 | 5.69 | 83 | 7 | 2 | 186.2 | 237 | 81 | 44 | 0 | 7 | 2 | 5 | 52 | 9 | 1 | .173 |
| 1 yr. | 0 | 0 | – | 0.00 | 2 | 0 | 0 | 3 | 2 | 0 | 0 | 0 | 0 | 0 | 0 | 0 | 0 | 0 | – |

## Dutch McCall

**McCALL, ROBERT LEONARD**   BL TL 6'1½"   185 lbs.
B. Dec. 27, 1920, Columbia, Tenn.

| | W | L | PCT | ERA | G | GS | CG | IP | H | BB | SO | ShO | W | L | SV | AB | H | HR | BA |
|---|---|---|---|---|---|---|---|---|---|---|---|---|---|---|---|---|---|---|---|
| 1948 CHI N | 4 | 13 | .235 | 4.82 | 30 | 20 | 5 | 151.1 | 158 | 85 | 89 | 0 | 0 | 3 | 0 | 53 | 9 | 0 | .170 |

## George McConnell

**McCONNELL, GEORGE NEELY**   BR TR 6'3"   190 lbs.
B. Sept. 16, 1877, Shelbyville, Tenn.   D. May 10, 1964, Chattanooga, Tenn.

| | W | L | PCT | ERA | G | GS | CG | IP | H | BB | SO | ShO | W | L | SV | AB | H | HR | BA |
|---|---|---|---|---|---|---|---|---|---|---|---|---|---|---|---|---|---|---|---|
| 1909 NY A | 0 | 1 | .000 | 2.25 | 2 | 1 | 0 | 4 | 3 | 3 | 4 | 0 | 0 | 1 | 0 | 43 | 9 | 0 | .209 |
| 1912 | 8 | 12 | .400 | 2.75 | 23 | 20 | 19 | 176.2 | 172 | 52 | 91 | 0 | 0 | 0 | 0 | 91 | 27 | 0 | .297 |
| 1913 | 4 | 15 | .211 | 3.20 | 35 | 20 | 8 | 180 | 162 | 60 | 72 | 0 | 0 | 1 | 3 | 67 | 12 | 0 | .179 |
| 1914 CHI N | 0 | 1 | .000 | 1.29 | 1 | 0 | 0 | 7 | 3 | 3 | 3 | 0 | 0 | 0 | 0 | 2 | 0 | 0 | .000 |
| 1915 CHI F | 25 | 10 | .714 | 2.20 | 44 | 35 | 23 | 303 | 262 | 89 | 151 | 4 | 3 | 1 | 1 | 125 | 31 | 1 | .248 |
| 1916 CHI N | 4 | 12 | .250 | 2.57 | 28 | 20 | 8 | 171.1 | 137 | 35 | 82 | 1 | 0 | 2 | 0 | 57 | 9 | 0 | .158 |
| 6 yrs. | 41 | 51 | .446 | 2.60 | 133 | 97 | 58 | 842 | 739 | 242 | 403 | 5 | 3 | 5 | 4 | * | | | |
| 2 yrs. | 4 | 13 | .235 | 2.52 | 29 | 21 | 8 | 178.1 | 140 | 38 | 85 | 1 | 0 | 2 | 0 | 59 | 9 | 0 | .153 |

| | W | L | PCT | ERA | G | GS | CG | IP | H | BB | SO | ShO | Relief Pitching W | L | SV | BATTING AB | H | HR | BA |
|---|---|---|---|---|---|---|---|---|---|---|---|---|---|---|---|---|---|---|---|

## Jim McCormick

**McCORMICK, JAMES**
B. 1856, Glasgow, Scotland    D. Mar. 10, 1918, Paterson, N. J.
Manager 1879-80.

BR   TR   5'10½" 195 lbs.

| | W | L | PCT | ERA | G | GS | CG | IP | H | BB | SO | ShO | W | L | SV | AB | H | HR | BA |
|---|---|---|---|---|---|---|---|---|---|---|---|---|---|---|---|---|---|---|---|
| 1878 IND N | 5 | 8 | .385 | 1.69 | 14 | 14 | 12 | 117 | 128 | 15 | 36 | 1 | 0 | 0 | 0 | 56 | 8 | 0 | .143 |
| 1879 CLE N | 20 | 40 | .333 | 2.42 | 62 | 60 | 59 | 546.1 | 582 | 74 | 197 | 3 | 1 | 0 | 0 | 282 | 62 | 0 | .220 |
| 1880 | 45 | 28 | .616 | 1.85 | 74 | 74 | 72 | 657.2 | 585 | 75 | 260 | 7 | 0 | 0 | 0 | 289 | 71 | 0 | .246 |
| 1881 | 26 | 30 | .464 | 2.45 | 59 | 58 | 57 | 526 | 484 | 84 | 178 | 2 | 0 | 0 | 0 | 309 | 79 | 0 | .256 |
| 1882 | 36 | 29 | .554 | 2.37 | 68 | 67 | 65 | 595.2 | 550 | 103 | 200 | 4 | 1 | 0 | 0 | 262 | 57 | 2 | .218 |
| 1883 | 27 | 13 | .675 | 1.84 | 43 | 41 | 36 | 342 | 316 | 65 | 145 | 1 | 1 | 0 | 1 | 157 | 37 | 0 | .236 |
| 1884 2 teams | | | | | CLE | N | (42G 19–22) | | CIN | U | (26G 21–3) | | | | | | | | |
| "   total | 40 | 25 | .615 | 2.37 | 68 | 68 | 63 | 569 | 508 | 89 | 343 | 10 | 0 | 0 | 0 | 300 | 77 | 0 | .257 |
| 1885 2 teams | | | | | PRO | N | (4G 1–3) | | CHI | N | (24G 20–4) | | | | | | | | |
| "   total | 21 | 7 | .750 | 2.43 | 28 | 28 | 28 | 252 | 221 | 60 | 96 | 3 | 0 | 0 | 0 | 117 | 26 | 0 | .222 |
| 1886 CHI N | 31 | 11 | .738 | 2.82 | 42 | 42 | 38 | 347.2 | 341 | 100 | 172 | 2 | 0 | 0 | 0 | 174 | 41 | 2 | .236 |
| 1887 PIT N | 13 | 23 | .361 | 4.30 | 36 | 36 | 36 | 322.1 | 377 | 84 | 77 | 0 | 0 | 0 | 0 | 136 | 33 | 0 | .243 |
| 10 yrs. | 264 | 214 | .552 | 2.43 | 494 | 488 | 466 | 4275.2 | 4092 | 749 | 1704 | 33 | 3 | 0 | 1 | * | | | |
| | | | | | | | 10th | | | | | | | | | | | | |
| 2 yrs. | 51 | 15 | .773 | 2.67 | 66 | 66 | 62 | 562.2 | 528 | 140 | 260 | 5 | 0 | 0 | 0 | 277 | 64 | 2 | .231 |

## Lindy McDaniel

**McDANIEL, LYNDALL DALE**
Brother of Von McDaniel.
B. Dec. 13, 1935, Hollis, Okla.

BR   TR   6'3"     195 lbs.

| | W | L | PCT | ERA | G | GS | CG | IP | H | BB | SO | ShO | W | L | SV | AB | H | HR | BA |
|---|---|---|---|---|---|---|---|---|---|---|---|---|---|---|---|---|---|---|---|
| 1955 STL N | 0 | 0 | – | 4.74 | 4 | 2 | 0 | 19 | 22 | 7 | 7 | 0 | 0 | 0 | 0 | 5 | 1 | 0 | .200 |
| 1956 | 7 | 6 | .538 | 3.40 | 39 | 7 | 1 | 116.1 | 121 | 42 | 59 | 0 | 5 | 2 | 0 | 32 | 7 | 0 | .219 |
| 1957 | 15 | 9 | .625 | 3.49 | 30 | 26 | 10 | 191 | 196 | 53 | 75 | 1 | 3 | 0 | 0 | 74 | 19 | 1 | .257 |
| 1958 | 5 | 7 | .417 | 5.80 | 26 | 17 | 2 | 108.2 | 139 | 31 | 47 | 1 | 0 | 2 | 0 | 30 | 2 | 0 | .067 |
| 1959 | 14 | 12 | .538 | 3.82 | 62 | 7 | 1 | 132 | 144 | 41 | 86 | 0 | 13 | 8 | 15 | 29 | 1 | 0 | .034 |
| 1960 | 12 | 4 | .750 | 2.09 | 65 | 2 | 1 | 116.1 | 85 | 24 | 105 | 0 | 12 | 2 | 26 | 26 | 6 | 0 | .231 |
| 1961 | 10 | 6 | .625 | 4.87 | 55 | 0 | 0 | 94.1 | 117 | 31 | 69 | 0 | 10 | 6 | 9 | 17 | 4 | 0 | .235 |
| 1962 | 3 | 10 | .231 | 4.12 | 55 | 2 | 0 | 107 | 96 | 29 | 79 | 0 | 2 | 9 | 14 | 21 | 2 | 0 | .095 |
| 1963 CHI N | 13 | 7 | .650 | 2.86 | 57 | 0 | 0 | 88 | 82 | 27 | 75 | 0 | 13 | 7 | 22 | 22 | 2 | 1 | .091 |
| 1964 | 1 | 7 | .125 | 3.88 | 63 | 0 | 0 | 95 | 104 | 23 | 71 | 0 | 1 | 7 | 15 | 16 | 2 | 0 | .125 |
| 1965 | 5 | 6 | .455 | 2.59 | 71 | 0 | 0 | 128.2 | 115 | 47 | 92 | 0 | 5 | 6 | 2 | 8 | 0 | 0 | .000 |
| 1966 SF N | 10 | 5 | .667 | 2.66 | 64 | 0 | 0 | 121.2 | 103 | 35 | 93 | 0 | 10 | 5 | 6 | 22 | 2 | 0 | .091 |
| 1967 | 2 | 6 | .250 | 3.72 | 41 | 0 | 0 | 72.2 | 69 | 24 | 48 | 0 | 2 | 4 | 3 | 11 | 1 | 0 | .091 |
| 1968 2 teams | | | | | SF | N | (12G 0–0) | | NY | A | (24G 4–1) | | | | | | | | |
| "   total | 4 | 1 | .800 | 3.31 | 36 | 0 | 0 | 70.2 | 60 | 17 | 52 | 0 | 4 | 1 | 10 | 15 | 0 | 0 | .000 |
| 1969 NY A | 5 | 6 | .455 | 3.55 | 51 | 0 | 0 | 83.2 | 84 | 23 | 60 | 0 | 5 | 6 | 5 | 8 | 0 | 0 | .000 |
| 1970 | 9 | 5 | .643 | 2.01 | 62 | 0 | 0 | 112 | 88 | 23 | 81 | 0 | 9 | 5 | 29 | 24 | 4 | 0 | .167 |
| 1971 | 5 | 10 | .333 | 5.01 | 44 | 0 | 0 | 70 | 82 | 24 | 39 | 0 | 5 | 10 | 4 | 9 | 1 | 0 | .111 |
| 1972 | 3 | 1 | .750 | 2.25 | 37 | 0 | 0 | 68 | 54 | 25 | 47 | 0 | 3 | 1 | 0 | 7 | 2 | 1 | .286 |
| 1973 | 12 | 6 | .667 | 2.86 | 47 | 3 | 1 | 160.1 | 148 | 49 | 93 | 0 | 12 | 3 | 10 | 0 | 0 | | – |
| 1974 KC A | 1 | 4 | .200 | 3.45 | 38 | 5 | 2 | 107 | 109 | 24 | 47 | 0 | 0 | 2 | 1 | 0 | 0 | | – |
| 1975 | 5 | 1 | .833 | 4.15 | 40 | 0 | 0 | 78 | 81 | 24 | 40 | 0 | 5 | 1 | 1 | 0 | 0 | | – |
| 21 yrs. | 141 | 119 | .542 | 3.45 | 987 | 74 | 18 | 2140.1 | 2099 | 623 | 1361 | 2 | 119 | 87 | 172 | 376 | 56 | 3 | .149 |
| | | | | | | 2nd | | | | | | | 2nd | | | | | | |
| 3 yrs. | 19 | 20 | .487 | 3.06 | 191 | 0 | 0 | 311.2 | 301 | 97 | 238 | 0 | 19 | 20 | 39 | 46 | 4 | 1 | .087 |
| | | | | | | | | | | | | | | | 6th | | | | |

## Monte McFarland

**McFARLAND, LAMONT A.**
Brother of Chappie McFarland.
B. 1873, Illinois    D. Nov. 15, 1913, Peoria, Ill.

| | W | L | PCT | ERA | G | GS | CG | IP | H | BB | SO | ShO | W | L | SV | AB | H | HR | BA |
|---|---|---|---|---|---|---|---|---|---|---|---|---|---|---|---|---|---|---|---|
| 1895 CHI N | 2 | 0 | 1.000 | 5.14 | 2 | 2 | 2 | 14 | 21 | 5 | 5 | 0 | 0 | 0 | 0 | 7 | 1 | 0 | .143 |
| 1896 | 0 | 4 | .000 | 7.20 | 4 | 3 | 2 | 25 | 32 | 21 | 3 | 0 | 0 | 1 | 0 | 12 | 0 | 0 | .000 |
| 2 yrs. | 2 | 4 | .333 | 6.46 | 6 | 5 | 4 | 39 | 53 | 26 | 8 | 0 | 0 | 1 | 0 | 19 | 1 | 0 | .053 |
| 2 yrs. | 2 | 4 | .333 | 6.46 | 6 | 5 | 4 | 39 | 53 | 26 | 8 | 0 | 0 | 1 | 0 | 19 | 1 | 0 | .053 |

## Willie McGill

**McGILL, WILLIAM VANESS (Kid)**
B. Nov. 10, 1873, Atlanta, Ga.    D. Aug. 29, 1944, Indianapolis, Ind.

TL   5'6½" 170 lbs.

| | W | L | PCT | ERA | G | GS | CG | IP | H | BB | SO | ShO | W | L | SV | AB | H | HR | BA |
|---|---|---|---|---|---|---|---|---|---|---|---|---|---|---|---|---|---|---|---|
| 1890 CLE P | 11 | 9 | .550 | 4.12 | 24 | 20 | 19 | 183.2 | 92 | 96 | 82 | 0 | 1 | 0 | 0 | 68 | 10 | 0 | .147 |
| 1891 2 teams | | | | | C-M | AA | (8G 2–5) | | STL | AA | (35G 18–10) | | | | | | | | |
| "   total | 20 | 15 | .571 | 3.35 | 43 | 39 | 28 | 314 | 294 | 168 | 173 | 1 | 1 | 1 | 1 | 107 | 16 | 0 | .150 |
| 1892 CIN N | 1 | 1 | .500 | 5.29 | 3 | 3 | 1 | 17 | 18 | 5 | 7 | 0 | 0 | 0 | 0 | 7 | 2 | 0 | .286 |
| 1893 CHI N | 17 | 18 | .486 | 4.61 | 39 | 34 | 26 | 302.2 | 311 | 181 | 91 | 1 | 1 | 2 | 0 | 124 | 29 | 0 | .234 |
| 1894 | 7 | 19 | .269 | 5.84 | 27 | 23 | 22 | 208 | 272 | 117 | 58 | 0 | 2 | 1 | 0 | 82 | 20 | 0 | .244 |
| 1895 PHI N | 10 | 8 | .556 | 5.55 | 20 | 20 | 13 | 146 | 177 | 81 | 70 | 0 | 0 | 0 | 0 | 63 | 14 | 0 | .222 |
| 1896 | 5 | 4 | .556 | 5.31 | 12 | 11 | 7 | 79.2 | 87 | 53 | 29 | 0 | 0 | 0 | 0 | 29 | 6 | 0 | .207 |
| 7 yrs. | 71 | 74 | .490 | 4.59 | 168 | 150 | 116 | 1251 | 1381 | 701 | 510 | 2 | 5 | 4 | 1 | 480 | 97 | 0 | .202 |
| 2 yrs. | 24 | 37 | .393 | 5.11 | 66 | 57 | 48 | 510.2 | 583 | 298 | 149 | 1 | 3 | 3 | 0 | 206 | 49 | 0 | .238 |

## Dan McGinn

**McGINN, DANIEL MICHAEL**
B. Nov. 29, 1943, Omaha, Neb.

BL   TL   6'     185 lbs.

| | W | L | PCT | ERA | G | GS | CG | IP | H | BB | SO | ShO | W | L | SV | AB | H | HR | BA |
|---|---|---|---|---|---|---|---|---|---|---|---|---|---|---|---|---|---|---|---|
| 1968 CIN N | 0 | 1 | .000 | 5.25 | 14 | 0 | 0 | 12 | 13 | 11 | 16 | 0 | 0 | 1 | 0 | 2 | 0 | 0 | .000 |
| 1969 MON N | 7 | 10 | .412 | 3.94 | 74 | 1 | 0 | 132.1 | 123 | 65 | 112 | 0 | 7 | 10 | 6 | 29 | 5 | 1 | .172 |
| 1970 | 7 | 10 | .412 | 5.43 | 52 | 19 | 3 | 131 | 154 | 78 | 83 | 2 | 2 | 1 | 0 | 35 | 4 | 0 | .114 |
| 1971 | 1 | 4 | .200 | 5.96 | 28 | 6 | 1 | 71 | 74 | 42 | 40 | 0 | 0 | 1 | 0 | 17 | 4 | 0 | .235 |
| 1972 CHI N | 0 | 5 | .000 | 5.86 | 42 | 2 | 0 | 63 | 78 | 29 | 42 | 0 | 0 | 3 | 4 | 8 | 2 | 0 | .250 |
| 5 yrs. | 15 | 30 | .333 | 5.10 | 210 | 28 | 4 | 409.1 | 442 | 225 | 293 | 2 | 9 | 16 | 10 | 91 | 15 | 1 | .165 |
| 1 yr. | 0 | 5 | .000 | 5.86 | 42 | 2 | 0 | 63 | 78 | 29 | 42 | 0 | 0 | 3 | 4 | 8 | 2 | 0 | .250 |

| | W | L | PCT | ERA | G | GS | CG | IP | H | BB | SO | ShO | Relief Pitching W | L | SV | BATTING AB | H | HR | BA |
|---|---|---|---|---|---|---|---|---|---|---|---|---|---|---|---|---|---|---|---|

## Gus McGinnis

**McGINNIS, AUGUST**
B. 1870, Barnesville, Ohio   Deceased.        5'10½" 197 lbs.

| | W | L | PCT | ERA | G | GS | CG | IP | H | BB | SO | ShO | RP W | L | SV | AB | H | HR | BA |
|---|---|---|---|---|---|---|---|---|---|---|---|---|---|---|---|---|---|---|---|
| 1893 2 teams | | | CHI | N | (13G 2–5) | | | PHI | N | (5G 1–3) | | | | | | | | | |
| " total | 3 | 8 | .273 | 4.99 | 18 | 9 | 7 | 104.2 | 124 | 48 | 25 | 1 | 1 | 1 | 0 | 40 | 9 | 0 | .225 |

## Lynn McGlothen

**McGLOTHEN, LYNN EVERETT**
B. Mar. 27, 1950, Monroe, La.   D. Aug. 14, 1984, Dubach, La.        BL TR 6'2"   185 lbs.

| | W | L | PCT | ERA | G | GS | CG | IP | H | BB | SO | ShO | RP W | L | SV | AB | H | HR | BA |
|---|---|---|---|---|---|---|---|---|---|---|---|---|---|---|---|---|---|---|---|
| 1972 BOS A | 8 | 7 | .533 | 3.41 | 22 | 22 | 4 | 145.1 | 135 | 59 | 112 | 1 | 0 | 0 | 0 | 53 | 10 | 0 | .189 |
| 1973 | 1 | 2 | .333 | 8.22 | 6 | 3 | 0 | 23 | 39 | 8 | 16 | 0 | 0 | 0 | 0 | 0 | 0 | 0 | – |
| 1974 STL N | 16 | 12 | .571 | 2.70 | 31 | 31 | 8 | 237 | 212 | 89 | 142 | 3 | 0 | 0 | 0 | 83 | 15 | 0 | .181 |
| 1975 | 15 | 13 | .536 | 3.92 | 35 | 34 | 9 | 239 | 231 | 97 | 146 | 2 | 0 | 0 | 0 | 80 | 7 | 0 | .088 |
| 1976 | 13 | 15 | .464 | 3.91 | 33 | 32 | 10 | 205 | 209 | 68 | 106 | 4 | 0 | 0 | 0 | 71 | 15 | 0 | .211 |
| 1977 SF N | 2 | 9 | .182 | 5.63 | 21 | 15 | 2 | 80 | 94 | 52 | 42 | 0 | 0 | 1 | 0 | 19 | 2 | 0 | .105 |
| 1978 2 teams | | | SF | N | (5G 0–0) | | | CHI | N | (49G 5–3) | | | | | | | | | |
| " total | 5 | 3 | .625 | 3.30 | 54 | 6 | 0 | 92.2 | 92 | 43 | 69 | 0 | 5 | 2 | 0 | 16 | 3 | 0 | .188 |
| 1979 CHI N | 13 | 14 | .481 | 4.12 | 42 | 29 | 6 | 212 | 236 | 55 | 147 | 1 | 3 | 1 | 2 | 71 | 16 | 0 | .225 |
| 1980 | 12 | 14 | .462 | 4.80 | 39 | 27 | 2 | 182 | 211 | 64 | 119 | 2 | 0 | 1 | 0 | 51 | 10 | 0 | .196 |
| 1981 2 teams | | | CHI | N | (20G 1–4) | | | CHI | A | (11G 0–0) | | | | | | | | | |
| " total | 1 | 4 | .200 | 4.56 | 31 | 6 | 0 | 77 | 85 | 35 | 38 | 0 | 1 | 1 | 0 | 12 | 1 | 0 | .083 |
| 1982 NY A | 0 | 0 | – | 10.80 | 4 | 0 | 0 | 5 | 9 | 2 | 2 | 0 | 0 | 0 | 0 | 0 | 0 | 0 | – |
| 11 yrs. | 86 | 93 | .480 | 3.98 | 318 | 201 | 41 | 1498 | 1553 | 572 | 939 | 13 | 9 | 6 | 2 | 456 | 79 | 0 | .173 |
| 4 yrs. | 31 | 35 | .470 | 4.25 | 150 | 63 | 8 | 529 | 595 | 186 | 352 | 3 | 1 | 1 | 0 | 147 | 30 | 0 | .204 |

## Harry McIntyre

**McINTYRE, JOHN REED (Rocks)**
B. Jan. 11, 1879, Dayton, Ohio   D. Jan. 9, 1949, Daytona Beach, Fla.        BR TR 5'11"   180 lbs.

| | W | L | PCT | ERA | G | GS | CG | IP | H | BB | SO | ShO | RP W | L | SV | AB | H | HR | BA |
|---|---|---|---|---|---|---|---|---|---|---|---|---|---|---|---|---|---|---|---|
| 1905 BKN N | 8 | 25 | .242 | 3.70 | 40 | 35 | 29 | 309 | 340 | 101 | 135 | 1 | 0 | 1 | 1 | 138 | 34 | 1 | .246 |
| 1906 | 13 | 21 | .382 | 2.97 | 39 | 31 | 25 | 276 | 254 | 89 | 121 | 4 | 2 | 2 | 3 | 103 | 18 | 0 | .175 |
| 1907 | 7 | 15 | .318 | 2.39 | 28 | 22 | 19 | 199.2 | 178 | 79 | 49 | 3 | 1 | 0 | 0 | 69 | 15 | 0 | .217 |
| 1908 | 11 | 20 | .355 | 2.69 | 40 | 35 | 26 | 288 | 259 | 90 | 108 | 4 | 0 | 1 | 2 | 100 | 20 | 0 | .200 |
| 1909 | 7 | 17 | .292 | 3.63 | 32 | 26 | 20 | 228 | 200 | 91 | 84 | 2 | 0 | 1 | 0 | 76 | 13 | 0 | .171 |
| 1910 CHI N | 13 | 9 | .591 | 3.07 | 28 | 19 | 10 | 176 | 152 | 50 | 65 | 2 | 4 | 1 | 0 | 66 | 17 | 1 | .258 |
| 1911 | 11 | 7 | .611 | 4.11 | 25 | 17 | 9 | 149 | 147 | 33 | 56 | 1 | 2 | 0 | 0 | 53 | 14 | 0 | .264 |
| 1912 | 1 | 2 | .333 | 3.80 | 4 | 3 | 2 | 23.2 | 22 | 6 | 8 | 0 | 1 | 0 | 0 | 10 | 3 | 0 | .300 |
| 1913 CIN N | 0 | 1 | .000 | 27.00 | 1 | 0 | 0 | 1 | 3 | 0 | 0 | 0 | 0 | 0 | 0 | 0 | 0 | 0 | – |
| 9 yrs. | 71 | 117 | .378 | 3.22 | 237 | 188 | 140 | 1650.1 | 1555 | 539 | 626 | 17 | 9 | 8 | 6 | 615 | 134 | 2 | .218 |
| 3 yrs. | 25 | 18 | .581 | 3.56 | 57 | 39 | 21 | 348.2 | 321 | 89 | 129 | 3 | 6 | 2 | 0 | 129 | 34 | 1 | .264 |

WORLD SERIES

| | W | L | PCT | ERA | G | GS | CG | IP | H | BB | SO | ShO | RP W | L | SV | AB | H | HR | BA |
|---|---|---|---|---|---|---|---|---|---|---|---|---|---|---|---|---|---|---|---|
| 1910 CHI N | 0 | 1 | .000 | 6.75 | 2 | 0 | 0 | 5.1 | 4 | 3 | 3 | 0 | 0 | 1 | 0 | 1 | 0 | 0 | .000 |

## Cal McLish

**McLISH, CALVIN COOLIDGE JULIUS CAESAR TUSKAHOMA (Buster)**
B. Dec. 1, 1925, Anadarko, Okla.        BR TR 6'   179 lbs.
BR 1944

| | W | L | PCT | ERA | G | GS | CG | IP | H | BB | SO | ShO | RP W | L | SV | AB | H | HR | BA |
|---|---|---|---|---|---|---|---|---|---|---|---|---|---|---|---|---|---|---|---|
| 1944 BKN N | 3 | 10 | .231 | 7.82 | 23 | 13 | 3 | 84 | 110 | 48 | 24 | 0 | 0 | 2 | 0 | 32 | 7 | 0 | .219 |
| 1946 | 0 | 0 | – | ∞ | 1 | 0 | 0 | 0 | 1 | 0 | 0 | 0 | 0 | 0 | 0 | 0 | 0 | 0 | – |
| 1947 PIT N | 0 | 0 | – | 18.00 | 1 | 0 | 0 | 1 | 2 | 0 | 0 | 0 | 0 | 0 | 0 | 0 | 0 | 0 | – |
| 1948 | 0 | 0 | – | 9.00 | 2 | 1 | 0 | 5 | 8 | 2 | 1 | 0 | 0 | 0 | 0 | 1 | 0 | 0 | .000 |
| 1949 CHI N | 1 | 1 | .500 | 5.87 | 8 | 2 | 0 | 23 | 31 | 12 | 6 | 0 | 0 | 0 | 0 | 9 | 3 | 1 | .333 |
| 1951 | 4 | 10 | .286 | 4.45 | 30 | 17 | 5 | 145.2 | 159 | 52 | 46 | 1 | 0 | 1 | 0 | 42 | 5 | 0 | .119 |
| 1956 CLE A | 2 | 4 | .333 | 4.96 | 37 | 2 | 0 | 61.2 | 67 | 32 | 27 | 0 | 1 | 3 | 1 | 9 | 1 | 0 | .111 |
| 1957 | 9 | 7 | .563 | 2.74 | 42 | 7 | 2 | 144.1 | 117 | 67 | 88 | 0 | 7 | 5 | 1 | 43 | 8 | 2 | .186 |
| 1958 | 16 | 8 | .667 | 2.99 | 39 | 30 | 13 | 225.2 | 214 | 70 | 97 | 0 | 0 | 0 | 1 | 64 | 6 | 0 | .094 |
| 1959 | 19 | 8 | .704 | 3.63 | 35 | 32 | 13 | 235.1 | 253 | 72 | 113 | 0 | 0 | 0 | 0 | 74 | 14 | 0 | .189 |
| 1960 CIN N | 4 | 14 | .222 | 4.16 | 37 | 21 | 2 | 151.1 | 170 | 48 | 56 | 1 | 0 | 0 | 1 | 41 | 2 | 0 | .049 |
| 1961 CHI A | 10 | 13 | .435 | 4.38 | 31 | 27 | 4 | 162.1 | 178 | 47 | 80 | 0 | 0 | 0 | 1 | 54 | 9 | 0 | .167 |
| 1962 PHI N | 11 | 5 | .688 | 4.25 | 32 | 24 | 5 | 154.2 | 184 | 45 | 71 | 1 | 1 | 0 | 1 | 51 | 4 | 0 | .078 |
| 1963 | 13 | 11 | .542 | 3.26 | 32 | 32 | 10 | 209.2 | 184 | 56 | 98 | 2 | 0 | 0 | 0 | 69 | 14 | 0 | .203 |
| 1964 | 0 | 1 | .000 | 3.38 | 2 | 1 | 0 | 5.1 | 6 | 1 | 6 | 0 | 0 | 0 | 0 | 1 | 0 | 0 | .000 |
| 15 yrs. | 92 | 92 | .500 | 4.01 | 352 | 209 | 57 | 1609 | 1684 | 552 | 713 | 5 | 9 | 14 | 6 | 490 | 73 | 3 | .149 |
| 2 yrs. | 5 | 11 | .313 | 4.64 | 38 | 19 | 5 | 168.2 | 190 | 64 | 52 | 1 | 0 | 1 | 0 | 51 | 8 | 1 | .157 |

## Cal McVey

**McVEY, CALVIN ALEXANDER**
B. Aug. 30, 1850, County, Iowa   D. Aug. 20, 1926, San Francisco, Calif.        BR TR 5'9"   170 lbs.
Manager 1873, 1878-79.

| | W | L | PCT | ERA | G | GS | CG | IP | H | BB | SO | ShO | RP W | L | SV | AB | H | HR | BA |
|---|---|---|---|---|---|---|---|---|---|---|---|---|---|---|---|---|---|---|---|
| 1876 CHI N | 5 | 1 | .833 | 1.52 | 11 | 6 | 5 | 59.1 | 57 | 2 | 9 | 0 | 0 | 0 | 2 | 308 | 107 | 0 | .347 |
| 1877 | 4 | 8 | .333 | 4.50 | 17 | 10 | 6 | 92 | 129 | 11 | 20 | 0 | 1 | 1 | 2 | 266 | 98 | 0 | .368 |
| 1879 CIN N | 0 | 2 | .000 | 8.36 | 3 | 1 | 1 | 14 | 34 | 2 | 7 | 0 | 0 | 1 | 0 | 354 | 105 | 0 | .297 |
| 3 yrs. | 9 | 11 | .450 | 3.76 | 31 | 17 | 12 | 165.1 | 220 | 15 | 36 | 0 | 1 | 2 | 4 | * | | | |
| 2 yrs. | 9 | 9 | .500 | 3.33 | 28 | 16 | 11 | 151.1 | 186 | 13 | 29 | 0 | 1 | 1 | 4 | 574 | 205 | 1 | .357 |

## George Meakim

**MEAKIM, GEORGE CLINTON**
B. July 11, 1865, Brooklyn, N. Y.   D. Feb. 17, 1923, Queens, N. Y.        BR TR 5'7½"   154 lbs.

| | W | L | PCT | ERA | G | GS | CG | IP | H | BB | SO | ShO | RP W | L | SV | AB | H | HR | BA |
|---|---|---|---|---|---|---|---|---|---|---|---|---|---|---|---|---|---|---|---|
| 1890 LOU AA | 12 | 7 | .632 | 2.91 | 28 | 21 | 16 | 192 | 173 | 63 | 123 | 3 | 1 | 0 | 1 | 72 | 11 | 0 | .153 |
| 1891 PHI AA | 1 | 4 | .200 | 6.94 | 6 | 6 | 4 | 35 | 51 | 22 | 13 | 0 | 0 | 0 | 0 | 15 | 3 | 0 | .200 |
| 1892 2 teams | | | CHI | N | (1G 0–1) | | | CIN | N | (3G 1–1) | | | | | | | | | |
| " total | 1 | 2 | .333 | 9.53 | 4 | 4 | 2 | 22.2 | 37 | 11 | 4 | 0 | 0 | 0 | 0 | 10 | 2 | 0 | .200 |
| 1895 LOU N | 1 | 0 | 1.000 | 2.57 | 1 | 1 | 1 | 7 | 7 | 4 | 2 | 0 | 0 | 0 | 0 | 3 | 1 | 0 | .333 |
| 4 yrs. | 15 | 13 | .536 | 4.03 | 39 | 32 | 23 | 256.2 | 268 | 100 | 142 | 3 | 1 | 0 | 1 | 100 | 17 | 0 | .170 |
| 1 yr. | 0 | 1 | .000 | 11.00 | 1 | 1 | 1 | 9 | 18 | 2 | 0 | 0 | 0 | 0 | 0 | 5 | 2 | 0 | .400 |

| | W | L | PCT | ERA | G | GS | CG | IP | H | BB | SO | ShO | Relief Pitching W | L | SV | BATTING AB | H | HR | BA |
|---|---|---|---|---|---|---|---|---|---|---|---|---|---|---|---|---|---|---|---|

## Russ Meers

**MEERS, RUSSELL HARLAN (Babe)**      BL TL 5'10" 170 lbs.
B. Nov. 28, 1918, Tilton, Ill.

| | W | L | PCT | ERA | G | GS | CG | IP | H | BB | SO | ShO | W | L | SV | AB | H | HR | BA |
|---|---|---|---|---|---|---|---|---|---|---|---|---|---|---|---|---|---|---|---|
| 1941 CHI N | 0 | 1 | .000 | 1.13 | 1 | 1 | 0 | 8 | 5 | 0 | 5 | 0 | 0 | 0 | 0 | 2 | 0 | 0 | .000 |
| 1946 | 1 | 2 | .333 | 3.18 | 7 | 2 | 0 | 11.1 | 10 | 10 | 2 | 0 | 1 | 0 | 0 | 1 | 1 | 0 | 1.000 |
| 1947 | 2 | 0 | 1.000 | 4.48 | 35 | 1 | 0 | 64.1 | 61 | 38 | 28 | 0 | 2 | 0 | 0 | 14 | 2 | 0 | .143 |
| 3 yrs. | 3 | 3 | .500 | 3.98 | 43 | 4 | 0 | 83.2 | 76 | 48 | 35 | 0 | 3 | 0 | 0 | 17 | 3 | 0 | .176 |
| 3 yrs. | 3 | 3 | .500 | 3.98 | 43 | 4 | 0 | 83.2 | 76 | 48 | 35 | 0 | 3 | 0 | 0 | 17 | 3 | 0 | .176 |

## Sam Mejias

**MEJIAS, SAMUEL ELIAS**      BR TR 6' 170 lbs.
B. May 9, 1953, Santiago, Dominican Republic

| | W | L | PCT | ERA | G | GS | CG | IP | H | BB | SO | ShO | W | L | SV | AB | H | HR | BA |
|---|---|---|---|---|---|---|---|---|---|---|---|---|---|---|---|---|---|---|---|
| 1978 MON N | 0 | 0 | – | 0.00 | 1 | 0 | 0 | 1 | 0 | 0 | 0 | 0 | 0 | 0 | 0 | * | | | |

## Jock Menefee

**MENEFEE, JOHN**      BR TR 6'
B. Jan. 16, 1868, West Virginia    D. Mar. 11, 1953, Belle Vernon, Pa.

| | W | L | PCT | ERA | G | GS | CG | IP | H | BB | SO | ShO | W | L | SV | AB | H | HR | BA |
|---|---|---|---|---|---|---|---|---|---|---|---|---|---|---|---|---|---|---|---|
| 1892 PIT N | 0 | 0 | – | 11.25 | 1 | 0 | 0 | 4 | 10 | 2 | 0 | 0 | 0 | 0 | 0 | 3 | 0 | 0 | .000 |
| 1893 LOU N | 8 | 7 | .533 | 4.24 | 15 | 15 | 14 | 129.1 | 150 | 40 | 30 | 1 | 0 | 0 | 0 | 73 | 20 | 0 | .274 |
| 1894 2 teams | | | LOU | N (28G 8–17) | | | PIT | N (13G 5–8) | | | | | | | | | | | |
| " total | 13 | 25 | .342 | 4.68 | 41 | 37 | 33 | 323.1 | 417 | 89 | 76 | 1 | 0 | 1 | 0 | 126 | 25 | 0 | .198 |
| 1895 PIT N | 0 | 1 | .000 | 16.20 | 2 | 1 | 0 | 1.2 | 2 | 7 | 0 | 0 | 0 | 0 | 0 | 0 | 0 | 0 | – |
| 1898 NY N | 0 | 1 | .000 | 4.82 | 1 | 1 | 1 | 9.1 | 11 | 2 | 3 | 0 | 0 | 0 | 0 | 5 | 0 | 0 | .000 |
| 1900 CHI N | 9 | 4 | .692 | 3.85 | 16 | 13 | 11 | 117 | 140 | 35 | 30 | 0 | 1 | 0 | 0 | 46 | 5 | 0 | .109 |
| 1901 | 8 | 13 | .381 | 3.80 | 21 | 20 | 19 | 182.1 | 201 | 34 | 55 | 0 | 0 | 1 | 0 | 152 | 39 | 0 | .257 |
| 1902 | 12 | 10 | .545 | 2.42 | 22 | 21 | 20 | 197.1 | 202 | 26 | 60 | 5 | 1 | 0 | 0 | 216 | 50 | 0 | .231 |
| 1903 | 8 | 8 | .500 | 3.00 | 20 | 17 | 13 | 147 | 157 | 38 | 39 | 1 | 1 | 1 | 0 | 64 | 13 | 0 | .203 |
| 9 yrs. | 58 | 69 | .457 | 3.81 | 139 | 125 | 111 | 1111.1 | 1290 | 273 | 293 | 8 | 3 | 3 | 0 | * | | | |
| 4 yrs. | 37 | 35 | .514 | 3.20 | 79 | 71 | 63 | 643.2 | 700 | 133 | 184 | 6 | 3 | 2 | 0 | 478 | 107 | 0 | .224 |

## Ron Meridith

**MERIDITH, RONALD KNOX**      BL TL 6' 175 lbs.
B. Nov. 26, 1956, San Pedro, Calif.

| | W | L | PCT | ERA | G | GS | CG | IP | H | BB | SO | ShO | W | L | SV | AB | H | HR | BA |
|---|---|---|---|---|---|---|---|---|---|---|---|---|---|---|---|---|---|---|---|
| 1984 CHI N | 0 | 0 | – | 3.38 | 3 | 0 | 0 | 5.1 | 6 | 2 | 4 | 0 | 0 | 0 | 0 | 0 | 0 | 0 | – |
| 1985 | 3 | 2 | .600 | 4.47 | 32 | 0 | 0 | 46.1 | 53 | 24 | 23 | 0 | 3 | 2 | 1 | 4 | 1 | 0 | .250 |
| 2 yrs. | 3 | 2 | .600 | 4.35 | 35 | 0 | 0 | 51.2 | 59 | 26 | 27 | 0 | 3 | 2 | 1 | 4 | 1 | 0 | .250 |
| 2 yrs. | 3 | 2 | .600 | 4.35 | 35 | 0 | 0 | 51.2 | 59 | 26 | 27 | 0 | 3 | 2 | 1 | 4 | 1 | 0 | .250 |

## Sam Mertes

**MERTES, SAMUEL BLAIR (Sandow)**      BR TR 5'10" 185 lbs.
B. Aug. 6, 1872, San Francisco, Calif.    D. Mar. 11, 1945, San Francisco, Calif.

| | W | L | PCT | ERA | G | GS | CG | IP | H | BB | SO | ShO | W | L | SV | AB | H | HR | BA |
|---|---|---|---|---|---|---|---|---|---|---|---|---|---|---|---|---|---|---|---|
| 1902 CHI A | 1 | 0 | 1.000 | 1.17 | 1 | 0 | 0 | 7.2 | 6 | 0 | 0 | 0 | 1 | 0 | 0 | * | | | |

## Russ Meyer

**MEYER, RUSSELL CHARLES (The Mad Monk)**      BB TR 6'1" 175 lbs.
B. Oct. 25, 1923, Peru, Ill.

| | W | L | PCT | ERA | G | GS | CG | IP | H | BB | SO | ShO | W | L | SV | AB | H | HR | BA |
|---|---|---|---|---|---|---|---|---|---|---|---|---|---|---|---|---|---|---|---|
| 1946 CHI N | 0 | 0 | – | 3.18 | 4 | 1 | 0 | 17 | 21 | 10 | 10 | 0 | 0 | 0 | 1 | 5 | 1 | 0 | .200 |
| 1947 | 3 | 2 | .600 | 3.40 | 23 | 2 | 1 | 45 | 43 | 14 | 22 | 0 | 3 | 1 | 0 | 12 | 3 | 0 | .250 |
| 1948 | 10 | 10 | .500 | 3.66 | 29 | 26 | 8 | 164.2 | 157 | 77 | 89 | 3 | 0 | 2 | 0 | 56 | 6 | 0 | .107 |
| 1949 PHI N | 17 | 8 | .680 | 3.08 | 37 | 28 | 14 | 213 | 199 | 70 | 78 | 2 | 2 | 1 | 1 | 70 | 10 | 0 | .143 |
| 1950 | 9 | 11 | .450 | 5.30 | 32 | 25 | 3 | 159.2 | 193 | 67 | 74 | 0 | 0 | 1 | 1 | 50 | 7 | 0 | .140 |
| 1951 | 8 | 9 | .471 | 3.48 | 28 | 24 | 7 | 168 | 172 | 55 | 65 | 2 | 0 | 1 | 0 | 48 | 5 | 0 | .104 |
| 1952 | 13 | 14 | .481 | 3.14 | 37 | 32 | 14 | 232.1 | 235 | 65 | 92 | 1 | 0 | 1 | 0 | 79 | 7 | 1 | .089 |
| 1953 BKN N | 15 | 5 | .750 | 4.56 | 34 | 32 | 10 | 191.1 | 201 | 63 | 106 | 2 | 0 | 1 | 0 | 75 | 11 | 0 | .147 |
| 1954 | 11 | 6 | .647 | 3.99 | 36 | 28 | 6 | 180.1 | 193 | 49 | 70 | 2 | 0 | 0 | 0 | 47 | 2 | 0 | .043 |
| 1955 | 6 | 2 | .750 | 5.42 | 18 | 11 | 2 | 73 | 86 | 31 | 26 | 1 | .1 | 1 | 0 | 27 | 1 | 0 | .037 |
| 1956 2 teams | | | CHI | N (20G 1–6) | | | CIN | N (1G 0–0) | | | | | | | | | | | |
| " total | 1 | 6 | .143 | 6.21 | 21 | 9 | 0 | 58 | 72 | 26 | 29 | 0 | 0 | 0 | 0 | 12 | 1 | 0 | .083 |
| 1957 BOS A | 0 | 0 | – | 5.40 | 2 | 1 | 0 | 5 | 10 | 3 | 1 | 0 | 0 | 0 | 0 | 1 | 1 | 0 | 1.000 |
| 1959 KC A | 1 | 0 | 1.000 | 4.50 | 18 | 0 | 0 | 24 | 24 | 11 | 10 | 0 | 1 | 0 | 1 | 2 | 0 | 0 | .000 |
| 13 yrs. | 94 | 73 | .563 | 3.99 | 319 | 219 | 65 | 1531.1 | 1606 | 541 | 672 | 13 | 7 | 10 | 5 | 484 | 55 | 1 | .114 |
| 4 yrs. | 14 | 18 | .438 | 4.12 | 76 | 38 | 9 | 283.2 | 292 | 127 | 149 | 3 | 3 | 4 | 1 | 85 | 11 | 0 | .129 |

**WORLD SERIES**

| | W | L | PCT | ERA | G | GS | CG | IP | H | BB | SO | ShO | W | L | SV | AB | H | HR | BA |
|---|---|---|---|---|---|---|---|---|---|---|---|---|---|---|---|---|---|---|---|
| 1950 PHI N | 0 | 1 | .000 | 5.40 | 2 | 0 | 0 | 1.2 | 4 | 0 | 1 | 0 | 0 | 0 | 0 | 0 | 0 | 0 | – |
| 1953 BKN N | 0 | 0 | – | 6.23 | 1 | 0 | 0 | 4.1 | 8 | 4 | 5 | 0 | 0 | 0 | 0 | 1 | 0 | 0 | .000 |
| 1955 | 0 | 0 | – | 0.00 | 1 | 0 | 0 | 5.2 | 4 | 2 | 4 | 0 | 0 | 0 | 0 | 2 | 0 | 0 | .000 |
| 3 yrs. | 0 | 1 | .000 | 3.09 | 4 | 0 | 0 | 11.2 | 16 | 6 | 10 | 0 | 0 | 0 | 0 | 3 | 0 | 0 | .000 |

## Pete Mikkelsen

**MIKKELSEN, PETER JAMES**      BR TR 6'2" 210 lbs.
B. Oct. 25, 1939, Staten Island, N. Y.

| | W | L | PCT | ERA | G | GS | CG | IP | H | BB | SO | ShO | W | L | SV | AB | H | HR | BA |
|---|---|---|---|---|---|---|---|---|---|---|---|---|---|---|---|---|---|---|---|
| 1964 NY A | 7 | 4 | .636 | 3.56 | 50 | 0 | 0 | 86 | 79 | 41 | 63 | 0 | 7 | 4 | 12 | 16 | 1 | 0 | .063 |
| 1965 | 4 | 9 | .308 | 3.28 | 41 | 3 | 0 | 82.1 | 78 | 36 | 69 | 0 | 4 | 6 | 1 | 10 | 1 | 0 | .100 |
| 1966 PIT N | 9 | 8 | .529 | 3.07 | 71 | 0 | 0 | 126 | 106 | 51 | 76 | 0 | 9 | 8 | 14 | 20 | 3 | 0 | .150 |
| 1967 2 teams | | | PIT | N (32G 1–2) | | | CHI | N (7G 0–0) | | | | | | | | | | | |
| " total | 1 | 2 | .333 | 4.55 | 39 | 0 | 0 | 63.1 | 59 | 24 | 30 | 0 | 1 | 2 | 2 | 4 | 0 | 0 | .000 |
| 1968 2 teams | | | CHI | N (3G 0–0) | | | STL | N (5G 0–0) | | | | | | | | | | | |
| " total | 0 | 0 | – | 2.61 | 8 | 0 | 0 | 20.2 | 17 | 8 | 13 | 0 | 0 | 0 | 0 | 4 | 1 | 0 | .250 |
| 1969 LA N | 7 | 5 | .583 | 2.78 | 48 | 0 | 0 | 81 | 57 | 30 | 51 | 0 | 7 | 5 | 4 | 6 | 1 | 0 | .167 |
| 1970 | 4 | 2 | .667 | 2.76 | 33 | 0 | 0 | 62 | 48 | 20 | 47 | 0 | 4 | 2 | 6 | 6 | 2 | 0 | .333 |
| 1971 | 8 | 5 | .615 | 3.65 | 41 | 0 | 0 | 74 | 67 | 17 | 46 | 0 | 8 | 5 | 5 | 10 | 2 | 0 | .200 |
| 1972 | 5 | 5 | .500 | 4.06 | 33 | 0 | 0 | 57.2 | 65 | 23 | 41 | 0 | 5 | 5 | 5 | 7 | 0 | 0 | .000 |
| 9 yrs. | 45 | 40 | .529 | 3.38 | 364 | 3 | 0 | 653 | 576 | 250 | 436 | 0 | 45 | 37 | 49 | 83 | 11 | 0 | .133 |
| 2 yrs. | 0 | 0 | – | 6.94 | 10 | 0 | 0 | 11.2 | 16 | 6 | 5 | 0 | 0 | 0 | 0 | 1 | 1 | 0 | 1.000 |

**WORLD SERIES**

| | W | L | PCT | ERA | G | GS | CG | IP | H | BB | SO | ShO | W | L | SV | AB | H | HR | BA |
|---|---|---|---|---|---|---|---|---|---|---|---|---|---|---|---|---|---|---|---|
| 1964 NY A | 0 | 1 | .000 | 5.79 | 4 | 0 | 0 | 4.2 | 2 | 4 | 2 | 4 | 0 | 1 | 0 | 0 | 0 | 0 | – |

| | W | L | PCT | ERA | G | GS | CG | IP | H | BB | SO | ShO | Relief Pitching W | L | SV | AB | H | HR | BA |
|---|---|---|---|---|---|---|---|---|---|---|---|---|---|---|---|---|---|---|---|

## John Miklos

**MIKLOS, JOHN JOSEPH (Hank)**
B. Nov. 27, 1910, Chicago, Ill.

BL TL 5'11" 185 lbs.

| | W | L | PCT | ERA | G | GS | CG | IP | H | BB | SO | ShO | W | L | SV | AB | H | HR | BA |
|---|---|---|---|---|---|---|---|---|---|---|---|---|---|---|---|---|---|---|---|
| 1944 CHI N | 0 | 0 | – | 7.71 | 2 | 0 | 0 | 7 | 9 | 3 | 0 | 0 | 0 | 0 | 0 | 2 | 0 | 0 | .000 |

## Bob Miller

**MILLER, ROBERT LANE**
B. Feb. 18, 1939, St. Louis, Mo.

BR TR 6'1" 180 lbs.

| | W | L | PCT | ERA | G | GS | CG | IP | H | BB | SO | ShO | W | L | SV | AB | H | HR | BA |
|---|---|---|---|---|---|---|---|---|---|---|---|---|---|---|---|---|---|---|---|
| 1957 STL N | 0 | 0 | – | 7.00 | 5 | 0 | 0 | 9 | 13 | 5 | 7 | 0 | 0 | 0 | 0 | 0 | 0 | 0 | – |
| 1959 | 4 | 3 | .571 | 3.31 | 11 | 10 | 3 | 70.2 | 66 | 21 | 43 | 0 | 0 | 0 | 0 | 24 | 5 | 0 | .208 |
| 1960 | 4 | 3 | .571 | 3.42 | 15 | 7 | 0 | 52.2 | 53 | 17 | 33 | 0 | 1 | 0 | 0 | 14 | 2 | 0 | .143 |
| 1961 | 1 | 3 | .250 | 4.24 | 34 | 5 | 0 | 74.1 | 82 | 46 | 39 | 0 | 1 | 1 | 3 | 14 | 5 | 0 | .357 |
| 1962 NY N | 1 | 12 | .077 | 4.89 | 33 | 21 | 1 | 143.2 | 146 | 62 | 91 | 0 | 0 | 1 | 1 | 41 | 5 | 0 | .122 |
| 1963 LA N | 10 | 8 | .556 | 2.89 | 42 | 23 | 2 | 187 | 171 | 65 | 125 | 0 | 4 | 2 | 1 | 57 | 4 | 0 | .070 |
| 1964 | 7 | 7 | .500 | 2.62 | 74 | 2 | 0 | 137.2 | 115 | 63 | 94 | 0 | 6 | 7 | 9 | 19 | 3 | 0 | .158 |
| 1965 | 6 | 7 | .462 | 2.97 | 61 | 1 | 0 | 103 | 82 | 26 | 77 | 0 | 6 | 6 | 9 | 16 | 0 | 0 | .000 |
| 1966 | 4 | 2 | .667 | 2.77 | 46 | 0 | 0 | 84.1 | 70 | 29 | 58 | 0 | 4 | 2 | 5 | 13 | 1 | 0 | .077 |
| 1967 | 2 | 9 | .182 | 4.31 | 52 | 4 | 0 | 85.2 | 88 | 27 | 32 | 0 | 2 | 6 | 0 | 8 | 1 | 0 | .125 |
| 1968 MIN A | 0 | 3 | .000 | 2.74 | 45 | 0 | 0 | 72.1 | 65 | 24 | 41 | 0 | 0 | 3 | 2 | 7 | 1 | 0 | .143 |
| 1969 | 5 | 5 | .500 | 3.02 | 48 | 11 | 1 | 119.1 | 118 | 32 | 57 | 0 | 4 | 3 | 3 | 31 | 0 | 0 | .000 |
| 1970 3 teams | | | CLE | A (15G 2–2) | | | CHI | N (7G 0–0) | | | CHI | | A (15G 4–6) | | | | | | |
| " total | 6 | 8 | .429 | 4.79 | 37 | 15 | 0 | 107 | 129 | 54 | 55 | 0 | 2 | 0 | 3 | 28 | 5 | 0 | .179 |
| 1971 3 teams | | | CHI | N (2G 0–0) | | | SD | N (38G 7–3) | | | PIT | | N (16G 1–2) | | | | | | |
| " total | 8 | 5 | .615 | 1.64 | 56 | 0 | 0 | 98.2 | 83 | 40 | 51 | 0 | 8 | 5 | 10 | 12 | 0 | 0 | .000 |
| 1972 PIT N | 5 | 2 | .714 | 2.65 | 36 | 0 | 0 | 54.1 | 54 | 24 | 18 | 0 | 5 | 2 | 3 | 4 | 0 | 0 | .000 |
| 1973 3 teams | | | DET | A (22G 4–2) | | | SD | N (18G 0–0) | | | NY | | N (1G 0–0) | | | | | | |
| " total | 4 | 2 | .667 | 3.67 | 41 | 0 | 0 | 73.2 | 63 | 34 | 39 | 0 | 4 | 2 | 1 | 2 | 0 | 0 | .000 |
| 1974 NY N | 2 | 2 | .500 | 3.58 | 58 | 0 | 0 | 78 | 89 | 39 | 35 | 0 | 2 | 2 | 2 | 9 | 1 | 0 | .111 |
| 17 yrs. | 69 | 81 | .460 | 3.37 | 694 | 99 | 7 | 1551.1 | 1487 | 608 | 895 | 0 | 45 | 43 | 52 | 299 | 33 | 0 | .110 |
| 2 yrs. | 0 | 0 | – | 5.06 | 9 | 1 | 0 | 16 | 16 | 7 | 6 | 0 | 0 | 0 | 2 | 1 | 0 | 0 | .000 |
| **LEAGUE CHAMPIONSHIP SERIES** | | | | | | | | | | | | | | | | | | | |
| 1969 MIN A | 0 | 1 | .000 | 5.40 | 1 | 1 | 0 | 1.2 | 5 | 0 | 0 | 0 | 0 | 0 | 0 | 0 | 0 | 0 | – |
| 1971 PIT N | 0 | 0 | – | 6.00 | 1 | 0 | 0 | 3 | 3 | 3 | 3 | 0 | 0 | 0 | 0 | 1 | 0 | 0 | .000 |
| 1972 | 0 | 0 | – | 0.00 | 1 | 0 | 0 | 1 | 0 | 0 | 1 | 0 | 0 | 0 | 0 | 0 | 0 | 0 | – |
| 3 yrs. | 0 | 1 | .000 | 4.76 | 3 | 1 | 0 | 5.2 | 8 | 3 | 4 | 0 | 0 | 0 | 0 | 1 | 0 | 0 | .000 |
| **WORLD SERIES** | | | | | | | | | | | | | | | | | | | |
| 1965 LA N | 0 | 0 | – | 0.00 | 2 | 0 | 0 | 1.1 | 0 | 0 | 0 | 0 | 0 | 0 | 0 | 0 | 0 | 0 | – |
| 1966 | 0 | 0 | – | 0.00 | 1 | 0 | 0 | 3 | 2 | 2 | 1 | 0 | 0 | 0 | 0 | 0 | 0 | 0 | – |
| 1971 PIT N | 0 | 1 | .000 | 3.86 | 3 | 0 | 0 | 4.2 | 7 | 1 | 2 | 0 | 0 | 0 | 0 | 0 | 0 | 0 | – |
| 3 yrs. | 0 | 1 | .000 | 2.00 | 6 | 0 | 0 | 9 | 9 | 3 | 3 | 0 | 0 | 0 | 0 | 0 | 0 | 0 | – |

## Ox Miller

**MILLER, JOHN ANTHONY**
B. May 4, 1915, Gause, Tex.

BR TR 6'1" 190 lbs.

| | W | L | PCT | ERA | G | GS | CG | IP | H | BB | SO | ShO | W | L | SV | AB | H | HR | BA |
|---|---|---|---|---|---|---|---|---|---|---|---|---|---|---|---|---|---|---|---|
| 1943 2 teams | | | WAS | A (3G 0–0) | | | STL | A (2G 0–0) | | | | | | | | | | | |
| " total | 0 | 0 | – | 11.25 | 5 | 0 | 0 | 12 | 17 | 8 | 4 | 0 | 0 | 0 | 0 | 2 | 0 | 0 | .000 |
| 1945 STL A | 2 | 1 | .667 | 1.59 | 4 | 3 | 3 | 28.1 | 23 | 5 | 4 | 0 | 0 | 0 | 0 | 11 | 2 | 0 | .182 |
| 1946 | 1 | 3 | .250 | 6.88 | 11 | 3 | 0 | 35.1 | 52 | 15 | 12 | 0 | 0 | 0 | 1 | 7 | 2 | 0 | .286 |
| 1947 CHI N | 1 | 2 | .333 | 10.13 | 4 | 4 | 1 | 16 | 31 | 5 | 7 | 0 | 0 | 0 | 0 | 7 | 3 | 1 | .429 |
| 4 yrs. | 4 | 6 | .400 | 6.38 | 24 | 10 | 4 | 91.2 | 123 | 33 | 27 | 0 | 0 | 0 | 1 | 27 | 7 | 1 | .259 |
| 1 yr. | 1 | 2 | .333 | 10.13 | 4 | 4 | 1 | 16 | 31 | 5 | 7 | 0 | 0 | 0 | 0 | 7 | 3 | 1 | .429 |

## George Milstead

**MILSTEAD, GEORGE EARL (Cowboy)**
B. Sept. 26, 1903, Cleburne, Tex.   D. Aug. 9, 1977, Cleburne, Tex.

BL TL 5'10" 144 lbs.

| | W | L | PCT | ERA | G | GS | CG | IP | H | BB | SO | ShO | W | L | SV | AB | H | HR | BA |
|---|---|---|---|---|---|---|---|---|---|---|---|---|---|---|---|---|---|---|---|
| 1924 CHI N | 1 | 1 | .500 | 6.07 | 13 | 2 | 1 | 29.2 | 41 | 13 | 6 | 0 | 0 | 0 | 0 | 6 | 1 | 0 | .167 |
| 1925 | 1 | 1 | .500 | 3.00 | 5 | 3 | 1 | 21 | 26 | 8 | 7 | 0 | 0 | 0 | 0 | 7 | 0 | 0 | .000 |
| 1926 | 1 | 5 | .167 | 3.58 | 18 | 4 | 0 | 55.1 | 63 | 24 | 14 | 0 | 1 | 2 | 2 | 19 | 1 | 0 | .053 |
| 3 yrs. | 3 | 7 | .300 | 4.16 | 36 | 9 | 2 | 106 | 130 | 45 | 27 | 0 | 1 | 2 | 2 | 32 | 2 | 0 | .063 |
| 3 yrs. | 3 | 7 | .300 | 4.16 | 36 | 9 | 2 | 106 | 130 | 45 | 27 | 0 | 1 | 2 | 2 | 32 | 2 | 0 | .063 |

## Paul Minner

**MINNER, PAUL EDISON (Lefty)**
B. July 30, 1923, New Wilmington, Pa.

BL TL 6'5" 200 lbs.

| | W | L | PCT | ERA | G | GS | CG | IP | H | BB | SO | ShO | W | L | SV | AB | H | HR | BA |
|---|---|---|---|---|---|---|---|---|---|---|---|---|---|---|---|---|---|---|---|
| 1946 BKN N | 0 | 1 | .000 | 6.75 | 3 | 0 | 0 | 4 | 6 | 3 | 3 | 0 | 0 | 1 | 0 | 0 | 0 | 0 | – |
| 1948 | 4 | 3 | .571 | 2.44 | 28 | 2 | 0 | 62.2 | 61 | 26 | 23 | 0 | 3 | 3 | 1 | 21 | 4 | 0 | .190 |
| 1949 | 3 | 1 | .750 | 3.80 | 27 | 1 | 0 | 47.1 | 49 | 18 | 17 | 0 | 3 | 1 | 2 | 14 | 3 | 0 | .214 |
| 1950 CHI N | 8 | 13 | .381 | 4.11 | 39 | 24 | 9 | 190.1 | 217 | 72 | 99 | 1 | 0 | 0 | 4 | 65 | 14 | 1 | .215 |
| 1951 | 6 | 17 | .261 | 3.79 | 33 | 28 | 14 | 201.2 | 219 | 64 | 68 | 3 | 0 | 0 | 1 | 71 | 18 | 1 | .254 |
| 1952 | 14 | 9 | .609 | 3.74 | 28 | 27 | 12 | 180.2 | 180 | 54 | 61 | 2 | 0 | 0 | 0 | 64 | 15 | 1 | .234 |
| 1953 | 12 | 15 | .444 | 4.21 | 31 | 27 | 9 | 201 | 227 | 40 | 64 | 2 | 2 | 0 | 1 | 68 | 15 | 1 | .221 |
| 1954 | 11 | 11 | .500 | 3.96 | 32 | 29 | 12 | 218 | 236 | 50 | 79 | 0 | 0 | 1 | 1 | 76 | 13 | 2 | .171 |
| 1955 | 9 | 9 | .500 | 3.48 | 22 | 22 | 7 | 157.2 | 173 | 47 | 53 | 1 | 0 | 0 | 0 | 56 | 13 | 0 | .232 |
| 1956 | 2 | 5 | .286 | 6.89 | 10 | 9 | 1 | 47 | 60 | 19 | 14 | 0 | 0 | 0 | 0 | 12 | 3 | 0 | .250 |
| 10 yrs. | 69 | 84 | .451 | 3.94 | 253 | 169 | 64 | 1310.1 | 1428 | 393 | 481 | 9 | 8 | 6 | 10 | 447 | 98 | 6 | .219 |
| 7 yrs. | 62 | 79 | .440 | 4.02 | 195 | 166 | 64 | 1196.1 | 1312 | 346 | 438 | 9 | 2 | 1 | 7 | 412 | 91 | 6 | .221 |
| **WORLD SERIES** | | | | | | | | | | | | | | | | | | | |
| 1949 BKN N | 0 | 0 | – | 0.00 | 1 | 0 | 0 | 1 | 1 | 0 | 0 | 0 | 0 | 0 | 0 | 0 | 0 | 0 | – |

## Fred Mitchell

**MITCHELL, FREDERICK FRANCIS**
Born Frederick Francis Yapp.
B. June 5, 1878, Cambridge, Mass.   D. Oct. 13, 1970, Newton, Mass.
Manager 1917-23.

BR TR 5'9½" 185 lbs.

| | W | L | PCT | ERA | G | GS | CG | IP | H | BB | SO | ShO | W | L | SV | AB | H | HR | BA |
|---|---|---|---|---|---|---|---|---|---|---|---|---|---|---|---|---|---|---|---|
| 1901 BOS A | 6 | 6 | .500 | 3.81 | 17 | 13 | 10 | 108.2 | 115 | 51 | 34 | 0 | 1 | 0 | 0 | 44 | 7 | 0 | .159 |

| | W | L | PCT | ERA | G | GS | CG | IP | H | BB | SO | ShO | Relief Pitching W | L | SV | BATTING AB | H | HR | BA |
|---|---|---|---|---|---|---|---|---|---|---|---|---|---|---|---|---|---|---|---|

## Fred Mitchell  continued

| | | | | | | | | | | | | | | | | | | | |
|---|---|---|---|---|---|---|---|---|---|---|---|---|---|---|---|---|---|---|---|
| 1902 2 teams | | BOS A (1G 0–1) | | | PHI A (18G 5–7) | | | | | | | | | | | | | | |
| " total | 5 | 8 | .385 | 3.87 | 19 | 14 | 9 | 111.2 | 128 | 64 | 24 | 0 | 1 | 1 | 1 | 49 | 9 | 0 | .184 |
| 1903 PHI N | 11 | 15 | .423 | 4.48 | 28 | 28 | 24 | 227 | 250 | 102 | 69 | 1 | 0 | 0 | 0 | 95 | 19 | 0 | .200 |
| 1904 2 teams | | PHI N (13G 4–7) | | | BKN N (8G 2–5) | | | | | | | | | | | | | | |
| " total | 6 | 12 | .333 | 3.56 | 21 | 21 | 19 | 174.2 | 206 | 48 | 45 | 1 | 0 | 0 | 0 | 106 | 24 | 0 | .226 |
| 1905 BKN N | 3 | 7 | .300 | 4.78 | 12 | 10 | 9 | 96 | 107 | 38 | 44 | 0 | 0 | 0 | 0 | 79 | 15 | 0 | .190 |
| 5 yrs. | 31 | 48 | .392 | 4.10 | 97 | 86 | 71 | 718 | 806 | 303 | 216 | 2 | 2 | 1 | 1 | * | | | |

## Bill Moisan

**MOISAN, WILLIAM JOSEPH**
B. July 30, 1925, Bradford, Mass.                    BL  TR  6'1"      170 lbs.

| | | | | | | | | | | | | | | | | | | | |
|---|---|---|---|---|---|---|---|---|---|---|---|---|---|---|---|---|---|---|---|
| 1953 CHI N | 0 | 0 | – | 5.40 | 3 | 0 | 0 | 5 | 5 | 2 | 1 | 0 | 0 | 0 | 0 | 0 | 0 | 0 | – |

## Donnie Moore

**MOORE, DONNIE RAY**
B. Feb. 13, 1954, Lubbock, Tex.                      BL  TR  6'       175 lbs.

| | | | | | | | | | | | | | | | | | | | |
|---|---|---|---|---|---|---|---|---|---|---|---|---|---|---|---|---|---|---|---|
| 1975 CHI N | 0 | 0 | – | 4.00 | 4 | 1 | 0 | 9 | 12 | 4 | 8 | 0 | 0 | 0 | 0 | 3 | 0 | 0 | .000 |
| 1977 | 4 | 2 | .667 | 4.04 | 27 | 1 | 0 | 49 | 51 | 18 | 34 | 0 | 3 | 2 | 0 | 10 | 3 | 0 | .300 |
| 1978 | 9 | 7 | .563 | 4.11 | 71 | 1 | 0 | 103 | 117 | 31 | 50 | 0 | 9 | 7 | 4 | 15 | 4 | 0 | .267 |
| 1979 | 1 | 4 | .200 | 5.18 | 39 | 1 | 0 | 73 | 95 | 25 | 43 | 0 | 1 | 3 | 1 | 13 | 2 | 0 | .154 |
| 1980 STL N | 1 | 1 | .500 | 6.14 | 11 | 0 | 0 | 22 | 25 | 5 | 10 | 0 | 1 | 0 | 0 | 4 | 3 | 0 | .750 |
| 1981 MIL A | 0 | 0 | – | 6.75 | 3 | 0 | 0 | 4 | 4 | 4 | 2 | 0 | 0 | 0 | 0 | 0 | 0 | 0 | – |
| 1982 ATL N | 3 | 1 | .750 | 4.23 | 16 | 0 | 0 | 27.2 | 32 | 7 | 17 | 0 | 3 | 1 | 1 | 1 | 0 | 0 | .000 |
| 1983 | 2 | 3 | .400 | 3.67 | 43 | 0 | 0 | 68.2 | 72 | 10 | 41 | 0 | 2 | 3 | 6 | 8 | 4 | 0 | .500 |
| 1984 | 4 | 5 | .444 | 2.94 | 47 | 0 | 0 | 64.1 | 63 | 18 | 47 | 0 | 4 | 5 | 16 | 3 | 0 | 0 | .000 |
| 1985 CAL A | 8 | 8 | .500 | 1.92 | 65 | 0 | 0 | 103 | 91 | 21 | 72 | 0 | 8 | 8 | 31 | 0 | 0 | 0 | – |
| 10 yrs. | 32 | 31 | .508 | 3.73 | 326 | 4 | 0 | 523.2 | 562 | 143 | 324 | 0 | 31 | 30 | 59 | 57 | 16 | 0 | .281 |
| 4 yrs. | 14 | 13 | .519 | 4.42 | 141 | 4 | 0 | 234 | 275 | 78 | 135 | 0 | 13 | 12 | 5 | 41 | 9 | 0 | .220 |

LEAGUE CHAMPIONSHIP SERIES

| | | | | | | | | | | | | | | | | | | | |
|---|---|---|---|---|---|---|---|---|---|---|---|---|---|---|---|---|---|---|---|
| 1982 ATL N | 0 | 0 | – | 0.00 | 2 | 0 | 0 | 2.2 | 2 | 1 | 0 | 0 | 0 | 0 | 0 | 0 | 0 | 0 | – |

## Earl Moore

**MOORE, EARL ALONZO (Crossfire)**
B. July 29, 1878, Pickerington, Ohio    D. Nov. 28, 1961, Columbus, Ohio        BR  TR  6'   195 lbs.

| | | | | | | | | | | | | | | | | | | | |
|---|---|---|---|---|---|---|---|---|---|---|---|---|---|---|---|---|---|---|---|
| 1901 CLE A | 16 | 14 | .533 | 2.90 | 31 | 30 | 28 | 251.1 | 234 | 107 | 99 | 4 | 0 | 0 | 0 | 99 | 16 | 0 | .162 |
| 1902 | 17 | 17 | .500 | 2.95 | 36 | 34 | 29 | 293 | 304 | 101 | 84 | 4 | 1 | 0 | 1 | 113 | 24 | 0 | .212 |
| 1903 | 19 | 9 | .679 | 1.77 | 29 | 27 | 27 | 238.2 | 189 | 56 | 142 | 3 | 1 | 1 | 1 | 84 | 8 | 0 | .095 |
| 1904 | 12 | 11 | .522 | 2.25 | 26 | 24 | 22 | 227.2 | 186 | 61 | 139 | 1 | 0 | 0 | 0 | 86 | 12 | 0 | .140 |
| 1905 | 15 | 15 | .500 | 2.64 | 31 | 30 | 28 | 269 | 232 | 92 | 131 | 3 | 0 | 0 | 0 | 94 | 10 | 0 | .106 |
| 1906 | 1 | 1 | .500 | 3.94 | 5 | 4 | 2 | 29.2 | 27 | 18 | 8 | 0 | 0 | 0 | 0 | 10 | 0 | 0 | .000 |
| 1907 2 teams | | CLE A (3G 1–1) | | | NY A (12G 2–6) | | | | | | | | | | | | | | |
| " total | 3 | 7 | .300 | 4.10 | 15 | 11 | 4 | 83.1 | 90 | 38 | 35 | 0 | 0 | 0 | 1 | 29 | 6 | 0 | .207 |
| 1908 PHI N | 2 | 1 | .667 | 0.00 | 3 | 3 | 3 | 26 | 20 | 8 | 16 | 1 | 0 | 0 | 0 | 9 | 2 | 0 | .222 |
| 1909 | 18 | 12 | .600 | 2.10 | 38 | 34 | 24 | 299.2 | 238 | 108 | 173 | 4 | 2 | 1 | 0 | 96 | 9 | 0 | .094 |
| 1910 | 22 | 15 | .595 | 2.58 | 46 | 35 | 19 | 283 | 228 | 121 | 185 | 6 | 3 | 3 | 0 | 87 | 20 | 0 | .230 |
| 1911 | 15 | 19 | .441 | 2.63 | 42 | 36 | 21 | 308.1 | 265 | 164 | 174 | 5 | 0 | 2 | 1 | 101 | 11 | 0 | .109 |
| 1912 | 9 | 14 | .391 | 3.31 | 31 | 24 | 10 | 182.1 | 186 | 77 | 79 | 1 | 2 | 0 | 0 | 56 | 6 | 0 | .107 |
| 1913 2 teams | | PHI N (12G 1–3) | | | CHI N (7G 1–1) | | | | | | | | | | | | | | |
| " total | 2 | 4 | .333 | 4.82 | 19 | 6 | 0 | 80.1 | 84 | 52 | 36 | 0 | 0 | 0 | 1 | 24 | 1 | 0 | .042 |
| 1914 BUF F | 10 | 14 | .417 | 4.30 | 36 | 27 | 14 | 194.2 | 184 | 99 | 96 | 2 | 0 | 1 | 0 | 56 | 9 | 0 | .161 |
| 14 yrs. | 161 | 153 | .513 | 2.78 | 388 | 325 | 231 | 2767 | 2467 | 1102 | 1397 | 34 | 8 | 9 | 7 | 944 | 134 | 0 | .142 |
| 1 yr. | 1 | 1 | .500 | 4.45 | 7 | 2 | 0 | 28.1 | 34 | 12 | 12 | 0 | 0 | 0 | 0 | 8 | 1 | 0 | .125 |

## Jake Mooty

**MOOTY, J T**
B. Apr. 13, 1913, Bennett, Tex.    D. Apr. 20, 1970, Fort Worth, Tex.        BR  TR  5'10½"  170 lbs.

| | | | | | | | | | | | | | | | | | | | |
|---|---|---|---|---|---|---|---|---|---|---|---|---|---|---|---|---|---|---|---|
| 1936 CIN N | 0 | 0 | – | 3.95 | 8 | 0 | 0 | 13.2 | 10 | 4 | 11 | 0 | 0 | 0 | 1 | 1 | 0 | 0 | .000 |
| 1937 | 0 | 3 | .000 | 8.31 | 14 | 2 | 0 | 39 | 54 | 22 | 11 | 0 | 0 | 1 | 1 | 8 | 0 | 0 | .000 |
| 1940 CHI N | 6 | 6 | .500 | 2.92 | 20 | 12 | 6 | 114 | 101 | 49 | 42 | 0 | 2 | 0 | 1 | 38 | 10 | 0 | .263 |
| 1941 | 8 | 9 | .471 | 3.35 | 33 | 14 | 7 | 153.1 | 143 | 56 | 45 | 1 | 0 | 3 | 4 | 50 | 10 | 0 | .200 |
| 1942 | 2 | 5 | .286 | 4.70 | 19 | 10 | 1 | 84.1 | 89 | 44 | 28 | 0 | 0 | 1 | 1 | 28 | 6 | 0 | .214 |
| 1943 | 0 | 0 | – | 0.00 | 2 | 0 | 0 | 1 | 2 | 1 | 1 | 0 | 0 | 0 | 0 | 0 | 0 | 0 | – |
| 1944 DET A | 0 | 0 | – | 4.45 | 15 | 0 | 0 | 28.1 | 35 | 18 | 7 | 0 | 0 | 0 | 0 | 7 | 1 | 0 | .143 |
| 7 yrs. | 16 | 23 | .410 | 4.03 | 111 | 38 | 14 | 433.2 | 434 | 194 | 145 | 1 | 5 | 2 | 8 | 132 | 27 | 0 | .205 |
| 4 yrs. | 16 | 20 | .444 | 3.52 | 74 | 36 | 14 | 352.2 | 335 | 150 | 116 | 1 | 5 | 1 | 6 | 116 | 26 | 0 | .224 |

## Seth Morehead

**MOREHEAD, SETH MARVIN (Moe)**
B. Aug. 15, 1934, Houston, Tex.                      BL  TL  6'½"     195 lbs.

| | | | | | | | | | | | | | | | | | | | |
|---|---|---|---|---|---|---|---|---|---|---|---|---|---|---|---|---|---|---|---|
| 1957 PHI N | 1 | 1 | .500 | 3.68 | 34 | 1 | 1 | 58.2 | 57 | 20 | 36 | 0 | 0 | 1 | 1 | 6 | 0 | 0 | .000 |
| 1958 | 1 | 6 | .143 | 5.85 | 27 | 11 | 0 | 92.1 | 121 | 26 | 54 | 0 | 0 | 0 | 0 | 22 | 4 | 0 | .182 |
| 1959 2 teams | | PHI N (3G 0–2) | | | CHI N (11G 0–1) | | | | | | | | | | | | | | |
| " total | 0 | 3 | .000 | 6.59 | 14 | 5 | 0 | 28.2 | 40 | 11 | 17 | 0 | 0 | 0 | 0 | 5 | 1 | 0 | .200 |
| 1960 CHI N | 2 | 9 | .182 | 3.94 | 45 | 7 | 2 | 123.1 | 123 | 46 | 64 | 0 | 2 | 4 | 4 | 29 | 4 | 0 | .138 |
| 1961 MIL N | 1 | 0 | 1.000 | 6.46 | 12 | 0 | 0 | 15.1 | 16 | 7 | 13 | 0 | 1 | 0 | 0 | 0 | 0 | 0 | – |
| 5 yrs. | 5 | 19 | .208 | 4.81 | 132 | 24 | 3 | 318.1 | 357 | 110 | 184 | 0 | 3 | 5 | 5 | 62 | 9 | 0 | .145 |
| 2 yrs. | 2 | 10 | .167 | 4.06 | 56 | 9 | 2 | 142 | 148 | 54 | 73 | 0 | 2 | 4 | 4 | 31 | 5 | 0 | .161 |

## Ed Morris

**MORRIS, WALTER EDWARD**
B. Dec. 7, 1899, Foshee, Ala.    D. Mar. 3, 1932, Century, Fla.        BR  TR  6'2"   185 lbs.

| | | | | | | | | | | | | | | | | | | | |
|---|---|---|---|---|---|---|---|---|---|---|---|---|---|---|---|---|---|---|---|
| 1922 CHI N | 0 | 0 | – | 8.25 | 5 | 0 | 0 | 12 | 22 | 6 | 5 | 0 | 0 | 0 | 0 | 4 | 1 | 0 | .250 |
| 1928 BOS A | 19 | 15 | .559 | 3.53 | 47 | 29 | 20 | 257.2 | 255 | 80 | 104 | 0 | 3 | 2 | 5 | 91 | 14 | 0 | .154 |
| 1929 | 14 | 14 | .500 | 4.45 | 33 | 26 | 17 | 208.1 | 227 | 95 | 73 | 2 | 2 | 1 | 1 | 69 | 16 | 1 | .232 |
| 1930 | 4 | 9 | .308 | 4.13 | 18 | 9 | 3 | 65.1 | 67 | 38 | 28 | 0 | 2 | 2 | 0 | 19 | 6 | 0 | .316 |

| | W | L | PCT | ERA | G | GS | CG | IP | H | BB | SO | ShO | Relief Pitching W | L | SV | BATTING AB | H | HR | BA |
|---|---|---|---|---|---|---|---|---|---|---|---|---|---|---|---|---|---|---|---|

## Ed Morris continued

| | W | L | PCT | ERA | G | GS | CG | IP | H | BB | SO | ShO | W | L | SV | AB | H | HR | BA |
|---|---|---|---|---|---|---|---|---|---|---|---|---|---|---|---|---|---|---|---|
| 1931 | 5 | 7 | .417 | 4.75 | 37 | 14 | 3 | 130.2 | 131 | 74 | 46 | 0 | 1 | 1 | 0 | 38 | 6 | 0 | .158 |
| 5 yrs. | 42 | 45 | .483 | 4.19 | 140 | 78 | 43 | 674 | 702 | 293 | 256 | 2 | 8 | 6 | 6 | 221 | 43 | 1 | .195 |
| 1 yr. | 0 | 0 | — | 8.25 | 5 | 0 | 0 | 12 | 22 | 6 | 5 | 0 | 0 | 0 | 0 | 4 | 1 | 0 | .250 |

## Deacon Morrissey

**MORRISSEY, MICHAEL JOSEPH**
B. May 5, 1876, Baltimore, Md.    D. Feb. 22, 1939, Baltimore, Md.    5'4"    140 lbs.

| | W | L | PCT | ERA | G | GS | CG | IP | H | BB | SO | ShO | W | L | SV | AB | H | HR | BA |
|---|---|---|---|---|---|---|---|---|---|---|---|---|---|---|---|---|---|---|---|
| 1901 BOS A | 0 | 0 | — | 2.08 | 1 | 0 | 0 | 4.1 | 5 | 2 | 1 | 0 | 0 | 0 | 0 | 3 | 0 | 0 | .000 |
| 1902 CHI N | 1 | 3 | .250 | 2.25 | 5 | 5 | 5 | 40 | 40 | 8 | 13 | 0 | 0 | 0 | 0 | 22 | 2 | 0 | .091 |
| 2 yrs. | 1 | 3 | .250 | 2.23 | 6 | 5 | 5 | 44.1 | 45 | 10 | 14 | 0 | 0 | 0 | 0 | 25 | 2 | 0 | .080 |
| 1 yr. | 1 | 3 | .250 | 2.25 | 5 | 5 | 5 | 40 | 40 | 8 | 13 | 0 | 0 | 0 | 0 | 22 | 2 | 0 | .091 |

## Paul Moskau

**MOSKAU, PAUL RICHARD**
B. Dec. 20, 1953, St. Joseph, Mo.    BR TR 6'2"    200 lbs.

| | W | L | PCT | ERA | G | GS | CG | IP | H | BB | SO | ShO | W | L | SV | AB | H | HR | BA |
|---|---|---|---|---|---|---|---|---|---|---|---|---|---|---|---|---|---|---|---|
| 1977 CIN N | 6 | 6 | .500 | 4.00 | 20 | 19 | 2 | 108 | 116 | 40 | 71 | 2 | 0 | 0 | 0 | 38 | 7 | 1 | .184 |
| 1978 | 6 | 4 | .600 | 3.97 | 26 | 25 | 2 | 145 | 139 | 57 | 88 | 1 | 0 | 0 | 1 | 49 | 10 | 1 | .204 |
| 1979 | 5 | 4 | .556 | 3.91 | 21 | 15 | 1 | 106 | 107 | 51 | 58 | 0 | 1 | 0 | 0 | 37 | 3 | 0 | .081 |
| 1980 | 9 | 7 | .563 | 4.00 | 33 | 19 | 0 | 153 | 147 | 41 | 94 | 0 | 5 | 0 | 2 | 44 | 7 | 0 | .159 |
| 1981 | 2 | 1 | .667 | 4.91 | 27 | 1 | 0 | 55 | 54 | 32 | 32 | 0 | 2 | 1 | 2 | 6 | 0 | 0 | .000 |
| 1982 PIT N | 1 | 3 | .250 | 4.37 | 13 | 5 | 0 | 35 | 43 | 8 | 15 | 0 | 0 | 0 | 0 | 11 | 1 | 0 | .091 |
| 1983 CHI N | 3 | 2 | .600 | 6.75 | 8 | 8 | 0 | 32 | 44 | 14 | 16 | 0 | 0 | 0 | 0 | 11 | 2 | 0 | .182 |
| 7 yrs. | 32 | 27 | .542 | 4.22 | 148 | 92 | 7 | 634 | 650 | 243 | 374 | 4 | 8 | 2 | 5 | 196 | 30 | 2 | .153 |
| 1 yr. | 3 | 2 | .600 | 6.75 | 8 | 8 | 0 | 32 | 44 | 14 | 16 | 0 | 0 | 0 | 0 | 11 | 2 | 0 | .182 |

## Jim Mosolf

**MOSOLF, JAMES FREDERICK**
B. Aug. 21, 1905, Puyallup, Wash.    D. Dec. 28, 1979, Salem, Ore.    BL TR 5'10"    186 lbs.

| | W | L | PCT | ERA | G | GS | CG | IP | H | BB | SO | ShO | W | L | SV | AB | H | HR | BA |
|---|---|---|---|---|---|---|---|---|---|---|---|---|---|---|---|---|---|---|---|
| 1930 PIT N | 0 | 0 | — | 27.00 | 1 | 0 | 0 | .1 | 1 | 0 | 1 | 0 | 0 | 0 | 0 | * | | | |

## Mal Moss

**MOSS, CHARLES MALCOLM**
B. Apr. 18, 1905, Sullivan, Ind.    D. Feb. 5, 1983, Savannah, Ga.    BR TL 6'    175 lbs.

| | W | L | PCT | ERA | G | GS | CG | IP | H | BB | SO | ShO | W | L | SV | AB | H | HR | BA |
|---|---|---|---|---|---|---|---|---|---|---|---|---|---|---|---|---|---|---|---|
| 1930 CHI N | 0 | 0 | — | 6.27 | 12 | 0 | 0 | 18.2 | 18 | 14 | 4 | 0 | 0 | 0 | 1 | 11 | 3 | 0 | .273 |

## Phil Mudrock

**MUDROCK, PHILIP RAY**
B. June 12, 1937, Louisville, Colo.    BR TR 6'1"    190 lbs.

| | W | L | PCT | ERA | G | GS | CG | IP | H | BB | SO | ShO | W | L | SV | AB | H | HR | BA |
|---|---|---|---|---|---|---|---|---|---|---|---|---|---|---|---|---|---|---|---|
| 1963 CHI N | 0 | 0 | — | 9.00 | 1 | 0 | 0 | 2 | 2 | 0 | 0 | 0 | 0 | 0 | 0 | 0 | 0 | 0 | — |

## Bob Muncrief

**MUNCRIEF, ROBERT CLEVELAND**
B. Jan. 28, 1916, Madill, Okla.    BR TR 6'2"    190 lbs.

| | W | L | PCT | ERA | G | GS | CG | IP | H | BB | SO | ShO | W | L | SV | AB | H | HR | BA |
|---|---|---|---|---|---|---|---|---|---|---|---|---|---|---|---|---|---|---|---|
| 1937 STL A | 0 | 0 | — | 4.50 | 1 | 1 | 0 | 2 | 3 | 2 | 4 | 0 | 0 | 0 | 0 | 0 | 0 | 0 | — |
| 1939 | 0 | 0 | — | 15.00 | 2 | 0 | 0 | 3 | 7 | 3 | 1 | 0 | 0 | 0 | 0 | 0 | 0 | 0 | — |
| 1941 | 13 | 9 | .591 | 3.65 | 36 | 24 | 12 | 214.1 | 221 | 53 | 67 | 2 | 1 | 0 | 1 | 76 | 18 | 0 | .237 |
| 1942 | 6 | 8 | .429 | 3.89 | 24 | 18 | 7 | 134.1 | 149 | 31 | 39 | 1 | 0 | 0 | 0 | 45 | 5 | 0 | .111 |
| 1943 | 13 | 12 | .520 | 2.81 | 35 | 27 | 12 | 205 | 211 | 48 | 80 | 3 | 1 | 1 | 1 | 66 | 10 | 0 | .152 |
| 1944 | 13 | 8 | .619 | 3.08 | 33 | 27 | 12 | 219.1 | 216 | 50 | 88 | 3 | 0 | 1 | 1 | 78 | 18 | 0 | .231 |
| 1945 | 13 | 4 | .765 | 2.72 | 27 | 15 | 10 | 145.2 | 132 | 44 | 54 | 0 | 3 | 2 | 1 | 45 | 3 | 0 | .067 |
| 1946 | 3 | 12 | .200 | 4.99 | 29 | 14 | 4 | 115.1 | 149 | 31 | 49 | 1 | 0 | 1 | 0 | 32 | 1 | 0 | .031 |
| 1947 | 8 | 14 | .364 | 4.90 | 31 | 23 | 7 | 176.1 | 210 | 51 | 74 | 0 | 2 | 1 | 0 | 57 | 6 | 0 | .105 |
| 1948 CLE A | 5 | 4 | .556 | 3.98 | 21 | 9 | 1 | 72.1 | 76 | 31 | 24 | 1 | 2 | 0 | 0 | 18 | 2 | 0 | .111 |
| 1949 2 teams | PIT N (13G 1–5) | | | | | CHI | N | (34G 5–6) | | | | | | | | | | | |
| " total | 6 | 11 | .353 | 5.12 | 47 | 7 | 2 | 110.2 | 124 | 44 | 47 | 0 | 4 | 7 | 5 | 21 | 5 | 0 | .238 |
| 1951 NY A | 0 | 0 | — | 9.00 | 2 | 0 | 0 | 3 | 5 | 4 | 2 | 0 | 0 | 0 | 0 | 0 | 0 | 0 | — |
| 12 yrs. | 80 | 82 | .494 | 3.80 | 288 | 165 | 67 | 1401.1 | 1503 | 392 | 525 | 11 | 13 | 13 | 9 | 438 | 68 | 0 | .155 |
| 1 yr. | 5 | 6 | .455 | 4.56 | 34 | 3 | 1 | 75 | 80 | 31 | 36 | 0 | 4 | 4 | 2 | 14 | 4 | 0 | .286 |

WORLD SERIES

| | W | L | PCT | ERA | G | GS | CG | IP | H | BB | SO | ShO | W | L | SV | AB | H | HR | BA |
|---|---|---|---|---|---|---|---|---|---|---|---|---|---|---|---|---|---|---|---|
| 1944 STL A | 0 | 1 | .000 | 1.35 | 2 | 0 | 0 | 6.2 | 5 | 4 | 4 | 0 | 0 | 1 | 0 | 1 | 0 | 0 | .000 |
| 1948 CLE A | 0 | 0 | — | 0.00 | 1 | 0 | 0 | 2 | 1 | 0 | 0 | 0 | 0 | 0 | 0 | 0 | 0 | 0 | — |
| 2 yrs. | 0 | 1 | .000 | 1.04 | 3 | 0 | 0 | 8.2 | 6 | 4 | 4 | 0 | 0 | 1 | 0 | 1 | 0 | 0 | .000 |

## Danny Murphy

**MURPHY, DANIEL FRANCIS**
B. Aug. 23, 1942, Beverly, Mass.    BL TR 5'11"    185 lbs.

| | W | L | PCT | ERA | G | GS | CG | IP | H | BB | SO | ShO | W | L | SV | AB | H | HR | BA |
|---|---|---|---|---|---|---|---|---|---|---|---|---|---|---|---|---|---|---|---|
| 1960 CHI N | 0 | 0 | — | 0.00 | 0 | 0 | 0 | | | 0 | 0 | 0 | 0 | 0 | 0 | 75 | 9 | 1 | .120 |
| 1961 | 0 | 0 | — | 0.00 | 0 | 0 | 0 | | 0 | 0 | 0 | 0 | 0 | 0 | 0 | 13 | 5 | 2 | .385 |
| 1962 | 0 | 0 | — | 0.00 | 0 | 0 | 0 | | 0 | 0 | 0 | 0 | 0 | 0 | 0 | 35 | 7 | 0 | .200 |
| 1969 CHI A | 2 | 1 | .667 | 2.01 | 17 | 0 | 0 | 31.1 | 28 | 10 | 16 | 0 | 2 | 1 | 4 | 1 | 0 | 0 | .000 |
| 1970 | 2 | 3 | .400 | 5.67 | 51 | 0 | 0 | 81 | 82 | 49 | 42 | 0 | 2 | 3 | 5 | 6 | 2 | 1 | .333 |
| 5 yrs. | 4 | 4 | .500 | 4.65 | 68 | 0 | 0 | 112.1 | 110 | 59 | 58 | 0 | 4 | 4 | 9 | * | | | |

## Buddy Napier

**NAPIER, SKELTON LeROY**
B. Dec. 18, 1889, Byronville, Ga.    D. Mar. 29, 1968, Hutchins, Tex.    BR TR 6'    180 lbs.

| | W | L | PCT | ERA | G | GS | CG | IP | H | BB | SO | ShO | W | L | SV | AB | H | HR | BA |
|---|---|---|---|---|---|---|---|---|---|---|---|---|---|---|---|---|---|---|---|
| 1912 STL A | 1 | 2 | .333 | 4.97 | 7 | 2 | 0 | 25.1 | 33 | 5 | 10 | 0 | 1 | 0 | 0 | 7 | 0 | 0 | .000 |
| 1918 CHI N | 0 | 0 | — | 5.40 | 1 | 0 | 0 | 6.2 | 10 | 4 | 2 | 0 | 0 | 0 | 0 | 3 | 1 | 0 | .333 |
| 1920 CIN N | 4 | 2 | .667 | 1.29 | 9 | 5 | 5 | 49 | 47 | 7 | 17 | 1 | 1 | 0 | 0 | 14 | 3 | 0 | .214 |
| 1921 | 0 | 2 | .000 | 5.56 | 22 | 6 | 1 | 56.2 | 72 | 13 | 14 | 0 | 0 | 0 | 1 | 14 | 2 | 0 | .143 |
| 4 yrs. | 5 | 6 | .455 | 3.92 | 39 | 13 | 6 | 137.2 | 162 | 29 | 43 | 1 | 2 | 0 | 1 | 38 | 6 | 0 | .158 |
| 1 yr. | 0 | 0 | — | 5.40 | 1 | 0 | 0 | 6.2 | 10 | 4 | 2 | 0 | 0 | 0 | 0 | 3 | 1 | 0 | .333 |

| | W | L | PCT | ERA | G | GS | CG | IP | H | BB | SO | ShO | Relief Pitching W | L | SV | BATTING AB | H | HR | BA |
|---|---|---|---|---|---|---|---|---|---|---|---|---|---|---|---|---|---|---|---|

## Art Nehf

**NEHF, ARTHUR NEUKOM**
B. July 31, 1892, Terre Haute, Ind.    D. Dec. 18, 1960, Phoenix, Ariz.
BL  TL  5'9½"  176 lbs.

| | W | L | PCT | ERA | G | GS | CG | IP | H | BB | SO | ShO | RP W | L | SV | AB | H | HR | BA |
|---|---|---|---|---|---|---|---|---|---|---|---|---|---|---|---|---|---|---|---|
| 1915 BOS N | 5 | 4 | .556 | 2.53 | 12 | 10 | 6 | 78.1 | 60 | 21 | 39 | 4 | 0 | 0 | 0 | 28 | 4 | 0 | .143 |
| 1916 | 7 | 5 | .583 | 2.01 | 22 | 12 | 6 | 121 | 110 | 20 | 36 | 1 | 1 | 1 | 0 | 40 | 5 | 0 | .125 |
| 1917 | 17 | 8 | .680 | 2.16 | 38 | 23 | 17 | 233.1 | 197 | 39 | 101 | 5 | 4 | 2 | 0 | 70 | 12 | 0 | .171 |
| 1918 | 15 | 15 | .500 | 2.69 | 32 | 31 | 28 | 284.1 | 274 | 76 | 96 | 2 | 0 | 0 | 0 | 95 | 16 | 0 | .168 · |
| 1919 2 teams | | | BOS | N (22G 8–9) | | NY | N (13G 9–2) | | | | | | | | | | | | |
| " total | 17 | 11 | .607 | 2.49 | 35 | 31 | 22 | 270.2 | 221 | 59 | 77 | 3 | 0 | 1 | 0 | 98 | 21 | 1 | .214 |
| 1920 NY N | 21 | 12 | .636 | 3.08 | 40 | 33 | 22 | 280.2 | 273 | 45 | 79 | 5 | 2 | 0 | 0 | 97 | 26 | 0 | .268 |
| 1921 | 20 | 10 | .667 | 3.63 | 41 | 34 | 18 | 260.2 | 266 | 55 | 67 | 2 | 1 | 1 | 1 | 89 | 18 | 0 | .202 |
| 1922 | 19 | 13 | .594 | 3.29 | 37 | 35 | 20 | 268.1 | 286 | 64 | 60 | 3 | 0 | 1 | 1 | 98 | 25 | 1 | .255 |
| 1923 | 13 | 10 | .565 | 4.50 | 34 | 27 | 7 | 196 | 219 | 49 | 50 | 1 | 1 | 1 | 2 | 63 | 12 | 0 | .190 |
| 1924 | 14 | 4 | .778 | 3.62 | 30 | 20 | 11 | 171.2 | 167 | 42 | 72 | 0 | 1 | 0 | 2 | 57 | 13 | 5 | .228 |
| 1925 | 11 | 9 | .550 | 3.77 | 29 | 20 | 8 | 155 | 193 | 50 | 63 | 1 | 4 | 1 | 1 | 51 | 11 | 0 | .216 |
| 1926 2 teams | | | NY | N (2G 0–0) | | CIN | N (7G 0–1) | | | | | | | | | | | | |
| " total | 0 | 1 | .000 | 4.34 | 9 | 0 | 0 | 18.2 | 27 | 6 | 4 | 0 | 0 | 1 | 0 | 6 | 1 | 0 | .167 |
| 1927 2 teams | | | CIN | N (21G 3–5) | | CHI | N (8G 1–1) | | | | | | | | | | | | |
| " total | 4 | 6 | .400 | 4.02 | 29 | 7 | 3 | 71.2 | 84 | 23 | 33 | 1 | 3 | 1 | 5 | 20 | 4 | 0 | .200 |
| 1928 CHI N | 13 | 7 | .650 | 2.65 | 31 | 21 | 10 | 176.2 | 190 | 52 | 40 | 2 | 0 | 2 | 0 | 58 | 11 | 1 | .190 |
| 1929 | 8 | 5 | .615 | 5.59 | 32 | 15 | 4 | 120.2 | 148 | 39 | 27 | 0 | 1 | 2 | 1 | 45 | 13 | 0 | .289 |
| 15 yrs. | 184 | 120 | .605 | 3.20 | 451 | 319 | 182 | 2707.2 | 2715 | 640 | 844 | /30 | 18 | 14 | 13 | 915 | 192 | 8 | .210 |
| 2 yrs. | 22 | 13 | .629 | 3.64 | 71 | 38 | 16 | 323.2 | 363 | 100 | 79 | 3 | 1 | 4 | 2 | 110 | 27 | 1 | .245 |

| WORLD SERIES | | | | | | | | | | | | | | | | | | | |
|---|---|---|---|---|---|---|---|---|---|---|---|---|---|---|---|---|---|---|---|
| 1921 NY N | 1 | 2 | .333 | 1.38 | 3 | 3 | 3 | 26 | 13 | 13 | 8 | 1 | 0 | 0 | 0 | 9 | 0 | 0 | .000 |
| 1922 | 1 | 0 | 1.000 | 2.25 | 2 | 2 | 1 | 16 | 11 | 3 | 6 | 0 | 0 | 0 | 0 | 3 | 0 | 0 | .000 |
| 1923 | 1 | 1 | .500 | 2.76 | 2 | 2 | 1 | 16.1 | 10 | 6 | 7 | 1 | 0 | 0 | 0 | 6 | 1 | 0 | .167 |
| 1924 | 1 | 1 | .500 | 1.83 | 3 | 2 | 1 | 19.2 | 15 | 9 | 7 | 0 | 0 | 0 | 0 | 7 | 3 | 0 | .429 |
| 1929 CHI N | 0 | 0 | – | 18.00 | 2 | 0 | 0 | 1 | 1 | 1 | 0 | 0 | 0 | 0 | 0 | 0 | 0 | 0 | – |
| 5 yrs. | 4 | 4 | .500 | 2.16 | 12 | 9 | 6 | 79 | 50 | 32 | 28 | 2 | 0 | 0 | 0 | 25 | 4 | 0 | .160 |
| | | | 7th | | | 7th | 6th | 6th | 7th | | | 2nd | | 4th | | | | | |

## Lynn Nelson

**NELSON, LYNN BERNARD (Line Drive)**
B. Feb. 24, 1905, Sheldon, N. D.    D. Feb. 15, 1955, Kansas City, Mo.
BL  TR  5'10½"  170 lbs.

| | W | L | PCT | ERA | G | GS | CG | IP | H | BB | SO | ShO | RP W | L | SV | AB | H | HR | BA |
|---|---|---|---|---|---|---|---|---|---|---|---|---|---|---|---|---|---|---|---|
| 1930 CHI N | 3 | 2 | .600 | 5.09 | 37 | 3 | 0 | 81.1 | 97 | 28 | 29 | 0 | 2 | 2 | 0 | 18 | 4 | 0 | .222 |
| 1933 | 5 | 5 | .500 | 3.21 | 24 | 3 | 3 | 75.2 | 65 | 30 | 20 | 0 | 4 | 3 | 1 | 21 | 5 | 0 | .238 |
| 1934 | 0 | 1 | .000 | 36.00 | 2 | 1 | 0 | 1 | 4 | 1 | 0 | 0 | 0 | 0 | 0 | 0 | 0 | 0 | – |
| 1937 PHI A | 4 | 9 | .308 | 5.90 | 30 | 4 | 1 | 116 | 140 | 51 | 49 | 0 | 4 | 7 | 2 | 113 | 40 | 4 | .354 |
| 1938 | 10 | 11 | .476 | 5.65 | 32 | 23 | 13 | 191 | 215 | 79 | 75 | 0 | 0 | 2 | 2 | 112 | 31 | 0 | .277 |
| 1939 | 10 | 13 | .435 | 4.78 | 35 | 24 | 12 | 197.2 | 233 | 64 | 75 | 2 | 2 | 0 | 1 | 80 | 15 | 0 | .188 |
| 1940 DET A | 1 | 1 | .500 | 10.93 | 6 | 2 | 0 | 14 | 23 | 9 | 7 | 0 | 1 | 0 | 0 | 23 | 8 | 1 | .348 |
| 7 yrs. | 33 | 42 | .440 | 5.25 | 166 | 60 | 29 | 676.2 | 777 | 262 | 255 | 2 | 13 | 14 | 6 | * | | | |
| 3 yrs. | 8 | 8 | .500 | 4.39 | 63 | 7 | 3 | 158 | 166 | 59 | 49 | 0 | 6 | 5 | 1 | 39 | 9 | 0 | .231 |

## Joel Newkirk

**NEWKIRK, JOEL INEZ (Sailor)**
Brother of Floyd Newkirk.
B. May 1, 1896, Kyana, Ind.    D. Jan. 22, 1966, Eldorado, Ill.
BR  TR  6'  180 lbs.

| | W | L | PCT | ERA | G | GS | CG | IP | H | BB | SO | ShO | RP W | L | SV | AB | H | HR | BA |
|---|---|---|---|---|---|---|---|---|---|---|---|---|---|---|---|---|---|---|---|
| 1919 CHI N | 0 | 0 | – | 13.50 | 1 | 0 | 0 | 2 | 3 | 1 | 0 | 0 | 0 | 0 | 0 | 1 | 0 | 0 | .000 |
| 1920 | 0 | 1 | .000 | 5.40 | 2 | 1 | 0 | 6.2 | 8 | 6 | 2 | 0 | 0 | 0 | 0 | 3 | 0 | 0 | .000 |
| 2 yrs. | 0 | 1 | .000 | 7.27 | 3 | 1 | 0 | 8.2 | 10 | 9 | 3 | 0 | 0 | 0 | 0 | 4 | 0 | 0 | .000 |
| 2 yrs. | 0 | 1 | .000 | 7.27 | 3 | 1 | 0 | 8.2 | 10 | 9 | 3 | 0 | 0 | 0 | 0 | 4 | 0 | 0 | .000 |

## Ray Newman

**NEWMAN, RAYMOND FRANCIS**
B. June 20, 1945, Evansville, Ind.
BL  TL  6'5"  205 lbs.

| | W | L | PCT | ERA | G | GS | CG | IP | H | BB | SO | ShO | RP W | L | SV | AB | H | HR | BA |
|---|---|---|---|---|---|---|---|---|---|---|---|---|---|---|---|---|---|---|---|
| 1971 CHI N | 1 | 2 | .333 | 3.55 | 30 | 0 | 0 | 38 | 30 | 17 | 35 | 0 | 1 | 2 | 2 | 6 | 0 | 0 | .000 |
| 1972 MIL A | 0 | 0 | – | 0.00 | 4 | 0 | 0 | 7 | 4 | 2 | 1 | 0 | 0 | 0 | 1 | 1 | 1 | 0 | 1.000 |
| 1973 | 2 | 1 | .667 | 2.95 | 11 | 0 | 0 | 18.1 | 19 | 5 | 10 | 0 | 2 | 1 | 1 | 0 | 0 | 0 | – |
| 3 yrs. | 3 | 3 | .500 | 2.98 | 45 | 0 | 0 | 63.1 | 53 | 24 | 46 | 0 | 3 | 3 | 4 | 7 | 1 | 0 | .143 |
| 1 yr. | 1 | 2 | .333 | 3.55 | 30 | 0 | 0 | 38 | 30 | 17 | 35 | 0 | 1 | 2 | 2 | 6 | 0 | 0 | .000 |

## Bobo Newsom

**NEWSOM, NORMAN LOUIS (Buck)**
B. Aug. 11, 1907, Hartsville, S. C.    D. Dec. 7, 1962, Orlando, Fla.
BR  TR  6'3"  200 lbs.

| | W | L | PCT | ERA | G | GS | CG | IP | H | BB | SO | ShO | RP W | L | SV | AB | H | HR | BA |
|---|---|---|---|---|---|---|---|---|---|---|---|---|---|---|---|---|---|---|---|
| 1929 BKN N | 0 | 3 | .000 | 10.61 | 3 | 2 | 0 | 9.1 | 15 | 5 | 6 | 0 | 0 | 1 | 0 | 2 | 0 | 0 | .000 |
| 1930 | 0 | 0 | – | 0.00 | 2 | 0 | 0 | 3 | 2 | 2 | 1 | 0 | 0 | 0 | 0 | 0 | 0 | 0 | – |
| 1932 CHI N | 0 | 0 | – | 0.00 | 1 | 0 | 0 | 1 | 1 | 0 | 0 | 0 | 0 | 0 | 0 | 0 | 0 | 0 | – |
| 1934 STL A | 16 | 20 | .444 | 4.01 | 47 | 32 | 15 | 262.1 | 259 | 149 | 135 | 2 | 3 | 4 | 5 | 93 | 17 | 0 | .183 |
| 1935 2 teams | | | STL | A (7G 0–6) | | WAS | A (28G 11–12) | | | | | | | | | | | | |
| " total | 11 | 18 | .379 | 4.52 | 35 | 29 | 18 | 241 | 276 | 97 | 87 | 2 | 0 | 2 | 3 | 84 | 23 | 0 | .274 |
| 1936 WAS A | 17 | 15 | .531 | 4.32 | 43 | 38 | 24 | 285.2 | 294 | 146 | 156 | 4 | 0 | 0 | 2 | 108 | 23 | 0 | .213 |
| 1937 2 teams | | | WAS | A (11G 3–4) | | BOS | A (30G 13–10) | | | | | | | | | | | | |
| " total | 16 | 14 | .533 | 4.74 | 41 | 37 | 17 | 275.1 | 271 | 167 | 166 | 1 | 1 | 1 | 0 | 100 | 22 | 1 | .220 |
| 1938 STL A | 20 | 16 | .556 | 5.08 | 44 | 40 | 31 | 329.2 | 334 | 192 | 226 | 0 | 0 | 0 | 0 | 124 | 31 | 0 | .250 |
| 1939 2 teams | | | STL | A (6G 3–1) | | DET | A (35G 17–10) | | | | | | | | | | | | |
| " total | 20 | 11 | .645 | 3.58 | 41 | 37 | 24 | 291.2 | 272 | 126 | 192 | 3 | 0 | 0 | 2 | 115 | 22 | 0 | .191 |
| 1940 DET A | 21 | 5 | .808 | 2.83 | 36 | 34 | 20 | 264 | 235 | 100 | 164 | 3 | 1 | 1 | 0 | 107 | 23 | 0 | .215 |
| 1941 | 12 | 20 | .375 | 4.60 | 43 | 36 | 12 | 250.1 | 265 | 118 | 175 | 2 | 1 | 1 | 2 | 88 | 9 | 0 | .102 |
| 1942 2 teams | | | WAS | A (30G 11–17) | | BKN | N (6G 2–2) | | | | | | | | | | | | |
| " total | 13 | 19 | .406 | 4.73 | 36 | 34 | 17 | 245.2 | 264 | 106 | 134 | 3 | 1 | 0 | 0 | 86 | 12 | 0 | .140 |
| 1943 3 teams | | | BKN | N (22G 9–4) | | STL | A (10G 1–6) | | WAS | A (6G 3–3) | | | | | | | | | |
| " total | 13 | 13 | .500 | 4.22 | 38 | 27 | 8 | 217.1 | 220 | 113 | 123 | 1 | 4 | 1 | 1 | 74 | 18 | 0 | .243 |
| 1944 PHI A | 13 | 15 | .464 | 2.82 | 37 | 33 | 18 | 265 | 243 | 82 | 142 | 2 | 0 | 0 | 1 | 88 | 10 | 0 | .114 |
| 1945 | 8 | 20 | .286 | 3.29 | 36 | 34 | 16 | 257.1 | 255 | 103 | 127 | 3 | 0 | 1 | 0 | 86 | 14 | 0 | .163 |
| 1946 2 teams | | | PHI | A (10G 3–5) | | WAS | A (24G 11–8) | | | | | | | | | | | | |
| " total | 14 | 13 | .519 | 2.93 | 34 | 31 | 17 | 236.2 | 224 | 90 | 114 | 3 | 1 | 0 | 0 | 81 | 12 | 0 | .148 |

| | W | L | PCT | ERA | G | GS | CG | IP | H | BB | SO | ShO | Relief Pitching W | L | SV | BATTING AB | H | HR | BA |
|---|---|---|---|---|---|---|---|---|---|---|---|---|---|---|---|---|---|---|---|

## Bobo Newsom continued

| | W | L | PCT | ERA | G | GS | CG | IP | H | BB | SO | ShO | W | L | SV | AB | H | HR | BA |
|---|---|---|---|---|---|---|---|---|---|---|---|---|---|---|---|---|---|---|---|
| 1947 2 teams | | | | WAS | A | (14G 4–6) | | NY | A | (17G 7–5) | | | | | | | | | |
| " total | 11 | 11 | .500 | 3.34 | 31 | 28 | 7 | 199.1 | 208 | 67 | 82 | 2 | 0 | 0 | 0 | 71 | 11 | 0 | .155 |
| 1948 NY N | 0 | 4 | .000 | 4.21 | 11 | 4 | 0 | 25.2 | 35 | 13 | 9 | 0 | 0 | 1 | 0 | 7 | 3 | 0 | .429 |
| 1952 2 teams | | | | WAS | A | (10G 1–1) | | PHI | A | (14G 3–3) | | | | | | | | | |
| " total | 4 | 4 | .500 | 3.88 | 24 | 5 | 1 | 60.1 | 54 | 32 | 27 | 0 | 3 | 2 | 3 | 17 | 2 | 0 | .118 |
| 1953 PHI A | 4 | 1 | .667 | 4.89 | 17 | 2 | 1 | 38.2 | 44 | 24 | 16 | 0 | 1 | 0 | 0 | 6 | 1 | 0 | .167 |
| 20 yrs. | 211 | 222 | .487 | 3.98 | 600 | 483 | 246 | 3759.1 | 3771 | 1732 4th | 2082 | 31 | 15 | 15 | 21 | 1337 | 253 | 1 | .189 |
| 1 yr. | 0 | 0 | – | 0.00 | 1 | 0 | 0 | 1 | 1 | 0 | 1 | 0 | 0 | 0 | 0 | 0 | 0 | 0 | – |
| WORLD SERIES | | | | | | | | | | | | | | | | | | | |
| 1940 DET A | 2 | 1 | .667 | 1.38 | 3 | 3 | 3 | 26 | 18 | 4 | 17 | 1 | 0 | 0 | 0 | 10 | 1 | 0 | .100 |
| 1947 NY A | 0 | 1 | .000 | 19.29 | 2 | 1 | 0 | 2.1 | 6 | 2 | 0 | 0 | 0 | 0 | 0 | 0 | 0 | 0 | – |
| 2 yrs. | 2 | 2 | .500 | 2.86 | 5 | 4 | 3 | 28.1 | 24 | 6 | 17 | 1 | 0 | 0 | 0 | 10 | 1 | 0 | .100 |

## Dolan Nichols

**NICHOLS, DOLAN LEVON (Nick)**
B. Feb. 28, 1930, Tishomingo, Miss.    BR TR 6'   195 lbs.

| | W | L | PCT | ERA | G | GS | CG | IP | H | BB | SO | ShO | W | L | SV | AB | H | HR | BA |
|---|---|---|---|---|---|---|---|---|---|---|---|---|---|---|---|---|---|---|---|
| 1958 CHI N | 0 | 4 | .000 | 5.01 | 24 | 0 | 0 | 41.1 | 46 | 16 | 9 | 0 | 0 | 4 | 1 | 5 | 0 | 0 | .000 |

## George Nicol

**NICOL, GEORGE EDWARD**
B. Oct. 17, 1870, Barry, Ill.    D. Aug. 10, 1924, Milwaukee, Wis.    TL 5'7"   155 lbs.

| | W | L | PCT | ERA | G | GS | CG | IP | H | BB | SO | ShO | W | L | SV | AB | H | HR | BA |
|---|---|---|---|---|---|---|---|---|---|---|---|---|---|---|---|---|---|---|---|
| 1890 STL AA | 2 | 1 | .667 | 4.76 | 3 | 3 | 2 | 17 | 11 | 19 | 16 | 0 | 0 | 0 | 0 | 7 | 2 | 0 | .286 |
| 1891 CHI N | 0 | 1 | .000 | 4.91 | 3 | 2 | 0 | 11 | 14 | 10 | 12 | 0 | 0 | 1 | 0 | 6 | 2 | 0 | .333 |
| 1894 2 teams | | | | PIT | N | (8G 3–4) | | LOU | N | (1G 0–1) | | | | | | | | | |
| " total | 3 | 5 | .375 | 7.93 | 9 | 6 | 4 | 53.1 | 76 | 38 | 14 | 0 | 2 | 0 | 0 | 128 | 47 | 0 | .367 |
| 3 yrs. | 5 | 7 | .417 | 6.86 | 15 | 11 | 6 | 81.1 | 101 | 67 | 42 | 0 | 2 | 1 | 0 | * | | | |
| 1 yr. | 0 | 1 | .000 | 4.91 | 3 | 2 | 0 | 11 | 14 | 10 | 12 | 0 | 0 | 1 | 0 | 6 | 2 | 0 | .333 |

## Joe Niekro

**NIEKRO, JOSEPH FRANKLIN**
Brother of Phil Niekro.
B. Nov. 7, 1944, Martins Ferry, Ohio.    BR TR 6'1"   185 lbs.

| | W | L | PCT | ERA | G | GS | CG | IP | H | BB | SO | ShO | W | L | SV | AB | H | HR | BA |
|---|---|---|---|---|---|---|---|---|---|---|---|---|---|---|---|---|---|---|---|
| 1967 CHI N | 10 | 7 | .588 | 3.34 | 36 | 22 | 7 | 169.2 | 171 | 32 | 77 | 2 | 1 | 1 | 0 | 46 | 9 | 0 | .196 |
| 1968 | 14 | 10 | .583 | 4.31 | 34 | 29 | 2 | 177.1 | 204 | 59 | 65 | 1 | 1 | 0 | 2 | 60 | 6 | 0 | .100 |
| 1969 2 teams | | | | CHI | N | (4G 0–1) | | SD | N | (37G 8–17) | | | | | | | | | |
| " total | 8 | 18 | .308 | 3.70 | 41 | 34 | 8 | 221.1 | 237 | 51 | 62 | 3 | 0 | 0 | 0 | 56 | 7 | 0 | .125 |
| 1970 DET A | 12 | 13 | .480 | 4.06 | 38 | 34 | 6 | 213 | 221 | 72 | 101 | 2 | 1 | 0 | 0 | 66 | 13 | 0 | .197 |
| 1971 | 6 | 7 | .462 | 4.50 | 31 | 15 | 0 | 122 | 136 | 49 | 43 | 0 | 2 | 0 | 1 | 30 | 4 | 0 | .133 |
| 1972 | 3 | 2 | .600 | 3.83 | 18 | 7 | 1 | 47 | 62 | 8 | 24 | 0 | 0 | 1 | 1 | 12 | 3 | 0 | .250 |
| 1973 ATL N | 2 | 4 | .333 | 4.13 | 20 | 0 | 0 | 24 | 23 | 11 | 12 | 0 | 2 | 4 | 3 | 3 | 1 | 0 | .333 |
| 1974 | 3 | 2 | .600 | 3.56 | 27 | 2 | 0 | 43 | 36 | 18 | 31 | 0 | 3 | 2 | 0 | 5 | 0 | 0 | .000 |
| 1975 HOU N | 6 | 4 | .600 | 3.07 | 40 | 4 | 1 | 88 | 79 | 39 | 54 | 1 | 3 | 4 | 4 | 14 | 3 | 0 | .214 |
| 1976 | 4 | 8 | .333 | 3.36 | 36 | 13 | 0 | 118 | 107 | 56 | 77 | 0 | 4 | 0 | 2 | 27 | 5 | 1 | .185 |
| 1977 | 13 | 8 | .619 | 3.03 | 44 | 14 | 9 | 181 | 155 | 64 | 101 | 2 | 4 | 4 | 5 | 50 | 7 | 0 | .140 |
| 1978 | 14 | 14 | .500 | 3.86 | 35 | 29 | 10 | 203 | 190 | 73 | 97 | 1 | 1 | 0 | 0 | 65 | 9 | 0 | .138 |
| 1979 | 21 | 11 | .656 | 3.00 | 38 | 38 | 11 | 264 | 221 | 107 | 119 | 5 | 0 | 0 | 0 | 83 | 10 | 0 | .120 |
| 1980 | 20 | 12 | .625 | 3.55 | 37 | 36 | 11 | 256 | 268 | 79 | 127 | 2 | 1 | 0 | 0 | 80 | 22 | 0 | .275 |
| 1981 | 9 | 9 | .500 | 2.82 | 24 | 24 | 5 | 166 | 150 | 47 | 77 | 2 | 0 | 0 | 0 | 51 | 9 | 0 | .176 |
| 1982 | 17 | 12 | .586 | 2.47 | 35 | 35 | 16 | 270 | 224 | 64 | 130 | 5 | 0 | 0 | 0 | 89 | 8 | 0 | .090 |
| 1983 | 15 | 14 | .517 | 3.48 | 38 | 38 | 9 | 263.2 | 238 | 101 | 152 | 1 | 0 | 0 | 0 | 85 | 8 | 0 | .094 |
| 1984 | 16 | 12 | .571 | 3.04 | 38 | 38 | 6 | 248.1 | 223 | 89 | 127 | 1 | 1 | 0 | 0 | 83 | 11 | 0 | .133 |
| 1985 2 teams | | | | HOU | N | (32G 9–12) | | NY | A | (3G 2–1) | | | | | | | | | |
| " total | 11 | 13 | .458 | 3.83 | 35 | 35 | 4 | 225.1 | 211 | 107 | 121 | 1 | 0 | 0 | 0 | 68 | 17 | 0 | .250 |
| 19 yrs. | 204 | 180 | .531 | 3.44 | 645 | 447 | 106 | 3300.2 | 3156 | 1126 | 1597 | 29 | 19 | 18 | 16 | 973 | 152 | 1 | .156 |
| 3 yrs. | 24 | 18 | .571 | 3.83 | 74 | 54 | 9 | 366.1 | 399 | 97 | 149 | 3 | 2 | 1 | 2 | 111 | 16 | 0 | .144 |
| DIVISIONAL PLAYOFF SERIES | | | | | | | | | | | | | | | | | | | |
| 1981 HOU N | 0 | 0 | – | 0.00 | 1 | 1 | 0 | 8 | 7 | 3 | 4 | 0 | 0 | 0 | 0 | 2 | 0 | 0 | .000 |
| LEAGUE CHAMPIONSHIP SERIES | | | | | | | | | | | | | | | | | | | |
| 1980 HOU N | 0 | 0 | – | 0.00 | 1 | 1 | 0 | 10 | 6 | 1 | 2 | 0 | 0 | 0 | 0 | 3 | 0 | 0 | .000 |

## Dickie Noles

**NOLES, DICKIE RAY**
B. Nov. 19, 1956, Charlotte, N. C.    BR TR 6'2"   160 lbs.

| | W | L | PCT | ERA | G | GS | CG | IP | H | BB | SO | ShO | W | L | SV | AB | H | HR | BA |
|---|---|---|---|---|---|---|---|---|---|---|---|---|---|---|---|---|---|---|---|
| 1979 PHI N | 3 | 4 | .429 | 3.80 | 14 | 14 | 0 | 90 | 80 | 38 | 42 | 0 | 0 | 0 | 0 | 30 | 3 | 0 | .100 |
| 1980 | 1 | 4 | .200 | 3.89 | 48 | 3 | 0 | 81 | 80 | 42 | 57 | 0 | 0 | 4 | 6 | 13 | 4 | 0 | .308 |
| 1981 | 2 | 2 | .500 | 4.19 | 13 | 8 | 0 | 58 | 57 | 23 | 34 | 0 | 0 | 0 | 0 | 19 | 2 | 0 | .105 |
| 1982 CHI N | 10 | 13 | .435 | 4.42 | 31 | 30 | 2 | 171 | 180 | 61 | 85 | 2 | 0 | 0 | 0 | 56 | 6 | 0 | .107 |
| 1983 | 5 | 10 | .333 | 4.72 | 24 | 18 | 1 | 116.1 | 133 | 37 | 59 | 1 | 0 | 1 | 0 | 38 | 9 | 0 | .237 |
| 1984 2 teams | | | | CHI | N | (21G 2–2) | | TEX | A | (18G 2–3) | | | | | | | | | |
| " total | 4 | 5 | .444 | 5.15 | 39 | 7 | 0 | 108.1 | 120 | 46 | 53 | 0 | 4 | 3 | 0 | 10 | 0 | 0 | .000 |
| 1985 TEX A | 4 | 8 | .333 | 5.06 | 28 | 13 | 0 | 110.1 | 129 | 33 | 59 | 0 | 1 | 1 | 1 | 0 | 0 | 0 | – |
| 7 yrs. | 29 | 46 | .387 | 4.52 | 197 | 93 | 3 | 735 | 779 | 280 | 389 | 3 | 5 | 9 | 7 | 166 | 24 | 0 | .145 |
| 3 yrs. | 17 | 25 | .405 | 4.63 | 76 | 49 | 3 | 338 | 373 | 114 | 158 | 3 | 2 | 2 | 0 | 104 | 15 | 0 | .144 |
| DIVISIONAL PLAYOFF SERIES | | | | | | | | | | | | | | | | | | | |
| 1981 PHI N | 0 | 0 | – | 4.50 | 1 | 1 | 0 | 4 | 4 | 2 | 5 | 0 | 0 | 0 | 0 | 0 | 0 | 0 | – |
| LEAGUE CHAMPIONSHIP SERIES | | | | | | | | | | | | | | | | | | | |
| 1980 PHI N | 0 | 0 | – | 0.00 | 2 | 0 | 0 | 2.2 | 1 | 3 | 0 | 0 | 0 | 0 | 0 | 0 | 0 | 0 | – |
| WORLD SERIES | | | | | | | | | | | | | | | | | | | |
| 1980 PHI N | 0 | 0 | – | 1.93 | 1 | 0 | 0 | 4.2 | 5 | 2 | 6 | 0 | 0 | 0 | 0 | 0 | 0 | 0 | – |

| | W | L | PCT | ERA | G | GS | CG | IP | H | BB | SO | ShO | Relief Pitching W | L | SV | BATTING AB | H | HR | BA |
|---|---|---|---|---|---|---|---|---|---|---|---|---|---|---|---|---|---|---|---|

## Wayne Nordhagen

**NORDHAGEN, WAYNE OREN**
B. July 4, 1948, Thief River Falls, Minn.　　　　　　　BR TR 6'2"　205 lbs.

| | W | L | PCT | ERA | G | GS | CG | IP | H | BB | SO | ShO | RP W | L | SV | AB | H | HR | BA |
|---|---|---|---|---|---|---|---|---|---|---|---|---|---|---|---|---|---|---|---|
| 1979 CHI A | 0 | 0 | – | 9.00 | 2 | 0 | 0 | 2 | 2 | 1 | 2 | 0 | 0 | 0 | 0 | * | | | |

## Fred Norman

**NORMAN, FREDIE HUBERT**
B. Aug. 20, 1942, San Antonio, Tex.　　　　　　　BL TL 5'8"　155 lbs.

| | W | L | PCT | ERA | G | GS | CG | IP | H | BB | SO | ShO | RP W | L | SV | AB | H | HR | BA |
|---|---|---|---|---|---|---|---|---|---|---|---|---|---|---|---|---|---|---|---|
| 1962 KC A | 0 | 0 | – | 2.25 | 2 | 0 | 0 | 4 | 4 | 1 | 2 | 0 | 0 | 0 | 0 | 0 | 0 | 0 | – |
| 1963 | 0 | 1 | .000 | 11.37 | 2 | 2 | 0 | 6.1 | 9 | 7 | 6 | 0 | 0 | 0 | 0 | 1 | 0 | 0 | .000 |
| 1964 CHI N | 0 | 4 | .000 | 6.54 | 8 | 5 | 0 | 31.2 | 34 | 21 | 20 | 0 | 0 | 0 | 0 | 11 | 1 | 0 | .091 |
| 1966 | 0 | 0 | – | 4.50 | 2 | 0 | 0 | 4 | 5 | 2 | 6 | 0 | 0 | 0 | 0 | 0 | 0 | 0 | – |
| 1967 | 0 | 0 | – | 0.00 | 1 | 0 | 0 | 1 | 0 | 0 | 3 | 0 | 0 | 0 | 0 | 0 | 0 | 0 | – |
| 1970 2 teams | | | LA | N | (30G 2–0) | | STL | N | (1G 0–0) | | | | | | | | | | |
| " total | 2 | 0 | 1.000 | 5.14 | 31 | 0 | 0 | 63 | 66 | 33 | 47 | 0 | 2 | 0 | 1 | 7 | 1 | 0 | .143 |
| 1971 2 teams | | | STL | N | (4G 0–0) | | SD | N | (20G 3–12) | | | | | | | | | | |
| " total | 3 | 12 | .200 | 3.57 | 24 | 18 | 5 | 131 | 121 | 63 | 81 | 0 | 0 | 0 | 0 | 38 | 9 | 0 | .237 |
| 1972 SD N | 9 | 11 | .450 | 3.44 | 42 | 28 | 10 | 211.2 | 195 | 88 | 167 | 6 | 1 | 0 | 2 | 64 | 8 | 0 | .125 |
| 1973 2 teams | | | SD | N | (12G 1–7) | | CIN | N | (24G 12–6) | | | | | | | | | | |
| " total | 13 | 13 | .500 | 3.60 | 36 | 35 | 8 | 240.1 | 208 | 101 | 161 | 3 | 0 | 0 | 0 | 80 | 6 | 0 | .075 |
| 1974 CIN N | 13 | 12 | .520 | 3.15 | 35 | 26 | 8 | 186 | 170 | 68 | 141 | 2 | 0 | 2 | 0 | 61 | 8 | 0 | .131 |
| 1975 | 12 | 4 | .750 | 3.73 | 34 | 26 | 2 | 188 | 163 | 84 | 119 | 0 | 1 | 0 | 0 | 60 | 7 | 0 | .117 |
| 1976 | 12 | 7 | .632 | 3.10 | 33 | 24 | 8 | 180 | 153 | 70 | 126 | 3 | 1 | 0 | 0 | 50 | 7 | 0 | .140 |
| 1977 | 14 | 13 | .519 | 3.38 | 35 | 34 | 8 | 221 | 200 | 98 | 160 | 1 | 0 | 0 | 0 | 73 | 8 | 0 | .110 |
| 1978 | 11 | 9 | .550 | 3.71 | 36 | 31 | 0 | 177 | 173 | 82 | 111 | 0 | 1 | 0 | 1 | 50 | 7 | 0 | .140 |
| 1979 | 11 | 13 | .458 | 3.65 | 34 | 31 | 5 | 195 | 193 | 57 | 95 | 0 | 0 | 1 | 0 | 59 | 9 | 0 | .153 |
| 1980 MON N | 4 | 4 | .500 | 4.05 | 48 | 8 | 2 | 98.6 | 96 | 40 | 58 | 0 | 1 | 0 | 4 | 20 | 1 | 0 | .050 |
| 16 yrs. | 104 | 103 | .502 | 3.64 | 403 | 268 | 56 | 1938.6 | 1790 | 815 | 1303 | 15 | 6 | 4 | 8 | 574 | 72 | 0 | .125 |
| 3 yrs. | 0 | 4 | .000 | 6.14 | 11 | 5 | 0 | 36.2 | 39 | 23 | 29 | 0 | 0 | 0 | 0 | 11 | 1 | 0 | .091 |

LEAGUE CHAMPIONSHIP SERIES

| | W | L | PCT | ERA | G | GS | CG | IP | H | BB | SO | ShO | RP W | L | SV | AB | H | HR | BA |
|---|---|---|---|---|---|---|---|---|---|---|---|---|---|---|---|---|---|---|---|
| 1973 CIN N | 0 | 0 | – | 1.80 | 1 | 1 | 0 | 5 | 1 | 3 | 3 | 0 | 0 | 0 | 0 | 1 | 0 | 0 | .000 |
| 1975 | 1 | 0 | 1.000 | 1.50 | 1 | 1 | 0 | 6 | 4 | 5 | 4 | 0 | 0 | 0 | 0 | 1 | 0 | 0 | .000 |
| 1979 | 0 | 0 | – | 18.00 | 1 | 0 | 0 | 2 | 4 | 1 | 1 | 0 | 0 | 0 | 0 | 1 | 0 | 0 | .000 |
| 3 yrs. | 1 | 0 | 1.000 | 4.15 | 3 | 2 | 0 | 13 | 9 | 9 | 8 | 0 | 0 | 0 | 0 | 3 | 0 | 0 | .000 |

WORLD SERIES

| | W | L | PCT | ERA | G | GS | CG | IP | H | BB | SO | ShO | RP W | L | SV | AB | H | HR | BA |
|---|---|---|---|---|---|---|---|---|---|---|---|---|---|---|---|---|---|---|---|
| 1975 CIN N | 0 | 1 | .000 | 9.00 | 2 | 1 | 0 | 4 | 8 | 3 | 2 | 0 | 0 | 0 | 0 | 1 | 0 | 0 | .000 |
| 1976 | 0 | 0 | – | 4.26 | 1 | 1 | 0 | 6.1 | 9 | 2 | 2 | 0 | 0 | 0 | 0 | 0 | 0 | 0 | – |
| 2 yrs. | 0 | 1 | .000 | 6.10 | 3 | 2 | 0 | 10.1 | 17 | 5 | 4 | 0 | 0 | 0 | 0 | 1 | 0 | 0 | .000 |

## Don Nottebart

**NOTTEBART, DONALD EDWARD**
B. Jan. 23, 1936, West Newton, Mass.　　　　　　　BR TR 6'1"　190 lbs.

| | W | L | PCT | ERA | G | GS | CG | IP | H | BB | SO | ShO | RP W | L | SV | AB | H | HR | BA |
|---|---|---|---|---|---|---|---|---|---|---|---|---|---|---|---|---|---|---|---|
| 1960 MIL N | 1 | 0 | 1.000 | 4.11 | 5 | 1 | 0 | 15.1 | 14 | 15 | 8 | 0 | 1 | 0 | 1 | 5 | 0 | 0 | .000 |
| 1961 | 6 | 7 | .462 | 4.06 | 38 | 11 | 2 | 126.1 | 117 | 48 | 66 | 0 | 3 | 2 | 3 | 38 | 7 | 0 | .184 |
| 1962 | 2 | 2 | .500 | 3.23 | 39 | 0 | 0 | 64 | 64 | 20 | 36 | 0 | 2 | 2 | 2 | 6 | 2 | 0 | .333 |
| 1963 HOU N | 11 | 8 | .579 | 3.17 | 31 | 27 | 9 | 193 | 170 | 39 | 118 | 2 | 0 | 0 | 0 | 66 | 11 | 0 | .167 |
| 1964 | 6 | 11 | .353 | 3.90 | 28 | 24 | 2 | 157 | 165 | 37 | 90 | 0 | 1 | 0 | 0 | 47 | 3 | 0 | .064 |
| 1965 | 4 | 15 | .211 | 4.67 | 29 | 25 | 3 | 158 | 166 | 55 | 77 | 0 | 0 | 1 | 0 | 48 | 5 | 0 | .104 |
| 1966 CIN N | 5 | 4 | .556 | 3.07 | 59 | 1 | 0 | 111.1 | 97 | 43 | 69 | 0 | 5 | 4 | 11 | 24 | 4 | 0 | .167 |
| 1967 | 0 | 3 | .000 | 1.93 | 47 | 0 | 0 | 79.1 | 75 | 19 | 48 | 0 | 0 | 3 | 4 | 3 | 0 | 0 | .000 |
| 1969 2 teams | | | NY | A | (4G 0–0) | | CHI | N | (16G 1–1) | | | | | | | | | | |
| " total | 1 | 1 | .500 | 6.38 | 20 | 0 | 0 | 24 | 34 | 7 | 13 | 0 | 1 | 1 | 0 | 1 | 0 | 0 | .000 |
| 9 yrs. | 36 | 51 | .414 | 3.65 | 296 | 89 | 16 | 928.1 | 902 | 283 | 525 | 2 | 13 | 13 | 21 | 238 | 32 | 0 | .134 |
| 1 yr. | 1 | 1 | .500 | 7.00 | 16 | 0 | 0 | 18 | 28 | 7 | 8 | 0 | 1 | 1 | 0 | 1 | 0 | 0 | .000 |

## Rich Nye

**NYE, RICHARD RAYMOND**
B. Aug. 4, 1944, Oakland, Calif.　　　　　　　BL TL 6'4"　185 lbs.

| | W | L | PCT | ERA | G | GS | CG | IP | H | BB | SO | ShO | RP W | L | SV | AB | H | HR | BA |
|---|---|---|---|---|---|---|---|---|---|---|---|---|---|---|---|---|---|---|---|
| 1966 CHI N | 0 | 2 | .000 | 2.12 | 3 | 2 | 0 | 17 | 16 | 7 | 9 | 0 | 0 | 0 | 0 | 4 | 1 | 0 | .250 |
| 1967 | 13 | 10 | .565 | 3.20 | 35 | 30 | 7 | 205 | 179 | 52 | 119 | 0 | 0 | 1 | 0 | 75 | 16 | 0 | .213 |
| 1968 | 7 | 12 | .368 | 3.80 | 27 | 20 | 6 | 132.2 | 145 | 34 | 74 | 1 | 1 | 0 | 1 | 44 | 8 | 0 | .182 |
| 1969 | 3 | 5 | .375 | 5.09 | 34 | 5 | 1 | 69 | 72 | 21 | 39 | 0 | 0 | 0 | 3 | 16 | 1 | 0 | .063 |
| 1970 2 teams | | | MON | N | (8G 3–2) | | STL | N | (6G 0–0) | | | | | | | | | | |
| " total | 3 | 2 | .600 | 4.14 | 14 | 6 | 2 | 54.1 | 60 | 26 | 26 | 0 | 0 | 0 | 0 | 19 | 4 | 0 | .211 |
| 5 yrs. | 26 | 31 | .456 | 3.71 | 113 | 63 | 16 | 478 | 472 | 140 | 267 | 1 | 1 | 1 | 4 | 158 | 30 | 0 | .190 |
| 4 yrs. | 23 | 29 | .442 | 3.65 | 99 | 57 | 14 | 423.2 | 412 | 114 | 241 | 1 | 1 | 1 | 4 | 139 | 26 | 0 | .187 |

## Vern Olsen

**OLSEN, VERN JARL**
B. Mar. 16, 1918, Hillsboro, Ore.　　　　　　　BR TL 6'½"　175 lbs.

| | W | L | PCT | ERA | G | GS | CG | IP | H | BB | SO | ShO | RP W | L | SV | AB | H | HR | BA |
|---|---|---|---|---|---|---|---|---|---|---|---|---|---|---|---|---|---|---|---|
| 1939 CHI N | 1 | 0 | 1.000 | 0.00 | 4 | 0 | 0 | 7.2 | 2 | 7 | 3 | 0 | 1 | 0 | 0 | 1 | 0 | 0 | .000 |
| 1940 | 13 | 9 | .591 | 2.97 | 34 | 20 | 9 | 172.2 | 172 | 62 | 71 | 4 | 2 | 1 | 0 | 57 | 15 | 0 | .263 |
| 1941 | 10 | 8 | .556 | 3.15 | 37 | 23 | 10 | 185.2 | 202 | 59 | 73 | 2 | 0 | 0 | 1 | 63 | 15 | 1 | .238 |
| 1942 | 6 | 9 | .400 | 4.49 | 32 | 17 | 4 | 140.1 | 161 | 55 | 46 | 1 | 0 | 1 | 1 | 48 | 9 | 0 | .188 |
| 1946 | 0 | 0 | – | 2.79 | 5 | 0 | 0 | 9.2 | 10 | 9 | 8 | 0 | 0 | 0 | 0 | 0 | 0 | 0 | – |
| 5 yrs. | 30 | 26 | .536 | 3.40 | 112 | 60 | 23 | 516 | 547 | 192 | 201 | 7 | 3 | 2 | 2 | 169 | 39 | 1 | .231 |
| 5 yrs. | 30 | 26 | .536 | 3.40 | 112 | 60 | 23 | 516 | 547 | 192 | 201 | 7 | 3 | 2 | 2 | 169 | 39 | 1 | .231 |

## Emmett O'Neill

**O'NEILL, ROBERT EMMETT (Pinky)**
B. Jan. 13, 1918, San Mateo, Calif.　　　　　　　BR TR 6'3"　185 lbs.

| | W | L | PCT | ERA | G | GS | CG | IP | H | BB | SO | ShO | RP W | L | SV | AB | H | HR | BA |
|---|---|---|---|---|---|---|---|---|---|---|---|---|---|---|---|---|---|---|---|
| 1943 BOS A | 1 | 4 | .200 | 4.53 | 11 | 5 | 1 | 57.2 | 56 | 46 | 20 | 0 | 1 | 0 | 0 | 16 | 3 | 0 | .188 |
| 1944 | 6 | 11 | .353 | 4.63 | 28 | 22 | 8 | 151.2 | 154 | 89 | 68 | 1 | 0 | 0 | 0 | 55 | 10 | 0 | .182 |
| 1945 | 8 | 11 | .421 | 5.15 | 24 | 22 | 10 | 141.2 | 134 | 117 | 55 | 1 | 0 | 0 | 0 | 50 | 9 | 1 | .180 |
| 1946 2 teams | | | CHI | N | (1G 0–0) | | CHI | A | (2G 0–0) | | | | | | | | | | |
| " total | 0 | 0 | – | 0.00 | 3 | 0 | 0 | 4.2 | 4 | 8 | 1 | 0 | 0 | 0 | 0 | 1 | 0 | 0 | .000 |
| 4 yrs. | 15 | 26 | .366 | 4.76 | 66 | 49 | 19 | 355.2 | 348 | 260 | 144 | 2 | 1 | 0 | 0 | 122 | 22 | 1 | .180 |
| 1 yr. | 0 | 0 | – | 0.00 | 1 | 0 | 0 | 3 | 1 | 6 | 0 | 0 | 0 | 0 | 0 | 0 | 0 | 0 | – |

| | W | L | PCT | ERA | G | GS | CG | IP | H | BB | SO | ShO | Relief Pitching W | L | SV | BATTING AB | H | HR | BA |
|---|---|---|---|---|---|---|---|---|---|---|---|---|---|---|---|---|---|---|---|

## Bob Osborn

**OSBORN, JOHN BODE**            BR TR 6'1"   175 lbs.
B. Apr. 17, 1903, San Diego, Tex.     D. Apr. 19, 1960, Paris, Ark.

| | W | L | PCT | ERA | G | GS | CG | IP | H | BB | SO | ShO | W | L | SV | AB | H | HR | BA |
|---|---|---|---|---|---|---|---|---|---|---|---|---|---|---|---|---|---|---|---|
| 1925 CHI N | 0 | 0 | — | 0.00 | 1 | 0 | 0 | 2 | 6 | 0 | 0 | 0 | 0 | 0 | 0 | 0 | 0 | 0 | — |
| 1926 | 6 | 5 | .545 | 3.63 | 31 | 15 | 6 | 136.1 | 157 | 58 | 43 | 0 | 2 | 0 | 1 | 41 | 6 | 0 | .146 |
| 1927 | 5 | 5 | .500 | 4.18 | 24 | 12 | 2 | 107.2 | 125 | 48 | 45 | 0 | 1 | 1 | 0 | 39 | 8 | 0 | .205 |
| 1929 | 0 | 0 | | 3.00 | 3 | 1 | 0 | 9 | 8 | 2 | 1 | 0 | 0 | 0 | 0 | 4 | 1 | 0 | .250 |
| 1930 | 10 | 6 | .625 | 4.97 | 35 | 13 | 3 | 126.2 | 147 | 53 | 42 | 0 | 5 | 3 | 1 | 42 | 4 | 0 | .095 |
| 1931 PIT N | 6 | 1 | .857 | 5.01 | 27 | 2 | 0 | 64.2 | 85 | 20 | 9 | 0 | 6 | 1 | 0 | 18 | 3 | 0 | .167 |
| 6 yrs. | 27 | 17 | .614 | 4.32 | 121 | 43 | 11 | 446.1 | 528 | 181 | 140 | 0 | 14 | 5 | 2 | 144 | 22 | 0 | .153 |
| 5 yrs. | 21 | 16 | .568 | 4.20 | 94 | 41 | 11 | 381.2 | 443 | 161 | 131 | 0 | 8 | 4 | 2 | 126 | 19 | 0 | .151 |

## Tiny Osborne

**OSBORNE, EARNEST PRESTON**        BL TR 6'4½"   215 lbs.
Father of Bobo Osborne.
B. Apr. 9, 1893, Porterdale, Ga.     D. Jan. 5, 1969, Atlanta, Ga.

| | W | L | PCT | ERA | G | GS | CG | IP | H | BB | SO | ShO | W | L | SV | AB | H | HR | BA |
|---|---|---|---|---|---|---|---|---|---|---|---|---|---|---|---|---|---|---|---|
| 1922 CHI N | 9 | 5 | .643 | 4.50 | 41 | 14 | 7 | 184 | 183 | 95 | 81 | 1 | 1 | 1 | 3 | 67 | 9 | 0 | .134 |
| 1923 | 8 | 15 | .348 | 4.56 | 37 | 25 | 8 | 179.2 | 174 | 89 | 69 | 1 | 1 | 3 | 1 | 60 | 12 | 0 | .200 |
| 1924 **2 teams** | | | CHI | N | (2G 0–0) | | BKN | N | (21G 6–5) | | | | | | | | | | |
| " total | 6 | 5 | .545 | 5.03 | 23 | 13 | 6 | 107.1 | 126 | 56 | 54 | 0 | 1 | 0 | 1 | 36 | 9 | 0 | .250 |
| 1925 BKN N | 8 | 15 | .348 | 4.94 | 41 | 22 | 10 | 175 | 210 | 75 | 59 | 0 | 2 | 4 | 1 | 57 | 14 | 0 | .246 |
| 4 yrs. | 31 | 40 | .437 | 4.72 | 142 | 74 | 31 | 646 | 693 | 315 | 263 | 2 | 6 | 8 | 6 | 220 | 44 | 0 | .200 |
| 3 yrs. | 17 | 20 | .459 | 4.52 | 80 | 39 | 15 | 366.2 | 360 | 186 | 152 | 2 | 3 | 4 | 5 | 127 | 21 | 0 | .165 |

## Orval Overall

**OVERALL, ORVAL**             BB TR 6'2"   214 lbs.
B. Feb. 2, 1881, Visalia, Calif.     D. July 14, 1947, Fresno, Calif.

| | W | L | PCT | ERA | G | GS | CG | IP | H | BB | SO | ShO | W | L | SV | AB | H | HR | BA |
|---|---|---|---|---|---|---|---|---|---|---|---|---|---|---|---|---|---|---|---|
| 1905 CIN N | 17 | 22 | .436 | 2.86 | 42 | 39 | 32 | 318 | 290 | 147 | 173 | 2 | 1 | 1 | 0 | 117 | 17 | 0 | .145 |
| 1906 **2 teams** | | | CIN | N | (13G 3–5) | | CHI | N | (18G 12–3) | | | | | | | | | | |
| " total | 15 | 8 | .652 | 2.74 | 31 | 24 | 19 | 226.1 | 193 | 97 | 127 | 2 | 2 | 0 | 1 | 84 | 15 | 0 | .179 |
| 1907 CHI N | 23 | 8 | .742 | 1.70 | 35 | 29 | 26 | 265.1 | 199 | 69 | 139 | 8 | 1 | 2 | 3 | 94 | 20 | 0 | .213 |
| 1908 | 15 | 11 | .577 | 1.92 | 37 | 27 | 16 | 225 | 165 | 78 | 167 | 4 | 3 | 0 | 2 | 70 | 9 | 0 | .129 |
| 1909 | 20 | 11 | .645 | 1.42 | 38 | 32 | 23 | 285 | 204 | 80 | 205 | 9 | 1 | 0 | 2 | 96 | 22 | 2 | .229 |
| 1910 | 12 | 6 | .667 | 2.68 | 23 | 21 | 11 | 144.2 | 106 | 54 | 92 | 4 | 0 | 1 | 1 | 41 | 5 | 0 | .122 |
| 1913 | 4 | 5 | .444 | 3.31 | 11 | 9 | 6 | 68 | 73 | 26 | 30 | 1 | 0 | 0 | 0 | 24 | 6 | 0 | .250 |
| 7 yrs. | 106 | 71 | .599 | 2.24 | 217 | 181 | 133 | 1532.1 | 1230 | 551 | 933 | 30 | 8 | 4 | 9 | 526 | 94 | 2 | .179 |
| | | | | **8th** | | | | | | | | | | | | | | | |
| 6 yrs. | 86 | 44 | .662 | 1.92 | 162 | 132 | 95 | 1132 | 863 | 358 | 727 | 28 | 7 | 3 | 9 | 378 | 71 | 2 | .188 |
| | | | **5th** | **3rd** | | | | | | | | **5th** | | | | | | | |

WORLD SERIES

| | W | L | PCT | ERA | G | GS | CG | IP | H | BB | SO | ShO | W | L | SV | AB | H | HR | BA |
|---|---|---|---|---|---|---|---|---|---|---|---|---|---|---|---|---|---|---|---|
| 1906 CHI N | 0 | 0 | | 1.50 | 2 | 1 | 0 | 12 | 10 | 3 | 8 | 0 | 0 | 0 | 0 | 4 | 1 | 0 | .250 |
| 1907 | 1 | 0 | 1.000 | 1.00 | 2 | 2 | 1 | 18 | 14 | 4 | 11 | 0 | 0 | 0 | 0 | 5 | 1 | 0 | .200 |
| 1908 | 2 | 0 | 1.000 | 0.98 | 3 | 2 | 2 | 18.1 | 7 | 7 | 15 | 1 | 0 | 0 | 0 | 6 | 2 | 0 | .333 |
| 1910 | 0 | 1 | .000 | 9.00 | 1 | 0 | 0 | 3 | 6 | 1 | 1 | 0 | 0 | 0 | 0 | 0 | 0 | 0 | .000 |
| 4 yrs. | 3 | 1 | .750 | 1.58 | 8 | 5 | 3 | 51.1 | 37 | 15 | 35 | 1 | 0 | 0 | 0 | 16 | 4 | 0 | .250 |

## Ernie Ovitz

**OVITZ, ERNEST GAYHART**        BR TR 5'8½"   156 lbs.
B. Oct. 7, 1885, Mineral Point, Wis.     D. Sept. 11, 1980, Green Bay, Wis.

| | W | L | PCT | ERA | G | GS | CG | IP | H | BB | SO | ShO | W | L | SV | AB | H | HR | BA |
|---|---|---|---|---|---|---|---|---|---|---|---|---|---|---|---|---|---|---|---|
| 1911 CHI N | 0 | 0 | — | 4.50 | 1 | 0 | 0 | 2 | 3 | 3 | 0 | 0 | 0 | 0 | 0 | 0 | 0 | 0 | — |

## Gene Packard

**PACKARD, EUGENE MILO**          BL TL 5'10"   155 lbs.
B. July 13, 1887, Colorado Springs, Colo.     D. May 19, 1959, Riverside, Calif.

| | W | L | PCT | ERA | G | GS | CG | IP | H | BB | SO | ShO | W | L | SV | AB | H | HR | BA |
|---|---|---|---|---|---|---|---|---|---|---|---|---|---|---|---|---|---|---|---|
| 1912 CIN N | 1 | 0 | 1.000 | 3.00 | 1 | 1 | 1 | 9 | 7 | 4 | 2 | 0 | 0 | 0 | 0 | 4 | 1 | 0 | .250 |
| 1913 | 7 | 11 | .389 | 2.97 | 39 | 21 | 9 | 190.2 | 208 | 64 | 73 | 2 | 1 | 2 | 0 | 61 | 11 | 0 | .180 |
| 1914 KC F | 21 | 13 | .618 | 2.89 | 42 | 34 | 24 | 302 | 282 | 88 | 154 | 4 | 3 | 0 | 4 | 116 | 28 | 1 | .241 |
| 1915 | 20 | 11 | .645 | 2.68 | 42 | 31 | 21 | 281.2 | 250 | 74 | 108 | 5 | 2 | 2 | 2 | 95 | 22 | 1 | .232 |
| 1916 CHI N | 10 | 6 | .625 | 2.78 | 37 | 15 | 5 | 155.1 | 154 | 38 | 36 | 2 | 4 | 1 | 5 | 54 | 7 | 0 | .130 |
| 1917 **2 teams** | | | CHI | N | (2G 0–0) | | STL | N | (34G 9–6) | | | | | | | | | | |
| " total | 9 | 6 | .600 | 2.55 | 36 | 11 | 6 | 155 | 141 | 25 | 45 | 0 | 6 | 0 | 2 | 52 | 15 | 0 | .288 |
| 1918 STL N | 12 | 12 | .500 | 3.50 | 30 | 23 | 10 | 182.1 | 184 | 33 | 46 | 1 | 3 | 1 | 2 | 69 | 12 | 0 | .174 |
| 1919 PHI N | 6 | 8 | .429 | 4.15 | 21 | 16 | 10 | 134.1 | 167 | 30 | 24 | 1 | 0 | 1 | 1 | 51 | 7 | 0 | .137 |
| 8 yrs. | 86 | 67 | .562 | 3.01 | 248 | 152 | 86 | 1410.1 | 1393 | 356 | 488 | 15 | 19 | 7 | 16 | 502 | 103 | 2 | .205 |
| 2 yrs. | 10 | 6 | .625 | 2.87 | 39 | 15 | 5 | 157 | 157 | 38 | 37 | 2 | 4 | 1 | 5 | 54 | 7 | 0 | .130 |

## Vance Page

**PAGE, VANCE LINWOOD**          BR TR 6'   180 lbs.
B. Sept. 15, 1905, Elm City, N. C.     D. July 14, 1951, Wilson, N. C.

| | W | L | PCT | ERA | G | GS | CG | IP | H | BB | SO | ShO | W | L | SV | AB | H | HR | BA |
|---|---|---|---|---|---|---|---|---|---|---|---|---|---|---|---|---|---|---|---|
| 1938 CHI N | 5 | 4 | .556 | 3.84 | 13 | 9 | 3 | 68 | 90 | 13 | 18 | 0 | 0 | 0 | 0 | 26 | 4 | 0 | .154 |
| 1939 | 7 | 7 | .500 | 3.88 | 27 | 17 | 8 | 139.1 | 169 | 37 | 43 | 1 | 1 | 0 | 1 | 47 | 12 | 0 | .255 |
| 1940 | 1 | 3 | .250 | 4.42 | 30 | 1 | 0 | 59 | 65 | 26 | 22 | 0 | 1 | 3 | 2 | 13 | 4 | 0 | .308 |
| 1941 | 2 | 2 | .500 | 4.28 | 25 | 3 | 1 | 48.1 | 48 | 30 | 17 | 0 | 2 | 2 | 1 | 7 | 2 | 0 | .286 |
| 4 yrs. | 15 | 16 | .484 | 4.03 | 95 | 30 | 12 | 314.2 | 372 | 106 | 100 | 1 | 4 | 5 | 5 | 93 | 22 | 0 | .237 |
| 4 yrs. | 15 | 16 | .484 | 4.03 | 95 | 30 | 12 | 314.2 | 372 | 106 | 100 | 1 | 4 | 5 | 5 | 93 | 22 | 0 | .237 |

WORLD SERIES

| | W | L | PCT | ERA | G | GS | CG | IP | H | BB | SO | ShO | W | L | SV | AB | H | HR | BA |
|---|---|---|---|---|---|---|---|---|---|---|---|---|---|---|---|---|---|---|---|
| 1938 CHI N | 0 | 0 | — | 13.50 | 1 | 0 | 0 | 1.1 | 2 | 0 | 0 | 0 | 0 | 0 | 0 | 0 | 0 | 0 | — |

## Milt Pappas

**PAPPAS, MILTON STEVEN (Gimpy)**        BR TR 6'3"   190 lbs.
B. May 11, 1939, Detroit, Mich.

| | W | L | PCT | ERA | G | GS | CG | IP | H | BB | SO | ShO | W | L | SV | AB | H | HR | BA |
|---|---|---|---|---|---|---|---|---|---|---|---|---|---|---|---|---|---|---|---|
| 1957 BAL A | 0 | 0 | — | 1.00 | 4 | 0 | 0 | 9 | 6 | 3 | 3 | 0 | 0 | 0 | 0 | 1 | 0 | 0 | .000 |
| 1958 | 10 | 10 | .500 | 4.06 | 31 | 21 | 3 | 135.1 | 135 | 48 | 72 | 0 | 1 | 1 | 0 | 42 | 6 | 1 | .143 |
| 1959 | 15 | 9 | .625 | 3.27 | 33 | 27 | 15 | 209.1 | 175 | 75 | 120 | 4 | 1 | 0 | 3 | 79 | 11 | 0 | .139 |
| 1960 | 15 | 11 | .577 | 3.37 | 30 | 27 | 11 | 205.2 | 184 | 83 | 126 | 3 | 2 | 1 | 0 | 70 | 3 | 1 | .043 |
| 1961 | 13 | 9 | .591 | 3.04 | 26 | 23 | 11 | 177.2 | 134 | 78 | 89 | 4 | 1 | 0 | 1 | 66 | 9 | 3 | .136 |
| 1962 | 12 | 10 | .545 | 4.03 | 35 | 32 | 9 | 205.1 | 200 | 75 | 130 | 1 | 0 | 0 | 0 | 69 | 6 | 4 | .087 |
| 1963 | 16 | 9 | .640 | 3.03 | 34 | 32 | 11 | 216.2 | 186 | 69 | 120 | 4 | 0 | 0 | 0 | 71 | 9 | 2 | .127 |

| | W | L | PCT | ERA | G | GS | CG | IP | H | BB | SO | ShO | Relief Pitching W | L | SV | BATTING AB | H | HR | BA |
|---|---|---|---|---|---|---|---|---|---|---|---|---|---|---|---|---|---|---|---|

## Milt Pappas continued

| | W | L | PCT | ERA | G | GS | CG | IP | H | BB | SO | ShO | W | L | SV | AB | H | HR | BA |
|---|---|---|---|---|---|---|---|---|---|---|---|---|---|---|---|---|---|---|---|
| 1964 | 16 | 7 | .696 | 2.97 | 37 | 36 | 13 | 251.2 | 225 | 48 | 157 | 7 | 0 | 0 | 0 | 93 | 12 | 0 | .129 |
| 1965 | 13 | 9 | .591 | 2.60 | 34 | 34 | 9 | 221.1 | 192 | 52 | 127 | 3 | 0 | 0 | 0 | 70 | 5 | 0 | .071 |
| 1966 CIN N | 12 | 11 | .522 | 4.29 | 33 | 32 | 6 | 209.2 | 224 | 39 | 133 | 2 | 0 | 1 | 0 | 75 | 8 | 1 | .107 |
| 1967 | 16 | 13 | .552 | 3.35 | 34 | 32 | 5 | 217.2 | 218 | 38 | 129 | 3 | 2 | 0 | 0 | 72 | 7 | 1 | .097 |
| 1968 2 teams | | CIN | N | (15G 2–5) | ATL | N | (22G 10–8) | | | | | | | | | | | | |
| " total | 12 | 13 | .480 | 3.47 | 37 | 30 | 3 | 184 | 181 | 32 | 118 | 1 | 0 | 1 | 0 | 53 | 7 | 1 | .132 |
| 1969 ATL N | 6 | 10 | .375 | 3.63 | 26 | 24 | 1 | 144 | 149 | 44 | 72 | 0 | 0 | 0 | 0 | 45 | 7 | 2 | .156 |
| 1970 2 teams | | ATL | N | (11G 2–2) | CHI | N | (21G 10–8) | | | | | | | | | | | | |
| " total | 12 | 10 | .545 | 3.34 | 32 | 23 | 7 | 180.1 | 179 | 43 | 105 | 2 | 1 | 0 | 0 | 60 | 12 | 0 | .200 |
| 1971 CHI N | 17 | 14 | .548 | 3.52 | 35 | 35 | 14 | 261 | 279 | 62 | 99 | 5 | 0 | 0 | 0 | 91 | 14 | 0 | .154 |
| 1972 | 17 | 7 | .708 | 2.77 | 29 | 28 | 10 | 195 | 187 | 29 | 80 | 3 | 0 | 0 | 0 | 68 | 13 | 1 | .191 |
| 1973 | 7 | 12 | .368 | 4.28 | 30 | 29 | 1 | 162 | 192 | 40 | 48 | 1 | 0 | 0 | 0 | 48 | 3 | 1 | .063 |
| 17 yrs. | 209 | 164 | .560 | 3.40 | 520 | 465 | 129 | 3185.2 | 3046 | 858 | 1728 | 43 | 8 | 4 | 4 | 1073 | 132 | 20 | .123 |
| 4 yrs. | 51 | 41 | .554 | 3.33 | 115 | 112 | 31 | 762.2 | 793 | 167 | 307 | 11 | 0 | 0 | 0 | 257 | 42 | 4 | .163 |

LEAGUE CHAMPIONSHIP SERIES

| | W | L | PCT | ERA | G | GS | CG | IP | H | BB | SO | ShO | W | L | SV | AB | H | HR | BA |
|---|---|---|---|---|---|---|---|---|---|---|---|---|---|---|---|---|---|---|---|
| 1969 ATL N | 0 | 0 | – | 11.57 | 1 | 0 | 0 | 2.1 | 4 | 0 | 4 | 0 | 0 | 0 | 0 | 1 | 0 | 0 | .000 |

## Doc Parker

**PARKER, HARLEY PARK**           BR  TR  6'2"    200 lbs.
Brother of Jay Parker.
B. June 14, 1874, Theresa, N. Y.    D. Mar. 3, 1941, Chicago, Ill.

| | W | L | PCT | ERA | G | GS | CG | IP | H | BB | SO | ShO | W | L | SV | AB | H | HR | BA |
|---|---|---|---|---|---|---|---|---|---|---|---|---|---|---|---|---|---|---|---|
| 1893 CHI N | 0 | 0 | – | 13.50 | 1 | 0 | 0 | 2 | 5 | 1 | 0 | 0 | 0 | 0 | 0 | 1 | 0 | 0 | .000 |
| 1895 | 4 | 2 | .667 | 3.68 | 7 | 6 | 5 | 51.1 | 65 | 9 | 9 | 1 | 0 | 0 | 0 | 22 | 7 | 0 | .318 |
| 1896 | 1 | 5 | .167 | 6.16 | 9 | 7 | 7 | 73 | 100 | 27 | 15 | 0 | 0 | 0 | 0 | 36 | 10 | 0 | .278 |
| 1901 CIN N | 0 | 1 | .000 | 15.75 | 1 | 1 | 1 | 8 | 26 | 2 | 0 | 0 | 0 | 0 | 0 | 3 | 0 | 0 | .000 |
| 4 yrs. | 5 | 8 | .385 | 5.90 | 18 | 14 | 13 | 134.1 | 196 | 39 | 24 | 1 | 0 | 0 | 0 | 62 | 17 | 0 | .274 |
| 3 yrs. | 5 | 7 | .417 | 5.27 | 17 | 13 | 12 | 126.1 | 170 | 37 | 24 | 1 | 0 | 0 | 1 | 59 | 17 | 0 | .288 |

## Roy Parmelee

**PARMELEE, LeROY EARL (Bud)**        BR  TR  6'1"    190 lbs.
B. Apr. 25, 1907, Lambertville, Mich.    D. Aug. 31, 1981, Monroe, Mich.

| | W | L | PCT | ERA | G | GS | CG | IP | H | BB | SO | ShO | W | L | SV | AB | H | HR | BA |
|---|---|---|---|---|---|---|---|---|---|---|---|---|---|---|---|---|---|---|---|
| 1929 NY N | 1 | 0 | 1.000 | 9.00 | 2 | 1 | 0 | 7 | 13 | 3 | 1 | 0 | 0 | 0 | 0 | 2 | 1 | 0 | .500 |
| 1930 | 0 | 1 | .000 | 9.43 | 11 | 1 | 0 | 21 | 18 | 26 | 19 | 0 | 0 | 0 | 0 | 4 | 1 | 0 | .250 |
| 1931 | 2 | 2 | .500 | 3.68 | 13 | 5 | 4 | 58.2 | 47 | 33 | 30 | 0 | 0 | 0 | 0 | 20 | 4 | 0 | .200 |
| 1932 | 0 | 3 | .000 | 3.91 | 8 | 3 | 0 | 25.1 | 25 | 14 | 23 | 0 | 0 | 0 | 0 | 5 | 2 | 0 | .400 |
| 1933 | 13 | 8 | .619 | 3.17 | 32 | 32 | 14 | 218.1 | 191 | 77 | 132 | 3 | 0 | 0 | 0 | 81 | 19 | 1 | .235 |
| 1934 | 10 | 6 | .625 | 3.42 | 22 | 20 | 7 | 152.2 | 134 | 60 | 83 | 3 | 0 | 0 | 0 | 55 | 11 | 2 | .200 |
| 1935 | 14 | 10 | .583 | 4.22 | 34 | 31 | 13 | 226 | 214 | 97 | 79 | 0 | 1 | 0 | 0 | 86 | 18 | 0 | .209 |
| 1936 STL N | 11 | 11 | .500 | 4.56 | 37 | 28 | 9 | 221 | 226 | 107 | 79 | 0 | 0 | 1 | 2 | 76 | 15 | 0 | .197 |
| 1937 PHI N | 7 | 8 | .467 | 5.13 | 33 | 18 | 8 | 145.2 | 165 | 79 | 55 | 0 | 1 | 0 | 0 | 52 | 9 | 2 | .173 |
| 1939 PHI A | 1 | 6 | .143 | 6.45 | 14 | 5 | 0 | 44.2 | 42 | 35 | 13 | 0 | 1 | 2 | 1 | 15 | 2 | 0 | .133 |
| 10 yrs. | 59 | 55 | .518 | 4.27 | 206 | 144 | 55 | 1120.1 | 1075 | 531 | 514 | 6 | 2 | 4 | 3 | 396 | 82 | 5 | .207 |
| 1 yr. | 7 | 8 | .467 | 5.13 | 33 | 18 | 8 | 145.2 | 165 | 79 | 55 | 0 | 1 | 0 | 0 | 52 | 9 | 2 | .173 |

## Tom Parrott

**PARROTT, THOMAS WILLIAM (Tacky Tom)**     BR  TR  6'2"    170 lbs.
Brother of Jiggs Parrott.
B. Apr. 10, 1868, Portland, Ore.    D. Jan. 1, 1932, Dundee, Ore.

| | W | L | PCT | ERA | G | GS | CG | IP | H | BB | SO | ShO | W | L | SV | AB | H | HR | BA |
|---|---|---|---|---|---|---|---|---|---|---|---|---|---|---|---|---|---|---|---|
| 1893 2 teams | | CHI | N | (4G 0–3) | CIN | N | (22G 10–7) | | | | | | | | | | | | |
| " total | 10 | 10 | .500 | 4.48 | 26 | 20 | 13 | 181 | 209 | 87 | 40 | 1 | 3 | 0 | 0 | 95 | 20 | 1 | .211 |
| 1894 CIN N | 17 | 19 | .472 | 5.60 | 41 | 36 | 31 | 308.2 | 402 | 126 | 61 | 1 | 0 | 1 | 1 | 229 | 74 | 4 | .323 |
| 1895 | 11 | 18 | .379 | 5.47 | 41 | 31 | 23 | 263.1 | 382 | 76 | 57 | 0 | 3 | 1 | 3 | 201 | 69 | 3 | .343 |
| 1896 STL N | 1 | 1 | .500 | 6.21 | 7 | 2 | 2 | 42 | 62 | 18 | 8 | 0 | 0 | 0 | 0 | 474 | 138 | 7 | .291 |
| 4 yrs. | 39 | 48 | .448 | 5.33 | 115 | 89 | 69 | 795 | 1055 | 307 | 166 | 2 | 6 | 2 | 4 | * | | | .259 |
| 1 yr. | 0 | 3 | .000 | 6.67 | 4 | 3 | 2 | 27 | 35 | 17 | 7 | 0 | 0 | 0 | 0 | 27 | 7 | 0 | .259 |

## Claude Passeau

**PASSEAU, CLAUDE WILLIAM**          BR  TR  6'3"    198 lbs.
B. Apr. 9, 1909, Waynesboro, Miss.

| | W | L | PCT | ERA | G | GS | CG | IP | H | BB | SO | ShO | W | L | SV | AB | H | HR | BA |
|---|---|---|---|---|---|---|---|---|---|---|---|---|---|---|---|---|---|---|---|
| 1935 PIT N | 0 | 1 | .000 | 12.00 | 1 | 1 | 0 | 3 | 7 | 2 | 1 | 0 | 0 | 0 | 0 | 1 | 0 | 0 | .000 |
| 1936 PHI N | 11 | 15 | .423 | 3.48 | 49 | 21 | 8 | 217.1 | 247 | 55 | 85 | 2 | 3 | 7 | 3 | 78 | 22 | 2 | .282 |
| 1937 | 14 | 18 | .438 | 4.34 | 50 | 34 | 18 | 292.1 | 348 | 79 | 135 | 1 | 2 | 1 | 2 | 107 | 21 | 1 | .196 |
| 1938 | 11 | 18 | .379 | 4.52 | 44 | 33 | 15 | 239 | 281 | 93 | 100 | 0 | 0 | 0 | 1 | 80 | 13 | 0 | .163 |
| 1939 2 teams | | PHI | N | (8G 2–4) | CHI | N | (34G 13–9) | | | | | | | | | | | | |
| " total | 15 | 13 | .536 | 3.28 | 42 | 35 | 17 | 274.1 | 269 | 73 | 137 | 2 | 1 | 2 | 3 | 97 | 16 | 1 | .165 |
| 1940 CHI N | 20 | 13 | .606 | 2.50 | 46 | 31 | 20 | 280.2 | 259 | 59 | 124 | 4 | 1 | 1 | 5 | 98 | 20 | 1 | .204 |
| 1941 | 14 | 14 | .500 | 3.35 | 34 | 30 | 20 | 231 | 262 | 52 | 80 | 3 | 1 | 1 | 0 | 86 | 19 | 3 | .221 |
| 1942 | 19 | 14 | .576 | 2.68 | 35 | 34 | 24 | 278.1 | 284 | 74 | 89 | 3 | 0 | 0 | 0 | 105 | 19 | 2 | .181 |
| 1943 | 15 | 12 | .556 | 2.91 | 35 | 31 | 18 | 257 | 245 | 66 | 93 | 2 | 0 | 1 | 1 | 96 | 19 | 0 | .198 |
| 1944 | 15 | 9 | .625 | 2.89 | 34 | 27 | 18 | 227 | 234 | 50 | 89 | 2 | 0 | 0 | 0 | 80 | 13 | 0 | .163 |
| 1945 | 17 | 9 | .654 | 2.46 | 34 | 27 | 19 | 227 | 205 | 59 | 98 | 5 | 1 | 0 | 0 | 91 | 17 | 2 | .187 |
| 1946 | 9 | 8 | .529 | 3.13 | 21 | 21 | 10 | 129.1 | 118 | 42 | 47 | 2 | 0 | 0 | 0 | 49 | 10 | 3 | .204 |
| 1947 | 2 | 6 | .250 | 6.25 | 19 | 6 | 1 | 63.1 | 97 | 24 | 26 | 1 | 1 | 0 | 2 | 14 | 0 | 0 | .000 |
| 13 yrs. | 162 | 150 | .519 | 3.32 | 444 | 331 | 188 | 2719.2 | 2856 | 728 | 1104 | 27 | 13 | 13 | 21 | 982 | 189 | 15 | .192 |
| 9 yrs. | 124 | 94 | .569 | 2.96 | 292 | 234 | 143 | 1914.2 | 1919 | 474 | 754 | 23 | 8 | 5 | 15 | 696 | 129 | 12 | .185 |
| | | | | 10th | | | | | | | | 8th | | | | | | | |

WORLD SERIES

| | W | L | PCT | ERA | G | GS | CG | IP | H | BB | SO | ShO | W | L | SV | AB | H | HR | BA |
|---|---|---|---|---|---|---|---|---|---|---|---|---|---|---|---|---|---|---|---|
| 1945 CHI N | 1 | 0 | 1.000 | 2.70 | 3 | 2 | 1 | 16.2 | 7 | 8 | 3 | 1 | 0 | 0 | 0 | 7 | 0 | 0 | .000 |

## Reggie Patterson

**PATTERSON, REGINALD ALLEN**        BR  TR  6'4"    180 lbs.
B. Nov. 7, 1958, Birmingham, Ala.

| | W | L | PCT | ERA | G | GS | CG | IP | H | BB | SO | ShO | W | L | SV | AB | H | HR | BA |
|---|---|---|---|---|---|---|---|---|---|---|---|---|---|---|---|---|---|---|---|
| 1981 CHI A | 0 | 1 | .000 | 14.14 | 6 | 1 | 0 | 7 | 14 | 6 | 2 | 0 | 0 | 0 | 0 | 0 | 0 | 0 | – |
| 1983 CHI N | 1 | 2 | .333 | 4.82 | 5 | 2 | 0 | 18.2 | 17 | 6 | 10 | 0 | 0 | 1 | 0 | 6 | 0 | 0 | .000 |
| 1984 | 0 | 1 | .000 | 10.50 | 3 | 1 | 0 | 6 | 10 | 2 | 5 | 0 | 0 | 0 | 0 | 2 | 0 | 0 | .000 |

| | W | L | PCT | ERA | G | GS | CG | IP | H | BB | SO | ShO | Relief Pitching W | L | SV | BATTING AB | H | HR | BA |
|---|---|---|---|---|---|---|---|---|---|---|---|---|---|---|---|---|---|---|---|

## Reggie Patterson continued

| | W | L | PCT | ERA | G | GS | CG | IP | H | BB | SO | ShO | W | L | SV | AB | H | HR | BA |
|---|---|---|---|---|---|---|---|---|---|---|---|---|---|---|---|---|---|---|---|
| 1985 | 3 | 0 | 1.000 | 3.00 | 8 | 5 | 1 | 39 | 36 | 10 | 17 | 0 | 0 | 0 | 0 | 10 | 1 | 0 | .100 |
| 4 yrs. | 4 | 4 | .500 | 5.22 | 22 | 9 | 1 | 70.2 | 77 | 24 | 34 | 0 | 0 | 1 | 0 | 18 | 1 | 0 | .056 |
| 3 yrs. | 4 | 3 | .571 | 4.24 | 16 | 8 | 1 | 63.2 | 63 | 18 | 32 | 0 | 0 | 1 | 0 | 18 | 1 | 0 | .056 |

## Mike Paul

**PAUL, MICHAEL GEORGE**    BL TL 6'   175 lbs.
B. Apr. 18, 1945, Detroit, Mich.

| | W | L | PCT | ERA | G | GS | CG | IP | H | BB | SO | ShO | W | L | SV | AB | H | HR | BA |
|---|---|---|---|---|---|---|---|---|---|---|---|---|---|---|---|---|---|---|---|
| 1968 CLE A | 5 | 8 | .385 | 3.93 | 36 | 7 | 0 | 91.2 | 72 | 35 | 87 | 0 | 2 | 5 | 3 | 24 | 4 | 0 | .167 |
| 1969 | 5 | 10 | .333 | 3.61 | 47 | 12 | 0 | 117.1 | 104 | 54 | 98 | 0 | 4 | 3 | 2 | 27 | 0 | 0 | .000 |
| 1970 | 2 | 8 | .200 | 4.81 | 30 | 15 | 1 | 88 | 91 | 45 | 70 | 0 | 0 | 1 | 0 | 26 | 4 | 0 | .154 |
| 1971 | 2 | 7 | .222 | 5.95 | 17 | 12 | 1 | 62 | 78 | 14 | 33 | 0 | 0 | 0 | 0 | 19 | 1 | 0 | .053 |
| 1972 TEX A | 8 | 9 | .471 | 2.17 | 49 | 20 | 2 | 162 | 149 | 52 | 108 | 1 | 1 | 1 | 1 | 48 | 8 | 0 | .167 |
| 1973 2 teams | | | | | TEX A (36G 5–4) | | | | CHI N (11G 0–1) | | | | | | | | | | |
| " total | 5 | 5 | .500 | 4.71 | 47 | 11 | 1 | 105 | 121 | 45 | 55 | 0 | 1 | 1 | 2 | 4 | 0 | 0 | .000 |
| 1974 CHI N | 0 | 1 | .000 | 36.00 | 2 | 0 | 0 | 1 | 4 | 1 | 1 | 0 | 0 | 1 | 0 | 0 | 0 | 0 | – |
| 7 yrs. | 27 | 48 | .360 | 3.92 | 228 | 77 | 5 | 627 | 619 | 246 | 452 | 1 | 8 | 12 | 8 | 148 | 17 | 0 | .115 |
| 2 yrs. | 0 | 2 | .000 | 5.21 | 13 | 1 | 0 | 19 | 21 | 10 | 7 | 0 | 0 | 1 | 0 | 4 | 0 | 0 | – |

## George Pearce

**PEARCE, GEORGE THOMAS**    BL TL 5'10½" 175 lbs.
B. Jan. 10, 1888, Aurora, Ill.   D. Oct. 11, 1935, Van Buren, N. Y.

| | W | L | PCT | ERA | G | GS | CG | IP | H | BB | SO | ShO | W | L | SV | AB | H | HR | BA |
|---|---|---|---|---|---|---|---|---|---|---|---|---|---|---|---|---|---|---|---|
| 1912 CHI N | 0 | 0 | – | 5.52 | 3 | 2 | 0 | 14.2 | 15 | 12 | 9 | 0 | 0 | 0 | 0 | 6 | 1 | 0 | .167 |
| 1913 | 13 | 5 | .722 | 2.31 | 25 | 21 | 14 | 163.1 | 137 | 59 | 73 | 3 | 1 | 0 | 0 | 55 | 4 | 0 | .073 |
| 1914 | 8 | 12 | .400 | 3.51 | 30 | 16 | 4 | 141 | 122 | 65 | 78 | 0 | 2 | 3 | 1 | 45 | 4 | 0 | .089 |
| 1915 | 13 | 9 | .591 | 3.32 | 36 | 20 | 8 | 176 | 158 | 77 | 96 | 2 | 4 | 1 | 0 | 56 | 11 | 0 | .196 |
| 1916 | 0 | 0 | – | 2.08 | 4 | 1 | 0 | 4.1 | 6 | 1 | 0 | 0 | 0 | 0 | 0 | 0 | 0 | 0 | – |
| 1917 STL N | 1 | 1 | .500 | 3.48 | 5 | 0 | 0 | 10.1 | 7 | 3 | 4 | 0 | 1 | 1 | 0 | 4 | 0 | 0 | .000 |
| 6 yrs. | 35 | 27 | .565 | 3.11 | 103 | 60 | 26 | 509.2 | 445 | 217 | 260 | 5 | 8 | 5 | 1 | 166 | 20 | 0 | .120 |
| 5 yrs. | 34 | 26 | .567 | 3.10 | 98 | 60 | 26 | 499.1 | 438 | 214 | 256 | 5 | 7 | 4 | 1 | 162 | 20 | 0 | .123 |

## Ken Penner

**PENNER, KENNETH WILLIAM**    BL TR 5'11½" 170 lbs.
B. Apr. 24, 1896, Booneville, Ind.   D. May 28, 1959, Sacramento, Calif.

| | W | L | PCT | ERA | G | GS | CG | IP | H | BB | SO | ShO | W | L | SV | AB | H | HR | BA |
|---|---|---|---|---|---|---|---|---|---|---|---|---|---|---|---|---|---|---|---|
| 1916 CLE A | 1 | 0 | 1.000 | 4.26 | 4 | 2 | 0 | 12.2 | 14 | 4 | 5 | 0 | 0 | 0 | 0 | 0 | 0 | 0 | .000 |
| 1929 CHI N | 0 | 1 | .000 | 2.84 | 5 | 0 | 0 | 12.2 | 14 | 6 | 3 | 0 | 0 | 1 | 0 | 4 | 1 | 0 | .250 |
| 2 yrs. | 1 | 1 | .500 | 3.55 | 9 | 2 | 0 | 25.1 | *28 | 10 | 8 | 0 | 0 | 1 | 0 | 6 | 1 | 0 | .167 |
| 1 yr. | 0 | 1 | .000 | 2.84 | 5 | 0 | 0 | 12.2 | 14 | 6 | 3 | 0 | 0 | 1 | 0 | 4 | 1 | 0 | .250 |

## Harry Perkowski

**PERKOWSKI, HARRY WALTER**    BL TL 6'2½" 196 lbs.
B. Sept. 6, 1922, Dante, Va.

| | W | L | PCT | ERA | G | GS | CG | IP | H | BB | SO | ShO | W | L | SV | AB | H | HR | BA |
|---|---|---|---|---|---|---|---|---|---|---|---|---|---|---|---|---|---|---|---|
| 1947 CIN N | 0 | 0 | – | 3.68 | 3 | 1 | 0 | 7.1 | 12 | 3 | 2 | 0 | 0 | 0 | 0 | 1 | 0 | 0 | .000 |
| 1949 | 1 | 1 | .500 | 4.56 | 5 | 3 | 2 | 23.2 | 21 | 14 | 3 | 0 | 0 | 0 | 0 | 9 | 3 | 0 | .333 |
| 1950 | 0 | 0 | – | 5.24 | 22 | 0 | 0 | 34.1 | 36 | 23 | 19 | 0 | 0 | 0 | 0 | 22 | 7 | 0 | .318 |
| 1951 | 3 | 6 | .333 | 2.82 | 35 | 7 | 1 | 102 | 96 | 46 | 56 | 0 | 0 | 2 | 1 | 25 | 1 | 0 | .040 |
| 1952 | 12 | 10 | .545 | 3.80 | 33 | 24 | 11 | 194 | 197 | 89 | 86 | 1 | 0 | 2 | 0 | 75 | 12 | 0 | .160 |
| 1953 | 12 | 11 | .522 | 4.52 | 33 | 25 | 7 | 193 | 204 | 62 | 70 | 2 | 2 | 0 | 2 | 69 | 14 | 0 | .203 |
| 1954 | 2 | 8 | .200 | 6.11 | 28 | 12 | 3 | 95.2 | 100 | 62 | 32 | 1 | 0 | 2 | 0 | 25 | 4 | 1 | .160 |
| 1955 CHI N | 3 | 4 | .429 | 5.29 | 25 | 4 | 0 | 47.2 | 53 | 25 | 28 | 0 | 3 | 1 | 2 | 13 | 2 | 0 | .154 |
| 8 yrs. | 33 | 40 | .452 | 4.37 | 184 | 76 | 24 | 697.2 | 719 | 324 | 296 | 4 | 5 | 7 | 5 | 239 | 43 | 1 | .180 |
| 1 yr. | 3 | 4 | .429 | 5.29 | 25 | 4 | 0 | 47.2 | 53 | 25 | 28 | 0 | 3 | 1 | 2 | 13 | 2 | 0 | .154 |

## Jon Perlman

**PERLMAN, JONATHAN SAMUEL**    BL TR 6'3" 185 lbs.
B. Dec. 13, 1956, Dallas, Tex.

| | W | L | PCT | ERA | G | GS | CG | IP | H | BB | SO | ShO | W | L | SV | AB | H | HR | BA |
|---|---|---|---|---|---|---|---|---|---|---|---|---|---|---|---|---|---|---|---|
| 1985 CHI N | 1 | 0 | 1.000 | 11.42 | 6 | 0 | 0 | 8.2 | 10 | 8 | 4 | 0 | 1 | 0 | 0 | 1 | 0 | 0 | .000 |

## Scott Perry

**PERRY, HERBERT SCOTT**    BL TR 6'1" 195 lbs.
B. Apr. 17, 1891, Dennison, Tex.   D. Oct. 27, 1959, Kansas City, Mo.

| | W | L | PCT | ERA | G | GS | CG | IP | H | BB | SO | ShO | W | L | SV | AB | H | HR | BA |
|---|---|---|---|---|---|---|---|---|---|---|---|---|---|---|---|---|---|---|---|
| 1915 STL A | 0 | 0 | – | 13.50 | 1 | 1 | 0 | 2 | 5 | 1 | 0 | 0 | 0 | 0 | 0 | 0 | 0 | 0 | – |
| 1916 CHI N | 2 | 1 | .667 | 2.54 | 4 | 3 | 2 | 28.1 | 30 | 3 | 10 | 1 | 0 | 0 | 0 | 11 | 3 | 0 | .273 |
| 1917 CIN N | 0 | 0 | – | 6.75 | 4 | 1 | 0 | 13.1 | 17 | 8 | 4 | 0 | 0 | 0 | 0 | 5 | 0 | 0 | .000 |
| 1918 PHI A | 21 | 19 | .525 | 1.98 | 44 | 36 | 30 | 332.1 | 295 | 111 | 81 | 4 | 4 | 2 | 1 | 112 | 15 | 0 | .134 |
| 1919 | 4 | 17 | .190 | 3.58 | 25 | 21 | 12 | 183.2 | 193 | 72 | 38 | 0 | 0 | 2 | 1 | 59 | 8 | 0 | .136 |
| 1920 | 11 | 25 | .306 | 3.62 | 42 | 34 | 20 | 263.2 | 310 | 65 | 79 | 1 | 1 | 2 | 1 | 83 | 13 | 1 | .157 |
| 1921 | 3 | 6 | .333 | 4.11 | 12 | 8 | 5 | 70 | 77 | 24 | 19 | 0 | 0 | 1 | 1 | 26 | 1 | 0 | .038 |
| 7 yrs. | 41 | 68 | .376 | 3.07 | 132 | 104 | 69 | 893.1 | 927 | 284 | 231 | 6 | 5 | 7 | 4 | 296 | 40 | 1 | .135 |
| 1 yr. | 2 | 1 | .667 | 2.54 | 4 | 3 | 2 | 28.1 | 30 | 3 | 10 | 1 | 0 | 0 | 0 | 11 | 3 | 0 | .273 |

## Johnny Peters

**PETERS, JOHN PAUL**    BR TR 180 lbs.
B. Apr. 8, 1850, Louisiana, Mo.   D. Jan. 4, 1924, St. Louis, Mo.

| | W | L | PCT | ERA | G | GS | CG | IP | H | BB | SO | ShO | W | L | SV | AB | H | HR | BA |
|---|---|---|---|---|---|---|---|---|---|---|---|---|---|---|---|---|---|---|---|
| 1876 CHI N | 0 | 0 | – | 0.00 | 1 | 0 | 0 | 1 | 1 | 1 | 0 | 0 | 0 | 0 | 1 | * | | | |

## Bob Pettit

**PETTIT, ROBERT HENRY**    BL 5'9" 160 lbs.
B. July 19, 1861, Williamstown, Mass.   D. Nov. 1, 1910, Derby, Conn.

| | W | L | PCT | ERA | G | GS | CG | IP | H | BB | SO | ShO | W | L | SV | AB | H | HR | BA |
|---|---|---|---|---|---|---|---|---|---|---|---|---|---|---|---|---|---|---|---|
| 1887 CHI N | 0 | 0 | – | 0.00 | 1 | 0 | 0 | 1 | 3 | 2 | 0 | 0 | 0 | 0 | 1 | * | | | |

## Jesse Petty

**PETTY, JESSE LEE (The Silver Fox)**    BR TL 6' 195 lbs.
B. Nov. 23, 1894, Orr, Okla.   D. Oct. 23, 1971, St. Paul, Minn.

| | W | L | PCT | ERA | G | GS | CG | IP | H | BB | SO | ShO | W | L | SV | AB | H | HR | BA |
|---|---|---|---|---|---|---|---|---|---|---|---|---|---|---|---|---|---|---|---|
| 1921 CLE A | 0 | 0 | – | 2.00 | 4 | 0 | 0 | 9 | 10 | 0 | 0 | 0 | 0 | 0 | 0 | 2 | 0 | 0 | .000 |
| 1925 BKN N | 9 | 9 | .500 | 4.88 | 28 | 22 | 7 | 153 | 188 | 47 | 39 | 0 | 3 | 0 | 0 | 50 | 7 | 0 | .140 |

| | W | L | PCT | ERA | G | GS | CG | IP | H | BB | SO | ShO | Relief Pitching W | L | SV | BATTING AB | H | HR | BA |
|---|---|---|---|---|---|---|---|---|---|---|---|---|---|---|---|---|---|---|---|

## Jesse Petty continued

| | W | L | PCT | ERA | G | GS | CG | IP | H | BB | SO | ShO | W | L | SV | AB | H | HR | BA |
|---|---|---|---|---|---|---|---|---|---|---|---|---|---|---|---|---|---|---|---|
| 1926 | 17 | 17 | .500 | 2.84 | 38 | 33 | 23 | 275.2 | 246 | 79 | 101 | 1 | 2 | 1 | 1 | 97 | 17 | 0 | .175 |
| 1927 | 13 | 18 | .419 | 2.98 | 42 | 33 | 19 | 271.2 | 263 | 53 | 101 | 2 | 2 | 1 | 1 | 91 | 9 | 0 | .099 |
| 1928 | 15 | 15 | .500 | 4.04 | 40 | 31 | 15 | 234 | 264 | 56 | 74 | 2 | 1 | 2 | 1 | 81 | 9 | 0 | .111 |
| 1929 **PIT N** | 11 | 10 | .524 | 3.71 | 36 | 25 | 12 | 184.1 | 197 | 42 | 58 | 1 | 1 | 0 | 0 | 67 | 7 | 0 | .104 |
| 1930 **2 teams** | | | PIT N | (10G 1–6) | | | CHI N | (9G 1–3) | | | | | | | | | | | |
| " total | 2 | 9 | .182 | 5.69 | 19 | 10 | 0 | 80.2 | 118 | 19 | 34 | 0 | 1 | 1 | 1 | 25 | 4 | 0 | .160 |
| 7 yrs. | 67 | 78 | .462 | 3.68 | 207 | 154 | 76 | 1208.1 | 1286 | 296 | 407 | 6 | 10 | 5 | 4 | 413 | 53 | 0 | .128 |
| 1 yr. | 1 | 3 | .250 | 2.97 | 9 | 3 | 0 | 39.1 | 51 | 6 | 18 | 0 | 1 | 0 | 0 | 13 | 3 | 0 | .231 |

## Big Jeff Pfeffer

**PFEFFER, FRANCIS XAVIER**       BR TR
Brother of Jeff Pfeffer.
B. Mar. 31, 1882, Champaign, Ill.    D. Dec. 19, 1954, Kankakee, Ill.

| | W | L | PCT | ERA | G | GS | CG | IP | H | BB | SO | ShO | W | L | SV | AB | H | HR | BA |
|---|---|---|---|---|---|---|---|---|---|---|---|---|---|---|---|---|---|---|---|
| 1905 **CHI N** | 4 | 5 | .444 | 2.50 | 15 | 11 | 9 | 101 | 84 | 36 | 56 | 0 | 0 | 0 | 0 | 40 | 8 | 0 | .200 |
| 1906 **BOS N** | 13 | 22 | .371 | 2.95 | 35 | 35 | 33 | 302.1 | 270 | 114 | 158 | 4 | 0 | 0 | 0 | 158 | 31 | 1 | .196 |
| 1907 | 6 | 8 | .429 | 3.00 | 19 | 16 | 12 | 144 | 129 | 61 | 65 | 1 | 0 | 0 | 0 | 60 | 15 | 0 | .250 |
| 1908 | 0 | 0 | — | 12.60 | 4 | 0 | 0 | 10 | 18 | 8 | 3 | 0 | 0 | 0 | 0 | 2 | 0 | 0 | .000 |
| 1910 **CHI N** | 1 | 0 | 1.000 | 3.27 | 13 | 1 | 1 | 41.1 | 43 | 16 | 11 | 0 | 0 | 0 | 0 | 17 | 3 | 0 | .176 |
| 1911 **BOS N** | 7 | 5 | .583 | 4.73 | 26 | 6 | 4 | 97 | 116 | 57 | 24 | 1 | 4 | 2 | 2 | 46 | 9 | 1 | .196 |
| 6 yrs. | 31 | 40 | .437 | 3.30 | 112 | 69 | 59 | 695.2 | 660 | 292 | 317 | 6 | 4 | 2 | 2 | * | | | |
| 2 yrs. | 5 | 5 | .500 | 2.72 | 28 | 12 | 10 | 142.1 | 127 | 52 | 67 | 0 | 0 | 0 | 0 | 57 | 11 | 0 | .193 |

## Fred Pfeffer

**PFEFFER, NATHANIEL FREDERICK (Dandelion Fritz)**     BR TR 5'10½" 184 lbs.
B. Mar. 17, 1860, Louisville, Ky.    D. Apr. 10, 1932, Chicago, Ill.
Manager 1892.

| | W | L | PCT | ERA | G | GS | CG | IP | H | BB | SO | ShO | W | L | SV | AB | H | HR | BA |
|---|---|---|---|---|---|---|---|---|---|---|---|---|---|---|---|---|---|---|---|
| 1884 **CHI N** | 0 | 0 | — | 9.00 | 1 | 0 | 0 | 1 | 3 | 1 | 0 | 0 | 0 | 0 | 0 | 467 | 135 | 25 | .289 |
| 1885 | 2 | 1 | .667 | 2.56 | 5 | 2 | 2 | 31.2 | 26 | 8 | 13 | 0 | 1 | 0 | 2 | 469 | 113 | 6 | .241 |
| 1892 **LOU N** | 0 | 0 | — | 1.80 | 1 | 0 | 0 | 5 | 4 | 5 | 0 | 0 | 0 | 0 | 0 | 470 | 121 | 2 | .257 |
| 1894 | 0 | 0 | — | 2.57 | 1 | 0 | 0 | 7 | 8 | 6 | 0 | 0 | 0 | 0 | 0 | 409 | 126 | 5 | .308 |
| 4 yrs. | 2 | 1 | .667 | 2.62 | 8 | 2 | 2 | 44.2 | 41 | 20 | 13 | 0 | 1 | 0 | 2 | * | | | |
| 2 yrs. | 2 | 1 | .667 | 2.76 | 6 | 2 | 2 | 32.2 | 29 | 9 | 13 | 0 | 1 | 0 | 2 | 4280 | 1080 | 79 | .252 |

## Jack Pfiester

**PFIESTER, JOHN ALBERT (Jack the Giant Killer)**     BR TL 5'11" 180 lbs.
Born John Albert Hagenbush.
B. May 24, 1878, Cincinnati, Ohio    D. Sept. 3, 1953, Twightwee, Ohio

| | W | L | PCT | ERA | G | GS | CG | IP | H | BB | SO | ShO | W | L | SV | AB | H | HR | BA |
|---|---|---|---|---|---|---|---|---|---|---|---|---|---|---|---|---|---|---|---|
| 1903 **PIT N** | 0 | 3 | .000 | 6.16 | 3 | 3 | 2 | 19 | 26 | 10 | 15 | 0 | 0 | 0 | 0 | 6 | 0 | 0 | .000 |
| 1904 | 1 | 1 | .500 | 7.20 | 3 | 2 | 1 | 20 | 28 | 9 | 6 | 0 | 0 | 0 | 0 | 7 | 2 | 0 | .286 |
| 1906 **CHI N** | 20 | 8 | .714 | 1.56 | 31 | 29 | 20 | 241.2 | 173 | 63 | 153 | 4 | 1 | 0 | 0 | 84 | 4 | 0 | .048 |
| 1907 | 15 | 9 | .625 | 1.15 | 30 | 22 | 13 | 195 | 143 | 48 | 90 | 3 | 2 | 1 | 0 | 64 | 6 | 0 | .094 |
| 1908 | 12 | 10 | .545 | 2.00 | 33 | 29 | 18 | 252 | 204 | 70 | 117 | 3 | 0 | 1 | 0 | 79 | 8 | 0 | .101 |
| 1909 | 17 | 6 | .739 | 2.43 | 29 | 25 | 13 | 196.2 | 179 | 49 | 73 | 5 | 1 | 0 | 0 | 65 | 11 | 0 | .169 |
| 1910 | 6 | 3 | .667 | 1.79 | 14 | 13 | 5 | 100.1 | 82 | 26 | 34 | 2 | 0 | 0 | 0 | 33 | 3 | 0 | .091 |
| 1911 | 0 | 4 | .000 | 4.01 | 6 | 5 | 3 | 33.2 | 34 | 18 | 15 | 0 | 0 | 0 | 0 | 11 | 2 | 0 | .182 |
| 8 yrs. | 71 | 44 | .617 | 2.04 | 149 | 128 | 75 | 1058.1 | 869 | 293 | 503 | 17 | 4 | 2 | 0 | 349 | 36 | 0 | .103 |
| 6 yrs. | 70 | 40 | .636 | 1.86 | 143 | 123 | 72 | 1019.1 | 815 | 274 | 482 | 17 | 4 | 2 | 0 | 336 | 34 | 0 | .101 |
| | | | | **6th** | **2nd** | | | | | | | | | | | | | | |

**WORLD SERIES**

| | W | L | PCT | ERA | G | GS | CG | IP | H | BB | SO | ShO | W | L | SV | AB | H | HR | BA |
|---|---|---|---|---|---|---|---|---|---|---|---|---|---|---|---|---|---|---|---|
| 1906 **CHI N** | 0 | 2 | .000 | 6.10 | 2 | 1 | 1 | 10.1 | 7 | 3 | 11 | 0 | 0 | 0 | 0 | 2 | 0 | 0 | .000 |
| 1907 | 1 | 0 | 1.000 | 1.00 | 1 | 1 | 1 | 9 | 9 | 1 | 3 | 0 | 0 | 0 | 0 | 2 | 0 | 0 | .000 |
| 1908 | 0 | 1 | .000 | 7.88 | 1 | 1 | 0 | 8 | 10 | 3 | 1 | 0 | 0 | 0 | 0 | 2 | 0 | 0 | .000 |
| 1910 | 0 | 0 | — | 0.00 | 1 | 0 | 0 | 6.2 | 9 | 1 | 1 | 0 | 0 | 0 | 0 | 2 | 0 | 0 | .000 |
| 4 yrs. | 1 | 3 | .250 | 3.97 | 5 | 3 | 2 | 34 | 35 | 8 | 16 | 0 | 0 | 0 | 0 | 8 | 0 | 0 | .000 |

## Taylor Phillips

**PHILLIPS, WILLIAM TAYLOR (Tay)**     BL TL 5'11" 185 lbs.
B. June 18, 1933, Atlanta, Ga.

| | W | L | PCT | ERA | G | GS | CG | IP | H | BB | SO | ShO | W | L | SV | AB | H | HR | BA |
|---|---|---|---|---|---|---|---|---|---|---|---|---|---|---|---|---|---|---|---|
| 1956 **MIL N** | 5 | 3 | .625 | 2.26 | 23 | 6 | 3 | 87.2 | 69 | 33 | 36 | 0 | 2 | 1 | 2 | 21 | 0 | 0 | .000 |
| 1957 | 3 | 2 | .600 | 5.55 | 27 | 6 | 0 | 73 | 82 | 40 | 36 | 0 | 2 | 1 | 2 | 20 | 2 | 0 | .100 |
| 1958 **CHI N** | 7 | 10 | .412 | 4.76 | 39 | 27 | 5 | 170.1 | 178 | 79 | 102 | 1 | 1 | 0 | 1 | 54 | 3 | 0 | .056 |
| 1959 **2 teams** | | | CHI N | (7G 0–2) | | | PHI N | (32G 1–4) | | | | | | | | | | | |
| " total | 1 | 6 | .143 | 5.54 | 39 | 5 | 1 | 79.2 | 94 | 42 | 40 | 0 | 0 | 3 | 1 | 15 | 1 | 0 | .067 |
| 1960 **PHI N** | 0 | 1 | .000 | 8.36 | 10 | 1 | 0 | 14 | 21 | 4 | 6 | 0 | 0 | 0 | 0 | 1 | 0 | 0 | .000 |
| 1963 **CHI A** | 0 | 0 | — | 10.29 | 9 | 0 | 0 | 14 | 16 | 13 | 10 | 0 | 0 | 0 | 0 | 2 | 0 | 0 | .000 |
| 6 yrs. | 16 | 22 | .421 | 4.82 | 147 | 45 | 9 | 438.2 | 460 | 211 | 233 | 1 | 5 | 5 | 6 | 113 | 6 | 0 | .053 |
| 2 yrs. | 7 | 12 | .368 | 5.01 | 46 | 29 | 5 | 187 | 200 | 90 | 107 | 1 | 1 | 0 | 1 | 58 | 3 | 0 | .052 |

## Tom Phoebus

**PHOEBUS, THOMAS HAROLD**     BR TR 5'8" 185 lbs.
B. Apr. 7, 1942, Baltimore, Md.

| | W | L | PCT | ERA | G | GS | CG | IP | H | BB | SO | ShO | W | L | SV | AB | H | HR | BA |
|---|---|---|---|---|---|---|---|---|---|---|---|---|---|---|---|---|---|---|---|
| 1966 **BAL A** | 2 | 1 | .667 | 1.23 | 3 | 3 | 2 | 22 | 16 | 6 | 17 | 2 | 0 | 0 | 0 | 6 | 1 | 0 | .167 |
| 1967 | 14 | 9 | .609 | 3.33 | 33 | 33 | 7 | 208 | 177 | 114 | 179 | 4 | 0 | 0 | 0 | 76 | 11 | 1 | .145 |
| 1968 | 15 | 15 | .500 | 2.62 | 36 | 36 | 9 | 240.2 | 186 | 105 | 193 | 3 | 0 | 0 | 0 | 82 | 15 | 1 | .183 |
| 1969 | 14 | 7 | .667 | 3.52 | 35 | 33 | 6 | 202 | 180 | 87 | 117 | 2 | 0 | 0 | 0 | 75 | 15 | 0 | .200 |
| 1970 | 5 | 5 | .500 | 3.07 | 27 | 21 | 3 | 135 | 106 | 62 | 72 | 0 | 0 | 0 | 0 | 43 | 7 | 0 | .163 |
| 1971 **SD N** | 3 | 11 | .214 | 4.47 | 29 | 21 | 2 | 133 | 144 | 64 | 80 | 0 | 0 | 0 | 0 | 36 | 6 | 0 | .167 |
| 1972 **2 teams** | | | SD N | (1G 0–1) | | | CHI N | (37G 3–3) | | | | | | | | | | | |
| " total | 3 | 4 | .429 | 4.04 | 38 | 2 | 0 | 89 | 79 | 51 | 67 | 0 | 3 | 2 | 6 | 17 | 2 | 0 | .118 |
| 7 yrs. | 56 | 52 | .519 | 3.33 | 201 | 149 | 29 | 1029.2 | 888 | 489 | 725 | 11 | 3 | 2 | 6 | 335 | 57 | 2 | .170 |
| 1 yr. | 3 | 3 | .500 | 3.78 | 37 | 1 | 0 | 83.1 | 76 | 45 | 59 | 0 | 3 | 2 | 6 | 15 | 2 | 0 | .133 |

**WORLD SERIES**

| | W | L | PCT | ERA | G | GS | CG | IP | H | BB | SO | ShO | W | L | SV | AB | H | HR | BA |
|---|---|---|---|---|---|---|---|---|---|---|---|---|---|---|---|---|---|---|---|
| 1970 **BAL A** | 1 | 0 | 1.000 | 0.00 | 1 | 0 | 0 | 1.2 | 1 | 1 | 0 | 0 | 1 | 0 | 0 | 0 | 0 | 0 | — |

| | W | L | PCT | ERA | G | GS | CG | IP | H | BB | SO | ShO | Relief Pitching W | L | SV | BATTING AB | H | HR | BA |
|---|---|---|---|---|---|---|---|---|---|---|---|---|---|---|---|---|---|---|---|

## Bill Phyle

**PHYLE, WILLIAM JOSEPH** TR
B. June 25, 1875, Duluth, Minn.   D. Aug. 6, 1953, Los Angeles, Calif.

| | W | L | PCT | ERA | G | GS | CG | IP | H | BB | SO | ShO | W | L | SV | AB | H | HR | BA |
|---|---|---|---|---|---|---|---|---|---|---|---|---|---|---|---|---|---|---|---|
| 1898 CHI N | 2 | 1 | .667 | 0.78 | 3 | 3 | 3 | 23 | 24 | 6 | 4 | 2 | 0 | 0 | 0 | 9 | 1 | 0 | .111 |
| 1899 | 1 | 8 | .111 | 4.20 | 10 | 9 | 9 | 83.2 | 92 | 29 | 10 | 0 | 0 | 0 | 1 | 34 | 6 | 0 | .176 |
| 1901 NY N | 7 | 10 | .412 | 4.27 | 24 | 19 | 16 | 168.2 | 208 | 54 | 62 | 0 | 0 | 0 | 1 | 66 | 12 | 0 | .182 |
| 1906 STL N | 0 | 0 | – | 0.00 | 2 | 0 | 0 | 0 | 0 | 0 | 0 | 0 | 0 | 0 | 0 | 73 | 13 | 0 | .178 |
| 4 yrs. | 10 | 19 | .345 | 3.96 | 37 | 31 | 28 | 275.1 | 324 | 89 | 76 | 2 | 0 | 0 | 2 | 182 | 32 | 0 | .176 |
| 2 yrs. | 3 | 9 | .250 | 3.46 | 13 | 12 | 12 | 106.2 | 116 | 35 | 14 | 2 | 0 | 0 | 1 | 43 | 7 | 0 | .163 |

## Ray Pierce

**PIERCE, RAYMOND LESTER (Lefty)** BL TL 5'7" 156 lbs.
B. June 6, 1897, Emporia, Kans.   D. May 4, 1963, Denver, Colo.

| | W | L | PCT | ERA | G | GS | CG | IP | H | BB | SO | ShO | W | L | SV | AB | H | HR | BA |
|---|---|---|---|---|---|---|---|---|---|---|---|---|---|---|---|---|---|---|---|
| 1924 CHI N | 0 | 0 | – | 7.36 | 6 | 0 | 0 | 7.1 | 7 | 4 | 2 | 0 | 0 | 0 | 0 | 0 | 0 | 0 | – |
| 1925 PHI N | 5 | 4 | .556 | 5.50 | 23 | 8 | 4 | 90 | 134 | 24 | 18 | 0 | 1 | 1 | 0 | 28 | 5 | 0 | .179 |
| 1926 | 2 | 7 | .222 | 5.63 | 37 | 7 | 1 | 84.2 | 128 | 35 | 18 | 0 | 2 | 2 | 0 | 24 | 3 | 0 | .125 |
| 3 yrs. | 7 | 11 | .389 | 5.64 | 66 | 15 | 5 | 182 | 269 | 63 | 38 | 0 | 3 | 3 | 0 | 52 | 8 | 0 | .154 |
| 1 yr. | 0 | 0 | – | 7.36 | 6 | 0 | 0 | 7.1 | 7 | 4 | 2 | 0 | 0 | 0 | 0 | 0 | 0 | 0 | – |

## Bill Piercy

**PIERCY, WILLIAM BENTON (Wild Bill)** BR TR 6'1½" 170 lbs.
B. May 2, 1896, El Monte, Calif.   D. Aug. 28, 1951, Long Beach, Calif.

| | W | L | PCT | ERA | G | GS | CG | IP | H | BB | SO | ShO | W | L | SV | AB | H | HR | BA |
|---|---|---|---|---|---|---|---|---|---|---|---|---|---|---|---|---|---|---|---|
| 1917 NY A | 0 | 1 | .000 | 3.00 | 1 | 1 | 1 | 9 | 9 | 2 | 4 | 0 | 0 | 0 | 0 | 2 | 0 | 0 | .000 |
| 1921 | 5 | 4 | .556 | 2.98 | 14 | 10 | 5 | 81.2 | 82 | 28 | 35 | 1 | 1 | 1 | 0 | 28 | 6 | 0 | .214 |
| 1922 BOS A | 3 | 9 | .250 | 4.67 | 29 | 12 | 7 | 121.1 | 140 | 62 | 24 | 1 | 0 | 1 | 0 | 34 | 5 | 0 | .147 |
| 1923 | 8 | 17 | .320 | 3.41 | 30 | 24 | 11 | 187.1 | 193 | 73 | 51 | 0 | 0 | 4 | 0 | 53 | 7 | 0 | .132 |
| 1924 | 5 | 7 | .417 | 6.20 | 22 | 17 | 3 | 114.2 | 147 | 64 | 20 | 0 | 0 | 0 | 0 | 36 | 5 | 0 | .139 |
| 1926 CHI N | 6 | 5 | .545 | 4.48 | 19 | 5 | 1 | 90.1 | 96 | 37 | 31 | 0 | 4 | 3 | 0 | 35 | 9 | 0 | .257 |
| 6 yrs. | 27 | 43 | .386 | 4.29 | 115 | 69 | 28 | 604.1 | 667 | 266 | 165 | 2 | 5 | 9 | 0 | 188 | 32 | 0 | .170 |
| 1 yr. | 6 | 5 | .545 | 4.48 | 19 | 5 | 1 | 90.1 | 96 | 37 | 31 | 0 | 4 | 3 | 0 | 35 | 9 | 0 | .257 |

WORLD SERIES

| | W | L | PCT | ERA | G | GS | CG | IP | H | BB | SO | ShO | W | L | SV | AB | H | HR | BA |
|---|---|---|---|---|---|---|---|---|---|---|---|---|---|---|---|---|---|---|---|
| 1921 NY A | 0 | 0 | – | 0.00 | 1 | 0 | 0 | 1 | 2 | 0 | 2 | 0 | 0 | 0 | 0 | 0 | 0 | 0 | – |

## George Piktuzis

**PIKTUZIS, GEORGE RICHARD** BR TL 6'2" 200 lbs.
B. Jan. 3, 1932, Chicago, Ill.

| | W | L | PCT | ERA | G | GS | CG | IP | H | BB | SO | ShO | W | L | SV | AB | H | HR | BA |
|---|---|---|---|---|---|---|---|---|---|---|---|---|---|---|---|---|---|---|---|
| 1956 CHI N | 0 | 0 | – | 7.20 | 2 | 0 | 0 | 5 | 6 | 2 | 3 | 0 | 0 | 0 | 0 | 0 | 0 | 0 | – |

## Horacio Pina

**PINA, HORACIO GARCIA** BR TR 6'2" 177 lbs.
B. Mar. 12, 1945, Coahuila, Mexico

| | W | L | PCT | ERA | G | GS | CG | IP | H | BB | SO | ShO | W | L | SV | AB | H | HR | BA |
|---|---|---|---|---|---|---|---|---|---|---|---|---|---|---|---|---|---|---|---|
| 1968 CLE A | 1 | 1 | .500 | 1.72 | 12 | 3 | 0 | 31.1 | 24 | 15 | 24 | 0 | 0 | 0 | 2 | 6 | 0 | 0 | .000 |
| 1969 | 4 | 2 | .667 | 5.21 | 31 | 4 | 0 | 46.2 | 44 | 27 | 32 | 0 | 3 | 1 | 1 | 6 | 3 | 0 | .500 |
| 1970 WAS A | 5 | 3 | .625 | 2.79 | 61 | 0 | 0 | 71 | 66 | 35 | 41 | 0 | 5 | 3 | 6 | 3 | 0 | 0 | .000 |
| 1971 | 1 | 1 | .500 | 3.57 | 56 | 0 | 0 | 58 | 47 | 31 | 38 | 0 | 1 | 1 | 2 | 1 | 0 | 0 | .000 |
| 1972 TEX A | 2 | 7 | .222 | 3.20 | 60 | 0 | 0 | 76 | 61 | 43 | 60 | 0 | 2 | 7 | 15 | 5 | 1 | 0 | .200 |
| 1973 OAK A | 6 | 3 | .667 | 2.76 | 47 | 0 | 0 | 88 | 58 | 34 | 41 | 0 | 6 | 3 | 8 | 0 | 0 | 0 | – |
| 1974 2 teams | | | | | CHI N (34G 3–4) | | | | CAL A (11G 1–2) | | | | | | | | | | |
| " total | 4 | 6 | .400 | 3.66 | 45 | 0 | 0 | 59 | 58 | 31 | 38 | 0 | 4 | 6 | 4 | 5 | 1 | 0 | .200 |
| 1978 PHI N | 0 | 0 | – | 0.00 | 2 | 0 | 0 | 2 | 0 | 0 | 4 | 0 | 0 | 0 | 0 | 1 | 0 | 0 | .000 |
| 8 yrs. | 23 | 23 | .500 | 3.25 | 314 | 7 | 0 | 432 | 358 | 216 | 278 | 0 | 21 | 21 | 38 | 27 | 5 | 0 | .185 |
| 1 yr. | 3 | 4 | .429 | 4.02 | 34 | 0 | 0 | 47 | 49 | 28 | 32 | 0 | 3 | 4 | 4 | 5 | 1 | 0 | .200 |

LEAGUE CHAMPIONSHIP SERIES

| | W | L | PCT | ERA | G | GS | CG | IP | H | BB | SO | ShO | W | L | SV | AB | H | HR | BA |
|---|---|---|---|---|---|---|---|---|---|---|---|---|---|---|---|---|---|---|---|
| 1973 OAK A | 0 | 0 | – | 0.00 | 1 | 0 | 0 | 2 | 3 | 1 | 1 | 0 | 0 | 0 | 0 | 0 | 0 | 0 | – |

WORLD SERIES

| | W | L | PCT | ERA | G | GS | CG | IP | H | BB | SO | ShO | W | L | SV | AB | H | HR | BA |
|---|---|---|---|---|---|---|---|---|---|---|---|---|---|---|---|---|---|---|---|
| 1973 OAK A | 0 | 0 | – | 0.00 | 2 | 0 | 0 | 3 | 6 | 2 | 0 | 0 | 0 | 0 | 0 | 0 | 0 | 0 | – |

## Juan Pizarro

**PIZARRO, JUAN CORDOVA** BL TL 5'11" 170 lbs.
B. Feb. 7, 1938, Santurce, Puerto Rico

| | W | L | PCT | ERA | G | GS | CG | IP | H | BB | SO | ShO | W | L | SV | AB | H | HR | BA |
|---|---|---|---|---|---|---|---|---|---|---|---|---|---|---|---|---|---|---|---|
| 1957 MIL N | 5 | 6 | .455 | 4.62 | 24 | 10 | 3 | 99.1 | 99 | 51 | 68 | 0 | 3 | 1 | 0 | 36 | 9 | 1 | .250 |
| 1958 | 6 | 4 | .600 | 2.70 | 26 | 10 | 7 | 96.2 | 75 | 47 | 84 | 1 | 1 | 1 | 1 | 32 | 8 | 0 | .250 |
| 1959 | 6 | 2 | .750 | 3.77 | 29 | 14 | 6 | 133.2 | 117 | 70 | 126 | 2 | 0 | 0 | 0 | 41 | 5 | 0 | .122 |
| 1960 | 6 | 7 | .462 | 4.55 | 21 | 17 | 3 | 114.2 | 105 | 72 | 88 | 0 | 1 | 1 | 0 | 40 | 11 | 0 | .275 |
| 1961 CHI A | 14 | 7 | .667 | 3.05 | 39 | 25 | 12 | 194.2 | 164 | 89 | 188 | 1 | 0 | 0 | 2 | 69 | 17 | 0 | .246 |
| 1962 | 12 | 14 | .462 | 3.81 | 36 | 32 | 9 | 203.1 | 182 | 97 | 173 | 1 | 3 | 0 | 1 | 69 | 11 | 0 | .159 |
| 1963 | 16 | 8 | .667 | 2.39 | 32 | 28 | 10 | 214.2 | 177 | 63 | 163 | 3 | 2 | 0 | 1 | 73 | 13 | 2 | .178 |
| 1964 | 19 | 9 | .679 | 2.56 | 33 | 33 | 11 | 239 | 193 | 55 | 162 | 4 | 0 | 0 | 0 | 90 | 19 | 3 | .211 |
| 1965 | 6 | 3 | .667 | 3.43 | 18 | 12 | 9 | 97 | 96 | 37 | 65 | 1 | 0 | 0 | 0 | 34 | 8 | 1 | .235 |
| 1966 | 8 | 6 | .571 | 3.76 | 34 | 9 | 1 | 88.2 | 91 | 39 | 42 | 0 | 4 | 2 | 3 | 26 | 4 | 0 | .154 |
| 1967 PIT N | 8 | 10 | .444 | 3.95 | 50 | 9 | 1 | 107 | 99 | 52 | 96 | 1 | 7 | 5 | 9 | 27 | 7 | 0 | .259 |
| 1968 2 teams | | | | | PIT N (12G 1–1) | | | | BOS A (19G 6–8) | | | | | | | | | | |
| " total | 7 | 9 | .438 | 3.56 | 31 | 12 | 6 | 118.2 | 111 | 54 | 90 | 0 | 2 | 3 | 2 | 33 | 5 | 0 | .152 |
| 1969 3 teams | | | | | BOS A (6G 0–1) | | | CLE A (48G 3–3) | | | | OAK A (3G 1–1) | | | | | | | |
| " total | 4 | 5 | .444 | 3.35 | 57 | 4 | 1 | 99.1 | 84 | 58 | 52 | 0 | 3 | 5 | 7 | 20 | 5 | 0 | .250 |
| 1970 CHI N | 0 | 0 | – | 4.50 | 12 | 0 | 0 | 16 | 16 | 9 | 14 | 0 | 0 | 0 | 1 | 3 | 0 | 0 | .000 |
| 1971 | 6 | 5 | .538 | 3.48 | 16 | 14 | 7 | 101 | 78 | 40 | 67 | 3 | 0 | 0 | 0 | 34 | 6 | 1 | .176 |
| 1972 | 4 | 5 | .444 | 3.97 | 16 | 7 | 1 | 59 | 66 | 32 | 24 | 0 | 3 | 0 | 1 | 21 | 3 | 0 | .143 |
| 1973 2 teams | | | | | CHI N (2G 0–1) | | | | HOU N (15G 2–2) | | | | | | | | | | |
| " total | 2 | 3 | .400 | 7.24 | 17 | 1 | 0 | 27.1 | 34 | 12 | 13 | 0 | 2 | 2 | 0 | 4 | 0 | 0 | .000 |
| 1974 PIT N | 2 | 2 | .500 | 1.88 | 7 | 2 | 0 | 24 | 20 | 11 | 7 | 0 | 2 | 0 | 0 | 6 | 2 | 0 | .333 |
| 18 yrs. | 131 | 105 | .555 | 3.43 | 488 | 245 | 79 | 2034 | 1807 | 888 | 1522 | 17 | 31 | 20 | 28 | 658 | 133 | 8 | .202 |
| 4 yrs. | 11 | 12 | .478 | 3.90 | 46 | 21 | 7 | 180 | 166 | 82 | 108 | 3 | 3 | 1 | 2 | 59 | 9 | 1 | .153 |

LEAGUE CHAMPIONSHIP SERIES

| | W | L | PCT | ERA | G | GS | CG | IP | H | BB | SO | ShO | W | L | SV | AB | H | HR | BA |
|---|---|---|---|---|---|---|---|---|---|---|---|---|---|---|---|---|---|---|---|
| 1974 PIT N | 0 | 0 | – | 0.00 | 1 | 0 | 0 | .2 | 0 | 1 | 0 | 0 | 0 | 0 | 0 | 0 | 0 | 0 | – |

WORLD SERIES

| | W | L | PCT | ERA | G | GS | CG | IP | H | BB | SO | ShO | W | L | SV | AB | H | HR | BA |
|---|---|---|---|---|---|---|---|---|---|---|---|---|---|---|---|---|---|---|---|
| 1957 MIL N | 0 | 0 | – | 10.80 | 1 | 0 | 0 | 1.2 | 3 | 2 | 1 | 0 | 0 | 0 | 0 | 1 | 0 | 0 | .000 |

| | W | L | PCT | ERA | G | GS | CG | IP | H | BB | SO | ShO | Relief Pitching W | L | SV | BATTING AB | H | HR | BA |
|---|---|---|---|---|---|---|---|---|---|---|---|---|---|---|---|---|---|---|---|

## Juan Pizarro continued

| | W | L | PCT | ERA | G | GS | CG | IP | H | BB | SO | ShO | W | L | SV | AB | H | HR | BA |
|---|---|---|---|---|---|---|---|---|---|---|---|---|---|---|---|---|---|---|---|
| 1958 | 0 | 0 | – | 5.40 | 1 | 0 | 0 | 1.2 | 2 | 1 | 3 | 0 | 0 | 0 | 0 | 0 | 0 | 0 | – |
| 2 yrs. | 0 | 0 | – | 8.10 | 2 | 0 | 0 | 3.1 | 5 | 3 | 4 | 0 | 0 | 0 | 0 | 1 | 0 | 0 | .000 |

## Tom Poholsky

**POHOLSKY, THOMAS GEORGE**                BR TR 6'3" 205 lbs.
B. Aug. 26, 1929, Detroit, Mich.

| | W | L | PCT | ERA | G | GS | CG | IP | H | BB | SO | ShO | W | L | SV | AB | H | HR | BA |
|---|---|---|---|---|---|---|---|---|---|---|---|---|---|---|---|---|---|---|---|
| 1950 STL N | 0 | 0 | – | 3.68 | 5 | 1 | 0 | 14.2 | 16 | 3 | 2 | 0 | 0 | 0 | 0 | 2 | 0 | 0 | .000 |
| 1951 | 7 | 13 | .350 | 4.43 | 38 | 26 | 10 | 195 | 204 | 68 | 70 | 1 | 1 | 2 | 1 | 67 | 14 | 0 | .209 |
| 1954 | 5 | 7 | .417 | 3.06 | 25 | 13 | 4 | 106 | 101 | 20 | 55 | 0 | 0 | 2 | 0 | 27 | 4 | 0 | .148 |
| 1955 | 9 | 11 | .450 | 3.81 | 30 | 24 | 8 | 151 | 143 | 35 | 66 | 2 | 0 | 0 | 0 | 44 | 8 | 0 | .182 |
| 1956 | 9 | 14 | .391 | 3.59 | 33 | 29 | 7 | 203 | 210 | 44 | 95 | 2 | 0 | 0 | 0 | 69 | 11 | 0 | .159 |
| 1957 CHI N | 1 | 7 | .125 | 4.93 | 28 | 11 | 1 | 84 | 117 | 22 | 28 | 0 | 0 | 0 | 0 | 19 | 2 | 0 | .105 |
| 6 yrs. | 31 | 52 | .373 | 3.93 | 159 | 104 | 30 | 753.2 | 791 | 192 | 316 | 5 | 1 | 4 | 1 | 228 | 39 | 0 | .171 |
| 1 yr. | 1 | 7 | .125 | 4.93 | 28 | 11 | 1 | 84 | 117 | 22 | 28 | 0 | 0 | 0 | 0 | 19 | 2 | 0 | .105 |

## Howie Pollet

**POLLET, HOWARD JOSEPH**                BL TL 6'1½" 175 lbs.
B. June 26, 1921, New Orleans, La.    D. Aug. 8, 1974, Houston, Tex.

| | W | L | PCT | ERA | G | GS | CG | IP | H | BB | SO | ShO | W | L | SV | AB | H | HR | BA |
|---|---|---|---|---|---|---|---|---|---|---|---|---|---|---|---|---|---|---|---|
| 1941 STL N | 5 | 2 | .714 | 1.93 | 9 | 8 | 6 | 70 | 55 | 27 | 37 | 2 | 0 | 0 | 0 | 28 | 5 | 0 | .179 |
| 1942 | 7 | 5 | .583 | 2.88 | 27 | 13 | 5 | 109.1 | 102 | 39 | 42 | 2 | 0 | 1 | 0 | 31 | 7 | 0 | .226 |
| 1943 | 8 | 4 | .667 | 1.75 | 16 | 14 | 12 | 118.1 | 83 | 32 | 61 | 5 | 0 | 0 | 0 | 43 | 7 | 0 | .163 |
| 1946 | 21 | 10 | .677 | 2.10 | 40 | 32 | 22 | 266 | 228 | 86 | 107 | 4 | 0 | 0 | 5 | 87 | 14 | 0 | .161 |
| 1947 | 9 | 11 | .450 | 4.34 | 37 | 24 | 9 | 176.1 | 195 | 87 | 73 | 0 | 1 | 0 | 2 | 65 | 15 | 0 | .231 |
| 1948 | 13 | 8 | .619 | 4.54 | 36 | 26 | 11 | 186.1 | 216 | 67 | 80 | 0 | 2 | 0 | 0 | 68 | 8 | 0 | .118 |
| 1949 | 20 | 9 | .690 | 2.77 | 39 | 28 | 17 | 230.2 | 228 | 59 | 108 | 5 | 3 | 1 | 1 | 82 | 16 | 0 | .195 |
| 1950 | 14 | 13 | .519 | 3.29 | 37 | 30 | 14 | 232.1 | 228 | 68 | 117 | 2 | 1 | 1 | 2 | 84 | 12 | 0 | .143 |
| 1951 2 teams | | | STL | N | (6G 0–3) | | PIT | N | (21G 6–10) | | | | | | | | | | |
| " total | 6 | 13 | .316 | 4.98 | 27 | 23 | 4 | 141 | 151 | 59 | 57 | 1 | 0 | 2 | 1 | 37 | 5 | 0 | .135 |
| 1952 PIT N | 7 | 16 | .304 | 4.12 | 31 | 30 | 9 | 214 | 217 | 71 | 90 | 1 | 0 | 0 | 0 | 68 | 13 | 0 | .191 |
| 1953 2 teams | | | PIT | N | (5G 1–1) | | CHI | N | (25G 5–6) | | | | | | | | | | |
| " total | 6 | 7 | .462 | 4.79 | 30 | 18 | 2 | 124 | 147 | 50 | 53 | 0 | 0 | 1 | 1 | 34 | 5 | 0 | .147 |
| 1954 CHI N | 8 | 10 | .444 | 3.58 | 20 | 20 | 4 | 128.1 | 131 | 54 | 58 | 2 | 0 | 0 | 0 | 47 | 13 | 0 | .277 |
| 1955 | 4 | 3 | .571 | 5.61 | 24 | 7 | 1 | 61 | 62 | 27 | 27 | 1 | 3 | 0 | 5 | 15 | 6 | 0 | .400 |
| 1956 2 teams | | | CHI | A | (11G 3–1) | | PIT | N | (19G 0–4) | | | | | | | | | | |
| " total | 3 | 5 | .375 | 3.62 | 30 | 4 | 0 | 49.2 | 45 | 19 | 24 | 0 | 3 | 4 | 3 | 9 | 3 | 0 | .333 |
| 14 yrs. | 131 | 116 | .530 | 3.51 | 403 | 277 | 116 | 2107.1 | 2088 | 745 | 934 | 25 | 13 | 10 | 20 | 698 | 129 | 0 | .185 |
| 3 yrs. | 17 | 19 | .472 | 4.19 | 69 | 43 | 7 | 300.2 | 313 | 125 | 130 | 3 | 3 | 0 | 6 | 93 | 23 | 0 | .247 |
| WORLD SERIES | | | | | | | | | | | | | | | | | | | |
| 1942 STL N | 0 | 0 | – | 0.00 | 1 | 0 | 0 | .1 | 0 | 0 | 0 | 0 | 0 | 0 | 0 | 0 | 0 | 0 | – |
| 1946 | 0 | 1 | .000 | 3.48 | 2 | 2 | 1 | 10.1 | 12 | 4 | 3 | 0 | 0 | 0 | 0 | 4 | 0 | 0 | .000 |
| 2 yrs. | 0 | 1 | .000 | 3.38 | 3 | 2 | 1 | 10.2 | 12 | 4 | 3 | 0 | 0 | 0 | 0 | 4 | 0 | 0 | .000 |

## Elmer Ponder

**PONDER, CHARLES ELMER**                BR TR 6' 178 lbs.
B. June 26, 1893, Reed, Okla.    D. Apr. 20, 1974, Albuquerque, N. M.

| | W | L | PCT | ERA | G | GS | CG | IP | H | BB | SO | ShO | W | L | SV | AB | H | HR | BA |
|---|---|---|---|---|---|---|---|---|---|---|---|---|---|---|---|---|---|---|---|
| 1917 PIT N | 1 | 1 | .500 | 1.69 | 3 | 2 | 1 | 21.1 | 12 | 6 | 11 | 1 | 0 | 0 | 0 | 7 | 0 | 0 | .000 |
| 1919 | 0 | 5 | .000 | 3.99 | 9 | 5 | 0 | 47.1 | 55 | 6 | 6 | 0 | 0 | 0 | 0 | 15 | 2 | 0 | .133 |
| 1920 | 11 | 15 | .423 | 2.62 | 33 | 23 | 13 | 196 | 182 | 40 | 62 | 2 | 3 | 3 | 0 | 59 | 7 | 0 | .119 |
| 1921 2 teams | | | PIT | N | (8G 2–0) | | CHI | N | (16G 3–6) | | | | | | | | | | |
| " total | 5 | 6 | .455 | 4.18 | 24 | 12 | 6 | 114 | 146 | 20 | 34 | 0 | 1 | 0 | 0 | 43 | 4 | 0 | .093 |
| 4 yrs. | 17 | 27 | .386 | 3.21 | 69 | 42 | 20 | 378.2 | 395 | 72 | 113 | 3 | 4 | 3 | 0 | 124 | 13 | 0 | .105 |
| 1 yr. | 3 | 6 | .333 | 4.74 | 16 | 11 | 5 | 89.1 | 117 | 17 | 31 | 0 | 0 | 0 | 0 | 33 | 4 | 0 | .121 |

## Tom Poorman

**POORMAN, THOMAS IVERSON**                BL TR 5'10½" 170 lbs.
B. Oct. 14, 1857, Lock Haven, Pa.    D. Feb. 18, 1905, Lock Haven, Pa.

| | W | L | PCT | ERA | G | GS | CG | IP | H | BB | SO | ShO | W | L | SV | AB | H | HR | BA |
|---|---|---|---|---|---|---|---|---|---|---|---|---|---|---|---|---|---|---|---|
| 1880 2 teams | | | BUF | N | (11G 1–8) | | CHI | N | (2G 2–0) | | | | | | | | | | |
| " total | 3 | 8 | .273 | 3.87 | 13 | 10 | 9 | 100 | 129 | 27 | 13 | 0 | 1 | 0 | 1 | 95 | 16 | 0 | .168 |
| 1884 TOL AA | 0 | 1 | .000 | 3.00 | 1 | 1 | 1 | 9 | 13 | 2 | 0 | 0 | 0 | 0 | 0 | 382 | 89 | 0 | .233 |
| 1887 PHI AA | 0 | 0 | – | 40.50 | 1 | 0 | 0 | .2 | 5 | 1 | 1 | 0 | 0 | 0 | 0 | 585 | 155 | 4 | .265 |
| 3 yrs. | 3 | 9 | .250 | 4.02 | 15 | 11 | 10 | 109.2 | 147 | 30 | 14 | 0 | 1 | 0 | 1 | * | | | |
| 1 yr. | 2 | 0 | 1.000 | 2.40 | 2 | 1 | 0 | 15 | 12 | 8 | 0 | 0 | 1 | 0 | 0 | 25 | 5 | 0 | .200 |

## Bob Porterfield

**PORTERFIELD, ERWIN COOLIDGE**                BR TR 6' 190 lbs.
B. Aug. 10, 1923, Newport, Va.    D. Apr. 28, 1980, Charlotte, N. C.

| | W | L | PCT | ERA | G | GS | CG | IP | H | BB | SO | ShO | W | L | SV | AB | H | HR | BA |
|---|---|---|---|---|---|---|---|---|---|---|---|---|---|---|---|---|---|---|---|
| 1948 NY A | 5 | 3 | .625 | 4.50 | 16 | 12 | 2 | 78 | 85 | 34 | 30 | 1 | 1 | 0 | 0 | 24 | 6 | 0 | .250 |
| 1949 | 2 | 5 | .286 | 4.06 | 12 | 8 | 3 | 57.2 | 53 | 29 | 25 | 0 | 0 | 2 | 0 | 19 | 1 | 0 | .053 |
| 1950 | 1 | 1 | .500 | 8.69 | 10 | 2 | 0 | 19.2 | 28 | 8 | 9 | 0 | 1 | 0 | 1 | 3 | 1 | 0 | .333 |
| 1951 2 teams | | | NY | A | (2G 0–0) | | WAS | A | (19G 9–8) | | | | | | | | | | |
| " total | 9 | 8 | .529 | 3.50 | 21 | 19 | 10 | 136.1 | 114 | 57 | 55 | 3 | 0 | 0 | 0 | 46 | 6 | 0 | .130 |
| 1952 WAS A | 13 | 14 | .481 | 2.72 | 31 | 29 | 15 | 231.1 | 222 | 85 | 80 | 3 | 1 | 0 | 0 | 79 | 15 | 0 | .190 |
| 1953 | 22 | 10 | .688 | 3.35 | 34 | 32 | 24 | 255 | 243 | 73 | 77 | 9 | 1 | 0 | 0 | 98 | 25 | 3 | .255 |
| 1954 | 13 | 15 | .464 | 3.32 | 32 | 31 | 21 | 244 | 249 | 77 | 82 | 2 | 1 | 0 | 0 | 88 | 9 | 1 | .102 |
| 1955 | 10 | 17 | .370 | 4.45 | 30 | 27 | 8 | 178 | 197 | 55 | 74 | 2 | 0 | 1 | 0 | 63 | 12 | 0 | .190 |
| 1956 BOS A | 3 | 12 | .200 | 5.14 | 25 | 18 | 4 | 126 | 127 | 64 | 53 | 1 | 0 | 2 | 0 | 43 | 14 | 1 | .326 |
| 1957 | 4 | 4 | .500 | 4.05 | 28 | 9 | 3 | 102.1 | 107 | 30 | 28 | 1 | 1 | 0 | 1 | 29 | 5 | 0 | .172 |
| 1958 2 teams | | | BOS | A | (2G 0–0) | | PIT | N | (37G 4–6) | | | | | | | | | | |
| " total | 4 | 6 | .400 | 3.34 | 39 | 6 | 2 | 91.2 | 81 | 19 | 40 | 1 | 2 | 3 | 5 | 20 | 1 | 1 | .050 |
| 1959 2 teams | | | PIT | N | (36G 1–2) | | CHI | N | (4G 0–0) | | | | | | | | | | |
| " total | 1 | 2 | .333 | 5.29 | 40 | 0 | 0 | 47.2 | 65 | 22 | 19 | 0 | 1 | 2 | 1 | 4 | 0 | 0 | .000 |
| 12 yrs. | 87 | 97 | .473 | 3.79 | 318 | 193 | 92 | 1567.2 | 1571 | 553 | 572 | 23 | 9 | 10 | 8 | 516 | 95 | 6 | .184 |
| 1 yr. | 0 | 0 | – | 11.37 | 4 | 0 | 0 | 6.1 | 14 | 3 | 0 | 0 | 0 | 0 | 0 | 1 | 0 | 0 | .000 |

| | W | L | PCT | ERA | G | GS | CG | IP | H | BB | SO | ShO | Relief Pitching W | L | SV | BATTING AB | H | HR | BA |
|---|---|---|---|---|---|---|---|---|---|---|---|---|---|---|---|---|---|---|---|

## Bill Powell

**POWELL, WILLIAM BURRIS**    BR TR 6'2½" 182 lbs.
B. May 8, 1885, Grafton, W. Va.    D. Sept. 28, 1967, East Liverpool, Ohio

| | W | L | PCT | ERA | G | GS | CG | IP | H | BB | SO | ShO | W | L | SV | AB | H | HR | BA |
|---|---|---|---|---|---|---|---|---|---|---|---|---|---|---|---|---|---|---|---|
| 1909 PIT N | 0 | 1 | .000 | 3.68 | 3 | 1 | 0 | 7.1 | 7 | 6 | 2 | 0 | 0 | 0 | 0 | 4 | 1 | 0 | .250 |
| 1910 | 4 | 6 | .400 | 2.40 | 12 | 9 | 4 | 75 | 65 | 34 | 23 | 2 | 1 | 0 | 0 | 23 | 6 | 0 | .261 |
| 1912 CHI N | 0 | 0 | — | 9.00 | 1 | 0 | 0 | 2 | 2 | 1 | 0 | 0 | 0 | 0 | 0 | 0 | 0 | 0 | — |
| 1913 CIN N | 0 | 1 | .000 | 54.00 | 1 | 1 | 0 | .1 | 2 | 2 | 0 | 0 | 0 | 0 | 0 | 0 | 0 | 0 | — |
| 4 yrs. | 4 | 8 | .333 | 2.87 | 17 | 11 | 4 | 84.2 | 76 | 43 | 25 | 2 | 1 | 0 | 0 | 27 | 7 | 0 | .259 |
| 1 yr. | 0 | 0 | — | 9.00 | 1 | 0 | 0 | 2 | 2 | 1 | 0 | 0 | 0 | 0 | 0 | 0 | 0 | 0 | — |

## Willie Prall

**PRALL, WILFRED ANTHONY**    BL TL 6'3" 200 lbs.
B. Apr. 20, 1950, Hackensack, N. J.

| | W | L | PCT | ERA | G | GS | CG | IP | H | BB | SO | ShO | W | L | SV | AB | H | HR | BA |
|---|---|---|---|---|---|---|---|---|---|---|---|---|---|---|---|---|---|---|---|
| 1975 CHI N | 0 | 2 | .000 | 8.40 | 3 | 3 | 0 | 15 | 21 | 8 | 7 | 0 | 0 | 0 | 0 | 4 | 0 | 0 | .000 |

## Mike Prendergast

**PRENDERGAST, MICHAEL THOMAS (Iron Mike)**    BR TR 5'9½" 165 lbs.
B. Dec. 15, 1888, Arlington, Ill.    D. Nov. 18, 1967, Omaha, Neb.

| | W | L | PCT | ERA | G | GS | CG | IP | H | BB | SO | ShO | W | L | SV | AB | H | HR | BA |
|---|---|---|---|---|---|---|---|---|---|---|---|---|---|---|---|---|---|---|---|
| 1914 CHI F | 5 | 9 | .357 | 2.38 | 30 | 19 | 7 | 136 | 131 | 40 | 71 | 1 | 0 | 1 | 0 | 37 | 4 | 0 | .108 |
| 1915 | 14 | 12 | .538 | 2.48 | 42 | 30 | 16 | 253.2 | 220 | 67 | 95 | 3 | 2 | 3 | 0 | 80 | 6 | 0 | .075 |
| 1916 CHI N | 6 | 11 | .353 | 2.31 | 35 | 10 | 4 | 152 | 127 | 23 | 56 | 2 | 3 | 4 | 2 | 46 | 7 | 0 | .152 |
| 1917 | 3 | 6 | .333 | 3.35 | 35 | 8 | 1 | 99.1 | 112 | 21 | 43 | 0 | 1 | 1 | 1 | 28 | 7 | 0 | .250 |
| 1918 PHI N | 13 | 14 | .481 | 2.89 | 33 | 30 | 20 | 252.1 | 257 | 46 | 41 | 0 | 0 | 1 | 1 | 85 | 7 | 0 | .082 |
| 1919 | 0 | 1 | .000 | 8.40 | 5 | 0 | 0 | 15 | 20 | 10 | 5 | 0 | 0 | 1 | 0 | 3 | 1 | 0 | .333 |
| 6 yrs. | 41 | 53 | .436 | 2.74 | 180 | 97 | 48 | 908.1 | 867 | 207 | 311 | 6 | 6 | 10 | 4 | 279 | 32 | 0 | .115 |
| 2 yrs. | 9 | 17 | .346 | 2.72 | 70 | 18 | 5 | 251.1 | 239 | 44 | 99 | 2 | 4 | 5 | 3 | 74 | 14 | 0 | .189 |

## Tot Pressnell

**PRESSNELL, FOREST CHARLES**    BR TR 5'10½" 175 lbs.
B. Aug. 8, 1906, Findlay, Ohio

| | W | L | PCT | ERA | G | GS | CG | IP | H | BB | SO | ShO | W | L | SV | AB | H | HR | BA |
|---|---|---|---|---|---|---|---|---|---|---|---|---|---|---|---|---|---|---|---|
| 1938 BKN N | 11 | 14 | .440 | 3.56 | 43 | 19 | 6 | 192 | 209 | 56 | 57 | 1 | 4 | 3 | 3 | 63 | 9 | 0 | .143 |
| 1939 | 9 | 7 | .563 | 4.02 | 31 | 18 | 10 | 156.2 | 171 | 33 | 43 | 2 | 0 | 0 | 2 | 51 | 10 | 0 | .196 |
| 1940 | 6 | 5 | .545 | 3.69 | 24 | 4 | 1 | 68.1 | 58 | 17 | 21 | 1 | 4 | 4 | 2 | 17 | 0 | 0 | .000 |
| 1941 CHI N | 5 | 3 | .625 | 3.09 | 29 | 1 | 0 | 70 | 69 | 23 | 27 | 0 | 5 | 2 | 1 | 15 | 3 | 0 | .200 |
| 1942 | 1 | 1 | .500 | 5.49 | 27 | 0 | 0 | 39.1 | 40 | 5 | 9 | 0 | 1 | 1 | 4 | 3 | 2 | 0 | .667 |
| 5 yrs. | 32 | 30 | .516 | 3.80 | 154 | 42 | 17 | 526.1 | 547 | 134 | 157 | 4 | 14 | 10 | 12 | 149 | 24 | 0 | .161 |
| 2 yrs. | 6 | 4 | .600 | 3.95 | 56 | 1 | 0 | 109.1 | 109 | 28 | 36 | 0 | 6 | 3 | 5 | 18 | 5 | 0 | .278 |

## Ray Prim

**PRIM, RAYMOND LEE (Pop)**    BR TL 6' 178 lbs.
B. Dec. 30, 1906, Salitpa, Ala.

| | W | L | PCT | ERA | G | GS | CG | IP | H | BB | SO | ShO | W | L | SV | AB | H | HR | BA |
|---|---|---|---|---|---|---|---|---|---|---|---|---|---|---|---|---|---|---|---|
| 1933 WAS A | 0 | 1 | .000 | 3.14 | 2 | 1 | 0 | 14.1 | 13 | 2 | 6 | 0 | 0 | 0 | 0 | 5 | 0 | 0 | .000 |
| 1934 | 0 | 2 | .000 | 6.75 | 8 | 1 | 0 | 14.2 | 19 | 8 | 3 | 0 | 0 | 1 | 0 | 3 | 0 | 0 | .000 |
| 1935 PHI N | 3 | 4 | .429 | 5.77 | 29 | 6 | 1 | 73.1 | 110 | 15 | 27 | 0 | 3 | 1 | 0 | 24 | 2 | 0 | .083 |
| 1943 CHI N | 4 | 3 | .571 | 2.55 | 29 | 5 | 0 | 60 | 67 | 14 | 27 | 0 | 2 | 1 | 1 | 12 | 2 | 0 | .167 |
| 1945 | 13 | 8 | .619 | 2.40 | 34 | 19 | 9 | 165.1 | 142 | 23 | 88 | 2 | 3 | 2 | 2 | 51 | 13 | 0 | .255 |
| 1946 | 2 | 3 | .400 | 5.79 | 14 | 2 | 0 | 23.1 | 28 | 10 | 10 | 0 | 0 | 0 | 1 | 5 | 1 | 0 | .200 |
| 6 yrs. | 22 | 21 | .512 | 3.56 | 116 | 34 | 10 | 351 | 379 | 72 | 161 | 2 | 8 | 5 | 4 | 100 | 18 | 0 | .180 |
| 3 yrs. | 19 | 14 | .576 | 2.75 | 77 | 26 | 9 | 248.2 | 237 | 47 | 125 | 2 | 5 | 3 | 4 | 68 | 16 | 0 | .235 |

**WORLD SERIES**

| | W | L | PCT | ERA | G | GS | CG | IP | H | BB | SO | ShO | W | L | SV | AB | H | HR | BA |
|---|---|---|---|---|---|---|---|---|---|---|---|---|---|---|---|---|---|---|---|
| 1945 CHI N | 0 | 1 | .000 | 9.00 | 2 | 1 | 0 | 4 | 4 | 1 | 1 | 0 | 0 | 0 | 0 | 0 | 0 | 0 | — |

## Don Prince

**PRINCE, DONALD MARK**    BR TR 6'4" 200 lbs.
B. Apr. 5, 1938, Clarkton, N. C.

| | W | L | PCT | ERA | G | GS | CG | IP | H | BB | SO | ShO | W | L | SV | AB | H | HR | BA |
|---|---|---|---|---|---|---|---|---|---|---|---|---|---|---|---|---|---|---|---|
| 1962 CHI N | 0 | 0 | — | 0.00 | 1 | 0 | 0 | 1 | 0 | 1 | 0 | 0 | 0 | 0 | 0 | 0 | 0 | 0 | — |

## Mike Proly

**PROLY, MICHAEL JAMES**    BR TR 6' 185 lbs.
B. Dec. 15, 1950, Jamaica, N. Y.

| | W | L | PCT | ERA | G | GS | CG | IP | H | BB | SO | ShO | W | L | SV | AB | H | HR | BA |
|---|---|---|---|---|---|---|---|---|---|---|---|---|---|---|---|---|---|---|---|
| 1976 STL N | 1 | 0 | 1.000 | 3.71 | 14 | 0 | 0 | 17 | 21 | 6 | 4 | 0 | 1 | 0 | 0 | 0 | 0 | 0 | — |
| 1978 CHI A | 5 | 2 | .714 | 2.74 | 14 | 6 | 2 | 65.2 | 63 | 12 | 19 | 0 | 0 | 0 | 1 | 0 | 0 | 0 | — |
| 1979 | 3 | 8 | .273 | 3.89 | 38 | 6 | 0 | 88 | 89 | 40 | 32 | 0 | 3 | 4 | 9 | 0 | 0 | 0 | — |
| 1980 | 5 | 10 | .333 | 3.06 | 62 | 3 | 0 | 147 | 136 | 58 | 56 | 0 | 4 | 4 | 8 | 0 | 0 | 0 | — |
| 1981 PHI N | 2 | 1 | .667 | 3.86 | 35 | 2 | 0 | 63 | 66 | 19 | 19 | 0 | 2 | 1 | 2 | 7 | 0 | 0 | .000 |
| 1982 CHI N | 5 | 3 | .625 | 2.30 | 44 | 1 | 0 | 82 | 77 | 22 | 24 | 0 | 4 | 3 | 1 | 14 | 4 | 0 | .286 |
| 1983 | 1 | 5 | .167 | 3.58 | 60 | 0 | 0 | 83 | 79 | 38 | 31 | 0 | 1 | 5 | 1 | 11 | 1 | 0 | .091 |
| 7 yrs. | 22 | 29 | .431 | 3.23 | 267 | 18 | 2 | 545.2 | 531 | 195 | 185 | 0 | 15 | 17 | 22 | 32 | 5 | 0 | .156 |
| 2 yrs. | 6 | 8 | .429 | 2.95 | 104 | 1 | 0 | 165 | 156 | 60 | 55 | 0 | 5 | 8 | 2 | 25 | 5 | 0 | .200 |

## John Pyecha

**PYECHA, JOHN NICHOLAS**    BR TR 6'5" 200 lbs.
B. Nov. 25, 1931, Aliquippa, Pa.

| | W | L | PCT | ERA | G | GS | CG | IP | H | BB | SO | ShO | W | L | SV | AB | H | HR | BA |
|---|---|---|---|---|---|---|---|---|---|---|---|---|---|---|---|---|---|---|---|
| 1954 CHI N | 0 | 1 | .000 | 10.13 | 1 | 0 | 0 | 2.2 | 4 | 2 | 2 | 0 | 0 | 1 | 0 | 1 | 0 | 0 | .000 |

## Shadow Pyle

**PYLE, HARRY THOMAS**    5'8" 136 lbs.
B. Oct. 30, 1861, Reading, Pa.    D. Nov. 26, 1908, Reading, Pa.

| | W | L | PCT | ERA | G | GS | CG | IP | H | BB | SO | ShO | W | L | SV | AB | H | HR | BA |
|---|---|---|---|---|---|---|---|---|---|---|---|---|---|---|---|---|---|---|---|
| 1884 PHI N | 0 | 1 | .000 | 4.00 | 1 | 1 | 1 | 9 | 9 | 6 | 4 | 0 | 0 | 0 | 0 | 4 | 0 | 0 | .000 |
| 1887 CHI N | 1 | 3 | .250 | 4.73 | 4 | 4 | 3 | 26.2 | 32 | 21 | 5 | 0 | 0 | 0 | 0 | 16 | 3 | 1 | .188 |
| 2 yrs. | 1 | 4 | .200 | 4.54 | 5 | 5 | 4 | 35.2 | 41 | 27 | 9 | 0 | 0 | 0 | 0 | 20 | 3 | 1 | .150 |
| 1 yr. | 1 | 3 | .250 | 4.73 | 4 | 4 | 3 | 26.2 | 32 | 21 | 5 | 0 | 0 | 0 | 0 | 16 | 3 | 1 | .188 |

## Wimpy Quinn

**QUINN, WELLINGTON HUNT**    BR TR 6'2" 187 lbs.
B. May 14, 1918, Birmingham, Ala.    D. Sept. 1, 1954, Los Angeles, Calif.

| | W | L | PCT | ERA | G | GS | CG | IP | H | BB | SO | ShO | W | L | SV | AB | H | HR | BA |
|---|---|---|---|---|---|---|---|---|---|---|---|---|---|---|---|---|---|---|---|
| 1941 CHI N | 0 | 0 | — | 7.20 | 3 | 0 | 0 | 5 | 3 | 3 | 2 | 0 | 0 | 0 | 0 | 2 | 1 | 0 | .500 |

| | W | L | PCT | ERA | G | GS | CG | IP | H | BB | SO | ShO | Relief Pitching W | L | SV | BATTING AB | H | HR | BA |
|---|---|---|---|---|---|---|---|---|---|---|---|---|---|---|---|---|---|---|---|

## Dick Radatz

RADATZ, RICHARD RAYMOND (The Monster)  BR TR 6'6"  230 lbs.
B. Apr. 2, 1937, Detroit, Mich.

| | W | L | PCT | ERA | G | GS | CG | IP | H | BB | SO | ShO | W | L | SV | AB | H | HR | BA |
|---|---|---|---|---|---|---|---|---|---|---|---|---|---|---|---|---|---|---|---|
| 1962 BOS A | 9 | 6 | .600 | 2.24 | 62 | 0 | 0 | 124.2 | 95 | 40 | 144 | 0 | 9 | 6 | 24 | 31 | 3 | 0 | .097 |
| 1963 | 15 | 6 | .714 | 1.97 | 66 | 0 | 0 | 132.1 | 94 | 51 | 162 | 0 | 15 | 6 | 25 | 29 | 2 | 0 | .069 |
| 1964 | 16 | 9 | .640 | 2.29 | 79 | 0 | 0 | 157 | 103 | 58 | 181 | 0 | 16 | 9 | 29 | 37 | 6 | 0 | .162 |
| 1965 | 9 | 11 | .450 | 3.91 | 63 | 0 | 0 | 124.1 | 104 | 53 | 121 | 0 | 9 | 11 | 22 | 27 | 5 | 1 | .185 |
| 1966 2 teams | | | | BOS A (16G 0-2) | | | | CLE A (39G 0-3) | | | | | | | | | | | |
| " total | 0 | 5 | .000 | 4.64 | 55 | 0 | 0 | 75.2 | 73 | 45 | 68 | 0 | 0 | 5 | 14 | 11 | 1 | 0 | .091 |
| 1967 2 teams | | | | CLE A (3G 0-0) | | | | CHI N (20G 1-0) | | | | | | | | | | | |
| " total | 1 | 0 | 1.000 | 6.49 | 23 | 0 | 0 | 26.1 | 17 | 26 | 19 | 0 | 1 | 0 | 5 | 4 | 1 | 0 | .250 |
| 1969 2 teams | | | | DET A (11G 2-2) | | | | MON N (22G 0-4) | | | | | | | | | | | |
| " total | 2 | 6 | .250 | 4.89 | 33 | 0 | 0 | 53.1 | 46 | 23 | 50 | 0 | 2 | 6 | 3 | 6 | 1 | 0 | .167 |
| 7 yrs. | 52 | 43 | .547 | 3.13 | 381 | 0 | 0 | 693.2 | 532 | 296 | 745 | 0 | 52 | 43 | 122 | 145 | 19 | 1 | .131 |
| 1 yr. | 1 | 0 | 1.000 | 6.56 | 20 | 0 | 0 | 23.1 | 12 | 24 | 18 | 0 | 1 | 0 | 5 | 4 | 1 | 0 | .250 |

## Ken Raffensberger

RAFFENSBERGER, KENNETH DAVID  BR TL 6'2"  185 lbs.
B. Aug. 8, 1917, York, Pa.

| | W | L | PCT | ERA | G | GS | CG | IP | H | BB | SO | ShO | W | L | SV | AB | H | HR | BA |
|---|---|---|---|---|---|---|---|---|---|---|---|---|---|---|---|---|---|---|---|---|
| 1939 STL N | 0 | 0 | — | 0.00 | 1 | 0 | 0 | 1 | 2 | 0 | 1 | 0 | 0 | 0 | 0 | 0 | 0 | 0 | — |
| 1940 CHI N | 7 | 9 | .438 | 3.38 | 43 | 10 | 3 | 114.2 | 120 | 29 | 55 | 0 | 4 | 4 | 3 | 30 | 5 | 0 | .167 |
| 1941 | 0 | 1 | .000 | 4.50 | 10 | 1 | 0 | 18 | 17 | 7 | 5 | 0 | 0 | 1 | 0 | 5 | 0 | 0 | .000 |
| 1943 PHI N | 0 | 1 | .000 | 1.13 | 1 | 1 | 1 | 8 | 7 | 2 | 3 | 0 | 0 | 0 | 0 | 3 | 0 | 0 | .000 |
| 1944 | 13 | 20 | .394 | 3.06 | 37 | 31 | 18 | 258.2 | 257 | 45 | 136 | 3 | 1 | 2 | 0 | 80 | 11 | 0 | .138 |
| 1945 | 0 | 3 | .000 | 4.44 | 5 | 4 | 1 | 24.1 | 28 | 14 | 6 | 0 | 0 | 0 | 0 | 8 | 0 | 0 | .000 |
| 1946 | 8 | 15 | .348 | 3.63 | 39 | 23 | 14 | 196 | 203 | 39 | 73 | 2 | 0 | 0 | 6 | 60 | 10 | 0 | .167 |
| 1947 2 teams | | | | PHI N (10G 2-6) | | | | CIN N (19G 6-5) | | | | | | | | | | | |
| " total | 8 | 11 | .421 | 4.51 | 29 | 22 | 10 | 147.2 | 182 | 37 | 54 | 1 | 1 | 2 | 1 | 52 | 10 | 0 | .192 |
| 1948 CIN N | 11 | 12 | .478 | 3.84 | 40 | 24 | 7 | 180.1 | 187 | 37 | 57 | 4 | 3 | 0 | 0 | 62 | 7 | 0 | .113 |
| 1949 | 18 | 17 | .514 | 3.39 | 41 | 38 | 20 | 284 | 289 | 80 | 103 | 5 | 1 | 1 | 0 | 90 | 16 | 1 | .178 |
| 1950 | 14 | 19 | .424 | 4.26 | 38 | 35 | 18 | 239 | 271 | 40 | 87 | 4 | 0 | 0 | 0 | 82 | 11 | 1 | .134 |
| 1951 | 16 | 17 | .485 | 3.44 | 42 | 33 | 14 | 248.2 | 232 | 38 | 81 | 5 | 2 | 2 | 5 | 82 | 10 | 0 | .122 |
| 1952 | 17 | 13 | .567 | 2.81 | 38 | 33 | 18 | 247 | 247 | 45 | 93 | 6 | 0 | 2 | 1 | 75 | 8 | 1 | .107 |
| 1953 | 7 | 14 | .333 | 3.93 | 26 | 26 | 9 | 174 | 200 | 33 | 47 | 1 | 0 | 0 | 0 | 57 | 8 | 1 | .140 |
| 1954 | 0 | 2 | .000 | 7.84 | 6 | 1 | 0 | 10.1 | 15 | 3 | 5 | 0 | 0 | 2 | 0 | 2 | 1 | 0 | .500 |
| 15 yrs. | 119 | 154 | .436 | 3.60 | 396 | 282 | 133 | 2151.2 | 2257 | 449 | 806 | 31 | 12 | 16 | 16 | 688 | 97 | 4 | .141 |
| 2 yrs. | 7 | 10 | .412 | 3.53 | 53 | 11 | 3 | 132.2 | 137 | 36 | 60 | 0 | 4 | 5 | 3 | 35 | 5 | 0 | .143 |

## Pat Ragan

RAGAN, DON CARLOS PATRICK  BR TR 5'10½" 185 lbs.
B. Nov. 15, 1888, Blanchard, Iowa  D. Sept. 4, 1956, Los Angeles, Calif.

| | W | L | PCT | ERA | G | GS | CG | IP | H | BB | SO | ShO | W | L | SV | AB | H | HR | BA |
|---|---|---|---|---|---|---|---|---|---|---|---|---|---|---|---|---|---|---|---|---|
| 1909 2 teams | | | | CIN N (2G 0-1) | | | | CHI N (2G 0-0) | | | | | | | | | | | |
| " total | 0 | 1 | .000 | 3.09 | 4 | 0 | 0 | 11.2 | 11 | 5 | 4 | 0 | 0 | 1 | 0 | 4 | 1 | 0 | .250 |
| 1911 BKN N | 4 | 3 | .571 | 2.11 | 22 | 7 | 5 | 93.2 | 81 | 31 | 39 | 2 | 0 | 0 | 1 | 29 | 4 | 0 | .138 |
| 1912 | 7 | 18 | .280 | 3.63 | 36 | 26 | 12 | 208 | 211 | 65 | 101 | 1 | 1 | 2 | 1 | 67 | 4 | 0 | .060 |
| 1913 | 15 | 18 | .455 | 3.77 | 44 | 32 | 14 | 264.2 | 284 | 64 | 109 | 0 | 3 | 3 | 0 | 91 | 15 | 0 | .165 |
| 1914 | 10 | 15 | .400 | 2.98 | 38 | 26 | 14 | 208.1 | 214 | 85 | 106 | 1 | 1 | 2 | 3 | 75 | 10 | 0 | .133 |
| 1915 2 teams | | | | BKN N (5G 1-0) | | | | BOS N (33G 15-12) | | | | | | | | | | | |
| " total | 16 | 12 | .571 | 2.34 | 38 | 26 | 13 | 246.2 | 219 | 67 | 88 | 3 | 4 | 1 | 0 | 86 | 13 | 0 | .151 |
| 1916 BOS N | 9 | 9 | .500 | 2.08 | 28 | 23 | 14 | 182 | 143 | 47 | 94 | 3 | 0 | 0 | 0 | 60 | 13 | 0 | .217 |
| 1917 | 6 | 9 | .400 | 2.93 | 30 | 13 | 5 | 147.2 | 138 | 35 | 61 | 1 | 3 | 2 | 1 | 48 | 6 | 1 | .125 |
| 1918 | 8 | 17 | .320 | 3.23 | 30 | 25 | 15 | 206.1 | 212 | 54 | 68 | 2 | 0 | 2 | 0 | 71 | 13 | 0 | .183 |
| 1919 3 teams | | | | BOS N (4G 0-2) | | | NY N (7G 1-0) | | | CHI A (1G 0-0) | | | | | | | | | |
| " total | 1 | 2 | .333 | 3.44 | 12 | 4 | 1 | 36.2 | 36 | 17 | 10 | 0 | 0 | 0 | 0 | 11 | 4 | 0 | .364 |
| 1923 PHI N | 0 | 0 | — | 6.00 | 1 | 0 | 0 | 3 | 6 | 0 | 0 | 0 | 0 | 0 | 0 | 2 | 1 | 0 | .500 |
| 11 yrs. | 76 | 104 | .422 | 2.99 | 283 | 182 | 93 | 1608.2 | 1555 | 470 | 680 | 13 | 12 | 13 | 6 | 544 | 84 | 1 | .154 |
| 1 yr. | 0 | 0 | — | 2.45 | 2 | 0 | 0 | 3.2 | 4 | 1 | 2 | 0 | 0 | 0 | 0 | 2 | 0 | 0 | .000 |

## Chuck Rainey

RAINEY, CHARLES DAVID  BR TR 5'11"  220 lbs.
B. July 14, 1954, San Diego, Calif.

| | W | L | PCT | ERA | G | GS | CG | IP | H | BB | SO | ShO | W | L | SV | AB | H | HR | BA |
|---|---|---|---|---|---|---|---|---|---|---|---|---|---|---|---|---|---|---|---|---|
| 1979 BOS A | 8 | 5 | .615 | 3.81 | 20 | 16 | 4 | 104 | 97 | 41 | 41 | 1 | 0 | 0 | 1 | 0 | 0 | 0 | — |
| 1980 | 8 | 3 | .727 | 4.86 | 16 | 13 | 2 | 87 | 92 | 41 | 43 | 1 | 0 | 0 | 0 | 0 | 0 | 0 | — |
| 1981 | 0 | 1 | .000 | 2.70 | 11 | 2 | 0 | 40 | 39 | 13 | 20 | 0 | 0 | 0 | 0 | 0 | 0 | 0 | — |
| 1982 | 7 | 5 | .583 | 5.02 | 27 | 25 | 3 | 129 | 146 | 63 | 57 | 3 | 0 | 0 | 0 | 0 | 0 | 0 | — |
| 1983 CHI N | 14 | 13 | .519 | 4.48 | 34 | 34 | 1 | 191 | 219 | 74 | 84 | 1 | 0 | 0 | 0 | 56 | 9 | 0 | .161 |
| 1984 2 teams | | | | CHI N (17G 5-7) | | | | OAK A (16G 1-1) | | | | | | | | | | | |
| " total | 6 | 8 | .429 | 4.92 | 33 | 16 | 0 | 119 | 145 | 55 | 55 | 0 | 0 | 0 | 0 | 31 | 3 | 0 | .097 |
| 6 yrs. | 43 | 35 | .551 | 4.50 | 141 | 106 | 10 | 670 | 738 | 287 | 300 | 6 | 1 | 1 | 2 | 87 | 12 | 0 | .138 |
| 2 yrs. | 19 | 20 | .487 | 4.41 | 51 | 50 | 1 | 279.1 | 321 | 112 | 129 | 1 | 0 | 0 | 0 | 87 | 12 | 0 | .138 |

## Willie Ramsdell

RAMSDELL, JAMES WILLARD (Willie the Knuck)  BR TR 5'11"  165 lbs.
B. Apr. 4, 1916, Williamsburg, Kans.  D. Oct. 8, 1969, Wichita, Kans.

| | W | L | PCT | ERA | G | GS | CG | IP | H | BB | SO | ShO | W | L | SV | AB | H | HR | BA |
|---|---|---|---|---|---|---|---|---|---|---|---|---|---|---|---|---|---|---|---|---|
| 1947 BKN N | 1 | 1 | .500 | 6.75 | 2 | 0 | 0 | 2.2 | 4 | 3 | 3 | 0 | 1 | 1 | 0 | 1 | 1 | 0 | 1.000 |
| 1948 | 4 | 4 | .500 | 5.19 | 27 | 1 | 0 | 50.1 | 48 | 41 | 34 | 0 | 4 | 3 | 4 | 11 | 1 | 0 | .091 |
| 1950 2 teams | | | | BKN N (5G 1-2) | | | | CIN N (27G 7-12) | | | | | | | | | | | |
| " total | 8 | 14 | .364 | 3.68 | 32 | 22 | 8 | 163.2 | 158 | 77 | 85 | 1 | 1 | 3 | 1 | 53 | 10 | 0 | .189 |
| 1951 CIN N | 9 | 17 | .346 | 4.04 | 31 | 31 | 10 | 196 | 204 | 70 | 88 | 1 | 0 | 0 | 0 | 58 | 9 | 0 | .155 |
| 1952 CHI N | 2 | 3 | .400 | 2.42 | 19 | 4 | 0 | 67 | 41 | 24 | 30 | 0 | 2 | 0 | 0 | 18 | 1 | 0 | .056 |
| 5 yrs. | 24 | 39 | .381 | 3.83 | 111 | 58 | 18 | 479.2 | 455 | 215 | 240 | 2 | 8 | 7 | 5 | 141 | 22 | 0 | .156 |
| 1 yr. | 2 | 3 | .400 | 2.42 | 19 | 4 | 0 | 67 | 41 | 24 | 30 | 0 | 2 | 0 | 0 | 18 | 1 | 0 | .056 |

## Frank Reberger

REBERGER, FRANK BEALL (Crane)  BL TR 6'5"  200 lbs.
B. June 7, 1944, Caldwell, Ida.

| | W | L | PCT | ERA | G | GS | CG | IP | H | BB | SO | ShO | W | L | SV | AB | H | HR | BA |
|---|---|---|---|---|---|---|---|---|---|---|---|---|---|---|---|---|---|---|---|---|
| 1968 CHI N | 0 | 1 | .000 | 4.50 | 3 | 1 | 0 | 6 | 9 | 2 | 3 | 0 | 0 | 1 | 0 | 0 | 0 | 0 | — |
| 1969 SD N | 1 | 2 | .333 | 3.58 | 67 | 0 | 0 | 88 | 83 | 41 | 65 | 0 | 1 | 2 | 6 | 5 | 1 | 0 | .200 |
| 1970 SF N | 7 | 8 | .467 | 5.57 | 45 | 18 | 3 | 152 | 178 | 98 | 117 | 0 | 1 | 2 | 2 | 47 | 11 | 0 | .234 |

| | W | L | PCT | ERA | G | GS | CG | IP | H | BB | SO | ShO | Relief Pitching W | L | SV | BATTING AB | H | HR | BA |
|---|---|---|---|---|---|---|---|---|---|---|---|---|---|---|---|---|---|---|---|

## Frank Reberger continued

| | W | L | PCT | ERA | G | GS | CG | IP | H | BB | SO | ShO | W | L | SV | AB | H | HR | BA |
|---|---|---|---|---|---|---|---|---|---|---|---|---|---|---|---|---|---|---|---|
| 1971 | 3 | 0 | 1.000 | 3.89 | 13 | 7 | 0 | 44 | 37 | 19 | 21 | 0 | 0 | 0 | 0 | 13 | 3 | 0 | .231 |
| 1972 | 3 | 4 | .429 | 4.00 | 20 | 11 | 2 | 99 | 97 | 37 | 52 | 0 | 0 | 0 | 0 | 35 | 8 | 0 | .229 |
| 5 yrs. | 14 | 15 | .483 | 4.51 | 148 | 37 | 5 | 389 | 404 | 197 | 258 | 0 | 2 | 5 | 8 | 100 | 23 | 0 | .230 |
| 1 yr. | 0 | 1 | .000 | 4.50 | 3 | 1 | 0 | 6 | 9 | 2 | 3 | 0 | 0 | 1 | 0 | 0 | 0 | 0 | — |

## Phil Regan

**REGAN, PHILIP RAYMOND (The Vulture)**    BR TR 6'3"   200 lbs.
B. Apr. 6, 1937, Otsego, Mich.

| | W | L | PCT | ERA | G | GS | CG | IP | H | BB | SO | ShO | W | L | SV | AB | H | HR | BA |
|---|---|---|---|---|---|---|---|---|---|---|---|---|---|---|---|---|---|---|---|
| 1960 DET A | 0 | 4 | .000 | 4.50 | 17 | 7 | 0 | 68 | 70 | 25 | 38 | 0 | 0 | 0 | 1 | 17 | 1 | 0 | .059 |
| 1961 | 10 | 7 | .588 | 5.25 | 32 | 16 | 6 | 120 | 134 | 41 | 46 | 0 | 2 | 2 | 2 | 40 | 3 | 0 | .075 |
| 1962 | 11 | 9 | .550 | 4.04 | 35 | 23 | 6 | 171.1 | 169 | 64 | 87 | 0 | 1 | 2 | 0 | 63 | 13 | 0 | .206 |
| 1963 | 15 | 9 | .625 | 3.86 | 38 | 27 | 5 | 189 | 179 | 59 | 115 | 1 | 2 | 1 | 1 | 63 | 9 | 1 | .143 |
| 1964 | 5 | 10 | .333 | 5.03 | 32 | 21 | 2 | 146.2 | 162 | 49 | 91 | 0 | 1 | 0 | 1 | 41 | 13 | 0 | .317 |
| 1965 | 1 | 5 | .167 | 5.05 | 16 | 7 | 1 | 51.2 | 57 | 20 | 37 | 0 | 0 | 0 | 0 | 12 | 1 | 0 | .083 |
| 1966 LA N | 14 | 1 | .933 | 1.62 | 65 | 0 | 0 | 116.2 | 85 | 24 | 88 | 0 | 14 | 1 | 21 | 21 | 3 | 0 | .143 |
| 1967 | 6 | 9 | .400 | 2.99 | 55 | 3 | 0 | 96.1 | 108 | 32 | 53 | 0 | 5 | 7 | 6 | 10 | 1 | 0 | .100 |
| 1968 2 teams | | | LA | N (5G 2–0) | | CHI | N (68G 10–5) | | | | | | | | | | | | |
| " total | 12 | 5 | .706 | 2.27 | 73 | 0 | 0 | 134.2 | 119 | 25 | 67 | 0 | 12 | 5 | 25 | 21 | 3 | 0 | .143 |
| 1969 CHI N | 12 | 6 | .667 | 3.70 | 71 | 0 | 0 | 112 | 120 | 35 | 56 | 0 | 12 | 6 | 17 | 15 | 1 | 0 | .067 |
| 1970 | 5 | 9 | .357 | 4.74 | 54 | 0 | 0 | 76 | 81 | 32 | 31 | 0 | 5 | 9 | 12 | 9 | 0 | 0 | .000 |
| 1971 | 5 | 5 | .500 | 3.95 | 48 | 1 | 0 | 73 | 84 | 33 | 28 | 0 | 4 | 5 | 6 | 8 | 0 | 0 | .000 |
| 1972 2 teams | | | CHI | N (5G 0–1) | | CHI | A (10G 0–1) | | | | | | | | | | | | |
| " total | 0 | 2 | .000 | 3.63 | 15 | 0 | 0 | 17.1 | 24 | 8 | 6 | 0 | 0 | 2 | 0 | 1 | 1 | 0 | 1.000 |
| 13 yrs. | 96 | 81 | .542 | 3.84 | 551 | 105 | 20 | 1372.2 | 1392 | 447 | 743 | 1 | 58 | 40 | 92 | 321 | 49 | 1 | .153 |
| 5 yrs. | 32 | 26 | .552 | 3.44 | 246 | 1 | 0 | 392 | 400 | 126 | 177 | 0 | 31 | 26 | 60 | 52 | 4 | 0 | .077 |
| | | | | | | | | | | | | | 5th | | 4th | | | | |

**WORLD SERIES**

| | W | L | PCT | ERA | G | GS | CG | IP | H | BB | SO | ShO | W | L | SV | AB | H | HR | BA |
|---|---|---|---|---|---|---|---|---|---|---|---|---|---|---|---|---|---|---|---|
| 1966 LA N | 0 | 0 | — | 0.00 | 2 | 0 | 0 | 1.2 | 0 | 1 | 2 | 0 | 0 | 0 | 0 | 0 | 0 | 0 | — |

## Laurie Reis

**REIS, LAWRENCE P.**    BL TR   160 lbs.
B. Nov. 20, 1858, Illinois    D. Jan. 24, 1921, Chicago, Ill.

| | W | L | PCT | ERA | G | GS | CG | IP | H | BB | SO | ShO | W | L | SV | AB | H | HR | BA |
|---|---|---|---|---|---|---|---|---|---|---|---|---|---|---|---|---|---|---|---|
| 1877 CHI N | 3 | 1 | .750 | 0.75 | 4 | 4 | 4 | 36 | 29 | 6 | 11 | 1 | 0 | 0 | 0 | 16 | 2 | 0 | .125 |
| 1878 | 1 | 3 | .250 | 3.25 | 4 | 4 | 4 | 36 | 55 | 4 | 8 | 0 | 0 | 0 | 0 | 20 | 3 | 0 | .150 |
| 2 yrs. | 4 | 4 | .500 | 2.00 | 8 | 8 | 8 | 72 | 84 | 10 | 19 | 1 | 0 | 0 | 0 | 36 | 5 | 0 | .139 |
| 2 yrs. | 4 | 4 | .500 | 2.00 | 8 | 8 | 8 | 72 | 84 | 10 | 19 | 1 | 0 | 0 | 0 | 36 | 5 | 0 | .139 |

## Steve Renko

**RENKO, STEVEN**    BR TR 6'5"   230 lbs.
B. Dec. 10, 1944, Kansas City, Kans.

| | W | L | PCT | ERA | G | GS | CG | IP | H | BB | SO | ShO | W | L | SV | AB | H | HR | BA |
|---|---|---|---|---|---|---|---|---|---|---|---|---|---|---|---|---|---|---|---|
| 1969 MON N | 6 | 7 | .462 | 4.02 | 18 | 15 | 4 | 103 | 94 | 50 | 68 | 0 | 0 | 0 | 0 | 36 | 6 | 1 | .167 |
| 1970 | 13 | 11 | .542 | 4.32 | 41 | 33 | 7 | 223 | 203 | 104 | 142 | 1 | 0 | 0 | 1 | 80 | 16 | 1 | .200 |
| 1971 | 15 | 14 | .517 | 3.75 | 40 | 37 | 9 | 276 | 256 | 135 | 129 | 3 | 0 | 0 | 0 | 100 | 21 | 2 | .210 |
| 1972 | 1 | 10 | .091 | 5.20 | 30 | 12 | 0 | 97 | 96 | 67 | 66 | 0 | 0 | 0 | 0 | 24 | 7 | 0 | .292 |
| 1973 | 15 | 11 | .577 | 2.81 | 36 | 34 | 9 | 249.2 | 201 | 108 | 164 | 0 | 0 | 0 | 1 | 88 | 24 | 0 | .273 |
| 1974 | 12 | 16 | .429 | 4.03 | 37 | 35 | 8 | 228 | 222 | 81 | 138 | 1 | 0 | 0 | 0 | 81 | 17 | 1 | .210 |
| 1975 | 6 | 12 | .333 | 4.08 | 31 | 25 | 3 | 170 | 175 | 76 | 99 | 1 | 0 | 0 | 1 | 54 | 15 | 1 | .278 |
| 1976 2 teams | | | MON | N (5G 0–1) | | CHI | N (28G 8–11) | | | | | | | | | | | | |
| " total | 8 | 12 | .400 | 3.98 | 33 | 28 | 4 | 176.1 | 179 | 46 | 116 | 0 | 0 | 0 | 0 | 56 | 6 | 0 | .107 |
| 1977 2 teams | | | CHI | N (13G 2–2) | | CHI | A (8G 5–0) | | | | | | | | | | | | |
| " total | 7 | 2 | .778 | 4.07 | 21 | 16 | 0 | 104 | 106 | 38 | 70 | 0 | 0 | 0 | 0 | 12 | 2 | 0 | .167 |
| 1978 OAK A | 6 | 12 | .333 | 4.29 | 27 | 25 | 3 | 151 | 152 | 67 | 89 | 1 | 0 | 0 | 0 | 0 | 0 | 0 | — |
| 1979 BOS A | 11 | 9 | .550 | 4.11 | 27 | 27 | 4 | 171 | 174 | 53 | 99 | 1 | 0 | 0 | 0 | 0 | 0 | 0 | — |
| 1980 | 9 | 9 | .500 | 4.20 | 32 | 23 | 1 | 165 | 180 | 56 | 90 | 0 | 2 | 0 | 0 | 0 | 0 | 0 | — |
| 1981 CAL A | 8 | 4 | .667 | 3.44 | 22 | 15 | 0 | 102 | 93 | 42 | 50 | 0 | 1 | 0 | 1 | 0 | 0 | 0 | — |
| 1982 | 11 | 6 | .647 | 4.44 | 31 | 23 | 4 | 156 | 163 | 51 | 81 | 0 | 3 | 1 | 0 | 0 | 0 | 0 | — |
| 1983 KC A | 6 | 11 | .353 | 4.30 | 25 | 17 | 1 | 121.1 | 144 | 36 | 54 | 0 | 0 | 1 | 0 | 0 | 0 | 0 | — |
| 15 yrs. | 134 | 146 | .479 | 4.00 | 451 | 365 | 57 | 2493.1 | 2438 | 1010 | 1455 | 8 | 6 | 4 | 6 | 531 | 114 | 6 | .215 |
| 2 yrs. | 10 | 13 | .435 | 4.03 | 41 | 35 | 4 | 214.1 | 215 | 64 | 146 | 0 | 0 | 0 | 1 | 65 | 7 | 0 | .108 |

## Ed Reulbach

**REULBACH, EDWARD MARVIN (Big Ed)**    BR TR 6'1"   190 lbs.
B. Dec. 1, 1882, Detroit, Mich.    D. July 17, 1961, Glens Falls, N. Y.

| | W | L | PCT | ERA | G | GS | CG | IP | H | BB | SO | ShO | W | L | SV | AB | H | HR | BA |
|---|---|---|---|---|---|---|---|---|---|---|---|---|---|---|---|---|---|---|---|
| 1905 CHI N | 18 | 13 | .581 | 1.42 | 34 | 29 | 28 | 292 | 208 | 73 | 152 | 5 | 2 | 1 | 1 | 110 | 14 | 0 | .127 |
| 1906 | 19 | 4 | .826 | 1.65 | 33 | 24 | 20 | 218 | 129 | 92 | 94 | 6 | 1 | 0 | 2 | 83 | 13 | 0 | .157 |
| 1907 | 17 | 4 | .810 | 1.69 | 27 | 22 | 16 | 192 | 147 | 64 | 96 | 4 | 2 | 0 | 0 | 63 | 11 | 1 | .175 |
| 1908 | 24 | 7 | .774 | 2.03 | 46 | 35 | 25 | 297.2 | 227 | 106 | 133 | 7 | 3 | 0 | 1 | 99 | 23 | 0 | .232 |
| 1909 | 19 | 10 | .655 | 1.78 | 35 | 32 | 23 | 262.2 | 194 | 82 | 105 | 6 | 0 | 1 | 0 | 86 | 12 | 0 | .140 |
| 1910 | 12 | 8 | .600 | 3.12 | 24 | 23 | 13 | 173.1 | 161 | 49 | 55 | 1 | 0 | 1 | 0 | 56 | 6 | 0 | .107 |
| 1911 | 16 | 9 | .640 | 2.96 | 33 | 29 | 15 | 221.2 | 191 | 103 | 79 | 2 | 1 | 0 | 0 | 67 | 6 | 0 | .090 |
| 1912 | 10 | 6 | .625 | 3.78 | 39 | 19 | 8 | 169 | 161 | 60 | 75 | 0 | 3 | 1 | 3 | 55 | 6 | 0 | .109 |
| 1913 2 teams | | | CHI | N (9G 1–3) | | BKN | N (15G 7–6) | | | | | | | | | | | | |
| " total | 8 | 9 | .471 | 2.66 | 24 | 14 | 9 | 148.2 | 118 | 56 | 56 | 2 | 1 | 0 | 0 | 41 | 6 | 0 | .146 |
| 1914 BKN N | 11 | 18 | .379 | 2.64 | 44 | 29 | 14 | 256 | 228 | 83 | 119 | 3 | 1 | 3 | 3 | 74 | 9 | 0 | .122 |
| 1915 NWK F | 20 | 10 | .667 | 2.23 | 33 | 30 | 23 | 270 | 233 | 69 | 117 | 4 | 1 | 0 | 1 | 92 | 18 | 0 | .196 |
| 1916 BOS N | 7 | 6 | .538 | 2.47 | 21 | 11 | 6 | 109.1 | 99 | 41 | 47 | 0 | 2 | 1 | 0 | 33 | 3 | 0 | .091 |
| 1917 | 0 | 1 | .000 | 2.82 | 5 | 2 | 0 | 22.1 | 21 | 15 | 9 | 0 | 0 | 0 | 0 | 3 | 0 | 0 | .000 |
| 13 yrs. | 181 | 105 | .633 | 2.28 | 398 | 299 | 200 | 2632.2 | 2117 | 892 | 1137 | 40 | 17 | 8 | 11 | 862 | 127 | 1 | .147 |
| 9 yrs. | 136 | 64 | .680 | 2.24 | 280 | 215 | 149 | 1865 | 1459 | 650 | 799 | 31 | 12 | 4 | 7 | 631 | 94 | 1 | .149 |
| | | | 10th | 3rd | 5th | | | | | | | | 7th | | 3rd | | | | |

**WORLD SERIES**

| | W | L | PCT | ERA | G | GS | CG | IP | H | BB | SO | ShO | W | L | SV | AB | H | HR | BA |
|---|---|---|---|---|---|---|---|---|---|---|---|---|---|---|---|---|---|---|---|
| 1906 CHI N | 1 | 0 | 1.000 | 2.45 | 2 | 2 | 1 | 11 | 6 | 8 | 4 | 0 | 0 | 0 | 0 | 3 | 0 | 0 | .000 |
| 1907 | 1 | 0 | 1.000 | 0.75 | 2 | 1 | 1 | 12 | 6 | 3 | 4 | 0 | 0 | 0 | 0 | 5 | 1 | 0 | .200 |
| 1908 | 0 | 0 | — | 4.70 | 2 | 1 | 0 | 7.2 | 9 | 1 | 5 | 0 | 0 | 0 | 0 | 3 | 0 | 0 | .000 |

| | W | L | PCT | ERA | G | GS | CG | IP | H | BB | SO | ShO | Relief Pitching W | L | SV | BATTING AB | H | HR | BA |
|---|---|---|---|---|---|---|---|---|---|---|---|---|---|---|---|---|---|---|---|

## Ed Reulbach continued

| | W | L | PCT | ERA | G | GS | CG | IP | H | BB | SO | ShO | W | L | SV | AB | H | HR | BA |
|---|---|---|---|---|---|---|---|---|---|---|---|---|---|---|---|---|---|---|---|
| 1910 | 0 | 0 | – | 13.50 | 1 | 1 | 0 | 2 | 3 | 2 | 0 | 0 | 0 | 0 | 0 | 0 | 0 | 0 | – |
| 4 yrs. | 2 | 0 | 1.000 | 3.03 | 7 | 5 | 2 | 32.2 | 24 | 14 | 13 | 0 | 0 | 0 | 0 | 11 | 1 | 0 | .091 |
| | | | 1st | | | | | | | | | | | | | | | | |

## Paul Reuschel

**REUSCHEL, PAUL RICHARD**　　　　　　　BR TR 6'4"　225 lbs.
Brother of Rick Reuschel.
B. Jan. 12, 1947, Quincy, Ill.

| | W | L | PCT | ERA | G | GS | CG | IP | H | BB | SO | ShO | W | L | SV | AB | H | HR | BA |
|---|---|---|---|---|---|---|---|---|---|---|---|---|---|---|---|---|---|---|---|
| 1975 CHI N | 1 | 3 | .250 | 3.50 | 28 | 0 | 0 | 36 | 44 | 13 | 12 | 0 | 1 | 3 | 5 | 4 | 0 | 0 | .000 |
| 1976 | 4 | 2 | .667 | 4.55 | 50 | 2 | 0 | 87 | 94 | 33 | 55 | 0 | 3 | 1 | 3 | 13 | 2 | 0 | .154 |
| 1977 | 5 | 6 | .455 | 4.37 | 69 | 0 | 0 | 107 | 105 | 40 | 62 | 0 | 5 | 6 | 4 | 11 | 0 | 0 | .000 |
| 1978 2 teams | | | CHI N | (16G 2–0) | | | CLE | A | (18G 2–4) | | | | | | | | | | |
| " total | 4 | 4 | .500 | 3.59 | 34 | 6 | 1 | 117.2 | 124 | 35 | 37 | 0 | 4 | 0 | 0 | 4 | 0 | 0 | .000 |
| 1979 CLE A | 2 | 1 | .667 | 8.00 | 17 | 1 | 0 | 45 | 73 | 11 | 22 | 0 | 2 | 1 | 1 | 0 | 0 | 0 | – |
| 5 yrs. | 16 | 16 | .500 | 4.52 | 198 | 9 | 1 | 392.2 | 440 | 132 | 188 | 0 | 15 | 11 | 13 | 32 | 2 | 0 | .063 |
| 4 yrs. | 12 | 11 | .522 | 4.40 | 163 | 2 | 0 | 258 | 272 | 99 | 142 | 0 | 11 | 10 | 12 | 32 | 2 | 0 | .063 |

## Rick Reuschel

**REUSCHEL, RICKY EUGENE**　　　　　　　BR TR 6'3"　215 lbs.
Brother of Paul Reuschel.
B. May 16, 1949, Quincy, Ill.

| | W | L | PCT | ERA | G | GS | CG | IP | H | BB | SO | ShO | W | L | SV | AB | H | HR | BA |
|---|---|---|---|---|---|---|---|---|---|---|---|---|---|---|---|---|---|---|---|
| 1972 CHI N | 10 | 8 | .556 | 2.93 | 21 | 18 | 5 | 129 | 127 | 29 | 87 | 4 | 1 | 0 | 0 | 44 | 6 | 0 | .136 |
| 1973 | 14 | 15 | .483 | 3.00 | 36 | 36 | 7 | 237 | 244 | 62 | 168 | 3 | 0 | 0 | 0 | 73 | 9 | 0 | .123 |
| 1974 | 13 | 12 | .520 | 4.29 | 41 | 38 | 8 | 241 | 262 | 83 | 160 | 2 | 1 | 0 | 0 | 86 | 19 | 0 | .221 |
| 1975 | 11 | 17 | .393 | 3.73 | 38 | 37 | 6 | 234 | 244 | 67 | 155 | 0 | 0 | 0 | 1 | 77 | 16 | 1 | .208 |
| 1976 | 14 | 12 | .538 | 3.46 | 38 | 37 | 9 | 260 | 260 | 64 | 146 | 2 | 0 | 0 | 1 | 83 | 19 | 0 | .229 |
| 1977 | 20 | 10 | .667 | 2.79 | 39 | 37 | 8 | 252 | 233 | 74 | 166 | 4 | 1 | 0 | 1 | 87 | 18 | 1 | .207 |
| 1978 | 14 | 15 | .483 | 3.41 | 35 | 35 | 9 | 243 | 235 | 54 | 115 | 1 | 0 | 0 | 0 | 73 | 10 | 0 | .137 |
| 1979 | 18 | 12 | .600 | 3.62 | 36 | 36 | 5 | 239 | 251 | 75 | 125 | 1 | 0 | 0 | 0 | 79 | 13 | 0 | .165 |
| 1980 | 11 | 13 | .458 | 3.40 | 38 | 38 | 6 | 257 | 281 | 76 | 140 | 0 | 0 | 0 | 0 | 82 | 13 | 0 | .159 |
| 1981 2 teams | | | CHI N | (13G 4–7) | | | NY | A | (12G 4–4) | | | | | | | | | | |
| " total | 8 | 11 | .421 | 3.10 | 25 | 24 | 4 | 157 | 162 | 33 | 75 | 0 | 0 | 0 | 0 | 25 | 2 | 0 | .080 |
| 1983 CHI N | 1 | 1 | .500 | 3.92 | 4 | 4 | 0 | 20.2 | 18 | 10 | 9 | 0 | 0 | 0 | 0 | 7 | 1 | 0 | .143 |
| 1984 | 5 | 5 | .500 | 5.17 | 19 | 14 | 1 | 92.1 | 123 | 23 | 43 | 0 | 1 | 0 | 0 | 29 | 7 | 0 | .241 |
| 1985 PIT N | 14 | 8 | .636 | 2.27 | 31 | 26 | 9 | 194 | 153 | 52 | 138 | 1 | 2 | 0 | 1 | 59 | 10 | 1 | .169 |
| 13 yrs. | 153 | 139 | .524 | 3.38 | 401 | 380 | 77 | 2556 | 2593 | 702 | 1527 | 18 | 6 | 0 | 4 | 804 | 143 | 3 | .178 |
| 12 yrs. | 135 | 127 | .515 | 3.50 | 358 | 343 | 65 | 2291 | 2365 | 640 | 1367 | 17 | 4 | 0 | 3 | 745 | 133 | 2 | .179 |
| | | | 5th | | | | 7th | | | 6th | | | 8th | 3rd | | | | | |

DIVISIONAL PLAYOFF SERIES

| | W | L | PCT | ERA | G | GS | CG | IP | H | BB | SO | ShO | W | L | SV | AB | H | HR | BA |
|---|---|---|---|---|---|---|---|---|---|---|---|---|---|---|---|---|---|---|---|
| 1981 NY A | 0 | 1 | .000 | 3.00 | 1 | 1 | 0 | 6 | 4 | 1 | 3 | 0 | 0 | 0 | 0 | 0 | 0 | 0 | – |

WORLD SERIES

| | W | L | PCT | ERA | G | GS | CG | IP | H | BB | SO | ShO | W | L | SV | AB | H | HR | BA |
|---|---|---|---|---|---|---|---|---|---|---|---|---|---|---|---|---|---|---|---|
| 1981 NY A | 0 | 0 | – | 4.91 | 2 | 1 | 0 | 3.2 | 7 | 3 | 2 | 0 | 0 | 0 | 0 | 0 | 0 | 0 | .000 |

## Archie Reynolds

**REYNOLDS, ARCHIE EDWARD**　　　　　　　BR TR 6'2"　205 lbs.
B. Jan. 3, 1946, Glendale, Calif.

| | W | L | PCT | ERA | G | GS | CG | IP | H | BB | SO | ShO | W | L | SV | AB | H | HR | BA |
|---|---|---|---|---|---|---|---|---|---|---|---|---|---|---|---|---|---|---|---|
| 1968 CHI N | 0 | 1 | .000 | 6.75 | 7 | 1 | 0 | 13.1 | 14 | 7 | 6 | 0 | 0 | 1 | 0 | 2 | 1 | 0 | .500 |
| 1969 | 0 | 1 | .000 | 2.57 | 2 | 2 | 0 | 7 | 11 | 7 | 4 | 0 | 0 | 0 | 0 | 1 | 0 | 0 | .000 |
| 1970 | 0 | 2 | .000 | 6.60 | 7 | 1 | 0 | 15 | 17 | 9 | 9 | 0 | 0 | 1 | 0 | 2 | 0 | 0 | .000 |
| 1971 CAL A | 0 | 3 | .000 | 4.67 | 15 | 1 | 0 | 27 | 32 | 18 | 15 | 0 | 0 | 3 | 0 | 2 | 0 | 0 | .000 |
| 1972 MIL A | 0 | 1 | .000 | 7.11 | 5 | 2 | 0 | 19 | 26 | 8 | 13 | 0 | 0 | 1 | 0 | 4 | 2 | 0 | .500 |
| 5 yrs. | 0 | 8 | .000 | 5.75 | 36 | 7 | 0 | 81.1 | 100 | 49 | 47 | 0 | 0 | 6 | 0 | 11 | 3 | 0 | .273 |
| 3 yrs. | 0 | 4 | .000 | 5.86 | 16 | 4 | 0 | 35.1 | 42 | 23 | 19 | 0 | 0 | 2 | 0 | 5 | 1 | 0 | .200 |

## Bob Rhoads

**RHOADS, ROBERT BARTON (Dusty)**　　　　　　　BR TR 6'1"　215 lbs.
B. Oct. 4, 1879, Wooster, Ohio　　D. Feb. 12, 1967, San Bernardino, Calif.

| | W | L | PCT | ERA | G | GS | CG | IP | H | BB | SO | ShO | W | L | SV | AB | H | HR | BA |
|---|---|---|---|---|---|---|---|---|---|---|---|---|---|---|---|---|---|---|---|
| 1902 CHI N | 4 | 8 | .333 | 3.20 | 16 | 12 | 12 | 118 | 131 | 42 | 43 | 1 | 0 | 0 | 1 | 45 | 10 | 0 | .222 |
| 1903 2 teams | | | STL | N | (17G 5–8) | | | CLE | A | (5G 2–3) | | | | | | | | | |
| " total | 7 | 11 | .389 | 4.76 | 22 | 18 | 17 | 170 | 209 | 50 | 73 | 1 | 0 | 0 | 0 | 67 | 9 | 1 | .134 |
| 1904 CLE A | 10 | 9 | .526 | 2.87 | 22 | 19 | 18 | 175.1 | 175 | 48 | 72 | 0 | 0 | 0 | 0 | 92 | 18 | 0 | .196 |
| 1905 | 16 | 9 | .640 | 2.83 | 28 | 26 | 24 | 235 | 219 | 55 | 61 | 4 | 1 | 0 | 0 | 95 | 21 | 1 | .221 |
| 1906 | 22 | 10 | .688 | 1.80 | 38 | 34 | 31 | 315 | 259 | 92 | 89 | 7 | 1 | 0 | 1 | 118 | 19 | 0 | .161 |
| 1907 | 15 | 14 | .517 | 2.29 | 35 | 31 | 23 | 275 | 258 | 84 | 76 | 5 | 1 | 0 | 1 | 92 | 17 | 0 | .185 |
| 1908 | 18 | 12 | .600 | 1.77 | 37 | 30 | 20 | 270 | 229 | 73 | 62 | 1 | 2 | 2 | 0 | 90 | 20 | 0 | .222 |
| 1909 | 5 | 9 | .357 | 2.90 | 20 | 15 | 9 | 133.1 | 124 | 50 | 46 | 2 | 0 | 1 | 0 | 43 | 7 | 0 | .163 |
| 8 yrs. | 97 | 82 | .542 | 2.61 | 218 | 185 | 154 | 1691.2 | 1604 | 494 | 522 | 21 | 5 | 3 | 3 | 642 | 121 | 2 | .188 |
| 1 yr. | 4 | 8 | .333 | 3.20 | 16 | 12 | 12 | 118 | 131 | 42 | 43 | 1 | 0 | 0 | 1 | 45 | 10 | 0 | .222 |

## Lew Richie

**RICHIE, LEWIS A.**　　　　　　　BR TR
B. Aug. 23, 1883, Ambler, Pa.　　D. Aug. 15, 1936, South Mountain, Pa.

| | W | L | PCT | ERA | G | GS | CG | IP | H | BB | SO | ShO | W | L | SV | AB | H | HR | BA |
|---|---|---|---|---|---|---|---|---|---|---|---|---|---|---|---|---|---|---|---|
| 1906 PHI N | 9 | 11 | .450 | 2.41 | 33 | 22 | 14 | 205.2 | 170 | 79 | 65 | 3 | 0 | 1 | 0 | 60 | 3 | 0 | .050 |
| 1907 | 6 | 6 | .500 | 1.77 | 25 | 12 | 9 | 117 | 88 | 38 | 40 | 2 | 2 | 0 | 0 | 43 | 7 | 0 | .163 |
| 1908 | 7 | 10 | .412 | 1.83 | 25 | 15 | 13 | 157.2 | 125 | 49 | 58 | 2 | 1 | 1 | 1 | 52 | 11 | 0 | .212 |
| 1909 2 teams | | | PHI | N | (11G 1–1) | | | BOS | N | (22G 7–7) | | | | | | | | | |
| " total | 8 | 8 | .500 | 2.24 | 33 | 14 | 9 | 176.2 | 158 | 62 | 53 | 2 | 3 | 2 | 3 | 60 | 9 | 0 | .150 |
| 1910 2 teams | | | BOS | N | (4G 0–3) | | | CHI | N | (30G 11–4) | | | | | | | | | |
| " total | 11 | 7 | .611 | 2.71 | 34 | 13 | 8 | 146.1 | 137 | 60 | 60 | 3 | 5 | 2 | 3 | 44 | 9 | 0 | .205 |
| 1911 CHI N | 15 | 11 | .577 | 2.31 | 36 | 28 | 18 | 253 | 213 | 103 | 78 | 4 | 0 | 1 | 1 | 91 | 14 | 0 | .154 |
| 1912 | 16 | 8 | .667 | 2.95 | 39 | 27 | 15 | 238 | 222 | 74 | 69 | 4 | 2 | 2 | 0 | 76 | 10 | 0 | .132 |
| 1913 | 2 | 4 | .333 | 5.82 | 16 | 6 | 1 | 65 | 77 | 30 | 15 | 0 | 1 | 0 | 1 | 17 | 2 | 0 | .118 |
| 8 yrs. | 74 | 65 | .532 | 2.54 | 241 | 137 | 87 | 1359.1 | 1190 | 495 | 438 | 20 | 13 | 10 | 8 | 443 | 65 | 0 | .147 |
| 4 yrs. | 44 | 27 | .620 | 2.94 | 121 | 72 | 42 | 686 | 629 | 258 | 215 | 11 | 7 | 5 | 4 | 224 | 35 | 0 | .156 |

WORLD SERIES

| | W | L | PCT | ERA | G | GS | CG | IP | H | BB | SO | ShO | W | L | SV | AB | H | HR | BA |
|---|---|---|---|---|---|---|---|---|---|---|---|---|---|---|---|---|---|---|---|
| 1910 CHI N | 0 | 0 | – | 0.00 | 1 | 0 | 0 | 1 | 1 | 0 | 0 | 0 | 0 | 0 | 0 | 0 | 0 | 0 | – |

| | W | L | PCT | ERA | G | GS | CG | IP | H | BB | SO | ShO | Relief Pitching W | L | SV | BATTING AB | H | HR | BA |
|---|---|---|---|---|---|---|---|---|---|---|---|---|---|---|---|---|---|---|---|

## Beryl Richmond

RICHMOND, BERYL JUSTICE
B. Aug. 24, 1907, Glen Easton, W. Va.
D. Apr. 24, 1980, Cameron, W. Va.

BB TL 6'1" 185 lbs.
BR 1933

| | W | L | PCT | ERA | G | GS | CG | IP | H | BB | SO | ShO | W | L | SV | AB | H | HR | BA |
|---|---|---|---|---|---|---|---|---|---|---|---|---|---|---|---|---|---|---|---|
| 1933 CHI N | 0 | 0 | – | 1.93 | 4 | 0 | 0 | 4.2 | 10 | 2 | 2 | 0 | 0 | 0 | 0 | 1 | 0 | 0 | .000 |
| 1934 CIN N | 1 | 2 | .333 | 3.72 | 6 | 2 | 1 | 19.1 | 23 | 10 | 9 | 0 | 0 | 1 | 0 | 5 | 0 | 0 | .000 |
| 2 yrs. | 1 | 2 | .333 | 3.38 | 10 | 2 | 1 | 24 | 33 | 12 | 11 | 0 | 0 | 1 | 0 | 6 | 0 | 0 | .000 |
| 1 yr. | 0 | 0 | – | 1.93 | 4 | 0 | 0 | 4.2 | 10 | 2 | 2 | 0 | 0 | 0 | 0 | 1 | 0 | 0 | .000 |

## Reggie Richter

RICHTER, EMIL HENRY
B. Sept. 14, 1888, Dusseldorf, Germany    D. Aug. 2, 1934, Winfield, Ill.

BR TR 6'2" 180 lbs.

| | W | L | PCT | ERA | G | GS | CG | IP | H | BB | SO | ShO | W | L | SV | AB | H | HR | BA |
|---|---|---|---|---|---|---|---|---|---|---|---|---|---|---|---|---|---|---|---|
| 1911 CHI N | 1 | 3 | .250 | 3.13 | 22 | 5 | 0 | 54.2 | 62 | 20 | 34 | 0 | 0 | 1 | 2 | 10 | 1 | 0 | .100 |

## George Riley

RILEY, GEORGE MICHAEL
B. Oct. 6, 1956, Philadelphia, Pa.

BL TL 6'2" 210 lbs.

| | W | L | PCT | ERA | G | GS | CG | IP | H | BB | SO | ShO | W | L | SV | AB | H | HR | BA |
|---|---|---|---|---|---|---|---|---|---|---|---|---|---|---|---|---|---|---|---|
| 1979 CHI N | 0 | 1 | .000 | 5.54 | 4 | 1 | 0 | 13 | 16 | 6 | 5 | 0 | 0 | 0 | 0 | 2 | 0 | 0 | .000 |
| 1980 | 0 | 4 | .000 | 5.75 | 22 | 0 | 0 | 36 | 41 | 20 | 18 | 0 | 0 | 4 | 0 | 1 | 0 | 0 | .000 |
| 1984 SF N | 1 | 0 | 1.000 | 3.99 | 5 | 4 | 0 | 29.1 | 39 | 7 | 12 | 0 | 0 | 0 | 0 | 10 | 1 | 0 | .100 |
| 3 yrs. | 1 | 5 | .167 | 5.06 | 31 | 5 | 0 | 78.1 | 96 | 33 | 35 | 0 | 0 | 4 | 0 | 13 | 1 | 0 | .077 |
| 2 yrs. | 0 | 5 | .000 | 5.69 | 26 | 1 | 0 | 49 | 57 | 26 | 23 | 0 | 0 | 4 | 0 | 3 | 0 | 0 | .000 |

## Allen Ripley

RIPLEY, ALLEN STEVENS
Son of Walt Ripley.
B. Oct. 18, 1952, Norwood, Mass.

BR TR 6'3" 190 lbs.

| | W | L | PCT | ERA | G | GS | CG | IP | H | BB | SO | ShO | W | L | SV | AB | H | HR | BA |
|---|---|---|---|---|---|---|---|---|---|---|---|---|---|---|---|---|---|---|---|
| 1978 BOS A | 2 | 5 | .286 | 5.55 | 15 | 11 | 1 | 73 | 92 | 22 | 26 | 0 | 0 | 0 | 0 | 0 | 0 | 0 | – |
| 1979 | 3 | 1 | .750 | 5.12 | 16 | 3 | 0 | 65 | 77 | 25 | 34 | 0 | 2 | 0 | 1 | 0 | 0 | 0 | – |
| 1980 SF N | 9 | 10 | .474 | 4.14 | 23 | 20 | 2 | 113 | 119 | 36 | 65 | 0 | 1 | 1 | 0 | 40 | 6 | 0 | .150 |
| 1981 | 4 | 4 | .500 | 4.05 | 19 | 14 | 1 | 91 | 103 | 27 | 47 | 0 | 0 | 0 | 0 | 30 | 4 | 0 | .133 |
| 1982 CHI N | 5 | 7 | .417 | 4.26 | 28 | 19 | 0 | 122.2 | 130 | 38 | 57 | 0 | 0 | 1 | 0 | 38 | 5 | 0 | .132 |
| 5 yrs. | 23 | 27 | .460 | 4.51 | 101 | 67 | 4 | 464.2 | 521 | 148 | 229 | 0 | 3 | 2 | 1 | 108 | 15 | 0 | .139 |
| 1 yr. | 5 | 7 | .417 | 4.26 | 28 | 19 | 0 | 122.2 | 130 | 38 | 57 | 0 | 0 | 1 | 0 | 38 | 5 | 0 | .132 |

## Skel Roach

ROACH, SKEL
Born Rudolph C. Weichbrodt.
B. Oct. 20, 1871, Germany    D. Mar. 9, 1958, Oak Park, Ill.

BR TR

| | W | L | PCT | ERA | G | GS | CG | IP | H | BB | SO | ShO | W | L | SV | AB | H | HR | BA |
|---|---|---|---|---|---|---|---|---|---|---|---|---|---|---|---|---|---|---|---|
| 1899 CHI N | 1 | 0 | 1.000 | 3.00 | 1 | 1 | 1 | 9 | 13 | 1 | 0 | 0 | 0 | 0 | 0 | 4 | 0 | 0 | .000 |

## Dave Roberts

ROBERTS, DAVID ARTHUR
B. Sept. 11, 1944, Gallipolis, Ohio

BL TL 6'3" 195 lbs.

| | W | L | PCT | ERA | G | GS | CG | IP | H | BB | SO | ShO | W | L | SV | AB | H | HR | BA |
|---|---|---|---|---|---|---|---|---|---|---|---|---|---|---|---|---|---|---|---|
| 1969 SD N | 0 | 3 | .000 | 4.78 | 22 | 5 | 0 | 49 | 65 | 19 | 19 | 0 | 0 | 0 | 1 | 15 | 4 | 0 | .267 |
| 1970 | 8 | 14 | .364 | 3.81 | 43 | 21 | 3 | 182 | 182 | 43 | 102 | 2 | 4 | 0 | 1 | 59 | 9 | 2 | .153 |
| 1971 | 14 | 17 | .452 | 2.10 | 37 | 34 | 14 | 270 | 238 | 61 | 135 | 2 | 0 | 1 | 0 | 86 | 19 | 0 | .221 |
| 1972 HOU N | 12 | 7 | .632 | 4.50 | 35 | 28 | 7 | 192 | 227 | 57 | 111 | 3 | 1 | 0 | 2 | 67 | 16 | 2 | .239 |
| 1973 | 17 | 11 | .607 | 2.85 | 39 | 36 | 12 | 249.1 | 264 | 62 | 119 | 6 | 0 | 0 | 0 | 85 | 11 | 0 | .129 |
| 1974 | 10 | 12 | .455 | 3.40 | 34 | 30 | 8 | 204 | 216 | 65 | 72 | 2 | 1 | 0 | 1 | 73 | 16 | 1 | .219 |
| 1975 | 8 | 14 | .364 | 4.27 | 32 | 27 | 7 | 198 | 182 | 73 | 101 | 0 | 2 | 0 | 1 | 63 | 9 | 0 | .143 |
| 1976 DET A | 16 | 17 | .485 | 4.00 | 36 | 36 | 18 | 252 | 254 | 63 | 79 | 4 | 0 | 0 | 0 | 0 | 0 | 0 | – |
| 1977 2 teams | | | | | DET | N (22G 4–10) | | | CHI | N (17G 1–1) | | | | | | | | | |
| " total | 5 | 11 | .313 | 4.60 | 39 | 28 | 6 | 182 | 198 | 53 | 69 | 0 | 0 | 0 | 1 | 17 | 1 | 0 | .059 |
| 1978 CHI N | 6 | 8 | .429 | 5.26 | 35 | 20 | 2 | 142 | 159 | 56 | 54 | 1 | 1 | 0 | 1 | 52 | 17 | 2 | .327 |
| 1979 2 teams | | | | | SF | N (26G 0–2) | | | PIT | N (21G 5–2) | | | | | | | | | |
| " total | 5 | 4 | .556 | 2.90 | 47 | 4 | 0 | 80.2 | 89 | 30 | 38 | 0 | 5 | 2 | 4 | 10 | 0 | 0 | .000 |
| 1980 2 teams | | | | | PIT | N (2G 0–1) | | | SEA | A (37G 2–3) | | | | | | | | | |
| " total | 2 | 4 | .333 | 4.39 | 39 | 4 | 0 | 82 | 88 | 28 | 48 | 0 | 0 | 2 | 3 | 0 | 0 | 0 | – |
| 1981 NY N | 0 | 3 | .000 | 9.60 | 7 | 4 | 0 | 15 | 26 | 5 | 10 | 0 | 0 | 0 | 0 | 4 | 1 | 0 | .250 |
| 13 yrs. | 103 | 125 | .452 | 3.78 | 445 | 277 | 77 | 2098 | 2188 | 615 | 957 | 20 | 14 | 5 | 15 | 531 | 103 | 7 | .194 |
| 2 yrs. | 7 | 9 | .438 | 4.71 | 52 | 26 | 3 | 195 | 214 | 68 | 77 | 1 | 1 | 0 | 2 | 69 | 18 | 2 | .261 |

**LEAGUE CHAMPIONSHIP SERIES**

| | W | L | PCT | ERA | G | GS | CG | IP | H | BB | SO | ShO | W | L | SV | AB | H | HR | BA |
|---|---|---|---|---|---|---|---|---|---|---|---|---|---|---|---|---|---|---|---|
| 1979 PIT N | 0 | 0 | – | 0.00 | 1 | 0 | 0 | 0 | 0 | 1 | 0 | 0 | 0 | 0 | 0 | 0 | 0 | 0 | – |

## Robin Roberts

ROBERTS, ROBIN EVAN
B. Sept. 30, 1926, Springfield, Ill.
Hall of Fame 1976.

BB TR 6' 190 lbs.
BL 1948-52

| | W | L | PCT | ERA | G | GS | CG | IP | H | BB | SO | ShO | W | L | SV | AB | H | HR | BA |
|---|---|---|---|---|---|---|---|---|---|---|---|---|---|---|---|---|---|---|---|
| 1948 PHI N | 7 | 9 | .438 | 3.19 | 20 | 20 | 9 | 146.2 | 148 | 61 | 84 | 0 | 0 | 0 | 0 | 44 | 11 | 1 | .250 |
| 1949 | 15 | 15 | .500 | 3.69 | 43 | 31 | 11 | 226.2 | 229 | 75 | 95 | 3 | 3 | 2 | 4 | 67 | 5 | 0 | .075 |
| 1950 | 20 | 11 | .645 | 3.02 | 40 | 39 | 21 | 304.1 | 282 | 77 | 146 | 5 | 0 | 0 | 1 | 102 | 12 | 0 | .118 |
| 1951 | 21 | 15 | .583 | 3.03 | 44 | 39 | 22 | 315 | 284 | 64 | 127 | 6 | 0 | 1 | 2 | 87 | 15 | 0 | .172 |
| 1952 | 28 | 7 | .800 | 2.59 | 39 | 37 | 30 | 330 | 292 | 45 | 148 | 3 | 0 | 0 | 0 | 112 | 14 | 0 | .125 |
| 1953 | 23 | 16 | .590 | 2.75 | 44 | 41 | 33 | 346.2 | 324 | 61 | 198 | 5 | 0 | 0 | 0 | 123 | 22 | 1 | .179 |
| 1954 | 23 | 15 | .605 | 2.97 | 45 | 38 | 29 | 336.2 | 289 | 56 | 185 | 4 | 3 | 0 | 4 | 122 | 15 | 0 | .123 |
| 1955 | 23 | 14 | .622 | 3.28 | 41 | 38 | 26 | 305 | 292 | 53 | 160 | 1 | 0 | 0 | 1 | 107 | 27 | 2 | .252 |
| 1956 | 19 | 18 | .514 | 4.45 | 43 | 37 | 22 | 297.1 | 328 | 40 | 157 | 1 | 2 | 0 | 3 | 100 | 20 | 1 | .200 |
| 1957 | 10 | 22 | .313 | 4.07 | 39 | 32 | 14 | 249.2 | 246 | 43 | 128 | 2 | 1 | 2 | 2 | 80 | 13 | 0 | .163 |
| 1958 | 17 | 14 | .548 | 3.24 | 35 | 34 | 21 | 269.2 | 270 | 51 | 130 | 1 | 0 | 0 | 0 | 99 | 20 | 0 | .202 |
| 1959 | 15 | 17 | .469 | 4.27 | 35 | 35 | 19 | 257.1 | 267 | 35 | 137 | 2 | 0 | 0 | 0 | 89 | 17 | 0 | .191 |
| 1960 | 12 | 16 | .429 | 4.02 | 35 | 33 | 13 | 237.1 | 256 | 34 | 122 | 2 | 0 | 0 | 0 | 79 | 12 | 0 | .152 |
| 1961 | 1 | 10 | .091 | 5.85 | 26 | 18 | 2 | 117 | 154 | 23 | 54 | 0 | 0 | 0 | 0 | 33 | 3 | 0 | .091 |
| 1962 BAL A | 10 | 9 | .526 | 2.78 | 27 | 25 | 6 | 191.1 | 176 | 41 | 102 | 0 | 0 | 0 | 0 | 52 | 10 | 0 | .192 |
| 1963 | 14 | 13 | .519 | 3.33 | 35 | 35 | 9 | 251.1 | 230 | 40 | 124 | 2 | 0 | 0 | 0 | 79 | 16 | 0 | .203 |
| 1964 | 13 | 7 | .650 | 2.91 | 31 | 31 | 8 | 204 | 203 | 52 | 109 | 4 | 0 | 0 | 0 | 68 | 9 | 0 | .132 |

| | W | L | PCT | ERA | G | GS | CG | IP | H | BB | SO | ShO | Relief Pitching W | L | SV | BATTING AB | H | HR | BA |
|---|---|---|---|---|---|---|---|---|---|---|---|---|---|---|---|---|---|---|---|

## Robin Roberts continued

| | W | L | PCT | ERA | G | GS | CG | IP | H | BB | SO | ShO | W | L | SV | AB | H | HR | BA |
|---|---|---|---|---|---|---|---|---|---|---|---|---|---|---|---|---|---|---|---|
| 1965 **2 teams** | **BAL** | **A** | (20G 5–7) | | **HOU** | **N** | (10G 5–2) | | | | | | | | | | | | |
| " total | 10 | 9 | .526 | 2.78 | 30 | 25 | 8 | 190.2 | 171 | 30 | 97 | 3 | 1 | 0 | 0 | 56 | 11 | 0 | .196 |
| 1966 **2 teams** | **HOU** | **N** | (13G 3–5) | | **CHI** | **N** | (11G 2–3) | | | | | | | | | | | | |
| " total | 5 | 8 | .385 | 4.82 | 24 | 21 | 2 | 112 | 141 | 21 | 54 | 1 | 1 | 0 | 1 | 26 | 3 | 0 | .115 |
| 19 yrs. | 286 | 245 | .539 | 3.41 | 676 | 609 | 305 | 4688.2 | 4582 | 902 | 2357 | 45 | 11 | 5 | 25 | 1525 | 255 | 5 | .167 |
| | | 8th | | | | | | | | | | | | | | | | | |
| 1 yr. | 2 | 3 | .400 | 6.14 | 11 | 9 | 1 | 48.1 | 62 | 11 | 28 | 0 | 1 | 0 | 0 | 10 | 2 | 0 | .200 |
| WORLD SERIES | | | | | | | | | | | | | | | | | | | |
| 1950 **PHI N** | 0 | 1 | .000 | 1.64 | 2 | 1 | 1 | 11 | 11 | 3 | 5 | 0 | 0 | 0 | 0 | 2 | 0 | 0 | .000 |

## Freddy Rodriguez

**RODRIGUEZ, FERNANDO PEDRO**   BR TR 6'   180 lbs.
B. Apr. 29, 1928, Havana, Cuba

| | W | L | PCT | ERA | G | GS | CG | IP | H | BB | SO | ShO | W | L | SV | AB | H | HR | BA |
|---|---|---|---|---|---|---|---|---|---|---|---|---|---|---|---|---|---|---|---|
| 1958 **CHI N** | 0 | 0 | – | 7.36 | 7 | 0 | 0 | 7.1 | 8 | 5 | 5 | 0 | 0 | 0 | 2 | 1 | 0 | 0 | .000 |
| 1959 **PHI N** | 0 | 0 | – | 13.50 | 1 | 0 | 0 | 2 | 4 | 0 | 1 | 0 | 0 | 0 | 0 | 0 | 0 | 0 | – |
| 2 yrs. | 0 | 0 | – | 8.68 | 8 | 0 | 0 | 9.1 | 12 | 5 | 6 | 0 | 0 | 0 | 2 | 1 | 0 | 0 | .000 |
| 1 yr. | 0 | 0 | – | 7.36 | 7 | 0 | 0 | 7.1 | 8 | 5 | 5 | 0 | 0 | 0 | 2 | 1 | 0 | 0 | .000 |

## Roberto Rodriguez

**RODRIGUEZ, ROBERTO MUNOZ (Bobby)**   BR TR 6'3"   185 lbs.
B. Feb. 5, 1943, Caracas, Venezuela

| | W | L | PCT | ERA | G | GS | CG | IP | H | BB | SO | ShO | W | L | SV | AB | H | HR | BA |
|---|---|---|---|---|---|---|---|---|---|---|---|---|---|---|---|---|---|---|---|
| 1967 **KC A** | 1 | 1 | .500 | 3.57 | 15 | 5 | 0 | 40.1 | 42 | 14 | 29 | 0 | 0 | 0 | 2 | 9 | 0 | 0 | .000 |
| 1970 **3 teams** | **OAK** | **A** | (6G 0–0) | | **SD** | **N** | (10G 0–0) | | **CHI** | **N** | (26G 3–2) | | | | | | | | |
| " total | 3 | 2 | .600 | 5.53 | 42 | 0 | 0 | 71.2 | 86 | 23 | 62 | 0 | 3 | 2 | 5 | 12 | 1 | 1 | .083 |
| 2 yrs. | 4 | 3 | .571 | 4.82 | 57 | 5 | 0 | 112 | 128 | 37 | 91 | 0 | 3 | 2 | 7 | 21 | 1 | 1 | .048 |
| 1 yr. | 3 | 2 | .600 | 5.82 | 26 | 0 | 0 | 43.1 | 50 | 15 | 46 | 0 | 3 | 2 | 2 | 8 | 1 | 1 | .125 |

## Charlie Root

**ROOT, CHARLES HENRY (Chinski)**   BR TR 5'10½" 190 lbs.
B. Mar. 17, 1899, Middletown, Ohio   D. Nov. 5, 1970, Hollister, Calif.

| | W | L | PCT | ERA | G | GS | CG | IP | H | BB | SO | ShO | W | L | SV | AB | H | HR | BA |
|---|---|---|---|---|---|---|---|---|---|---|---|---|---|---|---|---|---|---|---|
| 1923 **STL A** | 0 | 4 | .000 | 5.70 | 27 | 2 | 0 | 60 | 68 | 18 | 27 | 0 | 0 | 2 | 0 | 13 | 1 | 0 | .077 |
| 1926 **CHI N** | 18 | 17 | .514 | 2.82 | 42 | 32 | 21 | 271.1 | 267 | 62 | 127 | 2 | 2 | 3 | 2 | 91 | 13 | 1 | .143 |
| 1927 | **26** | 15 | .634 | 3.76 | **48** | 36 | 21 | **309** | 296 | **117** | 145 | 4 | 5 | 2 | 2 | 122 | 27 | 0 | .221 |
| 1928 | 14 | 18 | .438 | 3.57 | 40 | 30 | 13 | 237 | 214 | 73 | 122 | 1 | 1 | 2 | 2 | 73 | 13 | 0 | .178 |
| 1929 | 19 | 6 | **.760** | 3.47 | 43 | 31 | 19 | 272 | 286 | 83 | 124 | 4 | 2 | 0 | 5 | 96 | 15 | 1 | .156 |
| 1930 | 16 | 14 | .533 | 4.33 | 37 | 30 | 15 | 220.1 | 247 | 63 | 124 | 4 | 0 | 1 | 3 | 80 | 21 | 0 | .263 |
| 1931 | 17 | 14 | .548 | 3.48 | 39 | 31 | 19 | 251 | 240 | 71 | 131 | 3 | 2 | 1 | 2 | 90 | 20 | 0 | .222 |
| 1932 | 15 | 10 | .600 | 3.58 | 39 | 23 | 11 | 216.1 | 211 | 55 | 96 | 0 | 3 | 2 | 3 | 76 | 13 | 1 | .171 |
| 1933 | 15 | 10 | .600 | 2.60 | 35 | 30 | 20 | 242.1 | 232 | 61 | 86 | 2 | 1 | 1 | 0 | 85 | 8 | 0 | .094 |
| 1934 | 4 | 7 | .364 | 4.28 | 34 | 9 | 2 | 117.2 | 141 | 53 | 46 | 0 | 3 | 2 | 0 | 40 | 7 | 2 | .175 |
| 1935 | 15 | 8 | .652 | 3.08 | 38 | 18 | 11 | 201.1 | 193 | 47 | 94 | 1 | 5 | 3 | 2 | 69 | 14 | 1 | .203 |
| 1936 | 3 | 6 | .333 | 4.15 | 33 | 4 | 0 | 73.2 | 81 | 20 | 32 | 0 | 2 | 5 | 1 | 15 | 5 | 0 | .333 |
| 1937 | 13 | 5 | .722 | 3.38 | 43 | 15 | 5 | 178.2 | 173 | 32 | 74 | 0 | 8 | 0 | 5 | 67 | 12 | 1 | .179 |
| 1938 | 8 | 7 | .533 | 2.86 | 44 | 11 | 5 | 160.2 | 163 | 30 | 70 | 0 | 4 | 1 | 8 | 48 | 8 | 0 | .167 |
| 1939 | 8 | 8 | .500 | 4.03 | 35 | 16 | 8 | 167.1 | 189 | 34 | 65 | 0 | 1 | 1 | 4 | 57 | 10 | 1 | .175 |
| 1940 | 2 | 4 | .333 | 3.82 | 36 | 8 | 1 | 113 | 118 | 33 | 50 | 0 | 2 | 0 | 1 | 31 | 4 | 0 | .129 |
| 1941 | 8 | 7 | .533 | 5.40 | 19 | 15 | 6 | 106.2 | 133 | 37 | 46 | 0 | 1 | 0 | 0 | 33 | 5 | 1 | .152 |
| 17 yrs. | 201 | 160 | .557 | 3.58 | 632 | 341 | 177 | 3198.1 | 3252 | 889 | 1459 | 21 | 42 | 26 | 40 | 1086 | 196 | 11 | .180 |
| 16 yrs. | 201 | 156 | .563 | 3.54 | 605 | 339 | 177 | 3138.1 | 3184 | 871 | 1432 | 21 | 42 | 24 | 40 | 1073 | 195 | 11 | .182 |
| | 1st | 1st | | | 1st | | | 1st | | | 2nd | | 2nd 10th | | 2nd | | | 5th | |
| WORLD SERIES | | | | | | | | | | | | | | | | | | | |
| 1929 **CHI N** | 0 | 1 | .000 | 4.73 | 2 | 2 | 0 | 13.1 | 12 | 2 | 8 | 0 | 0 | 0 | 0 | 5 | 0 | 0 | .000 |
| 1932 | 0 | 1 | .000 | 10.38 | 1 | 1 | 0 | 4.1 | 6 | 3 | 4 | 0 | 0 | 0 | 0 | 2 | 0 | 0 | .000 |
| 1935 | 0 | 1 | .000 | 18.00 | 2 | 1 | 0 | 2 | 5 | 1 | 2 | 0 | 0 | 0 | 0 | 0 | 0 | 0 | – |
| 1938 | 0 | 0 | – | 3.00 | 1 | 0 | 0 | 3 | 3 | 0 | 1 | 0 | 0 | 0 | 0 | 0 | 0 | 0 | – |
| 4 yrs. | 0 | 3 | .000 | 6.75 | 6 | 4 | 0 | 22.2 | 26 | 6 | 15 | 0 | 0 | 0 | 0 | 7 | 0 | 0 | .000 |

## Gary Ross

**ROSS, GARY DOUGLAS**   BR TR 6'1"   185 lbs.
B. Sept. 16, 1947, McKeesport, Pa.

| | W | L | PCT | ERA | G | GS | CG | IP | H | BB | SO | ShO | W | L | SV | AB | H | HR | BA |
|---|---|---|---|---|---|---|---|---|---|---|---|---|---|---|---|---|---|---|---|
| 1968 **CHI N** | 1 | 1 | .500 | 4.17 | 13 | 5 | 1 | 41 | 44 | 25 | 31 | 0 | 0 | 0 | 0 | 11 | 1 | 0 | .091 |
| 1969 **2 teams** | **CHI** | **N** | (2G 0–0) | | **SD** | **N** | (46G 3–12) | | | | | | | | | | | | |
| " total | 3 | 12 | .200 | 4.35 | 48 | 18 | 2 | 111.2 | 105 | 58 | 60 | 0 | 0 | 0 | 3 | 23 | 0 | 0 | .000 |
| 1970 **SD N** | 2 | 3 | .400 | 5.23 | 33 | 2 | 0 | 62 | 72 | 36 | 39 | 0 | 2 | 3 | 1 | 8 | 4 | 0 | .500 |
| 1971 | 1 | 3 | .250 | 3.00 | 13 | 0 | 0 | 24 | 27 | 11 | 13 | 0 | 1 | 3 | 0 | 1 | 0 | 0 | .000 |
| 1972 | 4 | 3 | .571 | 2.45 | 60 | 0 | 0 | 91.2 | 87 | 49 | 46 | 0 | 4 | 3 | 3 | 13 | 2 | 0 | .154 |
| 1973 | 4 | 4 | .500 | 5.42 | 58 | 0 | 0 | 76.1 | 93 | 33 | 44 | 0 | 4 | 4 | 0 | 4 | 0 | 0 | .000 |
| 1974 | 0 | 0 | – | 4.50 | 9 | 0 | 0 | 18 | 23 | 6 | 11 | 0 | 0 | 0 | 0 | 1 | 0 | 0 | .000 |
| 1975 **CAL A** | 0 | 1 | .000 | 5.40 | 1 | 1 | 0 | 5 | 6 | 1 | 4 | 0 | 0 | 0 | 0 | 0 | 0 | 0 | – |
| 1976 | 8 | 16 | .333 | 3.00 | 34 | 31 | 7 | 225 | 224 | 58 | 100 | 2 | 0 | 0 | 0 | 0 | 0 | 0 | – |
| 1977 | 2 | 4 | .333 | 5.59 | 14 | 12 | 0 | 58 | 83 | 11 | 30 | 0 | 0 | 0 | 0 | 0 | 0 | 0 | – |
| 10 yrs. | 25 | 47 | .347 | 3.93 | 283 | 59 | 8 | 712.2 | 764 | 288 | 378 | 2 | 11 | 13 | 7 | 61 | 7 | 0 | .115 |
| 2 yrs. | 1 | 1 | .500 | 4.60 | 15 | 6 | 1 | 43 | 45 | 27 | 33 | 0 | 0 | 0 | 0 | 11 | 1 | 0 | .091 |

## Jack Rowan

**ROWAN, JOHN ALBERT**   BR TR 6'1"   210 lbs.
B. June 16, 1886, New Castle, Pa.   D. Sept. 29, 1966, Dayton, Ohio

| | W | L | PCT | ERA | G | GS | CG | IP | H | BB | SO | ShO | W | L | SV | AB | H | HR | BA |
|---|---|---|---|---|---|---|---|---|---|---|---|---|---|---|---|---|---|---|---|
| 1906 **DET A** | 0 | 1 | .000 | 11.00 | 1 | 1 | 1 | 9 | 15 | 6 | 0 | 0 | 0 | 0 | 0 | 4 | 1 | 0 | .250 |
| 1908 **CIN N** | 3 | 3 | .500 | 1.82 | 8 | 7 | 4 | 49.1 | 46 | 16 | 24 | 1 | 1 | 0 | 0 | 14 | 1 | 0 | .071 |
| 1909 | 11 | 12 | .478 | 2.79 | 38 | 23 | 14 | 225.2 | 185 | 104 | 81 | 0 | 3 | 0 | 0 | 65 | 6 | 0 | .092 |
| 1910 | 14 | 13 | .519 | 2.93 | 42 | 30 | 18 | 261 | 242 | 105 | 108 | 4 | 3 | 3 | 1 | 83 | 19 | 0 | .229 |
| 1911 **2 teams** | **PHI** | **N** | (12G 2–4) | | **CHI** | **N** | (1G 0–0) | | | | | | | | | | | | |
| " total | 2 | 4 | .333 | 4.72 | 13 | 6 | 2 | 47.2 | 60 | 22 | 17 | 0 | 0 | 1 | 0 | 14 | 1 | 0 | .071 |
| 1913 **CIN N** | 0 | 4 | .000 | 3.00 | 5 | 5 | 5 | 39 | 37 | 9 | 21 | 0 | 0 | 0 | 0 | 11 | 2 | 0 | .182 |

| | W | L | PCT | ERA | G | GS | CG | IP | H | BB | SO | ShO | Relief Pitching W | L | SV | BATTING AB | H | HR | BA |
|---|---|---|---|---|---|---|---|---|---|---|---|---|---|---|---|---|---|---|---|

## Jack Rowan continued

| | W | L | PCT | ERA | G | GS | CG | IP | H | BB | SO | ShO | W | L | SV | AB | H | HR | BA |
|---|---|---|---|---|---|---|---|---|---|---|---|---|---|---|---|---|---|---|---|
| 1914 | 1 | 3 | .250 | 3.46 | 12 | 2 | 0 | 39 | 38 | 10 | 16 | 0 | 1 | 1 | 1 | 8 | 0 | 0 | .000 |
| 7 yrs. | 31 | 40 | .437 | 3.07 | 119 | 74 | 44 | 670.2 | 623 | 272 | 267 | 5 | 8 | 5 | 2 | 199 | 30 | 0 | .151 |
| 1 yr. | 0 | 0 | – | 4.50 | 1 | 0 | 0 | 2 | 1 | 2 | 0 | 0 | 0 | 0 | 0 | 1 | 0 | 0 | .000 |

## Dave Rowe

**ROWE, DAVID**    BR TR 5'9"   180 lbs.
Brother of Jack Rowe.
B. Feb., 1856, Jacksonville, Ill.   Deceased.
Manager 1886, 1888.

| | W | L | PCT | ERA | G | GS | CG | IP | H | BB | SO | ShO | W | L | SV | AB | H | HR | BA |
|---|---|---|---|---|---|---|---|---|---|---|---|---|---|---|---|---|---|---|---|
| 1877 CHI N | 0 | 1 | .000 | 18.00 | 1 | 1 | 0 | 1 | 3 | 2 | 0 | 0 | 0 | 0 | 0 | 7 | 2 | 0 | .286 |
| 1882 CLE N | 0 | 1 | .000 | 12.00 | 1 | 1 | 1 | 9 | 29 | 7 | 0 | 0 | 0 | 0 | 0 | 97 | 25 | 1 | .258 |
| 1883 BAL AA | 0 | 0 | – | 20.25 | 1 | 0 | 0 | 4 | 12 | 2 | 1 | 0 | 0 | 0 | 0 | 256 | 80 | 0 | .313 |
| 1884 STL U | 1 | 0 | 1.000 | 2.00 | 1 | 1 | 1 | 9 | 10 | 0 | 2 | 0 | 0 | 0 | 0 | 485 | 142 | 3 | .293 |
| 4 yrs. | 1 | 2 | .333 | 9.78 | 4 | 3 | 2 | 23 | 54 | 11 | 3 | 0 | 0 | 0 | 0 | * | | | |
| 1 yr. | 0 | 1 | .000 | 18.00 | 1 | 1 | 0 | 1 | 3 | 2 | 0 | 0 | 0 | 0 | 0 | 7 | 2 | 0 | .286 |

## Luther Roy

**ROY, LUTHER FRANKLIN**    BR TR 5'10½" 161 lbs.
Brother of Charlie Roy.
B. July 29, 1902, Ooltewah, Tenn.   D. July 24, 1963, Grand Rapids, Mich.

| | W | L | PCT | ERA | G | GS | CG | IP | H | BB | SO | ShO | W | L | SV | AB | H | HR | BA |
|---|---|---|---|---|---|---|---|---|---|---|---|---|---|---|---|---|---|---|---|
| 1924 CLE A | 0 | 5 | .000 | 7.77 | 16 | 5 | 2 | 48.2 | 62 | 31 | 14 | 0 | 0 | 1 | 0 | 15 | 4 | 0 | .267 |
| 1925 | 0 | 0 | – | 3.60 | 6 | 1 | 0 | 10 | 14 | 11 | 1 | 0 | 0 | 0 | 0 | 2 | 0 | 0 | .000 |
| 1927 CHI N | 3 | 1 | .750 | 2.29 | 11 | 0 | 0 | 19.2 | 14 | 11 | 5 | 0 | 3 | 1 | 0 | 3 | 1 | 0 | .333 |
| 1929 2 teams | | | | PHI N | (21G 3–6) | | | BKN | N | (2G 0–0) | | | | | | | | | |
| " total | 3 | 6 | .333 | 8.29 | 23 | 12 | 1 | 92.1 | 141 | 39 | 16 | 0 | 1 | 1 | 0 | 33 | 9 | 0 | .273 |
| 4 yrs. | 6 | 12 | .333 | 7.17 | 56 | 18 | 3 | 170.2 | 231 | 92 | 36 | 0 | 4 | 3 | 0 | 53 | 14 | 0 | .264 |
| 1 yr. | 3 | 1 | .750 | 2.29 | 11 | 0 | 0 | 19.2 | 14 | 11 | 5 | 0 | 3 | 1 | 0 | 3 | 1 | 0 | .333 |

## Dutch Ruether

**RUETHER, WALTER HENRY**    BL TL 6'1½" 180 lbs.
B. Sept. 13, 1893, Alameda, Calif.   D. May 16, 1970, Phoenix, Ariz.

| | W | L | PCT | ERA | G | GS | CG | IP | H | BB | SO | ShO | W | L | SV | AB | H | HR | BA |
|---|---|---|---|---|---|---|---|---|---|---|---|---|---|---|---|---|---|---|---|
| 1917 2 teams | | | | CHI N | (10G 2–0) | | | CIN | N | (7G 1–2) | | | | | | | | | |
| " total | 3 | 2 | .600 | 3.00 | 17 | 8 | 2 | 72 | 80 | 26 | 35 | 1 | 0 | 0 | 0 | 68 | 17 | 0 | .250 |
| 1918 CIN N | 0 | 1 | .000 | 2.70 | 2 | 2 | 1 | 10 | 10 | 3 | 10 | 0 | 0 | 0 | 0 | 3 | 0 | 0 | .000 |
| 1919 | 19 | 6 | .760 | 1.82 | 33 | 29 | 20 | 242.2 | 195 | 83 | 78 | 3 | 0 | 0 | 0 | 92 | 24 | 0 | .261 |
| 1920 | 16 | 12 | .571 | 2.47 | 37 | 33 | 23 | 265.2 | 235 | 96 | 99 | 5 | 0 | 1 | 3 | 104 | 20 | 0 | .192 |
| 1921 BKN N | 10 | 13 | .435 | 4.26 | 36 | 27 | 12 | 211.1 | 247 | 67 | 78 | 1 | 0 | 0 | 2 | 97 | 34 | 2 | .351 |
| 1922 | 21 | 12 | .636 | 3.53 | 35 | 35 | 26 | 267.1 | 290 | 92 | 89 | 2 | 0 | 0 | 0 | 125 | 26 | 2 | .208 |
| 1923 | 15 | 14 | .517 | 4.22 | 34 | 34 | 20 | 275 | 308 | 86 | 87 | 0 | 0 | 0 | 0 | 117 | 32 | 0 | .274 |
| 1924 | 8 | 13 | .381 | 3.94 | 30 | 21 | 13 | 166.2 | 189 | 45 | 65 | 2 | 0 | 0 | 0 | 62 | 15 | 0 | .242 |
| 1925 WAS A | 18 | 7 | .720 | 3.87 | 30 | 29 | 16 | 223.1 | 241 | 105 | 68 | 1 | 0 | 1 | 0 | 108 | 36 | 1 | .333 |
| 1926 2 teams | | | | WAS | A | (23G 12–6) | | NY | A | (5G 2–3) | | | | | | | | | |
| " total | 14 | 9 | .609 | 4.60 | 28 | 28 | 10 | 205.1 | 246 | 84 | 56 | 0 | 0 | 0 | 0 | 113 | 25 | 1 | .221 |
| 1927 NY A | 13 | 6 | .684 | 3.38 | 27 | 26 | 12 | 184 | 202 | 52 | 45 | 3 | 0 | 0 | 0 | 80 | 21 | 1 | .263 |
| 11 yrs. | 137 | 95 | .591 | 3.50 | 309 | 272 | 155 | 2123.1 | 2243 | 739 | 710 | 18 | 1 | 3 | 8 | * | | | |
| 1 yr. | 2 | 0 | 1.000 | 2.48 | 10 | 4 | 1 | 36.1 | 37 | 12 | 23 | 0 | 0 | 0 | 0 | 44 | 12 | 0 | .273 |

**WORLD SERIES**

| | W | L | PCT | ERA | G | GS | CG | IP | H | BB | SO | ShO | W | L | SV | AB | H | HR | BA |
|---|---|---|---|---|---|---|---|---|---|---|---|---|---|---|---|---|---|---|---|
| 1919 CIN N | 1 | 0 | 1.000 | 2.57 | 2 | 2 | 1 | 14 | 12 | 4 | 1 | 0 | 0 | 0 | 0 | 6 | 4 | 0 | .667 |
| 1926 NY A | 0 | 1 | .000 | 8.31 | 1 | 1 | 0 | 4.1 | 7 | 2 | 1 | 0 | 0 | 0 | 0 | 4 | 0 | 0 | .000 |
| 2 yrs. | 1 | 1 | .500 | 3.93 | 3 | 3 | 1 | 18.1 | 19 | 6 | 2 | 0 | 0 | 0 | 0 | 11 | 4 | 0 | .364 |

## Bob Rush

**RUSH, ROBERT RANSOM**    BR TR 6'4"   205 lbs.
B. Dec. 21, 1925, Battle Creek, Mich.

| | W | L | PCT | ERA | G | GS | CG | IP | H | BB | SO | ShO | W | L | SV | AB | H | HR | BA |
|---|---|---|---|---|---|---|---|---|---|---|---|---|---|---|---|---|---|---|---|
| 1948 CHI N | 5 | 11 | .313 | 3.92 | 36 | 16 | 4 | 133.1 | 153 | 37 | 72 | 0 | 2 | 0 | 0 | 39 | 5 | 0 | .128 |
| 1949 | 10 | 18 | .357 | 4.07 | 35 | 27 | 9 | 201 | 197 | 79 | 80 | 1 | 2 | 0 | 4 | 63 | 2 | 0 | .032 |
| 1950 | 13 | 20 | .394 | 3.71 | 39 | 34 | 19 | 254.2 | 261 | 93 | 93 | 1 | 0 | 2 | 1 | 90 | 15 | 1 | .167 |
| 1951 | 11 | 12 | .478 | 3.83 | 37 | 29 | 12 | 211.1 | 219 | 68 | 129 | 2 | 2 | 0 | 2 | 68 | 13 | 0 | .191 |
| 1952 | 17 | 13 | .567 | 2.70 | 34 | 32 | 17 | 250.1 | 205 | 81 | 157 | 4 | 0 | 2 | 0 | 96 | 28 | 0 | .292 |
| 1953 | 9 | 14 | .391 | 4.54 | 29 | 28 | 8 | 166.2 | 177 | 66 | 84 | 1 | 0 | 0 | 0 | 54 | 6 | 0 | .111 |
| 1954 | 13 | 15 | .464 | 3.77 | 33 | 32 | 11 | 236.1 | 213 | 103 | 124 | 0 | 0 | 0 | 0 | 83 | 23 | 2 | .277 |
| 1955 | 13 | 11 | .542 | 3.50 | 33 | 33 | 14 | 234 | 204 | 73 | 130 | 3 | 0 | 0 | 0 | 82 | 9 | 1 | .110 |
| 1956 | 13 | 10 | .565 | 3.19 | 32 | 32 | 13 | 239.2 | 210 | 59 | 104 | 1 | 0 | 0 | 0 | 82 | 8 | 0 | .098 |
| 1957 | 6 | 16 | .273 | 4.38 | 31 | 29 | 5 | 205.1 | 211 | 66 | 103 | 0 | 0 | 0 | 0 | 69 | 14 | 0 | .203 |
| 1958 MIL N | 10 | 6 | .625 | 3.42 | 28 | 20 | 5 | 147.1 | 142 | 31 | 84 | 2 | 3 | 1 | 0 | 45 | 9 | 0 | .200 |
| 1959 | 5 | 6 | .455 | 2.40 | 31 | 9 | 1 | 101.1 | 102 | 23 | 64 | 1 | 3 | 2 | 0 | 32 | 6 | 0 | .188 |
| 1960 2 teams | | | | MIL | N | (10G 2–0) | | CHI | A | (9G 0–0) | | | | | | | | | |
| " total | 2 | 0 | 1.000 | 4.91 | 19 | 0 | 0 | 29.1 | 40 | 10 | 20 | 0 | 2 | 0 | 1 | 4 | 2 | 0 | .500 |
| 13 yrs. | 127 | 152 | .455 | 3.65 | 417 | 321 | 118 | 2410.2 | 2334 | 789 | 1244 | 16 | 14 | 7 | 8 | 807 | 140 | 4 | .173 |
| 10 yrs. | 110 | 140 | .440 | 3.71 | 339 | 292 | 112 | 2132.2 | 2050 | 725 | 1076 | 13 | 6 | 4 | 7 | 726 | 123 | 4 | .169 |
| | | | 3rd | | | 9th | | | | | 4th | 7th | | | | | | | | |

**WORLD SERIES**

| | W | L | PCT | ERA | G | GS | CG | IP | H | BB | SO | ShO | W | L | SV | AB | H | HR | BA |
|---|---|---|---|---|---|---|---|---|---|---|---|---|---|---|---|---|---|---|---|
| 1958 MIL N | 0 | 1 | .000 | 3.00 | 1 | 1 | 0 | 6 | 3 | 5 | 2 | 0 | 0 | 0 | 0 | 0 | 0 | 0 | .000 |

## Jack Russell

**RUSSELL, JACK ERWIN**    BR TR 6'1½" 178 lbs.
B. Oct. 24, 1905, Paris, Tex.

| | W | L | PCT | ERA | G | GS | CG | IP | H | BB | SO | ShO | W | L | SV | AB | H | HR | BA |
|---|---|---|---|---|---|---|---|---|---|---|---|---|---|---|---|---|---|---|---|
| 1926 BOS A | 0 | 5 | .000 | 3.58 | 36 | 5 | 1 | 98 | 94 | 24 | 17 | 0 | 0 | 0 | 0 | 21 | 4 | 0 | .190 |
| 1927 | 4 | 9 | .308 | 4.10 | 34 | 15 | 4 | 147 | 172 | 40 | 25 | 1 | 1 | 1 | 0 | 48 | 6 | 0 | .125 |
| 1928 | 11 | 14 | .440 | 3.84 | 32 | 26 | 10 | 201.1 | 233 | 41 | 27 | 2 | 1 | 0 | 0 | 62 | 13 | 0 | .210 |
| 1929 | 6 | 18 | .250 | 3.94 | 35 | 32 | 13 | 226.1 | 263 | 40 | 37 | 0 | 0 | 0 | 0 | 70 | 9 | 0 | .129 |
| 1930 | 9 | 20 | .310 | 5.45 | 35 | 30 | 15 | 229.2 | 302 | 53 | 35 | 0 | 0 | 0 | 0 | 79 | 14 | 1 | .177 |
| 1931 | 10 | 18 | .357 | 5.16 | 36 | 31 | 13 | 232 | 298 | 65 | 45 | 0 | 0 | 1 | 0 | 82 | 16 | 0 | .195 |

| | W | L | PCT | ERA | G | GS | CG | IP | H | BB | SO | ShO | Relief Pitching W | L | SV | BATTING AB | H | HR | BA |
|---|---|---|---|---|---|---|---|---|---|---|---|---|---|---|---|---|---|---|---|

## Jack Russell continued

| | W | L | PCT | ERA | G | GS | CG | IP | H | BB | SO | ShO | W | L | SV | AB | H | HR | BA |
|---|---|---|---|---|---|---|---|---|---|---|---|---|---|---|---|---|---|---|---|
| 1932 2 teams | | | **BOS** | **A** (11G 1–7) | | **CLE** | **A** (18G 5–7) | | | | | | | | | | | | |
| " total | 6 | 14 | .300 | 5.25 | 29 | 17 | 7 | 152.2 | 207 | 42 | 34 | 0 | 0 | 3 | 1 | 51 | 13 | 0 | .255 |
| 1933 WAS A | 12 | 6 | .667 | 2.69 | 50 | 3 | 2 | 124 | 119 | 32 | 28 | 0 | 11 | 4 | 13 | 34 | 5 | 0 | .147 |
| 1934 | 5 | 10 | .333 | 4.17 | 54 | 9 | 3 | 157.2 | 179 | 56 | 38 | 0 | 2 | 7 | 7 | 44 | 7 | 0 | .159 |
| 1935 | 4 | 9 | .308 | 5.71 | 43 | 7 | 2 | 126 | 170 | 37 | 30 | 0 | 4 | 5 | 3 | 35 | 7 | 0 | .200 |
| 1936 2 teams | | | **WAS** | **A** (18G 3–2) | | **BOS** | **A** (23G 0–3) | | | | | | | | | | | | |
| " total | 3 | 5 | .375 | 6.02 | 41 | 7 | 1 | 89.2 | 123 | 41 | 15 | 0 | 1 | 4 | 3 | 22 | 2 | 0 | .091 |
| 1937 DET A | 2 | 5 | .286 | 7.59 | 25 | 0 | 0 | 40.1 | 63 | 20 | 10 | 0 | 2 | 5 | 4 | 7 | 0 | 0 | .000 |
| 1938 CHI N | 6 | 1 | .857 | 3.34 | 42 | 0 | 0 | 102.1 | 100 | 30 | 29 | 0 | 6 | 1 | 3 | 32 | 7 | 0 | .219 |
| 1939 | 4 | 3 | .571 | 3.67 | 39 | 0 | 0 | 68.2 | 78 | 24 | 32 | 0 | 4 | 3 | 3 | 17 | 0 | 0 | .000 |
| 1940 STL N | 3 | 4 | .429 | 2.50 | 26 | 0 | 0 | 54 | 53 | 26 | 16 | 0 | 3 | 4 | 1 | 13 | 0 | 0 | .000 |
| 15 yrs. | 85 | 141 | .376 | 4.47 | 557 | 182 | 71 | 2049.2 | 2454 | 571 | 418 | 3 | 35 | 40 | 38 | 617 | 103 | 1 | .167 |
| 2 yrs. | 10 | 4 | .714 | 3.47 | 81 | 0 | 0 | 171 | 178 | 54 | 61 | 0 | 10 | 4 | 6 | 49 | 7 | 0 | .143 |

**WORLD SERIES**

| | W | L | PCT | ERA | G | GS | CG | IP | H | BB | SO | ShO | W | L | SV | AB | H | HR | BA |
|---|---|---|---|---|---|---|---|---|---|---|---|---|---|---|---|---|---|---|---|
| 1933 WAS A | 0 | 1 | .000 | 0.87 | 3 | 0 | 0 | 10.1 | 8 | 0 | 7 | 0 | 0 | 1 | 0 | 2 | 0 | 0 | .000 |
| 1938 CHI N | 0 | 0 | – | 0.00 | 2 | 0 | 0 | 1.2 | 1 | 1 | 0 | 0 | 0 | 0 | 0 | 0 | 0 | 0 | – |
| 2 yrs. | 0 | 1 | .000 | 0.75 | 5 | 0 | 0 | 12 | 9 | 1 | 7 | 0 | 0 | 1 | 0 | 2 | 0 | 0 | .000 |

## Dick Ruthven

RUTHVEN, RICHARD DAVID                BR TR 6'3"      190 lbs.
B. Mar. 27, 1951, Sacramento, Calif.

| | W | L | PCT | ERA | G | GS | CG | IP | H | BB | SO | ShO | W | L | SV | AB | H | HR | BA |
|---|---|---|---|---|---|---|---|---|---|---|---|---|---|---|---|---|---|---|---|
| 1973 PHI N | 6 | 9 | .400 | 4.21 | 25 | 23 | 3 | 128.1 | 125 | 75 | 98 | 1 | 1 | 0 | 0 | 38 | 5 | 0 | .132 |
| 1974 | 9 | 13 | .409 | 4.01 | 35 | 35 | 6 | 213 | 182 | 116 | 153 | 0 | 0 | 0 | 0 | 68 | 13 | 0 | .191 |
| 1975 | 2 | 2 | .500 | 4.17 | 11 | 7 | 0 | 41 | 37 | 22 | 26 | 0 | 0 | 0 | 0 | 13 | 2 | 0 | .154 |
| 1976 ATL N | 14 | 17 | .452 | 4.20 | 36 | 36 | 8 | 240 | 255 | 90 | 142 | 4 | 0 | 0 | 0 | 76 | 13 | 0 | .171 |
| 1977 | 7 | 13 | .350 | 4.23 | 25 | 23 | 6 | 151 | 158 | 62 | 84 | 2 | 0 | 0 | 0 | 45 | 12 | 1 | .267 |
| 1978 2 teams | | | **ATL** | **N** (13G 2–6) | | **PHI** | **N** (20G 13–5) | | | | | | | | | | | | |
| " total | 15 | 11 | .577 | 3.38 | 33 | 33 | 11 | 231.2 | 214 | 56 | 120 | 3 | 0 | 0 | 0 | 77 | 17 | 0 | .221 |
| 1979 PHI N | 7 | 5 | .583 | 4.28 | 20 | 20 | 3 | 122 | 121 | 37 | 58 | 2 | 0 | 0 | 0 | 41 | 6 | 0 | .146 |
| 1980 | 17 | 10 | .630 | 3.55 | 33 | 33 | 6 | 223 | 241 | 74 | 86 | 1 | 0 | 0 | 0 | 68 | 16 | 0 | .235 |
| 1981 | 12 | 7 | .632 | 5.14 | 23 | 22 | 5 | 147 | 162 | 54 | 80 | 0 | 0 | 0 | 0 | 50 | 7 | 0 | .140 |
| 1982 | 11 | 11 | .500 | 3.79 | 33 | 31 | 8 | 204.1 | 189 | 59 | 115 | 2 | 0 | 0 | 0 | 64 | 7 | 0 | .109 |
| 1983 2 teams | | | **PHI** | **N** (7G 1–3) | | **CHI** | **N** (25G 12–9) | | | | | | | | | | | | |
| " total | 13 | 12 | .520 | 4.38 | 32 | 32 | 5 | 183 | 202 | 38 | 99 | 2 | 0 | 0 | 0 | 62 | 13 | 0 | .210 |
| 1984 CHI N | 6 | 10 | .375 | 5.04 | 23 | 22 | 0 | 126.2 | 154 | 41 | 55 | 0 | 0 | 0 | 0 | 44 | 7 | 0 | .159 |
| 1985 | 4 | 7 | .364 | 4.53 | 20 | 15 | 0 | 87.1 | 103 | 37 | 26 | 0 | 0 | 0 | 0 | 24 | 5 | 0 | .208 |
| 13 yrs. | 123 | 127 | .492 | 4.13 | 349 | 332 | 61 | 2098.1 | 2143 | 761 | 1142 | 17 | 1 | 0 | 1 | 670 | 123 | 1 | .184 |
| 3 yrs. | 22 | 26 | .458 | 4.53 | 68 | 62 | 5 | 363.1 | 413 | 106 | 154 | 2 | 0 | 0 | 0 | 121 | 24 | 0 | .198 |

**DIVISIONAL PLAYOFF SERIES**

| | W | L | PCT | ERA | G | GS | CG | IP | H | BB | SO | ShO | W | L | SV | AB | H | HR | BA |
|---|---|---|---|---|---|---|---|---|---|---|---|---|---|---|---|---|---|---|---|
| 1981 PHI N | 0 | 1 | .000 | 4.50 | 1 | 1 | 0 | 4 | 3 | 1 | 0 | 0 | 0 | 0 | 0 | 1 | 0 | 0 | .000 |

**LEAGUE CHAMPIONSHIP SERIES**

| | W | L | PCT | ERA | G | GS | CG | IP | H | BB | SO | ShO | W | L | SV | AB | H | HR | BA |
|---|---|---|---|---|---|---|---|---|---|---|---|---|---|---|---|---|---|---|---|
| 1978 PHI N | 0 | 1 | .000 | 5.79 | 1 | 1 | 0 | 4.2 | 6 | 0 | 3 | 0 | 0 | 0 | 0 | 1 | 0 | 0 | .000 |
| 1980 | 1 | 0 | 1.000 | 2.00 | 2 | 1 | 0 | 9 | 3 | 5 | 4 | 0 | 1 | 0 | 0 | 2 | 0 | 0 | .000 |
| 2 yrs. | 1 | 1 | .500 | 3.29 | 3 | 2 | 0 | 13.2 | 9 | 5 | 7 | 0 | 1 | 0 | 0 | 3 | 0 | 0 | .000 |

**WORLD SERIES**

| | W | L | PCT | ERA | G | GS | CG | IP | H | BB | SO | ShO | W | L | SV | AB | H | HR | BA |
|---|---|---|---|---|---|---|---|---|---|---|---|---|---|---|---|---|---|---|---|
| 1980 PHI N | 0 | 0 | – | 3.00 | 1 | 1 | 0 | 9 | 9 | 1 | 7 | 0 | 0 | 0 | 0 | 0 | 0 | 0 | – |

## Jimmy Ryan

RYAN, JAMES E.                        BR TL 5'9"      162 lbs.
B. Feb. 11, 1863, Clinton, Mass.    D. Oct. 26, 1923, Chicago, Ill.

| | W | L | PCT | ERA | G | GS | CG | IP | H | BB | SO | ShO | W | L | SV | AB | H | HR | BA |
|---|---|---|---|---|---|---|---|---|---|---|---|---|---|---|---|---|---|---|---|
| 1886 CHI N | 0 | 0 | – | 4.63 | 5 | 0 | 0 | 23.1 | 19 | 13 | 15 | 0 | 0 | 0 | 1 | 327 | 100 | 4 | .306 |
| 1887 | 2 | 1 | .667 | 4.20 | 8 | 3 | 2 | 45 | 53 | 17 | 14 | 0 | 1 | 0 | 0 | 508 | 145 | 11 | .285 |
| 1888 | 4 | 0 | 1.000 | 3.05 | 8 | 2 | 1 | 38.1 | 47 | 12 | 11 | 0 | 3 | 0 | 0 | 549 | 182 | 16 | .332 |
| 1891 | 0 | 0 | – | 1.59 | 2 | 0 | 0 | 5.2 | 11 | 2 | 2 | 0 | 0 | 0 | 0 | 505 | 145 | 9 | .287 |
| 1893 | 0 | 0 | – | 0.00 | 1 | 0 | 0 | 4.2 | 3 | 0 | 1 | 0 | 0 | 0 | 1 | 341 | 102 | 3 | .299 |
| 5 yrs. | 6 | 1 | .857 | 3.62 | 24 | 5 | 3 | 117 | 133 | 44 | 43 | 0 | 4 | 0 | 2 | * | | | |
| 5 yrs. | 6 | 1 | .857 | 3.62 | 24 | 5 | 3 | 117 | 133 | 44 | 43 | 0 | 4 | 0 | 2 | 6770 | 2102 | 99 | .310 |

## Jim St. Vrain

ST. VRAIN, JAMES MARCELLIN                         TL
B. June 6, 1871, Ralls County, Mo.    D. June 12, 1937, Butte, Mont.

| | W | L | PCT | ERA | G | GS | CG | IP | H | BB | SO | ShO | W | L | SV | AB | H | HR | BA |
|---|---|---|---|---|---|---|---|---|---|---|---|---|---|---|---|---|---|---|---|
| 1902 CHI N | 4 | 6 | .400 | 2.08 | 12 | 11 | 10 | 95 | 88 | 25 | 51 | 1 | 0 | 0 | 0 | 31 | 3 | 0 | .097 |

## Scott Sanderson

SANDERSON, SCOTT DOUGLAS              BR TR 6'5"      195 lbs.
B. July 22, 1956, Dearborn, Mich.

| | W | L | PCT | ERA | G | GS | CG | IP | H | BB | SO | ShO | W | L | SV | AB | H | HR | BA |
|---|---|---|---|---|---|---|---|---|---|---|---|---|---|---|---|---|---|---|---|
| 1978 MON N | 4 | 2 | .667 | 2.51 | 10 | 9 | 1 | 61 | 52 | 21 | 50 | 1 | 0 | 0 | 0 | 19 | 2 | 0 | .105 |
| 1979 | 9 | 8 | .529 | 3.43 | 34 | 24 | 5 | 168 | 148 | 54 | 138 | 3 | 1 | 1 | 1 | 50 | 8 | 0 | .160 |
| 1980 | 16 | 11 | .593 | 3.11 | 33 | 33 | 7 | 211 | 206 | 56 | 125 | 3 | 0 | 0 | 0 | 64 | 5 | 0 | .078 |
| 1981 | 9 | 7 | .563 | 2.96 | 22 | 22 | 4 | 137 | 122 | 31 | 77 | 1 | 0 | 0 | 0 | 35 | 4 | 0 | .114 |
| 1982 | 12 | 12 | .500 | 3.46 | 32 | 32 | 7 | 224 | 212 | 58 | 158 | 0 | 0 | 0 | 0 | 57 | 8 | 1 | .140 |
| 1983 | 6 | 7 | .462 | 4.65 | 18 | 16 | 0 | 81.1 | 98 | 20 | 55 | 0 | 0 | 0 | 1 | 28 | 4 | 0 | .143 |
| 1984 CHI N | 8 | 5 | .615 | 3.14 | 24 | 24 | 3 | 140.2 | 140 | 24 | 76 | 0 | 0 | 0 | 0 | 42 | 5 | 0 | .119 |
| 1985 | 5 | 6 | .455 | 3.12 | 19 | 19 | 2 | 121 | 100 | 27 | 80 | 0 | 0 | 0 | 0 | 31 | 2 | 0 | .065 |
| 8 yrs. | 69 | 58 | .543 | 3.29 | 192 | 179 | 29 | 1144 | 1078 | 291 | 759 | 8 | 1 | 1 | 2 | 326 | 38 | 1 | .117 |
| 2 yrs. | 13 | 11 | .542 | 3.13 | 43 | 43 | 5 | 261.2 | 240 | 51 | 156 | 0 | 0 | 0 | 0 | 73 | 7 | 0 | .096 |

**DIVISIONAL PLAYOFF SERIES**

| | W | L | PCT | ERA | G | GS | CG | IP | H | BB | SO | ShO | W | L | SV | AB | H | HR | BA |
|---|---|---|---|---|---|---|---|---|---|---|---|---|---|---|---|---|---|---|---|
| 1981 MON N | 0 | 0 | – | 6.75 | 1 | 1 | 0 | 2.2 | 4 | 2 | 2 | 0 | 0 | 0 | 0 | 1 | 0 | 0 | .000 |

**LEAGUE CHAMPIONSHIP SERIES**

| | W | L | PCT | ERA | G | GS | CG | IP | H | BB | SO | ShO | W | L | SV | AB | H | HR | BA |
|---|---|---|---|---|---|---|---|---|---|---|---|---|---|---|---|---|---|---|---|
| 1984 CHI N | 0 | 0 | – | 5.79 | 1 | 1 | 0 | 4.2 | 6 | 1 | 2 | 0 | 0 | 0 | 0 | 2 | 0 | 0 | .000 |

## Germany Schaefer

SCHAEFER, HERMAN A.                   BR TR
B. Feb. 4, 1878, Chicago, Ill.    D. May 16, 1919, Saranac Lake, N. Y.

| | W | L | PCT | ERA | G | GS | CG | IP | H | BB | SO | ShO | W | L | SV | AB | H | HR | BA |
|---|---|---|---|---|---|---|---|---|---|---|---|---|---|---|---|---|---|---|---|
| 1912 WAS A | 0 | 0 | – | 0.00 | 1 | 0 | 0 | .2 | 1 | 0 | 0 | 0 | 0 | 0 | 0 | 166 | 41 | 0 | .247 |

| | W | L | PCT | ERA | G | GS | CG | IP | H | BB | SO | ShO | Relief Pitching W | L | SV | BATTING AB | H | HR | BA |
|---|---|---|---|---|---|---|---|---|---|---|---|---|---|---|---|---|---|---|---|

## Germany Schaefer continued

| | W | L | PCT | ERA | G | GS | CG | IP | H | BB | SO | ShO | W | L | SV | AB | H | HR | BA |
|---|---|---|---|---|---|---|---|---|---|---|---|---|---|---|---|---|---|---|---|
| 1913 | 0 | 0 | — | 54.00 | 1 | 0 | 0 | .1 | 2 | 0 | 0 | 0 | 0 | 0 | 0 | 100 | 32 | 0 | .320 |
| 2 yrs. | 0 | 0 | — | 18.00 | 2 | 0 | 0 | 1 | 3 | 0 | 0 | 0 | 0 | 0 | 0 | * | | | |

## Joe Schaffernoth

**SCHAFFERNOTH, JOSEPH ARTHUR**
B. Aug. 6, 1937, Trenton, N. J.　　BR TR 6'4½" 195 lbs.

| | W | L | PCT | ERA | G | GS | CG | IP | H | BB | SO | ShO | W | L | SV | AB | H | HR | BA |
|---|---|---|---|---|---|---|---|---|---|---|---|---|---|---|---|---|---|---|---|
| 1959 CHI N | 1 | 0 | 1.000 | 8.22 | 5 | 1 | 0 | 7.2 | 11 | 4 | 3 | 0 | 1 | 0 | 0 | 3 | 0 | 0 | .000 |
| 1960 | 2 | 3 | .400 | 2.78 | 33 | 0 | 0 | 55 | 46 | 17 | 33 | 0 | 2 | 3 | 3 | 7 | 2 | 0 | .286 |
| 1961 2 teams | | | CHI | N | (21G | 0–4) | | CLE | A | (15G | 0–1) | | | | | | | | |
| " total | 0 | 5 | .000 | 5.86 | 36 | 0 | 0 | 55.1 | 59 | 32 | 32 | 0 | 0 | 5 | 0 | 6 | 0 | 0 | .000 |
| 3 yrs. | 3 | 8 | .273 | 4.58 | 74 | 1 | 0 | 118 | 116 | 53 | 68 | 0 | 3 | 8 | 3 | 16 | 2 | 0 | .125 |
| 3 yrs. | 3 | 7 | .300 | 4.54 | 59 | 1 | 0 | 101 | 100 | 39 | 59 | 0 | 3 | 7 | 3 | 15 | 2 | 0 | .133 |

## Freddy Schmidt

**SCHMIDT, FREDERICK ALBERT**
B. Feb. 9, 1916, Hartford, Conn.　　BR TR 6'1" 185 lbs.

| | W | L | PCT | ERA | G | GS | CG | IP | H | BB | SO | ShO | W | L | SV | AB | H | HR | BA |
|---|---|---|---|---|---|---|---|---|---|---|---|---|---|---|---|---|---|---|---|
| 1944 STL N | 7 | 3 | .700 | 3.15 | 37 | 9 | 3 | 114.1 | 94 | 58 | 58 | 2 | 3 | 0 | 5 | 34 | 7 | 0 | .206 |
| 1946 | 1 | 0 | 1.000 | 3.29 | 16 | 0 | 0 | 27.1 | 27 | 15 | 14 | 0 | 1 | 0 | 0 | 1 | 0 | 0 | .000 |
| 1947 3 teams | | | STL | N | (2G | 0–0) | | PHI | N | (29G | 5–8) | | CHI | N | (1G | 0–0) | | | |
| " total | 5 | 8 | .385 | 4.73 | 32 | 6 | 0 | 83.2 | 85 | 49 | 26 | 0 | 5 | 4 | 0 | 22 | 1 | 0 | .045 |
| 3 yrs. | 13 | 11 | .542 | 3.75 | 85 | 15 | 3 | 225.1 | 206 | 122 | 98 | 2 | 9 | 4 | 5 | 57 | 8 | 0 | .140 |
| 1 yr. | 0 | 0 | — | 9.00 | 1 | 1 | 0 | 3 | 4 | 5 | 0 | 0 | 0 | 0 | 0 | 2 | 0 | 0 | .000 |

WORLD SERIES

| | W | L | PCT | ERA | G | GS | CG | IP | H | BB | SO | ShO | W | L | SV | AB | H | HR | BA |
|---|---|---|---|---|---|---|---|---|---|---|---|---|---|---|---|---|---|---|---|
| 1944 STL N | 0 | 0 | — | 0.00 | 1 | 0 | 0 | 3.1 | 1 | 1 | 1 | 0 | 0 | 0 | 0 | 1 | 0 | 0 | .000 |

## Johnny Schmitz

**SCHMITZ, JOHN ALBERT (Bear Tracks)**
B. Nov. 27, 1920, Wausau, Wis.　　BR TL 6' 170 lbs.

| | W | L | PCT | ERA | G | GS | CG | IP | H | BB | SO | ShO | W | L | SV | AB | H | HR | BA |
|---|---|---|---|---|---|---|---|---|---|---|---|---|---|---|---|---|---|---|---|
| 1941 CHI N | 2 | 0 | 1.000 | 1.31 | 5 | 3 | 1 | 20.2 | 12 | 9 | 11 | 0 | 1 | 0 | 0 | 7 | 4 | 0 | .571 |
| 1942 | 3 | 7 | .300 | 3.43 | 23 | 10 | 1 | 86.2 | 70 | 45 | 51 | 0 | 0 | 1 | 2 | 26 | 4 | 0 | .154 |
| 1946 | 11 | 11 | .500 | 2.61 | 41 | 31 | 14 | 224.1 | 184 | 94 | 135 | 3 | 1 | 1 | 2 | 70 | 9 | 1 | .129 |
| 1947 | 13 | 18 | .419 | 3.22 | 38 | 28 | 10 | 207 | 209 | 80 | 97 | 3 | 1 | 3 | 4 | 68 | 9 | 0 | .132 |
| 1948 | 18 | 13 | .581 | 2.64 | 34 | 30 | 18 | 242 | 186 | 97 | 100 | 2 | 3 | 0 | 1 | 84 | 11 | 0 | .131 |
| 1949 | 11 | 13 | .458 | 4.35 | 36 | 31 | 9 | 207 | 227 | 92 | 75 | 3 | 1 | 1 | 3 | 70 | 10 | 0 | .143 |
| 1950 | 10 | 16 | .385 | 4.99 | 39 | 27 | 8 | 193 | 217 | 91 | 75 | 3 | 1 | 1 | 0 | 67 | 8 | 0 | .119 |
| 1951 2 teams | | | CHI | N | (8G | 1–2) | | BKN | N | (16G | 1–4) | | | | | | | | |
| " total | 2 | 6 | .250 | 5.99 | 24 | 10 | 0 | 73.2 | 77 | 43 | 26 | 0 | 0 | 2 | 0 | 24 | 5 | 1 | .208 |
| 1952 3 teams | | | BKN | N | (10G | 1–1) | | NY | A | (5G | 1–1) | | CIN | N | (3G | 1–0) | | | |
| " total | 3 | 2 | .600 | 3.71 | 18 | 5 | 2 | 53.1 | 47 | 30 | 17 | 0 | 1 | 1 | 1 | 13 | 4 | 0 | .308 |
| 1953 2 teams | | | NY | A | (3G | 0–0) | | WAS | A | (24G | 2–7) | | | | | | | | |
| " total | 2 | 7 | .222 | 3.62 | 27 | 13 | 5 | 112 | 120 | 40 | 39 | 0 | 1 | 1 | 4 | 34 | 2 | 0 | .059 |
| 1954 WAS A | 11 | 8 | .579 | 2.91 | 29 | 23 | 12 | 185.1 | 176 | 64 | 56 | 2 | 0 | 1 | 1 | 60 | 7 | 0 | .117 |
| 1955 | 7 | 10 | .412 | 3.71 | 32 | 21 | 6 | 165 | 187 | 54 | 49 | 1 | 0 | 0 | 1 | 54 | 10 | 0 | .185 |
| 1956 2 teams | | | BOS | A | (2G | 0–0) | | BAL | A | (18G | 0–3) | | | | | | | | |
| " total | 0 | 3 | .000 | 3.59 | 20 | 3 | 0 | 42.2 | 54 | 18 | 15 | 0 | 0 | 0 | 0 | 10 | 0 | 0 | .000 |
| 13 yrs. | 93 | 114 | .449 | 3.55 | 366 | 235 | 86 | 1812.2 | 1766 | 757 | 746 | 17 | 10 | 13 | 19 | 587 | 83 | 2 | .141 |
| 8 yrs. | 69 | 80 | .463 | 3.52 | 224 | 163 | 61 | 1198.2 | 1127 | 523 | 550 | 14 | 8 | 9 | 12 | 398 | 56 | 1 | .141 |

## Ed Schorr

**SCHORR, EDWARD WALTER**
B. Feb. 16, 1891, Bremen, Ohio　　D. Sept. 12, 1969, Atlantic City, N. J.　　BR TR 6'2½" 180 lbs.

| | W | L | PCT | ERA | G | GS | CG | IP | H | BB | SO | ShO | W | L | SV | AB | H | HR | BA |
|---|---|---|---|---|---|---|---|---|---|---|---|---|---|---|---|---|---|---|---|
| 1915 CHI N | 0 | 0 | — | 7.50 | 2 | 0 | 0 | 6 | 9 | 5 | 3 | 0 | 0 | 0 | 0 | 1 | 0 | 0 | .500 |

## Al Schroll

**SCHROLL, ALBERT BRINGHURST (Bull)**
B. Mar. 22, 1933, New Orleans, La.　　BR TR 6'2" 210 lbs.

| | W | L | PCT | ERA | G | GS | CG | IP | H | BB | SO | ShO | W | L | SV | AB | H | HR | BA |
|---|---|---|---|---|---|---|---|---|---|---|---|---|---|---|---|---|---|---|---|
| 1958 BOS A | 0 | 0 | — | 4.50 | 5 | 0 | 0 | 10 | 6 | 4 | 7 | 0 | 0 | 0 | 0 | 1 | 1 | 0 | 1.000 |
| 1959 2 teams | | | PHI | N | (3G | 1–1) | | BOS | A | (14G | 1–4) | | | | | | | | |
| " total | 2 | 5 | .286 | 5.37 | 17 | 5 | 1 | 55.1 | 59 | 28 | 30 | 0 | 1 | 2 | 0 | 13 | 2 | 0 | .154 |
| 1960 CHI N | 0 | 0 | — | 10.13 | 2 | 0 | 0 | 2.2 | 3 | 5 | 2 | 0 | 0 | 0 | 0 | 1 | 1 | 0 | 1.000 |
| 1961 MIN A | 4 | 4 | .500 | 5.22 | 11 | 8 | 2 | 50 | 53 | 27 | 24 | 0 | 1 | 0 | 0 | 18 | 5 | 1 | .278 |
| 4 yrs. | 6 | 9 | .400 | 5.34 | 35 | 13 | 3 | 118 | 121 | 64 | 63 | 0 | 2 | 2 | 0 | 33 | 9 | 1 | .273 |
| 1 yr. | 0 | 0 | — | 10.13 | 2 | 0 | 0 | 2.2 | 3 | 5 | 2 | 0 | 0 | 0 | 0 | 1 | 1 | 0 | 1.000 |

## Barney Schultz

**SCHULTZ, GEORGE WARREN**
B. Aug. 15, 1926, Beverly, N. J.　　BR TR 6'2" 200 lbs.

| | W | L | PCT | ERA | G | GS | CG | IP | H | BB | SO | ShO | W | L | SV | AB | H | HR | BA |
|---|---|---|---|---|---|---|---|---|---|---|---|---|---|---|---|---|---|---|---|
| 1955 STL N | 1 | 2 | .333 | 7.89 | 19 | 0 | 0 | 29.2 | 28 | 15 | 19 | 0 | 1 | 2 | 4 | 4 | 0 | 0 | .000 |
| 1959 DET A | 1 | 2 | .333 | 4.42 | 13 | 0 | 0 | 18.1 | 17 | 14 | 17 | 0 | 1 | 2 | 0 | 2 | 2 | 0 | 1.000 |
| 1961 CHI N | 7 | 6 | .538 | 2.70 | 41 | 0 | 0 | 66.2 | 57 | 25 | 59 | 0 | 7 | 6 | 7 | 10 | 1 | 0 | .100 |
| 1962 | 5 | 5 | .500 | 3.82 | 51 | 0 | 0 | 77.2 | 66 | 23 | 58 | 0 | 5 | 5 | 5 | 5 | 0 | 0 | .000 |
| 1963 2 teams | | | CHI | N | (15G | 1–0) | | STL | N | (24G | 2–0) | | | | | | | | |
| " total | 3 | 0 | 1.000 | 3.59 | 39 | 0 | 0 | 62.2 | 61 | 17 | 44 | 0 | 3 | 0 | 3 | 4 | 0 | 0 | .000 |
| 1964 STL N | 1 | 3 | .250 | 1.64 | 30 | 0 | 0 | 49.1 | 35 | 11 | 29 | 0 | 1 | 3 | 14 | 6 | 1 | 0 | .167 |
| 1965 | 2 | 2 | .500 | 3.83 | 34 | 0 | 0 | 42.1 | 39 | 11 | 38 | 0 | 2 | 2 | 2 | 2 | 0 | 0 | .000 |
| 7 yrs. | 20 | 20 | .500 | 3.63 | 227 | 0 | 0 | 346.2 | 303 | 116 | 264 | 0 | 20 | 20 | 35 | 33 | 4 | 0 | .121 |
| 3 yrs. | 13 | 11 | .542 | 3.36 | 107 | 0 | 0 | 171.2 | 148 | 57 | 135 | 0 | 13 | 11 | 14 | 19 | 1 | 0 | .053 |

WORLD SERIES

| | W | L | PCT | ERA | G | GS | CG | IP | H | BB | SO | ShO | W | L | SV | AB | H | HR | BA |
|---|---|---|---|---|---|---|---|---|---|---|---|---|---|---|---|---|---|---|---|
| 1964 STL N | 0 | 1 | .000 | 18.00 | 4 | 0 | 0 | 4 | 9 | 3 | 1 | 0 | 0 | 1 | 1 | 1 | 0 | 0 | .000 |

## Bob Schultz

**SCHULTZ, ROBERT DUFFY (Bill)**
B. Nov. 27, 1923, Louisville, Ky.　　D. Mar. 31, 1979, Nashville, Tenn.　　BR TL 6'3" 200 lbs.

| | W | L | PCT | ERA | G | GS | CG | IP | H | BB | SO | ShO | W | L | SV | AB | H | HR | BA |
|---|---|---|---|---|---|---|---|---|---|---|---|---|---|---|---|---|---|---|---|
| 1951 CHI N | 3 | 6 | .333 | 5.24 | 17 | 10 | 2 | 77.1 | 75 | 51 | 27 | 0 | 1 | 0 | 0 | 29 | 4 | 0 | .138 |
| 1952 | 6 | 3 | .667 | 4.01 | 29 | 5 | 1 | 74 | 63 | 51 | 31 | 0 | 4 | 0 | 0 | 18 | 4 | 0 | .222 |

| | W | L | PCT | ERA | G | GS | CG | IP | H | BB | SO | ShO | Relief Pitching W | L | SV | BATTING AB | H | HR | BA |
|---|---|---|---|---|---|---|---|---|---|---|---|---|---|---|---|---|---|---|---|

## Bob Schultz continued

| | W | L | PCT | ERA | G | GS | CG | IP | H | BB | SO | ShO | W | L | SV | AB | H | HR | BA |
|---|---|---|---|---|---|---|---|---|---|---|---|---|---|---|---|---|---|---|---|
| 1953 2 teams | CHI | N | (7G 0–2) | | PIT | N | (11G 0–2) | | | | | | | | | | | | |
| " total | 0 | 4 | .000 | 7.12 | 18 | 4 | 0 | 30.1 | 39 | 21 | 9 | 0 | 0 | 1 | 0 | 5 | 0 | 0 | .000 |
| 1955 DET A | 0 | 0 | – | 20.25 | 1 | 0 | 0 | 1.1 | 2 | 2 | 0 | 0 | 0 | 0 | 0 | 0 | 0 | 0 | – |
| 4 yrs. | 9 | 13 | .409 | 5.16 | 65 | 19 | 3 | 183 | 179 | 125 | 67 | 0 | 5 | 1 | 0 | 52 | 8 | 0 | .154 |
| 3 yrs. | 9 | 11 | .450 | 4.69 | 53 | 17 | 3 | 163 | 151 | 113 | 62 | 0 | 5 | 1 | 0 | 50 | 8 | 0 | .160 |

## Buddy Schultz

**SCHULTZ, CHARLES BUDD**
B. Sept. 19, 1950, Cleveland, Ohio　　　　　　　　BR TL 6'　　170 lbs.

| | W | L | PCT | ERA | G | GS | CG | IP | H | BB | SO | ShO | W | L | SV | AB | H | HR | BA |
|---|---|---|---|---|---|---|---|---|---|---|---|---|---|---|---|---|---|---|---|
| 1975 CHI N | 2 | 0 | 1.000 | 6.00 | 6 | 0 | 0 | 6 | 11 | 5 | 4 | 0 | 2 | 0 | 0 | | | | |
| 1976 | 1 | 1 | .500 | 6.00 | 29 | 0 | 0 | 24 | 37 | 9 | 15 | 0 | 1 | 1 | 2 | 4 | 0 | 0 | .000 |
| 1977 STL N | 6 | 1 | .857 | 2.33 | 40 | 3 | 0 | 85 | 76 | 24 | 66 | 0 | 4 | 1 | 1 | 12 | 2 | 0 | .167 |
| 1978 | 2 | 4 | .333 | 3.80 | 62 | 0 | 0 | 83 | 68 | 36 | 70 | 0 | 2 | 4 | 6 | 5 | 1 | 0 | .200 |
| 1979 | 4 | 3 | .571 | 4.50 | 31 | 0 | 0 | 42 | 40 | 14 | 38 | 0 | 4 | 3 | 3 | 4 | 0 | 0 | .000 |
| 5 yrs. | 15 | 9 | .625 | 3.68 | 168 | 3 | 0 | 240 | 232 | 88 | 193 | 0 | 13 | 9 | 12 | 25 | 3 | 0 | .120 |
| 2 yrs. | 3 | 1 | .750 | 6.00 | 35 | 0 | 0 | 30 | 48 | 14 | 19 | 0 | 3 | 1 | 2 | 4 | 0 | 0 | .000 |

## Don Schulze

**SCHULZE, DONALD ARTHUR**
B. Sept. 27, 1962, Roselle, Ill.　　　　　　　　　BR TR 6'3"　　215 lbs.

| | W | L | PCT | ERA | G | GS | CG | IP | H | BB | SO | ShO | W | L | SV | AB | H | HR | BA |
|---|---|---|---|---|---|---|---|---|---|---|---|---|---|---|---|---|---|---|---|
| 1983 CHI N | 0 | 1 | .000 | 7.07 | 4 | 3 | 0 | 14 | 19 | 7 | 8 | 0 | 0 | 0 | 0 | 1 | 0 | 0 | .000 |
| 1984 2 teams | CHI | N | (1G 0–0) | | CLE | A | (19G 3–6) | | | | | | | | | | | | |
| " total | 3 | 6 | .333 | 5.08 | 20 | 15 | 2 | 88.2 | 113 | 28 | 41 | 0 | 0 | 0 | 0 | 0 | 0 | 0 | – |
| 1985 CLE A | 4 | 10 | .286 | 6.01 | 19 | 18 | 1 | 94.1 | 128 | 19 | 37 | 0 | 0 | 0 | 0 | 0 | 0 | 0 | – |
| 3 yrs. | 7 | 17 | .292 | 5.66 | 43 | 36 | 3 | 197 | 260 | 54 | 86 | 0 | 0 | 0 | 0 | 1 | 0 | 0 | .000 |
| 2 yrs. | 0 | 1 | .000 | 7.94 | 5 | 4 | 0 | 17 | 27 | 8 | 10 | 0 | 0 | 0 | 0 | 1 | 0 | 0 | .000 |

## Wayne Schurr

**SCHURR, WAYNE ALLEN**
B. Aug. 6, 1937, Garrett, Ind.　　　　　　　　　　BR TR 6'4"　　185 lbs.

| | W | L | PCT | ERA | G | GS | CG | IP | H | BB | SO | ShO | W | L | SV | AB | H | HR | BA |
|---|---|---|---|---|---|---|---|---|---|---|---|---|---|---|---|---|---|---|---|
| 1964 CHI N | 0 | 0 | – | 3.72 | 26 | 0 | 0 | 48.1 | 57 | 11 | 29 | 0 | 0 | 0 | 0 | 5 | 0 | 0 | .000 |

## Rudy Schwenck

**SCHWENCK, RUDOLPH CHRISTIAN**
B. Apr. 6, 1884, Louisville, Ky.　　D. Nov. 27, 1941, Anchorage, Ky.　　5'6"

| | W | L | PCT | ERA | G | GS | CG | IP | H | BB | SO | ShO | W | L | SV | AB | H | HR | BA |
|---|---|---|---|---|---|---|---|---|---|---|---|---|---|---|---|---|---|---|---|
| 1909 CHI N | 1 | 1 | .500 | 13.50 | 3 | 2 | 0 | 4 | 16 | 3 | 3 | 0 | 0 | 0 | 0 | 4 | 1 | 0 | .250 |

## Dick Scott

**SCOTT, RICHARD LEWIS**
B. Mar. 15, 1933, Portsmouth, N. H.　　　　　　BR TL 6'2"　　185 lbs.

| | W | L | PCT | ERA | G | GS | CG | IP | H | BB | SO | ShO | W | L | SV | AB | H | HR | BA |
|---|---|---|---|---|---|---|---|---|---|---|---|---|---|---|---|---|---|---|---|
| 1963 LA N | 0 | 0 | – | 6.75 | 9 | 0 | 0 | 12 | 17 | 3 | 6 | 0 | 0 | 0 | 2 | 0 | 0 | 0 | – |
| 1964 CHI N | 0 | 0 | – | 12.46 | 3 | 0 | 0 | 4.1 | 10 | 1 | 1 | 0 | 0 | 0 | 0 | 0 | 0 | 0 | – |
| 2 yrs. | 0 | 0 | – | 8.27 | 12 | 0 | 0 | 16.1 | 27 | 4 | 7 | 0 | 0 | 0 | 2 | 0 | 0 | 0 | – |
| 1 yr. | 0 | 0 | – | 12.46 | 3 | 0 | 0 | 4.1 | 10 | 1 | 1 | 0 | 0 | 0 | 0 | 0 | 0 | 0 | – |

## Milt Scott

**SCOTT, MILTON PARKER (Mikado Milt)**
B. Jan. 17, 1866, Chicago, Ill.　　D. Nov. 3, 1938, Baltimore, Md.　　5'9"　　160 lbs.

| | W | L | PCT | ERA | G | GS | CG | IP | H | BB | SO | ShO | W | L | SV | AB | H | HR | BA |
|---|---|---|---|---|---|---|---|---|---|---|---|---|---|---|---|---|---|---|---|
| 1886 BAL AA | 0 | 0 | – | 3.00 | 1 | 0 | 0 | 3 | 2 | 2 | 0 | 0 | 0 | 0 | 0 | * | | | |

## Tom Seaton

**SEATON, THOMAS GORDON**
B. Aug. 30, 1887, Blair, Neb.　　D. Apr. 10, 1940, El Paso, Tex.　　BL TR 6'　　175 lbs.

| | W | L | PCT | ERA | G | GS | CG | IP | H | BB | SO | ShO | W | L | SV | AB | H | HR | BA |
|---|---|---|---|---|---|---|---|---|---|---|---|---|---|---|---|---|---|---|---|
| 1912 PHI N | 16 | 12 | .571 | 3.28 | 44 | 27 | 16 | 255 | 246 | 106 | 118 | 2 | 3 | 1 | 2 | 83 | 18 | 0 | .217 |
| 1913 | 27 | 12 | .692 | 2.60 | 52 | 35 | 21 | 322.1 | 262 | 136 | 168 | 6 | 5 | 5 | 1 | 110 | 12 | 1 | .109 |
| 1914 BKN F | 25 | 13 | .658 | 3.03 | 44 | 38 | 26 | 302.2 | 299 | 102 | 172 | 7 | 2 | 0 | 2 | 107 | 22 | 1 | .206 |
| 1915 2 teams | BKN | F | (32G 11–17) | | NWK | F | (12G 3–6) | | | | | | | | | | | | |
| " total | 15 | 17 | .469 | 3.92 | 44 | 33 | 20 | 264.1 | 260 | 120 | 114 | 0 | 1 | 1 | 4 | 92 | 20 | 2 | .217 |
| 1916 CHI N | 6 | 6 | .500 | 3.27 | 31 | 14 | 4 | 121 | 108 | 43 | 45 | 0 | 3 | 2 | 1 | 38 | 7 | 0 | .184 |
| 1917 | 5 | 4 | .556 | 2.53 | 16 | 9 | 3 | 74.2 | 60 | 23 | 27 | 1 | 1 | 1 | 1 | 21 | 5 | 0 | .238 |
| 6 yrs. | 94 | 64 | .595 | 3.14 | 231 | 156 | 90 | 1340 | 1235 | 530 | 644 | 16 | 15 | 10 | 11 | 451 | 84 | 4 | .186 |
| 2 yrs. | 11 | 10 | .524 | 2.99 | 47 | 23 | 7 | 195.2 | 168 | 66 | 72 | 1 | 4 | 3 | 2 | 59 | 12 | 0 | .203 |

## Herman Segelke

**SEGELKE, HERMAN NEILS**
B. Apr. 24, 1958, San Mateo, Calif.　　　　　　BR TR 6'4"　　215 lbs.

| | W | L | PCT | ERA | G | GS | CG | IP | H | BB | SO | ShO | W | L | SV | AB | H | HR | BA |
|---|---|---|---|---|---|---|---|---|---|---|---|---|---|---|---|---|---|---|---|
| 1982 CHI N | 0 | 0 | – | 8.31 | 3 | 0 | 0 | 4.1 | 6 | 6 | 4 | 0 | 0 | 0 | 0 | 0 | 0 | 0 | – |

## Dick Selma

**SELMA, RICHARD JAY**
B. Nov. 4, 1943, Santa Ana, Calif.　　　　　　BR TR 5'11"　　160 lbs.
　　　　　　　　　　　　　　　　　　　　　　BB 1966

| | W | L | PCT | ERA | G | GS | CG | IP | H | BB | SO | ShO | W | L | SV | AB | H | HR | BA |
|---|---|---|---|---|---|---|---|---|---|---|---|---|---|---|---|---|---|---|---|
| 1965 NY N | 2 | 1 | .667 | 3.71 | 4 | 4 | 1 | 26.2 | 22 | 9 | 26 | 1 | 0 | 0 | 0 | 9 | 2 | 0 | .222 |
| 1966 | 4 | 6 | .400 | 4.24 | 30 | 7 | 0 | 80.2 | 84 | 39 | 58 | 0 | 4 | 2 | 1 | 14 | 1 | 0 | .071 |
| 1967 | 2 | 4 | .333 | 2.77 | 38 | 4 | 0 | 81.1 | 71 | 36 | 52 | 0 | 2 | 3 | 2 | 22 | 2 | 0 | .091 |
| 1968 | 9 | 10 | .474 | 2.75 | 34 | 23 | 4 | 170.1 | 148 | 54 | 117 | 3 | 0 | 0 | 0 | 58 | 12 | 0 | .207 |
| 1969 2 teams | SD | N | (4G 2–2) | | CHI | N | (36G 10–8) | | | | | | | | | | | | |
| " total | 12 | 10 | .545 | 3.68 | 40 | 28 | 5 | 190.2 | 156 | 81 | 181 | 2 | 3 | 1 | 1 | 59 | 10 | 0 | .169 |
| 1970 PHI N | 8 | 9 | .471 | 2.75 | 73 | 0 | 0 | 134 | 108 | 59 | 153 | 0 | 8 | 9 | 22 | 20 | 3 | 0 | .150 |
| 1971 | 0 | 2 | .000 | 3.24 | 17 | 0 | 0 | 25 | 21 | 8 | 15 | 0 | 0 | 2 | 1 | 1 | 1 | 0 | 1.000 |
| 1972 | 4 | 9 | .182 | 5.56 | 46 | 10 | 1 | 98.2 | 91 | 73 | 58 | 0 | 1 | 1 | 0 | 20 | 4 | 0 | .200 |
| 1973 | 1 | 1 | .500 | 5.63 | 6 | 0 | 0 | 8 | 6 | 5 | 4 | 0 | 1 | 1 | 0 | 0 | 0 | 0 | – |
| 1974 2 teams | CAL | A | (18G 2–2) | | MIL | A | (2G 0–0) | | | | | | | | | | | | |
| " total | 2 | 2 | .500 | 6.48 | 20 | 0 | 0 | 25 | 27 | 17 | 17 | 0 | 2 | 2 | 1 | 0 | 0 | 0 | – |
| 10 yrs. | 42 | 54 | .438 | 3.62 | 307 | 76 | 11 | 840.1 | 734 | 381 | 681 | 6 | 21 | 20 | 31 | 203 | 35 | 0 | .172 |
| 1 yr. | 10 | 8 | .556 | 3.63 | 36 | 25 | 4 | 168.2 | 137 | 72 | 161 | 2 | 2 | 1 | 1 | 52 | 8 | 0 | .154 |

| | | W | L | PCT | ERA | G | GS | CG | IP | H | BB | SO | ShO | Relief Pitching W | L | SV | BATTING AB | H | HR | BA |
|---|---|---|---|---|---|---|---|---|---|---|---|---|---|---|---|---|---|---|---|---|

## Manny Seoane

**SEOANE, MANUEL MODESTO**
B. June 26, 1955, Tampa, Fla.  BR TR 6'3"  187 lbs.

| | | W | L | PCT | ERA | G | GS | CG | IP | H | BB | SO | ShO | W | L | SV | AB | H | HR | BA |
|---|---|---|---|---|---|---|---|---|---|---|---|---|---|---|---|---|---|---|---|---|
| 1977 | PHI N | 0 | 0 | — | 6.00 | 2 | 1 | 0 | 6 | 11 | 3 | 4 | 0 | 0 | 0 | 0 | 2 | 1 | 0 | .500 |
| 1978 | CHI N | 1 | 0 | 1.000 | 5.63 | 7 | 1 | 0 | 8 | 11 | 6 | 5 | 0 | 1 | 0 | 0 | 0 | 0 | 0 | |
| | 2 yrs. | 1 | 0 | 1.000 | 5.79 | 9 | 2 | 0 | 14 | 22 | 9 | 9 | 0 | 1 | 0 | 0 | 2 | 1 | 0 | .500 |
| | 1 yr. | 1 | 0 | 1.000 | 5.63 | 7 | 1 | 0 | 8 | 11 | 6 | 5 | 0 | 1 | 0 | 0 | 0 | 0 | 0 | |

## Bobby Shantz

**SHANTZ, ROBERT CLAYTON**
Brother of Billy Shantz.
B. Sept. 26, 1925, Pottstown, Pa.  BR TL 5'6"  139 lbs.

| | | W | L | PCT | ERA | G | GS | CG | IP | H | BB | SO | ShO | W | L | SV | AB | H | HR | BA |
|---|---|---|---|---|---|---|---|---|---|---|---|---|---|---|---|---|---|---|---|---|
| 1949 | PHI A | 6 | 8 | .429 | 3.40 | 33 | 7 | 4 | 127 | 100 | 74 | 58 | 1 | 3 | 4 | 2 | 37 | 7 | 0 | .189 |
| 1950 | | 8 | 14 | .364 | 4.61 | 36 | 23 | 6 | 214.2 | 251 | 85 | 93 | 1 | 2 | 0 | 0 | 66 | 11 | 1 | .167 |
| 1951 | | 18 | 10 | .643 | 3.94 | 32 | 25 | 13 | 205.1 | 213 | 70 | 77 | 4 | 2 | 1 | 0 | 72 | 18 | 0 | .250 |
| 1952 | | 24 | 7 | .774 | 2.48 | 33 | 33 | 27 | 279.2 | 230 | 63 | 152 | 5 | 0 | 0 | 0 | 96 | 19 | 0 | .198 |
| 1953 | | 5 | 9 | .357 | 4.09 | 16 | 16 | 6 | 105.2 | 107 | 26 | 58 | 0 | 0 | 0 | 0 | 38 | 9 | 0 | .237 |
| 1954 | | 1 | 0 | 1.000 | 7.88 | 2 | 1 | 0 | 8 | 12 | 3 | 3 | 0 | 0 | 0 | 0 | 3 | 1 | 0 | .333 |
| 1955 | KC A | 5 | 10 | .333 | 4.54 | 23 | 17 | 4 | 125 | 124 | 66 | 58 | 1 | 2 | 0 | 0 | 41 | 6 | 0 | .146 |
| 1956 | | 2 | 7 | .222 | 4.35 | 45 | 2 | 1 | 101.1 | 95 | 37 | 67 | 0 | 1 | 6 | 9 | 22 | 2 | 0 | .091 |
| 1957 | NY A | 11 | 5 | .688 | 2.45 | 30 | 21 | 9 | 173 | 157 | 40 | 72 | 1 | 1 | 0 | 5 | 56 | 10 | 0 | .179 |
| 1958 | | 7 | 6 | .538 | 3.36 | 33 | 13 | 3 | 126 | 127 | 35 | 80 | 0 | 5 | 5 | 0 | 35 | 8 | 0 | .229 |
| 1959 | | 7 | 3 | .700 | 2.38 | 33 | 4 | 2 | 94.2 | 64 | 33 | 66 | 2 | 5 | 1 | 3 | 23 | 5 | 0 | .217 |
| 1960 | | 5 | 4 | .556 | 2.79 | 42 | 0 | 0 | 67.2 | 57 | 24 | 54 | 0 | 5 | 4 | 11 | 10 | 1 | 0 | .100 |
| 1961 | PIT N | 6 | 3 | .667 | 3.32 | 43 | 6 | 2 | 89.1 | 91 | 26 | 61 | 1 | 3 | 1 | 2 | 16 | 7 | 0 | .438 |
| 1962 | 2 teams | | | | | HOU N (3G 1-1) | | | | STL N (28G 5-3) | | | | | | | | | | | |
| " | total | 6 | 4 | .600 | 1.95 | 31 | 3 | 1 | 78.1 | 60 | 25 | 61 | 0 | 5 | 3 | 4 | 21 | 2 | 0 | .095 |
| 1963 | STL N | 6 | 4 | .600 | 2.61 | 55 | 0 | 0 | 79.1 | 55 | 17 | 70 | 0 | 6 | 4 | 11 | 7 | 1 | 0 | .143 |
| 1964 | 3 teams | | | | | STL N (16G 1-3) | | | | CHI N (20G 0-1) | | | | | PHI N (14G 1-1) | | | | | | |
| " | total | 2 | 5 | .286 | 3.12 | 50 | 0 | 0 | 60.2 | 52 | 19 | 42 | 0 | 2 | 5 | 1 | 5 | 0 | 0 | .000 |
| | 16 yrs. | 119 | 99 | .546 | 3.38 | 537 | 171 | 78 | 1935.2 | 1795 | 643 | 1072 | 16 | 42 | 34 | 48 | 548 | 107 | 1 | .195 |
| | 1 yr. | 0 | 1 | .000 | 5.56 | 20 | 0 | 0 | 11.1 | 15 | 6 | 12 | 0 | 0 | 1 | 1 | 0 | 0 | 0 | |

**WORLD SERIES**

| | | W | L | PCT | ERA | G | GS | CG | IP | H | BB | SO | ShO | W | L | SV | AB | H | HR | BA |
|---|---|---|---|---|---|---|---|---|---|---|---|---|---|---|---|---|---|---|---|---|
| 1957 | NY A | 0 | 1 | .000 | 4.05 | 3 | 1 | 0 | 6.2 | 8 | 2 | 7 | 0 | 0 | 0 | 0 | 1 | 0 | 0 | .000 |
| 1960 | | 0 | 0 | — | 4.26 | 3 | 0 | 0 | 6.1 | 4 | 1 | 1 | 0 | 0 | 0 | 1 | 3 | 1 | 0 | .333 |
| | 2 yrs. | 0 | 1 | .000 | 4.15 | 6 | 1 | 0 | 13 | 12 | 3 | 8 | 0 | 0 | 0 | 1 | 4 | 1 | 0 | .250 |

## Bob Shaw

**SHAW, ROBERT JOHN**
B. June 29, 1933, New York, N. Y.  BR TR 6'2"  195 lbs.

| | | W | L | PCT | ERA | G | GS | CG | IP | H | BB | SO | ShO | W | L | SV | AB | H | HR | BA |
|---|---|---|---|---|---|---|---|---|---|---|---|---|---|---|---|---|---|---|---|---|
| 1957 | DET A | 0 | 1 | .000 | 7.45 | 7 | 0 | 0 | 9.2 | 11 | 7 | 4 | 0 | 0 | 1 | 0 | 2 | 0 | 0 | .000 |
| 1958 | 2 teams | | | | | DET A (11G 1-2) | | | | CHI A (29G 4-2) | | | | | | | | | | | |
| " | total | 5 | 4 | .556 | 4.76 | 40 | 5 | 0 | 90.2 | 99 | 41 | 35 | 0 | 5 | 1 | 1 | 22 | 3 | 0 | .136 |
| 1959 | CHI A | 18 | 6 | .750 | 2.69 | 47 | 26 | 8 | 230.2 | 217 | 54 | 89 | 3 | 2 | 0 | 3 | 73 | 9 | 0 | .123 |
| 1960 | | 13 | 13 | .500 | 4.06 | 36 | 32 | 7 | 192.2 | 221 | 62 | 46 | 1 | 1 | 1 | 0 | 58 | 8 | 0 | .138 |
| 1961 | 2 teams | | | | | CHI A (14G 3-4) | | | | KC A (26G 9-10) | | | | | | | | | | | |
| " | total | 12 | 14 | .462 | 4.14 | 40 | 34 | 9 | 221.2 | 250 | 78 | 91 | 0 | 1 | 0 | 0 | 73 | 11 | 0 | .151 |
| 1962 | MIL N | 15 | 9 | .625 | 2.80 | 38 | 29 | 12 | 225 | 223 | 44 | 124 | 3 | 1 | 0 | 2 | 73 | 10 | 0 | .137 |
| 1963 | | 7 | 11 | .389 | 2.66 | 48 | 16 | 3 | 159 | 144 | 55 | 105 | 3 | 3 | 5 | 13 | 41 | 5 | 0 | .122 |
| 1964 | SF N | 7 | 6 | .538 | 3.76 | 61 | 1 | 0 | 93.1 | 105 | 31 | 57 | 0 | 7 | 5 | 11 | 13 | 0 | 0 | .000 |
| 1965 | | 16 | 9 | .640 | 2.64 | 42 | 33 | 6 | 235 | 213 | 53 | 148 | 1 | 1 | 1 | 2 | 79 | 8 | 0 | .101 |
| 1966 | 2 teams | | | | | SF N (13G 1-4) | | | | NY N (26G 11-10) | | | | | | | | | | | |
| " | total | 12 | 14 | .462 | 4.29 | 39 | 31 | 7 | 199.1 | 216 | 49 | 125 | 2 | 0 | 1 | 0 | 56 | 13 | 0 | .232 |
| 1967 | 2 teams | | | | | NY N (23G 3-9) | | | | CHI N (9G 0-2) | | | | | | | | | | | |
| " | total | 3 | 11 | .214 | 4.61 | 32 | 16 | 3 | 121 | 138 | 37 | 56 | 1 | 1 | 2 | 0 | 29 | 2 | 0 | .069 |
| | 11 yrs. | 108 | 98 | .524 | 3.52 | 430 | 223 | 55 | 1778 | 1837 | 511 | 880 | 14 | 22 | 17 | 32 | 519 | 69 | 0 | .133 |
| | 1 yr. | 0 | 2 | .000 | 6.04 | 9 | 3 | 0 | 22.1 | 33 | 9 | 7 | 0 | 0 | 1 | 0 | 4 | 1 | 0 | .250 |

**WORLD SERIES**

| | | W | L | PCT | ERA | G | GS | CG | IP | H | BB | SO | ShO | W | L | SV | AB | H | HR | BA |
|---|---|---|---|---|---|---|---|---|---|---|---|---|---|---|---|---|---|---|---|---|
| 1959 | CHI A | 1 | 1 | .500 | 2.57 | 2 | 2 | 0 | 14 | 17 | 2 | 2 | 0 | 0 | 0 | 0 | 4 | 1 | 0 | .250 |

## Sam Shaw

**SHAW, SAMUEL E.**
B. May, 1864, Baltimore, Md.  Deceased.  BR TR 5'5"  140 lbs.

| | | W | L | PCT | ERA | G | GS | CG | IP | H | BB | SO | ShO | W | L | SV | AB | H | HR | BA |
|---|---|---|---|---|---|---|---|---|---|---|---|---|---|---|---|---|---|---|---|---|
| 1888 | BAL AA | 2 | 4 | .333 | 3.40 | 6 | 6 | 6 | 53 | 65 | 15 | 22 | 0 | 0 | 0 | 0 | 20 | 3 | 0 | .150 |
| 1893 | CHI N | 1 | 0 | 1.000 | 5.63 | 2 | 2 | 1 | 16 | 12 | 13 | 1 | 0 | 0 | 0 | 0 | 7 | 2 | 0 | .286 |
| | 2 yrs. | 3 | 4 | .429 | 3.91 | 8 | 8 | 7 | 69 | 77 | 28 | 23 | 0 | 0 | 0 | 0 | 27 | 5 | 0 | .185 |
| | 1 yr. | 1 | 0 | 1.000 | 5.63 | 2 | 2 | 1 | 16 | 12 | 13 | 1 | 0 | 0 | 0 | 0 | 7 | 2 | 0 | .286 |

## Al Shealy

**SHEALY, ALBERT BERLEY**
B. May 24, 1900, Chapin, S. C.  D. Mar. 7, 1967, Hagerstown, Md.  BR TR 5'11"  175 lbs.

| | | W | L | PCT | ERA | G | GS | CG | IP | H | BB | SO | ShO | W | L | SV | AB | H | HR | BA |
|---|---|---|---|---|---|---|---|---|---|---|---|---|---|---|---|---|---|---|---|---|
| 1928 | NY A | 8 | 6 | .571 | 5.06 | 23 | 12 | 3 | 96 | 124 | 42 | 39 | 0 | 2 | 1 | 2 | 38 | 9 | 1 | .237 |
| 1930 | CHI N | 0 | 0 | — | 8.00 | 24 | 0 | 0 | 27 | 37 | 14 | 14 | 0 | 0 | 0 | 0 | 5 | 3 | 0 | .600 |
| | 2 yrs. | 8 | 6 | .571 | 5.71 | 47 | 12 | 3 | 123 | 161 | 56 | 53 | 0 | 2 | 1 | 2 | 43 | 12 | 1 | .279 |
| | 1 yr. | 0 | 0 | — | 8.00 | 24 | 0 | 0 | 27 | 37 | 14 | 14 | 0 | 0 | 0 | 0 | 5 | 3 | 0 | .600 |

## Clyde Shoun

**SHOUN, CLYDE MITCHELL (Hardrock)**
B. Mar. 20, 1912, Mountain City, Tenn.  D. Mar. 20, 1968, Mountain Home, Tenn.  BL TL 6'1"  188 lbs.

| | | W | L | PCT | ERA | G | GS | CG | IP | H | BB | SO | ShO | W | L | SV | AB | H | HR | BA |
|---|---|---|---|---|---|---|---|---|---|---|---|---|---|---|---|---|---|---|---|---|
| 1935 | CHI N | 1 | 0 | 1.000 | 2.84 | 5 | 1 | 0 | 12.2 | 14 | 5 | 9 | 0 | 1 | 0 | 0 | 3 | 0 | 0 | .000 |
| 1936 | | 0 | 0 | — | 12.46 | 4 | 0 | 0 | 4.1 | 3 | 6 | 1 | 0 | 0 | 0 | 0 | 0 | 0 | 0 | |
| 1937 | | 7 | 7 | .500 | 5.61 | 37 | 9 | 2 | 93 | 118 | 45 | 43 | 0 | 3 | 4 | 3 | 29 | 4 | 0 | .138 |
| 1938 | STL N | 6 | 6 | .500 | 4.14 | 40 | 12 | 3 | 117.1 | 130 | 43 | 37 | 0 | 2 | 2 | 1 | 31 | 8 | 0 | .258 |
| 1939 | | 3 | 1 | .750 | 3.76 | 53 | 2 | 0 | 103 | 98 | 42 | 50 | 0 | 3 | 1 | 9 | 26 | 3 | 0 | .115 |
| 1940 | | 13 | 11 | .542 | 3.92 | 54 | 19 | 13 | 197.1 | 193 | 46 | 82 | 1 | 3 | 4 | 5 | 63 | 12 | 0 | .190 |
| 1941 | | 3 | 5 | .375 | 5.66 | 26 | 6 | 0 | 70 | 98 | 20 | 34 | 0 | 3 | 0 | 0 | 22 | 4 | 0 | .182 |

| | W | L | PCT | ERA | G | GS | CG | IP | H | BB | SO | ShO | Relief Pitching W | L | SV | BATTING AB | H | HR | BA |
|---|---|---|---|---|---|---|---|---|---|---|---|---|---|---|---|---|---|---|---|

## Clyde Shoun continued

| | W | L | PCT | ERA | G | GS | CG | IP | H | BB | SO | ShO | W | L | SV | AB | H | HR | BA |
|---|---|---|---|---|---|---|---|---|---|---|---|---|---|---|---|---|---|---|---|
| 1942 2 teams | | STL | N | (2G 0–0) | | CIN | N | (34G 1–3) | | | | | | | | | | | |
| " total | 1 | 3 | .250 | 2.18 | 36 | 0 | 0 | 74.1 | 56 | 24 | 32 | 0 | 1 | 3 | 0 | 13 | 4 | 0 | .308 |
| 1943 CIN N | 14 | 5 | .737 | 3.06 | 45 | 5 | 2 | 147 | 131 | 46 | 61 | 0 | 13 | 3 | 7 | 42 | 13 | 0 | .310 |
| 1944 | 13 | 10 | .565 | 3.02 | 38 | 21 | 12 | 202.2 | 193 | 42 | 55 | 1 | 3 | 2 | 2 | 67 | 15 | 0 | .224 |
| 1946 | 1 | 6 | .143 | 4.10 | 27 | 5 | 0 | 79 | 87 | 26 | 20 | 0 | 1 | 3 | 0 | 21 | 2 | 0 | .095 |
| 1947 2 teams | | CIN | N | (10G 0–0) | | BOS | N | (26G 5–3) | | | | | | | | | | | |
| " total | 5 | 3 | .625 | 4.50 | 36 | 3 | 1 | 88 | 89 | 26 | 30 | 1 | 4 | 1 | 1 | 19 | 3 | 0 | .158 |
| 1948 BOS N | 5 | 1 | .833 | 4.01 | 36 | 2 | 1 | 74 | 77 | 20 | 25 | 0 | 4 | 1 | 4 | 21 | 4 | 0 | .190 |
| 1949 2 teams | | BOS | N | (1G 0–0) | | CHI | A | (16G 1–1) | | | | | | | | | | | |
| " total | 1 | 1 | .500 | 5.55 | 17 | 0 | 0 | 24.1 | 38 | 13 | 8 | 0 | 1 | 1 | 0 | 5 | 1 | 0 | .200 |
| 14 yrs. | 73 | 59 | .553 | 3.91 | 454 | 85 | 34 | 1287 | 1325 | 404 | 483 | 3 | 41 | 25 | 29 | 362 | 73 | 0 | .202 |
| 3 yrs. | 8 | 7 | .533 | 5.56 | 46 | 10 | 2 | 110 | 135 | 56 | 49 | 0 | 3 | 3 | 0 | 32 | 4 | 0 | .125 |

## Walter Signer

**SIGNER, WALTER DONALD ALOYSIUS**          BR  TR  6'          165 lbs.
B. Oct. 12, 1910, New York, N. Y.     D. July 23, 1974, Greenwich, Conn.

| | W | L | PCT | ERA | G | GS | CG | IP | H | BB | SO | ShO | W | L | SV | AB | H | HR | BA |
|---|---|---|---|---|---|---|---|---|---|---|---|---|---|---|---|---|---|---|---|
| 1943 CHI N | 2 | 1 | .667 | 2.88 | 4 | 2 | 1 | 25 | 24 | 4 | 5 | 0 | 1 | 0 | 0 | 8 | 2 | 0 | .250 |
| 1945 | 0 | 0 | – | 3.38 | 6 | 0 | 0 | 8 | 11 | 5 | 0 | 0 | 0 | 0 | 1 | 1 | 0 | 0 | .000 |
| 2 yrs. | 2 | 1 | .667 | 3.00 | 10 | 2 | 1 | 33 | 35 | 9 | 5 | 0 | 1 | 0 | 1 | 9 | 2 | 0 | .222 |
| 2 yrs. | 2 | 1 | .667 | 3.00 | 10 | 2 | 1 | 33 | 35 | 9 | 5 | 0 | 1 | 0 | 1 | 9 | 2 | 0 | .222 |

## Curt Simmons

**SIMMONS, CURTIS THOMAS**          BL  TL  5'11"          175 lbs.
B. May 19, 1929, Egypt, Pa.

| | W | L | PCT | ERA | G | GS | CG | IP | H | BB | SO | ShO | W | L | SV | AB | H | HR | BA |
|---|---|---|---|---|---|---|---|---|---|---|---|---|---|---|---|---|---|---|---|
| 1947 PHI N | 1 | 0 | 1.000 | 1.00 | 1 | 1 | 1 | 9 | 5 | 6 | 9 | 0 | 0 | 0 | 0 | 2 | 1 | 0 | .500 |
| 1948 | 7 | 13 | .350 | 4.87 | 31 | 22 | 7 | 170 | 169 | 108 | 86 | 0 | 0 | 0 | 0 | 51 | 7 | 0 | .137 |
| 1949 | 4 | 10 | .286 | 4.59 | 38 | 14 | 2 | 131.1 | 133 | 55 | 83 | 0 | 1 | 3 | 1 | 41 | 7 | 0 | .171 |
| 1950 | 17 | 8 | .680 | 3.40 | 31 | 27 | 11 | 214.2 | 178 | 88 | 146 | 2 | 2 | 0 | 1 | 77 | 12 | 0 | .156 |
| 1952 | 14 | 8 | .636 | 2.82 | 28 | 28 | 15 | 201.1 | 170 | 70 | 141 | 6 | 0 | 0 | 0 | 67 | 11 | 1 | .164 |
| 1953 | 16 | 13 | .552 | 3.21 | 32 | 30 | 19 | 238 | 211 | 82 | 138 | 4 | 0 | 0 | 0 | 93 | 13 | 0 | .140 |
| 1954 | 14 | 15 | .483 | 2.81 | 34 | 33 | 21 | 253 | 226 | 98 | 125 | 3 | 0 | 0 | 1 | 91 | 16 | 0 | .176 |
| 1955 | 8 | 8 | .500 | 4.92 | 25 | 22 | 3 | 130 | 148 | 50 | 58 | 0 | 1 | 1 | 0 | 46 | 8 | 0 | .174 |
| 1956 | 15 | 10 | .600 | 3.36 | 33 | 27 | 14 | 198 | 186 | 65 | 88 | 0 | 1 | 0 | 0 | 72 | 17 | 0 | .236 |
| 1957 | 12 | 11 | .522 | 3.44 | 32 | 29 | 9 | 212 | 214 | 50 | 92 | 2 | 0 | 0 | 0 | 71 | 17 | 0 | .239 |
| 1958 | 7 | 14 | .333 | 4.38 | 29 | 27 | 7 | 168.1 | 196 | 40 | 78 | 1 | 0 | 0 | 1 | 59 | 12 | 0 | .203 |
| 1959 | 0 | 0 | – | 4.50 | 7 | 0 | 0 | 10 | 16 | 0 | 4 | 0 | 0 | 0 | 0 | 0 | 0 | 0 | – |
| 1960 2 teams | | PHI | N | (4G 0–0) | | STL | N | (23G 7–4) | | | | | | | | | | | |
| " total | 7 | 4 | .636 | 3.06 | 27 | 19 | 3 | 156 | 162 | 37 | 67 | 1 | 0 | 0 | 0 | 47 | 10 | 0 | .213 |
| 1961 STL N | 9 | 10 | .474 | 3.13 | 30 | 29 | 6 | 195.2 | 203 | 64 | 99 | 2 | 0 | 0 | 0 | 66 | 20 | 0 | .303 |
| 1962 | 10 | 10 | .500 | 3.51 | 31 | 22 | 9 | 154 | 167 | 32 | 74 | 4 | 0 | 3 | 0 | 50 | 8 | 0 | .160 |
| 1963 | 15 | 9 | .625 | 2.48 | 32 | 32 | 11 | 232.2 | 209 | 48 | 127 | 6 | 0 | 0 | 0 | 81 | 13 | 0 | .160 |
| 1964 | 18 | 9 | .667 | 3.43 | 34 | 34 | 12 | 244 | 233 | 49 | 104 | 3 | 0 | 0 | 0 | 94 | 10 | 0 | .106 |
| 1965 | 9 | 15 | .375 | 4.08 | 34 | 32 | 5 | 203 | 229 | 54 | 96 | 0 | 0 | 0 | 0 | 64 | 3 | 0 | .047 |
| 1966 2 teams | | STL | N | (10G 1–1) | | CHI | N | (19G 4–7) | | | | | | | | | | | |
| " total | 5 | 8 | .385 | 4.23 | 29 | 15 | 4 | 110.2 | 114 | 35 | 38 | 1 | 2 | 2 | 0 | 26 | 3 | 0 | .115 |
| 1967 2 teams | | CHI | N | (17G 3–7) | | CAL | A | (14G 2–1) | | | | | | | | | | | |
| " total | 5 | 8 | .385 | 4.24 | 31 | 18 | 4 | 116.2 | 144 | 32 | 44 | 1 | 1 | 0 | 1 | 37 | 6 | 0 | .162 |
| 20 yrs. | 193 | 183 | .513 | 3.54 | 569 | 461 | 163 | 3348.1 | 3313 | 1063 | 1697 | 36 | 8 | 9 | 5 | 1135 | 194 | 1 | .171 |
| 2 yrs. | 7 | 14 | .333 | 4.52 | 36 | 24 | 6 | 159.1 | 179 | 44 | 55 | 1 | 2 | 2 | 0 | 46 | 6 | 0 | .130 |

| WORLD SERIES | | | | | | | | | | | | | | | | | | | |
|---|---|---|---|---|---|---|---|---|---|---|---|---|---|---|---|---|---|---|---|
| 1964 STL N | 0 | 1 | .000 | 2.51 | 2 | 2 | 0 | 14.1 | 11 | 3 | 8 | 0 | 0 | 0 | 0 | 4 | 2 | 0 | .500 |

## Duke Simpson

**SIMPSON, THOMAS LEO**          BR  TR  6'1½"          190 lbs.
B. Sept. 15, 1927, Columbus, Ohio

| | W | L | PCT | ERA | G | GS | CG | IP | H | BB | SO | ShO | W | L | SV | AB | H | HR | BA |
|---|---|---|---|---|---|---|---|---|---|---|---|---|---|---|---|---|---|---|---|
| 1953 CHI N | 1 | 2 | .333 | 8.00 | 30 | 1 | 0 | 45 | 60 | 25 | 21 | 0 | 1 | 1 | 0 | 8 | 2 | 0 | .250 |

## Elmer Singleton

**SINGLETON, BERT ELMER (Smoky)**          BR  TR  6'2"          174 lbs.
B. June 26, 1918, Ogden, Utah                                                 BB 1957-58

| | W | L | PCT | ERA | G | GS | CG | IP | H | BB | SO | ShO | W | L | SV | AB | H | HR | BA |
|---|---|---|---|---|---|---|---|---|---|---|---|---|---|---|---|---|---|---|---|
| 1945 BOS N | 1 | 4 | .200 | 4.82 | 7 | 5 | 1 | 37.1 | 35 | 14 | 14 | 0 | 0 | 0 | 0 | 11 | 0 | 0 | .000 |
| 1946 | 0 | 1 | .000 | 3.74 | 15 | 2 | 0 | 33.2 | 27 | 21 | 17 | 0 | 0 | 0 | 1 | 4 | 0 | 0 | .000 |
| 1947 PIT N | 2 | 2 | .500 | 6.31 | 36 | 3 | 0 | 67 | 70 | 39 | 24 | 0 | 2 | 0 | 1 | 13 | 4 | 0 | .308 |
| 1948 | 4 | 6 | .400 | 4.97 | 38 | 5 | 1 | 92.1 | 90 | 40 | 53 | 0 | 3 | 4 | 2 | 23 | 2 | 0 | .087 |
| 1950 WAS A | 1 | 2 | .333 | 5.20 | 21 | 1 | 0 | 36.1 | 39 | 17 | 19 | 0 | 1 | 2 | 0 | 7 | 3 | 0 | .429 |
| 1957 CHI N | 0 | 1 | .000 | 6.75 | 5 | 2 | 0 | 13.1 | 20 | 2 | 6 | 0 | 0 | 1 | 0 | 3 | 0 | 0 | .000 |
| 1958 | 1 | 0 | 1.000 | 0.00 | 2 | 0 | 0 | 4.2 | 1 | 1 | 2 | 0 | 1 | 0 | 0 | 1 | 0 | 0 | .000 |
| 1959 | 2 | 1 | .667 | 2.72 | 21 | 1 | 0 | 43 | 40 | 12 | 25 | 0 | 1 | 1 | 0 | 6 | 0 | 0 | .000 |
| 8 yrs. | 11 | 17 | .393 | 4.83 | 145 | 19 | 2 | 327.2 | 322 | 146 | 160 | 0 | 8 | 8 | 4 | 68 | 9 | 0 | .132 |
| 3 yrs. | 3 | 2 | .600 | 3.39 | 28 | 3 | 0 | 61 | 61 | 15 | 33 | 0 | 2 | 2 | 0 | 10 | 0 | 0 | .000 |

## Cy Slapnicka

**SLAPNICKA, CYRIL CHARLES**          BB  TR  5'10"          165 lbs.
B. Mar. 23, 1886, Cedar Rapids, Iowa     D. Oct. 20, 1979, Cedar Rapids, Iowa

| | W | L | PCT | ERA | G | GS | CG | IP | H | BB | SO | ShO | W | L | SV | AB | H | HR | BA |
|---|---|---|---|---|---|---|---|---|---|---|---|---|---|---|---|---|---|---|---|
| 1911 CHI N | 0 | 2 | .000 | 3.38 | 3 | 2 | 1 | 24 | 21 | 7 | 10 | 0 | 0 | 0 | 0 | 9 | 2 | 0 | .222 |
| 1918 PIT N | 1 | 4 | .200 | 4.74 | 7 | 6 | 4 | 49.1 | 50 | 22 | 3 | 0 | 0 | 0 | 1 | 14 | 1 | 0 | .071 |
| 2 yrs. | 1 | 6 | .143 | 4.30 | 10 | 8 | 5 | 73.1 | 71 | 29 | 13 | 0 | 0 | 0 | 1 | 23 | 3 | 0 | .130 |
| 1 yr. | 0 | 2 | .000 | 3.38 | 3 | 2 | 1 | 24 | 21 | 7 | 10 | 0 | 0 | 0 | 0 | 9 | 2 | 0 | .222 |

## Sterling Slaughter

**SLAUGHTER, STERLING FEORE**          BR  TR  5'11"          165 lbs.
B. Nov. 18, 1941, Danville, Ill.

| | W | L | PCT | ERA | G | GS | CG | IP | H | BB | SO | ShO | W | L | SV | AB | H | HR | BA |
|---|---|---|---|---|---|---|---|---|---|---|---|---|---|---|---|---|---|---|---|
| 1964 CHI N | 2 | 4 | .333 | 5.75 | 20 | 6 | 1 | 51.2 | 64 | 32 | 32 | 0 | 0 | 2 | 0 | 12 | 1 | 0 | .083 |

| | W | L | PCT | ERA | G | GS | CG | IP | H | BB | SO | ShO | Relief Pitching W | L | SV | BATTING AB | H | HR | BA |
|---|---|---|---|---|---|---|---|---|---|---|---|---|---|---|---|---|---|---|---|

## Dwain Sloat

**SLOAT, DWAIN CLIFFORD (Lefty)**
B. Dec. 1, 1918, Nokomis, Ill.                                    BR TL 6'          168 lbs.

| | W | L | PCT | ERA | G | GS | CG | IP | H | BB | SO | ShO | W | L | SV | AB | H | HR | BA |
|---|---|---|---|---|---|---|---|---|---|---|---|---|---|---|---|---|---|---|---|
| 1948 BKN N | 0 | 1 | .000 | 6.14 | 4 | 1 | 0 | 7.1 | 7 | 8 | 1 | 0 | 0 | 0 | 0 | 1 | 0 | 0 | .000 |
| 1949 CHI N | 0 | 0 | — | 7.00 | 5 | 1 | 0 | 9 | 14 | 3 | 3 | 0 | 0 | 0 | 0 | 0 | 0 | 0 | — |
| 2 yrs. | 0 | 1 | .000 | 6.61 | 9 | 2 | 0 | 16.1 | 21 | 11 | 4 | 0 | 0 | 0 | 0 | 1 | 0 | 0 | .000 |
| 1 yr. | 0 | 0 | — | 7.00 | 5 | 1 | 0 | 9 | 14 | 3 | 3 | 0 | 0 | 0 | 0 | 0 | 0 | 0 | — |

## Bob Smith

**SMITH, ROBERT ELDRIDGE**
B. Apr. 22, 1898, Rogersville, Tenn.                              BR TR 5'10"       175 lbs.

| | W | L | PCT | ERA | G | GS | CG | IP | H | BB | SO | ShO | W | L | SV | AB | H | HR | BA |
|---|---|---|---|---|---|---|---|---|---|---|---|---|---|---|---|---|---|---|---|
| 1923 BOS N | 0 | 0 | — | 0.00 | 0 | 0 | 0 | | 0 | 0 | 0 | 0 | 0 | 0 | 0 | 375 | 94 | 0 | .251 |
| 1924 | 0 | 0 | — | 0.00 | 0 | 0 | 0 | | 0 | 0 | 0 | 0 | 0 | 0 | 0 | 347 | 79 | 2 | .228 |
| 1925 | 5 | 3 | .625 | 4.47 | 13 | 10 | 6 | 92.2 | 110 | 36 | 19 | 0 | 0 | 1 | 0 | 174 | 49 | 0 | .282 |
| 1926 | 10 | 13 | .435 | 3.91 | 33 | 23 | 14 | 193.1 | 199 | 75 | 44 | 4 | 2 | 0 | 1 | 84 | 25 | 0 | .298 |
| 1927 | 10 | 18 | .357 | 3.76 | 41 | 32 | 16 | 260.2 | 297 | 75 | 81 | 1 | 2 | 2 | 3 | 109 | 27 | 1 | .248 |
| 1928 | 13 | 17 | .433 | 3.87 | 38 | 25 | 14 | 244.1 | 274 | 74 | 59 | 0 | 2 | 2 | 2 | 92 | 23 | 1 | .250 |
| 1929 | 11 | 17 | .393 | 4.68 | 34 | 29 | 19 | 231 | 256 | 71 | 65 | 1 | 0 | 1 | 3 | 99 | 17 | 1 | .172 |
| 1930 | 10 | 14 | .417 | 4.26 | 38 | 24 | 14 | 219.2 | 247 | 85 | 84 | 2 | 2 | 0 | 5 | 81 | 19 | 0 | .235 |
| 1931 CHI N | 15 | 12 | .556 | 3.22 | 36 | 29 | 18 | 240.1 | 239 | 62 | 63 | 2 | 0 | 0 | 2 | 87 | 19 | 0 | .218 |
| 1932 | 4 | 3 | .571 | 4.61 | 34 | 11 | 4 | 119 | 148 | 36 | 35 | 1 | 0 | 1 | 2 | 42 | 10 | 0 | .238 |
| 1933 2 teams | | | CIN | N | (16G 4–4) | | | BOS | N | (14G 4–3) | | | | | | | | | |
| "      total | 8 | 7 | .533 | 2.65 | 30 | 10 | 7 | 132.1 | 143 | 18 | 34 | 1 | 3 | 2 | 1 | 45 | 9 | 0 | .200 |
| 1934 BOS N | 6 | 9 | .400 | 4.66 | 39 | 5 | 3 | 121.2 | 133 | 36 | 26 | 0 | 4 | 6 | 5 | 36 | 9 | 0 | .250 |
| 1935 | 8 | 18 | .308 | 3.94 | 46 | 20 | 8 | 203.1 | 232 | 61 | 58 | 2 | 3 | 3 | 5 | 63 | 17 | 0 | .270 |
| 1936 | 6 | 7 | .462 | 3.77 | 35 | 11 | 5 | 136 | 142 | 35 | 36 | 2 | 2 | 1 | 8 | 45 | 10 | 0 | .222 |
| 1937 | 0 | 1 | .000 | 4.09 | 18 | 0 | 0 | 44 | 52 | 6 | 14 | 0 | 0 | 1 | 3 | 10 | 2 | 0 | .200 |
| 15 yrs. | 106 | 139 | .433 | 3.95 | 435 | 229 | 128 | 2238.1 | 2472 | 670 | 618 | 16 | 20 | 20 | 40 | * | | | .225 |
| 2 yrs. | 19 | 15 | .559 | 3.68 | 70 | 40 | 22 | 359.1 | 387 | 98 | 98 | 3 | 0 | 1 | 4 | 129 | 29 | 0 | .225 |

WORLD SERIES

| | W | L | PCT | ERA | G | GS | CG | IP | H | BB | SO | ShO | W | L | SV | AB | H | HR | BA |
|---|---|---|---|---|---|---|---|---|---|---|---|---|---|---|---|---|---|---|---|
| 1932 CHI N | 0 | 0 | — | 9.00 | 1 | 0 | 0 | 1 | 2 | 0 | 1 | 0 | 0 | 0 | 0 | 0 | 0 | 0 | — |

## Charlie Smith

**SMITH, CHARLES EDWIN**
Brother of Fred Smith.
B. Apr. 20, 1880, Cleveland, Ohio    D. Jan. 3, 1929, Wickliffe, Ohio                BR TR

| | W | L | PCT | ERA | G | GS | CG | IP | H | BB | SO | ShO | W | L | SV | AB | H | HR | BA |
|---|---|---|---|---|---|---|---|---|---|---|---|---|---|---|---|---|---|---|---|
| 1902 CLE A | 2 | 1 | .667 | 4.05 | 3 | 3 | 2 | 20 | 23 | 5 | 5 | 1 | 0 | 0 | 0 | 8 | 1 | 0 | .125 |
| 1906 WAS A | 9 | 16 | .360 | 2.91 | 33 | 22 | 17 | 235.1 | 250 | 75 | 105 | 2 | 3 | 2 | 0 | 87 | 16 | 1 | .184 |
| 1907 | 10 | 20 | .333 | 2.61 | 36 | 31 | 21 | 258.2 | 254 | 51 | 119 | 3 | 0 | 3 | 0 | 84 | 12 | 0 | .143 |
| 1908 | 9 | 13 | .409 | 2.40 | 26 | 22 | 13 | 184 | 166 | 60 | 83 | 1 | 0 | 1 | 1 | 65 | 8 | 0 | .123 |
| 1909 2 teams | | | WAS | A | (23G 3–12) | | | BOS | A | (3G 3–0) | | | | | | | | | |
| "      total | 6 | 12 | .333 | 3.11 | 26 | 18 | 9 | 170.2 | 163 | 39 | 83 | 1 | 0 | 2 | 0 | 55 | 10 | 0 | .182 |
| 1910 BOS A | 11 | 6 | .647 | 2.30 | 24 | 18 | 11 | 156.1 | 141 | 35 | 53 | 0 | 1 | 1 | 1 | 44 | 5 | 0 | .114 |
| 1911 2 teams | | | BOS | A | (1G 0–0) | | | CHI | N | (7G 3–2) | | | | | | | | | |
| "      total | 3 | 2 | .600 | 1.80 | 8 | 6 | 3 | 40 | 33 | 8 | 11 | 1 | 0 | 0 | 0 | 13 | 1 | 0 | .077 |
| 1912 CHI N | 7 | 4 | .636 | 4.21 | 21 | 5 | 1 | 94 | 92 | 31 | 47 | 0 | 6 | 1 | 1 | 35 | 9 | 0 | .257 |
| 1913 | 7 | 9 | .438 | 2.55 | 20 | 17 | 8 | 137.2 | 138 | 34 | 47 | 1 | 1 | 0 | 0 | 45 | 4 | 0 | .089 |
| 1914 | 2 | 4 | .333 | 3.86 | 16 | 5 | 1 | 53.2 | 49 | 15 | 17 | 0 | 1 | 0 | 0 | 11 | 1 | 0 | .091 |
| 10 yrs. | 66 | 87 | .431 | 2.81 | 213 | 147 | 86 | 1350.1 | 1309 | 353 | 570 | 10 | 12 | 10 | 3 | 447 | 67 | 1 | .150 |
| 4 yrs. | 19 | 19 | .500 | 3.12 | 64 | 32 | 13 | 323.1 | 310 | 87 | 122 | 2 | 8 | 1 | 1 | 104 | 15 | 0 | .144 |

## Lee Smith

**SMITH, LEE ARTHUR JR.**
B. Dec. 4, 1957, Jamestown, La.                                   BR TR 6'5"        220 lbs.

| | W | L | PCT | ERA | G | GS | CG | IP | H | BB | SO | ShO | W | L | SV | AB | H | HR | BA |
|---|---|---|---|---|---|---|---|---|---|---|---|---|---|---|---|---|---|---|---|
| 1980 CHI N | 2 | 0 | 1.000 | 2.86 | 18 | 0 | 0 | 22 | 21 | 14 | 17 | 0 | 2 | 0 | 0 | | | | — |
| 1981 | 3 | 6 | .333 | 3.49 | 40 | 1 | 0 | 67 | 57 | 31 | 50 | 0 | 3 | 5 | 1 | 9 | 0 | 0 | .000 |
| 1982 | 2 | 5 | .286 | 2.69 | 72 | 5 | 0 | 117 | 105 | 37 | 99 | 0 | 2 | 1 | 17 | 16 | 1 | 1 | .063 |
| 1983 | 4 | 10 | .286 | 1.65 | 66 | 0 | 0 | 103.1 | 70 | 41 | 91 | 0 | 4 | 10 | 29 | 9 | 1 | 0 | .111 |
| 1984 | 9 | 7 | .563 | 3.65 | 69 | 0 | 0 | 101 | 98 | 35 | 86 | 0 | 9 | 7 | 33 | 13 | 1 | 0 | .077 |
| 1985 | 7 | 4 | .636 | 3.04 | 65 | 0 | 0 | 97.2 | 87 | 32 | 112 | 0 | 7 | 4 | 33 | 6 | 0 | 0 | .000 |
| 6 yrs. | 27 | 32 | .458 | 2.85 | 330 | 6 | 0 | 508 | 438 | 190 | 455 | 0 | 27 | 27 | 113 | 53 | 3 | 1 | .057 |
| 6 yrs. | 27 | 32 | .458 | 2.85 | 330 | 6 | 0 | 508 | 438 | 190 | 455 | 0 | 27 | 27 | 113 | 53 | 3 | 1 | .057 |
| | | | | | | | | 10th | | | | | 7th | 2nd | | | | | |

LEAGUE CHAMPIONSHIP SERIES

| | W | L | PCT | ERA | G | GS | CG | IP | H | BB | SO | ShO | W | L | SV | AB | H | HR | BA |
|---|---|---|---|---|---|---|---|---|---|---|---|---|---|---|---|---|---|---|---|
| 1984 CHI N | 0 | 1 | .000 | 9.00 | 2 | 0 | 0 | 2 | 3 | 0 | 3 | 0 | 0 | 1 | 1 | 0 | 0 | 0 | — |

## Riverboat Smith

**SMITH, ROBERT WALKUP**
B. May 13, 1928, Clarence, Mo.                                    BL TL 6'          185 lbs.
                                                                 BB 1959

| | W | L | PCT | ERA | G | GS | CG | IP | H | BB | SO | ShO | W | L | SV | AB | H | HR | BA |
|---|---|---|---|---|---|---|---|---|---|---|---|---|---|---|---|---|---|---|---|
| 1958 BOS A | 4 | 3 | .571 | 3.78 | 17 | 7 | 1 | 66.2 | 61 | 45 | 43 | 0 | 1 | 1 | 0 | 19 | 2 | 0 | .105 |
| 1959 2 teams | | | CHI | N | (1G 0–0) | | | CLE | A | (12G 0–1) | | | | | | | | | |
| "      total | 0 | 1 | .000 | 6.90 | 13 | 3 | 0 | 30 | 36 | 14 | 17 | 0 | 0 | 0 | 0 | 6 | 0 | 0 | .000 |
| 2 yrs. | 4 | 4 | .500 | 4.75 | 30 | 10 | 1 | 96.2 | 97 | 59 | 60 | 0 | 1 | 1 | 0 | 25 | 2 | 0 | .080 |
| 1 yr. | 0 | 0 | — | 81.00 | 1 | 0 | 0 | .2 | 5 | 2 | 0 | 0 | 0 | 0 | 0 | 0 | 0 | 0 | — |

## Willie Smith

**SMITH, WILLIE (Wonderful Willie)**
B. Feb. 11, 1939, Anniston, Ala.                                  BL TL 6'          182 lbs.

| | W | L | PCT | ERA | G | GS | CG | IP | H | BB | SO | ShO | W | L | SV | AB | H | HR | BA |
|---|---|---|---|---|---|---|---|---|---|---|---|---|---|---|---|---|---|---|---|
| 1963 DET A | 1 | 0 | 1.000 | 4.57 | 11 | 2 | 0 | 21.2 | 24 | 13 | 16 | 0 | 1 | 0 | 2 | 8 | 1 | 0 | .125 |
| 1964 LA  A | 1 | 4 | .200 | 2.84 | 15 | 1 | 0 | 31.2 | 34 | 10 | 20 | 0 | 1 | 4 | 0 | 359 | 108 | 11 | .301 |
| 1968 2 teams | | | CLE | A | (2G 0–0) | | | CHI | N | (1G 0–0) | | | | | | | | | |
| "      total | 0 | 0 | — | 0.00 | 3 | 0 | 0 | 7.2 | 2 | 1 | 3 | 0 | 0 | 0 | 0 | 184 | 45 | 5 | .245 |
| 3 yrs. | 2 | 4 | .333 | 3.10 | 29 | 3 | 0 | 61 | 60 | 24 | 39 | 0 | 2 | 4 | 2 | * | | | .244 |
| 1 yr. | 0 | 0 | — | 0.00 | 1 | 0 | 0 | 2.2 | 2 | 0 | 2 | 0 | 0 | 0 | 0 | 504 | 123 | 19 | .244 |

| | W | L | PCT | ERA | G | GS | CG | IP | H | BB | SO | ShO | Relief Pitching W | L | SV | BATTING AB | H | HR | BA |
|---|---|---|---|---|---|---|---|---|---|---|---|---|---|---|---|---|---|---|---|

## Marcelino Solis

**SOLIS, MARCELINO**
B. July 19, 1930, San Luis Potosi, Mexico
BL TL 6'1"  185 lbs.

| | W | L | PCT | ERA | G | GS | CG | IP | H | BB | SO | ShO | W | L | SV | AB | H | HR | BA |
|---|---|---|---|---|---|---|---|---|---|---|---|---|---|---|---|---|---|---|---|
| 1958 CHI N | 3 | 3 | .500 | 6.06 | 15 | 4 | 0 | 52 | 74 | 20 | 15 | 0 | 3 | 1 | 0 | 20 | 5 | 0 | .250 |

## Eddie Solomon

**SOLOMON, EDDIE JR (Buddy)**
B. Feb. 9, 1951, Perry, Ga.
BR TR 6'3½"  198 lbs.

| | W | L | PCT | ERA | G | GS | CG | IP | H | BB | SO | ShO | W | L | SV | AB | H | HR | BA |
|---|---|---|---|---|---|---|---|---|---|---|---|---|---|---|---|---|---|---|---|
| 1973 LA N | 0 | 0 | — | 7.11 | 4 | 0 | 0 | 6.1 | 10 | 4 | 6 | 0 | 0 | 0 | 0 | 1 | 0 | 0 | .000 |
| 1974 | 0 | 0 | — | 1.35 | 4 | 0 | 0 | 6.2 | 5 | 2 | 2 | 0 | 0 | 0 | 1 | 0 | 0 | 0 | |
| 1975 CHI N | 0 | 0 | — | 1.29 | 6 | 0 | 0 | 7 | 7 | 6 | 3 | 0 | 0 | 0 | 0 | 0 | 0 | 0 | |
| 1976 STL N | 1 | 1 | .500 | 4.86 | 26 | 2 | 0 | 37 | 45 | 16 | 19 | 0 | 0 | 1 | 0 | 5 | 2 | 0 | .400 |
| 1977 ATL N | 6 | 6 | .500 | 4.55 | 18 | 16 | 0 | 89 | 110 | 34 | 54 | 0 | 0 | 0 | 0 | 31 | 4 | 0 | .129 |
| 1978 | 4 | 6 | .400 | 4.08 | 37 | 8 | 0 | 106 | 98 | 50 | 64 | 0 | 1 | 3 | 2 | 29 | 4 | 0 | .138 |
| 1979 | 7 | 14 | .333 | 4.21 | 31 | 30 | 4 | 186 | 184 | 51 | 96 | 0 | 0 | 0 | 0 | 64 | 13 | 0 | .203 |
| 1980 PIT N | 7 | 3 | .700 | 2.70 | 26 | 12 | 2 | 100 | 96 | 37 | 35 | 0 | 2 | 0 | 0 | 32 | 7 | 0 | .219 |
| 1981 | 8 | 6 | .571 | 3.12 | 22 | 17 | 2 | 127 | 133 | 27 | 38 | 0 | 1 | 1 | 1 | 43 | 7 | 0 | .163 |
| 1982 2 teams | | | PIT N | (11G 2-6) | | CHI A | (6G 1-0) | | | | | | | | | | | | |
| " total | 3 | 6 | .333 | 6.33 | 17 | 10 | 0 | 54 | 76 | 20 | 20 | 0 | 2 | 0 | 0 | 15 | 2 | 0 | .133 |
| 10 yrs. | 36 | 42 | .462 | 3.99 | 191 | 95 | 8 | 719 | 764 | 247 | 337 | 0 | 6 | 5 | 4 | 220 | 39 | 0 | .177 |
| 1 yr. | 0 | 0 | — | 1.29 | 6 | 0 | 0 | 7 | 7 | 6 | 3 | 0 | 0 | 0 | 0 | 0 | 0 | 0 | |

LEAGUE CHAMPIONSHIP SERIES

| | W | L | PCT | ERA | G | GS | CG | IP | H | BB | SO | ShO | W | L | SV | AB | H | HR | BA |
|---|---|---|---|---|---|---|---|---|---|---|---|---|---|---|---|---|---|---|---|
| 1974 LA N | 0 | 0 | — | 0.00 | 1 | 0 | 0 | 2 | 2 | 1 | 1 | 0 | 0 | 0 | 0 | 0 | 0 | 0 | — |

## Rudy Sommers

**SOMMERS, RUDOLPH**
B. Oct. 30, 1888, Cincinnati, Ohio    D. Mar. 18, 1949, Louisville, Ky.
BL TL 5'11"  170 lbs.

| | W | L | PCT | ERA | G | GS | CG | IP | H | BB | SO | ShO | W | L | SV | AB | H | HR | BA |
|---|---|---|---|---|---|---|---|---|---|---|---|---|---|---|---|---|---|---|---|
| 1912 CHI N | 0 | 1 | .000 | 3.00 | 1 | 0 | 0 | 3 | 4 | 2 | 2 | 0 | 0 | 0 | 0 | 0 | 0 | 0 | — |
| 1914 BKN F | 4 | 7 | .364 | 4.06 | 23 | 8 | 2 | 82 | 88 | 34 | 40 | 0 | 3 | 0 | 0 | 24 | 6 | 0 | .250 |
| 1926 BOS A | 0 | 0 | — | 13.50 | 2 | 0 | 0 | 2 | 3 | 3 | 0 | 0 | 0 | 0 | 0 | 0 | 0 | 0 | — |
| 1927 | 0 | 0 | — | 8.36 | 7 | 0 | 0 | 14 | 18 | 14 | 2 | 0 | 0 | 1 | 0 | 2 | 1 | 0 | .500 |
| 4 yrs. | 4 | 8 | .333 | 4.81 | 33 | 8 | 2 | 101 | 113 | 53 | 44 | 0 | 3 | 1 | 0 | 26 | 7 | 0 | .269 |
| 1 yr. | 0 | 1 | .000 | 3.00 | 1 | 0 | 0 | 3 | 4 | 2 | 2 | 0 | 0 | 1 | 0 | 0 | 0 | 0 | — |

## Lary Sorensen

**SORENSEN, LARY ALAN**
B. Oct. 4, 1955, Detroit, Mich.
BR TR 6'2"  200 lbs.

| | W | L | PCT | ERA | G | GS | CG | IP | H | BB | SO | ShO | W | L | SV | AB | H | HR | BA |
|---|---|---|---|---|---|---|---|---|---|---|---|---|---|---|---|---|---|---|---|
| 1977 MIL A | 7 | 10 | .412 | 4.37 | 23 | 20 | 9 | 142 | 147 | 36 | 57 | 0 | 0 | 1 | 0 | 0 | 0 | 0 | — |
| 1978 | 18 | 12 | .600 | 3.21 | 37 | 36 | 17 | 280.2 | 277 | 50 | 78 | 3 | 0 | 0 | 1 | 0 | 0 | 0 | — |
| 1979 | 15 | 14 | .517 | 3.98 | 34 | 34 | 16 | 235 | 250 | 42 | 63 | 2 | 0 | 0 | 0 | 0 | 0 | 0 | — |
| 1980 | 12 | 10 | .545 | 3.67 | 35 | 29 | 8 | 196 | 242 | 45 | 54 | 2 | 0 | 1 | 1 | 0 | 0 | 0 | — |
| 1981 STL N | 7 | 7 | .500 | 3.28 | 23 | 23 | 3 | 140 | 149 | 26 | 52 | 1 | 0 | 0 | 0 | 46 | 3 | 0 | .065 |
| 1982 CLE A | 10 | 15 | .400 | 5.61 | 32 | 30 | 6 | 189.1 | 251 | 55 | 62 | 1 | 0 | 0 | 0 | 0 | 0 | 0 | — |
| 1983 | 12 | 11 | .522 | 4.24 | 36 | 34 | 8 | 222.2 | 238 | 65 | 76 | 1 | 0 | 0 | 0 | 0 | 0 | 0 | — |
| 1984 OAK A | 6 | 13 | .316 | 4.91 | 46 | 21 | 2 | 183.1 | 240 | 44 | 63 | 0 | 1 | 2 | 1 | 0 | 0 | 0 | .000 |
| 1985 CHI N | 3 | 7 | .300 | 4.26 | 45 | 3 | 0 | 82.1 | 86 | 24 | 34 | 0 | 3 | 5 | 0 | 6 | 0 | 0 | .058 |
| 9 yrs. | 90 | 99 | .476 | 4.12 | 311 | 230 | 69 | 1671.1 | 1880 | 387 | 539 | 10 | 4 | 9 | 3 | 52 | 3 | 0 | .000 |
| 1 yr. | 3 | 7 | .300 | 4.26 | 45 | 3 | 0 | 82.1 | 86 | 24 | 34 | 0 | 3 | 5 | 0 | 6 | 0 | 0 | .000 |

## Al Spalding

**SPALDING, ALBERT GOODWILL**
B. Sept. 2, 1850, Byron, Ill.    D. Sept. 9, 1915, Point Loma, Calif.
Manager 1876-77.
Hall of Fame 1939.
BR TR 6'1"  170 lbs.

| | W | L | PCT | ERA | G | GS | CG | IP | H | BB | SO | ShO | W | L | SV | AB | H | HR | BA |
|---|---|---|---|---|---|---|---|---|---|---|---|---|---|---|---|---|---|---|---|
| 1876 CHI N | 47 | 13 | .783 | 1.75 | 61 | 60 | 53 | 528.2 | 542 | 26 | 39 | 8 | 0 | 0 | 0 | 292 | 91 | 0 | .312 |
| 1877 | 1 | 0 | 1.000 | 3.27 | 4 | 1 | 0 | 11 | 17 | 0 | 2 | 0 | 1 | 0 | 1 | 254 | 65 | 0 | .256 |
| 1878 | 0 | 0 | — | 0.00 | 0 | 0 | 0 | 0 | 0 | 0 | 0 | 0 | 0 | 0 | 0 | 4 | 2 | 0 | .500 |
| 3 yrs. | 48 | 13 | .787 | 1.78 | 65 | 61 | 53 | 539.2 | 559 | 26 | 41 | 8 | 1 | 0 | 1 | * | | | |
| 2 yrs. | 48 | 13 | .787 | 1.78 | 65 | 61 | 53 | 539.2 | 559 | 26 | 41 | 8 | 1 | 0 | 1 | 550 | 158 | 0 | .287 |

## Carl Spongburg

**SPONGBURG, CARL GUSTAVE**
B. May 21, 1884, Idaho Falls, Ida.    D. July 21, 1938, Los Angeles, Calif.
BR TR

| | W | L | PCT | ERA | G | GS | CG | IP | H | BB | SO | ShO | W | L | SV | AB | H | HR | BA |
|---|---|---|---|---|---|---|---|---|---|---|---|---|---|---|---|---|---|---|---|
| 1908 CHI N | 0 | 0 | — | 9.00 | 1 | 0 | 0 | 7 | 9 | 6 | 4 | 0 | 0 | 0 | 0 | 3 | 2 | 0 | .667 |

## Charlie Sprague

**SPRAGUE, CHARLES WELLINGTON**
B. Oct. 10, 1864, Cleveland, Ohio    D. Dec. 31, 1912, Des Moines, Iowa
BL TL 5'11"  150 lbs.

| | W | L | PCT | ERA | G | GS | CG | IP | H | BB | SO | ShO | W | L | SV | AB | H | HR | BA |
|---|---|---|---|---|---|---|---|---|---|---|---|---|---|---|---|---|---|---|---|
| 1887 CHI N | 1 | 0 | 1.000 | 4.91 | 3 | 3 | 2 | 22 | 24 | 13 | 9 | 0 | 0 | 0 | 0 | 13 | 2 | 0 | .154 |
| 1889 CLE N | 0 | 2 | .000 | 8.47 | 2 | 2 | 2 | 17 | 27 | 10 | 8 | 0 | 0 | 0 | 0 | 7 | 1 | 0 | .143 |
| 1890 TOL AA | 9 | 5 | .643 | 3.89 | 19 | 12 | 9 | 122.2 | 111 | 78 | 59 | 0 | 1 | 2 | 0 | 199 | 47 | 0 | .236 |
| 3 yrs. | 10 | 7 | .588 | 4.51 | 24 | 17 | 13 | 161.2 | 162 | 101 | 76 | 0 | 1 | 2 | 0 | * | | | |
| 1 yr. | 1 | 0 | 1.000 | 4.91 | 3 | 3 | 2 | 22 | 24 | 13 | 9 | 0 | 0 | 0 | 0 | 13 | 2 | 0 | .154 |

## Jack Spring

**SPRING, JACK RUSSELL**
B. Mar. 11, 1933, Spokane, Wash.
BR TL 6'1"  175 lbs.

| | W | L | PCT | ERA | G | GS | CG | IP | H | BB | SO | ShO | W | L | SV | AB | H | HR | BA |
|---|---|---|---|---|---|---|---|---|---|---|---|---|---|---|---|---|---|---|---|
| 1955 PHI N | 0 | 1 | .000 | 6.75 | 2 | 0 | 0 | 2.2 | 2 | 1 | 2 | 0 | 0 | 1 | 0 | 1 | 0 | 0 | .000 |
| 1957 BOS A | 0 | 0 | — | 0.00 | 1 | 0 | 0 | 1 | 0 | 1 | 2 | 0 | 0 | 0 | 0 | 0 | 0 | 0 | — |
| 1958 WAS A | 0 | 0 | — | 14.14 | 3 | 1 | 0 | 7 | 16 | 7 | 1 | 0 | 0 | 0 | 0 | 2 | 0 | 0 | .000 |
| 1961 LA A | 3 | 0 | 1.000 | 4.26 | 18 | 4 | 0 | 38 | 35 | 15 | 27 | 0 | 0 | 0 | 0 | 8 | 0 | 0 | — |
| 1962 | 4 | 2 | .667 | 4.02 | 57 | 0 | 0 | 65 | 66 | 30 | 31 | 0 | 4 | 2 | 6 | 11 | 1 | 0 | .091 |
| 1963 | 1 | 0 | 1.000 | 3.05 | 45 | 0 | 0 | 38.1 | 40 | 9 | 13 | 0 | 1 | 0 | 3 | 3 | 1 | 0 | .333 |
| 1964 3 teams | | | LA A | (6G 1-0) | | CHI N | (7G 0-0) | | STL N | (2G 0-0) | | | | | | | | | |
| " total | 1 | 0 | 1.000 | 4.38 | 15 | 0 | 0 | 12.1 | 15 | 6 | 1 | 0 | 1 | 0 | 0 | 0 | 0 | 0 | — |

| | W | L | PCT | ERA | G | GS | CG | IP | H | BB | SO | ShO | Relief Pitching W | L | SV | BATTING AB | H | HR | BA |
|---|---|---|---|---|---|---|---|---|---|---|---|---|---|---|---|---|---|---|---|

## Jack Spring continued

| | W | L | PCT | ERA | G | GS | CG | IP | H | BB | SO | ShO | W | L | SV | AB | H | HR | BA |
|---|---|---|---|---|---|---|---|---|---|---|---|---|---|---|---|---|---|---|---|
| 1965 CLE A | 1 | 2 | .333 | 3.74 | 14 | 0 | 0 | 21.2 | 21 | 10 | 9 | 0 | 1 | 2 | 0 | 3 | 1 | 0 | .333 |
| 8 yrs. | 12 | 5 | .706 | 4.26 | 155 | 5 | 0 | 186 | 195 | 78 | 86 | 0 | 9 | 5 | 8 | 28 | 3 | 0 | .107 |
| 1 yr. | 0 | 0 | – | 6.00 | 7 | 0 | 0 | 6 | 4 | 2 | 1 | 0 | 0 | 0 | 0 | 0 | 0 | 0 | |

## Eddie Stack

**STACK, WILLIAM EDWARD**    BR TR
B. Oct. 24, 1887, Chicago, Ill.    D. Aug. 28, 1958, Chicago, Ill.

| | W | L | PCT | ERA | G | GS | CG | IP | H | BB | SO | ShO | W | L | SV | AB | H | HR | BA |
|---|---|---|---|---|---|---|---|---|---|---|---|---|---|---|---|---|---|---|---|
| 1910 PHI N | 6 | 7 | .462 | 4.00 | 20 | 16 | 7 | 117 | 115 | 34 | 48 | 1 | 0 | 0 | 0 | 36 | 3 | 0 | .083 |
| 1911 | 5 | 5 | .500 | 3.59 | 13 | 10 | 5 | 77.2 | 67 | 41 | 36 | 0 | 0 | 0 | 0 | 24 | 2 | 0 | .083 |
| 1912 BKN N | 7 | 5 | .583 | 3.36 | 28 | 17 | 4 | 142 | 139 | 55 | 45 | 0 | 2 | 1 | 1 | 52 | 7 | 0 | .135 |
| 1913 2 teams | | BKN | N (23G 4–4) | | CHI | N (11G 4–2) | | | | | | | | | | | | | |
| " total | 8 | 6 | .571 | 3.07 | 34 | 16 | 7 | 138 | 135 | 47 | 62 | 2 | 0 | 1 | 1 | 41 | 5 | 0 | .122 |
| 1914 CHI N | 0 | 1 | .000 | 4.96 | 7 | 1 | 0 | 16.1 | 13 | 11 | 9 | 0 | 0 | 0 | 0 | 4 | 0 | 0 | .000 |
| 5 yrs. | 26 | 24 | .520 | 3.52 | 102 | 60 | 23 | 491 | 469 | 188 | 200 | 3 | 2 | 2 | 2 | 157 | 17 | 0 | .108 |
| 2 yrs. | 4 | 3 | .571 | 4.41 | 18 | 8 | 3 | 67.1 | 69 | 26 | 37 | 1 | 0 | 0 | 1 | 20 | 1 | 0 | .050 |

## Pete Standridge

**STANDRIDGE, ALFRED PETER**    BR TR 5'10½" 165 lbs.
B. Apr. 25, 1891, Seattle, Wash.    D. Aug. 2, 1963, San Francisco, Calif.

| | W | L | PCT | ERA | G | GS | CG | IP | H | BB | SO | ShO | W | L | SV | AB | H | HR | BA |
|---|---|---|---|---|---|---|---|---|---|---|---|---|---|---|---|---|---|---|---|
| 1911 STL N | 0 | 0 | – | 9.64 | 2 | 0 | 0 | 4.2 | 4 | 4 | 3 | 0 | 0 | 0 | 0 | 1 | 0 | 0 | .000 |
| 1915 CHI N | 4 | 1 | .800 | 3.61 | 29 | 3 | 2 | 112.1 | 120 | 36 | 42 | 0 | 2 | 1 | 0 | 40 | 9 | 0 | .225 |
| 2 yrs. | 4 | 1 | .800 | 3.85 | 31 | 3 | 2 | 117 | 124 | 40 | 45 | 0 | 2 | 1 | 0 | 41 | 9 | 0 | .220 |
| 1 yr. | 4 | 1 | .800 | 3.61 | 29 | 3 | 2 | 112.1 | 120 | 36 | 42 | 0 | 2 | 1 | 0 | 40 | 9 | 0 | .225 |

## Joe Stanley

**STANLEY, JOSEPH BERNARD**    BB TR 5'9½" 150 lbs.
Brother of Buck Stanley.
B. Apr. 2, 1881, Washington, D. C.    D. Sept. 13, 1967, Detroit, Mich.

| | W | L | PCT | ERA | G | GS | CG | IP | H | BB | SO | ShO | W | L | SV | AB | H | HR | BA |
|---|---|---|---|---|---|---|---|---|---|---|---|---|---|---|---|---|---|---|---|
| 1897 WAS N | 0 | 0 | – | 0.00 | 1 | 0 | 0 | .2 | 0 | 0 | 0 | 0 | 0 | 0 | 0 | 1 | 0 | 0 | .000 |
| 1903 BOS N | 0 | 0 | – | 9.00 | 1 | 0 | 0 | 4 | 4 | 4 | 4 | 0 | 0 | 0 | 0 | 308 | 77 | 1 | .250 |
| 1906 WAS A | 0 | 0 | – | 12.00 | 1 | 0 | 0 | 3 | 3 | 1 | 0 | 0 | 0 | 0 | 0 | 221 | 36 | 0 | .163 |
| 3 yrs. | 0 | 0 | – | 9.39 | 3 | 0 | 0 | 7.2 | 7 | 5 | 4 | 0 | 0 | 0 | 0 | * | | | |

## Ray Starr

**STARR, RAYMOND FRANCIS (Iron Man)**    BR TR 6'1" 178 lbs.
B. Apr. 23, 1906, Nowata, Okla.    D. Feb. 9, 1963, Baylis, Ill.

| | W | L | PCT | ERA | G | GS | CG | IP | H | BB | SO | ShO | W | L | SV | AB | H | HR | BA |
|---|---|---|---|---|---|---|---|---|---|---|---|---|---|---|---|---|---|---|---|
| 1932 STL N | 1 | 1 | .500 | 2.70 | 3 | 2 | 1 | 20 | 19 | 10 | 6 | 1 | 0 | 0 | 0 | 4 | 1 | 0 | .250 |
| 1933 2 teams | | NY | N (6G 0–1) | | BOS | N (9G 0–1) | | | | | | | | | | | | | |
| " total | 0 | 2 | .000 | 4.35 | 15 | 3 | 0 | 41.1 | 51 | 19 | 17 | 0 | 0 | 1 | 0 | 10 | 1 | 0 | .100 |
| 1941 CIN N | 3 | 2 | .600 | 2.65 | 7 | 4 | 3 | 34 | 28 | 6 | 11 | 2 | 1 | 1 | 0 | 11 | 2 | 0 | .182 |
| 1942 | 15 | 13 | .536 | 2.67 | 37 | 33 | 17 | 276.2 | 228 | 106 | 83 | 4 | 0 | 0 | 0 | 88 | 8 | 0 | .091 |
| 1943 | 11 | 10 | .524 | 3.64 | 36 | 33 | 9 | 217.1 | 201 | 91 | 42 | 2 | 1 | 0 | 1 | 74 | 9 | 0 | .122 |
| 1944 PIT N | 6 | 5 | .545 | 5.02 | 27 | 12 | 5 | 89.2 | 116 | 36 | 25 | 0 | 2 | 3 | 3 | 22 | 3 | 0 | .136 |
| 1945 2 teams | | PIT | N (4G 0–2) | | CHI | N (9G 1–0) | | | | | | | | | | | | | |
| " total | 1 | 2 | .333 | 8.10 | 13 | 1 | 0 | 20 | 27 | 11 | 5 | 0 | 1 | 2 | 0 | 3 | 2 | 0 | .667 |
| 7 yrs. | 37 | 35 | .514 | 3.53 | 138 | 88 | 35 | 699 | 670 | 279 | 189 | 9 | 5 | 6 | 4 | 212 | 26 | 0 | .123 |
| 1 yr. | 1 | 0 | 1.000 | 7.43 | 9 | 1 | 0 | 13.1 | 17 | 7 | 5 | 0 | 1 | 0 | 0 | 2 | 1 | 0 | .500 |

## Ed Stauffer

**STAUFFER, CHARLES EDWARD**    BR TR 5'11" 185 lbs.
B. Jan. 10, 1898, Emsworth, Pa.    D. July 2, 1979, St. Petersburg, Fla.

| | W | L | PCT | ERA | G | GS | CG | IP | H | BB | SO | ShO | W | L | SV | AB | H | HR | BA |
|---|---|---|---|---|---|---|---|---|---|---|---|---|---|---|---|---|---|---|---|
| 1923 CHI N | 0 | 0 | – | 13.50 | 1 | 0 | 0 | 2 | 5 | 1 | 0 | 0 | 0 | 0 | 0 | 0 | 0 | 0 | |
| 1925 STL A | 0 | 1 | .000 | 5.34 | 20 | 1 | 0 | 30.1 | 34 | 21 | 13 | 0 | 0 | 0 | 0 | 4 | 1 | 0 | .250 |
| 2 yrs. | 0 | 1 | .000 | 5.85 | 21 | 1 | 0 | 32.1 | 39 | 22 | 13 | 0 | 0 | 0 | 0 | 4 | 1 | 0 | .250 |
| 1 yr. | 0 | 0 | – | 13.50 | 1 | 0 | 0 | 2 | 5 | 1 | 0 | 0 | 0 | 0 | 0 | 0 | 0 | 0 | |

## Morrie Steevens

**STEEVENS, MORRIS DALE**    BL TL 6'2" 175 lbs.
B. Oct. 7, 1940, Salem, Ill.

| | W | L | PCT | ERA | G | GS | CG | IP | H | BB | SO | ShO | W | L | SV | AB | H | HR | BA |
|---|---|---|---|---|---|---|---|---|---|---|---|---|---|---|---|---|---|---|---|
| 1962 CHI N | 0 | 1 | .000 | 2.40 | 12 | 1 | 0 | 15 | 10 | 11 | 5 | 0 | 0 | 0 | 0 | 1 | 0 | 0 | .000 |
| 1964 PHI N | 0 | 0 | – | 3.38 | 4 | 0 | 0 | 2.2 | 5 | 1 | 3 | 0 | 0 | 0 | 0 | 0 | 0 | 0 | – |
| 1965 | 0 | 1 | .000 | 16.88 | 6 | 0 | 0 | 2.2 | 5 | 4 | 3 | 0 | 0 | 1 | 0 | 0 | 0 | 0 | – |
| 3 yrs. | 0 | 2 | .000 | 4.43 | 22 | 1 | 0 | 20.1 | 20 | 16 | 11 | 0 | 0 | 1 | 0 | 1 | 0 | 0 | .000 |
| 1 yr. | 0 | 1 | .000 | 2.40 | 12 | 1 | 0 | 15 | 10 | 11 | 5 | 0 | 0 | 0 | 0 | 1 | 0 | 0 | .000 |

## Ed Stein

**STEIN, EDWARD F.**    TR 5'11" 170 lbs.
B. Sept. 5, 1869, Detroit, Mich.    D. May 10, 1928, Detroit, Mich.

| | W | L | PCT | ERA | G | GS | CG | IP | H | BB | SO | ShO | W | L | SV | AB | H | HR | BA |
|---|---|---|---|---|---|---|---|---|---|---|---|---|---|---|---|---|---|---|---|
| 1890 CHI N | 12 | 6 | .667 | 3.81 | 20 | 18 | 14 | 160.2 | 147 | 83 | 65 | 1 | 0 | 1 | 0 | 59 | 9 | 0 | .153 |
| 1891 | 7 | 6 | .538 | 3.74 | 14 | 10 | 9 | 101 | 99 | 57 | 38 | 1 | 2 | 1 | 0 | 43 | 7 | 0 | .163 |
| 1892 BKN N | 27 | 16 | .628 | 2.84 | 48 | 42 | 38 | 377.1 | 310 | 150 | 190 | 6 | 3 | 0 | 1 | 144 | 31 | 0 | .215 |
| 1893 | 19 | 15 | .559 | 3.77 | 37 | 34 | 28 | 298.1 | 294 | 119 | 81 | 1 | 2 | 0 | 0 | 118 | 25 | 0 | .212 |
| 1894 | 27 | 14 | .659 | 4.54 | 45 | 41 | 38 | 359 | 396 | 171 | 84 | 2 | 2 | 0 | 1 | 146 | 38 | 2 | .260 |
| 1895 | 15 | 13 | .536 | 4.72 | 32 | 27 | 24 | 255.1 | 282 | 93 | 55 | 1 | 0 | 1 | 0 | 104 | 26 | 0 | .250 |
| 1896 | 3 | 6 | .333 | 4.88 | 17 | 10 | 6 | 90.1 | 130 | 51 | 16 | 0 | 1 | 0 | 0 | 39 | 10 | 0 | .256 |
| 1898 | 0 | 2 | .000 | 5.48 | 3 | 2 | 2 | 23 | 39 | 9 | 6 | 0 | 0 | 0 | 0 | 10 | 4 | 0 | .400 |
| 8 yrs. | 110 | 78 | .585 | 3.96 | 216 | 184 | 159 | 1665 | 1697 | 733 | 535 | 12 | 11 | 3 | 3 | 663 | 150 | 2 | .226 |
| 2 yrs. | 19 | 12 | .613 | 3.78 | 34 | 28 | 23 | 261.2 | 246 | 140 | 103 | 2 | 2 | 2 | 0 | 102 | 16 | 0 | .157 |

## Randy Stein

**STEIN, WILLIAM RANDOLPH**    BR TR 6'4" 210 lbs.
B. Mar. 7, 1953, Pomona, Calif.

| | W | L | PCT | ERA | G | GS | CG | IP | H | BB | SO | ShO | W | L | SV | AB | H | HR | BA |
|---|---|---|---|---|---|---|---|---|---|---|---|---|---|---|---|---|---|---|---|
| 1978 MIL A | 3 | 2 | .600 | 5.33 | 31 | 1 | 0 | 72.2 | 78 | 39 | 42 | 0 | 3 | 1 | 1 | 0 | 0 | 0 | – |
| 1979 SEA A | 2 | 3 | .400 | 5.93 | 23 | 1 | 0 | 41 | 48 | 27 | 39 | 0 | 2 | 2 | 0 | 0 | 0 | 0 | – |
| 1981 | 0 | 1 | .000 | 11.00 | 5 | 0 | 0 | 9 | 18 | 8 | 6 | 0 | 0 | 1 | 0 | 0 | 0 | 0 | – |

| | W | L | PCT | ERA | G | GS | CG | IP | H | BB | SO | ShO | Relief Pitching W | L | SV | BATTING AB | H | HR | BA |
|---|---|---|---|---|---|---|---|---|---|---|---|---|---|---|---|---|---|---|---|

## Randy Stein continued

| | W | L | PCT | ERA | G | GS | CG | IP | H | BB | SO | ShO | W | L | SV | AB | H | HR | BA |
|---|---|---|---|---|---|---|---|---|---|---|---|---|---|---|---|---|---|---|---|
| 1982 CHI N | 0 | 0 | — | 3.48 | 6 | 0 | 0 | 10.1 | 7 | 7 | 6 | 0 | 0 | 0 | 0 | 0 | 0 | 0 | — |
| 4 yrs. | 5 | 6 | .455 | 5.75 | 65 | 2 | 0 | 133 | 151 | 81 | 93 | 0 | 5 | 4 | 1 | 0 | 0 | 0 | — |
| 1 yr. | 0 | 0 | — | 3.48 | 6 | 0 | 0 | 10.1 | 7 | 7 | 6 | 0 | 0 | 0 | 0 | 0 | 0 | 0 | — |

## Earl Stephenson

STEPHENSON, CHESTER EARL  BL TL 6'3" 175 lbs.
B. July 31, 1947, Benson, N. C.

| | W | L | PCT | ERA | G | GS | CG | IP | H | BB | SO | ShO | W | L | SV | AB | H | HR | BA |
|---|---|---|---|---|---|---|---|---|---|---|---|---|---|---|---|---|---|---|---|
| 1971 CHI N | 1 | 0 | 1.000 | 4.50 | 16 | 0 | 0 | 20 | 24 | 11 | 11 | 0 | 1 | 1 | 1 | 2 | 0 | 0 | .000 |
| 1972 MIL A | 3 | 5 | .375 | 3.26 | 35 | 8 | 1 | 80 | 79 | 33 | 33 | 0 | 1 | 0 | 0 | 18 | 0 | 0 | .000 |
| 1977 BAL A | 0 | 0 | — | 9.00 | 1 | 0 | 0 | 3 | 5 | 0 | 2 | 0 | 0 | 0 | 0 | 0 | 0 | 0 | — |
| 1978 | 0 | 0 | — | 2.79 | 2 | 0 | 0 | 9.2 | 10 | 5 | 4 | 0 | 0 | 0 | 0 | 0 | 0 | 0 | — |
| 4 yrs. | 4 | 5 | .444 | 3.59 | 54 | 8 | 1 | 112.2 | 118 | 49 | 50 | 0 | 2 | 1 | 1 | 20 | 0 | 0 | .000 |
| 1 yr. | 1 | 0 | 1.000 | 4.50 | 16 | 0 | 0 | 20 | 24 | 11 | 11 | 0 | 1 | 1 | 1 | 2 | 0 | 0 | .000 |

## Mack Stewart

STEWART, WILLIAM MACKLIN  BR TR 6' 167 lbs.
B. Sept. 23, 1914, Stevenson, Ala.  D. Mar. 21, 1960, Macon, Ga.

| | W | L | PCT | ERA | G | GS | CG | IP | H | BB | SO | ShO | W | L | SV | AB | H | HR | BA |
|---|---|---|---|---|---|---|---|---|---|---|---|---|---|---|---|---|---|---|---|
| 1944 CHI N | 0 | 0 | — | 1.46 | 8 | 0 | 0 | 12.1 | 11 | 4 | 3 | 0 | 0 | 0 | 0 | 1 | 0 | 0 | .000 |
| 1945 | 0 | 1 | .000 | 4.76 | 16 | 1 | 0 | 28.1 | 37 | 14 | 9 | 0 | 0 | 0 | 0 | 3 | 1 | 0 | .333 |
| 2 yrs. | 0 | 1 | .000 | 3.76 | 24 | 1 | 0 | 40.2 | 48 | 18 | 12 | 0 | 0 | 0 | 0 | 4 | 1 | 0 | .250 |
| 2 yrs. | 0 | 1 | .000 | 3.76 | 24 | 1 | 0 | 40.2 | 48 | 18 | 12 | 0 | 0 | 0 | 0 | 4 | 1 | 0 | .250 |

## Tim Stoddard

STODDARD, TIMOTHY PAUL  BR TR 6'7" 230 lbs.
B. Jan. 24, 1953, East Chicago, Ind.

| | W | L | PCT | ERA | G | GS | CG | IP | H | BB | SO | ShO | W | L | SV | AB | H | HR | BA |
|---|---|---|---|---|---|---|---|---|---|---|---|---|---|---|---|---|---|---|---|
| 1975 CHI A | 0 | 0 | — | 9.00 | 1 | 0 | 0 | 1 | 2 | 0 | 0 | 0 | 0 | 0 | 0 | 0 | 0 | 0 | — |
| 1978 BAL A | 0 | 1 | .000 | 6.00 | 8 | 0 | 0 | 18 | 22 | 8 | 14 | 0 | 0 | 1 | 0 | 0 | 0 | 0 | — |
| 1979 | 3 | 1 | .750 | 1.71 | 29 | 0 | 0 | 58 | 44 | 19 | 47 | 0 | 3 | 1 | 3 | 0 | 0 | 0 | — |
| 1980 | 5 | 3 | .625 | 2.51 | 64 | 0 | 0 | 86 | 72 | 38 | 64 | 0 | 5 | 3 | 26 | 0 | 0 | 0 | — |
| 1981 | 4 | 2 | .667 | 3.89 | 31 | 0 | 0 | 37 | 38 | 18 | 32 | 0 | 4 | 2 | 7 | 0 | 0 | 0 | — |
| 1982 | 3 | 4 | .429 | 4.02 | 50 | 0 | 0 | 56 | 53 | 29 | 42 | 0 | 3 | 4 | 12 | 0 | 0 | 0 | — |
| 1983 | 4 | 3 | .571 | 6.09 | 47 | 0 | 0 | 57.2 | 65 | 29 | 50 | 0 | 4 | 3 | 9 | 0 | 0 | 0 | — |
| 1984 CHI N | 10 | 6 | .625 | 3.82 | 58 | 0 | 0 | 92 | 77 | 57 | 87 | 0 | 10 | 6 | 7 | 11 | 1 | 0 | .091 |
| 1985 SD N | 1 | 6 | .143 | 4.65 | 44 | 0 | 0 | 60 | 63 | 37 | 42 | 0 | 1 | 6 | 1 | 5 | 0 | 0 | .000 |
| 9 yrs. | 30 | 26 | .536 | 3.83 | 332 | 0 | 0 | 465.2 | 436 | 235 | 378 | 0 | 30 | 26 | 65 | 16 | 1 | 0 | .063 |
| 1 yr. | 10 | 6 | .625 | 3.82 | 58 | 0 | 0 | 92 | 77 | 57 | 87 | 0 | 10 | 6 | 7 | 11 | 1 | 0 | .091 |

LEAGUE CHAMPIONSHIP SERIES

| | W | L | PCT | ERA | G | GS | CG | IP | H | BB | SO | ShO | W | L | SV | AB | H | HR | BA |
|---|---|---|---|---|---|---|---|---|---|---|---|---|---|---|---|---|---|---|---|
| 1984 CHI N | 0 | 0 | — | 4.50 | 2 | 0 | 0 | 2 | 1 | 2 | 2 | 0 | 0 | 0 | 0 | 0 | 0 | 0 | — |

WORLD SERIES

| | W | L | PCT | ERA | G | GS | CG | IP | H | BB | SO | ShO | W | L | SV | AB | H | HR | BA |
|---|---|---|---|---|---|---|---|---|---|---|---|---|---|---|---|---|---|---|---|
| 1979 BAL A | 1 | 0 | 1.000 | 5.40 | 4 | 0 | 0 | 5 | 6 | 1 | 3 | 0 | 1 | 0 | 0 | 1 | 1 | 0 | 1.000 |

## Steve Stone

STONE, STEVEN MICHAEL  BR TR 5'10" 175 lbs.
B. July 14, 1947, Cleveland, Ohio

| | W | L | PCT | ERA | G | GS | CG | IP | H | BB | SO | ShO | W | L | SV | AB | H | HR | BA |
|---|---|---|---|---|---|---|---|---|---|---|---|---|---|---|---|---|---|---|---|
| 1971 SF N | 5 | 9 | .357 | 4.14 | 24 | 19 | 2 | 111 | 110 | 55 | 63 | 2 | 0 | 0 | 0 | 34 | 0 | 0 | .000 |
| 1972 | 6 | 8 | .429 | 2.98 | 27 | 16 | 4 | 124 | 97 | 49 | 85 | 1 | 1 | 0 | 0 | 34 | 4 | 0 | .118 |
| 1973 CHI A | 6 | 11 | .353 | 4.24 | 36 | 22 | 3 | 176.1 | 163 | 82 | 138 | 0 | 0 | 1 | 1 | 0 | 0 | 0 | — |
| 1974 CHI N | 8 | 6 | .571 | 4.13 | 38 | 23 | 1 | 170 | 185 | 64 | 90 | 0 | 1 | 1 | 0 | 58 | 7 | 0 | .121 |
| 1975 | 12 | 8 | .600 | 3.95 | 33 | 32 | 6 | 214 | 198 | 80 | 139 | 1 | 0 | 0 | 0 | 72 | 8 | 0 | .111 |
| 1976 | 3 | 6 | .333 | 4.08 | 17 | 15 | 1 | 75 | 70 | 21 | 33 | 1 | 0 | 0 | 0 | 21 | 3 | 0 | .143 |
| 1977 CHI A | 15 | 12 | .556 | 4.52 | 31 | 31 | 8 | 207 | 228 | 80 | 124 | 0 | 0 | 0 | 0 | 0 | 0 | 0 | — |
| 1978 | 12 | 12 | .500 | 4.37 | 30 | 30 | 6 | 212 | 196 | 84 | 118 | 1 | 0 | 0 | 0 | 0 | 0 | 0 | — |
| 1979 BAL A | 11 | 7 | .611 | 3.77 | 32 | 32 | 3 | 186 | 173 | 73 | 96 | 0 | 0 | 0 | 0 | 0 | 0 | 0 | — |
| 1980 | 25 | 7 | .781 | 3.23 | 37 | 37 | 9 | 251 | 224 | 101 | 149 | 1 | 0 | 0 | 0 | 0 | 0 | 0 | — |
| 1981 | 4 | 7 | .364 | 4.57 | 15 | 12 | 0 | 63 | 63 | 27 | 30 | 0 | 0 | 1 | 0 | 0 | 0 | 0 | — |
| 11 yrs. | 107 | 93 | .535 | 3.96 | 320 | 269 | 43 | 1789.1 | 1707 | 716 | 1065 | 7 | 2 | 3 | 1 | 219 | 22 | 0 | .100 |
| 3 yrs. | 23 | 20 | .535 | 4.04 | 88 | 70 | 8 | 459 | 453 | 165 | 262 | 2 | 1 | 1 | 0 | 151 | 18 | 0 | .119 |

WORLD SERIES

| | W | L | PCT | ERA | G | GS | CG | IP | H | BB | SO | ShO | W | L | SV | AB | H | HR | BA |
|---|---|---|---|---|---|---|---|---|---|---|---|---|---|---|---|---|---|---|---|
| 1979 BAL A | 0 | 0 | — | 9.00 | 1 | 0 | 0 | 2 | 4 | 2 | 2 | 0 | 0 | 0 | 0 | 0 | 0 | 0 | — |

## Bill Stoneman

STONEMAN, WILLIAM HAMBLY  BR TR 5'10" 170 lbs.
B. Apr. 7, 1944, Oak Park, Ill.

| | W | L | PCT | ERA | G | GS | CG | IP | H | BB | SO | ShO | W | L | SV | AB | H | HR | BA |
|---|---|---|---|---|---|---|---|---|---|---|---|---|---|---|---|---|---|---|---|
| 1967 CHI N | 2 | 4 | .333 | 3.29 | 28 | 2 | 0 | 63 | 51 | 22 | 52 | 0 | 2 | 4 | 4 | 13 | 0 | 0 | .000 |
| 1968 | 0 | 1 | .000 | 5.52 | 18 | 0 | 0 | 29.1 | 35 | 14 | 18 | 0 | 0 | 1 | 0 | 4 | 0 | 0 | .000 |
| 1969 MON N | 11 | 19 | .367 | 4.39 | 42 | 36 | 8 | 235.2 | 233 | 123 | 185 | 5 | 0 | 0 | 0 | 73 | 4 | 0 | .055 |
| 1970 | 7 | 15 | .318 | 4.59 | 40 | 30 | 5 | 208 | 209 | 109 | 176 | 3 | 0 | 0 | 0 | 60 | 6 | 0 | .100 |
| 1971 | 17 | 16 | .515 | 3.14 | 39 | 39 | 20 | 295 | 243 | 146 | 251 | 3 | 0 | 0 | 0 | 93 | 12 | 0 | .129 |
| 1972 | 12 | 14 | .462 | 2.98 | 36 | 35 | 13 | 250.2 | 213 | 102 | 171 | 4 | 0 | 0 | 0 | 75 | 6 | 0 | .080 |
| 1973 | 4 | 8 | .333 | 6.80 | 29 | 17 | 0 | 96.2 | 120 | 55 | 48 | 0 | 1 | 0 | 1 | 20 | 1 | 0 | .050 |
| 1974 CAL A | 1 | 8 | .111 | 6.10 | 13 | 11 | 0 | 59 | 78 | 31 | 33 | 0 | 0 | 0 | 0 | 0 | 0 | 0 | — |
| 8 yrs. | 54 | 85 | .388 | 4.08 | 245 | 170 | 46 | 1237.1 | 1182 | 602 | 934 | 15 | 3 | 5 | 5 | 338 | 29 | 0 | .086 |
| 2 yrs. | 2 | 5 | .286 | 4.00 | 46 | 2 | 0 | 92.1 | 86 | 36 | 70 | 0 | 2 | 5 | 4 | 17 | 0 | 0 | .000 |

## Scott Stratton

STRATTON, C. SCOTT  BL TR 6' 180 lbs.
B. Oct. 2, 1869, Campbellsburg, Ky.  D. Mar. 8, 1939, Louisville, Ky.

| | W | L | PCT | ERA | G | GS | CG | IP | H | BB | SO | ShO | W | L | SV | AB | H | HR | BA |
|---|---|---|---|---|---|---|---|---|---|---|---|---|---|---|---|---|---|---|---|
| 1888 LOU AA | 10 | 17 | .370 | 3.64 | 33 | 28 | 28 | 269.2 | 287 | 53 | 97 | 2 | 0 | 0 | 0 | 249 | 64 | 1 | .257 |
| 1889 | 3 | 13 | .188 | 3.23 | 19 | 17 | 13 | 133.2 | 157 | 42 | 42 | 0 | 0 | 1 | 1 | 229 | 66 | 4 | .288 |
| 1890 | 34 | 14 | .708 | 2.36 | 50 | 49 | 44 | 431 | 398 | 61 | 207 | 4 | 0 | 0 | 0 | 189 | 61 | 0 | .323 |
| 1891 2 teams | | | PIT N (2G 0–2) | | | LOU AA (20G 6–13) | | | | | | | | | | | | | |
| " total | 6 | 15 | .286 | 3.92 | 22 | 22 | 22 | 190.1 | 220 | 39 | 57 | 1 | 0 | 0 | 0 | 123 | 28 | 0 | .228 |
| 1892 LOU N | 21 | 19 | .525 | 2.92 | 42 | 40 | 39 | 351.2 | 342 | 70 | 93 | 2 | 0 | 0 | 0 | 219 | 56 | 0 | .256 |
| 1893 | 12 | 24 | .333 | 5.45 | 38 | 36 | 35 | 323.2 | 451 | 104 | 44 | 1 | 0 | 0 | 0 | 221 | 50 | 0 | .226 |

| | W | L | PCT | ERA | G | GS | CG | IP | H | BB | SO | ShO | Relief Pitching W | L | SV | BATTING AB | H | HR | BA |
|---|---|---|---|---|---|---|---|---|---|---|---|---|---|---|---|---|---|---|---|

## Scott Stratton continued

| | W | L | PCT | ERA | G | GS | CG | IP | H | BB | SO | ShO | W | L | SV | AB | H | HR | BA |
|---|---|---|---|---|---|---|---|---|---|---|---|---|---|---|---|---|---|---|---|
| 1894 2 teams | | | LOU | N | (7G 1–5) | | | CHI | N | (15G 8–5) | | | | | | | | | |
| " total | 9 | 10 | .474 | 6.65 | 22 | 17 | 15 | 162.1 | 270 | 53 | 26 | 0 | 2 | 1 | 0 | 133 | 48 | 3 | .361 |
| 1895 CHI N | 2 | 3 | .400 | 9.60 | 5 | 5 | 3 | 30 | 51 | 14 | 4 | 0 | 0 | 0 | 0 | 24 | 7 | 0 | .292 |
| 8 yrs. | 97 | 115 | .458 | 3.88 | 231 | 214 | 199 | 1892.1 | 2176 | 436 | 570 | 10 | 2 | 2 | 1 | * | | | |
| 2 yrs. | 10 | 8 | .556 | 6.75 | 20 | 17 | 14 | 149.1 | 249 | 54 | 27 | 0 | 1 | 1 | 0 | 120 | 43 | 3 | .358 |

## George Stueland

**STUELAND, GEORGE ANTON**     BB TR 6'1½" 174 lbs.
B. Mar. 2, 1899, Renwick, Iowa    BR 1925
D. Sept. 9, 1964, Onawa, Iowa

| | W | L | PCT | ERA | G | GS | CG | IP | H | BB | SO | ShO | W | L | SV | AB | H | HR | BA |
|---|---|---|---|---|---|---|---|---|---|---|---|---|---|---|---|---|---|---|---|
| 1921 CHI N | 0 | 1 | .000 | 5.73 | 2 | 1 | 0 | 11 | 7 | 4 | 0 | 0 | 0 | 0 | 0 | 3 | 1 | 0 | .333 |
| 1922 | 9 | 4 | .692 | 5.92 | 34 | 12 | 4 | 111 | 129 | 48 | 43 | 0 | 3 | 1 | 0 | 31 | 4 | 0 | .129 |
| 1923 | 0 | 1 | .000 | 5.63 | 6 | 0 | 0 | 8 | 11 | 5 | 2 | 0 | 0 | 1 | 0 | 0 | 0 | 0 | |
| 1925 | 0 | 0 | – | 3.00 | 2 | 0 | 0 | 3 | 2 | 3 | 2 | 0 | 0 | 0 | 0 | 1 | 1 | 0 | 1.000 |
| 4 yrs. | 9 | 6 | .600 | 5.82 | 44 | 13 | 4 | 133 | 153 | 63 | 51 | 0 | 3 | 2 | 0 | 35 | 6 | 0 | .171 |
| 4 yrs. | 9 | 6 | .600 | 5.82 | 44 | 13 | 4 | 133 | 153 | 63 | 51 | 0 | 3 | 2 | 0 | 35 | 6 | 0 | .171 |

## Marty Sullivan

**SULLIVAN, MARTIN C.**    BR TR
B. Oct. 20, 1862, Lowell, Mass.    D. Jan. 6, 1894, Lowell, Mass.

| | W | L | PCT | ERA | G | GS | CG | IP | H | BB | SO | ShO | W | L | SV | AB | H | HR | BA |
|---|---|---|---|---|---|---|---|---|---|---|---|---|---|---|---|---|---|---|---|
| 1887 CHI N | 0 | 0 | – | 7.71 | 1 | 0 | 0 | 2.1 | 6 | 1 | 1 | 0 | 0 | 0 | 0 | * | | | |

## Mike Sullivan

**SULLIVAN, MICHAEL JOSEPH (Big Mike)**    BL 6'1" 210 lbs.
B. Oct. 23, 1866, Boston, Mass.    D. June 14, 1906, Boston, Mass.

| | W | L | PCT | ERA | G | GS | CG | IP | H | BB | SO | ShO | W | L | SV | AB | H | HR | BA |
|---|---|---|---|---|---|---|---|---|---|---|---|---|---|---|---|---|---|---|---|
| 1889 WAS N | 0 | 3 | .000 | 7.24 | 9 | 3 | 3 | 41 | 47 | 32 | 15 | 0 | 0 | 0 | 0 | 19 | 1 | 0 | .053 |
| 1890 CHI N | 5 | 6 | .455 | 4.59 | 12 | 10 | 10 | 96 | 108 | 58 | 33 | 0 | 0 | 0 | 0 | 40 | 5 | 0 | .125 |
| 1891 2 teams | | | PHI | AA | (2G 0–2) | | | NY | N | (3G 1–2) | | | | | | | | | |
| " total | 1 | 4 | .200 | 3.43 | 5 | 5 | 5 | 42 | 41 | 18 | 18 | 0 | 0 | 0 | 0 | 17 | 2 | 0 | .118 |
| 1892 CIN N | 12 | 4 | .750 | 3.08 | 21 | 16 | 15 | 166.1 | 179 | 74 | 56 | 0 | 2 | 0 | 0 | 74 | 13 | 0 | .176 |
| 1893 | 8 | 11 | .421 | 5.05 | 27 | 18 | 14 | 183.2 | 200 | 103 | 40 | 0 | 2 | 2 | 1 | 79 | 16 | 1 | .203 |
| 1894 2 teams | | | WAS | N | (20G 2–10) | | | CLE | N | (13G 6–5) | | | | | | | | | |
| " total | 8 | 15 | .348 | 6.48 | 33 | 23 | 20 | 208.1 | 294 | 121 | 40 | 0 | 0 | 2 | 1 | 101 | 22 | 1 | .218 |
| 1895 CLE N | 1 | 2 | .333 | 8.42 | 4 | 3 | 2 | 31 | 42 | 16 | 5 | 0 | 0 | 0 | 0 | 15 | 2 | 0 | .133 |
| 1896 NY N | 10 | 13 | .435 | 4.66 | 25 | 22 | 18 | 185.1 | 188 | 71 | 42 | 0 | 3 | 0 | 0 | 77 | 16 | 0 | .208 |
| 1897 | 8 | 7 | .533 | 5.09 | 23 | 16 | 11 | 148.2 | 183 | 71 | 35 | 1 | 2 | 1 | 2 | 66 | 18 | 0 | .273 |
| 1898 BOS N | 0 | 1 | .000 | 12.00 | 3 | 2 | 0 | 12 | 19 | 9 | 1 | 0 | 0 | 0 | 0 | 3 | 1 | 0 | .333 |
| 1899 | 1 | 0 | 1.000 | 5.00 | 1 | 1 | 1 | 9 | 10 | 4 | 1 | 0 | 0 | 0 | 0 | 3 | 1 | 0 | .333 |
| 11 yrs. | 54 | 66 | .450 | 5.11 | 163 | 121 | 99 | 1123.1 | 1311 | 577 | 286 | 1 | 9 | 5 | 4 | 494 | 97 | 2 | .196 |
| 1 yr. | 5 | 6 | .455 | 4.59 | 12 | 10 | 10 | 96 | 108 | 58 | 33 | 0 | 0 | 0 | 0 | 40 | 5 | 0 | .125 |

## Billy Sunday

**SUNDAY, WILLIAM ASHLEY (The Evangelist)**    BL TR 5'10" 160 lbs.
B. Nov. 19, 1862, Ames, Iowa    D. Nov. 6, 1935, Chicago, Ill.

| | W | L | PCT | ERA | G | GS | CG | IP | H | BB | SO | ShO | W | L | SV | AB | H | HR | BA |
|---|---|---|---|---|---|---|---|---|---|---|---|---|---|---|---|---|---|---|---|
| 1890 PHI N | 0 | 0 | – | ∞ | 1 | 0 | 0 | | 2 | 0 | 0 | 0 | 0 | 0 | 0 | * | | | |

## Rick Sutcliffe

**SUTCLIFFE, RICHARD LEE**    BL TR 6'7" 215 lbs.
B. June 21, 1956, Independence, Mo.

| | W | L | PCT | ERA | G | GS | CG | IP | H | BB | SO | ShO | W | L | SV | AB | H | HR | BA |
|---|---|---|---|---|---|---|---|---|---|---|---|---|---|---|---|---|---|---|---|
| 1976 LA N | 0 | 0 | – | 0.00 | 1 | 1 | 0 | 5 | 2 | 1 | 3 | 0 | 0 | 0 | 0 | 1 | 0 | 0 | .000 |
| 1978 | 0 | 0 | – | 0.00 | 2 | 0 | 0 | 2 | 2 | 1 | 0 | 0 | 0 | 0 | 0 | 0 | 0 | 0 | |
| 1979 | 17 | 10 | .630 | 3.46 | 39 | 30 | 5 | 242 | 217 | 97 | 117 | 1 | 1 | 2 | 0 | 85 | 21 | 1 | .247 |
| 1980 | 3 | 9 | .250 | 5.56 | 42 | 10 | 1 | 110 | 122 | 55 | 59 | 1 | 2 | 5 | 5 | 27 | 4 | 0 | .148 |
| 1981 | 2 | 2 | .500 | 4.02 | 14 | 6 | 0 | 47 | 41 | 20 | 16 | 0 | 0 | 0 | 0 | 11 | 2 | 0 | .182 |
| 1982 CLE A | 14 | 8 | .636 | 2.96 | 34 | 27 | 6 | 216 | 174 | 98 | 142 | 1 | 2 | 1 | 1 | 0 | 0 | 0 | |
| 1983 | 17 | 11 | .607 | 4.29 | 36 | 35 | 10 | 243.1 | 251 | 102 | 160 | 2 | 1 | 0 | 0 | 0 | 0 | 0 | |
| 1984 2 teams | | | CLE | A | (15G 4–5) | | | CHI | N | (20G 16–1) | | | | | | | | | |
| " total | 20 | 6 | .769 | 3.64 | 35 | 35 | 9 | 244.2 | 234 | 85 | 213 | 3 | 0 | 0 | 0 | 56 | 14 | 0 | .250 |
| 1985 CHI N | 8 | 8 | .500 | 3.18 | 20 | 20 | 6 | 130 | 119 | 44 | 102 | 3 | 0 | 0 | 0 | 43 | 10 | 1 | .233 |
| 9 yrs. | 81 | 54 | .600 | 3.73 | 223 | 164 | 37 | 1240 | 1162 | 503 | 812 | 11 | 6 | 8 | 6 | 223 | 51 | 2 | .229 |
| 2 yrs. | 24 | 9 | .727 | 2.92 | 40 | 40 | 13 | 280.1 | 242 | 83 | 257 | 6 | 0 | 0 | 0 | 99 | 24 | 1 | .242 |

**LEAGUE CHAMPIONSHIP SERIES**

| | W | L | PCT | ERA | G | GS | CG | IP | H | BB | SO | ShO | W | L | SV | AB | H | HR | BA |
|---|---|---|---|---|---|---|---|---|---|---|---|---|---|---|---|---|---|---|---|
| 1984 CHI N | 1 | 1 | .500 | 3.38 | 2 | 2 | 0 | 13.1 | 9 | 8 | 10 | 0 | 0 | 0 | 0 | 6 | 3 | 1 | .500 |

## Bruce Sutter

**SUTTER, HOWARD BRUCE**    BR TR 6'2" 190 lbs.
B. Jan. 8, 1953, Lancaster, Pa.

| | W | L | PCT | ERA | G | GS | CG | IP | H | BB | SO | ShO | W | L | SV | AB | H | HR | BA |
|---|---|---|---|---|---|---|---|---|---|---|---|---|---|---|---|---|---|---|---|
| 1976 CHI N | 6 | 3 | .667 | 2.71 | 52 | 0 | 0 | 83 | 63 | 26 | 73 | 0 | 6 | 3 | 10 | 8 | 0 | 0 | .000 |
| 1977 | 7 | 3 | .700 | 1.35 | 62 | 0 | 0 | 107 | 69 | 23 | 129 | 0 | 7 | 3 | 31 | 20 | 3 | 0 | .150 |
| 1978 | 8 | 10 | .444 | 3.18 | 64 | 0 | 0 | 99 | 82 | 34 | 106 | 0 | 8 | 10 | 27 | 13 | 1 | 0 | .077 |
| 1979 | 6 | 6 | .500 | 2.23 | 62 | 0 | 0 | 101 | 67 | 32 | 110 | 0 | 6 | 6 | 37 | 12 | 3 | 0 | .250 |
| 1980 | 5 | 8 | .385 | 2.65 | 60 | 0 | 0 | 102 | 90 | 34 | 76 | 0 | 5 | 8 | 28 | 9 | 1 | 0 | .111 |
| 1981 STL N | 3 | 5 | .375 | 2.63 | 48 | 0 | 0 | 82 | 64 | 24 | 57 | 0 | 3 | 5 | 25 | 9 | 0 | 0 | .000 |
| 1982 | 9 | 8 | .529 | 2.90 | 70 | 0 | 0 | 102.1 | 88 | 34 | 61 | 0 | 9 | 8 | 36 | 8 | 1 | 0 | .125 |
| 1983 | 9 | 10 | .474 | 4.23 | 60 | 0 | 0 | 89.1 | 90 | 30 | 64 | 0 | 9 | 10 | 21 | 7 | 0 | 0 | .000 |
| 1984 | 5 | 7 | .417 | 1.54 | 71 | 0 | 0 | 122.2 | 109 | 23 | 77 | 0 | 5 | 7 | 45¹ | 10 | 0 | 0 | .000 |
| 1985 ATL N | 7 | 7 | .500 | 4.48 | 58 | 0 | 0 | 88.1 | 91 | 29 | 52 | 0 | 7 | 7 | 23 | 4 | 0 | 0 | .000 |
| 10 yrs. | 65 | 67 | .492 | 2.72 | 607 | 0 | 0 | 976.2 | 813 | 289 | 805 | 0 | 65 | 67 | 283 2nd | 100 | 9 | 0 | .090 |
| 5 yrs. | 32 | 30 | .516 | 2.40 | 300 | 0 | 0 | 492 | 371 | 149 | 494 | 0 | 32 4th | 30 | 133 1st | 62 | 8 | 0 | .129 |

**LEAGUE CHAMPIONSHIP SERIES**

| | W | L | PCT | ERA | G | GS | CG | IP | H | BB | SO | ShO | W | L | SV | AB | H | HR | BA |
|---|---|---|---|---|---|---|---|---|---|---|---|---|---|---|---|---|---|---|---|
| 1982 STL N | 1 | 0 | 1.000 | 0.00 | 2 | 0 | 0 | 4.1 | 0 | 1 | 0 | 0 | 1 | 0 | 1 | 1 | 0 | 0 | .000 |

**WORLD SERIES**

| | W | L | PCT | ERA | G | GS | CG | IP | H | BB | SO | ShO | W | L | SV | AB | H | HR | BA |
|---|---|---|---|---|---|---|---|---|---|---|---|---|---|---|---|---|---|---|---|
| 1982 STL N | 1 | 0 | 1.000 | 4.70 | 4 | 0 | 0 | 7.2 | 6 | 3 | 6 | 0 | 1 | 0 | 2 10th | 0 | 0 | 0 | – |

| | W | L | PCT | ERA | G | GS | CG | IP | H | BB | SO | ShO | Relief W | Relief L | Relief SV | AB | H | HR | BA |
|---|---|---|---|---|---|---|---|---|---|---|---|---|---|---|---|---|---|---|---|

## Les Sweetland

SWEETLAND, LESTER LEO (Sugar)
B. Aug. 15, 1901, St. Ignace, Mich.
D. Mar. 4, 1974, Melbourne, Fla.
BB TL 5'11½" 155 lbs.
BL 1927, BR 1928-29

| | W | L | PCT | ERA | G | GS | CG | IP | H | BB | SO | ShO | Rel W | Rel L | Rel SV | AB | H | HR | BA |
|---|---|---|---|---|---|---|---|---|---|---|---|---|---|---|---|---|---|---|---|
| 1927 PHI N | 2 | 10 | .167 | 6.16 | 21 | 13 | 6 | 103.2 | 147 | 53 | 21 | 0 | 0 | 1 | 0 | 38 | 12 | 0 | .316 |
| 1928 | 3 | 15 | .167 | 6.58 | 37 | 18 | 5 | 135.1 | 163 | 97 | 23 | 0 | 1 | 3 | 2 | 47 | 9 | 0 | .191 |
| 1929 | 13 | 11 | .542 | 5.11 | 43 | 25 | 10 | 204.1 | 255 | 87 | 47 | 2 | 2 | 0 | 2 | 89 | 26 | 0 | .292 |
| 1930 | 7 | 15 | .318 | 7.71 | 34 | 25 | 8 | 167 | 271 | 60 | 36 | 1 | 0 | 2 | 0 | 57 | 16 | 0 | .281 |
| 1931 CHI N | 8 | 7 | .533 | 5.04 | 26 | 14 | 9 | 130.1 | 156 | 61 | 32 | 0 | 1 | 1 | 0 | 56 | 15 | 0 | .268 |
| 5 yrs. | 33 | 58 | .363 | 6.10 | 161 | 95 | 38 | 740.2 | 992 | 358 | 159 | 3 | 4 | 7 | 4 | 287 | 78 | 0 | .272 |
| 1 yr. | 8 | 7 | .533 | 5.04 | 26 | 14 | 9 | 130.1 | 156 | 61 | 32 | 0 | 1 | 1 | 0 | 56 | 15 | 0 | .268 |

## Jack Taylor

TAYLOR, JOHN W.
B. Jan. 14, 1874, Straightville, Ohio   D. Mar. 4, 1938, Columbus, Ohio
BR TR 5'10" 170 lbs.

| | W | L | PCT | ERA | G | GS | CG | IP | H | BB | SO | ShO | Rel W | Rel L | Rel SV | AB | H | HR | BA |
|---|---|---|---|---|---|---|---|---|---|---|---|---|---|---|---|---|---|---|---|
| 1898 CHI N | 5 | 0 | 1.000 | 2.20 | 5 | 5 | 5 | 41 | 32 | 10 | 11 | 0 | 0 | 0 | 0 | 15 | 3 | 0 | .200 |
| 1899 | 18 | 21 | .462 | 3.76 | 41 | 39 | 39 | 354.2 | 380 | 84 | 67 | 1 | 1 | 0 | 0 | 139 | 37 | 0 | .266 |
| 1900 | 10 | 17 | .370 | 2.55 | 28 | 26 | 25 | 222.1 | 226 | 58 | 57 | 2 | 1 | 0 | 1 | 81 | 19 | 1 | .235 |
| 1901 | 13 | 19 | .406 | 3.36 | 33 | 31 | 30 | 275.2 | 341 | 44 | 68 | 0 | 1 | 0 | 0 | 106 | 23 | 0 | .217 |
| 1902 | 22 | 11 | .667 | 1.33 | 36 | 33 | 33 | 324.2 | 271 | 43 | 83 | 8 | 1 | 0 | 1 | 186 | 44 | 0 | .237 |
| 1903 | 21 | 14 | .600 | 2.45 | 37 | 33 | 33 | 312.1 | 277 | 57 | 83 | 1 | 1 | 1 | 1 | 126 | 28 | 0 | .222 |
| 1904 STL N | 21 | 19 | .525 | 2.22 | 41 | 39 | 39 | 352 | 297 | 82 | 103 | 2 | 0 | 0 | 1 | 133 | 28 | 1 | .211 |
| 1905 | 15 | 21 | .417 | 3.44 | 37 | 34 | 34 | 309 | 302 | 85 | 102 | 3 | 1 | 1 | 1 | 121 | 23 | 0 | .190 |
| 1906 2 teams | | | STL N (17G 8-9) | | | | CHI N (17G 12-3) | | | | | | | | | | | | |
| " total | 20 | 12 | .625 | 1.99 | 34 | 33 | 32 | 302.1 | 249 | 86 | 61 | 3 | 0 | 0 | 0 | 106 | 22 | 0 | .208 |
| 1907 CHI N | 6 | 5 | .545 | 3.29 | 18 | 13 | 8 | 123 | 127 | 33 | 22 | 0 | 1 | 0 | 0 | 47 | 9 | 0 | .191 |
| 10 yrs. | 151 | 139 | .521 | 2.66 | 310 | 286 | 278 | 2617 | 2502 | 582 | 657 | 20 | 7 | 2 | 5 | * | | | .231 |
| 8 yrs. | 107 | 90 | .543 | 2.66 | 215 | 196 | 188 | 1801 | 1770 | 368 | 425 | 14 | 6 | 1 | 3 | 753 | 174 | 1 | .231 |
| | | | | | | | | 5th | | | | | | | | | | | |

## Bud Teachout

TEACHOUT, ARTHUR JOHN
B. Feb. 27, 1904, Los Angeles, Calif.   D. May 11, 1985, Laguna Beach, Calif.
BR TL 6'2" 183 lbs.

| | W | L | PCT | ERA | G | GS | CG | IP | H | BB | SO | ShO | Rel W | Rel L | Rel SV | AB | H | HR | BA |
|---|---|---|---|---|---|---|---|---|---|---|---|---|---|---|---|---|---|---|---|
| 1930 CHI N | 11 | 4 | .733 | 4.06 | 40 | 16 | 6 | 153 | 178 | 48 | 59 | 0 | 4 | 1 | 0 | 63 | 17 | 0 | .270 |
| 1931 | 1 | 2 | .333 | 5.72 | 27 | 3 | 1 | 61.1 | 79 | 28 | 14 | 0 | 1 | 0 | 0 | 21 | 5 | 0 | .238 |
| 1932 STL N | 0 | 0 | — | 0.00 | 1 | 0 | 0 | 2 | 2 | 0 | 0 | 0 | 0 | 0 | 0 | 0 | 0 | 0 | — |
| 3 yrs. | 12 | 6 | .667 | 4.51 | 68 | 19 | 7 | 215.1 | 259 | 76 | 73 | 0 | 5 | 1 | 0 | 84 | 22 | 0 | .262 |
| 2 yrs. | 12 | 6 | .667 | 4.53 | 67 | 19 | 7 | 214.1 | 257 | 76 | 73 | 0 | 5 | 1 | 0 | 84 | 22 | 0 | .262 |

## Patsy Tebeau

TEBEAU, OLIVER WENDELL
Brother of White Wings Tebeau.
B. Dec. 5, 1864, St. Louis, Mo.   D. May 15, 1918, St. Louis, Mo.
Manager 1890-1900.
BR TR 5'8" 163 lbs.

| | W | L | PCT | ERA | G | GS | CG | IP | H | BB | SO | ShO | Rel W | Rel L | Rel SV | AB | H | HR | BA |
|---|---|---|---|---|---|---|---|---|---|---|---|---|---|---|---|---|---|---|---|
| 1896 CLE N | 0 | 0 | — | 0.00 | 1 | 0 | 0 | | 1 | 0 | 0 | 0 | 0 | 0 | 0 | * | | | |

## John Tener

TENER, JOHN KINLEY
B. July 25, 1863, Tyrone County, Ireland   D. May 19, 1946, Pittsburgh, Pa.
BR TR 6'4" 180 lbs.

| | W | L | PCT | ERA | G | GS | CG | IP | H | BB | SO | ShO | Rel W | Rel L | Rel SV | AB | H | HR | BA |
|---|---|---|---|---|---|---|---|---|---|---|---|---|---|---|---|---|---|---|---|
| 1885 BAL AA | 0 | 0 | — | 0.00 | 0 | 0 | 0 | | | | | | | | | 4 | 0 | 0 | .000 |
| 1888 CHI N | 7 | 5 | .583 | 2.74 | 12 | 12 | 11 | 102 | 90 | 25 | 39 | 1 | 0 | 0 | 0 | 46 | 9 | 0 | .196 |
| 1889 | 15 | 15 | .500 | 3.64 | 35 | 30 | 28 | 287 | 302 | 105 | 105 | 1 | 1 | 2 | 0 | 150 | 41 | 1 | .273 |
| 1890 PIT P | 3 | 11 | .214 | 7.31 | 14 | 14 | 13 | 117 | 160 | 70 | 30 | 0 | 0 | 0 | 0 | 63 | 12 | 2 | .190 |
| 4 yrs. | 25 | 31 | .446 | 4.30 | 61 | 56 | 52 | 506 | 552 | 200 | 174 | 2 | 1 | 2 | 0 | 263 | 62 | 3 | .236 |
| 2 yrs. | 22 | 20 | .524 | 3.40 | 47 | 42 | 39 | 389 | 392 | 130 | 144 | 2 | 1 | 2 | 0 | 196 | 50 | 1 | .255 |

## Adonis Terry

TERRY, WILLIAM H
B. Aug. 7, 1864, Westfield, Mass.   D. Feb. 24, 1915, Milwaukee, Wis.
BR TR 168 lbs.

| | W | L | PCT | ERA | G | GS | CG | IP | H | BB | SO | ShO | Rel W | Rel L | Rel SV | AB | H | HR | BA |
|---|---|---|---|---|---|---|---|---|---|---|---|---|---|---|---|---|---|---|---|
| 1884 BKN AA | 20 | 35 | .364 | 3.49 | 57 | 56 | 55 | 485 | 487 | 75 | 233 | 3 | 0 | 0 | 0 | 240 | 56 | 0 | .233 |
| 1885 | 6 | 17 | .261 | 4.26 | 25 | 23 | 23 | 209 | 213 | 42 | 96 | 0 | 0 | 0 | 1 | 264 | 45 | 1 | .170 |
| 1886 | 18 | 16 | .529 | 3.09 | 34 | 34 | 32 | 288.1 | 263 | 115 | 162 | 5 | 0 | 0 | 0 | 299 | 71 | 2 | .237 |
| 1887 | 16 | 16 | .500 | 4.02 | 40 | 35 | 35 | 318 | 331 | 99 | 138 | 1 | 0 | 0 | 3 | 352 | 103 | 3 | .293 |
| 1888 | 13 | 8 | .619 | 2.03 | 23 | 23 | 20 | 195 | 145 | 67 | 138 | 2 | 0 | 0 | 0 | 115 | 29 | 0 | .252 |
| 1889 | 22 | 15 | .595 | 3.29 | 41 | 39 | 35 | 326 | 285 | 126 | 186 | 2 | 0 | 0 | 0 | 160 | 48 | 2 | .300 |
| 1890 BKN N | 26 | 16 | .619 | 2.94 | 46 | 44 | 38 | 370 | 362 | 133 | 185 | 1 | 0 | 0 | 0 | 363 | 101 | 4 | .278 |
| 1891 | 6 | 16 | .273 | 4.22 | 25 | 22 | 18 | 194 | 207 | 80 | 65 | 1 | 0 | 0 | 1 | 91 | 19 | 0 | .209 |
| 1892 2 teams | | | BAL N (1G 0-1) | | | | PIT N (30G 17-7) | | | | | | | | | | | | |
| " total | 17 | 8 | .680 | 2.57 | 31 | 27 | 25 | 249 | 192 | 113 | 98 | 2 | 0 | 0 | 1 | 104 | 16 | 2 | .154 |
| 1893 PIT N | 12 | 8 | .600 | 4.45 | 22 | 19 | 14 | 170 | 177 | 99 | 52 | 0 | 2 | 1 | 0 | 71 | 18 | 0 | .254 |
| 1894 2 teams | | | PIT N (1G 0-1) | | | | CHI N (23G 5-11) | | | | | | | | | | | | |
| " total | 5 | 12 | .294 | 6.09 | 24 | 22 | 16 | 164 | 234 | 127 | 39 | 0 | 0 | 0 | 0 | 95 | 33 | 0 | .347 |
| 1895 CHI N | 21 | 14 | .600 | 4.80 | 38 | 34 | 31 | 311.1 | 346 | 131 | 88 | 0 | 2 | 0 | 0 | 137 | 30 | 1 | .219 |
| 1896 | 15 | 13 | .536 | 4.28 | 30 | 28 | 25 | 235.1 | 268 | 88 | 74 | 1 | 1 | 1 | 0 | 99 | 26 | 0 | .263 |
| 1897 | 0 | 1 | .000 | 10.13 | 1 | 1 | 1 | 8 | 14 | 6 | 1 | 0 | 0 | 0 | 0 | 3 | 0 | 0 | .000 |
| 14 yrs. | 197 | 195 | .503 | 3.72 | 441 | 407 | 368 | 3523 | 3521 | 1301 | 1555 | 18 | 5 | 2 | 6 | * | | | .266 |
| 4 yrs. | 41 | 39 | .513 | 4.93 | 92 | 84 | 73 | 718 | 857 | 348 | 202 | 1 | 3 | 1 | 0 | 334 | 89 | 1 | .266 |

## Walter Thornton

THORNTON, WALTER MILLER
B. Feb. 18, 1875, Lewiston, Me.   D. July 14, 1960, Los Angeles, Calif.
TL 6'1" 180 lbs.

| | W | L | PCT | ERA | G | GS | CG | IP | H | BB | SO | ShO | Rel W | Rel L | Rel SV | AB | H | HR | BA |
|---|---|---|---|---|---|---|---|---|---|---|---|---|---|---|---|---|---|---|---|
| 1895 CHI N | 2 | 0 | 1.000 | 6.08 | 7 | 2 | 2 | 40 | 58 | 31 | 13 | 0 | 0 | 0 | 1 | 22 | 7 | 1 | .318 |
| 1896 | 2 | 1 | .667 | 5.70 | 5 | 5 | 2 | 23.2 | 30 | 13 | 10 | 0 | 0 | 0 | 0 | 22 | 8 | 0 | .364 |
| 1897 | 6 | 7 | .462 | 4.70 | 16 | 16 | 15 | 130.1 | 164 | 51 | 55 | 0 | 0 | 0 | 0 | 265 | 85 | 0 | .321 |
| 1898 | 13 | 10 | .565 | 3.34 | 28 | 25 | 21 | 215.1 | 226 | 56 | 56 | 2 | 0 | 0 | 0 | 210 | 62 | 0 | .295 |
| 4 yrs. | 23 | 18 | .561 | 4.18 | 56 | 48 | 40 | 409.1 | 478 | 151 | 134 | 2 | 0 | 0 | 1 | * | 162 | 1 | .312 |
| 4 yrs. | 23 | 18 | .561 | 4.18 | 56 | 48 | 40 | 409.1 | 478 | 151 | 134 | 2 | 0 | 0 | 1 | 519 | 162 | 1 | .312 |

| | W | L | PCT | ERA | G | GS | CG | IP | H | BB | SO | ShO | Relief Pitching W | L | SV | BATTING AB | H | HR | BA |
|---|---|---|---|---|---|---|---|---|---|---|---|---|---|---|---|---|---|---|---|

## Bob Thorpe

**THORPE, ROBERT JOSEPH**
B. Jan. 12, 1935, San Diego, Calif.   D. Mar. 17, 1960, San Diego, Calif.
BR TR 6'1"   170 lbs.

| | W | L | PCT | ERA | G | GS | CG | IP | H | BB | SO | ShO | W | L | SV | AB | H | HR | BA |
|---|---|---|---|---|---|---|---|---|---|---|---|---|---|---|---|---|---|---|---|
| 1955 CHI N | 0 | 0 | — | 3.00 | 2 | 0 | 0 | 3 | 4 | 0 | 0 | 0 | 0 | 0 | 0 | 0 | 0 | 0 | — |

## Dick Tidrow

**TIDROW, RICHARD WILLIAM (Dirt)**
B. May 14, 1947, San Francisco, Calif.
BR TR 6'4"   210 lbs.

| | W | L | PCT | ERA | G | GS | CG | IP | H | BB | SO | ShO | W | L | SV | AB | H | HR | BA |
|---|---|---|---|---|---|---|---|---|---|---|---|---|---|---|---|---|---|---|---|
| 1972 CLE A | 14 | 15 | .483 | 2.77 | 39 | 34 | 10 | 237 | 200 | 70 | 123 | 3 | 1 | 0 | 0 | 70 | 7 | 0 | .100 |
| 1973 | 14 | 16 | .467 | 4.42 | 42 | 40 | 13 | 274.2 | 289 | 95 | 138 | 2 | 0 | 0 | 0 | 0 | 0 | 0 | — |
| 1974 2 teams | | | | | CLE A (4G 1–3) | | | NY A (33G 11–9) | | | | | | | | | | | |
| " total | 12 | 12 | .500 | 4.16 | 37 | 29 | 5 | 210 | 226 | 66 | 108 | 0 | 2 | 0 | 1 | 0 | 0 | 0 | — |
| 1975 NY A | 6 | 3 | .667 | 3.13 | 37 | 0 | 0 | 69 | 65 | 31 | 38 | 0 | 6 | 3 | 5 | 0 | 0 | 0 | — |
| 1976 | 4 | 5 | .444 | 2.63 | 47 | 2 | 0 | 92.1 | 80 | 24 | 65 | 0 | 4 | 5 | 10 | 0 | 0 | 0 | — |
| 1977 | 11 | 4 | .733 | 3.16 | 49 | 7 | 0 | 151 | 143 | 41 | 83 | 0 | 4 | 4 | 5 | 0 | 0 | 0 | — |
| 1978 | 7 | 11 | .389 | 3.84 | 31 | 25 | 4 | 185.1 | 191 | 53 | 73 | 0 | 0 | 1 | 0 | 0 | 0 | 0 | — |
| 1979 2 teams | | | | | NY A (14G 2–1) | | | CHI N (63G 11–5) | | | | | | | | | | | |
| " total | 13 | 6 | .684 | 3.64 | 77 | 0 | 0 | 126 | 124 | 46 | 75 | 0 | 13 | 6 | 6 | 10 | 2 | 0 | .200 |
| 1980 CHI N | 6 | 5 | .545 | 2.79 | 84 | 0 | 0 | 116 | 97 | 53 | 97 | 0 | 6 | 5 | 6 | 4 | 0 | 0 | .000 |
| 1981 | 3 | 10 | .231 | 5.04 | 51 | 0 | 0 | 75 | 73 | 30 | 39 | 0 | 3 | 10 | 9 | 5 | 0 | 0 | .000 |
| 1982 | 8 | 3 | .727 | 3.39 | 65 | 0 | 0 | 103.2 | 106 | 29 | 62 | 0 | 8 | 3 | 6 | 6 | 0 | 0 | .000 |
| 1983 CHI A | 2 | 4 | .333 | 4.22 | 50 | 1 | 0 | 91.2 | 86 | 34 | 66 | 0 | 2 | 4 | 7 | 0 | 0 | 0 | — |
| 1984 NY N | 0 | 1 | .000 | 9.19 | 11 | 0 | 0 | 15.2 | 25 | 7 | 8 | 0 | 0 | 0 | 0 | 0 | 0 | 0 | — |
| 13 yrs. | 100 | 94 | .515 | 3.68 | 620 | 138 | 32 | 1747.1 | 1705 | 579 | 975 | 5 | 51 | 41 | 55 | 95 | 9 | 0 | .095 |
| 4 yrs. | 28 | 23 | .549 | 3.35 | 263 | 0 | 0 | 397.2 | 362 | 154 | 266 | 0 | 28 | 23 | 25 | 25 | 2 | 0 | .080 |
| | | | | | | | | | | | | | | 6th | | | | | |

### LEAGUE CHAMPIONSHIP SERIES

| | W | L | PCT | ERA | G | GS | CG | IP | H | BB | SO | ShO | W | L | SV | AB | H | HR | BA |
|---|---|---|---|---|---|---|---|---|---|---|---|---|---|---|---|---|---|---|---|
| 1976 NY A | 1 | 0 | 1.000 | 3.68 | 3 | 0 | 0 | 7.1 | 6 | 4 | 0 | 0 | 1 | 0 | 0 | 0 | 0 | 0 | — |
| 1977 | 0 | 0 | — | 3.86 | 2 | 0 | 0 | 7 | 6 | 3 | 3 | 0 | 0 | 0 | 0 | 0 | 0 | 0 | — |
| 1978 | 0 | 0 | — | 4.76 | 1 | 0 | 0 | 5.2 | 8 | 2 | 1 | 0 | 0 | 0 | 0 | 0 | 0 | 0 | — |
| 1983 CHI A | 0 | 0 | — | 3.00 | 1 | 0 | 0 | 3 | 1 | 3 | 3 | 0 | 0 | 0 | 0 | 0 | 0 | 0 | — |
| 4 yrs. | 1 | 0 | 1.000 | 3.91 | 7 | 0 | 0 | 23 | 21 | 12 | 7 | 0 | 1 | 0 | 0 | 0 | 0 | 0 | — |

### WORLD SERIES

| | W | L | PCT | ERA | G | GS | CG | IP | H | BB | SO | ShO | W | L | SV | AB | H | HR | BA |
|---|---|---|---|---|---|---|---|---|---|---|---|---|---|---|---|---|---|---|---|
| 1976 NY A | 0 | 0 | — | 7.71 | 2 | 0 | 0 | 2.1 | 5 | 1 | 1 | 0 | 0 | 0 | 0 | 0 | 0 | 0 | — |
| 1977 | 0 | 0 | — | 4.91 | 2 | 0 | 0 | 3.2 | 5 | 0 | 1 | 0 | 0 | 0 | 0 | 1 | 0 | 0 | .000 |
| 1978 | 0 | 0 | — | 1.93 | 2 | 0 | 0 | 4.2 | 4 | 0 | 5 | 0 | 0 | 0 | 0 | 0 | 0 | 0 | — |
| 3 yrs. | 0 | 0 | — | 4.22 | 6 | 0 | 0 | 10.2 | 14 | 1 | 7 | 0 | 0 | 0 | 0 | 1 | 0 | 0 | .000 |

## Bobby Tiefenauer

**TIEFENAUER, BOBBY GENE**
B. Oct. 10, 1929, Desloge, Mo.
BR TR 6'2"   185 lbs.

| | W | L | PCT | ERA | G | GS | CG | IP | H | BB | SO | ShO | W | L | SV | AB | H | HR | BA |
|---|---|---|---|---|---|---|---|---|---|---|---|---|---|---|---|---|---|---|---|
| 1952 STL N | 0 | 0 | — | 7.88 | 6 | 0 | 0 | 8 | 12 | 7 | 3 | 0 | 0 | 0 | 0 | 1 | 0 | 0 | .000 |
| 1955 | 1 | 4 | .200 | 4.41 | 18 | 0 | 0 | 32.2 | 31 | 10 | 16 | 0 | 1 | 4 | 0 | 5 | 0 | 0 | .000 |
| 1960 CLE A | 0 | 1 | .000 | 2.00 | 6 | 0 | 0 | 9 | 8 | 3 | 2 | 0 | 0 | 1 | 0 | 1 | 0 | 0 | .000 |
| 1961 STL N | 0 | 0 | — | 6.23 | 3 | 0 | 0 | 4.1 | 9 | 4 | 3 | 0 | 0 | 0 | 0 | 0 | 0 | 0 | — |
| 1962 HOU N | 2 | 4 | .333 | 4.34 | 43 | 0 | 0 | 85 | 91 | 21 | 60 | 0 | 2 | 4 | 1 | 9 | 1 | 0 | .111 |
| 1963 MIL N | 1 | 1 | .500 | 1.21 | 12 | 0 | 0 | 29.2 | 20 | 4 | 22 | 0 | 1 | 1 | 2 | 5 | 0 | 0 | .000 |
| 1964 | 4 | 6 | .400 | 3.21 | 46 | 0 | 0 | 73 | 61 | 15 | 48 | 0 | 4 | 6 | 13 | 14 | 0 | 0 | .000 |
| 1965 3 teams | | | | | MIL N (6G 0–1) | | | NY A (10G 1–1) | | | | | CLE A (15G 0–5) | | | | | | |
| " total | 1 | 7 | .125 | 4.71 | 31 | 0 | 0 | 49.2 | 51 | 18 | 35 | 0 | 1 | 7 | 6 | 3 | 0 | 0 | .000 |
| 1967 CLE A | 0 | 1 | .000 | 0.79 | 5 | 0 | 0 | 11.1 | 9 | 3 | 6 | 0 | 0 | 1 | 0 | 0 | 0 | 0 | — |
| 1968 CHI N | 0 | 0 | — | 6.08 | 9 | 0 | 0 | 13.1 | 20 | 2 | 9 | 0 | 0 | 1 | 1 | 1 | 0 | 0 | .000 |
| 10 yrs. | 9 | 25 | .265 | 3.84 | 179 | 0 | 0 | 316 | 312 | 87 | 204 | 0 | 9 | 25 | 23 | 39 | 1 | 0 | .026 |
| 1 yr. | 0 | 1 | .000 | 6.08 | 9 | 0 | 0 | 13.1 | 20 | 2 | 9 | 0 | 0 | 1 | 1 | 1 | 0 | 0 | .000 |

## Ben Tincup

**TINCUP, AUSTIN BEN**
B. Dec. 14, 1890, Adair, Okla.   D. July 5, 1980, Claremore, Okla.
BL TR 6'1"   180 lbs.

| | W | L | PCT | ERA | G | GS | CG | IP | H | BB | SO | ShO | W | L | SV | AB | H | HR | BA |
|---|---|---|---|---|---|---|---|---|---|---|---|---|---|---|---|---|---|---|---|
| 1914 PHI N | 7 | 10 | .412 | 2.61 | 28 | 17 | 9 | 155 | 165 | 62 | 108 | 3 | 2 | 1 | 1 | 53 | 9 | 0 | .170 |
| 1915 | 0 | 0 | — | 2.03 | 10 | 0 | 0 | 31 | 26 | 9 | 10 | 0 | 0 | 0 | 0 | 9 | 0 | 0 | .000 |
| 1916 | 0 | 0 | — | 0.00 | 0 | 0 | 0 | 0 | 0 | 0 | 0 | 0 | 0 | 0 | 0 | 1 | 0 | 0 | .000 |
| 1918 | 0 | 1 | .000 | 7.56 | 8 | 1 | 0 | 16.2 | 24 | 6 | 6 | 0 | 0 | 0 | 0 | 8 | 1 | 0 | .125 |
| 1928 CHI N | 0 | 0 | — | 7.00 | 2 | 0 | 0 | 9 | 14 | 1 | 3 | 0 | 0 | 0 | 0 | 3 | 0 | 0 | .000 |
| 5 yrs. | 7 | 11 | .389 | 3.10 | 48 | 18 | 9 | 211.2 | 229 | 78 | 127 | 3 | 2 | 1 | 1 | 74 | 10 | 0 | .135 |
| 1 yr. | 0 | 0 | — | 7.00 | 2 | 0 | 0 | 9 | 14 | 1 | 3 | 0 | 0 | 0 | 0 | 3 | 0 | 0 | .000 |

## Bud Tinning

**TINNING, LYLE FORREST**
B. Mar. 12, 1906, Pilger, Neb.
D. Jan. 17, 1961, Evansville, Ind.
BB TR 6'   198 lbs.
BR 1934-35

| | W | L | PCT | ERA | G | GS | CG | IP | H | BB | SO | ShO | W | L | SV | AB | H | HR | BA |
|---|---|---|---|---|---|---|---|---|---|---|---|---|---|---|---|---|---|---|---|
| 1932 CHI N | 5 | 3 | .625 | 2.80 | 24 | 7 | 2 | 93.1 | 93 | 24 | 30 | 0 | 4 | 0 | 0 | 23 | 2 | 0 | .087 |
| 1933 | 13 | 6 | .684 | 3.18 | 32 | 21 | 10 | 175.1 | 169 | 60 | 59 | 3 | 1 | 0 | 1 | 67 | 14 | 0 | .209 |
| 1934 | 4 | 6 | .400 | 3.34 | 39 | 7 | 1 | 129.1 | 134 | 46 | 44 | 1 | 3 | 1 | 3 | 39 | 7 | 0 | .179 |
| 1935 STL N | 0 | 0 | — | 5.87 | 4 | 0 | 0 | 7.2 | 9 | 5 | 2 | 0 | 0 | 0 | 0 | 1 | 0 | 0 | .000 |
| 4 yrs. | 22 | 15 | .595 | 3.19 | 99 | 35 | 13 | 405.2 | 405 | 135 | 135 | 4 | 8 | 1 | 4 | 130 | 23 | 0 | .177 |
| 3 yrs. | 22 | 15 | .595 | 3.14 | 95 | 35 | 13 | 398 | 396 | 130 | 133 | 4 | 8 | 1 | 4 | 129 | 23 | 0 | .178 |

### WORLD SERIES

| | W | L | PCT | ERA | G | GS | CG | IP | H | BB | SO | ShO | W | L | SV | AB | H | HR | BA |
|---|---|---|---|---|---|---|---|---|---|---|---|---|---|---|---|---|---|---|---|
| 1932 CHI N | 0 | 0 | — | 0.00 | 2 | 0 | 0 | 2.1 | 0 | 0 | 3 | 0 | 0 | 0 | 0 | 0 | 0 | 0 | — |

## Jim Todd

**TODD, JAMES RICHARD JR.**
B. Sept. 21, 1947, Lancaster, Pa.
BL TR 6'2"   190 lbs.

| | W | L | PCT | ERA | G | GS | CG | IP | H | BB | SO | ShO | W | L | SV | AB | H | HR | BA |
|---|---|---|---|---|---|---|---|---|---|---|---|---|---|---|---|---|---|---|---|
| 1974 CHI N | 4 | 2 | .667 | 3.89 | 43 | 6 | 0 | 88 | 82 | 41 | 42 | 0 | 3 | 0 | 3 | 16 | 1 | 0 | .063 |
| 1975 OAK A | 8 | 3 | .727 | 2.29 | 58 | 0 | 0 | 122 | 104 | 33 | 50 | 0 | 8 | 3 | 12 | 0 | 0 | 0 | — |
| 1976 | 7 | 8 | .467 | 3.80 | 49 | 0 | 0 | 83 | 87 | 34 | 22 | 0 | 7 | 8 | 4 | 0 | 0 | 0 | — |
| 1977 CHI N | 1 | 1 | .500 | 9.00 | 20 | 0 | 0 | 31 | 47 | 19 | 17 | 0 | 1 | 1 | 0 | 1 | 0 | 0 | .000 |
| 1978 SEA A | 3 | 4 | .429 | 3.88 | 49 | 2 | 0 | 106.2 | 113 | 61 | 37 | 0 | 3 | 3 | 3 | 0 | 0 | 0 | — |

| | W | L | PCT | ERA | G | GS | CG | IP | H | BB | SO | ShO | Relief Pitching W | L | SV | BATTING AB | H | HR | BA |
|---|---|---|---|---|---|---|---|---|---|---|---|---|---|---|---|---|---|---|---|

## Jim Todd continued

| | W | L | PCT | ERA | G | GS | CG | IP | H | BB | SO | ShO | W | L | SV | AB | H | HR | BA |
|---|---|---|---|---|---|---|---|---|---|---|---|---|---|---|---|---|---|---|---|
| 1979 OAK A | 2 | 5 | .286 | 6.56 | 51 | 0 | 0 | 81 | 108 | 51 | 26 | 0 | 2 | 5 | 2 | 0 | 0 | 0 | – |
| 6 yrs. | 25 | 23 | .521 | 4.22 | 270 | 8 | 0 | 511.2 | 541 | 239 | 194 | 0 | 24 | 20 | 24 | 17 | 1 | 0 | .059 |
| 2 yrs. | 5 | 3 | .625 | 5.22 | 63 | 6 | 0 | 119 | 129 | 60 | 59 | 0 | 4 | 1 | 3 | 17 | 1 | 0 | .059 |

LEAGUE CHAMPIONSHIP SERIES

| | W | L | PCT | ERA | G | GS | CG | IP | H | BB | SO | ShO | W | L | SV | AB | H | HR | BA |
|---|---|---|---|---|---|---|---|---|---|---|---|---|---|---|---|---|---|---|---|
| 1975 OAK A | 0 | 0 | – | 9.00 | 3 | 0 | 0 | 1 | 3 | 0 | 0 | 0 | 0 | 0 | 0 | 0 | 0 | 0 | – |

## Ron Tompkins

TOMPKINS, RONALD EVERETT (Stretch)
B. Nov. 27, 1944, San Diego, Calif.    BR TR 6'4" 198 lbs.

| | W | L | PCT | ERA | G | GS | CG | IP | H | BB | SO | ShO | W | L | SV | AB | H | HR | BA |
|---|---|---|---|---|---|---|---|---|---|---|---|---|---|---|---|---|---|---|---|
| 1965 KC A | 0 | 0 | | 3.48 | 5 | 1 | 0 | 10.1 | 9 | 3 | 4 | 0 | 0 | 0 | 0 | 1 | 0 | 0 | .000 |
| 1971 CHI N | 0 | 2 | .000 | 4.05 | 35 | 0 | 0 | 40 | 31 | 21 | 20 | 0 | 0 | 2 | 3 | 0 | 0 | 0 | – |
| 2 yrs. | 0 | 2 | .000 | 3.93 | 40 | 1 | 0 | 50.1 | 40 | 24 | 24 | 0 | 0 | 2 | 3 | 1 | 0 | 0 | .000 |
| 1 yr. | 0 | 2 | .000 | 4.05 | 35 | 0 | 0 | 40 | 31 | 21 | 20 | 0 | 0 | 2 | 3 | 0 | 0 | 0 | – |

## Fred Toney

TONEY, FRED ALEXANDRA
B. Dec. 11, 1888, Nashville, Tenn.   D. Mar. 11, 1953, Nashville, Tenn.    BR TR 6'6" 245 lbs.

| | W | L | PCT | ERA | G | GS | CG | IP | H | BB | SO | ShO | W | L | SV | AB | H | HR | BA |
|---|---|---|---|---|---|---|---|---|---|---|---|---|---|---|---|---|---|---|---|
| 1911 CHI N | 1 | 1 | .500 | 2.42 | 18 | 4 | 1 | 67 | 55 | 35 | 27 | 0 | 0 | 0 | 0 | 18 | 2 | 0 | .111 |
| 1912 | 1 | 2 | .333 | 5.25 | 9 | 2 | 0 | 24 | 21 | 11 | 9 | 0 | 1 | 0 | 0 | 5 | 0 | 0 | .000 |
| 1913 | 2 | 2 | .500 | 6.00 | 7 | 5 | 2 | 39 | 52 | 22 | 12 | 0 | 0 | 0 | 0 | 12 | 3 | 0 | .250 |
| 1915 CIN N | 15 | 6 | .714 | 1.58 | 36 | 23 | 18 | 222.2 | 160 | 73 | 108 | 6 | 1 | 1 | 2 | 74 | 7 | 0 | .095 |
| 1916 | 14 | 17 | .452 | 2.28 | 41 | 38 | 21 | 300 | 247 | 78 | 146 | 3 | 0 | 0 | 1 | 99 | 12 | 0 | .121 |
| 1917 | 24 | 16 | .600 | 2.20 | 43 | 42 | 31 | 339.2 | 300 | 77 | 123 | 7 | 0 | 0 | 1 | 116 | 13 | 0 | .112 |
| 1918 2 teams | | | CIN | N | (21G | 6–10) | NY | N | (11G | 6–2) | | | | | | | | | |
| " total | 12 | 12 | .500 | 2.43 | 32 | 28 | 16 | 222 | 203 | 38 | 51 | 2 | 0 | 0 | 3 | 74 | 15 | 0 | .203 |
| 1919 NY N | 13 | 6 | .684 | 1.84 | 24 | 20 | 14 | 181 | 157 | 35 | 40 | 4 | 0 | 1 | 1 | 66 | 15 | 0 | .227 |
| 1920 | 21 | 11 | .656 | 2.65 | 42 | 37 | 17 | 278.1 | 266 | 57 | 81 | 4 | 2 | 0 | 1 | 96 | 23 | 0 | .240 |
| 1921 | 18 | 11 | .621 | 3.61 | 42 | 32 | 16 | 249.1 | 274 | 65 | 63 | 1 | 3 | 0 | 3 | 86 | 18 | 3 | .209 |
| 1922 | 5 | 6 | .455 | 4.17 | 13 | 12 | 6 | 86.1 | 91 | 31 | 10 | 0 | 0 | 0 | 0 | 30 | 2 | 0 | .067 |
| 1923 STL N | 11 | 12 | .478 | 3.84 | 29 | 28 | 16 | 196.2 | 211 | 61 | 48 | 1 | 0 | 0 | 0 | 69 | 8 | 0 | .116 |
| 12 yrs. | 137 | 102 | .573 | 2.69 | 336 | 271 | 158 | 2206 | 2037 | 583 | 718 | 28 | 7 | 2 | 12 | 745 | 118 | 3 | .158 |
| 3 yrs. | 4 | 5 | .444 | 4.02 | 34 | 11 | 3 | 130 | 128 | 68 | 48 | 0 | 1 | 0 | 0 | 35 | 5 | 0 | .143 |

WORLD SERIES

| | W | L | PCT | ERA | G | GS | CG | IP | H | BB | SO | ShO | W | L | SV | AB | H | HR | BA |
|---|---|---|---|---|---|---|---|---|---|---|---|---|---|---|---|---|---|---|---|
| 1921 NY N | 0 | 0 | – | 23.63 | 2 | 2 | 0 | 2.2 | 7 | 3 | 1 | 0 | 0 | 0 | 0 | 0 | 0 | 0 | – |

## Hector Torres

TORRES, HECTOR EPITACIO
B. Sept. 16, 1945, Monterrey, Mexico    BR TR 6' 175 lbs.

| | W | L | PCT | ERA | G | GS | CG | IP | H | BB | SO | ShO | W | L | SV | AB | H | HR | BA |
|---|---|---|---|---|---|---|---|---|---|---|---|---|---|---|---|---|---|---|---|
| 1972 MON N | 0 | 0 | – | 27.00 | 1 | 0 | 0 | .2 | 5 | 0 | 0 | 0 | 0 | 0 | 0 | * | | | |

## Paul Toth

TOTH, PAUL LOUIS
B. June 30, 1935, McRoberts, Ky.    BR TR 6'1" 175 lbs.

| | W | L | PCT | ERA | G | GS | CG | IP | H | BB | SO | ShO | W | L | SV | AB | H | HR | BA |
|---|---|---|---|---|---|---|---|---|---|---|---|---|---|---|---|---|---|---|---|
| 1962 2 teams | | | STL | N | (6G | 1–0) | CHI | N | (6G | 3–1) | | | | | | | | | |
| " total | 4 | 1 | .800 | 4.62 | 12 | 5 | 2 | 50.2 | 47 | 14 | 16 | 0 | 0 | 0 | 0 | 16 | 4 | 0 | .250 |
| 1963 CHI N | 5 | 9 | .357 | 3.10 | 27 | 14 | 3 | 130.2 | 115 | 35 | 66 | 2 | 1 | 3 | 0 | 39 | 1 | 0 | .026 |
| 1964 | 0 | 2 | .000 | 8.44 | 4 | 2 | 0 | 10.2 | 15 | 5 | 0 | 0 | 0 | 0 | 0 | 3 | 1 | 0 | .333 |
| 3 yrs. | 9 | 12 | .429 | 3.80 | 43 | 21 | 5 | 192 | 177 | 54 | 82 | 2 | 1 | 3 | 0 | 58 | 6 | 0 | .103 |
| 3 yrs. | 8 | 12 | .400 | 3.64 | 37 | 20 | 4 | 175.1 | 159 | 50 | 77 | 2 | 1 | 3 | 0 | 53 | 4 | 0 | .075 |

## Bill Tremel

TREMEL, WILLIAM LEONARD (Mumbles)
B. July 4, 1929, Lilly, Pa.    BR TR 5'11" 180 lbs.

| | W | L | PCT | ERA | G | GS | CG | IP | H | BB | SO | ShO | W | L | SV | AB | H | HR | BA |
|---|---|---|---|---|---|---|---|---|---|---|---|---|---|---|---|---|---|---|---|
| 1954 CHI N | 1 | 2 | .333 | 4.21 | 33 | 0 | 0 | 51.1 | 45 | 28 | 21 | 0 | 1 | 2 | 4 | 8 | 2 | 0 | .250 |
| 1955 | 3 | 0 | 1.000 | 3.72 | 23 | 0 | 0 | 38.2 | 33 | 18 | 13 | 0 | 3 | 0 | 2 | 7 | 2 | 0 | .286 |
| 1956 | 0 | 0 | | 13.50 | 1 | 0 | 0 | .2 | 3 | 0 | 0 | 0 | 0 | 0 | 0 | 0 | 0 | 0 | – |
| 3 yrs. | 4 | 2 | .667 | 4.07 | 57 | 0 | 0 | 90.2 | 81 | 46 | 34 | 0 | 4 | 2 | 6 | 15 | 4 | 0 | .267 |
| 3 yrs. | 4 | 2 | .667 | 4.07 | 57 | 0 | 0 | 90.2 | 81 | 46 | 34 | 0 | 4 | 2 | 6 | 15 | 4 | 0 | .267 |

## Steve Trout

TROUT, STEVEN RUSSELL (Rainbow)
Son of Dizzy Trout.
B. July 30, 1957, Detroit, Mich.    BL TL 6'4" 195 lbs.

| | W | L | PCT | ERA | G | GS | CG | IP | H | BB | SO | ShO | W | L | SV | AB | H | HR | BA |
|---|---|---|---|---|---|---|---|---|---|---|---|---|---|---|---|---|---|---|---|
| 1978 CHI A | 3 | 0 | 1.000 | 4.03 | 4 | 3 | 1 | 22.1 | 19 | 11 | 11 | 0 | 0 | 0 | 0 | 0 | 0 | 0 | – |
| 1979 | 11 | 8 | .579 | 3.89 | 34 | 18 | 6 | 155 | 165 | 59 | 76 | 2 | 1 | 2 | 4 | 0 | 0 | 0 | – |
| 1980 | 9 | 16 | .360 | 3.69 | 32 | 30 | 7 | 200 | 229 | 49 | 89 | 2 | 0 | 0 | 0 | 0 | 0 | 0 | – |
| 1981 | 8 | 7 | .533 | 3.46 | 20 | 18 | 3 | 125 | 122 | 38 | 54 | 0 | 1 | 0 | 0 | 0 | 0 | 0 | – |
| 1982 | 6 | 9 | .400 | 4.26 | 25 | 19 | 2 | 120.1 | 130 | 50 | 62 | 0 | 0 | 0 | 0 | 0 | 0 | 0 | – |
| 1983 CHI N | 10 | 14 | .417 | 4.65 | 34 | 32 | 1 | 180 | 217 | 59 | 80 | 0 | 1 | 0 | 0 | 62 | 12 | 0 | .194 |
| 1984 | 13 | 7 | .650 | 3.41 | 32 | 31 | 6 | 190 | 205 | 59 | 81 | 2 | 0 | 1 | 0 | 61 | 8 | 0 | .131 |
| 1985 | 9 | 7 | .563 | 3.39 | 24 | 24 | 3 | 140.2 | 142 | 63 | 44 | 1 | 0 | 0 | 0 | 46 | 5 | 0 | .109 |
| 8 yrs. | 69 | 68 | .504 | 3.83 | 205 | 175 | 29 | 1133.1 | 1229 | 388 | 497 | 7 | 3 | 3 | 4 | 169 | 25 | 0 | .148 |
| 3 yrs. | 32 | 28 | .533 | 3.84 | 90 | 87 | 10 | 510.2 | 564 | 181 | 205 | 3 | 1 | 1 | 0 | 169 | 25 | 0 | .148 |

LEAGUE CHAMPIONSHIP SERIES

| | W | L | PCT | ERA | G | GS | CG | IP | H | BB | SO | ShO | W | L | SV | AB | H | HR | BA |
|---|---|---|---|---|---|---|---|---|---|---|---|---|---|---|---|---|---|---|---|
| 1984 CHI N | 1 | 0 | 1.000 | 2.00 | 2 | 1 | 0 | 9 | 5 | 3 | 3 | 0 | 0 | 0 | 0 | 2 | 1 | 0 | .500 |

## Ted Turner

TURNER, THEODORE HOLTOP
B. May 4, 1892, Laurenceburg, Ky.   D. Feb. 4, 1958, Laurenceburg, Ky.    BR TR 6' 180 lbs.

| | W | L | PCT | ERA | G | GS | CG | IP | H | BB | SO | ShO | W | L | SV | AB | H | HR | BA |
|---|---|---|---|---|---|---|---|---|---|---|---|---|---|---|---|---|---|---|---|
| 1920 CHI N | 0 | 0 | – | 13.50 | 1 | 0 | 0 | 1.1 | 2 | 1 | 0 | 0 | 0 | 0 | 0 | 1 | 0 | 0 | .000 |

| | W | L | PCT | ERA | G | GS | CG | IP | H | BB | SO | ShO | Relief Pitching W | L | SV | BATTING AB | H | HR | BA |
|---|---|---|---|---|---|---|---|---|---|---|---|---|---|---|---|---|---|---|---|

## Lefty Tyler

**TYLER, GEORGE ALBERT**  BL TL 6' 175 lbs.
Brother of Fred Tyler.
B. Dec. 14, 1889, Derry, N. H.    D. Sept. 29, 1953, Lowell, Mass.

| | W | L | PCT | ERA | G | GS | CG | IP | H | BB | SO | ShO | W | L | SV | AB | H | HR | BA |
|---|---|---|---|---|---|---|---|---|---|---|---|---|---|---|---|---|---|---|---|
| 1910 **BOS N** | 0 | 0 | — | 2.38 | 2 | 0 | 0 | 11.1 | 11 | 6 | 6 | 0 | 0 | 0 | 0 | 4 | 2 | 0 | .500 |
| 1911 | 7 | 10 | .412 | 5.06 | 28 | 20 | 10 | 165.1 | 150 | 109 | 90 | 1 | 1 | 0 | 0 | 61 | 10 | 0 | .164 |
| 1912 | 12 | **22** | .353 | 4.18 | 42 | 31 | 18 | 256.1 | 262 | 126 | 144 | 1 | 2 | 3 | 0 | 96 | 19 | 0 | .198 |
| 1913 | 16 | 17 | .485 | 2.79 | 39 | 34 | **28** | 290.1 | 245 | 108 | 143 | 4 | 1 | 0 | 2 | 102 | 21 | 0 | .206 |
| 1914 | 16 | 14 | .533 | 2.69 | 38 | 34 | 21 | 271.1 | 247 | 101 | 140 | 6 | 0 | 1 | 2 | 94 | 19 | 0 | .202 |
| 1915 | 10 | 9 | .526 | 2.86 | 32 | 24 | 15 | 204.2 | 182 | 84 | 89 | 1 | 0 | 0 | 0 | 88 | 23 | 1 | .261 |
| 1916 | 17 | 10 | .630 | 2.02 | 34 | 28 | 21 | 249.1 | 200 | 58 | 117 | 6 | 2 | 1 | 1 | 93 | 19 | 3 | .204 |
| 1917 | 14 | 12 | .538 | 2.52 | 32 | 28 | 22 | 239 | 203 | 86 | 98 | 4 | 1 | 1 | 1 | 134 | 31 | 0 | .231 |
| 1918 **CHI N** | 19 | 9 | .679 | 2.00 | 33 | 30 | 22 | 269.1 | 218 | 67 | 102 | **8** | 1 | 1 | 1 | 100 | 21 | 0 | .210 |
| 1919 | 2 | 2 | .500 | 2.10 | 6 | 5 | 3 | 30 | 20 | 13 | 9 | 0 | 0 | 0 | 0 | 7 | 1 | 0 | .143 |
| 1920 | 11 | 12 | .478 | 3.31 | 27 | 27 | 18 | 193 | 193 | 57 | 57 | 2 | 0 | 0 | 0 | 65 | 17 | 0 | .262 |
| 1921 | 3 | 2 | .600 | 3.24 | 10 | 6 | 4 | 50 | 59 | 14 | 8 | 0 | 1 | 0 | 0 | 26 | 6 | 0 | .231 |
| 12 yrs. | 127 | 119 | .516 | 2.95 | 323 | 267 | 182 | 2230 | 1990 | 829 | 1003 | 33 | 9 | 7 | 7 | * | | | |
| 4 yrs. | 35 | 25 | .583 | 2.59 | 76 | 68 | 47 | 542.1 | 490 | 151 | 176 | 10 | 2 | 1 | 1 | 198 | 45 | 0 | .227 |

WORLD SERIES
| 1914 **BOS N** | 0 | 0 | — | 3.60 | 1 | 1 | 0 | 10 | 8 | 3 | 4 | 0 | 0 | 0 | 0 | 3 | 0 | 0 | .000 |
| 1918 **CHI N** | 1 | 1 | .500 | 1.17 | 3 | 3 | 1 | 23 | 14 | 11 | 4 | 0 | 0 | 0 | 0 | 5 | 1 | 0 | .200 |
| 2 yrs. | 1 | 1 | .500 | 1.91 | 4 | 4 | 1 | 33 | 22 | 14 | 8 | 0 | 0 | 0 | 0 | 8 | 1 | 0 | .125 |

## John Upham

**UPHAM, JOHN LESLIE**  BL TL 6' 180 lbs.
B. Dec. 29, 1941, Windsor, Ont., Canada

| 1967 **CHI N** | 0 | 1 | .000 | 33.75 | 5 | 0 | 0 | 1.1 | 4 | 2 | 2 | 0 | 0 | 1 | 0 | 3 | 2 | 0 | .667 |
| 1968 | 0 | 0 | — | 0.00 | 2 | 0 | 0 | 7 | 2 | 3 | 2 | 0 | 0 | 0 | 0 | 10 | 2 | 0 | .200 |
| 2 yrs. | 0 | 1 | .000 | 5.40 | 7 | 0 | 0 | 8.1 | 6 | 5 | 4 | 0 | 0 | 1 | 0 | * | | | |
| 2 yrs. | 0 | 1 | .000 | 5.40 | 7 | 0 | 0 | 8.1 | 6 | 5 | 4 | 0 | 0 | 1 | 0 | 13 | 4 | 0 | .308 |

## Vito Valentinetti

**VALENTINETTI, VITO JOHN**  BR TR 6' 195 lbs.
B. Sept. 16, 1928, West New York, N. J.

| 1954 **CHI A** | 0 | 0 | — | 54.00 | 1 | 0 | 0 | 1.1 | 2 | 1 | 0 | 0 | 0 | 0 | 0 | 0 | 0 | 0 | — |
| 1956 **CHI N** | 6 | 4 | .600 | 3.78 | 42 | 2 | 0 | 95.1 | 84 | 36 | 26 | 0 | 6 | 3 | 1 | 20 | 2 | 0 | .100 |
| 1957 2 teams | | | | | **CHI N** (9G 0-0) | | | | **CLE A** (11G 2-2) | | | | | | | | | | |
| " total | 2 | 2 | .500 | 4.04 | 20 | 2 | 1 | 35.2 | 38 | 20 | 17 | 0 | 1 | 2 | 0 | 7 | 1 | 0 | .143 |
| 1958 2 teams | | | | | **DET A** (15G 1-0) | | | | **WAS A** (23G 4-6) | | | | | | | | | | |
| " total | 5 | 6 | .455 | 4.80 | 38 | 10 | 2 | 114.1 | 124 | 54 | 43 | 0 | 1 | 1 | 2 | 28 | 9 | 0 | .321 |
| 1959 **WAS A** | 0 | 2 | .000 | 10.13 | 7 | 1 | 0 | 10.2 | 16 | 10 | 7 | 0 | 0 | 0 | 0 | 0 | 0 | 0 | — |
| 5 yrs. | 13 | 14 | .481 | 4.73 | 108 | 15 | 3 | 257 | 266 | 122 | 94 | 0 | 8 | 7 | 3 | 55 | 12 | 0 | .218 |
| 2 yrs. | 6 | 4 | .600 | 3.61 | 51 | 2 | 0 | 107.1 | 96 | 43 | 34 | 0 | 6 | 3 | 1 | 22 | 2 | 0 | .091 |

## Hy Vandenberg

**VANDENBERG, HAROLD HARRIS**  BR TR 6'2½" 195 lbs.
B. Mar. 17, 1906, Abilene, Kans.

| 1935 **BOS A** | 0 | 0 | — | 20.25 | 3 | 0 | 0 | 5.1 | 15 | 4 | 2 | 0 | 0 | 0 | 0 | 1 | 1 | 0 | 1.000 |
| 1937 **NY N** | 0 | 1 | .000 | 7.88 | 1 | 1 | 0 | 8 | 10 | 6 | 2 | 0 | 0 | 0 | 0 | 4 | 0 | 0 | .000 |
| 1938 | 0 | 1 | .000 | 7.50 | 6 | 1 | 0 | 18 | 28 | 12 | 7 | 0 | 0 | 1 | 0 | 4 | 0 | 0 | .000 |
| 1939 | 0 | 0 | — | 5.68 | 2 | 1 | 0 | 6.1 | 10 | 6 | 3 | 0 | 0 | 0 | 0 | 2 | 0 | 0 | .000 |
| 1940 | 1 | 1 | .500 | 3.90 | 13 | 3 | 1 | 32.1 | 27 | 16 | 17 | 0 | 0 | 1 | 1 | 8 | 1 | 0 | .125 |
| 1944 **CHI N** | 7 | 4 | .636 | 3.63 | 35 | 9 | 2 | 126.1 | 123 | 51 | 54 | 0 | 4 | 2 | 2 | 38 | 9 | 0 | .237 |
| 1945 | 6 | 3 | .667 | 3.49 | 30 | 7 | 3 | 95.1 | 91 | 33 | 35 | 1 | 2 | 1 | 2 | 32 | 4 | 0 | .125 |
| 7 yrs. | 14 | 10 | .583 | 4.32 | 90 | 22 | 7 | 291.2 | 304 | 128 | 120 | 1 | 6 | 5 | 5 | 89 | 15 | 0 | .169 |
| 2 yrs. | 13 | 7 | .650 | 3.57 | 65 | 16 | 5 | 221.2 | 214 | 84 | 89 | 1 | 6 | 3 | 4 | 70 | 13 | 0 | .186 |

WORLD SERIES
| 1945 **CHI N** | 0 | 0 | — | 0.00 | 3 | 0 | 0 | 6 | 1 | 3 | 3 | 0 | 0 | 0 | 0 | 1 | 0 | 0 | .000 |

## Johnny Vander Meer

**VANDER MEER, JOHN SAMUEL (The Dutch Master, Double No-Hit)**  BR TL 6'1" 190 lbs.
B. Nov. 2, 1914, Prospect Park, N. J.  BB 1937-42

| 1937 **CIN N** | 3 | 5 | .375 | 3.84 | 19 | 9 | 4 | 84.1 | 63 | 69 | 52 | 0 | 0 | 0 | 0 | 23 | 5 | 0 | .217 |
| 1938 | 15 | 10 | .600 | 3.12 | 32 | 29 | 16 | 225.1 | 177 | 103 | 125 | 3 | 0 | 0 | 0 | 83 | 15 | 0 | .181 |
| 1939 | 5 | 9 | .357 | 4.67 | 30 | 21 | 8 | 129 | 128 | 95 | 102 | 0 | 0 | 2 | 0 | 36 | 4 | 0 | .111 |
| 1940 | 3 | 1 | .750 | 3.75 | 10 | 7 | 2 | 48 | 38 | 41 | 41 | 0 | 0 | 0 | 0 | 20 | 6 | 0 | .300 |
| 1941 | 16 | 13 | .552 | 2.82 | 33 | 32 | 18 | 226.1 | 172 | 126 | **202** | 6 | 0 | 0 | 0 | 76 | 10 | 0 | .132 |
| 1942 | 18 | 12 | .600 | 2.43 | 33 | 33 | 21 | 244 | 188 | 102 | **186** | 4 | 0 | 0 | 0 | 75 | 11 | 0 | .147 |
| 1943 | 15 | 16 | .484 | 2.87 | 36 | **36** | 21 | 289 | 228 | **162** | **174** | 3 | 0 | 0 | 0 | 95 | 13 | 0 | .137 |
| 1946 | 10 | 12 | .455 | 3.17 | 29 | 25 | 11 | 204.1 | 175 | 78 | 94 | 5 | 1 | 0 | 0 | 73 | 18 | 0 | .247 |
| 1947 | 9 | 14 | .391 | 4.40 | 30 | 29 | 9 | 186 | 186 | 87 | 79 | 3 | 0 | 0 | 0 | 57 | 5 | 0 | .088 |
| 1948 | 17 | 14 | .548 | 3.41 | 33 | 33 | 14 | 232 | 204 | **124** | 120 | 3 | 0 | 0 | 0 | 78 | 11 | 1 | .141 |
| 1949 | 5 | 10 | .333 | 4.90 | 28 | 24 | 7 | 159.2 | 172 | 85 | 76 | 3 | 0 | 0 | 0 | 52 | 4 | 0 | .077 |
| 1950 **CHI N** | 3 | 4 | .429 | 3.79 | 32 | 6 | 0 | 73.2 | 60 | 59 | 41 | 0 | 3 | 1 | 1 | 16 | 2 | 0 | .125 |
| 1951 **CLE A** | 0 | 1 | .000 | 18.00 | 1 | 0 | 0 | 2 | 0 | 2 | 0 | 0 | 0 | 0 | 0 | 1 | 0 | 0 | .000 |
| 13 yrs. | 119 | 121 | .496 | 3.44 | 346 | 285 | 131 | 2104.2 | 1799 | 1132 | 1294 | 30 | 4 | 3 | 2 | 685 | 104 | 1 | .152 |
| 1 yr. | 3 | 4 | .429 | 3.79 | 32 | 6 | 0 | 73.2 | 60 | 59 | 41 | 0 | 3 | 1 | 1 | 16 | 2 | 0 | .125 |

WORLD SERIES
| 1940 **CIN N** | 0 | 0 | — | 0.00 | 1 | 0 | 0 | 3 | 2 | 3 | 2 | 0 | 0 | 0 | 0 | 0 | 0 | 0 | — |

## George Van Haltren

**VAN HALTREN, GEORGE EDWARD MARTIN**  BL TL 5'11" 170 lbs.
B. Mar. 30, 1866, St. Louis, Mo.    D. Sept. 29, 1945, Oakland, Calif.
Manager 1891-92.

| 1887 **CHI N** | 11 | 7 | .611 | 3.86 | 20 | 18 | 18 | 161 | 177 | 66 | 76 | 1 | 0 | 0 | 1 | 172 | 35 | 3 | .203 |
| 1888 | 13 | 13 | .500 | 3.52 | 30 | 24 | 24 | 245.2 | 263 | 60 | 139 | 4 | 0 | 2 | 1 | 318 | 90 | 4 | .283 |

| | W | L | PCT | ERA | G | GS | CG | IP | H | BB | SO | ShO | Relief Pitching W | L | SV | BATTING AB | H | HR | BA |
|---|---|---|---|---|---|---|---|---|---|---|---|---|---|---|---|---|---|---|---|

## George Van Haltren  continued

| | W | L | PCT | ERA | G | GS | CG | IP | H | BB | SO | ShO | W | L | SV | AB | H | HR | BA |
|---|---|---|---|---|---|---|---|---|---|---|---|---|---|---|---|---|---|---|---|
| 1890 BKN P | 15 | 10 | .600 | 4.28 | 28 | 25 | 23 | 223 | 272 | 89 | 48 | 0 | 0 | 0 | 2 | 376 | 126 | 5 | .335 |
| 1891 BAL AA | 0 | 1 | .000 | 5.09 | 6 | 1 | 0 | 23 | 38 | 10 | 7 | 0 | 0 | 0 | 0 | 566 | 180 | 9 | .318 |
| 1892 BAL N | 0 | 0 | — | 9.20 | 4 | 0 | 0 | 14.2 | 28 | 7 | 5 | 0 | 0 | 0 | 0 | 611 | 179 | 7 | .293 |
| 1895 NY N | 0 | 0 | — | 12.60 | 1 | 0 | 0 | 5 | 13 | 2 | 1 | 0 | 0 | 0 | 0 | 521 | 177 | 8 | .340 |
| 1896 | 1 | 0 | 1.000 | 2.25 | 2 | 0 | 0 | 8 | 5 | 1 | 3 | 0 | 1 | 0 | 0 | 562 | 197 | 5 | .351 |
| 1900 | 0 | 0 | — | 0.00 | 1 | 0 | 0 | 3 | 1 | 3 | 0 | 0 | 0 | 0 | 0 | 571 | 180 | 1 | .315 |
| 1901 | 0 | 0 | — | 3.00 | 1 | 0 | 0 | 6 | 12 | 6 | 2 | 0 | 0 | 0 | 0 | 544 | 186 | 1 | .342 |
| 9 yrs. | 40 | 31 | .563 | 4.05 | 93 | 68 | 65 | 689.1 | 809 | 244 | 281 | 5 | 1 | 2 | 4 | * | | | |
| 2 yrs. | 24 | 20 | .545 | 3.65 | 50 | 42 | 42 | 406.2 | 440 | 126 | 215 | 5 | 0 | 2 | 2 | 1033 | 293 | 16 | .284 |

## Ike Van Zandt

**VAN ZANDT, CHARLES ISAAC**  BL
B. 1877, Brooklyn, N. Y.   D. Sept. 14, 1908, Nashua, N. H.

| | W | L | PCT | ERA | G | GS | CG | IP | H | BB | SO | ShO | W | L | SV | AB | H | HR | BA |
|---|---|---|---|---|---|---|---|---|---|---|---|---|---|---|---|---|---|---|---|
| 1901 NY N | 0 | 0 | — | 7.11 | 2 | 0 | 0 | 12.2 | 16 | 8 | 2 | 0 | 0 | 0 | 0 | 6 | 1 | 0 | .167 |
| 1905 STL A | 0 | 0 | — | 0.00 | 1 | 0 | 0 | 6.2 | 2 | 2 | 3 | 0 | 0 | 0 | 0 | 322 | 75 | 1 | .233 |
| 2 yrs. | 0 | 0 | — | 4.66 | 3 | 0 | 0 | 19.1 | 18 | 10 | 5 | 0 | 0 | 0 | 0 | * | | | |

## Andy Varga

**VARGA, ANDREW WILLIAM**  BR TL 6'4"  187 lbs.
B. Dec. 11, 1930, Chicago, Ill.

| | W | L | PCT | ERA | G | GS | CG | IP | H | BB | SO | ShO | W | L | SV | AB | H | HR | BA |
|---|---|---|---|---|---|---|---|---|---|---|---|---|---|---|---|---|---|---|---|
| 1950 CHI N | 0 | 0 | — | 0.00 | 1 | 0 | 0 | 1 | 0 | 1 | 0 | 0 | 0 | 0 | 0 | 0 | 0 | 0 | — |
| 1951 | 0 | 0 | — | 3.00 | 2 | 0 | 0 | 3 | 2 | 6 | 1 | 0 | 0 | 0 | 0 | 0 | 0 | 0 | — |
| 2 yrs. | 0 | 0 | — | 2.25 | 3 | 0 | 0 | 4 | 2 | 7 | 1 | 0 | 0 | 0 | 0 | 0 | 0 | 0 | — |
| 2 yrs. | 0 | 0 | — | 2.25 | 3 | 0 | 0 | 4 | 2 | 7 | 1 | 0 | 0 | 0 | 0 | 0 | 0 | 0 | — |

## Hippo Vaughn

**VAUGHN, JAMES LESLIE**  BB TL 6'4"  215 lbs.
B. Apr. 9, 1888, Weatherford, Tex.   D. May 29, 1966, Chicago, Ill.

| | W | L | PCT | ERA | G | GS | CG | IP | H | BB | SO | ShO | W | L | SV | AB | H | HR | BA |
|---|---|---|---|---|---|---|---|---|---|---|---|---|---|---|---|---|---|---|---|
| 1908 NY A | 0 | 0 | — | 3.86 | 2 | 0 | 0 | 2.1 | 1 | 4 | 2 | 0 | 0 | 0 | 0 | 1 | 0 | 0 | .000 |
| 1910 | 13 | 11 | .542 | 1.83 | 30 | 25 | 18 | 221.2 | 190 | 58 | 107 | 5 | 4 | 0 | 1 | 75 | 10 | 0 | .133 |
| 1911 | 8 | 10 | .444 | 4.39 | 26 | 18 | 11 | 145.2 | 158 | 54 | 74 | 0 | 1 | 2 | 0 | 49 | 7 | 0 | .143 |
| 1912 2 teams | | | | **NY A** (15G 2–8) | | | | **WAS A** (12G 4–3) | | | | | | | | | | | |
| "    total | 6 | 11 | .353 | 3.88 | 27 | 18 | 9 | 144 | 141 | 80 | 95 | 1 | 1 | 2 | 0 | 51 | 8 | 0 | .157 |
| 1913 CHI N | 5 | 1 | .833 | 1.45 | 7 | 6 | 5 | 56 | 37 | 27 | 36 | 2 | 0 | 0 | 0 | 21 | 4 | 0 | .190 |
| 1914 | 21 | 13 | .618 | 2.05 | 42 | 35 | 23 | 293.2 | 236 | 109 | 165 | 4 | 0 | 1 | 1 | 97 | 14 | 1 | .144 |
| 1915 | 20 | 12 | .625 | 2.87 | 41 | 34 | 18 | 269.2 | 240 | 77 | 148 | 4 | 4 | 1 | 0 | 86 | 14 | 0 | .163 |
| 1916 | 17 | 14 | .548 | 2.20 | 44 | 35 | 21 | 294 | 269 | 67 | 144 | 4 | 1 | 2 | 1 | 104 | 14 | 0 | .135 |
| 1917 | 23 | 13 | .639 | 2.01 | 41 | 39 | 27 | 295.2 | 255 | 91 | 195 | 5 | 0 | 0 | 0 | 100 | 16 | 0 | .160 |
| 1918 | **22** | 10 | .688 | **1.74** | 35 | **33** | 27 | **290.1** | 216 | 76 | **148** | **8** | 0 | 2 | 0 | 96 | 23 | 0 | .240 |
| 1919 | 21 | 14 | .600 | 1.79 | 38 | **37** | 25 | **306.2** | 264 | 62 | **141** | 4 | 0 | 0 | 1 | 98 | 17 | 0 | .173 |
| 1920 | 19 | 16 | .543 | 2.54 | 40 | 38 | 24 | 301 | 301 | 81 | 131 | 4 | 0 | 0 | 0 | 102 | 22 | 1 | .216 |
| 1921 | 3 | 11 | .214 | 6.01 | 17 | 14 | 7 | 109.1 | 153 | 31 | 30 | 0 | 0 | 2 | 0 | 41 | 10 | 1 | .244 |
| 13 yrs. | 178 | 136 | .567 | 2.49 | 390 | 332 | 215 | 2730 | 2461 | 817 | 1416 | 41 | 11 | 12 | 5 | 921 | 159 | 3 | .173 |
| 9 yrs. | 151 | 104 | .592 | 2.33 | 305 | 271 | 177 | 2216.1 | 1971 | 621 | 1138 | 35 | 5 | 8 | 4 | 745 | 134 | 3 | .180 |
| | 8th | 8th | | 7th | | | | 7th | 8th | | 9th | 5th | 2nd | | | | | | |

WORLD SERIES

| | W | L | PCT | ERA | G | GS | CG | IP | H | BB | SO | ShO | W | L | SV | AB | H | HR | BA |
|---|---|---|---|---|---|---|---|---|---|---|---|---|---|---|---|---|---|---|---|
| 1918 CHI N | 1 | 2 | .333 | 1.00 | 3 | 3 | 3 | 27 | 17 | 5 | 17 | 1 | 0 | 0 | 0 | 10 | 0 | 0 | .000 |
| | | | | 6th | | | | | | | | | | | | | | | |

## Joe Vernon

**VERNON, JOSEPH HENRY**  BR TR 5'11"  160 lbs.
B. Nov. 25, 1889, Mansfield, Mass.   D. Mar. 13, 1955, Philadelphia, Pa.

| | W | L | PCT | ERA | G | GS | CG | IP | H | BB | SO | ShO | W | L | SV | AB | H | HR | BA |
|---|---|---|---|---|---|---|---|---|---|---|---|---|---|---|---|---|---|---|---|
| 1912 CHI N | 0 | 0 | — | 11.25 | 1 | 0 | 0 | 4 | 4 | 6 | 1 | 0 | 0 | 0 | 0 | 2 | 0 | 0 | .000 |
| 1914 BKN F | 0 | 0 | — | 10.80 | 1 | 1 | 0 | 3.1 | 4 | 5 | 0 | 0 | 0 | 0 | 0 | 1 | 0 | 0 | .000 |
| 2 yrs. | 0 | 0 | — | 11.05 | 2 | 1 | 0 | 7.1 | 8 | 11 | 1 | 0 | 0 | 0 | 0 | 3 | 0 | 0 | .000 |
| 1 yr. | 0 | 0 | — | 11.25 | 1 | 0 | 0 | 4 | 4 | 6 | 1 | 0 | 0 | 0 | 0 | 2 | 0 | 0 | .000 |

## Tom Vickery

**VICKERY, THOMAS GILL**  6'  170 lbs.
B. May 5, 1867, Milford, N. J.   D. Mar. 21, 1921, Milford, N. J.

| | W | L | PCT | ERA | G | GS | CG | IP | H | BB | SO | ShO | W | L | SV | AB | H | HR | BA |
|---|---|---|---|---|---|---|---|---|---|---|---|---|---|---|---|---|---|---|---|
| 1890 PHI N | 24 | 22 | .522 | 3.44 | 46 | 46 | 41 | 382 | 405 | 184 | 162 | 1 | 0 | 0 | 0 | 159 | 33 | 0 | .208 |
| 1891 CHI N | 5 | 5 | .500 | 4.07 | 14 | 12 | 7 | 79.2 | 72 | 44 | 39 | 0 | 0 | 0 | 0 | 39 | 7 | 0 | .179 |
| 1892 BAL N | 8 | 10 | .444 | 3.53 | 24 | 21 | 17 | 176 | 189 | 87 | 49 | 0 | 0 | 0 | 0 | 74 | 18 | 0 | .243 |
| 1893 PHI N | 4 | 5 | .444 | 5.40 | 13 | 11 | 7 | 80 | 100 | 37 | 15 | 0 | 1 | 1 | 0 | 35 | 11 | 0 | .314 |
| 4 yrs. | 41 | 42 | .494 | 3.75 | 97 | 90 | 72 | 717.2 | 766 | 352 | 265 | 1 | 1 | 1 | 0 | 307 | 69 | 0 | .225 |
| 1 yr. | 5 | 5 | .500 | 4.07 | 14 | 12 | 7 | 79.2 | 72 | 44 | 39 | 0 | 0 | 0 | 0 | 39 | 7 | 0 | .179 |

## Bill Voiselle

**VOISELLE, WILLIAM SYMMES (Big Bill, Ninety-Six)**  BR TR 6'4"  200 lbs.
B. Jan. 29, 1919, Greenwood, S. C.

| | W | L | PCT | ERA | G | GS | CG | IP | H | BB | SO | ShO | W | L | SV | AB | H | HR | BA |
|---|---|---|---|---|---|---|---|---|---|---|---|---|---|---|---|---|---|---|---|
| 1942 NY N | 0 | 1 | .000 | 2.00 | 2 | 1 | 0 | 9 | 6 | 4 | 5 | 0 | 0 | 0 | 0 | 2 | 0 | 0 | .000 |
| 1943 | 1 | 2 | .333 | 2.03 | 4 | 4 | 3 | 31 | 18 | 14 | 19 | 0 | 0 | 0 | 0 | 9 | 1 | 0 | .111 |
| 1944 | 21 | 16 | .568 | 3.02 | 43 | **41** | 25 | **312.2** | 276 | 118 | **161** | 1 | 1 | 0 | 0 | 105 | 22 | 0 | .210 |
| 1945 | 14 | 14 | .500 | 4.49 | 41 | **35** | 14 | 232.1 | 249 | 97 | 115 | 4 | 1 | 0 | 0 | 79 | 10 | 0 | .127 |
| 1946 | 9 | 15 | .375 | 3.74 | 36 | 25 | 10 | 178 | 171 | 85 | 89 | 2 | 1 | 1 | 0 | 55 | 9 | 0 | .164 |
| 1947 2 teams | | | | **NY N** (11G 1–4) | | | | **BOS N** (22G 8–7) | | | | | | | | | | | |
| "    total | 9 | 11 | .450 | 4.40 | 33 | 25 | 9 | 174 | 190 | 73 | 71 | 0 | 1 | 1 | 0 | 68 | 11 | 0 | .162 |
| 1948 BOS N | 13 | 13 | .500 | 3.63 | 37 | 30 | 9 | 215.2 | 226 | 90 | 89 | 2 | 2 | 0 | 2 | 72 | 7 | 0 | .097 |
| 1949 | 7 | 8 | .467 | 4.04 | 30 | 22 | 5 | 169.1 | 170 | 78 | 63 | 4 | 1 | 0 | 1 | 61 | 7 | 0 | .115 |
| 1950 CHI N | 0 | 4 | .000 | 5.79 | 19 | 7 | 0 | 51.1 | 64 | 29 | 25 | 0 | 0 | 0 | 0 | 13 | 1 | 0 | .077 |
| 9 yrs. | 74 | 84 | .468 | 3.83 | 245 | 190 | 74 | 1373.1 | 1370 | 588 | 637 | 13 | 7 | 2 | 3 | 464 | 68 | 0 | .147 |
| 1 yr. | 0 | 4 | .000 | 5.79 | 19 | 7 | 0 | 51.1 | 64 | 29 | 25 | 0 | 0 | 0 | 0 | 13 | 1 | 0 | .077 |

WORLD SERIES

| | W | L | PCT | ERA | G | GS | CG | IP | H | BB | SO | ShO | W | L | SV | AB | H | HR | BA |
|---|---|---|---|---|---|---|---|---|---|---|---|---|---|---|---|---|---|---|---|
| 1948 BOS N | 0 | 1 | .000 | 2.53 | 2 | 1 | 0 | 10.2 | 8 | 2 | 2 | 0 | 0 | 0 | 0 | 2 | 0 | 0 | .000 |

| | W | L | PCT | ERA | G | GS | CG | IP | H | BB | SO | ShO | W | L | SV | AB | H | HR | BA |
|---|---|---|---|---|---|---|---|---|---|---|---|---|---|---|---|---|---|---|---|
| | | | | | | | | | | | | | **Relief Pitching** | | | **BATTING** | | | |

## Rube Waddell

**WADDELL, GEORGE EDWARD**   BR TL 6'1½" 196 lbs.
B. Oct. 13, 1876, Bradford, Pa.   D. Apr. 1, 1914, San Antonio, Tex.
Hall of Fame 1946.

| | W | L | PCT | ERA | G | GS | CG | IP | H | BB | SO | ShO | W | L | SV | AB | H | HR | BA |
|---|---|---|---|---|---|---|---|---|---|---|---|---|---|---|---|---|---|---|---|
| 1897 LOU N | 0 | 1 | .000 | 3.21 | 2 | 1 | 1 | 14 | 17 | 6 | 5 | 0 | 0 | 0 | 0 | 6 | 0 | 0 | .000 |
| 1899 | 7 | 2 | .778 | 3.08 | 10 | 9 | 9 | 79 | 69 | 14 | 44 | 1 | 0 | 0 | 1 | 34 | 8 | 0 | .235 |
| 1900 PIT N | 8 | 13 | .381 | 2.37 | 29 | 22 | 16 | 208.2 | 176 | 55 | 130 | 2 | 0 | 3 | 0 | 81 | 14 | 0 | .173 |
| 1901 2 teams | | | | | | PIT N (2G 0–2) | | | CHI N (29G 13–15) | | | | | | | | | | |
| " total | 13 | 17 | .433 | 3.01 | 31 | 30 | 26 | 251.1 | 249 | 75 | 172 | 0 | 0 | 1 | 0 | 101 | 25 | 2 | .248 |
| 1902 PHI A | 24 | 7 | .774 | 2.05 | 33 | 27 | 26 | 276.1 | 224 | 64 | 210 | 3 | 5 | 0 | 0 | 112 | 32 | 1 | .286 |
| 1903 | 21 | 16 | .568 | 2.44 | 39 | 38 | 34 | 324 | 274 | 85 | 302 | 4 | 0 | 0 | 0 | 115 | 14 | 0 | .122 |
| 1904 | 25 | 19 | .568 | 1.62 | 46 | 46 | 39 | 383 | 307 | 91 | 349 | 8 | 0 | 0 | 0 | 139 | 17 | 0 | .122 |
| 1905 | 26 | 11 | .703 | 1.48 | 46 | 34 | 27 | 328.2 | 231 | 90 | 287 | 7 | 8 | 0 | 0 | 116 | 20 | 0 | .172 |
| 1906 | 15 | 17 | .469 | 2.21 | 43 | 34 | 22 | 272.2 | 221 | 92 | 196 | 8 | 2 | 0 | 0 | 86 | 14 | 0 | .163 |
| 1907 | 19 | 13 | .594 | 2.15 | 44 | 33 | 20 | 284.2 | 234 | 73 | 232 | 7 | 3 | 0 | 0 | 97 | 12 | 0 | .124 |
| 1908 STL A | 19 | 14 | .576 | 1.89 | 43 | 36 | 25 | 285.2 | 223 | 90 | 232 | 5 | 1 | 1 | 3 | 91 | 10 | 1 | .110 |
| 1909 | 11 | 14 | .440 | 2.37 | 31 | 28 | 16 | 220.1 | 204 | 57 | 141 | 5 | 1 | 0 | 0 | 75 | 5 | 0 | .067 |
| 1910 | 3 | 1 | .750 | 3.55 | 10 | 2 | 0 | 33 | 31 | 11 | 16 | 0 | 2 | 1 | 1 | 9 | 1 | 0 | .111 |
| 13 yrs. | 191 | 145 | .568 | 2.16 6th | 407 | 340 | 261 | 2961.1 | 2460 | 803 | 2316 | 50 | 22 | 6 | 5 | 1062 | 172 | 4 | .162 |
| 1 yr. | 13 | 15 | .464 | 2.81 | 29 | 28 | 26 | 243.2 | 239 | 66 | 168 | 0 | 0 | 0 | 0 | 98 | 25 | 2 | .255 |

## Ben Wade

**WADE, BENJAMIN STYRON**   BR TR 6'3" 195 lbs.
Brother of Jake Wade.
B. Nov. 26, 1922, Morehead City, N. C.

| | W | L | PCT | ERA | G | GS | CG | IP | H | BB | SO | ShO | W | L | SV | AB | H | HR | BA |
|---|---|---|---|---|---|---|---|---|---|---|---|---|---|---|---|---|---|---|---|
| 1948 CHI N | 0 | 1 | .000 | 7.20 | 2 | 0 | 0 | 5 | 4 | 4 | 1 | 0 | 0 | 1 | 0 | 2 | 0 | 0 | .000 |
| 1952 BKN N | 11 | 9 | .550 | 3.60 | 37 | 24 | 5 | 180 | 166 | 94 | 118 | 1 | 2 | 0 | 3 | 60 | 7 | 3 | .117 |
| 1953 | 7 | 5 | .583 | 3.79 | 32 | 0 | 0 | 90.1 | 79 | 33 | 65 | 0 | 7 | 5 | 3 | 24 | 4 | 1 | .167 |
| 1954 2 teams | | | | | | BKN N (23G 1–1) | | | STL N (13G 0–0) | | | | | | | | | | |
| " total | 1 | 1 | .500 | 7.28 | 36 | 0 | 0 | 68 | 89 | 36 | 44 | 0 | 1 | 1 | 3 | 8 | 0 | 0 | .000 |
| 1955 PIT N | 0 | 1 | .000 | 3.21 | 11 | 1 | 0 | 28 | 26 | 14 | 7 | 0 | 0 | 1 | 1 | 4 | 0 | 0 | .000 |
| 5 yrs. | 19 | 17 | .528 | 4.34 | 118 | 25 | 5 | 371.1 | 364 | 181 | 235 | 1 | 10 | 8 | 10 | 98 | 11 | 4 | .112 |
| 1 yr. | 0 | 1 | .000 | 7.20 | 2 | 0 | 0 | 5 | 4 | 4 | 1 | 0 | 0 | 1 | 0 | 2 | 0 | 0 | .000 |

WORLD SERIES

| | W | L | PCT | ERA | G | GS | CG | IP | H | BB | SO | ShO | W | L | SV | AB | H | HR | BA |
|---|---|---|---|---|---|---|---|---|---|---|---|---|---|---|---|---|---|---|---|
| 1953 BKN N | 0 | 0 | – | 15.43 | 2 | 0 | 0 | 2.1 | 4 | 1 | 2 | 0 | 0 | 0 | 0 | 0 | 0 | 0 | – |

## Roy Walker

**WALKER, JAMES ROY (Dixie)**   BR TR 6'1½" 180 lbs.
B. Apr. 13, 1893, Lawrenceburg, Tenn.   BB 1922
D. Feb. 10, 1962, New Orleans, La.

| | W | L | PCT | ERA | G | GS | CG | IP | H | BB | SO | ShO | W | L | SV | AB | H | HR | BA |
|---|---|---|---|---|---|---|---|---|---|---|---|---|---|---|---|---|---|---|---|
| 1912 CLE A | 0 | 0 | – | 0.00 | 2 | 0 | 0 | 3 | 0 | 3 | 1 | 0 | 0 | 0 | 0 | 0 | 0 | 0 | – |
| 1915 | 4 | 9 | .308 | 3.98 | 25 | 15 | 4 | 131 | 122 | 65 | 57 | 0 | 0 | 1 | 1 | 38 | 5 | 0 | .132 |
| 1917 CHI N | 0 | 1 | .000 | 3.86 | 2 | 1 | 0 | 7 | 8 | 5 | 4 | 0 | 0 | 0 | 0 | 1 | 0 | 0 | .000 |
| 1918 | 1 | 3 | .250 | 2.70 | 13 | 7 | 2 | 43.1 | 50 | 15 | 20 | 0 | 0 | 0 | 1 | 11 | 0 | 0 | .000 |
| 1921 STL N | 11 | 12 | .478 | 4.22 | 38 | 24 | 11 | 170.2 | 194 | 53 | 52 | 0 | 2 | 0 | 3 | 54 | 11 | 0 | .204 |
| 1922 | 1 | 2 | .333 | 4.78 | 12 | 2 | 0 | 32 | 34 | 15 | 14 | 0 | 1 | 0 | 0 | 7 | 1 | 0 | .143 |
| 6 yrs. | 17 | 27 | .386 | 3.98 | 92 | 49 | 17 | 387 | 408 | 156 | 148 | 0 | 3 | 2 | 5 | 111 | 17 | 0 | .153 |
| 2 yrs. | 1 | 4 | .200 | 2.86 | 15 | 8 | 2 | 50.1 | 58 | 20 | 24 | 0 | 0 | 0 | 0 | 12 | 0 | 0 | .000 |

## Dick Ward

**WARD, RICHARD (Ole)**   BR TR 6'1" 198 lbs.
B. May 21, 1909, Herrick, S. D.   D. May 31, 1966, Freeland, Wash.

| | W | L | PCT | ERA | G | GS | CG | IP | H | BB | SO | ShO | W | L | SV | AB | H | HR | BA |
|---|---|---|---|---|---|---|---|---|---|---|---|---|---|---|---|---|---|---|---|
| 1934 CHI N | 0 | 0 | – | 3.18 | 3 | 0 | 0 | 5.2 | 9 | 2 | 1 | 0 | 0 | 0 | 0 | 1 | 0 | 0 | .000 |
| 1935 STL N | 0 | 0 | – | 0.00 | 1 | 0 | 0 | 0 | 0 | 1 | 0 | 0 | 0 | 0 | 0 | 0 | 0 | 0 | – |
| 2 yrs. | 0 | 0 | – | 3.18 | 4 | 0 | 0 | 5.2 | 9 | 3 | 1 | 0 | 0 | 0 | 0 | 1 | 0 | 0 | .000 |
| 1 yr. | 0 | 0 | – | 3.18 | 3 | 0 | 0 | 5.2 | 9 | 2 | 1 | 0 | 0 | 0 | 0 | 1 | 0 | 0 | .000 |

## Lon Warneke

**WARNEKE, LONNIE (The Arkansas Humming Bird)**   BR TR 6'2" 185 lbs.
B. Mar. 28, 1909, Mt. Ida, Ark.   D. June 23, 1976, Hot Springs, Ark.

| | W | L | PCT | ERA | G | GS | CG | IP | H | BB | SO | ShO | W | L | SV | AB | H | HR | BA |
|---|---|---|---|---|---|---|---|---|---|---|---|---|---|---|---|---|---|---|---|
| 1930 CHI N | 0 | 0 | – | 33.75 | 1 | 0 | 0 | 1.1 | 2 | 5 | 0 | 0 | 0 | 0 | 0 | 0 | 0 | 0 | – |
| 1931 | 2 | 4 | .333 | 3.22 | 20 | 7 | 3 | 64.1 | 67 | 37 | 27 | 0 | 0 | 1 | 0 | 19 | 5 | 0 | .263 |
| 1932 | 22 | 6 | .786 | 2.37 | 35 | 32 | 25 | 277 | 247 | 64 | 106 | 4 | 0 | 0 | 0 | 99 | 19 | 0 | .192 |
| 1933 | 18 | 13 | .581 | 2.00 | 36 | 34 | 26 | 287.1 | 262 | 75 | 133 | 4 | 0 | 0 | 1 | 100 | 30 | 2 | .300 |
| 1934 | 22 | 10 | .688 | 3.21 | 43 | 35 | 23 | 291.1 | 273 | 66 | 143 | 3 | 2 | 1 | 3 | 113 | 22 | 0 | .195 |
| 1935 | 20 | 13 | .606 | 3.06 | 42 | 30 | 20 | 261.2 | 255 | 50 | 120 | 1 | 4 | 3 | 4 | 91 | 20 | 0 | .220 |
| 1936 | 16 | 13 | .552 | 3.44 | 40 | 29 | 13 | 240.2 | 246 | 76 | 113 | 4 | 1 | 5 | 1 | 84 | 17 | 1 | .202 |
| 1937 STL N | 18 | 11 | .621 | 4.53 | 36 | 33 | 18 | 238.2 | 280 | 69 | 87 | 2 | 0 | 0 | 0 | 80 | 21 | 0 | .263 |
| 1938 | 13 | 8 | .619 | 3.97 | 31 | 26 | 12 | 197 | 199 | 64 | 89 | 4 | 2 | 0 | 0 | 71 | 23 | 0 | .324 |
| 1939 | 13 | 7 | .650 | 3.78 | 34 | 21 | 6 | 162 | 160 | 49 | 59 | 3 | 3 | 1 | 2 | 52 | 10 | 0 | .192 |
| 1940 | 16 | 10 | .615 | 3.14 | 33 | 31 | 17 | 232 | 235 | 47 | 85 | 1 | 0 | 0 | 0 | 86 | 18 | 1 | .209 |
| 1941 | 17 | 9 | .654 | 3.15 | 37 | 30 | 12 | 246 | 227 | 82 | 83 | 4 | 3 | 1 | 0 | 77 | 9 | 0 | .117 |
| 1942 2 teams | | | | | | STL N (12G 6–4) | | | CHI N (15G 5–7) | | | | | | | | | | |
| " total | 11 | 11 | .500 | 2.73 | 27 | 24 | 14 | 181 | 173 | 36 | 59 | 1 | 0 | 0 | 2 | 62 | 16 | 0 | .258 |
| 1943 CHI N | 4 | 5 | .444 | 3.16 | 21 | 10 | 4 | 88.1 | 82 | 18 | 30 | 0 | 1 | 0 | 0 | 26 | 5 | 0 | .192 |
| 1945 | 1 | 1 | .500 | 3.86 | 9 | 1 | 0 | 14 | 16 | 1 | 4 | 0 | 1 | 0 | 0 | 2 | 0 | 0 | .000 |
| 15 yrs. | 193 | 121 | .615 | 3.18 | 445 | 343 | 192 | 2782.2 | 2726 | 739 | 1140 | 31 | 17 | 12 | 13 | 962 | 215 | 4 | .223 |
| 10 yrs. | 110 | 72 | .604 | 2.84 | 262 | 190 | 122 | 1625 | 1549 | 413 | 706 | 17 | 9 | 10 | 11 | 566 | 124 | 3 | .219 |

WORLD SERIES

| | W | L | PCT | ERA | G | GS | CG | IP | H | BB | SO | ShO | W | L | SV | AB | H | HR | BA |
|---|---|---|---|---|---|---|---|---|---|---|---|---|---|---|---|---|---|---|---|
| 1932 CHI N | 0 | 1 | .000 | 5.91 | 2 | 1 | 1 | 10.2 | 15 | 5 | 8 | 0 | 0 | 0 | 0 | 4 | 0 | 0 | .000 |
| 1935 | 2 | 0 | 1.000 | 0.54 | 3 | 2 | 1 | 16.2 | 9 | 4 | 5 | 1 | 0 | 0 | 0 | 5 | 1 | 0 | .200 |
| 2 yrs. | 2 | 1 | .667 | 2.63 | 5 | 3 | 2 | 27.1 | 24 | 9 | 13 | 1 | 0 | 0 | 0 | 9 | 1 | 0 | .111 |

## Jack Warner

**WARNER, JACK DYER**   BR TR 5'11" 190 lbs.
B. July 12, 1940, Brandywine, W. Va.

| | W | L | PCT | ERA | G | GS | CG | IP | H | BB | SO | ShO | W | L | SV | AB | H | HR | BA |
|---|---|---|---|---|---|---|---|---|---|---|---|---|---|---|---|---|---|---|---|
| 1962 CHI N | 0 | 0 | – | 7.71 | 7 | 0 | 0 | 7 | 9 | 0 | 3 | 0 | 0 | 0 | 0 | 0 | 0 | 0 | – |

| | W | L | PCT | ERA | G | GS | CG | IP | H | BB | SO | ShO | W | L | SV | AB | H | HR | BA |
|---|---|---|---|---|---|---|---|---|---|---|---|---|---|---|---|---|---|---|---|
| | | | | | | | | | | | | | Relief Pitching | | | BATTING | | | |

### Jack Warner continued

| | W | L | PCT | ERA | G | GS | CG | IP | H | BB | SO | ShO | W | L | SV | AB | H | HR | BA |
|---|---|---|---|---|---|---|---|---|---|---|---|---|---|---|---|---|---|---|---|
| 1963 | 0 | 1 | .000 | 2.78 | 8 | 0 | 0 | 22.2 | 21 | 8 | 7 | 0 | 0 | 1 | 0 | 4 | 1 | 0 | .250 |
| 1964 | 0 | 0 | — | 2.89 | 7 | 0 | 0 | 9.1 | 12 | 4 | 6 | 0 | 0 | 0 | 0 | 0 | 0 | 0 | — |
| 1965 | 0 | 1 | .000 | 8.62 | 11 | 0 | 0 | 15.2 | 22 | 9 | 7 | 0 | 0 | 1 | 0 | 1 | 0 | 0 | .000 |
| 4 yrs. | 0 | 2 | .000 | 5.10 | 33 | 0 | 0 | 54.2 | 64 | 21 | 23 | 0 | 0 | 2 | 0 | 5 | 1 | 0 | .200 |
| 4 yrs. | 0 | 2 | .000 | 5.10 | 33 | 0 | 0 | 54.2 | 64 | 21 | 23 | 0 | 0 | 2 | 0 | 5 | 1 | 0 | .200 |

## Doc Watson

WATSON, CHARLES JOHN         BR TL 5'10½" 170 lbs.
B. Jan. 30, 1885, Kensington, Ohio     D. Dec. 30, 1949, San Diego, Calif.

| | W | L | PCT | ERA | G | GS | CG | IP | H | BB | SO | ShO | W | L | SV | AB | H | HR | BA |
|---|---|---|---|---|---|---|---|---|---|---|---|---|---|---|---|---|---|---|---|
| 1913 CHI N | 1 | 0 | 1.000 | 1.00 | 1 | 1 | 1 | 9 | 8 | 6 | 1 | 0 | 0 | 0 | 0 | 2 | 0 | 0 | .000 |
| 1914 2 teams | | | CHI F (26G 9–11) | | STL | F (9G 3–4) | | | | | | | | | | | | | |
| " total | 12 | 15 | .444 | 2.01 | 35 | 25 | 14 | 228 | 186 | 73 | 87 | 5 | 1 | 3 | 1 | 70 | 7 | 0 | .100 |
| 1915 STL F | 7 | 10 | .412 | 3.98 | 33 | 20 | 6 | 135.2 | 132 | 58 | 45 | 0 | 2 | 0 | 0 | 40 | 5 | 0 | .125 |
| 3 yrs. | 20 | 25 | .444 | 2.70 | 69 | 46 | 21 | 372.2 | 326 | 137 | 133 | 5 | 3 | 3 | 1 | 112 | 12 | 0 | .107 |
| 1 yr. | 1 | 0 | 1.000 | 1.00 | 1 | 1 | 1 | 9 | 8 | 6 | 1 | 0 | 0 | 0 | 0 | 2 | 0 | 0 | .000 |

## Eddie Watt

WATT, EDWARD DEAN         BR TR 5'10" 183 lbs.
B. Apr. 4, 1942, Lamonie, Iowa

| | W | L | PCT | ERA | G | GS | CG | IP | H | BB | SO | ShO | W | L | SV | AB | H | HR | BA |
|---|---|---|---|---|---|---|---|---|---|---|---|---|---|---|---|---|---|---|---|
| 1966 BAL A | 9 | 7 | .563 | 3.83 | 43 | 13 | 1 | 145.2 | 123 | 44 | 102 | 0 | 7 | 2 | 4 | 46 | 14 | 2 | .304 |
| 1967 | 3 | 5 | .375 | 2.26 | 49 | 0 | 0 | 103.2 | 67 | 37 | 93 | 0 | 3 | 5 | 8 | 22 | 4 | 1 | .182 |
| 1968 | 5 | 5 | .500 | 2.27 | 59 | 0 | 0 | 83.1 | 63 | 35 | 72 | 0 | 5 | 5 | 11 | 8 | 0 | 0 | .000 |
| 1969 | 5 | 2 | .714 | 1.65 | 56 | 0 | 0 | 71 | 49 | 26 | 46 | 0 | 5 | 2 | 16 | 8 | 0 | 0 | .000 |
| 1970 | 7 | 7 | .500 | 3.27 | 53 | 0 | 0 | 55 | 44 | 29 | 33 | 0 | 7 | 7 | 12 | 8 | 1 | 0 | .125 |
| 1971 | 3 | 1 | .750 | 1.80 | 35 | 0 | 0 | 40 | 39 | 8 | 26 | 0 | 3 | 1 | 11 | 5 | 0 | 0 | .000 |
| 1972 | 2 | 3 | .400 | 2.15 | 38 | 0 | 0 | 46 | 30 | 20 | 23 | 0 | 2 | 3 | 7 | 2 | 0 | 0 | .000 |
| 1973 | 3 | 4 | .429 | 3.30 | 30 | 0 | 0 | 71 | 62 | 21 | 38 | 0 | 3 | 4 | 5 | 0 | 0 | 0 | — |
| 1974 PHI N | 1 | 1 | .500 | 4.03 | 42 | 0 | 0 | 38 | 39 | 26 | 23 | 0 | 1 | 1 | 6 | 1 | 0 | 0 | .000 |
| 1975 CHI N | 0 | 1 | .000 | 13.50 | 6 | 0 | 0 | 6 | 14 | 8 | 6 | 0 | 0 | 1 | 0 | 0 | 0 | 0 | — |
| 10 yrs. | 38 | 36 | .514 | 2.91 | 411 | 13 | 1 | 659.2 | 530 | 254 | 462 | 0 | 36 | 31 | 80 | 100 | 19 | 3 | .190 |
| 1 yr. | 0 | 1 | .000 | 13.50 | 6 | 0 | 0 | 6 | 14 | 8 | 6 | 0 | 0 | 1 | 0 | 0 | 0 | 0 | — |

LEAGUE CHAMPIONSHIP SERIES

| | W | L | PCT | ERA | G | GS | CG | IP | H | BB | SO | ShO | W | L | SV | AB | H | HR | BA |
|---|---|---|---|---|---|---|---|---|---|---|---|---|---|---|---|---|---|---|---|
| 1969 BAL A | 0 | 0 | — | 0.00 | 1 | 0 | 0 | 2 | 0 | 0 | 2 | 0 | 0 | 0 | 0 | 0 | 0 | 0 | — |
| 1971 | 0 | 0 | — | 0.00 | 1 | 0 | 0 | 2 | 2 | 0 | 1 | 0 | 0 | 0 | 1 | 0 | 0 | 0 | — |
| 1973 | 0 | 0 | — | 0.00 | 1 | 0 | 0 | .1 | 0 | 1 | 0 | 0 | 0 | 0 | 0 | 0 | 0 | 0 | — |
| 3 yrs. | 0 | 0 | — | 0.00 | 3 | 0 | 0 | 4.1 | 2 | 1 | 3 | 0 | 0 | 0 | 1 | 0 | 0 | 0 | — |

WORLD SERIES

| | W | L | PCT | ERA | G | GS | CG | IP | H | BB | SO | ShO | W | L | SV | AB | H | HR | BA |
|---|---|---|---|---|---|---|---|---|---|---|---|---|---|---|---|---|---|---|---|
| 1969 BAL A | 0 | 1 | .000 | 3.00 | 2 | 0 | 0 | 3 | 4 | 0 | 3 | 0 | 0 | 1 | 0 | 0 | 0 | 0 | — |
| 1970 | 0 | 1 | .000 | 9.00 | 1 | 0 | 0 | 1 | 2 | 1 | 3 | 0 | 0 | 1 | 0 | 0 | 0 | 0 | — |
| 1971 | 0 | 1 | .000 | 3.86 | 2 | 0 | 0 | 2.1 | 4 | 0 | 2 | 0 | 0 | 0 | 0 | 0 | 0 | 0 | — |
| 3 yrs. | 0 | 3 | .000 | 4.26 | 5 | 0 | 0 | 6.1 | 10 | 1 | 8 | 0 | 0 | 2 | 0 | 0 | 0 | 0 | — |
| | | | | | | | | | | | | 2nd | | | | | | | |

## Harry Weaver

WEAVER, HARRY ABRAHAM         BR TR 5'11" 160 lbs.
B. Feb. 26, 1892, Clarendon, Pa.     D. May 30, 1983, Rochester, N. Y.

| | W | L | PCT | ERA | G | GS | CG | IP | H | BB | SO | ShO | W | L | SV | AB | H | HR | BA |
|---|---|---|---|---|---|---|---|---|---|---|---|---|---|---|---|---|---|---|---|
| 1915 PHI A | 0 | 2 | .000 | 3.00 | 2 | 2 | 2 | 18 | 18 | 10 | 1 | 0 | 0 | 0 | 0 | 6 | 1 | 0 | .167 |
| 1916 | 0 | 0 | — | 10.13 | 3 | 0 | 0 | 8 | 14 | 5 | 2 | 0 | 0 | 0 | 0 | 2 | 1 | 0 | .500 |
| 1917 CHI N | 1 | 1 | .500 | 2.75 | 4 | 2 | 1 | 19.2 | 17 | 7 | 8 | 0 | 0 | 0 | 0 | 5 | 1 | 0 | .200 |
| 1918 | 2 | 2 | .500 | 2.20 | 8 | 3 | 1 | 32.2 | 27 | 7 | 9 | 1 | 1 | 0 | 1 | 8 | 2 | 0 | .250 |
| 1919 | 0 | 1 | .000 | 10.80 | 2 | 1 | 0 | 3.1 | 6 | 2 | 1 | 0 | 0 | 1 | 0 | 1 | 0 | 0 | .000 |
| 5 yrs. | 3 | 6 | .333 | 3.64 | 19 | 8 | 4 | 81.2 | 82 | 31 | 21 | 1 | 1 | 1 | 1 | 22 | 5 | 0 | .227 |
| 3 yrs. | 3 | 4 | .429 | 2.91 | 14 | 6 | 2 | 55.2 | 50 | 16 | 18 | 1 | 1 | 1 | 1 | 14 | 3 | 0 | .214 |

## Jim Weaver

WEAVER, JAMES DEMENT (Big Jim)         BR TR 6'6" 230 lbs.
B. Nov. 25, 1903, Fulton, Ky.     D. Feb. 16, 1984, Lakeland, Fla.

| | W | L | PCT | ERA | G | GS | CG | IP | H | BB | SO | ShO | W | L | SV | AB | H | HR | BA |
|---|---|---|---|---|---|---|---|---|---|---|---|---|---|---|---|---|---|---|---|
| 1928 WAS A | 0 | 0 | — | 1.50 | 3 | 0 | 0 | 6 | 2 | 6 | 2 | 0 | 0 | 0 | 0 | 1 | 0 | 0 | .000 |
| 1931 NY A | 2 | 1 | .667 | 5.31 | 17 | 5 | 2 | 57.2 | 66 | 29 | 28 | 0 | 0 | 1 | 0 | 20 | 1 | 0 | .050 |
| 1934 2 teams | | | STL A (5G 2–0) | | CHI | N (27G 11–9) | | | | | | | | | | | | | |
| " total | 13 | 9 | .591 | 4.18 | 32 | 25 | 10 | 178.2 | 180 | 74 | 109 | 1 | 2 | 0 | 0 | 59 | 4 | 0 | .068 |
| 1935 PIT N | 14 | 8 | .636 | 3.42 | 33 | 22 | 11 | 176.1 | 177 | 58 | 87 | 4 | 2 | 0 | 0 | 56 | 4 | 0 | .071 |
| 1936 | 14 | 8 | .636 | 4.31 | 38 | 31 | 11 | 225.2 | 239 | 74 | 108 | 1 | 0 | 0 | 0 | 79 | 8 | 0 | .101 |
| 1937 | 8 | 5 | .615 | 3.20 | 32 | 9 | 2 | 109.2 | 106 | 31 | 44 | 1 | 5 | 4 | 0 | 27 | 4 | 0 | .148 |
| 1938 2 teams | | | STL A (1G 0–1) | | CIN | N (30G 6–4) | | | | | | | | | | | | | |
| " total | 6 | 5 | .545 | 3.43 | 31 | 16 | 2 | 136.1 | 118 | 63 | 68 | 0 | 1 | 3 | 3 | 46 | 9 | 0 | .196 |
| 1939 CIN N | 0 | 0 | — | 3.00 | 3 | 0 | 0 | 3 | 3 | 1 | 3 | 0 | 0 | 0 | 0 | 1 | 0 | 0 | .000 |
| 8 yrs. | 57 | 36 | .613 | 3.88 | 189 | 108 | 38 | 893.1 | 891 | 336 | 449 | 7 | 10 | 5 | 3 | 289 | 30 | 0 | .104 |
| 1 yr. | 11 | 9 | .550 | 3.91 | 27 | 20 | 8 | 159 | 163 | 54 | 98 | 1 | 2 | 0 | 0 | 52 | 3 | 0 | .058 |

## Orlie Weaver

WEAVER, ORVILLE FOREST         BR TR 6' 180 lbs.
B. June 4, 1886, Newport, Ky.     D. Nov. 28, 1970, New Orleans, La.

| | W | L | PCT | ERA | G | GS | CG | IP | H | BB | SO | ShO | W | L | SV | AB | H | HR | BA |
|---|---|---|---|---|---|---|---|---|---|---|---|---|---|---|---|---|---|---|---|
| 1910 CHI N | 1 | 2 | .333 | 3.66 | 7 | 2 | 2 | 32 | 34 | 15 | 22 | 0 | 0 | 1 | 0 | 13 | 2 | 0 | .154 |
| 1911 2 teams | | | CHI N (6G 3–2) | | BOS | N (27G 3–12) | | | | | | | | | | | | | |
| " total | 6 | 14 | .300 | 5.30 | 33 | 21 | 5 | 164.2 | 169 | 101 | 70 | 1 | 1 | 1 | 0 | 58 | 6 | 0 | .103 |
| 2 yrs. | 7 | 16 | .304 | 5.03 | 40 | 23 | 7 | 196.2 | 203 | 116 | 92 | 1 | 1 | 2 | 0 | 71 | 8 | 0 | .113 |
| 2 yrs. | 4 | 4 | .500 | 2.74 | 13 | 6 | 3 | 75.2 | 63 | 32 | 42 | 1 | 1 | 1 | 0 | 30 | 3 | 0 | .100 |

## Jake Weimer

WEIMER, JACOB (Tornado Jake)         BL TL 5'11" 175 lbs.
B. Nov. 29, 1873, Ottumwa, Iowa     D. June 17, 1928, Chicago, Ill.

| | W | L | PCT | ERA | G | GS | CG | IP | H | BB | SO | ShO | W | L | SV | AB | H | HR | BA |
|---|---|---|---|---|---|---|---|---|---|---|---|---|---|---|---|---|---|---|---|
| 1903 CHI N | 21 | 9 | .700 | 2.30 | 35 | 33 | 27 | 282 | 241 | 104 | 128 | 3 | 0 | 0 | 0 | 107 | 21 | 0 | .196 |
| 1904 | 20 | 14 | .588 | 1.91 | 37 | 37 | 31 | 307 | 229 | 97 | 177 | 5 | 0 | 0 | 0 | 115 | 21 | 0 | .183 |
| 1905 | 18 | 12 | .600 | 2.27 | 33 | 30 | 26 | 250 | 212 | 80 | 107 | 2 | 1 | 1 | 1 | 92 | 19 | 0 | .207 |
| 1906 CIN N | 20 | 14 | .588 | 2.22 | 41 | 39 | 31 | 304.2 | 263 | 99 | 141 | 7 | 1 | 1 | 0 | 108 | 29 | 0 | .269 |

| | W | L | PCT | ERA | G | GS | CG | IP | H | BB | SO | ShO | Relief Pitching W | L | SV | BATTING AB | H | HR | BA |
|---|---|---|---|---|---|---|---|---|---|---|---|---|---|---|---|---|---|---|---|

## Jake Weimer continued

| | W | L | PCT | ERA | G | GS | CG | IP | H | BB | SO | ShO | W | L | SV | AB | H | HR | BA |
|---|---|---|---|---|---|---|---|---|---|---|---|---|---|---|---|---|---|---|---|
| 1907 | 11 | 14 | .440 | 2.41 | 29 | 26 | 19 | 209 | 165 | 63 | 67 | 3 | 2 | 1 | 0 | 72 | 14 | 1 | .194 |
| 1908 | 8 | 7 | .533 | 2.39 | 15 | 15 | 9 | 116.2 | 110 | 50 | 36 | 2 | 0 | 0 | 0 | 45 | 11 | 0 | .244 |
| 1909 NY N | 0 | 0 | — | 9.00 | 1 | 0 | 0 | 3 | 7 | 0 | 1 | 0 | 0 | 0 | 0 | 1 | 0 | 0 | .000 |
| 7 yrs. | 98 | 70 | .583 | 2.23 | 191 | 180 | 143 | 1472.1 | 1227 | 493 | 657 | 22 | 4 | 2 | 2 | 540 | 115 | 1 | .213 |
| 3 yrs. | 59 | 35 | .628 | 2.15 | 105 | 100 | 84 | 839 | 682 | 281 | 412 | 10 | 1 | 1 | 1 | 314 | 61 | 0 | .194 |
| | | | | 8th | 4th | | | | | | | | | | | | | | |

## Lefty Weinert

**WEINERT, PHILIP WALTER**
B. Apr. 21, 1901, Philadelphia, Pa.   D. Apr. 17, 1973, Rockledge, Fla.
BL TL 6'1"   195 lbs.

| | W | L | PCT | ERA | G | GS | CG | IP | H | BB | SO | ShO | W | L | SV | AB | H | HR | BA |
|---|---|---|---|---|---|---|---|---|---|---|---|---|---|---|---|---|---|---|---|
| 1919 PHI N | 0 | 0 | — | 18.00 | 1 | 0 | 0 | 4 | 11 | 2 | 0 | 0 | 0 | 0 | 0 | 2 | 2 | 0 | 1.000 |
| 1920 | 1 | 1 | .500 | 6.14 | 10 | 2 | 0 | 22 | 27 | 19 | 10 | 0 | 1 | 0 | 0 | 5 | 0 | 0 | .000 |
| 1921 | 1 | 0 | 1.000 | 1.46 | 8 | 0 | 0 | 12.1 | 8 | 5 | 2 | 0 | 1 | 0 | 0 | 1 | 1 | 0 | 1.000 |
| 1922 | 8 | 11 | .421 | 3.40 | 34 | 22 | 10 | 166.2 | 189 | 70 | 58 | 0 | 3 | 1 | 1 | 58 | 14 | 0 | .241 |
| 1923 | 4 | 17 | .190 | 5.42 | 38 | 20 | 8 | 156 | 207 | 81 | 46 | 0 | 0 | 2 | 1 | 59 | 19 | 0 | .322 |
| 1924 | 0 | 1 | .000 | 2.45 | 8 | 1 | 0 | 14.2 | 10 | 11 | 7 | 0 | 0 | 0 | 0 | 4 | 0 | 0 | .000 |
| 1927 CHI N | 1 | 1 | .500 | 4.58 | 5 | 3 | 1 | 19.2 | 21 | 6 | 5 | 0 | 0 | 0 | 0 | 5 | 1 | 0 | .200 |
| 1928 | 1 | 0 | 1.000 | 5.29 | 10 | 1 | 0 | 17 | 24 | 9 | 8 | 0 | 1 | 0 | 0 | 2 | 0 | 0 | .000 |
| 1931 NY A | 2 | 2 | .500 | 6.20 | 17 | 0 | 0 | 24.2 | 31 | 19 | 24 | 0 | 2 | 2 | 0 | 6 | 0 | 0 | .000 |
| 9 yrs. | 18 | 33 | .353 | 4.59 | 131 | 49 | 19 | 437 | 528 | 222 | 160 | 0 | 8 | 5 | 2 | 142 | 37 | 0 | .261 |
| 2 yrs. | 2 | 1 | .667 | 4.91 | 15 | 4 | 1 | 36.2 | 45 | 15 | 13 | 0 | 1 | 0 | 0 | 7 | 1 | 0 | .143 |

## Johnny Welch

**WELCH, JOHN VERNON**
B. Dec. 2, 1906, Washington, D. C.   D. Sept. 2, 1940, St. Louis, Mo.
BL TR 6'3"   184 lbs.

| | W | L | PCT | ERA | G | GS | CG | IP | H | BB | SO | ShO | W | L | SV | AB | H | HR | BA |
|---|---|---|---|---|---|---|---|---|---|---|---|---|---|---|---|---|---|---|---|
| 1926 CHI N | 0 | 0 | — | 2.08 | 3 | 0 | 0 | 4.1 | 5 | 1 | 0 | 0 | 0 | 0 | 0 | 1 | 1 | 0 | 1.000 |
| 1927 | 0 | 0 | — | 9.00 | 1 | 0 | 0 | 1 | 0 | 3 | 1 | 0 | 0 | 0 | 0 | 1 | 0 | 0 | — |
| 1928 | 0 | 0 | — | 15.75 | 3 | 0 | 0 | 4 | 13 | 0 | 2 | 0 | 0 | 0 | 0 | 0 | 0 | 0 | — |
| 1931 | 2 | 1 | .667 | 3.74 | 8 | 3 | 1 | 33.2 | 39 | 10 | 7 | 0 | 1 | 1 | 0 | 12 | 5 | 0 | .417 |
| 1932 BOS A | 4 | 6 | .400 | 5.23 | 20 | 8 | 3 | 72.1 | 93 | 38 | 26 | 1 | 1 | 1 | 0 | 36 | 9 | 1 | .250 |
| 1933 | 4 | 9 | .308 | 4.60 | 47 | 7 | 1 | 129 | 142 | 67 | 68 | 0 | 3 | 5 | 3 | 37 | 6 | 0 | .162 |
| 1934 | 13 | 15 | .464 | 4.49 | 41 | 28 | 13 | 206.1 | 223 | 76 | 91 | 1 | 3 | 6 | 0 | 74 | 15 | 0 | .203 |
| 1935 | 10 | 9 | .526 | 4.47 | 31 | 19 | 10 | 143 | 155 | 53 | 48 | 1 | 2 | 0 | 2 | 50 | 9 | 0 | .180 |
| 1936 2 teams | | | | BOS | A | (9G 2–1) | | PIT | N | (9G 0–0) | | | | | | | | | |
| " total | 2 | 1 | .667 | 5.10 | 18 | 4 | 1 | 54.2 | 65 | 14 | 14 | 0 | 0 | 0 | 0 | 18 | 5 | 0 | .278 |
| 9 yrs. | 35 | 41 | .461 | 4.66 | 172 | 63 | 24 | 648.1 | 735 | 262 | 257 | 3 | 10 | 13 | 6 | 228 | 50 | 1 | .219 |
| 4 yrs. | 2 | 1 | .667 | 4.81 | 15 | 3 | 1 | 43 | 57 | 14 | 10 | 0 | 1 | 1 | 0 | 13 | 6 | 0 | .462 |

## Rip Wheeler

**WHEELER, FLOYD CLARK**
B. Mar. 2, 1898, Marion, Ky.   D. Sept. 18, 1969, Marion, Ky.
BR TR 6'   180 lbs.

| | W | L | PCT | ERA | G | GS | CG | IP | H | BB | SO | ShO | W | L | SV | AB | H | HR | BA |
|---|---|---|---|---|---|---|---|---|---|---|---|---|---|---|---|---|---|---|---|
| 1921 PIT N | 0 | 0 | — | 9.00 | 1 | 0 | 0 | 3 | 6 | 1 | 0 | 0 | 0 | 0 | 0 | 1 | 0 | 0 | .000 |
| 1922 | 0 | 0 | — | 0.00 | 1 | 0 | 0 | 1 | 1 | 2 | 0 | 0 | 0 | 0 | 0 | 0 | 0 | 0 | — |
| 1923 CHI N | 1 | 2 | .333 | 4.88 | 3 | 3 | 1 | 24 | 28 | 5 | 5 | 0 | 0 | 0 | 0 | 9 | 1 | 0 | .111 |
| 1924 | 3 | 6 | .333 | 3.91 | 29 | 4 | 0 | 101.1 | 103 | 21 | 16 | 0 | 2 | 3 | 0 | 32 | 7 | 0 | .219 |
| 4 yrs. | 4 | 8 | .333 | 4.18 | 34 | 7 | 1 | 129.1 | 138 | 29 | 21 | 0 | 2 | 3 | 0 | 42 | 8 | 0 | .190 |
| 2 yrs. | 4 | 8 | .333 | 4.09 | 32 | 7 | 1 | 125.1 | 131 | 26 | 21 | 0 | 2 | 3 | 0 | 41 | 8 | 0 | .195 |

## Deacon White

**WHITE, JAMES LAURIE**
Brother of Will White.
B. Dec. 7, 1847, Caton, N. Y.   D. July 7, 1939, Aurora, Ill.
Manager 1879.
BL TR 5'11"   175 lbs.

| | W | L | PCT | ERA | G | GS | CG | IP | H | BB | SO | ShO | W | L | SV | AB | H | HR | BA |
|---|---|---|---|---|---|---|---|---|---|---|---|---|---|---|---|---|---|---|---|
| 1876 CHI N | 0 | 0 | — | 0.00 | 1 | 0 | 0 | 2 | 1 | 0 | 3 | 0 | 0 | 0 | 1 | 303 | 104 | 1 | .343 |
| 1890 BUF P | 0 | 0 | — | 9.00 | 1 | 0 | 0 | 8 | 18 | 2 | 0 | 0 | 0 | 0 | 0 | 439 | 114 | 0 | .260 |
| 2 yrs. | 0 | 0 | — | 7.20 | 2 | 0 | 0 | 10 | 19 | 2 | 3 | 0 | 0 | 0 | 1 | * | | | |
| 1 yr. | 0 | 0 | — | 0.00 | 1 | 0 | 0 | 2 | 1 | 0 | 3 | 0 | 0 | 0 | 1 | 303 | 104 | 1 | .343 |

## Earl Whitehill

**WHITEHILL, EARL OLIVER**
B. Feb. 7, 1899, Cedar Rapids, Iowa   D. Oct. 22, 1954, Omaha, Neb.
BL TL 5'9½"   174 lbs.

| | W | L | PCT | ERA | G | GS | CG | IP | H | BB | SO | ShO | W | L | SV | AB | H | HR | BA |
|---|---|---|---|---|---|---|---|---|---|---|---|---|---|---|---|---|---|---|---|
| 1923 DET A | 2 | 0 | 1.000 | 2.73 | 8 | 3 | 2 | 33 | 22 | 15 | 19 | 1 | 2 | 0 | 0 | 11 | 4 | 0 | .364 |
| 1924 | 17 | 9 | .654 | 3.86 | 35 | 32 | 16 | 233 | 260 | 79 | 65 | 2 | 0 | 2 | 0 | 89 | 19 | 0 | .213 |
| 1925 | 11 | 11 | .500 | 4.66 | 35 | 33 | 15 | 239.1 | 267 | 88 | 83 | 1 | 0 | 0 | 2 | 87 | 19 | 0 | .218 |
| 1926 | 16 | 13 | .552 | 3.99 | 36 | 34 | 13 | 252.1 | 271 | 79 | 109 | 0 | 2 | 0 | 0 | 91 | 23 | 0 | .253 |
| 1927 | 16 | 14 | .533 | 3.36 | 41 | 31 | 17 | 236 | 238 | 105 | 95 | 3 | 3 | 1 | 3 | 78 | 16 | 0 | .205 |
| 1928 | 11 | 16 | .407 | 4.31 | 31 | 30 | 12 | 196.1 | 214 | 78 | 93 | 1 | 1 | 0 | 0 | 67 | 13 | 0 | .194 |
| 1929 | 14 | 15 | .483 | 4.62 | 38 | 28 | 18 | 245.1 | 267 | 96 | 103 | 1 | 4 | 1 | 1 | 90 | 23 | 3 | .256 |
| 1930 | 17 | 13 | .567 | 4.24 | 34 | 31 | 16 | 220.2 | 248 | 80 | 109 | 0 | 0 | 1 | 0 | 83 | 16 | 0 | .193 |
| 1931 | 13 | 16 | .448 | 4.06 | 34 | 34 | 22 | 272.1 | 287 | 118 | 81 | 0 | 0 | 0 | 1 | 97 | 15 | 0 | .155 |
| 1932 | 16 | 12 | .571 | 4.54 | 33 | 31 | 17 | 244 | 255 | 93 | 81 | 3 | 1 | 0 | 0 | 90 | 22 | 0 | .244 |
| 1933 WAS A | 22 | 8 | .733 | 3.33 | 39 | 37 | 19 | 270 | 271 | 100 | 96 | 2 | 0 | 0 | 1 | 108 | 24 | 0 | .222 |
| 1934 | 14 | 11 | .560 | 4.52 | 32 | 31 | 15 | 235 | 269 | 94 | 96 | 0 | 0 | 0 | 0 | 85 | 17 | 1 | .200 |
| 1935 | 14 | 13 | .519 | 4.29 | 34 | 34 | 19 | 279.1 | 318 | 104 | 102 | 1 | 0 | 0 | 0 | 104 | 19 | 0 | .183 |
| 1936 | 14 | 11 | .560 | 4.87 | 28 | 28 | 14 | 212.1 | 252 | 89 | 63 | 0 | 0 | 0 | 0 | 77 | 13 | 0 | .169 |
| 1937 CLE A | 8 | 8 | .500 | 6.49 | 33 | 22 | 6 | 147 | 189 | 80 | 53 | 1 | 0 | 0 | 2 | 49 | 11 | 0 | .224 |
| 1938 | 9 | 8 | .529 | 5.56 | 26 | 23 | 4 | 160.1 | 187 | 83 | 60 | 0 | 1 | 0 | 0 | 56 | 7 | 0 | .125 |
| 1939 CHI N | 4 | 7 | .364 | 5.14 | 24 | 11 | 2 | 89.1 | 102 | 50 | 42 | 1 | 0 | 1 | 1 | 29 | 3 | 0 | .103 |
| 17 yrs. | 218 | 185 | .541 | 4.36 | 541 | 473 | 227 | 3565.2 | 3917 | 1431 | 1350 | 17 | 14 | 6 | 11 | 1291 | 264 | 4 | .204 |
| 1 yr. | 4 | 7 | .364 | 5.14 | 24 | 11 | 2 | 89.1 | 102 | 50 | 42 | 1 | 0 | 1 | 1 | 29 | 3 | 0 | .103 |

| WORLD SERIES | | | | | | | | | | | | | | | | | | | |
|---|---|---|---|---|---|---|---|---|---|---|---|---|---|---|---|---|---|---|---|
| 1933 WAS A | 1 | 0 | 1.000 | 0.00 | 1 | 1 | 1 | 9 | 5 | 2 | 2 | 1 | 0 | 0 | 0 | 3 | 0 | 0 | .000 |

| | W | L | PCT | ERA | G | GS | CG | IP | H | BB | SO | ShO | Relief Pitching W | L | SV | BATTING AB | H | HR | BA |
|---|---|---|---|---|---|---|---|---|---|---|---|---|---|---|---|---|---|---|---|

## Bob Wicker

**WICKER, ROBERT KITRIDGE**      BR TR 6'1"   195 lbs.
B. May 25, 1878, Bedford, Ind.     D. Jan. 22, 1955, Evanston, Ill.

| | W | L | PCT | ERA | G | GS | CG | IP | H | BB | SO | ShO | W | L | SV | AB | H | HR | BA |
|---|---|---|---|---|---|---|---|---|---|---|---|---|---|---|---|---|---|---|---|
| 1901 STL N | 0 | 0 | – | 0.00 | 1 | 0 | 0 | 3 | 4 | 1 | 2 | 0 | 0 | 0 | 0 | 3 | 1 | 0 | .333 |
| 1902 | 5 | 13 | .278 | 3.19 | 22 | 16 | 14 | 152.1 | 159 | 45 | 78 | 1 | 1 | 2 | 0 | 77 | 18 | 0 | .234 |
| 1903 2 teams | | | STL | N (1G 0–0) | | | CHI | N (32G 19–10) | | | | | | | | | | | |
| " total | 19 | 10 | .655 | 2.96 | 33 | 27 | 24 | 252 | 240 | 77 | 113 | 1 | 1 | 1 | 1 | 100 | 24 | 0 | .240 |
| 1904 CHI N | 17 | 8 | .680 | 2.67 | 30 | 27 | 23 | 229 | 201 | 58 | 99 | 4 | 0 | 1 | 0 | 155 | 34 | 0 | .219 |
| 1905 | 13 | 7 | .650 | 2.02 | 22 | 22 | 17 | 178 | 139 | 47 | 86 | 4 | 0 | 0 | 0 | 72 | 10 | 0 | .139 |
| 1906 2 teams | | | CHI | N (10G 3–5) | | | CIN | N (20G 6–14) | | | | | | | | | | | |
| " total | 9 | 19 | .321 | 2.79 | 30 | 25 | 19 | 222.1 | 220 | 65 | 94 | 0 | 1 | 3 | 0 | 70 | 11 | 0 | .157 |
| 6 yrs. | 63 | 57 | .525 | 2.73 | 138 | 117 | 97 | 1036.2 | 963 | 293 | 472 | 10 | 3 | 7 | 1 | * | | 0 | .203 |
| 4 yrs. | 52 | 30 | .634 | 2.66 | 94 | 84 | 69 | 726.1 | 646 | 198 | 320 | 9 | 1 | 3 | 1 | 345 | 70 | 0 | .203 |

## Charlie Wiedemeyer

**WIEDEMEYER, CHARLES JOHN**      BL TL 6'3"   180 lbs.
B. Jan. 31, 1914, Chicago, Ill.     D. Oct. 27, 1979, Lake Geneva, Fla.

| | W | L | PCT | ERA | G | GS | CG | IP | H | BB | SO | ShO | W | L | SV | AB | H | HR | BA |
|---|---|---|---|---|---|---|---|---|---|---|---|---|---|---|---|---|---|---|---|
| 1934 CHI N | 0 | 0 | – | 9.72 | 4 | 1 | 0 | 8.1 | 16 | 4 | 2 | 0 | 0 | 0 | 0 | 1 | 0 | 0 | .000 |

## Milt Wilcox

**WILCOX, MILTON EDWARD**      BR TR 6'2"   185 lbs.
B. Apr. 20, 1950, Honolulu, Hawaii

| | W | L | PCT | ERA | G | GS | CG | IP | H | BB | SO | ShO | W | L | SV | AB | H | HR | BA |
|---|---|---|---|---|---|---|---|---|---|---|---|---|---|---|---|---|---|---|---|
| 1970 CIN N | 3 | 1 | .750 | 2.45 | 5 | 2 | 1 | 22 | 19 | 7 | 13 | 1 | 1 | 1 | 1 | 5 | 1 | 0 | .200 |
| 1971 | 2 | 2 | .500 | 3.35 | 18 | 3 | 0 | 43 | 43 | 17 | 21 | 0 | 2 | 1 | 1 | 9 | 0 | 0 | .000 |
| 1972 CLE A | 7 | 14 | .333 | 3.40 | 32 | 27 | 4 | 156 | 145 | 72 | 90 | 2 | 0 | 1 | 0 | 45 | 9 | 0 | .200 |
| 1973 | 8 | 10 | .444 | 5.83 | 26 | 19 | 4 | 134.1 | 143 | 68 | 82 | 0 | 0 | 0 | 0 | 0 | 0 | 0 | – |
| 1974 | 2 | 2 | .500 | 4.69 | 41 | 2 | 1 | 71 | 74 | 24 | 33 | 0 | 1 | 1 | 4 | 0 | 0 | 0 | – |
| 1975 CHI N | 0 | 1 | .000 | 5.68 | 25 | 0 | 0 | 38 | 50 | 17 | 21 | 0 | 0 | 1 | 0 | 3 | 1 | 0 | .333 |
| 1977 DET A | 6 | 2 | .750 | 3.65 | 20 | 13 | 1 | 106 | 96 | 37 | 82 | 0 | 1 | 0 | 0 | 0 | 0 | 0 | – |
| 1978 | 13 | 12 | .520 | 3.76 | 29 | 27 | 16 | 215.1 | 208 | 68 | 132 | 2 | 0 | 1 | 0 | 0 | 0 | 0 | – |
| 1979 | 12 | 10 | .545 | 4.36 | 33 | 29 | 7 | 196 | 201 | 73 | 109 | 0 | 1 | 0 | 0 | 0 | 0 | 0 | – |
| 1980 | 13 | 11 | .542 | 4.48 | 32 | 31 | 13 | 199 | 201 | 68 | 97 | 1 | 1 | 0 | 0 | 0 | 0 | 0 | – |
| 1981 | 12 | 9 | .571 | 3.04 | 24 | 24 | 8 | 166 | 152 | 52 | 79 | 1 | 0 | 0 | 0 | 0 | 0 | 0 | – |
| 1982 | 12 | 10 | .545 | 3.62 | 29 | 29 | 9 | 193.2 | 187 | 85 | 112 | 1 | 0 | 0 | 0 | 0 | 0 | 0 | – |
| 1983 | 11 | 10 | .524 | 3.97 | 26 | 26 | 9 | 186 | 164 | 74 | 101 | 2 | 0 | 0 | 0 | 0 | 0 | 0 | – |
| 1984 | 17 | 8 | .680 | 4.00 | 33 | 33 | 0 | 193.2 | 183 | 66 | 119 | 0 | 0 | 0 | 0 | 0 | 0 | 0 | – |
| 1985 | 1 | 3 | .250 | 4.85 | 8 | 8 | 0 | 39 | 54 | 21 | 20 | 0 | 0 | 0 | 0 | 0 | 0 | 0 | – |
| 15 yrs. | 119 | 105 | .531 | 4.04 | 381 | 273 | 73 | 1959 | 1917 | 742 | 1111 | 10 | 7 | 6 | 6 | 62 | 11 | 0 | .177 |
| 1 yr. | 0 | 1 | .000 | 5.68 | 25 | 0 | 0 | 38 | 50 | 17 | 21 | 0 | 0 | 1 | 0 | 3 | 1 | 0 | .333 |

LEAGUE CHAMPIONSHIP SERIES

| | W | L | PCT | ERA | G | GS | CG | IP | H | BB | SO | ShO | W | L | SV | AB | H | HR | BA |
|---|---|---|---|---|---|---|---|---|---|---|---|---|---|---|---|---|---|---|---|
| 1970 CIN N | 1 | 0 | 1.000 | 0.00 | 1 | 0 | 0 | 3 | 1 | 2 | 5 | 0 | 0 | 0 | 0 | 0 | 0 | 0 | – |
| 1984 DET A | 1 | 0 | 1.000 | 0.00 | 1 | 1 | 0 | 8 | 2 | 2 | 8 | 0 | 0 | 0 | 0 | 0 | 0 | 0 | – |
| 2 yrs. | 2 | 0 | 1.000 | 0.00 | 2 | 1 | 0 | 11 | 3 | 4 | 13 | 0 | 1 | 0 | 0 | 0 | 0 | 0 | – |

WORLD SERIES

| | W | L | PCT | ERA | G | GS | CG | IP | H | BB | SO | ShO | W | L | SV | AB | H | HR | BA |
|---|---|---|---|---|---|---|---|---|---|---|---|---|---|---|---|---|---|---|---|
| 1970 CIN N | 0 | 1 | .000 | 9.00 | 2 | 0 | 0 | 2 | 3 | 0 | 2 | 0 | 0 | 0 | 0 | 0 | 0 | 0 | – |
| 1984 DET A | 1 | 0 | 1.000 | 1.50 | 1 | 1 | 0 | 6 | 7 | 2 | 4 | 0 | 0 | 0 | 0 | 0 | 0 | 0 | – |
| 2 yrs. | 1 | 1 | .500 | 3.38 | 3 | 1 | 0 | 8 | 10 | 2 | 6 | 0 | 0 | 0 | 0 | 0 | 0 | 0 | – |

## Hoyt Wilhelm

**WILHELM, JAMES HOYT**      BR TR 6'   190 lbs.
B. July 26, 1923, Huntersville, N. C.
Hall of Fame 1985.

| | W | L | PCT | ERA | G | GS | CG | IP | H | BB | SO | ShO | W | L | SV | AB | H | HR | BA |
|---|---|---|---|---|---|---|---|---|---|---|---|---|---|---|---|---|---|---|---|
| 1952 NY N | 15 | 3 | .833 | 2.43 | 71 | 0 | 0 | 159.1 | 127 | 57 | 108 | 0 | 15 | 3 | 11 | 38 | 6 | 1 | .158 |
| 1953 | 7 | 8 | .467 | 3.04 | 68 | 0 | 0 | 145 | 127 | 77 | 71 | 0 | 7 | 8 | 15 | 33 | 5 | 0 | .152 |
| 1954 | 12 | 4 | .750 | 2.10 | 57 | 0 | 0 | 111.1 | 77 | 52 | 64 | 0 | 12 | 4 | 7 | 21 | 1 | 0 | .048 |
| 1955 | 4 | 1 | .800 | 3.93 | 59 | 0 | 0 | 103 | 104 | 40 | 71 | 0 | 4 | 1 | 0 | 19 | 3 | 0 | .158 |
| 1956 | 4 | 9 | .308 | 3.83 | 64 | 0 | 0 | 89.1 | 97 | 43 | 71 | 0 | 4 | 9 | 8 | 9 | 2 | 0 | .222 |
| 1957 2 teams | | | STL | N (40G 1–4) | | | CLE | A (2G 1–0) | | | | | | | | | | | |
| " total | 2 | 4 | .333 | 4.14 | 42 | 0 | 0 | 58.2 | 54 | 22 | 29 | 0 | 2 | 4 | 12 | 6 | 0 | 0 | .000 |
| 1958 2 teams | | | CLE | A (30G 2–7) | | | BAL | A (9G 1–3) | | | | | | | | | | | |
| " total | 3 | 10 | .231 | 2.34 | 39 | 10 | 4 | 131 | 95 | 45 | 92 | 1 | 2 | 4 | 5 | 32 | 3 | 0 | .094 |
| 1959 BAL A | 15 | 11 | .577 | 2.19 | 32 | 27 | 13 | 226 | 178 | 77 | 139 | 3 | 0 | 1 | 0 | 76 | 4 | 0 | .053 |
| 1960 | 11 | 8 | .579 | 3.31 | 41 | 11 | 3 | 147 | 125 | 39 | 107 | 1 | 7 | 5 | 7 | 42 | 3 | 0 | .071 |
| 1961 | 9 | 7 | .563 | 2.30 | 51 | 1 | 0 | 109.2 | 89 | 41 | 87 | 0 | 9 | 7 | 18 | 20 | 1 | 0 | .050 |
| 1962 | 7 | 10 | .412 | 1.94 | 52 | 0 | 0 | 93 | 64 | 34 | 90 | 0 | 7 | 10 | 15 | 16 | 2 | 0 | .125 |
| 1963 CHI A | 5 | 8 | .385 | 2.64 | 55 | 3 | 0 | 136.1 | 106 | 30 | 111 | 0 | 5 | 7 | 21 | 29 | 2 | 0 | .069 |
| 1964 | 12 | 9 | .571 | 1.99 | 73 | 0 | 0 | 131.1 | 94 | 30 | 95 | 0 | 12 | 9 | 27 | 21 | 3 | 0 | .143 |
| 1965 | 7 | 7 | .500 | 1.81 | 66 | 0 | 0 | 144 | 88 | 32 | 106 | 0 | 7 | 7 | 20 | 22 | 0 | 0 | .000 |
| 1966 | 5 | 2 | .714 | 1.66 | 46 | 0 | 0 | 81.1 | 50 | 17 | 61 | 0 | 5 | 2 | 6 | 8 | 1 | 0 | .125 |
| 1967 | 8 | 3 | .727 | 1.31 | 49 | 0 | 0 | 89 | 58 | 34 | 76 | 0 | 8 | 3 | 12 | 13 | 1 | 0 | .077 |
| 1968 | 4 | 4 | .500 | 1.73 | 72 | 0 | 0 | 93.2 | 69 | 24 | 72 | 0 | 4 | 4 | 12 | 3 | 0 | 0 | .000 |
| 1969 2 teams | | | CAL | A (44G 5–7) | | | ATL | N (8G 2–0) | | | | | | | | | | | |
| " total | 7 | 7 | .500 | 2.20 | 52 | 0 | 0 | 77.2 | 50 | 22 | 67 | 0 | 7 | 7 | 14 | 9 | 0 | 0 | .000 |
| 1970 2 teams | | | ATL | N (50G 6–4) | | | CHI | N (3G 0–1) | | | | | | | | | | | |
| " total | 6 | 5 | .545 | 3.40 | 53 | 0 | 0 | 82 | 73 | 42 | 68 | 0 | 6 | 5 | 13 | 11 | 1 | 0 | .091 |
| 1971 2 teams | | | ATL | N (3G 0–0) | | | LA | N (9G 0–1) | | | | | | | | | | | |
| " total | 0 | 1 | .000 | 2.70 | 12 | 0 | 0 | 20 | 12 | 5 | 16 | 0 | 0 | 1 | 3 | 3 | 0 | 0 | .000 |
| 1972 LA N | 0 | 1 | .000 | 4.62 | 16 | 0 | 0 | 25.1 | 20 | 15 | 9 | 0 | 0 | 1 | 0 | 1 | 0 | 0 | .000 |
| 21 yrs. | 143 | 122 | .540 | 2.52 | 1070 1st | 52 | 20 | 2254 | 1757 | 778 | 1610 | 5 | 123 1st | 102 | 227 5th | 432 | 38 | 1 | .088 |
| 1 yr. | 0 | 1 | .000 | 9.82 | 3 | 0 | 0 | 3.2 | 4 | 3 | 1 | 0 | 0 | 1 | 0 | 0 | 0 | 0 | – |

WORLD SERIES

| | W | L | PCT | ERA | G | GS | CG | IP | H | BB | SO | ShO | W | L | SV | AB | H | HR | BA |
|---|---|---|---|---|---|---|---|---|---|---|---|---|---|---|---|---|---|---|---|
| 1954 NY N | 0 | 0 | – | 0.00 | 2 | 0 | 0 | 2.1 | 1 | 0 | 3 | 0 | 0 | 0 | 0 | 1 | 0 | 0 | .000 |

| | W | L | PCT | ERA | G | GS | CG | IP | H | BB | SO | ShO | Relief Pitching W | L | SV | BATTING AB | H | HR | BA |
|---|---|---|---|---|---|---|---|---|---|---|---|---|---|---|---|---|---|---|---|

# Pop Williams

**WILLIAMS, WALTER MERRILL**    BR TR 5'11" 190 lbs.
B. May 19, 1874, Bowdoinham, Me.    D. Aug. 4, 1959, Topsham, Me.

| | W | L | PCT | ERA | G | GS | CG | IP | H | BB | SO | ShO | W | L | SV | AB | H | HR | BA |
|---|---|---|---|---|---|---|---|---|---|---|---|---|---|---|---|---|---|---|---|
| 1898 **WAS N** | 0 | 2 | .000 | 8.47 | 2 | 2 | 2 | 17 | 32 | 7 | 3 | 0 | 0 | 0 | 0 | 8 | 3 | 0 | .375 |
| 1902 **CHI N** | 12 | 16 | .429 | 2.51 | 31 | 31 | 26 | 254.1 | 259 | 63 | 94 | 1 | 0 | 0 | 0 | 116 | 23 | 0 | .198 |
| 1903 **3 teams** | | | **CHI N** (1G 0–1) | | | | **PHI N** (2G 1–1) | | | **BOS N** (10G 4–5) | | | | | | | | | |
| " total | 5 | 7 | .417 | 3.99 | 13 | 13 | 12 | 106 | 127 | 43 | 30 | 1 | 0 | 0 | 0 | 51 | 12 | 0 | .235 |
| 3 yrs. | 17 | 25 | .405 | 3.20 | 46 | 46 | 40 | 377.1 | 418 | 113 | 127 | 2 | 0 | 0 | 0 | 175 | 38 | 0 | .217 |
| 2 yrs. | 12 | 17 | .414 | 2.57 | 32 | 32 | 27 | 259.1 | 268 | 63 | 96 | 1 | 0 | 0 | 0 | 118 | 23 | 0 | .195 |

# Wash Williams

**WILLIAMS, WASHINGTON J.**    5'11" 180 lbs.
B. Philadelphia, Pa.    D. Jan. 9, 1890, Philadelphia, Pa.

| | W | L | PCT | ERA | G | GS | CG | IP | H | BB | SO | ShO | W | L | SV | AB | H | HR | BA |
|---|---|---|---|---|---|---|---|---|---|---|---|---|---|---|---|---|---|---|---|
| 1885 **CHI N** | 0 | 0 | – | 13.50 | 1 | 1 | 0 | 2 | 2 | 5 | 0 | 0 | 0 | 0 | 0 | * | | | |

# Ned Williamson

**WILLIAMSON, EDWARD NAGLE**    BR TR 5'11" 170 lbs.
B. Oct. 24, 1857, Philadelphia, Pa.    D. Mar. 3, 1894, Hot Springs, Ark.

| | W | L | PCT | ERA | G | GS | CG | IP | H | BB | SO | ShO | W | L | SV | AB | H | HR | BA |
|---|---|---|---|---|---|---|---|---|---|---|---|---|---|---|---|---|---|---|---|
| 1881 **CHI N** | 1 | 1 | .500 | 2.00 | 3 | 1 | 1 | 18 | 14 | 0 | 2 | 0 | 0 | 0 | 0 | 343 | 92 | 1 | .268 |
| 1882 | 0 | 0 | – | 6.00 | 1 | 0 | 0 | 3 | 9 | 1 | 0 | 0 | 0 | 0 | 0 | 348 | 98 | 3 | .282 |
| 1883 | 0 | 0 | – | 9.00 | 1 | 0 | 0 | 1 | 1 | 1 | 1 | 0 | 0 | 0 | 0 | 402 | 111 | 2 | .276 |
| 1884 | 0 | 0 | – | 18.00 | 2 | 0 | 0 | 2 | 8 | 2 | 0 | 0 | 0 | 0 | 0 | 417 | 116 | 27 | .278 |
| 1885 | 0 | 0 | – | 0.00 | 2 | 0 | 0 | 6 | 2 | 0 | 3 | 0 | 0 | 0 | 2 | 407 | 97 | 3 | .238 |
| 1886 | 0 | 0 | – | 0.00 | 2 | 0 | 0 | 2 | 1 | 0 | 1 | 0 | 0 | 0 | 1 | 430 | 93 | 6 | .216 |
| 1887 | 0 | 0 | – | 9.00 | 1 | 0 | 0 | 2 | 3 | 1 | 0 | 0 | 0 | 0 | 0 | 439 | 117 | 9 | .267 |
| 7 yrs. | 1 | 1 | .500 | 3.34 | 12 | 1 | 1 | 35 | 38 | 5 | 7 | 0 | 0 | 0 | 3 | * | | | |
| 7 yrs. | 1 | 1 | .500 | 3.34 | 12 | 1 | 1 | 35 | 38 | 5 | 7 | 0 | 0 | 0 | 3 | 4042 | 1050 | 61 | .260 |

# Jim Willis

**WILLIS, JAMES GLADDEN**    BL TR 6'3" 175 lbs.
B. Mar. 20, 1927, Doyline, La.

| | W | L | PCT | ERA | G | GS | CG | IP | H | BB | SO | ShO | W | L | SV | AB | H | HR | BA |
|---|---|---|---|---|---|---|---|---|---|---|---|---|---|---|---|---|---|---|---|
| 1953 **CHI N** | 2 | 1 | .667 | 3.12 | 13 | 3 | 2 | 43.1 | 37 | 17 | 15 | 0 | 0 | 0 | 0 | 9 | 0 | 0 | .000 |
| 1954 | 0 | 1 | .000 | 3.91 | 14 | 1 | 0 | 23 | 22 | 18 | 5 | 0 | 0 | 0 | 0 | 5 | 0 | 0 | .000 |
| 2 yrs. | 2 | 2 | .500 | 3.39 | 27 | 4 | 2 | 66.1 | 59 | 35 | 20 | 0 | 0 | 0 | 0 | 14 | 0 | 0 | .000 |
| 2 yrs. | 2 | 2 | .500 | 3.39 | 27 | 4 | 2 | 66.1 | 59 | 35 | 20 | 0 | 0 | 0 | 0 | 14 | 0 | 0 | .000 |

# Harry Wolter

**WOLTER, HARRY MEIGS**    BL TL 5'10" 175 lbs.
B. July 11, 1884, Monterey, Calif.    D. July 7, 1970, Palo Alto, Calif.

| | W | L | PCT | ERA | G | GS | CG | IP | H | BB | SO | ShO | W | L | SV | AB | H | HR | BA |
|---|---|---|---|---|---|---|---|---|---|---|---|---|---|---|---|---|---|---|---|
| 1907 **3 teams** | | | **CIN N** (0G 0–0) | | | | **PIT N** (1G 0–0) | | | **STL N** (3G 1–2) | | | | | | | | | |
| " total | 1 | 2 | .333 | 4.32 | 4 | 3 | 1 | 25 | 30 | 20 | 8 | 0 | 0 | 0 | 0 | 63 | 18 | 0 | .286 |
| 1909 **BOS A** | 4 | 4 | .500 | 3.91 | 10 | 6 | 0 | 53 | 53 | 28 | 20 | 0 | 1 | 1 | 0 | 119 | 29 | 2 | .244 |
| 2 yrs. | 5 | 6 | .455 | 4.04 | 14 | 9 | 1 | 78 | 83 | 48 | 28 | 0 | 1 | 1 | 0 | * | | | |

# Walt Woods

**WOODS, WALTER SYDNEY**    TR 5'9½" 165 lbs.
B. Apr. 28, 1875, Rye, N. H.    D. Oct. 30, 1951, Portsmouth, N. H.

| | W | L | PCT | ERA | G | GS | CG | IP | H | BB | SO | ShO | W | L | SV | AB | H | HR | BA |
|---|---|---|---|---|---|---|---|---|---|---|---|---|---|---|---|---|---|---|---|
| 1898 **CHI N** | 9 | 13 | .409 | 3.14 | 27 | 22 | 18 | 215 | 224 | 59 | 26 | 3 | 0 | 1 | 0 | 154 | 27 | 0 | .175 |
| 1899 **LOU N** | 9 | 13 | .409 | 3.28 | 26 | 21 | 17 | 186.1 | 216 | 37 | 21 | 0 | 2 | 1 | 0 | 126 | 19 | 1 | .151 |
| 1900 **PIT N** | 0 | 0 | – | 21.00 | 1 | 0 | 0 | 3 | 9 | 1 | 1 | 0 | 0 | 0 | 0 | 1 | 0 | 0 | .000 |
| 3 yrs. | 18 | 26 | .409 | 3.34 | 54 | 43 | 35 | 404.1 | 449 | 97 | 48 | 3 | 2 | 2 | 0 | * | | | |
| 1 yr. | 9 | 13 | .409 | 3.14 | 27 | 22 | 18 | 215 | 224 | 59 | 26 | 3 | 0 | 1 | 0 | 154 | 27 | 0 | .175 |

# Bob Wright

**WRIGHT, ROBERT CASSIUS**    BR TR 6'1½" 175 lbs.
B. Dec. 13, 1891, Greensburg, Ind.

| | W | L | PCT | ERA | G | GS | CG | IP | H | BB | SO | ShO | W | L | SV | AB | H | HR | BA |
|---|---|---|---|---|---|---|---|---|---|---|---|---|---|---|---|---|---|---|---|
| 1915 **CHI N** | 0 | 0 | – | 2.25 | 2 | 0 | 0 | 4 | 6 | 0 | 3 | 0 | 0 | 0 | 0 | 0 | 0 | 0 | |

# Dave Wright

**WRIGHT, DAVID WILLIAM**    BR TR 6' 185 lbs.
B. Aug. 27, 1875, Dennison, Ohio    D. Jan. 18, 1946, Dennison, Ohio

| | W | L | PCT | ERA | G | GS | CG | IP | H | BB | SO | ShO | W | L | SV | AB | H | HR | BA |
|---|---|---|---|---|---|---|---|---|---|---|---|---|---|---|---|---|---|---|---|
| 1895 **PIT N** | 0 | 0 | – | 27.00 | 1 | 0 | 0 | 2 | 6 | 1 | 0 | 0 | 0 | 0 | 0 | 1 | 0 | 0 | .000 |
| 1897 **CHI N** | 1 | 0 | 1.000 | 15.43 | 1 | 1 | 1 | 7 | 17 | 2 | 4 | 0 | 0 | 0 | 0 | 3 | 1 | 0 | .333 |
| 2 yrs. | 1 | 0 | 1.000 | 18.00 | 2 | 1 | 1 | 9 | 23 | 3 | 4 | 0 | 0 | 0 | 0 | 4 | 1 | 0 | .250 |
| 1 yr. | 1 | 0 | 1.000 | 15.43 | 1 | 1 | 1 | 7 | 17 | 2 | 4 | 0 | 0 | 0 | 0 | 3 | 1 | 0 | .333 |

# Mel Wright

**WRIGHT, MELVIN JAMES**    BR TR 6'3" 210 lbs.
B. May 11, 1928, Manila, Ark.    D. May 16, 1983, Houston, Tex.

| | W | L | PCT | ERA | G | GS | CG | IP | H | BB | SO | ShO | W | L | SV | AB | H | HR | BA |
|---|---|---|---|---|---|---|---|---|---|---|---|---|---|---|---|---|---|---|---|
| 1954 **STL N** | 0 | 0 | – | 10.45 | 9 | 0 | 0 | 10.1 | 16 | 11 | 4 | 0 | 0 | 0 | 0 | 1 | 0 | 0 | .000 |
| 1955 | 2 | 2 | .500 | 6.19 | 29 | 0 | 0 | 36.1 | 44 | 9 | 18 | 0 | 2 | 2 | 1 | 6 | 0 | 0 | .000 |
| 1960 **CHI N** | 0 | 1 | .000 | 4.96 | 9 | 0 | 0 | 16.1 | 17 | 3 | 8 | 0 | 0 | 1 | 2 | 2 | 0 | 0 | .000 |
| 1961 | 0 | 1 | .000 | 10.71 | 11 | 0 | 0 | 21 | 42 | 4 | 6 | 0 | 0 | 1 | 0 | 2 | 0 | 0 | .000 |
| 4 yrs. | 2 | 4 | .333 | 7.61 | 58 | 0 | 0 | 84 | 119 | 27 | 36 | 0 | 2 | 4 | 3 | 11 | 0 | 0 | .000 |
| 2 yrs. | 0 | 2 | .000 | 8.20 | 20 | 0 | 0 | 37.1 | 59 | 7 | 14 | 0 | 0 | 2 | 2 | 4 | 0 | 0 | .000 |

# Hank Wyse

**WYSE, HENRY WASHINGTON (Hooks)**    BR TR 5'11½" 185 lbs.
B. Mar. 1, 1918, Lunsford, Ark.

| | W | L | PCT | ERA | G | GS | CG | IP | H | BB | SO | ShO | W | L | SV | AB | H | HR | BA |
|---|---|---|---|---|---|---|---|---|---|---|---|---|---|---|---|---|---|---|---|
| 1942 **CHI N** | 2 | 1 | .667 | 1.93 | 4 | 4 | 1 | 28 | 33 | 6 | 8 | 1 | 0 | 0 | 0 | 8 | 1 | 0 | .125 |
| 1943 | 9 | 7 | .563 | 2.94 | 38 | 15 | 8 | 156 | 160 | 34 | 45 | 2 | 1 | 2 | 5 | 50 | 4 | 0 | .080 |
| 1944 | 16 | 15 | .516 | 3.15 | 41 | 34 | 14 | 257.1 | 277 | 57 | 86 | 3 | 2 | 1 | 1 | 90 | 16 | 0 | .178 |
| 1945 | 22 | 10 | .688 | 2.68 | 38 | 34 | 23 | 278.1 | 272 | 55 | 77 | 2 | 1 | 0 | 0 | 101 | 17 | 0 | .168 |
| 1946 | 14 | 12 | .538 | 2.68 | 40 | 27 | 12 | 201.1 | 206 | 52 | 52 | 2 | 0 | 0 | 1 | 74 | 18 | 0 | .243 |
| 1947 | 6 | 9 | .400 | 4.31 | 37 | 19 | 5 | 142 | 158 | 64 | 53 | 1 | 1 | 0 | 1 | 45 | 5 | 0 | .111 |
| 1950 **PHI A** | 9 | 14 | .391 | 5.85 | 41 | 23 | 4 | 170.2 | 192 | 87 | 33 | 0 | 1 | 4 | 0 | 59 | 9 | 0 | .153 |

| | W | L | PCT | ERA | G | GS | CG | IP | H | BB | SO | ShO | Relief Pitching W | L | SV | BATTING AB | H | HR | BA |
|---|---|---|---|---|---|---|---|---|---|---|---|---|---|---|---|---|---|---|---|

## Hank Wyse continued

| | W | L | PCT | ERA | G | GS | CG | IP | H | BB | SO | ShO | W | L | SV | AB | H | HR | BA |
|---|---|---|---|---|---|---|---|---|---|---|---|---|---|---|---|---|---|---|---|
| 1951 **2 teams** | PHI | A | (9G 1–2) | **WAS** | **A** | (3G 0–0) | | | | | | | | | | | | | |
| " **total** | 1 | 2 | .333 | 8.63 | 12 | 3 | 0 | 24 | 41 | 18 | 8 | 0 | 1 | 1 | 0 | 8 | 1 | 0 | .125 |
| 8 yrs. | 79 | 70 | .530 | 3.52 | 251 | 159 | 67 | 1257.2 | 1339 | 373 | 362 | 11 | 7 | 8 | 8 | 435 | 71 | 0 | .163 |
| 6 yrs. | 69 | 54 | .561 | 3.03 | 198 | 133 | 63 | 1063 | 1106 | 268 | 321 | 11 | 5 | 3 | 8 | 368 | 61 | 0 | .166 |
| WORLD SERIES | | | | | | | | | | | | | | | | | | | |
| 1945 CHI N | 0 | 1 | .000 | 7.04 | 3 | 1 | 0 | 7.2 | 8 | 4 | 1 | 0 | 0 | 0 | 0 | 3 | 0 | 0 | .000 |

## Carroll Yerkes

**YERKES, CHARLES CARROLL (Lefty)**   BR TL 5'11" 162 lbs.
B. June 13, 1903, McSherrystown, Pa.   D. Dec. 20, 1950, Oakland, Calif.

| | W | L | PCT | ERA | G | GS | CG | IP | H | BB | SO | ShO | W | L | SV | AB | H | HR | BA |
|---|---|---|---|---|---|---|---|---|---|---|---|---|---|---|---|---|---|---|---|
| 1927 PHI A | 0 | 0 | – | 0.00 | 1 | 0 | 0 | 1 | 0 | 1 | 0 | 0 | 0 | 0 | 0 | 0 | 0 | 0 | – |
| 1928 | 0 | 1 | .000 | 2.08 | 2 | 1 | 1 | 8.2 | 7 | 2 | 1 | 0 | 0 | 0 | 0 | 3 | 0 | 0 | .000 |
| 1929 | 1 | 0 | 1.000 | 4.58 | 19 | 2 | 0 | 37.1 | 47 | 13 | 11 | 0 | 1 | 0 | 1 | 10 | 0 | 0 | .000 |
| 1932 CHI N | 0 | 0 | – | 3.00 | 2 | 0 | 0 | 9 | 5 | 3 | 4 | 0 | 0 | 0 | 0 | 3 | 1 | 0 | .333 |
| 1933 | 0 | 0 | – | 4.50 | 1 | 0 | 0 | 2 | 2 | 1 | 0 | 0 | 0 | 0 | 0 | 0 | 0 | 0 | – |
| 5 yrs. | 1 | 1 | .500 | 3.88 | 25 | 3 | 1 | 58 | 61 | 20 | 16 | 0 | 1 | 0 | 1 | 16 | 1 | 0 | .063 |
| 2 yrs. | 0 | 0 | – | 3.27 | 3 | 0 | 0 | 11 | 7 | 4 | 4 | 0 | 0 | 0 | 0 | 3 | 1 | 0 | .333 |

## Lefty York

**YORK, JAMES EDWARD**   BL TL 5'10" 185 lbs.
B. Nov. 1, 1892, West Fork, Ark.   D. Apr. 9, 1961, York, Pa.

| | W | L | PCT | ERA | G | GS | CG | IP | H | BB | SO | ShO | W | L | SV | AB | H | HR | BA |
|---|---|---|---|---|---|---|---|---|---|---|---|---|---|---|---|---|---|---|---|
| 1919 PHI A | 0 | 2 | .000 | 24.92 | 2 | 2 | 0 | 4.1 | 13 | 5 | 2 | 0 | 0 | 0 | 0 | 1 | 0 | 0 | .000 |
| 1921 CHI N | 5 | 9 | .357 | 4.73 | 40 | 10 | 4 | 139 | 170 | 63 | 57 | 1 | 4 | 0 | 1 | 39 | 5 | 0 | .128 |
| 2 yrs. | 5 | 11 | .313 | 5.34 | 42 | 12 | 4 | 143.1 | 183 | 68 | 59 | 1 | 4 | 0 | 1 | 40 | 5 | 0 | .125 |
| 1 yr. | 5 | 9 | .357 | 4.73 | 40 | 10 | 4 | 139 | 170 | 63 | 57 | 1 | 4 | 0 | 1 | 39 | 5 | 0 | .128 |

## Gus Yost

**YOST, GUS**   6'5"
B. Toronto, Ont., Canada   D. Oct. 16, 1895, Toronto, Ont., Canada

| | W | L | PCT | ERA | G | GS | CG | IP | H | BB | SO | ShO | W | L | SV | AB | H | HR | BA |
|---|---|---|---|---|---|---|---|---|---|---|---|---|---|---|---|---|---|---|---|
| 1893 CHI N | 0 | 1 | .000 | 13.50 | 1 | 1 | 0 | 2.2 | 3 | 8 | 1 | 0 | 0 | 0 | 0 | 1 | 0 | 0 | .000 |

## Zip Zabel

**ZABEL, GEORGE WASHINGTON**   BR TR 6'1½" 185 lbs.
B. Feb. 18, 1891, Wetmore, Kans.   D. May 31, 1970, Beloit, Wis.

| | W | L | PCT | ERA | G | GS | CG | IP | H | BB | SO | ShO | W | L | SV | AB | H | HR | BA |
|---|---|---|---|---|---|---|---|---|---|---|---|---|---|---|---|---|---|---|---|
| 1913 CHI N | 1 | 0 | 1.000 | 0.00 | 1 | 1 | 0 | 5 | 3 | 1 | 0 | 0 | 0 | 0 | 0 | 2 | 0 | 0 | .000 |
| 1914 | 4 | 4 | .500 | 2.18 | 29 | 7 | 2 | 128 | 104 | 45 | 50 | 0 | 2 | 0 | 1 | 38 | 7 | 0 | .184 |
| 1915 | 7 | 10 | .412 | 3.20 | 36 | 17 | 8 | 163 | 124 | 84 | 60 | 3 | 2 | 2 | 0 | 54 | 4 | 0 | .074 |
| 3 yrs. | 12 | 14 | .462 | 2.71 | 66 | 25 | 10 | 296 | 231 | 130 | 110 | 3 | 4 | 2 | 1 | 94 | 11 | 0 | .117 |
| 3 yrs. | 12 | 14 | .462 | 2.71 | 66 | 25 | 10 | 296 | 231 | 130 | 110 | 3 | 4 | 2 | 1 | 94 | 11 | 0 | .117 |

## Geoff Zahn

**ZAHN, GEOFFREY CLAYTON**   BL TL 6'1" 180 lbs.
B. Dec. 19, 1946, Baltimore, Md.

| | W | L | PCT | ERA | G | GS | CG | IP | H | BB | SO | ShO | W | L | SV | AB | H | HR | BA |
|---|---|---|---|---|---|---|---|---|---|---|---|---|---|---|---|---|---|---|---|
| 1973 LA N | 1 | 0 | 1.000 | 1.35 | 6 | 1 | 0 | 13.1 | 5 | 2 | 9 | 0 | 0 | 0 | 0 | 2 | 0 | 0 | .000 |
| 1974 | 3 | 5 | .375 | 2.03 | 21 | 10 | 1 | 80 | 78 | 16 | 33 | 0 | 0 | 1 | 0 | 23 | 4 | 0 | .174 |
| 1975 **2 teams** | LA | N | (2G 0–1) | CHI | N | (16G 2–7) | | | | | | | | | | | | | |
| " **total** | 2 | 8 | .200 | 4.66 | 18 | 10 | 0 | 65.2 | 69 | 31 | 22 | 0 | 2 | 1 | 1 | 15 | 2 | 0 | .133 |
| 1976 CHI N | 0 | 1 | .000 | 11.25 | 3 | 2 | 0 | 8 | 16 | 2 | 4 | 0 | 0 | 0 | 0 | 3 | 0 | 0 | .000 |
| 1977 MIN A | 12 | 14 | .462 | 4.68 | 34 | 32 | 7 | 198 | 234 | 66 | 88 | 1 | 0 | 0 | 0 | 0 | 0 | 0 | – |
| 1978 | 14 | 14 | .500 | 3.03 | 35 | 35 | 12 | 252.1 | 260 | 81 | 106 | 1 | 0 | 0 | 0 | 0 | 0 | 0 | – |
| 1979 | 13 | 7 | .650 | 3.57 | 26 | 24 | 4 | 169 | 181 | 41 | 58 | 0 | 0 | 0 | 0 | 0 | 0 | 0 | – |
| 1980 | 14 | 18 | .438 | 4.40 | 38 | 35 | 13 | 233 | 273 | 66 | 96 | 5 | 0 | 1 | 0 | 0 | 0 | 0 | – |
| 1981 CAL A | 10 | 11 | .476 | 4.42 | 25 | 25 | 9 | 161 | 181 | 43 | 52 | 0 | 0 | 0 | 0 | 0 | 0 | 0 | – |
| 1982 | 18 | 8 | .692 | 3.73 | 34 | 34 | 12 | 229.1 | 225 | 65 | 81 | 4 | 0 | 0 | 0 | 0 | 0 | 0 | – |
| 1983 | 9 | 11 | .450 | 3.33 | 29 | 28 | 11 | 203 | 212 | 51 | 81 | 3 | 0 | 0 | 0 | 0 | 0 | 0 | – |
| 1984 | 13 | 10 | .565 | 3.12 | 28 | 27 | 9 | 199.1 | 200 | 48 | 61 | 5 | 0 | 0 | 0 | 0 | 0 | 0 | – |
| 1985 | 2 | 2 | .500 | 4.38 | 7 | 7 | 1 | 37 | 44 | 14 | 14 | 1 | 0 | 0 | 0 | 0 | 0 | 0 | – |
| 13 yrs. | 111 | 109 | .505 | 3.74 | 304 | 270 | 79 | 1849 | 1978 | 526 | 705 | 20 | 2 | 3 | 1 | 43 | 6 | 0 | .140 |
| 2 yrs. | 2 | 8 | .200 | 5.22 | 19 | 12 | 0 | 70.2 | 83 | 28 | 25 | 0 | 2 | 0 | 1 | 18 | 2 | 0 | .111 |
| LEAGUE CHAMPIONSHIP SERIES | | | | | | | | | | | | | | | | | | | |
| 1982 CAL A | 0 | 1 | .000 | 7.36 | 1 | 1 | 0 | 3.2 | 4 | 1 | 2 | 0 | 0 | 0 | 0 | 0 | 0 | 0 | – |

## Oscar Zamora

**ZAMORA, OSCAR JOSE**   BR TR 5'10" 178 lbs.
B. Sept. 23, 1944, Camaguey, Cuba

| | W | L | PCT | ERA | G | GS | CG | IP | H | BB | SO | ShO | W | L | SV | AB | H | HR | BA |
|---|---|---|---|---|---|---|---|---|---|---|---|---|---|---|---|---|---|---|---|
| 1974 CHI N | 3 | 9 | .250 | 3.11 | 56 | 0 | 0 | 84 | 82 | 19 | 38 | 0 | 3 | 9 | 10 | 11 | 2 | 0 | .182 |
| 1975 | 5 | 2 | .714 | 5.07 | 52 | 0 | 0 | 71 | 84 | 15 | 28 | 0 | 5 | 2 | 10 | 6 | 1 | 0 | .167 |
| 1976 | 5 | 3 | .625 | 5.24 | 40 | 2 | 0 | 55 | 70 | 17 | 27 | 0 | 5 | 2 | 3 | 9 | 0 | 0 | .000 |
| 1978 HOU N | 0 | 0 | – | 7.20 | 10 | 0 | 0 | 15 | 20 | 7 | 6 | 0 | 0 | 0 | 0 | 2 | 0 | 0 | .000 |
| 4 yrs. | 13 | 14 | .481 | 4.52 | 158 | 2 | 0 | 225 | 256 | 58 | 99 | 0 | 13 | 13 | 23 | 28 | 3 | 0 | .107 |
| 3 yrs. | 13 | 14 | .481 | 4.33 | 148 | 2 | 0 | 210 | 236 | 51 | 93 | 0 | 13 | 13 | 23 | 26 | 3 | 0 | .115 |

## Bob Zick

**ZICK, ROBERT GEORGE**   BL TR 6' 168 lbs.
B. Apr. 26, 1927, Chicago, Ill.

| | W | L | PCT | ERA | G | GS | CG | IP | H | BB | SO | ShO | W | L | SV | AB | H | HR | BA |
|---|---|---|---|---|---|---|---|---|---|---|---|---|---|---|---|---|---|---|---|
| 1954 CHI N | 0 | 0 | – | 8.27 | 8 | 0 | 0 | 16.1 | 23 | 7 | 9 | 0 | 0 | 0 | 0 | 4 | 1 | 0 | .250 |

# Manager Register

The Manager Register is an alphabetical listing of every man who has managed the Chicago Cubs. Included are facts about the managers and their year-by-year managerial records for the regular season, League Championship Series, and the World Series.

Most of the information in this section is self-explanatory. That which is not is explained as follows:

*Games Managed* includes tie games.

*Lifetime Total*. The first total shown after the regular season's statistics is the manager's total lifetime record in the major leagues.

*Cubs Lifetime Total*. The second line is the manager's total lifetime record with the Cubs.

*Blank space* appearing beneath a team and league means that the team and league are the same.

*Standing*. The figures in this column indicate the standing of the team at the end of the season and when there was a managerial change. The four possible cases are as follows:

> *Only Manager for the Team That Year*. Indicated by a single bold-faced figure that appears in the extreme left-hand column and shows the final standing of the team.
>
> *Manager Started Season, But Did Not Finish*. Indicated by two figures: the first is bold-faced and shows the standing of the team when this manager left; the second shows the final standing of the team.

*Manager Finished Season, But Did Not Start.* Indicated by two figures: the first shows the standing of the team when this manager started; the second is bold-faced and shows the final standing of the team.

*Manager Did Not Start or Finish Season.* Indicated by three figures: the first shows the standing of the team when this manager started; the second is bold-faced and shows the standing of the team when this manager left; the third shows the final standing of the team.

*1981 Split Season Indicator.* The managers' records for the 1981 split season are given separately for each half. "(1st)" or "(2nd)" will appear to the right of the standings to indicate which half.

| | G | W | L | PCT | Standing | | | | G | W | L | PCT | Standing |
|---|---|---|---|---|---|---|---|---|---|---|---|---|---|

## Joey Amalfitano

**AMALFITANO, JOHN JOSEPH**
B. Jan. 23, 1934, San Pedro, Calif.

| | | G | W | L | PCT | Standing | |
|---|---|---|---|---|---|---|---|
| 1979 | CHI N | 7 | 2 | 5 | .286 | 5 | 5 |
| 1980 | | 72 | 26 | 46 | .361 | 6 | 6 |
| 1981 | | 54 | 15 | 37 | .288 | 6 | (1st) |
| 1981 | | 52 | 23 | 28 | .451 | 5 | (2nd) |
| 3 yrs. | | 185 | 66 | 116 | .363 | | |
| 4 yrs. | | 185 | 66 | 116 | .363 | | |

## Cap Anson

**ANSON, ADRIAN CONSTANTINE (Pop)**
B. Apr. 17, 1852, Marshalltown, Iowa
D. Apr. 14, 1922, Chicago, Ill.
Hall of Fame 1939.

| | | G | W | L | PCT | Standing | | |
|---|---|---|---|---|---|---|---|---|
| 1879 | CHI N | 83 | 46 | 33 | .582 | 4 | | |
| 1880 | | 86 | 67 | 17 | .798 | 1 | | |
| 1881 | | 84 | 56 | 28 | .667 | 1 | | |
| 1882 | | 84 | 55 | 29 | .655 | 1 | | |
| 1883 | | 98 | 59 | 39 | .602 | 2 | | |
| 1884 | | 113 | 62 | 50 | .554 | 4 | | |
| 1885 | | 113 | 87 | 25 | .777 | 1 | | |
| 1886 | | 126 | 90 | 34 | .726 | 1 | | |
| 1887 | | 127 | 71 | 50 | .587 | 3 | | |
| 1888 | | 135 | 77 | 58 | .570 | 2 | | |
| 1889 | | 136 | 67 | 65 | .508 | 3 | | |
| 1890 | | 139 | 84 | 53 | .613 | 2 | | |
| 1891 | | 137 | 82 | 53 | .607 | 2 | | |
| 1892 | | 147 | 70 | 76 | .479 | 7 | | |
| 1893 | | 128 | 56 | 71 | .441 | 9 | | |
| 1894 | | 135 | 57 | 75 | .432 | 8 | | |
| 1895 | | 133 | 72 | 58 | .554 | 4 | | |
| 1896 | | 132 | 71 | 57 | .555 | 5 | | |
| 1897 | | 138 | 59 | 73 | .447 | 9 | | |
| 1898 | NY N | 22 | 9 | 13 | .409 | 6 | 7 | 7 |
| 20 yrs. | | 2296 | 1297 | 957 | .575 | | | |
| 19 yrs. | | 2274 | 1288 | 944 | .577 | | | |

## Lou Boudreau

**BOUDREAU, LOUIS**
B. July 17, 1917, Harvey, Ill.
Hall of Fame 1970.

| | | G | W | L | PCT | Standing | |
|---|---|---|---|---|---|---|---|
| 1942 | CLE A | 156 | 75 | 79 | .487 | 4 | |
| 1943 | | 153 | 82 | 71 | .536 | 3 | |
| 1944 | | 155 | 72 | 82 | .468 | 5 | |
| 1945 | | 147 | 73 | 72 | .503 | 5 | |
| 1946 | | 156 | 68 | 86 | .442 | 6 | |
| 1947 | | 157 | 80 | 74 | .519 | 4 | |
| 1948 | | 156 | 97 | 58 | .626 | 1 | |
| 1949 | | 154 | 89 | 65 | .578 | 3 | |
| 1950 | | 155 | 92 | 62 | .597 | 4 | |
| 1952 | BOS A | 154 | 76 | 78 | .494 | 6 | |
| 1953 | | 153 | 84 | 69 | .549 | 4 | |
| 1954 | | 156 | 69 | 85 | .448 | 4 | |
| 1955 | KC A | 155 | 63 | 91 | .409 | 6 | |
| 1956 | | 154 | 52 | 102 | .338 | 8 | |
| 1957 | | 104 | 36 | 67 | .350 | 8 | 7 |
| 1960 | CHI N | 139 | 54 | 83 | .394 | 8 | 7 |
| 16 yrs. | | 2404 | 1162 | 1224 | .487 | | |
| 1 yr. | | 139 | 54 | 83 | .394 | | |

WORLD SERIES

| | | G | W | L | PCT | |
|---|---|---|---|---|---|---|
| 1948 | CLE A | 6 | 4 | 2 | .667 | |

## Roger Bresnahan

**BRESNAHAN, ROGER PHILIP (The Duke of Tralee)**
B. June 11, 1879, Toledo, Ohio
D. Dec. 4, 1944, Toledo, Ohio
Hall of Fame 1945.

| | | G | W | L | PCT | Standing | |
|---|---|---|---|---|---|---|---|
| 1909 | STL N | 154 | 54 | 98 | .355 | 7 | |
| 1910 | | 153 | 63 | 90 | .412 | 7 | |
| 1911 | | 158 | 75 | 74 | .503 | 5 | |
| 1912 | | 153 | 63 | 90 | .412 | 6 | |
| 1915 | CHI N | 156 | 73 | 80 | .477 | 4 | |
| 5 yrs. | | 774 | 328 | 432 | .432 | | |
| 1 yr. | | 156 | 73 | 80 | .477 | | |

## Tom Burns

**BURNS, THOMAS EVERETT**
B. Mar. 30, 1857, Honesdale, Pa.
D. Mar. 19, 1902, Jersey City, N. J.

| | | G | W | L | PCT | Standing | |
|---|---|---|---|---|---|---|---|
| 1892 | PIT N | 56 | 25 | 30 | .455 | 9 | 6 |
| 1898 | CHI N | 152 | 85 | 65 | .567 | 4 | |
| 1899 | | 152 | 75 | 73 | .507 | 8 | |
| 3 yrs. | | 360 | 185 | 168 | .524 | | |
| 2 yrs. | | 304 | 160 | 138 | .537 | | |

## Phil Cavarretta

**CAVARRETTA, PHILIP JOSEPH**
B. July 19, 1916, Chicago, Ill.

| | | G | W | L | PCT | Standing | |
|---|---|---|---|---|---|---|---|
| 1951 | CHI N | 74 | 27 | 47 | .365 | 7 | 8 |
| 1952 | | 155 | 77 | 77 | .500 | 5 | |
| 1953 | | 155 | 65 | 89 | .422 | 7 | |
| 3 yrs. | | 384 | 169 | 213 | .442 | | |
| 3 yrs. | | 384 | 169 | 213 | .442 | | |

## Frank Chance

**CHANCE, FRANK LEROY (Husk, The Peerless Leader)**
B. Sept. 9, 1877, Fresno, Calif.
D. Sept. 14, 1924, Los Angeles, Calif.
Hall of Fame 1946.

| | | G | W | L | PCT | Standing | |
|---|---|---|---|---|---|---|---|
| 1905 | CHI N | 65 | 40 | 23 | .635 | 4 | 3 |
| 1906 | | 154 | 116 | 36 | .763 | 1 | |
| 1907 | | 155 | 107 | 45 | .704 | 1 | |
| 1908 | | 158 | 99 | 55 | .643 | 1 | |
| 1909 | | 155 | 104 | 49 | .680 | 2 | |
| 1910 | | 154 | 104 | 50 | .675 | 1 | |
| 1911 | | 157 | 92 | 62 | .597 | 2 | |
| 1912 | | 152 | 91 | 59 | .607 | 3 | |
| 1913 | NY A | 153 | 57 | 94 | .377 | 7 | |
| 1914 | | 140 | 61 | 76 | .445 | 7 | 6 |
| 1923 | BOS A | 154 | 61 | 91 | .401 | 8 | |
| 11 yrs. | | 1597 | 932 | 640 | .593 | | |
| | | | | | | 6th | |
| 8 yrs. | | 1150 | 753 | 379 | .665 | | |

WORLD SERIES

| | | G | W | L | PCT | |
|---|---|---|---|---|---|---|
| 1906 | CHI N | 6 | 2 | 4 | .333 | |
| 1907 | | 5 | 4 | 0 | 1.000 | |
| 1908 | | 5 | 4 | 1 | .800 | |
| 1910 | | 5 | 1 | 4 | .200 | |
| 4 yrs. | | 21 | 11 | 9 | .550 | |
| | | | 9th | | 5th | |
| 4 yrs. | | 21 | 11 | 9 | .550 | |

## Harry Craft

**CRAFT, HARRY FRANCIS**
B. Apr. 19, 1915, Ellisville, Miss.

| | | G | W | L | PCT | Standing | | |
|---|---|---|---|---|---|---|---|---|
| 1957 | KC A | 50 | 23 | 27 | .460 | 8 | 7 | |
| 1958 | | 156 | 73 | 81 | .474 | 7 | | |
| 1959 | | 154 | 66 | 88 | .429 | 7 | | |
| 1961 | CHI N | 16 | 7 | 9 | .438 | 7 | 7 | 7 |
| 1962 | HOU N | 162 | 64 | 96 | .400 | 8 | | |
| 1963 | | 162 | 66 | 96 | .407 | 9 | | |
| 1964 | | 149 | 61 | 88 | .409 | 9 | 9 | |
| 7 yrs. | | 849 | 360 | 485 | .426 | | | |
| 1 yr. | | 16 | 7 | 9 | .438 | | | |

## Leo Durocher

**DUROCHER, LEO ERNEST (The Lip)**
B. July 27, 1905, W. Springfield, Mass.

| | | G | W | L | PCT | Standing | |
|---|---|---|---|---|---|---|---|
| 1939 | BKN N | 157 | 84 | 69 | .549 | 3 | |
| 1940 | | 156 | 88 | 65 | .575 | 2 | |
| 1941 | | 157 | 100 | 54 | .649 | 1 | |
| 1942 | | 155 | 104 | 50 | .675 | 2 | |
| 1943 | | 153 | 81 | 72 | .529 | 3 | |
| 1944 | | 155 | 63 | 91 | .409 | 7 | |
| 1945 | | 155 | 87 | 67 | .565 | 3 | |
| 1946 | | 157 | 96 | 60 | .615 | 2 | |
| 1948 | | 75 | 37 | 38 | .493 | 5 | 3 |
| 1948 | NY N | 79 | 41 | 38 | .519 | 4 | 5 |
| 1949 | | 156 | 73 | 81 | .474 | 5 | |

| | G | W | L | PCT | Standing | | |
|---|---|---|---|---|---|---|---|

## Leo Durocher continued

| | | | G | W | L | PCT | Standing | | |
|---|---|---|---|---|---|---|---|---|---|
| 1950 | | | 154 | 86 | 68 | .558 | 3 | | |
| 1951 | | | 157 | 98 | 59 | .624 | 1 | | |
| 1952 | | | 154 | 92 | 62 | .597 | 2 | | |
| 1953 | | | 155 | 70 | 84 | .455 | 5 | | |
| 1954 | | | 154 | 97 | 57 | .630 | 1 | | |
| 1955 | | | 154 | 80 | 74 | .519 | 3 | | |
| 1966 | CHI | N | 162 | 59 | 103 | .364 | 10 | | |
| 1967 | | | 162 | 87 | 74 | .540 | 3 | | |
| 1968 | | | 163 | 84 | 78 | .519 | 3 | | |
| 1969 | | | 163 | 92 | 70 | .568 | 2 | | |
| 1970 | | | 162 | 84 | 78 | .519 | 2 | | |
| 1971 | | | 162 | 83 | 79 | .512 | 3 | | |
| 1972 | | | 90 | 46 | 44 | .511 | 4 | 2 | |
| 1972 | HOU | N | 31 | 16 | 15 | .516 | 2 | 2 | |
| 1973 | | | 162 | 82 | 80 | .506 | 4 | | |
| 24 yrs. | | | 3740 | 2010 | 1710 | .540 | | | |
| | | | | 5th | 6th | 7th | | | |
| 7 yrs. | | | 1064 | 535 | 526 | .504 | | | |

WORLD SERIES

| | | | G | W | L | PCT | |
|---|---|---|---|---|---|---|---|
| 1941 | BKN | N | 5 | 1 | 4 | .200 | |
| 1951 | NY | N | 6 | 2 | 4 | .333 | |
| 1954 | | | 4 | 4 | 0 | 1.000 | |
| 3 yrs. | | | 15 | 7 | 8 | .467 | |

## Lee Elia

**ELIA, LEE CONSTANTINE**
B. July 16, 1937, Philadelphia, Pa.

| | | | G | W | L | PCT | Standing | |
|---|---|---|---|---|---|---|---|---|
| 1982 | CHI | N | 162 | 73 | 89 | .451 | 5 | |
| 1983 | | | 123 | 54 | 69 | .439 | 5 | 5 |
| 2 yrs. | | | 285 | 127 | 158 | .446 | | |
| 2 yrs. | | | 285 | 127 | 158 | .446 | | |

## Johnny Evers

**EVERS, JOHN JOSEPH (The Trojan, The Crab)**
Brother of Joe Evers.
B. July 21, 1881, Troy, N.Y.
D. Mar. 28, 1947, Albany, N.Y.
Hall of Fame 1946.

| | | | G | W | L | PCT | Standing | |
|---|---|---|---|---|---|---|---|---|
| 1913 | CHI | N | 154 | 88 | 65 | .575 | 3 | |
| 1921 | | | 98 | 42 | 56 | .429 | 7 | 7 |
| 1924 | CHI | A | 154 | 66 | 87 | .431 | 8 | |
| 3 yrs. | | | 406 | 196 | 208 | .485 | | |
| 2 yrs. | | | 252 | 130 | 121 | .518 | | |

## Bob Ferguson

**FERGUSON, ROBERT V. (Death to Flying Things)**
B. Jan. 31, 1845, Brooklyn, N.Y.
D. May 3, 1894, Brooklyn, N.Y.

| | | | G | W | L | PCT | Standing | | |
|---|---|---|---|---|---|---|---|---|---|
| 1876 | HAR | N | 69 | 47 | 21 | .691 | 3 | | |
| 1877 | | | 60 | 31 | 27 | .534 | 3 | | |
| 1878 | CHI | N | 61 | 30 | 30 | .500 | 4 | | |
| 1879 | TRO | N | 18 | 7 | 10 | .412 | 8 | 8 | |
| 1880 | | | 83 | 41 | 42 | .494 | 4 | | |
| 1881 | | | 85 | 39 | 45 | .464 | 5 | | |
| 1882 | | | 85 | 35 | 48 | .422 | 7 | | |
| 1883 | PHI | N | 17 | 4 | 13 | .235 | 8 | 8 | |
| 1884 | PIT | AA | 26 | 5 | 21 | .192 | 12 | 12 | 11 |
| 1886 | NY | AA | 119 | 47 | 70 | .402 | 8 | 7 | |
| 1887 | | | 30 | 6 | 24 | .200 | 8 | 7 | |
| 11 yrs. | | | 653 | 292 | 351 | .454 | | | |
| 1 yr. | | | 61 | 30 | 30 | .500 | | | |

## Charlie Fox

**FOX, CHARLES FRANCIS (Irish)**
B. Oct. 7, 1921, New York, N.Y.

| | | | G | W | L | PCT | Standing | | |
|---|---|---|---|---|---|---|---|---|---|
| 1970 | SF | N | 118 | 67 | 51 | .568 | 5 | 3 | |
| 1971 | | | 162 | 90 | 72 | .556 | 1 | | |
| 1972 | | | 155 | 69 | 86 | .445 | 5 | | |
| 1973 | | | 162 | 88 | 74 | .543 | 3 | | |
| 1974 | | | 76 | 34 | 42 | .447 | 5 | 5 | |
| 1976 | MON | N | 34 | 12 | 22 | .353 | 6 | 6 | |
| 1983 | CHI | N | 39 | 17 | 22 | .436 | 5 | 5 | |
| 7 yrs. | | | 746 | 377 | 369 | .505 | | | |
| 1 yr. | | | 39 | 17 | 22 | .436 | | | |

## Charlie Fox continued

LEAGUE CHAMPIONSHIP SERIES

| | | | G | W | L | PCT | |
|---|---|---|---|---|---|---|---|
| 1971 | SF | N | 4 | 1 | 3 | .250 | |

## Herman Franks

**FRANKS, HERMAN LOUIS**
B. Jan. 4, 1914, Price, Utah

| | | | G | W | L | PCT | Standing | |
|---|---|---|---|---|---|---|---|---|
| 1965 | SF | N | 163 | 95 | 67 | .586 | 2 | |
| 1966 | | | 161 | 93 | 68 | .578 | 2 | |
| 1967 | | | 162 | 91 | 71 | .562 | 2 | |
| 1968 | | | 163 | 88 | 74 | .543 | 2 | |
| 1977 | CHI | N | 162 | 81 | 81 | .500 | 4 | |
| 1978 | | | 162 | 79 | 83 | .488 | 3 | |
| 1979 | | | 155 | 78 | 77 | .503 | 5 | 5 |
| 7 yrs. | | | 1128 | 605 | 521 | .537 | | |
| 3 yrs. | | | 479 | 238 | 241 | .497 | | |

## Jim Frey

**FREY, JAMES GOTTFRIED**
B. May 26, 1931, Cleveland, Ohio

| | | | G | W | L | PCT | Standing | | |
|---|---|---|---|---|---|---|---|---|---|
| 1980 | KC | A | 162 | 97 | 65 | .599 | 1 | | |
| 1981 | | | 50 | 20 | 30 | .400 | 5 | | (1st) |
| 1981 | | | 20 | 10 | 10 | .500 | 2 | 1 | (2nd) |
| 1984 | CHI | N | 161 | 96 | 65 | .596 | 1 | | |
| 1985 | | | 162 | 77 | 84 | .478 | 4 | | |
| 4 yrs. | | | 555 | 300 | 254 | .542 | | | |
| 2 yrs. | | | 323 | 173 | 149 | .537 | | | |

LEAGUE CHAMPIONSHIP SERIES

| | | | G | W | L | PCT | |
|---|---|---|---|---|---|---|---|
| 1980 | KC | A | 3 | 3 | 0 | 1.000 | |
| 1984 | CHI | N | 5 | 2 | 3 | .400 | |
| 2 yrs. | | | 8 | 5 | 3 | .625 | |
| 1 yr. | | | 5 | 2 | 3 | .400 | |

WORLD SERIES

| | | | G | W | L | PCT | |
|---|---|---|---|---|---|---|---|
| 1980 | KC | A | 6 | 2 | 4 | .333 | |

## Frankie Frisch

**FRISCH, FRANK FRANCIS (The Fordham Flash)**
B. Sept. 9, 1898, Bronx, N.Y.
D. Mar. 12, 1973, Wilmington, Del.
Hall of Fame 1947.

| | | | G | W | L | PCT | Standing | | |
|---|---|---|---|---|---|---|---|---|---|
| 1933 | STL | N | 63 | 36 | 26 | .581 | 5 | 5 | |
| 1934 | | | 154 | 95 | 58 | .621 | 1 | | |
| 1935 | | | 154 | 96 | 58 | .623 | 2 | | |
| 1936 | | | 155 | 87 | 67 | .565 | 2 | | |
| 1937 | | | 157 | 81 | 73 | .526 | 4 | | |
| 1938 | | | 138 | 62 | 72 | .463 | 6 | 6 | |
| 1940 | PIT | N | 156 | 78 | 76 | .506 | 4 | | |
| 1941 | | | 156 | 81 | 73 | .526 | 4 | | |
| 1942 | | | 151 | 66 | 81 | .449 | 5 | | |
| 1943 | | | 157 | 80 | 74 | .519 | 4 | | |
| 1944 | | | 158 | 90 | 63 | .588 | 2 | | |
| 1945 | | | 155 | 82 | 72 | .532 | 4 | | |
| 1946 | | | 152 | 62 | 89 | .411 | 7 | 7 | |
| 1949 | CHI | N | 104 | 42 | 62 | .404 | 8 | 8 | |
| 1950 | | | 154 | 64 | 89 | .418 | 7 | | |
| 1951 | | | 81 | 35 | 45 | .438 | 7 | 8 | |
| 16 yrs. | | | 2245 | 1137 | 1078 | .513 | | | |
| 3 yrs. | | | 339 | 141 | 196 | .418 | | | |

WORLD SERIES

| | | | G | W | L | PCT | |
|---|---|---|---|---|---|---|---|
| 1934 | STL | N | 7 | 4 | 3 | .571 | |

## George Gibson

**GIBSON, GEORGE (Moon)**
B. July 22, 1880, London, Ont., Canada
D. Jan. 25, 1967, London, Ont., Canada

| | | | G | W | L | PCT | Standing | | |
|---|---|---|---|---|---|---|---|---|---|
| 1920 | PIT | N | 155 | 79 | 75 | .513 | 4 | | |
| 1921 | | | 154 | 90 | 63 | .588 | 2 | | |
| 1922 | | | 65 | 32 | 33 | .492 | 5 | 3 | |
| 1925 | CHI | N | 26 | 12 | 14 | .462 | 8 | 8 | |
| 1932 | PIT | N | 154 | 86 | 68 | .558 | 2 | | |
| 1933 | | | 154 | 87 | 67 | .565 | 2 | | |
| 1934 | | | 52 | 27 | 24 | .529 | 4 | 5 | |
| 7 yrs. | | | 760 | 413 | 344 | .546 | | | |
| 1 yr. | | | 26 | 12 | 14 | .462 | | | |

| | G | W | L | PCT | Standing | | | | G | W | L | PCT | Standing | |
|---|---|---|---|---|---|---|---|---|---|---|---|---|---|---|

# Preston Gomez
**GOMEZ, PEDRO MARTINEZ**
B. Apr. 20, 1923, Central Preston, Cuba

| | | G | W | L | PCT | Standing | |
|---|---|---|---|---|---|---|---|
| 1969 | SD N | 162 | 52 | 110 | .321 | 6 | |
| 1970 | | 162 | 63 | 99 | .389 | 6 | |
| 1971 | | 161 | 61 | 100 | .379 | 6 | |
| 1972 | | 11 | 4 | 7 | .364 | 4 | 6 |
| 1974 | HOU N | 162 | 81 | 81 | .500 | 4 | |
| 1975 | | 128 | 47 | 80 | .370 | 6 | 6 |
| 1980 | CHI N | 90 | 38 | 52 | .422 | 6 | 6 |
| 7 yrs. | | 876 | 346 | 529 | .395 | | |
| 1 yr. | | 90 | 38 | 52 | .422 | | |

# Charlie Grimm
**GRIMM, CHARLES JOHN (Jolly Cholly)**
B. Aug. 28, 1898, St. Louis, Mo.
D. Nov. 15, 1983, Scottsdale, Ariz.

| | | G | W | L | PCT | Standing | |
|---|---|---|---|---|---|---|---|
| 1932 | CHI N | 57 | 37 | 20 | .649 | 2 | 1 |
| 1933 | | 154 | 86 | 68 | .558 | 3 | |
| 1934 | | 152 | 86 | 65 | .570 | 3 | |
| 1935 | | 154 | 100 | 54 | .649 | 1 | |
| 1936 | | 154 | 87 | 67 | .565 | 2 | |
| 1937 | | 154 | 93 | 61 | .604 | 2 | |
| 1938 | | 81 | 45 | 36 | .556 | 3 | 1 |
| 1944 | | 146 | 74 | 69 | .517 | 8 | 4 |
| 1945 | | 155 | 98 | 56 | .636 | 1 | |
| 1946 | | 155 | 82 | 71 | .536 | 3 | |
| 1947 | | 155 | 69 | 85 | .448 | 6 | |
| 1948 | | 155 | 64 | 90 | .416 | 8 | |
| 1949 | | 50 | 19 | 31 | .380 | 8 | 8 |
| 1952 | BOS N | 120 | 51 | 67 | .432 | 6 | 7 |
| 1953 | MIL N | 157 | 92 | 62 | .597 | 2 | |
| 1954 | | 154 | 89 | 65 | .578 | 3 | |
| 1955 | | 154 | 85 | 69 | .552 | 2 | |
| 1956 | | 46 | 24 | 22 | .522 | 5 | 2 |
| 1960 | CHI N | 17 | 6 | 11 | .353 | 8 | 7 |
| 19 yrs. | | 2370 | 1287 | 1069 | .546 | | |
| 14 yrs. | | 1739 | 946 | 784 | .547 | | |

WORLD SERIES

| | | G | W | L | PCT | | |
|---|---|---|---|---|---|---|---|
| 1932 | CHI N | 4 | 0 | 4 | .000 | | |
| 1935 | | 6 | 2 | 4 | .333 | | |
| 1945 | | 7 | 3 | 4 | .429 | | |
| 3 yrs. | | 17 | 5 | 12 | .294 | | |
| | | | | | | 10th | |
| 3 yrs. | | 17 | 5 | 12 | .294 | | |

# Stan Hack
**HACK, STANLEY CAMFIELD (Smiling Stan)**
B. Dec. 6, 1909, Sacramento, Calif.
D. Dec. 15, 1979, Dickson, Ill.

| | | G | W | L | PCT | Standing | |
|---|---|---|---|---|---|---|---|
| 1954 | CHI N | 154 | 64 | 90 | .416 | 7 | |
| 1955 | | 154 | 72 | 81 | .471 | 6 | |
| 1956 | | 157 | 60 | 94 | .390 | 8 | |
| 1958 | STL N | 10 | 3 | 7 | .300 | 5 | 5 |
| 4 yrs. | | 475 | 199 | 272 | .423 | | |
| 3 yrs. | | 465 | 196 | 265 | .425 | | |

# Gabby Hartnett
**HARTNETT, CHARLES LEO**
B. Dec. 20, 1900, Woonsocket, R. I.
D. Dec. 20, 1972, Park Ridge, Ill.
Hall of Fame 1955.

| | | G | W | L | PCT | Standing | |
|---|---|---|---|---|---|---|---|
| 1938 | CHI N | 73 | 44 | 27 | .620 | 3 | 1 |
| 1939 | | 156 | 84 | 70 | .545 | 4 | |
| 1940 | | 154 | 75 | 79 | .487 | 5 | |
| 3 yrs. | | 383 | 203 | 176 | .536 | | |
| 3 yrs. | | 383 | 203 | 176 | .536 | | |

WORLD SERIES

| | | G | W | L | PCT | | |
|---|---|---|---|---|---|---|---|
| 1938 | CHI N | 4 | 0 | 4 | .000 | | |

# Vedie Himsl
**HIMSL, AVITUS BERNARD**
B. Apr. 2, 1917, Plevna, Mont.

| | | G | W | L | PCT | Standing | |
|---|---|---|---|---|---|---|---|
| 1961 | CHI N | 32 | 10 | 21 | .323 | 7 | 7 |

# Rogers Hornsby
**HORNSBY, ROGERS (Rajah)**
B. Apr. 27, 1896, Winters, Tex.
D. Jan. 5, 1963, Chicago, Ill.
Hall of Fame 1942.

| | | G | W | L | PCT | Standing | |
|---|---|---|---|---|---|---|---|
| 1925 | STL N | 115 | 64 | 51 | .557 | 8 | 4 |
| 1926 | | 156 | 89 | 65 | .578 | 1 | |
| 1928 | BOS N | 122 | 39 | 83 | .320 | 7 | 7 |
| 1930 | CHI N | 4 | 4 | 0 | 1.000 | 2 | 2 |
| 1931 | | 156 | 84 | 70 | .545 | 3 | |
| 1932 | | 97 | 53 | 44 | .546 | 2 | 1 |
| 1933 | STL A | 56 | 20 | 34 | .370 | 8 | 8 |
| 1934 | | 154 | 67 | 85 | .441 | 6 | |
| 1935 | | 155 | 65 | 87 | .428 | 7 | |
| 1936 | | 155 | 57 | 95 | .375 | 7 | |
| 1937 | | 76 | 25 | 50 | .333 | 8 | 8 |
| 1952 | | 50 | 22 | 28 | .440 | 7 | 7 |
| 1952 | CIN N | 51 | 27 | 24 | .529 | 7 | 6 |
| 1953 | | 147 | 64 | 82 | .438 | 6 | 6 |
| 13 yrs. | | 1494 | 680 | 798 | .460 | | |
| 3 yrs. | | 257 | 141 | 114 | .553 | | |

WORLD SERIES

| | | G | W | L | PCT | | |
|---|---|---|---|---|---|---|---|
| 1926 | STL N | 7 | 4 | 3 | .571 | | |

# Roy Johnson
**JOHNSON, ROY CLEVELAND**
Brother of Bob Johnson.
B. Feb. 23, 1903, Pryor, Okla.
D. Sept. 11, 1973, Tacoma, Wash.

| | | G | W | L | PCT | Standing | |
|---|---|---|---|---|---|---|---|
| 1944 | CHI N | 1 | 0 | 1 | .000 | 8 | 8 | 4 |

# Bob Kennedy
**KENNEDY, ROBERT DANIEL**
Father of Terry Kennedy.
B. Aug. 18, 1920, Chicago, Ill.

| | | G | W | L | PCT | Standing | |
|---|---|---|---|---|---|---|---|
| 1963 | CHI N | 162 | 82 | 80 | .506 | 7 | |
| 1964 | | 162 | 76 | 86 | .469 | 8 | |
| 1965 | | 58 | 24 | 32 | .429 | 9 | 8 |
| 1968 | OAK A | 163 | 82 | 80 | .506 | 6 | |
| 4 yrs. | | 545 | 264 | 278 | .487 | | |
| 3 yrs. | | 382 | 182 | 198 | .479 | | |

# Bill Killefer
**KILLEFER, WILLIAM LAVIER (Reindeer Bill)**
Brother of Red Killefer.
B. Oct. 10, 1887, Bloomingdale, Mich.
D. July 2, 1960, Elsmere, Del.

| | | G | W | L | PCT | Standing | |
|---|---|---|---|---|---|---|---|
| 1921 | CHI N | 55 | 22 | 33 | .400 | 7 | 7 |
| 1922 | | 156 | 80 | 74 | .519 | 5 | |
| 1923 | | 154 | 83 | 71 | .539 | 4 | |
| 1924 | | 154 | 81 | 72 | .529 | 5 | |
| 1925 | | 75 | 33 | 42 | .440 | 7 | 8 |
| 1930 | STL A | 154 | 64 | 90 | .416 | 6 | |
| 1931 | | 154 | 63 | 91 | .409 | 5 | |
| 1932 | | 154 | 63 | 91 | .409 | 6 | |
| 1933 | | 93 | 34 | 59 | .366 | 8 | 8 |
| 9 yrs. | | 1149 | 523 | 623 | .456 | | |
| 5 yrs. | | 594 | 299 | 292 | .506 | | |

# Lou Klein
**KLEIN, LOUIS FRANK**
B. Oct. 22, 1918, New Orleans, La.
D. June 20, 1976, Metairie, La.

| | | G | W | L | PCT | Standing | |
|---|---|---|---|---|---|---|---|
| 1961 | CHI N | 12 | 5 | 7 | .417 | 7 | 7 | |
| 1962 | | 30 | 12 | 18 | .400 | 9 | 9 | 9 |
| 1965 | | 106 | 48 | 58 | .453 | 9 | 8 | |
| 3 yrs. | | 148 | 65 | 83 | .439 | | |
| 3 yrs. | | 148 | 65 | 83 | .439 | | |

# Whitey Lockman
**LOCKMAN, CARROLL WALTER**
B. July 25, 1926, Lowell, N. C.

| | | G | W | L | PCT | Standing | |
|---|---|---|---|---|---|---|---|
| 1972 | CHI N | 65 | 39 | 26 | .600 | 4 | 2 |
| 1973 | | 161 | 77 | 84 | .478 | 5 | |

| | G | W | L | PCT | Standing | | |
|---|---|---|---|---|---|---|---|

## Whitey Lockman continued

| | | G | W | L | PCT | Standing | |
|---|---|---|---|---|---|---|---|
| 1974 | | 93 | 41 | 52 | .441 | 5 | 6 |
| 3 yrs. | | 319 | 157 | 162 | .492 | | |
| 3 yrs. | | 319 | 157 | 162 | .492 | | |

## Tom Loftus

**LOFTUS, THOMAS JOSEPH**
B. Nov. 15, 1856, Jefferson City, Mo.
D. Apr. 16, 1910, Concord, Mass.

| | | G | W | L | PCT | Standing | |
|---|---|---|---|---|---|---|---|
| 1884 | MIL U | 12 | 8 | 4 | .667 | 2 | |
| 1888 | CLE AA | 74 | 31 | 41 | .431 | 7 | 6 |
| 1889 | CLE N | 136 | 61 | 72 | .459 | 6 | |
| 1890 | CIN N | 134 | 77 | 55 | .583 | 4 | |
| 1891 | | 138 | 56 | 81 | .409 | 7 | |
| 1900 | CHI N | 146 | 65 | 75 | .464 | 5 | |
| 1901 | | 140 | 53 | 86 | .381 | 6 | |
| 1902 | WAS A | 138 | 61 | 75 | .449 | 6 | |
| 1903 | | 140 | 43 | 94 | .314 | 8 | |
| 9 yrs. | | 1058 | 455 | 583 | .438 | | |
| 2 yrs. | | 286 | 118 | 161 | .423 | | |

## Rabbit Maranville

**MARANVILLE, WALTER JAMES VINCENT**
B. Nov. 11, 1891, Springfield, Mass.
D. Jan. 5, 1954, New York, N. Y.
Hall of Fame 1954.

| | | G | W | L | PCT | Standing | | |
|---|---|---|---|---|---|---|---|---|
| 1925 | CHI N | 53 | 23 | 30 | .434 | 7 | 8 | 8 |

## Jim Marshall

**MARSHALL, RUFUS JAMES**
B. May 25, 1932, Danville, Ill.

| | | G | W | L | PCT | Standing | |
|---|---|---|---|---|---|---|---|
| 1974 | CHI N | 69 | 25 | 44 | .362 | 5 | 6 |
| 1975 | | 162 | 75 | 87 | .463 | 5 | |
| 1976 | | 162 | 75 | 87 | .463 | 4 | |
| 1979 | OAK A | 162 | 54 | 108 | .333 | 7 | |
| 4 yrs. | | 555 | 229 | 326 | .413 | | |
| 3 yrs. | | 393 | 175 | 218 | .445 | | |

## Joe McCarthy

**McCARTHY, JOSEPH VINCENT (Marse Joe)**
B. Apr. 21, 1887, Philadelphia, Pa.
D. Jan. 3, 1978, Buffalo, N. Y.
Hall of Fame 1957.

| | | G | W | L | PCT | Standing | |
|---|---|---|---|---|---|---|---|
| 1926 | CHI N | 155 | 82 | 72 | .532 | 4 | |
| 1927 | | 153 | 85 | 68 | .556 | 4 | |
| 1928 | | 154 | 91 | 63 | .591 | 3 | |
| 1929 | | 156 | 98 | 54 | .645 | 1 | |
| 1930 | | 152 | 86 | 64 | .573 | 2 | 2 |
| 1931 | NY A | 155 | 94 | 59 | .614 | 2 | |
| 1932 | | 155 | 107 | 47 | .695 | 1 | |
| 1933 | | 152 | 91 | 59 | .607 | 2 | |
| 1934 | | 154 | 94 | 60 | .610 | 2 | |
| 1935 | | 149 | 89 | 60 | .597 | 2 | |
| 1936 | | 155 | 102 | 51 | .667 | 1 | |
| 1937 | | 157 | 102 | 52 | .662 | 1 | |
| 1938 | | 157 | 99 | 53 | .651 | 1 | |
| 1939 | | 152 | 106 | 45 | .702 | 1 | |
| 1940 | | 155 | 88 | 66 | .571 | 3 | |
| 1941 | | 156 | 101 | 53 | .656 | 1 | |
| 1942 | | 154 | 103 | 51 | .669 | 1 | |
| 1943 | | 155 | 98 | 56 | .636 | 1 | |
| 1944 | | 154 | 83 | 71 | .539 | 3 | |
| 1945 | | 152 | 81 | 71 | .533 | 4 | |
| 1946 | | 35 | 22 | 13 | .629 | 2 | 3 |
| 1948 | BOS A | 155 | 96 | 59 | .619 | 2 | |
| 1949 | | 155 | 96 | 58 | .623 | 2 | |
| 1950 | | 62 | 32 | 30 | .516 | 4 | 3 |
| 24 yrs. | | 3489 | 2126 | 1335 | .614 | | |
| | | | 9th | 4th | | 1st | |
| 5 yrs. | | 770 | 442 | 321 | .579 | | |

WORLD SERIES

| | | G | W | L | PCT | |
|---|---|---|---|---|---|---|
| 1929 | CHI N | 5 | 1 | 4 | .200 | |
| 1932 | NY A | 4 | 4 | 0 | 1.000 | |
| 1936 | | 6 | 4 | 2 | .667 | |
| 1937 | | 5 | 4 | 1 | .800 | |
| 1938 | | 4 | 4 | 0 | 1.000 | |

## Joe McCarthy continued

| | | G | W | L | PCT | |
|---|---|---|---|---|---|---|
| 1939 | | 4 | 4 | 0 | 1.000 | |
| 1941 | | 5 | 4 | 1 | .800 | |
| 1942 | | 5 | 1 | 4 | .200 | |
| 1943 | | 5 | 4 | 1 | .800 | |
| 9 yrs. | | 43 | 30 | 13 | .698 | |
| | | 3rd | 2nd | 8th | | 1st |
| 1 yr. | | 5 | 1 | 4 | .200 | |

## Charlie Metro

**METRO, CHARLES**
Born Charles Moreskonich.
B. Apr. 28, 1919, Nanty-Glo, Pa.

| | | G | W | L | PCT | Standing | | |
|---|---|---|---|---|---|---|---|---|
| 1962 | CHI N | 112 | 43 | 69 | .384 | 9 | 9 | |
| 1970 | KC A | 54 | 19 | 35 | .352 | 6 | 4 | |
| 2 yrs. | | 166 | 62 | 104 | .373 | | | |
| 1 yr. | | 112 | 43 | 69 | .384 | | | |

## Fred Mitchell

**MITCHELL, FREDERICK FRANCIS**
Born Frederick Francis Yapp.
B. June 5, 1878, Cambridge, Mass.
D. Oct. 13, 1970, Newton, Mass.

| | | G | W | L | PCT | Standing | |
|---|---|---|---|---|---|---|---|
| 1917 | CHI N | 157 | 74 | 80 | .481 | 5 | |
| 1918 | | 131 | 84 | 45 | .651 | 1 | |
| 1919 | | 140 | 75 | 65 | .536 | 3 | |
| 1920 | | 154 | 75 | 79 | .487 | 5 | |
| 1921 | BOS N | 153 | 79 | 74 | .516 | 4 | |
| 1922 | | 154 | 53 | 100 | .346 | 8 | |
| 1923 | | 155 | 54 | 100 | .351 | 7 | |
| 7 yrs. | | 1044 | 494 | 543 | .476 | | |
| 4 yrs. | | 582 | 308 | 269 | .534 | | |

WORLD SERIES

| | | G | W | L | PCT | |
|---|---|---|---|---|---|---|
| 1918 | CHI N | 6 | 2 | 4 | .333 | |

## Hank O'Day

**O'DAY, HENRY FRANCIS**
B. July 8, 1862, Chicago, Ill.
D. July 2, 1935, Chicago, Ill.

| | | G | W | L | PCT | Standing | |
|---|---|---|---|---|---|---|---|
| 1912 | CIN N | 155 | 75 | 78 | .490 | 4 | |
| 1914 | CHI N | 156 | 78 | 76 | .506 | 4 | |
| 2 yrs. | | 311 | 153 | 154 | .498 | | |
| 1 yr. | | 156 | 78 | 76 | .506 | | |

## Bob Scheffing

**SCHEFFING, ROBERT BODEN**
B. Aug. 11, 1915, Overland, Mo.
D. Oct. 26, 1985, Scottsdale, Ariz.

| | | G | W | L | PCT | Standing | |
|---|---|---|---|---|---|---|---|
| 1957 | CHI N | 156 | 62 | 92 | .403 | 7 | |
| 1958 | | 154 | 72 | 82 | .468 | 5 | |
| 1959 | | 155 | 74 | 80 | .481 | 5 | |
| 1961 | DET A | 163 | 101 | 61 | .623 | 2 | |
| 1962 | | 161 | 85 | 76 | .528 | 4 | |
| 1963 | | 60 | 24 | 36 | .400 | 9 | 5 |
| 6 yrs. | | 849 | 418 | 427 | .495 | | |
| 3 yrs. | | 465 | 208 | 254 | .450 | | |

## Frank Selee

**SELEE, FRANK GIBSON**
B. Oct. 26, 1859, Amherst, N. H.
D. July 5, 1909, Denver, Colo.

| | | G | W | L | PCT | Standing | |
|---|---|---|---|---|---|---|---|
| 1890 | BOS N | 134 | 76 | 57 | .571 | 5 | |
| 1891 | | 140 | 87 | 51 | .630 | 1 | |
| 1892 | | 152 | 102 | 48 | .680 | 1 | |
| 1893 | | 131 | 86 | 43 | .667 | 1 | |
| 1894 | | 133 | 83 | 49 | .629 | 3 | |
| 1895 | | 132 | 71 | 60 | .542 | 5 | |
| 1896 | | 132 | 74 | 57 | .565 | 4 | |
| 1897 | | 135 | 93 | 39 | .705 | 1 | |
| 1898 | | 152 | 102 | 47 | .685 | 1 | |
| 1899 | | 153 | 95 | 57 | .625 | 2 | |
| 1900 | | 142 | 66 | 72 | .478 | 4 | |
| 1901 | | 140 | 69 | 69 | .500 | 5 | |

| | G | W | L | PCT | Standing | | | G | W | L | PCT | Standing |
|---|---|---|---|---|---|---|---|---|---|---|---|---|

## Frank Selee  continued

| | | G | W | L | PCT | Standing |
|---|---|---|---|---|---|---|
| 1902 | CHI N | 141 | 68 | 69 | .496 | 5 |
| 1903 | | 139 | 82 | 56 | .594 | 3 |
| 1904 | | 156 | 93 | 60 | .608 | 2 |
| 1905 | | 90 | 52 | 38 | .578 | 4  3 |
| 16 yrs. | | 2202 | 1299 | 872 | .598 | |
| | | | | | | 4th |
| 4 yrs. | | 526 | 295 | 223 | .569 | |

## Al Spalding
**SPALDING, ALBERT GOODWILL**
B. Sept. 2, 1850, Byron, Ill.
D. Sept. 9, 1915, Point Loma, Calif.
Hall of Fame 1939.

| | | G | W | L | PCT | Standing |
|---|---|---|---|---|---|---|
| 1876 | CHI N | 66 | 52 | 14 | .788 | 1 |
| 1877 | | 60 | 26 | 33 | .441 | 5 |
| 2 yrs. | | 126 | 78 | 47 | .624 | |
| 2 yrs. | | 126 | 78 | 47 | .624 | |

## El Tappe
**TAPPE, ELVIN WALTER**
B. May 21, 1927, Quincy, Ill.

| | | G | W | L | PCT | Standing |
|---|---|---|---|---|---|---|
| 1961 | CHI N | 96 | 42 | 53 | .442 | 7  7  7 |
| 1962 | | 20 | 4 | 16 | .200 | 9  9 |
| 2 yrs. | | 116 | 46 | 69 | .400 | |
| 2 yrs. | | 116 | 46 | 69 | .400 | |

## Joe Tinker
**TINKER, JOSEPH BERT**
B. July 27, 1880, Muscotah, Kans.
D. July 27, 1948, Orlando, Fla.
Hall of Fame 1946.

| | | G | W | L | PCT | Standing |
|---|---|---|---|---|---|---|
| 1913 | CIN N | 156 | 64 | 89 | .418 | 7 |
| 1914 | CHI F | 157 | 87 | 67 | .565 | 2 |
| 1915 | | 155 | 86 | 66 | .566 | 1 |
| 1916 | CHI N | 156 | 67 | 86 | .438 | 5 |
| 4 yrs. | | 624 | 304 | 308 | .497 | |
| 1 yr. | | 156 | 67 | 86 | .438 | |

## Jimmie Wilson
**WILSON, JAMES (Ace)**
B. July 23, 1900, Philadelphia, Pa.
D. May 31, 1947, Bradenton, Fla.

| | | G | W | L | PCT | Standing |
|---|---|---|---|---|---|---|
| 1934 | PHI N | 149 | 56 | 93 | .376 | 7 |
| 1935 | | 156 | 64 | 89 | .418 | 7 |
| 1936 | | 154 | 54 | 100 | .351 | 8 |
| 1937 | | 155 | 61 | 92 | .399 | 7 |
| 1938 | | 149 | 45 | 103 | .304 | 8  8 |
| 1941 | CHI N | 155 | 70 | 84 | .455 | 6 |
| 1942 | | 155 | 68 | 86 | .442 | 6 |
| 1943 | | 154 | 74 | 79 | .484 | 5 |
| 1944 | | 10 | 1 | 9 | .100 | 8  4 |
| 9 yrs. | | 1237 | 493 | 735 | .401 | |
| 4 yrs. | | 474 | 213 | 258 | .452 | |

# Cubs World Series Highlights
and Summaries

This section provides information on the ten World Series and one League Championship Series the Cubs have played in through 1985. Included are facts about the individual games; most of the information is self-explanatory. That which may appear unfamiliar is listed below.

## INDIVIDUAL GAME INFORMATION

*Innings Pitched.* Pitchers are listed in the order of appearance. In parentheses, following each pitcher's name, are the number of innings he pitched in the game. For example: Doe (2.1) would mean that he pitched 2⅓ innings.

*Winning and Losing Pitchers.* Indicated by bold-faced print.

*Saves.* The pitcher who is credited with a Save is indicated by the abbreviation SV, which appears in bold-faced print after his innings pitched.

*Home Runs.* Players are listed in the order their home runs were hit.

| NE SCORES & PITCHERS (inn. pit.) | HOME RUNS (men on) | HIGHLIGHTS |
|---|---|---|

## Chicago (A.L.) defeats Chicago (N.L.) 4 games to 2

**GAME 1 - OCTOBER 9**

CHI A 000 011 000   2 4 1
CHI N 000 001 000   1 4 2
Altrock (9)
Brown (9)

Isbell scored Jones with the tie-breaking run on a single in the sixth in a game played in bitterly cold weather and snow flurries.

**GAME 2 - OCTOBER 10**

CHI N 031 001 020   7 10 2
CHI A 000 010 000   1 1 2
Reulbach (9)
White (3), Owen (6)

Reulbach pitched six no-hit innings before yielding a single to Donahue. He finished with a one-hitter, but walked six and hit one batter.

**GAME 3 - OCTOBER 11**

CHI A 000 003 000   3 4 1
CHI N 000 000 000   0 2 2
Walsh (9)
Pfiester (9)

Rohe's three-run triple in the sixth broke open the game and aided Walsh's record 12-strikeout pitching performance.

**GAME 4 - OCTOBER 12**

CHI N 000 000 100   1 7 1
CHI A 000 000 000   0 2 1
Brown (9)
Altrock (9)

Evers singled in Chance in the seventh to back up Brown's two-hitter.

**GAME 5 - OCTOBER 13**

CHI A 102 401 000   8 12 6
CHI N 300 102 000   6 6 0
Walsh (6.1), White (2.2) SV
Reulbach (2), **Pfiester** (1.1),
   Overall (5.2)

Isbell hit four doubles, scored three runs and drove in two to pace the White Sox' twelve-hit attack.

**GAME 6 - OCTOBER 14**

CHI N 100 010 001   3 7 0
CHI A 340 000 01x   8 14 3
Brown (1.2), Overall (6.1)
White (9)

The White Sox jumped to a 7-1 lead after two innings and won the Series as Hahn contributed four hits and Donahue and Davis each drove in three runs.

### Team Totals

| | | W | AB | H | 2B | 3B | HR | R | RBI | BA | BB | SO | ERA |
|---|---|---|---|---|---|---|---|---|---|---|---|---|---|
| CHI | A | 4 | 187 | 37 | 10 | 3 | 0 | 22 | 19 | .198 | 18 | 35 | 1.67 |
| CHI | N | 2 | 184 | 36 | 9 | 0 | 0 | 18 | 11 | .196 | 18 | 27 | 3.40 |

### Individual Batting

**CHICAGO (A.L.)**

| | AB | H | 2B | 3B | HR | R | RBI | BA |
|---|---|---|---|---|---|---|---|---|
| F. Isbell, 2b | 26 | 8 | 4 | 0 | 0 | 4 | 4 | .308 |
| E. Hahn, of | 22 | 6 | 0 | 0 | 0 | 4 | 0 | .273 |
| F. Jones, of | 21 | 2 | 0 | 0 | 0 | 4 | 0 | .095 |
| G. Rohe, 3b | 21 | 7 | 1 | 2 | 0 | 2 | 4 | .333 |
| B. Sullivan, c | 21 | 0 | 0 | 0 | 0 | 0 | 0 | .000 |
| P. Dougherty, of | 20 | 2 | 0 | 0 | 0 | 1 | 1 | .100 |
| J. Donahue, 1b | 18 | 6 | 2 | 1 | 0 | 0 | 4 | .333 |
| G. Davis, ss | 13 | 4 | 3 | 0 | 0 | 4 | 6 | .308 |
| L. Tannehill, ss | 9 | 1 | 0 | 0 | 0 | 1 | 0 | .111 |
| N. Altrock, p | 4 | 1 | 0 | 0 | 0 | 0 | 0 | .250 |
| E. Walsh, p | 4 | 0 | 0 | 0 | 0 | 1 | 0 | .000 |
| D. White, p | 3 | 0 | 0 | 0 | 0 | 0 | 0 | .000 |
| F. Owen, p | 2 | 0 | 0 | 0 | 0 | 0 | 0 | .000 |
| E. McFarland | 1 | 0 | 0 | 0 | 0 | 0 | 0 | .000 |
| B. O'Neill, of | 1 | 0 | 0 | 0 | 0 | 1 | 0 | .000 |
| B. Towne | 1 | 0 | 0 | 0 | 0 | 0 | 0 | .000 |

**Errors:** F. Isbell (5), G. Rohe (3), G. Davis (2), J. Donahue, P. Dougherty, B. Sullivan, E. Walsh
**Stolen bases:** P. Dougherty (2), G. Rohe (2), G. Davis, F. Isbell

**CHICAGO (N.L.)**

| | AB | H | 2B | 3B | HR | R | RBI | BA |
|---|---|---|---|---|---|---|---|---|
| W. Schulte, of | 26 | 7 | 3 | 0 | 0 | 1 | 3 | .269 |
| S. Hofman, of | 23 | 7 | 1 | 0 | 0 | 3 | 2 | .304 |
| F. Chance, 1b | 21 | 5 | 1 | 0 | 0 | 3 | 0 | .238 |
| J. Sheckard, of | 21 | 0 | 0 | 0 | 0 | 0 | 1 | .000 |
| J. Evers, 2b | 20 | 3 | 1 | 0 | 0 | 2 | 1 | .150 |
| H. Steinfeldt, 3b | 20 | 5 | 1 | 0 | 0 | 2 | 2 | .250 |
| J. Tinker, ss | 18 | 3 | 0 | 0 | 0 | 4 | 1 | .167 |
| J. Kling, c | 17 | 3 | 1 | 0 | 0 | 2 | 0 | .176 |
| T. Brown, p | 6 | 2 | 0 | 0 | 0 | 0 | 0 | .333 |
| O. Overall, p | 4 | 1 | 1 | 0 | 0 | 1 | 0 | .250 |
| E. Reulbach, p | 3 | 0 | 0 | 0 | 0 | 0 | 1 | .000 |
| P. Moran | 2 | 0 | 0 | 0 | 0 | 0 | 0 | .000 |
| J. Pfiester, p | 2 | 0 | 0 | 0 | 0 | 0 | 0 | .000 |
| D. Gessler | 1 | 0 | 0 | 0 | 0 | 0 | 0 | .000 |

**Errors:** J. Tinker (2), T. Brown, J. Evers, J. Kling, J. Pfiester, H. Steinfeldt
**Stolen bases:** F. Chance (2), J. Evers (2), J. Tinker (2), S. Hofman, J. Sheckard

### Individual Pitching

**CHICAGO (A.L.)**

| | W | L | ERA | IP | H | BB | SO | SV |
|---|---|---|---|---|---|---|---|---|
| N. Altrock | 1 | 1 | 1.00 | 18 | 11 | 2 | 5 | 0 |
| E. Walsh | 2 | 0 | 1.80 | 15 | 7 | 6 | 17 | 0 |
| D. White | 1 | 1 | 1.80 | 15 | 12 | 7 | 4 | 1 |
| F. Owen | 0 | 0 | 3.00 | 6 | 6 | 3 | 2 | 0 |

**CHICAGO (N.L.)**

| | W | L | ERA | IP | H | BB | SO | SV |
|---|---|---|---|---|---|---|---|---|
| T. Brown | 1 | 2 | 3.66 | 19.2 | 14 | 4 | 12 | 0 |
| O. Overall | 0 | 0 | 1.50 | 12 | 10 | 3 | 8 | 0 |
| E. Reulbach | 1 | 0 | 2.45 | 11 | 6 | 8 | 4 | 0 |
| J. Pfiester | 0 | 2 | 6.10 | 10.1 | 7 | 3 | 11 | 0 |

| LINE SCORES & PITCHERS (inn. pit.) | HOME RUNS (men on) | HIGHLIGHTS |
|---|---|---|

## Chicago (N.L.) defeats Detroit (A.L.) 4 games to 0

**GAME 1 - OCTOBER 8**

```
DET  A  000 000 030 000   3  9  3
CHI  N  000 100 002 000   3 10  5
Donovan (12)
Overall (9), Reulbach (3)
```

Schmidt's third-strike passed ball with two out in the ninth allowed the Cubs to even the game, which ended after 12 in a 3-3 tie. Donovan struck out 12 and the Cubs stole seven bases.

**GAME 2 - OCTOBER 9**

```
DET  A  010 000 000   1  9  1
CHI  N  010 200 00x   3  9  1
Mullin (8)
Pfiester (9)
```

Slagle drove in the go-ahead run with a single in the fourth, then scored an insurance run on Sheckard's double.

**GAME 3 - OCTOBER 10**

```
DET  A  000 001 000   1  6  1
CHI  N  010 310 00x   5 10  1
Siever (4), Killian (4)
Reulbach (9)
```

Evers's three hits led the Cubs' attack as Reulbach subdued the Tigers on six scattered hits.

**GAME 4 - OCTOBER 11**

```
CHI  N  000 020 301   6  7  2
DET  A  000 100 000   1  5  2
Overall (9)
Donovan (9)
```

Overall aided his own cause with a go-ahead two-run single in the fifth as he held the Tigers to five hits.

**GAME 5 - OCTOBER 12**

```
CHI  N  110 000 000   2  7  1
DET  A  000 000 000   0  7  2
Brown (9)
Mullin (9)
```

The Cubs swept the Series behind Brown's shutout. The Cubs swiped 18 bases in the five games, and held batting champ Ty Cobb to a .200 average.

### Team Totals

|  |  | W | AB | H | 2B | 3B | HR | R | RBI | BA | BB | SO | ERA |
|---|---|---|---|---|---|---|---|---|---|---|---|---|---|
| CHI | N | 4 | 167 | 43 | 6 | 1 | 0 | 19 | 16 | .257 | 12 | 25 | 0.75 |
| DET | A | 0 | 172 | 36 | 1 | 2 | 0 | 6 | 6 | .209 | 9 | 22 | 1.96 |

### Individual Batting

#### CHICAGO (N.L.)

| | AB | H | 2B | 3B | HR | R | RBI | BA |
|---|---|---|---|---|---|---|---|---|
| J. Slagle, of | 22 | 6 | 0 | 0 | 0 | 3 | 4 | .273 |
| J. Sheckard, of | 21 | 5 | 2 | 0 | 0 | 0 | 2 | .238 |
| J. Evers, 2b, ss | 20 | 7 | 2 | 0 | 0 | 2 | 1 | .350 |
| W. Schulte, of | 20 | 5 | 0 | 0 | 0 | 3 | 2 | .250 |
| J. Kling, c | 19 | 4 | 0 | 0 | 0 | 2 | 1 | .211 |
| H. Steinfeldt, 3b | 17 | 8 | 1 | 1 | 0 | 2 | 2 | .471 |
| F. Chance, 1b | 14 | 3 | 1 | 0 | 0 | 3 | 0 | .214 |
| J. Tinker, ss | 13 | 2 | 0 | 0 | 0 | 4 | 1 | .154 |
| D. Howard, 1b | 5 | 1 | 0 | 0 | 0 | 0 | 0 | .200 |
| O. Overall, p | 5 | 1 | 0 | 0 | 0 | 0 | 2 | .200 |
| E. Reulbach, p | 5 | 1 | 0 | 0 | 0 | 0 | 1 | .200 |
| T. Brown, p | 3 | 0 | 0 | 0 | 0 | 0 | 0 | .000 |
| J. Pfiester, p | 2 | 0 | 0 | 0 | 0 | 0 | 0 | .000 |
| H. Zimmerman, 2b | 1 | 0 | 0 | 0 | 0 | 0 | 0 | .000 |
| P. Moran | 0 | 0 | 0 | 0 | 0 | 0 | 0 | — |

**Errors:** J. Evers (3), J. Tinker (3), W. Schulte (2), J. Kling, J. Slagle
**Stolen bases:** J. Slagle (6), F. Chance (3), J. Evers (3), J. Tinker (2), D. Howard, W. Schulte, J. Sheckard, H. Steinfeldt

#### DETROIT (A.L.)

| | AB | H | 2B | 3B | HR | R | RBI | BA |
|---|---|---|---|---|---|---|---|---|
| S. Crawford, of | 21 | 5 | 1 | 0 | 0 | 1 | 2 | .238 |
| G. Schaefer, 2b | 21 | 3 | 0 | 0 | 1 | 1 | 0 | .143 |
| T. Cobb, of | 20 | 4 | 0 | 1 | 0 | 1 | 1 | .200 |
| B. Coughlin, 3b | 20 | 5 | 0 | 0 | 0 | 0 | 0 | .250 |
| C. Rossman, 1b | 20 | 8 | 0 | 1 | 0 | 1 | 2 | .400 |
| D. Jones, of | 17 | 6 | 0 | 0 | 0 | 1 | 0 | .353 |
| C. O'Leary, ss | 17 | 1 | 0 | 0 | 0 | 0 | 0 | .059 |
| B. Schmidt, c | 12 | 2 | 0 | 0 | 0 | 0 | 0 | .167 |
| W. Donovan, p | 8 | 0 | 0 | 0 | 0 | 0 | 0 | .000 |
| G. Mullin, p | 6 | 0 | 0 | 0 | 0 | 0 | 0 | .000 |
| F. Payne, c | 4 | 1 | 0 | 0 | 0 | 0 | 1 | .250 |
| J. Archer, c | 3 | 0 | 0 | 0 | 0 | 0 | 0 | .000 |
| E. Killian, p | 2 | 1 | 0 | 0 | 0 | 1 | 0 | .500 |
| E. Siever, p | 1 | 0 | 0 | 0 | 0 | 0 | 0 | .000 |

**Errors:** B. Coughlin (2), C. O'Leary (2), B. Schmidt (2), D. Jones, F. Payne, C. Rossman
**Stolen bases:** D. Jones (3), C. Rossman (2), B. Coughlin, G. Schaefer

### Individual Pitching

#### CHICAGO (N.L.)

| | W | L | ERA | IP | H | BB | SO | SV |
|---|---|---|---|---|---|---|---|---|
| O. Overall | 1 | 0 | 1.00 | 18 | 14 | 4 | 11 | 0 |
| E. Reulbach | 1 | 0 | 0.75 | 12 | 6 | 3 | 4 | 0 |
| T. Brown | 1 | 0 | 0.00 | 9 | 7 | 1 | 4 | 0 |
| J. Pfiester | 1 | 0 | 1.00 | 9 | 9 | 1 | 3 | 0 |

#### DETROIT (A.L.)

| | W | L | ERA | IP | H | BB | SO | SV |
|---|---|---|---|---|---|---|---|---|
| W. Donovan | 0 | 1 | 1.29 | 21 | 17 | 5 | 16 | 0 |
| G. Mullin | 0 | 2 | 2.12 | 17 | 16 | 6 | 7 | 0 |
| E. Killian | 0 | 0 | 2.25 | 4 | 3 | 1 | 1 | 0 |
| E. Siever | 0 | 1 | 4.50 | 4 | 7 | 0 | 1 | 0 |

LINE SCORES & PITCHERS (inn. pit.)        HOME RUNS (men on)        HIGHLIGHTS

## Chicago (N.L.) defeats Detroit (A.L.) 4 games to 1

**GAME 1 - OCTOBER 10**
CHI  N  004 000 105   10 14  2
DET  A  100 000 320    6 10  4
Reulbach (6.2), Overall (0.1),
  **Brown** (2)
Killian (2.1), **Summers** (6.2)

Five Cub runs in the ninth, four scoring
on two-run singles by Hofman and Kling,
broke open a game played in heavy rain.

**GAME 2 - OCTOBER 11**
DET  A  000 000 001   1  4  1
CHI  N  000 000 06x   6  7  1
Donovan (8)
**Overall** (9)

Tinker (1 on)

Donovan held the Cubs to one hit in seven
innings, but Tinker's homer sparked a
six-run rally that broke up a scoreless
deadlock.

**GAME 3 - OCTOBER 12**
DET  A  100 005 020   8 11  4
CHI  N  000 300 000   3  7  2
**Mullin** (9)
Pfiester (8), Reulbach (1)

Cobb's four hits led the Detroit attack
to a come-from-behind victory.

**GAME 4 - OCTOBER 13**
CHI  A  002 000 001   3 10  0
DET  N  000 000 000   0  4  1
**Brown** (9)
**Summers** (8), Winter (1)

Back-to-back scoring singles by
Steinfeldt and Hofman in the third gave
Brown all the runs he needed to subdue
the Tigers.

**GAME 5 - OCTOBER 14**
CHI  N  100 010 000   2 10  0
DET  A  000 000 000   0  3  0
**Overall** (9)
Donovan (9)

Three hits and one RBI each by Evers and
Chance aided Overall's 10-strikeout
pitching in the Series clincher.

## Team Totals

|       |   | W | AB  | H  | 2B | 3B | HR | R  | RBI | BA   | BB | SO | ERA  |
|-------|---|---|-----|----|----|----|----|----|-----|------|----|----|------|
| CHI   | N | 4 | 164 | 48 | 4  | 2  | 1  | 24 | 20  | .293 | 13 | 26 | 2.60 |
| DET   | A | 1 | 158 | 32 | 5  | 0  | 0  | 15 | 14  | .203 | 12 | 26 | 3.48 |

## Individual Batting

### CHICAGO (N.L.)

|                   | AB | H | 2B | 3B | HR | R | RBI | BA   |
|-------------------|----|---|----|----|----|---|-----|------|
| J. Sheckard, of   | 21 | 5 | 2  | 0  | 0  | 2 | 1   | .238 |
| J. Evers, 2b      | 20 | 7 | 1  | 0  | 0  | 5 | 2   | .350 |
| F. Chance, 1b     | 19 | 8 | 0  | 0  | 0  | 4 | 2   | .421 |
| S. Hofman, of     | 19 | 6 | 0  | 1  | 0  | 2 | 4   | .316 |
| J. Tinker, ss     | 19 | 5 | 0  | 0  | 1  | 2 | 5   | .263 |
| W. Schulte, of    | 18 | 7 | 0  | 1  | 0  | 4 | 2   | .389 |
| J. Kling, c       | 16 | 4 | 1  | 0  | 0  | 2 | 1   | .250 |
| H. Steinfeldt, 3b | 16 | 4 | 0  | 0  | 0  | 3 | 3   | .250 |
| O. Overall, p     | 6  | 2 | 0  | 0  | 0  | 0 | 0   | .333 |
| T. Brown, p       | 4  | 0 | 0  | 0  | 0  | 0 | 0   | .000 |
| E. Reulbach, p    | 3  | 0 | 0  | 0  | 0  | 0 | 0   | .000 |
| J. Pfiester, p    | 2  | 0 | 0  | 0  | 0  | 0 | 0   | .000 |
| D. Howard         | 1  | 0 | 0  | 0  | 0  | 0 | 0   | .000 |

**Errors:** F. Chance (3), J. Evers, H. Steinfeldt
**Stolen bases:** F. Chance (5), J. Evers (2), S. Hofman (2),
W. Schulte (2), J. Sheckard, H. Steinfeldt,
J. Tinker

### DETROIT (A.L.)

|                     | AB | H | 2B | 3B | HR | R | RBI | BA   |
|---------------------|----|---|----|----|----|---|-----|------|
| S. Crawford, of     | 21 | 5 | 1  | 0  | 0  | 2 | 1   | .238 |
| T. Cobb, of         | 19 | 7 | 1  | 0  | 0  | 3 | 4   | .368 |
| C. O'Leary, ss      | 19 | 3 | 0  | 0  | 0  | 2 | 0   | .158 |
| C. Rossman, 1b      | 19 | 4 | 0  | 0  | 0  | 3 | 3   | .211 |
| M. McIntyre, of     | 18 | 4 | 1  | 0  | 0  | 2 | 0   | .222 |
| G. Schaefer, 3b, 2b | 16 | 2 | 0  | 0  | 0  | 0 | 0   | .125 |
| B. Schmidt, c       | 14 | 1 | 0  | 0  | 0  | 0 | 1   | .071 |
| B. Coughlin, 3b     | 8  | 1 | 0  | 0  | 0  | 0 | 1   | .125 |
| R. Downs, 2b        | 6  | 1 | 1  | 0  | 0  | 1 | 1   | .167 |
| E. Summers, p       | 5  | 1 | 0  | 0  | 0  | 0 | 1   | .200 |
| W. Donovan, p       | 4  | 0 | 0  | 0  | 0  | 0 | 0   | .000 |
| I. Thomas, c        | 4  | 2 | 1  | 0  | 0  | 0 | 1   | .500 |
| G. Mullin, p        | 3  | 1 | 0  | 0  | 0  | 1 | 1   | .333 |
| D. Jones            | 2  | 0 | 0  | 0  | 0  | 1 | 0   | .000 |

**Errors:** T. Cobb (2), C. Rossman (2), B. Coughlin,
W. Donovan, R. Downs, M. McIntyre,
C. O'Leary, G. Schaefer
**Stolen bases:** T. Cobb (2), W. Donovan, M. McIntyre

## Individual Pitching

### CHICAGO (N.L.)

|             | W | L | ERA  | IP   | H  | BB | SO | SV |
|-------------|---|---|------|------|----|----|----|----|
| O. Overall  | 2 | 0 | 0.98 | 18.1 | 7  | 7  | 15 | 0  |
| T. Brown    | 2 | 0 | 0.00 | 11   | 6  | 1  | 5  | 0  |
| J. Pfiester | 0 | 1 | 7.88 | 8    | 10 | 3  | 1  | 0  |
| E. Reulbach | 0 | 0 | 4.70 | 7.2  | 9  | 1  | 5  | 0  |

### DETROIT (A.L.)

|             | W | L | ERA  | IP   | H  | BB | SO | SV |
|-------------|---|---|------|------|----|----|----|----|
| W. Donovan  | 0 | 2 | 4.24 | 17   | 17 | 4  | 10 | 0  |
| E. Summers  | 0 | 2 | 4.30 | 14.2 | 18 | 4  | 7  | 0  |
| G. Mullin   | 1 | 0 | 1.00 | 9    | 7  | 1  | 8  | 0  |
| E. Killian  | 0 | 0 | 7.71 | 2.1  | 5  | 3  | 1  | 0  |
| G. Winter   | 0 | 0 | 0.00 | 1    | 1  | 1  | 0  | 0  |

**LINE SCORES & PITCHERS (inn. pit.)**      **HOME RUNS (men on)**      **HIGHLIGHTS**

## Philadelphia (A.L.) defeats Chicago (N.L.) 4 games to 1

### GAME 1 - OCTOBER 17

```
CHI  N   000 000 001    1  3  1
PHI  A   021 000 01x    4  7  2
```
**Overall** (3), McIntire (5)
Bender (9)

Baker's single, two doubles, and two RBIs paced the Athletics' attack. Bender lost his shutout in the ninth thanks to errors by Thomas and Strunk.

### GAME 2 - OCTOBER 18

```
CHI  N   100 000 101    3  8  3
PHI  A   002 010 06x    9 14  4
```
**Brown** (7), Richie (1)
Coombs (9)

The Athletics broke open the game with a six-run seventh featuring four Athletics doubles. Everyone in the Philadelphia lineup contributed at least one hit.

### GAME 3 - OCTOBER 20

```
PHI  A   125 000 400   12 15  1
CHI  N   120 000 020    5  6  5
```
**Coombs** (9)
Reulbach (2), **McIntire** (0.1)
  Pfiester (6.2)

Murphy (2 on)

Murphy's three-run homer sparked a five-run third inning to put the game out of reach of the Cubs. Coombs aided his own cause with three hits and three RBIs.

### GAME 4 - OCTOBER 22

```
PHI  A   001 200 000 0    3 11  3
CHI  N   100 100 001 1    4  9  1
```
Bender (9.2)
Cole (8), **Brown** (2)

Chance's triple with one out in the ninth tied the game and Sheckard's game-winning single in the bottom of the tenth prevented a Series sweep.

### GAME 5 - OCTOBER 23

```
PHI  A   100 010 050    7  9  1
CHI  N   010 000 010    2  9  2
```
**Coombs** (9)
Brown (9)

A tight 2-1 game is broken up as the Athletics scored five times in the eighth to win the Series. Coombs posted his third victory and Collins led the offense with three hits and two RBIs.

### Team Totals

|      |   | W | AB | H | 2B | 3B | HR | R | RBI | BA | BB | SO | ERA |
|------|---|---|----|---|----|----|----|---|-----|------|----|----|------|
| PHI | A | 4 | 177 | 56 | 19 | 1 | 1 | 35 | 29 | .316 | 17 | 24 | 2.76 |
| CHI | N | 1 | 158 | 35 | 11 | 1 | 0 | 15 | 13 | .222 | 18 | 31 | 4.70 |

### Individual Batting

#### PHILADELPHIA (A.L.)

|              | AB | H | 2B | 3B | HR | R | RBI | BA |
|--------------|----|---|----|----|----|---|-----|------|
| F. Baker, 3b | 22 | 9 | 3 | 0 | 0 | 6 | 4 | .409 |
| B. Lord, of | 22 | 4 | 2 | 0 | 0 | 3 | 1 | .182 |
| E. Collins, 2b | 21 | 9 | 4 | 0 | 0 | 5 | 3 | .429 |
| D. Murphy, of | 20 | 7 | 3 | 0 | 1 | 6 | 8 | .350 |
| A. Strunk, of | 18 | 5 | 1 | 1 | 0 | 2 | 2 | .278 |
| J. Barry, ss | 17 | 4 | 2 | 0 | 0 | 3 | 3 | .235 |
| H. Davis, 1b | 17 | 6 | 3 | 0 | 0 | 5 | 2 | .353 |
| J. Coombs, p | 13 | 5 | 1 | 0 | 0 | 0 | 3 | .385 |
| I. Thomas, c | 12 | 3 | 0 | 0 | 0 | 2 | 1 | .250 |
| C. Bender, p | 6 | 2 | 0 | 0 | 0 | 1 | 1 | .333 |
| T. Hartsel, of | 5 | 1 | 0 | 0 | 0 | 2 | 0 | .200 |
| J. Lapp, c | 4 | 1 | 0 | 0 | 0 | 0 | 1 | .250 |

**Errors:** F. Baker (3), H. Davis (3), J. Coombs (2), E. Collins, A. Strunk, I. Thomas
**Stolen bases:** E. Collins (4), T. Hartsel (2), D. Murphy

#### CHICAGO (N.L.)

|                 | AB | H | 2B | 3B | HR | R | RBI | BA |
|-----------------|----|---|----|----|----|---|-----|------|
| H. Steinfeldt, 3b | 20 | 2 | 1 | 0 | 0 | 1 | .100 |
| J. Tinker, ss | 18 | 6 | 2 | 0 | 0 | 2 | 0 | .333 |
| F. Chance, 1b | 17 | 6 | 1 | 1 | 0 | 1 | 4 | .353 |
| W. Schulte, of | 17 | 6 | 3 | 0 | 0 | 3 | 2 | .353 |
| H. Zimmerman, 2b | 17 | 4 | 1 | 0 | 0 | 0 | 2 | .235 |
| S. Hofman, of | 15 | 4 | 0 | 0 | 0 | 2 | 2 | .267 |
| J. Sheckard, of | 14 | 4 | 2 | 0 | 0 | 5 | 1 | .286 |
| J. Kling, c | 13 | 1 | 0 | 0 | 0 | 0 | 1 | .077 |
| J. Archer, 1b, c | 11 | 2 | 1 | 0 | 0 | 1 | 0 | .182 |
| T. Brown, p | 7 | 0 | 0 | 0 | 0 | 0 | 0 | .000 |
| G. Beaumont | 2 | 0 | 0 | 0 | 0 | 1 | 0 | .000 |
| K. Cole, p | 2 | 0 | 0 | 0 | 0 | 0 | 0 | .000 |
| J. Pfiester, p | 2 | 0 | 0 | 0 | 0 | 0 | 0 | .000 |
| H. McIntyre, p | 1 | 0 | 0 | 0 | 0 | 0 | 0 | .000 |
| T. Needham | 1 | 0 | 0 | 0 | 0 | 0 | 0 | .000 |
| O. Overall, p | 1 | 0 | 0 | 0 | 0 | 0 | 0 | .000 |
| J. Kane | 0 | 0 | 0 | 0 | 0 | 0 | 0 | – |

**Errors:** H. Steinfeldt (4), J. Tinker (2), T. Brown, S. Hofman, H. McIntyre, W. Schulte, J. Sheckard, H. Zimmerman
**Stolen bases:** J. Sheckard, J. Tinker, H. Zimmerman

### Individual Pitching

#### PHILADELPHIA (A.L.)

|           | W | L | ERA | IP | H | BB | SO | SV |
|-----------|---|---|------|-----|----|----|----|----|
| J. Coombs | 3 | 0 | 3.33 | 27 | 23 | 14 | 17 | 0 |
| C. Bender | 1 | 1 | 1.93 | 18.2 | 12 | 4 | 14 | 0 |

#### CHICAGO (N.L.)

|             | W | L | ERA | IP | H | BB | SO | SV |
|-------------|---|---|-------|-----|----|----|----|----|
| T. Brown | 1 | 2 | 5.00 | 18 | 23 | 7 | 14 | 0 |
| K. Cole | 0 | 0 | 3.38 | 8 | 10 | 3 | 5 | 0 |
| J. Pfiester | 0 | 0 | 0.00 | 6.2 | 9 | 1 | 1 | 0 |
| H. McIntyre | 0 | 1 | 6.75 | 5.1 | 4 | 3 | 3 | 0 |
| O. Overall | 0 | 1 | 9.00 | 3 | 6 | 1 | 1 | 0 |
| E. Reulbach | 0 | 0 | 13.50 | 2 | 3 | 2 | 0 | 0 |
| L. Richie | 0 | 0 | 0.00 | 1 | 1 | 0 | 0 | 0 |

| LINE SCORES & PITCHERS (inn. pit.) | HOME RUNS (men on) | HIGHLIGHTS |
|---|---|---|

## Boston (A.L.) defeats Chicago (N.L.) 4 games to 2

**GAME 1 - SEPTEMBER 5**
```
BOS A  000 100 000    1  5  0
CHI N  000 000 000    0  6  0
Ruth (9)
Vaughn (9)
```
Ruth and Vaughn allowed just eleven singles between them, but Boston packaged two of them with a walk in the fourth for the game's only run.

**GAME 2 - SEPTEMBER 6**
```
BOS A  000 000 001    1  6  1
CHI N  030 000 00x    3  7  1
Bush (8)
Tyler (9)
```
Tyler went the distance and singled in two runs in the second. The shutout was spoiled when Strunk and Whiteman tripled in the ninth.

**GAME 3 - SEPTEMBER 7**
```
BOS A  000 200 000    2  7  0
CHI N  000 010 000    1  7  1
Mays (9)
Vaughn (9)
```
Scott singled home McInnis with the deciding run in the fourth. Pick tried to score from second on a passed ball with two out in the bottom of the ninth, but got caught in a rundown and retired.

**GAME 4 - SEPTEMBER 9**
```
CHI N  000 000 020    2  7  1
BOS A  000 200 01x    3  4  0
Tyler (7), Douglas (1)
Ruth (8), Bush (1) SV
```
Schang scored the go-ahead run in the eighth on Killefer's passed ball and Douglas's wild throw. Ruth's record scoreless inning streak dating back to the 1916 Series was stopped in the eighth after 29.2 innings.

**GAME 5 - SEPTEMBER 10**
```
CHI N  001 000 020    3  7  0
BOS A  000 000 000    0  5  0
Vaughn (9)
Jones (9)
```
Vaughn stopped Boston on five hits after two hard-luck losses.

**GAME 6 - SEPTEMBER 11**
```
CHI N  000 100 000    1  3  2
BOS A  002 000 00x    2  5  0
Tyler (7), Hendrix (1)
Mays (9)
```
Flack's error in the third let in two runs as Mays subdued Chicago on three hits.

## Team Totals

|       |   | W | AB | H | 2B | 3B | HR | R | RBI | BA | BB | SO | ERA |
|-------|---|---|----|----|----|----|----|----|-----|------|----|----|------|
| BOS | A | 4 | 172 | 32 | 2 | 3 | 0 | 9 | 6 | .186 | 16 | 21 | 1.70 |
| CHI | N | 2 | 176 | 37 | 5 | 1 | 0 | 10 | 10 | .210 | 18 | 14 | 1.04 |

## Individual Batting

### BOSTON (A.L.)

| | AB | H | 2B | 3B | HR | R | RBI | BA |
|---|----|----|----|----|----|----|-----|------|
| A. Strunk, of | 23 | 4 | 1 | 1 | 0 | 1 | 0 | .174 |
| H. Hooper, of | 20 | 4 | 0 | 0 | 0 | 0 | 0 | .200 |
| S. McInnis, 1b | 20 | 5 | 0 | 0 | 0 | 2 | 1 | .250 |
| E. Scott, ss | 20 | 2 | 0 | 0 | 0 | 0 | 0 | .100 |
| G. Whiteman, of | 20 | 5 | 0 | 1 | 0 | 2 | 1 | .250 |
| D. Shean, 2b | 19 | 4 | 1 | 0 | 0 | 2 | 0 | .211 |
| F. Thomas, 3b | 17 | 2 | 0 | 0 | 0 | 0 | 1 | .118 |
| S. Agnew, c | 9 | 0 | 0 | 0 | 0 | 0 | 0 | .000 |
| W. Schang, c | 9 | 4 | 0 | 0 | 0 | 1 | 1 | .444 |
| C. Mays, p | 5 | 1 | 0 | 0 | 0 | 1 | 0 | .200 |
| B. Ruth, of, p | 5 | 1 | 0 | 1 | 0 | 0 | 2 | .200 |
| J. Bush, p | 2 | 0 | 0 | 0 | 0 | 0 | 0 | .000 |
| J. Dubuc | 1 | 0 | 0 | 0 | 0 | 0 | 0 | .000 |
| S. Jones, p | 1 | 0 | 0 | 0 | 0 | 0 | 0 | .000 |
| H. Miller | 1 | 0 | 0 | 0 | 0 | 0 | 0 | .000 |

**Errors:** G. Whiteman

**Stolen bases:** W. Schang, D. Shean, G. Whiteman

### CHICAGO (N.L.)

| | AB | H | 2B | 3B | HR | R | RBI | BA |
|---|----|----|----|----|----|----|-----|------|
| L. Mann, of | 22 | 5 | 2 | 0 | 0 | 2 | 2 | .227 |
| C. Hollocher, ss | 21 | 4 | 0 | 1 | 0 | 2 | 0 | .190 |
| D. Paskert, of | 21 | 4 | 1 | 0 | 0 | 0 | 2 | .190 |
| M. Flack, of | 19 | 5 | 0 | 0 | 0 | 2 | 1 | .263 |
| F. Merkle, 1b | 18 | 5 | 0 | 0 | 0 | 1 | 1 | .278 |
| C. Pick, 2b | 18 | 7 | 1 | 0 | 0 | 0 | 0 | .389 |
| C. Deal, 3b | 17 | 3 | 0 | 0 | 0 | 0 | 0 | .176 |
| B. Killefer, c | 17 | 2 | 1 | 0 | 0 | 2 | 2 | .118 |
| H. Vaughn, p | 10 | 0 | 0 | 0 | 0 | 0 | 0 | .000 |
| L. Tyler, p | 5 | 1 | 0 | 0 | 0 | 0 | 2 | .200 |
| B. O'Farrell, c | 3 | 0 | 0 | 0 | 0 | 0 | 0 | .000 |
| T. Barber | 2 | 0 | 0 | 0 | 0 | 0 | 0 | .000 |
| C. Hendrix, p | 1 | 1 | 0 | 0 | 0 | 0 | 0 | 1.000 |
| B. McCabe | 1 | 0 | 0 | 0 | 0 | 1 | 0 | .000 |
| C. Wortman, 2b | 1 | 0 | 0 | 0 | 0 | 0 | 0 | .000 |
| R. Zeider, 3b | 0 | 0 | 0 | 0 | 0 | 0 | 0 | .— |

**Errors:** C. Deal, P. Douglas, M. Flack, C. Hollocher, L. Tyler

**Stolen bases:** C. Hollocher (2), M. Flack

## Individual Pitching

### BOSTON (A.L.)

| | W | L | ERA | IP | H | BB | SO | SV |
|---|---|---|------|----|----|----|----|----|
| C. Mays | 2 | 0 | 1.00 | 18 | 10 | 3 | 5 | 0 |
| B. Ruth | 2 | 0 | 1.06 | 17 | 13 | 7 | 4 | 0 |
| J. Bush | 0 | 1 | 3.00 | 9 | 7 | 3 | 0 | 1 |
| S. Jones | 0 | 1 | 3.00 | 9 | 7 | 5 | 5 | 0 |

### CHICAGO (N.L.)

| | W | L | ERA | IP | H | BB | SO | SV |
|---|---|---|------|----|----|----|----|----|
| H. Vaughn | 1 | 2 | 1.00 | 27 | 17 | 5 | 17 | 0 |
| L. Tyler | 1 | 1 | 1.17 | 23 | 14 | 11 | 4 | 0 |
| P. Douglas | 0 | 1 | 0.00 | 1 | 1 | 0 | 0 | 0 |
| C. Hendrix | 0 | 0 | 0.00 | 1 | 0 | 0 | 0 | 0 |

| LINE SCORES & PITCHERS (inn. pit.) | HOME RUNS (men on) | HIGHLIGHTS |
|---|---|---|

## Philadelphia (A.L.) defeats Chicago (N.L.) 4 games to 1

### GAME 1 - OCTOBER 8

PHI  A  000 000 102   3  6  1
CHI  N  000 000 001   1  8  2
**Ehmke** (9)
**Root** (7), Bush (2)

Foxx

Ehmke struck out 13, surpassing the Series record of 12 set by Walsh in 1906. Foxx's home run in the seventh broke a scoreless deadlock, and Miller's two-run single in the ninth applied the crusher.

### GAME 2 - OCTOBER 9

PHI  A  003 300 120   9 12  0

CHI  N  000 030 000   3 10  1
**Earnshaw** (4.2), Grove (4.1) **SV**
**Malone** (3.2), Blake (1.1), Carlson (3), Nehf (1)

Foxx (2 on),
Simmons (1 on)

Foxx again took charge, his three-run homer in the third launching the scoring. Earnshaw got credit for the win despite being relieved by Grove in the fifth.

### GAME 3 - OCTOBER 11

CHI  N  000 003 000   3  6  1
PHI  A  000 010 000   1  9  1
**Bush** (9)
**Earnshaw** (9)

A two-run single in the sixth by Cuyler gives the National League its first Series victory after ten straight setbacks. Earnshaw, on one day's rest, struck out ten, but lost on two unearned runs.

### GAME 4 - OCTOBER 12

CHI  N  000 205  1 00   8 10  2
PHI  A  000 000 (10)0x  10 15  2
**Root** (6.1), Nehf (0), **Blake** (0), Malone (0.2), Carlson (1)
**Quinn** (5), Walberg (1), **Rommel** (1), Grove (2) **SV**

Grimm (1 on),
Simmons, Haas (2 on)

A fabulous ten-run seventh overcame an 8-0 deficit and lifted the A's to an incredible triumph. Wilson contributed to the scoring binge by losing two balls in the sun.

### GAME 5 - OCTOBER 14

CHI  N  000 200 000   2  8  0
PHI  A  000 000 003   3  6  0
**Malone** (8.2)
Ehmke (3.2), **Walberg** (5.1)

Haas (1 on)

Three runs in the last of the ninth brought a dramatic end to the Series. A two-run homer by Haas tied the score before Simmons and Miller doubled to score the winning run.

## Team Totals

|      |   | W | AB | H | 2B | 3B | HR | R | RBI | BA | BB | SO | ERA |
|------|---|---|----|---|----|----|----|---|-----|-----|----|----|-----|
| PHI  | A | 4 | 171 | 48 | 5 | 0 | 6 | 26 | 26 | .281 | 13 | 27 | 2.40 |
| CHI  | N | 1 | 173 | 43 | 6 | 2 | 1 | 17 | 15 | .249 | 13 | 50 | 4.33 |

## Individual Batting

### PHILADELPHIA (A.L.)

| | AB | H | 2B | 3B | HR | R | RBI | BA |
|---|----|----|----|----|----|---|-----|-----|
| M. Bishop, 2b | 21 | 4 | 0 | 0 | 0 | 2 | 1 | .190 |
| M. Haas, of | 21 | 5 | 0 | 0 | 2 | 3 | 6 | .238 |
| J. Foxx, 1b | 20 | 7 | 1 | 0 | 2 | 5 | 5 | .350 |
| A. Simmons, of | 20 | 6 | 1 | 0 | 2 | 6 | 5 | .300 |
| J. Dykes, 3b | 19 | 8 | 1 | 0 | 0 | 2 | 4 | .421 |
| B. Miller, of | 19 | 7 | 1 | 0 | 0 | 1 | 4 | .368 |
| J. Boley, ss | 17 | 4 | 0 | 0 | 0 | 1 | 1 | .235 |
| M. Cochrane, c | 15 | 6 | 1 | 0 | 0 | 5 | 0 | .400 |
| G. Earnshaw, p | 5 | 0 | 0 | 0 | 0 | 1 | 0 | .000 |
| H. Ehmke, p | 5 | 1 | 0 | 0 | 0 | 0 | 0 | .200 |
| G. Burns | 2 | 0 | 0 | 0 | 0 | 0 | 0 | .000 |
| L. Grove, p | 2 | 0 | 0 | 0 | 0 | 0 | 0 | .000 |
| J. Quinn, p | 2 | 0 | 0 | 0 | 0 | 0 | 0 | .000 |
| W. French | 1 | 0 | 0 | 0 | 0 | 0 | 0 | .000 |
| H. Summa | 1 | 0 | 0 | 0 | 0 | 0 | 0 | .000 |
| R. Walberg, p | 1 | 0 | 0 | 0 | 0 | 0 | 0 | .000 |

**Errors:** J. Dykes (2), B. Miller, R. Walberg

### CHICAGO (N.L.)

| | AB | H | 2B | 3B | HR | R | RBI | BA |
|---|----|----|----|----|----|---|-----|-----|
| W. English, ss | 21 | 4 | 2 | 0 | 0 | 4 | 0 | .190 |
| R. Hornsby, 2b | 21 | 5 | 1 | 1 | 0 | 4 | 1 | .238 |
| K. Cuyler, of | 20 | 6 | 1 | 0 | 0 | 4 | 4 | .300 |
| N. McMillan, 3b | 20 | 2 | 0 | 0 | 0 | 0 | 0 | .100 |
| R. Stephenson, of | 19 | 6 | 1 | 0 | 0 | 3 | 3 | .316 |
| C. Grimm, 1b | 18 | 7 | 0 | 0 | 1 | 2 | 4 | .389 |
| Z. Taylor, c | 17 | 3 | 0 | 0 | 0 | 0 | 3 | .176 |
| H. Wilson, of | 17 | 8 | 0 | 1 | 0 | 2 | 0 | .471 |
| C. Root, p | 5 | 0 | 0 | 0 | 0 | 0 | 0 | .000 |
| P. Malone, p | 4 | 1 | 1 | 0 | 0 | 0 | 0 | .250 |
| G. Bush, p | 3 | 0 | 0 | 0 | 0 | 1 | 0 | .000 |
| G. Hartnett | 3 | 0 | 0 | 0 | 0 | 0 | 0 | .000 |
| F. Blair | 1 | 0 | 0 | 0 | 0 | 0 | 0 | .000 |
| S. Blake, p | 1 | 1 | 0 | 0 | 0 | 0 | 0 | 1.000 |
| M. Gonzalez, c | 1 | 0 | 0 | 0 | 0 | 0 | 0 | .000 |
| C. Heathcote | 1 | 0 | 0 | 0 | 0 | 0 | 0 | .000 |
| C. Tolson | 1 | 0 | 0 | 0 | 0 | 0 | 0 | .000 |

**Errors:** W. English (4), K. Cuyler, R. Hornsby, H. Wilson
**Stolen bases:** N. McMillan

## Individual Pitching

### PHILADELPHIA (A.L.)

| | W | L | ERA | IP | H | BB | SO | SV |
|---|---|---|-----|----|----|----|----|----|
| G. Earnshaw | 1 | 1 | 2.63 | 13.2 | 14 | 6 | 17 | 0 |
| H. Ehmke | 1 | 0 | 1.42 | 12.2 | 14 | 3 | 13 | 0 |
| L. Grove | 0 | 0 | 0.00 | 6.1 | 3 | 1 | 10 | 2 |
| R. Walberg | 1 | 0 | 0.00 | 6.1 | 3 | 0 | 8 | 0 |
| J. Quinn | 0 | 0 | 9.00 | 5 | 7 | 2 | 2 | 0 |
| E. Rommel | 1 | 0 | 9.00 | 1 | 2 | 1 | 0 | 0 |

### CHICAGO (N.L.)

| | W | L | ERA | IP | H | BB | SO | SV |
|---|---|---|-----|----|----|----|----|----|
| P. Malone | 0 | 2 | 4.15 | 13 | 12 | 7 | 11 | 0 |
| C. Root | 0 | 1 | 4.73 | 13.1 | 12 | 2 | 8 | 0 |
| G. Bush | 1 | 0 | 0.82 | 11 | 12 | 2 | 4 | 0 |
| H. Carlson | 0 | 0 | 6.75 | 4 | 7 | 1 | 3 | 0 |
| S. Blake | 0 | 1 | 13.50 | 1.1 | 4 | 0 | 1 | 0 |
| A. Nehf | 0 | 0 | 18.00 | 1 | 1 | 1 | 0 | 0 |

| LINE SCORES & PITCHERS (inn. pit.) | HOME RUNS (men on) | HIGHLIGHTS |
|---|---|---|

## New York (A.L.) defeats Chicago (N.L.) 4 games to 0

**GAME 1 - SEPTEMBER 28**

```
CHI  N  200 000 220    6 10  1
NY   A  000 305 31x   12  8  2
Bush (5.1), Grimes (1.2), Smith (1)
Ruffing (9)
```

Gehrig (1 on)

Bush retired the first nine batters, but the Yanks exploded, thanks to Gehrig's two-run homer in the fourth, and two-run singles by Dickey and Combs. Ruffing struck out ten in going the distance.

**GAME 2 - SEPTEMBER 29**

```
CHI  N  101 000 000    2  9  0
NY   A  202 010 00x    5 10  1
Warneke (8)
Gomez (9)
```

Chapman's single in the third gave the Yankees the lead, and Gomez shut the Cubs down. Gehrig had three hits and scored two runs.

**GAME 3 - OCTOBER 1**

```
NY   A  301 020 001    7  8  1

CHI  N  102 100 001    5  9  4
Pipgras (8), Pennock (1) SV
Root (4.1), Malone (2.2), May (1.1),
Tinning (0.2)
```

Ruth (2 on), Gehrig,
Ruth, Gehrig
Cuyler, Hartnett

In a home run carnival which featured two homers each by Ruth and Gehrig, the Yankees took a commanding three-game lead in the Series. Back-to-back home runs in the fifth by the two sluggers decided the game.

**GAME 4 - OCTOBER 2**

```
NY   A  102 002 404   13 19  4

CHI  N  400 001 001    6  9  1
W. Moore (5.1),
Pennock (3) SV
Bush (0.1), Warneke (2.2), May (3.1),
Tinning (1.2), Grimes (1)
```

Lazzeri (1 on), Combs,
Lazzeri (1 on)
Demaree (2 on)

The Yankees came back from a 4-1 first inning deficit to sweep the Series. The Cubs held Ruth to just one single, but six other Yankees had two or more hits on the day.

### Team Totals

|   |   | W | AB | H | 2B | 3B | HR | R | RBI | BA | BB | SO | ERA |
|---|---|---|----|---|----|----|----|---|-----|----|----|----|----|
| NY | A | 4 | 144 | 45 | 6 | 0 | 8 | 37 | 36 | .313 | 23 | 26 | 3.25 |
| CHI | N | 0 | 146 | 37 | 8 | 2 | 3 | 19 | 16 | .253 | 11 | 24 | 9.26 |

### Individual Batting

**NEW YORK (A.L.)**

|  | AB | H | 2B | 3B | HR | R | RBI | BA |
|---|---|---|---|---|---|---|---|---|
| B. Chapman, of | 17 | 5 | 1 | 0 | 0 | 1 | 6 | .294 |
| L. Gehrig, 1b | 17 | 9 | 1 | 0 | 3 | 9 | 8 | .529 |
| T. Lazzeri, 2b | 17 | 5 | 0 | 0 | 2 | 4 | 5 | .294 |
| E. Combs, of | 16 | 6 | 2 | 0 | 1 | 8 | 4 | .375 |
| B. Dickey, c | 16 | 7 | 0 | 0 | 0 | 2 | 4 | .438 |
| F. Crosetti, ss | 15 | 2 | 1 | 0 | 0 | 2 | 0 | .133 |
| B. Ruth, of | 15 | 5 | 0 | 0 | 2 | 6 | 6 | .333 |
| J. Sewell, 3b | 15 | 5 | 1 | 0 | 0 | 4 | 3 | .333 |
| G. Pipgras, p | 5 | 0 | 0 | 0 | 0 | 0 | 0 | .000 |
| R. Ruffing, p | 4 | 0 | 0 | 0 | 0 | 0 | 0 | .000 |
| L. Gomez, p | 3 | 0 | 0 | 0 | 0 | 0 | 0 | .000 |
| W. Moore, p | 3 | 1 | 0 | 0 | 0 | 0 | 0 | .333 |
| H. Pennock, p | 1 | 0 | 0 | 0 | 0 | 0 | 0 | .000 |
| S. Byrd, of | 0 | 0 | 0 | 0 | 0 | 0 | 0 | — |
| M. Hoag | 0 | 0 | 0 | 0 | 0 | 1 | 0 | — |

**Errors:** F. Crosetti (4), L. Gehrig, T. Lazzeri, B. Ruth, J. Sewell

**CHICAGO (N.L.)**

|  | AB | H | 2B | 3B | HR | R | RBI | BA |
|---|---|---|---|---|---|---|---|---|
| K. Cuyler, of | 18 | 5 | 1 | 1 | 1 | 2 | 2 | .278 |
| B. Herman, 2b | 18 | 4 | 1 | 0 | 0 | 5 | 1 | .222 |
| R. Stephenson, of | 18 | 8 | 1 | 0 | 0 | 2 | 4 | .444 |
| W. English, 3b | 17 | 3 | 0 | 0 | 0 | 2 | 1 | .176 |
| G. Hartnett, c | 16 | 5 | 2 | 0 | 1 | 2 | 1 | .313 |
| C. Grimm, 1b | 15 | 5 | 2 | 0 | 0 | 2 | 1 | .333 |
| B. Jurges, ss | 11 | 4 | 1 | 0 | 0 | 1 | 1 | .364 |
| F. Demaree, of | 7 | 2 | 0 | 0 | 1 | 1 | 4 | .286 |
| J. Moore, of | 7 | 0 | 0 | 0 | 0 | 1 | 0 | .000 |
| M. Koenig, ss | 4 | 1 | 0 | 1 | 0 | 1 | 1 | .250 |
| L. Warneke, p | 4 | 0 | 0 | 0 | 0 | 0 | 0 | .000 |
| R. Hemsley, c | 3 | 0 | 0 | 0 | 0 | 0 | 0 | .000 |
| M. Gudat | 2 | 0 | 0 | 0 | 0 | 0 | 0 | .000 |
| J. May, p | 2 | 0 | 0 | 0 | 0 | 0 | 0 | .000 |
| C. Root, p | 2 | 0 | 0 | 0 | 0 | 0 | 0 | .000 |
| G. Bush, p | 1 | 0 | 0 | 0 | 0 | 0 | 0 | .000 |
| B. Grimes, p | 1 | 0 | 0 | 0 | 0 | 0 | 0 | .000 |
| S. Hack | 0 | 0 | 0 | 0 | 0 | 0 | 0 | — |

**Errors:** B. Jurges (2), F. Demaree, W. English, G. Hartnett, B. Herman
**Stolen bases:** K. Cuyler, B. Jurges

### Individual Pitching

**NEW YORK (A.L.)**

|  | W | L | ERA | IP | H | BB | SO | SV |
|---|---|---|---|---|---|---|---|---|
| L. Gomez | 1 | 0 | 1.00 | 9 | 9 | 1 | 8 | 0 |
| R. Ruffing | 1 | 0 | 4.00 | 9 | 10 | 6 | 10 | 0 |
| G. Pipgras | 1 | 0 | 4.50 | 8 | 9 | 3 | 1 | 0 |
| W. Moore | 1 | 0 | 0.00 | 5.1 | 2 | 0 | 1 | 0 |
| H. Pennock | 0 | 0 | 2.25 | 4 | 2 | 1 | 4 | 2 |
| J. Allen | 0 | 0 | 40.50 | 0.2 | 5 | 0 | 0 | 0 |

**CHICAGO (N.L.)**

|  | W | L | ERA | IP | H | BB | SO | SV |
|---|---|---|---|---|---|---|---|---|
| L. Warneke | 0 | 1 | 5.91 | 10.2 | 15 | 5 | 8 | 0 |
| G. Bush | 0 | 1 | 14.29 | 5.2 | 5 | 6 | 2 | 0 |
| J. May | 0 | 1 | 11.57 | 4.2 | 9 | 3 | 4 | 0 |
| C. Root | 0 | 1 | 10.38 | 4.1 | 6 | 3 | 4 | 0 |
| B. Grimes | 0 | 0 | 23.63 | 2.2 | 7 | 2 | 0 | 0 |
| P. Malone | 0 | 0 | 0.00 | 2.2 | 1 | 4 | 4 | 0 |
| B. Tinning | 0 | 0 | 0.00 | 2.1 | 0 | 0 | 3 | 0 |
| B. Smith | 0 | 0 | 9.00 | 1 | 2 | 0 | 1 | 0 |

| LINE SCORES & PITCHERS (inn. pit.) | HOME RUNS (men on) | HIGHLIGHTS |
| --- | --- | --- |

## Detroit (A.L.) defeats Chicago (N.L.) 4 games to 2

**GAME 1 - OCTOBER 2**

| | | | | | |
| --- | --- | --- | --- | --- | --- |
| CHI | N | 200 000 001 | 3 7 0 | | |
| DET | A | 000 000 000 | 0 4 3 | | |

Warneke (9)
Rowe (9)

Demaree

Chicago scored twice in the first on hits by Galan and Hartnett and Rowe's error as Warneke pitched a four-hit shutout.

**GAME 2 - OCTOBER 3**

| | | | | |
| --- | --- | --- | --- | --- |
| CHI | N | 000 010 200 | 3 6 1 | |
| DET | A | 400 300 10x | 8 9 2 | |

Root (0), Henshaw (3.2), Kowalik (4.1)
Bridges (9)

Greenberg (1 on)

Hits by the first four batters in the Tiger first, capped by Greenberg's homer, chased Root and ensured the victory.

**GAME 3 - OCTOBER 4**

| | | | | |
| --- | --- | --- | --- | --- |
| DET | A | 000 001 040 01 | 6 12 2 | |
| CHI | N | 020 010 002 00 | 5 10 3 | |

Auker (6), Hogsett (1), **Rowe** (4)
Lee (7.1), Warneke (1.2), **French** (2)

Demaree

White's single scored Owen with the winning run in the eleventh after the Cubs tied the game in the ninth on singles by Hack, Klein, and O'Dea and a long fly by Galan.

**GAME 4 - OCTOBER 5**

| | | | | |
| --- | --- | --- | --- | --- |
| DET | A | 001 001 000 | 2 7 0 | |
| CHI | N | 010 000 000 | 1 5 2 | |

Crowder (9)
Carleton (7), Root (2)

Hartnett

The Tigers scored the winning run in the sixth on errors by Galan and Jurges.

**GAME 5 - OCTOBER 6**

| | | | | |
| --- | --- | --- | --- | --- |
| DET | A | 000 000 001 | 1 7 1 | |
| CHI | N | 002 000 10x | 3 8 0 | |

Rowe (8)
Warneke (6), Lee (3) **SV**

Klein (1 on)

The Cubs scored twice in the third on Herman's triple and Klein's homer. Warneke left after six shutout innings because of a sore shoulder. Lee had to retire Clifton with two out and runners on second and third in the ninth to preserve the victory.

**GAME 6 - OCTOBER 7**

| | | | | |
| --- | --- | --- | --- | --- |
| CHI | N | 001 020 000 | 3 12 0 | |
| DET | A | 100 101 001 | 4 12 1 | |

French (8.2)
Bridges (9)

Herman (1 on)

The Tigers won in the ninth inning when Cochrane singled, Gehringer's grounder moved him to second, and Goslin's single brought him in for the Series-ending run.

### Team Totals

| | | W | AB | H | 2B | 3B | HR | R | RBI | BA | BB | SO | ERA |
| --- | --- | --- | --- | --- | --- | --- | --- | --- | --- | --- | --- | --- | --- |
| DET | A | 4 | 206 | 51 | 11 | 1 | 1 | 21 | 18 | .248 | 25 | 27 | 2.29 |
| CHI | N | 2 | 202 | 48 | 6 | 2 | 5 | 18 | 17 | .238 | 11 | 29 | 2.81 |

### Individual Batting

**DETROIT (A.L.)**

| | AB | H | 2B | 3B | HR | R | RBI | BA |
| --- | --- | --- | --- | --- | --- | --- | --- | --- |
| P. Fox, of | 26 | 10 | 3 | 1 | 0 | 1 | 4 | .385 |
| M. Cochrane, c | 24 | 7 | 1 | 0 | 0 | 3 | 1 | .292 |
| C. Gehringer, 2b | 24 | 9 | 3 | 0 | 0 | 4 | 4 | .375 |
| B. Rogell, ss | 24 | 7 | 2 | 0 | 0 | 1 | 1 | .292 |
| G. Goslin, of | 22 | 6 | 1 | 0 | 0 | 2 | 3 | .273 |
| M. Owen, 3b, 1b | 20 | 1 | 0 | 0 | 0 | 2 | 1 | .050 |
| J. White, of | 19 | 5 | 0 | 0 | 0 | 3 | 1 | .263 |
| F. Clifton, 3b | 16 | 0 | 0 | 0 | 0 | 1 | 0 | .000 |
| T. Bridges, p | 8 | 1 | 0 | 0 | 0 | 1 | 1 | .125 |
| S. Rowe, p | 8 | 2 | 1 | 0 | 0 | 0 | 0 | .250 |
| H. Greenberg, 1b | 6 | 1 | 0 | 0 | 1 | 1 | 2 | .167 |
| G. Walker, of | 4 | 1 | 0 | 0 | 0 | 1 | 0 | .250 |
| G. Crowder, p | 3 | 1 | 0 | 0 | 0 | 0 | 0 | .333 |
| E. Auker, p | 2 | 0 | 0 | 0 | 0 | 0 | 0 | .000 |

**Errors:** H. Greenberg (3), F. Clifton, M. Cochrane, P. Fox, G. Goslin, M. Owen, S. Rowe
**Stolen bases:** C. Gehringer

**CHICAGO (N.L.)**

| | AB | H | 2B | 3B | HR | R | RBI | BA |
| --- | --- | --- | --- | --- | --- | --- | --- | --- |
| A. Galan, of | 25 | 4 | 1 | 0 | 0 | 2 | 2 | .160 |
| P. Cavarretta, 1b | 24 | 3 | 0 | 0 | 0 | 1 | 0 | .125 |
| F. Demaree, of | 24 | 6 | 1 | 0 | 2 | 2 | 2 | .250 |
| G. Hartnett, c | 24 | 7 | 0 | 0 | 1 | 1 | 2 | .292 |
| B. Herman, 2b | 24 | 8 | 2 | 1 | 1 | 3 | 6 | .333 |
| S. Hack, ss, 3b | 22 | 5 | 1 | 1 | 0 | 2 | 0 | .227 |
| B. Jurges, ss | 16 | 4 | 0 | 0 | 0 | 3 | 1 | .250 |
| F. Lindstrom, 3b, of | 15 | 3 | 1 | 0 | 0 | 0 | 0 | .200 |
| C. Klein, of | 12 | 4 | 0 | 0 | 1 | 2 | 2 | .333 |
| L. Warneke, p | 5 | 1 | 0 | 0 | 0 | 0 | 0 | .200 |
| L. French, p | 4 | 1 | 0 | 0 | 0 | 1 | 0 | .250 |
| F. Kowalik, p | 2 | 1 | 0 | 0 | 0 | 1 | 0 | .500 |
| T. Carleton, p | 1 | 0 | 0 | 0 | 0 | 0 | 0 | .000 |
| R. Henshaw, p | 1 | 0 | 0 | 0 | 0 | 0 | 0 | .000 |
| B. Lee, p | 1 | 0 | 0 | 0 | 0 | 0 | 1 | .000 |
| K. O'Dea | 1 | 1 | 0 | 0 | 0 | 0 | 1 | 1.000 |
| W. Stephenson | 1 | 0 | 0 | 0 | 0 | 0 | 0 | .000 |

**Errors:** P. Cavarretta, A. Galan, B. Herman, B. Jurges, F. Kowalik, F. Lindstrom
**Stolen bases:** S. Hack

### Individual Pitching

**DETROIT (A.L.)**

| | W | L | ERA | IP | H | BB | SO | SV |
| --- | --- | --- | --- | --- | --- | --- | --- | --- |
| S. Rowe | 1 | 2 | 2.57 | 21 | 19 | 1 | 14 | 0 |
| T. Bridges | 2 | 0 | 2.50 | 18 | 18 | 4 | 9 | 0 |
| G. Crowder | 1 | 0 | 1.00 | 9 | 5 | 3 | 5 | 0 |
| E. Auker | 0 | 0 | 3.00 | 6 | 6 | 2 | 1 | 0 |
| C. Hogsett | 0 | 0 | 0.00 | 1 | 0 | 1 | 0 | 0 |

**CHICAGO (N.L.)**

| | W | L | ERA | IP | H | BB | SO | SV |
| --- | --- | --- | --- | --- | --- | --- | --- | --- |
| L. Warneke | 2 | 0 | 0.54 | 16.2 | 9 | 4 | 5 | 0 |
| L. French | 0 | 2 | 3.38 | 10.2 | 15 | 2 | 8 | 0 |
| B. Lee | 0 | 0 | 3.48 | 10.1 | 11 | 5 | 5 | 1 |
| T. Carleton | 0 | 1 | 1.29 | 7 | 6 | 7 | 4 | 0 |
| F. Kowalik | 0 | 0 | 2.08 | 4.1 | 3 | 1 | 1 | 0 |
| R. Henshaw | 0 | 0 | 7.36 | 3.2 | 2 | 5 | 2 | 0 |
| C. Root | 0 | 1 | 18.00 | 2 | 5 | 1 | 2 | 0 |

| LINE SCORES & PITCHERS (inn. pit.) | HOME RUNS (men on) | HIGHLIGHTS |
|---|---|---|

## New York (A.L.) defeats Chicago (N.L.) 4 games to 0

**GAME 1 - OCTOBER 5**

```
NY   A  020 000 100    3 12  1
CHI  N  001 000 000    1  9  1
```
**Ruffing** (9)
**Lee** (8), Russell (1)

Dickey's four singles led the New York attack in support of Ruffing's nine-hit effort.

**GAME 2 - OCTOBER 6**

```
NY   A  020 000 022    6  7  2
CHI  N  102 000 000    3 11  0
```
**Gomez** (7), Murphy (2) **SV**
**Dean** (8), French (1)

Crosetti (1 on),
DiMaggio (1 on)

Crosetti batted in the tying and winning runs with an eighth-inning homer after Dizzy Dean, with no fastball left due to a sore arm, had held the Yankees to five hits in the first seven innings.

**GAME 3 - OCTOBER 8**

```
CHI  N  000 010 010    2  5  1
NY   A  000 022 01x    5  7  2
```
**Bryant** (5.1), Russell (0.2), French (2)
**Pearson** (9)

Marty
Gordon, Dickey

Gordon's homer in the fifth was the first Yankee hit off Bryant, and his two-run single in the sixth gave the Yankees a three-run cushion.

**GAME 4 - OCTOBER 9**

```
CHI  N  000 100 020    3  8  1
NY   A  030 001 04x    8 11  1
```
**Lee** (3), Root (3), Page (1.1),
   French (0.1), Carleton (0), Dean (0.1)
**Ruffing** (9)

O'Dea (1 on)
Henrich

New York scored three runs in the second on a two-out error by Jurges, two singles, and Crosetti's triple. Four more in the eighth ensured the clincher after O'Dea's homer in the top of the eighth narrowed the lead to one run.

## Team Totals

| | | W | AB | H | 2B | 3B | HR | R | RBI | BA | BB | SO | ERA |
|---|---|---|---|---|---|---|---|---|---|---|---|---|---|
| NY | A | 4 | 135 | 37 | 6 | 1 | 5 | 22 | 21 | .274 | 11 | 16 | 1.75 |
| CHI | N | 0 | 136 | 33 | 4 | 1 | 2 | 9 | 8 | .243 | 6 | 26 | 5.03 |

## Individual Batting

### NEW YORK (A.L.)

| | AB | H | 2B | 3B | HR | R | RBI | BA |
|---|---|---|---|---|---|---|---|---|
| R. Rolfe, 3b | 18 | 3 | 0 | 0 | 0 | 0 | 1 | .167 |
| F. Crosetti, ss | 16 | 4 | 2 | 1 | 1 | 1 | 6 | .250 |
| T. Henrich, of | 16 | 4 | 1 | 0 | 1 | 3 | 1 | .250 |
| B. Dickey, c | 15 | 6 | 0 | 0 | 1 | 2 | 2 | .400 |
| J. DiMaggio, of | 15 | 4 | 0 | 0 | 1 | 4 | 2 | .267 |
| J. Gordon, 2b | 15 | 6 | 2 | 0 | 1 | 3 | 6 | .400 |
| L. Gehrig, 1b | 14 | 4 | 0 | 0 | 0 | 4 | 0 | .286 |
| G. Selkirk, of | 10 | 2 | 0 | 0 | 0 | 1 | 0 | .200 |
| R. Ruffing, p | 6 | 1 | 0 | 0 | 0 | 1 | 1 | .167 |
| M. Hoag, of | 5 | 2 | 1 | 0 | 0 | 3 | 1 | .400 |
| M. Pearson, p | 3 | 1 | 0 | 0 | 0 | 1 | 0 | .333 |
| L. Gomez, p | 2 | 0 | 0 | 0 | 0 | 0 | 0 | .000 |

**Errors:** J. Gordon (2), R. Rolfe (2), F. Crosetti, T. Henrich
**Stolen bases:** B. Dickey, J. Gordon, R. Rolfe

### CHICAGO (N.L.)

| | AB | H | 2B | 3B | HR | R | RBI | BA |
|---|---|---|---|---|---|---|---|---|
| S. Hack, 3b | 17 | 8 | 1 | 0 | 0 | 3 | 1 | .471 |
| B. Herman, 2b | 16 | 3 | 0 | 0 | 0 | 1 | 0 | .188 |
| R. Collins, 1b | 15 | 2 | 0 | 0 | 0 | 1 | 0 | .133 |
| P. Cavarretta, of | 13 | 6 | 1 | 0 | 0 | 1 | 0 | .462 |
| B. Jurges, ss | 13 | 3 | 1 | 0 | 0 | 0 | 0 | .231 |
| J. Marty, of | 12 | 6 | 1 | 0 | 1 | 1 | 5 | .500 |
| C. Reynolds, of | 12 | 0 | 0 | 0 | 0 | 0 | 0 | .000 |
| G. Hartnett, c | 11 | 1 | 0 | 1 | 0 | 0 | 0 | .091 |
| F. Demaree, of | 10 | 1 | 0 | 0 | 0 | 1 | 0 | .100 |
| K. O'Dea, c | 5 | 1 | 0 | 0 | 1 | 1 | 2 | .200 |
| D. Dean, p | 3 | 2 | 0 | 0 | 0 | 0 | 0 | .667 |
| B. Lee, p | 3 | 0 | 0 | 0 | 0 | 0 | 0 | .000 |
| C. Bryant, p | 2 | 0 | 0 | 0 | 0 | 0 | 0 | .000 |
| A. Galan | 2 | 0 | 0 | 0 | 0 | 0 | 0 | .000 |
| T. Lazzeri | 2 | 0 | 0 | 0 | 0 | 0 | 0 | .000 |

**Errors:** B. Herman (2), B. Jurges

## Individual Pitching

### NEW YORK (A.L.)

| | W | L | ERA | IP | H | BB | SO | SV |
|---|---|---|---|---|---|---|---|---|
| R. Ruffing | 2 | 0 | 1.50 | 18 | 17 | 2 | 11 | 0 |
| M. Pearson | 1 | 0 | 1.00 | 9 | 5 | 2 | 9 | 0 |
| L. Gomez | 1 | 0 | 3.86 | 7 | 9 | 1 | 5 | 0 |
| J. Murphy | 0 | 0 | 0.00 | 2 | 2 | 1 | 1 | 1 |

### CHICAGO (N.L.)

| | W | L | ERA | IP | H | BB | SO | SV |
|---|---|---|---|---|---|---|---|---|
| B. Lee | 0 | 2 | 2.45 | 11 | 15 | 1 | 8 | 0 |
| D. Dean | 0 | 1 | 6.48 | 8.1 | 8 | 1 | 2 | 0 |
| C. Bryant | 0 | 1 | 6.75 | 5.1 | 6 | 5 | 3 | 0 |
| L. French | 0 | 0 | 2.70 | 3.1 | 1 | 1 | 2 | 0 |
| C. Root | 0 | 0 | 3.00 | 3 | 3 | 0 | 1 | 0 |
| V. Page | 0 | 0 | 13.50 | 1.1 | 2 | 0 | 0 | 0 |
| J. Russell | 0 | 0 | 0.00 | 1.2 | 1 | 1 | 0 | 0 |
| T. Carleton | 0 | 0 | ∞ | 0.0 | 1 | 2 | 0 | 0 |

| LINE SCORES & PITCHERS (inn. pit.) | HOME RUNS (men on) | HIGHLIGHTS |
|---|---|---|

## Detroit (A.L.) defeats Chicago (N.L.) 4 games to 3

**GAME 1 - OCTOBER 3**

CHI N 403 000 200   9 13 0
DET A 000 000 000   0 6 0
**Borowy** (9)
**Newhouser** (2.2), Benton (1.1),
  Tobin (3), Mueller (2)

Cavarretta

Newhouser gave up seven hits and eight runs in the first three innings as Cavarretta and Pafko scored three runs each and Nicholson had three RBIs.

**GAME 2 - OCTOBER 4**

CHI N 000 100 000   1 7 0
DET A 000 040 00x   4 7 0
**Wyse** (6), Erickson (2)
**Trucks** (9)

Greenberg (2 on)

Greenberg's homer with two on in the fifth broke open the game.

**GAME 3 - OCTOBER 5**

CHI N 000 200 100   3 8 0
DET A 000 000 000   0 1 2
**Passeau** (9)
**Overmire** (6), Benton (3)

Passeau allowed only a single to York in the third and a walk to Swift in the sixth.

**GAME 4 - OCTOBER 6**

DET A 000 400 000   4 7 1
CHI N 000 001 000   1 5 1
**Trout** (9)
**Prim** (3.1), Derringer (1.2)
  Vandenburg (2), Erickson (2)

Prim retired the first ten batters in the game, but the Tigers knocked him out with four in the fourth.

**GAME 5 - OCTOBER 7**

DET A 001 004 102   8 11 0
CHI N 000 000 201   4 7 2
**Newhouser** (9)
**Borowy** (5), Vandenburg (0.2), Chipman (0.1),
  Derringer (2), Erickson (1)

Newhouser benefitted from another four-run Tiger rally and struck out nine Cubs in the victory. Greenberg's three doubles keyed the attack.

**GAME 6 - OCTOBER 8**

DET A 010 000 240 000   7 13 1
CHI N 000 041 200 001   8 15 3
**Trucks** (4.1), Caster (0.2), Bridges (1.2),
  Benton (0.1), **Trout** (4.2)
Passeau (6.2), Wyse (0.2), Prim (0.2),
  **Borowy** (4)

Greenberg

Hack's drive bounced past Greenberg for a double and brought home the winning run in the twelfth after Greenberg tied the game with a homer in the eighth. Borowy held the Tigers hitless over the last four innings.

**GAME 7 - OCTOBER 10**

DET A 510 000 120   9 9 1
CHI N 100 100 010   3 10 0
**Newhouser** (9)
**Borowy** (0), Derringer (1.2),
  Vandenberg (3.1), Erickson (2),
  Passeau (1), Wyse (1)

The Cubs gambled and sent in Borowy with only a day's rest. The Tigers hit three successive singles to knock him out in the first, and went on to score five in the frame to sew up the Series.

### Team Totals

| | | W | AB | H | 2B | 3B | HR | R | RBI | BA | BB | SO | ERA |
|---|---|---|---|---|---|---|---|---|---|---|---|---|---|
| DET | A | 4 | 242 | 54 | 10 | 0 | 2 | 32 | 32 | .223 | 33 | 22 | 3.84 |
| CHI | N | 3 | 246 | 65 | 16 | 3 | 1 | 29 | 27 | .264 | 19 | 48 | 4.15 |

### Individual Batting

**DETROIT (A.L.)**

| | AB | H | 2B | 3B | HR | R | RBI | BA |
|---|---|---|---|---|---|---|---|---|
| D. Cramer, of | 29 | 11 | 0 | 0 | 0 | 7 | 4 | .379 |
| E. Mayo, 2b | 28 | 7 | 1 | 0 | 0 | 4 | 2 | .250 |
| J. Outlaw, 3b | 28 | 5 | 0 | 0 | 0 | 1 | 3 | .179 |
| R. York, 1b | 28 | 5 | 1 | 0 | 0 | 1 | 3 | .179 |
| S. Webb, ss | 27 | 5 | 0 | 0 | 0 | 4 | 1 | .185 |
| H. Greenberg, of | 23 | 7 | 3 | 0 | 2 | 7 | 7 | .304 |
| R. Cullenbine, of | 22 | 5 | 2 | 0 | 0 | 5 | 4 | .227 |
| P. Richards, c | 19 | 4 | 2 | 0 | 0 | 0 | 6 | .211 |
| H. Newhouser, p | 8 | 0 | 0 | 0 | 0 | 0 | 1 | .000 |
| D. Trout, p | 6 | 1 | 0 | 0 | 0 | 0 | 0 | .167 |
| B. Swift, c | 4 | 1 | 0 | 0 | 0 | 1 | 0 | .250 |
| V. Trucks, p | 4 | 0 | 0 | 0 | 0 | 0 | 0 | .000 |
| J. Hoover, ss | 3 | 1 | 0 | 0 | 0 | 1 | 1 | .333 |
| C. Hostetler | 3 | 0 | 0 | 0 | 0 | 0 | 0 | .000 |
| J. McHale | 3 | 0 | 0 | 0 | 0 | 0 | 0 | .000 |
| H. Walker | 2 | 1 | 0 | 0 | 0 | 1 | 0 | .500 |
| R. Borom | 1 | 0 | 0 | 0 | 0 | 0 | 0 | .000 |
| Z. Eaton | 1 | 0 | 0 | 0 | 0 | 0 | 0 | .000 |
| B. Maier | 1 | 1 | 0 | 0 | 0 | 0 | 1 | 1.000 |
| S. Overmire, p | 1 | 0 | 0 | 0 | 0 | 0 | 0 | .000 |
| J. Tobin, p | 1 | 0 | 0 | 0 | 0 | 0 | 0 | .000 |
| E. Mierkowicz, of | 0 | 0 | 0 | 0 | 0 | 0 | 0 | — |

**Errors:** E. Mayo, H. Newhouser, P. Richards, S. Webb, R. York.
**Stolen bases:** D. Cramer, R. Cullenbine, J. Outlaw

**CHICAGO (N.L.)**

| | AB | H | 2B | 3B | HR | R | RBI | BA |
|---|---|---|---|---|---|---|---|---|
| S. Hack, 3b | 30 | 11 | 3 | 0 | 0 | 1 | 4 | .367 |
| D. Johnson, 2b | 29 | 5 | 2 | 1 | 0 | 4 | 0 | .172 |
| P. Lowrey, of | 29 | 9 | 1 | 0 | 0 | 4 | 0 | .310 |
| B. Nicholson, of | 28 | 6 | 1 | 1 | 0 | 1 | 8 | .214 |
| A. Pafko, of | 28 | 6 | 2 | 1 | 0 | 5 | 2 | .214 |
| P. Cavarretta, 1b | 26 | 11 | 2 | 0 | 1 | 7 | 5 | .423 |
| M. Livingston, c | 22 | 8 | 3 | 0 | 0 | 3 | 4 | .364 |
| R. Hughes, ss | 17 | 5 | 1 | 0 | 0 | 1 | 3 | .294 |
| C. Passeau, p | 7 | 0 | 0 | 0 | 0 | 1 | 1 | .000 |
| P. Gillespie, c | 6 | 0 | 0 | 0 | 0 | 0 | 0 | .000 |
| H. Borowy, p | 5 | 1 | 1 | 0 | 0 | 1 | 0 | .200 |
| F. Secory | 5 | 2 | 0 | 0 | 0 | 0 | 0 | .400 |
| H. Wyse, p | 3 | 0 | 0 | 0 | 0 | 0 | 0 | .000 |
| H. Becker | 2 | 1 | 0 | 0 | 0 | 0 | 0 | .500 |
| L. Merullo, ss | 2 | 0 | 0 | 0 | 0 | 0 | 0 | .000 |
| E. Sauer | 2 | 0 | 0 | 0 | 0 | 0 | 0 | .000 |
| D. Williams, c | 2 | 0 | 0 | 0 | 0 | 0 | 0 | .000 |
| McCullough | 1 | 0 | 0 | 0 | 0 | 0 | 0 | .000 |
| B. Schuster, ss | 1 | 0 | 0 | 0 | 0 | 1 | 0 | .000 |
| H. Vandenberg, p | 1 | 0 | 0 | 0 | 0 | 0 | 0 | .000 |
| C. Block | 0 | 0 | 0 | 0 | 0 | 0 | 0 | — |

**Errors:** S. Hack (3), D. Johnson, B. Nicholson, A. Pafko.
**Stolen bases:** P. Lowrey

### Individual Pitching

**DETROIT (A.L.)**

| | W | L | ERA | IP | H | BB | SO | SV |
|---|---|---|---|---|---|---|---|---|
| H. Newhouser | 2 | 1 | 6.10 | 20.2 | 25 | 4 | 22 | 0 |
| D. Trout | 1 | 1 | 0.66 | 13.2 | 9 | 3 | 9 | 0 |
| V. Trucks | 1 | 0 | 3.38 | 13.1 | 14 | 5 | 7 | 0 |
| S. Overmire | 0 | 1 | 3.00 | 6 | 4 | 2 | 2 | 0 |
| A. Benton | 0 | 0 | 1.93 | 4.2 | 6 | 0 | 5 | 0 |
| J. Tobin | 0 | 0 | 6.00 | 3 | 4 | 1 | 0 | 0 |
| L. Mueller | 0 | 0 | 0.00 | 2 | 0 | 1 | 1 | 0 |
| T. Bridges | 0 | 0 | 16.20 | 1.2 | 3 | 3 | 1 | 0 |

**CHICAGO (N.L.)**

| | W | L | ERA | IP | H | BB | SO | SV |
|---|---|---|---|---|---|---|---|---|
| H. Borowy | 2 | 2 | 4.00 | 18 | 21 | 6 | 8 | 0 |
| C. Passeau | 1 | 0 | 2.70 | 16.2 | 7 | 3 | 3 | 0 |
| P. Erickson | 0 | 0 | 3.86 | 7 | 8 | 3 | 5 | 0 |
| H. Wyse | 0 | 1 | 7.04 | 7.2 | 8 | 4 | 1 | 0 |
| H. Vandenberg | 0 | 0 | 0.00 | 6 | 1 | 3 | 0 | 0 |
| P. Derringer | 0 | 0 | 6.75 | 5.1 | 5 | 7 | 1 | 0 |
| R. Prim | 0 | 0 | 9.00 | 4 | 4 | 1 | 1 | 0 |
| B. Chipman | 0 | 0 | 0.00 | 0.1 | 0 | 1 | 0 | 0 |

| LINE SCORES & PITCHERS (inn. pit.) | HOME RUNS (men on) | HIGHLIGHTS |
|---|---|---|

## San Diego (West) defeats Chicago (East) 3 games to 2

**GAME 1 - OCTOBER 2**

```
SD  W  000 000 000    0  6  1
CHI E  203 062 00x   13 16  0
```
**Show** (4), Harris (2), Booker (2)
**Sutcliffe** (7), Brusstar (2)

Dernier, Matthews, Sutcliffe, Matthews (2 on), Cey

In the first playoff appearance for both clubs, the Cubs set NL LCS records for runs, hits, home runs, and total bases in battering the Padres. A strike by major league umpires caused the league to call in college and former pro umps to work the games.

**GAME 2 - OCTOBER 3**

```
SD  W  000 101 000    2  5  0
CHI E  102 100 00x    4  8  1
```
**Thurmond** (3.2), Hawkins (1.1),
  Dravecky (2), Lefferts (1)
**Trout** (8.1), Smith (0.2) **SV**

Trout scattered five hits before yielding to Lee Smith, who nailed down the win. Sandberg and Moreland each had two hits for the Cubs.

**GAME 3 - OCTOBER 4**

```
CHI E  010 000 000    1  5  0
SD  W  000 034 00x    7 11  0
```
**Eckersley** (5.1), Frazier (1.2),
  Stoddard (1)
**Whitson** (8), Gossage (1)

McReynolds (2 on)

Templeton's two-run double in the fifth gave the Padres their first lead of the series, and McReynolds's homer in the sixth put the game away. Whitson allowed five hits over eight innings to keep San Diego's hopes alive.

**GAME 4 - OCTOBER 6**

```
CHI E  000 300 020    5  8  1
SD  W  002 010 202    7 11  0
```
Sanderson (4.2), Brusstar (1.1),
  Stoddard (1), **Smith** (1.1)
Lollar (4.1), Hawkins (0.2), Dravecky (2)
  Gossage (1), **Lefferts** (1)

Davis (1 on), Durham
Garvey (1 on)

Garvey capped a four-for-five, five RBI game with his two run homer in the bottom of the ninth to win one of the most dramatic LCS games ever played.

**GAME 5 - OCTOBER 7**

```
CHI E  210 000 000    3  5  1
SD  W  000 002 40x    6  8  0
```
**Sutcliffe** (6.1), Trout (0.2),
  Brusstar (1)
Show (1.1), Hawkins (1.2), Dravecky (2)
  **Lefferts** (2), Gossage (2) **SV**

Durham (1 on), Davis

The Padres became the first National League team to come back from two games down to win the series. Durham's error allowed Martinez to score the tying run and then three straight singles capped the four run rally that won the game.

### Team Totals

|     |   | W | AB | H | 2B | 3B | HR | R | RBI | BA | BB | SO | ERA |
|---|---|---|---|---|---|---|---|---|---|---|---|---|---|
| SD | W | 3 | 155 | 41 | 5 | 1 | 2 | 22 | 20 | .265 | 14 | 22 | 5.23 |
| CHI | E | 2 | 162 | 42 | 11 | 0 | 9 | 26 | 25 | .259 | 20 | 28 | 4.25 |

### Individual Batting

**SAN DIEGO (WEST)**

|                 | AB | H | 2B | 3B | HR | R | RBI | BA |
|---|---|---|---|---|---|---|---|---|
| S. Garvey, 1b   | 20 | 8 | 1 | 0 | 1 | 1 | 7 | .400 |
| A. Wiggins, 2b  | 19 | 6 | 0 | 0 | 0 | 4 | 1 | .316 |
| T. Gwynn, of    | 19 | 7 | 3 | 0 | 0 | 6 | 3 | .368 |
| T. Kennedy, c   | 18 | 4 | 0 | 0 | 0 | 2 | 1 | .222 |
| C. Martinez, of | 17 | 3 | 0 | 0 | 0 | 1 | 0 | .176 |
| G. Templeton, ss| 15 | 5 | 1 | 0 | 0 | 2 | 3 | .333 |
| G. Nettles, 3b  | 14 | 2 | 0 | 0 | 0 | 1 | 2 | .143 |
| McReynolds, of  | 10 | 3 | 0 | 0 | 1 | 2 | 4 | .300 |
| L. Salazar, 3b, of | 5 | 1 | 0 | 1 | 0 | 0 | 0 | .200 |
| B. Brown, of    | 4 | 0 | 0 | 0 | 0 | 1 | 0 | .000 |
| E. Whitson, p   | 3 | 0 | 0 | 0 | 0 | 0 | 0 | .000 |
| K. Bevacqua     | 2 | 0 | 0 | 0 | 0 | 0 | 0 | .000 |
| C. Summers      | 2 | 0 | 0 | 0 | 0 | 0 | 0 | .000 |
| T. Flannery     | 2 | 1 | 0 | 0 | 0 | 2 | 0 | .500 |
| M. Ramirez      | 2 | 0 | 0 | 0 | 0 | 0 | 0 | .000 |
| T. Lollar, p    | 1 | 0 | 0 | 0 | 0 | 0 | 0 | .000 |
| E. Show, p      | 1 | 0 | 0 | 0 | 0 | 0 | 0 | .000 |
| M. Thurmond, p  | 1 | 1 | 0 | 0 | 0 | 0 | 0 | 1.000 |

**Errors:** G. Templeton
**Stolen bases:** G. Templeton, B. Brown

**CHICAGO (EAST)**

|                 | AB | H | 2B | 3B | HR | R | RBI | BA |
|---|---|---|---|---|---|---|---|---|
| L. Durham, 1b   | 20 | 3 | 0 | 0 | 2 | 2 | 4 | .150 |
| R. Cey, 3b      | 19 | 3 | 1 | 0 | 1 | 3 | 3 | .158 |
| R. Sandberg, 2b | 19 | 7 | 2 | 0 | 0 | 3 | 2 | .368 |
| K. Moreland, of | 18 | 6 | 2 | 0 | 0 | 3 | 2 | .333 |
| J. Davis, c     | 18 | 7 | 2 | 0 | 2 | 3 | 6 | .389 |
| B. Dernier, of  | 17 | 4 | 2 | 0 | 1 | 5 | 1 | .235 |
| L. Bowa, ss     | 15 | 3 | 1 | 0 | 0 | 1 | 1 | .200 |
| G. Matthews, of | 15 | 3 | 0 | 0 | 2 | 4 | 5 | .200 |
| R. Sutcliffe, p | 6 | 3 | 0 | 0 | 1 | 1 | 1 | .500 |
| D. Eckersley, p | 2 | 0 | 0 | 0 | 0 | 0 | 0 | .000 |
| T. Bosley       | 2 | 0 | 0 | 0 | 0 | 0 | 0 | .000 |
| S. Trout, p     | 2 | 1 | 0 | 0 | 0 | 0 | 0 | .500 |
| S. Sanderson, p | 2 | 0 | 0 | 0 | 0 | 0 | 0 | .000 |
| R. Hebner       | 1 | 0 | 0 | 0 | 0 | 0 | 0 | .000 |
| G. Woods, of    | 1 | 0 | 0 | 0 | 0 | 0 | 0 | .000 |
| W. Brusstar, p  | 1 | 0 | 0 | 0 | 0 | 0 | 0 | .000 |
| D. Lopes, of    | 1 | 0 | 0 | 0 | 0 | 0 | 0 | .000 |
| S. Lake, c      | 1 | 1 | 1 | 0 | 0 | 0 | 0 | 1.000 |
| H. Cotto, of    | 1 | 1 | 0 | 0 | 0 | 1 | 0 | 1.000 |
| T. Veryzer, 3b, ss | 1 | 0 | 0 | 0 | 0 | 0 | 0 | .000 |

**Errors:** S. Trout, L. Durham, R. Sandberg
**Stolen bases:** R. Sandberg (3), B. Dernier (2), G. Matthews

### Individual Pitching

**SAN DIEGO (WEST)**

|             | W | L | ERA | IP | H | BB | SO | SV |
|---|---|---|---|---|---|---|---|---|
| E. Whitson  | 1 | 0 | 1.13 | 8 | 5 | 2 | 6 | 0 |
| D. Dravecky | 0 | 0 | 0.00 | 6 | 2 | 0 | 5 | 0 |
| E. Show     | 0 | 1 | 13.50 | 5.1 | 8 | 4 | 2 | 0 |
| T. Lollar   | 0 | 0 | 6.23 | 4.1 | 3 | 4 | 3 | 0 |
| G. Gossage  | 0 | 0 | 4.50 | 4 | 5 | 1 | 5 | 1 |
| C. Lefferts | 2 | 0 | 0.00 | 4 | 1 | 1 | 1 | 0 |
| A. Hawkins  | 0 | 0 | 0.00 | 3.2 | 0 | 2 | 1 | 0 |
| M. Thurmond | 0 | 1 | 9.82 | 3.2 | 7 | 2 | 1 | 0 |
| G. Harris   | 0 | 0 | 31.50 | 2 | 9 | 3 | 2 | 0 |
| G. Booker   | 0 | 0 | 0.00 | 2 | 2 | 1 | 2 | 0 |

**CHICAGO (EAST)**

|              | W | L | ERA | IP | H | BB | SO | SV |
|---|---|---|---|---|---|---|---|---|
| R. Sutcliffe | 1 | 1 | 3.38 | 13.1 | 9 | 8 | 10 | 0 |
| S. Trout     | 1 | 0 | 2.00 | 9 | 5 | 3 | 3 | 0 |
| D. Eckersley | 0 | 1 | 8.44 | 5.1 | 9 | 0 | 0 | 0 |
| W. Brusstar  | 0 | 0 | 0.00 | 4.2 | 6 | 0 | 1 | 0 |
| S. Sanderson | 0 | 0 | 5.79 | 4.2 | 6 | 1 | 2 | 0 |
| T. Stoddard  | 0 | 0 | 4.50 | 2 | 1 | 2 | 2 | 0 |
| L. Smith     | 0 | 1 | 9.00 | 2 | 3 | 0 | 3 | 1 |
| G. Frazier   | 0 | 0 | 10.80 | 1.2 | 2 | 0 | 1 | 0 |

# Macmillan Brings You the Best in Baseball Books

*The Baseball Encyclopedia,* edited by Joseph L. Reichler

The complete and official record of major league baseball—every player, every record, every statistic in the history of the game. Now in its sixth edition. "I cannot imagine life without it."—Jonathan Yardley, *The Washington Post Book World*

*The 1986 Baseball Encyclopedia Update*

Keep your *Encyclopedia* current with the *1986 Update.* Complete career listings for everyone who played at least one game in the 1985 season, standings and leaders for the '85 season, and World Series and League Championship Series highlights.

*The 1986 Elias Baseball Analyst,* by Seymour Siwoff, Steve Hirdt, and Peter Hirdt

The most complete, detailed analysis of player performance ever, from the secret files of the Elias Sports Bureau. Complete batting and pitching performance at home and on the road, vs. lefties and righties, with men on base and bases empty, even with runners in scoring position in the late innings of close ball games! "The best book of baseball statistics ever created. By a multiple of about 10."—Thomas Boswell, *The Washington Post*

*Baseball America,* by Donald Honig

Donald Honig, our leading baseball historian, portrays the lives of the game's greatest stars: how they were shaped by their times, and how their lives and legends reflect the changes in our society over the past hundred years. *"Baseball America* is part history, part biography, part drama, and a complete pleasure."—Ira Berkow, sports columnist, *The New York Times*

*Weaver on Strategy,* by Earl Weaver with Terry Pluto

A guide for armchair managers, by baseball's master tactician. "Once in a lifetime, a genuine, 24-karat genius comes along, and we ought to listen. *Weaver on Strategy* is gold, burnished by the master."—Tony Kubek

*A Baseball Winter: The Off-Season Life of the Summer Game,*
        edited by Terry Pluto and Jeffrey Neuman

An in-depth look at the events of a baseball off-season, from the last out of the World Series to the first pitch of opening day. A unique, involving, fresh, and innovative look at the overlooked end of the year-round business of baseball. "The inside information here gives the best look I've ever seen at how a baseball team really operates."—Brooks Robinson

*Voices from Cooperstown,* by Anthony J. Connor

The thoughts and reminiscences of sixty-five Hall of Famers, skillfully blended to create a touching portrait of a life in the game. "Through the recollections of these old-time craftsmen, who happen to have played baseball and played it with love, we have a lively informal history of an epoch that will never come again."—Studs Terkel

*The World Series,* by Richard M. Cohen, David S. Neft, and Jordan A. Deutsch

Complete play-by-play of every World Series game ever, from the first Series in 1903 through the Royals' come-from-behind triumph in 1985.
(Available in August)